ISBN 978-1-5285-6201-0
PIBN 10931128

FB &c Ltd, Dalton House, 60 Windsor Avenue, London, SW19 2RR.
Company number 08720141. Registered in England and Wales.

INDEX TO

The Florists' Exchange, Vol. XXII, 1906

ILLUSTRATED ARTICLES MARKED WITH AN (*) ASTERISK

SUPPLEMENT WITH THIS ISSUE

THE FLORISTS' EXCHANGE

We are a straight shoot and aim to grow into a vigorous plant

A WEEKLY MEDIUM OF INTERCHANGE FOR FLORISTS, NURSERYMEN, SEEDSMEN AND THE TRADE IN GENERAL

Vol. XXII. No. 1 NEW YORK AND CHICAGO, JULY 7, 1906 One Dollar Per Year

HYDRANGEAS

For Summer Blooming.

We have a magnificent lot of Hydrangea Otaksa grown especially for **JULY AND AUGUST FLOWERING.** The plants are just coming into bloom, just beginning to show color, and will be in perfection during July and August, when they are in great demand at watering places and other summer resorts. There is nothing showier or more satisfactory for lawn decoration. We make a specialty of them, and find an increasing demand for them from year to year. They can be shipped anywhere safely by freight.

Large plants in tubs, $2.00 to $3.00 each, according to size; Very large specimens, in half barrels, $5.00 and $7.50 each.

F. R. PIERSON CO., Tarrytown-on-Hudson, N. Y.

ONLY **$5.00** PER HUNDRED

from 2¼ inch pots in thousand lots;

$6.00 in smaller lots.

Richmond, Killarney and Beauty

Grafted Stock

Bride, Bridesmaid, Killarney and Richmond

Exceptionally Fine, Large Plants

SEND FOR SAMPLES.

W. H. ELLIOTT, BRIGHTON, MASS.

Mention The Florists' Exchange when writing.

SOW NOW Vaughan's Primrose Seed

If you have not received our list of Primula and Perennial Seeds, please write for same.

CHINESE PRIMULAS

With Fringed Foliage

	250 seeds	1000 seeds
Chiswick Red, bright red	$0.50	$1.75
Kermesina Splendens, crimson	.50	1.75
Alba Magnifica, snow white, of excellent form and habit	.50	1.70
Glowing Coal, the darkest red	.50	1.75
Peach Blossom, beautiful white with pink hue	.50	1.70
Blue, a clear sky-blue	.50	1.70
Upright Deep Velvety Red	.50	1.90
Rosea, a bright pink	.35	1.50
Bridesmaid, brightest pink	.50	1.75
Mont Blanc, large, pure milk-white flowers	.50	
Striata, white and lilac-striped	.35	1.30
Mixed, a splendid variety. ¼ oz., $3.00	.35	1.25

VAUGHAN'S INTERNATIONAL PRIMULA MIXTURE : : :

THIS mixture is composed of the most salable colors of single

Flowering Chinese Primulas : : : :

the best whites, pinks and reds, with a sprinkling of other colors enough to give a large variety of colors, the most important shades predominating. We have taken special pains to make this mixture as complete as possible and unreservedly recommend it to everyone.

Pkt. of 250 seeds...$0 50
5 Pkts., 1250 seeds.. 2 00
Per 1-16 oz.......... 3 50

Obconica Grandiflora, mixed, 1-16 oz., 60c.; Trade pkt., 25c.
Obconica Grandiflora, large flowering, pink, 1-16 oz., 85c.; Trade pkt., 25c.
Obconica Grandiflora, large flowering, pure white, 1-16 oz., 85c.; Trade pkt., 25c.

CALCEOLARIA HYBRIDA

Our mixture is composed of the choicest selections of the tigered, marbled, spotted and variegated varieties and we know will give entire satisfaction.
Trade pkt., 1000 seeds, 50c.; 3 trade pkts., $1.25.

CINERARIA

Vaughan's Columbian Mixture

It consists of a mixture made up by ourselves of the choicest English, French and German strains and cannot be excelled in variety of colors, size, shape and substance of flowers and perfect habit of plant.
Trade pkt., 1000 seeds, 50c.; 3 pkts., $1.25.
"Old Rose," A splendid strain, producing large flowers, which range in color from pink to rich coppery red. Trade pkt., 50c.
Large Flowering White, Crimson, Blue, Blood-Red; each, per trade pkt., 500 seeds, 35c.
Hybrida, fine large flowering mixed, 500 seeds, trade pkt. .... 25c.
Hybrida Grandiflora Nana, best mixed dwarf, trade pkt. .... 25c.
Hybrida Plenissima, extra choice double mixed, trade pkt. .... 50c.
Hybrida Plenissima, double white, trade pkt. .... 50c.

DOUBLE CHINESE PRIMROSES

White, pink, flesh, red, and striped; each, per 150 seeds, 35c.; Double mixed, 200 seeds, 35c.; 1000 seeds, $1.50.

NEW GIANT PRIMULAS

This new strain is a vast improvement on the older varieties, the flowers being considerably larger.
Giant Pink, Pure White and Copper Color; each, pkt. of 250 seeds .... 50c.
Giant Mixed, includes this year a number of new shades; pkt. of 250 seeds .... 50c.

10 Per Cent Special Cash Discount On orders over $2.00 fo Flower seeds if the cash is enclosed. This discount does not apply to Asparagus Seed.

Vaughan's Seed Store 14 BARCLAY ST., NEW YORK

CHICAGO, 84-86 Randolph Street
Greenhouses, Western Springs, Ill

MAJESTY MIGNONETTE

(Greenhouse Matured Seed)

THE *grandest of all Mignonettes* for indoor *forcing*—Easy to grow, strong constitution—and throwing up a *quantity of flower spikes* which grow to an immense size; the *lateral shoots*—too—are *as large as many Mignonettes* now grown under glass.

The seed I offer has been saved for me by a *leading grower of Mignonette*—who makes a *specialty* of this useful cut flower for the *New York market*, from *selected spikes only*—*under glass.*

Trial pkt., 30c.; half trade pkt., 60c.; trade pkt. containing about 1,000 seeds, $1.00.

Sweet Peas for Christmas and Thanksgiving Flowering

Boddington's Christmas Early Pink.—This is the earliest and most profitable and useful Sweet Pea in cultivation. 60c. per lb.; 15c. per oz.

Boddington's Christmas Early White.—A companion to Christmas Early Pink. Just as free and profuse a bloomer, and is, without doubt, the finest early white for indoor planting. 75c. per lb.; 20c. per oz.

PANSY SEED

Boddington's Challenge Mixture

This mixture contains all the finest *Giant* strains—of the leading Pansy Specialists in the world—the *Giant* self colors, the *Giant* striped and margined, and the *Giant* blotched—all carefully mixed in proportion—the *finest* that money can buy—the finest your money can buy. *A Florist*, who has grown it, said "Why don't you call it *Defiance!*"

Price ¼ trade pkt. 40c, trade pkt. 75c, ¼ oz. $1.50, ½ oz. $2.50, oz. $5.00. (For named varieties and to color see catalogue.)

ARTHUR T. BODDINGTON

342 West 14th Street New York City

Mention The Florists' Exchange when writing.

CANES FOR YOUR MUMS

6 to 8 feet, can be cut to any length, 1000 $6.00.

Mastica for glazing purposes, 1 gal. $1.25; Case of 6 gals., $6.75.

Glazing Points. Perfection, 1000 55c.

Fine Ground Rose Bone. 200 lbs. $4.00.

Wm. Elliott & Sons 201 Fulton St. NEW YORK

Mention The Florists' Exchange when writing.

FOR IMMEDIATE SOWING

We offer

PRIMULA OBCONICA RAWSON'S NEW GIANT
Pure White, Pink, Crimson, Superb Mixture .... per 100 seeds. 50c.; per 1000 seeds, $4.00

CINERARIA GRANDIFLORA
Rawson's Superfine .... Liberal Trade Pkt. 1.00

CINERARIA GRANDIFLORA DWARF
Rawson's Superfine .... Liberal Trade Pkt. 1.00

MIGNONETTE RAWSON'S MAMMOTH FRAGRANT
One of the finest Greenhouse Mignonettes in existence .... ¼ oz. 50.; per oz., 1.50

CANDYTUFT, RAWSON'S GIANT WHITE
.... Per oz. 30c.; per lb., 4.00

And the most complete collection of choice and desirable perennial flower seeds. Our catalogue free upon application. RAWSON'S INTERESTING BULB CATALOGUE out JULY 15. Write for it.

W. W. RAWSON & COMPANY
5 Union St., Boston, Mass.

Mention The Florists' Exchange when writing

TURNIP SEED.

SEVEN TOP

VERY SCARCE THIS SEASON

We offer hardy Northern-grown, all the produce of Bloomsdale Seed Farms:

WHOLESALE PRICES { 100 pounds at 20 cts. per lb. / 500 " " 19 " " / 1000 " " 18 " "

Fifteen Dollars for one hundred pounds of other leading sorts.
Write for New Wholesale Priced Card of Seeds for Mid Summer Sowing.

Bristol, Penna. **D. LANDRETH SEED COMPANY.**

PACIFIC SEED GROWERS' CO.
411-415 SANSOME STREET
SAN FRANCISCO, CAL.
Specialties:
Onion, Carrot, Lettuce, Sweet Peas

Mention The Florists' Exchange when writing.

Thorburn's Bulbs

LILIUM HARRISII

LILIUM LONGIFLORUM

and all other BULBS for Florists. Send us your requirements for special prices.

CYCAS REVOLUTA STEMS just arrived from Japan. Sizes and prices on application.

ASPARAGUS PLUMOSUS NANUS, $3.00 per 1000 seeds. Special prices en large quantities.

J. M. THORBURN & CO.
36 Cortlandt Street, New York.

Mention The Florists' Exchange when writing.

New Crop of my

Christmas Flowering

SWEET PEA SEED

Christmas Pink and Florence Denzer, pure white, will be ready August 1st.

Those two well known varieties are raised by over 2000 florists all over the world. Here is one out of many letters received:

Dear Sir: My sweet peas, which I raised from your seed, received the highest award at the Carnation Exhibit in Boston, being over 18 inches long. JOHN T. GALK. Tewkesbury, Mass.

Price 1-4 lb. 75c.; per lb. $7.00
MAILED FREE

New Christmas Flowering Hybrids, 20 to 30 colors, mostly blue, salmon, purple lavender, in mixtures; also Mrs. Edie Wild, carmine, separate color. 1 Trade pkt., $1.00, 5 Trade pkts. $4.00; not more than 5 pkts. taken in order to each customer just now. Those new hybrids are just as free bloomers as Cristmas Pink and Florence Denzer, some much larger, and received first-class Certificate of Merit by the Mass. Horticultural Society, Boston, March 24. Seed ready in Sept.

All seed originated with me is sold in my original sealed pkts., with cultural directions, to the growers, but none for seedsmen for propagating.

Orders filled strictly in rotation.

ANT. C. ZVOLANEK
BOUND BROOK, N. J.

MUSHROOM SPAWN

Tissue Pure Culture, 10 lbs. $1.00; 100 lbs. $8.00; 1000 lbs. $75.00. Best English, 10 lbs. 75c.; 100 lbs. $6.00; 1000 lbs. $56.00.

STUMPP & WALTER CO.
50 Barclay Street, New York.

A BED OF MUSHROOMS

Raised from our Spawn, will bear longer and yield better than from any other variety of Spawn. This is proven by facts. Full particulars and information how to succeed in mushroom raising free. We warrant you it using our method of growing mushrooms that all will go well.

KNUD GUNDESTRUP & CO., MUSHROOM SPECIALISTS 4273 Milwaukee Ave., CHICAGO

Mention The Florists' Exchange when writing.

PANSY SEED

Brown's Extra Select Superb Giant Prize PANSIES, awarded Silver Medal, St. Louis Exposition 1904. My own grown new 1906 crop ready. Price mixed seed 3000 seeds, $1.00; ¼ oz., $1.50; ½ oz., $2.50., 1 oz., $5.00; ¼ lb., $14.00; ⅛ lb., $25.00; 1 lb., $50.00. Cash with order.

PETER BROWN
Lancaster, Pa.

Mention The Florists' Exchange when writing.

Pansy Seed

THE JENNINGS STRAIN

New crop now ready, saved from finest selected stock, large flowering and great variety of fancy colors. By mail one pkt., 4000 seed, $1.00; ½ oz., $2.50; 1 oz., $5.00, 2 oz., $9.00; 3 oz., $12.00. Cash with order.

E. B. JENNINGS,
Lock Box 254 Southport, Conn.

Grower of the Finest Pansies.

Mention The Florists' Exchange when writing.

XXX SEEDS

CHINESE PRIMROSE

Finest grown, mixed, 500 seeds. $1.00; ½ pkt., 50c.

Primula Obconica Grand. Finest large flowering mixed, 1000 seeds, 50c.

CINERARIA. Finest large-flowering, dwf. mxd., 1000 seeds, 50c.

DAISY, double Giant mixed, 1000 Seeds 25c.

GIANT PANSY. The best large flowering varieties, critically selected, 5000 seeds $1.00; half pkt., 50c.; per oz. $3.50. 500 seeds of Giant Mme. Perret, pansy seed added to every $1.00 pkt. of Giant Pansy. Cash. Liberal extra count of seeds in all packets.

JOHN F. RUPP, Shiremanstown, Pa.
The Home of Primroses

Mention The Florists' Exchange when writing.

SEED BAGS

All packet sizes carried in stock in **MANILLA, AMBER LAID,** and **UNBLEACHED PAPERS.**
Printing done with cuts and cultural directions.
Large lots at very low rates.
Send for samples and discount sheet.
Our intimate acquaintance with the packet trade and our large facilities enable us to meet all requirements satisfactorily.

Address

The Brown Bag Filling Machine Co.,
Fitchburg, Mass.

H. H. HICKS,
Importer of and dealer in
MUSHROOM SPAWN
KENNETT SQUARE, PA.

Invoices of Barter's English Mushroom Spawn received monthly. Am. Pure Culture Spawn always on hand. When writing for prices state quantity wanted.

Mention The Florists' Exchange when writing.

MUSHROOM SPAWN

Originators and growers of **superior strains** of **Tissue-Culture Pure Spawn.**
Send for our booklet.

PURE CULTURE SPAWN CO.
PACIFIC, MO.

Mention the Florists' Exchange when writing

BURPEE'S SEEDS

PHILADELPHIA

Blue List of Wholesale Prices mailed only to those who plant for profit.

Mention The Florists' Exchange when writing.

NOW READY

Zirngiebel's Prize Pansy Seeds,

in trade packages; $1.00 each.
GIANT MARKET, 2000 SEEDS.
GIANT FANCY, 600 SEEDS.
Full directions with each package.

Augustus Zirngiebel, Needham, Mass.

Mention The Florists' Exchange when writing.

ROEMER'S SUPERB PRIZE PANSIES

The finest strain of Pansies in the World. Introducer and Grower of all the leading Novelties Highest Award, International Exhibition Dusseldorf, 1906. Catalogue free on application.

FRED. ROEMER, Seed Grower,
Quedlinburg, Germany.

Mention the Florists' Exchange when writing.

Giant Cinerarias

Mixture of perfect colors.

Dwarf Hybrids / Semi-Dwarf Hybrids } Each separate Tr. Pkt. $0.50 6 Tr. Pkts. $2.50

O. V. ZANGEN, Seedsman, HOBOKEN, N. J.

Mention The Florists' Exchange when writing.

Catalog Engravings

and ILLUSTRATIONS

that print EASILY. That's the kind we make—have been since '73

JAS. M. BRYANT, Horticultural Engraving and Printing
706 Chestnut Street, PHILADELPHIA, PA.

Write for our Catalogue of Stock Engravings.

Mention The Florists' Exchange when writing.

ADVERTISING IN THE FLORISTS' EXCHANGE
- - - IS SURE TO BRING RESULTS - - -

Seed Trade Report.

AMERICAN SEED TRADE ASSOCIATION

Henry W. Wood, Richmond, Va., president; C. S. Burge, Toledo, O., first vice-president; G. B. McVay, Birmingham, Ala., second vice-president; C. E. Kendel, Cleveland, O., secretary and treasurer; J. H. Ford, Ravenna, O., assistant secretary.

In the list of those killed in the railroad accident, which occurred at Salisbury, England, on July 1, appears the name of Louis Goeppinger. Mr. Goeppinger, who was the traveling representative of the seed house of Peignaux & H. Lorin, Angers, France, was returning from his annual trip to the United States, having sailed from New York on the steamer New York on June 23. He had visited this country annually for a number of years, and was well known among the American wholesale seed houses.

DENVER, COL.—The Post, in its June 28 issue, illustrates the new seed warehouse of F. Barteldes Company. The building is located on the southeast corner of Sixteenth and Wynkoop streets; cost, $50,000. The building will be 50x125 feet in extent, with five stories and basement. The structure will be the heaviest in Denver, each floor being calculated to carry a pressure of 600 pounds to the square foot. Mill construction will be used throughout. The offices will be on the second floor, connected by bridge with the Sixteenth street viaduct. The exterior will be of dark red pressed brick, with red stone trimmings. The building will be completed September 1.

See page 14 for conclusion of report of convention of the American Seed Trade Association at Toledo, O., last week.

CANADIAN SEED GROWERS' ASSOCIATION.—The third annual convention of this organization opened in Ottawa on Wednesday, June 27. The attendance was large. In the afternoon a paper was read by the district representative of the seed branch of the Department of Agriculture. At night Professor J. W. Robertson delivered the presidential address, and addresses were also delivered by Hon. Sydney Fisher and Hon. W. R. Motherwell of Regina. The following officers were elected: President, Professor James W. Robertson. Board of directors, Prof. C. A. Zavitz, Guelph; Hon. W. R. Motherwell, Regina, and Messrs. Thomas A. Peters, Fredericton, N. B.; C. A. Bigault, Quebec; Thomas H. Woolford, Cardston, Alberta; Hugh W. Gibson, Wolseley, Sask; W. G. Davidson, Bethel, Que.; Thomas C. Waugh, North Bedegue, Prince Edward Island; J. O. Duke, Olinda, Ontario, and John Money, Valley River, Manitoba. Secretary-treasurer, E. H. Newman.

TOLEDO, O.—Two meetings for the election of officers have recently been held by The Henry Philipps Seed & Implement Company. The same officers were elected in both meetings for different positions. One was held on the 21st of June and at the latter meeting of June 28th the following officers are reported as elected: President Paul A. Philipps; vice-president, Henry West; secretary and treasurer, Mrs. E. West Philipps. Previous to these meetings the officers were as follows: President, Mrs. E. West Philipps; vice-president, Paul A. Philipps; secretary and treasurer, Henry Philipps, Jr.

The Churchill Grain & Seed Company was incorporated on July 2 with a capital of $50,000, by Joseph Baker, Charles E. Cameron, Lloyd T. Williams, F. L. Geddes and Walter E. Stone. The concern will remain practically unchanged from the old firm of Churchill & Company, the company merely reorganizing into a stock corporation. SCH.

A RUST-RESISTING CANTALOUPE.—In a recent bulletin of the Colorado Experimental Station, P. K. Blinn reports the discovery by a local grower of a rust-resisting cantaloupe which promises to be of immense value to the Rockyford cantaloupe industry. In this case seed of the Rockyford variety was purchased from five different seedsmen. They were planted and cultivated under similar conditions. When rust attacked the field just before the melons began to ripen, it developed rapidly and soon destroyed all the vines except those grown from the seed of one seedsman. Many of the hills from this strain of Rockyford seed remained green throughout the season and produced a good crop of melons. Further observations in the muskmelon fields of that neighborhood also showed that wherever this strain of Rockyford seed had been used many hills were unaffected with rust, while with other strains of seed of the same variety the vines were all dead.

Mr. Blinn selected a quantity of seed from the rust-resistant hills and planted them in comparison with ordinary seed. "On the rust-resisting hills the melons were hidden under a healthy growth of vines, and were large, solidly netted, with thick, firm flesh, small seed cavity completely filled with seed. On the rusted hills the plants were almost devoid of leaves and the small melons were prematurely ripe, with thin, watery flesh, large, open seed cavity, and practically of no market value."

In tracing back the history of this strain of seed it was found that some years before a seedsman had saved the first lot from a single healthy melon taken from a field of rusted vines. It had therefore been developed by the simple process of saving seed from the best melons produced by plants which withstood attacks of rust when surrounding plants were destroyed by this disease.

European Notes.

Summer commences to-day, so the calendars inform us, and they at any rate are infallible; but those who, like the writer, have been enjoying (?) the bleak northeast wind known as the "mistral," which has been traveling over southern France at the rate of from 40 to 60 Rilometres per hour for many days past, begin to wonder where Summer comes in. There is no lack of bright sunshine, and in the shelter of the cypress hedges it is undoubtedly hot, but the living force of the sun's rays appears to be absent.

The vegetation is almost stationary, for while the canal water reaches the roots, the leaves, stems and flowers are smothered in dust. For nearly five weeks not one drop of rain has fallen, neither has there been one dewy night. As a result of all this the wheat harvest is upon us, and of our many cultures in this region only onion and carrot appear to benefit.

In other parts of Europe more favorable conditions appear to prevail. In Italy, England and western France copious rains have fallen, and we may hope with the advent of Summer to see a change for the better ere long.

EUROPEAN SEEDS.

CATALOGUES RECEIVED.

PETERSON NURSERY (Wm. A. Peterson, Proprietor), Chicago. Catalogue of Peonies and German Iris. Illustrated. The peonies are listed under colors. The Peterson firm has been established since 1856 and has given special attention to Peonies for the past 20 years, the nomenclature being carefully studied.

A. DESSERT, a Chenonceaux, France. —General Catalogue of Peonies. Illustrated. M. Dessert has made a specialty of Ponies for more than sixty years, and his collections are very comprehensive and interesting.

NURSERY DEPARTMENT.

Conducted by Joseph Meehan.

AMERICAN ASSOCIATION OF NURSERYMEN, Orlando Harrison, Berlin, Md., president; J. W. Hill, Des Moines, Ia., vice-president; George C. Seager, Rochester, N. Y., secretary; C. L. Yates, Rochester, N. Y., treasurer.

LAWRENCE, KANS.—The National Nurseries, which have been doing a good business in Lawrence for some years, have found the need of increased shipping facilities and to that end have purchased two acres of ground on the Haskell road for the purpose of erecting a large packing shed. E. H. Balco, proprietor and manager, is greatly pleased with the growth of the business, and intends to add to the equipment of the nurseries as fast as necessary.

Horticultural Notes.

The reason Rhododendron maximum, our native sort, does not make the appearance the hybrid varieties do is not altogether because of its lack of varied color, but not flowering before July the trusses of blossoms are hidden by the young shoots made since Spring opened.

A little pruning by finger and thumb when trees and shrubs are growing effects the object a good deal better than pruning at any other time. The side shoots push out at once, accomplishing bushiness the same season.

Objections are often made to the manetti rose as a stock for budding. Try the Prairie rose, R. setigera. It does not sucker, and in the South, where it has been tried, it is much esteemed.

Quercus Robur fastigiata, salisburia, Lombardy poplar, Van Geerti poplar, deciduous cypress, white cedar, native Arbor vitæ are all slender, tall growing trees, well suited to many situations, while out of place in others. Just where to place a tree of the proper kind demands the skill of the planter.

Zero weather does not hurt the hardy orange, Citrus trifoliata. It stands quite uninjured in the neighborhood of Philadelphia, where it meets zero weather almost every Winter. Its pretty blossoms in Spring, and its oranges in Autumn, make it sought for for ornamental purposes; and those who want a formidable hedge plant could get nothing as good.

Laurus nobilis, the sweet bay, is becoming a great favorite. The standard forms are much used near buildings. Florists find a good sale for them. They can be housed in barns or stables in Winter; in fact, they have been known to live out all Winter in Philadelphia when in sheltered positions.

Rhododendron cuttings made of half ripened wood and placed in a bed of sand and peat in a greenhouse will root. It is hardly worth doing this in the case of ordinary kinds, but it would be if the variety be a valuable one.

In the japonica section of Hydrangea Hortensia, which contains those with flat heads of flowers, two of them, the Imperatrice Eugenie and acuminata, are very good ones. The former is rose colored, the latter blue. All the japonica type are rather hardier than Hortensia proper.

Red Jacket gooseberry is the result of efforts to improve our native sorts. Given a partially shaded position and a moist soil, it thrives and bears prodigious crops of fruit, which ripen with us in the last days of July.

The correspondent who inquired if he could gather ripe currants before July 1, as his family left for the seashore at that date, can surely do so anywhere in Pennsylvania. In Philadelphia this fruit is ripe toward the close of June, while the latest varieties of strawberries are still to be had.

A writer in "Park and Cemetery" states that the superintendent of Audubon Park, New Orleans, has adopted a plan to cure and preserve trees with hollow trunks that is "original," by filling the hollows with cement. The plan is a good one, but it is by no means "original"; it has been in practice in these parts many a year.

Our native beech makes a grand tree when set out where it can grow at will untrammeled. When of some age it takes on the drooping character of its lower branches which so distinguishes the pin oak. This, with its white bark, gives it a character that calls for its planting.

Forming Standard Shrubs.

Standard shrubs are not to the liking of everyone. Their artificial appearance sometimes jars those who believe nature should be allowed full sway with such growths. For all this, there is a great call for these standards, and the demand will continue, for there are positions where the use of standards is much in place, just as much so as are flowering pot plants in our conservatories and dwellings.

In the case of shrubs, it is the best plan to cut to the ground some strong plants in early Spring, and then select for the standard the strongest shoot of each cut down plant. With many shrubs no stake will be required to insure a straight growth. Very often it is the best way to let the shoot grow at will without pruning for the first season, topping it at the required height the Spring following. At the same time, the shoots should be cut off from the stem from the ground to near the top where the head is looked for.

Wistarias are beautiful objects when in standard form. Although a vine, the wistaria shoots become as tough as desired in time, quite able to sustain a head of branches and flowers. Any young one-year-old flexible shoot may be tied to a stake and in a few years will be stiff enough to sustain a head. And as in the case of shrubs, a strong plant can be cut down, and its young shoot tied to a stake as it grows. Wistarias are greatly appreciated when in standard form; they are then practically a weeping shrub; and everyone knows how much they are appreciated when in blossom.

There is yet ample time this season to take in hand many of the shrubs and vines desirable for the formation of standards.

Syringa Vulgaris

Variations in Junipers.

Our common red cedar, Juniperus virginiana, grows practically over all of our country. But its character changes according to the climate it meets with, and this is why there are some dozen or more Juniperus under different names, all of which are but variations of virginiana. It is right that they should bear different names, for those who know the red cedar of Pennsylvania, say, and then see its representative in New Mexico, would hardly credit that climate had caused them to appear so widely dissimilar. These remarks are suggested by having seen lately the seeds of Juniperus virginiana from Utah. These berries are almost of the size of small marbles, and there is no wonder it passes under the name of Juniper utahense. In Wisconsin there is a juniper which nurserymen sell as sabina, but it is not sabina but a dwarf form of the common juniper, Juniperus communis, and goes under the name of Juniperus prostrata. Sabina has foliage more like that of the red cedar, and one would fancy it a variety of the latter were it not that it is counted as a distinct species and from Europe.

Mazzard Cherry Seed.

What has come to be called Mazzard cherry is really but the degenerate sweet cherry of our gardens. Birds carry off the fruit from cultivated trees, drop the stones along fence rows and the borders of woods, and the seedlings that spring up from them produce fruit which we call Mazzard cherry. In a botanical way it is known as Cerasus avium. These wild trees give the stones which are so much valued for producing seedlings for budding and grafting—Mazzard stocks. The cherries are ripe now, and in the vicinity of the older cities there are many trees from which the fruit may be gathered and the stones saved. The proper way to treat the stones is to mix them with damp sand as soon as they are freed of pulp. In this way they may be kept until Fall when they can be sown in beds prepared for them; or they may be allowed to remain in the sand until Spring and be sown then. But in the latter case, they must be in a cold place, either outdoors or in a cold shed. If in a warm building the stones would sprout before Spring opened.

Whatever is done do not let the stones become dry. To grow, they must be kept moist from the time they are gathered until sown. This applies as well to all stone fruits.

Syringa Vulgaris, Common Lilac.

Lilacs are so common in every garden that it would seem an easy task to discover a nice one to photograph, but we were some time in finding one, because they are usually crowded with other shrubs. The one pictured is a fair representative of a comparatively young bush, and it has been caught when very full of flowers. It represents the old common lilac from which all of the great number of valuable sorts of to-day have sprung. Old sort as it is, it is still the one customers all ask the nurseryman for. There mey be better ones—there are better —but there are none that represent home as this one does. Every one remembers the lilac bush in his mother's garden, and it was the old style purple one, and so it is that this sort appeals to those planting a garden far more than any other variety.

The number of varieties in cultivation to-day is very great, and with all due regard to the oldest one of all many of them are much superior. None excel it in grateful fragrance, but they do in size of panicle, and many of them in excellence of color. There are paler colored ones and darker colored sorts, some of the latter almost crimson; and some of them, while of just the old color, have larger flowers and larger panicles.

The white lilac, almost as old as the common one, has also been greatly improved not only in size of panicle and of flower, but in the way of double forms. The improved lilacs, both double and single, are so numerous that many who have large grounds now have beds made wholly of lilacs. By mixing with them the new Chinese one, Ligustrum oblata, they get the earliest of all to flower, and then by not forgetting those grown as Hungarian lilacs, viz., S. Josikæ and S. Rosa, very late flowering species, there is a continuance of flowers for many weeks.

Hemlock Hedges.

One visiting the older estates in the midst of us will hardly fail to find thereon a hemlock spruce hedge or the remains of one. It and the Norway spruce and Arbor vitæ were the three evergreens a hedge was chosen from. There is today no better evergreen for a hedge than the hemlock. Always beautiful, it is especially so in early Summer when its lovely pendant shoots of green foliage are displaying their lengthening growths. As a hedge or as a single tree, there is absolutely no evergreen that equals it in beauty.

Many gardeners prune it twice a year, but unless desired of an exceedingly level outline, once a season is sufficient. This should be cone when the new growth is nearly completed for the season. The little made later will really thicken the hedge. Many plant with the idea that the hedge can always be kept at the same height, say four feet; but this is not possible. Both height and width must advance a little, or the hedge would die. So prune as one will, a hedge will become very large in time. There are some hemlock hedges in this vicinity over 50 years old. There is life in them yet, but pruning has been so severe of late years, trying to keep back extension, that the vitality of the plants is low. Such old hedges should be taken out, fresh soil put in and young plants set.

When hemlocks can be had with balls of soil attached to the roots, not one should fail. And even without the ball, there need be but little loss in transplanting, if care be exercised that not a root be allowed to dry. It is the drying of the root that causes the loss of so many evergreens. Spring, or very early Fall, is the best time to plant.

JOSEPH MEEHAN.

Propagation of Crimson Rambler.

(141) When is the proper time to propagate Crimson Rambler rose?
Long Island N. P.

—We propagate these roses both Winter and Summer, but consider May and June the best time to propagate them in order to have the best results.

JACKSON & PERKINS CO.

The Study of Rose Growing.

(142) Is there any advantage in learning rose growing in Europe, and where? F. C. D.
New Jersey.

—For the cultivation of roses indoors it would be of little use to any one to go to Europe in order to study the same. The best indoor roses are grown right here in America.

Compost for Carnations.

(143) Would it be advisable to put either wood ashes or leaf mold in the carnation benches when making up new beds? M. & D.
Massachusetts.

—We would not advise mixing any leaf mold with carnation soil. Wood ashes will be beneficial to a certain extent, and they should be spread on the ground before the plowing is done in order that the soil may have the full benefit from them. Where the soil is particularly heavy, and the carnations are already planted in the benches, it might be advisable to scatter very thinly over the surface a little of the wood ashes, though they should be used quite sparingly at such a time.

Geraniums for General Business.

(144) Kindly name six geraniums most desirable for a general business, and state what percentage of each should be grown. K. & K.
Indiana.

—If we were limited to six varieties of geraniums for general purposes, we would grow General Grant and Alphonse Ricard for scarlet, and would let these two varieties constitute half of the total number we grew. The other four varieties we would grow in equal proportions; and they would be: For salmon pink, Beaute Poitevine; white, La Favorite; pink, Mrs. Frances Perkins; and crimson, S. A. Nutt.

Wants to Start in Business.

(145) Do you think a greenhouse 24x150 feet, well looked after, would raise enough stock to be profitable? With a very little encouragement I will embark in the business, as I have the name of being a good gardener, and above all I like the work; but do not know whether I could make it pay where artificial heat has to be supplied. C. A. D.

—A greenhouse 24x150 feet would be large enough to maintain a small business, and should be quite profitable if run to the best advantage.

LIST OF ADVERTISERS

PONTIAC, MICH.—During the recent wind storm which passed over this section 26 of the ventilators in the Pontiac Floral Company's greenhouses were blown off and shattered; damage about $200.

INDEX TO STOCK ADVERTISED

Contents.

FIRMS WHO ARE BUILDING

KNIGHTSTOWN, IND.—B. F. Hensley, West View, is building three new greenhouses, each 200 by 26 feet. Also a boiler room 50 by 60 feet. One house will be devoted exclusively to the Richmond rose.

INDIANAPOLIS, IND.—H. W. Rieman has been granted a permit to erect greenhouses at 1207 South East street, to cost $2,000.

NEW LONDON, WIS.—E. H. Olson has begun work on two new greenhouses, each 75 by 20 feet. It is his intention to build two more structures of the same size next Spring.

REVIEW OF THE MARKET

NEW YORK.—The cut flower market is just about as near rock bottom as possible. It does not seem that there is any fixed price on any line of flowers. There is yet a steady supply of roses; much greater than can be cleared out satisfactorily. The same can also be said of carnations. Lilies still keep plentiful, and the call for them is so poor that they have been selling at prices ranging from $1 to $3 per 100. Sweet peas are a glut; some of them do not average $1 per hundred bunches.

Of course there is never much business around the fourth of July, and this year is no exception to the rule. The weather is extremely hot, and however good the flowers may be or of whatever kind, does not seem to matter; there is practically no call for anything.

CHICAGO.—The few days' spurt in the closing June week, attributable to the school graduations, as well as, to a certain extent, to the dilatory bridal arrangements, offered quite a relief to the wholesale market last week and a very generous aid to many retailers. Otherwise there is little to be said beyond the fact that the Summer conditions of trade have arrived, and although good stock is generally sold at a fair price much has to be sacrificed. It appears to be a dribbling business without much certainty of results to be forecasted a day in advance. At present those who are getting in a fair proportion of good stock in the entire cut are readily able to clear themselves by sacrificing the lower grades.

There are few specialties to attract the attention of the observer, conditions varying slightly from different points of view. As a general rule, colored stock both in roses and carnations is off, though there are a few good American Beauty and Liberty and some Mrs. Lawson carnations which are up to what might be called a fancy grade.

Lilium candidum were much more freely offered last week than ever before, and other outside stock, including sweet peas (of various grades), Shasta daisies, delphiniums, goat's beard spiraea and numerous kindred selections, which if not immediately available have had to take the inevitable chance in the "survival of the fittest," with the exception of L. candidum which being of more substance have to a considerable extent been placed in cold storage.

W. K. W.

BOSTON.—There is practically no call whatever for flowers. Last week ended school exercises which took up a lot of the surplus stock; but now that these are over there is little doing. Growers have not yet thrown out their old plants of carnations, consequently are sending to market all they can of whatsoever flowers there are. The result is obvious—no demand and carnations everywhere at almost any price. Then there is the same story about roses; the supply is far above the demand. Peonies are now past, having held on longer in this market than in many others. Sweet peas are plentiful and of good quality. Lily of the valley still comes in, with a moderate demand. In green goods and other lines there is practically no change, nor is any looked for for some time to come. J. W. D.

PITTSBURG.—Cutflower trade the past few weeks was fair, principally for wedding orders and school commencements. Stock is plentiful but not of the best; the hot weather has had a bad effect on stock under glass. Prices are satisfactory for both roses and carnations; other stock is rather cheap. Candidum lilies were much used being abundant and of good quality. Sweet peas are also very plentiful and in good demand. L. S. Neff is cutting quantities of white hardy phlox, of which he sold thousands of plants the past season. Peonies are still in evidence; the Pittsburg Cut Flower Company received some nice shipments of these the past week which arrived in fine shape. The plant season is about ended; only a few o fth gardeners are yet to be seen about the markets. E. C. R.

CINCINNATI.—The retail trade is quieting down. Sweet peas are coming in lively and prices have dropped somewhat in consequence. Asters will soon begin to cut a figure and they will be welcomed. Roses are about of the same quality as last week, with the exception of American Beauty which are good for this time of year. Carnations are becoming small in size, and the cuts are also diminishing. E. G. G.

DETROIT.—The commission houses are kept fairly well cleaned out. Good roses are very scarce and carnations bring a good price. June weddings are numerous, calling for many decorations. HARRY.

INDIANAPOLIS.—Trade last week was satisfactory with the retailers; wedding decorations were numerous and funeral work, in generous amounts, arrived daily. Counter business, too, was better than for some time. Stock has been plentiful enough, but the variety has been lacking; roses, carnations, sweet peas and lilies are about all the florist has to offer, with the exception of field flowers which have a limited use. Carnations are no longer a burden as poor grades are readily taken at $1 a 100. Sweet peas, the quality of which has greatly improved, sell at 20c. to 35c. a 100; white ones are at times scarce, so are shipped in at 25c. a 100.

Smilax and asparagus have been scarce for some time, but relief is in sight. Shasta daisies this season are fine, at 50c. a 100; the smaller field daisies find a market at 15c.

Large quantities of roses, especially Kaiserin Augusta Victoria and Bride, were called for for decorations on Wednesday. Madame Abel Chatenay is almost always in brisk demand at $5 to $8. American Beauty have been selling better at $5 to $25 a 100; those cut from new stock are most promising.

L. auratum and L. longiflorum bridge a wide gap for funeral work, at $12.50 to $15 a 100. China asters made their debut this week, but will not be cut in quantity for some time. I. B.

NEW BEDFORD, MASS.—The usual Summer dullness has at last struck us. Outside of funeral work there is not much doing. Carnations are now bringing 35c. per dozen; the quality is very good considering the time of year and the hot weather. Outdoor sweet peas are now coming into bloom. Other outdoor flowers give plenty to cut from for cheap bouquets. The bedding out season is about through with; from all reports, it has been very satisfactory, and fairly good prices have been realized for stock sold. The growers are now giving attention to their greenhouses and will soon be housing carnations. H. A. Jahn is working up a big stock of his new white seedling carnation; it is a beauty, and a winner. He will disseminate it in two years' time. This variety will then have had 6 years' trial before being introduced to the trade—surely a good enough test for any variety.

Great interest is being shown in the dahlia show to be held in the Fall. So far the weather has been very nice for the growing of young carnation stock in the field; the young plants are looking fine and healthy. Wm. S. Brown will be very strong on asters this year.

HORTICO.

MINNEAPOLIS—The market the past week has been somewhat unsettled, on account of the shortage of roses of different varieties. It appears that a great many of the growers have not kept a sufficient number of old roses in the benches to supply the demand; the larger dealers therefore have experienced some trouble in getting supplies of some varieties with which to fill orders. Trade has been very fair and, if anything, has kept up much better this season than in past seasons. From all appearances the June weddings did not strike the most of the trade until the latter part of the month and then they came thick and fast. All dealers have been favored with their share; some of the larger ones have had as many as six and eight wedding outfits to make in a single day.

Moline, Ill.

Florists of the three cities held their annual picnic on the north bank of Rock river about a half-mile east of the Watch Tower, June 28. There was a great feast and a great crowd of members of the Tri-city association and their families and invited friends, and the excitement over the sports was at high temperature which put the torrid weather into the shade.

The annual quoits contest developed keen rivalry between the three cities. Messrs. Temple and Pauly for Davenport, won.

In the running race Mr. Pauly of Davenport finished first in competition with Mr. Knees of Moline and Gaetjer of Rock Island.

The boys' and girls' races were won by Davenport, and the fat men's race narrowed down to Messrs. Arp and Boehm of Davenport who are the only ones capable of meeting the conditions, and they divided the prize between them without undergoing the exhaustion of the race.

THE WEEK'S WORK.

Timme's Timely Teachings.

Outdoor Roses.

Rose growing in the open entails unceasing attention and watchful care. It is at this time that insects of varying species attack foliage, buds and new shoots, when disorders peculiar to roses most readily gain a start, if not detected in time and waylaid in their course of depredation. The first few and often widely separated signs of danger, betraying the onset of trouble, are usually of so trifling and unsuspicious an appearance as to yield no immediate conception as to their portentous meaning, and the novice in open air rose culture is very apt to heedlessly pass them by, while the eyes of the more experienced grower, trained by the vigils of a never-ending warfare, soon descry the presence of the enemy under cover.

The June bug is one of the early callers and a marauder that defies the common tactics of the rose grower. Although due in June it is often away into July before it makes its appearance, staying a considerable time, and doing much damage. The fresh shoots are its favorite diet. In some seasons and in some localities it becomes a common plague, hard to combat. Dustings and sprayings of deadly decoctions are of little avail in its case. Gathering in the bugs by hand during the night with the aid of a lantern and drowning them in a handy vessel of turpentine or kerosene is the best way to rout them and to bring about a noticeable scarcity of June bugs, alive and kicking.

Roses out of doors are hardly ever troubled by red spider, if well attended to, but when once infested it will be found that the evil is much harder to fight in the open than under glass. Syringing, forceful and often, in any event a great help to roses in hot and dry weather, is the remedy here as well as indoors. The rose slug must be dealt with promptly, as soon as its presence is noticed. Slug shot, tobacco dust or hellebore, blown on and through the bushes with a powder gun from time to time, when the plants are wet, will keep this pest in check, as also canker worms, greenfly and caterpillars. Fir tree oil is also good, but remedies that spot and injure the foliage should not be used. Bordeaux mixture, the sure going remedy for most fungoid diseases, has this fault. It leaves defacing streaks and blotches all over the foliage and should therefore not be employed in fighting rust on roses that are to yield blooms for cutting, or on roses massed for effect. Varieties especially susceptible to rust, black spot or blight, and never-do-wells in certain localities, should not be grown there. There are plenty of others.

Mildew.

Some of our best roses always suffer more or less from mildew at about this time of the year, notably moss roses, some varieties of the hybrid perpetual class and nearly all of the multiflora section, of which Crimson Rambler is the most striking example. In some seasons mildew on roses takes the form of a deep-seated, wide-spreading disease, if not checked in time. In the disfigurement of roses and rose gardens through careless culture or causes beyond our control in field culture, mildew is a factor much to be feared. It must be understood that mildew not merely disfigures, but that, in doing so, it is most active in blocking the free circulation of sap, in hindering proper development, in destroying inherent vigor and health. And mildew not only attacks the foliage, but very often also the wood. In severe cases the malady is by no means eliminated with the shedding of the leaves in Autumn; colonies of vital spores being carried over into the following season. In a season especially marked by the prevalence of mildew on outdoor roses, a deal of future trouble to the grower is in constant preparation. Roses intended for forcing and pot culture, usually suffer most. Their wood, after such a Summer, should receive a washing with copper soap, after the wood is pruned down and any time before the new growth is started. The spread of mildew on roses under field culture can, however, be kept in check to a considerable extent by a timely use of such remedies as copperine, fostite, grapedust and powdered sulphur, employed in mild but frequent applications rather than in over-doses.

Roses for Pot Culture.

If the ground in which roses, intended for forcing and to be potted up next Fall, are now making their best growth, underwent proper manipulation, before the roses were planted, very little in the way of top cultivation, beyond keeping the surface clear of weeds, will be found needful at this time of the season. Deep and frequent hoeing is not advisable. Most varieties coming under this head thrive best in heavy, well firmed soil, no more disturbed by fork or hoe than what is necessary to keep down weeds and to maintain a loose, broken up thin surface layer. Watering and sprinkling at the close of hot and windy days does much good while the roses are making a fast growth, but when this is nearing final development, unless the season is an extremely dry one, watering should be discontinued, to allow the wood to gain complete maturity. There is little sense in keeping up the regular watering until the very end of the season, as is so often seen and probably deemed necessary.

Roses for Cutting.

The blooms of any rose when cut at the proper moment are desirable material for the decorative floral artist. But the number of varieties is small that with a fair profit could be cultivated in the open for that especial purpose. Hybrid perpetual roses in well chosen varieties, favorably placed and properly cared for, produce from the second and third year after planting a rich array of choice flowers that indeed would be of high value for cutting, did they in appreciable numbers come at any other time than just in the month of roses, when there is anyway an over-abundance of everything in the line of cut flowers. Roses to be profitable or at least of some value to the commercial florist as yielders of cut blooms must bring flowers or buds of good form, size and color throughout the Summer, but especially at the season of dearth and brisk demand. Stems must be of fair length and the foliage bright and perfect. Roses with these attributes are to be found in the tea and hybrid tea classes. But the varieties combining all these qualities under open air culture are by no means plentiful, and the few that do exist do not thrive equally well in all localities; and where they do, it is owing to good culture and often to the nicest of special care.

In most climates and sections within the zone of successful rose culture, especially those favored by equable seasons and fanned by lake or ocean breezes, tea and hybrid tea roses can be grown to perfection out of doors and be safely carried through the Winters under a good covering of dry leaves. An open, porous, gritty soil suits these better than a heavy loam, and it should be liberally fertilized before and after planting, as is proper with all roses. Essential to entire success are watering and spraying during the hot Summer and the immediate removal of suckers from the stocks of grafted roses, which, especially in the first season after planting, will be a great source of annoyance. Roses on their own roots give less trouble, and some varieties should not be grown otherwise in permanent open borders.

It is not advisable to start with more than two or three good sorts, if the cut product is to be disposed of at the wholesale market. In fact, one fine kind, as for instance Maman Cochet, or at the most, both of its forms, the pink and the white, is all sufficient. This is a rose of vigorous constitution, a free and continuous producer of large, well-formed buds and flowers, and the foliage is fine. At first the stems are rather short, but they increase in length from week to week, until, at the height of the season no fault can be found on this score.

Carnations for Pot Culture.

While it is true that the shapeliest and most easily managed specimens of potted roses are those raised under continuous all time pot treatment, it is otherwise with carnations. A healthier, stouter, more compact and freer flowering carnation, ready for the pot in the Fall and quickly taking to it, is obtained by open field culture. Those retail plant growers who of late have gone in largely for potted carnations, and there are now many of them, should follow my advice, based on years of experimental experience, and plant their carnations out in the free ground of a well prepared border, instead of shifting them from pot to pot, a process deleterious to the plants and troublesome to the grower. Even now, late as it is, plants, probably now in four inch pots, may still be planted out and would soon show the unmistakable marks of betterment by field culture. Watering is only necessary in long continuing spells of very dry weather; but pinching back right along should be done until they are potted up in the Fall. If they are intended for the plant trade in Winter, coming handy as the house-varieties do even for Christmas, the potting up should take place not later than September, after which all cutting back must be discontinued; but the transfer to the house may be delayed until quite late in October. Potted carnations raised for the trade in early Spring—a time when many more could be sold than are raised—need not be potted up before November. For this trade none answer the purpose better, none are more profitable or easier to grow, than the hardy garden carnations Dwarf Vienna and Grenadin, raised from seeds the previous Spring, planted out early, potted up in November, stored away under a bench in the coolest house and cleaned and started afresh in early March. A small percentage of these two varieties comes single-flowered, but even these, when covered with flowers and buds, are attractive and far too good to throw away. Carnations taken from the rank and file of our standard forcing varieties to be worked into good potted plants for the Spring trade, are treated similar to the hardy garden sorts. There is no need of selecting the finest and newest of our forcing varieties for this kind of work. Any free flowering kind of a sturdy, compact bush form fully answers the purpose.

FRED. W. TIMME.

FOUNDED IN 1888

FLORISTS' EXCHANGE

A Weekly Medium of Interchange for Florists, Nurserymen, Seedsmen and the Trade in general

Exclusively a Trade Paper.

Entered at New York Post Office as Second Class Matter

Published EVERY SATURDAY by

A. T. DE LA MARE PTG. AND PUB. CO. LTD.

2, 4, 6 and 8 Duane Street,

P. O. Box 1697. Telephone 3765 John. **NEW YORK.**

CHICAGO OFFICE: 127 East Berwyn Avenue.

ILLUSTRATIONS.

Electrotypes of the illustrations used in this paper can usually be supplied by the publishers. Price on application.

YEARLY SUBSCRIPTIONS.

United States, Canada, and Mexico, $1.00. Foreign countries in postal union, $2.50. Payable in advance. Remit by Express Money Order Draft on New York. Post Office Money Order or Registered Letter.

The address label indicates the date when subscription expires and is our only receipt therefore.

REGISTERED CABLE ADDRESS:

Florex, New York.

ADVERTISING RATES.

One-half inch, 75c.; ¾-inch, $1.00; 1-inch, $1.25, special positions extra. Send for Rate Card showing discount of 10c., 15c., 25c., or 35c., per inch on continuous advertising. For rates on Wants, etc., see column for Classified Advertisements.

Copy must reach this office 12 o'clock Wednesday to secure insertion in issue of following Saturday.

Orders from unknown parties must be accompanied with cash or satisfactory references.

The Index to Volume XXI of the Florists' Exchange accompanies this issue as a supplement. Should you fail to receive a copy kindly advise this office.

Society of American Florists and Ornamental Horticulturists.

Department of Plant Registration.

Charles G. Roebling, Trenton, N. J., submits for registration Cattleya Charles G. Roebling; a stray seedling. Flower pure white, six inches across with slight trace of yellow in throat. Probably raised from Cattleya Harrisonæ alba Cattleya Mendelii Bluntii, which parents it resembles very much. Bulbs are eighteen inches long and two-leaved; quite strong growing. Flowers are of good substance.

Also Cattleya Kinkora, C. Mendelii Morganii × Cattleya intermedia alba. Flowers pure white, with richly colored lip. Bulbs are two-leaved, slender, about ten inches long.

WM. J. STEWART,
Secretary.

Chrysanthemum Society of America.

Special Prizes.

W. Wells of Merstham, Surrey, England, offers gold, silver gilt and silver medals for six varieties of chrysanthemums two of each on 12-inch stems. The following varieties are eligible in this competition; Mrs. H. Partridge, Mrs. D. Willis James, Merstham Crimson, Mary Ann Pockett, Beatrice May, T. Richardson, Mrs. Heaume, E. J. Brooks, Mrs. F. F. Thompson, Mrs. Wm. Knox, Mrs. J. E. Dunn and Miss May Siddon.

Prizes of $50, $25 and $10 are offered for twelve blooms on 24 inch stems, for the best seedling or sport not yet in commerce. The color to be white, pink or yellow, the name to be given by the donor of the prize.

Charles H. Totty offers prizes of $12, $8 and $5 for twelve blooms in twelve varieties, stems not over 12 inches long, introductions of 1906. Open to all.

F. R. Pierson offers a silver cup for 36 chrysanthemums, six varieties, six blooms of each, introduced in America in 1905 and 1906.

Nathan Smith & Son offer $25 for best 24 blooms of American origin, introductions of 1904, 1905 and 1906; three varieties—white, pink, and yellow eight blooms of each, shown in separate vases.

Vaughan's Seed Store offers a silver cup, value $15, for the best specimen bush chrysanthemum plant, which has not received any other award. Open to private gardeners only.

Pittsburg, Pa. DAVID FRASER, secretary.

Dayton Convention Matters.

All plans for the coming convention are nearly completed. It remains for the executive committee to finish the official program and all the arrangements will have been made for the banner convention in the history of the Society of American Florists and Ornamental Horticulturists to be pulled off at the shortest notice.

The surprises will be many. To see the wonderful illumination of Far Hills will be worth a trip across the continent alone. The great exhibit promises to be the largest we have ever had. The housing of guests is well looked after. The amusements will be many and out of the ordinary.

Prices for all accommodations will be very reasonable and the service the best to be had. All points of interest in the Middle West are easily reached from fair Dayton at reasonable figures.

It is quite a compliment to be entertained by the great National Military Home, a thing which befalls but very few societies in a decennium. The great entertainment offered by The National Cash Register Company will surpass anything ever seen by any visitor. Of this we are confident. The work on the exhibition and meeting grounds is progressing finely, and visitors will find everything necessary to modern civilization, as far as money can make it. All we have to say is, "Come, and you will never regret it. You will see much and you will learn much."

Hotels.

The headquarters during the convention will be the Hotel Algonquin. All hotels are within one square of all street cars, taking you to the exhibition grounds within ten minutes. We give here a list and prices of the leading hotels:

AMERICAN PLAN.

Hotel.	Rate per Day.	Guests.
The Algonquin	$2.50 to $5.00	300
The Beckel	3.00 to 4.00	200
The Phillips	2.00 to 2.50	150
Hotel Daytonia	1.00 to 1.50	100
The Aldine	1.00 to 1.50	25
The Vendome	1.50	25

EUROPEAN PLAN.

Hotel.	Rate per Day.	Guests.
The Atlas	$1.00 to $2.00	75
The Wehner	.50 to .75	50
The Stag Hotel	.50	25
The Urban	.50 to 1.00	60

We have also on our list a number of smaller hotels and a whole lot of private houses, prices from 50c. to 75c. for single rooms. If a sufficient number of applications are made, a camp will be established, with well-furnished, double-roof tents, four cots to a tent, at a nominal cost of from 50c. to 75c. each. Anyone wanting accommodations, if no individual arrangements are preferred, should make application as soon as possible to J. B. Heiss, President of the Florists' Club, who will see that all are accommodated to the best satisfaction of all concerned.

DAYTON FLORISTS' CLUB.

New York Botanical Garden Notes.

From the June, 1906, number of the Journal of the New York Botanical Garden we take the following items:

Professor Murrill illustrates and describes a serious fungus disease of the chestnut the ravages of which have done considerable damage to these trees in the Zoölogical Park and elsewhere, threatening the extinction of this valuable tree in and about New York city. The spraying of young trees with copper sulfate solution, or strong Bordeaux mixture in the Spring before the buds open might be of advantage in killing the spores that have found lodgment among the branches during the Winter, but the real efficacy of this treatment is so doubtful that it could not be recommended for large trees, where the practical difficulties and expense of applying it are much increased. Nursery trees should be pruned of all affected branches as soon as they are discovered, and the wounds carefully dressed with tar or paint or other suitable substance. Vigilance and care should largely control the disease among young trees. With older trees all dead and infected wood should be cut out and burned and all wounds covered without delay. Particular attention should be paid to water, soil and other conditions of culture affecting the vitality of the tree; since anything that impairs its health renders it less able to resist fungus attack.

It is possible that the conspicuous ravages of the disease about New York city are largely due to the severe and prolonged Winter of 1903-'04, during which many trees of various kinds were killed or injured. The chestnut is peculiar, moreover, in its power to sprout from the stump almost indefinitely, and most of the trees now existing in this region are descendants of trees cut for lumber many decades ago. This repeated coppicing cannot fail at length to impair the vigor of each new generation of sprouts and render them peculiarly liable to speedy infection and vigorous attack.

On the afternoon of May 23, 1906, the Torrey Botanical Club held a special meeting at the museum building in honor of the tenth anniversary of the commencement of work in the development of the New York Botanical Garden, planting having been commenced in the Spring of 1896. Dr. Henry H. Rusby, president of the club, delivered an illustrated lecture on "The History of Botany in New York City."

The advantages of the Garden are being utilized successfully in correlation with the nature study work of the public schools of New York city. Lectures on plant life, etc., under the auspices of the Board of Education, have been delivered by various members of the Garden staff, at which the attendances numbered from 450 to 850, being composed of classes from the various schools of the Bronx Borough in charge of their teachers. After the lectures the pupils were divided into convenient groups, each under the charge of a guide and demonstrator, and the topics treated of in the lectures were further illustrated and enforced by study of the museum collections, and of the living plants in the greenhouses, and out of doors, in the forest and plantations.

OUR READERS' VIEWS

More About Geraniums.

Editor Florists' Exchange:

I see that geranium expert (?) has chosen a nom de plume for himself which is certainly a misnomer. Seeing he did not have the pluck to sign his own name, he might have had the modesty to choose something less suggestive of know-it-allness than "Expertus." "Viridis" would be far nearer the mark!

He still insists that Young Beginner should plant 500 plants as stock from which to raise 4,000 geraniums. Why he should advise him to start with thirty-year-old methods is more than I can see. If he was giving Young Beginner advice regarding chrysanthemum growing, would he advise him to plant them out in the field and lift them in the Fall, as was the custom 25 or 30 years ago? Would he advise growing carnations, roses or, in fact, any of our commercial plants or flowers by those thirty-year-old methods? If not, why should he advocate antiquated methods for geranium growing? The methods of growing geraniums have changed and improved just the same as everything else in the plant line, although "Expertus" does not seem to be aware of the fact.

Of course there are "geraniums and geraniums," just as there are roses and roses, carnations and carnations, also experts and experts. Those Fall rooted cuttings which "Expertus" recommends will occupy valuable bench room for eight or nine months, will require lots of attention and some labor, and will cost the grower about as much as he gets for them. The "other geraniums," taken from greenhouse grown plants make the ideal plants. The stock must be in a warm house, not "too warm," judiciously fed, not "over-stimulated." The cuttings from those plants need no stimulating if the soil is all right, a matter which every up-to-date grower will see to. Those plants will be ready for market from March on, and will "mislead and disappoint" no one, judging from the fact that the same customers come after the same stock year after year.

I beg to inform "Expertus" that there is nothing at all wonderful about making a plant multiply itself eighty-fold; it is like everything else, easily done when you know how. Expertus does not know how; therefore he is not an expert.

"Expertus" has been doing some figuring, probably on the side of a six-inch pot with a four-penny nail, and has evidently come to the conclusion that my figures are too big; 2,000,000 does look big; nevertheless, it is about right. I have on a list before me the names of 32 growers who will average 50,000 plants each; the other half million, more or less, will be easily found among the 115 or 120 other growers who sell mixed stock in the market. I can think of only one or two growers, who do not carry geraniums. Prices for some years have been quite satisfactory. Along about the end of June and in July quite a few geraniums are sold as law as $3 or $4 per hundred; and I guess there is just as much profit, or I might say as little loss, in selling them at that price as there is in selling Fall struck stock in May at the regular price.

I shall certainly keep my eye on the question box as advised, and pick out all the "good information" I can; also amusement, seeing "Expertus" is an "occasional contributor."

Concerning that other Doubting Thomas, who modestly signs himself, "Another Green One," I must say that I think he is a hopeless case. If he has been at it for 22 years and has not found out the "trick" for himself, it would take on operation with a hammer and chisel to get it into his head. It is said that an operation of that nature is necessary to put a joke into a Scotchman's head. Anyway, "where ignorance is bliss 'tis folly to be wise."

JOHN BIRNIE.

Judges and Exhibitors.

Editor Florists' Exchange:

The importance of a wise selection in the choice of judges for flower shows can hardly be over-estimated. Past observations compel us to say candidly that on occasions judges' decisions indicate that but little importance seemed to have been connected with their selection. This remark does not at all imply that those men were not capable, each in his own particular line of work; but that admission avails nothing to an exhibitor who may have failed to get his just dues.

An example of what I refer to came under my observation last Summer at an exhibition held in a small but rather horticulturally important New England city. The judges were, as I have already intimated, capable gardeners; but that fact did not deter them from making what I and many others considered some ludicrous awards. On exhibition there happened to be three tubs of Canterbury bells. It did not take the judges long to decide to award the exhibitor $10 for this exhibit; and I heard afterward that it was even thought to award a silver medal for it. Now, in contrast to that award, I may state that at the same exhibition Messrs. Lager & Hurrell, Summit, N. J., had a table of valuable and rare orchids and Julius Roehrs Company, a table of beautiful and rare stove and greenhouse plants. Both of these exhibits were passed by almost unnoticed by the judges; and it was a question if either exhibit would have been awarded anything, if the judges' attention had not been frequently called to the objects of their neglect.

Still another illustration of the decisions of those judges (all good men, I repeat). On one side of the exhibition hall (not far from, but covering twenty times as much floor space as the Canterbury bells referred to) was a group of specimen dracænas, I should say over a hundred in number. This group was awarded $10 by the judges—just as much as was awarded for the tubs of Canterbury bells grown from seed a few months before without any extra effort.

In the cases here instanced I do not believe the judges for a moment thought of favoring one exhibitor more than another, yet their awards in all these cases would lead anyone to think that all their decisions were arrived at without a moment's thought; whereas thoughtfulness should enter into decisions nearly as much as knowledge and rapidity of discernment.

In its effect, the decision of judges may mean a great deal one way or the other to an exhibitor; and for that reason alone it is the duty of organizations to safeguard the interests of exhibitors by selecting men for judges, who are known to be familiar with the objects on exhibition; or, if as in the case of rare plants, not expected to be familiar, the judges ought to be able to discern that the plants were rare, and recognize their merit, if they had any.

Next, in my opinion, to unfair decisions, comes what I term the foolish and exacting requirements of some schedules, and the action of judges in paying attention to them. I refer to exhibits of cut flowers and fruit where stated numbers are stipulated. On more than one occasion I have seen the best exhibit disqualified because there happened to be one too many (accidentally no doubt). It is usually the custom, if not the rule, for judges to count the articles. Why then disqualify if there are too many? Instead, would it not be more equitable to extract the best individual article in exhibits having too many?

Even though judges' decisions are sometimes, as I stated, not to our way of thinking, still I believe that in all cases their decisions should be final, otherwise endless contention invariably results. And to avoid this, as well as the other evil, it should be the aim of every society, and of every officer and member individually, to make all awards according to merit only; and this can only be attained by a wise selection of judges and thoughtful deliberation on the part of the judges themselves.

From the way medals are distributed by some societies, as we see by reading the lists of awards in the horticultural press, we might suppose some of those societies had a medal factory going day and night; or else we come to the conclusion that those societies have mysterious ways of their own to attract so many worthy novelties, unknown to people elsewhere. Indiscriminate medal-giving, be they silver, bronze or even leather medals, will in time work injury, because there is no use in closing our eyes to the fact that many medals are awarded to commonplace objects, thereby making awards to things of real merit practically valueless, except intrinsically.

In the matter of certificates, ocassionally we see awards made that would lead to suppose that when judges ran up against anything that caused them to doubt what award to make, if any, they ended their deliberations by ordering a first-class certificate to be given. Now, in my opinion, certificates should at least rank next to silver medals, and should only be awarded to objects showing unusual cultural skill in development, or to things that are rare and of merit besides.

H. Y.

Reflections on Current Topics.

MR. EDITOR.—Some time ago I was honored by the receipt of a postal card from Buffalo, bearing an undecipherable signature, but which from its tenor I glean was sent by my friend Scott. He informs me that he feels flattered by the reference to himself in this column—quite natural, having been mentioned in the same breath with Job—but he assures me that his acquaintance with Constantine was never a personal one. I am willing to believe this; for Scott is not the only person who talks and writes about men and things with which he has no personal acquaintance. Yet I admire his profound knowledge of history, both sacred and profane, especially the latter.

I observe that he has been casting aspersions on my old friend Noah and his better half, assuming that they were responsible for the perpetuation of certain undesirable insects, reptiles and quadrupeds, among them the musteline carnivores of the genus Mephitis, introduced into the ark by Noah as a "cheap disinfectant" when the patriarch had "the snakes." William, I'm astonished at this sacrilege. Besides, don't you know that the genus is purely an American one, materializing long after the flood, in the Oolite period? As well blame Mrs. Noah, who was no gardener, for introducing as a culinary vegetable the Symplocarpus fœtidus, (having been deceived by its common name of skunk's cabbage) with an eye to a feast at the end of the forty days' voyage; for didn't she already have Ham?

It is always a joy to read of that perennial pleasurable event—the outing to Waretown, the littoral retreat of Commodore John Westcott. This year the event has not stimulated any original poetry, I observe, although one chronicler accompanies his description of the affair with a choice quotation from Thomson. Now The Seasons, and other productions of that Scottish poet-philosopher, make good reading; but in celebration of a Waretown outing, they fall far short of the original sonnet of J. C. Vaughan, which the surroundings of the retreat inspired. I hope some day John Westcott will invite the S. A. F. down there, so that we all may partake of his hospitality, and among other things view those wonderful mosquitoes, which, so far as I have read, have been the only creations capable of puncturing George Watson's hide successfully.

I observe that the practice of intruding the faces and figures of persons, male and female, into photographs ostensibly supposed to portray plants and flowers, is again receiving attention. One objector to the practice says: "There may be cases where a grower's portrait might appear with his productions and still seem in good taste; it is, however, quite exceptional." This assertion does not altogether harmonize with the general objection taken; for if portraits of this kind are misfits at all it would seem they would be out of place in every case. It cannot be that the writer means us to infer that presentable portraits of plantsmen or growers are the exception and not the rule, and that the "physiogs" of most of those having plants photographed would mar the beauty of any picture in which they appeared? The practice seems to me to be a harmless one. The picture business in our trade papers is overdone, anyway, in my opinion; too many of those appearing being neither remarkable for their beauty nor their instructiveness. The object of some publishers, nowadays, seems to be to pander largely to the frailty of human nature along the lines of vanity, and evidently nothing so readily accomplishes this as the appearance of portraits in the papers, even to those showing the dogs of greenhouse owners, and the latest welcome cherubs kindly brought by the stork.

I have been reading, with a good deal of enjoyment, the criticisms, illnatured and otherwise, appearing in your New England contemporary on what seemed to be a bit of wellmeant advice proffered by a Rochester (N. Y.) paper regarding the school of instruction in horticulture and landscape gardening proposed to be established by the Boston Gardeners and Florists' Club. On reflection one wonders how, without such a school, our American gardens and parks have been developed to and maintained at their present state of perfection. But a remark by R. T. McGorum, in your contemporary, is enough to dampen the ardor of the promoters of the proposed educational institution. He says "Landscape gardening is an art which very few can master thoroughly." It is to be hoped that those who take the course of instruction to be provided will form part of the "very few," or the effort will surely be in vain; for "a little learning" in landscape work is worse than none; and of this we surely have sufficient evidence now.

Another ray of hope that the wellmeant intentions of our Boston friends may not be altogether futile is afforded in a quotation made by Mr. McGorum. He says: "Catch a Scotchman when he is young, and there can be something made out of him." May it so happen that the scholars for the most part next Fall are Scotch who have not exceeded the plastic age, or whose vision has not become affected by the "Gruns of the Greybaird."

There can be no question of the praiseworthiness of the Boston club's effort to assist young gardeners to a better knowledge of their profession in all its requirements; and provided the teachers are themselves competent, good only can result from the endeavor. Yet landscape gardeners, like poets, seem to be born not made; and we have it on the authority of the poet whom Mr. McGorum delights to quote—that there are many who go into college "stirks and come out asses." (P. S. I never went to college. J.) This statement, I hope, will not bring down the wrath of the editor of your New England contemporary on the head of JOB.

Japanese Pigmy Trees.

Messrs. Barr & Sons have been exhibiting these dwarf trees for some time past, and they favor us with the following advice: "Throughout Spring and Summer keep the Thuja obtusa in an airy sunny place, such as a balcony, terrace, or on sheltered banks or staging out of doors, selecting always a situation which, though dry, is not windswept. Give water once a day if required, or it may be necessary in very dry hot weather to water the plant twice a day, just to keep the soil damp without being sodden. Rain water should be used. The plant benefits by being put out in a soft warm rain. If the thuja is kept indoors for decoration it should be placed in a sunny window, and during the night be kept out of doors. Should the atmosphere be dry and hot, a light spraying overhead with rain water should be given in the evening. The dry heat from a gas stove or open fireplace must be avoided. During Winter keep the plant in a cool greenhouse, and give a watering once a week—just sufficient to prevent the soil becoming too dry. The dwarfed pines, larches, and junipers should be treated in a similar manner to the thujas.

"Dwarfed maples should be placed out of doors in early Spring in a warm sheltered spot protected from winds, and left exposed to all weathers until in full leaf. In favored localities the plants may remain plunged out of doors all the Winter; otherwise, when their leaves are shed and the wood is ripe remove them to a cool cellar where growth will not be excited until the following Spring.

"When these Japanese dwarfed trees commence making their new growth in March, April, May and June, give a little manure in the form of bonemeal once a month; to a vase 12 inches in diameter give three or four teaspoonfuls, spreading the bonemeal evenly round the edge of the vase or pan after first disturbing the surface soil; to smaller vases give in proportion. Repotting should take place every two or three years (in February or March), and this should be done by an experienced gardener accustomed to growing and potting heaths and New Holland plants. In the process of repotting a portion of the old soil should be removed from round the edges and bottom, and the thin old roots pruned. See to the crocking, so as to insure good drainage, and spread at the bottom of the pan or vase some good turfy loam; then drop the plant carefully in, filling up with good turfy loam round the sides. The plants should be firmly potted and well rammed round the edges to prevent the escape of water, which should soak through the whole of the ball of soil. Where the pans are very shallow it is advisable to replace a portion of the old soil each Spring with some good turfy loam and leaf soil. After a few years it may be found advisable to shift the trees into larger vases or pans, but as the great object is to keep them dwarf, the smaller the vase or pan used the better. These forest trees are capable of growing to a great size, and they can only be kept in their 'Tom Thumb' condition by discouraging growth. To maintain this dwarf stature pinch back the young growth from April to June with the thumb and finger. In the case of the thujas and other conifers (except pines) pinch out the points of the young growth all over the plants so as to keep the desired shape. In the case of the pines pinch out only the irregular growths. Maples should be pinched back to two or four leaves on each shoot." —Journal of Horticulture.

The French Chrysanthemum Society holds its annual congress at Caen on November 7 and 8 next. Among the subjects to be discussed are: The sterilization of composts! apparatus to employ; alphabetical nomenclature: rules to adopt; variations or sports, means to produce and fix them; insects and maladies of the chrysanthemum; means to employ to develop the taste for chrysanthemum culture; better methods of packing chrysanthemums (cut flowers and plants in pots).

WINDOW GLASS.—Window glass factories which were in operation the first of the week have remained in blast owing to favorable weather conditions, although the June output is usually not large enough to affect the market to any considerable extent. The demand generally is light in the East, while in the Middle West and on the Pacific Coast the activity is reported as being greater.—The Metal Worker.

The Brooklyn Eagle in a recent issue reproduced a number of the "wholesome chestnuts" of our esteemed contemporary, Horticulture, under the title of "Floral Tips for the Amateur Gardener." We compliment the Editor of the Eagle on his keen discernment, and correct estimate of current horticultural information.

Kniphofia or Tritoma—Which?

Two hundred years have elapsed since the introduction of the species Aloides or Uvaria. Besides Kniphofia and Tritoma, the genus has been known as Rudolphœmeria, Triclissa, Tritomanthe and Tritomium—Kniphofia having priority and Tritoma being better known and more generally used. They are all natives of South Africa and Abyssinia, except one from Madagascar.

It seems strange that a genus so remarkably distinct, so characteristically effective, and so easily cultivated has been so long in obtaining the recognition it so worthily deserves. Fifty years ago, in England, uvaria was a telling object during October and November, in mixed borders, where it had for companions such pompon chrysanthemums as Bob, La Neige, Drin Drin, Mustapha, Riquiqui, and taller kinds like Aregina, Vesta and Pio No; besides Michaelmas daisies, hypericums, erigerons, Belladonna amaryllis, sternbergia and others. Burchelli and Rooperi were little known at that time—soon to be followed by Uvaria grandiflora and caulescens. The total number of species is nearly a score and there are now catalogued upwards of three score kinds, including hybrids. Originally tritomas were looked upon as late flowering plants only; now they may be had in flower from June to December.

Where they are to be grown depends entirely upon the convenience and desire of the planter; but they must have full sunshine, rich soil, and frequent soakings of water; or, what is better, manure water. Don't try to grow tritomas in poverty hollow.

As individual clumps on rock work or on elevations where the foliage can have equal development, they are most beautiful. Let me recommend a plan of cultivation which is not much known, or not nearly as much appreciated as it should be, and that is, to plant all the late flowering kinds in the open ground in galvanized wire baskets of not less than 14 to 18 inches in diameter. I refer especially to such varieties as grandiflora, grandis, nobilis, Saundersii and speciosa. These flower in late October and all through November. Nobilis and grandis have scapes from 6 to 8 feet high. Of course, they will be lifted before frost and become companions of chrysanthemums, as they require about the same treatment. (Makers of November schedules will please take notice, and find a place in their exhibitions for them).

All tritomas in the Western States need protection. The surest way is to dig before sharp frost, reduce the foliage, pack in boxes of soil, make firm and keep in a light cellar or storeroom, where they will be safe from frost. South of Philadelphia they are hardy.

Propagation is by division, done at any time when there is some root action.

As cut flowers tritomas are very effective in large vases combined with their own foliage, bearing in mind to keep the scapes upright or nearly so.

Growing plants in wire baskets in the open, and then transferring them into tubs, or large pots, early in October, being careful not to damage the leaves either by twisting or bruising, feeding with liquid manure, keeping the plants uniform by judiciously staking, make telling specimens for decorations of all kinds, especially so under artificial light. Such kinds as grandis, nobilis and speciosa may be had in fine shape for Christmas. Who is going to do the tritoma justice?

The following selection contains only those that are known to be distinct and of the greatest merit. Several new varieties are now being offered which promise to be acquisitions.

Uvaria (Aloides) angustifolia, very free grower, flower stems 4 feet; flowers rosy peach, distinct. October.

Grandiflora glaucescens, foliage glaucous, flowers orange red changing to deep yellow; 6 feet. October and November.

Gigantea, magnificent plant 6 to 8 feet; large, bright red, and yellow flowers, October.

Meteor, 4 feet high, long scapes of uniform apricot color; distinct and effective. September.

Nobilis, a magnificent variety, 6 to 8 feet or more in height, immense heads of bright red shaded yellow. October and November.

Rubens, most brilliant deep coral red flowers, on nearly round heads; distinct and fine. October and November.

Sanguinea robusta, scapes 4 to 5 feet high; of a rich deep crimson, extra fine and showy. October and November.

Burchelli, (species), a handsome early flowering kind, dark red, fading to orange. August and September.

Caulescens, (species), a handsome plant with with blue green foliage, scape tall, flowers greenish yellow turning red. A beautiful plant. August to October.

Comosa, (species), foliage broad and aloe-like, with flowers apricot red; distinct. August.

Grandis, (species), a very distinct pale green leaved plant, the latest to bloom. The flowers are brilliant red and bright yellow in dense heads. November.

Leichtlinii, (species), a distinct plant of medium size; scapes 2 feet high; flowers deep brownish red. This sort is peculiar, owing to the flowers opening from the top of the scape instead of the bottom, as in other species. August.

Leichtlinii distachya, distinct and beautiful; scapes 2 to 3 feet high; flowers borne in dense heads, yellow at first changing to orange red, anthers extremely long, crimson, with black tips. A remarkable variety. August.

Leichtlinii sanguinea, of medium growth; flowers deep blood red perhaps the brightest of all; fine. August.

La Perle (variety), a beautiful and most charming variety, flowers bright red with white margins changing to carmine; anthers are orange colored and the stamens black; height 3 feet. Flowers in September and October.

Sceptre d'Or (variety), a very free grower; flower stems 3 feet high of a bright purple brown color. The flowers open ochre red, with yellow margins, changing to rich orange; distinct and handsome. September and October.

Pfitzeri (variety), one of the most beautiful and the one that has done much to make the tritoma more appreciated. It is of free growth, with fine foliage; the flowers are most freely produced on scapes from 18 inches to 3 feet high. July to October or later.

Macowanii (species), a lovely plant of fine habit and exceedingly free flowering; scapes 1½ to 2 feet; flowers bright apricot and buff. July to September.

Maxima (species), foliage light green, scapes 2½ feet high, quite stout, flowers very bright scarlet. October and November.

M. grandis, a dwarf plant with flower heads nearly a foot long; orange turning to yellow; scapes 2½ feet high. August.

M. globosa, a very striking late flowering kind with pale green foliage, heads of spherical form; color richest scarlet. August.

Mutabilis (species), begins to flower in June, of dwarf habit; flower heads nearly round; color orange, yellow and white, distinct.

Natalensis (species), a tall growing, very distinct kind, with long spikes of deep red flowers. October.

Præcox (species), a very handsome plant with deep green leaves and stout spikes of bright yellow and red; flowers in May.

Rooperii (species), one of the most beautiful; vigorous growing plants with handsome recurved leaves; flower spikes very stout 2½ to 3 feet high; flowers brilliant red and yellow, intensely bright. August.

Sarmentosa (species), a very interesting dwarf growing kind; foliage glaucous and drooping; flower scapes short and stout; color red with pale yellow tips. Nearly always in flower. May to November.

Saundersii, leaves very broad, deep sea green, finely recurved; flower stems 4 to 5 feet high, deep brown; head of flowers cone-shaped, 12 inches long; color pale orange red shading to rich crimson. One of the finest. August, September and October.

Serotina (species), foliage narrow deeply serrated, upright in growth, scape 3 feet high; flower heads conical; color yellow, tipped with red, distinct. August and September.

Speciosa (Baker), a remarkable plant; flower scapes 6 to 8 feet high; heads nearly one foot long, of the most brilliant scarlet. Truly beautiful and one of the latest to flower; should be in every collection. November to December.

JOHN THORPE.

Sweet Peas Grown by W. T. Brown, Hilton, N. J.
In foreground two daughters of Mr. Brown and daughter of Professor W. G. Johnson

Sweet Peas at Hilton, N. J.

Editor Florists' Exchange:

The accompanying illustration shows a patch of sweet peas growing on the place of W. T. Brown at Hilton, N. J. It was a splendid sight to see these long rows of sweet peas in full bloom. They were higher than one's head on June 9. He was picking and selling them in the local Newark market to his special customers. The rows were over 200 feet long.

We are indebted to Professor W. G. Johnson for the photograph.

English Horticultural Notes.

A HORTICULTURAL BENEFIT AND PROVIDENT SOCIETY.—Though this society (which is entirely controlled by and confined to horticulturists) is not so strong as it deserves to be, yet it is now advancing very favorably. Last year there were 105 new members. Its invested funds amount to £27,057, and if it wound up to-morrow it could pay £27 to every one of its 1,200 members. The society dates from 1864, but for many years it made practically no progress. Its aims are to provide sick pay to members, and those that pay 3s. per month, which is the higher scale, receive 18s. per week for 26 weeks, and half this sum for other 26 weeks, should they require it. There is also a convalescent fund, which eenables a person who is recovering from an illness to go to the seaside to enjoy the bracing, recuperative air. I believe I gave a copy of the rules to Professor F. A. Waugh, of Amherst, once, when he was in London, and half anticipated that he would have been instrumental in establishing a similar society in the United States. I now enclose a copy of the annual report, together with the rules, for the editor's consideration. There is no better institution of the kind in the United Kingdom, a fact that is vouched for by the Registrar of Friendly Societies. There is no death money—no payment for funeral expenses—but then the yearly installments paid in are credited to the account of each member. Should he become a lapsed member, his account remains to his credit all the same, though he ceases to get interest upon it, and he cannot withdraw it (nor can any member) until he has reached the age of 60 years. As an instance, I have been a member five years, and have paid in £2 yearly. This covers every expense (2s. 6d. for the management fund, and usually 3s. deduction for the sick pay expenses), leaving me with a comfortable balance to my credit, and should I die, the money is paid out on production of certificate to the party to whom it is willed. These, then, briefly, are the facts in connection with the United Horticultural Benefit and Provident Society. It will be seen that to a society like this, distance makes no object; nor would it in America.

J. HARRISON DICK.

Bureau of Credit.

(Paper read before the Convention of the American Seed Trade Association, Toledo, O., June 27, 1906, by W. S. Powell of the Bureau of Credit.)

Mr. Breck, Chairman of the Bureau of Credit, Wholesale Seedsmen's League, has asked me to come here and make you a report on what the bureau has done for its members during the past year, and to explain at some length the operation of the bureau, so that those using it may be better informed concerning its methods, and also that their number may be still further augmented from the ranks of the association.

It will be remembered that for three years the members of the American Seed Trade Association enjoyed the privileges and benefits of the Bureau of Credit without expense to them; a service which increased the expenses of the league to such an extent that the directors of the league, with the approval of your executive committee, voted to ask the members of this association to each pay $10 per year in addition to the regular collection fees, to assist in maintaining the bureau; the understanding between the officers of both the league and the association being that members not subscribing the $10 would not receive the further notification sheets of the Bureau of Credit, or be entitled to its services as a collection or mercantile agency. It will be of interest to you to learn that in response to communications on this subject, some 37 members of the association subscribed, and are now among our most valued coworkers; while on the other hand the names of some 97 members of the association who have not subscribed, have, in accordance with the above mentioned understanding been removed from the list of those to whom we mail our notification sheets and furnish special information, and from whom we can receive business.

As the membership of the association comprises some 140 members who are not members of the Wholesale Seedsmen's league, it seems that the members of the American Seed Trade Association do not fully understand the workings and advantages of our system, or the number of subscribers would be very much larger. This being the case, it has been deemed advisable to bring the matter more personally and directly before you, which task it is my very pleasant duty to preform.

Work Accomplished in 1905.

Last year 53 members of the league and association sent the bureau 821 claims, aggregating $26,065.32, and we collected and remitted to the members about $12,000, of which $5,312.75 was collected through the medium of the "Demand Letter" at an expense to creditors of only $275.09, while through the "Attorney's Department" was collected $6,600 from which the income from the bureau was $232.29. As the total receipts from fees and collections and subscriptions amounted to but $877.38, while the expenses of the bureau for the year were $1,258.02, a deficit of $380.64 had to be borne by the Wholesale Seedsmen League.

General Working Plan.

Now, to turn from matters past to things present and future; if you will bear with me a very few minutes I will try to explain as briefly as possible the general working of the Bureau of Credit, and a few of the many advantages which attend its use. In the first place, considered solely as a medium for the collection of overdue accounts that are beyond the usual methods of office collection, the Bureau of Credit is unquestionably far in advance of any ordinary commercial collection agency. For one thing, for instance, in the matter of fees. As the bureau is conducted for the good of the Seed Trade, and not as a mere private money making enterprise, it is entirely consistent for it to make a charge, as it does, smaller than that of ordinary agencies. As you all know, the fee on accounts collected through the medium of the "Demand Letter" and resulting correspondence is only 5 per cent or one half the charge of any other reputable collection agency. Further than this advantage in the matter of charges there is a very marked one of special effectiveness. Through its unique relation to and peculiar position in the Seed Trade, the Bureau of Credit can handle accounts in the trade to much better advantage than any outside collection agency possibly could, through the special action it takes with debtors, which affects their whole standing in the trade. The first step taken by the bureau makes clear to a debtor that his credit with practically the whole Seed Trade is cut off until he has paid the account then under discussion. He is told that unless payment is made within a specified time he will be reported to the entire membership as a delinquent, and that firms whose names appear on the back of that notification letter will refuse to sell him further goods, except for cash, until the debt is settled; and further than this, he is notified that if the debt remains unpaid at the expiration of the time specified, the matter will be immediately turned over to attorneys at his place with instructions to take most vigorous action to enforce payment. This combination is calculated to bring even the hardest debtor to a realization of the tenderness of his position, if he buys from firms in the trade, or if he has anything that is reachable by legal process. Beyond the fear of material consequences, there is in every man a moral objection to being made known to a whole trade as a man who refuses to pay his honest debts; who is to be avoided as a customer, and not to be trusted; and this psychological effect of the bureau's first "Demand Letter" has in many cases been sufficient in itself to secure settlement from a debtor who was absolutely uncollectible by any legal process.

Aid of Attorneys.

Please bear in mind, however, that our efforts are not confined to demands by any manner of means. When a debtor fails to pay or reply satisfactorily to the first demand, his account, after our special communication with member on the subject, is placed with our corresponding attorney at debtor's place, or at the nearest point to it, the attorney being instructed to act vigorously and severely, not however, incurring expenses or entering actual suit without specific authority from us; on which point, we, in each case, get special instructions from member before authorizing such action. Through the local attorneys, debtor is coaxed and worked after the most approved fashion, and if these methods prove ineffective, the advisability of suit is reported upon to member, and legal proceedings entered if he authorizes. Any account which is any way collectible, is collected by the Attorney's Department, and at the least possible expense. The fees for collection through the services of local attor-

dollars worth of business every year, gives us a decidedly greater influence with these attorneys than would be that of a commercial house which was sending out to attorneys the comparatively small amount of business neys vary from 10 per cent. to 5 per cent. of the amount collected, according to the size of the claim, with the usual minimum attorney's fee of $2. All these fees are contingent, no charges being made where a collection is not effected.

It has been asked by members, "If a claim needs the attention of an attorney at debtor's place, what is the advantage of sending it through the Bureau of Credit, rather than to an attorney direct?" In the first place, to keep in touch with the best and most reliable attorneys requires a system and care that is a department in itself, and which no business house would feel like maintaining as a part of its regular office force. A complete system of this sort of Bureau of Credit must needs maintain all the time, keeping a list of correspondent attorneys revised and corrected so as to be in touch with the best attorney at a place at any time; replacing, whenever necessary, the names of attorneys to whom it is deemed inadvisable, for various reasons, to send further business. Further than this, it will be readily understood that the fact that we pass to local attorneys many thousands of

which any one house would have. An account coming from us unquestionably receives more prompt and careful attention than the same account would coming to the attorney from the house direct.

The local attorney understands that unless the business coming from us is given careful and proper attention, our future business will be placed with some other attorney covering his point, with whom we are in touch, who will handle it to our satisfaction.

Attorneys' Fees.

One more, and not to be overlooked advantage, will be found in the matter of attorneys' fees. We have a set schedule of fees which are agreed upon between us and attorneys, on which special basis an attorney will not handle claim from a house direct. This is also true in many cases regarding the amount of money required to be advanced by a client for costs of suit; and then there are the advantages we are frequently able to get in special cases for members which are decidedly worthy of consideration. With ordinary collection agencies these advantages, when in the form of rebates, go into the treasury of the agency as profit. With the Bureau of Credit these savings and benefits acrne directly to the member owning the claim. Are not these considerations in themselves sufficient to influence every member on purely business principles to send his collection through the Bureau of Credit in preference to any outside agency, to say nothing of the other many advantages which the bureau offers him?

Co-operation of Members Needed.

Just one thing more: While the collection of bad accounts is indeed a very important item, there is another element of the bureau's scope which should not be overlooked. It is indeed good for us to be able to collect the bad accounts which you are unfortunate enough to have already contracted, but is it not equally good to be able to help you avoid taking on accounts which are known to be bad, and over the adjustment of which some of your fellow members have had trouble in the past? One of the most important duties of the Bureau of Credit, and one which from this time forth is to receive double care and energy, is the advice to members through our frequently issued notification sheets of delinquent debtors; bad pay, wrangling-over-condition, chronic-kicker, habitual-allowance-claimer, etc.; but in this matter, as in all others, we need every member's individual co-operation. If each firm represented here will send in to the Bureau of Credit for dissemination among the other members of this association, the names of the unsatisfactory buyers, bad pay customers, etc., it comes in contact with, we can cover the trade most thoroughly; and it is the question of a very short time when each member will find himself personally saved actual money by the warning of some other member's experience with which we acquaint him, that will certainly more than repay him for the small trouble he has gone to to do his share in this good work; leaving out of consideration the immense service he is rendering to the trade in general and to the members of this association in particular. Under the terms of its charter the Bureau of Credit is legally authorized to conduct a general mercantile agency business, in addition to the foregoing, which enables us to furnish members upon application with special reports on persons desiring credit at their hands.

To conclude we want the members to feel that every resource of the Bureau of Credit—the whole system, the working force, the position of influence which the bureau occupies in the collection world—are all at the disposition of each and every member, whether his accounts are large or whether they are small, whether they are many or whether they are few. We want every one individually to lend us the weight of his co-operation to the extent of passing through the Bureau of Credit whatever accounts he is obliged to go outside of his office force to collect. We do not ask for something that is to be unprofitable. We simply want the chance to benefit every member of this association. We want to save him actual money and give him better results than he can get through any other medium. We are doing it right now for others, and we can do it just as surely for you; and we will if you but furnish us with the opportunity.

Establishment of William Sim, Cliftondale, Mass.

THE AMERICAN SEED TRADE ASSOCIATION

TOLEDO (O.) CONVENTION

REPORT OF PROCEEDINGS CONCLUDED

The first business on Thursday morning was the adoption of the recommendation of the Executive Committee that a certain amount be placed at the disposal of the transportation committee for the furtherance of their work during the ensuing year.

H. W. Wood presented the report of the committee on President's address recommending that Mr. Page be reimbursed for his expense in attending the conference with the florists' and nurserymen's associations, and that G. B. McVay be repaid initiation fee and annual dues advanced by him in pursuance of the membership of the American Seed Trade Association and the American Merchants' and Manufacturers' Association.

In regard to the registration bureau, the committee recommended the following:

"WHEREAS the Department of Agriculture has about decided to allow Professor W. W. Tracy to devote most of his time to preparing lists and descriptions of standard varieties of vegetables.

"BE IT RESOLVED that a committee of five be appointed by the chair at this session to have discretionary powers in co-operating with Professor Tracy and to decide whether these descriptions, as amended and approved by the committee, shall be presented at the next annual meeting for the approval of this association; the committee also to have discretionary powers to make recommendations as to further work along this and the kindred lines named in President Grenell's address in regard to the registration bureau."

With respect to the recommendation of the president in regard to experiment stations many recommended that the same be referred to the committee on experiment stations.

In regard to the literary committee proposed the committee stated that Mr. Willard would make a statement with respect to that, and they believed it could be worked with the National Council of Horticulture.

The various recommendations of the committee were adopted.

Messrs. Wood, Willard, Woodruff, Cropp and Burpee were appointed a committee on registration bureau.

Invitations were extended to hold the next annual meeting in the cities of Chicago, Denver, Louisville, Niagara Falls, Milwaukee and Norfolk. Final action on these invitations is vested in the executive committee. A straw vote was taken as expressing the preference of the association, resulting however in no decisive expression, the votes being scattered, the largest number for any one point being recorded in favor of New York.

An invitation was received from the National Cash Register Company extending the courtesy of the management to the convention, and asking that a visit be made to their plant. Owing to lack of time the invitation was not accepted, but suitably acknowledged.

The following report by the Committee on Government Free Seed Distribution, Henry W. Wood, chairman, was received and unanimously adopted:

"RESOLVED that we endorse heartily the action taken by the Agricultural Committee of the House and also the Agricultural Committee of the Senate in opposition to the continuance of the distribution by the U. S. Department of Agriculture of the common varieties of garden and flower seeds.

"We consider it beneath the dignity of the representatives of the U. S. Government to distribute packets of seeds that can be bought at any village store.

"We are thoroughly in sympathy with the action of the National Grange and the other organizations representing the agricultural and horticutural interest of the country in condemning the Congressional free seed distribution as now conducted."

The special committee on seed adulteration, Messrs. Albert McCullough and Henry Nungesser, reported that in the short time allowed them they had been unable to formulate a satisfactory report, and asked that a standing committee be continued on this subject and a vigorous campaign waged against seed adulteration.

Mr. Wood believed that probably injustice had been done to many innocent seed dealers who have been published by the Department of Agriculture as selling adulterated seed. Mr. Wood discussed the bill introduced by Hon. South Trimble on the subject of seed adulteration. Mr. Wood believed that at present there are few people in this country who will knowingly mix products; although such a practice has prevailed in the past to some extent, it is to-day looked down upon by all in the trade. On the other hand, too stringent regulation is unjust, inasmuch as seeds are not put up hermetically as are canned foods, and there is much difficulty in locating the responsibility for adulteration, if any. The short time during which many seed commodities must be handled precludes the use of such elaborate machinery as was recommended by Mr. Trimble. Mr. Wood believed that if any attempt was made by dealers generally to send samples in for inspection as suggested by Mr. Trimble's Bill, that the facilities of the Department of Agriculture would be utterly inadequate to the task of examining and reporting on same.

Mr. Green, of Chicago, thought that the penalty for selling adulterated seeds should fall only on the people who are proven to be guilty, and that the innocent should not suffer with the guilty.

L. L. May made a strong speech in favor of sustaining all movements from whatever source they came that would tend to repress adulteration and maintain the integrity of the seed business. He believed that the entire seed trade had been benefited by the honest efforts made by the Government along the line of pure product.

Mr. Wood, of Kentucky, affirmed that he was in entire sympathy with every movement of the kind, but thought an injustice had been done in particular cases, no doubt, unwittingly.

Mr. May hoped that the Department would pursue its work still further and include the whole category of peas, beans, corn and everything else.

On motion of Mr. Willard, a vote of thanks was extended to Mr. Horace J. McFarland and Professor W. W. Tracy for their interest in the work of the association and the papers which they presented.

On motion of Mr. Burpee, the thanks of the convention were voted to the Toledo daily papers for courtesies extended; also to the local seedsmen of Toledo for their magnificent entertainment of the convention.

Captain Burnet Landreth during the convention related an interesting case of extraordinary vitality in radish seed, 50 per cent. of which grew after twenty years, storage in the Polar regions.

Another matter which Captain Landreth brought forward was a suggestion that a color scale be formulated and adopted by the Association, embracing, say a range of from 100 to 150 shades of the primary colors, each shade to be numbered. The suggestion was favorably received and on motion of Albert McCullough a committee of three was appointed to consider the matter and to report at the next annual meeting. Captain Landreth's idea is that the chart could be gotten up very cheaply and sold, say at as low as 5c., so that the means will be provided for accurate descriptions of colors of plants, flowers, fruit, etc., which in time might become nationally and perhaps internationally adopted. Mr. Page suggested as a practical difficulty that might arise the liability of the colors to fade, but Captain Landreth thought this could be easily provided for, inasmuch as the chart will be furnished so cheaply that a new supply could be obtained at any time.

Following the formal adjournment of the convention, when all present were invited into the parlors of the Boody House and Messrs. Burpee and Willard having escorted past President Grenell into the presence of the company assembled to do him honor, Albert McCullough, on behalf of the entire company, presented Mr. Grenell with an elegant cut glass punch bowl and glasses, the bowl resting on a mirrored base bordered with silver, accompanying the gift with appropriate remarks, to which Mr. Grenell gracefully responded.

In giving list of speakers at banquet, obtained in advance, the name of the toastmaster, W. H. Moorehouse, of Toledo, was inadvertently omitted.

Among the seedsmen present at the Toledo, (O.) convention the following were not included in the list published in our columns last week:

Adams, T. Lee, Kansas City, Mo.
Brown, Alfred J., Alfred J. Brown Seed Co., Grand Rapids, Mich.
Boller, Chas. A., Stecher Lith. Co., Rochester, N. Y.
Cropp, Carl, Vaughan's Seed Store, Chicago and New York.
Clark, C. S., Wakeman, O.
Collins, P. V., Northwestern Agriculturist, Minneapolis, Minn.
Crumbaugh, E. N., Crumbaugh & Kuehn, Toledo, O.
Clark, Arthur, E. B. Clark Co., Milford, Conn.
Dennison, Edward A., W. A. Dennison Seed Co., Ellisburg, N. Y.
Dennison, A. P., W. A. Dennison Seed Co., Ellisburg, N. Y.
Dungan, Edward C., Wm. Henry Maule, Philadelphia, Pa.
Dickinson, O. H. Springfield, Mass.
Davis, G. N., The Albert Dickinson Co., Chicago, Ill.
Edgerton, Geo. B., Harvey Seed Co., Buffalo, N. Y.
Fonda, W. T., Mandeville & King Co., Rochester, N. Y.
Goodwin, A. H., W. W. Barnard Co., Chicago, Ill.
Gillespie, J. L., American Seed Co., Detroit, Mich.
Gitteau, Abner, W. H. Moorhouse & Co., Toledo, O.
Keller, Jno. C., C. A. King & Co., Toledo, Ohio.
Kreagler, Geo. A., The Toledo Seed Co., Toledo, O.
Kipping, L. A., Archias Seeds, Sedalia, Mo.
Ludwig, T. J., The Livingston Seed Co., Columbus, O.
Leonard, S. F., Leonard Seed Co., Chicago, Ill.

C. E. Kendel, Secy.-Treas.

Henry W. Wood, President.

C. B. McVay, Second Vice-President.

J. H. Ford, Asst. Secy.

OFFICERS OF THE AMERICAN SEED TRADE ASSOCIATION.

Mangelsdorf, A. F., Mangelsdorf Bros. Co., Atchison, Kan.
Massie, C. C., Northrup, King & Co., Minneapolis, Minn.
Mayer, Fred, J. F. Zahm & Co., Toledo, Ohio.
Nicholson, Robert, Texas Seed & Floral Co., Dallas, Tex.
Norton, E. J., Greenfield, O.
Nungesser, Henry, Henry Nungesser & Co., New York, N. Y.
Pommer, R. W., D. I. Bushnell & Co., St. Louis, Mo.
Philipps, W. T., Toledo, O.
Philipps, Chas. J. S., H. Philipps Seed & Impt. Co., Toledo, O.
Philipps, Fred G., H. Philipps Seed & Impt. Co., Toledo, O.
Reeves, W. A., Leonard Seed Co., Chicago, Ill.
Scarlett, Wm. G., Wm. G. Scarlett & Co., Baltimore, Md.
Scoville, Louis P., Ravenswood Exchange Bank, Chicago, Ill.
Sperry, F. P., The Livingston Seed Co., Columbus, O.
Smith, C. W., Leonard Seed Co., Chicago, Ill.
Theilmann, E. E., The Theilmann Seed Co., Erie, Pa.
White, Frank B., Pres't. White's Class Advg. Co., Chicago, Ill.
Zentz, J. M., Leonard Seed Co., Chicago, Ill.

Little Girls' Race.

P. J. Foley Awarding the Prizes.

The Outing of The Chicago Florists' Club.

President-Elect Henry W. Wood.

Henry W. Wood, the president-elect of The American Seed Trade Association, is the present head of the well known firm of T. W. Wood & Sons, Richmond, Va. His active connection with the seed business dates back to the year 1879, at which time his father, the late T. W. Wood, founded the present business. The elder Mr. Wood continued as the head of the firm up to the time of his death, last year, but during the latter years of his life had practically given over the active management to his sons. From the very incipiency of this business, Henry W. Wood has always been actively engaged in it. In fact, the business was originally started from the desire of Henry in his boyhood days to learn and follow the seed business as an occupation. T. W. Wood having been engaged in the grain and seed business in England, and, after coming to this country, having engaged in farming, the experience obtained in this way gave a most excellent foundation for the starting of the present business.

The president-elect has always taken an active part in agricultural and business affairs, and was for two years president of the Virginia State Agricultural Society, conducting while in office a most successful ten-day exposition. He is at present a member of the Board of Directors of the Richmond Chamber of Commerce, also a member of the Richmond Grain and Cotton Exchange. He has been quite active in all matters pertaining to the interests of the seed trade, the firm of T. W. Wood & Sons having joined the American Seed Trade Association almost at its beginning. He is a member of the Board of Directors of the Wholesale Seedsmen's League, and took quite an active part in the campaign which was carried on against the free seed distribution during the present year.

Assistant Secretary J. H. Ford.

J. H. Ford, assistant secretary of the American Seed Trade Association, is the son of the late Frank Ford, seedsman, of Ravenna, O., in which city he was born on April 30, 1864. He was graduated from Ravenna High School in 1880, and in May, 1883, was taken into partnership by his father, the firm (now the Ford Seed Company) being styled Frank Ford & Son.

Mr. Ford has been identified with the seed and nursery trades ever since he was old enough to take an active part in business. Since the death of his father in 1897 he has been the manager of the seed house bearing his name, and is a hard worker in his chosen profession.

In November, 1885, Mr. Ford was married to Miss Edie Simons. He has been identified with the Disciple Church since February, 1885, and has been active in church, Sunday school, and Christian Endeavor work, having held various offices in all of these; at present he is elder and clerk of the church.

Chicago.

News Notes.

The extreme temperature which prevailed in the West last week produced an overwhelming effect on the participants in trade and the question of vacations was a prominent one. Side trips of temporary duration are evidently the plans of many of the leaders, with the general assurance of a very large representation at Dayton in August.

The family of W. E. Lynch, of E. H. Hunt's left for the East this week where they will spend the Summer visiting different New England points until their return in September.

The latter part of last week the Chicagoans who attended the Toledo convention of the American Seed Trade Association returned, accompanied by L. L. May, of St. Paul, Minn.; J. T. Buckbee, of Rockford, Ill.; and W. Atlee Burpee of Philadelphia, who is on his way to the Pacific coast. The consensus of opinion of those in attendance was that the meeting was a grand success and that the recent impetus given to the activity of the association's endeavors augurs well for its future prosperity.

Vaughan's Seed Store has received the first shipment of freesia bulbs, the California refracta and the new freesia Purity, both varieties being in excellent condition.

A letter received from P. J. Hauswirth reports the probability of his return to Chicago this week, and as there is no absolute need among the florists of San Francisco at the present time he suggests that the "Relief Fund" disposition be held in abeyance for the present. It is expected that at the meeting of the club next Thursday evening a full report will be made by the president as to the conditions in the stricken district and action taken as to the disposition of the funds.

J. A. Budlong's new houses in Bowmanville, which were erected and planted within a few weeks, the stock being one year old American Beauty plants taken from another range, are now showing a superb growth, giving every promise of most satisfactory results, cutting commencing at perhaps six weeks' distance. The grafted Bride, Bridesmaid and Richmond, (especially the latter), to which some of the new and a number of the old houses are to be devoted, could not be in a more satisfactory condition. At the present time this range is producing some high grade carnations for this season of the year, and the field plants for the coming year are very satisfactory. Though at an increased expense it is believed that the practice of growing the plants in plunged pots will prove profitable owing to more immediate and permanent establishment at the time of benching.

The Chicago Rose Company have been very successful in handling Lilium candidum and have, outside of present receipts, some excellent stock in storage.

The picnic given by the Chicago Florists' Club was such a pronounced success that there is a possibility of its being duplicated during the season, and there is more than a probability of an outing by the Retailers' Association, though just what form it will assume is yet to be decided.

Monday inaugurated the Summer season and the early closing hour is in vogue.

John P. Degnan, secretary of the Chicago Rose Company, has retired from active work in connection with the concern, and will soon start West for a vacation trip and a good rest, probably going as far as the Pacific coast. On his return to Chicago he expects to take up a connection with the line of business with which he has so long been identified, but possibly in a different form.

Mrs. C. I. Stewart returned from Omaha last week accompanied by Mr. Stewart's mother, who will spend the Summer in Chicago.

H. P. Rentfrew of St. Joseph, Mich., the candidum king, has been in town and quite active in forcing the sale of his favorite flower.

Frank A. Benthey, of New Castle, Ind., son of F. F. Benthey of the Benthey-Coatsworth Company, and secretary of the New Castle Florists' Club, was in town the first of the week. He reports the young stock in the greenhouses in excellent condition and the prospects of the local club, now numbering upwards of thirty members, as very promising when they reopen their rooms in September.

The J. B. Deamud Company having just settled up balancing their semi-annual accounts, report an unexpectedly satisfactory business, which is evidently the result of the indefatigable endeavors of the members of the house.

At Peter Reinberg's the planting of roses is practically completed and at this season the plants never looked better, especially noticeable being the three houses of their new seedling Mrs. Marshall Field, which are in perfect condition and give promise of wonderful results later in the year.

Even at the low ebb which prevails in the general lines C. W. McKellar reports a very satisfactory call for cattleyas, of which he is still carrying a good line.

Field daisies at one dollar per thousand are still in demand, large quantities being handled daily.

John Risch had a narrow escape Sunday evening, when driving his automobile to the garage. When turning into Thirty-third street boulevard he struck the curb and nearly overturned the machine, the only material damage, however, being a bursted tire.

Monday and Tuesday last Charles T. Neiglick moved from his old established stand at 239 North State street, corner of Chestnut, to his newly equipped establishment across the street, where may be seen one of the most perfectly up-to-date flower stores in the city.

Though some returns have been received from the Wietor-Sinner fishing expedition, they have not been heavy enough to affect the market price.

WILLIAM K. WOOD.

Phoenix Roebelenii

THE MOST GRACEFUL PALM OF ALL.

We have almost the entire stock of it in America.

SEEDLINGS, $5.00 per 100; $40.00 per 1000; $350.00 per 10,000. 4 in. pot plants, about 1 foot high; 12-15 leaves, $1.00 each; $80.00 per 100; $750.00 per 1000. 7 in. pot plants, about 2-2½ feet high, $5.00 each; $40.00 per 10; $350.00 per 100.

SPECIMEN PLANTS, $7.50-$10.00.

We also offer for sale—STOVE PLANTS, CALADIUMS, CROTONS and DRACAENAS in finest varieties at reasonable prices.

JOHN LEWIS CHILDS

FLORAL PARK - - - - - L. I., N. Y.

Mention The Florists' Exchange when writing.

FERNS IN FLATS

Now ready for 2 1-2 inch pots. Flats contain over 100 clumps, which can be divided. Varieties include ASPIDIUM TSUSSEMENSE, CRYTOMIUM FALCATUM, PTERIS MAYII, P. WIMSETTI, P. NANA COMPACTA, P. ADIANTOIDES, P. SERRULATA, LASTREAS, etc.

PRICES, $2.00 PER FLAT; 20 OR MORE FLATS AT $1.75.

CASH WITH ORDER FROM UNKNOWN PARTIES.

McHUTCHISON & CO.

17 Murray Street NEW YORK CITY

Mention The Florists' Exchange when writing.

FERNS.

NEPHROLEPIS BARROWSII, 2½ in. pots, $10.00 per 100.

NEPHROLEPIS SCOTTII, 4 in. pots, $15.00 per 100.

ASPARAGUS PLUMOSUS, 4 in. pots, $10.00 per 100.

HUGH GRAHAM CO.,

Logan Nurseries, York Road and Louden Street, PHILADELPHIA, PA.

Mention The Florists' Exchange when writing.

FERNS

You Must Have

Only 5000 left. Speak quick.

Bostons, 5 in., 20c.; 4 in., 15c., 3 in., ready for 4 in., 10c.

Piersonii, 5 in., 20c.; 4 in., 15c.; 3 in., 10c.

Scottii, 4 in., 15c.; 3 in., 10c.; **Foster**, 2½ in., 4c.

Baby Rambler Roses, 5 in., 20c.; 4 in., 15c.

Hydrangea Otaksa and Shasta Daisy, $2.50 per 100.

English Ivy, large leaved, 3½ in., long vines, 6c.

Started Caladiums, $5.00 per 100.

Asparagus Plumosus Nanus, 3½ in., 6c.; 2½ in., $2.50 per 100.

Asparagus Sprengerii, 3½ in., 6c.

2000 Mums left, 2½ in. pot plants. List free.

Cash please.

BENJAMIN CONNELL, West Grove, Pa.

Mention The Florists' Exchange when writing.

Adiantum Cuneatum

From 3 in. pots ready to shift, per 100 $5.00 per 1,000, $45.00

From 2½ in. pots ready to shift, per 100 $4.00; per 1000, $35.00.

Adiantum Hybridum

Similar to Croweanum. From 4 in. pots ready to shift, per 100, $10.00.

Seedlings in flats, nice clumps which can be divided and ready for 2½ in pots, per flat, $2.50.

Asparagus Sprengeri

In 2½ in. pots. Nice plants. Per 100, $2.50; per 1,000, $20.00

O. V. ZANGEN

Seedsman HOBOKEN, N. J.

Mention the Florists' Exchange when writing.

EMERSON C. McFADDEN

Wholesale Grower

Asparagus Plumosus Nanus, Etc.

Short Hills, N. J.

Tel. 28 A.

Mention The Florists' Exchange when writing.

NEPHROLEPIS SCOTTII

Small plants from the benches, $5.00 per 100; $50.00 per 1000. Plants large enough for 6 in. pots, $25.00 per 100. Plants large enough to go in 7 and 8 in. pots, $50.00 per 100.

Asparagus Plumosus Nanus, 2½ in., fine plants, $3.00 per 100.

JOHN SCOTT,

Rutland Road and East 45th Street;

BROOKLYN, N. Y.

Telephone 2890 Bedford.

Mention The Florists' Exchange when writing.

FERNS OUR SPECIALTY

CIBOTIUM SCHIEDEI

We have a large stock of this beautiful tree fern in 3 in. pots, ready for a shift, at $25.00 per 100. 25 plants at 100 rate.

FERN SEEDLINGS FROM FLATS

Eight to ten best market varieties at $1.00 per 100, or $8.50 per 1000. If by mail add 10c. for each hundred plants.

ASSORTED FERNS FOR DISHES

From 2¼ in. pots. The best and hardiest varieties in market at $3.00 per 100, or $25.00 per 1000. 250 plants at 1000 rate.

Adiantum Cuneatum, 2¼ in. pots, $3.50 per 100, $30.00 per 1000.

FERN SPORES

Gathered from our own stock. 35c. per trade package, $4.00 per doz. packages.

Gardenia Vietchii from 2¼ in. pots. $7.50 per 100, $70.00 per 1000; 500 at 1000 rate.

ANDERSON & CHRISTENSEN,

SHORT HILLS, N. J.

Mention The Florists' Exchange when writing.

FERN SEEDLINGS

FROM FLATS.

The first crop is now ready for potting, including the following varieties: Pteris Cretica Cristata, Pteris Cretica Albo-Lineata, Pteris Adiantoides, Pteris Argyraea, Pteris Mayii, Cyrtomium Falcatum, Aspidium Tsussemense, Onychium Japonica, Doodia Aspera. My selection, $1.00 per 100; $8.50 per 1000. If by mail, add 10c. per 100 for postage.

Mixed Ferns for dishes, 2¼ in., $3.00 per 100; $25.00 per 1000; 250 at 1000 rate; 3 in., $6.00 per 100.

Adiantum Cuneatum, 3 in., $6.00 per 100.

FRANK N. ESKESEN, MADISON, N. J.

Mention The Florists' Exchange when writing.

NEPHROLEPIS

Whitmani, 2¼ in., $25.00 per 100.

Boston Ferns, 2¼ in., $3.00 per 100.

Henry H. Barrows & Son, Whitman, Mass.

FERNS

Are now in fine shape. A good variety and nice bushy stock, 2½ in., $3.00 per 100; $25.00 per 1000.

Kentia Belmoreana, 4 in., clean and bushy, 25c.

Cocos Weddeliana, 10c.

Dracaena Indivisa, 4 in., strong, 12c.

Mme. Sallerol Geraniums, 2 in., $2.00 per 100.

English Ivy, 4 in., fine stock, $10.00 per 100.

H. WESTON, HEMPSTEAD, N. Y.

FERNS

8 in. Scottii Ferns, 40c. 8000 6 in. Boston Ferns, 40c. Large pans Boston Ferns, $1.00; $1.50; $2.00; $2.50. No C.O.D. Cash or reference.

W. C. SMITH,

61st & Market Sts. PHILADELPHIA, PA.

Mention The Florists' Exchange when writing.

O. K. ORCHIDS

A large shipment of CATTLEYA TRIANAE just arrived in splendid condition. This Cattleya is the most valuable one of all, because it blooms at Christmas time when flowers are expensive. In original cases, write for prices; cheaper in large quantities. Cash or satisfactory New York references required.

JOHN De BUCK,

Collector of Orchids,

P. O. Box 78. COLLEGE POINT, L. I., N. Y.

Mention The Florists' Exchange when writing.

ORCHIDS

Largest Importers, Exporters, Growers and Hybridists in the world.

Sander, St. Albans, England

and

235 Broadway, Room 1, New York City

Mention The Florists' Exchange when writing.

ORCHIDS

Arrived, large shipments of Cattleya Gigas and Cattleya Speciosissima, C. Mossiae, C. Percivaliana.

Write for Prices.

LAGER & HURRELL, Summit, N. J.

Growers and Importers

Mention The Florists' Exchange when writing.

COCOS PALMS.

Strong 2½ inch at $1.50 per dozen. Write for lowest prices on Kentias.

Jas. F. Barclay R. I. GREENHOUSES Pawtucket, R. I.

A FEW GOOD THINGS YOU WANT

Dracaena Indivisa, 4 and 5 in., $10.00 and $25.00 per 100.

Alternanthera, red and yellow, 2 in. pots, $2.00 per 100

Asparagus Sprengeri, 2 in., $2.50 per 100.

Geraniums, S. A. Nutt, Castellane, John Doyle, Perkins, Double Gen. Grant, Poitevine, Mme. Salleroi, 2 in. pots, $2.00 per 100; 3 in. pots $4.00 per 100.

Vinca Var., 2 in., $2.00 per 100; 3 in., $4.00 per 100.

Rex Begonia, nice plants, 2 and 3½ in., $6.00 per 100.

COLEUS, Verschaffeltii and Golden Bedder 2 inch, $2.00 per 100.

Cigar Plant, Heliotrope, Blue Ageratum, Lemon Verbena, Verbenas and Scarlet Sage, 2 in., $2.00 per 100. Cash with order.

GEO. M. EMMANS, Newton, N. J.

Mention The Florists' Exchange when writing.

LOOK HERE--BARGAINS

Cannas, Burbank and Henderson, big, strong, plants, 10 to 16 in. high at $3.50 per 100. **Geraniums**, mixed, 2 in. pots, $1.75 per 100. **Cuphea and Feverfew**, 2 in. pots, 75c per 100. **Selaginella Denticulata**, 2 in. pots, $1.25 per 100. **Moonvines**, strong, 2 in. pots, $1.00 per 100. **Moonvines**, from soil, 60c per 100. **Cryptomeria Japonica**, 2 in., $3.00 per 100.

E. I. Rawlings, Quakertown, Pa.

Mention The Florists' Exchange when writing.

SMILAX PLANTS.

Strictly No. 1 plants; from 2 in. pots, $1.00 per 100; $9.00 per 1000. Seedlings from boxes, $4.00 per 1000.

R. KILBOURN, CLINTON, N. Y.

Mention The Florists' Exchange when writing

		Per 100
Asparagus Plumosus,	2¼ in. pots,	$2.50
" **Sprengerii**,	" " "	2.00
Smilax........................	" " "	1.50

J. S. BLOOM,

RIEGELSVILLE, PA.

Mention The Florists' Exchange when writing.

REMEMBER

We are still Headquarters for

BAY TREES BOX TREES

...EVERGREENS...

Price Lists on application.

JULIUS ROEHRS CO.,

Exotic Nurseries, Rutherford, N. J.

Mention The Florists' Exchange when writing.

ROBERT CRAIG & CO.

ROSES, PALMS, CROTONS

CARNATIONS and Novelties in DECORATIVE PLANTS

Market and 49th Sts. PHILADELPHIA, PA.

Mention The Florists' Exchange when writing.

Decorative Plants

Latania Borbonica, 2¼ in. pots, $3.00; 3 in., $6.00; 4 in., $15.00 per 100. Large specimen plants from $2.00 to $5.00 each.

Kentia Belmoreana and Forsteriana, 2¼ in. pots, $8.00; 3 in., $15.00; 5 in., $50.00 per 100; 6 in., $15.00 per doz.; 7 in. and upward, $1.75 to $35.00 each.

Areca Lutescens, 3 in. $10.00; 4 in, $20.00 per 100; 6 in., $1.00 each and upward.

Pandanus Utilis, 2 in. pots, $3.00; 4 in., $20.00 per 100.

Phoenix Reclinata, 5 in. pots, $25.00 per 100.

Phoenix Canariensis, fine specimen plants, from $3.00 to $35.00 each.

Araucaria Excelsa, 5 in. pots, $65.00 per 100.

Assorted Ferns, 2¼ in. pots, $3.00 per 100.

Nephrolepis Compacta, 3 in. pots, $8.00; 4 in., $15.00 per 100.

Plants in Fine Condition.

JOHN BADER, Troy Hill, Allegheny, Pa.

Mention The Florists' Exchange when writing.

PLANT CULTURE

PRICE, $1.00.

The best book for the plant grower.

A. T. DE LA MARE PTG. & PUB. CO. LTD.

2-8 Duane Street, New York.

Bargains in CHOICE PLANTS

Asparagus Plumosus from 2½ in. pots, $5.00 per 100; 3½ in. pots, $10.00 per 100; 4½ in. pots, $20.00 per 100.

Pandanus Veitchii, 5 in. pots, $5.00 per doz.; 6 in. pots, $8.00 per doz.

Pandanus Sanderi, 6 in. pots, $1.00 each; 6½ in., $1.50 each; 7 in., $2.00 each.

Dracæna Terminalis, 5 and 5½ in. pots, $6.00 per doz.

Dracæna Terminalis, 4 in. pots, $3.00 per doz.

English Ivy, from 4 in. pots, $2.00 and $2.50 per doz.; $15.00 per 100. About 3 feet high and bushy.

Anthericum, variegated, per doz., $1.50; per 100, $12.00.

Gloxinias, in bloom, fine plants, $2.00 per doz.

Boston Ferns, 5 in. pots, $3.00 per doz.; 6 in. pots, $9.00 per doz.; 7 in. pots, $12.00 per doz.

Kentia Belmoreana and Forsteriana, $3.00, $4.00, $5.00, $6.00 per doz.; also by the 100. Also $1.00, $1.50, $2.00, $2.50, $3.00 each and by the doz.

Larger plants, combination, $6.00, $7.00, $8.00, $10.00, $12.00, $15.00, $18.00, $30.00 each.

Dracæna Fragrans, $6.00, $9.00, $12.00 per doz., 6 in., 6½ and 7 in. pots.

Latania Borbonica, $4.00, $5.00, $6.00 per doz., also by the 100.

Phœnix Canariensis, large plants, 6½ to 7 feet high, 11 in. pots, $12.00 to $14.00 per pair.

Scottii Fern, $7.00 per doz.

Bird's Nest Fern, large plants, 6½ in. pots, $1.50 each, $18.00 per doz.

Araucaria Excelsa, 50c., 75c., $1.00, $1.50, $2.00, $2.50 each.

Cut Flowers of Gardenias, $2.00 per doz. Also plants in pots, nice and bushy, one year old, $9.00 per doz., $65.00 per 100.

Aspidistra, green, $1.00 per pot, 10 to 12 leaves.

Cut Flowers of Lily of the Valley, $4.00 and $5.00 per 100.

Boxwood Pyramids, in pots, $1.50, $2.00 and $2.50 a pair; fine plants. Other sizes sold out.

Bay Trees, Pyramids.
55-60 in. high from top of tub, $14.00 per pair
65-70 in. high from top of tub, 15.00 per pair
72 in. high from top of tub, 18.00 per pair
84 in. high from top of tub, 20.00 per pair

Bay Trees, Standards. (with 4 feet stems.)
32 in. diameter of crown, $14.00 per pair
36 in. diameter of crown, 16.00 per pair

Peat for Orchid Planting, $2.00 per sack, containing one barrel.

Leaf-Mold, $1.00 per bag.

State if you want plants shipped without pots.

Cash with order or satisfactory New York references required.

ANTON SCHULTHEIS
19th St. & 4th Avenue, COLLEGE POINT, L. I., N. Y.

Mention The Florists' Exchange when writing.

LOOK! See Us Grow.

ARAUCARIA EXCELSA a specialty. 6,000 are in now, imported from Ghent, Belgium this Spring, 1906. Now planted in 5½ and 6 in. pots, well established, and ready for shipment to all parts of America. All these are grown for us by an Araucaria Specialist in Ghent, Belgium. **NO SEEDLINGS**, but Araucarias raised from top cuttings only are offered. This is now our 11th Anniversary, and our importations have grown from 250 in the first year to the remarkable number of **6,000 IN THE ELEVENTH YEAR.** My reputation as Araucaria Importer gains footway in every greenhouse and florist store in America. Our Araucarias need no *coaxing*, genuine facts tell in quality and cheapness.

Please Note Our Lowest Prices

10 to 12 in. high, 2-yr. old, 3 tiers, 5½ in. pots, $0.50; 12 to 14 in. high, 3 to 4 tiers, 5½ in. pots, $0.60; 14 to 16 in. high, 3-yr., 3 to 4 tiers, 6 in. pots, $0.75; 18 to 20 in., 3-yr., 4 to 5 tiers, 6 in. pots, $1.00; 20 to 40 in., 4-yr. old; 6 in. pots, 5 to 6 tiers, $1.25.

ARAUCARIA EXCELSA SPECIMEN, 7 in. pots, 3 to 4 feet high, $3.00 each.

ARAUCARIA COMPACTA ROBUSTA, 6 to 7 in. pots, unusually large, very beautiful, from $1.25, $1.50, $1.75, $2.00 each. **GLAUCA**, 6 in. pots, $1.00, $1.25, $1.50 each.

KENTIA FORSTERIANA, 7 in. pots, made-up plants, 1 large in center, 3 smaller sizes, 22 to 25 in. high around, gives them a good appearance, $2.00 each. 6 in. pots, single plants, 35 to 40 in. high, 5 to 6 good leaves, 4 year old, $1.25 to $1.50 each; 6 in. pots, 30 to 35 in. high, 4 year old, 5 good leaves, $1.00; 5½ in. pots, 3 year old, 25 to 30 in. high, 5 good leaves, 75c; made-up plants, 3 and 4 in. pots, 18 to 20 in high, 25 cts. to 30 cts. each.

KENTIA BELMOREANA, 5½ to 6 in. pots, bushy, fine plants, from 75 cts. to $1.00 to $1.25 each.

ARECA LUTESCENS, made-up, 25 cts.

COCOS WEDDELLIANA, 15 cts.

CYCAS REVOLUTA (Sago Palm), 6 in.-7 in. pots, with from 6 to 20 leaves per plant, 10cts. per leaf.

SOLANUM or JERUSALEM CHERRY, $5.00 per 100.

CASH WITH ORDER

When ordering, say whether the plants should be shipped in the pots or not

GODFREY ASCHMANN
Importer and Wholesale Grower of Pot Plants
1012 Ontario Street, - - PHILADELPHIA, PA.

Mention The Florists' Exchange when writing.

GERANIUMS ROOTED CUTTINGS

FALL DELIVERY. IN ANY QUANTITY.

I have almost 300,000 stock plants to work from and want your order now so that I can give it special attention when we come to take cuttings.

Send for Descriptive Price List

	Per 100	Per 1,000
SMILAX		
100,000 ready now, carefully cut back and grown with an air space around every pot	$1.50	$12.00
ASPARAGUS ROBUSTUS		
20,000 once repotted, fine strong plants and a great improvement over Plumosus in every respect. Try at least a hundred, next year you will want a thousand	$5.00	$40.00
ASPARAGUS SPRENGERII		
50,000 good strong plants once repotted into rose pots and a bargain at the price	$2.00	$15.00

ALBERT M. KERR,
Lancaster, Pa.

Mention The Florists' Exchange when writing.

TAKE NOTICE

We still have good stock in quantity as follows: In bud and bloom, **Geraniums**, S. A. Nutt, A. Ricard, John Doyle, Jean Viaud, La Favorite, Mme. Jaulin, Gloire de France and other good varieties, 3½ in. pots, $5.00 per 100. **Heliotrope**, Chieftain and Queen of Violets, 3½ in. pots, $5.00 per 100. **Cannas**, C. Henderson, F. Vaughan, Queen Charlotte, Duke and Martha Washington, green foliage, beautiful pink bloom, 4 in. pots, $5.00 per 100. **Begonia**, flowering, 3½ in. pots, $5.00 per 100. **Begonia Rex**, 3½ in. pots, $6.00 per 100. **Single Petunias**, large flowering, 3 in. pots, $1.50 per 100. **Nasturtiums**, 3 in. pots, $2.50 per 100. **Parlor Ivy, Ageratum**, Dwarf Blue, **Lobelia, Cuphea**, 2½ in. pots, $2.00 per 100. **Vinca Variegata**, 2½ in. pots, very good, $2.00 per 100. **Heliotrope**, 2½ in. pots, $2.00 per 100. **Rose Geranium**, 3½ in. pots, $6.00 per 100. **Centaurea Gymnocarpa**, 3 in. pots, $2.50 per 100. Cash with order.

W. J. CHINNICK, TRENTON, N. J.

GERANIUMS.

Nutt, Buchner, Doyle, Poitevine, Viaud, 3 in. pots, $3.00 per 100. 4 in. $5.00 per 100.
Cannas, 3 and 3½ in. pots, $4.00 and $5.00 per 100.
Fuchsias, 3 in. pots, $3.00 per 100.
Coleus, Verschaffeltii, Golden Bedder and other varieties, 2 in. pots, $1.00 per 100. Cash with order.

ERNEST HARRIS, Delanson, N. Y.

Mention The Florists' Exchange when writing.

3000 GERANIUMS

S. A. Nutt, all fine plants in bud and bloom. 4 in. pots, $4.00 and $5.00 per 100; **Double Petunias**, from 4 in. pots, $7.00 per 100.

COLEUS

Golden Bedder, 2½ in. pots, $2.00 per 100.

A. N. TOWELL
West 200th St. & Ft. Washington Ave.
New York City.

Mention The Florists' Exchange when writing.

Geraniums Geraniums

4in. pots at $6.00 per 100.
3in. pots at $4.00 per 100.
Heliotrope, 4 in. $4.00 per 100.
" 2 in. $3.00 per 100.
Lobelia, 2 in. $2.00 per 100.
Coleus, in variety, 2¼ in. pots, $2.00 per 100.

Don't get left, but get your order in. Cash must accompany same.

J. E. FELTHOUSEN,
154 VAN VRANKEN AVE., SCHENECTADY, N. Y.

GERANIUMS

2 in., $2.25 per 100; $18.00 per 1000. **S. A. Nutt, J. Viaud, White Swan, Ricard, E. G. Hill, Marquise de Castellane and Atkinson.**
Asparagus Sprengerii, 2 in., $2.00; $17.00 per 1000
Boston Ferns, 2 in., $3.00 per 100; 3 in., $5.00 per 100; 4 in., $8.00 per 100; 6 in. pans at $4.00 per doz.
Cissus Discolor at $3.00 per 100.

THE NATIONAL PLANT CO., DAYTON, O.

Mention The Florists' Exchange when writing.

CELERY PLANTS

600,000 A No. 1 TRANSPLANTED CELERY PLANTS. 9 choice varieties.

Send for Price List.

W. B. DU RIE, Rahway, N. J.

Mention The Florists' Exchange when writing.

BARGAIN

Geraniums, 8 varieties, in bloom, strong, 3 to 4 in., $2.50 to $3.50 per 100.
Asparagus Sprengerii, large, 4 in., $4.00 per 100; $35.00 per 1000.
Dracæna Indivisa, large, 4 in., $5.00 per 100; $45.00 per 1000.
Ferns, from flats, best varieties, ready for 2 to 3 in., $1.00 per 100. Large clumps for decorating and cutting, $6.00 to $8.00 per 100.
Cyclamen Gig., Hugh Low & Company's Prize Strain, including fringed and bearded varieties, 2-3 and 4 in., $4.00-$6.00 and $10.00 per 100. Cash.

WM. S. HERZOG, MORRIS PLAINS, N. J.

Mention The Florists' Exchange when writing.

GERANIUMS

Grand stock in bud and bloom. Best bedders in red, white and pink, also assorted colors. $7.00 per 100, 500 at $6.50 per 100.

COLEUS

Extra fine, red, yellow and assorted.
2½ inch, $3.00 per 100; $25.00 per 1000.
3 inch, $4.00 per 100; $35.00 per 1000.

THE H. WEBER & SONS CO.,
OAKLAND, MD.

Mention The Florists' Exchange when writing.

Jensen & Dekema

CARNATION SPECIALISTS

674 W. Foster Ave., CHICAGO.

Mention The Florists' Exchange when writing.

CARNATIONS

SMITH & GANNETT,
GENEVA, N. Y.

Mention The Florists' Exchange when writing.

CARNATIONS

Rooted Cuttings

All the new varieties of 1906. All the standard varieties worth growing.

WM. SWAYNE, Box 226, Kennett Square Pa.

Mention The Florists' Exchange when writing.

CANNAS

Allemania, Gray, Henderson, M. Washington, Metallica, from 3 in. pots, fine stock, $4.00 per 100

Shellroad Greenhouses, GRANGE, P. O. BALTIMORE, MD.

Mention The Florists' Exchange when writing.

RED SPORT.

The most profitable red carnation grown.

	Per 100	Per 1000
RED SPORT	$6.00	$40.00
QUEEN LOUISE	1.25	10.00

All cuttings well rooted, true to name, and perfectly healthy.

A. B. DAVIS & SON, Inc., Purcellville Va.

Mention The Florists' Exchange when writing.

CARNATIONS

We have the best list of Carnations in the country. Send for it.

We can quote lowest prices for best quality cuttings. Write us.

Chicago Carnation Co., Joliet, Ill.

Mention The Florists' Exchange when writing.

FIELD GROWN CARNATIONS

FROM JANUARY CUTTINGS.
Ready for delivery July 1.

	Per 100
WHITE LAWSON and ENCHANTRESS,	$8.00
RED LAWSON and HARRY FENN	7.00
MRS. OMWAKE our ENCHANTRESS SPORT	10.00

CASH PLEASE.

HENRY EICHHOLZ, Waynesboro, Pa

Mention the Florists' Exchange when writing.

HELEN GODDARD

The Coming Commercial Pink Carnation

Rooted cuttings, ready January 1, 1906. Price, $10.00 per 100; $75.00 per 1000.

S. J. GODDARD, Framingham, Mass.

Mention The Florists' Exchange when writing.

CARNATIONS

F. DORNER & SONS CO.
LA FAYETTE, IND.

Mention The Florists' Exchange when writing.

IVY LEAVED Geraniums

n full bud and bloom; white, light and dark pink, 2½ in. pots, $2.50 per 100.

NATHAN SMITH & SON,
ADRIAN, MICH.

Mention The Florists' Exchange when writing.

CLASSIFIED ADVERTISEMENTS

CASH WITH ORDER.

The columns under this heading are reserved for advertisements of Stock for Sale, Stock Wanted, Help Wanted, Situations Wanted or other Wants; also of Greenhouse, Land, Second-Hand Materials, etc., For Sale or Rent.

Our charge is 10 cts. per line (7 words to the line), set solid, without display. No advt. accepted for less than thirty cents.

Display advertisements in these columns, 15 cents per line; count 12 lines agate to the inch.

[If replies to Help Wanted, Situation Wanted, or other advertisements are to be addressed care of this office, advertisers add 10 cents to cover expense of forwarding.]

Copy must reach New York office 12 o'clock Wednesday, to secure insertion in issue of following Saturday.

Advertisers in the Western States desiring to advertise under initials, may save time by having their answer directed care our Chicago office at 127 E. Berwyn Ave.

SITUATIONS WANTED

SITUATION WANTED—First-class florist and gardener, single, 29, life experience, able to take charge and handle men. Address, Ability, care The Florists' Exchange.

SITUATION WANTED—By a gardener and florist; single man, with a thorough knowledge of the business. Address, James O'Brien, 128 Lexington Avenue, Jersey City, N. J.

SITUATION WANTED—By working foreman, competent, married man. Roses, carnations and mums a specialty. A No. 1 propagator. Address, Grower, care The Florists' Exchange.

SITUATION WANTED—By a young married man as grower of roses, carnations, mums and general stock. 11 years' experience; English, good references. Address, L. C., care The Florists' Exchange.

SITUATION WANTED—By single man who has some knowledge in roses, carnations and other stock. References. Willing, good worker and sober. Address, P. C., care The Florists' Exchange.

SITUATION WANTED—By a young man, good character, education and experience; as foreman of rose growing establishment. References given on application. Address, L. F., care The Florists' Exchange.

SITUATION WANTED—Thoroughly learned gardener, 24 years of age, German, single, wants a steady position; good grower of carnations, mums and bedding plants. Private or commercial. References. Address, L. D., care The Florists' Exchange.

SITUATION WANTED—Steady, by August 15, by a first-class all-around florist. A No. 1 orchid grower. Steady, sober and honest. 9 years in present position. Private place preferred. Please state wages. Address, L. B., care The Florists' Exchange.

SITUATION WANTED—As head gardener on private place by competent man with life experience in all branches of gardening. Expert grower of plants, cut flowers, fruit and vegetables under glass and outside. Excellent references. German-American, 42, married, small family. Address M. Schmidt, Suffern, N. Y.

HELP WANTED

WANTED—A first-class rose grower for Brides and Maids. Sober and reliable; good wages and steady place. Call on A. L. Thorne, Flushing Avenue, N. Y. City.

WANTED—Greenhouse men for general work; state salary and references in first letter. The Gasser Company, Wholesale Growers Cut Flowers, Cleveland, Ohio.

WANTED—Thoroughly first-class experienced rose and carnation growers. Apply stating age, married or single, references and wages expected. None but first-class men wanted. Lake View Rose Gardens, Jamestown, N. Y.

WANTED—An assistant florist in a rose and carnation establishment, good, steady place. Will pay from $10.00 to $12.00 per week to start. Give references and ability in first letter. Muskogee Carnation Company, Muskogee, Ind. Ter.

WANTED—Salesmen, men of ability and good character, to solicit orders for nursery stock from the Morris Nurseries, West Chester, Pa. Good pay and steady employment to successful salesmen. Address, P. A. Keene, 1 Madison Avenue, N. Y. City.

WANTED—At once, single middle aged man for general gardening in Cemetery and greenhouse work. German preferred; one who can speak English. $25.00 per month, board, room and washing. Steady position year around. Address, L. G., care The Florists' Exchange.

WANTED—Seedsmen; we require at once several young men for counter work. Only such need apply as have thorough experience in all branches of the seed business. We offer splendid chances for advancement. Apply in writing. W. W. Rawson & Company, Boston, Mass.

HELP WANTED

WANTED—A sober, experienced man to grow common flowers, vegetable plants and early vegetables under glass and outside. Small commercial house. A man past 50 preferred. A position for years to the right man. Address, Chas. G. Dolson, Box 176, Waverly, Penna.

GOOD OPPORTUNITY

Energetic young man, with thorough ornamental nursery training including hardy herbaceous plants, may find it to his advantage to correspond with us. Permanent position to right party. State experience, references, and salary expected. Position now open.

THE ELM CITY NURSERY CO.

NEW HAVEN, CONN.

Mention The Florists' Exchange when writing.

MISCELLANEOUS WANTS

WANTED TO BUY—Greenhouses to be taken down. State full particulars of same when writing. Address, F. W., care The Florists' Exchange.

WANTED—50 boxes, 10 x 12 and 12 x 12, double thick second-hand glass. James L. Stone, Trumansburg, N. Y.

WANTED TO BUY Palms or Ferns, or any saleable plants, if bargains, to sell over our retail counters.

MISSOURI FLORAL CO.

922 Main Street, Kansas City, Mo.

Mention The Florists' Exchange when writing.

FOR SALE OR RENT

FOR SALE—Greenhouse property, with or without a part or whole of valuable property and dwelling house; good retail trade, or would make a fine place for road house. Bargain. Address, F. W. Miles, Plainfield, N. J.

FOR RENT—Small greenhouses and florist business in prosperous running condition. Southern Connecticut. Full particulars and reason for renting to anyone interested. Address, L. E., care The Florists' Exchange.

FOR SALE—A fine established nursery business with a constituency reaching from the Atlantic to the Pacific, and from Manitoba to the Gulf. Old age of proprietor the only reason for sale. C. S. Harrison, York, Neb.

DESIRABLE greenhouse plant of three houses, 24x200 feet; propagating house, 100 feet; potting shed, stable and dwelling. Steam heat, city water. Highland, opposite Poughkeepsie. Joseph Wood, Spring Valley, New York.

FOR SALE—Greenhouses at Madison, N. J. Situated on North Street. One 162 x 36; two 150 x 18 feet, 8 in.; one 150 x 12. Heated by both hot water and steam. Place in first-class condition. For particulars address, 50 Park Avenue, Madison, New Jersey.

FOR SALE—Two acres of ground and four greenhouses consisting of 13,000 feet of glass, all stocked and in good order. Also one barn and dwelling nearly finished. Will sell very reasonable and on easy terms. Apply to Jos. Fisher, Schuyler Avenue, Kearney, New Jersey.

FOR RENT—Greenhouse plant containing three houses, 6 miles from Boston. All modern conveniences; new boilers, etc. Everything in first-class repair. Terms reasonable to responsible party. Excellent chance for a man who means business. Address or call, 820 Beale Street, Wollaston, Quincy, Mass.

To lease for a term of years, my establishment on Greene Avenue, consisting of about 7,000 feet of glass, office and salesroom. Stable and wagon shed. Horse and wagons. Place well stocked and heated with hot water. Every convenience, all in good condition. A good business in the best location in the city. Established for 40 years. Wishing to retire from business. This is a good opportunity for the right man. Come and see it. Richard Shannon, 341-349 Greene Avenue, Brooklyn, New York.

FOR SALE

A splendid wholesale business consisting of nine iron frame greenhouses and two dwelling houses. Everything in up-to-date condition, well heated. Two acres of ground and within half hour drive of New York City. For further particulars communicate with

O. V. ZANGEN, SEEDSMAN, HOBOKEN, N. J.

Mention The Florists' Exchange when writing.

FOR SALE OR RENT

FOR RENT OR SALE

About 12,000 feet of glass, hot water and steam heating—5 to 10 acres land—six-room residence, on electric car line, two miles from city and suburbs having 100,000 population—for lease or sale on easy terms, immediate possession.

BARTON MYERS, Norfolk, Virginia.

Mention The Florists' Exchange when writing.

PUBLIC SALE OF

Hostetter's Greenhouses on Saturday, July 14t 1906, pursuant to an order of the Orphan's Cour, of Lancaster County, Pa., will be sold at Public Sale on the premises No. 3 in the borough of Manheim, the following described real estate, late of Abraham Hostetter, deceased to wit:

A LOT OF GROUND

Situated in said borough, fronting on the east side of Grant street 180 feet, and extending of that width eastward to Pitt street 219 feet more or less. The buildings and improvements thereon erected are six greenhouses, in size, viz.: one 30 x 204 ft. three, 18 x 204 ft.; one, 22 x 204 ft.; and one 12 x 66 ft., all in good condition and almost new; and located within a few blocks of the railroad station. The soil is very well adapted for raising carnations, roses, violets, chrysanthemums, etc.; also at the same time will be sold 30,000 carnation plants, new and standard varieties—6,000 chrysanthemums; 2,000 violets; 30 boxes of glass, etc. The plant is equipped with two heating boilers, and all necessary piping and equipments for the successful cultivation of flowers or vegetables.

The plant is well located for the wholesale florist business, and worthy the attention of persons desiring to engage in the business.

Sale to commence at 1 o'clock p. m. on said day, when the conditions will be made known by the undersigned administrators of said deceased.

Manheim P. O., NATHAN HOSTETTER
Lancaster Co., Pa., CEPHAS HOSTETTER

Mention The Florists' Exchange when writing.

STOCK FOR SALE

FREESIA BULBS, No. 1 size, $3.00 per 1000. T. J. King, Newburyport, Mass.

ORCHIDS, just arrived, Cattleya Mendelii in very fine condition. C. Mertz, Norris Avenue, Jamaica, L. I., N. Y.

LETTUCE—Big Boston, Tennis Ball, Simpson and Boston Market. Also Wakefield Flat Dutch Cabbage. $1.00 per 100; $8.00 per 1000. Blake & Todd, Greensboro, N. C.

5,000 Strong 2 1-2 in. Smilax plants, $1.50 per 100; $10.00 per 1000. Sample plants, 10c. Cash with order. L. Epple, Pelham, N. Y.

ASTERS, ready to plant out. Fine stock, 9 colors and varieties. $2.00 per 1000. Cash. Shippensburg Floral Company, Shippensburg, Pa.

PRIMULA OBC. GRANDIFLORA, SEEDLINGS, 25c. per 100; 2¼ in. pots, $2.00 per 100. Cash please. A. Relyea & Son, Poughkeepsie, N. Y.

JERUSALEM CHERRIES, seedlings, 25c. per 100; 2½ in. pots, fine plants, $3.00 per 100. Cash please. A Relyea & Son, Poughkeepsie, N. Y.

SEEDS—All kinds of native tree and shrub seeds for sale at low prices: Betula Nigra, 50c. per lb. F. M. Crayton, Box 393, Biltmore, N. C.

CHRYSANTHEMUMS from small pots; white or pink Ivory, October sunshine, or other early varieties. Must be cheap. J. & W. Leach, Astoria, L. I. City, N. Y.

ALTERNANTHERAS, strong, bushy, $2.50 per 100; Salvia, $3.00 per 100; Geraniums, 3 1-2 in., $4.00 per 100; Ageratum, $2.00 per 100. Cash please. F. A. Peterson, Florist, Asbury Park, N. J.

MARIE LOUISE VIOLETS, strong Winter grown stock, ready for planting at once. Write me at once for sample. $2.00 per 100; $12.00 per 1000. Louis D. McCoy, Monsey, N. Y.

100,000 Sweet Potato Sprouts, extra fine. 500,000 Cabbage plants, several varieties, all $1.00 per 1000; $8.00 per 10,000. Orders filled same day as received. W. F. Allen, Salisbury, Md.

BABY RAMBLER roses, fine dormant stock, $25 per 100. 2 1-2 inch pot plants, extra well rooted $7 per 100, $65 per 1000. Orders booked for delivery now or any time up to late Spring. Samples free. Brown Brothers Co., Rochester, N. Y.

ASPARAGUS PLUMOSUS SEEDLINGS, strong, 3 in. $1.00 per 100; strong, 6 in. high, 2 1-2 in. pots, $4.00 per 100; GREVILLEA ROBUSTA, 6 in. high, from flats, $3.00 per 100; 10 in. high, 3 in. pots, $6.00 per 100; HIBISCUS, single and double red, from 2 in. pots, $5.00 per 100; LAURESTINUS, from 2 in. pots and STRAWBERRY GUAVA, from flats, $3.00 per 100; CHAMAEROPS EXCELSA palms, 1 year seed bed, $1.50 per 100.

NOTICE THIS: All prepaid at prices given for cash. PIONEER NURSERY, MONROVIA, CAL.

Thirty cents is the minimum charge for advertisements on this page.

STOCK FOR SALE

ROSES AND ASPARAGUS. 1000 one year old A No. 1 Asparagus Sprengerii. 2500 MAIDS from 2 1-2 and 4 in. pots. 800 BRIDES from 2 1-2 and 4 in pots. 70 PEARLS from 2 1-2 and 4 in. pots. 125 GOLDEN GATES from 2 1-4 in. pots. 100 KAISERINS from 2 1-4 in. pots. 500 RICHMONDS from 2 1-2 and 3 in. pots. All well rooted and healthy plants. Also 1 year old BRIDES, MAIDS and AMERICAN BEAUTIES from bench. Write for prices. We want to sell. Small or large orders. MADISON ROSE COMPANY, MADISON, N. J.

FOR SALE

FOR SALE—12 Hitchings hot water expansion tanks for 3 1-2 in. pipe, in good condition, cleaned, ready to set up. 1-3 price of new. Also horse lawn mower, easy running, $20.00. Address, K. D., care The Florists' Exchange.

FOR SALE—Stover fifty foot Steel Tower and Tank in use a short time. Good as new; price reasonable. Write for particulars. Wm. C. De Witt, R. F. D. No. 1, Phillipsburg, N. J.

FOR SALE—Florist's covered delivery wagon, newly painted. Plate glass sides. Coach gear guaranteed, in first class condition; a bargain if taken at once. Address K. V., care The Florists' Exchange.

BOILERS, BOILERS, BOILERS.
SEVERAL good second hand boilers on hand, also new No. 16 Hitchings at reduced cost. Write for list. Wm. H. Lutton, West Side Avenue Station, C. R. R. of N. J., Jersey City, N. J.

FOR SALE—One No. 26 Perfect Hot Water Boiler, capacity, 1200 square feet of radiation. In good condition. Price fifty ($50.00) dollars. Delivered F. O. B. New York. Address, A. B. Munro, 326 E. 28th Street, Flatbush, Brooklyn, New York.

FOR SALE—Brand new Kroeschell Boiler. We can ship any size at short notice. Why buy second-hand boiler and risk your stock when you can get a new Kroeschell Boiler at very reasonable figures. Write for our prices before buying anything. Kroeschell Brothers Company, 55 Erie Street, Chicago, Ill.

FOR SALE CHEAP

12 greenhouses to be torn down; glazed with 16 x 24 and 10 x 12 double thick glass. Heated with 2 in. wrought iron and 4 in. cast iron greenhouse pipe. One No. 17 sectional, two No. 16 and one No. 15 Hitchings boilers. Will sell together or separate.

METROPOLITAN MATERIAL COMPANY,
1398 METROPOLITAN AVE., BROOKLYN, N. Y.

FOR SALE

Greenhouse Material milled from Gulf Cypress, to any detail furnished, or our own patterns as desired, cut and spliced ready for erection. Estimates for complete constructions furnished.

V. E. REICH, Brooklyn, N. Y.

1429-1437 Metropolitan Ave.

Mention The Florists' Exchange when writing.

FOR SALE

PUMPS -Ericsson. Second-hand, from [illegible] up; all repairs; other makes; new; [illegible]

BOILERS One second-hand tubular hot water boiler 3 ft. in diameter 12 ft. long. Price $35.00. One No. 15 Hitchings as good as new, $50.00.

PIPE Good serviceable second-hand, with Threads; 2-in., 7 cts.; 1½-in., 5½ cts.; 1¼-in., 4 cts.; 1-in., 3 cts.; 2½ in., 10 cts.; 3 in., 14 cts.; 4 in., 19 cts. New 2-in. Standard, full lengths, with couplings, 8¼ cts. ft. Old and new fittings and valves. Old 4 inch cast iron 15c per foot.

STOCKS and DIES New Economy, best made No. 1 Threads, ½-in., ¾-in. 1-in. pipe, $3.00. No. 2 Threads, 1¼-in., 1½-in. 2-in. pipe, $4.00.

PIPE CUTTERS New Saunders Pattern. No. 1 cuts ⅛-in.-1-in. pipe, $1.00. No. 2 cuts 1-in.-2-in. pipe, $1.30.

STILLSON WRENCHES New. 18-in., grips ¼-in.-2-in. pipe, $1.65; 24-in. grips ¼-in.-2½ in. pipe, $2.40; 36-in., grips ½-in.-3½-in. pipe, $4.75.

PIPE VISES New. No. 1 Hinged, grips ⅛-in.-2 in. pipe, $2.00.

GARDEN HOSE New. 50 ft. lengths. ¾-in., guaranteed 100-lbs. pressure, 7½ cts. per ft.; ¾-in. not guaranteed, 4¾ cts. per ft., 25 ft. lengths, ½c. per ft. more.

HOT-BED SASH New. Cypress, 3 ft. x 6 ft., from 75 cts. up; glazed, complete, from $1.60 up. Second-hand, in good condition, all glass in, $1.00 each.

GLASS New American 10x12 single $1.80 per box; 12x12 single $1.90 per box; 10x12, 12x12, 10x16 double, $2.55 per box; 12x14, 12x20, 14x14, double, $2.75 per box; 16x16, 16x18, $3.10 per box; 16x24 double $3.30 per box. Second hand glass, 8 x 10, 8 x 12, and 10 x 12 single at $1.50 per box, double $1.75 per box.

Get our prices on New Gulf Cypress Building Material, Ventilating Apparatus, Oil, White Lead, Putty, Paint, Points, etc.

METROPOLITAN MATERIAL CO.

1398-1408 Metropolitan Avenue, BROOKLYN, N.Y.

Mention The Florists' Exchange when writing.

Newport, R. I.

News Notes.

John Marshall has several seedling carnations which he is growing on for the second year. One seedling Mr. Marshall is especially careful about resembles Robert Craig, and in the opinion of some a trifle larger than the latter variety, but last season it was not equal to Craig in stem. This year, in order if possible to definitely determine to his entire satisfaction the relative merits of both, Mr. Marshall intends growing his own seedling side by side with Robert Craig in the same bench. If Mr. Marshall's seedling develops in stem in a degree equal to what it has already done in size and substance of flower as well as in shade of color, it would certainly seem to be worth growing.

Carl Jurgens has just commenced the erection of a new greenhouse.

The Knights Templar of Rhode Island and southern Massachusetts had their annual outing in this city Monday. In the ranks of the visiting Sir Knights there were many members of the craft, while Washington Commandery of Newport had also a liberal sprinkling of gardeners and florists.

Newport dealers are early this season in finding out how scarce ferns are in the hands of local growers. Frequently orders are going out of town for this class of stock. There is no denying the fact that for some purposes nothing can take the place of the old Boston fern; the length and grace of the fronds of Nephrolepis bostoniensis make it indispensable for florists' uses.

Specimen plants of Latania borbonica were of late years but little in demand; this season there seems to be more call for them. Phœnix, too, seem to be finding berths this year. Perhaps the reason for both is that people do not care to see kentias spoiled so quickly as they invariably are when placed outdoors.

The house decorations for the Sands-Minott wedding were done by Joseph Leikens. Wadley & Smythe supplied the bouquets for the bride and bridesmaid. The bride's bouquet was of orchids and lily of the valley. Oscar Schultz supplied some of the plants used, besides all the outdoor flowers, of which there were large quantities in the whole decoration.

Outdoor roses are not up to the average of former years on many places here; while they are fully a week later in blooming than last year. Hybrid tea rose Gruss an Teplitz is becoming very deservedly popular here; it is not only a prolific bloomer, of good color and rich foliage, but it is also perfectly hardy—quite a commendation for the growing of large numbers of it. Bell Siebrecht is also a rose of the same type that the better it is known the more popular it will become. This rose is in color a beautiful pink, while Gruss an Teplitz is just as beautiful a scarlet.

The elm leaf beetle is in evidence in its early stages now in Newport, and systematic spraying with arsenate of lead is vigorously carried on to check the progress of the pest.

Last year the float of the Newport Horticultural Society in the carnival parade was voted to equal, if not surpass, everything in line. Had it not been for the timely advice and the vigorous work of Fred. M. Smythe, who arrived on the scene while the committee were in a quandary what to do, it is doubtful if the result would have been so satisfactory as to call forth such plaudits from the multitudes along the line of march. This year, in recognition of the highly artistic character of last year's float, the general committee voted to ask the Horticultural Society to build a floral throne as part of its float for the accommodation of the Queen of the Carnival. Plans are already drawn, and a model constructed for this float which will be distinctly floral. Immense quantities of flowers and green material will be used in its construction. A large order will in a few days be placed for Southern smilax. The carnival will run from August 6 to 11, inclusive; members of the craft having a week off then could do no better than spend it in Newport, where a good time is assured.

D. M.

New York.

News Notes.

The reports from Bermuda point to a shortage in the crop of bulbs for this season. One prominent grower in the islands has written his customers here, saying that owing to the drought the crop will not average 50 per cent. of its usual quantity. The grower in question states that after going through his own fields, and discovering that his crop was to be short, he visited other growers and found that they were similarly situated. Consequently, he is asking his customers to reduce their orders.

A florist named Harry Butler, whose home is at 310 West One Hundred and Seventeenth street, was driven insane by the extreme heat of last Saturday, and had to be taken to a hospital.

Wm. L. Hundertmark, a florist of Passaic, N. J., who has been remodeling his store, held an opening day last Saturday, June 30, and through a printed circular invited the general public to pay him a visit.

S. Burnett of Burnett Bros., seedsmen, 101 West street, sailed for Europe on the Caledonia, June 28, for a three months' business trip.

Charles H. Plumb, Detroit, Mich., and Peter Duff, Orange, N. J., sailed on Saturday last for Scotland.

John Heeremans, Madison, N. J., sailed on the Baltic on July 4, for a trip to England. David Fraser and family of Pittsburg, Secretary of the Chrysanthemum Society of America, were passengers on the same boat as was R. C. Pye, Nyack, N. Y.

Frank Hamilton has resigned his position as manager of the landscape department of the Cottage Gardens Company, Queens, N. Y. Mr. Hamilton's family has been in poor health for some time, and a change of climate is necessary to a restoration.

C. W. Ward, Cottage Gardens, Queens, N. Y., left for Detroit, Mich., last week.

The wholesale dealers have commenced closing at 4 p. m. each day, and will continue to do so during the months of July and August.

A meeting of the board of trustees of the National Association of Gardeners was held on June 12, when the incorporation of a gardeners' home was considered. In order to perfect the details of the scheme, the meeting was adjourned for two weeks. President J. M. Hunter entertained the board at dinner after the close of the meeting at Della's Hotel, Fort Lee, N. J. Those present were John M. Hunter, John Shore, James Bell, Frank Drew, W. E. Maynard, Hoff. Herlihy,, and J. J. Sipp.

F. Lautenschlager, representative of Kroeschell Brothers, Chicago, is in the city this week.

Mr. and Mrs. John H. Taylor, Bayside, L. I., are in Europe on a pleasure trip.

Theodore P. Lawlor and Patrick H. Lawlor, Flushing, N. Y., and Leo. B. Lawlor, of Brooklyn, N. Y., have formed a corporation to grow plants, vines, etc., to be known as the Flushing Nurseries, with a capital of $1,000.

The "Fourth" was a very quiet day so far as business went; the wholesale district was practically deserted, and most of the stores were closed up before midday.

Richard Cooper, an errand boy in the employ of William Kervan, 20 West Twenty-seventh street, was run over by an automobile on Tuesday morning last, and killed.

The Club Outing.

The sixth annual outing of the New York Florists' Club was held on Monday, July 2. The party numbering over three hundred left the dock at Thirty-first street and East River on the steamer Isabel, a little after 10 o'clock, and proceeded to Witzel's Point Grove. The weather, while rather warm, was ideal for the day's outing. The trip up the Sound on the boat was very enjoyable; music from Stowe's orchestra, together with guitar and vocal music was provided. Arrived at the grove, dinner was partaken of, after which the sports of the day commenced with the ladies' bowling match, the baseball game, and the children's races.

In the ladies' bowling match Mrs. R. Whitman won first prize with a score of 32; Miss A. Gaynor and Miss Foberg each made 31, and tied for second place. Mrs. A. Schmutz was next with 30; then came Mrs. Vocke with 29; Mrs. A. J. Schmutz with 28, and Mrs. Fenrich with 27.

The baseball game between the married and single men, was won by the benedicts with a score of six to four.

In the Press bowling contest J. H. Pepper carried off the prize with a score of 48.

In the bowling match open to all, the prizes were won in the following order: J. A. Manda, 96; A. Wilson, 85; R. Irwin, 82; J. Birnie, 78; C. Kukudi, 76; J. Donaldson, 73; W. C. Mansfield, 70; A. Zeller and H. Dailledouze each 66.

The prize for the handsomest baby went to Master Charles Albert, son of Frank H. Traendby.

In the girls' race for those under five years of age, the prize winners were: Margaret Wagner, first; Helen Manda, second; Evelyn Kessler, third.

Boys' race for those under five years of age—Franklin Adams, first; J. Scott, Jr., second; and J. Hiltman, third.

Girls' race for those under seven years of age—Eloise Schenck, first; Margaret Wagner, second; Agnes Kessler, third.

Boys' race for those under seven years—George Lenker, first; Ira Freiberg, second; Walter Pepper, third.

Girls' race for those under nine years—Ella Lenker, first; Olive Iler, second; Ethel Adams, third.

Boys' under nine years—Fred Pepper, first; Willie Manda, second; Walter Pepper, third.

Girls' race for those under twelve years—Freda Schenck, first; Carrie Bohler, second; Josephine Pesenecker, third.

Boys' race for those under twelve years—Lawrence Schenck, first; Will. Massman, second; Gustave Koppel, third.

Girls' race for those under fifteen years of age—Annie Birnie, first; Nellie Erhardt, second; Marion Iler, third.

Boys' race for those under fifteen years—Robert Young, first; W. Friedberg, second; W. Iler, third.

Young ladies' race—Agnes Birnie, first; Alice Gaynor, second; R. DuRie, third.

Married ladies' race—Mrs. F. Smith, first; Mrs. Worstadt, second; Mrs. Fenrich, third.

One-hundred-yard race for members of the New York Florists' Club only—Meyer Gottlieb, first; Joseph Fenrich, second.

One-hundred-yard race for young ladies of any age over twenty—A. Manda, first; Annie Gaynor, second; A. Roberts, third.

Potato race—Agnes Birnie, first; Mrs. Iler, second; Louise Doergler, third.

Race for married ladies of any age—Mrs. Smith.

Artificial fat man's race—F. H. Traendly, first; O. Bohmler, second.

Quarter-mile race open to all was won by F. Lautenschlager; and the 100-yard race open to growers only, by F. Smith.

The Tug-of-War between the growers and wholesalers was won easily by the growers.

The 220-yard race was won by N. Leavitt, the second prize going to H. Riechard.

In putting the weight, W. Bogart was first, and F. White second.

The consolation race for young ladies over 16 years was won by Marjorie Birnie; and for Chas. Webber's special race the winners were F. Smith and G. Burns.

Taking it all in all, the sixth annual outing was a success in every particular. The journey back was made in good season, allowing everybody to get home early in the evening.

Washington, D. C.

Florists' Club Outing.

As there are ony a few more weeks in which to make final preparations for the outing of the club, it will be necessary for those members and friends who contemplate going, and who have not notified the secretary of their intentions, to do so immediately. It is absolutely necessary to have all the data in before July 20, so that the committee may be able to charter the required number of private coaches to the beach; also the number of plates to be laid for the banquet. Tickets for the banquet can be secured from all the local florists and members of the committee.

The Senate has ratified a plan to create a World Institute, a treaty of much importance. It is the purpose of the institute to gather and disseminate accurate information of the condition of the world's visible supply of agricultural staples, for the common benefit of agriculture in all countries. The quantity of staples on hand in various producing countries and the condition of the growing crops are to be ascertained through the co-operation of the powers signatory to the protocol; and this information collated and translated into the equivalent measures and values of each nation, is to be transmitted by cable simultaneously to all countries. Through this agency the agriculturists throughout the world will be made acquainted with the state of the world's supply. It is expected that the International Institute will put an end to violent fluctuations in the price of food products by placing the world in possession of information now unavailable or guessed at.

With Congress adjourned, the White House deserted and the Cabinet families nearly all established at their Summer homes or on their vacation travels, things are quiet in Washington. The temperature has been hovering around the 100 mark. The last week of June witnessed a score of handsome weddings; the most interesting event of Wednesday, June 27, was the marriage of Miss Alwine Haas and Robert Martin Calfee, of Cleveland, O., which took place at the home of the bride's mother, 1432 Q street. The drawing room and dining room were banked with palms and ferns, the bride carrying a bouquet of lily of the valley.

The row of thick shade-producing elm trees along the walk in front of the White House grounds on Pennsylvania avenue, has been considerably marred by the removal last week of one of the largest and oldest trees of the number. The big elm, which was planted during the presidency of Abraham Lincoln, was denuded of a number of its large branches by the heavy wind storm last Saturday afternoon.

J. A. G.

Indianapolis.

News Notes.

Representatives of the Advance Ventilating Company are canvassing this section and exhibiting a sample of their improved apparatus.

The father of August and John Grande passed away on Monday, June 25. August Grande, Sr., had been an invalid for many years. Besides the two well-known sons, August and John, he is survived by a daughter, Mrs. Louis Hoerger, who is also active in the florist business.

John Rieman is sporting a fine new delivery wagon. He is preparing, also, to make improvements in his store.

A. Wiegand & Sons are to make extensive alterations in their store this Summer; the room proper is to be enlarged, new ice boxes are to be installed, and the conservatory given an overhauling.

A. Smith, formerly with Baur & Smith, has accepted employment at E. A. Nelson's place.

Clarence Thomas is enjoying his vacation.

Visitors: Richard Arms, Urbana, Ill.; Wilbur Byers, Franklin, Ind.

I. B.

HARTFORD, CONN.—The Connecticut Horticultural Society held a meeting at the rose garden in Elizabeth Park, Hartford, and the 19 members present afterward took a lunch at the park restaurant. The meeting was called principally to give the members an opportunity to see the roses while they are in their prime, and considerable time was spent in examining the various varieties. A communication was read from the New Haven Horticultural Society, inviting the Hartford Society to unite in an outing in July. The New London County Horticultural Society will also take part in the outing and a joint committee from the three societies will decide upon the time and place.

Joseph T. Simpson of Rochester, formerly in the florist business in this city thirty years ago, has been visiting relatives here.

DOYLESTOWN, PA.—Considerable damage was done by the hail at John E. Andre's rose houses, on the lower State road, about a mile southwest of Doylestown, on June 24. Much glass was broken and some plants injured.

Kansas City.

Trade News.

The past Spring business was greater in volume than any previous one. Every florist in the city, almost without exception, cleaned out of all his bedding stock and in many instances could have used more.

W. J. Barnes says that this has been the best season he has ever enjoyed. He handled two decorations last week in addition to filling some belated plant orders. Rumor has it that Mr. Barnes will establish a downtown store this Fall.

R. S. Brown & Son are sending in about the best carnations on the market. There was considerable funeral work during the week, which helped things out considerably. The outdoor planting is all over with.

Mrs. Annie Schneider opened a new flower store on Grand avenue last Saturday. A brass band was employed to furnish the music and the store was thronged with visitors all day. A large number of roses and carnations were given away during the day. Mrs. Schneider has a fine location and is thoroughly experienced in the business, her husband having started a flower store here in 1870.

The Wyandotte Seed House of Kansas City, Kas., reports a splendid business this Spring in seeds and bedding stock.

Lawrence Swager, who has conducted a flower store at 13th and Grand avenue, failed last week. The liabilities are reported at about $2,500, with the assets very small.

Al. Murray, formerly foreman at W. J. Barnes' place, is now foreman at the Hayes greenhouses at Topeka, Kan.

Chas. A. Schaeffer and James Bigham, formerly the Chas. A. Schaeffer Floral Company, will go into the real estate business in this city.

A fire at the Tenth street greenhouses of W. H. Humfeld one night last week did about $100 damage. The origin of the fire is unknown.

John Schneider, one of the old time florists of Kansas City, is again in the business after several years' retirement. He has opened up a place on Walnut street.

A. Freudenthal has been suffering from an attack of grip.

TRAVELER.

Wholesale Prices of Cut Flowers, New York, July 5, 1906

Prices quoted are by the hundred unless otherwise noted.

Roses	A. Beauty, fancy—special	8.00 to 15.00
	" extra	5.00 to 8.00
	" No. 1	4.00 to 5.00
	" No. 2	3.00 to 4.00
	" No. 3	1.00 to 1.50
	Bride, 'Maid, fancy—spe'l	3.00 to 4.00
	" extra	2.00 to 8.00
	" No. 1	1 00 to 2.00
	" No. 2	.50 to 1.00
	Golden Gate	1.00 to 5.00
	Liberty	...... to ......
	Mme. Abel Chatenay	1.00 to 6.00
Adiantum		.50 to .75
	Croweanum	.75 to 1.50
Asparagus		25.00 to 50 00
	" Plumosus, bunches	10.00 to 15.00
	" Sprengeri, bunches	10.00 to 15.00
Callas		...... to ......
Cattleyas		25.00 to 50.00
Daisies		.50 to 1.00
Gladiolus		2.00 to 4.00
		...... to ......

Carnations	Inf'r grades, all colors		.50 to 1 00
	Standard Varieties	White	.50 to 1 00
		Pink	.50 to 1 00
		Red	.50 to 1 00
		Yel. & Var.	.50 to 1 00
	*Fancy— (*The highest grades of standard var.)	White	1.00 to 2 00
		Pink	1.00 to 2.00
		Red	1.00 to 2 00
		Yel. & Var.	1.00 to 2 00
	Novelties		2.00 to 3 00
Lilies			1 00 to 4 00
Lily of the Valley			1.00 to 2 00
Mignonette			.50 to 1.00
			...... to ......
			...... to ......
			...... to ......
Pansies, per dozen bunches			.50 to .75
Smilax			8.00 to 10.00
Sweet Peas, per bunch			.01 to .02

Wholesale Prices of Cut Flowers—Per 100

Boston July 3, 1906	Buffalo July 2, 1906	Detroit July 1, 1906	Cincinnati June 30, 1906	Baltimore June 25, 1906	NAMES AND VARIETIES	Milwaukee June 15, 1906	Phil'delphia June 16, 1906	Pittsburg June 25, 1906	St. Louis July 2, 1906
10.00 to 20.00	20.00 to 25.00	10.00 to 35.00	... to 30.00	... to ...	ROSES: A. BEAUTY, fancy—special	25.00 to 30.00	15.00 to 20.00	20.00 to 25.00	15.00 to 20.00
6.00 to 10.00	12.00 to 20.00	... to ...	20.00 to 25.00	12.50 to 15.00	" extra	18.00 to 20.00	10.00 to 12.00	15.00 to 18.00	10.00 to 12.50
2.00 to 6.00	6.00 to 12.00	... to ...	10.00 to 15.00	5.00 to 8.00	" No. 1	12.50 to 15.00	6.00 to 8.00	8.00 to 10.00	6.00 to 8.00
1.00 to 2.00	3.00 to 6.00	... to ...	4.00 to 6.00	... to ...	" Culls and ordinary	6.00 to 10.00	1.00 to 4.00	2.00 to 3.00	3.00 to 5.00
... to ...	6.00 to 7.00	3.00 to 6.00	... to ...	... to ...	BRIDE, 'MAID, fancy-special	... to 8.00	6.00 to 10.00	... to 8.00	5.00 to 6.00
... to ...	5.00 to 6.00	... to ...	5.00 to 6.00	... to 4.00	" extra	... to 6.00	5.00 to 6.00	... to 6.00	3.00 to 4.00
2.00 to 4.00	4.00 to 5.00	... to ...	3.00 to 4.00	... to 3.00	" No. 1	... to 4.00	2.00 to 4.00	... to 4.00	... to 2.00
.50 to 1.00	3.00 to 4.00	... to ...	... to 2.00	... to 2.00	" No. 2	... to 2.00	... to 1.00	... to 2.00	... to ...
... to ...	2.00 to 3.00	4.00 to 8.00	... to ...	2.00 to 4.00	GOLDEN GATE	4.00 to 8.00	1.00 to 8.00	... to ...	2.00 to 5.00
2.00 to 8.00	3.00 to 8.00	... to ...	2.00 to 6.00	4.00 to 8.00	K. A. VICTORIA	4.00 to 8.00	2.00 to 8.00	4.00 to 12.00	2.00 to 6.00
2.00 to 12.00	3.00 to 8.00	... to ...	... to ...	... to ...	LIBERTY	4.00 to 10.00	2.00 to 12.00	... to ...	... to ...
... to ...	3.00 to 6.00	4.00 to 10.00	... to ...	... to ...	METEOR	4.00 to 6.00	... to ...	... to ...	... to ...
... to ...	3.00 to 5.00	4.00 to 10.00	... to ...	2.00 to 4.00	PERLE	... to ...	... to ...	4.00 to 6.00	2.00 to 4.00
... to ...	... to ...	... to 50.00	... to ...	... to ...	ORCHIDS—Cattleyas	... to ...	... to 50.00	... to ...	... to ...
... to ...	1.00 to 1.25	... to ...	... to .50	.50 to .75	CARNATIONS: Inferior grades, all colors	... to ...	... to ...	... to 1.00	.75 to 1.00
... to ...	1.25 to 1.50	... to 1.00	1.00 to 1.50	1.00 to 1.50	Standard Varieties: White	... to ...	1.50 to 2.00	... to 1.50	.75 to 1.00
... to ...	1.25 to 1.50	... to ...	1.00 to 1.50	1.00 to 1.50	Pink	1.00 to 2.00	1.50 to 2.00	... to 1.50	.75 to 1.00
... to ...	1.25 to 1.50	... to ...	1.00 to 1.50	1.00 to 1.50	Red	... to ...	1.50 to 2.00	... to 1.50	.75 to 1.00
... to ...	1.50 to 2.50	... to 3.00	1.00 to 1.50	1.00 to 1.50	Yellow and var	... to ...	1.50 to 2.00	... to 1.50	.75 to 1.00
.50 to 1.00	2.00 to 2.50	... to ...	... to ...	... to 3.00	Fancy Varieties: White	... to 3.00	2.00 to 3.00	... to 2.00	1.00 to 2.00
.50 to 1.50	2.00 to 2.50	... to ...	... to ...	... to 3.00	Pink	... to 3.00	2.00 to 3.00	... to 2.00	1.00 to 2.00
.50 to 1.50	2.00 to 2.50	... to ...	... to ...	... to 3.00	Red	... to 3.00	2.00 to 3.00	... to 2.00	1.00 to 2.00
.50 to 1.50	2.00 to 2.50	... to 1.50	... to ...	... to 3.00	Yellow and var	... to 3.00	2.00 to 3.00	... to 2.00	1.00 to 2.00
... to ...	... to ...	... to ...	... to ...	... to ...	Novelties	... to ...	... to ...	... to ...	... to ...
.75 to 1.00	1.00 to 2.00	... to 2.00	... to 1.00	... to 1.00	ADIANTUM	... to 1.00	... to 1.00	1.25 to 1.50	... to 1.00
... to 50.00	40.00 to 50.00	25.00 to 60.00	... to 50.00	25.00 to 50.00	ASPARAGUS, Plum. and Ten	20.00 to 30.00	... to 50.00	30.00 to 50.00	25.00 to 50.00
... to ...	1.00 to 2.00	20.00 to 30.00	... to 35.00	25.00 to 50.00	" Sprengeri, bunches	20.00 to 30.00	... to 50.00	20.00 to 30.00	25.00 to 50.00
4.00 to 6.00	8.00 to 10.00	... to 10.00	... to 1.00	6.00 to 8.00	CALLAS	... to ...	... to 8.00	8.00 to 12.00	... to ...
... to ...	... to ...	.75 to 1.50	... to ...	... to ...	DAISIES	... to .75	... to 1.00	1.00 to 1.50	.50 to 1.00
2.00 to 4.00	... to ...	8.00 to 10.00	... to 4.00	2.00 to 4.00	GLADIOLUS	... to ...	... to ...	6.00 to 10.00	... to 5.00
... to ...	... to ...	... to ...	... to 12.50	10.00 to 12.50	LILIES, Harrisii	... to ...	8.00 to 12.00	... to ...	... to ...
... to ...	10.00 to 12.00	... to ...	... to ...	10.00 to 12.50	" Longiflorum	... to 15.00	... to ...	10.00 to 20.00	... to ...
2.00 to 4.00	3.00 to 4.00	3.00 to 4.00	... to 4.00	1.00 to 2.00	LILY OF THE VALLEY	... to 3.00	2.00 to 4.00	2.00 to 4.00	3.00 to 4.00
... to ...	1.00 to 2.00	... to ...	... to ...	2.00 to 2.50	MIGNONETTE, ordinary	... to ...	1.00 to 2.00	... to ...	... to ...
... to ...	... to ...	... to ...	... to ...	... to ...	" fancy	... to 2.00	... to ...	... to ...	... to ...
... to ...	2.00 to 5.00	4.00 to 6.00	... to ...	... to ...	PEONIES	4.00 to 6.00	... to ...	6.00 to 8.00	... to ...
... to 12.50	... to 15.00	12.50 to 15.00	... to 15.00	12.50 to 20.00	SMILAX	... to 25.00	15.00 to 20.00	10.00 to 15.00	... to 15.00
... to ...	... to ...	... to ...	... to ...	... to ...	VIOLETS, ordinary	... to ...	... to ...	... to ...	... to ...
... to ...	... to ...	... to ...	... to ...	... to ...	" fancy	... to ...	... to ...	... to ...	... to ...
... to ...	... to ...	... to ...	... to ...	... to ...	NARCISSUS	... to ...	... to ...	... to ...	... to ...
.15 to .25	.40 to .50	.50 to .75	.25 to .35	.20 to .35	SWEET PEAS	... to 1.00	.40 to 1.00	.25 to 1.00	.15 to .20
... to ...	... to ...	... to ...	... to ...	... to ...		... to ...	... to ...	... to ...	... to ...
... to ...	... to ...	... to ...	... to ...	... to ...		... to ...	... to ...	... to ...	... to ...
... to ...	... to ...	... to ...	... to ...	... to ...		... to ...	... to ...	... to ...	... to ...

Columbus, O.

Trade Notes.

The striking feature of the past season has been the unprecedented demand for bedding plants. Although the variety called for was not large, the list included the well established favorites. Many of our local florists, although they had provided liberally, geraniums especially being grown by the thousands and tens of thousands, found themselves short of good stock.

Council's finance committee has decided in favor of remodeling the city's big greenhouse in Franklin Park in order to make it more available for practical results. This institution has been a sort of white elephant on the city's hands, as it has proved very expensive to heat. The result was the city has been obliged to buy each year a great many plants that should have been grown in the city greenhouses for the parks.

Club News.

At the last meeting of the Columbus Florists' Club it was decided to hold another chrysanthemum show the coming Fall. The plan to be carried out will be somewhat similar to that of last year, but probably on a larger scale. At the next meeting of the club it is intended to take up the subject of the Dayton convention, and see what can be done to make it interesting to the delegates and visitors who may come this way either before or after the meeting.

C. D. B.

Cincinnati, O.

News Notes.

The usual Summer lull has arrived, and July and August will see a general remodeling and getting ready for Fall business. June has been a good month. Stock has kept up fairly well, but the last few days it has been of very poor quality on account of the hot spell here—94 degrees in the shade for the past two days. Saturday last it was 90 degrees, with plenty of air. Picnics and early closings will help us enjoy the dull season.

George Heinl, of Toledo, was a caller on Friday, on his way home.

Weiland & Olinger are moving their ice box and fixtures from Louisville, Ky. Wm. Gardiner is now located at the Cincinnati house.

Charles Hoffmeister has gone to New Castle to look after the growing end of the business.

E. G. GILLETT.

Wholesale Prices of Cut Flowers, Chicago, July 3, 1906.

Prices quoted are by the hundred unless otherwise noted.

ROSES — American Beauty		
36-inch stems........per doz.	.... to	4.00
30-inch stems........ "	.... to	3.00
24-inch stems........ "	.... to	2.50
20-inch stems........ "	.... to	2.00
18-inch stems........ "	.... to	1.50
12-inch stems........ "	....	1.00
8-inch stems and shorts "	.50 to	.75
Bride' Maid, fancy special........	5.00 to	6.00
" extra........	4.00 to	5.00
" No. 1........	2.00 to	3.00
" No. 2........	.50 to	1.00
Golden Gate........	2.00 to	6.00
Carnot........	2.00 to	6.00
Uncle John........	2.00 to	8.00
Liberty........	2.00 to	8.00
Richmond........	2.00 to	6.00
Kaiserins........	2.00 to	6.00
Killarney........	2.00 to	8.00
Perle........	2.00 to	6.00
Chatenay........	2.00 to	6.00
Orchids—Cattleyas........	.... to	50.00
Smilax........	8.00 to	12.00
Lily of the Valley........	2.00 to	4.00
Sweet Peas........	.25 to	.50

CARNATIONS			
Inferior grades all colors		.25 to	.50
Standard Varieties	White........	1.00 to	1.50
	Pink........	1.00 to	1.50
	Red........	1.00 to	1.50
	Yellow & var........	1.00 to	1.50
*Fancy (The highest grades of Sta'd var)	White........	2.00 to	2.50
	Pink........	2.00 to	2.50
	Red........	2.00 to	2.50
	Yellow & var........	2.00 to	2.50
Novelties........		.... to	....
Adiantum........		.50 to	1.00
Asparagus, Plum. & Ten........		.35 to	.50
" Sprengeri, bunches.		.35 to	.50
Gladiolus........		2.00 to	6.00
Lilies, Longiflorum........		8.00 to	12.00
Harrisii........		8.00 to	12.00
Mignonette, ordinary........		1.00 to	2.00
....		.... to	....
Peonies........		2.00 to	6.00
Lilium Candidum, $1.00 per bunch			
Hardy Ferns per 1000........		1.00 to	1.50
Galax "		1.00 to	1.25

St. Louis.

News Notes.

Walter Retzer of Seattle, and J. M. Page of San Francisco, are visiting friends and relations in the city. Both were formerly students at Shaw's Garden, and have many acquaintances in the trade who were glad to see them.

Some of the wholesale houses are contemplating closing at 5 o'clock during the next two months. Why not all get in line?

H. M. Schisler of the Schisler-Cornell Seed Company attended the seedsmen's convention at Toledo, Ohio, last week. Mr. Pommer of the D. I. Bushnell Company spent a day at the meeting. Mr. Nichols of the St. Louis Seed Company was unable to attend owing to a rush of business.

S. Freund of Milwaukee, representing Hummel & Downing, florists' folding boxes, spent a few days with the trade last week.

Harry Balsley of Detroit spent Saturday in the city, coming from Kansas City, Mo., where he reports good trade in red pots.

Frank M. Ellis is still in Panama looking after his interest in the banana plantation. In a letter he states that it will be August before he returns home.

Fred C. Weber, Theo. Miller and Miss Newman are making splendid Summer shows in their windows, consisting of up-to-date cut stock, and blooming plants.

Charles Wors has the flower stands at Delmar Garden. He says trade has improved since the hot weather brought out better crowds.

Fred H. Meinhardt, who is state vice-president of the S. A. F. O. H., has got busy looking up new members. The next club meeting will find him ready with blank applications.

President Ammann of the Florists' Club says he would like to see a large attendance at the meeting next Thursday afternoon. This meeting is to take place at his home in Edwardsville, Ill.; and he gives the following instructions as to how to get there: The members should meet in a body at the bridge entrance at 12:30, and take the car marked Alton, Edwardsville and Granite City Connection. A car leaves every 20 minutes. After that there are two changes, one at East St. Louis and the other at Mitchell; then tell the conductor to leave you off at the greenhouses. This meeting will be an interesting one for all the members. The features will be the nomination of officers, the discussions by Messrs. Weber and Braun, and the entertainment furnished by President Ammann.

The florist bowlers are trying to organise a Summer league of three teams to bowl once a week. Two teams have already been formed. Those who have entered their names are: W. C. Smith, C. A. Kuehn, J. J. Beneke, Will Adies, Ed. Gerlach, Geo. Schriefer, Otto Brunig, James Arado, Henry Lohrenz, and A. G. Grieger. ST. PATRICK.

Detroit.

An Outing.

Twenty-two of Detroit's florists enjoyed a day's fishing at Algonac Thursday, June 28. There were ten boatloads of would-be fishermen, each boat being rowed by an Indian guide. All returned at 7 p. m. to enjoy an elaborate hotel dinner.

J. F. Sullivan has been home the past week suffering from stomach trouble. HARRY.

ROCHESTER, N. Y.—Burglars recently visited Joseph O. Pridmore's flower store at No. 356 Lyell avenue. They broke several panes of glass in the building and entered. The cash drawer was forced open. Less than a dollar was taken. The police are investigating.

San Francisco.

News Items.

All the florists already re-established in this city are fortunate in that they were so long in the trade before the city's disaster that they are well acquainted with every dealer in flowers in every city and hamlet throughout the State; as a consequence their shipping orders amount to more or less every day. If it were not for this business, their daily transactions would not foot up to exceed one-half what it does. And this last week, owing to school-closings throughout the State, the shipping of flowers was extra good, excelling this trade of the last few years. So say Sievers & Boland, Servrau Bros., Pelicano, Rossi & Co. and Alex. Mann, Jr.

It is unfortunate that our Fillmore street florist is out and injured, all owing to fluctuation in this unsettled city. Immediately after the shakeup and fire Fillmore street was grasped as the most available for the purposes of business by professional men, and every building that could be used for store or office purposes was pressed into service. As though by magic Fillmore street was soon the principal street of the city, rents quadrupled and those who had store leases running a year or more were offered for them fabulous prices. But now, what a change! With the work of restoration well under way, the activities of the city's life are drawing away from Fillmore street, mostly to a point half a mile further downtown to Van Ness avenue, the western line of the burned district, and to Golden Gate avenue and to temporary structures that have sprung up in or near old trade centers in the destroyed portion of the city, and I think the time is not far distant when the city that the fire forced out to Fillmore street will have moved back to or near its old haunts.

The lady writer who conducts bright society columns for a local daily paper, has this item this week: Mrs. Jack Sievers, the bride-wife of the junior member of John H. Sievers Co., the flower growers, in her charming, hospitable way, has cared for a large number of friends in her Sansalito home ever since the 18th of April. She has given refuge to a large number of strangers, too, and helped clothe many. ALVIN.

Ventura-by-the-Sea, Cal.

The Free Press of June 22 last contains the following item: "George W. Oliver of the Agricultural Department at Washington, is making his yearly visit to California and spent part of Friday afternoon and Saturday morning in Mrs. Shepherd's gardens. Mr. Oliver was enthusiastic in his admiration of the wonderful begonias and rare plants to be seen everywhere in this garden, and thinks Mrs. Shepherd's tree begonias and the wonderful climber 'Marjorie Daw' marvels of beauty, and valuable additions to the world of flowers. Mrs. Shepherd's new dahlia 'Pericles,' evidently a cross between Imperialis and the Mexican dahlia Maximillian, he considers a superb thing; but what interested him even more was Mrs. Shepherd's everblooming new rose 'Oriole.' This rose is a seedling from La Jonquille, and the stock is so limited that it has not been sold in the East and is not known to rosarians. It is a very vigorous growing rose, attaining a height of 6 feet in a few years, of rather slender habit, medium foliage, and bears its buds on long strong stems. It is perfectly healthy, never having mildew or any imperfections of that kind; but what makes it so wonderfully attractive is its unusual color, pure orange, much the shade of that of the Richardson.

"The Oriole is a most persistent and perpetual bloomer, and a large bunch of its splendid flowers would attract a crowd any place it was exhibited.

"Mr. Oliver tells Mrs. Shepherd that she should have this rose introduced in the East; that it would be enthusiastically received and too much cannot be said in its praise. It would be hardy in the East, south of New York, and very beautiful for cut flowers under glass, if it would preserve its fine rich color."

Boston.

Florists' Club Outing.

Unfortunately a rainy afternoon prevented a large gathering of the Gardeners and Florists' Club on Saturday at their outing to the establishment of William Sim, Cliftondale. Notwithstanding the severity of the elements about forty were present and were surprised indeed at the immense crops which Mr. Sim has in his houses at the present time. As is well known Mr. Sim is a grower of specialties and his specialty at this season is tomatoes. True, tomatoes are a little at variance from the routine crops of the general florist, but at this season of the year there is no question but many a florist might turn an honest and useful penny by cropping with tomatoes, instead of having empty benches as we too often see. Mr. Sim is also a violet grower, a sweet pea specialist and without question an expert on tomatoes. These are the main products of his large establishment, which, by the way, is only seven years old, having crept along until it now ranks among the larger plants in this locality. Of course, sweet peas and violets are Winter crops; so are chrysanthemums, which are not grown here any more, and as Mr. Sim never allows any of his houses to be without a crop we see vast houses of tomatoes. Cucumbers are grown in one house and melons are in another, but these are only side issues, from the main crop—tomatoes. I do not believe that any of those present ever saw more or finer grown tomatoes in one place. There were house after house of them, something like fifty thousand plants in all, and they were all in bearing, giving an enormous crop; and, what is more, it was hard to tell which plant had the best crop or the best shaped fruit. In one of the larger houses Mr. Sim said his yield would be about fifteen tons. His daily picking is now about 100 bushels, and at the time of the visit 125 bushels were ready for picking for Monday morning's market. Only one variety is grown—Comet. Others have been tried and are being tried, but Comet is the variety that is depended upon. The plants all showed intensive care and cultivation, for few bunches of fruit were set with less than six, and many of them seven and eight. Besides those in the houses large quantities were grown in the field.

As usual, the place was neatness throughout, not a weed being seen anywhere. As soon as these crops of tomatoes are finished the houses are filled with sweet peas or violets. Of the latter large fields were seen which would indicate that Mr. Sim is still going to hold the record as a violet grower.

The picnic of the Gardeners and Florists' Club will be held in Caledonian Grove, West Roxbury, on Wednesday, July 25. The committee in charge is actively at work and a very successful outing is assured.

There will be an exhibition of products of children's gardens at Horticultural Hall on Saturday, and as a good many prizes are offered, a very interesting exhibition is looked for.

J. W. D.

Lenox, Mass.

The annual rose and strawberry exhibition of the Lenox Horticultural Society took place in the Town Hall, Lenox, June 26. Unfortunately perennials and strawberries were scarce, the former owing to the recent rains; the latter to the lateness of the season. Roses were shown remarkably well, especially a large vase of Frau Karl Druschki, exhibited by E. Jenkins, for which he was awarded a first class certificate.

The principal exhibitors in pot plants were S. Carlquist, who had some remarkably fine tuberous begonias and gloxinias. E. Jenkins had standard geraniums, which were excellent; they stood 5 feet high and were literally covered with blooms; gloxinias and Acalypha Sanderiana. P. J. Donahue had some good plants of Nicotiana Sanderæ. In peonies F. Heeremans had the largest display. Perennials were shown by Miss A. Kneeland and Miss H. Parish. In vegetables E. Jenkins and D. Dunn were first in their respective classes, in which were some good celery, onions and potatoes for the time of year. F. Heeremans showed a collection of vegetables, not for competition, for which he was awarded a cultural commendation, and a diploma for lettuce, "Sutton's Favorite." In the fruit classes the awards were divided between A. H. Wingett and P. J. Donahue.

Messrs. F. Reynolds and E. Edwards were the judges.

GEORGE FOULSHAM, Sec'y.

Buffalo.

News Items.

Henry Wise, of Wise Brothers, of East Aurora, has taken charge of Wm. F. Kasting's greenhouse plant in Erie, Pa. Mr. Kasting is fortunate in securing such an able grower.

Mrs. Bailey, wife of the popular Jake, at Kasting's wholesale house, presented her husband with a nine-pound boy on Sunday last.

W. J. Palmer & Son have had the past week the three largest weddings of the season. The Howard wedding decoration used up an abundance of outdoor flowers; the bridal table was handsomely decorated with Bride roses, lily of the valley and white sweet peas, making a pretty effect. At the Gansom wedding specimen hydrangea plants and large quantities of American Beauty roses were used. The Davis wedding, at St. Paul's Church, required a large number of palms and hydrangeas, also one thousand pink peonies.

Charles Schnell, of S. A. Anderson's, who was married on June 27 to Miss Towers, has left for an extended wedding trip.

W. H. G.

Minneapolis.

News Notes.

A meeting of the Twin City florists was held at Nagel's greenhouses, June 28, to arrange for the picnic. The following officers were re-elected to fill the offices they held the past year: Olof Olson, chairman; E. Nagel, treasurer; Ralph Latham, secretary. The treasurer reported a balance on hand from last year, and the society in general is in a prosperous condition. Some favor a steamboat ride down the Mississippi River, while others favor a picnic at one of the nearby lakes.

Ralph Latham reports a good trade considering the time of the season.

The department stores continue to corral the most of the cheap trade; every day seems to be a banner day with them. Donaldsons and the Powers Mercantile appear to have about all they can do on Saturday. At the close prices at which they sell, it must take an immense number of sales to realize much of a profit. They offer good carnations at 25c., 35c. and 50c. per dozen; roses at from 75c. to $1 per dozen and all other flowers in the same proportion.

Rice Brothers, wholesale florists, say trade is about over with them; stock is not at all plentiful, and the demand from the country very light.

Trade with the Greeks this year has not been good, and another season it is very probable we shall have a much less number with us, a fact which will be appreciated by the florists.

PAUL.

NEW HAVEN, CONN.—During the severest part of the electrical storm that visited Edgewood this week, the Elm City Nursery Company's new tower was struck, the roof practically ruined. In the current's passage downward, one peculiar antic it cut up was the melting of several feet of brass chains connected with one of the valves. It is quite probable that the buildings were saved by the lightning's seeking the tower, which is close by.

Philadelphia.

Florists' Club Meeting.

While the attendance was very slim at the meeting on Tuesday last, yet those present were well rewarded as the meeting was a good one. Convention matters came in for considerable discussion. John Westcott as chairman of transportation committee reported that the fare, at one fare and a third would be $20.07. George C. Watson, chairman of hotel committee, gave a full list of all the hotels in Dayton with the capacity of each, and stated that the Algonquin was the most desirable, capacity 350, rates $2.50 and $3, American plan. All other hotels are smaller. Any one going to Dayton should get a room reserved as the capacity of the hotels will be fully taken up.

Following up a discussion at the June meeting about suits brought by commission men against the Adams Express Company, Edward Reid of the grievance committee made a very good report. He had investigated two cases recently nonsuited in this city. The express company is very careful to get its cases before one judge, and the nonsuit is almost always allowed, on the plea that it is the consignee who should sue, not the consignor. In one very able opinion by a prominent attorney it was stated that many courts had decided that as the consignor was equally interested in the shipment "viz., if it was not delivered he did not get his money," it was perfectly legal for him to sue. This opinion ended by saying if the cases could only be brought before a jury damages could be obtained in almost every case. Other members of the club took up the discussion, and several stated that the U. S. Express Company had treated them much better than the Adams.

Ernest Hemming of Thomas Meehan & Sons made a very able address on "Japanese Iris," giving the history of these flowers as being introduced here in 1858, and spoke at length on the various good points of the Iris. To get perfect results the plants should be treated as aquatics, flooded during the growing and flowering season and kept dry during Winter.

The reception and banquet of Hugh Dickson of Belfast, Ireland, will be given at Dooner's Hotel on Friday, July 6, at 7 p. m.

W. A. Leonard of Lansdowne will take a trip to England early in August to visit his father who is now 84.

The dissolution of Johnson & Stokes, seedsmen, has now taken place. The Johnson Seed Company is doing business at 217 Market street, and Walter A. Stokes is at 219. Previously the old firm occupied both stores. All stock on hand was divided equally, then all doorways between the two stores were walled up, and on Monday last two firms started up, where one had been before.

DAVID RUST.

Pittsburg.

News Notes.

T. P. Langhans of the Pittsburg CutFlower Company is spending a few days in the East. Other members of the trade are getting ready for their vacation this month. E. C. Ludwig and family expect to go to Atlantic City shortly for a long rest. Quite a few are going to the convention of the S. A. F. O. H. next month and will take in Cincinnati and other points.

The annual outing of the Florists' Club will be held Tuesday, July 10, and every member of the club should try his best to be there and bring a friend along if he desires. A boat ride on the Monongahela river to a point either up or down, which has not yet been decided upon as it depends upon the stage of water, when a stop will be made at some grove for several hours, returning in the evening to the city. Sports of all kinds will be indulged in for which about 30 prizes will be offered. A game of baseball between growers and retailers will also be on the program and will likely be a hotly contested affair. There will also be card playing on the boat and dancing, with plenty to eat and drink. The committee in charge promise a good time for everybody so don't fail to come and show them that you appreciate their efforts. The boat leaves the wharf at foot of Market street at 9:15 a. m., rain or shine. The committee is desirous of having the boat decorated nicely, and if any one wishes to donate greens or flowers, have them at Blind Brother's store early Tuesday morning, or bring them to the boat as early as possible. Some of the florists have promised to close up shop for the day so that their help may be able to attend; it is a pity that all will not do so. The boat ride of last year was a delightful affair and pleased all who went along, so from all indications this outing will eclipse last year's in point of attendance. Get boat tickets in good time from the committee.

E. C. REINEMAN.

HEATING.

Growers' Problems Solved by U. G. Scollay.

I would like to ask some questions in regard to heating an addition to a house. I enclose a rough sketch. No 1 is the old house which is 30 x 35 feet and 9 feet high at the center, even span, and contains about 400 feet of 2-inch pipe. No. 2 is the addition and is 24 by 30 feet, single span, on the south end of old house, and contains 1080 square feet of glass; 9 feet high at the highest point. How many feet of 2-inch pipe will I require to heat for carnations and bedding stock? Would two 2-inch flow pipes be sufficient, or would I need 3-inch pipe to supply the coils? The beds are solid; how would you arrange the piping? I am using a hot water boiler, 465 square inches of grate surface. By adding two sections I would increase the grate to 652 square inches, and the radiation to 1,300 square feet. Would that be large enough, or would you advise a new boiler for the addition? O. H. J. P.
Rhode Island.

—If you find it easier to connect from the boiler just as it is, with a separate main to the new addition, I would advise running a 3-inch flow and return main from the boiler, through the present house into the new section. You can run from this main three 2-inch pipes along the west, south and east sides to the doorway. Make this coil up in one flow and two returns. In addition to this I would advise connecting up four coils, running north and south, of four 2-inch pipes each. These can be hung on the sides of the beds. You do not show on your sketch the location of your benches, but I assume that they are laid out north and south. This applies to the benches other than the side ones. From one of the coils which I presume you have on the east side of the present house, you can make an extension into the new section, and run a short coil of, say, three or four 2-inch pipes from east to west to the present doorway on the south end of the old house. This latter coil will take care of the glass exposure above the roof of the old house. If you find it desirable to make any particular change in this layout, I would say that you will require at least 550 feet of 2-inch pipe in the new section; and at the same time I would mention that I consider you are quite short of surface in the present house, when you state that you have only 400 feet of 2-inch pipe in it. In my opinion you will save coal and attention if you will increase this by 100 feet. The present rating of your boiler, 900 square feet of radiation, if it is good, should be ample for the two houses; but if you will add the two sections mentioned and increase its capacity it will do you no harm, but rather will save you fuel and give less night work keeping up the temperature of the houses. It is always well to have at least 25 per cent. excess capacity. When I say excess capacity, I mean "capacity," and not many of the ordinary ratings according to catalogues. Not knowing the present layout of your heating plant I am compelled to make suggestions as I do, to simplify matters for you. A little more detail in many of the sketches submitted would help me materially to answer questions in a more intelligent way.

U. G. SCOLLAY.

THE FLORISTS' EXCHANGE

We are a straight shoot and aim to grow into a vigorous plant

A WEEKLY MEDIUM OF INTERCHANGE FOR FLORISTS, NURSERYMEN, SEEDSMEN AND THE TRADE IN GENERAL

Vol. XXII. No. 2 NEW YORK AND CHICAGO, JULY 14, 1906 One Dollar Per Year

HYDRANGEAS

For Summer Blooming.

We have a magnificent lot of Hydrangea Otaksa grown especially for **JULY AND AUGUST FLOWERING**. The plants are just coming into bloom, just beginning to show color, and will be in perfection during July and August, when they are in great demand at watering places and other summer resorts. There is nothing showier or more satisfactory for lawn decoration. We make a specialty of them, and find an increasing demand for them from year to year. They can be shipped anywhere safely by freight.

Large plants in tubs, $2.00 to $3.00 each, according to size; Very large specimens, in half barrels, $5.00 and $7.50 each.

F. R. PIERSON CO., Tarrytown-on-Hudson, N. Y.

ONLY **$5.00** PER HUNDRED

from 2¼ inch pots in thousand lots;

$6.00 in smaller lots.

Richmond, Killarney and Beauty

Grafted Stock

BRIDE and BRIDESMAID

$12.00 per 100

KILLARNEY and RICHMOND

$15.00 per 100

Exceptionally Fine, Large Plants

SEND FOR SAMPLES.

W. H. ELLIOTT, BRIGHTON, MASS.

Mention The Florists' Exchange when writing.

SOW NOW Vaughan's Primrose Seed

If you have not received our list of Primula and Perennial Seeds, please write for same.

CHINESE PRIMULAS
With Fringed Foliage

	250 seeds	1000 seeds
Chiswick Red, bright red	$0.50	$1.75
Kermesina Splendens, crimson	.50	1.75
Alba Magnifica, snow white, of excellent form and habit	.50	1.70
Glowing Coal, the darkest red	.50	1.75
Peach Blossom, beautiful white with pink hue	.50	1.70
Blue, a clear sky-blue	.50	1.70
Upright Deep Velvety Red	.50	1.90
Rosea, a bright pink	.35	1.50
Bridesmaid, brightest pink	.50	1.75
Mont Blanc, large, pure milk-white flowers	.50	
Striata, white and lilac-striped	.35	1.30
Mixed, a splendid variety. ⅛ oz., $3.00	.35	1.35

DOUBLE CHINESE PRIMROSES

White, pink, flesh, red and striped; each, per 150 seeds, 35c.; Double mixed, 500 seeds, 35c.; 1000 seeds, $1.50.

NEW GIANT PRIMULAS

This new strain is a vast improvement on the older varieties, the flowers being considerably larger.

Giant Pink, Pure White and Copper Color; each pkt. of 250 seeds ..... 50c.

Giant Mixed, includes this year a number of new shades; pkt. of 250 seeds ..... 50c.

VAUGHAN'S INTERNATIONAL PRIMULA MIXTURE : : :

THIS mixture is composed of the most salable colors of single

Flowering Chinese Primulas : : : :

the best whites, pinks and reds, with a sprinkling of other colors enough to give a large variety of colors, the most important shades predominating. We have taken special pains to make this mixture as complete as possible and unreservedly recommend it to everyone.

Pkt of 250 seeds ... $0 50
6 Pkts., 1250 seeds ... 2 50
Per 1-16 oz 2 50

Obconica Grandiflora, mixed, 1-16 oz., 60c.; Trade pkt., 25c.

Obconica Grandiflora, large flowering, pink, 1-16 oz., 85c.; Trade pkt., 25c.

Obconica Grandiflora, large flowering, pure white, 1-16 oz., 85c.; Trade pkt., 25c.

CALCEOLARIA HYBRIDA

Our mixture is composed of the choicest selections of the tigered, marbled, spotted and variegated varieties and we know will give entire satisfaction.

Trade pkt., 1000 seeds, 50c.; 3 trade pkts., $1.25.

CINERARIA

Vaughan's Columbian Mixture

It consists of a mixture made up by ourselves of the choicest English, French and German strains and cann t be excelled in variety of colors size, shape and substance of flowers and perfect habit of plant.

Trade pkt., 1000 seeds, 50c.; 3 pkts., $1.25.

"**Old Rose**," A splendid strain, producing large flowers, which range in color from pink to rich coppery red. Trade pkt., 50c.

Large Flowering White, Crimson Blue, Blood-Red; each, per trade pkt., 500 seeds, 35c.

Hybrida, fine large flowering mixed, 500 seeds, trade pkt ..... 25c.

Hybrida Grandiflora Nana, best mixed dwarf, trade pkt ..... 25c.

Hybrida Plenissima, extra choice double mixed trade pkt ..... 50c.

Hybrida Plenissima, double white, trade pkt ..... 50c.

10 Per Cent Special Cash Discount On orders over $2.00 for Flower seeds if the cash is enclosed. This discount does not apply to Asparagus Seed.

Vaughan's Seed Store 14 BARCLAY ST., NEW YORK

CHICAGO, 84-86 Randolph Street
Greenhouses, Western Springs, Ill

MAJESTY MIGNONETTE

(Greenhouse Matured Seed)

THE *grandest of all Mignonettes* for indoor *forcing*—Easy to grow, strong constitution—and throwing up a *quantity of flower spikes* which grow to an immense size; the *lateral shoots*—too—are *as large as many Mignonettes* now grown under glass.

The seed I offer has been saved for me by a *leading grower of Mignonette*—who makes a *specialty* of this useful cut flower for the *New York market*, from *selected spikes only—under glass.*

Trial pkt., 30c.; half trade pkt., 60c.; trade pkt. containing about 1,000 seeds, $1.00.

Sweet Peas for Christmas and Thanksgiving Flowering

Boddington's Christmas Early Pink.—This is the earliest and most profitable and useful Sweet Pea in cultivation. 60c. per lb.; 15c. per oz.

Boddington's Christmas Early White.—A companion to Christmas Early Pink. Just as free and profuse a bloomer, and is, without doubt, the finest early white for indoor planting. 75c. per lb.; 20c. per oz.

PANSY SEED

Boddington's Challenge Mixture

This mixture contains all the finest *Giant* strains—of the leading Pansy Specialists in the world—the *Giant* self colors, the *Giant* striped and margined, and the *Giant* blotched—all carefully mixed in proportion—the *finest* that money can buy—the finest your money can buy. *A Florist*, who has grown it, said "Why don't you call it *Defiance!*"

Price ⅛ trade pkt. 40c. trade pkt. 75c. ⅛ oz. $1.50. ¼ oz. $2.50. oz. $5.00. (For named varieties and to color see catalogue.)

ARTHUR T. BODDINGTON

342 West 14th Street *New York City*

Mention The Florists' Exchange when writing.

COOLING AND REFRESHING

New Pansy Seed

Extra Blended, Large Flowering, Trade Packet, $1.00

Primula Obconica, Trade Packet, 25c.
Candytuft, White Empress, Ounce, 20c.
Glazing Points, Peerless No. 2, postpaid, 75c
Mastica for glazing, gal., $1.25; 6 gallon cases, $6.75.
Fine Rose Bone, 200 lbs., $4.00.
Nitrate of Soda, 50 lbs., $2.00; 100 lbs., $3.50.
Sulphur, 25 lbs., 85c.

Wm. Elliott & Sons 201 Fulton St. NEW YORK

Mention The Florists' Exchange when writing.

FOR IMMEDIATE SOWING

We offer

PRIMULA OBCONICA RAWSON'S NEW GIANT
Pure White, Pink, Crimson, Superb Mixture .... per 100 seeds, 50c.; per 1000 seeds, $4.00

CINERARIA GRANDIFLORA
Rawson's Superfine .... Liberal Trade Pkt. 1.00

CINERARIA GRANDIFLORA DWARF
Rawson's Superfine .... Liberal Trade Pkt. 1.00

MIGNONETTE RAWSON'S MAMMOTH FRAGRANT
One of the finest Greenhouse Mignonettes in existence .... ¼ oz. 50.; per oz., 1.50

CANDYTUFT, RAWSON'S GIANT WHITE
.... Per oz. 80c.; per lb., 4.00

And the most complete collection of choice and desirable perennial flower seeds. Our catalogue free upon application. RAWSON'S INTERESTING BULB CATALOGUE out JULY 15. Write for it. : : :

W. W. RAWSON & COMPANY
5 Union St., Boston, Mass.

Mention The Florists' Exchange when writing.

PACIFIC SEED GROWERS' CO.
411-415 SANSOME STREET
SAN FRANCISCO, CAL.
Specialties:
Onion, Carrot, Lettuce, Sweet Peas

Mention The Florists' Exchange when writing.

Removal Notice

J. M. THORBURN & CO.
(Late of 36 Certlandt Street)
Have removed to their large new 5 story building at
33 BARCLAY STREET
Extending through to 38 Park Place.

Our WHOLESALE BULB CATALOGUE will be ready next week. Send for it and compare our prices before you order elsewhere. We handle only first size bulbs. : :

J. M. THORBURN & CO.
33 Barclay St. through to 38 Park Place
Established 1802 NEW YORK

Mention The Florists' Exchange when writing.

New Catalogue
COLORED SEED BAGS

Write for copy and prices, stating quantity you wish to purchase.

Herndon, Lester & Ivey Co,
Richmond, Va.

Mention The Florists' Exchange when writing.

New Crop of my
Christmas Flowering
SWEET PEA SEED

Christmas Pink and Florence Denzer, pure white, will be ready August 1st.

Those two well known varieties are raised by over 2000 florists all over the world. Here is one out of many letters received:

Dear Sir: My sweet peas, which I raised from your seed, received the highest award at the Carnation Exhibit in Boston, being over 18 inches long. JOHN T. GALE, Tewkesbury, Mass.

Price 1-4 lb. 75c.; per lb. $7.00
MAILED FREE

New Christmas Flowering Hybrids, 20 to 30 colors, mostly blue, salmon, purple lavender, in mixtures; also Mrs. Edie Wild, carmine, separate color. 1 Trade pkt., $1.00, 5 Trade pkts, $4.00; not more than 5 pkts. taken in order to each customer just now. Those new hybrids are just as free bloomers as Cristmas Pink and Florence Denzer, some much larger, and received first-class Certificate of Merit by the Mass. Horticultural Society, Boston, March 24. Seed ready in Sept.

All seed originated with me is sold in my original sealed pkts., with cultural directions, to the growers, but none for seedsmen for propagating.

Orders filled strictly in rotation.

ANT. C. ZVOLANEK
BOUND BROOK, N. J.

Pansy Seed
THE JENNINGS STRAIN

New crop now ready, saved from finest selected stock, large flowering and great variety of fancy colors. By mail one pkt., 4000 seed, $1.00; ¼ oz., $2.50; 1 oz., $5.00, 2 oz., $9.00; 3 oz., $12.00. Cash with order.

E. B. JENNINGS,
Lock Box 254 Southport, Conn.
Grower of the Finest Pansies.

Mention The Florists' Exchange when writing.

CINERARIA SEED

S. & W. Co.'s Giant Prize Strain, pkt., 50c.; 1-64 oz., $2.00

PANSY SEED

Non Plus Ultra, mixed, pkt., 25c.; ¼ oz., $1.50; per oz., $5.00

STUMPP & WALTER CO., 50 Barclay Street, New York

Mention The Florists' Exchange when writing.

A BED OF MUSHROOMS

Raised from our Spawn, will **bear longer and yield better** than from any other variety of Spawn. This is proven by facts. Full particulars and information how to succeed in mushroom raising free. We warrant you if using our method of growing mushrooms that all will go well.

KNUD GUNDESTRUP & CO., MUSHROOM SPECIALISTS, 4273 Milwaukee Ave., CHICAGO

Mention The Florists' Exchange when writing.

PRIMROSES

Improved Chinese: Finest grown, named or mixed. Strong 2 inch $2.00 per 100.

Cyclamen Giganteum: Finest mixed, strong 2½ inch $4.00 per 100.

XXX SEEDS

CHINESE PRIMROSE

Finest grown, mixed, 500 seeds, $1.00; ½ pkt., 50c.

Primula Obconica Grand. Finest large flowering mixed, 1000 seeds, 50c.

CINERARIA. Finest large-flowering, dwf. mxd., 1000 seeds, 50c.

DAISY, double Giant mixed, 1000 Seeds 25c.

GIANT PANSY. The best large flowering varieties, critically selected, 5000 seeds, $1.00; half pkt., 50c.; per oz, $3.50. 500 seeds of Giant Mme. Perret, pansy seed added to every $1.00 pkt. of Giant Pansy. Cash. Liberal extra count of seeds in all packets.

JOHN F. RUPP, Shiremanstown, Pa.
The Home of Primroses

Mention The Florists' Exchange when writing.

PANSY SEED

Brown's Extra Select Superb Giant Prize PANSIES, awarded Silver Medal, St. Louis Exposition 1904. My own grown new 1906 crop ready. Price mixed seed 3000 seeds, $1.00; ¼ oz., $1.50; ½ oz., $2.50., 1 oz., $5.00; ¼ lb., $14.00; ½ lb., $25.00; 1 lb., $50.00. Cash with order.

PETER BROWN
Lancaster, Pa.

Mention The Florists' Exchange when writing.

PANSY SEED

Schmidt's Famous Strain, large flowering and fancy colors; none better. Per pkt., 50c.; ¼ oz., $2.00; 1 oz., $8.50. Plants ready September.

J. C. SCHMIDT CO.
BRISTOL, PA.

Mention The Florists' Exchange when writing.

PANSY SEED

Of my own growing—**Crop of 1906.**
Unexcelled Mixture, ¼ oz., $1.00; oz., $3.00. **Parisian Mammoth,** imported, ¼ oz., $1.00; oz., $3.00. **Danish Exhibition,** imported, ¼ oz., $1.00; oz., $3.00. **Masterpiece,** fringed edge, imported, ¼ oz., $1.00; oz., $3.00. **Giant Mammoth,** extra fine, imported, ¼ oz., $1.50; oz., $5.50.

FRANCIS BRILL, HEMPSTEAD, L. I., N. Y.

Mention The Florists' Exchange when writing.

Catalog Engravings
and ILLUSTRATIONS

that print EASILY. That's the kind we make—have been since '73

JAS. M. BRYANT, Horticultural Engraving and Printing
706 Chestnut Street, PHILADELPHIA, PA.

Write for our Catalogue of Stock Engravings.

Mention The Florists' Exchange when writing.

MUSHROOM SPAWN

Originators and growers of **superior strains of Tissue-Culture Pure Spawn.**
Send for our booklet.

PURE CULTURE SPAWN CO.
PACIFIC, MO.

Mention the Florists' Exchange when writing.

H. H. HICKS,
Importer of and dealer in
MUSHROOM SPAWN
KENNETT SQUARE, PA.

"Invoices of Barter's English Mushroom Spawn received monthly. Am. Pure Culture Spawn always on hand. When writing for prices state quantity wanted.

Mention The Florists' Exchange when writing.

ROEMER'S SUPERB PRIZE PANSIES

"The finest strain of Pansies in the World." Introducer and Grower of all the leading Novelties Highest Award, International Exhibition Dusseldorf, 1906. Catalogue free on application.

FRED. ROEMER, Seed Grower,
Quedlinburg, Germany.

Mention the Florists' Exchange when writing.

NOW READY
Zirngiebel's Prize Pansy Seeds,

In trade packages; $1.00 each.
GIANT MARKET, 2000 SEEDS.
GIANT FANCY, 600 SEEDS.
Full directions with each package.

Augustus Zirngiebel, Needham, Mass.

Mention The Florists' Exchange when writing.

BURPEE'S SEEDS

PHILADELPHIA

Blue List of Wholesale Prices mailed only to those who plant for profit.

Mention The Florists' Exchange when writing.

Giant Cinerarias

Mixture of perfect colors.

Dwarf Hybrids, Semi-Dwarf Hybrids } Each separate Tr. Pkt. $0.50, 6 Tr. Pkts. $2.50

O. V. ZANGEN, Seedsman, HOBOKEN, N. J.

Mention The Florists' Exchange when writing.

C. C. MORSE & CO.

Seed Growers
815-817 Sansome Street,
SAN FRANCISCO, CAL.
Careful growers of California specialties

Mention The Florists' Exchange when writing.

PLANT CULTURE

PRICE, $1.00.
The best book for the plant grower.
A. T. DE LA MARE PTG. & PUB. CO. LTD.
2-8 Duane Street, New York.

Seed Trade Report.

AMERICAN SEED TRADE ASSOCIATION

Henry W. Wood, Richmond, Va., president; C. S. Burge, Toledo, O., first vice-president; G. B. McVay, Birmingham, Ala., second vice-president; C. E. Kendel, Cleveland, O., secretary and treasurer; J. H. Ford, Ravenna, O., assistant secretary.

The total value of grass seeds exported from the United States during the year ending June 30, 1905, was $2,002,622; that of all other seeds, $317,554. The value of the imports of seeds, other than flax seed or linseed, for the same period, was $3,138,932.

CHICAGO.—The local report from the cucumber centers is rather discouraging especially in the fields of White Spine where the crop is much below the average and the prospect for a good seed result is far from promising. However, recent rains may have relieved the threatening conditions.

A SWEET PEA FARM IN CALIFORNIA.—I wonder how many readers of The Florists' Exchange, who have never seen a sweet pea field of 160 acres can imagine what it looks like when in full bloom? The writer visited the John Bodger seed farm in Los Angeles county, June 25, and the sight of that field is one never to be forgotten. It is one half mile square, divided by a road running east and west. The rows are a quarter mile long. Where the sweet peas are grown in separate colors they give the field the appearance of a great floor laid in mosaics; where they are grown in mixtures, the light colors predominating, the 40 acres look like beautifully mottled cloth. The varieties are in lands 10 to 100 feet wide, according to quantity, and are separated by rows of lettuce, larkspur, candytuft, and scarlet flax. To the windward side of this great field the air is filled with the fragrance for miles. A crop of Yorkshire Hero peas from 40 acres was being threshed. This stock is for the local trade, and is the first produced in this part of the state. Forty acres Kentucky Wonder, 20 acres Scarlet Runner, and 100 acres Lima beans, are making a fine showing. Here the rules of the gardener in regard to covering seed are set aside, and all seeds are put down to the moist seed bed under a covering of two to five inches of dry finely pulverized soil. This system of planting is possible only in a climate where no rain falls after the seed is in the ground.

About July 1 the sweet pea harvest will begin, of the early varieties, and will close in about 20 days. The dwarf varieties are cut with a California bean cutter, which is a sled made of plank 24 inches wide, and 2 inches thick, shod with iron soles. From each sole depends a knife about 3 feet long, pointing diagonally to the rear of the sled, which cuts the beans or peas close to the ground and by means of iron rods on the knives leave the vines in small windrows where they are left to dry. Two rows are cut at a time; and three horses are required to draw the sled. The threshing is done in the field. The tall growing varieties are cut with a regular mowing machine, left to dry as is done with alfalfa hay for several days; they are then piled up for a week or two to cure, and afterward threshed according to the convenience of the grower, he having no fear of violent wind and rain to disperse the piles and damage the crop.

P. D. B.

CONGRESSIONAL DISTRIBUTION OF VEGETABLE AND FLOWER SEEDS.—In the Yearbook of the Department of Agriculture for 1905, just issued, Professor A. J. Pieters, Botanist in Charge of Seed and Plant Introduction and Distribution, Bureau of Plant Industry, tells of the Department's methods in the purchase of Congressional seeds. He says:

"This Office aims to get seeds of the best value. This, of course, does not mean the cheapest seed, as everyone knows that the value of vegetable seed is not measured solely by the price. Vitality and trueness to type, or purity of stock, are of the utmost importance, and of these the latter can be determined only by a field inspection. Experts must therefore be employed who know the general character of each grower's stock, and part of whose business it is to visit the principal growers at least once each year to keep posted on their work and on the quality of their stock. The objects kept in view are (1) to obtain good seeds—as good as those sold by the best mail-trade houses (though they are no better, since the seeds are bought mostly from the growers who supply the seed trade); and (2) to get these seeds at the best prices.

* * *

"The seed needed is secured in one of two ways: (1) It is bought outright, the seeds being on hand at the time of purchase, or (2) it is contracted for, the Department agreeing to pay a fixed sum for all seed of satisfactory quality delivered up to a given amount. All seeds offered are considered by a special committee which consults with the seed experts of the Bureau of Plant Industry and recommends purchases in accordance with the following considerations: (1) The known quality of the stocks offered; (2) the reputation of the firm making the offer; (3) the price, calculated upon delivery at Washington, D. C.

"The price, though important, is never the first consideration; good seeds must be secured at a fair price, and 'the best value' is the watchword in the work. The packeting of the seed is done by contract."

European Notes.

The heat wave which has caused us such terrible anxiety during the month now closing is fast subsiding in the more northerly parts of Europe, and in England and northern France copious rains have fallen. There is every probability that these will travel farther south, and in that case some of our crops that appear under present conditions to be hopelessly lost, may yet be partially saved. Beets, mangels and carrots which have benefited by the hot sun during the period of their inflorescence sadly needed the rain to develop the seed; the same is true of onion and leek, two of our most promising crops this year.

Radishes (Summer varieties) have gone never to return, so far as the French growers are concerned; the English and Dutch growers have been more fortunate, but the varieties grown in these two countries are principally the midseason and late. The forcing kinds are a specialty with the French growers, and, where these have not perished from heat and drought, the flowers and foliage are being devoured by maggot and fly. As regards mangels matters are slightly complicated owing to the rapidly increasing popularity of the giant half sugar varieties. The reason is not far to seek, as analysis has shown that they contain a very high percentage of nutritive matter, and being more solid are also more resistant to adverse influences. If properly stored at the time of lifting they will keep sound and sweet until the new crop is ready, and this quality in times of drought, like the present, renders them simply invaluable. The late George Taber, working in conjunction with an eminent agricultural chemist, developed his famous Gate Post mangel many years ago on the same lines as the above, and up to the present the only variety that approaches it in solidity and nutritive value is the Golden Tankard, the German variety Eckendorf being a good second.

While the crops of European onions are so very promising, the prospects for next year's crops are by no means favorable, as the drought has inflicted great injury on the growing plants. Up to the present leek has not suffered to the same extent.

The samples of extra early turnip which have already been threshed out are small and very red in color; the germination, however, is quite satisfactory. Rutabaga, where it is left standing, has improved considerably; the crop will in any case be small and inadequate.

In flower seeds nasturtiums are prospering; and sweet peas have gone to the wall. Wallflowers are finishing splendidly; the crop will be abundant and good. EUROPEAN SEEDS.

FRENCH SEED TRADE.—To the long period of nasty, rainy weather which we had here (and in most European countries as I hear) succeeded very nice, beautiful dry weather. We are now enjoying a lovely bright sun, such as we have not been seeing for a long time past. The result is that the soil has become so dry all of a sudden, that farmers are now anxiously waiting for some rain. As stated in my last report, most biennial plants, were planted some time since, in a pitiful condition, being so very small and tiny, that the question was whether they would get on or not. Besides they were stuck into a wet, badly prepared soil, in which they could not possibly find any strength at all. The sudden change in the weather, becoming so very hot and dry, terribly affected those young plants, which were either burnt down or forced to shoot up quickly to seed. We may easily realize that under such circumstances they will produce but a very small quantity of seeds.

Such is the case this season for swedes, turnips, carrots, beets, mangels, etc. Of course this will be no great inconvenience as regards swedes and turnips of which there are still such large stocks in warehouses. On the contrary it will be to the benefit of both dealer and the farmer, as it will lower the stocks and cause a certain advance in prices this year or next, and we all well know the rise in price is much needed by the farmers, who have now to grow these articles at such a low price that there cannot be any living for them under the circumstances.

I believe beets suffered most, and it is a great pity to see such small plants of beets in the fields, which have already shot up. Certainly the crop will be worse this year than it has been for a long time, and consequently a good rise in price is inevitable.

Mangels are not looking well either, but there was such a large acreage planted, that it would not be easy now to say what they will do later on.

Cabbages came out the best of all, as it looks, although a good deal of them perished through the Winter, and some others badly shot up to seed in some districts, the crop will not be so bad after all.

Leeks are looking pretty well for the present.

Onions have kept very small, they did not develop properly and a good many lots suffered last March in earth on account of long standing wet weather, and the stalks have become yellowish. Owing to the extraordinary high prices of last season, I think that, even if the plants get on nicely and do not get broken down by hail or storm, etc., the fall in price of onion seeds will not be so great as it was first expected from the large acreages planted.

Parsnips and parsleys do not look bad, for the present.

Mignonette, nasturtiums, etc., suffered terribly from hot weather, and a good many lots could not even be sown owing to drought.

Sweet peas which have to be sown already in March, on the contrary, had to stand a fearful wet period which hurt them terribly, so only a very poor crop of same is to be expected this year.

Cabbage, lettuces and Cos lettuces have just lately been transplanted under very good weather conditions.

Radishes are quite a failure with us; firstly the acreage planted was awfully small, then the prices paid to the growers were much higher than usual, so that no doubt we may reckon upon a big advance in prices.

Up to present time vines are looking beautiful and let us hope for a good wine year which is so much wanted in our country after these last two or three bad years.—French Seeds in Horticultural Advertiser.

June 22, 1906.

NARCISSUS TRUMPET MAJOR, FRENCH GROWN.—Since the need of early forcing trumpet daffodils has been felt, the French grown Trumpet Major may be considered as an acquisition in the long list to choose from. Though an early bloomer, yet the forcing must be done with a great deal of skill, acquired by much practical experience, as not every grower, able to force a good many other trumpet narcissus successfully, can make of this article a paying business.

It is not my intention to give complete cultural directions, leading directly to success, but only a very important hint how to obtain with less skill, a moderate turnout, leaving the perfection of the work to the grower, viz., make a selection of single crowned, round bulbs only.

Perhaps many may wonder at me giving such a simple hint, but if you look on the average French Trumpet Major, imported direct (mixed lots, as they are, of single and double crowned, split-up and mother bulbs), boxed and grown, you will be astonished at the great many disappointed faces at the time when the flowers should be harvested. It is not without reason that so many have abandoned this line, stating that in French trumpets there is no profit; the half or two thirds of them do not flower. Long experience, however, has taught that the greatest chance of fair blooming is to be secured from single crowned bulbs, and one has to see well to it that there is no second bulb in the same skin. I cannot give a warrant that all will have success by this method, but one can, with proper treatment, almost depend upon 80 per cent. of the bulbs flowering.

The quality of the Trumpet Major from France usually served is worthless or next to it. The really good forcing bulb of one single crown and sufficient size (11c. m. or by preference 12 c. m.) is difficult to obtain on account of the scarcity; and most of the time one has to pay a good price for them; but, at least, he can expect that his stock is worth the outlay. Only very few French bulb exporters are aware of the grade wanted.

The cause of so many bad bulbs being sent across the ocean may be found in the difficulty of raising them. It seems that they will not grow to any size without being apt to divide themselves, and if not actually split in two, yet the same skin contains, in many cases, more than one bulb. The raisers in France, thus having always a very limited crop, think it sparingly paid labor to grow them for your market. Their experience though does not go further than the culture on their own local ground, where they see flower, by natural growing, nearly every offset, big or little. It is difficult to convince them that the same result cannot be obtained when the bulbs are grown in artificial heat, less light and closed air. They like to market a great number of bulbs and the majority of exporters, being but little more instructed on this subject than their growers, supply the market with bulbs far too dear for the money.

France. R.

NURSERY DEPARTMENT.

Conducted by Joseph Meehan.

The total value of the nursery stock imported into the United States during the year ending June 30, 1906, was $1,512,066; exports of the same amounted to $219,223.

Horticultural Notes.

Among bush honeysuckles the one known as Lonicera Morrowi is a great favorite because of its bright red berries, which it bears in such immense quantities in the Summer months. All the bush honeysuckles are propagated either by seeds, soft wood cuttings in Summer or hard wood cuttings made in Winter and set out in Spring.

The best mulch of all for plants in Summer is that of fine dust. This is secured by frequent harrowings whenever the soil is in a suitable condition for it. Mulching of leaves, short grass and the like is apt to cause roots to approach the surface, which is not desirable.

Kœlreuteria paniculata, a Japanese tree, deserves to be better known than it is. Its compound leaves are pretty all Summer, but its immense panicles of yellow flowers, which come in Midsummer, give it its chief value.

Among Midsummer flowering shrubs of merit place the several vitexes. Of Vitex agnus-castus there are three colors—white, lilac, and deep lilac. Then there is another species, incisa. All are Summer blooming.

As soon as Summer flowering shrubs are out of bloom, give them a fair pruning back. Many of them, especially spiræas, if so treated, flower again in Autumn, some of them as freely as in their first display.

The false larch, so called, Pseudo larix Kæmpferi, is a beautiful tree. Though deciduous, as all larches are, it has an appearance in Summer of a fir, its foliage being between those of a larch and a fir. In late Autumn the foliage becomes of a yellow tinge.

Tsuga Mertensiana, the western hemlock spruce, is thought not hardy, but there are specimens of it about Philadelphia which thrive very well. Williamsoni, another one, considered synonymous with Hookeriana, is also hardy hereabout.

Paulownia plants are so easily raised from seeds that any other mode is not considered. But when desired it propagates readily from pieces of root, cut up and set outdoors in early Spring, or in a greenhouse.

In former days it was the custom of European nurserymen to remove the strip of wood from a bud before budding with it, and this may still be the rule. But our own nurserymen consider its removal entirely unnecessary, and insert the bud just as it is cut from the shoot furnishing it.

Root Pruning Trees.

The great superiority of transplanted trees over others not so treated is so apparent to all familiar with the subject that it is now far more common than it was for nurserymen to pay great attention to transplanting. A tree prepared in this way can be transplanted with almost entire safety. The cost of preparing is so little that it can easily be added to the price of the tree, and no customer whose trees live will ever find fault with the extra price paid. If the thought arises that a high price has been paid for a tree it is rarely expressed when the tree lives and flourishes.

At this season of the year actual transplanting cannot be done to any extent, but root pruning can; and it is just as good, often better. Sometimes when trees are but small a thrusting down of a spade around them will cut off the ends of roots, and be sufficient. When the trees are larger a trench is dug at a few feet from their center, circling the trees and severing the roots met with in the operation. If the trees are large and tap roots are supposed to exist, the digging goes under them until the roots are met with and cut. The soil is then thrown back; and, in one or two years if dug for transplanting there will be trees well supplied with roots.

When trees are large the root pruning is better than a transplanting. There is no disturbance of the roots in all their parts. A number will always be found undisturbed, the tree itself is still in solid ground; and no matter how large a tree or how many roots were cut, I have never known one so treated to die.

There is really no time in which this mode of pruning may not be done, nor no tree, evergreen or deciduous, on which it may not be practiced. This is a good time to do it, as roots are still forming; and even when growth is over for the season it may still be done, and all will then be ready for the next season's development.

English Walnuts for Profit.

One of the city papers contained a statement recently that the Department of Agriculture was making an effort to establish the industry of growing the English walnut for its nuts. Probably it was some reporter's mistake, as these nuts have been produced in California for many years past, and at the present time some of the nuts sold east are represented as of California growth. At any rate, it does not need the California climate to grow this walnut. The tree is hardy and fruitful in Eastern Pennsylvania, in New York, and as far as Connecticut, anyway, along the coast; and I am told of some nice trees of it at Rochester, New York, along the Lake.

There are some seedlings apparently hardier than others. When nuts come here from Southern Europe, the seedlings they produce seem less hardy than those raised from seeds obtained from the colder parts of Germany or from trees fruiting here; and this indicates the desirability of getting nuts from trees growing as far north as possible. There are in Germantown ancient English walnut trees, perhaps over 60 years old, which bear nuts annually, and from these nuts one would be justified in believing he would get a race of seedlings hardier than would be those from nuts from trees in a much warmer climate in Winter.

To have success in getting the nuts to grow they must be kept in a moist condition from gathering to sowing. Place them in slightly moist soil as soon as gathered there to remain until sown, in Fall or Spring, the latter season preferred.

Increasing Pterostyrax Hispidum.

A writer recently suggested that the Pterostyrax hispidum could be increased by grafting it on the Halesia tetraptera. So it could, and where one has but small plants of pterostyrax and can get many small halesias for stocks, the grafting may be practiced to advantage. But when of age to flower, which it is not long in reaching, there is no need to rely on grafting. Seeds are produced freely, and, sown in Spring, they germinate well, giving an abundance of seedlings in a short time. The young seedlings reach a height of four to five feet in four years, which is a good selling size; so it will be seen there is nothing to prevent one having a good supply of plants in a short time after seeds are available.

Too much cannot be said in favor of this beautiful tree. There is no doubt of its great popularity as soon as a general knowledge of its usefulness is spread abroad. Its racemes of white flowers are borne in great profusion, and droop as do those of the wistaria.

In addition to the modes of propagation already mentioned, there is that of root cuttings, which could be followed if desired; but of this it can be said as of some of the other methods, rely on seeds as the most satisfactory way of all.

Beauty of the Catalpa.

There are several trees which when bereft of foliage have not an appearance encouraging to buyers. One of them is the catalpa. It is so bare of twigs always that before it breaks into leaf it has not an attractive look. Even those who are engaged in the planting of trees and who therefore should know better, shun the tree too much. When in full display of flowers as it is here in late June, it is the most ornamental tree on a lawn. The panicles of white flowers are very large, and it rarely fails to have such a head of blossoms on every small branch it possesses.

The best catalpa of all to grow for the beauty of its flowers is the Eastern one, C. bignonioides; the reason is, that in growth the tree is round-headed, its lower branches sweeping the ground. Because of this habit there is a grand display of flowers visible, and obtainable, if need be; and the tree when it blossoms is almost alone in this respect, so few other trees bloom then.

The western one, C. speciosa, is an upright grower. It becomes tall, and is apt to have but few branches near the ground. Thus, while the best for timber growers it is not as ornamental as C. bignonioides for flowering purposes. Both want ample room to develop, to have them at their best.

To those who do appreciate these trees there is another thing that recommends them, which is, that pushing into growth late in Spring affords a chance to plant one later than could be done with almost any other tree.

Catalpas grow easily from either seeds or cuttings. Both need attention in Spring. Hard wood cuttings are made of suitable lengths in Winter, kept in a cool, moist place, and set out early in Spring. Practically every one may be expected to root. Seeds sown in Spring give plants a foot high by Fall.

JOSEPH MEEHAN.

Retinispora Obtusa Compacta Aurea.

Retinispora Obtusa Compacta Aurea.

It would be a great disappointment to landscape gardeners and all planters were there no retinisporas. It took but a short time after their introduction years ago to make them a necessity to every one that needed a few evergreens. The Norway spruce and the hemlock spruce as well as the Arbor vitæ and some pines were always among the principal evergreens on planters' lists, and they are still to be found there; but there is now included the retinispora.

The retinisporas all come to us from Japan, and the great variety of them introduced from that country enables one to select from a dozen or more of distinct sorts.

It would hardly be believed that all the sorts known are but varieties of two species—R. obtusa and R. pisifera, were it not that botanists assure us it is so. The well known and valued R. plumosa and its yellow-tinted variety, aurea, come from pisifera. The one we illustrate is a variety of the other species, R. obtusa, and in the appearance of growth of its small twigs, the relationship is apparent. But the species itself, R. obtusa, grows to a large size, a tree, in fact, and a handsome one at that. Then comes a break in its character and a dwarf form appears, which is called R. obtusa compacta. It grows much as the picture represents it. We think a little pruning has been given the one shown, but not much. Following this dwarf kind is one having its foliage golden tinted, and this gives us the one we illustrate—Retinispora obtusa compacta aurea—a long name, but more fittingly descriptive of the evergreen than the names of many trees are.

There is something extremely pretty in this evergreen when seen occupying a position on a lawn, such as this one does. The saucer-shaped arrangement of the ends of the twigs adds attraction to it, making of it, we think, one of the most desirable of dwarf evergreens. And the fact of the golden tipped foliage must not be lost sight of, for it is a great merit.

The golden Chinese Arbor vitæ, and many other dwarf forms of this one and of the American, are frequently met with on pleasure grounds, and all have their places, but none is to be preferred to the Retinispora obtusa compacta aurea when one of its shape suits the place to be filled. Some of the varieties of American Arbor vitæ are not of a good green color in Winter. This retinispora is. It is of a cheerful green hue the whole season through.

JOSEPH MEEHAN.

QUESTION BOX

Tile Window Boxes.

(2) Can you furnish the name of the company putting out the tile window boxes? WM. SWINBANK.
Sycamore, Ill.

—We cannot locate the manufacturers. If any such are in existence at the present time, perhaps some reader can supply the information.

Borers in Pines.

(1) I have some Pinus cembra and Pinus strobus attacked by a borer on the twigs and trunks causing them to turn brown and some have died. What treatment would you suggest for the already attacked trees, and what to prevent the pest spreading to others. A. P.
N. Y.

—There is really no way to prevent twig borers in trees. Nothing more can be done than burning the twigs as soon as the damage is discovered, to prevent an increase of the insect. It often happens that such pests are rampant for a year or two, then disappear; and let us hope that in a short time your trees will be free from attacks. J. M.

PLANT FOR NAME.—V. H. P.—Koelreuteria paniculata.

LIST OF ADVERTISERS

INDEX TO STOCK ADVERTISED

Contents.

PROVIDENCE, R. I.—The usual dullness, especially noticeable in Midsummer, is now apparent in the cut flower market. Stock of the first grades is not at all plentiful. Kaiserin Augusta Victoria, Bride and Bridesmaid are in good supply, especially shorts; $2 to $4 is asked: although a few fancies bring $6 per 100. Carnations are not very fancy; prime white and pink are in fair demand at $1.50 per 100; others sell at 75c. to $1 per 100. Sweet peas are short in stem, but good in bloom; 15c. to 35c. per 100 is the ruling price. Dahlias are here; early asters are also in, but the quality is poor and they move slowly.
G. S. W.

REVIEW OF THE MARKET

NEW YORK.—The cut flower business has assumed its ordinary Summer proportions, and there is very little doing in any line. The best selling stock in the market seems to be the roses that come from such growers as make a specialty of Kaiserin Augusta Victoria, Souvenir du President Carnot and kindred varieties, and who grow for Summer cutting only. The supply of American Beauty roses keeps up right along, and while one occasionally hears of lots selling at $3 per dozen, it is well understood that those buying by the hundred are able to purchase at prices much below that figure.

Carnations are getting scarcer, and it is just as well. There is little or no demand for them and prices are low.

Lily of the valley is, on some days, in fair demand, and prices fluctuate considerably.

Cattleyas are plentiful and are offered at figures that seem unusually low for such beautiful flowers. Lilies are bringing a little better prices than was possible one week ago, owing more to the diminution of the supply than to any increase in demand.

Sweet peas are not so much of a glut as they were, though there is plenty to go round, and no extravagant prices are asked for them.

Four o'clock is the closing time every day among the wholesale dealers, though the day's tradings seem to be finished long before that hour arrives.

CHICAGO.—This market has very little to offer of interest for the present. Although stories of varying effects may come from different sources, it is perfectly safe to say that Summer conditions are well established, and there is liable to be very little change in staple lines in the immediate future. Good stock finds a ready market, and the lower grades take their chances and generally suffer. In roses there is a slight improvement in the young stock of American Beauty, and the cut of the Summer roses, Souvenir du President Carnot, Kaiserin Augusta Victoria and La Detroit, are fully up to the expectations. Bride, Bridesmaid, as a rule, are only of what could be classed as mediocre.

Carnations are of not far above medium quality and although the call for shipping is fairly good the price holds low, taking a very creamy line of goods that will find a purchaser at two dollars per hundred.

Though peonies are practically out, there are one or two concerns who are offering very nice stock and expect the supply to hold through the middle of the month from cold storage.
W. K. W.

BOSTON.—The state of the cut flower business has not altered a great deal from last week; one day the demand would be good when all at once there would be a complete glut. All kinds of flowers are plentiful, but the quality is not alarming. The large quantities seen of many kinds are not of the best by any means. Roses sell at anywhere from $1 up to $6, while the poorer grades go in quantity at less. Carnations bring from 50c. to $1.50 though a few fancies may bring $2. Sweet peas are plentiful at 25c. and 35c. Candytuft and feverfew bring 25c. a bunch. Stocks in various colors bring 25c. a bunch. Heliotrope sells at 25c. Gypsophila sells very readily at 20c. and 25c. a bunch. Adiantum brings 50c. and $1, and there is no change in the prices of asparagus and other greens. J. W. D.

ST. LOUIS.—Since the first of July trade among the wholesalers and retailers has been very quiet, and the Summer dullness has set in for good. The market is very short on first class stock in almost everything; in seconds there is more than enough, plenty going to the waste pile. Only a few first class American Beauty roses are coming in, and they sell well at $2.50 per dozen; short ones are off color which hurts their sale. Bride and Bridesmaid are of very poor quality. Kaiserin Augusta Victoria, Ivory and Souvenir du President Carnot are in good demand at from $3 to $4 per 100; extra fancy sell at $5 and $6.

Carnations of extra good quality go at $2; others at from $1 to $1.50 per 100. The blooms are becoming very small and pale in color. Enchantress and Prosperity keep up better than the rest.

The largest overstock in the market at present is in sweet peas. In thousand lots the best of these bring $1; short ones 50c. In small lots white and lavender sell best at 25c. per 100. Outdoor stock needs a good rain. Asters are not yet in overstock, and sell well at $1, and $1.50 per 100.
ST. PATRICK

INDIANAPOLIS.—This month's business has not been as brisk as it should be, though it is a Summer month. An occasional spurt of funeral work is about all that keeps things moving. Several July wedding decorations, an unusual occurrence, are looked for next week.

Despite the small amount of business transacted there is a scarcity of good flowers. Sweet peas have suffered much from the rain, and are mostly short stemmed. 25c. per hundred is the wholesale price for them. Four varieties of lilies, auratum, longiflorum, rubrum and album, are now in the market, and are welcomed for funeral work. The first two bring $1.50 per dozen; the last 75c.

Good carnations are scarce. At times it is difficult to obtain any, even at good prices for the quality offered—$1.50 to $2 per 100. Excellent Shasta daisies are in the market at 50c. per 100. Shipped roses, with the exception of La France and Kaiserin Augusta Victoria, are much superior to the home-grown ones. Good Mme. Abel Chatenay are received at $6 to $7 per 100. American Beauty are finding a good market at $5 to $20 per 100.

Green goods remain scarce in this vicinity, especially smilax and adiantum, which have to be obtained from outside points.

Tomlinson Hall market reports a fair business for the season. Quantities of field-grown flowers are disposed of at low prices.
I. B.

COLUMBUS.—With July, and terribly hot weather, trade has fallen off greatly—Summer dullness has set in. But the craft are all satisfied, as certainly no one could find fault with the splendid run of business we have had all the year until now. June was full of good wedding decoration orders. It would seem as if more flowers than usual had been ordered for funerals this year; with us all, funeral work has been and is especially active. Roses are getting very poor and small; American Beauty are gone, as far as any good ones are concerned, what there are sell for $1.50 and $2 a dozen. Some very good Mme. Abel Chatenay and Kaiserin Augusta Victoria are to be had; they bring the same price as the poor Beauties; but the Kaiserin always was one of our best Summer roses.

Carnations of medium to poor quality have been in enormous supply; we heard of some purchases as low as $7.50 a thousand for fair stock; the average retail prices have been 25c. to 35c. a dozen, with a few fancy Enchantress and Mrs. Lawson bringing 75c.

There is one very important advance noted this season, and that is in the collections. Many members of the craft tell me that their customers never before were so prompt, both wholesale and retail. Sweet peas are coming in very short-stemmed now, but for some days have been in such enormous supply that they could not possibly be disposed of. We have tried to get at the rate of $1 a hundred for them in any size bunch the customer wanted, but lately it has been any price to get rid of them. Now that outdoor lily of the valley has gone, the growers again have a chance; the best valley brings 75c. to $1 the dozen.
F. W.

MINNEAPOLIS.—Business is reported by all of the trade to have been quiet the past week, practically all that has been done was in the funeral work line. Stock of all kinds is very scarce, and all outdoor flowers are being used to good advantage. What stock is on the market is somewhat inferior and in consequence is sold at a close figure. Roses are particularly scarce. The prices have dropped to a considerable extent on account of the inferior quality. American Beauty are carried in small numbers by the large dealers. For a fair quality of roses we are getting all the way from $1 to $1.50 per dozen. Carnations are sold at from 25c. to 75c. per dozen, the price depending entirely upon where they are purchased. The small dealers are only able to get 35c. and 35c. a dozen, while in the larger stores they sell at 50c. and 75c. per dozen, the quality in both cases being about the same.

The plant trade is over although an order now and then is booked for a box or bed. One of our largest growers found some difficulty in filling a $3 vase the past week; this goes to show that the plant trade this season has been indeed very heavy. The general report is that about twice as many plants were grown this season over any past year, and it is gratifying to know that all have been disposed of at a good figure, the sale of geraniums was very active. The greenhouses without exception are cleaned out of stock, and considerable work is being done repairing and building, although the latter is not as active as anticipated in the fore part of the season.
PAUL.

ROSES

All planting of young stock should be finished by the middle of this month if possible, if the plants are to make much headway before Fall. Time was, a few years ago, when we considered the middle of July early enough to bench our plants a good deal of the work being done as late as August; but like the carnation growers, nearly all of us start early.

There is one objection to very early planting. During the Summer the plants dry out rapidly and thus require a large quantity of water; and very frequently more is applied than the plants should actually have, the result being a very heavy growth entirely out of proportion to the root development, so that when Fall comes the soil has become more or less sour, and the roots are unable to support the plants. Thus a severe check is given the stock, from which it seldom recovers till Spring.

As has been suggested in these notes before, only the ball of the plant should be watered after planting for the first week or, two; then as the roots begin to spread, which can be easily seen by scratching away the soil in a few places, a larger area should be watered, till finally eight weeks after benching, the whole bench can be watered.

Another very important matter at this time of the year is to keep the surface of the benches loose by continual scratching. Do not wait for weeds to come, but go over the benches twice a week if possible. The value of this can easily be seen by leaving a small part of a bench untouched and noting results. No fertilizer of any kind should be given for some time to come, as the plants must not be forced at this season. The ventilators should be kept open day and night in fair weather; but if side ventilators are used as well these should be closed nights, as the plants can stand no draughts. There is no reason for any mildew appearing: as a precaution, however, a little sulphur can be dusted on the plants once a week, on a bright day.

Keep the young plants disbudded, nipping the shoots back far enough to insure strong breaks.

Now is the time to add to the appearance of the place by the liberal use of paint. Keep the houses in good repair: the outlay is small each year, while if neglected for a few years, it will cost more than double to get things back in shape. As for paints we still prefer to use lead and oil outside, with a small amount of turpentine added for indoors.

PENN.

DREER'S GIANT CYCLAMEN

Few things which can readily be grown by the florist produces better returns either as cut flowers or pot plants or gives as much satisfaction to the buyer as **CYCLAMEN**, provided they are of first class quality.

Our strain is grown for us by a life long specialist, and for size, freedom of bloom, purity of coloring, and habit of growth are perfection.

We offer new crop seed as follows:

Dreer's Giant Pure White.
" " White with carmine eye.
Dreer's Giant Rose.
" " Blood Rose

75c. per 100 seeds; $6.00 per 1000

Dreer's Giant Mixed

An even mixture of all the colors, 60c per 100 seeds; $5.00 per 1000. 250 seeds or more at 1000 rate.

For **Cineraria, Daisies, Pansy, Primulas** and other seasonable stock see our wholesale price list.

Henry A. Dreer
714 Chestnut Street,
Philadelphia, Pa.

Mention The Florists' Exchange when writing.

FERNS.

NEPHROLEPIS BARROWSII, 2½ in. pots. $10.00 per 100.
NEPHROLEPIS SCOTTII, 4 in. pots, $15.00 per 100.
ASPARAGUS PLUMOSUS, 4 in. pots, $10.00 per 100.

HUGH GRAHAM CO.,
Logan Nurseries, York Road and Louden Street, PHILADELPHIA, PA.

Mention The Florists' Exchange when writing.

FERNS IN FLATS

Now ready for 2 1-2 inch pots. Flats contain ove 100 clumps, which can be divided. Varieties include ASPIDIUM TSUSSEMENSE, CRYTOMIUM FALCATUM, PTERIS MAYII, T. WIMSETTI, T. NANA COMPACTA, T. ADIANTOIDES, T. SERRULATA, LASTREAS, etc.

PRICES, $2.00 PER FLAT; 20 OR MORE FLATS AT $1.75.
CASH WITH ORDER FROM UNKNOWN PARTIES.

McHUTCHISON & CO.
17 Murray Street - - - NEW YORK CITY

Mention The Florists' Exchange when writing.

FERNS
You Must Have

Only 5,000 left; speak quick.

Piersonii, 5 in., 20c.; 4 in., 15c.; 3 in., 10c.
Scottii, 5 in., 20c.; 4 in. 15c.; 3 in. 10c.
Bostons, 3 in., ready to shift, 10c.
Asparagus Plumosus Nanus, 3½ in. 6c; 2½ in., $2.50 per 100.
Asparagus Sprengerii, 3½ in., 6c.
20,000 Field Carnations.

Write me. Cash please.

BENJAMIN CONNELL, West Grove, Pa.
Mention The Florists' Exchange when writing.

FERNS OUR SPECIALTY

CIBOTIUM SCHIEDEI
We have a large stock of this beautiful tree fern in 3 in. pots, ready for a shift, at $26.00 per 100, 26 plants at 100 rate.

FERN SEEDLINGS FROM FLATS
Eight to ten best market varieties at $1.00 per 100, or $8.50 per 1000. If by mail add 10c. for each hundred plants.

ASSORTED FERNS FOR DISHES
From 2¼ in. pots. The best and hardiest varieties in market at $3.00 per 100, or $25.00 per 1000. 250 plants at 1000 rate.

Adiantum Cuneatum, 2¼ in. pots, $3.50 per 100, $30.00 per 1000.

FERN SPORES
Gathered from our own stock, 35c. per trade package. $4.00 per doz. packages.

Gardenia Vietchii from 2¼ in. pots, $7.50 per 100, $70.00 per 1000; 500 at 1000 rate.

ANDERSON & CHRISTENSEN,
SHORT HILLS, N. J.
Mention The Florists' Exchange when writing.

FERNS

6 in. **Scottii Ferns**, 40c. 8000 6 in. **Boston Ferns**, 40c. Large pans **Boston Ferns**, $1.00; $1.50; $2.00; $2.50. No C.O.D. Cash or reference.

W. C. SMITH,
61st & Market Sts. PHILADELPHIA, PA.
Mention The Florists' Exchange when writing.

FERNS

Are now in fine shape. A good variety and nice bushy stock, 2¼ in., $3.00 per 100; $25.00 per 1000.
Kentia Belmoreana, 4 in., clean and bushy, 20c.
Cocos Weddeliana, 10c.
Dracaena Indivisa, 4 in., strong, 12c.
Mme. Salleroi Geranium, 2 in., $2.00 per 100.
English Ivy, 4 in., fine stock, $10.00 per 100.

H. WESTON, HEMPSTEAD, N. Y.

GERANIUMS ROOTED CUTTINGS

FALL DELIVERY. IN ANY QUANTITY.

I have almost 200,000 stock plants to work from and want your order now so that I can give it special attention when we come to take cuttings.

Send for Descriptive Price List

	Per 100	Per 1,000
SMILAX — 100,000 ready now, carefully cut back and grown with an air space around every pot	$1.50	$12.00
ASPARAGUS ROBUSTUS — 20,000 once repotted, fine strong plants and a great improvement over Plumosus in every respect. Try at least a hundred, next year you will want a thousand	$5.00	$40.00
ASPARAGUS SPRENGERII — 50,000 good strong plants once repotted into rose pots and a bargain at the price	$2.00	$15.00

ALBERT M. HERR,
Lancaster, Pa.
Mention The Florists' Exchange when writing.

MOUNTAIN OF SNOW

This Geranium is unsurpassed for bedding and vase work. Its bright scarlet flowers and white and green foliage make it one of the most attractive plants for fine work. Large bushy plants 3½ and 4 in. pots, 5c. each.

Asparagus Sprengerii, big plants in 3 in. pots, plenty large enough to go in fours, 5c

Asparagus Plumosus Nanus, large, 3 in. stock. Only about 300 left, 6c. each.

R. G. HANFORD, Norwalk, Conn.
Mention The Florists' Exchange when writing.

BARGAIN

Geraniums, 8 varieties, in bloom, strong, 3 to 4 in., $2.50 to $3.50 per 100.
Asparagus Sprengerii, large, 4 in., $4.00 per 100; $35.00 per 1000.
Dracaena Indivisa, large, 4 in., $6.00 per 100; $45.00 per 1000.
Ferns, from flats, best varieties, ready for 2 to 3 in., $1.00 per 100. Large clumps for decorating and cutting, $6.00 to $8.00 per 100.
Cyclamen Gig., Hugh Low & Company's Prize Strain, including fringed and bearded varieties, 2-3 and 4 in., $4.00-$6.00 and $10.00 per 100. Cash.

WM. S. HERZOG, MORRIS PLAINS, N. J.

Adiantum Cuneatum

From 3 in. pots ready to shift, per 100, $5.00 per 1,000, $45.00.
From 2½ in. pots ready to shift, per 100 $4.00: per 1000, $35.00.

Adiantum Hybridum

Similar to Croweanum. From 4 in. pots ready to shift, per 100, $10.00.

Seedlings in flats, nice clumps which can be divided and ready for 2½ in pots, per flat, $2.50.

O. V. ZANGEN
Seedsman HOBOKEN, N. J.
Mention the Florists' Exchange when writing.

NEPHROLEPIS SCOTTII

Small plants from the benches, $5.00 per 100; $50.00 per 1000. Plants large enough for 6 in. pots, $25.00 per 100. Plants large enough to go in 7 and 8 in. pots, $50.00 per 100.

Asparagus Plumosus Nanus, 2¼ in., fine plants, $3.00 per 100.

JOHN SCOTT,
Rutland Road and East 45th Street;
BROOKLYN, N. Y.
Telephone 2890 Bedford.
Mention The Florists' Exchange when writing.

NEPHROLEPIS

Whitmani, 2¼ in., $25.00 per 100.
Boston Ferns, 2¼ in., $3.00 per 100.

Henry H. Barrows & Son, Whitman, Mass.

ORCHIDS

Largest Importers, Exporters, Growers and Hybridists in the world.

Sander, St. Albans, England
and
235 Broadway, Room 1, New York City

Mention The Florists' Exchange when writing.

Geraniums Geraniums

4 in. pots at $6.00 per 100.
3 in. pots at $4.00 per 100.
Heliotrope, 4 in. $4.00 per 100.
" 2 in. $3.00 per 100.
Lobelia, 2 in. $2.00 per 100.
Coleus, in variety, 2½ in. pots, $2.00 per 100.

Don't get left, but get your order in. Cash must accompany same.

J. E. FELTHOUSEN,
154 VAN VRANKEN AVE., SCHENECTADY, N. Y.

GERANIUMS

Grand stock in bud and bloom. Best bedders in red, white and pink, also assorted colors. $7.00 per 100, 500 at $6.50 per 100.

COLEUS

Extra fine, red, yellow and assorted.
2½ inch, $3.00 per 100; $25.00 per 1000.
3 inch, $4.00 per 100; $35.00 per 1000.

THE H. WEBER & SONS CO.,
OAKLAND, MD.

GERANIUMS.

Nutt, Buchner, Doyle, Poitevine, Viaud, 3 in. pots, $3.00 per 100. 4 in. $5.00 per 100.
Cannas, 3 and 3½ in. pots, $4.00 and $5.00 per 100.
Fuchsias, 3 in. pots, $3.00 per 100.
Coleus, Verschaffeltii, Golden Bedder and other varieties, 2 in. pots, $1.00 per 100. Cash with order.

ERNEST HARRIS, Delanson, N. Y.

FERN SEEDLINGS

FROM FLATS.

The first crop is now ready for potting, including the following varieties: **Pteris Cretica Cristata, Pteris Cretica Albo-Lineata, Pteris Adiantoides, Pteris Argyraea, Pteris Mayii, Cyrtomium Falcatum, Aspidium Tsussemense, Onychium Japonica, Doodia Aspera.** My selection, $1.00 per 100; $8.50 per 1000. If by mail, add 10c. per 100 for postage.

Mixed Ferns for dishes, 2¼ in., $3.00 per 100; $25.00 per 1000; 250 at 1000 rate; 3 in., $6.00 per 100.
Adiantum Cuneatum, 3 in., $6.00 per 100.

FRANK N. ESKESEN, MADISON, N. J.
Mention The Florists' Exchange when writing.

ORCHIDS

Arrived, large shipments of **Cattleya Gigas** and **Cattleya Speciosissima, C. Mossiae, C. Percivaliana.**

Write for Prices.

LAGER & HURRELL, Summit, N. J.
Growers and Importers
Mention The Florists' Exchange when writing.

GERANIUMS

2 in., $2.25 per 100; $18.00 per 1000. **S. A. Nutt, J. Viaud, White Swan, Ricard, E. G. Hill, Marquise de Castellane and Atkinson.**
Asparagus Sprengerii, 2 in., $2.00; $17.00 per 1000
Boston Ferns, 2 in., $3.00 per 100; 3 in., $5.00 per 100; 4 in., $8.00 per 100; 6 in. pans at $4.00 per doz.
Cissus Discolor at $3.00 per 100.

THE NATIONAL PLANT CO., DAYTON, O.
Mention The Florists' Exchange when writing.

CANNAS

Allemania, Gray, Henderson, M. Washington, Metallica, from 3 in. pots, fine stock, $4.00 per 100

Shellroad Greenhouses, GRANGE, P. O., BALTIMORE, MD.
Mention The Florists' Exchange when writing.

A RECORD TO BE PROUD OF

The Florists' Hail Association has paid 950 losses amounting to $96.000.00
For particulars address,

JOHN G. ESLER, Saddle River, N. J.
Mention the Florists' Exchange when writing.

FOUNDED IN 1888

THE FLORISTS' EXCHANGE

A Weekly Medium of Interchange for Florists, Nurserymen, Seedsmen and the Trade in general

Exclusively a Trade Paper.

Entered at New York Post Office as Second Class Matter

Published EVERY SATURDAY by

A. T. DE LA MARE PTG. AND PUB. CO. LTD.

2, 4, 6 and 8 Duane Street,

P. O. Box 1697. Telephone 3765 John. NEW YORK.

CHICAGO OFFICE: 127 East Berwyn Avenue.

ILLUSTRATIONS.

Electrotypes of the illustrations used in this paper can usually be supplied by the publishers. Price on application.

YEARLY SUBSCRIPTIONS.

United States, Canada, and Mexico, $1.00. Foreign countries in postal union, $2.50. Payable in advance. Remit by Express Money Order Draft on New York. Post Office Money Order or Registered Letter.

The address label indicates the date when subscription expires and is our only receipt therefore.

REGISTERED CABLE ADDRESS:

Florex, New York.

ADVERTISING RATES.

One-half inch, 75c.; ¾-inch, $1.00; 1-inch, $1.25, special positions extra. Send for Rate Card showing discount of 10c., 15c., 25c., or 35c., per inch on continuous advertising. For rates on Wants, etc., see column for Classified Advertisements.

Copy must reach this office 12 o'clock Wednesday to secure insertion in issue of following Saturday.

Orders from unknown parties must be accompanied with cash or satisfactory references.

Dayton Convention Notes.

Everything is progressing nicely. All local arrangements are so far completed. Every committee has been attending to its duties, and every one is alive to his responsibility, to greet all visitors as well as they know how. The report of the superintendent of exhibits shows up well as far as the number of exhibitors are concerned. Some of the larger firms have done nobly; but we regret that the large wholesale houses that should have advertising signs, have not so far responded. Refreshing was the letter of the firm of Bassett & Washburn, Chicago, with a check for $50.00 for a sign, and the statement that it is every florist's duty to help this convention along. Only a few more such and the local club will not have to worry about making both ends meet. All concessions are given free of charge, and the club has only one point in view, namely, to treat all visitors gloriously. Even the souvenir program was left to the private enterprise of Austin Shaw and Harry M. Altick; so nothing is coming from this source.

It is everybody's desire to make this the banner convention, but we must have the aid of all; exhibitors and advertisers must not stand back but come forward with a will becoming such a country as ours. This is a national affair, arranged not only for the benefit of the trade but also for the education of the masses. So far, nothing has been heard of landscape gardeners' plans, of enterprising firms and young men of push and enterprise. The Dayton Florists' Club will see that liberal prizes are offered for such work. Furthermore, there is need of electric signs of leading firms on the outside grounds; such can be offered at reasonable cost.

Wake up, gentlemen. This is a national convention. All eyes are centered for the time being on Dayton. You owe it to yourself, to your business, to the whole country, to show the world what our peerless art does for mankind.

THE DAYTON FLORISTS' CLUB.

[As regards the souvenir program, heretofore, so far as we know, the profits, if any, resulting from this feature of the annual convention have gone to the local club. We believe advertising patronage is accorded with this end in view, in the desire to help the local organization in defraying the expense of the entertainment of the national society. If "nothing is coming" to the Dayton Club from this source this year, it will establish a pernicious precedent. To convert the souvenir into a money-making scheme for private enterprise is to rob it of its generally accepted character, and is quite at variance with what we understand to be the original intent of these souvenirs. Ed.]

The Buffalo News says that President Wm. F. Kasting of the S. A. F. O. H., is regarded in Democratic circles as likely to run for the Assembly in the Third District. If he consents to make the run it is conceded he may have the nomination without asking for it.

Society of American Florists and Ornamental Horticulturists.

Department of Plant Registration.

Paul Niehoff, Lehighton, Pa., submits for registration rose Aurora; seedling from Bon Silene x Souvenir du President Carnot. Flowers large and full; color light pink with a deeper shading in the centre; growth very strong; foliage dark green; stems 4 to 5 feet long. Very prolific with no tendency to go dormant during Winter.

This is the rose which Mr. Niehoff recently exhibited under the name of Columbia. On being informed that another rose had already been registered with the S. A. F. as Columbia he withdrew his claim, and the rose will be disseminated as Aurora.

WM. J. STEWART,
Secretary.

Platt's Platitude.

Pursuant to a motion passed by the New Jersey Floricultural Society, the secretary of that organization entered into communication with the Hon. T. C. Platt, President of the United States Express Company, in regard to the recent advance in rates on cut flowers and returned empty boxes made by that corporation. The society bases its complaint on, among other things, the fact that "(1) other competing carriers have found the original rates remunerative; (2) the risk of carrying on a business in so perishable a commodity demands consideration."

Back comes the response from E. T. Platt, treasurer of the express company in question, advancing the stereotyped explanation of the increased tariff charges, that consignments of flowers "were being carried at a loss by this company," and naively adding: "You would hardly think that one-half a cent or even a cent a pound on flowers that are sold at such high prices in New York by the retailers could be considered a very exorbitant charge."

Evidently the worthy and ingenuous treasurer of the United States Express Company has been a victim of the alleged "high prices" for flowers sold in New York by the retailers, hence his apparent familiarity with these prices, and his conception that half a cent or a cent a pound extra for expressage is neither here nor there, in the final income to the florist. He does not know, or if he does, forgets that the New York retailer has little or nothing to do with the case; and that what the grower of flowers receives for his products, and what the retailer exacts who disposes of them to the public are entirely different matters. The retailers are not complaining of excessive express charges; it is the grower and shipper of the flowers to the market who has the grievance, on whom falls the burden of paying the express tariff. The grower's profits are small enough now, goodness knows; and the doubling of express rates for the conveyance of his flowers to market is not going to improve matters any.

Apart from that, the retail prices paid for any article of commerce have or should have no bearing on the rates charged by the common carriers of these articles, and should in no way influence the makers of these rates; on the other hand, express rates charged have much to do with the selling value of a commodity, and the action of the express company can only have one tendency, viz.; to make the alleged "high prices" of flowers still higher, though we fear the grower will not be a participant in the result.

The idea that seems to permeate the brain of Mr. Platt is that the New York retailers are getting too much money for their merchandise, and that part of their imagined immense profits is needed by the United States Express Company in its business. Unfortunately, the screws are being used on the wrong parties, but it is evident that the growers must look for relief elsewhere than to the United States Express Company; and this they should do.

Where Doctors Disagree.

There seems to be no unanimity of opinion among the Government authorities as to the value of the seed distributed free by Congressmen, under the auspices of a beneficent, paternal government, judging by the remarks of the various gentlemen who have had something to say on the subject.

Dr. Galloway, before the House Agricultural Committee, is reported to have said: "We send out seeds that must necessarily be better than the ordinary seed which the seedsmen can secure."

The views of his chief are not those of Professor A. J. Pieters, Botanist in Charge of Seed and Plant Introduction and Distribution, who naturally it would seem, is in closer touch with the work of seed distribution and the character of the seeds sent out from Washington than Dr. Galloway. Dr. Pieters in the Yearbook for 1905, just published, expresses the following opinion:

"The objects kept in view are (1) to obtain good seeds—as good as those sold by the mail-trade houses (though they are no better, since the seeds are bought mostly from the growers who supply the seed trade,) etc."

Dr. Galloway's remarks have been rather inelegantly characterized as "twaddle," "rot," etc., by practical seedsmen; and savored of adding insult to injury. On the other hand, those of his subordinate have the ring of common sense and fairness, and as such are to be commended.

OUR READERS' VIEWS

[Wholesome discussions on subjects that interest. Contributions to this column are always welcome.—Ed.]

Bureau of Credit.

Editor Florists' Exchange:

In common with many of your readers I was greatly interested in the paper entitled "The Bureau of Credit," read by Mr. W. S. Powell, its secretary, before the Toledo convention of the American Seed Trade Association. Perhaps I may be able to throw some additional light on the problem which this paper seeks to solve. My experience during the last three years as vice-president, treasurer and general manager of the National Florists' Board of Trade justifies me in saying that the plea put forth by Mr. Powell in behalf of his Bureau of Credit is one that should be carefully considered by those to whom it is addressed. The Board with which I am connected is doing among the florists and nurserymen, and to a limited extent among the seedsmen also, exactly the same work which the Bureau of Credit has undertaken among the latter alone.

The Florists' Board endeavors to warn the trade against delinquent debtors, whether hopelessly bad or only abnormally slow, through the medium of a Credit and Information List, a little quarterly, which, as the result of eight years' experience, now contains the names of nearly 5,500 persons with appropriate ratings. Besides this, we place at the disposal of our members, without charge to them, the information on which these ratings are based. Moreover, we give to our members, again without charge, except in certain rare instances, the privileges of obtaining a rating on any name not found in our book.

Our list is far from being a "black-list," for it contains the names of many of the best houses in the country. These ratings are continually changed as occasion may require. We regard our system of reporting as superior to any other, for it combines all the advantages of the credit report without any of its drawbacks.

Our method of procedure in the collection of accounts is so nearly identical with that pursued by the Bureau of Credit as to show that, either there is only one good method followed by the best collection agencies, or else our fame is such as to lead others to follow our example. A compliment that we appreciate!

I was interested in the statement that 53 members had placed with the credit bureau for collection accounts aggregating $26,000, an average of about $500 for each member. This is certainly a very high average and shows clearly the necessity of combined action on the part of the seedsmen against those who prey upon them. Our experience is, that in most instances the members of the Florists' Board guard themselves against such losses through the protection afforded by our book.

It is also interesting to note in Mr. Powell's report that about 47 per cent. of the value of these claims was collected through his bureau; and that of the money collected about 44 per cent. was sent in response to the first demand. But as shown in his report the cost of these first demand collections was much greater than it should be, for they should be made on the 3 per cent. basis, as we make them through our draft system. The fees retained on these collections by the credit bureau were just over 5 per cent., or about 40 per cent. greater than would have been the case under our system. The attorneys' fees do not vary, for all reputable lawyers charge at least 10 per cent. of the amount collected, except on very small accounts, when the charge is greater. The forwarder, or agency, is entitled to one-third of this fee and the remaining two-thirds are retained by the local attorneys. Every lawyer whom we employ is placed under bonds, so that our clients have a double security—that of the Board and of the Bonding Company.

The credit bureau and the Florists' Board are alike in that each at least claims to have at heart the good of its members; but they are unlike in that all obligations cease to a member of the Board on the payment of the annual membership fee of $10, which includes his subscription to the list. Should there be a deficiency in the Board's budget, its stockholders alone would suffer from it. Fortunately, however, there is no immediate danger of such a catastrophe.

What Mr. Powell says concerning the attitude of the local attorney toward the collection agency is undoubtedly correct. On the whole the Board can congratulate itself on the ability and fidelity of the lawyers it employs. Since the present management assumed control of the Board, over three years ago, we have made it our invariable rule to ask from a client for advances for costs, only the exact amount requested by a local attorney; and where, as in some few cases, the attorney in making his remittance has made any reduction in our favor, we always give our client the advantage of it, retaining only one-third of the regular fee. I infer, though it is not expressly so stated, that this is also done by the credit bureau. I hope so, for nothing else can be regarded as fair to the client.

Mr. Powell's words as to the necessity of co-operation in the trade meet with my fullest endorsement. One reason why all our trade agencies remain comparatively inefficient, is that those most interested do not work together for the common good. The few that do co-operate with us are entitled to our cordial thanks. To show my meaning, I would say that one of our number (a seed house by the way) received ratings from us on 81 separate names during the first quarter of this year at a cost to him of just $1. If all would do this, what a splendid benefit would accrue!

In closing I would say we are gratified that our latest competitor, hardly yet a rival, is following the well-beaten paths laid out by us, pursuing the same methods by which we have won success; and for the rest we shall meet the competition, if such it be, by giving to the ever-increasing number of those that trust us a better, more faithful and more efficient service.

New York. EDWARD MCK. WHITING.
National Florists' Board of Trade.

Concerning Geraniums.

Editor Florists' Exchange:

John Birnie is, I observe, still trying to mislead the young grower who sought advice about geraniums through your columns a few weeks ago. Instead of calling names and trying to exploit his fund of Scotch wit, Mr. Birnie should refer to the original question, and tender the grower better advice than was originally given; that is, if he can.

Mr. Birnie evidently thinks the young man intended embarking in the rooted cutting business; or else was going to supply the peddlers of New York City, men who retail geraniums at 6c. each and still make a profit on them. If Young Beginner follows my advice and plants 500 stock plants, he will be reasonably sure of securing the number he desires; though, if he be located where the Summers are not so long nor so favorable to plant growth as in New Jersey, and if he is not fortunate enough to own an up-to-date greenhouse establishment, such as Mr. Birnie seems to have, perhaps it would be well for him to plant a few more rather than less.

Mr. Birnie appears to be imbued with the idea that New Jersey covers the entire globe, and that nothing is right unless it conforms to his methods. He forgets that there are places far removed from the New York market, which is an excellent one for some things, though there is probably more poorly grown stock in the geranium line disposed of there than I had any idea of, judging from the number grown and the time allowed them in growing.

With reference to his mention of 30-year-old methods, I am free to confess that so far as the geranium goes, I am yet using methods that I learned over thirty years ago; but then I am growing for a class of trade which calls for good plants, and not rooted cuttings. Notwithstanding that, if Mr. Birnie will tell in what way his present methods differ from those he says were in vogue thirty years ago, I think it will be found that what appears to him to be a new method is not new at all, but something that, fifty years ago, every apprentice in a plant introducer's establishment was fully cognizant of.

Unlike Mr. Birnie, I get my amusement from the correspondence column and not from the Question Box of The Florists' Exchange, and I am particularly amused to read that because a man signs his name to communications appearing in public print he is possessed of "pluck;" whereas, to my mind, it but demonstrates his eager aim for notoriety.

Meantime, readers of your paper, along with myself, are waiting for Mr. Birnie to give some tangible proof of his assertion that my methods are not those of the expert, while his own (which I hope he will furnish) are, according to his way of thinking. And this information he will give if he desires to be helpful to his fellows, rather than be regarded as merely a carping, facetious critic, whose effusions neither edify nor enlighten.

EXPERTUS.

Editor Florists' Exchange:

May I have a word or two to say on geraniums? I don't know it all; but have grown plants to retail at $1.80 a dozen. I am getting ready to do the same thing next Spring.

As Mr. Birnie says take 50 stock plants. On the 28th of August select 50 plants that have 10 shoots on each plant. Take these 500 cuttings and put them in sand. About September 25 they will be ready for potting. Let them grow on uninterruptedly for ten weeks. Then top these plants and you will get 500 cuttings, making in all 1,000 cuttings.

Now, back to the stock plants. In a week after the cuttings were taken either pot up the stock plants or transplant them into a bench in the house. By the last of October these plants will have sent out new breaks suitable for cuttings. Suppose each shoot has two cuttings, making 20 to a plant or 1,000 to the 50 plants. Put these in the sand the first day of November. About the sixth of December they will be ready for potting. This added to the 1,000 earlier batch makes 2,000. Now on these 50 stock plants let us say there is a break on each shoot that is slow in growing, but by December first they are ready to put in the sand. That will make 2,500 so far.

Take the 1,000 cuttings that were put in the sand November 1. Potted up December 6 they may be ready for topping by the last of February. This brings the total up to 3,500. The cuttings from the others will be very small.

I would like to ask Mr. Birnie if he can do that in the cutting line. Although I follow this method, I have never been able to find plants to be perfect or to produce perfect cuttings each and every one. But by supposing a whole lot I get 3,500 cuttings by March. Supposing isn't doing. If Mr. Birnie can tell me how to get those 4,000 cuttings to fill 4-inch pots for Spring sales I will throw up the sponge. My plants have never reached the wholesale market yet, which speaks well for somebody.

The party who signed his name "Beginner" is not supposed to know as much as you or I; so why not let him take his 500 plants and he will see in time whether he can do with less. As for me, I will believe that 50 plants will produce 4,000 cuttings when I see it, not before. F. WEEPY.

Editor Florists' Exchange:

Noticing the "free for all fight" John Birnie has with the geranium experts in your "Readers' Column," I wish to state that when we introduced Mars, America, Dryden, etc., a few years ago, we got from 30 to 40 cuttings per plant a season; and it took from five to six weeks to have them rooted and established in 2¼-inch pots, losing hardly five per cent. in the operation. What a folly it is for "green experts" to buck up against John Birnie.

HENRY EICHHOLZ.

Editor Florists' Exchange:

In your issue of June 23, John Birnie criticizes some expert for answering a beginner in growing geraniums. Mr. Birnie says fifty plants properly manipulated would make 4,000 plants; but he does not say how to handle them to get such results. I would like to have him give us his plan.

WIS. F. S. WEIGAND.

Landscape Gardeners and Pictures.

Editor Florists' Exchange:

I see in last week's Florists' Exchange that Job makes some remarks, saying that the landscape department of the Boston Gardeners and Florists' Club should be "maistly Scotch." Age seems to be smoothing out the hard feelings he has had against that race. Time works wonders; and it is wonderful to see Job so changed after the wordy duels between himself and Birnie.

One thing in which I agree with Job is, that some

The Late Frederick A. Blake.

of the picture business is being overdone, in the trade papers, especially the portraits of some of our gallant fishermen florists. Getting one's picture taken on the sands beside the ocean, or beside some placid stream, holding a great catch, looks nice; but the little boy with the overalls and straw hat, who probably caught the fish with the bent pin and who parted with his burden for some coin, should also be included in the picture.

R. T. McGORUM.

English Horticultural Notes.

SWEET PEA MONT BLANC.—This is an ideal dwarf and early flowering sweet pea. Few possess it so far, but it seems likely to be widely sought after. The flowers are large and as white as those of Dorothy Eckford, the best white so far. It grows about 2 feet high and produces a great abundance of flowers on long, erect stalks, these coming earlier (in open-air culture) than any other variety I know of. Messrs. Benary were the introducers.

PEONIES.—Little headway is made with these in England, largely because our growers have no idea of how to stage them effectively, and they will not confine themselves to the best selected kinds. Instead, they prefer a hotch-potch mixture of all shades of colors. A beautiful new rosy pink variety has received an award of merit; it is named Mons. C. Leveque, and is indeed a splendid flower. The exhibitors were Messrs. Bath, Ltd., of Wisbech.

NEW POPPIES AND LUPINES are attracting attention. Messrs. Barr & Sons, of King street, Covent Garden, have the best collection of hybrid lupines that I am acquainted with; while W. J. Godfrey, of Exmouth, Devon, and Amos Perry, of Enfield, near London, are the chief specialists in the oriental poppies.

J. HARRISON DICK.

THE MONMOUTH COUNTY HORTICULTURAL SOCIETY held its monthly meeting on July 6. It was sweet pea night, and this flower was very well represented. W. W. Kennedy had seventeen varieties; H. A. Kettel twenty-one; George Hale, William Dowlen and N. Butterbach fifteen varieties each, George Kuhn, sixteen. William Dowlen read a short paper on sweet peas and a general discussion followed. Two new members were elected, and two proposed.

B.

Obituary

Frederick A. Blake.

Frederick A. Blake, one of the most enthusiastic horticulturists in Massachusetts, died very suddenly at his home in Rochdale, Mass., Sunday, July 1, aged 65 years. Mr. Blake was born in Lowell, Mass., and was educated in the schools of that city. He went to Worcester and at one time was bookkeeper for J. H. & G. M. Walker, manufacturers of boots and shoes. Later Mr. Blake went to Greenville (Rochdale) and associated with his brother-in-law, J. D. Clark, in the manufacture of woolen goods. After the death of Mr. Clark the firm name was changed to the J. D. Clark Company with Mr. Blake as president and general manager. About four years ago Mr. Blake retired from active business and devoted his time largely to horticultural pursuits. He was a member of the American Carnation Society, the American Peony Society, the Massachusetts Horticultural Society, the Worcester County Horticultural Society, the Worcester Agricultural Society, the Fruit Growers' Association, and other organizations. He was a very successful grower and exhibitor.

His greenhouses were conducted more on private lines than for market purposes, although he did ship many fine carnations to Welch Brothers in Boston. The Worcester Horticultural Society loses a valuable member for very seldom was there an exhibition where Mr. Blake did not take one or more of the leading premiums.

The deceased was a retiring man, not given to making a big stir in the business or social world, but having become acquainted with him one soon learned his sterling worth.

It was not generally known that Mr. Blake was musically inclined but such was the fact. For twenty years he was organist at the Baptist Church in Greenville. At his funeral which took place on July 3, the closing piece was the response "Heavenly Father, Hear," with the words and music composed by Mr. Blake himself

He was also a member of several Masonic organizations, but as a local paper expressed it "he was not addicted to the office holding habit," although ready at all times to lend a hand to make successful any affair that he might be connected with.

The funeral service was almost entirely of the Masonic order and was largely attended. The floral tributes were numerous and testified to the high esteem in which he was held. A widow survives him.

William C. Oberghaus.

William C. Oberghaus, gatekeeper for the past seventeen years at Shaw's Garden, St. Louis, died on Saturday, July 7. He had been a sufferer from heart disease for several years. His familiar face will be missed by thousands of visitors. Many S. A. F. O. H. delegates will no doubt remember him during the conventions of 1893 and 1904. It is estimated that he admitted nearly 2,000,000 persons during his long period of service at the garden.

"Billy," as he was familiarly known, was born in Syracuse, N. Y., in 1855, and was 51 years old at the time of his death. At an early age he became a trusted friend of the late Henry Shaw, and 17 years ago he was appointed gatekeeper. He lived in the old homestead in the garden near the entrance. He leaves a widow and four children, and a host of friends in the trade to mourn his loss. The funeral took place Monday afternoon. Services were held at Epiphany church, and interment was in St. Matthews cemetery.

ST. P.

Theodore S. Hubbard.

—Theodore S. Hubbard, died suddenly at his home, 65 Genesee street, Geneva, N. Y., on the evening of Thursday, July 5, 1906. He had been afflicted with arterial trouble for some time and was taken with cerebral hemorrhage and died almost instantly.

Mr. Hubbard was born in Cameron, Steuben County, in 1843, and spent his early life in that place. In 1866 he moved to Fredonia, where he founded the T. S. Hubbard Company, the largest producers of grapevines in the United States. He moved to Geneva in 1887, but still continued his connection with the Fredonia Company.

He was a member of the North Presbyterian Church and gave freely to all of the enterprises of that society. His generosity was not confined to the church, but he was one of the largest contributors to the building fund of the original Y. M. C. A., and also gave to their building fund after the fire. He is survived by his widow, two sons, T. Gilbert and Pomeroy, and one daughter.

Peonies at Cottage Gardens, L. I.

The accompanying illustrations of peonies are reproduced from photographs recently taken on the grounds of the Cottage Gardens Company, Queens, N. Y. We are indebted to Mr. Ward for the pictures, as well as the subjoined descriptions of the varieties:

Gloire de Charles Gombault (Gombault, 1866, introduced by A. Dessert, 1896), large globular flowers, extra full, deep fleshy pink collar, shaded apricot, with tuft of broad petals pink striated carmine, multicolor variety; color of a great freshness.

Mme. Lemonier (Calot, 1864), large very full flowers of a pretty lilac.

Mons. Barral (Calot, 1866), soft pink; perfect shape.

Mme. Forel (Crousse, 1881), late. Enormous, very full ball-shaped bloom on very long strong stems; perfect shape and splendid habit; color glossy ash-colored pink with silvery reflex with deeper rose center.

Meissonier (Crousse, 1886), late. Enormous full convex blooms on long stems; guard petals brilliant purple amaranth, center deep crimson; remarkable for its splendid coloring.

Mons. Boucharlat, aine (Calot, 1868), midseason. Medium-sized, well-formed blooms on erect stems; color bright, lilaceous pink with occasional carmine spots on the central petals; good grower; compact habit. Very valuable in landscape work.

Giganthea (Synonym for **Lamartine**, Calot, 1860), requires three to four years from division to show true character blooms. Large, early bloom on long stems; moderate grower; free bloomer; color the most exquisite shade of delicate rose-pink, tipped with silvery white and reflected with a silver sheen; the most exquisite fragrance of any peony. The finest of all peonies for cut flower purposes.

Peony Mons. Barral.

Growers, Cottage Gardens Company, Queens, N. Y.

Peonies in America.

Editor Florists' Exchange:

I wish to correct some views presented by Rev. C. S. Harrison in your issue of June 30 last. When one rushes into print care should be exercised before positive and authoritative statements are made, as very great injustice may be done to others by broad assertions, without knowing or trying to know what various other growers have at hand, many buyers being often guided by such notices.

I believe that my statistics and information relative to peonies in America are as definite as those of any grower. I acknowledge the two collections named by Mr. Harrison are very fine; but, for his future guidance, pardon me for asking his attention to several other very fine collections; specifically allow me to elaborate regarding my own. We have nearly every sort listed in America and Europe, something over 1,200 sorts and species, embracing about 125,000 commercial plants—one of the largest collections in the world, from a varietal standpoint. While our collection embraces tripl e the number of sorts found in any other American collection, we are only increasing the very best ones. There may be, and is, much difference as to what constitutes "the best" sorts. With me a peony must be a free, vigorous grower, hardy in bud, a good shipper, and of the right color. Many sorts from the standpoint of the exhibition table are very fine, but are not in the dividend class.

One may go into ecstacies; enthusiasm may be so stirred that one outrivals in dreaminess the allegories of the ancient poets (erroneously called "prophets" in these latter days) in describing or writing up novelties; but these must possess great merit to go beyond the novelty age. Many of the latest novelties will not be in a critical list five years hence; many should never have been sent out at all. This obtains because many seedling growers have a very limited collection of named sorts, hence send out many duplicates of older ones.

In regard to nomenclature, the reverend gentleman speaks about correcting names in rather a light vein. The larger becomes my experience, the more cautiously I venture an opinion as to the trueness of many sorts. The different seasonable conditions exert an influence on peonies. As an example, Delachii and F. Ortegai in a wet, cool season will come very dark and of a perfectly incurved anemone globe; in a hot, dry season they are much more crimson in color, more flat shaped, with little if any incurving. Many sorts vary from year to year. Heavy manuring, etc., all contribute to baffle one. Often we err on this account.

In our large list of reds many at first seem quite alike; when comparatively examined they are quite different. But the plants should be fully established before an opinion is offered. Some sorts always show up true; others will be quite variant yearly. As an example, Baroness Schroeder, we have picked up from five sources; some the first year came a deep pink, light pink, blush pink, pure white, flat shape, perfect globes, etc. When fully established they all came out typically. One point wherein I was confident was the root formation—texture, veinings, etc.

Some sorts will never be clarified. We have quite a number of instances where we have 3, 6 or 12 sorts that can be cut about the same time, which when bunched cannot be named apart by the most critical expert anywhere. The only differentiating points are the technical ones of leaf or root formations, or manner of growth in the earlier stages. No one but the critical grower who watches these features throughout the entire season, and especially notes the details, from root formation, etc., to the sear leaf in October, can say much about it.

As an instance, M. Guerin (two sorts), Giganthea roesa, Sydonia, and several others are very much alike; of some my doubts are if they are not the same they are duplicated. G. rosea and Sydonia can be bunched together and no one can pick them out. But their roots are radically dissimilar, one being a smooth, dark, finely-veined root, while Sydonia has a lighter, irregular "pimpled" root. For our distinguished friends to pass judgment on all these sorts without knowing all these technical differentiations and without having a large collection embracing all sorts, will simply put matters deeper into a chaotic abyss.

The matter of any one clarifying the nomenclature from the chaos existing, basing opinions on present descriptions, is in all seriousness a bit humorous or burlesquing in its effect. As an instance, a very large number of one English firm's sorts are either identical with or exact duplicates of French sorts. Even several of our American sorts are worthy of renaming by them with brilliantly glowing praise of their superiority, etc. Some of the most exacting Holland growers are sending Nec Plus Ultra for G. rosea; Eugene Verdier for L'Indispensable; Marie Lemoine for M. de Galhou, etc.

What is your authority? Whence your earliest description? The introducer, etc.? How far back have you a complete list? It is up to you, reverend sir, to elucidate.

In descriptions one will say fleshy white; another, fleshy pink; another, light pink, etc., and each will send the same sort. Now I claim, for one and the same sort that is too great a range for me to accept an opinion. Of course, not everyone is up on color, or has critical eyesight. One will call straw color what another will call creamy white or delicate canary, again, deep purple, dark purple, violaceous red, all describe the same variety.

I have reduced it to this point—buying from introducers whenever possible to do so, or from specialists having sorts from introducers for a long time following the original descriptions. This brings it a bit nearer definiteness; but even at that it is more or less problematical. This Spring we had clumps of John Richardson from the introducer blooming as Andre Lauries. Think what joy there is in paying $5 for a 15c. plant. With our disappointments and mix-ups we must see some joy, some recompense, yea, a brilliant future. Let us all have our say; but in the best of humor flavored with the most exacting care in the doing though thoroughly optimistic. I think such critical growers as Mr. Ward and others will say AMEN to my views.

When our descriptions shall embrace shape, form, more definiteness as to color and shadings, type of stem, leaf, petalage, height, etc., then we could be somewhat certain about our descriptions answering for sorts in hand. But this would be too expensive for general catalogues, where each word means money.

Referring to Mr. Ward's address I evidently got a better deal in buying than he. While some names are wrong, our stocks were only slightly mixed and these largely from two noted growers. The Holland growers' official list is badly off compared with the original descriptions. This is also true of many of our "largest" growers' lists.

As far as I know my literature anent the peony is second to none. There is much sloppiness in what has been going the rounds as peony matter. The task of clarifying the nomenclature of peonies is a very large one—larger and more difficult than many seem to realize.

For one I have always held to the opinion that all should send roots of doubtful sorts to one of our most critical growers, where the largest amount of experience could be utilized in disentangling the matter. This has been my position since the inception of the subject. I may be wrong, but this must be proven before I can change my position.

We need a manual, covering the ground very carefully, exactingly, broadly, critically, by those whose experience is the most definite.

Canaŀ Dover, O. C. BETSCHER.

The Florists' Exchange is in receipt of a pretty pictorial souvenir postal card from W. A. Peterson, of Peterson's Nurseries, Chicago, vice-president of The American Peony Society, who is now in Sweden.

Etherized Plants.

At Cornell University, Ithaca, N. Y., extensive experiments in the etherization of plants have been under way for some time, conducted by C. I. Lewis and J. E. Homett, the former looking after the bulbs, and the latter being intrusted with the forcing of shrubs and herbaceous plants, under the direction of Professor John Craig head of the Horticultural Department.

The objects of the work are to test the efficiency of ether on the forcing of such herbaceous perennials as aquilegias, golden glows and Astilbe japonica, bulbs of narcissus, tulip, hyacinth, Easter lily and of various miscellaneous plants, to determine, if possible, the number of hours plants should be exposed to ether to obtain best results, to acquire an idea of the amount of ether required, to test the use of ether on forcing of rhubarb and asparagus, to see if common shrubs respond alike to the action of ether, to determine whether it is possible to ripen berries, and thus make salable for Christmas such plants as the aucubas, and, finally, to obtain an idea of the efficiency of the forcing of plants by ether from the commercial standpoint.

The shrubs are obtained in the Fall shortly after cold weather has set in, and are placed in a room where the temperature is kept as near freezing as possible. When plants are required for use they are taken out a few hours before placing them in

Mme. Lemoiner

Gloire de Charles Gombault

Giganthea

ether, in order that they may become comparatively dry before etherization.

The etherizing apparatus consists of an airtight galvanized iron box, made especially for this purpose, 3 feet 3 inches by 2 feet 6 inches. It contains two trays, rendering it possible to have three tiers of bulbs or plants undergoing the experiment at once. The trays are composed of heavy wire mesh, in order that the ether may permeate every part of the box. In order to render the box absolutely airtight, the cover is so made that it fits down about five inches over the body of the box, resting on a flange or ridge which is overlaid with thick felt. Precautions being taken to clamp the lid on firmly, the box is practically airtight.

In placing such plants as aquilegias, golden glows and spiræas in the box, care must be taken to remove as much dirt as possible from the roots, giving the ether free access. Shrubs, lilacs, etc., are placed in the box without being potted. When the preliminary work is completed, a small ball of felt containing the required amount of ether is introduced into the airtight box, and the lid clamped down as rapidly as possible.

When removed, after twenty-four, thirty-six or forty-eight hours, as the case may be, the plants are aired before being placed in the forcing house. Other specimens of the same plant, known as check plants, are put at their side to enable the experimenter to make his comparisons.

The lilac has given the best results, etherized lilacs coming into bloom eight to ten days earlier than the untreated ones. With Japanese quince and deutzia the results are not as marked. Under the head of herbaceous plants, golden glows and aquilegias gave little or no results, while, on the other hand, Spiræa astilboides showed the action of ether in a most remarkable manner, the etherized plant coming into full bloom from ten days to three weeks before the unetherized. Rhubarb treated in a like manner was ready to cut five days before the untreated rhubarb, and yielded a much larger proportion of edible stocks. In the case of asparagus, a remarkable phenomenon was observed. The plant grew riotously, becoming tall and spindly, and was absolutely unfit for use. The Easter lily shows indication of blooming from one to three weeks before the unetherized sample.

The use of ether on plants marks a revolution in horticulture. The whole subject is still in the experimental stage, but its supporters predict more startling results to come. The specimens subjected not only grow with increased rapidity, varying with the particular specimen, but the flower seems to attain a fuller bloom and maturity.

Meissonier

Mons. Boucharlat, aine

Mme. Forel

PEONIES IN COLLECTION OF COTTAGE GARDENS COMPANY, QUEENS, L. I.

CLUB AND SOCIETY DOINGS.

THE COLUMBUS (OHIO) FLORISTS' CLUB held its regular meeting Monday evening, July 2. President Stephens was in the chair. The attendance was the very largest in a long time. The meeting was of a social nature, the club having voted to have a "smoker talk" and refreshments as well. The entertainment committee, composed of Messrs. Bauman, McKellar, and Reichart, attended to their duties in the most satisfactory manner. It was perhaps the most enjoyable and harmonious meeting of the year. These informal "smoke talks" do much to promote the prosperity of any club, and their cost is a very slight matter when compared with the pleasure derived from them. It was voted to hold the annual picnic at Buckeye Lake, Ohio, Thursday, July 12. The outing committee, which consists of Messrs. McKellar, Curry, Metzmaver, Reichart, and Bauman, will arrange all details, and provide a most attractive program, consisting of baseball, races, etc., for both young and old. It will be a regular old-time basket picnic. Had it not been for the convention in August at Dayton, we should not have had the outing so early, but so many are going to Dayton we decided to have it at once. Adjourned till July 17. F. W.

ELBERON (N. J.) HORTICULTURAL SOCIETY.—A meeting of this society was held on Monday, July 2, President W. D. Robertson in the chair. A good attendance of the members was present, considering the warm weather through which we were passing. Some fine exhibits were shown, notably a collection of cannas by A. Bauer, which was awarded a certificate of merit. The prize of the evening, which was donated by Mr. Kennedy of Oceanic for a collection of vegetables, was won by F. Dettlinger. Collections of cut flowers were shown by A. Bauer, H. Hall, and Ben. Wycoff, while W. D. Robertson exhibited a fine vase of Chrysanthemum maximum. Some good vegetables were also shown.

This young society holds its first flower show on Friday and Saturday, July 13 and 14. G. M.

NEW JERSEY FLORICULTURAL SOCIETY.—The regular monthly meeting and floral display of this society was held July 6. Orchids were the most prominent flowers, the exhibits of Lager & Hurrell and Julius Roehrs Company being of high merit and were suitably rewarded. A specimen hydrangea from Mr. J. Crosby Brown, showing the cultural skill of Peter Duff, had over two hundred blooms. A Scottii fern exhibited by the Colgates, grown by William Reid, received 90 points.

Reports were received relating to the recent effort of the society in maintaining a float; through the liberality of members in furnishing flowers, the outlay was kept within the allowance of $25. A congratulatory letter from the managers of the parade was ordered placed on file.

Letters were read to and from the United States Express Company in conformity with the motion of Harry O. May at the June meeting. The reply of Edward T. Platt as under was received with laughter:

"Yours of the 15th. ultimo, addressed to the Hon. T. C. Platt, President of this Company, has been referred to me. In reply I beg to state that the reason we had to increase our charges on shipments of flowers is due to the fact that such consignments were being carried at a loss by this company, and it was necessary for us to increase the rates. You would hardly think that one-half a cent or even a cent a pound on flowers that are sold at such high prices in New York by the retailers, could be considered a very exorbitant charge."

George Smith called attention to the gentleman's irrelevancy in excusing the exorbitant express charges on the ground of high prices received by New York retailers, when the burden came on the growers, and announced that the advanced rates were said to have cost the company already $40,000 per annum in the withdrawal of patronage.

The judges for the evening were E. Thomas, George von Qualen and Arthur T. Caparn.

A paper upon "The Dahlia" was read by Walter Gray of Maplewood, in absence of George K. Austin through sickness, who was announced to read a paper on "Orchids in the Open."

J. B. D.

Our London Letter.

BY A. HEMSLEY.

FLORAL DECORATIONS.—The Royal Horticultural Society had a special show of floral arrangements at their new hall on June 20. It was a matter of regret that none of our best London florists contributed. There were some very good arrangements, but on the whole they fell short of what might have been expected; and some of the provincial florists who came up expecting to see some of the work of our best London craftsmen were much disappointed. Messrs. Perkins & Sons, the well known florists of Coventry, took the lead and secured the society's gold medal for their various exhibits. Two bouquets of orchids in different classes were very well finished; also a large cross standing on a broad base. This was covered with double white stocks with a tine of forget-me-nots running from the center column at each angle. From the center of the cross hung Cymbidium Lowianum and odontoglossums. On one side was an anchor made of yellow roses and Erica Cavendishi with a rope of forget-me-nots. And on the other a heart of crimson carnations and Campanula pulla, these were supported from the center column of the cross. From Mr. W. Treseder, Cardiff, came a very large harp; the base was well made up with orchids of various sorts, and cattleyas were largely used for the frame, with strings of lily of the valley.

In tables decorated with roses, Madame Abel Chatenay was the favorite variety used; and the same variety was employed for the first prize bouquet. In one class sweet pea Gladys Unwin was used for the first prize table. Another first prize table was done with yellow irises, yellow and bronze aquilegias, Geum atrosanguineum and asparagus. Another went for a nice arrangement in which Odontoglossum crispum and lily of the valley were the only flowers used. The stands most favored were the rustic silver plated of various patterns with the small receptacles on branching irregular standards. In vases of flowers there were a good many exhibits, but nothing of exceptional merit.

THE ROYAL BOTANICAL SOCIETY.—The Summer show recently held at the beautiful gardens was a great success. The rhododendrons of Messrs. J. Waterer & Sons, Ltd., which filled the large tent were perhaps the leading feature. They were in superb condition. Varieties of special note were Gomer Waterer, a lovely blush mauve with bold trusses of large flowers. Mum, Moonshine and many others might be mentioned. A special large gold medal awarded. The Rambler roses from Messrs. W. Paul & Sons were well flowered and included fine specimens of The Farquhar, Lady Gay, Hiawatha, Debutante, Dorothy Perkins, and Philadelphia. A new hybrid tea, "Earl of Warwick," cream ground with blush pink shading, large full flowers, gained a certificate of merit. Geo. Mount was another good exhibitor of roses but his were chiefly large flowers of Captain Hayward Ulrich Brunner, Mme. Caroline Testout, Mrs. Sharman-Crawford, etc.—grand blooms on long stems. I should not omit Frau Karl Druschki which were extra fine. Gold medals were given for both of the above exhibits.

From Messrs. Kelway & Sons, Langport came peonies of the best sorts. Of those I noted Countess of Warwick, John Solano, Major Loder, Summer Day, and Maharajah as among the best. Delphiniums and pyrethrums were also very good. Poppies from Amos Perry included Mrs. Perry, salmon, and Queen Alexandra, two fine varieties of the oriental section. These gained certificates of merit, and the same distinction from the R. H. Society previously.

Sweet peas came from Messrs Watkins & Simpson in grand form. Mrs. A. Watkins, Frank Dolby, and E. J. Castle gained certificates of merit, but Nora Unwin, a pure white of the Gladys Unwin type, failed; yet I think it one of the best. Evelyn Byatt, previously certificated, was very fine. Helen Lewis also keeps up its character, and Bolton's Pink was equally good.

From W. J. Godfrey came two good ivy-leaved pelargoniums; they were Exmouth Gem and Lady Gertrude. Devonshire Lass should also be worth attention.

AT THE NURSERIES.—I find H. B. May has considerably extended the culture of stove plants; ixoras are among the more recent additions. He has had a grand lot of these this season and they have sold readily to the florists, one year old plants making from two shillings and sixpence to five shillings each.

Messrs. H. Low & Co. are going in stronger than ever for carnations. They send me blooms of about two dozen varieties of the malmaisons. Princess of Wales is one of the most profitable; their large stock of this, which I saw just before they were in flower, were very healthy. The blooms of Victory which they send are fine, also Candace.

At L. R. Russell's nursery I saw the finest lot of marantas, anthuriums, foliage varieties and other aroids that I have met with for a long ime. Aralia elegantissima Veitchii and others are also well done.

School Gardens in California.

The second year of school gardening work closed with the closing of our schools, June 29. A number of public spirited women two years ago conceived the idea of educating our future citizens in the knowledge of plant life by teaching the children how to care for plants and make the most of the great natural advantages with which we are endowed, in the beautifying of home grounds and public parks, and some system in street tree planting that shall eventually make our city the most beautiful in the world. When the subject was first presented to our board of education they looked upon it as a harmless fad of a few visionary idealists, and gave these earnest, thoughtful women permission to try their experiment in one school yard. The result was a revelation to those who were interested enough to go to see the work done, and the great benefit to the children thus engaged, that this year the idea was carried out in four schools. Vegetables as well as flowers were grown, and in the majority of cases the beds would have been a credit to any professional gardener. Eighty-five dollars in cash were distributed in amounts of $1 to $5 each for the best work done. Mayor McAleer was present at the entertainment given in the Bethlehem Institute by the children, and as each winner was called up for his or her award he gave each a hearty shake of the hand and a pleasant word of encouragement.

This year the work was not begun until February. The coming school year the campaign will be begun in October, for two principal reasons. First, it has been learned that boys and girls interested in this garden work are better pupils; are much more easily controlled, and have a respectful, dignified manner in the presence of their teachers and visitors who call to see their work, that children have not who are not thus interested.

Second, to teach the children and through them the parents that there is no necessity of ground lying idle in this delightful climate, during the Fall and Winter months, and that it is possible to have flowers and vegetables every day of the year in the open air. Then, too, the promoters of the scheme have the thought in mind of teaching the children perseverance, the habit of sticking to a job until it is finished—an accomplishment they must all have if they hope to be successful in life. P. D. BARNHART.

School Gardens at Los Angeles, Cal.

THE WEEK'S WORK.

Timme's Timely Teachings.

Nephrolepis.

Any time from quite early in the Spring until the end of this month the planting of Boston ferns into benches with a view to raising a stock of young ferns for next year is in season. It is now when a bench or part of one can best be spared for this purpose. Three or at most four inches of light, sandy soil is all sufficient. In letting all the runners strike root, a large number of young plants, ready for small pots, is quickly obtained. Frequent sprinkling and a light shading on bright days is about all that is needed in the way of care while the runners are rooting. Several batches of little plants might be taken out of the bench at intervals, if quantity is the main desideratum, one lot succeeding the other as long as there are runners, and, finally, the stock plants, when taken out, could be pulled apart and the divisions be started anew in small pots. But few growers find it necessary to resort to extreme measures in the multiplication of Boston ferns.

To grow this young stock into fine salable goods is of far greater importance than excessive propagation. Good plants may be raised by again making use of a bench. Now the full light and plenty of room are afforded, and all runners are removed. In early Fall the plants are potted up, either singly or several in one pot, in sizes deemed most desirable for the grower's particular trade. If this is done in good season, say in the middle of September, they will be nicely spread and fairly well established ferns by the time when the call for them is greatest. Constant pot culture, however, produces the best appearing Boston ferns. Grace and elegance replace the innate stiffness of its remote forerunner, the old sword fern. Then, too, plants raised in pots altogether keep better and last longer as parlor or living room subjects. Of course, this method of growing them up into good sized specimens requires a greater amount of care and attention—and skill too—than usually goes with bench culture; but I think it pays.

Fern Baskets.

In potting up Boston ferns and varieties that have sportingly sprung from the original type, some baskets of varying sizes and shapes should also be made up. There is no time or season when fern baskets, baskets of any kind, well stocked and overflowing with luxuriant vegetation, could not be sold at a fairly good price, or when they failed to be an attractive feature of store or greenhouse equipment. Boston ferns are as easily grown in baskets as in pots, but the baskets must be of durable construction or trouble will set in when the ferns are at their very best. Wire baskets with pretty wide meshes, lined with sheet moss, are mostly used; but a Boston fern will outlast any kind of basket made of ordinary iron wire, no matter of what number or how strong this is. Baskets of solid copper wire cost much more, but they will last long enough to give the fern a chance to grow into a thing of beauty. These ferns also do well and look fine in well designed bowls or baskets of the potter's handiwork.

Ferns in Variety.

The great popularity of the Boston fern may have lessened the sales in palms, dracænas, rubber trees and decorative plants of that class—no doubt it has; but ferns of other species are as much admired and as readily purchased as ever. The trade in foliage plants, ferns in particular, is a never-ceasing coming and going one not in any marked degree dependent on season or locality. A retail plant concern without its attractive and interesting collection of ferns can not be considered well equipped for business; it is a lame affair. No need of sumptuous display or stuffy arrangement. A well chosen, trimly kept and properly cared for assortment of ferns, ranging in size from three to six-inch pots, the varieties intermingling, will find a fit place and assert its charm and effectiveness on any ordinary bench or staging where plants may live and thrive. Here they gain in beauty and value from day to day, contented with the smallest share of the grower's attention. But when, as is the common practice, they are stood under benches or in any out-of-the-way corner, or when they are made to do duty as underbrush in crowded plant colonies, as a covering screen to pots of towering palms and the like, they soon lose their vigor, their peculiar grace and elegance of bearing.

This is a very good time to make a beginning with ferns, or to replenish the stock already on hand. I do not advise the raising of a future supply in this line from spores. This part might as well be left to the experienced specialist, who is so well equipped for his work in all respects as to be able to furnish the retailer with ferns in all sizes at a nominal cost, at far less than what the small grower could raise them for. In ordering two or 2 1-2-inch stock, fine, thrifty ferns are obtained, that, when received ,are usually ready for the 3, most of them for the 4-inch pots, and the latter is a good size for retailing. It is remarkable how rapidly and with what little labor and special care ferns of nearly all species grow into nice plants, salable at almost any stage of growth. What they need is a moderate amount of moisture at their roots at all times, a shading on sunny days and a sprinkling overhead in dry weather to create a fair degree of atmospheric humidity. A thorough drying out at any time is death to ferns, and constant drenching of the soil brings about the same result, only the process is slower. A steady temperature at any point between 50 and 60 degrees in Midwinter is about right for a collection of varying species.

Small ferns, as everybody knows, come extremely handy in filling baskets, hampers, pans and dishes of all kinds, now so much liked as holiday gifts and in fair demand at all seasons of the year. It is now time to also provide suitable stock for this kind of trade. Seedling ferns, yet in trays, are best for the purpose. They should now be ordered; their price is low and their size just right for 2 or 2 1-2-inch pots. They will need no farther transplanting after being potted up, until made use of as filling material.

Freesias.

The season when the planting of bulbs claims our attention is close at

C. S. Burge,
First Vice-President American Seed Trade Association.

hand. Freesias are among the first to arrive. Whenever it can be made possible select a bench for their culture with clear light overhead, in a house where a steady heat of about 52 degrees can easily be maintained in Winter. In a lower temperature freesias bloom too late for a good market, and the bulbs (for the following season) that are produced in a cool house, do not fully mature. The stock thus soon runs out and new bulbs will have to be purchased every year. The expense involved in the annual buying of bulbs in itself is not so much a matter of regret as the grower's inability in such a case to work up a carefully selected strain of freesias, superior to anything he can buy. With freesias this is possible to do; while any such attempt in the case of other bulbs would only be a profitless exploit.

As a by-culture among other crops freesias amount to little and the product in flowers is nothing to be proud of; nor can they be grown to perfection in shallow flats, but will do fairly well in pots. Where their culture is made somewhat of a specialty they are given benches all to themselves in a pretty warm, well lighted house, and the planting is done as soon as the corms can be obtained, or as soon as the benches can be had in readiness.

In planting the bulbs in rows they should be put about two inches apart and the rows six inches; or plant in evenly spaced hills, six or eight corms to a hill. Use a sandy, well enriched sod compost, avoiding the use of fresh manure. Press the corm into the soil to the depth of one inch below the surface. Freesias are moisture-loving plants. With a bench well-drained, over-watering is well-nigh impossible. They want a good wetting down right after being planted and should at no time ever afterward be allowed to become thoroughly dry. I here place especial stress on this point in their culture, because to its non-observance may be traced those discouraging failures with freesias, which last season I had occasion to witness, with their cause plainly set forth.

Pansies.

In line with freesias as a profitable side crop in cut flower production during the greater part of Winter are pansies. There is very little difference between the two as regards initial outlay, ease of culture, room taken up and ultimate returns. Good pansy flowers, which here means large blooms on long, stout stems, regardless of color, sell as fast as they can be picked in Midwinter or early Spring. If the growing of pansies for the Winter's flower market is on the program, then no time should be lost in making a start. Seeds of some good, vigorous strain must now be sown. A cold frame that can be darkened by the covering of boards until the plants are up is as good as any place for the purpose, better than flats or the inside of a greenhouse. If thinly sown, with plenty of room between the seedlings, they could remain undisturbed until large enough for the bench; otherwise they must be pricked off and given a chance to become stocky little bushes. In benching they are set five inches apart into the richest kind of thoroughly composted soil.

Hardy Perennials.

A well arranged and trimly kept border of hardy herbaceous perennials soon grows into a source of much pleasure and considerable profit to anyone who has made the raising and selling of plants his occupation. Such a collection, being a part of the stock in trade, should be well chosen and should chiefly consist of such varieties as are truly hardy, sure to do well and well known and liked by all classes of people. There are any number of kinds that will in every particular come up to these requirements.

This is the beginning of the season when the hardy border looks its brightest. Keeping the bed free of weeds, staking, tying, labeling and watering is work to be attended to at this time. Little in the way of shifting or replanting, or of propagating by division or cuttings can now be attempted. But seeds of various kinds may be sown at this time of the year. It is this one of the many ways in which to provide good stock for next year's sales, a way open to such retail florists whose lack of sufficient garden space forbids the maintenance of a hardy herbaceous border. The seeds of nearly all varieties, that may thus be raised to any advantage, germinate readily and quickly grow into sturdy little plants. All of them transplant easily when still small. A frame or a nicely prepared bit of ground will do finely for a seed bed; or the seeds may be started in trays or boxes. An early pricking off is advisable and soon after that a planting into cold frames or the open border, with sufficient space between plants to obviate future crowding. If that is done in good season, so as to afford sufficient time for re-establishment before Winter sets in, the stock will be all the better for it in the Spring.

Another way, and one now largely practiced by large and small growers, is to grow the seedlings, as also much of the young stock in this department obtained by division and from cuttings and intended to meet the demand in early Spring, in pots altogether, giving them a shift from time to time and placing them in cold frames during the Summer. Some kinds stay in these frames until disposed of in the Spring; others are taken to warmer quarters and grown slowly along, all of them being of salable size in the early part of Spring. There is no difficulty whatever in disposing of stock of this kind, firmly rooted and nicely started as it is when it comes out of the pots. It is a line of business not likely to be overdone in the near future.

Asters.

When asters begin to show buds it is time to set the hose a-playing. Little artificial watering is usually needed before that. The earlier sorts will soon be in, but the main crop of flowers is not due until the end of August and the first half of September. Of late the chief endeavor in aster growing has been to avoid the rush, to have them come either very early or quite late, neither attempt resulting in the production of fine flowers.

This season, so far, has been a dry one and in other respects has proved unfavorable to outdoor crops. Asters especially have suffered much from one cause or another, and it may all be that, with all sorts of trouble yet in store, the season will turn out to be a disastrous one for some of the growers while others, favorably located, well equipped with adequate means for watering and knowing the alpha and omega of present day aster culture, will reap a rich harvest. Such a season then, it would seem, is to be preferred to one of widespread abundance as far as the traffic in asters is concerned.

From now on asters should not be disturbed at the roots any more than is necessary to keep the ground from cracking and free of weeds. Watering is necessary, if perfect blooms on stiff stems are wanted, unless frequent showers supply the needed moisture. The aster bugs at their earliest appearance in single file must be picked off and destroyed. The pinching out of the first central bud always pays.

FRED. W. TIMME.

CHANGES IN BUSINESS.

ROCHESTER, N. H.—Melvin H. Folsom has opened a floral department at Preston's department store.

HARVARD, ILL.—H. W. Newitt is out with a proposition to establish a greenhouse business here provided the necessary encouragement is offered.

BATAVIA, N. Y.—Anson W. Bogue has started what will be known as the Genessee County Nurseries, at the corner of Richmond avenue and Oak street.

ROCHESTER, N. Y.—Otto Suecker has bought J. D. Fry's greenhouses, consisting of 5,000 square feet of glass. He raises cut flowers and bedding plants for the retail trade.

BUFFALO.—The J. G. Pickelman Company has been incorporated to carry on a florist business; capital, $2,500; incorporators, J. G. Pickelman, C. Pickelman, and J. F. Pallenson, Buffalo.

STAFFORD SPRINGS, Conn.—Joseph Braun of Westerly, R. I., has leased the greenhouses of the Stafford Floral Company for two years, with the privilege of buying the business. Mr. Braun has arrived in town and commenced his work.

HOWARD LAKE, MINN.—W. H. Eddy has enlarged his business by buying the entire stock of the Howard Lake Nursery and grounds of W. L. Taylor, and will now run the two under the name of The Howard Lake and Victor Nurseries.

COLORADO SPRINGS, COLO.—J. B. Braidwood of this city has sold his retail store to Miss Florence Kennedy who has been very successful at Cripple Creek for the past four years. William Clark assumes charge of the greenhouses once more.

EL PASO, ILL.—The new company organized by Charles Snyder for the erection of greenhouses here will be known as the El Paso Carnation Company. Considerably more than the bonus was raised and this money will be returned to the subscribers pro rata.

TILTON, ILL.—John Willius is moving his greenhouse from East Main street near the Soldier's Home to Tilton. Mr. Willius has an elegant home here and plenty of room for his large greenhouses. The old Duke greenhouse was recently sold and removed from Tilton.

GARDINER, MASS.—The greenhouses and other property on the East Templeton road, formerly owned by Arthur F. Johnson, are to be sold at public auction. Mr. Johnson expects to move to Amherst in the Fall where his son, Roger A. Johnson, is to become a student at Amherst college.

DES MOINES, IA.—Lozier, the florist, has purchased the business of the New York Floral Company located at 408 Sixth avenue and will consolidate it with his store at 317 Sixth avenue in the K. P. block. Mr. Lozier is operating a store in East Des Moines and announces that he expects to open branch stores in other cities.

YOUNGSTOWN, O.—The Walker Floral Company has been incorporated with a capital stock of $30,000 by John Walker, E. Hippard, I. T. Brant, C. H. Kennedy and B. F. Wirt. The company will operate the store on West Federal street formerly under the name of Walker & McLean. The business will be conducted as heretofore with Mr. Walker in charge of the greenhouses.

NORTH TONAWANDA, N. Y.—G. E. Towne and A. J. Howe, formerly with A. N. Pierson, Cromwell, Conn., have bought out the C. J. Pult greenhouses of this place, where they do a first class retail trade. The plant consists of six houses containing 12,000 square feet of glass. A general line of stock, such as roses, carnations, chrysanthemums, and bedding plants is grown.

C. S. Burge.

We have pleasure in presenting the portrait of C. S. Burge, of Toledo, O., first vice-president of The American Seed Trade Association. Mr. Burge has been connected with S. W. Flower & Co., Toledo, in the seed business since 1882, and has always taken an active part in the work of the Seed Trade Association.

ORDER PEONY PLANTS NOW.

Complete list ready for distribution. Ship September first. Stock Guaranteed true. It means something to carry away a silver cup and nine first prizes out of twelve awarded at the Exhibition of the American Peony Society. That is what we did.

PETERSON NURSERY, 1301 Stock Exchange Building, **CHICAGO, ILL.**

GROW MUSHROOMS

If you do not know how, procure that simple but complete and practical book called "How to Grow Mushrooms." The price is ten cents and it can be secured from this office

Special rates will be made to the trade who wish to supply their customers.

THE FLORISTS' EXCHANGE

2 Duane St., New York

PEONIES.

Queen Victoria (the cold storage flower) $9.00 per 100. **Festiva Maxima**, $30.00 per 100. **Fragrans** (the bloom producer), $6.00 per 100. For 1000 rates or other varieties, write.

GILBERT H. WILD,
SARCOXIE, MO.

Mention The Florists' Exchange when writing.

CELERY---CABBAGE

White Plume, Golden-Self, Golden Heart, fine plants, $1.50 per 1000.

Cabbage Plants—Flat Dutch and Drumhead $1.00 per 1000; 5000 for $4.00.

Cauliflower Plants, Early Snowball, $2.00 per 1000.

J. C. SCHMIDT CO., Bristol, Pa.

Mention The Florists' Exchange when writing.

PEONIES

A splendid collection of peonies, some of the choicest. Send for price list.
Send 25c. each for Peony and Phlox manuals.

C. S. HARRISON,
YORK, NEB.

Mention the Florists' Exchange when writing.

ASPARAGUS

Spengeri, extra strong, 3 in. pots, $5 per 100.
Extra Strong, 4 in. pots, $6 per 100.
Smilax, 2½ in. pots $2 per 100.
Cabbage Plants, Flat Dutch, Succession and Winningstadt, $1.50 per 1000. Cash with order.

S. G. BENJAMIN
Fishkill, N. J.

Mention The Florists' Exchange when writing.

CULTURAL DIRECTIONS

Specially written for the use of your amateur customers. Send Twenty-five cents for complete sample set, which amount will be deducted from order for first thousand.

The universal favor in which these Directions are held, as shown by the many orders received therefor, encourages us in the belief that these Leaflets are just the neat little factor to help promote business and establish better relations between the dealer and his customer.

TRY SOME!

BIG BUSINESS ASSISTANT

TO SAVE TIME, QUICKEN SALES, AND AID YOU PLEASE YOUR CUSTOMER, WE HAVE PREPARED

Cultural Directions

COVERING A NUMBER OF THOSE PLANTS AND BULBS MOST LARGELY IN DEMAND

THE "CULTURALS" have been written by experts; they are fuller, and contain more detailed directions than it is possible to embrace in a catalogue. Equipped with these, just hand one out with each sale, and save yourself considerable present and future trouble, as the customer will then be able to consult the directions, grow his plants, seeds or bulbs intelligently, and so receive satisfactory results, without having to continually resort to you for advice.

The following "Culturals" are now ready:

AMARYLLIS (Hippeastrum)	CROCUS, Snowdrop and Scilla Sibirica	MUSHROOM CULTURE
ANNUALS FROM SEED	DAHLIA	ONIONS
ASPARAGUS	FERNS	PALMS, House Culture of
ASTERS	FREESIA	PANSY
BEGONIA, TUBEROUS	GERANIUM	PEONIES
BULBS	GLADIOLUS	PERENNIALS, Hardy
CABBAGE and CAULIFLOWER	GLOXINIA	PRIMULA
CANNA	HOT BEDS and FRAMES	ROSE CULTURE
CARNATIONS, MONTHLY	HOUSE PLANTS, Care of	SWEET PEA, The
CELERY	HYACINTHS, Dutch and Roman	TOMATOES
CHINESE SACRED LILY	IRIS AND TRITOMA	TUBEROSE
CHRYSANTHEMUM	LAWNS	TULIP
CLIMBING PLANTS Hardy	LILY CULTURE for House and Garden	VEGETABLES
COLEUS, and other bedders		VIOLETS
		WATER GARDEN, How to make and Manage a

PRICE LIST

500 Cultural Directions for $1.50
1,000 - - - - - - 2.50

Printed on white paper, clear type, size 6 x 9½ inches, in an assortment, your selection of not less than 100 of each, delivered carriage paid.

Sufficient space will be left at the bottom of each leaflet for your name, address, etc. If you desire this imprint (3 lines) we will put same on for you at 50 cents for 500, 75 cents for 1000. Special quotations will be made on quantities of 5,000 "CULTURALS" or over.

A. T. De La Mare Ptg. and Pub. Co. Ltd.

Pubs. The Florists' Exchange. P. O. Box, 1697, NEW YORK

Mention The Florists' Exchange when writing.

LOOK! See Us Grow.

Always buy of Aschmann, the great Araucaria importer of America.
OUR MOTTO—Cheap, Good, Honest Dealings and Quick Sales.

ARAUCARIA EXCELSA a specialty. 5,000 are in now, imported from Ghent, Belgium this Spring, 1906. Now planted in 5½ and 6 in. pots, well established, and ready for shipment to all parts of America. All these are grown for us by an Araucaria Specialist in Ghent, Belgium. **NO SEEDLINGS**, but Araucarias raised from top cuttings only are offered. This is now our 11th Anniversary, and our importations have grown from 250 in the first year to the remarkable number of **6,000 IN THE ELEVENTH YEAR.** My reputation as Araucaria Importer gains footway in every greenhouse and florist store in America. Our Araucarias need no *coaxing*, genuine facts tell in quality and cheapness.

Please Note Our Lowest Prices

12 to 14 in. 5½ in. pots, 3 to 4 tiers, 2-yr. old. 50c. 14 to 16 in., 5½ in. pots, 3 to 4 tiers, 2-yr. old, 60c. 16 to 18 in. 5¼ 6 in. pots, 4 to 5 tiers, 3-yr. old. 75c. 18 to 20 in., 6 in. pots, 5 to 6 tiers, 4-yr. old, $1.00. 20 to 24 in. 6 in. to 7 in. pots, 5 to 6 tiers, 4-yr. old, $1.25. 36-40 to 50 in. 7 in. pots, specimen plants from $2.50 to $3.00 each.

ARAUCARIA COMPACTA ROBUSTA—have several thousand of them; can supply all wants. These plants were never so fine in shape and condition as this year. The set of the greenhouse, as broad as long, 12 to 20 in., in height, 3 to 4 perfect tiers, 20 to 30 inches across, 3-4-5 year old, 6 to 7 in. pots, $1.25, $1.50, $1.75, $2.00, $2.50 to $3.00 each.

ARAUCARIA EXCELSA GLAUCA—This variety on account of its beautiful Green-Blueish tiers, dwarf habit, fine compact shape, gives it a striking appearance, and anybody seeing them, must undoubtedly fall in love with them at sight. Plants, 6-7 inch pots, 3-4-5 perfect tiers, 3-4 year old, 15 to 25 inch high, from 15 to 30 in. across, $1.25, $1.50, $1.75, $2.00 to $2.50 each.

SOLANUM or JERUSALEM CHERRY, $5.00 per 100.

KENTIA FORSTERIANA, 7 in. pots, made-up plants, 1 large in center, 3 smaller sizes, 22 to 25 in. high around, gives them a good appearance, $2.00 each. 6 in. pots, single plants, 35 to 40 in. high, 5 to 6 good leaves, 4 year old, $1.25 to $1.50 each; 6 in. pots, 30 to 35 in. high, 4 year old, 5 good leaves, $1.00; 5¾ in. pots, 3 year old, 25 to 30 in. high, 5 good leaves, 75c. made-up plants, 3 and 4 in. pots, 18 to 20 in. high, 25 cts. to 30 cts. each.

KENTIA BELMOREANA, 5¾ to 6 in. pots, bushy, fine plants, from 75 cts. to $1.00 to $1.25 each.

ARECA LUTESCENS, made-up, 25 cts.

COCOS WEDDELIANA, 15 cts.

CYCAS REVOLUTA (Sago Palm), 6 in.-7 in. pots, with from 6 to 20 leaves per plant, 10 cts. per leaf.

CASH WITH ORDER

When ordering, say whether the plants should be shipped in the pots or not

GODFREY ASCHMANN

Importer and Wholesale Grower of Pot Plants

1012 Ontario Street, - - PHILADELPHIA, PA.

Mention The Florists' Exchange when writing.

YOUR

Fall Catalogue

We have been printing Trade Catalogues for the past fifteen years; have been accumulating stock cuts and photographs for the past fifteen years, and, equally important, perhaps most important of all, have been steadily improving in our knowledge as to what is required in the way of style, workmanship and finish in order to produce a catalogue that

Will Be Effective

Send in full specifications and we will promptly give you an estimate. We supply our stock cuts free to customers.

A. T. DE LA MARE PTG. & PUB. CO. Ltd.
2 to 8 Duane Street, New York City.

Louisville.

Society Meeting.

The July meeting of the Kentucky Society of Florists was to have been held at the store of Fred Haupt, on the night before the Fourth, but there was a very slender attendance. Members, there is no excuse for your not being able to give one night a month for the welfare of the society and your business interests. Encourage the officers in their endeavor by attending regularly.

Trade Notes.

There is quite a little building going on in Louisville this Summer. Jacob Schulz is rebuilding four houses. George Thompson is moving from his old place to a new one and is putting up three new houses. H. Kleinstarink has put a fine stone wall around his entire place and is rebuilding one house and adding three new ones, also a new boiler house. Frank Gottwald is also building.

Anders Rasmussen of New Albany, Ind., has returned from a trip to New York, where he went to dispose of his patented ventilator.

A country magistrate here has taken it upon himself to see that some of the old Blue laws on the statute books are enforced and every week swears out warrants against business people who keep their places of business open on Sunday. A great many houses close on Sunday to escape the annoyance of being haled before the court, and so it has been with the florist store men. During these Summer months it does not make much difference; and by Fall there will be something doing in political lines.

The bowlers among us are practising weekly, and while not yet in championship form we are steadily improving and should give a good account of ourselves in the S. A. F. O. H contest.

A. R. B.

Los Angeles, Cal.

News Notes.

Jacaranda ovalifolia has been in bloom for a month, and a gorgeous sight it is to see large trees covered with spikes of bloom 12 to 24 inches long. The flowers are a dark purple—about the size and very much the shape of those of the large flowering pentstemons. The tree sheds its beautiful, fern like foliage before the flowers appear. It is one of our most desirable shade trees, and is largely used as a street tree, standing well the dust and cramped quarters the curbing affords.

Tecoma Stans is just now coming into flower. The blooms are not so large as those of its near relative—Bignonia Tweediana—but are of the same beautiful golden color, and it has the merit of great profusion of bloom for three or four months. It is shrubby in habit of growth, and should be grown wherever it will endure the Winter climate.

The drouth resisting character of Plumbago capensis has only been discovered by the writer, never before having seen it growing away from other plants that required water. At present he has care of a 50 foot hedge that has not had a drop of water for two months, yet it is in vigorous condition, covered with its beautiful blue flowers. It seems to be as drouth-resistant as the lantana.

P. D. BARNHART.

MILWAUKEE, WIS.—The Milwaukee Retail Flower Dealers' Association has been organized to protect their interests. The association is composed of twenty-four members. Officers were elected as follows: President, Mrs. Frederick Davis; vice-president, William Edlefsen; secretary, A. B. Loufbourow; treasurer, Mrs. Ida Baumgarten.

CLASSIFIED ADVERTISEMENTS

CASH WITH ORDER.

The columns under this heading are reserved for advertisements of Stock for Sale, Stock Wanted, Help Wanted, Situations Wanted or other Wants; also of Greenhouse, Land, Second-Hand Materials, etc., For Sale or Rent.

Our charge is 10 cts. per line (7 words to the line), set solid, without display. No advt. accepted for less than thirty cents.

Display advertisements in these columns, 15 cents per line; count 12 lines agate to the inch.

[If replies to Help Wanted, Situation Wanted, or other advertisements are to be addressed care of this office, advertisers add 10 cents to cover expense of forwarding.]

Copy must reach New York office 12 o'clock Wednesday to secure insertion in issue of following Saturday.

Advertisers in the Western States desiring to advertise under initials, may save time by having their answer directed care our Chicago office at 127 E. Berwyn Ave.

SITUATIONS WANTED

SITUATION WANTED—By all-around florist. Wholesale or retail. State wages. Address, L. K., care The Florists' Exchange.

SITUATION WANTED—Traveler, thoroughly conversant with every branch of the trade and who can give best of references. S. P. D., Box 1697, New York.

SITUATION WANTED—By single man who has experience in carnations, mums and bedding plants. References, L. Geh, 150 Central Avenue, Brooklyn, New York.

SITUATION WANTED—By working foreman. Competent, married man. Roses, carnations and mums a specialty. A No. 1 propagator. Address, Grower, care The Florists' Exchange.

SITUATON WANTED—By practical all-around grower, 20 years experience, private or commercial. Reliable and not afraid of work. Age 37. Address, L. J., care The Florists' Exchange.

SITUATION WANTED—By a young married man as grower of roses, carnations, mums and general stock. 11 years' experience; English, good references. Address, L. C., care The Florists' Exchange.

SITUATION WANTED—By a young man, good character, education and experience; as foreman of rose growing establishment. References given on application. Address, L. F., care The Florists' Exchange.

SITUATION WANTED—By middle aged florist, life experience growing roses, carnations, violets, chrysanthemums, decorative and bedding plants. Single, sober, state wages by the week. L. H., care The Florists' Exchange.

SITUATION WANTED—As head gardener on private place by competent man with life experience in all branches of gardening. Expert grower of plants, cut flowers, fruit and vegetables under glass and outside. Excellent references. German-American, 42, married, small family. Address M. Schmidt, Suffern, N.

HELP WANTED

WANTED—Young man with experience in cut flowers, growing roses, carnations and mums. L. I. Neff, Pittsburg, Pa.

WANTED—A first class rose grower for Brides and Maids. Sober and reliable; good wages and steady place. Call on A. L. Thorne, Flushing, L. I.

WANTED—Gardeners, to pot plants, and do other work in greenhouses. Steady work and good wages to steady, able-bodied, reliable men. J. T. Lovett, Little Silver, N. J.

WANTED—An assistant, one who is competent to handle wholesale and retail business in owner's absence. Not afraid of work. Address, Flora T. Howell, Pine Bush, New York. L. B. 14.

WANTED—Florist with some experience in potting, watering and growing of above plants. Send copy of references and experience in first letter. Address, 3132 McHenry Avenue, Westwood, Cincinnati, Ohio.

WANTED—Thoroughly first-class experienced rose and carnation growers. Apply stating age, married or single, references and wages expected. None but first-class men wanted. Lake View Rose Gardens, Jamestown, N. Y.

WANTED—An A No. 1 grower of carnations and general pot plants to work under foreman in commercial place. Permanent position for the right man. Address, L. N., care The Florists' Exchange.

WANTED—Seedsmen; we require at once several young men for counter work. Only such need apply as have thorough experience in all branches of the seed business. We offer splendid chances for advancement. Apply in writing. W. W. Rawson & Company, Boston, Mass.

HELP WANTED

WANTED—An assistant florist in a rose and carnation establishment, good, steady place. Will pay from $10.00 to $12.00 per week to start. Give references and ability in first letter. Muskogee Carnation Company, Muskogee, Ind. Ter.

WANTED—At once, man as working foreman. Must be first class grower of roses, carnations and general stock. Married man preferred. Have house near greenhouse. Apply, stating wages and giving references, to Jos. R. Goldman, Middletown, O.

WANTED—Salesmen, men of ability and good character, to solicit orders for nursery stock from the Morris Nurseries, West Chester, Pa. Good pay and steady employment to successful salesmen. Address, F. A. Keene, 1 Madison Avenue, N. Y. City.

WANTED—A first class florist for roses, carnations, violets, pot plants and Easter stock for retail trade. Steady place; Wages to start, $45.00 per month and board. Good references and ability in first letter. Address, L. M., care The Florists' Exchange.

WANTED—Nurseryman and florist as manager and salesman for small commercial business in suburb of New York City. A thoroughly up-to-date, wide-awake young man, who can make sales and push the business along. In your first letter, please send copy of past references, also state salary expected, age, etc. Address, S., care Mr. A. McConnell, Windsor Arcade, 5th Avenue, New York City.

GOOD OPPORTUNITY

Energetic young man, with thorough ornamental nursery training including hardy herbaceous plants, may find it to his advantage to correspond with us. Permanent position to right party. State experience, references, and salary expected. Position now open.

THE ELM CITY NURSERY CO.
NEW HAVEN, CONN.
Mention The Florists' Exchange when writing.

WANTED

10 Greenhouse men who are accustomed to making cuttings. To the right men, wages no object. Only live men need apply. Address,

ELIZABETH NURSERY CO.
ELIZABETH, N. J.
Mention The Florists' Exchange when writing.

MISCELLANEOUS WANTS

WANTED TO BUY—Greenhouses to be taken down. State full particulars of same when writing. Address, F. W., care The Florists' Exchange.

WANTED TO BUY—A small retail place of two or three houses and dwelling house. Greenhouses must be in good repair and fully stocked. Southern New England preferred. Address, Greenhouse, care The Florists' Exchange.

WANTED TO BUY

Palms or Ferns, or any saleable plants, if bargains, to sell over our retail counters.

MISSOURI FLORAL CO.
922 Main Street, Kansas City, Mo.
Mention The Florists' Exchange when writing.

FOR SALE OR RENT

FOR SALE

A splendid wholesale business consisting of nine iron frame greenhouses and two dwelling houses. Everything in up-to-date condition. Well heated. Two acres of ground and within half hour drive of New York City. For further particulars communicate with

O. V. ZANGEN, SEEDSMAN, HOBOKEN, N. J.
Mention The Florists' Exchange when writing.

FOR SALE OR RENT

FOR SALE or will rent to a responsible party, a fine greenhouse property. 13,000 feet of glass. Fine residence. Address, Silas C. Howell, Lock Box 14, Pine Bush, New York.

FOR SALE—At a great sacrifice, 6 Hitchings's extra heavy cast iron, upright expansion tanks, 4-2 in. connections to each tank. Elizabeth Nursery Company, Elizabeth, N. J.

FOR SALE—Florists' place, a few miles out of Boston toward Brockton. Greenhouses, 5000 sq. ft. glass, stocked. Modern house and barn, 2 acres of land, $4800.00. Address, L. I., care The Florists' Exchange.

FOR RENT—Small greenhouses and florist business in prosperous running condition. Southern Connecticut. Full particulars and reason for renting to anyone interested. Address, L. E., care The Florists' Exchange.

FOR SALE—A fine established nursery business with a constituency reaching from the Atlantic to the Pacific, and from Manitoba to the Gulf. Old age of proprietor the only reason for sale. C. S. Harrison, York, Neb.

DESIRABLE greenhouse plant of three houses, 24x200 feet; propagating house, 100 feet; potting shed, stable and dwelling. Steam heat, city water. Highland, opposite Poughkeepsie. Joseph Wood, Spring Valley, New York.

FOR SALE—Greenhouses at Madison, N. J. Situated on North Street. One 162 x 36; two 150 x 18 feet, 8 in.; one 150 x 12. Heated by both hot water and steam. Place in first-class condition. For particulars address, 50 Park Avenue, Madison, New Jersey.

To lease for a term of years, my establishment on Greene Avenue, consisting of about 7,000 feet of glass, office and salesroom. Stable and wagon shed. Horse and Wagons. Place well stocked and heated with hot water. Every convenience, all in good condition. A good business in the best location in the city. Established for 40 years. Wishing to retire from business. This is a good opportunity for the right man. Come and see it. Richard Shannon, 341-349 Greene Avenue, Brooklyn, New York.

FOR SALE—Owing to failing health, I will sell my florist establishment, beautifully situated between Larchmont Manor and Mamaroneck, Westchester Co., New York, near railroad station; trolley lines within one minute walk. First class opportunity for the right man. Plenty of landscape and jobbing work. The place contains four acres, 2 greenhouses, 104 feet long and lots of sash; well stocked with trees and shrubs, etc.; horse, wagon and tools. Address, Box 44, Larchmont, New York.

FOR RENT—Owing to other business interests, we will offer for rent our greenhouse plant at Grafton, Mass., consisting of one house 142 x 32, one 75 x 18, with connecting house 15 x 10. These houses were built by Lord & Burnham within two years, and are thoroughly equipped in every respect. We also have in the field, 8,000 carnation plants in good condition, which can be purchased at a reasonable price. Norcross & Stratton, Grafton, Mass.; or J. E. Norcross, 33 Franklin Street, Boston, Mass.

STOCK FOR SALE

Giant Double Alyssum, 2 in., fine, $2.00 per 100. Fox & Rosen, Parkerford, Pa.

FREESIA BULBS, No. 1 size, $3.00 per 1000. T. J. King, Newburyport, Mass.

Quercus Alba, Q. Coccinea and Q. Rubra, $1.50 per bu. Fraxinus Americana, 14c. lb. Address, Box 393, Biltmore, N. C.

5,000 Strong 2 1-2 in. Smilax plants, $1.50 per 100; $10.00 per 1000. Sample plants, 10c. Cash with order. L. Epple, Pelham, N. Y.

PRIMULA—Chinese, finest fringed mixed, 2c. Asters, branching, 4 colors, $2.00 per 1,000. Cash. Shippensburg Floral Company, Shippensburg, Pa.

PRIMULA OBC. GRANDIFLORA, SEEDLINGS, 25c. per 100; 2½ in. pots, $2.00 per 100. Cash please. A. Relyea & Son, Poughkeepsie, N. Y.

THREE magnificent palms (Latania Borbonica), 18 feet high and 18 feet wide. Reason for selling, no place to store. Apply, L. T. Burden, Newport, R. I.

JERUSALEM CHERRIES, seedlings, 25c. per 100; 2½ in. pots, fine plants, $3.00 per 100. Cash please. A. Relyea & Son, Poughkeepsie, N. Y.

ASPARAGUS PLUMOSUS SEEDLINGS, strong, 3 in. $1.00 per 100; strong, 6 in. high, 2 1-2 in. pots, $4.00 per 100; GREVILLEA ROBUSTA, 6 in. high, from flats, $3.00 per 100; 10 in. high, 3 in. pots, $6.00 per 100; HIBISCUS, single and double red, from 2 in. pots, $5.00 per 100; LAURESTINUS, from 2 in. pots and STRAWBERRY GUAVA, from flats, $3.00 per 100; CHAMAEROPS EXCELSA palms, 1 year seed bed, $1.50 per 100.
NOTICE THIS: All prepaid at prices given for cash. PIONEER NURSERY, MONROVIA, CAL.

Thirty cents is the minimum charge for advertisements on this page.

STOCK FOR SALE

Surplus stock for sale.—700 smilax, 2 1-4 in. pots, $1.50 per 100 or $10.00 takes the lot. Park Floral Co., Trenton, N. J.

LETTUCE—Big Boston, Tennis Ball, Simpson and Boston Market. Also Wakefield Flat Dutch Cabbage. $1.00 per 100; $8.00 per 1000. Blake & Todd, Greensboro, N. C.

Roses, Brides and Bridesmaids, from 4 in. pots, $6.00 per 100; $50.00 per 1,000. American Beauty plants from 3 and 4 in. pots, $8.00 to $15.00 per 1000. All good, clean stock. L. A. Noe, Madison, N. J.

ALTERNANTHERAS, strong, bushy, $2.50 per 100; Salvia, $3.00 per 100; Geraniums, 3 1-2 in., $4.00 per 100; Ageratum, $2.00 per 100. Cash please. F. A. Peterson, Florist, Asbury Park, N. J.

Mums, Bonnaffon and other leading Varieties, R. C., $1.50 and $3.00 per 100; 2 1-2 in. pots, $2.50 and $3.00 per 100. Fine stock. Some nice 3 1-2 in. Nutt and Poitevine Geraniums left. Cash. Waverly Greenhouses, Tuckahoe, New York.

Brides, Maids, American Beauties and Richmonds, 4 in. pots, one year old. Bridesmaids, and asparagus, from bench, all clean, healthy and well-rooted. Send for our low prices on small or large orders. Madison Rose Company, Madison, N. J.

BABY RAMBLER roses, fine dormant stock, $25 per 100, 2 1-2 inch pot plants, extra well rooted $7 per 100, $65 per 1000. Orders booked for delivery now or any time up to late Spring. Samples free. Brown Brothers Co., Rochester, N. Y.

FOR SALE

FOR SALE CHEAP

12 greenhouses to be torn down; glazed with 16 x 24 and 16 x 18 double thick glass. Heated with 3 in. wrought iron and 4 in. cast iron greenhouse pipe. One No. 87 sectional, two No. 18, and one No. 16 Hitchings boilers. Will sell together or separate.

METROPOLITAN MATERIAL COMPANY,
1398 METROPOLITAN AVE., BROOKLYN, N. Y.

FOR SALE

Greenhouse Material milled from Gulf Cypress, to any detail furnished, or our own patterns as desired, cut and spliced ready for erection. Estimates for complete constructions furnished.

V. E. REICH, Brooklyn, N. Y.
1429-1437 Metropolitan Ave.
Mention The Florists' Exchange when writing.

FOR SALE

PUMPS Rider-Ericsson. Second-hand, from $40.00 up; all repairs; other makes; new; cheap.

BOILERS One second- and tubular hot water boiler 3 ft. 7in diameter 12 ft. long. Price $35.00. One No. 15 Hitchings as good as new, $80.00.

PIPE Good serviceable second-hand, with threads; 1-in., 7 cts.; 1¼-in., 5½ cts.; 1½-in., 4 cts.; 1-in., 3 cts.; 2½ in., 10 cts.; 3 in., 14 cts.; 4 in., 19 cts. New 2-in. Standard, full lengths, with couplings, 8¼ cts. ft. Old and new fittings and valves. Old 4 inch cast iron 15c per foot.

STOCKS and DIES New Economy, best made No. 1 Threads, ¼-in., ¾-in. 1-in. pipe, $3.00. No. 2 Threads, 1¼-in., 1½-in. 2-in. pipe, $4.00.

PIPE CUTTERS New Saunders Pattern. No. 1 cuts ¼-in.-1-in. pipe, $1.00. No. 2 cuts 1-in.-2-in. pipe, $1.30.

STILLSON WRENCHES New. 18-in., grips ¼-in.-2-in. pipe, $1.65; 24-in. grips ¼-in.-2½ in. pipe, $2.40; 36-in., grips ¼-in.-3½-in. pipe, $4.75.

PIPE VISES New. No. 1 Hinged, grips ¼-in.-2 in. pipe, $2.00.

GARDEN HOSE New. 50 ft. lengths. ¾-in., guaranteed 100-lbs. pressure, 7½ cts. per ft.; ¾-in. not guaranteed, 4¾ cts. per ft., 25 ft. lengths, ¼c. per ft. more.

HOT-BED SASH New. Cypress, 3-ft.x6 ft., from 75 cts. up; glazed, complete, from $1.60 up. Second-hand, in good condition, all glass in, $1.00 each.

GLASS New American 10x12 single $1.80 per box; 12x12 single $1.90 per box; 10x12, 12x12, 10x15 double, $1.95 per box; 12x14, 12x20, 14x14, double, $2.15 per box; 16x16, 16x18, $3.10 per box; 16x24 double $3.30 per box. Second hand glass, 8 x 10, 8 x 12, and 10 x 12 single at $1.50 per box, double $1.75 per box.

Get our prices on New Gulf Cypress Building Material, Ventilating Apparatus, Oil, White Lead, Putty, Paint, Points, etc.

METROPOLITAN MATERIAL CO.
1398-1408 Metropolitan Avenue, BROOKLYN, N.Y.
Mention The Florists' Exchange when writing.

HOW TO GROW MUSHROOMS

A practical treatise of instruction, giving full and complete details how to produce this luscious vegetable.

Price, - - - 10 cents.

A. T. De La Mare Ptg. & Pub. Co.,
2-8 Duane St. New York.

St. Paul.

News Notes.

The Twin City florists after some discussion have decided to hold their picnic at Shakopee, Minn., July 21. They have chartered a steamboat to take them down the river to Shakopee. A good program has been arranged including races of all kinds and a general good time is in store for all.

L. L. May & Company report trade as a coming in jerks; while business in cut flowers is quiet, funeral work comes in in good shape, and when it does come, it is in large amounts. On account of so many outdoor flowers, the profit at this time of the year is good.

Gus. Colberg of the Swanson Floral Company has just returned from a trip to Chicago.

C. F. Vogt is well satisfied with the business so far this month and instead of losing money during July, he anticipates a gain.

The florists in the resident districts are undoubtedly the worst off of any; people are away at the lakes and being located out of the business district they will have a hard time to make both ends meet for the next 60 days.

PAUL.

Minneapolis.

News Notes.

The trade seems to be in the hands of the department stores at this time of the year. While they do not succeed in getting as good a price as the florists, they set a figure just a little below and in this way catch certain customers that are looking for close figures.

Oscar Amundson of the Rosary says business is quiet, but as he has had a good season he is not worrying and is willing to rest for the next few months.

Rice Bros. wholesale florists, are not doing very much these days; while the country trade is somewhat active, the city business appears to be very much the other way.

PAUL.

DANVERS, MASS.—William Shirley, of the firm of Learnard & Shirley, florists, and family are at York Beach, Me., for a week.

Newport, R. I.

Trade Notes.

The Newport season has just opened, and if the vim characteristic of the opening counts for much the season all through will be a good one for florists. All the New York florists having stores on the avenue are here and at it in deep earnest. Leikens has had several good-sized decorations already, while Mr. Spaulding, of the J. M. Hodgson Company, had to leave New York sooner than he anticipated to prepare for a large and elaborate decoration for a dinner and entertainment given last week by Mrs. Stuyvesant Fish.

Messrs. Wadley & Smythe are doing a very good business in cut flowers at their casino stand besides securing a fair share of the other work going. The casino is such a splendid location for the sale of cut flowers that a lucrative business is assured, apart altogether from outside decorations.

Fadden's, the oldest established retail flower store in Newport, is very attractive at present, and apparently a good business is being done there.

Gibson's store looks much brighter and more attractive than usual; while further down the avenue Siebrecht & Son have a display of plants and flowers all so choice and inviting that no wonder their store trade is better than usual at this time of the year. Although this firm have for a number of years rented the once famous greenhouses of the late Mrs. Paran Stevens, their choice foliage plants and orchids are not grown there because their immense establishment at New Rochelle is better adapted for plant growing; besides for economic reasons the Newport greenhouses are practically closed in the Winter.

The J. M. Hodgson Company are the only New York and Newport retail florists strictly speaking who run greenhouses in Newport all the year round. This firm has a large area covered with glass, under which is housed an immense supply of miscellaneous stock for use in the Summer.

Hybrid perpetual roses are things of the past for a season, and even while they lasted, they were quite disappointing, solely because of the long spell of unfavorable weather. Although the number of hybrid perpetuals planted every Fall and Spring seems to be increasing instead of diminishing, there appears a marked tendency to increase the planting of hybrid teas outdoors. And this is only as it should be, considering their availability and adaptability for occasion and use. There have been quite large purchases of Baby Ramblers recently by retailers from out of town growers.

J. K. M. L. Farquhar made a hurried visit to Newport last week. Mr. Farquhar was in search of specimen palms and other foliage plants for the stocking of a large greenhouse on a place whereon the firm, of which Mr. Farquhar is a partner, has a large force of men grading and planting. While here, Mr. Farquhar gave a practical idea of the demand for young energetic gardeners by hiring several, and intimating a desire to run up against some more good ones who would be willing to work for good pay.

Harry A. Bunyard, representing A. T. Boddington, New York, visited Newport a few days ago and left behind him as evidence of good feeling an offer of a liberal premium for a well arranged as well as a well grown collection of vegetables to be competed for at the Horticultural Society's Show in August. Mr. Bunyard knows a thing or two about the arrangement of exhibits at flower shows, hence his idea that 25 points should count for arrangement in a collection of vegetables. He makes this a condition of the premium, and there is no question that the suggestion will be adopted by the committee when it meets.

D. M.

Hail Item.

The morning papers on Wednesday gave accounts of a hail storm at Washington and Morristown, N. J. The hail covered the ground to the depth of several inches. So far as we have been able to learn, Madison, Chatham, Murray Hill, Summit and Short Hills escaped. The loss to the Florists' Hail Association will probably be light.

Philadelphia.

Reception to Hugh Dickson.

The dinner and reception tendered by the Florists' Club of Philadelphia to Hugh Dickson of Newtonards, Belfast, Ireland, at Dooner's Hotel on July 6, was a very nice affair. The number present was not quite up to expectations, but taking into account the season of the year and the short notice at which the affair was gotten up, the committee did very well. Thomas B. Meehan, president of the club, presided. Robert Craig acted as toastmaster and introduced the guest of the evening, Mr. Dickson, who made a short speech thanking the club for the honor conferred upon him, stating that that honor really belonged to his two brothers who had done all the work on roses. Other speakers were Wm. F. Gude of Washington, D. C., who spoke on "Our Country from a Floricultural Point of View;" Dr. Robert Huey, who made a very good speech on the "History of the Rose," dwelling at length on the Dickson introductions and paying special tribute to Killarney. P. J. Lynch of the Dingee & Conard Company, West Grove, Pa., spoke of "The Rose in the Mail Order Trade." Antoine

Hugh Dickson

Wintzer of the Conard & Jones Company, West Grove, Pa., spoke of the work being done in the hybridisation of roses. Among those present were: Joseph Heacock, Robert Craig, Edwin Lonsdale, Thos. B. Meehan, Alex. B. Scott, S. S. Pennock, Wm. F. Gude, George Craig, C. E. Larzelen, Fred Hahman, Wm. K. Harris, John Westcott, George Burton, W. H. Vance, Edward Reid, Dr. Robert Huey, Dr. Tull, P. J. Lynch, Professor H. Dodds, W. A. Leonard, Robert Kift, A. Farenwald, John Welsh Young, Henry F. Michell, D. T. Connor, Wm. P. Craig, John Dunham, Robert A. Craig, Antoine Wintzer, and G. C. Watson. Several excellent songs were sung, the party breaking up about midnight.

News of the Week.

Convention bowling matters are now occupying the attention of club members and the first of five matches to select the team for Dayton will be rolled this week, two matches on the club alleys and three on neutral alleys. Our bowlers are going to Dayton this year determined that all elements of professionalism shall be eradicated from the bowling tournament, and that every member of any team shall be employed in the business and a member of his club. No more of this business of giving a man employment for two weeks to make him eligible. John Westcott says the prizes now up for competition were given for amateurs only.

On account of so many failures recently in the retail business the wholesale commission men have thought it advisable to organize to protect themselves, and have formed the Florists' Protective Association of Philadelphia, the object of which is to sell for cash only to anyone who owes a bill to any member of the association. All bills will be presented to customers on the first of each month and are to be due and payable by the 15th: if bills are not paid by the 20th, the delinquents are to be reported, and the party owing the bill can then buy for cash only. This will prevent a customer from running a three months' bill with one house and then going to another to do likewise. Any parties refusing c.o.d. shipments will also be reported, and sold to for cash in the future. All disputes as to bills will be referred to an arbitration committee. All business will be carried on strictly confidentially. The commission men of this city are more of a unit than ever before known; and by sticking to this association they hope to keep away from creditors' meetings.

DAVID RUST.

CANADIAN NEWS

OTTAWA.—Spring trade is over and all are satisfied with the results. Last week there has been a shortage of almost all kinds of bedding plants. Scarlet geraniums have been called for all through the Spring. Next in demand have been cannas and coleus. There has been a very large increase in the number of verandah vases; in fact, this has become the principal form of decoration around the city. Geraniums of any size and quality brought $1.50 per dozen; cannas, $1.50; and coleus, 75c and $1 per dozen. It seems as if one can never have a surplus of vines, however large his stock; but good 4-inch plants are very much more profitable for box filling than small ones.

Stock is now being thrown out, although not so many roses as formerly. Young plants are good and clean. The weather for carnations in the field has been fine, an occasional rain doing great good.

Wright is busy with his new range which is to be devoted to carnations.

Graham Brothers are busy replanting roses and changing benches to solid beds. These gentlemen have been badly handicapped owing to the illness of both, and having to move their seed and flower store to another location, temporarily, while their store on one of the best sites on Sparks street (lately purchased) is being made ready for them. This, when completed, will be one of the finest stores in Ottawa.

Business for Summer is very good. Peonies, now selling at $1 per dozen, are in good demand.

C. Scrim, who has been with Wm. H. Elliott of Brighton, Mass., has returned to Ottawa and joined the staff at Scrim's.

The next important thing to think about is the convention at Guelph. That should not bother us much, as a good business year takes away any question as to "can I afford it?" And, coming during Toronto exhibition week, with its cheap rates, makes it easy and pleasant. I am looking forward to my visit to Guelph.

E.

MONTREAL.—The bedding season is over and all are glad. Stock sold out clean, with cannas in short supply. More geraniums were disposed of than ever before. Hardy perennials were somewhat scarce owing to so much stock having been killed during the past Winter. Peonies and hybrid roses were in great demand for private planting; also all perennials yielding flowers suitable for cutting.

Weddings were very numerous during June. The big orders were pretty well divided among the florists who could take care of them. The demand for decorations at weddings is on the increase, and attention should be given this branch, as it is very profitable. School closings called for a lot of cut flowers.

Outdoor sweet peas are in and of very good quality. Carnations are really good for the season.

Business at the present writing is very quiet, and early closing is the rule.

The Florists' Club will go to Highgate Springs, Vermont, for the annual picnic next Wednesday.

Harris & Hopton and Jos. Bennett are building new houses.

W. C. H.

DALLAS TEX.—E. H. R. Green has purchased a carload of double strength glass for use at his greenhouses south of the city. The heavier glass will be used by him throughout the establishment as a precaution against the heavy hail which falls at times in this section of the State. It is double strength glass, 12 by 16 inches in size.

VICTORY

Strong healthy field grown plants, now ready, $15.00 per 100; $125.00 per 1000; 250 at 1000 rates. A discount for cash with order. GUTTMAN & WEBBER, 43 West 28th St., N. Y.

Field Grown CARNATIONS

For immediate delivery.

Our ENCHANTRESS SPORT

MRS. W. T. OMWAKE

Being the color of Fiancee we believe this the most desirable of all Enchantress Sports. First size, $10.00 per 100; 2nd size, $8.00 per 100. Rooted cuttings, Dec. and Jan. delivery, $5.00 per 100.

Red Lawson, the best red to date. 1st size, $8.00 per 100; 2nd size, $6.00 per 100.

Harry Fenn, the best dark red. 1st size, $7.00 per 100; 2nd size, $5.00 per 100. Samples, 25c.

HENRY EICHHOLZ, Waynesboro, Pa.

Mention the Florists' Exchange when writing.

Jensen & Dekema

CARNATION SPECIALISTS

674 W. Foster Ave., CHICAGO.

Mention The Florists' Exchange when writing.

CARNATIONS

We have the best list of Carnations in the country. Send for it.

We can quote lowest prices for best quality cuttings. Write us.

Chicago Carnation Co., Joliet, Ill.

Mention The Florists' Exchange when writing.

HELEN GODDARD

The Coming Commercial Pink Carnation

Rooted cuttings, ready January 1, 1906. Price, $10.00 per 100; $75.00 per 1000.

S. J. GODDARD, Framingham, Mass.

Mention The Florists' Exchange when writing.

CARNATIONS

F. DORNER & SONS CO.

LA FAYETTE, IND.

Mention The Florists' Exchange when writing.

RED SPORT.

The most profitable red carnation grown.

	Per 100	Per 1000
RED SPORT	$5.00	$40.00
QUEEN LOUISE	1.25	10.00

All cuttings well rooted, true to name, and perfectly healthy.

A. B. DAVIS & SON, Inc., Purcellville Va.

Mention The Florists' Exchange when writing.

CARNATIONS

SMITH & GANNETT,

GENEVA, N. Y.

Mention The Florists' Exchange when writing.

CARNATIONS

Rooted Cuttings

All the new varieties of 1906. All the standard varieties worth growing.

WM. SWAYNE, Box 226, Kennett Square Pa.

Mention The Florists' Exchange when writing.

10,000 Mme. F. Bergmann CHRYSANTHEMUMS

Still the best early 'mum. Large white and round as a ball. Plants in splendid condition. Price $2.50 per 100 or $20.00 per 1000.

Morton's Evergreen Lodge, Clarksville, Tenn.

Mention The Florists' Exchange when writing.

CHRYSANTHEMUMS.

300 Col. Appleton, 150 W. H. Reiman, 600 Ivory, 350 Dr. Enguehard, 600 Major Bonnaffon. Good stock from flats. $1.00 per 100; $18.00 per 1000. Cash with order.

JOHN WHITE

ELIZABETH, N. J.

Mention The Florists' Exchange when writing.

GRAFTED ROSES

Fine Stock from 3-in. pots.

Richmond, $2.50 per doz., $15.00 per 100, $125.00 per 1000.

Killarney, $2.50 per doz., $18.00 per 100, $150.00 per 1000.

Etoile De France, $3.00 per doz., $18.00 per 100.

Kaiserin, Carnot, Uncle John, Chatenay, $2.00 per doz., $15.00 per 100.

Bride, Bridesmaid, Golden Gate, Wootton, $2.00 per doz., $12.00 per 100.

ROSES OWN ROOTS

Fine Stock from 3-in. pots.

Richmond, $12.00 per 100; $100.00 per 1000.

Etoile De France, $12.00 per 100.

Sunrise, Perle, Sunset, Chatenay, $8.00 per 100.

Bride, Bridesmaid, Golden Gate, $7.00 per 100.

Killarney, La France, 2 yrs. old, from 6 in. pots, $25.00 per 100.

CANNAS

Best named varieties from 3½ in. pots, $6.00 and $8.00 per 100.

CHRYSANTHEMUMS

Gen. Hutton, H. A. Allen, Mrs. Wm. Duckham, Jennie Nonin. From 3 ½ in. pots $1.50 per doz. $8.00 per 100.

Mrs. A. T. Miller, Dora Stevens, Lady Cranston, Mrs. W. Higgie, Mrs. T. W. Pockett. From 3½ in. pots $1.00 per doz., $5.00 per 100.

Geo. Kalb, Mrs. McArthur, Maud Dean, Mrs. Coombe, Nagoya, Robt. Halliday, A. J. Balfour, Nellie Pockett. Price from 2½ in. pots, $3.50 per 100, $30.00 per 1000.

Autumn Glory, Ada Spaulding, Dorothy Devens, Harry May, Ivory, J. E. Lager, J. H. Troy, Mrs. S. T. Murdoch, Mrs. Humphrey, Mad. Fred Bergmann, Niveus, Thomas H. Brown, Xeno, Price from 2½ in. pots, $3.00 per 100, $25.00 per 1000.

800 hardy pompons, 12 fine varieties, pink, yellow, white and bronze, $25.00 per 100.

VIOLETS—Fine Stock

Marie Louise from 3 in. pots $4.00 per 100, 2 1-4 in. pots, $3.00 per 100; $25.00 per 1000.

Miscellaneous Plants – For varieties and prices see page 20, last issue.

Send for Catalogue.

Wood Bros., Fishkill, N. Y.

Mention The Florists' Exchange when writing.

VIOLETS. VIOLETS.

MARIE LOUISE Violets, clean and healthy in every particular, ready August 15th. 3 in. pots $5.00 per 100.

Cash with order.

WM. J. CHINNICK, TRENTON, N. J.

Mention The Florists' Exchange when writing.

CHRYSANTHEMUM STOCK 2 1-4 in. POTS

PINK	Per 100
A. J. Balfour	$2.50
Dr. Enguehard	3.00
Glory of Pacific	2.00
Leila Filkins	5.00
Maud Dean	2.50
Mrs. Coombes	2.50
Pink Ivory	2.00
Valerie Greenham	10.00
Wm. Duckham	2.50
YELLOW	
Appleton	2.50
C. J. Salter	3.00
Mrs. R. Thirkell	4.00

October Sunshine, Per 100	$2.50
Smilax from 2¼ inch pots	2.00
WHITE	
Ivory	2.00
Mme. Bergman	2.00
Alice Byron	3.00
Mrs. Henry Robinson	2.50
Polly Rose	2.00
Timothy Eaton	2.50
White Coombes	3.00
CRIMSON	
Black Hawk	2.00
John Shrimpton	2.00

MIGNONETTE SEED

Extra Selected ALLEN'S DEFIANCE $1.00 per trade pkt.

EDWARD J. TAYLOR, Southport, Conn.

Mention The Florists' Exchange when writing.

Begonia "Gloire de Lorraine" and "Turnford Hall"

NOW READY FOR DELIVERY. Propagated strictly from **single leaf**; this method gives much better results than from cuttings, $15.00 per 100, $140.00 per 1000, 4 inch pots, $40.00 per 100. **ADIANTUM FARLEYENSE**, fine specimens $18.00 to $24.00 per doz, 1¾ inch pots, $8.00 per 100; 2½ inch pots, $15.00 per 100. **PANDANUS VEITCHII**, 50c., $1.00, $1.50 and $2.50 each. Good value guaranteed. Cash with order from unknown correspondents.

J. A. PETERSON, McHenry Ave., Westwood, CINCINNATI, OHIO

Mention The Florists' Exchange when writing.

GREENHOUSE AND BEDDING PLANTS.

Geraniums, in variety, 40c. per doz. $2.00 per 100 and up.

WRITE FOR CATALOGUE.

	doz.	100
Achryanthes, Emersoni	$ .40	$2.00
Alternanthera, red and yellow	.40	2.00
Hardy English Ivy	.40	2.00
Lemon Verbena	.40	2.00
Smilax	.40	2.00

	doz.	100
Hardy Chrysanthemums, small flowered	$.40	$2.00
Hardy Chrysanthemums, Aster flowered	.50	3.00

DAHLIA ROOTS, we are booking orders for fall delivery, send for list.

A cordial invitation is extended to all interested in Horticulture to visit us, Cowenton Station, Philadelphia division B. & O. R. R. 12 miles north of Baltimore.

R. VINCENT Jr. & SON, WHITE MARSH, MD.

Mention The Florists' Exchange when writing.

SMILAX

	per 1000	per 100
2¼ in. pots	$12.00	$1.25
Asp. Plumosus, 2¼ in. pots, Aug. 1st		2.00
Cineraria, August 1st		2.00
Pansy Seed, large flowering, per oz., $4.00		

PRIMROSES

	per 100
Chinese, 2¼ in. pots, July 23rd	$2.00
Obconica, Rosea and Alba	2.00
Forbesi, fine for cut flowers	2.00
P. W. Narcissus, 13 ctm	1.25

CASH PLEASE

JOS. H. CUNNINGHAM, Delaware, O.

Mention The Florists' Exchange when writing.

Governor Herrick Violet

The finest single violet ever offered. Write me about it today.

Price: One dozen, $2.00; 100, $10.00; 1000 at $75.00 or 5000 or more at $60.00 per 1000. No. 1 Stock.

H. R. CARLTON, WILLOUGHBY, OHIO.

Mention The Florists' Exchange when writing.

MARIE LOUISE VIOLETS

Schuneman's famous Violets are well-known as the most fragrant of all Violets. Fine plants for benching at once, guaranteed the best stock in the market, none better. Only $2.00 per 100; $15.00 per 1000. Come and take a look at them. Only 17 miles from New York City. Money returned if not suited.

GEO. T. SCHUNEMAN, Violet Range.

BALDWINS, L. I., N. Y.

Mention The Florists' Exchange when writing.

FIELD GROWN VIOLETS

Strong, healthy, well-rooted plants of **Lady Campbell** (double), ready now at $2.50 per 100; $20.00 per 1000. **California** (single), ready by Aug. 15th, $3.00 per 100. Packed to carry safely, free of charge.

CHAS. BLACK, HIGHTSTOWN, N. J.

Mention The Florists' Exchange when writing.

MARIE LOUISE VIOLETS

Strong Plants, February or March struck, healthy and free from disease. Cash with order. Your money cheerfully refunded if not satisfactory. **$2.00 per 100, $15.00 per 1000.**

C. LAWRITZEN,

BOX 261 RHINEBECK, N. Y.

Mention The Florists' Exchange when writing.

ADVERTISING IN THE FLORISTS' EXCHANGE IS SURE TO BRING RESULTS

Wholesale Prices of Cut Flowers, New York, July 12, 1906

Prices quoted are by the hundred unless otherwise noted.

Roses — A. Beauty, fancy—special	10.00 to 20.00	Carnations — Inf'r grades, all colors	.50 to 1.00
" extra	6.00 to 10.00	Standard Varieties — White	.50 to 1.00
" No. 1	4.00 to 5.00	Pink	.50 to 1.00
" No. 2	3.00 to 4.00	Red	.50 to 1.00
" No. 3	1.00 to 1.50	Yel. & Var.	.50 to 1.00
Bride, 'Maid, fancy—spe'l	3.00 to 4.00	*Fancy— (*The highest grades of standard var.) White	1.00 to 2.00
" extra	2.00 to 3.00	Pink	1.00 to 2.00
" No. 1	1.00 to 2.00	Red	1.00 to 2.00
" No. 2	.50 to 1.00	Yel. & Var.	...... to ......
Golden Gate	1.00 to 5.00	Novelties	2.00 to 3.00
Liberty	...... to	Lilies	3.00 to 6.00
Mme. Abel Chatenay	1.00 to 6.00	Lily of the Valley	1.00 to 3.00
Adiantum	.50 to .75	Mignonette	...... to ......
Croweanum	.75 to 1.50		...... to ......
Asparagus	25.00 to 50.00		...... to ......
" Plumosus, bunches	10.00 to 15.00		...... to ......
" Sprengeri, bunches	10.00 to 15.00	Pansies, per dozen bunches	.50 to .75
Callas	...... to	Smilax	8.00 to 10.00
Cattleyas	25.00 to 50.00	Sweet Peas, per bunch	.01 to .03
Daisies	.50 to 1.00		
Gladiolus	2.00 to 4.00		
	...... to		

Wholesale Prices of Cut Flowers—Per 100

Boston July 9, 1906	Buffalo July 9, 1906	Detroit July 1, 1906	Cincinnati July 7, 1906	Baltimore June 25, 1906	NAMES AND VARIETIES	Milwaukee June 15, 1906	Phil'delphia June 16, 1906	Pittsburg July 10, 1906	St. Louis July 9, 1906
15.00 to 20.00	20.00 to 25.00	10.00 to 35.00	to 30.00	to	ROSES A. BEAUTY, fancy—special	25.00 to 30.00	15.00 to 20.00	20.00 to 25.00	15.00 to 20.00
10.00 to 15.00	12.00 to 20.00	to	20.00 to 25.00	12.50 to 15.00	" extra	18.00 to 20.00	10.00 to 12.00	15.00 to 18.00	10.00 to 12.50
4.00 to 10.00	6.00 to 12.00	to	10.00 to 15.00	5.00 to 8.00	" No. 1	12.50 to 15.00	6.00 to 8.00	8.00 to 10.00	6.00 to 8.00
1.00 to 4.00	3.00 to 6.00	to	to	to	" Culls and ordinary	6.00 to 10.00	1.00 to 4.00	2.00 to 3.00	3.00 to 5.00
to	6.00 to 7.00	5.00 to 6.00	to 6.00	to	BRIDE, 'MAID, fancy-special	to 8.00	6.00 to 10.00	to	4.00 to 5.00
2.00 to 4.00	5.00 to 6.00	to	to 5.00	to 4.00	" extra	to 6.00	5.00 to 6.00	to	2.00 to 3.00
1.00 to 2.00	4.00 to 5.00	to	3.00 to 4.00	to 3.00	" No. 1	to 4.00	2.00 to 4.00	to	to 2.00
to	3.00 to 4.00	to	to 2.00	to 2.00	" No. 2	to 2.00	to 1.00	to	to
to	2.00 to 3.00	4.00 to 8.00	to	2.00 to 4.00	GOLDEN GATE	4.00 to 8.00	1.00 to 8.00	to	2.00 to 4.00
1.00 to 6.00	3.00 to 8.00	to	2.00 to 6.00	4.00 to 8.00	K. A. VICTORIA	4.00 to 8.00	2.00 to 8.00	3.00 to 12.00	2.00 to 6.00
2.00 to 8.00	3.00 to 6.00	to	to	to	LIBERTY	4.00 to 10.00	2.00 to 12.00	to	to
to	3.00 to 6.00	4.00 to 10.00	to	to	METEOR	4.00 to 6.00	to	to	to
to	3.00 to 5.00	4.00 to 10.00	to	2.00 to 4.00	PERLE	to	to	4.00 to 6.00	2.00 to 4.00
to	to	to 50.00	to	to	ORCHIDS—Cattleyas	to	to 50.00	to	to
to	1.00 to 1.25	to	to	.50 to .75	CARNATIONS Inferior grades, all colors	to	to	to 1.00	to
to	1.25 to 1.50	to 1.00	to 1.00	1.00 to 1.50	Standard Varieties White	to	1.50 to 2.00	to 1.50	to 1.00
to	1.25 to 1.50	to	to 1.00	1.00 to 1.50	Standard Varieties Pink	1.00 to 2.00	1.50 to 2.00	to 1.50	to 1.00
to	1.25 to 1.50	to	to 1.00	1.00 to 1.50	Standard Varieties Red	to	1.50 to 2.00	to 1.50	to 1.00
to	1.50 to 2.50	to 3.00	to	1.00 to 1.50	Standard Varieties Yellow and var.	to	1.50 to 2.00	to	to 1.00
.50 to 1.00	2.00 to 2.50	to	to	to 3.00	Fancy Varieties White	to 3.00	2.00 to 3.00	to 2.00	1.00 to 1.50
.50 to 1.50	2.00 to 2.50	to	to	to 3.00	Fancy Varieties Pink	to 3.00	2.00 to 3.00	to 2.00	1.00 to 1.50
.50 to 1.50	2.00 to 2.50	to	to	to 3.00	Fancy Varieties Red	to 3.00	2.00 to 3.00	to 2.00	1.00 to 1.50
.50 to 1.50	2.00 to 2.50	to 1.50	to	to 3.00	Fancy Varieties Yellow and var	to 3.00	2.00 to 3.00	to	1.00 to 1.50
to	to	to	to	to	Novelties	to	to	to	to
.50 to 1.00	1.00 to 2.00	to 2.00	to	to 1.00	ADIANTUM	to 1.00	to 1.00	1.25 to 1.50	to 1.00
to 50.00	40.00 to 50.00	25.00 to 60.00	to 50.00	25.00 to 50.00	ASPARAGUS, Plum. and Ten	20.00 to 30.00	to 50.00	30.00 to 50.00	25.00 to 50.00
to	1.00 to 2.00	20.00 to 30.00	to 35.00	25.00 to 50.00	" Sprengeri, bunches	20.00 to 30.00	to 50.00	20.00 to 30.00	25.00 to 50.00
to	8.00 to 10.00	to 10.00	to 1.00	6.00 to 8.00	CALLAS	to	to 8.00	to	to
to	to	.75 to 1.50	to	to	DAISIES	to .75	to 1.00	to	.25 to .50
to	to	8.00 to 10.00	to	2.00 to 4.00	GLADIOLUS	to	to	4.00 to 8.00	to 5.00
to	to	to	to 12.00	10.00 to 12.50	LILIES, Harrisii	to	8.00 to 12.00	to	to
to	10.00 to 12.00	to	to	10.00 to 12.50	" Longiflorum	to 15.00	to	to	to
2.00 to 4.00	3.00 to 4.00	3.00 to 4.00	to 4.00	1.00 to 2.00	LILY OF THE VALLEY	to 3.00	2.00 to 4.00	2.00 to 4.00	to
to	1.00 to 2.00	to	to	2.00 to 2.50	MIGNONETTE, ordinary	to	1.00 to 2.00	to	to
to	to	to	to	to	" fancy	to 2.00	to	to	to
to	2.00 to 5.00	4.00 to 8.00	to	to	PEONIES	4.00 to 6.00	to	to	to
to 12.50	to 15.00	12.50 to 15.00	to 15.00	12.50 to 20.00	SMILAX	to 25.00	15.00 to 20.00	10.00 to 15.00	to 15.00
to	to	to	to	to	VIOLETS, ordinary	to	to	to	to
to	to	to	to	to	" fancy	to	to	to	to
to	to	to	to	to	NARCISSUS	to	to	to	to
.20 to .30	.40 to .50	.50 to .75	.35 to .50	.20 to .35	SWEET PEAS	to 1.00	.40 to 1.00	.10 to .50	.10 to .15
to	to	to	to	to		to	to	to	to
to	to	to	to	to		to	to	to	to
to	to	to	to	to		to	to	to	to

San Francisco.

News Notes.

Yesterday was Fourth of July in San Francisco and everybody took part in the usual manner of its observance, just the same as before the city's recent affliction and the usual din and noise were not a whit less than they used to be. Golden Gate Park was the rallying point, and the morning papers all agree that the greatest multitude of its history was gathered there. The voices of two thousand well drilled school children supplied the vocal music for the occasion and everyone of these tidily groomed lads and lassies wore a tiny bouquet with the California flower for its center. 'Midst a group of grown people occupying the right of the great platform that was crowded with the young choristers, the florists of the city were represented by Mr. Boland of Sievers & Boland.

Not only was there a great sale on Independence Day for the California flower, but florists tell me that trade generally was better than satisfactory. While the many thousands of people who went to parks to hear singing and Fourth of July orations took basket luncheons with them, there were other thousands who don't like to get into noisy crowds, that stayed at home. And these home-stayers to a considerable extent were entertainers and had with them at their dinner tables a few friends. And florists say it is incidentally rare that a Californian gives a dinner unaccompanied with a table decoration of flowers, not always elaborate, but always neat and tidy.

Also from the waterfront came a good supply of flower orders. Nearly every ship at anchor in the bay or lying alongside the wharves was decorated in honor of the Fourth, mostly of course with American flags and bunting. And it was pleasant to notice also that in graceful courtesy to the nationality of the port that was sheltering them nearly all the foreign vessels were decorated and made unstinted showing of flowers.

To the New San Francisco list of florists another of the ante-fire flower dealers, Charles Stappenbeck is to be added. He has opened a flower store in his residence in the Western Addition. The last look I had at his double size store at Polk and Sutter streets, I saw the roof of the store, which was a one story building, resting on his vases of flowers that covered the tables. This view was the day after the earthquake, before the fire reached the store.

ALVIN.

Wholesale Prices of Cut Flowers, Chicago, July 10, 1906.

Prices quoted are by the hundred unless otherwise noted.

ROSES American Beauty		
36-inch stems........per doz.	.... to	4.00
30-inch stems.......... "	.... to	3.00
24-inch stems.......... "	.... to	2.50
20-inch stems.......... "	.... to	2.00
18-inch stems.......... "	.... to	1.50
12-inch stems.......... "	....	1.00
8-inch stems and shorts "	.5	.75
Bride' Maid, fancy special......	5.00 to	6.00
" extra............	4.00 to	5.00
" No. 1............	2.00	3.00
" No. 2............	.50	1.00
Golden Gate..................	2.00	6.00
Carnot........................	2.00	6.00
Uncle John....................	2.00	8.00
Liberty.......................	2.00	8.00
Richmond......................	2.00	6.00
Kaiserine.....................	2.00	6.00
Killarney.....................	2.00	8.00
Perle.........................	2.00	6.00
Chatenay......................	2.00	6.00
Orchids—Cattleyas............	....	50.00
Smilax........................	8.00	12.00
Lily of the Valley............	2.00 to	4.00
Sweet Peas....................	.25 to	.50

CARNATIONS			
Inferior grades all colors		.25 to	.50
Standard Varieties	White........	.75 to	1.00
	Pink.........	.75 to	1.00
	Red..........	.75 to	1.00
	Yellow & var....	.75 to	1.00
*Fancy (The highest grades of Sta'd var)	White........	1.50 to	2.00
	Pink.........	1.50 to	2.00
	Red..........	1.50 to	2.00
	Yellow & var....	1.50 to	2.00
Novelties....................		.... to	....
Adiantum.....................		.50 to	1.00
Asparagus, Plum. & Ten.......		.35 to	.50
" Sprengeri, bunches.		.35 to	.50
Gladiolus....................		2.00 to	6.00
Lilies, Longiflorum..........		8.00 to	12.00
Harrisii.....................		8.00 to	12.00
Mignonette, ordinary.........		1.00 to	2.00
....		.... to	....
Peonies......................		2.00 to	6.00
Lilium Candidum, $1.00 per bunch			
Hardy Ferns per 1000.........		1.00 to	1.50
Galax "		1.00 to	1.25

New York.

The Week's News.

We are now in the dullest month of the year, and the mind turns toward vacations spent far away from the madding crowd more easily than to business matters.

Thanks to the efforts of the transportation committee of The New York Florists' Club—W. F. Sheridan, John B. Nugent, Jr., and F. H. Traendly—a splendid vacation trip will be afforded those who attend the annual convention of the S. A. F. O. H., to be held in Dayton, Ohio, commencing August 21. The committee has arranged to travel over the New York Central lines, on the train known as the South Western Limited, leaving Grand Central station at 2 p. m. on August 20, and arriving at Dayton at 8 o'clock the next morning. This train is considered the best equipped in the world for passenger traffic, and a comfortable and enjoyable journey is assured. The fare for the round trip will be $22.67.

Philadelphia wholesale florists are adopting a scheme which should commend itself to every wholesale dealer and grower in the business. Their plan of operation provides that all book accounts will be due on the 10th of the month following purchase. If not paid by the 20th, cash is to be demanded for all purchases until back bills are cleared up and the creditor reinstated. This is an excellent idea, and one that a majority of New York wholesale florists tried to adopt two or three years ago, but owing to a premature exploitation of the matter in a contemporary, the organization was not perfected. The Philadelphia dealers are to be congratulated on their perspicacity in seeking to provide a remedy against a long credit system, and we have no doubt that after their scheme gets into good working order, and the benefit derived therefrom is seen, dealers in other cities will adopt similar methods for their mutual protection.

Through the exploding of an oil lamp, Clarence Gerard, engineer for John Lewis Childs, Floral Park, L. I., received burns that caused his death on July 6. Mr. Gerard was 50 years of age, and leaves a widow and two children.

W. Mills of the State Nurseries Helena, Montana, sailed on the Celtic, on Friday, July 13, for a business and pleasure trip to Europe.

Joseph Fleischman has purchased 10 acres of land at Cedarhurst, L. I., and Herman Warendorff together with another gentleman not connected with the trade, has bought 45 acres, between Cedarhurst and Woodmere, L. I.

The annual meeting of the stockholders of the New York Market Florists' Association will be held on Monday, July 16, in room 804, at No. 257 Broadway, at 12 o'clock, for the election of officers and other business that may come before the meeting.

Jas. M. Thorburn & Company, seedsmen, have removed to their new five-story building at 33 Barclay street through to 38 Park place. Their new telephone numbers are 4065 and 4066 Cortlandt.

Chicago.

The Week's News.

M. Silverstone, proprietor of the St. Louis Palm and Floral Company, was a recent visitor.

Sam Graff, of Graff Brothers, Columbus, Ohio, for which concern he is the Chicago purchasing agent, states that their business for the season just closed was decidedly the best they have ever enjoyed.

A daughter was born to Henry Wietor of Wietor Brothers a few days since and is progressing nicely.

Irving Gingrich, treasurer-manager of the South Bend Floral Company, South Bend, Ind., spent a few days in Chicago last week and while here placed an order with the Foley Manufacturing Company for material for a large increase in their greenhouses.

A. L. Vaughan, of Vaughan & Sperry, left on Friday of last week with a party of six for Spirit Lake, Wis., for a fishing and camping tour of several weeks' duration. As they are to be located eighteen miles from a telegraph station it is expected that absolute rest from business cares will be secured.

J. F. and W. K. Kidwell will spend the month of July at Portage Lake, Mich.

At George Reinberg's greenhouses Foreman Arnold has the rose planting nearly completed, all the young stock being in, there remaining but a few houses of the new range to plant, which will be filled with old plants that were removed from benches in the Spring and have been kept in pots for the past two months. The general condition of the stock throughout was never better.

N. J. Wietor and John Sinner returned from Tomahawk Lake on Sunday, the latter having placed a twenty-two pound muskalonge to his credit.

Fred Sperry returned last Saturday from a trip across the lake where he spent a week rusticating at Otsego, Mich.

The eccentricities of the trade were well shown the other day when the J. B. Deamud Company received a telegraph order for 500 Shasta daisies from a party who had not been a regular customer. About two hours after 575 of the desired stock had been received from a consignor who was also irregular—none of these flowers having been in stock for two weeks or more. So it goes at times, but not always.

John Poehlmann is on deck again after his slight indisposition.

George Asmus and Mrs. Asmus entertained a party of the local fraternity and their ladies at their home on Warren avenue on July 4.

Leonard Kill expects to leave for Cincinnati on Thursday next accompanied by his family for a short outing.

Although the peonies which have been in cold storage are pretty well out of the market Kruchten & Johnson have a fine stock in hand which will probably last through the middle of the month.

C. L. Washburn will spend his vacation on the north shore of Lake Superior returning in time to attend the national convention at Dayton.

O. P. Bassett is off on an automobile tour through Wisconsin including especially the section of the state in which the most beautiful lakes abound.

John W. Beyer, manager and treasurer of the August F. Beyer flower store of South Bend, Indiana, has been spending a few days in Chicago.

Mrs. T. E. Waters has left for the East and will spend the Summer in Boston and vicinity.

Steve Minon of the Kennicott Brothers Company staff left last week for St. Joe, Mich., where he will spend a few weeks.

Bassett & Washburn report an unprecedented sale of Summer roses of which they have an excellent supply including as specialties, Kaiserin Augusta Victoria, Souvenir du President Carnot, and La Detroit.

Miss Gunterburg, who sells in the Flower Growers' Market for the House of the Good Shepherd, returned recently from an outing spent across the lake.

Poehlmann Brothers expect to cut from their young American Beauty stock within a very short time.

E. G. Hill, Richmond, Ind., was in town Monday.

J. J. Rohr of Naperville was in the city Monday. Having turned all his interest in his greenhouses over to his son, Charles F. Rohr, he expects to leave in August for Colorado Springs looking for and hoping to receive a relief from bronchial affections which have recently annoyed him.

Fred Strall, who has for some time been running a retail establishment in the Rand & McNally Building, was forced into insolvency this week.

C. M. Dickinson and family are vacationing among the lakes of Northern Wisconsin where Mr. Dickinson will have ample opportunity to enjoy to the fullest extent his fondness for the piscatorial art.

The A. L. Randall Company received word last week from Miss Tonner to the effect that she had reached Rome and Florence, in Italy, after a very pleasant voyage with the exception of one or two days on the ocean.

Percy Jones is still offering a choice line of cold storage peonies from the Klehm's Nurseries, which are now in perfect condition and bid fair to hold after the middle of the month.

Duncan A. Robertson of the Ernst Wienhoeber Floral Company is on a month's vacation, which he will spend in Colorado.

WM. K. WOOD

Cincinnati, O.

News Notes.

The celebration of July 4 seemed to be gone into more than usual in this city. The paper balloon appeared to have full sway, and tended to remind one that in a few years hence the air-ship will be seen flying through space in the same way. The only accident to a florist's family that I have heard of was that of Ben George. His little boy, Sidney, had his hand badly lacerated by a shooting cane.

Very little can be said as to business; house-cleaning keeps some of us busy.

The writer is remodeling his commission house entirely, having just installed a large cold storage box, and doubled his total capacity. When the work is finished I shall be pleased to have my friends stop in and look it over.

Gus. Meyer, of Sunderbruch & Meyer, has sailed for Europe to visit his parents for a couple of months.

B. P. Critchell's brother, of Chicago, was badly hurt in the boat train accident in England, but from last reports there are hopes of his recovery.

Programs and tickets are out for the Fourteenth annual outing of The Florists' Club of Cincinnati at Norwood Inn Park, July 19, and a good time is promised all. At the same time, don't forget that the S. A. F. O. H. meets in Dayton in August; only a few weeks away. You cannot afford to miss this meeting for one day at least. It is not definitely settled how the Cincinnati contingent will travel, but, most likely, they will leave Cincinnati on the morning of Tuesday, August 21, at 8:30 o'clock via C. H. and D. R. R. Fare for the round trip $2.20. Returning, we shall leave Dayton at 9 p. m., arriving at Cincinnati by 10:45, giving plenty of time to see the magnificent illumination of Far Hill, the home of John Patterson of the National Cash Register Company at Dayton; and to reach home by midnight after arriving in the city. The day, August 21, will be one long to be remembered, and we want the ladies especially to impress it upon their husbands that they are going also. H. M. Frank, superintendent of exhibits at Dayton, writes me that space is being taken rapidly, and if any of the craft in this vicinity want space, and have not already engaged it, they had better get busy. E. G. GILLETT.

St. Louis.

News Notes.

A. Bayhouse of the Bayhouse Floral Company, Boise, Idaho, was a caller the past week, and visited the different growers in the city.

A. S. Halstead, president of the St. Clair Floral Company, Belleville, left for Chicago, Monday night on business. He will also visit his daughter who lives in Detroit.

Mrs. Wm. Ellison and daughter are spending the Summer months at northern Summer resorts. Miss Allie is at present in Grand Rapids, Mich., visiting relatives.

Henry Edmunds of Belleville, Ill., returned home Saturday from a week's visit at Chicago.

Fred Weber, Jr., is enjoying himself at the northern lakes. He is expected back home some time this week.

Fred H. Meinhardt, state vice-president of the S. A. F. O. H., was hustling the past week in the society's interest. He will this year have charge of the transportation from here; those who are going to Dayton should advise him at once.

L. Bauman of the L. Bauman & Company, Chicago, was in town last week attending to the wants of the trade in his line.

President Ammann of the Florists' Club entertained the members at his place Thursday.

Mrs. F. M. Ellis and her daughters left last week to visit friends at Slater, Mo. It is said they will remain there until Mr. Ellis returns home from Panama.

Messrs. Beyer, Fillmore and Weber, the trustees of the club, have decided to hold the club's picnic at Romona Park, which is situated on the suburban line, and considered one of the most beautiful parks in the country. The date is set for Thursday, July 26. They are busy at work making out the program of games. There is a fine lake on the grounds for boating and fishing. This year we will again have the famous Colored Jubilee Band, which always is a great attraction for the young folks. A baseball game between the retailers and wholesalers has also been arranged. J. F. Ammann and E. W. Guy have been selected to act as umpires. Schriefer and Alves will pitch and catch for the wholesalers, and Beneke and Adles will do the same for the retailers. And let the best team win. ST. PATRICK.

The Michel Plant and Seed Company has filed a statement that it has made an increase in its capital stock from $25,000 to $30,000. Assets, $45,552.33; liabilities, $15,764.69.

Springfield, O.

Considering the importance of this locality in the growing and shipping of plants, and the prevailing goodwill among its florists, it seems strange that Springfield has thus far been without organisation of any kind. At the call of several concerns among whom the matter has been quietly discussed for some time past, a meeting was held Monday evening, July 2, in the offices of The Good & Reese Company, at which the following firms were represented: P. J. Agnew, American Rose & Plant Company, B. C. Blake & Son, Callander Cactus Company, Ferncliff Floral Company, Good & Reese Company, The Leedle Floral Company, McGregor Brothers Company, George H. Mellen Company, Charles Unglaub, Charles M. Niuffer, Springfield Floral Company, Schmidt & Botley, Highland Floral Company, and Harry C. Reeser, all of this city; also R. H. Murphy & Son and Reeser Floral Company of Urbana, and Fairview Floral Company of Beatty. John M. Good was elected temporary chairman and C. W. Schmidt, secretary.

After an informal discussion indicating general favor toward the project of forming a florists' club, a committee on constitution and by-laws was appointed, consisting of Charles C. Leedle, C. W. Schmidt and Leman Bradford. Committees on membership and nominations were also appointed, after which the meeting adjourned for two weeks at the end of which each committee is expected to report. GE DALE.

Boston.

A Summer Show.

The Saturday Summer show of the Massachusetts Horticultural Society at Horticultural Hall was exceptionally fine and was much ahead of any like show held. The arrangement of the hall, which was well filled, was very good and the collections of delphiniums, which were the main feature of the show, were indeed very attractive. Martin Sullivan, gardener to Mr. Wm. Whitmans, was an easy winner of the first prise in the collection of these flowers, which included the following varieties: J. S. Sargent, Mrs. Tree, Alfred, Persimmon, Gumis, Frank Hale, Coomassie, F. Carr, Christian DeWitt, Albert Edward, Windeline, Captain Percy Scott, and Dorothy Kelway. These are all superb varieties and anyone wishing a collection of these fine flowers will be amply repaid by that selection. Wm. Thatcher, gardener to Mrs. J. L. Gardner was the winner of the second prise.

The collections of Japan iris were very fine indeed, Wm. Thatcher and Martin Sullivan taking the honors in the order mentioned.

In hardy herbaceous plants the Bay State Nurseries took first honors being closely followed by the Blue Hills Nurseries. Each of these exhibitors also had collections for effect as did Robert Cameron of the Harvard Botanical Gardens, who put up a collection of some seventy-five varieties. The Boston Park Department made a display of Farquhar roses which was very fine indeed, and showed the value of this rose under intense cultivation. Duncan Finlayson showed a fine plant of Dendrobium thyrsiflorum, being awarded a First Class Certificate of merit for the same.

An interesting feature of the exhibition were the exhibits from children's gardens. These, which entirely filled the small side hall, were shown for the first time in Boston and the results are very satisfactory. The exhibits of vegetables were very fine at this exhibition; and the fruits shown were also very good, cherries and strawberries being the leaders.

News Notes.

Frank T. White of Holbrook surprised his many friends by returning from a week's absence on Friday bringing Mrs. White along with him. Mrs. White is a sister of Wm. Patterson of Wollaston, and as the young couple are well known in the trade they have the very best wishes of a host of friends.

Herbert Tyler, salesman for the Montrose Greenhouses will take a two weeks' vacation in Canada trying to overcome an ailment which has recently been threatening him.

W. A. Hastings of the A. H. Hews Company has started on an extended business trip through the New England states.

Mann Bros. are bringing in some very fine lilies at present including some superb auratum and the new philippinense.

Asters have made their appearance though not in great quantities as yet, Paul Richwagen and Mrs. Forbes being the first in the market with them this season.

Daniel Leamey, salesman for the Waban Rose Conservatories in the Park street market has gone on a two weeks vacation to New Hampshire. Wm. Morgan of the same establishment has been spending his vacation at Lake George, N. Y. Besides those Europe bound mentioned last week are J. T. Butterworth and Duncan Finlayson both of whom sailed on the Ivernia on Tuesday.

J. W. D.

Providence, R. I.

News of the Week.

The foliage of the massive elms which form the greater portion of natural beauty along leading highways in this vicinity, is now undergoing destruction by elm beetles. In some sections the result of the ravages of this pest causes the bereft trees to appear as though swept by fire. George Johnson & Company, florists, have a large force of men at work upon private estates, spraying with arsenate of lead solution. The popularity of elms as shade trees is rapidly declining, and each year numbers are cut down and replaced with American or European linden, either of which have elegant foliage and, thus far, have been free from destructive insects.

F. Macrae & Sons are making interior alterations and improvements about their establishment on Smith street. The greater portion of their houses is now devoted to carnations and Bride and Bridesmaid roses. Chrysanthemums, once a leading feature, are now grown only in small numbers; the verdict of Mr. Macrae in regard to them, as returning small profits, being exactly in accord with the general opinion among growers who cater to this market.

The first of a series of outings of the Florists' Club, to leading establishments where cut flowers are grown, occurs this month.

The innocent, greedy, ever-reading public were treated to something different from the usual routine of newspaper articles in last Sunday's edition of a leading newspaper. The subject involved, was: "Chrysanthemums; their Culture and Preparation for Exhibition." That the author is unmistakably a genius, evidently reared upon limited rations of adulterated food, is clearly evidenced as he proceeds thus: "The enormous blooms seen and admired at Winter exhibitions are not so natural a product as one may suppose. From the time the seeds are planted until the blossoms are shown in the exhibition hall, the plants are under the careful guidance of a skilled specialist. For many weeks before the show, the plants are fed daily rations of sweetened milk; this being done by a small tube placed in an incision in the center stalk. As the blossoms begin to unfold, the petals are curled and frilled by skilled specialists, to make them appear to the best advantage. The beautiful color blendings are mostly produced by mineral dyes." It is probable that such treatment would produce better goats than chrysanthemums. Wonder if John Birnie will try it on geraniums?

G. S. W.

Pittsburg.

News Notes.

The July meeting of the Florists' Club was better attended than anyone expected, as it was strictly a business meeting. The convention of the S. A. F. O. H. at Dayton, Ohio, and the annual outing were discussed and seemed to interest a good many members. Two new members were elected and one proposed. From present indications it looks as if a fair delegation from this city will go to Dayton. The fare one way is $7 and if we get the one and one-third fare, the round trip will cost about $9.35. The committee on transportation will report at next meeting in August and give particulars as to the fare and the railroad to be taken. The outing committee reported that arrangements had been completed for the annual picnic and a larger crowd than last year is expected.

J. Jones, President of the Florists' Club and foreman of the Schenley Park conservatories, will sail about the middle of the month for the old country and expects to take in England and Ireland and perhaps spend a few days in France.

David Fraser, secretary of the Chrysanthemum Society of America, sailed a few days ago for a few months stay.

The Pittsburg Rose & Carnation Company's two large new houses are well under way, one ready for glazing and the other almost completed as to the iron frame work. Both houses are of the same perfect construction as the balance of the plant, built to last, and the company has now one of the finest plants in the country. One house is already stocked with carnations which are in fine condition, promising an early crop.

Business the past week was very quiet, with an abundance of stock of all sorts. Sweet peas are in fair demand. Roses and carnations are showing the effects of hot weather.

Oscar Oehmler, who is with Gude Brothers of Washington, is here on a visit to his old home.

W. K. Boas, the paper box manufacturer of Philadelphia and B. Eschner of M. Rice & Company, also of Philadelphia, were in the city this week.

E. C. REINEMAN.

KALAMAZOO, MICH.—Business for the latter half of June has kept well up to expectations. Some good-sized wedding and funeral orders helping out the finish of the commencement season. People, however, are fast departing for the various Summer resorts, and from now on not much business is expected.

Mr. Fisher, of Fisher & Rockin, reports the firm as being well pleased with business done since the concern started up in the Spring, in fact it has exceeded their expectations.

Van Bochove & Brother have already finished replanting their young roses, which are taking on a nice growth. American Beauty and Richmond will be leaders with them next season, although Bride and Bridesmaid will also be planted largely. Ivory and Golden Gate will have only a small space here, as they are scarcely good enough for the requirements of the firm's trade.

Considerable overhauling and repairing is going on with all the growers, but new additions are not numerous just now. Fred Marker is preparing for the erection of another house, 20 by 50 feet; and Grofvert and De Smit will also build a propagating house this Summer. This seems to be the extent of building this year.

Indianapolis.

News Notes.

Alfred Pahud, the Crown Hill Cemetery florist, intends buying land further out in the near future. It is his intention to build a range of houses at the new place which will supply the needs of his present establishment.

The City Park Board is to erect the foundations and make other preparations for large conservatories at Riverside Park. The remainder of the greenhouses may be built this Summer, or the work may be left until next.

August Rieman is cutting large quantities of sweet peas.

John Bertermann and family are at South Haven, Mich.

A majority of the retailers are giving their store employees vacations. This leaves the remainder busy cleaning up for the Winter season, and attending to routine work.

I. B.

Kalamazoo, Mich.

The local papers announce the public sale of the lands, building, stock, etc., of the Central Nursery Company of this city by the sheriff in order to satisfy judgment claims by creditors. The company, which was comprised of a number of well known business men of the city, organized some six years ago with a capital stock of $50,000 and did quite a considerable business, but for various reasons failed to make a financial, success of the venture. We believe the liabilities amount to a considerable sum.

S. B.

TUSCOLA, ILL.—George Schmitt has received new glass to take the place of that broken by the storm of May 30. There were over 1200 panes broken in the greenhouse by the storm and the owner had no insurance.

THE FLORISTS' EXCHANGE

We are a straight shoot and aim to grow into a vigorous plant

A WEEKLY MEDIUM OF INTERCHANGE FOR FLORISTS, NURSERYMEN, SEEDSMEN AND THE TRADE IN GENERAL

Vol. XXII. No. 3 — NEW YORK AND CHICAGO, JULY 21, 1906 — One Dollar Per Year

PLANT NOW

Lilium Harrisii for Early Forcing

WE OFFER some extra choice Lilium Harrisii which has been grown for us from the original, pure stock. This is the kind of stock that you want for the very earliest forcing, and it is the true, original Harrisii. The small sizes—5-7s and 6-7s—are particularly desirable for this purpose, as they will flower more quickly than the larger bulbs. If you want to get a little of the original pure Harrisii, try a case or two of this. As our stock of this is limited, we can offer only a few cases to a single buyer. If you have been dissatisfied with the Harrisii that you have forced heretofore, try a case or two of this, and see if it is not more than worth the difference in price over the stock that you have been buying. In ordering, ask for the pure selected strain of original Harrisii, which we offer as follows:—

5 to 7 inch bulbs,	400 to the case,	$17.00	per case
6 to 7 " "	350 " " "	17.50	" "
7 to 9 " "	200 " " "	18.00	" "
9 to 11 " "	100 " " "	18.00	" "

Easter Comes Early Next Year—March 31st

and a great many growers will want to use Harrisii instead of Longiflorum so as to be sure to have the plants in flower in time as the season is going to be short for Japan Longiflorum. The crop of Harrisii this year is the shortest it has been in years, and in view of the extra demand, we advise those who have not already covered their requirements to lose no time doing so.

For the very earliest forcing—Christmas and later—we recommend the pure Harrisii offered above, but for later forcing, for Easter, our customers will find the regular stock offered below first-class stock—much better than the average stock usually offered. We can quote the regular stock as follows:—

6 to 7 inch bulbs,	350 to the case,	$14.00	per case.
7 to 9 " "	200 " " "	15.00	" "
9 to 11 " "	100 " " "	15.00	" "

Freesia Refracta Alba, the true white variety. Now ready. Finest Bermuda-grown stock. $1.00 per 100; $7.50 per 1,000.

Bermuda Buttercup Oxalis. $1.00 per 100; $7.50 per 1,000.

F. R. PIERSON CO., Tarrytown-on-Hudson, N. Y.

ONLY **$5.00** PER HUNDRED

from 2¼ inch pots in thousand lots;

$6.00 in smaller lots.

Richmond, Killarney and Beauty

Grafted Stock

BRIDE and BRIDESMAID
$12.00 per 100

KILLARNEY and RICHMOND
$15.00 per 100

Exceptionally Fine, Large Plants

SEND FOR SAMPLES.

W. H. ELLIOTT, BRIGHTON, MASS.

Mention The Florists' Exchange when writing.

Vaughan's Seed Store Vaughan's Seed Store Vaughan's Seed Store Vaughan's Seed Store

BERMUDA LILIES

VERY SCARCE THIS YEAR

We offer subject to being unsold

	100	1000
Lilium Harrisii, 5 and 7 in.	$5.00	$40.00
" " 6 and 7 in.	6.00	50.00
Lilium Doeli, for Easter or late forcing. 5 and 7 in.	4.00	35.00
" " " " " 6 and 7 in.	6.00	50.00

FREESIA

We have a fine stock of well cured healthy bulbs now ready.

WHITE FLOWERED BERMUDA

	100	1000
Choice, ⅜ to ½ in.	$0.65	$5.00
Mammoth, ½ to ¾ in.	1.00	7.50

CALIFORNIA GROWN

	100	1000
1st Quality, ⅜ to ½ in.	$0.45	$3.00
Choice, ½ to ¾ in.	0.65	5.00

Ready soon **Callas, Roman Hyacinths, Candidum, Paper White Narcissus, all Dutch Bulbs.**

We are headquarters. Write for prices

Vaughan's Seed Store

14 BARCLAY ST., NEW YORK

CHICAGO, 84-86 Randolph Street Greenhouses, Western Springs, Ill

Vaughan's Seed Store (border repeated)

Reseda „Majestät"

(Samen im Gewächshaus gereift)

Die **größte aller Reseden für Zimmerkultur** — leicht zu ziehen, starke Constitution und Wachsthum einer Menge von Knospen, welche immense Größe erreichen; die **Seitenschößlinge** — ebenfalls — sind so groß, **wie bei diesen Reseden, die jetzt unter Glas wachsen.**

Der von mir offerirte Samen ist von einem **der ersten Reseden-Züchter** für mich gezogen worden. Er befaßt sich speciell mit der Züchtung für den **New Yorker Markt, nur aus extra gewählten Blumen — unter Glas.**

Probe-Paket 30 Cts.; halbes Handels-Paket 60 Cts.; Handels-Paket, etwa 1000 Samen enthaltend, $1.00.

Blumen-Erbsen für Weihnachten u. Danksagungstag.

Boddington's frühe Weihnachts Rosafarbene. — Dies ist die früheste, profitabelste und nützlichste Blumenerbse, die gezogen wird. 60 Cts. per Pfd., 15 Cts. per Unze.

Boddington's frühe Weihnachts Weiße. — Schwester der Weihnachts Rosenfarbenen. Blüht ebenso frei und üppig und ist zweifellos die feinste Weiße für Zimmerkultur. 75 Cts. per Pfd.; 20 Cts. per Unze.

Stiefmütterchen-Samen.

Boddington's „Challenge" Mischung.

Diese Mischung enthält alle feinsten **Riesenblumen** — der ersten Stiefmütterchen-Specialisten der Welt — die **Riesen**-Selbstfärber, **Riesen**gestreifte und -geränderte, und die **Riesen**getupfte, alle sorgfältig im Verhältniß gemischt — **die feinsten,** die käuflich sind — die **feinsten,** die **Sie** für Geld haben können. Ein **Blumenzüchter,** welcher sie gezogen hat, sagte: „Weßhalb nennen Sie sie nicht Herausforderung"?

Preis: halbes Handels-Paket 40 Cts.; Handels-Paket 75 Cts.; viertel Unze $1.50, halbe Unze $2.50, Unze $5.00. (Namen der Arten und Farbe siehe Katalog.)

ARTHUR T. BODDINGTON

342 West 14. Strasse — New York City

Mention The Florists' Exchange when writing.

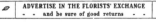

Seed Trade Report.

AMERICAN SEED TRADE ASSOCIATION

Henry W. Wood, Richmond, Va., president; C. S. Burge, Toledo, O., first vice-president; G. B. McVay, Birmingham, Ala., second vice-president; C. E. Kendel, Cleveland, O., secretary and treasurer; J. H. Ford, Ravenna, O., assistant secretary.

During the year 1905 California packed 56,170 cases of peas, and 73,275 cases of beans and other vegetables.

CHICAGO.—A. Setterberg is now superintendent of the seed department of the Sears, Roebuck Company, the position recently vacated by S. D. Dysinger.

On Monday, in conversation with probably the most close observer of the onion set industry in this section, the following interesting and important points were gleaned: Some fields are very fine, promising a full crop if sufficient rain reaches them this week, otherwise they may shrink; while other fields, especially of late planting and those most affected by the drouth, will go down to an average of 40 to 45 per cent. of what they should have produced under favorable conditions. As to varieties the yellows take the lead in general condition, with whites following closely, both of which may be said to be excellent. In reds the acreage is small and in some instances it is very evident that the seed was too poor to make good sets. With favorable weather the harvest will be at its height at the publication of this note, and within two weeks we shall be able to give a detailed account of the results.

W. W. Barnard is in Wisconsin closely watching the results of the seed crops of that section.

A. Ringier, of the W. W. Barnard Company, returned the first of the week from a business trip to Kansas City.

NEW KIND of POTATO in FRANCE.—The British vice-consul at Rouen reports that the cultivation in France of a new potato brought from Uruguay has been observed for some time with great interest. A variety of this potato, called the "Solanum commersonii violet," is said to possess excellence of taste as well as nutritive value, and is equal to the best table potato known in France. This variety is distinguished by its resistance to frost, also to disease, and its one great advantage is that it prospers most in a damp or swampy soil, where no other kind of potato would grow. Every kind of soil, whether clayey, calcareous, or silicious, seems equally adapted for its culture, provided it is damp. The price of this potato, which has now been placed on the market in a limited quantity for planting purposes, is 2 shillings (about 48 cents) per pound.

Correction.

In the advertisement of Ant. C. Zvolanek in last week's issue, page 30, the price per pound of Sweet Pea seed was given as $7.00, which was an error. It should have been $2.00 per pound.

SAMPLES of SEEDS for DEPARTMENT of AGRICULTURE.—The following circular has been distributed by the Treasury Department to officers of the Customs:

"At the instance of the Secretary of Agriculture, it is hereby directed that until July 1, 1907, 2-ounce samples of all importations of 100 pounds or more of grass, clover, and forage-plant seeds be prepared at the earliest practicable date after entry, and forwarded to the Seed Laboratory, Department of Agriculture, Washington, D. C., labeled with names and addresses of consignors and consignees, name of seed as given in the invoice, and quantity of the consignment."

G. B. McVay.

G. B. McVay, second vice-president of The American Seed Trade Association, whose portrait appeared in our issue of July 7, page 14, was raised on a farm in Texas, and educated in the public schools and University of that state. He was married in 1890 at the age of twenty years, and removed to Birmingham, Ala., where he now lives with a family of five children. In 1891 he secured a position with Amzi Godden, then a prominent retail druggist at Birmingham, as prescription clerk. Five years later the business was incorporated as the Amzi Godden Company and he was taken into the concern as secretary. In the meantime the company was pushing the seed business as a side line, having issued their first catalogue in 1893. A short time after the company sold out its retail drug stores and engaged in the wholesale drug business, opening up an exclusive seed business in another building. The company sold out their wholesale drug business in 1900, and have since devoted their entire time and energy to the seed business. August 1, 1905, the company was reorganized, under the name of Amzi Godden Seed Company, with paid in capital of $40,000.

Mr. McVay is president of the company. He is by profession a chemist and pharmacist, and at one time was president of the Alabama Pharmaceutical Association. Mr. McVay is also interested in the manufacture of fertilizers, being a director in the Jefferson Fertilizer Company.

European Notes.

The powers that be have decided that there is not to be any forcing radish at all this year, so that while rain has fallen nearly all around, the Anjou district still remains as dry as a bone. Of course, beet and carrot are suffering very much, but having been planted early they got a hold of the land before the drought set in. Onion and leek are now at their best; another ten days will see both these crops practically safe from disease.

Peas are maturing rapidly all around. Loud also are the complaints of the quality of many of the stocks received from your side last year; this is especially true of the extra earlies.

The reports respecting the onion crop from Germany are rather conflicting, but in no case is it claimed to be first rate. The cold spell in May seriously retarded the development both in Germany and Holland, and now it is affirmed, the mildew has been developed by the almost tropical heat. A heavy rainfall during the past 24 hours has cooled the air, cleansed the plants and in some cases submerged them, so that no great surplus of onion will be found in Germany this year.

Cabbage is in the balance everywhere, but the acreage is so moderate that it does not cause us much anxiety.

Recent callers include Lem W. Bowen of Detroit, who, with his two sons, is making his usual trip, a la automobile; William Ewing, of Montreal, who has set his foot upon his native heath once more; F. J. D. McKay, representing T. W. Wood & Sons, Richmond, Va.; and, last, but not least, W. J. Bryan, of Lincoln, Neb., whose speech at the Independence Day banquet in London has raised him very high in the estimation of his own countrymen and evoked the highest respect of all English speaking peoples, his free silver heresy notwithstanding.

George H. Dicks, who is looking after the cultures of Cooper, Taber & Company in France, is the proud father of a baby daughter that he has not yet seen. His venerable pater, who is even more elevated at the new dignity, will attend to the cigar department during his forthcoming visit to the land of the free.

This week's notes must have a tragic ending in recording the untimely death of the well known and highly respected Louis Goeppinger, who was killed in the terrible railway smash at Salisbury last Sunday morning. For many years past he had made London his home; it is fitting that his body should rest within her borders R. I. P.

EUROPEAN SEEDS.

NOTES FROM HOLLAND.—Now that the general crop of tulips may be said to have been lifted, it appears that, although with few exceptions the crop is a decided short one, those fields that have not suffered in May from the so-called blight in the foliage, have proved to produce a very superior crop to the places that suffered so much during the latter part of May last. At present it is still doubtful what really causes this blight in the foliage; but that it spreads with great rapidity wherever it makes its appearance, and in consequence, affects the growth of the foliage, and more or less the satisfactory crop of the tulips is without doubt. One of the largest growers is at present engaged in making minute and extensive trials in this respect, and we may shortly expect to see the publication of the results of these trials in the trade papers. The many complaints that have been heard lately from both England and Germany in regard to bedding tulips partly failing to come, or only making a weakly and unsatisfactory growth, go to show that this point should receive a more careful investigation to ascertain the real cause.

The hyacinth crop, which has only been lifted partially, has not given any cause for complaint; but as the main crop of salable bulbs will not be out of the ground until the middle of July, nothing definite can yet be said. It is, however, very likely that the crocus crop will be a very poor one, and that quantities on hand will be sold out early in the season. Narcissus and iris are all looking well and promise to give a fine crop; but it should not be overlooked that owing to the prevailing low prices, the stocks of these are not as large as what they used to be, and should there be anything like a fair demand there will not be any surplus left on the hands of the growers, as was the case during the last two seasons. The cleaning and curing of all these millions of bulbs is now requiring the help of many hundreds of hands, and if the present dry and warm weather will only continue, this process may be expected to be finished within two or three weeks.—Correspondent Horticultural Trade Journal.

CATALOGUES RECEIVED.

HUBERT & COMPANY, Guernsey, England.—Trade Catalogue of Bulbs; also Tuberous Rooted, Herbaceous and Decorative Plants.

HENRY A. DREER, Philadelphia.—Midsummer Catalogue of Seeds, Bulbs, Plants, Implements, etc. Illustrated.

M. HERB, Naples, Italy.—General Catalogue of Bulbs and Seeds for Autumu Sowing.

H. H. BERGER & COMPANY, New York.—Autumn Price List of Bulbs, Seeds, and Plants. Illustrated. This firm makes a specialty of Japanese plants and bulbs. The list, which is a very complete one, will be found of much interest.

NURSERY DEPARTMENT.

Conducted by Joseph Meehan.

AMERICAN ASSOCIATION OF NURSERYMEN, Orlando Harrison, Berlin, Md., president; J. W. Hill, Des Moines, Ia., vice-president; George C. Seager, Rochester, N. Y., secretary; C. L. Yates, Rochester, N. Y., treasurer.

Horticultural Notes.

Crepe myrtle, Lagerstrœmia indica, can be increased by soft wood cuttings made and placed in the greenhouse in Summer, as well as by hard wood cuttings set out in early Spring. In the South, where the plants seed freely, they are easily raised from cuttings.

The lovely flowering apples and crabs are readily increased by budding. The months of July and August usually find stocks in good condition for budding. Bud a good number of Bechtel's crab.

European bird cherry, Cerasus padus, forms a large, handsome tree, beautiful when in flower, and the delight of robins when in fruit. Those who wish to encourage birds, should plant a tree of this cherry.

Cutings of shrubs in course of propagation under glass at this season need close watching that fungus does not get among them. Shade to the glass is beter than shade close to the cuttings; and little fungus generates where there is plenty of light.

Stocks of fruit trees desired for budding or grafting should never be obtained from suckers, as stocks so raised take the suckering character with them. This is seen in the Morello cherry in old gardens. Where set out from suckers they form thickets by suckering.

Common hop vine is often used to cover a trellis desired to be quickly covered. It is good for this purpose, but a prettier one, if not quite as rampant a grower, is the golden-leaved hop. Its golden tinted foliage is most attractive.

Hoya carnosa, known as the wax plant and honey plant, is too seldom seen in greenhouse collections. It is an interesting lawn plant, and when in flower is a good seller. It always interests young gardeners to be told that the old flower heads are not to be cut off, as new flowers come from them the next season.

European houses are offering a golden-leaved form of the Dimorphanthus mandshuricus. The Dimorphanthus is closely allied to aralia, and it can be well understood how beautiful a golden-leaved form of it must be.

As all persmmons are not fruit bearing, the fruit bearing sorts of Japanese varieties are usually grafted on seedlings of our native sorts. Strong two-year seedlings are good for the purpose.

Teas' weeping mulberry grows readily from cuttings, but such plants are of a trailing nature only, of the nature of a vine, in fact. In this condition they are very good for planting along banks, to prevent the soil washing out.

During July and August the Magnolia tripetala is at its best display. The conical seed pods are then ripe and are of a deep pink color. The beauty of the tree then is far greater than when it is in flower in May. In many ways it is the most ornamental of all magnolias.

Scarlet Bergamot.

In our gardens, in a cultivated state, is often seen the scarlet bergamot, but rarely is it seen in such situations in the full glory of growth as it is to be found when in a half swampy place in a wild state. As seen in an average garden, it is in the full sun and in an ordinary position as to soil. What it demands to make the grand display it is capable of making, is low, damp ground. Low ground is usually deep as well, and all these things combined will give plants and flowers of wonderful growth. It is then that the scarlet blaze of the flowers is so prominent and so beautiful. In its wild state the plant makes a height of from 2 to 3 feet, producing numerous shoots, each one crowned with its head of scarlet flowers, arranged in a circular row on the flat heads, and even the bracts which are numerous, are of a dull red color.

In nature this scarlet bergamot, Monarda didyma, is often met with in groups of a hundred plants or more. It flowers in July in Pennsylvania, and where the plants are accessible, many persons travel a long distance to see them when in bloom.

There are several bergamots in cultivation, all worthy, but none so good for dazzling display as the one of which we write.

Hydrangea Hortensia Japonica.

Because of the great beauty of Hydrangea Hortensia when in flower, there is a universal regret that it is not reliably hardy north of Baltimore. It will live outdoors all winter in Pennsylvania, but the life will be only at the root, unless in a well sheltered place, in which case it will sometimes keep alive enough of its branches to give some flowers in Summer. When killed to the ground, it makes a thicket of growth in Summer, but this growth rarely flowers until the Summer following.

There is a section of this hydrangea known as Hydrangea Hortensia japonica, which has proved hardier than the type, and which bears flowers of much beauty. There are several varieties of it, all of great merit. A good blue flowered one is called acuminata; another, not so blue, cœrulea, and a rose colored one Imperatrice Eugenie; and there is still another, Thunbergii. Besides, in other ways, these all differ from Hortensia proper in having flat heads of flowers instead of rounded ones as it has. These japonica varieties are not absolutely hardy in Philadelphia, but that they are nearly so is evidenced by the many showy specimens of them in flower so often seen in gardens here. The color of these hydrangeas differs so much from that of any other shrub flowering in Midsummer that this alone is an inducement to secure plants for the lawn.

Florists who sell pot plants would find a good sale for these hydrangeas, without doubt. In addition to their beauty, to be able to say that they are hardy would greatly aid their sale.

At this time of the year there are numerous young shoots on the plants, giving wood for cuttings to be propagated just as the common form is.

Red Berried Holly.

Professor Massey, in the Practical Farmer, suggests that the red berried holly, Ilex Cassine, might prove hardy if planted in Philadelphia, as it is a native of Virginia southward. Some years ago small plants were tried at Germantown, Pa., but without success. But there is no doubt it could be planted in a sheltered place where it would live. The writer has often studied the requirements of these southern plants and has succeded in finding them, and thus has carried the plants through the Winter. This red berried holly, and many another southern shrub and tree could be had to live here when one has large grounds, containing a variety of situations. Occasionally this holly, Ilex Cassine, is to be found in the collections of Christmas greens that come from the South to our florists. They know it under its local name, Youpon.

Another red berried holly which has endured our Winters is the Ilex cornuta of Japan. It is more nearly like the hollies of our Christmas time than is the Cassine; as it has large, prickly, holly-like leaves, while those of the latter are small comparatively, and not prickly as the others are. Ilex Cassine occupies low ground naturally, but when hardiness is in question it is better to set the plants in positions where their wood will ripen well before Winter sets in.

Many of the beautiful trees and shrubs of the South could be grown in pots or tubs and sold for decorative purposes for Christmas and other occasions, just as is now done with such as come from Europe.

Fraxinus Ornus—Flowering Ash, Manna Ash.

To those acquainted with the beauty of the Fraxinus ornus when in flower it is always a surprise to find so many collections of trees without it being represented in them. We really think it a beautiful tree and one all collections should contain; and aside from its other merits there are so very few trees flowering when it does, in early June. All ash trees flower, and we have said before very many of them are worth considering for their blossoms, but there are none of them bearing flowers as beautiful as this. A glance at the illustration will satisfy any one, we are sure, that we are not overpraising the tree in this respect. Every prominent twig is generally capped with a cluster of blossoms, such as the picture displays. The flowers are fleecy white, prettier we think, than those of the white fringe, as the Chionanthus virginica is called, and they well cause the tree itself to be known under the common name of manna ash.

In England, where the tree is much valued in landscape gardening work, its flowers are of a greenish white, but under our bright skies they are almost white, having but little green in them; and when a tree stands out alone and is in flower it is conspicuous and beautiful. The clusters of flowers are shorter than the leaves so that they present an attractive appearance the foliage partly overlapping them.

The flowering ash makes but a small tree, 20 to 30 feet, which allows of its being planted in positions in which large growing ash trees could not be permitted; and it commences to flower when it is quite young. In some lists it is to be found under the name Ornus europæa, but botanists agree that it is rightly placed in Fraxinus.

Seeds follow the flowers freely, and even these are not unattractive, they come in such large numbers.

JOSEPH MEEHAN.

Fraxinus Ornus—Flowering Ash (Manna Ash.)

Pear Blight.

Nurserymen are rarely troubled with pear blight on the pear trees they sell, for the reason that the blight starts in the blossoms of the tree and trees are sold before they are of a flowering age, as a rule. It had been discovered years ago that as soon as a branch was stricken, shown by its blackened leaves and branches, it called for the cutting off of the branch at once as the only way to prevent the disease spreading to the whole tree. Further knowledge soon followed, to cut several inches below the part already dead, as the poisoned sap worked downward, and a portion would possibly be below the part already killed. It transpired later that the disease entered the tree through the flowers almost entirely, accounting for its rarely appearing on young trees not of a flowering age. The cut off branches must be burned, to prevent any spread of the disease to other trees.

Peonies Dying.

Some specimens of peony attacked by the fungus Botrytis paeoniae (Sclerotinia paeoniae) were recently submitted to the Scientific Committee of the Royal Horticultural Society of England. The character of the disease, and suggested remedy, are described as follows: "The shoots droop before the flower opens, and just above the surface of the soil a white web of fungal thread may be seen spreading over the surface of the stem. Later resting bodies or hard lumps (sclerotia) of a black color are formed both above and below the surface of the soil. The diseased shoots should be removed and burned as soon as discovered, and fresh stable manure should not be used for mulching. If plants have been attacked, it is well to remove the old soil from about them, and replace it with fresh soil with which lime has been mixed. This should be done in the Spring."

Grapes Splitting.

(3). Could you give me some information as to why the berries of Foster's White Muscadine, and Madresfield Court grapes split in the last swelling? I have them in the same house with Black Hamburg and Bowood Muscats. The latter finish up well every year, but the former two varieties will split, under good treatment and different conditions. I have tried the border, wet, dry; kept off laterals and let them on, with the same results. Also have given an abundance of air day and night, on favorable occasions. VITIS.

—Foster's Seedling and Madresfield Court grapes are both subject to splitting just as they commence to color, more especially near the salt air, as then we usually get more moisture in the atmosphere. However, Vitis has tried most of the remedies known for the prevention of this evil.

In cultivating grapes that are subject to give split berries, they can be handled better by planting them at one end of the house rather than having them mixed with other varieties. Four years ago Foster's Seedling split badly with me. The season following I let up sooner with the moisture under those canes, with the result that I have not been bothered with splitting since. But, of course, our canes are planted at the end of grapery. In the case of Madresfield Court, as the fruit begins to color, putting salt hay on the border is a capital preventive—just enough to hold the moisture down; also if the border is watered before they take on their second swelling. This should carry them through the dangerous period. My experience is, there must be no moisture to lodge on the bunches at the coloring stage, or the berries will surely split. In fact I keep on a crack of bottom air as well as top. This allows better circulation. I also leave the laterals for the two or three weeks the fruit is coloring. If all those remedies fail, there is only one more that I know of, and that is, cut the wood at the back of the bunch—a slanting cut a third through. This will check the sap somewhat, and will not harm the fruit. WM. TURNER.

California Violet.

(4) I have a lot of California violet seedlings. Would they make plants true to the original if grown?
Conn. INQUIRER.

—The character of the seedlings will depend upon whether any cross-fertilization took place at the time of flowering. The only way to determine their value is to grow them along until they begin to bloom.

Yellowing of Rose Leaves.

(5) Would you kindly inform me as to the cause of the lower leaves on young rose plants, just set in the beds, turning yellow and falling off, and a remedy. C. G. R.

—The trouble with the young roses no doubt arises from the soil being kept too wet.

Remedy for Red Spider.

(6) Is there any remedy for red spider other than syringing? C. G. R.

—Spray the plants thoroughly every day, but allow as little water as possible to fall on the soil, and the red spider will soon disappear. There is no better remedy.

Club Root

(7) What is club root; and would you please give a means of identification of it, also a preventive?
New York. C. G. R.

—To identify club root, examine the roots carefully, and if they are attacked with this trouble, little knots or balls will be found; the plants also get yellow and sickly and cease to grow. A liberal sprinkling of lime on the soil will sometimes check the trouble, though there is no absolute cure for it.

Bordeaux Mixture.

(8) Is Bordeaux mixture good to use for bugs and insects? The bugs we refer to are those usually found on elm trees, which do so much damage. Why I cannot name them is that as yet I have not been able to discover which ones do the most damage, but ask this question in regard to the use of the mixture for the destroying of the general run of bugs. T. & H.

—Bordeaux mixture has been proved an excellent insecticide as well as a fungicide, and can be recommended for beetles, etc. When using Bordeaux mixture for insects, a little Paris green may be added with good effect.

Hyacinths vs. Mushrooms.

(9) Which will be likely to pay the better under the benches for the Fall and Winter—one crop of hyacinths, or a bed of mushrooms?
A NEW BEGINNER.
New Jersey.

—We would not advise growing either hyacinths or mushrooms under the benches. Hyacinths should either be kept in a cold cellar or buried outdoors until within three or four weeks of the time they are needed to flower. Mushrooms, if grown under the benches, create too much filth and vermin, and are a menace to whatever is being grown upon the benches.

H. L., Albany, N. Y., is respectfully reminded that all anonymous communications go to the balaam box. Your signature should appear on your letter, not necessarily for publication, but as an evidence of good faith.

LIST OF ADVERTISERS

MINNEAPOLIS, MINN.—T. H. Hall, 3910 Lyndale avenue, will add to his plant four greenhouses, each 24 feet wide and 95, 95, 119 and 119 feet, respectively, long, with a brick boiler house 24x30 feet.

SALINA, KAN.—Edward Jatro has nearly completed the construction of four new greenhouses.

INDEX TO STOCK ADVERTISED

Contents.

OWENSBORO, KY.—The Nanz Floral Company has been incorporated with a capital stock of $2,000. The incorporators are R. W. Nanz, Miss Katherine Nanz and Mrs. C. G. Nanz. The officers are R. W. Nanz, president and general manager, and Katherine Nanz, secretary. The new organization will continue to conduct the greenhouse business of the late C. G. Nanz, but will enlarge the business and their facilities for handling it. A new greenhouse 25 by 100 feet in dimensions will be constructed in connection with the houses already standing on South Walnut street. A store in the central part of the city will be opened for the purpose of bringing the products of the greenhouses in closer touch with the retail trade. A location has not yet been selected for the downtown store, but several well located sites are being considered.

REVIEW OF THE MARKET

NEW YORK.—Considering that the month is July, and that we are in the midst of a rather heated spell of weather, the cut flower business is keeping up fairly well. Roses that are of good quality—and there is a moderate supply coming in daily—are selling out nicely every day, and prices in the main are quite satisfactory. The carnation supply is now down to its minimum, and few are seen; they are not missed, however, as plenty of other stock is available.

Lilies are not so numerous as has been the rule for several weeks back, and prices are much firmer.

Cattleyas are still too plentiful for the demand and values show no improvement.

Adiantum is in rather poor demand and prices have dropped considerably. Asparagus and smilax are also in too heavy supply for present needs, and clearances have to be made at a sacrifice of values. Gladioli are more in evidence again; and a limited supply of purple asters are reaching the market every day. Sweet peas are clearing out somewhat better than they were, the supply having diminished materially.

CHICAGO.—There is not a great deal to offer that is new or interesting in connection with market conditions here this week. Summer conditions appear to be perfectly established and trade runs along at a low ebb. The shipping business is generally said to be a little better than at the corresponding season in previous years, and meritorious stock finds ready sale at prices which now show but slight variation from week to week.

The middle of July may be said to have wound up the peony stock from cold storage, and the magnitude of this business has been very great. The handlers of these goods from this section have certainly reduced this art to a science, and goods seen last week which had been five weeks in storage were in as perfect condition as could be desired.

Some growers are offering a line of roses from young stock which are creditable, though most of the stock coming in is nothing to boast about.

Sweet peas are showing up in continued large supply and on the average a little better in quality than a week ago.

Carnations are dropping off in quality as well as quantity, and will probably not show much improvement in the immediate future though rains may help the outside grown flowers which are now coming in suffering for the want of water. Greens are in full supply. W. K. W.

ST. LOUIS.—The demand for flowers, both wholesale and retail, is reported very slow. In retail circles business is about as dull as it can be and nothing much is looked for, except funeral work, which, too, seems to have fallen off.

According to the daily press the death rate is very small, which speaks well for the health of our city.

Stock is quite plentiful, but not of the very best quality. Outdoor flowers have suffered greatly from the long dry spell, but the good soaking rain of Sunday will soon put asters in good shape.

There are more poor roses coming in than good ones, with prices ranging from $3 to $5 per 100. Carnations are in good demand, but are becoming very scarce; Enchantress is about the only good carnation obtainable. Red and pink are scarce; white are coming in better from the field. Sweet peas continue a glut, at very low prices; lots of 5,000 going at 50c. per 1000. Asters sell well at $1 to $1.50 per 100. Gladioli bring 2c. to 3c. per stalk.

Everything in greens is in plenty for all demands. ST. PATRICK.

INDIANAPOLIS.—The long Summer days are interrupted occasionally with spurts of funeral work. Besides this and a small decoration now and then there is little flower business to attend to. Stock is plentiful enough, but a variety is lacking. Asters have become a factor in the market at $1 to $1.50 per 100. Those in the field are most promising, and it will be but a few days until an abundance is marketable. Copious rains lately have caused disaster to the sweet peas; a few are sold at 25c. per 100. Lilies are still a mainstay for funeral work. Lilium auratum and L. longiflorum wholesale at $1.50 to $2 per dozen. Lilium album and L. rubrum sell at $5 per 100. Gladioli were noticeable in quantities the past week; the were readily sold at $2 to $4 per 100y

Carnations are scarce, and, high quality considered, $1.50 to $2 per 100 is the price for them. The finest Shasta daisies are yet brought to the store men at 50c. per 100. Swainsona is much used, at 25c. per bunch of fifteen sprays.

Roses in general have much improved. Few mildewed ones are now being received. Bridesmaid, Bride and Golden Gate bring $3 to $5 per 100; La France and Madame Abel Chatenay are the most select pink at $7. Excellent Kaiserin Augusta Victoria sell at $5 to $6. Quite a few Richmond are shipped in, but this rose opens too quickly at this season to elicit any favorable comment. New crop, medium-sized American Beauty are satisfactory at $5 per 100. I. B.

BOSTON.—There is little to be said about the market these days for there is little doing. Sometimes everything is cleaned up; then again a glut is on in all lines. Carnations remain practically the same, selling at 50c., 75c., $1 and sometimes $1.50. Roses bring from $1 to $6 for the best grades. Liliums, such as auratum, longiflorum and candidum, are quite plenty. Auratum sell at $1 per dozen. Asters are now quite abundant at $1. Sweet peas are good at 15c., 25c. and 35c. Gladioli of the best grades bring $6 and $8. Feverfew, candytuft, and gypsophila sell at two bunches for 25c. Lily of the valley holds its own at $2 to $4, while asparagus, ferns and smilax remain unchanged. J. W. D.

CINCINNATI, O.—Summer dullness is with us, and not much is doing except funeral work. American Beauty roses are the only really good stock coming to this market, and they fetch $3, $2.50, $2, $1.75, $1.50, and $1 per dozen. The writer is the only one handling this stock. Gladioli are beginning to come in and sell at 2c. and 3c. Asters are seen once in a while, but they are very poor as yet. The grasshoppers are doing lots of damage to the outdoor stock. Sweet peas are good and fetch 25c. to 50c. per 100. Carnations are on their last legs and $1 per 100 is about the top notch.

CHANGES IN BUSINESS.

NAMPA, IDAHO.—Louis Poland of Des Moines, Ia., is preparing to go into the florist business here.

SILVER CITY, N. M.—Miss Boulware has assumed charge of the greenhouse formerly conducted by Mrs. J. W. Hairston.

CELINA, O.—Ernsberger Brothers, of Decatur, Ill., will establish a branch of their business here, erecting 10,000 square feet of glass.

SOUTHINGTON, CONN.—Olson & Lunden have purchased the greenhouses at the corner of Main and Bristol streets from C. W. Blatchley.

ROCHESTER, N. Y.—The Charlton Nursery Company has purchased the retail nursery business of George Moulson & Son. J. M. Charlton is president Edward S. Osborne, secretary and treasurer.

BOSTON, MASS.—H. E. Fiske Seed Co. has been incorporated to deal in seeds, shrubs and nursery stock; capital, $30,000. President, P. H. Stratton, Cambridge, and treasurer, H. E. Fiske, Wollaston.

SHERMAN, TEX.—The Byrne Floral Company has been organized, and is composed of F. A. Byrne, president and manager, and Mrs. John Grant, secretary and treasurer.

It is stated 10,000 square feet of glass has been arranged for by the promoters. The new concern expects to be ready for business by the first of September.

FIRMS WHO ARE BUILDING.

SENECA FALLS, N. Y.—D. H. Ruthrauff will build a greenhouse, 80 x 11 feet.

COHOES, N. Y.—Sault Brothers are making additions to their greenhouse plant.

CHAMBERSBURG, PA.—Byer Brothers are building three carnation houses, each 25 by 100 feet.

SAUGUS, MASS.—J. G. Holmes is building a greenhouse 75 x 20 feet. The work is being done by W. F. Symmes, East Billerica, Mass., who makes a specialty of greenhouses building.

ROCKFORD, ILL.—New greenhouses are being built at the H. W. Buckbee plant on Kishwaukee street, replacing many of the old buildings. Considerable concrete construction is being used.

AMES, IA.—F. J. Olsau, the proprietor of Olsanville greenhouse, lying just west of the college campus, has commenced the erection of a much larger and more modern building near the site of the old one.

STERLING, ILL.—The Sterling Floral Company is having five of the old greenhouses, the first erected at the site of the present plant, torn down, and on the site of the same the company will erect thereon a new and modern greenhouse which will be used almost exclusively for the raising of carnations.

THE WEEK'S WORK.

Timme's Timely Teachings.

Palms.

The use of palms for outdoor decorative effects during the Summer has wrought the ruin of many a nice and valuable specimen. The practice, at all times a risky proceeding, very closely resembles reckless sacrifice. The gratifying results of many years of skilful labor and careful watching have often thus been thrown to the winds of one short season. It is an error to think that cultivated palms, home grown and reared under artificial conditions, must still be set down as natives of torrid zones, children from the sun-scorched and wind-swept coast stretches of tropical climes. There I have seen them, stumbled over their roots for days and, sorry to say it, failed to be gushingly impressed with their imposing grandeur. I beheld them with the eyes of the northern gardener, compared these hoboes in their rags and tatters, with those proud aristocrats in our conservatories and became well satisfied that a free and help-thyself existence greatly impairs the dignified bearing of any one of the many members of this royal family.

Why palms are so often employed in outdoor plant arrangements, especially on private places—mostly against the will of the gardener in charge—is easily explained by their great effectiveness either as single specimens or parts of a compact group. In such a case, a set of damaged and weather-beaten plants, if such there are, will do service for several seasons. It is hard to thus kill a palm outright, which would open a welcome way of ridding the place of some of the most unsightly of the lot. Instead they remain, for the greater part of the year a disgrace to the palm house. Such a state of affairs with no suggestion of hope for anything in the way of justified disposal of the unsightly stock, should never be tolerated on any commercial place. The damage done to faultlessly grown, perfect palms of the medium and larger sizes in the decoration of halls, churches and houses for the various festive occasions coming our way, is slight and usually well paid for, and cannot be compared with the great loss sustained by their use in all Summer lawn adornments. To lend out palms for the purpose at a small recompense is unwise; to induce customers to buy them outright looks more like real business.

At this season palms do their best growing and the cultivator's chief aim now must be to prevent this growth from becoming too soft and flabby, which under a too densely shaded glass and with an overplus of stagnant humidity in the house is only too likely to occur. Abundant ventilation day and night is therefore now in order. A fumigating now and then with any one of the different nicotine preparations will do no harm and is the safest means of keeping down most insects of the minute species; while forceful syringing prevents others from gaining a firm foothold. Badly infested plants should be given a thorough cleaning and be set by themselves. A scale ridden plant of any kind, laid on its side over an ant hill, is the cleanest thing on earth when taken up a few hours after. If there is anything else that ants are good for I do not know it, but I know of several things good for ants; slug shot, arsenical mixtures, heavily charged manure water, water all alone in oft-repeated drenchings, all will make life a burden to ants and either kill them or drive them away.

Palms of advanced age and size, being excessively root-bound, should now be repotted, if this operation, owing to pressure of work, had to be postponed earlier in the season. There should be no excuse for crowding these into closely packed quarters now, while vegetation is most active. A spreading and thinning out will expose moss-clad, mucky nooks and recesses to the wholesome free play of light and air. Young stock requires spacing, repotting, sorting into different grades and sizes and resetting at frequent intervals right along until early Fall, when a brief let up in the work from then until about February marks the end of one and the beginning of another season.

Ficus Elastica.

The propagation of rubber plants on extensive plans is carried on during a time when hard firing furnishes the needed even and continuous supply of heat. For the small grower, however, there is no better season for the increase of stock than the present, and no better course of procedure than mossing. By following this method, which is nothing but a form of layering, full fledged plants are obtained right at the start. Crippled and lanky plants, the branches of old unsalable specimens, anything unsightly in the rubber line is operated upon, the calling forth of roots at joints and below the leafy tops being the object. The place to be mossed for the formation of roots first undergoes some sort of mutilation, inflicted with a sharp knife. Cutting the wood almost half through on one side, inserting a bit of wood or gravel to keep the cut open, washing away the gum after the bleeding has stopped and then tying sphagnum moss in a good, thick layer firmly around this part of the wood, is all there is to the operation. Of course, it is understood that the moss must be kept moist either by frequent syringing or by pouring water on it from time to time. It will not be long at this season of the year before the white roots show through the ball of moss. Full time for the formation of abundant roots should be allowed before cutting away the rooted top from the wood below it. These tops are then potted, shaded for a few days and grown on as young thrifty stock.

Aspidistras.

If the stock in aspidistras is to be increased, now is the time to go at it. Large plants, not materially gaining in value as they grow older, can be made into a number of small ones, all of them of greater service for decorating or the general pot plant trade. The old, densely leaved clumps are divided into shapely tufts, just right for 3 or 4-inch pots. A sharp trimming in of the roots is advisable, and any pieces thus falling off, usually studded with latent eyes, may also be potted up. These now thrown upon their own resources, soon break into a bright and vigorous leafage.

Calceolarias.

It is time to make a beginning in the growing of calceolarias for next season's marketing. Clean leaf mold made gritty by the addition of a little sand, is the kind of soil in which to start the seeds. In sowing one must guard against scattering the minute grains too thickly, which might result in a wholesale damping off of the little seedlings, only too inclined at all times to yield to decay. The seeds want no covering, and are merely pressed into the surface of the soil, after which the trays are carefully watered with a fine spray can. Placed in a frame, shaded and not allowed to become dry, the trays will soon be covered with a lusty green. It is then time to provide for an abundance of ventilation and direct light. The sashes are of use only as a protection against heavy rains and should then be raised six or eight inches above the frame all around, and only in late Fall, when frost is threatening, should the frames be tightly shut. A frame shading of muslin, easily placed and removed, is the handiest device for shielding the seedlings against the fierce rays of the Midsummer sun. Great care must be exercised in spraying and watering to avoid extremes either way. The danger of loss through damping off is lessened by timely transplanting from box to box. When of good size, strudy and vigorous, the plants are potted up, but remain in the frame until this becomes too risky a place late in the season, when the plants are transferred to a safer place under glass. Transplanted from time to time they will reach their last shift about the first week in March.

Repairing.

As usual there is lots to do in setting things right for Winter. This is the time to hunt up defects in the heating apparatus, to build and repair benches, to replace broken glass. A new coat of paint all around would also be of benefit. The repainting of rafters inside and outside, with the glass left in, is at this time of the year the most strenuous job in the decorative line. There is something fascinating in staying away from it. With the full glare of the sun on the glass, almost blinding the performer, with the hornets and wasps nesting beneath the ridge pole, and the perspiration flowing in streams the work is anything but pleasant. A canvas covering over the plants below and a movable section of board covering overhead on the roof, to be shoved along as the work progresses, will render the work, at least the inside part of it, endurable. A repainting of this sort improves the appearance but not the durability of a house. It never reaches the seat of wood destroying decay, which is covered by the edges of the glass. To make a thorough going job of it—and an easy and rapid one, too—the removal of all the glass before painting is necessary, to be followed up with a good job of reglazing into a new bed of putty. There are many houses with shaking, rattling, putty-loosened glass, where such a radical measure in doing repairs would do a world of good. Now is a good time to go at it.

FRED. W. TIMME.

FOUNDED IN 1888

THE FLORISTS' EXCHANGE

A Weekly Medium of Interchange for Florists, Nurserymen Seedsmen and the Trade in general

Exclusively a Trade Paper.

Entered at New York Post Office as Second Class Matter

Published EVERY SATURDAY by

A. T. DE LA MARE PTG. AND PUB. CO. LTD.

2, 4, 6 and 8 Duane Street,

P. O. Box 1697. Telephone 3765 John. **NEW YORK.**

CHICAGO OFFICE: 127 East Berwyn Avenue.

ILLUSTRATIONS.

Electrotypes of the illustrations used in this paper can usually be supplied by the publishers. Price on application.

YEARLY SUBSCRIPTIONS.

United States, Canada, and Mexico, $1.00. Foreign countries in postal union, $2.50. Payable in advance. Remit by Express Money Order Draft on New York. Post Office Money Order or Registered Letter.

The address label indicates the date when subscription expires and is our only receipt therefore.

REGISTERED CABLE ADDRESS:

Florex, New York.

Society of American Florists and Ornamental Horticulturists.

Department of Plant Registration.

The E. G. Hill Company, Richmond, Ind., submit for registration Hydrangea arborescens alba grandiflora (the snowball hydrangea). An American shrub of exquisite beauty and perfect hardiness; leaf broadly ovate and pointed; blooming time, last week in June, and lasting on into August. The form of the bloom resembles that of hortensia, of fine size, borne in great profusion and continuously, and of the greatest purity of color. The plant attains a height of 4 feet, and specimens 4 feet in diameter have been noted.

WM. J. STEWART,
Secretary.

Floral Decorations in Parks and City or Village Squares.

The American Association of Park Superintendents has issued its first printed bulletin (June, 1906), which is devoted to the subject forming the heading of this note. Heretofore the very practical and serviceable discussions of the park men were distributed through the medium of mimeographed sheets. The printed bulletin is a great improvement on the former method.

We hope these bulletins will have a wide circulation because they contain the views of the leading men engaged in that particular branch of horticulture on the topics on which the pamphlets treat.

Florists throughout the country will no doubt appreciate the fact that the park men have been devoting their attention to the subject of flower beds in the public breathing spots. The object lessons in planting presented there; the educational character of such planting and other merits associated with it stimulate the people with a desire to possess plants and flowers which, as a natural sequence, must result in the greater development of the florist business.

It is gratifying to observe that the majority of the park superintendents contributing to the bulletin under consideration favor flower gardens in parks, though condemning everything that savors of the fantastic or incongruous. They also, and rightly criticise unfavorably the poor taste at times shown in the planting. "There are still glaring errors perpetrated under the name of gardening," says Superintendent J. A. Pettigrew of Boston; "and, sad to say, parks are not free from them."

We congratulate the park superintendents on their enterprise in the issuance of printed bulletins. All former issues are to appear in the new form.

A TEMPERATURE CHART.—The Madison Cooper Company of Watertown, N. Y., sends us a specimen of its new temperature chart. To those who are interested in cold storage or the storage of perishable products this chart should be useful for reference. The price of the chart is 25c.

Proceeds of the Dayton Souvenir Book.

Editor Florists' Exchange:

It is true that I have taken charge of this book individually, because the club, through its president, did not wish to accept the responsibility. Mr. Shaw, through an assistant, is aiding me on the advertising, as I believe he has done on several souvenir books, for which he will receive an ordinary commission, but the net proceeds of the publication will be expended for such features of the Dayton meeting as will be approved of by the executive committee of the S. A. F. and the Dayton Florists' Club.

I trust that the Souvenir Book will be supported, for while I am not printing it for profit, I would not enjoy doing the work and losing money besides.

H. M. ALTICK,
Vice-President, S. A. F. O. H.

[The getting out of a convention souvenir book is, as we understand it, purely a matter that concerns the local organization entertaining the S. A. F. O. H., and one with which the executive committee of the latter body has nothing to do, so that it does not need to approve of the expenditure of the profits, if any, from the book. We believe the Dayton Florists' Club can easily attend to that; but we had been assured by its president that "nothing was coming" to the club from the publication of the souvenir.

We are glad to receive Mr. Altick's explanation, but it is unfortunate that the arrangements for this matter were not clearly understood between him and the local florists' club, before the communication of the latter appeared in all the trade papers. So, too, is it unfortunate that the stationery concerning the souvenir, so far as we have seen, gives no evidence of emanating from the Dayton Florists' Club. However, "all's well that ends well," and we hope the publication of the souvenir will result in a big profit, as it should do under the circumstances now disclosed.—Ed.]

Government Work for the Florist and Gardener.

In a paper relating to the Business of Seed and Plant Introduction, prepared by Professor A. J. Pieters, Botanist in Charge, and appearing in the Yearbook of the Department of Agriculture, just issued, he tells of the work doing by the Government on behalf of the florist and ornamental gardener. Among other things he says: "Attention is being given to the matter of growing flower and field seeds, the latter especially where a new crop is introduced, for which home-grown seed will be wanted.

"There has long been a more or less desultory interest in the culture of Dutch bulbs—tulips, narcissi, and hyacinths—in the United States. Good bulbs of these kinds have been grown at various times but never in commercial quantities. This Office has undertaken to help along this industry by furnishing good stock in some cases and testing such American-grown bulbs as could be obtained. During the Spring of 1905, blooms of Emperor narcissus from American-grown bulbs, forced in the Department of Agriculture greenhouses, graced the table of the President of the United States. An expert propagator has been twice sent to the bulb growers to assist them with advice as to methods and to see what was being done. Besides this help given to those interested in bulb culture, a trial ground for bulbs has been maintained on the Potomac Flats, near Washington, so that the chief varieties could be compared and the questions of fertilizers, harvesting, and handling under conditions prevailing on the Atlantic coast could be studied. Here many thousands of bulbs are planted, the stocks of the leading Dutch dealers being compared as to quality.

"Special attention has also been given to the production of the Easter lily in the United States. The bulbs of this lily, so important to the florist, are now imported and a large percentage is usually diseased. If a place can be found in the United States where healthy stock can be grown and put on the market as early as the bulbs are now received from Bermuda, we shall solve a problem that will be worth much to the commercial florist. Substantial progress has already been made, full reports of which will be made public in due time. This is only mentioned here as one of the lines of work in which this Office is engaged."

Growing American Beauty Roses in Cuba.

Can the American Beauty rose be raised in Cuba and made a commercial success? That is the novel and interesting project Juan M. Ceballos, of Bay Shore and Manhattan, is experimenting upon. He has had shipped from his Cuban estates a quantity of Cuban soil. It has already reached this country and gone to the biggest growest of the American Beauty in the Union, a firm of rose men up the Hudson. They will test this soil and report to Mr. Ceballos upon its qualities.

Horticulturists who have heard of the plan predict that it will probably not succeed. Cuban grown American Beauties at the best, they say, would have to be grown under glass, and grown under glass there would be no advantage in raising them in Cuba, rather a disadvantage if they had to make the long sea voyage to America. It is not at all certain, they say beside, that the American Beauty would grow even under glass in Cuban soil. They call the experiment very problematical.

Experimenting with this soil, it is understood, will go on this Summer and Fall. A big new Cuban product may possibly come out of this. —Brooklyn Eagle.

BOOKS RECEIVED.

ENTOMOLOGY, WITH SPECIAL REFERENCE TO ITS BIOLOGICAL AND ECONOMIC ASPECTS. By Dr. Justus Watson Folsom, Instructor of Entomology at the University of Illinois. Publishers, P. Blakiston's Son & Company, Philadelphia, Pa. Price, $3, net.

To the lover of outdoor life there is probably no more fascinating study than that connected with insects. It was Jefferies who said: "The fields are but large open spaces after a time to many, unless they know a little of insects, when at once they become populous, and there is a link found between the birds and the flowers. It is like opening another book of endless pages, and colored illustrations on every page."

This is from the standpoint of the layman. On the other hand, the husbandman counts many of these creations among his most relentless foes; but still finds a study of their anatomy and habits essential in order to successfully combat the pests.

While the work before us has been written with the aim of giving a comprehensive and concise account of insects designed more especially for the use of students, yet it will be found of the greatest service and interest to the general reader.

It is a well printed volume of 485 pages, and is profusely illustrated, there being five plates, one of which is in color, showing protective mimicry among butterflies, and 300 other illustrations.

Probably the chapter of greatest direct interest to our readers is that which treats upon Insects in Relation to Plants. No other animals sustain such intimate and complex relations to plants as insects do, and the more luxuriant and varied the flora, the more abundant and diversified is its insect fauna. Dr. Folsom says the number of insects supported by one kind of plant is seldom small and often surprisingly large. The poison ivy (Rhus toxicodendron) is almost exempt from attacks, though even this plant is eaten by a leaf-mining caterpillar, two pyralid larvæ and the larva of a scolytid beetle. Horse-chestnut and buckeye have perhaps a dozen species at most; elm has eighty; birches have over one hundred; and so have maples; pines are known to harbor 170 species and may yield as many more; while our oaks sustain certainly 500 species of insects and probably twice as many.

Turning to cultivated plants, the clover is affected, directly or indirectly, by about 200 species, including predaceous insects, parasites, and flower-visitors. Clover grows so vigorously that it is able to withstand a great deal of injury from insects. Corn is attacked by about 200 species, of which 50 do notable injury and some 20 are pests. Apple insects number some 400 species. Not uncommonly an insect is restricted to a single species of plant. As regards number of food plants, the gypsy moth "holds the record," for its caterpillar will eat almost any plant. In Massachusetts, according to Forbush and Fernald, it fed in the field upon 78 species of plants, in captivity upon 458 species (20 under stress of hunger, the rest freely) and refused only 19 species, most of which (such as larkspur and red pepper) had poisonous or pungent juices, or were otherwise unsuitable as food. The migratory locust is notoriously omnivorous, and perhaps eats more kinds of plants than the gypsy moth.

No attempt has been made by the author to provide remedies for the different insect pests, though the various known parasites and bird enemies are enumerated. But a comprehensive and concise account of the work done by entomologists in different States, as well as by the State Experiment Stations, the United States Department of Agriculture and other institutions puts the reader in touch with the best available information on the subject of combating insect ravages. Then there is given an extensive and select list of works treating on entomological subjects, the literature on which now numbers scarcely less than 100,000 titles. A very complete index adds to the value of a very valuable, interesting and instructive work. Copies of the book can be secured through this office.

A Deluded Publisher.

Editor Florists' Exchange:

"The Boston paper wrote me yesterday to tak[e] my big advertisement out of your paper and giv[e] it to them. They promised me twice as good re-sults as from your paper. I refused.

"Pennsylvania. — —."

[A wise decision, indeed; and as you have had [a] taste of what the "Boston paper" actually can do fo[r] you in the way of bringing results from advertisin[g] in its columns, the stand you take is no doubt [a] most natural one. We hardly think that even th[e] party who made the statement you quote could him-self be cajoled into believing it. It looks to us lik[e] an attempt at a warm weather joke. We would [in] all kindness submit for the calm consideration [of] our esteemed but deluded contemporary, the sayin[g] of the late lamented Josh Billings: "It is better [to] kno less than so much that ain't so." Ed. F. E.]

The Revue de L'Horticulture Belge et Etranger for July, contains a colored plate of the Lobel[ia] Kathleen Mallard. A writer in the same journ[al] says this surpasses all the known varieties of lobeli[a]. Sander & Sons, St. Alban's, England, exhibited it [at] a recent meeting of the Royal Horticultural Socie[ty] where it was awarded a certificate of merit.

We are in receipt of an interesting illustrat[ed] pamphlet telling of the attractions of the conve[n]tion city, Dayton, O., and describing briefly the lan[d]scape gardening work of the National Cash Regist[er] Company.

OUR READERS' VIEWS

[Wholesome discussions on subjects that interest. Contributions to this column are always welcome.—Ed.]

Window Tile Boxes.

Editor Florists' Exchange:

Referring to the matter of tile window boxes, mentioned in your Question Box, we give the name of the manufacturers herewith—The United Mitch Co., Ltd., 151-157 High Street, Waltham, Mass.

VALENTIN BURGEVIN'S SONS.

[Thank you. Ed.]

Concerning Geraniums.

"What a great fire a little spark kindleth!"

Editor Florists' Exchange:

"Expertus" is down and out. He acknowledges the fact that he is a back number, admitting that he uses 30-year-old methods in growing geraniums. If he has any doubt about how far in the rear he is, a perusal of either the letter of Mr. Weepy or that of Mr. Eichholz will certainly convince him that he "ain't in it."

Who is "misleading" Young Beginner now? With the two beforementioned letters before him, he has no doubt come to the conclusion before this that the advice of "Expertus" is erroneous and "misleading" to a degree.

"Expertus" suggests that I should tender Young Beginner "better advice than was originally given." That is very easily done. I take it for granted that Young Beginner wants to start growing geraniums with up-to-date methods; I therefore advise him to use 50 plants as stock; those 50 plants, properly manipulated, as I said in a former letter, will give him considerably more than 4000 cuttings. Mr. Wiegand—that gentlemen out in the "wild and hairy," as the divine Sarah put it, please take notice.

Young Beginner can see by this time what a humbug it would be to use 500 plants as stock from which to raise 4,000 cuttings. Mr. Weepy explains in a very elaborate and comprehensive manner how he can get 3,500 cuttings from 50 plants; therefore, if Young Beginner uses Mr. Weepy's method, (which I don't approve) he would only need 60 plants for stock; and I am sure that if Mr. Weepy put the same energy into his propagating as he does into his figuring, he would, by using New York market methods, easily get the other 500 cuttings, that is, if he did not lose his temper when he reached 3,500. Anyway, Mr. Weepy is not the man to stick at a paltry 500 cuttings; he will "get there" without doubt, consequently he will not need that "sponge." Will he kindly pass it on to "Expertus," who no doubt by this time feels like throwing it sky high and retiring to his corner.

Mr. Eichholz records the fact that he got from 30 to 40 cuttings per plant "a few years ago" (no doubt he could do better now), which gives him from 1,500 to 2,000 cuttings per 50 plants. According to that, Young Beginner would need only 100 or at most 125 plants for stock, not 500. But Mr. Eichholz did not get half what he should have got; if, however, that gentlemen has occasion now, or at some future time, to raise geraniums in quantity he will undoubtedly adopt New York market methods with which he is probably conversant, seeing he asks for no information, like the "green experts."

However, Young Beginner will have to do something right away, and take somebody's advice at once. If he has been waiting for this controversy to be settled he may "get left," and have no geraniums at all next Spring. If he has not already done so, let him buy 50 good plants, which is unquestionably sufficient. He must see the utter futility of "Expertus's" advice, after reading the letters of Mr. Weepy and Mr. Eichholz. If he feels like spending the money, he can, of course, buy 60 plants which, according to Mr. Weepy's figures, would be all that is necessary. Even the amount of stock suggested by Mr. Eichholz (100 to 125) would be far more economical and far more business-like than 500!

Mr. Editor, with your permission I will change the subject and try to kill two birds with one stone. I see it recorded in The Florists' Exchange that Jersey bowlers took all the prizes worth having at the New York Florists' Club's outing. Such being the fact, and the convention so near, I would suggest that the New York Florists' Club bowling team might come over to Jersey and roll a few games, thus giving them the opportunity to get posted on the finer points of bowling. Flatbush, please take notice!

JOHN BIRNIE.

Editor Florists' Exchange:

The contention between John Birnie and Expertus about geraniums reminds me of the first week in June last, when we found we were short on geraniums, especially red, as there seems to be a fad for that color lately. We could have got the plants nearer home, but wanted especially at this time something up-to-date. We chose a New York house that we thought reliable, sent an express order for 500 nice, stocky, 3-inch plants in bloom or bud. To our great disappointment we got frail, long-jointed, drawn things, no good for our order. We saw the plants were no good for our present use, so we got some elsewhere near home. We potted up the foreign stock in 3-inch pots, gave them a good house and care; now for a week past they are about what we wanted then.

This confirms what Expertus says about New York grown geraniums. When we want geraniums again, we will not likely send to New York for them.

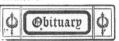

A CANADIAN.

The Holland Peony Society's List.

Editor Florists' Exchange:

Our attention has recently been called to the Holland list of peonies sent you by the Elm City Nursery Company; and of which you said it would be read with great interest by all peony growers. It assuredly gives a rather too long list of varieties, with descriptions whch are in some instances, to say the least, misleading. We see they have also dropped some of the finest old kinds. To name one only, Alex. Dumas; and we would like to ask for what reason, as this, with several others lacking, is among the best of any collection extant.

Unfortunately, a long list of names does not always contain a like number of varieties, but in many instances are merely repetitions, and some in question have many aliases.

Louis Van Houtte as given in the list should be Van Houtte, which is a good rose colored variety. Louis Van Houtte, however, is a dark purple, and is one of the very best of its color.

Prolifera tricolor is described incorrectly as being white. It, however, produces tri-colored-flowers,—hence its name, and is, we consider, a good variety.

Whitleyi (Queen Victoria) is given as soft rose, while The Florists' Exchange June 28 describes it as "pure white and one of the best for cutting," which we can affirm. We recently noticed a western grower quoting it as the "Drop White," of the Chicago market; and we note in several Holland catalogues, it is called a synonym of Festiva, to which we cannot agree. Anyway, it is one of the most useful of all the white peonies.

The Late Joseph J. Wood.

If the Holland growers will combine and give a list of procurable varieties true to name, with all the synonyms attached for each variety, then a right start will have been made; and also a list of growers who affirm the list and who will abide by the list, and not substitute other varieties. And we have no doubt but the entire stock of plants will then be worked off more easily than now. Then we will be getting out of the mist hitherto obscuring same.

President C. W. Ward of the American Peony Society in his annual address at Boston in June last made some interesting remarks about varieties and the way they are substituted, stating it to be impossible at times to get the kinds wanted. We in common with other purchasers have shared this, and the only way to do is to prove them before selling. Of course, this takes time, but it is time well spent. We have at times got the very opposite of what we ordered. For instance we ordered some Solfaterre (which name stands for yellow) and received an undesirable pink kind instead, while those who sent it took refuge in saying that there were two Solfaterres in Holland, the pink one being spelled with one letter less than the other. One may as well say that the name Snowball peony is applied to a pink as well as a white kind—preposterous on the face of it! We have also undesirable pink kinds sent us for Felix Crousse, etc. This way of doing business shows an amount of crass ignorance, or, an utter indifference to the wishes of the purchasers, whose interest they ought to seek before all others, and such business should be put an end to at once.

Two years ago, one of our wholesale customers wrote us asking if double peonies, P. tenuifolia fl. pl., could be furnished in pink, purple and white flowers. We replied no; there were no such kinds in existence, when he informed us that a large firm of American nurserymen had assured him that they could supply them. Comment on same is superfluous, but it shows the callousness of some to get trade.

JOHN CHARLTON & SONS.

Rochester, N. Y.

Obituary

Joseph J. Wood.

Joseph J. Wood, of Fishkill, N. Y., died at his home there on July 4. Mr. Wood was born in 1828, and had always been a resident of the neighborhood in which he died. For 18 years he had charge of the Rapalje estate, and in 1874 formed a partnership with J. Burrow to conduct a commercial florist business, under the title of Burrow & Wood. Later he and his brother bought out the interest of Mr. Burrow, and carried on the business under the firm name of I. C. Wood & Brother. The business grew and prospered, and in 1889 two sons of Mr. Wood took it over conducting it under the style of Wood Brothers, well known throughout the country as growers of miscellaneous florists' stock.

In 1855 the deceased married Rebecca J. Vernol, and last year they celebrated their golden wedding. He leaves a widow, one daughter, and four sons—Lewis E., Eugene V., Isaac J. and Howard E.

Mr. Wood was held in high esteem by all who knew him. He was a kind and devoted husband and father, and all his business dealings were characterized with the strictest integrity and honesty. The sympathy of the entire trade will go out to the stricken family, in this their first sad bereavement in fifty years.

Joseph Forsyth Johnson.

Joseph Forsyth Johnson, landscape gardener, died suddenly on Tuesday evening, July 17, at the Brooklyn Hospital in Raymond street, that city, whither he had been brought in a cab, in a dying state, by a friend. The coroner's inquest revealed that one of his lungs was completely gone, and that he was in a tubercular condition generally. He had been a sufferer from rheumatic trouble for some time. He was 67 years of age.

Mr. Johnson spent his childhood in the nurseries of his grandfather (John Forsyth), near Hull, England, and his apprenticeship with J. C. Niven, one of the foremost of English botanists and landscape artists. Mr. Johnson was in charge of the botanical garden, and originated the Whit-week Flower Shows at Manchester, in 1867. His management of the International Horticultural Exhibition, held in Belfast in 1874, was admitted by the English press to have been one of the highest artistic attainments. These exhibitions are laid out for landscape effect, and the effort led to his being given charge of the National Horticultural Exhibition for the Royal Horticultural Society of London, in 1878. He was elected on the jury of the International Exhibitions held at Paris, Brussels, Ghent, St. Petersburg and Amsterdam.

He was elected Curator of the Royal Botanical Gardens at Belfast, Ireland, in 1869, and was a director of the Alexandra Palace, London, in 1880. Numerous monuments to his skilled landscape work are scattered all over Great Britain.

The depression in land values and the closing of the Alexandra Palace induced him to come to America. His most notable work here was at Prospect Park, Brooklyn, where he advised the commissioners to thin out the trees, in order to obtain grand views of the land. His opinion was at that time treated with ridicule, but later his advice was put into practice. At Atlanta, Ga., he laid out the parks and exhibition grounds, the railroad gardens between Atlanta and Savannah, and carried successfully through numerous other important landscape works, in different parts of the country.

Mr. Johnson contributed a series of articles on landscape gardening, accompanied with plans, to American Gardening, which commanded wide attention. He was the author of a work on landscape gardening—Residential Sites and Environments—published by the A. T. De La Mare Printing and Publishing Co.

He was a charter member of the Epping Lodge, F. and A. M., London, England., and one of its first officers. Deceased was a member of the New York Florists' Club, and took a keen interest in all horticultural matters.

The funeral took place Wednesday, interment being in Evergreen Cemetery, Brooklyn, the services being in charge of the Masonic fraternity.

The Floral Committee of the Dutch Horticultural and Botanical Society at its June meeting awarded a certificate of merit to Pyrethrum roseum fl. pl as a new plant, exhibited by H. J. de Lang of Oegstgeest. The flowers are soft pale yellow, tinted salmon. Honorable mention was given to Pyrethrum roseum fl. pl., Fürst Bismarck, as a new plant shown by G. de Pree of Leyden. The flowers are rose colored, very double, and the plant a strong grower.

Some Tall Campanulas (Bell Flowers.)

How is it that we see so little of these very distinct and charming plants? Is it because they are cheap; or is it because they are not known?

Campanulas are as easily grown as chrysanthemums, cinerarias or geraniums if they receive proper care in the way of Winter protection, judicious watering and thorough drainage. Besides, the soil must be open, friable, and made moderately rich with decayed manure, and when growing rapidly the plants given manure water two or three times each week. A cold greenhouse, where the temperature can be controlled at between 35 and 45 degrees is a suitable place, or a frame with like provisions are ideal Winter quarters for campanulas. Light frost-proof cellars where potatoes will not freeze, may also be used for Winter storage. Avoid at all times during Winter water accumulating in the centers of the plants.

Propagating by division of the perennial species can be best done in early Spring. Many of these can also be raised from seed—which is to be recommended. Of course, this does not apply to many of the double flowering varieties which necessarily must be propagated by division or by cuttings. The biennial species are all raised from seed; and March is the best month of all to sow it, so as to raise strong plants before the next November.

The general Summer care should be similar to that given to stevias or carnations and perhaps the continuous growing in pots is to be recommended rather than planting in the open ground; 5 to 7-inch pots are convenient sizes to use for storing in. Early in March the plants should be shifted into larger pots, singly; or from 5 to 7, or 9 or more may be planted into shallow pots or tubs, the sizes of which shall be determined. In any event, the plants must be made as firm as possible and care must be taken to provide good drainage. A light cool house is best, where they are to be brought forward gently.

As soon as the flower spike begins to push, the plants may be exposed to a higher temperature when it is desired to have them earlier in bloom.

For all kinds of decorations, whether indoors or outdoors especially on verandahs, Summer porches, in hallways, campanulas are most suitable. After June 10 they are safe out of doors. Of course, those requiring supports by staking or otherwise must have the work neatly done, and at the proper time.

For the outdoor garden, these campanulas are unsurpassed. If after they have received the necessary protection during the Winter, hardened off in the Spring and planted in the open about the middle of May, in front of a wall or in the shelter of a shrubbery border, or in any place where they will not be thrashed by the wind, they will give as much pleasure as cannas, or gladioli, or dahlias. And remember, no other family can boast of such colors as these bellflowers. Some of the many dwarf campanulas are worthy of more attention than they now receive, and to which I may refer later. The following list contains distinct and easily obtained varieties, which are not at all miffy or particular, as some few kinds are:

Glomerata, a British species, bearing large clusters of single flowers on stems from 1 to 2½ feet high. The heads contain from 15 to 30 flowers each, according to the strength of the plants, which continue in flower for some time. The colors are bluish violet, with veined markings of white. It may be had in flower from May to September. There is a white variety and a double variety of this species, besides half a doze nother kinds, with variable purple flowers, the best of which are elliptica and nicaensis. These are best grown three or more plants in one pot or tub.

Grandis. This is a splendid species, introduced from Siberia in 1842. The flowers are very large, broad and saucer-shaped, arranged alternately on the stems, which are ffom 18 inches to three feet high. The color of the type is pale violet blue, but there are many shades, and also a pure white flowered variety. The leaves are long and lanceolate. A very distinct plant, flowering in June and July.

Cactiflora produces its flowers freely in rather loose heads, on numerous stems with from three to five flowers on each. The individual flowers are nearly upright. The colors are milky blue, tinged more or less with bright lavender. It flowers from June to September, and grows from two to six feet high. A charming plant.

Medium (Canterbury bells). It is impossible to praise this dear old plant sufficiently. And why one does not see thousands of it has been to me one source of regret. With so much effective and varied coloring, and architectural beauty, surely the time will arrive when it shall be as often seen as it deserves. It can be readily forced from April onward. Biennial, June and July.

M. calycantha and M. calycanthena are the most remarkable forms of medium, with their cup and saucer shaped flowers. No other species of plant is so diversified, while their colors are more extensive than the species proper. June and July.

Nobilis (species from China, 1844), characteristically distinct, with drooping scapes of crowded flowers; prevailing colors red, violet, or plum purple, blotched or spotted with cream color or white; foliage ample, ovate and toothed. End of June and July. Height, 2 to 3 feet.

Persicæfolia, a British species, one of the best known campanulas, owing to its adaptability for general purposes. The flowers are borne on terminal stalks, nearly always solitary, opening broadly, cup-shaped, the surfaces as if enameled. The species varies in color through blue and intermediate shades to pure white. There are also many varieties with double or semi-double flowers. The foliage is narrow and of bright, shining green. Flowers from June to September.

Pyramidalis—the chimney bellflower—is one of the oldest and most beautiful British species; it has been cultivated in gardens since 1596. When well grown and in flower, no plant is more effective. Specimens have been grown 6 feet high and 4 feet in diameter in large pots or tubs. Plants grown out of doors under favorable circumstances reach from 7 to 9 feet in height and 6 to 7 feet in diameter. The flowers are so numerous and so thickly arranged on the spikes as to present almost a solid mass from the time the plants begin to bloom in June till the beginning of September. There are many varieties, but none is more beautiful than the dark and light blue, and the pure white. One of the best of all garden plants.

Van Houttei is a hybrid introduced about the middle of the last century. The flowers are deep blue, pendulous and nearly 3 inches long, borne on the top of the spike. The lower ones are more round and open, nearly flat. There is yet another form of flowers intermediate between those described, which makes this one of the most interesting hybrids known. It flowers from June to August.

Another hybrid, Burghalti, has some of the characteristics of Van Houttei, and is also a distinct and valuable variety.

Versicolor (species from Greece, 1788) has flowers borne in long, spicate wreaths of various colors—from blue to white, arranged in somewhat rotate form, giving a very distinct expression. The lower leaves are heart-shaped, the upper ones more ovate. Height from 2 to 5 feet.

Vidalii, flowers freely in long racemes, wax-like in texture, pure white, disc broad, surrounded with a deep orange ring; leaves thick and fleshy, strap shaped and deeply toothed. A native of the Azores; introduced in 1851. It flowers in July, August and early September.

JOHN THORPE.

Field of Sweet Peas on Farm of John Bodger & Sons, Gardena, Cal.

(See page 31, issue of July 14, 1906).

Handling Cut Flowers.

(Paper read by J. H. Bath, Omaha, Neb., before the Nebraska State Horticultural Society.)

From a commercial viewpoint I think that growers, generally, give too little attention as to how their stock is handled after it is cut. Of first importance is to have the stock sorted and put in water as soon as possible, after being cut. I find it a good idea to have vessels of water in the greenhouses, conveniently situated, wherein the blooms may be placed awaiting their removal to the sorting room, and, if the cut is large, the petals are not soft when being sorted, thereby preventing a great deal of bruising they usually otherwise sustain.

After sorting, the long and short stemmed stock should be placed in separate jars of proper depths to keep them together and straight, and on hardening weak stems will be found to have straightened considerably.

Flowers kept in the cellar over night should always have their stems cut afresh, and the water refreshed if it is desired to hold them longer. The temperature of the cellar or ice chest should be from 45 to 50 degrees Fahrenheit all the year around.

Too much care cannot be used in packing flowers, whether the distance be one mile or one hundred. The damage comes not from the jar of wagons or cars, but the blooms bruise each other. Wax or manilla tissue paper or cotton cloth chould be placed between the layers. Always have a cushion of paper or air space at the head of the box when packing, because a very slight jar in a forward direction is sure to bruise the flowers badly.

I do not believe greenhouse employes receive enough instruction on the handling of cut flowers. They are almost invariably rough with them. The blooms can be handled rapidly and gently. I personally have seen a number of expert rose growers who treated the flowers after they were cut, in a most shameful manner, such as squeezing long and short together, or laying them down hard, almost dropping them, on the table. This probably is the result of mere thoughtlessness; but it takes no more time to handle them properly.

I believe that as many of the flowers as will permit should be broken off instead of cut with a knife, because more of the pore surface is brought in direct contact with the water in this manner. This applies particularly to chrysanthemums, lilacs, heavy-stemmed roses, and others having heavy stems.

On receipt of stock at the store, the flowers should always be gone over, the stems freshly clipped and bruised petals and deformed foliage removed. If they have been shipped from a distance, they should not be used until they have been chilled a second time.

In these days of fancy carnations we are troubled at times with many split calyces. This can be remedied, if carefully done, with a needle and thread, or with stemming wire, sewing the parted calyx together.

Too many flowers are usually placed in one vase. Put them in several vases, the flowers won't wilt, as otherwise; the foliage is not destroyed, and you have, apparently, a larger stock and an infinitely more artistic display for your customers' inspection.

As to preservatives, many have suggested the use of patented stuff, chloride of sodium, bicarbonate of soda, and even a rank poison, nux vomica, but I believe nature intended cool, clear water, and plenty of it, as the preservative par excellence, of cut flowers.

Flowers grown in a greenhouse should never be offered for sale until they have stood in water and have been kept in cellar or ice chest at a temperature of 50° for at least twelve hours, and twenty-four is better. This allows the stems to become filled with water, for the pith acts much as a sponge. Then, and not until then, will the cut flowers keep, and be satisfactory to the buyer.

Fresh air is as important as fresh water; for instance, at this time carnations will keep but one day at the store, and should I take some of the same lot to my home, where the air circulation is good, they will keep three to four days longer.

A draught will wilt a rose badly, and scarcely injure a carnation, so it is best to avoid draughts.

In conclusion I would say that common sense, coupled with an observing eye, should govern the care of cut flowers.

CLUB AND SOCIETY DOINGS.

Society for Horticultural Science.

(Summary of papers read at the Cornell Meeting, June 27-28.)

President L. H. Bailey's address was on "The Field for Experiment in Horticulture." Professor John Craig presented a paper on "Plant Growing by Artificial Light." Prof. Lazenby spoke on "Plant Growing under Different Colored Cloths." Unfortunately these papers have not yet come into the reviewer's hands, hence abstracts of them can not be given at this time.

W. T. Macoun spoke on "The Relation of Winter Apples to Hardiness of Trees." To withstand a test Winter at Ottawa, a tree or shrub must ripen its wood early. Winter-killing is liable to be more severe after a season when the growth has been strong than when it has been short. The more moderate the climate where a variety originates, the less resistant is it to Winter-killing. The hardiest two varieties of apples are those that have originated in Russia and are Summer or Autumn varieties. This is because these ripen their wood most thoroughly, whereas Winter varieties continue growth later in the season. Unless the fruit of a variety reaches a certain, but as yet undertermined, stage of development every season a certain time before it has to be picked, owing to danger from frost, that variety is not a safe one to plant. The basis for the production of the desired Winter apple for the north should be a variety which has withstood test Winters in a similar climate and is also the latest keeper of such varieties.

Professor William Stuart presented a general discussion of the use of anesthetics on the forcing of plants and summarized his own experiments with rhubarb. The experience of a number of investigators indicates that some plants will stand larger doses of anesthetics than others. As a rule these doses vary from 7 to 15 c. c. per cubic foot of air space. The time of treatment varies with the season of the year, the class of plants and the temperature at time of treatment. As a rule this variation is from 24 to 72 hours. Etherization of rhubarb plants for Winter forcing results in an increased yield. Freezing, at least early in the season, is a necessary process. Etherization does not seem to perform the same function as freezing. Actual freezing for late forcing may not be necessary.

In a paper on Pollination Methods, Prof. S. W. Fletcher presented a symposium of his own experience and that of a considerable number of other plant breeders. The ideal time to emasculate blossoms is as late as possible before the anthers dehisce, but may be done when the buds are still quite small. If complete accuracy is not essential and when working on blossoms that do not mature stamens and pistils simultaneously, the blossoms need not be emasculated. In crossing, select mature trees of moderate growth and perfectly sound. On such trees select buds borne high up on the outside of the tree on well nourished branches on the side of the tree opposite from the direction of severe prevailing winds. As to the instruments for emasculating in the majority of cases a small scalpel is to be preferred, specially for the stone and pome fruits. As to the location of the cut, the majority opinion is that it should be made at the insertion of the stamens above the nectary, though the author himself prefers to make it as high up as possible. The safest time to pollinate is near the beginning of the receptive condition of the pistils or perhaps twenty-four hours before. A receptive stigma usually glistens when it catches the sunlight and in most fruits it is beginning to be slightly brownish. Brush pollinating is often most practicable when many blossoms must be pollinated in a short time. For our common trees, however, some workers use the thumb or forefinger. As to the percentage of successes, seven pollinators of experience placed their averages variously at from 50 per cent. down.

Some phases of Pollination were presented by Prof. N. O. Booth. The period during which fresh pollen is available for study may be lengthened by forcing twigs in the laboratory. If pollen is taken from the orchard at the normal blooming season it is advisable to take twigs with still unopened buds and let them open indoors. This assures freedom from foreign pollen. Pollen of the same variety differs greatly in germination when trees are grown under different conditions. Determination of the percentage of the germinating pollen is an index to the capacity of such trees for self-pollination in such localities and hence for planting in solid blocks. Very few apple varieties have the pollen all good and none so far all bad, most varieties showing different proportions of mixed forms. Pollen from the same tree may differ with the condition of the tree. Tompkins King and Esopus Spitzenburg among others have notably weak pollen and are successfully raised only in neighborhoods where conditions are favorable for pollen production. Varieties with particularly strong pollen, as Jonathan and Ralls, are of wide adaptation and are often liable to overbear, the fruits being consequently under size.

Professor Fred. W. Card presented a symposium of experience as to the advantages of double-working apples on vigorous stocks. The value of top-working to increase hardiness of stock in a trying the South. Weak growing varieties are benefited by the practice. Early bearing can be promoted by climate is unquestioned. It markedly reduces injury from certain diseases. Northern Spy especially promises to reduce injury from the wooly aphis in top-working on a weak stock although at the expense of productiveness and doubtless of longevity. But for ordinary varieties in favorable regions the advantages of top-working are outweighed by the disadvantages.

Earle J. Owen discussed the importance of Selection in Plant Breeding, citing several striking examples of its application.

Professor L. C. Corbett raised the query, What is to be the future application of the term horticulture? To the already recognized subdivisions of horticultural interests in America, namely: olericulture, pomology, floriculture and landscape gardening, the author would add plant breeding and plant propagation. Under the latter head is comprised nursery work and the increasing of annual plants from seed or from herbaceous cuttings.

H. J. Eustace gave an account of investigations on apples decaying in commercial cold storage. Several varieties of apples were inoculated with black rot, brown rot, bitter rot, soft rot or blue rot and a species of alternaria and at once put in a cold storage under standard temperature conditions, that is, where the temperature was held constantly at 30 to 32 degrees F. At the end of two months none of these diseases had developed except the soft or blue rot. Later when the inoculated fruit was taken out of storage the other diseases also developed, showing that the low temperature of the cold storage simply retarded the fungi in their development but did not destroy them. In another experiment where the temperature ranged from 37 to 56 degrees, decays developed slowly except the soft rot; but when the temperature ranged from 54 to 65½ degrees all decays developed and in most cases very rapidly. Peaches similarly inoculated and held in cold storage two weeks had developed decays in about one-half of the specimens.

H. P. Gould described the recording of phenological data for pomological uses as has been carried on by the U. S. Department of Agriculture for several years past. The blanks used by the department collecting data were exhibited and described.

V. A. CLARK,
Secretary.

TARRYTOWN, (N. Y.) HORTICULTURAL SOCIETY.—The schedule of prizes for the eighth annual exhibition of this society has been issued. The show will be held in Music Hall from October 31 to November 1, inclusive. E. W. Neubrand is secretary, and James W. Smith manager. In addition to the regular premiums a number of special prizes are offered. The society's silver medal will be awarded for the best new decorative plant not now in commerce. Among trade firms donating special prizes we note the following: F. R. Pierson, Pierson U-Bar Company, Vaughan's Seed Store, Julius Roehrs Company, Henry A. Dreer, Arthur T. Boddington, Peter Henderson & Company, who offer a prize of $10 for the best essay on growing vegetables in the garden; and William F. McCord.

Scales of points for judging are included in the schedule, and are those of the national societies devoted to special flowers. The following is the scale for judging vegetables: Arrangement, 20 points; size, 10, form, 15; market value, 20; table qualities, 15; cleanness of growth, 20.

THE SOUTHERN CALIFORNIA HORTICULTURAL SOCIETY met in Symphony Hall, Saturday evening July 7. There were fifty people present to listen to a lecture, illustrated by stereopticon, given by Charles D. Willard, secretary of the Municipal League, on the subject, "New Civic Ideals." Howard & Smith had a fine display of tuberous begonias in 4-inch pots, and cut blooms of perennial phlox. This beautiful flower is not as extensively grown on this coast as it should be. The city parks had a fine lot of cut flowers among them a branch of a South African shrub known by the name of Dios cottonifolia. The beautiful pink flowers are borne in tufts on the ends of the branches. Theodore Payne was present with a fine collection of our native wild flowers. He was for years connected with The Germain Seed Company, and is now in business for himself at 327 South Main street, Los Angeles. He makes a specialty of native flower seeds, bulbs and plants, and is trying to educate Californians to appreciate and grow such plants indigenous to the State as are attractive either in foliage or flower. When this object shall have been accomplished our flower gardens and our streets will be more beautiful than they are at present, and that, too, with much less care and water than are necessary under our present system of planting.

There is a native horse chestnut, with pure white spikes of bloom, four inches in diameter, eighteen inches long, that would make a fine street tree, suitable to our dry atmosphere, yet I have never seen one in cultivation. A native maple, with dense foliage of a beautiful bronze color, is not found in cultivation outside of our parks, and there only in small numbers. Here as in the East native plants, no matter how beautiful they may be, are passed by by our growers for the products of far away lands, to the detriment of landscape work whether it be large or small.

P. D. BARNHART.

THE CHICAGO FLORISTS' CLUB met in Handel Hall, Thursday evening, July 12, with but a small attendance. In the absence of the president and vice-president, J. C. Vaughan occupied the chair. David Erickson was admitted to membership, and two applications were placed on file for action at the next meeting.

Mr. Vaughan, as chairman of the transportation committee in connection with the S. A. F. O. H. Convention, reported that the Central Traffic Association had granted a round trip fare from all sections to Dayton at a one and a third rate; with a further concession that the tickets were available for returning for one week after the close of the convention. This latter point was granted in the hope and the natural supposition that many of the delegates from the East would wish to extend their journey a few days, while many from the West would desire to spend a week in the eastern section. It is hoped that a still further reduction may be made to a one fare for the round trip; full particulars, however, will later be supplied through the trade papers and by committees.

The club voted to entertain the visitors who after enjoying the convention may desire to look a little into the magnitude of the cut flower business of the Central West by spending a few days in Chicago, and arrangements were placed on foot which will make the stay of visitors here a pleasant one.

Field of Sweet Peas on Farm of John Bodger & Sons, Gardena, Cal.

A list of the subscribers to the recent Florists' Club picnic was read by the secretary, and it was shown by the committee that a balance of $30 remained in the treasury, proving the event to have been a financial as well as social success.

The thanks of the club were extended to the subscribers, to Mr. Higinbotham, Mr. Hartshorne and the employes of the Chicago Carnation Company, who contributed to the pleasure of the club members and their friends on the occasion of their recent outing at Joliet, and to the Entertainment Committee of the club through whose endeavors one of the most pleasant and successful outings ever enjoyed was accomplished.

H. E. Philpott, of Winnipeg, entertained the meeting with a short talk of the progress of horticulture in Manitoba, which he stated was proportionally as great as in Chicago.

W. K. WOOD.

ST. LOUIS FLORISTS' CLUB.—The club held its regular July meeting last Thursday afternoon at the home of President Ammann in Edwardsville, Ill. The members, most of them accompanied by their wives and daughters, met at the bridge at 12.30, at starting time. The count was 42. Good connections were made, and the party arrived at Edwardsville at 2 o'clock. We were met at the station by President Ammann, wife and daughters, and escorted to their home a block away. An inspection tour was made through the big range of houses. After that we were invited into the cooling room to refresh the inner man. A field of carnation plants was then looked at; nearly 75,000 plants were seen, and voted very fine. The party then proceeded to the fair grounds, four blocks away, where the meeting was held, the ladies attending in a body. The meeting opened at 3 o'clock with President Ammann in the chair, and all the other officers present. Fred Meinhardt, who has charge of the transportation to Dayton, reported that the tround trip would cost $12.00—$9.00 going and $3 returning. The question of railroad will be left to the members who are to make the trip. Fred hopes for a large delegation, and those who contemplate going should send in their names to him at once.

The trustees reported that all arrangements were completed for the picnic which will be held at Ramona Park on Thursday, July 26. They were allowed $50; this, with the subscriptions, brings up the amount to over $100. A fine program of games has been arranged, including a baseball game and a badger fight.

Resolutions on the death of Wm. Schray were presented by the committee, and adopted.

The nomination of officers then took place. Frank Fillmore, E. W. Guy and Professor H. C. Irish were nominated for president; for vice-president, F. H. Weber, John Connon, and G. Augermuller, were the nominees. For secretary, Emil Schray and J. J. Beneke. Henry Lohrens, Chas. H. Jungel, A. G. Bentzen and R. Windt were placed in nomination for the office of treasurer. For one trustee to serve three years the nominees were: Wm. Winter, A. G. Fehr, C. A. Kuehn and R. J. Scott. Frank Fillmore led a discussion on "Growing Carnations in Pots."

A vote of thanks was tendered President Ammann for the entertainment. The secretary announced that the discussions for the August meeting would be by C. C. Sanders on "Growing Nursery Stock," and by A. Jablonsky on "Growing Begonia Gloire de Lorraine." These with the election of officers should make the next meeting a big attraction. The meeting then adjourned until August 9. After the adjournment refreshments were served. The July meeting will be long remembered as one of those good old-time outdoor gatherings. As one member remarked "the stay-at-homes again missed a rare treat."

ST. PATRICK.

NASSAU COUNTY HORTICULTURAL SOCIETY.—The July regular monthly meeting was held at the usual place on the evening of the 11th inst. The attendance was large, with President Harrison in the chair. There was one nomination to active membership. The prize for the best exhibit of sweet peas, three varieties, twenty-five of each, was awarded to John F. Johnston. In the competition for points, S. J. Trepass scored 92 1-3 with peaches, melons, and Nephrolepis Whitmanii; A. MacKenzie, 90 2-3 with adiantum, caladium and peaches; Felix Mense, 81 2-3 with hollyhocks, roses and stocks. H. F. Meyer made an exhibit of outdoor grown vegetables and fruits, including lima beans, tomatoes, sweet corn, cucumbers, peppers, and blackberries, and received special mention from the judges. A silver match safe will be given at next meeting for the best exhibit of six varieties of vegetables.

W. Willesen tendered his resignation as a member of the executive committee and F. Boulon, Sea Cliff was appointed to fill the vacancy.

J. F. J.

ELBERON (N. J.) HORTICULTURAL SOCIETY.—The first annual exhibition of this young progressive society was held last week, and was a pronounced success. Of the fifty-three classes in the premium list, all were filled with the exception of six. In addition there were several special classes, the exhibitors receiving a certificate of merit for their displays. The judges of the show were: Alexander MacKenzie of Glen Cove, L. I.; H. A. Kettel of Oceanic, and John Frankie, of Tuxedo Park. The competition was mostly among the local gardeners. Bobbink & Atkins, Rutherford, N. J. made an interesting display of hardy flowers.

Visiting horticulturists at the show included a delegation from the Monmouth County Horticultural Society, C. E. Ross, of F. R. Pierson Company, of Tarrytown, N. Y.; Harry Bunyard, of A. T. Boddington, New York, and John O'Dell, Rutherford, N. J.

The society was organized last November. At present it has seventy members living in Long Branch, Deal and Allenhurst. The present officers of the society to whom credit is due for the first flower show are:

President, William D. Robertson, vice-president; Herbert Hall, secretary, George Masson; treasurer, James Kennedy; executive committee, A. Bauer, H. Wood, A. Grieb, E. O'Rourke, Frederick Dettlinger and J. Ralliston.

Exhibition committee—James Kennedy, W. D. Robertson and Henry Postel.

Canadian Horticultural Association.

The ninth annual convention and exhibition of this association will be held on August 29 and 30, 1906, at Guelph, Ont.

Transportation.

The convention this year being held during the first week of the Toronto Industrial Exhibition the "certificate plan" will not be made use of. Members living at a distance will find it to their advantage to avail themselves of the low rates to Toronto at that time and procure an ordinary return ticket at Toronto for Guelph. It will be advisable, however, for each one to study the question of rates from his own locality in order to reach the destination at lowest cost.

GUELPH HOTELS.

Wellington	$2.00 per day.
King Edward	$1.00 to $2.50 per day.
Royal	$1.50 per day.
Commercial, Western and others	$1.00 per day.

The sessions will be held in the Gymnasium Hall of the Ontario Agricultural College, and the following program has been prepared:

At the opening session at 2 p. m., Wednesday, August 29, an address of welcome will be delivered by G. C. Creelman, Esq., president of the college. President Fendley will read his address and the officers' reports will be presented;

At the evening session 7.30 o'clock, Wednesday, the following papers will be read and discussed: "Fertilizers, their Nature and Use" by Professor R. Harcourt, O. A. C., Guelph, "Commercial Carnations" by J. Morgan, Hamilton.

The program for the second day, Thursday, August 30, is as follows: At the morning session opening at 10 o'clock, these papers will be read:

"A Review of Roses to present date and their special requirements" by J. H. Dunlop, Toronto.

"Greenhouse Insect Pests" Illustrated with natural and preserved specimens of plants and insects, by Professor Tennyson D. Jarvis, Entomologist, O. A. C.

Question Box.—"What is the best system of heating a 150 by 21 Greenhouse?"

Thursday afternoon, 2 o'clock—Address by Rev. P. C. L. Harris, President Guelph Horticultural Society.

Essay on "Conifers" by Geo. Vair, Normal School Gardens, Toronto.

3.30 p. m.—Tour of College Departmental Buildings and Grounds.

5.30 p. m.—"At Home" Members and friends of Canadian Horticultural Association and Executive of the Guelph Horticultural Society.

Thursday, August 30, 1906, fourth session 7 p. m. —Essay on "Business Pointers for the Retail Trade" by W. C. Hall, (of Messrs. Hall and Robinson,) Outremont, Que.

Copies of the program can be obtained from Secretary A. H. Ewing, Woodstock, Ont.

Hydrangea Arborescens Alba Grandiflora—The "Snowball Hydrangea."

Editor Florists' Exchange:

Some time ago we noted a paragraph in your paper headed "The Snowball Hydrangea," and since seeing the plant we can realize how this grand shrub has almost named itself by its points of resemblance in bloom to the flower of a fine viburnum, but there the similarity ceases, for this American hydrangea has a beauty of stem and habit, an elegance of foliage, not found in many of our garden shrubs. This added to the large size of its pure white panicles, its likeness in form to H. Hrtensia, its freedom both of growth and bloom, and its long flowering season—beginning in June and lasting well into August—mark it as of almost sensational value both to the florist and the amateur, for it adds beauty to the garden when the earlier shrubs have all passed.

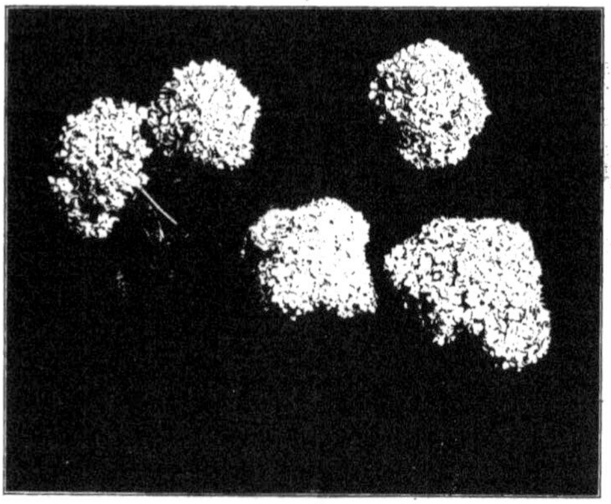

Hydraugea Arborescens Alba Grandiflora—The Snowball Hydrangea.

To the florist its value can be guessed, coming just when large, showy white flowers are the scarcest, and its refined beauty and fine keeping qualities make it fit for many uses. In the greenhouses, in early Spring, the young stock being grown on for planting out, furnishes quantities of small panicles that work up nicely in designs. The larger plants have as yet not been tried indoors, but out of doors in two to three years they attain a height of four feet and about the same breadth.

The stock held in this section of the country originated from a plant found growing wild in the woods of Ohio.

A hardy shrub, of perfect beauty, lasting over two months in continuous bloom, and pure white in color, will certainly find a warm welcome.

The name at the head of this paragraph has been forwarded for registry.

S. A. HILL.

Richmond, Ind.

New York.

The Week's News.

The transportation committee of the Florists' Club are perfecting arrangements with the New York Central railroad for the conveyance of the delegates who will attend the S. A. F. O. H. convention at Dayton, O., August 21-24, and a circular containing full information will be distributed in the near future. It is arranged that delegates wishing to stop over at Niagara Falls on the return journey will have that privilege, at no additional charge. The fare for the round trip is $22.67.

It would seem from present indications that this city will make no special efforts to have a representative bowling team in the annual tournament of the S. A. F. O. H. If other cities paid as little attention to bowling matters at the convention, as does New York, it would soon become apparent to those at the head of affairs that a bowling tournament was not an absolute necessity at these annual gatherings, and that the time devoted to that sport could perhaps be used to better purpose.

Wm. Scott, who has been superintendent at the Eastman Estate, Tarrytown, N. Y. and James T. Scott, who for the last two and one half years has been with the F. R. Pierson Company, Tarrytown, N. Y., have entered the commercial greenhouse and nursery business under the title of Elmsford Nurseries, Scott Brothers, proprietors, at Elmsford, N. Y. In their announcement, Scott Brothers state that their nurseries cover 30 acres of land and that a modern range of greenhouses is in course of construction. Their specialties will be grafted roses, up-to-date carnations, gardenias and foliage plants. Wm. Scott will devote his time to the growing department, and James T. Scott will have charge of the landscape and sales departments. For the present, and until their buildings are completed, which will be about October 1, their address is Scott Brothers, 42 Orchard street, Tarrytown, N. Y.

L. Kratz, florist at Montclair, N. J., has gone out of business, and A. D. Rose has purchased all the glass contained in his greenhouses.

Harry A. Bunyard has been appointed traveling representative of the S. A. F. O. H. by President W. F. Kasting.

Louis Schmutz has sailed for Europe on a pleasure trip; and Phil. Kessler leaves early next month on a similar errand.

J. B. Heiss, of Dayton, O., has been spending several days in the city looking up trade exhibits for the convention hall. He is using every effort to make the gathering in Dayton next month a success; and so far as we can learn he secured many orders for space during his stay here.

Mr. Heiss states that the entertainment features of the convention will be unsurpassed. To witness the electric illumination of Far Hills will itself be worth the journey. Then there are the buildings and grounds of the National Cash Register Company and an inspection of the company's plant which are all interesting and instructive. Concessions have been granted to caterers who will be present on the Fair Grounds, so that the delegates will experience no inconvenience in the way of securing meals nearby. This will also prove a benefit to exhibitors as it will tend to keep the conventionists on the grounds. The outdoor display has been somewhat disappointing, so far as outside firms are concerned; but the local men leapt into the breach, and now the surroundings of the convention hall are fairly attractive. A very large attendance is expected, and Mr. Heiss feels certain that everyone who makes the trip, will be amply repaid and be glad that he went to Dayton.

J. E. Hoffmire sailed for Europe on Thursday, July 19, on a business trip for McHutchison & Company, importers.

C. W. Ward is enjoying a vacation in the hills of New Hampshire.

Frank McMahon is on an automobile tour to the White Mountains.

James McManus left for Denver, Col., last Saturday for a short vacation.

Miss Smedley, bookkeeper for J. K. Allen, is back from a fortnight's vacation spent in the mountains.

A. H. Langjahr is taking a short respite from his business, at Asbury Park, N. J.

G. F. Neipp, Aqueduct, L. I., has sold his property to the Brooklyn Water Department, and will vacate within the next few months. Mr. Neipp will secure another location, and continue in the growing business on a larger scale. Although the sale of his property has been an advantageous one, Mr. Neipp feels too young to retire from business permanently.

The will of the late Ferdinand Boulon, Sea Cliff, has been admitted to probate. His estate is estimated to be worth about $50,000.

Philadelphia.

The Week's News.

The retail stores are doing a very good transient trade for Summer, and there is still a fair amount of shipping going on at the wholesale houses. Carnations are very scarce in this market; there are comparatively very few outdoor grown carnations no wcoming to this city.

John Westcott had the following party down at Waretown on Saturday and Sunday last: John Burton, George Craig, Robert Kift, William Graham and George M. Bainbridge.

J. Liddon, Pennock won a yacht race at Ocean City on Saturday last. The course was 12 miles. There were many yachts in the contest.

Victor Groshens, manager of the Hugh Graham Company nurseries at Logan, sailed on Saturday by the Red Star line for Antwerp. A. Leuthy of Boston went with him. These two gentlemen worked together years ago at Wills' near London.

Paul R. Klingsporn, lately with Dumont & Company, has bought the fixtures, etc., of the Charles P. Poryzees store on Fifteenth street above Chestnut. He opened the store on Tuesday as the Rosary Flower Shop.

A. B. Cartledge is cruising in Chesapeake Bay this week in his motor yacht.

W. R. Gibson, now of Savannah, Ga., is spending his vacation around this city.

At the Pennsylvania Horticultural Society's meeting on Tuesday prizes were offered for outdoor cut flowers, first being awarded to Mr. John W. Pepper, William Robertson, gardener; second to Mr. James W. Paul, Jr., Joseph Hurley, gardener; and third to Mrs. R. J. C. Walker, John McCleary, gardener. The competition was very keen. Henry F. Michell Company offered prizes for new varieties of potatoes, tomatoes and sweet corn.

Mr. and Mrs. John G. Eisele sailed for Europe on the 12th inst., for a three months' pleasure trip through Germany, France and Switzerland.

DAVID RUST.

Boston.

The Annual Picnic.

The annual picnic of the Gardeners and Florists' Club will be held Wednesday, July 25, at Waushakam Grove, South Framingham, instead of at Calendonian Grove as at first decided. This grove, which is some twenty miles from Boston, affords a fine opportunity for members and their families to have a day's outing in the country. The committee having the matter in charge is composed of Fred Palmer, chairman, David Lumsden, Ed. Hatch, Wm. Sim and Peter Miller, and from the well known ability of these men in handling such matters there is no question that the comforts of everyone will be looked after. Arrangements have been made with the Boston and Worcester Street Railway for two special cars to leave Park Square, Boston, direct to the grove at 8.30 a. m. Over $100 will be awarded in prizes for the various sports.

A rule this year will be that no contestant in these sports can take more than two prizes, not including the team events. Don't forget the date, Wednesday, July 25.

News Notes.

The second annual baseball game between the salesmen of the Park street and Music Hall flower markets will take place on Childs' farm, Waltham, at 1 p. m. August 5 next. Take car to Waltham Square, where a committee will be in waiting to escort the visitors to the grounds. H. C. Ward is manager of the Music Hall team, Thos. Mathews being captain, and the Park street team feels very much strengthened in having Wm. R. Nicholson as captain with J. F. Free as manager.

A. Leuthy of Roslindale sailed on his annual European trip on Saturday.

E. Sutermeister of Hyde Park is spending a few weeks in Portland, Me.

Arthur Kidder and family of Lincoln are at Rangeley Lakes for a month.

George Solomon of Houghton & Dutton's is on his honeymoon as well as vacation.

N. L. Silverman and family will spend July and August in Maine.

Edward Ragan with the David Fisher estate is away on his vacation.

Jos. Margolis and Chas. Robinson of H. M. Robinson & Company are spending a month at Brunswick, Me.

David Welch of Welch Brothers is at Lake Champlain. F. Wm. Freystedt of the same firm is at Peek's Island, Me., on his vacation.

Peter Fisher and family are spending a few weeks at Scituate.

W. W. Edgar and family are at Brant Rock.

A. Bloom of Welch Brothers is spending his vacation in New Hampshire. Lawrence Flynn of the same firm is back again from his vacation.

Henry M. Robinson & Company report a very good business in all kinds of supplies and have had much call for their new specialty, lyrata, for Summer decorations.

W. J. Collins of the Faulkner farm, Brookline, one of the popular young gardeners of the locality, was operated on for appendicitis on Saturday, and at last reports was getting along as comfortably as expected.

J. G. Leikens of Newport is the sole agent in that city for the handling of the popular Wellesley rose of which the Waban Rose Conservatories are making him tri-weekly shipments.

Mrs. Elizabeth Cartwright of Wellesley, mother of George, Elijah, Henry, Jarvis, and Richard Cartwright, all well known in the trade, sustained a serious injury last week by falling out of bed and breaking her leg. She is now in the Newton Hospital, and as she is 85 years of age she is in a rather critical condition, grave doubts being felt of her recovery.

Wm. Penn, the Bromfield street florist, is at Peek's Island.

Julius Zinn has returned from his annual outing.

Fred. Roberts of Doyle's Back Bay store, is in Nova Scotia trying to escape the humidity with which Boston is favored at present.

Bernard T. McGinty, manager of McCarthy flower department, has started on his vacation, Chris. Donovan having returned.

J. W. DUNCAN.

Pittsburg.

The Club Outing.

The thirteenth annual outing of the Florists' Club, held July 10, was attended by about 300 people and was a most enjoyable affair. The party left the wharf at Market street on the barge Beauty about half-past nine and reached Clairton shortly after noon, when a landing was made at Blair's beach until 6 p. m.; all arrived home about 10 o'clock. The weather was delightful, excepting a heavy shower, which lasted an hour, but did not do any harm, as all sought shelter on the boat and passed their time dancing, etc. The committee provided well for food and drink, and it was well they did so, as never was so much consumed heretofore at any outing. The sports of the day began shortly after landing and lasted until leaving time. The base ball game of eight innings had to be stopped, which was unfortunate, as the score was tied 8 to 8, and the parties had to cut the cards to see who was the winner. The growers won and received the prize—a case of black and tan health restorer given by H. H. Holmes Company, which was divided among the team. Other prizes were won as follows:

100 yard dash, boys 6-8 years, prize a watch donated by T. P. Langhans—Won by A. Burki.

100 yard dash, girls 6-8 years, handkerchiefs from E. C. Ludwig—Bertha Walters.

100 yard dash, boys 9-10 years, stick pin from J. W. Ludwig—N. Augney.

100 yard dash, girls 9-10 years, stick pin from Gustav Ludwig—Florence Ingham.

Three-legged race, 11-13 years, two knives from Pittsburg Cutflower Company, Limited—E. Mains and Ed. Ludwig.

100 yard dash, girls 11-13 years, picture from J. A. Elliott Company—Myrtle Kraus.

100 yard dash, men, box cigars from George Dimling—C. Stewart.

Egg and spoon race, silver belt pin from A. Loch—Lena Ludwig.

Potato race, $3 hat from H. L. Blind & Brother—Ed. McCallum.

Bag race, baseball glove from Joseph Jones—F. Holzman.

100 yard dash, growers only, brass syringe from W. C. Beckert—J. Wyland.

100 yard dash, for men, silver teapot from Pittsburg Florists' Exchange—A. Riley.

100 yard dash, women's race, card tray from William Loew—Mary Boss.

100 yard dash, for men, backward—A box of tobies from Valley Greenhouse Company was distributed among the crowd as there were no entries for this event.

100 yard dash, ladies, one dozen handkerchiefs from W. A. Clarke—Miss Lease.

100 yard dash, for fat men, pipe from John Bader—Ed. Smerchel.

100 yard dash, ladies, a floral album from E. C. Reineman—Carrie Jordan.

100 yard dash, girls 14-16 years, parasol from Mrs. E. A. Williams—Josephine Henderson.

20 yard peanut race, knife, from E. C. Ludwig—V. Mont.

Fat women's race, purse from Fred Burki—Mrs. Palmer.

Hopping race, for boys, knife from Fred Ruch—J. Boss.

Running broad jump, for boys, knife from C. Rieger—Master Geer.

100 yard dash, ladies from 17-20 years, vase from Breitenstein & Flemm—Annie Reibel.

Running broad jump, for men, $5 gold piece from A. W. Smith—J. Gerwig.

Tug of war, box of cigars from Randolph & McClements—A party of 12, mostly dealers, who won against growers; it was a bitter struggle.

For the cake walk, which was held aboard the boat, J. B. Murdoch & Company gave $5 and almost everybody took part in the affair.

The judges were Fred. Burki, J. L. Wyland and E. C. Reineman.

The baseball match was very exciting; both sides had strong batteries and not so many runs were made as usual.

The boat was decorated with greens, mostly oak branches, which Fred Burki sent in from his farm, and some flowers were sent by some of the members. The trip up the Monongahela river is quite interesting, particularly to those who never experienced going through several locks and passing the greatest steel works in the country.

Trade is almost at a standstill, stock is moving slowly, which makes one feel like closing up shop and getting away.

E. C. Ludwig and family are sojourning at Atlantic City, where they intend to stay for some weeks.

As regards the rates to the convention at Dayton, O., our railroad offices have not received notice on their weekly bulletins about the fare for the trip. We are all expecting the one and one-third fare as usual, and hope it will be granted, as quite a few intend to go and want a fair rate. The price one way from Pittsburg is $7, and if we get the one and one-third rate it will be under $10 for the round trip.

E. C. REINEMAN.

WORCESTER, MASS.—C. W. Moeckel has brought an action of tort against C. A. Cross & Company for injuries alleged to be occasioned to greenhouses occupied by the plaintiff and to plants therein, from an explosion on the premises of the defendant, March 21, 1904. The plaintiff got a verdict in the Superior court and the defendant carried the case to the Supreme court on exceptions, which exceptions were overruled.

CHICAGO.—The Globe Greenhouse Company will erect a store and flat building on Madison street, near Fifty-third avenue. It will be two story, 25x40 feet. In connection with this building is to be constructed a greenhouse, 38x60 feet, of glass and iron. The total cost will be $7,000.

LEBANON, O.—Daniel Whiskeyman, of this place, who recently opened up greenhouses on Queen street, west of Lancaster, is making extensive improvements. The main building is 210 feet long by 20 feet wide and will be divided into six sections.

GRAFTED ROSES

Fine Stock from 3-in. pots.

Richmond, $2.50 per doz., $15.00 per 100, $125.00 per 1000.

Killarney, $2.50 per doz., $18.00 per 100, $150.00 per 1000.

Etoile De France, $3.00 per doz., $18.00 per 100.

Kaiserin, Carnot, Uncle John, Chatenay, $2.00 per doz., $15.00 per 100.

Bride, Bridesmaid, Golden Gate, Wootton, $2.00 per doz., $12.00 per 100.

ROSES OWN ROOTS

Fine Stock from 3-in. pots.

Richmond, $12.00 per 100; $100.00 per 1000.

Etoile De France, $12.00 per 100.

Sunrise, Perle, Sunset, Chatenay, $8.00 per 100.

Bride, Bridesmaid, Golden Gate, $7.00 per 100.

CANNAS

Best named varieties from 3½ in. pots, $5.00 and $6.00 per 100.

CHRYSANTHEMUMS

H. A. Allen, Jennie Nonin. From 2½ in. pots $1.50 per doz., $8.00 per 100.

Mrs. A. T. Miller, Dora Stevens, Lady Cranston, Mrs. W. Higgie, Mrs. T. W. Pockett From 2½ in. pots $1.00 per doz., $5.00 per 100.

Geo. Kalb, Mrs. McArthur, Maud Dean, Mrs. Coombs, Nagoya, Robt. Halliday, A. J. Balfour, Nellie Pockett. Price from 2¼ in. pots, $3.50 per 100, $30.00 per 1000.

Autumn Glory, Ada Spaulding, Dorothy Devens, Glory Pacific Harry May, Ivory, J. E. Lager, J. H. Troy, Mrs. S. T. Murdoch, Mrs. Humphrey, Nivens, Thomas H. Brown, Xeno. Price from 2½ in. pots, $3.00 per 100, $25.00 per 1000.

800 hardy pompons, 12 fine varieties, pink, yellow, white and bronze, $1.50 per 100.

VIOLETS—Fine Stock

Marie Louise from 3 in. pots $4.00 per 100, 2 1-4 in. pots, $3.00 per 100; $25.00 per 1000.

Miscellaneous Plants.—For varieties and prices see page 20, July 7, issue.

Asparagus Plumosus Nanus from 3 inch pots $8.00 per 100; Sprengerii from 3 inch pots, $6.00 per 100.

Send for Catalogue.

Wood Bros., Fishkill, N. Y.

Mention The Florists' Exchange when writing.

Decorative Plants

Latania Borbonica, 2¼ in. pots, $3.00; 3 in: $6.00; 4 in., $15.00 per 100. Large specimen plants from $2.00 to $5.00 each.

Kentia Belmoreana and Forsteriana, 2¼ in. pots, $8.00; 3 in., $15.00; 5 in., $60.00 per 100; 6 in. $15.00 per doz.; 7 in. and upward, $1.75 to $35.00 each.

Areca Lutescens, 3 in. $10.00; 4 in. $20.00 per 100; 6 in., $1.00 each and upward.

Pandanus Utilis, 3 in. pots, $8.00; 4 in., $20.00 per 100.

Phœnix Reclinata, 5 in. pots, $35.00 per 100.

Phœnix Canariensis, fine specimen plants, from $3.00 to $35.00 each.

Araucaria Excelsa, 5 in. pots, $65.00 per 100.

Assorted Ferns, 2¼ in. pots, $3.00 per 100.

Nephrolepis Compacta, 3 in. pots, $8.00; 4 in., $15.00 per 100.

Plants in Fine Condition.

JOHN BADER, Troy Hill, Allegheny, Pa.

Mention The Florists' Exchange when writing.

ASPARAGUS

	Per 100
Sprengerii, 3 in.	$3.00
Abutilon Savitzii, 2 in.	2.50
" New French Dwarf, 2 in.	3.00
Jerusalem Cherries, 4 inches, full of bloom, strong	8.00

Cash with order, please.

GEO. J. HUGHES, BERLIN, N. J.

Mention The Florists' Exchange when writing.

	Per 100
Asparagus Plumosus, 2¼ in. pots,	$2.50
" Sprengerii, " " "	2.00
Smilax " " "	1.50

J. S. BLOOM,
RIEGELSVILLE, PA.

Mention The Florists' Exchange when writing.

A Few Good Things YOU WANT

Dracæna Indivisa, 4 and 5 in., $20.00 and $35.00 per 100.

Asparagus Sprengeri, 2 in., $2.50 per 100.

Geraniums, S. A. Nutt, Castellane, John Doyle, Perkins, Double Gen. Grant, Poitevine, Mme. Salleroi, 2 in. pots, $2.00 per 100; 3 in. pots $4.00 per 100. Rooted Cuttings, $1.00 per 100.

Vinca Var., 2 in., $2.00 per 100; 3 in., $4.00 per 100.

Rex Begonia, nice plants, 2 and 2½ in., $6.00 per 100.

Asparagus Plumosus, 2 in. $3.00 per 100.

GEO. M. EMMANS, Newton, N. J.

Mention The Florists' Exchange when writing.

ASPARAGUS

Sprengerii, extra strong, 3 in. pots, $5 per 100. Extra Strong, 4 in. pots, $6 per 100.

Smilax, 2½ in. pots $2 per 100.

Cabbage Plants, Flat Dutch, Succession and Winningstadt, $1.50 per 1000. Cash with order.

S. G. BENJAMIN, Fishkill, N. Y.

Mention The Florists' Exchange when writing.

EMERSON C. McFADDEN

Wholesale Grower

Asparagus Plumosus Nanus, Etc.

Short Hills, N. J.

Tel. 28 A.

Mention The Florists' Exchange when writing.

SMILAX PLANTS.

Strictly No. 1 plants; from 2 in. pots, $1.00 per 100; $9.00 per 1000. Seedlings from boxes, $4.00 per 1000.

R. KILBOURN, CLINTON, N. Y.

Mention The Florists' Exchange when writing.

CYCLAMEN

Splendens Giganteum Hybrids.

This strain has no equal or better. Perfect flowers of Giant type in five true colors well grown plants from 2½ in. pots $5.00 per 100, $45.00 per 1000; from 3 in. pots $7.00 per 100; $65.00 per 1000.

Primula. ***Obconica Grandiflora.*** The celebrated Ronsdorfer and Lattmans Hybrids most beautiful strain from 2½ in. pots, $3.00 per 100, including the fringed varieties.

Asparagus. ***Plumosus Nanus.*** From flats fine plants $1.50 per 100, $12.50 per 1000.

SATISFACTION GUARANTEED.

PAUL MADER, East Stroudsburg, Pa

Mention The Florists' Exchange when writing.

PEONIES

A splendid collection of peonies, some of the choicest. Send for price list.

Send 25c. each for Peony and Phlox manuals.

C. S. HARRISON,
YORK, NEB.

Mention the Florists' Exchange when writing.

PEONIES.

Queen Victoria (the cold storage flower) $9.00 per 100. **Festiva Maxima**, $30.00 per 100. **Fragrans** (the bloom producer), $6.00 per 100. For 1000 rates or other varieties, write.

GILBERT H. WILD,
SARCOXIE, MO.

Mention The Florists' Exchange when writing.

Commercial Violet Culture

Price, $1.50

The Florists' Exchange, 2-8 Duane St., New York.

Mention The Florists' Exchange when writing.

GERANIUMS ROOTED CUTTINGS

FALL DELIVERY. IN ANY QUANTITY.

I have almost 100,000 stock plants to work from and want your order now so that I can give it special attention when we come to take cuttings.

Send for Descriptive Price List

	Per 100	Per 1,000
SMILAX 100,000 ready now, carefully cut back and grown with an air space around every pot	$1.50	$12.00
ASPARAGUS ROBUSTUS. 20,000 once repotted. fine strong plants and a great improvement over Plumosus in every respect. Try at least a hundred, next year you will want a thousand	$5.00	$40.00
ASPARAGUS SPRENGERII 50,000 good strong plants once repotted into rose pots and a bargain at the price	$2.00	$15.00

ALBERT M. HERR,
Lancaster, Pa.

Mention The Florists' Exchange when writing.

Geraniums Geraniums

4 in. pots at $6.00 per 100.
3 in. pots at $4.00 per 100.
Heliotrope, 4 in. $4.00 per 100.
" 2 in. $3.00 per 100.
Lobelia, 2 in. $2.00 per 100.
Coleus, in variety, 2½ in. pots, $2.00 per 100.

Don't get left, but get your order in. Cash must accompany same.

J. E. FELTHOUSEN,
154 VAN VRANKEN AVE., SCHENECTADY, N. Y.

Mention The Florists' Exchange when writing.

MOUNTAIN OF SNOW

This **Geranium** is unsurpassed for bedding and vase work. Its bright scarlet flowers and white and green foliage make it one of the most attractive plants for fine work. Large bushy plants 3½ and 4 in. pots, 8c. each.

Asparagus Sprengerii, big plants in 3 in. pots, plenty large enough to go in fours. 5c

Asparagus Plumosus Nanus, large, 3 in. stock. Only about 300 left, 6c. each.

R. G. HANFORD, Norwalk, Conn.

Mention The Florists' Exchange when writing.

GERANIUMS

Grand stock in bud and bloom. Best bedders in red, white and pink, also assorted colors. $7.00 per 100, 500 at $6.50 per 100.

COLEUS

Extra fine, red, yellow and assorted.
2½ inch, $3.00 per 100; $25.00 per 1000.
3 inch, $4.00 per 100; $35.00 per 1000.

THE H. WEBER & SONS CO.,
OAKLAND, MD.

Mention The Florists' Exchange when writing.

BARGAIN GERANIUMS

Buchner and Dbl. Grant, strong, 3 and 4 in., $2.50 per 100; $20.00 per 1000, in bloom.

Ferns, from flats, large plants fill 2 and 3 in. pots at once, $1.00, $1.50 per 100; $8.00, $12.00 per 1000. Fine large clumps for cutting $4.00 per 100.

Dracæna Indivisa, large, 4 in., $5.00 per 100. Cash.

Standard 4 in. pots, used once, carefully packed, $5.00 per 1000.

WM. S. HERZOG, MORRIS PLAINS, N. J.

Mention The Florists' Exchange when writing.

CHRYSANTHEMUMS

Rooted cuttings from sand, **Polly Rose, William Duckham, Dr. Enguehard, American Beauty, Intensity, Marie Liger, Maud Dean**, $12.00 per 1000. **Polly Rose** and **Dr. Enguehard**, strong plants from soil, $18.00 per 1000. 250 at 1000 price. Cash with order.

G. P. NEIPP
JAMAICA P.O. AQUEDUCT, L. I.

Mention The Florists' Exchange when writing.

All NURSERYMEN, SEEDSMEN and FLORISTS

wishing to do business with Europe should send for the

"Horticultural Advertiser"

This is THE British Trade Paper, being read weekly by all Horticultural traders. It is also taken by over 1000 of the best Continental houses. Annual subscriptions to cover cost of postage, 75 cents. Money orders payable at Lowdham, Notts. Address

EDITORS OF THE "H. A."
Chilwell Nurseries, Lowdham, Notts

European Agents for THE AMERICAN CARNATION

Mention the Florists' Exchange when writing

GERANIUMS

S. A. Nutt, J. Viaud, White Swan, E. G. Hill, Atkinson, A. Ricard, Mad. De Castellane, **Asparagus Sprengerii**, all from 2 inc. pots, $2.00 per 100, $17.50 per 1000.

E. H. Trego, Telegraph, **Cissus Discolor**, **English Ivy, Boston Fern**, all from 2 in. pots $3.00 per 100, **Boston Fern**, 6 in. pan, $4.00 per doz. **Ivy Geraniums, Hibiscus, Fuchsia**, **Begonia**, in variety, named, from 2 in. pots, at $2.50 per 100.

THE NATIONAL PLANT CO., DAYTON, O

Mention The Florists' Exchange when writing

GERANIUMS.

Nutt, Poitevine, Buchner, Doyle, Ricard, Viaud, Brett, and others.

Rooted Cuttings. Orders booked for Fall delivery.

ERNEST HARRIS, Delanson, N. Y

Mention The Florists' Exchange when writing

DAHLIAS

Now is the time to place your order for Bulbs which will insure you getting named varieties in any quantity; delivery to be made this fall or early spring.

DAVID HERBERT & SON
Successors to L. K. PEACOCK, Inc.
ATCO, N. J.

Mention The Florists' Exchange when writing

10,000 Mme. F. Bergmann

CHRYSANTHEMUMS

Still the best early 'mum. Large white as round as a ball. Plants in splendid condition. Price $2.50 per 100 or $20.00 per 1000.

Morton's Evergreen Lodge, Clarksville, Ten

Mention The Florists' Exchange when writing

JERUSALEM CHERRIES

Strong stock from 2 in. pots, $2.00 per 1

CRYPTOMERIA JAPONICA, 2 pots, ready for 4 inch, $3.00 to $4.00 per 1

Write us for Geraniums, Cannas, Cuphea, Selaginellas, etc., all at reduced prices.

E. I. RAWLINGS, Quakertown, P

Mention The Florists' Exchange when writing

BEGONIA RE

BEST NAMED SORTS

An immense stock in fine condition immediate sales, 2½ inch, $5.00 per 100.

See ad. in Last Issue.

NATHAN SMITH & SON
ADRIAN, MICH.

CELERY---CABBA

White Plume, Golden-Self, Golden Heart plants, $1.50 per 1000.

Cabbage Plants—Flat Dutch and Drum $1.00 per 1000; 5000 for $4.00.

Cauliflower Plants, Early Snowball, $2.0 1000.

J. C. SCHMIDT CO., Bristol,

Mention The Florists' Exchange when wr

Phoenix Roebelenii

THE MOST GRACEFUL PALM OF ALL.

We have almost the entire stock of it in America.

SEEDLINGS, $5.00 per 100; $40.00 per 1000; $350.00 per 10,000. 4 in. pot plants, about 1 foot high; 12-15 leaves, $1.00 each; $80.00 per 100; $750.00 per 1000. 7 in. pot plants, about 2-2½ feet high, $5.00 each; $40.00 per 10; $350.00 per 100.

SPECIMEN PLANTS, $7.50-$10.00.

We also offer for sale—STOVE PLANTS, CALADIUMS, CROTONS and DRACAENAS in finest varieties at reasonable prices.

JOHN LEWIS CHILDS
FLORAL PARK - - - - - L. I., N. Y.

Mention The Florists' Exchange when writing

FERNS IN FLATS

Now ready for 2 1-2 inch pots. Flats contain over 100 clumps, which can be divided. Varieties include ASPIDIUM TSUSSEMENSE, CRYTOMIUM FALCATUM, PTERIS MAYII, WIMSETTI, NANA COMPACTA, ADIANTOIDES, SERRULATA, LASTREAS, etc.

PRICES, $2.00 PER FLAT; 20 OR MORE FLATS AT $1.75.
CASH WITH ORDER FROM UNKNOWN PARTIES.

McHUTCHISON & CO.
17 Murray Street - - - NEW YORK CITY

Mention The Florists' Exchange when writing.

FERNS.

POINSETTIAS, 2½ inch pots, $5.00 per 100.

ASPARAGUS PLUMOSUS, 4 in. pots, $10.00 per 100.

HUGH GRAHAM CO.,
Logan Nurseries, York Road and Louden Street, PHILADELPHIA, PA.

Mention The Florists' Exchange when writing.

FERNS

You Must Have

Only 5,000 left; speak quick.

Piersonii, 5 in., 20c.; 4 in., 15c.; 3 in., 10c.

Scotti, 5 in., 20c.; 4 in., 15c.; 3 in., 10c.

Bostons, 3 in., ready to shift, 10c.

Asparagus Plumosus Nanus, 3½ in. 6c; 2½ in., $2.50 per 100.

Asparagus Sprengerii, 3½ in., 6c.

20,000 Field Carnations.

Write me. Cash please.

BENJAMIN CONNELL, West Grove, Pa.

Mention The Florists' Exchange when writing

NEPHROLEPIS SCOTTII

Small plants from the benches, $5.00 per 100; $50.00 per 1000. Plants large enough for 6 in. pots, $25.00 per 100. Plants large enough to go in 7 and 8 in. pots, $50.00 per 100.

Asparagus Plumosus Nanus, 2¼ in., fine plants, $3.00 per 100.

JOHN SCOTT,
Rutland Road and East 45th Street;
BROOKLYN, N. Y.
Telephone 2890 Bedford.

Mention The Florists' Exchange when writing.

NEPHROLEPIS WHITMANI

is the fern to grow.

Having ordered a large quantity I can fill your orders at short notice. Price, $25.00 per 100; $200.00 per 1000.

S. S. SKIDELSKY,
824 No. 24 St., Philadelphia, Pa.

Mention The Florists' Exchange when writing.

FERNS OUR SPECIALTY

CIBOTIUM SCHIEDEI

We have a large stock of this beautiful tree fern in 3 in. pots, ready for a shift, at $25.00 per 100. 26 plants at 100 rate.

FERN SEEDLINGS FROM FLATS

Eight to ten best market varieties at $1.00 per 100, or $8.50 per 1000. If by mail add 10c. for each hundred plants.

ASSORTED FERNS FOR DISHES

From 2¼ in. pots. The best and hardiest varieties in market at $3.00 per 100, or $26.00 per 1000. 250 plants at 1000 rate.

Adiantum Cuneatum, 2¼ in. pots, $3.50 per 100, $30.00 per 1000.

FERN SPORES

Gathered from our own stock. 35c. per trade package. $4.00 per doz. packages.

Gardenia Vietchii from 2¼ in. pots, $7.50 per 100, $70.00 per 1000; 500 at 1000 rate.

ANDERSON & CHRISTENSEN,
SHORT HILLS, N. J.

Mention The Florists' Exchange when writing.

Adiantum Cuneatum

From 3 in. pots ready to shift, per 100, $5.00 per 1,000, $45.00

From 2½ in. pots ready to shift, per 100 $4.00; per 1000, $35.00.

Adiantum Hybridum

Similar to Croweanum. From 4 in. pots ready to shift, per 100, $10.00.

Seedlings in flats, nice clumps which can be divided and ready for 2½ in pots, per flat, $2.50.

O. V. ZANGEN
Seedsman HOBOKEN, N. J.

Mention the Florists' Exchange when writing.

FERN SEEDLINGS

FROM FLATS.

The first crop is now ready for potting, including the following varieties: Pteris Cretica Cristata, Pteris Cretica Albo-Lineata, Pteris Adiantoides, Pteris Argyraea, Pteris Mayii, Cyrtomium Falcatum, Aspidium Tsussemense, Onychium Japonica, Doodia Aspera. My selection, $1.00 per 100; $8.50 per 1000. If by mail, add 10c. per 100 for postage.

Mixed Ferns for dishes, 2¼ in., $3.00 per 100; $26.00 per 1000; 250 at 1000 rate; 3 in., $6.00 per 100.

Adiantum Cuneatum, 3 in., $6.00 per 100.

FRANK N. ESKESEN, MADISON, N. J.

Mention The Florists' Exchange when writing.

FERNS

6 in. **Scottii Ferns,** 40c. 8000 6 in. Boston Ferns, 40c. Large pans Boston Ferns, $1.00; $1.50; $2.00; $2.50. No C.O.D. Cash or reference.

W. C. SMITH,
61st & Market Sts. PHILADELPHIA, PA.

Mention The Florists' Exchange when writing.

NEPHROLEPIS

Whitmani, 2¼ in., $25.00 per 100.

Boston Ferns, 2¼ in., $3.00 per 100.

Henry H. Barrows & Son, Whitman, Mass.

REMEMBER

We are still Headquarters for

BAY TREES BOX TREES
...EVERGREENS...

Price Lists on application.

JULIUS ROEHRS CO.,
Exotic Nurseries, Rutherford, N. J.

Mention The Florists' Exchange when writing.

FERNS

Are now in fine shape. A good variety and nice bushy stock, 2½ in., $3.00 per 100; $25.00 per 1000.

Kentia Belmoreana, 4 in., clean and bushy, 25c.

Cocos Weddeliana, 10c.

Dracaena Indivisa, 4 in., strong, 12c.

Mme. Salleroi Geraniums, 2 in., $2.00 per 100.

English Ivy, 4 in., fine stock, $10.00 per 100.

H. WESTON, HEMPSTEAD, N. Y.

BOSTON FERNS

Taken from bench, $10.00 and $20.00 per 100.

5 and 6 inch **Pot Ferns,** from $3.00 per doz. up Extra fine stock.

Geraniums, 3½ inch stock, $4.00 per 100.

BOCK, THE FLORIST,
2394 MASS AVENUE NORTH CAMBRIDGE, MASS.

Mention The Florists' Exchange when writing.

ORCHIDS

Arrived, large shipments of Cattleya Gigas and Cattleya Speciosissima, C. Mossiae, C. Percivaliana.

Write for Prices.

LAGER & HURRELL, Summit, N. J.
Growers and Importers

Mention The Florists' Exchange when writing.

ORCHIDS

Largest Importers, Exporters, Growers and Hybridists in the world.

Sander, St. Albans, England
and
235 Broadway, Room 1, New York City

Mention The Florists' Exchange when writing.

ROBERT CRAIG & CO.

ROSES, PALMS, CROTONS

CARNATIONS and Novelties in DECORATIVE PLANTS

Market and 49th Sts. PHILADELPHIA, PA.

COCOS PALMS.

Strong 2¼ inch at $1.50 per dozen. Write for lowest prices on Kentias.

Jas. F. Barclay R. I. GREENHOUSES Pawtucket, R. I.

Mention The Florists' Exchange when writing.

LOOK! See Us Grow.

Always buy of Aschmann, the great Araucaria importer of America.

OUR MOTTO—Cheap, Good, Honest Dealings and Quick Sales.

ARAUCARIA EXCELSA a specialty. 6,000 are in now, imported from Ghent, Belgium this Spring, 1906. Now planted in 5½ and 6 in. pots, well established, and ready for shipment to all parts of America. All these are grown for us by an Araucaria Specialist in Ghent, Belgium. **NO SEEDLINGS,** but Araucarias raised from top cuttings only are offered. This is now our 11th Anniversary, and our importations have grown from 250 in the first year to the remarkable number of **6,000 IN THE ELEVENTH YEAR.** My reputation as Araucaria Importer gains footway in every greenhouse and florist store in America. Our Araucarias need no *coaxing*, genuine facts tell in quality and cheapness.

Please Note Our Lowest Prices

12 to 14 in. 5½ in. pots, 3 to 4 tiers, 2-yr. old, 50c. 14 to 16 in., 5½ in. pots, 3 to 4 tiers, 2-yr. old, 60c. 16 to 18 in. 5½ 6 in. pots, 4 to 5 tiers, 3-yr. old, 75c. 18 to 20 in., 6 in. pots, 5 to 6 tiers, 4-yr. old, $1.00. 20 to 24 in. 6 in. to 7 in. pots, 5 to 6 tiers, 4-yr. old, $1.25. 36-40 to 50 in. 7 in. pots, specimen plants from $2.50 to $3.00 each.

ARAUCARIA COMPACTA ROBUSTA—have several thousand of them; can supply all wants. These plants were never so fine in shape and condition as this year. The set of the greenhouse, as broad as long, 12 to 20 in., in height, 3 to 4 perfect tiers, 20 to 30 inches across, 3-4-5 year old, 6 to 7 in. pots, $1.25, $1.50, $1.75, $2.00, $2.50 to $3.00 each.

ARAUCARIA EXCELSA GLAUCA—This variety on account of its beautiful Green-Blueish tiers, dwarf habit, fine compact shape, gives it a striking appearance, and anybody seeing them, must undoubtedly fall in love with them at sight. Plants, 6-7 inch pots, 3-4-5 perfect tiers, 3-4 year old, 15 to 25 inch high, from 15 to 30 in. across, $1.25, $1.50, $1.75, $2.00 to $2.50 each.

SOLANUM or JERUSALEM CHERRY, $5.00 per 100.

KENTIA FORSTERIANA, 7 in. pots, made-up plants, 1 large in center, 3 smaller sizes, 22 to 25 in. high around, gives them a good appearance, $2.00 each. 6 in. pots, single plants, 35 to 40 in. high, 5 to 6 good leaves, 4 year old, $1.25 to $1.50 each; 6 in. pots, 30 to 35 in. high, 4 year old, 5 good leaves, $1.00; 5½ in. pots, 3 year old, 25 to 30 in. high, 5 good leaves, 75c. made-up plants, 3 and 4 in. pots, 18 to 20 in. high, 25 cts. to 30 cts. each.

KENTIA BELMOREANA, 5½ to 6 in. pots, bushy, fine plants, from 75 cts. to $1.00 to $1.25 each.

ARECA LUTESCENS, made-up, 25 cts.

COCOS WEDDELIANA, 15 cts.

CYCAS REVOLUTA (Sago Palm), 6 in.-7 in. pots, with from 6 to 20 leaves per plant, 10 cts. per leaf.

CASH WITH ORDER

When ordering, say whether the plants should be shipped in the pots or not

GODFREY ASCHMANN
Importer and Wholesale Grower of Pot Plants
1012 Ontario Street, - - PHILADELPHIA, PA.

Mention The Florists' Exchange when writing.

CLASSIFIED ADVERTISEMENTS

CASH WITH ORDER.

The columns under this heading are reserved for advertisements of Stock for Sale, Stock Wanted, Help Wanted, Situations Wanted or other Wants; also of Greenhouse, Land, Second-Hand Materials, etc., For Sale or Rent.

Our charge is 10 cts. per line (7 words to the line), set solid, without display. No advt. accepted for less than thirty cents.

Display advertisements in these columns, 15 cents per line; count 12 lines agate to the inch.

[If replies to Help Wanted, Situation Wanted, or other advertisements are to be addressed care of this office, advertisers add 10 cents to cover expense of forwarding.]

Copy must reach New York office 12 o'clock Wednesday to secure insertion in issue of following Saturday.

Advertisers in the Western States desiring to advertise under initials, may save time by having their answer directed care our Chicago office at 127 E. Berwyn Ave.

SITUATIONS WANTED

SITUATION WANTED—By all-around florist, wholesale or retail. State wages. Address, L. K., care The Florists' Exchange.

SITUATION WANTED—By florist, young man, 6 years' experience, good salesman and maker up. E. Richter, 724 10th Avenue, New York City.

SITUATION WANTED—By single Frenchman, 26 years old, in private or commercial place, who has had good experience in greenhouse and garden work; not afraid of work. Address J. A., P. O. Box 2, Glen Cove, Long Island.

SITUATION WANTED—Single man, 45 years old, desires steady position. Thoroughly understands outdoor work; good knowledge of general greenhouse stock. State wages. James O'Brien, 138 Lexington Avenue, Jersey City, N. J.

SITUATION WANTED—As working foreman in a first-class retail business, only in Eastern States to August 1. 23 years' practical experience in Europe and this country in general line of stock. Aged 39, single man. Address, B. Horn, General Delivery Office, Savannah, Ga.

SITUATION WANTED—By German, 35, single, reliable, nine years commercial, one year private, experience in this country. A. No. 1 carnation grower, also 'mums and general stock. Able to take charge. State wages. Address, L. P., care The Florists' Exchange.

SITUATION WANTED—As foreman or general manager, 20 years' experience. Sober, reliable and first-class on general cut flower stock and pot plants. Can plan, build and heat. Certificate as Carnationist from Mass. Hort. Society. First-class designer. Please correspond. L. S., care The Florists' Exchange.

HELP WANTED

WANTED—Gardeners, to pot plants, and do other work in greenhouses. Steady work and good wages to steady, able-bodied, reliable men. J. T. Lovett, Little Silver, N. J.

WANTED—Working foreman for general greenhouse work; state wages expected and where last employed. W. C. Goodrich, R. F. D. No. 2, Watervliet, New York.

WANTED—At once, two good men with some experience in growing roses, carnations and general stock. State wages and give reference. Address A. Stoeckle, Watertown, N. Y.

WANTED—Carnation grower who can produce first-class flowers. Steady place for reliable sober man, no night firing, age, married or single, wages and references. August 1st to 15th. Byer Brothers, Chambersburg, Pa.

WANTED—Young man as seedsman to solicit orders of market gardeners in the vicinity of Philadelphia and New York. Write stating experience and salary expected. Correspondence strictly confidential. Address, L. H., care The Florists' Exchange.

WANTED—Thoroughly first-class experienced rose and carnation growers. Apply stating age, married or single, references and wages expected. None but first-class men wanted. Lake View Rose Gardens, Jamestown, N. Y.

WANTED—An A No. 1 grower of carnations and general pot plants to work under foreman in commercial place. Permanent position for the right man. Address, L. N., care The Florists' Exchange.

WANTED—At once, section man and helper. Beauties, Brides and Maids on an up-to-date new commercial place. Only sober, industrious men need apply, with wages expected, etc. E. F. Hoehl, Manager of the Madison Cut Flower Company, Madison, N. J.

WANTED—One or two hustling salesmen for nursery stock. Those who have had experience in that line and a good record as salesmen for such stock. To such men I will pay a good salary and expenses. Nursery more than 50 years old. Address, P. A. Reese, 1 Madison Avenue, New York.

HELP WANTED

WANTED—Seedsmen; we require at once several young men for counter work. Only such need apply as have thorough experience in all branches of the seed business. We offer splendid chances for advancement. Apply in writing. W. W. Rawson & Company, Boston, Mass.

WANTED—A young man as assistant on a private place. First class experience in roses, carnations and general greenhouse stock required. Man from a commercial place preferred. Answer by mail only. Address, H. P., c/o A. T. Boddington, 342 West 14th street, City.

WANTED—Working foreman to grow roses and some Easter stock on moderate-sized place. Married, under 40, able to show credentials as to habits and ability to grow good stock, who can hustle himself and make others hustle. Such a man will find a permanent place, pleasant location and fair treatment. No "rounders" need apply. Pay, including house and fuel, $75 to $80 per month. Address, L. T., care The Florists' Exchange.

MISCELLANEOUS WANTS

WANTED TO BUY—Greenhouses to be taken down. State full particulars of same when writing. Address, F. W., care The Florists' Exchange.

WANTED TO BUY—A small retail place of two or three houses and dwelling house. Greenhouses must be in good repair and fully stocked. Southern New England preferred. Address, Greenhouse, care The Florists' Exchange.

WANTED TO BUY—Property, 5 acres or more with or without greenhouses and within reach of New York Market. Must be in healthy location with nice natural surroundings. G. F. Neipp, Aqueduct, L. I., N. Y.

FOR SALE OR RENT

FOR SALE or will rent to a responsible party, a fine greenhouse property. 13,000 feet of glass. Fine residence. Address, Silas O. Howell, Lock Box 14, Pine Bush, New York.

FOR SALE—At a great sacrifice, 6 Hitching's extra heavy cast iron, upright expansion tanks, 4-2 in. connections to each tank. Elizabeth Nursery Company, Elizabeth, N. J.

FOR SALE—Florists' place, a few miles out of Boston toward Brockton. Greenhouses, 5000 sq. ft. glass, stocked. Modern house and barn, 2 acres of land, $4800.00. Address, L. I., care The Florists' Exchange.

TO LEASE—Two greenhouses, a good boiler and everything for ready use, situated in a good locality. Terms reasonable. Mrs. M. Polambo, Greenleaf Avenue, West New Brighton, S. I.

DESIRABLE greenhouse plant of three houses, 24x200 feet; propagating house, 100 feet; potting shed, stable and dwelling. Steam heat, city water. Highland, opposite Poughkeepsie. Joseph Wood, Spring Valley, New York.

FOR RENT—Small greenhouse and florist business in prosperous running condition. Southern Connecticut. Full particulars and reason for renting to anyone interested. Address L. U. care The Florists' Exchange.

FOR SALE—A fine established nursery business with a constituency reaching from the Atlantic to the Pacific, and from Manitoba to the Gulf. Old age of proprietor the only reason for sale. C. S. Harrison, York, Neb.

FOR RENT—A greenhouse plant of fifteen thousand feet of glass, with an established trade. Reason for renting, am conducting a store and wish to devote my time entirely to same. Address, L. O., care The Florists' Exchange.

TO LET—greenhouse establishment in the city of Poughkeepsie, N. Y. 8000 feet of glass, city water, plenty of soil, fine location. For particulars come and see, or write to James Coleman, 212 Mansion street, Poughkeepsie, N. Y.

FOR SALE—Greenhouses at Madison, N. J. Situated on North Street. One 162 x 36; two 150 x 18 feet, 8 in.; one 150 x 12. Heated by both hot water and steam. Place in first-class condition. For particulars address, 60 Park Avenue, Madison, New Jersey.

FOR SALE—Two new greenhouses stocked, 4,000 feet glass, hot water heat. New 8 room steam heated house. Water and gas, grounds 150 by 185 feet. Town 4,000 inhabitants; good home trade. Two minutes from shipping station. One hour to New York. Address Jos. R. Walling, Box 203, Keyport, N. J.

FOR SALE—Owing to failing health, I will sell my florist establishment, beautifully situated between Larchmont Manor and Mamaroneck, Westchester Co., New York, near railroad station; trolley lines within one minute walk. First class opportunity for the right men. Plenty of landscape and jobbing work. The place contains four acres, 2 greenhouses, 104 feet long and lots of sash; well stocked with trees and shrubs, etc.; horse, wagon and tools. Address, Box 44, Larchmont, New York.

FOR SALE OR RENT

To lease for a term of years, my establishment on Greene Avenue, consisting of about 7,000 feet of glass, office and salesroom. Stable and wagon shed. Horse and wagons. Place well stocked and heated with hot water. Every convenience, all in good condition. A good business in the best location in the city. Established for 40 years. Wishing to retire from business. This is a good opportunity for the right man. Come and see it. Richard Shannon, 341-349 Greene Avenue, Brooklyn, New York.

FOR RENT—Owing to continued ill health, I am compelled to give up business for a while, and want a thoroughly reliable and competent man, well up in growing roses and other stock, to rent my place (10,000 feet glass). Will sell to the proper party; good business can be done. This is a fine opening for a man with small capital to secure an established trade. References exchanged. Full investigation desired. Possession at once. Don't answer unless you can fill the bill. For particulars address, "Important" care The Florists' Exchange.

FOR RENT—Owing to other business interests, we will offer for rent our greenhouse plant at Grafton, Mass., consisting of one house 142 x 32, one 75 x 18, with connecting house 15 x 10. These houses were built by Lord & Burnham within two years, and are thoroughly equipped in every respect. We also have in the field, 8,000 carnation plants in good condition, which can be purchased at a reasonable price. Norcross & Stratton, Grafton, Mass.; or J. E. Norcross, 33 Franklin Street, Boston, Mass.

FOR SALE

A splendid wholesale business consisting of nine iron frame greenhouses and two dwelling houses. Everything in up-to-date condition, well heated. Two acres of ground and within half hour drive of New York City. For further particulars communicate with

O. V. ZANGEN, SEEDSMAN, HOBOKEN, N. J.

Mention The Florists' Exchange when writing.

STOCK FOR SALE

Giant Double Alyssum, 2 in., fine, $2.00 per 100. Fox & Rosen, Parkerford, Pa.

FREESIA BULBS, No. 1 size, $3.00 per 1000. T. J. King, Newburyport, Mass.

Quercus Alba, Q. Coccinea and Q. Rubra, $1.50 per bu. Fraxinus Americana, 14c. lb. Address, Box 393, Biltmore, N. C.

Surplus stock for sale.—700 smilax, 2 1-4 in. pots, $1.50 per 100 or $10.00 takes the lot. Park Floral Co., Trenton, N. J.

PRIMULA—Chinese, finest fringed mixed, 2c. Asters, branching, 4 colors, $2.00 per 1,000. Cash. Shippensburg Floral Company, Shippensburg, Pa.

PEONY FESTIVA MAXIMA, and other best sorts in strong plants, 2 yr. old. Catalogue free. A. Dessert, Peony Specialist, Chenonceaux, France.

JERUSALEM CHERRIES, seedlings, 25c. per 100; 2½ in. pots, fine plants, $3.00 per 100. Cash please. A. Relyea & Son, Poughkeepsie, N. Y.

THREE magnificent palms (Latania Borbonica), 18 feet high and 18 feet wide. Reason for selling, no place to store. Apply, I. T. Burden, Newport, R. I.

MARIE LOUISE VIOLETS, strong Winter grown stock, ready for planting at once. Write me at once for sample. $2.00 per 100; $12.00 per 1000. Louis D. McCoy, Monsey, N. Y.

JARDINIERE FERNS, seedlings, good, strong, healthy stock, in variety only. Now ready for potting. Price, $1.50 per 100 by mail; $10.00 per 1000, F. O. B. Exp. B. Soltau, 199 Grant avenue, Jersey City, N. J.

Roses, Brides and Bridesmaids, from 4 in. pots, $6.00 per 100; $50.00 per 1,000. American Beauty plants from 3 and 4 in. pots, $8.00 to $15.00 per 1000. All good, clean stock. L. A. Noe, Madison, N. J.

ALTERNANTHERAS, strong, bushy, $2.50 per 100; Salvia, $3.00 per 100; Geraniums, 3 1-2 in., $4.00 per 100; Ageratum, $2.00 per 100. Cash please. P. A. Peterson, Florist, Asbury Park, N. J.

Mums, Bonnaffon and other leading varieties, R. C., $1.50 and $2.00 per 100; 2 1-2 in. pots, $2.50 and $3.00 per 100. Fine stock. Some nice 3 1-2 in. Nutt and Poitevine Geraniums left. Cash. Waverly Greenhouses, Tuckahoe, New York.

Brides, Maids, American Beauties and Richmonds, 4 in. pots, one year old. Bridesmaids, and asparagus, from bench, all clean, healthy and well-rooted. Send for our low prices on small or large orders. Madison Rose Company, Madison, N. J.

BABY RAMBLER roses, fine dormant stock, $25 per 100, 2 1-2 inch pot plants, extra well rooted $7 per 100, $65 per 1000. Orders booked for delivery now or any time up to late Spring. Samples free. Brown Brothers Co., Rochester, N. Y.

2500 BRIDESMAID plants, 3000 Brides, 1500 American Beauties, 1000 Meteors, all good, fine plants in 4 in. pots. Packed and shipped at express office. Maids, Brides and Meteors, 5c. each, American Beauties, 12c. each. Louis M. Noe, Madison, N. J.

FOR SALE

FOR SALE—Half price, 5000 wire carnation supports, used only 1 year; good as new, $10.00 per 1000. A. L. Thorne, Flushing, L. I.

FOR SALE—Cheap, all sizes greenhouse glass, new stock. Address, Glass, care The Florists' Exchange.

FOR SALE—1500 feet new 2 in. iron pipe, 8cts. ft. Lot of glass 16x18, A. double, all new. P. O. Box 120, Chatham, N. J.

FOR SALE—12 Hitchings hot water expansion tanks for 3 1-2 in. pipe, in good condition, cleaned, ready to set up. 1-3 price of new. Also horse lawn mower, easy running, $20.00. Address, K. D., care The Florists' Exchange.

FOR SALE—Stover fifty foot Steel Tower and Tank in use a short time. Good as new; price reasonable. Write for particulars. Wm. C. De Witt, R. F. D. No. 1, Phillipsburg, N. J.

FOR SALE—Two Lord and Burnham Ventilating Apparatus, with arms and pipe hangers. In use two seasons. Suitable for house 200 feet long. Cost, $65.00 new. $40.00 takes both machines. W. C. Pray, Kinkora, N. J.

BOILERS. BOILERS. BOILERS.

SEVERAL good second hand boilers on hand, also new No. 16 Hitchings at reduced cost. Write for list. Wm. H. Lutton, West Side Avenue Station, C. R. R. of N. J., Jersey City, N. J.

FOR SALE—Brand new Kroeschell Boiler. We can ship any size at short notice. Why buy second-hand boiler and risk your stock when you can get a new Kroeschell Boiler at very reasonable figures. Write for our prices before buying anything. Kroeschell Brothers Company, 55 Erie Street, Chicago, Ill.

FOR SALE CHEAP

12 greenhouses to be torn down; glazed with 16 x 24 and 10 x 12 double thick glass. Heated with 2 in. wrought iron and 4 in. cast iron greenhouse pipe. One No. 57 sectional, two No. 18 and one No. 16 Hitchings boilers. Will sell together or separate.

METROPOLITAN MATERIAL COMPANY,
1398 METROPOLITAN AVE., BROOKLYN, N. Y.

Mention The Florists' Exchange when writing.

FOR SALE

Greenhouse Material milled from Gulf Cypress, to any detail furnished, or our own patterns as desired, cut and spliced ready for erection. Estimates for complete constructions furnished.

V. E. REICH, Brooklyn, N. Y.
1429-1437 Metropolitan Ave.

Mention The Florists' Exchange when writing.

FOR SALE

PUMPS Rider-Ericsson. Second-hand, from $40.00 up; all repairs; other makes; new; cheap.

BOILERS One second-hand tubular hot water boiler 3 ft. in diameter 12 ft. long. Price $35.00. One No. 15 Hitchings as good as new, $60.00.

PIPE Good serviceable second-hand, with Threads; 2-in., 7 cts.; 1½-in., 5½ cts.; 1¼-in., 4 cts.; 1-in., 3 cts.; 2½ in., 10 cts.; 3 in., 14 cts.; 4 in., 19 cts. New 2-in. Standard, full lengths, with couplings; 8¼ cts. ft. Old and new fittings and valves. Old 4 inch cast iron 15c per foot.

STOCKS and DIES New Economy, best made No. 1 Threads, ¼-in., ¾-in., 1-in. pipe, $3.00. No. 2 Threads, 1¼-in., 1½-in., 2-in. pipe, $4.00.

PIPE CUTTERS New Saunders Pattern. No. 1 cuts ⅛-in.-1-in. pipe, $1.00. No. 2 cuts 1-in.-2-in. pipe, $1.30.

STILLSON WRENCHES New, 18-in., grips ¼-in.-2-in. pipe, $1.65; 24-in., grips ¼-in.-2½ in. pipe, $2.40; 36-in., grips ½-in.-3½-in. pipe, $4.75.

PIPE VISES New, No. 1 Hinged, grips ⅛-in.-3 in. pipe, $2.00.

GARDEN HOSE New. 50 ft. lengths. ¾-in., guaranteed 100-lbs. pressure, 7½ cts. per ft.; ¾-in. not guaranteed, 4¾ cts. per ft., 25 ft. lengths, ½c. per ft. more.

HOT-BED SASH New. Cypress, 3-ft.x6 ft., from 75 cts. up; glazed, complete, from $1.60 up. Second-hand, in good condition, all glass in, $1.00 each.

GLASS New American 10x12 single $1.80 per box; 12x12 single $1.90 per box; 10x12, 12x12, 10x15 double, $2.55 per box; 12x14, 12x20, 14x14, double, $2.75 per box; 16x16, 16x18, $3.10 per box; 16x24 double $3.20 per box. Second hand glass, 8 x 10, 8 x 12, and 10 x 12 single at $1.50 per box, double $1.75 per box.

Get our prices on New Gulf Cypress Building Material, Ventilating Apparatus, Oil, White Lead, Putty, Paint, Points, etc.

METROPOLITAN MATERIAL CO.
1398-1408 Metropolitan Avenue, BROOKLYN, N. Y.

Mention The Florists' Exchange when writing.

Thirty cents is the minimum charge for advertisements on this page.

San Francisco.

In the picturesque flower garden of the University of California I enjoyed a treat this week. The speaker was Professor Hugo de Vries of Amsterdam, a noted botanist, who told me The Florists' Exchange was no stranger to him, and that a representative of that paper was welcome to sit with his class. Nearly 200 pupils composed his audience—the botany class of advanced students at the Summer school of the university, who closely watched and attentively listened while the European savant discussed in the botanical garden his unique theories of evolution as illustrated in plant life and development.

Dr. de Vries used as an object lesson to illustrate the scientific truths he put forth Lamarck's evening primrose. This plant repeatedly originates new species, spontaneously, without the aid of any factors considered necessary in evolutionary process by Darwinian students. Professor de Vries told his students that this plant had much to do with providing material for his book on osmosis, wherein is expounded fully his theory of heredity. The development of this theory led him to the conclusion, differing from Darwin's, that evolution oftenest takes place by sudden leaps and bounds rather than by a slow and almost imperceptible but constant change.

All of San Francisco's florists were pleased this week on receiving a good wish visit made by P. J. Hauswirth, Chicago. This visiting gentleman of the trade is a prominent Order of Redmen member, and as a representative of the order has been in San Francisco some weeks distributing financial assistance to his brethren who were in distress as a result of the earthquake-fire, a goodly number of such being San Francisco florists. Mr. Hauswirth returned home this week.

The trade this week had to do with disfigured roses, a mildew effect of extreme hot weather we have now had for nine days. Carnations, too, were tarnished, but not so badly, and enough fairly good ones could be selected to satisfy the limited demand. Notwithstanding, it is a pleasure to report that three more ante-calamity florists have taken a stand this week for a new deal, all of them selecting sites at the corner of Polk and Sutter streets, one block within the burned district, from the Van Ness avenue fire line. This trio is Podesto & Baldocchi, Frank Shibeley and Charles Steppenbeck.

ALVIN.

Indianapolis.

News Notes.

A severe hailstorm passed over this section Thursday noon, July 12. Much damage was done to all forms of vegetation. In some places the hail covered the ground completely. At the County Workhouse farm the loss to vegetables alone was estimated conservatively at $5,000. About that amount was destroyed at the Insane Hospital grounds. A greenhouse at this place superintended by William Weber was practically annihilated, not a glass being left unbroken. The Indianapolis Water Company reports that the glass in its conservatories was destroyed. Only one commercial florist firm suffered to any extent. A. Wiegand & Sons lost several hundred panes of glass, beside 150 rubber and numerous other plants in hot beds. Some of their houses suffered severely; others lost little glass. This was accounted for by the fact that in some instances the glass was struck at right angles, at other times at an angle which would cause the ice to rebound without injury to the house.

Edward Bertemann and family are at South Haven, Mich.

E. N. Weygandt is making extensive improvements at his establishment on East Tenth street.

George Wiegand is enjoying his vacation.

It cannot be impressed upon the local florists too often that the Dayton convention will be but a few miles away this year, and that no one in the trade can afford to miss a national gathering of such great importance when it is placed veritably at his door. It is the intention of several to have a special car from Indianapolis for the opening day.

I. B.

Cincinnati, O.

Club Notes.

The Florists' Society held a meeting on Saturday evening last, but aside from paying the secretary and treasurer their salaries there was not much accomplished. The C. H. & D. railroad will be the official route to Dayton. The train leaves the C. H. & D. station at Baymiller and Sixth street at 8.15 a. m., August 21. Fare $2.20 round trip good returning at any time. Coming back you can leave at most any time; but the last C. H. & D. train leaves the Union station at 8.35 p. m. Two cents a mile is the rate in Ohio, and $1.10 is the price to Dayton from this city, and if you do not care to buy a round ticket the fare will be the same any way. But don't fail to go with the crowd on August 21, at 8.15 a. m.

E. G. GILLETT.

Washington, D. C.

Adrian J. Pieters, for several years Botanist in Charge of Seed and Plant Introduction and Distribution, United States Department of Agriculture, will leave the department about the middle of August next, to engage in commercial seed growing in California. The exact location has not been decided on, but it will be in the seed-growing belt of that State, probably the Santa Clara Valley. Mr. Pieters will aim to have seeds, both vegetable and flower, only of the highest standard and quality, in which he will undoubtedly succeed, as his experience in handling seeds, both foreign and domestic, has been very great. Preparations will be made this Fall for immediate operations in the Spring.

J. A. G.

A Reliable Friend.

We have answered many advertisements in your paper, and have received in every case stock as advertised. We think The Florists' Exchange the best friend we have, and watch for it every week.

TOWNE & HOWE.

New York.

Bargains in CHOICE PLANTS

English Ivy, from 4½ in. pots, $2.00 and $1.50 per doz. About 3 feet high and bushy.

Ivy, fan shaped, fine and bushy, $6.00 per doz., 75c. each.

Anthericum, variegated, per doz., $1.50; per 100, $12.00.

Boston Ferns, 5 in. pots, $3.00 per doz.; 6 in. pots, $6.00 per doz.; 7 in. pots, $12.00 per doz.

Kentia Belmoreana and Forsteriana, $3.00, $4.00, $5.00, $6.00 $9.00 per doz.; also by the 100. Also $1.00, $1.50, $2.00, $2.50, $3.00 each and by the 2 doz.

Phoenix Canariensis, large plants, 6½ to 7 feet high, 11 in. pots, $12.00 to $14.00 per pair.

Bird's Nest Fern, large plants, 6½ in. pots, $1.50 each, $18.00 per doz.

Araucaria Excelsa, 50c., 75c., $1.00, $1.50, $2.00, $2.50 each. Also by the 100.

Aspidistra, green, $1.00 per pot, 10 to 12 leaves.

Cut Flowers of Lily of the Valley, $4.00 and $5.00 per 100.

Boxwood Pyramids, in pots, $2.00 and $2.50 a pair, fine plants. Other sizes sold out.

Bay Trees, Pyramids.
- 55-60 in. high from top of tub, $14.00 per pair
- 65-70 in. high from top of tub, 16.00 per pair
- 72 in. high from top of tub, 18.00 per pair
- 84 in. high from top of tub, 20.00 per pair

Bay Trees, Standards (with 4 feet stems.)
- 32 in. diameter of crown, $14.00 per pair
- 36 in. diameter of crown, 16.00 per pair

Leaf-Mold, $1.00 per bag.

Asparagus Plumosus 3½ in. pots, $1.25 per doz.; per 100, $9.00; 4 in. pots, $2.00 per doz.; 4½ in. pots, $3.00 per doz.

Kentia Forsteriana, combinations, from $3.00, $4.00, $5.00, $8.00, $10.00, $15.00 to $20.00 each.

Dracæna Fragrans, $4.00 $6.00, $9.00, $12.00 $15.00, $24.00 per doz.

Latania Borbonica, from 5 in. pots, $4.00 per doz.; 6 in. $6.00 per doz.

Scottii Fern, 6½ in. pots: $7.00 per doz. Specimens $2.50 each. From the bench for 5½ and 6 in. pots, $5.00 per doz.; $40.00 per 100.

Piersoni Fern, 6½ in. pots, $9.00 per doz.

N. Elegantissima, from 4½ in. pots, $4.00 per doz.; $30.00 per 100.

Cattleya Trianae, 40 plants, 400 good bulbs, $16.00 per original case.

Orchid Peat, $1.00 per bag.

Rubbers, from 7 in. pots, 3 ft. high, $9.00 per doz.

Boston Ferns, specimens $3.00 each. 1 pair extra large, 14 in. pots, $15.00 the pair.

Areca Lutescens, 5½ in. pots, 9.00 per doz.; 3 in a pot.

Pandanus Veitchii, 5 in. pots, $6.00 per doz.; 6 in. pots, $9.00 per doz.; 6½ in., $12.00 per doz.; 7 in., $18 per doz.

Dracæna Terminalis, 4 in. pots, $3.00 per doz.; 5 in. pots, $6.00 per doz.; 6 in., $9.00 per doz.

Gardenia Veitchii, fine large Plants, 6½ in. pots, well budded, $9.00 per doz.

Cycas Revoluta, we have them in 5½, 6, 7 and 8 in. pots, very fine, 50c., 75c., $1.00, $1.50, $2.00 and $3.00 each.

Cibodium Scheidii, 6, 6½ and 7 in. pots, $1.50, $2.00 and $2.50 each.

Cash with order or satisfactory New York references required.

ANTON SCHULTHEIS

19th St. & 4th Avenue, COLLEGE POINT, L. I., N.Y.

Mention The Florists' Exchange when writing.

GREENHOUSE AND BEDDING PLANTS.

Geraniums, in variety, 40c. per doz. $2.00 per 100 and up.

WRITE FOR CATALOGUE.

	doz.	100
Achryanthes, Emersoni	$ .40	$2.00
Alternanthera, red and yellow	.40	2.00
Hardy English Ivy	.40	2.00
Lemon Verbena	.40	2.00
Smilax	.40	2.00
Hardy Chrysanthemums, small flowered	$.40	$2.00
Hardy Chrysanthemums, Aster flowered	.50	3.00

DAHLIA ROOTS, we are booking orders for fall delivery, send for list.

A cordial invitation is extended to all interested in Horticulture to visit us, Cowenton Station, Philadelphia division B. & O. R. R. 12 miles north of Baltimore.

R. VINCENT Jr. & SON, WHITE MARSH, MD.

Mention The Florists' Exchange when writing.

Begonia "Gloire de Lorraine" and "Turnford Hall"

NOW READY FOR DELIVERY. Propagated strictly from single leaf; this method gives much better results than from cuttings, $15.00 per 100, $140.00 per 1000, 4 inch pots, $40.00 per 100. **ADIANTUM FARLEYENSE**, fine specimens $18.00 to $24.00 per doz, 1¾ inch pots, $8.00 per 100; 2¼ inch pots, $15.00 per 100. **PANDANUS VEITCHII**, 50c., $1.00, $1.50 and $2.50 each. Good value guaranteed. Cash with order from unknown correspondents.

J. A. PETERSON, McHenry Ave., Westwood, CINCINNATI, OHIO

Mention The Florists' Exchange when writing.

SMILAX

	per 1000	per 100
2¼ in. pots	$12.00	$1.25
Asp. Plumosus, 2¼ in. pots, Aug. 1st		2.00
Cineraria, August 1st		2.00
Pansy Seed, large flowering, per oz., $4.00		

PRIMROSES

	per 100
Chinese, 2¼ in. pots, July 23rd	$2.00
Obconica, Rosea and Alba	2.00
Forbesi, fine for cut flowers	2.00
P. W. Narcissus, 13 ctm.	1.25

CASH PLEASE

JOS. H. CUNNINGHAM, Delaware, O.

Mention The Florists' Exchange when writing.

CHINESE PRIMROSES,

Christmas Peppers, Jerusalem Cherries, 2 in. and 2½ in. pots, $2.00 per 100.

STEVIA SERRATA, 2 in. 1½c.

GERANIUMS, 2½ in., Viaud, Bernandian and 7 other sorts, $1.60 per 100.

Cash, or C. O. D.

BYER BROS., Chambersburg, Pa.

Mention The Florists' Exchange when writing.

POINSETTIAS

2¼ in. pots, $5.00 per 100; $40.00 per 1000. Cash with order.

S. N. PENTECOST,

1790-1810 East 101 St., CLEVELAND, O.

Mention The Florists' Exchange when writing.

CULTURAL DIRECTIONS

Specially written for the use of your amateur customers. Send Twenty-five cents for complete sample set, which amount will be deducted from order for first thousand.

The universal favor in which these Directions are held, as shown by the many orders received therefor, encourages us in the belief that these Leaflets are just the neat little factor to help promote business and establish better relations between the dealer and his customer.

TRY SOME!

BIG BUSINESS ASSISTANT

TO SAVE TIME, QUICKEN SALES, AND AID YOU PLEASE YOUR CUSTOMER, WE HAVE PREPARED

Cultural Directions

COVERING A NUMBER OF THOSE PLANTS AND BULBS MOST LARGELY IN DEMAND

THE "CULTURALS" have been written by experts; they are fuller, and contain more detailed directions than it is possible to embrace in a catalogue. Equipped with these, just hand one out with each sale, and save yourself considerable present and future trouble, as the customer will then be able to consult the directions, grow his plants, seeds or bulbs intelligently, and so receive satisfactory results, without having to continually resort to you for advice.

The following "Culturals" are now ready:

AMARYLLIS (Hippeastrum)
ANNUALS FROM SEED
ASPARAGUS
ASTERS
BEGONIA, TUBEROUS
BULBS
CABBAGE and CAULIFLOWER
CANNA
CARNATIONS, MONTHLY
CELERY
CHINESE SACRED LILY
CHRYSANTHEMUM
CLIMBING PLANTS, Hardy
COLEUS, and other bedders
CROCUS, Snowdrop and Scilla Sibirica
DAHLIA
FERNS
FREESIA
GERANIUM
GLADIOLUS
GLOXINIA
HOT BEDS and FRAMES
HOUSE PLANTS, Care of
HYACINTHS, Dutch and Roman
IRIS AND TRITOMA
LAWNS
LILY CULTURE for House and Garden
MUSHROOM CULTURE
ONIONS
PALMS, House Culture of
PANSY
PEONIES
PERENNIALS, Hardy
PRIMULA
ROSE CULTURE
SWEET PEA, The
TOMATOES
TUBEROSE
TULIP
VEGETABLES
VIOLETS
WATER GARDEN, How to make and Manage a

PRICE LIST

500 Cultural Directions for $1.50
1,000 - - - - - - 2.50
Printed on white paper, clear type, size 6 x 9¼ inches, in an assortment, your selection of not less than 100 of each, delivered carriage paid.

Sufficient space will be left at the bottom of each leaflet for your name, address, etc. If you desire this imprint (3 lines) we will put same on for you at 50 cents for 500, 75 cents for 1000. Special quotations will be made on quantities of 5,000 "CULTURALS" or over.

A. T. De La Mare Ptg. and Pub. Co. Ltd.

Pubs. The Florists' Exchange. P. O. Box, 1697, NEW YORK

Mention The Florists' Exchange when writing.

YOUR

Fall Catalogue

We have been printing Trade Catalogues for the past fifteen years; have been accumulating stock cuts and photographs for the past fifteen years, and, equally important, perhaps most important of all, have been steadily improving in our knowledge as to what is required in the way of style, workmanship and finish in order to produce a catalogue that

Will Be Effective

Send in full specifications and we will promptly give you an estimate. We supply our stock cuts free to customers.

A. T. DE LA MARE PTG. & PUB. CO. Ltd.

2 to 8 Duane Street, New York City.

J. K. ALLEN
Wholesale Commission Dealer in **Cut Flowers**
106 West 28th St., NEW YORK
Open at 6 a. m. every day.
Telephone, 167 Madison Square.
Consignments Solicited.
Mention The Florists' Exchange when writing.

Wm. Stuart Allen Co.
Commission Merchants in CUT FLOWERS
ORCHIDS AT ALL SEASONS
53 WEST 28th STREET, NEW YORK
Telephone 356 Madison Square
Mention the Florists' Exchange when writing.

C. BONNET — G. H. BLAKE
BONNET & BLAKE
Wholesale Florists
106 Livingston Street, BROOKLYN, N. Y.
Telephone: 4638 Main.
Consignments solicited. Out-of-town orders carefully attended to. Give us a trial.
Mention The Florists' Exchange when writing.

CUT FLOWER EXCHANGE
Sixth Ave. and 26th St.
Coogan Building, NEW YORK
Open every Morning at Six o'clock for the Sale of Cut Flowers.
Wall Space for advertising purposes to Rent.
V. S. DORVAL, Jr., Secretary.
Mention the Florists' Exchange when writing.

Joseph S. Fenrich
...Wholesale Florist...
—THE RELIABLE HOUSE—
110 West 28th Street
Telephone 324-325 Madison Square.
Mention The Florists' Exchange when writing.

FORD BROS.
Wholesale Florists
48 WEST 28th ST., NEW YORK
Telephone, 3870-3871 Madison Square
Mention The Florists' Exchange when writing.

GROWERS, ATTENTION
Always Ready to Receive Fine Stock
WILLIAM H. GUNTHER
30 West 29th Street
'Phone, 551 Madison Square. NEW YORK
Violets, Roses, Carnations, Orchids
Established 1888
Mention the Florists' Exchange when writing.

ALEX. J. GUTTMAN
The Wholesale Florist of New York
43 WEST 28th STREET
Phones 1664-1665 Madison Square
Mention The Florists' Exchange when writing.

A. M. HENSHAW
..Wholesale Florist..
52 West 28th Street, NEW YORK
First class Roses and Carnations a specialty.
Consignments Solicited. Tel. 5583 Madison Sq.
Mention The Florists' Exchange when writing.

HICKS & CRAWBUCK, Inc.
Wholesale Florists
And Dealers in FLORISTS' SUPPLIES
76-78 Court Street
Phone, 3660-3661 Main BROOKLYN, N. Y.
Mention The Florists' Exchange when writing.

HEADQUARTERS FOR NOVELTIES
ORCHIDS A SPECIALTY
THE HIGHEST GRADE OF **VALLEY** ALWAYS ON HAND
GARDENIAS, DAISIES, ROSES, CARNATIONS.
JAMES McMANUS, Telephone 759 Mad. Sq. 42 W. 28th St., New York.

PHILIP F. KESSLER
Wholesale Florist
55-57 W. 26th St., NEW YORK.
Telephone, 2921-5243 Madison Square.
Mention the Florists' Exchange when writing.

JULIUS LANG
Wholesale Florist
53 WEST 30th STREET
NEW YORK
Consignments Solicited. Telephone: 280 Madison Sq.
Mention the Florists' Exchange when writing.

WILLIAM H. KUEBLER
Wholesale Commission Dealer in
CUT FLOWERS
28 Willoughby St.,
Telephone, 4591 Main. BROOKLYN, N. Y.
Mention the Florists' Exchange when writing.

FRANK MILLANG
Wholesale Commission Dealer in
CUT FLOWERS
55-57 West 26th Street, New York
Telephone Call: 299 Madison Square.
Mention the Florists' Exchange when writing.

ALFRED H. LANGJAHR
55 WEST 28th STREET, NEW YORK
Telephone, 4626-4627 Madison Square — Established 1891
SPECIAL VALLEY AND TOP GRADE ASPARAGUS
Consignments of First Class Stock Solicited.

Horace E. Froment
SUCCESSOR TO
W. GHORMLEY WHOLESALE COMMISSION FLORIST
Receiver and Shipper of all varieties of Cut Flowers
Telephones, 2200 and 2201 Madison Square. 57 West 28th St., NEW YORK

Wholesale Prices of Cut Flowers, New York, July 19, 1906

Prices quoted are by the hundred unless otherwise noted.

Roses	A. Beauty, fancy—special	10.00	to	25.00
	" extra	6.00	to	10.00
	" No. 1	4.00	to	5.00
	" No. 2	3.00	to	4.00
	" No. 3	1.00	to	1.50
	Bride, Maid, fancy—spe'l	3.00	to	4.00
	" extra	2.00	to	3.00
	" No. 1	1 00	to	2.00
	" No. 2	.50	to	1.00
	Golden Gate	1.00	to	5.00
	Liberty	......	to	......
	Mme. Abel Chatenay	1.00	to	6.00
Adiantum		.50	to	.75
	Croweanum	.50	to	1.00
Asparagus		25.00	to	50 00
	" Plumosus, bunches	10.00	to	15.00
	" Sprengerii, bunches	10.00	to	15.00
Cattleyas		25.00	to	50.00
Daisies		.50	to	1.00
Gladiolus		2.00	to	3.00
		....	to	.....

Carnations	Inf'r grades, all colors		.50	to	1.
	Standard Varieties	White	.50	to	1.
		Pink	.50	to	1
		Red	.50	to	1.0
		Yel. & Var.	.50	to	1.0
	*Fancy— (*The highest grades of standard var.)	White	1 00	to	2.0
		Pink	1 00	to	2.00
		Red	1 00	to	2.00
		Yel. & Var.	......	to	......
	Novelties		......	to	......
Lilies			5 00	to	8.00
Lily of the Valley			1.00	to	3.00
Mignonette			......	to	......
				to	......
				to	......
				to	......
Pansies, per dozen bunches			.50	to	.75
Smilax			8.00	to	10.00
Sweet Peas, per bunch			.01	to	.08

WALTER F. SHERIDAN
Wholesale Florist
Telephone, 902 Madison Square — 39 WEST 28TH ST., NEW YORK
ALL VARIETIES OF CUT FLOWERS IN SEASON

TOP GRADE FOR SHIPPING
American Beauty, Bridesmaid, Bride, Liberty, Meteor, Lily of the Valley, Carnations
Telephone, 1998 Madison Square — JOHN I. RAYNOR, 49 West 28th St., NEW YORK

Edw. C. Horan
55 West 28th St., NEW YORK
TELEPHONE, 1462-1463 MADISON SQUARE
CUT FLOWERS AT WHOLESALE
Mention The Florists' Exchange when writing.

JOHN YOUNG
Wholesale Florist
51 W. 28th St., NEW YORK
TELEPHONE: 4463-4464 MADISON SQUARE
Mention the Florists' Exchange when writing.

A. MOLTZ
Wholesale Florist
55-57 West 26th St., NEW YORK
1st Floor. Telephone, 2921-5243 Madison Sq.
Mention The Florists' Exchange when writing.

MOORE, HENTZ & NASH
WHOLESALE
GROWER — AGENT
COMMISSION FLORISTS
55 West 26th St., New York.
Telephone Call, 756 Madison Square
Mention The Florists' Exchange when writing.

GEORGE SALTFORD
Wholesale Florist
CONSIGNMENTS SOLICITED
49 West 29th Street, New York
TELEPHONE: 3393 MADISON SQUARE
Mention The Florists' Exchange when writing.

J. Seligman — Joseph J. Levy
JOHN SELIGMAN & COMPANY
Wholesale Florists
56 West 26th Street,
Tel. 4878 Madison New York.
Opposite New York Cut Flower Company
Mention The Florists' Exchange when writing.

SLINN & THOMPSON
Wholesale Florists
55 and 57 West 26th Street, NEW YORK
SPECIALTIES—Violets, Carnations and Roses
Shipping orders receive prompt attention. Consignments Solicited.
Telephone: 3864 Madison Square
Mention the Florists' Exchange when writing

FRANK H. TRAENDLY — CHARLES SCHENCK
TRAENDLY & SCHENCK
Wholesale Florists
44 WEST 28th STREET, NEW YORK
and CUT FLOWER EXCHANGE
Telephones: 798 and 799 MADISON SQUARE
CONSIGNMENTS SOLICITED
Mention the Florists' Exchange when writing.

A. L. YOUNG & CO.
WHOLESALE FLORISTS
54 West 28th St., NEW YORK
Telephone 3559 Madison Square.
Consignments of choice cut flowers solicited. Prompt payments. Give us a trial
Mention The Florists' Exchange when writing.

THOMAS YOUNG
Wholesale Florist
43 West 28th Street, NEW YORK
Telephone, 4850 Madison Square
Consignments of Choice Flowers solicited
Mention The Florists' Exchange when writing.

Wholesale Prices of Cut Flowers—Per 100

Boston July 17, 1906	Buffalo July 16, 1906	Detroit July 1, 1906	Cincinnati July 16, 1906	Baltimore July 16, 1906	NAMES AND VARIETIES	Milwaukee July 14, 1906	Phil'delphia July 17, 1906	Pittsburg July 18, 1906	St. Louis July 16, 1906
10.00 to 20.00	20.00 to 25.00	10.00 to 35.00	to 30.00	to	ROSES — A. BEAUTY, fancy—special	to 25.00	25.00 to 30.00	20.00 to 25.00	15.00 to 20.00
6.00 to 10.00	12.00 to 20.00	to	to 25.50	12.50 to 15.00	" extra	18.00 to 20.00	to 20.00	12.00 to 15.00	10.00 to 12.50
4.00 to 6.00	6.00 to 12.00	to	to 20.00	5.00 to 8.00	" No. 1	10.00 to 15.00	6.00 to 15.00	6.00 to 8.00	6.00 to 8.00
2.00 to 4.00	3.00 to 6.00	to	8.00 to 10.00	to	" Culls and ordinary	4.00 to 8.00	5.00 to 10.00	2.00 to 3.00	3.00 to 5.00
to	6.00 to 7.00	3.00 to 6.00	to 6.00	to	BRIDE, 'MAID, fancy-special	to 6.00	to 8.00	to 6.00	4.00 to 5.00
4.00 to 6.00	5.00 to 6.00	to	to 5.00	to 4.00	" extra	to 4.00	to 7.00	to 5.00	2.00 to 3.00
1.00 to 4.00	4.00 to 5.00	to	to 4.00	to 3.00	" No. 1	to 3.00	5.00 to 6.00	2.50 to 4.00	to 3.00
to	3.00 to 4.00	to	to 3.00	to 2.00	" No. 2	to 2.00	2.00 to 3.00	to 2.00	to 2.00
to	2.00 to 3.00	4.00 to 8.00	3.00 to 5.00	2.00 to 4.00	GOLDEN GATE	4.00 to 6.00	3.00 to 4.00	to	2.00 to 5.00
2.00 to 6.00	3.00 to 8.00	to	3.00 to 6.00	4.00 to 8.00	K. A. VICTORIA	4.00 to 8.00	3.00 to 5.00	3.00 to 12.00	2.00 to 6.00
2.00 to 8.00	3.00 to 8.00	to	to	to	LIBERTY	4.00 to 6.00	4.00 to 6.00	to	to
to	3.00 to 6.00	4.00 to 10.00	to	to	METEOR	to	to	to	to
to	3.00 to 5.00	4.00 to 10.00	to	2.00 to 4.00	PERLE	2.00 to 4.00	to	2.00 to 4.00	2.00 to 4.00
to	to	to 50.00	to	to	ORCHIDS—Cattleyas	to	to	to	to
to	1.00 to 1.25	to	to	.50 to .75	CARNATIONS — Inferior grades, all colors	to	to	to .75	to 1.00
to	1.25 to 1.50	to 1.00	to 1.00	1.00 to 1.50	Standard Varieties — White	to	to	to 1.00	to 1.00
to	1.25 to 1.50	to	to 1.00	1.00 to 1.50	Standard Varieties — Pink	to 1.00	1.00 to 1.50	to 1.00	to 1.00
to	1.25 to 1.50	to	to 1.00	1.00 to 1.50	Standard Varieties — Red	to	1.00 to 1.50	to 1.00	to 1.00
to	1.50 to 2.50	to 3.00	to	1.00 to 1.50	Standard Varieties — Yellow and var.	to	1.00 to 1.50	to	to 1.00
.50 to 1.00	2.00 to 2.50	to	to	to 3.00	Fancy Varieties — White	to	1.50 to 2.00	to 2.00	1.00 to 2.00
.50 to 1.50	2.00 to 2.50	to	to	to 8.00	Fancy Varieties — Pink	to	1.50 to 2.00	to 2.00	1.50 to 2.00
.50 to 1.50	2.00 to 2.50	to	to	to 8.00	Fancy Varieties — Red	to 1.00	1.50 to 2.00	to 2.00	1.00 to 2.00
.50 to 1.50	2.00 to 2.50	to 1.50	to	to 8.00	Fancy Varieties — Yellow and var.	to	1.50 to 2.00	to	1.00 to 2.00
to	to	to	to	to	Novelties	to	to	to	to
.50 to 1.00	1.00 to 2.00	to 2.00	to 1.00	to 1.00	ADIANTUM	to 1.00	to	1.25 to 1.50	to
to 50.00	40.00 to 50.00	25.00 to 60.00	to 50.00	25.00 to 50.00	ASPARAGUS, Plum. and Ten.	20.00 to 30.00	25.00 to 35.00	30.00 to 50.00	25.00 to 50.00
to	1.00 to 2.00	20.00 to 30.00	to 35.00	25.00 to 50.00	" Sprengeri, bunches	20.00 to 30.00	25.00 to 35.00	20.00 to 40.00	25.00 to 50.00
to	8.00 to 10.00	to 10.00	to 1.00	6.00 to 8.00	CALLAS	to	to 8.00	to	to
4.00 to 8.00	to	.75 to 1.50	to	to	DAISIES	to .40	to 1.00	.50 to 1.50	to
to	to	8.00 to 10.00	to 3.00	2.00 to 4.00	GLADIOLUS	to 3.00	to	6.00 to 8.00	3.00 to 5.00
2.00 to 4.00	to	to	to 12.50	10.00 to 12.50	LILIES, Harrisii	to	8.00 to 12.00	to	to
to	10.00 to 12.00	to	to	10.00 to 12.50	" Longiflorum	to 12.50	to	15.00 to 18.00	to
2.00 to 4.00	3.00 to 4.00	3.00 to 4.00	3.00 to 4.00	1.00 to 2.00	LILY OF THE VALLEY	to 3.00	3.00 to 4.00	2.00 to 4.00	to
to	1.00 to 2.00	to	to	2.00 to 2.50	MIGNONETTE, ordinary	to	1.00 to 2.00	to	to
to	to	to	to	to	" fancy	to 1.00	to	to	to
to	2.00 to 5.00	4.00 to 8.00	to	to	PEONIES	to	to	to	to
to 12.50	to 15.00	12.50 to 15.00	to 15.00	12.50 to 20.00	SMILAX	to 15.00	10.00 to 12.50	12.50 to 15.00	12.50 to 15.00
to	to	to	to	to	VIOLETS, ordinary	to	to	to	to
to	to	to	to	to	" fancy	to	to	to	to
to	to	to	to	to	NARCISSUS	to	to	to	to
.15 to .35	.40 to .50	.50 to .75	to .25	.20 to .35	SWEET PEAS	.25 to .50	.50 to .75	.25 to .50	.10 to .15
to	to	to	to	to		to	to	to	to
to	to	to	to	to		to	to	to	to
to	to	to	to	to		to	to	to	to

St. Louis.

News Notes.

The Florists' Club outing will take place next Thursday, July 26, at Ramona Park. The club invites all the florists to take part. The trustees are working hard to make this one of the best outings the club has ever had. The baseball game causes considerable talk in the wholesale district, and a number of bets have already been placed on the result. It has been reported that C. C. Sanders has sent to Dallas, Texas, for a badger to be used in the badger fight. The colored jubilee singers have been engaged. These events will be the features of the outing.

G. C. McClure has left his position at Shaw's Garden, and has returned to his home in Buffalo. G. H. Pring has taken Mr. McClure's position and is now in charge of the orchid houses at the Garden.

Berning is handling a fine lot of Lilium longiflorum giganteum; these are grown by James W. Dunford at Clayton.

City Forester Meyer has handed in his report to the Street Commissioner which shows that 13,153 trees have been located and placed on the books; 53 per cent. of these were found in good condition; 28 per cent. fair, and the remainder diseased by smoke, insects and gas mains.

All the city parks are in very fine condition this year, and Superintendent Ostertag has covered himself with glory the short time he has been in office.

W. J. Pilcher, who until recently was in the growing business at Kirkwood, left Monday morning for a trip west as far as Kansas City. They say he is to establish himself in the greenhouse business somewhere between here and Kansas City.

The present trustees, Carl Beyer, Frank Weber and F. J. Fillmore, are voted the best set of trustees the club has had; anything they go after must come, so their office has this sign out: "R. L. H."—Run like Hustlers.

ST. PATRICK.

PAWTUCKET, R. I.—James Barclay, proprietor of the Rhode Island Greenhouses on Main street, fell in one of his greenhouses last week and as he fell his left arm caught in one of the hooks supporting the steam pipe, causing a very painful injury. The hook entered the flesh to the bone, lacerating the arm severely. The injury was dressed by a physician.

Wholesale Prices of Cut Flowers, Chicago, July 17, 1906.

Prices quoted are by the hundred unless otherwise noted.

ROSES — American Beauty		
36-inch stems.........per doz.	.... to	4.00
30-inch stems.......... "	.... to	3.00
24-inch stems.......... "	.... to	2.50
20-inch stems.......... "	.... to	2.00
18-inch stems.......... "	.... to	1.50
12-inch stems.......... "	.... to	1.00
8-inch stems and shorts "	.50 to	.75
Bride Maid, fancy special	5.00 to	6.00
" extra	4.00 to	5.00
" No. 1	2.00 to	3.00
" No. 2	.50 to	1.00
Golden Gate	2.00 to	6.00
Carnot	2.00 to	6.00
Uncle John	2.00 to	8.00
Liberty	2.00 to	8.00
Richmond	2.00 to	6.00
Kaiserina	2.00 to	6.00
Killarney	3.00 to	8.00
Perle	2.00 to	6.00
Chatenay	2.00 to	6.00
Orchids—Cattleyas	.... to	50.00
SMILAX	8.00 to	12.00
LILY OF THE VALLEY	2.00 to	4.00
SWEET PEAS	.25 to	.50

CARNATIONS			
Inferior grades all colors		.25 to	.50
STANDARD VARIETIES	White	.75 to	1.00
	Pink	.75 to	1.00
	Red	.75 to	1.00
	Yellow & var.	.75 to	1.00
*FANCY (The highest grades of Sta'd var)	White	1.50 to	2.00
	Pink	1.50 to	2.00
	Red	1.50 to	2.00
	Yellow & var.	1.50 to	2.00
NOVELTIES		.... to	....
ADIANTUM		.50 to	1.00
ASPARAGUS, Plum. & Ten.		.35 to	.50
" Sprengeri, bunches		.35 to	.50
GLADIOLUS		2.00 to	6.00
LILIES, Longiflorum		8.00 to	12.00
HARRISII		8.00 to	12.00
MIGNONETTE, ordinary		1.00 to	2.00
....		.... to	....
....		.... to	....
HARDY FERNS per 1000		1.00 to	1.50
GALAX "		1.00 to	1.25

Chicago.

Trade Notes.

At the George Wittbold Company's Buckingham place houses the stock is in beautiful condition for this season, especially in the newly erected show house. Some of the older houses are being rebuilt and plans are already being formulated for very extensive alterations to be carried out next Spring. The concern has now, through the Summer months, practically the same physical equipment that is employed during the busy season, nominally seventy men and twenty-five well fed horses. Louis Wittbold takes pride in showing the perfect condition of the stock in the different houses as an absolute proof of the claims which he makes for his watering system, all of which seem to be fully justified.

Joseph Ziska, who has just graduated from school, has taken up greenhouse work at the establishment of the Chicago Rose Company.

The Benthey-Coatsworth Company reports roses as moving very satisfactorily for this time of the year, both as to quality and demand.

The report is quite general of large losses among aster plants in the field. Although there is a great deal of the yellows, more serious inroads are being made in some cases by a disease with which the growers are yet unacquainted.

A. L. Randall, who is spending nearly all his time during the Summer on his fruit farm at Benton Harbor, Mich., reports that he will not have over one-tenth of a normal peach crop, while all other fruit prospects are excellent.

George R. Scott of the Winterson Company took a business trip last week to Elgin and other towns in the western section. He reports that George Souster of Elgin is rebuilding several houses and that his stock generally is in good condition. He is cutting Portia carnation of remarkably fine quantity from the field.

H. E. Philpott of Winnipeg, Manitoba, was in town and attended the meeting on Thursday evening of the Chicago Florists' Club of which organization he is a member.

M. J. Hamlin, until recently connected with the Waverly Nursery Company, of Waverly, Mass., has associated himself with the Riverbank Nursery Company of Geneva, this state, where a specialty will be made of small ferns in large quantities, mushrooms and choice cut flowers. Additional glass is being erected, boilers and piping added, and it is expected that a larger increase in facilities will be made next season.

At Western Springs perhaps the most novel feature of the present week is the exhibition of Vaughan's annual hollyhocks which are now in their prime, a very large percentage being double, the height of the stocks running in many cases to eight feet and the colors including all the old and many new and pleasing shades. The next attraction will be ripe next week when the bulk of the sweet pea trials, including eighty-five varieties, will be on exhibition.

Mr. Brotherton, manager of the Jerome B. Rice Seed Co., of Cambridge, N. Y., was among recent callers.

H. B. Henry of Memphis, Tenn., a local grower and retailer, spent a few days the first of the week calling on his old friends in Chicago, where he was formerly located in the retail business.

Clarence Drisseler of the Wietor Brothers salesrooms left on Monday for his annual recuperation trip.

Statements which are misleading having been made in print regarding the Chicago Rose Company and its future plans we are authorized to state that the company will retain its headquarters at 56 and 58 Wabash avenue and continue to run its greenhouses and handle consignments of cut flowers and plants. The concern will also handle all lines of goods appertaining to the requirements of the trade. Joseph Ziska, the president of the company, will continue to manage the design business with which he has so long been associated; John Ziska, now treasurer, will look out for his department and John Sterrett will have charge of the wants of the buyers and sellers.

Miss Nellie C. Moore is spending a few weeks at Channel Lake, where as a disciple of Izaak Walton she reports an existence even more enchanting than that which she so much enjoys divided up between the Flower Growers' Market and Morton Grove.

Fred. H. Rowe, brother of Harry Rowe, has taken charge of the retail business of the Phœnix Nursery Company, of Bloomington, Ill., having until recently occupied a similar position with the Chicago Carnation Company at Joliet.

The mushroom industry is rapidly assuming a decided importance in this section, the season recently closed having been a very successful one. One concern reports having gathered two hundred and fifty pounds in a single day.

The bowling team of the Florists' Club has recently resumed practice, meeting every Tuesday evening at Bensinger's alleys, 114 Monroe street.

P. J. Hauswirth returned Sunday from a two months' trip to San Francisco and other points on the Pacific Coast, where, accompanied by Mrs. Hauswirth, he was delegated to disperse the funds donated to afflicted associates of the I. O. O. Red Men, as the representative of the highest ruler of the United States and Canada. As president of the Chicago Florists' Club he was also authorized to dispose of the funds recently collected by the club as occasion should dictate to his judgment. As a full report of his actions and opinion on this matter will be made at the next club meeting it can only be said at this time that he met with the Pacific Horticultural Society at a special meeting and the matter was thoroughly canvassed. Both Mr. and Mrs. Hauswirth returned in excellent health, and although the work was, on the whole, constant and arduous, Mr. Hauswirth says that it has given him an experience which he would not have missed for a great deal.

Some opportunity was given for side trips of a purely pleasure or social nature, including a day at Soquel, near Santa Cruz, where G. L. Grant was found in the midst of his miniature paradise enjoying to the fullest extent the landscape work in connection with his Pacific home. At present it is sufficient to say that the florists are rapidly recovering from their recent losses and that business is not, as might be supposed, at a standstill, many of the florists doing a fairly good trade. Carnations are selling well at a fair price and are of good quality, especially Enchantress and Prosperity, the latter being especially noticeable for a strength of stem not found in this section of the country.

Robert Newcomb severed his connection with the Central Floral Company and left on Tuesday evening for Phœnix, Arizona.

Messrs. Lubliner and Trinz left Sunday for Milwaukee, where they will spend a few days, after which the latter will proceed to Cincinnati.

The rains of Saturday and Sunday were most emphatically local, an inch and a half of precipitation having been reported in the business section, while at a short distance it took the form of a heavy dew. Sunday morning the storm was so heavy that many basements were flooded, there being at one time over six inches of water standing in the salesroom of the Kennicott Brothers Company.

The Central Floral Company, at their new store at 68 State street, are giving an interesting and attractive daily change of window display.

Alex. Newitt, floor manager of the J. B. Deamud Company, started Monday on a two weeks' vacation on the old farm at Joliet.

Tuesday evening saw a jolly party composed of Peter Reinberg, John Muno, and Adam Zender and the respective better halves, leave Chicago for Colorado Springs, Denver, and the interesting points of Colorado.

Wietor Brothers have started planting their carnations; their chrysanthemums are all planted, and they are cutting young American Beauty roses of excellent quality and in generous quantity.

Dr. Halstead of the St. Clair Floral Company, Belleville, Ill., was in town Saturday last. He speaks most confidently of the prospects of his new geranium Sycamore.

WILLIAM K. WOOD.

St. Paul.

News Notes.

From all appearances we are to have a big attendance at our annual outing, which includes a steamboat ride to Shakopee and a picnic there. About every florist in the Twin Cities will be present with their families, and an enjoyable time is looked forward to.

E. F. Lemke, one of our pioneer florists, has been doing a very nice business lately, and is well satisfied.

C. F. Vogt reports a heavy trade in funeral work, and is apparently well satisfied with the profits realized at this time of the season. He is having a large ice box built, which will be a good addition to his store.

Christ. Bussjaeger's daughter was married on the 11th. He rented a large hall which accommodated about 250 guests. The florists all put in toward a handsome present, which no doubt was greatly appreciated.

Considerable improvements are making by St. Paul florists, and this Fall will find us with some of the finest stores in the country, as about every dealer is doing something in the way of repairs.

The Greek fruit dealers are evidently convinced that the florist business is not what it is cracked up to be, as we hear of a number of ice boxes for sale by them. St. Paul trade does not patronize them.

L. L. May & Co. report a better July business than last season. Funeral work seems to be their main hold at this time of the year.

PAUL.

Omaha, Neb.

Trade Notes.

Trade is rather quiet, and were it not for funeral work, scarcely anything would be doing. Carnation plants in the field are looking well, as is most everything else in this section. Rose planting is going on merrily and this work is almost completed in many places.

George Sorenson, Florence, is adding two short houses. J. H. B.

The Summer meeting of the Nebraska State Horticultural Society was held at Hanscom Park pavilion, July 11 and 12. Mayor Dahlman welcomed the florists with an address, and James Y. Craig, president of the park board, also delivered an address of welcome Wednesday, to which Rev. C. S. Harrison responded. J. J. Hess, president of the Omaha Florists' Club, J. L. Coppoc, Chambers; Paul E. R. Getzschmann, Omaha, and W. R. Adams, superintendent of parks, were down for talks the first day of the meeting at the morning session. In the afternoon Ed. Williams, Grand Island; Irwin Frey, Lincoln; John Bath, Omaha, and M. Stauch of Council Bluffs spoke, while in the evening addresses were delivered by Judge Slabaugh, president of the Omaha Civic Improvement League and C. S. Harrison of York. Thursday the members of the society enjoyed a trolley ride around the city.

ROCHDALE, MASS.—In the will of the late F. A. Blake the following bequests are enumerated: Worcester Children's Friend Society, $2000; Trustees of the First Universalist Society, Worcester, $1000; Trustees of the Greenville Baptist cemetery, $500; Worcester County Horticultural Society, $1000. The will disposes of a large estate, and names his wife for executrix without giving surety on her official bond. The will was made June 5, 1908.

Baltimore.

News Notes.

The July meeting of the club was very well attended and much business transacted.

The store business is fairly good for this season of the year.

Severe storms have caused some damage to roadways, especially in the parks and cemeteries.

The lawns, trees, beds and shrubs are in perfect condition and almost entirely free from insects. The displays of geraniums, vincas and cannas are exceptionally fine everywhere; the large numbers in our public squares and parks in full bloom and the varieties of gay colors are commented upon.

The new swimming pool, with the great athletic fields and outdoor gymnasium, at Patterson Park, has been completed and thousands are in daily attendance. This feature of park athletic facilities is growing immensely popular with the youth of this city; the park board has expended $45,000 on these improvements in Patterson Park alone.

The new Florists' Exchange Building in Baltimore is being rapidly pushed to completion; the directors of the Exchange expect to occupy the building in October.

The club has accepted an invitation from the Maryland Horticultural Society to attend its Summer meeting August 8 and 9 at Orlando Harrison's nurseries in Berlin, Md., which is in close proximity to Ocean City, the famous seaside resort. A good time is assured, and a number of the Baltimore florists will attend. The following is part of the programme with the entertainment given the members by the firm of J. G. Harrison & Son: August 8; 1 p. m., dinner in Berlin Manor Grove; 2 p. m., meeting in Manor Grove, with remarks by President Cohill, and Mayor Orlando Harrison's address of welcome; address by President Sylvester, of Maryland Agricultural College, and Professor F. A. Waugh, of Massachusetts; 4-7 p. m., tour of the nurseries, over 1,000 acres; 8 p. m., train to Ocean City; 8.30 p. m., supper; 9 p. m., evening on the beach. Next day meetings, bathing, etc. C. L. SEYBOLD.

Newport, R. I.

Trade Notes.

There is no scarcity of choice cut flowers in Newport at present, notwithstanding that in general flowers are anything but at their best at this time of the year. But the Newport season, which is July, August and September, corresponds with November, December and January in New York, when at both seasons and in both places the highest prices are paid for the best class of stock.

American Beauty roses are worth as much retail here now as they were last Winter in New York. Lily of the valley and the best grade of carnations the same in proportion. Gardenias are always in good demand throughout the season, and it very often happens that there are not nearly enough to go round. This season, from what I can see, I think gardenias will be unusually scarce. Sweet peas, immense quantities of which are used up here, are below the average in crop and quality this season. Hollyhocks are just coming in; they will not be in very great demand for a week or more or until some big entertainments are given. A good pink variety of hollyhock is about all that is grown here; it is locally called the "Newport pink." I do not know whether or not we have a right to call it by that name, but I do know that it is the best pink hollyhock I ever saw.

Among the other common flowers used in great quantities here is antirrhinum, especially a very large yellow, which is in great favor with florists for window work as well as for customers' decorations. Gloxinias are used a good deal by florists, and the color most sought after is a brilliant red.

In plants, Adiantum Farleyense of good quality are picked up on sight; these are used very often for dinner table decoration for small and select parties, and when only the families themselves are dining. The sizes of plants used are those in from 4 to 6-inch pots; larger plants are of course also valuable, being in demand for room adornment.

Water lilies are grown but by one florist in Newport, Hodgson; but it is by no means the case that water lilies are never called for. When they are, however, those receiving the orders have to chase around pretty lively to get them.

Every year Henry A. Dreer, Philadelphia, puts up an elaborate exhibit of aquatics at our shows, which is, I think, having the effect of making water lilies popular with the people who could use the flowers for decorating. One instance of this I know. Shortly after seeing the Dreer exhibit at our show last year, Mrs. Pembroke Jones gave one of the largest entertainments ever given in Newport; in the decorations water lilies played an important part, resulting, as Mrs. Jones said, from the impression made on her by the flowers seen at the Casino show. D. M.

Providence, R. I.

News of the Week.

The first of a series of monthly outings of the Rhode Island Horticultural Society occurred on Wednesday, July 11. A party consisting of about one hundred members and guests were entertained at the home of Sam W. Lewis at Warwick, R. I. Mr. Lewis is one of the original founders of the society, having been a member for a period of over forty years, and the welcome extended to his lifelong associates upon this occasion, therefore, had more than usual significance. The latchstring was out; free-handed hospitality was extended to all and the freedom of the farm, with its wealth of gardens and groves was at the command of the party. At noon, a bountiful repast was served upon a high point of the farm, where, overlooking Narragansett bay, the company saw before them a most attractive view of Rhode Island's irregular coastline. After luncheon, the party were escorted to Drum rock, once an abiding place of the Narragansett Indians. The rock is located a short distance from the home of Mr. Lewis, and the path leading, as it does, through field and forest, makes the little journey the more interesting. The Indians used this natural sounding rock in calling members of the tribe to councils and war dances. The rock is still in perfect preservation in this respect, and a slight movement of a person standing upon it causes the rock to send forth a drumming sound audible fully a half-mile distant.

Carnation stock is making excellent growth in the field, the seasonable weather conditions and frequent showers of the past month being especially favorable toward promoting a steady and rapid growth. Stock planted May 1 is fully a month, in point of growth, in advance of stock planted at same time last year. Planting in houses has not begun as yet; the majority of growers in this vicinity regarding the month of July as most favorable toward bringing the plants to maturity.

Quite a number of the trade are from home this week. Souvenir postals received from Vermont, New Hampshire and isolated towns in Maine, tell of depopulated streams and ponds; the sonorous monotone of gigantic mosquitoes; the willing response to the dinner call and the inability of all but the "star" boarder to secure even a smell of that which made Milwaukee famous. Needless to say, in some instances, the vacation period will not be an extended one.

Business has been rather quiet. Pink and white carnations and Bride and Bridesmaid roses are selling fairly well. Outdoor stock is in no demand. A number of store men are cleaning house and making improvements throughout. G. S. W.

Buffalo.

News Items.

Vacation season has begun. George McClure, the landscape gardener, will leave for a three months' trip abroad on the 23d inst.

Philip Scott, of the Scott Floral Company, Denver, Col., is here visiting his old home and friends. He has also found time to don the mask and chest protector to play with his old team mates. When he resided in Buffalo he was considered one of the best amateur baseball catchers in this part of the State.

Steve Rebstock is again at Crystal Beach, superintending one of the largest concessions there.

Carl Humphreys, of W. J. Palmer's, is spending two weeks visiting relatives at Sodus Point, Syracuse and Rochester.

Ed. Walter, of the same firm, is spending a week at Angola.

James Walton is spending two weeks at Toledo, O.

W. H. Grever and family are spending two weeks at the "Sea Shell," Crystal Beach. W. H. G.

PORTLAND, MICH.—Says the Portland Review "Some enterprising man could make a barrel of money out of a greenhouse. The Lake Odessa Vegetable and Floral Company started one less than a year ago and are now arranging to build another to take care of the demand for their goods. It will be 30 by 90, with cement benches, where flowers and vegetables will be grown."

Columbus, O.

Club Outing.

Last Thursday was the appointed outing day for the Columbus Florists' Club, and bright and early a lively crowd of florists, their families and employes, took a special car for Buckeye Lake, a noted resort about 20 miles east of this city. The attendance was a little disappointing in one respect—that was the absence of greenhouse proprietors, and many establishments which were not represented at all. However, President Stephens, Vice-President Corry, Secretary McKellar and other active members were on hand and did everything in their power to make the day enjoyable.

In the grove at the north end of the lake the regulation boys', girls', ladies' and sack races were pulled off with great éclat; also a short but rapid baseball game occupied attention until dinner time. An elaborate spread from the baskets in waiting and boating and fishing were extensively indulged in during the afternoon. John Burns maintained his reputation as champion fisherman, with a fine catch; and Mr. Seibert kept things stirred up all along the line on the way home, thus preventing too much monotony. C. D. B.

The club's prizes were awarded as follows: Ladies' race, Mrs. Galbreth first; Miss Hoyeler, second.

Girls' race, Celia Oestreicher first.

Boys' race, Herman Quecke first.

Sack race, I. D. Seibert first; A. M. Hills second.

Three-legged race, Depray and Stephens first, against Hills and Bauman second.

The outing was a most marked success in every way, thanks to our able committee. F. W.

NEW BEDFORD, MASS.—Once in a while a little spurt of funeral work comes in, to liven up things. There is plenty of building and repairing going on, emptying and filling benches and other Summer work.

The uptown florists report trade very quiet; early closing is the general rule with them. A movement was started to close Wednesday afternoons, but somehow or other it fe[ll] through.

Carnations are pretty well played out; fairly good blooms bring 35c. per dozen. Roses of good quality are unknown just at present; a few short stemmed flowers are seen. Sweet peas of good quality are coming in; these bring 50c. per hundred. Asters are now in the market.

E. Y. Pierce's new house on Cottage street is almost completed. Roses are all planted in it.

H. A. Jahn, at Clark's Point, has his new seedling white carnation cuttings planted in one of the greenhouses. Growers, keep your eyes on this variety; it is a winner.

HORTICO.

Suspicion Spreading Everywhere.

A bug harangued a motley crew
  Of other bugs and ants,
And candidly advised them to
  Beware of potted plants.

Philadelphia Bulletin.

Mention The Florists' Exchange when writing.

WHOLESALE TRADE LIST

ABUTILON SAVITZII, 2 in. pots, $3.00 per 100.
ASPARAGUS PLUMOSUS, 2½ in. pots, $3.00 per 100.
ASPARAGUS SPRENGERII, 3 in. pots, $5.00 per 100.
ASPARAGUS SPRENGERII, 5 in. pots, $2.00 per doz.
ASTERS SEMPLE'S Branching and Boston Market strong plants, $1.00 per 100.
CHINESE PRIMROSES, 2 in. pots, $2.00 per 100.
CINERARIA HYBRIDA, 2 in pots, $2.00 per 100.
CLEMATIS MONTANA, strong plants, 4 in. pots, $1.50 per doz.
CLEMATIS MONTANA GRANDIFLORA, 4 in. pots, $2.00 per doz.
CLEMATIS PANICULATA, 4 in. pots, $1.50 per doz., $10.00 per 100; 3 in. pots, 75c. per doz.; $5.00 per 100.
DAISY, QUEEN ALEXANDRIA, 2½ in. pots, $3.00 per 100.
DRACÆNA INDIVISA, 5 in. pots, $2.00 per doz.
IVY, Hardy English, 4 in. pots, $1.50 per doz.; $10.00 per 100
Pair of **LATANIA BORBONICA**, 18 in. tubs, 8 perfect leaves on each plant, $15.00 per pair. Smaller pair in 14 in. tubs, 6 leaves, $10.00 per pair.
Pair of **PHOENIX RECLINATA**, 12 in. pots, $8.00 per pair.

C. EISELE, 11th & Roy Streets, PHILADELPHIA, PA.

Mention The Florists' Exchange when writing.

SUMMER IN WINTER

BY USING

Standard Greenhouse Boilers

One cent gets our Catalog

GIBLIN & CO., UTICA, N. Y.

Mention The Florists' Exchange when writing.

WEATHERED COMPANY.

Builders of Iron and Cypress Greenhouses, Greenhouse Heating and Ventilating Apparatus.

P. O. Address, Box 789, New York City.

Mention The Florists' Exchange when writing.

The Greenhouse Boiler

"Far Ahead of Any

steam boiler that I have ever seen or used in regard to heating and is very economical in coal."

This is the verdict of an old time florist.

Do not decide until you have my estimate on boiler or heating material.

JOHN A. PAYNE

Horticultural Architect and Builder

33 Clendenny Ave., Jersey City, N.J.

Sash opening apparatus and all kinds of greenhouse structural material.

Mention The Florists' Exchange when writing.

GREENHOUSES.

MATERIAL FURNISHED AND MEN TO SUPERINTEND ERECTION IF DESIRED.

CYPRESS SASH BARS
ANY LENGTH UP TO 32 FT. OR LONGER.

THE A. T. Stearns Lumber Co., NEPONSET, BOSTON, MASS.

Mention The Florists' Exchange when writing.

Dealers in Boilers get best results when they advertise here.

WE MADE A SUGGESTION

last week that you give a little hard sensed thought to the comparative lasting qualities of the Iron Frame House—against the wooden house, with its everlasting repair bill—we only mentioned the endurance side then, but now want to suggest a few things to think about on the shade question.

¶The wooden house requires a sash bar 1⅝" x 2½"

¶The Iron Frame sash bars are only 15/16" x 1⅞"

¶Wooden Houses require numerous heavy purlins and supporting members.

¶The Iron Frame simply requires a truss rod from rafter to rafter across the peak; or even in a 40 foot house, two small columns are all that is necessary.

¶The wooden house carries the sash bars from eave to ridge, which in connection with the bar of ventilating sash just about doubles the shade.

¶The Iron Frame bars are carried to the header only—giving one-half the shade.

¶"The man who looks ahead is the man who gets ahead."
—The man who has the lightest house, grows the best plants
—gets the best prices.
—The man whose repair bills are way down, has profits way up.
Send for our Iron Frame Circular.

Lord & Burnham Co.

Greenhouse Designers and Manufacturers.

1133 Broadway, corner 26th St., NEW YORK.

BOSTON BRANCH, 819 Tremont Building.

Mention The Florists' Exchange when writing.

Scollay Boilers

are best

for Green House Heating. Standard Cast Iron Green House Pipe and Fittings.

We are Headquarters for all sizes wrought iron pipe and fittings.

It will pay you to get our special quotations. We also contract for, and erect **Steam and Hot Water Heating** apparatus in all parts of the country.

Illustrated catalogues free on application.

JOHN A. SCOLLAY,

74-76 MYRTLE AVE., BOROUGH OF BROOKLYN, NEW YORK CITY.

Telephones 1492-1493 Main.

U. G. SCOLLAY, Manager.

Mention The Florists' Exchange when writing.

Greenhouse Material of Louisiana Cypress and Hot Bed Sash Washington Red Cedar

Greenhouse Hardware and Posts. Patent V and U Gutters.

OUR GRADE INVARIABLY THE BEST, OUR PRICES RIGHT.

Write for Catalogue and Estimate when figuring on your new houses.

A. DIETSCH CO., 615 to 621 Sheffield Avenue, CHICAGO, ILL.

Mention The Florists' Exchange when writing.

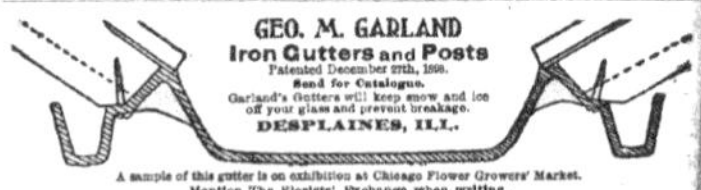

GEO. M. GARLAND

Iron Gutters and Posts

Patented December 27th, 1898.

Send for Catalogue.

Garland's Gutters will keep snow and ice off your glass and prevent breakage.

DESPLAINES, ILL.

A sample of this gutter is on exhibition at Chicago Flower Growers' Market.

Mention The Florists' Exchange when writing.

A. HERRMANN

Manufacturer of Floral Metal Designs

IMPORTER AND DEALER IN FLORISTS' SUPPLIES

FACTORY: 709 FIRST AVENUE, BETWEEN 40th AND 41st STREETS, NEW YORK

OFFICE AND WAREROOMS: 404, 406, 408, 410, 412 East 34th St.

WRITE FOR NEW CATALOGUE

Mention The Florists' Exchange when writing.

THE FLORISTS' SUPPLY HOUSE OF AMERICA

We have the largest assortment of Florists' Supplies in the country.

No order too large, none too small, to receive prompt attention.

SEND FOR CATALOGUE.

H. BAYERSDORFER & CO., 50, 52, 54, 56 North Fourth St., PHILADELPHIA, PA.

Mention The Florists' Exchange when writing.

THE FLORISTS' EXCHANGE

We are a straight shoot and aim to grow into a vigorous plant

A WEEKLY MEDIUM OF INTERCHANGE FOR FLORISTS, NURSERYMEN, SEEDSMEN AND THE TRADE IN GENERAL

Vol. XXII. No. 4 | NEW YORK AND CHICAGO, JULY 28, 1906 | One Dollar Per Year

PLANT NOW

Lilium Harrisii for Early Forcing

WE OFFER some extra choice Lilium Harrisii which has been grown for us from the original, pure stock. This is the kind of stock that you want for the very earliest forcing, and it is the true, original Harrisii. The small sizes—5-7s and 6-7s—are particularly desirable for this purpose, as they will flower more quickly than the larger bulbs. If you want to get a little of the original pure Harrisii, try a case or two of this. As our stock of this is limited, we can offer only a few cases to a single buyer. If you have been dissatisfied with the Harrisii that you have forced heretofore, try a case or two of this, and see if it is not more than worth the difference in price over the stock that you have been buying. In ordering, ask for the pure selected strain of original Harrisii, which we offer as follows:—

5 to 7	inch bulbs,	400	to the case,	$17.00	per case
6 to 7	" "	350	" " "	17.50	" "
7 to 9	" "	200	" " "	18.00	" "
9 to 11	" "	100	" " "	18.00	" "

Easter Comes Early Next Year—March 31st

and a great many growers will want to use Harrisii instead of Longiflorum so as to be sure to have the plants in flower in time, as the season is going to be short for Japan Longiflorum. The crop of Harrisii this year is the shortest it has been in years, and in view of the extra demand, we advise those who have not already covered their requirements to lose no time doing so.

For the very earliest forcing—Christmas and later—we recommend the pure Harrisii offered above, but for later forcing, for Easter, our customers will find the regular stock offered below first-class stock—much better than the average stock usually offered. We can quote the regular stock as follows:—

6 to 7	inch bulbs,	350	to the case,	$14.00	per case.
7 to 9	" "	200	" " "	15.00	" "
9 to 11	" "	100	" " "	15.00	" "

Freesia Refracta Alba, the true white variety. Now ready. Finest Bermuda-grown stock. $1.00 per 100; $7.50 per 1,000.

Bermuda Buttercup Oxalis. $1.00 per 100; $7.50 per 1,000.

F. R. PIERSON CO., Tarrytown-on-Hudson, N. Y.

NOW is the TIME

to secure

Richmond, Killarney and Beauty

Only a limited number left

$5.00 per 100

I have some very fine large plants of

GRAFTED { Bride, Bridesmaid, Killarney and Richmond

only $12.00 per 100

SEND FOR SAMPLES.

W. H. ELLIOTT, BRIGHTON, MASS.

Mention The Florists' Exchange when writing.

Vaughan's Seed Store Vaughan's Seed Store Vaughan's Seed Store Vaughan's Seed Store

BERMUDA LILIES

VERY SCARCE THIS YEAR

We offer subject to being unsold

	100	1000
Lilium Harrisii, 5 and 7 in.	$5.00	$40.00
" " 6 and 7 in.	6.00	50.00
Lilium Doeii, for Easter or late forcing, 5 and 7 in.	4.00	35.00
" " " " " 6 and 7 in.	6.00	50.00

FREESIA

We have a fine stock of well cured healthy bulbs now ready.

WHITE FLOWERED BERMUDA

	100	1000
Choice, 3/8 to 1/2 in.	$0.65	$5.00
Mammoth, 1/2 to 3/4 in.	1.00	9.00

CALIFORNIA GROWN

	100	1000
1st Quality, 3/8 to 1/2 in.	$0.45	$3.00
Choice, 1/2 to 3/4 in.	0.65	5.00

Ready soon Callas, Roman Hyacinths, Candidum, Paper White Narcissus, all Dutch Bulbs.

We are headquarters. Write for prices

Vaughan's Seed Store 14 BARCLAY ST., NEW YORK

CHICAGO, 84-86 Randolph Street Greenhouses, Western Springs, Ill

Oncidium Varicosum Rogersii

PRICE

	Per 12	Per 100
Small Pieces,	$3.50	$25.00
Large "	6.50	50.00
Ex. large pieces	9.50	75.00
Selected "	12.50	100.00
Ex. " "	15.50	125.00

ONCIDIUM VARICOSUM ROGERSII

DESCRIPTION—Flowers deep canary yellow, which are borne in great profusion—upon one or more spikes, during October, November and December—succeeds well in pots or upon blocks of wood in an ordinary greenhouse—all the above pieces offered will flower the first season—you get your money back in bloom and still have the plants.

ARTHUR T. BODDINGTON

342 West 14th Street, New York City

Mention The Florists' Exchange when writing.

CONTENTS AND INDEX TO ADVERTISERS PAGE 91

FRESH ILLINOIS CANES
1000 $6.00.

New Pansy Seed

Extra Blended, Large Flowering, Trade Packet, $1.00

Primula Obconica, Trade Packet, 25c.
Candytuft, White Empress Ounce, 20c.
Glazing Points, Peerless No. 2, postpaid. 75c
Mastica for glazing, gal., $1.25; 6 gallon cases, $6.75.
Fine Rose Bone, 200 lbs., $4.00.
Nitrate of Soda, 50 lbs., $2.00; 100 lbs., $3.50.
Sulphur, 25 lbs., 85c.

Wm. Elliott & Sons 201 Fulton St. NEW YORK

Mention The Florists' Exchange when writing.

Rawson's Wholesale Bulb Catalogue

Contains more choice and new varieties of Bulbs than any other catalogue in the United States. If you have not received one by this time, let us know and we shall mail you a copy at once.

W. W. RAWSON & CO.

5 UNION STREET, BOSTON, MASS.

Mention The Florists' Exchange when writing.

PACIFIC SEED GROWERS' CO.
411-415 SANSOME STREET
SAN FRANCISCO, CAL.
Specialties:
Onion, Carrot, Lettuce, Sweet Peas

Mention The Florists' Exchange when writing.

Thorburn's Bulbs

LILIUM HARRISII

LILIUM LONGIFLORUM

and all other bulbs for florists.
Send us your requirements for special prices.

CYCAS REVOLUTA STEMS

from Japan. Sizes and prices on application.
Asparagus plumosus nanus. $3.50 per 1000 seeds.

J. M. THORNBURN & CO.,
33 Barclay St., New York.

Mention The Florists' Exchange when writing.

ROEMER'S SUPERB PRIZE PANSIES

The finest strain of Pansies in the World. Introducer and Grower of all the leading Novelties Highest Award, International Exhibition Dusseldorf, 1906. Catalogue free on application.

FRED. ROEMER, Seed Grower, Quedlinburg, Germany.

Mention the Florists' Exchange when writing.

C. C. MORSE & CO.
Seed Growers
815-817 Sansome Street,
SAN FRANCISCO, CAL.
Careful growers of California specialties

Mention The Florists' Exchange when writing.

New Crop of my
Christmas Flowering
SWEET PEA SEED

Christmas Pink and Florence Denzer, pure white, will be ready August 1st.

Those two well known varieties are raised by over 2000 florists all over the world. Here is one out of many letters received:

Dear Sir: My sweet peas, which I raised from your seed, received the highest award at the Carnation Exhibit in Boston, being over 18 inches long. JOHN T. GALE, Tewkesbury, Mass.

Price 1-4 lb. 75c.; per lb. $2.00
MAILED FREE

New Christmas Flowering Hybrids, 20 to 30 colors, mostly blue, salmon, purple lavender, in mixtures; also Mrs. Edie Wild, carmine, separate color. 1 Trade pkt., $1.00, 5 Trade pkts, $4.00; not more than 5 pkts. taken in order to each customer just now. These new hybrids are just as free bloomers as Cristmas Pink and Florence Denzer, some much larger, and received first-class Certificate of Merit by the Mass. Horticultural Society, Boston, March 24. Seed ready in Sept.

All seed originated with me is sold in my original sealed pkts., with cultural directions, to the growers, but none for seedsmen for propagating.

Orders filled strictly in rotation.

ANT. C. ZVOLANEK
BOUND BROOK, N. J.

SEED BAGS

All packet sizes carried in stock in **MANILLA, AMBER LAID,** and **UNBLEACHED PAPERS.**
Printing done with cuts and cultural directions.
Large lots at very low rates.
Send for samples and discount sheet.
Our intimate acquaintance with the packet trade and our large facilities enable us to meet all requirements satisfactorily.

Address

The Brown Bag Filling Machine Co.,
Fitchburg, Mass.

CINERARIA SEED

S. & W. Co.'s Giant Prize Strain, pkt., 50c.; 1-64 oz., $2.00

PANSY SEED

Non Plus Ultra, mixed, pkt., 25c.; ¼ oz., $1.50; per oz., $5.00

STUMPP & WALTER CO., 50 Barclay Street, New York

Mention The Florists' Exchange when writing.

A BED OF MUSHROOMS

Raised from our Spawn, will **bear longer and yield better** than from any other variety of Spawn. This is proven by facts. Full particulars and information how to succeed in mushroom raising free. We warrant you if using our method of growing mushrooms that all will go well.

KNUD GUNDESTRUP & CO., MUSHROOM SPECIALISTS, 4273 Milwaukee Ave., CHICAGO

Mention The Florists' Exchange when writing.

PRIMROSES

Improved Chinese: Finest grown, named or mixed. Strong 2 inch $2.00 per 100.

XXX SEEDS
CHINESE PRIMROSE

Finest grown, mixed, 500 seeds $1.00; ½ pkt., 50c.

Cyclamen Giganteum: Finest Giant mixed, 200 seeds $1.00; ½ pkt., 50c.

DAISY, double Giant mixed, 1000 Seeds 25c.

GIANT PANSY. The best large flowering varieties, critically selected, 5000 seeds $1.00; half pkt., 50c.; per oz. $3.50. 500 seeds of Giant Mme. Perret, pansy seed added to every $1.00 pkt. of Giant Pansy. Cash. Liberal extra count of seeds in all packets.

JOHN F. RUPP, Shiremanstown, Pa.
The Home of Primroses

Mention The Florists' Exchange when writing.

The Choicest strains of Florists' Stocks

Including
Cineraria Calceolaria, Cyclamen, Pansy, Petunia, etc.,

CAN BE HAD FROM

JAMES VICK'S SONS
ROCHESTER, N. Y.

Mention The Florists' Exchange when writing.

Pansy Seed
THE JENNINGS STRAIN

New crop now ready, saved from finest selected stock, large flowering and great variety of fancy colors. By mail one pkt., 4000 seed, $1.00; ¼ oz., $2.50; 1 oz., $5.00, 2 oz., $9.00; 3 oz., $12.00. Cash with order.

E. B. JENNINGS,
Lock Box 254 Southport, Conn.
Grower of the Finest Pansies.

Mention The Florists' Exchange when writing.

PANSY SEED

Brown's Extra Select Superb Giant Prize PANSIES, awarded Silver Medal, St. Louis Exposition 1904. My own grown new 1906 crop ready. Price mixed seed 3000 seeds, $1.00; ¼ oz., $1.50; ½ oz., $2.50., 1 oz., $5.00; ¼ lb., $14.00; ½ lb., $25.00; 1 lb., $50.00. Cash with order.

PETER BROWN
Lancaster, Pa.

Mention The Florists' Exchange when writing.

H. H. HICKS,
Importer of and dealer in
MUSHROOM SPAWN
KENNETT SQUARE, PA.

Invoices of Barter's English Mushroom Spawn received monthly. Am. Pure Culture Spawn always on hand. When writing for prices state quantity wanted.

Mention The Florists' Exchange when writing.

MUSHROOM SPAWN

Originators and growers of **superior strains of Tissue-Culture Pure Spawn.**
Send for our booklet.

PURE CULTURE SPAWN CO.
PACIFIC, MO.

Mention the Florists' Exchange when writing.

PANSY SEED

Schmidt's Famous Strain, large flowering and fancy colors; none better. Per pkt., 50c.; ¼ oz., $2.00; 1 oz., $8.50. Plants ready September.

J. C. SCHMIDT CO.
BRISTOL, PA.

Mention The Florists' Exchange when writing.

Giant Cinerarias

Mixture of perfect colors

Dwarf Hybrids, Semi-Dwarf Hybrids — Each separate Tr. Pkt. $0.50, 6 Tr. Pkts. $2.50

O. V. ZANGEN, Seedsman, HOBOKEN, N. J.

Mention The Florists' Exchange when writing.

PANSY SEED

Of my own growing—**Crop of 1906.**

Unexcelled Mixture, ¼ oz., $1.00; oz., $8.00. **Parisian Mammoth,** imported, ¼ oz., $1.00; oz., $8.00. **Danish Exhibition,** imported, ¼ oz., $1.00; oz., $3.00. **Masterpiece,** fringed edge, imported, ¼ oz., $1.00; oz., $8.00. **Giant Mammoth,** extra fine, imported, ¼ oz., $1.50; oz., $5.50.

FRANCIS BRILL, HEMPSTEAD, L. I., N. Y.

Mention The Florists' Exchange when writing.

BURPEE'S SEEDS
PHILADELPHIA

Blue List of Wholesale Prices mailed only to those who plant for profit.

Mention The Florists' Exchange when writing.

Catalog Engravings
and ILLUSTRATIONS

that print EASILY. That's the kind we make—have been since '73

JAS. M. BRYANT, Horticultural Engraving and Printing
706 Chestnut Street, PHILADELPHIA, PA.

Write for our Catalogue of Stock Engravings.

Mention The Florists' Exchange when writing.

Seed Trade Report.

AMERICAN SEED TRADE ASSOCIATION

Henry W. Wood, Richmond, Va., president; C. S. Burge, Toledo, O., first vice-president; G. B. McVay, Birmingham, Ala., second vice-president; C. E. Kendel, Cleveland, O., secretary and treasurer; J. H. Ford, Ravenna, O., assistant secretary.

NEW ORLEANS, LA.—The J. Steckler Seed Company will soon vacate their present quarters and move into their own place, next door, which will be fitted up to accommodate their increasing trade. P. A.

NEW YORK.—The long established seed business of Alfred Bridgeman, 37 West Nineteenth street, has been purchased by W. C. Rickards, Jr., and A. J. Rickards, and, commencing August 1, will be conducted by them under the title of The Bridgeman Seed Company, Rickards Brothers, proprietors. W. C. Rickards has been in the employ of J. M. Thorburn & Company for the past 20 years; and his brother was three years with the same firm, and seven years with Stumpp & Walter Company.

The semi-annual meeting of the National Pickle Packers' Manufacturers' Association was held at the Palmer House in Chicago on Wednesday of last week. It was figured that there were at present enough pickles in storage to furnish every person in the United States with a dozen a day for more than a month. The new pure food law was endorsed. William Ballinger of Keokuk was elected president, and Frank A. Brown of Chicago, secretary-treasurer.

European Notes.

The hot, dry spell still persists throughout Western Europe, while in Germany and the whole of Holland copious rains, attended in the latter country by strong, cold winds, have fallen during the past six days. While this was badly needed for some of the crops, it has inflicted serious injury upon onion and spinach. Many of the onion stems are beaten down, and as the plants are only just beginning to bloom there is no possibility of the seed being developed. If the cold winds do not further develop the mildew, the losses caused by rain will not give us much anxiety, as we find on a closer inspection that a larger acreage has been planted than had been supposed.

As regards spinach, this plant takes such a slight hold of the ground that the injury caused by the heavy rains is all the more serious, for the plants beaten down cannot possibly recover. The loss may be fairly estimated at fully 3 cwt. per acre. This with a considerably smaller acreage makes the outlook for this article not very cheerful. EUROPEAN SEEDS.

FRENCH SEED CROPS.—The French seed growers were recently all praying for Summer weather, but now they have got it, do not seem from recent reports to be entirely satisfied. The drought succeeding suddenly to a cold wet period appears to have baked the soil like pie-crust, and growth is in consequence not so robust as the growers would like to see. From what we can gather this is one of these seasons when the first-rate cultivator, whose land is well worked and fertilized, is likely to reap full advantage from this industry. In a normal year the difference is not so marked, the indifferent cultivators merely coming in a little behind, but this season some of them will probably fail to get any crop at all.—Horticultural Advertiser.

CATALOGUES RECEIVED.

C. BETCHER, Canal Dover O.—Special List of Peonies.

SOAR BROTHERS, Little River, Fla.—Wholesale Price List of Trees, Bulbs, Seeds and Decorative Stock.

CRENSHAW BROTHERS SEED COMPANY, Tampa, Fla.—Fall Catalogue of Seeds, Bulbs, Plants and Poultry Supplies.

NEW YORK MARKET GARDENERS' ASSOCIATION, Richmond Borough, New York.—Illustrated Price List of Pansy and other seasonable Seeds and Bulbs.

NURSERY DEPARTMENT.

Conducted by Joseph Meehan.

AMERICAN ASSOCIATION OF NURSERYMEN.
Orlando Harrison, Berlin, Md., president; J. W. Hill, Des Moines, Ia., vice-president; George C. Seager, Rochester, N. Y., secretary; C. L. Yates, Rochester, N. Y., treasurer.

BARABOO, WIS.—Martin F. Foley, president of the Great Northern Nursery Company in this city, has announced his candidacy for state senator in the twenty-seventh district. Mr. Foley is the first candidate in the field and probably will be the only one from Sauk county.

American fruit growers are invited to participate in the Dominion fruit exhibit, which is to be held at Halifax this coming Autumn. It is said that the exhibits must arrive at Halifax before September 28. The superintendent of the agricultural department of the exhibition is G. Bigelow, of Wolfville, Nova Scotia.

The Pacific Coast Association of Nurserymen will meet in Salem, Ore., the first week in July, 1907. The following officers were elected: President—F. W. Powers, Chico, Cal., vice-presidents—W. D. Ingalls, North Yakima, Wash.; C. A. Howard, Riverside, Cal.; C. F. Lansing, Oregon; W. J. Henry, Vancouver, B. C., C. P. Hardwell, Caldwell, Ida; P. A. Dix, Salt Lake City, Utah. Secretary-treasurer— P. A. Tonneson, Tacoma. Committee on settlement of difficulties—S. A. Miller, Milton Ore.; W. D. Ingalls, North Yakima, Wash.; H. A. Lewis, Portland Ore.

Horticultural Notes.

Aster incisus, formerly called Calimeris incisa, is a capital early flowering species. Botanical works say of it that it blooms in August and September, but with us it flowers in July. The flowers are pale blue. It forms a compact clump of a height of two feet.

Erica vagans is a good hardy heath for the Northern States. It forms a bush rather more spreading than tall. The flowers are very light pink, almost white when well developed. It is a good one where such evergreens are valued.

Though the scarlet Clematis coccinea is but of herbaceous nature, it is a neat, pretty vine, and when rambling over brush, as sweet peas are often permitted to do, it forms a most attractive object.

Cemetery superintendents have been recommended to have a small nursery attached to their grounds, the same as those connected with parks have. This is good advice. Florists, too, would find a sample plot a source of profit to them. Many a sale would follow the showing of such to visitors.

Our native Rhododendron maximum deserves planting because of its late flowering. It is almost Midsummer before it blooms. The prevailing color is light pink to the bud, becoming white on full expansion; some are tinted purple. In its native haunts it grows to a height of 20 feet.

Not much has been heard of the Japanese wineberry of late, but it is both desirable as an ornamental and as a fruit. Those who have not got it in their collection should give it a trial. Its hairy stems, purplish red in color, are pretty.

Yellow locust timber is among the most durable known, a fact which has caused its extensive planting in many states. In some parts of the country the locust borer, Cyllene pictus, has been so destructive that it has caused a suspension of the planting of the tree.

The Colorado Douglas spruce, Pseudotsuga Douglasii is quite hardy in the Northern Atlantic States, but not so the one from Oregon and Washington. New Mexico and Arizona also give a hardy type, the tree flourishing there in the mountain regions.

A Summer Blooming Azalea.

A neglected azalea is the native one, A. viscosa. In general collections it is rarely met with. This should not be, for it is one well worthy a place wherever shrubs are grown. Its chief recommendation is, to me, its late flowering. It is long after all others are past blooming when the flowers of A. viscosa expand. In this vicinity it was in good display in Mid-July. There appears to be a difference in the time of blooming of the plants. When in nursery rows some are in flower and over long before others expand; and this can be observed every year.

Another point of merit possessed by this azalea is its delicious fragrance, of the odor of the honeysuckle. No other azalea approaches it in this respect; and then, too, its flowers are of a waxy white color, while its foliage is of a quite glaucous hue.

In its native haunts it flourishes on the edges of swamps, where such plants as clethra and the tall huckleberry grow, but it by no means demands a similar position in cultivation. It will grow, and grow well, in any ordinary garden location, even in the full sun, while preferring low ground, and partial shade.

Ampelopsis Veitchii and A. Virginica.

The two ampelopses, Veitchii and virginica, are the most popular of all vines for the covering of walls, as well as for all other purposes for which vines are used. Their self clinging tendencies are what make them so valuable. Before the advent of the Japanese one, Veitchii, our native species, virginica, was largely used. But the Japanese is superior in this way, that it does not push out branches which do not cling, but hang loosely from the wall, such as the native one does.

This is why it is preferred. It clings closely, clothing the walls of a house with an even sheet of green. The Virginia creeper is of a lovely orange yellow appearance in late Autumn, while Veitchii becomes of a bronze red hue.

When it comes to the clothing of a tree or something aside from a wall, the virginica, or Virginia creeper, as it is called, is often to be preferred. The hanging branches have a festooning effect which especially in the case of trees, creates a pleasing appearance.

There are several ways of propagating these vines. There is choice among cuttings, layers or seeds. Cuttings may be taken from half ripened wood struck indoors in Summer; or from hard wood, set outdoors in Spring. Seeds may be sown in Autumn outdoors, or in Spring if kept moist through the Winter; or indoor sowings may be made. Under vines on walls the seedlings spring up by hundreds in Spring, from berries that fall in Autumn.

Pot plants of these vines prove good sellers, especially in Summer, when digging them from the open ground is out of the question.

Pinus Mughus.

Red Berried Viburnum.

A shrub that has met with much favor since its introduction a few years ago is Viburnum tomentosum, the parent of the variety plicatum. Its flat heads of clear white flowers in early Spring are of pleasing appearance, and are unlike those of any other shrub flowering at that time. The berries which succeed them become of a deep scarlet color in July, at which time the bush is highly ornamental; and it is well worthy of its name—red berried viburnum.

This shrub does not commence flowering at as early an age as does V. plicatum. It takes a well established bush to flower well, and it is only with age that the best display of both flowers and fruit is made.

There is another very pretty red berried species—Viburnum Wrightii. The bunches of flowers are not as pretty as those of V. tomentosum, but the berries make as good a display.

This is the season to layer viburnums. Layered now, these would be nice young plants by Fall, which if set out in Spring would make good selling stock by the close of the growing season; and when layering no mistake will be made if a large number of those layered are composed of V. tomentosum.

Strawberries in Pots.

To get a crop of fruit from Fall planted strawberries it is necessary that the plants be well established and set with a good ball of earth. It is not difficult to obtain such plants when it is but a question of moving plants from one part of a garden to another; but for shipping a different method has to be employed, and here is where the pot plant comes in. A common way of getting pot plants is to sink pots to the level of the ground around old plants, allowing the young plants as they grow to root into them. In this way from one runner a half dozen plants can be had before the season closes.

But a better way to procure pot plants is to take the runners from the parent plants as soon as the first few white roots are visible on them. Cut off the plants, take them to a potting shed and pot them at once, placing them under cover in a greenhouse or a frame, where it will be damp and shady, and in a short time there will be pot plants ready to transplant. There is no trouble about the rooting; every plant will grow, the whole process being far more satisfactory than that of placing pots of soil around the plants outdoors.

When a variety of strawberry is new, the cutting of a runner to pot it may not be desired, as it may lessen the number of plants obtained. But as when one layer is cut off it permits of others forming from the old plants, its loss is not as great as one would suppose.

Pinus Mughus.

In nursery and other collections Pinus Mughus is often met with under such names as P. Pumilio, P. montana and P. carpatica, and while these names may really represent different looking plants, botanies agree that the name heading these notes should stand for all. That the trees do differ, those familiar with them know well. In any nursery row where a dozen or so only of plants appear, some will be found making a growth almost horizontal, hugging the ground, nearly. Others make a stiff, upright growth, and again others that in the course of years become in shape like the one pictured. This one, in fact, is a good representative of what is thought to be the typical Mughus. As seen in old grounds the trees are of the same outline, and the largest of them about 12 feet high and, generally rather wider than high. Many specimens are to be seen of the more spreading form, and these will be several feet wider than they are high.

The varying forms seen in seedling rows are very likely traceable to the gathering of seeds, from different trees, the trees representing different types.

In the whole list of hardy pines there is not another making the dwarf, dense growth of the one illustrated, and this fact makes it in great favor with planters.

The specimen photographed is near the summit of a very steep ascent, where a tall growing pine would be out of place, but where the P. Mughus is just right for the situation.

When this pine is young it should be frequently transplanted, to encourage it to form small roots, otherwise to transplant a good sized specimen is difficult. Spring is the only time the moving should be attempted; just as the buds show signs of swelling is a good time. JOSEPH MEEHAN.

Stigmaphyllon.

This plant seems peculiarly adapted, by its requirements and the uses for which it is available, for growers who are likewise retail florists. It will not do well in pots, but if planted in a bench in a somewhat shady part of a house and given some inducements in the way of a trellis, it will succeed admirably and flower almost continuously.

Stigmaphyllon is an excellent thing for baskets and other forms of decorative work by itself; or if used along with allamandas the two make very effective work, the former adding grace and lightness to the latter.

S. ciliatum is the variety grown in greenhouses. It has peculiarly shaped flowers of a pleasing yellow color produced on the vine in a way that makes it very adaptable for florists' work. Young plants can be raised from cuttings inserted in sand in bottom heat. Somewhat ripe wood should be used for the cuttings. M.

Growing Mignonette and Snapdragon with Carnations.

(10) Can mignonette and snapdragon be grown in the same house with carnations, in a temperature of 52 degrees? Which is the best snapdragon, giant or dwarf, and the most prolific? F. D. B.

—The mignonette might do fairly well in the same house as the carnations, but the snapdragon had better be planted in some other house, where the temperature can be run a little higher toward the flowering period. The tall growing snapdragon is the best one to grow for cut flower purposes.

Building an Icebox.

(11) Where can I find directions for building an icebox for holding flowers before shipping, that would be cheaper but as good as a refrigerator? F. D. B.

—Consult some local carpenter who has done that kind of work.

Taking the Bud.

(12) Is it yet too early to take the crown bud of Polly Rose chrysanthemums? They are good strong plants. R. P.
Conn.

—The tenth of August will be plenty early enough to take the bud, then good salable flowers can be safely expected. Buds taken during July have but a slim chance of developing into good blooms.

Fertilizer for Carnations.

(13) We have just benched a house of Boston Market carnations and would like to be informed as to the best time to apply bone meal and how much to use per square foot of bench. J. E. C.
Conn.

—If the soil in which the carnations are planted was well prepared, there will be no need to apply any fertilizer for six or eight weeks yet. After that time a little liquid manure once a week will be as beneficial as anything that can be employed. If, however, we had to use bone, we would afford a very light dusting over the surface, using a 5-inch potful to about 40 square feet of bench space.

Shading Violets.

(14) When is the proper time to remove shading from Princess of Wales violet plants. I grow them in beds in greenhouses and use cheese cloth for shading. Is the first of September too early?

Is the Governor Herrick violet larger or better than the Princess of Wales? Which do you consider the better for commercial use? CANADA.

—In the removal of shading when used for violet culture one must be governed entirely by circumstances. Remove the cheese cloth just as soon as the temperature can be kept down without it.

The new violet Governor Herrick, is claimed to be an improvement over all other single violets; but as it is not yet in general cultivation, being only introduced this season, we think it would be best, if particulars are wanted, to write to the introducer, H. R. Carlton, Willoughby, Ohio.

Time to Bud Roses.

(15) I would like to know the time to bud roses such as Baby Rambler on to a standard. G. H. W.

—If the standards are outdoors planted in a permanent position, they may be budded anytime from the middle of July to the middle of August.

Forcing Head Lettuce.

(16) Kindly give me some information as to the forcing of head lettuce. I have 100 feet of glass and want to use this for lettuce alone, but have never been successful with head lettuce. What seed or what variety is the best? What kind of treatment shall I give? How shall I arrange heat; and what about soil?
Penna. J. Y.

—There are different methods of raising head lettuce under glass. Good lettuce can be grown on raised benches provided there are 5 or 6 inches of soil, although solid beds are preferable, as the plants do not then need so much water, and the the conditions seem more adapted to them, the plants getting more natural moisture from the solid beds. Boston Market is one of the very best head lettuces for forcing purposes. Glass House can also be relied on to head up satisfactorily although a little under size. A temperature of 45 degrees at night, 55 to 60 degrees daytime during the forcing season would be about right for them. To be successful with lettuce it must be grown on without a check, and quickly; therefore, select a soil in which the plants will root readily. I don't know of anything better than a liberal coating of thoroughly decayed farmyard manure, intermixed with the soil; say, for four loads of soil one load of old manure. Then after the first crop of lettuce has been cut, a light coating of wood ashes forked in before planting again, would be beneficial.

It should take from six to eight weeks to mature a crop of lettuce from the time of planting; and if a continuous supply is the aim, seed should be sown every ten days from the first of September on. Avoid using a heavy soil; head lettuce will thrive better in a free working soil. WM. TURNER.

Time to Sow Seeds.

17) Kindly answer the following questions: When is the proper time to sow peony seed; hemlock, blue spruce, and white pine seed—Spring or Fall? Iris and phlox seed?
Conn. C. & L.

—If indoors peony seed might be sown now; but outdoors it should be sown very early in Spring.

Sow the evergreen seeds in Spring, early, outdoors.

Same answer as for No. 1.
J. M.

PLANT FOR NAME.—Kindly give me the name of the plant, a leaf of which I enclose. It came from a package of Government seed labeled "Japanese umbrella plant."
O. M. P.

—The name of the plant, a leaf of which you send, is Sterculia platanifolia. G. W. O.

GERANIUMS FOR NAME.—Of the two geranium flowers sent for name, the salmon pink one is Beaute Poitevine. The magenta pink variety we do not know, and would recommend that you send the flower for identification to the grower who supplied the plants.

LIST OF ADVERTISERS

INDEX TO STOCK ADVERTISED

Contents.

PAGE

FIRMS WHO ARE BUILDING.

COLUMBUS, O.—John R. Hellenthal will build a greenhouse to cost $600.

FOREST CITY, IA.—B. R. Anderson is erecting another greenhouse.

SO. PORTLAND, ME.——Minnott is building a new greenhouse.

TOPEKA, KAN.—B. E. Rodman will erect an addition to his greenhouse to cost $400.

BIDDEFORD, ME.—Charles S. Strout has completed a greenhouse 160 feet in length.

NEW ULM, MINN.—Christ Boock is adding a greenhouse, 20 x 100 feet, and will install a new boiler.

PHILADELPHIA, PA.—C. Mecky will build a range of eight greenhouses. The contract has been given to Benjamin Walker.

MASPETH, N. Y.—A. Sauerwald has sold his vegetable growing establishment, and will build greenhouses and enter the cut flower growers' ranks.

B.

FORT COLLINS, COL.—The Fort Collins Floral Company was dissolved on July 9, H. C. Pratt retiring. H. H. Orth will continue the business.

REVIEW OF THE MARKET

NEW YORK.—The cut flower business is extremely quiet just now. There is little demand for good roses, and while not so many are coming in, there is just about enough to fill all wants; consequently, but ordinary prices are realized for the best class of stock even. Inferior roses are arriving regularly, and there are quite a few that are bringing anywhere from 50c. to $2 per 100. The length of stem does not seem to make much difference in the value, as the chief use to which the flowers are put is for funeral work.

There is still a fair supply of carnations on hand, and the best grades of these have been selling fairly well during the last few days.

Lily of the valley does not move satisfactorily, and is not bringing quite such good prices as were obtained a week ago. Lilies are fairly plentiful; some of them are coming in very much spotted from some cause or other, and have no market value whatever. Flowers that are good and clean have been bringing as high as 6c. and 8c. each.

Cattelyas are still plentiful enough for all demands, and sell anywhere from 25c. to 60c. each, according to the variety.

Gladiolus is increasing every day, and it does not seem that prices are to get very high, as some of the gladiolus have already been disposed of at 50c. per 100.

There are still plenty of sweet peas to satisfy all buyers, though the supply is not nearly so heavy as formerly.

Greens such as adiantum, asparagus and similax are at a very low ebb, there being little demand for any of this material.

Dahlias are coming in regularly, though the supply is by no means heavy yet; still the poor condition of the market makes it impossible to realize anything like good values for them.

CHICAGO.—The market is in a perfectly comotose state. With a fair call for good stock for shipping purposes there is some evidence of activity during part of the day, but the languid feeling permeates the different channels of trade so frequently between daylight and dark that one is hardly safe to say that business is good or bad or even to say that there is any business.

Carnations are still getting poorer, if that were possible; and roses, especially from young stock, are improving in quality. Lilium auratum is showing up in good shape both as to quality and quantity.

There is little further to be said beyond the fact that Summer conditions prevail, and low prices predominate.

W. K. W.

ST. LOUIS.—The trade here has passed through another very dull week with nothing to do outside of funeral work. The wholesalers say that white stock sells fairly well, but colored in almost all lines goes begging. A nice lot of roses are coming in which are meeting with good demand. Bride and Bridesmaid are still mildewed, and this hurts their sale. Kaiserin Augusta Victoria and Ivory sell much better, also Souvenir du President Carnot; the price is $2 to $5 per 100. Carnations do not meet a good demand. Stock is small; select bring $2 per 100. A lot of short-stemmed flowers are coming in from the field that do not bring over 50c. per 100. Lily of the valley is scarce, and the call for it light. A fine lot of first-class asters are in; white and purple have the call at $1 to $2.50 per 100. These, with gladiolus spikes, which are a great glut, make up the retailers' window decorations, and in the West End some pretty displays are seen. Sweet peas show the effects of the hot weather and are noted for their short stems; 50c. to $1 per thousand is what they bring.

We are much in need of a good rain for the outdoor stock.

ST. PATRICK.

INDIANAPOLIS. — Funeral work saves the day, as extreme dullness prevails in all other lines. On account of the heavy rains cut flowers are much more plentiful than last week. Asters particularly are much benefited, and are brought to market in quantity at $1 to $1.50 per 100. Lilies continue plentiful, at last week's prices. Gladiolus is abundant at $4 to $6. Masses of Golden Glow are sold at $1 per 100 sprays; this flower is valuable for window decoration. Carnations are almost out of the market; $1 to $2 per 100 is the price for them. Enchantress in this vicinity has proven to be an admirable Summer carnation. Enough home-grown roses are to be had for all requirements, but, of course, the regular shipments are continued. Excellent La France and Kaiserin Augusta Victoria are selling at $4 to $7 a 100. Bridesmaid and Bride are much improved, at $3 to $4. Fine new crop American Beauty are received, at $3 to $15 a 100.

Tomlinson Hall Market reports a very fair business. Much hardy material which could be disposed of in no other way is sold here.

I. B.

ST. PAUL.—Trade is undoubtedly very quiet, all that is doing being in funeral work, which from reports appears to have been very active the past week. Some of the larger dealers at times had about all they could attend to. Stock is very scarce. The new crop of roses is not in as yet; the stock we are now getting is very inferior and could not be sold very well during the active season. It is hard to find a dealer with a good quality of roses on hand. Carnations are small and inferior, and are sold at close prices; the most of the dealers are offering them at 25c. and 35c. a dozen, while the large stores get 50c. and 75c. a dozen. Roses are selling for $1 and $1.50 per dozen; the actual worth of them is about 50c. a dozen.

Tiger lilies help out greatly in the funeral work, and appear to take very well with the trade.

Building is very quiet; the most of the growers are repairing the old houses, but very few new ones are being erected. Possibly the coming month will see quite a change, as a number of concerns contemplate building during August. The excessive heat the past week has prevented considerable work being done in some of the larger places; the help have been made sick by the heat under glass, and it was an impossibility to get the average amount of work done.

PAUL.

BOSTON.—The regular Summer routine continues. Flowers are coming in in goodly numbers, and prices continue practically unchanged. Sometimes a little variation takes place in the case of the better grades of roses which by the way, are now in rather short supply of such varieties as Kaiserin Augusta Victoria. Richmond has been doing fairly well for a Summer rose, though no large flowers of it have recently been seen. Killarney has been doing well. Not many Liberty are seen; and of other varieties only small grades are noticed.

Carnations are not so plentiful; Fair Maid is the prevailing variety at this season.

Lilies are plentiful at 35c. per dozen for lancifolium and auratum. Sweet peas are good at 15c. and 25c. Asters are quite abundant and continue at last week's prices. There is plenty of all kinds of material for the demands which are not large.

J. W. D.

NEW BEDFORD, MASS.—Funeral work continues quite plentiful, and uses up lots of stock; otherwise there is little doing in the cut flower line. Carnations now bring 35c. per dozen and these will soon be a thing of the past; most of the growers will throw out the old plants in a week or so. Some good sweet peas are coming into this market; they are of fine quality, 50c. per 100 is the price asked at retail. These flowers with asters, candytuft and other outdoor stock help to fill all orders at the present time.

We are having lots of rain here and as a result, plants in the field are looking fine, and making good growth.

H. V. Sowle has thrown out all of his old carnation plants, and will commence to plant new stock soon. He has a fine batch of carnations which he is growing in pots; they are certainly healthy and strong plants. His White Lawson plants are still in the bench and throwing some good flowers for this time of the year.

Chrysanthemums are all planted in this section, and in good shape. R. H. Woodhouse has a house of young roses which are hard to beat at the present time; stock is all grafted in which method he is a firm believer.

HORTICO.

WINONA, MINN.—Charles Siebrecht, who established and has engaged for the past ten years the Central greenhouse located at the corner of Howard and Washington streets, has removed to his former home at 624 East Wabasha street and will re-establish the greenhouses at that location. He has purchased from Youmans Brothers their greenhouse buildings on West Fourth street, formerly occupied by the Winona Floral Company and will during the Summer remove these to the new location.

MONTPELIER, VT.—Alex. Broadfoot has purchased the interest of Alexander Emslie, of Barre, in the Montpelier greenhouses, and will continue the business. Two years ago Mr. Emslie purchased the business from Ernest Jacobsen, now of San Francisco. A few months later Alderman Broadfoot entered the firm. Owing to the ill health of Mr. Emslie, most of the active work and management of the business has fallen on Alderman Broadfoot. The firm has built up a large business in this section of the state.

CROOKSTON, MINN.—Mrs. C. W. Vandermark has decided to sell out her greenhouse and nursery, and will retire from the business.

THE WEEK'S WORK.

Timme's Timely Teachings.

Lilium Harrisii.

If the flowers of Harrisii lilies or the flowering plants are wanted early, it is necessary to start in with bulbs from the first shipments, due to arrive the first or second week in August. There are few growers who, under stress of common reasoning, suppose that the early arrivals in Lilium Harrisii are not as fully ripened as the bulbs that are shipped here later in the season, and that all the trouble experienced in late years in the forcing of these lilies is due to the use of immature bulbs. But neither supposition is borne out by actual facts. The disease prevalent in Bermuda lilies has very little to do with the ripening of the bulbs, and its cause, not yet fully explained, must be looked for in quite another direction. If it is thought that the bulbs coming early are less reliable than those arriving later, attention is here called to the fact that last year and also the year before the greatest trouble was experienced with the later lots of Harrisii lilies, those planted late and forced for Easter, while the loss in early started bulbs, those that came in at Christmas and the early Winter months, amounted to little. An experienced lily grower can tell whether a bulb is well ripened or not, but no matter how experienced he may be he is unable with the closest of scrutiny to detect the slightest trace of the disease peculiar to these lilies, in a bulb, full of its germs. He plants it and deplores his ill luck, when growth is well under way and when it is too late to turn aside actual loss.

Size of Bulbs.

Harrisii lilies come in several graded sizes, ranging from the 5-7inch to mammoth bulbs of over a foot in circumference. These latter possess no special attraction for the commercial florist. In the growing of lilies for profit the two smaller grades, the 5-7 and 7-9inch bulbs, are preferred, and of these the small size finds most favor with the majority of growers, not merely because the bulbs cost less, but on account of the greater utility of the product in made-up floral work and in meeting the ever-increasing call for lilies in pots from people to whom size means little, price everything. To these patrons a lily is a lily, and your competitor will have their custom if he sells his lilies with one or two open flowers and a few green buds at a lower price than you ask for yours with four flowers and a number of well promising buds. For a closely discriminating trade—highly appreciated by every good florist—the larger sized lily bulbs undoubtedly guarantee best returns. While in bulbs of hyacinths and tulips solidity and exterior smoothness count for more than size, it is different with lilies. In wholesaling lilies the open flowers and white buds count; and whatever the ruling price of these may be, the product from the larger bulbs, although these cost twice as much as the small sized grade, often brings three and four fold the price obtainable for thinly flowered spikes. As far as the growing and forcing of the various sizes is concerned there is no advantage in handling the one over that of the other, nor is the one grade more susceptible to disease than the other; and, when similarly treated, their time of flowering is the same.

Starting the Bulbs.

Good garden loam with about one fourth of its bulk well decayed cow manure, thoroughly incorporated, is a good soil for Harrisii lilies. For the small bulbs 5-inch pots and for the larger 6-inch pots are used. A small handful of potsherds placed over the drainage hole forestalls stagnancy in the soil, most to be feared right after root formation has begun, when but a small part of the soil has as yet been penetrated by the roots. Here lies the only advantage in using small pots first and giving the lilies a shift into the right sized pots, after they have made a good start. In the starting of large bulbs, very large ones in particular, this still remains the proper way to do.

In planting, nothing of the bulb but the extreme tip should be showing.

good watering now finishes the job of planting. Outdoor frames, not now in use, provide the best place for the pots, because here they can be covered with sashes, which will prevent an overplus of moisture from pouring rains, should such occur, while in dry weather they greatly aid in holding moisture in and around the pots underneath them. This they will do, even when raised three or four inches above the frame, as they should be, to allow of a constant sweep of fresh air over the lilies. As an additional safeguard against rapid escape of moisture a layer of old, nicely broken up manure, or in place of this earth, ashes or sand, is spread directly on, between and over the pots, an inch or two in thickness. In very dry weather another good watering may, after all, become necessary before the lilies can be taken out for forcing. The pots should be examined from time to time to make certain that the soil in the pots has lost no moisture to a degree verging on dryness. It is somewhat difficult in the height of Summer to maintain that uniform humidity, essential to root formation, on which much of success depends. But if excesses cannot be avoided then rather a little too much water while the lilies are yet out of doors, than ever at any time too dry. In from three to five weeks most of the bulbs will have started to send out roots, some of them showing quite a profusion. It is then time to sort out the most advanced for very early forcing, being sure to select none but what show a good start in the formation of roots, even if backward in top growth. In another two or three weeks all of them may be taken out and housed.

Forcing the Early Lilies.

The forcing of Harrisii lilies for the early trade in Fall and Winter, when there is no necessity of bringing them into bloom all at one time, is an easy affair. In a temperature of from 60 to 65 degrees day and night they will finish up as they are needed for a steady flow of trade right along until Midwinter, the fastest ones being in time for Thanksgiving, the main lot for Christmas, and the slowest for the many festive occasions that enliven business after New Year's day. The lilies will stand a heat of 10 degrees higher, and if for special purposes there is need of some pushing to bring them in on time, hard forcing may safely be resorted to. A grading and separating once or twice, daily syringing, sufficient watering and fumigating twice a week, is work that goes with the forcing of lilies.

FRED. W. TIMME.

FOUNDED IN 1888

FLORISTS' EXCHANGE

A Weekly Medium of Interchange for Florists, Nurserymen, Seedsmen and the Trade in general

Exclusively a Trade Paper.

Entered at New York Post Office as Second Class Matter

Published EVERY SATURDAY by

A. T. DE LA MARE PTG. AND PUB. CO. LTD.

2, 4, 6 and 8 Duane Street,

P. O. Box 1697.
Telephone 3765 John.

NEW YORK.

CHICAGO OFFICE: 127 East Berwyn Avenue.

ILLUSTRATIONS.

Electrotypes of the illustrations used in this paper can usually be supplied by the publishers. Price on application.

YEARLY SUBSCRIPTIONS.

United States, Canada, and Mexico, $1.00. Foreign countries in postal union, $2.50. Payable in advance. Remit by Express Money Order Draft on New York. Post Office Money Order or Registered Letter.

The address label indicates the date when subscription expires and is our only receipt therefore.

REGISTERED CABLE ADDRESS:

Florex, New York.

ADVERTISING RATES.

One-half inch, 75c.; ¾-inch, $1.00; 1-inch, $1.25, special positions extra. Send for Rate Card showing discount of 10c., 15c., 25c., or 35c., per inch on continuous advertising. For rates on Wants, etc., see column for Classified Advertisements.

Copy must reach this office 12 o'clock Wednesday to secure insertion in issue of following Saturday.

Orders from unknown parties must be accompanied with cash or satisfactory references.

Horticulture and Its Chestnuts.

In complimenting the Editor of the Brooklyn Eagle on his characterization of the "wholesome chestnuts," of our Boston contemporary as "Floral Tips for the Amateur Gardener," we seem to have struck a hornet's nest, for the editor of that "nice little floricultural journal," as a Rochester (N. Y.) paper dubs it, attacks us with wasp-like ferocity, insinuating that we are envious (of what?), and asserting that we seem to "extract comfort out of little things which others heedlessly pass by," and other heinous crimes of that kind. And he has apparently been burning the midnight oil searching the columns of The Florists' Exchange for some phrase or sentence to prove, that because we live in a glass house, he is in a position to throw stones at us, which he does. His bricks, however, lose their force, because of the subterfuge he resorts to, in lifting a sentence or two from the text with which they were associated, showing the hard straits he is in to discover in our columns something to ridicule or belittle—a high tribute to The Florists' Exchange, surely. Then, too, what he has selected will stand comparison with the best in its line provided. One of the quotations is from the notes of our much esteemed correspondent, Joseph Meehan, whose contributions are always "luminous," but never "chestnutty" or platitudinal, as our readers will, we feel sure, readily admit; and were the whole sentence given, of which the other quotation is but a part, it would be found not so funny after all.

However, we sympathize with our youthful contemporary; although we cannot assume the responsibility of having "consigned it to the amateur ranks,' a classification that seems to be not so palatable to itself as the "chestnuts" it doles out are to those catering to the wants of the amateur gardener. In view of what has occurred, a good title for that edifying column might be "roasted chestnuts."

Meantime we assure our esteemed contemporary that our "profound interest" in its doings remains unabated, and that part of our vigilance will be directed toward discovering in its pages that "merit," undisclosed as yet, which "envy as its shade will pursue." We shall also continue to extract "comfort out of little things which others heedlessly pass by," among them Horticulture's brilliant editorials, never more entertaining or comforting than when its editor is smarting under some real or fancied wrong.

So, "Let there be gall enough in thy ink; though thou write with a goose-pen, no matter."

Reflections on Current Topics.

MR. EDITOR.—Notwithstanding the articles in our trade papers are all, more or less, of a serious nature, a few sentences are sometimes seen that smack of the humorous when nothing humorous is intended. Once in a while it is the "types" that are responsible for this; at other times the slovenly use of the blue pencil by editors. A case of the latter kind recently came under my observation, so obviously the result of sloveniiness both on the part of the writer and editor, and so grotesque in its character, that I here refer to it, in the hope of benefiting, if possible, those most concerned.

In your New England contemporary, the "boastin'" paper, a contributor, an old hand, by the way, at scribbling, describes his visit to certain famous gardens, where some large specimen hydrangeas were the first things that "struck" him; and he proceeds to tell of these plants and their receptacles as follows: "The tubs are so large that it takes eight men to lift some of them. They are six feet through and eight feet high. Considerable skill is shown in training them so as to evenly cover the plants with bloom, making them into perfect globes." Wonderful skill! Sturdy men! Gee Whiz! I thought Munchausen was dead, but his spirit seems to still survive in T. D. Hatfield! Or was the gardoner Scotch, with a "Greybaird" in his possession?

I notice that some experts are taking John Birnie to task because that gentleman asserts he can manipulate geraniums, numerically, to better advantage than the average mortal. The controversialists seem to take Birnie too seriously. They forget that he is so accustomed to the manipulation of that "windbag" about which we have heard so much, that it is second nature to him to be "breezy" in his scribblings. John apparently thinks he has a "secret," and being a representative of that "close race" he's evidently going to hold on to the secret. A humorist once said that "the Scotch rigidly keep the Sabbath—and everything else they can lay their hands on." And you'll observe Birnie never once goes back on his nationality.

There seems to be a little mix-up in regard to that Dayton souvenir book. I quite agree with you that it would be unfortunate if any individual "graft" were permitted in connection with an S. A. F. convention where the desire is to be mutually helpful. It seems a pity, too, that some one conueeted with the local organizations does not do the work of soliciting advertisements and thus save the commission paid to a hireling. There should be no difficulty connected with that work, as nearly all the leading florists seem willing to help along every convention; and what one man can do others surely can attempt if not accomplish. It is well that the Dayton matter has turned out as explained in your last week's issue, for not much commendation is coming to any one who takes advantage of an affair like an S. A. F. convention to Croker-like, work for "his own pocket all the time."

Speaking of the Dayton convention, I observe several candidates for the S. A. F. presidency and other offices have been mentioned. I still favor my first choice, the genial Chicago "Red Man." You'll find no harder worker, or one more unselfish, in the society's ranks; and although a keen sportsman, business with him goes ahead of pleasure always. He would dignify the office, and bring to it the experience of many years in society work. So far as I know, he eschews politics, so mere self-aggrandizement would not be the object of his election.

Your prolific-of-ideas Cincinnati correspondent, I notice, states that the present secretary is not to run again for that office, and he suggests that that official be made president of the national body next year. To my way of thinking, that would not be a tangible enough reward for long service. He should have a pension, with the title of "secretary-emeritus" all his remaining days. Almost twenty years of one's life spent in the society's service surely betokens meritorious endeavor which an honorary title cannot fully recompense, even with the Yearly salary coming all the time during that period. But youth will not abide with us always; and advancing years bring their drawbacks with them. This, also, in this day of young men; and that some worthy successor to the present incumbent may be found in the ranks of that class is the desire of every well-wisher of the S. A. F. I have no candidate to propose; but there are many young men available for the position. Perhaps John Birnie may be induced to take it, if he is not as old as

JOB.

The question of packing and shipping flowers, which was recently discussed by the express companics in the United States, which wanted to charge an extra half cent for transportation, says the Tribune, has called attention to the Colonial Exposition now being held in Marseilles. The Paris-Lyons Railroad has announced that it will organize, with the assistance of the general commissioner of the exposition, a national exhibition of baskets and cases for the packing and shipping of flowers, fruits, vegetables, etc. This exhibition will include a force of men and women, who will prepare, in the presence of a jury, packages of flowers, fruits and vegetables, which will be furnished by the commissionér of the exposition. This competition will probably be held on September 8, in the buildings of the Colonial Exposition at Marseilles.

The Dayton Souvenir.

To offset a wrong impression, created by a communication from a member of this club recently published in the trade papers, we wish to state that the reference made to the publication of the Dayton souvenir being left to "private enterprise," was made without the knowledge of the actual conditions, and does an injustice to H. M. Altick, in charge of this work.

We, therefore, by action of this club fully endorse H. M. Altick's statement of facts published in a recent issue of this paper, as correct in every respect, and herewith assure the patrons of the souvenir, and the members of the S. A. F. O. H. that their support of this publication will aid the Dayton Florists' Club in making a successful convention.

CHAS. LUTZENBERGER, Vice-President
J. B. HEISS, President
H. H. RITTER, Treasurer
HORACE M. FRANK, Secretary

Our Ignorance of Peonies.

In a recent issue of the "Gardeners' Chronicle," the editor, after facetiously commenting on the efforts making by the Cornell University, horticultural department, on behalf of the peony, and the fact that a student of that educational institution is engaged in the work, which, according to our English contemporary, is to gain for him the title of "Doctor of Peonies,' we are informed that the "peony is not universally appreciated in America," this being illustrated by the fact that at a recent dinner given in London, at which the tables were decorated with bowls of peonies, and where the company consisted largely of Americans, the flowers were unknown to the diners.

This condition is improving, however; largely through the endeavors of the American Peony Society, and the work doing at Cornell. And if our esteemed contemporary will only impress on the English peony growers the importance of that work and the necessity of emulating it over there, the final outcome will go a long way toward popularizing the peony both at home and abroad.

Obituary

Joseph H. Stewart.

Joseph H. Stewart, nurseryman, Medford, Oregon, died on Saturday, July 7, aged 72 years and six months. He was born in Washington County, Maine, and when twenty-one years of age, at Quincy, Ill., he was united in marriage to Miss Elizabeth Hyman, who now, as the faithful companion of years, survives him, sorrowing. After his marriage he resided for a time in Hannibal, Mo., but in 1860 removed to Quincy, Ill., where he established a nursery and engaged very successfully in fruit raising, taking many premiums at state exhibits and such like places. In 1870 he was elected to the state legislature, serving with great acceptability. In 1884 he made a trip to Oregon believing, from what he knew of the country that Oregon would be an unexcelled place for growing fine fruit, berries, etc. So much pleased was he that February, 1885, found him located in Rogue River Valley. He has been called the "father of the fruit industry in Oregon," and, as his old friend, Dr. Geary, once said, "Every fruit tree in Rogue River Valley will be a monument to his memory."

He was a man of affairs and took a keen interest in all public enterprises, advising, directing and often aiding with his influence and money. He was one of the organizers of the Medford Bank, which was organized in 1899 and served as president of it for two full years.

He leaves a widow, one son and three daughters to mourn their loss.

Miss F. E. Russ, florist, Medford, Oregon writes: Mr. Stewart's father, Wm. Stewart, was the first man to go into the nursery business in Adams County, Ill. He sold the grafts which Seth Llewellyn brought in an ox-wagon to Oregon. The following year one of these grafts bore a red apple, the first apple in Oregon. People came some 40 or 50 miles to see that red apple, and wore a path through the nursery to where it grew."

OUR READERS' VIEWS

[Wholesome discussions on subjects that interest. Contributions to this column are always welcome.—Ed.]

Concerning Geraniums.

Editor Florists' Exchange:

I see that facetious exponent of the New York market methods of growing geraniums, John Birnie, is pleased to say that I am down and out, just because I am using 30-year-old methods in producing these plants. After reading the communication signed "A Canadian," published under Mr. Birnie's letter in the issue of July 21, I have come to the conclusion that there are others who have had occasion to get acquainted with geraniums as grown for the New York market, much to their disadvantage; and are now fully aware of the utter uselessness of geraniums, such as are sold in the market of that city, for purposes to which good plants are put.

Mr. Eichholz, in his letter was, I feel sure, referring only to rooted cuttings, not bedding plants. No doubt Mr. Birnie has at some time or other bought rooted cuttings of both geraniums and carnations. If he has, he will have noticed that there is quite some difference between the rooted cuttings sent out by the introducer of a novelty, and the plants one would be expected to supply to a retail customer.

Of course, I realize the peculiar position in which Mr. Birnie is placed. He is growing for the cheapest market in the country; his clientele, the street pedlers, demand only a plant with two or three leaves and a flower, so that they can re-sell it at 5c. or 6c. But where else could such poorly manipulated stock be got rid of except in the crowded streets of New York, where there is no other home for the plant than the fire-escape, and where the economy of the customer would deter him from purchasing, if it was not for the loud voice of the pedler and the insignificant price asked for the plant?

I may be "down and out" but I am considerably removed from the position of having to market the products of my greenhouses at the prices demanded by such a class of buyers as those who attend the New York plant market daily during the Spring of the year. I have visited that market out of curiosity once or twice, and know somewhat of the stock there sold and the methods of selling it.

Mr. Birnie has evidently nothing new to tell about geraniums. He has given Young Beginner no practical instructions as yet; and I don't believe he can tell anything about the propagation of a geranium that was not known to every florist or gardener 30 years ago. The rooted cutting business is one thing, and the growing of plants for retail trade is another. The only trouble with Mr. Birnie seems to be, that he has been catering so long to a cheap market, he has forgot—if he ever knew—what a geranium looks like when it is well grown.

I do not believe that Young Beginner is waiting for this controversy to be ended before deciding how many geraniums to plant; he will have followed my advice long ago.

In conclusion, I will reiterate that to grow geraniums for a good market one must produce a much better article than is required to fill the bill in John Birnie's market, judging from my own and "A Canadian's" experience with the plants from Birnie's district.

To criticize without giving better information than that originally tendered reveals but a carping disgruntled spirit, and displays the tactics employed by a pot-house politician, or a desire, stimulated by fear of competition, to mislead any one likely to become a competitor.

In the meantime, Mr. Birnie, write out that method of extraordinary re-production of geraniums; let us see what it is like, then I can get a line upon how far out of date you really are. Don't waste time trying to find a quotation suitable for a head line to an effusion that evades the main issue. Just give us the plain facts, without either facetiousness or a poor attempt at wit.

EXPERTUS.

Editor Florists' Exchange:

The day on which we received The Florists' Exchange containing John Birnie's estimate of the fecundity of the geranium was comparatively speaking an uneventful one. True, our Jersey milker had broken into Deacon Jones' cabbage patch and cleaned out his cabbage and corn, and we had been threatened with a suit for damages; however, we succeeded in effecting a settlement by giving him 50 geraniums and a copy of Birnie's opinion of the possibilities of the same. Nothing had transpired to mar the peace of the domestic circle unless the fact that Johnny had the croup, Mary Ann the measles, and that Tommy had knocked the scab off where he was vaccinated a few days before, could be construed into any trouble. We had just finished putting together the pieces of our favorite bull pup which had been knocked galley west by a passing trolley car, while intently enjoying the peaceful occupation of shutting off the hot air from the circulating apparatus of neighbor McCarty's pet cat.

Pat, the hired man, had just finished putting a new seat in his jeans, that he had lost in clearing the last fence in a steeplechase with Farmer Swift's thoroughbred bull. Peace reigned. Pat had resumed his favorite seat on the edge of a flat under the old apple tree, and after filling his pet dudheen with a choice selection from the bale of tobacco stems in the shed, began to exhale its perfume on the desert air. Picking up the aforementioned Exchange he settled back in contentment. After a few minutes he sprang up with a yell. Asking him what bit him, he replied, "I want my pay raised. Be jabers, I am worrukin' for a millionaire. This business makes the insurance business look like thirty cents;" and he showed me Birnie's figures. I told him Birnie was only joking.

"Be hivins," says he, "a man that can joke like that this hot weather is a brave man, and its mine for a breath of the air he breathes;" and dancing a jig on the bottom of an upturned flat he broke into song.

Birnie, me bhoy, you're a brick.
  The divvle himself can't say more;
Because you can do the trick
  It makes the greenhorns sore.

Your thousand from fifty, I swow,
  Great jumpin', jiminy crips;
It beats all the sums I know,
  Beats something from nothing leaves six.

Don't tell them how you do it,
  For sure as guns if you do,
They'll say you've a bug in your bonnet;
  "Git, G'wan, Skiddoo."

Oh, don't tell them how you do it,
  For cert, between you and me,
They'll say you've the numbers mixed
  And say it is twenty-three.

What if you jolly the figures
  It's the trick of the high 'nancier.
But tell us, Oh tell us, friend Birnie,
  Was it whisky or was it beer?

Or was it the festive rarebit,
  Or lobster, or toothsome clam,
Which when you juggled those figures
  Made you not to care a ——. Wow?

With a wild yell Pat made for the gate. The last seen of him he was disappearing in the tall heather in the direction of Jersey City.

J. R. J.

Editor Florists' Exchange:

John Birnie is not the "red hot stuff" geranium grower I thought he was. He says I would need 125 stock plants to produce 4,000 plants, "but he may be able to do better to-day." Beg pardon! We, four years ago, did far better than Mr. Birnie is able to do to-day. We will say we got our top cut off the field-grown plants the middle of August, 12 from each plant. (Remember, we do not allow the plants to bloom in the field, but pinch out the tops to produce cuttings). These plants are rooted, 10 out of 12, by October 1, taken into house. These produce by November 1 another 10 top cuttings, which will be by January 1 doubled up again, and by March 1 again, giving eight weeks for each operation. We housed the old plants a week after the tops were taken—August 15. These plants by October 1 will each give at least 10 more cuttings, and will produce 10 each at least every eight weeks.

This will show you, after figuring up, that one good stock plant and its offspring will produce 100 plants by March 1. All these can be had in 4-inch pots by May 30; and the 100 top cuttings March 1, or even April 1, will be nice single plants in bloom in 3-inch pots by Decoration Day, which actually will make it 200 plants per stock plant, or double the number Mr. Birnie is able to raise. How is this, John, for slow Pennsylvania?

To do this, Young Beginner should grow his geraniums in a tempertature of from 50-55 degrees at least; and his knife must be ready for every cutting as soon as hard enough to be sure of rooting. The young plants and stock plants must be on benches near to the glass, and kept growing. Methods used 40 years ago, along benches or under benches, wont do nowadays. And the cuttings must be in charge of a man who can root cuttings 100 per cent. These are the results we got, and which lots of slow Pennsylvanians around Lancaster get to-day. If John Birnie can only grow 100 plants from a stock plant, and Expertus only 10, neither of them is up-to-date, in my estimation.

"A Canadian" complains of the grade of New York geraniums; but if I recollect right, it was John Birnie who thought William Scott, of Buffalo, another New Yorker, should have a medal for sidetracking the establishment of "a standard size of plants" at the St. Louis convention of the S. A. F. And here "A Canadian" again proves the necessity of such a measure, to protect himself. But what a lot of harm such a move would do New York geraniums, for instance!

Penna. HENRY EICHHOLZ.

Editor Florists' Exchange:

Will you ask John Birnie to quit writing letters in which there is nothing useful and just give us minute instructions on how to raise geraniums. He says, "not too much heat; not too much stimulant." Kindly ask him to use the thermometer, so we shall have a guide in our ignorance.

ANOTHER CANADIAN.

Editor Florists' Exchange:

In number 26 of your esteemed paper I asked John Birnie, politely as I thought, to give an account of his method of making geranium cuttings, signing my query: "Another Green One." The next edition brought his answer, consisting mainly of a stale joke, broadly told, and to my notion applied in a pretty ugly manner. Later Messrs. F. Weepy and F. S. Weigand put questions to Mr. Birnie, none of which was answered.

I now wish to ask, is there any reader of The Florists' Exchange who not only claims that he can do as Mr. Birnie does, but who is also willing to tell, in a straightforward and business-like manner, as Messrs. Eichholz and Weepy have done, how to start with 50 nice four-inch stock plants June 15 and obtain from these fifty plants, considerably more than four thousand ideal plants, to be ready for sale from March on?

Indianapolis. H. JUNGE.

Editor Florists' Exchange:

I think if John Birnie would have put the greatest part of his letter to the more useful purpose of instructing us "greenies," he would have done a world of good, with the same amount of labor. There are thousands of florists just in the same position as the one who asked the question as to how many stock plants it would require to produce 4000 geraniums. I am one who would very much like John Birnie, expert, to begin at A and go on to Z of geranium growing. Please ask the said John to tell us how to grow the best geraniums for the least money, said stock to be sold from May 15 on. Also to tell us the best kinds, their names and colors. If he does this we shall forget his light talk and look for something at another time which will be very profitable.

CANADIAN FLORIST.

Ontario.

Editor Florists' Exchange:

Here is our contribution to the "Geranium discussion" entitled,

"Tell Us How, Mr. Birnie, Tell Us How."

Tell us how, Mr. Birnie, tell us how,
As you write from week to week,—
Like the sphinx you will not speak,—
As to how, as to how.

Tell your fellow craftsmen old
How you grow plants eighty-fold,
Fit in six months to be sold.
Tell us how, Mr. Birnie, tell us how.

Read you how "Canadian" thought
Good geraniums could be bought,—
And the rubbish that he got—
In New York. In New York?

Tell us now, Mr. Birnie, tell us now;
Is that the kind of plants you grow
By your process, "eighty-fold,"
To be sold to young and old?
Tell us now! Tell us now.

Tell us how, Mr. Birnie, tell us how.
You've given us gas, you've given us chaff;
You've tried your best to make us laugh,
But now come down to facts
And tell us how, Mr. Birnie, tell us how.

MOUNTAIN FARMERS.

Editor Florists' Exchange

The gentleman signing himself "A Canadian" could not, had he tried, given a fuller indorsement of the New York geranium; neither could a more complete refutation of the slurs aimed at it by "Expertus" have been written. "A Canadian" found that he was short of geraniums in the first week of June; he sent an order to New York for 3-inch stock, probably receiving the plants in the second week of June, and by the 10th of July they were what he expected to get—"something up-to-date,"—evidently recuperating from their 1000 mile journey in three weeks. This completely refutes the assertion of "Expertus" on page 828 of The Florists' Exchange, that the New York market geranium, "if planted would, by the end of September, still be so small," etc. But then it is obvious that "Expertus" knows very little about up-to-date geranium growing.

But to the point "A Canadian's" "great disappointment" was altogether due to his own mistake in ordering 3-inch stock; he should have ordered plants from 4 1-4-inch pots, which is, and has been the standard size for geraniums for many years in the New York market. Many of the best growers use no 3-inch pots, shifting directly from 2 1-4 to 4 1-4, claiming that they thereby save a great amount of labor, and enabling them to handle a larger quantity of stock; and from observation I must say that geraniums grown in that manner are as good, and bring the same price, as those given two shifts.

I must thank "A Canadian" for his unintentional indorsement of the New York grown geranium; and I am sure that when he needs more up-to-date geraniums he will send to New York for them.

JOHN BIRNIE.

Harry A. Bayersdorfer, Philadelphia, Pa., sends The Florists' Exchange a souvenir postal card from gay Paree, with the information that he would sail on July 14 on the steamer New York, from Southampton, England, with a ship load of novelties.

Peonies in America.

Editor Florists' Exchange:

I was not aware that in my article "Aftermath of the Peony Show" I was putting a chip on my shoulder or throwing down the gauntlet to friend Betscher. He accuses me of "rushing into print." My rushing days are over. I write with deliberation. Yet censure it as he will, it is a sort of Godsend to him, inasmuch as it gives him a chance—a splendid chance—to advertise his own collection.

He strangely silent concerning the "several other" fine collections, while he gloriously elaborates his own. He speaks of ecstacies and enthusiasms. Hasn't he a little bit himself when he says he has "125,000 in 1200 sorts?" Come to think, if Thurlow, whom I mentioned, should cut his roots up real fine he might have that many. If one has 1200 kinds he has just about 800 too many.

I am reminded of a visit I once made. The lady of the house spoke of an event that happened the day before about 4 o'clock. The husband insisted that it was fifteen minutes past four, and they had it nip and tuck, back and forth, and then didn't settle it. Hadn't a committee better be appointed to accurately count and register both fields?

Our friend rather sneers at American born peonies. All must bear the import brand. I think Richardson's Milton Hill and Grandiflora, Terry's Etta, and Rosenfield's Golden aHrvest will last longer than five years, to say nothing of those splendid new ones seen at the Boston show, which went far ahead of most imported ones.

Mr. Betscher speaks of much "sloppiness" going the rounds as peony matter. Is that the reason why he himself rushes at it with such greediness?

Now, my dear sir, please don't pitch in quite so heavily. From the tone of your article one would really think you were the Great Mogul, throned on your own "Ipse dixit." I just imagine a deep bass voice coming all the way from Canal Dover, and it says:

"Fi fo fum!
I smell the blood of Harrison;
Dead or alive, I will have some."

Now I will leave it to the fraternity if there was anything in my short article to arouse so much bile. It looks to me as though Betscher seized the occasion to exploit himself and advertise his superior knowledge and business!

York, Neb. C. S. HARRISON.

Peonies in Holland.

Messrs. Endtz Van Nes & Company, Boskoop, Holland, send us a dozen photographs of peony blooms, of varieties regarded by that firm "as some of the very best." They include the following sorts: Mrs. Willock, Jeanne d' Arc, both of which are figured herewith) Boule de Niege, Madame de Verneville, Duchesse de Nemours, Thryne, Madame Crousse, Edouard Andre, Marie Lemoine, Mons. Jules Elie, Madame Emile Galle and Duke of Wellington.

The concern says: "Of one sort we are not sure, and that is Mrs. Willock. The same is a very fine flower, answering the description of the party from whom we bought it (Kelway, England); but we do not find the central petals narrow, at least not very. Neither are they broad, but middling.

"The description of Thryne is 'light flesh color; center, sulphur yellow turning to white with age.'"

American Peony Society.

The formation of a special society is no novelty in this country. What is noteworthy, however, is that such a society should be associated with a university. We can scarcely conceive our sedate universities, such as Oxford or Cambridge, interesting themselves in such, as they would judge, frivolous pursuits as peony growing. Our American cousins take wider views of the functions of a university, and so we find that the Peony Society is to meet at Cornell University next year, that a large collection of peonies, nearly 2,000 varieties, is being grown and studied in the college grounds; and that one of the advanced students is preparing a thesis on peonies for his doctor's degree in the university. The robes of a doctor of music in this country are gorgeous enough—what must be the apparel of a doctor of peonies? That the peony is not universally appreciated in America was illustrated by the fact that some time since we were dining at a public table decorated with bowls of peonies. The company consisted largely of Americans, to whom the flowers in question seemed to be quite unknown.—The Gardener's Chronicle.

English Holly.

The climate of New England is not especially favorable for growing many things that flourish in the British Isles, but the climate of the localities where holly succeeds best pretty nearly equals in severity that of the New England States. Knowing that, one might suppose that there would be no difficulty experienced with holly in those states. It is not severe frost that plays havoc with holly and many other things; it is the intense heat of the sun after freezing that does the damage, and holly more than most other plants requires shade to do well, and, I think, that if planted in a shady situation they will grow here. As a precaution, it will be well, for several Winters after planting, to put some spruce branches upon the south side of where the plants are growing, and to strew some litter or marsh hay among the branches and over the roots.

M.

Peony Mrs. Willock.

Eremurus.

About a dozen plants of eremurus, growing in the garden of Commodore Gerry, at Newport, R. I., made a gorgeous display, which lasted more than six weeks and has just ended. These plants are grown in a row in the vegetable garden, and were planted by Mr. Griffin, he having an idea that on some occasion he might be able to use the flowers in a large decoration, but so far circumstances did not favor the execution of this plan.

Seeing these beautiful plants develop and display their grandeur for so many weeks, I could not help wondering why more of them were not planted in clumps for the adornment of grounds, where they would show to double advantage. Although large plants of eremurmus are somewhat costly, still, if we consider the display they make they are not more so than many other things. Several of the flower spikes of the eremurus planted, I think two years ago, by Mr. Griffin, measured over 9 feet in height. The soil where these plants are grown is exceedingly rich, and it may be added that in growing this plant rich soil is absolutely necessary for success.

D. M.

Peony Jeanne d'Arc.

CLUB AND SOCIETY DOINGS.

THE COLUMBUS, (O.) FLORISTS' CLUB held its meeting on Tuesday evening, July 17, in Iroquois Hall. President Stephens occupied the chair. C. D. Batelle and Leo. Bauman were elected to membership. Plans for the attendance of our members at the Dayton convention were actively discussed. Much interest is manifested in this affair by the craft here; in fact, it looks now as if fifty would go. The writer would not be surprised if our club made an outing of the event, and went to the convention in a body, in a special car decorated for the occasion. That this matter might be worked up in proper shape; a committee, consisting of Messrs. Woodrow, McKellar, and Faxon, was appointed to formulate a plan to be submitted at the next meeting. Another matter in which our club is very much in earnest is the chrysanthemum show to be held this Fall, probably in the new Franklin Memorial Hall. This subject was discussed in its many phases, and very soon the various committees will be announced. The matter of childrens' gardens also came up, and from the reports so far received it would seem that the seeds distributed by our club in the early Spring are yielding excellent results. It is proposed this year to award Holland bulbs for prizes in place of money.

The meeting adjourned till Tuesday evening, August 7. F. W.

Trees at Skibo Castle, Scotland.

The nurserymen of Scotland and England and, to some extent, those of Ireland also have substantial reasons to be thankful that Andrew Carnegie purchased the estate of Skibo Castle in the Highlands of Scotland. Skibo was always noted for fine trees and extensive shrubberies, but since Mr. Carnegie obtained possession thousands upon thousands of trees and shrubs have been planted there. Mr. Carnegie is passionately fond of trees and shrubs; he is especially fond of rhododendrons, and he was quick to see that on his new estate there were many spots where rhododendrons would flourish as some had flourished on other parts before, with the result that these were planted in such numbers that one or two nurseries in Aberdeen and Edinburgh were all but cleaned out of this stock.

The gardens at Skibo were also noted for beautifully trained pear and apple trees on walls, but pears and apples did not satisfy Mr. Carnegie. He had most of those trees torn off, and then had the walls covered with glass, planting peach, apricot and nectarine trees where the pears and apples were. Mr. Carnegie thought an apple or pear was just as good coming off a standard tree that grew anywhere in the garden; while peaches he knew could not be produced in that climate, mild as it is, from trees grown in the open.

Although Mr. Carnegie has ample means to procure and plant whatever tree and shrub he desires, and cares but little whether it grows or not so far as returns are concerned, he does not, however, go about it in that way. Instead, the woods on his estate are treated in the best possible manner with a view to make them profitable where possible, and for that reason he has had sawmills erected in different parts of his estate in order that when trees are cut down during the progress of systematic thinning they may be manufactured into lumber for use in the building of cottages; and the soft pine is sawn into barrel staves to be shipped to ports where herring are packed. Mr. Carnegie is, by the care he is bestowing on his trees as well as by the numbers he is planting, doing a great work for arboriculture in Scotland. D. M.

Consul-General Roosevelt, writing from Brussels, tells of the development of the hothouse-grape industry and the extension of hothouse cultivation to other fruits and vegetables. He reports:

About forty years ago the cultivation of grapes under glass was practiced on a small scale at Hoeylaert, a village near Brussels, more as an experimental venture than as a business enterprise. From the beginning the experiment was accompanied by success, and from its small origin this method of cultivation rapidly developed until it now ranks as one of the most flourishing and lucrative industries in this district. To-day there are no less than 10,000 hothouses in the immediate vicinity of Brussels. The hothouses are usually from 65 to 82 feet in length, and about 26 feet in width. Heat is distributed through clay pipes.

The principal varieties of grapes are: Frankenthal, a blue, medium-size grape of fine flavor and very juicy; Big Colman, an immense purple grape of attractive appearance, somewhat too solid and lacking in juice, and the Black Alicante and Queen Victoria, both acceptable as to quality and flavor. These grapes are sold on the Belgian retail markets all the year round, at prices varying with the seasons, from about 15 cents to $1 per pound. In the last few years the cultivation of peaches, in connection with grapes, has also become quite profitable, and, although still practiced on a limited scale, has produced excellent results, the yield being first class in every respect.

The cultivation of strawberries, tomatoes, spinach, lettuce, asparagus, and chicory under glass is also carried on in this district by syndicates, which regulate production as well as prices. Grapes grown in this consular district are exported largely to England, Germany, Russia, and Denmark, and occasionally in small quantities to the United States.

Winter Flowering Sweet Peas

A Bit of History.

About twenty-five years ago I made my first experiments in raising sweet peas in Winter under glass. I tried all varieties which were at that date obtainable, but could never raise a plant which would give flowers before the latter part of April. After several years of such experiments I came to the conclusion that it was impossible to get sweet peas earlier than the time mentioned, from the present varieties, so I started cross-fertilization with others, among them the lathyrus, but the first few years without success. I obtained several new varieties, a few of which were double-flowered, but I did not succeed in getting a free-flowering plant until I made a cross with the European vetch, largely grown on farms in central Europe as green fodder. About October, 1891, I sowed some of this seed which I had hybridized with the vetch, and the following January 1, 1892, I was surprised to find two little plants, each with one open flower and several buds. The flowers were very small, color a reddish pink, and not of much value, the plants growing only to a height of 24 inches under glass. But I was satisfied with this for a start, and increased the seed all I possibly could. I crossed and recrossed each year, and each new hybrid showed improvement over the previous one, in size of flower, color, length of stem, and in the plant itself. The first seedling of value which appeared was obtained from Blanche Ferry; it came of the same color, but the plant was only 20 inches high, under glass, and produced only about 10 single flowers; but after much crossing and re-crossing with the parent variety, I secured fine long-stemmed, large flowers, plants over six feet high, which were covered with masses of bloom all Winter.

In 1897 almost every day I was able to send to the New York market several hundreds of fine blooms. This variety is now known as the famous Christmas Pink, but it is today a great improvement over what it was in 1897. Crossing this variety with Emily Henderson, I originated, in '95, Miss Florence Denzer, which is the best of all whites.

I now have 64 varieties in all existing colors, from lightest salmon to darkest pink and red, from lightest lavender to darkest blue and purple, also yellows and variegated. All these varieties, when grown under glass, begin to bloom when 3 to 4 feet high, and continue flowering all Winter, sometimes until June. The plants are covered with a mass of large, long-stemmed flowers. Height of plants, 8 to 15 feet.

Some New Varieties.

The following are good varieties which will soon be introduced:

Christmas Captain, standard purple, wings blue.

Christmas Comptes, lavender, similar to Countess of Radnor, but much larger.

Miss Helen Miller Gould, standard lilac, variegated; wings white. Very large open flowers.

Mrs. Alex. Wallace, lavender, similar to Lady Hamilton in Midwinter, changing to a somewhat darker color in warmer days; large and good keeper. This flower has been on the road for nine days and arrived at destination in good condition.

Mrs. Edie Wild, fine carmine, very beautiful, medium flowers, with long stems, coming in bloom five to eight days later. This variety will outclass Christmas red.

Wm. J. Stewart, fine blue during Winter months, somewhat darker in Spring.

Mrs. Wm. Sim, salmon orange in Winter, changing to a dark salmon color in Spring; extremely long stems.

Mrs. F. J. Dolansky, silvery salmon, similar to Gladys Unwin, but more hooded.

Christmas Meteor, scarlet, similar to King Edward in color, but with open flowers.

Miss Josie Reilly, standard lilac, wings lavender; very large, open flower.

J. K. Allen, white ground, spotted pink; changing sometimes more into pink; very large and strong grower.

Jack Hunter, yellow and salmon; extra long stems.

Watchung, or black seeded Denzer, pure white, almost the same as Florence Denzer, only blackseeded.

Those last named varieties are just as free bloomers, and sometimes come larger than Christmas Pink and Florence Denzer. They have been under trial for several years, and many specialists who have visited my establishment give it as their opinion that these varieties will outclass all the old Summer flowering sweet peas.

Growing Sweet Peas in Winter.

Select the highest light houses for sweet peas. Fill the benches, or well-drained solid beds, with good compost, about three parts sod and one part old horse manure. Drop four to five seeds about twelve by twenty inches apart, water thoroughly, keep always on the wet side and in a steady growing condition.

White seeded sweet peas, such as Florence Denzer, must be started in sand, as they seldom germinate if sown directly in soil. Or, soak them over night in water; next morning put them in damp sawdust or some similar material for two to four days until roots about 1-4 inch have started; as soon as this start has been made, sow them in moist soil which should stand a few days without watering. Plant either in the benches where they are to grow, or in pots. After the plants start to grow, which will be in two to three days, give them some water and in a few days more they can be watered just as heavily as black-seeded ones. If the space on the benches is not ready, sow in four or five inch pots, and then plant in benches after three or four weeks, but be very careful with the watering, as over-dry or pot-bound plants will never produce good flowers.

Supporting.

When the plants reach a height of 6 inches they should be given support, and the best method is this: Stretch one wire on bottom and another wire about 6 feet above that, and connect with strings, from time to time helping the plants to climb.

Temperature and Ventilating.

Ventilation is one of the most important points in growing sweet peas successfully. As soon as sown all the air possible should be allowed. The best temperature is 45 to 50 degrees at night, 56 degrees during cloudy and 65 to 70 degrees F. on bright sunny days. As soon as cool nights arrive, let the steam run in two to four pipes, at the same time the ventilators should be kept open as long as possible, especially when the first buds appear. This will prevent the dropping of the buds, especially during rainy or inclement weather.

Insects.

The first insect which will appear is the green worm, similar to the cabbage worm, these must be picked off every day before they become too numerous. They will be found almost always on the top or upper leaves. After several hard frosts the worm will disappear. The green fly is a very bad enemy of sweet peas, but light fumigating or syringing with a light solution of nicotine from time to time, will check them if done in time.

Sweet Peas the Year Round.

All of my Winter-blooming varieties will flower all the year round, if planted from time to time.

If you want a crop from November to April sow the seed the latter part of August or first part of September. October sowing will yield a crop from New Year's to June. November and December sowings will bring a crop from February until the hot weather comes. For Winter sowing I use my special Winter selected brand. The stock seed of this brand is raised during the Winter months from the best flowers in my greenhouses. For May and June crop sow the first part of March, in cold frames or in pots, and plant outdoors as soon as the weather permits. For July, August and September flowering sow in May and June two or three weeks apart. For October and November flowers sow the latter part of July or first part of August, in frames.

To obtain good long-stemmed flowers from outdoors, the soil must be well prepared and watered. If possible, protect the plants from the hot noonday sun. Good short old manure mulch will be found of great advantage.

ANT. C. ZVOLANEK.
Bound Brook, N. J.

SWEET PEAS

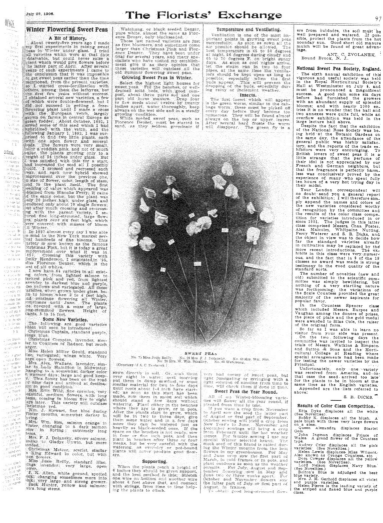

No 75 Miss Josie Reilly. No. 23 Mrs. F. J. Dolansky. No. 63 Mrs. Wm. Sim. No. 28 Mrs. W. Wm. Scialler. No. 66 Watchung.

(Courtesy of A. C. Zvolanek.)

National Sweet Pea Society, England.

The sixth annual exhibition of this vigorous and useful society was held in the Royal Horticultural Society's Hall at Westminster on July 5, and must be pronounced a magnificent success. A good rain some six days before had furnished the growers with an abundant supply of splendid blooms; and with nearly 1000 entries it is no wonder that the hall and two annexes were quite full, while an overflow exhibition was held in the large lecture hall above.

Despite the fact that the exhibition of the National Rose Society was being held at the Botanic Gardens on the same day, the attendance of the general public was highly satisfactory, and the reports of the trade exhibitors were very encouraging. To British lovers of sweet peas it is a little strange that the perfume of their idol is not appreciated by our French and German neighbors, but that the fragrance is perfectly harmless was conclusively proved by the experience of many who spent fully ten hours of a very hot trying day in their midst.

Your London correspondent will no doubt send you a general report of the exhibition; I will therefore simply append the names and colors of the new varieties considered worthy of recognition by the committee and the results of the color class competition for varieties introduced in or since 1901. The judges in this latter class comprised Messrs. Chas. Foster, Alex. Malcolm, Whitpaine Nutting, Percy Waterer and S. B. Dicks, and the object in view was to decide how far the standard varieties already in cultivation may be replaced by the more recent introductions. The exhibits in this class were very numerous, and the fact that in 9 of the 19 classes no award was made is strong testimony to the good quality of the standard sorts.

The number of novelties (new and old) submitted to the scientific committee was simply bewildering, but nothing of a very startling nature was forthcoming; the variations of the fickle Countess provided the great majority of the newer aspirants for popular favor.

In the Countess Spencer class which included Messrs. Burpee and Vaughan among the donors of prizes, the piece of plate and the gold medal were awarded to Silas Cole, the raiser of the original form.

So far as I was able to learn no visitor from your side was present.

On the two following days the committee was invited to inspect the trials of Messrs. Watkins & Simpson and Sutton & Sons and the Horticultural College at Reading where special arrangements had been made for testing the newer varieties by the Principal.

Unfortunately, only one variety was received from America, and in that case the seed arrived too late for the plants to be in bloom at the same time as the English varieties.

Appended are the lists referred to above:

S. B. DICKS.

Results of Color Class Competition.

Etta Dyke displaces all the white (See Novelties).

Bobby K. displaces all the blush. A pale blush with three very large flowers on a stem.

Queen Alexandra displaces Scarlet Gem.

John Ingman displaces Prince of Wales. A grand flower of the Countess type.

Audrey Crier displaces all the pink varieties. (See Novelties.)

Helen Lewis displaces Miss Wilmott. Also known as Orange Countess, etc.

Dora Cowper displaces all the yellow varieties. (See Novelties).

Lord Nelson displaces Navy Blue. (See Novelties.)

Bolton's Blue is adjudged the best blue variety.

Mrs. J. M. Gerhold displaces all violet and purple varieties.

Helen Pierce is the leading variety of the striped and flaked blue and purple class.

It was decided by the judges that a new color class for salmon red varieties should be formed with Henry Eckford for a start. It is a pity this variety burns so badly; perhaps California culture will improve it in this respect. In the meantime it should be grown in a half shady situation.

Novelties, Etc.

Etta Dyke. (A. M.), a pure white Countess.

Elsie Herbert. (A. M.), a very large flushed white of perfect form and good substance.

Maude Guest (A. M., very similar in color to the above but of the true Countess type.

Dora Cowper (A. M.), a giant and very substantial clear yellow, immensely superior to Mrs. Eckford.

Horace J. Wright (A. M.), a superb flower with dark purplish blue standard and slightly paler wings.

Lord Nelson (A. M.), a large, rich deep blue, somewhat in style of Navy Blue but much superior.

Audrey Crier (F. C. C., and silver medal as the best novelty of the year). A large delicate pink of the Countess type; a grand flower.

Princess Maud of Wales (A. M.), of Countess form with a color intermediate between those of Helen Lewis and John Ingman.

Queen of Norway (A. M.), may best be described as Dorothy Tennant on the Countess form.

A. M. signifies Award of Merit.

F. C. C. signifies First Class Certificate.

New York.

News Notes.

With the near approach of the convention of the S. A. F. O. H., and the probable endeavor of some one of our New York florists to be elected to the presidency of that body, one often hears the remark these days, "Who is to be the next president?" A. H. Langjahr is still spending his spare moments down on the sea beach, and we did not have the opportunity of finding out how far he had progressed in his candidacy for the office. We have also been informed that there are other men located in New York with ambitions for that honorable position, but as no open effort on their behalf has been made, we are unable to mention any names. One thing can be said, however, should any one of the New York aspirants be elected to the S. A. F. presidency, there is no doubt whatever that the office will be filled with dignity and efficiency.

James McManus, wholesale florist of 42 West Twenty-eighth street, returned on Monday last from a ten days' stay in Denver, Col., and reports having had a most enjoyable vacation.

George Saltford, wholesale florist, of 46 West Twenty-ninth street, leaves this week for a vacation to the Thousand Islands.

Anton Schultheis of College Point, L. I., writes to inform us that he has suffered no loss from hail, but that a cousin of his of the same name, located in Scranton, Pa., met with a severe loss from that cause.

Owing to ill health, C. S. Christianson has been compelled to retire, so has sold his well known and long established business, located at 67 East Tenth street, New York City, to George Wernz, who has been in his employ for many years, and Robert Koehne, who has had charge of Bloomingdale's cut flower department for the past nine years. The business will be conducted under the firm name of Wernz & Koehne, and it is hoped to build up a good trade.

John J. Perkins, wholesale florist of 50 West Twenty-eighth street, lost a valuable horse during the hot weather last week. Death is supposed to have been the result of the animal getting overheated.

M. Ford of Ford Brothers, 48 West Twenty-eighth street, is on a vacation in Pennsylvania.

W. C. Mansfield retail florist of Eighty-first street and Lexington avenue, has started on a fishing trip to the Thousand Islands.

H. E. Froment, 57 West Twenty-eighth street, has been making a valuable improvement in the rear of his store, putting in new tables of a more convenient size for the handling of such long stemmed roses as American Beauty, and others.

Benjamin Hammond of slug shot fame, Fishkill-on-the-Hudson, N. Y., who is president of the Board of Education of that town, recently delivered his annual address before that body.

Reports from the Hudson river violet districts are to the effect that the ravages of "black rot" are more extensive this season than has ever been known before, and that hundreds of thousands of plants are dying out on the benches. This is most unfortunate, as at this late date there is no means of making up the deficiency, nobody having any violet runners for sale. It would seem that there is a good opening for some one to establish a rooted cutting business in the violet industry, in order to meet just such emergencies as are confronting the violet growers this season.

Patrick Donegan, the well-known head salesman for Ford Brothers, is enjoying a well-earned vacation in Pennsylvania.

Utica, N. Y.

News Items.

George H. Benedict is building four new houses each 30 x 200 feet. Two will be planted to chrysanthemums, and two to roses. He is now cutting Kaiserin Augusta Victoria of good quality. Trade with him for the last year has been good. His carnations in the field are looking fine; this has been one of the best of years for growing outside.

The Utica Florists' Club on an Outing

Peter Crowe is rebuilding four of his fern houses. Adiantum Croweanum is very fine now; he is having a big cut, of good quality.

Frank McGowan, who has been on a trip to Philadelphia for about eight days, returned with a lot of new ideas. I believe he intends to repipe his houses for hot water. He is about to plant carnations; these will form the bulk of what he will grow; he has been cutting some very good ones.

C. F. Seltzer had the misfortune to hurt his hand very badly about a week ago, but I believe is getting along very nicely. He is making some repairs and throwing out a house of roses to make room for more carnations. Trade has been good with him this season.

Robert Boyce is about ready to plant in carnations. This year he planted everything out of doors and thinks he likes this method best. His plants are some of the best to be found around Utica.

C. F. Baker & Son are very busy potting ferns of which they grow thousands, sending them to all parts of the country. They are fine this year. This firm's carnations have all been planted in this season. Mr. Baker thinks that is the only way and the plants surely do look well, and he is bound to have an early crop. The concern has been repairing and painting and will soon have everything looking spick and span, as it always does at this place.

I called on John Owens of Whitesboro a few days ago and found himself and wife very busy with funeral work, but he said he would surely find time to attend the Florists' Club picnic at Otsego Lake.

Harry Brant has returned from his wedding trip. Dame Rumor has it that two more of our florists are to join the benedicts the latter part of August. Good luck to them.

At the next meeting of the Utica Florists' Club on August 7, the members will be entertained at the Beefsteak Club, Ilion, by Theo. Schesh. They will leave Utica on trolley at 8 p. m. A fine time is promised, and we will surely get it. We ought to have a big turnout. Mr. Schesch and wife are now at the seashore. We missed them very much at the picnic.

Dr. W. A. Rowlands is growing some chrysanthemums this year, one house, I think. His carnations are in good condition and he will soon begin to plant.

Mr. Martin of Spencer & Martin is at Fourth Lake, Adirondack Mountains, for a few days.

Frank Baker and family leave in a few days for the mountains for their Summer vacation.

Harry Seitz, who has been with Baker & Son for the past three years, has changed his business and left the florist's trade.

The Club Picnic.

On the morning of July 17, the florists, their sweethearts and wives assembled, a merry crowd, provided with good sized baskets, interesting looking enough. A trolley car had been chartered and everything was done by our genial secretary to make all comfortable. The ample car was sufficiently large to seat the party of 75, and the jolly crowd was soon on their way to Cooperstown; here the steamer Mohican was in waiting. The ride to Three Mile Point was all too short. Through the kindness of the Cooperstown florist and his wife the tables in the pavilion were ready for the guests, and in a very short time the florists and their wives were enjoying the contents of the baskets.

A tour of the pleasant grove, or a test of the fishing was then indulged in till summoned by the arrival of the boat Pathfinder when a trip was made around the lake. The beautiful wooded hills with their snugly tucked in cottages received unstinted praise. To many in the company the two hours' ride, with constantly changing scenery, the gentle lapping of the water and music in the air, made a combination affording rare pleasure. Readers of Cooper were especially interested in Natty Bumpo's Cave and other spots along the lake which that author has made famous in his Leatherstocking Tales. It was with a sigh of regret that the boat was left, and the party dispersed in Cooperstown, some to visit Cooper's grave, others to climb the mountain for a last view of the lake now earning the name of Glimmerglass, as it shone in the last rays of the setting sun. Nightfall once more found the party settled in the car for the homeward trip. When the last good night was said in Utica everyone voted the 1906 outing a decided success.

Among the out of town members present were Mr. and Mrs. Quinn of Norwich, N. Y.; Mr. and Mrs. E. J. Byam and two daughters, Rome, N. Y.; John Humphrey and sister, Rome, N. Y.; R. Kilbourn, Clinton, N. Y.; Joe Trandt, Canajoharie, N. Y.; Mr. and Mrs. Auld, New Hartford, N. Y.; Mr. and Mrs. John Owens, Whitesboro, N. Y.; Mr. and Mrs. George Benedict, Yorkville, N. Y.; and W. H. Alexander, Albany, N. Y.

QUIZ.

Buffalo.

News Notes.

The warm spell slightly moderated the past week, but not until half the help in about all the local stores had applied for their vacations. In most cases, it has not been hard to get away, owing to the slow trade.

Ben. Stafford has been spending his vacation in the East, visiting New York, Boston, Atlantic City and Philadelphia.

Miss Ruby Mark is spending three week sight-seeing in the Thousand Islands.

Joseph Sangster and wife, formerly with S. A. Anderson but now of Paterson, N. J., were visiting old friends in town the past week.

Miss Rowan is spending her vacation at Olcott Beach and reports having a very enjoyable time.

Miss Beatrice Smith, of F. H. Kramer's, Washington D. C., was in town the past week.

Wallace Eiss, bookkeeper for Wm. F. Kasting, is spending his vacation in the Muskoka Lakes. Jacob Bareley of the same firm is at one of the local summer resorts.

W. J. Palmer and family have been spending a couple of days in Toronto.

W. F. Kasting has returned from Erie, Pa., where he has been putting in some very strenuous work superintending the construction of his greenhouse plant located there. Mr. and Mrs. Kasting and family are now spending the remainder of the Summer season at the Half Past Twelve Club on Grand Island.

John Kraemer of the Washington Market, is at Crystal Beach.

W. H. G.

St. Paul.

News Notes.

The picnic given by the Twin City florists on Thursday, July 19 was a great success. The steamer Hiawatha and barge were comfortably filled, there being about 200 florists and their families on board. The original intention was to go up the river to Shakopee, but on account of the low water in the Minnesota river it was impossible to do this, so another course was adopted, and we went down to Red Rock, where the sports were held. The following is a list of the winners in the different events.

Boys' Race under 12—Elmer Bergstrom, Alfred May, Julius Stern.

Girls' Race under 12—Amestasia Dil[illegible] Olivia Hiersekorn, Elizabeth Sugar.

Boys' Race under 16—Louis Franse[illegible] Percy Armstrong, Capsol Kieper.

Young Ladies' Race—Helen Latham[illegible] Esther Holmberg, Ida Busch.

Married Ladies' Nail Driving Contest—Mrs. Busch, Mrs. Raasch, Mrs. P[illegible]vogel.

Obstacle Race for Employees—Ge[illegible] Raats, John Nylof, Robert Topel.

100 Yard Race for Employers—O. [illegible] Olson, Wm. Swanson, Carl Hangen.

Shooting Contest—Carl Peterson, [illegible] C. Hansen, Miss Hartman.

Prize Waltz on Boat—Julius Neutling and Miss Martha Guerenz; M[illegible] and Mrs. Hultgren; Otto Krinke a[illegible] Miss Lane.

Miss Lane.

Married Ladies' Race.—Mrs. Geo[illegible]mein, Mrs. Roach, Mrs. Jones.

The committee in charge, consisting of E. Nagel, Minneapolis; R. Latham, C. Henderson, Carl Hange[illegible] Henry Puvogel, N. C. Hansen and J. Olson, St. Paul, worked hard to have everything come off successfully, a[illegible] succeeded beyond a doubt. Socially and financially, the affair was a success, and all participants unquestionably enjoyed themselves. The prizes were beautiful, and, to a large extent were contributed by the different merchants of the Twin Cities.

The bowling contest between the Minneapolis and St. Paul Clubs is to be held at a later date; considerable rivalry exists, so that all may expect a pretty warm time.

PAUL.

Boston.

A Flower Show.

There was an exceedingly interesting exhibition at Horticultural Hall on Saturday. Sweet peas were the main attraction but there were many other flowers worthy of note. Displays of herbaceous flowers were made by the Blue Hills Nursery, by the Harvard Botanical Gardens and by R. & J. Farquhar & Company. In the collection of the latter were some fine vases of Hemerocallis aurantiaca major. Tailby & Son exhibited their hybrid calla; and Wm. Thatcher staged Clerodendron fallax which was quite attractive. Mrs. J. L. Gardner was the only exhibitor of achimenes which are usually an attraction at this show. In the classes for sweet peas the following awards were made. Display of named varieties filling thirty vases, 25 sprays of each—first W. J. Clemson. Best twelve varieties, named, six sprays of each—first, Joseph Thorpe; second, A. E. Hartshorn; third, Wm. Whitman. Fifty sprays, any named white variety—first, Oscar B. Kenrick, Dorothy Eckford; second, A. E. Hartshorn, same variety; third, W. J. Clemson, also with Dorothy Eckford. Light pink or blush—first, A. E. Hartshorn; Countess Spencer; second, E. L. Lewis, Gladys Unwin; third, W. J. Clemson. Any named rose colored variety—first, E. L. Lewis, American Queen. Any named blue or purple variety—first, E. L. Lewis, Helen Pierce. Any named lavender variety—first, A. E. Hartshorn, Mrs. Geo. Higginson; second, W. J. Clemson, Lady Grisel Hamilton; third, Oscar B. Kenrick, same variety. Any named red or crimson variety—first, Oscar B. Kenrick, King Edward VII. Any named orange or salmon variety—first, W. J. Clemson, Miss Wilmott; second, E. L. Lewis, same; third, Mrs. A. W. Blake, Lady Mary Currie. Any named variety, any other color—first, E. L. Lewis, Maid of Honor; second, E. L. Lewis, America; third, Oscar B. Kenrick, Stanley.

News Notes.

Lewis R. Jackson of Woburn is building another house, thus doubling his glass capacity.

Welch Brothers are making plans for greatly enlarging their floor space next Fall. Some new and entirely up-to-date methods of handling the wholesale business will be introduced.

The Waban Rose Conservatories have commenced their Summer cut of American Beauty, handling some very fine blooms for this season.

Among those off on vacation this week are: Gus Camp and Chas. Miller of Zinn's; Frank J. Norton of McMulkin's; and Frank Kelly of Whipple & Company. J. W. D.

Philadelphia.

Trade Notes.

The supply of cut flowers just now is very poor; with many things it is between seasons, and on account of so much cloudy and rainy weather the quality of outdoor stock is not up to the average. Asters are arriving in fair quantity, but are small and short in stem. The retail stores are busy in the early mornings only.

Next season, as Easter comes early, the social season here will start much earlier than usual; and as there will be a large list of debutantes, it may interest the trade to know that the dancing class of Mrs. Mason, which starts the social affairs, will commence December 3.

Our bowlers are now rolling a series of matches on outside alleys in order to decide who shall compose the team for Dayton. Some of the old standbys are not in good form; the team looks like Robertson, Falck, Connor, Adelberger, Graham and Dunlap or Batchelor for substitute.

J. Liddon Pennock again won the Saturday yacht race at Ocean City. One of his crew fell overboard, but Mr. Pennock had such a good lead, that he was able to come about, pick up his man, and still win out.

DAVID RUST.

EAST ST. LOUIS, ILL.—Reynolds Seed and Commission Company has increased its capital stock from $5,000 to $10,000.

Springfield, O.

At the second gathering of florists of Springfield and vicinity, held on Monday evening, July 16, reports were received from committees appointed at the initial meeting. A constitution and by-laws were adopted, the name of the organization to be "The Springfield Florists' Club," regular meeting to be held on the second Monday evening of each month. Officers to serve for one year were elected as follows: John M. Good, president; Roger H. Murphy, vice-president; Chas. W. Schmidt, secretary and Roy McGregor, treasurer. An entertainment committee was appointed which has since announced the first picnic to be held at Eichholz Park on Thursday, August 2.

The Daily News of 20th inst. states, "Big hay wagons were used to carry 56 of the employees and their families of the Good & Reese Company to Clifton Friday morning, where they are holding their picnic. The day is being spent in playing ball and other outdoor sports."

A new record was established this season by The Leedle Floral Company, which made its first shipment of young rose plants from early Summer propagation on July 11, new stock not ordinarily being expected to be in shipping condition until early Fall. GE. DALE.

MACOMB, ILL.—The Western Illinois Stoneware Company is planning to add a flower pot manufactory to its business.

Phoenix Roebelenii

THE MOST GRACEFUL PALM OF ALL.

We have almost the entire stock of it in America.

SEEDLINGS, $5.00 per 100; $40.00 per 1000; $350.00 per 10,000. 4 in. pot plants, about 1 foot high; 12-15 leaves, $1.00 each; $80.00 per 100; $750.00 per 1000; 7 in. pot plants, about 2-2½ feet high, $5.00 each; $40.00 per 10; $350.00 per 100.
SPECIMEN PLANTS, $7.50-$10.00.
We also offer for sale—**STOVE PLANTS, CALADIUMS, CROTONS** and **DRACAENAS** in finest varieties at reasonable prices.

JOHN LEWIS CHILDS
FLORAL PARK - - - - - L. I., N. Y.

Mention The Florists' Exchange when writing.

FERNS

	Doz	100
SCOTTII, 2¼ inch	$0.75	$5.00
BARROWSII, 2¼ inch	1.25	8.00

THE CONARD & JONES CO.
WEST GROVE, PA.

Mention The Florists' Exchange when writing.

CELERY---CABBAGE

White Plume, Golden-Self, Golden Heart, fine plants, $1.50 per 1000.

Cabbage Plants—Flat Dutch and Drumhead $1.00 per 1000; 5000 for $4.00.

Cauliflower Plants, Early Snowball, $2.00 per 1000.

J. C. SCHMIDT CO., Bristol, Pa.

Mention The Florists' Exchange when writing.

Decorative Plants

Latania Borbonica, 2¼ in. pots, $3.00; 3 in. $6.00; 4 in., $15.00 per 100. Large specimen plants from $2.00 to $5.00 each.

Kentia Belmoreana and Forsteriana, 2½ in. pots, $8.00; 3 in., $16.00; 5 in., $60.00 per 100; 6 in. $15.00 per doz.; 7 in. and upward, $1.75 to $36.00 each.

Areca Lutescens, 3 in. $10.00; 4 in. $20.00 per 100; 6 in., $1.00 each and upward.

Pandanus Utilis, 3 in. pots, $3.00; 4 in., $20.00 per 100.

Phœnix Reclinata, 6 in. pots, $35.00 per 100.

Phœnix Canariensis, fine specimen plants, from $3.00 to $35.00 each.

Araucaria Excelsa, 6 in. pots, $65.00 per 100.

Assorted Ferns, 2¼ in. pots, $3.00 per 100. **Nephrolepis Compacta**, 3 in. pots, $8.00; 4 in., $15.00 per 100.

Plants in Fine Condition.

JOHN BADER, Troy Hill, Allegheny, Pa.

Mention The Florists' Exchange when writing.

SMILAX PLANTS.

Strictly No. 1 plants; from 2 in. pots, $1.00 per 100; $9.00 per 1000. Seedlings from boxes, $4.00 per 1000.

R. KILBOURN, CLINTON, N. Y.

Mention The Florists' Exchange when writing.

ASPARAGUS

Sprengerii, extra strong, 3 in. pots, $5 per 100.
Extra Strong, 4 in. pots, $6 per 100.
Smilax, 2½ in. pots $2 per 100.
Cabbage Plants, Flat Dutch, Succession and Winningstadt, $1.50 per 1000. Cash with order.

S. G. BENJAMIN, Fishkill, N. Y.

Mention The Florists' Exchange when writing.

ORCHIDS

Arrived in superb condition **Cattleya Dowiana, C. Gigas, C. Mossiae, C. Percivaliana, C. Speciosissima, C. Eldorado, C. Superba, C. Labiata, C. Leopoldii** and many more.

Write for Prices.

LAGER & HURRELL, Summit, N. J.
Growers and Importers

Mention The Florists' Exchange when writing.

ORCHIDS

Largest Importers, Exporters, Growers and Hybridists in the world.

Sander, St. Albans, England
and
235 Broadway, Room 1, New York City

Mention The Florists' Exchange when writing.

COCOS PALMS.

Strong 2¼ inch at $1.50 per dozen. Write for lowest prices on Kentias.

Jas. F. Barclay R. I. GREENHOUSES Pawtucket, R. I.

Mention The Florists' Exchange when writing.

Commercial Violet Culture

Price, $1.50

The Florists' Exchange, 2-8 Duane St., New York

STUDER OFFERS

Latania Borbonica, Phoenix Canariensis, from 6 in. pots, 2½ feet tall, $5.00 per doz. **Latania**, from 5 in. pots, 2 foot size and **Kentia Belmoreana**, 20 in. tall, also **Chamærops Excelsa**, from 5 in. pots, $3.50 per doz. **Boston Ferns**, from 4 in. pots, $3.00 per doz.; all these fine plants ready for a shift. Red, Pink and White **Geraniums**, 4 in. pots, in bud and bloom $4.00 per 100. **Scarlet Sage**, 3 in., $3.00 per 100. Pot grown, best monthly hybrid, Moss and Climbing **Roses**, 4-5-6 in. pots, $1.00, $2.00 and $3.00 per doz. according to size.

CASH PLEASE.

N. STUDER, Anacostia, D.C.

Mention The Florists' Exchange when writing.

ASPARAGUS

	Per 100
Sprengerii, 3 in.	$3.00
Smilax, 2¼ in.	1.25
Primula Obconica, Grandiflora, Alba, Rosea and Hybrida, 2 in.	2.00

Cash with order, please.

GEO. J. HUGHES, BERLIN, N. J.

Mention The Florists' Exchange when writing.

A Few Good Things YOU WANT

Dracæna Indivisa, 4 and 5 in., $10.00 and $25.00 per 100.

Asparagus Sprengeri, 2 in., $2.50 per 100.

Geraniums, S. A. Nutt, Castellane, John Doyle, Perkins, Double Gen. Grant, Poitevine, Mme. Sallerol, 2 in. pots, $2.00 per 100; 3 in. pots $4.00 per 100. Rooted Cuttings, $1.00 per 100.

Vinca Var., 2 in., $2.00 per 100; 3 in., $4.00 per 100.
Rex Begonia, nice plants, 2 and 2½ in., $5.00 per 100.

Asparagus Plumosus, 2 in. $3.00 per 100.

GEO. M. EMMANS, Newton, N. J.

Mention The Florists' Exchange when writing.

		Per 100
Asparagus Plumosus,	2¼ in. pots,	$2.50
" **Sprengerii**,	" " "	2.00
Smilax	" " "	1.50

J. S. BLOOM,
RIEGELSVILLE, PA.

Mention The Florists' Exchange when writing.

ROBERT CRAIG & CO.

ROSES, PALMS, CROTONS

CARNATIONS and Novelties in DECORATIVE PLANTS

Market and 49th Sts. PHILADELPHIA, PA.

English Ivy, 4 in., 8c., 2 in., 2c. **Vinca**, 4 in., 5c. **German Ivy**, 2 in., $1.00 per 100. Cash.

J. H. DANN & SON, WESTFIELD, N. Y.

Mention The Florists' Exchange when writing.

REMEMBER

We are still Headquarters for

BAY TREES BOX TREES
...EVERGREENS...

Price Lists on application.

JULIUS ROEHRS CO.,
Exotic Nurseries, Rutherford, N. J.

Mention The Florists' Exchange when writing.

EMERSON C. McFADDEN

Wholesale Grower

Asparagus Plumosus Nanus, Etc.

Short Hills, N. J.
Tel. 28 A.

Mention The Florists' Exchange when writing.

ASPARAGUS SPRENGERI

Large plants from 3 in. pots 5c. each.

Asparagus Plumosus Nanus, about 200 fine plants left, 3 in. pots 5c. each, to close them out.

Liberal count on both.

R. G. HANFORD, Norwalk, Conn.

Mention The Florists' Exchange when writing.

MARIE LOUISE VIOLETS

YOUR LAST CHANCE. NO MORE AFTER THIS WEEK

Schuneman's famous Violets are well-known as the most fragrant of all Violets. Fine plants for benching at once, guaranteed the best stock in the market, none better. Only $2.00 per 100; $15.00 per 1000. Come and take a look at them. Only 17 miles from New York City. Money returned if not suited.

GEO. T. SCHUNEMAN

Dear Sir:—The violets arrived safely and in good condition.

Thanks for your promptness.

Mrs. F. W. Van Emburgh,
44 Westervelt Ave., North Plainfield, N. J.

GEO. T. SCHUNEMAN, Violet Range.
BALDWINS, L. I., N. Y.

Mention The Florists' Exchange when writing.

MARIE LOUISE VIOLETS

Strong Plants. February or March struck, healthy and free from disease. Cash with order. Your money cheerfully refunded if not satisfactory. **$2.00 per 100, $15.00 per 1000.**

C. LAWRITZEN,
BOX 261 RHINEBECK, N. Y.

Mention The Florists' Exchange when writing.

VIOLETS

MARIE LOUISE Violets, clean and healthy in every particular, ready August 15th. 3 in. pots. $5.00 per 100.

CASH WITH ORDER.

WM. J. CHINNICK,
TRENTON, N. J.

Mention The Florists' Exchange when writing.

BEGONIA REX

BEST NAMED SORTS

An immense stock in fine condition for immediate sales, 2½ inch, $5.00 per 100.

See ad. in Last Issue.

NATHAN SMITH & SON,
ADRIAN, MICH.

Mention The Florists' Exchange when writing.

Governor Herrick Violet

The finest single violet ever offered. Write me about it today.

Price: One dozen, $2.00; 100, $10.00; 1000 at $75.00 or 5000 or more at $60.00 per 1000. No. 1 Stock.

H. R. CARLTON, WILLOUGHBY, OHIO.

Mention The Florists' Exchange when writing.

FIELD GROWN VIOLETS

Strong, healthy, well-rooted plants of **Lady Campbell** (double), ready now at $2.50 per 100; $20.00 per 1000. **California** (single), ready by Aug. 15th, $3.00 per 100. Packed to carry safely, free of charge.

CHAS. BLACK, HIGHTSTOWN, N. J.

Mention The Florists' Exchange when writing.

Field Grown CARNATIONS

6000 **White Lawson** .... $6.00 per 100.
5000 **Enchantress** 5000 **Queen Louise**
1000 **Bountiful** 500 **The Belle**
5000 **Pink Lawson** 300 **Crisis**
1000 **Roosevelt** 200 **Richmond Gem**
2000 **Harlowarden** 500 **Flamingo**
1000 **Estelle** 200 **F. Burki**
100 **Eclipse**,
$5.00 per 100; $45.00 per 1000.
Limestone land, no stem rot.

CASH WITH ORDER.

Wells Fargo, American, Adams, U. S. Express.

W. SABRANSKY, KENTON, O.

Mention The Florists' Exchange when writing.

FIELD GROWN

Carnation Plants

Enchantress, $40.00 and $50.00 per 1000.
McGowan, $30.0 In field, no plants shipped.

WM. BELL, BAYSIDE, L. I.

Mention The Florists' Exchange when writing.

FIELD GROWN CARNATIONS

Good Healthy Stock.

PROSPERITY	$5.00	per 100.
LAWSON	5.00	" "
HARLOWARDEN	5.00	" "

Terms Cash.

RIDDELL & HERRICK, FARMINGDALE, L. I.

Mention The Florists' Exchange when writing.

FIELD-GROWN

Carnation Plants

Send for price and list of varieties.

Chicago Carnation Co., Joliet, Ill.

Mention The Florists' Exchange when writing.

CLASSIFIED ADVERTISEMENTS

CASH WITH ORDER.

The columns under this heading are reserved for advertisements of Stock for Sale, Stock Wanted, Help Wanted, Situations Wanted or other Wants; also of Greenhouse, Land, Second-Hand Materials, etc., For Sale or Rent.

Our charge is 10 cts. per line (7 words to the line), set solid, without display. No advt. accepted for less than thirty cents.

Display advertisements in these columns, 15 cents per line; count 12 lines agate to the inch.

[If replies to Help Wanted, Situation Wanted, or other advertisements are to be addressed care of this office, advertisers add 10 cents to cover expense of forwarding.]

Copy must reach New York office 12 o'clock Wednesday to secure insertion in issue of following Saturday.

Advertisers in the Western States desiring to advertise under initials, may save time by having their answer directed care our Chicago office at 127 E. Berwyn Ave.

SITUATIONS WANTED

SITUATION WANTED—By grower and propagator of roses, carnations, mums and other plants. 14 years experience. German, good references. State full particulars with wages. Address, Ohio, care The Florists' Exchange.

SITUATION WANTED—As working foreman by a practical grower of cut flowers and pot plants. German, aged 36, single, life experience. Best of references given. Please state wages. Address, L. Z., care The Florists' Exchange.

SITUATION WANTED—With a first-class seed house; well up in all branches. Flower seeds a specialty. Many years experience in Europe and America with best known houses. Highest references. Address, L. V., care The Florists' Exchange.

SITUATION WANTED—By practical, middle-aged florist, life experience growing roses, carnations, violets, chrysanthemums, decorative and bedding plants. Single, sober, state wages and particulars. Address, L. Y., care The Florists' Exchange.

SITUATION WANTED—As foreman or general manager, 20 years' experience. Sober, reliable and first-class on general cut flower stock and pot plants. Can plan, build and heat. Certificate as carnationist from Mass. Hort. Society. First-class designer. Please correspond. L. S., care The Florists' Exchange.

SITUATION WANTED—As working foreman on either private or commercial place by an expert in all branches of gardening. 12 years experience, roses, orchids, carnations a specialty. Fully understands landscape gardening, carpet bedding, as well as growing of pot plants, cut flowers, fruits and vegetables under glass or outside. German, 26, single, best of references; open for engagement August 1st. John Mihalik, care Geo. Cole, Far Hills, N. J.

HELP WANTED

WANTED—Single young man for general greenhouse work; steady position. State wages wanted to Chas. L. Stanley, Plainfield, N. J.

WANTED—An experienced rose grower. State wages expected and give references. Robt. Scott & Son, Sharon Hill, Del. Co., Pa.

WANTED—August 20, young man with good experience, for greenhouses on large private place. Apply to Carl Lindrath, Narberth, Pa.

WANTED—Man for general greenhouse work. Asparagus Plumosus a specialty. Wages, $10.00 per week. Apply to Emerson C. McFadden, Short Hills, N. J.

WANTED—At once a good grower of carnations and pot plants. State age, salary expected, and whether married or single. Address, L. X., care The Florists' Exchange.

WANTED—Working foreman for general greenhouse work; state wages expected and where last employed. W. C. Goodrich, R. F. D. No. 2, Watervliet, New York.

WANTED—Young man to work at garden work and in greenhouse. Must understand designing and be a good salesman. References required as to honesty. Address, M. C., care The Florists' Exchange.

WANTED—Thoroughly first-class experienced rose and carnation growers. Apply stating age, married or single, references and wages expected. None but first-class men wanted. Lake View Rose Gardens, Jamestown, N. Y.

WANTED—At once, section man and helper. Beauties, Brides and Maids on an up-to-date new commercial place. Only sober, industrious men need apply, with wages expected, etc. B. F. Hoehl, Manager of the Madison Cut Flower Company, Madison, N. J.

WANTED A working foreman to take charge of seven small houses. A single man preferred, who understands rose and carnation growing. Answer immediately, stating references and salary desired. Address A., 707 Calvert Building, Baltimore, Md.

Mention the Florists' Exchange when writing.

HELP WANTED

WANTED—One or two hustling salesmen for nursery stock. Those who have had experience in that line and a good record as salesmen for such stock. To such men I will pay a good salary and expenses. Nursery more than 50 years old. Address, P. A. Keene, 1 Madison Avenue, New York.

WANTED—Nursery foreman, to take full charge of a nursery embracing about 200 acres, where a general line of stock is raised, principally ornamental. Must be one thoroughly up-to-date, good, executive ability. Such a man can secure a first-class position. Apply with references to L. W., care The Florists' Exchange.

WANTED—Floral decorator and designer. One of New York's leading establishments will require a fully experienced head salesman, maker-up and designer, accustomed to high class work on or about September 15th. Applications received now. State experience and salary expected. Correspondence will be held strictly confidential. An exceptional opportunity. Address, Competent, care The Florists' Exchange.

WANTED—Working foreman to grow roses and some Easter stock on moderate-sized place. Married, under 40, able to show credentials as to habits and ability to grow good stock, who can hustle himself and make others hustle. Such a man will find a permanent place, pleasant location and fair treatment. No "rounders" need apply. Pay, including house and fuel, $75 to $80 per month. Address, L. T., care The Florists' Exchange.

MISCELLANEOUS WANTS

WANTED TO BUY—Greenhouses to be taken down. State full particulars of same when writing. Address, F. W., care The Florists' Exchange.

WANTED TO BUY—A small retail place of two or three houses and dwelling house. Greenhouses must be in good repair and fully stocked. Southern New England preferred. Address, Greenhouse, care The Florists' Exchange.

WANTED TO BUY—Property, 5 acres or more with or without greenhouses and within reach of New York Market. Must be in healthy location with nice natural surroundings. G. F. Neipp, Aqueduct, L. I., N. Y.

An Arboriculturist, experienced, 34 years of age, married, desires to communicate with some person engaged in this branch, with a view to forming a partnership. Has a small capital at disposition. Address, A. Z., Advertising offices of Swartsenburg, Gouda, Holland.

FOR SALE OR RENT

FOR SALE or will rent to a responsible party, a fine greenhouse property. 12,000 feet of glass. Fine residence. Address, Silas O. Howell, Lock Box 14, Pine Bush, New York.

DESIRABLE greenhouse plant of three houses, 24x200 feet; propagating house, 100 feet; potting shed, stable and dwelling. Steam heat, city water. Highland, opposite Poughkeepsie. Joseph Wood, Spring Valley, New York.

FOR RENT—Small greenhouse and florist business in prosperous running condition, Southern Connecticut. Full particulars and reason for renting to anyone interested. Address L. U. care The Florists' Exchange.

FOR SALE—A fine established nursery business with a constituency reaching from the Atlantic to the Pacific, and from Manitoba to the Gulf. Old age of proprietor the only reason for sale. C. S. Harrison, York, Neb.

FOR RENT—A greenhouse plant of fifteen thousand feet of glass, with an established trade. Reason for renting, am conducting a store and wish to devote my time entirely to same. Address, L. O., care The Florists' Exchange.

TO LET—greenhouse establishment in the city of Poughkeepsie, N. Y. 8000 feet of glass, city water, plenty of soil, fine location. For particulars, come and see, or write to James Coleman, 212 Mansion street, Poughkeepsie, N. Y.

FOR SALE—Greenhouses at Madison, N. J. Situated on North Street. One 162 x 86; two 150 x 18 feet, 8 in.; one 150 x 12. Heated by both hot water and steam. Place in first-class condition. For particulars address, 60 Park Avenue, Madison, New Jersey.

To lease for a term of years, my establishment on Greene Avenue, consisting of about 7,000 feet of glass, office and salesroom. Stable and wagon shed. Horse and wagons. Place well stocked and heated with hot water. Every convenience, all in good condition. A good business in the best location in the city. Established for 40 years. Wishing to retire from business. This is a good opportunity for the right man. Come and see it. Richard Shannon, 341-349 Greene Avenue, Brooklyn, New York.

Thirty cents is the minimum charge for advertisements on this page.

FOR SALE OR RENT

FOR SALE—Owing to failing health, I will sell my florist establishment, beautifully situated between Larchmont Manor and Mamaroneck, Westchester Co., New York, near railroad station; trolley lines within one minute walk. First class opportunity for the right man. Plenty of landscape and jobbing work. The place contains four acres, 2 greenhouses, 104 feet long and lots of sash; well stocked with trees and shrubs, etc.; horse, wagon and tools. Address, Box 44, Larchmont, New York.

STOCK FOR SALE

Quercus Alba, Q. Coccinea and Q. Rubra, $1.50 per bu. Fraxinus Americana, 14c. lb. Address, Box 893, Biltmore, N. C.

PEONY FESTIVA MAXIMA, and other best sorts in strong plants, 2 yr. old. Catalogue free. A. Dessert, Peony Specialist, Chenonceaux, France.

JERUSALEM CHERRIES, seedlings, 25c. per 100; 2½ in. pots, fine plants, $3.00 per 100. Cash please. A. Relyea & Son, Poughkeepsie, N. Y.

THREE magnificent palms (Latania Borbonica), 13 feet high and 13 feet wide. Reason for selling, no place to store. Apply, I. T. Burden, Newport, R. I.

PRIMULA, Chinese, finest fringed, mixed; Obconica Grandiflora, fringed, Alba Rosea, 2 in. 2c.; cash. Shippensburg Floral Company, Shippensburg, Pa.

MARIE LOUISE VIOLETS, strong Winter grown stock, ready for planting at once. Write me at once for sample. $2.00 per 100; $12.00 per 1000. Louis D. McCoy, Monsey, N. Y.

STOCK FOR SALE—Brides, Maids and American Beauties, in 4 in. pots; best of plants. Also 1 year old Asparagus. All at low bottom prices. Small or large orders. Madison Rose Company, Madison, N. J.

JARDINIERE FERNS, seedlings, good, strong, healthy stock, in variety only. Now ready for potting. Price, $1.50 per 100 by mail; $10.00 per 1000, F. O. B. Exp. B. Soltau, 199 Grant avenue, Jersey City, N. J.

BABY RAMBLER roses, fine dormant stock, $25 per 100. 2 1-2 inch pot plants, extra well rooted $7 per 100, $65 per 1000. Orders booked for delivery now or any time up to late Spring. Samples free. Brown Brothers Co., Rochester, N. Y.

2500 BRIDESMAID plants, 2000 Brides, 1500 American Beauties, 1000 Meteors, all good, fine plants in 4 in. pots. Packed and shipped at express office. Maids, Brides and Meteors, 5c. each. American Beauties, 12c. each. Louis M. Noe, Madison, N. J.

GIANT PANSY.—Mme. Perret, genuine gold medal, Parisian Bugnot, Cassier, Giant Trimardeau, Excelsior, Coquette de Porissy, Giant Beaconsfield, improved, etc. Forget-me-not, Victoria, Dwarf blue Bellis Perennis, Mignonette, giant red forcing, Hardy Larkspur, white, blue and mixed. Send for prices. Beaulieu, Pansy Specialist, Woodhaven, N. Y.

FOR SALE—Two horizontal tubular boilers 14 feet x 5 feet; 62 3 1-2 inch tubes; 70 horse power; grates, valves and all fittings complete. One locomotive boiler 28 feet x 5 feet, 150 horse power; 81 tubes 3 1-2 inches; with stack 80 feet high x 30 inches; with shaking grates. The two boilers were taken out to make room for one of larger capacity, and are in first-class condition. Insured by Hartford Steam Boiler Ins. & Ins. Co. at 100 pounds pressure. The locomotive boiler was bought for temporary use. Will be sold cheap. Apply to Plainfield Water Supply Co., Plainfield, N. J.

FOR SALE

FOR SALE—Cheap, all sizes greenhouse glass, new stock. Address, Glass, care The Florists' Exchange.

FOR SALE—One No. 6 Weathered Boiler in good condition, price $35.00. J. H. Fiesser, 415 Summit Avenue, West Hoboken, N. J.

FOR SALE—1500 feet new 2 in. iron pipe, 8cts. ft. Lot of glass 16x18, A. double, all new. P. O. Box 120, Chatham, N. J.

FOR SALE—12 Hitchings hot water expansion tanks for 3 1-2 in. pipe, in good condition, cleaned, ready to set up. 1-3 price of new. Also horse lawn mower, easy running, $20.00. Address, K. D., care The Florists' Exchange.

FOR SALE—Stover fifty foot Steel Tower and Tank in use a short time. Good as new; price reasonable. Write for particulars. Wm. C. De Witt, R. F. D. No. 1, Phillipsburg, N. J.

FOR SALE—Two Lord and Burnham Ventilating Apparatus, with arms and pipe hangers. In use two seasons. Suitable for house 200 feet long. Cost, $65.00 new. $40.00 takes both machines. W. C. Pray, Kinkora, N. J.

BOILERS, BOILERS, BOILERS.

SEVERAL good second hand boilers on hand, also new No. 16 Hitchings at reduced cost. Write for list. Wm. H. Lutton, West Side Avenue Station, C. R. R. of N. J., Jersey City, N. J.

FOR SALE

Greenhouse Material milled from Gulf Cypress, to any detail furnished, or our own patterns as desired, cut and spliced ready for erection. Estimates for complete constructions furnished.

V. E. REICH, Brooklyn, N. Y.

1429-1437 Metropolitan Ave.

Mention The Florists' Exchange when writing.

FOR SALE

PUMPS Rider-Ericsson. Second-hand, from $40.00 up; all repairs; other makes; new; cheap.

BOILERS One second-hand tubular hot water boiler 3 ft. in diameter 12 ft. long. Price $35.00. One No. 15 Hitchings as good as new, $60.00.

PIPE Good serviceable second-hand, with Threads; 2-in., 7 cts.; 1½-in., 5½ cts.; 1¼-in., 4 cts.; 1-in., 3 cts.; 2½ in., 10 cts.; 3 in., 14 cts.; 4 in., 19 cts. New 2-in. Standard, full lengths, with couplings, 8¼ cts. ft. Old and new fittings and valves. Old 4 inch cast iron 15c per foot.

STOCKS and DIES New Economy, best made No. 1 Threads, ¼-in., ¾-in., 1-in. pipe, $3.00. No. 2 Threads, 1¼-in., 1½-in., 2-in. pipe, $4.00.

PIPE CUTTERS New Saunders Pattern. No. 1 cuts ¼-in.-1-in. pipe, $1.00. No. 2 cuts 1-in.-2-in. pipe, $1.30.

STILLSON WRENCHES New. 18-in., grips ¼-in.-2-in. pipe, $1.65; 24-in. grips ¼-in.-2½ in. pipe, $2.40; 36-in., grips ¼-in.-3½-in. pipe, $4.75.

PIPE VISES New. No. 1 Hinged, grips ¼-in.-3 in. pipe, $2.00.

GARDEN HOSE New. 50 ft. lengths. ¾-in., guaranteed 100-lbs. pressure, 7½ cts. per ft.; ¾-in., not guaranteed, 4¾ cts. per ft., 25 ft. lengths, ½c. per ft. more.

HOT-BED SASH New. Cypress, 3-ft.x6 ft., from 75 cts. up; glazed, complete, from $1.60 up. Second-hand, in good condition, all glass in, $1.00 each.

GLASS New American 10x12 single $1.75 per box; 12x12 single $1.90 per box; 10x12, 12x12, 10x15 double, $2.40 per box; 12x14, 12x20, 14x14, double, $2.80 per box; 16x16, 16x18, $3.00 per box; 16x24 double $3.20 per box. Second hand glass, 8 x 10, 8 x 12, double, $1.50 per box; 10x12 double at $1.75 per box.

Old material, ridge, plates, gutters, bars, etc.

Get our prices on New Gulf Cypress Building Material, Ventilating Apparatus, Oil, White Lead, Putty, Paint, Points, etc.

METROPOLITAN MATERIAL CO.

1398-1408 Metropolitan Avenue, BROOKLYN, N.Y

Mention The Florists' Exchange when writing.

All NURSERYMEN, SEEDSMEN and FLORISTS

wishing to do business with Europe should send for the

"Horticultural Advertiser"

This is THE British Trade Paper, being read weekly by all Horticultural traders. It is also taken by over 1000 of the best Continental houses. Annual subscriptions to cover cost of postage, 75 cents. Money orders payable at Lowdham, Notts. Address

EDITORS OF THE "H. A."

Chilwell Nurseries, Lowdham, Notts

European Agents for THE AMERICAN CARNATIO

Mention the Florists' Exchange when writi

OUR ENDEAVOR

is to place THE FLORISTS' EXCHANGE in the hands of every reader within 1000 miles on Saturday of each week.

In order to effect this even distribution, which makes for the benefit of our advertisers, it is necessary that all advertising copy for current issue should reach us by

12 noon, on Wednesday.

Mention The Florists' Exchange when writ

Boston Club's Outing.

It was a large gathering of the Gardeners' and Florists' Club at Waushakum Grove, South Framingham, on Wednesday. The weather was perfect and the arrangements were carried out to the letter by the committee, so that every one present had a very enjoyable time. Special cars carried the party to and from Boston, and as the grounds were in excellent shape for the sporting events a very interesting afternoon was spent.

Unfortunately, a good many prominent members were unable to be present; this was caused mainly by their being out of town at this season.

The full list of events follows:

Baseball, Married vs. Single; Lord and Burnham prizes, nine pair cuff links—Single (Johnson, captain), 14; Married (Fischer, captain), 9.

Baseball, boys under 16; William E. Doyle prizes, nine ball gloves—Hodgson, captain, 16; Wheeler, captain, 3.

Baseball, girls, no age limit; Welch Brothers' prizes, nine chatelaine pins—Ella Palmer, captain, 10; Iva Wheeler, captain, 9.

Cricket, Commercial vs. Private Gardeners; Edward Hatch prizes, eleven pins—Private Gardeners winners. Score, 33-29.

50 yards race, boys under 10; Bay State Nurseries prizes, first, magnet watch; second, knife; third, Rugby ball—First, Thomas Iliffe; second, Theodore Palmer; third, Victor Lumsden.

50 yards race, girls under 10; H. M. Robinson & Company's prizes, first, locket and chain; second, brooch; third, brooch—First, Helen Bearse; second Lillian Bearse; third, Harriet Coles.

100 yards race, boys from 10 to 16 years; W. W. Edgar Company's prizes, first, football; second, catcher mit; third, junior ball—First, Geo. Palmer; second, James Harbison; third, Clarence Doten.

100 yards race, girls from 10 to 16 years; Braman, Dow & Company's prizes, first, tennis racquet; second, pair handy pins; third, locket—First, Florence Lumsden; second, Helen Bearse; third, Florence Eisenhardt.

50 yards race, married ladies; A. H. Hews & Company's prizes, first, suit case; second, umbrella; third, hammock—First, Mrs. Robert Edgar; second, Mrs. A. Eisenhardt; third, Mrs. T. Neal.

100 yards race, young ladies over 16 years; first, Houghton & Clark prize, manicure set; second, David Lumsden prize, camera—First, Ella Palmer; second, Ethel Roy.

100 yards, club members only; first, J. Breck & Son prize, barometer; second, T. J. Grey & Company prize, cup; third, D. Finlayson's prize, watch fob—First, Thomas Brown; second, A. E. Shedd; third, F. Cannell.

100 yards sack race, open to all; Daniel Iliffe prize.; first, clock; second, knife—First, Alexander Burr; second, J. McCarthy.

100 yards race, fat men over 200 lbs.; Schlegel & Fottler Company's prizes, first, clock; second, umbrella—First, W. R. Nicholson; second, James Wheeler.

50 yards race, men over 50 years; W. W. Rawson Company's prizes, first, umbrella; second, paper knife—First, William Miller; second, J. Keady.

Potato race for ladies; H. H. Barrows Sons' prizes, first, umbrella; second, collar box—First, Louise Eisenhardt; second, Jean Westwood.

100 yards 3-legged race, Henry Penn's prizes, first, two pair cuff buttons; second, two pins—First, Thomas Brown and Harry Coles; second, A. Lowe and A. F. McDermott.

240 yards handicap; first, T. J. Grey's prize, silver cup; second, William Sim's prize, military hair brush; third, William Sim's prize, watch fob—First, F. Cannell; second, A. E. Shedd; third, F. E. Palmer.

Quoit match; first, Julius Zinn's prize, meerschaum pipe; second, Alex. Montgomery's prize, clothes brush—First, William Munroe; second, William Robb.

High jump; H. H. Barrows Sons' prizes, first, umbrella; second, collar box—First, Frank Edgar, 4 ft. 9 in.; second, Frank McDermott, 4 ft. 8 in.

Long jump; Framingham Nurseries' prizes, first, Waterman fountain pen; second, shaving set—First, W. Johnson, 13 ft. 8 in.; second, Frank Edgar, 13 ft. 4 in.

Putting 16-lb shot; first, W. J. Stewart prize; second, Sporting Committee's prize, fancy silk suspenders—First, W. R. Nicholson, 25 ft. 1½ in.; second, D. McKenzie, 24 ft. 10 in.

Throwing 12-pound hammer; Sporting Committee's prizes, first, umbrella; second, clothes brush—First, William Munroe, 94 ft. 4 in.; second, William Robb, 93 ft. 6 in.

Tug of war, Commercial vs. Private Gardeners; sporting committee prize, box cigars—Private gardeners winners.

240 yards handicap, boys 10 to 16 years; A. F. Scott prizes, first, rod and reel; second, punching bag; third, knife—First, George Palmer; second, William Iliffe; third, James Harbison.

100 yards race, open to all; Shady Hills Nursery Company's prizes, first, umbrella; second, pocketbook—First, J. Lally; second, Thomas Brown.

J. W. DUNCAN.

Newport, R. I.

News Notes.

S. G. Harris, Tarrytown, N. Y., offers $15 in three premiums for a collection of hybrid tea roses, to be competed for at the Newport Horticultural Society's exhibition in August. Mr. Harris was a visitor here recently, and in course of conversation expressed his satisfaction with the state of trade. He predicts a great future for hybrid teas.

Last week Commodore and Mrs. Gerry gave the first of a series of dinner parties. On that occasion the table was, as usual, decorated elaborately, not with cut flowers but with ornamental foliage plants. Usually when plants in any great numbers are utilized for table decoration the effect is somewhat heavy if we may use that term, but in this case the plants selected for the purpose and their arrangement were such that an exceedingly graceful and beautiful effect was produced, helped perhaps by the ingenious introduction of a subdued illumination by electricity. Among the plants used in this decoration were finely colored crotons and dracaenas and choice caladiums.

John H. Cox is at present in Newport taking orders for plants, seeds and bulbs.

Newport gardeners read with interest the news of Scott Brothers launching in the nursery business. Both members of the new firm are well known here especially James T. Scott, who while with the F. R. Pierson Company was a frequent visitor. We wish them success. D. M.

Indianapolis.

The Geranium Discussion.

Several growers in this vicinity are losing sleep waiting for copies of The Florists' Exchange bearing information on the "Geranium Discussion." The writer has been requested to inform the florists in his notes that John Birnie must either prove that it is possible to grow eighty good geraniums from one plant, according to his own specifications, without any sidestepping or juggling of words, and also beg the pardon of "Another Green One" for saying he was a hopeless case, or profess his ignorance to the trade of our land by forever holding his peace on any subject pertaining to plant culture. Indiana boasts of a number of the best growers in this country, and their reputations as such will not, and cannot, be questioned by Birnie's clever arrangement of words.

Homer Wiegand is visiting Detroit.

John Hartje is preparing to sell his present establishment and to erect another range of houses on farm land west of the city.

John Grande is cutting large quantities of asters.

Visitors: A. Blomer, representing Randall & Co., Chicago. I. B.

BAY SHORE, N. Y.—The United Bay Shore Horticultural society was formed on Monday evening last by the union of the Suffolk County Horticultural Association and the Bay Shore Horticultural Society. Several meetings had previously been held with the object of getting together, and while many points were agreed upon, the final understanding was not reached until Monday. The new organization has every reason for succeeding and giving a monster exhibition on October 25, 26, and 27 next. The officers, chosen equally from the two former societies are as follows: President, Eugene P. Strong; vice-president, William Stuart; Secretary, William McCollum, treasurer, David McIntosh; corresponding secretary, M. J. Connellan; exhibition committee. John Tobin, chairman, George Jayne, Nathan Yesek, John Rogers, David McIntosh, Nicholas Reil and Alfred Rochane.

COLUMBIA CITY, Ind.—Albert J. Wagoner plans to remove his establishment from its present location on West Van Buren street to his twenty-five acre farm a quarter of a mile west of this city. His purpose is to erect a larger and thoroughly modern system of greenhouses upon a favorable site on this tract of land and to engage in the raising of flowers and plants on a larger scale than heretofore.

New Orleans.

News Notes.

The long drought was broken two weeks ago and rains have been of daily occurrence since.

The German Gardener's Club held its regular meeting last week. A paper on "Landscape Gardening" was read by President L. Muller. The membership consists of 25.

The outing of the Horticultural Society to Grand Isle was an enjoyable affair; unfortunately many members from one cause or another were prevented participating.

The principal feature of the annual meeting of the Horticultural Society was the election of officers. Otto Abele of the firm of Abele Brothers was elected president; C. L. Seeber, secretary of the Metairie Ridge Nursery Company, vice-president; John Eblen, reelected treasurer; C. R. Panter, reelected secretary. After adjournment the newly elected officers did the honors Dan Newsham was admitted to membership. P. A. Chopin, the retiring president, on behalf of himself and his wife thanked the members for their wedding gift. Chas. White, who was recently elected to life membership, sent a letter of appreciation. Owing to the hot weather there will be no meetings until October. A delegation of about 6 or 8 members will attend the S. A. F. O. H. convention at Dayton next month.

Otto Abele,
Pres.-elect New Orleans Horticultural Society.

Frank Faessel is trying a new wrinkle; he has done away with field planting, and has all his roses, chrysanthemums, asparagus, etc., planted on benches. They are certainly looking fine, and his experiment will be watched with interest. P. A.

Otto Abele.

Otto Abele, the newly elected president of the New Orleans Horticultural Society, was born in Gundelsheim, Germany, 33 years ago. Coming to this country when but a boy his love for nature induced him to enter the florists' business. After serving in several establishments he started in business on his own account, in landscape gardening and the growing of pot plants, and has been successful from the start. In 1894 he formed a partnership with his brother under the firm name of Abele Brothers.

He is a member of the German Gardeners' Club, the German Singing Society, and several other organizations. A.

MACON, GA.—The Georgia Horticultural Society will meet in this city on August 7 and 8. P. J. Berckmans, Augusta, Ga., is president.

MIDDLE VILLAGE, N. Y.—H. Pladeck sailed for Germany last week on the Kaiserin Auguste Victoria. B.

CANADIAN NEWS

TORONTO—After the best Spring business the plant trade has ever had in this city, with all good bedding stock cleared out, the growers are now nearly as busy as ever, for empty houses means plenty of work to fill them again quickly, as the margin of profit is still too small to allow much time for idleness. The cut flower trade also has been good, but is letting up now. The roses coming in are generally poor in quality and good carnations are about done. Some good asters are offered, and at present sell well. A considerable variety of hardy stock is also available, and much of it comes in handy. Some gladiolus is offered, also a few dahlias, but so far these do not find much favor.

There is likely to be a goodly number from this city in attendance at the C. H. A. convention at Guelph. It is only a few hours' ride from Toronto, and a good many of the boys will make the trip. We hear that there is likely to be quite a number of the trade from Western Ontario there.

The Toronto Horticultural Society had a very pleasant outing to Niagara Falls on July 6. The committee in charge of the arrangements carried out everything in good order, and Roderick Cameron, the genial gardener at Victoria park, did all that was possible to make everybody at home. It is always a treat for anyone interested in hardy plants and shrubs to meet Mr. Cameron; and on this occasion he was at his best.

THOS. MANTON.

LONDON, ONT.—Business is very slow at present, all that is doing being a little funeral work.

Fred Dicks is very busy replanting roses, carnations, and chrysanthemums. At Gammage & Sons carnations, chrysanthemums and roses are doing splendidly; this firm's stock of Begonia Gloire de Lorraine is something to be proud of, they having been successful in propagating from leaf cuttings during April and May. Stephens, Darch & Hunter and West are looking forward to a good Fall trade.

The London florists expect to hold their annual picnic very soon.

The weather still remains very warm, with not enough rain for outdoor stock.

On a recent visit to neighboring towns we found everything looking prosperous. H. L. Janzen, Berlin, Ont., is building a block of four new houses, of King construction; the houses are 300 feet long and 25 feet wide, with four benches to a house. In roses Mr. Janzen is growing Bride, Bridesmaid, Golden Gate, American Beauty and Richmond, all being in fine condition. Other stock in general is looking promising.

Mr. Iler, also of Berlin, reports a good Spring trade.

At Galt, Ont., Adam Dunn, A. J. Young, John Wells and P. A. Balling- all report trade good.

F. CHEESMAN.

CHANGES IN BUSINESS.

WEST CHESTER, PA.—Application has been made for the incorporation of the Morris Nursery Company by George Achelis, Peter A. Keene and Martha G. Lear. This extensive nursery has for years been known as the "Morris Nursery," having been started by the late Paschall Morris, but carried on by George Achelis for the past twenty-five or thirty years. It has very extensive property, many farms and lots hereabouts being leased and planted with trees, etc. The incorporation is for the purpose of extending the business.

OCONTO, WIS.—Sylvester's greenhouses are undergoing some of the usual Summer repairs new benches being put in. Mr. Sylvester is preparing for a still more extensive wholesale trade the coming Fall and Winter.

DAVENPORT, IA.—John Beimford has sold his greenhouses, but not the stock, to E. Friedericksen & Sons, who will move the houses to their plant in South Wilton, and greatly extend their business.

CHESTER, PA.—The store at 317 Market street has changed hands, the new owner being Elizabeth M. Bartow, the florist. Mrs Bartow is at present conducting her business at 315 Market street, and she will at once remove to her new headquarters.

Bargains in CHOICE PLANTS

English Ivy, from 4½ in. pots, $2.00 and $1.50 per doz. About 3 feet high and bushy.
Ivy, fan shaped, fine and bushy, $6.00 per doz., 75c. each.
Anthericum, variegated, per doz. $1.50; per 100, $12.00.
Boston Ferns, 5 in. pots, $3.00 per doz.; 6 in. pots, $9.00 per doz.; 7 in. pots, $12.00 per doz.
Kentia Belmoreana and Forsteriana, $3.00, $4.00, $5.00, $6.00 $9.00 per doz.; also by the 100. Also $1.00, $1.50, $2.00, $2.50, $3.00 each and by the 2 doz.
Phœnix Canariensis, large plants, 6½ to 7 feet high, 11 in. pots, $12.00 to $14.00 per pair.
Bird's Nest Fern, large plants, 6½ in. pots, $1.50 each, $18.00 per doz.
Araucaria Excelsa, 50c., 75c., $1.00, $1.50, $2.00, $2.50 each. Also by the 100.
Aspidistra, green, $1.00 per pot, 10 to 12 leaves.
Cut Flowers of Lily of the Valley, $4.00 and $5.00 per 100.
Boxwood Pyramids, in pots, $2.00 and $2.50 a pair, fine plants. Other sizes sold out.
Bay Trees, Pyramids.
55-60 in. high from top of tub, $14.00 per pair
65-70 in. high from top of tub, 15.00 per pair
72 in. high from top of tub, 18.00 per pair
84 in. high from top of tub, 20.00 per pair
Bay Trees, Standards. (with 4 feet stems.)
32 in. diameter of crown, $14.00 per pair
36 in. diameter of crown, 16.00 per pair
Leaf-Mold, $1.00 per bag.
Asparagus Plumosus 3½ in. pots, $1.25 per doz.; per 100, $9.00; 4 in. pots, $2.00 per doz.; 4½ in. pots, $3.00 per doz.
Kentia Forsteriana, combinations, from $3.00, $4.00, $5.00, $6.00, $10.00, $15.00 to $20.00 each.
Dracæna Fragrans, $4.00 $6.00, $9.00, $12.00 $15.00, $24.00 per doz.
Latania Borbonica, from 5 in. pots, $4.00 per doz.; 6 in. $6.00 per doz.
Scottii Fern, 6½ in. pots; $7.00 per doz. Specimens $2.50 each. From the bench for 5½ and 6 in. pots, $6.00 per doz.; $40.00 per 100.
Piersoni Fern, 5½ in. pots, $9.00 per doz.
N. Elegantissima, from 4½ in. pots, $4.00 per doz.; $30.00 per 100.
Cattleya Trianae, 40 plants, 400 good bulbs, $50.00 per original case.
Orchid Peat, $1.00 per bag.
Rubbers, from 7 in. pots, 3 ft. high, $9.00 per doz.
Boston Ferns, specimens $3.00 each. 1 pair extra large, 14 in. pots, $15.00 the pair.
Areca Lutescens, 5½ in. pots, 9.00 per doz., 3 in a pot.
Pandanus Veitchii, 5 in. pots, $6.00 per doz.; 6 in. pots, $9.00 per doz.; 6½ in., $12.00 per doz.; 7 in., $18 per doz.
Dracæna Terminalis, 4 in. pots, $3.00 per doz.; 5 in. pots, $5.00 per doz.; 6 in., $6.00 per doz.
Gardenia Veitchii, fine large Plants, 5½ in. pots, well budded, $9.00 per doz.
Cycas Revoluta, we have them in 5½, 6, 7 and 8 in. pots, very fine, 50c., 75c., $1.00, $1.50, $2.00 and $3.00 each.
Cibotium Scheidii, 6, 6½ and 7 in. pots, $1.50, $2.00 and $2.50 each.

Cash with order or satisfactory New York references required.

I wish to inform my many friends and customers that the report of my having suffered a loss by hail was erroneous.

I have had no loss, either from hail or any other cause. My stock is all in superb condition, and I can fill your orders on short notice.

ANTON SCHULTHEIS
19th St. & 4th Avenue, COLLEGE POINT, L. I., N. Y.

Mention The Florists' Exchange when writing.

GRAFTED ROSES

Fine Stock from 3-in. pots.

Richmond, $2.50 per doz., $15.00 per 100, $135.00 per 1000.
Killarney, $2.50 per doz., $18.00 per 100, $150.00 per 1000.
Etoile De France, $3.00 per doz., $18.00 per 100.
Kaiserin, Carnot, Uncle John, Chatenay, $2.00 per doz., $15.00 per 100.
Bride, Bridesmaid, Golden Gate, Wootton, $2.00 per doz., $12.00 per 100.

ROSES OWN ROOTS

Fine Stock from 3-in. pots.

Richmond, $12.00 per 100; $100.00 per 1000.
Etoile De France, $12.00 per 100.
Sunrise, Perle, Sunset, Chatenay, $8.00 per 100.
Bride, Bridesmaid, Golden Gate, $7.00 per 100.

CANNAS

Best named varieties from 3½ in. pots, $5.00 and $6.00 per 100.

CHRYSANTHEMUMS

H. A. Allen, Jennie Nonin. From 2¼ in. pots $1.50 per doz, $8.00 per 100.
Mrs. A. T. Miller, Dora Stevens, Lady Cranston, Mrs. W. Higgle, Mrs. T. W. Pockett From 3½ in. pots $4.00 per doz., $6.00 per 100.
Geo. Kalb, Mrs. McArthur, Maud Dean, Mrs. Coombe, Nagoya, Robt. Halliday, A. J. Balfour, Nellie Pockett. Price from 2½ in. pots, $3.50 per 100, $30.00 per 1000.
Autumn Glory, Ada Spaulding, Dorothy Devens, Glory Pacific Harry May, Ivory, J. E. Lager, J. H. Troy, Mrs. S. T. Murdoch, Mrs. Humphrey, Niveus, Thomas H. Brown, Xeno. Price from 2½ in. pots, $3.00 per 100, $25.00 per 1000.
800 hardy pompons, 12 fine varieties, pink, yellow, white and bronze, $2.50 per 100.

VIOLETS—Fine Stock

Marie Louise from 3 in. pots $4.00 per 100, 2 1-4 in. pots, $3.00 per 100; $25.00 per 1000.

Miscellaneous Plants—For varieties and prices see page 20, July 7, issue.
Asparagus Plumosus Nanus from 3 inch pots $8.00 per 100; Sprengerii from 3 inch pots, $6.00 per 100.

Send for Catalogue.

Wood Bros., Fishkill, N. Y.

Mention The Florists' Exchange when writing.

BARGAINS
Smilax and Asparagus

I need room and rather than handle the following stock a second time I offer it at these low prices, please send order in **now**.

ASPARAGUS SPRENGERII fine two inch pot stock at $1.50 per 100; $12.50 per 1000.
ASPARAGUS PLUMOSUS fine plants from two inch pots at $2.50 per 100; $20.00 per 1000.
ASPARAGUS ROBUSTUS extra strong fine plants, this variety is a great improvement over Plumosus and every grower should try at least a hundred. $3.50 per 100 $30.00 per 1000.
SMILAX as good as it can be grown, carefully cut back and with air space around each pot. $1.50 per 100 $12.50 per 1000.
GERANIUMS send for my list of rooted cuttings. I have almost 200,000 stock plants to work from and want your orders for fall delivery.

ALBERT M. HERR,
Lancaster, Pa.

Mention The Florists' Exchange when writing.

CYCLAMEN
SPLENDENS GIGANTEUM HYBRIDS

This strain has no equal or better. Perfect flowers of Giant type in five true colors well grown plants from 2½ in. pots $5.00 per 100, $45.00 per 1000; from 3 in. pots $7.00 per 100; $65.00 per 1000.

Asparagus. Plumosus Nanus. From flats fine plants $1.50 per 100, $12.50 per 1000

SATISFACTION GUARANTEED.

PAUL MADER, EAST STROUDSBURG, PA.

Mention The Florists' Exchange when writing.

JERUSALEM CHERRIES

Strong stock from 2 in. pots, $2.00 per 100.
CRYPTOMERIA JAPONICA, 2 in. pots, ready for 4 inch, $3.00 to $4.00 per 100.
Write us for Geraniums, Cannas, Cupheas, Selaginellas, etc., all at reduced prices.

E. I. RAWLINGS, Quakertown, Pa.

Mention The Florists' Exchange when writing.

LOOK! See Us Grow.

A GOOD INVESTMENT; BETTER THAN BONDS.

Have you any loose change? If so, make 100 per cent. on your money. Write an order to Godfrey Aschmann for his Araucaria excelsa, glauca or compacta. Prices will soon advance. This kind of bond never fails.

ARAUCARIA EXCELSA a specialty. 6,000 are in now, imported from Ghent, Belgium this Spring, 1906. Now planted in 5½ and 6 in. pots, well established, and ready for shipment to all parts of America. All these are grown for us by an Araucaria Specialist in Ghent, Belgium. **NO SEEDLINGS**, but Araucarias raised from top cuttings only are offered. This is now our 11th Anniversary, and our importations have grown from 250 in the first year to the remarkable number of **6,000 IN THE ELEVENTH YEAR.** My reputation as Araucaria Importer gains footway in every greenhouse and florist store in America. Our Araucarias need no *coaxing*, genuine facts tell in quality and cheapness.

Please Note Our Lowest Prices

12 to 14 in. 5½ in. pots, 3 to 4 tiers, 2-yr. old, 50c. 14 to 16 in., 5½ in. pots, 3 to 4 tiers, 2-yr. old, 60c. 16 to 18 in. 5½ to 6 in. pots, 4 to 5 tiers, 3-yr. old, 75c. 18 to 20 in., 6 in. pots, 5 to 6 tiers, 4-yr. old, $1.00. 20 to 24 in. 6 in. to 7 in. pots, 5 to 6 tiers, 4-yr. old, $1.25. 30-40 to 50 in. 7 in. pots, specimen plants from $2.50 to $3.00 each.

ARAUCARIA COMPACTA ROBUSTA — have several thousand of them; can supply all wants. These plants were never so fine in shape and condition as this year. The set of the greenhouse, as broad as long, 12 to 20 in., in height, 3 to 4 perfect tiers; 20 to 30 inches across, 3-4-5 year old, 6 to 7 in. pots, $1.25, $1.50, $1.75, $2.00, $2.50 to $3.00 each.
ARAUCARIA EXCELSA GLAUCA—This variety on account of its beautiful Green-Blueish tiers, dwarf habit, fine compact shape, gives it a striking appearance, and anybody seeing them, must undoubtedly fall in love with them at sight. Plants, 6-7 inch pots, 3-4-5 perfect tiers, 3-4 year old, 15 to 25 inch high, from 15 to 30 in. across, $1.25, $1.50, $1.75, $2.00 to $2.50 each.
SOLANUM or JERUSALEM CHERRY, $5.00 per 100.
KENTIA BELMOREANA, 5½ to 6 in. pots, bushy, fine plants, from 75 cts. to $1.00 to $1.25 each.
KENTIA FORSTERIANA, 7 in. pots, made-up plants, 1 large in center, 3 smaller sizes, 22 to 25 in. high around, gives them a good appearance, $2.00 each. 6 in. pots, single plants, 35 to 40 in. high, 5 to 6 good leaves, 4 year old, $1.25 to $1.50 each; 6 in. pots, 30 to 35 in. high, 4 year old, 5 good leaves, $1.00; 5½ in. pots, 3 year old, 25 to 30 in. high, 5 good leaves, 75c., made-up plants, 3 and 4 in. pots, 18 to 20 in. high, 25 cts. to 30 cts. each.
ARECA LUTESCENS, made-up, 25 cts.
COCOS WEDDELIANA, 15 cts.
CYCAS REVOLUTA (Sago Palm), 6 in.-7 in. pots, with from 6 to 20 leaves per plant, 10 cts. per leaf.
NEPHROLEPIS BARROWSII, 6 in. pots, strong, ready for 7-8 in., 75c. 4 in. pots, 25c.
NEPHROLEPIS SCOTTII, 6 in. pots, 50c.; 4 in. pots, 20c.
BOSTON FERNS, 4 in., 20c.
FERNS for dishes, a fine assortment, 2¼ in., $5.00 per 100

CASH WITH ORDER

When ordering, say whether the plants should be shipped in the pots or not

GODFREY ASCHMANN
Importer and Wholesale Grower of Pot Plants
1012 Ontario Street, - - PHILADELPHIA, PA.

Mention The Florists' Exchange when writing.

Begonia "Gloire de Lorraine" and "Turnford Hall"

NOW READY FOR DELIVERY. Propagated strictly from **single leaf**: this method gives much better results than from cuttings, $15.00 per 100, $140.00 per 1000, 4 inch pots, $40.00 per 100. **ADIANTUM FARLEYENSE**, fine specimens $18.00 to $24.00 per doz, 1¾ inch pots, $8.00 per 100; 2½ inch pots, $15.00 per 100. **PANDANUS VEITCHII**, 50c., $1.00, $1.50 and $2.50 each. Good value guaranteed. Cash with order from unknown correspondents.

J. A. PETERSON, McHenry Ave., Westwood, CINCINNATI, OHIO

Mention The Florists' Exchange when writing.

SMILAX

	per 1000	per 100
2¼ in. pots	$9.00	$1.00
Asp. Plumosus, 2¼ in. pots, Aug. 1st		2.00
Cineraria, August 1st		2.00
Pansy Seed, large flowering, per oz. $4.00		

PRIMROSES

	per 100
Chinese, 2¼ in. pots, July 23rd	$2.00
Obconica, Roses and Alba	2.00
Forbesi, fine for cut flowers	2.00
P. W. Narcissus, 13 ctm	1.25

CASH PLEASE

JOS. H. CUNNINGHAM, Delaware, O.

Mention The Florists' Exchange when writing.

CHINESE PRIMROSES

Finest mixed, strong, 2 in., 2c. Grand. flm. Alba, Rosea, Lilac.
Primula Obconica, Carmine, Hybrid, 2 in., 2c.
" " Double and new Red 2 in., 3c.
Asparagus Sprengerii, and Plumosus 2 in., 2c.
Christmas Peppers, Jerusalem Cherries, 2 in. and 2¼ in. pots, $2.00 per 100.
Ferns from Bench: Boston, Piersoni 4 in. 10c; 5 in., 12½c. Tarrytown, 3 in., 10c; 4 in., 15c; 5 in., 25c. Scottii, 3 in., 6c; 4 in., 12½c; 5 in., 15c.
Geraniums, 2¼ in. Viaud, Bernandinn and 7 other sorts, $1.50 per 100.

Cash or C. O. D.

BYER BROS. Chambersburg, Pa.

Mention The Florists' Exchange when writing.

CANNAS

Allemania, Gray, Henderson, M. Washington, Metallica, from 3 in. pots, fine stock, $4.00 per 100

Shellroad Greenhouses, GRANGE P. O. BALTIMORE, MD.

Mention The Florists' Exchange when writing.

POINSETTIAS

2¼ in. pots, $5.00 per 100; $40.00 per 1000. Cash with order.

S. N. PENTECOST,
1790-1810 East 101 St., CLEVELAND, O.

Mention The Florists' Exchange when writing.

50,000 Pansy Seedlings

Finest strain at $4.00 per 1000. Delivery beginning September 1st. Orders booked in rotation. Strictly cash with order.

J. CONDON, Horticulturist,
734 5th Ave., Brooklyn, N. Y.

Mention The Florists' Exchange when writing.

Stevia Serrata

True, winter blooming, strong, bushy, ready to shift, 3½ in. pots, $5.00 per 100; $45.00 per 1000.
ASPARAGUS SPRENGERII, 2 inch, very strong, $2.50 per 100; $20.00 per 1000.

DEAN FERRIS, Peekskill, N.Y.

Mention The Florists' Exchange when writing.

Wholesale Prices of Cut Flowers, New York, July 26, 1906
Prices quoted are by the hundred unless otherwise noted.

Roses—A. Beauty, fancy—special	10.00 to 20.00		Carnations—Inf'r grades, all colors		.50 to 1.00
" extra	6.00 to 10.00		Standard Varieties	White	1.00 to 2.00
" No. 1	4.00 to 5.00			Pink	1.00 to 2.00
" No. 2	3.00 to 4.00			Red	1.00 to 2.00
" No. 3	1.00 to 1.50			Yel. & Var.	1.00 to 2.00
Bride, Maid, fancy—spc'l	3.00 to 4.00		*Fancy— (*The highest grades of standard var.)	White	2.00 to 2.50
" extra	2.00 to 3.00			Pink	2.00 to 2.50
" No. 1	1.00 to 2.00			Red	2.00 to 2.50
" No. 2	.50 to 1.00			Yel. & Var.	...... to ......
Golden Gate	1.00 to 5.00		Novelties		...... to
Liberty	...... to		Lilies		5.00 to 8.00
Mme. Abel Chatenay	1.00 to 6.00		Lily of the Valley		1.00 to 2.00
Adiantum	.50 to .75		Mignonette		...... to ......
Crowbanum	.50 to 1.00		......		...... to ......
Asparagus	25.00 to 50.00		......		...... to ......
" Plumosus, bunches	10.00 to 15.00		......		...... to ......
" Sprengerii, bunches	10.00 to 15.00		Pansies, per dozen bunches		.50 to .75
Cattleyas	25.00 to 50.00		Smilax		8.00 to 10.00
Daisies	.50 to 1.00		Sweet Peas, per bunch		.01 to .03
Gladiolus	.50 to 1.00				
......	...... to				

Wholesale Prices of Cut Flowers—Per 100

Boston July 23, 1906	Buffalo July 25, 1906	Detroit July 22, 1906	Cincinnati July 21, 1906	Baltimore July 16, 1906	NAMES AND VARIETIES	Milwaukee July 14, 1906	Phil'delphia July 24, 1906	Pittsburg July 25, 1906	St. Louis July 23, 1906
10.00 to 20.00	20.00 to 25.00	10.00 to 35.00	20.00 to 30.00	to	Roses: A. BEAUTY, fancy—special	to 25.00	15.00 to 20.00	20.00 to 25.00	15.00 to 20.00
6.00 to 10.00	12.00 to 20.00	to	10.00 to 15.00	12.50 to 15.00	" extra	15.00 to 20.00	10.00 to 15.00	15.00 to 18.00	10.00 to 12.50
4.00 to 6.00	6.00 to 12.00	to	6.00 to 8.00	5.00 to 8.00	" No. 1	10.00 to 15.00	5.00 to 7.00	8.00 to 10.00	6.00 to 8.00
2.00 to 4.00	3.00 to 6.00	to	8.00 to 10.00	to	" Culls and ordinary	4.00 to 8.00	1.00 to 4.00	2.00 to 5.00	3.00 to 5.00
to	5.00 to 6.00	3.00 to 6.00	to 6.00	to	BRIDE, 'MAID, fancy-special	to 6.00	to	to	4.00 to 5.00
2.00 to 4.00	4.00 to 5.00	to	to 5.00	to 4.00	" extra	to 4.00	6.00 to 8.00	to 6.00	2.00 to 3.00
1.00 to 2.00	3.00 to 4.00	to	to 4.00	to 3.00	" No. 1	to 3.00	4.00 to 5.00	to 3.00	to
to	2.00 to 3.00	to	to 3.00	to 2.00	" No. 2	to 2.00	2.00 to 3.00	to 2.00	to
to	to	4.00 to 8.00	to 6.00	2.00 to 4.00	GOLDEN GATE	4.00 to 6.00	4.00 to 8.00	to	2.00 to 4.00
2.00 to 8.00	8.00 to 7.00	to	2.00 to 4.00	4.00 to 8.00	K. A. VICTORIA	4.00 to 8.00	4.00 to 6.00	4.00 to 12.00	2.00 to 6.00
to	3.00 to 7.00	to	to	to	LIBERTY	4.00 to 6.00	3.00 to 6.00	4.00 to 8.00	to
to	8.00 to 6.00	4.00 to 10.00	to	to	METEOR	to	to	to	to
to	3.00 to 5.00	4.00 to 10.00	to	2.00 to 4.00	PERLE	2.00 to 4.00	to	to	2.00 to 4.00
to	to	to 50.00	to	to	ORCHIDS—Cattleyas	to	to 50.00	to	to
to	.75 to 1.00	to	to .50	.50 to .75	Carnations: Inferior grades, all colors	to	.75 to 1.00	.50 to .75	.75 to 1.00
to	1.25 to 1.50	to 1.00	to 1.00	1.00 to 1.50	Standard Varieties: White	to	.75 to 1.00	to 1.00	.75 to 1.00
to	1.00 to 1.50	to	to 1.00	1.00 to 1.50	Standard Varieties: Pink	to 1.00	.75 to 1.00	to 1.00	.75 to 1.00
to	1.00 to 1.50	to	to 1.00	1.00 to 1.50	Standard Varieties: Red	to	.75 to 1.00	to 1.00	.75 to 1.00
to	1.00 to 1.50	to 3.00	to	1.00 to 1.50	Standard Varieties: Yellow and var.	to	.75 to 1.00	to	.75 to 1.00
.50 to 1.50	1.50 to 2.00	to	to	to 3.00	Fancy Varieties: White	to	2.00 to 2.50	to 2.00	1.50 to 2.00
.50 to 1.50	1.50 to 2.00	to	to	to 3.00	Fancy Varieties: Pink	to	2.00 to 2.50	to 2.00	1.50 to 2.00
.50 to 1.50	1.50 to 2.00	to	to	to 3.00	Fancy Varieties: Red	to 1.50	2.00 to 2.50	to 2.00	1.50 to 2.00
.50 to 1.50	1.50 to 2.00	to 1.50	to	to 3.00	Fancy Varieties: Yellow and var	to	2.00 to 2.50	to	1.50 to 2.00
to	to	to	to	to	Novelties	to	to	to	to
.50 to .75	.50 to 1.00	to 2.00	to 1.00	to 1.00	ADIANTUM	to 1.00	to 1.00	1.25 to 1.50	to 1.00
to 50.00	to	25.00 to 60.00	to 50.00	25.00 to 50.00	ASPARAGUS, Plum. and Ten.	20.00 to 30.00	25.00 to 35.00	25.00 to 50.00	25.00 to 50.00
to	to	20.00 to 30.00	to 35.00	25.00 to 50.00	" Sprengeri, bunches	20.00 to 30.00	25.00 to 35.00	20.00 to 30.00	25.00 to 50.00
to	to	to	2.00 to 4.00	to	ASTERS	to	to	to	to
to	8.00 to 10.00	to 10.00	to 1.00	6.00 to 8.00	CALLAS	to	to	to	to
to	to	.75 to 1.50	to	to	DAISIES	to .40	3.00 to 4.00	.50 to 1.00	.25 to .50
to	2.00 to 4.00	8.00 to 10.00	to	2.00 to 4.00	GLADIOLUS	to 8.00	8.00 to 12.00	5.00 to 6.00	to 2.00
to	to	to	2.00 to 4.00	10.00 to 12.50	LILIES, Harrisii	to	to	to	to
2.00 to 4.00	12.00 to 15.00	to	to 15.00	10.00 to 12.50	" Longiflorum	to 12.50	2.00 to 4.00	15.00 to 18.00	to
to	3.00 to 4.00	3.00 to 4.00	to	1.00 to 2.00	LILY OF THE VALLEY	to 3.00	1.00 to 2.00	2.00 to 4.00	to
to	to	to	to 4.00	2.00 to 2.50	MIGNONETTE, ordinary	to	to	to	to
to	to	to	to	to	" fancy	to 1.00	to	to	to
to 12.50	to	4.00 to 8.00	to	to	PEONIES	to	15.00 to 20.00	to	to 12.50
to	to 15.00	12.50 to 15.00	to	12.50 to 20.00	SMILAX	to 15.00	to	12.50 to 15.00	to
to	to	to	to 15.00	to	VIOLETS, ordinary	to	to	to	to
to	to	to	to	to	" fancy	to	to	to	to
to	to	to	to	to	NARCISSUS	to	to	to	to
.15 to .25	.15 to .25	.50 to .75	.25 to .35	.20 to .35	SWEET PEAS	.25 to .50	to .50	.15 to .25	.10 to .15

St. Louis.

News Items.

Last week we had with us S. B. Beal, of L. L. May & Co., St Paul, Minn. selling seeds for early Spring delivery. George M. Kellogg, Pleasant Hill, Mo., also called and reported things at his place in fine shape.

Our four wholesale houses will close half day Thursday of this week to enable their employees and families to attend the picnic of the Florists' Club.

The Park Department has a good fat bank account, as at the recent bond election $670,000 was given them for much needed improvements. Commissioner Aul and Superintendent Ostertag can now do justice to their work.

Growers of ginseng in this state are having a good sale for their product, according to Chief Clerk of the State Labor Bureau, J. H. Nolen, who reports that the sale of ginseng amounted to $105,648, representing 17,608 pounds, the bulk of which was sent to China.

Carew Sanders, a cousin of Edgar Sanders, of Chicago, who is 78 years old, has been very sick the past week, though at this writing is much improved. Mr. Sanders is one of the oldest members of the local Florists' Club.

After a stay of six months looking after his banana plantation interests in Panama, Frank Ellis is expected home next week. Another trip will be necessary before the end of this year.

The younger element in the Florists' Club are out hustling and say by the end of one year the membership will be 125; six new applications are in their hands for our next meeting. A number of entertainments will be given this coming season.

The bowling club, which started its Monday night matches, is developing a number of good bowlers to take the places of the older ones who have dropped out. Among the new ones are Eddie Gerlach, George Schriefer, Julius Koenig, Otto Bruenig, W. C. Smith, C. Geiger, Henry Lohrenz, and Robert Meinhardt; these, with C. A. Kuehn and J. J. Beneke make two teams, and bowl Monday nights at the Palace Alleys. All florists are invited to attend and have a good time. If enough can be secured a third team will be made up.

ST. PATRICK.

ELMIRA, N. Y.—Early on the morning of July 24, four masked men overpowered James Barton, night watchman at the United States Cut Flower Company's plant north of this city, and blew open the safe. They secured $12 from the safe and took $6 and a revolver from the night watchman.

Wholesale Prices of Cut Flowers, Chicago, July 24, 1906.

Prices quoted are by the hundred unless otherwise noted.

ROSES — American Beauty			CARNATIONS		
36-inch stems.......per doz.	...... to	4.00	Inferior grades all colors	.25 to	.50
30-inch stems "	...... to	3.00	STANDARD VARIETIES White	.75 to	1.00
24-inch stems "	...... to	2.50	Pink	.75 to	1.00
20-inch stems "	...... to	2.00	Red	.75 to	1.00
18-inch stems "	...... to	1.50	Yellow & var.	.75 to	1.00
12-inch stems "	...... to	1.00	*FANCY (The highest grades of Stan'd var) White	1.50 to	2.00
8-inch stems and shorts "	.50 to	.75	Pink	1.50 to	2.00
Bride Maid, fancy special	5.00 to	6.00	Red	1.50 to	2.00
" extra	4.00 to	5.00	Yellow & var	1.50 to	2.00
" No. 1	2.00 to	3.00	NOVELTIES	...... to	......
" No. 2	.50 to	1.00	ADIANTUM	.50 to	1.00
Golden Gate	2.00 to	6.00	ASPARAGUS, Plum. & Ten.	.35 to	.50
Carnot	2.00 to	6.00	" Sprengeri, bunches	.35 to	.50
Uncle John	2.00 to	8.00	GLADIOLUS	2.00 to	6.00
Liberty	2.00 to	8.00	LILIES, Longiflorum	8.00 to	12.00
Richmond	2.00 to	6.00	Harrisii	8.00 to	12.00
Kaiserins	2.00 to	6.00	Auratum	8.00 to	10.00
Killarney	3.00 to	8.00	Nymphaea	...... to	1.00
Perle	2.00 to	6.00	MIGNONETTE, ordinary	1.00 to	2.00
Chatenay	2.00 to	6.00	......	...... to	......
Orchids—Cattleyas	...... to	50.00	......	...... to	......
SMILAX	8.00 to	12.00			
LILY OF THE VALLEY	2.00 to	4.00	HARDY FERNS per 1000	1.00 to	1.50
SWEET PEAS	.25 to	.50	GALAX "	1.00 to	1.25

Chicago.

News Notes.

At E. H. Hunt's painting and renovating are in order during the good old Summer days.

E. G. Hill and F. H. Howard of Howard & Smith, Los Angeles, Cal., were recent visitors at the Bassett & Washburn establishment, Hinsdale, and were much interested in the original system pursued there in the cultivation of Summer roses which has proved such a noted success. A range of 140,000 square feet of glass is devoted entirely to these products, and during the Winter a heavy layer of corn stalks is placed on the roofs so that it is possible to maintain that great desideratum in the cultivation of this class—an equable temperature of 28 degrees throughout the Winter months, and with this roof protection not even during the hot days of last January did the heat penetrate to disturb the even conditions within the houses. By this means the freezing and thawing so detrimental to later results are entirely obviated.

Peter Reinberg is cutting an extra fine line of American Beauty roses from his young stock, and reports that this crop is in superior condition and considerably in advance of previous years.

L. Coatsworth of the Benthey-Coatsworth Company will participate in the festivities connected with the reunion of the Coatsworth family at Kingsville, Ont., which will be inaugurated on August 9. Later he will visit Toronto and take a hand in the grand golf tournament, returning in time to share in the convention proceedings at Dayton.

Joe Beavet of Lubliner & Trinz left last week for his annual outing which includes a week at Toledo, O., and another week at Put-in-Bay.

Richard F. Gloede of Evanston was in town last week exploiting the excellent qualities of his three new geraniums Mrs. Richard F. Gloede, Illinois, and Kenilworth, from all of which there are great expectations.

F. Copeman, representing D. M. Ferry & Co., of Detroit, was in this city last week on his yearly tour of inspection.

Fred. C. Fischer has sold out his retail establishment at 614 Dempster street, Evanston, to his sons John and Sebastian, who will continue the business under the firm name of Fischer Brothers, the father continuing as a grower at the old stand.

Two or three of the younger generation of florists are killing time this month as jurors, among them being Sebastian Fischer and Mr. Swanson.

Mr. Forsburg of the J. C. Rennison concern of Sioux City, Iowa, was in town renewing old associations last week.

John L. Parker of Birmingham, Ala., came up from the South last week to see what was going on at headquarters.

Frank Hagan of the George Reinberg office staff is off on his vacation at Fox Lake.

Ed. Hauswirth and his family returned last Saturday from a pleasant outing of a few days spent in Milwaukee.

At the Eaton Flower Shop, although recently opened, appearances prove a very encouraging condition. Constant improvements are being installed. Charles H. Grant formerly with Small in New York has been added to the clerical force and a delivery automobile has been ordered which will soon be on duty.

Gus Alles, bookkeeper and floor manager of Wietor Brothers' office, started on his vacation Monday.

John Risch and H. D. Rogers returned Monday from a pleasant trip to Spring Lake, Mich., where they enjoyed themselves thoroughly and during the trip had the pleasure of spending a few hours in Grand Rapids, Muskegon, Grand Haven, South Haven and other interesting points.

At Anton Thèn's greenhouses on Winnemac avenue the miscellaneous crops which are grown to supply the two retail stores run by this concern, are in excellent condition, giving promise of maintaining the reputation for producing high grade stock which Mr. Then and his sons have established. Among the general assortment to be cultivated the coming season will be included 8,000 chrysanthemums, and in carnations, two houses each of Enchantress, Cardinal, and Lady Bountiful, and one house each of Harlowarden, Bride, Mrs. T. W. Lawson, White Lawson, and Winnemac, the latter being a yellow seedling produced at this place. Mr. Then now has about 55,000 feet of glass and is planning for a substantial increase next Spring. Here also are to be found 100,000 carnation plants in the field and the concern will enter the competition of supplying field grown stock this Fall.

A collision between the Chicago Rose Company's double horse delivery wagon and an electric car on Sunday morning came near having serious results. John Sterrett was thrown backward against the back of the seat and was only saved from vital injury by that iron constitution which has sustained him through many physical battles.

Word was received at Vaughan & Sperry's a few days ago from Mr. Vaughan who is rusticating at Spirit Lake that his record was an 8-pound bass, but the number that he has entangled makes up for the size, as he reports having taken 60 pounds of fish in one day.

Bernard Zalinger, floor manager in the Flower Growers' Market for Sinner Brothers, left the first of the week for an outing at South Haven, Mich.

The J. B. Deamud Company point with justifiable pride to a list of 85 shipments made on Saturday and Sunday last. Though the amounts are not to be compared with Winter returns the plenitude of orders is absolute proof that the concern is well recommended.

WILLIAM K. WOOD.

Cincinnati, O.

News Notes.

An abundance of rain has helped the carnations in the field, and this Fall will find the houses well stocked with fine plants.

E. G. Hill of Richmond, Ind., was here one day this week and he tells me they are just completing their new range of houses which are 500 feet long by 28 feet wide. The houses are all planted with carnations, holding eighty thousand plants. This range of houses will be well worth seeing.

The annual outing of the Cincinnati Florists' Society took place on Thursday of last week, over a hundred people being present. All seemed to enjoy themselves. Ben George and D. Rusconi treated the party to lobsters. Park Superintendent Rodgers is quite a baseball enthusiast and in playing the game overdid himself; it required about half an hour to bring him to, as he was "all in." The day was very hot and running was more than he could stand.

Harry M. Altick, vice-president S. A. F. O. H., was present. I am very sorry the report was heralded broadcast that the Dayton convention souvenir was a private enterprise, for such is not the case, as Mr. Altick has already explained. I hope those advertisers who were induced to withdraw their advertisements will reinstate them.

C. E. Critchell and wife are in New York seeing the sights.

C. J. Ohmer, nephew of the writer, will leave on his vacation July 28 going from Cincinnati to Old Point Comfort, thence by steamer to Boston and back to New York; he will also visit the coast resorts—Long Branch, Asbury Park, and Atlantic City; likewise Philadelphia, etc.

The trustees of the Jabez Elliott Flower Market have nicely painted the stands in the market.

At present writing, the less said about business the better. Fortunately, the National League is playing a series of games here and you can find the florists well represented at League Park almost any afternoon.

Don't forget the florists' train for Dayton leaves the C. H. & D. station on August 21 at 8.15 a. m. You are expected.

E. G. GILLETT.

Columbus, O.

News Items.

Mr. Siebert of the Fifth Avenue Floral Company, is taking a well earned vacation on the upper lakes. Perhaps when he returns he may be induced to tell The Florists' Exchange how he worked it when he raised those fine geraniums.

Mr. Metzmaier, the South Fourth street florist, is still traveling around on crutches, the result of a severe attack of rheumatism.

John R. Hellenthal points with pride to his fine new carnation house, dimensions, 30 x 140 feet, now about ready for planting. The stock in the field shows up very fine, although the effects of the excessively wet weather are feared.

C. D. B.

HEATING.

Growers' Problems Solved by U. G. Scollay.

Noticing quite a good many answers in The Florists' Exchange in regard to steam and hot water heating, we beg to consult you with respect to the enclosed sketch. We are desirous to know the exact amount of piping required for the houses to be heated by steam, and the size of pipe you would suggest to be used. What size horse power boiler will it require?

Kentucky. C. G. N.

Your sketch while nicely laid out, shows only the elevations, and the alley way is placed so peculiarly that it rather puzzles me. I take it that it is in rear of shed and the 75x20 foot house is therefore the one that is detached. I also take it that this house is to the north of the shed. If this is correct, I would lay your job out as follows: basing calculations on temperatures, outside zero, inside 55 to 60 degrees Fahr. In 75x20 foot house place eight lines of 1¼-inch pipe under the benches, supplying same with 2-inch overhead steam main, returning from coils to boiler with 1½-inch. In 100x20 foot house place eight lines 1¼-inch pipe under benches, supplying same with 2½-inch overhead main, returning with 1½-inch from coils. In 27x100 foot house, place twelve lines 1¼-inch pipe under benches, with 3-inch overhead steam supply, and 2-inch return from coils. Your boiler should have a capacity of not less than 20 h. p. and be tapped for 4-inch steam supply, and 2½-inch return. The area of the smoke outlet should be not less than 288 square inches, unless you have an unusually good draft in stack or chimney, in which case you can get along with less area. Your boiler will, of course, be placed in the pit, which you seem to have located at the southwest corner of the shed. Start from the boiler with 4-inch steam main branches to 100x20 foot house with 2½ inch, and to 100x27 foot house with 3-inch. These mains in houses to be overhead, dropping to far end and connecting to coils, which latter will all grade from far end toward boilers. For the 75x20 foot house run 2-inch from the boiler. This may be run overhead outdoors across the alley keeping it as high as possible, and covering it; or it may run underground, provided your boiler is at sufficient depth for the purpose. If you run underground, we presume, of course, you would probably protect them, both steam and return pipes. This can be done by placing them in a trench or incasing them each in larger size piping. After entering the house you will, of course, run your main and coils in the same manner as described for the other houses. We think the above fully answers your questions.

U. G. SCOLLAY.

I send you a plan of my greenhouses and ask your advice in regard to piping the same to keep the desired temperature. I have been using the 4-inch cast iron pipe, but have lately had trouble with water in my boiler pit, and can't very well use the pipe as it is now, for the reason that I cannot get rise enough for the flows at the boiler. Therefore I have concluded to put in smaller pipe with overhead flow. House No 1 I use to grow geraniums and other bedding plants that require about the same temperature; house No. 2 for smilax, begonias and plants of that order. No. 3 for palms and ferns; Nos. 4, 5 and 6 for carnations. I have in use a boiler, which has a rating to heat 18,500 feet of glass, so that there is plenty of boiler capacity. At present I am using a small cast iron boiler with the other one; it (the small boiler) is under the office and partly heats the carnation houses. Houses Nos. 1 and 2 are two feet lower than the other four houses. I hope I have made the plan accurate enough, that you can understand it all right.

V. A. S.

Set the boiler as low as possible. Run from the boiler into house number 1 with 6-inch supply main; place the tee 6x5x2½ inches, the latter opening to supply overhead main for house number 1. Continue 5-inch into house number 2, and turn south with elbow and continue 5-inch to a point opposite the center of house number 3; place tee 5x5x2½ inches using the 2½-inch opening for palm house and office. Continue 5-inch south to a point opposite center of house number 4, placing there a 5x4½x3½-inch tee the 3½-inch opening to supply house number 4. Continue 4½ inch to a point opposite the ridge of house number 5, and place a tee 4½x3½x3, the latter to be used to supply house number 5. Continue 3½-inch to a point opposite the center of house number 6, and place tee 3½x3x2½ inches, allowing the 2½-inch to supply house number 6. Continue the 3-inch to the far end of house number 1 to supply the coils in that house. The return mains and branch mains in all cases to be run with area corresponding to the flow mains.

In house number 1 under the east bench place four lines of 2-inch pipe, and under the west bench three lines, feeding each of these coils from the overhead main with 2-inch connections. In house number 2 under the east bench place six lines, and under the west bench three lines; also place on each side of the center solid bed one line. (It is understood that in all cases we will refer to lines of 2-inch pipe). Feed the six pipe coil with 2½-nch connections; the three pipe coil with 2-inch, and the line on the solid bed with 1½ or 2-inch as you find convenient.

In house number 6 place four lines under the south bench, three lines under the north bench, and connect each of these coils with 2-inch form the main. In house number 5 place five lines under the north bench and three under the south bench, and two under the center bench. Feed the five pipe coil with 2½-inch, the others each with 2-inch. In house number 4 place four lines under each side bench, and two under the center bench. Feed each coil with 2-inch. In house number 3 run two coils of seven pipes each from a point opposite the doorway leading to the office each way, thence along the sides easterly to the main return. I do not know the exact layout of your office, but would suggest that you place in it not less than 200 feet of 2-inch pipe.

Be sure and place full opening gate valves on all connections, between overhead mains and coils, such valves to be also of the same size as the connections specified. Let the highest point of the flow main be just above the boiler if possible and air vent it from that point. Let your main drop from this down to the far end of house number 2 at a grade of not less than one inch in ten feet. If in any case you have to jump up from the main supply line with your branch mains, be sure and air vent at the highest point of each "jump".

Previous articles in The Florists' Exchange have frequently given full particulars concerning the location and connection of expansion tanks.

If your houses are adequately piped at present with 4-inch cast iron pipe, you might overcome the difficulty in circulation you speak of, by using a special circulator to accelerate the flow of the water. This has been done very successfullly.

Concerning water in boiler pits I might say that I have frequently overcome this trouble by using an ejector. Any good plumber can tell you what the latter is, and how to apply it. If you have no such source of information convenient to you, write me again, and I will go into that phase of the matter.

According to the rating of your present boiler, I consider it will have about all it can do to take care of your present amount of glass.

U. G. SCOLLAY.

ROCHESTER, N. Y.—Fire did $25 damage in an upper room in the rear of the building occupied by the J. B. Keller Sons, florists in Clinton avenue north, at 12 o'clock July 10. The fire was discovered before it had had an opportunity to spread. A hole had been burned in the floor.

WOBURN, MASS.—J. W. Howard, florist, alleges that owing to the poor condition of Russell street in the western section of the city, his stock of cut roses were bruised in transportation, and he asks for relief in the sum of $500 from the board of public works.

SOUTH BEND, IND.—The South Bend Floral Company is making arrangements to greatly enlarge its present capacity and to add new lines to its business operations. These improvements were brought about through a partial reorganization of the company, several new stockholders investing in the concern, among them being Mrs. Irving Gingrich, Clem W. William and Arthur Studebaker. A new heating plant embracing the vacuum steam system is one of the improvements that will be made. Three new greenhouses 30 by 206 feet of iron and glass construction will be added. The King Construction Company, of North Tonawanda, N. Y., has the contract for the iron work and the Foley Manufacturing Company, of Chicago, the contract for the wood work. The improvements will be completed by September 1. The present buildings will be used for carnations. Rose, chrysanthemum and lettuce culture will receive attention in the three new greenhouses. Palms and ferns will also be carried.

Chrysanthemum smoking is the latest thing in England, Cigarettes made of chrysanthemum leaves and cascarilla bark have been found to give relief in cases of epilepsy, and one doctor recommended them as a substitute for tobacco.

San Francisco.

News Items.

The sign of Joe Goldstone, florist and decorator, was erected this week at 1814 Post street, near Fillmore. This young man has been in the trade for years and lost his Sixth street store in the big fire.

Last week I reported the opening of a flower store by Podesta & Baldocchi at Polk and Sutter streets, the new site selected by several other florists, as stated. These gentlemen prefer not to be grouped with the other corner stores, so, to be more particular I re-announce that Podesta & Baldocchi are on Sutter street, three doors from Polk, at 1206 Sutter.

I noticed some additional help this week in the flower store of Clies & Jacobsen. They reported an extra good run of trade all the week. Mr. Cleis has just returned from a fishing vacation in Santa Cruz mountains, and in a day or two Mr. Jacobsen will start on his annual outing, going this time for deer shooting in Sonoma county.

Before the current month expires the Merchants' Association of San Francisco will sit down at a notable dinner, and Florist F. A. Miller, president of the San Francisco Floral Society, whose place of business, including his Hayes Valley Nurseries was licked out of sight by the great fire, and Thomas Cox, head of the Cox Seed Company, who was also a total loser to the extent of thousands of dollars by the holocaust, will attend this dinner as representatives of the trade. This collation will be given in the banquet hall of the St. Francis Hotel and the tables are to be decorated with an abundance of flowers. On all sides of the hotel extend ruins. Gutted office buildings, ragged business blocks, Nob Hill wrecks, trampled Union square and the ruins of club structures are in full view. Millions of dollars went up in smoke in the neighborhood and the magnificent hostelry where the dinner will occur danced up and down with the quake but didn't mind it much, but to the following fire yielded everything but its steel and stone and cement.

Mrs. Mabel Osgood Wright, who lives in beautiful accord with her husband at Fairfield, Conn., was my former school-mate friend back in Ohio. She has written another book that was issued from the press this month by the Macmillan Company, New York. "The Garden, You and I" is its title. ALVIN.

DAVENPORT, IA.—The Tri-City Florists' Club met July 12 with Henry Pauli on Eastern avenue for a regular business session. But little business was transacted at the meeting. Mr. Pauli is building several new greenhouses, which proved of considerable interest to the guests. The usual papers and discussions were dispensed with on account of the heat. On August 9, the next regular meeting date, the florists will gather at Fejervary park.

Mention The Florists' Exchange when writing

WHOLESALE TRADE LIST

AMPELOPSIS VEITCHII, 4 inch pots, long runners $1.50 per doz; $10.00 per 100.
ASPARAGUS PLUMOSUS, 2½ in. pots, $3.00 per 100; 4 inch pots $1.50 per doz.; $10.00 per 100.
ASPARAGUS SPRENGERII, 4 in. pots, $1.00 per doz.
CINERARIA HYBRIDA, 3 in pots, $2.00 per 100.
CLEMATIS MONTANA, strong plants, 4 in. pots, $1.50 per doz.
CLEMATIS MONTANA GRANDIFLORA, 4 in. pots, $2.00 per doz.
CLEMATIS PANICULATA, 4 in. pots, $1.50 per doz., $10.00 per 100; 3 in. pots, 75c. per doz.; $5.00 per 100.
DAISY, QUEEN ALEXANDRIA, 3¼ in. pots, $3.00 per 100.
DRACÆNA INDIVISA, 5 in. pots, $2.00 per doz.
IVY, Hardy English, 4 in. pots, $1.50 per doz.; $10.00 per 100.
The real **BRIDAL MYRTLE**, elegant round shaped Plants 5 in. pots $3.00 per doz.
Pair of **LATANIA BORBONICA**, 18 in. tubs, 8 perfect leaves on each plant, $15.00 per pair. Smaller pair in 14 in. tubs, 6 leaves, $10.00 per pair.
Pair of **PHOENIX RECLINATA**, 12 in. pots, $8.00 per pair.

C. EISELE, 11th & Roy Streets, PHILADELPHIA, PA.

Mention The Florists' Exchange when writing.

PLANT CULTURE

PRICE, $1.00.

The best book for the plant grower.

A. T. DE LA MARE PTG. & PUB. CO. LTD.
2-8 Duane Street, New York.

The Greenhouse Boiler

"24° BELOW ZERO

and we had no difficulty in maintaining a temperature of 60°" is the testimony of a well known Pennsylvania florist who is using my **GREENHOUSE BOILER.**

Let me quote you prices.

JOHN A. PAYNE
Horticultural Architect and Builder
33 Clendenny Ave., Jersey City, N.J.

Sash opening apparatus and all kinds of greenhouse structural material.

Mention The Florists' Exchange when writing.

SUMMER IN WINTER
BY USING
Standard Greenhouse Boilers
One cent gets our Catalog
GIBLIN & CO., UTICA, N. Y.

Mention The Florists' Exchange when writing.

ARE YOU GOING TO BUILD

Assure yourself of **HONEST COMPETITION** figures by obtaining an estimate from me on **Iron Frame** or **Sash bar** greenhouses. My prices are the lowest for the best class of **work.**

FRANK VAN ASSCHE
(FORMERLY SUPT. FOR WEATHERED)
FACTORY: Fulton and Rose Ave., Jersey City, N. J.

"The test of years is the real test."

Scollay Boilers
ARE BEST

See our advertisement in next issue.
Catalogues sent on application.

JOHN A. SCOLLAY,
74-76 MYRTLE AVE.,
BOROUGH OF BROOKLYN,
NEW YORK CITY.
Telephones 1492-1493 Main.
U. G. SCOLLAY, Manager.

Mention The Florists' Exchange when writing.

A. HERRMANN
Manufacturer of Floral Metal Designs
IMPORTER AND DEALER IN FLORISTS' SUPPLIES
FACTORY: 709 FIRST AVENUE, BETWEEN 40th AND 41st STREETS, NEW YORK
OFFICE AND WAREROOMS: 404, 406, 408, 410, 412 East 34th St.
WRITE FOR NEW CATALOGUE

Mention The Florists' Exchange when writing.

THE MAN WHO LOOKS AHEAD IS THE MAN WHO GETS AHEAD

Take for instance the case of priming your greenhouse materials: We prime coat by dipping and allowing the oil and pigment to soak thoroughly into every stick—done that way because if the wood isn't **oil satisfied** in the prime, it takes it out of the next coat—when you take the oil out of a paint, you take the binder out—the life of the paint is gone. Give the wood in priming all the oil it wants and the following coats will retain all the oil they need.

¶ We believe the only way to stay right is to start right—so first let us prime your materials—then always paint them with our Ideal Greenhouse White Lead which makes the "Paint that Stays Put."

Lord & Burnham Co.
Greenhouse Designers and Manufacturers.
1133 Broadway, corner 26th St., NEW YORK.
BOSTON BRANCH, 819 Tremont Building.

Mention The Florists' Exchange when writing.

The Best Advertisement

is to furnish the best grade of material at reasonable prices.

That's what causes the constant growth of our business.

La. Cypress and Washington Red Cedar

GREENHOUSE MATERIAL.
GREENHOUSE HARDWARE AND POSTS.

A. DIETSCH CO., 615 Sheffield Ave., CHICAGO.

Mention The Florists' Exchange when writing

THE FLORISTS' SUPPLY HOUSE OF AMERICA

We have the largest assortment of Florists' Supplies in the country.
No order too large, none too small, to receive prompt attention.
SEND FOR CATALOGUE.

H. BAYERSDORFER & CO., 50, 52, 54, 56 North Fourth St., PHILADELPHIA, PA.

Mention The Florists' Exchange when writing.

THE FLORISTS' EXCHANGE

We are a straight shoot and aim to grow into a vigorous plant

A WEEKLY MEDIUM OF INTERCHANGE FOR FLORISTS, NURSERYMEN, SEEDSMEN AND THE TRADE IN GENERAL

Vol XXII. No. 5 — NEW YORK AND CHICAGO, AUGUST 4, 1906 — One Dollar Per Year

PLANT NOW

Lilium Harrisii for Early Forcing

WE OFFER some extra choice Lilium Harrisii which has been grown for us from the original, pure stock. This is the kind of stock that you want for the very earliest forcing, and it is the true, original Harrisii. The small sizes—5-7s and 6-7s—are particularly desirable for this purpose, as they will flower more quickly than the larger bulbs. If you want to get a little of the original pure Harrisii, try a case or two of this. As our stock of this is limited, we can offer only a few cases to a single buyer. If you have been dissatisfied with the Harrisii that you have forced heretofore; try a case or two of this, and see if it is not more than worth the difference in price over the stock that you have been buying. In ordering, ask for the pure selected strain of original Harrisii, which we offer as follows :—

5 to 7 inch bulbs, 400 to the case, $17.00 per case
6 to 7 " " 350 " " " 17.50 " "
7 to 9 " " 200 " " " 20.00 " "

Easter Comes Early Next Year—March 31st

and a great many growers will want to use Harrisii instead of Longiflorum so as to be sure to have the plants in flower in time, as the season is going to be short for Japan Longiflorum. The crop of Harrisii this year is the shortest it has been in years, and in view of the extra demand, we advise those who have not already covered their requirements to ose no time doing so.

For the very earliest forcing—Christmas and later—we recommend the pure Harrisii offered above, but for later forcing, for Easter, our customers will find the regular stock offered below first-class stock—much better than the average stock usually offered. We can quote the regular stock as follows :—

6 to 7 inch bulbs, 335 to the case, $13.50 per case.

Freesia Refracta Alba, the true white variety. Now ready. Finest Bermuda-grown stock. $1.00 per 100; $7.50 per 1,000.

Bermuda Buttercup Oxalis. $1.00 per 100; $7.50 per 1,000.

F. R. PIERSON CO., Tarrytown-on-Hudson, N. Y.

Mention The Florists' Exchange when writing.

NOW is the TIME

to secure

Richmond, Killarney and Beauty

Only a limited number left

$5.00 per 100

I have some very fine large plants of

GRAFTED { **Bride, Bridesmaid, Killarney and Richmond**

only $12.00 per 100

SEND FOR SAMPLES.

W. H. ELLIOTT, BRIGHTON, MASS.

Mention The Florists' Exchange when writing.

SOW NOW.

VAUGHAN'S INTERNATIONAL PRIMULA MIXTURE.

This mixture is composed of the most salable colors, the best whites, pinks and reds, with a sprinkling of other colors enough to give a large variety of colors, the most important shades predominating. We have taken special pains to make this mixture as complete as possible, and unreservedly recommend it to everyone.

Pkt. of 250 seeds	50c
5 pkts. 1250 seeds	$2.00
Per 1-16 oz	2.50

NEW GIANT PRIMULAS.

This new strain is a vast improvement on the older varieties, the flowers being considerably larger.

Giant Pink, Blue, Pure White and Copper Color, each pkt. of 250 seeds.............50c

Giant Mixed, includes this year a number of new shades, pkt., 250 seeds.............50c

Primula Obconica Grandiflora, mixed, 1-16 oz., 60c; Trade pkt., 25c.

Primula Obconica, large flowering, pink, 1-16 oz., 85c; Trade pkt., 25c.

Primula Obconica, large flowering, white, 1-16 oz., 85c; Trade pkt., 25c.

CHINESE PRIMULAS.

	250 seeds	1000 seeds
Chiswick Red, bright red	$0.50	$1.75
Alba Magnifica, snow white, of excellent form and habit	.50	1.70
Glowing Coal, the darkest red	.50	1.75
Blue, a clear sky-blue	.50	1.70
Upright Deep Velvety Red	.50	1.90
Bridesmaid, brightest pink	.50	1.75
Mont Blanc, large, pure milk white	.50	
Mixed, a splendid variety, ¼ oz. $8.00	.35	1.25

CALCEOLARIA HYBRIDA.

Our mixture is composed of the choicest selections of the tigered, marbled, spotted and variegated varieties and we know will give entire satisfaction.

Trade pkt., 1000 seeds, 50c; 3 pkts., $1.25

CINERARIA.

Vaughan's Columbian Mixture.

It consists of a mixture made up by ourselves of the choicest English, French and German strains and cannot be excelled in variety of colors, size, shape and substance of flowers and perfect habit of plant.

Trade pkt., 1000 seeds, 50c; 3 pkts., $1.25

FALL BULBS ARRIVING

Freesia, Lilies, Callas, Roman Hyacinths, Candidum, Paper White Narcissus, all Dutch Bulbs.

We are headquarters. Write for prices

Vaughan's Seed Store — 14 BARCLAY ST., NEW YORK

CHICAGO, 84-86 Randolph Street Greenhouses, Western Springs, Ill

Vaughan's Seed Store — Vaughan's Seed Store

CYCLAMEN SEED

Boddington's Gigantic Cyclamen

Gigantic White Butterfly	Gigantic Cherry Red
Gigantic Pink	Gigantic Crimson
Gigantic White	Gigantic Rose
Gigantic Crimson and White	Gigantic Salmon

Princess May, *Lovely Pink and Crimson.*

Salmon Queen, *Deep Salmon.*

Price, 50c per trade pkt.; 100 seeds, $1.25; 1000 seeds, $12.00.

GIGANTIC MIXED in equal proportions as above, same price.

Ordinary Giant Strains, 75c per 100; $6.00 per 1000.

Fall Bulb Catalogue and herbaceous seed list now ready—both free.

ARTHUR T. BODDINGTON

342 West 14th Street, New York City.

Mention The Florists' Exchange when writing.

CONTENTS AND INDEX TO ADVERTISERS, PAGE 119

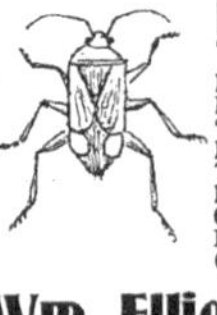

INSECTICIDES

Havana Tobacco Stems, 100 lbs. $1.25.
Havana Tobacco Dust, 100 lbs $2.00.
"Nico Fumes" Tobacco Paper, 24 sheets 75 cts.
Nicoticide, pints, $2.25.
To-bak-ine Fumigating Paper, box 60 cts.
Rose Bone, 200 lbs. $4.00.
Glazing Points, Peerless No. 2 postpaid, 75 cts.
Mastica for Glazing, gal. $1.25.
Canes, $6.00 per 1000.

Wm. Elliott & Sons, New York.

Mention The Florists' Exchange when writing.

LILIUM PHILIPPINENSE

This lily was awarded a "Gold Medal" by the Massachusetts Horticultural Society. For description see our Bulb Catalogue. WE CAN DELIVER 100,000 OF THESE BULBS BY SEPTEMBER! It can easily be forced into flower inside of nine weeks. Considering this being a novelty we offer Lilium Philippinense at these remarkably low prices: Per dozen, $2.00; per 100, $12.00, per 1000, $100.00; per 10,000, $900.00.

W. W. RAWSON & CO.

5 UNION STREET, BOSTON, MASS.

Mention The Florists' Exchange when writing

PACIFIC SEED GROWERS' CO.
411-415 SANSOME STREET
SAN FRANCISCO, CAL.
Specialties:
Onion, Carrot, Lettuce, Sweet Peas

Mention The Florists' Exchange when writing.

Thorburn's Bulbs

LILIUM HARRISII

LILIUM LONGIFLORUM

and all other bulbs for florists.
Send us your requirements for special prices.

CYCAS REVOLUTA STEMS

from Japan. Sizes and prices on application.
Asparagus plumosus nanus, $3.50 per 1000 seeds.

J. M. THORBURN & CO.,
33 Barclay St., New York.

Mention The Florists' Exchange when writing.

PANSY SEED

Schmidt's Famous Strain, large flowering and fancy colors; none better. Per pkt., 50c.; ½ oz., $2.00; 1 oz., $3.50. Plants ready September.

J. C. SCHMIDT CO.
BRISTOL, PA.

Mention The Florists' Exchange when writing.

MUSHROOM SPAWN

Originators and growers of **superior strains of Tissue-Culture Pure Spawn.**
Send for our booklet.

PURE CULTURE SPAWN CO.
PACIFIC, MO.

Mention the Florists' Exchange when writing.

New Crop of my

Christmas Flowering SWEET PEA SEED

Christmas Pink and Florence Denzer, pure white, will be ready August 1st.

Those two well known varieties are raised by over 2000 florists all over the world. Here is one out of many letters received:

Dear Sir: My sweet peas, which I raised from your seed, received the highest award at the Carnation Exhibit in Boston, being over 18 inches long. JOHN T. GALE, Tewkesbury, Mass.

Price 1-4 lb. 75c.; per lb. $2.00
MAILED FREE

New Christmas Flowering Hybrids, 20 to 30 colors, mostly blue, salmon, purple, lavender, in mixtures; also Mrs. Edie Wild, carmine, separate color. 1 Trade pkt., $1.00, 5 Trade pkts, $4.00; not more than 5 pkts. taken in order to each customer just now. These new hybrids are just as free bloomers as Cristmas Pink and Florence Denzer, some much larger, and received first-class Certificate of Merit by the Mass. Horticultural Society, Boston, March 24. Seed ready in Sept.

All seed originated with me is sold in my original sealed pkts., with cultural directions, to the growers, but none for seedsmen for propagating.

Orders filled strictly in rotation.

ANT. C. ZVOLANEK
BOUND BROOK, N. J.

Mention The Florists' Exchange when writing.

PANSY SEED

Brown's Extra Select Superb Giant Prize PANSIES, awarded Silver Medal, St. Louis Exposition 1904. My own grown new 1906 crop ready. Price mixed seed 3000 seeds, $1.00; ¼ oz., $1.50; ½ oz., $2.50., 1 oz., $5.00; ¼ lb., $14.00; ⅓ lb., $25.00; 1 lb., $50.00. Cash with order.

PETER BROWN
Lancaster, Pa.

Mention The Florists' Exchange when writing.

PANSY SEED

Famous Strains of Mammoth Mixed Pansies

S. & W. Co.'s
NON PLUS ULTRA

Our Non Plus Ultra Pansy is a mixture containing the largest, handsomest, most perfect varieties ever sent out. The beautiful coloring and variety of marking give a bed of these pansies a most brilliant appearance; the seed having been saved from the greatest assortment of types, including only the best of Giant Cassier's, Bugnot's, Trimardeau, and Giant English, French and German strains. Finest mixed, per trade pkt., 25c.; ¼ oz., $1.50; per oz., $5.00.

Very Large Flowering Varieties

These are remarkably large Pansies, which, for size of flower and robust growth, eclipse all other strains. Their range of color has heretofore been limited, but this season we are able to offer several grand new varieties.

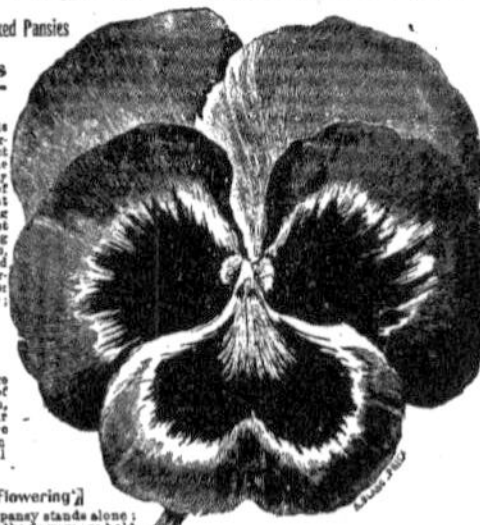

Pansy—Non Plus Ultra

Cassier's Large-Flowering

In form, color and size this pansy stands alone; the plants are very robust and the flowers are held well above the foliage, and should be grown amongst all other pansies, as they add to the effect on account of their robust habits.

Per pkt., 15c.; per oz., $2.50

S. & W. Co.'s Giant Purple
" " Pres. Carnot
" " Rosy Lilac
" " Lord Beaconsfield
" " Kaiser Wilhelm
" " Yellow, black eye
" " Pure Yellow

S. & W. Co's. White, dark eye
" " Snow White
" " Fire King
" " Light Blue, white center
" " Aurical Aeliora
" " King of the Blacks
" " Victoria Red

Per 500 seeds, 25c.; ¼ oz., 75c.; 1 oz., $2.30; ¼ lb., $8.00

STUMPP & WALTER CO., **50 Barclay Street, New York**

Mention The Florists' Exchange when writing.

BURPEE'S SEEDS

PHILADELPHIA

Blue List of Wholesale Prices mailed only to those who plant for profit.

Mention The Florists' Exchange when writing.

The Choicest strains of Florists' Stocks

Including

Cineraria Calceolaria, Cyclamen, Pansy, Petunia, etc.,

CAN BE HAD FROM

JAMES VICK'S SONS
ROCHESTER, N. Y.

Mention The Florists' Exchange when writing.

PRIMROSES

Improved Chinese: Finest grown, named or mixed. Strong 2 inch $2.00 per 100.

XXX SEEDS

CHINESE PRIMROSE

Finest grown, mixed, 500 seeds, $1.00; ½ pkt., 50c.

Cyclamen Giganteum: Finest Giant mixed, 200 seeds $1.00; ½ pkt., 50c.

DAISY, double Giant mixed, 1000 Seeds 25c.

GIANT PANSY. The best large flowering varieties, critically selected, 5000 seeds, $1.00; half pkt., 50c.; per oz. $3.50. 500 seeds of Giant Mme. Perret, pansy seed added to every $1.00 pkt. of Giant Pansy. Cash. Liberal extra count of seeds in all packets.

JOHN F. RUPP, Shiremanstown, Pa.
The Home of Primroses

CINERARIA

Large Flowering Prize, Splendid Mixed T. P. $0.50
Large Flowering, Semi Dwarf Prize, Splendid Mixed, T. P. $0.50

PANSY, Superb Mixed.
oz. $4.50. ¼ oz. $1.15 ⅛ oz. $0.60

W. C. BECKERT,
Allegheny, Pa.

Mention the Florists' Exchange when writing.

Giant Cinerarias

Mixture of perfect colors

Dwarf Hybrids, Semi-Dwarf Hybrids } Each separate Tr. Pkt. $0.50, 6 Tr. Pkts. $2.50

O. V. ZANGEN, Seedsman, HOBOKEN, N. J.

Mention The Florists' Exchange when writing.

Pansy Seed

THE JENNINGS STRAIN

New crop now ready, saved from finest selected stock, large flowering and great variety of fancy colors. By mail one pkt., 4000 seed, $1.00; ¼ oz., $2.50; 1 oz., $5.00, 2 oz., $9.00; 3 oz., $12.00. Cash with order.

E. B. JENNINGS
Lock Box 254 Southport, Conn.

Grower of the Finest Pansies.

Mention The Florists' Exchange when writing

Catalog Engravings and ILLUSTRATIONS

that print EASILY. That's the kind we make—have been since '73

JAS. M. BRYANT, Horticultural Engraving and Printing
706 Chestnut Street, PHILADELPHIA, PA.

Write for our Catalogue of Stock Engravings

Seed Trade Report.

AMERICAN SEED TRADE ASSOCIATION

Henry W. Wood, Richmond, Va., president; C. S. Burge, Toledo, O., first vice-president; G. B. McVay, Birmingham, Ala., second vice-president; C. E. Kendel, Cleveland, O., secretary and treasurer; J. H. Ford, Ravenna, O., assistant secretary.

TROY, N. Y.—Josiah Young has succeeded to the seed firm of Young & Halstead.

NEW YORK.—The steamship Quebec brought consignments of lily bulbs from Bermuda on July 28. The cases are opening up in fine condition.

CLARINDA, IA.—The A. A. Berry Seed Company, held its annual meeting Tuesday, July 10, and declared a dividend. The statement showed that the company had done 40 per cent. more business than the previous year.

European Notes.

As the drought still persists throughout Western France it is no wonder that growers have steadily set their faces against accepting beet cultures for 1907 unless a much higher figure is paid than has been customary of late. As there cannot possibly be any surplus from this year's crops, the growers are bound to get their own way, if provision is to be made for 1907 deliveries. It is a far cry ahead, but those who demand strictly French grown early varieties of radish next year will have to pay more, and for the same reason. Those who have counted upon Dutch grown seed to make up the deficiency this year will be disappointed, as the acreage in that country is very small and the plants are badly injured by vermin.

To the list of shortages we must add all varieties of dandelion. The crop of these is absurdly small, and the prices demanded by the growers (and paid to them) are out of all proportion to the real value of the article. At the same time there is no possibility of the prices going down, and he who calls the tune will have to pay the piper.

It is reported that the crop of Lucerne on your side is very small, and some very heavy purchases of yearling seed have recently been made for shipment to America. As the Provence crop is bound to be small, the farmer will have to pay higher prices next year. Bright, clean samples of Trifolium incarnatum are now on the market. As there is a fairly good supply of fodder in England, thanks to a few warm showers, the demand can hardly be very great, but there will be a good home trade in the article on account of the drought.

Sweet pea cranks in England are frantic with delight at the awarding of a gold medal by the Floral Committee of the Royal Horticultural Society to C. W. Breadmore's exhibit of sweet peas.

EUROPEAN SEEDS.

SEED CROPS IN MOROCCO.—Consul Hoffman Philip, of Tangier, reports that the general outlook for the various seed crops in Morocco for the coming season is excellent, and that the rainfall has been abundant in all districts. He says: "In respect to the probable yields of canary, coriander, and fenugreek seeds, inquiries incline me to believe that they will be considerable and equal to the demand of average years. The drought of last season will to a certain extent preclude this years's yield from being exceptionally large, owing to the resulting poverty among the agriculturists and the special attention devoted to crops of cereals, etc. There has also been considerable damage by locusts to the crops in the extreme southerly districts. However, I see no reason to suppose that this year's seed crop will not be a liberal one, and I should advise the particular attention of our business houses to Morocco as an exceptionally good source of supply in this direction and one capable of great development."

The Garden, He and She.

HE

Come into the garden, Maud.
Let us see how our seeds have grown:
You remember the day when we planted them.
How swiftly the weeks have flown!
Let us see if the cabbage is in bloom,
Let us hunt for the parsley stalks,
And look at the lettuce vines and try
To discover the hollyhocks.

SHE.

I have been in the garden, dear,
The lettuce is not in bloom,
And the pickle stalks and the cabbage vines
I guess have gone up the flume.
The horrid man at the seedstore must
Have swindled us on the seeds;
I looked through the garden yesterday,
And there's nothing there but weeds.

—Chicago Record-Herald.

San Francisco.

A begonia exhibition of the Siever's Nurseries was visited by thousands of people last week. One house, 150 feet in length, was devoted to these plants in bloom, which were greatly admired, many being purchased for spot cash.

ALVIN.

BLOOMINGTON, ILL.—A. N. Carpenter, a pioneer landscape gardener died here July 22, aged 78 years. He was born in Bristol County, Mass.

URBANA, O.—A new boiler and furnace are being installed by the Murphy Greenhouses in Oakland street.

CATALOGUES RECEIVED.

CHARLES D. BALL, Holmesburg, Pa. —Wholesale Price List of Palms and Decorative Plants, Autumn, 1906.

GEORGE HOLLIS, South Weymouth, Mass.—Price List of Peonies, including seedlings of his own raising.

A. SARTORIUS & COMPANY, 45 Murray street, New York.—Catalogue of Paints, etc.

AUG. GRAVEREAU, Neauphle-le-Chateau, France. Catalogue of Pansy and other Flower Seeds; also catalogue of named Gladiolus. H. Beaulieu, Woodhaven, N. Y., American agent.

W. W. RAWSON & COMPANY, Boston, Mass.—Wholesale Price List of Bulbs for Fall Planting.

J. M. THORBURN & COMPANY, 33 Barclay street, New York.—Wholesale Trade Price-List of High-Class Bulbs for Forcing and Outdoor Planting, etc.

THE PERENNIAL GARDENS COMPANY, Toledo, O.—Wholesale Price List of Flower Seeds, Bulbs and Plants. Illustrated. A novelty enumerated in this list is "The New Everblooming Pink Baby Rambler rose (Anna Mueller), color an intense brilliant rose."

COTTAGE GARDENS COMPANY, Queens, N. Y.—Peony Catalogue 1906. Handsomely illustrated and well printed. The firm's stock of Peonies now consists of upward of 50,000 plants, comprising, approximately, 400 varieties, selected with care, and embracing all the choicest and most desirable sorts.

Milwaukee.

News Items.

Trade has been very quiet during the month of July. Stock has been plentiful in both roses and carnations, but the quality has deteriorated the past few weeks. Outdoor stock is now coming in abundantly.

There will be some increase in glass, and additions will be put mostly into carnations.

There will probably be no more than two or three of the trade from here attending the Dayton convention.

M.

NURSERY DEPARTMENT.

Conducted by Joseph Meehan.

AMERICAN ASSOCIATION OF NURSERYMEN.
Orlando Harrison, Berlin, Md., president; J. W. Hill, Des Moines, Ia., vice-president; George C. Seager, Rochester, N. Y., secretary; C. L. Yates, Rochester, N. Y., treasurer.

The Kentucky Nursery Company, Louisville, Ky., has been incorporated with a capital stock of $30,000. Incorporators: F. Boone Gardiner, M. L. Gardiner, and R. L. Cullen.

Some of the leading Eastern nurserymen were in New York last week, comparing notes, and talking over prices. It seems that there is no surplus of any stocks. Among those noted were Messrs. Wm. C. Barry and C. Maloy, Rochester, N. Y.; Thomas B. Meehan, Dreshertown, Pa., and Wm. Warner Harper, Andorra Nurseries, Chestnut Hill, Pa.

The July number of House and Garden contains an excellent portrait of Frederick W. Kelsey, nurseryman, New York, author of "The First County Park System in America," together with extensive extracts from that interesting volume.

The Newark Advertiser in a recent editorial says Mr. Kelsey has made the county park system known far and wide by the descriptions and illustrations in his book. "Mr. Kelsey, who helped to create the system and to develop it, has now made it known not only in New York, but throughtout the country, numerous critical notices of his volume in newspapers and periodicals carrying the advertisement among millions of readers. It is seldom that a writer is enabled to gratify a literary taste and at the same time confer great benefits upon the community in which he lives."

OTTAWA, KAN.—The new packing house which is being built by A. Willis at his nursery on Cherry street, will be completed by September 1. The building now being put up is an even hundred feet square and sixteen feet high in the clear. It is frost proof. It joins the present house on the east and the two combined will make one house two hundred feet long and one hundred feet wide.

VACCINATING TREES.—According to Consul-General Guenther, of Frankfort, German papers state that it happens frequently that the roots of fruit trees are more exhausted than the parts above the ground, and so the life of the tree is threatened.

In order to prolong its life in such cases it has been recommended to vaccinate the trunk of the tree with a solution of sulphate of iron, the same article which is used in the so-called anæmia or chlorosis (Bleichsucht) of the grapevine. A Russian scientist, Mr. Sigismund Monrjetzki, has now made minute scientific experiments with reference to the results of such vaccinations, and by employing colored solutions he has shown that the solution never enters into the old wood. It only follows the young growth, but it penetrates into the roots down to a depth of 1 meter (about 39 inches), while on the other hand it penetrates up to the top of the tree. It is therefore deemed best to vaccinate the tree through a single opening of the neck of the root, and it should serve not only for the introduction of nutritive substances, but also of such liquids which, by killing certain bacteria, tend to cure diseases of the plant.

[There seems some merit in the introduction of foreign substances to trees. Trees sprayed with compounds for killing fungi and insects appear to grow better than trees not sprayed, and does not this indicate absorption of the substances by the bark? It is known bark does absorb moisture to the benefit of the tree. J. M.]

Seasonable Topics.

There are planters who think much of the Hydrangea paniculata, because of its upright flowering shoots. Aside from this advantage, it is hardly worth planting. The sterile flowers are few, and its flowering precedes that of H. paniculata grandiflora but a week or two. When grandiflora does come it is infinitely, better both for ornament and for florists' use.

Monarda fistulosa var. purpurea is the handsomest of all, unless it be M. didyma. It is of a bushy habit, bears dark rose colored flowers, and when massed makes a handsome display. The pleasant odor of the leaves is perceptible as the plants are passed by.

At a meeting of the Missouri State Horticultural Society the following pie cherries were named as the best in the order listed: Early Richmond, Montmorency, Ostheim and English Morello. Mahaleb stocks are preferred but early Richmond does best on its own stock—from seedlings it is presumed.

While the grape flourishes on high ground, and such a position is generally recommended for it, in its wild state it is always found in low ground, along water courses usually. And blights and all ailments pass the plants by there.

Galtonia (Hyacinthus) candicans is a fine plant for setting in clumps or other massings. Its tall spikes of white flowers look not unlike those of the yucca when seen from a distance. They are funnel-shaped, drooping, fragrant appearing freely in the upper half of its 4 foot scape. It flowers in the open border in Midsummer.

Veronica virginica is a pretty wild plant not over common in our woods. It is a useful border plant, where it is sometimes seen. The flowers and flower spike are not unlike those of miniature snake root (cimicifuga) the flowers being white, too, as are those of the other. Its old name is Septandra virginica.

The fruit of the mulberry is a great delight to fowls, and when a customer wants a tree to plant in a chicken yard, recommend the mulberry. As the fruit ripens in succession, there is food for fowls for a period of about six weeks.

Evergreen Seedlings.

A Manitoba correspondent writes me asking if it is possible to raise evergreens from seed, and if so, how to protect them in Winter.

To have the best success with evergreen seeds they should be sown at the earliest date possible in Spring. The soil should be good and fine, and the seeds covered to about their own depth. Germination should be looked for in from four to six weeks. Seed beds are best shaded, but the shade must not be too thick. A skeleton frame, the slats an inch apart, is a good contrivance. This frame can be raised from the ground a little as the seeds advance in growth. This is necessary because if shaded too much they are liable to damp off; and if not shaded at all the sun burns them off. In two months from the time the seedlings are out of the ground the frame can be elevated to be a foot above them in which position it could remain all Summer.

In Winter, if deep snows prevail, no other protection would be required; otherwise, a light covering of forest leaves, kept in place by brush, corn stalks or the like is advisable. The Manitoba snows should be sufficient protection for the seedlings.

Evergreen seedlings are too small at the close of one year's growth for transplanting. It is better to let them stand another year before transplanting them. When done, let it be early in Spring, that they may get a good root-hold before hot weather sets in.

Beauty of Trumpet Vines.

Considering how beautiful trumpet vines are when in flower they are seen far too seldom in collections. The common one, Tecoma radicans, is often used as a climber, a position it fills well, though it is not the only one it could occupy. The others, the golden variety of radicans and the grandiflora, a Chinese species, are still, uncommon in collections. Now, while all these are excellent climbers they are also equally desirable for using as shrubs or as tub plants, uses to which they are seldom put.

Branch of Caragana Arborescens.

In some of our parks examples of what ornamental bushes they make can be met with. All that is required is to set out a plant, placing a strong stake alongside it to support it for a year or two, and then let it grow at will. It is surprising how quickly such a plant flowers. Lacking something to climb to it turns its attention to flowering, as all such vines do in similar circumstances, and in two to three years it blooms.

Caragana Arborescens.

Caragana Arborescens—Siberian Pea.

Siberian pea, as the caragana is usually called, is one of the oldest known shrubs in cultivation, yet it is by no means common in collections. It was introduced to botanic gardens as long ago as 150 years and over. By those acquainted with it, it is greatly esteemed; and it deserves to be because of its pretty foliage, bright yellow flowers and its hardiness.

Coming from Siberia, as it does, no one need question its hardiness; and, indeed the demands for it from far off Manitoba have caused its reputation for hardiness to be well understood by all nurserymen, as shrubs for that cold Canadian region must necessarily be very hardy to withstand the climate there.

The yellow flowers come about the time the foliage is well expanded, a period when many other of the very early shrubs have flowered; and for this reason and because the flowers are not seen at a long distance off, as they are on shrubs that bloom before the leaves come, many fail to notice the plant as they would do otherwise. A good use for it is found in cutting small branches of it and setting them in vases of water for room ornamentation. Then the yellow blossoms interspersed with green leaves are a charming sight.

The shrub, belonging to leguminous plants, has flowers pea-shaped; and, looking at them, at first glance one would be excused for taking them to be laburnum blossoms, only they are smaller and are not borne in racemes, coming in fascicles of but a few flowers each.

Our photograph is a very good one as showing the habit of growth of the caragana. The branches are almost upright; and in this, too, the plant resembles a laburnum.

There are several other species of the caragana, two of which, frutescens and jubata, are also from Siberia, and of these two there are varieties in cultivation; but of all the known species and varieties the one of our notes, C. arborescens, is the only one fairly well known here. And it is the only tall growing one of the whole of the hardy sorts, reaching, in time, a height of from 15 to 20 feet, and if desired it can be grown to a single stem, forming a small tree. JOSEPH MEEHAN.

THE WEEK'S WORK.

Timme's Timely Teachings.

Rambler Roses.

Roses of the Crimson Rambler class that were planted in the field in the Spring are now drawing near the close of their season's growing. But the end is not yet; they are still gaining in headway, the canes growing longer and stronger from day to day, thus giving plain warning that the terminal growth is not far off. What these roses now need most is water, plenty of it, overhead and at the roots, to bring about an even and perfect finish. A drying out now not only interferes with a nice, uniform setting of future flowering growth all along the canes, but it tends to ripen off the wood altogether too soon, often throwing it into a new growth after the first good rains in early Fall—a most undesirable bit of misbehavior on the part of roses destined to pose as the finest of stock for an early Spring trade. Therefore, spare not in the matter of syringing and watering, not until the roses show unmistakable signs of having reached a point when no more growth worth looking for will be forth coming. It is then time to gradually let up in watering; not entirely, should the weather be extremely dry, but just in occasional moderate applications slowly approaching the stage of complete withholding, thus inaugurating a normal and thoroughgoing process of ripening. The observance of just such seemingly unimportant details of culture does more in bringing success and gratifying returns than the nicest kind of forcing later on, or the bedecking with gaudy ribbons and frills still later.

Roses in Pots.

There is no doubt that roses grown in pots all Summer are much easier to manage and give greater satisfaction when forced the following Winter than roses grown in the open field and potted up in November. That hard wooded shrubs—and a rose is nothing else—should first be firmly established in their pots and be provided with a solid ball of active roots before ever being subjected to forcing, is a point not questioned by good gardeners. And it should also be perfectly plain, that a rose, dug up and potted in late Fall, dormant and inactive as it is at that time, cannot put forth working fibers in sufficiency for Spring forcing to render it fully equipped for the ordeal. With proper care and treatment impartially conferred, a remarkable difference between pot-grown and field-grown plants is noticed at once, when comparing the one with the other, both at their best in early Spring. It is then when potted roses of the hybrid perpetual and hybrid tea classes, that had been in pots ever since the previous Spring, show their great superiority over those potted up in the Fall. They were worth and brought nearly twice as much as others last Spring. This not even considering the greater ease with which they are forced, outweighs all objections that might be raised against the adoption of a method entailing much extra care and labor. The essence of advancement in any trade, ours included, lies in the production of a better article from year to year, not in the searching for and finding of easy methods alone, especially not when these tend to decrease the commercial value of the output.

Summer Treatment of Potted Roses.

I have found that potted roses intended for next Winter's forcing or for the plant trade in the Spring, do better if kept constantly in the greenhouse during the hottest part of Summer than they would anywhere out of doors. Only when they have completed their growth are they removed to outdoor frames to fully ripen out their wood. There are two sets of them, the one being roses that were potted up early as one and two year old dormant plants. Some of these required another shift into larger pots since, while most of them do not need this and are forced, flowered and sold next Spring in the same pot into which they were put a year before. The other set is composed of young roses propagated last Winter. These make a steady and most rapid growth up until about the middle or end of August. By that time they have undergone the last of the many shiftings from pot to pot that are necessary to keep them in good shape, and at a rapid headway. In all other respects the treatment of the two lots is alike. They grow in the very richest kind of well-composted soil, three parts of sod to two parts of manure, with a little crushed bone in the bottom of the pot at the last transplanting. When growing fast they need a deal of water and a sprinkling once or twice a day, and they should have it, even after the growth is completed, until they begin to shed the first leaves, when less is needed and none at all after all the leaves have fallen or are ready to drop. Fast growing roses in a sunny and well-ventilated greenhouse are never troubled much by insects or disease during the Summer and throughout are pretty clean stock. They need no stopping or cutting back until brought forward for forcing next Winter, but all buds are nipped off as they appear during the Summer. In September, or a little earlier, they are transferred to cold frames or, should these be occupied otherwise, to any well exposed place in the garden. To prevent angle worms and other troublesome rummagers from finding their way into the pots, it is well to stand the roses on boards or planks, with a thin layer of earth or ashes between board and pots. Some coarse manure or litter strewn loosely between and over the pots lightens the labor of keeping up a moderate degree of moisture at the roots. In long lasting spells of heavy rain, possible but not likely to occur at that season, the plants could be laid on their sides. They are housed quite late in the Fall, and if they have a good freezing they will be fit subjects for forcing at any time after the New Year. Roses reared in this fashion, that remain unsold on the grower's hands in the Spring, should then be replanted into a larger pot and grown on. These will finish their growth and ripen their wood much sooner the second year than they did in the first, making them excellent stock for very early forcing.

Some weeks ago I had a deal to say about roses but somehow missed to hit the right spot with some growers, as was evidenced by several letters of inquiry that have reached me since. "How best to work up a good stock in potted roses for Spring sales when there is no room for field culture?" was the purport of the questions asked. I hope the subject has here been fully covered.

FRED W. TIMME.

Don'ts for Advertisers.

In an address on Advertising by F. D. Coburn, secretary of the Kansas State Board of Agriculture, at a banquet given in Chicago by White's Class Advertising Company are found the following terse suggestions about advertising:

Don't lie. Live up to your annoucements.

Don't be stingy in your appropriation.

Don't be brusque, gruff, "smart" nor exacting with the solicitor. He may be fully as much of a gentleman as yourself, and if he is not you have a fine opportunity to show him an example of a true gentleman's behavior.

Don't try to tell too much in a small space. Give your announcement daylight and breathing room. A stuffed advertisment is liable to have a short reach.

Don't fail, if not located at a well-known point, always to announce your direction and distance from some well-known point, and the railroads that reach you.

Don't forget the value of the short and friendly reading notice.

Don't forget that they cost the publisher money.

Don't demand something for nothing, especially long-winded puffs of yourself and what you have. Pay your way, and pleasantly; the prompt payment is doubly sanctified. The haggler, the skin-flint, the knocker and bluffer may carry his point at times, but in the long run he will lose out—in standing if not in money.

Don't, if the publisher makes an error of commission or omission (and these errors are common to most of us), try to regulate him by rudeness until other means have failed. He may know how to be quite as rude as you, and, besides he has a club. There are few instances in which a publisher is not glad to rectify in good measure any mistakes for which his office is responsible.

Don't drop out. Keep something doing. Change your copy and stay alive.

Don't forget to award the other fellow the same square deal you ask for yourself.

LIST OF ADVERTISERS

INDEX TO STOCK ADVERTISED

Contents.

FIRMS WHO ARE BUILDING.

DECATUR, ILL.—N. Bommersback is adding several new greenhouses to his extensive plant.

WASHINGTON, IA.—The Keck Floral Company, has been incorporated with a capital of $20,000; E. C. Keck and others incorporators.

ELWOOD, MO.—Walter Blubaugh is adding another greenhouse to his plant, and will install steam heating.

OAKLAND, R. I.—Amos F. Darling is erecting an addition to his already extensive plant.

READING, PA.—B. Frank Hain is building two greenhouses.

DES MOINES, IA.—The Iowa Seed Company has just broken ground for the erection of six new greenhouses, each 180 foot long, for the growing of carnations. This will give them about 50,000 feet of glass.

REVIEW OF THE MARKET

NEW YORK.—The market has been in a very stagnated condition the past week, so much so that there is practically nothing doing. It is therefore but of little information to compare supply and demand. Roses of fairly good quality have had to go to the dump pile, there being no buyers. Perhaps the greatest glut is in asters which it has been impossible to dispose of at any price. Every wholesale house has been flooded with these flowers. Gladioli were also seen in immense quantities, and there has been little or no outlet for them, except for window display. To sum up, the expected dull trade at this particular season has gone beyond the anticipations of the most pessimistic and to repeat, there's absolutely nothing doing. Prices remain unchanged from those quoted in last week's issue.

CHICAGO.—Little can be said regarding the general market conditions that is not perfectly familiar to everyone conversant with the Midsummer season of previous years. While good stock is extremely scarce and anything that could be classed as fancy is even scarce, there is a correspondingly light call from local and shipping consumers.

Summer roses and in many cases American Beauty show up to a higher standard than they usually have done at the first of August, but the general line of teas is hardly to be considered as a staple article.

Carnations are of varied conditions. Though there are some coming in that warrant and readily bring $2 per hundred, the bulk of the offerings are so inferior that 75c. to $1 covers the price of most of the output.

Sweet peas, though plentiful, are poor; and the aster season, which is now opening, never did so under more unauspicious conditions. It is perhaps too much to say that the crop is a failure, but at the present tiem there are multitudes of asters being shipped in. Good asters readily bring $1 per hundred and where a dealer has them really good, $1.50 is gladly paid. The best, of which there are very few, bring $2 per hundred.

An over supply of Lilium auratum has reduced the price somewhat.

W. K. W.

BOSTON.—On account of many of the growers clearing out their houses flowers have not been so plentiful the past week. There have been enough however, for all demands. Asters are the most plentiful at the present time and the quality is good; prices range from 50c. to $1. Roses are of rather poor quality except those grown specially for Summer use. Carnations are small, selling at from 50c. to $1.50. Lilies are of good quality at $3 for speciosums while longiflorum bring $1.50 per dozen. Sweet peas fetch 20c. and 25c. Candytuft, feverfew and gypsophila sell at 15c. per bunch. Corn flowers bring 15c.; gladiolus, 50c. per dozen. There is no change in greens of any kind.

J. W. D.

ST. LOUIS.—In the cut flower trade nothing was doing last week except funeral work. As most of the buyers at the wholesale houses ask for white flowers, much colored stock is going to waste. Good first-class roses are always in demand, but very few come in at present; fancy are as high as $8 per 100, from that down to $1.50. American Beauty are very poor, being off color. But few good carnations are arriving; white from the field are best. Asters are selling fairly well, that is, white and purple, the best bringing $2 per 100; the bulk sell for $1. There are too many gladioli and many are given away in order to dispose of them. The hot weather is getting the best of sweet peas and stock is poor at 15c. per 100. In the green market there is plenty of everything. ST. PATRICK.

CINCINNATI.—While the Summer dullness is with us, still, for July, we have very little room for complaint. Asters are now coming into the market from all quarters, and are selling at $1 to $1.50 and $2 per 100. White are in the lead. American Beauty roses are still on top and the only real good roses coming into the market. They fetch from $1 to $2.50 per dozen, clearing out nicely nearly every day. Sweet peas are about done. Gladiolus are coming in quite lively, and sell at $1 to $2 per 100. Carnations are about over until the new crop starts, and this will be some time yet. E. G. G.

INDIANAPOLIS.—Several batches of funeral work have taken some of the dullness away, so there is no complaint from the trade. Stock is plentiful, more so than in other Summers, on account of recent rains. Asters, gladioli, daisies, golden glow, and other outdoor flowers are cut in large quantities, and the quality is fine. Asters wholesale at $1 per 100; gladioli $2 to $3. Three kinds of lilies are still factors in this market; L. longiflorum at $2 per dozen; L. auratum at $1.50 and L. rubrum at 50c. Liberal quantities of roses have been used for funeral work; this is satisfactory for local growers as it saves shipping. Select Kaiserin Augusta Victoria have a heavy call at $6 per 100. Medium grade Bridesmaid and Bride bring $3 to $4. Good Madame Abel Chatenay are shipped in at $7. Carnations, good ones, are scarce. Many customers through force of habit inquire for them, but it is not difficult to sell a substitute.

Green goods are scarce. Smilax and asparagus are shipped at current prices.

Tomlinson Hall market growers report a satisfactory business, more so than usual because of the quantity of field flowers at this season. I. B.

CHANGES IN BUSINESS.

PHILADELPHIA, PA.—The Chase Nurseries have been incorporated, capital $250,000.

JONESBORO, IND.—Elbert Jay of Kokomo is contemplating erecting greenhouses here and embarking in the florist business.

WABAN, MASS.—Prof. F. W. Rane, of New Hampshire with an associate has purchased of Wm. C. Strong a considerable amount of land on Moffat road beyond the E. W. Conant place, with the intention of building several large greenhouses and carrying on the business of flower raising scientifically. He has also brought the two houses further on behind the Van Norman estate.

BOSTON, MASS.—Munson-Walker Company, landscape gardeners; have been incorporated; capital $25,000; president, Chester L. Whitaker, 8 Fairview ter., Somerville; treasurer, James E. Whitaker, 8 Fairview ter., Somerville.

Frost Insecticide Company, Arlington, Mass., has been incorporated, capital $10,000; president, Harold L. Frost, 200 Pleasant street, Arlington; treasurer, Charles H. Higgins, 7 Swan street, Arlington.

GOSHEN, IND.—The Colonial Flower Shop is to be the name of a modern floral establishment to be opened at 210 North Main street about September 1, by Miss Dora Brown. The building will be modernised and specially fitted for the purpose. Miss Brown has resigned her position with the Goshen Floral Company and will go to Detroit, Chicago and other cities seeking the up-to-date methods of the business. She will also make a trip to an Indian reservation to select novelties in hampers, baskets, etc.

BUSINESS DIFFICULTIES.

GALVESTON, TEX.—A petition in voluntary bankruptcy has been filed in the United States Court by Charles Eicholt, florist. Total liabilities are scheduled at $7,218.95 and total assets at $5,503.64, $4,760 of whch is claimed as exempt, and of this $474.65 is stock in trade and $200 is household goods.

NOTICE.

The annual meeting of the FLORISTS' HAIL ASSOCIATION will be held at Fair Grounds Pavilion, Dayton, Ohio, at 3 p.m., August 22, 1906.

JOHN G. ESLER, Secretary.

Saddle River, N. J.

Mention the Florists' Exchange when writing.

Bees and Wasps Attacking Peaches.

(18) What can be done to prevent bees and wasps stinging peaches when the fruit is about to ripen? I had a case where a lot of bees attacked a peach tree and ruined nearly all the fruit on it. A. H.
Penna.

—The only remedy to keep wasps and bees from attacking fruit is to wrap up the fruit in little muslin bags. This is rather a tedious task, but sometimes it is necessary when perfect fruit is desired. In regions where wasps and bees are very numerous.

Herbicide.

(19) Can you tell me the name of the manufacturers of the weed killer called Herbicide? Y.
New York

—Perhaps some reader can give the desired information.

Too Much Constitution.

(20) What is meant by a carnation plant having "too much constitution?" H. & H.

—We did not think such a thing was possible.

An Expert.

(21) What is an expert in any line of the florist business? H. & H.

—Consult some up-to-date dictionary.

Scale on Palms.

(22) What is the most effective way of removing scales on kentia leaves without injuring the foliage? SUBSCRIBER.

—Either of the following methods may be used for this purpose without injury to the foliage, if the work be carefully done: Dip the plant in strong soapsuds, lay it on its side to avoid having the soap drain into the soil, and allow it to remain for about an hour, then wipe off the scales with a sponge. Either whale oil soap or ivory soap will answer for the purpose. Or dip the plant twice or three times at intervals of two days in a solution of tobacco extract, the solution being in the proportion of 1 part of Roseleaf Extract to 40 parts of warm water. The latter treatment will sometimes clean off all the scale, though its success depends upon the species of scale, some of these insects being much harder to kill than others. W. H. T.

Providence, R. I.

News of the Week.

Planting in of carnation stock is now occupying the attention of growers. Stock everywhere is in superh condition as a result of an ideal growing season, and some excellent flowers will undoubtedly be seen later. The excessive heat and oppressive atmosphere in the houses make planting a disagreeable task. One enterprising grower, whose houses are electric lighted, has overcome the difficulties caused by the heat, by persuading his force to work nights instead of days.

James F. Barclay of the Rhode Island Greenhouses, Pawtucket, R. I., is reported as slowly recovering from his recent accident.

J. F. Jordan, proprietor of the Park Avenue Greenhouses, Auburn, R. I., is making improvements and alterations, suggested by experience during the past Winter. A propagating house that formerly extended north and south has been taken down, and will be reconstructed so as to extend east and west and thus be in accord with the range of carnation houses. He has also made changes in the heating apparatus and increased the height of the chimney.

A novelty in the line of growing plants, which commands ready sale among the stores in this vicinity, also at the fashionable shore resorts, is seen in the form of what is labeled the "Janpanese air plant." The habit of growth is evidently similar to that of the Japanese fern ball, and it is the unique holder in which the plant is contained that unquestionably assists its sale. A shell, once the abode of a monster clam, but now filled with sphagnum moss, suspended by cord, seems to furnish abundant nourishment and proper conditions toward promoting perfect growth.

W. H. Tarbox, East Greenwich, R. I. is cutting superb dahlias from the earlier flowering varieties, grown at his farm. He is disposing of the product among local stores.

The usual Midsummer quietness prevails among the stores. Funeral work keeps pink and white carnations and roses cleaned out fairly well. About the only presentable roses in sight are Bride and Bridesmaid, grown inside. The attractive prices offered at Newport, and Narragansett Pier for fancy roses, very closely approach the Midwinter schedule, hence considerable stock goes to these places.

Carnations are practically done; another week will probably present nothing but short-stemmed field blossoms. Enchantress and Fair Maid have proved exceptional Summer bloomers. Outdoor stock is very abundant; purple and white asters are about the only stock of this nature that sells at a profitable figure.

G. S. W.

AMES, IA.—The marriage of A. F. Irwin, associate professor of horticulture at Ames, and Miss Mary Turner took place recently at Oskaloosa. The ceremony was performed by President A. Rosenberger of Penn college. The bride was for several years connected with the Oskaloosa Saturday Globe and for the past year has been stenographer for President Storms at Ames.

NEW BRITAIN, CONN.—Arthur Vols will build a flower store, 12 by 24 feet, on Edson street.

FOUNDED IN 1888

FLORISTS' EXCHANGE

A Weekly Medium of Interchange for Florists, Nurserymen Seedsmen and the Trade in general

Exclusively a Trade Paper.

Entered at New York Post Office as Second Class Matter

Published EVERY SATURDAY by

A. T. DE LA MARE PTG. AND PUB. CO. LTD.

2, 4, 6 and 8 Duane Street,

P. O. Box 1697.
Telephone 3765 John.
NEW YORK.

CHICAGO OFFICE: 127 East Berwyn Avenue.

ILLUSTRATIONS.

Electrotypes of the illustrations used in this paper can usually be supplied by the publishers. Price on application.

YEARLY SUBSCRIPTIONS.

United States, Canada, and Mexico, $1.00. Foreign countries in postal union, $2.50. Payable in advance. Remit by Express Money Order Draft on New York. Post Office Money Order or Registered Letter.

The address label indicates the date when subscription expires and is our only receipt therefore.

REGISTERED CABLE ADDRESS:

Florex, New York.

ADVERTISING RATES.

One-half inch, 75c.; ¾-inch, $1.00; 1-inch, $1.25, special positions extra. Send for Rate Card showing discount of 10c., 15c., 25c., or 35c., per inch on continuous advertising. For rates on Wants, etc., see column for Classified Advertisements.

Copy must reach this office 12 o'clock Wednesday to secure insertion in issue of following Saturday.

Orders from unknown parties must be accompanied with cash or satisfactory references.

The S. A. F. Presidency.

Editor Florists' Exchange:

Would it not be wise for the members of the S. A. F. O. H. to give some attention to the selection of a suitable and logical candidate to fill the position of president for the ensuing year, rather than to leave it altogether to canvassing and buttonholing members at the last moment? or until they have unwittingly pledged themselves to friends on personal grounds alone? It seems to me that the best interests of the society often point to some man, who would never dream of seeking the position himself in any way.

I am expressing my belief that H. B. Beatty, for so many years a faithful member and efficient officer, serving as he has done year after year, and never wavering in his devotion to the best interests of the society, is such a man. He is too modest a gentlemen to seek the office. Let us see to it that the office seeks the man.

Cleveland, O. ADAM GRAHAM.

Job's Choice of S. A. F. President.

Editor Florists' Exchange:

I was rather amused at Job in his article regarding officers of the S. A. F. O. H., especially the president. In the beginning of his article he says, "I still favor my first choice the genial Chicago 'Red Man;'" and farther down the column Job says, "I have no candidate to propose." It's not hard to see through a wall with a hole in it. I have named my choice for president, and he is William J. Stewart, not saying but what the genial Chicago "Red Man" is all that Job claims for him. Both are good fellows, and very capable.

E. G. GILLETT.

Unionized Flowers.

The Chicago American of July 22 contained the following item: "The Florists' Union will open a flower store in the downtown district. The union has adopted a union label, and every rose or bunch of flowers sold will have the label attached. Members of unions will be urged to purchase flowers for funerals, weddings and parties."

Exhibitions.

The schedule of prizes has been issued for the eleventh annual flower show of the Morris County Gardeners and Florists' Society, to be held in the Assembly Rooms, Madison, N. J., November 1 and 2 next. Some $450 in cash are offered as premiums. Copies of the schedule can be obtained from Secretary E. Reagan, box 315, Morristown, N. J.

S. A. F. Officers.

In another column of this week's issue will be found a communication from Adam Graham, Cleveland, O., an ex-president of the S. A. F. O. H., offering the suggestion that some prior consideration be given by delegates to the forthcoming Dayton convention to the matter of choosing the chief executive officer of the national society, in preference to the haphazard method of selection and nomination of candidates at the convention which has heretofore prevailed, much to the annoyance of some whose names have been placed before the assemblage, and who have felt compelled to "stand," out of courtesy to those putting their names in nomination rather than from personal ambition or choice.

We fully endorse the plan proposed by Mr. Graham—one which we have several times previously urged.

The presidency of the S. A. F. is an office to which many may aspire, and well be proud of filling, but it is also one the duties connected with which not every person is capable of properly carrying out in all their phases. For that reason, the society has seen to it that its leaders have largely been among the brainiest men in the business, men whose individual qualifications have placed them in the forefront of their compeers, men who have dignified and honored the high position to which they were elected.

The same satisfactory standard must be maintained, if the S. A. F. is to be looked up to and regarded as worthy of the place it has filled and now fills at the head of the progressive horticultural organisations of the country. And it is because of this fact, that the choice of a president should receive the fullest and best consideration of the members previous to the annual meeting—a consideration which the importance of the subject demands.

There are occasions throughout the year, outside of the annual convention, when the president of the national society appears in public. It is therefore meet that he should be a man capable of acting well his part when called upon, at every function at which he is present, able to hold his end up with credit to himself as well as to the great body he represents and of which he is the chief executive officer. There can be no greater humiliation to the society, no more sorry spectacle to those having its best interests at heart, than the public performance of a leader lacking these essential requisites.

Mr. Graham presents the name of Treasurer H. B. Beatty for the presidency. This proposition is also a case of "the office seeking the man;" a method that rarely fails in the choice of an officer who will fill the bill in the most satisfactory manner.

It has also been publicly reported, without refutation, that the present incumbent of the secretary's office will not again seek re-election. That being so, it is, we think, likewise imperative that the matter of a successor to Mr. Stewart be well and previously considered, to the end that the best available talent be secured. Upon the efficiency of its secretary, and the complete and faithful performance of his work, the success of the society in its every aspect most largely depends. The duties are arduous, more so than appears on the surface. Their full carrying out demands native qualities of no mean order, and the closest application, the most unflagging devotion to the work in hand. Therefore, the choice of a secretary should have the best thought of every member who desires to see the society not only retain its present status, but advance in its sphere as far as individual and collective effort can contribute to that end.

We understand that Phil J. Hauswirth, of Chicago, has been prevailed upon by his many friends to allow his name to be put forward as a candidate for the secretaryship. This is another case of the "office seeking the man;" as such it will, we feel sure, receive the consideration it deserves.

Dayton Convention Notes.

It is only three weeks more until this convention opens. Affairs are in tip-top shape; peace and harmony reign all the way around, and the twenty-second convention of the S. A. F. O. H. promises to be the most successful in the society's history as far as exhibition, lectures, entertainment, etc., are concerned.

The exhibition probably will be the largest in the history of the society. This is chiefly due to the untiring efforts of the superintendent of exhibits to gain this end. The trade all over the country has shown up well in exhibits as well as in advertisements.

We cannot do more than urge all to come prepared to treat exhibitors and advertisers liberally. Come prepared, gentlemen, to buy at least part of some man's exhibit. It is a tremendous task, and a very great expense to which these gentlemen go, to make a display at our conventions. It is the solemn duty of everybody to draw the channels of trade during this convention to the exhibitors and advertisers.

Glaring banners will stare you in the face informing you of the leaders in the parade. A large bulletin board will be put up in the office, where you may leave your name, and the time of appointment with the ones you desire to meet and have not known. If you have a greenhouse to build; if you require a figure on fittings or pipes; if you have to buy glass or paint or putty; if you do not see the exhibits, you will see the banners of the representative firms dealing in these materials floating in the exhibition hall.

If you have steamboat orders to send out of New York harbor, gigantic signs will inform you of the names of the parties able to fill these orders. If you do not know them, leave your name and address at the office, and the respective gentlemen will be pleased to meet you. Save for the convention—all your supply orders, and plant and import orders. You will meet representatives of firms in these lines, and every one of them is worthy of your patronage.

The president of the Dayton Florists' Club, J. B. Heiss, has been in New York for one week, because there was an undercurrent of a wrong impression that this convention was more or less a western affair. Mr. Heiss was received by the craft gloriously, was aided in the undertaking of this convention liberally, and the New York craftsmen grasped the opportunity at a moment and saw the advantage of exhibiting and advertising at the convention. Mr. Heiss would like to extend his personal thanks to advertisers and exhibitors for their liberal contributions, and for the cordial treatment he received from all the members in New York.

It would be desirable if some of the leading firms would put up large electric signs, which can be furnished by the Dayton Club in 10-inch letters at $5 a letter, burning for four nights, these signs to be placed in the outside grounds. Some other firms ought to come forward and do as the enterprising New York brethren have done—put signs and banners pertaining to their firm and business in the exhibition hall. Such signs can be furnished, 15 ft. x 6 ft., for $15; larger in proportion.

To conclude, there is no question that this will be the largest and best convention in the history of the S. A. F. The Dayton Club is straining every nerve to make the whole affair a grand success. The way it looks now, it may be that some of the entertainments will have to be cut out on account of lack of time. However, all the arrangements will be decided later and the results published.

The officers of the Dayton Florists' Club met July 27 at the exhibition grounds, with all the concessionists, to make final contracts for lighting the ground surrounding the buildings laid out for this occasion. Everybody was astonished to see how well things show up. All were unanimous in their praise of Messrs. Freudenberger and Hassey. Both of these gentlemen enjoy in this section of the country the very best reputation, one as a landscape gardener the other as a decorator; but what we beheld left our expectations far far behind. The beautifying of the grounds is chiefly due to the untiring efforts of Mr. Freudenberger. These unassuming young men, having in charge besides about 800 acres of park land, (in addition to making one new park,) one park of about 1200 acres, the other of 400 acres have spent every spare moment in the most unselfish way for the benefit of the craft and this association.

A thousand thanks are due to Mr. Patterson of the National Cash Register Company, for his generosity in turning over to Mr. Freudenberger his men, teams, tools, and materials free of charge to beautify the outdoor surroundings. The name of John H. Patterson should be written in gilded letters in connection with every future convention of the national society. It is through his untiring efforts that the city of Dayton is in the matter of landscaping what it is to-day. There are no more slums; no more tenements. This, verily, is a "City of Homes," through Mr. Patterson's efforts in making the people love all that is great and good in nature, by surrounding their homes with beautiful flowers, shrubs and trees. Where will you find another man who will ask his most humble neighbor to, "Please fix up your property;" and if the poverty racket is brought forth will ask this very man to give him permission to fix up his property at his own expense and tell him to come to get his seeds and shrubs to improve his property? However, I do not want to say too much; visitors to the convention will judge for themselves.

At one of the last meetings of the Dayton club changes were made on the committee of interior decoration, and Mr. Freudenberger was chosen unanimously as chairman of same.

People are waking up now to the beauty of perennials and it is with regret that we say that the contemplated outdoor exhibit has not shown up as well as was anticipated. A large lot of ground was gotten ready for such an exhibit, but exhibitors stayed out, and finally the Dayton club passed a resolution to fill up the empty exhibition spaces. The smallest and most humble brought whatever he had, and Mr. Freudenberger planted as ornamentally as he could these empty spaces intended for exhibitors originally, with the material that was forthcoming from the members of the Dayton Florists' Club. And when you come here, ladies and gentlemen, you will see that his efforts have not been in vain.

As I said before, people are waking up to the value of perennials. Now, you gentlemen who neglected to make an outdoor exhibit send some plants for indoors. They will be well protected. If you can't send plants, send cut flowers. Your exhibit will open up new avenues of trade, and will be quite instructive to a great many members who are not well versed on the beauty and value of perennials.

Here is a pointer for you gentlemen of the horticultural building trade. Contracts will be let out this Fall by one large concern alone for a $20,0[illegible] conservatory. The eyes of this firm are centered on this convention. Now, gentlemen, be alive to the situation and be in the swim.

As previously stated, the Dayton Florists' Club will offer a few prizes for the best plans for landscape gardening. Now, you large enterprising landscape architects, take a few hundred feet of exhibition space and show the world samples of work you have done in the past. Show them plans of parks that ought to be constructed now, even unfinished. Make the trade familiar with what you are doing, and don't hide your light under a bushel. We have to introduce novel features at every convention, and this will be one most beneficial to all the trade. Come forward, if it is only with a few pencil sketches, and instruct the members of this association on what can be done with a small amount of money to make even the most humble home a thing of beauty. Show them what you are doing to elevate citizenship and make better men and women of us all.

J. B. HEISS.

To Dayton from New York, Boston and the East.

The New York Central Lines have been selected by the New York Florists' Club as the official route to Dayton convention. Rate of fare and one-third, on the certificate plan, has been authorized for the round trip. When purchasing ticket to Dayton, ask agent for a certificate, which, when properly vised at the meeting, will entitle you to ticket at one-third fare returning.

			R. R. Tkt.	B'th.
MONDAY, AUGUST 20th.				
Lv. New York, N. Y. Central	2:04	p.m.	$17.25	$4.00
Lv. Boston, B. & A. R. R.	10:45	a.m.	19.25	.....
Lv. Worcester, B. & A. R. R.	11:55	a.m.	18.25	.....
Lv. Springfield, B. & A. R. R.	1:11	p.m.	17.25	.....
Lv. Pittsfield, B. & A. R. R.	2:59	p.m.	16.92	.....
Ar. Albany, B. & A. R. R.	4:15	p.m.	.....	.....
Lv. Albany, N. Y. Central	5:03	p.m.	15.75	4.00
Lv. Schenectady, N. Y. Central	5:36	p.m.	15.50	4.00
Lv. Utica, N. Y. Central	7:09	p.m.	14.49	3.50
Lv. Syracuse, N. Y. Central	8:24	p.m.	13.43	3.00
Lv. Rochester, N. Y. Central	10:00	p.m.	11.83	2.50
Ar. Buffalo, N. Y. Central	11:37	p.m.	.....	.....
Lv. Buffalo, L. S. & M. S.	11:52	p.m.	10.45	2.50
TUESDAY, AUGUST, 21st.				
Ar. Dayton, Big 4	8:55	a.m.	.....	.....

The members from New England points will note from above schedule that they will join the New York Florists' Club at Albany, thus affording an opportunity of traveling together, adding materially to the enjoyment of the trip.

Certain privileges are granted in connection with tickets reading via these lines without additional cost. These tickets will be accepted for passage by the C. & B. Steamboat Line between Cleveland and Buffalo, also by the Hudson River Day Line or People's Night Line from Albany to New York, upon notice to the conductor; permission to stopover at Niagara Falls for a period not exceeding ten days, but tickets must be deposited with depot agent at Niagara Falls immediately upon arrival.

Exclusive Pullman sleepers to run through without change will be arranged if a sufficient number of applications are made to the committee in charge, consequently communicate at the earliest possible date with Walter F. Sheridan, 39 West Twenty-eighth street, New York City.

FRANK H. TRAENDLY,
JOHN B. NUGENT, Jr.,
WALTER F. SHERIDAN,
Transportation Committee.

Or tickets may be purchased from Alex. Macfarlane, Ticket Agent, New York Central, 1216 Broadway, New York.

Chicago to Dayton—via Big Four.

The Chicago Florists' Club has concluded arrangements for the special train over the Cleveland, Cincinnati, Chicago and St. Louis Ry., leaving Michigan Central Passenger station, Twelfth street, Chicago, at 12:45 noon, Monday, August 20, and due to arrive in Dayton, via Kankakee, La Fayette and Indianapolis, about 8:40 p. m., practically a daylight ride all the way.

The train will consist of three or more new day coaches, one combination car, one dining car to serve luncheon and dinner a la carte.

The rate by the certificate plan for the round trip is only $9.70. These tickets are good on all trains August 17 to 23 and for the return trip the validated certificates will be honored up to and including August 31.

The Chicago Florists' Club cordially invites the florists of the northwest and southwest, delegates to the convention, to join this special train at Chicago Monday noon as above stated, and see that when they buy their tickets and secure their certificates for the same that these tickets read "via Big Four Route" from Chicago to Dayton.

Delegates who can join us at any point along our route are requested to do so. The committee will be glad to hear as early as possible from all who decide to join our party, so that the necessary arrangements can be made in time. Delegates buying tickets at Chicago will secure them at the city ticket office of the Big Four, 238 S. Clark street, with certificates.

P. J. HAUSWIRTH,
President.
L. H. WINTERSON,
Secretary.
J. C. VAUGHAN,
WILLIS N. RUDD,
GEORGE ASMUS,
Committee on Transportation.

Peter H. Murphy, a florist of Springfield, O., died on July 23, aged 86 years. Death resulted from heart failure. A widow survives him.

Deceased was a veteran of the Civil War, having enlisted in the Sixty-sixth regiment in Urbana, O. He was a member of Mitchell Post G. A. R.

Concerning Geraniums.

Editor Florists' Exchange:

I see Expertus is still at it, although in a very weak and insipid fashion; he is evidently at his last gasp. He ought to have retired while he could do so with at least a little dignity; now it is too late. His last effusion is only a tiresome repetition and rehash of his former letters, which consist mainly of mean, unwarranted and spiteful slurs aimed at the New York market geraniums and the men who grow them. Several of those growers by the way, hold the cultural certificate of the New York Florists' Club for geraniums exhibited in market shape in the club room, and those geraniums were not grown for exhibition purposes, but were picked up at a moment's notice and expressed directly to the club room. And it is well known that the New York Florists' Club does not bestow its certificate upon anything that does not deserve it.

The New York plant market is, I believe, the largest market of its kind in this country, and it is to be expected that among over 200 growers all grades of stock are represented, from the indifferent to the very finest. This Expertus must know, he having, as he says, visited the market "once or twice." He must also admit—unless he is intentionally traducing the New York market geranium—that the majority of the stock exposed for sale there is of exceptionally fine quality. But probably Expertus was looking through green spectacles! His uncalled for slap at our "clientele" is in a line with the rest of his scurrilous screeds—misleading and unfair. Representatives of all the retail stores of New York, both great and small, are to be seen at our market during the season, their automobiles and fancy wagons being one of the "sights" there in the early morning.

The peddler to whom Expertus has a marked antipathy, (probably because he "works" the neighborhood in which Expertus is located with better stock than he can produce) fills, in the plant market, the place occupied by the Greek in the cut flower markets and the commission district—a cleaner up of what is left. I have often seen geraniums so high in price for weeks at a time that they were out of the reach of the peddler altogether, supply and demand determining the price in the plant market as it does in the cut flower market, and everywhere else.

I see no use in wasting more good ink on Expertus as I have other fish to fry. The New York geranium has an established reputation which neither Expertus nor any one else can hurt; the demand for it is increasing, and it maintains its reputation wherever it is sent.

The next on the docket is "J. R. J." Nothing much there, only a record of some domestic calamities and a so-called song, which is on a par with that memorable effort Job made to emulate that now historic masterpiece of Vaughan's after the Barnegat blowout. One line of that song I want to take notice of. "Was it whiskey or was it beer?" I beg to inform "J. R. J." that it was neither, I am "temperate in all things," and extremely temperate in temperance itself. Concerning his domestic "trouble"—he won't be out of the woods in that line until he cuts his own wisdom teeth. "Pat" has not arrived here yet, and I don't expect to see him now, most probably the next news of him will come from Lancaster, Pa.

I am extremely sorry that I have lost the high opinion that Mr. Eichholz had of me two weeks ago, and not from any fault of mine. His own figures on page 39 of The Florists' Exchange are "30 to 40 cuttings per plant a season." I made no exact figures at that time, merely mentally averaging it 35 and wrote down 100 to 125. I have made closer calculation since then and find that he would only need 114¼ plants for 4,000 cuttings. But I see in last week's issue he puts a chip on his shoulder, and proceeds to give the modus operandi for raising "200 plants per stock plant," and I don't doubt his word for a moment. I have always maintained throughout this discussion that considerably more than 4,000 cuttings can be raised from 50 plants, and now Mr. Eichholz proves conclusively that I am right, raising as he did 10,000 cuttings per 50 plants. That is all right; the only thing I find fault with is the method he uses. Had he used New York market methods he would have got better results with considerably less labor and expense.

However we have got a geranium grower on Staten Island working on a machine which will, he claims, when perfected, revolutionize geranium growing. All one will have to do is to put the pot, the soil and the cutting in at one end of the machine, and the geranium comes out at the other, full grown in full flower and all ready for market.

Young Beginner will observe that he will only require 20 stock plants for 4,000 cuttings, using Mr. Eichholz's method.

"Another Canadian" should have known better than to mention either "heat" or "stimulant" in such weather as we are having in Jersey just now; my thermometer is in the ice box.

Apparently Mr. Junge and I are on the "outs;" but I take the liberty to refer him to Mr. Eichholz's letter for an answer to his question. I might also say that I don't see anything wrong with his nom-de-plume.

"Canadian Florist" evidently labors under the misapprehension that I am one of those penny a line Gamaliels, who dole out perennial doses of, "Hints," "Notes," etc., of doubtful value, at so much a dose.

That last piece of poetry I am setting to music on A minor, so that it can be played on the bagpipes. Its name will be "The Farmer's Prayer."

Another scribe signing himself I. B. in the Indianapolis news notes of last issue, throws down the gauntlet and challenges me to "prove that it is possible to grow eighty good geraniums from one plant." Mr. Eichholz has done that for me. I therefore refer him also to that gentleman's letter on page 95, which conclusively proves that it can be done.

Job's squib is hardly worth notice, but in case he might feel slighted I will state that there is no "secret" about New York market methods in propagating geraniums. I have never asserted that I can "manipulate geraniums, numerically, to better advantage than the average mortal," neither have I ever claimed that those methods were exclusively my own. They are methods used in common by florists who grow geraniums for the New York market, no one has a monopoly of them. Many of those growers manage very easily to raise and sell from fifty to seventy-five thousand geraniums annually from space that would look incredible to the uninitiated, and they don't have to carry 500 stock plants for every 4,000 cuttings either. JOHN BIRNIE.

Obituary

Mrs. Christina Maitre.

Mrs. Christina Maitre, New Orleans, La., died Friday, July 27. She had been in the florist business in that city with her husband, the late R. Maitre, since 1857.

Deceased was born in Bavaria, and was 64 years of age. Her only surviving daughter is the wife of Mathew Cook, florist, New Orleans.

Mrs. Maitre was a woman of charming personality, widely known, and greatly esteemed.

Alexander Emslie.

Alexander Emslie, the well known florist, of Montpelier, Vt., died on Wednesday evening, July 25, after a long illness with consumption. He was taken sick a year ago last June and since that time had been able to do little work. His twin brother with whom he was associated in the greenhouse business, died less than a year ago.

Mr. Emslie was born in Aberdeen, Scotland, 38 years ago, coming to this country when a young man. About six years ago, with his brother, he went into the greenhouse business building houses on the road from Montpelier to Barre. His business increased rapidly and he was obliged to build additions from time to time. Three years ago last July he purchased the greenhouse in Montpelier owned by Ernest Jacobsen who had worked up a large and extensive business. About two years ago Mr. Emslie went into partnership with Alexander Broadfoot and new houses were built and the business increased with rapid strides. Within the past month Mr. Broadfoot acquired Mr. Emslie's interest in the business and is now the sole proprietor.

Mr. Emslie was an honest man and had the respect of all who knew and did business with him. He was industrious and built up a good business both in Barre and Montpelier.

He was a member of Clan Gordon, No. 12, O. S. C., was an Odd Fellow and a Mason. He leaves a widow and two children, two brothers, George and William, who will conduct the Barre greenhouses, and some other brothers and sisters in Scotland.

James Weir, Jr.

James Weir, Jr., florist, Greenwood Cemetery, Brooklyn, N. Y., died suddenly on board the sloop yacht Senta, on which he was cruising, and while acting as helmsman, on Wednesday, August 1. The coroner's inquest revealed that Mr. Weir had succumbed to a rupture of the heart. He was 62 years of age.

Deceased was born near London, England, and was the son of the late James Weir of Bay Ridge, N. Y., one of the pioneer florists in the vicinity of New York. After leaving school James Weir, Jr., worked in his father's greenhouses, in the early days of the business going to Washington market with the products.

About 42 years ago he embarked in the florist's business on his own account, at Twenty-fifth street, Brooklyn, opposite the main entrance of Greenwood Cemetery, and succeeded in building up a large trade.

Mr. Weir was interested in politics. He was for many years a member of the Putnam Democratic Club, and was Alderman from the Eighth Ward, Brooklyn, from 1879 to 1883. He also served on the Brooklyn Board of Education on which his term of office would have terminated next year.

He was a keen sportsman and was a member of several athletic and yachting clubs.

Mr. Weir was naturally a quiet, unassuming man, and was held in the highest esteem by all who knew him. He leaves a widow; one son James E., who was associated with him in business, and three daughters to mourn his loss, also a sister and two brothers, John Weir, the well known Brooklyn retailer, and Fred Weir, in charge of the greenhouses at Bay Ridge, both of the firm of James Weir's Sons.

Funeral services will be held to-day (Saturday) at 2 p. m., at his late residence, 236 Twenty-fifth street, Brooklyn, N. Y.; interment in Greenwood Cemetery.

SOCIETY OF AMERICAN FLORISTS AND ORNAMENTAL HORTICULTURISTS

Incorporated by Special Act of Congress
And approved by President McKinley, March 4, 1901.

PRELIMINARY PROGRAM OF THE TWENTY-SECOND ANNUAL MEETING AND EXHIBITION

TO BE HELD AT
DAYTON, OHIO
AUGUST 21, 22, 23 AND 24, 1906

Opening Session, Tuesday, Aug. 21, 2 P. M.

The opening session will be devoted to an address of welcome by Mayor Chas. F. Snyder, response by ex-president Patrick O'Mara; the annual address of the President, and reports of Secretary, Treasurer, State Vice-Presidents, Committees, and other officials of the society.

President's Reception, 7 P. M.

This always-popular social feature will be held on Tuesday evening at Far Hills, the private estate of Mr. John H. Patterson, under the auspices of the Dayton Florists' Club. Music, refreshments, and grand illumination of the grounds.

Second Day, Wednesday, Aug. 22, 9.30 A. M.

Following reports of judges at the morning session, Wednesday, August 22, the prize essays prepared by members on the subject of "The Best Method of Marketing the Product of the Wholesale Plant and Flower Grower," will be presented and the awards announced.

Bowling Tournament, 1.30 P. M.

The bowling contests between teams representing the various Florists' Clubs, will take place at the Bowling Alleys, Fairview Park. Preliminary individual rolling and the ladies' contest will take place at Lakeside Park. Many valuable trophies have been donated. For instructions as to entries, etc., address George Asmus, 897 Madison ave., Chicago, Ill.

Promenade Concert.

There will be a promenade concert at the Exhibition Building during the afternoon for the entertainment of those who do not attend the bowling tournament.

Florists' Hall Association of America, 3 P. M.

Annual Meeting at Convention Hall.

Illustrated Lecture, 8 P. M.

Title and lecturer to be announced later.

Question Box.

The Question Box will be opened after the close of the lecture, and a general discussion will be in order upon a number of practical topics.

American Carnation Society.

There will be a meeting of members of the American Carnation Society at the Algonquin Hotel, immediately after the adjournment of the evening session of the S. A. F.

Third Day, Thursday Aug. 23, 9.30 A. M.

Subjects for discussion at the morning session, Thursday, August 23, will be:

"Recent Improvements in Retailers' Methods of Offering Flowers." Essayist to be announced later.

"The Ideal Private Gardener and his work," by Fred E. Palmer, Brookline, Mass.

Election of Officers.

During the discussion the election of officers for 1907 will take place, the polls being kept open two hours.

Helianthemum Vulgare, The Rock Rose.

Photo by W. H. Waite.

Selection of Next Meeting Place and Nomination of Officers.

The selection of the location of the next meeting (polls open one hour), nomination of officers and roll-call of States for Nomination for State Vice-Presidents for next year will take place at this session.

Address.

"Teaching Horticulture in the Public Schools," by E. V. Hallock, N. Y.

Amendments to Constitution and By-Laws.

The Executive Board recommends the passage of the following amendments:

Article 11, section 2, to be amended by striking out in paragraph (d) the words "12 o'clock noon" and inserting "11 a. m."

The following to be added to paragraph (d) "In case of failure to elect on first ballot, the president shall order a new ballot immediately, polls to remain open one hour; should this ballot fail to elect, the president shall order a third ballot, polls to remain open one hour; this ballot shall be limited to the two candidates receiving the highest vote on preceding ballot."

Question Box.

The Question Box will be opened during the voting.

Exhibitors' Day.

By vote of the Executive Board, Thursday afternoon will be devoted exclusively to the interests of the exhibitors. There will be band concerts in the Exhibition Hall, and in the grounds outside, noon and evening.

Evening Session, 7.30 P. M.

The main topic for this evening, as assigned by the Executive Board will be addresses and a discussion on the unfinished business.

Friday, Aug 24, Dayton Florists' Day.

The program as arranged for the fourth day, Friday, is as follows: At 10 a. m., a trip to the National Cash Register Co., the model factory of the world. In the afternoon at 2.00 o'clock, a street car ride to Soldiers' Home; band concert at the Home by Uncle Sam's band; address at Memorial Hall.

The Trade Exhibition.

The trade exhibition will be located in the central pavilion at the Fair Grounds. Growers of plants, seeds, bulbs, shrubs and trees, dealers in florists' supplies, greenhouse requisites, building material for greenhouse construction, heating apparatus, etc., can here meet the best buyers in the horticultural profession, and no better opportunity for directing attention to the special merits of their goods can be found.

N. B. Exhibitors are reminded that the duties of the judges are limited to the consideration of and making of awards to Novelties and Improved Devices only. Exhibitors are required to make previous entry of all such exhibits with the superintendent in writing. Full rules and regulations, together with diagrams of the exhibition hall, may be obtained from Horace M. Frank, Superintendent, 112 South Main street, Dayton, O., to whom all applications for space should be made as early as possible.

Outdoor Exhibition.

This convention offers the first opportunity in the society's history to make a display of outdoor planted material. There is yet room for the placing of others and dealers having pot-grown stock to offer can have same properly set out, labelled and cared for without extra charge, until the Convention, by making prompt application to Harry M. Altick, Vice-president, who has charge of this department.

Bulbs for Testing.

American growers of any forcing bulbs, plants or seeds of sorts not yet grown in this country in commercial quantity, or dealers controlling stocks of such goods, are invited to send samples of their product to the trade exhibition, where they will be given space free of charge, provided the bulbs then become the property of the society for testing purposes as to their forcing qualities, results of said testing and awards for quality to be published the following season. Please make entries with the secretary.

Badge Book.

In accordance with the instructions voted by the society last year in Washington, a system of numbered badges and key-book to correspond has been put into operation this year under the direction of the Executive Board. It is believed that the members will find these numbers valuable as a convenient means of identification of one another. The names of all new members joining prior to July 15 this year, have been included in the list. Each member of the society will be supplied with a copy of the book.

Hotels in Dayton.

All hotels are within one square of all street cars, taking you to the exhibition grounds within ten minutes. Following is a list with capacity and prices of the leading hotels:

Hotel	Capacity	Per day
AMERICAN PLAN		
The Algonquin	300	$2.50 to $5.00
The Beckel	200	$3.00 to $4.00
The Phillips	150	$2.00 to $2.50
Hotel Daytonia	100	$1.00 to $1.50
The Aldine	25	$1.00 to $1.50
The Vendome	25	$1.50
EUROPEAN PLAN		
The Atlas	75	$1.00 to $2.00
The Wehner	50	.50 to 75
The Stag Hotel	25	.50
The Urban	60	.50 to $1.00

The hotel committee has also on its list a number of smaller hotels and a whole lot of private houses, prices from 50c. to 75c. for single rooms. If enough applications are made a camp will be established, with well-furnished double-roof tents, four cots to a tent, at a nominal cost of from 50c. to 75c. each. Any wanting accommodations, if no individual arrangements are preferred, should make application as soon as possible to J. B. Heiss, Chairman of Hotel Committee, who will see that all are satisfactorily accommodated.

Helianthemum Vulgare, the Rock Rose.

Wherever hardy, the rock rose ought to find a place in the garden; few more showy plants are to be found than when large masses of those under consideration are in flower. They are shrubby in habit, yet so low that they are especially suitable as rock plants. They are not partial to soils, thriving well in rather poor dry ground, although I do not recommend poor dry soils for them. I merely mention it because they will thrive where many other plants would not. They deserve good care and cultivation and will well repay the cultivator. There are many varieties of H. vulgare, the clump illustrated being a beautiful dark red variety called amabile. They are easily propagated by cuttings or from seed.

Clematises for Pots.

Among the best varieties that have been exhibited as forced plants within the last two years says the Journal of Horticulture, England, are the following: —Albert Victor, lavender; Countess of Lovelace, mauve, double; Fair Rosamond, white, with slight purplish bar in centre of petals; Fair Queen, blush, with pink bar; Lady Caroline Nevill, pale mauve; Lord Nevill, rich plum; Lord Wolseley, reddish purple; Lucy Lemoine, double white; Marcel Moser, rosy mauve, purple bar; Marie Lefebvre, French white; Mrs. Bateman; Mrs. George Jackman, satiny white; Mrs. S. C. Baker, soft pink, reddish bar; purpurea elegans, deep violet; Venus Victrix, pale lavender; Ville de Lyon, rosy crimson.

Some old Favorites—Now Crassulas.

How deserving of further culture are these plants: Once Crassula coccinea, then kalosanthes, now crassula again; once Rochea falcata, then kalosanthes, now crassula. This changing of names makes no difference to the plants, as they will always be beautiful whatever they are called.

These succulent plants seemingly have been forgotten by those who once knew them—and in these rapid times very few have even noticed them or even know their names. How beautiful and responsive they are, may be readily found out by those who will give them good care and attention. Because these plants will not die right out is perhaps the reason why one sees once in a great while, a wretched specimen with a scrap of flower on it. The man who can grow first-class geraniums, either specimens 3 feet in diameter, or in 5-inch pots with five trusses on each—a la Birnie or ?—can do these subjects.

No starvation, should be the motto. Once I helped to grow specimen crassulas of the first four mentioned in the list herewith given. The soil composition was half Epping Forest loam, one-quarter sheep droppings, one-quarter broken pots, passed through two sieves so that nothing but one-half-inch size was kept. The sheep droppings were spread on the bottom of an iron pan, the loam was placed over them and then the receptacle was put on the top of the furnace of the flue (no hot water) to get dried and blended. The broken pots were added when the potting was done, the whole rammed hard, watered when necessary and kept in the pelargonium house in full light on the front bench (house was lean-to; pots and size No. 1). The plants when in bloom were 3 feet high and more through, with 35 to 50 trusses on each. They were heavy, but they were as beautiful as they were weighty.

Propagation is effected by cuttings, preferably in the Spring. Where possible stock plants should be kept so that a full year's growth may be made on the plants before the cuttings are taken. This applies particularly to coccinea and falcata. Plunge or plant out the stock plants in the full sun during the Summer. All young plants should also be plunged or planted out in the very sunniest place in well-drained positions. Take up in September, place in a sunny house, keep rather dry in Winter, temperature 50 to 55 degrees, and they will come along as freely as any other plant. Pot firmly when necessary in good rich sandy soil.

Specimens of any size may be had by putting a number of plants together. When coming into flower give one or two good soakings of manure water. The plants of coccinea and versicolor must be carefully staked and tied, otherwise they are liable to snap off at the ground line; the leaves of these being very heavy, the plants are easily overbalanced.

Nearly all crassulas last in flower for a month or six weeks, which is a great recommendation for their culture.

The following is a list of the best sorts:

Coccinea, flowers brilliant scarlet, an inch or more long and nearly as wide, borne in dense heads of from 20 to 40 flowers each, depending upon the culture given. The leaves are thick and of the brightest shining green. The perfume is delicious, like honey nectar, with a dash of pineapple—once inhaled never forgotten: height 1 to 4 feet. Introduced from Table Mountain, 1710.

Fine varieties of coccinea are: Madame Kerchove, brilliant scarlet with pure white centers; Etna, deep fulgent red, distinct; Vesuvius, most brilliant scarlet, the same shade as that of the Quorn huntsman's coat.

Falcata, flowers bright coral crimson, individually small, borne in dense heads 4 to 7 inches across, depending, like coccinea, on the strength and culture given. The leaves are thick, of a pleasing silvery green, and are variously scimitar-shaped; height 1 to 6 or more feet. Introduced 1795.

Jasminea, flowers opening white, changing to deep rose color, borne in compact heads 2 to 3 inches across, resembling very much those of the common jessamine. A fine commercial plant, flowering in April, May and June. Requires liberal treatment. Introduced 1815.

Versicolor, flowers borne in rather loose heads; tubes long, with shorter limbs, segments recurving; color bright red on the outside with pure white center inside on first opening, the whole of the flower maturing to coral red. Deliciously scented, in the evening only. Blooms nearly all Summer. The leaves are lance-shaped, quite thick; growth upright. Introduced 1741.

JOHN THORPE.

Achillea Ptarmica, "The Pearl."

This well known plant needs little description as it is already so popular on account of the snowy whiteness of its blossoms, and its usefulness as material in cut flower work. "The Pearl" is the double flowering form of A. ptarmica.

JOHN F. JOHNSTON.

Long Island.

Railroad to Give Away Bouquets.

The Union Pacific is to follow the plan of the Michigan Central Railroad and give away bouquets to passengers on its trains; it is planning to establish greenhouses at Ogden, Utah, Denver, Col., Cheyenne, Wyo., and Grand Island, Neb., in which the stock will be grown for the purpose mentioned, as well as to supply the dining cars.

A Nebraska Peony Farm.

The World-Herald of Omaha, Neb., in its edition of Sunday, July 22, contains an illustrated account of the peony farm of J. F. Rosenfield, West Point, Neb. There are eight acres devoted to peonies, and Mr. Rosenfield has 400 varieties, half that number being of his own origination. In connection with the work of hybridization, Mr. Rosenfield keeps some fifteen or twenty hives of honey bees. The varieties which it is desired to cross are planted near together, and the bees do the rest.

Mr. Rosenfield believes that Nebraska is a natural abode for the peony. Flowers are shipped as far as California, and "there is scarcely a state in the Union where Nebraska peonies are not in demand."

The same newspaper contains some remarks by the veteran C. S. Harrison on his favorite plant.

Mr. Harrison says: "What tremendous strides have already been made; and the successes of the past are only prophecies of the future. Fifty years ago there were only twenty-five varieties. Now there are over 2,000 named, besides thousands of others in the background. An interest is being awakened unknown before.

"To show the awakening interest, in the Fall of 1904, the leading papers of the West, aggregating a circulation of over 300,000, published special illustrated issues awakening an interest in the great empire of the Northwest where such flowers are so much needed and where they succeed so well."

Liliums in England.

The Japanese lilium trade is now engaging the attention of growers in England, this being the season when the orders are placed for the bulbs for the following Autumn delivery. Prices this year are again very high, and crop reports received from Yokohama are very pessimistic. If anything like true, the supply of bulbs on the English markets will again be very short.

It is difficult to determine how a profit is made out of growing the bulbs, considering the best prices paid by the English growers. This year as much as £8 to £10 per 1,000 is being asked and obtained by the importers for Longiflorum multiflorum 7x9; and for Lancifolium album Kratzeri., 9x10, £21 per 1,000 is being given by some of the larger growers. Sufficient orders are already booked to make the price go even higher. Just what is causing these high prices to continue is somewhat of a mystery. No doubt the war in the far East prevented bulb cultivation and exportation, to a great extent. Also Germany has for some years been a good customer at gradually improving prices, I presume; and from reports I have heard the American demand has greatly increased during the last few years. But in England the cultivation has been steadily declining for some years, and before the idea of retarding became general had almost died out. Since the different sorts have been successfully and profitably retarded the cultivation has been greatly stimulated and is now rapidly increasing again. This fact no doubt has a lot to do with the advanced price.

Retarded longiflorum lilies have been on the London markets all through the Winter and Spring. At times really fancy prices have been realized both on cut flowers and pot plants, and some one or two growers have made a little pile of money out of their cultivation.

As to Varieties.

There still exists very great doubt as to which are the best varieties to grow and handle, only a few growers, for instance, being able to distinguish the difference between Lilium longiflorum eximium, L. long. multiflorum and L. long. giganteum; and if the wrong varieties are procured for any special purpose or time of flowering, much loss, trouble and vexation will result.

For retarding purposes for blooming very late, that is, for keeping in ice, say, beyond six months after the actual process of retarding growth has set in, the longiflorum giganteum is the best, and in fact is, taken all round, the best for all purposes. Although its price is a long way above that of the other two sorts, it is the cheapest in the long run, at least for late retarding, being far more reliable and able to withstand the deteriorating effects of long storage in ice much better than the others. This variety can be easily distinguished (once a grower becomes familiar with its chief characteristics) by having a more or less black stem. The growth is altogether more robust and strong; the leaves are slightly larger and the bloom is made of much stouter material and has altogether more substance. But the most noticeable distinguishing feature is, of course, the black stem. The blooms are larger and, if anything, a little whiter and will stand much longer when cut than those of the other sorts.

There is much talk among the growers here on which are the best sorts to grow, some favoring one and some another sort; but it is now more and more being recognized that the multiflorum and giganteum are the best for all purposes. The multiflorum type is somewhat more difficult to distinguish from the common eximium; and even when growers order all multiflorum they frequently get the other variety, in many cases not knowing the difference. A frequent practice with either the merchants in Europe or the packers in Japan, probably the latter, is to mix half eximium with the multiflorum, when all the latter are ordered, and either the ignorance of the grower fails to detect the mixture or if any difference is noticed it is put down to some portion of the batch not having been cultivated or grown so well as the others, for after all is said and done the multiflorum is no more than a very much improved and glorified type of eximium. But the multiflorum can be easily distinguished, being a much stronger grower and also having the leaves set somewhat closer together on the stem than the other sort. The leaves also are somewhat broader and longer. The same size bulb will produce double the number of blooms, which are of much greater substance in the petal and somewhat more expanded at the mouth. Also, the multiflorum have a tendency, in many cases, to make a branching growth, thus considerably increasing the quantity of bloom. This variety is also the best (probably of all three) for retarding, for taking out of the ice chamber during the first six months of the retarding process, although not so reliable as giganteum for use during the latter half of the retarding process. The eximium is probably the least valuable of any of the species, although still used in very large numbers, probably on account of its cheapness and owing to the bulbs being much easier of cultivation and propagation in Japan and elsewhere. It does not produce half the number of blooms of the other varieties, and the flowers have not nearly as much substance in the petals, in some instances being almost transparent. Neither does it appear to possess sufficient constitution to withstand the process of retarding quite successfully, not even under the most careful and expert treatment.

The other varieties grown, both fresh and retarded, are L. lancifolium speciosum album Kratzerii, Mel-

Photo by J. F. Johnston. Achillea The Pearl.

pomene and rubrum, the latter two, of course, being the colored spotted varieties, rubrum being used by far in the greater portion of the two colored sorts.

It seems to be generally considered now that album and Kratzerii are one and the same thing, and the two names are now linked together and the bulbs bought as one and the same variety, although I personally do not agree with these statements. I remember years ago when I bloomed my first batch of these sorts from Yokohama, and the Kratzerii was bloomed for the first time and a fancy price was given for it, album was white with a green stripe down the center of each petal, Kratzerii pure white with an entire absence of the green stripe in any shape or form. I am of opinion that the true Kratzerii is never obtained or used in quantity by any grower, but the variety grown under that name is nothing more than the old album.

The three varieties of lancifolium mentioned above are all good for retarding; in fact, I think better blooms are obtained than when grown from fresh bulbs, but, unlike the longiflorum the demand for bloom is always limited owing to the cost, which I think will never be reduced under any system of cultivation, all the lancifoliums being very particular as to their requirements, an expert at the business being needed to do them at all successfully. They too, require specially constructed houses, and are a long time on hand from the period of potting to cutting the bloom. Here they are grown successfully in conjunction with roses and chrysanthemums, roses occupying the houses in late Winter and early Spring, liliums during late Spring, all Summer and early Autumn, and chrysanthemums during late Autumn and early Winter. The broad lofty houses required for the liliums admirably suit both roses and chrysanthemums. One grower near London has 12 houses used entirely for these three crops, the dimensions of the structures being somewhere about 36 feet wide by 250 feet long and as high in proportion.

Bulbs Bloomed the Second Year.

By far the finest blooms and biggest crops are obtained on bulbs that are bloomed the second year, although very few growers can successfully carry the bulbs through the resting period without considerably diminishing their size and strength of constitution. But if they are grown properly during the first year they need little more than gradually drying off in their flowering pots, and, when quite dry, turning the pots on their sides, withholding all water until the time comes round to shake them out and repot. If they show any signs of disease, or the scales fall away or the bulb is much wasted, they are not worth the expense of growing on again; but if they do come through successfully the improved blooms and increased number resulting will be a surprise to the grower. Of course, this only applies to fresh bulbs, retarded ones being totally useless the second year.

The Retarding Process.

The art of retarding seems to be gaining perfection more and more each year. At one time the bulk put in cold storage was a failure, but experience has brought about many improvements, and only a very small percentage of stored bulbs is a failure.

Unlike lily of the valley, liliums in my experience (although I am informed it is not the experience of some others) are more successful in a dry atmosphere. A wet atmosphere in the cold rooms, such as successful valley retarding requires, causes liliums to rot, more or less, and while lily of the valley take 4 to 6 degrees of wet frost, a lilium is successful in 8 to 10 degrees of moderately dry atmosphere, although it must not be as dry as the air in our English cold air stores which are principally used for storing provisions.

Married Ladies' Race, Mrs. Robert Edgar leading.

One Hundred Yards Dash—the Start.

BOSTON GARDENERS AND FLORISTS' CLUB OUTING

The Tug of War, Boston Club Outing.

Many materials have been tried for packing the bulbs for retarding, but ordinary clay seems to be the most suitable. It is always necessary to be particular to examine every bulb for any trace of disease or fungoid trouble, and discard those affected before putting a batch in cold stores, otherwise one bad bulb in a case will rot the whole lot in the course of two or three months. For retarding, the larger sizes should be used, 7x9 in giganteum being the very smallest that can be retarded with success; and generally speaking, it is the same with the other two longiflorum varieties. In the case of lancifoliums, 7x9 is too small, especially in album to successfully retard, and is the smallest size to successfully force in fresh bulbs.

An European Supply a Question.

It does not seem likely that the growing of liliums will ever be a commercial success in Europe. Several attempts have been made in Cambridgeshire and Lincolnshire, England, but so far fithout success. In one or two instances the bulbs, more especially the lancifoliums, have thrived all right and made samples fully equal to any grown in Japan, but the cost of production was far greater than the figure at which they can be bought in that country. But it my be, that, as time goes on, cheaper methods will be utilized. Certainly the fact of them growing to perfection in England at all seems to indicate that climate, soil and other natural conditions are right, and it only rests with the grower to use these circumstances more economically for the growth of liliums here for this work to become a commercial success.

In one or two districts in Holland some fine samples are produced, far better, in my opinion, than any grown in Japan, but here again the cost of production is greater than the price for which the bulbs can be brought from Japan, consequently the culture has not reached as yet much beyond the experimental stage. I have hopes, however, that sooner or later these bulbs will be produced in sufficient quantities both in Holland and England to supply the European markets, and at much less than is at present paid to the far eastern growers.

ENGLISH CORRESPONDENT.

Uses for Ivy.

English ivy is being used more and more of late, partly because of its value and partly because it is now better understood how hardy it is in many situations where it was looked on before as being of a partly unreliable nature. In Eastern Pennsylvania it is in common use, as it fills so many places well that other vines would not answer for. For covering the trunks of trees there is nothing as good. It clings to the bark well, and when it gets from the soil what food it needs, it grows fast and soon covers the whole trunk. It never harms a tree unless when it is permitted to extend itself so far as to cover the foliage of the tree. When it does this, it will kill a tree, as will anything else that destroys its foliage.

For covering the ground under trees this ivy is in great demand. It is well suited in such a situation. The shade it gets in Winter is just what it wants; as often it is the sun in Winter that causes the plant to fail when fully exposed to it. It is the protection the ground affords that causes the ivy to thrive so well when used on graves. When so used there is soon an ivy-covered mound which in every respect seems most appropriate. Walls of all kinds are often made beautiful by the use of ivy. There is no other evergreen to take its place. Euonymus radicans is evergreen and hardy, but its foliage is very small, and it sets so close to a wall that it fails to create the effect that the English ivy does. For low walls the latter is excellent, such walls as are often used to form the boundary of a terrace, for example.

There may be a difference in the hardiness of ivies, as many suppose, but the well doing or not of plants is often more dependent on situation than anything else. The English ivy needs as much shade in Winter as possible, to do its best.

JOSEPH MEEHAN.

LOOK! See Us Grow.

A GOOD INVESTMENT; BETTER THAN BONDS.
Have you any loose change? If so, make 100 per cent. on your money. Write an order to Godfrey Aschmann for his Araucaria excelsa, glauca or compacta. Prices will soon advance. This kind of bond never fails.

ARAUCARIA EXCELSA a specialty. 6,000 are in now, imported from Ghent, Belgium this Spring, 1906. Now planted in 5½ and 6 in. pots, well established, and ready for shipment to all parts of America. All these are grown for us by an Araucaria Specialist in Ghent, Belgium. **NO SEEDLINGS,** but Araucarias raised from top cuttings only are offered. This is now our 11th Anniversary, and our importations have grown from 250 in the first year to the remarkable number of **6,000 IN THE ELEVENTH YEAR.** My reputation as Araucaria Importer gains footway in every greenhouse and florist store in America. Our Araucarias need no *coaxing*, genuine facts tell in quality and cheapness.

Please Note Our Lowest Prices

12 to 14 in. 5½ in. pots, 3 to 4 tiers, 2-yr. old, 50c. 14 to 16 in., 5½ in. pots, 3 to 4 tiers, 2-yr. old, 60c. 16 to 18 in. 5½ to 6 in. pots, 4 to 5 tiers, 3-yr. old, 75c. 18 to 20 in., 6 in. pots, 5 to 6 tiers, 4-yr. old, $1.00. 20 to 24 in. 6 in. to 7 in. pots, 5 to 6 tiers, 4-yr. old, $1.25. 36-40 to 50 in. 7 in. pots, specimen plants from $2.50 to $3.00 each.

ARAUCARIA COMPACTA ROBUSTA – have several thousand of them; can supply all wants. These plants were never so fine in shape and condition as this year. The set of the greenhouse, as broad as long, 12 to 20 in., in height, 3 to 4 perfect tiers, 20 to 30 inches across. 3-4-5 year old, 6 to 7 in. pots, $1.25, $1.50, $1.75, $2.00, $2.50 to $3.00 each.

ARAUCARIA EXCELSA GLAUCA—This variety on account of its beautiful Green-Blueish tiers, dwarf habit, fine compact shape, gives it a striking appearance, and anybody seeing them, must undoubtedly fall in love with them at sight. Plants, 6-7 inch pots, 3-4-5 perfect tiers, 3-4 year old, 15 to 25 inch high, from 15 to 30 in. across, $1.25, $1.50, $1.75, $2.00 to $2.50 each.

SOLANUM or JERUSALEM CHERRY, $5.00 per 100.

KENTIA BELMOREANA, 5½ to 6 in. pots, bushy, fine plants, from 75 cts. to $1.00 to $1.25 each.

KENTIA FORSTERIANA, 7 in. pots, made-up plants, 1 large in center, 3 smaller sizes, 22 to 25 in. high around, gives them a good appearance, $2.00 each. 6 in. pots, single plants, 35 to 40 in. high, 5 to 6 good leaves, 4 year old, $1.25 to $1.50 each; 6 in. pots, 30 to 35 in. high, 4 year old, 5 good leaves, $1.00; 5½ in. pots, 3 year old, 25 to 30 in. high, 5 good leaves, 75c. made-up plants, 3 and 4 in. pots, 18 to 20 in. high, 25 cts. to 30 cts. each.

ARECA LUTESCENS, made-up, 25 cts.

COCOS WEDDELIANA, 15 cts.

CYCAS REVOLUTA (Sago Palm), 6 in.-7 in. pots, with from 6 to 20 leaves per plant, 10 cts. per leaf.

NEPHROLEPIS BARROWSII, 6 in. pots, strong, ready for 7-8 in., 75c. 4 in. pots, 25c.

NEPHROLEPIS SCOTTII, 6 in. pots, 50c.; 4 in. pots, 20c.

BOSTON FERNS, 4 in., 20c.

FERNS for dishes, a fine assortment, 2½ in., $5.00 per 100.

CASH WITH ORDER

When ordering, say whether the plants should be shipped in the pots or not

GODFREY ASCHMANN
Importer and Wholesale Grower of Pot Plants
1012 Ontario Street, - - PHILADELPHIA, PA.

Mention The Florists' Exchange when writing.

Begonia "Gloire deLorraine" and "Turnford Hall"

NOW READY FOR DELIVERY. Propagated strictly from **single leaf**; this method gives much better results than from cuttings, $15.00 per 100, $140.00 per 1000, 4 inch pots, $40.00 per 100. **ADIANTUM FARLEYENSE,** fine specimens $18.00 to $24.00 per doz, 1¾ inch pots, $8.00 per 100; 2½ inch pots, $15.00 per 100. **PANDANUS VEITCHII,** 50c., $1.00, $1.50 and $2.50 each. Good value guaranteed. Cash with order from unknown correspondents.

J. A. PETERSON, McHenry Ave., Westwood, CINCINNATI, OHIO

Mention The Florists' Exchange when writing.

DRACAENA TERMINALIS

Matured canes always ready for shipment. Delivered to any part of the United States for 10 cents a foot. Send cash for a trial order.

PORTO RICO PINEAPPLE CO., RIO PIEDRAS, PORTO RICO.

Mention The Florists' Exchange when writing.

CHINESE PRIMROSES

Finest mixed, strong, 2 in., 2c.
Primula Obconica, Carmine, Hybrid, 2 in., 2c.
" " Double and new Red 2 in., 3c.
Grand. fim. Alba, Rosea, Lilac.
Asparagus Sprengerii, and Plumosus 2 in., 2c.
Christmas Peppers, Jerusalem Cherries, 2 in. and 2½ in. pots, $2.00 per 100.

Ferns from Bench:
Boston, Piersoni, 4 in. 10c; 5 in. 12½c.
Tarrytown, 3 in., 10c; 4 in., 15c; 5 in., 25c.
Scottii, 3 in., 8c; 4 in., 12½c; 5 in., 15c.

Geraniums, 2½ in. Viaud, Bernandian and 7 other sorts, $1.50 per 100.
Cash or C. O. D.

BYER BROS. Chambersburg, Pa.

A FEW BARGAINS TO MAKE ROOM

Asparagus Plumosus Nanus, 2½ in. pots, fine stock, $5.00 per 100. **Asparagus Sprengerii,** 3 in. pots, fine stock, $4.00 per 100. **Fine Croweanum Fern,** 3 in. pots, fine Stock, $4.00 per 100. **Smilax,** 2 in. pots, strong stock, $1.50 per 100. 50-6 in. pans and 50-8 in. pans of Cypripedium Insigne, fine strong stock that will bloom this season. Write for price. Cash with order.

JOSEPH TOWELL, PATERSON, N. J.

Mention The Florists' Exchange when writing.

POINSETTIAS

2½ in. pots, $5.00 per 100; $40.00 per 1000. Cash with order.

S. N. PENTECOST,
1790-1810 East 101 St., CLEVELAND, O.

Mention The Florists' Exchange when writing.

50,000 Pansy Seedlings

Finest strain at $4.00 per 1000. Delivery beginning September 1st. Orders booked in rotation. Strictly cash with order.

J. CONDON, Horticulturist,
734 5th Ave., Brooklyn, N. Y.

Mention The Florists' Exchange when writing.

Primula Obconica Grandiflora

2 1-2 in., $2.50 per 100. Ask for list (seedlings of hardy plants)

BAUDISCH & CO.,
537 Fulton Street UNION HILL, N. J.

Mention The Florists' Exchange when writing.

CARNATIONS

	per 1000	per 100
500 Queen Louis, field grown		$4.00
Smilax	$9.00	1.00
Asp. Plumosus, 2½ in. pots, Aug. 15th		2.00
Cineraria, Sept. 15th		2.00
Pansy Seed, large flowering, per oz., $4.00		

PRIMROSES

	per 100
Chinese, 2½ in. pots, Aug. 10th	$2.00
Obconica, Rosea and Alba, Aug. 10th	2.00
Forbesi, fine for cut flowers	2.00
P. W. Narcissus, 13 ctm., Sept.	1.25

CASH PLEASE

JOS. H. CUNNINGHAM, Delaware, O.

Mention The Florists' Exchange when writing.

FIELD GROWN Carnation Plants

Enchantress, $40.00 and $50.00 per 1000.
McGowan, $30.00 in field, no plants shipped.

WM. BELL, BAYSIDE, L. I.

Mention The Florists' Exchange when writing.

FIELD-GROWN Carnation Plants

Send for price and list of varieties.

Chicago Carnation Co., Joliet, Ill.

Mention The Florists' Exchange when writing.

FIELD GROWN CARNATIONS

Good Healthy Stock.

PROSPERITY	$5.00	per 100.
LAWSON	5.00	" "
HARLOWARDEN	5.00	" "

Terms Cash.

RIDDELL & HERRICK, FARMINGDALE, L. I.

Mention The Florists' Exchange when writing.

CARNATIONS

Fine field plants, ready to ship. Enchantress, Pink and White Lawson, Queen, Boston Market, $6.00 per 100; $45.00 per 1000.

Ardisia crenulata, strong, bushy plants from bench, well berried, ready for 5-6 in. pots, $8.00 and $9.00 per doz.

Geraniums, 12 varieties. Have order booked for Fall delivery; can fill orders from 100-100,000. Get my prices. Standard, 4 in. pots, $9.00 per 1000; 5000, $40.00 saucers 80c. 100. Cash.

WM. S. HERZOG, MORRIS PLAINS, N. J.

Mention The Florists' Exchange when writing.

BEGONIA REX

BEST NAMED SORTS

An immense stock in fine condition for immediate sales, 2½ inch, $5.00 per 100.
See ad. in Last Issue.

NATHAN SMITH & SON,
ADRIAN, MICH.

Mention The Florists' Exchange when writing.

CHRYSANTHEMUMS

R. C. from sand. **Dr. Enguehard, Wm. Duckham, Am. Beauty,** $1.20 per 100. A good assortment of the best standard varieties in the best condition from soil on account of removal, $20.00 per 1000.
Cash with order.

G. F. NEIPP,
AQUEDUCT, L. I., N. Y.
JAMAICA P. O.

Mention The Florists' Exchange when writing.

A Few Good Things YOU WANT

Dracæna Indivisa, 4 and 5 in., $10.00 and $25.00 per 100.

Asparagus Sprengeri, 2 in., $2.50 per 100.

Geraniums, S. A. Nutt, Castellane, John Doyle, Perkins, Double Gen. Grant, Poitevine, Mme. Salleroi, 2 in. pots, $2.00 per 100; 3 in. pots $4.00 per 100. Rooted Cuttings, $1.00 per 100.

Rex Begonia, nice plants, 2 and 2½ in., $6.00 per 100.

Asparagus Plumosus, 2 in. $3.00 per 100.

GEO. M. EMMANS, Newton, N. J.

Mention The Florists' Exchange when writing.

Boston.

Picnic Echoes.

In addition to the contributors of prizes mentioned in the list of last week were the following: W. H. Elliott, R & J. Farquhar & Company, Holly-Castle Company, Thomas Roland, A. T. Stearns Lumber Company, and P. Feinstein.

The private gardeners had the greatest pull.

Secretary Craig, who was unavoidably absent, was greatly missed.

President Wheeler worked hard to make the affair enjoyable for everyone.

Many of the older members were missed, but as one of them told the writer "I could not get there in person, but was present in spirit."

The weather man favored the craft, for it was the only day this year in July that was comfortable and free from rain.

News Notes.

Edward McMulkin and family are spending the Summer at Scituate.

Frank T. White has gone to New Hampshire.

Herbert Tyler has resigned his position as salesman for the Montrose Greenhouses and will remove to Quebec where he has secured a position.

Samuel Beck who represents Jas. Tulis in the Park street market, and Frank Silverman have gone to Maine for a few weeks.

Robt. T. McGorum has rented a stall in the Park Street Flower Market and will be represented by J. S. Manter.

Henry M. Robinson & Company, owing to their increasing business, have had to take larger quarters for a store-house for their ferns, galax, etc.

Jos. White of Doyle's has started on a bicycle trip through Maine.

John Riley of Galvin's has gone to Saratoga.

J. A. Cartwright of the Waban Rose Conservatories has started on his vacation, and so have Harry Kelly of Newman's and W. J. F. Flynn of Robinson's.

H. M. Robinson and family have gone to Savoy for a month.

M. Barrett of McMulkin's is on the sick list.

Visitors this week included C. U. Fohn and James Cumming, Hartford, Conn.

J. W. DUNCAN.

CANNAS

Allemania, Gray, Henderson, M. Washington, Metallica, from 3 in. pots, fine stock, $4.00 per 100

Shellroad Greenhouses, GRANGE, P. O. BALTIMORE, MD.

Mention The Florists' Exchange when writing.

CELERY---CABBAGE

White Plume, Golden-Self, Golden Heart, fine plants, $1.50 per 1000.

Cabbage Plants—Flat Dutch and Drumhead $1.00 per 1000; 5000 for $4.00.

Cauliflower Plants, Early Snowball, $2.00 per 1000.

J. C. SCHMIDT CO., Bristol, Pa.

Mention The Florists' Exchange when writing.

REMEMBER

We are still Headquarters for

BAY TREES BOX TREES
...EVERGREENS...

Price Lists on application.

JULIUS ROEHRS CO.,
Exotic Nurseries, Rutherford, N. J.

Mention The Florists' Exchange when writing.

Phoenix Roebelenii

THE MOST GRACEFUL PALM OF ALL.

We have almost the entire stock of it in America.

SEEDLINGS, $5.00 per 100; $40.00 per 1000; $350.00 per 10,000. 4 in. pot plants, about 1 foot high; 12-15 leaves, $1.00 each; $80.00 per 100; $750.00 per 1000. 7 in. pot plants, about 2-2½ feet high, $5.00 each; $40.00 per 10; $350.00 per 100.

SPECIMEN PLANTS, $7.50-$10.00.

We also offer for sale—STOVE PLANTS, CALADIUMS, CROTONS and DRACAENAS in finest varieties at reasonable prices.

JOHN LEWIS CHILDS

FLORAL PARK - - - - - L. I., N. Y.

Mention The Florists' Exchange when writing.

NEPHROLEPIS SCOTTII

Small plants from the benches, $5.00 per 100; $50.00 per 1000. Plants large enough for 6 in. pots, $25.00 per 100. Plants large enough to go in 7 and 8 in. pots, $50.00 per 100.

Asparagus Plumosus Nanus, 2¼ in., fine plants, $3.00 per 100.

JOHN SCOTT,

Rutland Road and East 45th Street; BROOKLYN, N. Y.

Telephone 2890 Bedford.

Mention The Florists' Exchange when writing.

BOSTON FERNS

Taken from bench, $10.00 and $20.00 per 100.
5 and 6 inch **Pot Ferns**, from $3.00 per doz. up
Extra fine stock.
Geraniums, 3½ inch stock, $4.00 per 100.

BOCK, THE FLORIST,

2394 MASS AVENUE NORTH CAMBRIDGE, MASS.

Mention The Florists' Exchange when writing.

Decorative Plants

Latania Borbonica, 2½ in. pots, $3.00; 3 in.; $6.00; 4 in., $15.00 per 100. Large specimen plants from $2.00 to $5.00 each.

Kentia Belmoreana and Forsteriana, 2½ in. pots, $8.00; 3 in., $15.00; 5 in., $60.00 per 100; 6 in. $15.00 per doz.; 7 in. and upward, $1.75 to $35.00 each.

Areca Lutescens, 3 in. $10.00; 4 in. $20.00 per 100; 8 in., $1.00 each and upward.

Pandanus Utilis, 2 in. pots, $3.00; 4 in., $20.00 per 100.

Phœnix Reclinata, 5 in. pots, $35.00 per 100.

Phœnix Canariensis, fine specimen plants, from $3.00 to $35.00 each.

Araucaria Excelsa, 5 in. pots, $65.00 per 100.

Assorted Ferns, 2½ in. pots, $3.00 per 100.
Nephrolepis Compacta, 3 in. pots, $8.00; 4 in., $16.00 per 100.

Plants in Fine Condition.

JOHN BADER, Troy Hill, Allegheny, Pa.

Mention The Florists' Exchange when writing.

FERNS IN FLATS

Now ready for 2 1-2 inch pots. Flats contain over 100 clumps, which can be divided. Varieties include ASPIDIUM TSUSSEMENSE, CRYTOMIUM FALCATUM, PTERIS MAYII, WIMSETTI, NANA COMPACTA, ADIANTOIDES, SERRULATA, LASTREAS, etc.

PRICES, $2.00 PER FLAT; 20 OR MORE FLATS AT $1.75.
CASH WITH ORDER FROM UNKNOWN PARTIES.

McHUTCHISON & CO.

17 Murray Street - - - NEW YORK CITY

Mention The Florists' Exchange when writing.

FERNS.

POINSETTIAS, 2½ inch pots, $5.00 per 100.

ASPARAGUS PLUMOSUS, 4 in. pots, $10.00 per 100.

HUGH GRAHAM CO.,

Logan Nurseries, York Road and Louden Street, PHILADELPHIA, PA.

Mention The Florists' Exchange when writing.

FERNS

Are now in fine shape. A good variety and nice bushy stock, 2½ in., $3.00 per 100; $25.00 per 1000.
Kentia Belmoreana, 4 in., clean and bushy, 25c.
Cocos Weddeliana, 10c.
Dracaena Indivisa, 4 in., strong, 12c.
Mme. Salleroi Geraniums, 2 in., $2.00 per 100.
English Ivy, 4 in., fine stock, $10.00 per 100.

H. WESTON, HEMPSTEAD, N. Y.

FERNS

Dos. 100

	Doz.	100
SCOTTII, 2½ inch	$0.75	$5.00
BARROWSII, 2½ inch	1.25	8.00

THE CONARD & JONES CO.

WEST GROVE, PA.

Mention The Florists' Exchange when writing.

COCOS PALMS.

Strong 2½ inch at $1.50 per dozen. Write for lowest prices on **Kentias.**

Jas. F. Barclay R. I. GREENHOUSES Pawtucket, R. I.

Mention The Florists' Exchange when writing.

SMILAX PLANTS.

Strictly No. 1 plants; from 2 in. pots, $1.00 per 100; $9.00 per 1000. Seedlings from boxes; $4.00 per 1000.

R. KILBOURN, CLINTON, N. Y.

Mention The Florists' Exchange when writing.

ASPARAGUS

Sprengerii, extra strong, 3 in. pots, $5 per 100.
Extra Strong, 4 in. pots, $6 per 100.
Smilax, 2½ in. pots $2 per 100.
Cabbage Plants, Flat Dutch, Succession and Winningstadt, $1.50 per 1000. Cash with order.

S. G. BENJAMIN, Fishkill, N. Y.

Mention The Florists' Exchange when writing.

		Per 100
Asparagus Plumosus,	2¼ in. pots,	$2.50
" **Sprengerii,**	" " "	2.00
Smilax......................	" " "	1.50

J. S. BLOOM,

RIEGELSVILLE, PA.

Mention The Florists' Exchange when writing.

ASPARAGUS SPRENGERI

Large plants from 3 in. pots 5c. each.

Asparagus Plumosus Nanus, about 200 fine plants left, 3 in. pots 5c. each, to close them out.

Liberal count on both.

R. G. HANFORD, Norwalk, Conn.

Mention The Florists' Exchange when writing.

EMERSON C. McFADDEN

Wholesale Grower

Asparagus Plumosus Nanus, Etc.

Short Hills, N. J.

Tel. 28 A.

Mention The Florists' Exchange when writing.

NEPHROLEPIS

Whitmani, 2¼ in., $25.00 per 100.
Barrowsii, $10.00 per 100.

Henry H. Barrows & Son, Whitman, Mass.

FERNS

You Must Have

Only 5,000 left; speak quick.

Piersonii, 5 in., 20c.; 4 in., 15c.; 3 in., 10c.

Scotti, 5 in., 20c.; 4 in., 15c.; 3 in., 10c.

Bostons, 3 in., ready to shift, 10c.

Asparagus Plumosus Nanus, 3½ in. 6c; 2½ in., $2.50 per 100.

Asparagus Sprengerii, 3½ in., 6c.

20,000 Field Carnations.

Write me. Cash please.

BENJAMIN CONNELL, West Grove, Pa.

Mention The Florists' Exchange when writing.

FERN SEEDLINGS

FROM FLATS.

The first crop is now ready for potting, including the following varieties: **Pteris Cretica Cristata, Pteris Cretica Albo-Lineata, Pteris Adiantoides, Pteris Argyraea, Pteris Mayii, Cyrtomium Falcatum, Aspidium Tsussemense, Onychium Japonica, Doodia Aspera.** My selection, $1.00 per 100; $8.50 per 1000. If by mail, add 10c. per 100 for postage.

Mixed Ferns for dishes, 2½ in., $3.00 per 100; $25.00 per 1000; 250 at 1000 rate; 3 in., $6.00 per 100.

Adiantum Cuneatum, 3 in., $6.00 per 100.

FRANK N. ESKESEN, MADISON, N. J.

Mention The Florists' Exchange when writing.

Adiantum Cuneatum

From 2½ in. pots ready to shift, per 100 $4.00; per 1000, $35.00.

Asparagus Plumosus Nanus

true kind, from 2½ in. pots, per 100, $3.00; per 1000, $25.00.

Ferns in Flats

Each flat contains about 110 divisible clumps, standard varieties as: Aspidium Tsussemense, Cyrtomium Falcatum, Lastraea Aristata Variegata, Pteris Adiantoides Cretica Albolineata, Gilberti, Mayi, Magnifica, Serrulata, Serr. Crist., Nana Compacta, Wimsetti, Adiantum Cuneatum, per flat, $2.00; per 12 flats, buyers' selection, $22.00; my own selection, $20.00. For larger quantities ask special quotation.

O. V. ZANGEN

Seedsman HOBOKEN, N. J.

Mention the Florists' Exchange when writing.

FERNS OUR SPECIALTY

CIBOTIUM SCHIEDEI

We have a large stock of this beautiful tree fern in 3 in. pots, ready for a shift, at $35.00 per 100. 25 plants at 100 rate.

FERN SEEDLINGS FROM FLATS

Eight to ten best market varieties at $1.00 per 100, or $8.50 per 1000. If by mail add 10c. for each hundred plants.

ASSORTED FERNS FOR DISHES

From 2½ in. pots. The best and hardiest varieties in market at $3.00 per 100, or $25.00 per 1000. 250 plants at 1000 rate.

Adiantum Cuneatum, 2½ in. pots, $3.50 per 100, $30.00 per 1000.

FERN SPORES

Gathered from our own stock. 35c. per trade package, $4.00 per doz. packages.

Gardenia Vietchii from 2½ in. pots, $7.50 per 100, $70.00 per 1000; 400 at 1000 rate.

ANDERSON & CHRISTENSEN,

SHORT HILLS, N. J.

Mention The Florists' Exchange when writing.

NEPHROLEPIS WHITMANI

is the fern to grow.

Having ordered a large quantity I can fill your orders at short notice. Price, $25.00 per 100; $200.00 per 1000.

S. S. SKIDELSKY,

824 No. 24 St., Philadelphia, Pa.

Mention The Florists' Exchange when writing.

ROBERT CRAIG & CO.

ROSES, PALMS, CROTONS

CARNATIONS and Novelties in DECORATIVE PLANTS

Market and 49th Sts. PHILADELPHIA, PA.

Mention The Florists' Exchange when writing.

ORCHIDS

Largest Importers, Exporters, Growers and Hybridists in the world.

Sander, St. Albans, England

and

235 Broadway, Room 1, New York City

Mention The Florists' Exchange when writing.

ORCHIDS

Arrived in superb condition **Cattleya Dowiana, C. Gigas, C. Mossiae, C. Percivaliana, C. Speciosissima, C. Eldorado, C. Superba, C. Labiata, C. Leopoldii** and many more.

Write for Prices.

LAGER & HURRELL, Summit, N. J.

Growers and Importers

Mention The Florists' Exchange when writing.

STUDER OFFERS

Latania Borbonica, Phoenix Canariensis, from 6 in. pots, 2½ feet tall, $5.00 per doz. **Latania**, from 5 in. pots, 2 foot size and **Kentia Belmoreana**, 20 in. tall, also **Chamærops Excelsa**, from 5 in. pots, $3.50 per doz. **Boston Ferns**, from 4 in. pots, $3.00 per doz.; all these fine plants ready for a shift. Red, Pink and White **Geraniums**, 4 in. pots, in bud and bloom $4.00 per 100. **Scarlet Sage**, 3 in., $3.00 per 100. Pot grown, best monthly hybrid, Moss and Climbing **Roses**, 4-5-6 in. pots, $1.00, $2.00 and $3.00 per doz. according to size.

CASH PLEASE.

N. STUDER, Anacostia, D. C.

Mention The Florists' Exchange when writing.

VICTORY

Strong healthy field grown plants, now ready, $15.00 per 100; $125.00 per 1000; 250 at 1000 rates. A discount for cash with order. GUTTMAN & WEBBER, 43 West 28th St., N. Y

CARNATIONS

	1st size per 100	2d size per 100
Glendale	$12.00	—
Victory	12.00	—
Robt. Craig	12.00	—
Enchantress	8.00	—
Lady Bountiful	—	$6.00
Belle	8.00	6.00
White Lawson	—	7.00
Boston Market	7.00	5.00
White Cloud	7.00	—

FIELD PLANTS

	1st size per 100	2d size per 100
Nelson Fisher	—	$6.00
Prosperity	6.00	—
Flamingo	8.00	6.00
Cardinal	—	6.00
Crane	—	5.00
Estelle	2d size $5.00;	3d size $3.50

CHRYSANTHEMUMS--Surplus Stock

250 **Jerome Jones,** 150 **Yellow Jones,** 350 **Alice Byron,** 600 **Yellow Eaton,** 600 **Timothy Eaton,** 300 **Appleton,** 200 **Marie Liger,** 300 **White Bonnaffon,** 300 **Golden Wedding,** 250 **Robinson,** 250 **Mme. Douillet,** 200 **V. Morel,** 500 **Wm. Duckham,** 250 **Dr. Enguehard,** 125 **Paul Sahut.** The above in rooted cuttings at $1.25 per 100.

250, 3 in. **Dr. Enguehard,** 200, 3 in. **Ben Wells,** 300, 2 in. **Monrovia,** 150, 2 in. **Yellow Eaton,** 75, 2 in. **T. Eaton,** 125, 2 in. **Golden Wedding,** 25, 2 in. **Et. Bonnefond,** at $2.50 per 100.

400, 4 in. **Maids,** 250, 4 in. **Brides** at $7.00 per 100. 500, 2½ in. **Gates,** 300, 2½ in. **Brides,** 150, 2½ in. **Perle,** at $3.50 per 100.

Rex Begonia 4 in. 12c. 5 in. 20c. **Vinca Variegata** 3 in. $6.00 per 100. **Richmond Roses** 2 in. $5.00. 3 in. $8.00 per 100. **Asparagus Plumosus** 2 in. $2.00 per 100 **Cash or C. O. D.**

W. J. & M. S. VESEY, Fort Wayne, Ind.

Mention The Florists' Exchange when writing.

Field Grown Carnations

Fine Sturdy Plants
Grown on Clay Soil

PINK LAWSON, QUEEN LOUISE, FLORA HILL, BOSTON MARKET, FAIRMAID

$5.00 per 100; $45.00 per 1000.

SPEAK QUICK; *before they are all gone.*

The Calla Cut Flower Co., Calla, Ohio.

Mention The Florists' Exchange when writing.

100,000 FIELD GROWN CARNATION PLANTS

30,000 LAWSON

	Per 100
LAWSON	$5.00
ENCHANTRESS	7.00
QUEEN LOUISE	5.00
MAY NAYLOR (White)	5.00
BRADT	5.00
PROSPERITY	4.00

EXTRA SELECTED DEFIANCE MIGNONETTE SEED, $1.00 PER TRADE PACKET.

EDWARD J. TAYLOR, Southport, Conn.

Mention The Florists' Exchange when writing.

ANNOUNCEMENT

ANSWERING MANY ENQUIRIES

My New (Orange Scarlet) Carnation BEACON

will be DISSEMINATED jointly by

THE COTTAGE GARDENS CO., QUEENS, N. Y. AND PETER FISHER, ELLIS, MASS.

SEASON OF 1906-7

PRICES.

Per	100	$12.00	50 at 200 rate
"	1,000	100.00	250 at 1000 rate
"	2,500	95.00	per 1000
"	5,000	90.00	"
"	10,000	80.00	"

Orders of 20,000 (or more) when cash accompanies, or is sent prior to shipments, $75.00 per 1000.

No order of more than 5,000 accepted, for shipment at one time.

Orders will be RECEIVED NOW and BOOKED strictly in ROTATION.

Send for descriptive circular and mention the Florists' Exchange.

PETER FISHER, Ellis, Mass.

Mention The Florists' Exchange when writing.

Field Grown CARNATIONS

6000 **White Lawson** .... $6.00 per 100.
5000 **Enchantress** 5000 **Queen Louise**
1000 **Bountiful** 500 **The Belle**
5000 **Pink Lawson** 300 **Crisis**
1000 **Roosevelt** 200 **Richmond Gem**
2000 **Harlowarden** 500 **Flamingo**
1000 **Estelle** 200 **F. Burki**
100 **Eclipse.**

$5.00 per 100; $45.00 per 1000.
Limestone land, no stem rot.

CASH WITH ORDER.

Wells Fargo, American, Adams, U. S. Express

W. SABRANSKY, KENTON, O.

Mention The Florists' Exchange when writing.

ABUNDANCE

Healthy, stocky, field grown plants. First size, $12.00 per 100; $100.00 per 1000. Second size, $10.00 per 100; $75.00 per 1000; 250 at a 1000 rates. Delivery 15th of August.

CASH WITH ORDER.

Abundance Carnation is an easy lifter, takes hold quickly, and makes good-sized stems on first crop.

Freesia Purity bulbs all sold out clean.

RUDOLPH FISCHER, Great Neck, L.I. N.Y.

Mention The Florists' Exchange when writing.

CARNATIONS

Excellent Field Grown

The Queen	$8.00	per 100
Crimson Glow, (new)	12.00	" 1'0
Lieut. Peary, medium size	8.00	" 100

Cash or references with order.

DAILLEDOUZE BROTHERS

Flatbush, Brooklyn, N. Y.

Mention The Florists' Exchange when writing.

50,000 Large, Healthy, Bushy Carnation Plants

Pink Lawson, Enchantress, Adonis, Flamingo, Crusader, Mrs. Patten, Neptune, Queen Louise, Roosevelt, Harry Fenn, Genevieve Lord, White Cloud, Prosperity, Ad. Cervera, Boston Market, Joost, Flora Hill, Ethel Crocker.

$4.00 per 100.

FIANCEE 10c.; OUTOROON, No. 1—No. 2; RED LAWSON, LADY BOUNTIFUL, 8c.
ROBERT CRAIG Carnation, 12c.
ASPARAGUS PLUMOSUS, strong 2 1-2 in. 3c; 4in.8c.
" SPRENGERI, 2 1-2 in. 2c.
SMILAX, 2 1-2 in. 2c.
PARSLEY PLANTS, $1.00 per 100.
Cash Please.

F. B. RINE, Lewisburg, Pa.

Mention The Florists' Exchange when writing.

CARNATIONS

PLANTS FROM FIELD.

Fair Maid, Queen, Mrs. Patten, Harlowarden, $5.00 per 100; $45.00 per 1000. Strong and healthy.

Satisfaction guaranteed. Cash with Order.

HUGH CHESNEY, Farmington, Ct.

Mention The Florists' Exchange when writing.

CARNATIONS

Rooted Cuttings

All the new varieties of 1906. All the standard varieties worth growing.

WM. SWAYNE, Box 226, Kennett Square Pa.

Mention The Florists' Exchange when writing.

CARNATIONS

SMITH & GANNETT,

GENEVA, N. Y.

Mention The Florists' Exchange when writing.

CARNATIONS

F. DORNER & SONS CO.
LA FAYETTE, IND.

CARNATIONS

Hardy double, early flowering, extra mixed, per oz., $2.50. **Wallflowers,** double dwarf, and single, mixed, extra trade packet, 25c. **Pansy,** giant fancy, **Woodhaven brand,** per oz., $10.00. Fine mixed for florists, per oz., $5.00. Good mixed, per oz., $2.00. **Daisy,** Snowball, Longfellow, Giant mixed, red, pink, white, quilled red, etc. **Lettuce,** la sans Rivale, etc.

BEAULIEU, WOODHAVEN, N. Y.

Mention The Florists' Exchange when writing.

CARNATIONS

FINE FIELD GROWN PLANTS
CORRESPONDENCE SOLICITED

A. B. DAVIS & SON, Inc., Purcellville Va.

Mention The Florists' Exchange when writing.

CARNATIONS

Field-grown plants; ready now. **Prosperity** and **Genevieve Lord,** $6.00 per 100.

THE H. WEBER & SONS CO.,
OAKLAND, MD.

Mention The Florists' Exchange when writing.

"MRS. OMWAKE"

SPORT OF ENCHANTRESS

$10.00 per 100. Cash.

HENRY EICHHOLZ, Waynesboro, Pa.

ENCHANTRESS

Field-grown, ready August 15, $6.00 per 100; $50.00 per 1000.

WHITE BROTHERS, Gasport, N. Y.

Mention The Florists' Exchange when writing.

Jensen & Dekema

CARNATION SPECIALISTS

674 W. Foster Ave., CHICAGO.

S. J. GODDARD

Framingham, Mass.

Rooted Carnation Cuttings a Specialty

Correspondence Solicited.

CLASSIFIED ADVERTISEMENTS

CASH WITH ORDER.

The columns under this heading are reserved for advertisements of Stock for Sale, Stock Wanted, Help Wanted, Situations Wanted or other Wants; also of Greenhouse, Land, Second-Hand Materials, etc., For Sale or Rent.

Our charge is 10 cts. per line (7 words to the line), set solid, without display. No advt. accepted for less than thirty cents.

Display advertisements in these columns, 15 cents per line; count 12 lines agate to the inch.

[If replies to Help Wanted, Situation Wanted, or other advertisements are to be addressed care of this office, advertisers add 10 cents to cover expense of forwarding.]

Copy must reach New York office 12 o'clock Wednesday to secure insertion in issue of following Saturday.

Advertisers in the Western States desiring to advertise under initials, may save time by having their answer directed care our Chicago office at 127 E. Berwyn Ave.

SITUATIONS WANTED

SITUATION WANTED—Young man, 4 years' experience, wishes position in greenhouses or store. R. Richter, 724 10th Avenue, New York City.

SITUATION WANTED—As foreman of a rose establishment. References, stating character, intelligence and ability given on application. Address, M. P., care The Florists' Exchange.

SITUATION WANTED—Good grower of commercial stock wants position, wholesale or retail. Long experience in charge; first-class references. N. E. preferred. Address, M. Q., care The Florists' Exchange.

SITUATION WANTED—As assistant gardener on private place by young Scotsman; single, honest and sober. Good references if desired. Please state wages with board in first letter. Address, M. T., care The Florists' Exchange.

SITUATION WANTED—Gardener, Scotch, 28 years of age, unmarried, life experience on other side, twelve months in this country as greenhouse man on private place, wishes situation as second gardener on private place. Disengaged end of August. Address, M. L., care The Florists' Exchange.

SITUATION WANTED—As working foreman on private or commercial place. 16 years' experience here and abroad in every line of the trade. German, married, small family. Please state particulars in first letter. Open for engagement September 1st. J. Hoffman, Chichester, Ulster County, New York.

HELP WANTED

WANTED—A thoroughly competent man to take charge of a section of Beauties. Apply Frank Dolan, care of John Young Company, Bedford Station, New York.

WANTED—August 20, young man with good experience, for greenhouses on large private place. Apply to Carl Liedreth, Narberth, Pa.

WANTED—A good salesman to superintend an exhibit in the Florist Convention at Dayton. Reply to M. O., care The Florists' Exchange.

WANTED—An experienced gardener; both inside and outside work. Apply Peter Denyse, 79th street and Sixth avenue, Brooklyn, N. Y.

WANTED—Gardener for New York store; one who understands about plants and outdoor work. Address, M. W., care The Florists' Exchange.

WANTED—An assistant for greenhouse on private place. Please state age and experience in first letter. Address, T. B., care The Florists' Exchange.

WANTED—Good man for general greenhouse work. Good wages and steady position to the right man. Address, M. V., care The Florists' Exchange.

WANTED—Man for general greenhouse work. Asparagus Plumosus a specialty. Wages, $10.00 per week. Apply to Emerson C. McFadden, Short Hills, N. J.

WANTED—At once, an assistant, competent to handle wholesale and retail business in owner's absence. $30.00 per month, board and room. Address, Flora T. Howell, Pine Bush, N. Y.

WANTED—Married man for rose section $15.00 per week. Single man on chrysanthemums, $14.00 per week. Please state age, experience and send references. Address, M. G., care The Florists' Exchange.

WANTED—A first-class man for retail florist in Chicago; no greenhouse work. Must be a good salesman and designer. State wages, references. Address, M. D., care The Florists' Exchange.

WANTED—Thoroughly first-class experienced rose and carnation growers. Apply stating age, married or single, references and wages expected. None but first-class men wanted. Lake View Rose Gardens, Jamestown, N. Y.

WANTED—A young man, single, with experience in roses, carnations, and general greenhouse stock; one with European experience preferred. Fair wages to right party. Address, stating nationality, age, and with copy of references. M. K., care The Florists' Exchange.

HELP WANTED

WANTED—Young man as seedsman to solicit orders of market gardeners in the vicinity of Philadelphia and New York. Write stating experience and salary expected. Correspondence strictly confidential. Address, L. H., care The Florists' Exchange.

WANTED—Good all-around man for jobbing, garden work and make himself useful in florists store. Steady work all the year round to right man. Young men preferred. References required. Apply at once. Address, M. F., care The Florists' Exchange.

WANTED—An energetic young man to assist in landscape work; fair knowledge of stock, trimming, etc. essential. Dutch or German preferred. State wages expected with references. A. Van Leeuwen, Jr., Worcester, Mass.

WANTED

At once by a large New York seed house, one or two good counter hands. Apply giving full particulars and stating salary wanted to **P. O. Box 1697, NEW York City.**

Mention The Florists' Exchange when writing.

MISCELLANEOUS WANTS

WANTED TO BUY—Greenhouses to be taken down. State full particulars of same when writing. Address, F. W., care The Florists' Exchange.

WANTED—8000 choice carnation plants. Write us promptly, giving varieties and lowest spot cash prices. Reeds Lake Floral Company, Michigan Trust Blk., Grand Rapids, Mich.

WANTED TO RENT—A range of greenhouses, about 10,000 feet. Must be of modern construction and in good repair, with dwelling, good water and soil supply. Address, M. L., care The Florists' Exchange.

PARTNERS with capital and experience, with first-class references, for greenhouse and florist store in central states. Fine opening for right parties. Present investment, $35,000. Year's business, $23,000. Address, M. U., care The Florists' Exchange.

SHADE TREES Wanted; nursery grown. Also evergreens and hardy shrubs. Any size, kind, quantity. Describe fully and name lowest prices delivered New York. Address, M. R., care The Florists' Exchange.

TO EXCHANGE—1200 to 1500 Ethel Croker carnation plants, field grown, now ready to plant in; fine stocky plants. For some good red or white field grown plants or will sell for $4.00 per 100. Chas. L. Baum, 317 West Clinch Street, Knoxville, Tenn.

WANTED TO BUY OR LEASE—With privilege of purchase 2 to 5 years, a range of commercial greenhouses, with 2 to 10 acres of land attached, if possible, within one hour of New York City. State terms. Strictly, mutually confidential. Address, M. N., care The Florists' Exchange.

FOR SALE OR RENT

FOR SALE—One horizontal boiler; 40 horse power; all complete; good condition; cheap. Alex. B. Garden, Anacostia, D. C.

FOR SALE—Two greenhouses to be taken down and removed. Nearly new. For particulars address, W. C. Merritt, Washingtonville, N. Y.

FOR SALE—Three greenhouses of about 6,000 feet of glass. Good established retail business, or would rent for term of years. George Main, Gloversville, New York.

FOR SALE—Greenhouse, 20 x 40 feet, including pipes and boiler, in fine condition. Price low to quick buyer. Address, Mrs. W. T. Duryea, Amityville, L. I.

FOR SALE or will rent to a responsible party, a fine greenhouse property. 13,000 feet of glass. Fine residence. Address, Silas C. Howell, Lock Box 14, Pine Bush, New York.

TO LEASE—Two greenhouses, a good boiler, and everything for ready use. Situated in a good locality. Terms reasonable. Single man preferred. Mrs. M. Palumbo, Greenleaf Avenue, West New Brighton, S. I.

FOR RENT—Small greenhouse and florist business in prosperous running condition. Southern Connecticut. Full particulars and reason for renting to any one interested. Address, M. R., care The Florists' Exchange.

FOR SALE—A fine established nursery business with a constituency reaching from the Atlantic to the Pacific, and from Manitoba to the Gulf. Old age of proprietor the only reason for sale. C. S. Harrison, York, Neb.

DESIRABLE greenhouse plant of three houses, 24x200 feet; propagating house, 100 feet; potting shed, stable and dwelling. Steam heat, city water. Highland, opposite Poughkeepsie. Joseph Wood, Spring Valley, New York.

TO LEASE—For a term of years a small commercial greenhouse plant, about 4,000 feet of glass, well stocked with good varieties of chrysanthemums, and heated with Furman Hot Water Sectional Boiler. Five minutes from station, and 25 minutes from New York City market. For further particulars address, M. H., care The Florists' Exchange.

FOR SALE OR RENT

TO LET—greenhouse establishment in the city of Poughkeepsie, N. Y. 8000 feet of glass, city water, plenty of soil, fine location. For particulars, come and see, or write to James Coleman, 212 Mansion street, Poughkeepsie, N. Y.

FOR SALE OR RENT—Two places, Secaucus and West Hoboken, two or three miles from New York. Good wholesale business; nice place; established since 1856; fifteen greenhouses stocked; heated with Hitchings boilers; house, stable and as much property as desired. Going to retire. For particulars address, Weigand Brothers, West Hoboken, N. J.

FOR SALE—Owing to failing health, I will sell my florist establishment, beautifully situated between Larchmont Manor and Mamaroneck, Westchester Co., New York, near railroad station; trolley lines within one minute walk. First class opportunity for the right man. Plenty of landscape and jobbing work. The place contains four acres, 2 greenhouses, 104 feet long and lots of sash; well stocked with trees and shrubs, etc.; horse, wagon and tools. Address, Box 44, Larchmont, New York.

To lease for a term of years, my establishment on Greene Avenue, consisting of about 7,000 feet of glass, office and salesroom. Stable and wagon shed. Horse and wagons. Place well stocked and heated with hot water. Every convenience, all in good condition. A good business in the best location in the city. Established for 40 years. Wishing to retire from business. This is a good opportunity for the right man. Come and see it. Richard Shannon, 341-349 Greene Avenue, Brooklyn, New York.

Valuable Greenhouses to Lease.

The houses formerly owned by the late F. A. Blake, of Rochdale, Mass., will be leased on easy terms to responsible party. They consist of seven houses having floor area of 6800 sq. ft., with boiler house, barn and two to three acres of good land. The stock, consisting of 2600 choice carnations in the field, and a large and select variety of other plants, will be sold cheap for cash to lessee. Situated nine miles from Worcester and fifty-three miles from Boston. Address,

MRS. F. A. BLAKE, ROCHDALE, MASS.

Mention The Florists' Exchange when writing.

STOCK FOR SALE

JERUSALEM CHERRIES, 2 1-2-in. pots only, $3 per 100. Cash please. A. Relyea & Son, Poughkeepsie, New York.

Quercus Alba, Q. Coccinea and Q. Rubra, $1.50 per bu. Fraxinus Americana, 14c. lb. Address, Box 893, Biltmore, N. C.

PEONY FESTIVA MAXIMA, and other best sorts in strong plants, 2 yr. old. Catalogue free. A. Dessert, Peony Specialist, Chenonceaux, France.

SEEDS, pansy, new crop, $1.00 per packet; $4.00 per oz.; $12.00 per 1-4 lb. Pansy plants, $4.00 per 1,000. Cash. B. Soltau, 199 Grant avenue, Jersey City, N. J.

5000 2 1-4 in. Asparagus Sprengerii, good strong plants, ready to shift, $1.75 per 100. Reeds Lake Floral Company, Michigan Trust Blk., Grand Rapids, Mich.

PRIMULA, Chinese, finest fringed, mixed; Obconica Grandiflora, fringed, Alba Rosea, 2 in. 2c.; cash. Shippensburg Floral Company, Shippensburg, Pa.

BABY RAMBLER ROSES, H. P. and Rambler roses, field grown, 2 year stock, for sale cheap. Write for list. Schaufelberger & Hill, Penfield, New York.

20,000 Retinispora plumosa aurea, 4 to 6 inches, transplanted. Also 4,000 Retinispora Squarrosa Veitchii, 6 inches, transplanted. Address, Rhode Island Nurseries, Newport, R. I.

CARNATIONS, first-class, field grown plants. Buchantress, Lawson, Queen, $6.00 per 100; $50.00 per 1000. Cash with order please. Mrs. P. F. Conley, Princeton Avenue, & Updike Street, Providence, R. I.

STOCK FOR SALE—Brides, Maids and American Beauties, in 4 in. pots; best of plants. Also 1 year old Asparagus. All at low bottom prices. Small or large orders. Madison Rose Company, Madison, N. J.

JARDINIERE FERNS, seedlings, good, strong, healthy stock, in variety only. Now ready for potting. Price, $1.50 per 100 by mail; $10.00 per 1000, F. O. B. Exp. B. Soltau, 199 Grant avenue, Jersey City, N. J.

BABY RAMBLER roses, fine dormant stock, $25 per 100. 2 1-2 inch pot plants, extra well rooted $7 per 100, $65 per 1000. Orders booked for delivery now or any time up to late Spring. Samples free. Brown Brothers Co., Rochester, N. Y.

2500 BRIDESMAID plants, 2000 Brides, 1500 American Beauties, 1000 Meteors, all good, fine plants in 4 in. pots. Packed and shipped at express office. Maids, Brides and Meteors, 5c. each. American Beauties, 12c. each. Louis M. Noe, Madison, N. J.

STOCK FOR SALE

YUCCA FILAMENTOSA, $1.00 lb.; Amorpha fruticosa, 25c. lb.; Ampelopsis quinquefolia, 75c. lb.; Azalea arborescens, $2.00 lb.; Corylus rostrata, 50c. lb.; Crataegus crus-galli, 25c. lb.; Juglans cineren, $1.00 bu.; Juglans nigra, $1.00 bu.; Cornus florida, 20c. lb. F. M. Crayton, Box 893, Biltmore, N. C.

GIANT PANSY.—Mme. Perret, genuine gold medal, Parisian Bugnot, Cassier, Giant Trimardeau, Excelsior, Coquette de Poriesy, Giant Beaconsfield, improved, etc. Forget-me-not, Victoria, Dwarf blue Bellis Perennis, Mignonette, giant red forcing, Hardy Larkspur, white, blue and mixed. Send for prices. Beaulieu, Pansy Specialist, Woodhaven, N. Y.

FOR SALE

FOR SALE—Cheap, all sizes greenhouse glass, new stock. Address, Glass, care The Florists' Exchange.

FOR SALE—One No. 6 Weathered Boiler in good condition, price $35.00. J. H. Flesser, 415 Summit Avenue, West Hoboken, N. J.

FOR SALE—1500 feet new 2 in. iron pipe, 8cts. ft. Lot of glass 16x18, A. double, all new. P. O. Box 120, Chatham, N. J.

FOR SALE—12 Hitchings hot water expansion tanks for 3 1-2 in. pipe, in good condition, cleaned, ready to set up. 1-3 price of new. Also horse lawn mower, easy running, $20.00. Address, K. D., care The Florists' Exchange.

FOR SALE—Stover fifty foot Steel Tower and Tank in use a short time. Good as new; price reasonable. Write for particulars. Wm. C. De Witt, R. F. D. No. 1, Phillipsburg, N. J.

10,000 5 in. pots, as good as new, cost $12.00 per 1000; will sell for $9.00 per 1000. Cash with all orders please. Dean & Parse, 46 to 52 Ashwood Avenue, Summit, New Jersey.

BOILERS, BOILERS, BOILERS.

SEVERAL good second hand boilers on hand, also new No. 16 Hitchings at reduced cost. Write for list. Wm. H. Lutton, West Side Avenue Station, C. R. R. of N. J., Jersey City, N. J.

FOR SALE

Greenhouse Material milled from Gulf Cypress, to any detail furnished, or our own patterns as desired, cut and spliced ready for erection. Estimates for complete constructions furnished.

V. E. REICH, Brooklyn, N. Y.

1429-1437 Metropolitan Ave.

Mention The Florists' Exchange when writing.

FOR SALE

PUMPS Rider-Ericsson. Second-hand, from $40.00 up; all repairs; other makes; new; cheap.

BOILERS One second-hand tubular hot water boiler 3 ft in diameter 12 ft. long. Price $35.00. One No. 16 Hitchings as good as new, $60.00.

PIPE Good serviceable second-hand, with Threads; 2-in., 7 cts.; 1½-in., 4½ cts.; 1¼-in., 4 cts.; 1-in., 3 cts.; 3½ in., 10 cts.; 3 in., 14 cts.; 4 in., 19 cts. New 2-in. Standard, full lengths, with couplings, 8¼ cts. ft. Old and new fittings and valves. Old 4 inch cast iron 15c per foot.

STOCKS and DIES New Econ my, best made No. 1 Threads, ¼-in., ¾-in. 1-in. pipe, $3.00. No. 2 Threads, 1¼-in., 1½-in. 2-in. pipe, $4.00.

PIPE CUTTERS New Saunders Pattern. No. 1 cuts ⅛-in.-1-in. pipe, $1.00. No. 2 cuts 1-in.-2-in. pipe, $1.30.

STILLSON WRENCHES New, 18-in., grips ¼-in.-2-in. pipe, $1.65; 24-in. grips ¼-in.-2½ in. pipe, $2.40; 36-in., grips ½-in.-3½-in. pipe, $4.75.

PIPE VISES New, No. 1 Hinged, grips ⅛-in.-2 in. pipe, $2.00.

GARDEN HOSE New, 50 ft. lengths. ¾-in., guaranteed 100-lbs. pressure, 7½ cts. per ft.; ¾-in. not guaranteed, 4¾ cts. per ft., 25 ft. lengths, ½c. per ft. more.

HOT-BED SASH New, Cypress, 3-ft. x6 ft., from 75 cts. up; glazed, complete, from $1.90 up. Second-hand, in good condition, all glass in, $1.00 each.

GLASS New American 10x12 single $1.75 per box; 12x12 single $1.90 per box; 10x12, 12x12, 10x16 double, $2.40 per box; 12x14, 12x20, 14x14, double, $2.60 per box; 16x16, 16x18, $3.00 per box; 16x24 double $3.20 per box. Second hand glass, 8 x 10, 9 x 12, double, $1.50 per box; 10x12 double at $1.75 per box.

Old material, ridge, plates, gutters, bars, etc.

Get our prices on New Gulf Cypress Building Material, Ventilating Apparatus, Oil, White Lead, Putty, Paint, Points, etc.

METROPOLITAN MATERIAL CO.

1398-1408 Metropolitan Avenue, BROOKLYN, N.Y

Mention The Florists' Exchange when writing.

Thirty cents is the minimum charge for advertisements on this page.

New York.

The Week's News.

As the date of the Dayton convention draws nearer, it is safe to predict that a representative delegation will leave here for the convention city. In view of the fact that the train by which the conventionites will travel is limited as to the number of coaches, it will be well for all intending going to make speedy application for tickets, both railroad and sleeping car, so that no disappointment may occur. Full information regarding the trip has been distributed in circulars issued by the transportation committee of the Florists' Club, composed of Messrs. Walter F. Sheridan, Frank H. Traendly and John B. Nugent, Jr., all of Twenty-eighth street, either of whom will answer any inquiries in the meantime, and to whom applications for tickets, etc., should be sent.

The recent organization of the Philadelphia wholesale florists, and its reported satisfactory workings, is being discussed by the New York brethren. Probably similar action may be taken "in the street," at no distant date. It would seem there is need of such co-operation.

The news having come East that Phil. J. Hauswirth of Chicago was likely to be a candidate for the office of secretary of the S. A. F., the present incumbent according to reports retiring, much satisfaction is expressed thereanent. It is generally believed that Mr. Hauswirth would prove a most efficient and capable officer.

As stated in our market report this week, inactivity prevails in Twenty-eighth street. John I. Raynor, who has been in the business for many years, gives it as his opinion that never before in his experience has trade been so dull at this season of the year. A noticeable fact in this usually busy mart, is the devotion to duty of the wholesalers. While one or more of the assistants are gone on their annual vacation, the heads of the various houses, with but few exceptions, stick close to their desks during these dull dog days. Some of them are taking a respite by going home early, or staying with their families one or two days a week when business is expected to be least exciting.

Horace E. Froment will go on his vacation after all his boys have had their outing, probably this month.

There are so many assistants in the wholesale houses these times that it is impossible to keep tab on all their whereabouts during vacation time. It can safely be said that all who are away are enjoying themselves, and that those who have returned feel fully refreshed and ready for the rush when it comes.

Owing to lack of time we were unable to discover how many wholesaler babies had had birthdays at this particular time, but as several of these "Amoosin' little Kusses," the male portion of whom are looked upon as likely to succeed to the business of their progenitors, "advented" on this terrestrial ball about a year ago, the natural sequence is that this is just about the time when they would have a birthday. We shall endeavor to dig up a list of these darlings, and hope to lay it before our readers in a future issue.

James McManus, the orchid man, has now got fully rested from his recent trip West. Jimmy went to Denver, Col., and other points, and participated in the Elks' parade in the city named. The "Best People on Earth," of whom Mr. McManus is one, were pelted with snowballs by the enthusiastic citizens in the morning, but that little discomfort was compensated for by the high balls dispensed as night drew on. Mr. McManus speaks enthusiastically of his 12 days' journey, and says if the S. A. F. should ever decide to hold its convention in Denver, it will provide its members with an educational treat of no mean order.

Owing to a change in the help arrangements at the establishment of the Hinode Florist Company, Whitestone, L. I., James B. Kidd, who has been superintendent there for some time, has left that concern. He is anxious to return to his first love, "the seed business," and is now open for an engagement in that branch. Mr. Kidd has had many years experience, both behind the counter and on the road, and is a capable seedsman.

A. L. Young & Company, 54 West Twenty-eighth street, are receiving quantities of cut sprays of Clethra alnifolia, a native shrub; the white, fragrant flowers come in handy in funeral work.

S. S. Butterfield of the staff of this paper has, with his family, gone on a short vacation to Jamestown, N. Y.

John Nash of Moore, Hentz & Nash, wholesalers, will leave on his vacation next week, on the return of John Kral, his assistant. The latter, in company with the youngest son of Mr. Nash, has been enjoying himself making short trips on the Sound in his yacht.

John Birnie was in town the other day. He is state vice-president of the S. A. F. for New Jersey, but fears he will be unable to be present at the Dayton convention, where he would have liked to say something on the propagation of geraniums.

Wm. H. Gunther, wholesaler, is spending a few days at Sea Girt.

A visitor in the wholesale district this week was C. P. Critchell of Cincinnati, O. He was accompanied by his wife. It is understood that Mr. Critchell picked up many valuable pointers which he can turn to profitable account in his business in the Western city.

Over in Brooklyn business is very quiet, and the wholesale dealers are taking advantage of that condition to rest up a little. George H. Crawbuck has gone with his family to East Quogue, L. I., his partner, F. Hicks, having returned from his vacation. George H. Blake, of Bonnet & Blake, is at Rochester, N. Y., combining business with pleasure. This firm expects soon to receive consignments of those up-state asters, which gave so much satisfaction last year. William H. Kuebler intends spending his vacation in Maine.

A. T. Boddington, seedsman, 334 West Fourteenth street, has just received a large shipment of Oncidium varicosum Rogersii in splendid condition.

A Brooklyn court has decided that an express company is legally bound to heed the injunction, "This Side Up—Handle With Care!" when it is placed by the shippers on a box or package. Of course shippers are expected to place the label only on one side of the box.

Frank Hamilton has started in business on his own account as landscape gardener, with an office at 55 Liberty street, the one occupied by the late Joseph Forsyth Johnson.

Benjamin F. Dorrance, Dorranceton, Pa., was also a visitor.

St. Louis.

Club Picnic.

The St. Louis Florists' Club picnic, held last Thursday, was a great success in every way, especially so in the matter of attendance. The florists with their families began to arrive early at Ramona Park, and by the time the heavy rain storm came up, there were fully two hundred people on the grounds. The storm lasted about an hour, when the sun appeared and dried up the grounds putting them in good condition for the games. After lunch, the trustees started the sports, chairman Beyer announcer. Twelve men took part in the 100 yard dash, and A. Hartmann won after a hard race, his prize being a silk umbrella; R. Windler was second. In the boys' race, John Bentzen won a baseball and bat. Fred M. Alves won the hop stey and jump from a field ofeleve n, his jump being 36 feet; be was presented with a tie pin for his work. The little girls' race was next; Alice Jablonsky had five competitors but she outran them all, and won a brooch. In the single ladies' race Eugenia Beeb won over eight competitors, and was given a prize of a fine fan. The running broad jump, in which ten took part, was won by Fred Alves with a jump of 15 feet 6 inches, this being his second victory of the day. A. Hartmann came second. In the old men's race 50 years or over, J. J. Beneke had it all his own way and won as he pleased, the prize was a box of cigars. E. W. Guy, second. Carl Beyer had the fat men's race won before it started. H. Berning and Fred Ammann were the other runners. Carl won a beer mug. Seventeen ladies took part in the egg and spoon race for married women; Mrs. C. Beyer was the winner receiving a gold bracelet, the best prize of the day. Adolph Steidle and Dora Miller divided a box of candy in the potato race for boys and girls; eleven others tried for the same box. The Steidle brothers contested for combination fishing pole in the sack race for boys under 18 years, Vogel winning by a good margin. Beyer and Beneke were in charge of the tug-of-war, six men on a side. Beyer's side having the hardest pullers won out, and got a box of cigars to be divided among the winners. The great baseball game between the wholesalers and retailers came off next, and was watched by a large crowd, both sides having rooters.

The Wholesale and Retail Baseball Teams After the Game.
ST. LOUIS FLORISTS' CLUB PICNIC.

Beneke and Weber and Shriefer and Alves were the batteries. After five hard innings, the wholesalers won by a score of 10 to 2. The retailers had poor support; both pitchers and catchers worked in great style. The players of the wholesalers won a box of cigars.

News Notes.

James S. Wilson of Vaughan's Greenhouses, Western Springs, Ill., was among our visitors; he is a St. Louis boy, and came here to attend the picnic and see his brother and many friends. Another caller was H. E. Philpott, of Winnipeg, Canada, who visited the different growers and Shaw's Garden. Mr. Philpott, in company with J. S. Wilson, left Sunday night for Chicago. B. Eschner, of M. Rice & Co., Philadelphia, spent a few days here the past week. S. S. Skidelsky was here, and also talked up the S. A. F. convention to us.

Fred Alves, of Augermuller, and Otto Berning, were the baseball players who were hurt at the picnic; Alves will be laid up for at least ten days and Berning about a week.

One of the most important meetings of the year will be that of the Florists' Club, on next Thursday, at the regular meeting hall. The annual election of officers will take place and the payment of yearly dues will be in order. Fred H. Meinhardt will be on hand at the meeting. All those who intend going to the S. A. F. convention at Dayton, O., should hand in their names to him that night.

ST. PATRICK.

Bargains in CHOICE PLANTS

English Ivy, from 4½ in. pots, $2.00 and $1.50 per doz. About 3 feet high and bushy.
Ivy, fan shaped, fine and bushy, $6.00 per doz., 75c. each.
Anthericum, variegated, per doz., $1.50; per 100, $12.00.
Boston Ferns, 5 in. pots, $3.00 per doz.; 6 in. pots, $9.00 per doz.; 7 in. pots, $12.00 per doz.
Kentia Belmoreana and Forsteriana, $3.00, $4.00, $5.00, $6.00 $9.00 per doz.; also by the 100. Also $1.00, $1.50, $2.00, $2.50, $3.00 each and by the 2 doz.
Phœnix Canariensis, large plants, 6½ to 7 feet high, 11 in. pots, $12.00 to $14.00 per pair.
Bird's Nest Fern, large plants, 6½ in. pots, $1.50 each, $18.00 per doz.
Araucaria Excelsa, 50c., 75c., $1.00, $1.50, $2.00, $2.50 each. Also by the 100.
Aspidistra, green, $1.00 per pot, 10 to 12 leaves.
Cut Flowers of Lily of the Valley, $4.00 and $5.00 per 100.
Boxwood Pyramids, in pots, $2.00 and $1.50 a pair, fine plants. Other sizes sold out.
Bay Trees, Pyramids.
54-60 in. high from top of tub, $14.00 per pair
66-70 in. high from top of tub, 15.00 per pair
72 in. high from top of tub, 18.00 per pair
84 in. high from top of tub, 20.00 per pair
Bay Trees, Standards. (with 4 feet stems.)
32 in. diameter of crown, $14.00 per pair
36 in. diameter of crown, 16.00 per pair
Leaf-Mold, $1.00 per bag.
Asparagus Plumosus 3½ in. pots, $1.25 per doz.; per 100, $9.00; 4 in. pots, $2.00 per doz.; 4½ in. pots, $3.00 per doz.
Kentia Forsteriana, combinations, from $3.00, $4.00, $5.00, $6.00, $10.00, $15.00 to $20.00 each.
Dracæna Fragrans, $4.00 $6.00, $8.00, $12.00 $15.00, $24.00 per doz.
Latania Borbonica, from 5 in. pots, $4.00 per doz.; 6 in. $6.00 per doz.
Scottii Fern, 6½ in. pots; $7.00 per doz. Specimens $2.50 each. From the bench for 6½ and 8 in. pots, $5.00 per doz.; $40.00 per 100.
Piersoni Fern, 5½ in. pots, $9.00 per doz.
N. Elegantissima, from 4½ in. pots, $4.00 per doz.; $30.00 per 100.
Cattleya Trianae, 40 plants, 400 good bulbs, $50.00 per original case.
Orchid Peat, $1.00 per bag.
Rubbers, from 7 in. pots, 3 ft. high, $9.00 per doz.
Boston Ferns, specimens $3.00 each. 1 pair extra large, 14 in. pots, $15.00 the pair.
Areca Lutescens, 5½ in. pots, 9.00 per doz.; 3 in a pot.
Pandanus Veitchii, 5 in. pots, $6.00 per doz.; 6 in. pots, $9.00 per doz.; 6½ in., $12.00 per doz.; 7 in., $18 per doz.
Dracæna Terminalis, 4 in. pots, $3.00 per doz.; 5 in. pots, $5.00 per doz.; 6 in., $8.00 per doz.
Gardenia Veitchii, fine large Plants, 5½ in. pots, well budded, $9.00 per doz.
Cycas Revoluta, we have them in 5½, 6, 7 and 8 in. pots, very fine, 50c., 75c., $1.00, $1.50, $2.00 and $3.00 each.
Cibotium Scheidii, 6, 6½ and 7 in. pots, $1.50, $2.00 and $2.50 each.

Cash with order or satisfactory New York references required.

I wish to inform my many friends and customers that the report of my having suffered a loss by hail was erroneous.

I have had no loss, either from hail or any other cause. My stock is all in superb condition, and I can fill your orders on short notice.

ANTON SCHULTHEIS
19th St. & 4th Avenue, COLLEGE POINT, L. I., N.Y.

Mention The Florists' Exchange when writing.

GRAFTED ROSES

Fine Stock from 3-in. pots.

Richmond, $2.50 per doz., $15.00 per 100, $125.00 per 1000.
Killarney, $3.00 per doz., $15.00 per 100,
Etoile De France, $3.00 per doz., $18.00 per 100.
Kaiserin, Carnot, Uncle John, Chatenay, $2.00 per doz., $15.00 per 100.
Bride, Bridesmaid, Golden Gate, Wootton, $2.00 per doz., $12.00 per 100.

ROSES OWN ROOTS

Fine Stock from 3-in. pots.

Richmond, $10.00 per 100; $90.00 per 1000.
Etoile De France, $12.00 per 100.
Sunrise, Perle, Sunset, Chatenay, $8.00 per 100.
Bride, Bridesmaid, Golden Gate, $7.00 per 100.
Asparagus Plumosus Nanus from 3 inch pots, $8.00 per 100; **Sprengerii** from 3 inch pots, $6.00 per 100.

RUBBER PLANTS

Fine stock 2 feet high, 60c. each; $6.00 a doz.; 2½ to 3 feet high, 80c. each; $8.00 a doz.

Send for Catalogue.

Wood Bros., Fishkill, N. Y.

Mention The Florists' Exchange when writing.

Stevia Serrata

True, winter blooming, strong, bushy, ready to shift, 3½ in. pots, $5.00 per 100; $45.00 per 1000.

ASPARAGUS SPRENGERII, 2 inch, very strong, $2.50 per 100; $20.00 per 1000.

DEAN FERRIS, Peekskill, N.Y.

Mention The Florists' Exchange when writing.

Transplanted Celery Plants

Strong stock, bushy and well hardened, $2.00 per 1000; $17.50 per 10,000. 100 prepaid, 35c. W. Plume, G. Pascal, Golden Self Blanching, Dwarf Golden Heart, Boston Market and Winter Queen. Prompt shipment.

R. KILBOURN, CLINTON, N. Y.

Mention The Florists' Exchange when writing.

BARGAINS
Smilax and Asparagus

I need room and rather than handle the following stock a second time I offer it at these low prices, please send order in now.

ASPARAGUS SPRENGERII
fine two inch pot stock at $1.50 per 100; $12.50 per 1000.

ASPARAGUS PLUMOSUS
fine plants from two inch pots at $2.50 per 100; $20.00 per 1000.

ASPARAGUS ROBUSTUS
extra strong fine plants, this variety is a great improvement over Plumosus and every grower should try at least a hundred. $3.50 per 100; $30.00 per 1000.

SMILAX
as good as it can be grown, carefully cut back and with air space around each pot. $1.50 per 100; $12.50 per 1000.

GERANIUMS
send for my list of rooted cuttings. I have almost 200,000 stock plants to work from and want your orders for fall delivery.

ALBERT M. HERR,
Lancaster, Pa.

Mention The Florists' Exchange when writing.

CYCLAMEN

SPLENDENS GIGANTEUM HYBRIDS

This strain has no equal or better. Perfect flowers of Giant type in five true colors well grown plants from 2½ in. pots $5.00 per 100, $45.00 per 1000; from 3 in. pots $7.00 per 100; $65.00 per 1000.

Asparagus. Plumosus Nanus.

From flats fine plants $1.50 per 100. $12.50 per 1000.

SATISFACTION GUARANTEED.

PAUL MADER, EAST STROUDSBURG, PA.

SURPLUS STOCK—CHEAP

200 **The Bride** roses, 2 in. pots, $1.75 per 100.
500 **Bridesmaid** roses, 2 in. pots, $2.00 per 100.
1000 **Cannas**, red and yellow, strong, $8.00 per 100.
50 **Dracaena indivisa**, 3½ in., 6c. each.
2000 **Cuphea**, Cigar Plant, 2 in. pots, 75c. per 100.
2000 **Feverfew**, Double White, 2 in. pots, 50c. per 100.
10000 **Jerusalem Cherries**, big and strong, ready for 4 in. pots, from 2 in. pots at $2.00 per 100. You will never get better or cheaper stock than this. **E. I. Rawlings, Quakertown, Pa.**

Mention The Florists' Exchange when writing.

CULTURAL DIRECTIONS

Specially written for the use of your amateur customers. Send Twenty-five cents for complete sample set, which amount will be deducted from order for first thousand.

The universal favor in which these Directions are held, as shown by the many orders received therefor, encourages us in the belief that these Leaflets are just the neat little factor to help promote business and establish better relations between the dealer and his customer.

TRY SOME!

BIG BUSINESS ASSISTANT

TO SAVE TIME, QUICKEN SALES, AND AID YOU PLEASE YOUR CUSTOMER, WE HAVE PREPARED

Cultural Directions

COVERING A NUMBER OF THOSE PLANTS AND BULBS MOST LARGELY IN DEMAND

THE "CULTURALS" have been written by experts; they are fuller, and contain more detailed directions than it is possible to embrace in a catalogue. Equipped with these, just hand one out with each sale, and save yourself considerable present and future trouble, as the customer will then be able to consult the directions, grow his plants, seeds or bulbs intelligently, and so receive satisfactory results, without having to continually resort to you for advice.

The following "Culturals" are now ready:

AMARYLLIS (Hippeastrum)
ANNUALS FROM SEED
ASPARAGUS
ASTERS
BEGONIA, TUBEROUS
BULBS
CABBAGE and CAULIFLOWER
CANNA
CARNATIONS, MONTHLY
CELERY
CHINESE SACRED LILY
CHRYSANTHEMUM
CLIMBING PLANTS, Hardy
COLEUS, and other bedders
CROCUS, Snowdrop and Scilla Sibirica
DAHLIA
FERNS
FREESIA
GERANIUM
GLADIOLUS
GLOXINIA
HOT BEDS and FRAMES
HOUSE PLANTS, Care of
HYACINTHS, Dutch and Roman
IRIS AND TRITOMA
LAWNS
LILY CULTURE for House and Garden
MUSHROOM CULTURE
ONIONS
PALMS, House Culture of
PANSY
PEONIES
PERENNIALS, Hardy
PRIMULA
ROSE CULTURE
SWEET PEA, The
TOMATOES
TUBEROSE
TULIP
VEGETABLES
VIOLETS
WATER GARDEN, How to make and Manage a

PRICE LIST

500 Cultural Directions for $1.50
1,000 - - - - - 2.50
Printed on white paper, clear type, size 6 x 9½ inches, in an assortment, your selection of not less than 100 of each, delivered carriage paid.

Sufficient space will be left at the bottom of each leaflet for your name, address, etc. If you desire this imprint (3 lines) we will put same on for you at 50 cents for 500, 75 cents for 1000. Special quotations will be made on quantities of 5,000 "CULTURALS" or over.

A. T. De La Mare Ptg. and Pub. Co. Ltd.
Pubs. The Florists' Exchange. P. O. Box, 1697, NEW YORK

YOUR Fall Catalogue

We have been printing Trade Catalogues for the past fifteen years; have been accumulating stock cuts and photographs for the past fifteen years, and, equally important, perhaps most important of all, have been steadily improving in our knowledge as to what is required in the way of style, workmanship and finish in order to produce a catalogue that

Will Be Effective

Send in full specifications and we will promptly give you an estimate. We supply our stock cuts free to customers.

A. T. DE LA MARE PTG. & PUB. CO. Ltd.
2 to 8 Duane Street, New York City.

J. K. ALLEN

Wholesale Commission Dealer in **Cut Flowers**

106 West 28th St., NEW YORK

Open at 6 a. m. every day.
Telephone, 167 Madison Square.
Consignments Solicited.

Mention The Florists' Exchange when writing.

Wm. Stuart Allen Co.

Commission Merchants in CUT FLOWERS
ORCHIDS AT ALL SEASONS

53 WEST 28th STREET, NEW YORK

Telephone 356 Madison Square

Mention the Florists' Exchange when writing

C. BONNET G. H. BLAKE

BONNET & BLAKE

Wholesale Florists

106 Livingston Street, BROOKLYN, N. Y.

Telephone: 4638 Main.

Consignments solicited. Out-of-town orders carefully attended to. Give us a trial.

Mention The Florists' Exchange when writing.

CUT FLOWER EXCHANGE

Sixth Ave. and 26th St.
Coogan Building, NEW YORK
Open every Morning at Six o'clock for the Sale of Cut Flowers.
Wall Space for advertising purposes to Rent.
V. S. DORVAL, Jr., Secretary.

Mention the Florists' Exchange when writing

Joseph S. Fenrich

...Wholesale Florist...

—THE RELIABLE HOUSE—

110 West 28th Street

Telephone 324-325 Madison Square.

Mention The Florists' Exchange when writing.

FORD BROS.

Wholesale Florists

48 WEST 28th ST., NEW YORK

Telephone, 3870-3871 Madison Square

Mention The Florists' Exchange when writing.

GROWERS, ATTENTION!
Always Ready to Receive Fine Stock

WILLIAM H. GUNTHER

30 West 29th Street
'Phone, 551 Madison Square. NEW YORK

Violets, Roses, Carnations, Orchids

Established 1888

Mention the Florists' Exchange when writing

ALEX. J. GUTTMAN

The Wholesale Florist of New York

43 WEST 28th STREET

Phones 1664-1665 Madison Square

Mention The Florists' Exchange when writing

A. M. HENSHAW

..Wholesale Florist..

52 West 28th Street, NEW YORK

First class Roses and Carnations a specialty.

Consignments Solicited. Tel. 5583 Madison Sq.

Mention The Florists' Exchange when writing.

HICKS & CRAWBUCK, Inc.

Wholesale Florists

And Dealers in FLORISTS' SUPPLIES

76-78 Court Street

Phone, 3660-3661 Main BROOKLYN, N. Y.

Mention The Florists' Exchange when writing.

HEADQUARTERS FOR NOVELTIES

ORCHIDS A SPECIALTY

THE HIGHEST GRADE OF **VALLEY** ALWAYS ON HAND

GARDENIAS, DAISIES, ROSES, CARNATIONS.

JAMES McMANUS, Telephone 759 Mad. Sq. 42 W. 28th St., New York.

PHILIP F. KESSLER

Wholesale Florist

55-57 W. 26th St., NEW YORK.

Telephone, 2921-5243 Madison Square.

Mention the Florists' Exchange when writing

JULIUS LANG

Wholesale Florist

53 WEST 30th STREET
NEW YORK

Consignments Solicited. Telephone: 280 Madison Sq.

Mention the Florists' Exchange when writing

WILLIAM H. KUEBLER

Wholesale Commission Dealer in

CUT FLOWERS

28 Willoughby St.,

Telephone, 4591 Main. BROOKLYN, N. Y.

Mention the Florists' Exchange when writing

FRANK MILLANG

Wholesale Commission Dealer in

CUT FLOWERS

55-57 West 26th Street, New York

Telephone Call: 299 Madison Square.

Mention the Florists' Exchange when writing.

ALFRED H. LANGJAHR

55 WEST 28th STREET, NEW YORK

Telephone, 4626-4627 Madison Square Established 1891

SPECIAL VALLEY AND TOP GRADE ASPARAGUS

Consignments of First Class Stock Solicited.

Horace E. Froment

SUCCESSOR TO

W. GHORMLEY

WHOLESALE COMMISSION FLORIST

Receiver and Shipper of all varieties of Cut Flowers

Telephones, 2200 and 2201 Madison Square. 157 West 28th St., NEW YORK

Wholesale Prices of Cut Flowers, New York, August 2, 1906

Prices quoted are by the hundred unless otherwise noted.

Roses	A. Beauty, fancy—special	10.00 to	20.00
	" extra	6.00 to	10.00
	" No. 1	4.00 to	5.00
	" No. 2	3.00 to	4.00
	" No. 3	1.00 to	1.50
	Bride, Maid, fancy—spe'l	3.00 to	4.00
	" extra	2.00 to	3.00
	" No. 1	1.00 to	2.00
	" No. 2	.50 to	1.00
	Golden Gate	1.00 to	5.00
	Liberty	..... to	.....
	Mme. Abel Chatenay	1.00 to	6.00
Adiantum		.50 to	.75
	Croweanum	.50 to	1.00
Asparagus		25.00 to	50.00
	" Plumosus, bunches	10.00 to	15.00
	" Sprengerii, bunches	10.00 to	15.00
Cattleyas		25.00 to	50.00
Daisies		.50 to	1.00
Gladiolus		.50 to	1.00
		..... to	.....

Carnations	Inf'r grades, all colors	.50 to	1.00
	Standard Varieties — White	1.00 to	2.00
	Standard Varieties — Pink	1.00 to	2.00
	Standard Varieties — Red	1.00 to	2.00
	Standard Varieties — Yel. & Var.	1.00 to	2.00
	*Fancy— (*The highest grades of standard var.) — White	2.00 to	2.50
	*Fancy — Pink	2.00 to	2.50
	*Fancy — Red	2.00 to	2.50
	*Fancy — Yel. & Var.	..... to	.....
	Novelties	..... to	.....
Lilies		5.00 to	8.00
Lily of the Valley		1.00 to	2.00
Mignonette		..... to	.....
		..... to	.....
		..... to	.....
		..... to	.....
Pansies, per dozen bunches		.50 to	.75
Smilax		8.00 to	10.00
Sweet Peas, per bunch		.01 to	.03

WALTER F. SHERIDAN

Wholesale Florist

Telephone, 1902 Madison Square — 39 WEST 28TH ST., NEW YORK

ALL VARIETIES OF CUT FLOWERS IN SEASON

TOP GRADE FOR SHIPPING

American Beauty, Bridesmaid, Bride, Liberty, Meteor, Lily of the Valley, Carnations

Telephone, 1998 Madison Square — JOHN I. RAYNOR, 49 West 28th St., NEW YORK

Edw. C. Horan

55 West 28th St., NEW YORK

TELEPHONE, 1462-1463 MADISON SQUARE

CUT FLOWERS AT WHOLESALE

Mention The Florists' Exchange when writing.

JOHN YOUNG

Wholesale Florist

51 W. 28th St., NEW YORK

TELEPHONE: 4463-4464 MADISON SQUARE

Mention the Florists' Exchange when writing

A. MOLTZ

Wholesale Florist

55-57 West 26th St., NEW YORK

1st Floor. Telephone, 2921-5243 Madison Sq.

Mention The Florists' Exchange when writing.

MOORE, HENTZ & NASH
WHOLESALE
GROWER AGENT
COMMISSION FLORISTS
55 West 26th St., New York

Telephone Call,
756 Madison Square

Mention The Florists' Exchange when writing.

GEORGE SALTFORD

Wholesale Florist

CONSIGNMENTS SOLICITED

46 West 29th Street, New York

TELEPHONE: 3393 MADISON SQUARE

Mention The Florists' Exchange when writing.

J. Seligman Joseph J. Levy

JOHN SELIGMAN & COMPANY

Wholesale Florists

56 West 26th Street,

Tel. 4878 Madison New York.

Opposite New York Cut Flower Company

Mention The Florists' Exchange when writing.

B. S. SLINN, JR.

Wholesale Florist

55 and 57 West 26th Street, NEW YORK

SPECIALTIES—Violets, Carnations and Roses. Shipping orders receive prompt attention. Consignment Solicited.

Telephone: 3864 Madison Square

Mention the Florists' Exchange when writing.

FRANK H. TRAENDLY CHARLES SCHENCK

TRAENDLY & SCHENCK

Wholesale Florists

44 WEST 28th STREET, NEW YORK
and CUT FLOWER EXCHANGE

Telephones: 798 and 799 MADISON SQUARE

CONSIGNMENTS SOLICITED

Mention the Florists' Exchange when writing.

A. L. YOUNG & CO.

WHOLESALE FLORISTS

54 West 28th St., NEW YORK

Telephone 3559 Madison Square.

Consignments of choice cut flowers solicited. Prompt payments. Give us a trial.

Mention The Florists' Exchange when writing.

THOMAS YOUNG

Wholesale Florist

43 West 28th Street, NEW YORK

Telephone, 4850 Madison Square

Consignments of Choice Flowers solicited

Mention The Florists' Exchange when writing.

Wholesale Prices of Cut Flowers—Per 100

Boston July 30, 1906	Buffalo July 30, 1906	Detroit July 22, 1906	Cincinnati July 28, 1906	Baltimore July 16, 1906	NAMES AND VARIETIES	Milwaukee July 28, 1906	Phil'delphia July 24, 1906	Pittsburg July 31, 1906	St. Louis July 30, 1906
15.00 to 20.00	20.00 to 25.00	10.00 to 35.00	75.00 to 80.00	to	ROSES: A. BEAUTY, fancy—special	to 25.00	15.00 to 20.00	20.00 to 25.00	15.00 to 20.00
10.00 to 15.00	12.00 to 20.00	to	to 20.00	12.50 to 15.00	" extra	15.00 to 18.00	10.00 to 15.00	15.00 to 18.00	10.00 to 12.50
2.00 to 10.00	6.00 to 12.00	to	16.00 to 15.00	5.00 to 8.00	" No. 1	10.00 to 12.50	5.00 to 7.00	8.00 to 12.00	6.00 to 8.00
2.00 to 4.00	3.00 to 6.00	to	to	to	" Culls and ordinary	4.00 to 6.00	1.00 to 4.00	3.00 to 4.00	3.00 to 5.00
to	5.00 to 6.00	3.00 to 6.00	3.00 to 5.00	to	BRIDE, 'MAID, fancy-special	to 6.00	to	to	4.00 to 5.00
3.00 to 5.00	4.00 to 5.00	to	2.00 to 3.00	to 4.00	" extra	to 5.00	6.00 to 8.00	to 6.00	2.00 to 3.00
2.00 to 3.00	3.00 to 4.00	to	1.00 to 2.00	to 3.00	" No. 1	to 4.00	4.00 to 5.00	to 4.00	to
.50 to 2.00	2.00 to 3.00	to	to	to 2.00	" No. 2	to 2.00	2.00 to 3.00	to 2.00	to
to	to	4.00 to 8.00	to	2.00 to 4.00	GOLDEN GATE	4.00 to 6.00	4.00 to 8.00	to	2.00 to 4.00
2.00 to 6.00	3.00 to 7.00	to	2.00 to 5.00	4.00 to 8.00	K. A. VICTORIA	4.00 to 8.00	4.00 to 6.00	4.00 to 12.00	2.00 to 5.00
to	3.00 to 7.00	to	to	to	LIBERTY	4.00 to 6.00	3.00 to 6.00	2.00 to 8.00	to
to	3.00 to 6.00	4.00 to 10.00	to	to	METEOR	to	to	to	to
to	3.00 to 5.00	4.00 to 10.00	to	2.00 to 4.00	PERLE	4.00 to 6.00	to	to	2.00 to 4.00
to	to	to 50.00	to	to	ORCHIDS—Cattleyas	to	to 50.00	to	to
to	.75 to 1.00	to	to .50	.50 to .75	CARNATIONS: Inferior grades, all colors	to 1.00	.75 to 1.00	.75 to 1.00	.75 to 1.00
to	1.25 to 1.50	to 1.00	to 1.00	1.00 to 1.50	Standard Varieties: White	to 1.00	.75 to 1.00	to 2.00	.75 to 1.00
to	1.00 to 1.50	to	to 1.00	1.00 to 1.50	Pink	to 1.00	.75 to 1.00	to 2.00	.75 to 1.00
to	1.00 to 1.50	to	to 1.00	1.00 to 1.50	Red	to 1.00	.75 to 1.00	to 2.00	.75 to 1.00
to	1.00 to 1.50	to 3.00	to	1.00 to 1.50	Yellow and var.	to 1.00	.75 to 1.00	to	.75 to 1.00
.50 to 1.00	1.50 to 2.00	to	to	to 3.00	Fancy Varieties: White	1.50 to 2.00	2.00 to 2.50	to	1.00 to 1.50
.50 to 1.50	1.50 to 2.00	to	to	to 3.00	Pink	1.50 to 2.00	2.00 to 2.50	to	1.00 to 1.50
.50 to 1.50	1.50 to 2.00	to	to	to 3.00	Red	1.50 to 2.00	2.00 to 2.50	to	1.00 to 1.50
.50 to 1.50	1.50 to 2.00	to 1.50	to	to 3.00	Yellow and var.	1.50 to 2.00	2.00 to 2.50	to	1.00 to 1.50
to	to	to	to	to	Novelties	to	to	to	to
.75 to 1.00	.50 to 1.00	to 2.00	to	to 1.00	ADIANTUM	to 1.00	to 1.00	1.25 to 1.50	to
to 50.00	to	25.00 to 60.00	to 50.00	25.00 to 50.00	ASPARAGUS, Plum. and Ten.	20.00 to 30.00	25.00 to 35.00	to	25.00 to 40.00
to	to	20.00 to 30.00	to 35.00	25.00 to 50.00	" Sprengeri, bunches	20.00 to 30.00	25.00 to 35.00	15.00 to 25.00	25.00 to 50.00
.50 to 1.00	.50 to 2.00	to	1.00 to 2.00	to	ASTERS	.50 to 1.00	to	.75 to 2.50	.50 to 2.50
to	8.00 to 10.00	to 10.00	to 1.00	6.00 to 8.00	CALLAS	to	to	to	to
to	to	.75 to 1.50	to	to	DAISIES	to .40	3.00 to 4.00	to	to
4.00 to 6.00	1.00 to 3.00	8.00 to 10.00	2.00 to 3.00	2.00 to 4.00	GLADIOLUS	to	8.00 to 12.00	4.00 to 6.00	to
to	to	to	12.00 to 15.00	10.00 to 12.50	LILIES, Harrisii	to 12.50	to	to	to
6.00 to 8.00	12.00 to 15.00	to	to	10.00 to 12.50	" Longiflorum	to 12.50	2.00 to 4.00	15.00 to 18.00	to
2.00 to 4.00	3.00 to 4.00	3.00 to 4.00	3.00 to 4.00	1.00 to 2.00	LILY OF THE VALLEY	to	1.00 to 2.00	2.00 to 4.00	to
to	to	to	to	2.00 to 2.50	MIGNONETTE, ordinary	to	to	to	to
to	to	to	to	to	" fancy	to	to	to	to
to	to	4.00 to 8.00	to	to	PEONIES	to	15.00 to 20.00	to	to
to 12.50	to 15.00	12.50 to 15.00	12.00 to 15.00	12.50 to 20.00	SMILAX	to 15.00	to	10.00 to 12.50	to 12.50
to	to	to	to	to	VIOLETS, ordinary	to	to	to	to
to	to	to	to	to	" fancy	to	to	to	to
to	to	to	to	to	NARCISSUS	to	to	to	to
.20 to .25	.15 to .25	.50 to .75	to .35	.20 to .35	SWEET PEAS	.25 to .50	to .50	.25 to .40	.10 to .15
to	to	to	to	to		to	to	to	to
to	to	to	to	to		to	to	to	to

Kalamazoo, Mich.

The News.

Extremely hot weather and drought have prevailed during the past few weeks, and business has declined till almost imperceptible. Growers were becoming somewhat worried over the drought, but were greatly relieved July 29 when copious rains fell and the ground was well watered; at present writing it looks as if nice stock will be lifted for the season's planting. In this vicinity this work is usually done about the middle and latter end of August, with the exception of a few benches for early work. This year, however, the Van Bochoves have already got a good start with the work and will continue to plant until their 60,000 plants are all housed.

Roses are growing quite thriftily notwithstanding the heat; and most of the other stock is in a promising condition.

H. Heithouse has bought some ground on the west side and intends to erect a small greenhouse establishment at once. He will grow principally bedding stock and vegetable plants for Spring sales. He has been identified with the trade here for many years. S. B.

Toledo, O.

Club News.

Only 15 members attended the last meeting of the florists' club held on Thursday, but they had a lively time. Our Detroit neighbors asked us to join them on a water trip from Detroit to Cleveland, or meet them at Cleveland and go from there to the convention city. Some liked the idea very much, but most were against it, as we would like to go to Dayton by the new trolley line, which makes the trip in 4½ hours. It is hard to say how many of us will attend; they do not dare to go away for such a long time, as they do not believe they can depend enough on their help.

Business is very slow, slower than in former years at this time. Planting carnations in the houses is now in order, and the plants look well and promise good returns.

We have had pretty severe hailstorms of late, but no glass was broken.

A new stimulus has been given to our club meeting by the offering of prizes; $3 have been offered by our president Mr. Bayer for the best cut flowers of asters, one dozen each of white, pink, purple and lavender of any kind; it is not necessary that the four dozen come from one party. The club offered a prize of $1 for the best collection of cannas of at least six good varieties. This it is hoped will bring about a very much larger attendance than there has been lately; and the competition is expected to be very keen. Sch.

Wholesale Prices of Cut Flowers, Chicago, Aug. 1, 1906.

Prices quoted are by the hundred unless otherwise noted.

ROSES — American Beauty		
36-inch stems.........per doz.	.... to	4.00
30-inch stems .... "	.... to	3.00
24-inch stems.......... "	.... to	2.50
20-inch stems.......... "	.... to	2.00
18-inch stems.......... "	.... to	1.50
12-inch stems.......... "	.... to	1.00
8-inch stems and shorts "	.50 to	.75
Bride Maid, fancy special......	5.00 to	6.00
" extra..............	4.00 to	5.00
" No. 1..............	2.00 to	3.00
" No. 2..............	.50 to	1.00
Golden Gate..................	2.00 to	6.00
Carnot.......................	2.00 to	6.00
Uncle John...................	2.00 to	8.00
Liberty......................	2.00 to	8.00
Richmond.....................	2.00 to	8.00
Kaiserina....................	2.00 to	8.00
Killarney....................	3.00 to	8.00
Perle........................	2.00 to	6.00
Chatenay.....................	2.00 to	6.00
Orchids—Cattleyas...........	.... to	50.00
SMILAX.......................	8.00 to	12.00
LILY OF THE VALLEY............	2.00 to	4.00
SWEET PEAS....................	.25 to	.50

CARNATIONS			
Inferior grades all colors		.25 to	.50
STANDARD VARIETIES	White........	.75 to	1.00
	Pink........	.75 to	1.00
	Red........	.75 to	1.00
	Yellow & var....	.75 to	1.00
*FANCY (The highest grades of Sta'd var)	White........	1.50 to	2.00
	Pink........	1.50 to	2.00
	Red........	1.50 to	2.00
	Yellow & var....	1.50 to	2.00
NOVELTIES..................		.... to	....
ADIANTUM..................		.50 to	1.00
ASPARAGUS, Plum. & Ten......		.35 to	.50
" Sprengeri, bunches.		.35 to	.50
GLADIOLUS..................		2.00 to	6.00
LILIES, Longiflorum.......		8.00 to	12.00
HARRISII..................		8.00 to	12.00
AURATUM..................		6.00 to	8.00
NYMPHAEA..................		.... to	1.00
MIGNONETTE, ordinary.......		1.00 to	2.00
....		.... to	....
....		.... to	....
HARDY FERNS per 1000......		1.00 to	1.50
GALAX "		1.00 to	1.25
ASTERS....................		.50 to	1.00

Chicago.

News Notes.

Under the caption, "A Trip to Chicago," the following notice has been sent out by the Chicago Florists' Club, "Convention visitors who may decide to make a further western trip during the week following the Dayton meeting are cordially invited by the Chicago Florists' Club to advise its secretary when they will be in the city in order that an afternoon or evening visit with the club can be arranged. P. J. Hauswirth, president, L. H. Winterson, secretary, No. 47 Wabash avenue."

A. L. Vaughan returned from Spirit Lake with a good coat of tan, and a remarkable freedom from his old rheumatic enemy.

Miss Nellie C. Moore, the city representative of the concern of N. C. Moore, has returned from her camping trip at Channel Lake in buoyant spirits over her piscatorial success. Not only did the finny tribe respond to her alluring bait but a turtle weighing 29 pounds was numbered among her conquests. A report of this capture was forwarded to Morton Grove and preparations were set in progress for a florists' turtle banquet, but unfortunately for the epicures a loud splashing aroused the campers at night as the turtle escaped to his natural element.

H. C. Blewitt of Desplaines was a recent visitor, and reports having had excellent success with his sweet pea crop this Summer; but like many others his thousands of aster plants are practically a failure.

The Chicago Rose Company has had a very successful run on the novelty of grass growing heads. Being on the ground floor a good window display of this feature has proved a great attraction to visitors to the city many of whom have called in and procured a card, and orders are being continually received from all sections of the Central, Western, and South Western states.

Mr. Washburn of A. Washburn & Sons, of Bloomington, Ill., was a recent visitor.

Joe Trinz leaves on Saturday of this week for a month's trip East, taking in New York City and Saratoga.

Wm. F. Hackencamp, Jr., of Quincy, Ill., passed through Chicago a few days ago on his way to Buffalo.

Mr. Le Borieus is getting ready to establish a range of houses for commercial purposes at Duluth and was in town a few days ago looking up material.

Within a small fraction of three inches of rain was the reported precipitation in this city on Saturday last resulting in many flooded basements in the business section among them being the Kennicott Brothers Company's which was also inundated a week or two previously.

Fred Sperry left on Saturday last for an outing at Michigan City.

Mrs. T. E. Waters has returned from her Eastern vacation.

Charles Balluff of the Eaton Flower Shop, accompanied by his wife, left on Monday for his annual fishing expedition to Lake Butte Des Mortes, Oshkosh, Wis., where he has visited now for so many years that he can almost give the genealogical pedigree of a fish as soon as he makes a strike.

Miss Klunder, cashier for H. E. Klunder accompanied by a young lady associate is off for a two weeks' recreation trip to Ottawa Beach, Miss Klunder expecting later to visit a former friend and school-mate in Providence, R. I.

S. E. Morris of the Manistee Floral Company of Manistee, Mich., visited Chicago last week.

The unprecedented call for greenhouse material goes on unabated, indicating a phenomenal increase in the business from nearly all sections. Another noticeable feature in this line is that collections never before were so good—all showing a remarkably prosperous condition of the trade.

The Fleischmann Floral Company has increased its capital stock from $10,000 to $100,000.

At a meeting of the Retail Florists' Association held on Thursday evening of last week it was decided to hold their first annual picnic on August 15 at some convenient grounds, presumably at one of the northwest parks, the full particulars of which are still undecided. We can only say at this writing that every endeavor will be exerted to make this occasion one of pleasure and interest; and as the details are in the hands of some of the enterprising members of the craft, success is assured.

The E. F. Winterson Company is this week exhibiting some very handsome specimens of nymphæas of the hybrid varieties, and undoubtedly a ready market would spontaneously create itself for this class of goods wherever introduced in this section, if they could be delivered in salable condition.

The next meeting of the Chicago Florists' Club will be held in Handel Hall on Thursday evening, August 9, and it is hoped will be attended by every member and all their friends. The arrangements for the excursion to Dayton will there and then be completed. Although without the permission and even against the desire of the president of the local club, he is to be formally presented to the country as the next secretary of the S. A. F. O. H. Little more can be said. Job wanted the "Red Man" for president. Personally he desires no office, but it appears that his friends have forced him as a candidate for the position where he can put in his time keeping the books.

H. E. Philpott and James Wilson returned Monday from St. Louis where they enjoyed the associations of olden days and participated with the florists' club in the picnic pleasures. Mr. Philpott, after a few days in Chicago, will proceed to Milwaukee and cruise around among his old friends until the meeting of the national society at Dayton.

Charles W. Crawford, bookkeeper for Charles Freuh & Sons of Saginaw was in Chicago on Sunday last.

Dry weather is forcing the dahlia crop in ahead of time, and the flowers are correspondingly of inferior quality. It is hoped that recent rains may save them above the point which the asters have reached.

Alex. Newett, floor manager, and Miss Florence Emmett, secretary of the J. B. Deamud Company, returned from their vacations the latter part of last week.

Peter Reinberg and party returned from Colorado on Saturday night last. While in Denver they called on Henry Weiland, a son of Mathew Weiland, one of the oldest florists in Chicago. The young man has purchased a location in Denver, where his health has much improved, and next Spring will erect a range of houses.

Fred Heinl of Terre Haute, Ind., was in Chicago first of the week.

WILLIAM K. WOOD.

HARTFORD, CONN.—One of the choicest exhibitions that has yet been made by the Connecticut Horticultural Society was that of July 13th. A Japanese dwarf hollyhock was the object of much admiration. J. F Huss and J. A. Weber of the Walter Goodwin estate, were the exhibitors. A committee consisting of J. F. Huss, Charles Peterson, Alexander Cummings, P. Zuger and W. W. Hunt was appointed by the society to make arrangements for the entertainment of the members of the New Haven Horticultural Society. Seven new members were received, as follows: Alexander Reganzy, Walter Crawford, Neil Nelson, James D. Ralph, Alexander Cummings, Jr., and Eugene A. Walter.

Delegates, representing the Bridgeport, New Haven and New London Horticultural societies, and numbering about thirty-five, visited this city, Wednesday, and were met at the railroad station by a special committee of the Connecticut Horticultural society, of which John F. Huss of the Goodwin estate was chairman. The visitors first visited Bushnell Park and afterwards went to the Goodwin estate to see the work of Superintendent Huss. Elizabeth Park was the next place visited, and a lunch was served by the Hartford Florists' Club. During the rest of the day other parks in the city were visited.

ROME, N. Y.—Robert J. Wilson in the employ of E. J. Byam, went to Troy, July 23, where his wife is visiting, and she met him at the depot. As she stepped out of the carriage she tripped and fell and broke her right ankle.

Jamestown, N. Y.

Fire broke out in the Lakeview Rose Gardens shortly after 7 o'clock on Sunday morning, July 29. The fire department was called out, and when the firemen arrived, it was found that the blaze had started in the packing room through poor insulation of the electric wires. About 1,250 feet of hose had to be laid before a stream of water could be obtained, but the fire was soon extinguished thereafter.

The delay in getting water may seem strange at a greenhouse establishment, but an explanation of this is found in the fact that the different section men are in the habit of hiding their hose from each other to prevent its being purloined; and, the fire breaking out early on a Sunday morning, before any of the help arrived, no hose could be found, so superintendent Chas. Roney had no other alternative than to call out the fire department.

The damage to plants and building was but slight; and is fully covered by insurance.

Baltimore.

News Notes.

Business conditions at this time are exceptionally good; stock is moving rapidly, and fair prices are obtained. Plenty of rain and a few cool days have had a tendency to improve the quality of both indoor and outdoor flowers.

The last meeting of the Gardeners' Club was an enthusiastic one. A large delegation will take in the Ocean City trip and the Summer meeting of the Maryland Horticultural Society.

We are also getting up a good party to attend the S. A. F. convention in Dayton, O. The bowlers are practicing diligently, but are playing the little duck pins; the heavy game has suffered since the little pins and balls have been in such favor as a Summer game in this locality.

Among a number of interesting questions before the club was one, "Where can practical and theoretic landscape gardening be learned in this country?" A number of members took part in this discussion.

C. L. SEYBOLD.

Utica, N. Y.

News Notes.

Theo. Schesch, Ilion, N. Y., is at St. Elizabeth Hospital this city. He has undergone a very painful operation on one of his eyes, but is getting along very nicely. He has the best wishes of all the Utica florists for his speedy recovery.

Mr. and Mrs. Wm. Wagner, florist, Cooperstown, are in the city on a short visit to Mr. Wagner's mother and friends.

Mr. and Mrs. John M. Matti are at Otter Lake, Adirondack Mountains. Chas. M. Matthews and J. C. Spencer of Spencer & Martin are at the same place.

Summer trade is on now in good earnest, and we could all go afishing. Asters are coming in of fine quality and there are some fairly good roses. Spencer & Martin are showing some extra fine water lilies in white and pink, and some of the Mexican type.

QUIZ.

Manchester, Mass.

Society Meeting.

The regular meeting of the North Shore Horticultural Society was held Friday evening with a large and appreciative attendance. Thos. Connally was speaker of the evening and gave an interesting talk on a recent trip to California. It was sweet pea night and there were many fine exhibits on the tables, in fact so many that it was decided to hold a regular sweet pea exhibition next year. Those having exhibits at this meeting were F. E. Cole, gardener at the Spaulding estate; W. E. Allen, gardener to Mrs. W. Scott Fitz; Thos Jack, gardener to W. B. Walker; Mr. Scott, gardener to Mrs. Higginson; James Salter, gardener to Mrs. Dexter and Arthur Jackson.

At the next meeting David Wakefield will give a talk on fertilizers, and as he is quite an expert in their proper use having shown good results in raising various crops a very instructive evening is anticipated.

J. W. D.

Twin Cities.

News Notes.

The florists of the Twin Cities will have a bowling contest Friday, August 3, to be held in Pfister's alleys, St. Paul. As the bowlers have a reasonable amount of cash on hand from the picnic we can expect some very fine team and individual contests, as each city is doing their best to pick out the best bowlers.

Ashton Kerschner, formerly with the State Nursery of Helena, Montana, has been with us for the past week or ten days. He reports trade in the West on the boom and expects large improvements within the next few years. The State Nursery has about 200,000 feet of glass and the stock grown is of the best quality.

PAUL.

KNOXVILLE, ILL.—H. S. McGowen, florist of Santa Cruz, has been in town several days looking up a location. He sold his business at Santa Cruz and has been investigating the advantages offered him by this valley.

HEATING.

Growers' Problems Solved by U. G. Scollay.

How many 2-inch pipe will be required to heat two houses, as shown on accompanying plan, to 70 degrees, hot water heating? The boiler will have to be set on the ground level as we are on the beach here and cannot go over a foot deep before we get water. The dwelling house adjoins the small house. The place is protected pretty well by dwelling houses. I have a lot of 2-inch pipe and want to use it.

New Jersey. W. J. H.

—Your proposition is very impractical. It is almost an impossibility to successfully warm any building the way you propose, unless you arrange to place an electrical circulator on the main return pipe near the boiler, and then you will have the danger of the apparatus not doing its work satisfactorily in case any derangement should occur in the working of the circulator. Your best plan is to have an iron tank made and sink it in the ground, this tank to be used as a boiler pit. You can procure a low height hot water boiler, so that the tank need not be very deep; the pipes can be kept up as near the bottom of the bench as is feasible; this would save extra depth of pit. You do not mention what you intend to grow, but the temperature stated (70 degrees) is rather high and is unusual except in special cases. In the larger house, to maintain 70 degrees in zero weather you will require eighteen lines of 2-inch pipe, and in the smaller house fourteen lines. This is based on a good circulation and temperature of water in the pipes averaging 160 degrees. I cannot very well lay out any plan for you until I know whether you will use a circulator, or have a pit sunk as described. Let me know, and I will give you any suggestions possible. Your case, I should think, calls for one of the first class heating concerns, to install the heating for you.

U. G. SCOLLAY.

REPLYING to A. M. B., Pa.—It will give you no advantage to change the location of your expansion tank, except in case you elevate it, and then the only advantage would be that you could get the temperature of the water in the pipes somewhat higher, owing to the increased pressure. This, of course, would depend on the power of the boiler, and your manner of firing. As you state the present heating apparatus works satisfactorily, I would not suggest making any change.

Answering your question relative to residence heating, I would say that if this arrangement of expansion tank works at all satisfactorily there is no harm in leaving it connected to the water closet tank. I might say, however, that I have seen jobs of this kind cause severe physical discomfort. If you do not see the point, write me personally.

U. G. SCOLLAY.

I have two houses, 17 x 80 and 18 x 70 feet respectively heated by brick flues, fire grate 16 x 30 inches. By erecting a house between these two, 80 feet long, 11 wide with 4 foot side can it be arranged to use these furnaces for hot water? How many rows and what size piping would be required to keep the house at a carnation temperature; and can it be safely heated by these furnaces? The houses have a furnace in each; fire grate 16 x 30.

New York. D. H. R.

—The two furnaces that heat your present two houses can be arranged with pipe coils in them to carry some additional pipes for hot water. I personally would not advise you to try and heat so much glass with them; however, if you want to take the chance I would recommend placing in the new house six lines of 4-inch or nine lines of 2-inch pipe. If you desire to follow this arrangement you can take from each furnace three lines of 4-inch, and in case you use 2-inch, four lines from one furnace and five from the other. Your best plan would be to heat your whole establishment by hot water; but in case you do not wish to go to this expense I would suggest getting a boiler of, say, 600 feet 4-inch pipe rating, to economically heat the new house. This will not cost much, and the expense of altering the furnaces and putting coils in them, would probably amount to the cost of the boiler. I have figured liberally on heating surfaces, for you sometimes get very cold weather in your vicinity.

U. G. SCOLLAY.

REPLYING to E. J. H., Pa.—In house 75 x 27 feet space twelve lines of 4-inch pipe. In palm house ten lines, in forcing house 4 lines, under benches on east, south, and west sides, and two on north side of doorway, all 4-inch. I would recommend at least seven valves. Let your chimney have an area of at least 12 x 12 inches. It, of course, being assumed that your boiler has good easy capacity for the above job. You do not state what it is, so I cannot tell. As you have the boiler pit 7 feet deep, I would suggest that you run your mains across the palm house below grade, so that you can avoid the doorways. From these mains run a separate set to take care of the 75 x 27 foot house. If your boiler will permit it, you could run the mains for this house separately, and I would suggest not less than 4-inch for this house alone. You can distribute the pipes in the large carnation house four under each side bench, two under the outer center benches. You can put them up in two flow and two returns each for side benches and one flow and one return for center benches. The expansion tank can be located in the shed, and the ends of the circulation closed with air cocks. Let the rise of the pipes in the 95 foot run, be at least six inches more if you can get it.

The height of your chimney will be governed by surroundings. If there are no buildings around the boiler room, I should think that if you clear the ridge of the highest greenhouse by three or four feet you will have no trouble.

U. G. SCOLLAY.

I am building 2 side-hill greenhouses, the upper one is 20 by 90 feet; the lower one, 20 by 60 feet, connected as shown in accompanying diagram. How many feet of 1 1-2-inch pipe will it take for each house to heat to 60 degrees zero weather? I am using a boiler rated at 6,000 square feet of radiation. The boiler is situated 6 feet below the level of the lowest house.

Montana. W. E. M.

—The following layout is the simplest proposition that I can offer you The difference of the grade in the two houses will compel you to act along the lines I suggest. In the 60 by 20 foot house, sixteen lines 1½-inch pipe, and also 3-inch main to feed the 90 by 20 house running along the west wall of same from west to east to the far end of this house. From this main take off the 1½-inch pipe and grade them all toward the boiler. You can place six pipes under the south bench, three under each of the center benches and four under the north bench. These can all be taken off this said main at the far end with 2-inch connections to each coil. In the 90 by 20 foot house I would suggest that you run a separate 4-inch main from the boiler across the small house up to and into the 90 by 20 house. This main will only run across the west end of the 90 by 20 house. From this main you can take the branches for the sixteen pipe 1½-inch which are to go in this house. They are to be laid out in the same proportion as the other house. The pipes in this house will all rise from west to east, and the air vent be placed on the end of each of the four coils.

The air vent in the 60 by 20 foot house will be at the highest point on the 3-inch main at the far end, which main will be hung on the north wall, and on the far end, and the coils will then in this house not need venting, except at the point above mentioned.

I would suggest that the 3-inch main of the small house be run on the same level and grade as the 1½-inch pipes will be in the larger house. This will even up your circulation, and you should have no trouble. The 3-inch main in this house will about make up for the extra amount of glass that you have in it.

U. G. SCOLLAY.

SOUTH BEND, IND.—The South Bend Floral Company held its annual stockholders' meeting recently. Clem W. Studebaker was elected president; William Studebaker, secretary, and Irving W. Gingrich, treasurer and manager of the company.

Cincinnati, O.

News Notes.

W. E. Hall writes me under date of July 27, that a heavy hail storm had passed over his district, but Will being one of those lucky boys, the storm only smashed about fifty panes of glass. He is cutting and shipping some good asters to this market, as is also our esteemed friend George Bayer of Toledo, O.

Fred Gear leaves in a short time for a trip through Yellowstone Park.

C. J. Ohmer left at noon Monday for Boston.

As Cincinnati will run a special over the C., H. & D. R. R. to Dayton, leaving here at 8:15 a. m., we shall be more than pleased to have all the florists tributary to Cincinnati to go with us. It would be nice if Indianapolis and Chicago could join us at Hamilton, and all travel together to the convention city.

Mrs. Anne Garges leaves next Thursday for Atlantic City and New York. Mrs. Garges and daughter have a store on Central avenue. She is the daughter of Mr. and Mrs. Magrie, late of College Hill, who were among the pioneer florist families of this city. Mrs. Garges was in the employ of L. L. May & Company of Minneapolis, Minn.

Nicholas Weber, florist, having a store in Mohawk, Cincinnati, leaves Monday for a two weeks' trip to Milwaukee, Chicago, and other points accompanied by his wife and child.

Wm. Lodder of Hamilton, O., was also a caller. E. G. GILLETT.

Philadelphia.

News Notes.

Next Tuesday the Florists' Club meets, and as this is the last meeting before the convention a good attendance is expected. If you are going to Dayton, why don't you send word to John Westcott, so that he can talk business with the railroads? The rate is fixed; it will be $20.67 for the round trip, but accommodations depend upon the number which the committee can guarantee.

H. Bayersdorfer had a very successful trip in Europe. He has secured many sterling novelties, and has also been given the American agency for several lines of standard goods.

The Henry F. Michell Company has booked a large number of bulb orders this season. Several of these are filled in Holland and are shipped direct to the customers.

Paul Berkowitz and wife left on Wednesday for Altoona, Pa., for a two weeks' vacation; most of his time will be spent in the Allegheny mountains.

There has been a number of changes among employees of the wholesale commission houses the past week. John Wilson of the Leo Niessen Company has gone back to his old employers, Habermehl's Sons, in the retail store at Twenty-second and Diamond streets. Robert Glass of Leo. Neissen Company has gone with Samuel S. Pennock. Clarence Watson, formerly with Mr. Pennock, is now with the Leo Niessen Company.

Bayersdorfer & Company have had a very busy Summer; their packing department has been kept going at full capacity right along. Just now they are very busy, as four steamers are in with lots of new goods. The steamer Marquette has 150 cases of baskets on board; and other steamers now in with goods are the Amerika, Mississippi and the Armenia. One of these brought a lot of the well known Tone ware vases which are being shipped off in original cases.

The Chrysanthemum Society of America goes to Chicago, the American Rose Society to Washington; now, to make a fair deal, why should not the S. A. F. go to Boston next year?

DAVID RUST.

CONVENTION NUMBER NEXT WEEK.

THE FLORISTS' EXCHANGE

We are a ... aim to grow into a vigorous plant

A WEEKLY MEDIUM OF INTERCHANGE FOR FLORISTS, NURSERYMEN, SEEDSMEN AND THE TRADE IN GENERAL

Vol. XXII. No. 6 — NEW YORK AND CHICAGO, AUGUST 11, 1906 — One Dollar Per Year

HITE ROMAN HYACINTHS

11 to 12 cmt. $2.25 per 100; $18.00 per 1000
12 to 15 cmt. $2.50 per 100; $22.00 per 1000.
Paper Whites, 13 up $1.75 per 100; $9.00 per 1000.
Freesias, Ex. selected, 85c. 100; $7.50 per 1000.
Harrisii, 5 to 7 $3.75 per 100; $35.00 per 1000.
Canes, 6 to 9 feet, $6.00 per 1000.

Wm. Elliott & Sons, 201 Fulton Street, New York

Mention The Florists' Exchange when writing.

LILIUM PHILIPPINENSE

This lily was awarded a "Gold Medal" by the Massachusetts Horticultural Society. For description see our Bulb Catalogue. WE CAN DELIVER 100,000 OF THESE BULBS BY SEPTEMBER! It can easily be forced into flower inside of nine weeks. Considering this being a novelty we offer Lilium Philippinense at these remarkably low prices: Per dozen, $2.00; per 100, $12.00, per 1000, $100.00; per 10,000, $900.00.

W. W. RAWSON & CO.

5 UNION STREET, BOSTON, MASS.

Mention The Florists' Exchange when writing.

PACIFIC SEED GROWERS' CO.
411-415 SANSOME STREET
SAN FRANCISCO, CAL.
Specialties:
Onion, Carrot, Lettuce, Sweet Peas

Mention The Florists' Exchange when writing.

Thorburn's Bulbs

LILIUM HARRISII

LILIUM LONGIFLORUM

and all other bulbs for florists.
Send us your requirements for special prices.

CYCAS REVOLUTA STEMS

from Japan. Sizes and prices on application.
Asparagus plumosus nanus, $3.50 per 1000 seeds.

J. M. THORBURN & CO.,
33 Barclay St., New York.

Mention The Florists' Exchange when writing.

NOW READY

Zirngiebel's Prize Pansy Seeds,

in trade packages: $1.00 each.
GIANT MARKET, 2000 SEEDS.
GIANT FANCY, 600 SEEDS.
Full directions with each package.

Augustus Zirngiebel, Needham, Mass

Mention The Florists' Exchange when writing.

PANSY SEED

Of my own growing, crop of 1906, "**My Giant Market,**" the finest and largest variety of fancy colors to be had. In trade pkt. of 5000 seeds, $1.00 Plants ready September 1st. Cash with order.

E. A BLINN, CROMWELL, CONN.

Mention The Florists' Exchange when writing.

New Crop of my

Christmas Flowering SWEET PEA SEED

Christmas Pink and Florence Denzer, pure white, will be ready August 1st.

Those two well known varieties are raised by over 2000 florists all over the world. Here is one out of many letters received:

Dear Sir: My sweet peas, which I raised from your seed, received the highest award at the Carnation Exhibit in Boston, being over 18 inches long. JOHN T. GALE,
Tewkesbury, Mass.

Price 1-4 lb. 75c.; per lb. $2.00
MAILED FREE

New Christmas Flowering Hybrids, 20 to 30 colors, mostly blue, salmon, purple, lavender, in mixtures; also Mrs. Edie Wild, carmine, separate color. 1 Trade pkt., $1.00. 5 Trade pkts, $4.00; not more than 5 pkts. taken in order to each customer just now. These new hybrids are just as free bloomers as Cristmas Pink and Florence Denzer, some much larger, and received first-class Certificate of Merit by the Mass. Horticultural Society, Boston, March 24. Seed ready in Sept.
All seed originated with me is sold in my original sealed pkts., with cultural directions, to the growers, but none for seedsmen for propagating.
Orders filled strictly in rotation.

ANT. C. ZVOLANEK
BOUND BROOK, N. J.

Mention The Florists' Exchange when writing.

PANSY SEED

Brown's Extra Select Superb Giant Prize PANSIES, awarded Silver Medal, St. Louis Exposition 1904. My own grown new 1906 crop ready. Price mixed seed 3000 seeds, $1.00; ¼ oz., $1.50; ½ oz., $2.50., 1 oz., $5.00; ¼ lb., $14.00; ½ lb., $25.00; 1 lb., $50.00. Cash with order.

PETER BROWN
Lancaster, Pa.

Mention The Florists' Exchange when writing.

PANSY SEED

Famous Strains of Mammoth Mixed Pansies

S. & W. Co.'s NON PLUS ULTRA

Our Non Plus Ultra Pansy is a mixture containing the largest, handsomest, most perfect varieties ever sent out. The beautiful coloring and variety of marking give a bed of these pansies a most brilliant appearance; the seed having been saved from the greatest assortment of types, including only the best of Giant Cassier's, Bugnot's, Trimardeau, and Giant English, French and German strains. Finest mixed, per trade pkt., 25c.; ¼ oz., $1.50; per oz., $4.50.

Very Large Flowering Varieties

These are remarkably large Pansies, which, for size of flower and robust growth, eclipse all other strains. Their range of color has heretofore been limited, but this season we are able to offer several grand new varieties.

Pansy—Non Plus Ultra

Cassier's Large-Flowering

In form, color and size this pansy stands alone; the plants are very robust and the flowers are held well above the foliage, and should be grown amongst all other pansies, as they add to the effect on account of their robust habits.

Per pkt., 15c.; per oz. $2.50

S. & W. Co.'s Giant Purple	S. & W. Co's. White, dark eye
" " Pres. Carnot	" " Snow White
" " Rosy Lilac	" " Fire King
" " Lord Beaconsfield	" " Light Blue, white center
" " Kaiser Wilhelm	" " Aurical Aefiora
" " Yellow, black eye	" " King of the Blacks
" " Pure Yellow	" " Victoria Red

Per 500 seeds, 25c.; ¼ oz., 75c.; 1 oz., $2.50; ¼ lb., $8.00

CINERARIA, S. & W. Co.'s GIANT

Prize Strain, per pkt. 50c.; per 1000 seed $1.00.

PRIMULA—Sinensis.

Alba Magnifica	Rose Queen
Ruby Queen	Magenta Queen
Giant Blue	Scarlet Salmon
Giant Crimson	Mixed

per pkt. 50c.; per 1000 seeds $1.50.

FERNS IN FLATS

The cheapest and most convenient way to buy Ferns. These flats contain about 110 small clumps, when divided will make 2 to 3 plants each, making about 250 plants to the flat.
The following varieties we still have for sale.

Adiantum Cuneatum
Aspidium Tsussemense
Crytomium Falcatum
Lomaria Gibba
Pteris Adiantoides
Pteris Magnifica
Pteris Wimsettii
Pteris Cretica Albolineata
— Mixed —
$2.00 per flat.

STUMPP & WALTER CO., 50 Barclay St., New York

Mention The Florists' Exchange when writing.

PRIMROSES

Improved Chinese: Finest grown, named or mixed. Strong 2 inch. $2.00 per 100.

XXX SEEDS

CHINESE PRIMROSE

Finest grown, mixed, 500 seeds, $1.00; ½ pkt., 50c.
Cyclamen Giganteum: Finest Giant mixed, 200 seeds $1.00; ½ pkt., 50c.
DAISY: Double Giant mixed, 1000 Seeds 25c.

GIANT PANSY. The best large flowering varieties, critically selected, 5000 seeds $1.00; half pkt., 50c.; 500 seeds of Giant Mme. Perret, pansy seed added to every $1.00 pkt. of Giant Pansy. Cash. Liberal extra count of seeds in all packets.

JOHN F. RUPP, Shiremanstown, Pa.
The Home of Primroses

Mention The Florists' Exchange when writing.

Pansy Seed

THE JENNINGS STRAIN

New crop now ready, saved from finest selected stock, large flowering and great variety of fancy colors. By mail one pkt., 4000 seed, $1.00; ¼ oz., $2.50; 1 oz., $5.00, 2 oz., $9.00; 3 oz., $12.00. Cash with order.

E. B. JENNINGS,
Lock Box 254 Southport, Conn.
Grower of the Finest Pansies.

Mention The Florists' Exchange when writing.

Commercial Violet Culture

Price, $1.50

The Florists' Exchange, 2-8 Duane St., New York

Seed Trade Report.

AMERICAN SEED TRADE ASSOCIATION

Henry W. Wood, Richmond, Va., president; C. S. Burge, Toledo, O., first vice-president; G. B. McVay, Birmingham, Ala., second vice-president; C. E. Kendel, Cleveland, O., secretary and treasurer; J. H. Ford, Ravenna, O., assistant secretary.

NEW YORK.—S. B. Dicks representing Cooper, Taber & Co., London, arrived per s. s. Campania to-day and can be heard of care of R. J. Godwin's Sons, 16-18 Exchange Place, New York City.

NEW YORK.—Maurice Fuld, manager for W. W. Rawson & Company, seedsmen, Boston, Mass., was in town this week.

O. H. R. Weise of Sachs & Company, seedsmen, Quedlinburg, is in town on his annual tour of the United States.

CHICAGO.—The harvest of onion sets is now nearly completed. Everybody connected with this important branch in this section is now busy, and as the crop as a whole is light the work will soon be completed.

TO INCREASE IOWA'S CORN CROP.—An appropriation by the Iowa legislature of $35,000 is to be expended to increase the yield of corn in that State by 5,000,000 bushels. Professor P. G. Holden, of the Iowa State Agricultural College at Ames, is to have charge of the matter. Last year there were about 9,000,000 acres of corn in Iowa, and the average yield was 36 bushels to the acre. The year before the yield was 32 bushels. Professor Holden believes that by the proper selection of the seed corn one-third can be added to the yield of the State, and that the proposed increase of 5,000,000 bushels is a very conservative figure. To accomplish this he has planned to go into every section of the State and reach practically every farmer until he has the seed corn theories thoroughly inculcated into them.

Farmers' Bulletin 254 of the Department of Agriculture, Washington, D. C., is devoted to Cucumbers. Professor L. C. Corbett, the author, gives full cultural directions for outdoors and for forcing, also other valuable information.

European Notes.

It should have been stated in last week's notes that the acreage of radish left standing in Holland is very small, as one large grower informed the writer that he had arranged to grow a good quantity, but the season was against him from the first. At any rate, there is very little standing now, and that looks very bad at present and is now beyond revival.

Spinach is ripening up very rapidly for which growers are grateful as the Summer trade has quite exhausted last season's stocks. If the storms which are flying round just now are only temporary we may be able to ship this article inside of three weeks.

The aforesaid storms are very acceptable to all except the early farmers who are now busy cutting their grain crops.

Mangel and broad beans are in several places infested with aphis; the storms will not only wash these down, but also help the development of the seed. EUROPEAN SEEDS.

QUEDLINBURG SEED CROPS.—The weather during the whole of June, alternative rain and sunshine, was favorable to the growing seed crops, and brought them a good deal forward, though they are at present about a week or two behind the usual time.

Harvest crops.—Corn salad, good; turnips and forget-me-not (Myosotis alpestris varieties), middling and pretty good.

Present state of growing crops—Vegetable seeds: Beans, dwarf or kidney and runner, partly good, partly middling, and the delicate varieties below middling. Beetroots, carrots, cress, chervil, chicory, leek, lettuces, onions, parsley, parsnips and radishes good. Peas, round-seeded varieties, good; wrinkled marrow varieties, middling. Cabbage, white, red and savoy, Kohlrabi and spinach, middling and pretty good. Cucumber, ridge varieties, these have seriously suffered from the unfavorable weather and they stand rather thin.

Farm Seeds—Mangels, sugar beets and swedes, partly good and partly middling.

Flower Seeds—open-ground cultures.—Pansies, although they look very well, the yield of the crop appears to turn out below middling owing to frequent heavy rains that caused part of the flowers to pass away without setting seed. Stocks, wallflowers, asters, larkspurs, balsams, carnations, mignonette, nasturtiums, sweet peas, snapdragons, scabious, Canterbury bells, sweet william, sweet sultan, chinese pink (Dianthus chinensis and varieties), lobelias, lupins, helichrysum, marigold, petunias, polyanthus, violets, zinnias and the miscellaneous flowers are partly good and partly middling while hollyhocks and Drummondi phlox stand rather thin.

Principal pot-grown flower seeds: Stocks, annual, Autumn and Winter, double wallflowers, large-flowered petunias, begonias, calceolarias, cinerarias, cyclamen, gloxinias, Primula chinensis and obconica, pelargoniums, etc., and partly good and partly middling.

On the whole the present state of the growing seed crops may be considered as satisfactory.— Horticultural Trade Journal.

HOLLAND SEED CROPS.—Sluis & Groot, seed-growers and merchants, Enkhuizen, Holland, make the following report for July, 1906: Generally speaking, crops, owing to exceptionally cold weather in the Spring, are somewhat backward. Cauliflower stands fairly good, white cabbage, red cabbage, Savoy, Brussels sprouts, and borecole very small plantations and general stand a middling one, a part even considerably under middling. Turnip, exceptionally small acreage; stand fairly good. Swedes, very small plantation, with poor prospects of crop. Kohlrabi, little sown; stand fair. Mangel-Wurzel, sugar beet, and beet fairly good. Carrot as a whole promises a fair crop; stand rather thin. Parsnips and scorzonera, very good, not much planted. Corn salad, excellent crop. Radish, Summer, suffered considerably from insects, so that a considerable acreage was lost; what was left is fairly good. Radish, Winter, not much planted; stand pretty promising. Onion, small plantations; stand good. Garlic bulbs, good. Celeriac and parsley, middling stand. Borage, looks good but rather late. Chervil, average crop, but a considerable acreage was lost. Chervil, curled, a total failure almost. Spinach, promises an average crop. Cucumbers, pretty good. Peas, generally very good. Dwarf beans and running beans promise a middling crop although rather late owing to very cold weather in the Spring. English beans, excellent crop.

Flower seeds.—Prospects of the growing crops are not so favorable as last year being somewhat backward, owing to the cold weather in May. We expect, however, that if the weather continues favorable, the crop as a whole will be still an average one. Antirrhinum is excellent. Calliopsis looks good; small plantation. Campanula, owing to the dry weather of last Autumn most of the plants remained too small and consequently did not run to seed. Very small crop in several sorts. Candytuft, middling crop. Centaurea, very good stand, not much sown. Convolvulus, stand very good. Dianthus look very promising. Eschscholtzia, very good. Gypsophila, good. Helichrysum looks promising up till now. Lobelia, stand fair. Mignonette, average crop, rather thin. Mimulus, excellent crop. Myosotis, fairly good. Nasturtium, very fairly good. Nemophila, good. Pansies, average crop; small plantations. Papaver, good crop. Petunia, fairly good, rather late. Phlox, average crop. Rhodanthe, pretty good. Stocks, Virginian, little sown. Stand very good as yet. Sweet peas, little sown; look good. Ten-weeks stocks, rather late. Verbena, very good. Wallflower, crop apparently under middling.

MARKET FOR AMERICAN SEEDS—Consul Maxwell Blake writes from Funchal that during the first half of this year the heavy rains and unusual cold weather destroyed certain Madeira Island crops and seriously threatened the maturity of others. The low temperature resisted the efforts of the seeds even as late as May, a month when generally the soil is very warm. The potato crop was practically destroyed, beans also rotted in the soil, and the sweet potato, perhaps the most essential article of food in the diet of the peasant, has been very greatly damaged. All seeds for next year's crops will, as a consequence, be short of the demand and thus very much dearer. Here is offered a splendid opportunity for the market of American seeds, as it is generally admitted that the seeds of our drier climate have never failed of good results whenever they have been used in Madeira. Seeds are admitted duty free. There is, however, a small octroi tax. [The Funchal dealers in seeds are named by the consul, and the names can be secured from the Bureau of Manufactures. Correspondence with them should be in Portuguese.]

CATALOGUES RECEIVED.

HERBST & COMPANY, Rathenov, Germany.—Price List of roses.

D. A. KOSTER, Boskoop, Holland.—General Catalogue of Nursery Stock for 1906-7.

HENRY F. MICHELL COMPANY, Philadelphia, Pa.—Wholesale Catalogue and Price List of Bulbs, Seeds, and Seasonable Supplies. Illustrated.

ARTHUR T. BODDINGTON, New York City.—Price List of Seeds of the Best Hardy Perennials and Old-fashioned Flowers. Also Catalogue of Bulbs for Forcing and Planting.

NURSERY DEPARTMENT.

Conducted by Joseph Meehan.

AMERICAN ASSOCIATION OF NURSERYMEN, Orlando Harrison, Berlin, Md., president; J. W. Hill, Des Moines, Ia., vice-president; George C. Seager, Rochester, N. Y., secretary; C. L. Yates, Rochester, N. Y., treasurer.

THE SOUTHERN NURSERYMEN'S ASSOCIATION holds its annual meeting on Lookout Mountain, Tenn., Wednesday and Thursday, August 15 and 16. A very interesting program has been prepared, copies of which can be obtained from Secretary Charles T. Smith, Concord, Ga. Orlando Harrison, Berlin, Md., is president.

Lagerstroemia Indica.

In your notes on lagerstrœmia in The Florists' Exchange of July 21, you mention the fact that in the South these plants are easily raised from hardwood cuttings. That is correct as to all the varieties except the white. This does not readily strike root; in fact, the percentage is so small as hardly to justify planting hardwood cuttings. My personal experience in the South taught me that very good success was had with root cuttings, and that was the only way I grew the white crepe myrtle.

Your notes are always so full of pith and good points that I can best show my interest and appreciation by mentioning my own experience when it differs from yours.

Newark, N. Y. JOHN WATSON,
of Jackson & Perkins Company.

[Mr. Watson has our thanks for his note concerning the lagerstrœmia, and for his kind expression of appreciation of the horticultural department. The last word in the paragraph he refers to in July 21 issue should read "seeds" instead of "cuttings" as printed. J. M.]

Seasonable Topics.

Rehmannia angulata is a perennial of much merit. It blooms abundantly in July and August, the flowers, not unlike those of a foxglove in general appearance, being of a rosy purple color, and produced abundantly. The leaves are incised. Being a native of Japan and China it should prove well adapted to our climate. Its tall spikes, two to three feet high, are excellent for cutting purposes.

Veronica longifolia subsessilis is a most useful subject for cut flower work. It forms spikes of purplish blue blossoms on stems two feet high. The half drooping undeveloped ends of the flower heads add grace to a vase of mixed cut flowers. It is a Japanese perennial.

Some of the early flowering magnolias, such as Soulangeana and Lennei, are now as full of flowers almost as they were in early Spring. It is not rare to see a few flowers on the trees at this season, Midsummer, but it is rare to see so many. The Summer has been wet and warm, causing growth to continue, and forcing out the flowers which drier weather would have kept dormant until Spring.

With the nice growing weather the rains and heat provide, if the old flower heads of many spiræas are cut off, notably those of Anthony Waterer, a display of blooms will follow almost the equal of the first one.

Continual cultivation among trees is a most profitable operation. Soil so worked will contain moisture long after that with a hard crust is dust dry. Nursery trees when in ground harrowed all Summer make a fine, strong growth, even when rains come seldom.

In the Middle Atlantic States generally there have been numerous rains, with hot weather, and every nurseryman met with is pleased with the way his stock is growing. Evergreens are looking better than they have done for years. There was a drought in May, injuring some newly set stock; but June and July brought the very best sort of weather.

Polygonum lanigerum is a new species in collection of this well known genus. It has leaves of silvery whiteness, on both sides, and making a height of 5 to 6 feet it forms a conspicuous clump. The flowers, which are of a light orange, are not to be valued as are the silvery leaves. It is a perennial, from the tropics of the old world, but whether hardy here remains to be proved.

The common rudbeckia of our fields, R. hirta, is a showy perennial, and its heads of yellow flowers are larger when under cultivation than when in a wild state. The one known as speciosa (Newmanni) may be said to be an improved form of hirta in appearance.

English Ivy.

A correspondent sends us a sprig of ivy of which he says he has plants purchased for English ivy. He is in doubts of its being the true sort, and asks if it is Hedera helix. The leaves on the sprig he sends are not such as are found on what is looked upon as the typical English ivy, though it is Hedera helix. This botanical name covers a host of varieties of ivy, nearly all varieties of English ivy. The latter ivy has a leaf of moderate size, angular and three or five-lobed. Many of the varieties have much larger leaves, some of them hardly lobed at all; and although useful in many ways, are not thought as pretty as those with deeply lobed foliage. There is now in my garden a variety secured from an English wood; the leaves are very small and finely divided, yet approaching in character the typical English ivy. The one sent me by the correspondent referred to has almost entire leaves, and seems of robust growth. It reminds me of one sometimes found in collections under the name of Hedera helix Regneriana, of which there is a tree form now rather common.

Beauty of Viburnum Lantana.

There are many trees and shrubs of far more beauty when in fruit than they are when in flower. References have been made before to the Viburnum cassinoides, V. tomentosum, V. Wrightii, Magnolia macrophylla, M. tripetala, Vitus heterophylla and others, all of which bear berries of greater attraction to many than are the flowers. Just now on lawns hereabout the Eglish shrub or small tree, Viburnum Lantana, is displaying its attractive heads of fruit. Early in Spring it bore white flowers, in large flat heads. The green berries which followed became red in early July; now at the close of the month they are of a shining black. As the red and the black berries are mingled on the same heads they form a pleasing combination.

Those who sell shrubs make no mistake when they recommend this one; and it thrives well in almost all ordinary places. In Britain, where it is common, it rejoices in a chalky soil, where it is usually met with. There it is called "wayfaring tree."

All these shrubs with handsome berries do much to add to the pleasure of one's grounds; and many who recognize this, use their efforts to get together as good a collection of them as they can.

Flowering Branches of Cornus Mas.

Cornus Mas, European Dogwood.

In many collections of shrubs the European dogwood, Cornus Mas, is the very first of all to flower, and for this reason it is held in high esteem by all, especially those who know of its beauty of bloom and fruit as well. The flower buds form in Autumn, in the same way as those of our native one, Cornus florida, so it is known long before Spring arrives whether flowers are coming or not. But there is no need of looking for the buds beforehand, for if the bush be in a favorable place for it, an open one, and it is large enough to bloom, it will never miss flowering every Spring. In the Middle States early April is the time for it to flower; sometimes warm days in late March, will bring it into bloom.

The flowers of this dogwood are not at all like those of our large white one. They are quite small, yellow and borne in little clusters, such as our illustrations show. It is the large numbers of the flowers that cause the fine display. Just a sight of the bush photographed and of the twigs as well will show one how thickly the flowers are studded along the branches. The bush pictured was such a sight that many went out of their way to see it.

It is, of course, the earliness of its blooming that makes the dogwood so much observed. There is absolutely no other flowering shrub making a display equal to it then; and remembering how the first flowers of Spring charm us all it will be understood why the European dogwood is so much sought for.

The beauty of this dogwood does not end with its flowering. Berries are formed, which become of the size of small plums, and by Summer time these ripen, and are then of a bright red color. Their appearance has suggested for this dogwood the common name, Cornelian cherry. A good deal of pulp covers the bony seeds, and those who wish can make tarts of the berries as do some of the housekeepers of Europe.

There is a variegated leaved variety of this dogwood, as well as one with leaves marked with white and red.

This shrub is known i nthe trade as English dogwood. Curiously, while quite common in English gardens, it is not a native of that part of Europe.

JOSEPH MEEHAN.

Cornus Mas—European Dogwood.

ROSES

Plants that were benched in May or June will now be making a pretty good growth, and tying will become necessary; though it seems to benefit the plants to allow them to lie around for a while, without any support as they break much stronger. Still tying must not be put off too long. Wire stakes are the best for general use, except where American Beauty is grown, when wires run lengthwise of the bench will be found much more convenient, and better in every way. We use but one stake to a plant. Care must be taken, however, not to tie the plants too close, or to bunch them up. Tie each shoot separately; of course where two stakes are used to a plant the shoots can be spread a little more, allowing of a better circulation of air. The stakes should be at least three feet long, and where the bench is too close to the glass, the stakes can be slanted; but roses should have at least three feet of head room, to do well. The wires on the Beauty benches should be in 3 to 4 tiers, the first 15 inches above the soil, the others 18 inches apart. Where a bench holds three rows of plants, there should be four of wire, and where there are four rows of plants put five of wire. There is thus a better chance to spread the plants, and less danger of spot and red spider later on. When tying the strong bottom shoots of this rose great care must be taken not to pull the knots too tight; always allow for future growth.

Syringing must now be carefully attended to, so that the plants are clean when the short days come. Never neglect an opportunity to fumigate the houses two or three times a week, whenever the temperature is below 70 or 72 degrees, or green fly and thrips will flourish. The dark muggy and stormy weather of the past week has greatly softened the plants; therefore to overcome this leave on all the air possible, night and day; when clear the ventilators should be wide open at all time.

From now on however, the doors and side ventilators should be kept closed. Keep the soil loose, though in the early houses scratching must be carefully done, as the roots are getting very near the surface. A little air-slaked lime, applied lightly, will be beneficial, especially where the green scum is in evidence.

It is still too early for feeding or mulching, though manure for the first mulch should now be turned over frequently. Remember that the more decayed it is, the better it will be. As there is really nourishment enough in the soil for some time yet the idea of this early mulch is merely to protect the fine feeding roots which will ere long be right on the surface of the soil. Keep the benches a little on the dry side, never allow them to get soggy. Before syringing, make sure the soil is not too dry, otherwise the foliage will scald.

PENN.

LIST OF ADVERTISERS

INDEX TO STOCK ADVERTISED

Contents.

PAGE

REVIEW OF THE MARKET

NEW YORK.—Business in cut flowers is at a very low ebb, there being very little doing in any line. The heavy rain storms have spoiled the aster supply for the time being, and many of these flowers are offered at fifteen or twenty cents a hundred so that clearances can be made; but even then it is a difficult matter to move them.

Roses are coming in more plentifully, but the weather is so warm that they open out quite a good deal by the time they reach the city; and business in general is so poor, that excepting for a few of special grade, there is practically no demand for them and prices are anything but what they should be.

Carnations are conspicuous by their absence; but there is plenty of other stock to more than make up the carnation deficiency. Of lilies and gladiolus there is an abundance and of lily of the valley and cattleyas there is enough to supply all demands, with no change in values.

Supplies of Hydrangea paniculata grandiflora are coming in heavily, but as yet the retailers are not finding much use for these flowers. Green material of all kinds is selling very poorly, and the average prices are lower than has been the rule for a long time.

During the latter part of the week American Beauty roses became so plentiful that special and other grades had to be sold by the box; and it was believed that the average prices would not be over $3 per hundred.

CHICAGO.—The market is in a comatose state. "Nothing doing," is the slightly slangy expression which greets the reportorial inquiry as to market conditions in nine cases out of ten.

W. K. W.

BOSTON.—A week of excessively warm weather has caused business to be quiet. In fact very little has been done to make any changes from reports of a week ago. There are few good roses, except American Beauty; all other varieties have very small blooms. Carnations are poor; asters are the most plentiful of any flowers at present, and there has not been any extra demand for them. Sweet peas are beginning to show the effects of the warm weather. Lilies are good with prices as a week ago.

J. W. D.

PHILADELPHIA.—There are probably more flowers on hand just now than have been seen before at this time of year. New crop American Beauty roses are here before all the old crop blooms have disappeared. Among those cutting from new plants are Alfred Burton, Robert Scott & Son, George Burton and Meyers & Samtman. There is also a very large quantity of tea roses yet coming in; David Anderson is cutting as many flowers of these as he did three months ago. Asters are piling up every day, and the very best quality flowers only are selling.

Robert Scott & Son are sending in some very good Liberty and Killarney roses.

Most of the street peddlers are now at the seashore resorts, and judging from the way they are buying, business is good with them. They purchase a better quality of stock for that trade.

D. R.

ST. LOUIS.—Business is dull. Plenty of stock is on hand, but first class grade flowers are scarce. Plenty of roses are to be had, very much off color and soft. Carnations are in the same condition; there is hardly any use to quote prices, as one's own figure will buy most of the stock. So many asters are coming in that quantities go to waste. Asters bring 25c. to $1 per 100; white and purple sell best. The supply of gladioli is shortening up somewhat, but more than enough is in the market at 1c. to 2c. per stalk in small lots. Lily of the valley is scarce, and but little called for. The green market is in good condition.

ST. PATRICK.

ST. PAUL.—The usual quiet times prevail throughout the trade, although we have had much better business this year than we have had during July in any year for some time past. Stock is still remarkably scarce. Roses of good quality are indeed hard to obtain, and it will be some time before we will have any great number of them. Carnations are also scarce and of very poor quality. Asters are helping out wonderfully in the funeral work line, and sweet peas are also brought into play nicely. It is noticeable, however, that sweet peas this season are much inferior to those of past years, no doubt due to the continued rains we have had during the plants' best blooming season. Funeral work seems to be about all the florists have to depend on at this time and judging by calling at four of the larger places they have been kept quite busy with it during the week. Prices remain firm no doubt due to the shortage of stock.

PAUL.

MINNEAPOLIS.—Business is very quiet with the majority of the dealers. One or two are in all probability favored a little more than the rest, but there is none of them doing a very active trade; indeed, if conditions were otherwise, it would be a very hard matter to meet the demand, as all stock is extremely scarce. Roses are very scarce, and those arriving are very small and inferior and one could not very well ask more than $1 per dozen for them. Bride and Bridesmaid are very small and were it not for the fact that all dealers have about the same quality of stock they could not be sold at all.

Carnations are of very inferior quality and vary in price. No American Beauty to speak of are grown in this section and what we get comes from an outside point. Lilies help out wonderfully particularly in funeral work, which seems to have been good with some of the trade.

Carnations are looking very fine in some of the fields and several growers will undoubtedly have some good strong plants. Young stock of roses as a rule looks very good, and the prospects are for good stock this Fall. Owing to the heavy improvements made by the growers we can reasonbly expect to get more roses this year than in the past season.

PAUL.

INDIANAPOLIS.—The lowest ebb has apparently been reached in the year's business; all lines, even funeral work, have fallen off perceptibly. Although the cut is comparatively light, flowers are plentiful; at the market, vase after vase of choice asters stood without a buyer at 75c. to $1 a 100. A limited quantity of light colored gladioli is sold at $2 to $3 a 100. Longiflorum lilies move well at times for $2 a dozen; L. rubrum sells as well as any flower at $5 a 100. A few Enchantress, White Cloud and Mrs. Lawson carnations relieve this market, going at $1.50 per 100. The various roses are plentiful at same prices as quoted last week. The severe dry spell has caused much damage to carnations remaining in the field.

I. B.

CINCINNATI, O.—The past week has seen the largest glut of asters that this market has had in many years; consequently the prices have gone all to pieces. Then there has been no demand to move the stock. Gladioli have suffered from the same cause. One of the finest gladiolus that I have seen this season is a light Daybreak pink shade and has a fine truss of flowers; this sells readily at 3c. and in some markets would command a much higher price. Roses and carnations are not of much force and very few are coming into the market. Sweet peas are about gone.

E. G. G.

NEW BEDFORD, MASS.—Trade the past week has been very quiet. Flowers are quite plentiful, asters are now in full swing; and there is an abundance of sweet peas coming into market just now. A few carnations are still to be seen; these are fairly good. The prices asked are: 35c. per dozen; asters, 35c. per dozen; sweet peas, 50c. per hundred.

R. H. Woodhouse has a patch of phlox which is grand; some fine colors are to be seen in it.

S. S. Peckham has discontinued his Walnut street greenhouses and will devote his whole attention to his Sixth street store and conservatory and his range of glass in Fairhaven.

E. Y. Pierce on Cottage street has his new house planted to roses which are looking well. He will commence to house his carnations next week.

We have had plenty of rain lately and stock in the field is looking in good condition.

HORTICO.

CHANGES IN BUSINESS.

GRAFTON, MASS. — Norcross & Stratton have rented their greenhouses on South street, to Thomas Heskey, Hopedale, formerly head gardener for Draper estate, Hopedale. Mr. Heskey will begin work soon to get ready for Winter business.

GRUNDY CENTER, IA.—Roy McCullough has leased the greenhouse plant of Theo. Soners, who has retired from the business on account of ill health.

WHEELING, W. VA.—Misses Clara Forbes and Mary Donahey will shortly open a flower store in Market street, this city. Miss Forbes has been for years manager of the Wheeling Greenhouse Company. Miss Donahey recently resigned as high school teacher in the Martins Ferry school.

BUFFALO, N. Y.—The Central Park Floral Company has been incorporated; capital, $2,000. Incorporators: Julius A. Goehle, Henry Hart, Clara C. Hamocher, Buffalo, N. Y.

NEXT SATURDAY

AUGUST 18, 1906

THE DAYTON CONVENTION

EDITION WILL BE PUBLISHED

Beautifully illustrated; replete with information and interesting from cover to cover.

This issue appeals to every advertiser who has goods to offer at this season for the reason that the Trade generally look for this particular number of The Florists' Exchange to advise them of what is new, of what is attractive, and of what is a bargain. It marks, too, the preliminary opening of the Fall season.

The judicious use of our columns, if commenced with this issue and persisted in, should have its good effect on each individual advertiser's business throughout the Fall and Winter.

Advertisements received until Wednesday, August 15

We do not solicit advertising that would not be profitable, but we do ask for a full measure of that business which is seasonable and appropriate. Copy should be forwarded us without delay.

THE FLORISTS' EXCHANGE,
P. O. BOX 1697.
Nos. 2 to 8 DUANE STREET, NEW YORK CITY.

GET THE BEST

IT DON'T PAY TO BUY POOR STOCK

	100	1000		100	1000
RICHMOND ROSE, 2½ inch	$5.00	$40.00	3½ inch	$6.50	$56.00
AMERICAN BEAUTIES, 3 inch	5.00	40.00	3½ inch	6.50	55.00
BRIDESMAIDS, 3½ inch	5.00	45.00			
CHATENAY, 2½ inch	3.50	30.00	3½ inch	5.00	45.00
UNCLE JOHN, 2½ inch	3.50	30.00	3½ inch	5.00	45.00
GOLDEN GATES, 2½ inch	3.50	30.00	3½ inch	4.50	
KAISERIN, 2½ inch	3.50	30.00			
SUNRISE, 3½ inch	5.50	50.00			
PERLES, 3½ inch	6.00	55.00			

SATISFACTION ABSOLUTELY GUARANTEED

SPRENGERI, 2 inch .... $2.20 per 100; $18.00 per 1000
PLUMOSUS, 2 inch .... 2.50 " 22.00 "
YELLOW SNAPDRAGON, 3½ inch .... 5.00 " 45.00 "

FIELD GROWN CARNATION PLANTS

FREE FROM STEM ROT OR OTHER DISEASES. STRONG HEALTHY PLANTS

	100	1000		100	1000
MRS. THOS. LAWSON	5.00	$45.00	RED SPORT OF MACEO	$4.00	$35.00
WHITE LAWSON	6.00	50.00	QUEEN	4.00	35.00
WOLCOTT	4.00	35.00	PATTEN	4.00	35.00
PROSPERITY	4.00	35.00	ELSIE MARTIN	4.00	35.00
THE BELLE	4.00	35.00	HARLOWARDEN	4.00	35.00
BOUNTIFUL	6.00	55.00	FIANCEE	4.00	35.00
ENCHANTRESS	6.00	55.00	CARDINAL	6.00	50.00
PHYLLIS	4.00				

POEHLMANN BROS. COMPANY, MORTON GROVE, ILL.

Mention The Florists' Exchange when writing.

LOOK! See Us Grow.

A GOOD INVESTMENT; BETTER THAN BONDS.

Have you any loose change? If so, make 100 per cent. on your money. Write an order to Godfrey Aschmann for his Araucaria excelsa, glauca or compacta. Prices will soon advance. This kind of bond never fails.

ARAUCARIA EXCELSA a specialty. 6,000 are in now, imported from Ghent, Belgium this Spring, 1906. Now planted in 5½ and 6 in.-pots, well established, and ready for shipment to all parts of America. All these are grown for us by an Araucaria Specialist in Ghent, Belgium. **NO SEEDLINGS**, but Araucarias raised from top cuttings only are offered. This is now our 11th Anniversary, and our importations have grown from 250 in the first year to the remarkable number of **6,000 IN THE ELEVENTH YEAR.** My reputation as Araucaria Importer gains footway in every greenhouse and florist store in America. Our Araucarias need no *coaxing*, genuine facts tell in quality and cheapness.

Please Note Our Lowest Prices

12 to 14 in. 5½ in. pots, 3 to 4 tiers, 2-yr. old, 50c. 14 to 16 in., 5½ in. pots, 3 to 4 tiers, 2-yr. old, 60c. 16 to 18 in. 5½ to 6 in. pots, 4 to 5 tiers, 3-yr. old, 75c. 18 to 20 in., 6 in. pots, 5 to 6 tiers, 4-yr. old, $1.00. 20 to 24 in. 6 in. to 7 in. pots, 5 to 6 tiers, 4-yr. old, $1.25. 36-40 to 50 in. 7 in. pots, specimen plants from $2.50 to $3.00 each.

ARAUCARIA COMPACTA ROBUSTA—have several thousand of them; can supply all wants. These plants were never so fine in shape and condition as this year. The set of the greenhouse, as broad as long, 12 to 20 in. in height, 3 to 4 perfect tiers, 20 to 30 inches across, 3-4-5 year old, 6 to 7 in. pots, $1.25, $1.50, $1.75, $2.00, $2.50 to $3.00 each.

ARAUCARIA EXCELSA GLAUCA—This variety on account of its beautiful Green-Blueish tiers, dwarf habit, fine compact shape, gives it a striking appearance, and anybody seeing them, must undoubtedly fall in love with them at sight. Plants, 6-7 inch pots, 3-4-5 perfect tiers, 3-4 year old, 15 to 25 inch high, from 15 to 30 in. across, $1.25, $1.50, $1.75, $2.00 to $2.50 each.

SOLANUM or JERUSALEM CHERRY, $5.00 per 100.

KENTIA BELMOREANA, 5½ to 6 in. pots, bushy, fine plants, from 75 cts. to $1.00 to $1.25 each.

KENTIA FORSTERIANA, 7 in. pots, made-up plants, 1 large in center, 3 smaller sizes, 22 to 25 in. high around, gives them a good appearance, $2.00 each. 6 in. pots, single plants, 35 to 40 in. high, 5 to 6 good leaves, 4 year old, $1.25 to $1.50 each; 6 in. pots, 30 to 35 in. high, 4 year old, 5 good leaves, $1.00; 5½ in. pots, 3 year old, 25 to 30 in. high, 5 good leaves, 75c. made-up plants, 3 and 4 in. pots, 18 to 20 in. high, 25 cts. to 30 cts. each.

ARECA LUTESCENS, made-up, 25 cts.

COCOS WEDDELIANA, 15 cts.

CYCAS REVOLUTA (Sago Palm), 6 in.-7 in. pots, with from 6 to 20 leaves per plant, 10 cts. per leaf.

NEPHROLEPIS BARROWSII, 6 in. pots, strong, ready for 7-8 in., 75c. 4 in. pots, 25c.

NEPHROLEPIS SCOTTII, 6 in. pots, 50c.; 4 in. pots, 20c.

BOSTON FERNS, 4 in., 20c.

FERNS for dishes, a fine assortment, 2½ in., $5.00 per 100.

CASH WITH ORDER

When ordering, say whether the plants should be shipped in the pots or not

GODFREY ASCHMANN

Importer and Wholesale Grower of Pot Plants

1012 Ontario Street, - - PHILADELPHIA, PA.

Mention The Florists' Exchange when writing.

DRACAENA TERMINALIS Matured canes always ready for shipment. Delivered to any part of the United States for 10 cents a foot. Send cash for a trial order.

PORTO RICO PINEAPPLE CO., RIO PIEDRAS, PORTO RICO.

Mention The Florists' Exchange when writing.

Dreer's Kentias

Nearly Three Acres to select from.

KENTIA FORSTERIANA—MADE-UP PLANTS

			Each
5 in. pots, 4 plants in a pot,	18 to 18	inches	$0.60
6 " 3 " "	20 to 24	"	1.00
7 " 3 " "	24 to 28	"	1.50
7 " 3 " "	28 to 30	"	2.00
7-in. tubs, 4 plants in a tub,	34 to 36	"	2.50
7 " 4 " "	36 to 40	"	3.00
8-in pots, 3 plants in a pot,	36 to 40	"	3.00
9 " 4 " "	3½	feet	4.00
9-in. tubs, 4 plants in a tub,	3½ to 4	"	5.00
10-in. pots, 4 plants in a pot,	4	"	6.00
9-in. tubs, 4 plants in a tub,	4½	"	7.50
12 " 4 " "	7 to 8	"	15.00
13 " 6 " "	very heavy 5½ to 6 feet		15.00
14 " 4 " "	8 to 9 feet		25.00

We call special attention to the $15.00 plants which for decorative purposes will be found one of the best values we have ever offered, they have been grown in small tubs and are in a very convenient shape for handling.

KENTIA FORSTERIANA—SINGLE PLANTS

				Per doz.	Per 100	Per 1000
2½ in. pts.	4 leaves,	8 to 10 in.	high	$1.50	$10.00	$90.00
3 "	5 "	12 to 15	"	2.00	15.00	140.00
4 "	5 "	15	"	4.50	35.00	
						Each
6 "	6 "	24 to 28	"			$1.00
6 "	6 "	28 to 30	"			1.25
6 "	6 "	30 to 32	"			1.50
7 "	6 "	34 to 36	"			2.00
7 "	6 "	36 to 40	"			2.50
9 "	6 "	46 to 48	"			3.50
7 in. tubs,	6 "	48	"			4.00
8 "	6 "	4½	ft. high			5.00
10 "	6 to 7 "	5 to 5½	"			10.00
10 "	6 to 7 "	8½ to 9	"			15.00

The $10.00 and $15.00 plants are tall handsome specimens, grand stock for decorating and of excellent value.

KENTIA BELMOREANA

				Per doz.	Per 100	Per 1000
2½ in. pts,	4 leaves,	8 to 10 in.	high	$1.50	$10.00	$90.00
3 "	5 "	12	"	2.00	15.00	140.00
						Each
6 "	6 "	20 to 24	"			$1.00
6 "	6 "	24 to 26	"			1.25
6 "	6 to 7 "	26 to 28	"			1.50
7 "	6 "	30 to 32	"			2.00
7 "	6 "	36 to 40	"			3.00
9 in. tubs,	6 to 7 "	46 to 48	"	very heavy		7.50

K. Belmoreana at $1.00, $1.25, $1.50 and $2.00 each are scarce and values are not as good as in past seasons, the plants as sent out however, are full market value.

HENRY A. DREER,

714 Chestnut St., PHILADELPHIA, PENNA.

Mention The Florists' Exchange when writing.

Seaforthia Elegans

ONE of the finest housepalms and exceedingly useful to the florist for decorating. We grow in quantity. Note ne prices:—

8 in. pots, 4 to 6 leaves, 4 to 4½ ft. high, $2.00 each.
9 in. pots, 5 or 6 leaves, about 5 ft. high, $3.75 each.
12 in. pots (or tubs) 5 to 7 leaves, 5-6 ft. high, $4.75 each.

These can be sent by freight safely now up to cold weather. Ask for our illustrated catalogue.

REASONER BROS.
Royal-Palm Nurseries
ONECO, FLORIDA

Mention The Florists' Exchange when writing.

COCOS PALMS.

Strong 2¼ inch at $1.50 per dozen. Write for lowest prices on Kentias.

Jas. F. Barclay R. I. GREENHOUSES Pawtucket, R. I.

Mention The Florists' Exchange when writing.

ORCHIDS

Arrived in superb condition Cattleya Dowiana, C. Gigas, C. Mossiae, C. Percivaliana, C. Speciosissima, C. Eldorado, C. Superba, C. Labiata, C. Leopoldii and many more. Write for Prices.

LAGER & HURRELL, Summit, N. J.
Growers and Importers

ORCHIDS

Largest Importers, Exporters, Growers and Hybridists in the world.

Sander, St. Albans, England
and
235 Broadway, Room 1, New York City

Mention The Florists' Exchange when writing.

POINSETTIAS

2½ in. pots, $5.00 per 100; $40.00 per 1000. Cash with order.

S. N. PENTECOST,
1790-1810 East 101 St., CLEVELAND, O.

Mention The Florists' Exchange when writing.

FOUNDED IN 1888

FLORISTS' EXCHANGE

A Weekly Medium of Interchange for Florists, Nurserymen Seedsmen and the Trade in general

Exclusively a Trade Paper.

Entered at New York Post Office as Second Class Matter

Published EVERY SATURDAY by

A. T. DE LA MARE PTG. AND PUB. CO. LTD.

2, 4, 6 and 8 Duane Street,

P. O. Box 1697.
Telephone 3765 John. NEW YORK.

CHICAGO OFFICE: 127 East Berwyn Avenue.

ILLUSTRATIONS.

Electrotypes of the illustrations used in this paper can usually be supplied by the publishers. Price on application.

YEARLY SUBSCRIPTIONS.

United States, Canada, and Mexico, $1.00. Foreign countries in postal union, $2.50. Payable in advance. Remit by Express Money Order Draft on New York. Post Office Money Order or Registered Letter.

The address label indicates the date when subscription expires and is our only receipt therefore.

REGISTERED CABLE ADDRESS:

Florex, New York.

ADVERTISING RATES.

One-half inch, 75c.; ¾-inch, $1.00; 1-inch, $1.25, special positions extra. Send for Rate Card showing discount of 10c., 15c., 25c., or 35c., per inch on continuous advertising. For rates on Wants, etc., see column for Classified Advertisements.

Copy must reach this office 12 o'clock Wednesday to secure insertion in issue of following Saturday.

Orders from unknown parties must be accompanied with cash or satisfactory references.

Society of American Florists and Ornamental Horticulturists.

W. F. Gude, Washington, D. C., will contribute the paper on "Recent Improvements in Retailers' Methods of Offering Flowers," at the S. A. F. convention at Dayton, O.

The Western Passenger Association, controlling territory west of Chicago declines to give extension on return certificates from Dayton; therefore, certificates from that territory will be available only up to August 28.

Department of Plant Registration.

Lager & Hurrell, Summit, N. J., submit for registration orchid seedling Laelio-Cattleya Lady Bernice, Cattleya gigas atropurpurea × Lælia purpurata. Flowers large, 7 inches across; sepals and petals lilac with numerous and delicate mottles and veins of rosy purple overlaid, these accentuating more toward the tips of the petals. Lip wavy, 2 inches across, dark purple with a minute margin of rose. Lower part of throat with numerous yellow and reddish-brown longitudinal veins; upper part or sides of tube, orange yellow.

W. J. STEWART,
Secretary.

American Rose Society.

The executive committee recently held a meeting at the Fifth avenue hotel, New York City, and took up the matter of preparing the way for the next annual meeting and show at Washington. The Washington Florists' Club has joined hands to make a strong effort for a handsome showing.

The committee went over the prize schedule of last year and spent some time in devising means to secure ample prizes for the exhibit.

The effort is being made to gather together and put into permanent form, the history of the organization which was first started at Atlantic City in 1894, and the present organization which was put in force March 13, 1899, W. C. Barry of Rochester, N. Y., being the first president of the society. The motto proposed at the executive meeting for the organization was, "A Rose for Every Home; a Bush for Every Garden."

The sense of the committee is that the society should be broadened to make it as comprehensive as its name, that American represents no section, but takes in the entire bound of the zone where roses grow.

BENJAMIN HAMMOND,
Secretary.

The latest addition to labor's ranks in the United Brotherhood of Rural, Horticultural and Agricultural Wage Earners of America. The headquarters is in Dallas, Tex.

Convention Notes.

The preliminary official program is at hand. The Entertainment Committee met Wednesday last week and made final arrangements for all entertainments.

Ladies and Gentlemen, you certainly will be treated admirably. The Dayton Florists' Club held an overflowing meeting July 30 and further details were arranged for this great convention. Everybody is prepared to give you a most hearty welcome.

Miss Bessie Evangeline Dornbusch has composed for our convention a most beautiful poem, which she read before the club, and deafening applause was her reward. This young lady, a daughter of one of our members, possesses no mean poetical ability and is a most excellent elocutionist. It was decided that she should deliver her poem immediately before the illustrated lecture on landscape gardening at Far Hills, and following the banquet, all in the open air on the big lawn.

Quite a few more surprises have been added on the Exhibition Grounds, and even the members of the club are in the dark as to what these surprises are. However, I can tell you this much—they are wonderful.

The generosity of Mr. John H. Patterson of the National Cash Register Company is something commendable. He has given the National Society free access to everything he has, and naturally is quite a help, through our local club; for without the aid of Mr. Patterson the local Florists' Club would have to raise in the neighborhood of $10,000 to provide the decorations and give the entertainment you will receive in Dayton.

All members who are still hesitating about making an exhibit, should please hurry up. Time is short, and space is getting scarce. If you want to be a leader in the parade, be a generous exhibitor or advertiser.

The president's reception will take place at Far Hills at seven o'clock in the evening of August 21, the first day of the convention. Mr. John H. Patterson has given over for this night, for the use of the national society, his palatial home and most beautiful park—Far Hills. The illumination of Far Hills will be such as we have never seen before; it certainly will be quite unique in its way. Imagine large oak and elm trees, for instance, each one decorated in different colors with multitudes of lights. The planting of the shrubbery will be illustrated in fire and flame, natural like, large climbers such as clematis, Crimson Rambler roses, etc., will have their flowers reproduced by electricity. The celebrated ational Cash Register band will furnish the music for the night's entertainment. Mr. Patterson will provide everybody with a dainty lunch on the big lawn, to be followed by the recitation of a poem by Miss Dornbusch, and then the grand illustrated lecture on "Landscape Gardening and Garden Architecture" will commence, delivered by an expert in this line. The slides are absolutely true to nature, some of them procured under the greatest difficulties, and colored by the foremost artists in the world.

Many requests are being received from members for cards of admission for non-members of the association for the entertainment and president's reception at Far Hills. Members desiring to bring a friend for this occasion must send in their names at once; they will receive the cards at the secretary's office in the exhibition building. We must know how many people we have to entertain at the banquet. This lunch is a compliment of Mr. Patterson to the S. A. F. and the Dayton Florists' Club, and we do not desire to put him to any unnecessary expense preparing for a lot of people that will never show up.

The inspection hall will be a thing of beauty, and the exhibition large. When you arrive in Dayton, make free use of the bureau of information at the depot. It will be conducted by the merchants' police of Dayton, under the supervision of the Dayton Florists' Club. Do not forget to register at once with Secretary Stewart at the exhibition hall. The club has made arrangements with the Xenia Traction line to give a five minutes service from the Algonquin Hotel to the Fair Grounds. Signs on the cars will inform you that this is the official line. Take no other. Members will benefit the national association and the local Florists' Club in part by patronizing this line only. Arrangements have been made with this official line to sell six tickets for 25 cents or 25 tickets for $1 with the privilege of transferring to any line in the City of Dayton, either way. You can procure your tickets from the conductor, or at the office of the secretary in the exposition hall.

In order to reach Far Hills for the presidents' reception, special arrangements have been made with the Oak Wood line which will give a two minute service either coming or going to Far Hills until 11:30 p. m.

All visitors are requested to stay during the whole of the convention if possible, for the last day will be just as instructive and entertaining as the first one.

As I stated before, you will find on the ground everything for the inner man, all at the most reasonable prices. The bills of fare, etc., are under the supervision of the Florists' Club. However all concessions are given free of charge; but should there be any discourtesy or inattention on the part of waiters, please report at once to the chairman, J. B. Heiss. A book for registering complaints will be found at the secretary's desk, and anything wrong will be remedied at once.

On arriving in the city you may leave your baggage checks, or baggage, at the depot with the official baggage master at the Union Station, who will see that your goods are delivered to your hotel or boarding-house at once.

From all indications, this convention will be a hummer. Come one and all. All the boys here will receive you in the most generous spirit and with open hearts; and we shall see that the city is turned over to you. Those who want to be assisted in securing accommodations in hotels or private houses, should not wait until the last day, for the Chairman on Hotels has other duties to perform besides looking out for your comfort. Please make up your minds in time, and send your communications, if you desire to be assisted, to J. B. HEISS.

Philadelphia to Seek 1907 Convention.

The Florists' Culb of Philadelphia at its meeting on Tuesday evening decided to invite the S. A. F. to hold the 1907 convention in that city. A committee was appointed, with Robert Craig as chairman, to take charge of the matter and extend the invitation at the Dayton meeting. The transportation committee of the club has not yet decided upon the route to Dayton; we are waiting to hear from Baltimore and Washington. If we can unite with the delegation from these cities the B. & O. route may be selected—B. & O. via Columbus. The train leaves Philadelphia 4:30 p. m. Monday, arriving at in Dayton 12:10 noon Tuesday, with one hour for breakfast at Columbus. Pennsylvania R. R. train leaves Philadelphia 4:30 p. m. Monday, arriving at Dayton 9 a. m. Tuesday. Members will be notified when the route is selected. DAVID RUST.

S. A. F. Shooting Contest.

In addition to the regular bowling tournament, for which elegant team and individual prizes have been provided, a suitable number of prizes will be provided for competition by the trap shooters. The skill of the florist shooters having been exploited in this city has called forth a challenge from one of our local clubs for a friendly team shoot, either five men or ten men teams. We hope that all florists skilled in this sport will bring their guns with them to that we may qualify a team that will uphold our reputation and that will be able to hustle these local shooters, and there are some "good ones."

H. M. ALTICK.
Chairman Local Committee on Sports.

The Prevention of Commercial Corruption

The House of Commons lately passed through its final stages a bill, the necessity for which is generally acknowledged. The facts brought to light startled the public at the time, but many of them now are only too familiar. The late Lord Chief Justice Russell of Killowen gave instances of goods being wilfully destroyed by corrupt employes in order that they might get a fresh commission on a fresh order. He showed that throughout our commercial and industrial life the practice of secret commissions was creating, and still is creating, gross dishonesty, and he demonstrated that without an amendment of the law the evil would grow worse, for the dishonest would drag down the honest. The present Government, to its credit, declined to allow the opposition of a few members to stop so important a measure. Whether the bill will do all that is hoped from it remains to be seen, but it at any rate, says the Daily Graphic, stamps as a crime, a form of corruption which is a disgrace to the character of our commercial life. We do not see how foreign dealers are to be prevented from offering illicit commissions and discounts, or how the consciences of the recipients are to be awakened.—The Gardeners' Chronicle, England.

There will always be, we fear, different and differing views held on the very objectionable practice of giving and receiving commissions; and the evil has become so common and is so deeply engrained in mankind generally that it will be difficult to eradicate it, even though the effort be backed by law.

Not long ago, after the appearance of some comments on the subject of "Gardeners' Graft" in our columns, we received a communication setting forth that the man who knew where to purchase goods profitably to his employer was entitled to any commission that the seller might see fit to give the gardener. The writer of that letter evidently did not consider that the wages he was receiving from his employer were paid him to do the very best he could for those he was serving, both in the buying of goods and in every other way. A Philadelphia firm recently announced publicly by advertisement that it paid a certain commission to all gardeners buying of that particular concern. That seems to us to be one way of minimizing "graft;" for employers are thereby made aware that gardeners purchasing goods in that seed store would receive a "rake-off;" and, no doubt, would see to it that the same was credited to the actual buyer, and not his agent.

As our London contemporary says there will be a difficulty in awakening the consciences of the recipients of commissions whether given by local or foreign tradesmen, for there are some men, too many, alas, with whom the eighth commandment is a dead letter; men who are willing to sink their manhood to the lowest level provided they can work for their own pockets all the time. For such men law has no terrors, and Dante's Inferno is but a chimera. So what's the use?

The Late James Hartshorne

Obituary

James Hartshorne.

James Hartshorne died at Joliet, Ill., on Monday, August 6, from the result of an operation.

Mr. Hartshorne was born in Shropshire, England, on April 8, 1868. Coming to America in 1888, he first located at Boston, directly afterward securing the position of second foreman in the gardens of the late Charles Burley, Esq. of Exeter, N. H. The horticultural development of the World's Fair led him to strike out for Chicago in 1892 with the thought of finding employment in that section of the Fair. Instead of taking part in this, however, the late John C. Ure, then having considerable to do with the exposition matters, more particularly those connected with the Illinois and other state buildings and grounds, engaged Mr. Hartshorne to operate his greenhouses at Arygle Park. Here he did good work as a carnation and chrysanthemum grower, and in 1896 carried off some 20 premiums for exhibits of the Divine Flower at the Chicago Fall show. Nor was it as a specialist in carnations alone that he showed his skill, for he won other premiums, his groups of ornamental palms, ferns and other plants at the Chicago exhibitions being highly praised. In many other ways he proved himself to be a good all-round plantsman.

In 1897, Mr. Hartshorne was engaged by H. N. Higinbotham, Esq., of Chicago, as gardener both at his city residence and his delightful country home at Joliet, Ill. In the following year, the Chicago Carnation Company was formed and Mr. Hartshorne was appointed manager. Mr. Hartshorne here maintained his record as a first-class carnation grower, and placed upon the market several new varieties among them Harlowarden, Her Majesty, Bon Homme Richard, and others. He also purchased from Fred Dorner & Sons Company and distributed to the trade the carnation Fiancee. Last year he secured from Richard Witterstaetter, of Cincinnati, O., the variety Aristocrat, which is to be introduced into the trade this season.

Mr. Hartshorne was also a member of the Chicago Peony Farm Company, a concern devoted to the cultivation of that now popular flower.

Like all progressive men, Mr. Hartshorne believed in association among his compeers. He early joined the Chicago Florists' Club, taking an active part in its affairs, and in 1899 was elected its president. He was also a member of the Chicago Horticultural Society, the Society of American Florists, The Chrysanthemum Society of America on the seedling committee of which he served in 1899. He was likewise a member of the American Carnation Society, and was elected its president at Detroit, occupying the chair with much acceptance at the Chicago meeting of that organization in 1905. Mr. Hartshorne was also a member of the American Association of Nurserymen. He was a Master Mason.

A widow and two children are left to mourn his loss.

Edward D. Clark.

Edward D. Clark, nearly forty years a resident of Providence, R. I., and one of the pioneer and most widely known florists in the city, died of acute Bright's disease, at his home on Laurel avenue, July 26.

Mr. Clark was born in London, England, in 1851. His early education was acquired in the schools of the city of his birth. When about eighteen years of age he came to America, locating at Providence and there securing employment as apprentice in a machine shop. Eventually, becoming interested in horticulture, in 1876, he established a modest greenhouse plant at the corner of Wickenden and Governor streets. A few years later, his business had so increased, as to outgrow the facilities offered there, and a range of rose houses was built at Tockwotten street. For about twenty years he conducted a prosperous wholesale and retail trade at this location, acquiring exceptional abilities as a rose grower. About two years ago, a large and modern carnation range was also erected at his residence.

In the passing of Mr. Clark the trade is deprived of an honored and respected brother; one whose life was characterized by the strictest fidelity. Although of a quiet and retiring disposition, seldom interesting himself in society or public affairs, Mr. Clark was one of the organizers and most active members of the Providence Florists and Gardeners' Club, and his best interests were ever keenly alive to all that concerned modern horticulture. He leaves a widow, three sons and one daughter. The funeral, which occurred July 29, was very largely attended. A beautiful array of floral designs from friends and business associates, silently, but expressively attested the degree of esteem in which he was held. The business will be conducted by the sons.

W.

The Late Edward D. Clark

OUR READERS' VIEWS

[Wholesome discussions on subjects that interest. Contributions to this column are always welcome.—Ed.]

A Definition.

Editor Florists' Exchange:

In answer to H. F. H., I would say, that the true definition of the term—"expert florist," is—"arrogant ass." Detailed explanation on application.

HARRY SMITH, Jr.

Herbicide.

Editor Florists' Exchange:

I notice in the August 4 issue Question Box (19) "Y" asks for the name of the manufacturer of the weed killer called Herbicide. This material is manufactured and sold by Reade Manufacturing Co., (Agricultural Manufacturing Chemists) 546 West 22d street, New York. I tried some of this last week and it was most effectual.

Saxton, Pa. E. S. CREMER.

[We are much obliged to our correspondent for the information. Ed. F. E.]

The Late James Weir, Jr.

Associate Bowlers and Shooters.

The Florists' Exchange:

Having several strong associate bowlers in Baltimore the question has been raised there whether or not associate members of bowling and shooting teams should be allowed to take part in the convention prize contests. A number of the larger cities have heretofore put up exceptionally strong teams with associates, and the cry of unfairness was heard on every side at almost every convention. A very large number of the S. A. F. "sports" will be glad to receive the desired information through the trade papers from the Committee on Sports for the Dayton meeting. We think that all persons who are not directly identified with our profession should be debarred from participation in the regular contests. We do think, however, that those associate members should be given a chance for certain trophies should they desire to take part among themselves under a seperate rule.

BALTIMORE GARDENERS' CLUB.

Concerning Geraniums.

Editor Florists Exchange:

I have read the wordy articles of John Birnie on Expertus's method of growing geraniums but notwithstanding all the space Mr. Birnie has occupied in your valuable paper, he has not given us any information as to where Expertus was wrong, nor has he tried to teach a great many of your readers how to grow geraniums in the cheapest and most approved way. After following his windy screeds for a number of weeks in which he criticises everyone who has made any suggestions on the topic, he all at once starts off with "Expertus is down and out," and finishes with "come over to Jersey and learn how to bowl." Well, I have learned he comes from New Jersey; and if the thousand geraniums I got from a New Jersey firm last Spring were raised on John Birnie's plan, I don't want any more such stuff. Neither do I want the crop of white fly I got with them.

Now, Mr. Editor, if John Birnie is so smart as to use up your space for a number of weeks and say nothing, will you be kind enough to send out some one from your office, after the style of Upton Sinclair, and let us know of the wonderful secret Mr. Birnie has in connection with geraniums. Peter Henderson would have told us all about the matter in ten lines, and not have tried to be smart either.

CANADA.

OUR CONVENTION NUMBER

Will be issued next week. It will be handsomely illustrated, and will contain lots of interesting information concerning the Gem City. Every Trade Exhibitor should tell in that issue what he will have to offer the delegates. Send in copy for your ads. EARLY.

Our London Letter.

BY A. HEMSLEY.

THE ROYAL HORTICULTURAL SOCIETY.—Since my last notes we have had another grand show, held in the grounds connected with Holland House, Kensington. It proved a great success in every way, yet there were few special things in the way of novelties. Water lilies have been a feature at most of our London shows. The varieties of Marliacea are the most prominent and improved varieties being added. Of those who have exhibited well are Messrs. Cutbush & Sons; their pond at the R. H. S. show was superb. Amos Perry has been showing well a crimson variety James Brydon, which recently gained an award of merit. Messrs. R. Wallace & Company make a specialty of water lilies. Messrs. Barr & Sons have a large collection of all the best sorts. Other firms also do them well. In the market the blooms are in demand, and it seems likely that these lovely water flowers will continue to grow in favor.

PEONIES have been very prominent at the exhibitions and also in the market. Growers now understand that the flowers must be cut before they are too far advanced, consequently the blooms last better. In the market we only get a limited number of sorts. The colors most favored are the soft shades of pink, and the pure whites. The crimsons are largely grown, but do not make such good prices. I find among growers who give special attention to peony culture and have large stocks of the choicer sorts, Messrs. Kelway & Sons still keep up their prestige, and have shown some remarkably fine varieties. Messrs. R. H. Bath, Ltd. grow an extensive collection, and have secured awards for some fine new varieties this season. Peonies have been a prominent feature with most other hardy plant growers.

HEUCHERAS.—Of these we are now getting quite a large number of varieties; one of the best I have seen is H. crizioides gracillima. Atrosanguinea is another useful sort. Others may be useful in a collection but are not decided enough in color for florist's work.

While on hardy flowers I must refer to Coreopsis grandiflora. Though by no means a new plant it has come much into favor recently. Raised from carefully selected seed there is room for further improvement. I have before me some blooms received from H. J. Jones, and I find that though from a selected stock, there are some much better than others, and it seems possible to make considerable improvement. I am rather gone on this selection business. It was what was taught me in my earliest experience. Many an evening I have spent in going through beds of annuals, putting a stick to anything a little better than the rest. Seed saved from these, if not coming quite up to the mark was always a long way in advance of the ordinary stock. If you start cross-fertilizing you don't know what you may get; and if you do make a distinct break it may not prove satisfactory the following year, but if you carefully select from year to year you must be going the right way. Another point is, that where there are branching spikes, always save from the terminal stems and cut away the laterals. I believe that in stocks of the Ten-week and intermediate types a much larger percentage of doubles are secured where all the side shoots are cut away and seed saved from the main stems only.

SWEET PEAS.—We are getting a multiplicity of names and some improved varieties, yet I cannot see that we can afford to do away with some of the older sorts. With Bolton's Pink and all the others of similar shade. I do not think we can part with our old friend Miss Willmot. We have several new whites, but for the present we must be loyal to Dorothy Eckford. In those of a mauve or lavender shade we have some promising candidates for favor. Lady Cooper, Miss H. C. Phillbrick, and Romolo Piazzaini are promising, but we cannot yet discard Lady Grizel Hamilton. Dora Cowper is a good cream, but the Hon. Mrs. Kenyon has stood the test, and, though not quite of an ideal color, it has sold well in the market. In the deep reds I think King Edward VII and Queen Alexandra are decided improvements on Mars and Salopian. Elsie Herbert and White Wonder may prove good whites. Nora Unwin, which I saw some weeks ago, was another promising white. Evelyn Byatt was good from most exhibitors at the National Sweet Pea Society's show. The only variety to gain a first class certificate was Miss Audrey Crier, a pretty rose pink with a nearly white base. The varieties John Ingman, George Herbert, and Messrs. Cannell's Rosy Morn, which recently gained an award of merit, are too much alike. Gladys Unwin has found favor in the market, and Paradise, which is a deeper shade, should prove valuable. But all of these and the Spencer family have rather a withered look after they have been packed. I have seen no other pea that has such a fresh appearance, when the boxes are opened, as Miss Willmott. In deep colored varieties Horace Wright and Lord Nelson are good. Helen Pierce, dark blue veined on white, finds many admirers, and Helen Lewis is a good variety.

GERANIUMS.—For the bedding sorts this name has not yet quite died out, but many growers now give them their proper appellation—pelargoniums. I was interested in the correspondence in The Florists' Exchange in regard to the number of plants required for propagating a certain quantity. Our growers get an immense lot from a few plants. Old stools are planted out during the Summer and a good batch of cuttings is taken from them in the Autumn; later they are taken up and potted, kept in a cool dry house until January, when they are plunged where there is a good bottom heat and a fairly warm surface. It is only a short time before there are plenty of nice short cuttings taken off and rooted on a warm bench. They root in a short time and there will be another batch of cuttings ready by the time the first can be removed. The ordinary market sorts are rooted in shallow boxes, and a good many of them are sold early to those who can pot them off and grow them on for bedding. Most of the Autumn struck plants are grown on for 5-inch pots, and are used chiefly for window box work, etc.; but during the last few years, these large plants are used by many for bedding, especially for London work where an immediate effect is required. The Spring struck plants, however, or at least the earlier batches, make quite good plants by the middle of May, and being dwarf they are preferred by many.

Agave Americana in Flower. The Plant is Ten Years old

Photo by R. H. Mesick, Los Angeles, Cal.

Some Interesting Plants.

A beautiful sight is Jasminum azoricum, just now in bloom, with its star-shaped, pure white flowers, closely set on the stem, against a background of dark green foliage. It is the most beautiful, though not the most fragrant member of the family, and along the coast section of this State should be more extensively planted. It should be given a trial in the warm, dry interior valleys.

The photograph herewith shows a century plant, Agave americana, now ten years old. The height of the stem may be estimated by the picture of the young lady beside it. Orioles by the dozen flock from daylight until noon to the blossoms and feed upon the nectar they contain.

A bed of Commelina cœlestis, a plant resembling wandering jew, Tradescantia discolor, is a beautiful thing indeed. The flowers have but two petals which are of the color of those of Salvia patens, are about one inch in diameter, borne on stems a foot high. The sheath holding the buds is shaped exactly like a clam-shell, closed tightly to prevent evaporation of the fluid during the warm dry part of the day.

Stigmaphyllon ciliatum in partial shade is a beautiful vine, both in foliage and flower, adapted to this climate. It is not a rank grower as are bignonias. It does not seed freely, but is readily propagated from hardwood cuttings planted in the Spring.

Lemon verbena, which grows to be a good sized tree here, is also propagated in the same way; so also are fuchsias.

Mandevilla suaveolens is another of our desirable vines now in full bloom. Its pure white fragrant flowers are desirable as cut flowers. It is not adapted to the interior valleys of the State.

Los Angeles, Cal.

P. D. BARNHART.

Comparative Experiments with Various Insecticides for the San Jose Scale.

Comparative experiments with various insecticides for the control of the San Jose scale were begun in January, 1905, in two orchards near Richview, Ill., one containing 780 apple and peach trees badly infested by the San Jose scale, and the other, 680 peach trees generally but less heavily infested. A part of the insecticides was applied January 3 to 10, and a part from March 21 to 24, with the object of testing by comparison the effect of Spring and Midwinter sprayings. The results of treatment were tested by critical inspection made during the latter part of May, and September 5 to 8.

For the purpose of these comparisons each tree in both orchards was first carefully graded in January, and again at the dates of inspection above mentioned, as to the the amount of infestation, figured on a scale of six degrees. The results of treatment were determined by a comparison of conditions previous to treatment with those at the later dates of inspection, and also with those of check plots left untreated, but examined and graded with the rest.

Seventeen preparations with a lime and sulphur basis were used in these experiments, including various forms of the California wash and the Oregon wash, and mixtures of lime and sulphur without salt or blue vitriol. These preparations varied in the kind of lime used in making them, in the proportions of the various ingredients, and in the length of time during which the mixtures were boiled to procure their solution. Two compounds were also used, supposed to be solutions of lime and sulphur, and known respectively as "Calcothion" and "Con Sol." Eleven of these mixtures were applied to plots varying in size from 34 to 141 trees, and six were applied to plots containing from 5 to 12 trees.

In addition to these experiments with lime and sulphur mixtures, an ordinary whale-oil-soap solution was used on 117 trees, a solution of "Tak-a-nap" soap on 8, a kerosene preparation known as "Scalecide" on 31, another sold as "Frutolin" on 3, and several variations of a 20-per cent. kerosene and water mixture made by hydrated lime in lieu of soap were applied to 5 trees. A solution of caustic soda was applied to three trees, and Bowker's Tree Soap to a single tree.

The cheapest and most efficient of the eleven lime and sulphur mixtures thoroughly tested against the San Jose scale were those made without salt or blue vitrol, and dissolved by boiling together. They cost from 84 cents to $1.03 per hundred gallons of the fluid ready for spraying, varying according to the proportions of the chemicals used. Infested trees once treated with these solutions in March bore about one-fifth as many living scales the following September as the companion check trees not treated. The next in value were the ordinary California wash, made with lime, sulphur, and salt at an expense of from 94 cents to $1.07 per hundred gallons, and the Oregon wash of lime, sulphur, and blue vitriol, made at virtually the same cost.

There was a marked and very important difference in the final effect of these mixtures dependent upon the time of their application, the Midwinter treatment yielding a result far inferior to that of early Spring.

A cold solution of lime and sulphur made with soda was found less than one-third as effective as the other lime and sulphur washes, dissolved by boiling. It costs from $1.24 to $1.44 per hundred gallons, varying according to the proportions of the ingredients. The petroleum preparation called "Scalecide" was found somewhat less efficient than the ordinary lime and sulphur mixtures, and costs about two and a half times as much as the raw materials of those preparations. It has only the advantage that it may be prepared for use by simply diluting with water. Whale-oil soap compared very well with the California wash, but at a cost about eight times as great.

Experiments with the other insecticides were made on too small a scale to warrant final conclusions, but, so far as they go, they indicate that these mixtures have an insecticide value less than that of the ordinary Oregon wash.

The general outcome of these experiments establishes the simple lime and sulphur washes prepared by boiling as superior, on the whole, to all the other mixtures tested, and shows that January applications of these preparations are scarcely more than half as efficient as those made in March.—Abstract from Bulletin 107, University of Illinois Agricultural Experiment Station.

Some Dwarf Campanulas (Bell Flowers).

The dwarf campanulas have become greater favorites in Europe than almost any other dwarf Summer flowering plant. There is so much to recommend them with their beautifully shaped variously disposed trim flowers and their many, varied and expressively formed leaves and stems. The kinds here enumerated are interestingly distinct; many of them are suitable alike for pot culture, borders and rockeries. There are but few campanulas that do better on elevated surfaces, than at the ground level, many thriving much better on, or in rockeries than in any other place.

In mentioning rockeries, it is surprising there are not more made. I mean rockeries suitable for alpine plants generally. However, it is campanulas we have now under consideration. Rockeries suitable for these may be made separately, or they may be made on the front of borders to form a margin. Wherever they may be they must have full sunshine and be away from the dripping of trees. A foot above the ordinary surface level is the lowest elevation permissible; and the soil which must be rich and sandy, is to be not less than two feet deep. The higher the elevation, the deeper must be the good soil. Some stones must be two or more feet long, even if they are not thick, so that they may be deeply placed, upright or nearly so, in the soil for the roots of the plants to follow the water as it trickles down. The bays or plateaus for each group must be of a size suitable to the plants' requirements, some large and some small. The soil must be made firm; and stones must be so placed on the margins of the bays that a depth of not less than two inches for the small bays, and not less than three inches, for the large bays, shall be made so as to hold these depths of water. The secret in rock work cultivation is to have the water go through the soil and not just over the surface. A careless man cannot make a rockwork a success.

Various kinds of stone can be used in rockeries, preferably sandstone, limestone or tufa—last of all furnace clinkers. Good leaf mold, very gritty sand, and old mortar may be used advantageously for many kinds.

Many of these campanulas are not hardy but they are all perpetual and are easily propagated by division. In fact, they are extremely prolific in underground stolons which when separated make plants very easily. They may be also readily raised from seed, where the types of the species are desired only. The difficult varieties, like those of carpathica, must necessarily be propagated by divisions or cuttings. Plantings of carefully hardened off plants may be made early in April firmly done and thoroughly watered.

I must again mention planting in wire baskets. These baskets are readily made by any handy man; they can be made of any desired shape or size—they should be made of the best galvanized wire, or what is better copper wire, of sufficient diameter to accord with the size required; the depth also can be determined in the same manner. The wires in the smallest baskets need not be closer together than 1½ inches and in the larger ones in proportion. Where a number of baskets are required a wire worker is the man to do the work.

The Summer cultivation should be such as is given to other temporary plants, not forgetting to afford an occasional soaking of manure water, or a taste of nitrate of soda in weak solution during the season.

The Winter protection of campanulas is best afforded where they can be stored in their baskets, these packed in boxes with comparatively dry soil and placed in a deep, light cold frame or cold greenhouse. They must be kept dry, as dry as one keeps an agave, until March, when if it is desirable they may then be divided as required, placed in new soil again in baskets and made ready to go out of doors just as soon as the weather will permit.

For pot culture treat as you would geraniums. For border culture plant only in dry deep sandy soil and protect them so that coarser growing plants do not smother them.

The descriptive list which follows is of perpetual kinds only, but there are several interesting annual species, which are effective and harmonizing—such as dichotoma, blue purple; erinus, blue and rose; Loefflingii, violet blue; ramosissima, blue and white.

Allioni, flowers, if raised from seed vary from light blue to pure white. The flowers are half pendant, more than an inch in diameter, produced freely, singly, on slender stems; leaves lance shaped on stem, at base they are more rounded. Height of plant three to six inches. A little gem for rockwork only. Introduced from Piedmont Alps, 1820. Flowers from July to September.

Alpina, flowers deep blue, rather numerous, arranged loosely along the whole stem; flowering July and August. Leaves variously shaped, toothed and having woolly surfaces. Height 4 to 10 inches. Introduced 1779. Rockery.

Barbata, flowers pendant, in loose racemes rising from the axils of the larger leaves; corolla pale blue with lighter center, somewhat hairy; outer surfaces glabrous and shining; leaves few, tongue-shaped, somewhat villose. Flowers in June and July. Height from 10 to 20 inches. A fine plant for rockeries. Introduced from the European Alps, 1752. There is also a white variety of this species quite pleasing and distinct.

Cœspitosa, flowers drooping, sometimes three and four at the top of each stem; the corolla is deep blue, often with white markings. Flowering from May to August. Leaves more or less oval, toothed and shining; stems numerous. Very free. Height 4 to 6 inches. Europe 1813. Rockery.

Carpathica, a delightful species with many beautiful varieties, suitable alike for borders, rockwork or pots. The species has deep blue, widely open flowers 2 to 2 1-2 inches across borne on long stems with several flowers branching from each, and terminating with an erect flower. Blooms from June to August. Leaves of various sizes, more or less oval. Transylvania, 1774. The best varieties of carpathica are alba, pure white; pelviformis, deep lilac, distinct; turbinata, deepest purple, and Hendersoni, mauve.

Caucasica, a little gem, with flowers of the richest violet blue, gracefully drooping, in three or more together on elegant slender stems. Flowers July and August. Leaves variously interesting in shape and size. Height 6 to 10 inches. Caucasus, 1804. Rockery.

Cenisia, flowers, deep gentian blue, an inch or more in diameter, borne singly on very slender stems, standing erect. June and July. Leaves ovate, lanceolate and deeply toothed. A free growing little gem, 6 to 9 inches high. Pots and rockery. Italy. 1775. I wrote labels for this in 1853.

Isophylla, a beautiful free flowering species bearing good sized open salver-shaped flowers in round heads; color lavender blue and silvery white. August. Leaves heart shaped and toothed. Good for borders, rockwork or pots. Height 8 to 16 inches. Italy, 1868. A white variety (alba) of this species is also a very charming plant.

Nitida, a bright little plant, with blue or blue and white flowers in loose racemes, with distinct corollas. Blooms nearly all Summer. Leaves in rosettes, leathery, very dark shining green; 6 to 12 inches. Good for borders or rockwork; a native species. There are double blue and double white varieties of this species.

Portenschlagiana, flowers truly bell-shaped, light blue purple in color, erect, or nearly so, some disposed at the ends of the shoots with others in the axils of the secondary leaves. June and July. Leaves deep green, peculiarly kidney-shaped; 5 to 12 inches high. Good for borders, rockwork or pots. Europe, 1811.

Pusilla, flowers of medium size, bell-shaped, pendant, on very slender stems; colors, from deep blue to pure white. July and August. Leaves round, in loose tufts, distinctly toothed; height 6 inches. Europe, 1779. Rockery.

Rotundifolia, the harebell and bluebell of Europe. Bearing solitary drooping bell-shaped flowers on slender stems, of a deep blue color. June to August. Lower leaves variously rounded and toothed; 10 to 16 inches high. Britain. Rockeries and borders.

Waldsteiniana, a gem of gems, growing 6 to 10 inches high, each shoot surmounted with large spreading violet blue wide open flowers, of thick texture. June and July. Leaves deep green, variously shaped; height 6 to 10 inches. Suitable for pots, rockwork or borders. Exquisite. Hungary, 1824.

JOHN THORPE.

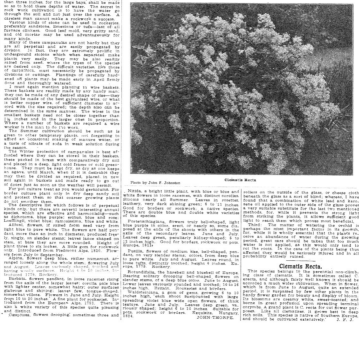

Photo by John F. Johnston — Clematis Recta

The Culture of Orchids, as Viewed by a Private Gardener.

(Read before the New Jersey Floricultural Society by Arthur W. Bodwell.)

In the growing or cultivation of the orchid I have decided to divide my subject into three main points and will ask you to consider; first, the matter of airing or ventilation.

The orchid may be grown in earthen pots and pans, or in baskets, especially provided for the purpose. From my personal experience I prefer the use of the basket as it allows the air to circulate freely about the roots and prevents an over abundance of moisture. As with all other subjects that have life and the possibility of growth the most essential quality for orchids is an abundance of fresh air.

In the case of modern houses where top ventilation is ample I would suggest that the ventilators at the top of the house be kept open at all times in the Summer months, thus assuring an abundance of fresh air. In cases where the houses are not modern, side ventilation may be used, but I much prefer top ventilation, for, I believe, that ventilation from the side serves to absorb the moisture in the house, which is a decided requisite to the orchid.

Second: The matter of light is of great importance to the growing of the orchid; for while it should receive an abundance of light, care should be exercised as to the manner in which the light is allowed to reach the plant, as the strong rays would, in all probability, prove quite injurious. For the purpose of protecting the plants some use shade rollers on the outside of the glass, or cheese cloth beneath the glass as a sort of blind; whereas, I have found that a combination of white lead and kerosene oil applied to the outer side of the glass proves a very suitable substitute for the last two mentioned methods, for, while it prevents the strong light from striking the plants, it allows sufficient good light to reach them which proves most beneficial.

Third: The matter of watering the orchid is perhaps the most important factor in its growth, for, while it is wholly essential that the plants receive an abundance of water during the growing period, great care should be taken that too much water is not applied, as this would only tend to rot the roots. In the case of the plants being thus affected they would be seriously injured and in all probability entirely ruined.

Clematis Recta.

This species belongs to the perennial non-climbing class of clematis. It is sometimes called C. erecta, and although fairly well known it should be accorded a much wider cultivation. When in flower, which is from June to August, quite an extended period, it is surpassed by few other plants in the hardy flower garden for beauty and display of bloom. Its blossoms are creamy white, sweet-scented, and borne in great profusion upon spreading terminal corymbs. A grand plant is C. recta for cut flower purposes. Like all clematises, it grows best in deep rich soils. This species is native of Southern Europe, and should be cultivated extensively.

J. F. J.

Floriculture in Mexico.

Editor Florists' Exchange:

I am inclosing herewith some extracts from a letter received from a valued correspondent in Mexico. I have omitted the names of persons and places, but with these exceptions the letter is sent to you just as received. It seems to me that it would be very ineresting to your readers to have some insight into the condition of the florist's business in some parts of Mexico. This location, I should say, is not near the capital.

A. J. PIETERS.

Botanist in Charge. Bureau of Plant Industry. Dep. of Agriculture, Washington, D. C.

"It will give you an idea of the chance I have of making a living out of floriculture here if I tell you of a very characteristic experience I had to-day. The swellest confectionery and ice cream store here gives to-night one of its regular tri-weekly evening concerts and sent a boy to me this afternoon for 'flowers to be presented to the ladies at the concert', without specifying the quantity or saying how much they wished to pay. This is a copy of my bill, sent with the flowers:

12 doz. carnations at 3c., per doz.	.36
7 doz. carnations at 1c. per doz.	.07
22 La France roses at 50c. per 100	.11
30 Choicest roses Asstd. at 40c. per 100	.12
20 Standard fine roses asstd. at 30c. per 100	.06
	72

"It is true that there were only five first class flowers among the carnations, but the La France roses were superb, and among the '30 choicest' were five buds of Kaiserin, Pierre Notting, Antoine Rivoire, Cochet, Testout, Sunrise, Etoile, Prince of Bulgaria, President Carnot, and Golden Gate, and I think I was right in being disgusted when the boy brought me the money and a polite intimation from the house that my charges seemed a little high. I venture to say that the lot I sold for 72c. silver, would bring $15 gold readily in any of the northern cities.

"I can cut daily about 1500 rose buds, mostly La Reine, at times equal to American Beauty, but all I can get for them in the market is 8 cents per 100; and as the delivery baskets carry only 350 to 400 rose buds, representing 28c. to 32c. value, it really isn't worth the trouble to market them, as the cost of cutting and delivering a basketful is about 13c., leaving but 15c. to 19c. for me, or say 75c. if I sold all the 1500. At this season one sees sitting along the edge of the sidewalk near the market, a string of Indians offering two bunches of roses containing five flowers each, for 1c., and on Sunday, I saw one criminal selling the oldfashioned Scotch pinks in bunches of about 15 flowers at one cent also.

"It makes me envious to read of the prices paid for flowers in the United States, especially for violets which I sell during the season at $1 per kilogram of some 3,000 flowers, of which I pay 50c. for the picking, while I occasionally find in my copy of the N. Y. Sun a note about violets selling for perhaps $2.50 gold per 100. At any rate my 4,000 flowers per day would bring $100 gold, while I get here $1.33 silver, when I sell all the flowers ready for picking, but I never manage to sell an average of two-fifths of them.

"It is about the same with every other sort of flowers, the most valuable being the Easter lily (blooming here in May) which sometimes sells for 3 cents per flower on the streets, though more commonly for 1 cent per flower. Tuberoses bring 1½c to 2c per stalk, gladiolus, 2c per stalk (except the common red, which sells for ½c), chrysanthemums 3c to 5c per dozen, cactus dahlias 5c per dozen (and very hard to get that much; and so on ad nauseam.

"The orchids for which the New Yorkers pay from $1 to $5 gold per spray, sell here for 3 sprays for 1c.; so what can one expect with other flowers? As an experiment I yesterday made up two bunches of six of my choicest roses each and told the woman to whom I delivered them to sell them for the best price obtainable, and she managed to get 2c for one bunch and 3c for the other. In the evening I plodded through clouds of dust for six blocks to the Chinese railway beanery for supper and during the meal read in the Sun about a convention of New York florists, every single delegate to which showed up in overcoats lined with genuine Russian sable. After the convention I assume that they adjourned to Sherry's and filled up on broiled lobster with drawn butter with an accompaniment of sparkling Burgundy, that being my idea of the best use to which a multi-millionaire can put his surplus cash.

"The fact is, as I need scarcely say, that I have got to quit. Of course expenses here do not compare with those north, but at best my labor is (three men and one woman, area cultivated 3¼ acres) $1.95 per day, my board 90c, and the total of light, wash, street cars, club, newspaper, etc., is at least $1.25 per day—an aggregate of at least $4.10 per day. As my rent is one-half of the gross receipts I would have to sell more than 10,000 Reina rosebuds every day to keep even. I would not grumble if I were taking it easy and letting some one else attend to my business, but the fact is that I begin work, hard physical work, at 5 a. m. and keep it up without intermission until 6:15 p. m. and almost every night spend an hour or two transplanting, propagating and potting. Work in the garden at this season isn't fattening, either, for my chemical thermometer laid on the ground in full sun showed at 11:15 this morning, 79½ degrees centigrade, the boiling point of water here is about 92½ centigrade.

"I have about unburdened myself, and it is only fair to state that the great difficulty for me was caused by the unusually favorable season and the resulting oversupply of roses, for the usual price paid for the common sorts has been from 75c to $1 per 100 instead of the 8c now current. At the same time I must confess that the people here are notorious all over civilized Mexico for their stinginess, and I'll certify to their utter want of good taste in the rose line.

"They'll rave over the poor weakling Sunrise and admire the Prince of Bulgaria, but secretly they prefer a big 'rosa Fe Blanca' (Lamarque). American Beauty and Paul Neyron are not wanted because they 'look just like a Reina.' As a fact, a well developed Reina blossom is splendid, and when an American woman here gets a chance to wander through a rose garden and cut what she likes, the chances are ten to one that she will cut little except Reinas, to the open-mouthed astonishment of the 'gente.' There is one little flower that our people will pay for, a good camellia; alba plena imbricata, will usually fetch $1 to $1.50, but only from men in love."

Peonies in America.

Editor Florists' Exchange:

In reply to our esteemed friend from Nebraska, C. S. Harrison, I have little to say, as our circular covers every phase of the subject very much more to the point than he comes back at me askance. All the matter written for the magazines and periodicals for peony propaganda gives unstinted merit to our American growers where, by comparison, it it due.

In the November, 1904, "Mayflower" we brought the work of the various American seedling raisers before the public. Mr. Terry of Iowa who brought out some of the very best sorts, was then unknown to many of the foremost eastern specialists, because the peony was in a state of coma; perhaps a "dead one" would be more expressively to the point. In our circular we give American sorts listed the very highest endorsement. What more can we do? If there is anything more that you know of that we can do, let us have it; we certainly could use something more emphatic if we knew how.

We have no desire to be Moguls, nor gullers, monopolists or anything of the kind. We simply reviewed the fields of horticulture for the most promising investment, development and evolution. After giving various plants a very careful study, we considered the peony the one plant that would be worthy of unlimited work, that could be popularised. With this end in view we began the task of getting up a collection of peonies. We then made up a program to secure, regardless of the work, trouble and reasonableness of expense, a complete list of commercial and private sorts, European and American herbaceous sorts; to secure only in a large way those that proved of the very best economic values, from reliable growers; to increase nothing in quantity unless of the highest merit; to prove every sort in our list; to have a list that the world would have to accept as at the top in every way; to have the best and most authoritative literature anent the peony getable.

With a complement of all the above we knew we could make he very weightiest claims that language could convey.... We have the collection to preclude the necessity of buyers going abroad for a single obtainable sort.

We are accomplishing our mission; it is purely a cold business proposition, no Mogul, I-am-the-whole-cheese idea. We believe in planning on the very broadest basis in whatever fields we attempt to explore or exploit; then we feel we can be honest in making the very greatest claims no one can refute. We can prove every claim we make.

My good sir, is there a single statement, fact, idea or principle that you can gainsay, controvert, take exception to? We are without bias, prejudice, sentiment in this matter. We desire to be exactingly correct in every statement we may make. Is that wrong?

We have builded our collection of peonies (We may as well include our other growings as they have been brought together on the same lines) to have the most representative, and one of the largest on earth.

We are willing to pay our share to bring about the visit of the committee suggested. We would like nothing better than the cap-sheaf this committee would have to award us; we know this because we have the proof. And if our friend from the land of the "peerless leader" will come here next Summer he will do the "Ipse dixit" for us. C. BETSCHER.

Liliums in England.

Editor Florists' Exchange:

Permit me to make a few remarks concerning "Liliums in England," of which English Correspondent writes at some length in your issue of August 4.

It is hardly possible for anyone to tell the difference between the bulbs of L. lancifolium album and those of the Kratzerii, but, I should think, that anybody growing a batch of the latter, when he got his blooms out, could instantly see if he had been deceived, inasmuch as the pollen of the Kratzerii is yellow in contrast to the rest of the lancifoliums, a fact which English Correspondent has overlooked.

Liliums may be retarded successfully in 8 to 10 degrees of frost, but it is certainly unnecessary expense to keep your chambers down to 22 to 24 degrees above zero. A well known firm of London nurserymen, with whom I was employed less than two years ago, kept their bulb chambers considerably warmer. They also very successfully retarded lily of the valley in the same dry air as the liliums, but at a different temperature.

I cannot see that lancifoliums require specially constructed houses, nor such a very particular treatment, as long as they are not overwatered or kept too dry when in bud. The firm referred to has about 20 houses originally built for cucumber-growing, which are now exclusively used for the growing of retarded liliums; and the place the products hold in the London market proves that they are making a success of it. Anybody acquainted with that style of house knows that it is neither broad nor lofty; 12½ feet wide, from 4 to 5 feet from the ground to the gutter plate and from 10 to 12 feet to the ridge. No staging isneeded for the growing of liliums in those houses, it being so much easier for "the man with the knife" to get about the stock; at the same time gets a fairer view of the bloom he is cutting. As liliums require very frequent fumigating to keep them even comparatively clean, it will save a good deal on that account not to have the houses so very lofty.

I do not think it at all advisable to use larger sizes of longiflorum for retarding than the 7-9 bulbs. The others do not retard as well, besides, for the cut flower business at least, it is not of much use to have more than say from 4 to 5 buds on each stem. If you have more than that, you cannot count all the buds and be fair to your customers; or you must cut your first best blooms short, and for those you cannot obtain a very good price. For lancifolium album about the same price is paid for short as for long; not so with Melpomene or rubrum. I do not think more than six pence a dozen was ever gotten for short blooms of these, unless that has taken place since I left London.

English Correspondent seems to overlook altogether L. auratum and tigrinum. True, not very large numbers of these varieties are retarded; still sufficient for comment.

Of late years much disease has been found in auratum bulbs, but if good sound stock is obtained, they retard very successfully and are always in demand in the London market. I do not know why, but the fact remains, that when retarded the almost offensive strong smell of the auratum disappears and with that the only objection anybody could have to the beautiful golden lily of Japan. L. tigrinum is not retarded in very large numbers, but still is in some demand at a reasonable price.

Mass. JOHN NISSEN.

Hardy Edible Oranges.

From reports appearing in horticultural papers from time to time it seems that the efforts to produce a hybrid orange hardier than before known are meeting with some success, and that there are varieties now so produced that will stand much farther North than the old race of trees would. This is good news, and indicates that we of the Northern States may yet have one we will be able to grow in our gardens. One of the parents of these hardier sorts is the Japanese species, Citrus trifoliata, known as the hardy orange. This one is hardy to New York City and further along the coast. The writer has mentioned before that seeds of common orange and lemon thrown out in the garden develop seedlings, when in city yards, that endure the Winters of Philadelphia. This indicates greater hardiness in them than is generally supposed. Some of these seedlings might be expected to produce fruit fit to eat. The grafting of those with edible fruit on stocks of the "hardy orange" does not make the product of the cion hardier than it was. Stocks do not influence trees in the way of hardiness. They may cause trees to grow late in the season, the wood not ripening well, making them less hardy; or they may cause a short, stocky growth, well ripened, which would be in the interest of hardiness. In other ways stocks exert no influence.

When to Prune Privet Hedges.

A Massachusetts correspondent writes me to tell him if it would hurt a privet hedge to prune it now, and also what is the proper time to prune it. This question often comes up. Recently an employer asked the same question, and gave as a reason for his inquiry that his gardener frequently trimmed his hedge.

There is no set time for trimming a privet hedge, excepting that the last pruning for the season should be given just before final growth stops. There are then little shoots made where the ends have been cut off which thicken the hedge; and it is not too late for the wood to ripen well before Winter sets in.

Aside from this one can prune a privet hedge as often as desired. How often depends on the taste for neatness. To keep a fairly level surface such a hedge would need a half dozen clippings through the Summer. A privet hedge is in view from where these lines are being written. It has been clipped but once, but badly needs another trimming, and it will get a third one later. This very hedge could take four clippings readily were a quite even surface much desired through the season.

When hedges are young it is better not to clip too often. Strong plants are wanted, to insure a vigorous hedge in the future, and frequent clippings do not permit of the roots gathering great strength.

Although these notes refer to the privet they apply in the main to all hedges.

JOSEPH MEEHAN.

THE WEEK'S WORK.

Timme's Timely Teachings.

Callas.

It is time to start callas. Roots that were grown in pots or benches last season, that have had a good rest and are now showing the beginning of a sturdy crown growth, a broad, hard button of yellowish green, are good for another season. They should now be cleaned and freed of dry soil and dry roots, and planted without delay. If they are soft and flabby, or showing spots of mouldy decay and perhaps have already started a thin, spindly bit of growth, it will not pay to bother with them, and a start should be made with new roots. These are cheap enough and most growers use none but fresh roots every year.

The old Richardia æthiopica, or lily of the Nile, once highly prized as a very effective and most easily managed house plant, now goes a-begging for a small remnant of the old time favor; but as material for high class made up floral work its flowers hold a place peculiarly their own and not likely ever to be lost. Its cousin, Richardia alba maculata, certainly a fine thing when well grown, is now also rarely seen among the commercial florists' potted stock, this mainly because it proved a failure as a living room and parlor plant. It is by no means as easily grown as the old calla. But I think if pot plant growers would go in a little deeper for that fine, free flowering and easily raised little beauty, which made its debut some years ago as "Little Gem" and has since been rogued and given just recognition as a pure and distinct variety, there would be little trouble in finding admirers and buyers in plenty for all of it that could be raised for some time to come. It grows astonishingly fast and produces its pure white, shovel-formed little flowers in unstinted abundance; the foliage is clean and bright, and forms an appropriate setting to the flowers. In short, it is a good pot plant.

Callas for cutting are best grown in benches. Use a rich, heavy loam and plant the roots a foot or a little more apart. If they are very long, lay them in a slanting position, always exposing the crown above ground though The soil at planting should be rather moist, and if surfaced with a thin layer of moss or rooted manure, would stay moist until growth has made somewhat of a start. If this can be managed and very little in the way of watering becomes needful at this initial stage, decay will not interfere with a prompt and vigorous start. After this has been secured, watering in regular quantities becomes necessary, these to be increased as growth progresses; but always remembering that callas, although mighty thirsty when doing their best, are not aquatic plants and that overwatering is possible and harmful too. Liquid manure does no harm, but in all my trials with and without, before and after, I noticed between the variously treated lots no difference either in number or size of flowers. The most spotless and most substantial blooms on strongest stalks are grown in a temperature of from 58 to 60 degrees. In 65 degrees and higher the flowers are less pure in color and also lack durability; but the stems, though not so stout, are longer, and, no doubt, the bloom is produced in a more rapid succession.

French Bulbs.

Roman hyacinths and Paper White narcissus, due to arrive this month, should be planted as soon as they can be had. If they are not wanted for very early forcing they can be held back after they are rooted and will then give better results in late forcing than any held over dry and out of ground. Then, too, the work of boxing, burying and again unearthing in summery weather has something of genuine pleasure in it, an element entirely lacking when the cold norther blows through your whiskers and the merry tingle in the points of your dirt-bedaubed and cold-benumbed fingers calls forth the use of a brand of language that is most harmful to hyacinths and narcissi.

This class of bulbs may be planted in any sort of ordinary good soil, unsparingly enriched with very old manure, either from the compost heap or from worn-out hot beds. I have forced these bulbs for years with something like unusual success in soil taken out of carnation and rose benches some time previous to being made use of for bulbs. Boxes of from three to four inches in depth, not too heavy to handle when filled, holding from forty to fifty bulbs, closely set of course, are used instead of shallow trays or flats, in which it is difficult to grow anything in hyacinths or other deep-rooting bulbs worth carrying to an over-stocked market. In planting it is only necessary to press the bulbs far enough into the soil to hold their position against watering and the immediate handling of the boxes. Were it not for possible displacement, they would root and grow lustily, if merely placed on the surface of the soil, base down. The boxes, as also pots and dishes, if such are used, after being thoroughly watered, are covered with fresh soil, which I find to be the handiest and best, or in lieu of this, with coal ashes or sand. Tan bark, sawdust or manure should not be used, of any one of the first named materials is just as handy. A layer of three or four inches is all sufficient; more will do no harm, but is not necessary.

The boxes containing Paper White narcissi should be taken out and removed to a cool greenhouse in about five weeks, while Roman hyacinths must stay two or three weeks longer. In a carnation house the narcissi will make a slowly progressing but steady and exceedingly fine growth, and the flower spikes will make a better showing when marketed than the product obtained by harder forcing. The boxes of narcissi should stand on the coolest but also lightest bench of the house, never under the bench except for a week or so after being brought in from outdoors. Roman hyacinths, on the other hand, like a warm bottom to stand on and also a reasonable amount of heat, coupled with moisture overhead. A pretty warm bench in an intermediate or rose house is a good place for the boxes. A forcing of four weeks for the earliest and three weeks for the later stock should bring well rooted Roman hyacinths into full bloom, ready for cutting. Water at the roots and in frequent sprayings must not be spared during this process. A heavy shading for the first two weeks will aid in holding uniform heat and moisture and will give length to the flower spikes. After that they want more light and a gradual let-up in heat.

Mignonette.

There are several ways in which to start a good plantation of mignonette for next Winter's cutting. Mignonette is good florist's stock and now of sufficient importance to justify thorough going proceedings. Its culture for a Winter's market, when it is as good a paying crop as any we raise, cannot be said to be particularly difficult. If there is any one of the details more trying and less easy than others, it is the starting of the little seedlings at this time of the year, and next to that the difficulty in obtaining a true and uniformly excellent strain of seed. This is no fault of the seed growers or the seed dealers. It is owing to the fact that all improved forms of mignonette are no fixed types, though they are regarded as distinct varieties. They are ever ready to revert to the old, original mignonette, and a goodly percentage of the seeds born by the finer sorts every season has turned tail, as it were. This difficulty is not entirely overcome by careful selection, not by growing one's own seed from year to year, and although in this way one may build up a good strain in the course of time, it will not be so very much better than those offered by seed firms to fully pay for the extra trouble in raising it.

As to the troublesome starting of seedlings in mid-Summer, I have found, after trying several methods, that to sow the seeds where the plants are wanted is still the best course to pursue. It is best for the plants and saves a deal of labor also. It is just as easy, with a little forethought and prudent management, to have the benches in readiness now as at any time later on. If mignonette is to be grown on benches now taken up by chrysanthemums, it is best to start the seeds a month from now in 3 or 4-inch pots and to transplant into the benches when these are cleared off. Or the grower might wait until then and sow his seeds directly into the soil of the bench, which will bring him a crop of mignonette in early Spring, not very much later than that from pot-raised seedlings. If there is any choice between beds or benches at all, he should select for mignonette a solid bed in a house exceptionally well equipped with means for ventilation and for holding a steady heat in mid-Winter of about 50 degrees.

A heavy but somewhat gritty loam generously enriched with old manure is a good soil for mignonette. Have it well solidified by giving it a good tramping over before or after sowing. Mark out spaces a foot each way; let them be an inch or two deeper than the surrounding level of the soil, thinly scatter six or eight seeds in each depression, give them a good firming down into the soil, cover them by merely leveling the soil over and around them with your hand and then water well and cover all with paper in single thickness, this to be removed when the plants are peeping through the soil. Now afford plenty of clear light and pure air, but water sparingly until the seedlings are three or four inches high. Then pull out all but one, this to be the sturdiest, straightest and least branched of the lot; kill very worm and slug you happen to meet during the performance and in a week or two after this level off the bed by drawing the higher soil up and against the plants.

Geraniums.

It is well to start in a little early with propagating geraniums so that another good crop of cuttings may be had before frost puts a stop to outdoor growth. The stock plants could, however, be lifted in good season, be potted up or planted in benches and be made to produce material for propagation away into Winter, if this way of providing sufficient stock for next Spring must be resorted to. But, mind you, there is such a thing as over-propagating geraniums as well as carnations and other leading florist's stock. Anybody can work up a lot of geraniums, astonishingly great in number, and shockingly away off in quality, from a few stock plants, but such ways are not those of the good grower. It is strange that practiced florists still persist in loading up their greenhouses with unpromising, rubbishy "stuff" of such things as geraniums, when they know that every old woman and every baby in the land can tell a good geranium from a poor one, and when it is the easiest thing on earth to provide good stock in this line.

The greater part of the poorly grown and delusively enticing stock in geraniums offered every Spring is obtained by rooting either too hard or too sappy wood from plants that have already furnished several crops of cuttings. The cuttng in two of nicely progressing little plants in order to gain a top cutting always means the making of two poor plants out of one good one, because the upper part is too short and soft and the lower stump too hard to ever make an even all-around break, and it will never—not in time—fully recover from the setback it received in the operation. Lanky, fast-growing young plants, not scarce in some varieties, can and, of course must be, dealt with in that way, but even most of these, had they been stopped in time and afforded sufficient room, light and air, would not have grown up to lanky sticks. A thrifty, stocky little geranium must be stopped by pinching away the top at the highest, clearly defined joint, thus causing no check in growth, because very little of working foliage has been taken away. Don't wait, aiming at a cutting, until the plant is too tall, lest the break will be too high, or, if a cutting is obtained, the break will be slow and not at all of a character to presage the making of a fine plant.

There is little choice between the rooting of cuttings in a regular sand bed or placing them at once in small pots in sandy soil. A thousand cuttings from the sand, when rooted, are quickly potted up and usually present a better appearance than those rooted in pots. Sturdy, short-jointed top cuttings of from three to four inches in length, make, without question, the best stock for next Spring's marketing. It matters little whether they are struck now or a month later, they will be good geraniums if potted, repotted and stopped in time and given room light and air in a house averaging 55 degrees of heat. A good grade of geraniums may be grown from cuttings struck in mid-Winter, if these were taken from vigorous stock plants and treated as advised for the early made stock. This sort of stock will likely be smaller, perhaps less branched, and consequently cheaper, than that started now or in the Fall, but it need not be poor stock for all that. I have seen 3-inch geraniums sold at retail in the Spring at a price satisfactory to grower and buyer, every plant of which was worth three of the 4-inch geraniums offered here and there.

FRED W. TIMME.

QUESTION BOX

Pruning Privet and Arbor Vitae

(23) I send you samples of privet. Would it do to prune the plants now? If not when is the best time to do so? I have also some Arbor vitæ which I would like to prune. Kindly let me know whether this can be done now, or the best time to do the work.

Mass. J. J. L.

—When young, that is when it has been planted but a year or two, it is better to let the hedge grow as it will the first season, pruning it into shape in early Spring. But when it is a well formed hedge, prune it whenever you wish through the Summer, when keeping it in good shape requires it. With us three prunings is the rule. One is given about mid-June, another toward the close of July, and the third in mid-September.

Two prunings suffice for Arbor vitæ one in late June, another in early August. Prune both the privet and the Arbor vitæ now, if you so desire. J. M.

Ipswich, Mass.

Benjamin Fewkes, the veteran florist, met with a very serious accident on Saturday, July 28. In company with his wife and Miss Kellett of Somerville, a young lady guest, Mr. Fewkes was driving down to his cottage at Fox island near Sagamore Hill. Where the hill slopes down to Fox Creek, the landing place for hill and island, a small pier is to be built, and a derrick had been set up. Just as Mr. Fewkes drove past this point, the guide chair of the derrick broke and the boom in falling struck the rear of the wagon. This frightened the horse and he jumped, throwing Mr. Fewkes out upon the ground, and breaking one arm, and one leg above the knee. His forehead also was cut by its contact with a sharp stone and his face and head considerably bruised. The horse ran down the bank, out on the marsh where he turned about and making his way back to the cottage was stopped. Mrs. Fewkes and Miss Kellett kept their seats bravely and were uninjured. Mr. Fewkes is 82 years of age. The latest bulletin reports him as comfortable as possible under the circumstances.

New Bedford, Mass.

Trade News.

There is not much improvement in trade as yet; the usual Summer dullness seems to have struck us. A little funeral work comes in now and then. A good supply of asters is now in the market; these bring 35c. per dozen. A few carnations are still to be seen. Fair Maid is looking well. As an all round carnation this variety cannot be beat. It is to be regretted that it is not grown more extensively than it is. It has a better color and is a better shipper than Enchantress, being fully as free a bloomer as that variety.

R. H. Woodhouse has his violets all planted. The plants are some of the best the writer has seen, Princess of Wales is the variety grown. George N. Borden, his foreman, has gone to Jolly Island, N. H., for three weeks.

Wm. Livesey has added another 14 feet to his greenhouse, also a lean-to 8 feet by 64 feet long, on the south side, for violets, etc. HORTICO.

St. Paul.

The News.

Improvements of all kinds among the store men seem to be the order of the day and some are going into them rather deeply. By the time the Fall trade opens up, we can expect to see about as fine a lot of stores as any city of our size can boast of.

L. L. May & Company have had an unusually heavy week in the funeral work line; counter trade for loose cut flowers is small. Their carnation plants in the field look fine and have every appearance of being good for a large crop, after being transplanted.

The Swanson Floral Company apparently are doing a nice trade; their place is very attractive and being in a good location is much admired.

Holm & Olson's place is nearing completion and will be a very attractive store when completed. They will have a floor space of 150 by 50 feet, also a conservatory in the rear.

H. Krinke & Son's continue to put up an attractive display of potted plants, the lateness of the season, however, makes the sale indeed slow.

The Twin City florists bowling contest was pulled off successfully Friday evening, August 3, at Pfister's alleys. A fine programme was arranged and prizes were won by the following: Ladies Prizes—Mrs. Bulow, Miss K. Hansen, Miss Will, Mrs. N. C. Hansen, Miss F. Johnson, Miss Seegar; and booby, Miss Schulz.

Gentlemen's Prizes—Oscar Carlson, P. Hansen, H. Schieman, O. J. Olson, C. Hansen, Jr., F. Schulze, and booby, E. P. Holm. Oscar Carlson made the most strikes for which a special prize was given. O. J. Olson made the most spares.

B. Eschner of Rice & Company, Philadelphia, kindly contributed a $5 gold piece for one of the prizes. After the bowling was over about 50 sat down to a nice lunch which was enjoyed by all. PAUL.

CARNATIONS

	Per 100	Per 1000
FIANCEE	$6 00	
LAWSON	6 00	$50 00
NELSON FISHER	7 00	60 00
GUARDIAN ANGEL	4 00	35 00
MORNING GLORY	4 00	35 00
LIEUT. PEARY	8 00	75 00
FRED BURKI	$7 00	$60 00
BOSTON MARKET	5 00	45 00
FLORA HILL	5 00	45 00
WHITE CLOUD	5 00	45 00
CHICAGO (Red Bradt)	5 00	45 00
HARLOWARDEN	6 00	50 00

WIETOR BROS. 51 Wabash Ave., **CHICAGO**

Mention The Florists' Exchange when writing.

100,000 FIELD GROWN CARNATION PLANTS

30,000 LAWSON

	Per 100
LAWSON	$5.00
ENCHANTRESS	7.00
QUEEN LOUISE	5.00
MAY NAYLOR (White)	5.00
BRADT	5.00
PROSPERITY	4.00

EXTRA SELECTED DEFIANCE MIGNONETTE SEED, $1.00 PER TRADE PACKET.

EDWARD J. TAYLOR, Southport, Conn.

Mention The Florists' Exchange when writing.

Field Grown Carnation Plants

ALL THE STANDARD VARIETIES

List and prices on application.

Rose plants 1000 Liberty 3 in. pots .... $5.00 per 100
1000 " 2¼ " " .... 4.00 " 100

THE LEO NIESSEN COMPANY, 1217 Arch St. Philadelphia, Pa.

Mention The Florists' Exchange when writing.

CARNATIONS FIELD PLANTS

	1st size per 100	2d size per 100
Glendale	$12.00	—
Victory	12.00	—
Robt. Craig	12.00	—
Enchantress	8.00	—
Lady Bountiful	—	$6.00
Belle	8.00	6.00
Boston Market	7.00	5.00
White Cloud	7.00	—
Nelson Fisher	—	$6.00
Prosperity	6.00	—
Flamingo	8.00	6.00
Cardinal	—	6.00
Crane	—	5.00
Estelle	2d size $5.00;	3d size $3.50

400 4 in. **Maids,** 250, 4 in. **Brides** at $7.00 per 100. 500, 2½ in. **Gates,** 300, 2½ in. **Brides,** 150, 2½ in. **Perle,** at $3.50 per 100.
Rex Begonia 4 in. 12c. 5 in. 20c. **Vinca Variegata** 3 in. $6.00 per 100. **Richmond Roses** 2 in. $5.00. 3 in. $8.00 per 100. **Asparagus Plumosus** 2 in. $2.00 per 100 **Cash or C. O. D.**

W. J. & M. S. VESEY, Fort Wayne, Ind.

Mention The Florists' Exchange when writing.

CARNATIONS

	per 1000	per 100
500 **Queen Louis,** field grown		$4.00
Smilax	$9.00	1.00
Asp. Plumosus, 2½ in. pots. Aug. 15th		2.00
Cineraria, Sept. 15th		2.00
Pansy Seed, large flowering, per oz., $4.00		

PRIMROSES

	per 100
Chinese, 2½ in. pots, Aug. 10th	$2.00
Obconica, Roses and Albs, Aug. 10th	2.00
Forbesi, fine for cut flowers	2.00
P. W. Narcissus, 13 ctm., Sept.	1.25

CASH PLEASE

JOS. H. CUNNINGHAM, Delaware, O.

Mention The Florists' Exchange when writing.

ABUNDANCE

Healthy, stocky, field grown plants. First size, $12.00 per 100; $100.00 per 1000. Second size, $10.00 per 100; $75.00 per 1000; 250 at a 1000 rates. Delivery 15th of August.

CASH WITH ORDER.

Abundance Carnation is an easy lifter, takes hold quickly, and makes good-sized stems on first crop.

Freesia Purity bulbs all sold out clean.

RUDOLPH FISCHER, Great Neck, L.I. N.Y.

Mention The Florists' Exchange when writing.

"MRS. OMWAKE"

SPORT OF ENCHANTRESS

$10.00 per 100. Cash.

HENRY EICHHOLZ, Waynesboro, Pa.

CARNATIONS

Excellent Field Grown

The Queen .... $8.00 per 100
Crimson Glow, (new) .... 12.00 " 100
Lieut. Peary, medium size .... 8.00 " 100

Cash or references with order.

DAILLEDOUZE BROTHERS
Flatbush, Brooklyn, N. Y.

CARNATIONS

F. DORNER & SONS CO.
LA FAYETTE, IND.

Mention The Florists' Exchange when writing.

50,000 Large, Healthy, Bushy Carnation Plants

Pink Lawson, Enchantress, Adonis, Flamingo, Crusader, Mrs. Patten, Neptune, Queen Louise, Roosevelt, Harry Fenn, Genevieve Lord, White Cloud, Prosperity, Ad. Cervera, Boston Market, Joost, Flora Hill, Ethel Crocker.
$4.00 per 100.
FIANCEE, 10c.; OCTOROON, No. 1—No. 2; RED LAWSON, LADY BOUNTIFUL, 8c.
ROBERT CRAIG Carnation, 12c.
ASPARAGUS PLUMOSUS, strong 2 1-2 in. 3c; 4 in. 8c
" SPRENGERI, 2 1-2 in. 2c.
SMILAX, 2 1-2 in. $1.50 per 100.
PARSLEY PLANTS, $2.00 per 1000.
Cash Please.

F. B. RINE, Lewisburg, Pa.

Mention The Florists' Exchange when writing.

Field Grown CARNATIONS

6000 White Lawson .... $6.00 per 100.
1000 Roosevelt 2000 Harlowarden
5000 Queen Louise 300 Crisis
500 Flamingo 200 F. Burki
100 Eclipse.
$5.00 per 100; $45.00 per 1000.
Limestone land, no stem rot.

CASH WITH ORDER.

Wells Fargo, American, Adams, U. S. Express

W. SABRANSKY, KENTON, O.

Mention The Florists' Exchange when writing.

FIELD-GROWN Carnation Plants

Send for price and list of varieties.

Chicago Carnation Co., Joliet, Ill.

Mention The Florists' Exchange when writing.

CARNATIONS

PLANTS FROM FIELD.

Fair Maid, Queen, Mrs. Patten, Harlowarden, $5.00 per 100; $45.00 per 1000. Strong and healthy.
Satisfaction guaranteed. Cash with Order.

HUGH CHESNEY, Farmington, Ct.

Mention The Florists' Exchange when writing.

CARNATIONS

Field Grown plants for August 27 and later delivery.

THE H. WEBER & SONS CO.,
OAKLAND, MD.

Mention The Florists' Exchange when writing.

FINE FIELD-GROWN CARNATION PLANTS

Prosperity	per	100	$6.00
Mrs. T. W. Lawson	"	"	6.00
Queen Louise	"	"	4.50
White Cloud	"	"	4.50
Smilax Plants	"	"	1.50

Cash please.

R. I. HART, Hackettstown, N. J.

Mention the Florists' Exchange when writing.

CARNATIONS

Fine field plants, ready to ship. Enchantress, Pink and White Lawson, Queen, Boston Market, $6.00 per 100; $45.00 per 1000.

Ardisia crenulata, strong, bushy plants from bench, well berried, ready for 5-6 in. pots, $6.00 and $9.00 per doz.

Geraniums, 12 varieties. Have order booked for Fall delivery; can fill orders from 100-100,000. Get my prices. Standard, 6 in. pots, $9.00 per 1000; 5000, $40.00 saucers 60c. 100. Cash.

WM. S. HERZOG, MORRIS PLAINS, N. J.

Mention The Florists' Exchange when writing.

PLANT CULTURE

PRICE, $1.00.

The best book for the plant grower.

A. T. DE LA MARE PTG. & PUB. CO. LTD.

S. J. GODDARD

Framingham, Mass.

Rooted Carnation Cuttings a Specialty

Correspondence Solicited.

CARNATIONS

FINE FIELD GROWN PLANTS
CORRESPONDENCE SOLICITED

A. B. DAVIS & SON, Inc., Purcellville Va.

Mention The Florists' Exchange when writing.

FIELD GROWN Carnation Plants

Enchantress, $40.00 and $50.00 per 1000.
McGowan, $30.0'. Cash with order.

WM. BELL, BAYSIDE, L. I.

Mention The Florists' Exchange when writing.

ENCHANTRESS

Field-grown, ready August 15, $6.00 per 100; $50.00 per 1000.

WHITE BROTHERS, Gasport, N. Y.

Mention The Florists' Exchange when writing.

CARNATIONS

SMITH & GANNETT,
GENEVA, N. Y.

Mention The Florists' Exchange when writing.

FIELD GROWN CARNATION PLANTS

Queen Louise, Queen, Lawson, Enchantress, Harlowarden, Mrs. Patten, Fiancee, $6.00 per 100; $50.00 per 1000.

S. J. REUTER, Westerly, R. I.

Jensen & Dekema

CARNATION SPECIALISTS

674 W. Foster Ave., CHICAGO.

CARNATIONS

Rooted Cuttings

All the new varieties of 1906. All the standard varieties worth growing.

WM. SWAYNE, Box 226, Kennett Square Pa.

Mention The Florists' Exchange when writing.

Carnations

Enchantress, Patten and N. Fisher the leaders. Also Vesper, Queen and Boston Market.

ISAAC A. PASSMORE West Chester, Pa.

Mention The Florists' Exchange when writing.

CULTURAL DIRECTIONS

Specially written for the use of your amateur customers. Send Twenty-five cents for complete sample set, which amount will be deducted from order for first thousand.

The universal favor in which these Directions are held, as shown by the many orders received therefor, encourages us in the belief that these Leaflets are just the neat little factor to help promote business and establish better relations between the dealer and his customer.

TRY SOME!

BIG BUSINESS ASSISTANT

TO SAVE TIME, QUICKEN SALES, AND AID YOU PLEASE YOUR CUSTOMER, WE HAVE PREPARED

Cultural Directions

COVERING A NUMBER OF THOSE PLANTS AND BULBS MOST LARGELY IN DEMAND

THE "CULTURALS" have been written by experts; they are fuller, and contain more detailed directions than it is possible to embrace in a catalogue.

Equipped with these, just hand one out with each sale, and save yourself considerable present and future trouble, as the customer will then be able to consult the directions, grow his plants, seeds or bulbs intelligently, and so receive satisfactory results, without having to continually resort to you for advice.

The following "Culturals" are now ready:

AMARYLLIS (Hippeastrum)
ANNUALS FROM SEED
ASPARAGUS
ASTERS
BEGONIA, TUBEROUS
BULBS
CABBAGE and CAULIFLOWER
CANNA
CARNATIONS, MONTHLY
CELERY
CHINESE SACRED LILY
CHRYSANTHEMUM
CLIMBING PLANTS, Hardy
COLEUS, and other bedders
CROCUS, Snowdrop and Scilla Sibirica
DAHLIA
FERNS
FREESIA
GERANIUM
GLADIOLUS
GLOXINIA
HOT BEDS and FRAMES
HOUSE PLANTS, Care of
HYACINTHS, Dutch and Roman
IRIS AND TRITOMA
LAWNS
LILY CULTURE for House and Garden
MUSHROOM CULTURE
ONIONS
PALMS, House Culture of
PANSY
PEONIES
PERENNIALS, Hardy
PRIMULA
ROSE CULTURE
SWEET PEA, The
TOMATOES
TUBEROSE
TULIP
VEGETABLES
VIOLETS
WATER GARDEN, How to make and Manage a

PRICE LIST

500 Cultural Directions for $1.50
1,000 - - - - - 2.50
Printed on white paper, clear type, size 6 x 9½ inches, in an assortment, your selection of not less than 100 of each, delivered carriage paid.

Sufficient space will be left at the bottom of each leaflet for your name, address, etc. If you desire this imprint (3 lines) we will put same on for you at 50 cents for 500, 75 cents for 1000. Special quotations will be made on quantities of 5,000 "CULTURALS" or over.

A. T. De La Mare Ptg. and Pub. Co. Ltd.
Pubs. The Florists' Exchange. P. O. Box, 1697, NEW YORK

YOUR Fall Catalogue

We have been printing Trade Catalogues for the past fifteen years; have been accumulating stock cuts and photographs for the past fifteen years, and, equally important, perhaps most important of all, have been steadily improving in our knowledge as to what is required in the way of style, workmanship and finish in order to produce a catalogue that

Will Be Effective

Send in full specifications and we will promptly give you an estimate. We supply our stock cuts free to customers.

A. T. DE LA MARE PTG. & PUB. CO. Ltd.
2 to 8 Duane Street, New York City.

FERNS.

POINSETTIAS, 2½ inch pots, $5.00 per 100.
ASPARAGUS PLUMOSUS, 4 in. pots, $10.00 per 100.

HUGH GRAHAM CO.,
Logan Nurseries, York Road and Louden Street, PHILADELPHIA, PA.

Mention The Florists' Exchange when writing.

FERNS OUR SPECIALTY

CIBOTIUM SCHIEDEI

We have a large stock of this beautiful tree fern in 3 in. pots, ready for a shift, at $25.00 per 100. 25 plants at 100 rate.

FERN SEEDLINGS FROM FLATS

Eight to ten best market varieties at $1.00 per 100, or $8.50 per 1000. If by mail add 10c. for each hundred plants.

ASSORTED FERNS FOR DISHES

From 2¼ in. pots. The best and hardiest varieties in market at $3.00 per 100, or $25.00 per 1000. 250 plants at 1000 rate.

Adiantum Cuneatum, 2¼ in. pots, $3.50 per 100, $30.00 per 1000.

FERN SPORES

Gathered from our own stock. 35c. per trade package. $4.00 per doz packages.

Gardenia Vietchii from 2¼ in. pots. $7.50 per 100. $70.00 per 1000; 500 at 1000 rate.

ANDERSON & CHRISTENSEN,
SHORT HILLS, N. J.

Mention The Florists' Exchange when writing.

FERNS You Must Have

Only 5,000 left; speak quick.

Piersoni, 5 in., 20c.; 4 in., 15c.; 3 in., 10c.
Scottii, 5 in., 20c.; 4 in., 15c.; 3 in., 10c.
Bostons, 3 in., ready to shift, 10c.
Asparagus Plumosus Nanus, 3½ in. 6c; 2½ in., $2.50 per 100.
Asparagus Sprengerii, 3½ in., 6c.
20,000 Field Carnations.
Hydrangeas Otaksa and Vinca maj., variegated, strong 2½ in., $2.50 per 100.

Write me. Cash please.

BENJAMIN CONNELL, West Grove, Pa.

Mention The Florists' Exchange when writing.

FERNS

Are now in fine shape. A good variety and nice bushy stock, 2¼ in., $3.00 per 100; $25.00 per 1000.
Kentia Belmoreana, 4 in., clean and bushy, 25c.
Cocos Weddeliana, 10c.
Dracaena Indivisa, 4 in., strong, 12c.
Mme. Salleroi Geraniums, 2 in., $2.00 per 100.
English Ivy, 4 in., fine stock, $10.00 per 100.

H. WESTON, HEMPSTEAD, N. Y.

Mention The Florists' Exchange when writing.

BOSTON FERNS

Taken from bench, $10.00 and $20.00 per 100.
5 and 6 inch Pot Ferns, from $3.00 per doz. up Extra fine stock.
Geraniums, 3½ inch stock, $4.00 per 100.

BOCK, THE FLORIST,
2394 MASS AVENUE NORTH CAMBRIDGE, MASS.

Mention The Florists' Exchange when writing.

ROBERT CRAIG & CO.

ROSES, PALMS, CROTONS

CARNATIONS and Novelties in DECORATIVE PLANTS

Market and 49th Sts. PHILADELPHIA, PA.

Mention The Florists' Exchange when writing.

THE UNSOLICITED TESTIMONIALS from advertisers who use our columns, on the unparalleled success, and the large returns therefrom, afford a guarantee of the efficacy of advertising in THE FLORISTS' EXCHANGE such as no other similar periodical can boast of.

Mention The Florists' Exchange when writing.

Adiantum Cuneatum

From 2¼ in. pots ready to shift, per 100 $4.00; per 1000, $35.00.

Asparagus Plumosus Nanus

true kind, from 2¼ in. pots, per 100, $3.00; per 1000, $25.00.

Ferns in Flats

Each flat contains about 110 divisible clumps, standard varieties as: Aspargus Tsussemense, Cyrtomium Falcatum, Lastraea Aristata Variegata, Pteris Adiantoides Cretica Albolineata, Gilbertii, Mayi, Magnifica, Serrulata, Serr. Crist., Nana Compacta, Wimsetti, Adiantum Cuneatum, per flat, $2.00; per 12 flats, buyers' selection, $22.00; my own selection, $20.00. For larger quantities ask special quotation.

O. V. ZANGEN
Seedsman HOBOKEN, N. J.

Mention the Florists' Exchange when writing.

NEPHROLEPIS SCOTTII

Small plants from the benches, $5.00 per 100; $50.00 per 1000. Plants large enough for 6 in. pots, $25.00 per 100. Plants large enough to go in 7 and 8 in. pots, $50.00 per 100.

Asparagus Plumosus Nanus, 2¼ in., fine plants, $3.00 per 100.

JOHN SCOTT,
Rutland Road and East 45th Street; BROOKLYN, N. Y.
Telephone 2890 Bedford.

Mention The Florists' Exchange when writing.

FERN SEEDLINGS

FROM FLATS.

The first crop is now ready for potting, including the following varieties: Pteris Cretica Cristata, Pteris Cretica Albo-Lineata, Pteris Adiantoides, Pteris Argyraea, Pteris Mayii, Cyrtomium Falcatum, Aspidium Tsussemense, Onychium Japonica, Doodia Aspera. My selection, $1.00 per 100; $8.50 per 1000. If by mail, add 10c. per 100 for postage.

M Ferns for dishes, 2¼ in., $3.00 per 100; $36.00 per 1000; 250 at 1000 rate; 3 in., $6.00 per 100.
Adiantum Cuneatum, 3 in., $6.00 per 100.

FRANK N. ESKESEN, MADISON, N. J.

Mention The Florists' Exchange when writing.

NEPHROLEPIS WHITMANI

is the fern to grow.

Having ordered a large quantity I can fill your orders at short notice. Price, $25.00 per 100; $200.00 per 1000.

S. S. SKIDELSKY,
824 No. 24 St., Philadelphia, Pa.

Mention The Florists' Exchange when writing.

NEPHROLEPIS

Whitmani, 2¼ in., $25.00 per 100.
Barrowsii, $10.00 per 100.

Henry H. Barrows & Son, Whitman, Mass.

Mention The Florists' Exchange when writing.

FERNS

	Doz.	100
SCOTTII, 2¼ inch	$0.75	$6.00
BARROWSII, 2¼ inch	1.25	8.00

THE CONARD & JONES CO.
WEST GROVE, PA.

Mention The Florists' Exchange when writing.

CLASSIFIED ADVERTISEMENTS

CASH WITH ORDER.

The columns under this heading are reserved for advertisements of Stock for Sale, Stock Wanted, Help Wanted, Situations Wanted or other Wants; also of Greenhouse, Land, Second-Hand Materials, etc., For Sale or Rent.

Our charge is 10 cts. per line (7 words to the line), set solid, without display. No advt. accepted for less than thirty cents.

Display advertisements in these columns, 15 cents per line; count 12 lines agate to the inch.

[If replies to Help Wanted, Situation Wanted, or other advertisements are to be addressed care of this office, advertisers add 10 cents to cover expense of forwarding.]

Copy must reach New York office 12 o'clock Wednesday to secure insertion in issue of following Saturday.

Advertisers in the Western States desiring to advertise under initials, may save time by having their answer directed care our Chicago office at 127 E. Berwyn Ave.

SITUATIONS WANTED

SITUATION WANTED—By A1 rose and carnation grower, only first-class place wanted. Married. F. Stevens, Chatham, N. J.

SITUATION WANTED—By young man 8 years' experience in greenhouses; good references. L. Geb, 150 Central Ave., Brooklyn, N. Y.

SITUATION WANTED—By first class designer and decorator, quick worker, good salesman. Good references. Address, N. A., care Florists' Exchange.

SITUATION WANTED—As foreman of a rose establishment. References, stating character, intelligence and ability given on application. Address, M. P., care The Florists' Exchange.

SITUATION WANTED—As working foreman by a good pot-plant and cut flower grower. German; age 37. Life-time experience, best of reference given. Please state wages. Address, N. B., care The Florists' Exchange.

SITUATION WANTED—By a practical middle-aged florist, life experience growing roses, carnations, violets, chrysanthemums, decorative and bedding plants. Single, sober, state wages and particulars. Address, M. Z., care The Florists' Exchange.

SITUATION WANTED—By florist, Norwegian, age 24, speaking some English. Specialty, hothouse and bedding plants. Well recommended. Prefers place near New York, private or commercial. Address, E. P., 8 State street, New York.

SITUATION WANTED—As working foreman on private or commercial place. 16 years' experience here and abroad in every line of the trade. German, married, small family. Please state particulars in first letter. Open for engagement September 1st. L. Hoffman, Chichester, Ulster County, New York.

HELP WANTED

WANTED—Strong young man to learn florist trade. Must be respectable, and handy with tools. George Allen, Princeton, N. J.

WANTED—A good reliable grower of carnations, chrysanthemums, and bedding plants. Apply with references and wages wanted to Converse Greenhouses, Webster, Mass.

WANTED—A thoroughly competent man to take charge of a section of Beauties. Apply Frank Dolan, care of John Young Company, Bedford Station, New York.

WATED—Good man for general greenhouse work. Good wages and steady position to the right man. Address, M. V., care The Florists' Exchange.

WANTED—Assistant for rose houses, young man who has had one or two years' experience preferred. Address, Robert Miller, Rose grower, East Brookfield, Mass.

WANTED—Working foreman, for general greenhouse work. State where last employed. Wages $30 per month, board and room to start with. Address G, care Florists' Exchange.

WANTED—Married man for rose section $15.00 per week. Single man on chrysanthemums, $14.00 per week. Please state age, experience and send references. Address, M. G., care The Florists' Exchange.

WANTED—A first-class man for retail florist in Chicago; no greenhouse work. Must be a good salesman and designer. State wages, references. Address, M. D., care The Florists' Exchange.

WANTED—A first class plantman, one who is up on bedding and choice store-stock, with a fair knowledge of chrysanthemums and bulb forcing. A permanent place and good salary to a capable man. Honaker, The Florist, Lexington, Ky.

Thirty cents is the minimum charge for advertisements on this page.

MISCELLANEOUS WANTS

WANTED—To buy, second-hand Dean steam or hot-water heater, style "C." Address Box 72, Shrewsbury, Mass.

WANTED TO BUY—Greenhouses to be taken down. State full particulars of same when writing. Address, F. W., care The Florists' Exchange.

SHADE TREES wanted; nursery grown. Also evergreens and hardy shrubs. Any size, kind, quantity. Describe fully and name lowest prices delivered New York. Address, M. E., care The Florists' Exchange.

PARTNERS with capital and experience, with first-class references, for greenhouse and florist store in central states. Fine opening for right parties. Present investment, $35,000. Year's business, $23,000. Address, M. U., care The Florists' Exchange.

NURSERY CATALOGUES WANTED
FRANK HAMILTON, Landscape Gardener
Bryant Building, 55 Liberty Street, New York
Mention The Florists' Exchange when writing.

WANTED TO RENT

A range of 8,000 to 12,000 ft. of Greenhouses to be used for commercial growing for New York market, or in part for a local trade. With good water and soil supply, 2 to 10 acres of land. Situated not more than one hour from New York. Would take lease of 3 to 5 years with privilege of purchase within that period of time.

Address M. N., care of Florists' Exchange.

Mention The Florists' Exchange when writing.

FOR SALE OR RENT

FOR SALE—One horizontal boiler; 40 horse power; all complete; good condition; cheap. Alex. B. Garden, Anacostia, D. C.

FOR SALE—Two greenhouses to be taken down and removed. Nearly new. For particulars address, W. C. Merritt, Washingtonville, N. Y.

FOR SALE—Three greenhouses of about 6,000 feet of glass. Good established retail business, or would rent for term of years. George Main, Gloversville, New York.

FOR SALE—Greenhouse comprising over 8,000 square feet of glass situated in Northern New Jersey. Including all stock, horse, wagons, and harness, etc. Doing good retail business. Address, B., care Florists' Exchange.

FOR SALE—A fine established florist, plant and seed business in prosperous running condition located in the best residential part of the Bronx; full particulars. S. Ch. Nagels Seed Store, 654 East 154th Street, New York.

FOR SALE—House, 7 rooms, steam heat, 1 stable, 5 greenhouses, well stocked; steam heat, Kearney, N. J., 5 minutes from Erie R. R. depot, and 5 minutes from N. Y. trolley. J. G. Perry, Schuyler Avenue, Kearney, New Jersey.

FOR RENT—Small greenhouse and florist business in prosperous running condition. Southern Connecticut. Full particulars and reason for renting to any one interested. Address, M. R., care The Florists' Exchange.

FOR SALE—A fine established nursery business with a constituency reaching from the Atlantic to the Pacific, and from Manitoba to the Gulf. Old age of proprietor the only reason for sale. C. S. Harrison, York, Neb.

DESIRABLE greenhouse plant of three houses, 24x200 feet; propagating house, 100 feet; potting shed, stable and dwelling. Steam heat, city water. Highland, opposite Poughkeepsie. Joseph Wood, Spring Valley, New York.

TO LET—greenhouse establishment in the city of Poughkeepsie, N. Y. 8000 feet of glass, city water, plenty of soil, fine location. For particulars, come and see, or write to James Coleman, 212 Marmion street, Poughkeepsie, N. Y.

FOR SALE—A paying greenhouse establishment of 7,800 feet glass, with nearly one acre of ground, six room cottage house in a growing city of 15,000. Only one other establishment in the city. In central Ohio. Reason for selling ill-health. Full particulars on application. Or will sell material in greenhouses alone. Address, M. X., care Florists' Exchange.

TO LEASE—For a term of years a small commercial greenhouse plant, about 4,000 feet of glass, well stocked with good varieties of chrysanthemums, and heated with Furman Hot Water Sectional Boiler. Five minutes from station, and 25 minutes from New York City market. For further particulars address, M. H., care The Florists' Exchange.

FOR SALE—On account of failing health, a florist business well established, situated near trolley and railroad station, fifteen minutes drive from a city of over 100,000 inhabitants and thirty minutes from New York City. Three greenhouses (plenty market stock on hand) plenty of sashes, dwelling house of six rooms, barn, horse, three wagons and sleigh, tools, etc. A gold mine for the right man. Must be seen to be appreciated. Address, M. Y., care Florists' Exchange.

FOR SALE OR RENT

FOR SALE—Owing to failing health, I will sell my florist establishment, beautifully situated between Larchmont Manor and Mamaroneck, Westchester Co., New York, near railroad station; trolley lines within one minute walk. First class opportunity for the right man. Plenty of landscape and jobbing work. The place contains four acres, 2 greenhouses, 104 feet long and lots of sash; well stocked with trees and shrubs, etc.; horse, wagon and tools. Address, Box 44, Larchmont, New York.

To lease for a term of years, my establishment on Greene Avenue, consisting of about 7,000 feet of glass, office and salesroom. Stable and wagon shed. Horse and wagons. Place well stocked and heated with hot water. Every convenience, all in good condition. A good business in the best location in the city. Established for 40 years. Wishing to retire from business. This is a good opportunity for the right man. Come and see it. Richard Shannon, 341-349 Greene Avenue, Brooklyn, New York.

Valuable Greenhouses to Lease.

The houses formerly owned by the late F. A. Blake, of Rochdale, Mass., will be leased on easy terms to responsible party. They consist of seven houses having floor area of 6800 sq. ft., with boiler house, barn and two to three acres of good land. The stock, consisting of 2600 choice carnations in the field, and a large and select variety of other plants, will be sold cheap for cash to lessee. Situated nine miles from Worcester and fifty-three miles from Boston. Address,

MRS. F. A. BLAKE,
ROCHDALE, MASS.

Mention The Florists' Exchange when writing.

STOCK FOR SALE

JERUSALEM CHERRIES, 2 1-2-in. pots only, $3 per 100. Cash please. A. Relyea & Son, Poughkeepsie, New York.

PEONY FESTIVA MAXIMA, and other best sorts in strong plants, 2 yr. old. Catalogue free. A. Dessert, Peony Specialist, Chenonceaux, France.

SEEDS, pansy, new crop, $1.00 per packet; $4.00 per oz.; $12.00 per 1-4 lb. Pansy plants, $4.00 per 1,000. Cash. B. Soltau, 199 Grant avenue, Jersey City, N. J.

PRIMULA: Chinese fringed mixed, 1 3-4 c. Obconica grandiflora fringed, Alba, Rosea, 2 in., 2c. Cash. Shippensburg Floral Co., Shippensburg, Pa.

BABY RAMBLER ROSES, H. P. and Rambler roses, field grown, 2 year stock, for sale cheap. write for list. Schaufelberger & Hill, Penfield, New York.

20,000 Retinispora plumosa aurea, 4 to 6 inches, transplanted. Also 4,000 Retinispora Squarrosa Veitchii, 6 inches, transplanted. Address, Rhode Island Nurseries, Newport, R. I.

QUEEN LOUISE and C. A. Dana carnations, $5.00 per 100; $35.00 per 1,000. Giant Double Alyssum, 2 in., $2.00 per 100. Will exchange either for A. plumosus nanus. Fox & Rosen, Parkerford, Pa.

CARNATION PLANTS, nice field-grown. Enchantress, Mrs. T. W. Lawson, $6.00 per 100; Joost, New Daybreak, or Prosperity, Wolcott, $5.00 per 100. For cash. M. J. Schaaf, Dansville, N. Y.

CARNATIONS, first-class, field grown plants. Enchantress, Lawson, Queen, $6.00 per 100; $50.00 per 1000. Cash with order please. Mrs. P. F. Conley, Princeton Avenue, & Updike Street, Providence, R. I.

STOCK FOR SALE—Brides, Maids and American Beauties, in 4 in. pots; best of plants. Also 1 year old Asparagus. All at low bottom prices. Small or large orders. Madison Rose Company, Madison, N. J.

JARDINIERE FERNS, seedlings, good, strong, healthy stock, in variety only. Now ready for potting. Price, $1.50 per 100 by mail; $10.00 per 1000, F. O. B. Exp. B. Soltau, 199 Grant avenue, Jersey City, N. J.

BABY RAMBLER roses, fine dormant stock, $25 per 100. 2 1-2 inch pot plants, extra well rooted $7 per 100, $65 per 1000. Orders booked for delivery now or any time up to late Spring. Samples free. Brown Brothers Co., Rochester, N. Y.

2500 BRIDESMAID plants, 2000 Brides, 1500 American Beauties, 1000 Meteors, all good, fine plants in 4 in. pots. Packed and shipped at express office. Maids, Brides and Meteors, 5c. each. American Beauties, 12c. each. Louis M. Noe, Madison, N. J.

YUCCA FILAMENTOSA, $1.00 lb.; Amorpha fruticosa, 25c. lb.; Ampelopsis quinquefolia, 75c. lb.; Azalea arborescens, $2.00 lb.; Corylus rostrata, 50c. lb.; Crataegus crus-galli, 25c. lb.; Juglans cinerea, $1.00 bu.; Juglans nigra, $1.00 bu.; Cornus florida, 20c. lb. F. M. Crayton, Box 393, Biltmore, N. C.

FOR SALE

FOR SALE—Cheap, all sizes greenhouse glass, new stock. Address, Glass, care The Florists' Exchange.

FOR SALE—Rafters and ventilating apparatus for greenhouses. 90 Palisade Ave., West Hoboken, N. J.

FOR SALE—5,000 3 1-2 inch pots at half price. Platform, spring wagon, 1 set of harness, 72 hot bed sash. Will sell cheap. Frank Albright, 13 Pringle St. and Forest Ave., Brooklyn, N. Y.

FOR SALE—12 Hitchings hot water expansion tanks for 3 1-2 in. pipe, in good condition, cleaned, ready to set up. 1-3 price of new. Also horse lawn mower, easy running, $20.00. Address, K. D., care The Florists' Exchange.

FOR SALE—Stover fifty foot Steel Tower and Tank in use a short time. Good as new; price reasonable. Write for particulars. Wm. C. De Witt, R. F. D. No. 1, Phillipsburg, N. J.

10,000 5 in. pots, as good as new, cost $12.00 per 1000; will sell for $9.00 per 1000. Cash with all orders please. Dean & Parse, 46 to 52 Ashwood Avenue, Summit, New Jersey.

BOILERS, BOILERS, BOILERS.

SEVERAL good second hand boilers on hand, also new No. 16 Hitchings at reduced cost. Write for list. Wm. H. Lutton, West Side Avenue Station, C. R. R. of N. J., Jersey City, N. J.

FOR SALE—Six 4 inch gate valves, good as new, at $4.00. Large lot calla clumps, 16 large azalea indica plants in 12 x 14 inch pots for cutting; 100 large clumps Adiantum Cuneatum, 20 boxes 8 x 10 double thick glass, clean, $2.25 box. J. Geist, Melrose, Mass. Tel. 333-5.

FOR SALE

Greenhouse Material milled from Gulf Cypress, to any detail furnished, or our own patterns as desired, cut and spliced ready for erection. Estimates for complete constructions furnished.

V. E. REICH, Brooklyn, N. Y.
1429-1437 Metropolitan Ave.

Mention The Florists' Exchange when writing.

FOR SALE

PUMPS Rider-Ericsson. Second-hand, from $40.00 up; all repairs; other makes; new; cheap.

BOILERS One second-hand tubular hot water boiler 3 ft. in diameter 12 ft. long. Price $35.00. One No. 16 Hitchings as good as new, $60.00.

PIPE Good serviceable second-hand, with Threads; 2-in., 7 cts.; 1½-in., 5½ cts.; 1¼-in., 4 cts.; 1-in., 3 cts.; 2½ in., 10 cts.; 3 in., 14 cts.; 4 in., 19 cts. New 2-in. Standard, full lengths, with couplings, 8¼ cts. ft. Old and new fittings and valves. Old 4 inch cast iron 15c per foot.

STOCKS and DIES New Economy, best made No. 1 Threads, ½-in., ¾-in. 1-in. pipe, $3.00. No. 2 Threads, 1¼-in., 1½-in. 2-in. pipe, $4.00.

PIPE CUTTERS New Saunders Pattern. No. 1 cuts ⅛-in.-1-in. pipe, $1.00. No. 2 cuts 1-in.-2-in. pipe, $1.30.

STILLSON WRENCHES New. 18-in., grips ¼-in.-2-in. pipe, $1.65; 24-in. grips ¼-in.-2½ in. pipe, $2.40; 36-in., grips ½-in.-3½-in. pipe, $4.75.

PIPE VISES New. No. 1 Hinged, grips ⅛-in.-2 in. pipe, $2.00.

GARDEN HOSE New. 50 ft. lengths. ¾-in., guaranteed 100-lbs. pressure, 7½ cts. per ft.; ¾-in. not guaranteed, 4¾ cts. per ft., 25 ft. lengths, ½c. per ft. more.

HOT-BED SASH New. Cypress, 3-ft.x6 ft., from 75 cts. up; glazed, complete, from $1.60 up. Second-hand, in good condition, all glass in, $1.00 each.

GLASS New American 10x12 single $1.75 per box; 12x12 single $1.90 per box; 10x12, 12x12, 10x15 double, $2.40 per box; 12x14, 12x20, 14x14, double, $2.90 per box; 16x16, 18x18, $3.00 per box; 16x24 double $3.30 per box. Second hand glass, 8 x 10, 8 x 12, double, $1.60 per box.

Old material, ridge, plates, gutters, bars, etc.

Get our prices on New Gulf Cypress Building Material, Ventilating Apparatus, Oil, White Lead, Putty, Paint, Points, etc.

METROPOLITAN MATERIAL CO.

1398-1408 Metropolitan Avenue, BROOKLYN, N.Y

Mention The Florists' Exchange when writing.

OUR ENDEAVOR

is to place THE FLORISTS' EXCHANGE in the hands of every reader within 1000 miles on Saturday of each week.

In order to effect this even distribution, which makes for the benefit of our advertisers, it is necessary that all advertising copy for current issue should reach us by

12 noon, on Wednesday.

New York.

News Notes.

Funeral services over the remains of the late James Weir, Jr., who died on his yacht in Geering Harbor, Greenpoint, Wednesday of last week were held at his late home, 236 Twenty-fifth street, Brooklyn, N. Y., Saturday afternoon last. The outpouring of mourning friends attested the general esteem for the deceased, and the floral tokens were numerous. Three carriages were needed to take all the pieces to the place of interment in Greenwood. Among the floral pieces was one made to resemble the club flag, from the Shelter Island Yacht Club, and there was an anchor twelve feet in length from the employees of Mr. Weir.

Several of Mr. Weir's old employees are now in business for themselves. Thomas E. Langton, retailer Flatbush avenue, Brooklyn, was Mr. Weir's first workman; and the late Anthony Wollmers, Twenty-fifth street, was also in the employ of Mr. Weir.

The Richmond County Agricultural Society will hold its annual Fair September 5 to 8 inclusive, on the grounds near Midland Beach, S. I. A. C. Nellis is manager of the Agricultural, Horticultural and Floricultural departments; and premiums are offered for fruits, vegetables, cut flowers, potted plants and floral designs.

It is refreshing to note John Birnie's able defense of the New York geranium growers. Seeing that this city is noted for having the best of everything either floriculturally or otherwise, it does not seem possible that we can be behind other cities in the cultivation of geraniums, or any other plants for that matter.

The weather has been extremely warm this week, and the early closing among the wholesale stores is a feature that is much enjoyed by all the salesmen. What a grand feature it would be to the help in the retail stores if an early closing system could be adopted in that branch of the business.

Charles Carlin, the veteran buyer for Thorley, is away on his usual two months' vacation. 'Tis but few of us who are wealthy enough to make our vacation last the sixth part of a year.

Vaughan's Seed Store handled this week two carloads of French bulbs.

Beaulieu, Woodhaven, N. Y., has secured the agency for the great French insecticide, Le Foudroyant, a sure remedy for all insect pests.

William Lutton of Jersey City has secured the contract for the erection and heating complete of the range of glass for the Huntington Nursery Company, Huntington, Long Island, N. Y. He also has several large contracts on hand and a large staff of men working, and has just completed the additional range of 10,000 square feet of glass for Jacob Hauck of Bloomfield, N. J.

On Wednesday of this week, 2,500 cases of French bulbs arrived at this port on the steamer Gallia of the Fabre Line. This is believed to be the largest consignment of French bulbs that ever reached here on one ship. They were despatched from Marseilles.

Visitors this week included Messrs. Schoenhut, Buffalo, N. Y.; Vick of Vick & Hill, Barnard, N. Y.; and G. J. Nor Dell, Long Branch, N. J.; H. Pfister, Washington; C. Dehn, Saratoga, N. Y.

Pittsburg.

Trade Notes.

The first dull Summer month is past and trade was about the same as is usual at this time of year. In the Allegheny Market business was fairly good; considerable funeral work helping out. The commission houses have little to do, a few hours each morning generally winds up business for the day. There is plenty of stock, not particularly choice as regards roses and carnations. Asters are coming stronger and of good quality. Sweet peas are abundant.

W. Clark of the Pittsburg Cut Flower Company is spending his vacation, and T. P. Langhans, of the same company, is ready to leave for the Thousand Islands to put in three weeks' fishing, etc.

John Bader received a nice lot of Whitmanii fern last week, and expects to grow it heavily; he thinks this is the best thing out in ferns, more distinct and true than some other varieties lately introduced. It certainly is a beautiful fern if it retains an upright habit, but it looks to be of the drooping sort.

The first Lilium Harrisii bulbs have arrived and look fine.

Close to the city there have been severe hailstorms lately, but we have not heard of any loss of glass to any extent.

The next meeting of the Florists' Club will take place Tuesday, August 7, and will be a business one. The reports of the picnic committee and of the transportation committee of the S. A. F. convention to Dayton, will be heard. All those expecting to go to Dayton should be present at that meeting so that arrangements can be made. The fare will be $9.35 (one and one-third rate) on the certificate plan.

E. C. REINEMAN.

JACKSONVILLE, FLA.—Edward Young, of the firm of Hofmann & Young, who has been florist at the Central Hospital for the Insane for several years, has resigned his position and will hereafter devote his entire time to the growing business of his firm. His successor at the hospital is Harry Heinl who has entered upon his duties.

Bargains in CHOICE PLANTS

English Ivy, from 4½ in. pots, $2.00 and $1.50 per doz. About 3 feet high and bushy.

Anthericum, variegated, per doz., $1.50; per 100, $12.00.

Kentia Belmoreana and Forsteriana, $3.00, $4.00, $5.00, $6.00 $9.00 per doz.; also by the 100. Also $1.00, $1.50, $2.00, $2.50, $3.00 each and by the 2 doz.

Phœnix Canariensis, large plants, 6½ to 7 feet high, 11 in. pots, $12.00 to $14.00 per pair.

Bird's Nest Fern, large plants, 6½ in. pots, $1.50 each, $15.00 per doz.

Araucaria Excelsa, 50c., 75c., $1.00, $1.50, $2.00, $2.50 each. Also by the 100.

Cut Flowers of Lily of the Valley, $4.00 and $5.00 per 100.

Boxwood Pyramids, in pots, $2.00 and $2.50 a pair, fine plants. Other sizes sold out.

Bay Trees, Pyramids.
55-60 in. high from top of tub, $14.00 per pair
65-70 in. high from top of tub, 15.00 per pair

Leaf-Mold, $1.00 per bag.

Asparagus Plumosus 3½ in. pots, $1.25 per doz.; per 100, $9.00; 4 in. pots, $2.00 per doz.; 4½ in. pots, $3.00 per doz.

Kentia Forsteriana, combinations, from $3.00, $4.00, $5.00, $6.00, $10.00, $15.00 to $20.00 each.

Piersoni Fern, 5½ in. pots, $9.00 per doz.

N. Elegantissima, from 4½ in. pots, $4.00 per doz.; $30.00 per 100.

Cattleya Trianae, 40 plants, 400 good bulbs, $50.00 per original case.

Orchid Peat, $1.00 per bag.

Rubbers, from 7 in. pots, 3 ft. high, $9.00 per doz.

Pandanus Veitchii, 5 in. pots, $6.00 per doz.; 6 in. pots, $9.00 per doz.; 6½ in., $12.00 per doz.; 7 in., $18 per doz.

Dracæna Terminalis, 4 in. pots, $3.00 per doz.; 5 in. pots, $5.00 per doz.; 6 in., $9.00 per doz.

Gardenia Veitchii, fine large Plants, 5½ in. pots, well budded, $9.00 per doz.

Cycas Revoluta, we have them in 5½, 6, 7 and 8 in. pots, very fine, 50c., 75c., $1.00, $1.50, $2.00 and $3.00 each.

Cibotium Scheidii, 6, 6½ and 7 in. pots, $1.50, $2.00 and $2.50 each.

Dracæna Fragrans. From 5 in. pots, $4.00 per doz.; 6 in. pots from $6.00 to $9.00 per doz.; 7 in. pots, $18.00 per doz.; 8 in. pots, $24.00 per. doz.

Livistona Sinensis, superior to Latania borbonica, larger fan, compact and dark green foliage. 5 in. pot, $4.00 per doz.; 6 in. pots, $6.00 per doz., 7 in. pots, $12.00 per doz.

Areca Lutescens. 6½ in. pots, 3 in a pot, 30 ins. high, doz. $9.00.

Boston Ferns. 5 in. pots, $3.00 per doz.; 6 in. pots, $6.00 per doz.; 7 in. pots, $12.00 per doz. Specimens, 9 in. pots, $3.00 each.

Scottii Fern. 5 in. pots, $3.00 per doz.; 5½ in. pots, $5.00 per doz.; 6½ in. pots, $8.00 doz.

Large Scottii, 10 in. pans, $2.50 each.

Fern Balls, $9.00 per doz.

Crotons, in variety, 4 in. pots, $3.00 per doz.

Aspidistra green, 5½ in. pots, 8 leaves and over, $9.00 per doz.; 6½ in. pots, 15 to 25 leaves, $1.50 and $2.00 each.

Johnsonii Fern, 6 in. pots, $9.00 per doz. (Sword fern.)

Lygodium Scandens, climbing fern, 30 ins. high, per doz., $6.00.

English Ivy, fan-shaped, 2 feet wide, 3 to 4 feet high, 6½ in. pots, $6.00 per doz.; selected, $9.00 per doz.

Primula Obconica, finest pink strain, bushy plants from 4 in. pots ready to go in 5 in. pots, $1.50 per doz.; $10.00 per 100.

Daisy Plants, for Christmas blooming from 6 in. pots $6.00 per doz.

Begonia Rex, 4 in. pots, $1.50 per doz.; selected $2.00 per doz.

Cash with order or satisfactory New York references required.

ANTON SCHULTHEIS
19th St. & 4th Avenue, COLLEGE POINT, N.Y.

Mention The Florists' Exchange when writing.

GRAND EXHIBITION OF GLADIOLUS BLOOMS

. . . AT . . .

HORTICULTURAL HALL,
BOSTON, MASS.

On Saturday, August 18

ALSO AT

Exhibition Hall, Dayton, O.

During S. A. F. Convention, August, 21-24. Named kinds a specialty. Do not miss seeing "AMERICA"

JOHN LEWIS CHILDS, Floral Park, L. I. N. Y.

Mention The Florists' Exchange when writing.

BROTHER FLORISTS

ARE YOU GOING TO DAYTON?

If so, don't fail to see the display of CANNAS planted in the City parks. We feel sure that they will interest you at least, but if you should spend a few minutes or hours in looking them over and should conclude that you had wasted your time just put in your bill for the same and we will give you check in full. We have been told that no one will see them, but we think "PERHAPS." There are but 188 different varieties of them and all but 17 are of our own originating. There are but 1445 of them, and they comprise all the Cannas, we believe, that are in the city parks. Probably this small display wont cut much ice, in comparison with those at the fair grounds but we hope that You will go and see them any way. . . . .

Southern Floral Nursery Co., Bucatunna, Miss. and Fruitdale, Ala.

Mention The Florists' Exchange when writing.

Beautiful and Rare Gladioli

Cut spikes, all colors imaginable in any quantity,— 100 ACRES from which to select, write for prices.

ARTHUR COWEE, Gladiolus Specialist, Meadowvale Farm, Berlin, N. Y.

Mention The Florists' Exchange when writing.

CHINESE PRIMROSES

Finest mixed, strong, 2 in., 2c.

Primula Obconica, Carmine, Hybrid, 2 in., 2c.
" " Double and new Red 2 in., 3c.
Grand. fim. Alba, Rosea, Lilac.

Asparagus Sprengerii, and **Plumosus** 2 in., 2c.

Christmas Peppers, Jerusalem Cherries, 2 in. and 2¼ in. pots, $2.00 per 100.

Ferns from Bench
- Boston, Piersoni, 4 in. 10c; 5 in. 12½c.
- Tarrytown, 3 in., 10c; 4 in., 15c; 5 in., 25c.
- Scottii, 3 in., 8c; 4 in., 12½c; 5 in., 15c.

Geraniums, 2¼ in. Vlaud, Bernandian and 7 other sorts, $1.50 per 100.

Cash or C. O. D.

BYER BROS. Chambersburg, Pa.

Mention The Florists' Exchange when writing.

Decorative Plants

Latania Borbonica, 2¼ in. pots, $3.00; 3 in. $6.00; 4 in., $15.00 per 100. Large specimen plants from $2.00 to $5.00 each.

Kentia Belmoreana and Forsteriana, 2¼ in. pots, $8.00; 3 in., $15.00; 5 in., $50.00 per 100; 6 in. $15.00 per doz.; 7 in. and upward, $1.75 to $36.00 each.

Areca Lutescens, 3 in. $10.00; 4 in. $20.00 per 100; 6 in., $1.00 each and upward.

Pandanus Utilis, 3 in. pots, $3.00; 4 in., $20.00 per 100.

Phœnix Reclinata, 6 in. pots, $25.00 per 100.

Phœnix Canariensis, fine specimen plants, from $3.00 to $35.00 each.

Araucaria Excelsa, 6 in. pots, $65.00 per 100.

Assorted Ferns, 2¼ in. pots, $3.00 per 100.

Nephrolepis Compacta, 3 in. pots, $8.00; 4 in., $15.00 per 100.

Plants in Fine Condition.

JOHN BADER, Troy Hill, Allegheny, Pa.

AMPELOPSIS VEITCHII

Fine plants from 2½ in. pots, $3.00 per 100.

E. C. HAINES, Bedford Station, N. Y.

Mention The Florists' Exchange when writing.

A Few Good Things YOU WANT

Dracæna Indivisa, 4 and 5 in., $10.00 and $25.00 per 100.

Asparagus Sprengeri, 2 in., $2.50 per 100.

Geraniums, S. A. Nutt, Castellane, John Doyle, Perkins, Double Gen. Grant, Poitevine, Mme. Sallerol, 2 in. pots, $2.00 per 100; 3 in. pots $4.00 per 100. Rooted Cuttings, $1.00 per 100.

Rex Begonia, nice plants, 3 and 3½ in., $5.00 per 100.

Asparagus Plumosus, 2 in. $3.00 per 100.

Boston Fern 5 in. 30c each.

Pierson Fern 6 in. 50c each.

GEO. M. EMMANS, Newton, N. J.

Mention The Florists' Exchange when writing.

50,000 Pansy Seedlings

Finest strain at $4.00 per 1000. Delivery beginning September 1st. Orders booked in rotation. Strictly cash with order.

J. CONDON, Horticulturist,
734 5th Ave., Brooklyn, N. Y.

Mention The Florists' Exchange when writing.

SURPLUS STOCK—CHEAP

- 200 **The Bride** roses, 2 in. pots, $1.75 per 100.
- 500 **Bridesmaid** roses, 2 in. pots, $2.00 per 100.
- 1000 **Cannas**, red and yellow, strong, $3.00 per 100.
- 50 **Dracaena Indivisa**, 34 in., 6c. each.
- 3000 **Cuphea**, Cigar Plant, 2 in. pots, 75c. per 100.
- 2000 **Feverfew**, Double White, 2 in. pots, 50c. per 100.
- 10000 **Jerusalem Cherries**, big and strong, ready for 4 in. pots, from 2 in. pots at $2.00 per 100.

You will never get better or cheaper stock than this. **E. I. Rawlings, Quakertown, Pa.**

Mention The Florists' Exchange when writing.

Primula Obconica Grandiflora

2 1-2 in., $2.50 per 100. Ask for list (seedlings of hardy plants)

BAUDISCH & CO.,
537 Fulton Street UNION HILL, N. J.

Mention The Florists' Exchange when writing.

CYCLAMEN

SPLENDENS GIGANTEUM HYBRIDS

This strain has no equal or better. Perfect flowers of Giant type in five true colors well grown plants from 3 in. pots $7.00 per 100; $65.00 per 1000.

Asparagus. Plumosus Nanus.

From flats fine plants $1.50 per 100, $12.50 per 1000.

SATISFACTION GUARANTEED.

PAUL MADER, EAST STROUDSBURG, PA

Mention The Florists' Exchange when writing.

CYCLAMENS

Strong plants, $5.00 per 100, $45.00 per 1000.

ASPARAGUS

Sprengerii in 2¼ pots, $2.50 per 100, $20.00 per 1000, also in flats at 75c per 100; **Plumosus Nanus** in 2¼ pots, $3.00 per 100.

F. A. GIFFORD, Westbury Sta., L. I

Mention The Florists' Exchange when writing.

GARDENIA VEITCHII

500 strong, bushy plants from 3 inch pots, ready for a shift, at $12.00 per 100, or will make a special low price for the lot if taken at once for cash.

MADSEN & CHRISTENSEN, WOODRIDGE, N. J.

Mention The Florists' Exchange when writing.

DORSETT VIOLETS

Extra strong field grown plants. Price $4.00 per 100. Sample free.

PAUL THOMSON, West Hartford, Conn.

Mention The Florists' Exchange when writing.

VIOLETS

MARIE LOUISE Violets, clean and healthy in every particular, ready August 15th, 3 in. pots $5.00 per 100.

CASH WITH ORDER.

WM. J. CHINNICK,
TRENTON, N. J.

Mention The Florists' Exchange when writing.

FIELD GROWN VIOLETS

Strong, healthy, well-rooted plants of **Lady Campbell** (double), ready now at $2.50 per 100; $20.00 per 1000. **California** (single), ready by Aug. 15th, $3.00 per 100. Packed to carry safely, free of charge.

CHAS. BLACK, HIGHTSTOWN, N. J.

Mention The Florists' Exchange when writing.

Governor Herrick Violet

The finest single violet ever offered. Write me about it today.

Price: One dozen, $2.00; 100, $10.00; 1000 at $75.00 or 5000 or more at $60.00 per 1000. No. 1 Stock.

H. R. CARLTON, WILLOUGHBY, OHIO.

Mention The Florists' Exchange when writing.

VIOLETS, SMILAX

Lady Campbell and **California** out of 2½ in. healthy stock plants, $2.00 per 100; $17.50 per 1,000

Smilax, fine bushy plants 2½ in., $1.25 per 100; $10.00 per 1000

J. C. SCHMIDT CO., Bristol, Pa.

Mention The Florists' Exchange when writing.

CHRISTMAS PEPPERS

Fine stocky plants in bud and bloom, 3 and 3½ inch pots, $5.00 per 100. Cash with order.

D. H. RUTHRAUFF, Seneca Falls, N. Y

Mention The Florists' Exchange when writing

J. K. ALLEN

Wholesale Commission Dealer in Cut Flowers

106 West 28th St., NEW YORK

Open at 6 a. m. every day.
Telephone, 167 Madison Square.
Consignments Solicited.

Mention The Florists' Exchange when writing.

Wm. Stuart Allen Co.

Commission Merchants in CUT FLOWERS

ORCHIDS AT ALL SEASONS

53 WEST 28th STREET, NEW YORK

Telephone 356 Madison Square

Mention the Florists' Exchange when writing.

C. BONNET G. H. BLAKE

BONNET & BLAKE

Wholesale Florists

106 Livingston Street, BROOKLYN, N. Y.

Telephone: 4638 Main.

Consignments solicited. Out-of-town orders carefully attended to. Give us a trial.

Mention The Florists' Exchange when writing.

CUT FLOWER EXCHANGE

Sixth Ave. and 26th St.

Coogan Building, NEW YORK

Open every Morning at Six o'clock for the Sale of Cut Flowers.

Wall Space for advertising purposes to Rent.

V. S. DORVAL, Jr., Secretary.

Mention the Florists' Exchange when writing.

Joseph S. Fenrich

...Wholesale Florist...

—THE RELIABLE HOUSE—

110 West 28th Street

Telephone 324-325 Madison Square.

Mention The Florists' Exchange when writing.

FORD BROS.

Wholesale Florists

48 WEST 28th ST., NEW YORK

Telephone, 3870-3871 Madison Square

Mention The Florists' Exchange when writing.

GROWERS, ATTENTION!

Always Ready to Receive Fine Stock

WILLIAM H. GUNTHER

30 West 29th Street

'Phone, 551 Madison Square. NEW YORK

Violets, Roses, Carnations, Orchids

Established 1888

Mention the Florists' Exchange when writing.

ALEX. J. GUTTMAN

The Wholesale Florist of New York

43 WEST 28th STREET

Phones 1664-1665 Madison Square

Mention The Florists' Exchange when writing.

A. M. HENSHAW

..Wholesale Florist..

52 West 28th Street, NEW YORK

First class Roses and Carnations a specialty.

Consignments Solicited. Tel. 5583 Madison Sq.

Mention The Florists' Exchange when writing.

HICKS & CRAWBUCK, Inc.

Wholesale Florists

And Dealers in FLORISTS' SUPPLIES

76-78 Court Street

Phone, 3660-3661 Main BROOKLYN, N. Y.

Mention The Florists' Exchange when writing.

HEADQUARTERS FOR NOVELTIES

ORCHIDS A SPECIALTY

THE HIGHEST GRADE OF VALLEY ALWAYS ON HAND

CARDENIAS, DAISIES, ROSES, CARNATIONS.

JAMES McMANUS, Telephone 759 Mad. Sq. 42 W. 28th St., New York.

PHILIP F. KESSLER

Wholesale Florist

55-57 W. 26th St., NEW YORK.

Telephone, 2921-5243 Madison Square.

Mention the Florists' Exchange when writing.

JULIUS LANG

Wholesale Florist

53 WEST 30th STREET NEW YORK

Consignments Solicited. Telephone: 280 Madison Sq.

Mention the Florists' Exchange when writing

WILLIAM H. KUEBLER

Wholesale Commission Dealer in

CUT FLOWERS

28 Willoughby St.,

Telephone, 4591 Main. BROOKLYN, N. Y.

Mention the Florists' Exchange when writing.

FRANK MILLANG

Wholesale Commission Dealer in

CUT FLOWERS

55-57 West 26th Street, New York

Telephone Call: 299 Madison Square.

Mention the Florists' Exchange when writing

ALFRED H. LANGJAHR

55 WEST 28th STREET, NEW YORK

Telephone, 4626-4627 Madison Square Established 1891

SPECIAL VALLEY AND TOP GRADE ASPARAGUS

Consignments of First Class Stock Solicited.

Horace E. Froment

SUCCESSOR TO

W. GHORMLEY WHOLESALE COMMISSION FLORIST

Receiver and Shipper of all varieties of Cut Flowers

Telephones, 2200 and 2201 Madison Square. 157 West 28th St., NEW YORK

Wholesale Prices of Cut Flowers, New York, August 9, 1906

Prices quoted are by the hundred unless otherwise noted.

Roses	A. BEAUTY, fancy—special	10.00 to	20.00
	" extra	6.00 to	10.00
	" No. 1	4.00 to	5.00
	" No. 2	3.00 to	4.00
	" No. 3	1.00 to	1.50
	Bride, Maid, fancy—spe'l	3.00 to	4.00
	" extra	2.00 to	3.00
	" No. 1	1 00 to	2.00
	" No. 2	.50 to	1.00
	Golden Gate	1.00 to	5.00
	Liberty	...... to	......
	Mme. Abel Chatenay	1.00 to	6.00
ADIANTUM		.50 to	.75
CROWEANUM		.50 to	1.00
ASPARAGUS		25.00 to	50 00
"	Plumosus, bunches	8.00 to	15.00
"	Sprengeril, bunches	8.00 to	15.00
ASTERS		.15 to	.75
CATTLEYAS		50.00 to	60.00
DAISIES		.50 to	1.00
GLADIOLUS		.50 to	1.00
		...... to	......

Carnations	Inf'r grades, all colors		.50 to	1.00
	STANDARD VARIETIES	White	1 00 to	2.00
		Pink	1.00 to	2 00
		Red	1.00 to	2.00
		Yel. & Var.	1.00 to	2.00
	*FANCY— (*The highest grades of standard var.)	White	2.00 to	2 50
		Pink	2.00 to	2.50
		Red	2 00 to	2 50
		Yel. & Var.	...... to	......
	NOVELTIES		...... to	......
LILIES			5 00 to	6.00
LILY OF THE VALLEY			1.00 to	3 00
MIGNONETTE			...... to	......
			...... to	......
			...... to	......
			...... to	......
PANSIES, per dozen bunches			.50 to	.75
SMILAX			8.00 to	10.00
SWEET PEAS, per bunch			.01 to	.03

WALTER F. SHERIDAN

Wholesale Florist

Telephone, 902 Madison Square 39 WEST 28TH ST., NEW YORK

ALL VARIETIES OF CUT FLOWERS IN SEASON

TOP GRADE FOR SHIPPING

American Beauty, Bridesmaid, Bride, Liberty, Meteor, Lily of the Valley, Carnations

Telephone, 1998 Madison Square JOHN I. RAYNOR, 49 West 28th St., NEW YORK

Edw. C. Horan

55 West 28th St., NEW YORK

TELEPHONE, 1462-1463 MADISON SQUARE

CUT FLOWERS AT WHOLESALE

Mention The Florists' Exchange when writing.

JOHN YOUNG

Wholesale Florist

51 W. 28th St., NEW YORK

TELEPHONE: 4463-4464 MADISON SQUARE

Mention the Florists' Exchange when writing.

A. MOLTZ

Wholesale Florist

55-57 West 26th St., NEW YORK

1st Floor. Telephone, 2921-5243 Madison Sq.

Mention The Florists' Exchange when writing.

MOORE, HENTZ & NASH
WHOLESALE
GROWER AGENT
COMMISSION FLORISTS
55 West 26th St., New York

Telephone Call, 756 Madison Square

Mention The Florists' Exchange when writing.

GEORGE SALTFORD

Wholesale Florist

CONSIGNMENTS SOLICITED

46 West 29th Street, New York

TELEPHONE: 3393 MADISON SQUARE

Mention The Florists' Exchange when writing.

J. Seligman Joseph J. Levy

JOHN SELIGMAN & COMPANY

Wholesale Florists

56 West 26th Street,

Tel. 4878 Madison New York.

Opposite New York Cut Flower Company

Mention The Florists' Exchange when writing.

B. S. SLINN, JR.

Wholesale Florist

55 and 57 West 26th Street, NEW YORK

SPECIALTIES—Violets, Carnations and Roses

Shipping orders receive prompt attention. Consignment Solicited.

Telephone: 3864 Madison Square

Mention the Florists' Exchange when writing.

FRANK H. TRAENDLY CHARLES SCHENCK

TRAENDLY & SCHENCK

Wholesale Florists

44 WEST 28th STREET, NEW YORK

and CUT FLOWER EXCHANGE

Telephones: 798 and 799 MADISON SQUARE

CONSIGNMENTS SOLICITED

Mention the Florists' Exchange when writing.

A. L. YOUNG & CO.

WHOLESALE FLORISTS

54 West 28th St., NEW YORK

Telephone 3559 Madison Square.

Consignments of choice cut flowers solicited. Prompt payments. Give us a trial.

Mention The Florists' Exchange when writing.

THOMAS YOUNG

Wholesale Florist

43 West 28th Street, NEW YORK

Telephone, 4850 Madison Square

Consignments of Choice Flowers solicited

Mention The Florists' Exchange when writing.

Wholesale Prices of Cut Flowers—Per 100

Boston Aug. 8, 1906	Buffalo Aug. 7, 1906	Detroit Aug. 5, 1906	Cincinnati Aug. 4, 1906	Baltimore Aug. 6, 1906	NAMES AND VARIETIES	Milwaukee July 28, 1906	Phil'delphia July 24, 1906	Pittsburg Aug. 8, 1906	St. Louis Aug. 6, 1906
10.00 to 20.00	20.00 to 25.00	10.00 to 35.00	25.00 to 30.00	to	ROSES — A. BEAUTY, fancy—special	to 25.00	15.00 to 20.00	20.00 to 25.00	15.00 to 20.00
6.00 to 15.00	12.00 to 20.00	to	to 20.00	12.50 to 15.00	" extra	15.00 to 18.00	10.00 to 15.00	12.00 to 15.00	10.00 to 12.50
4.00 to 6.00	6.00 to 12.00	to	10.00 to 15.00	5.00 to 8.00	" No. 1	10.00 to 12.50	5.00 to 7.00	8.00 to 10.00	6.00 to 8.00
2.00 to 4.00	3.00 to 6.00	to	to	to	" Culls and ordinary	4.00 to 6.00	1.00 to 4.00	4.00 to 5.00	3.00 to 5.00
to	5.00 to 6.00	3.00 to 6.00	2.00 to 3.00	to	BRIDE, 'MAID, fancy-special	to 6.00	to	to	4.00 to 5.00
3.00 to 5.00	4.00 to 5.00	to	2.00 to 3.00	to 4.00	" extra	to 5.00	6.00 to 8.00	to 6.00	2.00 to 3.00
2.00 to 4.00	3.00 to 4.00	to	1.00 to 2.00	to 3.00	" No. 1	to 4.00	4.00 to 5.00	to 4.00	to
1.00 to 2.00	2.00 to 3.00	to	to 1.00	to 2.00	" No. 2	to 2.00	2.00 to 3.00	to 2.00	to
to	to	4.00 to 8.00	to	2.00 to 4.00	GOLDEN GATE	4.00 to 6.00	4.00 to 8.00	to	2.00 to 4.00
2.00 to 6.00	3.00 to 7.00	to	2.00 to 5.00	4.00 to 8.00	K. A. VICTORIA	4.00 to 8.00	4.00 to 6.00	2.00 to 12.00	2.00 to 6.00
4.00 to 8.00	3.00 to 7.00	to	to	to	LIBERTY	4.00 to 6.00	5.00 to 6.00	3.00 to 8.00	to
to	3.00 to 6.00	4.00 to 10.00	to	to	METEOR	to	to	to	to
to	3.00 to 5.00	4.00 to 10.00	to	2.00 to 4.00	PERLE	4.00 to 6.00	to	to	2.00 to 4.00
to	to	to 50.00	to	to	ORCHIDS—Cattleyas	to	to 50.00	to	to
to	.50 to 1.00	to	to	.50 to .75	CARNATIONS — Inferior grades, all colors	to 1.00	.75 to 1.00	.50 to .75	.50 to .75
to	1.00 to 1.25	to 1.00	to 1.00	1.00 to 1.50	Standard Varieties — White	to 1.00	.75 to 1.00	to 1.00	.50 to .75
to	1.00 to 1.25	to	to 1.00	1.00 to 1.50	Pink	to 1.00	.75 to 1.00	to 1.00	.50 to .75
to	1.00 to 1.25	to	to 1.00	1.00 to 1.50	Red	to 1.00	.75 to 1.00	to 1.00	.50 to .75
to	to	to 3.00	to	1.00 to 1.50	Yellow and var.	to 1.00	.75 to 1.00	to	.50 to .75
.50 to 1.50	1.50 to 2.00	to	to	to 3.00	Fancy Varieties — White	1.50 to 2.00	2.00 to 2.50	to 2.00	1.00 to 1.50
.50 to 1.50	1.50 to 2.00	to	to	to 3.00	Pink	1.50 to 2.00	2.00 to 2.50	to 2.00	1.00 to 1.50
.50 to 1.50	1.50 to 2.00	to	to	to 3.00	Red	1.50 to 2.00	2.00 to 2.50	to 2.00	1.00 to 1.50
.50 to 1.50	1.50 to 2.00	to 1.50	to	to 3.00	Yellow and var	1.50 to 2.00	2.00 to 2.50	to 2.00	1.00 to 1.50
.50 to 1.00	to	to	to	to	Novelties	to	to	to	to
to	.50 to 1.00	to 2.00	to	to 1.00	ADIANTUM	to 1.00	to 1.00	1.25 to 1.50	to
to 50.00	to	25.00 to 60.00	25.00 to 50.00	25.00 to 50.00	ASPARAGUS, Plum. and Ten	20.00 to 30.00	25.00 to 35.00	30.00 to 40.00	25.00 to 50.00
to	to	20.00 to 30.00	25.00 to 35.00	25.00 to 50.00	" Sprengeri, bunches	20.00 to 30.00	25.00 to 35.00	1.00 to 2.00	25.00 to 50.00
.50 to 1.00	.50 to 2.00	to	.50 to 2.00	to	ASTERS	.50 to 1.00	to	.50 to 2.00	.50 to 2.50
to	8.00 to 10.00	to 10.00	to 1.00	6.00 to 8.00	CALLAS	to	to	to	to
6.00 to 8.00	to	.75 to 1.50	to	to	DAISIES	to .40	3.00 to 4.00	to .50	to
4.00 to 6.00	1.00 to 3.00	8.00 to 10.00	1.00 to 4.00	2.00 to 4.00	GLADIOLUS	to	8.00 to 12.00	3.00 to 7.00	to 2.00
to	to	to	12.00 to 15.00	10.00 to 12.50	LILIES, Harrisii	to 12.50	to	to	to
2.00 to 4.00	12.00 to 15.00	to	to 12.50	10.00 to 12.50	" Longiflorum	to 12.50	2.00 to 4.00	12.50 to 15.00	to
to	3.00 to 4.00	3.00 to 4.00	to 4.00	1.00 to 2.00	LILY OF THE VALLEY	to	1.00 to 2.00	2.00 to 4.00	to
to	to	to	to	2.00 to 2.50	MIGNONETTE, ordinary	to	to	to	to
to	to	to	to	to	" fancy	to	to	to	to
to	to	4.00 to 8.00	to	to	PEONIES	to	15.00 to 20.00	to	to
to 12.50	to 15.00	12.50 to 15.00	to 15.00	12.50 to 20.00	SMILAX	to 15.00	to	10.00 to 12.50	to 12.50
to	to	to	to	to	VIOLETS, ordinary	to	to	to	to
to	to	to	to	to	" fancy	to	to	to	to
to	to	to	to	to	NARCISSUS	to	to	to	to
.20 to .25	.15 to .25	.50 to .75	to .35	.20 to .35	SWEET PEAS	.25 to .50	to .50	.10 to .50	.10 to .15
to	to	to	to	to		to	to	to	to
to	to	to	to	to		to	to	to	to

Boston.

News Notes.

At Horticultural Hall on Saturday there was an unusually good show for this season of the year. It was phlox day and the exhibits of these were much finer than any that have been seen in Boston for several years back. Worthy of special note were the fine displays made by T. C. Thurlow and W. N. Craig. Robert Cameron of the Harvard Botanical Gardens had an excellent display of annuals and also perennials. J. B. Lawrence, A. E. Johnson, Jos Thorpe, W. G. Winsor and Towle's Dahlia Gardens staged very fine exhibits of dahlias, showing many well developed flowers for so early in the season. A first-class certificate was awarded to the Blue Hill's Nurseries for Gypsophila paniculata flora plena which is certainly an addition among hardy flowers that will be welcomed by many. Lager & Hurrell, Summit, N. J. were awarded honorable mention for Vanda Miss Agnes Joachim.

At the meeting of the Board of Trustees of the Massachusetts Horticultural Society held on Saturday, T. D. Hatfield was elected on the committee on plants and flowers in place of James Wheeler, who resigned recently.

B. T. McGinty has resigned his position with N. F. McCarthy & Company and is now salesman for F. A. Lake and others in the Music Hall market.

Thos Pegler, who has been salesman for Oscar Dorr of Foxboro, has acquired the Brown Greenhouses at Wollaston and will make the growing of violets a specialty.

J. W. DUNCAN.

Philadelphia.

News Items.

W. J. Sherry of the Johnson Seed Company is off on his vacation, which he will spend along the New England coast, leaving New York on Saturday by Fall River line steamer.

Edward Reid is on his annual tour among his southern customers, having left New York on Friday by Clyde Line steamer for Jacksonville, Fla.

A. L. Pennock is up from Florida for two weeks to look after some business affairs.

The Johnson Seed Company have had the front of their store torn out this week and are putting in a new double show window.

DAVID RUST.

FINDLAY, O.—S. J. McMichaels is adding another greenhouse to his establishment on Larkins street.

Wholesale Prices of Cut Flowers, Chicago, Aug. 8, 1906.

Prices quoted are by the hundred unless otherwise noted.

ROSES American Beauty		
36-inch stems..........per doz.	.... to	4.00
30-inch stems.......... "	.... to	3.00
24-inch stems.......... "	.... to	2.50
20-inch stems.......... "	.... to	2.00
18-inch stems.......... "	.... to	1.50
12-inch stems.......... "	.... to	1.00
8-inch stems and shorts "	.50 to	.75
Bride Maid, fancy special......	5.00 to	6.00
" extra........	4.00 to	5.00
" No. 1........	2.00 to	3.00
" No. 2........	.50 to	1.00
Golden Gate........	2.00 to	6.00
Carnot........	2.00 to	6.00
Uncle John........	2.00 to	8.00
Liberty........	2.00 to	8.00
Richmond........	2.00 to	8.00
Kaiserine........	2.00 to	8.00
Killarney........	3.00 to	8.00
Perle........	2.00 to	6.00
Chatenay........	2.00 to	6.00
Orchids—Cattleyas........	.... to	50.00
Smilax........	8.00 to	12.00
Lily of the Valley........	2.00 to	4.00
Sweet Peas........	.25 to	.50

CARNATIONS			
Inferior grades all colors		.25 to	.50
Standard Varieties	White........	.75 to	1.00
	Pink........	.75 to	1.00
	Red........	.75 to	1.00
	Yellow & var....	.75 to	1.00
*Fancy (The highest grades of Sta'd var)	White........	1.50 to	2.00
	Pink........	1.50 to	2.00
	Red........	1.50 to	2.00
	Yellow & var....	1.50 to	2.00
Novelties........		.... to	....
Adiantum........		.50 to	1.00
Asparagus, Plum. & Ten........		.35 to	.50
" Sprengeri, bunches.		.35 to	.50
Gladiolus........		2.00 to	6.00
Lilies, Longiflorum........		8.00 to	12.00
Harrisii........		8.00 to	12.00
Auratum........		6.00 to	8.00
Nymphaea........		.... to	1.00
Mignonette, ordinary........		1.00 to	2.00
Tuberoses, Spikes........		4.00 to	8.00
....		.... to	....
....		.... to	....
Hardy Ferns per 1000........		1.00 to	1.50
Galax "		1.00 to	1.25
Asters........		.50 to	1.00

Chicago.

News Notes.

A week or two ago Joseph Gutzloe, an old time gardener of this city, made a complaint at the Chicago Avenue police station about the burning of rubbish near his home. His story was questioned, and after an exciting scene he was incarcerated and the following morning committed to jail. Fortunately one of his influencial customers became conversant with the facts and obtained his release, and the arresting officer is now under suspension. These facts have been pretty well ventilated by the daily and trade papers, but there is a fact in connection with Mr. Gutzloe's career which is not generally known and which forms an important epoch in the history of commercial horticulture in Chicago. A few d?ys ago I called on our old time friend Mugar Sanders who I am happy to report to his unlimited list of admirers is in the best of spirits and with the exception of the right pedal promoter, in the best of health, and recalling the matter in which Mr. Gutzloe was implicated Mr. Sanders referred to his notes, taken several years ago, from which I make the following excerpt. "Joseph Gutzloe, a German gardener, tree planter, etc., living yet on the North side, opened up a sort of wholesale flower store in a deep basement on the west side of Madison street, between La Salle street and Fifth avenue, it is my belief one year or so before any other effort was made in Chicago in the wholesale cut flower business, Otto Frese says it was after Mr. Vaughan started. It was probably in 1877." Other parties have informed me that Mr. Gutzloe was undoubtedly the first wholesale cut flower dealer in Chicago, being, in a small way the founder of a business which now runs into the plural millions annually.

Andrew Anderson of Batavia, this state, was looking up his old acquaintances in Chicago last week.

B. F. Vandervate of Galena, Ill., was in town last week procuring material to replace his recent loss caused by a severe hail storm.

William Lubliner left on Monday last for his annual outing of two weeks which will be spent at Grey's Lake in Southern Illinois.

E. N. Zetlitz of the Lima Floral Company of Lima, Ohio was in this city a few days ago on a trip combining business and pleasure.

S. S. Skidelsky of Philadelphia is making his annual round up through this section and left Chicago last Saturday for Milwaukee.

E. F. Winterson returned last week from a two weeks' sojourn at Mount Clemens, Mich., where by a close application to the famous baths he succeeded in reducing his avoirdupois to the extent of seventeen pounds and in entirely eradicating the rheumatic trouble with which he has been severely afflicted recently.

At the J. B. Deamud Company's headquarters extensive improvements are under way including new flooring and alterations in the bench and table arrangements.

H. E. Klunder is making an excellent display of nymphæas and other aquatics including the Egyptian lotus, all of which attract a great deal of attention at the State street store.

W. L. Rock of Kansas City returned through Chicago the first of the week from a vacation spent in the northern part of Michigan.

William Graff of Columbus, Ohio, was in town the first of the week.

C. S. Ford of Philadelphia reached town on Sunday last from Cincinnati on a hasty western trip which culminates at the convention at Dayton.

L. H. Winterson of the E. F. Winterson Company and secretary of our local florists' club has made plans to visit Dayton, and, accompanied by Mrs. Winterson, will extend his tour through the East taking in Buffalo, Albany, the Hudson, New York and Philadelphia.

Mr. and Mrs. Charles W. McKellar spent a few days this week in Michigan.

Otto Goerish of the A. L. Randall staff left on Monday for a vacation trip in Michigan.

C. W. Erne of E. H. Hunt's returned the first of the week from a pleasant vacation spent in Michigan.

O. J. Friedman is spending his vacation at Charlevoix, Mich.

Among our recent visitors we had the pleasure of meeting H. H. Frey of Lincoln, Neb., who accompanied by his son and partner spent a few days in Chicago looking up material for an extensive addition to their plant and also making calls on the growers and wholesalers in and about Chicago.

G. L. Grant is in town renewing old associations and proving by physical evidence that the glorious climate of the Pacific Coast is all that the press agents of the railroads claim. As usual he will spend a few days in the Garden city, and after a few trips to inspect the success of his friends in neighboring localities will proceed to Dayton to participate in the convention proceedings.

Erick Johnson of the Randall Company returned the first of the week from Manitowac, Wis.

Fred W. Timme has left on a European trip embracing Scotland, France, Germany and Switzerland, if possible. He will be gone eight or ten weeks. WILLIAM K. WOOD.

St. Louis.

News Items.

John Gibson, in business at Olney, Ill., called on the various growers here the past week.

Vincent Gorley, of Grim & Gorley, had his automobile smashed last week while out riding with a young lady. The latter was badly hurt, the auto was a mass of kindling wood, but Vincent came out without a scratch.

Gearge Augermuller and Charles Schoule were on a fishing trip recently, but all they caught were bad colds, though they had a number of fish stories to tell us.

Gustave H. Kirk, an old employee of Stumpp & Walter Company, New York, called on the trade the past week. Mr. Kirk is now in the show business, but says he will be back in the trade in New York this Fall.

D. I. Bushnell, one of our local seedsmen, has just returned from an extensive trip having visited the principal cities of Europe.

The Shaw banquet takes place next Tuesday night, at 7 o'clock, at the Jefferson Hotel.

At Kalish & Sons, Delmar and Taylor streets, all hands are busy making improvements; they will build in the rear of their place two small show houses each 35 by 20 feet.

ST. PATRICK.

Buffalo.

he News.

Business has been fairly good. A number of funerals, also one large wedding used up a quantity of stock, which is very plentiful at present.

W. J. Palmer, vice-president of the American Carnation Society, will leave for the northern part of Canada for a month's outing, after a very busy season.

Mr. and Mrs. Myers (the former with L. H. Neubeck) will leave on a well-earned vacation, visiting relatives in Utica, N. Y. Ed. Armbrust, of the same firm, has left for an extended stay at East Norfolk, Mass.

Mr. and Mrs. Charles Sandiford are spending their vacation visiting their old home and friends at Boston, Mass., and vicinity. Mr. Sanford is exhibiting to his legion of admirers a house of fine cantaloupe, showing his ability as a grower.

W. J. Palmer & Son had the Setchworth-Wilson wedding, a large affair for this time of year, managed by E. A. Slattery.

Arthur Beyer has launched his new motor boat, one of the finest of its kind in this city.

R. E. Boettger is sending in some of his fine quality asters, which find a ready sale. W. H. G.

Cincinnati, O.

The Fall Festival.

Commencing September 28 the Fall Festival will be in full blast; and it will be of interest to all who can, to run down to Cincinnati immediately after the S. A. F. O. H. meeting. The festival is a World's Fair on a smaller scale. The first floral display will not be given until September 6; this will be made exclusively by W. K. Partridge, he receiving $700 for making it. The first intention of the Fall Festival Board was to make this show a competitive one; but our florists here said the trouble was more than the premium was worth; therefore, Mr. Partridge came to the front and said he would make it alone. The next exhibition will take place September 20 and competition will be open to all. The exhibits will be table decorations, baskets and bridal bouquets, for which the directors offer $500. We should like to see some outside talent compete, just to make it interesting. The Fall Festival will be on for four weeks, so all have a chance to see it. Don't fail to come to Cincinnati after the convention.

News Notes.

C. S. Ford of Philadelphia and New York was a caller last Friday, Ben Eschner is slated to appear in the near future, and Martin Reukauf will be in either before or immediately after.

The Hamilton County Fair is slated for August 13 to 18 inclusive, and is always quite an event. Quite a number of the craft make entries for the various prizes, J. T. Conger, George & Allan, Henry Schwarz, E. Kyrk & Company and others generally make it interesting for one another.

This is the season of the year for vacations. Miss Laura Murphy, daughter of William Murphy, has just returned from Birmingham, Ala. Fred Gear and wife are now doing Yellowstone Park. William Murphy and wife leave on the 15th for Erie, Pa., thence by boat to Chicago, whence Mr. Murphy will go to Los Angeles, Cal. C. E. Critchell and wife have just returned from a trip East. C. J. Ohmer is now in the East and will return about the 13th. Nicholas Weber and wife left on Monday, August 6 for Chicago and Milwaukee. L. H. Kyrk and wife will leave shortly for a visit in Seneca County near Tiffin. Mrs. Garges and Miss Laura Steigler are at Atlantic City and will visit New York before returning home.

Quite a little party of ladies and gentlemen of the craft were entertained by Mr. and Mrs. Gus. Adrian, at their home in Clifton last Saturday afternoon and evening.

Carnation men around here are all very busy planting their houses. One grower tells me that his plants taken from the sand, and planted immediately in the field without potting, are just as good as any plants on his place. The quality of the carnation stock in this section is better than it has been in years.

E. G. GILLETT.

Springfield, O.

Probably the most violent hail storm on record visited this locality on July 27, its duration having been about 45 minutes, and the sizes of the hailstones ranging from those of hickory nuts to hulled walnuts according to the various eyewitnesses. West of town, the ravines were said to have been piled full of hailstones. Nearly every florist here suffered slight loss of glass in hotbed sash, but all houses withstood the bombardment with the exception of several of the oldest houses of the George H. Mellen Company in which single strength glass was broken to the extent of approximately $100. We learn of only one concern here carrying hail insurance, but this recent experience will doubtless cause a more general demand for this sort of protection.

At Urbana, the Reeser Floral Company sustained a loss variously reported at from 300 to 700 lights of glass.

On Thursday, August 2, the first picnic of the Springfield Florists' Club was held at Eichols park, a romantic spot on the Springfield, Troy and Piqua Electric Railway. Athletic sports began with quoits, Ward Welch and Charlie Schmidt proving a pair invincible against all opposing pitchers. Refreshments were abundant for a big noontime lunch and were partaken of at the pleasure of each member or guest throughout the day. Ball was the leading attraction, a double header between the "South Enders" and the "'Tother Enders" resulting in favor of the latter to the tune of 10 to 9 and 21 to 4. Jack Good, pitcher for the vanquished, claimed it would have been otherwise had he been supported by a catcher other than Ward Welch who succumbed to "that tired feeling" and stretched at full length under a shade tree about the middle of the second game. Gus. Schneider and Charlie Schmidt worked together well as battery for the victors, and umpire Jimmy Maxwell announced amusing decisions in his rare old Scottish brogue. The closing event was a boat race which culminated in the capsizing of one boat and a thorough ducking for two muscular rowers.

GE DALE.

Indianapolis.

News Items.

It is generally understood that several good positions are to be offered for growers by the local park commissioners, and hustling is being done to secure them.

No definite arrangements have been made for the Dayton trip; the Chicago special reaches Indianapolis Monday afternoon, and without doubt many will board that train. Owing to the close proximity of the convention city, and the convenience of the traction line, many will travel from here to Dayton as often as business will permit while the convention is on.

Homer Wiegand is taking part of his outing at Niagara Falls and in Canada.

Edward Bertermann has been visiting Chicago retailers.

Sidney Smith is urging all who can to attend the Dayton convention so that something may be done in a concerted way.

Henry Duderstadt is spending his vacation in the country.

Bertermann Brothers Company have their new range of houses at Cumberland about completed.

P. D. Craig of Anderson visited the trade here this week. He informed the writer that Mrs. Craig would make the next trip with him.

Thos. Knipe of Kokomo visited several growers this week obtaining stock for his new place. His many friends wish him great success.

Rodenbeck Brothers are erecting another greenhouse.

E. A. Nelson has returned from a fishing trip.

Bertermann Brothers Company are having their store re-finished.

Clarence Thomas is on the sick list.

I. B.

Bucatunna, Miss.

At the meeting of the stockholders of the Southern Floral Nursery Company on July 14 for the organization of the company, the following board of directors were chosen: J. B. Bridge, Alex. B. Brown, and L. H. Read. The directors then elected J. B. Bridge, president; L. H. Read, vice-president and general manager, and Alex. B. Brown, secretary and treasurer. The prospects of the new company are very bright, the concern having assumed the entire business of the old firm of the same name with headquarters at Fruitdale, Ala. The wonderful growth of the business during the past two years made necessary the present changes, and it is hoped that with the addition of the new grounds that have been secured here and the addition of new capital, the company will be enabled to build up one of the largest nursery establishments in the South. The new firm has orders already booked for fifteen per cent. more cannas than the sale for the past year.

The company will not confine its efforts entirely to the nursery business, for in taking out its charter the right to operate a printing and publishing department, as well as a real estate and homeseekers' department was included.

The business of the company will be conducted on the co-operative plan all stockholders being allowed a special discount on anything they may desire to purchase from the concern.

Los Angeles, Cal.

At a special meeting of the Southern California Horticultural Society held recently, President Walter Raymond announced the week ending November 3 as the time for holding the next flower show of the society; the place, Blanchard and Symphony Halls. The idea of having a botanical display of such things as grow in Southern California in the open was discussed and decided upon the specimens to be numbered, a catalogue issued containing their names, both common and scientific, with their nativity, the numbers in the catalogue to correspond with those on the exhibits. This method will enable the student of plant life to learn the names and, to some extent, study the character of the flora found here, collected as it is from all over the world. In some cases photographs will be used, since no part of the subject can be displayed in the show. For instance there is a specimen of Jubea spectabilis over three feet in diameter; one of Cocos plumosa twenty-five feet high; a large cinnamon tree, an Araucaria excelsa, tweny-five feet high, with ten feet spread at the base, thoroughly furnished from the ground up which has escaped the ravages of the tree butcher. These with many other interesting specimens growing here may be studied from the pictures. Their location will be given and those who care to do so may study them where they grow.

The writer has been placed in charge of this part of the program and solicits the co-operation of every reader of The Florists' Exchange in Southern California. Let me know by October 15 what you have that will be in bloom at that time, that I may be able to have the catalogue issued and ready for distribution when the show opens.

Lagerstrœmia indica in several colors is now in bloom. It is one of our most beautiful flowering small trees. No one who has not seen its great panicles of bloom can have any idea of its grace and beauty. The petals are beautifully crinkled with petioles a quarter of an inch long, and it is no misnomer to call it crape myrtle. If given room to develop, and the knife and shears kept from it, it forms a fine pyramidal shaped head. Good specimens ten years old may be seen here, 20 feet high and 10 feet in diameter. It sheds its bark annually which always gives the tree a neat, clean appearance. Being deciduous, there is a prejudice against it on this coast, where evergreen trees are in favor. This error is gradually dawning upon the minds of planters, and the time will come when both deciduous and evergreen trees and shrubs will share honors in beautifying our landscape.

The eucalyptus family of trees provide us with bloom the entire year, different varieties flowering at different seasons. At present E. ficifolia is in bloom. The flowers are a brilliant scarlet, which makes it one of our most attractive small trees at this season of the year. Eucalpyti blooms have no petals nor sepals. The delicate stamens, and pistils are enclosed in capsules the upper half of which drops off and the flower blooms out full at once. These capsules differ greatly in size and appearance in the different varieties. This valuable species of drought-resisting trees will, in the years that are to come, change the appearance of our hills and plains from one of desolation, during the dry Summer months, to beautiful evergreen forests, and that too, to the financial advantage of the planters.

P. D. BARNHART.

EVANSVILLE, IND., will have a flower show and carnival in October. It is not certain at the present time whether the show will be given under the auspices of the Retail Merchants' Association or the Indiana Florists' Association.

EXETER, MASS.—Harry F. Hall, for several years assistant horticulturist at the New Hampshire college, has resigned to accept a position at Woburn, Mass. Last June Mr. Hall received the degree of B. S.

Detroit.

Club News.

The Detroit Florists' Club met Wednesday, August 1, for the election of officers for the insuing year. Wm. Dilger was re-elected president; E. A. Scribner, vice-president; J. F. Sullivan, secretary; Walter Taepke, treasurer; and W. B. Brown, librarian. After the election attention was directed to the forthcoming S. A. F. convention and aroused much enthusiasm among the members who will do all in their power to maintain Detroit's reputation as one of the leading cities in numbers attending national conventions. Philip Breitmeyer spoke in behalf of the S. A. F. He told of the points of interest in and the preparations made for visitors to Dayton. He also stated that Detroit would again be there with a bowling team. J. F. Sullivan made a stirring speech asking for a large attendance at Dayton. He also stated that the Toledo Club wished to join the Detroit brethren en route to the convention city and he was authorized to extend to them a cordial invitation. R. H. Ellis of Leamington, Ontario, was also invited to join the Detroit delegation. It was decided that we would travel over the C. H. & D leaving by the 12:35 train from Detroit on Monday, August 20. Geo. A. Rackham moved that the secretary be authorized to communicate with railroads. Hotels were also discussed, and it was practically decided that all of us would stop at the same house the necessary accommodations having previously been secured.

J. F. Sullivan, who appears to be the heaviest loser about Detroit this year, brought forward a suggestion that the club formally petition the S. A. F. asking that society to appropriate a sum of money for the purpose of finding a cure for the aster disease so prevalent all over the country. Unless immediate steps are taken to eliminate this disease, it seems altogether feasible that in a short time the aster will no longer be looked upon as a commercial flower. Mr. Sullivan said that he did not want anybody's cure, but somebody's cure that was authentic. He would have the matter placed in the hands of some reliable university, such as Cornell, so as to obtain a correct diagnosis of the disease and, if such a thing be possible, a positive cure. Ed. Beard moved that the secretary draw up a formal petition to the S. A. F. in the name of the Detroit Florists' Club embracing the gist of Mr. Sullivan's talk.

A vote of thanks was tendered Mr. and Mrs. Wm. Brown for energetic work done to make a success of the club outing.

Charles Olschefski was unanimously elected a club member.

After October 1 the club will occupy the Michigan Cut Flower Exchange parlors for its meetings.

HARRY.

San Francisco.

News reached here this week from Washington, D. C., that the Carnegie Institute delegation of scientists, who recently spent a few days here visiting Luther Burbank, had returned home and formed an organization for the purpose of carrying on a scientific analysis of the striking results in plant breeding secured by Burbank. Various members of the scientific staff of the institution will take up their residence with Mr. Burbank at his California home and make a close study of his more noted plants. The work is undertaken for the purpose of gaining information on heredity and evolution and making a written record of the facts learned. Burbank has never reduced the results of his work to writing and it will be the plan of the committee to make of his discoveries a permanent contribution to the library of science.

ALVIN.

WORCESTER, MASS.—O. B. Hadwen, president of the Worcester County Horticultural Society, celebrated his 82nd. birthday on August 2.

Orange, N. J.

Society Meeting.

The cultivation of the orchid as viewed by a private gardener, with practical examples of his own work, consumed the brief time of the New Jersey Floricultural Society at its regular monthly meeting on the third instant. The paper was prepared and read by Arthur W. Bodwell and was followed by a lively discussion participated in by John E. Lager, Jos. A. Manda, Henry Hurrell, George von Qualen and others. The orchid flowers were shown from the conservatories of William Barr and Henry Graves. Lager & Hurrell, Summit, N. J., had an interesting exhibit, including Lælio-Cattleya "Lady Bernice," flowered and exhibited for the first time. Jos. A. Manda also contributed some fine flowers.

The society decided to hold a special Fall exhibition in a public hall to which admission will be charged.

J. B. D.

Grand Rapids.

Trade Notes

A heavy rain has just arrived in the nick of time to save our crops especially carnations, from drying up. Business is quiet. On account of throwing out old plants and replanting, stock is scarce. Crabb & Hunter have five carnation houses planted. Cross, Smith, and the Grand Rapids Floral Company have also started planting. Cross has added one large rose house to his establishment so as to be able to supply his retail trade; he intends opening in the fall a store at the stand recently occupied by Miss Hartnet, who has removed to the Prythian Temple.

Mr. Diedricks, lately with Van Bochove Brothers, is now foreman for Charles Chadwick.

Jacob Dutmers of the Manistee Floral Company has acquired an interest in the Reed's Lake Greenhouses and will grow cut flowers for the wholesale market. John Steenman will take his former position with the Manistee Floral Company.

American Beauty roses, very scarce, sell for $1.50 to $2.50 per dozen; other roses $1; carnations 30c.; L. auratum and L. Harrisii, $2 to $2.25.

A good sized delegation will go from here to the Dayton convention, via Cincinnati.

G. F. CRABB.

S. A. F. O. H. CONVENTION REPORT NEXT WEEK.

THE FLORISTS' EXCHANGE

We are a straight shoot and aim to grow into a vigorous plant

A WEEKLY MEDIUM OF INTERCHANGE FOR FLORISTS, NURSERYMEN, SEEDSMEN AND THE TRADE IN GENERAL

Vol XXII. No. 7 NEW YORK AND CHICAGO, AUGUST 18, 1906 One Dollar Per Year

HITE ROMAN HYACINTHS

11 to 12 cmt. $2.25 per 100; $18.00 per 1000.
12 to 15 cmt. $2.50 per 100; $22.00 per 1000.
Paper Whites, 13 up $1.75 per 100; $9.00 per 1000.
Freesias, Ex. selected, 85c. 100; $7.50 per 1000.
Harrisii, 5 to 7 $3.75 per 100; $35.00 per 1000.
Canes, 6 to 9 feet, $6.00 per 1000.

Wm. Elliott & Sons, 201 Fulton Street, New York

Mention The Florists' Exchange when writing.

PACIFIC SEED GROWERS' CO.
109 MARKET STREET
SAN FRANCISCO, CAL.
Specialties:
Onion, Carrot, Lettuce, Sweet Peas

Mention The Florists' Exchange when writing.

Thorburn's Bulbs

LILIUM HARRISII

LILIUM LONGIFLORUM

and all other bulbs for florists.
Send us your requirements for special prices.

CYCAS REVOLUTA STEMS

from Japan. Sizes and prices on application.
Asparagus plumosus nanus, $3.50 per 1000 seeds.

J. M. THORBURN & CO.,

33 Barclay St., New York.

Mention The Florists' Exchange when writing.

PANSY SEED

Brown's Extra Select Superb Giant Prize PANSIES, awarded Silver Medal, St. Louis Exposition 1904. My own grown new 1906 crop ready. Price mixed seed 3000 seeds, $1.00; ¼ oz., $1.50; ½ oz., $2.50., 1 oz., $5.00; ¼ lb., $14.00; ⅓ lb., $25.00; 1 lb., $50.00. Cash with order.

PETER BROWN
Lancaster, Pa.

Mention The Florists' Exchange when writing.

Giant Pansy, Daisy, Forget-me-not, Hardy Carnation and single and double Wallflower. I do not praise my seed. I let my customers do that. Send for prices.

LE FOUDROYANT

Sure death to Red Spider, Thrips, Mealy Bug, Aphis, etc. Does not injure the foliage. Has been used in France with great success for the last five years, and in the Department of Agriculture, Washington, D. C. See electro in Florists' Exchange, issue Aug. 11, page 165.

Pansy, Giant Mme. Perret, true, gold medal at the Pan American; oz., $6.00. Cecile Davey, pure white, oz., $3.00. Marguerite Davey, oz., $4.00. Giant genuine Trimardeau, fine mixed, oz., $2.50. Lord Beaconsfields improved, oz., $1.50. Parisian improved, Graveraux, trade pkt., $1.00. The Woodhaven Mixture, oz., $10.00. These are genuine articles and 1906 crops, etc.

Beaulieu, Pansy Specialist

WOODHAVEN, N. Y.

Mention The Florists' Exchange when writing.

New Crop of my

Christmas Flowering SWEET PEA SEED

Christmas Pink and Florence Denzer, pure white, will be ready August 1st.

Those two well known varieties are raised by over 2000 florists all over the world. Here is one out of many letters received:

Dear Sir: My sweet peas, which I raised from your seed, received the highest award at the Carnation Exhibit in Boston, being over 18 inches long. JOHN T. GALE, Tewkesbury, Mass.

Price 1-4 lb. 75c.; per lb. $2.00
MAILED FREE

New Christmas Flowering Hybrids, 20 to 30 colors, mostly blue, salmon, purple, lavender, in mixtures; also Mrs. Edie Wild, carmine, separate color, 1 Trade pkt., $1.00, 5 Trade pkts, $4.00; not more than 5 pkts. taken in order to each customer just now. These new hybrids are just as free bloomers as Cristmas Pink and Florence Denzer, some much larger, and received first-class Certificate of Merit by the Mass. Horticultural Society, Boston, March 24. Seed ready in Sept.

All seed originated with me is sold in my original sealed pkts., with cultural directions, to the growers, but none for seedsmen for propagating.

Orders filled strictly in rotation.

ANT. C. ZVOLANEK
BOUND BROOK, N. J.

Mention The Florists' Exchange when writing.

The Choicest strains of Florists' Stocks

Including

Cineraria Calceolaria, Cyclamen, Pansy, Petunia, etc.,

CAN BE HAD FROM

JAMES VICK'S SONS
ROCHESTER, N. Y.

Mention The Florists' Exchange when writing.

PANSY SEED

Of my own growing, crop of 1906, "**My Giant Market,**" the finest and largest variety of fancy colors to be had. In trade pkt. of 6000 seeds, $1.00. Plants ready September 1st. Cash with order.

F. A BLINN, CROMWELL, CONN.

Mention The Florists' Exchange when writing.

PANSY SEED

Famous Strains of Mammoth Mixed Pansies

S. & W. Co.'s NON PLUS ULTRA

Our Non Plus Ultra Pansy is a mixture containing the largest, handsomest, most perfect varieties ever sent out. The beautiful coloring and variety of marking give a bed of these pansies a most brilliant appearance; the seed having been saved from the greatest assortment of types, including only the best of Giant Cassier's, Bugnot's, Trimardeau, and Giant English, French and German strains. Finest mixed, per trade pkt., 25c.; ¼ oz., $1.50; per oz., $5.00.

Very Large Flowering Varieties

These are remarkably large Pansies, which, for size of flower and robust growth, eclipse all other strains. Their range of color has heretofore been limited, but this season we are able to offer several grand new varieties.

Pansy—Non Plus Ultra

Cassier's Large-Flowering

In form, color and size this pansy stands alone; the plants are very robust and the flowers are held well above the foliage, and should be grown amongst all other pansies, as they add to the effect on account of their robust habits.

Per pkt., 15c.; per oz. $2.50

S. & W. Co.'s Giant Purple	S. & W. Co's. White, dark eye
" " Pres. Carnot	" " Snow White
" " Rosy Lilac	" " Fire King
" " Lord Beaconsfield	" " Light Blue, white center
" " Kaiser Wilhelm	" " Aurical Aeflora
" " Yellow, black eye	" " King of the Blacks
" " Pure Yellow	" " Victoria Red

Per 500 seeds, 25c.; ¼ oz., 75c.; 1 oz., $2.50; ¼ lb., $8.00

CINERARIA, S. & W. Co.'s GIANT

Prize Strain, per pkt. 50c.; per 1000 seed $1.00.

PRIMULA--Sinensis.

Alba Magnifica	Rose Queen	Ruby Queen	Magenta Queen
Giant Blue	Scarlet Salmon	Giant Crimson	Mixed

Per pkt. 50c.; per 1000 seeds $1.50.

FERNS IN FLATS

The cheapest and most convenient way to buy Ferns. These flats contain about 110 small clumps, when divided will make 2 to 3 plants each, making about 250 plants to the flat.

The following varieties we still have for sale.

Adiantum Cuneatum, Aspidium Tsussemense, Crytomium Falcatum, Lomaria Gibba, Pteris Adiantoides, Pteris Magnifica, Pteris Wimsettii, Pteris Cretica Albolineata.

— Mixed —
$2.00 per flat.

Stumpp & Walter Co.
50 Barclay Street, New York.

Mention The Florists' Exchange when writing.

BURPEE'S SEEDS

PHILADELPHIA

Blue List of Wholesale Prices mailed only to those who plant for profit.

Giant Cinerarias

Mixture of perfect colors

Dwarf Hybrids } Each separate Tr. Pkt. $0.50
Semi-Dwarf Hybrids } 6 Tr. Pkts. $2.50

O. V. ZANGEN, Seedsman, HOBOKEN, N.J.

Seed Trade Report.

AMERICAN SEED TRADE ASSOCIATION

Henry W. Wood, Richmond, Va., president; C. S. Burge, Toledo, O., first vice-president; G. B. McVay, Birmingham, Ala., second vice-president; C. E. Kendel, Cleveland, O., secretary and treasurer; J. H. Ford, Ravenna, O., assistant secretary.

MONTREAL, QUEB.—It is rumored that Wm. Rennie, seedsman, Toronto, Ont., will open a branch store in this city.

LAWRENCE, KANS.—The old firm of F. Barteldes & Company has incorporated under the name of The Barteldes Seed Company, with a fully paid up capital of $300,000. F. W. Barteldes is president, Max Wilhelmi, vice-president, and J. Uhrlaub, secretary and treasurer. The managers of the house in Denver will remain as before; C. R. Root, H. Warnecke and J. Wiesel. The manager of the Oklahoma City house will as formerly be C. F. Eltzholtz.

MILLINGTON, MICH.—The Sioux City Seed and Nursery Company will, shortly, commence raising their elevator one story, making a three story building of it. This will fill a long felt want as the company has for several seasons past been very much crowded for room.

T. E. Johns who has just returned from a tour of inspection of the crops of this concern says the outlook for the largest crop of beans in the history of the company is the finest in years. The recent rains saved the late planted crop.

CHICAGO.—A hasty glance at the stores is quite sufficient to satisfy the most credulous that this city has had its share of the seed trade during the season just closed, and that each one in the trade is making preparations for the Fall business, which will soon open. As was intimated in this column a few weeks ago, the firm of Hollenback is soon to take in a new partner in the person of Miss Bertha Kurz. The announcement is "At Home after October 15." Charlie is happy, as well he may be, for a more charming, able and willing "assistant" could not be found in the long list of Chicago possibilities.

AGAINST FREE SEEDS.—Henry W. Wood of Richmond, Va., president of the American Seed Trade Association, has issued an address to the public in which he declares the seed dealers will attack at the next session of Congress an appropriation for free seed distribution. Mr. Wood calls attention to the fact that the total packet seed trade last year was only 120,000,000 packets, of which the Government distributed 40,000,000. This, he says, is interference with a legitimate industry. The State grangers are being enlisted in the fight against free seeds and many of them have adopted resolutions asking Congress to forego the custom.

BURNING FREE SEEDS.—No better example of the waste occasioned by the free distribution of seeds has been afforded, we think, than the recent burning of hundreds of packets of Government seeds at Woodside, Long Island. The story of the burning and samples of the scorched packets, were brought to this office by H. Beaulieu, seedsman, Woodhaven, N. Y. The packets bear the franks of "Chas. A. Bowne, M. C.," and "J. E. Rider, M. C."

We respectfully direct the attention of the officials of the Department of Agriculture to this wanton destruction of Government seed; also submit the matter to our legislators for their consideration, as showing the use to which the parties located in the rural district named have put the Congressional seeds. This burning of free seed seems to us a decided practical rebuke to those Congressmen and Senators who clamor for this pernicious waste of the people's money.

SEED CROPS ON LONG ISLAND.—The season is past, the harvest is over but the anxiety of the farmers and the fears of the seedsmen, for whom the crops were grown, are simply intense. The outlook for a crop when the plants were set in April was by no means a hopeful one. From the first, in nearly every field a marked improvement was plainly visible; this continued until the crops were cut, and, in nearly every instance, the seed was safely secured, although the excessive rainy weather caused the seed to be so wet that it is now about as damp as when threshed, and, at the present writing there is no dry weather in sight. How long these conditions will continne, no one can say, no one knows. The farmers are doing their best to save the crops, and we think there will be but little loss from heating, which is the danger to be feared.

The yield of cabbage seed will be an average one, but the acreage is small when compared with that of previous years, a fact due to the high price of potatoes, which has caused many farmers to abandon seed growing for the more profitable one, the potato industry. If there is a shortage of any varieties it will be of the Wakefield and the early Flat Dutch sorts. There is an increasing demand for the Wakefield at the South, where the crop has been very profitable the past year.

Kale of the various kinds has been and is now a study. The regular Siberian type ripened its seed early, and has been delivered in splendid condition. The "slow-seeding" has proved true to name being more than two weeks behind at the harvest, and the seed will not be in condition to keep in bags until we have had at least two weeks of clear drying weather, of which we have not had a single day.

Scotch kale has shown some strange freaks this season. That which was grown on high, dry soils ripened at the usual time, but that on heavy soils kept on growing for a much longer period than usual, and the crop will be a fairly good one, but will not be fit for shipment for at least too weeks yet.

Spinach, so far as we can learn, has been a light crop and secured under difficulties. This crop is but little grown on Long Island, as foreign grown seed can be had at a much lower price; but those who want the best come here without regard to price.

Rutabaga has given a satisfactory yield and finds a ready market when the best is appreciated. The Purple Top Globe turnip is considerably grown in some sections. The growers get more for the growing than is paid for either kale or cabbage, and the local dealers have no trouble in getting one dollar per pound.

Brussels sprouts have done unusually well this season, although there is never much grown for seed purposes because of the uncertainty of a crop, and the demand being rather limited, there is a great satisfaction in knowing that there will be sufficient for at least two years, although there is a constantly increasing demand for the Long Island strain, because of its superior quality.

Bristol County (R. I.) seed growers state that the seed crop will be extremely light owing to the incessant rainfall throughout the season. Potatoes are rotting badly, and in many fields blight is seen. Onion sets are good, but seed onions are seriously damaged. Corn is growing luxuriantly, but blasting badly; in some fields scarcely a stalk shows signs of producing seed. It is probable that no tomato seed will be harvested.

G. S. W.

RAYMOND, MISS.—Galthis, Mc-urin & Company are building a new seed house.

Herlofson & Company, Christiana, Norway, want illustrated catalogues, price lists, etc., of different modern types of fruit tree and garden sprayers, watering cans, garden implements, lawn mowers, greenhouse heating apparatus, etc.

European Notes.

The heat throughout Europe during the past week has been of quite an exceptional character. The region lying between Berlin and Vienna has been literally baked, while in Paris and London the average maximum has been exceeded by many degrees. At the moment of writing a southwest storm of great severity is raging and the hail which accompanics it will make our spinach growers look blue, and, at the same time, further delay shipments. The greatest shrinkage will probably be in Germany where hail storms have been very frequent and destructive of late.

Alarming reports of damage to the onion crops by hail in Italy are just to hand, one firm reporting that the whole of its crops of the colored varieties have been destroyed. This will only affect dealers on your side indirectly, but European firms will be hard pressed, as owing to the poor crops of these varieties last year stocks are entirely cleaned out, and as there has been a revival in the demand during the past two years the difficulty is increased. No reports of any damage to the extra early silver-skinned varieties have reached us, so it may be presumed tha they are safe.

In flower seeds early asters are making a fine display, and the later kinds are rapidly making up for lost time. Nasturtiums were never before more promising; we even expect to harvest a fair crop of that dainty weakling Queen of Tom Thumb.

Sweet peas are literally borne down with seed pods. German stocks and wallflowers are in a poor way, but the single wallflowers in England are exceptionally good. Pansies, owing to lack of moisture, are in a bad way, and now that a prudent purchase has removed the surplus which has embarrassed the trade during the past season, there is hope that the crop, although small, will be profitable.

EUROPEAN SEEDS.

CATALOGUES RECEIVED.

F. & F. Nurseries, Springfield, N. J.—Catalogue of Trees, Shrubs, Evergreens, Vines, Roses, Plants and Bulbs. This firm has now 250 acres under cultivation.

NURSERY DEPARTMENT.

Conducted by Joseph Meehan.

AMERICAN ASSOCIATION OF NURSERYMEN, Orlando Harrison, Berlin, Md., president; J. W. Hill, Des Moines, Ia., vice-president; George C. Seager, Rochester, N. Y., secretary; C. L. Yates, Rochester, N. Y., treasurer.

HUNTSVILLE, ALABAMA.—One of the largest single orders ever received by a nursery company says the Memphis (Tenn.) Commercial, has been booked by the Chase Nursery Company, of this city. The order comes from Western Colorado, and is for 75,000 Elberta peach trees. The order will be filled jointly by the Chase and Alabama Nursery Companies.

SNOW HILL, MD.—The firm of W. M. Peters' Sons was mutually dissolved on June 27, Reese C. Peters buying the plant at Ironshire, Md., which comprises about the entire plant of the above firm. Reese C. Peters has associated with him his two sons, Alfred W. Peters and Norman M. Peters, and will carry on the nursery business under the firm name of R. C. Peters' Sons, succeeding the firm of W. M. Peters' Sons.

Kemble Mansion and Grounds.

We have had photographs taken of the Kemble Mansion and grounds in order to show the very fine hydrangeas which ornament the drive, as well as to give an idea of the beauty and extent of the grounds. But as our illustration is more to display the hydrangeas than anything else, it is to them we desire particularly to refer.

As will be seen by the picture the plants are of the Hortensia type. It is not everybody who can grow them as well as these have been grown. This type of hydrangeas needs treating in an exactly opposite way to that required by the one known as the hardy hydrangea, H. paniculata grandiflora. The Hortensia is not hardy in a necessary way. It is hardy this far, that in many Winters it will be killed to the ground, and then, though it will start freely from the ground when Spring comes and form a large bush by Fall, it will not flower the same season. Now, the hardy one, paniculata grandiflora, might freeze back as much as it desired, and would flower none the worse for it. But to return to Hortensia. These must be grown on all Summer, encouraged to make numbers of strong young shoots. It is these young shoots, preserved particularly to their topmost bud, which give the flowers such as these plants have at the Kemble grounds. The top bud is the one of all the others to preserve, as it is the one that gives the flower head. The whole secret of successful growing of this hydrangea is to treat the plants that they will grow well one season and then preserve them from freezing, that the shoots will not be injured. The best place for wintering the plants is a quite cold cellar, or a closed shed where hard freezings will not occur. A little freezing will not hurt the plants when in the shade; in fact, in mild Winters, when in a shady place, many a plant goes through the Winters of Philadelphia unharmed. The mistake is sometimes made of keeping these hydrangeas in a warm place in Winter. It takes but a temperature a few degrees above freezing to start the plants growing when in a cellar, especially if kept moist at the same time. As this growth is detrimental to their well being, it must be prevented by affording them as little water as will keep them from shriveling. In the case of but a plant or two, or more if desired, burying them outdoors in advance of Winter will preserve them very well.

The Kemble grounds are at Laverock, Montgomery Co., Pa., both the mansion and grounds occupying a commanding height.

JOSEPH MEEHAN.

Seasonable Suggestions.

Wier's cut-leaved maple makes a grand avenue tree, and should be pushed for use in this way by those interested. The droop of the branches takes away the formal character so many shade trees have.

Cercidiphyllum japonicum is a handsomely shaped tree, and its glaucous green leaves are considered an attraction. It prefers a partly damp situation. At the Amherst Agricultural College, Mass., there are trees that bear seeds, as Francis Canning mentions.

Mr. Reasoner, of Florida, says the prairie rose, R. setigera, makes an excellent stock for budding purposes in the South. No doubt it would do as well in the North, and it is easily had from seeds.

Peaches are ripening, and those who wish stones for sowing will be looking out for a supply. If kept from becoming very dry and sown in Fall, the pits sprout well in Spring. If not treated in this way, and sown dry in Spring, they will not grow for a year.

The rare Franklin tree, Gordonia pubescens, is but little known outside of Philadelphia and its environs. Its lovely white flowers, encircling their clusters of yellow stamens, expand from early August until frost. This season the first flowers expanded August 5.

A reliable old perennial plant is the Physostegia virginica, a plant old gardeners know under the name of dracocephalum. It grows from 2½ to 3 feet high, and through July bears a profusion of light pink flowers. When massed, it creates a fine effect.

Bambusa Metake makes an exceedingly ornamental plant for lawns. Being evergreen and quickly forming a good sized clump, it is very valuable. Visitors to Arlington, Va., will see some fine clumps near the Lee mansion. Bambusa Metake as well as B. aurea and B. argentea, are all from Japan.

Sambucus racemosa is one of the red berried elders. It ripens its fruit in June, nearly two months ahead of the common elderberry. Its large clusters of red berries are exceedingly ornamental. The bush should be in all collections where red berried subjects are valued.

Mr. Vry, writing from St. Paul, Minn., says that in his younger days Acer tartaricum was much used for hedges in Holland. Its habit of growth would fit it for this purpose. Its variety, Ginnala, should suit better still, its growth being green while yet of compact nature.

Kemble Mansion and Grounds, Laverock, Pa.

Increasing Wild Roses.

There is a great demand for our wild roses from those who have the forming of large pleasure grounds. Hundreds are planted where but one used to be, and there are cases where a thousand have been planted in one place. Many private establishments as well as parks make plantations wholly of roses, which is the cause of the great demand. In view of this call it is a pleasure to know that there is no difficulty in increasing stock rapidly. Seeds of all species are to be had without trouble, and, sown at the right time, they grow freely. The four most prominent sorts in the trade are carolina, nitida, setigera and blanda. Of these, carolina is the one found generally in damp situations, often in swamps. Blanda and nitida are found on higher ground, and neither grows as tall as carolina, which is often found six feet tall. Setigera is the wild prairie rose. All of the flowers are pink, some of brighter shades than others, and all bloom in June, setigera the latest of all.

Seeds of these roses are better sown in Autumn, but will keep until Spring, to be sown then, if desired. They may be sown pulp and all, or washed free of pulp and sown. The latter is the better plan.

Beds should be prepared in Autumn and seeds sown as soon as ready. These and all seeds sown at that time should be covered with light, fine soil, and after this should have a covering of forest leaves. This keeps them moist through the Winter as well as shaded, and is considered of great value by those who follow the practice.

Old-Time Grapes.

It must be very gratifying to the relatives of those who raised some of the older varieties of grapes to find them to-day in the very first rank of good kinds. In a recent discussion on grapes at a meeting of the Missouri Horticultural Society, all these old kinds were at the top of the list as profitable, market varieties: Concord, Moore's Early, Worden, Niagara, Brighton, Delaware and Ives' Seedling. One speaker, Dr. Whitten, who said he had 200 varieties, named for general use Moore's Early, Worden and Concord for black; Moore's Diamond and Niagara for white; Wyoming for red. Several other speakers named Moore's Early as the best early black grape, and this accords with the experience of those here who are acquainted with this variety. It bears a good sized bunch of berries which are never too crowded, so that all become of a good size. Nurserymen who have handled it always have well satisfied customers. Concord and Moore's Early for black, Niagara and Campbell's Early for white, and Brighton and Salem for red are good old reliable sorts to have for selling to the average customer.

Transplanting Evergreens in August.

A letter came to me recently in which the writer of it said he was puzzled to know whether it were better to plant evergreens in August than in Spring. He had read in his favorite paper that August was better than Spring, while other writers had said Spring was the proper season.

When time, labor and care are considered, Spring is the best time of all. Nevertheless, with extra care there need be no failures when the trees are set in August. Why more planting is not done then is because work of that kind is at a standstill. Owners of grounds are away, and landscape gardeners do not care to solicit the work, as it requires more care than Spring planting does. Nurserymen often set out stock then, as then men are at hand to attend to the requirements of the trees.

When August comes evergreen have their shoots fairly well ripened. If they are then carefully dug, with some ball to the roots, and set carefully in their new positions and good after treatment is afforded them, every one should live. When the holes are half filled with soil water should be poured in, and not once only but several times a day, and this should be kept up for two or three days, so that the tree be in almost a pool of water. After this the whole of the soil needed can be filled in. Success depends on a thorough drenching with water. With the wet, warm weather we have been experiencing no safer time could have been selected for the transplanting of evergreens. Even in ordinary Summers, with care taken to drench the trees transplantd both at the root and overhead, August is a good month for the work. The present season August, so far, has been unusually favorable.

Stigmaphyllon Ciliatum.

In a recetn number of The Florists' Exchange your correspondent, "M" referring to the beautiful Brazilian vine, Stigmaphyllon ciliatum, said of it among other things "Stigmaphyllon is an excellent thing for baskets and other forms of decorative work by itself; or if used along with allamandas the two make very effective work, the former adding grace and lightness to the latter." This will be fully endorsed by all who are familiar with this vine. And I would add that strong vines set outdoors in Summer grow surprisingly well. Some years ago when visiting the White House grounds, Washington, D. C., there was seen a vigorous vine trained along the railing near the mansion, growing and flowering in an interesting way.

JOSEPH MEEHAN.

EVERGREENS
DWARF BOX

PRICES UPON APPLICATION.

HIRAM T. JONES,

Union County Nurseries, Elizabeth, N. J.

Mention the Florists' Exchange when writing.

KOSTER & CO.

Hollandia Nurseries BOSKOOP, HOLLAND

Hardy Azaleas, Box Trees, Clematis, Conifers, Hydrangeas, Peonies.

Pot-Grown Plants for Forcing.

RHODODENDRONS, H. P. ROSES, Etc.

Catalogue free on demand.

Mention the Florists' Exchange when writing

Large Assortment **PEONIES** Very best Varieties

LOW PRICES

THE KIND THAT FLORISTS LIKE

"We make a specialty of growing stocky transplanted shrubbery and trees"

FULL ASSORTMENT OF Ornamentals, Fruits, Roses, Clematis, and Herbaceous Plants. Write for our fall wholesale trade list.

W. & T. SMITH CO., GENEVA, N. Y.

PLANT HERBACEOUS PERENNIALS NOW.

PLANT "BAY STATE FIELD GROWN" STOCK

We make a specialty of furnishing **Complete List for Formal Gardens and Border Planting**. If you do not see in this list just what you want, **write us**. We have many other varieties and novelties not mentioned here.

Our complete descriptive Catalog and Trade List Mailed Free.

		Per 10	Per 100
5000	**ACHILLEA**—Aegyptica, Millefolium, M. roseum, Ptarmica, Ptarmica fl. pl.	$1.00	$8.00
100	**ACORUS**—calamus variegatus		
500	**AGROSTEMMA**—Coronaria, Coronaria alba	.80	6.00
500	**AJUGA**—metallica crispa, reptans	1.00	8.00
25000	**ALTHÆA ROSEA**—(Hollyhock) Large assortment of colors and shades, both double and single	1.00	8.00
200	**ALYSSUM**—saxatile compactum	1.00	8.00
200	**AMSONIA**—Tabernaemontana	1.20	10.00
500	**ANCHUSA**—Italica, sempervirens	.80	6.00
3000	**ANEMONE**—Japonica, Jap. alba, Queen Charlotte, Whirlwind, Pennsylvanicum, etc.	1.00	8.00
1000	**ANTHEMIS**—Kelwayi, tinctoria	1.00	8.00
500	**APOIS**—tuberosa	.80	6.00
4000	**AQUILEGIA**—coerulea' Canadensis, chrysantha, vulgaris alba, flora plena	1.00	8.00
	alba fl. pl.	2.00	15.00
500	**ARABIS**—albida, alpina fl. pl.	.80	6.00
3000	**ARMERIA**—formosa, Lauchiana, maritima, maritima alba	1.00	8.00
500	**ARTEMESIA**—Dracunculus, pontica, Stellariana	1.00	8.00
1500	**ASCLEPIAS**—incarnata, tuberosa	.80	6.00
10000	**ASTERS**—(Michaelmas Daisies) 25 of the finest named varieties	.80	6.00
1000	**ASTILBE**—Japonica, multiflora	1.00	8.00
350	**AUBRETIA**—deltoides	2.00	15.00
100	**BAPTISIA**—australis, tinctoria	1.00	8.00
600	**BELLIS**—perennis	.80	6.00
800	**BOCCONIA**—cordata	.80	6.00
5000	**BOLTONIA**—asteroides, atisquama	.80	6.00
200	**CALLIRHOE**—involucrata	1.20	10.00
10000	**CAMPANULA**—carpatica, carpatica alba, macrantha, media, persicifolia, grandiflora, pyramidalis, pulcherrima, rotundifolia	1.00	8.00
200	**CASSIA**—Marylandica	1.00	8.00
100	**CATANANCHE**—coerulea	1.00	
1000	**CENTAUREA**—macrocephala, montana, montana alba	1.20	10.00
1000	**CERASTIUM**—Boissierii	1.00	8.00
1000	**CHELONE**—glabra, Lyoni	.80	6.00
3000	**CHRYSANTHEMUM**—Shasta Daisy, maximum, uliginosum	1.00	8.00
2000	**CHRYSANTHEMUM**—Hardy Pompon Varieties, 17 named varieties	1.00	8.00
100	**CIMICIFUGA**—racemosa	1.00	
500	**CLEMATIS**—Davidiana, recta	1.00	8.00
2000	**COREOPSIS**—delphinifolium, grandiflora, lanceolata	1.00	8.00
10000	**DELPHINIUM**—24 Named Varieties	1.00	8.00
3000	**DIANTHUS**—barbatus, deltoides, Heddewigi, plumarius, etc.	1.00	8.00
1000	**DIANTHUS**—Named Hybrids	1.50	12.00
500	**DICENTRA**—eximia, spectabilis	1.00	8.00
1000	**DICTAMNUS**—fraxinella, alba	1.50	12.00
1000	**DIGITALIS**—in Variety	1.00	8.00
200	**DORONICUM**—plantagineum excelsum	1.20	10.00
200	**ECHINACEA**—purpurea	1.20	10.00
300	**ECHINOPS**—pumilum, Ritro	1.00	8.00
500	**EPILOBIUM**—angustifolium	.80	6.00
200	**EPIMEDIUM**—macranthum, Muschianum	1.50	12.00
200	**ERIGERON**—speciosus	1.50	12.00
400	**ERYNGIUM**—alpinum, Amethystinum	1.50	12.00
600	**EULALIA**—Japonica, gracillima, Variegata, zebrina	1.00	8.00
300	**EUPATORIUM**—purpureum	1.00	8.00
3000	**FUNKIA**—lancifolia, marginata, ovata, Variegata	1.00	8.00
3000	**GAILLARDIA**—aristata, grandiflorum	.80	6.00
2000	**GALIUM**—boreale	.80	6.00
200	**GALEGA**—officinalis alba, rubra	1.00	
500	**GERANIUM**—sanguineum, album	.80	6.00
1000	**GYPSOPHILA**—acutifolia, paniculata, Stevenii	1.50	12.00
4000	**HELENIUM**—autumnale, grandicephalum striatum, pumilum, magnificum	1.00	8.00
	Hoopesii	1.50	
1000	**HELIANTHEMUM**—hyssopifolium, vulgare citrinum, flore pleno	1.00	8.00
3000	**HELIANTHUS**—decapetalus, mollis, rigida, etc.	.80	7.00
500	**HELIOPSIS**—lævis, Pitcheriana	1.00	8.00
2000	**HEMEROCALLIS**—flava, fulva, Sieboldi, Thunbergiana	1.00	8.00
1500	**HEUCHERA**—Americana, sanguinea	1.00	8.00
600	**HIBISCUS**—moscheutos, Crimson Eye	1.00	8.00
1000	**IBERIS**—corræfolia, sempervirens	1.00	8.00
500	**INCARVILLEA**—Delavayi	1.20	10.00
2000	**IRIS**—Alpine, 30 Named Varieties	2.50	20.00
5000	**IRIS**—German, 30 Named Varieties	1.00	8.00
25000	**IRIS**—Kæmpferii, 27 Named Varieties	1.20	10.00
3000	**IRIS**—orientalis, pseudacorus, Sibirica etc.	1.00	8.00
200	**LATHYRUS**—latifolius	1.00	8.00
2000	**LIATRIS**—pycnostachya, spicata	1.00	8.00
5000	**LILIUM**—All the leading varieties		
500	**LINUM**—flavum, perenne	1.00	8.00
1000	**LOBELIA**—cardinalis, syphilitica	1.00	7.00
2000	**LUPINUS**—perennis, polyphyllus, albus	.80	6.00
4000	**LYCHNIS**—Chalcedonica, alba, Haageana, plenissima, viscaria, flore pleno etc.	1.00	8.00
1000	**LYSIMACHIA**—clethroides, nummularia	.80	6.00
500	**LYTHRUM**—alatum roseum Superbum	1.00	8.00
1000	**MALVA**—moschata, moschata alba	.80	6.00
2000	**MONARDA**—didyma, fistulosa	1.00	8.00
600	**MYOSOTIS**—palustris, semperflorens	1.00	8.00
250	**ŒNOTHERA**—in Variety	1.00	
500	**OPUNTIA**—Missouriensis	1.50	
25000	**PÆONIAS**—125 Named Varieties	2.00	15.00
2000	**PAPAVER**—nudicaule and oriental poppies	1.00	8.00
100	**PARDANTHUS**—Chinensis	1.00	
3000	**PENSTEMON**—barbatus Torreyi, diffusus, digitalis, ovatum	1.00	8.00
200	**PHALARIS**—spectabilis, arundinacea	1.00	
10000	**PHLOX**—27 Named Varieties	1.00	8.00
2000	**PHLOX**—amœna	1.00	8.00
5000	**PHLOX**—subulata, subulata alba, The Bride	.80	6.00
2000	**PHYSOSTEGIA**—speciosa, Virginiana, alba, rubra	1.00	8.00
2000	**PLATYCODON**—grandiflora, alba, Mariesii	1.00	8.00
100	**PLUMBAGO**—larpentæ	1.00	
100	**POLEMONIUM**—cæruleum	1.00	
100	**POLYGONATUM**—commutatum, multiflorum	1.50	
100	**POLYGONUM**—Baldschuanicum, Sieboldi	1.50	
1000	**POTENTILLA**—Named varieties, both double and single	1.00	8.00
150	**PRIMULA**—veris superba	1.00	
500	**PYRETHRUM**—roseum in colors, uliginosum	1.00	8.00
2500	**RANUNCULUS**—acris fl. pl., repens	.80	6.00
2000	**RUDBECKIA**—fulgida, Golden Glow	.80	6.00
600	**SALVIA**—azurea, grandiflora, pratensis	1.00	8.00
200	**SAPONARIA**—ocymoides, officinalis fl. pl.	1.00	8.00
300	**SCABIOSA**—Caucasia	1.20	10.00
2000	**SEDUM**—acre, album, Sieboldii	.80	6.00
	spectabile	1.20	9.00
800	**SEMPERVIVUM**—in variety	.80	6.00
200	**SILENE**—Maritima	.80	6.00
1500	**SPIRÆA**—astilboides, filipendula, palmata, palmata alba, venusta, ulmaria fl. pl.	1.00	8.00
500	**STACHYS**—lanata, rosea grandiflora	.80	6.00
100	**STATICE**—latifolia	.80	
4000	**STOKESIA**—cyanea	.80	6.00
150	**TIARELLA**—cordifolia	1.00	
900	**TRADESCANTIA**—Virginica, alba	.80	6.00
2000	**TRITOMA**—Pfitzerii, uvaria grandiflora	1.00	8.00
200	**TUNICA**—saxifraga	1.00	8.00
3000	**VERONICA**—gentianoides, longifolia, spicata	.80	6.00
	longifolia subsessilis	1.20	10.00
1000	**VIOLA**—cornuta in variety, Double Russian, Wellsiana	1.50	12.00
5000	**VINCA**—Minor		4.00
2000	**YUCCA**—filamentosa	1.00	8.00

THE BAY STATE NURSERIES, W. H. WYMAN, Prop. NORTH ABINGTON, MASS.

PANSY

Holmes' Mammoth Exhibition Strain. Positively unsurpassed in size and markings. Satisfaction guaranteed or money refunded. New crop seed in any quantity.

Special Price trade pkt., 30c.; ⅛ oz., 60 c.; ¼ oz., $1.00; 1 oz., $4.00.

We are headquarters for florists' supplies. Quick service.

HOLMES SEED CO. Harrisburg, Pa., **SEED**

Mention The Florists' Exchange when writing.

BULBS FOR FLORISTS

Lilium Harrisii, Roman Hyacinths Paper White Narcissus, Freesias

Send for special prices.

New Crop **Mushroom Spawn—English and Pure Culture.**

WEEBER & DON, Seed Merchants and Growers

114 Chambers Street, NEW YORK

Mention The Florists' Exchange when writing.

JOHN SCHEEPERS & CO.

DEALERS AND IMPORTERS OF BULBS AND PLANTS.

2, 4 and 6 OLD SLIP, NEW YORK CITY.

Mention The Florists' Exchange when writing.

Trees and Shrubs

We make specially low prices on nursery stock to **Parks, Cemeteries,** etc.

Wholesale price list on application.

We carry immense quantities of the finest named varieties of peonies.

PETERSON NURSERY

505 W. PETERSON AVE., CHICAGO, ILL

LARGE TREES

OAKS AND MAPLES

PINES AND HEMLOCKS

ANDORRA NURSERIES

WM. WARNER HARPER, PROPRIETOR

Chestnut Hill, Philadelphia, Pa.

P. OUWERKERK

216 Jane Street

WEEHAWKEN HEIGHTS, N. J.

P. O. No. 1, Hoboken, N. J.

JUST RECEIVED FROM OUR HOLLAND NURSERIES

Rhododendrons, Azaleas, Spiræa Japonica, Lilium Speciosum, Peonies, Bleeding Heart, Pot-Grown Lilacs, Hydrangea in sorts, Clematis and H. P. Roses in the best sorts.

PRICES MODERATE

F. & F. NURSERIES

SPRINGFIELD NEW JERSEY

Wholesale Growers

TREES AND PLANTS in full assortment.

Trade Catalogue Free

AMERICAN **TREE SEEDS** AND PLANTS

Our Descriptive Catalogue of American Seeds and Plants is ready for mailing. Ask for it.

OTTO KATZENSTEIN & CO.

Tree Seeds and Plants Specialists, ATLANTA, GA

BERBERIS THUNBERGII

85,000 2 year transplanted 18 to 24 inch, fine bushy plants at $60.00 per 1000.

100,000 2 yr. seedlings, 6 to 12 in., $10.00 per 1000.

50,000 1 yr. seedlings, 4 to 8 in., $8.00 per 1000.

5,000 **MYRTLE** at $50.00 per 1000.

Would give discount to party buying entire lot of Berberis.

OAK HILL NURSERIES, Roslindale, Mass.

Catalog Engravings

and ILLUSTRATIONS

that print EASILY. That's the kind we make—have been since '73

JAS. M. BRYANT, Horticultural Engraving and Printing

706 Chestnut Street, PHILADELPHIA, PA.

Write for our Catalogue of Stock Engravings

Mention the Florists' Exchange when writing.

DAHLIAS

Now is the time to place your order for Bulbs which will insure you getting named varieties in any quantity; delivery to be made this fall or early spring.

DAVID HERBERT & SON,

Successors to L. K. PEACOCK, Inc.

ATCO, N. J.

Mention The Florists' Exchange when writing.

A BED OF MUSHROOMS

Raised from our Spawn, will **bear longer and yield better** than from any other variety of Spawn. This is proven by facts. Full particulars and information how to succeed in mushroom raising free. We warrant you if using our method of growing mushrooms that all will go well.

KNUD GUNDESTRUP & CO., MUSHROOM SPECIALISTS 4273 Milwaukee Ave., CHICAGO

Mention The Florists' Exchange when writing.

ADVERTISE IN THE FLORISTS' EXCHANGE - - and be sure of good returns - -

Henderson's Superior

Lilium Harrisii Bulbs

Are pronounced by Florists who have forced them

"Superior and Thoroughly Satisfactory"

"Please ship us 1000 Lilium Harrisii bulbs —6 to 7 inch size. We are giving you this order on the strength of getting bulbs equal in health to those we got from you last year, which produced the finest plants we had last season."
CLARK BROS., Florists, Portland Oregon.

"We have been more successful with your Harrisii bulbs than have any of the other florists in the vicinity of Wheeling with bulbs from other sources."
OSCAR WRIGHT, Moundsville, W. Va.

If you had the time and we had the space we could quote many more similar reports.

Prices of Henderson's Superior Lilium Harrisii Bulbs

NOW READY FOR SHIPMENT	Doz.	100	1000
First Size Bulbs (5 to 7 inches in circumference)	$0.60	$4.00	$38.00
Intermediate Size (6 to 7 inches in circumference)	0.85	5.00	45.00
Extra Size Bulbs (7 to 9 inches in circumference)	1.25	8.00	75.00

9 to 11 inch bulbs sold out

Our Florists' Catalogue of Bulbs, Plants and Seeds for Autumn Planting mailed free to Florists on application.

PETER HENDERSON & CO.
35 & 37 Cortlandt Street, NEW YORK

Mention The Florists' Exchange when writing

PEONIES

Queen Victoria (the cold storage flower) $9.00 per 100. Festiva Maxima, $30.00 per 100. Fragrans (the bloom producer) $6.00 per 100. For 1000 rates or other varieties, write.

GILBERT H. WILD
SARCOXIE, MO.

PAEONIAS FOR FALL DELIVERY

We are booking orders NOW from a large and well-assorted stock, carefully selected from hundreds of varieties tested. All have bloomed with us and we guarantee them true to name.

SEND FOR SPECIAL LIST WITH PRICES

We are headquarters, also, for ROSES, CLEMATIS, AMPELOPSIS, and HYDRANGEAS.
Use printed stationery: we sell at wholesale only.

JACKSON & PERKINS CO.
NEWARK, WAYNE CO., NEW YORK.

Sea Cliff Nurseries.
Dwarf and trained fruit trees a specialty.
Write for quotations.
FD. BOULON & SON,
SEA CLIFF, L. I., N. Y.

1500 Trumphet vines, 1-3 ft. trans. 4c.
1000 Norway Spruce with ball 1½-2 ft. 10c.
Send for surplus list.

Ellsworth Brown & Co.
SEABROOK, N. H.
Mention The Florists' Exchange when writing.

H. DEN OUDEN & SON,
BOSKOOP, HOLLAND.

Wholesale growers of nursery stock for the American trade. Catalogue free on demand. Also views in our nurseries.

Mention The Florists' Exchange when writing

THE AMERICAN CARNATION
Price, $3.50
A. T. DE LA MARE PTG. & PUB. CO. LTD.
2-8 Duane Street, New York

160,000 California Grown Bulbs

	Per 100	Per 1000
Narcissus Paper White	$1.50	$10.00
Narcissus Grand Monarque	2.00	15.00
Narcissus Grand Primo	2.00	14.00
Narcissus Gloriosus	2.00	15.00
Narcissus Incomparabilis Cynosure	1.50	10.00
Narcissus Incomparabilis Figaro	$1.50	$10.00
Narcissus Incomparabilis Dontle	1.50	10.00
Calla Lily Bulbs, 1-inch dia.	2.50	20.00
Calla Lily Bulbs, 1½-inch dia.	3.50	30.00
Calla Lily Bulbs, 2-inch dia.	6.00	50.00

Freight prepaid if cash is sent with order. 250 at 1000 rate.

A. MITTING, 17 to 23 Kennan St., **Santa Cruz, Cal.**

Mention The Florists' Exchange when writing.

SEND TO
THE MOON COMPANY
For Your { TREES, SHRUBS, VINES and SMALL FRUITS
Descriptive Illustrated Catalogue Free
THE WM. H. MOON CO.
Morrisville Pa.
Mention the Florists' Exchange when writing

VAN DER WEIJDEN & CO.
The Nurseries, BOSKOOP, HOLLAND.

First class nursery and florist stock such as: Conifers, Blue Spruces, Koster, extra blue, fine shape, 1-4 ft. Boxwood Pyramids and bush form Specimen, 1-5 ft., our own growing. Hardy Rhododendrons, 18-24 in. (clumps). Best varieties of Azalea Mollis, Magnolia, Peonies, Clematis, Roses, dwarf and standard, very best varieties. Baby Rambler, also standards, etc., etc. Catalogue free on demand. Prices are very reasonable, and stock of the best grade. Send us a part of your orders; you will be satisfied. No agents. For the trade only.

Mention The Florists' Exchange when writing.

STORRS & HARRISON CO.
NURSERYMEN, FLORISTS and SEEDSMEN
SEND FOR CATALOGUE
PAINESVILLE OHIO,
Mention the Florists' Exchange when writing.

EVERGREENS
Spruce, Firs, Arborvitae and Pines in variety.
HARDY PHLOX
A very desirable Assortment.
PÆONIA CLUMPS
Double and Single Pink, Mixed
HARDY PLANTS
In variety. Send for Trade List.
SOUTHWORTH BROS.,
BEVERLY, MASS.

Holland Nursery Stock
Ask for Our Catalogue. It will interest you.
ENDTZ, VAN NES & CO. BOSKOOP, HOLLAND
Mention The Florists' Exchange when writing.

LILIUM PHILIPPINENSE

THE BEST CHRISTMAS LILY YET INTRODUCED

This Lily was awarded a "Gold Medal" by the Massachusetts Horticultural Society

Will force easily into flower inside of nine weeks

We can deliver over 100,000 of these Bulbs by September 1

All our Bulbs will be absolutely true, sound and of flowering size

OUR PRICES:

dozen, $2.00; per 100, $12.00; per 1,000, $100.00; per 10,000, $900.00

Every Florist should at least try this valuable novelty

Do not Delay but Order At Once

W. W. RAWSON & CO., 5 UNION STREET BOSTON, MASS.

THE BEST OF ALL

ROSES

Strong and healthy

AMERICAN BEAUTY
RICHMOND
BRIDES
BRIDESMAIDS
CHATENAY
UNCLE JOHN

CARNATIONS

Field-grown Plants	per 100	per 1000
ENCHANTRESS, Light Pink	$6.00	$50.00
LAWSON, Pink	5.00	40.00
FLAMINGO, Red	5.00	40.00
Mrs. M. A. PATTEN, Variegated	6.00	50.00
BOSTON MARKET, White	5.00	40.00
QUEEN LOUISE	5.00	40.00
WHITE CLOUD	5.00	40.00

LIBERTY, Bench Plants, $3.00 per 100; $30.00 per 1000

GEORGE REINBERG, 35 RANDOLPH ST., **CHICAGO**

AFTER JUNE 1 ADDRESS ALL COMMUNICATIONS TO 35 RANDOLPH STREET

GET THE BEST

IT DON'T PAY TO BUY POOR STOCK

	100	1000		100	1000
RICHMOND ROSE, 2½ inch	$5.00	$40.00	3½ inch	$6.50	$55.00
AMERICAN BEAUTIES, 3 inch	5.00	40.00	3½ inch	6.50	56.00
BRIDESMAIDS, 3½ inch	5.00	45.00			
CHATENAY, 2½ inch	3.50	30.00	3½ inch	5.00	45.00
UNCLE JOHN, 2½ inch	3.50	30.00	3½ inch	5.00	45.00
GOLDEN GATES, 2½ inch	3.50	30.00	3½ inch	4.50	
KAISERIN, 2½ inch	3.50	30.00			
SUNRISE, 3½ inch	5.50	60.00			
PERLES, 3½ inch	6.00	55.00			

SATISFACTION ABSOLUTELY GUARANTEED

SPRENGERI, 2 inch	$2.20 per 100;	$18.00 per 1000.
PLUMOSUS, 2 inch	2.50 "	22.00 "
YELLOW SNAPDRAGON, 3½ inch	5.00 "	45.00 "

FIELD GROWN CARNATION PLANTS

FREE FROM STEM ROT OR OTHER DISEASES. STRONG HEALTHY PLANTS

	100	1000		100	1000
MRS. THOS. LAWSON	$5.00	$45.00	RED SPORT OF MACEO	$4.00	$35.00
WHITE LAWSON	6.00	50.00	QUEEN	4.00	35.00
WOLCOTT	4.00	35.00	PATTEN	4.00	35.00
PROSPERITY	4.00	35.00	ELSIE MARTIN	4.00	35.00
THE BELLE	4.00	35.00	HARLOWARDEN	4.00	35.00
BOUNTIFUL	6.00	55.00	FIANCEE	4.00	35.00
PHYLLIS	4.00				

POEHLMANN BROS. COMPANY, MORTON GROVE, ILL.

Mention The Florists' Exchange when writing.

GRAFTED ROSES

It is getting late in the season, and we are reaching the end of our supply. We have left, in grafted stock, 3 in. pots at $18.00 per 100; $150.00 per 1000:

KILLARNEY, RICHMOND, ROSALIND ORR ENGLISH, MORGAN, WOOTTON.

On own roots, 3 inch pots, at $8.00 per 100; $75.00 per 1000:

KILLARNEY, BRIDE, LIBERTY, TESTOUT

RICHMOND own root, 2½ inch pots, $6.00 per 100; $50.00 per 1000.

A. N. PIERSON;
CROMWELL, CONN.

Mention The Florists' Exchange when writing.

GRAFTED ROSES

Fine Stock from 3-in. pots.

Richmond, $2.50 per doz., $15.00 per 100, $125.00 per 1000.

Killarney, $2.00 per doz., $15.00 per 100.

Etoile De France, $3.00 per doz., $18.00 per 100.

Kaiserin, Carnot, Uncle John, Chatenay, $2.00 per doz., $15.00 per 100.

Bride, Bridesmaid, Golden Gate, Wootton, $2.00 per doz., $12.00 per 100.

ROSES OWN ROOTS

Fine Stock from 3-in. pots.

Richmond, $10.00 per 100; $90.00 per 1000.

Etoile De France, $12.00 per 100.

Sunrise, Perle, Sunset, Chatenay, $8.00 per 100.

Bride, Bridesmaid, Golden Gate, $7.00 per 100.

Asparagus Plumosus Nanus from 3 inch pots, $8.00 per 100; Sprengerii from 3 inch pots, $6.00 per 100.

RUBBER PLANTS

Fine stock 2 feet high, 50c. each; $5.00 a doz.; 2½ to 3 feet high, 60c. each; $6.00 a doz.

Send for Catalogue.

Wood Bros., Fishkill, N. Y.

Mention The Florists' Exchange when writing.

ROSES

200 Liberty, grafted, 3 and 4 inch pots, $10.00 per 100.

Smilax Plants 2½ inch pots, $2.00 per 100.

JAMES E. BEACH.
2019 Park Ave., Bridgeport, Conn.

Mention The Florists' Exchange when writing.

Strong plants 2½ in. pots. **ROSES** On own roots 4 in. pots.

	100	1000	
Cr. Rambler, Wood,	$2.50	$20.	Baby Rambler,
La France, Meteor,	2.50	20.	Crimson "
G. Gate, Notting,	2.50	20.	Clarta, Masson,
Diesbach, Masson,	3.00	25.	Diesbach, Wood,
Laing, Caprice,	$3.00	25.	Neyron, Laing,

100 best sorts for fall 1906 and spring 1907.

THE LEEDLE FLORAL COMPANY SPRINGFIELD, OHIO

Mention The Florists' Exchange when writing.

LIST OF ADVERTISERS

INDEX TO STOCK ADVERTISED

Contents.

REVIEW OF THE MARKET

NEW YORK.—The cut flower business is rather unsatisfactory at the present time, but as this condition is not unusual for mid-August, no complaints are heard. There is plenty of everything coming into the market; particularly are there full supplies of such flowers as gladiolus, hydrangeas and asters. The latter as yet do not seem to be quite up to the quality usually seen at this time of the year.

American Beauty roses, that up to within the last ten days have seemed to do so well all Summer, are now coming in much too plentifully for the demand, and although a few small lots can be cleared out at our quoted prices, the bulk of this stock has to be sold at greatly reduced figures. Of Bride and Bridesmaid roses the flowers coming in at present are mostly from young plants, and are necessarily short in stem, clearing out at about 25c. per 100.

Carnations are scarcer this Summer than has been the rule for several years; in fact, there are very few to be seen on the market. Dahlias are becoming more abundant every day, the majority of them being as yet quite short-stemmed. Cattleyas are scarcer now than they have been for some time, though there is little change in their market values. Lily of the valley is selling slowly, and no better prices than were obtained in several weeks past are recorded. Lilies are still in plentiful supply, and can be had at anywhere from $4 to $5 per 100.

In green material the demand is no better than has been the rule for several weeks, and prices remain the same.

BOSTON.—Slight changes prevail in the cut flower business. While there seems to be always a little doing, there are a great many times when "nothing doing" is the slogan. Asters of all colors remain very plentiful and the quality is comparatively good. Carnations are best from out of doors and they are of better quality than they have been. Prices do not vary. Roses remain practically unchanged; the call has not been great and the quality has not improved much. Sweet peas are played out as only flowers of poor quality are now seen. Gladiolus are good, and plentiful. Lilies are abundant and sell fairly well; longiflorum bring $1.50 per dozen, while lancifolium bring $3 and $4 per 100. Other staples, like asparagus and ferns, remain without change. J. W. D.

BUFFALO, N. Y.—The weather has been extremely hot for the past four weeks. This has also been one of the most rainless seasons in the past decade; all the growers in this vicinity are complaining about the drought, especially the asters growers. Plants that ought to be three feet high have grown about half the size, with no prospects of any more growth. Within the past week we have had a few showers, but they amounted to very little. Good roses are very scarce. Kaiserin Augusta Victoria seems to be the best Summer rose, and gives better satisfaction to the majority than any other similar kind; but, not enough are coming in to supply the demand. They are bringing from $1 to $2 retail. There has been a dearth of pink roses. Souvenir du President Carnot, Killarney and Mme. Abel Chatenay have good flowers, but the stems are very short. The blooms bring from 60c. to $1.50 per dozen retail. A few American Beauty are seen, but the flowers are poor, retailing at from $2 to $6 per dozen. Asters sell at from 25c. to 75c. per dozen, but very few are coming in, and those received are poor in quality owing to the dry season. Gladioli are very good, but not many are sold by the retailers, being used more for decorative purposes. They bring $1 for the best. W. H. G.

INDIANAPOLIS.—A large number of funeral orders have used up quantities of field flowers; a number of out-of-town orders have helped materially. Asters are still in too large quantity; 50c. to $1 a 100 is asked. The large Semple variety is being cut now; and is in demand at better prices. Home-grown gladioli, though not up to standard quality, are plentiful at $1.50 to $3 a 100. Out-of-town growers are offering them as low as $1.

Rubrum and longiflorum lilies are plentiful at current prices. New crop carnations for funeral work are to be had at the buyer's price. A few Enchantress bring $1. Satisfactory roses are obtained with difficulty. A few good Kaiserin Augusta Victoria and La France sell at $3 to $6. Red roses—Liberty and Richmond—open so quickly that few care to handle them.

Business is exceedingly quiet at Tomlinson Hall market. Some stock is wholesaled in the morning, but much goes to waste. I. B.

ST. LOUIS.—We a pleased to report that business was good last week, occasioned by funeral orders. White stock of all kinds was in big demand, and plenty of it was available in the early part of the week, but toward the end flowers were scarce. The demand was greatest Friday and Saturday. Asters have been in heavy supply, with a scarcity of good white; prices ranged from 25c. to $1.50 per 100. In rose, American Beauty are showing up better in quality, with fancies at $3 per dozen; others at from 50c. to $2 per dozen. Kaiserin Augusta Victoria, Bride, Bridesmaid, Golden Gate and Souvenir du President Carnot sell well when fancy, but there is too much stock of inferior quality; prices are from $2 to $5 per 100. Carnations are of better quality, being mostly field-grown, with o stems; pink and red are ver- scarce; white plentiful, at 50c. to $1 per 100.

Lily of the valley brings $3 per 100 and is of fair quality. Outdoor stock, such as gladioli, hydrangeas, tuberoses, sweet peas, cornflowers, and others sell slowly; rains have put them in good shape again. There is plenty of all kinds of greens. ST. PATRICK.

PROVIDENCE, R. I.—Business continues very quiet, with plenty of stock to fill all orders. Some fairly good Bride and Bridesmaid roses are coming in; all on short stems, however. Prices range from $2 to $5 per 100. Carnations are very poor stock in all grades; white is most in demand. Queen of the Market asters are about done; continued rainstorms have ruined early asters. The branching sorts are now quite plentiful and of fair quality. Dahlias were never finer; immense stocks are spoiling in the field owing to the dullness of the market. G. S. W.

CHANGES IN BUSINESS.

ARGOS, IND.—The Argos Floral and Plant Company was organized August 9, to deal in cut flowers, flower and vegetable plants, bulbs, seeds, etc. Wm. E. Hand is president and general manager, Noah E. Bundy, secretary and treasurer.

WHITMAN, MASS.—M. L. Belcher has purchased of Robert Moir the store that he has conducted for so many years in the Jenkins building, and he will take possession at once. Mr. Belcher is an experienced florist, and has extensive greenhouses at South Wymouth.

BROOKLYN, N. Y.—Alfred A. Hyatt has purchased the business of Tracy & Son at 252 Court street, and after completing alterations will continue the same under the name of A. A. Hyatt & Company. Samuel J. Heming, designer with Tracy & Son, will still retain his position with the new firm.

DENISON, TEX.—Will B. Munson has leased his greenhouse plant to Messrs. C. E. Majors and T. P. Gorman, who will operate it on their own account under the style of the Munson Greenhouses growing a general line of plants, with carnations and roses as specialties. Mr. Munson will devote all his attention to his nursery interests.

BLOOMINGTON, ILL.—The Phoenix Nursery Company has contracted for a greenhouse to be erected on its grounds east of Linden street and a little way north of the Kankakee branch of the Illinois Central. The plant will be a large one covering 3,000 square feet and will replace the old greenhouse owned by the company just north of the street car barns, which is being dismantled.

FIRMS WHO ARE BUILDING.

NEWTON HIGHLANDS, MASS.—Arthur Hewkes has begun the erection of a new greenhouse.

TEMPLETON, MASS.—Geo. W. Sutherland is erecting a small new greenhouse to be used for raising violets.

WAKEFIELD, MASS.—F. C. Bisacre of Swampscott, has purchased a house and lot, corner of Richmond and Spruce streets, and in the Spring will build greenhouses.

CHESHIRE, CONN.—Miss Nettie Smith is having the Clover Leaf greenhouse thoroughly repaired and alterations made for preparation for her Fall and Winter trade.

PITTSFIELD, MASS.—A. J. Loder, the florist, has purchased the Leighton house located on Lancey street; also the vacant lots adjoining the property. It is Mr. Loder's intention to erect a commodious greenhouse on the grounds as his present quarters are not large enough to meet the growing demands of his increased business.

FULL REPORT OF
THE DAYTON CONVENTION
An Advertiser's Opportunity

THE issue of THE FLORISTS' EXCHANGE for next Saturday, August 25, will contain a full and complete report of the proceedings of the Convention of the S. A. F. and O. H. at Dayton, Ohio, August 21 to 24.

Every reader is anxious to know just what was done, who was there, what Firms made exhibits, what new Goods were shown, how the election of new officers went, the next place of meeting, and the current news and gossip.

Advertisements received until Wednesday, August 22

Recognizing a special value to this issue of Aug. 25, some of our keen advertisers have already taken extra space therein; we therefore solicit further enlarged and new business from those whose advertising at this season would be timely.

THE FLORISTS' EXCHANGE
P. O. BOX 1697
Nos. 2 to 8 DUANE STREET, NEW YORK CITY

ORCHIDS ORCHIDS

WE collect, import, grow and sell ORCHIDS EXCLUSIVELY; hence we are in a position to supply this class of plants of better grades and lower prices than any other house, and if you intend buying ORCHIDS we respectfully solicit your orders. We can supply you with established ORCHIDS, or with freshly imported UNESTABLISHED plants, whichever you prefer. Ask for our list of FRESHLY IMPORTED ORCHIDS

LAGER & HURRELL
SUMMIT, N. J.

THE AMERICAN CARNATION
PRICE, $3.50. SEND FOR A COPY
A. T. DE LA MARE Ptg. & Pub. Co. Ltd., 2 Duane St., N.Y.

Dreer's Kentias

Nearly Three Acres to select from.

KENTIA FORSTERIANA—MADE-UP PLANTS

			Each
5 in. pots, 4 plants in a pot,	15 to 18	inches	$0.60
6 " 3 " "	20 to 24	"	1.00
7 " 3 " "	24 to 28	"	1.50
7 " 3 " "	28 to 30	"	2.00
7-in. tubs, 4 plants in a tub,	34 to 36	"	2.50
7 " 4 " "	36 to 40	"	3.00
8-in pots, 3 plants in a pot,	36 to 40	"	3.00
9 " 4 " "	3½	feet	4.00
9-in. tubs, 4 plants in a tub,	3½ to 4	"	5.00
10-in. pots, 4 plants in a pot,	4	"	6.00
9-in. tubs, 4 plants in a tub,	4½	"	7.50
12 " 4 " "	7 to 8	"	15.00
13 " 6 " "	very heavy 5½ to 6 feet		15.00
14 " 4 " "	8 to 9 feet		25.00

We call special attention to the $15.00 plants which for decorative purposes will be found one of the best values we have ever offered, they have been grown in small tubs and are in a very convenient shape for handling.

KENTIA FORSTERIANA—SINGLE PLANTS

	Per doz.	Per 100	Per 1000
2½ in. pts, 4 leaves, 8 to 10in. high	$1.50	$10.00	$90.00
3 " 5 " 12 to 15 "	2.00	15.00	140.00
4 " 5 " 15 "	4.50	35.00	

	Each
6 " 6 " 24 to 28 "	$1.00
6 " 6 " 28 to 30 "	1.25
6 " 6 " 30 to 32 "	1.50
7 " 6 " 34 to 36 "	2.00
7 " 6 " 36 to 40 "	2.50
9 " 6 " 46 to 48 "	3.50
7 in. tubs 6 " 48 "	4.00
8 " 6 " 4½ ft. high	5.00
10 " 6 to 7 " 8 to 8½ "	10.00
10 " 6 to 7 " 8½ to 9 "	15.00

The $10.00 and $15.00 plants are tall handsome specimens, grand stock for decorating and of excellent value.

KENTIA BELMOREANA

	Per doz.	Per 100	Per 1000
2½in. pts, 4 leaves, 8 to 10in. high	$1.50	$10.00	$90.00
3 " 5 " 12 "	2.00	15.00	140.00

	Each
6 " 6 " 20 to 24 "	$1.00
6 " 6 " 24 to 26 "	1.25
6 " 6 to 7 " 26 to 28 "	1.50
7 " 6 " 30 to 32 "	2.00
7 " 6 " 36 to 40 "	3.00
9 in. tubs, 6 to 7 " 46 to 48 " very heavy	7.50

K. Belmoreana at $1.00, $1.25, $1.50 and $2.00 each are scarce and values are not as good as in past seasons, the plants as sent out however, are full market value.

HENRY A. DREER,
714 Chestnut St., PHILADELPHIA, PENNA.
Mention The Florists' Exchange when writing.

ROSE PLANTS

	100	1000
LIBERTY	$3.00	$25.00
CHATENAY	2.50	22.50

RICHMOND

2½ in. pots, $5.00 per 100; $40.00 per 1000
3 in. pots, $6.00 per 100; $50.00 per 1000

CARNATIONS

STRONG, HEALTHY, FIELD GROWN PLANTS

	100	1000
LAWSON	$5.00	$40.00
NELSON	3.00	25.00
GUARDIAN ANGEL	3.00	25.00
NELSON FISHER	7.00	50.00
ENCHANTRESS	7.00	60.00
MRS. PATTEN	6.00	50.00
MORNING GLORY	$4.00	$30.00
BOSTON MARKET	5.00	40.00
LADY BOUNTIFUL	6.00	50.00
FLORA HILL	3.00	25.00
ESTELLE	5.00	40.00
FIANCEE	7.00	60.00

PETER REINBERG, 51 Wabash Ave., CHICAGO
Mention The Florists' Exchange when writing.

PEONIES

$6.00 to $10.00 per 100

EDWARD SWAYNE
WEST CHESTER, PA.
Mention the Florists' Exchange when writing.

POINSETTIA

2½ in. pots, $5.00 per 100; $40.00 per 1000. C with order.

S. N. PENTECOST,
1790-1810 East 101 St., CLEVELAND
Mention The Florists' Exchange when wri

FERNS.

POINSETTIAS, 2½ inch pots, $5.00 per 100.

ASPARAGUS PLUMOSUS, 4 in. pots, $10.00 per 100.

HUGH GRAHAM CO.,
Logan Nurseries, York Road and Louden Street, PHILADELPHIA, PA.

Mention The Florists' Exchange when writing.

FERNS OUR SPECIALTY

CIBOTIUM SCHIEDEI
We have a large stock of this beautiful tree fern in 3 in. pots, ready for a shift, at $25.00 per 100. 25 plants at 100 rate.

FERN SEEDLINGS FROM FLATS
Eight to ten best market varieties at $1.00 per 100, or $8.50 per 1000. If by mail add 10c. for each hundred plants.

ASSORTED FERNS FOR DISHES
From 2¼ in. pots. The best and hardiest varieties in market at $3.00 per 100, or $25.00 per 1000. 250 plants at 1000 rate.

Adiantum Cuneatum, 2¼ in. pots, $3.50 per 100, $30.00 per 1000.

FERN SPORES
Gathered from our own stock. 35c. per trade package, $4.00 per doz. packages.

Gardenia Veitchii from 2¼ in. pots. $7.50 per 100. $70.00 per 1000; 500 at 1000 rate.

ANDERSON & CHRISTENSEN,
SHORT HILLS, N. J.

Mention The Florists' Exchange when writing.

Adiantum Cuneatum
From 2¼ in. pots ready to shift, per 100 $4.00; per 1000, $35.00.

Asparagus Plumosus Nanus
true kind, from 2½ in. pots, per 100, $3.00; per 1000, $25.00.

Ferns in Flats
Each flat contains about 110 divisible clumps, standard varieties as: Asparagus Tsussemense, Cyrtomium Falcatum, Lastraea Aristata Variegata, Pteris Adiantoides Cretica Albolineata, Gilberti, Mayi, Magnifica, Serrulata, Serr. Crist., Nana Compacta, Wimsetti, Adiantum Cuneatum, per flat, $2.00; per 12 flats, buyers' selection, $22.00; my own selection, $20.00. For larger quantities ask special quotation.

O. V. ZANGEN
Seedsman HOBOKEN, N. J.

Mention the Florists' Exchange when writing.

NEPHROLEPIS SCOTTII

Small plants from the benches, $5.00 per 100; $50.00 per 1000. Plants large enough for 6 in. pots, $25.00 per 100. Plants large enough to go in 7 and 8 in. pots, $50.00 per 100.

Asparagus Plumosus Nanus, 2¼ in., fine plants, $3.00 per 100.

JOHN SCOTT,
Rutland Road and East 45th Street;
BROOKLYN, N. Y.
Telephone 2890 Bedford.

Mention The Florists' Exchange when writing.

Ferns From Bench

Boston, Piersoni, 4 in. 10c.; 5 in., 12½c.
Tarrytown, 3 in., 10c.; 4 in., 15c.; 5 in., 25c.
Scottii, 3 in., 8c.; 4 in., 12½c.; 5 in., 15c.

CHINESE PRIMROSES
Finest mixed, strong, 2 in., 2c.
Primula Obconica, Carmine, Hybrid, Grand. fim. Alba, Rosea, Lilac. 2 in., 2c.
" " Double and new Red 2 in., 3c.
Asparagus Sprengerii, and **Plumosus** 2 in., 2c.
Jerusalem Cherries, 2 in. and 2½ in. pots, $2.00 per 100.
Flowering Begonias, 8 kinds, 2 in. 2½c.
Cash or C. O. D.

BYER BROS. Chambersburg, Pa.

Mention The Florists' Exchange when writing.

FERNS You Must Have

Only 5,000 left; speak quick.

Piersoni, 5 in., 20c.; 4 in., 15c.; 3 in., 10c.
Scottii, 5 in., 20c.; 4 in., 15c.; 3 in., 10c.
Bostons, 3 in., ready to shift, 10c.
Asparagus Plumosus Nanus, 3½ in. 6c; 2½ in., $2.50 per 100.
Asparagus Sprengerii, 3½ in., 6c.
20,000 Field Carnations.
Hydrangeas Otaksa and **Vinca** maj., variegated, strong 2½ in., $2.50 per 100.
Write me. Cash please.

BENJAMIN CONNELL, West Grove, Pa.

Mention The Florists' Exchange when writing.

FERN SEEDLINGS
FROM FLATS

Are now in fine shape for potting, including the following varieties: **Pteris Cretica Cristata, Pteris Cretica Albo-Lineata, Pteris Adiantoides, Pteris Argyraea, Pteris Mayii, Cyrtomium Falcatum, Aspidium Tsussemense, Onychium Japonica, Doodia Aspera.** My selection, $1.00 per 100; $8.50 per 1000. If by mail add 10c. per 100 for postage.

Assorted Ferns for dishes, fine stocky plants from 2¼ in. pots at $3.00 per 100; $25.00 per 1000; 250 at 1000 rate; 3 in. $6.00 per 100.

Adiantum Cuneatum, 5 in. $20.00 per 100.

FRANK N. ESKESEN, MADISON, N. J.

Mention The Florists' Exchange when writing.

BOSTON FERNS

Taken from bench, $10.00 and $20.00 per 100.
5 and 6 inch **Pot Ferns,** from $3.00 per doz. up
Extra fine stock.
Geraniums, 3½ inch stock, $4.00 per 100.

BOCK, THE FLORIST,
2394 MASS AVENUE NORTH CAMBRIDGE, MASS.

Mention The Florists' Exchange when writing.

FERNS

Are now in fine shape. A good variety and nice bushy stock, 2¼ in., $3.00 per 100; $25.00 per 1000.
Kentia Belmoreana, 4 in., clean and bushy, 25c. 5 in. 50c.; 6 in. 75c.
Boston Ferns, Piersoni and **Scottii,** from bench, 25c. each.
Cocos Weddeliana, 10c.

H. WESTON, HEMPSTEAD, N. Y.

Mention The Florists' Exchange when writing.

NEPHROLEPIS WHITMANI

is the fern to grow.

Having ordered a large quantity I can fill your orders at short notice. Price, $25.00 per 100; $200.00 per 1000.

S. S. SKIDELSKY,
824 No. 24 St., Philadelphia, Pa.

Mention The Florists' Exchange when writing.

FERNS

	Doz.	100
SCOTTII, 2½ inch	$0.75	$5.00
BARROWSII, 2½ inch	1.25	8.00

THE CONARD & JONES CO.
WEST GROVE, PA.

Mention The Florists' Exchange when writing.

NEPHROLEPIS

Whitmani, 2¼ in., $25.00 per 100.
Barrowsii, $10.00 per 100.

Henry H. Barrows & Son, Whitman, Mass.

Mention The Florists' Exchange when writing.

OUR LITTLE PET

From Aschmann in Philadelphia I bought
An Araucaria, a pet for our little girl;
Now we have two pets, the pride of our thought:
The little girl so sweet, a head full of curls,
And the Araucaria with it s everlasting green,
A more joyful home you never have seen.

Watch us Grow!!

ARAUCARIA EXCELSA, the best of all decorative plants nature produces: a specialty. Every man in business life, to be successful, must adopt one thing as his specialty, and that specialty, whatever he may select, and of whatever nature it may be, he must guard, study and push to such an extent, that it not only benefits himself; but he must conduct it so, that every one who seeks his aid, service or his articles, whatever he advertises or practices, will **share a slice** of his **activity and prosperity.** I made the importation and cultivation of Araucaria as a special study in my life. The following figures will show you my success in business: In the first year I began with an import of 250; in the eleventh year (now 1906) my importation has grown up to 6,000 (come and see it). On account of the Araucaria growing yearly in favor as a much admired decorative plant for the arbor, bed room, dining and sitting rooms, stores, hotels, lawns and porches by the plant-consuming peoples all over the country, the **outlook** will be of an importation of at least 8,000 to 10,000 in the Spring of 1907. To secure this vast amount for 1907, I am now on the ocean, per steamer New Amsterdam, sailing from Hoboken, August 15, striking for Belgium and making contracts for next year. I shall also at the same time bring over with me a large lot of choice Azalea Indica, Palms, etc. for Christmas and Easter forcing. No money will be spared in obtaining for my customers the cream of the Belgium greenhouses.

Please note lowest price now going for August and September:

ARAUCARIA EXCELSA

12 to 14 in. 5½ in. pots, 3 to 4 tiers, 2-yr. old, 50c. 14 to 16 in., 5½ in. pots, 3 to 4 tiers, 2-yr. old, 60c. 16 to 18 in. 5½ to 6 in. pots, 4 to 5 tiers, 3-yr. old, 75c. 18 to 20 in., 6 in. pots, 5 to 6 tiers, 4-yr. old, $1.00. 20 to 24 in. 6 in. to 7 in. pots, 5 to 6 tiers, 4-yr. old, $1.25. 36-40 to 50 in. 7 in. pots, specimen plants from $2.50 to $3.00 each.

ARAUCARIA COMPACTA ROBUSTA — have several thousand of them; can supply all wants. These plants were never so fine in shape and condition as this year. The set of the greenhouse, as broad as long, 12 to 20 in., in height, 3 to 4 perfect tiers, 20 to 30 inches across, 3-4-5 year old, 6 to 7 in. pots, $1.25, $1.50, $1.75, $2.00, $2.50 to $3.00 each.

ARAUCARIA EXCELSA GLAUCA — This variety on account of its beautiful Green-Blueish tiers, dwarf habit, fine compact shape, gives it a striking appearance, and anybody seeing them, must undoubtedly fall in love with them at sight. Plants, 6-7 inch pots, 3-4-5 perfect tiers, 3-4 year old, 15 to 25 inch high, from 15 to 30 in. across, $1.25, $1.50, $1.75, $2.00 to $2.50 each.

SOLANUM or JERUSALEM CHERRY, $5.00 per 100.

KENTIA BELMOREANA, 5½ to 6 in. pots, bushy, fine plants, from 75 cts. to $1.00 to $1.25 each.

KENTIA FORSTERIANA, 7 in. pots, made-up plants, 1 large in center, 3 smaller sizes, 22 to 26 in. high around, gives them a good appearance, $2.00 each. 6 in. pots, single plants, 35 to 40 in. high, 5 to 6 good leaves, 4 year old, $1.25 to $1.50 each; 6 in. pots, 30 to 35 in. high, 4 year old, 5 good leaves, $1.00; 5½ in. pots, 3 year old, 25 to 30 in. high, 5 good leaves, 75c. made-up plants, 3 and 4 in. pots, 18 to 20 in. high, 25 cts. to 30 cts. each.

ARECA LUTESCENS, made-up, 25 cts.

COCOS WEDDELIANA, 15 cts.

CYCAS REVOLUTA (Sago Palm), 6 in.-7 in. pots, with from 6 to 20 leaves per plant, 10 cts. per leaf.

NEPHROLEPIS BARROWSII, 6 in. pots, strong, ready for 7-8 in., 50c. 4 in. pots, ready for 6-7 in., 25c.

NEPHROLEPIS SCOTTII, 6 in. pots, large, ready for 6-7 in. 50c; 5½ in. pots, 40c.; 5 in. 35c.; 4 in. 20c. to 25c.

BOSTON FERNS, 4 in. 20c. to 25c. I have them by the thousand, 5 in.: 30c. to 35c.

FERNS for dishes, a fine assortment, 2¼ in., $5.00 per 100; 3 in., $6.00 per 100.

FICUS ELASTICA, 6 in., 50c.

ASPARAGUS PLUMOSUS NANUS, 3 in., 6c; 4 in., 10c.

CASH WITH ORDER

When ordering, say whether the plants should be shipped in the pots or not

GODFREY ASCHMANN
Importer and Wholesale Grower of Pot Plants
1012 Ontario Street, - - PHILADELPHIA, PA.

Mention The Florists' Exchange when writing.

DRACAENA TERMINALIS

Matured canes always ready for shipment. Delivered to any part of the United States for 10 cents a foot. Send cash for a trial order.

PORTO RICO PINEAPPLE CO., RIO PIEDRAS, PORTO RICO.

Mention The Florists' Exchange when writing.

ROBERT CRAIG & CO.

ROSES, PALMS, CROTONS

CARNATIONS and Novelties in DECORATIVE PLANTS

Market and 49th Sts. PHILADELPHIA, PA.

Mention The Florists' Exchange when writing.

ORCHIDS

Largest Importers, Exporters, Growers and Hybridists in the world.

Sander, St. Albans, England
and
235 Broadway, Room 1, New York City

Mention The Florists' Exchange when writing.

COCOS PALMS.

Strong 2¼ inch at $1.50 per dozen. Write for lowest prices on Kentias.

Jas. F. Barclay R. I. GREENHOUSES Pawtucket, R. I.

Mention The Florists' Exchange when writing.

ASPARAGUS SPRENGERI

Large plants from 3 in. pots 5c. each.
Asparagus Plumosus Nanus, about 200 fine plants left, 3 in. pots 5c. each, to close them out.
Liberal count on both.

R. G. HANFORD, Norwalk, Conn.

Mention The Florists' Exchange when writing.

Familiar Sights at S.A.F. Convention

Will be the Out Door Exhibits
Prominent among which are Our Displays
All adjacent to Convention Hall

Do not miss our beds of **Novelty Cannas, Geraniums, Salvias, etc.**; also Groups of **Hardy Perennials**, such as **Boltonia, Rudbeckia Triloba, Helianthus, Phlox** and others.

Your inspection invited and all inquiries cheerfully answered.

When home from Convention we would be pleased to receive your orders for

FALL STOCK

Field Clumps of **Violets, Carnations, Phlox**, 4 in. **Roses**, offered in the several previous issues of this paper.

NATHAN SMITH & SON, Adrian, Mich.

Mention The Florists' Exchange when writing.

WHOLESALE TRADE LIST

AMPELOPSIS VEITCHII, 4 inch pots, long runners $1.50 per doz; $10.00 per 100.
ASPARAGUS PLUMOSUS, 2½ in. pots, $3.00 per 100.
ASPARAGUS SPRENGERII, 5 in. pots, $2.00 per doz.
CLEMATIS PANICULATA, 4 in. pots, $1.50 per doz., $10.00 per 100; 3 in. pots, 75c. per doz.; $6.00 per 100.
DRACÆNA INDIVISA, 6 in. pots, $3.00 per doz.
IVY, Hardy English, 4 in. pots, $1.50 per doz.; $10.00 per 100.
POINSETTIAS, fine plants, 3 in. pots, $6.00 per 100.
The real **BRIDAL MYRTLE**, elegant round shaped plants 6 in. pots $3.00 per doz.
STEVIA, dwarf and tall, 2½ in. pots, $3.00 per 100.

C. EISELE, 11th & Roy Streets, PHILADELPHIA, PA.

Mention The Florists' Exchange when writing.

Decorative Plants

Latania Borbonica, 2½ in. pots, $3.00; 3 in.; $6.00; 4 in., $15.00 per 100. Large specimen plants from $2.00 to $5.00 each.

Kentia Belmoreana and Forsteriana, 2½ in. pots, $8.00; 3 in., $15.00; 5 in., $60.00 per 100; 6 in. $15.00 per doz.; 7 in. and upward, $1.75 to $35.00 each.

Areca Lutescens, 3 in. $10.00; 4 in. $20.00 per 100; 8 in., $1.00 each and upward.

Pandanus Utilis, 3 in. pots, $3.00; 4 in., $20.00 per 100.

Phœnix Reclinata, 5 in. pots, $35.00 per 100.

Phœnix Canariensis, fine specimen plants, from $3.00 to $35.00 each.

Araucaria Excelsa, 5 in. pots, $65.00 per 100.

Assorted Ferns, 2¼ in. pots, $3.00 per 100. **Nephrolepis Compacta**, 3 in. pots, $8.00; 4 in., $15.00 per 100.

Plants in Fine Condition.

JOHN BADER, Troy Hill, Allegheny, Pa.

Mention The Florists' Exchange when writing.

SMILAX PLANTS

From 2 in. pots, strong and bushy ready for shift, $1.00 per 100; $9.00 per 1000. 3 in., very fine, $2.00 per 100; $18.00 per 1000.

Seedlings, from boxes, $4.00 per 1000. Can ship at once.

R. KILBOURN, CLINTON, N. Y.

Mention The Florists' Exchange when writing.

Sphagnum Moss and Cedar Poles

Moss, 5 barrel bale, $1.25; 2 bales, $2.25; 5 bales, $5.00; 10 bales, $9.50. **Poles**, 2 in. butt, 8 ft. long, $15.00 per 1000; 2½ in. butt, 10 to 12 feet long, $22.50 per 1000.

H. R. AKERS, Chatsworth, N. J.

Mention The Florists' Exchange when writing.

ASPARAGUS

	Per 100
Sprengerii, 3 in.	$3.00
" 2 in.	1.50
Plumosus Nanus, 2 in.	2.00
Primula Obconica, Grandiflora Alba, Rosea and Hybrida, 2 in.	2.00
" " **Robusta and Compacta**, 2 in.	3.00
Smilax, nice, 2½ in.	1.25
Paris Daisy, white and yellow, 3 in., bushy,	3.00

Orders booked for early September delivery of

Cineraria Grand flora Hybrida, Michell's Giant Prize, 2 in.	2.00
" **Stellata**, Sutton's, 2 in.	2.50
Calceolaria, James Superb mixed, 2 in.	3.00

Cash with order, please.

GEO. J. HUGHES, BERLIN, N. J.

Mention The Florists' Exchange when writing.

EMERSON C. McFADDEN

Wholesale Grower

Asparagus Plumosus Nanus, Etc.

Short Hills, N. J.

Tel. 28 A.

Mention The Florists' Exchange when writing.

SURPLUS STOCK—CHEAP

200 **The Bride** roses, 2 in. pots, $1.75 per 100.
500 **Bridesmaid** roses, 2 in. pots, $2.00 per 100.
1000 **Cannas**, red and yellow, strong, $8.00 per 100.
50 **Dracaena Indivisa**, 3½ in., 6c. each.
2000 **Cuphea**, Cigar Plant, 2 in. pots, 75c. per 100.
2000 **Feverfew**, Double White, 2 in. pots, 50c. per 100.
10000 **Jerusalem Cherries**, big and strong, ready for 4 in. pots, from 2 in. pots at $2.00 per 100. You will never get better or cheaper stock than this. **E. I. Rawlings, Quakertown, Pa.**

Mention The Florists' Exchange when writing.

A FEW BARGAINS TO MAKE ROOM

Asparagus Plumosus Nanus, 2½ in. pots, fine stock, $3.00 per 100. **Asparagus Sprengerii**, 4 in. pots, fine stock, $4.00 per 100. 5-6 in. pans and 10-2 in. pans of **Cypripedium Insigne**, fine strong stock that will bloom this season. Write for price. Cash with order.

JOSEPH TOWELL, PATERSON, N. J.

Mention The Florists' Exchange when writing.

ASPARAGUS

Sprengerii, extra strong, 3 in. pots, $5 per 100. Extra Strong, 4 in. pots, $6 per 100.
Smilax, 2½ in. pots $2 per 100.
Cabbage Plants, Flat Dutch, Succession and Winningstadt, $1.50 per 1000. Cash with order.

S. G. BENJAMIN, Fishkill, N. Y.

Mention The Florists' Exchange when writing.

Dwyer's Pot Grown Strawberry Plants

Strong, healthy plants from selected stock of choicest fruiting varieties sure to give satisfaction and **PRODUCE A FULL CROP IN 1907**. We also have a full line of Fruits and Ornamental Trees, Plants, Vines, etc., for Fall Planting.
We do Landscape Gardening in all its branches. **Catalogue Free**

T. J. DWYER & CO., P. O. Box 6 Cornwall, New York

Mention The Florists' Exchange when writing.

BROTHER FLORISTS

ARE YOU GOING TO DAYTON?

If so, don't fail to see the display of CANNAS planted in the City parks. We feel sure that they will interest you at least, but if you should spend a few minutes or hours in looking them over and should conclude that you had wasted your time just put in your bill for the same and we will give you check in full. We have been told that no one will see them, but we think "PERHAPS." There are but 188 different varieties of them and all but 17 are of our own originating. There are but 1445 of them, and they comprise all the Cannas, we believe, that are in the city parks. Probably this small display wont cut much ice, in comparison with those at the fair grounds but we hope that You will go and see them any way. . . . .

Southern Floral Nursery Co., Bucatunna, Miss. and Fruitdale, Ala.

Mention The Florists' Exchange when writing.

A Few Good Things YOU WANT

Dracæna Indivisa, 4 and 5 in., $10.00 and $25.00 per 100.

Asparagus Sprengeri, 2 in., $2.50 per 100.

Geraniums, S. A. Nutt, Castellane, John Doyle, Perkins, Double Gen. Grant, Poitevine, Mme. Salleroi, 2 in. pots, $2.00 per 100; 3 in. pots $4.00 per 100. Rooted Cuttings, $1.00 per 100.

Rex Begonia, nice plants, 2 and 2½ in., $6.00 per 100.

Asparagus Plumosus, 2 in. $3.00 per 100.
Boston Fern 5 in. 30c each.
Pierson Fern 6 in. 50c each.

GEO. M. EMMANS, Newton, N. J.

Mention The Florists' Exchange when writing.

2,000 **Smilax**, 2½ in., strong, cut back, per 100, $1.50; the lot for $17.50.
200 **Asparagus Plumosus**, $2.50 per 100.
1,000 **Asparagus Sprengerii**, 2½ in., $2.00 per 100; the lot for $17.00. This is strong and ready for a shift.

J. S. BLOOM, RIEGELSVILLE, PA.

Mention The Florists' Exchange when writing.

Stevia Serrata

True, winter blooming, strong, bushy, ready to shift, 3½ in. pots, $5.00 per 100; $45.00 per 1000.
ASPARAGUS SPRENGERII, 2 inch, very strong, $2.50 per 100; $20.00 per 1000.

DEAN FERRIS, Peekskill, N.Y.

Mention The Florists' Exchange when writing.

Primula Obconica Grandiflora

2 1-2 in., $2.50 per 100. Ask for list (seedlings of hardy plants)

BAUDISCH & CO.,
537 Fulton Street UNION HILL, N. J.

Mention The Florists' Exchange when writing.

GARDENIA VEITCHII

500 strong, bushy plants from 3 inch pots, ready for a shift, at $12.00 per 100, or will make a special low price for the lot if taken at once for cash.

MADSEN & CHRISTENSEN, WOODRIDGE, N. J.

Mention The Florists' Exchange when writing.

VIOLETS

MARIE LOUISE Violets, clean and healthy in every particular, ready August 15th, 3 in. pots $5.00 per 100.

CASH WITH ORDER.

WM. J. CHINNICK, TRENTON, N. J.

Mention The Florists' Exchange when writing.

Asparagus Robustus.

An Asparagus that is worthh a trial by every florist, similar in habit and appearance to Plumosus, but superior to that variety in every way.

Price per 100 $3.50; per 1000 $30.00.

This price is good only for orders received on or before Aug. 27th.

Asparagus Sprengerii.

Extra fine, good strong plants from rose pots, I have a surplus of these and want them cleaned up by August 27th, the price being good only for orders received on or before that date.

Price per 100 $1.50; per 1000 $12.50.

A few thousand very good seconds at $1.00 per 100.

Asparagus Plumosus and Smilax.

Plumosus very fine stock at $2.00 per 100.

Smilax good seconds at $1.00 per 100

Geraniums

Rooted Cuttings.

Orders accepted for delivery on and after Nov. 1st, at $10.00 and $12.50 per per 1000. I will have fourteen houses planted to stock plants, send for list of varieties.

At Dayton I will be stopping at the Algonquin Hotel and will have samples of **Robustus** and **Sprengerii** with me.

ALBERT M. HERR, Lancaster, Pa.

Mention The Florists' Exchange when writing.

VIOLETS, SMILAX

Lady Campbell and **California** out of 2½ in. healthy stock plants, $2.00 per 100; $17.50 per 1,000

Smilax, fine bushy plants 2½ in., $1.25 per 100; $10.00 per 1000

J. C. SCHMIDT CO., Bristol, Pa.

Mention The Florists' Exchange when writing.

Governor Herrick Violet

The finest single violet ever offered. Write me about it today.

Price: One dozen, $2.00; 100, $10.00; 1000 at $75.00 or 5000 or more at $60.00 per 1000. No. 1 Stock.

H. R. CARLTON, WILLOUGHBY, OHIO.

Mention The Florists' Exchange when writing.

WASHINGTON, PA.—William R. Smith, Superintendent of the U. S. Botanic Garden, Washington, D. C., was a recent visitor here. He came at the request of the managers of the Washington Cemetery for consultation in reference to the improvement and beautifying of the grounds. Mr. Smith declared the cemetery was susceptible of being made one of the most attractive in the country. He left for Pittsburg, Pa., where he is to be the guest of his friend William Falconer, Superintendent of the Allegheny Cemetery.

NORTH ABINGTON, MASS.—Work has begun on the building of a new greenhouse on Adams street by Sidney Littlefield. The greenhouse will be about 300 feet long and 50 feet wide. It will be connected with another large greenhouse, which was erected some time ago.

The Bay State Nursery Company is also making many improvements at its plant on Adams street and now is arranging for the erection of a large cold storage cellar, which will be 127 feet long and 45 feet wide. The business of this concern is growing rapidly and goods are being shipped to all parts of the United States.

VICTORY

Strong healthy field grown plants, now ready. First size, $15.00 per 100; Second size, $12.00 per 100; Third size, $10.00 per 100. A discount for cash with order. GUTTMAN & WEBBER, 43 West 28th St., N. Y

CARNATIONS

	Per 100	Per 1000		Per 100	Per 1000		Per 100	Per 1000
FIANCEE	$6 00		MORNING GLORY	$4 00	$35 00	FLORA HILL	$5 00	$45 00
LAWSON	6 00	$50 00	LIEUT. PEARY	8 00	75 00	WHITE CLOUD	5 00	45 00
NELSON FISHER	7 00	60 00	FRED BURKI	7 00	60 00	CHICAGO (Red Bradt)	5 00	45 00
GUARDIAN ANGEL	4 00	35 00	BOSTON MARKET	5 00	45 00	HARLOWARDEN	6 00	50 00

WIETOR BROS., 51 Wabash Ave., CHICAGO

Mention The Florists' Exchange when writing.

150,000 FIELD GROWN CARNATIONS

VERY FINE; PERFECTLY HEALTHY.

Lady Bountiful, Cardinal, Buttercup,
Price, $7.00 per 100.

Enchantress, Lawson, Queen, Flamingo, Roosevelt, M. A. Patten,
Price, $6.00 per 100.

Queen Louise, E. A. Nelson, Eldorado, Flora Hill, Portia, Crocker, J. H. Manley, Prosperity, Dorothy,
Price, $5.00 per 100.

J. L. DILLON, Bloomsburg, Pa.

Mention The Florists' Exchange when writing.

100,000 FIELD GROWN CARNATION PLANTS

30,000 LAWSON

	Per 100
LAWSON	$5.00
ELDORADO	5.00
ESTELLE	5.00
MAY NAYLOR (White)	5.00
BRADT	5.00
PROSPERITY	4.00
LAWSON SECONDS	3.50

EXTRA SELECTED DEFIANCE MIGNONETTE SEED, $1.00 PER TRADE PACKET

EDWARD J. TAYLOR, Southport, Conn.

Mention The Florists' Exchange when writing.

Field Grown Carnation Plants

THE LARGEST AND FINEST WE EVER HAD.

THE QUEEN, FAIR MAID, MRS. PATTEN — $5.00 per 100
WHITE LAWSON, PINK LAWSON, NELSON FISHER — $6.00 per 100
ENCHANTRESS, $7.00 per 100.

H. F. LITTLEFIELD, - - WORCESTER, MASS.

Mention The Florists' Exchange when writing.

Field Grown Carnation Plants

ALL THE STANDARD VARIETIES

List and prices on application.

Rose plants 1000 Liberty 3 in. pots .... $5.00 per 100
1000 " 2¼ " " .... 4.00 " 100

THE LEO NIESSEN COMPANY, 1217 Arch St. Philadelphia, Pa.

Mention The Florists' Exchange when writing.

CARNATIONS | FIELD PLANTS

	1st size per 100	2d size per 100
Glendale	$12.00	
Robt. Craig	12.00	
Bountiful	8.00	$6.00
Belle	7.00	5.00
Mrs. Lawson	6.00	

	1st size per 100	2d size per 100
Boston Market	$6.00	$5.00
White Cloud	6.00	
Nelson Fisher		6.00
Flamingo	7.00	5.00
Crane		5.00
Estelle	2d size $5.00; 3d size $3.50	

ROSES, 300 4 in. **Maids**, 150 4 in. **Brides**, $7.00 per 100. 500, 2½ in. **Gates**, 300, 2½ in. **Brides**, 150, 2½ in. **Perle**, $3.50 per 100. **Richmond**, 2 in. at $5.00; 3 in. at $8.00.
FERNS, **Boston** and **Piersoni**, 2½ in., $4.00 per 100; 4 in., $10.00; 5 in., $20.00; 6 in., $35.00, 7 in., $80.00
ASPARAGUS PLUMOSUS, 2 in., $2.00 per 100. **SPRENGERII**, 3 in., $6.00 per 100. Cash or C. O. D

W. J. & M. S. VESEY, Fort Wayne, Ind.

Mention The Florists' Exchange when writing.

MABELLE

New Pink Carnation for 1907

Color.—A peculiar shade of lovely pink, with a faint yellowish cast; several shades lighter than the Lawson. Unlike most pinks, the brightest sun does not injure the color.

Size.—Three to four inches in diameter when established.

Odor.—Pleasing, but not strong.

Stems.—Invariably strong, but always graceful, ranging from 12 to 30 inches during the season.

Habit, etc.—A very quick active grower, making specimen plants in a short time, even from late cuttings. On account of its rapid growth, requires supporting very soon after benching. Gets away rapidly, blooms early and gives long stems right from the start.

Productiveness.—Prodigious is the best word we know of to use here. It is the most incessant bloomer early and late, we have ever grown.

STOCK LIMITED.

Delivery January 5th to 10th and later.

Price, $12.00 per 100, $100. per 1000.

THE H. WEBER & SONS CO., OAKLAND, MD.

Mention The Florists' Exchange when writing.

ENCHANTRESS

Field-grown, ready August 15, $6,00 per 100; $50.00 per 1000.

WHITE BROTHERS, Gasport, N. Y.

Mention The Florists' Exchange when writing.

CARNATIONS

Let us have your order now for the coming new Carnations: January delivery. **Aristocrat, Windsor, White Enchantress, Helen M. Gould, Beacon** and **Rose Pink Enchantress.**

WM. SWAYNE, Box 226, Kennett Square, Pa

Mention The Florists' Exchange when writing

CARNATIONS

Second size field plants Enchantress, Lawson, Boston Market, Queen etc., $3.00 per 100; $25.00 per 1000.

Ardisia crenulata, strong, bushy plants from bench, well berried, ready for 5-6 in. pots, $6. and $9.00 per doz.

Geraniums, 12 varieties. Have order books for Fall delivery; can fill orders from 100-100,000. Get my prices. Standard, 5 in. pots, $0.00 per 1000; 6000, $40.00, saucers 5c. 10c. Cash.

WM. S. HERZOG, MORRIS PLAINS, N. J.

Mention The Florists' Exchange when writing

CARNATIONS

May Naylor, Marion & Joost, fine, field-grown plants, $4.00 per 100.
Alyssum, double Giant, for Winter flowering 2½ in. pots, $1.50 per 100.

J. C. SCHMIDT CO BRISTOL, PA.

Mention The Florists' Exchange when writing

CARNATIONS

Strong, Field Grown

	Per 100	1000		Per 100
Cervera	$4.00	$35.00	W. Scott	$3.50
Queen Louise	4.00		McGowan	3.50
Fr. Joost	3.50		Goethe	4.00

ISABELLE GREENHOUSES BABYLON, L. I., N. Y.

Mention The Florists' Exchange when writing

CARNATIONS

	per 1000	per 100
500 Queen Louise, field grown		$4.00
Asp. Plumosus, 2¼ in. pots, Aug. 15th		2.00
Cineraria, Sept. 15th		2.00
Pansy Seed, large flowering, per oz., $4.00		

PRIMROSES

	per 100
Chinese, 2¼ in. pots, Aug. 10th	$2.00
Obconica, Rosea and Alba, Aug. 10th	2.00
P. W. Narcissus, 13 ctm., Sept.	1.25

5 varieties Cannas, field grown clumps, $15.00 per 100.

CASH PLEASE

JOS. H. CUNNINGHAM, Delaware, O.

Mention The Florists' Exchange when writing.

FIELD GROWN

CARNATIONS

	100	1000
ENCHANTRESS	$7.00	$60.00
QUEEN LOUISE	5.00	45.00
BOSTON MARKET	5.00	45.00
WHITE LAWSON	6.00	
FLAMINGO	6.00	

Cash with order please.

FARNAM P. CAIRD,
271 RIVER ST., TROY, N. Y.

Mention The Florists' Exchange when writing.

FIELD GROWN

CARNATION PLANTS

Extra fine; grown on new ground; no diseases; no stem rot, of the following varieties:

JOOST — FLORA HILL
WHITE CLOUD — PERU
GLACIER — QUEEN LOUISE

At $5.00 per 100; $40.00 per 1000.
Cash with order please.

C. W. ESPY & SON
BROOKVILLE, PA.

Mention The Florists' Exchange when writing.

FIELD GROWN

CARNATIONS

VICTORY, ROBT. CRAIG, JOHN E. HAINES....$15.00 per 100.
FIANCEE, MRS. BRADT, DAHEIM, MRS. M. A. PATTEN, PROSPERITY....$6.00 per 100.

CHARLES H. TOTTY
MADISON, N. J.

Mention The Florists' Exchange when writing.

SURPLUS CARNATIONS

1200	Lawson	$6.00 per 100
1400	Joost	4.00 " "
800	Norway	5.00 " "
125	Queen Louise	5.00 " "

THE CHATHAM FLORAL CO., CHATHAM, N. Y.

Mention The Florists' Exchange when writing.

FIELD GROWN

Carnation Plants

McGowan, $30.0 per 1000. Cash with order.

WM. BELL, BAYSIDE, L. I.

Mention The Florists' Exchange when writing.

CARNATIONS

PLANTS FROM FIELD

Fair Maid, Queen, Mrs. Patten, $5.00 per 100; $45.00 per 1000. Strong and healthy.

Satisfaction guaranteed. Cash with Order.

HUGH CHESNEY, Farmington, Ct.

Mention The Florists' Exchange when writing.

50,000 Large, Healthy, Bushy Carnation Plants

Adonis, Flamingo, Crusader, Mrs. Patten, Neptune, Queen Louise, Roosevelt, Harry Fenn, Genevieve Lord, White Cloud, Prosperity, Ad. Cervera, Joost, Flora Hill, Ethel Crocker.

$4.00 per 100.

FIANCEE, 10c.; OUTOROON, No. 1—No. 2; RED LAWSON, LADY BOUNTIFUL, 8c.
ROBERT CRAIG Carnation, 12c.
ASPARAGUS PLUMOSUS, strong 2 1-2 in. 3c; 4in. 8c.
" SPRENGERI, 2 1-2 in. 2c.
SMILAX, 2 1-2 in. $1.50 per 100.
PARSLEY PLANTS, $3.00 per 1000.

Cash Please.

F. B. RINE, Lewisburg, Pa.

Mention The Florists' Exchange when writing.

ABUNDANCE

Healthy, stocky, field grown plants. First size, $12.00 per 100; $100.00 per 1000. Second size, $10 00 per 100; $75.00 per 1000; 250 at a 1000 rates. Delivery 15th of August.

CASH WITH ORDER.

Abundance Carnation is an easy lifter, takes hold quickly, and makes good-sized stems on first crop.

Freesia Purity bulbs all sold out clean.

RUDOLPH FISCHER, Great Neck, L.I. N.Y.

Mention The Florists' Exchange when writing.

CARNATIONS

Excellent Field Grown

The Queen	$8.00 per	100
Crimson Glow, (new)	12.00 "	100
Lieut. Peary, medium size	8.00 "	100

Cash or references with order.

DAILLEDOUZE BROTHERS
Flatbush, Brooklyn, N. Y.

Mention The Florists' Exchange when writing.

Field Grown CARNATIONS

6000 White Lawson .... $6.00 per 100.
1000 Roosevelt — 2000 Harlowarden
5000 Queen Louise — 300 Crisis
500 Flamingo — 200 F. Burki
100 Eclipse.

$5.00 per 100; $45.00 per 1000.
Limestone land, no stem rot.

CASH WITH ORDER.

Wells Fargo, American, Adams, U. S. Express

W. SABRANSKY, KENTON, O.

Mention The Florists' Exchange when writing.

FINE FIELD-GROWN

CARNATION PLANTS

Prosperity	per 100	$6.00
Mrs. T. W. Lawson	" "	6.00
Queen Louise	" "	4.50
White Cloud	" "	4.50
Smilax Plants	" "	1.50

Cash please.

R. I. HART, Hackettstown, N. J.

Mention the Florists' Exchange when writing.

CARNATIONS

Field Grown plants for August 27 and later delivery.

THE H. WEBER & SONS CO.,
OAKLAND, MD.

Mention The Florists' Exchange when writing.

HOW TO GROW MUSHROOMS

Price, - - - 10 cents.

A. T. De La Mare Ptg. & Pub. Co.,
2-8 Duane St. New York.

AUCTION SALE

THE ENTIRE HORTICULTURAL ESTABLISHMENT OF

G. J. NOR DEL

(Known as Nor Del's Greenhouses)

Belmont Ave., Long Branch, N. J.

8 greenhouses, pipe (4 inch), 3 boilers, **3 Excellent Horses,** sound, gentle, in finest possible condition; 3 trucks (single and double), delivery wagon (glass sides), farm wagon, dump cart, sleigh, buggy, runabout, wagon bodies, harness, tools, etc., etc.

Also a large variety of **Palms, Hydrangeas, Ferns** and **miscellaneous plants** of every variety and description. **Fine Rubbers, Specimen Cycas,** etc.

Farm tools, including harrow, single horse mower, iron lawn roller, implements of every character, etc. Rustic vases, tubs, boxes, etc. Fine quality jardinieres, pedestals, pans, wire work, office furniture, etc.

An unparalleled opportunity to secure the equipment of a modern up-to-date florist's plant. Everything in fine order and tip top condition, and practically as good as new. Reached from New York by C. R. R. of N. J., Penn. R. R., or via boats of the Patten Line (low freight rates via Patten Line, pier being but a short distance from greenhouses.) This sale absolutely unreserved, (Mr. Nor Del retiring from business.) Will positively be held

THURSDAY, AUGUST 23, 1906

Beginning promptly at 12 NOON. For further details address

G. J. NOR DEL, Belmont Ave., Long Branch, N. J.

J. P. CLEARY, Auctioneer

Mention The Florists' Exchange when writing.

FIELD-GROWN

Carnation Plants

Send for price and list of varieties.

Chicago Carnation Co., Joliet, Ill.

Mention The Florists' Exchange when writing.

FIELD GROWN CARNATIONS

Strong, healthy plants; now ready. **Fair Maid, Joost, Boston Market, Louise and Eventide** (Prolific bright scarlet), No. 1 plants, $4.00 per 100.

Pink and White Lawson at $5.00 per 100. **Delicacy,** white, slightly variegated, flowers being perfect and good size, very strong and prolific, $5.00 per per 100. Packed to carry safely.

CHAS. BLACK, HIGHTSTOWN, N. J.

Mention The Florists' Exchange when writing.

CARNATIONS

Good, strong, healthy, field grown carnation plants from new soil. A No. 1 plants in every way; well branched and free from disease. **Enchantress, Boston Market, Lady Bountiful, Mrs. M. A. Patten, Nelson Fisher,** Ethel Ward. Prices on application.

VALLEY VIEW GREENHOUSES, Marlborough, N.Y.
VELIE BROS., Props.

Mention The Florists' Exchange when writing.

FIELD GROWN

CARNATIONS and VIOLETS

Extra strong plants of Mrs. Lawson, Queen, Boston Market, Fair Maid and Harlowarden, No. 1, $6.00 per 100; $50.00 per 1000; No. 2, $5.00 per 100; $45.00 per 1000. CAMPBELL VIOLETS, large clumps, $5.00 per 100; $45.00 per 1000. PRINCESS OF WALES, $6.00 per 100; $50.00 per 1000. No better stock at any price. Cash with order please.

R. ENGELMAN & SON, Pittsfield, Mass.

Mention The Florists' Exchange when writing.

CARNATION PLANTS

ALL SOLD.

HENRY EICHHOLZ,
WAYNESBORO, PA.

Mention The Florists' Exchange when writing.

CARNATIONS

FINE FIELD GROWN PLANTS
CORRESPONDENCE SOLICITED

A. B. DAVIS & SON, Inc., Purcellville Va.

Mention The Florists' Exchange when writing.

CARNATIONS

F. DORNER & SONS CO.
LA FAYETTE, IND.

Mention The Florists' Exchange when writing.

CARNATIONS

SMITH & GANNETT,
GENEVA, N. Y.

Mention The Florists' Exchange when writing.

Jensen & Dekema

CARNATION SPECIALISTS

674 W. Foster Ave., CHICAGO.

Mention The Florists' Exchange when writing.

S. J. GODDARD

Framingham, Mass.

Rooted Carnation Cuttings a Specialty

Correspondence Solicited.

Mention The Florists' Exchange when writing.

Baltimore.

An Outing to Berlin, Md.

The horticulturists of Maryland together with sixty Baltimore florists attended the Summer meeting of the Maryland Horticultural Society, at Berlin and Ocean City, on the invitation of Mayor Orlando Harrison on August 8 and 9. Over 500 members were royally entertained by the Messrs. Harrison & Sons. A glorious time was had which will ever be remembered by those who participated. Mr. Harrison who is Mayor of Berlin, president of the American Association of Nurserymen and vice-president of the Maryland Horticultural Society, received his guests at his Berlin Manor Grove, and made a speech of welcome, in which he stated that it was a great pleasure to welcome horticulturists, as they are men and women of high moral worth. He claimed the soil is the basis of all wealth, and everyone who aided in its development is a public benefactor and a blessing to future generations. Maryland, he declared, is primarily a horticultural state.

Captain R. W. Silvester, president of Maryland Agricultural College, Dr. E. J. Dirickson, Professor Beattie, U. S. Department of Agriculture and Professor Waugh of Massachusetts, also spoke most interestingly on different matters. Messrs. R. Vincent and N. F. Flitton spoke on behalf of the Gardeners' Club of Baltimore.

The Harrison Nurseries were a great revelation to the visitors. Every vehicle in the town was utilized for passengers, numerous carriages and even two hay wagons were used in the seven mile drive over the nurseries. Over 1,000 acres are covered with millions of peach, apple, pear and plum trees, all in the very best condition. These immense fields covering 14 farms are perfectly level, and the clean dark green color of the foliage indicates a vigorous, healthy growth making a novel and very pretty picture. An idea of the immensity of these nurseries can be had when it is known that there are 3,000,000 apple trees ready for budding and over one and one-half million ready for market, together with 200,000 pears and 200,000 plum trees. Sixty acres are used each year for growing strawberries; 250 men, 64 horses and mules are employed. The colored boys are experts in tying buds and will tie 3,500 a day; negro men will put in that many buds and small boys go ahead in the rows stripping the lower branches of the seedlings making them ready for the budders and tyers. The method is perfect and 90 per cent. of the budded trees grow. Young colored women gather the branches containing suitable buds. It was a surprise to the members of the Gardeners' Club to see how the colored people attended to their work with such quickness and perfection. The entire nursery is kept as clean as a market garden by the use of up-to-date implements. Cow peas are sowed among the trees for a Winter mulch.

At Ocean City the members enjoyed themselves on the boardwalk, in the surf, bowling and with other amusements.

The Gardeners and Florists' Club held its meeting on Monday last. About twenty members have promised to attend the S. A. F. Dayton convention and it was decided by about 12 to 15 to join the Philadelphia delegation at Harrisburg, Pa., Monday, August 20. The rest will leave several days sooner by the B. & O. route.

The club passed resolutions of thanks to Messrs. Harrison & Sons, Berlin, Md., for the kind hospitality extended to the members on the occasion of the Summer meeting of the State Horticultural Society. As a token of appreciation the club sent to the Harrison firm an artistic silver water pitcher handsomely chased in fruits and flowers with the following engraving: "To J. G. Harrison & Sons, Berlin, Md., from the Gardeners' Club of Baltimore, August 8 and 9, 1906."

Active building operations are under way at I. H. Moss's fine nurseries in Govanstown, Md.

J. M. Rider, carnation grower, Brooklyn, Md., has suffered quite a loss by fire; his extensive barns, with both hay and implements, have been entirely consumed. The loss was but partially covered by insurance.

A good big representation from the Gardeners' Club will attend the S. A. F. convention. The next meeting of the club will be on Monday and the invitation on the part of the Philadelphia Florists' Club will be accepted to travel with them to Dayton. The Washington brethren have also been invited to join the same train, and it goes without saying that with Commodore Westcott, restored to health and vigor, at the head of the eastern delegation, a good time will be enjoyed en route.

CHAS. L. SEYBOLD.

Chicago.

The Late James Hartshorne.

James Hartshorne, who died in Joliet, Ill., on Monday of last week and was buried on Wednesday, was one of the most lovable and one of the most beloved members of our craft. In perfect health and spirits up to the Saturday preceding his death, the shock was intensified by its suddenness. News reached Chicago Sunday that he was seriously ill and had been operated on for some intestinal complaint. Monday morning a message was received stating that he was failing, and in the afternoon word reached here of his death.

Wednesday morning, twenty-eight members of the Chicago Florists' Club boarded the train for Joliet, and attended the last sad rites to the departed. Entirely covered with the flowers, in a beautiful assortment of designs, of which he was such a true admirer, the casket was brought out to the front of the old homestead and there the religious service was performed by Pastor Joseph C. Dent of the First Baptist church of Joliet, after which the body was taken to the cemetery, across the street from the greenhouses which he had been so instrumental in constructing.

The Masonic fraternity to which Mr. Hartshorne was allied then took charge of the body and at the cemetery performed the ritual service of the order.

A widow and five children survive.

The W. W. Barnard & Company have received the first consignment of bulbs and within a few days will have their catalogue in circulation.

Mrs. Edward Kaust left on Wednesday of last week for a vacation at her former home in Minnesota, where Mr. Kanst will join her.

H. E. Philpot of Winnepeg, Manitoba, a member of the Chicago Florists' Club, who has been here for several weeks, has made plans to proceed from the Dayton meeting to Guelph, Canada, and from there to Toronto stopping at Chicago on his return.

Florists' Club.

The monthly meeting was held in Handel Hall on Thursday evening, August 9, all of the Officers being present and with a fairly good attendance. The members proceeded to make arrangements for the trip to the annual convention at Dayton. President Hauswirth made a report of his experience in California and a few remarks were made by G. L. Grant and H. E. Philpot.

Remarks appropriate to the death of James Hartshorne were made by several members, and a committee of three, composed of George Asmus, L. H. Winterson, and W. K. Wood, were selected to draft resolutions.

W. K. WOOD.

DAYTON, O.—The Montgomery County Horticultural Society held its its regular monthly meeting recently at the residence of Charles T. Ohmer, in Ohmer Park. At the time of the organization of the Horticultural society 36 years ago, N. Ohmer, father of Chas. T. Ohmer, was elected its president. Mr. Ohmer served in this capacity for a period of 33 years. Since Mr. Ohmer's death three years ago the meetings have not been held at the Ohmer homestead, but as several requests were made by Mr. Ohmer to hold the meeting there, he very gladly consented. The guests were from all parts of the country, and numbered several hundred. A fine display of canna flowers was made by W. T. Engle.

Providence, R. I.

News of the Week.

A terrific electrical storm, leaving in its wake destruction that would do credit to a minature cyclone, passed over this vicinity, Monday evening, August 6. The storm was intensely severe in the towns of Norwood and Apponaug and several growers report damage from high winds and hail. At the nursery of Nathan Pierce & Son, a quantity of greenhouse glass was smashed and outdoor stock seriously damaged. Upon the estate of W. E. Wood, the wind and congealed particles were particularly active and destructive, laying low immense fields of asters and dahlias; while the frame for a modern carnation house, 48 by 300 feet, likewise went down before the gale.

A party of growers and store men went fishing down the bay, last Thursday. Although the results were not of such a serious nature as to affect market prices, yet almost an even hundred denizens of the briny deep were deprived of liberty and gratuitously distributed among friends. It is hoped that cottagers along shore will not fear a shipwreck has occurred, should the lost glassware eventually drift ashore.

The Midsummer exhibition of the Rhode Island Horticultural Society, takes place August 15 at Falstaff Club Hall, Westminster street. Special inducements are offered for displays of dahlias and asters, which undoubtedly will bring out a creditable showing. Admission will be complimentary to all.

The owners of the building occupied by John J. Johnston, florist, at 202 Westminister street, have entered suit for possession of the store. Mr. Johnston has been located there for several years and the present controversy is the outcome of the desire of a neighboring store to eject Mr. Johnston and gain possession of the store before his lease had expired.

William Hay, who maintains the honor of being the best rose grower in Rhode Island, is building another greenhouse to increase his range on Dyer avenue. T. O'Connor is building a carnation house at his establishment on Blackstone boulevard. Solid beds extend along the sides, while benches occupy the center space. Mr. O'Connor states that he has no preference between the two methods as concerns results. W. E. Wood is preparing for a modern range of rose and carnation houses upon his recently acquired property near Apponaug, R. I. G. S. Whitford, is adding three new greenhouses to his range; one for propagating, another for violets and a third for carnations.

G. S. W.

A Return Trap for Greenhouses.

A return trap built to solve the florist's steam heating problem, has been placed on the market by the Morehead Manufacturing Company, of Detroit, Mich. The Morehead Return Trap is a simple, effective and inexpensive device for returning all condensation in steam pipes to the boilers regardless of the position of the latter, whether above or below the coils. It performs this function in a positive and thorough manner. Once installed, it requires little or no attention, and can be relied upon under all conditions.

The trap consists of a cylinder steel

Morehead Return Trap

tank receiver of suitable capacity, swung on a brass trunion and actuated by a counter weight. Two smaller counter weights, in turn actuated by the larger, automatically operate a steam admission and an air relief valve. A steam port and two water connections, the latter provided with check valves for maintaining a flow in one direction, completes the list of trap parts.

The condensation in the returns is forced into the trap tank by the steam pressure from behind. When the tank has received a requisite amount of water, it tilts, automatically opening the live steam valve admitting steam at boiler pressure to the tank, thereby equalizing the pressure in the system and permitting the contents to flow into the boiler by gravity.

All moving and adjustable parts are entirely outside, consequently easily accessible.

In line with this subject, the Morehead Manufacturing Company are distributing an attractive booklet devoted to the interests of florists and greenhouse owners in general.

FOUNDED IN 1888

THE FLORISTS' EXCHANGE

A Weekly Medium of Interchange for Florists, Nurserymen Seedsmen and the Trade in general

Exclusively a Trade Paper.

Entered at New York Post Office as Second Class Matter

Published EVERY SATURDAY by

A. T. DE LA MARE PTG. AND PUB. CO. LTD.

2, 4, 6 and 8 Duane Street,

P. O. Box 1697.
Telephone 3765 John. NEW YORK.

CHICAGO OFFICE: 127 East Berwyn Avenue.

ILLUSTRATIONS.

Electrotypes of the illustrations used in this paper can usually be supplied by the publishers. Price on application.

YEARLY SUBSCRIPTIONS.

United States, Canada, and Mexico, $1.00. Foreign countries in postal union, $2.50. Payable in advance. Remit by Express Money Order Draft on New York. Post Office Money Order or Registered Letter.

The address label indicates the date when subscription expires and is our only receipt therefore.

REGISTERED CABLE ADDRESS:
Florex, New York.

ADVERTISING RATES.

One-half inch, 75c.; ¾-inch, $1.00; 1-inch, $1.25, special positions extra. Send for Rate Card showing discount of 10c., 15c., 25c., or 35c., per inch on continuous advertising. For rates on Wants, etc., see column for Classified Advertisements.

Copy must reach this office 12 o'clock Wednesday to secure insertion in issue of following Saturday.

Orders from unknown parties must be accompanied with cash or satisfactory references.

To Advertisers.

Under the heading "No 'Baiting' Advertising Rates, "our oldest Chicago contemporary remarks: "We have received several requests lately to insert trial advertisements free of charge 'as other trade papers offer,' etc.

The Florists' Exchange states here, most emphatically, that it does not conduct its business on any such unbusiness-like plan as is here referred to. As we have many times before said, all our advertisers pay for whatever advertising they are pleased to give us, and no advertisement is inserted in our columns without authority.

Our contemporary's statement must and does refer to "some other fellow."

The Garden, Reasons Why.

I've been down to see the man, Maud,
Who cheated us so on the seeds.
I told him what a fraud he was,
Of our garden full of weeds.

Now what do you think he said, Maud—
That his seeds are the best in the land;
Fresh and tested, and with half a chance
Would grow things fine and grand.
That the fault was all our own, dear,
Or else the late Spring was to blame.
That we planted too deep, or the rain was too wet;
The ground was too cold he was ready to bet;
Or a thousand reasons equally lame.

He asked when we bought the seeds, Maud;
Then I knew we had made a mistake.
'Twas a year ago we bought from him,
And our garden took the cake.
This Spring we used free government seeds
That our congressman kindly sent.
They have filled our yard full of weeds,
And the seedsman is innocent.

—G. G. B., in answer to "The Garden, He and She."

Obituary

Max Limprecht.

Max Limprecht, who for many years conducted a florists' supply and evergreen business at 119 West Thirtieth street, New York, died at his home in Hudson Heights, N. J., on Friday, August 10, after an illness of locomotor ataxia lasting three months. The funeral was held at his home on Monday, August 13, interment being in Hudson Heights cemetery. At the time of his death Mr. Limprecht was forty-four years old. He leaves a widow, one son and two daughters who will carry on the business under the firm name of Limprecht Florists' Supply Company.

Convention Notes.

As soon as you arrive in Dayton, Ohio, make free use of the Information Bureau at the Union Station. You cannot miss it. Members of the Dayton Florists' Club will be at the depot at all times to help you along as much as possible. Leave your baggage at the Information Bureau with the baggage master, and he will deliver it to your hotel or boarding house at once.

In the office of the Exhibition Building you will find a United States postoffice established; so address all your letters to the exhibition hall, reading: "Convention, Society of American Florists, Fair Grounds, Dayton, Ohio." Furthermore, for your convenience you will find a telegraph office at the secretary's office, besides telephones; the use of which latter is free.

A large bulletin board will be provided, on which you may post notice if you want to meet some one. Keep your eye on the bulletin board.

A book of complaints you will also find at the secretary's office, and a box where you may deposit suggestions for the running of future conventions. Make free with suggestions and do a little thinking yourself, for a handful of men can't do it all. You may know something that will be of advantage in the future.

Patronize the exhibitors and advertisers well. Have cheerful words for everybody, and at least make these fellows feel good. A few nice words for everybody don't cost you anything. Let this convention be run a little more on the patriarchal style, and be one family. Try to stay together and get acquainted with each other.

Have as good a time as you possibly can. The Dayton Florists' Club will do all in its power to give you such a time. Take free part in all discussions, and don't hide your light under a bushel. Boost the National Flower Show. If there is anything you want, make your needs known to the chairman of the Dayton Florists' Club, who will do his best to see that you get what you desire, if at all possible.

We would like to direct your attention to a novel feature of this convention, that is the exhibits of plants for parks and suburban and city homes, made by some of the largest concerns in the United States; also to some undiscovered talent. You will be surprised what talent is slumbering among those engaged in the art of landscape gardening and garden architecture. As the national society has made no provision for prizes for such exhibits, the Dayton Florists' Club will do so, in the shape of gold, silver, and bronze medals. Any young man who has not yet exhibited should not fail to make his entry, but come forward. It may be the making of him; it may bring him fame and fortune.

We regret to say that, through some misunderstanding, a large southern concern has placed its exhibits of cannas in the public parks. However, the same concern will exhibit its cut flowers in the exhibition hall; and all desiring to see these plants in the beds will be taken to the respective parks in a private conveyance by our genial park superintendent, Mr. Killworth.

Another point to which we would like to call attention is the street car service. Take only the yellow car that is marked the "Xenia Traction Line" and don't crowd the cars. You will only have to wait a minute or two for another one.

The chairman of the Dayton Florists' Club has paid a great deal of attention to the musical program, has selected every piece personally and is quite satisfied that you will get, either in orchestra or band music, the best that can be produced. We have avoided the classics, and only chosen such pieces as will make you feel good. Ladies, make free use of the dancing platforms, and select your partners.

As this is our last communication before the convention, the members of the Dayton Florists' Club hope to see you all in person, and have a good time together.

J. B. HEISS.

Hybridization Conference.

The second hybridization congress inaugurated by the Royal Horticultural Society was held in London, England, from July 31 to August 3. The proceedings opened with a conversazione, at which 150 foreign guests and members of the society were present. Sir Trevor Lawrence, president of the R. H. S. delivered an address of welcome, in the course of which he said: "Nowadays there are few parts of the earth to be explored, but in turn there are developments in another direction toward the addition of new types of plants. This was the process of hybridization and cross-breeding." He pleaded for a greater application of the scientific spirit, believing with Huxley that it is more valuable than any other.

The band of the Royal Horse Guards was in attendance.

At the conference proper, Professor W. Bateson, F. R. S., V. M. H., presided. It may be remembered that Professor Bateson was one of the leading spirits at the International Hybridization Conference held in New York in 1902. In a very able address he pleaded for co-operation with the practical men. He also deprecated the desire to place scientific investigations always upon a purely economic footing, and went on to discuss the present and former standpoints on the subject of pure breeds and reversions. It used to be thought that the pure individual would breed pure for generations. But no stock could be guaranteed to always continue true. Sometimes a reversion or degeneration would occur to the original or to an earlier type. Their present knowledge of the separatability or distinctness of characters was such that practical breeders could turn it to a good account, and results that formerly required, say twelve years to deduce, could be attained in four.

In the matter of recessive characters, these could never, and would never occur unless they came into contact at the same time in the hybrid. Recessives, however, breed true when kept by themselves. Then he turned to the case presented by Ten-week stocks. These are notoriously complex. The features to be followed are smoothness (glabrous) and hairiness, and thirdly, color. To get the color purple and the character of hairiness in one plant four "elements" must be present simultaneously, two to make the hairiness and two the purple.

Professor Johannsen of Copenhagen, Denmark, dealt with the subject, "Does Hybridization Increase Fluctuating Variability." He believes fluctuations are not inherited. It was pointed out that the sporting tendency would greatly alter any rules of heredity.

C. C. Hurst of Hinckley, a Mendelian student, discussed the crossing of antirrhinums from Mendel's standpoint. In his experiments he had used a red, a white, and a yellow variety respectively. These were fixed and named kinds well known in gardens. The results, briefly told, were that white×yellow gave all white, white therefore dominant, sap-yellow recessive. These white hybrids at the second generation gave a pure Mendelian result, three whites and one yellow. When red was crossed with yellow, red dominant, and there was no trace of yellow at all. Red crossed white gave red, but not crimson, like the Crimson King parent; it was a carmine. The next generation resulted in twelve red, three white, and one yellow, this really being composed of nine carmines, three crimsons, three whites, and one yellow.

A discussion took place on the subject of the necessity of an authoritative color chart. It was stated that experimenters and hybridizers, especially those whose aim was scientific, should adopt an international color code. The translation of colors into color terms was a matter requiring critical consideration.

Following an able paper on "Certain Complications Occurring in the Cross-breeding of Stocks," by Miss Saunders, was an interesting discussion on the doubling of these flowers. The old-fashioned theory of cramping the roots to produce doubling was alluded to. It was stated by Miss Saunders, and by others, that double stocks are absolutely seedless, therefore the seeds have to come from singles. Curiously, these singles furnish from 60 per cent. even to over 80 per cent. of doubles. It was true, said Mr. Dean and Mr. Sutton, that stocks for seed were usually grown in pots. M. de Vilmorin, on being asked to speak, said that he had carried out most careful and exhaustive trials to ascertain the pros and cons of doubling, but his results were negative. They knew nothing for certain; only this, that certain singles gave a higher percentage of doubles than others, and so the seed growers selected from these and tried to build up a strain that would invariably yield a high percentage of doubles. Mr. Bateson also said that he had noticed this fact, that in a certain strain of Brompton stocks the singles were all white and the doubles were all cream. In Professor Hugo de Vries' work "Mutations and Variability" there is an interesting chapter bearing upon this question, the facts of which were corroborated by M. de Vilmorin. What physiological factor produces doubling is therefore still unknown, but Miss Saunders is attacking the question, and we may hope to learn her results in time. She did state this, that she has never found a red glabrous Ten-week stock that does not produce doubles.

Dr. John H. Wilson of St. Andrews, Scotland, discussed "The Infertility of Hybrids." His conclusion so far is that infertility is very great. He described his results in the hybridizing of foxgloves (Digitalis purpurea alba × D. lutea). This gave a heavily fasciated flower, but the reciprocal cross gave no fasciation at all. A red tuberous begonia upon B. coccinea furnished a plant that refuses to grow and will not flower. B. heraclifolia × B. coccinea gave an intermediate type with no segregation in the seedlings. Passifloras had also been uniformly infertile, only one exception having occurred. The gooseberry and black currant hybrid had also fruited once, but he thought the pollination must have been from an outside species. The Logan berry, which Dr. Wilson doubts of being a hybrid, though the reputed parents are Rubus idæus and R. ursinus, can usually be raised from seed. He also showed wheats and potatoes, the latter a seedless cross between Solanum Commersoni and S. tuberosum. The pods swelled, but they were infertile. Mr. Sutton, however, had had a few seeds from this cross.

Various papers on orchid hybridization were presented. Mr. Rolfe of Kew, speaking on "Hybrid Cattleyas," said that Cattleya Leopoldi crossed with C. intermedia had given progeny which was then crossed with Lælia purpurata. There was now a hybrid genus—the Lælio-cattleya. Mendelian principles applied to hybrid cattleyas was very interesting. Mr. de Barris Crawshay treated of "Odontoglossum Hybrids," showing by means of paintings that very different flowers can arise from absolutely the same cross. As many as four distinct certificated varieties have arisen from the same seed pod. The flowers are different very often when the same cross is made by different growers. O. crispum and O. Harryanum he found to be the best and most often used parents. There are now forty-nine certificated hybrid odontoglossums, and Mr. Crawshay hoped that the future would see the production of some beautiful and improved novelties. Selection and in-breeding is now to be pursued.

On the subject of "The Influence of the Pollen Parent," Mr. Chittenden remarked that one of the great necessities in the present state of hybridization was reliable rules. It had all along been advanced that the pollen parent governs the color factor in hybrids. He has put this to the test. He had the evidence of reciprocal crosses to draw upon, and these did not bear out the theory. He had also checked the results as seen in 183 hybrids scattered through 67 genera. Of these, 42 followed the pollen (male) parent in color, 46 followed the mother in color, and the rest were intermediate.—Abridged from Report of the Conference appearing in the Journal of Horticulture, London, Eng.

OUR READERS' VIEWS

Growing American Beauty Roses in Cuba

Editor Florists' Exchange:

Referring to the article in your issue of July 21, I would state that there need be no doubt on that point, as I am growing American Beauty roses here now, and have been doing so since last Fall. I took a few plants with me from New Jersey. When I arrived at the place of which I am in charge I found six plants in bloom. I sent at once to the United States for 50 more, which I received in fair condition. I planted them in the borders without any special care, and was surprised to have them in bloom in six weeks. Of course, they were dormant when shipped, but in the six days' journey they had shown signs of growth, in bud and roots too. They were well supplied with water but beyond that they have had very little attention except staking to keep them from being damaged by the wind which we get here on the coast, but never enough to harm the blooms.

I fail to see the object to be attained by shipping Cuban soil to the United States, mentioned in the article referred to, as I have seen American Beauty roses grown in all kinds of soil in America. It is not a matter of soil, but climate. The plants bloom here all the year round. To-day, August 9, I cut some fine blooms.

It would be a great advantage to grow the flowers here if they would stand the four days' journey to New York under cold storage treatment. The soil around Havana is a rich, red clay; in fact, I have never seen better soil for rose growing either in America or Europe. How would carnations travel? I am growing them here with every success.

Havana, Cuba. CHAS. SHAW, Florist.

The New York Greek Flower Merchant.

Editor Florists' Exchange:

I have read with interest the letter "Concerning Geraniums" in your publication. One remark in John Birnie's letter published in The Florists' Exchange of August 4 convinces me that this gentleman knows very little about the flower market of New York. Mr. Birnie says, that "the place occupied by the Greek in the cut flower market and the commission district is as a cleaner up of what is left."

A more unwarranted and false assertion is hardly possible when speaking of the flower market in New York, seeing that the retail flower business in this Metropolis is almost entirely in the hands of Greek merchants; experts in flower lore and honest in their dealings.

Mr. Birnie had no reason whatever to take the Greeks into the "geranium" discussion, and it would be well for him in future to limit his observations to what is known to him.

New York. A. COVA.

Concerning Geraniums.

Editor Florists' Exchange:

In John Birnie's last letter, he says he has come to the conclusion that he will waste no more ink on me. I am glad to know that he has at last realized the utter uselessness of the ink he has been using; his characterizing it as waste is the smartest thing he has said yet.

I will not burden your columns with any further lengthy letter on the subject of geraniums; I think enough has been said on that subject. It is plainly evident, however, that nothing of value can be gleaned from Mr. Birnie. His visions of antomobiles and fancy wagons, (whatever the latter may be) attending the New York plant market, are but beautiful dreams; and I suppose are neither misleading nor unfair! But Mr. Editor, when you published pictures of this market a little over a year ago, you certainly left out automobiles and fancy wagons.

I can imagine the geraniums alleged to have been certificated by the New York Florists' Club, being picked up at a moment's notice. I can see how anxiously Mr. Birnie would avoid picking out his best plants for such a purpose. Especially does this seem possible, when, if I remember rightly, I have seen announcements in The Florists' Exchange about those exhibitions of the New York Florists' Club; and I think there were usually several weeks elapsing between the date of notice and that of th exhibition.

To conclue; let me say I have too much respect for plant growers in general to cast a slur at any of them; at the same time, if to tell the truth is to be guilty of writing "scurrilous screeds," I am perfectly willing to let it go at that. I sincerely hope the New York geranium market will not suffer from this prolonged discussion and my only regret is that the trade has benefited so little by what Birnie has said, and taken so much space to say on the subject, due no doubt to the fact that he has nothing of practical value to vouchsafe.

EXPERTUS.

To a Geranium.

Geranium, beauteous with the glow of many blooms in one,
 Flower most beloved that in my garden grows,
Redder than heart's blood, thy day has just begun
 When it is saddened by the dying rose,
And brilliancy left o'er from Summer's noon
 Is still thine own when first the aster wakes.
Full many a fickle, fragile blossom, in the boon
 Of one rare breath of fleeting fragrance breaks,
Then vanishes; but thou, from glad June's jubilee
 Until the Autumn whispers of the end,
In soft bestowal of thy spiced perfume, art constancy,
 Oh, flower of all that blow, the truest friend!

—Boston American.

Professor H. C. Irish,
Pres.-elect, St. Louis Florists' Club

H. C. Irish.

H. C. Irish, president-elect of the St. Louis Florists' Club, was born on a farm, near Janesville, Rock County, Wis., on April 22, 1868. After the death of his parents, in 1884, he moved to Spink County, South Dakota, where, with a brother, he operated a farm for four years. In 1888 he entered South Dakota Agricultural College, from which he was graduated in 1891, his expenses for his college course being met by teaching school during the long vacation, and working a few hours each day in the horticultural department under the direction of Prof. C. A. Keffer, now of the University of Tennessee. After leaving college, Mr. Irish taught school for one year, and then did post-graduate work at the Iowa State College of Agriculture and Mechanic Arts, specializing in botany and horticulture under L. H. Pammel and the late Professor J. L. Budd. The year 1894 was spent in practical nursery work with C. L. Watrous, of Des Moines, Iowa. In the Autmun of 1894, Mr. Irish went to the Missouri Botanical Garden, as horticultural assistant, occupying that position until the beginning of 1903 when he was made superintendent. The early part of the years 1896 and 1898 was spent in special and post-graduate work at Cornell University with Professor L. H. Bailey, leave of absence having been granted Mr. Irish by the Garden for that purpose.

He has contributed articles on various horticultural topics to the press, and monographed the genus capsicum (red peppers) and garden beans, these being published in the reports of the Missouri Botanical Garden.

Mr. Irish is a member of several national horticultural bodies, and many state horticultural societies. He has been secretary of the St. Louis County Horticultural Society and the Englemann Botanical Club of St. Louis, and is secretary of the preliminary organization of the National Council of Horticulture. ST. PATRICK.

CLUB AND SOCIETY DOINGS.

ST. LOUIS FLORISTS' CLUB.—We had a lively time at our club meeting Thursday afternoon, August 9, the election of officers for the ensuing year occurring at that time. The attendance was not as large as was expected. The balloting was keen and caused much excitement among the members, taking as many as three ballots in some cases, before the candidate was elected. The president arriving somewhat late, the meeting opened with Vice-president Steidle in the chair. The trustees reported they had $38.98 left from the recent outing, which money was placed in the entertainment fund. A vote of thanks was tendered the trustees for the able manner in which they had conducted the outing. Fred. H. Meinhardt, who is in charge of the transportation to Dayton, said the delegation from St. Louis would probably number 25, and would travel over the Vandalia Road, leaving Monday night, August 20, at 8.15, arriving at 8. a. m. next day at Dayton. The fare will be $12.00 for the round trip. Any intending to go to the convention, who have not yet sent in their names, should do so at once.

The secretary was instructed to send the club's sympathy to the bereaved family of the late James Hartshorne, also to the Chicago Florists' Club which has lost one of its foremost members.

Eight made application for membership, as follows: Edwin Denker, of St. Charles, Mo.; Frank Vennemann, of Kirkwood, Mo.; Chas. Fullgraf, and G. H. Pring, of Shaw's Garden; William C. Young, F. Hettemann, C. W. Wors, and Fred Alves of Augermuller's.

The election of officers resulted as follows: President, Professor H. C. Irish, Superintendent of Shaw's Garden, elected on the first ballot; E. W. Guy and F. Fillmore, both ex-presidents, were the other candidates. Three ballots were taken for the election of vice-president, John Connon, of Webster Grove, Mo., being successful. For secretary, the candidates were Emil Schray, who has held that office for the past fifteen years, and J. J. Beneke. Mr. Schray moved that the ballot be made unanimons for Mr. Beneke, and the latter was elected secretary. There were four candidates for the office of treasurer, A. J. Bentzen being successful; Fred H. Meinhardt, who has held the position for two years, was not a candidate for re-election.

There were five candidates for the office of one trustee to serve three years; William C. Smith won on the second ballot. The election gives us an entirely new set of officers, with the exception of Frank Weber and Carl Beyer, two trustees who hold over.

The treasurer's report showed that the club is in good financial standing.

At the next meeting Emil Schray will lead a discussion on "Growing Chrysanthemums for Cut Flowers." E. W. Guy of Belleville will lead on "Growing Bulbous Stock."

The club adjourned to meet on Thursday, September 13, at 2 p. m. in the regular meeting hall.

ST. PATRICK.

NASSAU COUNTY (N. Y.) HORTICULTURAL SOCIETY.—This society met at the usual place and time on Wednesday 8th inst. There was a very large attendance, President Harrison being in the chair. One new member was elected and one nominated to active membership. In the competition for points S. J. Trepass scored 92 1-3; H. Meyer, 87; Felix Mense, 81 1-3. The silver match safe, given for the best six varieties of vegetables, was awarded to S. J. Trepass. Others in the competition were: T. Harrison, Peter Ewen and H. Matz. Some good pears were exhibited by James Holloway; cannas and Dendrobium thyrsiflorum by F. Boulon & Son, and canna King Humbert by Peter Ewen.

The subjects for competition at next meeting are dahlias, in three classes, each with a box of cigars as a prize, as follows: best collection of single dahlias; best six varieties show dahlias; and best collection of cactus dahlias, all to be correctly named.

A very interesting and able paper, entitled "How to Grow American Beauty Roses," was read by C. Bertanzel, Glenhead, for which he received a very hearty vote of thanks. J. F. J.

THE WASHINGTON (D. C.) FLORISTS' CLUB held a largely attended meeting on July 7. Matters concerning the exhibition of the American Rose Society occupied the attention of the members for the greater part of the session. Z. D. Blackistone was elected vice-president.

The delegates from this city to the S. A. F. convention will travel by the C. & O. Railroad. The bowling team will be composed of Wm. Ernest, captain, George Cooke, J. J. Barry, S. Simmons, George Shaffer and Robert McLennan. Mc.

GLADIOLUS AMERICA.—The Florists' Exchange has received from John Lewis Childs, Floral Park, N. Y., a basket of flowers of that beautiful gladiolus, America. The lively pink shade possessed by this variety, together with the size of the individual segments, places America, we believe, at the head of all gladioli for commercial purposes.

The Coming Man With the Hoe
A. N. C. R. Boy Gardener

Society of American Florists *and* Ornamental Horticulturists

Incorporated by Special Act of Congress

Charter Signed by William McKinley, President of the United States, Mch. 4, 1901

TWENTY-SECOND ANNUAL MEETING AND EXHIBITION

To be Held at

DAYTON, OHIO, AUGUST 21, 22, 23 AND 24, 1906

Officers of the S. A. F. for 1906.

President, W. F. Kasting, Buffalo, N. Y.; vice-president, H. M. Altiok, Dayton, O.; secretary, Wm. J. Stewart, Boston, Mass.; Treasurer, H. B. Beatty, Pittsburg, Pa.

Directors for one year, H. H. Ritter, Dayton, Ohio; Theo. Wirth, Minneapolis.

For two years, V. H. Hallock, Queens, N. Y.; W. H. Elliott, Brighton, Mass.

For three years, F. H. Traendly, New York, N. Y.; Phil. J. Hauswirth, Chicago, Ill.

Botanist, Prof. L. H. Pammel, Ames, Iowa.

Pathologist, Dr. B. M. Duggar, Columbia, Mo.

Entomologist, Prof. Herbert Osborn, Columbus, Ohio.

Superintendent of Exhibition, Horace M. Frank, Dayton, Ohio.

Plant Registration in charge of Secretary.

Legislative Committee, Elmer D. Smith, Adrian, Mich.; J. A. Valentine, Denver, Colo.; Benj. Hammond, Fishkill-on-Hudson, N. Y.

Convention Sports Manager, George Asmus, Chicago, Ill.

Officers of Dayton Florists' Club.

President, J. B. Heiss; Vice-president, Chas. Lutzenburger; Secretary, Horace M. Frank; Treasurer, H. H. Ritter.

Chairmen of Convention Committees.

Exhibits—Horace M. Frank, 112 South Main street.

Reception—F. W. Ritter, 832 River street.

Hotels—J. B. Heiss, 112 Main street.

Entertainment—Chas. Lutzenburger, National Plant Co., Philadelphia street.

Finance—H. H. Ritter, 435 West Grand avenue.

Ladies—The Misses M. and L. Johnson, 142 South Jefferson street.

Bowling—Harry M. Altick.

ONCE more the great State of Ohio is to be favored with a visit from the Society of American Florists and Ornamental Horticulturists, Dayton being the place of meeting in this Year of our Lord, 1906.

The S. A. F. is no stranger to Ohio's Gem City, for here in the Opera House, on Friday, August 14, 1885, the organization, then holding its first meeting in Cincinnati, O., assembled for the purpose of transacting the unfinished business of that memorable and historical gathering. The society was drawn to Dayton at that time, on invitation, for the purpose of viewing the world renowned Soldiers' Home, and its interesting environs, a pleasure which will again be experienced this year.

At the time of the first visit of the S. A. F. to Dayton the society was in its swaddling clothes. The great work it had been formed to accomplish was new and its scope and character practically unknown to it. The initial meeting at Cincinnati, however, demonstrated the manner of men of which the organization was composed, their earnestness, their desire to see their chosen profession progress and rank with the foremost in the land in the carrying out of its particular work; and last but by no means least, the capabilities of the men engaged in the furtherance of that work.

The present year's visitation to Dayton sees the society a husky young man, with a long list of practical, helpful deeds to its credit, with ambition unwaning, with the same energy that characterized it at its beginning undiminished, with many members in its ranks imbued with the same progressive spirit as the original promoters possessed, ever alert to take hold of and carry forward to a successful culmination every feature that makes for the welfare and betterment of the craft which the association champions.

It is needless here to recapitulate the helpful accomplishments of the S. A. F. during the twenty-two years of its existence. Suffice it to say, that there is no one engaged in the florist industry to-day who is not reaping some pronounced personal benefit from the results of the society's endeavors.

William F. Kasting, President S. A. F. O. H.

We shall leave it to others more familiar with the details of these, perhaps, than we are, to dilate upon the criticisms that have been passed upon the S. A. F., justly and unjustly, the causes of dissatisfaction with some of its workings, and those responsible therefor. Our object now is solely to draw attention to its excellent qualities, which are many; and these, as we have said, are self-evident to all who will but look for them, whose vision is not obscured by bias or ignorance, or both.

The program arranged by the executive committee of the society for the coming meeting has already been published in our columns (See page 124, issue of August 4). From that program it will be learned that only a few papers are to be read; but that those to be presented deal with questions that affect members engaged in every branch of the business—the grower, the retailer, the private and landscape gardener, and all interested in the broader lines of horticultural development. Some very helpful hints on that most important subject, "The Best Method of Marketing the Product of the Wholesale Plant and Flower Grower," will no doubt be brought out in the essays to be submitted in the competition for cash prizes, generously donated by President Kasting.

A very important topic to be discussed at Dayton is that of the National Flower Show proposed to be held under the auspices of the S. A. F. O. H. It may be remembered that an effort was inaugurated last year to obtain a guarantee fund of $10,000 for the purposes of this exhibition. The latest published report of the committee intrusted with the work of raising that fund shows that 47 concerns have contributed in the aggregate the sum of $4,050, so far. In view of the importance of the suggested show not only to the society itself, but also to the trade in general, it seems to us there should be no difficulty or delay in securing the amount of money desired, if members will but give the subject the tangible consideration it deserves. We hope every delegate present at Dayton will have gone to the convention prepared to support, both morally and financially, the proposed undertaking.

The trade exhibit this year promises to break all records. This is always a strong factor in adding to the profitableness of the annual convention, and we are pleased to note its continual development and expansion. It is a matter for regret that more enthusiasm has not been shown in the outdoor feature of the trade display. The apathy, however, may be partly attributed to the novelty of the enterprise; and should the officers of the organization, in their wisdom, deem this feature worthy of perpetuation, doubtless the outdoor exhibit, as the years pass and its great benefit becomes more apparent, will develop into as interesting and as helpful an adjunct of the annual meetings as the indoor trade exhibit has done and is doing. By vote of the excontive board the Thursday afternoon of the convention will be devoted exclusively to the interests of the exhibitors—an excellent idea, sure to be fraught with fruitful consequences to the firms whose business acumen and enterprise command for them every attention and encouragement possible.

From what has already appeared in our columns there seems to be considerable interest abroad in the selection of the society's officers for the coming year. There can be no more potent sign of the worth of an organization than fair-minded, spirited rivalry for its elective offices. But as we have previously mentioned the choice of men to fill these offices is of the greatest importance, demanding the best thought of the members, both before and during the meeting. While it is true that no very bad breaks have been made in connection with this matter (We have reference more particularly to the presidency), still the evident trend of the times renders it imperative that an effort be made to secure the best available men for all the offices in the society's gift. These are likely to come from among the members whose interest in the organization is centered in the advancement and promotion of the real work which first called the association into existence, and which is the avowed object of its being, rather than from the ranks of those whose affiliation with the society is largely, if not wholly, to satisfy self indulgence, and who find greater pleasure and profit evidently in sharing in the extraneous functions that accompany an annual convention, than in participation in the actual work that goes to build up the association, and to make that work of the greatest practical benefit to its membership.

As will have been inferred from what has been stated, the hospitality of the Dayton brethren is no unknown quantity to the older members of the S. A. F.; many of whom are still with us, who have the most pleasant recollections of their first visit there. The craft of the present day will have equally pleasant remembrances of the trip to the Gem City this year. And the entertainment to be provided, the many courtesies to be shown, are all the more to be appreciated seeing that the S. A. F. goes to Dayton practically an unbidden guest so far as the local florists themselves are concerned. Nevertheless, a most cordial welcome and a very enjoyable educational and profitable time awaits every delegate to the 1906 convention of the S. A. F. O. H. May their number be a large one.

William J. Stewart
Secretary S. A. F. O. H.

From the "National Cyclopedia of American Biography," by permission of James T. White & Co.

GENERAL JONATHAN DAYTON,
FOUNDER OF THE CITY.

DAYTON--THE GEM CITY OF OHIO

S. A. F. O. H. MEETING PLACE, 1906

"Education, Religion, and Morality are Characteristics of its Citizens."

Dayton is the oldest of those marvelous interior cities of Ohio which owe their origin to the defeat of the allied tribes of Indians under the Miami chief Little Turtle in 1794. The rush of travel down the Ohio, which had come with the close of the Revolution, had been checked by a border warfare which lasted until Mad Anthony Wayne, by the victory of The Fallen Timbers on the Maumee and the establishment of a chain of forts extending along the western frontier of the future State, had broken the backbone of the confederacy and freed the country of the Indian terror. Then the tide of immigration, now unimpeded, began to ascend the affluents of the great river, and settlements were quickly formed on the Miami, the Scioto and the Muskingum. The first of these was Dayton. The confluence of the Big Miami, the Mad River, and Stillwater and Wolf creeks had pointed out to Jonathan Dayton, a distinguished veteran of the Revolution, the site of an important center of agri-

H. M. Altick
Vice-President S.A.F.O.H.

culture, industry and trade, and within three weeks of the signing of the treaty of Fort Greenville by the confederate tribes he had bou-ht the tract. Colonel Ludlow, the surveyor who had laid out the then prosperous village of Cincinnati, was sent to mark off the new town in the interior; and in April, 1796, sixteen immigrants settled at Dayton. The locality was already known to explorers and to hunters and trappers, and had twice been the skirmish-ground upon which the whites had defeated the redskins; and when it was noised abroad that a clearing had been effected upon the fertile lands at the mouth of Mad River, and that exemption from the horrors of savage warfare was now assured throughout the interminable forest of the Miami country, many of the fresh immigrants who began to flock across the mountains selected their farms here and put up their log houses near those of the handful who had felled the first trees at Dayton. Where they came from or how they got here will ever remain a mystery; but Dayton grew, and kept on growing, in spite of the destructive floods of 1805, and other years, and hardly noticing the Tecumseh uprising that terrified the more nothern part of the country. And when neighbor Harrison, who had fought beside Mad Anthony, and had whipped Tecumseh at Tippecanoe and again at the Thames, ran his uproarious political campaign of 1840, Dayton gave him the biggest of all the big "hard-cider and log-cabin" demonstrations of that demonstrative year, and then celebrated his election by incorporating herself into a city—as thirty-five years earlier she had defied the Dayton flood by building anew and becoming an incorporated village.

The Dayton jollification fixed and crystallized the name "Buckeye" in the English language as the accepted sobriquet of Ohio and its people. The Ohio buckeye, or American horse-chestnut—so called from its resemblance to the common horse-chestnut—was highly prized by the pioneers as the sure guide to a rich soil, as the lightest wood for their hastily built cabins, as the best tree of the forest to arrest the bullet of the native, as the easiest to be dug out into cradles and troughs and the like, as the quickest to be got out of the way for the first crop of corn, as furnishing the best fibre for the homemade hat of the settler and the most easily carved bowl and spoon for his mush and milk, as the slowest-burning wood for the indispensable backlog in the fireplace, as leaving the very best ashes for the making of soft soap, as being most efficacious in the cure of the inevitable chills and fever, and for its ready adaptation to many other wants and conveniences of life in the backwoods, as well as for the exceeding beauty of its early flower on the one hand and the touch-me-not character of its prickly and astringent nut on the other. When a Miami Indian admired a white man of fine build and commanding presence, he called him "netuck," that is, a "big buckeye." And when the Netucks of Ohio gathered at Dayton to whoop her up for Tippecanoe, they came with their cabin buckeye logs, and sporting canes of buckeye branches, and with garlands of buckeye adorn-

H. B. Beatty
Treasurer S. A. F. O. H.

The City of Dayton—Looking North from Reibold Building

ing their wives and sweethearts, and singing, as the bands played the "Blue Bells of Scotland"—

Oh where, tell me where
  Was your buckeye cabin made?
'Twas built among the merry boys
  Who wield the plough and spade,
Where the log cabins stand
  In the bonnie buckeye shade.

Oh what, tell me what
  Is to be your cabin's fate?
We'll wheel it to the capital
  And place it there elate,
For a token and a sign
  Of the bonnie Buckeye State.

Until the great Dayton demonstration of 1840, Ohio was hardly known at the national capital; since that time, she has given six Presidents, native or resident within the State, to the United States. The Dayton convention was the largest political meeting ever held in this country; the present day, with its cheap transportation and increased population, has not furnished its equal. The multitude covered ten acres by actual measurement, and at no time were more than two thirds of the people on the grounds. While Harrison was speaking, the crowd was measured by three separate civil engineers, whose estimates, allowing four to the square yard, were respectively 77,600, 75,000, and 80,000, the constant change of pressure and resistance accounting for the slight difference. At the same time more than 20,000 were sauntering about the environs, scattered around the refreshment booths, and lying in groups upon the plain discussing politics and making speeches among themselves. Thus this historic gathering, which was of the deepest national concern and notoriety, was swelled, including the citizens of the little town itself, to more than one hundred thousand of these sturdy Buckeyes, with their bands and drum corps, and their log cabins on wheels, and drinking hard cider and eating ginger-bread and corn dodgers and bacon, and yelling for "Tippecanoe, and Tyler too!" with all the might and main of their multitudinous throats and lungs.

Five years after Dayton had become an incorporated village, it had but 383 inhabitants. In 1841, when it took out a city charter, it had 6,067. The Directory for 1905 contains, exclusive of banks, corporations and business firms, 54,893 names, representing, say the publishers, a population of at least 113,000. According to the latest estimate, furnished semi-officially to The Florists' Exchange, it may be said that in the one hundred and ten years, ending April 1, 1906, since Mrs. Thompson, wife of Samuel Thompson, set the foot of the first settler on Dayton soil, Dayton has grown to a city of 115,000 souls, not to mention her immense floating population.

Dayton is a handsome city, regularly laid out with wide streets crossing at right angles. Main and Third streets are the dividing lines of all streets crossing them. Main runs north and south, and all streets crossing it prefix East or West to their names; and similarly Third runs east and west, all streets crossing it prefixing North and South to their names. The city is noted for its numerous elegant public buildings and private residences. Among the public edifices is the court house of Montgomery county, a monument of architectural beauty and skill, successfully modeled after the Parthenon and built of Dayton marble.

The county is of a gently undulating surface, having a soil of great fertility, drained and supplied with good water power by the Miami and Mad rivers and their branches, and is in easy communication by electric railways and macadamized roads converging from all directions in the city. The whole surrounding country has long been noted for its great crops of the finest wheat and corn, and for its numerous excellent horses, sheep and cattle; and the marble and limestone quarried in the vicinity find ready sale for local use and in the markets of other cities. Beautiful and fertile as is the whole Miami Valley, no other part of it equals the region immediately surrounding Dayton.

The city building, containing the city hall and council chamber and the market house beneath, runs from Main street through to Jefferson, between Third and Fourth. The mayor is elected biennially, and the council is only a legislative body. The annual income of the city is about $1,625,000. The expenditure for the schools is about $290,000 a year, for the police department $70,000, fire department $75,000, street lighting $50,000, and for the operation of the water-works about $40,000.

Dayton has an almost inexhaustible supply of the purest water from tube wells erected on both sides of Mad River, and carried throughout the city by means of 133 miles of street mains and delivered by 1,300 fire hydrants and 15,503 service taps. The sewerage, both underground and surface, is complete; the sanitary system extends throughout the area of the city, and there are about 70 miles of Storm sewerage.

"Old Log Cabin," First House in Dayton (still standing)

Dayton has 95 churches; many of her religious edifices are models of architectural beauty and elegance of design. Several of the denominations, and of the moral and social institutions, have important educational adjuncts; and the public schools of the city have long been noted for their superior appointments. The normal school, the manual training school, and the numerous kindergartens have a united attendance of about three thousand.

Dayton's library was established in 1805, and was the earliest incorporated library in Ohio. The beautiful new building on Third street, between St. Clair street and the Canal, contains, besides the library, a valuable museum of archæological, ethnographical and natural history collections. The number of volumes in the main building and the branches, not counting many thousands of valuable pamphlets, is 65,000. The Catholic Free Circulation Library has 3,500; and the National Cash Register Library 2,000.

Dayton owes the beginning of her phenomenal success as a business center to the opening of the Miami Canal from Cincinnati and the advent of a canal boat in Dayton on the 25th of January, 1829, and to the completion of the canal thence to Lake Erie. The latest potent force in the development of the city has been the electric lines of railway, of which Dayton has more than any other city in the State. The steam railroads bring about 125 trains a day into the Union Station which was opened in 1900. About 50 newspapers and periodicals,

Looking South from Dayton View, showing River and Bridge

Main Street, Dayton—Looking South.

Main Street, Dayton—Looking North.

including five dailies, are published in Dayton. There are nine banks, 20 building and loan associations, and not less than 240 incorporated companies engaged in the widely diversified business enterprises of this wonderful city.

The building and loan associations have been largely instrumental in the erection of more than 20,000 beautiful and convenient dwellings in the city. A large number of the incorporated companies keep from 500 to 2,500 employees at work. The water-power is artificially distributed. The busy manufactories have an output of about $50,000,000 a year.

The Soldiers' Home.

Dayton enjoys the worldwide reputation of being the site of the largest and best appointed military hospital in existence. Nothing could speak louder for the salubrity of the locality as a place of residence or a health resort than the choice of Dayton by the Government for so important an institution.

On a hill adjoining the city on the west is seen a plot of ground of 652 acres, handsomely laid out with avenues, artificial lakes, flower beds and groups of trees and shrubbery, and crowned with many imposing buildings known collectively as the Central National Soldiers' Home. Here are library, reading hall, music hall, and all the most comfortable and homelike accommodations for about 6,800 of our veteran volunteers, including the Government hospital, which has an average of 600 patients, all of whom were soldiers in the civil war and in our recent war with Spain.

The Home was the direct outcome of the civil war. The Dayton Light Guards had been among the first of the militia companies of the country to respond to the call of President Lincoln for volunteers; and when at the close of the war, Congress authorized the establishment of the Central Home at Dayton, the citizens of the town immediately subscribed the sum of $20,000 toward the foundation.

This Home is a unique place; a city of graybearded men, few women, and no children except those of the officers' families. On the gentle slopes of the great valley, the spot, from its location, its fine buildings, its greenhouses, its flower beds, and the display of the triumphs of landscape gardening, is one of great beauty; and these features render it a place of attraction for visitors, who come from all over the civilized world at the rate of more than 100,000 annually.

The visitor enters a large open space over which waves the American flag surrounded with siege guns, mortars, pyramids of shot and a battery set

Dayton Court House.

in battle position. In front is the headquarters building, in which are the executive offices and the library. To the right is Memorial Hall and the church; and beyond these is the hospital; while away in front of this is the soldiers' monument surrounded with the graves of thousands of veterans who have been buried with military honors in this beautiful place. Sixteen thousand old soldiers gave one dollar each to pay for the monument. Keeping the same position, to the left the visitor sees a rustic arbor, fountains, springs, lakes, flower garden, conservatory, and beyond these are rustic bridges, groves of forest trees, a park, and officers' residences embowered in trees and flowers. To the left, again, is the city of the soldiers, perfect in all its appointments; and beyond the woods and the more immediate confines are the vegetable garden and the broad acres of the Home farm. The church, a fine Gothic structure, is said to have been the first church ever erected by the Government of the United States. The noted Putnam Library was given by a lady whose son was killed at Ball's Bluff; and the Thomas Library was donated by old soldiers in honor of General Thomas.

Dayton Public Library and Park.

A RECENT VISIT TO DAYTON.

Just at this time the eyes of all horticulturally inclined are centered on one spot. This spot is located near the center of Ohio and is called Dayton. "the Gem City." Well may she bear this name, for Dayton is a city of homes; and here the great S. A. F. O. H. will assemble on August 21.

Dayton is a clean city; her streets are wide, Main street being 80 feet from curb to curb. Her people love everything that is beautiful, flowers coming first; and flower beds and window boxes are seen in profusion on all of her residence streets. The city is situated on the Miami River over which have recently been constructed three of the handsomest and longest concrete bridges in the world. Dayton is also a great manufacturing center, and within her gates is the "model factory of the world," also the Barney and Smith Car Works, the Davis Sewing Machine Company, Paper Box Factory (for florists' use), flour mills, Ohmer Street Car Register Company, and other industries too numerous to mention.

The hotels are of a high class, as are the amusement parks.

The Florists of Dayton.

Within her gates Dayton has some good people engaged in the florist's business. H. H. Ritter is the pioneer. His greenhouses and residence are situated over the river in North Dayton, he also has a store in the city, in charge of his son.

J. B. Heiss, president of the Dayton Florists' Club, has an extensive plant situated in East Dayton on Philadelphia and Fifth streets.

Farther along you will find the National Plant Company's establishment. This concern has a large range of glass and does a wholesale cut flower and catalogue plant business.

Gus. Horlacher is situated on the Smithville road and grows a general stock. Walter Horlacher, his brother, is located at the entrance of Woodland Cemetery; he grows cut flowers and a general collection of bedding plants.

John Boehner is another good fellow who grows a general stock and is making money; his range of glass is situated on South Brown street.

W. G. Matthews needs no introduction to most of the florists of the United States. I think he is an Elk; anyway he does a good business. His greenhouses are just across the Main street bridge; he also has a store near the Phillips House.

The Miami Floral Company has the largest plant in Dayton. This concern grows cut flowers exclusively, and its establishment is situated to the southwest of the city. George Bartholomew is in charge and he is pretty well known, especially by the Chicago brethren.

C. M. Schaeffer recently started on the north side with a number of houses.

J. H. Broxey is located south of Dayton near the entrance of Calvary Cemetery and grows a general stock. One word regarding this cemetery: The natural lay of the land is ideal, and the site is one of the handsomest in Ohio. Anyone wishing a beautiful view of Dayton and the surrounding country would be well repaid by a visit to Calvary.

W. J. Engle is a peony as well as a pansy grower; he also deals in other outdoor stock. He is located a short distance out of the city on a traction line.

Those having stores in the city are the Misses Johnson on Jefferson street; Mrs. J. F. Young on Fifth street; and Mrs. B. Hendricks on East Fifth street. J. B. Heiss also has a store. This comprises the greater part of the Dayton florists.

The Soldiers' Home.

I will now ask your attention for a few moments to Dayton's National Soldiers' Home—the beauty spot of Ohio. As you approach the Home, Grotto Lake first strikes the eye ;and as the car stops at the main entrance you must take off your hat to a majestic old American white ash, whose branches spread for 66 feet and whose shape any tree might well be proud of. On either side of the driveway entrance is concrete work artistically arranged for beauty and durability. Passing up the avenue, to the right you will notice large beds of roses in bloom; also the propagating houses; while to the left you will see Grotto Lake with its majestic white and black swans, and its wild mallard ducks. Before you are the large show greenhouses and the office of the chief gardener. These houses were recently built by Lord & Burnham Company, and are very fine. In the palm house are some splendid specimens. One plant of Corypha australis has fifty perfect leaves, is 25 feet high, with a spread of 25 feet. There are many other plants to be seen here that will astonish you.

Gate and Lodge National Soldiers' Home, Dayton, O.

Directly west of the rose beds and propagating houses mentioned is a place that will amuse the children as well as their guardians—the home of the alligators. There are many of them, and one is a very large specimen. I will tell you of a little incident that happened here. Two women, I will not say ladies, were abusing the guard who had asked them to make a small dog, which one woman carried in her arms, stop barking. During the fracas the women stood near the fence surrounding the enclosure, when suddenly the dog sprang from the woman's arms into the pond and in less time than it takes me to tell, the big alligator's mouth opened wide and down went the dog. So, children especially, don't miss seeing the big alligator.

Many amusing incidents occur here during a year. A party of ladies, with their old soldier quide, were "seeing the Home." They asked him if he got enough to eat. "That's my business," said the old man. "How long have you been here?" said one lady. Pointing to a large cannon standing near hé said, "I came here when that cannon was a pisto."

But to return to' my knitting. The Home has ten greenhouses of various sizes, costing about $30,000.

To the south of the large greenhouses you will discover the grotto, the lily ponds containing all the new varieties of aquatics; while under the trees you will see tuberous rooted begonias and out in the open, carpet bedding artistically arranged, with banana plants dotted here and there throughout. There are many other things of interest in this grotto, but I will leave them for you to discover later.

The number of tulips bought and planted on the grounds is 78,000; while the grand total of bedding plants will exceed 300,000.

Birdseye View of Soldiers' Home, Dayton, O.

Conservatory, National Soldiers' Home, Dayton, O.

I have given you but a small inkling of what you will see at this beautiful spot. The Home makes and distributes all of the clothing used by the different soldiers' homes in the United States, employing in the city of Dayton over 400 women in the manufacture of this clothing. The inmates of the Home number 6,800 at this writing and the cemetery contains over 9,000 graves.

The landscape work is now in charge of Herman Haerlin, Jr., who is a native of Cincinnati. Mr. Haerlin is a civil engineer, and runs his own lines and sets his grades. His position is chief gardener, and under him, taking care of the grounds, are 165 men. A man well fitted for this position is he, having been raised in the business under the guidance of his late father, H. Haerlin, Sr. The grounds of the Home comprise 652 acres. Mr. Haerlin is introducing into the Home economic, medicinal and useful trees, changing grades, laying out new beds and in many ways beautifying the grounds. On walking around you will notice many beautiful specimen trees.

Just at the entrance to the Home is Lakeview Park. Here one can shoot the chutes, ride on the scenic railway or merry-go-round, skate or bowl. At this park the individual and ladies' bowling contests of the S. A. F. will take place, while the team competition will be held at the other end of the car line, at Fairview Park.

The National Cash Register Company.

And now a few words on the only model factory in the world—the National Cash Register Company. To listen to a lecture that is delivered here twice a day will surely repay anyone many times over for the journey. Then to see the vast army of men and women employed here as they leave their work is a sight well worth seeing. The whole plant is educational, and anyone visiting the factory and not learning something must surely be dense, indeed. Forty-five hundred people are employed here; and 500,000 registers have been sold throughout the world since the institution was started. The landscape work is marvelous. The home of J. H. Patterson, where the president's reception will be held, is simply a dream. Wait and see for yourself! This factory itself is worth traveling from any part of the United States to see, even if there were no S. A. F. O. H. meeting in sight.

A visit to the Fair Grounds shows progress, and everything will be ready August 21.

E. G. GILLETT.

Points of Interest About Dayton and How to Reach Them.

National Military Home, Parent Institution of the Government—Electric cars of City Railway on Third and Fifth streets, and People's Railway westward on Third street.

Dayton State Insane Asylum—People's Railway, southward on Wayne avenue.

National Cash Register—Oakwood Street Railway, southward on Main street.

Miami Valley Hospital, and Woodland Cemetery—Oakwood Street Railway, southward on Main street.

St. Elizabeth Hospital—People's Railway, westward on Third and Washington streets.

Car Works and Water Works—People's Railway, northward on Jefferson and eastward on First street.

Fair Grounds—Xenia Traction Line.

Athletic Park of the Y. M. C. A., and Outing Park of the W. C. A.—People's Railway, northward on Main street.

Widows' Home—City Railway, eastward on Third or Fifth streets.

Cooper Park and Public Library, Van Cleve Park and Log Cabin, Soldiers' Monument, Post Office, Young Men's Christian Association, Women's Christian Association and Young Women's League Buildings—Five minutes walk from Court House.

Boulevard—By electric cars westward from Main street, or ten minutes walk through the fine residence section of Monument avenue, First, Second, Third, Fourth, and Fifth streets.

Dayton View Suburb—Oakwood Street Railway northward on Main street.

Union R. R. Station—People's electric car westward at Court House, or eight minutes walk.

The National Cash Register Company and its Welfare Work

One of the great attractions of Dayton is the "model factory" of the National Cash Register Company, its beautiful environs, and the homes of its operatives, all of whom are imbued with a love of gardening, inspired by the example provided by the president of the company, Mr. J. H. Patterson, a model citizen and master. Delegates to the forthcoming convention will be under many obligations to Mr. Patterson and his company, for courtesies shown, and for an earnest endeavor to make their visit to the Gem City both educational and pleasant.

From a booklet entitled "Nature, the Factory and the Home," recently issued by the National Cash Register Company, we take the subjoined extracts, which will show the character of the work done and doing, in a horticultural way, by this enterprising, considerate firm.

Like the outskirts of most American towns, the N. C. R. neighborhood nine years ago was dreary and uninteresting to the eye. Weather-stained cottages, built for shelter, not for beauty, straggled along ill-kept streets. The new factory, despite its substantial architecture, lost much of its pleasing character by reason of its unsightly setting. Trees, shrubs and flowers were almost unknown. Front yards were little squares of clay or neglected sod jealously fenced in. Back yards were given over to rubbish, broken furniture, piles of empty cans and boxes. The worst yards and dwellings were ugly. The best were commonplace.

Work done in such surroundings cannot be of the first quality. Health and cheerfulness are the two essentials of sustained effort. The company had already realized this and had begun welfare work for employees. The beautifying of the factory premises and the betterment of the neighborhood marked a great step forward in its effort to make labor safe, pleasant and healthful for the men and women employed at the N. C. R.

The change began with a general clearing up. Rubbish was removed from the grounds. Fences were torn down. Walks were straightened and rebuilt. The spaces about the buildings were sodded. Flowers, trees and shrubbery were planted. Conventional models were followed and the improvement was marked from the beginning. But the results were not entirely satisfactory.

To carry the work further it was decided that the aid of an expert in landscape gardening was needed. To secure a competent man was the problem. President Patterson had had an unfortunate experience

National Soldiers' Home, Dayton, O.—View North From Governor's Quarters.

with a landscape gardener, who began his "improvements" by chopping down the most valuable tree on the president's grounds. The absence of trees about the factory reassured the management, however, and the Olmsted Brothers, of Brookline, Massachusetts, were asked to submit plans.

Mr. John C. Olmsted came to Dayton. He viewed the factory grounds, noted the direction of possible growth, and began planting. He did not stop with the N. C. R. buildings and lawns. He extended his plans to cover the neighborhood. He showed by actual example how simple and easy the art of the gardener is, applying it on the one hand to the spreading factory grounds, on the other to the tiny plots usually allotted to modest town dwellings. He planted vines and shrubs and a dreary place became a pleasant picture. He showed that one could be an artist when using Nature's colors in tree and flower as well as when employing brush and paint on canvas. The aim of both is beauty.

Within a year a radical change had taken place in the appearance and in the spirit of the neighborhood. A definite idea of the thing to be taught had also been developed. This idea stands for good taste and beauty in the house and in its surroundings. It means green, smooth lawns, whether the premises be large or small, vine-covered houses, clean streets and alleys, the removal of nuisances, the improvement of working and living conditions, the rousing of interest in the physical, moral and intellectual welfare of the community and the creation of a public opinion which will demand that these ideals be put into practice in every day life.

Interest in the decorative use of shrubbery and flowers had always existed in Dayton. The Soldiers' Home, with its park-like grounds, had been to many residents an example of what could be done to improve their surroundings. The trouble was that all such effort had been haphazard, without plan or purpose. Nature's way of planting was never studied and knowledge of the first principles of outdoor art was completely lacking. To remedy this deficiency and to spread the teachings of Mr. Olmsted and Professor L. H. Bailey, of Cornell University, who analyzed what the Olmsteds had done and formulated the principles on which they worked, a systematic campaign of education was planned and executed.

Beginning with its own employees and residents of the factory neighborhood, the N. C. R. Company's teaching was in time extended to the whole city and ultimately to the people of the entire country. Simple booklets on landscape gardening, telling what to plant and how to plant it, were printed and distributed by thousands. Stereopticon lectures on outdoor art, illustrated with striking colored pictures, were delivered in every quarter of the city and in all the chief cities of the state.

Pictures teach more forcibly than words, and thousands of lantern slides were accumulated to show every phase of landscape gardening. The lessons of the lecture room were further illustrated by practical examples of planting. The vines and plants recommended by the company's gardeners were shown clinging to the factory walls or blooming on the borders of the factory lawns. Car-load lots of these were brought to Dayton and sold at actual cost to all who applied for them. To make sure that the best vines and shrubs would be used, a N. C. R. gardener talked with each purchaser and suggested the plants most suitable for the case. To the doubtful, object lessons in planting were given. Close watch was also kept of the neighborhood during the season, and the vines and shrubs which failed to thrive were given expert attention.

Out of the mass of material thus accumulated three primary rules were formulated as the basis of all outdoor art. These rules are:

a. Keep center of lawn open.
b. Plant in masses.
c. Avoid straight lines.

These simple principles—the A B C of landscape gardening—were the foundation of all the instruc-

Partial View of National Cash Register Company's Plant, Dayton, O.

N. C. R. Cottages facing the Factory

Some Backyards in South Park, Dayton, O., before and after planting

N. C. R. Extension, Showing Window Box Decorations.

tion given in turn to the N. C. R. neighborhood, the community and the state.

The illustrated lecture on landscape gardening was given for all N. C. R. employees and the N. C. R. neighborhood clubs. It was delivered in the public schools, before Sunday schools, improvement associations, business men's organizations. Its effect was widespread and immediate. The district about the factory, long known as "Slidertown," grew to be like a park in the number and beauty of its trees and shrubs. Fences were first hidden under vines and finally removed. Rickety sheds came down. Yards were cleared. "Slidertown" was forgotten and South Park became one of the show neighborhoods of the city. Of the organization of the N. C. R. Boys' Gardens, which had much to do with this transformation, an account is given elsewhere.

Not content with preaching the gospel of outdoor art, the company offered rewards for its practice. A series of substantial yearly prizes was established for the best-kept premises, the most beautiful vine effects and the most decorative window boxes. A committee, unacquainted with the contestants, selected the winners. The prizes were awarded in a big mass meeting which was itself a great factor in promoting enthusiasm for the work.

Of late years this system of prizes has extended to cover all Dayton. To encourage the interest of the children of the city the prizes are awarded only for yards and window boxes arranged and tended by pupils of the city schools. Two prizes have been allotted to each of the seventeen districts into which the city is divided.

In this work of interesting children, the Patterson School in Wyoming street has blazed the way for the other Dayton schools by beautifying its neighborhood and establishing a flower and vegetable garden for pupils. A huge adjoining lot also has been made into a miniature park, and window boxes secured for all the school windows. The Men's Improvement Club of Rubicon has carried neighborhood work to the southern limits of the city, offering on its own account a series of children's prizes for the best front gardens and window boxes.

Briefly, this is the history of one phase of N. C. R. welfare work which has, by reason of its effects, been its own reward. Slowly the results were obtained, because much of the work was along untried paths. The outcome, however, has justified the patient effort. To-day the factory has none of the dreary atmosphere of the old days. The visitor, on approaching, looks across broad lawns bordered by masses of shrubbery to buildings whose walls are relieved of monotony by clinging vines.

The N. C. R. neighborhood has felt the effects of the movement not less than the factory itself. From a section of Dayton once shunned it has come to rank as one of the most desirable of neighborhoods. Prettier dwellings, well-kept grounds, paved streets and many other improvements have followed in the wake of the landscape gardening. The value of property in South Park has been increased fourfold as the result of all this activity.

The Boys' Gardens.

No better account of the origin and purpose of the N. C. R. Boys' Gardens can be given than President Patterson's own explanation of the reasons for establishing them:

N. C. R. Boys' Gardens—Looking Toward Officers' Club.

How a N. C. R. Alley was Beautified.

"I asked one of our foreman in 1896 why he built his house on a $2,000 lot three miles from the factory, when he could have bought a lot near the factory equally good for $500. His reply was: 'I don't like the neighborhood.'

"Upon investigation, we found that three boys gave the neighborhood its bad reputation. We made an estimate of the value of the land these boys influenced in South Park within a radius of four blocks of the factory. The estimate showed that the three boys cost the property owners in the district $30,000. Ten thousand dollars for a bad boy! Studying further the cause of the trouble, we soon found that the boys were made bad by idleness. Nothing to do was the secret of their difficulty, as it is of most of the evils city life holds for boys and young men.

"The boys who were reared on farms—and I am thankful that I was one of them—were compelled to work. They had gardens to plant and cultivate, calves and fowls to feed, wood to carry in, and many other things to do. But improved machinery has cheapened farm products. It requires fewer people now to do the work. Hence the boys have been driven by the great progress of civilization to the cities. The little village blacksmith and wagon making shops have been swept away by the great industrial organizations in the cities. The little factories are gone, and the boys are here. What are we going to do with them? We must make men out of them."

Here was the problem, the solution and the outline of a policy. The company lost no time in determining to establish the Boys' Gardens. They were begun in the Spring of 1897.

Near the factory was a plot of ground adapted to the purpose. Two acres of this were plowed and forty lots, 10 feet by 130 feet each, were laid out. Seeds of various kinds were provided as well as all necessary tools and equipment. A competent gardener was secured to instruct the boys. The age limit of the gardeners was fixed at ten to fourteen years. The members of the neighborhood boys' club were given the preference in allotting gardens.

The famous recipe for rabbit stew, which began with the direction, "First catch your rabbit," seemed likely to be paraphrased in the makng of the Boys' Gardens. It was wholly a new enterprise and at first there was difficulty in "catching" the small boy, or, rather, in getting the small boy to "catch" the idea. But this obstacle was overcome, and, with the forty boys started, interest developed rapidly. By the time the seeds began to sprout, the young gardeners had become enthusiastic. Even a dry season and the necessity of carrying water did not diminish their interest.

Meanwhile the company had announced a series of prizes, amounting to $50, for the best gardens of the year. It had been agreed from the first that the boys were to own whatever they might raise. This proved profitable to many of the youngsters, some of them clearing good sums from the products of their little farm. Others kept their families supplied during the entire summer with the best of vegetables.

Only two or three dropped out of the class during the Summer, and so the results of the first year were highly satisfactory. The next season there was no difficulty in forming the class. On the contrary, applicants were far in excess of the garden plots available. Results, too, were more marked. Crops were larger and the influence of the work on the conduct of the boys was greater. More than any other effort of the N. C. R. towards neighborhood betterment the Boys' Gardens are responsible for the improvement of conditions in South Park.

Since then the project has grown continuously. The location of the gardens has been changed, and the space devoted to them enlarged. Last year the plots numbered 72. Pipes have been laid and ten hydrants obviate the work of water carrying.

A definite course of instruction is given in gardening. It covers a period of two years, at the end of which diplomas are awarded to those students who have successfully completed the work. In addition, prizes are awarded each year. Special bronze medals are given the prize-winners. The diplomas and medals are awarded at a banquet given by President Patterson to the young gardeners each year at the Officers' Club. The prizes take the form either of cash awards or of trips to various cities where the boys can study the park systems and other examples of landscape gardening.

System is a prominent feature in every department of the N. C. R. organization. So in the development of the Boys' Gardens project an effort has been made to systematize its administrative and educational functions. This has gone on slowly as problems have arisen. An outline of the plan of organization may be welcome to those who are interested in school and neighborhood gardens for children.

Application for membership in the gardening classes is made by card each Spring. This year there were three times as many applicants as there were gardens to assign. In consequence, a movement has been started to promote home gardens for those boys who failed to secure company lots.

N. C. R. Boy Gardeners and Their Products.

The application cards returned to the company are filed and kept as a permanent record. They are changed as the applicant is admitted to a class and as he progresses through the various degrees. Applicants, first-year classes, second-year classes and graduates are the divisions under which cards are filed.

Each boy to whom a plot is allotted receives notice summing up the simple conditions on which gardens are held. This card the boy signs and presents to the head gardener on the day he is instructed to report for work. Last Spring the young gardeners reported in March and began their work by helping to raise cabbage and tomato plants in hotbeds provided for their use and instruction. Thus each year the scope of the instruction is broadened to give the boys the greatest possible benefit. The first outdoor planting this year was done April 21.

With each garden and note book goes a set of tools—a rake, hoe, spade and trowel—each numbered to correspond with the garden and note book. Separate racks are provided in the tool house for each boy's outfit and he is required to keep the tools in place and in good order. All the young gardeners pay dues of ten cents each month, as it has been found advisable to let the boys feel that they are making some return for the privileges received.

The work of plowing and laying out the gardens is done by the company before the boys are given possession. This leaves only the easier preparation of the ground to the youngsters, which, with the planting, occupies the first four weeks. All necessary seeds, bulbs and sets are furnished by the company. An elective in the work is given by allowing one of the divisions in the individual gardens to be cultivated as the boy may desire. Over this strip the instructor exercises no authority. Whether the youth fills it full of growing things or leaves it uncultivated, no instruction or suggestion as to planting is offered. As a test of the boy's character and ability as a gardener this is excellent.

The instructor has a garden of his own which he cultivates in competition with the boys, the object being to demonstrate to them the most effective methods of cultivation.

Although considerable oral instruction is necessary, much of the teaching is done by example. A blackboard is used with good effect to convey to the boys the special directions for each day.

Scientific gardening is taught in a simple, practical way, so that the minds of the boys can grasp and apply its principles. The gardeners raise several crops of lettuce and three or four plantings of radishes, thus learning to secure two crops from the same ground. Every inch of space is utilized to get the best possible results with the widest variety of vegetables. Three co-operative plots were planted this Spring, all the boys sharing in the work and the product. Watermelons and muskmelons were planted in one of these, popcorn in another, and Spanish peanuts in the third.

A certain standard of progress is required in all gardens. If one boy lags behind the others in planting or cultivation, he is required to work extra time till he catches up. Promptness in beginning and stopping work is insisted upon. The gardeners' working hours are from 6:30 to 7:30 a. m. and from 4 to 5 p. m. If any boy wishes to work overtime, he must stop work with the others, report to the garden house, and receive permission to continue working after the others have quit for the day.

The prizes for the best records in gardening are awarded to the young farmers by three judges chosen from among those officers of the company who have no sons or relatives in the contest. This committee inspects the gardens at intervals, determining independently the number of points to be given. The judging is done entirely by numbers and at the lunch hour, when the boys are not at work. Members of the committee do not know by any chance to whom a particular garden belongs, and therefore no personal prejudice or favor ever creeps into the awards.

The prizes are of three sorts—cash, medals and educational trips. The cash prizes awarded for the best all-round records are as follows:

First Prize	$12 00
Second Prize	10 00
Third Prize	6 00
Fourth Prize	4 00
Fifth, Sixth, Seventh, Eighth Prizes, $2 each,	8 00
Ninth, Tenth, Eleventh, Twelfth Prizes, $1 "	4 00
Three prizes for best account books, $3, $2, $1	6 00

Exhibition Building, Fair Grounds, Dayton, O.

Where Convention and Trade Display of S. A. F. O. H. will be held.

The Camp at Far Hills, Dayton, O.

Each gardener is graded on five separate counts: 1. Value of product from his garden. 2. Condition of garden and tools. 3. Regularity of attendance. 4. Deportment. 5. Condition of account book. In awarding the prizes these five points are counted in the following ratios: 30 per cent. for value of product, 20 per cent. for condition of garden and tools, 20 per cent. for attendance, 20 per cent. for deportment, 10 per cent. for account book. Experience has shown that the best results for the boys themselves are not attained when the prizes are awarded for product alone.

All vegetables raised are weighed and their value fixed at market prices. The condition of the garden and tools is determined by the judges, who inspect the gardens regularly. The grade for attendance is based on the number of hours spent in the gardens. The rating for deportment is determined by a system of demerits—each boy having to his credit 100 merits at the beginning of the term. In the account books the dates of planting and the weight and value of all products harvested are kept. These books are graded on neatness, completeness and accuracy. To facilitate the keeping of the accounts each gardener, when his products are weighed, receives a duplicate slip stating the variety, the weight and the market value of the vegetables.

The medals awarded to the young gardeners are of bronze and were designed at Mr. Patterson's order in Paris. They are beautiful examples of work in low relief and are valued by the boys.

The last division of awards—the educational trips—is perhaps the most valuable of all. The effect of personal experiences can never be wiped out of one's character. Observing the way parks are laid out and cared for, and how artistic gardeners accomplish beautiful results, the prize-winners are helped to form right ideas in much besides gardening and flower planting. On these trips the youngsters are afforded every opportunity to study the city parks and greenhouses. Besides these special prizes, to every gardener who passes satisfactorily through the two-years course, a diploma signed by the company officers is awarded.

The boys are encouraged to make a beginning on home gardening at the same time that they are receiving the benefits of the company gardens. For this purpose additional seeds and plants are furnished to those who want them. This helps to get the garden habit firmly established at a time when the interest in such work is predominant over interest in all other occupations.

Besides teaching the boys how to plant and cultivate vegetables, the instructor gives the gardeners short talks which awaken in them a keener realization of their own kinship to all life and growth. These lectures are given out of doors in the atmosphere of the garden and at such times as are best adapted for letting the boys make their own interpretation of the facts given. Some of the subjects which are informally covered in this way are: Seed germination; the relation of water, air and temperature to germination; roots, stems, buds, sap, leaves; propagation by layering, grafting and budding; cross-fertilization and methods of improving varieties. They are also taught how to choose the varieties of flowers, fruits and vegetables best adapted for planting in particular localities.

Budding and grafting are also taught. In connection with the garden, a nursery of both peach and apple seedlings is maintained. Budding is done in July and grafting in the early Spring. Both involve considerable practice work which forms an excellent phase of manual training. As soon as the members of the class have learned the necessary operations, they are each allowed to transform several of the trees in the nursery. In the Autumn the budded stock it dug up and given to the boys who performed the budding. When planted in their own home yards these trees form life-long reminders of the years spent at the N. C. R. gardens. Besides gathering the fruit of the trees in future years the boys are given an excellent lesson in the realization of what stupendous results may be the outcome of slight present actions.

"Form, not reform," has been the animating principle in this gardening project. Teaching the boys to work, and teaching them interest in Nature, were believed by the company to be the right steps in forming character. Instruction only puts facts into the mind, while education develops the mind. Education brings out and strengthens character, trains one to meet and overcome difficulties, and cultivates courage, industry and ability. It is this sort of education the gardens give. The practice in measuring, in watching for things to come up, in learning to observe what they look at and to understand what they see, the increased love for Nature and things beautiful, the development of their bodies in the pure open air, the fixing of habits of industry, the prevention of idling on the streets—these are some of the benfits of the Boys' Gardens. They are benefits of far greater importance, both to the boys and to the state, than the value of the crops raised, which is considerable, while the cost of making the gardens is small.

There is no kind of teaching that squares itself with educational thought better than gardening. It educates because it deals with things and not with words. It cultivates observation, and keeps the senses keen. It shows that effect follows cause. It gives full play to all the motor activities. It broadens the mind and deepens thinking. When it is considered that sixty-five per cent. of American exports are products of the farm, it is easily understood what benefit children receive by being taught practically the fundamental importance of agriculture in social life. The value of the moral training is beyond any concrete estimate. By impressing children with the idea that personal, sustained effort is necessary to achieve a result they are given the first great lesson in citizenship.

The Trade Exhibition.

The trade exhibition will be located in the central pavilion at the Fair Grounds. Growers of plants, seeds, bulbs, shrubs and trees, dealers in florists' supplies, greenhouse requisites, building material for greenhouse construction, heating apparatus, etc., can here meet the best buyers in the horticultural profession, and no better opportunity for directing attention to the special merits of their goods can be found.

N. B. Exhibitors are reminded that the duties of the judges are limited to the consideration of and making of awards to Novelties and Improved Devices only. Exhibitors are required to make previous entry of all such exhibits with the superintendent in writing. Full rules and regulations, together with diagrams of the exhibition hall, may be obtained from Horace M. Frank, Superintendent, 112 South Main street, Dayton, O., to whom all applications for space should be made as early as possible.

Outdoor Exhibition.

This convention offers the first opportunity in the society's history to make a display of outdoor planted material. There is yet room for the placing of others and dealers having pot-grown stock to offer can have same properly set out, labelled and cared for without extra charge, until the Convention, by making prompt application to Harry M. Altick, Vice-president, who has charge of this department.

Water Lily Pond, Soldiers' Home, Dayton, O.

F. W. Ritter.
Chairman Reception Committee Dayton Florists' Club

H. Haerlin, Jr.
Supt. of Grounds, Soldiers' Home, Dayton, O.

Bulbs for Testing.

American growers of any forcing bulbs, plants or seeds of sorts not yet grown in this country in commercial quantity, or dealers controlling stocks of such goods, are invited to send samples of their product to the trade exhibition, where they will be given space free of charge, provided the bulbs then become the property of the society for testing purposes as to their forcing qualities, results of said testing and awards for quality to be published the following season. **Please make entries with the secretary.**

Badge Book.

In accordance with the instructions voted by the society last year in Washington, a system of numbered badges and key-book to correspond has been put into operation this year under the direction of the Executive Board. It is believed that the members will find these numbers valuable as a conveulent means of identification of one another. The names of all new members joining prior to July 15 this year, have been included in the list. Each member of the society will be supplied with a copy of the book.

Horace M. Frank, Secretary — J. B. Heiss, President — C. Lutzenberger, Vice-President — H. H. Ritter, Treasurer

Officers of the Dayton Florists' Club

The Misses M. and L. Johnson,
On Ladies' Committee Dayton Florists' Club

Welcome to Dayton.

Comrades, come let us join together
 Ere the season passes by;
Let us join our hands in friendship
 'Neath the Summer's azure sky.
For we know you'll ne'er regret it,
 Just our city once to see
In its thriving wealth and beauty
 Is an opportunity.

And the art of horticulture
 Draws us nearer to our God;
For there's beauty in the blossom,
 And there's rest within the sod.
And the heart and hand united
 Is a joy you will admit.
We ask you to come and join us
 In the bond of friendship.

Dayton, Ohio. BESSIE E. DORNBUSCH.

ALL ABOARD FOR DAYTON.

To Dayton from New York, Boston and the East.

The New York Central Lines have been selected by the New York Florists' Club as the official route to Dayton convention. Rate of fare and one-third, on the certificate plan, has been authorized for the round trip. When purchasing ticket to Dayton, ask agent for a certificate, which, when properly vised at the meeting, will entitle you to ticket at one-third fare returning.

		R. R. Tkt.	B'th.
MONDAY, AUGUST 20th.			
Lv. New York, N. Y. Central	2:04 p.m.	$17.25	$4.00
Lv. Boston, B. & A. R. R.	10:45 a.m.	19.25	.....
Lv. Worcester, B. & A. R. R.	11:55 a.m.	18.25	.....
Lv. Springfield, B. & A. R. R.	1:11 p.m.	17.25	.....
Lv. Pittsfield, B. & A. R. R.	2:59 p.m.	16.92	.....
Ar. Albany, B. & A. R. R.	4:15 p.m.	.....	.....
Lv. Albany, N. Y. Central	5:05 p.m.	15.75	4.00
Lv. Schenectady, N. Y. Central	5:36 p.m.	15.50	4.00
Lv. Utica, N. Y. Central	7:09 p.m.	14.49	3.50
Lv. Syracuse, N. Y. Central	8:24 p.m.	13.43	3.00
Lv. Rochester, N. Y. Central	10:00 p.m.	11.83	2.50
Ar. Buffalo, N. Y. Central	11:37 p.m.	.....	.....
Lv. Buffalo, L. S. & M. S.	11:52 p.m.	10.45	2.50
TUESDAY, AUGUST, 21st.			
Ar. Dayton, Big 4	8:55 a.m.	.....	.....

The members from New England points will note from above schedule that they will join the New York Florists' Club at Albany, thus affording an opportunity of traveling together, adding materially to the enjoyment of the trip.

Certain privileges are granted in connection with tickets reading via these lines without additional cost. These tickets will be accepted for passage by the C. & B. Steamboat Line between Cleveland and Buffalo, also by the Hudson River Day Line or People's Night Line from Albany to New York, upon notice to the conductor; permission to stopover at Niagara Falls for a period not exceeding ten days, but tickets must be deposited with depot agent at Niagara Falls immediately upon arrival.

Exclusive Pullman sleepers to run through without change will be arranged if a sufficient number of applications are made to the committee in charge, consequently communicate at the earliest possible date with Walter F. Sheridan, 39 West Twenty-eighth street, New York City.

FRANK H. TRAENDLY,
JOHN B. NUGENT, Jr.,
WALTER F. SHERIDAN,
Transportation Committee.

Or tickets may be purchased from Alex. Macfarlane, Ticket Agent, New York Central, 1216 Broadway, New York.

Chicago to Dayton—via Big Four.

The Chicago Florists' Club has concluded arrangements for the special train over the Cleveland, Cincinnati, Chicago and St. Louis Ry., leaving Michigan Central Passenger station, Twelfth street, Chicago, at 12:45 noon, Monday, August 20, and due to arrive in Dayton, via Kankakee, La Fayette and Indianapolis, about 8:40 p. m., practically a daylight ride all the way.

The train will consist of three or more new day coaches, one combination car, one dining car to serve luncheon and dinner a la carte.

The rate by the certificate plan for the round trip is only $9.70. These tickets are good on all trains August 17 to 23 and for the return trip the validated certificates will be honored up to and including August 31.

The Chicago Florists' Club cordially invites the florists of the northwest and southwest, delegates to the convention, to join this special train at Chicago Monday noon as above stated, and see that when they buy their tickets and secure their certificates for the same that these tickets read "via Big Four Route" from Chicago to Dayton.

Delegates who can join us at any point along our route are requested to do so. The committee will be glad to hear as early as possible from all who decide to join our party, so that the necessary arrangements can be made in time. Delegates buying tickets at Chicago will secure them at the city ticket office of the Big Four, 238 S. Clark street, with certificates.

P. J. HAUSWIRTH,
President.
L. H. WINTERSON,
Secretary.
J. C. VAUGHAN,
WILLIS N. RUDD,
GEORGE ASMUS,
Committee on Transportation.

Delegates to the Dayton convention should buy their tickets from lines represented by the Western Passenger Association, but keep in mind that traveling on their tickets they must leave Dayton no later than August 28. This is three days earlier than the limit allowed by the Central Passenger Association. This association covers most lines running west from Chicago. Always take certificates when buying tickets.
J. C. VAUGHAN.

Union Station, Dayton, O.

Hotel Algonquin, Dayton, O.

CINCINNATI.—The special train for our delegates to Dayton will leave this city over the C. H. & D. R. R., at 8:15 a. m. Tuesday, August 21. We shall be more than pleased to have all the florists tributary to Cincinnati join us.

DETROIT.—We have decided to travel over the C. H. & D. leaving by the 12:35 noon train, Monday, August 20.

PHILADELPHIA, PA.—Delegates will depart on Monday, August 20, at 4:30 p. m., by Pennsylvania Railroad, from Broad street station, arriving in Dayton at 9 a. m. Tuesday. Fare, $20.67 for the round trip. The Baltimore delegation will join us.

ST. LOUIS.—The conventionites will travel over the Vandalia Road, leaving Monday, August 20, at 8:15, arriving at Dayton at 8 a. m. next day. The fare will be $12 for the round trip.

WASHINGTON, D. C.—The delegates to the S. A. F. convention will travel by the B. & O. Railroad.

Hotels in Dayton.

All hotels are within one square of all street cars, taking you to the exhibition grounds within ten minutes. Following is a list with capacity and prices of the leading hotels:

Hotel	Capacity	Per day
AMERICAN PLAN		
The Algonquin	300	$2.50 to $5.00
The Beckel	200	$2.00 to $4.00
The Phillips	150	$2.00 to $2.50
Hotel Daytonia	100	$1.00 to $1.50
The Aldine	25	$1.00 to $1.50
The Vendome	25	$1.50
EUROPEAN PLAN		
The Atlas	75	$1.00 to $2.00
The Wehner	50	.50 to 75
The Stag Hotel	25	.50
The Urban	60	.50 to $1.00

The hotel committee has also on its list a number of smaller hotels and a whole lot of private houses, prices from 50c. to 75c. for single rooms. If enough applications are made a camp will be established, with well-furnished double-roof tents, four cots to a tent, at a nominal cost of from 50c. to 75c. each. Any wanting accommodations, if no individual arrangements are preferred, should make application as soon as possible to J. B. Heiss, Chairman of Hotel Committee, who will see that all are satisfactorily accommodated.

The Algonquin hotel will be headquarters of the S. A. F. O. H., and already preparations are being made for the accommodation of the many who have asked for rooms at the hotel.

The Bowling.

Wednesday, August 22, has been set aside for all ten pin contests, and the alleys at Lakeside and Fairview parks will be the scenes of battle. The team contests will begin at the Fairview park alleys at 1:30 and continue until 7:30 p. m. Each team will roll two games, total pins to count. There are no less than three "perpetual" trophies to be contested for by the winners. In addition to this, the Crawford, McGregor & Canby Company of Dayton have added a handsome silver cup to the list of prizes. There will be no less than three special team and individual prizes.

George Asmus,
Convention Sports Manager

At the conclusion of the team contests the individual player of each team having scored the greatest number of pins, along with the five "unattached" players making the best record in the "try outs" will roll for the individual championship.

While the "star" rollers are striving for the honors at the Fairview alleys, about 40 "unattached" bowlers, but members of the S. A. F., will roll a "try out" series at the Lakeside park alleys, beginning at 1:30 p. m. At 4:00 p. m. the women's contest will be started. Already no less than 30 of the fair sex have entered, and a spirited contest is looked for. Some very handsome prizes have been provided for this particular competition. The bowling competition is in charge of Harry Altick of this city, George Asmus of Chicago, and Sam Karpf, secretary of the American Bowling Congress.

Inasmuch as the "star" rollers will remain in this city nearly a week, it is probable that a number of special matches will be arranged with some of the local bowlers to be played at both the parks and the Headquarters alleys.—Dayton News.

Associate Bowlers and Shooters.

Editor Florists' Exchange:

Regarding the inquiry of the Baltimore Gardeners' Club as to the eligibility of associate bowlers in teams bowling at the S. A. F. O. H. convention, I would state that this question has come up for several years, and it was generally decided at a captains' meeting called prior to the contest, where the names of the contestants on each team are presented by the respective captains; and at that time if there is any protest against any player or players it is there considered. The chairman of the committee on sports does not think that this question comes under his jurisdiction. There is a permanent organization of the bowling clubs, which was inaugurated some years back, to regulate the game at our tournaments; and I believe this subject should come up at their meeting this year in Dayton.

Trusting that the matter referred to by the Baltimore Gardeners' Club will be settled amicably and equably.

Chicago. GEORGE ASMUS.
Chairman of Committee on Sports.

Mrs. J. F. Young,
Florist, Dayton, O.

CLASSIFIED ADVERTISEMENTS

CASH WITH ORDER.

The columns under this heading are reserved for advertisements of Stock for Sale, Stock Wanted, Help Wanted, Situations Wanted or other Wants; also of Greenhouse, Land, Second-Hand Materials, etc., For Sale or Rent.

Our charge is 10 cts. per line (7 words to the line), set solid, without display. No advt. accepted for less than thirty cents.

Display advertisements in these columns, 15 cents per line; count 12 lines agate to the inch.

[If replies to Help Wanted, Situation Wanted, or other advertisements are to be addressed care of this office, advertisers add 10 cents to cover expense of forwarding.]

Copy must reach New York office 12 o'clock Wednesday to secure insertion in issue of following Saturday.

Advertisers in the Western States desiring to advertise under initials, may save time by having their answer directed care our Chicago office at 127 E. Berwyn Ave.

SITUATIONS WANTED

SITUATION WANTED—A No 1 Beauty and tea rose grower. Best of references. 15 years experience; married. A. J. Ayres, Murray Hill, New Jersey.

SITUATION WANTED—As foreman of a rose establishment. References, stating character, intelligence and ability given on application. Address, M. P., care The Florists' Exchange.

SITUATION WANTED — First-class orchid grower and gardener with thorough experience needs situation. References first-class. Appy, N. H., care The Florists' Exchange.

SITUATION WANTED—As foreman by single man of 29. Well up in palms, ferns and pot plants. Roses, carnations and cut flowers in general. 14 years experience. Best of references. Address, N. E., care The Florists' Exchange.

SITUATION WANTED—As foreman by grower of roses, carnations, chrysanthemums and general stock. Roses a specialty; A No. 1 references. Aged 36, single, only a first-class place wanted. N. D., care The Florists' Exchange.

SITUATION WANTED—By young man, willing, honest and strictly sober. 23 years of age with one year private experience in greenhouses. At present employed; desires position on small business place. Chas A. Peterson, Rocky Dill Farm, White Plains, New York.

SITUATION WANTED—As foreman in good private place by Englishman, aged 27, single, life experience in first-class places (1 1-2 years in this country); disengaged early September. Good references. C. Young, Rahallion, Sea Bright, N. J.

SITUATION WANTED—American, 30 years old, 10 years experience in stores and greenhouses, designing and decorating, bedding out, etc. Willing to go West or South. Good references. Strictly temperate. Go now or a little later. Address, Florist, 247 Cumberland av., Portland, Maine.

TO IMPORTERS of plants, etc.—Advertiser with 20 years experience as a buyer of all kinds of high grade nursery produce on the London, England, market, seeks position with an American house to represent them in London. First-class references. Address, A. B., care Corneille & Company, 120 Hudson street, New York City.

SITUATION WANTED—As working foreman in a small or large commercial or private place. 26 years experience, good grower in cut flowers and pot plants, also landscape gardening, vegetables, etc. German, 40 years of age, married, best of references. Please state particulars in first letter. Address, B. Y., Post-Office, Newark, N. J.

SITUATION WANTED—Able Italian gardener, with five years experience in this country, specialist in pot flowers and ferns, understanding thoroughly all kinds of greenhouse work, desires situation as working foreman, either with employer or private family. Can furnish best of references and certificates as to his ability. Wages, $14 per week. Address, Labor Information Office for Italians, 59 Lafayette street, New York City.

HELP WANTED

WANTED—A good steady man to grow carnations and pot plants. State age and experience when answering. Arthur H. Bool, Ithaca, N. Y.

WANTED—A gardener for New York store, one who understands plants and outdoor work. Steady position for competent man. Address, N. L., care The Florists' Exchange.

WANTED—September 1, young or middle aged man of experience in general nursery work. Must be able to take charge of shipping and propagating. State wages wanted, age, nationality and references. C. R. Fish & Company, West Side Nurseries, Worcester, Mass.

HELP WANTED

WANTED—A thoroughly competent man to take charge of a section of Beauties. Apply Frank Dolan, care of John Young Company, Bedford Station, New York.

WANTED—Assistant for rose houses, young man who has had one or two years' experience preferred. Address, Robert Miller, Rose grower, East Brookfield, Mass.

WANTED—A first-class man for retail florist in Chicago; no greenhouse work. Must be a good salesman and designer. State wages. References. Address, M. D., care The Florists' Exchange.

WANTED—Man for general greenhouse work. Steady place; state age, experience and wages expected with room and board if single, without if married. Chas. Frost, Box 24, Kenilworth, N. J.

WANTED—An energetic young man to assist in landscape work; fair knowledge of stock, trimming, etc., essential. Dutch or German preferred. State wages expected with references. A. Van Leeuwen, Jr., Worcester, Mass.

WANTED—Experienced grower of chrysanthemums, carnations and bedding stock. State where last employed and wages expected with board per month. Address, N. F., care The Florists' Exchange.

WANTED—Salesman, to represent a well established Eastern nursery where nothing but the highest grade of specimen stock is carried. Must be thoroughly experienced and capable of commanding the best class of trade. Territory, Long Isand, vicinity of New York and Southern Connecticut. Good salary to competent party. Interview will be arranged for. Address, N. C., care The Florists' Exchange.

WANTED

Salesman, designer and decorator; must be up-to-date and able to take charge of first-class trade. None but A No. 1 need apply. Good wages to right party.

HOFFMAN
61 Massachusetts Ave. BOSTON, MASS.

FOREMAN WANTED

In Ornamental Nursery. State Salary and Experience. Address, E., Care THE FLORISTS' EXCHANGE.

MISCELLANEOUS WANTS

WANTED—To buy, second-hand Dean steam or hot-water heater, style "C." Address Box 72, Shrewsbury, Mass.

WANTED TO BUY—Greenhouses to be taken down. State full particulars of same when writing. Address, F. W., care The Florists' Exchange.

H. MILLER, dealer in Plants, bulbs, seeds, etc., 784 Broadway, Brooklyn, N. Y. Send me your wholesale catalogues.

WANTED—20,000 Retinispora plumosa aurea, 4 to 6 inches, transplanted. Also 4,000 Retinispora Squarrosa Veitchii, 6 inches, transplanted. Address Rhode Island Nurseries, Newport, R. I.

WANTED—For export to Europe, dried moss, dried flowers, artificial leaves, thistle fruit, and othr material for making wreaths. Kindly send samples and prices to osepb Fisher, 1022 Main Street, Cincinnati, Ohio.

WE will exchange 400 strings of smilax, value 10c. each for Mrs. T. W. Lawson and Enchantress carnation plants. The smilax will be ready September 15, and we will ship as wanted until October 15. Joseph E. Cornell & Company, Danbury, Ct.

FOR SALE OR RENT

FOR SALE—Three greenhouses of about 6,000 feet of glass. Good established retail business, or would rent for term of years. George Main, Gloversville, New York.

FOR SALE—Greenhouse plant, 40,000 square feet of glass; well stocked with roses, carnations, mums and smilax; all in good condition. Brisk wholesale trade. Outside city lines; taxes are small; steam heat; plenty of water; comfortable dwelling with modern improvements; all buildings in good order; 23 acres of farm and garden land. Trolley line passes; fifteen minutes from R. R. station driving. Good reason for selling. For price and all information address Florist, P. O., General Delivery, Albany, New York.

FOR SALE OR RENT

FOR SALE or will rent to a responsible party, a fine greenhouse property. 13,000 feet of glass. Fine residence. Address, Silas C. Howell, Lock Box 14, Pine Bush, New York.

FOR RENT—Small greenhouse and florist business in prosperous running condition. Southern Connecticut. Full particulars and reason for renting to anyone interested. Address, N. G., care The Florists' Exchange.

FOR SALE—Greenhouse comprising over 5,000 square feet of glass situated in Northern New Jersey. Including all stock, horse, wagons, and harness, etc. Doing good retail business. Address, B., care Florists' Exchange.

DESIRABLE greenhouse plant of three houses, 24x200 feet; propagating house, 100 feet; potting shed, stable and dwelling. Steam heat, city water. Highland, opposite Poughkeepsie. Joseph Wood, Spring Valley, New York.

FOR SALE—House, 7 rooms, steam heat, 1 stable, 5 greenhouses, well stocked; steam heat, Kearney, N. J., 5 minutes from Erie R. R. depot, and 5 minutes from N. Y. trolley. J. G. Perry, Schuyler Avenue, Kearney, New Jersey.

FOR SALE—A paying greenhouse establishment of 7,500 feet glass, with nearly one acre of ground, six room cottage house in a growing city of 15,000. Only one other establishment in the city. In Central Ohio. Reason for selling ill-health. Full particulars on application. Or will sell material in greenhouses alone. Address, M. X., care Florists' Exchange.

FOR SALE—At a bargain on account of removal and having two places, I will sell four greenhouses, two houses 16 x 80, other two 22 x 80. Boiler house, 16 x 20, with one large boiler to heat the place and another in reserve. Both boilers can burn buckwheat coal at a small cost. Only three or four years in use. Price only $1500. Hill Top Greenhouses, 15-16 Gray avenue, Utica, New York.

FOR SALE—An old established florist business. Consisting of store and seven greenhouses. Situated on the corner of Broadway and Orchard streets in the city of Kingston, N. Y. Population, 26,000. Cash sales for 1905 over $6000. Over $3000 spent in repairs put on place last year. All heated by hot water and place as good as new. Object for selling: wish to go into other business. Apply for particulars to M. B. Myers, Real Estate Agent, Kingston, New York.

FOR SALE—Owing to failing health, I will sell my florist establishment, beautifully situated between Larchmont Manor and Mamaroneck, Westchester Co., New York, near railroad station; trolley lines within one minute walk. First class opportunity for the right man. Plenty of landscape and jobbing work. The place contains four acres, 2 greenhouses, 104 feet long and lots of sash; well stocked with trees and shrubs, etc.; horse, wagon and tools. Address, Box 44, Larchmont, New York.

FOR SALE—On account of failing health, a florist business well established, situated near trolley and railroad station, fifteen minutes drive from a city of over 100,000 inhabitants and thirty minutes from New York City. Three greenhouses (plenty market stock on hand) plenty of sashes, dwelling house of six rooms, barn, horse, three wagons and sleigh, tools, etc. A gold mine for the right man. Must be seen to be appreciated. Address, M. Y., care Florists' Exchange.

STOCK FOR SALE

JERUSALEM CHERRIES, 2 1-2-in. pots only, $3 per 100. Cash please. A. Relyea & Son, Poughkeepsie, New York.

PEONY FESTIVA MAXIMA, and other best sorts in strong plants, 2 yr. old. Catalogue free. A. Dessert, Peony Specialist, Chenonceaux, France.

SEEDS, pansy, new crop, $1.00 per packet; $4.00 per oz.; $12.00 per 1-4 lb. Pansy plants, $4.00 per 1,000. Cash. B. Soltau, 199 Grant avenue, Jersey City, N. J.

PRIMULA, Chinese, finest fringed, mixed, 1 3-4 c. Cash. Our Giant pansies ready next month. Shippensburg Floral Company, Shippensburg, Pa.

BABY RAMBLER ROSES, H. P. and Rambler roses, field grown, 2 year stock, for sale cheap. Write for list. Schaufelberger & Hill, Penfield, New York.

QUEEN LOUISE and C. A. Dana Carnations, $5.00 per 100; $35.00 per 1,000. Giant Double Alyssum, 2 in., $2.00 per 100. Will exchange either for A. plumosus nanus. Fox & Rosen, Parkerford, Pa.

CARNATIONS, field plants. Enchantress, $6 per 100; $50 per 1000; Boston Market, $5 per 100; $40 per 1000; Lawson, $5 per 100; $40 per 1000; Red Lawson, $6 per 100; $50 per 1000. The J. A. Budlong & Son Co., Auburn, R. I.

CARNATIONS, first-class, field grown plants. Enchantress, Lawson, Queen, $6.00 per 100; $50.00 per 1000. Cash with order please. Mrs. P. F. Conley, Princeton Avenue, & Updike Street, Providence, R. I.

STOCK FOR SALE—Brides, Maids and American Beauties, in 4 in. pots; best of plants. Also 1 year old Asparagus. All at low bottom prices. Small or large orders. Madison Rose Company, Madison, N. J.

STOCK FOR SALE

JARDINIERE FERNS, seedlings, good, strong, healthy stock, in variety only. Now ready for potting. Price, $1.50 per 100 by mail; $10.00 per 1000, F. O. B. Exp. B. Soltau, 199 Grant avenue, Jersey City, N. J.

CARNATION PLANTS, nice field-grown. Enchantress, Mrs. T. W. Lawson, $6.00 per 100; Joost, New Daybreak, orProsperity, Wolcott, $5.00 per 100. For cash. M. J. Schaaf, Dansville, N. Y.

BABY RAMBLER roses, fine dormant stock, $25 per 100. 2 1-2 inch pot plants, extra well rooted $7 per 100, $65 per 1000. Orders booked for delivery now or any time up to late Spring. Samples free. Brown Brothers Co., Rochester, N. Y.

YUCCA FILAMENTOSA, $1.00 lb.; Amorpha fruticosa, 25c. lb.; Ampelopsis quinquefolia, 75c. lb.; Azalea arborescens, $2.00 lb.; Corylus rostrata, 50c. lb.; Crataegus crus-galli, 25c. lb.; Juglans cinerea, $1.00 bu.; Juglans nigra, $1.00 bu.; Cornus florida, 20c. lb. F. M. Crayton, Box 393, Biltmore, N. C.

LATANIA BORBONICA, 2 1-2 in., 4 leaves, $4.00 per 100. Chamaerops excelsa, 2 in., $3.00 per 100. Sable Palmetto, 2 in., $3.00 per 100. N. Bostoniensis and Piersoni runners, $1.50 per 100. N. Barrowsii runners, $5.00 per 100. N. Anna Foster and Scottii runners, $3.00 per 100. B. M. Wichers & Co., Gretna, La.

BERBERIS THUNBERGII, 3000, 16 to 20 in. at $55.00 per 1000; 3000 Laurel Leaf Willow, 4 to 5 ft., at $75.00 per 1000; 3000 6 to 7 ft. Laurel Leaf Willow at $120.00 per 1000; 3000 Golden Willow, 4 to 5 ft., $75.00 per 1000; 3000 Golden Willow, 6 to 7 ft., $120.00 per 1000. Pierce Nursery, Beverly Farms, Mass.

FOR SALE

FOR SALE—One horizontal boiler; 40 horse power; all complete; good condition; cheap. Alex. B. Garden, Anacostia, D. C.

FOR SALE—Glass, about 65 boxes, 10 x 12, extra double thick, $1.85; also about 15 boxes 16 x 20, $2.50. I Suesserman, 229 Livingston Street, Newark, N. J.

FOR SALE—12 Hitchings hot water expansion tanks for 3 1-2 in. pipe, in good condition, cleaned, ready to set up. 1-3 price of new. Also horse lawn mower, easy running, $20.00. Address, K. D., care The Florists' Exchange.

FOR SALE—Stover fifty foot Steel Tower and Tank in use a short time. Good as new; price reasonable. Write for particulars. Wm. C. De Witt, R. F. D. No. 1, Phillipsburg, N. J.

10,000 5 in. pots, as good as new, cost $12.00 per 1000; will sell for $9.00 per 1000. Cash with all orders please. Dean & Parse, 46 to 52 Ashwood Avenue, Summit, New Jersey.

BOILERS, BOILERS, BOILERS.

SEVERAL good second hand boilers on hand, also new No. 16 Hitchings at reduced cost. Write for list. Wm. H. Lutton, West Side Avenue Station, C. R. R. of N. J., Jersey City, N. J.

FOR SALE—Six 4 inch gate valves, good as new, at $4.00. Large lot calla clumps, 16 large azalea indica plants in 12 x 14 inch pots for cutting; 100 large clumps Adiantum Cuneatum. 20 boxes 8 x 10 double thick glass. Clean, $2.25 box. J. Geist, Melrose, Mass. Tel. 333-5.

FOR SALE

PUMPS Rider-Ericsson. Second-hand, from $40.00 up; all repairs; other makes; new; cheap.

BOILERS One second-hand tubular hot water boiler 3 ft. in diameter 12 ft. long. Price $35.00. One No. 15 Hitchings as good as new, $60.00.

PIPE Good serviceable second-hand, with Threads; 2-in., 7 cts.; 1½-in., 5½ cts.; 1¼-in., 4 cts.; 1-in., 3 cts.; 2½ in., 10 cts.; 3 in., 14 cts.; 4 in., 19 cts. New 2-in. Standard, full lengths, with couplings, 8½ cts. ft. Old and new fittings and valves. Old 4 inch cast iron 15c per foot.

STOCKS and DIES New Economy, best made No. 1 Threads, ¼-in., ¾-in. 1-in. pipe, $3.00. No. 2 Threads, 1¼-in., 1½-in. 2-in. pipe, $4.00.

PIPE CUTTERS New Saunders Pattern, No. 1 cuts ⅛-in.-1-in. pipe $1.00. No. 2 cuts 1-in.-2-in. pipe, $1.30.

STILLSON WRENCHES New. 18-in., grips ¼-in.-2-in. pipe, $1.65; 24-in. grips ¼-in.-2½ in. pipe, $2.40; 36-in., grips ½-in.-3½-in. pipe, $4.75.

PIPE VISES New. No. 1 Hinged, grips ⅛-in.-2 in. pipe, $2.00.

GARDEN HOSE New. 50 ft. lengths, ¾-in., guaranteed 100-lbs. pressure, 7½ cts. per ft.; ¾-in. not guaranteed, 4½ cts. per ft., 25 ft. lengths, ½c. per ft. more.

HOT-BED SASH New. Cypress, 3-ft.x6 ft., from 75 cts. up; glazed, complete, from $1.60 up. Second-hand, in good condition, all glass in, $1.00 each.

GLASS New American 10x12 single $1.75 per box; 12x12 single $1.90 per box; 10x12 $2.55, 12x12, 10x15 double $2.65 per box; 12x14, 12x20, 14x14, double, $2.75 per box; 12x16, 18x18, $3.10 per box; 16x24 double $3.25 per box. Second hand glass, 8 x 10, 8 x 12, double, $1.65 per box. Single $1.50.

Old material, ridge, plates, gutters, bars, etc.

Get our prices on New Gulf Cypress Building Material, Ventilating Apparatus, Oil, White Lead, Putty, Paint, Points, etc.

METROPOLITAN MATERIAL CO.

1398-1408 Metropolitan Avenue, BROOKLYN, N.Y.

Mention The Florists' Exchange when writing.

Wholesale Prices of Cut Flowers, New York, August 16, 1906

Prices quoted are by the hundred unless otherwise noted.

Roses	A. Beauty, fancy—special	6.00 to	15.00
	" extra	5.00 to	6.00
	" No. 1	4.00 to	5.00
	" No. 2	3.00 to	4.00
	" No. 3	1.00 to	1.50
	Bride, Maid, fancy—spe'l	3.00 to	4.00
	" extra	2.00 to	3.00
	" No. 1	1.00 to	2.00
	" No. 2	.25 to	.50
	Golden Gate	1.00 to	5.00
	Liberty	...... to	.....
	Mme. Abel Chatenay	1.00 to	6.00
Adiantum		.50 to	.75
	Croweanum	.50 to	1.00
Asparagus		25.00 to	50.00
	" Plumosus, bunches	8.00 to	15.00
	" Sprengerii, bunches	8.00 to	15.00
Asters		.25 to	1.00
Cattleyas		50.00 to	60.00
Daisies		.50 to	1.00
Gladiolus		.50 to	1.00
		...... to	.....

Carnations	Inf'r grades, all colors	.50 to	1.00
	Standard Varieties — White	1.00 to	2.00
	Standard Varieties — Pink	1.00 to	2.00
	Standard Varieties — Red	1.00 to	2.00
	Standard Varieties — Yel. & Var.	1.00 to	2.00
	*Fancy— (*The highest grades of standard var.) — White	2.00 to	2.50
	*Fancy — Pink	2.00 to	2.50
	*Fancy — Red	2.00 to	2.50
	*Fancy — Yel. & Var.	...... to	.....
	Novelties	...... to	.....
Dahlias, per bunch		.05 to	.10
Lilies		4.00 to	6.00
Lily of the Valley		1.00 to	3.00
Mignonette		...... to	.....
		...... to	.....
		...... to	.....
		...... to	.....
Pansies, per dozen bunches		.50 to	.75
Smilax		8.00 to	10.00
Sweet Peas, per bunch		.01 to	.03

Wholesale Prices of Cut Flowers—Per 100

Boston Aug. 14, 1906	Buffalo Aug. 13, 1906	Detroit Aug. 5, 1906	Cincinnati Aug. 11, 1906	Baltimore Aug. 6, 1906	NAMES AND VARIETIES	Milwaukee July 28, 1906	Phil'delphia July 24, 1906	Pittsburg Aug. 14, 1906	St. Louis Aug. 13, 1906
10.00 to 20.00	20.00 to 25.00	10.00 to 35.00	... to ...	... to ...	ROSES—A. BEAUTY, fancy—special	... to 25.00	15.00 to 20.00	25.00 to 30.00	15.00 to 20.00
6.00 to 10.00	12.00 to 20.00	... to ...	... to ...	12.50 to 15.00	" extra	15.00 to 18.00	10.00 to 15.00	... to 20.00	10.00 to 12.50
2.00 to 6.00	6.00 to 12.00	... to ...	... to ...	5.00 to 8.00	" No. 1	10.00 to 12.50	5.00 to 7.00	12.50 to 15.00	6.00 to 8.00
2.00 to 4.00	3.00 to 6.00	... to ...	... to ...	... to ...	" Culls and ordinary	4.00 to 6.00	1.00 to 4.00	3.00 to 5.00	3.00 to 5.00
... to ...	5.00 to 6.00	3.00 to 6.00	2.00 to 4.00	... to ...	BRIDE, 'MAID, fancy-special	... to 6.00	... to ...	... to ...	4.00 to 5.00
... to ...	4.00 to 5.00	... to ...	2.00 to 5.00	... to 4.00	" extra	... to 5.00	6.00 to 8.00	... to 6.00	2.00 to 3.00
2.00 to 6.00	3.00 to 4.00	... to ...	1.00 to 2.00	... to 3.00	" No. 1	... to 4.00	4.00 to 5.00	... to 4.00	... to ...
1.00 to 2.00	2.00 to 3.00	... to ...	... to ...	... to 2.00	" No. 2	... to 2.00	2.00 to 3.00	2.00 to 3.00	... to ...
... to ...	... to ...	4.00 to 8.00	... to ...	2.00 to 4.00	GOLDEN GATE	4.00 to 6.00	4.00 to 5.00	... to ...	2.00 to 4.00
2.00 to 8.00	3.00 to 7.00	... to ...	2.00 to 6.00	4.00 to 8.00	K. A. VICTORIA	4.00 to 8.00	4.00 to 6.00	... to ...	2.00 to 6.00
2.00 to 8.00	3.00 to 7.00	... to ...	... to ...	... to ...	LIBERTY	4.00 to 5.00	3.00 to 6.00	... to ...	... to ...
... to ...	3.00 to 6.00	4.00 to 10.00	... to ...	... to ...	METEOR	... to ...	... to ...	... to ...	... to ...
... to ...	3.00 to 5.00	4.00 to 10.00	... to ...	2.00 to 4.00	PERLE	4.00 to 6.00	... to ...	... to ...	2.00 to 4.00
... to ...	... to ...	... to 50.00	... to ...	... to ...	ORCHIDS—Cattleyas	... to ...	... to 50.00	... to ...	... to ...
... to ...	.50 to 1.00	... to ...	... to ...	.50 to .75	CARNATIONS—Inferior grades, all colors	... to 1.00	.75 to 1.00	.75 to 1.00	.50 to .75
... to ...	1.00 to 1.25	... to 1.00	... to 1.00	1.00 to 1.50	Standard Varieties—White	... to 1.00	.75 to 1.00	... to ...	.50 to .75
... to ...	1.00 to 1.25	... to ...	... to 1.00	1.00 to 1.50	Pink	... to 1.00	.75 to 1.00	... to ...	.50 to .75
... to ...	1.00 to 1.25	... to ...	... to 1.00	1.00 to 1.50	Red	... to 1.00	.75 to 1.00	... to ...	.50 to .75
... to ...	... to ...	... to 3.00	... to 1.00	1.00 to 1.50	Yellow and var.	... to 1.00	.75 to 1.00	... to ...	.50 to .75
.50 to 1.50	1.50 to 2.00	... to ...	... to ...	... to 3.00	Fancy Varieties—White	1.50 to 2.00	2.00 to 2.50	... to ...	.75 to 1.00
.50 to 1.50	1.50 to 2.00	... to ...	... to ...	... to 3.00	Pink	1.50 to 2.00	2.00 to 2.50	... to ...	.75 to 1.00
.50 to 1.50	1.50 to 2.00	... to ...	... to ...	... to 3.00	Red	1.50 to 2.00	2.00 to 2.50	... to ...	.75 to 1.00
.50 to 1.50	1.50 to 2.00	... to 1.50	... to ...	... to 3.00	Yellow and var.	1.50 to 2.00	2.00 to 2.50	... to ...	.75 to 1.00
... to ...	... to ...	... to ...	... to ...	... to ...	Novelties	... to ...	... to ...	... to ...	... to ...
.50 to 1.00	.50 to 1.00	... to 2.00	... to ...	... to 1.00	ADIANTUM	... to 1.00	... to 1.00	1.25 to 1.50	... to 1.00
... to 50.00	... to ...	25.00 to 60.00	35.00 to 50.00	25.00 to 50.00	ASPARAGUS, Plum. and Ten.	20.00 to 30.00	25.00 to 35.00	... to 50.00	25.00 to 50.00
... to ...	... to ...	20.00 to 30.00	25.00 to 35.00	25.00 to 50.00	" Sprengeri, bunches	20.00 to 30.00	25.00 to 35.00	... to 50.00	25.00 to 50.00
.75 to 1.00	.50 to 2.00	... to ...	.50 to 2.00	... to ...	ASTERS	.50 to 1.00	... to ...	.50 to 2.00	.35 to 5.00
... to ...	8.00 to 10.00	... to 10.00	... to ...	6.00 to 8.00	CALLAS	... to ...	... to ...	... to ...	... to ...
... to ...	... to ...	.75 to 1.50	... to ...	... to ...	DAISIES	... to .40	3.00 to 4.00	... to ...	... to ...
3.00 to 5.00	1.00 to 3.00	8.00 to 10.00	1.00 to 4.00	2.00 to 4.00	GLADIOLUS	... to ...	8.00 to 12.00	2.00 to 4.00	... to 2.00
... to ...	... to ...	... to ...	... to ...	10.00 to 12.50	LILIES, Harrisii	... to 12.50	... to ...	... to ...	... to ...
6.00 to 8.00	12.00 to 15.00	... to ...	... to 15.00	10.00 to 12.50	" Longiflorum	... to 12.50	2.00 to 4.00	15.00 to 18.00	... to ...
2.00 to 5.00	3.00 to 4.00	3.00 to 4.00	... to 4.00	1.00 to 2.00	LILY OF THE VALLEY	... to ...	1.00 to 2.00	2.00 to 4.00	3.00 to 4.00
... to ...	... to ...	... to ...	... to ...	2.00 to 2.50	MIGNONETTE, ordinary	... to ...	... to ...	... to ...	... to ...
... to ...	... to ...	... to ...	... to ...	... to ...	" fancy	... to ...	... to ...	... to ...	... to ...
... to ...	... to ...	4.00 to 8.00	... to ...	... to ...	PEONIES	... to ...	15.00 to 20.00	... to ...	... to ...
... to 12.50	... to 15.00	12.50 to 15.00	... to 15.00	12.50 to 20.00	SMILAX	... to 15.00	... to ...	12.50 to 15.00	... to 12.50
... to ...	... to ...	... to ...	... to ...	... to ...	VIOLETS, ordinary	... to ...	... to ...	... to ...	... to ...
... to ...	... to ...	... to ...	... to ...	... to ...	" fancy	... to ...	... to ...	... to ...	... to ...
... to ...	... to ...	... to ...	... to ...	... to ...	NARCISSUS	... to ...	... to ...	... to ...	... to ...
.15 to .25	.15 to .25	.50 to .75	... to ...	.20 to .35	SWEET PEAS	.25 to .50	... to .50	.40 to .50	... to ...
... to ...	... to ...	... to ...	... to ...	... to ...		... to ...	... to ...	... to ...	... to ...
... to ...	... to ...	... to ...	... to ...	... to ...		... to ...	... to ...	... to ...	... to ...

Buffalo.

News Notes.

The Florists' Club held a meeting on Wednesday, 8th inst., and decided to hold the annual picnic at the Old Fort, Erie Grove, which is in close proximity to our city, and can easily be reached by boarding the boat at the foot of Ferry street and connecting with the car at the Canadian side of the river. A special fast service has been promised by the management. The committee, Messrs. Legg, Scott and Bruecker, have decided to hold the affair on Wednesday, September 5, which will give the members attending the S. A. F. O. H. convention ample time to recuperate.

Mrs. W. J. Palmer and daughter have been spending their vacation at Hanlon's Point, near Toronto.

Jos. Speidel has returned from his much needed vacation.

Wm. Scott, President Kasting, D. B. Long and Charles Guenther will represent Buffalo at the S. A. F. convention.

Roland Cloudsley will spend his vacation motoring down the canal toward Seneca and Cayuga Lakes.

Captain Jas. Braik, the assistant park superintendent has been selected by the Scottish Society to judge in its bagpipe competition. Captain Braik is one of the most competent authorities on bagpipe music.

Emil Bruecker and wife are spending their vacation at Angola, N. Y.

W. H. G.

Indianapolis.

News Jottings.

It had been the wish of a number of the trade here to entertain those aboard the Chicago special to Dayton, but Secretary Winterson states that, while very grateful for the invitation, the Chicago florists find it will be impossible to delay the special at Indianapolis. Perchance the honor will be ours at some future time.

The news of genial Jimmie Hartshorne's death was received in this city with much sorrow. His many friends here, for he made them wherever he went, deplore the fact that such a young and promising career should be thus early terminated.

C. O. Betscher, Canal Dover, O., is cutting excellent gladioli.

Walter Bertermann is visiting Atlantic City and other eastern points.

John Rieman is having his store thoroughly refinished.

I. B.

Philadelphia.

Godfrey Aschmann sailed Wednesday last for Europe. He will visit Holland, France, Germany, and Switzerland. The trip is a business one; and Mr. Aschmann hopes, as usual, to secure the best of what is going abroad.

Wholesale Prices of Cut Flowers, Chicago, Aug. 15, 1906.

Prices quoted are by the hundred unless otherwise noted.

ROSES — American Beauty		
36-inch stems..........per doz.	.... to	4.00
30-inch stems.......... "	.... to	3.00
24-inch stems.......... "	.... to	2.50
20-inch stems.......... "	.... to	2.00
18-inch stems.......... "	.... to	1.50
12-inch stems.......... "	.... to	1.00
8-inch stems and shorts "	.50 to	.75
Bride Maid, fancy special......	5.00 to	6.00
" extra.............	4.00 to	5.00
" No. 1.............	2.00 to	3.00
" No. 2.............	.50 to	1.00
Golden Gate....................	2.00 to	6.00
Carnot.........................	2.00 to	6.00
Uncle John.....................	2.00 to	8.00
Liberty........................	2.00 to	8.00
Richmond.......................	2.00 to	8.00
Kaiserins......................	2.00 to	8.00
Killarney......................	3.00 to	8.00
Perle..........................	2.00 to	6.00
Chatenay.......................	2.00 to	6.00
Orchids—Cattleyas..........	.... to	50.00
Smilax.........................	8.00 to	12.00
Lily of the Valley.............	2.00 to	4.00
Sweet Peas.....................	.25 to	.50

CARNATIONS			
Inferior grades all colors		.25 to	.50
Standard Varieties	White..........	.75 to	1.00
	Pink...........	.75 to	1.00
	Red............	.75 to	1.00
	Yellow & var....	.75 to	1.00
*Fancy (The highest grades of Sta'd var)	White..........	1.50 to	2.00
	Pink...........	1.50 to	2.00
	Red............	1.50 to	2.00
	Yellow & var....	1.50 to	2.00
Novelties...................		.... to	....
Adiantum....................		.50 to	1.00
Asparagus, Plum. & Ten......		.35 to	.50
" Sprengeri, bunches.		.35 to	.50
Gladiolus...................		2.00 to	6.00
Lilies, Longiflorum.........		8.00 to	12.00
Harrisii....................		8.00 to	12.00
Auratum.....................		6.00 to	8.00
Nymphaea....................		.... to	1.00
Mignonette, ordinary........		1.00 to	2.00
Tuberoses, Spikes...........		4.00 to	8.00
....		.... to	....
....		.... to	....
Hardy Ferns per 1000........		1.00 to	1.50
Galax "		1.00 to	1.25
Asters......................		.50 to	1.00

New York.

News Notes.

Convention matters are creating considerable interest in this city, and we expect that a delegation of between twenty-five and thirty will depart on Monday next for Dayton, O. The train will leave the Grand Central station at 2.04 p. m.; but whether or not among the delegates there will be a bowling team, we are unable to say. It is rumored in Twenty-eighth street that if H. B. Beatty is a candidate for the presidency of the S. A. F. O. H., Alfred H. Langjahr, wholesale florist of this city, will make an effort to obtain the office of treasurer. Mr. Langjahr has been a long and faithful worker for the society, and his aspirations to hold a prominent office are commendable.

Thomas A. Stevenson who for over twenty years conducted a florist business in San Francisco, Cal., has been in town this week and speaks very discouragingly of the outlook for florists in that city so recently devastated by earthquake and fire. Mr. Stevenson believes that it will be fully fifty years before San Francisco regains her old-time business-like aspect, and he has no intention of again commencing business in that city, but would prefer if possible to locate with some prominent retailer in New York.

E. C. Earnshaw is traveling in England in the interests of the Bonora Company, and the latest advice from him is to the effect that he is selling a large quantity of that fertilizer among the prominent private estates and greenhouse establishments of that country.

A. Dacre, who for some time has managed the retail store of Robert G. Wilson, 48 West Thirtieth street, took over that business into his own hands on Wednesday, August 15. Mr. Wilson has a large retail store at Fulton st., and Greene avenue, Brooklyn, and the one he has been running in New York was operated as a branch store.

H. Miller will open on the first of September, a plant, bulb and seed store at 784 Broadway, Brooklyn, N. Y.

The Pierson U-Bar Company has secured the contract to build four greenhouses at Princeton, N. J., for M. Taylor Pyne, the cost being $8,100.

J. B. Kidd is again to be seen behind the counters of Wm. Elliott & Sons, seedsmen, 201 Fulton street, this city.

Miss Catherine Behan, who has charge of the office of John Young's wholesale florist store at 51 West Twenty-eighth street, is enjoying a two weeks' vacation in Sullivan County, New York.

J. K. Allen, wholesale florist of 106 West Twenty-eighth street, is away visiting the lake regions of New Jersey.

Horace E. Froment, wholesale florist of 57 West Twenty-eighth street, left on Monday for Lake George to enjoy a few days' recreation.

G. J. Nor Dell, Long Branch, N. J., will on Thursday, August 23, sell at auction his eight greenhouses and the stock contained therein; also tools, wagons and everything pertaining to a first-class florist establishment. J. P. Cleary will be the auctioneer.

Robert Leach of Jersey City has been handing around the cigars in celebration of an interesting event that happened at his home recently. It is a daughter.

Alexander McConnell, retail florist of Windsor Arcade, 571 Fifth avenue, has sent out a neat little booklet drawing attention to his removal from Forty-fifth street and Fifth avenue.

Arthur T. Boddington, seedsman, 342 West Fourteenth street, has been appointed the sole agent in the United States and Canada for the Edward's Cyaniding Machine, manufactured in England. This contrivance makes the use of cyanic acid gas possible without the usual dangers which hitherto have prevented general fumigating with this gas. Mr. Boddington will place the machine on the market immediately.

Lindenhurst, a portion of the estate of the late J. M. Hodgson at Newport, R. I., will be sold at auction to-day, Saturday, August 18, at 12 o'clock, noon.

Visitors this week were J. F. Huss, Hartford, Conn.; and Mr. and Mrs. I. Quint, Boston, Mass.

Boston.

News of the Week.

The semi-annual meeting of the directors of the Boston Co-operative Flower Growers' Association was held on Saturday evening.

Albert F. S. Mohegan of Cambridge has opened a new store at 10 Norfolk street, near Massachusetts avenue.

P. W. Firth and family of East Boston are spending a few weeks at Provincetown.

Wm. McAlpin of the J. A. Budlong & Sons Company is spending his vacation at New London, Conn.

Wm. Patterson of Quincy has been suffering with a broken foot for the past two weeks, from an accident received at that time.

Welch Brothers will remove October 1 from their present quarters, which their increasing business has outgrown, to 226 Devonshire street near Franklin street where they will occupy the entire first floor and basement, a total of twelve thousand feet of floor space. The location is convenient to both stations and near the offices of the American, National, Adams and New York and Boston express companies, and the premises will be fitted up with a complete cold storage plant, new counters, etc., thus making one of the best equipped wholesale houses in the country for the handling of cut flowers direct from the grower.

So far as can be learned only a few Bostonians will attend the S. A. F. O. H. Convention at Dayton.

J. W. DUNCAN.

Philadelphia.

The News.

The most important transaction in cut flower circles in this city is being consumated this week. It is the consolidation of the business of Samuel S. Pennock and the Philadelphia Wholesale Flower Market. The majority of the stock of the Flower Market is now held by Charles E. Meehan, there being only 191 shares outstanding, so it is probable that these will be liquidated. The new firm will take the name of the S. S. Pennock, Meehan Company. It will be capitalized at $60,000, and in the company will be Samuel S. Pennock, Charles E. Meehan, R. E. Faust and E. Fancourt, the larger amount of stock being held by the first two named gentlemen.

Samuel S. Pennock needs no introduction to our readers. He has been in the wholesale cut flower commission business for 30 years, and has shown a wonderful capacity for business. Starting in a small way with about four employees he has built up a very large trade, having about 20 employees. He owns his present building. This he has financed in such a way that by renting the upper floors his own business pays no rent. He has worked up a very large shipping trade and has always been very conscientious in his dealings, so that he has the entire confidence of his consignors and his customers.

Charles E. Meehan, the son of Joseph Meehan, began as a boy with Burton & Lonsdale, growers. He then was salesman for John Burton, afterward building greenhouses in Germantown. He always sold his own product, coming in every day with his wagon. When the Flower Market was started he was elected manager, and as time went on and the stall feature of the market did not take well here, he started out to work up a commission business which has now developed to over $30,000 per year. He is, without a doubt, one of the best cut flower salesmen we have.

R. E. Faust is bookkeeper for S. S. Pennock. E. Fancourt is in charge of the ribbon and supply department of S. S. Pennock.

The new arrangement will probably go into effect September 1. The business will be carried on at the S. S. Pennock establishment, 1612-16 Ludlow street. Extensive improvements have been made there this Summer, so that the place now has facilities second to none in this country for the handling of cut flowers in large quantities. It will probably be October 1 before Charles E. Meehan can wind up the Flower Market affairs and take his place at the new stand. The consolidation is certainly a good one, and a good business move; and the new company will undoubtedly do a very extensive trade.

John Welsh Young (Phil.) left on Tuesday for Camden, Me., for his annual vacation.

Robert Kift could not resist any longer, and has now joined the florist colony at Ocean City with his family.

Our delegation to Dayton will leave on Monday, August 20 at 4:30 p. m. by Pennsylvania R. R. from Broad street station arriving in Dayton at 9 a. m. Tuesday. At present it looks as if a good delegation will go from this city.

DAVID RUST.

San Francisco.

A recent meeting was held at the home of J. W. Bagge, President of the Pacific Coast Horticultural Society. A communication was read from P. J. Hauswirth, President of the Chicago Florists' Club, and with the communication was a draft for $150 issued by his club to the order of the Pacific Coast Society for use in helping any of the trade in need, sufferers by the recent calamity. This was a second assistance that has come from the Chicago trade. Another communication was read from the Park Commissioners, offering the society the use of the Park Lodge in Golden Gate Park for the society's meetings until it is able to procure a new hall.

H. Plath's nursery, formerly the Union Nursery is now called "The Ferneries." This gentleman is working up quite a large stock of young ferns for the Fall trade, as he is expecting an excessive demand for them. Ferns for dishes have been used more and more of late, and he has never been able to grow sufficient to fill all orders. Mr. Plath is of the opinion that there will be no lack of flowers next Winter, as most of the growers are getting their houses into shape again. At present, he said, the growers are experiencing a great deal of trouble in getting good help; it seems as if much of the old help has been scared away by the late earthquake-fire.

Near "The Ferneries" are the Ferrari Bros. who are hard at work planting their houses with carnations and roses, and likewise Schwerin Bros.

Trade at San Jose is fair, considering the great damage done there by the earthquake. Chas. Navelet of that city is doing considerable business, and is making improvements both in his store and at his nursery.

In San Jose is the Garden City Pottery, D. Raymond, manager. This plant has just increased its capacity by installing two electric motors. It is supplying almost the entire Pacific Coast with flower pots. The price has been reduced considerably, which is of great benefit to the growers as heretofore flower pots have been a great deal higher here than in the East.

At San Mateo the old firm of carnation growers, Fick & Faber, is no more, Chas. Fick having bought out his partner. Things are looking very prosperous; one of the large houses is being devoted to growing cucumbers, tomatoes and lettuce for the Winter. Mr. Fick is expecting a good trade among the wealthy people of San Mateo and Burlingame.

At Burlingame, where for many years C. Mitten has served as manager at E. W. McLellan & Co.'s wholesale nursery, there is a change. Mr. Mitten has resigned his position on account of Mr. McLellan replacing his white help with Japanese.

ALVIN.

SIOUX FALLS, S. D.—A recent fire in the residence portion of the Nudd & Thomas greenhouse plant caused damage to the extent of $100. The exploding of a gasoline stove was the cause of the blaze. Mrs. Nudd who was in the room at the time of the explosion was severely burned. Her injuries were such that the attendance of a physician was necessary.

BOONE, IA.—J. Loehrer is building another greenhouse, which will give him in all 4,000 square feet of glass. He will also open a store downtown. Mr. Loehrer complains of the competition of the Iowa State College of Agriculture, an institution maintained by the people of the State, including, of course, the florists.

PLANT FOR NAME, S. Bros., Fla. —The plant sent for name is Clerodendron fœtidum. G. W. O.

Topping Carnations.

(24) With our six houses of carnations all planted and mostly well established in their new quarters, with an average of some 8 to 10 flowering stems 2 to 6 inches in length, what is the proper date to discontinue topping them in order to begin cutting heavily about December 1? J. L. O'Q' & CO.

N. C.

—As there is such a diversity of habit among the different varieties of carnations, no exact information as to when the stopping should cease can be given. A safe rule to go by, however, would be to do no pinching back after the first of September.

Easter Lilies.

(25) Last season we planted our Easter lilies in 5-inch pots, covering the bulbs about one inch, and placed them directly on the bench with full light. We have never had better success than by this method. Would you advise a repetition of this plan, or did we just have luck in this instance?

Conn. J. E. C. & CO.

—Seeing that the bulbs did so well last season we would certainly follow the same mode of culture, if the bench space be available.

Trouble with Asters and Sweet Peas.

(26) I am having trouble with asters. A worm seems to bore into the stalk, and the plants, which are just nicely blossoming, immediately wither and die. Can you tell me what the worm is called, and if there is any preventive, or cure.

I also am losing my sweet peas; something is cutting the stalk about six inches from, or below, the flower stem. I find nothing but a green louse. Does that cause the trouble, and is there any cure before it is too late? A SUBSCRIBER.

—For the grub that attacks the aster plants there is no remedy that will stop its progress now. Next year, give the land a good dressing of lime in the Spring.

It must be caterpillars that are injuring the sweet peas. We would dust the vines over with Slug Shot, or strong tobacco powder.

Rose Bug on Peach Trees.

(27) Kindly give me a remedy for the rose bug on peach trees. They eat the young peaches which are thereby rendered unsalable. I would like to know what I can do next Spring, if the bugs appear.

Mass. READER.

—We know of no remedy for the rose bugs excepting to pick them off by hand.

Treatment of Bay Trees.

(28) Please give me in brief the proper treatment of bay trees, for out of door decoration, and treatment of same in Winter. Does it injure them to pinch out the young shoots soon after they appear in Spring? I have a pair of bays that are not doing well. They were sunk in the ground in tubs. They began to turn brown and I removed them from the tubs to the open ground. Was this a good thing to do? G. J. B.

—Bay trees, such as are imported and used for decorative purposes, should be kept in the tubs, watered whenever they require it without being kept either too wet or dry, and should not be pruned excepting that which is absolutely necessary to keep them in the form in which they have been grown. During Winter they can be kept in any light shed where actual freezing does not occur, and should be afforded only water enough to keep them from getting dust dry.

It was a mistake to pinch out the young shoots; also to take them from the tubs and plant them in the open ground. If the foliage falls, it would be better to buy new plants than to spend time, (probably two or three years) in trying to get the trees into good shape again.

Sweet Peas and Roses, Outdoors.

(29) I have two acres of level land, the best of soil. I desire to put one acre in sweet peas to cut from, and to have the flowers as early in the Spring and as late in the Fall as possible. What varieties are the best in red, white, lavender, white and lavender? How should they be cultivated to produce a continuous crop?

The other acre I wish to utilize for outdoor roses to obtain buds for funeral work all Summer long. What varieties will produce best in white, pink and yellow? What cultivation should they receive? I have plenty of help and everything needed to produce good results.

Penna. H. C. H.

—For us to name what would be the best varieties of sweet peas, in color, to be grown by the acre, might be but misleading and bring dissappointment; and we would recommend that you grow several varieties of each color, and consult any of the prominent seed houses as to the best varieties to sow.

For the acre of roses, we would plant Pink Maman Cochet, White Maman Cochet and for yellow Franz Deegen. We would buy one or two year old plants and set them out as early in the Spring as possible, manuring and ploughing the land in the Fall previous. As yellow roses never do very well outdoors, we would plant but a small proportion of that color.

Storing Hardy Ferns Over Winter.

(30) What is the best plan to store hardy ferns over Winter? I live near a woodland where hundreds of thousands of the best can be picked. Have lots of storage room. H. S. Y.

—Hardy ferns picked when dry late in Autumn, can be packed in boxes and stored in any cellar where the temperature is between 30 and 45 degrees, and will keep all through the Winter.

Bone and Ashes.

(31) Can you tell us where we can get raw ground bone and Canada hardwood ashes at trade prices? F.

—Any of the seed firms whose advertisements appear in our columns can supply the articles desired.

Wants Wild Peach Pits.

(32) Can you tell me where I can obtain some first class wild peach pits? I cannot find any offerings of these in your paper.

N. Y. C. H. WEEKS.

Chrysanthemums.

(33) We have Glory of the Pacific, Ivory, Wm. Duckham, Major Bonnaffon and Robert Halliday in 2½ inch pots just about ready for a shift. Will we be able to bloom these in 4-inch pots, and would a single stem be better than three breaks? We also have Alice Byron, Colonel Appleton, White Bonnaffon and Jeanne Nonin just potted in 2½ inch pots. How would you treat these from now on to obtain best results? Out of the whole bunch what kinds will we be able to get for Thanksgiving?

South Dakota. N. & T.

—The plants in 2½ inch pots just ready for a shift can be flowered in 4-inch pots though I would not take more than one flower from each plant; and even then these plants should have quite a little liquid fertilizer to finish the blooms or they will be very small. If the plants were far enough advanced to go into 6 inch pots they would be a whole lot better. The last lot just potted in 2½ inch pots I would plant out on a bench, if they were mine, wherever I could find room; unless, of course, it was calculated to flower them in pots and sell them as pot plants. Of all the kinds mentioned the ones that will keep for Thanksgiving are Jeanne Nonin, White Bonnaffon and possibly some of the Colonel Appleton, as the plants are so late. The others are all early to midseason.

CHARLES H. TOTTY.

Cincinnati.

It was with regret profound that the sad news was flashed over the wires to the craft in this city last week that James Hartshorne of Joliet, Ill., had passed to the great beyond. To know Jimmie was to like him. He was a carnation enthusiast whom the craft will greatly miss. The sad news was wired by Mrs. Hartshorne to R. Witterstaetter, Monday afternoon, August 6, the telegram stating that Mr. Hartshorne had died at 2 p. m. but giving no further particulars.

Business is Dull.

It is too warm to discuss business and even if we were so inclined there is no business to discuss. I will only drop this remark, that asters have ceased to be a glut, and good stock is selling at $1, $1.50 and $2; purple and lavender are very scarce. Pretty gladiolus, how is does go begging, with few exceptions! America sells, and this is one of the finest varieties I have ever seen. Dahlias are commencing to come in, and a little later some really fine ones will be seen.

Scott's Slap at Convention Bowlers.

I see our friend William Scott is taking Harry M. Altick to task regarding the convention shooting, but Mr. Altick has not been asleep, and Brother Scott will again get a chance to use his double barreled gun. But, oh, what a slap he gives the bowlers! He says: "Don't cater to a lot of crazy kids, and abolish the sport of gentlemen." That is pretty hot shot; but, of course, we know it's a joke.

E. G. GILLETT.

BRYN MAWR, PA.—In a fit of insanity, supposed to have been caused by the heat, William H. Schalliol, a florist, of Bryn Mawr, on August 8 jumped from a swiftly moving train and alighted unhurt, held up a hackman, terrorized citizens, and finally gave battle to four policemen, before he was overpowered and locked up in the police station. A brother of the insane man said Schalliol had been subject to such attacks before, for which he had been treated in an institution.

HINSDALE, MASS.—L. B. Brague will have the usual display of his specialties—cut ferns, sphagum moss, bouquet green, etc.—at the S. A. F. convention at Dayton.

St. Louis.

News Notes.

Mr. and Mrs. F. C. Weber and daughter Adele are on a river trip down South; they will return in time to take in the Dayton convention.

Phil. Goble, of Des Paires and S. B. Erker, of Oakland, Missouri, each have built two new houses to be used for growing violets and carnations. These four houses were built by Arnold Schiedegger, of Kirkwood, who is also in the growing business.

Mrs. A. C. Canfield of Springfield, Ill., was a visitor last week. Others who paid us a visit were George M. Kellogg of Pleasant Hill, and Emil Denker of St. Charles.

Hugo Gross of Kirkwood was all smiles last week when seen at the commission houses. Hugo says it is a big boy, and everything is well at home.

Henry Ostertag of Ostertag Brothers reports the loss, from heat, of three valuable horses.

In his report for July City Forester Meyer states that 81¼ miles of trees were inspected and 10,693 trees located. William Jordan, his assistant, is doing good work for the office.

The delegation from this city to the Dayton convention will be larger than anticipated; Fred H. Meinhardt has the names of 25, but 30 and perhaps 35 will probably start on Monday next, a number of ladies being included.

Alexander Waldbart, Jr., son of Alexander Waldbart, and nephew of George Waldbart, prominent florists, aged 31 years, fell from a second story window on Friday last and sustained internal injuries which will probably result fatally. He is being cared for at his father's home, 1061 Hamilton avenue. ST. PATRICK.

St. Paul.

News Notes.

The Twin cities will send in all about 8 or 10 florists to the S. A. F. convention at Dayton.

The Swanson Floral Company reports a very fair business during the dull season; funeral work has no doubt added greatly to the sales. Gus. Colberg of this concern contemplates taking in the convention.

L. L. May & Company are very busy making improvements both in their greenhouses and at their retail store. They are putting in new boilers. Their retail store is being completely renovated.

August Swanson and wife are enjoying their vacation at Isle Royale.

C. F. Vogt reports a fair trade but says good stock is hard to get.

Holm & Olson's new store is about completed. They contemplate moving within the next two weeks. Their new ice box is a large one, being about 30 feet long; in fact, possibly the largest in this section.

The Greeks evidently have found that St. Paul citizens will not buy from them. About six of them were handling flowers a short time ago and there is but one left. PAUL.

Detroit.

News Notes.

The firm of John Breitmeyer's Sons sustained a heavy loss by fire at their Mt. Clemens plant on August 4, 1906. They lost two big barns and the contents, upon which they carried but little insurance. The fire broke out about two o'clock in the morning and was well under way before any help was summoned. Fortunately the wind blew away from the buildings. Nothing is known concerning the origin of the fire. The loss is estimated at $3,500. The product of about 26 acres of hay was stored in one barn, and four horses two of which were fancy stock. The firm will commence to rebuild immediately. HARRY.

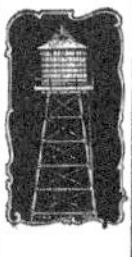

"*Absolutely Safe and Reliable. Ask Your Friends.*"

No Surplus Material

goes into our

Tank and Tower Plants

That is why they are so graceful.
But every inch of material used has been tested to at least four times the utmost strain that can be applied in service.

W. E. CALDWELL CO., Louisville, Ky.

Mention The Florists' Exchange when writing.

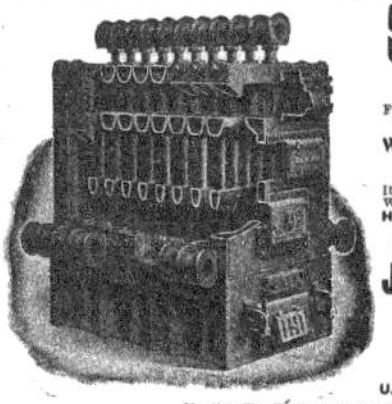

SCOLLAY BOILERS

ARE BEST

For Green House heating. Standard Cast Iron Green House Pipe and Fittings.

We are Headquarters for all sizes wrought iron pipe and fittings.

It will pay you to get our special quotation. We also contract for, and erect **Steam and Hot Water Heating** apparatus in all parts of the country.

Illustrated catalogues free on application.

JOHN A. SCOLLAY,
74-76 MYRTLE AVE.,
BOROUGH OF BROOKLYN,
NEW YORK CITY.
Telephones 1492-1493 Main.
U. G. SCOLLAY, Manager.

Mention The Florists' Exchange when writing.

KROESCHELL BROS. CO.

IMPROVED

Greenhouse Boiler

33 ERIE STREET, CHICAGO

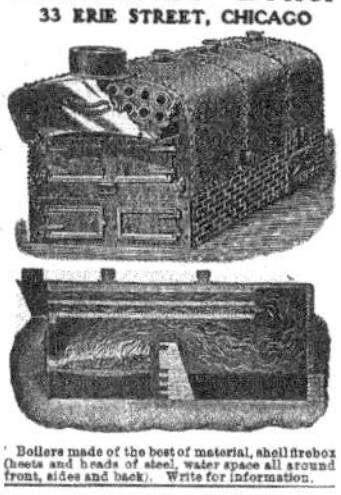

Boilers made of the best of material, shell firebox (sheets and heads of steel, water space all around front, sides and back). Write for information.

THE

GREENHOUSE COMPANY

222-228 Kearney Ave., JERSEY CITY, N. J.

Greenhouse Designers, Builders and Heating Engineers

Mention The Florists' Exchange when writing.

SUMMER IN WINTER

BY USING

Standard Greenhouse Boilers

One cent gets our Catalog

GIBLIN & CO., UTICA, N. Y.

Mention The Florists' Exchange when writing.

PLANT CULTURE

PRICE, $1.00.

The best book for the plant grower.

A. T. DE LA MARE PTG. & PUB. CO. LTD.

GREENHOUSES.

MATERIAL FURNISHED AND MEN TO SUPERINTEND ERECTION IF DESIRED.

CYPRESS SASH BARS ANY LENGTH UP TO 32 FT. OR LONGER.

THE A. T. STEARNS LUMBER CO., NEPONSET, BOSTON, MASS.

Mention The Florists' Exchange when writing.

The STANDARD VENTILATING MACHINERY

The original machine with self oiling cups; the most powerful, least complicated, very compact, with ease of operation.

The New Duplex Gutter over six miles in use and highly recommended; the only **drip proof** gutter in the market.

The Standard Return Steam Trap has no equal for simplicity or its workings. Catalogue free.

E. HIPPARD, Youngstown, O.

Mention The Florists' Exchange when writing.

GROW GOOD FLOWERS

By using

MOREHEAD RETURN TRAP

Every pipe in the greenhouse of equal temperature.

Condensation in steam pipes returned to the boilers whether located above or below Coils.

SEND FOR CATALOGUE

MOREHEAD MFG. CO.
1049 Grand Ave., DETROIT, MICH.

Mention The Florists' Exchange when writing.

THE HEART OF THE MATTER IS ALL HEART SUN DRIED CYPRESS

GREENHOUSE MATERIAL

IS THE VERY BEST—

FOLEY MFG. CO. 471 W. 22ND ST. CHICAGO,

HAVE IT, RIGHT FROM THE GULF OF MEXICO, AND WILL MAKE YOU RIGHT PRICES—

SEND FOR SKETCHES ESTIMATES AND CATALOGUE FREE—

HOT-BED SASH, VENTILATING APPARATUS, FITTINGS AND MANY OTHER THINGS—

If you are having delay in getting your roof material, send your orders TO US and don't be in trouble. We will handle any order in the time agreed. Try us.

FOLEY MANUFACTURING COMPANY, 471 W. 22nd ST., CHICAGO.

Mention The Florists' Exchange when writing.

ARE YOU GOING TO BUILD

Assure yourself of **HONEST COMPETITION** figures by obtaining an estimate from me on **Iron Frame** or **Sash bar** greenhouses. My prices are the lowest for the best class of **work.**

FRANK VAN ASSCHE

(FORMERLY SUPT. FOR WEATHERED)

FACTORY: Fulton and Rose Ave., Jersey City, N. J.

Mention The Florists' Exchange when writing.

Greenhouse Material — **Hot Bed Sash**

of Louisiana Cypress and Washington Red Cedar

Greenhouse Hardware and Posts. Patent V and U Gutters.

OUR GRADE INVARIABLY THE BEST, OUR PRICES RIGHT.

Write for Catalogue and Estimate when figuring on your new houses.

A. DIETSCH CO., 615 to 621 Sheffield Avenue, CHICAGO, ILL.

Mention The Florists' Exchange when writing.

GEO. M. GARLAND

Iron Gutters and Posts

Patented December 27th, 1898.

Send for Catalogue.

Garland's Gutters will keep snow and ice off your glass and prevent breakage.

DESPLAINES, ILL.

A sample of this gutter is on exhibition at Chicago Flower Growers' Market.

Mention The Florists' Exchange when writing.

EUREKA GREENHOUSES

Send for catalogue
Get the best

Greenhouse Material, Composition Posts

DILLON GREENHOUSE MFG. CO., Bloomsburg, Pa.

Mention The Florists' Exchange when writing.

THE JENNINGS IMPROVED IRON GUTTER

PATENT IRON BENCH FITTINGS AND ROOF SUPPORTS. VENTILATING APPARATUS. IMPROVED VAPORIZING PANS for Tobacco Extracts, Etc.

SEND FOR CIRCULARS

DILLER, CASKEY & CO.

Successors to JENNINGS BROS

S. W. CORNER SIXTH AND BERK STS., PHILADELPHIA, PA.

Mention The Florists' Exchange when writing.

S. A. F. O. H. CONVENTION REPORT NUMBER.

THE FLORISTS' EXCHANG

We are a straight shoot and aim to grow into a vigorous plant

A WEEKLY MEDIUM OF INTERCHANGE FOR FLORISTS, NURSERYMEN, SEEDSMEN AND THE TRADE IN GENERAL

ol. XXII. No. 8 — NEW YORK AND CHICAGO, AUGUST 25, 1906 — One Dollar

NEW CROP

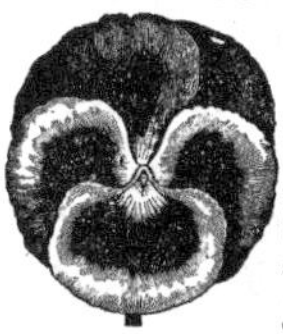

Johnson's Prize Winner Pansies

FROM THE WORLD'S FAMOUS GROWERS.

"These superb Giant Pansies are veritable **Prize Winners** wherever exhibited. Their extraordinary size, vigorous, compact habit, long stiff stems, heavy texture, wide range of magnificent colors, and distinctive markings have made them famous with the most critical Pansy Growers of the United States and Canada."

"**Johnson's Kingly Prize Winner Pansies** are the product of the **World's Leading Pansy Specialists**, and absolutely unsurpassed in quality by any strain extant. We offer seed as follows: 1000 seeds 30c.; 2000 seeds 50c.; 5000 seeds $1.00; ¼ oz. $1.25; per oz. $5.00."

PURE WHITE FREESIAS Per 100 $1.00 Per 1000 $7.00

Selected Bulbs, superior in quality to those grown in Bermuda, France or California. Florists realize as high as 75c. a dozen for the large pure white flowers.

See our Pansy offer in last week's Florists' Exchange.

JOHNSON SEED CO., Herbert W. Johnson (of the late firm of Johnson & Stokes), President **217 Market St., Philadelphia, Pa**

Mention The Florists' Exchange when writing.

Want Reliable Bulbs?

Look up our Ad. Aug. 18th

H. H. BERGER & CO.

17 BARCLAY ST., NEW YORK

Mention the Florists' Exchange when writing.

BULBS FOR FLORISTS

Lilium Harrisii, Roman Hyacinths Paper White Narcissus, Freesias

Send for special prices.

New Crop **Mushroom Spawn—English and Pure Culture.**

WEEBER & DON, Seed Merchants and Growers

114 Chambers Street, NEW YORK

Mention The Florists' Exchange when writing.

LILIUM PHILIPPINENSE

This lily was awarded a "Gold Medal" by the Massachusetts Horticultural Society. For description see our Bulb Catalogue. WE CAN DELIVER 100,000 OF THESE BULBS BY SEPTEMBER! It can easily be forced into flower inside of nine weeks. Considering this being a novelty we offer Lilium Philippinense at these remarkably low prices: Per dozen; $2.00; per 100, $12.00, per 1000, $100.00; per 10,000, $900.00.

W. W. RAWSON & CO.

5 UNION STREET, BOSTON, MASS.

Mention The Florists' Exchange when writing

160,000 California Grown Bulbs

	Per 100	Per 1000
Narcissus Paper White	$1.50	$10.00
Narcissus Grand Monarque	2.00	15.00
Narcissus Grand Primo	2.00	14.00
Narcissus Gloriosus	2.00	15.00
Narcissus Incomparabilis Cynosure	1.50	10.00
Narcissus Incomparabilis Figaro	$1.50	$10.00
Narcissus Incomparabilis Dontie	1.50	10.00
Calla Lily Bulbs, 1-inch dia	2.50	20.00
Calla Lily Bulbs, 1½-inch dia	3.50	30.00
Calla Lily Bulbs, 2-inch dia	6.00	50.00

Freight prepaid if cash is sent with order. 250 at 1000 rate.

A. MITTING, 17 to 23 Kennan St., **Santa Cruz, Cal.**

Mention The Florists' Exchange when writing.

$tokes $tandard $eeds.

ARE MONEY MAKERS

$tokes $eed $tore.

219 Market Street, Philadelphia

—Send for Catalogues—

Mention The Florists' Exchange when writing.

PANSY SEED

Brown's Extra Select Superb Giant Prize PANSIES, awarded Silver Medal, St. Louis Exposition 1904. My own grown new 1906 crop ready. Price mixed seed 1000 seeds, $1.00; ¼ oz., $1.50; ½ oz., $2.50., 1 oz., $5.00; ¼ lb., $14.00; ½ lb., $25.00; 1 lb., $50.00. Cash with order.

PETER BROWN

Lancaster, Pa.

Mention The Florists' Exchange when writing.

Pansy Seed

THE JENNINGS STRAIN

New crop now ready, saved from finest selected stock, large flowering and great variety of fancy colors. By mail one pkt., 4000 seed, $1.00; ½ oz., $2.50; 1 oz., $5.00, 2 oz., $9.00; 3 oz., $12.00. Cash with order.

E. B. JENNINGS,

Lock Box 254 **Southport, Conn.**

Grower of the Finest Pansies.

Mention The Florists' Exchange when writing.

CYCLAMEN SEED

NEW CROP

Michell's Giant Strain

Grown for us by one of the leading growers in Europe, and for size or blooms and free flowering qualities, cannot be excelled.

	100 Seeds	1000 Seeds
Giant White	$ .75	$6.00
Giant Pink	.75	6.00
Giant Red	.75	6.00
Giant White with Red Eye	.75	6.00
Giant Mixed	.60	5.00

ASPARAGUS PLUMOSUS NANUS

New Crop Greenhouse Grown

100 seeds	$ .60
500 seeds	2.25
1000 seeds	4.00
5000 seeds	19.00

Send for wholesale Bulb Catalogue, and write us for Special Prices on Bulbs in large quantities.

HENRY F. MICHELL CO.

1018 Market St., Philadelphia, Pa.

Mention The Florists' Exchange when writing.

PRIMROSES

Improved Chinese: Finest grown, named or mixed. Strong 2 inch, $2.00 per 100.

XXX SEEDS

CHINESE PRIMROSE

Finest grown, mixed, 500 seeds, $1.00; ½ pkt., 50c.

Cyclamen Giganteum: Finest Giant mixed, 200 seeds $1.00; ½ pkt., 50c.

DAISY: Double Giant mixed, 1000 Seeds 25c.

GIANT PANSY. The best large flowering varieties, critically selected, 5000 seeds, $1.00; half pkt., 50c.; 500 seeds of Giant Mme. Perret, pansy seed added to every $1.00 pkt. of Giant Pansy. Cash. Liberal extra count of seeds in all packets.

JOHN F. RUPP, Shiremanstown, Pa.

The Home of Primroses

Mention The Florists' Exchange when writing.

CINERARIA

Large Flowering Prize, Splendid Mixed T. P. $0.50

Large Flowering, Semi Dwarf Prize, Splendid Mixed, T. P. $0.50

PANSY, Superb Mixed.

oz. $4.50. ¼ oz. $1.15 ⅛ oz. $0.60

W. C. BECKERT,

Allegheny, Pa.

Mention the Florists' Exchange when writing.

Commercial Violet Culture.

Price, $1.50

The Florists' Exchange, 2-8 Duane St., New York

PRIVET AND EVERGREENS

If in want of fine large **Privet**, we have it; also **Evergreens**, extra fine stock. Call and see them.

THE ELIZABETH NURSERY CO.,

ELIZABETH, N. J.

Mention The Florists' Exchange when writing.

NOW READY

Zirngiebel's Prize Pansy Seeds,

in trade packages; $1.00 each.

GIANT MARKET, 2000 SEEDS.

GIANT FANCY, 600 SEEDS.

Full directions with each package.

Augustus Zirngiebel, Needham, Mass

Mention The Florists' Exchange when writing.

Catalog Engravings

and ILLUSTRATIONS

that print EASILY. That's the kind we make—have been since '73

JAS. M. BRYANT, Horticultural Engraving and Printing

706 Chestnut Street, PHILADELPHIA, PA.

Write for our Catalogue of Stock Engravings

Mention the Florists' Exchange when writing.

Seed Trade Report.

AMERICAN SEED TRADE ASSOCIATION

Henry W. Wood, Richmond, Va., president; C. S. Burge, Toledo, O., first vice-president; G. B. McVay, Birmingham, Ala., second vice-president; C. E. Kendel, Cleveland, O., secretary and treasurer; J. H. Ford, Ravenna, O., assistant secretary.

SAGINAW, W. S., MICH.—The Michigan condition of the bean crop indicates less yield than was anticipated two weeks ago. Extremely hot weather has cut off some fields, which will not pod, marking many vacancies in the pods of all, and materially reducing the yield. While the crop may fill contract orders, the surplus in growers' hands will not be as large as expected. Peas will be a fair crop on the whole, and samples will be fine. W. H. GRENELL.

MARBLEHEAD, MASS.—Onion seed has failed in some of the seed growing centers to a degree that make seed growers hesitate to make wholesale quotations. Our own crop promises extra well to date, but who can foretell what a week at the end of the season may bring forth? Have known a crop that was exceptionally promising up to within a week of ripening blasted to utter failure. Cucumbers in this section have blasted badly and the pickle men are at their wits' end. Several acres planted on our farm for seed are an utter failure and we feel fortunate in having carried over a surplus from the crop of last season. The long continuance of hot moist weather has rusted beans in this region badly; and early planted squash show wilted leaves and are almost at a standstill.

J. J. H. GREGORY.

BOSTON.—The Boston seed trade will be represented in the near future by a new firm The H. E. Fiske Seed Company of which H. E. Fiske is president and manager and W. C. Briggs treasurer. They will be general dealers in seeds, bulbs and plants and make a specialty of seeds for market gardeners' and florists' use. They will be in one of the best locations of Boston, opposite Faneuil Hall, in the building formerly occupied by W. W. Rawson & Co., which is being rebuilt and remodeled for the new firm. H. E. Fiske is well known in the Boston trade. He was for seventeen years with W. W. Rawson & Co., 12 years of which time he was manager, and his many friends wish him success in his new enterprize. John Clark formerly with W. W. Rawson & Co., and well known among the florist trade, will be with the new firm. J. W. D.

CHICAGO.—Four of the largest growers of onion sets, who cultivated two hundred and fifty acres, estimating a total product of 85,000 bushels, have completed their harvest, amounting all told, to about 65,000 bushels. The next ten important producers, with an acreage averaging about twelve each or perhaps one hundred and twenty-five in all, placed their combined expectations at above 45,000 bushels, but have less than 35,000 bushels to show for their labor.

Fifty to seventy-five small growers, with from one to two acres each, mostly producers of whites, in part for the pickle market have a residue of sets which will this year form an unimportant factor in the onion set market.

So, in fact, Chicago has for her home resources practically, in round numbers, but 100,000 bushels, of which there are already contracts in force, that will cover 65,000 bushels of this output.

There is one point of congratulation in connection with the shortage, and that is, the quality is of a very high standard, never having been excelled.

FREMONT, NEB.—We regret we cannot now give you a recent report of the conditions of the corn and vine seed crops. We are now engaged in sending out requests for growers reports of the present crop conditions, and will not have answers in sufficient numbers to make any estimates of the probable yields of the crops for two weeks or more. We believe from present indications and former reports that the sweet and field corn crops will be an average crop, but the acerage is, we think, considerably smaller than usual.

The cucumber and muskmelon and, in some cases, the watermelon crops have been damaged somewhat by the aphis and unfavorable weather conditions, and we do not look for many large crops, while in some cases the crops will be nearly total failures.

The pumpkin and squash crops are looking better than any other vine seed crops but, like the cucumber, the acreage is not as large as usual, with a few exceptions.

We have been having a week of extremely hot, dry weather, which has forced the corn ahead fast and helped the late crops, but if these conditions continue for another week we believe the corn will be checked and the growth of the ears and kernels shortened.

Should the hot, dry weather continne it will also shorten the cucumber and melon crops, as it is now about the time the second setting of fruit should set on the vines, and the second setting is the crop which is depended upon more largely for the seed crop, and with hot, dry weather for the next week or ten days the second setting will probably be light and the crops smaller.

If we have cooler weather and some good showers the crops will be helped materially, but we will have to get them soon.

However we believe that with a few exceptions there will be sufficient seed to fill most varieties nearly in full, as we understand the contract orders are generally somewhat smaller than has been the case for several years.

WESTERN SEED & IRRIGATION COMPANY.

European Notes.

The rains that would have been most acceptable to us in the middle of July, occur with distressing frequency just now, when we are harvesting our spinach and taking off the prime heads of our parsnip crop. Shipments of the former will consequently have to be delayed, for this seed soon loses its vitality if packed whenever so slightly out of condition.

A fair estimate of the European crop of spinach shows about 60 per cent. of last year's crop now standing. Dealers should handle this article with caution if there is any probability of an equal trade next Summer to that which has just concluded. No one will carry over any great surplus. The same remark applies to parsnip, for which the demand is exceptionally heavy. At present it does not seem possible that all the orders can be filled.

Considerable surprise has been expressed at the failure in the forcing radishes, which all the houses are now reporting; the writer can only say that ample notice of the possibility of the failure has been given in this column for many weeks past. Yearling seed of these varieties being of such indifferent germinating quality makes the shortage all the more severe.

Turnips, except the Aberdeen varieties are all coming in much better than estimated, and the rains before referred to, are all in favor of the young plants for next season's crops.

EUROPEAN SEEDS.

NOTES FROM ERFURT.—Our meteorological record for the present Summer is a mixture of thunderstorms and torrential rains, with a few hot days thrown in. This has not aided vegetation to catch up the ground lost through the late commencement of Spring and things in general are nearly a fortnight behind the usual time. In some places the rains have badly laid the crops. Warmer and drier weather, however, now seems to have set in to the great relief of our seed growers.

Peas have made a luxuriant growth, and if the weather favors the development of the pods, they should turn out a good crop. Beans did not come up as well as usual owing to unfavorable conditions of harvesting last Autumn ,and any attempt to judge their prospects as yet would be premature. Neither onion, carrot nor cucumber are in very good shape, while lettuce, radish, spinach and mangel wurzel are looking all right so far. Cabbage, kale and beet are also doing favorably, though the acreage of these is smaller than usual.

Flower seeds are mostly longing for some warm and not too moist weather. Perennials are yielding well, but some biennials, such as forget-me-not, will naturally be short, owing to the loss of so many plants during the Winter. Pansies are not seeding well and badly need some consistent sunshine, the damp atmosphere having hindered the setting of the pods. Sweet peas, though late, look healthy, and the same may be said in general of the annuals, which have, however, a considerable amount of lee-way to make up. Some of the more delicate kinds of asters have suffered by the wet and look as if insects had been at them, but on the whole this important culture is in a fairly promising condition. Ten-weeks stocks are coming along all right, but double wallflowers will only be a small crop. The large-flowering petunias now make a grand show on the stages, and form the admiration of numerous visitors, of whom we have had several from England and America, and the same may be said of the stage carnations. Cinerarias, calceolarias and primulas have all yielded satisfactorily.

A sweet pea show, the first of its kind in Germany, was recently held in Erfurt, with the view of bringing this beautiful flower more into popular favor, for although very largely grown here for export it is comparatively seldom met with in German gardens.—Horticultural Trade Journal.

CATALOGUES RECEIVED.

WILLIAM BULL & SONS, Chelsea, London, Eng.—Catalogue of Bulbs.

THE ELM CITY NURSERY COMPANY, New Haven, Conn.—Price List of Bulbs, Peonies, Herbaceous Plants, etc.

T. C. THURLOW & COMPANY, West Newbury, Mass.—Select List of Peonies, Iris and Phlox.

CENTRAL PARK NURSERY, Topeka, Kan.—Colored Illustration of new Canna Topeka, originated by Oscar Roehr; proposed official flower of 1911 Exposition.

SCHLEGEL & FOTTLER COMPANY, Boston, Mass.—Illustrated Catalogue of Bulbs and Plants, Autumn, 1906.

LUTHER BURBANK, Santa Rosa, Cal.—Price List of Novelties.

NURSERY DEPARTMENT.

Conducted by Joseph Meehan.

AMERICAN ASSOCIATION OF NURSERYMEN, Orlando Harrison, Berlin, Md., president; J. W. Hill, Des Moines, Ia., vice-president; George C. Seager, Rochester, N. Y., secretary; C. L. Yates, Rochester, N. Y., treasurer.

Nurserymen will find some useful information in Bulletin 58, Bureau of Entomology, Department of Agriculture, Washington, D. C., which treats on "The Western Pine-Destroying Bark Beetle."

Fruit of Silver Thorn.

There are some half dozen silver thorns common in cultivation, all of them possessing meritorious characters, usually either in foliage or fruit, sometimes in both. The one pictured is known as Elæagnus umbellata. Like all the family it has a beautiful silvery color on the under side of its leaves, a feature which gives the name silver thorn to all the species. There is great variation in the time of ripening of the berries of the different species. The first to ripen is the now well known Elæagnus longpipes. Its fruit is ripe within a month or two of the opening of Spring. The next is the one known as E. parvifolia; the fruit of it does not ripen until Midsummer. The next, and last of those most common, is the one of our sketch, Elæagnus umbellata. This ripens very late; in fact, it is barely ripe before October, but when it is ripe, it excels in beauty all the others. The berries are nearly always so thickly studded along the stems as to present a mass of salmon color—salmon being their color when ripe and nearly every season the weight of berries is so great that branches bend over with it. An idea of how thickly they stud the branches may be gained by a glance at the illustration. The branch shown was cut from a bush about six feet in height, the branches of which were bent over that some of them touched the ground. The photograph was taken late in October, and the display on the bush was kept up fully a month later, when hard freezing put an end to it, although there is some color to the berries until well into December. When E. longpipes was first introduced and our nurserymen sent to Europe for more of it, almost invariably they received our umbellata instead. This was pardonable, perhaps, for there is a close resemblance in the color of the young shoots of each, a cinnamon color being their characteristic; and there is general confusion in nurseries over the names of other of the species.

There is no mistake in saying that E. umbellata is a highly ornamental species and one which all should plant. Like all the species, the dull yellow flowers are quite fragrant, and like them, too, there are sterile and fertile plants, which suggests when procuring them to be sure they are some raised from cuttings from a seed bearing plant, which mode of raising them is adapted by many nurserymen.

JOSEPH MEEHAN.

Seasonable Suggestions.

Triphasia trifoliata is a spiny shrub from Southern China, sometimes used as a hedge in Cuba and the West Indies. It is occasionally confounded with the hardy orange, but it is quite distinct from it. The fruit is of about the size of the Missouri currant, Ribes aureum.

Japan persimmon thrives in Philadelphia when in sheltered positions, but is not reliable to ripen its fruit. But the fruit comes to this market every season, in good quantities, so its cultivation so far North is but for curiosity sake. As all do not produce perfect flowers, when grafting, wood from fruit-bearing trees must be used.

Three of our native azaleas—nudiflora, calendulacea and Vaseyi—are worthy of all the attention they receive. They are now planted far oftener than they were, being beautiful, and, of course, hardy. But viscosa, the July blooming species, needs more attention than it receives. The flowers are white and very fragrant.

August and September is the season when the Magnolia tripetala is in the height of its beauty. The "pods" of fruit are now ripe, of a carmine color, and about three inches in length. The seeds, freed of pulp and sown in October, grow freely in Spring.

Those who have planted climbing Clothilde Soupert rose and have been disappointed in its flowering, as so many have been, would find it an excellent stock on which to bud some other good rose, say Gloire de Dijon. The latter variety is quite hardy about Philadelphia, blooming from June to frost, and has a delicious perfume. Budding is in order now.

Pyrus japonica suffers so much from the attacks of the San Jose scale that it disheartens growers of it. Spraying it when in leaf might hurt the foliage; besides there is no need to do it then. A thorough spraying in March or April, just before the foliage develops, with Scalecide, will destroy all the scale the material touches.

Pretty plants for florists' uses are the achilleas. There is a dwarf yellow one, Achillea tomentosa, that makes a great showing of its heads of flowers. The A. millifolium rubrum is taller growing, making a height of 18 inches or more when it displays its heads of rose red flowers. Another, A. ptarmica plena, is of use to florists because of its double white flowers.

Viburnum tomentosum flowers better as it gets age. It then bears berries as well. These berries become very ornamental when ripening, being first of a bright red color, then changing to black before shriveling.

Green Wood Cuttings of Trees and Shrubs.

With the ripening of the wood of trees and shrubs it is a favorable time to make cuttings of those of which an increased supply is destined. With many trees and shrubs the wood is in good condition for cutting making in August. The desired conditions are when a half-ripened stage is reached. It is then that roots are made sooner than at any other time. When too green, cuttings are difficult to keep fresh without a great deal of water, and to give them an abundance of water increases the chance of their rotting. Therefore, the half ripened state brings the greatest satisfaction.

Elæagnus Umbellata—Silver Thorn

Many greenhouses are comparatively empty at this season of the year, affording room for boxes of cuttings. With the roof shaded, it is not necessary to have additional shading material placed over the boxes. This is an advantage, as it permits of air getting to the cuttings, lessening the risk of fungus attacking them, for fungus likes a close atmosphere and darkness.

Because of the difference in the time required for rooting, it is better to have but one kind of tree or shrub in a box instead of many. Those that require potting sooner than others can then be properly treated without disturbing the later rooting ones.

A far greater number of plants can be had, propagated from soft wood cuttings, than from hard wood; and really, though the hard wood ones, rooted from cuttings set in Spring, are larger at the start, it is not often that they are more salable by Autumn than are the green wood ones rooted in the preceding Summer. Take the common privet, for example. Strike the cuttings now, and pot them or transplant them to boxes or frames as soon as rooted. In Spring, set them in nursery rows, and let them grow on until Autumn. Take cuttings from privet shrubs in Winter; make them and keep them in a cold cellar until Spring, then set them in the nursery near those that were raised from green wood cutings and though they may be taller than the others, by Fall they will not be as bushy nor better plants to sell.

Black Hamburg Grapes Outdoors.

My notes of last season on the fruiting of the Black Hamburg grape outdoors have excited a good deal of interest, as I have recently had two letters concerning them, in addition to those received soon after the notes appeared.

I would say that my experience with this grape leads me to advise against anyone planting it in the North, excepting as a matter of interest. The fruit can be ripened, of course—it ripens outdoors in the South of England—but it lacks the flavor of those ripened in California or under glass. In fact, I quite agree with Professor Massy, who, mentioning that he had ripened this grape in Maryland, said of its fruit that he preferred a bunch of Concord.

The leaves of the Black Hamburg are not fitted to thrive in our climate as do those of our native grapes. Mildews attack them; and though true Bordeaux mixture will control this, the fruit is not worth the trouble.

A Tree for City Streets.

In towns or cities of small size there is no difficulty in finding suitable trees for the sidewalks. There are many trees that will thrive in such situations almost as well as on a lawn or in their wild positions. It is the city of large size, with miles on every side closely built up, that finds it difficult to select a tree suitable. The smoke from its chimneys, its asphalt and other tight pavements, the continual disturbance of the ground for all kinds of purposes affect trees so injuriously that to name a good one to withstand these adverse conditions is almost impossible. With good soil under the pavements, there is a large number of trees to select from, as there are many to fit any ordinary position. In the older cities where adverse conditions prevail, there is a tree coming to the front that is very promising. In appearance it is not unlike the old ailanthus, so much planted in times past, making much the same growth, excepting that it is less lofty and makes a rounder, more spreading head. It is said to be able to flourish under ill conditions as the ailanthus will, which is a good recommendation. Its name is Cedrela sinensis. The suckering habit of the ailanthus has always been against its use. While it cannot be said that the cedrela never suckers, it does so to such a small extent that it need not be considered. Were its roots to be badly mutilated, it might sucker, just as many other trees do under like conditions; but no one thinks of calling them suckering trees.

A tree like this, with all the merits of the ailanthus, and none of its objections, for there is no disagreeable odor to its flowers, is something long desired; and there will be, certainly, a great demand for this coming tree—Cedrela sinensis.

Waiting for the Leaves to Fall.

It was the old way to wait until all leaves had fallen from trees before planting them, and many good planters still adhere to this practice. The fall of the leaf certainly indicates that its work is over; but practically that work is over in advance of the leaf falling, and there is no perceptible gain in waiting for this to happen. On the other hand, early planting is of such decided advantage to many trees that it far outweighs any consideration of harm.

Landscape gardeners now start their plantings a month or six weeks ahead of the time for the dropping of the leaves. With us, late September is an excellent time for the work. The tree must be stripped of every leaf; it means work, but it pays. The wood is well ripened by September, and success follows the transplanting.

Should the soil be fairly moist, no watering is required, but in the experience of many who follow the September planting it pays to pour in a pailful of water to each tree.

Many nurserymen urge their customers to plant in September. This lessens their profits, as it takes time to hand-pick the leaves, but, on the other hand, it pays in the satisfaction given to the customer of having the trees live; and there is no trouble later on in adjusting claims for dead trees. Try the planting in late September.

JOSEPH MEEHAN.

Last Season's Rose Trade in Germany.

The business done in general in standard, and also in bush roses for forcing, in spite of the low prices obtained was satisfactory. Half-standard roses in consequence of the cheapness of standards were but little in demand, but forcing plants, with stems of 30-35c.m. high, found ready sale. In the Spring, as a consequence of the warm weather at the beginning of April, trade was influenced unfavorably, and large numbers of plants remained unsold. Prices of 50mk per 100 standards and 12mk per 100 dwarfs were not uncommon, and even at such low prices plants were unsalable. There was a better demand for novelties, and of these the red-flowered hybrid teas were greatly preferred. Climbing and polyantha enjoyed a rising popularity. Of hybrid teas, the variety Liberty was much in demand, and large stocks of out of doors worked plants have been raised for the approaching Autumn. In consequence of the abundant showers the condition of the roses is satisfactory; still complaints are general of the bad growth of buds, the results of the wet Summer and Winter of last year. The stocks of finished plants for the autumnal sales are of very good quality, and sufficient in quantity to meet the usual demands, especially as regards standards.

The present condition of wildling and Rosa canina stocks is extremely good, the Spring weather having had a very favorable influence on growth—From The German Trade Press.

CARNATIONS

	1st size per 100	2d size per 100
Glendale	$12.00	
Robt. Craig	12.00	
Bountiful	8.00	$6.00
Belle	7.00	5.00

FIELD PLANTS

	1st size per 100	2d size per 100
Boston Market	$6.00	$5.00
White Cloud	6.00	
Nelson Fisher		6.00
Flamingo	7.00	5.00
Crane		5.00
Estelle	2d size $5.00;	3d size $3.50

ROSES, 200 4 in. **Maids,** 150 4 in. **Brides,** $7.00 per 100. 500. 2½ in. **Gates,** 300. 2½ in. **Brides.** 150. 2½ in. **Perle,** $3.50 per 100. **Richmond,** 2 in. at $5.00; 3 in. at $8.00.

FERNS, Boston and **Piersoni,** 2½ in., $4.00 per 100; 4 in., $10.00; 5 in., $20.00; 6 in., $35.00, 7 in., $80.00.

ASPARAGUS PLUMOSUS, 2 in., $2.00 per 100. **SPRENGERII,** 3 in., $6.00 per 100. Cash or C. O. D.

W. J. & M. S. VESEY, Fort Wayne, Ind.

Mention The Florists' Exchange when writing.

Field Grown Carnation Plants

THE LARGEST AND FINEST WE EVER HAD.

THE QUEEN, FAIR MAID, MRS. PATTEN — $5.00 per 100

WHITE LAWSON, PINK LAWSON, NELSON FISHER — $6.00 per 100

ENCHANTRESS, $7.00 per 100.

H. F. LITTLEFIELD, - - WORCESTER, MASS.

Mention The Florists' Exchange when writing.

Field Grown Carnation Plants

ALL THE STANDARD VARIETIES

List and prices on application.

Rose plants 1000 Liberty 3 in. pots ....$5.00 per 100
1000 " " 2¼ " " .... 4.00 " 100

THE LEO NIESSEN COMPANY, 1217 Arch St. Philadelphia, Pa.

Mention The Florists' Exchange when writing.

CARNATIONS

	per 1000	per 100
500 **Queen Louise,** field grown		$4.00
Asp. Plumosus, 2½ in. pots. Aug. 15th		2.00
Cineraria, Sept. 15th		2.00
Pansy Seed, large flowering, per oz., $4.00		

PRIMROSES

	per 100
Chinese, 2½ in. pots, Aug. 10th	$2.00
Obconica, Rosea and Alba, Aug. 10th	2.00
P. W. Narcissus, 13 ctm., Sept.	1.25

5 varieties Cannas, field grown clumps, $15.00 per 100.

CASH PLEASE

JOS. H. CUNNINGHAM, Delaware, O.

Mention The Florists' Exchange when writing.

BUSHY

FIELD CARNATIONS

Mrs. T. W. Lawson, Harlowarden, Avondale, Glacier, Ethel Crocker and many others, 1st size, $6.00 per 100; $55.00 per 1000.

Enchantress, Lady Bountiful, $7.00 per 100; $60.00 per 1000.

NATHAN SMITH & SON, Adrian, Mich

Mention The Florists' Exchange when writing.

FIELD GROWN

CARNATIONS

VICTORY, ROBT. CRAIG, JOHN E. HAINES ....$15.00 per 100.

FIANCEE, MRS. BRADT, HARLOWARDEN, MRS. M. A. PATTEN, PROSPERITY....$6.00 per 100.

CHARLES H. TOTTY

MADISON, N. J.

Mention The Florists' Exchange when writing.

GERANIUMS.

Nutt, Poitevine, Buchner, Doyle, Ricard Viand, Brett, and others.

Rooted Cuttings. Orders booked for Fall delivery.

ERNEST HARRIS, Delanson, N. Y.

Mention The Florists' Exchange when writing.

ENCHANTRESS

Field-grown, ready Sept. 1, $6.00 per 100; $50.00 per 1000.

WHITE BROTHERS, Gasport, N. Y.

Mention The Florists' Exchange when writing.

CARNATIONS

PLANTS FROM FIELD

Fair Maid, Queen, Mrs. Patten, $5.00 per 100; $45.00 per 1000. Strong and healthy.

Satisfaction guaranteed. Cash with Order.

HUGH CHESNEY, Farmington, Ct.

Mention The Florists' Exchange when writing.

FIELD GROWN CARNATIONS

Strong, healthy plants; now ready. **Fair Maid, Joost, Boston Market, Louise** and **Eventide** (Prolific bright scarlet), No. 1 plants, $4.00 per 100.

Pink and White Lawson at $5.00 per 100. **Delicacy,** white, slightly variegated, flowers being perfect and good size, very strong and prolific, $5.00 per per 100. Packed to carry safely.

CHAS. BLACK, HIGHTSTOWN, N. J.

Mention The Florists' Exchange when writing.

CARNATIONS

Second size field plants Enchantress, Lawson, Boston Market, Queen, etc., $3.00 per 100; $25.00 per 1000.

Ardisia crenulata, strong, bushy plants from bench, well berried, ready for 5-6 in. pots, $6.00 and $8.00 per doz.

Geraniums, 12 varieties. Have order booked for Fall delivery; can fill orders from 100-100,000. Get my prices. Standard, 4 in. pots, $9.00 per 1000; 5000, $40.00, saucers 50c. 100. Cash.

WM. S. HERZOG, MORRIS PLAINS, N. J.

Mention The Florists' Exchange when writing.

ABUNDANCE

Healthy, stocky, field grown plants. First size. $12.00 per 100; $100.00 per 1000. Second size, $10.00 per 100; $75.00 per 1000; 250 at a 1000 rates. Delivery 15th of August.

CASH WITH ORDER.

RUDOLPH FISCHER, Great Neck, L.I., N.Y.

Mention The Florists' Exchange when writing.

FIELD GROWN

CARNATIONS and VIOLETS

Extra strong plants of Mrs. Lawson, Queen, Boston Market, Fair Maid and Harlowarden, No. 1, $6.00 per 100; $50.00 per 1000; No. 2, $5.00 per 100; $45.00 per 1000. CAMPBELL VIOLETS, large clumps, $5.00 per 100; $45.00 per 1000. PRINCESS OF WALES, $6.00 per 100; $50.00 per 1000. No better stock at any price. Cash with order please.

R. ENGELMAN & SON, Pittsfield, Mass.

Mention The Florists' Exchange when writing.

CARNATIONS

ENCHANTRESS	$50.00 per 1,000
QUEEN LOUISE	40.00 " "
LAWSON	40.00 " "

Good, strong, healthy plants. Cash with order.

HENRY KRUSCHKA

616 Cookman Ave., Asbury Park, N. J.

Mention The Florists' Exchange when writing.

FIELD-GROWN

Carnation Plants

Send for price and list of varieties.

Chicago Carnation Co., Joliet, Ill.

Mention The Florists' Exchange when writing.

Field Grown Carnations

$4.00 per 100

Fair Maid, Gov. Wolcott, Marquis, Prosperity, Roosevelt, N. Fisher, E. Crocker, G. Lord. 2nd size Queen Louise, $3.00 per 100.

Boston Ferns, 6 in. pans, $4.00 per doz.

THE NATIONAL PLANT CO. Dayton, O.

Mention The Florists' Exchange when writing.

CARNATIONS

Good, strong, healthy, field grown carnation plants from new soil. A No. 1 plants in every way; well branched and free from disease. **Enchantress, Boston Market, Lady Bountiful, Mrs. M. A. Patten, Nelson Fisher, Ethel Ward.** Prices on application.

VALLEY VIEW GREENHOUSES, Marlborough, N.Y.

VELIE BROS., Props.

Mention The Florists' Exchange when writing.

CHRYSANTHEMUMS

Extra strong plants, in 3 in. pots, of **Jones, Dr. Enguehard,** Perrin, **Mrs. Coombs, October Sunshine, Alice Byron, Ivory, Appleton,** etc. These plants have been cut back, and are in fine condition. $5.00 per 100 or the lot of about 200 for $9.00.

R. G. HANFORD, Norwalk, Conn.

Mention The Florists' Exchange when writing.

BABY MUMS

FIELD GROWN

(1) size, very heavy plants to pot up	15c each
(2) size, heavy plants	12c "
(3) size, good sized plants	10c "
Smaller sized plants	8c "

Cash.

HENRY EICHHOLZ, Waynesboro, Pa.

Mention The Florists' Exchange when writing.

The Heather

IN LORE, LYRIC AND LAY

By ALEX. WALLACE

Editor of THE FLORISTS' EXCHANGE

Tells the Story of Scotland's Famous Mountain Flower in Prose and Poetry. Full cloth, 380 pages, freely illustrated, including frontispiece in color.

PRICE $1.50, Postpaid

Send for free Sample Pages and Extracts from Reviews.

A. T. De La Mare Ptg. & Pub. Co. Ltd.

4-8 Duane Street, NEW YORK

GERANIUMS

From 2 in. pots ready for immediate delivery

Alliance, Lemoine 1905. Hybrid, Ivy and Zonal, semi-double, lilac, white, upper petals feathered and blotched crimson maroon, 25c. each; $2.00 per doz. **Fleuve Blanc,** the semi-double Bruant, that promises to become the standard white, flowers and foliage equal to Alph. Ricard, $1.50 per doz.; $10.00 per 100. **Cactus Geraniums,** four varieties, petals curled and twisted similar to the Cactus Dahlia, $2.00 per doz.; $15.00 per 100. **Double Dryden,** $1.00 per doz.; $5.00 per 100. **S. A. Nutt, La Pilote, Beaute Poitevine, Mme. Barney, Centaur, Miss Kendell, Mme. Jaulin, Jean Viaud, Mme. Charrotte,** 40c. per doz.; $2.00 per 100; $18.00 per 1000. **Ville Poitiers, Marquise de Castellane, Berthe de Preailly, M. Joli de Bammeville, Thomas Meehan,** 50c. per doz.; $3.00 per 100; $25.00 per 1000. Send for Geranium catalogue, let us figure on your future supply. **Alternantheras,** red and yellow, $2.00 per 100; $15.00 per 1000. **Hardy English Ivy,** $2.00 per 100; $15.00 per 1000. **Smilax,** $2.00 per 100; $15.00 per 1000. **Dahlia Roots,** we are booking orders for fall delivery; send for list.

A cordial invitation is extended to all interested in Horticulture to visit us. Cowenton Station, Philadelphia division, B. & O. R. R., 12 miles north of Baltimore.

R. VINCENT Jr. & SON,

WHITE MARSH, MD.

Mention The Florists' Exchange when writing.

GERANIUMS

ROOTED CUTTINGS

Orders booked for delivery Nov. 1st and after. I will have fourteen houses planted to stock plants and think I can supply you with the right kind of cuttings.

	per 100	per 1000
S. A. Nutt Perkins, Buchner, Doyle	$1.25	$10.00
Viaud, Jaulin, Poitevine, L. Francis	1.50	12.50
Ricard, Castellane, Trego	1.50	12.50
Peter Henderson	2.00	15.00
White Poitevine	3.00	25.00

ALBERT M. HERR, Lancaster, Pa.

Mention the Florists' Exchange when writing.

ORCHIDS

Arrived in superb condition **Cattleya Dowiana, C. Gigas, C. Mossiae, C. Percivaliana, C. Speciosissima, C. Eldorado, C. Superba, C. Labiata, C. Leopoldii** and many more.

Write for Prices.

LAGER & HURRELL, Summit, N. J.

Growers and Importers

COCOS PALMS.

Strong 2¼ inch at $1.50 per dozen. Write for lowest prices on **Kentias.**

Jas. F. Barclay R. I. GREENHOUSES Pawtucket, R. I.

Mention The Florists' Exchange when writing.

ORCHIDS

Largest Importers, Exporters, Growers and Hybridists in the world.

Sander, St. Albans, England

and

235 Broadway, Room 1, New York City

Mention The Florists' Exchange when writing.

ROBERT CRAIG & CO.

ROSES, PALMS, CROTONS

CARNATIONS and Novelties in DECORATIVE PLANTS

Market and 49th Sts. PHILADELPHIA, PA.

Mention The Florists' Exchange when writing.

Exhibition at Newport, R. I.

The Newport Horticultural Society's exhibition held Monday, Tuesday and Wednesday last week was successful from almost every point of view. It was a good general exhibition. Foliage plants, palms and ferns in the large specimen stages were well shown by private growers. Out-of-town commercial growers exhibited rare and choice plants in greater variety than usual. In the group classes there was fair competition. For a group of palms, ferns and foliage plants, Colin Robertson, gardener for Mrs. Goelet, was first. In the class for a group of the same kind, 50 square feet, James Boyd, gardener for Mrs. Astor, was first. In the group of palms, ferns and flowering plants, Colin Robertson was first with palms, nephrolepis in variety and anthuriums. James Robertson took second with palms, ferns and begonias; Gibson Brothers third, with palms, ferns and Lilium speciosum rubrum. In the gateway decoration, F. L. Beigler was first with small retinosporas.

In the class for a table of flowering plants and ferns, James Boyd was first with gloxinias, and Adiantum cuneatum; John Marshall second, with begonias, gloxinias and A. Farleyense. John Marshall took first for a table of decorative foliage plants. James Boyd second. Colin Robertson was first for crotons, James Boyd first for dracænas in 8-inch pots; David McIntosh first for dracænas in 6-inch pots.

The F. E. Conine Nursery Company, Stratford, Conn., captured the S. G. Harris prize for hybrid tea roses. The same firm had on exhibition a collection of everblooming roses for which they were awarded a first-class certificate of merit, and a gratuity of $5. James Crawshaw, Providence, R. I., showed a nice asparagus, A. plumosus Crawshawii, which seems a good thing for commercial purposes; it was awarded a certificate and a gratuity of $5. H. A. Jahn, New Bedford, showed some good cactus dahlias, taking three first prizes. Andrew J. Fish, also from New Bedford, took two firsts and some seconds.

The largest and most successful exhibitors in cactus dahlias were James Robertson, James Boyd, Colin Robertson, Andrew Christensen, and John Marshall.

James Boyd took first for peaches and nectarines; and James Robertson and Alex. Anderson took the bulk of the prizes for grapes, black and white.

John Lewis Childs, Floral Park, N. Y., put up the best and largest exhibit of gladoili ever seen here. Among the varieties attracting great attention were Canary Bird, yellow; F. L. Oakley and Fantastic, red; L. S. Hendrickson and Melrose, pink; these are only a few of the many good ones in this grand exhibit which received a certificate of merit and a gratuity of $10. Vaughan's Seed Store showed a vase of gladiolus, Mrs. Francis King, which is a very good variety, probably one of the very best reds; it shows up well at night under any kind of light. It received a certificate of merit.

Roses were rather disappointing both in quality and in the number of entries staged. John Marshall took first for American Beauty; Colin Robertson first for tea roses with Bridesmaid.

In the classes for made-up work, baskets and center pieces, some good examples were shown. John Marshall took first in baskets with allamandas; Gibson Brothers, first for a center piece made up with a seedling yellow dahlia and Adiantum cuneatum.

Henry A. Dreer, Inc., Philadelphia, had a good exhibit of aquatics for which they received a certificate of merit and a gratuity of $10. They also staged a few choice ferns and foliage plants. New plants in Dreer's exhibit included: Pteris Childsii, Pteris Wimsetti grandis; Marantas Mosella, insignis, hieroglyphica and Kummeriana; Asparagus Ducheni and myrtle-leaved smilax. This firm also made a fine display of nelumbiums, 10 varieties; of nymphæas, in hardy varieties, Andreana, James Brydon, W. B. Shaw, Wm. Doogue, the Marliaceas and Laydekeri, etc.; tender varieties; dentata magnifica and superba, Mrs. C. W. Ward, Frank Trelease, Sturtevanti, George Hunter, Jubilee, Kewensis, Rubra rosea, etc.

The Julius Roehrs Company's (Rutherford, N. J.) exhibit consisted of a fine group of choice foliage, table plants and rare palms, sprinkled here and there with the beautiful Dendrobium Phalænopsis Schrœderianum. Among the foliage were fine narrow foliaged crotons, such as Daviesii, Aighburthiensis, Mrs. H. B. May, Chelsonii, etc.; also several of the best varieties of marantas, diffenbachias, Curmeria Lindenii, new begonia rex var. Our Queen, Her Majesty, etc.; heliconias in several varieties. Among the choice palms worth mentioning were the rare Cyrtostachys Renda, Phœnix Roebelinii, Licuala horrida, Kentia Lindenii, etc. This group was awarded a silver medal and gratuity of $10.

Lager & Hurrell, Summit, N. J., as usual were here with a group of orchids. Although this is rather a poor season for these plants, they succeeded in making a very fine exhibit consisting of Lælia elegans, Cattleya gigas, C. Harrisoniæ, Dendrobium thyrsiflorum, Phalaenopsis Rienstadtianum lucidum varicosum, Oncidium Marshallianum, and O. macrochilum. For this exhibit the society awarded a silver medal and a gratuity of $5.

The judges for plants, fruits and flowers were Bruce Butterton, Alex. Fraser, and Stewart Ritchie; for baskets and table decorations, Richard Merrit, William Galvin, and Ralph Armstrong. D. M.

Rose Mrs. E. G. Hill.

This rose is pictured in the Revue de L'Horticulture Belge, from which the accompanying illustration is reproduced. A correspondent of that periodical, after regretting the prevailing fashion of naming flowers, because the designation in most cases conveys nothing of the plant's origin, says: "In the case before us, the designation of this variety, in the language of Horace and Virgil, would be elegantissima maxima. This rose will take its place among the most handsome, on account of the graceful incurving of its exterior petals. At first the flower has a globular aspect, later becoming "vase" shaped. The bushes are of exceptional vigor and exceedingly floriferous. Rose Mrs. E. G. Hill is carried on a very long stem of the requisite rigidity. The flower is extraordinarily large, very full, and expands easily. The lower part of the petals, (that turned toward the outside) is of a red, recalling the shade of the most beautiful coral; the upper part white and well marked. This rose forms an excellent acquisition both for outdoors and as a cut flower.

Rose Mrs. E. G. Mills
From Revue de L' Horticulture Belge

Practical Plant Breeding.

(Paper prepared by H. H. Groff, Simcoe, Ont., and read before the Royal Horticultural Society and International Plant Breeders' Conference, London, England.)

By way of introduction and for the information of this conference I will state that my business profession is that of banking, as was that of my late father, but in a private way we were both interested in the advanced products of horticulture in all its departments.

For many years my interest also extended to several types of pure bred animals and birds, during which time I gained valuable experience in breeding poultry, pigeons, rabbits, dogs, cattle and horses. The knowledge gained during my experiments with animate life has been of incalculable value in enabling me to determine the best system and practice likely to assure the most satisfactory results, during my past fifteen years of practical experience in plant breeding.

There are two classes of plant breeders, both of which are doing good work of more or less value from the scientific and economic view-point, in the interest of advanced knowledge and our advancing civilization.

The first of these is the breeder who works for the purpose of proving his theories, and who by a limited number of recorded crosses is able to place the simple analysis of his investigations in presentable form for educative purposes.

The second, or the breeder for practical results cannot do this without placing limitations upon his activity, which means his experience and success, as it is only the man who makes many crosses who may hope to approach even the border of a field of limitless possibilities in results.

Such a worker will secure innumerable examples and illustrations of the points valued by the theoretical breeder, but such being relatively barren of practical results will soon be forgotten, and it matters little that this is so, for the only value that such records would be is, that on a repetition of the cross a duplicate result could be secured, and a type thereby multiplied. This however is practically impossible in crossbreeding.

As has been stated by me before the American Breeders' Association: "The only admissible system to be practiced for the purpose of producing the highest average in types of economic value is that of breeding from domestic specific types as sires on selected females, according to the practice of animal breeders. The use of wild species with the hopes of attaining a similar ratio of such results is relatively absurd, as the only value that any wild species can be to the breeder for practical results is as foundation or laboratory stock, to be discarded yearly with their early hybrids as he advances step by step towards his ideal."

Now here it may be well to state that if the breeder uses his full opportunity, this ideal will be a progressive quality, and his standard will advance yearly as he sees the results attained by unlocking the treasures of ages of the past in scientific, though unrecorded, practical plant breeding; and, too, by the same means, he hastens evolution and draws the natural harvest of the eons of the future to meet the scientific harvest from the eons of the past, within the area of his trial grounds as well as within the grasp of his mental and physical activity.

I have spoken of limitations, and the man who will most feel the restricting force of these limitations is he who specializes his specialty, and by the production of innumerable examples of the possible practical results he desires to attain, opens up new and improved avenues for further advancement, until he becomes mentally stalled between these results and the horizon of the visible field, a horizon which will broaden as he advances, to an eternity of possibility beyond the conception of the human mind.

I have frequently stated, that the plant breeder, with the full complement of the chemical constituents of his laboratory stock in a condition of control, can do anything he may wish to do in producing types of his specialty at will. Not only is this so, but he will be surprised to find in the early course of his practice that he will develop more advanced types, and thus will have forced upon his recognition the interesting fact that he can do all he had hoped to accomplish and far more, and further, that the advancing years of his activity extend the visible field of possible satisfaction; and still further, that these possibilities broaden infinitely with each succeeding year of production and added knowledge.

The foregoing evidence and argument could be multiplied and prolonged indefinitely were it needful, but I will pass on to the subject of this address—the results to accrue from the practical aspect of plant breeding—for this is the great and valuable end of all our effort, mental or physical, theoretical or practical. Barren of results, the armchair scientist may cease to theorize, and the field worker abandon his labors and investigations while grilling under the Summer sun, for results are the standard by which man's work is judged.

By practical plant breeding I mean the application of that knowledge of the science which will enable the worker to secure the highest ratio of economic value in advanced results of an aesthetic or utilitarian character.

This is one of the most important features of plant breeding, as the value of the knowledge of what may be done by crossing is small when compared with that of the practice which will give manifold results of value to mankind, and the highest average of quality for the time and area occupied by the operator.

English Critic Arouses Burbank.

The New York Herald in a recent issue published the following item from its Santa Rosa, Cal., correspondent:

"Luther Burbank is indignant at the charges made by T. D. Cooke, editor of the London Garden, who called Mr. Burbank a 'poor imitator' and said the 'horticultural wizard's creations were little thought of, except by misguided persons.

"'I have been wilfully misrepresented,' Mr. Burbank said, 'by would-be plant breeders. There are men in New York and across the water who eat my plums day after day, and smack their lips, and at the same time find fault with me for producing them.'

"Mr. Cooke declared Mr. Burbank's Shasta Daisy was simply Chrysanthemum maximum, and was a favorite in English gardens thirty years ago.

"'Is that so?' said Mr. Burbank in reply. 'But England sent to America for improved varieties of daisy, and I have the assurance of many of the leading seedsmen of England and Europe that nothing can or does compare with my Shasta daisy.'

"As to the commercial value of his fruit and other productions, Mr. Burbank said the reports would show that annually two hundred to eight hundred carloads exclusively of Burbank fruits he had produced and distributed through seedsmen from his experimental grounds here and at Sebastopol, in this county, were sent East and to England."

"His gladioli are poor," says the critical Mr. Cook. To this Mr. Burbank replies: "If he wants to know about gladiolus, let him look at Bailey's Cyclopedia of Horticulture. All growers acknowledge that my gladioli are the basis of all the best stock in America or Europe."

"He is a mere beginner with hippeastrums," continues Mr. Cook, the critic. Here is what Burbank says in reply to this: "Dr. Hugo De Vries, the great

Dutch scientist and acknowledged authority, who has visited Santa Rosa, says that my hippeastrums are marvels. Professor James Ward of Cambridge, England, says that my amaryllis is magnificent and superior to any other.

"As to my blackberries, they have been little introduced in England up to the present time. My Himalaya blackberry is recognized as being the best for shipping purposes. It would take a thousand pages to answer and give proof. If it were required I could do it. As I said before, I have been wilfully misrepresented, and underlying it all is a spirit of jealousy. I ask again, has there been another inventor of fruits whose products have come into general use as rapidly as mine have?

"I have just received a statement made by Prof. Woodward of the Carnegie Institution at Washington, D. C., made since his return East a few weeks ago after a visit of several days here and at my experimental farm, and among other things he says: 'I know I shall be regarded as a crazy man when I tell you that the work being done by this one man will produce more wealth than the entire endowment of the Carnegie Institution, which is $10,000,000,' said President Woodward. 'But I accept this risk and make the statement. I will go further, and give it as my deliberata opinion that Burbank's discoveries will return five times $10,000,000. His potato alone has been worth millions to this country. He is now at work perfecting a new variety of potato that is expected to be an immense benefit to the country. He is not seeking to invent a freak; but merely to invent a fine, large palatable, vigorous potato of good keeping qualities. This, of course, is only one of a thousand of experiments which he he is now making.'"

And, finally, with a renewed warmth of feeling, Mr. Burbank said: "I have 380,000 species of plant life upon which I am operating at the present time, and "I challenge all England or any Englishman to produce a plum that is equal to the Wickson plum—one that is equal in size, quality, as productive and possessing such good shipping qualities. I challenge any Englishman to produce any daisy like the Shasta daisy, either in size, color or any other feature, and one that will bloom in six months instead of eighteen months. I challenge and ask any Englishman to produce a potato that has been grown as extensively, is as productive and still holds its own as the Burbank potato, which I invented."

ALVIN.

The letter which called forth Mr. Burbank's protest was sent by Mr. Cook to the Daily Mail, London, and is as follows:

"I hope you will allow me space to protest against the extraordinary statement that Mr. Luther Burbank has produced more new plant life, fruits, grasses, trees and flowers than any other man who ever lived. We are weary of this perpetual adoration of an American nurseryman whose wonderful creations are thought little of except by press interviewers and writers of books.

"It is unfair to the great hybridists of the past and of to-day that this untried experimentalist should be regarded by the lay mind as a pioneer in the production of new fruits and flowers. Here is the opinion of the well-known curator of the Royal Gardens, Kew:

"'Burbank is a child, a beginner, a rank outsider among the great plant breeders of to-day, such as Lemoine, Benury, Vervaine, Duval and Marliac, of continental fame, or Waterer, Veitch, Sander, Charlesworth, Paul, Cannell, Laxton and Engleheart of our own country. He is a poor imitator of the late Mr. Rivers, a record of whose works among fruits was published about thirty-five years ago. If Mr. Burbank desires to know what Rivers did and how scientifically, how careful he was, he should consult his Darwin.

"Now let us see what Mr. Burbank has actually given. Acknowledged authorities on plant breeding in the United States have little to say of Burbank's work. His admirers crack up his creations among fruits, but the dealers in America ignore them. The Shasta daisy is simply Chrysanthemum maximum, a favorite in English gardens thirty years ago. His gladioli are poor beside Kelway's and Lemoine's; his richardias are a long way behind what has been bred in England; he is a mere beginner with hippeastrums; he is all behind with poppies; the dahlias of his raising would not be looked at the second time by Mr. Cannell; his blackberries, plums, tomatoes (worthless mongrels); his potatoes (where are they?)—these and other Burbankian creations, so called appear to be things of no real account.

"And the spineless cactus, what is it? What is its origin? Mr. Burbank has hopes with regard to it, but has any one who knows anything of the genus opuntia seen it? How does it differ from the spineless sorts that we know in European gardens?"

The Artistic Salad.

The salad of to-day is a rapid evolution from the dictionary definition: "Leaves eaten raw," or "A preparation of uncooked herbs usually dressed with salt, vinegar and oil and eaten for giving a relish to other food," one reads in an article on "Salads—Artistic and Hygienic" in the June "Delineator." An up-to-date salad includes many combinations of vegetables or of fruit, sometimes both vegetables and fruit together. It owes its present honorable position to discoveries of its many enticing varieties and æsthetic possibilities. Used with the addition of nuts it becomes a very important part of the meal, not merely something to arouse a jaded appetite. Among the many discoveries of salad material may be mentioned tips of asparagus, uncooked potatoes, both Irish and sweet, cut in small tubes, grated carrots and grated beets. All the possible combinations of these ingredients are set forth in detail and in a way to tempt the palate, and there are, in addition, a variety of recipes for vegetables, pastry, etc.

Hardy Plant Notes.

One of the prettiest and most interesting blue hardy flowering perennials that has come under my observation during the past few years is an anchusa, probably a variety of Anchusa italica though apparently not quite so hardy as the species. I had the pleasure of seeing this beautiful plant in bloom last Summer in England and although it was the latter part of July the plant gave abundant proof of its beauty and utility for the border, for it was still very showy and blooming profusely and gave good evidence of continuing to keep up a goodly display of flowers for some weeks to come.

A few plants of it have already appeared on our shores. I had the pleasure of again making the acquaintance of this plant on the grounds of Frederick J. Rea of South Norwood, Mass., early in July and my former impressions concerning it were much strengthened although I was assured it was then past its prime; but the abundance of bloom it then showed did not bear out this statement.

The plant had not made the proportions it is said to reach, but young plants in the greenhouse accounted for this. It was not more than three feet high, while our European friends claim it will grow 6 to 7 feet high and more through. This may be so from older and more firmly established plants, but we can scarcely expect to obtain this height or width for a few years to come, as the plants have been used very heavily for propagation purposes and will be thus somewhat weakened in constitution. For when we consider it must be propagated by side or base unflowered shoots taken with a short heel attached or division of the roots, which can be divided into very small pieces an inch or two in length and placed in sand or sandy loam where they soon grow, we can see there will be nothing but small pot plants for a year or two at least.

We are also given to understand that the plants produce little or no seed, and what is produced is not to be relied upon as it reverts to the small flowers of the type. But as the anchusas are coarse, rapid growing plants they will soon overcome this and make a good report of themselves; and as soon as more stock can be secured and stronger divisions or cuttings obtained we may then expect to get good results from them, as they are well adapted to our climate, growing and flowering very profusely in both the border and open spots. Dense humidity seems to be its only foe that I know of, and this does not apparently affect its flowering qualities but simply causes its lower leaves to decay.

When planted in good deep rich soil the plants are not only robust of growth in foliage but of root also, and in light soils will send their roots down two or three feet in a single season, at least I have known seedlings do this; and if this plant assumes the gigantic proportions it is said to do I see no reason why it should be any exception to the rule.

There is some doubt expressed as to its being a true perennial; in some parts of England it seems it has failed to appear the second year. One very reputable writer and grower says it simply flowers itself to death, but this argument should not deter its cultivation; as once in possession of a good strong plant nothing is more easy of propagation. At the end of each flowering season where it is known to die or disappear, just dig up the roots, and if not ready to use store them in sand, as this seems to prevent decay. Cut up as desired and place in pots or boxes in sand or sandy soil where they will soon show signs of growth. If it is desired to hold over the roots for future use keep them in a cool place, free from excessive moisture when nearly every piece of root will grow, and towards Spring if strong plants are desired, they may be potted up and grown on in a cool greenhouse until the proper season arrives for planting out. Those that do not bloom the first year will carry over safely in the border without these necessary precautions, as it is only the very heavy flowering plants that succumb.

It appears that there are three large flowered varieties now in possession of hardy plant dealers and these will doubtless be offered by them. They are respectively named, A. italica var. Dropmore, A. italica magnifica and A. italica superba. It is with the first named variety with which this article deals, though the characteristics in all three are much the same. But the Dropmore variety produces much the largest flowers some being nearly one and a half inches in diameter, according to the raiser's description, though the ones I saw came nearer to the inch mark. But these were not on very vigorous plants, and I can readily imagine they will be much larger on stronger and more vigorous plants. Even this is a wonderful advance, and considering the plant's long period of flowering and the deep rich color of its flowers, these will make it much in demand as soon as its merits are known. In fact, all three varieties are decided improvements and worthy of cultivation.

HERBERT GREENSMITH.

Flower Garden and Fountain, Soldiers' Home, Dayton, O.

OUTLOOK FOR BOILER TRADE.—The boiler trade, which has not been in a satisfactory state for some time, as far as prices are concerned, has a much better outlook. Manufacturers are confident that this year will be a good one and they will not only be able to dispose of all their stock, but there will be urgent inquiries for more boilers than they can make. Stocks at the present time are low considering the season of the year and there is an excellent demand from the interior. Trade in the the New England States, which has been dull during the Summer months, shows promise of becoming more active. While no definite figures are named regarding the probable advance in boilers, it is believed that it will not be less than the advance in radiators which is announced as 5 per cent.—The Metal Worker.

NEWARK, N. Y.—The Jackson & Perkins Co., florists and nurserymen, has been incorporated; capital, $100,000. Incorporators: C. H. Perkins, G. C. Perkins, E. A. Miller, Newark, N. Y.

St. Louis.

The Shaw Banquet.

The Seventeenth Annual Shaw Banquet to gardeners, florists and nurserymen, as provided for in the will of the late Henry Shaw, took place on Tuesday evening, August 14, at the Jefferson Hotel. Owing to the meeting of the Apple Growers' Congress, the Banquet was held earlier than usual, so that these men could also attend. The hall was decorated with palms, the tables with pink asters.

Professor William Trelease acted as toastmaster, and the speakers from the head table were President Dunlap, of the Apple Growers' Congress, James Gurney, Doctor Burrell, Prof. Irish, president-elect of the Florists' Club, Walter Williams and others. Covers were laid for 250 persons, the guests being seated at round tables, six to each. Among those present of our local club were Henry Young, Will C. Young, Carl Beyer, Theo. Miller, J. J. Beneke, John Connon, E. W. Guy, C. C. Sanders, Fred H. Meinhardt, F. W. Ude, Jr., Edwin Denker, James W. Dunford, Frank J. Fillmore, R. F. Tesson, Henry Lohrenz, H. C. Pring, C. Fulgraf, F. W. Taylor, George Frow and Phil. Giehle.

The guests voted this the best affair yet given by the Shaw Trustees.

The Apple Growers' Congress.

The fourth annual meeting of the American Apple Growers' Congress was held on Tuesday and Wednesday, August 14 and 15, at Planters Hotel. The Congress has several thousand members, and the delegates, coming from all parts of the country numbered nearly one thousand. After the meeting, the delegates inspected the Ozark regions, starting on Thursday and returning Saturday morning, being much pleased with what they saw and heard. The following places were visited: Lebanon, Mo., Marionville, Rogers, Ark., Bentonville, Ark.

The next congress will meet in St. Louis, August 13 and 14, 1907.

The following officers were elected: President, H. M. Dunlap, Savoy, Ill.; vice-president, W. R. Wilkinson, St. Louis; secretary, T. C. Wilson, Hannibal, Mo.; treasurer, Wesley Green, Des Moines, Iowa, all the said officers serving their second term.

News of the Week.

Charlie Ford, who represents A. Herrmann, of New York, solicited orders for supplies from the trade last week. Henry Emmonds, of Belleville, was a visitor, and reports he is cutting nearly a thousand everblooming tuberoses daily, which he consigns to Berning. He is building a new house 35 x 150 for roses. Mr. Emmonds is one of the most prosperous florists in Belleville. Henry Aue, who has returned from Europe, says he will tell the members at the next club meeting all about his trip.

Louis A. Giger is to be married soon.

A number of the trade are enjoying themselves this week at the Dayton S. A. F. Convention. Fred Meinhardt reported the following as delegates: Mr. and Mrs. Theo. Miller and daughter; Mr. and Mrs. F. C. Weber and daughter; Mr. and Mrs. F. H. Meinhardt, the Misses Meinhardt; Otto John Koenig, J. J. Beneke, C. A. Kuehn, E. W. Guy, F. J. Ammann, George Walbart, W. C. Young, F. W. Ude, Jr., George Augermuller, H. A. Halstead, George M. Kellogg, Emil Denker. The bowling team to represent St. Louis at Dayton is to be selected from the following: C. A. Kuehn, J. J. Beneke, Theo. Miller, E. W. Guy, F. H. Meinhardt, W. C. Young and F. C. Weber.

The last bowling match rolled on last Monday night, between the retailers and wholesalers, resulted in the retailers winning two of the three games played, though the wholesalers totaled more pins; the totals were, 1703 to 1667. Three men were on a side.

ST. PATRICK.

Boston.

Massachusetts Horticultural Show.

The last of the Saturday shows of the season was held at Horticultural Hall on the 18th and, like its predecessors, had many attractions worthy of note. It is to be regretted that the Massachusetts Horticultural Society do not hold more of these exhibitions or keep them open to the public, for a longer period. It seems hardly worth while for many exhibitors to bring in such fine specimens as have been shown this season to be on the exhibition tables only four hours for the public to see.

Gladioli were the feature of the exhibition on Saturday and it is doubtful if ever better blooms were shown anywhere than those by J. K. Alexander. He was, of course, easily the winner of the first prize, and the varieties he exhibited included King Edward VII, Grace, Rufus, Perfection, White Perfection, The Queen, Yellow Globe, Howard, Bluebird, Fusiler, America and Daisy Leland.

John Lewis Childs had a large exhibit of some 75 varieties of gladioli which alone occupied much space. Among the most notable varieties of his collection were Bluejay, Contrast, Attraction, Blanche, Helen, Cardinal, Los Angeles and Melrose.

Dahlias were shown by many exhibitors in fine form but perhaps the most noticeable collection, was that of cactus varieties from W. W. Rawson & Co. This firm make a specialty of growing tubers of these varieties.

The Blue Hills Nurseries exhibited a hybrid Rosa Rugosa, var. Conrad F. Meyer, which was awarded honorable mention, and the same award was made to Walter Hunnewell (T. D. Hatfield, gardener) for vase of Senecio Clivorum.

Perennial phloxes were exhibited in better shape than any seen for some time, T. C. Thurlow exhibiting over fifty varieties.

In the prize collections of phloxes the prize winners were: first, F. W. Spinney; second, W. C. Winter; third William Whitman. Other notable exhibitors of dahlias and other flowers were: Towles' Dahlia Gardens; Mrs J. B. Lawrence, H. E. Johnson, W. G. Winsor, Mrs. A. W. Blake, H. B. Watts, Harvard Botanical Gardens Blue Hills Nurseries and W. J. Clemson.

News Notes.

The North Shore Horticultural Society will hold their annual Summer show on the 29 and 30, and from present indications will be the most attractive exhibition ever held by this progressive organization.

W. H. Knapp has returned from three weeks' stay in Jeffrey, N. H.

We regret to announce the illness of W. N. Craig, the genial secretary of the Gardeners' and Florists' Club who is confined to his home with sciatica.

G. A. Sutherland, the Hawley street wholesaler, is spending a few weeks in Maine.

O. S. Hendrickson, manager of the wholesale department of John Lewis Childs was in town this week.

An interesting ball game took place on the grounds of the Waban Rose Conservatories at Natick on Saturday between the Waban Rose employees captained by J. Gallagher, and salesmen of the Flower Markets, captained by Ed Curley. The former were easy winners. After the game Mr. Montgomery entertained the players to refreshments at the greenhouses.

P. J. Donohue of the Waban Rose Conservatories is spending his vacation at Old Orchard, Maine.

J. W. DUNCAN.

LIST OF ADVERTISERS

INDEX TO STOCK ADVERTISED

Contents.

PAGE

REVIEW OF THE MARKET

NEW YORK.—The cut flower business shows no improvement over last week, in fact, it is more quiet if anything, than it was at that time.

The supply of American Beauty roses keeps on steadily, and, as there is little demand for them in quantity, the prices realized are anything but satisfactory. Of Bride and Bridesmaid roses, there is little of extra quality coming in as yet, though this is perhaps just as well, as there is so little demand for anything in the rose line.

A few carnations are to be seen here and there, but they are limited in number. Asters are plentiful, and they seem to be of somewhat better quality than was the rule one week ago; prices are no doubt averaging a little better.

Of gladioli there are thousands, dahlias are getting more plentiful and speciosum lilies are coming in in quantity, though there does not seem to be any active demand for them. Harrisii lilies are still in plentiful enough supply for the call, and no change in prices is noted this week.

There is an abundance of Hydrangea P. G. coming in, and as this lasts so long when used for window display, and which purpose seems to be the only one that it is used for at this time, it kills the demand for many other kinds of flowers.

There is no change in the market conditions of smilax, asparagus, adiantum and other green material.

CHICAGO.—This market shows a gradually strengthening tendency. The general quality of stock, with the exception of carnations and sweet peas, is somewhat better than it was a week or two ago, the demand is fully as good, if not better, so that though there is no increase in prices, there is less tendency to cut.

There are no special features which are worthy of mention, everything running along in the even tenor of Midsummer dullness. W. K. W.

ST. LOUIS.—A little funeral work now and then keeps us from forgetting that we are in business; other lines of trade being very dull. Extra fancy stock of all kinds is very scarce, and a change would be welcome. The opening of the local schools marks the beginning of Fall trade, and will bring many of our society people home from the eastern and northern watering places.

Stock and prices are not good. A fair price could be had for fancy roses and carnations, but these are limited to a few hundred, hardly enough to supply one first-class establishment. American Beauty bring from 75c. to $3 per dozen; other roses, $2 to $5 per 100. Carnations, 50c. to $1 per 100. Asters, fancy, $2 to $5; other grades from 50c. to $1 per 100. Tuberroses, gladioli stalks, $1 to $2 per 100. The market is supplied with greens at usual prices.

ST. PATRICK.

BOSTON.—Trade is quiet. Roses are improving in quality but there is little call for them. Asters are very plentiful. There is quite a contrast from a year ago when one or two growers brought all that came to market at this season and now the market is overstocked with them.

Carnations are best from outside stock. Gladiolus are in good supply; sweet pears are more plentiful but they are of poor quality. Candituft and feverfew sells at 20c. and 25c per bunch. Lilies are good, but not a great demand.

J. W. D.

INDIANAPOLIS.—Despite extremely hot weather, business keeps up fairly well; all the retailers were busy with funeral work the past week.

It is noticeable this Summer that more flowers are sent to the hospitals and sick people than formerly.

The decorating season promises to open up earlier this Fall, as numerous orders are already booked for early September.

Select stock is exceedingly scarce and fancy prices are paid; even asters, so plentiful a week ago, are now readily taken at $1 to $2 per 100. Quantities of gladioli are shipped in at $1.50 to $2 per 100; home-grown bring $2 to $3.

Cold storage Longiflorum lilies may be had at $2 a dozen; a few L. rubrum remain at 50c. a dozen. Tuberoses sell well at 75c a dozen stalks.

Hardy hydrangeas are much appreciated for design work at $1 a dozen sprays.

Kaiserin Augusta Victoria, La France, and American Beauty are the best roses now being received. The damp weather seems to have caused havoc with the Bride and Bridesmaid as they are much mildewed.

Tomlinson Hall Market reports business as real good; of course not much stock is brought there now, but no trouble is experienced in disposing of the decreased quantity. I. B.

NEW BEDFORD, MASS.—Trade is fair, with plenty of flowers. Funeral work is what helps the florists these long Summer days. Asters are in good supply. Queen of the Market is all over the late ones, Vick's and Semple's are also coming in. These latter bring 35c. per dozen, retail. A few carnations are still to be seen from the old plants; 35c. per dozen is the price asked. R. H. Woodhouse and E. Y. Pierce have commenced to house their carnation plants. Stock is not quite so large as in other years, which is probably due to excess of rain and lack of sufficient sunshine. Young rose stock is looking fine.

E. Y. Pierce's new violet house is almost completed.

ST. PAUL.—Trade the past week was very quiet, the G. A. R. Encampment made a little spurt in business, but as that was about evenly distributed among the trade, there was no one florist that benefited a great deal.

Funeral work seems about all that is going on, and as some prominent old settlers have dropped off recently, some of the dealers have had fairly good business along that line.

Stock is easing up considerably though little difficulty is experienced in getting all that is wanted.

Roses are coming in nicely and prices are very low, some very good stock is purchased at the rate of $3.00 per 100.

Outdoor flowers seem to sell fairly well, asters especially, and the florist with only a fair trade, can make out very well. Some very fine asters have been thrown on the market at 1c. each, which are in turn retailed at 35c. and 50c. per dozen.

Gladioli are very good this season and command a fair price.

Sweet peas are in abundance and come in nicely for funeral designs and sprays.

The majority in the trade have had a very fair Summer business, and from reports, sales during July and up to the present date in August, have exceeded those of a year ago.

A noticeable fact is that all of the trade are making improvements, especially in their retail departments.

The greenhouse men are all very busy with their planting for the Fall trade, but the excessive heat has retarded their work to some extent.

PAUL.

Buffalo.

W. J. Palmer has returned from his vacation, spent in the north woods of Canada.

Miss Ruby Mark has returned from her trip through the Thousand Islands.

The motor boat seems to be the most popular way of traveling from the florist viewpoint. Arthur Beyer and party left for a three weeks' trip to visit points on the Hudson River, Lake Champlain and down to New York city.

Miss Mae Pendergast, who enjoys the distinction of being the only lady cahier in the florist business in Buffalo, left for a long rest at Thousand Islands.

Wm. Kalish and wife, of St. Louis, Mo., stopped here on their return from a trip through the St. Lawrence River.

H. W. Jones, with Blackistone, Washington, D. C., was a recent caller.

A. Richert has been spending his vacation at Olcott Beach.

E. A. Slattery was called out of town the past week to attend a funeral at Clayton, N. Y. W. H. G.

Hartford, Conn.

Carl U. Fohn, who has been forester at Keney Park during the past three years, has been appointed superintendent on the extensive property of Gen. Palmer at Colorado Springs, Col., and left Hartford on 17th inst. to assume his new duties.

Mr. Fohn has been an active and popular member of the Florists Club and the Connecticut Horticultural Society and his many friends in both bodies presented him on the evening preceding his departure, with a massive silver loving cup.

In horticultural and social circles here, Carl will be much missed and he carries with him to the West, the warmest good wishes of the entire "craft" of Hartford.

ALEX. CUMMING.

The Hybridization Conference.

At the banquet tendered the delegates by the Horticultural Club, London, Professor Bateson said, among other things, when he asked himself the meaning of all that princely hospitality he really could give no answer. He wondered sometimes whether they really had a valid position; but he felt, after all, that science and practice in horticulture should go hand in hand, and they were there that night to declare their belief that the promises made on behalf of that union would yet be fulfilled. He never could believe that all their efforts would be wasted, and there was a solidarity in their union which would last for many a day to come. The great thing was not to promise too much. Science could not do the impossible. They could not get a yellow pea from a white, or a red from a yellow, if the white and the yellow were non-existent; but if the colors were there, science would get at them. He believed, however, if the scientific were successfully combined with the practical, they would be able to produce something very remarkable. One thing was taught them by science, and that was patience. He did not refer to that patience necessary to watch a seed grow, but to that patience which was needed when scientists were speaking about matters which were absolutely unintelligible. (Laughter.) The present union of science with the practical was most bizarre—each got something from the other. He felt every confidence that that union would last for many years, and would be extraordinarily prolific. The day was past when their subjects would suffer from want of interest. There would be quite sufficient interest to carry them over the dead point, and then their work would become a living reality. If some things could only be understood, he believed that quite a new era for plants and animals would begin.

The session on Wednesday, August 1, opened at 10.30 a. m. Dr. E. Tschermak of Vienna gave an address on "The Bearing of Hybridization on the Origin of New Forms."

On Thursday, August 4, Dr. Erwin Smith read an interesting paper on "The Work of the United States Department of Agriculture in Plant Breeding." He told, among other things, of the effort to secure an edible orange which will be hardy as far as New York. They have already obtained a frost-resisting hybrid from Citrus trifoliata, but the quality of its fruit requires to be improved.

A vote of thanks was tendered by the Conference to the U. S. Department of Agriculture.

John H. Troy, New York, read a paper on "Florists' Ideals in the United States of America;" and a paper was contributed by James Douglas on "Cross-fertilization of the Auricula and of the Carnation."

Mons. C. G. Van Tuberger, Jr. of Haarlem, Holland, delivered an address on "Hybrids and Hybridization among Bulbous Plants. He said in part:

Lilium.—Very numerous crosses among various species were effected by me, and many seedlings are still under observation. A good and noteworthy race has sprung from the crossing of Lilium Martagon album with Lilium Hansoni. It is of particular interest to note, that whereas Lilium Martagon album, if raised from seed almost comes perfectly true, scarcely ten among a thousand plants reverting to the typical purple Martagon lily; out of the mingling of Lilium Martagon album with Lilium Hansoni not a single white Martagon occurred. All plants (several hundreds) that showed no influence of the pollen parent (Lil. Hansoni) reverted to the typical purple Martagon lily. Those that showed the influence of Lil. Hansoni developed into stately, tall growing lilies with broad, dark green foliage in whorls and pyramidal spikes, composed of very numerous flowers. The ground color of the flowers of these hybrids is a more or less pronounced pale buff-brown, either flushed with crimson or with deep orange and with purple spots. The individual size of the flowers much exceeds that of either parent. I named this strain Lilium mar-han, and I have already distributed two or three distinct varieties of it, while others are still in course of propagation. As far as is known to me the cross effected by Mr. Powell, of Southborough, between Lil. Martagon dalmaticum and Hansoni either produced true hybrids or gave dalmaticum pure. Other crosses which gave good results were effected between Lil. paradinum and Parryi and also between Lil. pardalinum x Humbodtl. These, however, have lately also been raised in America.

Brunsvigia Josephinæ, fertilized with pollen of Amaryllis belladonna, though raised from seed of the brunsvigia, show no influence of the mother parent, the bulb and foliage being that of an Amaryllis belladonna.

Colchicum.—Some very interesting plants came out of a cross between C. Sibthorpi and the double white flowered form of Colchicum autumnale. The seedlings either produced a large, broad petaled form of C. Sibthorpi or gave perfectly double flowered C. Sibthorpi, the flowers being composed of hundreds of narrow petals of a lilac red, faintly chequered white. These double flowers are perfectly sterile, whereas in the double white flowered Colchicum autumnale one occasionally finds a good pistil with potent pollen.

Eremurus.—Some very strong growing hardy hybrids, capable of resisting severe late Spring frosts, which will kill or hopelessly damage flower spikes and foliage of robustus and himalaicus, have been raised in my nursery by crossing E. himalaicus with early flowered forms of E. robustus, the result giving a fair percentage of immensely strong growing plants throwing spikes seven to eight feet in height with flowers of a pale rose color. These hybrids flower a little later than E. himalaicus and before E. robustus are out. Though not so showy as a finely developed specimen of E. robustus, the hybrid which I named Eremurus himrob, has the particular advantage of being capable to safely escape the so often deadly injurious effects of late Spring frosts. A very interesting and delicately beautiful plant is Eremurus Turbegni, which was produced by crossing E. himalaicus with pollen of an early flowered form of E. bungei. In this plant the foliage has the deep green color of that of E. bungei, but being almost as broad as that of E. himalaicus, while the spikes and individual flowers most resemble those of E. himalaicus, the color being a delicate pale primrose yellow. Seedlings of this hybrid either produce true E. Tubergeni or E. himalaicus, but I have not observed any E. Bungei to reappear among them. Hybrids between E. Bungei with robustus or Olgæ (the latter were also raised in Sir Michael Foster's garden at Shelford) give plants in which a coppery salmon yellow of the flowers predominates. In habit of growth and color of the flowers some of the seedlings cannot be distinguished from E. Warei, which I have always regarded to be a natural hybrid between E. Bungei and some rosy colored sort, and not a true species.

Hymenocallis.—With a view of ascertaining the correctness of the supposed parentage of H. macrostephana, after some years' trial I managed to have the two supposed parents Hymenoocallis speciosa and Hyenocallis (Ismene) calathina in flower at the same time. The results showed absolutely different plants from H. macrostephana, being much broader and thinner in the leaf; the formation and size of the inflorescence and of the individual flowers also being quite different. When in good condition this hybrid hymenocallis, the first authentically on record between the evergreen section hymenocallis and the deciduous ismenes, is a magnificent plant with an umbel of over a foot and a half across, with large, snowy white individual flowers, exceeding in size even the so large flowered H. macrostephana. This hybrid has been distributed under the name of H. daphne. Crosses between the white H. calathina and the yellow, green banded H. Amancaes gave charming mules of a delicate sulphur yellow. These, however, have also at various times been raised in England.

Mons. Van Tubergen also treated at some length upon Irises and Gladioli.

Mr. H. H. Groff, of Ontario, submitted a paper on "Practical Plant Breeding." This paper will appear in a future issue.

An exposition of his work upon Amaryllisæ, Cactacema, Gesneraceæ, and the genus Senecio, was given by A. Worsley, of Isleworth. Briefly he stated that in no single case of hybrid Amaryllisæ was the progeny other than fairly well equiposed. But he had had offspring from crosses which altogether resembled the female. These he regarded as not hybrids at all. They were akin to the reproductions that occur between zygopetalum and odontoglossum, where no actual sexual fusion has occurred. In crosses with Achimenes(?) Cooperi and A. Aikermani, the hybrids were equipoised. In one cross the white stigma of Cooperi was apparent in the seedlings, but in the reverse of the cross, the red stigma of Aikermani was dominant. This was interesting, because one usually finds the stigmas the same. In gloxinia x isoloma (male) the hybrids were seven-petalled, but spotted like the gloxinia. They were infertile.

Then he alluded to color changes in cinerarias. He stated what numbers of white, crimson, blue, pink seedlings he had from a crimson and white cross, but there was no new color. What appeared distinct was analysible into the primary colors of the parent flowers. This, however, he found, that wherever you get a color that varies greatly from the ancestral color, the plants were sterile, whereas the seedlings with colors nearly like unto the parent were fertile. Orange coloration underlies red in nearly every case. Orange and white produces pink.

Lastly, Mr. Worsley alluded to the Logan berry. Some folks doubted whether it was a hybrid. If the stipules were examined, however, they would be found to be intermediate between the reputed species of blackberry and raspberry (R. idæus x R. ursinus). Mr. Worsley's paper will also contain a complete list (with remarks) of all the known hybrid Cactaceæ.

In the discussion, Mr. Bateson referred to the belief held by Darwin and others that the cineraria was self-sterile. Mr. Worsley contradicted this. A tiny spider sometimes was found to be instrumental in pollenating the stigmas. In hybridizing he placed his plants upon inverted pots, and these in turn were surrounded by saucers of water. This prevented the spiders.

Herr F. Bürger, of Halberstadt, Germany, submitted a paper which was read by the assistant secretary, though Herr Bürger was present. The latter had acted upon the axiom "New seed, much growth: old seed, much flower," and had chosen for cross-breeding purposes plant showing signs of decay. His objects were mainly to get a new dwarf, compact type of growth, with bouquet flowers, and foliage which would resist the attacks of aphides. He also introduced the large scarlet Pelargonium grandiflorum, but seemingly with small success. He thought it probable that the pollen tube was too large to find entrance to the ovule chamber. No zonal had ever been made the seed bearer. He summarised his findings in this rule:—Every hybrid that has inherited equal numbers of characters from both parents in infertile, and only those are fertile which mostly follow the female. P. Peltatum was another of the species employed, but Herr Bürger is still struggling to get more of the zonal strain into his race of hybrids. There is a decided co-relation between certain colors and sterility.

A paper on "The Derivation of Some Recent Varieties of Roses" was next contributed by Arthur William Paul, of Waltham Cross. The necessary time was not available for the reading of the paper in full, but extracts were read, and the paper will appear with the others in the report of the conference. After alluding to the more or less haphazard methods by which fresh varieties of roses were obtained in the early days of raising roses from seed, Mr. Paul proceeded to describe methods pursued by the more skilful raisers of new varieties at the present time, instancing the particular crosses by which some of the most distinct of recent varieties have been obtained. During the last ten of twelve years the greatest advances appear to have been obtained in the hybrid Tea, dwarf polyantha, Chinese multiflora (rambler), Wichuriana, and rugosa classes; the varieties of Rose lutea have been used with good effect for hybridizing purposes, and some good new varieties have also been obtained in the hybrid perpetual and Tea-scented sections. Some of the most important of the croses cited were the following: —

H. T. Gruss an Teplitz—[Bourbon Sir J. Paxton×Noisette Fellenberg]×Tea Papa Gontier×Bourbon Gloire des Rosamanes.

H. T., Caloline Testout—Tea Madame re Tartas×H. T. Lady Mary Fitzwilliam.

H. T., Antoine Rivoire—Tea Dr. Grill×H. T. Lady Mary Fitzwilliam.

H. T., Earl of Warwick—Tea The Queen×H. T. Belle Siebrecht.

H. T. Richmond—H. T. Lady Battersea×H. P. Général Jacqueminot.

H. T., Konigin Carola—H. T. Caroline Testout×H. T. Viscountess Folkestone. In the flowers of this variety the colors and characteristics of both parents are clearly discernible.

H. T., Etoile de France—H. T. Madame Abel Chatenay×H. P. Fisher Holmes.

H. T., Madame Jules Gravereaux—Noisette Reve d'Or ×H. T. Viscountess Folkestone.

Polyantha, Eugénie Lamesch—Multiflora Aglaia×Noisette W. A. Richardson. It is somewhat remarkable that the result of this cross between two strong-growing varieies should be a dwarf-growing Rose.

Polyantha, Aschenbrodel—Polyanthat Petite Léonie× Austrian Copper.

Multiflora, Helène—[Hybrid Tea seedling×Aglaia]× Crimson Rambler.

Multiflora, Kathleen—Crimson Rambler×Felicité Perpetué.

Multiflora, Philadelphia Rambler—Crimson Rambler ×H. P. Victor Hugo.

Multiflora, Trier—Multiflora Aglaia×H. P. Mrs. Sharman Crawford.

Wichuriaiana, Jersey Baeuty—R. Wichuriaiana×Tea Perle des Jardins.

Wichuraiana, Pink Pearl—R. Wichuraiana×H. T. The Meteor.

Rugosa, Madame Georges Bruant—R. Rugosa×Tea Sombreuil.

Rugosa, Conrad Ferdinand Meyer [Tea Gloire de Dijon×H. P. Duc de Rohan]×Rugosa Germanica.

H. Briar, Soleil d'Or—H. P. Antoine Ducher×Persian Yellow.

H. Briar, Gottfried Keller—[H. P. Pierrre Notfing×Tea Madame Berard]×Persian Yellow×[Tea Madame Berard ×Persian Yellow]. Flowers of Gottfried Keller crossed with H. P. Charles Lefebvre, at Waltham Cross have produced seedlings of Brian-like foliage and habit of growth.

H. P., Frau Karl Druschki—H. P. eMrveille de Lyon ×H. T. Caroline Testout.

Hybridization Conference in London.

The third international conference on plant breeding has been held. The first of the series was opened at Chiswick, London, England, over 7 years ago. The second was in New York in 1902. The Royal Horticultural Society was the leader in this far-reaching movement so fruitful in achievement and in possibilities. By the courtesy of our French neighbors, it is proposed that the next conference be held in Paris in 1910.

The practical plant breeder asks "what do these conferences mean; what do they amount to?" First of all let me use the name that has been suggested for the new science. This name is "Genetics," that is the study or "elucidation of the phenomena of heredity and variation, in other words, the physiology of descent." Well, then, these conferences amount to this: they being together workers, both practical and scientific, from all the ends of the earth. They show the worker among orchids what the workers among roses, sweet peas, stocks, and even mice, rabbits and fowls, are doing. The scientist who is engrossed or lost in the idiosyncrasies of orchids, may be assisted by a discovery made by a brother worker in an entirely different field. The knowledge thus gained may be all that is required to clear away his own obstacles.

What has the present conference done? It has set the scientists homeward with many new problems, one being this—why do single stocks produce doubles; and why are doubles sterile? Also what are the physiological laws that govern doubling in stocks? These questions were suggested by a discussion which arose out of a very scientific paper by Miss Saunders of Newnham College, Cambridge, on "Certain Complications Occurring in the Cross-breeding of Stocks." The discussion on doubling was started by a gardener (Mr. Robert Fenn) and was assisted by Mr. Arthur W. Sutton (Reading), Monsieur Phillip de Vilmorin (Paris), Herr von Dieppe and others.

But indeed in a conference lasting over five sessions and occupying nearly a week, there were dozens of most important suggestions, questions, and hints made and answered. These I cannot all deal with, but I shall briefly outline the findings in some of the more important papers. There were exactly 45 of these, most of which were either read, or an address was given in their place. In the great majority of cases the speakers were present in person, there being about 70 or 80 foreign delegates and friends.

Professor William Bateson, M. A., F. R. S., of Cambridge was president of the conference. He is a thinker and investigator who "has been foremost in reducing to law and order the chaotic mass of detail relating to variation and heredity. We have learned from him that these matters may be coordinated and reduced to system and numerical proportion." His chairmanship received the highest praise.

One very important point has been brought to light in these Mendelian researches, and that is that in hybridization there is juxtaposition but no actual blending or fusion of parental characters: the male cells remain unaffected, the female cells are unchanged, though some characters may be "dominant," others latent or "recessive," till, by a socalled process of reversion, the latent character may reappear.

Also among other things, we have at last a critical appreciation of the physiological meaning of the term pure-bred. An individual is pure-bred when the two cells, male and female, from which it develops, are alike in composition. The several features or physiological characteristics may be treated as distinct in the cell divisions by which the germ-cells are formed. This conception of the unity and distinctness of characters provides the solid foundation which makes the science of genetics possible.

In the matter of reversion, it is now stated that any given reversionary character is merely a "recessive," for if kept to themselves they can be bred true. Reversion on crossing is rather more complex, and reversionary forms by crossing are found never to breed true in the first generation, though in the second generation there must be a small but definite percentage which are then pure-bred and will continue to breed true. Reversion or crossing is due to the meeting of long-parted factors. Conversely, variation is often due to the elimination or separation of factors. In other cases it may be due to the addition of new factors. In short, as Mr. Bateson said, with a critical knowledge of the meaning of "pure-bred" and "reversion," a new era begins.

I may state here, for the benefit of those who are interested in this most important subject, that all of the papers, together with the discussions, will be published in one volume shortly, and may be had at a moderate charge by all who are not Fellows of the Royal Horticultural Society.

Dr. Wilson of St. Andrews, Scotland, demonstrated the almost invariable infertility of hybrids. Mr. Chittenden of Chelmford, Essex, by statistics showed that the female parent in hybrids has the greater influence in transmitting the colors of her flowers. Hitherto it has always been regarded as the province of the male to impart color. Mr. Biffin of Cambridge showed that rusts and diseases (in wheat at all events) can be treated as Mendelian factors, and the ratio of infected to immune plants in the second generation of his hybridizing came out as practically 3 to 1. This discovery will have an important bearing upon the future direction of experiments into the heredity of diseases—diseases either of plants or animals.

The addresses and papers were highly technical and highly scientific. The work has already gone far and deep. Future experiments will mainly be in the direction of cytogeny, histology and physiological research. The great need is workers, and suitable monetary provision for these workers.

Ere concluding, I would mention that among the American delegates present were Dr. Erwin Smith of the Department of Agriculture, Washington: Dr. Hansen, South Dakota Agricultural College: John H. Troy, New York: Mr. Murrill, Botanical Gardens, New York; while C. Willis Ward, New York, sent a paper on "Carnations." Dr. C. A. Zavitz of Guelph, Canada, and H. H. Groff, Ontario, each had addresses, the former being present at the conference.

The meeting opened on Monday, July 31 with a conversazione: on Wednesday a special train took the company to Sir Trevor Lawrence's residence in Surrey, and on Friday the British Museum of National History, with Kew Gardens and Gunnersbury Gardens (Leopold de Rothschild, Esq.) were visited ere the company finally dispersed. A grand banquet was also included on Thursday evening, so that altogether this was one of the greatest meetings that the Royal Horticultural Society has ever inaugurated. There can be no doubt of this, that the results accruing from this conference will extend round the world. J. HARRISON DICK.

Our London Letter.

BY A. HEMSLEY.

THE ROYAL HORTICULTURAL SOCIETY.—We continue to get good shows at all the fortnightly meetings. On July 31 one of the most interesting exhibits was from H. B. May, who sent a large collection of ferns consisting entirely of varieties mostly raised by himself. There were some remarkable varieties of nephrolepis. During the last few years some remarkably distinct sorts have been raised. The one most likely to be of value for florists work is N. exaltata superba, a very fine crested form, with fronds standing up well.

I met J. H. Troy of New York, who read a paper at the conference on Hybridization and Plant Breeding. I was unable to attend the conference, but I understood there were some papers given which touched on the practical side of the question, but the scientific disclosures did not convey much to assist the practical workers. Mr. Troy seemed rather surprised to find that we have such good displays so often. He was interested in the American carnations which were well shown for so late in the season. We are likely to have some good things among the English varieties for next season.

SEED GROWING.—This season has been exceptionally favorable for some crops. When recently visiting Messrs. Dobbies Seed Farm, at Mark's Tey, Essex, I found they had made great advance in converting what was a very badly cultivated farm into a profitable seed growing ground. Some crops had suffered from the continual drought. The sweet peas had done well early in the season. The trial batch of new varieties revealed the fact that the orange shades, such as Henry Eckford, Evelyn Byatt, and others, would not stand the sun not even so well as Queen Alexandra, Scarlet Gem, King Edward, etc. Among other things noted I found the old time antirrhinums were receiving special attention and some very distinct shades of color were being grown. These after several years of careful selection have been fixed, and the white, yellow, pink, and other shades come very true from seed. The African marigolds are still great favorites, especially in the north of England, where Messrs. Dobbie have such a large trade. The strain which is grown for seeding at Mark's Tey is certainly as fine as could be found. W. Cuthbertson (the head of the firm) gives much of his time to selecting and improving the strains of the numerous flowers grown from seed. The special feature at the time of my visit was a trial of potatoes. The great boom in potatoes has died out, yet there is still money in growing for seed, and the object of the trials was to prove the superiority of Scotch grown seed. Some were grown in ground manured with artificial fertilizers, and some with farm yard manure, the latter proving best with all of the 25 sorts grown. From sixty sets, the average excess in weight was nearly 20 pounds; 86 pounds was the greatest weight from farm yard manure, the same variety giving only 62 pounds from artificial manure. Prizes offered for best samples of some special varieties brought exhibitors from all parts. From the samples seen it would seem that Midlothian Early does well in all districts. I should say that though the trials were conducted at Mark's Tey, Messrs Dobbies' ordinary crops of potatoes are all grown in Scotland.

I recently visited H. J. Jones's new nursery at Keston. Here I found the sweet peas doing well, and some very distinct new varieties, this result of careful crossing, and also some selections from Countess Spencer. It is really remarkable how this variety sports. It gives all shades of color, from pure white to deep purple. It is suggested that this is owing to the keel opening before fertilization takes place thus admitting pollen from others being conveyed. Of course, there is always plenty of spare pollen floating about which is liberated after those with the close keels are fertilized.

The only drawback about sweet peas now is, that we are getting far too many varieties. I find Helen Lewis is one of the greatest favorites among recent additions. Cannells "Rosy Morn" may prove valuable, but it requires to be grown with George Herbert and John Iugman. I think it would be difficult to sort them out if grown under the same conditions. In this I may be wrong, but I should not like to say one is much better than the other until it has been further proved. Chas. Breedmore's Etta Dyke is one of the best whites of the Spencer type. Dora Cowper a good creamy yellow, but it requires to be grown with the Hon. Mrs. Kenyon before saying too much about it. The latter has been a great favorite with florists this season, and has sold well in the market.

COVENT GARDEN MARKET.—The season being now over, we can look back on what has been a tolerably favorable one to growers. The greatest drawback was the cold, and frosty nights which came so late in the season. I am afraid there is little that is new or novel to record. Among the best new things we have for cut bloom is Gypsophila paniculata flore-pleno. This is much appreciated, and I find that growers who took it up early are increasing their stock, finding it a profitable plant to grow. It is one of the few things where the flowers being double the light graceful form is not destroyed.

Statices are much appreciated. Since the long stemmed large flowers have been more the fashion it has become necessary to use some light material among them, and the gypsophilas, statices, etc., have been more in demand. The best yellow statice is Bonduella; Sinuata both white and blue are useful, Tomentella superba, incana, and latifolia are also useful, and there are others of garden origin which are good. The very distinct species S. Suworowii is another which is coming to the front. The tall branching spikes of pink flowers are very pretty and keep their color well when dried.

Peonies are more extensively grown for market than formerly, but we do not want the immense flowers. It is the medium sized blooms of pure white, clear pink, and bright reds, which are in most demand. I find that those who pack carefully do best with them.

While on packing I may say that it seems strange to me that there should be so many who pay little regard to conditions. We have many who are careful, and whose flowers arrive in splendid condition. Some may cut and bunch well, but pack in hot, dry boxes, which extract all the moisture from the flowers before they reach the market. Cool boxes, properly lined with paper, and made as nearly air-tight as possible, secure flowers travelling well; but if the flowers are wet, and shut up close in warm boxes they, will be spoiled. We have no trouble with firms who properly understand their business, but I am frequently shown samples received by commission men where really good material has been spoiled by the packing, then the senders complain of the returns they get.

Cold-Resisting Fruits.

The address on this suject was delivered in American-English by Prof. N. E. Hansen, of the South Dakota Agricultural College, U. S. A. Briefly stated, he and his colleagues are trying to discover what hardiness means. They want to discover some underlying philosophy for cold resistance. Plants that extend over a wide area vary greatly in hardiness. Conifers from the west side of the Rockies are tender compared with those from the east side. Scots pine from western Europe is not so hardy as that from the Russian steppes. According to De Candolle it has taken 5000 years for species to reach their present limits. What did hardiness mean? Chemical and physiological examination of the wood structure and of the leaves failed to give them an answer. Cold resistance, then, could not be studied through the microscope. There was something secret and inherent in the plant itself. It has cost the Northern States £20,000,000 to discover that the apples of Western Europe were not hardy in Dakota. The Russian race of Pyrus Malus was the hardiest, and so in Dakota they were hybridizing with these. Selection alone does not bring about a hardier race; and hardiness cannot always be transmitted by hybridization. Among strawberries, a species from Alaska was being tried, and this was so hardy that it still lived though mercury was frozen. A raspberry which they have named Sunbeam, with stands 41 degrees below zero. The Kieffer pear was a subject that gave them hope. By its introduction pear culture had been made possible much farther south in America. Its heat resistance came from the Chinese pear. That Dr. Hansen and his colleagues have a difficult task before them is very evident.

George Paul brought forward a proposal with regard to Copyright in Plants. He stated that he had brought forward a similar resolution seven years ago. A nurseryman raises a new plant for which he may only get £50 or £100. Out of this small sum he has to pay probably £25 for advertising it, and also the expenses of his catalogue. He has only a few months in which he can have the sole sale of a novelty, after which the price goes down, since every nurseryman has a stock and can manufacture it. He thought the State should guarantee copyright in plants, just as they guarantee copyright in books, music, or inventions. A plea for legislation coming from this conference would be of value.

Mr. Bateson asked whether a law, even if passed, could be enforced. He asked Mr. Paul whether he thought it possible that he or anyone else could guarantee that they were sole proprietors of plant novelties. Prof. Wittmack, of Berlin, said the Prussian Agricultural Society was trying to enforce a rule with the same object in view as expressed by Mr. Paul, only it was a recommendation alone, and by a society not the Government. The rule was that no nurseryman could sell another's novelties until after three years. James Douglas opposed the proposition. He said that Mr. Paul was suggesting Protection—the very thing that the country had so emphatically voted against at the recent Parliamentary elections. The matter cut both ways. If Mr. Paul raised a rose, and had to sell it to other nurserymen, he also was privileged to buy and sell their novelties, and so the results were squared. Mr. Druery pointed out that while the infringement of book copyright could be proved, there was a difference when plants were the subject. Mr. Paul's suggestion was read to the meeting, but was lost.

A vote of thanks to Mr. Bateson concluded the conference.—Abridged from Journal of Horticulture, London.

FOUNDED IN 1888

FLORISTS' EXCHANGE

A Weekly Medium of Interchange for Florists, Nurserymen Seedsmen and the Trade in general

Exclusively a Trade Paper.

Entered at New York Post Office as Second Class Matter

Published EVERY SATURDAY by

A. T. DE LA MARE PTG. AND PUB. CO. LTD.

2' 4, 6 and 8 Duane Street,

P. O. Box 1697.
Telephone 3768 John. NEW YORK.

CHICAGO OFFICE: 127 East Berwyn Avenue.

ILLUSTRATIONS.

Electrotypes of the illustrations used in this paper can usually be supplied by the publishers. Price on application.

YEARLY SUBSCRIPTIONS.

United States, Canada, and Mexico, $1.00. Foreign countries in postal union, $2.50. Payable in advance. Remit by Express Money Order Draft on New York. Post Office Money Order or Registered Letter.

The address label indicates the date when subscription expires and is our only receipt therefore.

REGISTERED CABLE ADDRESS:
Florex, New York.

ADVERTISING RATES.

One-half inch, 75c.; ¾-inch, $1.00; 1-inch, $1.25, special positions extra. Send for Rate Card showing discount of 10c., 15c., 25c., or 35c., per inch on continuous advertising. For rates on Wants, etc., see column for Classified Advertisements.

Copy must reach this office 12 o'clock Wednesday to secure insertion in issue of following Saturday.

Orders from unknown parties must be accompanied with cash or satisfactory references.

President Kasting made an efficient presiding officer, putting through the business with dispatch.

George S. Whitford, Phenix, R. I., is no longer correspondent of The Florists' Exchange for Providence, R. I., and district.

To Dayton on a Bicycle.

Emil Leuly, who left West Hoboken on his wheel August 12, arrived in time for the Convention, after covering a distance of 1,000 miles. Mr. Leuly reached Buffalo in four days, five hours, and Cleveland in six days, five hours. From Cleveland the roads were poor.

This is Mr. Leuly's fifth Convention trip.

Cash Register Company Entertainment.

On Tuesday evening the National Cash Register Co. entertained the members of the S. A. F. in their Welfare Hall, which proved a most enjoyable event. After a substantial lunch, William Pflum, acting general manager of the company, in a neat speech told of the work horticulture had done for the company, and regretted the absence in Europe of Mr. Patterson, the head of the concern, who would have enjoyed the privilege of meeting so many men and women engaged in an industry in which he took great personal interest. He spoke of civic improvement work, but from an æsthetic and commercial aspect. Real estate in the vicinity of the factory had doubled in value since the work of beautifying the surroundings had been instituted. Such environs produced also better workmen. No class of men had a better opportunity to further such work than florists, and he hoped all present would seize it. He referred to the necessity of beginning with the young and asked the delegates not to be backward in giving both criticisms and suggestions on the examples of work seen.

President Kasting appointed Messrs. Stewart and Altick as a committee to send a cablegram to Mr. Patterson, who is now in Berlin, expressing the Society's appreciation of his hospitality and endeavor to make the visit pleasant and profitable.

A lecture, illustrated by stereopticon was then delivered by A. M. Thomas of The National Cash Register Co., showing views of the factory, many of the studies being colored. He also took his audience on an imaginary trip through the gardens of Cairo, Egypt, Japan, China, Mexico and Lower California, afterward throwing on the screen many beautiful representations of flowers in color, the work being of a very artistic and high class. Pictures showing scenes connected with the factory, and the great train robbery closed an entertainment unequalled in the history of the S. A. F.

Among officers of the company who were untiring in their endeavors to make the evening a pleasant one were A. D. Sinclair, acting manager of the Publicity Department, and Charles M. Steele, his assistant.

President-Elect William J. Stewart.

The name of William J. Stewart of Boston, Mass., has been before the horticultural world for more than a generation both in the capacity of merchant and as secretary of the S. A. F. On his retirement from the office this year his friends in the society immediately went to work to recompense his long and faithful service by elevating him to the presidency.

Mr. Stewart was born in Cambridge Mass, on March 17, 1849. He inherits his love of flowers from his father, who held the position of gardener in Mount Auburn Cemetery, Mass. William attended the public schools of his native town, where he resided until his marriage when he removed to Winchester, Mass., where he has a comfortable home, beautifully surrounded with plants, trees, and flowers, many of which are rare specimens—the gift of his admirers and friends. When he attained his majority he suffered from ill health and his doctor recommended some outdoor employment as a means of restoration. So William went to work for a time in the the botanical garden of Harvard University, Cambridge, Mass. He afterward secured employment in Boston in the retail flower business, and later operated a wholesale commission cut flower house in that city, working up a large trade, especially in the South and West. Subsequently Mr. Stewart disposed of that business and secured employment more congenial to his tastes as eastern correspondent of the American Florist, Chicago, a position he held until quite recently, when he became manager and editor of Horticulture, a gardening periodical, published in Boston.

Mr. Stewart has been a member of the S. A. F. since the Cincinnati meeting in 1885, and was one of the first essayists of the organization. His fidelity to the Society's interests was recognised by a set of resolutions unanimously passed by the organization at its present meeting.

Vice-President Elect John Westcott.

John Westcott, the newly elected vice-president of the S. A. F., has always been an ardent supporter of the Society, and the honor bestowed upon him is well deserved.

Mr. Westcott was born on the banks of the Delaware, near Philadelphia, Pa., and his first work was begun as assistant gardener at the well known estates of Alex. Brown and Caleb Cope. In 1861 he engaged in the florist business in Brooklyn, N. Y., and during the Civil War he served his country in the ranks.

In 1868 he returned to Philadelphia, and spent some time with A. L. Pennock at the old Twelfth street store. He was taken into partnership, in 1870, the firm then being Pennock Brothers, where he remained until 1892 at which time he bought the old Ferguson plale at Laurel Hill, Pa., where he is still located.

Mr. Westcott has always entered fully into the sports of the society, and is known wherever he travels as a jolly good fellow. The welfare of his fellowman is his ruling passion; unselfish, generous to a fault, and the members of the S A. F. O. H. can be assured of the duties of the office of vice-president being well taken care of while in the hands of John Westcott.

Secretary-Elect Phil. J. Hauswirth.

We think it can safely be said that there is no more popular member in the ranks of the S. A. F. O. H., than the newly elected secretary, Phil. J. Hauswirth, of Chicago. This popularity has come about through Mr. Hauswirth's unvarying amiability, his willingness when called upon to share in the work connected with everything that tends to the pleasure or profit of the craft, and his untiring energy and unselfish devotion in the carrying out of that work.

Mr. Hauswirth is a German by birth, and first saw the light on December 18, 1861. He came to this country when a boy, in company with his aunt, who in 1871 married Charles Reisig, one of the pioneer florists of Chicago. Phil began work in the establishment of Mr. Reisig in 1873, and continued in his employ for almost 18 years, both in greenhouse and store. In 1892 Mr. Hauswirth succeeded his uncle, who was then well advanced in years, in the conduct of the store connected with the Auditorium Hotel, on the Wabash avenue side, later moving to the Michigan avenue side, where he is now located, and where he carries on a thriving and lucrative business, in which he is assisted by his amiable wife and his son E. J.

For many years Mr. Hauswirth has been associated with the S. A. F., in the sporting branch of which he takes great delight. He is a keen bowler, and has acted as manager of the convention tournament on several occasions.

Mr. Hauswirth has also creditably managed various flower shows among them the World's Fair Exhibition at St. Louis in 1903, and the recent show of the American Carnation Society in Chicago.

Mr. Hauswirth is held in high esteem by the craft of his home town, as indeed he is throughout the country. He is president of the Chicago Florists' Club this year. For years he has been an active member of the Red Men, and is at present chairman of finance in the Great Council of the United States. As such, accompanied by Mrs. Hauswirth, he lately went to San Francisco to distribute relief to the brethren in the stricken city. He is also a prominent Elk.

The Florists' Exchange feels sure that Mr. Hauswirth will prove a worthy and efficient successor to the able retiring official who has so long held the office of secretary of the S. A. F..

THE AWARDS

Plant Section.

CHILDS, JOHN LEWIS, Floral Park, N. Y. Phoenix Roebleni, a handsome small species of Phoenix. The judges believed that this variety was perviously exhibited.

COWEE, ARTHUR, Berlin, N. Y. For new varieties of gladiolus. Certificate of Merit.

CRAIG, ROBT. CO., Philadelphia. Ficus Pandurata. Certificate of Merit.

DREER, H. A., Philadelphia. Bougainvillea Sanderiana, Wm. K. Harris, a new variegated plant. Certificate of Merit. We consider it a most elegant plant especially adapted for verandas, boxes and porches.

JANESVILLE FLORAL CO., Janesville, Wis. New fern Nephrolepis Amerpohlii. Certificate of Merit. No large specimens shown.

STORRS & HARRISON CO., Painesville, Ohio. Fern, N. Leedsii, a sport; a little more robust than the Tarrytown, otherwise not much different. Certificate of Merit.

ULLRICH, LEWIS, Tiffin, Ohio. New seedling single red geranium Tiffin. Honorable Mention. Good single geranium, evidently a fine bloomer.

VICK'S SONS, JAS., Rochester, N. Y. Asters, particularly the new Daybreak colors, and Vick's Violet King. Honorable Mention.

WINDMILLER, F., of The Livingston Seed Co., Columbus, Ohio. New hybrids of begonia semperflorens, especially valuable as bedding plants. Honorable Mention. A free flowering semperflorens type.

Miscellaneous Supplies.

BAYERSDORFER, H. & CO., Philadelphia, Pa. Imported Stone Ware in Grecian effects, and other novelties. Highly Commended.

BEAVEN, E. A., Evergreen, Ala. Sheet moss chemically treated, a very useful article. Highly Commended.

BROXEY, J. H., Dayton. Carnation support—best support to date. Certificate of Merit.

DAYTON PAPER NOVELTY CO., Dayton. New designs in folding boxes. Highly Commended.

DAYTON SUPPLY CO., Dayton. Spraying appliance. Highly Commended.

HEIM SUPPORT CO., Connersville, Ind. Carnation support. Special Mention.

HERENDEEN MFG. CO., Geneva, N. Y. Sectional boiler. Certificate of Merit. The manufacturers say it will burn hard and soft coal.

KASTING, WM. F., Buffalo, N. Y. Patented cement indestructible bench. Certificate of Merit. We believe that cement is the material which will be exclusively used for greenhouse benches, and this seems the most practical and cheapest bench yet invented.

KING CONSTRUCTION CO., Toronto, Canada. New gutter and ventilator. Certificate of Merit for gutters; also attachment to ventilator.

KROESCHELL BROS. CO., Chicago. Rocking grate for all kinds of boilers. Certificate of Merit.

LORD & BURNHAM CO., New York. Dust proof oil cup for ventilating apparatus and new truss house gutter. Former awarded Certificate of Merit; latter Highly Commended. Also new form of Burnham boiler, said to be adapted for hard and soft coal.

MOOREHEAD MANUFACTURING CO., Detroit, Mich. Steam trap. Certificate of Merit.

PENNOCK, S. S., Philadelphia, Pa. Ribbons. Highly Commended.

REED & KEELER, New York. Cycas holders, new casket and other standing designs. Highly Commended.

RICE, M. & CO., Philadelphia, Pa. Novelties in Baskets for table decorations and novel effects in Bark pot covers. Highly Commended

SCHLOSS BROS., New York. A fine exhibit of fancy ribbons in color and texture. Highly Commended.

SIM, WM., Cliftondale, Mass. Flower pole. Honorable Mention.

STERN, S. B. & CO., Montgaomery, Ala. Naturally prepared Christmas trees, varigated magnolia foliage, etc. Highly Commended.

THADEN, H. & Co., Atlanta, Ga. Truss for greenhouses. Highly commended as a strong and cheap truss.

VAUGHAN'S SEED STORE, New York and Chicago. Gladiolus "Mrs Francis King." Certificate of Merit.

WERTHEIMER BROS. New York. Ribbons. Highly Commended.

YANKEE HOSE & PIPE CLAMP CO., Dayton. Hose Mender. Highly Commended.

WINDOW GLASS.—According to reports the American Window Glass Company has disposed of stocks in Chicago to Chicago jobbers, and has discontinued its distributing branch in that city. Business is somewhat quiet, and quotatons from jobbers' lists are as follows: Greater New York, single, 90 and 5; double, 90 and 10 per cent. discount. Eastern District, excepting Boston, 90 and 10 per cent. for all sizes of single and double strength. Boston quotations are reported as being 90 and 15 per cent. for all sizes of single and double strength.
—The Metal Worker.

Obituary

Henry Charles Johnson.

Henry Charles Johnson, son of Charles Johnson, died on the 17th instant, at the home of his parents, Marietta, Pa. He had been in usual good health when, in January last, he caught a severe cold, which culminated in heart trouble and a complication of diseases and ended his life.

Mr. Johnson was born December 23, 1872, in the same house in which he died, and was in the 34th year of his age. He was trained in the seed business, being one of the best posted young seedsmen of the day. From 1893 to 1896 he was of the firm of E. & H. Johnson, seedsmen, Riverside, Cal. In 1896, with his father, and his brother Ethelbert, deceased in 1903, he founded the Johnson & Musser Seed Company, Los Angeles, Cal. He left this firm in 1900 to become a member of the T. H. Thompson Seed Company, Houston, Texas. Subsequently he organized, and was secretary and treasurer of, The Southern Rice Milling Company, at Houston, Texas. For the past two years, and up to his death, he was on the staff of William Henry Maule, the Philadelphia seedsman, occupying the position of head of one of the most important departments in that establishment.

The funeral took place in Marietta on the 20th instant.

Mr. Johnson possessed a genial, kindly, thoughtful nature, which endeared him to all who knew him. He is survived by a widow and one child, five years of age, and both parents. C. J.

Roger O'Mara.

Roger O'Mara, who was the oldest employee (in years of service) of the Peter Henderson Company, died at his home, 400 Grand avenue, Jersey City, on Thursday, August 16, from heart failure, after an illness of five days, and was interred in the Holy Name Cemetery on Saturday, August 18.

The deceased was 58 years of age; he was born at Borris-O-Leigh, Tipperary County, Ireland, in 1848, the oldest of a family of eight children, and came to America when a boy. In 1863 he entered the employ of the late Peter Henderson, and went through every department in the greenhouse business, from fireman to propagator, finally to the position of order clerk. For several years he sold the cut flowers from the establishment, to the trade in New York, and was one of the famous quartette of cut flower salesmen through whose hands the supply for New York went, previous to the establishment of wholesale commission houses. In 1890 when Peter Henderson died, Mr. O'Mara took charge of the plant counter in the store, which position he faithfully held until his death.

Mr. O'Mara was possessed of a most lovable disposition, his gentlemanly bearing and efforts to please were a pleasure to all who came in contact with him. He was unmarried and leaves one sister and two brothers, Daniel and Patrick, to mourn his loss.

Southern Nurserymen's Convention Held in Chattanooga, Tenn., August 15-16, 1906.

The eighth annual meeting of the Southern Nurserymen's Association at Lookout Inn has adjourned, after having discussed a number of questions, electing officers, passing resolutions condemning the free distribution of seeds, giving the labor question a few thoughts and several other questions of more or less interest to the people at large. The next meeting will be held at Richmond, Va., because of the fact that the Jamestown exposition is to be held there next summer.

The officers elected for the ensuing year are as follows: President, John A. Young, Greensboro, N. C.; vice-president, C. N. Griffin, Jacksonville, Fla.; secretary-treasurer, C. T. Smith, Concord, Ga.

"What fertilizers give the best results on nursery stock and how applied?" was discussed by J. C. Hale, of Winchester; William Griffin, of Jacksonville, Fla.; W. T. Hood, of Richmond, Va., and others.

"Should the Large Orchards get the Benefit of the Wholesale Prices on Trees?" precipitated a warm discussion, in which R. C. Berckmans, of Augusta, Ga., took the position that the orchardist should not get the benefit of wholesale prices. W. T. Hood also discussed the subject at length.

"Grading Nursery Stock" was discussed by W. A. Easterley, of Cleveland, Tenn., who said that it is a question as to the adoption of a uniform standard of grading. He stated that it seems the nurserymen have different systems of grading. J. W. Shadow, of Winchester, advocated the grading by calibre system. Herbert Chase, of Cleveland, took the position that the system should be left to the person doing the grading. It should depend upon the judgment of the individual. R. C. Chase, of Huntsville, also discussed the subject, advocating the calibre system of grading. "One-eighth of an inch is close enough to grade," said Wm. Griffin, of Jacksonville.

"Should Nurserymen Grow More Ornamental Stock etc.," was a subject taken up by R. C. Berckman's of Augusta, Ga., who said that the demand for ornamental stock in the South is increasing. "New towns, new mills, etc., want ornamental stock," said he. "All of the cities are planting with maple or other varieties, and the time has come when nurserymen should pay more attention to the growing of ornamental stock.

J. C. Hale, of the nominating committee, reported the selection of the new officers, who were elected by a unanimous vote.

A paper on "Upon What Reasonings Depend the Determination of a Nurseryman to Plant and Bud One Million Apple Seedlings," prepared by G. A. Harrison of Berlin, Md., was read by Secretary Smith.

President Harrison appointed a committee on the free distribution of seeds by the government, which reported as follows:

"We beg leave to submit the following resolution:

"Resolved: That the Southern Nurserymen's Association now assembled do as a body condemn, and disapprove of the free distribution of seed by the government, and that they exert every means to bring about a discontinuance of this bureau and that each member of this association be requested to write their representatives in Congress and Senate, requesting that he bring all pressure to bear on the condemnation and abolishment of this useless expenditure."

Before the close of the meeting Prsident Harrison appointed standing committees for the year, including the legislation committee which is composed of the following:

J. A. Young, Greensboro, N. C.; Robt. Chase, Huntsville, Ala.; E. W. Kirkpatrick, Sherman, Texas; C. M. Griffin, Jacksonville, Fla.; J. I. Harrison, Cleveland, Tenn., F. M. Downer, Bowling Green, Ky.

This committee was appointed to act in conjunction with a similar committee of the National Association.

Teaching Horticulture in the Public Schools.

(Abstract of Committee's Report.)

Great Need of Standardizing and Centralizing the Controlling Power.

After careful research and study of reports and methods now in vogue, we wish particularly to call your attention to two matters: first, the absence of text-books in all the present methods of teaching horticulture, and second, the lack of concerted action among the different associations conducting that work, be they civic, philanthropic, or educational.

This state of affairs we consider fortunate. The first because it does not require any great preparation, and makes possible the starting of an S. A. F. method sooner than it could otherwise be started, since no elaborate system of text-books is essential. The second, inasmuch as individual persons and organizations have accomplished so much and demonstrated so thoroughly that the interest of the people is already all that could be desired that we feel confident if this work can be placed upon a methodical, systematic, concerted plan—in other words, if the entire school system of horticulture can be standardised suitably for each grade of school, suggested by the S. A. F. and adopted by the different boards of education—we see no reason why this teaching of horticulture should not cover the entire land in a few years.

Text-Books.

In all the methods of teaching by the different organizations at present, we find no text-books are given to the pupils. Leaflets are compiled and issued to the teachers and also to pupils, in some cases by the boards of education, for the guidance and help of each.

Leaflets.—These leaflets of instruction for the use of teachers should emanate from a committee of the S. A. F. They should be placed in the hands of the State Boards of Education who will attend to distributing the different grades of leaflets to the different grades of schools; namely the rural common schools, the union and high schools, and the primary and grammar grades, compiled with special reference to the conditions prevailing in each grade.

We also suggest, for schools that have become somewhat advanced in garden work, and for pupils that have shown interest, that leaflets and small, simple pamphlets be prepared, containing plain illustrations of flowers, giving the botanical parts, also botanical names of the common trees, plants and flowers, and others giving simple explanations of what is meant by "annuals," "biennial," "hardy," "perennial," and other matters that are met with in every-day life. Even these simple leaflets and pamphlets are not to be given out to the pupils until they show sufficient interest in their work. This plan can be elaborated as conditions seem to require.

Lack of Concerted Action.

NEED OF STANDARDIZING.

On careful perusal of all documents and reports that we could obtain we find no two schools or organizations conducting their garden-work on the same lines, but each pursuing its work according to its own ideas, and as seems best to it. Great good has undoubtedly come from these disunited efforts, but greater good will undoubtedly come from concerted action, emanating from some central authority, thoroughly standardizing their work.

We have suggested dividing the schools into three classes, so that we can better meet the conditions and environment known to exist in schools of each class. In this case, we should issue three series of leaflets of instructions, diagrams, and routine work. The latter could be taken largely from the methods now in force in the various school-gardens.

Instructions to Teachers.

Besides placing the leaflets and pamphlets in the hands of the different teachers, we suggest that one of the trustees should familiarize himself with the proposed methods, using some of the fuller reports of some of the specially conducted schools of this nature, to get a general idea of how the plots are laid out and cared for near the schools, or plots loaned by people a little distance from the school and the home-garden.

If no trustee feels equal to this simple task, he could easily call to his assistant a florist, a market-gardener, or even a good farmer in the community to help start the work. If the teachers lack in knowledge of any particular subject, they should be given to understand that they could call upon the trustee who would find a person competent to explain.

A committee of the Massachusetts Horticultural Society comments very favorably on the system of children's home-gardens, stating that the society first offered three prizes, then ten, and were much surprised when they received over two hundred entries for the ten awards. The committee visited the home-gardens as far as possible, and found it was very encouraging to the children to do so. They state: "We still feel the children's home-garden movement is a very important one." This committee also gives prizes in connection with the home-garden system for best reports of work for the year.

Your committee, in view of the reports on these methods, suggest as an intermediate plan, where conditions seem to favor the method, a Demonstration Plot in the school-grounds, where the teacher can fully demonstrate with each pupil the preparation of the soil, the application of fertilizers, and the planting of each kind of seed, both of vegetable and flowers. By this means, the depth and distance of planting seed of the standard kinds can be easily learned by the pupils.

The Demonstration Plot could be used throughout the season for simple talks, during the growth of the plants, even to the method of killing potato bugs. The object of this Demonstration Plot is that it may be used in connection with the children's home-garden system. All instruction and knowledge, as it were, which the children carry home to use in their gardens, will come from this plot.

State Teachers.

The State might employ a few experienced garden directors or teachers to visit as many schools during the year as practicable. Schools should be able to call for this special aid where the subject is not sufficiently understood. The Committee on School Gardens of the Massachusetts Horticultural Society, after investigation, says: "The great lesson learned was that children's gardens are successfully carried on when under the leadership of an experienced director or teacher. No matter how enthusiastically the work is undertaken, without a proper understanding of gardening it is usually a failure." The same committee says: "There is a crying need for an institution in this State similar to that at Hartford, Conn., where school garden work can be taught."

In the course of time this study could be added to the curriculum of all normal schools, as it already belongs to that of several, these schools to furnish teachers with sufficient knowledge of the subject to follow the methods laid down.

Lectures.

In educational matter of the present day, be it ever so low or so high, much instruction is imparted to the pupils by lectures and talks. In the rural schools it is not absolutley necessary that the talks or lectures should be given at specified periods. They could be worked in at times best suited to the convenience of the teacher.

At most of these lectures, the teacher should have one or two potted plants or some flowers, and some varieties of the common seeds; and it would not take any great length of time, not more than a year or two, perhaps, to make most of the pupils familiar with the treatment of the common and most useful plants.

Appropriations for Carrying on the Work.

In the matter of appropriations, all the different kinds of school-garden work derive their financial aid from different sources, which is of necessity a varying and somewhat uncertain amount. For carrying on this work, we want a certain appropriation for each grade of school. By way of illustration, but not a suggestion, we would say five dollars each for the rural schools, ten for the primary and grammar schools, and twenty for the union and high schools. We confidently believe that even an amount as small as this would be felt in a community, but we feel that by correlating garden-work with other studies, the different boards of education would appropriate a larger sum.

But what must be made plain is that the appropriation should be a fixed factor in the expense of conducting the schools.

Public Meetings.

At least once a year there should be a public meeting in the form of a conference, where all persons interested should be invited to come and make suggestions, and lend their aid to this movement. The children should have a chance to talk a little on their ideas and work.

At meetings of this kind, questions of civic improvement and general betterment of surroundings could be discussed.

To be continued.

The Coming Man with the Hoe
A. N. C. R. Boy Gardener

Society of American Florists *and* Ornamental Horticulturists

Incorporated by Special Act of Congress

Charter Signed by William McKinley, President of the United States, Mch. 4, 1901

FULL REPORT OF

TWENTY-SECOND ANNUAL MEETING AND EXHIBITION

Held at

DAYTON, OHIO, AUGUST 21, 22, 23 AND 24, 1906

1907 CONVENTION CITY
PHILADELPHIA

OFFICERS FOR 1907

WM. J. STEWART	President
JOHN WESTCOTT	Vice-President
P. J. HAUSWORTH	Secretary
H. B. BEATTY	Treasurer

THE OPENING SESSION.

Tuesday Afternoon, August 21, 1906.

Seldom if ever has the National Society met under more unfavorable weather conditions than those experienced at Dayton. On Tuesday the delegates were sweltering in one of the hottest days of the year. When the hour arrived at which the convention should have opened a violent thunderstorm traveled over the city, bringing with it a heavy downpour of rain, which lowered the temperature, affording much needed relief to perspiring humanity. The Convention Hall was located on the Fair Grounds, opposite the Exhibition Building, and the structure bearing that honorable designation was a shingle covered enclosure with openings at various places. Through an unfortunate and unavoidable oversight not enough seats were provided for the delegates, many of whom stood throughout the whole of the first session, which commenced at 3.20 instead of 2 p. m. as intended. The attendance under the existing weather conditions was most gratifyingly large.

On the platform besides President Kasting and Secretary Stewart were Ex-Presidents Lonsdale, Breitmeyer, Vaughan; and Elliott, Hallock, Traendly and Hauswirth of the Executive Committee. The proceedings were opened by Mr. Altick, who apologized for local conditions, regretted wet weather and introduced Judge Charles W. Dale, who in absence of the Mayor welcomed the delegates to Dayton. The judge said he did not know of a body of men who brought more sunshine and happiness to a community than the Florists. All indications pointed to the fact that their work was progressing everywhere especially in the Convention City which is essentially a city of homes. Here in connection with every cottage and house, one could see flowers and plants indicating a wealth of refinement and culture within. He spoke of the great work doing by the National Cash Register Co. and to beneficial results, present and future, and hoped that the day would come when citizens of Dayton would show their appreciation by some substantial recognition of that great and glorious work. The judge concluded by extending a hearty welcome to Dayton and handing over the keys of city.

Professor John W. Cowell, responded. He thanked Judge Dale and the citizens of Dayton for their kind welcome. The convention had in one respect at least received one of the warmest receptions it had ever been their lot to have. He spoke of the beauty of the city, which he said was well governed and well "registered." Our society had come here to learn, and might be able to impart something of comfort in return and, like the cruise of oil and the handful of meal in the parable, knowledge extends as we impart it and leaves our capital untouched and often increased. The Professor then went on to tell of the aims and objects of the National Society and expressed the pleasure it gave him in being selected to respond on behalf of the organization to the hospitable welcome given. (Applause.)

Patrick O'Mara, New York, was to have responded to the address of welcome. Mr. O'Mara suffered a sad bereavement in the death of his brother last week and was unable to be present at the convention.

President Kasting was then introduced by Mr. Altick and read his address, which was heartily applauded.

The President's Address.

Twenty-two years ago, I am told, while this society then new-born was holding its first meeting in the city of Cincinnati, there came an invitation to visit this city and view the horticultural wonders as set forth at the Soldiers' Home and other places. To-day we come again, increased an hundred fold, to see not only the Soldiers' Home but to see and admire the thousands of plantations in the streets, squares, and about the homes of the people; plantations that have made the name of Dayton known the world over and have been an incentive for other municipalities and an object lesson in civic cleanliness and good taste.

Amid such surroundings, I trust our deliberations as a society may be immeasurably pleasant and profitable, and that as individuals we may carry away impressions and ideas that will enable us to improve our own environment, and add to the beauty and general attractiveness of the localities which we severally represent.

Twenty-two years is not a long time in the history of a nation or even of a society, but it is time enough, I think, to prove the solidity of our organization, and time enough for us to have profited by our experiences. If there was a need for an organization of this character twenty-two years ago, how much greater is the need to-day, with the enormous expansion of our business that has come in two decades. The wisdom of the Fathers has been amply demonstrated. We cannot afford, however, to stand still and rest upon the records of the past—we must put forth new efforts and keep pace with the great procession.

The question comes home to us: Are we making the most of our opportunities as a society with such broad aims and splendid possibilities? Would it not be well to pause in our congratulations and our commendations and indulge in a season of introspection, and see if we cannot profit by example and still further augment our usefulness. Let us take a leaf from the history of our Host City and clean up our backyard and put our front in such condition that it may be an example to all men, to the end that we may become a greater power for good in the years that are to come. Let us take an example too by the work that the National Cash Register Company has done, and in our wider dwelling place be leaders in improvement and education.

There are certain questions that seem to be perennial sources of discussion, which crop up annually for our consideration. Occasionally one is settled; but its place is immediately taken, and it is only by constantly hammering at them that they are brought into shape and disposed of.

I propose briefly to refer to the more important of these problems, not with the idea of giving you any fresh argument, but rather that they may not be allowed to rest until they are solved.

Among the questions discussed by my predecessors, perhaps none are of more general importance than those pertaining to education.

We as professors of garden art and craft will continue to be looked up to as those having authority to speak, and it devolves upon us to be prepared, so far as we may, to lead in all matters relating to horticultural pursuits. How we can best reach the people who are interested in garden matters, and increase their love for vernal surroundings, as well as to implant desire where no desire exists, are questions of vital importance and worthy of our most earnest consideration. Exhibitions as a factor in education are of the greatest value. It is by the eye more than by the ear that people are instructed. The value of local displays of plants and flowers, happily on the increase, have done much to stimulate a more general love for flowers and incidently have increased the demands for the product of our art. Probably still more far reaching on account of its greater publicity and more elaborate and comprehensive display would be an exhibition of national character, where the entire country would be represented.

National Flower Show.

This question of a National Flower Show was again before the executive committee of the society at its recent meeting in this city and was discussed at some length, and I believe no one dissented from the statement that such a show would be of the greatest benefit to our interests. The result of this discussion will appear in committee's report.

I trust that the details of plans for such an exhibition may be perfected in the near future and that an exhibition may be held in one of the great centers of the country. Perhaps it is unfortunate in some respects that our interests have been drawn away or divided by the organization of special societies devoted to the culture of individual flowers.

I mean that in many cases the interests in the special has overcome the interest in the general and to an extent has weakened the S. A. F. when it comes to a question of combination of all interests in one grand exhibition. Everyone with the welfare of our society at heart must labor for the closer union between these vigorous offspring and the Mother Society.

Trade Exhibitions.

Trade exhibitions, as they are now conducted at our annual meetings, are undoubtedy of great benefit to our members. They should be fostered, and the exhibitors should be encouraged in every way consistent with the proper disposal of the business of the convention.

I deem this subject of so much importance that I would recommend that special time should be given to the examination of the exhibits. The exhibitors come to our meeting under a great expense, they contribute largely to the success of our meetings both in interest and financially, and I believe they should have more consideration at the hands of the makers of the program.

We can well afford to call one day "Exhibitors' Day."

We have made an experiment with outdoor exhibits and while the result to date is not satisfactory, yet I believe the idea is good, and that this outdoor exhibition can be made an important adjunct. In order to make an exhibit of this kind a success time must be taken for proper preparation. A manager, preferably a local man, must be appointed and the ground be available a year before the date of meeting, or better still a year and a half. It would then be possible for Fall planting or even Spring planting to be done and plants could be properly established and prepared. This would enable our nurserymen to make an exhibit of trees, shrubs and such other hardy material as they might desire to show. A good exhibition of this character would add greatly to the interest of our meetings.

The Experiment Stations.

The experiment stations are doing much valuable educational work and their publications are far reaching. Every member of this society should avail himself of his opportunity to obtain the bulletins of his State Stations, and use his best endeavor to see that these stations are provided with sufficient funds to carry on their work.

Any one who has been familiar with the work of these institutions for the last twenty years, cannot have failed to notice the improvement in the quality of work done.

The complaint made by many that not enough work is done for the benefit of the florist and gardener is not so just as it was years ago, and in many instances more work along these lines would be done if it were called for.

If you don't ask for it, you don't get it.

Horticultural Education.

Horticultural education as provided in the public schools, is perhaps rather disappointing to many. But it must be remembered that in the common schools only the merest rudiments are possible and just how much horticultural instruction is given will depend largely upon the people of the locality.

Nature study is in many cases really a primary course in horticulture. Some of the states are showing considerable activity along this line, and probably the great need at the present time is a more efficient plan of work and better prepared instructors. The way to stimulate the work is by arousing public sentiment in behalf of the value of such study.

Mr. Hallock who has given this subject much thought will discuss the question at the meeting.

Free Seed Distribution.

Free seed distribution by the Federal Government still continues; but the efforts being made will if continued, I doubt not effect a discontinuance of the practice and the "hoary fraud" will be done away with.

Members of this society should give their representatives in Congress no rest until this practice is abolished.

Parcels Post.

A parcels post would be to the great advantage of most people in the trade and a great boom to the general public. The elements opposed to such public convenience are well known, and so far they have had influence enough to prevent the passage of a law establishing it. The agitation should be vigorously continued, and every means taken to impress our law makers with the necessity for such a method of transportation.

We are behind most civilized countries in this respect.

The Tariff.

The tariff on many articles which are of necessity imported or which might be imported to our great advantage still continues to vex us. Some of the duties imposed are indefensible as a whole and others should be greatly modified. This subject has been before us often and some action has been taken in regard to it. I would recommend the appointment of a committee whose duty it should be to lay before the proper authorities our views on the subject, and urge a revision of the duties whenevr possible.

Secretary's Office.

To return to our more immediate concerns it seems to me that we might profitably make some improvements in the conduct of our business affairs. The secretary's office is one of the most important, as well as one of the most permanent within the society, and some changes in the manner of business might be well undertaken. In the first pace, the secretary should give bonds, as is now required of the treasurer. His books and vouchers should be presented at the meeting of the executive committee for audit in connection with the accounts of the treasurer, and not be passed upon in bulk in the hurry of the annual convention. His accounts as published should be itemized, for every member has a right to know just how his money is being spent and to whom it is paid. The secretary is now the purchasing agent of the society and no check is kept upon his expenditures. I would suggest that all bills be approved by the president before going to the treasurer for payment.

The secretary should be paid an adequate salary sufficient to remunerate him for his time and incidental expenses, and this should cover them all, so that bills for extra help, etc., would not be presented to the society.

Amendment to the By-Laws.

The amendment to the by-Laws, in regard to manner of conducting election will come before you at this meeting and should not fail of action as recommended by the executive committee.

Membership.

Membership in the society should stand high. I cannot approve of the suggestion that the dues of certain members should be made less than that of others. While it is desirable to include in our membership everyone engaged in ornamental gardening, whether he be on a private estate, in a public position, or a wholesale warehouse, and an effort should be made to induce all to join; yet it should be understood that all come in on an equal footing and with equal responsibilities before the law.

The so called "private gardener" of to-day may be a public gardener to-morrow; the employee of to-day may be, and indeed he probably will be, an employer to-morrow. Nor should it be forgotten that many an employee is better able to pay dues than are some employers.

It seems to me that this society should keep in closer touch with the local organization. It should have its accredited agent at the local flower shows and other gatherings of the craft. This would, I believe, tend to add new material to our membership list and add to the prestige of our socrety.

In order to do this it would be necessary to have some one detailed for the purpose, and probably the secretary of our society would be most available for the purpose.

State Vice-Presidents.

More care should be taken in the selection of the state vice-presidents. At the present time one or two men from a locality get together and place in nomination the person who might suit them best, which as a rule is equivalent to the appointment for this office made by the president. This should be left entirely to the selection of the president when he takes office. If he should not be acquainted sufficiently with a person from that territory or locality, it would be then the duty of the president to ascertain from the local society if there be one or a few other members in the craft, which is the best man for him to appoint.

The office should stand for something and men should be appointed who will give some time to the interest of the society.

Business Methods.

Business methods need more study on the part of many men engaged in trade, and this is just as true of the flower trade as of any other. No man can hope to succeed who does his business in a loose and slipshod manner. No matter how small the business, a set of books should be kept so that the standing of the business can be found at a moment's notice.

Fair dealing both in buying and selling should be the rule, and a man's word should be a little better than his bond. Do not abuse your credit and you will find business very much easier. It is true in business as in other things that "A good name is better than riches."

I have alluded elsewhere to the trade exhibitions, and now I wish to add a few words in regard to their management.

I believe that the society should take entire charge of these exhibits. It should appoint a manager, pay all expenses and receive any profits that may arise from such exhitions. I am well aware that the custom has been otherwise, for the reason that the money realized was needed for the local people to help on the entertainment. Now this is all wrong. Is it not time that this society adopted an attitude of independence and dignity? Is it not time that this society selected its own place of meeting without putting it up to be auctioned off?

Would it not be possible for us to go in peace and quiet to some central point and hold our convention and entertain ourselves? There are many places that we could visit with profit to ourselves, where to be entertained by the local members of our trade would mean ruin to them. This entertainment has, in my opinion, grown to be a great evil, and an unjust tax upon the communities visited. It has reached a point in the emulation of hosts where it behooves us to stop and consider the cost. To-day there are only a few of the larger cities that dare invite a convention, because they cannot make the lavish preparations that have become customary. A reform in this direction is needed.

Sports.

Perhaps another reform is needed in the matter of sports? Do we not give rather too much valuable time to our games? It is true that they are enjoyable to many, but it hardly seems necessary to travel a thousand miles to play a game of baseball or shoot a few clay pigeons. I think we have gone a little too far, and, have suffered in the attendance at our meetings because of the time taken for these contests. I do not mean to decry the social value of our meetings, but is there not a better way of enjoying each other's society and one less embarrassing to the business of the convention.

I believe that these contests should be curtailed and so arranged as not to interfere with the working of the society as they do at present. Take a day for them if necessary, but let that day be after the business of the meeting is completed.

Horticultural Press.

One factor in the general success of our business that has received but scant notice from us, is the horticultural press. While it may be said that these publications are purely commercial enterprises, and outside of our societies, yet they contribute a great deal to our success as a society, and contain from time to time the condensed essence of the brains of our more prominent members. They are certainly worthy of our support in every way, and no man in our business can hope to be posted in the doings of our craft without the weekly perusal of these papers, advertisements and all.

A word more and I am finished. It has occurred to me that many good ideas are broached after the work of our committee is done. How easy it would be for every member of this society having opinions in regard to the management of the business of the society to put his ideas in writing and send the same to the secretary at any time previous to the meeting of the executive committee.

In surrendering the office of president to my successor, I want to thank you for your loyalty and consideration, which has made the work a joy, and will leave with me a most pleasant memory.

Secretary Stewart read a telegram from Theodore Wirth, Minneapolis, member of the Board of Directors, regretting his inability to be present and hoping the convention would be a successful one. The secretary then read his report, and at its close Benjamin Hammond, Fishkill, N. Y., moved that the Society pass a set of resolutions expressing its regret at losing the services of Mr. Stewart who had held the position of secretary for so many years, serving with fidelity in all the branches and ramifications of the office.

Report of Secretary.

I find it hard to realise that this is my nineteenth annual report as secretary. Twenty years seems a long period to look forward to, but very short in retrospect. Some of us who are awakening to the fact that the years count up very rapidly, and that conventions come around with alarming frequency of late, can, however, take some comfort from Emerson who wrote "We do not count a man's years until he has nothing else to count." It is to be hoped that each and every one of us may be immune from year-counting for many a year to come. To quote again from the same writer "Nothing great was ever achieved without enthusiasm." Dayton has been long on enthusiasm for many months—hence this truly great convention opening and, as nothing is more infectious than healthy enthusiasm, it is not difficult to forecast what kind of a convention this, which we are now entering upon, is to be.

You all know that the executive board met here last Spring, that we had a good time as executive boards always do and that we worked long and hard as executive boards also always do. The program as printed discloses but scantily the quantity and quality of oratory which is promised as various important subjects are brought forward, and he who thinks to stay away from any of the sessions little realizes what he will miss.

Among the recommendations of the executive board are, first, the proposition that at all future trade exhibitions the net profits therefrom be equally divided between the national society and the local organization. As this is a matter to be adjusted by the executive board each year, the main reason for referring to it here is that organizations planning to invite the society to visit their city may know before extending any invitation and govern themselves accordingly. The outdoor exhibition wisely planned, earnestly urged and generously carried out so far as the society and its Dayton friends are concerned, has not received the support that should have been given it by the plant growers and nursery trade generally. The project is on right lines, however, and should have another opportunity next year.

Recognizing the need of some better method of instruction in horticulture for young men a subcommittee was appointed to confer with Agricultural College officials and it was voted to recommend to the society the appropriation of a sum not to exceed $150 toward the carrying out of some practical plan of co-operation between the society and the college.

According to instructions by the society the scheme of numbered badges and a key book for members has been put in operation, and the name of every member registered up to July 15, 1906, appears therein.

Other important transactions by the executive board are fully disclosed in the various items of the official program which you have before you.

Express Rate Matters.

Acting on the complaint of members living in New Jersey an effort was made by your secretary and also by the chairman of the legislative committee to get from the manager of the United States Express Company a statement as to the reasons for the increased transportation charges made since last May upon flower shipments from New Jersey points to New York City, but we were met with a very decided refusal to give any explanation. A second request did not even receive the courtesy of an answer. Your secretary, in the meantime, had been making some investigations as to our privileges under the new Interstate Commerce Act, and on August 7, 1906, wrote the following letter:

Mr. T. M. Jones, Mgr., BOSTON, August, 7, 1906.
U. S. Express Company,
39 Broadway,
New York, N. Y.

Dear Sir:—

Referring to my letter of May 11, 1906, which thus far remains unanswered, I beg to state that in view of the universal sentiment of protest on the part of flower growers who are members of our society and whose interests are affected by the advanced rates on flowers shipped from producers in your territory to the New York wholesale market, I deem it to be my duty to submit this matter to the Interstate Commerce Commission for investigation and adjustment as is my privilege under the provisions of Section 13 of the amended Interstate Commerce Act, unless I receive some assurance from you that the increased charges complained of will be given prompt reconsideration by your company.

It would give me much pleasure to be able to report to our society at its convention in Dayton, Ohio, August 21-24, that the United States Express Company had taken this question under advisement and hoped to be able to announce a rate which would be generally accepted as just and reasonable.

Yours respectfully,
(Signed) WM. J. STEWART, Secretary.

This letter shared the same fate as its predecessor, no acknowledgment having thus far been received. I believe we have a good case; I know that the Interstate Commerce Commission will give us a prompt and courteous hearing, and hope we shall be able to arrange for the appearance of our legislative committee with necessary witnesses before that body at an early date.

Domestic-Grown Bulbs.

Regarding the domestic-grown narcissus bulbs exhibited by a Virginia grower last year which were submitted to J. F. Sullivan for testing, that gentleman reports that he gave them identically the same treatment that was given the foreign-grown bulbs of the same varieties and found the flowering qualities to be of substantially the same good value.

S. A. F. Medals Awarded.

Medals have been delivered during the past year as follows:

Robert Craig & Son, Philadelphia, a bronze medal for Ficus pandurata exhibited at the Washington convention.

Louis Wittbold, a bronze medal for mechanical watering system exhibited at the Washington convention.

Dennison School, Washington, D. C., through Miss Susan B. Sipe, bronze medal for superior work in gardening, October 16, 1905.

Through the American Carnation Society, January 24, 1906, a silver medal to Cottage Gardens Company for carnation Mrs. C. W. Ward and a bronze medal to Cottage Gardens Company for carnation Robert Craig.

Through the Cincinnati Florists' Society, March 10, 1906, a silver medal to R. Witterstaetter for carnation Afterglow; and a bronze medal to Minneapolis Floral Company for rose Miss Kate Moulton.

New Plant Names Registered.

New plant names have been registered since my last report as follows:

August 26, 1905—Canna, Uncle Sam, by Conard & Jones Co., West Grove, Pa.

October 14, 1905—Rose, Triumph, by Peter Henderson & Co., New York.

October 28, 1905—Canna, Vesuvius, by Peter Henderson & Co., New York.

November 11, 1905—Cannas, Prince of India, Jupiter, Venus, by Conard & Jones Co., West Grove, Pa.

December 23, 1905—Carnations, Winsor, Helen M. Gould, White Enchantress, by F. R. Pierson Co., Tarrytown-on-Hudson, N. Y.

January 27, 1906—Rose, Helen Good, by United States Nursery Co., Rich, Miss.

February 17, 1906—Sweet peas, Mrs. Alex. Wallace, J. K. Allen, Christmas Enchantress, Jack Hunter, Mrs. C. Wild, Christmas Meteor, by A. C. Zvolanek, Bound Brook, N. J.

February 24, 1906—Roses, Christine Wright, Columbia, by Hoopes, Brother & Thomas, West Chester, Pa.

March 10, 1906—Canna, Superior, by Wm. Schray & Sons, St. Louis, Mo.

March 10, 1906—Alternanthera aurea robusta, by Wm. Schray & Sons, St. Louis, Mo.

March 10, 1906—Sweet peas, Secretary William J. Stewart, Mrs. W. W. Smalley, by A. C. Zvolanek, Bound Brook, N. J.

March 24, 1906—Cannas, Dr. Wm. Saunders, Ottawa, by Conard & Jones Co., West Grove, Pa.

April 7, 1906—Sweet peas, Mrs. Wm. Sim, Mrs. F. J. Dolansky, Samuel J. Trepass, Maxwelton, Caroline Whitney, by A. C. Zvolanek, Bound Brook, N. J.

April 21, 1906—Sweet peas, Mrs. J. F. Hannay, Marion Staniford, Miss Jossie Reiley, by A. C. Zvolanek, Bound Brook, N. J.

April 28, 1906—Cannas, Mount Washington, Mount Zion, Henry George, Telegraph, Inman's Choice, Britta, Golden Cluster, Sensation, Uwanta, Thelma, Gold Mine, Pansy Read, Crown of Gold, Admiral Togo, Queen of Orange, The American Duchess, Golden Dawn, Royal Neighbor, Golden Express, Amalgamated, Ohio, Buckeye, Dayton, Nymphaea, Leader, Royal Bronze, Fairhope, by The Southern Floral Nursery Co., Fruitdale, Ala.

May 5, 1906—H. P. Rose, Charles Wagner, by Conard & Jones Co., West Grove, Pa.

May 12, 1906—Dendrobium nobile, Mrs. Lars Anderson, by Duncan Finlayson, Jamaica Plain, Mass.

June 9, 1906—Cannas, Queen of Beauty, Flashlight, Majestic, Bronze King, Giraffe, Moonlight, Blushing Belle, Southern Pride, Alabama, Mississippi, Bucatunna, Gen. Kuroki, Tom. L. Johnson, Emerald, Perfection, Daybreak, Sunbeam, Jumbo, Gov. Patterson, Chautauqua, Jr., by The Southern Floral Nursery Co., Fruitdale, Ala.

June 23, 1906—Nephrolepis Fruckii, and Berryii, by Henry C. Fruck, Grosse Point Farms, Mich.

July 14, 1906—Rose, Aurora, by Paul Niehoff, Lehighton, Pa.

July 21, 1906—Hydrangea arborescens alba grandiflora, by The E. G. Hill Co., Richmond, Ind.

August 11, 1906—Laelio—Cattleya, Lady Bernice, by Lager & Hurrell, Summit, N. J.

Necrology.

We have lost nine members by death since my last report:

C. G. Nanz, Louisville, Ky., August 17, 1905.
J. C. Rennison, Sioux City, Ia., February 24, 1906.
Aug. Rhotert, New York, N. Y., April 9, 1906.
C. H. Kunzman, Louisville, Ky., May 22, 1906.
George H. Rowden, Wallingford, Conn., May 17, 1906.
Hans Bartels, Milwaukee, Wis., April 30, 1906.
Abraham Hostetter, Manheim, Pa., April 18, 1906.
William Schray, St. Louis, Mo., May 15, 1906.
James Hartshorne, Joliet, Ill., August 6, 1906.

Membership Statistics.

Other membreship statistics are as follows:

Whole number of members as per printed report for 1905 was 889, of whom 114 were life members. This included 4 life members and 173 annual members who had been added or reinstated during the year. The acquisitions are credited as follows: Alabama, Colorado, Iowa, Louisiana, New Hampshire, Rhode Island, one each: California, Missouri, North Carolina, Virginia, Ontario, Manitoba, two each: Indiana, Wisconsin, three each: Connecticut, Georgia, Kentucky, four each: New Jersey, eight: Illinois, 10: Maryland, Michigan, 12 each: District of Columbia, Ohio, 13 each: Massachusetts, 18: New York, 26: Pennsylvania, 29.

The number of lapses during the year of members who had paid dues for the previous year but either resigned or failed to respond in 1905, was 111. These delinquencies are chargeable to the various States as follows: California, Kentucky, Maryland, Maine, Rhode Island, Texas, Ontario, one each. Colorado, Georgia, Kansas, Oklahoma, South Calolina, Tennessee, two each: Connecticut, Iowa, Minnesota, New Jersey, three each: Indiana, four: Michigan, five: Wisconsin, seven: Ohio, eight: Pennsylvania, nine: New York, twelve: Missouri thirteen: Illinois, twenty-two: The list of names of delinquents in each State was sent from the secretary's office to its respective vice-president. A few of the vice-presidents reported; from the majority no response was recived.

Valedictory.

It is, I think, generally known among the members that I have decided not to be a candidate for re-election to this office which with rare and generous confidence you have placed in my keeping for so many years. Since that day nineteen years ago, in Chicago, when I had the privilege of thanking you for the honor you had conferred in unanimously selecting me as the successor in office of such men as E. G. Hill and Edwin Lonsdale, many changes have come about. Very many loyal workers for the society whose friendships were so dear to us have been called away never to return. In meditating on the changed conditions and tremendous horticultural growth of this epoch in the society's history I feel that, while the ambitions and aims of the pioneers have in some respects fallen short of realization, yet, as societies go, this society has done well. The balance in the treasury as reported at the Chicago convention nineteen years ago, was $32.35. With this, our treasurer's report which you are about to listen to, will compare favorably.

Our membership, however, is not what it should be. Everyone identified with any department of horticulture is a sharer in the general benefits which the existence and the direct work of the society has made possible, and it is much to be regretted that thus far no effective means has been found of bringing the great mass of those engaged in those pursuits to do their share toward the support of the institution which has done so much for them and might do so much more if it could only have the necessary backing.

In seeking to be relieved from the responsibilities of the secretaryship I can assure you that my interest in the society's welfare will continue unabated, and I shall be ready at all times in the ranks to do whatever lies in my power for the grand old society whose burdens and whose joys have been so peculiarly my own for so many years.

The report of Treasurer Beatty was then read by the secretary, an abstract of which follows:

Treasurer's Report; Year 1905.

1905.			
Jan. 1.	Balance general fund	$2,923.07	
	Balance life membership fund	2,819.96	
	Cash on hand		$5,743.03
Dec. 31.	Total receipts, year 1905, general fund	2,403.44	
	Total receipts, year 1905, life mem. f'd	911.56	
	Total receipts, 1905		$3,315.00
			$9,058.03
Dec. 31.	Total disbursements, year 1905, general fund		$1,843.55
	Cash on hand Dec. 31, 1905		$7,214.48
Dec. 31.	Balance—Home Trust Co. of Pittsburgh		1,184.89
	Balance—Citizens Banking Co. of Oil City		2,298.07
	Balance — Germania Savings Bank of Pittsburgh		3,731.52
			$7,214.48

Edwin Lonsdale announced that the Peony Committee was not ready to report.

The reports for the various States were ordered printed in the report of the proceedings.

[Abstracts from these reports appear in this issue on another page.]

Alex. Wallace read the report of the Committee on the National Council of Horticulture, which was largely a summary of what has already appeared in our columns concerning the work of the Council in the distribution of information on horticultural subjects. Through the daily newspapers, the committee recommended, in view of the importance and usefulness of the work of the council of the trade generally, that the society vote a sum of money for the consideration of the Board of Directors for the purposes of the press bureau of the Council.

Messrs. Niessen, Breitmeyer and Vaughan supplemented the committee report and on motion of George Watson the Society recommended to the Executive Board to appropriate the sum of $200 and appoint two delegates to attend the meeting of the Council. Carried.

Naming of Judges.

The following gentlemen were named as judges of the Kasting Prize Essays: C. T. Guenther, Hamburg, N. Y.; F. C. Weber, St. Louis, and E. F. Winterson, Chicago, as a substitute for J. B. Nugent, New York. It seems that the essays had miscarried in the mail in transit to the committee members and were not then available for adjudication.

Exhibition Judges were appointed as follows: William Scott, Buffalo; Harry Papworth, New Orleans, and Charles Vick, Rochester.

Judges on landscape plans, for which the Dayton Florists' Club offered gold and silver medals, were named as follows: Professor Cowell, Buffalo; Edwin Lonsdale, Philadelphia; and H. D. Sealy, Elkhart, Ind.

A communication from the Detroit Florists' Club, relative to the aster disease was read, in which it was suggested that the Society of American Florists appropriate some sum sufficient to engage the services of Cornell University, or some similar institution, to take up the question in a scientific way and prescribe a remedy, if possible. Discussion of this matter was held over until the Wednesday evening session.

A letter from Beaulieu, Woodhaven, N. Y., regarding a parcels post and the abolishment of free seeds by the Government was also held over.

Call for Congress of Horticulture.

The following call for a National Congress of Horticulture was read. The National Council of Horticulture, embracing as it does, the broad interests of horticulture, has had under consideration the matter of a National Congress of Horticulture to convene at Jamestown, Virginia, some time during the exposition period. In view therefore of the interest manifested by a large number of persons representing various branches of horticultural activity, a Congress of Horticulture is called to convene at the Jamestown Exposition during the week of August 19-24, 1907.

The purpose of such a gathering is to consider the more or less scattered branches, and interest into more closer union, with a view that such a gathering would add inspiration and profit to all participants and others in attendance, and should be means of dignifying and advancing horticulture in all of its details. In addition to representatives of the boarder interests, it is proposed to include in the assemblage leading specialists of the various divisions of horticultural work who will consider topics of interest to the specialists, either before regular or special meetings of the several national societies, in case they arrange to hold a meeting at this time. Otherwise such topics will be presented before departmental or sectional meetings of the Congress representating the particular subject. The exposition, situated as it is, in the midst of a field, rich in horticultural products and easily accessible to a very large number who are interested in one or more branches of this great industry should insure an attendance commensurate with the interest involved. The Exposition Company, together with the Norfolk Horticultural Society, guarantees every possible courtesy and facilities, and which will make the meeting place ample and convenient.

Societies arranging to meet in affiliation with this Congress may hold their regular sessions independently and without conflicting with any of the sessions of the Congress. All persons interested in any phase of horticulture are therefore asked to cooperate in this movement, and all local, State and national societies are invited and urged to be present, either by holding their regular session or by duly authorized delegates. It is hoped that this congress will bring together a multitude of horticulturists that could hardly be expected to come together in any other manner, and that a goodly number of the national societies will decide to hold a regular session during the week in which the congress is in session.

It was announced that it had been impossible to secure a party to give an illustrated lecture on Wednesday evening, as originally intended by the Executive Committee. The meeting adjourned at 5.30.

President's Reception.

The president's reception was held in the Welfare Hall of the National Cash Register Co. Accompanying President Kasting on the platform were Mrs. Kasting, Secretary Stewart, H. M. Altick and wife, Treasurer Beatty and wife, and P. J. Hauswirth and wife.

Wednesday August 22.

The weather conditions were hardly so oppressive s those of yesterday, still they were warm enough) be uncomfortable.

This morning's session opened at 10:30 a. m. The ecretary read a telegram from Miss Perle Fulmer,)es Moines, Ia., regretting her inability to be present at the convention, the first time she had been bsent in eight consecutive years.

A communication was read from F. R. Pierson, 'arrytown, in reference to the work of the committe to confer with committees of the Seed and Nursery :ade associations. This committee was endeavoring to ecure pound rate for mailing catalogues, but the ıatter was meantime in abeyance. Secretary 'owles of the Postal Reform League made a lengthy ddress on the work of that organization in its eneavor to secure the amalgamation of third and ourth class mail matter, and cognate subjects. The eason why the postal service is in the unsatisfactory ondition in which it stands to-day is, Mr Cowles aid, because legislation has been for many years ast in the of men who would have wiped out the ostoffice if they could have done so. "What can ou expect of a postoffice controlled by Senators 'latt and Depew of New York?"

Benjamin Hammond, also spoke on this subject, nd on motion of William Scott, Buffalo, the fol›wing resolution was passed:

Resolved, That the S. A. F. O. H., assembled in nnual convention at Dayton endorse by unanimous ote the pending postal bill 4549 now before Conress.

On motion of Mr. Hallock a vote of thanks was ›ndered Mr. Cowles for his able address.

J. B. Heiss, Dayton, addressed the convention, :ating that an endeavor would be made to give an ut door illumination at Farhills, Thursday evening the weather permitted.

Several State Vice-president's reports were handed ı. President Kasting announced that Leo Niessen, tate Vice-president for Eastern Pennsylvania had :cured members, life and annual, to the amount of 70 during the past year.

The essays in the Kasting competition having vidently been lost, it was decided to award the rizes after the convention.

Philadelphia in 1907.

The selection of the next place of meeting resulted ı the choice of Philadelphia by a majority of ıirty votes. Its nearest competitor was Niagara alls. Two hundred thirty-five votes were cast, of 'hich the city chosen received 131. Messrs. Pap'orth, Foley and Niessen acted as tellers.

Nomination of Officers.

Nomination of officers was next in order. For resident the name of Wm. J. Stewart was presented y Colonel Castle of the Holly-Castle Co., Boston, 'ho eloquently extolled the fitness of his nominee ›r the position. E. G. Gillett and P. Breitmeyer ›conded the nomination. No other candidate was resented. For vice-president the names of John /estcott, S. S. Pennock and Leo Niessen were pre›nted. Mr. Westcott and Mr. Neissen desired to ithdraw, but the president ruled that their names ıust go on ballot. For secretary, H. M. Altick was roposed by Wm. Scott, of Buffalo, seconded by J. 'ulmer, Des Moines, Ia., Phil Hauswirth was put in omination by W. P. Gude, of Washington, seconded y P. J. Foley, Chicago, J. Bertermann, Indianapolis, nd J. F. Ammann, St. Louis. For treasurer, H. B. eatty, was proposed by W. W. Coles, Kokomo, Ind.

The amendment of Atrticle II, section 2, of the onstitution and By-Laws, by striking out in pararaph (d) the words "12 o'clock noon" and insertıg "11 a. m." as recommended by the Executive oard was passed with the following addition by J. . Esler: "After 11 a. m. insert the words 'or until ll legal voters in line at that time shall have had n opportunity to cast their votes.'"

On motion of Wm. Scott, of Buffalo, the secretary 'as instructed to send a telegram of sympathy to atrick O'Mara on his recent bereavement.

E. V. Hallock then delivered his address on Teachıg Horticulture in the Public Schools, an able pre›ntation of the subject, which was well received nd fully discussed by Messrs. Scott, Hammond, 'almer, Hall and Gude.

It was generally believed that the Society could o good work along lines suggested by the comıittee, and the amount asked in the report to carry ut the proposition was recommended for the best onsideration of the Board of Directors. The Comıittee was continued with W. J. Palmer, Brookline, lass., and Prof. Cowell, Buffalo, added.

Wednesday Evening Session.

The evening session opened at 8:30 with a large atendance. The report of the Exhibition Judges was ead by Wm. Scott, and will be found in another colmn.

-Professor Cowell read the report of the Judges on .andscape Gardening Plans. The following gentleıen were declared the winners: Gold medals, Mr. chieb of the National Cash Register Co., Dayton, nd Gordon H. Taylor, 156 Fifth ave., New York; ilver medals, Mr. Schieb and Mr. Freidenberger of he National Cash Register Co.; bronze medals, Olm:ed Brothers, Brookline, Mass., and Mr. Freidenerger. The committee expressed the opinion that n exhibition of this character seemed to them 'orthy of continuance and recommended that the matter be referred to the Executive Committee to formulate a definite plan as to how such a competition should be conducted.

F. E. Palmer, Brookline, Mass, then read his paper on the Ideal Gardener, which was well received and a vote of thanks tendered. [This address will be found in full on page 234.]

A discussion of the president's address then took place. On motion of Mr. Vaughan, it was decided that the Executive Committee be asked to put into effect the president's suggestion regarding the secretary's office.

Under the heading of Private Gardeners, relative to the secretary representing the society at flower shows, etc, a motion was passed recommending the appropriaiton of $200 for travelling expenses and the carrying out of the president's suggestion, a report of the result of the work to be made at the next convention.

The suggestion that a committee on tariff be appointed brought out a lengthy discussion, participated in by Colonel Castle, Messrs. Hill, Hammond, Vaughan, Scott, Wintzer, Elliott, Lenker, Craig, Esler and others. It was the consensus of opinion that a revision of the tariff on glass, lumber and other building materials was necessary. Finally, after much oratory and an airing of political views on protection and other cognate subjects, a motion was passed to the effect that it was the opinion of the Society that the tariff on greenhouse glass should be reduced. The matter was referred to the joint committee of the Florist, Seed and Nursery Trades for considera-

William J. Stewart
President-elect S. A. F. O. H.

tion and the formulation of some practical plan to bring the subject before the committee of Ways and Means at Washington. The meeting adjourned at 10:35.

American Carnation Society.

A meeting of the American Carnation Society was held in the Hotel Algonquin on Wednesday evening. President John H. Dunlop occupied the chair and all the other officers of the organization were present except J. F. Wilcox of Council Bluffs, Ia.

Last year's premium list was practically adopted. Some changes in the classification were made. The Daybreak shade of pink was changed to Enchantress shade, and Scott shade to pink between Lawson and Enchantress.

A proposed program of papers to be read at the meeting was prepared. Among the subjects to be dealt with are "New Systems of Watering and Greenhouse Construction," Mr. King of Toronto being the probable essayist; "Are There Too Many New Carnations Introduced?" "American Carnations and Their Prospects in Europe." For the latter an endeavor will be made to secure essayists in London, England, and Copenhagen, Denmark. Another paper will be "Carnations from a Canadian Point of View."

Each of the members of the executive committee pledged himself to put a question in the box so as to insure a lively meeting. A label will be printed and furnished to the exhibitors so that their flowers will go through to Toronto without any drawback being experienced.

Florists' Hall Association.

Of the proposed amendments to the By-Laws, Article V, Section 7, was adopted, reading as follows. "Any risk upon which three or more consecutive losses shall have been paid in the five years preceding the levying of an assessment, shall be considered a hazardous risk for that assessment, and an additional 10 per cent. of the gross amount of such assessment shall be added thereto."

Article V, Section 8, which reads as follows, was adopted: "Any risk upon which three or more consecutive losses shall have been paid in the 12 months preceding the levying of an assessment, shall be considered an extra hazardous risk for that assessment, and an additional 25 per cent of the gross amount of such assessment shall be added thereto."

Directors elected: Elmer D. Smith, Joseph Heacock, F. E Dorner. Officers elected, E. G. Hill, President; P. H. Ritter, Vice-President; John G. Esler, Secretary; Albert M. Herr, Treasurer.

The investment of the reserve fund was left in the hands of the president, secretary and treasurer, who are to constitute a finance committee.

[Secretary Esler's report will be found on page 235.]

The Great Bowling Match.

Seven teams competed in the Annual Bowling Tournament, and the Ladies' Bowling Prizes were hotly contested for. The list of prize winners and individual scores are as follows:

PHILADELPHIA.

Names—	First.	Second.	Third.	Total.
Robertson	160	177	146	483
Falck	131	154	167	452
Graham	181	164	128	473
Adelberger	166	115	151	432
Connor	183	181	146	510
Totals	821	791	738	2350

WASHINGTON.

Names—	First.	Second.	Third.	Total.
Cook	162	165	139	466
Simmonds	165	144	183	492
Berry	144	123	122	389
Wiedeman	147	134	119	400
Ernest	159	212	156	527
Totals	777	778	719	2274

CLEVELAND.

Names—	First.	Second.	Third.	Total.
Hart	169	158	139	466
Schmitt-Bates	90	114	159	363
R. Neigel	145	142	137	424
Bloy	109	162	122	393
C. Graham	156	140	200	496
Totals	669	716	757	2142

CHICAGO.

Names—	First.	Second.	Third.	Total.
Bergman	150	119	152	421
Scott	112	93	105	310
Wilson	106	167	106	379
Winterson	158	166	143	467
Asmus	186	156	146	488
Totals	712	711	652	2065

NEW YORK.

Names—	First.	Second.	Third.	Total.
Guttman, A. J.	123	135	127	385
Donaldson, J.	153	170	159	482
Scott, J.	95	161	81	337
Enggren, E. L.	132	115	112	359
Zeller, A.	130	137	127	394
Totals	633	718	606	1957

BALTIMORE.

Names—	First.	Second.	Third.	Total.
Richmond	138	138	146	422
Moss	151	134	107	392
Seidewitz	54	86	93	233
Weber	137	108	133	378
Seybold	182	183	160	525
Totals	662	649	639	1950

DETROIT.

Names—	First.	Second.	Third.	Total.
Sullivan	153	169	157	479
Taepke	100	120	146	366
Watson	92	127	146	365
Rahaley	104	138	129	137
Dunn	117	133	118	368
Totals	566	687	696	1949

Philadelphia, finishing first, won: (a) The Beatty trophy to be won twice by same team. (b) The Kasting cup. (Perpetual Prize.) (c) To each member, one silver match box donated by H. B. Beatty, Pittsburg, Pa.

Washington, finishing second, won: (a) The Crawford, McGregor & Canby Co. trophy, donated by the Crawford, McGregor & Canby Co., Dayton, O. (b) To each member, one pair of gold sleeve buttons.

Cleveland, finishing third, won: One prize cup.

Detroit, finishing last, won: Consolation prize, one prize cup.

Individual team prizes. Single high game score, Ernest, 212, gold cuff buttons. High average team

Report continued on page 232

THE EXHIBITION

Plant Exhibits.

The exhibition of plants was fully up to the standard of previous years, though there was possibly a slight monotony in the similarity of the offerings in the respective classes.

Frank Huntsman, Cincinnati, well grown aspidistras.

Joseph Heacock Co., Wyncote, Pa., a collection of palms and decorative plants.

Davis Brothers, Morrison, Ill., showed a table of Nephrolepis in various forms.

Charles D. Ball, Holmesburg, Philadelphia, a good showing of palms, Pandanus, etc.

Lewis Ulrich, Tiffin, Ohio, a brilliant display of his new seedling geranium "Tiffin."

The Hinode Florist Co., of Whitestone, N. Y., a varied assortment of Japanese Dwarf trees.

The Cushman Gladiolus Co., Sylvania, Ohio, showed a choice assortment of their blooms.

A. H. Cushman of the Cushman Gladiolus Co., Sylvania, O., in addition to their gladiolus showed also an interesting collection of dahlias, especially noticeable among which were Jean Charmant, a decorative variety, old rose pink in color; and Sylvia, a decorative with light center, surrounded by lilac pink.

Lager & Hurrell, Summit, N. J., a collection of dormant florists' orchids, largely imported Cattleyas.

Storrs & Harrison Co., Painesville, Ohio, ferns, and some dormant rose stock of excellent quality.

C. S. Ford, Philadelphia, a creditable exhibition of palms, ferns, and a general line of tropical plants.

F. R. Pierson Co., Tarrytown, N. Y., showed a table of their popular product, Nephrolepis Elegantissima.

H. R. Carlton, Willoughby, Ohio, exhibited some small pot grown plants of new single violet Governor Herrick.

Livingston Seed Co., Columbus, Ohio, an attractive display of Livingston's new hybrid semperflorens begonia.

Samuel S. Pennock, Philadelphia, an interesting exhibit of the Bird's Nest fern, Asplenium Nidus aris.

Henry H. Barrows & Son, Whitman, Mass., who grow Nephrolepis only, made a fine showing of their favorite, Whitmani.

J. A. Peterson, Westwood, Ohio, had some handsome Adiantum Farleyense, Pandanus Veitchii and Begonia Gloire de Lorraine.

Robert Craig & Son, Philadelphia, a nice assortment of plants, including crotons, cyclamen, small asparagus and Gardenia Vietchii.

Metairie Ridge Nursery Co., New Orleans, La., a fine line of tropical plants, of which the Pandanus Veitchii were especially noticeable.

Henry A. Dreer, Philadelphia, made an extensive display of their specialties, including small ferns and palms, Araucarias, and other decorative plants.

Vaughan's Seed Store, New York and Chicago, a notable showing of palms, ferns, Dracænas and Caladiums, making a specialty of Dracæna Amabilis.

Arthur Cowee, gladiolus specialist of Meadowdale Farm, Berlin, N. Y., exhibited a large pyramidal bank of his favorite product, including a fine assortment of Groff's Hybrids, of which he is the disseminator.

Chris. Winterich, Defiance, Ohio, made a fine showing of Cyclamen Giganteum in four to six-inch pots, with remarkably beautiful foliage, in some cases almost resembling caladiums.

John Lewis Childs, Floral Park, N. Y., made an excellent showing of gladioli, embracing 75 varieties. A specialty was his latest attraction, "America," which is unquestionably a flower of unusual quality.

Julius Roehrs Co., Rutherford, N. J., fine collection of decorative plants.

John Scott, Brooklyn, an excellent display of Nephrolepis Scottii, crotons and other decorative plants.

James Vicks Sons, Rochester, exhibited a beautiful assortment of asters.

Henry A. Dreer, Philadelphia had an attractive exhibit. The new Bougainvillea was shown by Wm. K. Harris of Philadelphia.

Nathan Smith & Son, Adrian, Mich., a handsome collection of phlox.

The Crowl Fern Co., Millington, Mass., an excellent assortment of their hardy cut ferns and festooning material.

H. J. Smith, Hinsdale, Mass., a creditable assortment of hardy greens.

Janesville Floral Co., Janesville, Wis., Nephrolepis Amerpohli in splendid form.

W. E. Gravett, Lancaster, O., exhibited his new white seedling aster.

A. C. Oelschig, Savannah, Ga., showed a sample lot of ficus elastica.

William Sim, Cliftondale, Mass., attracted a great deal of attention with his exhibit of the new forcing tomato "Comet" which has proved equally successful as a field variety.

An especially handsome addition to the exhibit of Robert Craig of Philadelphia was his collection of specimen plants of ficus pandurata.

Trade Exhibit.

The trade exhibit has maintained its reputation as being a most desirable part of the convention and that part which goes so far toward the defraying of expenses thereof. The representation has been as full as ever.

More instructive than ever, and that which is a pleasure to record, the firms exhibiting has expressed themselves as very well pleased with the amount of business that they are transacting.

J. H. Broxey, Dayton, Ohio, Gem Support, an adjustable support for carnations, ferns, etc., possessing considerable merit.

Yankee Hose and Pipe Clamp Co., Dayton, Ohio, a very new and effective device fo rmending hose.

Dayton Supply Co., Dayton, Ohio, an exhibit of sprayers for any purpose where it is desired to apply liquids in the form of a mist or spray, manufactured in knapsack, tripod with bucket equipment, in tanks of various sizes on wheels, and in the barrel form. These sprayers are of great power and can be used as well for whitewashing.

S. H. Shoup, Dayton, Ohio, wire designs.

The Heim Support Co., Connorsville, Ind., carnation supports, manufactured out of galvanized steel wire and by means of the double twist, made perfectly rigid and substantial. Also steel wire rose stakes and steel wire clips for roses and chrysanthemums.

A. Q. Wolf & Bro., Dayton, Ohio, Wolf ventilating apparatus and dump sieve pulverisers and ventilators.

Ionia Pottery Co., Ionia, Mich., a very creditable display of flower pots and florists' ware.

A. Dietsch Co., Chicago, greenhouse material. Adapted to houses of single construction is shown a new style eave plate of iron construction, selling at a very reasonable figure.

Louis Wittbold, Chicago, Wittbold improved watering system for fields or greenhouses; also a special rose nozzle for sprinkling roses.

W. H. Elverson Pottery Co., West Brighton, Pa., a full line of florists' flower pots.

The Advance Co., Richmond, Ind. The specialties of this company indicate their workmanlike finish and mechanical construction to be well up on modern requirements. Their specialties are ventilating apparatus, column brackets, pipe carriers and gutter brackets.

H. F. Michell Co., Philadelphia, fine oak jardinieres, bound in brass and with brass handles.

Herendeen Mfg. Co., Geneva, N. Y., Furman boilers. This company made a fine exhibit of their two representative boilers, the Furman New Sectional, Size A—83, and the Round Sectional, Size 24-2.

Holly-Castle Co., Boston, Mass. This exhibit, the Holly Electric Circulator, is an automatic device which places the circulation absolutely under the control of the user.

Lord & Burnham Co., New York, among the interesting exhibits we noted an improved ventilating apparatus showing dust proof oil cups; section of a truss construction for sash bar houses, including their new cast iron gutter; a new clamp fitting pipe bench arrangement, readily put up or taken apart, very strong, no more expansive than a good all wooden bench, and far more durable; also one of their Burnham Sectional boilers, No. 630; also pipe hangers for both steam and hot water.

King Construction Co., North Tonawanda, N. Y., section of greenhouse of the typical King construction.

Hippard Co., Youngstown, Ohio, Standard return steam trap, showing an improvement over last year, as in the new machine the fulcrum is automatically shifted from one center to another, thus altering the leverage as required and making the working operation perfect. Mr. Hippard reports remarkable success and great satisfaction to users.

C. L. Kimmel, Dayton, Ohio, an exhibit of field and garden seed, attractively done up in bottles; also Dr. Hess' Instant Louse Killer, said to work annihilation on melon bugs, and to be a remedy for all kinds of bugs or lice.

Oakwood Pottery Co., Dayton, flower pots and vases.

Wertheimer Bros., New York, an attractive display of ribbons, chiffons, violet ties.

Reed & Keller, New York, florists' supplies and wire designs; glassware, baskets and vases; flower holders for orchids and table decorations occupied prominence. A special line was shown in casket designs of wire work.

Bayersdorfer & Co., Philadelphia, as usual, and following their custom of many years, this firm made an exhibit surpassing in bewildering variety and extent, if such is possible, all that have gone before, and including every requirement of the retail florist in supplies.

Hummel & Downing Co., Milwaukee, paper boxes.

Rosedale Pottery Co., Zanesville, Ohio, flower pots and jardinieres.

A. H. Hews & Co., North Cambridge, Mass. An exhibit of their world-renowned florist pottery ware had gone astray at this writing.

Kroeschell Bros., Chicago. A boiler exhibit intended for the convention had not materialized at this writing.

Baumann & Co., Chicago, artificial and metal funeral designs, wreaths, crosses, baskets and florists' supplies generally.

Daniel B. Long, Buffalo, N. Y., literature for the use of florists, photographs of made-up work, etc.

C. S. Ford, Philadelphia, a general line of florists' supplies. Shows a new form of Christmas tree holder on stand, which looks like a good thing.

J. Stern & Co., Philadelphia, Florists' supplies.

Schloss Brothers, New York, ribbons and chiffons in every shade and width for florists use.

Benjamin Hammond, Fishkill, N. Y., a very neatly arranged and comprehensive exhibit of all the Hammond specialties. These goods have a splendid reputation the country over, and we are pleased to see them represented in the trade exhibit. Greenhouse white paint, Tremlows Old English Glazing Putty and Mount Beacon Shading Mixture are special favorites with all florists. Insecticide and fungicide remedies are represented by Slug Shot, Grape Dust, Bordeaux Mixture, Thrip Juice, and Horicum for scale, etc.

S. S. Pennock Co., Philadelphia, Pa. A trade exhibition without this firm's representation would be incomplete. In addition to showing the full general line of florists ribbon, telling specialties are shown in a new ribbon, matching Autumn foliage for chrysanthemums; also another style for foliage, shading from light to dark; and still another is a two toned striped loire in white and pink and blue for debutantes and bridal work; for violets something new in two widths and patterns is shown that is very effective. Also noted was a fine assortment of pins for the corsage.

Dayton Paper Novelty Co., Dayton, Ohio., Paper flower boxes. A new folding violet box "That's a wonder," cupid holding a bouquet of violets, stamped in colors. The firm reports a large sale of their boxes for long stemmed flowers, finished in enameled paper, with customer's name embossed.

M Rice & Co., Philadelphia, Pa., Florists supplies.

Lowe Bros., Dayton, O., paints and implements.

Dayton Fruit Tree Label Co., Dayton, Wooden labels for the trade.

National Cash Register Co., Department of Gardening, Agriculture and Landscape Gardening, an exhibit of garden and estate plans and of photographs showing results accomplished. Well worthy of study.

C. W. Skinner, Troy, Ohio, made an interesting exhibit on the fair grounds of his system of irrigation.

Kramer Bros. Foundry Co., Dayton, Vases for private grounds and cemeteries, iron settees and chairs.

J. A. Evans, Richmond, Ind. This house shows improvement on their twentieth century arm over that of 1905. In place of riveting the X part of the arm onto the wrought iron post, they use a bracket fastened to the wrought iron part of the arm, which receives the X part, this is a considerable improvement.

Foley Mfg Co., Chicago, Ill., an exhibit of the concentric principle of making gutter sills and cutting the ends of the sash bars. The bars can always be made to fit the sill for any pitch, and water from condensation grooves in the bars is allowed to drop free of the sills into the drip conductor sections of eaves plate. New style of header and the V shaped gutter were also shown.

W. F. Kasting, of Buffalo, N. Y., the indestructible greenhouse bench, entirely throughout of cement construction with iron bracing for the legs. Also the florists' soil pulverizer and sod crusher.

Hews & Co., North Cambridge, Mass., a full representative line of florists' standard flower pots and pans, azalea pots, fern dishes, rose pots, and vases for cut flowers. This firm gave away 5,000 souvenir miniature flower pots and saucers.

Moorehead Mfg. Co., Detroit, Mich. This company made an exhibit of the Moorehead tilting return trap, which we understand is gaining steadily in trade favor.

H. A. Dreer, Philadelphia, Pa. Deer's peerless glazing points. Over sixty-nine millions sold in seven years.

An interesting feature of the Exhibition Hall was the arrangement of trade signs around the balcony. Spaces here were taken by Breitmeyer Sons of Detroit; Bassett & Washburn, Chicago; Hitchings & Co., New York; Stump & Walter Co., New York; W. F. Kasting, Buffalo; Young & Nugent, New York; The E. G. Hill Co., Richmond, Ind.; H. R. Carlton, Willoughby, Ohio, and the trade papers.

When it is considered that the above firms make their contribution toward defraying the expenses of the convention in this liberal manner, they should be highly complimented.

H. Thaden Co., Atlanta, Ga., demonstrated the virtue of treir new bracing truss, for greenhouse roofs, which is a new idea in greenhouse construction doing away with posts and cross trussing. They also showed their improved victory tie, for holding wire supports, the object of which is to do away with string supports, and save tie and labor.

E. A. Beaven, Evergreen, Ala., attracted a great deal of attention with his exhibit of fadeless sheet moss, and also exhibited everything that is worth while in southern evergreens.

Outdoor Exhibits.

The grounds surrounding the fair building were extensively embellished and decorated by a beautiful assortment of growing plants, the beds and designing being under the general charge of the landscape architect of the National Cash Register Co.

Four outdoor trade displays were made, as follows:

Nathan Smith & Son, Adrian, Mich. occupied large section with cannas, coleus, and salvias. N ticable among the former were the Empress, Oscoda, Musafolia, Martha Washington and Dr. Robt. Funcke.

Holland and California bulbs were shown in large assortment by Vaughan's Seed Store, F. R. Pierson Co. and Arthur T. Boddington.

Vaughan's Seed Store, New York and Chicago, had a fine assortment of bedding plants, including larkspurs, asters and cannas, with a good display of Baby Rambler roses.

Henry A. Dreer, Philadelphia, had a handsome collection, including Crimson fountain grass, petunias and the new ageratum Inimitable.

Gus. Obermeyer, Parkersburg, W. Va., had a large bed of his beautiful canna West Virginia.

Reports of State Vice-Presidents.

We herewith give the most important points brought out in the reports of the various vice-presidents:

ALABAMA.—Reports from the various florists in all parts of the State to whom I have sent circulars state that business has ben exceptionally good during the past season. Prices about the same as last year for cut flowers, palms, ferns and decorative plants, but bedding plants sold as low as 25c. per dozen for geraniums. Bulbous stock sold better last year; narcissi and Dutch hyacinths were the leaders with little demand for lily of the valley.

There has been approximately twenty-five thousand (25,000) feet of new glass ercted during the past year. Birmingham claims about fifteen thousand feet.

The growers of our State are awakening to the fact that competition is the life of trade. A few years ago there were not twenty thousand feet of glass in the whole State devoted to cut flower growing. Most of our growers have at this date, August 1, all roses and carnations planted for cut flowers, while there are over 200,000 feet devoted to the above in this State. Prospects are looking bright for the coming season.

There has been established during the past season in our State an enterprising company in the nursery and floral business under the name of the Southern Nursery and Floral Company.

I think we should have a change of vice-presidents each year, the same as the president. I think this might put new life and new ideas into our business.

HUGH SEALES.

FLORIDA.—The past year has been a very prosperous one in this State in all lines of business, and I am confident that while the florists and horticulturists have contributed to that posperity, they have also received their share of it, and while I do not note any great advancement in florist lines I consider the business in a good sound condition. Some new glass has been put up in St. Augustine and Tampa. The demand, however is not large locally, for Florida has no large cities, neither is the demand steady as in more thickly populated States. Then we are so far from a good market and our express rates are so high that the grower with a surplus is up against a loss, consequently the disposition of the craft is to go slow, keeping a weather eye on general conditions and only increase the supply as fast as the local demand promises to use it.

In conversation and correspondence with the florists of the State the impression seems to prevail that cost of attendng the conventions, on account of the long distance we have to travel and in view of the restricted limitation placed on the tickets by the railroads, is too much for what we receive. If there was a longer time allowed, (say 30 days) on the transportation, a man could stay away long enough to get his money's worth.

Every year we are finding it possible to do, to grow, and to produce in Florida things that have heretofore been considered impossible, and are fast demonstrating to the outside world that Florida sand, (which is poor enough, God knows), will grow something besides oranges and pineapples.

C. D. MILLS.

KENTUCKY.—Trade has been steadily on the increase in all lines, both in the production and sale. The past Winter was not a very cold one, but was steady and about the same quantity of coal was consumed, which maintains a good price, especially about Louisville. In the western part of the State coal is very cheap, and there has probably been more building in that section than any other. We have had plenty of rain, but not enough to cause much loss. The holidays were very satisfactory in every respect, and the increase averaged about twenty per cent. for the State. The demand for plants for bedding continues on the increase, and there are a number of firms that do this class of work almost exclusively.

The nursery and seed businesses are active, and we now have several very large concerns in the State.

The S. A. F. membership is slowly but steadily increasing, and I hope, sometime in the near future, to see the convention landed for Louisville—"The Gateway to the South."

FRED L. SCHULZ.

LOUSIANA.—Within the past year horticulture in its many branches has made considerable headway and it appears that the growers of this state are beginning to reap what justly belongs to them in a horticultural way. For many years the profession in our state has been conducted in a rather modest way, when we consider the natural advantages we possess and the adaptability of our soil and climate, to the growth of many trees, plants, flowers, etc., we formerly purchased from northern firms. Where it was the custom a few years ago to send to our northren brethren for such stock as bay trees, azaleas, auracarias, etc. in dozen and half hundred lots, we now import direct from Belgium in 500 and 1000 lots. Arecas and kentias are grown in 10,000 lots, from seed imported direct from the tropics and often grown to salable sizes without spending a cent for coal, being wintered over in cold frames and summered outdoors with a slight lath protection against the rays of the sun, thus producing stronger and healthier plants than can be purchased elsewhere.

That there has been a general awakening is evidenced by the organization of the Society of Southern Florists, which was born of the New Orleans Horticultural Society and formally organized at Chattanooga, Tenn., on May 22 last. Being president of the New Orleans Horticultural Society at the time this movement to organize a southern society was launched, I say that I do not believe it will in any way effect the usefulness or membership of our national society, but owing to the vastness of the territory covered by the national society, and entirely different methods being required for our southern climate, it has been deemed necessary to call together in annual convention, southern growers and dealers, where methods strictly southern would be discussed.

It is not so very long ago that the bulk of the plant business of our State was done by Northern firms through their catalogues, and our local firms catered strictly to the trade in the immediate vicinity of their establishments, but at present we have several firms who spend thousands of dollars on their own catalogues, and ship to nearly every State in the South and to Central America also.

It has long been the custom for our retail florists to send to northern cut flower centers for their supply of choice cut flowers, but within the past year, there has been constructed by the Metairie Ridge Nursery Company, Ltd. in the suburbs of New Orleans, a magnificent range of glass for the growth of fancy cut flowers.

There is a steady increase in the interest displayed by the public in the cultivation of plants and flowers, and to show to what an extent it has developed I might mention the organization of the N. C. Floral Society, an organization composed of plant and flower lovers that numbers among its members many prominent society leaders, and whose purpose it is to increase the cultivation of plants and flowers among the people and by its system of dues guarantee to the New Orleans Horticultural Society that it will incur no financial loss at any of its future flower shows. This society will no doubt be of great benefit to us and will encourage our exhibitors to greater efforts.

After a careful summary of the business in all its branches, I can report great progress made, and if we are to judge the future of horticulture in Louisiana by the progress it has made in the past year, then the outlook is indeed very bright.

P. A .CHOPIN.

View of Entertainment at Welfare Hall, Tuesday Evening.

Courtesy of National Cash Register Co.

MASSACHUSETTS. (EAST).—Trade during the past year, taken all in all, has been the most prosperous our florists have ever experienced. Prices in the cut flower markets have not shown any advance but an increasingly large volume has been disposed of not only in Boston, but in the many other cities in this part of the old Bay State. Carnations have proved more popular than roses, and have frequently cleared out well when many roses were unsold. First class stock never fails to sell, no matter what the flower may be. Single violets meet with a rapidly increasing sale and not much higher price than the doubles; this is not surprising when their fine color, length of stem and size are considered. Orchids are meeting with more favor at the better class of retail stores, and many more would be sold were there not so many private collections amongst our wealthy flower lovers. Chrysanthemums have considerably declined in popularity and do not now prove a very remunerative crop. The taste for big blooms which originated in Boston has largely died out and medium sizes or undisbudded sprays are preferred by many of the most critical buyers. We believe this tendency toward smaller blooms will gradually spread to the cities.

A moderate amount of glass roof has been built during the past year, but quite a number of new firms have started which goes to show that business is in a healthy state. A considerable area of glass devoted exclusively to the framing of cucumber, tomatoes and lettuce, has been erected. Massachusetts is noted for these productions and prices during the past season have generally been satisfactory, quite a number of florists find it profitable to grow catch crops of tomatoes and cucumbers during the summer months.

There is a constant growth in the number of private estates requiring the services of skilled gardeners, and a good many houses have built for the culture of flowers and fruits on these estates. The steady addition to the numbers of greenhouses on private estates seems to make no difference to florists trade, as we seldom hear of any of them selling their productions as is commonly done in some states.

We have had during the present year some notable exhibitions and conventions at Horticultural Hall, Boston. In January, the Carnation Society gave us a rich treat; in March, the American Rose Society produced the finest exhibition of the Queen of Flowers probably ever held in America; in June, the smaller but none the less excellent Peony Society met with us, and provided another good show. The regular exhibitions of the Massachusetts Horticultural Society have also been of a high standard.

The Gardeners & Florists' Club of Boston continues to grow and prosper, it now has—August, 1906—over 330 members, with prospects of a heavy increase the coming Fall. Membership is pretty equally divided between commercial growers and private gardeners. Meetings are always very largely attended. The North Shore Horticultural Society and other clubs and societies in this part of the State are all in a prosperous condition.

The demand for good pot plants in flower has been very noticeable at the holidays, some of our best growers are realizing the needs of our market and are producing better stock than has been brought in from other plant growing centers. Ornamental trees and shrubs of the more popular sorts should prove a remunerative branch for some florists, the demand for these shows a wonderful advance.

Conditions for the coming season are very promising, and we look for good business during the season of 1906-7.

WILLIAM. N. CRAIG.

NEW JERSEY.—The part of New Jersey in which I am located is so near New York City that it is practically a part of it, therefore all stock, both cut flowers and plants, find its way there, the cut flowers to the commission district or the several markets established near there; the plants are disseminated from the plant market at Spring and Canal streets. Everything is sold at wholesale at all the places mentioned.

The demand for cut flowers of all kinds is on the increase especially the finer grades, the carnation being evidently considerably ahead as to popularity. The chrysanthemum is still a favorite in its season, but does not seem to hurt the sale of other flowers as it used to do. Carnations, roses, etc., have brought remunerative prices, and been in good demand all through the chrysanthemum season for several years.

The decorative plant business is also on the increase. Several New Jersey firms have gone out of the cut flower business and now grow decorative plants exclusively.

The demand for bedding plants increases every year, the geranium decidely in the lead. There is also a marked increase in the demand for window box and vase plants. The shipping trade is also growing.

The prospects for the coming season are good. Carnations in the field, although small owing to the dry weather in early Summer, are healthy, and many growers are busy at the present time getting them housed.

I hear of very little new glass being built on commercial places in New Jersey this season.

I am sorry to state that after strenuous efforts I have been unable to land one new member for the S. A. F. O. H.

JOHN BIRNIE.

TEXAS.—From a commercial view point, all the evidence at hand speaks of progress. Texas is beginning to realize that she can grow cut flowers, and one prominent grower of Dallas has made a start in the right direction having put up this year 100,000 square feet of glass, with the intention of doubling it next year. These houses are up-to-date, and no expense has been spared to make them the best in the country. He will grow all the new kinds of roses and carnations along with the best standard sorts, also the general run of cut flowers, and greens, doing a wholesale business only.

All over the State reports come in of new houses going up for retail use, but one of the great things the florist of this State have to contend with, is to get expert help; there is a good chance for such help down here, and after getting used to the weather, and the State, could get good wages.

In cut flowers, carnations have been grown more extensively than any other flower. Roses under glass up to the present haven't been a success, although a San Antonio grower does them well, and I think some of the other growers will take up rose culture in the near future. Roses do fine out in the open ground, and can be cut up to November. Small roses out of 2-inch pots were in great demand, the orders for some kinds have been hard to fill. Bedding plants were about all sold out this Spring.

All the houses sending out catalogues report a good business the past season, and are now busy getting up their elaborate Spring catalogues, with the expectation of 1907 being the best ever.

HARRY DONNELLY.

Bowling Tournament.

(Continued from page 229.)

contest, C. Seybold, scarf pin. Greatest number of strikes, E. F. Winterson, Meerschaum pipe. Greatest number of spares, V. Bergman, leather wallet. High average man on winning team, Connor, library set. The greatest number of strikes was made by Mr. Seybold, but as no contestant could take two prizes, the award was made to Mr. E. F. Winterson.

Men's preliminary individual bowling contest: Benecke, first, 370 points, camera; Mansfield, second, 334, bowling ball and bag; Holton, third, 317, umbrella; Pollworth, fourth, 314, pair of bowling shoes; Rasmussen, fifth, 310, pocketbook.

Individual bowling contest for the championship of the S. A. F.: Mr. Ernest having scored the highest number of points was awarded the diamond studded medal, emblematic of the championship, donated by the Bruswick Balke Collender Company, Chicago, Ill. Scores: Ernest, 363; Seybold, 347; Asmus, 344; Mansfield, 317; C. Graham, 320; Benecke, 298; Connor, 328; Pollworth, 295; Rasmussen, 271; Donaldson, 262.

Ladies' individual contest, two games, total pins to count: First prize won by Mrs. Weber, 316 points, set of combs, donated by H. B. Beatty of Pittsburg; second, Mrs. Hauswirth, 272, diamond studded shirtwaist set, donated by Mr. Beatty; third, Mrs. Scott, 270, diamond studded hair brooch, donated by Mr. Beatty; fourth, Mrs. Miller, 264, cut glass vase; fifth, Mrs. McKeller, 256, mayonnaise set; sixth, Mrs. Kill, 243, prize cup; seventh, Mrs. Asmus, 233, hat pin; ninth, Mrs. Whitman, 220, cut glass olive dish; tenth, Mrs. Reinecke, 220, library set; eleventh, Mrs. Critchell, 219, silver filigree cologne bottle; twelfth, Mrs. T. H. Meinhardt, 209, cut glass dish.

Phil. J. Hauswirth,
Secretary-elect S. A. F. O. H.

Thursday, August 23,

Morning Session.

The absorbing feature of this morning's session was the election of officers. The attendance was again large and weather conditions slightly more moderate and agreeable.

John G. Elser was appointed inspector of election and Messrs. Gillett, Sullivan and Meinhardt tellers. The polls remained open one hour.

A letter was read from E. Albertson, of the American Association of Nurserymen, explaining the efforts making by that body to secure a uniform tag, and other matters, and asking for the cooperation of florists selling nursery stock, in the matter of membership and contributions to the nurserymen's guarantee fund. The letter was referred to the Board of Directors.

The president announced the illness of J. V. Laner, Erie, Pa., at his hotel.

Irwin Bertermann read his paper on retailers methods of offering flowers. (See page 234.)

He was followed by William F. Gude of Washington on the same subject.

Votes of thanks were tendered the essayists

The question box was then opened. Regarding the aster disease, Mr. Bissett suggested that members whose plants are affected by this trouble should send specimens to the pathological division of the Department of Agriculure who will freely prescribe a remedy, if any such be known.

Another question which created considerable discussion was, "Is a Stove Plant in the United States a Green House Plant?" After sereval opinions had been given, the question was laid on the table.

"Is it to the benefit of the trade for originators of new cannas to name and disseminate a long list of varieties having no desirable merits over existing varieties," was another question asked. The discussion, participated in by Messrs. Vaughan Bissett Watson, Read, Wintzer, Hagenburger, Stewart, Wallace and others, resulted in a motion being passed to appoint a canna committee and that they cooperate with the Board of Directors with a view to making such changes in the by-laws regarding registration generally as will meet the exigencies of the case.

The next question asked was, "Would it not be wise to hold our meeting at the end of July or first week in August?" Nothing definite was arrived at.

President Kasting and Robert Craig were appointed deleates to the National Council of Horticulture.

The judges recommended that the Executive Committee make it a rule that the moment an exhibit is staged or permission has been given to stage it, the exhibitor be compelled to enter same.

Election of Officers.

The election of officers resulted as follows: 248 votes cast, 2 rejected. For president, W. J. Stewart, 245; J. A. Valentine, 1. Vice-president, S. S. Pennock, 70; Nessen, 42; John Westcott, 129. Secretary, P. J. Hauswirth, 181; H. M. Altick, 62. On motion of latter, the vote for secretary made unanimous. Treasurer, Beatty, 246.

W. S. Powell of the Bureau of Credit of the wholesale Seedmen's League read a paper on the workings of that institution, inviting florists to take advantage of the bureau.

The matter loncerning the stem of rot asters was referred o the Cociety's pathologist, Prof. Duggar, who will be asked to report on the subject through the trade press. Meeting adjourned at 1:15 p. m.

Interest in the meetings continudd unabated and the closing session of Thursday saw another large and enthusiastic audience. George Asmus, chairman of Sports Committee, read the result of the bowling competition, which will be found in another column.

The report of the superintendent of the trade exbibit, Horace E. Frank, was read by the secretary.

An invitation was extended by the Society of Southern Florists and Ornamental Horticulturists, which will hold its first annual meeting and convention in New Orleans in November next, to S. A. F. members to be present, and also to send exhibits for that occasion.

Philip J. Hauswirth made a report on the selection of a badge design for the life members. He showed several drawings of designs, the one favored by him being a rose leaf in green with the word "Life" across it. On motion of Mr. Lonsdale, the matter was referred to the Executive Committee with full power to act.

Mr. Carmody, on behalf of the society, presented to Mr. and Mrs. Kastings, a case of silverware as a token of appreciation and esteem. The president made a suitable reply, expressing his heartfelt thanks for the testimonial of good will.

In a neat speech, Robert Craig, presented to retiring Secretary Stewart a purse of gold ($180) as expression of the Society's appreciation of Mr. Stewart's twenty years of service in the position. The recipient feelingly replied.

The officers-elect were then introduced, each one promising his best efforts on behalf of the Soliety.

Messrs. Bissett, Hallock and Hauswirth were appointed a committee on Final Resolutions.

Discussion on Proposed Exhibition.

A discussion then ensued on the question of bolding an additional flower show under the auspices of the Society. Robert Craig outlined the proposition of the committee in charge of the show, Messrs Hill and Lonsdale being other members. He referred to the anticipated difficulty in getting a suitable manager. A proposed schedule had been prepared and after consideration the committee had decided that Chicago would be the most suitable city in which to hold the exhibition, and the date November, 1908. It had been suggested to offer three or four thousand dollars in premiums for novelties, hoth domestic and foreign. It was also proposed to hold the annual meeting for 1908 during the time of the suggested show. An endeavor would be made to interest the private gardeners of the country in the project. Mr. Hill also spoke on the subject. He believed such a show would be the means of doubling the membership of the Society and told of the interest shown by European firms in the project, several of whom would in all likelihood send over exhibits of their newest plants. "We believe the exhibition would do great good to every man in the profession. If the society could have a thousand life members at $25 each it would form a good spinal column for the S. A. F." (Applause). J. C. Vaughan also made a few remarks, urging the cooperation of Eastern growers in the exhibition. The securing of the necessary guarantee fund was progressing most favorably.

A suggestion that the designation "International" be applied to the exhibition was also discussed, but no final action taken thereon.

The following resolutions on the show project was adopted.

Resolved, that if this proposed exhibition be held, it shall be in the month of November, 1908, and that the date of the annual meeting be changed from August to November so that the annual meeting and exhibition be held at the same time and place, and that the executive committee be empowered to prepare for and to hold the proposed exhibition.

Mr. Vaughan suggested that in order to obviate a change in the constitution and by-laws a few members of the society could meet in August and adjourn till November, 1908.

A desire was also expressed that the members present their views on the change of date of meeting either to the Board of Directors or through the trade press.

The meeting then adjourned until 9:30 a. m. Friday to transact the unfinished business.

Shooting Tournament.

The following are the scores made at the shooting tournament.

Brown, Richmond, Va., 17; Seybold, Baltimore, 14; Rogers, Cincinnati, 13; Hippard, Youngstown, 12; Altick, Dayton, 12; Scott, Buffalo, 11.

Young, St. Louis, 10; Reimels, Woodhaven, 9; Herendeen, Geneva, 7; Rasmussen, 6.

Team shoot, Dayton, 190. Florists team, 173.

Thursday evening Entertainment.

After adjournment on Thursday evening the delegates witnessed the electric illumination of Far Hills, the estate of President Patterson of the National Cash Register Co., which also provided this treat. The outlines of the various trees and shrubs were portrayed by large and small electric lights in soft tones of color, the green foliage shining through the lights creating a most beautiful effect. The illumination, which extended for half a mile, was quite unique and thoroughly enjoyed by all present.

Friday, August 24, Dayton Florist Day.—At ten o'clock in the morning, the delegates were treated to a trip to the National Cash Register Company's works and there thoroughly inspected one of the model factories of the world.

In the afternoon the Soldiers' National Military Home was visited, as a compliment to the society from Governor Thomas, commander of the home, a band concert was there given by the celebrated Federal Band, at Memorial Hall on the grounds, addresses and closing exercises were made. In the evening a farewell concert and ball was given at the exhibition grounds.

New York to Dayton.

The New York delegation left via the New York Central railroad, at 2.3 p. m. on Monday, August 20. The travelers filled one Pullman, and an overflow had to be accommodated in other cars. The weather was warm without doubt, for wilted shirts and collars soon bore testimony thereto. Although neglige was soon apparent so far as the men of the party were concerned, how the ladies managed to keep cool and looking neat as ever all through a day and night of extreme heat, your scribe has not been able to discover. A rain storm encountered just beyond Albany alleviated weather conditions for a while and the substantial liquids and viands provided in great abundance by the New York Florists' Club and served with grace and his customary good will by Frank H. Traendly, New York, assisted by Victor S. Dorval of Long Island, helped much to while away the time and heat torridity. The names of all whom will be found in our list of delegates, published in another column.

Philadelphia.

The delegation for the S. A. F. Convention from this city left Broad street station at 4.30 p. m. Monday in a special Pullman car. Those who went

John Westcott,
Vice-President-elect S. A. F. O. H.

were John Westcott and wife, Robert Craig and wife, John Sibson and wife, William Swayne and wife, Julius Wolf, Jr., and wife, C. Turnley, F. Adelberger, William Robertson, John A. Ruppert, George C. Watson, Edwin Lonsdale, William Falck, D. T. Connor, Leo Niessen, William Graham, Antoine Wintzer, William De Shields, Samuel Dunlap and Alfred Burton.

DAVID RUST.

Reception of Visiting Ladies.

e visiting ladies were accorded the most cordial itality by the local auxiliary, through a comee consisting of Miss Minnie Johnson, chairman, Louise Johnson, Mrs. Young, Mrs. C. M. Schae- Mrs. Dornbush, Mrs. Hendricks, Mrs. Smith, Mrs. vnlee, Mrs. Heiss, Mrs. H. H. Ritter, Mrs. F. M. er, Miss Ritter and Miss Young.

the opening day of the convention a reception given in the parlor of the Algonquin Hotel. On day was the bowling contest, and a delightful afoon at Lakeside Park with it's many attractions. theater party at Dayton's handsome new theater, National, was enjoyed on Thursday and the d of entertainment closed on Friday afternoon a street car ride over the combined city lines, wed by a trip through the grounds of the Nal Military Home.

iday was Dayton Florists' Club Day. The visitmade a tour of the world famed factory of the onal Cash Register Company, after which they ed the National Soldiers' Home. A full account ese trips will appear in next issue; also fuller re- of various discussions.

even teams competed in the Annual Bowling nament, and the Ladies' Bowling Prizes were contested for. The list of prize winners and inual scores are as follows:

Delegates Registered at Dayton Convention, August 21 to 24, 1906.

, Otto, New Orleans, La.
ham & Son, W. W., representing E. H. Hunt, Chicago, Ill.
erman, J. F., Edwardsville, Ill.
ng, E. C., Chicago, Ill.
, J. K., New York, N. Y.
us, George, Chicago, Ill.
k, H. M., Dayton, Ohio.
e, Otto, New Orleans, La
rpohl, Edw., Janesville, Wis.
ner, August R., Louisville, Ky.
neman, S. S., Webb City, Mo.
y, J. J., Washington, D. C.
holme, Gustav, Syracuse, N. Y.
ty, H. B., Pittsburg, Pa.
l, O L., Dixon, Ill.
rlein, Peter, Elmhurst, N. Y.
n, F. P., Buffalo, N. Y.
t, Peter, Washington, D. C.
ker, Frank, Fremont, Ohio.
owitz, Paul, Philadelphia, Pa.
n, Mrs. R., Detroit, Mich.
tle, W. R., Washington, D. C.
ke, J. J., St. Louis, Mo.
le, John, West Hoboken, N. J.
ermann, Irwin C., Indianapolis, Ind.
Samuel, Phila., Pa.
ue, L. B., Hinsdale, Mass.
o, Edward, Mansfield, Ohio.
ber, A. F., Kansas City, Mo.
nner, Charles F., Cincinnati, Ohio.
ndenburg, Gus., East Liverpool, Ohio.
ven, E. A., Philadelphia, Pa.
ck, Charles H., Boston, Mass.
sen, A. C., Hinsdale, Ill.
mann, Ludolf, Chicago, Ill.
itmeyer, P., Detroit, Mich.
ton, Alfred, Philadelphia, Pa.
termann, John, Indianapolis, Ind.
er, George, Toledo, Ohio.
hler, Oscar, West Hoboken, N. J.
ringer, Rudolf G., Bay City, Mich.
lock, Mrs. E. M. and Son, Elkhart, Ind.
l, Charles D., Jr., Philadelphia, Pa.
l, Jr., Charles D., Philadelphia, Pa.
wn, H., Richmond, Va.
tels, P. C., North Olmstead, Ohio.
yard, Harry A., New York City.
m, C. L., Knoxville, Tenn.
hm, T., New Orleans, La.
hner, John, Dayton, Ohio.
ingsley, William, Indianapolis, Ind.
they, F. F., Chicago, Ill.
ckman, George H.,
ant, L. D., Kingston, Mass.
rows, Henry H., Jr., Whitman, Mass.
ker, Michael, Chicago, Ill.
, Asher M., North Olmstead, Ohio.
ningham, J. H., Delaware, Ohio.
rell, John F., Buffalo, N. Y.
k, J. A., Baltimore, Md.
berg, Gust. A., St Paul, Minn.
nor, D. T., Philadelphia, Pa.
hman, E. H., Sylvania, Ohio.
k, M., New Orleans, La.
lton, H. R. and Son, Willoughby, Ohio.
mody, J. D., Evansville, Ind.
ns, J. A., Richmond, Ind.
ig, William B., Philadelphia, Pa.
tle, William W., Boston, Mass.
es, W. H. and Son, Kokoma, Ind.
tchell, C. E., Cincinnati, Ohio.
rles McCullough, Cincinnati, Ohio.
ndler, Aleda, Berlin, N. Y.
vee, Arthur, Berlin, N. Y.
k, George H., Washington, D. C.
ey, S. W., Urbana, Ohio.
ker, Edwin, St. Charles, Mo.
ris, J. W., Morrison, Ill.
aldson, John, Elmhurst, N. Y.
lley, Charles P., Parkersburg, W. Va.
n, John, Detroit, Mich.
lap John H., Toronto, Ont.
La Mare, A. T., New York, N. Y.
val, E. J., Woodside, N. Y.
duck, Theodore, Washington, D. C.
ger, William, Detroit, Mich.
mud, J. B., Chicago, Ill.
ion, J. L., Bloomsburg, Pa.
ris, F. P.,
hner, B., Philadelphia, Pa.
ott, W. H., Boston, Mass.
er, John G., Saddle River, N. J.
on, Mrs. E. L., Chicago, Ill.
on, Miss M. M., Chicago, Ill.
s, R. H., Leamington, Ont.
ree, George, Lima, Ohio.
gren, E. L., Aqueduct, L. I.
est, William H., Washington, D. C.
e, Charles, New Orleans, La.
Forest, Jacob, Greenfield, Ind.
Falek, William, Philadelphia, Pa.
Ford, C. S., Philadelphia, Pa.
Frauenfelder, Conradp Chicago, Ill.
Falconer, D., Chatham, N. J.
Fruck, Henry C., Grosse Pointe Farms, Mich.
Frank, H. M., Dayton, Ohio.
Frischkoon, Augustus, Alleghany, Pa.
Fleming, H. Glenn, Fairmont, W. Va.
Fotheringham, J. R., Tarrytown, N. Y.
Fulmer, J. T. D., Des Moines, Ia.
George, A. B., Painesville, Ohio.
Gammage, W. W., London, Ont.
Gause, G. R., Richmond, Ind.
Gompf, Frank, Logan, Ohio.
Gilbert, J. J., Philadelphia, Pa.
Gerlach, William, Jr., Lexington, Ky.
Goudy, Jos. J., Philadelphia, Pa.
Goldman, Jos. R., Middletown, Ohio.
Gravitt, W. E., Lancaster, Ohio.
Grant, G. L., Chicago, Ill.
Geiger, William, Newark, Ohio.
Grave, Vernon D., Richmond, Ind.
Guenther, C. T., Hamburg, N. Y.
Graham, C J., Cleveland, Ohio.
Gingricht, Irving, South Bend, Ind.
Gasser, The J. M. Co., Cleveland, Ohio.
Goodline, J. F., Zanesville, Ohio.
Graham, M., Philadelphia, Pa.
Gillett, E. G., Cincinnati, Ohio.
Hippard, E., Youngstown, Ohio.
Hagenburger, Carl and wife, Mentor, Ohio.
Harris, William K., Philadelphia, Pa.
Halstead, A. S., Belleville, Ill.
Holton, F. H., Milwaukee, Wis.
Huntsman, Frank, Cincinnati, Ohio.
Harbison, Arthur, Harrodsburg, Ky.
Hart, B. T., Cleveland, Ohio.
Hey, Albert T., Springfield, Ohio.
Hart, A E., Cleveland, Ohio.
Haentze, E., Fond du Lac, Wis.
Hoffman, James, St. Paul, Minn.
Hess, Conrad, Baltimore, Md.
Harbison, S. M., Danville, Ky.
Heinl, Fred, Terrehaute, Ind.
Hellenthal, Joseph J., Columbus, Ohio.
Hennon, Charles, Elwood City,
Hoffmeister, Aug. F., Cincinnati, Ohio.
Henderson, Lewis, Omaha, Neb.
Haentze, E., Jr., Fond du Lac, Wis.
Hartshorne, William, Joliet, Ill.
Hauswirth, P. J., Chicago, Ill.
Haentze, E. Jr., Fond du Lac, Wis.
Holly, E. P., Boston, Mass.
Herr, Albert M., Lancaster, Pa.
Hallock, E. V., New York, N. Y.
Herendeen, F. W., Geneva, N. Y.
Hendrickson, Isaac S., Floral Park, N. Y.
Howard, H. B., Chicago, Ill.
Hammond Benj, Fishkill-on-Hudson, N. Y.
Hill, E. G., Richmond, Ind.
Irish, H. C., St. Louis, Mo.
Imley, John D., Zanesville, Ohio.
Ingram, Charles, Oxford, Ohio.
Imler, William E., Toledo, Ohio.
Joseph, Rosa, Pataskala, Ohio.
Johnson, May, Berlin N. Y.
Jackson, J. E., Gainesville, Ga.
Johnson, Charles H., Chicago, Ill.
Jensen, J. E., Chicago, Ill.
Jones, James E., Richmond, Ind.
Jacob, Fred, Hamilton, Ohio.
Kyle, W. P., Chicago, Ill.
Koenig, Otto G., St. Louis, Mo.
Krut, Anton, Jr., Butler, Pa.
Kakuda, A., New York, N. Y.
Kuhl, George A., Pekin, Ill.
Kruger, Mr. and Mrs. A., Meadville, Pa.
Keplinger, J. H., Baltimore, Md.
Knofe, H. H., Detroit, Mich.
Karl, George S., Baltimore, Md.
Kasting, William F., Buffalo, N. Y.
Koenig, John L., St. Louis, Mo.
Kill, Mr. and Mrs. Leonard, Chicago, Ill.
Kellogg, Gearge M., Pleasant Hill, Mo.
Keubler, William H., Brooklyn, N. Y.
Keuhn, C. A., St. Louis, Mo.
Kunzelman, H., Cincinnati, Ohio.
Karns, James H., Philadelphia, Pa.
Kyrk, Louis H., Cincinnati, Ohio.
Lamborn, L. L., Alliance, Ohio.
Ludwig, Gustav, Alleghany, Pa.
Lengner, A. F., Joliet, Ill.
Long, Daniel B., Buffalo, N. Y.
Luffman, Miss A. K., Spokane, Wash.
Langjahr, A. H., New York, N. Y.
Linn, William, Cliftondale, Mass.
Loew, William, Pittsburg, Pa.
Lovett, Lester C., Little Silver, N. J.
Lanser, Arthur H., Wayne, Pa.
Luffman, G. E., Birmingham, Ala.
Lonsdale, Edwin, Philadelphia, Pa
Luonda, G., Omaha, Neb.
Lautenschlager, F., Chicago, Ill.
Langhorn, A., Wheeling, W. Va.
Leach, John S., Hartford City, Ind.
Meinhardt, Matilda, St. Louis, Mo.
McKinstry, D. S., Kankakee, Ind.
Mineca, E., New Salem, Mass.
Murray, Samuel, Kansas City, Mo.
Meinhardt, Fred H., St. Louis, Mo.
Miller, J. L., Lynn, Mass.
Meehan, Charles E., Philadelphia, Pa.
Maynard, Mr. and Mrs. C. H., Detroit, Mich.
Miller, Theodore, St. Louis, Mo.
McLennan, Robert, Washington, D. C.
Mansfield, Lockport, N. Y.
Mansfield, Thomas, Lockport, N. Y.
Mueller, Charles P., Wichita, Kan.
Miller, William, Lynn, Mass.
Matthews, W. G., Dayton, Ohio.
Moon, Henry T., Morrisville, Pa.
Moss, I. H., Baltimore, Md.
Michael, Theodore, Detroit, Mich.
Moore, George F., Rushville, Ind.
Merkle, John, Mentor, Ohio.
Moore, Allister, Milwaukee, Wis.
McKellar, Charles W., Chicago, Ill.
McLean, George, Youngstown, Ohio.
Nickols, John, Scottdale, Pa.
Newsham, J. A., New Orleans, La.
Newbury, C. E., Mitchell, S. D.
Newsham, J. A., New Orleans, La.
Nieman, Lev., Philadelphia, Pa.
Oldham, L. A., Cambridge, Ohio.
Obermeyer, Gus., Parkersburg, W. Va.
Palmer, F. E., Brookline, Mass.
Palinsky, W. L., Chicago, Ill.
Poehlmann, Adolph H., Morton Grove, Ill.
Peterson, A., Hoopeston, W. Va.
Poehlmann, John W., Chicago, Ill.
Pollworth, C. C., Milwaukee, Wis.
Poehlmann, August F. Morton Grove, Ill.
Pochelon, Albert, Detroit, Mich.
Ponting, Fred, Cleveland, Ohio.
Philpott, H. E., Winnepeg, Manitoba.
Posta, George, Hunburg, Ga.
Peterson, J. A., Cincinnati, Ohio.
Papworth, Harry, New Orleans, La.
Rahany, F. L., New Orleans, La.
Richmond, M., Baltimore, Md.
Recorder, C. J., Hinsdale, Ill.
Rosnosky, J., Philadelphia, Pa.
Rashaley, Robert M., Detroit, Mich.
Renkauf, Martin, Philadelphia, Pa.
Roth, C. A., Columbus, Ohio.
Ringler, A., Chicago, Ill.
Roehrs, Julius, Rutherford, N. J.
Reimels, John, Long Island, N. Y.
Ritter, H. H., Dayton, Ohio.
Reineman, E. C., Pittsburg, Pa.
Rackham, George R., Detroit, Mich.
Rasmussen, A., Albany, Ind.
Ruppert, John A., Riverton, N. J.
Rohrer, H. R., Lancaster, Pa.
Reade, L. H., Fruitdale, Ala.
Rehm, Thomas, New Orleans, La.
Sibson, John F., Germantown, Pa.
Simmond, S., Washington, D. C.
Schulz, Jacob, Louisville, Ky.
Small, Dan. E., Kokomo, Ind.
Seele, H. D., Elkhart, Ind.
Strong, R. O., Jr., Cincinnati, Ohio.
Scribner, E. A., Detroit, Mich.
Stoehr, R. C., Dayton, Ohio.
Smith F., Indianapolis, Ind.
Struck, George, F., Summit, N. J.
Stevens, J. H., Chicago, Ill.
Stewart, William J., Boston, Mass.
Shaw, J. Austin, New York.
Smith, J. N., Marietta, Ohio.
Schmitt, J. W., Springfield, Ohio.
Schellhorn, C., Washington, D. C.
Schmitt, Charles A., Cleveland, Ohio.
Scott, George B., Chicago, Ill.
Seidewitz, Edwin A., Baltimore, Md.
Schramn, Chas. A. Toledo, Ohio.
Smith, Elmer D., Adrain, Mich.
Sackett, E. R., Fostoria, Ohio.
Schummer, Michael, Chicago, Ill.
Schupp, Phillip C., Jr., Chicago, Ill.
Sandeford, Robert, Chicago, Ill.
Schluraff, G. R., Erie, Pa.
Smith, H. P., Piqua, Ohio.
Scott, John, Brooklyn, N. Y.
Schloss, Emil, New York, N. Y.
Skidelsky, S. S., Philadelphia, Pa.
Swayne, William, Kennett Square, Pa.
Smith, H. J., Hinsdale, Mass.
Sanbransky, J. F., Kenton, Ohio.
Sonenschmidt, C., Indianapolis, Ind.
Schwab, Henry, Zanesville, Ohio.
Stool, O A., Oxford, Mich.
Seybold, Chas L., Baltimore, Md.
Sullivan, J. F., Detroit, Mich.
Thaden, H., Atlanta, Ga.
Turnley, C. W., Haddonfield, N. J.
Triffenger, C. H., Van Wert, Ohio.
Taplin, W. H., Philadelphia, Pa.
Traendley, Frank H., New York, N. Y.
Tobler, H., Traverse City, Mich.
Telogel, Ralph, Mt. Morris, N. Y.
Turner, William M., Wilkinsburg, Pa.
Ude, F. W., Jr., Kirkwood, Mo.
Unger, R. W., Detroit, Mich.
Ullrich, E. J., Tiffin, Ohio.
Virgin, U. J., New Orleans, La.
Vaughan, A. L., Chicago, Ill.
Vaughan, J. C., Chicago, Ill.
Vicks, F. W., Rochester, N. Y.
Vincent, Richard, Jr., White Marsh, Md.
Vincent, Richard A., White Marsh, Md.
Vick, Charles H., Rochester, N. Y.
Williams, Sohner, Danville, Ill.
Winters, Richard, Columbus, Ohio.
Winterend, Christ., Defiance, Ohio.
Windtmueller, Fred, Columbus, Ohio.
Wintzer, Antoine, West Grove, Pa.
Wallace, Alex., New York.
Whitcomb, Ansel H., Lawrence, Kan.
Watson, Robert, Detroit, Mich.
Washburn, C. L., Hinsdale, Ill.
Watson, George C., New York, N. Y.
Wood, William K., Chicago, Ill.
Wilson, James S., Western Springs, Ill.
Wiegand, A., Indianapolis, Ind.
Walker, Herbert G., Louisville, Ky.
Weber, Mr. and Mrs. Fred C., St. Louis, Mo.
Westcott John, Philadelphia, Pa.
Winterson, L. H., Chicago, Ill.
Wolf, J., Jr., Philadelphia, Pa.
Weber, Charles, New York, N. Y.
Winterson, E. F., Chicago, Ill.
Weaver, A., Massillon, Ohio.
Washburn, C. L., Bloomington, Ill.
Young, William C., St. Louis, Mo.
Yale, T. G., Wellington, Ohio.
Young, H., Ada, Ohio.
Zettler, L. J., Canton, Ohio.
Zeller, Alfred L., Brooklyn, N. Y.

GEORGIA STATE VICE-PRESIDENT'S REPORT.—For several years past there has been no room for complaint in the sale of cut flowers and plants. The past season shows a very decided increased in all branches of the trade, especially so in the line of bedding plants, palms, ferns, etc., the supply in the South being inadequate. Judging from reports received there must be an increase of about 25 per cent. of sales in the state. Additions to old places continue; there have been added to places in Atlanta about 100,000 square feet of glass thepast season, and yet there is room for more.

There is a fine opening for a number of small growers in and near Atlanta to grow each some few special things, and these openings will have to be filled by parties from East, North or West, as experienced help is a scarce article here.

To very much promote the interest of this society here, it will be necessary to hold a meeting somewhere in the South in the near future. J. E. JACKSON.

Recent Improvements in Retailers' Methods of Offering Flowers.

BY IRWIN BERTERMANN, INDIANAPOLIS.

In the time of the great Roman, Nero, the methods of arranging and presenting flowers were in keeping with that wonderful period. The Romans understood how to combine flowers with statuary, make wreaths and designs for classic pieces, to furnish sparkling fountains with plants, to use artistic vases, to blend colors and to decorate in a manner the leading florists of this great country are earnestly striving after. To be sure they did not watch or have the details of the present times—paper boxes of various hues, green, pink and white wax paper, pins to match the various flowers, cords, tassels, gauze, mattings and many other accessories were unknown to them, but the beauty and detail of their flower arrangements are a standard which all of us may look to.

Interior Fittings.

A compartment the size of a small room refrigerated by the establishment's plant, with glass shelving on either side and backed by mirrors, is the "proper caper" these days. This enables the store man to take his customers into the box, without disturbing the flowers or causing them to suffer from different temperatures.

The Window Display.

The florist's window is now also an all important point. It has long been recognized as his most efficient advertising medium, but it has only been of late years that expert trimmers were employed and the minutest details carefully observed. The flowers in the window must be arranged so that the colors blend or separate parts of the arrangement must contain a massing of one variety. The florist's window must attract the eye of those passing, and surpass in beauty and artistic value all the windows in the city, for in arrangement and neatness it must be equal to them and the beauty of the contents naturally surpass all others.

Commercial vs Idealistic.

The subject of the writer does not permit of a sermon, but this is a most opportune time to impress upon my listeners that so much is sacrificed for commercialism in the present day. Everything is made and arranged according to the ledger account. In this we find our German and French brother far superior. Not only is the commercial side of the florist's business taken into consideration in Europe, but the idealistic side is also well atended to. It is not only necessary to arrange a wreath or basket hurriedly, but it is also necessary to arrange it in an idealistic and artistic manner. I would refer every American retailer to the Bindekunst, a German trade paper. The illustrations therein will easily convince the reader that we are far behind in detail and smybolical work. The Berlin and Parisian florists not only put forth work which earns the dollar, but arrange pieces which signify much more than is found in our ordinary run of baskets, wreaths, pillows, etc.

Arrangement of Stores.

Great improvement has been noticed in late years in the arrangement of the flower stores. It is essential that the arrangement of the up-to-date flower store be such that it is just a trifle beyond the finest customer who enters, if it is to elicit, particularly from the feminine flower expert, the admiration, respect and last but not least, the patronage. Hampers and baskets, also vases and boxes of flowers are at all times in plain view and furnish suggestions and ideas to any one entering. Often times many of these arrangements go to waste, but they give prestige to the retailer who has energy enough to gain ideas and present them to his customers in a practical manner.

No Apology these Days.

An apology is no longer a necessity in the flower business as it was years ago. Suitable stock can be had at all times, though of course this varies with the season. The store man who takes it for granted that a customer should know without being shown, how to use flowers, is lost. It takes constant arrangement and a lot of new ideas to please the better class of customers. It was but a few years back that all customers looked alike to the clerk as they entered the store room. It is now necessary to grasp the idea of catering to different classes of people. The rich, the poor, the artistic, those of poor taste, those who want a lot for their money, those who want only the best, arranged in the most artistic manner, those who want certain color combinations, these qualities must all be grasped at a glance by the clerk, or he will lose many a customer who would have been well satisfied had the clerk been a better judge of human nature. The clerk no longer presents his wares in the timid way of years gone by; he knows the value of his stock and is not to be bluffed by any customer, but stands firmly by any position he may take.

Advantage Taken of Individual Plants.

Advantage is now taken of the peculiarities of each plant; a ribbon bow or cord placed in the proper manner and to the advantage of the plant, a pot cover in perfect harmony, a bit of moss or a little foliage, enhances the value from ten to fifty per cent. It is the neat and natty plant or flower that attracts and sells quicker and at a better figure than a more expensive plant carelessly arranged.

Interurban Railroads a Help.

One of the most recent improvements the retailer has is the great net work of interurban systems which are being built throughout the country. This is particularly true of my own state, Indiana. The close proximity of the greenhouse and the store, due to the electric lines, makes it possible for the retailer to have fresh stock at all times. There is no longer room for old stock as this is many times due to carelessness in ordering. It only takes a telephone call and fresh stock will be on hand in a few hours, whereas in years gone by large amounts had to be ordered at one time.

Improvement in Designs.

As we all know the day of the stereotype flower piece is a thing of the past. The florist now confines his funeral work almost entirely to baskets, bunches, wreaths and blankets. The view is now taken by those who are accustomed to buying flowers that offerings are sent to lighten the suffering of the bereaved, not to make it look more funereal like. As many colors are used as is consistent with good taste.

Public Appreciates Flower Seasons.

The general public now appreciates the various flowers seasons. They understand that chrysanthemums are not to be had in March, or Alpine violets in July. They look for the store man to have select, seasonable stock on hand at all times. It is possible for him to keep things moving lively almost the entire year. The dull Summer season is not nearly what it used to be, and the energetic tradesman can make much of it by handling and arranging the choicest seasonable stock. Seasonable novelties are now always sought for in the flower shops. Small turkeys, ducks, and various novelties must be on hand at Thanksgiving. Chimes, bells, wreaths, etc., must be on hand for Christmas and so on for every festive period. The public has learned to know that the flower shop is the proper place to obtain novelties which are not to be had elsewhere.

Flowers are no longer offered in receptacles which were formerly supposed to heighten the beauty of the contents by contrast with their shabbiness. The grower now affords good glass vases and his swell brother, the retailer, finer articles, not excluding cut-glass, or precious metals.

The growth of the retailer has been such that the modus operendi is patterned after the larger department stores and matters are systemized so that, for instance, an employee who supposedly does nothing but wait on customers, does not hide the broom or emerge from the cellar looking as if he had been in an encounter with the coal pile or moss bin.

The Telephone an Aid.

The use of the telephone, long distance and local, in offering flowers is increasing in enlightenment of the public in regard to them. A fair estimate of the amount sold in this manner is 40 per cent. of the gross sales, so the importance of having the 'phone answered in a proper manner is readily seen. The brainiest, shrewdest, best informed and most resourceful man in the establishment is now employed to answer the telephone. The fisherman at the 'phone must offer the most tempting bait, play with the game, hook the fish, reel it in and place it securely in the net before his work is accomplished. In many instances two or three telephones are placed in one store so that the impatient customer may not turn to a competitor.

The Art Progresses.

The art, and it is one, of arranging boxes of select long stem flowers, skillfully finished with violets, mignonette, pansies, and lily of the valley has now reached the point where to the uninitiated "Excelsior" need no longer be proclaimed. It is here where proof of skill and descernment of color and deftness in arrangement are most apparent. Often times choice boxes are lined with silk and the exterior ornamented with bows of ribbon or bunches of violets, valley and roses, softened with sprays of maidenhair ferns and A. Farlevense. This perfection in the make-up of cut flower boxes is one we may justly feel proud of. For the custom of sending fine boxes of beautiful flowers, like the American Beauty, originated with us—the Americans.

ELBERON (N. J.) HORTICULTURAL SOCIETY.—A meeting of this society was held on August 6, President W. D. Robertson in the chair. Three new members were proposed. A letter of thanks was received from the Board of Education of Ocean township thanking the society for the able manner in which it had beautified the grounds of the public school. Three prizes were awarded at this meeting for a collection of 25 varieties of cut flowers, the winners being, A. Bauer, J. Kennedy and A. Greib. W. D. Robertson exhibited a fine vase of Gypsophila paniculata, and H. Hall showed a decorative table plant. A specimen of Stanhopea graeolens was shown by the Lakeside Gardens. F. Dettlinger and B. Wyckoff staged some nice cut flowers. A bowling match was arranged between the Monmouth County Horticultural Society and the Elberon Horticultural Society to be played on August 10. G. M.

The Ideal Private Gardener and His Work.

(By F. E. Palmer, Bro kline, Mass.)

The title of this essay was selected by the executive committee of the Society of American Florists, and assigned to the Boston Gardeners and Florists' Club, as a fitting subject for its contribution to the literature of this convention. This was perfectly natural, for when questions of a philosophical nature are to be discussed, where else would one turn but to the "Athens of America," the erudite city of the old Bay State. It may be taken for granted, also that the Gardeners and Florists' Club of Boston, with its young and virile membership of 325 (this includes ladies), is perfectly able to handle any question that may be presented to it; but when it comes to the individual to whom this essay is assigned, every thoughtful person will agree that, while being greatly honored he is, nevertheless, confronted with a duty both difficult and onerous.

A Common Ideal Impossible.

In the first place, an ideal which would be common to a number of men is difficult of conception, in fact, impossible. Ideals are essentially individual, and are more characteristic of the man even, than his physical features. They change with him from day to day, as he grows in wisdom, always tantalizingly ahead like the desert mirage, yet always incentive to better work and nobler aims. With these thoughts in one's mind it is hard to get down to earth, where even the ideal gardener belongs.

Types of Other Days.

Before attempting to draw the picture of a present day ideal private gardener, it will be interesting and perhaps helpful, to cast a retrospective glance at types of other days and their environment. They are not so far removed as to be unfamiliar to most of us, indeed many honored examples are with us yet; and as the procession of bygone forms and faces is conjured up, we bow our heads in reverence. Many of them were splendid exponents of the true gardening spirit, were faithful servants, staunch friends of the young gardeners who were committed to their charge, though sometimes severe withal. They bring down to modern times, perhaps more than any other retainer, the spirit of those feudal days in which the extensive private garden had its birth and early nourishment.

Under old world conditions to this day, the number of private gardens of any size is a fixed quantity; new creations are few and far between and are largely offset by the decay and abandonment of old establishments; so, consequently, the market for head gardeners has always been a dull one. A satisfactory and satisfied incumbent held his position often for life. Not much was required of him in the way of technical or scientific knowledge, in fact, too much of that sort of thing would have spoiled him. He was essentially a retainer, although by common consent ranking considerably above the domestics, conservative to a degree, which is always characteristic of those who lack ambition because of the absence of opportunity, that baneful blight of the old world, supremely happy if a modest pension awaited him, or fortunate if able to end his days as the proprietor of a small grocery or public house.

One can easily realize that under the above conditions, there must have been constantly in existence a small army of rejected ones among the body of journeymen gardeners. Head positions not always being awarded with regard to merit, the under gardeners had little incentive to acquire an education above the common, the chances being that they would end their days in the ranks with the laborer. These things may explain the anomalous condition that has undoubtedly existed up to the present time and still exists, viz: that of a large number of intelligent men, engaged in a pursuit so near to nature, so lofty as to transcend almost all others—and if including agriculture, which it naturally does, so important in the world of economics as to comprehend all the necessary things of life within its scope; and yet who are so poorly equipped with technical and scientific education as to render them, as a class, marked in this respect.

It finds its most harmful expression in a conservatism which is positively suicidal in this new day and country. Failing to recognize the opportunity that is now before them of lifting themselves and their craft from the realm of drudgery and servitude into that of science and art where it properly belongs, cherishing the ideal of 'my lord' and 'my lady' who never interfered, the long hours of labor with small pay, the willing helpers who kept going fourteen hours per day if ordered to do so, no horse power, horses had to go to rest early,—no hose, nothing, in fact, that savored of innovation and that required new study; those were indeed good old days.

Present Conditions.

Let us turn, however, to the conditions which confront us in this marvellous age and country. The ordinary slow processes of evolution and national growth have been entirely ignored. Development along economic, social and art lines has been so rapid as to defy the average observer and student to trace it. The nation, from a condition of extreme crudity and devouring energy which might aptly be compared to the caterpillar stage, has suddenly emerged into a state of refinement and keen appreciation of beauty and art that is as startling and interesting to contemplate as the bursting forth of the perfect butterfly. Let us hope that this simile may not obtain in its ephemeral sense.

uring this period of strenuous commercial activ- the earth has been made to yield her treasures t bountifully. Nothing in the world's history pares with the development of the natural re- ces of this country during the last fifty years. struggle has been terrific, and the confusion 1 as that of the mighty rapids and whirlpool of gara. Out of this maelstrom and into the quiet ers of work well done, victory achieved, and for- s made have drifted thousands of men who are seeking rest, recreation, and happiness, the end which all previous effort has been but the means. k to nature is the word, and to the soil which e them their material wealth, they again look those more subtle elements that satisfy the soul. se are the men who have built themselves gar- s and who are looking for partners, rather than hired help, to enable them to accomplish this . It is perfectly fitting and proper to consider ideal gardener in the former relationship rather n the latter, and no intelligent proprietor will de- r to the spirit of such association.

The Gardener's Duties.

What kind of a personality will he have who ll fill the measure of this desire for hap- ess, and at the same time seize the op- tunity to exalt the status of his beloved fession, and raise himself to the high social, nomic and educational plane to which he natur- y and properly belongs? Let us consider the last rt of this theme first and discover what duties will required of him or, in other words, what is his rk, and afterwards try and fit the man to it.

The common idea among young gardeners who ready and feel qualified to take charge of im- rtant places, is, that the measure of these duties ould be included within the following limits; to able to grow the regular run of greenhouse stock ccessfully, including orchids, so that when exhibi- n times come around they may gather in some izes and nail the cards up in the potting shed to great glory of the house, and their own emolu- nt. Incidentally, they expect to supply the house h flowers in limited quantities of their own selec- n, and to grow fruit under glass. They consider kitchen garden to be part of their sphere, al- ugh, as a rule, having had very little experience that department, also the pleasure grounds with ich they have had still less. At first sight, it does em that the list includes about all that should be quired of he average gardener, and if he were a aster in every branch mentioned, he would cer- inly be pretty well equipped as a workman.

The duties of the ideal gardener, however, cover a uch wider range. He has formed a partnership ith the proprietor, the object of which is to pro- ice a certain indefinable, intangible thing called appiness. Primarily the happiness of the latter id also that of his own, as a natural corollary. ith this in view, he will seek to discover the bent his employer and, having found it, to guide it to practical channels. His common sense will ten come into conflict with whimsical desires, but ith plenty of tact and a desire to serve, this will ot be a serious source of trouble. He will be re- uired to plan and lay out an entirely new place, ect greenhouses, put in water supply, survey and ade land, build drives, handle large bodies of men telligently, to study up-to-date methods, and ap- iances such as labor saving machinery, insecti- des, and fertilizers; scoffing at nothing because its strangeness, but testing desirable things in- lligently with a view to conducting the place wih onomy and facility. One of his most delicate ities will be to preserve peace and harmony among s fellow employees, listening to the complaints of s subordinates with a judicial and kindly ear, and eading their cause with their employer. To the ounger gardeners under his charge he owes a pe- iliar and sacred duty. Having trod the path be- re them, he is in a position to know their desires nd ambitions, and should use every effort for their pbuilding into ideal men and gardeners. Short ours of labor, liberal wages, libraries, opportunities attend lectures and exhibitions, encouragement to rm or join clubs, and above all, a kindly personal terest in their welfare, easily lie within his power promote.

In providing the various garden products, he hould study the trend of fashionable taste and try nd forestall the demand in this respect, it being ways extremely pleasing to the proprietor to find imself the possessor of the newest things in flowers, uits and vegetables. On the other hand, it is ad taste on the gardeners' part, to persistently at- mpt to force his own particular hobby on an un- illing employer; this is undoubtedly a rock on hich many a good man splits. It is the duty, and hould be the pleasure, of the gardener to treat iends of the proprietor with courtesy and respect; is admonition is particularly applicable in cases hen married children, or other relatives, locate ermanently on the home estate and whose presence ere is often considered by the gardener as an in- rusion. Generally this involves merely the pro- uction of more garden stuff of every kind, which eans more labor, a matter which the ideal gar- ener can easily adjust by frankly explaining it to is employer. A thousand other duties might be numerated which attach to the ideal gardener of -day, which in years gone by were supposed to be utside of his province. Far from considering these dded burdens, however, he should welcome them s indications of increased opportunities and tributes his advanced intelligence.

The Gardener's Personality.

To successfully meet these requirements, what kind of man is needed? Certainly one with a most complete education in the knowledge and cultivation of plants that can be conceived. This should have begun in the lowest grades of the grammar school, and continued through every step of school life, not as a theory or dry recital of facts, but out in the garden and field. Happily this important feature in the education of every child, whether destined for the horticultural profession or not, is beginning to be recognized by our public educators. In the case of the ideal gardener, of course, this study should never cease; it should include a knowledge of the lower organisms both vegetable and animal, which we call diseases, also that of the insect and animal world in general, in so far as it affects plant life for good or ill.

A knowledge of physics, especially that branch pertaining to mechanics, of chemistry to the extent that he may appreciate the relative values of different elements in soil, air and water. To know the effects of various chemicals on insect life, and the poisons that are contained in many plants with their antidotes, would be extremely useful. The fundamental laws of art wherein it is shown that harmony of colors and forms follow as fixed and well defined rules as those that exist in the phenomena of sound, should be understood. This would naturallay include a study of the principles of landscape gardening; of elementary land surveying and the use of the instruments connected therewith.

All these and a hundred other things may be enumerated as contributing to the mental equipment of a modern first rate gardener. It is a pretty formidable curriculum, especially to the man whose lines of prospective have not carried him much beyond the potting bench, whose chief ambition is to drop into an easy job where the boss is away most of the time, and where no embarrassing questions are asked. Let it not be supposed for a moment, however, that the mere acquisition of all this knowledge in itself constitutes an ideal man. These things are simply tools to be used as means to an end, which is wisdom, and this finds its highest expression in the ability and desire to serve. If in the course of all these years of study and application he has not discovered that his own measure of happiness is commensurate with the service which he renders others, then his time and labor have been largely wasted. Unselfish service is the philosopher's stone. He who possesses it scatters happiness where'er he goes, to his employer, his fellow laborers, in fact, to all with whom he comes in contact. He possesses a pleasing personality, is interesting in conversation, and tactful in manner. Of him, his employer makes a friend and companion. He is not only an ideal gardener, but an ideal man.

Florists' Hall Association.

Secretary John G. Esler, Saddle River, N. J., in his report states that there are now 1,416 members in the Florists' Hall Association, with insurance on an equivalent of 25,056,546 square feet of glass.

The total receipts for the year ending August 1, 1906, as per Treasurer's report, have been $18,744.50. The total expenditure, $8,244.66. The cash balance at the close of the year is $15,150.49, of which $2,709.92 belongs to the Reserve Fund for future investment, leaving $12,440.57 on hand for the Emergency Fund. The Reserve Fund now consists of $13,400 invested in excellent securities, nearly all of which would command a premium, and $2,709.92 cash, making a total reserve fund on hand August 1, 1906, of $16,109.92.

Sixty-eight losses representing a breakage of 37,321 square feet of single thick glass and 21,046 square feet of double thick glass have been paid during the year; 1,019 losses have been adjusted since the organization of the Association, involving a total expenditure of a little over $101,000.00.

A series of hail storms in Central New York, Northern New Jersey, Eastern Pennsylvania and Delaware, did large damage, but the members of the F. H. A., with two exceptions, were not touched.

The apparent danger last year of an extra assessment did not materialize, and the Association commences the new year with a handsome balance both in Reserve and Emergency Funds.

The unadjusted losses at the close of the year, will aggregate less than $500 which is the only liability of the Association.

By addressing the Secretary, a duplicate of any adjustment of loss can be obtained, by any member of the Association, at any time.

In these days of insurance investigation it might be well to mention, that the F. H. A. has never paid a cent for office rent, fuel or light, and that the officials of the Association are both ready and willing, at any time, to give an account of their stewardship.

Undernoted is a list of the losses from August 1, 1905, to August 1, 1906:

1905		
Aug. 3.	W. J. Palmer, Buffalo, N. Y.	$46.15
Aug. 19.	Stella M. Springer, New Hampton, Ia.	15.20
Aug. 19.	O. G. McCormick, Logansport, Ind.	16.34
Aug. 19.	Pratt-Ford Greenhouse Co., Anoka, Minn.	36.91
Aug. 28.	John Tine, Somerville, N. J.	61.01
Aug. 28.	John Wunder, Winona, Minn.	31.53
Aug. 28.	Ed. Kirschner, Winona, Minn.	86.94
Aug. 28.	R. J. Groves, Atchison, Kansas	50.80
Aug. 31.	Anderson Floral Co., St. Cloud, Minn.	11.20
Aug. 31.	Newby & Co., Logansport, Ind.	120.54
Sept. 2.	Nelson Jarrett, Drakemore, Mo.	29.04
Sept. 7.	W. L. Rock Flower Co., Kansas City, Mo.	602.00
Sept. 11.	John S. Morris, Mirriam, Kansas	13.70
Sept. 18.	Templin & Co., Florence, Colo.	71.62
Sept. 25.	Joseph Tossini, Sioux Falls, S. D.	50.40
Sept. 25.	C. H. Frey, Lincoln, Neb.	99.30
Sept. 25.	Dole Floral Co., Beatrice, Neb.	10.60
Oct. 2.	Chapin Bros., Lincoln, Neb.	405.06
Oct. 31.	T. L. Eagle, Coffeyville, Kansas	16.09
Nov. 10.	C. H. Frey, Lincoln, Neb.	44.35
Nov. 18.	Wm. Schick, Wichita, Kansas	22.70
1906		
April 13.	E. H. R. Green, Terrill, Texas	27.23
May 9.	Will B. Munson, Dennison, Texas	250.00
May 9.	G. A. Kishpaugh, Iola, Kansas	34.72
May 12.	Pliny Hyde, Parsons, Kansas	7.35
May 12.	Okla. Agricultural College, Stillwater, Okla.	68.74
May 14.	J. W. Margrave & Co., Hiawatha, Kansas	9.10
May 15.	The Park Floral Co., Denver, Col.	107.80
May 18.	C. C. Wonneman, Mexico, Mo.	48.58
May 18.	Albert Mathews, Kinsman, Ohio	66.04
May 21.	Chas. A. Simonson, McPherson, Kansas	6.25
May 21.	N. S. Kalme, Alcott, Col.	11.70
May 21.	R. M. Nugent, Columbus, Kansas	9.80
May 23.	Andrew Brethaur, Allegheny, Pa.	62.18
May 26.	F. E. Blake, Columbus, Kansas	118.40
May 28.	The Knidler Floral Co., St. Cloud, Minn.	2.55
June 1.	Anderson Floral Co., St. Cloud, Minn.	7.47
June 2.	Mrs. Sarah E. Staton, Columbus, Kansas	9.90
June 8.	R. D. Backus, Iola, Kansas	14.78
June 8.	Mrs. M. P. Church, Roswell, N. M.	124.74
June 11.	Marshall Floral Co., Marshall, Mo.	21.84
June 12.	Hiram Meyers, Wellington, Kansas	89.90
June 16.	F. R. Ripley, Colorado City, Colo.	258.80
June 18.	Mrs. Cal. Richardson, Waverly, Ill.	200.88
June 19.	C. H. Meyer, Waterloo, N. Y.	478.80
June 20.	W. H. Niver, Hutchinson, Kansas	4.76
June 20.	Frank H. Oldham, Webb City, Mo.	16.50
June 20.	Herbert M. Mills, Auburn, N. Y.	8.11
June 20.	W. F. Smith, Arkansas City, Kansas	13.20
June 20.	Z. K. Jewett, Sparta, Wis.	9.35
June 23.	M. E. Wright, Pittsburg, Kansas	13.65
June 25.	Dole Floral Co., Beatrice, Nebraska	8.93
June 25.	Edney Smith Est., Waterloo, N. Y.	155.41
July 5.	Souderton Budg & Loan Association, Silverdale, Pa.	14.94
July 9.	W. J. McCune, Dixon, Ill.	51.31
July 9.	Walter S. Hall, Osage, Iowa	16.38
July 9.	Mrs. Mary E. Eaton, Lyons, Iowa	26.42
July 12.	Nichols Bros., Atlantic, Iowa	77.60
July 12.	Frank Banning, Kinsman, Ohio	20.12
July 16.	Henry Gaethje, Rock Island, Ill.	40.54
July 16.	R. C. Bovey, Dixon, Ill.	81.47
July 16.	G. C. Chapman, Sherman, Texas	15.68
July 18.	W. R. Perry, Cresco, Iowa	54.64
July 19.	N. H. Long & Co., Dixon, Ill.	100.28
July 26.	H. Barsch, Minneapolis, Minn.	30.24
July 26.	Edward Tees, Joplin, Mo.	9.74
July 26.	O. L. Baird, Dixon, Ill.	17.72
		$4,612.51

From the report of Treasurer Albert M. Herr, Lancaster, Pa., we take the subjoined extract:

Recapitulation.

To balance on hand Aug. 1, 1905	$4,650.65
Total Receipts for year ending Aug. 1, 1906	18,744.50
	$23,395.15
By Losses paid for year ending Aug. 1, 1906	4,612.51
By Expenses and Investments	3,632.15
By Balance on hand	15,150.49
	$23,395.15

American Sweet Chestnuts.

Because of the great interest now taken in forestry matters nurserymen are receiving inquiries for seedlings of native forest trees in quantities never dreamed of a few years ago. Many oaks, pines, yellow locust, catalpa, larch, and other well known valuable forest trees are now sought for by thousands each, and as this demand will be sure to increase from year to year as the timber supply lessens, this is the time to sow seeds to meet the call.

Among trees much sought for is the sweet chestnut of our woods, Castanea americana. The supply of this wood has not diminished as rapidly as that of some other sorts, because of the power it has of reproducing itself from sprouts. The cutting down of a tree does not end its life. It sends up many sprouts, one or two of the strongest of which are allowed to grow, and a tree stands where one did before.

It is the planting of entirely new tracts that is occupying the attention of planters now. This planting is better done with seedlings than with seeds, and it is now time that nurserymen were making plans for the sowing of the seeds. At this writing, Mid-August, the mature trees in this vicinity are full of burrs, so that a good crop may reasonably be expected.

The best success follows the sowing of the chestnuts as soon as they are ripe. Beds should be prepared for them in advance, that there may be no delay in getting seeds into the ground. If permitted to become dry through lying about for weeks after collected, they will not grow. Beds should be formed well away from grassy fields where mice are apt to lodge, or there will be but few chestnuts left when Spring comes. The center of a well cultivated field is a good spot. When sown and covered with soil a mulching of straw, hay, leaves or the like should be placed over all, kept on with sticks, to hold the soil moist and prevent frequent freezings and thawings.

CLASSIFIED ADVERTISEMENTS

CASH WITH ORDER.

The columns under this heading are reserved for advertisements of Stock for Sale, Stock Wanted, Help Wanted, Situations Wanted or other Wants; also of Greenhouse, Land, Second-Hand Materials, etc., For Sale or Rent.

Our charge is 10 cts. per line (7 words to the line), set solid, without display. No advt. accepted for less than thirty cents.

Display advertisements in these columns, 15 cents per line; count 12 lines agate to the inch.

[If replies to Help Wanted, Situation Wanted, or other advertisements are to be addressed care of this office, advertisers add 10 cents to cover expense of forwarding.]

Copy must reach New York office 12 o'clock Wednesday to secure insertion in issue of following Saturday.

Advertisers in the Western States desiring to advertise under initials, may save time by having their answer directed care our Chicago office at 127 E. Berwyn Ave.

SITUATIONS WANTED

SITUATION WANTED—As foreman. 25 years' experience. Wages or percentage. Address N. J., care The Forists' Exchange.

SITUATION WANTED — Experienced greenhouse hand, German, 19, lately landed, wishes position. W. Stoffreger, 136 Webster avenue, Yonkers, N. Y.

SITUATION WANTED—By an A No. 1 carnation and mum grower. Also good grower of bedding stock. Good references. J. P. Hersey, 29 South Main St., Attleboro, Mass.

SITUATION WANTED—By a first-class designer, decorator; good salesman, quick worker. Best references. New York or Pittsburg. Address, N. T., care The Florists' Exchange.

SITUATION WANTED—By September 1, growing roses, carnations, violets and pot plants. Wish a first-class place. Best of references from last employer. State wages. Address, James Stewart, Westport, Conn.

SITUATION WANTED—By a first-class rose grower and propagator; bedding plants and nursery work also. Life experience. Good references. Address, N. R., care The Florists' Exchange.

SITUATION WANTED—As working foreman on commercial place, German, married, A No. 1 references, good man, and not afraid of work. Address, Gardener, care Frank Fcly, 1136 State street, New Haven, Ct.

SITUATION WANTED—German, 30 years old, 18 years' experience, married, small family, not afraid of work, A No. 1 references, wishes steady private or commercial place. Address, Florist, 5th and Garden Streets, Hoboken, N. J.

SITUATION WANTED—Florist, in florist store, good designer and maker-up. 17 Years' experience in store and design work. Best references as to honesty and ability. Strictly temperate. Address, N. S., care The Florists' Exchange.

SITUATION WANTED—By married man, 16 years' experience in growing cut flowers, palms, ferns, bedding plants, and design work. Can show good references. Good retail place preferred. Please state wages. Address, N. P., care The Florists' Exchange.

SITUATION WANTED—Swede, aged 34, single, strictly sober, 16 years' experience in carnations, chrysanthemums, palms, ferns and general line of pot and bedding stock. Also fruit and vegetables under glass and outside. Best of references. Private or commercial. Address, N. Q., care The Florists' Exchange.

SITUATION WANTED—As manager or foreman on a large commercial place where first-class roses are wanted. Capable of taking charge of any sized place with all kinds of cut flowers. Strictly sober; long experience. State full particulars with wages in first letter. Address, N. W., care The Florists' Exchange.

HELP WANTED

WANTED—Thoroughly experienced man for retail florist store. Good salesman and designer. Address, N. K., care The Florists' Exchange.

WANTED—Good all-around florist to assist in greenhouses. State experience and wages expected. Address, N. V., care The Florists' Exchange.

WANTED—A good steady man to grow carnations, mums, pot plants, etc. Steady work. Apply to D. Y. Mellis, Holy Cross Cemetery, Flatbush, L. I., N. Y.

WANTED—A thoroughly competent man to take charge of a section of Beauties. Apply Frank Dolan, care of John Young Company, Bedford Station, New York.

WANTED—A first-class man for retail florist in Chicago; no greenhouse work. Must be a good salesman and designer. State wages. References. Address, M. D., care The Florists' Exchange.

HELP WANTED

WANTED—Good, all-around greenhouse man; able to take care of section. Address, Louis Dupuy, Whitestone, L. I.

WANTED—An experienced grower of plants and cut flowers. Married man preferred. Steady place; good wages. Vicinity of New York City. Address, N. L., care The Florists' Exchange.

WANTED—Young man with good knowledge of commercial greenhouse work, including filling orders, shipping, etc. Good wages and steady position. Apply to Florist, P. O. Box 1721, New York.

WANTED—A single man who understands roses and violets on a private place. Good place for a man who knows his business. Wages, $35 to $40 and board. Alex. Lothian, care Eldridge, Great Neck, L. I.

WANTED—At once, a good reliable grower of carnations and bedding plants. German preferred; wages $30 per month, board and room, to start with. Address, N. N., care The Florists' Exchange.

WANTED—An energetic young man to assist in landscape work; fair knowledge of stock, trimming, etc., essential. Dutch or German preferred. State wages expected with references. A. Van Leeuwen, Jr., Worcester, Mass.

WANTED—Sober, reliable man, able to take charge of 20,000 feet of glass. Mums, carnations and general line stock. State wages and references. William Hoffman, 673 East avenue, Pawtucket, R. I.

WANTED—Thoroughly, first-class experienced carnation grower. Apply stating age, married or single, references and wages expected. None but first-class man wanted; must be sober. Deyer Bros., Chambersburg, Pa.

WANTED—Experienced grower of chrysanthemums, carnations, and bedding stock. State where last employed and wages expected, with board per month. Address, Jacob Hauck, 51 Montgomery street, Bloomfield, N. J.

WANTED—Philadelphia seedsman, two of them, by a well-known Philadelphia seed house; widely experienced men in selling to professional gardeners employed on gentlemens' establishments in the vicinity of Philadelphia. None others need apply. Address, N. M., care The Florists' Exchange.

WANTED—September 1, young or middle aged man of experience in general nursery work. Must be able to take charge of shipping and propagating. State wages wanted, age, nationality and references. C. R. Fish & Company, West Side Nurseries, Worcester, Mass.

WANTED—Salesman, one who is a hustler, and understands all about nursery stock, and a fair knowledge of landscape work. To travel. Must have a good record. Steady employment and good pay. Address with references, P. A. Keene, The Morris Nursery Company, 1 Madison avenue, New York.

WANTED

Experienced grower of carnations, violets, Chrysanthemums and bedding stock. Single man preferred. Wages $35.00 per month with board.

SAXE & FLOTO, Waterbury, Conn.

Mention The Florists' Exchange when writing

WANTED

Salesman, designer and decorator: must be up-to-date and able to take charge of first-class trade. None but A No. 1 need apply. Good wages to right party.

HOFFMAN

61 Massachusetts Ave. BOSTON, MASS.

FOREMAN WANTED

In Ornamental Nursery. State Salary and Experience. Address, E., Care THE FLORISTS' EXCHANGE.

MISCELLANEOUS WANTS

WANTED TO BUY—Some second hand greenhouse bars in good condition. Address, N. U., care The Florists' Exchange.

WANTED—Cabbage plants; state variety and price; about 10,000 needed. White Hill Plantation Company, Pretoria, Ga.

WANTED TO BUY—Greenhouses to be taken down. State full particulars of same when writing. Address, F. W., care The Florists' Exchange.

WANTED—20,000 Retinispora plumosa aurea, 4 to 6 inches, transplanted. Also 4,000 Retinispora Squarrosa Veitchii, 6 inches, transplanted. Address Rhode Island Nurseries, Newport, R. I.

MISCELLANEOUS WANTS

WANTED—For export to Europe, dried moss, dried flowers, artificial leaves, thistle fruit, and othr material for making wreaths. Kindly send samples and prices to oseph Fisher, 1022 Main Street, Cincinnati, Ohio.

FOR SALE OR RENT

FOR SALE or will rent to a responsible party, a fine greenhouse property. 13,000 feet of glass. Fine residence. Address, Silas C. Howell, Lock Box 14, Pine Bush, New York.

FOR RENT—Small greenhouse and florist business in prosperous running condition. Southern Connecticut. Full particulars and reason for renting to anyone interested. Address, N. G., care The Florists' Exchange.

FOR SALE—Greenhouse comprising over 8,000 square feet of glass situated in Northern New Jersey. Including all stock, horse, wagons, and harness, etc. Doing good retail business. Address, B., care Florists' Exchange.

DESIRABLE greenhouse plant of three houses, 24x200 feet; propagating house, 100 feet; potting shed, stable and dwelling. Steam heat, city water. Highland, opposite Poughkeepsie. Joseph Wood, Spring Valley, New York.

FOR SALE—House, 7 rooms, steam heat, 1 stable, 5 greenhouses, well stocked; steam heat, Kearney, N. J., 5 minutes from Erie R. R. depot, and 5 minutes from N. Y. trolley. J. G. Perry, Schuyler Avenue, Kearney, New Jersey.

FOR RENT—On account of death, in upper Montclair, N. J., a florist's business, consisting of four greenhouses partly stocked and with carnations in field ready for planting. This is a splendid opportunity as there is a good market for everything grown. Trolley cars pass the door. Apply to Mrs. Robt. MacInnes, 676 Valley Road, Upper Montclair, N. J.

FOR SALE—A paying greenhouse establishment of 7,500 feet glass, with nearly one acre of ground, six room cottage house in a growing city of 15,000. Only one other establishment in the city. In central Ohio. Reason for selling ill-health. Full particulars on application. Or will sell material in greenhouses alone. Address, M. X., care Florists' Exchange.

FOR SALE—At a bargain on account of removal and having two places, I will sell four greenhouses, two houses 16 x 80, other two 22 x 80. Boiler house, 16 x 20, with one large boiler to heat the place and another in reserve. Both boilers can burn buckwheat coal at a small cost. Only three or four years in use. Price only $1500. Hill Top Greenhouses, 15-16 Gray avenue, Utica, New York.

FOR SALE—Owing to failing health, I will sell my florist establishment, beautifully situated between Larchmont Manor and Mamaroneck, Westchester Co., New York, near railroad station; trolley lines within one minute walk. First class opportunity for the right man. Plenty of landscape and jobbing work. The place contains four acres, 2 greenhouses, 104 feet long and lots of sash; well stocked with trees and shrubs, etc.; horse, wagon and tools. Address, Box 44, Larchmont, New York.

STOCK FOR SALE

15,000 strong, healthy, field-grown violet plants of Farquhar, Lady Campbell, La France and California, $5 per 100; $45 per 1000. Richard Langle, orth street, White Plains, N. Y.

SEEDS, pansy, new crop, $1.00 per packet; $4.00 per oz.; $12.00 per 1-4 lb. Pansy plants, $4.00 per 1,000. Cash. B. Soltau, 199 Grant avenue, Jersey City, N. J.

PRIMULA, Chinese, finest fringed, mixed, 1 3-4 c. Cash. Our Giant pansies ready next month. Shippensburg Floral Company, Shippensburg, Pa.

BABY RAMBLER ROSES, H. P. and Rambler roses, field grown, 2 year stock, for sale cheap. write for list. Schaufelberger & Hill, Penfield, New York.

JARDINIERE FERNS, seedlings, good, strong, healthy stock, in variety only. Now ready for potting. Price, $1.50 per 100 by mail; $10.00 per 1000, F. O. B. Exp. B. Soltau, 199 Grant avenue, Jersey City, N. J.

CARNATION PLANTS, nice field-grown, Enchantress, Mrs. T. W. Lawson, $6.00 per 100; Joost, New Daybreak, ocPsperity, Wolcott, $5.00 per 100. For cash. M. J. Schaaf, Dansville, N. Y.

BABY RAMBLER roses, fine dormant stock, $25 per 100, 2 1-2 inch pot plants, extra well rooted $7 per 100, $65 per 1000. Orders booked for delivery now or any time up to late Spring. Samples free. Brown Brothers Co., Rochester, N. Y.

YUCCA FILAMENTOSA, $1.00 lb.; Amorpha fruticosa, 25c. lb.; Ampelopsis quinquefolia, 75c. lb.; Azalea arborescens, $2.00 lb.; Corylus rostrata, 50c. lb.; Crataegus crus-galli, 25c. lb.; Juglans cinerea, $1.00 bu.; Juglans nigra, $1.00 bu.; Cornus florida, 20c. lb. F. M. Crayton, Box 393, Biltmore, N. C.

Thirty cents is the minimum charge for advertisements on this page.

STOCK FOR SALE

CARNATIONS, first-class, field grown plants. Enchantress, Lawson, Queen, $6.00 per 100; $50.00 per 1000. Cash with order please. Mrs. P. F. Conley, Princeton Avenue, & Updike Street, Providence, R. I.

CARNATIONS, field plants. Enchantress, $6 per 100; $50 per 1000; Boston Market, $5 per 100; $40 per 1000; Lawson, $5 per 100; $40 per 1000; Red Lawson, $6 per 100; $50 per 1000. The J. A. Budlong & Son Co., Auburn, R. I.

FOR SALE

FOR SALE—One horizontal boiler; 40 horse power; all complete; good condition; cheap. Alex. B. Garden, Anacostia, D. C.

FOR SALE—150 sash, 8½ x 8; 150 3⅓ x 6, in good condition also rafter to fit sashes. For particulars apply J. H. Fiesser, Hamilton avenue, North Bergen, N. J.

5,000 5-inch pots, as good as new, cost $12 per 1,000; will sell for $9 per 1,000. Cash with all orders please. Dean & Parse, 46 to 52 Ashwood avenue, Summit, New Jersey.

BOILERS, BOILERS, BOILERS.

SEVERAL good second hand boilers on hand, also new No. 16 Hitchings at reduced cost. Write for list. Wm. H. Lutton, West Side Avenue Station, C. R. R. of N. J., Jersey City, N. J.

FOR SALE—50 cypress hot bed sash, size 3 x 6, glazed with 10 x 12 glass, painted white, and in perfect condition. Most all of them new this season; none over three years old. $1.00 each. J. V. Cutler, Wassaic, N. Y.

FOR SALE—Glass, about 65 boxes, 10 x 12, extra double thick, $1.85; also about 15 boxes 16 x 20, $2.50. I. Suesserman, 229 Livingston Street, Newark, N. J.

FOR SALE—Stover fifty foot Steel Tower and Tank in use a short time. Good as new; price reasonable. Write for particulars. Wm. C. De Witt, R. F. D. No. 1, Phillipsburg, N. J.

FOR SALE—12 Hitchings hot water expansion tanks for 3 1-2 in. pipe, in good condition, cleaned, ready to set up. 1-3 price of new. Also horse lawn mower, easy running, $20.00. Address, K. D., care The Florists' Exchange.

FOR SALE—Six 4-inch gate valves at $4 each. 500 Calla bulbs, $6 per 100; 16 large Azalea indica for cutting; 100 large Adiantum cuneatum; 10 boxes 8 by 10, dbl., imported glass, $2.25 box; 8 boxes, 6 by 8, dbl., $1.75 box. J. Geist, Melrose, Mass.

FOR SALE No. 8 Furman Hot Water Boiler, at a sacrifice.

Good as new. Apply to

J. J. McMANMON,

6 Prescott St., LOWELL, MASS.

Mention The Florists' Exchange when writing.

FOR SALE

PUMPS Rider-Ericsson. Second-hand, from $40.00 up; all repairs; other makes; new; cheap.

BOILERS One second-hand tubular hot water boiler 3 ft. in diameter 12 ft. long. Price $35.00. One No. 16 Hitchings as good as new, $80.00.

PIPE Good serviceable second-hand, with Threads; 2-in., 7 cts.; 1½-in., 5½ cts.; 1¼-in., 4 cts.; 1-in., 3 cts.; 2½ in., 10 cts.; 3 in., 14 cts.; 4 in., 19 cts. New 2-in. Standard, full lengths, with couplings, 8½ cts. ft. Old and new fittings and valves. Old 4 inch cast iron 15c per foot.

STOCKS and DIES New Economy, best made No. 1 Threads, ¼-in., ¾-in., 1-in. pipe, $3.00. No. 2 Threads, 1¼-in., 1½-in., 2-in. pipe, $4.00.

PIPE CUTTERS New Saunders Pattern. No. 1 cuts ⅛-in.-1-in. pipe, $1.00. No. 2 cuts 1-in.-2-in. pipe, $1.30.

STILLSON WRENCHES New. 18-in., grips ¼-in.-2-in. pipe, $1.65; 24-in. grips ¼-in.-2½ in. pipe, $2.40; 36-in., grips ¼-in.-3½-in. pipe, $4.75.

PIPE VISES New. No. 1 Hinged, grips ⅛-in.-3 in. pipe, $2.00.

GARDEN HOSE New. 50 ft. lengths. ¾-in., guaranteed 100-lbs. pressure, 7½ cts. per ft.; ¾-in. not guaranteed, 4½ cts. per ft., 25 ft. lengths, ½c. per ft. more.

HOT-BED SASH New. Cypress, 3-ft.x6 ft., from 75 cts. up; glazed, complete, from $1.60 up. Second-hand, in good condition, all glass in, $1.00 each.

GLASS New American 10x12 single $1.75 per box; 12x12 single $1.90 per box; 10x12 $2.55, 12x12, 10x16 double $2.65 per box; 12x14, 12x20, 14x14, double, $2.75 per box; 16x16, 16x18, $3.10 per box; 16x24 double $3.25 per box. Second hand glass, 8 x 10, 8 x 12, double, $1.65 per box. Single $1.50.

Old material, ridge, plates, gutters, bars, etc.

Get our prices on New Gulf Cypress Building Material, Ventilating Apparatus, Oil, White Lead, Putty, Paint, Points, etc.

METROPOLITAN MATERIAL CO.

1398-1408 Metropolitan Avenue, BROOKLYN, N.Y

Mention The Florists' Exchange when writing.

OUR LITTLE PET

From Aschmann in Philadelphia I bought
An Araucaria, a pet for our little girl;
Now we have two pets, the pride of our thought:
The little girl so sweet, a head full of curls,
And the Araucaria with it s everlasting green,
A more joyful home you never have seen.

Watch us Grow!!

ARAUCARIA EXCELSA, the best of all decorative plants nature produces: a specialty. Every man in business life: to be successful, must adopt one thing as his specialty, and that specialty, whatever he may select, and of whatever nature it may be, he must guard, study and push to such an extent, that it not only benefits himself; but he must conduct it so, that every one who seeks his aid, service or his articles, whatever he advertises or practices, will **share a slice** of his **activity and prosperity.** I made the importation and cultivation of Araucaria as a special study in my life. The following figures will show you my success in business: In the first year I began with an import of 250; in the eleventh year (now 1906) my importation has grown up to 6,000 (come and see it). On account of the Araucaria growing yearly in favor as a much admired decorative plant for the arbor, bed room, dining and sitting rooms, stores, hotels, lawns and porches by the plant-consuming peoples all over the country, **the outlook** will be of an importation of at least 8,000 to 10,000 in the Spring of 1907. To secure this vast amount for 1907, I am now on the ocean, per steamer New Amsterdam, sailing from Hoboken, August 15, striking for Belgium and making contracts for next year. I shall also at the same time bring over with me a large lot of choice Azalea Indica, Palms, etc. for Christmas and Easter forcing. No money will be spared in obtaining for my customers the cream of the Belgium greenhouses.

Please note lowest price now going for August and September:

ARAUCARIA EXCELSA

12 to 14 in. 5½ in. pots, 3 to 4 tiers, 2-yr. old, 50c. 14 to 16 in., 5½ in. pots, 3 to 4 tiers, 2-yr. old, 60c. 16 to 18 in. 5¾ to 6 in. pots, 4 to 5 tiers, 3-yr. old, 75c. 18 to 20 in., 6 in. pots, 5 to 6 tiers, 4-yr. old, $1.00. 20 to 24 in. 6 in. to 7 in. pots, 5 to 6 tiers, 4-yr. old, $1.25. 36-40 to 50 in. 7 in. pots, specimen plants from $2.50 to $3.00 each.

ARAUCARIA COMPACTA ROBUSTA — have several thousand of them; can supply all wants. These plants were never so fine in shape and condition as this year. The set of the greenhouse, as broad as long, 12 to 20 in., in height, 3 to 4 perfect tiers, 20 to 30 inches across, 3-4-5 year old, 6 to 7 in. pots, $1.25, $1.50, $1.75, $2.00, $2.50 to $3.00 each.

ARAUCARIA EXCELSA GLAUCA — This variety on account of its beautiful Green-Blueish tiers, dwarf habit, fine compact shape, gives it a striking appearance, and anybody seeing them, must undoubtedly fall in love with them at sight. Plants, 6-7 inch pots, 3-4-5 perfect tiers, 3-4 year old, 15 to 25 inch high, from 15 to 30 in. across, $1.25, $1.50, $1.75, $2.00 to $2.50 each.

SOLANUM or JERUSALEM CHERRY, $5.00 per 100.

KENTIA BELMOREANA, 5½ to 6 in. pots, bushy, fine plants, from 75 cts. to $1.00 to $1.25 each.

KENTIA FORSTERIANA, 7 in. pots, made-up plants, 1 large in center, 3 smaller sizes, 22 to 25 in. high around, gives them a good appearance, $2.00 each. 6 in. pots, single plants, 35 to 40 in. high, 5 to 6 good leaves, 4 year old, $1.25 to $1.50 each; 6 in. pots, 30 to 35 in. high, 4 year old, 5 good leaves, $1.00; 5½ in. pots, 3 year old, 25 to 30 in. high, 5 good leaves, 75c. made-up plants, 3 and 4 in. pots, 18 to 20 in. high, 25 cts. to 30 cts. each.

ARECA LUTESCENS, made-up, 25 cts.

COCOS WEDDELIANA, 15 cts.

CYCAS REVOLUTA (Sago Palm), 6 in.-7 in. pots, with from 6 to 20 leaves per plant, 10 cts. per leaf.

NEPHROLEPIS BARROWSII, 6 in. pots, strong, ready for 7-8 in., 50c. 4 in. pots, ready for 6-7 in., 25c.

NEPHROLEPIS SCOTTII, 6 in. pots, large, ready for 6-7 in. 50c.; 5½ in. pots, 40c.; 5 in. 35c.; 4 in. 20c. to 25c.

BOSTON FERNS, 4 in., 20c. to 25c. I have them by the thousand, 5 in.; 30c. to 35c.

FERNS for dishes, a fine assortment, 2½ in., $5.00 per 100; 3 in., $6.00 per 100.

FICUS ELASTICA, 5 in., 50c.

ASPARAGUS PLUMOSUS NANUS, 3 in., 5c.; 4 in., 10c.

CASH WITH ORDER

When ordering, say whether the plants should be shipped in the pots or not

GODFREY ASCHMANN

Importer and Wholesale Grower of Pot Plants

1012 Ontario Street, - - PHILADELPHIA, PA.

Mention The Florists' Exchange when writing.

STUDER OFFERS

Latania Borbonica, Phoenix Canariensis, from 6 in. pots, 2½ feet tall, $5.00 per dozen. **Latania,** from 5 in. pots, 2 ft. size. **Kentia Belmoreana,** from 4 in. pots, 20 in. high, and **Chamaerops Excelsa** (a very useful and hardy palm), from 5 in. pots, $3.50 per doz. **Ferns,** bostons, from 4 in. pots, $2.50 per doz.; from 5 in., $4.00 per doz. Over ten thousand pot grown **Roses,** of all good varieties, 4-5-6 in. pots, $1.00-$2.00-$3.00 per doz. Pot Grown Roses forced better than field-grown or imported ones. **Adiantum Cuneatum,** 2-3-4 in., $3.00-$5.00-$7.00 per 100. **Asparagus Plumosus,** 2-3 in. pots, $3.00-$5.00 per 100. All plants grown in smallest pots, ready for a shift now. Will send two each size palms, ten in all, and six ferns for $3.50 as sample.

Discount on all stock 10% on the hundred and 5% for cash with order

N. STUDER, ANACOSTA, D.C.

Mention the Florists' Exchange when writing.

CYCLAMENS

Strong plants, $6.00 per 100; $45.00 per 1000.

ASPARAGUS

Sprengeri in 2½ pots, $2.50 per 100, $20.00 per 1000, also in flats at 75c. per 100; Plumosus Nanus in 2½ pots, $3.00 per 100.

F. A. GIFFORD, Westbury Sta., L. I.

Mention The Florists' Exchange when writing.

50,000 Pansy Seedlings

Finest strain at $4.00 per 1000. Delivery beginning September 1st. Orders booked in rotation. Strictly cash with order.

J. CONDON, Horticulturist,

734 5th Ave., Brooklyn, N. Y.

Mention The Florists' Exchange when writing.

POINSETTIAS

2½ in. pots, $5.00 per 100; $40.00 per 1000. Cash with order.

S. N. PENTECOST,

1790-1810 East 101 St., CLEVELAND, O.

Mention The Florists' Exchange when writing.

2,000 **Smilax,** 2½ in., strong, cut back, per 100, $1.50; the lot for $17.50.
200 **Asparagus Plumosus,** $2.50 per 100.
1,000 **Asparagus Sprengerii,** 2½ in., $2.00 per 100; the lot for $17.00. This is strong and ready for a shift.

J. S. BLOOM,

RIEGELSVILLE, PA.

Mention The Florists' Exchange when writing.

Dwyer's Pot Grown Strawberry Plants

Strong, healthy plants from selected stock of choicest fruiting varieties sure to give satisfaction and **PRODUCE A FULL CROP IN 1907.** We also have a full line of Fruits and Ornamental Trees, Plants, Vines, etc., for Fall Planting.
We do Landscape Gardening in all its branches. **Catalogue Free**

T. J. DWYER & CO., P. O. Box 6 Cornwall, New York

Mention The Florists' Exchange when writing.

Beautiful and Rare Gladioli

Cut spikes, all colors imaginable in any quantity,—
100 ACRES from which to select, write for prices.

ARTHUR COWEE, Gladiolus Specialist, Meadowvale Farm, Berlin, N. Y

Mention The Florists' Exchange when writing.

DRACAENA TERMINALIS

Matured canes always ready for shipment. Delivered to any part of the United States for 10 cents a foot. Send cash for a trial order.

PORTO RICO PINEAPPLE CO., RIO PIEDRAS, PORTO RICO.

Mention The Florists' Exchange when writing.

A Few Good Things YOU WANT

Dracaena Indivisa, 4 and 6 in., $10.00 and $25.00 per 100.

Asparagus Sprengeri, 2 in., $2.50 per 100.

Geraniums, S. A. Nutt, Castellane, John Doyle, Perkins, Double Gen. Grant, Poitevine, Mme. Sallerol, 2 in. pots, $2.00 per 100; 3 in. pots $4.00 per 100. Rooted Cuttings, $1.00 per 100.

Rex Begonia, nice plants, 2 and 2½ in., $5.00 per 100.

Asparagus Plumosus, 2 in. $3.00 per 100.
Boston Fern 5 in. 30c each.
Pierson Fern 6 in. 40c each.

GEO. M. EMMANS, Newton, N. J.

Mention The Florists' Exchange when writing.

Decorative Plants

Latania Borbonica, 2½ in. pots, $3.00; 3 in., $6.00; 4 in., $15.00 per 100. Large specimen plants from $2.00 to $5.00 each.

Kentia Belmoreana and Forsteriana, 2½ in. pots, $8.00; 3 in., $15.00; 5 in., $60.00 per 100; 6 in. $12.00 per doz.; 7 in. and upward, $1.75 to $36.00 each.

Areca Lutescens, 3 in. $10.00; 4 in. $20.00 per 100; 6 in., $1.00 each and upward.

Pandanus Utilis, 3 in. pots, $3.00; 4 in., $20.00 per 100.

Phoenix Reclinata, 5 in. pots, $35.00 per 100.

Phoenix Canariensis, fine specimen plants, from $3.00 to $35.00 each.

Araucaria Excelsa, 5 in. pots, $65.00 per 100.

Assorted Ferns, 2½ in. pots, $3.00 per 100.
Nephrolepis Compacta, 3 in. pots, $8.00; 4 in., $15.00 per 100.

Plants in Fine Condition.

JOHN BADER, Troy Hill, Allegheny, Pa.

Mention The Florists' Exchange when writing.

SURPLUS STOCK—CHEAP

200 **The Bride** roses, 2 in. pots, $1.75 per 100.
500 **Bridesmaid** roses, 2 in. pots, $2.00 per 100.
1000 **Cannas,** red and yellow, strong, $3.00 per 100.
50 **Dracaena Indivisa,** 3½ in., 6c. each.
2000 **Cuphea,** Cigar Plant, 2 in. pots, 75c. per 100.
2000 **Feverfew,** Double White, 2 in. pots, 60c. per 100.
10000 **Jerusalem Cherries,** big and strong, ready for 4 in. pots, from 2 in. pots at $2.00 per 100. You will never get better or cheaper stock than this. **E. I. Rawlings, Quakertown, Pa.**

Mention The Florists' Exchange when writing.

Stevia Serrata

True, winter blooming, strong, bushy, ready to shift, 2½ in. pots, $5.00 per 100; $45.00 per 1000.

ASPARAGUS SPRENGERII, 2 inch, very strong, $2.50 per 100; $20.00 per 1000.

DEAN FERRIS, Peekskill, N.Y.

Mention The Florists' Exchange when writing.

ASPARAGUS

Robustus $5.00 per 100; $40.00 per 1000.
Sprengerii $2.00 per 100; $15.00 per 1000.

ALBERT M. HERR

LANCASTER, PA.

Mention The Florists' Exchange when writing.

ASPARAGUS

		Per 100
Sprengerii, 3 in.		$3.00
" 2 in.		1.50
Plumosus Nanus, 2 in.		2.00
Primula Obconica, Grandiflora Alba, Rosea and Hybrida, 2 in.		2.00
" " **Robusta and Compacta,** 2 in.		3.00
Smilax, nice, 2½ in.		1.25
Paris Daisy, white and yellow, 3 in., bushy,		3.00

Orders booked for early September delivery of

Cineraria Grandiflora Hybrida, Michell's Giant Prize, 2 in.		2.00
" " **Stellata,** Sutton's, 2 in.		2.50
Calceolaria, James Superb mixed, 2 in.		3.00

Cash with order, please.

GEO. J. HUGHES, BERLIN, N. J.

Mention The Florists' Exchange when writing.

SMILAX PLANTS

Strong, Bushy Plants, many times cut back and ready for shift.

2 in. pots	$1.00 per 100,	$9.00	per 1000
3 in. pots	2.00 "	18.00	"
Seedlings from flats		4.00	"

We have grown Smilax Plants for the trade 18 years, and never had finer stock.

Send for Samples

R. KILBOURN

CLINTON, N. Y.

Mention The Florists' Exchange when writing.

EMERSON C. McFADDEN

Wholesale Grower

Asparagus Plumosus Nanus, Etc.

Short Hills, N. J.

Tel. 28 A.

Mention The Florists' Exchange when writing.

ASPARAGUS

Sprengerii, extra strong, 3 in. pots, $5 per 100.
Extra Strong, 4 in. pots, $6 per 100.
Smilax, 2½ in. pots $2 per 100.
Cabbage Plants, Flat Dutch, Succession and Winningstadt, $1.50 per 1000. Cash with order.

S. G. BENJAMIN, Fishkill, N. Y.

Mention The Florists' Exchange when writing.

CANNAS

300,000 roots for Fall delivery in 100 leading kinds, $8.00 to $20.00 per 1000. Write for our list. Send in your orders early.

SHELLROAD GREENHOUSES

Largest Canna Growers . Grange, Baltimore, Md.

Mention The Florists' Exchange when writing.

Wholesale Prices of Cut Flowers, New York, August 23, 1906

Prices quoted are by the hundred unless otherwise noted.

Roses	A. BEAUTY, fancy—special	6.00 to	15.00
	" extra	5.00 to	6.00
	" No. 1	4.00 to	5.00
	" No. 2	3.00 to	4.00
	" No. 3	1.00 to	1.50
	Bride, Maid, fancy—spe'l	3.00 to	4.00
	" extra	2.00 to	3.00
	" No. 1	1.00 to	2.00
	" No. 2	.25 to	.50
	Golden Gate	1.00 to	5.00
	Liberty	...... to	......
	Mme. Abel Chatenay	1.00 to	6.00
ADIANTUM		.50 to	.75
	CROWEANUM	.50 to	1.00
ASPARAGUS		25.00 to	50.00
	" Plumosus, bunches	8.00 to	15.00
	" Sprengerii, bunches	8.00 to	15.00
ASTERS		.25 to	3.00
CATTLEYAS		50.00 to	60.00
DAISIES		...... to	......
GLADIOLUS		.50 to	1.00
		...... to	......

Carnations	Inf'r grades, all colors		.50 to	1.00
	STANDARD VARIETIES	White	1.00 to	2.00
		Pink	1.00 to	2.00
		Red	1.00 to	2.00
		Yel. & Var.	...... to	......
	*FANCY— (*The highest grades of standard var.)	White	2.00 to	2.50
		Pink	2.00 to	2.50
		Red	2.00 to	2.50
		Yel. & Var.	...... to	......
	NOVELTIES		...... to	......
DAHLIAS, per bunch			.05 to	.15
LILIES			4.00 to	6.00
LILY OF THE VALLEY			1.00 to	3.00
MIGNONETTE			...... to	......
			...... to	......
			...... to	......
			...... to	......
PANSIES, per dozen bunches			.50 to	.75
SMILAX			8.00 to	10.00
SWEET PEAS, per bunch			...... to	......

Wholesale Prices of Cut Flowers—Per 100

Boston Aug. 20, 1906	Buffalo Aug. 13, 1906	Detroit Aug. 5, 1906	Cincinnati Aug. 20, 1906	Baltimore Aug. 6, 1906	NAMES AND VARIETIES	Milwaukee July 28, 1906	Phil'delphia July 24, 1906	Pittsburg Aug. 20, 1906	St. Louis Aug. 20, 1906
to	20.00 to 25.00	10.00 to 35.00	to 30.00	to	ROSES — A. BEAUTY, fancy—special	to 25.00	15.00 to 20.00	20.00 to 25.00	15.00 to 20.00
10.00 to 20.00	12.00 to 20.00	to	20.00 to 25.00	12.50 to 15.00	" extra	15.00 to 18.00	10.00 to 15.00	15.00 to 18.00	10.00 to 12.50
4.00 to 10.00	6.00 to 12.00	to	to 15.00	5.00 to 8.00	" No. 1	10.00 to 12.50	5.00 to 7.00	10.00 to 12.00	6.00 to 8.00
2.00 to 4.00	3.00 to 6.00	to	to	to	" Culls and ordinary	4.00 to 6.00	1.00 to 4.00	3.00 to 4.00	3.00 to 5.00
to	5.00 to 6.00	3.00 to 6.00	4.00 to 6.00	to	BRIDE, 'MAID, fancy-special	to 6.00	to	to 6.00	to
4.00 to 6.00	4.00 to 5.00	to	2.00 to 4.00	to 4.00	" extra	to 5.00	6.00 to 8.00	to 4.00	2.00 to 4.00
2.00 to 4.00	3.00 to 4.00	to	1.00 to 2.00	to 3.00	" No. 1	to 4.00	4.00 to 5.00	to 3.00	to
to 2.00	2.00 to 3.00	to	to	to 2.00	" No. 2	to 2.00	2.00 to 3.00	to 2.00	to
to	to	4.00 to 8.00	to	2.00 to 4.00	GOLDEN GATE	4.00 to 6.00	4.00 to 8.00	to	2.00 to 4.00
1 to 6.00	3.00 to 7.00	to	2.00 to 6.00	4.00 to 8.00	K. A. VICTORIA	4.00 to 8.00	4.00 to 6.00	3.00 to 12.00	2.00 to 6.00
1.00 to 8.00	3.00 to 7.00	to	to	to	LIBERTY	4.00 to 6.00	3.00 to 6.00	to	to
.00 to	3.00 to 6.00	4.00 to 10.00	to	to	METEOR	to	to	to	to
to	3.00 to 6.00	4.00 to 10.00	to	2.00 to 4.00	PERLE	4.00 to 6.00	to	to	2.00 to 3.00
to	to	to 50.00	to	to	ORCHIDS—Cattleyas	to	to 50.00	to	to
to	.50 to 1.00	to	to	.50 to .75	CARNATIONS — Inferior grades, all colors	to 1.00	.75 to 1.00	.75 to 1.00	to .50
to	1.00 to 1.25	to 1.00	to 1.00	1.00 to 1.50	Standard Varieties — White	to 1.00	.75 to 1.00	to	to .50
to	1.00 to 1.25	to	to 1.00	1.00 to 1.50	Standard Varieties — Pink	to 1.00	.75 to 1.00	to	to .50
to	1.00 to 1.25	to	to 1.00	1.00 to 1.50	Standard Varieties — Red	to 1.00	.75 to 1.00	to	to
to	to	to 8.00	to 1.00	1.00 to 1.50	Standard Varieties — Yellow and var.	to 1.00	.75 to 1.00	to	to
.50 to 1.50	1.50 to 2.00	to	to	to 3.00	Fancy Varieties — White	1.50 to 2.00	2.00 to 2.50	to	1.00 to 1.50
.50 to 1.50	1.50 to 2.00	to	to	to 3.00	Fancy Varieties — Pink	1.50 to 2.00	2.00 to 2.50	to	1.00 to 1.50
.50 to 1.50	1.50 to 2.00	to	to	to 3.00	Fancy Varieties — Red	1.50 to 2.00	2.00 to 2.50	to	to
.50 to 1.50	1.50 to 2.00	to 1.50	to	to 3.00	Fancy Varieties — Yellow and var	1.50 to 2.00	2.00 to 2.50	to	to
to	to	to	to	to	Novelties	to	to	to	to
.75 to 1.00	.50 to 1.00	to 2.00	to 1.00	to 1.00	ADIANTUM	to 1.00	to 1.00	1.25 to 1.50	to 1.00
to 50.00	to	25.00 to 60.00	to 50.00	25.00 to 50.00	ASPARAGUS, Plum. and Ten	20.00 to 30.00	25.00 to 35.00	40.00 to 50.00	25.00 to 40.00
to	to	20.00 to 30.00	to 35.00	25.00 to 50.00	" Sprengeri, bunches	20.00 to 30.00	25.00 to 35.00	to 50.00	10.00 to 20.00
.35 to .75	.50 to 2.00	to	1.00 to 3.00	to	ASTERS	.50 to 1.00	to	.50 to 2.00	.50 to 5.00
to	8.00 to 10.00	to 10.00	to	6.00 to 8.00	CALLAS	to	to	to	to
to	to	.75 to 1.50	to	to	DAISIES	to .40	3.00 to 4.00	to	to
3.00 to 5.00	1.00 to 3.00	8.00 to 10.00	1.00 to 3.00	2.00 to 4.00	GLADIOLUS	to	8.00 to 12.00	2.00 to 4.00	to 2.00
to	to	to	to	10.00 to 12.50	LILIES, Harrisii	to 12.50	to	15.00 to 18.00	to
4.00 to 8.00	12.00 to 15.00	to	12.00 to 15.00	10.00 to 12.50	" Longiflorum	to 12.50	2.00 to 4.00	to	to
2.00 to 4.00	3.00 to 4.00	3.00 to 4.00	to 4.00	1.00 to 2.00	LILY OF THE VALLEY	to	1.00 to 2.00	2.00 to 4.00	to
to	to	to	to	2.00 to 2.50	MIGNONETTE, ordinary	to	to	to	to
to	to	to	to	to	" fancy	to	to	to	to
to	to	4.00 to 8.00	to	to	PEONIES	to	15.00 to 20.00	to	to
10.00 to 12.50	to 15.00	12.50 to 15.00	to 15.00	12.50 to 20.00	SMILAX	to 15.00	to	12.50 to 15.00	to 12.50
to	to	to	to	to	VIOLETS, ordinary	to	to	to	to
to	to	to	to	to	" fancy	to	to	to	to
to	to	to	to	to	NARCISSUS	to	to	to	to
.20 to .25	.15 to .25	.50 to .75	to	.20 to .35	SWEET PEAS	.25 to .50	to .50	.10 to .50	to
to	to	to	to	to		to	to	to	to
to	to	to	to	to		to	to	to	to

Davenport, Ia.

The Tri-city Florists' Club met at Fjervary park in Davenport, recently and discussed the chrysanthemum. John T. Temple was named as delegate to represent the association at the next national convention of the Society of American Florists, which will be held at Dayton, O., during the week of August 26. At the national convention this year it is probable that the society will become affiliated with the Society of American Florists. Luncheon followed the business meeting at the park.

The News.

The junior member of the Stuppy Floral Company of St. Joseph, Mo., was a recent visitor.

W. G. Mathews and his foreman were in the city last week.

William A. Peterson is expected to return from his recent sojourn in Europe within a few days.

Louis Wittbold has received this Summer some very encouraging patronage in connection with his new watering system, and reports from places where it has been tried are universal in their commendatory nature. The even and excellent condition of the crops at the Wittbold establishment, where the system is thoroughly inaugurated, seem convincing beyond peradventure of the practicability of the invention.

Philadelphia.

H. Bayersdorfer & Company have for several years been handicapped for want of room and while they have from time to time rented additional warehouses near by, it was rather inconvenient, so in order to overcome this, and also to keep up with the march of progress, they have this week rented the five story building, 1129 Arch street, where they will have five floors each 29 by 135 feet. It will probably be two months before they can occupy the building, as it has to be fitted up for their requirements. Electric elevators will be installed and a lot of work done on the fifth floor, which will be used as a factory. The firm will retain some of their present quarters, to be used for storage purposes.

DAVID RUST.

FIRMS WHO ARE BUILDING

EAST MANSFIELD, MASS.—John W. Conrod is erecting a new greenhouse 147x30 feet. He is also adding a 50 foot addition to another house.

American Carnations—An Australian Criticism.

A recent contributor to the "Sydney Morning Herald" says that "the great impetus given to carnation-growing in America was due to the formation of a Carnation Society." What nonsense! The "impetus" comes from the public demand for something in the way of floral decorations for the season when flowers are of the greater value. The formation of a society came as an after-thought. The demand brought the society into existence, the society did not create the demand.

The presence of thousands of carnation ranges (the glass houses for Winter propagation of these flowers are called by this name) all over the States and Canada is the result of having found a type of flower that suits the public eye. Connoisseurs are not called in to "tivitate" the petals, or to put "paper collars" and "bangles'" on the many thousands of blooms sent in from these immense establishments. The flowers are just as Nature made them. They stand or fall on their own stems, and with their own petal arrangement, and their own perfume, three qualities which some of our "over-boomed" Colonial varieties know little of.

Further on in the article the contributor makes another stumble tilting "blind-eye" at the edge of the flowers which our "cousins" seem to prefer. Here it is: "The society by holding its shows at such a period of the year (the exhibitions are all held in Midwinter), must naturally bring the American carnation only before the public, thereby suppressing any taste for the refined type of the English flower, with its smooth-edged petal, being engendered."

The carnation exhibitions are held in Midwinter purposely to demonstrate the possibilities of the various flowers.

Where is the sense in growing flowers when even the novice has his yard full? American growers are a little more "slick" than the "Herald" contributor imagines. They are open-minded business people who know when a flower harvest is of the greatest value. Their concern lies mostly in producing carnations that are to pass muster on the tables of the people, carnations that are to give pleasure to the milk-maid or the millionaire; carnations that are hardy, and perfumy, even if they are a little serrated on the edge!

The English shell-petalled flower is an obsolete form as far as trade purposes go. It would have passed "out into the night" long ago, had it not been cleverly engineered, and manipulated to such an extent that "its own mother wouldn't know it."

Further on in the same article, another blunder. "American raisers have two methods of introducing new varieties into commerce, viz., "Boom method," and the "business method," etc.

We have not room to reprint all this paragraph, but we just have time to say that quite a number of our Sydney growers have, to our knowledge, done quite as much booming in their own small way as any American firm. And often with varieties that have not lived a year! If they could get the ear of the press they would do so still.

The article to which we refer was written to decry the American and to bolster up something raised in the Commonwealth. Being Australian, we are fond of our own; but we don't let our fondness blind our eyes and heads at the same time. Neither do we forget our common sense, or parade our prejudices.

There's nothing in Australia to compare with the big carnation movement that has taken place in America, and is now taking place in England. Readers of "The Amateur Gardener" know what we have said about the triumph of the American. Our small voice has always gone out in favor of the utility flower. It always will.

Instead of the carnation being in the ascendant, it is losing ground. Three years ago 500 plants were sold where 20 are sold now! All around the trade the story is the same. "We are tired of the carnation, as the Carnation Society knows it," has been, and is still, the burden of the nurseryman's complaint. The "faking" had killed that type of flower. Our public is now too wise to be led after the "sublime and heavenly bedder, or so-called 'perpetual' that require a lot of handling." Every trade grower to whom we have spoken has told us the same story. This is not imagination; it is plain, hard fact. The day of the dresser is done, and the winter-blooming varieties are what we want.

Winter-bloomers, you know, are quite often good spring-bloomers as well. You have just to make up your mind as to which season you want them to flower, and to grow them accordingly. For Winter flowers the propagating must be done not later than November. Get the layers or cuttings attended to at the time the other plants are in bloom, and you will get flowers when the "Springs" and "hybrid" perpetuals are idling.

For a good Winter flower we have never seen any thing in Colonials to compare with a bright scarlet self raised by Mr. Weston, gardener at Admiralty House. On Monday, June 18th, we saw fully a hundred nice plants in the garden borders, and saw hundreds of opening and fully opened flowers. Mr. Weston assures us that he has cut fully seventy dozen blooms from that hundred plants during the last two months. This statement is absolute truth, and not "boom" bosh. Other so-called good cold-season flowers were growing in company with the scarlet, but they did not show the same free-blooming habit. There are doubtless very many fine but these fine things are not grown purposely to things among the varieties sent out by our growers, bloom at this season of the year.

And yet some of our folk think they can teach Uncle Jonathan's carnationists points! Possibly they can, but it will be in holding great opinions of little things. But we are a lot younger than the Americans. Some day we may think and act as men.

Let us tell you of another experience. At Croydon, in the nursery of H. Gazzard, we saw several of the much-maligned serrated-edge flowers. One, a sweetly pretty pink, was quite "O. K." The edge neither kept it from growing nor from flowering. It will not be long before Mr. Gazzard has a big stock of the American forms. In the corner of one of his houses we saw the beginning of the stock which will soon be increased to supply the demands of the flower-loving, but not flower-faking, people.

Just to end this carnation talk, let us tell you that the carnation dressing began something like 80 years ago with one named Kit, who was eminent for his skill in dressing wigs as well as flowers. Kit, in the season, had as many applications to dress flowers as to dress heads, and it is humorously told of him that he "could both shave and lay a carnation with the greatest nicety."

Christopher Nunn was also an artist in this work. "The novices of garden work, who trusted to Dame Nature to open, expand, and perfect their flowers, were no match for Nunn, for he began where she left off, and perfected what she had left imperfect. His arrangements of the petals was admirable." No doubt it was. So are the "arrangements' that one meets at every November exhibition of the Carnation Society. If the society is to live, it must take a firm stand against the abuses which have reduced its membership to the present low ebb (28 is the last C. S. roll-call); it must look with broadened mind upon the advancements which have been made abroad; it must tell the full story every time one of its members sets out to enlighten the morning paper readers in regard to the ways of the useful carnation, and it should try and stop thinking that flowers raised by men and women outside the "pale" are valueless.

Looking matters fairly in the face, we ask what influence can be exerted by any society of 28, when the members are divided into two or three sections? The carnation tug-of-war has gone on for six years; by the end of another six the old rope will not be able to stand the strain. Possibly an infusion of some new "fringe-edged members" would leaven and liven the carnation lump.—The Amateur Gardener, Australia.

Wholesale Prices of Cut Flowers, Chicago, Aug. 22, 1906.

Prices quoted are by the hundred unless otherwise noted.

ROSES — American Beauty			
36-inch stems .... per doz.		to	4.00
30-inch stems .... "		to	3.00
24-inch stems .... "		to	2.50
20-inch stems .... "		to	2.00
18-inch stems .... "		to	1.50
12-inch stems .... "		to	1.00
8-inch stems and shorts "	.50	to	.75
Bride Maid, fancy special	5.00	to	6.00
" extra	4.00	to	5.00
" No. 1	2.00	to	3.00
" No. 2	.50	to	1.00
Golden Gate	2.00	to	6.00
Carnot	2.00	to	6.00
Uncle John	2.00	to	8.00
Liberty	2.00	to	8.00
Richmond	2.00	to	8.00
Kaiserina	2.00	to	8.00
Killarney	3.00	to	8.00
Perle	2.00	to	6.00
Chatenay	2.00	to	6.00
Orchids—Cattleyas		to	50.00
SMILAX	8.00	to	12.00
LILY OF THE VALLEY	2.00	to	4.00
SWEET PEAS	.25	to	.50

CARNATIONS				
Inferior grades all colors		.25	to	.50
STANDARD VARIETIES	White	.75	to	1.00
	Pink	.75	to	1.00
	Red	.75	to	1.00
	Yellow & var.	.75	to	1.00
*FANCY (The highest grades of Sta'd var)	White	1.50	to	2.00
	Pink	1.50	to	2.00
	Red	1.50	to	2.00
	Yellow & var.	1.50	to	2.00
NOVELTIES			to	
ADIANTUM		.50	to	1.00
ASPARAGUS, Plum. & Ten.		.35	to	.50
" Sprengeri, bunches		.35	to	.50
GLADIOLUS		2.00	to	6.00
LILIES, Longiflorum		8.00	to	12.00
HARRISII		8.00	to	12.00
AURATUM		6.00	to	8.00
NYMPHAEA			to	1.00
MIGNONETTE, ordinary		1.00	to	2.00
TUBEROSES, SPIKES		4.00	to	8.00
			to	
			to	
HARDY FERNS per 1000		1.00	to	1.5
GALAX "		1.00	to	1.20
ASTERS		.50	to	1.00

Lenox, (Mass.)

LENOX (MASS.) HORTICULTURAL SOCIETY.—The Lenox Horticultural Society held their exhibition of annuals and perennials in the Lenox town hall, Wednesday, August 15.

This was the best Summer exhibition in the history of the society. The hall was filled to the doors. Particularly fine were the collections of phlox decussata, there being upwards of 60 varieties shown, and all excellent varieties. All the classes for annuals and perennials was filled.

M. T. Reynolds, gardener to Mrs. Edith Wharton, won in the class for twenty varieties of annuals. Mr. Reynolds has won this class for three years successively.

R. Spears, gardener to Mrs. John Parsons, won in the class for twenty varieties of perennials, among which were Stenanthium robustum, Spirea davidiana, Rudbeckia maxima, Rudbeckia pupurea, Funkia subcordata gradniflora and Helianthus dowelliana. In sweet peas, Thos. Proctor, gardener to R. W. Patterson, was the principal exhibitor, who had some remarkably fine flowers.

In vegetables, F. Hareman, gardener to W. D. Sloane; and A. H. Wingett, gardener to Chas. Lanier, were first in their respective classes.

Mrs. W. B. O. Field won the table decoration (ladies' class) with dark blue Larkspur.

The following is the list of special awards: First class certificate to A. H. Wingett for new dahlia, Chas. Lanier; this is a fine dahlia, its color is apricot yellow, and it is a very large flower. First class certificate to M. T. Reynolds for seedling Phlox. This is a white Phlox of extra large size, with a blush pink eye. First class certificate to S. Carlquist for Rubus rosaefolius (strawberry and raspberry.)

The following were awarded diplomas: E. J. Norman for exhibit of berries; D. Dunn for exhibit of potted plants; A. Jenkins for collection of perennials; W. D. Curtis for collection of phlox; Geo. W. Folsom for Lilium auratum. Messrs. Geo. Thompson and A. G. Loveless were the judges.

GEO. FOULSHAM, Sec.

LEE, ILL.—The address of J. L. Lutz, Sr., has been changed from this town to Steward, R. F. D., Route 1. Lee County, Ill. All mail directed to Mr. Lutz should be addressed accordingly.

PITTSBURG, PA.—E. C. Ludwig and wife attended the convention of the Eagles at Milwaukee, Wis., going thence to the S. A. F. convention at Dayton, O.

Chicago.

To-day (Saturday) Miss Bertha Hurz and Charles Hollenback, will be married at the home of the brides' parents. It is needless to say that the best wishes of all in the trade surround them.

Charles Schneider, of the Central Floral Company, has been attracting a great deal of interest at his recently acquired store on State street, by the originality of his window designs. For the past two weeks or more these have been composed of many forms of our beautiful native flowers, which, it seems, are unknown to the urban population.

On Sunday last, an original advertising idea was propounded, three thousand specimens of Liatris Spicata with the common names of Button-Snakeroot or Blazing-Star and the advertisement of the concern, all printed on a small card and attached were distributed to all comers, resulting in a bargain counter rush which in one or two cases, came near proving perilous and, while the writer stood a few minutes on Monday, it was most interesting to see the young and the old come up and ask questions about "the wild flowers.

Edward Reiss, of Terre Haute, Ind. was a recent visitor.

A. B. Haven, representing the Haven Seed Company of Lodi, California, spent a few days in Chicago last week.

Last Saturday we had as callers Mr. N. B. Stover of the Grandeville Floral Co. of Grandeville, Mich., accompanied by Mrs. Stover and son.

Mr. and Mrs. Newberry of Mitchell, So. Dakota, spent last week in the Garden City of the West.

Bassett & Washburn's Beauties have taken advantage of the cool season and are now presenting themselves in a far advanced condition compared to preceding seasons.

O. P. Bassett, who is a most enthusiastic automboilist, notwithstanding the fact that he is one tenth of a decade beyond the allotted three score years and ten, sarted on his machine on Friday of last week for a 500 mile spin of ten days duration, into farthest Wisconsin.

Scheiden & Schoos, of Evanston, have leased the space in the Flower Growers' Market recently vacated by John Krachten and on which his lease expires in September, for the purpose of selling their own stock and doing a general commission business.

The Foley Mfg. Company is offering a free souvenir to all who cut out the coupon attached to the firm's advertisement in this issue of The Florists' Exchange and fill in their name and address, together with the amount of glass operated.

W. K. WOOD.

New York.

Between forty and fifty people left here over the Grand Central Railroad on Monday afternoon to attend the Convention of the S. A. F. O. H. at Dayton, Ohio. The day was warm and sultry, but the committee had provided plenty of refreshments, and no doubt weather conditions were soon forgotten after the different packages were opened and distributed among the travelers.

Mr. and Mrs. W. H. Elliott, of Brighton, Mass., came to New York on Monday, and joined the New York delegation on its journey to Dayton, O.

The retail trade throughout the city is rather quiet just now, the only work that seems to be going on is for funeral purposes.

John Lewis Childs, Floral Park, N. Y., has just made a generous gift in the shape of a check to pay for the new Womens' Building that is being erected on the Fair Grounds at Riverhead, L. I.

Mrs. U. G. Scollay, wife of U. G. Scollay, so well known to our readers through his communications on heating problems, recently lost two valuable diamond rings from their residence, 315 Greene Avenue, Brooklyn. The matter was placed in the hands of detectives with the result that the rings were found in a pawn shop, and where also it was learned that the rings had been brought there by a negro. Arrest of the negro who runs the elevator in the residence followed.

The will of the well-known florist, James Weir, who died recently has just been filed for probate. Mr. Weir was known as James Weir, Jr. With the petition for its probate there was filed no schedule of the value of the estate, but it is believed to be considerable.

By the terms of the will the widow Margaret A. Weir, gets the property at 236 Twenty-fifth street, Brooklyn, the household effects and $5,000. All the remaining estate is given to the four children, who are to pay their mother $2,500 a year for life. Specific bequests of $5,000 are made to the daughters, and the son, James E. Weir, is given the property at 228 Twenty-fifth street, Brooklyn. The son is also given the opportunity to purchase the good will of the florist business for $30,000 and have 10 years in which to pay for it. The widow and son are named as executors.

Louis F. S. Hess, College Point, N. Y., has obtained the contract to erect three greenhouses for W. Finger, Bayside, N. Y.; also for the erection of several greenhouses at Long Branch, N. J.

C. Bonnet of the firm of Bonnet & Blake, wholesale florists of Brooklyn, left on Saturday for a two weeks' vecation.

J. Nash of the firm of Moore, Hentz & Nash, wholesale florists, is taking a vacation at Asbury Park, N. J.

A. Hansen, seed grower of Copenhagen, Denmark was a visitor this week.

San Francisco.

News Items.

With upward of four square miles burned out of the center of this great harbor town it is now a distinctly trisected community, with retail business centers of activity in Valencia and Mission streets on the South Side. Fillmore and Divisedero streets on the West Side and Van Ness avenue and Polk streets on the North Side. Oakland, seven miles across the bay, with its two hundred thousand inhabitants, is the [illegible] Side. Before the burning the West Side was outfitted with flower stores inferior to those in all other sections of city. It then had but three. Now it is more numerously supplied than any other part of this trisected city the number being nine. The first one of the burnt-out florists to re-establish on the West Side was Alex. Mann, Jr., the "West Side Florist," who, according to what I read of him in a daily paper this week, guess he is all right. This is the daily paper item referred to:

"Alexander Mann will be the owner of a three-story store and hotel building which will be built on the South side of Post street, east of Fillmore. It will cover a lot 100x137 feet, and cost in the neighborhood of $32,000."

The near approaching season of expected good cheer for San Francisco and round the bay florists started auspiciously in Oakland this week with the swell wedding of Miss Emelie Louise Chamberlain and Dr. Howard J. Lackey, son of the late Alfred Lackey, who with the late Senator Fair and other smart financiers harvested untold millons in the flush days of the Comstock mines, and with other nabobs subsequently, built the million-dollar homes on Nob Hill that helped illuminate the sky at the time of the city's late disaster. A nice amount of this Comstock wealth came down through a natural inheritance course and made Oakland's swell wedding scene this week a veritable bower of huckleberry and costly flowers, pink blossoms and greenery, a combination so popular with brides this Summer, predominating. It is a picturesque chruch scene, and all credit for the superb decoration is due Manager John M. Holland and assistants, of the Oakland store of "Gill, the Florist."

Five new creations, the work of Luther Burbank, are announced this week as prepared for the market, and according to a bulletin received by Professor E. J. Wickson of the Department of Agriculture at the State University, will be commonly grown within a year. The new plants are listed in a catalogue just issued by Burbank and his experiments have been carried on on such large plans that a stock of seeds of the new creations has been prepared and will be at once placed on the market. The first and most wonderful of the new creations is the improved Australian star flower, a variety of unusual beauty and color, and is of the nature of the old-fashioned everlasting flowers. The Shirley poppy, a new variety of which has been named the Santa Rosa strain, is an enlargement of the regular cultivated poppy which is commonly grown in California gardens. It is larger and more beautiful than anything which has ever been offered, and the colors, particularly, are blended in a new manner. The California wind poppy is another variety of the common cultivated poppy, differing slightly from the Shirley poppy. The Heuchera cristata is a new foliage plant, which is considered by Burbank one of the most wonderful of his creations. It has large leaves of peculiar shape and brilliancy, and is one of the most striking foliage plants known. The Patagonia vegetable squash is a variety of garden vegetable which has been imported from Chili by Burbank and greatly improved. It is an apple shaped squash, very sweet to the taste, and is expected to be a favorite garden squash. ALVIN.

SAN FRANCISCO.—It really is too bad that since so large a portion of beautiful San Francisco was made desolate, the city has lost by departure tens of thousands of good citizens. And now another one of this class of long-time residents is going to leave us; and florists tell me if they learn the date of his departure for New York, his section of the overland car will be profusely decorated with flowers.

The news this week is that William J. Dingee, a Golden Gate Park Commissioner, has bought for more than $1,000,000 the palatial residence at 855 Fifth Avenue, New York, and that he will take up his home there within the next few weeks.

A few weeks ago this department of The Florists' Exchange noted that Mr. Dingee's home conservatories of rare plants and fancy blooms was a choice visiting spot in San Francisco; that his boyhood training was in the West Grove, (Penn.) Nurseries, so much advertised even to this day in The Florists' Exchange; and it was incidentally noted that he had just then sold his controlling interest in the Oakland Water Works Company for $11,000,000. Prominent florists say that Mr. Dingee was never known to pass their stands without buying a fine bunch of flowers, and that he passed them very often, particularly since the earthquake fire.

ALVIN.

NEW BEDFORD, MASS.—The past week saw a little spurt in the cut flower business, funeral work being chiefly the cause of this. Stock is none too plentiful, but in a few days, there will be plenty of asters in bloom. A good many of the growers here lost almost their entire crop during the wet weather, disease being very prevalent. Asters bring 35c. per dozen; carnations same price; the few that are being brought in are of fair quality. Wm. Livesey is still cutting good Fair Maid. Roses are very scarce just now, until the new plants come into bloom.

E. Y. Pierce's new house of roses is

E. T. Pierce's new house of roses is coming along well; he has planted Bride, Bridesmaid, Richmond and a few American Beauty. Mr. Pierce has housed some of his young carnation plants; his Boston Market are looking fine.

R. H. Woodhouse has also commenced to house his plants; he is putting on an addition to his residence.

Joe Pierce, grower for E. Y. Pierce, has gone on a two weeks' vacation; he will visit places in New Hampshire.

The Horticultural Society held its monthly meeting August 18. The subject for the evening was "The Dahlia."

Most of the florists here have sown their pansy seed and everyone is busy making preparations for the coming season which it is hoped will be a prosperous one.

E. S. Haskell had a reception decoration on August 11 at Nonquitt a Summer resort. HORTICO.

St. Paul.

J. W. Hoffman, manager of L. L. May & Co's retail department, in company with Gus. Colberg, of the Swanson Floral Co., left for Dayton, Ohio, Saturday, Aug. 18, to attend the convention of the S. A. F. O. H.

C. L. Reese, of the Reese Floral Co. of Springfield, Ohio, was in town and called on the leading dealers.

C. F. Vogt has been kept very busy with funeral work; stock is cheap, and prices on that kind of work is kept up nicely, so that the profits are very good.

Holm & Olson, intend moving into their new store the coming week, they have ordered some very fine fixtures, including an ice box, 30 feet long. PAUL.

Hydrangea Otaksa.

(34) I have Hydrangea otaksa, just given a needed shift into 5-inch from 4-inch pots. The plants have strong single stem 8 to 10 inches high. Will these produce only one flower? Can they yet be cut back to branch for more flowers? Will they need a shift when bringing them in to force for Easter and later? A. M. B.

—The hydrangeas should have been pinched back in the early stages of their growth so as to have developed several shoots. To do this now would spoil them for flowering next Spring. There will be but one flower to each stem; and if the plants have been recently repotted, there will be no need to give them another shift when started next year.

Callas, Geraniums.

(35) Can I, without doing harm, cut off a part of calla bulbs when planting, as they are too long for a 6-inch pot?

I send you a few geraniums leaves and would like to know the cause of the trouble which affects them. The plants are outside and grew well for sometime. W. A. P.

Mass.

—Where the calla tubers are very large, a part of the lower portion can be cut away without doing injury.

The geranium leaves seem to have suffered from dry weather only. Picking off the dead leaves and supplying the plants with water during dry times will no doubt bring the plants along all right.

Grasshoppers Eating Carnations.

(36) Please tell me what kind of a bug, or worm it is, that is eating the ends of my carnation plants. The plants are in the field, and a great many of them are like the sample enclosed. A. B. C.

New York.

—The carnation tips seem to have been eaten by grasshoppers.

Mignonette Following Asters.

(37) We have a house of asters just beginning to bloom, and they ought to be out of the way in four weeks time. We want to put in mignonette after they are gone. Now if we sow the seed in the bed, will it bloom in time to get a good paying crop; or would it be better to sow now in pots, and plant in as soon as the asters are out of the way?

New York. X. Y. Z.

—We would sow the mignonette at this time, two or three seeds together in thumb pots, then plant in the benches whenever space in the latter was available.

Shasta Daisies.

(38) When can Shasta daisies be divided? E. S.

—Early in the Spring will be the best time to divide the clumps of the Shasta daisies.

Plants for Spring and Summer Sales.

(39) Name a few plants suitable for Spring or early Summer sales that can be started now from seeds and wintered in cold frames or hot beds? SOUTHERN OHIO.

—A few things that could be started now and be useful for next Spring and Summer sales are pansies, antirrhinum, hollyhock, and Dianthus barbatus.

Plants to Follow Late 'Mums.

(40) Could you advise me what to plant in benches to follow late chrysanthemums, and to be off before third week in March—something to flower, suitable for a retail florist. Please state when to sow seed, etc.

Ohio. C. S. B.

—The best things we could recommend for filling the greenhouse space for such a short period would be verbenas or similar soft wooded plants. These if sown late in December or early in January, would by the middle of March be salable for Spring bedding, and could be cleared out timely for that purpose.

Carnations Drying Up.

(41) My carnations in the field seem to be drying up: leaves turning brown at the bottom and continuing doing so until they die. I have examined them carefully, and can find no cause. The ground is not dry, as we have had lots of rain. The plants just look as if they had been burned or scalded. I have never had an experience like this before.

New Jersey. E. N. C.

—The trouble with the carnations in the field, from the description given, is evidently stem rot, for which we know of no remedy.

Cincinnati.

CINCINNATI.—S. Skidelsky was here Friday, and many others are expected on Sunday, Monday and Tuesday. Everybody in Cincinnati who is a florist will not be at home on Tuesday, August 21; their address will be Dayton, O.

The Convention Number of The Florists' Exchange has just arrived, and its a dandy. Can any florist read that number without wishing he or she were a member of the S. A. F. O. H. if they are not already a member?

Business is very summerish.

Visitors in town: Geo. F. Crabb, Grand Rapids, Mich.

E. G. GILLETT.

CHANGES IN BUSINESS.

MORRISON, ILL.—The C. D. Gallentine Company has been incorporated to operate greenhouses; capital $30,000. Incorporators: Charles D. Gallentine, Joseph J. Gallentine, Olive D. Gallentine.

YOUNGSTOWN, O.—The Templin Company, who for years have conducted a seed business and greenhouses at Calla, has purchased the old stand of the Walker-McLean Company, which for some time has been in the hands of a receiver. The Templin Company will make this city their headquarters in the future, and will also have their shipping point here. The company has carried on a mail order business of wonderful proportions, and intends sending out 500,000 catalogues this season.

MILWAUKEE, WIS.—Clyde Young, of Washington, Ia., has bought a greenhouse plant in North Milwaukee, and will shortly take possession of same.

SEATTLE, WASH.—The Washington Floral Company has been incorporated with a capital of $25,000, by Christian Hoffmeister, K. L. Arnold and W. H. White.

Los Angeles, Cal.

The attendance at the last monthly meeting of our Horticultural Society was small, yet considerable interest was taken in the address given by our aquatic plant grower, E. D. Sturtevant, who illustrated his lecture by specimens from his pond—nymphæas, nelumbiums, saggitarias and Eichhornia azurea. The writer displayed some cutflowers of Stigmaphyllon ciliatum, Crassulas coccinea and falcata, Lobelias cardinalis and Queen Victoria and a branch of Melaleuca acuminata from a tree 20 feet high with as much spread of top. Such exhibits as these give lovers of plants and flowers a better idea of their forms and colors than is possible to obtain from illustrated, printed descriptions.

A discussion of the premium list for the next flower show brought out some helpful suggestions to the committee who has that matter in charge. The president announced that there would be no cash prizes given at this exhibition of Southern California products but that quite a number of fine cups, donated by public spirited citizens, will be the awards for the best displays in the different classes.

Fred. Howard of Howard & Smith, has gone to Europe to study plant life there and the methods of growers over the sea. If he finds any novelties which he thinks will suit our climate he will bring them along. His purpose also is to visit the principal firms of the Atlantic States and learn how they do plants there. Climatic conditions, however, are so vastly different in the two sections of the country—the Atlantic and Pacific coast—that what will succeed in the one may be a failure in the other.

Clerodendron fragrans is one of our most desirable flowering shrubs. The foliage is like that of the catalpa. The flowers are very double, pure white or with a peach blossom color, very fragrant; borne in corymbs four inches in diameter, on the point of the new growth.

The tensile strength of Phormium tenax is something amazing. The leaves grow from 4 to 6 feet long and could be used by nurserymen as a substitute for twine, in tying small bundles of stock. It propagates easily from seed or divisions of the plant. Why it should be called New Zeland flax is one of the mysteries of plant nomenclature, since it bears no resemblance whatever to the Linum family.

Lobelia Queen Victoria has proven to be the best of all the scarlet flowering varieties tried here. The flowers are not so numerous as on cardinalis but very much larger, and more brilliant. The dark bronze colored stalks and foliage add to its effect among ferns and light colored foliage plants.

P. D. BARNHART.

SAGINAW, MICH.—The florist business has made more progress in Saginaw the past ten years than almost any other line, not only in volume but in quality of product. The William Roethke Floral Co., which is just completing new and commodious greenhouses, will cut the popular carnation from 32,000 new plants, and 22,000 chrysanthemum plants and 22,000 roses will help supply the demand of Saginaw and other parts of the State during the coming Fall and Winter. The season has been a good one for the growing of most plants that florists cultivate.

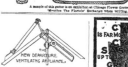

H AND C O

SUDDEN CHANGES

are severe tests on a boiler. A change of, say, 10 or 15 degrees colder in an hour—a change that your boiler must meet promptly and without endless shaking and poking—without an extravagant coal consumption—the Hitching Boilers are made that way—the right way for greenhouse boilers.

HITCHINGS & COMPANY

GREENHOUSE DESIGNERS AND BUILDERS

Manufacturers of Heating and Ventilating Apparatus

1170 Broadway - - New York

H AND C O

Mention The Florists' Exchange when writing.

Not Luck or "Happen So"

has been responsible for the remarkable growth of our business and given us so large a number of satisfied customers. It is not the result of getting promiscuous orders here, there, anywhere, anyhow—all profit or no profit at all—it is clearly due to the high quality of our material and the "square deal." Please bear in mind that of the forty years we have been in this business every one has seen an increase of orders. The manufacture of greenhouse material is our whole business—not a side line. We print this in the hope that you will inquire further. Our catalogue will be sent if you are interested.

John C. Moninger Co., Chicago

115 E. BLACKHAWK STREET

Mention The Florists' Exchange when writing.

GREENHOUSE LUMBER

BUILD WELL

There is a pleasant sense of satisfaction in knowing that when your order for Cypress is placed with us you will receive material upon which you can absolutely rely, and that shipment will be promptly made.

ESTIMATES AND PLANS

Furnished without charge. Let us hear from you if you contemplate building.

HOT BED SASH

CEDAR POSTS, IRON FITTINGS, ETC., ETC.

LOCKLAND LUMBER Co.

LOCKLAND, O.

KROESCHELL BROS. CO.

IMPROVED

Greenhouse Boiler

33 ERIE STREET, CHICAGO

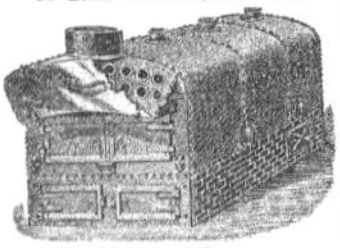

Boilers made of the best of material, shell firebox sheets and heads of steel, water space all around front, sides and back). Write for information.

SUMMER IN WINTER

BY USING

Standard Greenhouse Boilers

One cent gets our Catalog

GIBLIN & CO., UTICA, N. Y.

HEATING

THE GREENHOUSE

thoroughly and economically during the coming Winter is the problem now engrossing the mind of the Florist who takes time by the forelock.

I am in a position to help you to the best solution of this problem, I have done it for others, I can do it for you.

It will be to your advantage to consult me and get quotations on your heating plant either erected complete or for material ready for erection.

I have the largest line of greenhouse boilers on the market and can give prompt shipments.

WRITE ME TO-DAY

John A. Payne

Horticultural Architect and Builder

33 Clendenny Ave.

JERSEY CITY, N. J.

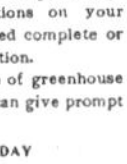

Sash opening apparatus and all kinds of greenhouse structural material.

THE AMERICAN CARNATION

Price $3.50

A. T. DE LA MARE PTG & PUB CO. LTD

2-8 Duane Street, New York.

The Best Advertisement

is to furnish the best grade of material at reasonable prices.

That's what causes the constant growth of our business.

La. Cypress and Washington Red Cedar

GREENHOUSE MATERIAL.

GREENHOUSE HARDWARE AND POSTS.

A. DIETSCH CO., 615 Sheffield Ave., CHICAGO.

THE JENNINGS IMPROVED IRON GUTTER

PATENT IRON BENCH FITTINGS AND ROOF SUPPORTS. VENTILATING APPARATUS. IMPROVED VAPORIZING PANS for Tobacco Extracts, Etc.

SEND FOR CIRCULARS

DILLER, CASKEY & CO.

Successors to JENNINGS BROS

S. W. CORNER SIXTH AND BERK STS., PHILADELPHIA, PA.

TILE DRAINED LAND IS MORE PRODUCTIVE

Earliest and easiest worked. Carries off surplus water; admits air to the soil. Increases the value. Acres of swampy land reclaimed and made fertile. Jackson's Round Drain Tile meets every requirement. We also make Sewer Pipe, Red and Fire Brick, Chimney Tops, Encaustic Side Walk Tile, etc. Write for what you want and prices. JOHN H. JACKSON, 50 Third Ave., Albany, N.Y.

Scollay Boilers

Hot Water and Steam

6 Patterns, Made in 60 Various Sizes. Capacities 150 to 10,000 Square Feet Heating Surface

Cast Iron Greenhouse Pipe

Special Cast Iron Greenhouse Pipe Fittings

Expansion Tanks, Stop Valves, etc.

Wrought Iron Pipe and Fittings of all Sizes

Brass Valves of any Description

...FULL LINE OF...

Engineers' Supplies Tools, Etc.

From Wm. H. Maher, Florist
Newport, R. I.

"The Scollay Boiler put in on March 19th was to replace one put in by you in **1876**. The old boiler was used each year, for about eight months, and has proved to be a very good one." The above boiler was in use nearly **30 years.** This speaks for itself.

John A. Scollay

U. G. Scollay
Manager

Hot Water and Steam Heating Engineer and Contractor

LONG DISTANCE TELEPHONE 1492-1493 MAIN

72-76 Myrtle Avenue, Borough of Brooklyn, New York City

Mention The Florists' Exchange when writing.

THE FLORISTS' EXCHANGE

We are a straight shoot and aim to grow into a vigorous plant

A WEEKLY MEDIUM OF INTERCHANGE FOR FLORISTS, NURSERYMEN, SEEDSMEN AND THE TRADE IN GENERAL

Vol. XXII. No. 9 | NEW YORK AND CHICAGO, SEPTEMBER 1, 1906 | One Dollar Per Year

CONTENTS AND INDEX TO ADVERTISERS. PAGE 257

LABOR DAY ITEMS

	100	1000
Narcissus Paper White	$1.75	$9.00
Lilium Candidum, extra forcing bulbs	6.00	50.00
Lilium Longiflorum Jap. 6 to 8	3.00	24.00
Lilium Longiflorum Jap. 7 to 9	4.50	40.00
Lilium Longiflorum Multiflorum Jap. 6 to 8	3.50	30.00
Lilium Longiflorum Multiflorum Jap. 7 to 9	5.00	45.00
Freesias, selected French	.75	6.00
White Romans, 11 to 12 cmt	2.25	18.00
White Romans, 12 to 15 cmt	2.50	22.00
Harrisii, 5 to 7 cmt	3.75	35.00
Canes, 6 to 9 ft		6.00

Cineraria, choice mixed, Williams, tr. pkt. 50c.
Calceolaria, choice mixed, Williams, tr. pkt. 50c.
Pansy Rainbow, blended, tr. pkt. $1.00.
Primula Sinensis, ⅛ tr. pkt. 50c.

Wm. Elliott & Sons, 201 Fulton Street New York

Mention The Florists' Exchange when writing.

C. C. MORSE & CO.

SEED GROWERS

171-173 Clay St., San Francisco, California

OUR SPECIALTIES

ONION LETTUCE SWEET PEAS

Also Carrot, Celery, Celeriac, Cucumber, Endive, Leek, Mustard, Parsley, Parsnip, Radish, Salsify, Spinach, Tomato and

FLOWER SEEDS

Growers for the trade on contract. Warehouses at Santa Clara; Farms and Farm headquarters Carnadero, near Gilroy.

Registered Cable Address: MORSEED, SAN FRANCISCO.

Mention The Florists' Exchange when writing.

PACIFIC SEED GROWERS' CO.

109 MARKET STREET
SAN FRANCISCO, CAL.
Specialties:
Onion, Carrot, Lettuce, Sweet Peas

Mention The Florists' Exchange when writing.

PEONIES

Strong plants, with 5 to 6 eyes, ready for shipment about September 10th.

	Each	Doz.
Agida	$ .20	$ 2.00
Canary	.50	5.00
Festiva Maxima	.50	4.00
Fragrans	.25	2.75
Hamlet	.20	2.00
Humei Carnea	.40	4.00
Lady Leon Bramwell	.50	5.00
Mary Lemoine	1.00	10.00
Mme. Calot	.20	2.00
Theo. Roosevelt	2.00	20.00
Queen Victoria	.25	2.75
Richardson's Rubra Superba	.40	4.00

WHITE ROMAN HYACINTHS

	Per 100	Per 1000
11x15	$2.25	$20.00
12x15	2.60	22.00
13x15	3.00	27.50
15 & up	4.00	38.00
BLUE ROMAN HYACINTHS	2.60	22.50
Pink " "	2.50	22.50
Dark Rose " "	2.75	25.00
White Italian "	2.50	22.50

NARCISSUS

Paper White Grandiflora (1250 to case)	1.00	9.00
Trumpet Major French	1.00	9.00
Jonquils Campernelles	.65	5.50
Double Roman	1.00	9.00
LILIUM HARRISII, 5x7	6.00	43.50
" " 6x7	6.50	60.00
" CANDIDUM 24 cmt	7.00	65.00
" " 22 "	6.00	55.00
FREESIA BULBS, 4½ cmt	.80	7.00
" " 5½ "	1.00	9.00
ORNITHOGALUM ARABICUM	1.50	12.00

STUMPP & WALTER CO.

50 Barclay St., NEW YORK

Mention The Florists' Exchange when writing.

Thorburn's Bulbs

HYACINTHS, TULIPS, NARCISSUS, CROCUS, LILIES and all other BULBS for FLORISTS

Send for our Wholesale Florists' Bulb List Now Ready.

J. M. THORBURN & CO.

33 BARCLAY ST., through to 32 PARK PLACE

NEW YORK

Mention The Florists' Exchange when writing.

MY GIANT CYCLAMEN

Are Ahead in Growth and Flowers

Bloodred, Carmine, Pink, Pure White, White with Carmine Eye. Each color separate. Tr. pkt., $1.00, 1000 seeds, $6.00. An even mixture of the above 5 colors, tr. pkt., 75c.; 1000 seeds, $5.00.

Silver Leaved New Hybrids. With semi-double flowers. Tr. pkt., $1.00; 1000 seeds, $10.00.

Snowball. New, the real pure white and largest in existence. Tr. pkt., $1.00, 1000 seeds, $15.00.

For larger quantities, special quotations.

O. V. ZANGEN, Seedsman, **HOBOKEN, N. J.**

Mention The Florists' Exchange when writing.

New Crop of my

Christmas Flowering SWEET PEA SEED

Christmas Pink and Florence Denzer, pure white, will be ready August 1st.

Those two well known varieties are raised by over 2000 florists all over the world. Here is one out of many letters received:

Dear Sir: My sweet peas, which I raised from your seed, received the highest award at the Carnation Exhibit in Boston, being over 18 inches long. JOHN T. GALE, Tewkesbury, Mass.

Price 1-4 lb. 75c.; per lb. $2.00
MAILED FREE

New Christmas Flowering Hybrids, 20 to 30 colors, mostly blue, salmon, purple lavender, in mixtures; also Mrs. Edie Wild, carmine, separate color. 1 Trade pkt., $1.00, 5 Trade pkts, $4.00; not more than 5 pkts. taken in order to each customer just now. These new hybrids are just as free bloomers as Cristmas Pink and Florence Denzer, some much larger, and received first-class Certificate of Merit by the Mass. Horticultural Society, Boston, March 24. Seed ready in Sept.

All seed originated with me is sold in my original sealed pkts., with cultural directions, to the growers, but none for seedsmen for propagating.

Orders filled strictly in rotation.

ANT. C. ZVOLANEK

BOUND BROOK, N. J.

Mention The Florists' Exchange when writing.

CINERARIA

Large Flowering Prize, Splendid Mixed T. P. $0.50

Large Flowering, Semi Dwarf Prize, Splendid Mixed, T. P. $0.50

PANSY, Superb Mixed.

oz. $4.50. ¼ oz. $1.15 ⅛ oz. $0.60

W. C. BECKERT,
Allegheny, Pa.

Mention the Florists' Exchange when writing.

The Choicest strains of Florists' Stocks

Including

Cineraria, Calceolaria, Cyclamen, Pansy, Petunia, etc.,

CAN BE HAD FROM

JAMES VICK'S SONS
ROCHESTER, N. Y.

Pansy Seed

THE JENNINGS STRAIN

New crop now ready, saved from finest selected stock, large flowering and great variety of fancy colors. By mail one pkt., 4000 seed, $1.00; ¼ oz., $2.50; 1 oz., $5.00, 2 oz., $9.00; 3 oz., $12.00. Cash with order.

Good strong Pansy Plants now ready, 60c. per 100 by mail. $4.00 per 1000 by express, 2000 $7.00.

E. B. JENNINGS,
Lock Box 254 Southport, Conn.
Grower of the Finest Pansies.

PANSY SEED

Of my own growing, crop of 1906, "**My Giant Market,**" the finest and largest variety of fancy colors to be had. In trade pkt. of 5000 seeds, $1.00. Plants ready September 1st. Cash with order.

E. A BLINN, CROMWELL, CONN.

Mention The Florists' Exchange when writing.

PRIMROSES

Improved Chinese: Finest grown, named or mixed. Strong 2 inch. $2.00 per 100.

XXX SEEDS

CHINESE PRIMROSE

Finest grown, mixed, 500 seeds, $1.00; ½ pkt., 50c.

Cyclamen Giganteum: Finest Giant mixed, 200 seeds $1.00; ½ pkt., 50c.

DAISY: Double Giant mixed, 1000 Seeds 25c.

GIANT PANSY. The best large flowering varieties, critically selected. 5000 seeds, $1.00; half pkt., 50c.; 500 seeds of Giant **Mme. Perret**, pansy seed added to every $1.00 pkt. of Giant Pansy. Cash. Liberal extra count of seeds in all packets.

JOHN F. RUPP, Shiremanstown, Pa.
The Home of Primroses

Giant, Madame Perret, genuine gold medal. **Cecile Davy, Marguerite Davy, Lord Beaconsfield, Cassier, Bugnot Giant Trimardeau,** mixed and in colors. **English mixed Daisy, Double Giant Forget-Me-Not,** dwarf blue, **Mignonette** for forcing, **Hollyhocks,** hardy **Carnations,** endive for Winter, extra good Escarole, round or green. Extra Chervil forcing radish, lettuce, Sans Rivale, or improved Big Boston; never gets red. Forcing lettuce, etc. Send for prices. Only choice varieties.

Ask for the Foudrogant, the best insecticide so far.

BEAULIEU, Woodhaven, N. Y.

BURPEE'S SEEDS

PHILADELPHIA

Blue List of Wholesale Prices mailed only to those who plant for profit.

Seed Trade Report.

AMERICAN SEED TRADE ASSOCIATION

Henry W. Wood, Richmond, Va., president; C. S. Burge, Toledo, O., first vice-president; G. B. McVay, Birmingham, Ala., second vice-president; C. E. Kendel, Cleveland, O., secretary and treasurer; J. H. Ford, Ravenna, O., assistant secretary.

CONDEMN FREE SEEDS.—The Douglas County (Kan.) Horticultural Society at its recent meeting passed the following resolutions condemning the free distribution of seeds by the Government.

"Resolved that the Douglas County Horticultural Society does hereby condemn the free seed distribution of the United States Agricultural department through Members of Congress. That we would favor a test of rare varieties from foreign countries. That we consider success in vegetable planting dependent upon the careful selection of varieties based upon class of soil. That the Government seeds we have tried have proved inferior. That we know the people at large consider free Govern seeds a sort of graft looking toward influencing votes, and that we petition our Congressmen to restore the distribution to its original intention, or to respond to the sober good sense of the people."

LOUISVILLE, KY.—Nothing new has developed in the situation around here lately in regard to grass seed crops or onion sets. As previously reported, orchard grass has turned out a better grade than usual; Kentucky blue and red top are short and prices higher. Onion sets have turned out a fairly good crop, though not so large as last year, due to the unfavorable season. The weather has been so very hot that very few sets have been bought as yet, but we expect a good fair movement of them in September. The crop of Winter oats is a good deal shorter than usual; quality is good. Seed wheat has turned out remarkably well.

SHEBOYGAN, WIS.—The pea crop in this vicinity, so far as delivered, proved to be about equal to our expectations, and is a fair average crop, and nearly all of it having been harvested under favorable conditions, we have a bright, sound, handsome sample, and as there was plenty of bright sunny weather, the berry is of good size and high vitality. In the section North from here, including Sturgeon Bay, all crops suffered from the drouth, which set in just as pods were filling, and the yield is materially shortened on this account; and although deliveries in that section have hardly begun, we expect about two-thirds of an average crop of bright, sound peas.

Beans in this State, so far as our observation extends, promise to be a fair crop, and with brighter weather than for the past two seasons, there is less rust and blight than usual; and we are looking for a crop of good quality and fair average yield, should no unfavorable conditions arise before or during harvest.

JOHN H. ALLAN SEED CO.

European Notes.

Up to this date, August 15, the drought in the west of France, which has continued for the past three months, still persists; and while it cannot injure crops that are practically non-existent, it is very seriously increasing the shortage on beets and mangels, and also affecting the leeks and onions which, until now, have made a middling stand. The outlook for a trade in these articles next year is very promising as, owing to reduced plantations and the reductions caused by drought, the growers confidently expect good prices for their bulbs during the coming Winter.

The most serious effects of the drought (however, concern the crops of beet, mangel, turnip, rutabaga and Winter radish for next season. The sowing time is passing rapidly and in very few cases has it been possible to get the land into condition for the purpose up to now.

EUROPEAN SEEDS.

American harvests for this year will be the largest on record, according to the following estimates based on data of the Department of Agriculture: Winter wheat, 493,434,000 bushels; Spring wheat, 278,830,000 bushels, against 428,462,834 and 264,516,655 bushels, respectively, in 1905. The total corn crop for 1906 is estimated at 2,713,194,000, against 2,707,993,540 bushels last year.

NURSERY DEPARTMENT.

Conducted by Joseph Meehan.

AMERICAN ASSOCIATION OF NURSERYMEN, Orlando Harrison, Berlin, Md., president; J. W. Hill, Des Moines, Ia., vice-president; George C. Seager, Rochester, N. Y., secretary; C. L. Yates; Rochester, N. Y., treasurer.

On Monday, August 20, H. Harold Hume, well-known throughout Florida and the South as an authority on horticultural subjects, returned to Florida to make the State his home permanently. He will be associated with G. L. Taber, in the Glen Saint Mary Nurseries, at Glen Saint Mary, Florida, a nursery concern which, for a quarter of a century, has enjoyed the confidence and patronage of Southern horticulturists. His connections with Mr. Taber's nurseries will add prestige to the business and his past record is a token of what may be expected from that concern.

News of Prof. Hume's return to Florida will be welcome to the many fruit growers and nurserymen of the South. From 1899 to 1904, Prof. Hume was horticulturist of the Florida Experiment Station and professor of horticulture in the University of Florida. Since that time he has been horticulturist to the North Carolina Department of Agriculture and Experiment Station.

As a writer, lecturer and investigator of horticultural problems, Prof. Hume has won an enviable reputation. During his connection with the Florida Experiment Station, some 18 bulletins were written by him on various subjects. His monograph of citrus fruits, published in 1904, is the standard work on orange culture to-day, and his new work "The Pecan and Its Culture," is now nearly ready for distribution.

Seasonable Notes.

Shapely bushes do not result when "chaste shrubs," Vitex agnus-castus, are let grow as they will. But give them the knife now and again and shrubs of pleasing shape are easily had. There are several colors of them, white, lilac, etc. They bloom in August.

In the Middle States, one rarely sees a good balsam fir in cultivation. They thrive for a year or two, then lose their vigor, and though alive are no ornament. It is rare to see one in as healthy a condition as when in a wild state.

Currant cuttings made and set out now will be nicely rooted before the season is over. They should receive a good mulching before Winter sets in, where danger from being hoisted out by frost exists.

Of the two Judas trees, the native one, Cercis canadensis and the Japanese C. japonica, the latter has much handsomer flowers than the former. But the canadensis is the taller grower, often making a small tree. Both seed freely and seedlings soon appear from Spring sown seeds.

Euonymus Sielboldianus is a beautiful shrub, evergreen when well sheltered or where Winters are not over severe. Its small greenish white flowers are not unattractive, and following these are small red berries. It propagates readily from green wood cuttings made at this season of the year.

Liatris pycnostachya, the Kansas Gay Feather, is an excellent plant to set in a half-wild place such as many large grounds contain. Its spikes of flowers make a height of three to four feet. The flowers are lilac-colored. Once planted, the liatris takes care of itself.

Clematis flammula is not the rapid grower the C. paniculata is, but as it blooms earlier in the season there is room for both; and then it is very fragrant. C. paniculata opens its first flowers in the third week in August in the vicinity of New York city, and is in full display about September 1.

Jasminum nudiflorum flowers in the earliest days of Spring, before its leaves appear, at which season it is a most welcome visitor. As a bush it is desirable all Summer long. The long slender branches droop gracefully from all sides, making it desirable for many situations.

Althæas flower from the growth of the same season. This Summer has been so warm and moist that a strong growth has been made, and numerous large flowers have resulted. There are many striking colors among the kinds now in cultivation. If need be, the althæa can be increased by grafting it on seedling stocks as well as by hard wood cuttings, the common way.

Platycodon grandiflorum is an old herbaceous plant that can always be recommended to one interested in such plants. There is a blue and a white variety of it, and sometimes a flower half white and half blue will appear. Many know this plant under its old name of campanula.

The fruiting hazel is a good shrub to set in low ground as it flourishes well there with sufficient drainage. In company with the alder and the willow, its catkins are among the first evidences of Spring shrubs and trees present.

Most planters know how hard it is to get fern-leaved beeches to live when transplanted. The chief reason is they carry so many twigs and branches, far out of proportion to their roots. The remedy is to prune the tops severely; without this it is safe to say many would die.

Red Berried Viburnum.

Reference has been made before to the red berries of a few of the virburnums, but there are so many of them, and all of such an ornamental appearance, that it is without doubt a fact that these shrubs are not nearly as well appreciated as they should be. Here is a list that comes to mind as I write in which the whole of them bear red berries at certain stages of growth:

Viburnum cassinoides, cotinifolium dilitatum, Lantana, opulus, Sieboldi, tomentosum and Wrightii. In the case of a few of these the red colored berries give way to black in the end, but the others maintain the red color until almost the last. And in the case of sterilis, sometimes called oxycoccos, the clusters of red berries hang on all Winter, being very ornamental.

Besides their red berries, these shrubs all bear pretty clusters of white flowers in early Spring, nearly all of them having large corymbs of flowers, for which feature alone many of them are planted.

What needs attention as well, in connection with these viburnums, is their beauty of growth, as a rule. Everyone of them makes a shapely shrub naturally, and when a slight pruning is given them from time to time, it makes the few tall growing species become of more compact growth.

Of the list, cassinoides and opulus are natives; the rest European or Japanese.

Rhus Cotinus, Mist Bush

These notes on viburnums are suggested from a conviction that nurserymen might push the sales of them to the satisfaction of customers and to their own profit.

Fall Planted Magnolias.

There is something in the disturbance of the roots of magnolias in Autumn acting against the well-doing of the trees when transplanted. It is cheaper to throw away the trees than to transplant them then, as the labor of planting will be saved, for all such planted trees will die. It is the same with the tulip tree, liriodendron. These trees have fleshy roots or more nearly so than most trees, and it is evident that trees with roots of this nature do not like disturbance in the Fall. When possible to secure a ball of soil with a tree the case is different. It is then no more of a disturbance than the planting of a tub specimen would be.

It sometimes happens that a customer very much desires a plant to be set in Autumn, plans seeming to demand it. The only chance of success would lie in the cutting back of the shrub or tree almost to the ground and then placing a thick mulch about it before Winter set in, enough of the mulch to keep the frost from the roots. And as to cutting back the plants, even when planted in Spring, a nice specimen is had in less time from a cut down plant than from an unpruned one.

Variegated Euonymus Radicans.

The beauty and hardiness of the Euonymus radicans variegata commend it to all who have use for a small-leaved self-clinging vine. In Japan, travelers tell us it is found covering the trunks of trees; and being of evergreen character, it there takes the place of English ivy, which is so useful for the same purpose when climates are not too severe.

The vine, as its name implies, is a climber, nevertheless those who wish it in bush shape can have it so. Just as with wistaria, trumpet vine, or any other vine, all it needs is support for a year or two after which it will stand erect itself. Even when not so supported, it forms a bush, but a more spreading one than when it has a stake to support it.

For low walls it is an excellent vine, soon covering the surface and forming a pretty picture with its green and white leaves; and it is easily kept within bounds.

As an edging to walks and beds it is in demand. With care the first year after planting it becomes well established, and in time will form a broad band of variegated foliage, often harmonizing nicely with plants within a bed when it is used. In the Northern States, Spring is the best season to plant it.

Rhus Cotinus.

One of the best known shrubs in old collections is the Rhus cotinus, an illustration of which appears with this. It rarely makes a compact bush without being pruned, but the one photographed fairly represents its growth when in good condition and in a comparatively young state. The misty looking arrangement of its heads of flowers is what has made it a favorite with planters, and is what suggested its common name, mist shrub. But this is not the only common name it owns. It is also called smoke bush, purple fringe and it, is the name it is the best known Venetian sumach. Mist bush, or mist tree, as some catalogue have under in this vicinity. It is a native of the South of Europe, extending to the Caucasus and it proves hardy over a large portion of the Northern States.

To have the mist bush in the best condition, a good annual pruning should be given it in early Spring. It both keeps it in good shape and in good condition for flowering. The bush displayed shows fairly well, and it would have been still better, perhaps, without its back ground of the large tulip tree. But in the way of planting, the bush is well placed, the tulip tree behind it, a Magnolia tripetala on its right, and a pathway along its front, suggest its being in a good position.

There is another rhus closely approaching cotinus in general character, but in some respects it is better. It is a native of the colder parts of Alabama, and is known as Rhus cotinoides. The growth is rather stronger than in the older species, and the foliage larger, longer and of a very pleasing shade of green.

All members of the rhus family go under the common name of sumach, although among gardeners this name stands for those of them that change to a beautiful color in Autumn, principally the R. glabra and R. typhina.

Sowing Seeds of Elaeagnus Longipes.

Seeds of Elæagnus longipes are ripening now, and many who have seed-bearing bushes will wish to increase their stock of plants. The seed should be gathered, washed free of pulp and placed in damp soil at once, to be kept in that condition until October, when it should be sown outdoors. Some may think why not sow outdoors at once. It is better not, because of its then being out of control and if hot, dry weather should catch it the seeds would spoil. When under cover it can be seen to that the conditions required are secured.

Although the fruit of this elæagnus can be eaten, it is rarely used; nor is the shrub planted for the use of its fruit. Its ornamental features are what recommend it. In early Spring there are its yellowish white flowers, and in August, its dark-red fruit.

Other species of elæagnus ripen their fruit later, some in September, and one, umbellatus, not until October.

JOSEPH MEEHAN.

EVERGREENS

DWARF BOX.

PRICES UPON APPLICATION.

HIRAM T. JONES,

Union County Nurseries, Elizabeth, N. J.

Mention the Florists' Exchange when writing.

STORRS & HARRISON CO.

NURSERYMEN, FLORISTS and SEEDSMEN

SEND FOR CATALOGUE

PAINESVILLE OHIO,

Mention the Florists' Exchange when writing.

HERBACEOUS PERENNIALS

for Summer and Autumn Planting. We offer NINE HUNDRED and SIXTY-SEVEN VARIETIES of STRONG FIELD-GROWN PLANTS. Send for Catalog and Trade List.

BAY STATE NURSERIES, NORTH ABINGTON, MASS.

Mention the Florists' Exchange when writing.

F. & F. NURSERIES

SPRINGFIELD NEW JERSEY

Wholesale Growers — **TREES AND PLANTS** in full assortment. — Trade Catalogue Free

AMERICAN **TREE SEEDS** AND PLANTS

Our Descriptive Catalogue of American Seeds and Plants is ready for mailing. Ask for it.

OTTO KATZENSTEIN & CO.

Tree Seeds and Plants Specialists, ATLANTA, GA

P. OUWERKERK

216 Jane Street

WEEHAWKEN HEIGHTS, N. J.

P. O. No. 1, Hoboken, N. J.

JUST RECEIVED FROM OUR HOLLAND NURSERIES

Rhododendrons, Azaleas, Spiræa Japonica, Lilium Speciosum, Peonies, Bleeding Heart, Pot-Grown Lilacs, Hydrangea in sorts, Clematis and H. P. Roses in the best sorts.

PRICES MODERATE

Mention The Florists' Exchange when writing.

NURSERY STOCK

CHEAP

BERBERIS THUNBERGII, all sizes.
ROSA LUCIDA, 3 years.
VIBURNUM CASSINOIDES, 2 years.
VIBURNUM DENTATUM, 2 years.
PRUNUS MARITIMA, 2 years.

WRITE FOR PRICES.

LITTLEFIELD & WYMAN

Successors to SIDNEY LITTLEFIELD

NORTH ABINGTON, MASS.

Mention The Florists' Exchange when writing.

Sea Cliff Nurseries.

Dwarf and trained fruit trees a specialty.
Write for quotations.

FD. BOULON & SON,

SEA CLIFF, L. I., N. Y.

Mention The Florists' Exchange when writing.

H. DEN OUDEN & SON,

BOSKOOP, HOLLAND.

Wholesale growers of nursery stock for the American trade. Catalogue free on demand. Also views in our nurseries.

Mention The Florists' Exchange when writing.

PEONIES

$6.00 to $10.00 per 100

EDWARD SWAYNE

WEST CHESTER, PA.

Mention the Florists' Exchange when writing.

1500 Trumphet vines, 1-3 ft. trans. 4c.
1000 Norway Spruce with ball 1½-2 ft. 10c.
Send for surplus list.

Ellsworth Brown & Co.

SEABROOK, N. H.

Mention The Florists' Exchange when writing.

GRAFTED ROSES

Killarney and Richmond grafted 3 in. pots at $15.00 per 100; $120.00 per 1000.

ASPARAGUS PLUMOSUS NANUS

2 in. pots, $3.00 per 100; $25.00 per 1,000.
2½ in. pots, $4.50 per 100; $40.00 per 1,000.
3 in. pots, $7.00 per 100; $65.00 per 1,000.
4 in. pots, $10.00 to $12.00 per 100.

ASPARAGUS SPRENGERI

2 in. pots, $3.00 per 100; $25.00 per 1,000.
2½ in. pots, $4.50 per 100; $40.00 per 1,000.
3 in. pots, $7.00 per 100; $65.00 per 1,000.

SMILAX

2¼ in. pots, $2.50 per 100; $20.00 per 1,000.

GARDENIAS

3 in. pots, $12.00 per 100, 4 in. pots, $20.00 per 100.
5 in. pots, $35.00 per 100; 6 in. pots, $60.00 per 100.
7 in. pots, $75.00 per 100.
8 in. pots, $2.00 each.
10 in. pots, $3.00 each.

VIOLET PLANTS

Lady Hume Campbell, $6.00 per 100.; $50.00 per 1000.

A. N. PIERSON

Cromwell, Conn.

Mention The Florists' Exchange when writing.

ROSES

Strong plants 2½ in. pots. — On own roots 4 in. pots.

	100	1000		100
Cr. Rambler, Wood,	$2.50	$20.	Baby Rambler,	$20.
La France, Meteor,	2.50	20.	Crimson "	6.
G. Gate, Notting,	2.50	20.	Charta, Masson,	7.
Diesbach, Masson,	3.00	25.	Diesbach, Wood,	7.
Laing, Caprice,	3.00	25.	Neyron, Laing,	8.

106 best sorts for fall 1906 and spring 1907.

THE LEEDLE FLORAL COMPANY, SPRINGFIELD, OHIO.

Mention The Florists' Exchange when writing.

Queen Beatrice Rose

Four to one shot. Four times as many flowers as Maid.

F. H. KRAMER, 916 F St. Washington, D. C.

Mention The Florists' Exchange when writing.

Roses and Smilax

250 **BRIDES**, 3½ in. pots, good stock, $10.00 for the lot. Cash. 400 **SMILAX**, 2½ in. pots, good stock, $10.00 for the lot. Cash.

JOHN WHITE

Waverly Place, ELIZABETH, N. J.

Mention the Florists' Exchange when writing.

ROSES

250 Golden Gates, 85 Brides, 90 Bridesmaids, 4 in. pots, fine plants, $5.00 per 100 or $15.00 for the lot.

SPY HILL CONSERVATORIES, Fishkill-on-Hudson, N. Y.

Mention the Florists' Exchange when writing.

VIOLET CULTURE

Price, $1.50 Postpaid

A. T. De La Mare Ptg. & Pub. Co. Ltd., New York

Large Assortment **PEONIES** Very best Varieties

LOW PRICES

THE KIND THAT FLORISTS LIKE

"We make a specialty of growing stocky transplanted shrubbery and trees"

FULL ASSORTMENT OF Ornamentals, Fruits, Roses, Clematis, and Herbaceous Plants. Write for our fall wholesale trade list.

W. & T. SMITH CO., GENEVA, N. Y.

Mention The Florists' Exchange when writing.

PAEONIAS

We offer under mentioned varieties, of our OWN STOCK, GUARANTEED TRUE TO NAME, in strong one year old clumps with three and more eyes. (No Divisions.)

	Per 100		Per 100
400 Boule de Neige, white	$18.00	800 Festiva, white	$7.00
500 Claire Dubois, pink	12.00	200 Illustration, pink	7.00
500 Comte de Niepperg, red	12.00	500 Louis van Houtte, red	7.00
600 Duchess de Nemours, white	18.00	500 Madame de Verneville, white	12.00
500 Duke of Wellington, white	14.00	400 Madame Emile Galle, soft lilac	16.00
500 Edward Andrea, red	14.00	500 Madame Forel, pink	14.00
4,000 Festiva Maxima, white	14.00		

Ask our trade list for full description of the flowers.
All kinds of forcing plants and nursery stock for sale.

ENDTZ VAN NES & CO., Boskoop, Holland

Mention The Florists' Exchange when writing.

PEONIES

Queen Victoria (the cold storage flower) $9.00 per 100. **Festiva Maxima**, $30.00 per 100. **Fragrans** (the bloom producer) $6.00 per 100. For 1000 rates or other varieties, write

GILBERT H. WILD, SARCOXIE, MO.

Mention The Florists' Exchange when writing.

GET THE BEST

IT DON'T PAY TO BUY POOR STOCK

	100	1000		100	1000
RICHMOND ROSE, 2½ inch	$5.00	$40.00	3½ inch	$6.50	$55.00
AMERICAN BEAUTIES, 3 inch	5.00	40.00	3½ inch	6.50	55.00
BRIDESMAIDS, 2½ inch	5.00	45.00			
CHATENAY, 2½ inch	3.50	30.00	3½ inch	5.00	45.00
UNCLE JOHN, 2½ inch	3.50	30.00	3½ inch	5.00	45.00
GOLDEN GATES, 2½ inch	3.50	30.00	3½ inch	4.50	
KAISERIN, 2½ inch	3.50	30.00			
SUNRISE, 3½ inch	5.50	50.00			
PERLES, 3½ inch	6.00	55.00			

SATISFACTION ABSOLUTELY GUARANTEED

SPRENGERI, 2 inch ... $2.20 per 100; $18.00 per 1000.
PLUMOSUS, 2 inch ... 2.50 " 22.00 "
YELLOW SNAPDRAGON, 3½ inch ... 5.00 " 45.00 "

FIELD GROWN CARNATION PLANTS

FREE FROM STEM ROT OR OTHER DISEASES. STRONG HEALTHY PLANTS

	100	1000		100	1000
MRS. THOS. LAWSON	$5.00	$45.00	THE BELLE	$4.00	$35.00
WHITE LAWSON	6.00	50.00	RED SPORT OF MACEO	4.00	35.00
WOLCOTT	4.00	35.00	ELSIE MARTIN	4.00	35.00
PROSPERITY	4.00	35.00	FIANCEE	4.00	35.00

POEHLMANN BROS. COMPANY, MORTON GROVE, ILL.

Mention The Florists' Exchange when writing.

Grafted Roses

Extra fine plants, free from mildew.

Killarney, 3½ in. pots, $18.00 per 100.

Liberty, Kaiserin, Maids, Wootton, 3½ in. pots, $12.00 per 100.

Own Root Roses

Richmond, Perle, 3 in. pots, $7.00 per 100

Brides, Golden Gates, Liberty, Maids, Kaiserin, Wootton, 3 in. pots $6.00 per 100.

J. L. DILLON

Bloomsburg, Pa.

Mention The Florists' Exchange when writing.

Dwyer's Pot Grown Strawberry Plants

Strong, healthy plants from selected stock of choicest fruiting varieties sure to give satisfaction and PRODUCE A FULL CROP IN 1907. We also have a full line of Fruits and Ornamental Trees, Plants, Vines, etc., for Fall Planting. We do Landscape Gardening in all its branches. Catalogue Free

T. J. DWYER & CO., P. O. Box 6 Cornwall, New York

Mention The Florists' Exchange when writing.

CHRYSANTHEMUMS

Extra strong plants, in 3 in. pots, of **Jones, Dr. Enguehard, Perrin, Mrs. Coombs, October Sunshine, Alice Byron, Ivory, Appleton**, etc. These plants have been cut back, and are in fine condition. $5.00 per 100 or the lot of about 200 for $9.00.

R. G. HANFORD, Norwalk, Conn.

Mention The Florists' Exchange when writing.

BABY MUMS

FIELD GROWN

(1) size, very heavy plants to pot up ... 15c each
(2) size, heavy plants ... 12c
(3) size, good sized plants ... 10c
Smaller sized plants ... 8c

Cash.

HENRY EICHHOLZ, Waynesboro, Pa.

Mention The Florists' Exchange when writing.

OUR LITTLE PET

From Aschmann in Philadelphia I bought
An Araucaria, a pet for our little girl;
Now we have two pets, the pride of our thought:
The little girl so sweet, a head full of curls,
And the Araucaria with its everlasting green,
A more joyful home you never have seen.

Watch us Grow!!

ARAUCARIA EXCELSA, the best of all decorative plants nature produces; a specialty. Every man in business life, to be successful, must adopt one thing as his specialty, and that specialty, whatever he may select, and of whatever nature it may be, he must guard, study and push to such an extent, that it not only benefits himself; but he must conduct it so, that every one who seeks his aid, service or his articles, whatever he advertises or practices, will **share a slice of his activity and prosperity.** I made the importation and cultivation of Araucaria as a special study in my life. The following figures will show you my success in business: In the first year I began with an import of 250; in the eleventh year (now 1906) my importation has grown up to 6,000 (come and see it). On account of the Araucaria growing yearly in favor as a much admired decorative plant for the arbor, bed room, dining and sitting rooms, stores, hotels, lawns and porches by the plant-consuming peoples all over the country, the **outlook** will be of an importation of at least 8,000 to 10,000 in the Spring of 1907. To secure this vast amount for 1907, I am now on the ocean, per steamer New Amsterdam, sailing from Hoboken, August 15, striking for Belgium and making contracts for next year. I shall also at the same time bring over with me a large lot of choice Azalea Indica, Palms, etc. for Christmas and Easter forcing. No money will be spared in obtaining for my customers the cream of the Belgium greenhouses.

Please note lowest price now going for August and September:

ARAUCARIA EXCELSA

12 to 14 in. 5½ in. pots, 3 to 4 tiers, 2-yr. old, 50c. 14 to 16 in., 5½ in. pots, 3 to 4 tiers, 2-yr. old, 60c. 16 to 18 in. 5½ to 6 in. pots, 4 to 5 tiers, 3-yr. old, 75c. 18 to 20 in., 6 in. pots, 5 to 6 tiers, 4-yr. old, $1.00. 20 to 24 in. 6 in. to 7 in. pots, 5 to 6 tiers, 4-yr. old, $1.25. 36-40 to 50 in. 7 in. pots, specimen plants from $2.50 to $3.00 each.

ARAUCARIA COMPACTA ROBUSTA — have several thousand of them; can supply all wants. These plants were never so fine in shape and condition as this year. The set of the greenhouse, as broad as long, 12 to 20 in. in height, 3 to 4 perfect tiers, 20 to 30 inches across, 3-4-5 year old, 6 to 7 in. pots, $1.25, $1.50, $1.75, $2.00, $2.50 to $3.00 each.

ARAUCARIA EXCELSA GLAUCA—This variety on account of its beautiful Green-Blueish tiers, dwarf habit, fine compact shape, gives it a striking appearance, and anybody seeing them, must undoubtedly fall in love with them at sight. Plants, 6-7 inch pots, 3-4-5 perfect tiers, 3-4 year old, 15 to 25 inch high, from 15 to 30 in. across, $1.25, $1.50, $1.75, $2.00 to $2.50 each.

KENTIA BELMOREANA, 5½ to 6 in. pots, bushy, fine plants, from 75 cts. to $1.00 to $1.25 each.

KENTIA FORSTERIANA, 7 in. pots, made-up plants, 1 large in center, 3 smaller sizes, 22 to 25 in. high around, gives them a good appearance, $2.00 each. 6 in. pots, single plants, 35 to 40 in. high, 5 to 6 good leaves, 4 year old, $1.25 to $1.50 each; 6 in. pots, 30 to 35 in. high, 4 year old, 5 good leaves, $1.00; 5½ in. pots, 3 year old, 25 to 30 in. high, 5 good leaves, 75c. made-up plants, 3 and 4 in. pots, 18 to 20 in. high, 25 cts. to 30 cts. each.

ARECA LUTESCENS, made-up, 25 cts.

COCOS WEDDELIANA, 15 cts.

CYCAS REVOLUTA (Sago Palm), 6 in.-7 in. pots, with from 6 to 20 leaves per plant, 10 cts. per leaf.

NEPHROLEPIS BARROWSII, 6 in. pots, strong, ready for 7-8 in., 50c. 4 in. pots, ready for 6-7 in., 25c.

NEPHROLEPIS SCOTTII, 6 in. pots, large, ready for 6-7 in. 50c.; 5½ in. pots, 40c.; 5 in. 35c.; 4 in. 20c. to 25c.

BOSTON FERNS, 4 in., 20c. to 25c. I have them by the thousand, 5 in; 30c. to 35c.

FERNS for dishes, a fine assortment, 2¼ in., $5.00 per 100; 3 in., $6.00 per 100.

FICUS ELASTICA, 6 in., 50c.

ASPARAGUS PLUMOSUS NANUS, 3 in., 6c.; 4 in., 10c.

CASH WITH ORDER

When ordering, say whether the plants should be shipped in the pots or not

GODFREY ASCHMANN

Importer and Wholesale Grower of Pot Plants

1012 Ontario Street, - - PHILADELPHIA, PA.

Mention The Florists' Exchange when writing.

ASPARAGUS

	Per 100
Sprengeri, 3 in.	$3.00
" 2 in.	1.50
Plumosus Nanus, 2 in.	2.00
Primula Obconica, Grandiflora Alba, Rosea and Hybrida, 2 in	2.00
" " **Robusta and Compacta,** 2 in.	3.00
Smilax, nice, 2½ in.	1.25
Paris Daisy, white and yellow, 3 in., bushy,	3.00

Orders booked for early September delivery of

Cineraria Grandiflora Hybrida, Michell's Giant Prize, 2 in.	2.00
" **Stellata,** Sutton's, 2 in.	2.50
Calceolaria, James Superb mixed, 2 in.	3.00

Cash with order, please.

GEO. J. HUGHES, BERLIN, N. J.

Mention The Florists' Exchange when writing.

2,000 **Smilax,** 2½ in., strong, cut back, per 100, $1.50; the lot for $17.50.

200 **Asparagus Plumosus,** $2.50 per 100.

1,000 **Asparagus Sprengeri,** 2½ in., $2.00 per 100; the lot for $17.00. This is strong and ready for a shift.

J. S. BLOOM,

RIEGELSVILLE, PA.

Mention The Florists' Exchange when writing.

SMILAX PLANTS

Strong, Bushy Plants, many times cut back and ready for shift.

2 in. pots	$1.00 per 100,	$9.00	per 1000
3 in. pots	2.00 "	18.00	"
Seedlings from flats	4.00		"

We have grown Smilax Plants for the trade 18 years, and never had finer stock.

Send for Samples

R. KILBOURN

CLINTON, N. Y.

Mention The Florists' Exchange when writing.

EMERSON C. McFADDEN

Wholesale Grower

Asparagus Plumosus Nanus, Etc.

Short Hills, N. J.

Tel. 28 A.

Mention The Florists' Exchange when writing.

The American Carnation

Price, $3.50

A. T. DE LA MARE PTG. & PUB. CO.,

2 Duane Street, New York

Begonia "Gloire de Lorraine" and "Turnford Hall"

very strong, 2¼ in. pots, $15.00 per 100; 3 inch, $25.00 per 100; 4 inch, $40.00 per 100.

Pandanus Veitchii, 12 to 14 inches high from top of soil	$ 75.00 per 100
" " 18 " 24 " " " " " "	100.00 " "
" " 24 " 26 " " " " " "	150.00 " "

Adiantum Farleyense, fine specimens, $1.00, $1.50 to $2.00 each.
" " 2¼ inch, fine stock, $15.00 per 100

Cash with order from unknown correspondents. Good value guaranteed.

J. A. PETERSON, McHenry Ave., Cincinnati, Ohio

Mention The Florists' Exchange when writing.

ASPARAGUS

	per 100
Plumosus Nanus, 2¼ in. pots	$2.00
Plumosus Seedlings,	1.00
Sprengerii Seedlings,	1.00
Pansy Seed, large flowering, per oz.	4.00

PRIMROSES

	per 100
Chinese, 2½ in. pots	$2.00
Obconica Alba, and Rosea	2.00
Cannas, 5 var., field, cheap	15.00

Pansy Plants, Oct. 1st, $3.00 per 1000; 50c. per 100.

CASH PLEASE.

JOS. H. CUNNINGHAM, Delaware, O.

Mention The Florists' Exchange when writing.

LUDVIG MOSBÆK,

ONARGA, ILL.

60,000 ASPARAGUS PL. N and SPRENGERII, very strong and fine plants, ready for a shift, 4 in., $10.00; 3 in., $5.00; 2½ in. $2.50 per 100.

40,000 FERNS, pot grown, excellent. Anna Foster, Boston, Piersoni, and Sword, 6 in., $40.00; 4 in., $15.00; 3 in., $8.00 per 100.

GERANIUMS, stock plants, 2½ in., and R. C. and other **Bedding Plants,** including 10,000 **CANNAS,** for Fall delivery.

200,000 PANSIES, seedlings of the well-known Florists' International Mixture, $3.00 per 1000.

Mention The Florists' Exchange when writing.

ASPARAGUS

Robustus $5.00 per 100; $40.00 per 1000.

Sprengeri $2.00 per 100; $15.00 per 1000.

ALBERT M. HERR

LANCASTER, PA.

Mention The Florists' Exchange when writing.

Stevia Serrata

True, winter blooming, strong, bushy, ready to shift, 2½ in. pots, $5.00 per 100; $45.00 per 1000.

ASPARAGUS SPRENGERII, 2 inch, very strong, $2.50 per 100; $20.00 per 1000.

DEAN FERRIS, Peekskill, N.Y.

Mention The Florists' Exchange when writing.

PRIMULA OBCONICA

Strong 4 inch, $6.00 per 100.

Ardisia crenulata, strong bushy plants from bench, well berried, ready for 5-6 in. pots, $6.00 and $9.00 per doz.

Geraniums, 12 varieties. Have order booked for Fall delivery; can fill orders from 100-100,000. Get my prices. Standard, 5 in. pots, $9.00 per 1000; $500, $40.00, saucers 50c. 100. Wanted 2 inch pots in exchange. Cash.

WM. S. HERZOG, MORRIS PLAINS, N. J.

Mention The Florists' Exchange when writing.

Primula Obconica Grandiflora

2 1-2 in., $2.50 per 100. Ask for list (seedlings of hardy plants)

BAUDISCH & CO.,

537 Fulton Street UNION HILL, N. J.

Mention The Florists' Exchange when writing.

CYCLAMEN

SPLENDENS GIGANTEUM HYBRIDS

This strain has no equal or better. Perfect flowers of Giant type in five true colors well grown plants from 3 in. pots $7.00, from 4 in. pots $15.00 per 100.

***Asparagus* Plumosus Nanus**

Good stock transplanted from flats, $1.50, from 2½ in. pots, $2.50, from 2½ in. pots, $3.00 per 100. In quantity of 500 or more less 10%.

SATISFACTION GUARANTEED

PAUL MADER, EAST STROUDSBURG, PA

Mention The Florists' Exchange when writing.

PANSIES

Brown's Extra Select Superb Giant Prize Pansies. Awarded Silver Medal, St. Louis Exposition, 1904.

PLANTS, mixed colors, in any quantity, $3.00 per 1000.

CASH WITH ORDER.

PETER BROWN, Lancaster, Pa.

Mention The Florists' Exchange when writing.

PANSIES

FINE STRAIN, $3.50 PER 1000

DAISIES (Bellis). Mixed $2.50 per 1000.

FORGET-ME-NOT Hardy blue, $3.00 per 1000.

ALEX. HAESELER

27 South St., HESHANTICUT, R. I.

Mention The Florists' Exchange when writing.

50,000 Pansy Seedlings

Finest strain at $3.50 per 1000. Delivery beginning September 1st. Orders booked in rotation. Strictly cash with order.

J. CONDON, Horticulturist

734 5th Ave., Brooklyn, N. Y.

Mention The Florists' Exchange when writing.

POINSETTIAS

2½ in. pots, $5.00 per 100; $40.00 per 1000, Cash with order.

S. N. PENTECOST,

1790-1810 East 101 St., CLEVELAND, O.

Mention The Florists' Exchange when writing.

SURPLUS STOCK—CHEAP

200 **The Bride** roses, 2 in. pots, $1.75 per 100.
500 **Bridesmaid** roses, 2 in. pots, $2.00 per 100.
1000 **Cannas,** red and yellow, strong, $3.00 per 100.
50 **Dracaena Indivisa,** 3½ in., 6c. each.
2000 **Cuphea,** Cigar Plant, 2 in. pots, 75c. per 100.
2000 **Feverfew,** Double White, 2 in. pots, 50c. per 100.
10000 **Jerusalem Cherries,** big and strong, ready for 4 in. pots, from 2 in. pots at $2.00 per 100. You will never get better or cheaper stock than this. **E. I. Rawlings, Quakertown, Pa.**

Mention The Florists' Exchange when writing.

CYCLAMENS

Strong plants, $5.00 per 100; $45.00 per 1000.

ASPARAGUS

Sprengerii in 2½ pots, $2.50 per 100, $20.00 per 1000, also in flats at 75c. per 100; Plumosus Nanus in 2½ pots, $3.00 per 100.

F. A. GIFFORD, Westbury Sta., L. I.

Mention The Florists' Exchange when writing.

2000	Achilea (The Pearl)	3c.
8000	Iris Sibirica	3c.
1000	Foxglove	3c.

ELLSWORTH BROWN & CO., SEABROOK, N. H.

Mention The Florists' Exchange when writing.

LIST OF ADVERTISERS

INDEX TO STOCK ADVERTISED

Contents.

REVIEW OF THE MARKET

NEW YORK.—The cut flower business is still in its Summer condition, and there is very little of the various stocks coming in daily that can be moved at satisfactory prices. American Beauty roses continue to arrive in quantities that exceed the regular demand, making prices unstable and erratic. Bride and Bridesmaid roses are mostly of the short-stemmed grades, yet they are cleared out from day to day at some price or other.

But few carnations are coming in, excepting such as are being cut from plants in the field. Asters are plentiful, and more of the large, long-stemmed flowers are seen than formerly. The best of the white and light pink colors are those that are fetching the top figures, the purple ones, not realizing quite so much. There are a great many coming in that are small and short of stem; which have had their color marred by the rains. Such stock has hardly any market value, and is cleared out at almost any figure a buyer will offer.

Dahlias, while increasing in numbers, have not yet reached their usual standard of quality, and it can hardly be said that fixed prices obtain.

The supply of longiflorum lilies continues adequate for all needs, and no change in prices has occurred. There is an abundance of speciosum lilies in the market, and it is found difficult to get rid of them, even when offered at one dollar per hundred.

Tritomas are coming in, in numbers, and are being used effectively by retail men for window display.

Cattleyas are rather short in supply just now, which, of course is a usual thing for this time of the year.

Lily of the valley is going very slow, there being very little demand for it.

Gladiolus and hydrangeas are both very plentiful, and are still selling at low figures. The trade in green material of all kinds continues quite slow, and prices have undergone no change.

CHICAGO.—The market has but little of novelty or interest to offer as everything is still in what may be termed a comatose state. Roses are improving somewhat in quality and notably in quantity, so that there is no variation in price and probably there will be none for the next six weeks or until the demand becomes more stable. Carnations from young stock are appearing with good heads, but as may be expected with short stems. Asters are of various qualities, though an influx of the inferior grades has slightly demoralized the price; superior brands are readily taken up at a profitable figure. Dahlias have made their appearance in quantities sufficiently large to be quoted.
W. K. W.

ST. LOUIS.—White flowers were in slight demand last week, but the hot weather had a depressing effect on business, and even the occasional funeral design order was lost sight of. The stock coming in the market may be classed as of the lower grades. There is a big demand for extra good American Beauty roses, but few are seen; $3 per dozen is the top price. Some good Kaiserin Augusta Victoria, Bride and Souvenir du President Carnot are to be had, but, like American Beauty, the supply is limited; price, $5 per 100, and as low as $1. Carnations, when good, have been considered a novelty in this market for the past month, and hardly bring over $1 per 100; plenty of the poor grades are in. Asters continue to be plentiful; those of the long, fancy varieties bring $2 to $3 per 100; others from 50c. to $1. Tuberose stalks are very plentiful and bring from $1 to $3 per 100. Other outdoor stock sells very slowly. Plenty of smilax and other greens are in this market.
ST. PATRICK.

INDIANAPOLIS.—Many funeral orders kept the store men busy last week; several decorations also helped break the Summer dullness. Medium and fancy stock of all kinds is in much demand. Semple asters are now in full sway, but the bugs and disease have blighted many; the balance are readily disposed of at $1 to $1.50 per 100. Auratum and longiflorum lilies still hold at $2 a dozen. Home-grown roses, particularly Bridesmaid and Bride, are plentiful enough at $2 to $4 per 100, but the quality is lacking, so many shipped ones are received at slightly higher prices. Medium and short-stemmed American Beauty are put to good use; $5 to $15 a 100 is the price. A variety of outdoor stock aids in giving characeter to flower work; hardy hydrangeas, especially, are almost indispensable at this time. Short-stemmed carnations are often sold at good figures as there are many occasions when they can be used to good advantage.

Tomlinson Hall Market reports a good week, all high grade stock obtainable was wholesaled there at satisfactory prices.
I. B.

MINNEAPOLIS.—Business is much improved since last report. Stock is still very scarce, particularly carnations. Roses are coming in much better, and there is a noticeable improvement in the quality; furthermore, we are getting a much better selection to buy from. Asters have taken the place of carnations and have more than made good especially in funeral designs. Loose cut flowers have sold fairly well the past week, which goes to show that some of the cut flower buyers have already returned from the Summer resorts. Upon interviewing all of the retail dealers, all have without exception claimed to have made expenses during the dull season, and some have made a little money, which must be considered a good state of affairs. A great many store improvements have been made, and if stocks are carried to fill the larger ice boxes that have been purchased, cut flower buyers will not have any difficulty in having their wants supplied. One box has been ordered which is 30 feet long, 11 feet wide, and about the same height; almost a carload of flowers can be handled in it.
PAUL.

ST. PAUL.—Trade conditions have not changed much during the past week. There is very little business being done, except funeral work. Stock continues very scarce. While we have been receiving more Bride and Bridesmaid, red roses are indeed hard to secure; and while the call for them is not at all heavy it is sometimes difficult to get even the few that are needed. It appears that the new roses have not done very much so far in producing a very large crop. Carnations remain about the same, hard to get and the stock that is brought in is small and inferior. In sweet peas the quality is improving greatly; all dealers carry these flowers in large numbers. Asters are coming in nicely and the quality is very fine. Considerable outdoor stock is used to good advantage in different arrangements. Prices keep up very well and a comparison of figures with those of a year ago shows that we are getting much better values. Furthermore, the business has kept up longer into the dull season. Roses are selling for $1 and $1.50 per dozen. Carnations bring 50c. and 75c. a dozen; asters, 50c., 75c. and $1 per dozen. Sweet peas, 25c. a bunch of 25.

From present prospects we will have another good season. Crop conditions in the Northwest were never better, which is all that is necessary to give the florists and all other merchants a prosperous year.
PAUL.

BOSTON.—There is little improvement in business. The demand is about the same as during the Summer dullness. Roses are of better quality, the varieties most popular being Kaiserin Augusta Victoria, Souvenir du President Carnot, Wellesley and American Beauty; but there is not a very great demand for the latter variety at present. Carnations are improving every day. Asters still remain the most plentiful; and gladioli are also seen in large numbers. Lilies are plentiful enough for all demands; and lily of the valley is continually used in limited quantity.
J. W. D.

CHANGES IN BUSINESS.

WINSTON-SALEM, N. C.—Robert E. Grunert will start in the florist business here and will erect one greenhouse, 32x18 feet, as a beginning, with some cold frames. He will make a specialty of roses and violets, but will also grow a general collection of plants. The establishment will be known as the West Salem Greenhouses.

DAVENPORT, IA.—The Davenport Nursery Company has filed articles of incorporation. The officers are Adolph Arp, president; H. G. Bryant, vice-president; Margaretha Arp, secretary and treasurer. The capital stock is $25,000, of which $15,000 is subscribed.

STREATOR, ILL.—Geo. A. Whitcomb of Morrison, Ill., and his son George, of Cleveland, have secured an option on two tracts of land near here on which they propose the erection of greenhouses covering 200,000 square feet.

LOUISVILLE, KY.—Charles M. Reimers has sold out his business, and is now located in Los Angeles, Cal. He does not anticipate embarking in any other business venture for a year or so.

FINDLAY, O.—J. J. Waaland and E. R. Sackett have purchased the Barnd & Karg Floral Company interest. The greenhouse will be used by the purchasers for propagating purposes.

SEATTLE, WASH.—The Washington Floral Co. was recently incorporated, with a capital of $25,000, by C. Hoffmeister, K. L. Arnold and W. H. White.

ATCO, N. J.—The firm of Peacock Dahlia Farms has been incorporated; capital, 25,000. Incorporators, M. L. Peacock, S. C. Southard, Atco, N. J.; and C. G. Stevenson, Camden, N. J.

ROSES

The plants in the early plant houses, if proper care has been a corded them, should now be makir a pretty good growth; and a lig mulch becomes necessary to prote the young feeding roots, which ca be found very near the surface of t soil. As previously suggested th mulch should consist of nothing b thoroughly rotted cow manure, we pulverized, and spread on the bench about one-half inch thick. Befo this is applied, give the benches fair coating of bone meal about pounds to a 100x20 foot house, a rub it in very lightly; then afford t mulch. When this is put on, t benches should be fairly dry so th when the manure is leveled, the plar can receive a good soaking. Aft mulching, greater care will have be exercised in watering, as the co dition of the bench cannot be told the appearance of the manure top; therefore, before watering, r your fingers in the soil clear to t bottom, so as to make sure of t quantity of water needed.

From now on the ventilators w have to be looked after a little clos for as the nights get cooler, the ve tilators must not remain wide op No set rule can be laid down for th the point being, on dry clear eve ings, to leave on more air, and damp weather a little less, thou it is safer at all times to have on little more than not enough.

A little sulphur should be dust over the plants once a week on cle days, as a preventive of mildew, a on cloudy, damp days air-slaked li alone will be of some benefit. G the lime fresh, and to slake it, spre it out in a box, quite thinly, and a barrel of lime use about 30 qua of water. Allow this to stand ov night, and it is then ready for u Lime slaked too long is not as go

Look over the houses frequent and where a weak plant appears, ke it disbudded. With a little extra ca the plants will soon catch up to th more robust neighbors.

As roses are very plentiful in t market, disbud all the short st stock any way, being careful to back far enough to insure a go break. Some growers advise j pinching out the bud; but this if f lowed up will soon produce a plant full of blind wood.

The heating apparatus, if not o hauled before this time, should ceive some attention. Do not w until the last minute to make necessary repairs, as delays are of dangerous.

PENN

Plant Notes.

Pansies have always been popular, and it is safe to say that they always will be, and the growers who raise good plants from select strains of seed will continue to find the business profitable as they have done in the past; but like everything else in the plant line, pansies nowadays have to be well grown and show good aristocratic breeding, in the shape of blooms of good size, substance and color, to find purchasers.

For these reasons the first consideration in pansy growing is to procure the best seed obtainable, and when thinking about the matter, although a dollar or two in difference between one kind of seed and another may seem quite a consideration, yet if that kind of economy is practiced, it will in due season be found to be false economy.

Pansies at all stages like good soil. The seed should be sown in a frame, the soil in which should be rich and mellow, and the surface over which the seeds are sown should be sifted. After the seed is sown, shade the glass just slightly, and until the plants begin to show above the surface. Whenever the seedlings are large enough to handle, they should be transplanted and each plant given room enough so that in course of growth they will not become crowded. Always attend carefully to watering and airing.

Plants of every kind, whether in pots or planted in benches, are benefited by having the surface soil stirred, and that at frequent intervals; and inseparable as this treatment is in success with plants in general, I have found that violets, whether in benches or in the open ground, appreciate this kind attention to their wants more than any other species of plants.

Violets detest water lodging around them, but again they like a good supply of water, and this supply can be given them more safely and at more frequent intervals if the soil is kept stirred as before noted. When watering violets it ought to be done thoroughly, and not again until the soil beneath the surface is found to be dry; and then shortly after watering, or when the surface in spots appears dry, the stirring process should commence. This stirring of the soil not only admits of the plants receiving more water than they otherwise would, but it also keeps everything sweet around the plants; and we have in addition to commend this treatment, the assurance from scientists that living organisms necessary for the nourishment of the roots require it for their own preservation.

Many make the mistake of lifting field-grown hydrangeas too early, when the wood is soft and not nearly matured; but as each locality, in temperature and other climatic conditions, is different in one or more particulars from the other, it is impossible to advise as to the exact date for lifting and potting.

While it is necessary to preserve all the roots possible when lifting the plants, I do not think it is at all indispensable for their future success to preserve much of the soil that adheres to the roots; in fact, I shake most of it from the roots, and give them instead a compost as rich as I can make it. After the plants are potted they should be placed in as exposed a situation as can be found for them outdoors. Until then, safety demands their removal to other quarters. These quarters should be, if possible, somewhat shady and cool. Give the plants a good watering directly after potting; subsequent watering should be infrequent. A cool cellar is a good place for resting hydrangeas, but care should be taken that frost does not reach them.

M. I.

Rose Lady Gay.

(42) Can you give us the names of some growers who are propagating the new rose Lady Gray? It seems to have created a veritable sensation on the other side of the water, but doesn't appear to be at all well-known on this side, although of American origin. Can you tell us who is growing it?

JACKSON & PERKINS CO.
Newark, New York.

Boston.

News Notes.

The Massachusetts Horticultural Society has issued a circular offering the following prizes to be awarded at the chrysanthemum show November 2, 3 and 4. For the best decorated dinner table laid for six covers for the second and third days of the exhibition three prizes:

First, $75 and a silver gilt medal;
Second, $50 and a silver medal;
Third, $35 and a bronze medal.

The judges are to be three ladies appointed by the committee on exhibitions. Tables will be furnished by the society, but all table supplies must be provided by the exhibitors. Entries must be made one week previous to the exhibition. This is an innovation in recent Boston shows and there is no doubt that these valuable prizes will excite keen competition among the floral artists of the city.

The preliminary schedule of the exhibitions in March and May of next year has also been issued and copies may be had from the secretary, W. P. Rich, 300 Massachusetts avenue.

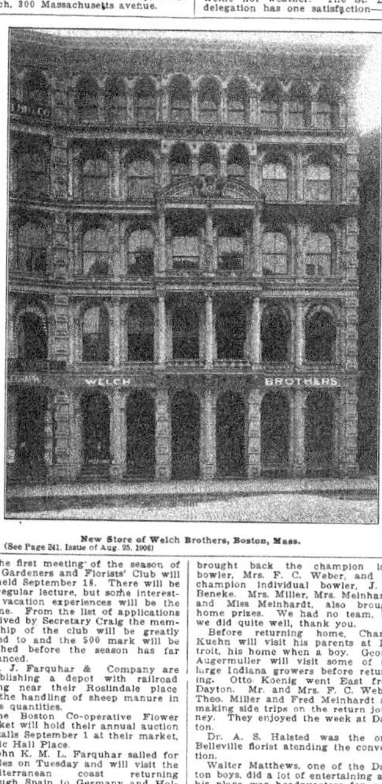

New Store of Welch Brothers, Boston, Mass.
(See Page 241, Issue of Aug. 25, 1906)

The first meeting of the season of the Gardeners and Florists' Club will be held September 18. There will be no regular lecture, but some interesting vacation experiences will be the theme. From the list of applications received by Secretary Craig the membership of the club will be greatly added to and the 500 mark will be reached before the season has far advanced.

R. J. Farquhar & Company are establishing a depot with railroad siding near their Roslindale place for the handling of sheep manure in large quantities.

The Boston Co-operative Flower Market will hold their annual auction of stalls September 1 at their market, Music Hall Place.

John K. M. L. Farquhar sailed for Naples on Tuesday and will visit the Mediterranean coast returning through Spain to Germany and Holland, where he will make selections of plants, etc., for the firm's next season's trade.

Wm. Doogue, superintendent of the Public Grounds Department, is seriously ill at his home in Dorchester.

The Boston Co-operative Flower Growers' Association will hold their auction sale of choice of stalls on Saturday morning, September 8, at their old established market on Park street.

John Dunbar, Rochester, N. Y., was a visitor this week.

J. W. DUNCAN.

St. Louis.

The Week's News.

Mrs. Brix, wife of Adolph Brix, has returned from a two months' stay in Europe.

Charles Fleckenstein, formerly in the cut flower commission business here, was in the city a few days ago attending the funeral of his father-in-law.

The first of the conventionites to return were J. J. Beneke, John L. Koenig, and H. Kruse. They report a pleasant time, the only thing marring their happiness was the extreme hot weather. The St. Louis delegation has one satisfaction—they brought back the champion lady bowler, Mrs. F. C. Weber, and the champion individual bowler, J. J. Beneke. Mrs. Miller, Mrs. Meinhardt, and Miss Meinhardt, also brought home prizes. We had no team, but we did quite well, thank you.

Before returning home, Charles Kuehn will visit his parents at Detroit, his home when a boy. George Augermuller will visit some of the large Indiana growers before returning. Otto Koenig went East from Dayton. Mr. and Mrs. F. C. Weber, Theo. Miller and Fred Meinhardt are making side trips on the return journey. They enjoyed the week at Dayton.

Dr. A. S. Halsted was the only Belleville florist atending the convention.

Walter Matthews, one of the Dayton boys, did a lot of entertaining and his place was headquarters for most of the delegates.

Mr. and Mrs. Carl Beyer are off on a trip East; they will visit Detroit, Buffalo and Niagara Falls.

ST. PATRICK.

Chicago.

Convention aftermath shows that Chicago was one of the best represented districts at Dayton, nearly all of the wholesale and commission houses having one or more delegates in attendance; the retail trade and growing interests were also in fairly good evidence. As the delegates come home singly or in parties they are unanimous in their praise of Dayton and the arrangements so ably carried out by the local club, the most severe criticism being lodged on the shoulders of the dispenser of the temperature and humidity, who not being a member of any of our organizations is exempt from censure.

A few minutes before J. B. Deamud boarded the train to return to his native heath he received a wire to the effect that Mrs. Deamud was seriously ill. We are pleased to report that she is improving.

A. L. Randall was in the city for two days last week and reports an excellent crop of grapes and pears on his Michigan fruit farm. Mr. Randall will return to office duty about September 20 when W. W. Randall accompanied by Mrs. Randall, will spend a few weeks in recuperation.

William E. Lynch of the E. A. Hunt Co., returned with his family from the East on Friday of last week, but has been confined to his house up to the present writing (Monday). He is, however, reported as being on the mend.

Miss Letta Bake of Ottumwa, Ia., was a recent visitor.

H. Roth of Lafayette, Ind., spent Saturday last in Chicago.

Augustus Caspers was a recent visitor to Chicago from Rochelle, Ill.

Poehlmann Brothers' stock from the Morton Grove houses is coming in exceptionally heavy for this season of the year and of especially fine quality. A beautiful crop of longiflorum lilies is one of their every day features, in addition to a complete supply of all florists' requirements.

With the opening of the Fall season, C. W. McKellar is receiving a new crop of orchids which are more than up to date.

J. W. Ensweiler has the sympathy of his friends in the trade on account of the recent loss of his youngest child.

Louis Coatsworth returned from Canada and spent a few days in town and went back to help celebrate the family reunion.

There has been not a little criticism of the second-class band wagons that the "Big 4" gave the Chicago delegation for their special to Dayton.

F. P. Davis, of Mobile, Ala., spent a few days with us last week.

E. V. Hallock continued his Western tour to Chicago and dropped off at many points to call on his old friends and associates.

WM. K. WOOD.

Indianapolis.

News Notes.

Walter Bertermann and Homer Wiegand and wife have returned from the East.

About twenty local florists will accept the hospitality of the Dayton Florists Club this week.

Irwin Bertermann, at the instance of the Evansville Retail Merchants' Association visited Evansville last week.

Henry Rieman has his extensive improvements about completed.

Visitors, Mr. Murphy, with J. C. Vaughan.

I. B.

WHEELING, W. VA.—The recent financial difficulties of the Schreiber-Mabis Company still has its echoes. One of the most regrettable after results is that of the veteran florist, Franz Laupp, who has been compelled to cease his business career. He has been located at 1327 Market street for the past sixteen years, always doing a prosperous business and making many friends. In all he was in the business, at various locations, for forty years. His affairs will be continued to a certain extent at the Island greenhouse, at the upper end of North Front street, by his wife, Mrs. Louise Laupp.

FOUNDED IN 1888

THE FLORISTS' EXCHANGE

A Weekly Medium of Interchange for Florists, Nurserymen Seedsmen and the Trade in general

Exclusively a Trade Paper.

Entered at New York Post Office as Second Class Matter

Published EVERY SATURDAY by

A. T. DE LA MARE PTG. AND PUB. CO. LTD.

2, 4, 6 and 8 Duane Street,

P. O. Box 1697.
Telephone 3765 John. **NEW YORK.**

CHICAGO OFFICE: 127 East Berwyn Avenue.

ILLUSTRATIONS.

Electrotypes of the illustrations used in this paper can usually be supplied by the publishers. Price on application.

YEARLY SUBSCRIPTIONS.

United States, Canada, and Mexico, $1.00. Foreign countries in postal union, $2.50. Payable in advance. Remit by Express Money Order Draft on New York. Post Office Money Order or Registered Letter.

The address label indicates the date when subscription expires and is our only receipt therefore.

REGISTERED CABLE ADDRESS:
Florex, New York.

ADVERTISING RATES.

One-half inch, 75c.; ¾-inch, $1.00; 1-inch, $1.25, special positions extra. Send for Rate Card showing discount of 10c., 15c., 25c., or 35c., per inch on continuous advertising. For rates on Wants, etc., see column for Classified Advertisements.

Copy must reach this office 12 o'clock Wednesday to secure insertion in issue of following Saturday.

Orders from unknown parties must be accompanied with cash or satisfactory references.

BOOKS RECEIVED.

DWARF FRUIT TREES—By F. A. Waugh, Professor of Horticulture and Landscape Gardening, Massachusetts Agricultural College. Illustrated, 225 Pages, 5x7 inches, Cloth. Price Postpaid 50 Cents. Published by Orange Judd Company, New York.

This is a serviceable little volume, and comes at an opportune time when interest in outdoor gardening in America is at high tide. Among the subjects now demanding attention is that of dwarf fruit trees, which are annually being cultivated in gardens in larger numbers. These dwarf trees have a great advantage in the fact that they come into bearing very early. One has to wait ten years for fruit from a common apple tree, while a dwarf tree of the same variety will bear in three years. The fruit is also of the highest quality. Even in strictly commercial operations the dwarf trees have their plan. They make the best of "fillers" for temporary planting between permanent standard trees in a new orchard, and there are some commercial orchards of dwarf trees, particularly of pears, long and favorably known in America, as profit yielding enterprises.

So far as the outdoor culture and management of these dwarf trees is concerned, Professor Waugh seems entirely at home, and the instruction he provides will be found of the greatest value. As much can hardly be said of his treatment of fruit trees under glass, however, to which a few pages of the book are devoted. He says "Sometimes wooden tubs are substituted for pots. These look better but are not so good in any other way." This statement is somewhat indefinite and misleading. Experienced growers of fruit under glass in this country prefer, on account of climatic conditions, tubs to pots, for the reason that during the hot weather the tubs are cooler for the roots than are pots.

The author also says that "all kinds of fruit trees can be grown in pots. Those which give the best returns are plums and nectarines." This is all right so far as nectarines are concerned; but whoever accepts the statement in its relation to plums as affording "best returns" will be disappointed. The pear, however, is wonderfully improved by pot culture.

The book, as a whole, is worth many times its cost to those who have an interest in this system of growing fruit trees. Copies of the volume can be obtained from The Florists' Exchange at the price named—50c each.

The Young & Bennett Company, Springfield, O., has purchased The Mayflower, published at Floral Park, N. Y., and will consolidate it with Floral Life.

S. A. F. Convention, 1906.

Take it all in all, as conventions go, the Dayton meeting of the S. A. F. O. H., held last week, may be regarded as having been a great success. With a large attendance that, notwithstanding the torrid weather, stuck close to business during business hours; with a very extensive and comprehensive trade display generally satisfactory to the exhibitors in the amount of business done; with hospitality and entertainments interesting, unique, and most enjoyable in their character, the convention of 1906 will long remain a very pleasant memory.

President Kasting made an acceptable chairman, putting through the work with commendable dispatch. Quick to grasp any situation that presented itself, strictly constitutional; forceful and energetic, yet withal quite diplomatic, he surprised even those who know him best by his able conduct of affairs. His address contained a number of very practical recommendations, several of which were or will be put in operation, chief among them being the change proposed to be made in relation to the secretary's office, placing that official under bonds, the auditing of his accounts by the executive committee, and the presentation of these accounts in itemized form. That these formalities have not been insisted upon heretofore, manifests either implicit confidence by the society in its secretary, or an incomprehensible indifference on the part of its Board of Directors to the disposition of its funds by that official.

The appropriation of $200 made by the society to ensure the presence of its secretary at flower shows and other gatherings of the craft, will no doubt add considerably to the membership, personal canvass being at all times preferable to solicitation by correspondence.

The little bit of advice proffered by the president on the subject of "Business Methods," is well-meant, and should be taken in the spirit in which it is given. No man, we think, can gainsay the president's statement, "Do not abuse your credit and you will find business very much easier."

We are in hearty accord with Mr. Kasting's suggestion that the S. A. F. O. H. should take entire charge of its trade exhibit, receiving any profits that accrue therefrom. This is something we have several times advocated, as well as the appointment of a permanent manager of the trade exhibit. A new superintendent of exhibition with every convention does not, in our opinion, conduce to that general allround satisfaction to exhibitors that a permanent manager, well equipped for the office, and conversant with the details of its requirements, is likely to afford. We again enter a plea for a permanent superintendent of exhibits. But be in no hurry in selecting your man. The best available only can fill the bill.

As regards the profits from the trade exhibit; these form the only asset accruing from a convention, and it does not seem right or proper that they should be handed over to somebody else. The entertainment of the delegates is entirely outside the province of the society proper; and while the hospitalities extended are highly appreciated always, whether on a lavish or meagre scale, the funds that by right belong to the organization should not be diverted to this purpose, while other and more useful and profitable avenues of expenditure are available. By all means let the trade exhibit profits find their way into the S. A. F. exchequer.

Reverting to the entertainment: it is rather impolite to criticize those whose satisfied guests we have been for these many years, yet it cannot be gainsaid that the practice has reached a position that has become burdensome. So long ago as the first Philadelphia convention in 1886 the committee on final resolutions on that occasion, commenting on the hospitalities extended said: "And to the Florists' Club of Philadelphia we extend our most grateful thanks for the royal way that we have been entertained, but while fully appreciating its great kindness, that has involved so much labor and expense, we most earnestly trust that this kind attention should not be taken as a precedent for future conventions; and that at the meeting to be held in Chicago, next August, the delegates there will best please those of the society in general by an entire omission of these courtesies." These recommendations were signed by Peter Henderson, John H. Taylor and W. J. Stewart. But the advice then given seems to have gone unheeded; and now another note of warning has been sounded. Will the reform said by President Kasting to be necessary, a statement endorsed by many members of the society, come about next year at the city which first set the pace that as the years have passed has neared the killing point?

In regard to the sports: they are all right in their place. But let them take place, as in former years, on the Friday of the convention—entertainment day. There is no necessity of the business of the society being interfered with by them, neither do we believe the bowlers themselves would stand for such interference. And they, we feel sure, would be willing to forego whatever other entertainment is agoing on the Friday so long as they can indulge their own predilections. To be otherwise minded would savor of anything but unselfishness—a characteristic common to all fair and square sportsmen

It is gratifying to note the disposition of the society to appropriate sums of money for the carrying out of objects tending to broaden its work as well as to increase its membership. Very little can be accomplished without judicious expenditure of funds, and the work mapped out, entailing disbursements of money, is sure to bring its own reward.

We sincerely hope that the little assistance lent by the society toward postal reform, the establishment of a parcels post system in America, the revision of the tariff and other things of that sort may be productive of good; though what was done at the sessions could easily have been accomplished with less waste of time and certainly with greatly diminished oratorical effort. The approaching of Congress on matters vital to the trade is no new thing to the S. A. F. O. H., which at this late day needs no instruction on how to go about it.

One of the most practical matters discussed by the delegates was that dealing with the registration of new plants. This is something that, in our opinion, needs emendation. Though not intended, there can be no question that the registration of a new plant with the society, such registration exploiting as it does in many cases the superiority of the novelty registered over existing sorts, over the signature of the society's secretary, forms a quasi-official endorsement of that novelty, and so appears to the majority of those who read the registration record.

We think also too much is taken for granted in connection with registration as at present carried out. If as interpreted by the secretary, registration is merely to safeguard priority of name, the simple appellation would be all-sufficient. But it does more than that; it also affords a means of identification through a description of the novelty more or less complete, which description is recorded on the books of the society without verification as to its correctness. This looks like doing things in a too slipshod manner, unworthy a national organization like the S. A. F. Hence it comes about that a man who has taken advantage of the registration department of the society complacently states in open meeting that he estimates the value of such registration as equivalent to so much free advertising—and nothing more.

The appointment of a canna committee to inspect all new varieties of this plant previous to registration is a step in the right directioin. But this preliminary should not, and cannot in justice to the membership, be confined to cannas; it should be made generally applicable in the case of every new plant for which registration is sought. Thus may we come to the point where registration of new plants by the S. A. F. will mean something, be an indication of the progress we are making, rather than a mere baptismal record of names attached to more or less fugacious denizens of the plant world.

The selection of Philadelphia augurs well for a record-breaking attendance next year and a very successful gathering in every particular.

Finally, as regards the proposed National Flower Show, under the auspices of the S. A. F. O. H.; the proposition is an excellent one, and we hope to see it carried out. We have our doubts, however, as to the practicability of a change of date of meeting for the year in which the show is to be held—1908—so that the exhibition and annual convention shall be held at the same time (November) and place—Chicago. We cannot forget the oft-repeated refrain that the convention trip is the only outing the majority of the florists take; that many delegates bring with them their wives and families; and that the ladies lend éclat to the gatherings. Such a trip

"When chill November's surly blast
Makes fields and forests bare,"

would not be of the enjoyable nature of that afforded during Mid-summer—heat and other drawbacks included. There are also many who might not find it convenient to attend in November.

While we thoroughly approve of the exhibition being held at that time, we would urge that the change of the date of the annual meeting be seriously considered. Meantime we should be pleased to publish the views of the members interested on this important matter.

A Warning.

Editor Florists' Exchange

It has come to my positive knowledge that certain irresponsible parties have sold bulbs for Fischer's giant Freesia Purity. For the benefit of those who have bought Purity not direct from me, I will give the names of the dealers who are selling Freesia Purity this season. They are: Arthur T. Boddington, New York; Peter Henderson & Company, New York; Stumpp & Walter Company, New York; Vaughan's Seed Store, New York and Chicago; W. W. Ranson & Company, Boston; Henry F. Michell Company, Philadelphia; and Hosea Waterer, Philadelphia.

Anybody who bought Freesia Purity from any other source did not get what they paid for.

Great Neck, L. I. RUDOLPH FISCHER.

OUR READERS' VIEWS

Concerning Geraniums.

Editor Florists' Exchange:

I see Expertus still has a little "wind" left in his carcass, but he is getting more harmless all the time. The first part of his letter is an abortive attempt to ridicule and contradict part of my last letter. His conclusion is as near as he dare come to an apology to the growers, "something which is altogether superfluous" the growers, and all who have read his effusion, have got his size to a nicety. A florist who can only raise eight cuttings from a stock plant is not likelyyto do much good or harm to the geranium business either in the market or elsewhere.

But if Expertus is really anxious for information of "practical value" regarding geranium growing, let him turn to page 152 of The Florists' Exchange, "Our London Letter," last paragraph under the caption "Geraniums." There he will find the whole thing in a nut shell.—written in a professional, comprehensive and florist-like manner. Mr. Hemsley states, "Our growers get an immense lot from a fewyplants." (not 8 cuttings.) It will also be observed that all the cuttings are taken directly from the stock plants, none of this topping humbug, nor taking cuttings from cuttings. London is evidently far ahead of Pennsylvania in geranium growing.

There is one practice London growers might change with advantage to themselves, that is, planting, "old stools" for stock. New York market growers plant out clean, vigorous, selected young plants for stock and find that it pays.

A gentleman signing himself "A. Cova" calls me down in a rather autocratic and domineering manner, for making the assertion that the Greek is a cleaner up of what is left, and from observation and inquiry, I find that I have nothing to take back.

Mr. Cova is evidently not one of the common or garden variety of Greek, he takes himself quite seriously, and, dogmatically claims, that "the retail flower business in this metropolis is in the hands of Greek merchants."

I am inclined to be a little sceptical regarding that statement, and I guess it will be news to many others. I have been a frequent visitor at the places where plants and flowers are sold in New York City for many years, and I find that the same old buyers, or their representatives, are there as of old, and, I notice that the best is always for them. Where the rest goes is not hard to guess.

An interesting bit of "flower lore" relating to the Greek will be found in the St. Paul "News Notes" on page 204 of The Florists' Exchange.

JOHN BIRNIE.

Appreciation from Australia.

Editor Florists' Exchange:

Having taken The Florists' Exchange for more than a year, I feel like writing a line or two to convey my warm appreciation of your great efforts to extend the art of horticulture by placing in the hands of your people, and our people, something which, as far as I can see, is head and shoulders above anything else I know. I like the style of your contributors, and I like their matter. Particularly interested am I in your carnation trade and your articles on this subject. If the secretary (I have forgotten his name) would mail me anything in the shape of the society's bulletins or the publishers would send me notices or review copies of their publications, some business might result. . . .

With greetings to American Horticulturists from an Australian.

J. G. LOCKLEY, Editor "Amateur Gardener."
Sydney, N. S. W.

Editor Florists' Exchange:

Please receive $2.50, subscription for your paper to 1907. I am pleased to say it is still up to the standard for useful information pertaining to horticulture and floriculture.

Of course, your seasons do not correspond with ours; and the climatic conditions being so very different the cultivation of plants vary so much on account of this that your style does not suit us. Take carnations for an example. All we do in the open border during Midwinter is to cover the blooms with a pot or small board to protect them from the rain or sun. At our carnation meeting (of 100 members) we had some fine flowers of American kinds, as well as seedlings. Being the introducer of the American carnation into Australia, I am writing a short paper on them, giving you credit where it is due, and discounting where it is not. However, you can rest assured the flower has come to stay with us; also it is likely to be improved upon by the look of the seedlings which are being raised wholesale.

I will forward a copy of my paper so that your readers may judge how and what we are doing with the American carnation.

I should be pleased to see in the reports of your shows what varieties took the first or second prizes. In many cases this is done, but some merely say so and so took first with 100 white or 100 pink and no name is attached to the variety. This information to your readers is of great help in selecting or knowing which one is best of its class.

Again, when a new variety comes out it should be stated if an improvement on any variety the name of such, (which would be a guide to the grower) and where the improvement comes in. I have had several new sorts out and find they are little or no better than older sorts.

I must say the E. G. Hill Company have treated me well. They pack light and with great care; but the long distance, five weeks' journey, is too much for plants to risk.

Australia. JAMES BEGGS.

Insects Stinging Fruits.

Editor Florists' Exchange:

In a recent issue of The Florists' Exchange, I noted among queries in the "Question Box" a remedy or method of preventing bees and other insects from destroying fruit on trees. Your correspondent is mistaken in thinking that bees sting ripening fruit. Such is not the case: as during my experience of over twenty years as a beekeeper, I have noted that a worker bee never stings anything unless attacked in the hive. The damage to fruit is caused by the tongue of the bee, which makes an incision in the covering or skin and extracts the juices or fruit acids. The task of covering fruit with muslin is most laborious, and unless your correspondent is located near some one who keeps bees for pleasure or profit, I suggest the following effective remedy: Upon a shallow plate or dish, place a quantity of honey slightly thinned with water, add a pinch of Paris green and place where the insects are most abundant. They will soon "load up" and start for home: it will be their last journey, however, as the poison will have done its fatal work before they will have reached their destination.

Rhode Island. G. S. W.

The Late William McMillan

Pelargoniums vs. Lady Washingtons.

Editor Florists' Exchange:

We sometimes see writers that say the designation Lady Washington is wrongly applied to pelargoniums, our friend William Scott, being the latest who recently admonished us on the subject.

This misapplication arose here at Rochester, N. Y., in the early fifties. In 1849 the late Josiah Salter, one of the celebrated Salter family of London, England, came to this country. Mr. Salter was a good all-around gardener knowing his business well. He had been engaged with his uncle John Salter who did as much, perhaps more than any other man, with the chrysanthemum, at Versailles, Paris, where he had a nursery. On the breaking out of the French revolution many Frenchmen left France, the Salters among them, and the next year found Mr. Salter at Rochester, N. Y., engaged in gardening. Mr. Salter brought with him from England, among other seeds, some choice pelargonium seed, I believe the Dobson strain, then about the best in Europe. He raised some good seedlings, many of them perhaps equal to any then in Europe.

One of his seedlings he called George Washington, another Lady Washington, another an unusually robust, grower, color rosy pink with black blotches on upper petals, he named Wm. H. Seward. All these varieties, no doubt like many other good things, are now lost to the trade, other varieties taking their place. Visitors to the greenhouses under Mr. Salter's charge, soon got to know and call them all Lady Washingtons from one variety, named Lady Washington; and when I succeeded to these greenhouses, on East avenue, in this city, in Fall of 1857, all visitors knew all pelargoniums as Lady Washingtons only, an erroneous term, which has now spread all over the country; like the term "Golden Glow," as applied to Rudbeckia laciniata fl. pl.

Of course, gardening and florist work in the early fifties was done quite differently in many respects to what prevails now, and sometimes I think for the worse under present methods.

JOHN CHARLTON.
Rochester, N. Y.

For General Information.

STOVE.—A plant-house devoted to the cultivation of subjects requiring a high temperature, many of which are amongst the most beautiful, either for their flowers or for their fine foliage.—Nicholson's Dictionary of Gardening.

STOVE PLANTS.—The term "stove" applied to plants undoubtedly originated from the method of heating the structures in which plants were grown before the advent of hot water and steam. Glasshouses such as then existed were heated by stoves and flues, usually made of bricks. Such structures came to be called stove-houses or stoves, and the plants grown in them "stove plants." (A "greenhouse" was in those days an unheated glasshouse in which plants were merely kept alive over Winter.) These terms still exist in England, but are applied to strictly tropical plants or those requiring a warm temperature for their successful culture in glasshouses. In this country such plants are spoken of as warmhouse or tropical plants.

In England, at the present time, more distinction is made in the names applied to plant houses than in this country. For instance, "greenhouse" in England now means the coolest glasshouse only, while in this country the name is usually indiscriminately applied to all glasshouses. The names applied to plant houses in England are therefore: Stove, for tropical plants; intermediate house, for plants hailing from warm-temperate climates; greenhouse, for those plants requiring the least degree of heat. A conservatory or show house is one in which plants are placed while in flower and usually kept at a cool temperature.

In practice such terms may be greatly modified to suit local conditions; for example, at the Botanic Gardens of Smith College, Northampton, Mass., the glasshouses are named cool-temperate house, warm-temperate house, tropical house, palm house, acacia and succulent house, experiment house and propagating house, the temperatures and moisture conditions being regulated to suit the requirements of each class of plants.

The cultivation of stove plants is too heterogeneous a subject to be treated exhaustively in a single book, because the stove contains thousands of dissimilar plant treasures from the tropics, especially those found at low altitudes. In general, the stove is the house which requires the most expense and care, the greatest heat and highest atmospheric moisture.—Bailey's Cyclopedia of American Horticulture.

Obituary

William McMillan.

William McMillan, Boston, who died last week, came to America from Scotland in 1886. After a short time spent with friends, he obtained a situation with W. W. Rawson & Co., seedsmen, Boston, Mass. His genial ways, ready wit and good nature won for him at once the respect of his employers and the good-will of his fellow employees. It was but a few years before the market gardeners of Boston found in him a friend whom they could always depend upon to give them just what they wanted. "If Mac put up the order it must be all right." This confidence showed his employers the esteem in which he was held by customers, and he was given charge of the vegetable seed department, which position he held, until suddenly taken ill on December 31, 1899. Most of the time since then he has been at the hospital. On pleasant days he was able to spend some hours out-of-doors until ten days ago, when he was suddenly stricken with a paralytic attack from which he never recovered, and passed away Wednesday, August 22. The funeral service was held at Forest Hills Cemetery, where interment was made on Friday, August 24 at 2.30 p. m. There were several beautiful floral designs; mute testimonials of affection, from friends and past employers. His immediate relations are in Scotland and England, except one brother who is in the West.

F. J. Neiglick.

Frank J. Neiglick died after an operation in Chicago on Friday of last week. Though quiet and unassuming he was well known to all the oldtime florists of that city having been to "the manner born" and having spent his life in close affiliation with the trade in the Garden City. The father of the deceased, P. N. Neiglick, is one of the oldest representatives in the trade and a brother, Charles T., is the well known State street florist. Mr. Neiglick was thirty-one years of age, and his demise will be a sad blow to many associates in the profession.

W. K. W.

The S.A.F.O.H. Dayton Convention

August 21-24, 1906

Continuation of Proceedings

The meeting announced for Friday at 9.30 a. m. did not convene until 12 noon, and was largely devoted to the passing of final resolutions presented by the committee, an informal discussion on the proposed National Flower Show and the reading of the judges' report on the outdoor exhibits.

The committee on Final Resolutions recommended that the society's thanks be tendered to President J. B. Heiss and the other membrs of the Dayton Florists' Club for the admirable manner in which their work connected with the convention had been carried out; to the ladies of the Dayton Florists' Club for the favors extended to the visiting ladies; to Horace M. Frank, superintendent of the trade exhibit, for his attention to the interests of exhibitors; to H. M. Altick, for his masterful handling of the sports and pastimes; to the postmaster at Dayton for the installation of postal service at the exhibition hall; to the Home Telephone Company and to the Bell Telephone Company for the free use of their respective telephone instruments, and to the daily press of Dayton for the lengthy and instructive reports of the proceedings. Separate resolutions were passed tendering thanks to the National Cash Register Company for hospitalities extended the delegates, and also to John H. Patterson for the great interest he had taken in the convention.

The discussion on the National Flower Show question elicited the fact that preparations for the holding of the exhibition were placed, by resolution, in the hands of the Executive Committee, and it was decided that a meeting of this committee be called by the president, at an early date, to further discuss the question, after which the meeting adjourned.

Judges' Awards at Dayton Exhibition.

Corrected Official Report.

CERTIFICATE OF MERIT.

W. F. Kasting, Buffalo, N. Y. Most practical and cheapest Indestructible Cement Greenhouse Bench.

H. A. Dreer, Philadelphia, Pa. Bougainvillea W. K. Harris. Highly commended at Washington, 1905, as Bougainvillea Sanderiana variegata.

Morehead Mfg. Co., Detroit, Mich. The Morehead Trap.

J. H. Broxey, Dayton, O. The Gem. Considerad the best carnation support to date.

King Construction Co., N. Tonawanda, N. Y. New Gutter and Spring Attachment to Ventilator.

Lord & Burnham Co., Irvington, N. Y. Dust-Proof Gear.

Herendeen Mfg. Co., Geneva, N. Y. New Three-piece Sectional Boiler B. & A. Series.

Kroeschell Bros., Chicago, Ill. Scale bearing shaking grate.

Kroeschell Bros., Chicago, Ill. Ideal Chain Wrench.

Vaughan's Seed Store, Chicago. Gladiolus Mrs. Frances W. King.

Edw. Amerophl, Janesville, Wis. Nephrolepis Amerpohlii. Very distinct; one of the best novelties in exhibition.

Arthur Cowee, Berlin, N. Y. Sixteen new gladioli all of great merit particularly Peace, Nilreb, 605, Scarsdale, and Cremida.

HONORABLE MENTION.

Wm. Sim, Cliftondale, Mass. For tomatoes of remarkable fertility and uniformity of size and color.

Fred Windmiller, Columbus, O. A free-flowering type of Begonia semperflorens.

Louis Ullrich, Tiffin, O. Zonal Geranium Tiffin, Single, scarlet.

James Vick's Sons, Rochester, N. Y. Asters, Vick's Violet King and twd new varieties of Daybreak color.

Hein Support Co., Connersville, Ind. Carnation Support.

Storrs & Harrison Co., Painesville, O. Nephrolepis Leedsii. A sport from Piersoni a little more robust than the Tarrytown.

HIGHLY COMMENDED.

Dayton Supply Co., Dayton, O. Simplicity Spray Pump. A most useful implement.

Wertheimer Bros., New York, N. Y. New and original Designs in Ribbon for American Beauty Roses.

E. A. Beaven, Evergreen, Ala. Fadeless Sheet Moss. A very useful article. Chemically treated.

H. Thaden, Atlanta, Ga. Equalizing Truss.

M. Rice & Co., Philadelphia, Pa. Novelty Adjustable Plant Baskets and Birch Bark Pot Covers.

J. Stern & Co., Philadelphia, Pa. Magnolia and Cycas Wreaths.

S. S. Pennock, Philadelphia, Pa. Pearl Pins and New Ribbon Designs.

H. Bayersdorfer & Co., Philadelphia, Pa. Imported Tone Ware of Grecian Effect and other Novelties.

Reed & Keller, New York, N. Y. New Forms for Design Work, Baskets, Cycas Holders, etc.

Schloss Bros., New York, N. Y. New Ribbon Novelties.

C. C. Myers, Dayton, O. The Yankee Hose and Pipe Clamp.

Dayton Paper Novelty Co., Dayton, O. Embossed Violet Box of New Design.

Lord & Burham Co., Irvington, N. Y. New Greenhouse Gutter.

The Trade Exhibit—View from Gallery showing center of Hall.

Report of Judges on Outdoor Exhibit.

The committee appointed to judge the outdoor exhibit of plants, beg to submit the following: An exhibit of Canna King Humbert, by the Vaughan Seed Store, Chicago and New York. This is an extra fine exhibit in fine shape. The canna is of fine habit, free flowering, flowers large of good color, and dark bronze leathery foliage.

The same firm makes an exhibit of Baby Rambler rose, also a bed of cannas composed of two unnamed varieties with Papa Nardy and David Harum.

Nathan Smith & Son, of Adrian, Mich., makes several interesting exhibits. A bed of Canna Imperial Gardener Hoppe, as growing here, is no improvoment over existing varieties. Canna Express, is a free bloomer, of dwarf habit and crimson color.

By the same firm Canna Director Holtz, yellow ground, heavily spotted red on smaller petals, others slightly spotted, a very effective color, plants of good habit; your committee thinks very highly of this variety, and recommend a certificate of merit. Also Canna Oscoda; this is not as effective as others in commerce. Canna Martha Washington, by the same firm. Salvia splendens Triumph, of good compact habit, early in flower, and of good color.

The same firm makes a very interesting display of hardy herbaceous plants. Very effective at the present time are Hibiscus Crimson Eye Rudbeckia triloba, Boltonia latisquama, Boltonia asteroides, Helenium autumnalis superbum, and Phlox Mrs. Dwyer, etc.

W. F. Kasting, Buffalo, N. Y., an exhibit of canna Mrs. Kasting, fine color, brilliant red; the flower spike carried well above the foliage, making it very effective.

H. A. Dreer, Philadelphia, make a very interesting exhibit of Delphinium Belladona, petunias, Pennisetum macrophyllum atrosanguineum, and ageratum Inimitable.

Gus Obermayer, Parkersburg, W. Va., showed canna West Virginia. This is an improved Souvenir d'Antoine Crozy, fine habit and free in flower.

Your committee recommend that the society's silver medal be awarded to Mr. John Freudenburger, for his care, planting, and tasteful arrangement of the outdoor exhibit.

PETER BISSET.
EDWIN LONSDALE.
WM. MILLER,
Judges.

A report of the society's committee on outdoor exhibit states that 2800 square feet of space was regularly entered by five exhibitors, also that the labor and care connected with this exhibit were kindly furnished by the National Cash Register Company, who kept from two to four men continually at the work. The society feels under great obligations to the company for their interest and for the good to the community made possible by their generosity. The interest awakened among the citizens of Dayton should prove of benefit to the local florists; and the feature of the 1906 convention, begun in a small way, should be continued, if possible, to ascertain its merits as a business proposition.

This committee was composed of H. M. Altick and W. J. Stewart.

Friday, Entertainment Day.

On Friday, after being photographed on the Fair Grounds, the convention delegates visited the model factory of the National Cash Register Company, and were escorted in groups of 20 by a representative of that firm through the various departments, the workings of the concern being fully explained. The tidiness of the surroundings of the operatives, the methodical manner in which the work was carried out in all its details, were highly complimented and the lecture and visit very much enjoyed by all present.

In the afternoon the conventionites were taken in street cars on a trolley ride through the city, and it was remarked that the influence of the National Cash Register Company in a horticultural way was seen throughout the whole of Dayton, almost every little cottage and home being surrounded with plants and flowers. The cars proceeded to the Soldiers' Home, and while there the visitors were presented to Governor Thomas and his staff, who welcomed the florists with a hearty handshake. They were then photographed, and afterward proceeded to Memorial Hall, where brief addresses were made by President Kasting of the S. A. F., and President Heiss and Vice-president Lützenberger, of the Dayton Florists' Club. The party then dispersed, each taking his or her own way through the grounds, visiting the grotto, the flower garden, the barracks, buildings, and other interesting features of this magnificent institution.

Throughout the grounds were observed, sitting on benches in groups and separately, hundreds of men who had given their services to their country during its most critical period. Some of the old soldiers were without arms, others without legs, and some were totally blind; many were old and decrepit using canes and crutches as an aid to locomotion. It was a pathetic, yet a most pleasurable sight to see these old battle-scarred veterans passing their time amid such beautiful surroundings provided by a grateful country, waiting patiently for the last roll-call that should muster them out forever.

Superintendent Haerlin was indefatigable in his endeavors to make the visit of the delegates a pleasant one, and took great pains to explain his work in improving and introducing new landscape features into the grounds.

On return to the city, the delegates were taken to the Fair Grounds where a final promenade concert was enjoyed.

A great many remained in Dayton till the following day, but the larger number departed for their homes by the evening trains on Friday, after having enjoyed a most pleasurable sojourn in the Gem City of Ohio, barring the heat.

L. Ullrich's New Geranium Tiffin

Advertising Signs in Exhibition Building

Stove vs. Greenhouse Plants.

The discussion on what constituted a stove plant in the United States, evoked by an inquiry in the Question Box asking that a stove plant be defined, and stating that an exhibitor at a flower show had been disqualified because he had shown such right in disqualifying the plants in question as stove plants.

Robert Craig said he believed the judge was plants as anthuriums, marantas and others in a group calling for stove plants, brought out the following:

Professor Irish, on being called on, said: "It seems to me that the plants in question should be classed as greenhouse plants. A stove house, as I understand it, is one which has a temperature of 82 degrees or over. I would like to ask Mr. Craig why he thinks the judges should reject these plants as stove plants.

Mr. Hallock asked Mr. Craig to define the line of demarcation between a greenhouse and a stove plant.

Mr. Craig stated that among gardeners there are greenhouse and stove plants. Greenhouse plants are commonly recognized as those growing in a temperature of 68 degrees or less, a stove plant in 75 degrees or more.

Mr. Bisset: There is no question at all but Mr. Craig is right. Greenhouse plants and stove plants are entirely distinct. The schedule was in error; it should have stated the temperature in which the plants were to be grown.

Mr. Stewart explained that the schedule of the Massachusetts Horticultural Society called for groups of stove and greenhouse plants. He thought it was necessary to make the classification specific where plants run so closely into each other as the ones under consideration.

Professor Irish was of the opinion that all were greenhouse plants; stove plants being simply a division of greenhouse plants. In Europe they had what they called the temperate house, the cool house, and the hot or stove house, but all were greenhouse plants. This view was held also by George Watson.

Antoine Wintzer thought that the distinction between greenhouse and stove plants was problematcal, which no man could define; it was a question of locality and conditions. In plant catalogues it was common to find the coleus classified as a greenhouse plant, but no one in this country would think of taking the coleus out of the bedding plant class. The same may be said of Cissus discolor; this plant could be planted in June, trained to a trellis, and would grow beautifully until Fall. Cannas were classified as tropical plants, but he had found by experience that the canna will really thrive and develop in a temperature that would be detrimental to the rose. Still we do not classify the tea rose as a stove plant. Well grown cannas will sustain a temperature of 40 degrees without suffering any detriment in foliage, while the same degree would be fatal to the rose.

Mr. Craig: There is no doubt that Professor Irish is right from his point of view, that gardeners recognize a cool house, an intermediate and a stove house. Mr. Stewart's statement about the Boston schedules (and they study out things carefully there) shows that there are stove and greenhouse plants recognized at these exhibitions; if it were otherwise the designation greenhouse plants would be big enough. Nicholson in his dictionary will tell you that such and such a plant is a stove house plant, or a greenhouse plant, or an intermediate house plant.

Mr. Hallock: I think all these gentlemen are all right in their definitions. I think the inquirer felt sore and wanted to get back at the judges. Some one should give him advice to conform to the schedule, and also suggest to the managers that they classify these two classes of plants as one.

Mr. Fulmer mentioned a case at one of the Iowa State Fairs were exception had been taken to Cycas revoluta being classified as a palm. This matter will come up at times, and is similar to the question as to when a pig becomes a shoat.

Mr. Watson thought the inquirer wanted to get the S. A. F. into a hole; it was too fine a point, and the trouble was owing largely to the fault of the schedule.

C. W. Turnley: "Thus far shalt thou go and no farther." A greenhouse is limited to a certain temperature. Should any florist attempt to grow marantas in a cool greenhouse temperature he would see what his success would amount to. Years ago in company with John Dick, now deceased, I was passing through his establishment, and asked him what the little enclosure that I observed was for. He said, "That is our stove house." And this was in a greenhouse, showing the difference between the temperature of a stove house and a greenhouse. Our boiler men figure upon the temperature of a greenhouse, and if you want a hot house that temperature must be increased. The speaker thought there was a decided difference between the temperature of a greenhouse and that of a stove house.

The discussion closed by the matter being laid on the table.

Portion of Outdoor Exhibit of Nathan Smith & Son, Adrian, Mich.

Registration of Cannas.

"Is it to the benefit of the trade for originators of new cannas to name and disseminate a long list of varieties having no desirable merits over existing kinds?"

Mr. Vaughan was of opinion that the society ought to revive the canna committee, and would prefer to have the approval of this canna committee in order to secure registration of new varieties by the secretary. Americans are doing very careful work on the canna, and it was necessary to throw away thousands of seedlings in order to get one of merit. A new canna, to be meritorious these days and worthy of introduction, ought to have about 15

Reed & Keller's Exhibit.

Exhibit of S. S. Pennock.

good points; lacking any one of these points it was worthless to the trade. This registering of cannas that have not been inspected by a committee, gives the varieties a half-way endorsement of the society, and a great many people may assume that cannas have merit because they have been registered. He believed it should not be too easy to register new varieties on the books of the association, and moved for the appointment of a canna committee composed of men who knew the canna, and who themselves were not commercially interested in the new varieties.

Peter Bisset: I think Mr. Vaughan is in the right direction. There is no doubt, from the reading of the secretary's report, that a whole lot of things have been registered that have no earthly value. It is far too easy for any gentleman to get seddlings registered that have little semblance of worth. We ought to charge a fee for registration or have a competent committee pass upon every plant that is submitted for registration. I think Mr. Vaughan should go a little further and have a general committee appointed.

Mr. Vaughan: I think the society should first take up the canna committee, and then take up the subject of a general inspection committee.

George Watson took exception to the leaving out of men commercially interested in the canna from the committee because then the society would be debarred of the best brains of the canna intellect. He did not believe there was any member of the society appointed on the committee who would be dishonorable enough to use his position for his own benefit.

Mr. Stewart said in connection with the registration matter he had always taken it for granted that registration had nothing to do with the merits or demerits of a variety; registration did not register the qualities or otherwise of any variety, nor should it be looked upon as any endorsement of it as having any value. Registration simply registered the name, giving the party registering the prior use of that name and that he be protected in that use as far as the society could protect him. If, as had been suggested, there should be a registration committee to pass upon the quality of the variety as to whether it was worthy of attention or not, he believed it would be a good thing. There were long lists of varieties now submitted for registration that burdened the secretary's report, but under the constitution the secretary could not do otherwise than register them.

Mr. Watson thought that the registration gave a fictitious value in the minds of the general public, and the appointment of a committee, and the inspection of varieties by that committee, would tend to eliminate this.

L. H. Read considered that the secretary was right in his interpretation of the constitution; he did not believe that the society had any right to deny registration to any one who produced a new plant and intended to put it on the market. If new plants were not to be registered they could be introduced without registration. All that registration did, it seemed to him, was to give a little advertising to the plants registered, perhaps.

C. Hagenburger thought that the matter should be left at it now stands. The more new cannas or other plants obtained and registered, the better for the S. A. F. Almost every man who obtained a new plant thought that he had got something good, but many of them had been mistaken in their judgment.

Antoine Wintzer thought it would be to the interests of the S. A. F. to see to it that the registration of plants was put on a high plane. Any one registering, say, a strain of pansies inferior to previous strains obtained would be going backward. Any grower could go into a canna field and get a lot of seedlings of any variety and originate new kinds indefinitely. He referred to a grower in Philadelphia who, some years ago, registered some 20 to 30 names of cannas, and not one of these were afterward put in commerce. This was a great injustice to other originators who were prevented using the names that had already been bestowed on such varieties. Originators of new cannas ought to be willing to test their plants for at least three years. The firm of which he is a member, practiced the plan of testing its new kinds from three to five years. He believed all new varieties ought to be inspected either by a canna committee or by some disinterested party, and that every plant should go on its own merits. The standard ought to be elevated. American florists had suffered considerably from the indiscriminate naming of cannas and other plants by foreign plantsmen. He could distribute ten thousand canna seeds and guarantee that each plant resulting would be superior to many he had seen in some of the parks. No doubt every disseminator of new cannas was perfectly honest in his intentions, but it would be a good thing for him to go round and see what other people are doing. The society could take such cannas as King Humbert and Louisiana and base the new varieties on the standard of these sorts.

Mr. Bisset stated, as showing the view of the registration matter held by outsiders that it had been brought to his attention by a party interested in the subject of new plants that the first place to which he would refer for a list of these would be to the records of the S. A. F.

Secretary Stewart thought possibly the gentleman whom Mr. Bisset had in mind had more particular reference to the list of new plants which the secretary published distinct from those registered; that list comprised new introductions by American houses, and by foreign houses, in the introduction of which American firms were interested.

Alex. Wallace asked the secretary to read the clause in the constitution authorising the registration of plants, which provided for the registration of new plants only, so that all plants registered were understood to be new as far as the parties registering knew.

The matter ended by the adoption of a resolution to appoint a canna committee of five members.

Discussion on the National Flower Show.

Robert Craig: You will all recollect that at Washington last year the subject of a National Flower Show was taken up and the project met with great favor. Among the recommendations made was one that it was necessary to have a guarantee fund of $10,000 in order to make the show something like what it should be. In a very few minutes we had about $3,000 subscribed by reliable people in the room. Since that time we find that the raising of this guarantee fund is the easiest part of the whole matter. The project has met with much favor by the large growers in the country, and by the representative amateur gardeners, so that we will have no difficulty in carrying out this idea, provided (and here comes the great difficulty) we can find a man to take charge of the exhibition. It has often been said that all the best work of the world has to be done by one man. Now it is evident that our busy commercial men have their own private interests to look after, and for the workings and carrying forward of this project they do not have the time. The committee think, after very careful consideration of the subject, that the society will have to employ some competent person who can control the time and take this matter in charge in order that it may become the success that it is possible to make such a show, and which such a show should be. The committee were instructed to prepare a schedule, a preliminary schedule at least, giving in detail how this amount of $8,000 or some of it, should be expended. They have done that in a way, subject of course to modification by the executive committee or any subsequent committee that may be appointed to carry out this plan, if it be undertaken. This schedule was gotten up with the idea that the show be held in March, and that there should be an annual meeting of the society held in conjunction with the show, but after considerable conferences, the committee decided to recommend that this exhibition, if it be held at all, should be held in the month of November instead of in March, and they thought if this were done, you might probably give up your Summer meeting. They thought very favorably of that idea, and have instructed me to present a resolution for your consideration bearing on that point. Among the matters of detail that the committee considered was the place of meeting. Where is the best place to hold this show? It was first thought that New York would be a good place, but experience in the past has shown that it is very difficult to make a flower show there pay. Of course the society wants, if possible, to realize enough money so that the guarantors will not lose anything, or at least not much. The committee has calculated that an exhibition in Philadelphia, or New York, or in fact any Eastern city, would not pay so well, as such a show would in some city in the Middle West. Indianapolis was talked of as being a convenient railroad center, and having other desirable features, but finally, after further consideration, we decided that Chicago is really the best place to carry this exhibition to a successful issue.

The committee have taken the Boston, Pennsylvania, and other schedules as a basis for the premium list. They have decided to recommend, if the project is undertaken, that from $3,000 to $4,000 of this money shall be spent for premiums for novelties, both here and abroad. In Europe there are collections of rex begonias better than anything we have here; there are collections of amaryllis, of crotons, etc., and the committee would like to see premiums offered so as to encourage these foreign growers to come over here and educate us up-to-date.

View from the Gallery Showing Advertising Signs.

Mr. Craig then went on to tell that the present date of the annual meeting was not seasonable for exhibiting plants or cut flowers, and continuing said, "If we decide to have the show in November we can have collections of flowers, roses and carnations, as well as of foliage and flowering plants. Now, gentlemen, I hope there will be an earnest consideration of this matter. It has been thought by members of the committee that 1908 would be the right time to prepare for this. Get the schedule out so that it can be sent to Europe and broadcast all over this country. Make a list so that private gardeners can exhibit collections of half a dozen new things in flowering and foliage plants well done. In considering this question the committee calculated that the private gardeners of America could put up first-class exhibits of six or a dozen plants and could show the people of America something of the possibilities of our great art. (Applause.)"

Mr. Hill: Mr. Craig has pretty well covered this question of a proposed National Flower Show, but I might say one thing in regard to the time proposed to hold the exhibition. We have had a good time here; we have enjoyed ourselves, but oh, my! it has been warm; and we have had just such experiences heretofore in other cities. The committee, in considering this matter, thought if we could hold our annual meeting in November and in connection therewith hold this flower show, that, in all probability, we could double the membership of this society. In case we do have a show, there will be given such an incentive to the florists of the country that they will really make up their minds that they cannot afford to stay away. After telling his phenomenon story, Mr. Hill went on to say: "I do not believe there will be any difficulty in getting a splendid exhibit from the European growers if we were to carry out the show as outlined by Mr. Craig. One or two gentlemen over there expressed to me when visiting their places last year that they would be delighted to make an exhibit in this country. I think we can make it to their interest to do so. There are lots of things all over Europe we could use in our business." Mr. Hill then spoke of the interest taken by the public in the Temple Show, London, which he visited, and also in the National Show in Paris. The Frenchman, if nothing, is artistic; he wished that we could have some Frenchman over here to show us how to arrange plants in our exhibition halls; they do it so artistically. Whatever a Frenchman touches in the way of a group of plants he makes a thing of beauty out of it. At the Paris show they had magnificent rhododendrons and azaleas six to seven feet high, filled with flowers, showing a wealth of bloom. The speaker then referred to the influence that such a show would have on the American plantsmen. He said the American people at the present time are in advance of the florists.

Exhibit of A. T. Boddington, New York.

They talk about teaching the school teachers, to get them to inculcate floriculture and horticulture in the minds of the young. The florists themselves need to be awakened as some of their places are really a shame to the profession. He confessed to being remiss in this matter himself, but if we go into this National Flower Show, Mr. Hill believed it would be educational in character: "it will bring great good to every man in the profession, and will double the membership." In speaking with Secretary-elect Hauswirth, Mr. Hill had stated that if the secretary could start out with one thousand life members at $25 a piece, that would make a good column for this S. A. F. "Let us start out with the idea that we are to be something, that we are to do something, and we shall get there. If we can inaugurate this show, it will do us individualy and collectively a world of good." (Applause.)

J. C. Vaughan endorsed what the previous speakers had said. He believed the society should hold its annual meeting at the time of the show, and that the two together would make a success of the affair. He did not believe they would experience any difficulty in getting the full amount of the guarantee fund; already there were between five and six thousand dollars subscribed, and that without any definite explanation to the guarantors as to how the exhibition was to be carried out. He thought that there had not been the unity between the East and West that should have been, and in order to make the show the success it ought to be, there must be more enthusiasm shown by the Eastern men in the project. He hoped that they would bring from five to six carloads of exhibits, and then there would be no doubt of the success of the undertaking.

Mr. Lonsdale: Since an effort will be made to encourage exhibits from abroad, I think we ought to refer to this show in the future as the International Flower Show. This was objected to by Messrs. Hallock and Watson.

Exhibit of Benjamin Hammond, Fishkill-on-Hudson, N. Y.

A resolution was then submitted by Mr. Craig, and adopted by the society, as follows:

Resolved, that if this proposed exhibition be held it shall be in the month of November, 1908, in the city of Chicago, and that the date of the annual meeting shall be changed from August to November, so that the exhibition and annual meeting shall be held at the same time and place, and that the executive committee be empowered to prepare for and to hold the proposed exhibition.

It was also suggested that in order to obviate any change in the constitution a meeting be held in August for the purpose of adjourning until November in 1908.

Expressions of opinions were asked on the subject of holding the annual meeting in November, but none was forthcoming. It was therefore recommended that those having anything to say on the subject should send their views either to the Executive Committee or express them through the trade papers.

Our Gem City.

(Poem composed by Miss Bessie Dornbusch, Dayton, O., for S. A. F. O. H.)

Scarcely a hundred years have fled
Since the pioneer his cattle led
Through the dense primeval wood
To where Dayton in her infancy stood.
There she lay one vast extent
Of forest trees, that gently bent
O'er fair Miami's sunlit tide,
Whose murmuring waters as they glide,
Repeat to us a tale of old—
Of settlers grim and warriors bold.
They'll tell you in a whisper low,
As down their winding course they go,
How on her shaded wooded brink
The lowing herds came down to drink;
And how the children strolled along
Singing a light and happy song,
Gathering roses or violets blue;
That on her winding banks they grew,
And stopped to play within the sand
Where dwellings, now, and factories stand.
Old Newcom tavern, too, can tell
Of how the forest tree once fell
To make room for cornfields wide
That graced Miami on every side.
And just beyond us on the hill
Another cabin stands with us still,
And it can tell you of long ago,
When that fair city, there below
Was just a struggling little town,
Ne'er dreaming of future renown;
That a little boy came here to play,
And longed that he some future day
Might build a home beneath these trees
To drink in the beauty and the breeze.
And this you see his dream fulfills,
For we stand to-night on beautiful Far Hills,
And there the city stretched below
In all its splendor and its glow—
Our Gem City, there she lies,
And she's all her name implies,
With her parks of shrub and flower,
She's the city of the hour.
And while to him her fame she owes,
With the flower her beauty grows.
Cultivate, then, each flower that blows;
And let Miami onward roll
Past city, town or shaded knoll,
And spread the news to far off lands
How our fair city in beauty stands;
And teach the lesson near and far
That beauty holds a magic power,
Can cultivate the mind and soul,
And lead us to a blissful goal.

Gladiolus Exhibit of Ar.hur Cowee, Berlin, N. Y.

Recent Improvements in Retailers' Methods of Offering Flowers for Sale.

(By Wm. F. Gude, Washington, D. C.)

Being requested to read a paper and lead a discussion on "Recent Improvements in Retailers' Methods of Offering Flowers for Sale," I do so reluctantly. Personally, I should much prefer the discussion to reading a paper. However, I know no better way to open this subject than to give you my own personal experience of the past twenty years in the retail florist's business at the national capital where we think we have some up-to-date flower stores.

There is, probably, no business or profession that has seen a greater change, in the last decade, than the retail florist's or one that has made greater strides. I am sure that no class of men have worked harder or longer hours than they.

Right here, I want to say we too often hear the cry, "Things are not as they used to be." This expression is too commonly used by a great many people engaged in the retail florist's business. "Things are not as they used to be" is not true in the sense in which it is spoken. While I do not doubt it is absolutely a fact in a great many cases, among the men who make that remark, because they have the same old fogey methods and manner of doing business used years ago, yet the wideawake florist, with the proper push, has gone ahead and adopted new and modern methods, with the inevitable result that he makes more money with less work, while the old-timer has been left with his old-fashioned ideas, little or no progress, long hours and small pay. The former has reason to thank the powers that be that, "things are not as they used to be."

Some Old-Time Methods

Sending flowers in old shoe and hat boxes; delivering funeral designs in a farm wagon; sending a man in his greenhouse togs to a fashionable home to carry plants and to decorate; tying bunches with narrow, cheap ribbon, cut swallow-tailed; sending bridal bouquets wrapped in paper; telling a patron the flowers he wants are out of date because they are not in stock.

I have been in flower-shops when a customer would leave an order for a wedding, birthday, or funeral, and explicitly state the time he wanted the flowers delivered; in many cases, to my personal knowledge, the flowers were sent after the occasion was over so that the sentimental effect was entirely lost, the occasion to use the flowers forever gone. The result invariably is, the next time the customer in question wants to buy flowers he tries some place where he has reason to expect that his purchase will be delivered when and where he wants it in up-to-date condition.

Again the old-fashioned way of delivering flowers, wrapped in any old piece of paper and deliver-

A Dayton View of the Florists.

The florists are with us this week. Holding a convention. Getting together to compare notes. Looking at each other's product. Figuring upon the cost of production. Devising ways and means of making two roses bloom where only one bloms now. A useful lot are they, these florists, and the millions of money they have invested in their business makes an industry as staid and staple as the railroads and as important to modern society as the carpet looms.

The first florist was probably a crippled old woman of the jungles. She was unable to join in the chase—as primeval woman was expected to do, until man found that he could induce her to stay at home and do the harder work of preparing the skins for clothing and caring for the children who would be needed when the neighboring band made war upon the tribe. This crippled old woman found a flower blooming by the side of the tent and, having the soul of a poet, she stuck a stick in the ground to prevent the children breaking it down. When the drouth came, she poured a little water upon the plant. When the bugs alighted upon it, she picked them off. When the frosts came she dug up the flower and carried it into the tent and throughout the long Winter, she watched it and cared for it—for she had no other children she could call her own, and the rest of the band of savages ignored her in her infirmities.

When the sun of Spring came bright and warm, the crippled old woman carried her flower to the light and planted it again in the ground. It grew and bloomed and bore a wondrous odor and a brilliant hue—more odorous than the flowers of the wood, more brilliant than the plants of the dell. And the savages wondered at the thing, for a miracle had been wrought.

And so, taking their cue from this crippled old savage, these florists are engaged in caring for the plants, in improving their odor and their color. While the rest of us savages are busily engaged in hunting food and in preparing the clothing, these men of miracle are raising flowers, and they say to us, in the justness of the heavens, "Give us of your food and raiment and we will give you of our flowers." It is an exchange as equitable as the traffic of the gods of old.

It is a blessed thing that we are able to secure within the day more than enough food and clothing for our own use and that we can spare something to exchange with the florist for their flowers. It has long ago been said that man could not live by bread alone. If he could it would be a mighty poor living.

The tent of the savage, the one beside which grew the flower, was a better tent than any of the rest in the jungle. It was the tent to which the savages went in the quiet of eventide. It was the tent where charity was most abundant; the tent where peace prevailed; the tent wherein were born the ideas that were of most benefit to the world; the ten from which issued the children who were best prepared for the struggles they were to encounter.

And it has been so ever since. The home surrounded by flowers is a better home than any other. From it issue men and women who lead the purest lives. In such a home is more harmony, more of love and charity. Thieves are not born amid the flowers. Criminals do not wear a blossom in their coats. The man who seeks to destroy the peace of the community does not visit the flower gardens when the dews are upon the blooms. It is in the churches and the schools and the hospitals and the orphan asylms that one expects to see the blooming things—not in the jails and prisons.

That is why we appreciate these florists. Because we know they are making the world better as well as brighter. They are as much missionaries as those who carry the Bible. They probably cure as many diseases as the physicians. Certainly they entertain as well as the artists or the musicians. And may we learn the lessons that they seek to teach."—Dayton News.

The S. A. F. Group Picture.

Copies of the group picture of the S. A. F. O. H. delegates, taken at the Soldiers' Home, Dayton, on Friday, August 24, can be secured from the photographer, A. L. Bowersox, 137 South Main street, Dayton, Ohio, at the following prices: 16x20 size, $1.50; smaller size, $1.00.

The photograph is a good one, and will form an excellent souvenir of the 1906 convention of the S. A. F.

Exhibit of H. Bayersdorfer & Co., Philadelphia, Pa.

ed by some ragged, dirty messenger, is not conducive to bringing the retail florist's business up to the plane of the modern up-to-date requirements which it so justly deserves.

Also the old-fashioned method of tying flowers on toothpicks with wires without any foliage, which was so popular years ago, has been almost entirely eliminated and a more natural system is now demanded by the average buying community. So much for the old methods.

Up-to-Date Methods.

The present up-to-date method followed by us is to have the flowers received fresh every morning, then properly assorted and arranged in large storage rooms where mirrors on all sides show them off to the best advantage.

One of the most important items is booking orders. In a great many establishments the old way of taking orders for any kind of flowers for commencements and debutantes' receptions, etc., knowing it is a question whether they can be secured, then substituting another kind at the last minute is an expensive one. What a great disappointment to a mother thinking she has a pleasant surprise for her daughter at the graduating exercises or some other function, when she orders a bunch of pink roses, and red carnations are received instead. Her patronage is then lost; she has no more confidence in that establishment.

Employees.

We have an up-to-date corps of clerks and employees who are able, capable and willing to wait on customers intelligently, and do not try to sell them a pink rose for a white one, or callas for lily of the valley. They do not work any more as they used to do. They used to get up at 5 o'clock in the morning and work until 10 or 11 o'clock at night for a very small compensation. It is fortunate that "things are not as they used to be" in this case. Employees in a retail florist's store should come in for full consideration and just treatment, because it is impossible for any one man to wait on every customer that comes to inquire about flowers. There are naturally in the retail florist's trade, as in all other kinds of business, customers with all sorts of ideas and in many cases hard to please. All of these should be studied and their peculiar fancies catered to, as much as possible, if they are willing to pay the price, because a satisfied customer is the best possible advertisement that anyone can have. Right here the employee who goes to extra trouble to cater to the whims of this particular class of customer, and does not run or hide when he or she comes in, is entitled to a great deal of consideration which, alas, he often does not receive. I have found invariably by studying the clerks' interests they are in a much better position to study the employer's interests; for it is only too true that florists work longer hours for less money than almost any other class of working men, requiring an equal amount of intelligence. The clerks and employees in a retail florist's store can do very much toward increasing or decreasing the sales and profits by strict attention or inattention to details in the business. It has always been our aim to keep the employees satisfied and where we succeeed in doing that, they invariably succeed in satisfying us.

Putting Up Orders.

This, in our estimation, is one of the most important items connected with the retail florist's trade. As time cuts quite a figure in this part of

window bottom of sand, gravel and zinc has given place to tile and mirror effects. A florist's window is the same now as that of the other up-to-date merchant who displays his finest goods to tempt the business, if the flowers are put up too early they will be apt to wither, and if too late they cannot be delivered in time; hence, this branch of the business requires constant care and exercise of judgment in order that the flowers may reach the parties interested in the best possible condition. Another very important item, is to send the customers exactly the quality and quantity promised for a given amount of money and not try to slight them with the thought or idea that they will never know the difference. This might do once in a while, but one is bound to be caught in the act some time, and with a very ugly reflection on the integrity of the house. Here it may be well to state that the politeness and intelligence of the driver or messenger who may happen to deliver the flowers will either reflect credit or discredit upon the establishment.

Window Display.

The old methods of trying to show the public how many plants a florist can put in a window was buried with the paper collar for bouquets. The the public to buy. A customer can form a pretty good idea of the florist's ability to create and execute artistic effects by his window display. For instance, when we have a surplus of any particular kind of flower a window tastefully arranged with vases, baskets, etc., of this same flower has time and again been the means of cleaning up the entire surplus at a good profit.

A window display on January 29, President McKinley's birthday, with a portrait of him, a few American flags and a nice assortment of carnations tastefully arranged will demonstrate what a window decoration can do. I would advise you to try it January 29 next.

Use of Ribbons.

The use of ribbons in the retail florist's business, has grown faster than the business itself, because by the present methods ribbons can be used to great advantage on nearly all arrangements of flowers, and when properly used are a great acquisition to any up-to-date floral arrangement.

Delivery of Flowers in Vases and Jardinieres.

In our city in particular there is a large demand for bunches of flowers at all seasons of the year, to be sent to the various offices or departments of the local municipal and United States government. In these cases it is often necessary to have a suitable vase or jardinere to offer to go with the bunch of flowers, that these may be delivered in good presentable condition, and their lasting qualities preserved by the stems being kept in water while in the office of the recipient.

In conclusion, to manage and operate an up-to-date flower store.

First, it is necessary to be conservative in buying. When I say buying, I mean not only cut flower stock, but plants, ribbons, jardinieres, florists' supplies of all kinds, and especially boxes and paper to suit all sizes of bunches and qualities of flowers. This is very important.

Second, having the necessary receptacles and supplies to go with the flowers; be sure to have good fresh stock at all times to show your customers and give them what you claim to sell.

Third, after the former two be sure to deliver the flowers as promised, on time and in good condition.

Teaching Horticulture in the Public Schools

(Concluded from page 225)

Relation of School-Gardens to Experiment Stations and Agricultural Colleges.

To some it may appear that the experiment stations and agricultural colleges conflict or compete with our movement. This is not the case. We should be content to call ourselves the common soldiers of this common cause, and we should also be content to be officered by experts from those institutions. They commence at the top and work down. We are commencing at the bottom, and will work up. We wish to call on those institutions for lectures, demonstrators, and instructors. We can work hand in hand with them, and we probably could not succeed without them.

Summary and Recommendations

Your committee now believes the work can be taken up with the end plainly in view. Whether it is on the exact lines laid down in this report, or better ideas from the succeeding committee, is of little consequence.

We have, available, so many detailed reports of the workings of the various associations taking up the matter of school-gardens, so much data and so many working plans, that a committee should be able to proceed with their duties understandingly.

But we must be doubly sure of the ground we take. We can not afford to make many mistakes at the outset or on fundamental lines. Our work must be humanitarian, logical, and in a manner to interest. Our progress must be slow and sure.

Our motives are altruistic and must remain so, or our efforts will fail. Neither this association nor any other association has any selfish motive concealed. No person or persons will have any advantages over any other person or persons. We shall work in an open field. In the advancement of horticulture we are sure to prosper and added wealth and comfort will accrue to the individual, the community, the State, and the Nation.

When the time comes, and we ask of the State a recognition in the matter of school appropriations, let us do so with the consciousness of a righteous cause, and a knowledge that not one penny will be diverted from its proper use. We believe it possible that some of the money now appropriated by the Agricultural Department for distributing the commonest of all common seeds can be diverted to the boards of education of the different States, for the purpose of school-gardens.

Recommendations.

Finally, your committee recommends that a new committee of five be appointed by the executive committee, the president and the vice-persident of this society to carry on the work as laid down in the report of your first committee, or on any other lines they deem best. And that they be authorized to spend a sum not to exceed one hundred dollars for preparing leaflets, diagrams, routine instructions, etc., during the coming year.

Respectfully submitted, at the Conveiltion of the Society of American Florists and Ornamental Horticulturists at Dayton, Ohio, August 21, 1906.

ALEXANDER WALLACE,
BENJAMIN HAMMOND,
EDWARD V. HALLOCK,
Committee.

For help in preparation of this pamphlet, acknowledgment and many thanks are due to all those who have kindly aided us in furnishing reports of their work and other material, or by their personal letters of information. If they are not

The S. A. F. O. H. Conventionites in front of Memorial Hall, Soldiers' Home, Dayton, O., August 24, 1906; Governor Thomas and Staff on left of Picture

separately mentioned in this place, or their work is not referred to elsewhere, it is through lack of space and not through intentional oversight.

Plan Suggested—Outline.

I. GROUND.

1. Utilize school grounds.
2. Obtain more, if possible, from school authorities or private sources.
3. Give each child a plot of his own.
   Teach children to care for their own; to respect rights of others.

II. INSTRUCTION.

1. Distribute leaflets among teachers.
   Printed rules or advice in simple form.
2. Employ teachers trained in garden-work.
   By Normal school methods.
3. Appoint qualified persons in charge of a district or township.
   To receive instruction from and report to Experiment Station.

III. DISTRIBUTION OF SEEDS.

1. Follow some generally approved plan, modified, where necessary.
   That of Cleveland Home Gardening Association, for example.

IV. TIME ALLOTTED FOR GARDEN-WORK.

1. Out of doors, use period devoted to nature study.
2. In class-room, combine lessons in gardening with other studies.
3. Interest children to work out of school—afternoons, Saturdays, at home.

V. EXHIBITIONS.

1. Of best material available.
2. Impromptu displays; special Horticultural Shows; Annual Fairs, etc.

Note.—We favor exhibitions of the best material each community has available, from a few vases of flowers in the school-room, impromptu displays at local picnics, and special exhibitions gotten up by school children in their own neighborhoods, to the usual agricultural fairs, with the new interest and enthusiasm the young people can put in this direction. Who can tell but it will create a revival of interest in our county fairs which seem to have failed in attracting the people as formerly.

VI. PRIZES.

1. Must vary in amount and methods.
2. Offered by Members of Civic Agricultural and Horticultural Associations, etc.

Note.—No exact rule can be suggested in regard to the number of prizes or the particular subjects to award prizes for. This matter must be in the hands of the governing board of each district. The amount of prizes should bear a well balanced relation to the amount of appropriation. We favor the offering of prizes and honorable mention, and we feel sure that many interested persons in each neighborhood would give something in the form of prizes to their favorite schools.

The committee's report is accompanied with many extracts from gardening and other periodicals treating on the subject of school gardens, etc.

Bowlers Celebrate Their Victory.

The Philadelphia bowlers celebrated their victory on Thursday evening, August 23, at the Algonquin Hotel, by filling the Beatty cup with a sparkling liquid. All the bowlers of prominence were present, as well as some of the celebrities of the S. A. F. Adam Graham of Cleveland acted as toastmaster. Speech, song and story passed the hours until 3 a. m.; when the enjoyable affair broke up. A very pleasant feature of the occasion was the subscription put in operation on behalf of the widow and children of James Hartshorne of Joliet, Ill., who, it is understood, have been left not too well provided for. The sum of $225 was realized.

Massachusetts Horticultural Society.

The schedule of the 1907 Spring exhibitions of the Massachusetts Horticultural Society has been issued. Some noteworthy features of interest are the bringing out of several old-time favorites which have not been seen in the lists for many years as well as some novelties which appear for the first time. Among these are camellias, schizanthus, imantophyllums (clivias), fibrous begonias, forced lilies, and Darwin and late single tulips.

In addition to the numerous classes of Spring bulbous plants are the classes of Indian azaleas, ericas, acacias "Easter plants," herbaceous spiræas, and climbing and Rambler roses. There is also a class of forced bulbs for amateurs only. The very liberal prizes offered should inspire a good competition at these exhibitions.

For the March exhibition the Julius Roehrs Company of Rutherford, N. J., offers special prizes to the amount of $25 for the best groups of hard wooded flowering greenhouse plants, such as acacias, camellias, azaleas, rhododendrons, etc., to be competed for by private gardeners only.

Accompanying this preliminary schedule is a circular announcing three special prizes for decorated dinner tables to be awarded at the chrysanthemum show of November 2-4, 1906. These prizes are for the best decorated tables laid for six covers, and the judges are to be three ladies selected by the committee on exhibitions. The prizes offered are as follows:

First, $75 and a Gilt Medal.
Second, $50 and a Silver Medal.
Third, $35 and a Bronze Medal.

Copies of the schedule and circular and any further information desired concerning these exhibitions can be obtained on application to the secretary, Wm. P. Rich, 300 Massachusetts avenue, Boston.

Belgian Glass Industry.

Consular Agent W. D. Shaughnessy, of Charleroi, advises that the situation of the Belgian window-glass market is assuming a troublesome aspect.

Prices are declining and several factories are only producing for their warehouses, notwithstanding that they already contain very large stocks. This unsettled state is due to falling off of usual orders from nearly all important export centers and demands of the others for small amounts. Further orders are not expected for some time. The stock at the works is therefore increasing in spite of the fact that eleven factories are closed for much-needed repairs. Operators are also confronted by demands of workmen for less hours and 15 per cent. increase in wages. Unless an agreement is effected it is expected that the men will declare a strike in September, at which time the present contracts expire. The trouble arose over the application of a Belgian law which gives to men working at blast furnaces one-half holiday per week. The labor union claims that this law does not apply to them and that they are entitled to a whole day, the companies opposing it. Orders have been issued to members of the union not to renew their contracts for four months, nor even for one day, unless satisfactory agreements are made with the companies. As the labor is 50 per cent. of the cost price, the companies claim they cannot afford to pay higher wages, stating that they are losing money.

Plant Notes from Southern California.

A bed of several hundred stalks of Hedychium coronarium on the Hollenbeck Home grounds, just now coming into bloom, fills the air surrounding with its delightful fragrance. The flowers are pure white, over two inches wide, and as beautiful in construction as a Vanda cœrulea. It is the stalks that came through the Winter without harm, though unprotected, except that the roots were kept comparatively dry, that are blooming now. The new ones of this season's growth, up to this time, will give a succession of flowers until December, when the temperature drops too low for its further development. It would be well worth while for Southern California florists to give this desirable plant a temporary protection during the Winter. As a cut flower it has no superior, and for decorating it could be used to great advantage. It requires about four inches of water a week and plenty of fertilizer for its best development, therefore is best adapted to the side of a lily and fish pond which can be made to overflow when fresh water is turned into the pond.

Cuphea llavea is one of our most desirable bedding plants, as yet too little known. It stands our bright sunlight and dry atmosphere to perfection. With slight protection during the Winter it grows to be quite a good-sized trailing shrub, and for fine effect in a mixed border. It harmonizes with Vinca alba, which is also perennial here. The system and methods of flower garden work are not carried out on this coast as they are in the East—indeed it may be truthfully stated that because of favorable climatic conditions we have no system—but a promiscuous way of doing things in that line of work that astonishes professional gardeners who drop in on us at all seasons of the year.

P. D. BARNHART.

John Scott's Exhibit of Nephrolepis Scottii

This does not apply to the plate-glass market, as the trust controlling all the plate-glass works has been able to keep the market firm and uphold profitable prices. It is the desire of the window glass companies, after the present troubles are settled, to also form a syndicate.

The manufacture of glass under its numerous and diversified applications is one of the most important branches of industrial activity of Belgium, and is most thickly settled in the basin of Charleroi. The export of window glass to the United States for the fiscal year ending June 30 amounted to $1,053,823, against $328,579 during the same period of 1905, an increase of over 70 per cent. In plate glass the export to the United States for the fiscal year ending June 30 was $834,955, against $483,425 in 1905, an increase of nearly 50 per cent.

Window glass is classified according to thickness. The qualities usually manufactured are of 14 to 28 ounces, viz. of 1½ to 3 millimeters thickness. Window panes are made of white or colored glass and are plain, straited, or fluted, and diamond shaped. Metallified window glass is also manufactured as well as mousseline—obtained by engraving with sand blast. There are 25 window-glass works in Belgium, all in the province of Hainaut, three of which are controlled by American companies. The annual production amounts approximately to about 30,000,000 square meters, 90 per cent. of which are exported.

A Dahlia Exhibition.

Members of the Baltimore and Washington Florists' Clubs will visit the establishment of R. Vincent, Jr., & Son, White Marsh, Md., on September 19, and inspect the firm's dahlia fields.

Plant Diseases.

The Maine Agricultural Experiment Station will shortly begin a systematic survey of the State with reference to those diseases of plants (blight, rust, etc.), which are caused by parasitic fungi. To make this survey as comprehensive as possible, correspondents are invited to send to the Station specimens of such diseased plants as come to their notice. These should be accompanied with the name and address of the collector, the date and place of collection; and if possible the name of the plant upon which the fungus is growing.

In most cases, especially where the distance is short, the specimens should be shipped green. Where the plants are to be shipped some distance, and the disease is one which progresses very rapidly, as is the case with the late blight of the potato, the specimens should be dried before mailing. This may be done by placing between two pieces of newspapers, with sheets of blotting or other absorbent paper above and below, the whole being placed on a flat surface and covered with a weight. The absorbent paper should be replaced twice daily with dried sheets, without disturbing the newspaper covering, until the specimens are dry. Dried specimens for mailing should be placed between pieces of pasteboard or in small flat pasteboard boxes.

Please address all correspondence on this topic to the Maine Agricultural Experiment Station, Orono, Maine. The receipt of all specimens will be acknowledged and a report upon the nature of its disease with treatment, if any can be suggested, will be sent as soon as possible after the specimens are identified.

CHAS. D. WOOD,
Director.

Convention Snap Shots.

Adam Graham was in a listless mood.

The new election amendment worked fine.

William H. Elliot's badge number was 23. He didn't skidoo.

The Roosters were out in force to greet J. K. Allen at Cleveland.

What President Kasting lacked in polish he made up in push.

President Kasting ranked with the best as a presiding officer.

John T. Temple of Davenport, Iowa, and Mr. Haentze of Fond du Lac, Wisconsin, were among the old timers who were missing.

The trade exhibition increases, which speaks well for the men who first conceived the idea.

The rhetoric of the Boston colonel turned out to be the prognostication of anything but an air castle.

The discussion on the tariff added a few degrees to the already high temperature, but—that was all.

John Birnie said that he never looked into the smiling face of the sergeant-at-arms without becoming thirsty.

Interest by outsiders in the convention sports seems to be waning—a straw that shows how the wind is blowing.

Several of the ladies became ill during their stay in Dayton, among them Mrs. Kasting and Mrs. Wm. H. Elliott.

Carmody was blamed for the lid having been lifted from the lower regions. He didn't deny the warm accusation.

The café on the Fair grounds was well patronized. Large potations of lemonade were disposed of by the caterers.

The illumination at Far Hills was beautiful beyond description, and was more than appreciated by those who were present.

The Crozy man from Iowa was missed. He'll be pleased to learn that another canna committee is to be appointed.

The Dayton Florists' Club covered themselves with glory. President Heiss and his lieutenants have reason to feel proud.

The Dayton Convention was an exposition of the idea that interesting topics can hold the convention better than essays.

Would a November meeting of the S. A. F. be as enjoyable as one in Midsummer, heat and all? That is now the question?

John G. Esler wanted every man in line at the hour of election to have a chance to cast his ballot. The recommendation went through.

When Cash Register methods prevail the hideous ice houses that mar the beauty of the Hudson, will be covered with Ampelopsis Veitchii.

The influence of the National Cash Register Company, horticulturally, was everywhere visible in the beautiful gardens and grounds of Dayton.

One of the sights next year will be a review of the bowling trophies that have floated to Philadelphia and that, like whirlpool driftwood, remain.

E. G. Hill says the American people are ahead of the florists in the tidiness of their surroundings. A cleaning up of front and back yards is recommended.

An admirer of Phil Foley after that gentleman's speech endorsing Niagara Falls, said "That is the first time I ever knew Mr. Foley was a humorist."

The $250 purse for the widow of Jimmy Hartshorne at an informal gathering, was the best evidence in the world that "florists' hearts are in the right place."

Several of the New York members availed themselves of the privilege of a sail down Lake Erie and the Hudson River. A few traveled as far as Toronto.

Professor Cowell, who has traveled extensively in the tropics, stated he never, while sojourning there, experienced heat equal to that showered on the delegates at Dayton.

The election of John Westcott to the vice-presidency of the society was a well-merited compliment. Some day the organization will make him president—or, at least, it should.

The United States presidential election would interfere with the proposed National Flower Show in 1908. What is the matter with postponing the presidential election?

Hot Scotch songs were a feature of the trip from New York to Dayton. Birnie regretted having left his bagpipes behind; but he made up for the omission by his vocal efforts.

Phil. Hauswirth, the new secretary, is a man who has traveled widely, has broad ideas, is cosmopolitan, and will be likely to lead the S. A. F. to green fields and pastures new.

The Beatty Cup was handed over to the winners with appropriate exercises, which consisted of floods of oratory, volumes of song, and a goodly sufficiency of other things.

When the heat had all but overcome the sergeant-at-arms he immediately arrested some one, and the temperature subsequently fell. We understand arrests were on that account quite frequent.

Emil Leuly beat his own record. He made the 1000-mile ride to Dayton in ten days. Mr. Leuly is one of the many features of the convention. Everybody inquired "has Leuly arrived?"

F. W. Herendeen, of Furman boiler fame, Geneva, N. Y., made the journey to Dayton in his automobile. Many of the delegates enjoyed a trip in Mr. Herendeen's horseless carriage during the convention.

The resolution drawn up to be sent to John H. Patterson of the National Cash Register Company, is said to be worthy of a Sentator Ingalls. It is reported being indeed flowery, as becomes a florists' organization.

"Enjoying your hospitalities. Congratulations on your eminent services to humanity.—SOCIETY OF AMERICAN FLORISTS," was the message sent to John H. Patterson at Berlin, Germany.

Carmody said he was familiar with castings, but the case of silverware presented to the president proved to be the best castings of the real stuff he had ever handled; and they were handed to a Kasting also thoroughly genuine.

There are always some ambitions thwarted at every convention, and that of Dayton proved no exception to the rule. Yet nothing is more admirable than a loser possessed of the real manly spirit; nothing more lamentable than the sore candidate who lacks it.

The S. A. F. should provide printed stationary for the use of the judges on exhibits, on which awards could be made under the respective classes. The Dayton awards were a mere jumble, indiscriminately announced, and on that account lacking force and interest.

Secretary Stewart now becomes President Stewart, and Treasurer Beatty should become President Beatty, in 1908. The presidency of the S. A. F. is a handsome reward for old and tried officers, and Beatty is the man to handle the big show of 1908—pre-eminently so above all others.

The idea that somebody will receive a benefit from the meeting of the S. A. F. O. H. has been exploded by the visit to Dayton. The S. A. F. has learned that the N. C. R. Co., is by its daily lectures doing far more for the advancement of horticulture than they can return in advertisement.

Which leads us to remark that the S. A. F. O. H. has been at times very narrow, stupid, and foolish.

John Westcott struggling in the toils of the vice-presidency was one of the occasions when his friends nearly had him tied down tight. By the way John Westcott and John G. Esler seem to be two of the S. A. F. old guard who do not seem to have an official bee in their bonnets, and they are both as happy as kings at that.

Several of the late retirers were drawn toward the Algonquin Hotel Thursday night by the echoes of sweet music and other weird sounds that were borne from that hostelry far away on the midnight air.

"They sang of love, and not of fame;
Forgot was each one's glory;
But all sang Annie Laurie,"
Each heart recalled a different name.

CATALOGUES RECEIVED.

WEEBER & DON, New York.—Fall Catalogue of Bulbs, Roots, and Seeds.

FOREST NURSERY COMPANY, Irving College, Tenn.—Price List of Nursery Stock.

GEORGE H. PETERSON, Fair Lawn, N. J.—The Peony Blue Book, an interesting booklet.

W. W. BARNARD & COMPANY, Chicago.—Catalogue of Bulbs and Seeds for Fall Planting.

P. J. BERCKMANS COMPANY, Augusta, Ga.—Wholesale Catalogue of Ornamental Nursery Stock, Fruit Trees, etc.

LORD & BURNHAM CO., New York, are distributing some very interesting literature setting forth the merits of their various well-known specialties. Among the pamphlets being sent out are the following: Hot Bed Sash and Frames; Truss Construction for Sash Bar Houses;; Iron Frame Greenhouse; Pleasure and Profit of Cold Frames; and Paint that Stays Put, and Something about Putty. Much valuable information is contained in the various publications, copies of which can be obtained on application to the firm.

Philadelphia.

Echoes of the Dayton Gathering.

All are now home from Dayton. The main delegation arrived at Broad street station at noon on Saturday. Everyone feels jubilant, and well they may, as this city certainly got the lion's share of what was given out. This week the only topic of discussion is convention past and future. Everyone here is desirous to make the 1907 meeting such that it will last forever in the memory of all who attend. Nothing will be left undone by our club. Work is already started for next year, and will be kept up continuously.

The election of Wm. J. Stewart to the presidency is very well received here. He is a member of our club, and has been among us so much that he could scarcely be more familiar did he reside here. Therefore, this again is more incentive for concerted action and for every fellow to put his shoulder to the wheel.

On Monday last John Wescott gathered together some twenty members at the club room to start the ball rolling. It was an instruction meeting, for all present got their orders from the vice-president elect. He said, "No one can talk today; I am dictator. You elected me against my wish, and now I will worst you all. In our club we have factions. You must all cut that out this next year. We want no altercations, but all must work as a unit. We have factions in the S. A. F. These are composed of followers of each of the four trade papers, and I have promised to do my best to bring these together by the next convention. We want united action in everything."

We all feel very glad that our bowlers won. We did not feel confident that we had sent a winning team, as we really expected stronger oppesotion from the West. But it is a great pleasure to finally win the H. B. Beatty trophy, as the donor is an old member of our club and is greatly respected in this city.

All those who made exhibits at Dayton are well pleased. Not only were the exhibits disposed of, but a large number of orders were booked.

News Notes.

The failure of the Real Estate Trust Company of this city will affect several firms in the trade, but it is felt that a whole dollar will be paid; the only disadvantage will be the delay.

Edward Reid returned on Sunday from his annual tour among his Southern customers; he had a very successful trip.

Al. Campbell will open his new commission house on Monday, at 1510 Sansom street.

Bayersdorfer & Company have 93 cases of supplies on the steamer Manitou, which has just arrived.

The continued wet weather has been very disastrous to carnations. Stem rot has set in, and growers around here have lost from six to eight thousand plants. There is scarcely a carnation man that has not one empty house.

Our club meets on Tuesday next; and in view of convention matters the meeting is expected to be a very important one. A large attendance is expected.

Victor Groshens, manager of the Logan establishment of the Hugh Graham Company, has returned from his trip to Europe, and has secured some grand stock for next season.

Come to Philadelphia in 1907 and take in that trip down Lovers' Lane. Niagara isn't in it. DAVID RUST.

Minneapolis.

News Notes.

Rice Bros. have moved into their new location, across the street from their old stand. They report a good season's trade and from the increase in business over last year, they anticipate good results this coming year.

Ralph Latham says it is the best Summer that he has had. Oscar Amundson of The Rosary is well pleased with trade, Ashton Kirschner has been assisting him for the past month.

A long felt want has as we believe, been supplied, in the way of a pot manufactory. PAUL.

Indianapolis.

Convention Aftermath.

The pilgrims who journeyed to Dayton are loud in their praise of the various features of the 1906 convention. Taking into consideration the size of the "Gem City" and the number of florists who had to battle with this immense undertaking, it must be said of them that their part was most creditably performed. The entertainment at Welfare Hall was one which could not be readily duplicated in the largest cities of our country. Not a florist who visited Far Hills but was deeply impressed with the wonderful illumination; not a decorator visited Mr. Patterson's estate who did not have opportunities to grasp ideas which alone were worth the trip to Dayton. Imagine (even the writer thinks he is imagining) oak trees, a hundred or more feet in height, containing bunches of electric lighted grapes of various hues, other trees and shrubs treated with electric flowers and lanterns in a most wonderful manner. The driveway, leading from the lodge to the residence, gave evidence of some of the most expert landscape gardening. The writer wishes to mention that in his opinion the trade exhibit and S. A. F. meetings were, in many respects, superior to any of the late conventions.

Visitors: W. N. Brothers, Peoria, Ill.; C. Frauenfelder, Chicago; Jas. Culbert, Ronwell, Ill. I. B.

SWEET PEAS.—The Horticultural Advertiser, England, of recent date, contains the following item: "Complaints are reaching us from various quarters that stocks of sweet peas have been badly mixed the last two years, rogues being sufficiently numerous in many cases to quite spoil the effect where a uniform tint was desired. It is suggested that culture on the huge farms in California lacks the individual care given by our own growers, and that to obtain pure stocks we must return to home grown seeds."

SPURRY SEED FREE OF DUTY.—It was decided August 28, by the Board of United States General Appraisers that so-called field spurry seed is free of duty. Henry Nungesser & Co. of New York imported the seed, which was returned for duty by Collector Stranahan on the basis of 20 per cent. The board reverses the collector's action.

FIRMS WHO ARE BUILDING.

WEST PITTSTON, PA.—Robert Ellis is rebuilding his greenhouses.

EASTON, MASS.—James H. Leach is adding a large greenhouse to his plant.

PRINCETON, ILL.—Wm. Trimble will build a greenhouse, 30 by 200 feet.

PUSCELL, IND.—Wm. High is rebuilding and improving his greenhouse plant. He is enjoying a splendid trade.

DIGHTON, MASS.—Josiah T. Place has broken ground for his new 100 by 25 foot greenhouse at the Dighton nursery.

CORTLAND, N. Y.—F. M. & N. M. Pratt have added a new house, 20x75, now filled with chrysanthemums and carnations.

PHILADELPHIA, PA.—Albert Schmitz will rebuilt his greenhouses which are located on the North side of Connarroe street.

MASPETH, N. Y.—John Schmieg is building a new house, 100x20 feet, for carnations; Jacob & Sons are supplying the boiler and building material.

WESTFIELD, MASS.—Henry Barton contemplates adding another greenhouse to his plant. Mr. Barton recently returned from a two weeks yachting excursion to Maine.

BLOOMINGTON, ILL.—The Phœnix Nursery Company is building three iron frame greenhouses. The new houses will have ventilating apparatus of the latest type and when completed will be models of modern ideas in greenhouse construction.

BUSINESS DIFFICULTIES.

RACINE, WIS.—Rudolph J. Mohr has filed a petition in bankruptcy showing liabilities of $2,567.77 and assets of $772.34.

CARNATIONS

	Per 100	Per 1000
FIANCEE	$6 00	
LAWSON	6 00	$50 00
NELSON FISHER	7 00	60 00
GUARDIAN ANGEL	4 00	35 00
MORNING GLORY	$4 00	$35 00
LIEUT. PEARY	8 00	75 00
FRED BURKI	7 00	60 00
BOSTON MARKET	5 00	45 00
FLORA HILL	$5 00	$45 00
WHITE CLOUD	5 00	45 00
CHICAGO (Red Bradt)	5 00	45 00
HARLOWARDEN	6 00	50 00

WIETOR BROS., 51 Wabash Ave., CHICAGO

Mention The Florists' Exchange when writing.

FIELD... GROWN CARNATION PLANTS

		Per 100	Per 1000
WHITE	Lady Bountiful, favorite white	$ 7.00	$ 60.00
	White Lawson	7.00	60.00
PINK	Mrs. Thos. W. Lawson	6.00	50.00
	Enchantress	7.00	
	Fair Maid	5.00	
SCARLET	Cardinal, best scarlet	7.00	60.00
	Skyrocket	7.00	60.00
	Crusader	6.00	50.00
VARIEGATED	Glendale, (new)	12.00	100.00
	Prosperity	5.00	40.00
CRIMSON	Harlowarden	5.00	40.00

CHICAGO CARNATION CO., Joliet, Ill.

Mention The Florists' Exchange when writing.

Field Grown Carnation Plants

THE LARGEST AND FINEST WE EVER HAD

THE QUEEN	$5.00 per 100	BOSTON MARKET	$5.00 per 100
FAIR MAID	5.00 "	FIANCEE -	5.00 "
QUEEN LOUISE	5.00 "	ENCHANTRESS	6.00 "

J. D. COCKCROFT

NORTHPORT, - - L. I., N. Y.

Mention The Florists' Exchange when writing.

Field Grown Carnation Plants

ALL THE STANDARD VARIETIES

List and prices on application.

Rose plants 1000 Liberty 3 in. pots ..... $5.00 per 100

1000 " 2¼ " " ..... 4.00 " 100

THE LEO NIESSEN COMPANY, 1217 Arch St. Philadelphia, Pa.

Mention The Florists' Exchange when writing.

Field Grown Carnation Plants

THE LARGEST AND FINEST WE EVER HAD.

THE QUEEN, FAIR MAID, MRS. PATTEN } $5.00 per 100

WHITE LAWSON, PINK LAWSON, NELSON FISHER } $6.00 per 100

ENCHANTRESS, $7.00 per 100.

H. F. LITTLEFIELD, - - WORCESTER, MASS.

Mention The Florists' Exchange when writing.

CARNATIONS

LARGE PLANTS

Queen Louise, Genevieve Lord, Enchantress, Harlowarden, The Queen, Crane, Flamingo, Lawson.

First size, $35.00 per 1000; Second size $30.00 per 1000.

FRANK NIQUET, Florist

PATCHOGUE, N. Y.

Mention The Florists' Exchange when writing.

CARNATIONS

FINE FIELD GROWN PLANTS

CORRESPONDENCE SOLICITED

A. B. DAVIS & SON, Inc., Purcellville Va.

Mention The Florists' Exchange when writing.

THE AMERICAN CARNATION

Price $3.50

A. T. DE LA MARE PTG & PUB CO. LTD

2-8 Duane Street, New York.

FIELD GROWN CARNATION PLANTS

Mrs Bradt ..... $5.00 per 100

Prosperity ..... 4.00 " "

Naylor (white) ..... 5.00 " "

Estelle ..... 5.00 " "

Eldorado ..... 5.00 " "

EDWARD J. TAYLOR, Southport, Conn.

Mention The Florists' Exchange when writing.

The Model EXTENSION

CARNATION SUPPORT

Endorsed by all the leading carnation growers as the best support on the market. Made with 2 or 3 circles. Write for prices and circulars.

We have special low prices to offer and can save you money on

Galvanized Wire ROSE STAKES

Write us for prices before ordering elsewhere. Prompt shipment guaranteed.

IGOE BROS.

226 North 9th Street

BROOKLYN, N. Y.

Mention The Florists' Exchange when writing.

FIELD GROWN Carnations

Extra fine healthy plants

	100	1000
QUEEN	$5.00	$45.00
FAIR MAID	5.00	45.00
LAWSON	6.00	50.00
FLORIANA	5.00	

250 Field-grown Jerusalem Cherries, stocky plants, $5.00 per 100.

CASH WITH ORDER

W. A. DAWSON, Willimantic, Conn.

Mention The Florists' Exchange when writing.

CARNATIONS

ENCHANTRESS ..... $50.00 per 1,000

QUEEN LOUISE ..... 40.00 " "

LAWSON ..... 40.00 " "

Good, strong, healthy plants. Cash with order.

HENRY KRUSCHKA

616 Cookman Ave., Asbury Park, N. J.

Mention The Florists' Exchange when writing.

FIELD GROWN

CARNATIONS and VIOLETS

Extra strong plants of Queen, Boston Market, Fair Maid and Patten No. 1, $6.00 per 100; $50.00 per 1000; No. 2, $5.00 per 100; $45.00 per 1000. CAMPBELL VIOLETS, large clumps, $5.00 per 100; $45.00 per 1000. PRINCESS OF WALES, $6.00 per 100; $50.00 per 1000. No better stock at any price. Cash with order please.

R. ENGELMAN & SON, Pittsfield, Mass.

Mention The Florists' Exchange when writing.

ABUNDANCE

Healthy, stocky, field grown plants. First size, $12.00 per 100; $100.00 per 1000. Second size, $10.00 per 100; $75.00 per 1000; 250 at a 1000 rates. Delivery 15th of August.

CASH WITH ORDER.

RUDOLPH FISCHER, Great Neck, L.I., N.Y.

Mention The Florists' Exchange when writing.

Field Grown Carnations

$4.00 per 100

Fair Maid, Gov. Wolcott, Marquis, Prosperity, Roosevelt, N. Fisher, E. Crocker, G. Lord. 2nd size Queen Louise, $3.00 per 100.

Boston Ferns, 6 in. pans, $4.00 per doz.

THE NATIONAL PLANT CO. Dayton, O.

Mention The Florists' Exchange when writing.

CARNATIONS

Good, strong, healthy, field grown carnation plants from new soil. A No. 1 plants in every way; well branched and free from disease. Enchantress, Boston Market, Lady Bountiful, Mrs. M. A. Patten, Nelson Fisher, Ethel Ward. Prices on application.

VALLEY VIEW GREENHOUSES, Marlborough, N.Y.

VELIE BROS., Props.

Mention The Florists' Exchange when writing

CARNATIONS

PLANTS FROM FIELD

Fair Maid, Queen, Mrs. Patten $5.00 per 100; $45.00 per 1000. Strong and healthy.

Satisfaction guaranteed. Cash with Order

HUGH CHESNEY, Farmington, C[illegible]

Mention The Florists' Exchange when writing

FIELD GROWN CARNATIONS

VICTORY, JOHN J. HAINES, $2.[illegible] per doz.; $15.00 per 100.

FIANCEE, G. LORD, GOV. ROOSEVELT, $6.00 per 100.

CHARLES H. TOTTY

MADISON, N. J.

Mention The Florists' Exchange when writing

FIELD GROWN CARNATION PLANTS

HARRY FENN $6.00 per 100. Fine plants [illegible] healthy stock.

E. WINKLER

WAKEFIELD, MASS.

Mention The Florists' Exchange when writing

40,000 extra fine field-grown Carnation plants. For particulars see under Stock for Sale.

M. J. SCHAAF

DANSVILLE, N. Y.

Mention the Florists' Exchange when writing

CLASSIFIED ADVERTISEMENTS

CASH WITH ORDER.

The columns under this heading are reserved for advertisements of Stock for Sale, Stock Wanted, Help Wanted, Situations Wanted or other Wants; also of Greenhouse, Land, Second-Hand Materials, etc., For Sale or Rent.

Our charge is 10 cts. per line (7 words to the line), set solid, without display. No advt. accepted for less than thirty cents.

Display advertisements in these columns, 15 cents per line; count 12 lines agate to the inch.

[If replies to Help Wanted, Situation Wanted, or other advertisements are to be addressed care of this office, advertisers add 10 cents to cover expense of forwarding.]

Copy must reach New York office 12 o'clock Wednesday to secure insertion in issue of following Saturday.

Advertisers in the Western States desiring to advertise under initials, may save time by having their answer directed care our Chicago office at 127 E. Berwyn Ave.

SITUATIONS WANTED

SITUATION WANTED—By three experienced young gardeners; in or outside work. Massachusetts preferred. Please state particulars. Address, N. Y., care The Florists' Exchange.

SITUATION WANTED—By a thoroughly competent plantsman and grower to travel. Varied experience, and best of references. Address N. E., care The Florists' Exchange.

SITUATION WANTED—In greenhouses, experienced in carnations, chrysanthemums and bedding plants. Good references. L. Geh, 150 Central Avenue, Brooklyn, N. Y.

SITUATION WANTED—By middle aged married man, grower of roses, carnations and general stock. 13 years' experience. Address, O. G., care The Florists' Exchange.

SITUATION WANTED—By a young man of good character, education, and experience as foreman of Eastern rose growing establishment. References on application. Address, O. C., care The Florists' Exchange.

SITUATION WANTED—In florist store good designer and maker-up. 17 years' experience in store and design work. Best references as to honesty and ability. Strictly temperate. Address, N. S., care The Florists' Exchange.

SITUATION WANTED—As working foreman, good grower of roses, carnations, chrysanthemums and general assortment of in and outdoor cut flowers and plants. Good designer. Good references. Address, Box 172, Holyoke, Mass.

SITUATION WANTED—Florist, 24 years of age, German, one year in this country, good references, seeks position with florist or landscape gardener. Address, A. Moser, care Jos. Schluderman, 162 East 88th street, New York City.

SITUATION WANTED—As working foreman; a good grower of roses, carnations, mums, Easter stock, and general line of bedding plants. German, aged 36, single, life time experience, best of references given. State full particulars and wages. Address, O. H., Care The Florists' Exchange.

SITUATION WANTED—As carnation grower; A No. 1 man who can produce results. Carnations my specialty for years, but can also handle general line of bedding stock, etc. First-class references. Married. Address, O. B., care The Florists' Exchange.

SITUATION WANTED—By German, single man, all around grower of Easter and bedding stock, general cut flowers, also perennial plants. Good propagator; rapid potter. Address, H. K., P. O. Box 268, East Hampton, L. I., N. Y.

SITUATION WANTED—Swede, aged 34, single, strictly sober, 16 years' experience in carnations, chrysanthemums, palms, ferns and general line of pot and bedding stock. Also fruit and vegetables under glass and outside. Best of references. Private or commercial. Address, N. Q., care The Florists' Exchange.

SITUATION WANTED—By young up-to-date florist as foreman or manager on commercial place. Strictly sober, honest and good worker. References. Address, O. A., care The Florists' Exchange.

HELP WANTED

WANTED—A young man to take charge of retail store in suburban town. Good maker-up and window dresser, and good general knowledge of store work. One preferred who has had experience in New York store, and can furnish good references. Address, E. H., care The Florists' Exchange.

WANTED—Head gardener, 35-40, married, with not more than two children. German preferred; to take charge of gentlemen's place; must be competent in all branches of gardening, and capable of handling men. Steady position, free apartments, fuel, light and vegetables. State age, wages, etc. Address with references, O. I., care The Florists' Exchange.

Thirty cents is the minimum charge for advertisements on this page.

HELP WANTED

WANTED—A competent florist of sober habits to take charge of commercial greenhouses. About 8,000 feet of glass. Full particulars on application. J. Terrill & Son, Picton, Ont., Canada.

WANTED—Florist and gardener, with experience in growing choice pot plants. Give experience, copy of references, age, etc. Wages, $60.00 per month. Address, O. D., care The Florists' Exchange.

WANTED—A thoroughly competent man to take charge of a section of Beauties. Apply Frank Dolan, care of John Young Company, Bedford Station, New York.

WANTED—A first-class man for retail florist in Chicago; no greenhouse work. Must be a good salesman and designer. State wages, References. Address, M. D., care The Florists' Exchange.

WANTED—At once, a good reliable grower of carnations and bedding plants. German preferred; wages $30 per month, board and room, to start with. Address, N. N., care The Florists' Exchange.

WANTED—An energetic young man to assist in landscape work; fair knowledge of stock, trimming, etc., essential. Dutch or German preferred. State wages expected with references. A. Van Leeuwen, Jr., Worcester, Mass.

WANTED—Two young men as assistants for growing choice stove and greenhouse plants. Wages, $25.00 per month, and board. Send copy of references and give experience. J. A. Peterson, McHenry avenue, Westwood, Cincinnati, O.

WANTED—At once, a good sober, industrious man, who thoroughly understands decorating, and will take care of two show houses, one for decorating, the other for selling purpose. Apply Chas. T. Siebert, Baum & Beatty streets, Pittsburg, Pa.

WANTED—September 1, young or middle aged man of experience in general nursery work. Must be able to take charge of shipping and propagating. State wages wanted, age, nationality and references. C. R. Fish & Company, West Side Nurseries, Worcester, Mass.

WANTED—Philadelphia seedsman, two of them, by a well-known Philadelphia seed house; widely experienced men in selling to professional gardeners employed on gentlemens' establishments in the vicinity of Philadelphia. None others need apply. Address, N. M., care The Florists' Exchange.

WANTED—Salesman, one who is a hustler, and understands all about nursery stock, and a fair knowledge of landscape work. To travel. Must have a good record. Steady employment and good pay. Address with references, P. A. Keene, The Morris Nursery Company, 1 Madison avenue, New York.

WANTED—Manager for wholesale commission business. Must be experienced, capable, and of unquestioned integrity. One preferred to purchase share in business. Applicants will be notified of place for interview in Philadelphia, September 9th. Address, O. F., care The Florists' Exchange.

MISCELLANEOUS WANTS

WANTED—1000 field-grown Enchantress and 500 Harry Fenn or Lawsons. Must be nice and clean. State prices for cash. Dauphin Bros., R. F. D. 1, Ballston, Va.

WANTED TO BUY—Greenhouses to be taken down. State full particulars of same when writing. Address, F. W., care The Florists' Exchange.

WANTED—20,000 Retinispora plumosa aurea, 4 to 6 inches, transplanted. Also 4,000 Retinispora Squarrosa Veitchii, 6 inches, transplanted. Address Rhode Island Nurseries, Newport, R. I.

WANTED TO RENT—Between 10 and 25,000 feet of glass, in good condition. Wholesale or retail. State full particulars. Address, N. X., care The Florists' Exchange.

WANTED TO RENT—With privilege of buying, one or two greenhouses with some land. New England preferred. Address, O. E., care The Florists' Exchange.

FOR SALE OR RENT

FOR SALE or will rent to a responsible party, a fine greenhouse property, 12,000 feet of glass. Fine residence. Address, Silas C. Howell, Lock Box 14, Pine Bush, New York.

FOR SALE OR RENT—Four greenhouses, about 7000 feet of glass, good established retail business, six miles from Philadelphia, also dwelling house, if wanted; this is an excellent opportunity. Apply Michell's Seed Store, 1018 Market street, Philadelphia, Pa.

FOR SALE—Owing to the ill health of the principal owner, it has become advisable to offer for sale the entire stock of the best known florist establishment in southern California. A long time lease hold on the grounds may be obtained. A fine opportunity to step into an established business, incorporated. For particulars, write to Box 94, Ventura, Cal.

FOR SALE OR RENT

FOR SALE—At a bargain, or will rent eight greenhouses in center of flourishing city of 20,000 inhabitants. J. H. Ives, 103 Elm street, Danbury, Conn.

DESIRABLE greenhouse plant of three houses, 24x200 feet; propagating house, 100 feet; potting shed, stable and dwelling. Steam heat, city water. Highland, opposite Poughkeepsie, Joseph Wood, Spring Valley, New York.

TO RENT—Greenhouses heated with Hitchings boilers, ¾ of an hour from New York. Business established since 1856. Plenty of soil, good water, house, stable; fine place. Going to retire. For particulars address, M. Weigand, West Hoboken, N. J.

FOR SALE—House, 7 rooms, steam heat, 1 stable, 5 greenhouses, well stocked; steam heat, Kearney, N. J., 5 minutes from Erie R. R. depot, and 5 minutes from N. Y. trolley. J. G. Perry, Schuyler Avenue, Kearney, New Jersey.

FOR SALE—At a bargain on account of removal and having two places, I will sell four greenhouses, two houses 16 x 80, other two 22 x 80. Boiler house, 16 x 20, with one large boiler to heat the place and another in reserve. Both boilers can burn buckwheat coal at a small cost. Only three or four years in use. Price only $1500. Hill Top Greenhouses, 15-16 Gray avenue, Utica, New York.

FOR SALE—Owing to failing health, I will sell my florist establishment, beautifully situated between Larchmont Manor and Mamaroneck, Westchester Co., New York, near railroad station; trolley lines within one minute walk. First class opportunity for the right man. Plenty of landscape and jobbing work. The place contains four acres, 2 greenhouses, 104 feet long and lots of sash; well stocked with trees and shrubs, etc.; horse, wagon and tools. Address, Box 44, Larchmont, New York.

STOCK FOR SALE

FOR SALE—Queen Louise and C. A. Dana carnations, fine stock, $5.00 per 100; $25.00 per 1000. Fox & Rosen, Parkerford, Pa.

PRIMULA, Chinese, finest fringed, mixed, 1 3-4 c. Cash. Our Giant pansies ready next month. Shippensburg Floral Company, Shippensburg, Pa.

STRONG, field-grown carnation plants: Joost, pink; Challenger, scarlet; Harlowarden, crimson; Gov. Wolcott and Edith Foster, white. $5.00 per 100. Cash. Hansen & Lundsted, Passaic, N. J.

16,000 strong, healthy, field-grown violet plants of Farquhar, Lady Campbell, La France and California, $5 per 100; $45 per 1000. Richard Langle, North street, White Plains, N. Y.

BABY RAMBLER roses, fine dormant stock, $25 per 100, 2 1-2 inch pot plants, extra well rooted $7 per 100, $65 per 1000. Orders booked for delivery now or any time up to late Spring. Samples free. Brown Brothers Co., Rochester, N. Y.

CARNATIONS, first-class, field grown plants. Enchantress, Lawson, Queen, $6.00 per 100; $50.00 per 1000. Cash with order please. Mrs. P. F. Conley, Princeton Avenue, & Updike Street, Providence, R. I.

CARNATIONS—Extra fine, field-grown plants: Enchantress, Mrs. T. W. Lawson, $6.00 per 100; $50.00 per 1000. Joost, New Daybreak, Prosperity, Wolcott, $5.00 per 100; $40.00 per 1000. Terms cash. M. J. Schaaf, Dansville, N. Y.

CARNATIONS, field plants. Enchantress, $6 per 100; $50 per 1000; Boston Market, $5 per 100; $40 per 1000; Lawson, $5 per 100; $40 per 1000; Red Lawson, $6 per 100; $50 per 1000. The J. A. Budlong & Son Co., Auburn, R. I.

FOR SALE

FOR SALE—60 cypress hot bed sash, size 3 x 6, glazed with 10 x 12 glass, painted white, and in perfect condition. Most all of them new this season; none over three years old. $1.00 each. J. V. Cutler, Wassaic, N. Y.

FOR SALE—12 Hitchings hot water expansion tanks for 3 1-2 in. pipe, in good condition, cleaned, ready to set up. 1-3 price of new. Also horse lawn mower, easy running, $20.00. Address, K. D., care The Florists' Exchange.

FOR SALE BOILERS—On account of removal, one Furman, steam or hot water, 12 sections, capacity, 8000 feet glass, $200.00. One Furman boiler, 9 sections, capacity, 6000 feet of glass, $150.00. Two extra boilers, steam or hot water, 12 sections each, to be bricked in together, capacity, 11,000 feet of glass, $200.00. One Henderson Thermo steam boiler, No. 841, capacity, 9000 feet of glass, $200.00. One Henderson Thermo steam boiler, No. 728, capacity, 5000 feet of glass, $125.00. One Novelty hot water boiler, five sections, used one season, $60.00. All boilers are as good as new, being used from one to four years only. G. F. Neipp, Aqueduct, L. I., N. Y.

STOCK FOR SALE

BOILERS, BOILERS, BOILERS.

SEVERAL good second hand boilers on hand, also new No. 16 Hitchings at reduced cost. Write for list. Wm. H. Lettou, West Side Avenue Station, C. R. R. of N. J., Jersey City, N. J.

FOR SALE—3000 feet of good 2-inch pipe; 2 large hot water boilers, good as new; lot of valves, 4-inch, 3½ and 2½ inches. All to be sold cheap for cash. Nelson & Johnson, Prospect street, Framingham, Mass.

FOR SALE—One Lord & Burnham steam dome, No. 5 boiler, in good order, price, $65.00. One Scollay, 7 section boiler in good order, price, $75.00. Inquire of V. E. Reich, 1429 Metropolitan avenue, Brooklyn, N. Y.

FOR SALE—One 20 H. P. horizontal tubular boiler; one 40½ barrel white cedar tank; one 8-foot galvanized water wheel; one No. 2 Gawthrop Ram; two new windmill pumps; also a coal and lumber yard; doing a good business. Apply to Harry J. McFarland, Route No. 8, Marshalton, Pa.

FOR SALE

Greenhouse Material milled from Gulf Cypress, to any detail furnished, or our own patterns as desired, cut and spliced ready for erection. Estimates for complete constructions furnished.

V. E. REICH, Brooklyn, N. Y.

1429-1437 Metropolitan Ave.

Mention The Florists' Exchange when writing.

FOR SALE

PUMPS Rider-Ericsson. Second-hand, from $40.00 up; all repairs; other makes; new; cheap.

BOILERS One second-hand tubular hot water boiler 3 ft. in diameter 12 ft. long. Price $36.00. One No. 17 Hitchings in first class condition, $125.00; and also 6 section round boiler, $75.00; No. 6 at $75.00; No. 6 Weathered at $75.00.

PIPE Good serviceable second-hand, with Threads; 2-in., 7 cts.; 1½-in., 5¼ cts.; 1¼-in., 4 cts.; 1-in., 3 cts.; 2½ in., 10 cts.; 3 in., 14 cts.; 4 in., 19 cts. New 2-in. Standard, full lengths, with couplings, 8¼ cts. ft. Old and new fittings and valves. Old 4 inch cast iron 15c per foot.

STOCKS and DIES New Economy, best made No. 1 Threads, ¼-in., ¾-in. 1-in. pipe, $3.00. No. 2 Threads, 1¼-in., 1½-in. 2-in. pipe, $4.00.

PIPE CUTTERS New Saunders Pattern. No. 1 cuts ¼-in.-1-in. pipe, $1.00. No. 2 cuts 1-in.-2-in. pipe, $1.30.

STILLSON WRENCHES New. 18-in., grips [illegible]-in.-2-in. pipe, $1.65; 24-in. grips ¼-in.-2½ in. pipe, $2.40; 36-in., grips ¼-in.-3½-in. pipe, $4.75.

PIPE VISES New. No. 1 Hinged, grips ¼-in.-2 in. pipe, $2.00.

GARDEN HOSE New. 50 ft. lengths. ¾-in., guaranteed 100-lbs. pressure, 7½ cts. per ft.; ¾-in. not guaranteed, 4¼ cts. per ft., 25 ft. lengths, ½c. per ft. more.

HOT-BED SASH New. Cypress, 3-ft.x6 ft., from 75 cts. up; glazed, complete, from $1.60 up. Second-hand, in good condition, all glass in, $1.00 each.

GLASS New American 10x12 single $1.75 per box; 12x12 single $1.90 per box; 10x12 $2.55, 12x12, 10x15 double $2.65 per box; 12x14, 12x20, 14x14, double, $2.75 per box; 16x16, 18x18, $3.10 per box; 16x24 double $3.25 per box. Second hand glass, 8 x 10, 8 x 14, double, $1.85 per box. Single $1.50.

Old material, ridge, plates, gutters, bars, etc.

Get our prices on New Gulf Cypress Building Material, Ventilating Apparatus, Oil, White Lead, Putty, Paint, Points, etc.

METROPOLITAN MATERIAL CO.

1398-1408 Metropolitan Avenue, BROOKLYN, N.Y

Mention The Florists' Exchange when writing.

OUR ENDEAVOR

is to place THE FLORISTS' EXCHANGE in the hands of every reader within 1000 miles on Saturday of each week.

In order to effect this even distribution, which makes for the benefit of our advertisers, it is necessary that all advertising copy for current issue should reach us by

12 noon, on Wednesday.

Wholesale Prices of Cut Flowers, New York, August 30, 1906
Prices quoted are by the hundred unless otherwise noted

Roses	A. Beauty, fancy—special	6.00 to	15.00
	" extra	5.00 to	6.00
	" No. 1	4.00 to	5.00
	" No. 2	3.00 to	4.00
	" No. 3	1.00 to	1.50
	Bride, Maid, fancy—spc'l	3.00 to	4.00
	" extra	2.00 to	3.00
	" No. 1	1.00 to	2.00
	" No. 2	.25 to	.50
	Golden Gate	1.00 to	5.00
	Liberty	.... to	.....
	Mme. Abel Chatenay	1.00 to	6.00
Adiantum		.50 to	.75
	Croweanum	.50 to	1.00
Asparagus		25.00 to	50.00
	" Plumosus, bunches	8.00 to	15.00
	" Sprengeri, bunches	8.00 to	15.00
Asters		.25 to	8.00
Cattleyas		50.00 to	60.00
Daisies		.... to	....
Gladiolus		.50 to	1.00
		.... to	....

Carnations	Inf'r grades, all colors	.50 to	1.00
	Standard Varieties — White	1.00 to	2.00
	Standard Varieties — Pink	1.00 to	2.00
	Standard Varieties — Red	1.00 to	2.00
	Standard Varieties — Yel. & Var.	.... to	....
	*Fancy— (*The highest grades of standard var.) — White	.... to	....
	*Fancy — Pink	.... to	....
	*Fancy — Red	.... to	....
	*Fancy — Yel. & Var.	.... to	....
	Novelties	.... to	....
Dahlias, per bunch		.05 to	.15
Lilies		4.00 to	6.00
Lily of the Valley		1.00 to	3.00
Mignonette		.... to	....
		.... to	....
		.... to	....
		.... to	....
Pansies, per dozen bunches		.50 to	.75
Smilax		8.00 to	10.00
Sweet Peas, per bunch		.... to	....

Wholesale Prices of Cut Flowers—Per 100

Boston Aug. 28, 1906	Buffalo Aug. 13, 1906	Detroit Aug. 5, 1906	Cincinnati Aug. 20, 1906	Baltimore Aug. 6, 1906	NAMES AND VARIETIES	Milwaukee July 28, 1906	Phil'delphia July 24, 1906	Pittsburg Aug. 28, 1906	St. Louis Aug. 27, 1909
to	20.00 to 25.00	10.00 to 25.00	to 30.00	to	ROSES — A. BEAUTY, fancy—special	to 25.00	15.00 to 20.00	20.00 to 25.00	15.00 to 20.00
10.00 to 20.00	12.00 to 20.00	to	20.00 to 25.00	12.50 to 15.00	" extra	15.00 to 18.00	10.00 to 15.00	12.00 to 15.00	10.00 to 12.50
4.00 to 10.00	6.00 to 12.00	to	to 15.00	5.00 to 8.00	" No. 1	10.00 to 12.50	5.00 to 7.00	8.00 to 10.00	6.00 to 8.00
2.00 to 4.00	3.00 to 6.00	to	to	to	" Culls and ordinary	4.00 to 6.00	1.00 to 4.00	4.00 to 5.00	3.00 to 5.00
to	5.00 to 6.00	3.00 to 6.00	4.00 to 6.00	to	BRIDE, 'MAID, fancy-special	to 6.00	to	2.00 to 6.00	to
4.00 to 6.00	4.00 to 5.00	to	2.00 to 4.00	to 4.00	" extra	to 5.00	6.00 to 8.00	to	to
2.00 to 4.00	3.00 to 4.00	to	1.00 to 2.00	to 3.00	" No. 1	to 4.00	4.00 to 5.00	to	to
.50 to 2.00	2.00 to 3.00	to	to	to 2.00	" No. 2	to 2.00	2.00 to 3.00	to	to
to	to	4.00 to 8.00	to	2.00 to 4.00	GOLDEN GATE	4.00 to 5.00	4.00 to 8.00	to	2.00 to 4.00
2.00 to 6.00	3.00 to 7.00	to	2.00 to 6.00	4.00 to 8.00	K. A. VICTORIA	4.00 to 8.00	4.00 to 6.00	to	2.00 to 6.00
to	3.00 to 7.00	to	to	to	LIBERTY	4.00 to 6.00	3.00 to 6.00	to	to
to	3.00 to 6.00	4.00 to 10.00	to	to	METEOR	to	to	to	to
to	3.00 to 5.00	4.00 to 10.00	to	2.00 to 4.00	PERLE	4.00 to 6.00	to	to	2.00 to 3.00
to	to	to 50.00	to	to	ORCHIDS—Cattleyas	to	to 50.00	to	to
to	.50 to 1.00	to	to	.50 to .75	CARNATIONS — Inferior grades, all colors	to 1.00	.75 to 1.00	.75 to 1.00	to .50
to	1.00 to 1.25	to 1.00	to 1.00	1.00 to 1.50	Standard Varieties { White	to 1.00	.75 to 1.00	to	to .50
to	1.00 to 1.25	to	to 1.00	1.00 to 1.50	Pink	to 1.00	.75 to 1.00	to	to .50
to	1.00 to 1.25	to	to 1.00	1.00 to 1.50	Red	to 1.00	.75 to 1.00	to	to
to	to	to 3.00	to 1.00	1.00 to 1.50	Yellow and var.	to 1.00	.75 to 1.00	to	to
.50 to 1.50	1.50 to 2.00	to	to	to 3.00	Fancy Varieties { White	1.50 to 2.00	2.00 to 2.50	to	.75 to 1.00
.50 to 1.50	1.50 to 2.00	to	to	to 3.00	Pink	1.50 to 2.00	2.00 to 2.50	to	.75 to 1.00
.50 to 1.50	1.50 to 2.00	to	to	to 3.00	Red	1.50 to 2.00	2.00 to 2.50	to	to
.50 to 1.50	1.50 to 2.00	to 1.50	to	to 3.00	Yellow and var.	1.50 to 2.00	2.00 to 2.50	to	to
to	to	to	to	to	Novelties	to	to	to	to
.75 to 1.00	.50 to 1.00	to 2.00	to 1.00	to 1.00	ADIANTUM	to 1.00	to 1.00	1.25 to 1.50	to 1.00
to 50.00	to	25.00 to 60.00	to 50.00	25.00 to 50.00	ASPARAGUS, Plum. and Ten.	20.00 to 30.00	25.00 to 35.00	30.00 to 50.00	25.00 to 50.00
to	to	20.00 to 30.00	to 35.00	25.00 to 50.00	" Sprengeri, bunches	20.00 to 30.00	25.00 to 35.00	20.00 to 40.00	25.00 to 50.00
.75 to 1.00	.50 to 2.00	to	1.00 to 3.00	to	ASTERS	.50 to 1.00	to	.50 to 2.00	1.00 to 3.00
to	8.00 to 10.00	to 10.00	to	6.00 to 8.00	CALLAS	to	to	to	to
to	to	.75 to 1.50	to	to	DAISIES	to .40	3.00 to 4.00	to .50	1.50 to 2.00
to	1.00 to 3.00	8.00 to 10.00	1.00 to 3.00	2.00 to 4.00	GLADIOLUS	to	8.00 to 12.00	2.00 to 4.00	to
to	to	to	to	10.00 to 12.50	LILIES, Harrisii	to 12.50	to	15.00 to 18.00	to
4.00 to 8.00	12.00 to 15.00	to	12.00 to 15.00	10.00 to 12.50	" Longiflorum	to 12.50	2.00 to 4.00	to	to
2.00 to 4.00	3.00 to 4.00	3.00 to 4.00	to 4.00	1.00 to 2.00	LILY OF THE VALLEY	to	1.00 to 2.00	2.00 to 4.00	to
to	to	to	to	2.00 to 2.50	MIGNONETTE, ordinary	to	to	to	to
to	to	to	to	to	" fancy	to	to	to	to
to	to	4.00 to 8.00	to	to	PEONIES	to	15.00 to 20.00	to	to
10.00 to 12.50	to 15.00	12.50 to 15.00	to 15.00	12.50 to 20.00	SMILAX	to 15.00	to	12.50 to 18.00	to 12.50
to	to	to	to	to	VIOLETS, ordinary	to	to	to	to
to	to	to	to	to	" fancy	to	to	to	to
to	to	to	to	to	NARCISSUS	to	to	to	.10 to .15
.20 to .25	.15 to .25	.50 to .75	to	.20 to .35	SWEET PEAS	.25 to .50	to .50	to	to
to	to	to	to	to		to	to	to	to
to	to	to	to	to		to	to	to	to

Buffalo.

News Notes.

Wm. Scott, D. B. Long, Wm. F. Kasting and C. T. Guenther, the local florists who attended the S. A. F. O. H. meeting have returned. All report having a good time, but all claim the weather was too hot for people living in this city of even temperature, which never goes above 85 degrees.

Among the out of town returning florists who attended the convention and stopped off here to visit our city and also Niagara Falls were Alex. J. Guttman and C. Weber of the firm of Guttman and Weber; John H. Dunlop of Tôronto, and Peter Beurelein and wife of Elmhurst, N. Y.

All is in readiness for the florist picnic which will be held at Fort Erie Grove, September 5. Those who intend participating in the games will arrive early so that the games can be started on time. These this year will be unusually interesting. The East Side florists will play the West Side. There will also be on the program a hundred yard dash, boys' race, ladies' race, running hop step and jump, sack race, three leg race, half mile run (open handicap), old men's race.

Mr. and Mrs. Jerry Brookins and son and Mr. Briggs, Mr. Brookins' father in law, had a very narrow escape from death on Saturday night, August 24. While returning from their Summer home at Angola their automobile crashed into a telegraph pole, throwing out the occupants but not injuring any of them to any extent. Mr. Briggs, who is a man advanced in age, received a severe shock.

W. H. G.

Utica, N. Y.

Trade for the month of August has been the best in years.

It has been very dry in our locality for the past two months; in consequence everything out of doors is poor.

Henry Martin, junior member of the firm of Spencer & Martin, on August 22, took unto himself a wife. They are now on their wedding trip in Ohio, and will be at home September 15.

J. C. Spencer and family leave soon for their camp—Glenwood on Otsego Lake, Cooperstown, N. Y.—for two weeks.

Frank Baker an family have returned from Port Leyden, where they have been spending the Summer.

Theo. Schesch of Ilion, who was in our St. Elisabeth Hospital undergoing a very painful operation on his eye, has been at home for nearly a week, and is recuperating nicely which all the florists in Utica are very glad to hear.

A. Newman of S. A. Weller, Zanesville, Ohio, was calling on the trade this week.

QUIZ.

Wholesale Prices of Cut Flowers, Chicago, Aug. 29, 1906

Prices quoted are by the hundred unless otherwise noted

ROSES — American Beauty		
36-inch stems ....per doz.	...... to	4.00
30-inch stems .... "	...... to	3.00
24-inch stems .... "	...... to	2.50
20-inch stems .... "	...... to	2.00
18-inch stems .... "	...... to	1.50
12-inch stems .... "	...... to	1.00
8-inch stems and shorts "	.50 to	.75
Bride Maid, fancy special	5.00 to	6.00
" extra	4.00 to	5.00
" No. 1	2.00 to	3.00
" No. 2	.50 to	1.00
Golden Gate	2.00 to	5.00
Carnot	2.00 to	6.00
Uncle John	2.00 to	8.00
Liberty	2.00 to	8.00
Richmond	2.00 to	8.00
Kaiserine	2.00 to	8.00
Killarney	3.00 to	8.00
Perle	2.00 to	6.00
Chatenay	2.00 to	6.00
Orchids—Cattleyas	...... to	50.00
SMILAX	8.00 to	12.00
LILY OF THE VALLEY	2.00 to	4.00
DAHLIAS	2.00 to	3.00

CARNATIONS		
Inferior grades all colors	.25 to	.50
STANDARD VARIETIES White	.75 to	1.00
STANDARD VARIETIES Pink	.75 to	1.00
STANDARD VARIETIES Red	.75 to	1.00
STANDARD VARIETIES Yellow & var	.75 to	1.00
*FANCY (The highest grades of Sta'd var) White	1.50 to	2.00
*FANCY Pink	1.50 to	2.00
*FANCY Red	1.50 to	2.00
*FANCY Yellow & var	1.50 to	2.00
NOVELTIES	...... to	......
ADIANTUM	.50 to	1.00
ASPARAGUS, Plum. & Ten.	.35 to	.50
" Sprengeri, bunches	.35 to	.50
GLADIOLUS	2.00 to	6.00
LILIES, Longiflorum	8.00 to	12.00
HARRISII	8.00 to	12.00
AURATUM	6.00 to	8.00
NYMPHAEA	...... to	1.00
MIGNONETTE, ordinary	1.00 to	2.00
TUBEROSES, SPIKES	4.00 to	8.00
......	...... to	......
......	...... to	......
HARDY FERNS per 1000	1.00 to	1.50
GALAX "	1.00 to	1.25
ASTERS	.50 to	2.50

New York.

News Notes.

Most of the delegates who attended the S. A. F. convention in Dayton last week, have returned, and it seems to be the general opinion that Dayton was a rather warm place; in fact, some are free to admit that it was very hot down there, and that they were glad to get back to old New York again where the weather is always tempered by refreshing sea breezes. We are sorry to see that our bowling team was so far from the front in the recent tournament of the S. A. F. O. H. though perhaps, the club's failure to win any of the trophies is but a sign of progress in other matters. We think it was Mr. O'Mara who remarked one evening at the alleys a year or two ago, that "the more intellectual a man became, the worse his bowling got to be."

The building in which is located the Broadway store of Chas. Thorley is undergoing a general reconstruction, and for the time being the usual attractive window display there is hidden from the street by a mass of ladders and builders' scaffolding.

Over in Brooklyn, there are rumors that some of the side-walk florists are likely to lose their stands owing to the efforts making by fruit dealers to obtain them. Just who will be the victors is at present uncertain, as it seems to be a question as to who will stand the highest rent. Unlike New York, the season for flowers in Brooklyn lasts all the year round, and through the Summer months it would seem that nearly all the stock that reaches the New York wholesale markets is eventually disposed of across the bridge.

News comes from Poughkeepsie and the neighboring violet regions, that the plants are not so much affected by disease as they were thought to be a few weeks ago, and that the prospects for large crops of flowers for the coming Winter are very bright indeed. At Rhinebeck, some 30 new greenhouses have been built for violet growing, and all indications point to an increased supply of blooms.

Wm. H. Gunther, who for many years has conducted a wholesale florist business at 30 West 29th street, has taken into partnership his younger brother John, and hereafter the firm title will be Gunther Brothers. John has been in the store as an employee since he was a boy, is thoroughly familiar with the wholesale flower business in every detail; and it goes without saying that success will attend the partnership of the Gunther Brothers.

Chas Kleingenbeck, who for 13 years has been in the florist business at Middle Village, N. Y., died August 18, at the age of 56 years. He leaves a widow, six sons, and three daughters. The business will be continued by his son Joseph.

The annual exhibition of the Schwæbischer Sængerbund of Brooklyn, N. Y., will be held in Ridgewood Park, Myrtle avenue, Brooklyn, on September 2, 3, 4 and 9.

E. F. Hoehl, for some time manager of the Madison Rose Company, Madison, N. J., is no longer with that firm.

H. E. Froment is back at business again after a pleasant vacation spent at Lake George.

Some of the leading wholesale florists will continue closing their stores at 4 p. m. daily until September 15.

Monday next, September 3, is Labor Day, and a general holiday in this city.

H. Holton, of the firm of Holton & Hunkel, Milwaukee, Wis., was in town this week.

Louisville.

Convention Echoes.

It is much easier to tell after the convention who were there, than to guess before it, who is going, so I will now tell that Mr. and Mrs. Anders Rasmussen, Mr. and Mrs. S. J. Thompson, Mrs. Jefferies, Jacob Schulz, Joseph Molck, Henry Fuchs, Louis Kirch and August R. Baumer have returned home safely and have only pleasant things to say about the meeting, the Dayton florists, the N. C. R. and the Soldiers' Home. All of our conventionites spent some time in Cincinnati, visiting the different growers and places of interest, and several made side trips to Richmond, Ind.

The past week has been the warmest of the Summer and business has suffered accordingly, it being the quietest week of the Summer.

Members of the Kentucky Society of Florists will make note, that the September meeting of the society will be held Tuesday evening the fourth. Be sure and be present as those who attended the convention will be expected to tell the stay-at-homes all about it.

Fred L. Schulz intends to open a wholesale house here, on October 1, in the store room formerly occupied by Weiland & Olinger.

Some time ago I mentioned that we were experiencing a spasm of reform in our city, and that one of our city magistrates was enforcing all the old "Blue Laws" on the statute books, but that he had not molested any of the florists. This is all changed now, for last week he swore out a warrant against Fred Haupt for doing business on Sunday. Mr. Haupt's trial was postponed until this week when the judge will tell us whether we may or may not sell flowers on Sunday.

A. R. B.

San Francisco.

News Notes.

This last week of August will see two or three more weddings that promise well for the cut flower trade, also several quiet home affairs, and then the round of September events will be ushered in with the more elaborate Fall weddings, the reopening of the various clubs and many delightful afternoon teas and card parties, for many of which the florists already have memoranda to attend to, florally.

The beautiful Palm Garden of the world-wide famous Palace Hotel of this city, which was considerably toppled by the April earthquake and burned to ashes next day by the unquenchable fire, is to be replaced, even grander than before. "It was a magnet of great attraction," was the remark made this week by one of the trustees of the hotel estate. And it was also said this week by these authorities that preparatory work will be commenced forthwith to replace the hotel on the old site, palm garden and all, on the lines of the original, but more elaborate. Three days ago the insurance loss on the Palace Hotel building was adjusted by New York, Hartford and London men at $1,302,610.22, and checks are now being drawn, aggregating this amount, by the ninety-eight companies involved in the loss. Incidentally, the adjusters say, this is the largest loss upon a single risk ever adjusted in this country, and they instance the Baltimore conflagration, two years ago, which produced the record loss up to that time, being $771,000 paid upon the Equitable Life Insurance Company's building.

Communications received at the University of California by friends of Dr. Hugo de Vries, the eminent botanist of the University of Amsterdam, who gave a course of lectures at the Summer session, state that the professor is preparing an article for publication in defense of Luther Burbank of Santa Rosa. Professor de Vries is a strong personal friend of Burbank, and while in California this Summer passed several days at Burbank's gardens and experiment station near Santa Rosa. At that time he spoke highly of the work done by Burbank and stated that he had the greatest admiration for his ability and felt interest in his work. The article which is being prepared by Professor de Vries in defense of the Santa Rosa "wizard" is called forth chiefly by recent adverse comments by an English botanist on the work of Burbank. Dr. de Vries is one of the most noted botanical authorities of the present day, and his defense of Burbank is expected to carry great weight.

Orchids of nearly every variety and numbering about 7,000, landed here this week from Manila. They were collected by Manuel D'Yriarte, a wealthy Filipino, and are in transit to the White House conservatories. D'Yriarte met the Taft party during its visit to the Far East, and so great was the admiration of those members for his gardens and particularly his orchids that he determined to send some of the choicest of the latter that could be found in the Philippines.

ALVIN.

Newport, R. I.

Horticultural Society Meeting.

At a meeting of the Horticultural Society Tuesday evening last there was quite a large attendance. The exhibits were not over numerous, but there were some good things among them. Paul Volquardson showed a large vase of Spiræa Davidii, for which he was awarded a certificate of merit and a gratuity of $5. This is a new variety of spiræa recently introduced by Henry A. Dreer of Philadelphia. The spikes are tall and graceful; in color it is mauve, with a suggestion of pink. It looks a good thing for herbaceous borders and for planting in clumps, but its color is against it for general decorative work in the cut state although for decorating light rooms it will be all right.

Stewart Ritchie showed some very good sweet peas of the varieties Dorothy Eckford and Florence Spencer, for which he received a certificate of merit and a gratuity. Andrew Christensen had on exhibition a superb specimen of Nephrolepis Scottii which showed good culture. A certificate and $5 of a gratuity was awarded. Gibson Brothers exhibited some tuberous rooted begonias; Samuel Speers, strawberries, and some fruit from a seedling gooseberry. John Marshall and John S. Stoddard showed collections of dahlias. A social session followed the completion of the work of the committee on awards.

Trade and News Notes.

The first half of the Newport season is gone, and while a few in the trade have no reason to complain of the state of business during that time there are others without material reasons for satisfaction. At the beginning of the season it looked as though things would boom from start to finish but they did not. The people who in former years gave two or more large entertainments in July were this year contented with a series of affairs much more modest than satisfied their ambitions and ideas of hospitality in former years. Then again there are more florists doing business here than was the case a few years ago, for which reason alone they all cannot expect to do as much business as was done in years past by half the number. There are several newcomers here this season among the cottagers but none of them have so far ventured the giving of entertainments on a sensational or startling scale. But they may do so before the season is over.

The florists of Newport and New York owe a lasting debt of gratitude to Mrs. Stuyvesant Fish for she it was who first set the laudable example of transforming her house and its immediate surroundings into a flower garden on the occasion of a large entertainment, and her example has been followed by many others to the delight of florists, because when an order for such a decoration comes in whoever gets it is not bound down to a low figure, but is given full scope to go ahead and show what he can do for his own credit and incidentally for the reputation of the entertainer, the result usually being something much better than anything that preceded it, in the accomplishment of which great quantities of material were used and much of that material could have been left in the hands of the growers had the hospitality of someone not attained such large proportions.

The kinds of material I have reference to are hydrangeas, hollyhocks in large quantities, lilies, and various other kinds of outdoor flowers that are only used in large quantities here when the decorations are on a large scale. Of course it is understood that choicer flowers are also made use of on such occasions; sometimes five thousand roses are used in one decoration.

Mrs. Fish already this season gave three such entertainments. Hodgson had the first; and Wadley & Smythe had the other two.

Joseph Leikens has just got an order from Mrs. O. H. P. Belmont for a plant and flower decoration which by all accounts will surpass everything heretofore attempted in Newport. Mrs. Belmont has had a large force of men for some time employed turning what were the coach house and stable at Belcourt into a ball room. This when completed will give her a ball room extending the whole length of this immense building. The scheme of decorating the ball room includes a border of plants placed in boxes along the entire length of the walls, with vines to grow up and cover the enamel brick work. A green painted trellis is now being erected to which the vines are to be tied. The whole roof will be festooned with green and flowers. Mr. Leikens calculates that the undertaking will keep him moving rapidly from now until the first of September when the entertainment comes off.

Mrs. W. B. Leeds entertained last week, when the decorations consisted mainly of water lilies. These are growing in popularity greatly of late years; and no wonder, because very effective work can be done with them when quantities are at command.

Leikens had a decoration for Mrs. E. C. Knight, Jr., a few evenings ago that was very much admired. Killarney roses and lily of the valley were principally used. The table was decorated in the style of Prince of Wales' feathers so much in evidence here lately and which makes a very pleasing and novel decoration. The decoration at Mrs. Knight's entertainment was considered one of the most successful of this mode of arrangement, because for one reason it was the largest yet attempted with roses.

Roses are much improved in appearance lately, American Beauty especially.

Jurgens' is a busy place at present with the work of supplying a large portion of the material used by the florists and preparing for Winter. Mr. Jurgens supplies not only Newport with the best lily of the valley, but also supplies the best handled by florists in other cities now as he has done for thirty or more years. Last week Mr. Jurgens received a very large consignment of bulbs, etc., from Europe.

William Jurgens is a very successful grower of Kaiserin Augusta Victroia roses and lily of the valley.

While it is no doubt the case that growers everywhere are getting busy now, but in few places are they so kept at it in July and August as they are here in Newport. In most other sections the cut flower demand is down to the minimum during these months, but here it is the reverse. That being a fact and other preparatory work also demanding attention, they have all they can attend to.

Stewart Ritchie has finished planting carnations including the stock required for his big new house. Mr. Ritchie is aiming at another big one for the near future.

Oscar Schultz is one of the busiest of the busy at present. He supplies a great deal of the outdoor material used by the avenue florists, and because his capacity was inadequate for the demand, he has recently considerably increased his establishment in area and stock.

Gibson Bros. are doing a good business at their avenue stand. This firm had at their nursery on Bliss road a great display of Lilium speciosum rubrum lately. I have noticed that occasionally Gibsons use a white Nicotiana Sanderæ in pots for decorating.

V. A. Vanicek of the Rhode Island Nurseries has just purchased a farm comprising forty acres adjoining his nursery grounds. In making this purchase Mr. Vanicek had in view the increasing demand for large specimen trees for the accommodation of which he heretofore was cramped for room. It is really amazing the rapidity with which Mr. Vanicek has developed his business. It is only twelve years ago since he started on a very small scale on Vernon avenue; to-day he has over one hundred acres devoted to nursery stock.

D. M.

Springfield, O.

As a fore-runner of the Dayton Convention, numerous delegations from distant eastern and southern points journeyed to Springfield a day in advance (Monday), and visited the extensive greenhouses of The Good & Reese Co., The McGregor Bros. Co., and other plant growing establishments. This affords to members of the S. A. F. an opportunity of seeing the sources of supply from which they have drawn for many years past and more fully realizing the importance of this market in the shipment of plants.

In the matter of rainfall, thunderstorms and oppressive atmosphere, July and August have been record breakers in this locality. The crops of weeds have come on persistently and heavily, and in some cases noticed, out-of-door plants are practically "out-o'-sight." During such weather, constant vigilance has been necessary, particularly about the propagating frames, where the careless or incompetent grower would be likely to suffer loss of cuttings, while the trained and painstaking expert would successfully carry his crop through all danger.

The Leedle Floral Company is erecting two new houses 20 x 152 feet and a "lean-to" 10 x 105 feet. The space gained will be devoted to the housing of rose plants which are being propagated in large quantities for the floral and nursery trade.

GEO. DALE.

PORTLAND, ME.—Hiram W. Dyer, who for many years was foreman at the greenhouses of Niles Nelson at South Portland has been engaged by J. W. Minott to take charge of the houses at Pleasantdale. The plant of Mr. Minott has steadily grown to be one of the largest in this section of the State and during the present season a new and very large house has been added to take care of the largely increasing business of the firm.

Cromwell, Conn.

E. H. R. Green, president of the Green Floral and Nursery Company, of Dallas, Texas, was a visitor in town last week. Mr. Green is better known, perhaps, as a railroad man than as a florist, but he is rapidly acquiring a leading position in the latter field, having the largest plant in Texas, with 125,000 square feet of glass. Many times a millionaire, he still derives much of his prominence from being the son of Mrs. Hetty Green of New York, reputed to be the richest woman in the world. He came here to look over the Pierson plant, preparatory to making some extensive additions to his own. On his return to Texas he will at once begin the construction of two new houses, each to be one thousand feet long and proportionally wide. These will be planted with Killarney, Richmond, Bride and Bridesmaid roses. Mr. Green is a man of strong and pleasing personality, and displays an intimate knowledge of floriculture and the details of general greenhouse work that is surprising in one who did not start at the bottom and obtain his information from hard work and long experience. His entering this field was not only by accident, but by his enterprise and grasp of the situation; he has made it a profitable investment. The future will no doubt know him as one of the leading florists of the country.

Wallace R. Pierson has passed most of the month of August at Watch Hill.

Magnus Pierson is adding a new house about 200 feet long, to his plant in the western part of the town. This will give him about 20,000 square feet of glass in all. The new house will be devoted largely to house plants and bedding stock.

A. N. Pierson has erected two new houses, 400 feet long, one 54 feet and the other 40 feet wide. The first has been planted with Killarney roses and the second is now filled with chrysanthemums. He is at work on a third house of the same length to be planted mostly with roses.

H.

SALT LAKE CITY, UTAH.—At a meeting of the Salt Lake Horticulture Society, held in that city recently, resolutions were adopted against the present government system of seed distribution. The members decided that they preferred the old system, that of giving choice seeds to a few leading gardeners in the different localities.

CANADIAN NEWS

OTTAWA.—The weather has been excessively warm with no let up. On Sunday last we expected a cold wave after having a visit from a genuine cyclone, which did immense damage to trees, shrubbery, plate glass windows, fences and cheap erections; but, strange to say, none to the greenhouses. Crops in the field need rain very much, otherwise they are looking well. Asters are very good; but the dry weather has made sweet peas short in the stem. Crops inside are looking fine but this very warm weather necessitates a strict watch for red spider. Business for Summer is fair, and stock fairly plentiful.

A visit from D. MacRorie of the Manda establishment was a pleasant feature; he seemed to be doing a good business in orchids, etc., in Canada.

R. Wright, of Alymer, is making good headway with his new carnation range and hopes to be able to attend the convention at Guelph.

Mrs. and Miss Scrim have gone to Muskoka lakes for a few weeks' rest. The rest of us took a day off and went to see Barnum's circus.

This week we shall most of us be off to the Guelph convention and Toronto exhibition, and expect to meet the majority of the florists of Canada there, and have the best convention yet; perhaps we will decide the Birnie geranium question. Our tickets allow a stop-over at the Dale estate establishment—another treat—and the thought of it all makes me feel young again. E.

Montreal.

The weather has turned very cool much to the satisfaction of tile bench makers, soil handlers, carnation planters and all greenhouse workers. Carnations are mostly all planted and doing well. Roses and chrysanthemums are very promising, but the bug has again tackled the latter. Asters in the field that looked promising a week ago are fast taking on that yellow diseased look.

The tradesmen who are going to the convention are hustling to get everything in good shape before starting for Guelph.

Retail trade has been very good, funeral work plentiful, and the prospects excellent for a brisk Fall business. The store men are busy painting and otherwise renovating their places of business.

J. D. Sinclair of Toronto will open a branch florists' supply and wholesale cut flower store here.

It is rumored that Rennie seedsmen, Toronto, will also open a branch here.

Mr. and Mrs. Simmonds, Toronto, were visitors last week on their way to Murray Bay, Que. W. C. H.

The New Bedford Horticultural Society held its annual Clambake at Padmaram, about three miles from the city, August 21, at 7.30 p. m. The members of the society and their friends left on a special car for the scene of action and all report having had an enjoyable evening.

IT'S WORTH SERIOUS THOUGHT

this showing up of your plants and flowers in the right surroundings—surroundings that set them off to best possible advantage and give to your customer an impression of the thorough way you do things. Then why not have a

U-BAR SHOW ROOM GREENHOUSE

where your plants can have almost an outdoor setting—so light and free from supporting parts are they—the most attractive, cheeriest places imaginable.

Pierson U-Bar Co.

Designers and Builders
U-Bar Greenhouses
Metropolitan Building

4th Ave. & 23d St., New York

KROESCHELL BROS. CO.

IMPROVED

Greenhouse Boiler

33 ERIE STREET, CHICAGO

Boilers made of the best of material, shell firebox sheets and heads of steel, water space all around front, sides and back). Write for information.

WEATHERED COMPANY.

Builders of Iron and Cypress Greenhouses, Greenhouse Heating and Ventilating Apparatus.

P. O. Address, Box 789, New York City.

Mention The Florists' Exchange when writing.

PLANT CULTURE

PRICE, $1.00.

The best book for the plant grower.

A. T. DE LA MARE PTG. & PUB. CO. LTD.

"Absolutely Safe and Reliable. Ask Your Friends."

We delight in having our BLUFFS CALLED by visits to our plant. There we have no trouble in proving our claims to prospective purchasers of

TANKS AND TOWERS

W. E. Caldwell Co.

LOUISVILLE, KY.

Mention The Florists' Exchange when writing.

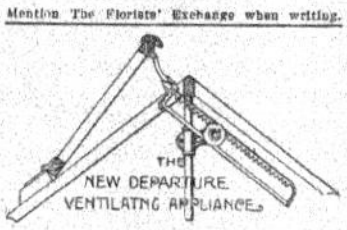

CHEAPEST and BEST

If you doubt it try them and be convinced. Send for descriptive Price Circular.

J. D. Carmody, Evansville, Ind.

Mention The Florists' Exchange when writing.

The STANDARD VENTILATING MACHINERY

The original ma hine with self oiling cups; the most powerful least complicated, very compact, with ease of operation.

The New Duplex Gutter over six miles in use and highly recommended; the only drip proof gutter in the market.

The Standard Return Steam Trap has no equal for simplicity or its workings. Catalogue free.

E. HIPPARD, Youngstown, O.

Mention The Florists' Exchange when writing

SUMMER IN WINTER

BY USING

Standard Greenhouse Boilers

One cent gets our Catalog

GIBLIN & CO., UTICA, N. Y.

Mention The Florists' Exchange when writing.

Our Material is the Best

and it is also the cheapest. The most important thing about this statement is that it's true. The next most important thing is that we can prove it. Of course you don't believe us, but if we are right you are losing money every time you build with other material. It will cost you nothing to inquire and it may save you "lots of money," also time and trouble. Why not write today? We will send you a catalogue and will be glad to talk the matter over any time.

John C. Moninger Co., Chicago

115 E. BLACKHAWK STREET

Mention The Florists' Exchange when writing.

GREENHOUSE LUMBER

BUILD WELL

There is a pleasant sense of satisfaction in knowing that when your order for Cypress is placed with us you will receive material upon which you can absolutely rely, and that shipment will be promptly made.

ESTIMATES AND PLANS

Furnished without charge. Let us hear from you if you contemplate building.

HOT BED SASH

CEDAR POSTS, IRON FITTINGS, ETC., ETC.

LOCKLAND LUMBER CO.

LOCKLAND, O.

Mention The Florists' Exchange When writing.

THE JENNINGS IMPROVED IRON GUTTER

PATENT IRON BENCH FITTINGS AND ROOF SUPPORTS. VENTILATING APPARATUS. IMPROVED VAPORIZING PANS for Tobacco Extracts, Etc.

SEND FOR CIRCULARS

DILLER, CASKEY & CO.

Successors to JENNINGS BROS

S. W. CORNER SIXTH AND BERK STS., PHILADELPHIA, PA.

Mention The Florists' Exchange when writing.

THE AMERICAN CARNATION

PRICE, $3.50. SEND FOR A COPY

A. T. DE LA MARE Ptg. & Pub. Co. Ltd., 2 Duane St., N.Y.

FURMAN BOILERS FOR GREENHOUSE HEATING

Valuable Catalogue on Modern Steam and Hot-Water Heating, mailed free upon request. Address

THE HERENDEEN MANUFACTURING CO.

Dept. F, GENEVA, N. Y.

196 Pearl Street, NEW YORK — OKLAHOMA CITY, O. T.

Furman Boilers have been awarded the Certificate of Merit at Five different Florists' Conventions. Have a record of 20 years. Over 25,000 in use.

SELLING AGENTS:

EDW. S. DEAN, Bloomington, Ill. — E. K. BARR, La Crosse, Wis.

Mention The Florists' Exchange when writing.

THE FLORISTS' EXCHANGE

We are a straight shoot and aim to grow into a vigorous plant

A WEEKLY MEDIUM OF INTERCHANGE FOR FLORISTS, NURSERYMEN, SEEDSMEN AND THE TRADE IN GENERAL

Vol. XXII. No. 10 — NEW YORK AND CHICAGO, SEPTEMBER 8, 1906 — One Dollar Per Year

NOW READY

Narcissus Paper White Grandiflora
---and---
White Roman Hyacinths

We offer the finest bulbs for immediate delivery, as follows:

Narcissus Paper White Grandiflora, finest quality bulbs, 13 c/m and up, 1,250 bulbs to the case, $11.25 per case; less quantities at $1.00 per 100.

Paper White Grandiflora Narcissus is always a money-maker. Plant at once for earliest crop, which is the most profitable.

White Roman Hyacinths, finest quality bulbs, 12 to 15 c/m, about 1,800 bulbs to the case, $2.50 per 100, $23.00 per 1,000.

Freesia Refracta Alba. Finest Bermuda-grown bulbs, ½ inch up, $7.50 per 1,000.

Bermuda Buttercup Oxalis. $1.00 per 100, $7.50 per $1,000.

Lilium Harrisii. 5 to 7 inch bulbs, 400 to the case, $16.00 per case; less quantities, $5.00 per 100. Larger sized bulbs all sold out.

F. R. PIERSON CO., Tarrytown-on-Hudson, N. Y.

Mention The Florists' Exchange when writing.

Vaughan's Bulbs

COMPLETE LINE FALL FORCING and BEDDING BULBS NOW READY.

French Roman Hyacinths, Paper White Narcissus.

FRENCH TRUMPET MAJOR FOR XMAS FORCING.

Freesia, Oxalis, Chinese Lilies, Thick Petaled Lilium Candidum, Dutch Hyacinths Bedding and Forcing, Tulips, Daffodils, etc., etc.

WE ARE AMERICAN HEADQUARTERS.

WRITE FOR FLORIST CATALOGUE.

Send us your list for pricing before buying.

Vaughan's Seed Store — 14 BARCLAY ST. NEW YORK — CHICAGO, 84-86 Randolph Street. Greenhouses, Western Springs, Ill.

Mention The Florists' Exchange when writing.

Headquarters for

Asparagus Plumosus Nanus

Cut strings, 50 cts. each

Rose Plants

own root stock

Richmond, Killarney and Beauty

$5.00 per 100

W. H. ELLIOTT

Brighton, Mass.

Mention The Florists' Exchange when writing.

BODDINGTON'S BULBS BLOOM

	Per 100	Per 1000
NARCISSUS PAPER WHITE GRANDIFLORA, (French grown) 13 ctms. and up, about 1,300 to a case, $11 00 per case	$ 1.00	$ 9.00
NARCISSUS PAPER WHITE GRANDIFLORA, 14 ctms. and up, about 1 00 to a case	1.25	11.00
ROMANS, (French grown) 11 to 12 ctms., 2,500 to a case	2.00	18.00
(Quality Brand) 12 to 15 ctms., 2,000 to a case	2.50	22.50
" " 13 to 15 ctms., 1,750 to a case	3.00	27.50
FREESIAS, (French grown) Large Bulbs	.75	6.00
Mammoth Bulbs	.85	7.50
CALLAS, (Japan grown, the best) 1½ to 1¾ inches in diameter	4.75	45.00
1¾ to 2 " " "	6.75	65.00
2 to 2½ " " "	10.00	95.00
LILIUM CANDIDUM, (French grown) 22 ctms. and up, 75c. per doz	5.00	45.00
LILIUM LONGIFLORUM MULTIFLORUM, (Boddington's Early Easter flowering type) 6-8 inch, 400 bulbs in a case	3.50	30.00
7-9 " 300 " " "	5.00	45.00
9-10 " 200 " " "	8.50	80.00
Monster, 100 " " "	15.00	

Cases of all bulbs furnished at the thousand rate.

HOLLAND GROWN BULBS

Everything that a florist may need, either for forcing, planting out, or for retailing in the store.

Fall Bulb Catalogue Free. — **Write for Special Prices on Quantities.**

ARTHUR T. BODDINGTON

342 West 14th Street — New York City

Mention The Florists' Exchange when writing.

CONTENTS AND INDEX TO ADVERTISERS, PAGE 287

INDIAN SUMMER

FREESIAS SELECTED, 85c. a 100; $7.50 a 1000.

	100	1000
Narcissus Paper White	$1.75	$9.00
Lilium Candidum, extra forcing bulbs	6.00	50.00
Lilium Longiflorum Jap. 6 to 8	3.00	24.00
Lilium Longiflorum Jap. 7 to 9	4.50	40.00
Lilium Longiflorum Multiflorum Jap. 6 to 8	3.50	30.00
Lilium Longiflorum Multiflorum Jap. 7 to 9	5.00	45.00
Freesias, selected French	.75	6.00
White Romans, 11 to 12 cmt.	2.25	18.00
White Romans, 12 to 15 cmt.	2.50	22.00
Harrisii, 5 to 7 cmt.	3.75	35.00
Canes, 6 to 9 ft.		6.00

Cineraria, choice mixed, Williams, tr. pkt. 50c.
Calceolaria, choice mixed, Williams, tr. pkt. 50c.
Pansy Rainbow, blended, tr. pkt. $1.00.
Primula Sinensis, ⅛ tr. pkt. 50c.

WM. ELLIOTT & SONS, 201 FULTON ST., NEW YORK

Mention The Florists' Exchange when writing.

PACIFIC SEED GROWERS' CO.
109 MARKET STREET
SAN FRANCISCO, CAL.
Specialties:
Onion, Carrot, Lettuce, Sweet Peas

Mention The Florists' Exchange when writing.

Thorburn's Bulbs

HYACINTHS, TULIPS, NARCISSUS, CROCUS, LILIES and all other BULBS for FLORISTS

Send for our Wholesale Florists' Bulb List Now Ready.

J. M. THORBURN & CO.
33 BARCLAY ST., through to 32 PARK PLACE
NEW YORK

Mention The Florists' Exchange when writing.

CINERARIA

Large Flowering Prize, Splendid Mixed T. P. $0.50

Large Flowering, Semi Dwarf Prize, Splendid Mixed, T. P. $0.50

PANSY, Superb Mixed.

oz. $4.50. ¼ oz. $1.15 ⅛ oz. $0.60

W. C. BECKERT,
Allegheny, Pa.

Mention the Florists' Exchange when writing.

PRIMROSES

Improved Chinese: Finest grown, named or mixed. Strong 2 inch. $2.00 per 100.

XXX SEEDS

CHINESE PRIMROSE

Finest grown, mixed, 500 seeds, $1.00; ½ pkt., 50c.
Cyclamen Giganteum: Finest Giant mixed, 200 seeds $1.00; ½ pkt., 50c.
DAISY: Double Giant mixed, 1000 Seeds 25c.

GIANT PANSY. The best large flowering varieties, critically selected, 5000 seeds, $1.00; half pkt., 50c.; 500 seeds of Giant Mme. Perret, pansy seed added to every $1.00 pkt. of Giant Pansy. Cash. Liberal extra count of seeds in all packets.

JOHN F. RUPP, Shiremanstown, Pa.
The Home of Primroses

Mention the Florists' Exchange when writing.

New Crop of my

Christmas Flowering

SWEET PEA SEED

Christmas Pink and Florence Denzer, pure white, will be ready August 1st.

Those two well known varieties are raised by over 2000 florists all over the world. Here is one out of many letters received:

Dear Sir: My sweet peas, which I raised from your seed, received the highest award at the Carnation Exhibit in Boston, being over 18 inches long. JOHN T. GALE, Tewksbury, Mass.

Price 1-4 lb. 75c.; per lb. $2.00
MAILED FREE

New Christmas Flowering Hybrids, 20 to 30 colors, mostly blue, salmon, purple lavender, in mixtures; also Mrs. Edie Wild, carmine, separate color. 1 Trade pkt., $1.00, 5 Trade pkts. $4.00; not more than 5 pkts. taken in order to each customer just now. These new hybrids are just as free bloomers as Cristmas Pink and Florence Denzer, some much larger, and received first-class Certificate of Merit by the Mass. Horticultural Society, Boston, March 24. Seed ready in Sept.

All seed originated with me is sold in my original sealed pkts., with cultural directions, to the growers, but none for seedsmen for propagating.

Orders filled strictly in rotation.

ANT. C. ZVOLANEK
BOUND BROOK, N. J.

Mention The Florists' Exchange when writing.

MY GIANT CYCLAMEN

Are Ahead in Growth and Flowers

Bloodred, Carmine, Pink, Pure White, White with Carmine Eye.
Each color separate. Tr. pkt., $1.00, 1000 seeds, $6.00. An even mixture of the above 5 colors, tr. pkt., 75c.; 1000 seeds, $5.00.

Silver Leaved New Hybrids.
With semi-double flowers. Tr. pkt., $1.00; 1000 seeds, $10.00.

Snowball.
New, the real pure white and largest in existence. Tr. pkt., $1.00, 1000 seeds, $15.00.

For larger quantities, special quotations.

O. V. ZANGEN, Seedsman, **HOBOKEN, N. J.**

Mention The Florists' Exchange when writing.

SEED PANSY PLANTS

THE JENNINGS STRAIN

50,000 plants now ready. From finest selected stock, large flowering, fancy colors, in great variety. Stock is first-class in every respect. 100 by mail, 60c.; by express, 500, $2.00; 1000 $4.00; 2000, $7.00; 3000, $10.00. Seed, $1.00 per pkt. of 4000; 1 oz., $5.00; 2 oz., $9.00; 3 oz., $12.00. Cash with order.

E. B. JENNINGS,
Lock Box 264 **Southport, Conn.**
Grower of the Finest Pansies

Mention The Florists' Exchange when writing.

S. & W. CO.'S BULBS

Roman Hyacinths

	Cases contain	100	1000
Pure White, 11x15	2000	$2.25	$20.00
Pure White, 12x15	1800	2.50	22.00
Pure White, 13x15	1250	3.00	27.50
Pure White, 15 and up	1000	4.00	38.00

Lilium Harrisii

5x7, 400 to case, $4.50 per 100
6x7, 335 to case, 5.50 per 100

Lilium Candidum

22 ctm. bulbs $4.50 per 100; $42.50 per 1000
24 ctm. bulbs 6.00 per 100; 50.00 per 1000

Freesia Bulbs

½ to ¾ in. bulbs, per 1000 $6.00
¾ in. and up extra, per 1000 9.00

Narcissus P. W. grandiflora

13 ctm. and up $9.00 per 1000

Stumpp & Walter Co.,

50 Barclay St., New York

Mention The Florists' Exchange when writing.

C. C. MORSE & CO.

SEED GROWERS
171-173 Clay St., San Francisco, California

OUR SPECIALTIES
ONION LETTUCE SWEET PEAS

Also Carrot, Celery, Celeriac, Cucumber, Endive, Leek, Mustard, Parsley, Parsnip, Radish, Salsify, Spinach, Tomato and

FLOWER SEEDS

Growers for the trade on contract. Warehouses at Santa Clara; Farms and Farm headquarters Carnadero, near Gilroy.

Registered Cable Address: MORSEED, SAN FRANCISCO.

Mention The Florists' Exchange when writing.

Stokes Standard Seeds.

ARE MONEY MAKERS

Stokes Seed Store.

219 Market Street, Philadelphia

—Send for Catalogues—

Mention The Florists' Exchange when writing.

LILIUM PHILIPPINENSE

This lily was awarded a "Gold Medal" by the Massachusetts Horticultural Society. For description see our Bulb Catalogue. WE CAN DELIVER 100,000 OF THESE BULBS BY SEPTEMBER! It can easily b forced into flower inside of nine weeks. Considering this being a novelt we offer Lilium Philippinense at these remarkably low prices: Per dozen $2.00; per 100, $12.00, per 1000, $100.00; per 10,000, $900.0

W. W. RAWSON & CO.
5 UNION STREET, BOSTON, MASS.

Mention The Florists' Exchange when writing

The Choicest strains of Florists' Stocks

Including
Cineraria, Calceolaria, Cyclamen, Pansy, Petunia, etc.,

CAN BE HAD FROM

JAMES VICK'S SONS
ROCHESTER, N. Y.

Catalog Engraving

and ILLUSTRATIONS

that print EASILY. That's the kind we make—have been since '73

JAS. M. BRYANT, Horticultural Engraving and Print
706 Chestnut Street, PHILADELPHIA, PA.

Write for our Catalogue of Stock Engravin

Mention the Florists' Exchange when writ

BURPEE'S SEED

PHILADELPHIA

Blue List of Wholesale Price mailed only to those who plant for profit.

THE AMERICAN CARNATION

Price $3.50. Send for Sample Pages

A. T. DELAMARE PTG. & PUB. CO., Ltd., 2-8 DUANE STREET, NEW YO

Seed Trade Report.

AMERICAN SEED TRADE ASSOCIATION

Henry W. Wood, Richmond, Va., president; C. S. Burge, Toledo, O., first vice-president; G. B. McVay, Birmingham, Ala., second vice-president; C. E. Kendel, Cleveland, O., secretary and treasurer; J. H. Ford, Ravenna, O., assistant secretary.

NOTES FROM HOLLAND.—Now that both hyacinth and tulip crops have been lifted, the disappointment as regards the hyacinths is certainly much keener than could have been expected. Notwithstanding that the crops have been looking well until the time of lifting, it is found that first size hyacinths do not come up to the usual mark and in consequence real large bulbs are at present scarce, and being sold at high prices. The trade generally in hyacinths is brisk and considering their slow moving last Autumn the present prices realized by the growers are satisfactory and no surplus is likely to remain on their hands.

Tulips of nearly all varieties are at present selling at fancy prices, not only caused by brisk demand, but principally caused by the enormous numbers that are being bought for the large cultures that are being started in the north of the country and whereby many millions of tulips are being taken off the market, causing an unprecedented sharp rise in the prices. Those of the foreign dealers who have secured their requirements early in the season will now reap the benefit of "early ordering" as many orders are now being refused, owing to stocks being completely sold out, and cannot even be had at much higher prices.—Horticultural Trade Journal.

Mr. Hjalmar Hartmann left Bremen, August 28, on S. S. Kaiser Wilhelm der Grosse for a trip through the United States and Canada, in the interest of Hjalmar Hartmann & Co., seed growers, Copenhagen, Denmark.

CHICAGO.—C. W. Scott, of the Vaughan Seed Store, has returned from Bermuda and reports a very pleasant and successful trip, though there is a marked shortage of longiflorum bulbs, especially in the large sizes.

European Notes.

The drought is responsible for many strange occurrences this year, not the least remarkable of which is the suddenness with which the harvest has closed what threatened to be a very protracted season. In Essex and Kent, England, the farmers have already commenced (Aug. 21) to cut their mangel, and the grain harvest is complete. Nasturtiums are drying up fast, in fact they are being picked in almost every place. Spinach, reduced in quantity by storms, is in bags ready for shipment. Peas and broad beans are practically matured and promise to be very good samples and fairly good crops.

The reverse side to this picture is the fact, slightly referred to last week, that for want of a good ground rain we are unable to put out cabbages and plants of other round seed crops for next season, and the young plants of swede turnip and mangel have either been eaten off by fly or are at a standstill.

As regards the French crops there is practically nothing new to report. Beets can be sown later than in England or Germany, but it will soon be too late, even here.

German growers are sadly troubled over the practical failure of the pansy crop. Prices of this article are bound to rise even if the Dutch growers should flood the market again. Already the choice, large flowered strains are away "out of sight." German stocks in pots have not done so well as usual; it is too early to talk about open ground seed; pure white and canary yellbw (two of our principal colors) are bound to be very scarce indeed.

Asters are not strong anywhere and in some parts they are even weak; they sadly need a return of dry, bright weather. Lately there has been much rain and only a few fine days between: this has seriously affected the carnations, and the outlook leaves much to be desired.

EUROPEAN SEEDS.

NURSERY STOCK

CHEAP

BERBERIS THUNBERGII, all sizes.
ROSA LUCIDA, 3 years.
VIBURNUM CASSINOIDES, 2 years.
VIBURNUM DENTATUM, 2 years.
PRUNUS MARITIMA, 2 years.

WRITE FOR PRICES.

LITTLEFIELD & WYMAN

Successors to SIDNEY LITTLEFIELD

NORTH ABINGTON, MASS.

Mention The Florists' Exchange when writing.

FALL SPECIALTIES:

PEONY—DORCHESTER (Richardson). Latest and best paying clear pink Peony. $25.00 per 100 for strong 3 to 5 eye divisions.
PEONY—QUEEN VICTORIA. One of the largest blocks of this popular white to be found. $12.00 per 100; $100.00 per 1000; for strong 3 to 5 eye divisions.
FORCING GRADE of FIELD-GROWN ROSES. Home grown, low budded plants, selected for pot culture: Magna Charta, Crimson Rambler, Paul Neyron, Dorothy Perkins, etc. $12.00 per 100; $100.00 per 1000.
HYDRANGEA—HORTENSIA and OTAKSA. Bushy young plants, with several flower shoots,—good for 6 to 7 inch pots.—$12.00 per 100. Extra heavy specimens for 10 to 12 inch pots or tubs, $60.00 per 100.
DRACAENA INDIVISA. (Field grown.) 5 inch pot size, $15.00 per 100. 6 inch pot size, $25.00 per 100.
CHRISTMAS PEPPER. Set with young fruits, 4 inch pots, bushy; $12.00 per 100.
PRIMULA—CHINENSIS. Strong 2½ inch, $3.00 per 100.
PRIMULA—OB CONICA GRANDIFLORA. 2½ inch, $2.50 per 100.

Send for Catalogue No. 5 for full list of Bulbs, Seeds, Palms, Ferns, Araucarias, etc.

The STORRS & HARRISON CO.,
PAINESVILLE, OHIO.

Mention The Florists' Exchange when writing.

PAEONIAS

We offer under mentioned varieties, of our **OWN STOCK, GUARANTEED TRUE TO NAME,** in strong one year old clumps with three and more eyes. (No Divisions.)

	Per 100
400 **Boule de Neige,** white	$18.00
500 **Claire Dubois,** pink	12.00
500 **Comte de Niepperg,** red	12.00
600 **Duchess de Nemours,** white	18.00
600 **Duke of Wellington,** white	14.00
300 **Edward Andrea,** red	14.00
4,000 **Festiva Maxima,** white	14.00
600 **Festiva,** white	$7.00
300 **Illustration,** pink	7.00
500 **Louis van Houtte,** red	7.00
500 **Madame de Verneville,** white	12.00
400 **Madame Emile Galle,** soft lilac	16.:0
500 **Madame Forel,** pink	14.00

Ask our trade list for full description of the flowers.
All kinds of forcing plants and nursery stock for sale.

ENDTZ VAN NES & CO., Boskoop, Holland

Mention The Florists' Exchange when writing.

PEONIES

Queen Victoria (the cold storage flower) $9.00 per 100. **Festiva Maxima,** $30.00 per 100. **Fragrans** (late Rose) $6.00 per 100. For 1000 rates or other varieties, write.

Large stock of M. L. Rhubarb and Lucretia Dewberry Plants. Write for prices.

GILBERT H. WILD, SARCOXIE, MO.

Mention The Florists' Exchange when writing.

Dwyer's Pot Grown Strawberry Plants

Strong, healthy plants from selected stock of choicest fruiting varieties sure to give satisfaction and **PRODUCE A FULL CROP IN 1907.** We also have a full line of Fruits and Ornamental Trees, Plants, Vines, etc., for Fall Planting.
We do Landscape Gardening in all its branches. **CatalogueFree**

T. J. DWYER & CO., P. O. Box 6 Cornwall, New York

Mention The Florists' Exchange when writing.

PEONIES

$6.00 to $10.00 per 100

EDWARD SWAYNE
WEST CHESTER, PA.

Mention the Florists' Exchange when writing.

1500 **Trumphet Vines,** 1-3 ft. traps. 4c.
1000 **Norway Spruce** with ball 1½-2 ft. 10c.
Send for surplus list.

Ellsworth Brown & Co.
SEABROOK, N. H.

Mention The Florists' Exchange when writing.

H. DEN OUDEN & SON,
BOSKOOP, HOLLAND.

Wholesale growers of nursery stock for the American trade. Catalogue free on demand. Also views in our nurseries.

Mention The Florists' Exchange when writing.

CANNAS

300,000 roots for Fall delivery in 100 leading kinds, $8.00 to $20.00 per 1000. Write for our list. Send in your orders early.

SHELLROAD GREENHOUSES

Largest Canna Growers Grange, Baltimore, Md.

Mention The Florists' Exchange when writing.

Shade Trees, Shrubs and Herbaceous Perennials

We have a surplus of the following nursery stock that we wish to close out. **TREES,** all perfect: each one a specimen. **SHRUBS,** all large, thrifty stock and very bushy. **HERBACEOUS PERENNIALS,** field-grown, 2 year old. We have many more varieties not mentioned here. Write for prices.

TREES	Per 100	Per 1000
Betula alba (White Birch), 10 to 12	$75.00	
Populus fastigiata (Lombardy Poplar), branched from the ground, 14 to 16	90.00	
Platanus occidentalis (American Plane or Button Ball) 14 to 16	100.00	
Salix aurea (Golden Bark Willow), branched to the ground, 12 to 14	25.00	
SHRUBS		
Ceanothus Americanus 2 to 2 1-2	15.00	
Comptonia asplenifolia, 4	12.00	
Cornus alba sanguinea, 5 to 6	20.00	
Cornus stolonifera, 3 1-2 to 4	15.00	
Deutzia, Pride of Rochester, large clumps, 4 feet	20.00	
Euonymus Americanus, bushy, branched from the ground, 3 1-2 to 4	25.00	
Forsythia fortunei, 4 to 5	20.00	
Ligustrum ovalifolium (California Privet), 3 1-2 to 4	6.00	$40.00
Ligustrum ovalifolium, 4 to 5	7.00	60.00
Ligustrum ovalifolium, extra choice, 5 to 6	10.00	80.00
Rhus glabra, 4 to 5	15.00	100.00
Sambucus Canadensis, 4 to 5	10.00	80.00
Spiraea Leutell, 3 to 4	12.00	100.00
Spiraea prunifolia, very large and bushy, 4 to 5	15.00	100.00
Spiraea aurea, 6 to 7	25.00	
Spiraea cimicifolia, 3	18.00	
Syringa vulgaris, 4	15.00	120.00
Syringa vulgaris alba, 4	15.00	120.00
Herbaceous Perennials		
Aster Novoea Angliæ	4.00	10.00
Callirpsis lanceolata	4.	30.00
Dianthus barbatus	4.	30.00
Dianthus Chinensis grandiflora	4.	30.00
Gaillardia grandiflora	5	40.00
Helianthus Maximiliani	5.	40.00
Helianthus multiflorus	8.00	60.00
Lobelia syphilitica	8.00	60.00
Monarda didyma, red, white and pink	4.	30.00
Phlox decussata, red, white and pink	5	30.00
Phlox decussata, mixed seedlings	3	20.00
Rudbeckia laciniata (Golden Glow)	3	120.00
Rudbeckia hirta	8.00	120.00
Spiraea japonica	8.00	70.00

VALLEY FARMS NURSERY CO., BROOKFIELD CENTRE, CONN.

Mention The Florists' Exchange when writing.

HARDY PHLOX

Now is the time to plant to get the best results next year.

WE OFFERTHE FOLLOWING VARIETIES

MARIE STUART (Miss Lingard). Pure white, the earliest of all phlox, and the best variety for the Florist's use. Price, $3.00 per hundred, $25.00 per thousand.
PRINCESS LOUISE. White with pink eye, early and continuous bloom. Price, $3.00 per hundred, $25.00 per thousand.

	per 100	per 1000
BRILLIANT—Rose pink	$4.00	$35.00
LUMINEAUX—Fine pink	4.00	35.00
ECLAIREUR—Brilliant magenta	4.00	35.00
DORA WINGELLER—Red	4.00	35.00
METEOR—Fine pink	5.00	
COQUELICOT—Scarlet	6.00	

All the above are strong divided roots.

COTTAGE GARDENS CONPANY, QUEENS, N. Y.

Mention The Florists' Exchange when writing.

HYDRANGEAS for FORCING

Otaksa and Thos. Hogg, with 7 to 12 Flowering Crowns, $12.00 per 100; with 5 to 6 Flowering Clowns, $9.00 per 100; with 4 Flowering Crowns, $7.00 per 100.

Japonica Rosea, (new), with 7 to 12 Flowering Crowns, $20.00 per 100; with 5 to 6 Flowering Crowns, $13.00 per 100; with 4 Flowering Crowns, $10.00 per 100.

We especially recommend the new Japonica Rosea; color, fine, rich pink, about the shade of Gloire de Lorraine Begonia; coloring is even, and does not show the white or washed-out shadings sometimes seen in Otaksa; foliage, uniform deep green, and does not streak nor yellow. Has taken medals in Europe and is a distinct acquisition.

Our plants are grown **outdoors** in beds and slat-houses; will be taken inside before frost and available for delivery next month, when wanted.

ROSES, field-grown, well-rooted, **especially suited for Forcing.** Write for prices. Full line of Ornamentals, Shrubs, Shades, Vines, etc.

JACKSON & PERKINS CO.
WHOLESALE NURSERYMEN AND FLORISTS
NEWARK, WAYNE CO., NEW YORK

Mention The Florists' Exchange when writing.

PLANT

Herbaceous Perennials

this month and save the rush of Spring work. We offer the following list of field grown stock:

	Per doz.	Per 100
Achillea, the Pearl	$ .75	$6.
Agrostemma, Coronaria	.75	6.
Anthemis, Tinctoria Kelwayii	.75	6.00
Aquilegia, Coerulea Canadensis	.75	6.00
Artemesia Abrotanum Purshiana, Stelleriana	.75	6.
Arabis, Alpina	.75	5.00
Boltonia, Asteroides, Latisquama	.75	6.00
Campanula, Grosseki, Punctata, Rapunculus	.75	6.00
Caryopteris, Mastacanthus	.75	6.00
Clematis, Davidiana	.75	6.00
Coreopsis, Rosea	.75	6.00
Delphinium, Chinensis	.75	6.00
Digitalis Gloxinaeflora White, Purple, Rose	.75	6.00
Eupatorium, Ageratoides, Cœlestinum	.75	6
Funkia, Coerulea	.75	6
Helianthus, Multiflorus Maximus	.75	6
Heliopsis, Scaber Major	1.00	8.00
Hibiscus, Moscheutos, Crimson Eye	.75	6.00
Hollyhocks, Double White, Pink, Yellow, Single, Mixed and Allegheny Fringed	1.00	8
Liatris, Pycnostachya	.90	7
Mentha, Piperita	.60	4
Myosotis, Palustris Semperflorens	.60	4
Pardanthus, Sinensis	.90	7
Physostegia, Virginica	.75	6.
Phlox, 10 varieties true to name	1.00	8.
Rudbeckia, Golden Glow, Newmanii	.75	6.00
Salvia, Azurea Grandiflora	.90	7.00
Sedum, Acre	.75	6.00
Stokesia, Cyanea	.75	6.00
Tritoma, Pfitzeri	1.70	8.00

EDWARD J. TAYLOR, Southport, Conn.

P. OUWERKERK

216 Jane Street

WEEHAWKEN HEIGHTS, N. J.

P. O. No. 1, Hoboken, N. J.

JUST RECEIVED FROM OUR HOLLAND NURSERIES

Rhododendrons, Azaleas, Spiræa Japonica, Lilium Speciosum, Peonies, Bleeding Heart, Pot-Grown Lilacs, Hydrangea in sorts, Clematis and H. P. Roses in the best sorts.

PRICES MODERATE

Mention The Florists' Exchange when writing

LARGE TREES
OAKS AND MAPLES
PINES AND HEMLOCKS
ANDORRA NURSERIES
WM. WARNER HARPER, PROPRIETOR
Chestnut Hill, Philadelphia, Pa.

Mention The Florists' Exchange when writing

VIOLET CULTURE

Price, $1 50 Postpaid

A.T. De La Mare Ptg. & Pub. Co. Ltd., New York

NURSERY DEPARTMENT.

Conducted by Joseph Meehan.

AMERICAN ASSOCIATION OF NURSERYMEN
Orlando Harrison, Berlin, Md., president; J. W. Hill, Des Moines, Ia., vice-president; George C. Seager, Rochester, N. Y., secretary; C. L. Yates, Rochester, N. Y., treasurer.

WICHITA, KANS.—Prof. E. A. Popenoe, of the State Agricultural College has been inspecting the stock of the Wichita Nursery, which he pronounced in perfect condition.

WOODWARD, IA.—J. L. Todd & Son have rented a tract of 80 acres and will establish a nursery for small fruits.

AUSTIN, TEX.—The annual inspection of the nurseries of the State is now in progress. The present inspector is Capt. A. W. Orr. It is suggested by Commissioner of Agriculture W. J. Clay that a license should be charged the nurserymen and that the inspectors should be paid by the State.

Berberis Thunbergii.

Because of the great beauty of a hedge of Japanese barberry (Berberis Thunbergii), it is in connection with its use for that purpose that it is generally thought of and, certainly, a more ornamental one than it makes can hardly be produced by any other shrub. But great as are its merits in that line, could a more useful shrub for bush purposes be desired by a planter? Here is an illustration of one which had been set out with nothing to disturb its growing as it wished, and what a beautiful object it has become! And, too, it has reached its present shape entirely unaided by pruning or anything else. What gives value to it is that there is no other shrub which can be mentioned of the same character as it, therefore no other one could fill its place. It really seems that every feature it has is good, and that in no one particular would anything else do as well. The leaves, first, are small and neat, green as desired in Summer, but when Autumn comes changing to a bronzy scarlet. Next, we have the flowers, cream white, not over conspicuous. Next come the berries, a bright scarlet when ripe, which is in late Summer, and these are so numerous usually, that the whole bush is a blaze of color. It is all these qualities combined that call for the extensive planting of this barberry. And, indeed, the end of praising it is not yet, for the red of the berries is not lost with freezing weather, as is the case with nearly all other berries, but they are still on the bushes when Spring brings around the flowering period again.

The bit of branch illustrated separately shows how thickly it is studded with berries, and this sprig is typical of all in the bush. And as the berries are still on the bush when it flowers again in Spring, and still of their scarlet color, they are often mistaken for flowers when viewed at a little distance away, by those unacquainted with the fact that the scarlet berries hang on in good condition from the previous season.

Berberis Thunbergii (Japan Barberry).

Hedges of Berberis Thunbergii.

It is no wonder the Berberis Thunbergii is so popular for hedges. Wherever seen they are beautiful. It matters not whether but an ornamental hedge or a defensive one is required this barberry is available for both. Its growth is dense, spreading, and spiny enough that the one handling it has to be careful how he does it. Its habit of growth is such that it becomes bushy without the artificial aid of pruning; and this alone is enough to recommend it as it is such a saving of labor. For a year or two after planting there is no need to prune it at all, afterwards to go over it once a year is enough, and then only to nip off the ends that are getting out of line. The habit of this barberry is to form a spreading bush. Left alone as a single lawn plant it is seen with a spread of growth equaling its height. It is helped in appearance by having its shoots at the sides kept back a little, and it adds to its compactness as well.

It is greatly in favor of this plant that it transplants well. When planting a hedge, and plants are in good condition, it is not necessary to consider the probability of some dying. Whole lines of hedges are set out without the loss of a plant, especially when the planting is done in Spring. The neat, small, pretty leaves of this hedge plant recommend it; when Summer comes there are the bright red berries, and these berries remain red until Spring, no matter how hard the freezings they meet with.

Picea Pungens and Varieties.

Picea pungens of Colorado has become synonymous to many with the Colorado Blue Spruce, causing many planters to overlook the common green form, a most desirable evergreen. There are two or even more distinct kinds of Picea pungens. The fine green form is accepted as the type, and the blue ones as varieties. The seeds of this Picea, as collected in Colorado, are sold as collected from bluest trees. Maybe they are, but the seedlings from them are of all shades from green to silver. Those with deep silver foliage are lovely objects on a lawn, especially from the time growth starts in Spring until toward Autumn. Those of the best type of blue show a silvery green the whole time until Winter approaches, when, with the hardening of growth, the color become less silvery. But let no one think the common green Picea pungens is not worth planting. It is a handsome hardy evergreen, valuable in all plantings, and makes a tree of broad, conical outline, just as do the silver-leaved ones, now to be seen on so many estates.

When securing seedlings from Colorado, the best types of green and of the silver foliaged ones can be marked in the rows as they grow, and when the next transplanting occurs, which should be in two or three years, the different types can be set out, each by itself.

The bluest types are increased by grafting or inarching. The Norway spruce makes a good stock for it. The greater number of those in cultivation are worked on this stock.

Unless often transplanted the Colorado Blue Spruce makes but few roots, whether from seed or grafted. Care is required in transplanting them; and always a ball of earth should be had with them whenever possible.

Transplanting Trees.

Taking advantage of the almost every day rains we have been having in this part of the country nurserymen and other planters are setting out evergreens, as practically every tree will grow. The wood is nearly ripe, or in such condition that it is quite safe to plant. Get a ball of earth with each plant as far as can be done and success will follow the planting. Where rains are not occurring, give a bucketful or two of water after planting, and all will go well.

It may be that a few deciduous trees are wanted for a planting. These could be set out, too, but the greater part of the foliage would have to be stripped off. A few leaves should be left on the ends of the branches. Such trees would make roots almost at once and the most of them would push forth fresh foliage. It is as well to defer planting deciduous trees until the close of September, but when certain work calls for the setting out of such trees now, there need be no hesitancy about doing it.

The value of the Autumn months for setting out trees has been greatly overlooked; and the present season is so uncommonly favorable for the work that it has tempted us to refer to it again.

Fruit of Japan Barberry (Berberis Thunbergii).

Seasonable Suggestions.

Buddleias are of an open, drooping growth, requiring pruning if a compact bush is required; but many persons prefer them in their natural growth. B. curviflora and B. intermedia are good for early Summer blooming.

Callicarpas are as useful as pot shrubs as they are in the open ground. Their chief beauty lies in their violet colored berries. When under cover, free from frost, these berries keep in good condition until late in Winter, making useful objects for window ornamentation. C. Americana is native and C. purpurea, Japanese.

Though abundant in many parts of the country, up to a recent date it was difficult to get trees of Quercus falcata in nurseries. It is a pleasure to note that it is now appearing in the lists of our prominent firms. It is one of the most distinct species of the many indigenous ones.

Not only are beach plums, Prunus maritima, valuable for their fruit, but the bush itself is an excellent one for planting near the sea. It delights in such a situation, the soil and air being just to its liking. To propagate it, preserve the stones in damp sand as soon as free from pulp and sow in October.

A lover of damp ground is the Asclepias incarnata, one of our native milkweeds; and a pretty pink flowered one it is. Though doing its best in damp ground, it will grow in ordinary situations. Those forming thickets of hardy perennials should not overlook this Summer flowering plant.

Other pretty perennials to recommend to customers for planting in half wild places are found among the asters. The A. Novæ Angliæ, A. patens, A. Novi-Belgii varieties, and A. amethystinus are particularly good, and when wholly native ones are not required the Asiatic one, tataricus, is desirable.

Rhamnus Cathartica, at one time much praised for hedging, is now rarely used for the purpose, better subjects being employed. The Rhamnus Caroliniana, commonly called Carolina buckthorn, makes a desirable large bush. Its foliage is of a lustrous green and at a certain stage of their ripening its large berries are of a pretty red color.

Andromeda Japonica is a neat leaved small evergreen, flowering early in Spring. Owing to its dwarf growth it is useful for so many purposes that there is good sale for it. Its leaves are handsomer than those of our native A. floribunda, a species it is often associated with in plantings.

JOSEPH MEEHAN.

A NEW INSECTICIDE.—One of the best means to make use of against aphides (green fly, etc.) on plants in the open air and under glass, says a German trade paper, is Hart-petroleum (Fels Naphtha?) in the proportion of 2 per cent. in water. This substance has been used with good effect on apple trees.

LIST OF ADVERTISERS

INDEX TO STOCK ADVERTISED

Contents.

PAGE

Smoking Out the Greenfly.

"Such a splendid idea occurred to me to-day, dear!" said a young wife to her husband when he came home from business in the evening. "Indeed! What's that?" he asked. "Well, you see—the gardener told me that the plants in the conservatory were being eaten up by greenfly, and the only thing that would cure them was tobacco smoke; so I gave him a handful of your cigars, and he's been in the greenhouse smoking all the afternoon."—Exchange.

REVIEW OF THE MARKET

NEW YORK.—Now that September is here business is expected to liven up a little. The supply of American Beauty roses is not so large as has been the rule for several weeks, and prices are, if anything, a little firmer. Bride and Bridesmaid roses are slightly more plentiful, and where the quality is all right there is not much effort needed to dispose of them, though averages are necessarily low owing to the greater portion of them being short-stemmed. There are a few Richmond coming in, but for hot weather purposes this rose is rather at a disadvantage as it blows open quickly.

Carnations are not at all plentiful as yet and such as are coming in are from outdoors.

Lilies are bringing a trifle better prices than they were last week. There is no change in prices of either lily of the valley or orchids. The latter have not been very plentiful lately, but Mr. McManus informs us that within the next few days he will have a supply of Cattleya labiata.

Dahlias are getting more plentiful every day, and some of the red varieties are to be had with fairly good stems. The poor demand there is as yet, however, makes it impossible to clean them out at satisfactory prices.

The supply of gladiolus is beginning to taper off a little, though there are plenty as yet for all purposes, and prices remain the same.

The market values for such stock as asparagus, smilax and adiantum fern of the several varieties have not changed.

CHICAGO.—The cooler weather with which we have been favored has tended to give a more encouraging tone to the market though up to the present time the assurance is more prospective than absolute. There is no change in prices but there is evidently less cutting than has been evident for several weeks past. Stock is gradually improving in quality and the general impression is expressed that it is superior to the early September condition of previous years. W. K. W.

PHILADELPHIA.—The cut flower market shows a better condition this week; roses are moving much better; for the new crop American Beauty prices range from $1.50 to $3.00. There has been a good demand for white roses. Asters are moving very good, in fact there are not sufficient of first quality flowers; these are selling at $2.00 per 100, and several of the commission house could use more.

Dahlias are coming in but so far the demand is poor; they are bought chiefly for window decoration at the retail stores. There is a very good demand for Adiantum Croweanum, but asparagus and smilax are moving slow.

Some American Beauty roses have been shipped here from growers who usually consign to New York, but the stock is not as good as we have from our local men. DAVID RUST.

BOSTON.—With the cooler weather of September a marked change is noticeable, more activity being at once displayed. Stock, too, will soon improve, for recently with the extreme hot weather there was little first class material in the market at all.

Asters are not so plentiful as they were; last season there was only a limited quantity supplied by a few growers but this season almost every one seems to have been raising asters. A glut on the market of these flowers the whole season has been the result. In roses, American Beauty are the best to be had, and there has been some exceptionally good blooms of these recently. Brides and Bridesmaids have been very poor, as they generally are during the Summer, but they will soon improve. Killarney is good and, by the way, this same rose is grand from out-of-doors at this season.

Carnations are beginning to improve; prices have advanced a little. Lilies still make their appearance selling at unchanged prices. Gladiolus are good and very popular. Hydrangeas are much in use for decorations. Lily of the valley has a steady demand. Asparagus and other greens have a continuous demand at unchanged prices. J. W. D.

ST. LOUIS.—A careful review of the business done during the month of August shows an increase over the previous month. The bulk of trade was funeral work; very little of anything else was going on among the retailers. The supply of better stock in all varieties is continually increasing, and the demand is becoming more regular each day. Prices are still at a low ebb, but with cooler weather and better stock they will be advanced.

Some of the wholesalers are beginning with shipping orders. Society folk are coming home from their Summer trips. This, with the opening of the schools, should make some difference to the trade this month. Last Monday (Labor Day) kept some of us busy, but generally speaking not much is expected on this holiday.

In looking through commission houses last Monday morning, we found prices on American Beauties from $1.50 to $3 per dozen; short stemmed ones $3 to $6 per 100; other roses from $3 to $4 for choice, and $1 to $2 for seconds per 100. Carnations, the very best fancy, are selling at $1.50; others, 50c. to 75c. per 100. Asters bring from 50c. to $2 per 100, and tuberose stalks from $1 to $3 per 100.

There are plenty of greens of all kinds. ST. PATRICK.

FIRMS INCORPORATED.

TOLEDO, OHIO.—The Schover Floral Company is incorporated with a capital of $10,000. The incorporators are: Frank J. Schwen, James C. Griblin, Albert Joseph and John J. Schwen.

FIRMS WHO ARE BUILDING.

CLEVELAND, O.—The Cleveland Cut Flower Co. is erecting new boiler sheds at their establishment on Eddy road.

DULUTH, MINN.—W. W. Seeking is building a new greenhouse on East Third street, the cost of which will be $1,000.

DIGHTON, MASS.—The Dighton Nursery Co. are building a house 100 feet long, 25 feet wide, 9 feet high in the peak, 2 1-2 feet high at sides.

FORT WAYNE, IND.—Sealed proposals will be received by the Board of Park Commissioners at their office, room 2, City Hall, until 3 p. m. Monday, September 10, 1906, for the construction and heating of a greenhouse in Lawton Park.

PAMPHLETS RECEIVED.

From the South Carolina Agri. Expt. Station a bulletin has been issued (No. 119) giving an analysis of commercial fertilizers.

From the Maryland Agricultural College comes an exhaustive report on, together with an analysis of, commercial fertilizers sold in Maryland.

Circular No. 19, of the Department of Agriculture, on Standards of Purity for Food Products.

San Francisco.

Florists who are in the society swim and are reckoned as pretty safe forecasters as to which way the society cat is going to jump this Fall and Winter, announce that the past week has indeed been a busy one for the society "eclat" on both sides of the bay, and the portents all point to a busy Winter season, with very little opportunity for indulging in the protracted beauty sleep. Weddings and engagements the past week offered the chief items of interest to cut-flower dealers and growers.

"The Woru Sisters, Florists," was one of the pretty store signs that was burned by the earthquake-fire. These orphan sisters were ne plus ultra in the floral trade as artistic designers of bloom bunches and original pieces of floral architecture, and they made plenty of money in the business, and recreated by taking trips across the sea. I am told by the trade that old citizens, who bought flowers in profusion, patronized "the Woru girls" for the love they bore their parents whom everybody knew as most estimable people, who were always doing something philanthropic for the city. Since the fire, these sisters have not resumed business, and this week the trade is talking of the sad fate that has befallen them, and the daily papers are exploiting the trouble. A superior judge has rendered a decision and uttered strong denunciations of the elder of the sisters, and taken from her a valuable estate and given it to a 15-year old grandson of Miss Woru's mother. The court's decision is that the young lady obtained the estate by undue influence for the purpose of defrauding the said grandson. ALVIN.

FERNS.

POINSETTIAS, 2½ inch pots, $5.00 per 100.

ASPARAGUS PLUMOSUS, 4 in. pots, $10.00 per 100.

HUGH GRAHAM CO.,
Logan Nurseries, York Road and Louden Street, PHILADELPHIA, PA.

Mention The Florists' Exchange when writing.

FERNS OUR SPECIALTY

CIBOTIUM SCHIEDEI

We have a large stock of this beautiful tree fern in 3 in. pots, ready for a shift, at $25.00 per 100. 25 plants at 100 rate.

FERN SEEDLINGS FROM FLATS

Eight to ten best market varieties at $1.00 per 100, or $8.50 per 1000. If by mail add 10c. for each hundred Plants.

ASSORTED FERNS FOR DISHES

From 2¼ in. pots. The best and hardiest varieties in market at $3.00 per 100, or $26.00 per 1000. 250 plants at 1000 rate.

Adiantum Cuneatum, 2¼ in. pots, $3.50 per 100, $30.00 per 1000

FERN SPORES

Gathered from our own stock. 35c. per trade package, $4.00 per doz. packages.

Gardenia Veitchii from 2¼ in. pots. $7.50 per 100, $70.00 per 1000; 400 at 1000 rate.

ANDERSON & CHRISTENSEN,
SHORT HILLS, N. J.

Mention The Florists' Exchange when writing.

FERNS *and* CARNATIONS

SPEAK QUICK

10,000 Healthy Field Grown Carnations, best commercial sorts, including **ELBON,** a fine, true red. **Send for list as they must be sold.**

1,000 **PIERSONI FERNS,** for 4 in. 15c.
1,000 " " for 3 in. 10c.
1,000 **BOSTON** " 3 in. ready for 4 in., 10c.
SCOTTII FERNS, 4 in., 20c.; 3 in., 10c.
ANNA FOSTER, 2½ in., 4c.
1,000 **ASPARAGUS PLUMOSUS NANUS,** 3½ in., 6c.; 2½ in., $2.50 per 100.
200 **ASPARAGUS SPRENGERII,** 3½ in., 6c.
1,000 **HYDRANGEA OTAKSA,** 2½ in., $2.50 per 100.
1,000 **VINCA MAJOR** var. 2½ in., $2.50 per 100.
All A No. 1 Stock. Cash please.

BENJ. CONNELL
WEST GROVE, PA.

Mention The Florists' Exchange when writing.

FERNS

	Doz	100
SCOTTII, 2½ inch	$0.75	$5.00
BARROWSII, 2½ inch	1.25	8.00

THE CONARD & JONES CO.
WEST GROVE, PA.

Mention The Florists' Exchange when writing.

BOSTON FERNS

Taken from bench, $10.00 and $20.00 per 100.
5 and 6 inch **Pot Ferns,** from $3.00 per doz. up
Extra fine stock.
Geraniums, 3½ inch stock, $4.00 per 100.

BOCK, THE FLORIST,
2394 MASS AVENUE NORTH CAMBRIDGE, MASS.

Mention The Florists' Exchange when writing.

FERNS

Are now in fine shape. A good variety and nice bushy stock, 2¼ in., $3.00 per 100; $25.00 per 1000.

Kentia Belmoreana, 4 in., clean and bushy, 25c. 5 in. 50c.; 6 in., 75c.

Boston Ferns, Piersoni and **Scottii,** from bench, 25c. each.

Cocos Weddeliana, 10c.

H. WESTON, HEMPSTEAD, N. Y.

Mention The Florists' Exchange when writing.

NEPHROLEPIS

Whitmani, 2¼ in., $25.00 per 100.
Barrowsii, $10.00 per 100.

Henry H. Barrows & Son, Whitman, Mass.

Mention The Florists' Exchange when writing.

Ferns From Bench

BOSTON, PIERSONI, 4 in. 10c.; 5 in. 12½c. Boston 6 in. 15 cts.
TARRYTOWN, 3 in., 10c.; 4 in., 15c.; 5 in., 25c. Runners $20.00 per 1000.
SCOTTII, 3 in., 8c.; 4 in., 12½c.

CHINESE PRIMROSES

Finest mixed, strong, 2 in., 2c.
Primula Obconica, Hybrid, Alba, Rosea, 2 in., ... 2c.
Asparagus Sprengerii, and **Plumosus** 2 in., 2c.
Jerusalem Cherries, field grown, ready for 4 in. 3 cts.
Flowering Begonias, 8 kinds, 2 in. 2½c.
Begonia Rex, 3 in. 6c.

Cash or C. O. D.

BYER BROS., Chambersburg, Pa.

Mention The Florists' Exchange when writing.

NEPHROLEPIS SCOTTII

Small plants from the benches, $5.00 per 100; $50.00 per 1000. Plants large enough for 6 in. pots, $25.00 per 100. Plants large enough to go in 7 and 8 in. pots, $50.00 per 100.

Asparagus Plumosus Nanus, 2¼ in., fine plants, $3.00 per 100.

JOHN SCOTT,
Rutland Road and East 45th Street;
BROOKLYN, N. Y.
Telephone 2890 Bedford.

Mention The Florists' Exchange when writing.

FERNS

Several hundred Tarrytown Ferns.

N. PIERSONI ELEGANTISSIMA, from 2½ in. pots, $10.00 per 100; extra nice and strong Stock.

R. ENGELMAN & SON
PITTSFIELD, MASS.

Mention The Florists' Exchange when writing.

Fern Seedlings

From flats, ten of the best varieties, at $1.00 per 100; $8.50 per 1000; if by mail add 10c. per 100. Ferns for dishes, good stocky plants from 2¼ in. pots, $3.00 per 100; $25.00 per 1000; 250 plants at 1000 rate.

Adiantum Cuneatum, 5 in. pots, $20.00 per 100.

FRANK N. ESKESEN, MADISON, N. J.

ROBERT CRAIG & CO.

ROSES, PALMS, CROTONS

CARNATIONS and Novelties in DECORATIVE PLANTS

Market and 49th Sts. PHILADELPHIA, PA.

COCOS PALMS.

Strong 2¼ inch at $1.50 per dozen. Write for lowest prices on **Kentias.**

Jas. F. Barclay R. I. GREENHOUSES Pawtucket, R. I.

BOSTON AND SCOTTII FERN

From 25c., 50c., 75c., $1.00 and $2.00 Each.
Asparagus Plumosus from $3.00 to $5.00 per 100
Cycas Revoluta in different sizes.

P. WAGNER,
Cor. Troy Ave. & Midwood St., Flatbush, Brooklyn, N.Y.

Mention The Florists' Exchange when writing.

Bargains in CHOICE PLANTS

Anthericum, variegated, per doz., $1.50; per 100, $12.00.
Araucaria Excelsa, 50c., 75c., $1.00, $1.50, $2.00, $2.50 each. Also by the 100.
Areca Lutescens, 6 in. pots, $12.00 per doz.
Asparagus Plumosus 3½ in. pots, $1.25 per doz.; per 100, $9.00; 4 in. pots, $2.00 per doz.; 4½ in. pots, $3.00 per doz.
Aspidistra green, 5½ in. pots, 8 leaves and over, $9.00 per doz.; 6½ in. pots, 15 to 25 leaves, $1.50 and $2.00 each.
Bay Trees, Pyramids.
55-60 in. high from top of tub, $14.00 per pair.
65-70 in. high from top of tub, 15.00 per pair.
Begonia Rex, 4 in. pots, $2.00 per doz.
Bird's Nest Fern, large plants, 6½ in. pots $1.50 each, $18.00 per doz.
Boston Ferns. 5 in. pots, $3.00 per doz.; 6 in. pots, $6.00 per doz.; 7 in. pots, $12.00 per doz. Specimens, 9 in. pots, $3.00 each.
Boston Ferns, 8 in. pots, $15.00 per doz.; 13 in. pots, $5.00 each.
Cibotium Schiedii, 6, 6½ and 7 in. pots, $1.50, $2.00 and $2.50 each.
Crotons, in variety, 4 in. pots, $3.00 per doz.
Cut Flowers of Lily of the Valley, $4.00 and $5.00 per 100.
Cycas Revoluta, we have them in 5½, 6, 7 and 8 in. pots, very fine, 50c., 75c., $1.00, $1.50, $2.00 and $3.00 each.
Cyclamen Persicum, 4½ in. pots, $4.00 per doz.; 5 in. pots, $5.00 per doz.; 5½ in. pots, $6.00 per doz.; 6 in. pots, $9.00 per doz.
Dracæna Fragrans. From 5 in. pots, $4.00 per doz.; 6 in. pots from $6.00 to $9.00 per doz.; 7 in. pots, $18.00 per doz.; 8 in. pots, $24.00 per doz.
Dracæna Indivisa, from 4½ in. pots, $2.50 per doz.; $18.00 per 100.
Dracæna Terminalis, 6 in. pots, $12.00 per doz.
Dracæna Terminalis, 4 in. pots, $3.00 per doz.; 5 in. pots, $6.00 per doz.
English Ivy, from 4½ in. pots, $2.00 and $2.50 per doz. About 3 feet high and bushy.
English Ivy, fan-shaped, 2 feet wide, 3 to 4 feet high, 6½ in. pots, $6.00 per doz.; selected, $9.00 per doz.
Fern Balls, $9.00 per doz.
6 in. Fern Dishes with centers, $4.00 per doz.
Gardenia Veitchii, fine large Plants, 5½ in. pots, well budded, $9.00 per doz.
Johnsonii Fern, 6 in. pots, $9.00 per doz. (Sword fern.)
Kentia Belmoreana and **Forsteriana,** $3.00, $4.00, $5.00, $8.00, $9.00 per doz.; also by the 100. Also $1.00, $1.50, $2.00, $2.50, $3.00 each and by the 2 doz.
Kentia Forsteriana, combinations, from $3.00, $4.00, $5.00, $6.00, $10.00, $15.00 to $20.00 each.
Leaf-Mold, $1.00 per bag.
Livistona Sinensis, superior to **Latania** borbonica, larger fan, compact and dark green foliage. 5 in. pot, $4.00 per doz.; 6 in. pots, $6.00 per doz., 7 in. pots, $12.00 per doz.
Lygodium Scandens, climbing fern, 30 ins. high, per doz., $9.00.
N. Elegantissima, from 4½ in. pots, $4.00 per doz.
Pandanus Utilis, 4½ in., $4.00 per doz.
Pandanus Veitchii, 5 in. pots, $5.00 per doz.; 6 in. pots, $9.00 per doz.; 6½ in., $12.00 per doz.; 7 in., $18 per doz.
Phœnix Canariensis, large plants, 6½ to 7 f. high, 11 in. pots, $12.00 to $14.00 per pair.
Piersoni Fern, 6½ in. pots, $9.00 per doz.
Primula Obconica, 5 in. pots, $2.00 per doz.; $15.00 per 100.
Rubbers, from 7 in. pots, 3 ft. high, $9.00 per doz.
Scottii Fern, 5 in. pots, $3.00 per doz.; 5½ in. pots, $5.00 per doz.; 6½ in. pots, $8.00 doz.
Scottii Fern, 8 in. pots or pans, $12.00 per doz.; $75.00 per 100. 11 in. pans, $3.00 each.
Large Scottii, 10 in. pans, $2.50 each.

NOW READY AND IN BLOOM:

Erica Cucullata, 4½ in. pots, fine plants, pink Trumpet, lasting a long time, $6.00 doz.
Erica Gracilis, dark pink, very beautiful, 3 in. pots, $1.00 and $3.00 doz. $15.00 per 100.
Erica Gracilis Autumnalis, loaded with light pink flowers, from 5 in. pots, about a foot high and bushy, $6.00 per doz.; from 6½ in. pots, $9.00 per doz.

Cash with order or satisfactory New York references required.

ANTON SCHULTHEIS, 19th St. & 4th Avenue College Point, N. Y.

Mention The Florists' Exchange when writing.

DRACAENA TERMINALIS

Matured canes always ready for shipment. Delivered to any part of the United States for 10 cents a foot. Send cash for a trial order.

PORTO RICO PINEAPPLE CO., RIO PIEDRAS, PORTO RICO.

Mention The Florists' Exchange when writing.

ASPARAGUS

	Per 100
Sprengerii, 3 in.	$3.00
" 2 in.	1.50
Plumosus Nanus, 2 in.	2.00
Primula Obconica, Grandiflora Alba, Rosea and Hybrida, 2 in.	2.00
" " **Robusta and Compacta,** 2 in.	3.00
Smilax, nice, 2¼ in.	1.25
Paris Daisy, white and yellow, 3 in., bushy,	3.00

Orders booked for early September delivery of

Cineraria Grandiflora Hybrida, Michell's Giant Prize, 2 in.	2.00
Calceolaria, James Superb mixed, 2 in.	3.00
Primula Chinensis, 2 in.	2.00
Primula Buttercup, yellow, 2 in.	2.00

Cash with order, please.

GEO. J. HUGHES, BERLIN, N. J.

Mention The Florists' Exchange when writing.

SMILAX PLANTS

Strong, Bushy Plants, many times cut back and ready for shift.

2 in. pots	$1.00 per 100,	$9.00	per 1000
3 in. pots	2.00 "	18.00	"
Seedlings from flats		4.00	"

We have grown Smilax Plants for the trade 18 years, and never had finer stock.

Send for Samples

R. KILBOURN
CLINTON, N. Y.

Mention The Florists' Exchange when writing.

ORCHIDS

Largest Importers, Exporters, Growers and Hybridists in the world.

Sander, St. Albans, England
and
235 Broadway, Room 1, New York City

Mention The Florists' Exchange when writing.

EMERSON C. McFADDEN
Wholesale Grower
Asparagus Plumosus Nanus, Etc.
Short Hills, N. J.
Tel. 28 A.

Mention The Florists' Exchange when writing.

ORCHIDS

Arrived in superb condition **Cattleya Dowiana, C. Gigas, C. Mossiae, C. Percivaliana, C. Speciosissima, C. Eldorado, C. Superba, C. Labiata, C. Leopoldii** and many more.

Write for Prices.

LAGER & HURRELL, Summit, N. J.
Growers and Importers

Mention The Florists' Exchange when writing.

ASPARAGUS

Robustus $5.00 per 100; $40.00 per 1000.
Sprengerii $2.00 per 100; $15.00 per 1000.

ALBERT M. HERR
LANCASTER, PA.

Mention The Florists' Exchange when writing.

OUR LITTLE PET

From Aschmann in Philadelphia I bought
An Araucaria, a pet for our little girl;
Now we have two pets, the pride of our thought:
The little girl so sweet, a head full of curls,
And the Araucaria with it s everlasting green,
A more joyful home you never have seen.

Watch us Grow!!

ARAUCARIA EXCELSA, the best of all decorative plants nature produces; a specialty. Every man in business life, to be successful, must adopt one thing as his specialty, and that specialty, whatever he may select, and of whatever nature it may be, he must guard, study and push to such an extent that it not only benefits himself; but he must conduct it so, that every one who seeks his aid, service or his articles, whatever he advertises or practices, will share a slice of his activity and prosperity. I made the importation and cultivation of Araucaria as a special study in my life. The following figures will show you my success in business: In the first year I began with an import of 250; in the eleventh year (now 1906) my importation has grown up to 6,000 (come and see it). On account of the Araucaria growing yearly in favor as a much admired decorative plant for the arbor, bed room, dining and sitting rooms, stores, hotels, lawns and porches by the plant-consuming peoples all over the country, the outlook will be of an importation of at least 8,000 to 10,000 in the Spring of 1907. To secure this vast amount for 1907, I am now on the ocean, per steamer New Amsterdam, sailing from Hoboken, August 15, striking for Belgium and making contracts for next year. I shall also at the same time bring over with me a large lot of choice Azalea Indica, Palms, etc. for Christmas and Easter forcing. No money will be spared in obtaining for my customers the cream of the Belgium greenhouses.

Please note lowest price now going for August and September:

ARAUCARIA EXCELSA

12 to 14 in. 5½ in. pots, 3 to 4 tiers, 2-yr. old, 50c. 14 to 16 in., 5½ in. pots, 3 to 4 tiers, 2-yr. old, 60c. 16 to 18 in. 5½ to 6 in. pots, 4 to 5 tiers, 3-yr. old, 75c. 18 to 20 in., 6 in. pots, 5 to 6 tiers, 4-yr. old, $1.00. 20 to 24 in. 6 in. to 7 in. pots, 5 to 6 tiers, 4-yr. old, $1.25. 36-40 to 50 in. 7 in. pots, specimen plants from $2.50 to $3.00 each.

ARAUCARIA COMPACTA ROBUSTA — have several thousand of them; can supply all wants. These plants were never so fine in shape and condition as this year. The set of the greenhouse, as broad as long, 12 to 20 in., in height, 3 to 4 perfect tiers, 20 to 30 inches across, 3-4-5 year old, 6 to 7 in. pots. $1.25, $1.50, $1.75, $2.00, $2.50 to $3.00 each.

ARAUCARIA EXCELSA GLAUCA—This variety on account of its beautiful Green-Blueish tiers, dwarf habit, fine compact shape, gives it a striking appearance, and anybody seeing them, must undoubtedly fall in love with them at sight. Plants, 6-7 inch pots, 3-4-5 perfect tiers, 3-4 year old, 15 to 25 inch high, from 15 to 30 in. across, $1.25, $1.50, $1.75, $2.00 to $2.50 each.

KENTIA BELMOREANA, 5½ to 6 in. pots, bushy, fine plants, from 75 cts. to $1.00 to $1.25 each.

KENTIA FORSTERIANA, 7 in. pots, made-up plants, 1 large in center, 3 smaller sizes, 22 to 25 in. high around, gives them a good appearance, $2.00 each. 6 in. pots, single plants, 35 to 40 in. high, 5 to 6 good leaves, 4 year old, $1.25 to $1.50 each; 6 in. pots, 30 to 35 in. high, 4 year old, 5 good leaves, $1.00; 5½ in. pots, 3 year old, 25 to 30 in. high, 5 good leaves, 75c. made-up plants, 3 and 4 in. pots, 18 to 20 in. high, 25 cts. to 30 cts. each.

ARECA LUTESCENS, made-up, 25 cts.

COCOS WEDDELIANA, 15 cts.

CYCAS REVOLUTA (Sago Palm), 6 in.-7 in. pots, with from 6 to 20 leaves per plant, 10 cts. per leaf.

NEPHROLEPIS BARROWSII, 6 in. pots, strong, ready for 7-8 in., 50c. 4 in. pots, ready for 6-7 in., 25c.

NEPHROLEPIS SCOTTII, 6 in. pots, large, ready for 6-7 in. 50c.; 5½ in. pots, 40c.; 5 in. 35c.; 4 in. 20c. to 25c.

BOSTON FERNS, 4 in., 20c. to 25c. I have them by the thousand, 5 in.; 30c. to 35c.

FERNS for dishes, a fine assortment, 2¼ in., $5.00 per 100; 3 in., $6.00 per 100.

FICUS ELASTICA, 6 in., 50c.

ASPARAGUS PLUMOSUS NANUS, 3 in., 6c.; 4 in., 10c.

CASH WITH ORDER

When ordering, say whether the plants should be shipped in the pots or not

GODFREY ASCHMANN

Importer and Wholesale Grower of Pot Plants

1012 Ontario Street, - - PHILADELPHIA, PA.

Mention The Florists' Exchange when writing.

WE ARE HEADQUARTERS FOR

Princess Violet Stock

Orders booked for September delivery. Strong field-grown plants, $50.00 per 1000.

WILLIAM SIM, Cliftondale, Mass.

Mention The Florists' Exchange when writing.

VIOLETS

Princess of Wales Violets, fine healthy plants; price on application by

GLEN COVE GREENHOUSES

F. G. MENSE, Prop.

GLEN COVE, N. Y.

Mention The Florists' Exchange when writing.

Governor Herrick Violet

The finest single violet ever offered. Write me about it today.

Price: One dozen, $2.00; 100, $10.00; 1000 at $75.00 or 5000 or more at $60.00 per 1000. No. 1 Stock.

H. R. CARLTON, WILLOUGHBY OHIO.

Mention The Florists' Exchange when writing.

VIOLETS

MARIE LOUISE Violets, clean and healthy in every particular, ready August 15th. 3 in. pots $5.00 per 100.

CASH WITH ORDER.

WM. J. CHINNICK,

TRENTON, N. J.

Mention The Florists' Exchange when writing.

VIOLETS, SMILAX

Lady Campbell and California out of 2½ in. healthy stock plants, $2.00 per 100; $17.50 per 1,000

Smilax, fine bushy plants 2½ in., $1.25 per 100; $10.00 per 1000

J. C. SCHMIDT CO., Bristol, Pa.

Mention The Florists' Exchange when writing.

VIOLETS

MARIE LOUISE and **CAMPBELL,** good stock, heavily rooted, $3.50 per 100; $30.00 per 1000.

W. H. THOMAS

Convent Station, Morris County, N. J.

Mention The Florists' Exchange when writing.

Commercial Violet Culture

Price, $1.50

The Florists' Exchange, 2-8 Duane St., New York

Begonia "Gloire de Lorraine" and "Turnford Hall"

very strong, 2¼ in. pots, $15.00 per 100; 3 inch, $25.00 per 100; 4 inch, $40.00 per 100.

Pandanus Veitchii, 12 to 14 inches high from top of soil .... $75.00 per 100
" " 18 " 24 " " " " " " .... 100.00 " "
" " 24 " 26 " " " " " " .... 150.00 " "

Adiantum Farleyense, fine specimens, $1.00, $1.50 to $2.00 each.
" " 2¼ inch, fine stock, $15.00 per 100

Cash with order from unknown correspondents. Good value guaranteed.

J. A. PETERSON, McHenry Ave., Cincinnati, Ohio

Mention The Florists' Exchange when writing.

ASPARAGUS

	per 100
Plumosus Nanus, 2¼ in. pots	$2.00
Plumosus Seedlings,	1.00
Sprengerii Seedlings,	1.00
Vinca variegated from field, Oct.	5.00

PRIMROSES

	per 100
Chinese, 2¼ in. pots	$2.00
Obconica Alba, and Rosea	2.00
Cannas, 5 var., field clump	15.00

Pansy Plants, Oct. 1st, $3.00 per 1000; 50c. per 100.

CASH PLEASE.

JOS. H. CUNNINGHAM, Delaware, O.

Mention The Florists' Exchange when writing.

HERE'S A BARGAIN:

5000 Gloire De Lorraine Begonias, two inch pots ready at once for three, and full of Shoots. Seeing is believing. Give us a trial order. **$10. per 100. $90.00 per 1000.**

(Money refunded if not satisfactory. How's that?)

E. A. BUTLER & SON, Niagara Falls, N. Y.

Mention The Florists' Exchange when writing.

Decorative Plants

Latania Borbonica, 2½ in. pots, $3.00; 3 in.; $6.00; 4 in., $15.00 per 100. Large specimen plants from $2.00 to $5.00 each.

Kentia Belmoreana and Forsteriana, 2¼ in. pots, $8.00; 3 in., $15.00; 4 in., $25.00 per 100; 5 in., $50.00 per 100; 6 in., $15.00 per doz.; 7 in. and upward, $1.75 to $35.00 each.

Areca Lutescens, 3 in. $10.00; 4 in. $20.00 per 100; 8 in., $1.00 each and upward.

Pandanus Utilis, 2 in. pots, $3.00; 4 in., $20.00 per 100.

Phœnix Reclinata, 5 in. pots, $35.00 per 100.

Phœnix Canariensis, fine specimen plants, from $3.00 to $35.00 each.

Araucaria Excelsa, 5 in. pots, $65.00 per 100.

Assorted Ferns, 2¼ in. pots, $3.00 per 100.

Nephrolepis Compacta, 3 in. pots, $8.00; 4 in., $15.00 per 100.

Plants in Fine Condition.

JOHN BADER, Troy Hill, Allegheny, Pa.

Mention The Florists' Exchange when writing.

LUDVIG MOSBÆK,

ONARGA, ILL.

60,000 ASPARAGUS PL. N and SPRENGERII, very strong and fine plants, ready for a shift, 4 in., $10.00; 3 in., $5.00; 2¼ in. $2.50 per 100.

40,000 FERNS, pot grown, excellent. Anna Foster, Boston, Piersoni, and Sword, 6 in., $40.00; 4 in. $15.00; 3 in., $8.00 per 100.

GERANIUMS, stock plants, 2¼ in., and R. C. and other Bedding Plants, including 150,000 CANNAS, for Fall delivery.

200,000 PANSIES, seedlings of the well-known Florists' International Mixture, $3.00 per 1000.

Mention The Florists' Exchange when writing.

DIFFERENT STOCK

Carnations Ad Cevera, 4 cts. Mixed, mostly Lawson and Enchantress, 4c.

Asparagus Plumosus, strong, 2½ in., 3c.; 4 in., 8c.

Asparagus Sprengerii, 2½ in., 2c.

Ferns for Jardinieres, 2½ in., 3c.; Boston, 5 x 6 in., 25c.; Tarrytown ferns, 6 in., 50c.

Smilax, strong, 2½ in., $1.50 per 100.

Parsley Plants, large, $2.00 per 1000.

Rex Begonia, 4 in., 12c. Cash Please.

F. B. RINE, Lewisburg, Pa.

Mention The Florists' Exchange when writing.

2000 **Achilea** (The Pearl) .... 3c.
3000 **Iris Sibirica** .... 3c.
1000 **Foxglove** .... 3c.

ELLSWORTH BROWN & CO., SEABROOK, N. H.

Mention The Florists' Exchange when writing.

A Few Good Things YOU WANT

Dracæna Indivisa, 4 and 5 in., $10.00 and $25.00 per 100.

Asparagus Sprengeri, 2 in., $2.50 per 100.

Geraniums, S. A. Nutt, Castellane, John Doyle, Perkins, Double Gen. Grant, Poitevine, Mme. Salleroi, 2 in. pots, $2.00 per 100; 3 in. pots $4.00 per 100. Rooted Cuttings, $1.00 per 100.

Rex Begonia, nice plants, 2 and 2½ in., $6.00 per 100.

Asparagus Plumosus, 2 in. $3.00 per 100.

Boston Fern 5 in. 30c each.

Pierson Fern 6 in. 50c each.

GEO. M. EMMANS, Newton, N. J.

Mention The Florists' Exchange when writing.

Primula Obconica Grandiflora

2 1-2 in., $2.50 per 100. Ask for list (seedlings of hardy plants)

BAUDISCH & CO.,

537 Fulton Street UNION HILL, N. J.

Mention The Florists' Exchange when writing.

Stevia Serrata

True, winter blooming, strong, bushy, ready to shift, 3½ in. pots, $5.00 per 100; $45.00 per 1000.

ASPARAGUS SPRENGERII, 2 inch, very strong, $2.50 per 100; $20.00 per 1000.

DEAN FERRIS, Peekskill, N. Y.

Mention The Florists' Exchange when writing.

SURPLUS STOCK—CHEAP

200 **The Bride** roses, 2 in. pots, $1.75 per 100.
500 **Bridesmaid** roses, 2 in. pots, $2.00 per 100.
1000 **Cannas,** red and yellow, strong, $3.00 per 100.
50 **Dracaena Indivisa,** 3½ in., 6c. each.
2000 **Cuphea,** Cigar Plant, 2 in. pots, 75c. per 100.
2000 **Feverfew,** Double White, 2 in. pots, 50c. per 100.
10000 **Jerusalem Cherries,** big and strong, ready for 4 in. pots, from 2 in. pots at $2.00 per 100. You will never get better or cheaper stock than this. **E. I. Rawlings, Quakertown, Pa.**

Mention The Florists' Exchange when writing.

2,000 **Smilax,** 2½ in., strong, cut back, per 100, $1.50; the lot for $17.50.
200 **Asparagus Plumosus,** $2.50 per 100.
1,000 **Asparagus Sprengerii,** 2½ in., $2.00 per 100; the lot for $17.00. This is strong and ready for a shift.

J. S. BLOOM,

RIEGELSVILLE, PA.

Mention The Florists' Exchange when writing.

FOUNDED IN 1888

FLORISTS' EXCHANGE

A Weekly Medium of Interchange for Florists, Nurserymen Seedsmen and the Trade in general

Exclusively a Trade Paper.

Entered at New York Post Office as Second Class Matter

Published EVERY SATURDAY by

A. T. DE LA MARE PTG. AND PUB. CO. LTD.

2, 4, 6 and 8 Duane Street,

P. O. Box 1697. Telephone 3765 John. NEW YORK.

CHICAGO OFFICE: 127 East Berwyn Avenue.

ILLUSTRATIONS.

Electrotypes of the illustrations used in this paper can usually be supplied by the publishers. Price on application.

YEARLY SUBSCRIPTIONS.

United States, Canada, and Mexico, $1.00. Foreign countries in postal union, $2.50. Payable in advance. Remit by Express Money Order Draft on New York. Post Office Money Order or Registered Letter.

The address label indicates the date when subscription expires and is our only receipt therefore.

REGISTERED CABLE ADDRESS:

Florex, New York.

ADVERTISING RATES.

One-half inch, 75c.; ¾-inch, $1.00; 1-inch, $1.25, special positions extra. Send for Rate Card showing discount of 10c., 15c., 25c., or 35c., per inch on continuous advertising. For rates on Wants, etc., see column for Classified Advertisements.

Copy must reach this office 12 o'clock Wednesday to secure insertion in issue of following Saturday.

Orders from unknown parties must be accompanied with cash or satisfactory references.

A CORRECTION.

In the advertisement of Welch Bros., which appeared on page 241, issue of August 25, drawing attention to their forthcoming removal on October 1, the new address should have read 226 Devonshire Street (Winthrop Square).

John Westcott on Factions.

According to our Philadelphia correspondence in last week's issue of The Florists' Exchange, John Westcott, that prince of good, genial, jovial fellows, is reported to have made the following remark: "We have factions in the S. A. F. These are composed of followers of each of the four trade papers," etc.

This is news to us, as it will, doubtless, be to those of our readers not already in the know. Just why the trade papers, or any one of them, can be accused of being responsible for the alleged "factions in the S. A. F." is difficult to understand. If any such factions exist, their creation must be looked for elsewhere, we think, than to the cause ascribed by Mr. Westcott.

As far as we see—and this we can say in all truthfulness, so far as we ourselves are concerned—the aim of each of the trade papers is to advance as far as they possibly can the interests of the S. A. F. This is their common endeavor. And surely such a laudable object would be and is conducive to something more honorable than creating "factions" in the national society.

Furthermore, we can hardly see the connection between "followers of the four trade papers," and the S. A. F., the membership of which forms but a small percentage of the clientele of the trade papers.

Successful trade papers are not builded in influence or circulation through catering to factional feeling—but the very opposite. They must be conducted on a broad-minded basis; they must be absolutely impartial; they cannot afford to undertake a hand in the politics of their local or national organizations, although they have a perfect right (for the good of the cause) to criticize the actions of such bodies.

In fact, and although the trade paper through its various agencies and sources of information, becomes unwittingly the repository of all trade secrets, intrigues and gossips, it cannot afford to attempt for a moment to use any of this knowledge as stepping stones to advancement, nor to bruit them abroad privately. Summing all up, that trade paper is most successful which eschews politics and avoids engendering factional feeling through zealously guarding the rights of all, even of those of the very few whom it may have good reason to detest.

The successful trade paper is the modern exponent of the Golden Rule.

Canadian Horticultural Association.

The convention is over and another step forward has been taken by the trade in Canada.

The majority of the delegates from Montreal, Ottowa, and other Eastern and Northern points, about forty in number, left from the Union Station, Toronto, on the morning of Wednesday, August 29; others went out by a later train, whilst quite a party went up on Thursday.

The first session was opened with an address of welcome by Prof. Reynolds, who took the place of President Creelman of the O. A. C., detained by the death of his brother. Prof. Reynolds stated that the C. H. A. and O. A. C. has much the same objects in view—the beautifying of the home and the improvement of flowers, fruit and produce. He hoped the members would have a useful and a pleasant convention, and that their visit to the College would be a material benefit. In closing he gave the delegates the freedom of the College. A. G. Wilshire answered in a few well chosen words.

President Fendley then asked Hermann Simmers to read his address, which was done, and laid on the table for future discussion.

In his address President Fendley expressed the feeling that every delegate should make himself at home, and be benefitted by the convention. The florist trade was only in its infancy in Canada, and would be furthered greatly by close attention to the discussions. Florists should be taught to fill every available space around their premises and the public would take notice. The trade should have a telegraph code, and should be able to get the standing of every florist in the business, so that goods will not have to be sent C. O. D. where the orders come from dealers unknown to the florist.

The report of the secretary, A. H. Ewing, Woodstock, showed that there were 81 members in good standing. Out of these, 45 were resident in or near Montreal, 12 in Toronto, and 24 from other places covering Manitoba to Nova Scotia. The large number from Montreal is due to the fact that the convention was held in that city last year. This was the first time that the convention had been held in a small city, and it was a good move because the smaller city requires the benefits these meetings impart more than the larger ones, where the trade was wealthier. The aim of the association was to lift up and carry forward all that tends to advance the interests of horticulture.

The report of the treasurer, Hermann Simmers, Toronto, showed a balance on hand of $92.91.

The geranium question was presented from the question box and many and varied were the opinions offered, but it was quite evident that the matter depends on the varieties and the way in which they are handled.

The trade exhibit judges reported at this session. The exhibit was held in the convention hall at the O. A. C., and though not large was a good one. Gammage & Son, London, had an interesting exhibit of miscellaneous florist stock plants, in trade sizes, all in good health and condition; awarded a diploma. A. Gilchrist, of Toronto Junction, showed some nice plants of Nephrolepis Whitmani, for which a certificate of merit was awarded; he also exhibited another sport from N. Barrowsii, but the plant is as yet too small to judge much of its merits. Robert Brooks, of Fergus, put up a fine box of tuberous begonia blooms for which a certificate of merit was awarded. J. Campbell, of Simcoe, exhibited a vase of one of Groff's new gladiolus called "Peace," a beautiful light variety, for which a certificate of merit was awarded. William Colvin, Galt, was awarded a diploma for a collection of gladiolus. Other exhibitors were the Arnot Chemical Company, and the Blackie Company, of Halifax, N. B., both showing fertilizers. Cranston & Son, of Hamilton, and the Foster Company, also of same city, flower pots. The Morehead Steam Trap was the only device shown connected with heating, and the gentleman in charge of it was certainly an able exponent of its usefulness.

The judges of the trade exhibit were E. Mepsted, Ottawa, Geo. Robinson, Montreal, and T. Manton, Toronto.

At the evening session Professor Harcourt gave an interesting paper on fertilizers which was well discussed. John Morgan, of Hamilton, read a paper on commercial carnations which was also much appreciated.

H. B. Cowen, managing director of the Canadian Florist, spoke of the progress of the paper; many members complimented him on its continued appearance, and the society decided to continue to support it as the official organ of the association.

On Thursday morning, London was chosen as the next place of meeting. J. H. Dunlop read a very practical paper or review of roses to date; all rose growers were much interested and Mr. Dunlop received many thanks. Professor Jarvis's paper on insect pests was read by Doctor Bethune. This also was a practical and useful paper. At the next session George Vair, Toronto, read an instructive paper on conifers; this was thoroughly appreciated by the practical gardeners present.

As many members were unable to stay for the evening session, it was moved and carried that the rules be suspended, and the election of officers proceeded with then. W. J. Lawrence, of Eglinton, was nominated by Mr. Gammage; John Walsh, Montreal, was nominated by T. Manton, and Wm. Hunt, Guelph, was nominated by Mr. Brooks. On the first ballot Mr. Walsh lead but did not have a majority of votes, Mr. Hunt having the smallest number of votes retired; the next ballot was a tie; on the third ballot Mr. Lawrence had a majority; before the president could declare him elected Mr. Walsh's name was withdrawn and the election of Mr. Lawrence was made unanimous. Mr. Walsh was elected vice-president; Ed. Dale, Brampton, second vice-president; H. Simmers, Toronto, treasurer, re-elected; A. H. Ewing, secretary, re-elected. The executive committee new members elected for three years: W. Kehoe, Ottawa, A. G. Stephens and T. Dicks, London.

After this session Professor Hutt of the College conducted the delegates over a considerable part of the College buildings and grounds, and at about 5.30 p. m., a pleasant at home was held on the lawn, at which the members of Guelph and members of the C. H. A. were entertained with refreshments and music. J. H. Dunlop acted as leader and brought out a fine entertainment of music and speeches; W. J. Lawrence sang several songs which were much appreciated; the affair only came to an end by calling the members to the final session.

Mr. and Mrs. W. Fendley were presented with a handsome set of cut glass, the presentation being made in a happy way by the first president of the association, Mr. W. W. Gammage, of London.

At the last session, Mr. Hall of Montreal read an able paper on business pointers for the retail trade. It was decided to put up a trophy of some sort to cost $50 for the carnation meeting at Toronto next January.

The thanks of the members are due to Wm. Hunt and the members of the local committees for their arrangement of the trade exhibit, for the general assistance given the delegates, and to the managers of the O. A. C. for their uniform kindness.

On Friday, the delegates who could afford the time, called at Brampton where they were royally entertained by the florists there, the Dale estate, R. Jennings and President W. Fendley doing all that was possible to make things pleasant. All the stock in Brampton town looks in the pink of condition; the Dale estate has rebuilt a large block of houses; Mr. Jennings is rebuilding and will certainly soon have a model place, while Mr. Fendley's new establishment is in fine condition. THOS. MANTON.

Toronto Industrial Exhibition.

The Industrial Exhibition is in full swing. The show of plants last week was, I think, just about up to the average, for although one of the principal former exhibitors, Wm. Houston, of the City Prison, has dropped out, others have about filled the gap. The two principal prizes were for 40 specimen foliage plants and for a group of plants arranged for effect. Three lots were put up for the first named, J. Chambers, Exhibition Park, was first; D. Robertson, of Reservoir Park, second; T. Manton, third. In the groups the competition was very keen and it was almost anybody's money; T. Manton was first; Government House, second; Allan Gardens, third, and Sir Henry Pellatt, fourth. In all the groups there was some good bright stock, the last named exhibit being generally very good, but rather small and lacking in green to fill it out and bring into relief the fine colors of the various plants.

The crotons, dracænas and ferns shown were all good. The flowering plants were also rather better than usual here at this season, but at that, were by no means good. Fine collections of caladiums and begonias were seen. The orchids were fair. The successful exhibitors were: J. Chambers, Exhibition Park; D. Robertson, Reservoir Park; Sir Henry Pellatt, Allan Gardens, Government House, W. Fudger, Wm. Jay & Son, and T. Manton.

The cut flowers are not up to our usual show, the heavy rains of Saturday and Sunday having put a good many outdoor flowers out of business. In the design classes, there were three competitors only, and J. H. Dunlop has all the first prizes, T. Holland, two seconds, and T. Manton, two seconds and one third. The rose prizes are shared between the Toronto Floral Company, W. Muston, manager, and J. H. Dunlop. There is a good show of gladiolus, a small but fair show of cut and hardy flowers; some good asters, fair dahlias, a few good sweet peas, a collection of the last named coming from H. A. Dreer, Inc., Philadelphia, Pa.

We have had many visitors in town, among others being Mr. and Mrs. Geo. Robinson, Montreal; E. I. Mepsted, Ottawa; Mr. and Mrs. A. Wilshire, Montreal, Mr. and Mrs. Gullopton, Montreal, Mr. T Manseeld, Lockport, N. Y.; Dan McRorie, Orange, N. J., and several representatives of the Dale estate, Brampton. T. MANTON.

Proposed Ladies' Auxiliary S. A. F. O. H.

Every wife, daughter, and sister of the members of the S. A. F. and O. H., also the lady members thereof, will soon receive a letter from a lady member of the society, asking co-operation in forming an auxiliary for social and instructive advantages. [Capital idea. We trust the effort will result in success, and promise the movement all the aid in our power. Ed.]

The Convention—From the Seedsman's Standpoint.

(George C. Watson before the Florists' Club of Philadelphia, September 4, 1906.)

Many a man has dug a cavity for the other fellow and fallen into the hole himself. Your committee on subjects last month assigned one to a seedsman whose duty it would be to report on the convention. Unfortunately for the committee there were no Philadelphia seedsmen at the convention big enough for this job. Mr. J. Otto Thilow, of Dreer's, had designed to go, and had promised to make an address, but his plans had to be changed at the last minute. So you see the cavity! Somebody had to fill it! The rest of the committee insisted on my jumping in, and that must be my excuse for attempting—even in a remote way—to fill up this hole. I approach the subject with a meekness exceeding the meekness of Moses, and am sorry we do not have the unhackneyed and original views of Mr. Thilow instead of the overworked and well-known notions of yours truly.

To my mind the first and most important feature of a convention to a seedsman is the opportunity it affords him of meeting his customers. It must be remembered that the seedsmen—and in using that term I mean it in the broadest sense—is the very opposite of a specialist. To be a seedsman in the proper sense, one must have a working knowledge of horticulture, floriculture, agriculture, and arboriculture; because the seedsman is an auxiliary to all these different branches of the art of gardening. You will observe that I dignify the art of gardening by embracing under it the culinary, the ornamental, the farm, and the forest. Loudon did so, and no more illustrious example could be followed. To be a gardener in the true sense of that term one must have a working knowledge of all these four great sub-divisions of the art and, as the seedsman is the auxiliary and helper in the same field, it follows that he also must be equally well posted so as to fulfil his proper functions with ease and dexterity. Therefore, the seedsman, as I said before, is the very opposite of a specialist. He is all embracing. But that is the strongest reason why he should be present at a convention of specialists like that of the Society of American Florists. There he comes in personal contact with his customers, gaining valuable knowledge from their experience with various specialties in which he has a direct pecuniary interest. He is able also to get a line on what is lacking and can lay his plans for future progress, thus becoming not only an auxiliary but a pioneer in the onward march of the art of gardening. I have made it a point to attend as many of these conventions as I could during the past twenty years and I have never regretted having done so. In fact, I consider it impossible to become thoroughly posted in the profession of a seedsman without taking in as many as possible of these and other conventions bearing on any phase or branch of the art of gardening.

The second and less important phase of this subject from the seedsman's standpoint is the actual and immediate business that can be transacted. From my own experience, and from what I have heard of that of others, the immediate business returns are not adequate in proportion to the expense and, moreover, unless a good exhibit is put up, they will be almost nil. If one goes to a convention for purely business reasons, rather than for the purpose of keeping posted, a good exhibit is indispensable. Quite a number of our most wideawake houses keep regularly making such displays, year in and year out, and they must find it pays them either directly or indirectly, else they would not keep it up. At the same time there can be no gainsaying the fact that a great many of our prominent seed houses do not attend. Whether it be indifference, lack of time, or what, I do not know; but I feel sure many of them need stirring up on this very subject. I can remember well how surprised I was in Buffalo in 1901, when not a single one of the local seedsmen took advantage of the grand chance of making an exhibit at the minimum of cost. I was ashamed of them. And this apathy prevails to-day. The seed trade wants shaking up on this point. Imagine what a grand show Burpee could make with sweet peas for instance, or Maule with dahlias, or Thorburn or Henderson with a general collection of their specialties. I hope to see full advantage taken by such firms in the exhibition of 1907.

In conclusion, I may say that for extent, excellence, and variety, the Dayton exhibition compared very favorably with those of recent years. There was at least one local seedsman who put up an exhibit, and the Livingston Seed Company, of the neighboring city of Columbus, had a very interesting display of tomatoes—the subject that has made the name of Livingston famous—besides some good new hybrids of Begonia semperflorens.

W. J. Lawrence.

W. J. Lawrence, the newly elected president of the Canadian Horticultural Association, was born in 1866, and has been connected with the profession of horticulture all his life; his father was a practical gardener. Mr. Lawrence commenced as an apprentice, when about 14 years of age, under George Vair, Chestnut Park, at that time the best private place in Toronto, and where several well-known men in the profession have made their start; serving there

W. J. Lawrence, President-elect C. H. A.

five years, he then went to F. G. Foster, of Hamilton, for two years; returning to Toronto, he managed the store end of the business of the Jas. Fleming estate. He was foreman for J. H. Dunlop for some time, and commenced business for himself early in 1898, and has since then built up a large business; he has about 60,000 feet of glass up-to-date King Construction on several acres of ground; he has proved himself to be a grower of first-class stock. Mr. Lawrence has been president of the Gardeners & Florists' Association, is a councillor of North Toronto, and chairman of the Fire and Light Committee; he is a splendid singer and a good speaker, and will no doubt make a good executive officer.

THOS. MANTON.

OUR READERS' VIEWS

Carnations Drying Up.

Editor Florists' Exchange:

In your Question Box, of the issue of August 25, page 244, Mr. E. N. C. well describes a disease which has made its appearance within the last few years on carnations, especially the Lawson variety, and we think you make a great mistake in saying it is evidently stem rot.

Carnations dying from stem rot show no sign of leaves turning brown until after the plant has rotted completely at the stem, just above the ground. In the disease E. N. C. so well describes, the stems of the plants do not rot at all, the leaves brown and the plant finally dies, while the main stem remains so perfect as to shoot out young shoots. We noticed this first here last year in our Lawson carnations in the field, and the disease grew much worse after planting in, in fact they got so bad that we were obliged to throw all our Lawson variety out.

This year, so far, the disease is not so bad; we think, though, we see no signs of our plants improving and believe we will have to do same as last year, throw the Lawsons out. We very much regret that we are unable to do anything for the disease or to advise your subscriber.

JOHN STANLEY.

Whitford Station, Pa.

Catalpa Sphynx and Mixed Insecticides.

Editor Florists' Exchange:

You may remember that a few days ago I called on you with specimens of a caterpillar which was destroying catalpa trees. They had about the proportions (when full grown) of an ordinary cigarette. Black above, yellow below, without hair, a single horn projecting prominently from the front of the head at an angle of perhaps 50 degrees. At your suggestion I wrote to Prof. J. B. Smith, our state entomologist, and sent him the specimens which I showed you. The answer has come to hand. It is as follows: "During Prof. Smith's absence in Europe, I beg to acknowledge receipt of yours of the 20th. The specimen which you sent is the larva of the Catalpa Sphynx, a medium sized moth. A few years ago these insects were not to be found in New Jersey, but at the present time they are spreading over the State from the south northward. The injury can be prevented by spraying the trees with arsenate of lead, at the rate of one pound in 75 gallons of water, whenever the insects make their appearance. They confine their feeding to Catalpa trees."

(Signed) A. E. MESKE.

I mentioned, when visiting you, one or two other items that might perhaps serve you to fill an odd corner when it comes to "making up." One was that mixed insecticides, like mixed drinks, may produce undesirable results. In June, I had been using some rose leaf insecticide in my auto-spray, and there remained in the chamber perhaps half a gallon of the spraying solution. I wished to use some Paris green, so dumped in some, possibly a tablespoonful, filled the auto-spray up with water (capacity about 3½ gallons) and did my spraying. Some other plants on which I used this mixture did not seem to like it very well, but my Crimson Ramblers were nearly killed by it. The foliage was sadly burned, and many of the branches, some the size of a telegraph wire and larger, were killed. Those particular Ramblers do not seem yet to have recoverd from the dose. My theory is a chemical reaction between the rose leaf insecticide and the Paris green.

Another item was a note as to one of my white lilac bushes which, after having put forth its blooms in May as usual, unexpectedly put forth another crop of blooms about the end of July. The July blooms were smaller both as to individual flowers and as to size of the cluster, perhaps a little more compact, but a smaller edition of the May product. I have had the bush about eight years, and it never did that before.

New Jersey. W.

An Interested Reader.

Editor Florists' Exchange:

The S. A. F. Convention Number of The Florists' Exchange of August 25, was especially interesting to us; also the English Burbank criticism. The Ideal Gardener and his Work—Thank you, Mr. Palmer, we in these remote parts like to hear of a good high standard to be maintained in the calling; we always thought there should be dignity in the work of the gardener; I suppose we will all get about as much respect as we deserve.

We have had an exceptionally dry and hot Summer; it has affected the carnations from outside with red spider; they look brown and it will take some weeks of moist atmosphere in the houses to restore them. Our chrysanthemums and roses look well. We are now getting nice rains with cool nights; generally the Summer has been too dry. Hay short; potatoes ditto. J. B.

New Brunswick.

Rose Lady Gay.

Editor Florists' Exchange:

In last week's Florists' Exchange Mr. Perkins asks for the names of growers who are propagating Rose Lady Gay. While I am unable to give the names of any propagating this rose in this section because there are few, if any, growers of rose plants here, that is, commercially, I can, however, say that Lady Gay was shown at our exhibitions by Mr. Walsh of Wood's Hole, and the sensation its appearance created on these occasions could hardly be exceeded by the flutter its appearance made on the other side of the water. This is not only a beautiful rose but an exceedingly useful one. Those Mr. Walsh exhibited here were grown in seven-inch pots, as well as I can remember, and in exhibiting them they were placed on the steps leading to the stage of the Casino Theatre (a most fitting place for their display). During the time the exhibition was open these plants were greatly admired and numerous inquiries were made concerning both the plants and the raiser. The plants then exhibited by Mr. Walsh were about five feet high and covered with bloom from top to bottom. This inquiry brings to my mind an exhibition held several years ago when Rose Dorothy Perkins received similar attention and was equally admired. D. M.

Editor Florists' Exchange:

I notice an inquiry from Messrs. Jackson & Perkins, asking the name of some growers who are propagating the new rose, Lady Gay. It is one of Mr. M. H. Walsh's seedlings and, if I am not mistaken, is a Wichuraiana hybrid. It was noticed very flatteringly in the trade press after the rose show of the American Rose Society last Spring.

It will be pleasant news to Messrs. Jackson & Perkins to learn that it has been compared favorably with their own Wichuraiana seedling, Dorothy Perkins. Indeed, one of the daily papers had an item, a short time ago, as coming from London, to the effect that the name of the rose Dorothy Perkins had been changed to Lady Grey—yes, Grey, not Gay—and it was selling very much more plentifully since the name had been changed. Personally I do not believe the name has been changed, but that some reporter of a daily newspaper, whose knowledge of roses was not very extensive, made the story up "out of his own head," as the old lady said.

I did hear a florist say, on one occasion, that he could see no difference between Dorothy Perkins and Lady Gay,—but another florist, who was present at the time, pooh-poohed the idea, and declared that Lady Gay, was far superior to the better known Dorothy Perkins. All this goes to show that the two may have some points of resemblance. I have seen and grown Dorothy Perkins, but have not had the pleasure of seeing Mr. Walsh's Lady Gay.

One reason why Lady Gay is not being extensively advertised is because, being new, there is not much stock ready to be placed on the market. Every florist, who has realized its value is propagating it in large numbers, and no doubt Messrs. Jackson & Perkins will have an opportunity of securing all they may need of it the coming Spring.

EDWIN LONSDALE.

A Visit to Wisley

A visit to the Royal Horticultural Society's Gardens at Wisley, England, had always been looked forward to by me with very much pleasure, even before they came into the Society's hands. I had heard so much of the many beautiful things to be seen there that a visit to this wonder spot, the late home of the lamented G. W. Wilson, was long ago a foregone conclusion.

I left London on the London and Southwestern Railway in the early morning to Byfleet, said to be the nearest point to the Gardens. I walked leisurely on to the Gardens, some four miles distant, through very tortuous, narrow, winding lanes with mostly hawthorn or privet hedges, typical of English lanes, but in most cases not high enough to obstruct the beautiful rural scenery en route. Passing through several small villages, with their beautiful, neat, trim cottage gardens and vegetable patches attached, which would do credit to any community, I arrived on Wisley Common, tired and weary. They were having what they termed "American weather," and I can assure you, with coat on arm and handkerchief in hand, it was hot; the sun shone brilliantly and the roads were dry and dusty. I would therefore advise any intending visitors to take a rig, at least one way.

Wisley Common, though not large, is very beautiful. The white and purple heather was just commencing to bloom. Interspersed with these was an abundance of harebells (Campanula rotundifolia), Lotus corniculatus, the harefoot clover, Trifolium arvense, Ononis spinosa and various other indigenous plants, which recalled boyhood days spent on moor or common. Skirting on this moor and just at the entrance to the Horticultural Gardens, is as beautiful a grove of pines as one could wish to see.

Gunnera Scabra
At Wisley Experiment Gardens, R. H. S., England

Why such gardens were established here, so far away from anywhere, I cannot imagine. The reason given by the Society is, to get away from the smoky atmosphere and excessive surrounding drainage of London, which they claim was very seriously hampering their efforts at Chiswick; and I must say they have done it.

The site is exceedingly beautiful and picturesque, with many lovely landscape features, which can be so useful to such a society. The land, as I noticed it in my brief visit, contained some flat, though not exactly low, ground, one or two large ponds, some rough rock land and some high, rolling ground which will prove very useful to them in their various lines of work. A small patch of woodland, in which its late owner had spent much time and care on thinning out some of the trees, planting thousands of rhododendrons, making beautiful shady woodland paths of them going in all directions, which seemed to make a perfect maze and must present a lovely sight when in bloom.

Thousands upon thousands of bulbs in various assortment have been here naturalized. Great patches of primulas and polyanthus of many varieties and species are seen. Liliums in variety have various groupings, notable among these Lilium giganteum, out of bloom, but still showing how perfectly at home it was. There were also present in this woodland paradise many of our native American plants from California which are too tender to grow with us outside in the North. I also noticed quite a large plant of Dicksonia antarctica, I think it was, as well as a batch of camellias, pernettya, olearia, and various other shrubs from different climes, which would succumb in our northern climate, growing there with good results.

In the ponds were various water lilies, while around the outer edges various plantings and groupings suitable for such situations, which does good credit to the hand that put them there. Gunnera, manicata, and G. scabra, associated with large ferns Phormium tenax, and various iris, backed up by a beautiful background of shrubbery, made a very telling effect. The writer, an amateur or novice in photography, made here one of his first attempts at picture making. In the immediate neighborhood was a newly constructed rockery, or rock garden, which had only just been planted, but which will add much to the beauty of this corner when the plants once get established.

Growing along the hillsides here and, in fact, scattered almost all around the outer edges of the woodland and in various rocky places, was the willow-leafed gentian, which had naturalized itself and was growing and blooming in great profusion, struggling even with the taller grasses and other low-growing things and holding its supremacy. Gaultheria procumbens, associated with our little Cornus canadensis, was here growing more rank and profuse than I ever saw them home, and a pretty combination they made. These were mostly growing in rather low parts of the rock garden and on the low edges of the woodland in partial shade, where they had both moisture and peatty or boggy soil.

I omitted to mention in my woodland walks the many large patches of various azaleas I saw there, which add much charm and interest to the place.

Passing on out of this beautiful spot, which I can never find words to describe, I was led by my guide to the trial grounds, where dahlias, violas and border carnations are being tested. The violas were simply magnificent, and were one blaze of color. They had been collected from various sources and placed here side by side for comparative test. Four had been selected by the Society's council as being the best for bedding purposes and general effect. They were Royal Sovereign, a deep yellow and a rayless variety; Counselor Watters, a crimson purple, self colored variety, with a dwarf, free habit, and said to be a splendid variety for bedding purposes; Dr. McFarlane, upper petals mauve, under petals very dark, with a clear white eye; Isolde, bright yellow, without rays, large and extra fine, a perfect beauty. These, my guide told me, were the best four and most distinct in the whole collection, but I must confess there were many others which, perhaps to my inexperienced eye, were equally as beautiful. Allow me to say here that wherever you go in England, violas are used by thousands for bedding purposes.

The dahlias, while showing a very healthy look and giving good promise of an abundance of bloom, with the exception of a very few varieties were not in a fit state to show what they were, or make any comparison whatever.

The carnations were past their best, but they had bloomed profusely. The colors, compared with what we see here, were simply not in it. Of course, I admit they are a different race, and in this respect no comparison can be made.

Passing from here I was shown the new greenhouses, nearing completion, which are to be devoted to the testing of fruits, vegetables, stove, greenhouse and other plants and flowers found the most interesting for useful and ornamental purposes. Trials of new varieties of fruit, etc., are to be made side by side with older varieties to determine their more valuable properties and uses. I understand hybridization of plants and the raising of new varieties are to be carried on here on an extensive scale as soon as the plant gets into thorough working order, but at present much of this work is in crude form. Considerable time, thought and care must be exercised in laying the foundation of so great an institution as this aims to be.

Of one thing we are assured and that is that the beautiful wild garden which Mr. Wilson labored for so many years to establish is to be preserved and very carefully continued.

Another feature or idea Mr. Wilson carried out on this place was to make an imitation ditch throughout a low piece of land. The soil was simply thrown out on either side and I do not suppose was even uniformly levelled, but was planted with various hardy plants, with a judicious sprinkling of small trees and shrubs, giving the whole the appearance of a small streamlet, naturally in its wild state; and if so many cultivated forms of plants had not been so frequently interspersed, the effect might have been complete.

HERBERT GREENSMITH.

California Plant Notes.

Vines.

Of all the curious flowering vines cultivated on this coast, the Snail Vine (Phaseolus Caracalla) is the most so. The flowers are twisted like the shell of a snail, and about the size of one of these full-grown pests of some California gardens. The color at first is white and purple, the white changing to yellow with the age of the flower. They are delightfully fragrant and borne in clusters of 15 to 20 blooms, resembling a cluster of grapes. It is a rapid growing vine and, if not injured by frost, soon covers a large surface. It flowers on the new growth and, if cut to the ground, will bloom as freely though not quite as early as if left run wild. It would be a fine subject for large grounds on the Atlantic Coast, if grown in tubs, which could be stored in cellars during the Winter.

Another interesting vine, though seldom met with, is Vitis gongylodes. It makes a marvelous growth; 3 to 4 inches a day is the record, this season, of the one on Hollenbeck Home grounds. Of a dark green color, and metallic hue, the leaves are large, trifoliate, on petioles 6 to 8 inches long.

The stem has four parallel membranes, a quarter-inch high, giving it a quadrangular appearance; it will endure but little frost.

At this season of the year, Solanum Wendlandii is one of our most gorgeous flower vines. It is a vigorous grower and its light purple flowers, borne in umbels a foot or more in diameter, makes it very attractive.

Antigonon leptopus, just now coming into bloom, is another beautiful subject too little known on this coast. Its dark pink flowers are borne on the tendrils of the vine in the greatest profusion. The foliage is very pretty, of a light green color, having the appearance of crumpled tissue paper. It will endure the warm dry atmosphere and bright sunlight of the interior valleys of the State, but freezes to the ground every Winter, therefore does not make as large vines as in the South, yet blooms profusely.

Muehlenbeckia complexa, for covering rock work, pergolas, or unsightly trunks of trees, has no superior. Its black wiry stems and small kidney-shaped leaves gives a very pleasing effect in landscape work. The flowers are very minute and inconspicuous. It is one of the few vines absolutely free from insect pests or fungous diseases—and will stand several degrees of frost.

Gunnera Manicata
At Wisley Experiment Gardens, R. H. S., England

Other Good Things.

Among the varigated foliage plants grown here, there is none more beautiful than Acalypha marginata. In full sunlight the larger part of the leaf assumes a dark bronze, while the margin is of a dark-red color. In partial shade the leaf is dark green, the margin a creamy white. As a subject for the lawn, or grown in pots for decorative purposes, it has few equals.

Australian Hibiscus, Lagunaria Pattersoni, is one of our most beautiful flowering trees. Its shell pink flowers are borne in great profusion. If given room to develop, it forms a beautiful evergreen pyramid, and will grow to a height of 30 feet. It is easily propagated from seeds, which are furnished with irritating barbs; therefore, it is best for the collector to wear gloves while at work.

Duranta Plumieri is a beautiful evergreen shrub which is covered with its racemes, four to six inches long, of pale lavender colored flowers, during the early Summer months, followed by a bountiful crop of fruit which ripens during the Fall months and remains the entire Winter, giving the plant a beautiful orange color. There is also a white flowering variety.

Hibiscus mutabilis, just now coming into bloom, will give a display of its changeable colored flowers until December. They are very double, and have different shades of pink during different hours of the day. It grows readily from cuttings, and if allowed to do so forms a good sized tree, with globe-shaped top. It is deciduous, and will stand considerable frost.

Hibiscus sinensis, both double and single, is the glory of Southern California gardens the entire Summer and Fall.

Melaleuca decussata, with its globe-shaped, light purple flowers, is one of our most attractive drouth-resistant shrubs. An interesting feature of this subject is the bark which is made up of thin paper-like layers to the depth of an inch or more. This entire family of small trees and shrubs is one of the most desirable that we grow on this coast. Some have blooms of the most brilliant scarlet, cylindrical in shape, six inches long, two inches in diameter, and will live through our dry Summers without water. One member, M. leucadendron, bears pinnacles from 18 to 24 inches in length of creamy white flowers, so light and feathery in its make-up that plumosa would have been a more appropriate specific name.

P. D. BARNHART.

New Geraniums at Evanston, Ill.

It is an interesting visit to go out to Evanston, Ill., and examine the greenhouse establishment of Richard F. Gloede at 2012 to 2034 Grey avenue, now of considerable proportions, but erected entirely through the efforts of Mr. and Mrs. Gloede, who first went to the prairies and camped out, about a de-

Evanston, Ill.—Approach to the establishment of Richard F. Gloede.

cade and a half ago. Especially noticeable is the stock of three new geraniums which were duly entered and described, about a year ago, as follows: "Mrs. R. F. Gloede, a seedling, flower, semi-double, very large, color rose pink, foliage dark green, zoned, growth exceedingly strong; tested three years."

"Kenilworth, zonal growth and habit, tall and robust; flowers single, dark scarlet; foliage large and leathery, seedling three years old standing storm and rain, the owner claims it to be the best all-round geranium out.

"Illinois, a sport from Beaute Poitevine, semi-double, identical with parent in every particular with the exception of the petals, which are irregularly toothed and somewhat larger than in Poitevine and blossoms are somewhat more widely open."

All these geraniums as seen growing here, appear meritorious acquisitions to our already extensive list of this important flower.

Mr. Gloede also does a large landscape business and is at present erecting a new carnation house. There are here also many other floral attractions.

W. K. W.

New Geraniums at R. F. Gloede's, Evanston, Ill.

Practical Plant Breeding.

(Concluded from Page 218)

In my work on the canna, which embraced all available species and early European hybrids as well as the latest and best productions obtainable, I proved yearly the correctness and value of my contention, for seven years of select breeding gradually eliminated types of no commercial value, until in the last season not only were discards practically nil, but the value and quality of the selected seedlings were equal to those of the best novelties of European introduction.

The great value of the system advocated by me is the fact that the success of breeding depends much upon the removal of every influence adverse to increased multiplication of advanced types. This will be appreciated by those workers on bulky plants and trees of slow maturing habit, requiring a large acreage for development, and the fact that I am speaking from an experience with nearly a million new hybrid gladioli, a plant that requires comparatively little space, although needing from three to five years to mature from seed. Fifteen years of unbroken work on this now my sole specialty has also proven the value my views in practice. In the progression of my system the first five years only is known to commerce, having been discarded by me ten years ago; the second series of five years is little known commercially, and received the Pan-American Exposition Gold Medal and St. Louis World's Fair Grand Prize; while the third series of five years is all in my personal possession, and unknown outside of my trial grounds.

I mention the above to make my statement more clear, for the reason that while my Canadian and United States representatives use over one hundred acres in multiplying and maturing my introduced productions, five acres of my own breeding and trial grounds is ample for my personal supervision, in view of the yearly increased average of high quality developed under the system of breeding practiced by me. This means that in the daily work of selecting from thousands of seedlings blooming in series of yearly production, the object lesson is most apparent in passing from section to section, with

Convention Hall, Dayton, O., where the S. A. F. met last August.

their gradual but marked increased ratio of high quality, and newer and more valuable types.

It is therefore imperative that the breeder should specialize that he should use every obtainable wild species of his specialty, and in using each for the purpose dictated by his judgment and experience thus control and render amenable to his direction the vital forces and chemical constituents of this foundation stock. By using all obtainable species he multiplies the possibilities for practical results and increased diversity in the material to be evolved from the product of future years, and yearly discarding species and early hybrids as they are superseded in the course of his operations.

Wild species are only of value so far as they may supply some desirable quality for incorporation in a domestic type containing other good qualities such as size, vigor, vitality and adaptability. Illustrating from my specialty, the blotch of the small purpureo-auratus can be placed upon a six foot domestic type, free from the objectionable cowled habit of this species, the throat mottling of the weak growing Saundersii can be transmitted to a race of strength and vigor, with the added influence of its wide, open flowers, and so on indefinitely.

That the foregoing can be done is good reason for not developing race hybrids, with the consequent loss of the most important quality of general adaptability to changed conditions. The natural development of wild species is usually accomplished by restricted conditions of habitat, an influence of ages impossible of neutralization by a few season's crossing. So highly do I appreciate this feature of adaptability that in bringing my productions to maturity I grow on four kinds of soil—sandy, sandy loam, clay loam, and humus or vegetable deposit—and before use in breeding they are proven in this quality in order that it may be also transmitted in crossing. Breeding from wild species is therefore of little practical value, as the farther our removal from their many objectionable features the better, and when by proper selection their best qualities can be controlled and applied according to our knowledge and discretion.

As I have spoken lightly of the value of pedigree types from wild species, it is only fair that I should give good reasons for my objection. Plant breeding is in its infancy, and too little has been done of a practical character in quantity to secure the general results to be attained by specialization and selection from hundreds of thousands of composite hybrids.

Of what practical value is the knowledge of the component ratios of life forces in simple hybrids, in comparison with that knowledge giving results in the highest ratios of useful and valuable qualities?—thereby saving labor, time, space and expense, and giving in the place of curios, the highest possible percentage of quality in economic types.

My advice to plant breeders is to multiply types by many thousands, using special proven selections as sires, on the lines of practice by successful animal breeders. Select and develop domestic races and sections of such high quality, vitality and general adaptability, that their progeny will not only be of higher quality than the parents, but that this quality wil be produced in quantity in the highest possible ratio. This is practical plant breeding.

It is not necessary at a conference like this to detail many of the more simple effects of the influence of the vital forces directed by the operator in hybridization, such as control of color, form, and special markings in the flower, size, habit, vitality and reproductive powers in the plant, or the increase or diminution of the component chemical constituents affecting the commercial value of our productions.

The operations of crossing, to be practical, must be understood from the important aspect of its blending of diverse chemical constituents, and the critical breeder will be interesed in observing the daily decomposition set up by his experimental blending and the chemical action referred to, as this frequently causes partial or complete disintegration of the forms resulting from such crosses.

I have said daily for the reason that this influence is apparent from the germination of the seed, and its daily development during every season preceding the maturity and fixity of a type, until its dominancy and stability are assured. This lesson reads from one day to five years in my specialty. I do not mean that each single variety needs this daily scrutiny, but that in the daily development of many thousands of seedlings, some live one day, others two, and so on daily until the close of the season, the seed bed is an object lesson on the lines to which I have referred, and that stability is not assured even at full maturity.

For practical and valuable economic results it is therefore not sufficient that the breeder should be able to produce types of symmetry and beauty, but he must add the quality of stability and adaptability to changed conditions to ensure due satisfaction for the ultimate grower.

In closing I will record one of many unique results in my experience in exhaustive work on this one plant, for the purpose of illustrating the subtle yet distinct character of the vital forces directed by the plant breeder. From among some types showing a tendency to produce double and semi-double flowers I had selected one of proven value as a useful breeder, after some years of experimental proving. The influence of this type not only carried the tendency of petal multiplication, but the seeds produced twin corms from time to time, an effect not manifested in the offspring of nomal types. Experiences like this prove the contention advanced in the early part of this paper that the hybridist does not need to spend time in special analysis for the purpose of securing examples of an interesting character, but that the great secret of success and satisfaction is large production from high class composite parents bred for the purpose, and that by these means many new, valuable and interesting types can yearly be produced, in addition to the highest ratio of useful and beautiful varieties, developed by practical plant breeding.

Chicago.—A Section of J. A. Budlong's New Range, Six Weeks after Planting with American Beauty Rose Plants.

CLUB AND SOCIETY DOINGS.

NEWPORT HORTICULTURAL SOCIETY.—A regular meeting of this society was held Tuesday evening, President MacLellan in the chair. There was a good attendance of members. The secretary read his report of the exhibition recently held in the Casino, which was very satisfactory from every point of view. The treasurer was ordered to pay all the premiums awarded. The committee having in charge the float for the carnival made a final report showing all expenses in connection with it; the report was received and the bills ordered paid. The moving spirit of this committee was Mr. Bruce Butterton; it was he who this year planned the design and made the model which was in itself a marvel of ingenious construction. Mr. Butterton's labors did not by any means cease with the completion of the model. On the other hand he was indefatigable throughout the whole period the float was under construction, in his efforts to make what was undertaken a success, and it is gratifying to him, as well as to the society, that the float was a decided success. D. M.

THE NORTH SHORE HORTI. SOCIETY, MANCHESTER, MASS.—The Summer show of this society was successfully held on the grounds of the Essex Country Club, August 29 and 30, in a large tent erected for the purpose.

In a select colony, like the North Shore, where are located practically all the best Summer residences in Massachusetts, one expects to see the very highest of culture amongst the gardeners of such a locality. At this exhibition, however, such was not the case, and many of the gardeners of the neighborhood did not exhibit at all; whether they were jealous of the few that did or not is a question, but it would seem that more harmony should prevail in a progressive young society like this. Displays of special note were: a collection of dahlias from W. W. Rawson & Co., including some 250 varieties of show, fancy and cactus in all the latest sorts; display of aquatics from H. A. Dreer & Co., Riverton, N. J.; display of outdoor roses from the Blue Hills Nurseries—this lot included some exceptionally good blooms of Frau Karl Druschki and Killarney; display of native trees and shrubs from Robert Mitchell, and display of plants from the North Shore Ferneries.

The Lord & Burnham silver cup for the best display of foliage and flowering plants was won by Thos. Jack, gardener to W. B. Walker. The R. & J. Farquhar & Co. silver cup for the best collection of vegetables was also won by Mr. Jack. The Schlegel & Fotler special prize of $35 for the best collection of annuals was won by Herbert Shaw, gardener to Mrs. G. M. Lane. The W. E. Doyle silver and bronze medals for the best table of flowers were won by Mrs. W. Scott Fitz and Mrs. C. E. Cabot. Other prizes included a long list of all seasonable flowers and vegetables. The judges of the exhibition were John W. Duncan, Boston, Robert Cameron, Cambridge, and James Stuart, Brookline. J. W. D.

The florists' Club in Berlin has undertaken to call into existence a school for florists, bouquetists, etc.

A Model Trade Paper.

The columns of The Florists' Exchange contain more real, live and instructive reading matter, more news, and more helpful trade information, than can be found in any other journal. Assist us in our endeavors, please, by recommending it to your friends.

Posibilities from Parasites.

This year's lecture season of the Massachusetts Horticultural Society was opened Saturday morning, January 13, by Dr. L. O. Howard, chief of the bureau of entomology in Washington. His subject was "The Possibilities from Insect Parasites," and he illustrated it with stereopticon views.

The lecture consisted of a careful historical summary of all of the work that has been done in different parts of the world with the practical handling of the insect enefies of injurious insects, starting with the first attempt in 1855 by Dr. Asa Fitch, hen State entomoligists of New York, to import the European parasites of the wheat midge, and closing with the present attempt to import into New England the European and Japanese parasites of the gypsy moth and brown-tail moth. The excellent work carried on in California in this direction was described at some length, from the first overwhelming success of the importation of the Australian ladybird in 1889 to destroy the fluted scale, down to the latest importation of an ichieumon fly from Spain, which is a parasite of the codling moth of the apple. The work done in Hawaii, in Western Australia, and in South Africa received due attention, and the similar work carried on under the United States Department at Washington, naturally, was not disregarded.

Doctor Howard called attention to the fact that work of this kind cannot be done with success with native insects, but that in the case of imported insects, which flourish exceedingly, an effort to introduce their parasites from their native homes should not be neglected.

With regard to the gypsy moth and brown-tail moth, he expressed himself as hopeful of success. In Europe the standing of these two insects may be compared to that in this country of the tent caterpillar of the forest and the tussock moth. In America both of these insects occasionally multiply sufficiently to bring about considerable damage to vegetion, but invariably after excessive multiplication they are suddenly reduced in numbers, and, while always present, seldom multiply again to an injurious extent until after a period of some years. This is due largely to the work of native parasites, since both are native American insects. In Europe the gypsy moth and brown-tail moth situation, as stated, is practically the same, although with the brown-tail moth in many countries there are police measures in force requiring the destruction of the over-wintering nests on certain dates in the Autumn. Thus, it was pointed out, certain of the collectors engaged to gather, in different parts of Europe, the nests of the brown-tail moth were obliged to collect them early, before they were destroyed by the owners of gardens and orchards. He described in some detail his last summer's trip to organize the work of important parasites of these two insects, and stated that it was difficult in very many localities to find any specimens at all of the gypsy moth, although it is well understood that in almost any year it is liable to appear in considerable numbers. The work of last Summer showed that it was an easy thing to import parasitized specimens of both species into Massachusetts, and it now remains simply to bring over as many as possible, and to care for them as well as possible, in the confident hope that some of them will establish themselves and become permanent denizens of the United States. Surely, with the extraordinary abundance of food which they will find in eastern Massachusetts, there can be no reason, unless it be climatic, why they should not breed rapidly and eventually reduce both the gypsy moth and the brown-tail moth to approximately European conditions.

Obituary

Mrs. John White.

Mrs. Marion T. White, wife of John White, the West street florist of Pittsfield, Mass., died suddenly last week of heart trouble, aged 63. Mrs. White, although able to be about, was under the care of Dr. William W. Leavitt, and was apparently improving when stricken. Mrs. White was born in Carlisle, Eng., and had lived in Pittsfield nearly a quarter of a century. She was twice married. Her first husband, William Gray, superintendent of the Corning estate in Albany, died in 1887. Three years ago she married Mr. White. Besides her husband Mrs. White leaves an aunt in England and a niece, Miss Dolly Gray, the latter being with her when she passed away. At the funeral services Rev. Walter A. Wagner, pastor of the South Congregational church officiated. The body was taken to Troy for cremation.

The Late James Hartshorne.

The following resolutions were adopted by the members of the Toronto Gardeners & Florists' Association at their regular August meeting and sent to Mrs. Hartshorne.

The officials and members of the Toronto Gardeners & Florists' Association do most sincerely sympathize with you in the great affliction you have suffered through the death of your dear husband.

And the members of this association feel that they have lost a true and kind friend, one who was always ready to do his part (and more) in assisting any of his brother craftsmen.

The members desire that you should know of the great esteem and respect in which he was held by them. E. F. COLLINS, Secretary.

Birds's Eye View of a Portion of the Peter Reinberg Range, Chicago.

Dahlia Exhibition.

R. Vincent & Son, White Marsh, Md., one of the largest dahlia growing firms in the country, if not the largest, will be visited on Wednesday, Sept. 19, by members of the Baltimore and Washington Florists' Clubs, the train leaving Washington at 11.00 a. m., and Baltimore at 11.50 a. m., over the B. & O. R. R. to Cowenton, where they will be met by the Vincent wagons.

The invitation is open to florists from the North as well, and we would suggest that all desiring to go from New York, Philadelphia, or vicinity, promptly notify the office of this paper in order that arrangements may be made for the visitors to take the express train leaving W. 23d st. at 7.50 a. m., or Liberty st. at 8.00 a. m., via B. & O. R. R.; same train leaves Philadelphia, 24th and Chestnut sts. at 10.22 a. m. This is the fastest morning train out and will not stop at Cowenton (the station for White Marsh), unless previously arranged for.

An exhibition of cut flowers will be made in the packing shed and the blooming plants in the fields will also be inspected. All interested in growing dahlias are cordially invited.

Trade exhibits will be made by H. F. Michell Co. and Griffith, Turner & Co.

Dayton, O.

In a letter to W. J. Stewart, secretary of the S. A. F., Mr. John C. Freudenberger, landscape gardener to the National Cash Register Co., gives expression to his gratitude and hearty thanks to one and all for the handsome ring presented to him by that society.

Notes for Beginners.

The Retail Florist.

It is possible to start in business as a retailer in quite a respectable manner with but a very small capital. A retail florist proper, the one who buys his stock, flowers and plants at wholesale, and sells at retail, can, if need be, commence business in a most simple, unpretentious fashion by renting a small store, or part of a large one, or even by securing the privilege of selling his flowers from a stand on the street, or in some nook, hallway or niche facing the passing public. The quality of goods and service, in a case like this, are less to be relied upon as factors to bring trade, than choice of locality. A retail florist of the better, or best, class, however; the one catering to a first-class trade, from a well-appointed place of business, needs considerable capital when starting in, especially if he has selected a choice locality in the downtown district of any large city, where traffic of a character favorable to his trade is, at least, at first, his mainstay. Here a place suitable for his business is at all times most difficult to find, and, if found, is only obtainable by paying an exorbitant rent. In basements and upper stories, where space is easier to obtain, and the matter of rent less forbidding, the retail florists' business does not flourish, and for a long time after starting remains a losing affair.

Instead of crowding into these centers of busy city life, where competition is keen, and has to be properly met, a nice place, if ever so small at the beginning, in the midst of a fine residence section, should be chosen for the opening of a new business in plants and flowers. While competition will also exert itself here, and be felt by the new beginner, such a location will grant him ample room and freedom to win trade, and to build up a business on methods and principles of his own.

Self-Made Gardeners.

The greatest number of those, who turned from their original trade, or profession, to floriculture as their new occupation, men and women from nearly all walks of life, are to be found among the smaller growers and retail florists; and, strange as it may seem, and despite the fact that nearly all of them knew but little of their new business, and less of theoretical floriculture, with no practical experience at all in either, they all managed to make a fair headway after their tiny bark was once safely launched. It seems strange, because it is a preconceived idea that if a great amount of acquired knowledge and a wide experience are needed in all horticultural pursuits, this particular branch of the profession—the growing of plants and flowers of many kinds, and from all climes and quarters of the earth—could only successfully be undertaken by those unusually learned and practiced in the requirements and mysteries of plant life.

Anyone, however, who has had opportunities to study the question at close range, who has been an eye witness of the first beginning and subsequent growth of some of these concerns, started and conducted by non-gardeners, has learned to understand that just this very business, thought to be open only to the professionally well skilled and highly gifted, is the one of all in which the lack of preparatory studies and an experience of years of active practice form the least of serions obstacles to beginners graduated from other schools of industries of life, especially when these deficiencies are fully made up and counterbalanced by an ever-felt warm and undulled love for flowers and plants, by a pair of bright, observant eyes, a frequently exercised habit of correct thinking, and an ever-ready willingness to learn—qualities often lacking where knowledge and experience drudge wearily along, steeped in their dreary round of a disenchanting daily routine.

Home-Made Floriculture.

Many have gradually drifted into the florist's business. Naturally embued with a love for flowers, and fond of working among them, they soon mastered the elementary but nevertheless fundamental lessons in the art of propagating plants from "slips," seeds and by layering. Rude and ungardener-like though these attempts to multiply were, yet they resulted in a mass of plants—more than the highly pleased propagator knew what to do with. The neighbors' gardens were stocked up with the overflow; nearby as well as distant friends received their share; kitchens and basements became storehouses of all sorts of plants during the Winter, and the fame of the "lucky" gardener spread. But ere long he, or she, found out that plants had a money value, could be sold for cash. This discovery added a new charm to the horticultural exploits, and urged them on to increased activity and new and untried experiments. All-efficient nature, at times crushing their hopes and foiling their plans, more often aided and assisted them in their efforts. What was playfully begun as a pastime for pleasure, was now eagerly continued as a business for profit, and as the seasons rolled by the erstwhile carpenter or tailor, merchant or teacher, developed into the gardener and florist, and his place of business into one not easily overlooked.

The experience of all who began business in this manner, as far as I can learn, is identical in this one point: that when they had reached a stage in their career when outdoor and hot-bed gardening became insufficient for their trade, and failed to give satisfactory results in lines newly attempted, and out of the ordinary, their whole fervent yearning was for a greenhouse. Not unlike the small boy who thought he could read if he only had his grandpa's spectacles, so these embryo gardeners were confident that if they only had a greenhouse at their command their road to rapid progress would be at once cleared of all obstacles, and gardening become an occupation free from all care and difficulties. But as soon as the first greenhouse was up their real troubles began. In the course of time, however, they learned to combat and to overcome these troubles; they profited by lessons, for which they paid dearly, and at the same time they familiarized themselves with plants and the art of growing and handling them to advantage.

To-day it would be unjust and certainly untrue to derisively look upon these men and women as non-professional intruders, for they have learned their trade, belong to us, and should be honored as an active, wide-awake and progressive class of workers in the busy field of horticulture. And, after all, are we not, old or new, continually pondering over unsolved problems, daily taking in our lessons? And who will say he knows it all, or can even truthfuly claim to know more than the next one? Is not this beautiful trade of ours, more than any other, of the "live and learn" order, and are not those old and gray therein often called upon to undo their snugly tied bundle of revered knowledge to discard one or the other of their rusty dogmas for the smooth and bright new wrinkle of the non-gardener? FRED W. TIMME.

PLANT NOTES.

Propagating Geraniums.

There are three methods of procedure in propagating geraniums in the Fall from stock planted outdoors in the Summer, and each method has its advocates among the ranks of the growers for commercial purposes and for private use.

The first method, and perhaps the one most generally practised, is that of rooting the cuttings from now on in benches in sand and then potting them into very small pots whenever they are rooted.

The second method is that of putting the cuttings, when they are made, into small pots.

The third method is that of putting the cuttings when they are made into flats, say from fifty to a hundred cuttings in a flat.

There are, I am sure, among growers in this country, some placed in such positions and under such circumstances that each method is practised by them.

By rooting the cuttings in benches in sand, a greater number of plants can be raised in a given time than by either of the other methods, and if at all times the cuttings are kept cool enough or, more correctly speaking, if the temperature of the house is not allowed to get too high, good salable plants will also be the result, but it is only reasonable to admit that when at first each cutting is placed in a pot and then on a bench, and properly cared for until rooted, stockier and better furnished plants will be had than can be obtained from out of a batch of cuttings closely packed in a sand bench, where it is impossible for each cutting to have the same space and the same attention as that given the one in a pot, and besides there is no check given the latter like that given the former in the process of changing from the sand bench into a pot. The pot method of rooting, however, takes more room and a great deal more time at first start.

The other method is that of putting the cuttings, to the number of fifty or more (the number depending on the size of the flats), into flats; this method is one that is generally practised by private growers and by some commercial growers also, and it is a method possessing many points of advantage that commend it to both classes of growers whom, as I said before, may be placed in such positions that the adoption of either of the other methods would not in the end suit their circumstances. When cuttings are put in flats a good way of disposing of them for a time is to place them in cold frames, until the cuttings are rooted, when they may be taken into the greenhouse and placed in any cool airy place and allowed to remain until it is convenient to pot them and to find room for them when potted. And, right here, comes one great advantage of this method, which is, that they may remain in their first quarters, I mean in the flats, for an indefinite period, providing they were not overcrowded nor given too much water nor kept too warm. Still another point in favor of the flat method is that they can be removed from one house to another before it is found convenient to pot them.

Those adopting this method should, however, count on losing ten per cent. of the cuttings put in if these are allowed (as they often are) to remain in flats three or four months. In preparing for rooting cuttings in the way just mentioned, drainage may be made of the siftings of the leaf mould and loam used for the body of the compost, which should consist of loam, leaf mould and sand in nearly equal proportions up to within an inch and a half of the top, then put fully half an inch of good clean sand over the whole. The cuttings should be thoroughly watered after being put in the flats and then shaded for a day or two, but after that they should have full light and as much air as possible when the weather is favorable. The cuttings will require going over frequently in order to remove dead and decaying leaves or any that may damp off.

Hollyhocks.

If seed of hollyhocks is not already sown, no time should be lost in procuring the best seed that can be obtained and sowing it; I say the best seed because if it so happens that when the plants come into flower there are three or more shades of color where only one was looked for, the difference between the price of good seed and unreliable seed will not be half as much as the difference between flowers that are salable and flowers that are not. When the seedlings are fit to handle easily, they should be pricked off into flats, about two inches between the plants and the same or a little more between the rows. When they have made good roots and are showing signs of crowding, they should be potted, and then again repotted until they are in 3-inch or 3½-inch pots ready for early Spring sales or Spring planting.
M. I.

Cultural Notes.

CROCKING POTS.—A grower of plants to be successful cannot afford to underrate the smallest detail of the business, and very often it is because of underrating the importance of one of more of these seemingly trivial details that failure instead of success comes after months of otherwise painstaking labor.

The crocking of pots by some is considered a rather unimportant part of the grower's duties, whereas it is really one of the most essential in the whole routine of plant growing. A plant put into a pot that has preiously been carelessly crocked invariably lives and sometimes goes the length of dying to give evidence to prove what I say. There is no plant that does not require good drainage in some way or other, although plants of slow growth and those requiring less water than others need more careful crocking for the pots than plants that are gross feeders and require frequent shifting, and even with these greater perfection can be attained if care is exercised in making provision for the drainage of water. When the soil gets down and clogs up the hole in the bottom of the pot in a very short time the soil will become sour and repulsive to the roots of the plant, and instead of making vigorous and healthy roots the plant will soon lose the roots it had already made with the result that instead of a thrifty plant a miserable starving apology for one for a brief space of time prolongs its painful existence.

I knew a gardener (I know him now for that matter,) who always insisted on supervising the crocking of pots when plants of considerable value were being potted, even though the men considered the work in any shape beneath their dignity; sometimes they resented this overseeing up to the quitting point. The gardener in question, however, grew good plants, and this with the additional fact that he was a very busy man should argue in favor of the importance he attached to the first step in plant culture.

In a general way it is always advisable in crocking pots to place the first piece which ought to be the largest and scooped over the hole with a few others of medium size around and over that, and then to cover these with a thin layer of much smaller ones.

GOSHEN, IND.—Miss Dora Brown, opened a retail store in the Mehnert Building, North Main st., Monday, September 3.

NEW LONDON, CONN.—Thos. E. Burroughs who, for twenty years, has been located in this city has removed to Deep River, Conn.

GERANIUMS

From 2 in. pots ready for immediate delivery

Alliance, Lemoine 1905. Hybrid Ivy and Zonal, semi-double, lilac, white, upper petals feathered and blotched crimson maroon, 25c. each; $2.00 per doz. **Fleuve Blanc,** the semi-double Bruant, that promises to become the standard white, flowers and foliage equal to Alph. Ricard, $1.50 per doz.; $10.00 per 100. **Cactus Geraniums,** four varieties, petals curled and twisted similar to the Cactus Dahlia, $2.00 per doz.; $15.00 per 100. **Double Dryden,** $1.00 per doz.; $5.00 per 100. **S. A. Nutt, La Pilote, Beaute Poitevine, Mme. Barney, Centaur, Miss Kendell, Mme. Jaulin, Jean Viaud, Mme. Charrotte,** 40c. per doz.; $2.00 per 100; $18.00 per 1000. **Ville Poitiers, Marquise de Castellane, Berthe de Presilly, M. Jeli de Bammeville, Thomas Meehan,** 50c. per doz.; $3.00 per 100; $25.00 per 1000. Send for Geranium catalogue, let us figure on your future supply. **Alternantheras,** red and yellow, $2.00 per 100; $15.00 per 1000. **Hardy English Ivy,** $2.00 per 100; $15.00 per 1000. **Smilax,** $2.00 per 100; $15.00 per 1000. **Dahlia Roots,** we are booking orders for fall delivery; send for list.

A cordial invitation is extended to all interested in Horticulture to visit us. Cowenton Station, Philadelphia division, B. & O. R. R., 12 miles north of Baltimore.

R. VINCENT Jr. & SON,
WHITE MARSH, MD.

Mention The Florists' Exchange when writing.

GERANIUMS
ROOTED CUTTINGS

Orders booked for delivery Nov. 1st and after. I will have fourteen houses planted to stock plants and I can supply you with the right kind of cuttings.

	per 100	per 1000
S. A. Nutt Perkins, Buchner, Doyle	$1.25	$12.50
Viaud, Jaulin, Poitevine, L. Francis	1.50	15.00
Ricard, Castellane, Trego	1.50	15.00
Peter Henderson	2.00	20.00
Fleuve Blanc (White Poitevine)	5.00	50.00

These cuttings are carefully grown and will make a better plant than the average pot plant.

ALBERT M. HERR, Lancaster, Pa.

Mention the Florists' Exchange when writing.

Geraniums Geraniums

4 in. pots at $6.00 per 100.
3 in. pots at $4.00 per 100.
Heliotrope, 4 in. $4.00 per 100.
" 2 in. $3.00 per 100.
Lobelia, 2 in. $2.00 per 100.
Coleus, in variety, 2½ in. pots, $2.00 per 100.

Don't get left, but get your order in. Cash must accompany same.

J. E. FELTHOUSEN,
154 VAN VRANKEN AVE., SCHENECTADY, N. Y.

Mention The Florists' Exchange when writing.

GERANIUMS
TRANSPLANTED STOCK

Ricard, Poitevine, Doyle,
Viand, Castellane, Nutt,
Buchner, Perkins, Grant, dbl.

$15.00 per 1000. Cash with order.

PETER BROWN, Lancaster, Pa.

Mention The Florists' Exchange when writing.

GERANIUMS

Rooted cuttings, transplanted in soil, best varieties, mixed, to close out on account of removal, $10.00 per 1000.

CARNATION SUPPORTS, round, some new, some slightly used, $5.00 per 1000; $40.00 per 10,000. Cash with order.

G. F. NEIPP, Aqueduct, L. I., N. Y.

Mention The Florists' Exchange when writing.

CARNATIONS

May Naylor, Marion & Joost, fine, field-grown plants, $4.00 per 100.
Alyssum, double Giant, for Winter flowering, 2¼ in. pots, $1.50 per 100.

J. C. SCHMIDT CO.
BRISTOL, PA.

Mention The Florists' Exchange when writing.

S. J. GODDARD

Framingham, Mass.

Rooted Carnation Cuttings a Specialty

Correspondence Solicited.

Mention The Florists' Exchange when writing.

CARNATION PLANTS

Strong, field-grown, A No. 1

CERVERA	$3.00 per 100.
W. SCOTT	3.00 " "
QUEEN LOUISE	4.00 " "
McGOWAN	3.00 " "

ISABELLE GREENHOUSES
Box 97 Babylon, L. I., N. Y.

Mention the Florists' Exchange when writing.

FIELD GROWN CARNATIONS

Only 400 **Nelson Fisher** left, at 5c. All cleaned out of other varieties. These are O. K. in every way; well branched, and in good, healthy condition. Also about 200 **Smilax** from 3 in. pots at $3.00 per 100. Cash with order please.

VALLEY VIEW GREENHOUSES, Marlborough, N.Y.
VELIE BROS., Props.

Mention The Florists' Exchange when writing.

FIELD GROWN CARNATIONS

PROSPERITY, grown on new ground, strong, healthy plants, $5.00 per 100; $45.00 per 1000. Cash with order please.

P. KRATZER, ROSLYN, L. I., N. Y.

Mention The Florists' Exchange when writing.

2000 CHRYSANTHEMUMS
"THE BABY"

Fine for Thanksgiving Day. Field-grown plants to pot up. For 7 in. pots, 15c.; 6 in. 12c; 5 in., 10c.; 4 in., 8c. each. Cash.

HENRY EICHHOLZ, Waynesboro, Pa.

Mention The Florists' Exchange when writing.

CHRYSANTHEMUMS

Extra strong plants, in 3 in. pots, of **Jones, Dr. Enguehard,** Perrin, **Mrs. Coombs, October Sunshine, Alice Byron, Ivory, Appleton,** etc. These plants have been cut back, and are in fine condition. $5.00 per 100 or the lot of about 200 for $8.00.

R. G. HANFORD, Norwalk, Conn.

Mention The Florists' Exchange when writing.

GERANIUMS.

Nutt, Poitevine, Buchner, Doyle, Ricard Viand, Brett, and others.

Rooted Cuttings. Orders booked for Fall delivery.

ERNEST HARRIS, Delanson, N. Y.

Mention The Florists' Exchange when writing.

POINSETTIAS

2¼ in. pots, $5.00 per 100; $40.00 per 1000. Cash with order.

S. N. PENTECOST,
1790-1810 East 101 St., CLEVELAND, O.

Mention The Florists' Exchange when writing.

VINCAS

Good, from field....$3.00 and $4.00 per 100
Primula Obconica, 2½ in....3.00 "
" " 3 in....4.00 "
" Chinese, 2 in....2.00 "
Carnations, Joost, strong....3.00 "

J. H. DANN & SON, Westfield, N. Y.

Mention The Florists' Exchange when writing.

CARNATIONS

	Per 100
GLENDALE	$12.00
ROBT. CRAIG	12.00
BOUNTIFUL	8.00
DOROTHY WHITNEY	8.00
BELLE	7.00
FLAMINGO	7.00
FIANCEE	7.00
HARRY FENN	6.00

FIELD PLANTS

	Per 100
BOSTON MARKET	$6.00
WHITE CLOUD	6.00
NELSON FISHER	6.00
ENCHANTRESS	6.00
MRS. PATTEN	6.00
PROSPERITY	5.00
NELSON	5.00
ESTELLE	2nd size, $5.00; 3rd size, 3.50

ROSES, 200 4 in. **Maids,** 150 4 in. **Brides,** $6.00 per 100. 500 2½ in. **Gates,** 300, 2½ in. **Brides,** 150 2½ in. **Perles,** $2.50 per 100. **Richmond** own roots, fine 3 in. $5.00; 2 in. $4.00 per 100.

FERNS, Boston and **Piersoni,** 3 in., $6.00 per 100; 4 in., $10.00; 6 in., $35.00; 7 in., $60.00.

ASPARAGUS PLUMOSUS, 2 in., $2.00 per 100. **SPRENGERII,** 3 in., $6.00 per 100. Cash or C. O. D.

W. J. & M. S. VESEY, Fort Wayne, Ind.

Mention The Florists' Exchange when writing.

Field Grown CARNATIONS

Flamingo, Roosevelt, Crisis, Harlowarden
Price, $ 6.00 per 100.

E. A. Nelson, Flora Hill, Wm. Scott, Portia, Eldorado, Crocker, Queen Louise
Price, $5.00 per 100; $4.50 per 1000.

J. L. DILLON, Bloomsburg, Pa.

Mention The Florists' Exchange when writing.

CARNATIONS

Crisis Scarlet	$5.00 per 100	Cardinal	$7.00 per 100
Fiancee	5.00 "	Estelle	5.00 "
Joost	5.00 "	Queen	5.00 "
B. Market	5.00 "	Harlowarden	5.00 "

Second size $2.00 per 100 less. Cash with order.

SMITH & GANNETT, Geneva, N. Y.

Mention The Florists' Exchange when writing.

FIELD GROWN CARNATION PLANTS

Mrs Bradt	$5.00 per 100
Prosperity	4.00 " "
Naylor (white)	5.00 " "
Estelle	5.00 " "
Eldorado	5.00 " "

EDWARD J. TAYLOR, Southport, Conn.

Mention The Florists' Exchange when writing.

FIELD GROWN Carnations

Extra fine healthy plants

	100	1000
QUEEN	$5.00	$45.00
FAIR MAID	5.00	45.00
FLORIANA	5.00	

250 Field-grown Jerusalem Cherries, stocky plants, $5.00 per 100.

CASH WITH ORDER

W. A. DAWSON, Willimantic, Conn.

Mention The Florists' Exchange when writing.

CARNATIONS
FIELD GROWN

	100
500 Boston Market	$4.00
300 Queen Louise	3.50
200 Lieut. Peary	4.00
Asparagus Sprengerii, 3 in. pots	5.00
Asparagus Sprengerii, 4 in. pots	8.00

Cash with order.

S. G. BENJAMIN, Fishkill, N. Y.

Mention The Florists' Exchange when writing.

CARNATION PLANTS

Fine, healthy Stock.

1600 WHITE LAWSON	$60.00 per 1000
250 ESTELLE	4.00 " 100
1600 DOROTHY	35.00 " 1000

Stock grown and shipped from Toledo, Ohio.

S. S. Skidelsky,
824 No. 24th St., PHILADELPHIA, PA

Mention The Florists' Exchange when writing.

40,000 extra fine field-grown Carnation plants. For particulars see under Stock for Sale.

M. J. SCHAAF
DANSVILLE, N. Y.

Mention the Florists' Exchange when writing.

MABELLE--New Pink Carnation for 1907

Color.—A peculiar shade of lovely pink, with a faint yellowish cast; several shades lighter than the Lawson. Unlike most pinks, the brightest sun does not injure the color. **Size.**—Three to four inches in diameter when established. **Odor.**—Pleasing, but not strong. **Stems.**—Invariably strong, but always graceful, ranging from 18 to 30 inches during the season. **Habit, etc.**—A very quick active grower, making specimen plants in a short time, even from late cuttings. On account of its rapid growth, requires supporting very soon after benching. Gets away rapidly, blooms early and gives long stems right from the start. **Productiveness.**—Prodigious is the best word we know of to use here. It is the most incessant bloomer early and late, we have ever grown. Stock limited. Delivery Jan. 5th to 10th and later. Price, $12.00 per 100, $100.00 per 1000.

THE H. WEBER & SONS CO., OAKLAND, MD.

Mention The Florists' Exchange when writing.

Field Grown Carnations

Crane, Fair Maid, Gov. Wolcott, Roosevelt, Marquis. 6 inch pans **Boston Ferns,** $4.00 per doz. 3 in. **Standard Geraniums,** $2.00 per 100; $18.00 per 1000.

THE NATIONAL PLANT CO. Dayton, O.

Mention The Florists' Exchange when writing.

ENCHANTRESS

Ready Sept. 15, $5.50 per 100; $45.00 per 1000.

WHITE BROTHERS, Gasport, N. Y.

Mention The Florists' Exchange when writing.

CARNATIONS

Let us have your order now for the coming new Carnations: January delivery. Aristocrat, Windsor, White Enchantress, Helen M. Gould, Beacon and Rose Pink Enchantress.

WM. SWAYNE, Box 226, Kennett Square, Pa.

Mention The Florists' Exchange when writing.

CARNATIONS

	Per 100	Per 1000		Per 100	Per 1000		Per 100	Per 1000
FIANCEE	$6 00		MORNING GLORY	$4 00	$35 00	FLORA HILL	$5 00	$45 00
LAWSON	6 00	$50 00	LIEUT. PEARY	8 00	75 00	WHITE CLOUD	5 00	45 00
NELSON FISHER	7 00	60 00	FRED BURKI	7 00	60 00	CHICAGO (Red Bradt)	5 00	45 00
GUARDIAN ANGEL	4 00	35 00	BOSTON MARKET	5 00	45 00	HARLOWARDEN	6 00	50 00

WIETOR BROS., 51 Wabash Ave., CHICAGO

Mention The Florists' Exchange when writing.

CARNATIONS

STRONG, HEALTHY, FIELD GROWN PLANTS

	100	1000		100	1000
LAWSON	$5.00	$40.00	MORNING GLORY	$4.00	$30.00
NELSON	3.00	25.00	BOSTON MARKET	4.00	35.00
GUARDIAN ANGEL	3.00	25.00	LADY BOUNTIFUL	6.00	50.00
NELSON FISHER	7.00	60.00	FLORA HILL	3.00	25.00
ENCHANTRESS	7.00	60.00	ESTELLE	5.00	40.00
MRS. PATTEN	6.00	50.00	FIANCEE	7.00	60.00

QUEEN LOUISE, MRS. INE, HIGINBOTHAM, ARMAZINDY WHITE CLOUD, all at $3.00 per 100; $25.00 per 1000.

ROSE PLANTS

	100	1000
LIBERTY 3 in. pots	$3.00	$25.00
CHATENAY 2½ in. pots	2.50	22.50

PETER REINBERG, 51 Wabash Ave., CHICAGO

Mention The Florists' Exchange when writing.

IELD... ROWN CARNATION PLANTS

		Per 100	Per 1000
ITE	Lady Bountiful, favorite white	$ 7.00	$ 60.00
	White Lawson	7.00	60.00
IK	Mrs. Thos. W. Lawson	6.00	50.00
	Enchantress	7.00	
	Fair Maid	6.00	
ARLET	Cardinal, best scarlet	7.00	60.00
	Skyrocket	7.00	60.00
	Crusader	6.00	50.00
RIEGATED	Glendale, (new)	12.00	100.00
	Prosperity	5.00	40.00
IMSON	Harlowarden	5.00	40.00

HICAGO CARNATION CO., Joliet, Ill.

Mention The Florists' Exchange when writing.

ield Grown Carnation Plants

THE LARGEST AND FINEST WE EVER HAD

THE QUEEN	$5.00 per 100	BOSTON MARKET	$5.00 per 100
FAIR MAID	5.00 "	FIANCEE	5.00 "
QUEEN LOUISE	5.00 "	ENCHANTRESS	6.00 "

J. D. COCKCROFT

NORTHPORT, - - L. I., N. Y.

Mention The Florists' Exchange when writing.

ield Grown Carnation Plants

ALL THE STANDARD VARIETIES

List and prices on application.

se plants 1000 Liberty 3 in. pots .... $5.00 per 100
1000 " 2¼ " " .... 4.00 " 100

IE LEO NIESSEN COMPANY, 1217 Arch St. Philadelphia, Pa

Mention The Florists' Exchange when writing.

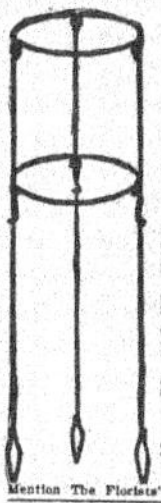

The Model EXTENSION

CARNATION SUPPORT

Endorsed by all the leading carnation growers as the best support on the market. Made with 2 or 3 circles. Write for prices and circulars.

We have special low prices to offer and can save you money on

Galvanized Wire ROSE STAKES

Write us for prices before ordering elsewhere. Prompt shipment guaranteed.

IGOE BROS.
226 North 9th Street
BROOKLYN, N.Y.

Mention The Florists' Exchange when writing.

FIELD GROWN

Carnation Plants

5000 Enchantress, 6c. each; $50.00 per 1000
Queen, 5c. each; $40.00 per 1000.
Lawson, white, 2nd size, $4.00 per 100.
" variegated, 2nd size, $5.00 per 100.
" pink, 2nd size, $3.50 per 100.
Lady Bountiful, 2nd size, $5.00 per 100.
Glacier, 2nd size, $3.50 per 100.

CASH

GOVE BROS., Biddeford, Me.

Mention The Florists' Exchange when writing.

CARNATIONS

Strong Field Grown Plants

Crimson Glow (new variety) $12.00 per 100

Cash or references with order.

DAILLEDOUZE BROTHERS
Flatbush, Brooklyn, N. Y.

Mention The Florists' Exchange when writing.

CARNATIONS

F. DORNER & SONS CO.
LA FAYETTE, IND.

Mention The Florists' Exchange when writing.

Jensen & Dekema

CARNATION SPECIALISTS

674 W. Foster Ave., CHICAGO.

Mention The Florists' Exchange when writing.

CARNATIONS

PLANTS FROM FIELD

Fair Maid, Queen, Mrs. Patten, $5.00 per 100; $45.00 per 1000. Strong and healthy.

Satisfaction guaranteed. Cash with Order.

HUGH CHESNEY, Farmington, Ct.

Mention The Florists' Exchange when writing.

FIELD GROWN CARNATIONS

VICTORY, JOHN J. HAINES, $2.00 per doz.; $15.00 per 100.
FIANCEE, G. LORD, GOV. ROOSEVELT, $6.00 per 100.

CHARLES H. TOTTY
MADISON, N. J.

Mention The Florists' Exchange when writing.

ABUNDANCE

Healthy, stocky, field grown plants. First size, $12.00 per 100; $100.00 per 1000. Second size, $10.00 per 100; $75.00 per 1000; 250 at a 1000 rates. Delivery 15th of August.

CASH WITH ORDER.

RUDOLPH FISCHER, Great Neck, L.I., N.Y.

Mention The Florists' Exchange when writing.

CARNATIONS

FINE FIELD GROWN PLANTS
CORRESPONDENCE SOLICITED

A. B. DAVIS & SON, Inc., Purcellville Va.

Mention The Florists' Exchange when writing.

Field Plants

CARNATIONS:—Harry Fenn,—fine plants at $4.50 per 100.
GERANIUMS:—S. A. Nutt ready for three inch pots, $2.00 per 100.

ALBERT M. HERR, Lancaster, Pa.

Mention The Florists' Exchange when writing.

CARNATIONS

ENCHANTRESS .... $50.00 per 1,000
QUEEN LOUISE .... 40.00 " "
LAWSON .... 40.00 " "

Good, strong, healthy plants. Cash with order.

HENRY KRUSCHKA
616 Cookman Ave., Asbury Park, N. J.

Mention The Florists' Exchange when writing.

ADVERTISE IN THE FLORISTS' EXCHANGE - - and be sure of good returns - -

CLASSIFIED ADVERTISEMENTS

CASH WITH ORDER.

The columns under this heading are reserved for advertisements of Stock for Sale, Stock Wanted, Help Wanted, Situations Wanted or other Wants; also of Greenhouse, Land, Second-Hand Materials, etc., For Sale or Rent.

Our charge is 10 cts. per line (7 words to the line), set solid, without display. No advt. accepted for less than thirty cents.

Display advertisements in these columns, 15 cents per line; count 12 lines agate to the inch.

[If replies to Help Wanted, Situation Wanted, or other advertisements are to be addressed care of this office, advertisers add 10 cents to cover expense of forwarding.]

Copy must reach New York office 12 o'clock Wednesday to secure insertion in issue of following Saturday.

Advertisers in the Western States desiring to advertise under initials, may save time by having their answer directed care our Chicago office at 127 E. Berwyn Ave.

SITUATIONS WANTED

SITUATION WANTED—By grower of roses, carnations, mums and general stock. West preferred. Address, D. H., 27 Slater St., Port Chester, N. Y.

SITUATION WANTED—By middle aged married man, grower of roses, carnations and general stock. 12 years' experience. Address, O. G., care The Florists' Exchange.

SITUATION WANTED—By a thoroughly competent plantsman and grower to travel. Varied experience, and best of references. Address N. Z., care The Florists' Exchange.

SITUATION WANTED—By florist and gardener in florist store. Good decorator and salesman; quick worker; strictly temperate. Address, O. R., care The Florists' Exchange.

SITUATION WANTED—Young German gardener and florist, three years in this country, wants position in greenhouse, nursery or retail flower store. Address, O. O., care The Florists' Exchange.

SITUATION WANTED—By a young man of good character, education, and experience as foreman of Eastern rose growing establishment. References on application. Address, O. C., care The Florists' Exchange.

SITUATION WANTED—By gardener and florist, German, single man, 34, grower of Easter bedding stock, carnations, mums, palms. Able to take charge. Address, O. S., care The Florists' Exchange.

SITUATION WANTED—Gardener, German, single, desires position in private family; take ful charge of greenhouses. Address, Pfaller, 731 Third avenue, care Donning, New York City.

SITUATION WANTED—As section man on first-class place to grow roses or carnations. Married man; please state particulars in first letter. Satisfactory references. Address, A. B. C., care The Florists' Exchange.

SITUATION WANTED—German, 30 years old, 16 years experience, married, small family, not afraid of work. A No. 1 references. Wishes steady private or commercial place. Address, Florist, 5th and Garden Streets, Hoboken, N. J.

SITUATION WANTED—As foreman, commercial or private, by German, 37, married, family, 21 years experience in landscape gardening and greenhouse management. Palms, ferns, carnations, mums, violets and general bedding stock. State full particulars. Address, O. N., care The Florists' Exchange.

SITUATION WANTED—A competent florist wishes a position on the first of October. To take charge of section; rose or carnation houses. Has first-class references; sober and honest, a Hollander by birth. Address, S. Heemskerk, care Dr. Hotchkiss, East Quogue, L. I.

SITUATION WANTED As superintendent or gardener by a thoroughly competent and practical man; experienced in all branches of horticulture, private and commercial, nursery and landscape work. Married, small family.

Address, O. Q., care THE FLORISTS' EXCHANGE

Mention The Florists' Exchange when writing.

SITUATIONS WANTED

SITUATION WANTED—Steady, from 1st or 15th of Oct., around New York or Brooklyn, by a young man, Swede, single and sober, as assistant in first-class commercial or private place. 5 years experience; one year in this country. No fireman. Address, O. L., care The Florists' Exchange.

SITUATION WANTED—By a young man, 21 years of age, having worked two years in the florist business, wants a position where roses, carnations and bedding stock are grown, and where he can learn to make-up designs. New York state preferred. First-class habits. Please give full particulars with wages in first letter. Address, Emil Simons, Fairport, N. Y.

HELP WANTED

WANTED—Single man to make himself generally useful. State wages wanted. Lebanon Greenhouses, Lebanon, Pa.

WANTED—A thoroughly competent man to take charge of a section of Beauties. Apply Frank Dolan, care of John Young Company, Bedford Station, New York.

WANTED—At once, a good night fireman. Must be good at potting and general greenhouse work. Steady position to the right man. Send references and state wages expected. Address, P. M. Olm, Bath, Me.

WANTED—A first-class man for retail florist in Chicago; no greenhouse work. Must be a good salesman and designer. State wages, References. Address, M. D., care The Florists' Exchange.

WANTED—Single man, understanding care of violets, to take charge of small commercial place. State experience, reference and wages with board. M. Halley, Box 199, Rhinebeck, N. Y.

WANTED—A practical gardener for private place where there are several greenhouses. German preferred. House furnished. Apply with references to J. M. Williams, 561 Hudson St., New York City.

WANTED—A man with some experience in growing carnations and general stock. Wages, $45.00 per month. State age and nationality when answering. Address, O. P., care The Florists' Exchange.

WANTED—Florist and gardener, with experience in growing choice pot plants. Give experience, copy of references, age, etc. Wages, $60.00 per month. Address, O. D., care The Florists' Exchange.

WANTED—Man for general greenhouse work. State in first letter age, references and wages expected, with room and board if single, without, if married. Chas. Frost, Box 24, Kenilworth, N. J.

WANTED—Sober, industrious young man, not over 25 years, for general greenhouse work. Good, steady place for the right man. State wages wanted per month with board and room Hugo Book, Worcester, Mass.

WANTED—An energetic young man to assist in landscape work; fair knowledge of stock, trimming, etc., essential. Dutch or German preferred. State wages expected with references. A. Van Leeuwen, Jr., Worcester, Mass.

WANTED—At once, a good sober young man who knows how to grow Dutch bulbs, palms and other decorative plants for retail florist. Assist in decorating, etc. 12 miles from New York City. Address, S. G., care The Florists' Exchange.

WANTED—At once, a good grower of all kinds of cut flowers, Easter and Christmas stock, and general bedding plants, to take charge. Wages, $75.00 per month, with house rent free. Address, O. T., care The Florists' Exchange.

WANTED—At once, a good sober, industrious man, who thoroughly understands decorating, and will take care of two show houses, one for decorating, the other for selling purposes. Apply Chas. T. Siebert, Baum & Beatty streets, Pittsburg, Pa.

WANTED—Salesman, one who is a hustler, and understands all about nursery stock, and a fair knowledge of landscape work. To travel. Must have a good record. Steady employment and good pay. Address with references, P. A. Keene, The Morris Nursery Company, 1 Madison avenue, New York.

WANTED—Manager for wholesale commission business. Must be experienced, capable, and of unquestioned integrity. One preferred to purchase share in business. Applicants will be notified of place for interview in Philadelphia, September 9th. Address, O. F., care The Florists' Exchange.

WANTED at once a young experienced Florist, must be good designer and window dresser. Apply stating Experience and salary wanted and if possible send Photo.

The Wright Floral Co. Ltd., Ottawa, Canada.

Mention The Florists' Exchange when writing.

Thirty cents is the minimum charge for advertisements on this page.

MISCELLANEOUS WANTS

WANTED—Partner with $2,000 to $3,000 capital to start wholesale business. Address, O. J., care The Florists' Exchange.

FOR SALE OR EXCHANGE—Extra, double thick glass, 10x12, $1.90 per box. Take roses or carnations. Wm. P. Kesteloo, Walden, N. Y.

WANTED—5,000 Acer Saccharinum, 1 to 3 feet. State price and size. V. A. Vaňicek, The Rhode Island Nurseries, Newport, R. I.

WANTED TO BUY—Greenhouses to be taken down. State full particulars of same when writing. Address, F. W., care The Florists' Exchange.

WANTED TO RENT—Between 10 and 25,000 feet of glass, in good condition. Wholesale or retail. State full particulars. Address, N. X., care The Florists' Exchange.

WANTED—A quantity of Clematis Paniculata Seedlings, in flats or transplanted. State size, and quantity, with lowest cash price.

PALISADES NURSERIES, Sparkill, New York

Mention The Florists' Exchange when writing.

FOR SALE OR RENT

FOR SALE—At a bargain, or will rent eight greenhouses in center of flourishing city of 20,000 inhabitants. J. H. Ives, 103 Elm street, Danbury, Conn.

FOR SALE or will rent to a responsible party, a fine greenhouse property, 13,000 feet of glass. Fine residence. Address, Silas C. Howell, Lock Box 14, Pine Bush, New York.

FOR SALE.—Greenhouses comprising over 8,000 square feet of glass, situated in Northern New Jersey. Including all stock, horse, wagons, harness, etc. Doing good retail business. Address, B., care The Florists' Exchange.

FOR SALE—Florist's business, corner lot, nearly 7 acres, 26 miles from Philadelphia, 3 hothouses, frame house, barn, outbuildings, on trolley, and near station. For particulars, address, O. M., care The Florists' Exchange.

DESIRABLE greenhouse plant of three houses, 24x200 feet; propagating house, 100 feet; potting shed, stable and dwelling. Steam heat, city water. Highland, opposite Poughkeepsie, Joseph Wood, Spring Valley, New York.

FOR SALE—Florist establishment, near city of 35,000 inhabitants, established 15 years, wholesale and retail. Stock in first-class condition. Fine living house of eleven rooms and bath, all improvements. Barn, shed and frames, 14 city lots to go with it; also with stocked nursery. Frank Knapper, 436 Bellevue avenue, Yonkers, N. Y.

FOR SALE—Owing to the ill health of the principal owner, it has become advisable to offer for sale the entire stock of the best known florist establishment in southern California. A long time lease held on the grounds may be obtained. A fine opportunity to step into an established business, incorporated. For particulars, write to Box 94, Ventura, Cal.

FOR SALE—At a bargain on account of removal and having two places, I will sell four greenhouses, two houses 16 x 80, other two 22 x 80. Boiler house, 16 x 20, with one large boiler to heat the place and another in reserve. Both boilers can burn buckwheat coal at a small cost. Only three or four years in use. Price only $1500. Hill Top Greenhouses, 15-16 Gray avenue, Utica, New York.

FOR SALE—Owing to failing health, I will sell my florist establishment, beautifully situated between Larchmont Manor and Mamaroneck, Westchester Co., New York, near railroad station; trolley lines within one minute walk. First class opportunity for the right man. Plenty of landscape and jobbing work. The place contains four acres, 2 greenhouses, 104 feet long and lots of sash; well stocked with trees and shrubs, etc.; horse, wagon and tools. Address, Box 44, Larchmont, New York.

STOCK FOR SALE

FOR SALE—Queen Louise and C. A. Dana carnations, fine stock, $5.00 per 100; $25.00 per 1000. Fox & Rosen, Parkerford, Pa.

STRONG, field-grown carnation plants: Joost, pink; Challenger, scarlet; Harlowarden, crimson; Gov. Wolcott and Edith Foster, white. $5.00 per 100. Cash. Hansen & Lundsted, Passaic, N. J.

15,000 strong, healthy, field-grown violet plants of Farquhar, Lady Campbell, La France and California, $5 per 100; $45 per 1000. Rickard Langle, North street, White Plains N. Y.

STOCK FOR SALE

JERUSALEM CHERRIES, full of fruit, fo[...] and 6 in. pots, $1.50 per doz. Smaller [...] bloom, $1.00 per doz. Ellis Bros., Keene, N. [...]

CANE STAKES (Japanese) for your Mums [...] ft. long, $6.00 per 1000; bundle of 2[...] $10.00. Arthur T. Boddington, 342 W. 1[...] St., N. Y.

Asparagus Sprengerii and Plumosus, 2 1-2 [...] extra fine stock, ready for 4 in., $3.00 [...] 100. Cash. William Hoffman, 673 East [...]enue, Pawtucket, R. I.

CARNATIONS, extra fine, field-grown, Ha[...] Warden, Estelle, Queen Louise, Law[...] White Lawson, Fred Burki, $6.00 per 1[...] $50.00 per 1000. Butz Bros., New Castle, [...]

GIANT PANSIES, mixed; double daisies [...] forget-me-nots, blue, 50c. per 100 mai[...] $2.50 per 1000 express. Cash. Shippensb[...] Floral Co., Shippensburg, Pa.

BABY RAMBLER roses, fine dormant st[...] $25 per 100. 2 1-2 inch pot plants, e[...] well rooted $7 per 100, $65 per 1000. Ord[...] booked for delivery now or any time up to [...] Spring. Samples free. Brown Brothers [...] Rochester, N. Y.

CARNATIONS—Extra fine, field-grown pla[...] Enchantress, Mrs. T. W. Lawson, $6.00 [...] 100; $50.00 per 1000. Joost, New Daybre[...] Prosperity, Wolcott, $5.00 per 100; $40.00 [...] 1000. Terms cash. M. J. Schaaf, Dansvi[...] N. Y.

2,000 Brides, 3,000 Bridesmaids, 1,000 Mete[...] 1,000 Beauties, out of 4 in. pots. No be[...] plants grown. Packed and delivered at [...] press office. Maids and Brides, 5c.; Met[...] 4c.; Beauties, 12c. each. Louis M. N[...] Madison, N. J.

Field-Grown carnation plants, strong [...] healthy: 100 Queen Louise; 150 Gov. W[...]cott; 175 Boston Market; 50 White Laws[...] 50 Thos. Lawson; 40 Prosperity; 60 Mrs. [...]ten; 40 Flamingo; 100 Dahelm; 30 Crane; [...] Estelle; 40 Floriana; 40 Marquis at $4.00 [...] 100. The whole lot for $30.00. Cash. He[...] Hansen, Catskill, N. Y.

FOR SALE

FOR SALE—12 Hitchings hot water expans[...] tanks for 3 1-2 in. pipe, in good conditi[...] cleaned, ready to set up. 1-3 price of n[...] Also horse lawn mower, easy running, $20. [...] Address, K. D., care The Florists' Exchan[...]

FOR SALE—50 cypress hot bed sash, siz[...] x 6, glazed with 10 x 12 glass, pain[...] white, and in perfect condition. Most all [...] them new this season; none over three y[...] old. $1.00 each. J. V. Cutler, Wassaic, N.[...]

FOR SALE—3000 feet of good 2-inch pipe[...] large hot water boilers, good as new; [...] of valves, 4-inch, 3½ and 2½ inches. Al[...] be sold cheap for cash. Nelson & Johns[...] Prospect street, Framingham, Mass.

FOR SALE

PUMPS Rider-Ericsson. Second-hand, f[...] $40.00 up; all repairs; other ma[...] new; cheap.

BOILERS One second-hand tubular hot w[...] boiler 3 ft. in diameter 12 ft. l[...] Price $36.00. One No. 17 Hitchings in first c[...] condition, $125.00; and also 5 section round bo[...] $75.00; No. 6 at $75.00; No. 9 Weathered at $75.00[...]

PIPE Good serviceable second-hand, [...] Threads; 2-in., 7 cts.; 1½-in., 5½ [...] 1¼-in., 4 cts.; 1-in., 3 cts.; 2½ in., 10 cts.; [...] 14 cts.; 4 in., 19 cts. New 2-in. Standard, [...] lengths, with couplings, 8¼ cts. ft. Old [...] new fittings and valves. Old 4 inch cast iro[...] per foot.

STOCKS and DIES New Economy, best m[...] No. 1 Threads, ¼-in., [...] 1-in. pipe, $3.00. No. 2 Threads, 1¼-in., 1[...] 2-in. pipe, $4.00.

PIPE CUTTERS New Saunders Pattern. N[...] cuts ⅛-in.-1-in. pipe, [...] No. 2 cuts 1-in.-2-in. pipe, $1.30.

STILLSON WRENCHES New. 18-in., grip[...] in.-2-in. pipe, [...] 24-in. grips ¼-in.-2½ in. pipe, $2.40; 36-in., [...] ½-in.-3½-in. pipe, $4.75.

PIPE VISES New. No. 1 Hinged, grips ⅛-[...] in. pipe, $2.00.

GARDEN HOSE New. 50 ft. lengths. ¾ [...] guaranteed 100-lbs. pres[...] 7½ cts. per ft.; ¾-in. not guaranteed, 4¾ [...] per ft., 25 ft. lengths, ½c. per ft. more.

HOT-BED SASH New. Cypress, 3-ft.x6 ft., [...] 75 cts. up; glazed, com[...] from $1.90 up. Second-hand, in good cond[...] all glass in, $1.00 each.

GLASS New American 10x12 single [...] per box; 12x12 single $1.9[...] box; 10x12 $2.55, 12x12, 10x15 do[...] $2.65 per box; 12x14, 12x20, 14x14, double, [...] per box; 16x16, 16x18, $3.10 per box; 16x24 do[...] $3.25 per box. Second hand glass, 8 x 10, [...] double, $1.65 per box. Single $1.50.

Old material, ridge, plates, gutters, bars, [...]

Get our prices on New Gulf Cypress B[...]ing Material, Ventilating Apparatus, [...] White Lead, Putty, Paint, Points, etc.

METROPOLITAN MATERIAL CO.

1398-1408 Metropolitan Avenue, BROOKLYN

Mention The Florists' Exchange when

Chicago.

A. L. Glaser of Dubuque, Iowa, accompanied by his son, was in Chicago last week.

John Stuppy of the Stuppy Floral Co., St. Joseph, Mo., visited us last week.

Duncan Robertson of the Ernst Wienhoeber Floral Co., has returned from his vacation spent in Colorado and is most enthusiastic in his praise of the Centennial State.

The J. B. Deamud Co. are on hand with a fine assortment of dahlias and gladioli and a constantly improving grade of roses.

Weiland & Risch report their greenhouses at Evanston in excellent condition and the crop in all lines, which is now beginning to come in, carries out their assertion.

J. A. Budlong is getting in some fine flowers from the young Beauty stock.

Vaughan & Sperry are receiving seasonable roses of exceptionally good quality for early September.

Zech & Mann are holding up well on their asters and are receiving carnations in plenty which, though still short-stemmed, are very creditable.

There is probably no more strenuous worker in Chicago, no man more closely devoted to his business, than George Reinberg, and it is with pleasure that we hear that he is about to take an outing to be spent in South Dakota.

F. F. Benthey went from Dayton to the Benthey-Coatsworth greenhouses at New Castle, Ind., and on his return to this city said he could not have wished to find their stock in a more satisfactory condition.

Anton G. Then while pursuing his duties at the greenhouse on Sunday, August 26, had the misfortune to step on a rusty nail and, a few days later, required the services of a physician to relieve his suffering. At last reports he was on the road to recovery.

Bryan Belcher of the George Reinberg greenhouse force is among the latest additions to the benedicts, having last week married Miss Blanche Garland, a daughter of the foreman at Jos. A. Seaman's establishment in Washington, Penn., who was formerly located in North Chicago.

Theo. Fabrucius, the well-known Lincoln avenue mushroom expert, had a narrow escape last week when a bale of hay fell on his back knocking him to the floor of the stable. After recovering consciousness he rapidly recuperated and the next day was about as usual.

Secretary of Agriculture James Wilson was at the Auditorium Hotel last week and received calls from several prominent horticulturists from this vicinity.

H. E. Philpott of Winnepeg, Manitoba, left Dayton and attended the meeting of the Canadian Society at Toronto, returning to Chicago on Friday of last week. If there is any thing of interest to a florist that gets by Brother Philpott, it must pass in an air ship.

R. H. Warder, superintendent of Lincoln Park, is about again attending to his duties after an illness extending over several weeks.

C. L. Washburn was telegraphed for the next day after he reached Dayton and, after the important matters were straightened out, he left for a hunting and fishing trip into Canada.

Wietor Brothers report an unusually large call for field-grown carnation plants of which their stock is, if possible, better than in previous years.

A recent call at Peter Reinberg's houses found everything in the most promising condition and, without making any derogatory comparison, it is safe to assert that handsomer young rose stock could not be found than that contained in the Foster avenue houses of their new specialty; Mrs. Marshall Field.

Harry G. Selfridge's collection of orchids, one of the finest in the West, has been forwarded from his Lake Geneva estate to the Lincoln Park greenhouses, where they will remain under Supt. Frey's care for the next few years, during the absence in London of the owner, where he is establishing a department store on American plans.

H. B. Sullivan of the Sunnyside Greenhouses, Rockford, this State, was in the city the first of the week.

The employees of the Poehlmann Bros. Co., with their families and friends, to the number of 200, enjoyed a picnic at Fink's Grove on Sunday last and, though the weather was slightly inclement, the occasion goes on record as a most delightful affair, all the sports, including races, bowling, music, etc., being most thoroughly enjoyed.

E. E. Pieser went to Pittsburg from Dayton, and from there proceeded through the Eastern cities, extending his tour into Canada.

Flint Kennicott had another severe attack of inflammatory rheumatism the latter part of last week, but was on deck attending to duty on Monday last.

Mr. and Mrs. J. B. Deamud left this week for an Eastern tour, their itinerary including New York, Saratoga, Philadelphia, Atlantic City and other points of interest, intending to be gone about two weeks.

L. H. Winterson and Mrs. Winterson are still touring in the East and report a most enjoyable trip.

J. B. Deamud Co. have received their first shipment of wild smilax and from now on will be prepared to supply all orders on reasonable notice.

Mr. and Mrs. George R. Scott, after leaving Dayton, spent a week touring neighboring States and, while in Indiana, Mr. Scott umpired three games of baseball.

Labor Day was quite generally observed in Chicago. As a rule, the retail stores kept their doors open through the usual hours, but the wholesale and commission men were nearly all closed by noon or shortly afterward.

P. J. Hauswirth, who has been entertaining a number of prominent members of the Improved Order of Red Men of different States for several days, left with the party on Friday for Niagara Falls, where the annual National conclave of the organization will be held.

Louis Coatsworth returned from New Orleans last Saturday and left this week again for Canada.

WILLIAM K. WOOD.

Philadelphia.

From present indications, it does not look as though this city will let up on its usual custom (the best for its guests), in entertaining the members of the S. A. F. next year. We have noticed the remarks in the Exchange on this question; this city has always been noted for its hospitality and it would be hard to abandon it, yet all interested can rest assured that the entertainment features will not retard in any respect the business of the convention. We are for the S. A. F. in every way and will do all we can to benefit the society. We cannot fail to bear in mind that if there had been no S. A. F. there would have been no Florists' Club here, as ours was the result of the organization of the trade, to prepare for the 1886 convention. Therefore, we stand by the parent organization, and will endeavor to render our hospitality on such lines as will benefit it still more.

Everyone is now home from the convention. Chas. E. Meehan was the last to arrive, coming in on Sunday. The Kasting and Beatty trophies were received on Tuesday, and are back in our show case, in the places they have occupied the past year. Even the Dayton people seemed to know their ultimate destination, as they took good care of the box we sent the trophies in, and shipped them back in it.

Will Rehder of Wilmington, N. C., was a visitor here on Tuesday.

The club meeting on Tuesday evening was well attended; the nomination of officers for the next year were as follows: President, Samuel S. Pennock; vice-president, Fred Hahman; treasurer, J. Wm. Colflesh; secretary, Edwin Lonsdale.

The evening was devoted mainly to the late Dayton convention. The subject for the next meeting will be a general discussion on the coming convention here in 1907. John Westcott presented the club with a portrait of H. B. Beatty and said it was a pleasure to have such a man as a member of our club, and as we now had the trophy presented by him, it was proper we should have his portrait to go with it. Thos. B. Meehan, as president of the club, accepted the gift, and a vote of thanks was given John Westcott.

Paul Klingspom, manager of the Rosary Flower Shop, 15th st., above Chestnut, will retire from that position on Saturday. Horace S. Dumont, the proprietor has, we understand, engaged Stuart McLean of Youngstown, Ohio, to manage the store; this young man is the son of Geo. McLean, formerly of this city.

L. R. Peacock of Atco, N J., is starting up a new dahlia business; he already has 15 acres in plants near Williamstown Junction, N. J., 2½ miles from his former farm at Atco.

DAVID RUST.

PORTSMOUTH, VA.—Messrs. D'Alcorn & Sons have received notice of a shipment of thirteen tons of daffodils, net weight without the cases, from their farm in England per S. S. Majestic. This is probably the largest shipment of daffodils ever sent to this country in one consignment. They are expecting several tons of narcissi and tulips to follow, having taken a farm at Portsmouth, Virginia, to plant the same. Mr. D'Alcorn has been very successful in this department in England, but thinks there is a much bigger future in this country. He traveled over 4,000 miles to find suitable soil and climate, and selected Portsmouth where he found a bulb farm already established. Although not exported with a view to sell he is advertising a few for sale as he would like them distributed over America, being anxious to know what State they are most adapted to.

OMRO, WIS.—The Omro Horticultural Society will hold a chrysanthemum show and fair, sometime in November next.

New York.

News Notes.

Last Monday (Labor Day), wholesale florists in the city closed their stores at noon, giving all hands a half holiday.

Next Monday, September 10, the New York Florists' Club will resume its annual monthly meetings after the summer vacation. Subjects for exhibition will be "Hardy Herbaceous Flowers," and it is hoped that a presentable showing will be made.

Several important things are to come before the members at this meeting, notably the report of the outing committee and the appointment of a nominating committee, and we shall, no doubt, be favored with short talks on the recent convention of the S. A. F. O. H. by the members of our club who were there.

The annual exhibition, of the Schwäbischer Sängerbund, which is being held this week in Ridgewood Park, is, we understand, to be the last exhibition of that society on those grounds. Ridgewood park will in all probability be cut up for building purposes before the time for the next annual meeting arrives.

The plant auction season will be opening shortly, and Mr. W. J. Elliott, the popular auctioneer of the firm of Wm. Elliott & Sons, 201 Fulton street, has been making tours among the growers of this vicinity, and expects to have a fine line of stock to be sold under the hammer during the coming season.

The authorities in Prospect Park, Brooklyn, had to draw a line at picnic parties for Labor Day, owing to the fact that the abuse of that privilege makes so much work for the park caretakers. Prospect park is one of the few places where "Keep off the Grass" signs are conspicuous by their absence, but it would seem of late that picnic parties have left so much refuse after them that something had to be done.

E. H. R. Green, a son of the richest woman in the world, Mrs. Hetty Green, is, we understand, going into the rose growing business on a large scale. Mr. Green has been spending some time at Cromwell, Conn., making a study of floriculture generally, and will likely locate somewhere in that locality.

The vacation season is drawing to a close, and the general home-coming of city dwellers is on. This means that the flower business will begin to improve in the near future.

G. F. Neipp, Aqueduct, N. Y., who recently sold his property there to the city of Brooklyn, has purchased six acres of land, on which are two greenhouses, at Chatham, N. J., and will locate there in a few weeks. On his newly acquired property, Mr. Neipp will add another greenhouse this Fall and next Spring will erect several more large houses.

Boston.

The sale of choice of stalls at the Music Hall Market of the Boston Cooperative Flower Market proved very successful on Saturday last. Prices ranged from $75 for first choice down to $15; about 90 stalls were sold. The market has been changed and greatly improved recently so that there is ample room for both growers and buyers, who patronize it.

W. N. Craig, who has been confined to his home for the past few weeks is able to be around again with the use of a cane.

Galvin had a very fine decoration at King's Chapel for the Williams-Jackson wedding on Thursday. Hydrangeas and clematis paniculata were both effectively used in large quantities.

The market of the Waban Rose Conservatories, on Somerset st., has been overhauled and repainted to a lighter color, giving it a very attractive appearance.

J. J. Slattery, of Galvin's, started on his vacation this week, visiting Atlantic City and Philadelphia, where he will look up the latest methods in vogue in his line.

NORTH ABINGTON, MASS.—Sidney Littlefield has purchased a 45-horse power boiler, which he will install in his new greenhouse.

Detroit.

Trade has been slow the past few weeks. Asters are small and poor, and good roses are scarce, especially Bride and Bridesmaid. But, at the same time, Detroit growers are very busy: Gust. H. Taepke has just finished an addition to his already large McClellan avenue plant; John Breitmeyer's Sons have added two houses to their Mack avenue establishment, and Frank Holznagle is also erecting three new houses and a boiler shed; B. Schroeter is just completing the installation of a new boiler. The Michigan Cut Flower Exchange has painted the floor of their parlor red, in anticipation of the red-hot discussions that the florists' Club will hold there after October.

Mt. Clemens florists have been awakened to the value of the Holly-Castle Circulator as a fuel saving device.

E. A. Scribner and wife have just returned from a prolonged trip through Cincinnati and Columbus.

HARRY.

Wholesale Prices of Cut Flowers, New York, Sept. 6, 1906

Prices quoted are by the hundred unless otherwise noted

Roses — A. Beauty, fancy—special	10.00	to	20.00
" extra	5.00	to	6.00
" No. 1	4.00	to	5.00
" No. 2	3.00	to	4.00
" No. 3	1.00	to	1.50
Bride, Maid, fancy—spe'l	3.00	to	4.00
" extra	2.00	to	3.00
" No. 1	1.00	to	1.50
" No. 2	......	to	.50
Golden Gate	1.00	to	......
Liberty	......	to	......
Mme. Abel Chatenay	......	to	......
Adiantum	.50	to	.75
Croweanum	.50	to	1.00
Asparagus	25.00	to	50.00
" Plumosus, bunches	8.00	to	15.00
" Sprengerii, bunches	8.00	to	15.00
Asters	.25	to	3.00
Cattleyas	50.00	to	60.00
Daisies	......	to	......
Gladiolus	.50	to	1.00
......	......	to	......

Carnations — Inf'r grades, all colors	.50	to	1.00
Standard Varieties — White	1.00	to	2.00
Standard Varieties — Pink	1.00	to	2.00
Standard Varieties — Red	1.00	to	2.00
Standard Varieties — Yel. & Var.	......	to	......
*Fancy— (*The highest grades of standard var.) White	......	to	......
*Fancy — Pink	......	to	......
*Fancy — Red	......	to	......
*Fancy — Yel. & Var.	......	to	......
Novelties	......	to	......
Dahlias, per bunch	.05	to	.15
Lilies	6.00	to	8.00
Lily of the Valley	1.00	to	3.00
Mignonette	......	to	......
......	......	to	......
......	......	to	......
......	......	to	......
Pansies, per dozen bunches	......	to	......
Smilax	8.00	to	10.00
Sweet Peas, per bunch	......	to	......

Wholesale Prices of Cut Flowers—Per 100

Boston Sept. 4, 1906	Buffalo Sept. 4, 1906	Detroit Aug. 5, 1906	Cincinnati Sept. 3, 1906	Baltimore Sept. 3, 1906	NAMES AND VARIETIES	Milwaukee July 25, 1906	Phil'delphia July 24, 1906	Pittsburg Sept. 5, 1906	St. Louis Aug. 27, 1909
10.00 to 20.00	20.00 to 25.00	10.00 to 35.00	to	to	ROSES — A. BEAUTY, fancy—special	to 25.00	15.00 to 20.00	20.00 to 25.00	15.00 to 20.00
6.00 to 10.00	12.00 to 20.00	to	20.00 to 30.00	to	" extra	15.00 to 18.00	10.00 to 15.00	12.00 to 15.00	10.00 to 12.50
1.00 to 6.00	6.00 to 12.00	to	10.00 to 15.00	to	" No. 1	10.00 to 12.50	5.00 to 7.00	8.00 to 10.00	6.00 to 8.00
to	3.00 to 6.00	to	3.00 to 4.00	to	" Culls and ordinary	4.00 to 6.00	1.00 to 4.00	3.00 to 4.00	3.00 to 5.00
to	5.00 to 6.00	3.00 to 6.00	to 4.00	to	BRIDE, 'MAID, fancy-special	to 6.00	to	to 6.00	to
2.00 to 4.00	4.00 to 5.00	to	2.00 to 3.00	to 4.00	" extra	to 5.00	6.00 to 8.00	to 4.00	to
1.00 to 2.00	3.00 to 4.00	to	1.00 to 2.00	to 3.00	" No. 1	to 4.00	4.00 to 5.00	to 2.00	to
.50 to 1.00	2.00 to 3.00	to	to	to 2.00	" No. 2	to 2.00	2.00 to 3.00	to	to
to	to	4.00 to 8.00	to	2.00 to 4.00	GOLDEN GATE	4.00 to 6.00	4.00 to 8.00	to	2.00 to 4.00
1.00 to 6.00	3.00 to 7.00	to	to	2.00 to 4.00	K. A. VICTORIA	4.00 to 5.00	4.00 to 6.00	4.00 to 12.00	2.00 to 6.00
1.00 to 6.00	3.00 to 7.00	to	to	2.00 to 3.00	LIBERTY	4.00 to 6.00	3.00 to 6.00	to	to
to	3.00 to 6.00	4.00 to 10.00	to	to	METEOR	to	to	to	to
to	3.00 to 5.00	4.00 to 10.00	to	2.00 to 3.00	PERLE	4.00 to 6.00	to	to	2.00 to 3.00
to	to	to 50.00	to	to	ORCHIDS—Cattleyas	to	to 50.00	to	to
to	.50 to 1.00	to	to	.50 to .75	CARNATIONS — Inferior grades, all colors	to 1.00	.75 to 1.00	.75 to 1.00	to .50
to	1.00 to 1.25	to 1.00	to 1.00	to 1.00	Standard Varieties — White	to 1.00	.75 to 1.00	.75 to 1.00	to .50
to	1.00 to 1.25	to	to 1.50	to 1.00	Standard Varieties — Pink	to 1.00	.75 to 1.00	.75 to 1.00	to .50
to	1.00 to 1.25	to	to 1.50	to 1.00	Standard Varieties — Red	to 1.00	.75 to 1.00	.75 to 1.00	to
to	to	to 3.00	to 1.50	to	Standard Varieties — Yellow and var.	to 1.00	.75 to 1.00	.75 to 1.00	to
1.00 to 2.00	1.50 to 2.00	to	to	to	Fancy Varieties — White	1.50 to 2.00	2.00 to 2.50	.75 to 1.00	.75 to 1.00
1.00 to 2.00	1.50 to 2.00	to	to	to	Fancy Varieties — Pink	1.50 to 2.00	2.00 to 2.50	.75 to 1.00	.75 to 1.00
1.00 to 2.00	1.50 to 2.00	to	to	to	Fancy Varieties — Red	1.50 to 2.00	2.00 to 2.50	.75 to 1.00	to
1.00 to 2.00	1.50 to 2.00	to 1.50	to	to	Fancy Varieties — Yellow and var.	1.50 to 2.00	2.00 to 2.50	.75 to 1.00	to
to	to	to	to	to	Novelties	to	to	to	to
.75 to 1.00	.50 to 1.00	to 2.00	to 1.00	to 1.00	ADIANTUM	to 1.00	to 1.00	1.00 to 1.50	to 1.00
to 50.00	to	25.00 to 60.00	35.00 to 50.00	25.00 to 50.00	ASPARAGUS, Plum. and Ten.	20.00 to 30.00	25.00 to 35.00	30.00 to 50.00	25.00 to 50.00
to	to	20.00 to 30.00	to 35.00	25.00 to 50.00	" Sprengeri, bunches	20.00 to 30.00	25.00 to 35.00	30.00 to 40.00	25.00 to 50.00
.50 to 1.00	.50 to 2.00	to	.50 to 1.50	to	ASTERS	.50 to 1.00	to	.50 to 2.50	1.00 to 3.00
to	8.00 to 10.00	to 10.00	to	6.00 to 8.00	CALLAS	to	to	to	to
to	to	.75 to 1.50	to	to	DAISIES	to .40	3.00 to 4.00	to	1.50 to 2.00
3.00 to 5.00	1.00 to 3.00	6.00 to 10.00	to	2.00 to 3.00	GLADIOLUS	to	8.00 to 12.00	2.00 to 3.00	to
to	to	to	to	to 10.00	LILIES, Harrisii	to 12.50	to	to	to
3.00 to 4.00	12.00 to 15.00	to	to 12.50	to	" Longiflorum	to 12.50	2.00 to 4.00	15.00 to 18.00	to
2.00 to 4.00	3.00 to 4.00	3.00 to 4.00	to 4.00	to	LILY OF THE VALLEY	to	1.00 to 2.00	2.00 to 4.00	to
to	to	to	to	to	MIGNONETTE, ordinary	to	to	to	to
to	to	to	to	to	" fancy	to	to	to	to
to	to	4.00 to 8.00	to	to	PEONIES	to	15.00 to 20.00	to	to
10.00 to 12.50	to 15.00	12.50 to 15.00	to 15.00	12.50 to 20.00	SMILAX	to 15.00	to	12.50 to 15.00	to 12.50
to	to	to	to	to	VIOLETS, ordinary	to	to	to	to
to	to	to	to	to	" fancy	to	to	to	to
to	to	to	to	to	NARCISSUS	to	to	to	.10 to .15
.15 to .25	.15 to .25	.50 to .75	to	to	SWEET PEAS	.25 to .50	to .50	to	to
to	to	to	to	to		to	to	to	to
to	to	to	to	to		to	to	to	to

FIRMS WHO ARE BUILDING.

PORTSMOUTH, VA.—D'Alcorn & Sons are building a greenhouse, 100x18 feet, for forcing bulbs.

OLYPHANT, PA.—E. J. Hull is building a new greenhouse.

HUNTINGTON, PA.—C. S. Fouse and W. S. Keith have purchased land at Mt. Union, and will start a seed and flower farm.

SACRED HEART, MINN.—W. Nichols, is erecting a large greenhouse, to be heated with steam. When completed, Mr. Nichols will engage in the florist business.

LEROY, N. J.—Wm. Barlow has installed a new boiler at his greenhouse establishment on Lathrop ave.

QUINCY, MASS.—Arnold & Johnson have removed to 1861 Hancock street.

GOSHEN, IND.—The Goshen Floral Company has moved to Washington street.

Edmonton, Canada.

From the Far Northwest.

Horticultural matters seem, like everything else, to be keeping right up to the times in this town of Edmonton, Province of Alberta, the most northwesterly of all the Canadian cities. We have now three up-to-date florists and there is probability of another at a very early date. Walter Ramsey is building five houses, 150x21-9 of the latest type of the King Construction Co. This block is practically finished, completion being delayed by non-arrival of a few minor parts from the East for the last house of the block. The house devoted to roses has been planted a month and the plants have grown magnificently. The black virgin soil of this part seems to suit all greenhouse plants to perfection. Carnations are doing fine; part of a house was planted from pots and part from plants from the field; these latter were of a size that I suppose would be called extras in the East, in fact they were almost too heavy. Chrysanthemums are growing very fast, and, in common with almost all plant life, are much dwarfer than in the East; the dwarfness is said to be caused by the altitude and the northerly location. One house will be devoted to lettuce and one to tomatoes the first season. The heating (low pressure steam) will be done by a "Florence" sectional heater.

Mr. Groos has quite an establishment on the old Ross place; he has several houses well filled with general lines and has this year added one house one hundred feet long; more would have been added were it not for the difficulty of procuring material. He has a splendid vegetable garden of several acres and is doing a rushing trade. Everything grown is of the highest grade, the seeds all being imported direct. Mr. Groos has a well appointed store on the main street in a central position.

Mr. Greenway, from London, Ont., has opened a growing establishment in the north end, corner First and Helmeck, and is growing a good assortment of popular plants. He is rather hampered for room at present, but says if business keeps on as it is, he will remedy this next Spring.

News has reached us that a well-known central Ontario florist is coming here to enter the business; we will be pleased to see him and wish him every success.

Generally Informative.

If a word about our city is permissible: the census of 1902 showed the city to have a population of 2300; the returns just out give a population for the city proper of between 12,000 and 13,000; this does not include the thousands that are living in tents and shacks of all sorts around the outskirts. Labor during the Summer, when the homesteaders are in, is plentiful and the best can be had for $2 a day. Building material and supplies of all kinds, owing to the building boom and distance from manufacturing centers, is very high priced. The cost of land in suitable localities is sky-high, for instance the ground covered by the five Ramsey houses (150x150) cost nearly $5,000. Coal is plentiful and at the mouth of the mine very cheap; the transportation, which has to be done by horse power at present, makes the cost higher than it otherwise would be. Vegetation of all kinds is very rank but dwarf. The growth and flower of common plants is all that could possibly be desired. For the sportsman, the locality is a paradise; wonderful stories reach us of success with the gun, and in the many lakes it is said fish are so plentiful that there is little sport in fishing. The climate during this Summer has been ideal: warm days and cool nights, with an occasional storm. There has been no damage from frost at present.

FRED BENNETT.

Wholesale Prices of Cut Flowers, Chicago, Sept. 5, 1906

Prices quoted are by the hundred unless otherwise noted

ROSES — American Beauty		
36-inch stems.........per doz.	.... to	4.00
30-inch stems........ "	.... to	3.00
24-inch stems........ "	.... to	2.50
20-inch stems........ "	.... to	2.00
18-inch stems........ "	.... to	1.50
12-inch stems........ "	.... to	1.00
8-inch stems and shorts "	.50 to	.75
Bride Maid, fancy special......	5.00 to	6.00
" extra........	4.00 to	5.00
" No. 1........	2.00 to	3.00
" No. 2........	.50 to	1.00
Golden Gate........	2.00 to	6.00
Carnot........	2.00 to	6.00
Uncle John........	2.00 to	8.00
Liberty........	3.00 to	8.00
Richmond........	2.00 to	8.00
Kaiserins........	2.00 to	8.00
Killarney........	3.00 to	8.00
Perle........	2.00 to	6.00
Chatenay........	2.00 to	6.00
Orchids—Cattleyas........	...... to	50.00
SMILAX........	8.00 to	12.00
LILY OF THE VALLEY........	2.00 to	4.00
DAHLIAS........	2.00 to	3.00

CARNATIONS		
Inferior grades all colors	.25 to	.50
STANDARD VARIETIES — White........	.75 to	1.00
STANDARD VARIETIES — Pink........	.75 to	1.00
STANDARD VARIETIES — Red........	.75 to	1.00
STANDARD VARIETIES — Yellow & var....	.75 to	1.00
*FANCY (The highest grades of Sta'd var) — White........	1.50 to	2.00
*FANCY — Pink........	1.50 to	2.00
*FANCY — Red........	1.50 to	2.00
*FANCY — Yellow & var....	1.50 to	2.00
NOVELTIES........	.... to	....
ADIANTUM........	.50 to	1.00
ASPARAGUS, Plum. & Ten........	.35 to	.50
" Sprengeri, bunches	.35 to	.50
GLADIOLUS........	2.00 to	6.00
LILIES, Longiflorum........	8.00 to	12.00
HARRISII........	8.00 to	12.00
AURATUM........	6.00 to	8.00
NYMPHAEA........	.... to	1.00
MIGNONETTE, ordinary........	1.00 to	2.00
TUBEROSES, SPIKES........	4.00 to	8.00
....	.... to	....
....	.... to	....
HARDY FERNS per 1000........	1.00 to	1.50
GALAX "	1.00 to	1.25
ASTERS........	.50 to	2.50

Newport, R. I.

Trade Notes.

Business was decidedly better during the latter part of last week than at any time during the Summer. The Horse Show at the Casino brought a great many visitors to the cottage colony where, in many cases, large dinners and elaborate entertainments were provided in their honor.

A Remarkable House and Table Decoration.

The most notable of these entertainments for various reasons, but chiefly because of the scale of magnificence on which the decorations were done, was the one given at Belcourt by Mrs. O. H. P. Belmont. In a forecast of this decoration, last week, in the Florists' Exchange, I announced that the work was entrusted to Joseph Leikens, and so it was understood at that time by the parties most directly interested, but "the best laid schemes o' mice an' men gang aft a-gley." Messrs. Wadley and Smythe finally got the job and completed it to the satisfaction of Mr. and Mrs. Belmont and to the delight of the guests.

The high ceiling was entirely covered with oak branches illuminated with myriads of small electric lights, the walls were covered with lattice work tacked behind which was green cheese cloth. Over the lattice work along the walls and arches, honeysuckle and other vines were tied in a manner that showed artistic conception of nature. These vines were supposed to have their roots embedded in soil in flower beds at regular spaces along the floor of the building and the beds were planted with dahlias, tuberous begonias, lilies, etc. At one end of the building, placed on high stone pedestals, were 12 of the largest orange trees procurable from Julius Roehrs, Rutherford, N. J.; these, with their own fruit and many more that did not belong to them, looked gorgeous, brightened by electric lights. Lilium speciosum rubrum was used in large numbers along the walls as backgrounds for dwarfer plants in the beds. Asparagus plumosus was also used in immense quantities in relieving the heavy effect of the oak branches.

There were ten tables set, on each of which was placed a very large center piece; four of these were made up tree shape, by being constructed in a frame of heavy wire on which the flowers and green were wired with regular florists' wire; these were certainly gorgeous when done with Killarney roses, and not far behind these were two done in the same style with Allamandas. But gorgeous and beautiful as were these, they were not more effective than two very large center pieces of Killarney and Bride roses, constructed in a somewhat different way: first about a hundred of the longest-stemmed roses were put in a silver vase, then about 50 short and medium stemmed flowers were tied to long wires, along with asparagus plumosus, and then placed among the other roses in the vase; the result was something stunning, especially so was the piece made of Killarney with upwards of two hundred flowers in its construction. In the middle of the room there was a large stone vase with a base forming a receptacle for growing plants; the top vase was filled with water lilies and the base with anthuriums.

Killarney roses were seen everywhere, and made use of in every conceivable way, and it has to be said of them that in masses, under electric light, they are unsurpassed in brilliancy of color and adaptability to various forms of decoration.

Mr. Smythe had a large force of men for several days engaged on the work, and the evening of the entertainment there were about twenty men there, among whom I noticed Mr. Albert Wadley and Mr. Edward Roehrs; the latter is spending his vacation in the congenial employment of Messrs. Wadley and Smythe.

D. M.

Syracuse, N. Y.

All the florists here are very satisfied with this Summer's trade, and look forward to a large call for the Fall and Winter, and are preparing themselves accordingly. There is a large increase in the planting of Romans and Paper Whites. Asters have, on the whole, been far from satisfactory this Summer.

After an absence of two years in England, it is a great pleasure to be back again with old friends and the first place I visited was that of L. E. Marquisee. Here I found everything in splendid condition; it has been my good fortune to be intimately acquainted with Mr. Marquisee for seventeen years, and I can truthfully say that I have never seen a more thrifty and promising stock than at the present time; his carnations are all that one could desire, not a sign of rust or disease; all are now benched. The varieties most largely planted are Lady Bountiful, Flamingo, Enchantress, Mrs. Patten, White Lawson, Mrs. Lawson, and one house 18x300 feet, planted with seedlings some of which are of great promise, and there is no doubt that several of them will give a good account of themselves.

C. Foederer, who has taken the Quigley houses, specialises in carnations; the following are his favorites: Enchantress, Marquis, Fair Maid, Queen Louise, Lawson.

Bard & Davis, the last florists to enter the lists, are very much encouraged with their success. Their four houses are of the most up-to-date pattern, the construction being light and strong; the glass is all 24x18, butted. They are now installing a new Scotch marine boiler of 75 h. p., which will be coupled on to the one in present use in case of a break-down.

Bob Bard is well-known as a rose specialist, and the varieties most largely planted are: Bride, Maid, Richmond, Perle and Hoste. Lilies are extensively grown here, and I noticed a fine batch of longiflorum, also of Valley in bloom.

It is always a pleasure to visit Gus Bartholme, for his compact place is neatness itself. In roses, Bride, Maid, Richmond, Ivory and Perle are chiefly grown; in carnations, Marquis he considers one of the most profitable; Lady Bountiful, Enchantress, Fair Maid, Queen Louise and Red Sport are also grown. Mr. Bartholme, with his wife, attended the convention at Dayton and was greatly pleased with all they saw and heard; in the future they will attend every one that is within easy distance.

The Wheadons, on Warren st., are greatly pleased with their Summer trade, which has been beyond their most sanguine expectations; funeral orders have been plentiful and large.

The New York State Fair will be held at Syracuse, September 10 to 15; it is expected the show of flowers will surpass any previous exhibition.

H. Y.

Fadeless Sheet Moss.

Last season I plunged in moss quite largely (for me) and after a couple of months I found that, instead of having a supply of nice green moss, such as I advertised to ship, I had quite a lot of russet which was practically worthless. This led to experiment on my part with dyes, restoratives, preservatives, etc., with the result that I finally found a combination restorative and preservative which gave the results you observed at the Dayton Convention. This combination I have filed a caveat on and will perfect its protection by letters patent as soon as possible.

The moss is chemically treated (not dyed) on scientific principles and is, in effect, perpetuated. The advantages are many, the most obvious of which is that it assures the florist of a perfectly natural green sheet moss, one that will keep indefinitely and at a price (when the waste in the ordinary grades sheet moss is taken into consideration) that is practically the same. It is much lighter for shipping, much cleaner, and there is no waste at all. To apply a very vulgar comparison to a very beautiful business, this moss is as staple as sugar or salt and, to our particular trade, quite as essential.

Ala. E. A. BEAVEN.

Frost Proofing Water Tanks.

(42) Will you kindly tell us the best method to make our outside tank frost proof? The tank is elevated about 15 feet, has 2000 gallons capacity; is 7 feet in diameter and 7 feet high. We would like to use it all Winter. LEBANON GREENHOUSES.

—Manufacturers of water tanks have various ways of frost proofing tanks outdoors we are not familiar with; but, in our experience, these methods are expensive, and we do not think you would care to tackle them. The best way we know of is to build a house about the tank, making it as weather or wind proof as possible. This should be done with double boarding at the very least, having paper between the boards. It is generally advisable to leave space enough between the tank and walls, so that a man may get around to make repairs, if such should be needed. We have seen tanks, many of them, kept from freezing in Winter by simply allowing water to be pumped into them steadily at night, and running the overflow back to the well again. Of course, in this case, we refer to instances where wind pumps were used and no expense was incurred for motive power; in most of such cases a top was put on the tanks. In very cold sections of the country we have seen it necessary to put a little heat around the tank, that is a coil of pipes, but this would be done only when the heat could be conveniently carried there from the heating apparatus of the greenhouses or dwelling house. The protection of the pipes leading to and from the tank, is, of course, the main consideration, as this is where the greatest part of the trouble comes in. These pipes should be incased in not less than two thicknesses of one-inch hair felt, covered with canvas. It is well also to put a layer of paper between the layers of felt; three thicknesses are very often used. A wood box should be built outside of this covering, leaving an air space of from one to two inches between the wood and felt.

U. G. SCOLLAY.

Too Much Tobacco.

(43) E. F. H., Del. The small insect with the chrysanthemum leaves was too badly crushed for identification. Whatever the insect might be, however, we could not find that he had done any damage to the leaves, which seem to be scorched as though they had been fumigated too heavily with tobacco.

Probably Thrip.

(44) I send you some chrysanthemum leaves; tell me, please, what kind of an insect is eating them and the remedy for same. Otherwise my plants are in a healthy condition and free from aphis. J. S.

—The chrysanthemum leaves seem to have been punctured in one or two places, probably with thrip, but, as the plants are healthy otherwise, a strong force of water, applied occasionally, will keep them clean.

Wallflowers for Winter.

(45) What is the best way to bring wallflowers in as cut flowers for Winter? My plants are two feet high, well branched and healthy; they are planted out in hot beds.

WOMEN FLORISTS.

—We would advise transferring the wallflowers to the greenhouse just before severe cold weather arrived, disturbing the roots as little as possible. Keep the house rather cool; say not over 50 degrees at night; and the plants free from aphis; they should commence to flower in the early part of the year.

Lang's Weeder.

(46) Please inform me of the name and address of manufacturers of the much advertised "Lang's Weeder?" T. F.

—Perhaps some dealer will supply the desired information.

Insurance Against Hail.

(47) Would you kindly inform me where I could insure our greenhouse glass against hail. It is all 16x24 double thick. P. S.

—The Florists' Hail Association, whose advertisement will be found in this issue, was organized especially for insurance of greenhouse glass against loss from hail storms. Write for particulars to its secretary, John G. Esler, Saddle River, N. J.

Utica, N. Y.

Trade is good for this time of year. Roses are improving in quality; Kaiserin, Liberty and Maman Cochet are fine and good keepers. We are getting very good asters from the western part of the State. Spencer & Martin are showing good quality Enchantress, also the new bright pink carnation Enchantress with fair length of stem. Gladioli sell well. Carnation planting is completed; Robert Boyce has some extra fine plants and so has Dr. W. A. Rowlands; it looks as if we shall have all we will want the coming Winter, especially of Enchantress. A number of wedding orders are booked for September.

Harry Brandt, of Brandt Brothers, is very sick at the hospital; it is the wish of all the florists that he will soon recover.

H. G. Martin and wife have returned from their wedding trip to Ohio.

Besides the outing on July 17, our club has had the pleasure of enjoying a beefsteak supper and camp fire treat, given by one of our best members, Theo. Schesch, at Ilion, New York, on August 31. At 6 p. m. about thirty members took the trolley to Ilion, fifteen miles East of Utica, where we were met by Mr. Schesch and his son, and escorted to the upper part of the town where the Beefsteak Club has a fine camp house in the woods. After a plentiful feast, we gathered round the camp fire and compared notes, meanwhile being entertained by songs by Harry Bishton, of Ilion, who was encored by long and hearty applause. At midnight, after three cheers for Brother Schesch, we departed on our homeward journey down the hill and through the woods, and Mr. Schesch's novel entertainment will not be forgotten. Mr. Schesch has almost recovered from the operation on his eyes.

J. C. Spencer left on Wednesday for his camp at Otsego Lake.

At this writing, Labor Day, we are having a much needed rain.

QUIZ.

Cincinnati.

August, as was to be expected, did not contribute much for the florist, with the exception of giving him time to take a vacation and attend the S. A. F. O. H. convention. The Dayton boys gave us all they promised, even to a hot old time. Quite a number of the craft passed through the Queen City, but, as I was taking a little vacation myself, I did not get a chance to see them. Business for September is starting out fairly well, and we hope it will continue. The writer is getting some good Beauty now and asters are holding out fairly well. American Beauty, of medium length, are selling at $1 per dozen. Brides and Bridesmaids are still small and 2 to 3 cents is about the limit. Asters and gladiolus are selling at 50c., $1.00, $1.50 and $2.00 per 100, and the market is well supplied. Labor Day did not cut any figure in the business.

Gus Bruner and wife are spending a few weeks at Clark's Lake, Mich. Julius Baer is wearing a broad smile; it's another boy. W. K. Partridge is very busy getting in shape for the Fall Festival Show, which takes place September 6; he will put up a fine exhibit. Baer and The Walnut Hill Floral Bazaar had the decorations for the opening of the Olympic Theater, September 2. E. G. GILLETT.

St. Louis.

Visitors the past week were Mr. Fancourt who sells ribbons for S. S. ennock of Philadelphia.

F. J. Farney is making his first trip or A. L. Randall Company, Chicago, elling florists' supplies.

C. A. Kuehn returned home on uesday of the past week after a few ays stay, at his old home in Deroit, visiting his parents.

Mr. and Mrs. F. C. Weber are pending a week at French Lick prings, Ind., since the Dayton Conention. They are expected home on Vednesday of this week.

Mr. and Mrs. Theo. Miller, George Valdbart, Mr. and Mrs. Meinhardt, Miss Tillie Meinhardt, A. S. Halsted nd Fred Ammann are all back from he convention after spending a few ays at points outside of Dayton. They all had a good time.

William Hucke, who makes his ome in Belleville, and late with Poehlmann Brothers, Chicago, has aken a position with the Muskogee Carnation Company at Muskogee, . T. Will is well known among the rade who wish him luck in his new osition.

The Florists' Club meeting will be held on next Thursday afternoon at 3 o'clock in its regular meeting hall on Grand avenue. This will be a most important meeting. A new set of officers will be installed to take charge of the club affairs the coming year. The only two old officers holding over are Carl Beyer and F. A. Weber, trustees. President Ammann, who will vacate the chair to Prof. H. C. Irish, the president-elect, hopes for a large attendance. Messrs. Schray and Guy will lead discussions which will be interesting to all members. There will also be eight applications for membership to be acted upon.

Frank Buckstat, prominent in the retail business here, has taken a position with Ostertag Brothers on Washington avenue. Henry Ostertag, of this firm, reports a number of large orders booked for Fall openings for this month.

George Angermuller is a happy father again; this time it's a girl; George reports mother and child doing well, and he is attending to the wants of the trade as usual.

Mr. L. H. Read, general manager of the Southern Floral Nursery Company of Fruitdale, Ala., was a visitor the past week.

Gustave Eggeling of the Eggeling Floral Company, has returned from his trip to Milwaukee, at which place he had a good time at the Eagle's Convention; Gus always has this wherever he goes.

Shaw's Garden held its second and last Sunday opening of the year last Sunday; the crowd was as large as usual. The St. Louis public always takes advantage of this great Sunday treat provided for by the late Henry Shaw, who stated in his will that the Garden should be open only on two Sundays in the year, the first in June and September.

As the season will soon open, a big general meeting of all florist bowlers will be called at the Palace Alleys, Monday night, to organize a Florists' League of three or four teams to bowl once a week. Suitable prizes will be hung up for the members of each team. Twenty-six names were presented Monday night, and these will receive notice of this big meeting. None but florists are eligible to join this league. ST. PATRICK.

Toronto.

Business has picked up considerably, and, with the opening of the exhibition this week, there is likely to be a continuation of this same pleasant state of affairs.

There are already enough plants in place in the Horticultural Building to assure a good show, and there is also a long list of entries to be heard from.

A quantity of good cut stock is coming in now; roses are improved very much; the American Beauty offered are fairly good, and the new cut of other roses is of fair quality and plentiful. A few carnations are offered but they are not extra good. Asters are of fine quality and plentiful. Gladioli are of exceptionally fine quality this season. Large quantities of perennials are offered.

The recent visit of the British Medical Association made things lively, and most of the boys got a share of the business going.

About twenty members turned out at the meeting of the G. and F. Association, August 21, owing to the extreme heat. President W. Wilshire was in the chair. The delegates to the Ontario Horticultural Exhibition reported arrangements for the Fall show in a very satisfactory condition. The secretary was instructed to send a letter of condolence to the widow of the late James Hartshorne. Mr. Hartshorne was well known here, and we feel as though we have lost a personal friend. Many kind words were said of him by the members and earnest sympathy expressed for his widow and children.

THOS. MANTON.

Cromwell, Conn.

The Connecticut Dairymen's Association, by invitation of A. N. Pierson, held a field meeting in Cromwell on Wednesday, September 5, that was largely attended and much enjoyed by those present. The guests began to arrive by teams and cars about 9:30 a. m., and were soon scattered over the place examining the greenhouses and barns. The dairy barn, equipped with the latest approved machinery, and with its herd of about one hundred cows, attracted a great deal of attention. Much interest was shown in the recently adopted method of milking by machinery. Mr. Pierson is growing about forty acres of corn for his two silos, which have a capacity of 500 tons. At 11.30, R. E. Buell, Director for Tolland County, gave a practical talk and illustration of the dairy cow. Lunch was served on the lawn fronting the greenhouses, at 12.30. Here, under the beautiful Maple trees, that make the center of the town so attractive, tables had been erected. After full justice had been done to the refreshments, Mr. Pierson welcomed his guests in a few well chosen words. The response was by H. O. Daniels, president of the association. Prof. L. A. Clinton, of Storrs Agri. College, then gave an address on "Soil Underdraining." Prof. E. H. Jenkins, of the Agri. Expt. Station, New Haven, talked on "The Corn Problem of Connecticut." The exercises closed with an address on "The Value of a Milk Record in Financing the Dairy Cow," by A. J. Pierpont, New Haven County Director. Cromwell and Mattabessett Granges, assisted in the entertainment. Interesting discussions followed the different addresses. H.

Indianapolis.

Cooler weather has brought with it brighter prospects of business. Funeral work has been very satisfactory for this season and all high grade stock is in demand. A few small weddings have also helped to break the monotony.

Roses are becoming more plentiful, but the quality is still a serious question when confronted by a customer who understands the possibilities of a rose. Carnations with stems 6 to 8 inches in length are numerous at 75c. per 100. Gladiolus are much used at $1 to $2 per 100.

Asters are improving again, and are more plentiful. $2 is the highest price for them, but the bulk is sold at $1 per 100. Cold storage Lilium longiflorum sell readily at $2 per dozen.

Field flowers are to be had in variety and quantity. The revenue obtained from these is not great, but they give variety to a retailer's stock, and are very appropriate for window trimming. Clematis paniculata and the hardy hydrangeas are particularly useful for this purpose.

Tomlinson Hall market reports a very quiet business the past week.

I. B.

HEATING.

Growers' Problems Solved by U. G. Scollay.

I have two greenhouses, each 16 feet wide, no wall between. Can I heat these houses by hanging 2-inch pipes on each wall and on the post in the middle to get from 52 to 56 degrees? If so, how many pipes (2-inch) would it require for water or steam? I have also one greenhouse, 10 feet wide. I wish to hang 2-inch pipes also on the walls of it. How many pipes would it require to heat that house to 56 degrees. F. G.

—Each of the 16-foot houses will require nine lines of 2-inch pipe for hot water, while the 10-foot house will take six lines same size pipe. These can, of course, be hung to posts by means of cast iron hook plates made for the purpose. You do not give the length of the houses, so it is hard for me to tell whether you should arrange your pipes so that each coil may be fed from a single 2-inch opening or not. Personally I do not usually allow, in my own installations, the feeding of more than 350 feet of 2-inch pipe from one opening 2-inch. If your houses are 150 feet long, I would suggest that you make a five-pipe side, into a two and a three-pipe coil. This will cost you more, but you will get better results. Should you determine to use steam, your houses will require six lines of 1¼-inch pipe in each of the two 16-foot houses and four lines, same size pipe, in the 10-foot house.

U. G. SCOLLAY.

Enclosed we send you a rough ground sketch of our place. When we started we installed a 25 h. p. boiler in the cellar under the shop, which worked well. Having made an addition, and expecting to make a further one, we put in a Scotch marine boiler of 75 h. p.; and having been advised by many in the craft to keep it above ground, we have done so. Now the problem is which is better—a trap or engine to inject the return water—and where should such be placed? We have a water pressure of 90 pounds. Also, can we still feed the coils without running an overhead pipe? B. D.

New York.

—From the very meager information you give, we can but give you a corresponding reply. We have used both traps and pumps with receiving tank, and find either to fully answer the requirements. In our own case, where we had a valuable outfit dependent on the working of mechanical means for returning condensation to the boiler, we are frank to say we would have both appliances. Should either go wrong temporarily, the other would be in readiness for use. As to pump and receiver, they can be procured from any good pump manufacturer. You will find in the advertising columns of The Florists' Exchange suitable traps offered. We cannot in fairness to such advertisers discuss the merits of various makes of goods in their line. I should say decidedly, your best plan is to run the overhead mains, keeping the steam as dry as possible until delivered to the coils. I might say, further, a low pressure gravity return steam job is considered the simplest. Had I had the chance you seem to have had with a deep cellar, I think I would have given some preference to that position for my boiler. However, you may have had some obstacles in the way, which are not clear to me from your letter.

U. G. SCOLLAY.

CONTENTS AND INDEX TO ADVERTISERS, PAGE 315

Seed Trade Report.

AMERICAN SEED TRADE ASSOCIATION

Henry W. Wood, Richmond, Va., president; C. S. Burge, Toledo, O., first vice-president; G. B. McVay, Birmingham, Ala., second vice-president; C. E. Kendel, Cleveland, O., secretary and treasurer; J. H. Ford, Ravenna, O., assistant secretary.

During the calendar year 1905, the value of the bulbs exported from Bermuda to the United States was $27,153.

Farmers' Bulletin No. 91 of the U. S. Department of Agriculture is devoted to the subject of "Potato Diseases and their Treatment," by Dr. R. T. Galloway.

ORANGE, CONN. — Watson S. Woodruff, the well known seed grower, is president of the Orange Fair Parade.

COLUMBUS, O.—On account of continued ill health, F. G. Johnson has resigned his position as secretary of The Livingston Seed Company, but it is understood still retains his stock in the concern. Josiah Livingston was elected to fill the vacancy.

B.

COUNCIL BLUFFS, IA.—A local newspaper says that the Shugart-Ouren Seed Company will this year raise over 100 acres of seed corn for the market. The firm was established in 1893. T. J. Shugart is president; F. R. Davis, vice-president; J. P. Davis, secretary; C. G. Ouren, treasurer.

MONTICELLO, FLA. — The weather conditions have been so unfavorable, that the melon seed crops will be very short, some fields a complete failure, and melons very shy of seed. As a whole, it has been the most unfavorable season I have ever experienced. D. H. GILBERT.

UNION, N. J.—The purchase of the Yellow Pine Company's property on the Hoboken shore front by the American Warehouse and Trading Company, which is the Eastern branch of the Albert Dickinson Company, seed growers of Chicago, is the largest real estate deal consummated this Summer.

CHICAGO.—Lowell Emerson, representing the Western Seed and Irrigation Company of Fremont. Neb., has spent a number of days in calling on his friends in this city.

Holland and other bulbs are now the great attraction at Vaughan's Seed Store and the stock on hand appears to be particularly sound.

The mushroom season is now fairly open and Knud Gundestrup & Co. of 4273 Milwaukee avenue report a very satisfactory demand for their guaranteed spawn from which the results have always proven entirely satisfactory.

WATERLOO, NEB. — Vine seed crops do not promise so well as three weeks ago; some damage has been done the late plantings by aphis, but the principal damage is from rust. Cucumbers have suffered mostly, and will, at best, be a light crop; 150 pounds to the acre will be a big yield, while more acres will yield 100 rather than 150 pounds. Musk melon vines have stood up better than cucumbers, but the fruit setting is very light and the average will not be over 50 per cent. of a crop. Water melons, squash and pumpkins promise well, although the first named is not making a heavy fruit setting. Both sugar and field corn are in fine shape and will make an average yield of probably better quality than for two years past; very little damage to the ears, and it promises to ripen in good season.

J. C. ROBINSON SEED CO.

VETCH SEED.—The protest of Currie Brothers, Milwaukee, Wis., against the assessment of duty on vetch seed by the collector of customs at Milwaukee, has been sustained, on the authority of a previous ruling on this class of seed.

AMERICAN SEED TRADE ASSOCIATION. — The report of the twenty-fourth annual convention, held at Toledo, O., June 26-28, 1906, has been distributed by Secretary Kendel. It contains a stenographic account of the proceedings, lists of officers and committees, etc. A fine portrait of Ex-president Wm. H. Grenell forms an excellent frontispiece.

ADULTERATED SEEDS. — A black list containing the names of ten firms found to be adulterating seed offered for sale to the Department of Agriculture has been made public by Secretary Wilson. The Secretary's action was taken in accordance with the terms of an act of Congress which requires him to buy seed in the open market and to publish the names and addresses of firms that sell or offer to sell adulterated seed to the Department. Samples submitted were found to contain from 7 per cent. to 53 per cent. of adulterants, most in yellow trefoil. Of 352 samples of seed of alfalfa nearly one-half were found to contain seed of the destructive parasitic plant dodder, nine samples were adulterated with yellow trefoil and nine with bur clover.

It is a noticeable fact that one or more of the firms listed have previously been posted by the Department as selling adulterated seed.

SPURRY AND SERADELLA SEED.—The seed of field spurry or common spurry (Spergula arvensis) and of seradella (Ornithopus sativus) are free of duty under the provision for "all flower and grass seeds" in paragraph 656, tariff act of 1897, and are not dutiable under the provision for "seeds of all kinds, not specially provided for," in paragraph 254 of said act. Before the United States General Appraisers, New York, August 27, 1906, in the matter of protests of Henry Nungesser & Co. against the assessment of duty by the collector of customs at the port of New York, the following opinion was rendered by Waite, General Appraiser: The merchandise is the seed of the field spurry (Spergula arvensis) and of a plant described as "seradella," whose scientific designation is Ornithopus sativus. Duty was assessed at 30 per cent ad valorem under the provision for "seeds of all kinds not specially provided for" in paragraph 254 of the tariff act of 1897. It is claimed in the protests that the seeds are free under paragraph 656, exempting among other things "all flower and grass seeds."

Spurry belongs to the order Caryophyllaceæ, which includes the carnations and pinks. The following description is taken from the International Encyclopedia (vol. 18, p. 475):

Spurry is a weed sometimes cultivated as a forage crop. Corn spurry or common spurry (Spergula arvensis) is an annual from 6 to 12 inches high, producing a tangled mass of succulent stems with numerous whorled linear leaves. It prefers sandy or stony soil, upon which it is often planted as a green manure and as a soiling crop for sheep and cattle. * * * Giant spurry (Spergula maxima), by many botanists not regarded as a species distinct from the above, is similar to, but larger than, common spurry.

The seed of Spergula arvensis, or common spurry, was held to be free as grass seed in Board decision In re Nungesser, G. A. 2597 (T. D. 15020). In a later decision, In re Salzer Seed Company, G. A. 5422 (T. D. 24676), the Board seems to have been unable to find on the evidence before it that the seed of Spergula maxima, or giant spurry, was a grass seed.

The Ornithopi, according to Paxton's Botanical Dictionary, are leguminous plants.

The evidence in this case shows that common spurry and seradella are used for forage purposes in much the same way as sainfoin, vetch, and clover, and that they may fairly be classed with the so-called "artificial grasses" that are now included in the accepted definitions of the term "grass," given its common rather than scientific meaning. The question presented in this case is practically identical with that considered in some detail in Board decision In re Willett Drug Company, G. A. 6350 (T. D. 27306). We think the reasons stated in that ruling justify us in sustaining the protests and reversing the collector's decision, which dispositiou of the cases is accordingly ordered.

CROPS IN CANADA.—The Crop Bulletin of the Ontario Department of Agriculture for August, 1906, contains the following information:

PEAS.—For about five or six years the depredation of the pea weevil (commonly called the "bug") were so great that in nearly every section of the Province the acreage given to peas shrank to alarmingly small proportions. Last year, however, the weevil gave but little trouble to pea growers, and this season the pest is usually mentioned only to remark its absence. Some correspondents speak of mildew and injury from rain in low-lying places, and complaint is also made by some that the intense heat at podding time prevented the peas from fully developing; but the general tone of the reports is most hopeful, and the pea crop may be regarded as one of the best for years. Correspondents predict a larger acreage for next year.

BEANS.—The growing of beans as a field crop is confined chiefly to Kent and adjoining counties. The crop was not fully matured as correspondents wrote, but gave promise of more than an average yield per acre. The raising of beans for selling in a green state to canning factories is on the increase.

PARCELS POST FOR DENMARK AND AMERICA.—Acting Postmaster-General Hitchcock has signed a parcels-post convention with Denmark, to take effect on October 1. It provides for the exchange and transmission through the postal services of both countries of parcels which weigh no more than 4 pounds and 6 ounces nor measure more than 3 feet 6 inches in length and 6 feet in length and girth combined. The value of the parcels carried is also limited to $50. Postage must be prepaid in full at the following rates: In the United States, on parcels for Denmark, 12 cents for each pound or fraction of a pound. In Denmark, on parcels for the United States, 60 ore for a parcel not exceeding 1 kilogram in weight, and 1 krona for other parcels. A delivery charge not exceeding 5 cents in the United States may be collected of the addressees of each parcel. The parcels-post regulations applicable to parcels for Norway apply also to parcels for Denmark. Parcels-post mails for Denmark will be made up at the New York post-office.

NURSERY DEPARTMENT.

Conducted by Joseph Meehan.

MONROE, MICH.—The firm of Ilgenfritz & Sons has been reorganized. The stock of Charles A. Ilgenfritz has been purchased by his brothers, who will continue the business under the old name. Charles A. Ilgenfritz will follow the business along lines of his own specialty.

Cedrela Sinensis.

Editor Nursery Department:

Referring to your accounts of Cedrela sinensis, we are not informed of its hardiness. Philadelphia climate might answer when Chicago will not. What can you give us about this or must they be proved?

Ill. JAMES KING.

—The Cedrela is so hardy here that, without doubt, it will prove so much further north. It comes from China, and many trees from there thrive where the Winters are very severe. If the Ailanthus is hardy at Chicago, there is little doubt the Cedrela will prove so. It was at one time classed with the Ailanthus in a botanical way, but except in appearance of its foliage it is quite distinct.

Propagation of Blackberries.

Are blackberries propagated from root cuttings, if so when is the proper time and how is it done?

SUBSCRIBER.

—Blackberries are propagated from root cuttings. The roots are best taken off from large plants just before Winter sets in. They are cut into lengths of about three inches, and are then buried in slightly damp sand or soil and kept in a cool cellar all Winter. As soon as Spring opens they are set in rows outdoors. There is no need to set them upright, they may lie lengthwise in the rows. Old plants may be dug up and have nearly all their roots cut off, and then, with their canes cut back one half or more, they are still fit for planting.

Seasonable Topics.

The Christmas fern, Aspidium acrostichoides, is the one of most use to florists, but for planting purposes the A. marginale and A. spinulosum are excellent ones to use. All three are evergreen sorts and of rather large growth.

Pueraria Thunbergiana (Dolichos Japonicus) is in full flower in the early days of September. The vine requires to be of some years' growth before it flowers, but, after commencing it blooms every year. It is the fastest growing and most rampant of all hardy vines. The flowers are of a rosy crimson color.

A few years ago a disease attacked the white birch, Betula alba, and its variety, the cut-leaved weeping, as well as our native one, B. populifolia. It swept through the country, destroying all the trees in its path. It is a pleasure to add that it seems to have disappeared, the trees set out since thriving unharmed.

Cutting off the tap roots of hickories when in their seedling state is something that should be done. Even with the side roots this produces these trees are difficult to transplant safely. Either root pruning or transplanting should be done every year until finally planted.

Fruit growers of Delaware claim the Oldmixon peach to be one of the best sorts yet. It is of good quality, good appearance, and a sure annual cropper, and one of the best of free stones. It ripens the first week in September. Nurserymen find it one of the best to recommend to customers.

At this season of the year, with the soil in the moist condition it is, the transplanting of herbaceous plants is work well done. Such plants become established before Winter sets in; and the work done now lessens that which it is usual to do in Spring.

Gordonia pubescens is perhaps the most rare hardy small tree in cultivation. It likes a half shady place and heat and moisture in Summer. Its camellia-like flowers are produced from early August until frost. It can be increased from soft wood cuttings.

Inquiries have come as to the hardiness of the Ulex Europæus, the gorse or furze of Europe. It will not endure the Winters of Philadelphia even; and when seen there it is a pot plant or one that has been entirely covered in Winter.

Transplanting Oaks in Autumn.

With the close of September the planting of many deciduous trees may be proceeded with, as the stripping of the leaves, which would then be necessary, would not greatly harm the trees, certainly not to an extent that would be worth considering. Leaves have pretty well performed their duty by that time, and but little would be gained by letting them remain longer on the trees, not enough to set against the gain of early planting.

Oak trees, and other trees for the matter of that, do very well when set out early in Autumn and well planted, better even than when set in Spring, in many cases. To the usual advice as to good planting there are two other points to be well considered. The first is that the trees must be closely pruned; and it must be understood that in the case of oaks this means pruning them almost to bare poles. It will not do at all to set them out with a lot of side branches to them. There are other trees that may be pruned unnecessarily close, but the oak must be cut in close. The younger the tree the less is this rule necessary, but with oak trees of a caliper of from 2 to 3 inches, the side branches must be cut to within six inches of the main stem. But little of the leader need be cut back, perhaps none. This retains the height of the trees, and very soon new shoots will form, which will push with vigor; and in two or three years later there will be a tree of far more satisfactory appearance than there would have been if the close pruning had not been done.

There is another and a most important matter to be attended to in the planting of oaks in Autumn. This is to so cover the ground about them that no frost will get to the roots. Where soil, sand, ashes, or the like, is available, a heap of any of these piled around a tree is sufficient, and is one of the best of ways of preventing the entry of frost. Forest leaves will answer, but soil is better as, in addition to keeping out frost, it prevents the tree swaying about in winds, greatly to its advantage. This covering need not be applied until the advent of frost.

California Privet in Flower. Shrub Shape.

Pacific Coast Douglas Fir.

Last season a traveler for an Oregon party made the rounds of the Middle States endeavoring to sell seeds of the Douglas Fir, Pseudotsuga Douglasii, from the Oregon trees. He met with but little success, because he found that it was well understood here that this tree would not endure our Winters. It is a pity it will not, for it is of more rapid growth than the one from Colorado, besides having foliage of a darker green. It is more than likely that its ability to stand the cold of our Winters would be sufficient were it set in a position sheltered by other trees and yet such a one admitting of its wood thoroughly ripening, as is the case with many other trees.

However, as the Colorado one does not fear zero and even lower temperature, no great grief need be experienced because the Pacific one is not available for our use. As the Douglas fir extends in growth from California to Alaska, and, in some positions much colder than others, without doubt there are some trees the seeds from which would give us seedlings of sufficient hardiness for our climate.

Those unacquainted with the Colorado form of the Douglas fir, and of the several other fine evergreens from that State, should secure some for their grounds.

Wrapping Roots of Evergreens.

The welldoing of transplanted evergreens, which is evident to everyone the past five years, is nearly altogether due to the digging of them with a ball of earth and wrapping the ball in sacking. Whether evergreens live or die when transplanted depends altogether on whether baled at the root or not. The complaints that imported evergreens were unsatisfactory, in that they did not live, led foreign growers to adopt the system recommended to them of sacking the balls of every evergreen; and it is rare now for any shipper abroad to send evergreens in any other way. The few firms that do ship in the old way are losing their customers on this side of the ocean.

Our own nurserymen find it pays them well to tie up in burlap the roots of all evergreens sold, no matter if to go but a very short distance from home. There are two very important reasons for doing this. Evergreens will not live if their rooots become dry. Deciduous stock may recover, but the resinous nature of the sap of evergreens prevents its circulating again if it becomes dry. This is why it is imperative that the roots be moist always. The keeping of a ball of soil to the roots ensures the moisture and the non-disturbance of many of them, and the plant goes into the ground almost as from a pot or tub. Nurserymen who have not yet adopted the plan of wrapping up the roots should do so at once. The cost of burlap sufficient for a tree, with that of labor added, is but a few cents, the whole of which can be added to the cost of the trees with perfect satisfaction to the customers, as the gratification of having living trees almost to a certainty makes the slight additional charge of no moment to them.

California Privet as a Shrub.

As a hedge plant the California privet is so much in demand that its merits as an ornamental shrub are often quite overlooked. It is a very good subject to be added to a collection where customers call for one; and, even as a single specimen, it can be used to good advantage. In the vicinity of New York city, when it is set near dwellings and in partially protected places, it keeps green the whole year through—a true evergreen, a better evergreen than any other hardy privet.

It is frequently so used in this city and in other ones further south, the lustrous green of its foliage being greatly in its favor as adding to its desirability. It forms a dense bush, especially when pruned, which makes it just what is often desired near an entrance way to give the privacy required.

When grown as a hedge the flowering of the privet occurs so sparingly that, as a flowering shrub, it is rarely thought of. Yet it is quite desirable in a flowering way. The illustration presented with this gives some idea of what it does in the flowering way. There are times when the flowering is so profuse as to almost hide the foliage. There is a strong odor to the flowers, generally agreeable when one is not too close to the bush, but too powerful, many think, when close to it.

To have an abundance of flowers there must be but little pruning done in Fall or Winter, the privet being a shrub that flowers on the shoots of the preceding season, therefore belonging to the class that are to be pruned as soon as flowering is over.

Cockspur Hawthorn Hedge.

Cockspur hawthorn (Cratægus crus-galli) is one of our native thorns, noted for its sharp spines and for its glossy green leaves. Single specimens of it are often found standing in meadows, and in such positions they are usually of much symmetry and beauty.

In former times this thorn was used as a hedge plant, as it is yet to some extent. In a lane leading to the old Bartram Botanic Gardens, now Bartram Park, Philadelphia, there are the remains of an old hedge, and another one formerly existed in Germantown. It certainly makes a very pretty hedge, especially in its earlier years, when the plants are vigorous and well furnished with fresh young growth. There must be many a hedge of it planted, for those nurserymen who raise the plants by the thousands say their sales of it are very good.

It may be that were it not so thorny it would be planted even more than it is, for the greater number of the hedges of shrubs set out to-day are not for defensive purposes, but simply as boundary plants, and there is no particular call for a plant to be of a thorny nature. The cockspur thorn is very pretty when clothed with its fresh growth. The foliage is of such a lustrous shining green that it attracts attention at once. It needs close pruning, twice a year, to bring forward its young growth, for it is the fresh green of the young shoots that attracts the most. This thorn is not difficult to transplant. Set out early in Spring, and closely pruned, practically every plant will live.

JOSEPH MEEHAN.

LIST OF ADVERTISERS

INDEX TO STOCK ADVERTISED

Contents.

REVIEW OF THE MARKET

NEW YORK.—The extremely warm weather experienced since Saturday has been anything but beneficial to either the flower business or to the flowers themselves. Last week trade seemed to be improving, but the recent hot spell appears to have stopped all progress, and the market is again in a very Summery condition. Roses of al lthe staple varieties are increasing in numbers, but prices all around are weaker than was the case a week ago. There is an increase in the supply of carnations, but owing to the very warm weather they do not arrive in very good condition, and many of them go to sleep very quickly.

Gladioli are not quite so much in evidence as they were. There is still an abundant supply of asters, which, by the way, are not up to the quality of recent years, and are not averaging as good prices. The demand for dahlias is limited as yet; prices show no improvement over those of last week. Lily of the valley and longiflorum lilies are plentiful enough for the call. Tuberoses are coming in in quantity, but are difficut to dispose of.

CHICAGO.—The market continues in a semidormant condition notwithstanding the fact that high class goods are readily taken up at more than a fair price. But a surplus of goods of less than medium grade continues, which tends to hold prices down, especially as the shipping demand is still limited. There is practically no change in prices, except in special sales of specialties or very select stock, which we cannot quote as a standard. W. K. W.

PHILADELPHIA.—Another hot spell arrived here on Sunday last and continues. This has had a very depressing effect on the cut flower market. Much more stock is arriving and the demand has fallen off, consequently all kinds of flowers are piling up at the wholesale houses. American Beauty roses are being held at from $1 to $3 per dozen. Tea roses are selling slowly at from $2 to $5 per 100. Among out door carnations William Scott and Ethel Crocker are moving fair at $1.50 per 100. Dahlias are now arriving in large quantities, but the demand, so far, is very limited. Some single and fancy cactus varieties are selling at $1.50 and $2 per 100; for the other kinds there are no prices, it depends how badly a man wants the flowers. Lily of the valley has been going very well at from $3 to $5 per 100. Of the large quantity of outdoor stock now in Tritoma Pfitzeri is selling best at $3 per 100. Asters are becoming a glut; they sell at from 75c. to $1.50 per 100.

DAVID RUST.

BOSTON.—Market conditions continue to improve. Roses are much better in quality and prices have advanced somewhat. Carnations are more plentiful than they have been. Asters have shortened up in supply, and some of good quality are yet to be seen. Gladioli are abundant. Lilies are plentiful enough for all demands. Candytuft and feverfew still appear in quantity. Sweet peas are to be had in limited numbers but the quality is poor. All greens remain at the same prices.

J. W. D.

PITTSBURG.—Trade is beginning to pick up; the last week it was fairly good, but there is entirely too much stock coming in for the demand. Asters are very plentiful and of good quality, selling at from 50c. to $3 per 100; the latter are choice, mostly Semple varieties. Gladioli are thinning out. Roses are fair and seem to be plentiful; but carnations are somewhat scarce, although there is no great demand for them as asters are too plentiful.

E. C. R.

INDIANAPOLIS.—Trade has been given a general impetus by continued cool weather, and the beginning of the Autumn business has been satisfactory. Decorations seem in vogue earlier than in other years, and some of the greenhouses have an appearance which augurs well for a prosperous plant trade. Many boxes of flowers, the majority for the sick-room, are ordered, but outside of these, the demand for cut stock is light. Amateur growers have flooded the market with asters, which sell as low as 50c. per 100. Fairly good carnations are being received at 50c. to $1. In roses, Bridesmaid, Bride and Golden Gate may be had in any quantity at $4 to $6 per 100; Richmond and Liberty show much improvement and bring $5 to $7. American Beauty are plentiful and very satisfactory for funeral work and counter trade; $4 to $25 a 100 is the price. Dahlias are numerous, but the quality is yet to be improved. Quantities of gladioli, tuberoses and golden rod are seen at Tomlinson Hall market, but business there is reported quiet.

I. B.

ST. LOUIS.—Retail and wholesale trade is showing activity. Roses are coming in with improved foliage and blooms, but the stems are short; the price for select Bride, Bridesmaid, Richmond, Souvenir du President Carnot, and Perle des Jardins is $5 per 100; for other grades, $2 to $3. Select American Beauty bring $3 to $4 per dozen; others, 75c. to $2. This rose is of extra good quality just now, with an excellent demand. Carnations are none too good, the very best bring only $1 per 100; field-grown 50c. Asters, which are very plentiful, sell at 50c. to $2 per 100; tuberoses, $3. Dahlias are very fine this year, but not many are used. Long sprays of Clematis paniculata are employed extensively. Everything in greens is plentiful.

ST. PATRICK.

CHANGES IN BUSINESS.

GRAND FORKS, N. D.—E. W. Kneeland has purchased property here, will build a greenhouse, and embark in the florist business.

RACINE, WIS.—A. J. Fidler, the Asylum avenue florist, has again resumed charge of his greenhouses which he disposed of last year to Rudolph Mohr of Chicago.

WOONSOCKET, R. I.—Mrs. James A. Staples has removed her flower store from Staples' drug store to the old location of Miss Cutler in the E. R. Darling store. The flower business has outgrown the old location and in order to better attend the wants of the increasing trade the removal was made necessary.

FIRMS WHO ARE BUILDING.

BELFAST, ME.—Willis E. Hamil o is building a rose house, 32x62 feet.t n

XENIA, O.—J. J. Lampert is adding several houses to his establishment.

TACOMA, WASH.—Louis Tschunko ir erecting three greenhouses at South Fiftieth street and Pacific avenue. The buildings will be 100x20x6 feet.

WATERLOO, IA.—Charles Sherwood is making an addition, 32x42 feet, to his greenhouse plant. It will be devoted to palms and ferns.

STREATOR, ILL.—The six greenhouses which have been in process of construction by Charles Leuter and Vincent Kangley, are now complete. Each house is 20x120 feet.

WIGGINVILLE, MASS.—Swanson & Dillgren are building a new greenhouse, 200x30 feet, for the cultivation of carnations. The house will be heated by a 35-horse-power boiler.

ASHTABULA, OHIO.—The Ashtabula Greenhouse Company has begun the rebuilding of its entire plant on Bunker Hill, a d when complete the new buildings and equipment will represent an outlay of $4,000.

LEBANON, PA.—C. D. and D. H. Mish have added two greenhouses to their plant.

C. Yost is also erecting a new greenhouse, and installing a 40-horse-power boiler.

PITTSFIELD, MASS.—Richard C. Engleman and son, Max Engleman, florists, have bought the Davis place adjoining their property near the Pleasure Pa k, and will erect several new greenhouses.

STERLING, ILL.—J. A. Swartley, proprietor of the Sterling Greenhouses, has let the contract for the erection of an addition to the plant. The new house will be 200 feet long and 46½ feet wide. It will be used exclusively for carnations.

FURMAN BOILER LITERATURE.—The Herendeen Manufacturing Company of Geneva, N. Y., are distributing their catalogues of Furman boilers, handsome publications containing much valuable information on heating matters generally; also a list of testimonials from florist firms who have installed these well-known heaters.

WHITE MARSH, MD.—Thomas Vincent of Richard Vincent, Jr. & Son, has been confined to his home with a severe illness since September 3.

Plant Notes.

CROTONS should now have as much light as they can possibly stand in order for them to develop their coloring to intensity. Some varieties do not stand as much sunlight as others, which peculiarity can easily be noted and such plants given shade as long as necessary. For Christmas sales crotons in 5 and 6 inch pots are good stock to have, but specimens in larger sized pots hardly pay considering the care and room necessary for the growing of good shapely plants of large size. The color of crotons will be intensified and the plants otherwise benefited if plants having their pots full of roots are given liquid manure two or three times a week. Cow manure is the best and safest to use even with it, it is advisable to water the plants almost immediately thereafter with pure water. When the soil is very dry (a condition that should never exist with crotons in their growing season) they should not receive manue ,water. The plants ought to be moved and turned around frequently if grown closely together, in order that they may have a symmetrical appearance.

CYCLAMEN grown in frames will require a great deal more attention from now on, and it will be much safer in a week or two to remove them to a greenhouse where temperature and air will be more under control. It will be necessary to shade the glass over cyclamen plants, but good growers have a decided objection to a permanent shading. Some removable covering for the glass will easily suggest itself to the grower. Cyclamen plants 5-inch pots are always the most salable, and when the plants are properly attended to from start to finish, plants good enough for almost any purpose can be grown in that size pot. Cyclamens require very careful watering and airing. Although in their growing season they are not averse to a temperature of 55 to 60 degrees at night, they require to be near the glass in a house that can be properly ventilated. When in flower a temperature 5 degrees lower than that stated answers their requirements. M. I.

OUR LITTLE PET

From Aschmann in Philadelphia I bought
An Araucaria, a pet for our little girl;
Now we have two pets, the pride of our thought:
The little girl so sweet, a head full of curls,
And the Araucaria with its everlasting green,
A more joyful home you never have seen.

Watch us Grow!!

ARAUCARIA EXCELSA, the best of all decorative plants nature produces; a specialty. Every man in business life, to be successful, must adopt one thing as his specialty, and that specialty, whatever he may select, and of whatever nature it may be, he must guard, study and push to such an extent, that it not only benefits himself, but he must conduct it so, that every one who seeks his aid, service or his articles, whatever he advertises or practices, will **share a slice of his activity and prosperity.** I made the importation and cultivation of Araucaria as a special study in my life. The following figures will show you my success in business: In the first year I began with an import of 250; in the eleventh year (now 1906) my importation has grown up to 6,000 (come and see it). On account of the Araucaria growing yearly in favor as a much admired decorative plant for the arbor, bed room, dining and sitting rooms, stores, hotels, lawns and porches by the plant-consuming peoples all over the country, **the outlook** will be of an importation of at least 8,000 to 10,000 in the Spring of 1907. To secure this vast amount for 1907, I am now in Belgium making contracts for next year. I shall also at the same time bring over with me a large lot of choice Azalea Indica, Palms, etc. for Christmas and Easter forcing. No money will be spared in obtaining for my customers the cream of the Belgium greenhouses.

Please note lowest price now going for September:

ARAUCARIA EXCELSA

12 to 14 in. 5½ in. pots, 3 to 4 tiers, 2-yr. old, 50c. 14 to 16 in., 5½ in. pots, 3 to 4 tiers, 2-yr. old, 60c. 16 to 18 in. 5½ to 6 in. pots, 4 to 5 tiers, 3-yr. old, 75c. 18 to 20 in., 6 in. pots, 5 to 6 tiers, 4-yr. old, $1.00. 20 to 24 in. 6 in. to 7 in. pots, 5 to 6 tiers, 4-yr. old, $1.25. 36-40 to 50 in. 7 in. pots, specimen plants from $2.50 to $3.00 each.

ARAUCARIA COMPACTA ROBUSTA — have several thousand of them; can supply all wants. These plants were never so fine in shape and condition as this year. The set of the greenhouse, as broad as long, 12 to 20 in., in height, 3 to 4 perfect tiers, 20 to 30 inches across, 3-4-5 year old, 6 to 7 in. pots, $1.25, $1.50, $1.75, $2.00, $2.50 to $3.00 each.

ARAUCARIA EXCELSA GLAUCA — This variety on account of its beautiful Green-Bluish tiers, dwarf habit, fine compact shape, gives it a striking appearance, and anybody seeing them, must undoubtedly fall in love with them at sight. Plants, 6-7 inch pots, 3-4-5 perfect tiers, 3-4 year old, 15 to 25 inch high, from 15 to 30 in. across, $1.25, $1.50, $1.75, $2.00 to $2.50 each.

KENTIA BELMOREANA, 5½ to 6 in. pots, bushy, fine plants, from 75 cts. to $1.00 to $1.25 each.

KENTIA FORSTERIANA, 7 in. pots, made-up plants, 1 large in center, 3 smaller sizes, 22 to 25 in. high around, gives them a good appearance, $2.00 each. 6 in. pots, single plants, 35 to 40 in. high, 5 to 6 good leaves, 4 year old, $1.25 to $1.50 each; 6 in. pots, 30 to 35 in. high, 4 year old, 5 good leaves, $1.00; 5½ in. pots, 3 year old, 25 to 30 in. high, 5 good leaves, 75c. made-up plants, 3 and 4 in. pots, 18 to 20 in. high, 25 cts. to 30 cts. each.

ARECA LUTESCENS, made-up, 25 cts.

COCOS WEDDELIANA, 15 cts.

NEPHROLEPIS BARROWSII, 6 in. pots, strong, ready for 7-8 in., 50c. 4 in. pots, ready for 6-7 in., 25c.

NEPHROLEPIS SCOTTII, 6 in. pots, large, ready for 6-7 in. 50c.; 5½ in. pots, 40c.; 5 in. 35c.; 4 in. 20c. to 25c.

BOSTON FERNS, 4 in., 20c. to 25c. I have them by the thousand. 5 in; 30c. to 35c.

FERNS for dishes, a fine assortment, 2¼ in., $5.00 per 100; 3 in., $6.00 per 100.

FICUS ELASTICA, 6 in., 50c.

ASPARAGUS PLUMOSUS NANUS, 3 in., 6c.; 4 in., 10c.

PRIMULA SINENSIS, in 4 in., pots ready to shift; will bloom for Christmas. $100 per 100.

CASH WITH ORDER

When ordering, say whether the plants should be shipped in the pots or not

GODFREY ASCHMANN

Importer and Wholesale Grower of Pot Plants

1012 Ontario Street, - - PHILADELPHIA, PA.

Mention The Florists' Exchange when writing.

AUCTION SALE

The entire establishment of **JOHN NICOL,** florist, Oak St., Jersey City, N. J., will be offered at public action on the premises, Wednesday, Sept. 19, 1906,

Beginning Promptly at 12 Noon.

Mr. Nicol is retiring from business, and everything used in the conduct of the horticultural business will be sold, absolutely without reserve.

Greenhouses, Sash, Boilers, Pipe, Tanks, Sheds, Store and Office Fixtures, Tools and Implements, Delivery Wagon, Wire Work, Brick, Lumber, etc.

Terms 25% cash; balance on removal of goods. All goods to be removed within one week after day of sale.

Greenhouses reached by Greenville car at Penn. R. R. Ferry.

Sale positive, rain or shine.

J. P. CLEARY, Auctioneer.

Mention The Florists' Exchange when writing.

Begonia "Gloire de Lorraine" and "Turnford Hall"

very strong, 2¼ in. pots, $15.00 per 100; 3 inch, $25.00 per 100; 4 inch, $40.00 per 100.

Pandanus Veitchii, 12 to 14 inches high from top of soil	$75.00	per 100
" " 18 " 24 " " " " " "	100.00	" "
" " 24 " 26 " " " " " "	150.00	" "

Adiantum Farleyense, fine specimens, $1.00, $1.50 to $2.00 each.
" " 2¼ inch, fine stock, $15.00 per 100.

Cash with order from unknown correspondents. Good value guaranteed.

J. A. PETERSON, McHenry Ave., Cincinnati, Ohio

Mention The Florists' Exchange when writing.

HERE'S A BARGAIN:

5000 Gloire De Lorraine Begonias, two inch pots ready at once for three, and full of Shoots. Seeing is believing. Give us a trial order. **$10. per 100. $90.00 per 1000.**

(Money refunded if not satisfactory. How's that?)

E. A. BUTLER & SON, Niagara Falls, N. Y.

Mention The Florists' Exchange when writing.

Extra Celestial Peppers

3 in. stock, $5.00 per 100; 5 in. stock, $10.00 per 100. This price only good 10 days as stock is worth double.

GEO. A. KUHL. Pekin, Ill.

Mention The Florists' Exchange when writing.

Stevia Serrata

True, winter blooming, strong, bushy, ready to shift, 3½ in. pots, $5.00 per 100; $45.00 per 1000.

ASPARAGUS SPRENGERII, 2 inch, very strong, $2.50 per 100; $20.00 per 1000.

DEAN FERRIS, Peekskill, N.Y.

Mention The Florists' Exchange when writing.

A Few Good Things YOU WANT

Dracaena Indivisa, 4 and 5 in., $10.00 and $25.00 per 100.

Asparagus Sprengeri, 3 in., $3.50 per 100.

Geraniums, S. A. Nutt, Castellane, John Doyle, Perkins, Double Gen. Grant, Poitevine, Mme. Salleroi, 2 in. pots, $2.00 per 100; 3 in. pots $4.00 per 100. Rooted Cuttings, $1.00 per 100.

Rex Begonia, nice plants, 2 and 2½ in., $5.00 per 100.

Asparagus Plumosus, 2 in. $3.00 per 100.

Boston Fern 5 in. 30c each.

Pierson Fern 6 in. 50c each.

GEO. M. EMMANS, Newton, N. J.

Mention The Florists' Exchange when writing.

Decorative Plants

Latania Borbonica, 2½ in. pots, $3.00; 3 in; $6.00; 4 in., $15.00 per 100. Large specimen plants from $2.00 to $5.00 each.

Kentia Belmoreana and Forsteriana, 2½ in. pots, $8.00; 3 in., $15.00; 4 in., $25.00 per 100; 5 in., $50.00 per 100; 6 in., $15.00 per doz.; 7 in. and upward, $1.75 to $36.00 each.

Areca Lutescens, 3 in. $10.00; 4 in. $20.00 per 100; 6 in., $1.00 each and upward.

Pandanus Utilis, 3 in. pots, $8.00; 4 in., $20.00 per 100.

Phoenix Reclinata, 5 in. pots, $35.00 per 100.

Phoenix Canariensis, fine specimen plants, from $3.00 to $35.00 each.

Araucaria Excelsa, 5 in. pots, $65.00 per 100.

Assorted Ferns, 2½ in. pots, $3.00 per 100.

Nephrolepis Compacta, 3 in. pots, $8.00; 4 in., $15.00 per 100.

Plants in Fine Condition.

JOHN BADER, Troy Hill, Allegheny, Pa.

Mention The Florists' Exchange when writing.

1500 Begonia Gloire de Lorraine

Strong 3 in., pots .... $15.00 per 100
200 4 in. pots .... $30.00 per 100

These will make excellent plants for Christmas.

S. S. SKIDELSKY,
824 No. 24 St., Philadelphia, Pa.

Mention The Florists' Exchange when writing.

DIFFERENT STOCK

Carnations Ad Covera, 4 cts. Mixed, mostly Lawson and Enchantress, 4c.

Asparagus Plumosus, strong, 2½ in., 3c.; 4 in., 8c.

Asparagus Sprengerii, 2½ in., 2c.

Ferns for Jardinieres, 2½ in., 3c.; Boston, 5 x 6 in., 25c.; Tarrytown ferns, 6 in., 50c.

Smilax, strong, 2½ in., $1.50 per 100.

Parsley Plants, large, $2.00 per 1000.

Rex Begonia, 4 in., 12c. **Cash Please.**

F. B. RINE, Lewisburg, Pa.

Mention The Florists' Exchange when writing.

Primula Obconica Grandiflora

2 1-2 in., $2.50 per 100. Ask for list (seedlings of hardy plants)

BAUDISCH & CO.,

537 Fulton Street UNION HILL, N. J.

Mention The Florists' Exchange when writing.

SURPLUS STOCK—CHEAP

300 **The Bride** roses, 2 in. pots, $1.75 per 100.
500 **Bridesmaid** roses, 2 in. pots, $2.00 per 100.
1000 **Cannas,** red and yellow, strong, $3.00 per 100.
50 **Dracaena Indivisa,** 3½ in., 6c. each.
2000 **Cuphea,** Cigar Plant, 2 in. pots, 75c. per 100.
2000 **Feverfew,** Double White, 2 in. pots, 60c. per 100.
10000 **Jerusalem Cherries,** big and strong, ready for 4 in. pots, from 2 in. pots at $2.00 per 100.

You will never get better or cheaper stock than this. **E. I. Rawlings, Quakertown, Pa.**

Mention The Florists' Exchange when writing.

PRIMULA OBCONICA

Strong 4 inch, $6.00 per 1000.

Cyclamen Giganteum, including fringed and bearded varieties, strong 3 in. $6.00, 4 in. $10.00, 5 in. $20.00 per 100.

Geraniums, 12 varieties. Have order booked for Fall delivery; can fill orders from 100-100,000. Get my prices. Standard, 5 in. pots, $9.00 per 1000; 5000, $40.00, saucers 50c. 100. Wanted 2 inch pots in exchange. Cash.

WM. S. HERZOG, MORRIS PLAINS, N. J.

Mention The Florists' Exchange when writing.

FOUNDED IN 1888

FLORISTS' EXCHANGE

A Weekly Medium of Interchange for Florists, Nurserymen Seedsmen and the Trade in general

Exclusively a Trade Paper.

Entered at New York Post Office as Second Class Matter

Published EVERY SATURDAY by

A. T. DE LA MARE PTG. AND PUB. CO. LTD.

2, 4, 6 and 8 Duane Street,

P. O. Box 1697.
Telephone 3765 John. NEW YORK.

CHICAGO OFFICE: 127 East Berwyn Avenue.

ILLUSTRATIONS.

Electrotypes of the illustrations used in this paper can usually be supplied by the publishers. Price on application.

YEARLY SUBSCRIPTIONS.

United States, Canada, and Mexico, $1.00. Foreign countries in postal union, $2.50. Payable in advance. Remit by Express Money Order Draft on New York. Post Office Money Order or Registered Letter.

The address label indicates the date when subscription expires and is our only receipt therefore.

REGISTERED CABLE ADDRESS:
Florex, New York.

ADVERTISING RATES.

One-half inch, 75c.; ¾-inch, $1.00; 1-inch, $1.25, special positions extra. Send for Rate Card showing discount of 10c., 15c., 25c., or 35c., per inch on continuous advertising. For rates on Wants, etc., see column for Classified Advertisements.

Copy must reach this office 12 o'clock Wednesday to secure insertion in issue of following Saturday.

Orders from unknown parties must be accompanied with cash or satisfactory references.

If advertisers would become members of the National Florists' Board of Trade they would at once be in a position to protect themselves against making bad debts. A word to the wise is sufficient.

Chrysanthemum Society of America.

The E. G. Hill Company offers a prize of $15 for the best 25 blooms of chrysanthemum Mary Mann; and $10 for best 15 blooms of any introduction of 1906. DAVID FRASER, Secretary.

American Carnation Society.

Varieties Registered.

By Baur & Smith, Indianapolis, Ind.—Pocahontas, a cross between a light red seedling and Governor Roosevelt; strong, upright grower, free flowering and produces flowers of very large size with good calyx and a long, strong stem. Color a bright shade of crimson.

ALBERT M. HERR, Secretary.

AMERICAN BREEDERS' ASSOCIATION.—The next meeting of this organization will be held at Columbus, O., January 15-18, 1907, inclusive. The Great Southern Hotel, corner Main and High streets, will be headquarters. Copies of the program announcement can be had of Secretary W. M. Hays, Washington, D. C.

The California Fruit Grower, published in Sacramento, Cal., in espousing the cause of Luther Burbank in connection with an English editor's recent criticism of that gentleman, makes use of the following language:

"What fools some men can make of themselves when they try! But, then, it is only by proving themselves unmitigated asses that some of them ever attain the notoriety which they crave. If they didn't do something to demonstrate to the world how little they really know, they would remain forever in decent obscurity. The latest example of what a fool a human being can be is a man named L. T. Cook.

"Until his recent violent attack of paresis L. T. Cook was a man whom nobody ever heard of. He happens to be the editor of an English publication called The Garden, but that's all. If he ever did anything worth doing, we haven't heard of it. But L. T. Cook yearned to be somebody, to do something that would attract attention. And he was evidently smart enough to know that nothing is so liable to attract attention as a violent attack upon some well-known character. So Mr. Cook proceeded to throw mud at Luther Burbank."

The Fruit Grower refers the critic to the Wickson plum, the sugar prune, and other of Burbank's "creations," and asks Mr. Cook to take a trip over to Ireland to find out where the Burbank potato is cultivated. The English editor is also advised to read what Professor Hugo De Vries of Holland has to say about Burbank and his work.

Notice to Subscribers.

Will any reader who has spare copies of The Florists' Exchange, issue of August 25, 1906, kindly send them to this office, and oblige the publishers.

Registration of Plants.

It is but natural that there should be divergent views on this subject, seeing that the object of plant registration is not specifically defined by the societies which adopt the practice.

Let it be assumed, as has been dogmatically asserted, that the primary and only purpose of registration is to safeguard priority of name, it cannot, we aver, be gainsaid that, as now conducted it carries with it the fact that a new plant has been obtained, a description of which, often with more or less embellishment, is promulgated broadcast, for the edification of the public, who may or may not be influenced by the registration in the purchase of that plant when it is put on the market.

The clause in the constitution of the S. A. F. O. H. regarding registration reads as follows: "He (the secretary) shall keep a registration book in which shall be recorded names and descriptions of new varieties of plants under the rules of the society, application for same having been duly made by the owner thereof, and shall give prompt public notice of each registration with the date of same in such horticulture journals as the executive board may direct."

By the carrying out of these instructions, the society, through its secretary, is made a party to the recording and dissemination of information concerning the correctness of which it has no official knowledge, the mere bald statement of the applicant for registration being taken for granted. This may be commendable credulity, but it seems to us to be neither good business methods, nor justice to the society itself, which is responsible for the distribution of particulars connected with a new plant, which may or may not be as set forth in the registration notice.

The Late James Warburton.

It is not so much the matter of curbing or controlling the raisers of new varieties in the giving of names to their plants, as it is the retaining of confidence in the work of the S. A. F. O. H., and the safeguarding of it from criticism that we believe a change in the registration system is an absolute necessity. That the plan, as at present pursued, has been abused there can, we think, be no question. That the existing system is loose and faulty is beyond cavil, when it has been possible to register new names for old plants as in the recent Japanese peonies case; or again, when the same name has been published for two varieties of new roses, viz.—"Columbia," an error subsequently rectified by the applicant having the prior right to the appellation.

We are ignorant of what "the rules of the society" are to which registration is subject; but we submit that one of these rules should be, that the newness of the candidate seeking registration should first of all be officially determined before the privilege of record is granted. For the society to estimate definitely the worth or worthlessness of a novelty before sufficient general test of same would be a foolhardy and dangerous procedure; but the official determining of the fact, whether or not the variety for which registration is sought conforms to the society's plan in its relation to newness is a simple, safe, and necessary undertaking.

Again, if registration is merely to protect the right of a raiser to a given name, why go beyond recording the mere appellation, or permit the publication of particulars, under the society's auspices, that will attach a fictitious value to registration in the minds of the reading public, which undoubtedly is now the case?

Furthermore, if priority alone is aimed at by registration, we do not feel quite satisfied that this is a matter which the society can control absolutely. The "Law of Priority," according to the Horticulturists' Rule Book (page 200), is set forth as follows: "Priority of publication is to be regarded as the fundamental principle of botanical nomenclature." It will thus be seen that the registration alone is not sufficient to establish priority, and the S. A. F. cannot control "publication."

Perhaps the makers of the society's constitution can tell the real purpose of registration had in view by them when they framed the clause, and whether, as now carried out, it means more than safeguarding priority or serves any more useful purpose, than has been asserted—providing a free advertisement for the varieties registered.

We quite agree with a contemporary that "American horticulture wants no dictators;" but those who would point the way in American horticulture should be actuated at all times by a desire to do things in such a manner as will beget confidence in their work, make for horticulture's best interests, without subjecting themselves, unnecessarily, to criticism or ridicule.

Obituary

George W. Patten.

George W. Patten, florist, Lowell, Mass., died at his home in Dracut on Saturday, September 1. He was 53 years of age, and had been engaged in the florist business for over thirty years. He is survived by his wife and one son, Percy, at present in the West. He was a member of the Lowell lodge of Odd Fellows and was a prominent member of the local society of Elks, where in 1900 and 1901 he was elected exalted ruler, being later appointed district deputy for Massachusetts by the grand exalted ruler of the United States.

The funeral was held on September 5, and was largely attended, many floral offerings testifying to the esteem in which the deceased was held in the community.

James Warburton.

James Warburton, an old time florist of Fall River, Mass., was found dead in his home on September 4, 1906. Death was due to gas asphyxiation.

Mr. Warburton came to Fall River from England in 1856 as an expert spinner. After spending many years at the loom he entered the florist business, and succeeded in building up a large trade. Some seven years ago the business was handed over to his son, Chatterton, by whom it is continued. The elder Mr. Warburton made a tour of the world in 1899. He was over 75 years of age.

Philip Faulk.

Philip Faulk, aged 85, one of the oldest truck gardeners in Allegheny County, Pa., died last week at his home in Ross township. He was born in Alsace, Europe, and came to Pittsburg when a young man, walking the distance from Philadelphia in Midwinter. He began gardening in 1845' selling his products in the Allegheny market. He was the senior member of the firm of P. Faulk & Son, florists and fruit growers. He is survived by seven sons and several daughters. Of the sons two of them are engaged in the florist business, namely Robert and Louis P., who stand in the Allegheny market.

E. C. R.

R. S. Johnston.

R. S. Johnston, proprietor of the Sussex Nurseries, near Stockley station, Del., one of the best known horticulturists of this peninsula, died August 28 at the age of 65 years. A widow and two daughters survive him.

H. Marshall Ward.

Professor H. Marshall Ward, author of many valuable treatises on trees, plants, and fungi, died at Torquay, England, on Sunday, August 26, 1906, after a long illness. He was 56 years of age.

Catalpa Sphinx, Etc.

Editor Florists' Exchange:

I have read the article on the catalpa sphinx and mixed insecticides in your issue of September 8, and now give you my experience with both of the matters mentioned. I always get rid of the catalpa caterpillar by spraying with tobacco water. A barrel filled with stems and water, allowed to stand over night will do; or better, till late the following afternoon.

As for Paris green, I have seen just the same thing mentioned by your correspondent happen with this substance and water alone. It is possible that the solution was too strong with the Paris green. I have used Paris green with the different tobacco solutions, but never experienced any damage from the mixtures. Where much spraying is done, it is well to try a little first and note the effect.

Conn. JULIUS RECK.

OUR READERS' VIEWS

The S. A. F. Convention.

Two Incidents at Dayton.

Editor Florists' Exchange:

After the bulk of members attending the S. A. F. Convention had left one of the largest hotels in Dayton, a man servant said to the writer, "Well, sir, you have had a good convention, but an unusually hot spell of weather. I have been employed here a good while and it's our business to attend to all who come, and to say nothing, but it is seldom you see such a lot of men as were here this week who size up as well, for when men get off in a crowd, away from home, they go it wild, generally. You may have a wild crowd with you, but if you did they stopped somewhere else; the florists who stopped here were certainly a clean lot of fellows."

At the Exhibition Hall a group of men were gathered and in the group was a young lad bright and alert. As is unfortunately not uncommon among some men, one of the party began to tell a questionable salacious story. As soon as its import was discernible, a rugged Scotchman, a real gentleman at heart, took that young lad immediately away by diverting his attention and leading the boy off to see sights worth seeing and free from impure insinuation. This incident was witnessed by one of the group who told of it at his hotel as a compliment to the thoughtful man. A gentleman who heard the incident, said: "I should like to meet that man and take my hat off to him. I honor a man of that calibre." The following morning, outside the Exhibition Hall, true to the word, the hat was doffed in respect to John Birnie, gentleman. VERITAS.

Registration of Plants.

Editor Florists' Exchange:

My idea has always been that registration was simply publication of the fact that a particular plant, or variety, had been given the name as registered and published; and the sole value of registration was to prevent duplication of names. I cannot imagine any condition of implied merit attaching to registration as at present followed by the S. A. F., unless the registered variety has been passed upon by a competent committee of judges, as, for example, the C. S. A. committee or the certificated varieties of carnations that have been passed upon by the American Carnation Society's judges. A. HERRINGTON.

New Jersey.

CLUB AND SOCIETY DOINGS.

NEW YORK FLORISTS' CLUB.—The first meeting of the New York Florists' Club since the Summer vacation was held on Monday evening, September 10, in the rooms corner of Twenty-third street and Eighth avenue. The night was extremely warm, which, no doubt, was the cause of the attendance being rather small. L. W. Wheeler announced that the outing committee was not prepared to make its final report. He assured the members however, that there would be a slight balance left in the hands of the committee.

Patrick O'Mara of the legislative committee reported on express matters to the effect that nothing further could be done at the present time, as the express companies had declared that they would only confer with the growers themselves. The growers had also failed to supply the committee with any specific details. Chas. H. Totty suggested that there was only one way to deal with the express companies, and that was to cut them out altogether, as had been done by the Madison growers.

For the transportation committee F. H. Traendly reported that the delegates had been chaperoned safely to the convention at Dayton. The bill for refreshments was ordered to be paid.

H. H. Barrows, Whitman, Mass., was elected to membership and three names were placed in nomination.

Secretary John Young reported that the letters of condolence he had sent to the San Francisco sufferers had been returned to him; he had again forwarded them, but had received no response as yet. The motion of L. W. Wheeler to amend the by-laws was withdrawn by that gentlemen. Treasurer Charles B. Weathered made his semi-annual report which showed a balance of $1,783.15.

A committee was appointed to draw up suitable resolutions on the death of Roger O'Mara, brother of Patrick O'Mara. President John Scott appointed on this committee Alexander Wallace, W. F. Sheridan and Charles B. Weathered. A committee was also appointed to perform a similar service connected with the death of James Weir, Jr., brother of John R. Weir; the president appointed E. V. Hallock, A. Zeller and John Birnie.

It was expected that descriptions of the recent convention of the S. A. F. O. H. at Dayton would be given by some of our members who were present at that gathering. F. H. Traendly was suffering too badly from hay fever to make a protracted speech, and the talk on Dayton was left chiefly in the hands of E. V. Hallock. Mr. Hallock in his remarks dwelt principally on the subject of the National Flower Show contemplated by the S. A. F. O. H., and the changing of the date of the annual meeting. Mr. Hallock was of the opinion that the executive committee could not do any work furthering the show, owing to the wording of the motion providing for the holding of such an exhibition as such motion was put before the convention. He asked for the opinion of the club as to whether it was desirable to change the meeting of the S. A. F. O. H. from August to November. This matter was discussed at length, P. O'Mara, A. J. Gutman, J. H. Pepper, Chas. Lenker, C. H. Totty and L. W. Wheeler all taking part. Finally, on motion of Mr. Birnie, it was decided unanimously that the date of the meeting of the S. A. F. O. H. had better not be changed.

Herbaceous flowers were on exhibition. J. T. Lovett of Little Silver, N. J., showed twenty-three vases of cut flowers which included over one hundred varieties. Among Mr. Lovett's exhibit were phlox in many varieties, Hyacinthus candicans, hibiscus, Crimson Eye, desmodium, Veronica longifolia subsessilis, delphiniums, Rudbeckia purpurea, etc. He was awarded the thanks of the club. Henri Beaulieu of Woodhaven, N. Y., showed some flowers of canna King Humbert, and several varieties of dahlias. The committee requested that they be shown again at the next meeting.

J. B. Nugent provided an excellent lunch of roast beef and accompanying liquids, which were appreciated very highly by all present.

NEW JERSEY FLORICULTURAL SOCIETY.—Lager & Hurrell, Joseph A. Manda, and the private estate of William Barr (Arthur W. Bodwell, gardener) made their usual contributions of orchids; and the Colgates (William Reid, gardener); John Crosby Brown (Peter Duff, gardener); Stewart Hartshorne (Arthur T. Caparn, gardener); William Runkle (D. Kindsgrab, gardener); Charles Hathaway (Max Schnyder, gardener); Col. H. A. Potter (William Phillips, gardener); A. T. Gillespie (Geo. Oakley, gardener), and Mrs. William Pierson (Chas. Ashmead, gardener), contributions of flowers and plants, at the regular monthly meeting of this society held on the 7th inst.

Alexander Wallace, Editor The Florists' Exchange, was present and made a few remarks concerning the convention and exhibition of the S. A. F. O. H. held at Dayton, O., last month. He referred particularly to the work, horticulturally, of the National Cash Register Company, and its influence on the citizens of Dayton; speaking also of the work along the line of civic improvement which he had witnessed among the Oranges during the day, praising the skill of the gardeners, and urging them to contribute, specimens of that skill to the forthcoming international flower show, to be held in Chicago in November, 1908, under the auspices of the Society of American Florists, for which premiums amounting to $10,000 will be awarded.

A large part of the business meeting was taken up in discussing arrangements, the hall, etc., for the usual Fall exhibit, but no decision was arrived at beyond the adoption of the schedule. The October meeting was voted a special dahlia night. Two new members were placed in nomination; and a vote of thanks was awarded the speaker of the evening.

In connection with the death of Henry Graves, prominent as an exhibitor of rare orchids at the meetings of the society, in many cases his entries being of plants never exhibited elsewhere, the following resolution was prepared by a committee consisting of Joseph B. Davis, William Reid and George Smith:

"Resolved, That in the death of Henry Graves, this society has lost a patron, and floriculture a sympathetic friend; and that in acknowledging this event publicly a just recognition is made of the value of his contributions of plants and flowers at our exhibitions, to the inspiration of our members and the education of the public generally." J. B. D.

The Start — The Finish

Buffalo Florists' Club Outing—Ladies' Race

Buffalo Florists' Club Outing.

The Buffalo Florists' Club held its annual picnic at Fort Erie Grove on September 5, and the affair was one of the most enjoyable in the club's history. William Scott told us about the recent convention, which he considered one of the best the S. A. F. has held so far. Past President Wm. F. Kasting also favored us with a speech.

The first event on the program was the base ball game between the East and West side florists, which was practically a walk-away for the West side team, the score being 10 to 4.

The hundred yard dash was won by Jimmie Longley. He was closely pushed by Conrad Baumgartner, Ed. Walther coming in a close third. Time eleven seconds.

The ladies' race was won by Miss Schlager. Miss Mark was second. In the boys' race Reinhard Klockhow came in first, closely followed by Jimmie Griffin and Billie Bixon. The hop-skip-and-jump was won by David Scott, 37 feet; Wm. H. Grever, second, 36 feet, 11 inches; Conrad Baumgartner, third, 34 feet; and Longley, fourth, 33 feet. In the hop race C. Baumgartner was first, Longley second, and Walther third. The old men's race was won by Mr. Sage of Bradford, who beat the gun in the start, and was never headed. Mr. McCarthy of Lockport ran a good race, and Mr. Ehmann, who was not in very good condition, was slightly winded at the finish. In the three-legged race, Walther and Grever ran first, Cramer and Ray second, Longley and Zimmerman third.

The half-mile race brought out a field of ten starters; the four winners were closely bunched at the finish—Longley first; Baumgartner, second; Zimmerman, third; and Walther, fourth. W. H. G.

SOUVENIR OF FOLEY MANUFACTURING COMPANY, Chicago.—We acknowledge, with thanks, receipt of a very useful souvenir being distributed by this well known firm to those who fill out the coupon in the concern's advertisement and forward it to Chicago. The souvenir is a neat steel tape measure, which gives the English system on one side and the metric system on the other. The tape is enclosed in an attractive metal covering, bearing the firm's advertisement.

They're Off!

A Review of Roses to Present Date and Their Requirements.

(A paper read by John H. Dunlop before the recent Convention of the Canadian Horticultural Association.)

The subject assigned me, or that I am asked to speak upon, is one of considerable magnitude: "A Review of Roses to Present Date and their Requirements." At first glance it would seem an easy task but as one analyzes the subject the first questions to confront you are: Are all soils alike? Are all conditions similar? Do all growers handle their plants in similar manner? The answer to each of these questions is a positive "No." Then, in that case, the paper will deal entirely with the condition, soil, etc., as existing at my greenhouses, and as far as I am able to learn through intercourse with those growing the varieties enumerated, and of the forcing varieties grown under glass for cut flowers.

Rose List Limited.

The rose growers have not been favored as other branches of the profession in the number of varieties put upon the market or disseminated by originators each season—look at the list of carnations and chrysanthemums—in fact, the number of varieties that have remained permanent or standard forcing varieties have been comparatively few.

There are so many points required in a rose to make it profitable; probably it is a good grower but the color may not be right; the flower may be too single or too double to open freely, in Winter it may have a tendency to be weak stemmed in dark weather or a shy bloomer at the same season. There are so many points to be considered in a forcing variety that there are very few that come up to the requirements of the ideal flower.

Look back for the past ten years, which is a comparatively short time, and note how many varieties have been introduced with glowing descriptions and how many are grown to-day. The majority have been tested and found wanting and discarded, as the critical public, to whose taste we cater, are capable of judging the variety and are not slow to detect the weak points no matter how much we would like to grow them. The patrons of our stores have to be considered and it is the popularity of the variety that we have to look to. But there is a better day coming; a good many of the supposed forcing varieties may have excellent points when grown in the open, and may be admirably adapted to out of door cultivation, and I think this is the part that is misleading. Almost all of the new varieties are raised in Eurppe, where the conditions are entirely different and unsuitable to the requirements of this country but I am sanguine of better things. Have we not men who feel the necessity, and have the courage to risk the raising of seedlings, who are spending time and money in the endeavor to give us something more and better suited to our requirements, who know the conditions and, I am proud to say, have achieved success and have overcome obstacles that have appeared unsurmountable?

Have we not Mr. Cook of Baltimore, who gave us Cornelia Cook and Wootton; Alex. Montgomery with Wellesley; E. G. Hill with Gen. MacArthur and Richmond? During the past week a visit was paid to this noted establishment, and there he has a house, 300 ft. in length, devoted to this year's seedlings, and to seedlings of one and two years, in limited quantities, under extended trial. We should be proud of the men who have the perseverance and skill to devote to this very important branch of our profession.

Some Recent Introductions.

Of the most recent introductions, and of what might be claimed the most important forcing varieties, I would name Richmond, originated by E. G. Hill, Richmond, Ind. This is an American seedling, a cross between Lady Battersea and Liberty. It is a hybrid tea with a much larger percentage of tea blood then most of the hybrid teas. The color, an ideal shade of bright crimson, delicately scented, of remarkably free growth and a free bloomer. This variety can be grown successfully with Bride or Bridesmaid; in fact, it is benefited by a few degrees less heat, say a night temperature of 55 degrees suits it better than 58 degrees. It does not require any particular culture or soil, as it has been grown successfully in both light and moderately heavy soil, but would recommend a clay loam where it is procurable, as I am inclined to think that there is more substance found in the flowers where the heavier soil is used. I would caution growers not to be too liberal in feeding Richmond. It was recommended at time of dissemination to feed it liberally but, as I said before, some soils being stronger and richer than others, caution and care must be exercised in feeding or disaster will be the result. I had a house of this variety last season where the instructions were carried out too closely and the result was that the variety got indigestion and had to be handled very carefully in order to put it in good working order again. There is nothing to be gained by this; better to be cautious and do a little underfeeding rather than overfeeding.

Madame Chatenay is a comparatively new variety but has found many admirers. It is of easy culture, being one of the strongest growing teas, easy to force and, like Richmond, is not particular as to soil. We have found a temperature of 55 degrees well suited. The variety takes well to feeding and, in the early Spring luxuriates in frequent waterings of liquid manure and a good mulch as the days grow longer. The color is of a soft peach pink on upper side of petal and a lighter shade on under side; it has a delicate perfume.

Killarney is a variety that has been neglected or overlooked. It originated with Dickson of Belfast. Although on the market for some three years its merits were not brought out until a year or so ago where it was grown in different sections in moderate quantities and the value became known; now it is being largely grown with excellent results as will be noted from the reports in the trade papers last season. It is a very free grower and has a fascinating appearance from the fact that the young growth is so showy, being a reddish plum color in comparison with the deep green of the matured foliage. The stems are stiff and erect at all seasons of the year. The bud is pointed, delicately scented and produced in profusion. The color is a deep shade of rose pink, although I have seen it very different in some sections, namely of a light wash pink. The odor is of the briar; when the hand is passed over the unopened bud it is like the odor of a briar hedge, which is always refreshing and appreciated. Similar temperature to Bride and Bridesmaid is best suited to Killarney.

Kate Moulton has only been disseminated and is in its first year's trial; its faults, if any, have not been discovered. I had a bunch sent me from Minneapolis, Minn., which arrived in good condition considering the long journey. It is of a bright, soft shade of pink, globular in form and good stem, although the neck was inclined to be weak; whether that is a fault or not remains to be seen. The variety appears to be a good grower.

Jacobina Magnifica.
Photo by W. H. Waite.

Wellesley, although on the market a couple of years, has not been grown around Toronto. I had an opportunity of seeing it at Natick, Mass., where it originated, and it appeared to be a promising variety. The color is a bright shade of medium dark pink of the Bridesmaid type, a good grower and a free bloomer. This is an American seedling, raised by that enthusiastic grower, Mr. Alex. Montgomery, who is also giving considerable time and thought to the raising of seedling roses. A visit to the Waban Conservatories is always a pleasant and profitable one. Here rose growing is a science and everything on the most approved plan.

Gen'l MacArthur is a variety raised by Mr. E. G. Hill, but was not intended for Winter forcing, or rather he did not consider it suitable. The stock was bought by The Storrs & Harrison Co. and Jno. N. May. It was received with considerable enthusiasm as the list of red forcing varieties was very meagre, the trade relying largely on Meteor which, of late, has shown considerable deterioration. MacArthur is of bright cherry red and very fragrant, a free grower and moderately free bloomer. There is quite a tendency to throw strong shoots which are too heavy for most purposes and are covered with large thorns resembling hardy roses. This variety has been grown successfully in the neighborhood, but most people prefer Richmond, and it looks as though MacArthur would be discarded before long. A temperature from 52 to 55 degrees is best suited to it and moderately heavy soil.

Franz Deegen, of comparatively recent introduction, is the best of the yellows, eliminating the habit of Perle, which is prone to come bullheaded and deformed in dark weather. Deegen opens as freely in Midwinter as at any other season of the year, with no deformed flowers. Of an exquisite shade of yellow, deepening to a deep shade of orange in the centre, a strong grower and continuous bloomer, this is a variety which improves with age, as plants undisturbed for four seasons are stronger and produce superior bloom to young plants. This variety is almost immune from mildew and for that reason can be grown where it would not be possible to grow Bride and Bridesmaid; of easy culture, a similar temperature to Bride is suitable for this variety; enjoys a fairly good feeding. This variety is benefited by being grafted.

Joey Hill, a French variety, introduced last season, is of the Perle type in appearance and habit. A soft shade of peach pink, but an entirely different shade from either Sunrise or Sunset in color, being a combination of both. Long pointed buds, good stems, and the most attractive variety of this color.

Rosalind Orr English has not proved itself as good as its companion Richmond; there is a tendency to black spot and the growth is unsatisfactory. The flower is medium in size and of a bright clear pink Hermosa shade. I expected better results from this variety but found others more satisfactory.

A Few Tested Preparations.

As this is an age of progress and improvement we are finding new ways and methods of fighting some of the pests that have been very troublesome in the past. Comparatively few growers will content themselves with burning tobacco for the extermination of the green fly. Although the preparations put on the market are comparatively expensive and increase the cost of producing bloom, yet the results are so much more satisfactory that to be up to date one feels that he should adopt them. There are a number of preparations, viz. Aphis Punk, To-Bak-Ine, Nico-Fume, and others. The preparations enumerated I can speak of from experience, having used them. For the best results I find the latter the most effective. It is easily applied and cheaper than the others. These preparations can be applied without injury to the bloom, which is not the case where tobacco is burned. I find Tobakine extract very effective with varieties like American Beauty, which are more subject to the attack of green fly than any other variety. On such the fly can be exterminated and kept in check where used regularly in the following manner and where steam heating is used. Take an ordinary oil can, fill with the liquid, start at the furthest end and drop on the hot pipes as quickly as possible, as the fumes are very sickening and you have to beat a hasty retreat. I well remember on a couple of occasions when necessity required, that I undertook to apply in the manner described; my recollection is not a pleasant one, as I had the worst case of sea sickness ever experienced, along with that giddiness which betokened an overdose of tanglefoot but, with a little care, this can be obviated. Tobakine is also a preventive of thrips when used in this way, a weekly application being sufficient to keep clear of both thrip and aphis.

There is also on the market Campbell's Sulphur Vaporizer; it helps to keep down mildew when firing ceases. It is an English patent and a trifle expensive, but very effective and eliminates almost all of the danger of ignition. We have all had our pet schemes of using sulphur; some of them have been costly, to wit, when the pan was placed over the coal oil stove and the flame set at what was thought just right to force the vapor from the sulphur on the pan and, just at that minute being called away to attend to some duty, on returning a couple of minutes later to our chagrin and dismay to find the pan had taken fire and the sulphur formed that deadly gas so fatal to plant life; perhaps that whole house ruined in those few minutes' absence. For this reason I am pleased to know that this vaporizer has reduced the danger minimum. We are using eight of them at present with excellent results.

I will not treat of the best houses for rose growing, as it is now well known that the lightest and airiest are most suitable for the purpose or, I might say, for the growing of any flower for Winter forcing. I hope I have not wearied you with the paper, which has been written with the wish that some benefit may result from its preparation.

Cement-Built Greenhouses.

What is described by the Guernsey Evening Press as a revolution in greenhouse building has been introduced into the Channel Islands. In the new method of building iron wires are covered with cement and walls so constructed are said to be practically everlasting and much cheaper than wood. It is claimed for concrete greenhouses that unlike wooden structures, they do not harbor plant pests, and the framework thus secured is more rigid than one of wood, and so will support a proportionately larger area of glass.

Jacobina Magnifica (Syn. Justicia Magnifica.)

This is a soft-wooded shrub and, when well grown, makes quite an attractive plant, especially for conservatory decoration. The flowers, which are of a rosy purple, are borne in dense terminal thryses. It is of simple culture, requiring temperate treatment in Winter. It is easily propagated from cuttings and the young plants bloom early and give largen flowers than old plants, although old plants cut back and allowed to break away make quite showy plants.

W. H. WAITE.

Influence of Acetylene Light on Plant Growth.

In a recent address before the International Acetylene Association Professor John Craig of Cornell University, Ithaca, N. Y., gave some interesting information concerning the effect of acetylene light on plant growth, the results of experiments made at Cornell by a student named M. J. Iorns, whose investigations covered two university years.

Professor Craig, in his introduction to the subject, says: "Acetylene more nearly approximates sunlight in its make-up than any other artificial illuminant used. It is composed of the same colors and in very similar degrees of intensity." This fact was established by Munsterberg.

The Experiments at Cornell.

The methods of conducting experiments with acetylene on plant growth at Cornell University were to add the acetylene illumination to the day light illumination by turning on the former after twilight fell. We endeavored to make comparisons on the influence of this light under different conditions, so that a warm, a medium and a cool house were used.

Temperature of warm house, 60 to 65 degrees at night; soil area, 235 square feet; 410 candlepower; five feet from ground.

Temperature of cool house, 45 to 50 degrees at night; soil area, 129 square feet; 350 candlepower; three feet from ground.

Temperature of medium house, 50 to 55 degrees at night; 100 square feet; 270 candlepower; two feet from bench.

Scope: The lights in two houses were run nearly 5,000 hours, during which time something over 2½ tons of carbide were used. In making the investigation, 150 plant forms, embracing 25 families, 50 genera and 65 species were employed.

General Results: Influence on top growth for culinary use: Most of the salad plants were studied. Lettuce, parsley and spinach were considerably hastened. The seeding period was also accelerated. The plants under acetylene were crisper and apparently more succulent than those grown under sun alone.

Plants Grown for Foliage.

Coleus: The vigor of the plant was increased, but no other marked change, either as to color or consistency of foliage, was noted.

Asparagus Sprengeri and plumosus: Very little, if any, difference was observed between the plants in sun and those in acetylene. Such difference as was noted was in favor of the acetylene plants.

Begonias, rex and tuberous: With both types the vegetative growth was considerably stronger under acetylene than under sun alone, but in most cases the flowering period was materially delayed. This might be an advantage in the case of the rex type, but would be a disadvantage in case of the tuberous varieties grown primarily for flowers.

Cobæa scandens: This produced 15 to 29 per cent. more vine under acetylene than under sun alone. No other modification was observed.

Ferns: These did not show any marked difference except in the matter of color, which was lighter in the plants under acetylene than those under sun.

Vegetable Summary (By Mr. Iorns.)

Comparing the results of the different vegetables, we find (1) that with the exception of the cucumbers, all the forms had a decided increase of the foliage parts.

(2) That the time of fruit maturing is variously affected. The strawberries and peas maturing earlier, the tomatoes and pole beans later, and the cucumbers and other forms practically unchanged.

(3) That there is, as a rule, an increase in the amount of fruit, also in size of individual fruits, the cucumber being the chief exception.

(4) That the chief beneficial effects of the light are to make up for deficiency of sunlight, give with few exceptions stronger, more vigorous top growth, and help overcome unfavorable conditions in certain other lines.

(5) That there seems to be a limit in rapidity of growth, beyond which plants cannot be forced at all proportional to the attendant expense. Just what conditions govern this limit or where the limit is in our forcing-house plants, is as yet unknown.

Photosynthetic processes are completed to the point of starch making; root systems increased in the main proportionately with top development.

Influence on Time of Blooming.

Mr. Iorns notes that with three exceptions all forms bloomed earlier under acetylene than under sun alone. Most notable differences are in the case of geraniums. In some cases plants under acetylene bloomed twenty days before those under sun light. In the case of carnations the blooming time was hastened, but the stems were elongated to an injurious extent. Therefore, from the standpoint of hastening the blooming, it is beneficial.

Lilium longiflorum was also greatly benefited. The per cent. of gain of plants under acetylene varied from 6 to 15. L. speciosum under acetylene bloomed two to three weeks ahead of those unlighted. In conjunction with either the effect was very marked.

Quantity of bloom: The influence on quantity of bloom is pronounced. In every case the amount of bloom was increased. In some plants two or three times as many blossoms were produced as in the sun.

Duration of bloom: Here we have an apparent contradiction. The addition of acetylene shortened the number of days which cucumber flowers remained on the vines, but in the case of lily and narcissus the flowers lasted a greater number of days than where only sun was used. This may be due in a measure to the innate character of the flower itself.

General Summary.

Between 90 and 95 per cent. of the plants experimented with responded favorably to the stimulus given by the acetylene light. The remainder were usually negative. There was no uniformity of results within a group of related plants. Lilies, for instance, gave markedly positive results, while some tulips failed to respond entirely.

No markedly injurious results were noted except where plants were growing under optimum conditions.

The general influence of acetylene seems to be that of weak or highly diluted sun light.

Under unfavorable conditions of temperature and sun light, acetylene can be used to considerable advantage in stimulating plant growth. It must not be regarded as a magic agent, with which miraculous plant growth may be wrought, but as a supplement or co-operative force to aid the gardener

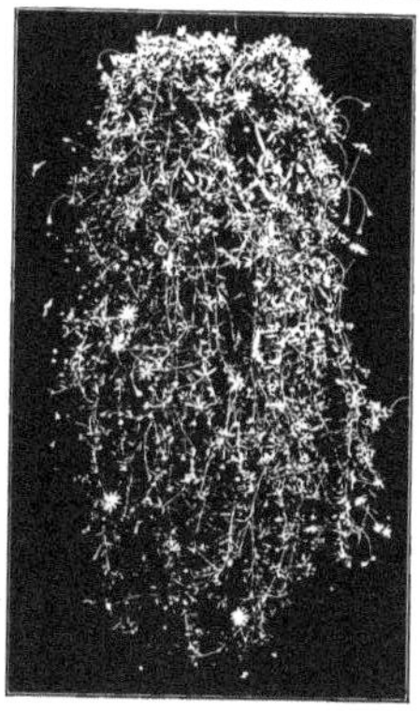

Othonna Capensis
Photo by John F. Johnston

under unfavorable conditions, or at times when natural stimuli must be augmented it promises to be useful.

Under such conditions, with certain forcing-house crops, I believe, it can be profitably applied.

In conclusion I would have it understood that I regard these experiments as merely preliminary. There are many questions yet to be answered. For instance, should acetylene be used only in the daytime, during the natural period of plant growth, or on dark days, when the sun light is deficient? What degree of illumination should be employed? If at night, is it best to run a weak light all night or a strong light in order to give a period of rest part of the time?

Why do some plants respond, and others not? What is the fundamental reason? Will the discovery of this reason give us further light in pursuing our investigations?—From the Acetylene Journal for September, 1906.

A Philadelphian Abroad.

A souvenir postal card from Paris, France, received from Godfrey Aschmann, of Philadelphia, Pa., informs us that Mr. Aschmann had already visited Holland and Belgium. From Paris he will go to Switzerland, and afterward to Italy. He says he has mailed some 500 souvenir postals to his customers, and expects to send from Switzerland as many more. Mr. Aschmann is on a business and pleasure trip combined.

Spraying for Scale Insects in the Fall.

On account of the unfavorable results which were obtained by many entomoligists and fruit growers in applying insecticides for scale insects during the Fall or early Winter, this operation has generally been postponed until late Winter or early Spring, just before the buds swell. The reasons commonly given for this practice included not only the experience which many had had in injuring the trees by early applications, but the belief that the insecticide would remain longer on the tree if applied in early Spring. In the case of the lime-sulphur wash it is obviously an advantage to have the insecticide upon the tree in a satisfactory condition at the time when the young scales are moving about.

According to experiments by J. B. Smith, entomologist of the New Jersey Station, it appears that all kinds of insecticides effective against scales may be applied with success in the early Fall, even before the trees have become thoroughly mature. In his experiments Doctor Smith used various preparations of soluble petroleum, lime and sulphur, whale-oil soap, kerosene limoid, and other preparations. The ordinary scale insects can not be kept in check in Summer for the reason that the foliage is injured when a sufficiently strong solution of a contact insecticide is used. If, however, applications are made in the Fall, after a part of the leaves have fallen off, or as soon as the leaves have turned yellow and the tree gives evidence of being nearly mature, a considerable percentage of the scale insects will still be active, and will be immediately destroyed by the insecticide. The application of ordinary treatments such as those just mentioned appears not to produce material injury to fruit trees, even including peach. For the latitude of New Jersey, Doctor Smith sets October 15 as about the right date to begin the Fall application of scale insecticides in average years. The purpose sought in applying the insecticides as early as possible is to catch the scale insects in an active condition while they are therefore exposed to the action of the remedy. As long as the sap circulates in the tree some of the scales are active, and since the trees appear not to be injured when treated after October 15 this seems to be a very good season for making the application. A few of the leaves are injured by early Fall applications, and, in general, the foliage may drop off somewhat sooner than it otherwise would. This appears not to be of any moment, however, since the trees come out in Spring in a thrifty condition and show no bad effects of the application.

A New Industry for California.

It is stated that a syndicate is arranging to purchase 15,000 acres of land near Marysville to be colonized with families from southern France, who will engage in the production of flowers for market and for perfumery, says the San Francisco Chronicle. The cultivation of flowers in the open, on a large scale, is new, so far as we know, in California. It is probably not commercially possible except in connection with a perfumery factory to utilize the culls and the surplus which the market will not take at remunerative prices. The industry is extensively pursued in southern France, whose climate is in some respects like our own, but less favorable for this purpose by reason of our freedom from Summer rains. It is probably not possible to introduce this industry into California at this time, except by the importation of the people to carry it on. Much technical skill is required in the manufacture of perfumes, but that is not difficult to provide either by importation or the more costly process of development. The trouble is to get the flowers picked. It requires a prodigious quantity of flowers to make a very trifling quantity of the concentrated perfume, and the wages possible to be earned at the rate per pound of leaves paid for picking in southern France would not be attractive to girls and women who can earn from one dollar per day upward in the canneries. Nevertheless, perfumery, as an article of luxury, carries a duty of 60 cents per pound and 45 per cent. ad valorem in addition, which is an excellent protective duty, although not intended as such, and will very likely enable wages to be paid, or prices for the leaves, which will be high enough to keep those familiar with the industry at work at it. The dispatch which calls our attention to the matter seems to intimate that the enterprise is promoted by the American Chamber of Commerce in Paris.

Othonna Capensis.

This is rather a peculiar looking little plant and highly interesting. When not in blossom it would be somewhat difficult for those unacquainted with it just what natural order of plants to place it in. Othonna crassifolia, it is sometimes called; in fact, probably best known by gardeners as such. And this older specific name of crassifolia seems most appropriate, as really the foliage resembles in a most marked degree some of the Sedum family. Therefore, when not in flower, one would naturally place this plant in the natural order of Crassulaceæ, or that to which the sedums belong, but it does not belong here. The order compositæ is its home, as can readily be seen when the plant opens its small yellow daisy-like flowers. Othonna capensis is an excellent plant for hanging baskets or used for trailing over the sides of flower boxes. What is more, it withstands, in a marked degree, extremes of temperature or moisture. There is no difficulty with its propagation as a piece of its stem, broken off, will root readily. JOHN F. JOHNSTON.

New York.

News of the Week.

Anton Schultheis, College Point, L. I., who had such a hard struggle with typhoid fever last Winter, has fully recovered his usual health, and has been enjoying himself this Summer at the mountains and seashore.

On Monday, September 10, A. J. Guttman celebrated the anniversary of his removal into Twenty-eighth street by treating everybody to cigars.

A. J. Tharp of Bedford Station, N. Y., devotes most of his time to the real estate business now that his sons are competent to take care of his florist interests. Since the beginning of the year Mr. Tharp has sold almost a half million dollars' worth of real estate in the district in which he lives.

Mrs. Messeburg, wife of Gus. Messeburg, is quite ill at her home in Flatbush, Brooklyn.

W. Ford of the firm of Ford Brothers, will spend Sunday with Mrs. Ford, who is staying with her parents in Pennsylvania.

J. B. Deamud of Chicago, with Mrs. Deamud, has been spending several days around New York, enjoying the attractions at Coney Island and other beach resorts, and looking over the violet industry around Rhinebeck and Poughkeepsie.

Traendly & Schenck are handling an exceptionally fine lot of Adiantum Farleyense in 6-inch pots from a Southern grower.

Several of the wholesale florists have been making tours around the violet districts, and the latest reports are that, although there has been some disease among the violet plants there will be no lack in the supply of these flowers during the coming Winter. It is also noticed that shipping will not begin quite so early this year; and from present market conditions it would seem that the violets can very well be spared for a few weeks yet.

Alfred Bunyard of The Rosary, was married on August 9 to Miss I. Hayes at the Marble Collegiate Church on Fifth avenue; the honeymoon was spent at Lake George.

A. T. Boddington, seedsman of 342 West Fourteenth street, is taking a vacation on the New England coast.

We are sorry to report that John Nicol, the well known florist of Oak street, Jersey City, who has been staying in Canada for some time, is quite ill, and will not resume his florist business. On Wednesday, September 19, the greenhouses of Mr. Nicol, together with stock and everything pertaining thereto, will be sold at auction, commencing at 12 o'clock noon. J. P. Cleary will be the auctionéer.

Wm. Elliott & Sons, 201 Fulton street, will commence their Fall auction season on Tuesday, September 18, at 11:30 a. m. They will offer a general assortment of decorative plants for indoor work, including palms, ferns, crotons, rubbers, etc.

S. Burnett of the firm of Burnett Brothers, 101 West street, will arrive to-day from Europe where he has been spending his vacation. While on the other side his mother and an aunt died; the sympathy of the trade will go out to the Burnett Brothers in their bereavement.

The gardeners and florists of Greater New York, a new title given to the park employees, held a picnic on Saturday, September 8, at 170th street and Amsterdam avenue.

Eddy Borque, manager for Chas. A. Dards, recently returned with his daughter and son from a month's sojourn at White Lake.

The sympathy of the trade is extended to Miss Laura Klein, manager of the cut flower department of Siegel & Cooper's department store, in the loss of her mother who died recently.

David Adams, representative of the J. M. Thorburn Company, seedsmen, has just returned from a vacation which he spent along the coast.

John Doughty of New Haven, Conn. was a visitor in town this week.

A. J. Vander Hock, florist, Jersey City, N. J., is back from a European trip.

Apropos of the visit of florists to the dahlia exhibition of R. Vincent, Jr. & Son, at White Marsh, Md., on Wednesday, September, 19, an arrangement has been made with the B. & O. officials whereby the fast express train leaving Liberty street at 8 a. m. will make a special stop at Cowenton.

Boston.

A Proposed Dahlia Society.

About twenty-five dahlia growers held a meeting during the recent exhibition at Horticultural Hall and talked over the formation of a dahlia society. It was finally agreed to form such a society and the following temporary officers were elected to select a date and place for next meeting for the regular organization of the society: President, H. F. Burt; secretary, M. Fuld; executive committee: J. H. Flint, N. L. Lindsay, A. E. Johnson, Mrs. H. A. Jahn and W. P. Lathrop.

The September Show.

The annual September exhibition of the Massachusetts Horticultural Society, which was held on Wednesday and Thursday of last week, while not up to former shows in the collection of plants was perhaps the best exhibition of dahlias ever seen in Boston. The small hall was entirely filled with dahlia blooms excepting the side tables which held fine collections of herbaceous plants from the Blue Hills Nurseries and the Bay State Nurseries. The most noticeable among these flowers was in the collection of the Blue Hills Nurseries in the shape of a vase of Liatris pycnostycha superba, for which a first class certificate was awarded. Another noticeable plant in the same collection was Lathyrus latifolius, "Pink Gem," of a very pleasing color; it received the award of honorable mention. W. W. Rawson & Company showed a lot of blooms of Lilium philippinense and a large collection of superb dahlia flowers. Joseph Breck & Sons also made an exhibit of dahlias and African marigolds, both lemon and orange, the varieties being "Breck's Sunburst."

H. A. Dreer made a very fine exbibit of aquatics, filling three large tanks; they received a first class certificate. The same firm also exhibited new plants, including Adiantum scutum ramosum, Adiantum macrophyllum album striatum, Asparagus Ducheni, Maranta Gaulleti and Pteris Childsii.

Lager & Hurrell, Summit, N. J., made a nice display of orchids in variety filling one table.

In the main hall the principal exhibit was a magnificent group of palms and foliage plants from the Harvard Botanical Gardens; Mr. Cameron's skill in arrangement added greatly to the effect of the display. Some noticeable plants in this group were Cocos Romans offiana, Licuala grandis, Anthurium crystallinum, Calatheas Veitchii and Makoyana, Nephrolepis acuta, Alpinia nutans variegata, Dracæna Sanderæ and Chamærops humilis.

R. and J. Farquhar & Company had a large group of foliage and ornamental plants; and a fine group came from George Barker, gardener to Mr. A. F. Estabrook.

In the competition classes for plants the prizes went to Mrs. Frederic Ayer (Geo. Page, gardener) to Mrs. J. L. Gardner (Wm. Thatcher, gardener) and to Mr. Wm. Whitman (Martin Sullivan, gardener).

As already mentioned the classes of dahlias formed a large part of the exhibition. The competition was keen, many of the classes having ten and twelve entries. Some of the finest blooms were in the class for amateurs only, J. H. Flint, the winner of the first prize, showing a superb lot though he was closely followed by W. F. Hall. In the regular classes the principal prize winners were: J. K. Alexander, Edgar W. Ela, W. H. Symonds, W. C. Winter, W. P. Lothrop, W. G. Winsor, W. D. Hathaway, Mrs. L. M. Towie, H. F. Burt, F. L. Tinkham, Mrs. H. A. Jahn and F. G. Baker.

News Notes.

The auction sale of stall choice in the Park street market of the Boston Co-operative Flower Growers Association on Saturday proved very satisfactory indeed; and while some of the stalls did not realize as much as last year, yet, on the whole, they averaged much more, as quite a few hundred dollars over last year was received for the same number of stalls. About 100 stalls were sold at prices ranging from $90 down to $15.

Secretary W. N. Craig in a lengthy circular to the members calls attention to the next meeting of the Gardeners and Florists' Club on Tuesday the 18th inst.; a close study of the same will convince the readers that they cannot miss this meeting—the first of the season.

The Worcester Conservatories have purchased the stock in the greenhouses of the late F. A. Blake, Rochdale, which included several seedling carnations of much promise.

Jos. Manter will now handle the products of Anderson & Williams in the Park street market.

Mann Brothers continue to bring to market lots of Lilium philippinense which sell readily.

H. H. Rogers of South Sudbury is sending in some very fine asters for so late in the season.

H. M. Robinson & Company are handling new crop Southern wild smilax, making a specialty of the same.

The bowling team of the Park street flower market held a meeting for the purpose of organization on Wednesday.

J. J. McCormack will open a cut flower department in the large store of the Henry Seigel Company.

James F. Quinn and wife have gone to Manchester, N. H., for a few weeks.

N. Silverman and J. J. McCormack have just returned from a visit to New York.

F. W. Fletcher, Auburndale, has been growing a lot of Physotegia virginiana which has been very popular on account of its pleasing color for window decorations.

James Wheeler is visiting in Buffalo and Niagara Falls. J. W. D.

Philadelphia.

News Notes.

The bowlers celebrated the recent victory at Dayton on Monday night last. The match was between the team that rolled at Dayton and a picked team of associate members of our club. The Dayton team won by a good margin.

John Westcott had as his guests at Waretown over Sunday Wm. Graham, Robert Kift, and George Coleman, steward of the Union League. Time hung heavily on their hands Sunday evening, so they took a stroll through the village and drifted into the Methodist Church. The minister seeing three strnagers called upon them, Kift for a prayer, and Coleman for a speech; they acquitted themselves like men.

Apropos of the visit of florists to the dahlia exhibition of R. Vincent, Jr. & Son, at White Marsh, Md., on Wednesday, September 19, an arrangement has been made with the B. & O. officials whereby the fast express train leaving Twenty-fourth and Chestnut streets at 10:22 a. m. will make a special stop at Cowenton.

Much discussion has taken place recently about carnations and stem rot. Most growers suppose that on low ground the rot is worst, but at the establishment of Mrs. R. C. Smith at Secane, Delaware County, Pa., there has been no stem rot in carnations, and but little trouble with violets. The ground here is perfectly low and level, with poor drainage. Growers all around have called upon this place to supply stock to fill empty space. DAVID RUST.

LOWELLVILLE, O.—The Darrow Garden Co. succeeds D. R. Darrow. The firm has built enough houses to more than double the glass formerly owned by Mr. Darrow.

ARLINGTON, MASS.—Alfred Wagland, florist, Broadway and Whitman streets, returned last week from a three months' sojourn in England.

Pittsburg.

News Items.

T. P. Langhans of the Pittsburg Cut Flower Company, who spent a month with his family near the Thousand Islands, is home again.

J. Jones, foreman of the Schenley Park conservatories and D. Fraser, gardener to Mr. H. C. Frick, are back from their trip to Europe, where they had a good time.

The September meeting of the Florists' Club was fairly well attended. The subject for discussion was "Gladiolus and Asters." A fair exhibit of blooms was made by the following: Frank Banning of Kinsman, Ohio, who showed a fine assortment of gladiolus, such as America, pink seedling No. 12, our best red, Mme. Monneret, Augusta, pink seedling No. 2, yellow seedling No. 1, a very fine bloom, and some others, all of them good sorts, which were admired by all present.

The Cushman Gladiolus Company of Sylvania, Ohio, showed some dahlias and a collection of gladiolus. Arthur Cowee of Berlin, N. Y., showed gladiolus. From the park conservatories came a fine lot of white, pink, lavender and purple asters, blooms as good as were ever grown in the city; the variety was Semple's branching. Also a few sprays of a scarlet geum, a pretty little thing.

President J. Jones told something about his trip to England and France, and stated that he did not see there anything better than our country can produce. Some carnations he had seen in Wales were bigger than anything he had ever laid his eyes on—as large as peonies and well-grown stocky plants. Clianthus Dampieri, which is difficult to grow here, does well in England. Some nice palms were seen in France, but he did not think much of the flower bedding in Paris.

A few words were said about the Dayton convention, and it seemed all were pleased who were there. W. Falconer was asked to tell something about the meeting of the cemetery superintendents, but he thought cemeteries were quiet places, and that a talk on them would not interest any one. E. C. REINEMAN.

Columbus, O.

News Notes.

At the last meeting of the Columbus Florists' Club it was decided to postpone the proposed chrysanthemum show for one year. This action was taken in view of the large expense of the undertaking and consequent risk.

The Franklin Park Commissioners, with a fund of $7,000 recently appropriated by Council, will arrange for extensive repairs on the park conservatory, including the purchase of two 60 horse power boilers. Superintendent Underwood is to be re-appointed, and an effort will be made to get a more liberal appropriation for maintenance.

T. E. Guy, who has a range of greenhouses at Arlington, a fine suburb northwest of the city, was the lucky purchaser of the Sonaker plant of that place, at administrator's sale recently. The two large greenhouses which he secured with but little competition of about two-thirds the appraisement, are fitted up as vegetable forcing houses.

Several of the local florists are interested in the question of better facilities in the way of a flower market, as the present arrangements around the Central market are very unsatisfactory. In this case as in other similar ones, the public boards seem to move with most aggravating slowness.

Jas. McKellar is back in his busy place at Graff Brothers after a pleasant vacation at the Magnetic Springs. C. D. B.

PITTSFIELD, MASS.—John White, florist who owns property on the section of South Church street, which it is proposed to abolish for the New York, New Haven Railroad, thinks that he should be paid as the closing of the highway there will cause him a lot of damage, he says.

SHERMAN, TEX.—The Texas Nursery Co. have added nearly 10,000 sq. ft. of glass to their plant.

ERNS *and* CARNATIONS

SPEAK QUICK

.000 Healthy Field Grown Carnations, best mercial sorts, including **ELBON,** a fine, true
Send for list as they must be sold.
)00 **PIERSONI FERNS,** for 4 in., 15c.
)00 " " for 3 in., 10c.
)00 **BOSTON** " 3 in. ready for 4 in., 10c.
COTTII FERNS, 4 in., 20c.; 3 in., 10c.
NNA FOSTER, 2½ in., 4c.
)00 **ASPARAGUS PLUMOSUS NANUS,** 3½ 6c.; 2½ in., $2.50 per 100.
0 **ASPARAGUS SPRENGERII,** 3½ in., 6c.
)00 **HYDRANGEA OTAKSA,** 2½ in., $2.50 per

)00 **VINCA MAJOR** var., 2½ in., $2.50 per 100.
l A No. 1 Stock. Cash please.

ENJ. CONNELL
WEST GROVE, PA.

tion The Florists' Exchange when writing.

erns From Bench

STON, PIERSONI, 4 in. 10c.; 5 in. ½c. Boston 6 in. 15 cts.
RRYTOWN, 3 in., 10c.; 4 in., 15c.; in., 25c. Runners $20.00 per 1000.
)TTII, 3 in., 8c.; 4 in., 12½c.

CHINESE PRIMROSES

hite, fine plants, 1½ cts.
mula Obconica, Hybrid Alba Rosea, 2 in., ts.
y and Floribunda Primroses, 2 in., 2 cts.
ay Plants, Giants, $3.00 per 100.
sies, double Snowball, Longfellow, elicata, $2.50 per 1000.
aragus Sprengerii, 2 in., 2 cts.
salem Cherries, field grown, ready, for 4 , 3 cts.
wering Begonias, 8 kinds, 2 in., 2½ cts.
onia Rex, 3 in., 6 cts.

Cash or C. O. D.

ER BROS., Chambersburg, Pa.

tion The Florists' Exchange when writing.

EPHROLEPIS SCOTTII

Small plants from the benches, $5.00 per); $50.00 per 1000. Plants large enough 6 in. pots, $25.00 per 100. Plants large ough to go in 7 and 8 in. pots, $50.00 per).

Asparagus Plumosus Nanus, 2¼ in., e plants, $3.00 per 100.

JOHN SCOTT,
tland Road and East 45th Street;
BROOKLYN, N. Y.
Telephone 2890 Bedford.

ntion The Florists' Exchange when writing.

FERNS

e now in fine shape. A good variety and nice shy stock, 2½ in., $3.00 per 100; $25.00 per 1000.
Kentia Belmoreana, 4 in., clean and bushy, 25c.), 50c.; 6 in. 75c.
Boston Ferns, Piersoni and Scottii, from ach, 25c. each.
Cocos Weddeliana, 10c.

. WESTON, HEMPSTEAD, N. Y.

ntion The Florists' Exchange when writing.

ORCHIDS

Arrived in superb condition **Cattleya Dowiana, Gigas, C. Mossiae, C. Percivaliana, C. Speciosissima, C. Eldorado, C. Superba, C. Labiata, Leopoldii** and many more.
Write for Prices.

AGER & HURRELL, Summit, N. J.
Growers and Importers

ntion The Florists' Exchange when writing.

ORCHIDS

Largest Importers, Exporters, Growers and Hybridists in the world.

Sander, St. Albans, England
and
235 Broadway, Room 1, New York City

ntion The Florists' Exchange when writing.

FERNS OUR SPECIALTY

Cibotium Schiedei: We have a grand stock of this magnificent tree fern in all sizes. 3 in. pots, $25.00 per 100; 4 in. pots, $45.00 per 100; 5 in. pots, $75.00 per 100; 7 in. pots, $1.70 each; 8 in. pots, $2.50 each.
Assorted Ferns, from 2¼ in. pots, all the best market varieties, $3.00 per 100, or $25.00 per 1000; 4 inch pots, $12.00 per 100. **Fern Seedlings,** from flats, $1.00 per 100 plants, or $8.50 per 1000. If by mail add 10c. each 100 plants.
Adiantum Cuneatum, 2 in. pots, $3.50 per 100
" 4 in. pots, 12.00 " "
" **Rhodophyllum** 4 in. pots $25.00 per 100
" **Lathomii,** 4 in. pots, $20.00 per 100
" **Regina,** 4 in. pots, $40.00 per 100
Fern Spores gathered from our own stock plants 35c. per trade package or $4.00 per doz. packages.

ANDERSON & CHRISTENSEN,
SHORT HILLS, N. J.

Mention the Florists' Exchange when writing

Fern Seedlings

From flats, ten of the best varieties, at $1.00 per 100; $8.50 per 1000; if by mail add 10c. per 100. Ferns for dishes, good stocky plants from 2¼ in. pots, $3.00 per 100; $25.00 per 1000; 250 plants at 1000 rate.
Adiantum Cuneatum, 5 in. pots, $20.00 per 100

FRANK N. ESKESEN, MADISON, N. J.

Mention The Florists' Exchange when writing.

FERNS

BOSTONS, 5 in. pots, $3.00 per doz.; 6 in. $6.00.; 7 in. $9.00; 8 in., $12.00 per doz. **PIERSONI,** at same price. **PIERSONI ELEGANTISSIMA,** 5 in. $4.00; 6 in. $9.00; 7 in. $12.00 per doz.
ASPARAGUS Plumosus Nanus and **ASSORTED FERNS,** 2 1-4 in., $3.50 per 100. Cash please.

H. HANSEN, 106 Avon St. Malden, Mass.

Mention The Florists' Exchange when writing.

BOSTON AND SCOTTII FERN

From 25c., 50c., 75c., $1.00 and $2.00 Each.
Asparagus Plumosus from $3.00 to $6.00 per 100
Cycas Revoluta in different sizes.

P. WAGNER,
Cor. Troy Ave. & Midwood St., Flatbush, Brooklyn, N.Y.

Mention The Florists' Exchange when writing.

ROBERT CRAIG & CO.

ROSES, PALMS, CROTONS

CARNATIONS and Novelties in DECORATIVE PLANTS

Market and 49th Sts. PHILADELPHIA, PA.

COCOS PALMS.

Strong 2½ inch at $1.60 per dozen. Write for lowest prices on **Kentias.**

Jas. F. Barclay R. I. GREENHOUSES Pawtucket, R. I.

ASPARAGUS

SPRENGERII, 500 very large; some of them will cut sprays one foot long now; are not stunted but healthy, $6.00 per 100; or $25.00 for the lot. Cash with order.

FILLOW & BANKS
WESTPORT - - - CONN.

Mention The Florists' Exchange when writing.

2,000 **Smilax,** 2½ in., strong, cut back, per 100, $1.50; the lot for $17.50.
200 **Asparagus Plumosus,** $2.50 per 100.
1,000 **Asparagus Sprengerii,** 2½ in., $2.00 per 100 the lot for $17.00. This is strong and ready for a shift.

J. S. BLOOM,
RIEGELSVILLE, PA.

Mention The Florists' Exchange when writing

EMERSON C. McFADDEN

Wholesale Grower

Asparagus Plumosus Nanus, Etc.
Short Hills, N. J.
Tel. 28 A.

Mention The Florists' Exchange when writing.

ASPARAGUS PLUMOSUS, 3 in., fine $5.50 per 100.
" **SPRENGERII,** 3 in., heavy, 4.50 per 100.

G. HANSON,
1024 S. Cameron St., HARRISBURG, PA.

Mention The Florists' Exchange when writing.

DRACAENA TERMINALIS

Matured canes always ready for shipment. Delivered to any part of the United States for 10 cents a foot. Send cash for a trial order.

PORTO RICO PINEAPPLE CO., RIO PIEDRAS, PORTO RICO.

Mention The Florists' Exchange when writing.

ASPARAGUS

	per 100
Plumosus Nanus, 2¼ in. pots	$2.00
Plumosus Seedlings,	1.00
Sprengerii, 2½ in. pots	2.00
Vinca variegated from field, Oct.	5.00

PRIMROSES

	per 100
Obconica Alba, and Rosea	2.00
Cannas, 5 var., field, clump	15.00

PANSY PLANTS, $3.00 per 1000; 50c. per 100.

CASH PLEASE.

JOS. H. CUNNINGHAM, Delaware, O.

Mention The Florists' Exchange when writing.

ASPARAGUS

	Per 100
Sprengerii, 3 in.	$3.00
" 2 in.	1.50
Plumosus Nanus, 2 in.	3.00
Primula Obconica Grandiflora Alba, Rosea and Hybrida, 2 in.	2.00
" " **Robusta and Compacta,** 3 in.	3.00
Smilax, fine 2¼ in. to close out	.75
Paris Daisy, white and yellow, 3 in., bushy,	3.00

Orders booked for early September delivery of

Cineraria Grandiflora Hybrida, Michell's Giant Prize, 2 in.	2.00
Calceolaria, James Superb mixed, 2 in.	3.00
Primula Chinensis, 2 in.	2.00
Primula Buttercup, yellow, 2 in.	2.00

Cash with order, please.

GEO. J. HUGHES, BERLIN, N. J.

Mention The Florists' Exchange when writing.

SMILAX PLANTS

Strong, Bushy Plants, many times cut back and ready for shift.

2 in. pots ......$1.00 per 100, $9.00 per 1000
Seedlings from flats............ 4.00 "

We have grown Smilax Plants for the trade 18 years, and never had finer stock.

Send for Samples

R. KILBOURN
CLINTON, N. Y.

Mention The Florists' Exchange when writing.

ASPARAGUS

Plumosus, 2½ and 3 in. strong plants, $25.00 per 1000.
Senecio Macroglossus, ever-blooming German Ivy; flowers, cream colored, large as a silver dollar, $3.00 per doz.

P. D. BARNHART,
573 S. Boyle Ave., Los Angeles, Cal.

Mention The Florists' Exchange when writing.

Asparagus Sprengerii

We have a large stock of strong plants in 4 in. and 5 in. pots and will close them out at $4.50 per 100.

CASH WITH ORDER

F. E. ALLEN & CO.
BROCKTON, MASS.

Mention the Florists' Exchange when writing.

VIOLETS

Campbell, field-grown plants, fine, $4.00 per 100; $35.00 per 1000
California, out of 2½ in., $2.00 per 100; $17.00 per 1000
Alyssum, double Giant, for winter flowering, 2½ in., $1.50 per 100
Dracena Indivisa, large field-grown plants, ready for 6 in., $7.00 per 100; $1.00 per doz.
Hydrangeas, for forcing, 5 to 9 flowering crowns, $7.00 per 100
Parsley, moss curled, large field-grown plants, $2.50 per 1000

J. C. SCHMIDT CO.
BRISTOL, PA.

Mention The Florists' Exchange when writing.

HEADQUARTERS FOR

Choice Plants

English Ivy, Anthericums, Kentias Forsteriana and Belmoreana, Phoenix Canariensis, Araucarias, Bay Trees and Boxwood Pyramids, Asparagus Plumosus, Bird's Nest, Scottii Elegantissima, Piersoni Boston and Johnsoni Ferns, Cattleya Trianæ Rubbers Dracænas Terminalis and Fragrans, Pandanus Veitchii, Gardenia Veitchii, Cycas Revoluta, Cibotium Schiedei Livistonii Sinensis, Areca Lutescens, Crotons, Aspidistras, Lygodium Scandens, Primula Obconica, Begonia Rex, Daisies, Fern Balls, Lily of the Valley, Cut Flowers, Leaf Mold, Orchid Peat, etc. Write for prices.

Anton Schultheis 19th St. and 4th Ave. College Point, L. I., N. Y.

Mention The Florists' Exchange when writing.

VIOLETS

FINE FIELD GROWN PLANTS
Marie Louise and Princess of Wales, $4.50 per 100; $40.00 per 1000

Carnations

Enchantress and Flamingo, $6.00 per 100; $50.00 per 1000
Queen Louise, $4.50 per 100; $40.00 per 1000

THE BOOL FLORAL CO.,
ITHACA, N. Y.

Mention The Florists' Exchange when writing.

WE ARE HEADQUARTERS FOR

Princess Violet Stock

Orders booked for September delivery.
Strong field-grown plants, $50.00 per 1000.

WILLIAM SIM, Cliftondale, Mass.

Mention The Florists' Exchange when writing.

Governor Herrick Violet

The finest single violet ever offered. Write me about it today.

Price: One dozen, $2.00; 100, $10.00; 1000 at $75.00 or 5000 or more at $60.00 per 1000. No. 1 Stock.

H. R. CARLTON, WILLOUGHBY OHIO.

Mention The Florists' Exchange when writing.

VIOLETS

MARIE LOUISE Violets, clean and healthy in every particular, ready August 15th. 3 in. pots $5.00 per 100.

CASH WITH ORDER.

WM. J. CHINNICK,
TRENTON, N. J.

Mention The Florists' Exchange when writing.

Commercial Violet Culture

PRICE, $1.50

The FLORISTS' EXCHANGE, 2-8 Duane St., New York

VICTORY

Strong healthy field grown plants, now ready. First size, $15.00 per 100; Second size, $12.00 per 100; Third size, $10.00 per 100. A discount for cash with order. GUTTMAN & WEBBER, 43 West 28th St., N. Y.

GERANIUMS

From 2 in. pots ready for immediate delivery

Alliance, Lemoine 1905. Hybrid, Ivy and Zonal, semi-double, lilac, white, upper petals feathered and blotched crimson maroon, 25c. each; $2.00 per doz. **Fleuve Blanc,** the semi-double Bruant, that promises to become the standard white, flowers and foliage equal to Alph. Ricard, $1.50 per doz.; $10.00 per 100. **Cactus Geraniums,** four varieties, petals curled and twisted similar to the Cactus Dahlia, $2.00 per doz.; $15.00 per 100. **Double Dryden,** $1.00 per doz.; $5.00 per 100. **S. A. Nutt, La Pilote, Beaute Poitevine, Mme. Barney, Centaur, Miss Kendell, Mme. Jaulin, Jean Viaud, Mme. Charrotte,** 40c. per doz.; $2.00 per 100; $18.00 per 1000. **Ville Poitiers, Marquise de Castellane, Berthe de Presilly, M. Joli de Bammeville, Thomas Meehan,** 50c. per doz.; $3.00 per 100; $25.00 per 1000. Send for Geranium catalogue, let us figure on your future supply. **Alternantheras,** red and yellow, $2.00 per 100; $15.00 per 1000. **Hardy English Ivy,** $2.00 per 100; $15.00 per 1000. **Smilax,** $2.00 per 100; $15.00 per 1000. **Dahlia Roots,** we are booking orders for fall delivery; send for list.

Rubbers, good stock from 4 in. pots, $2.00 per doz. $15.00 per 100.

Coleus, Lemon Verbenas and Giant Alyssum 40cts. doz. $2.00 per 100.

Ageratum, "Inimitable." Giant blue. $1.25 per doz. $8.00 per 100.

VEGETABLE PLANTS

Cabbage: Early Jersey and Charleston Wakefield. Succession and Early Summer. $1.00 per 1000. $8.50 per 10,000.

Lettuce. Grand Rapids, Big Boston and Boston Market. $1.00 per 1000. $8.10 per 10,000.

Parsley, Moss curled. $1.25 per 1000.

A cordial invitation is extended to all interested in Horticulture to visit us. Cowenton Station, Philadelphia division, B. & O. R. R., 12 miles north of Baltimore.

R. VINCENT Jr. & SON,
WHITE MARSH, MD.

Mention The Florists' Exchange when writing.

Geraniums Geraniums

4 in. pots at $6.00 per 100.
3 in. pots at $4.00 per 100.
Heliotrope, 4 in. $4.00 per 100.
" 2 in. $3.00 per 100.
Lobelia, 2 in. $2.00 per 100.
Coleus, in variety, 2½ in. pots, $2.00 per 100.

Don't get left, but get your order in. Cash must accompany same.

J. E. FELTHOUSEN,
154 VAN VRANKEN AVE., SCHENECTADY, N. Y.

Mention The Florists' Exchange when writing.

GERANIUMS

TRANSPLANTED STOCK

Ricard, Poitevine, Doyle,
Viaud, Castellane, Nutt,
Buchner, Perkins, Grant, dbl.

$15.00 per 1000. Cash with order.

PETER BROWN, Lancaster, Pa.

Mention The Florists' Exchange when writing.

GERANIUMS.

Nutt, Poitevine, Buchner, Doyle, Ricard Viaud, Brett, and others.

Rooted Cuttings. Orders booked for Fall delivery.

ERNEST HARRIS, Delanson, N. Y.

Mention The Florists' Exchange when writing.

Field Grown Carnation Plants

Only a few left. Write for list of variety and prices.

CHICAGO CARNATION CO.
JOLIET, Ill.

Mention the Florists' Exchange when writing.

A. B. DAVIS & SON, Inc.

PURCELLVILLE, VA.

WHOLESALE GROWERS OF CARNATIONS

Mention The Florists' Exchange when writing.

FIELD GROWN CARNATIONS

All sold out; nothing left but 200 Smilax, $2.00 per 100.

VALLEY VIEW GREENHOUSES, Marlborough, N.Y.
VELIE BROS., Props.

Mention The Florists' Exchange when writing.

ENCHANTRESS

SOLD

WHITE BROTHERS, Gasport, N. Y.

Mention The Florists' Exchange when writing.

GERANIUMS

ROOTED CUTTINGS

Orders booked for delivery Nov. 1st and after. I will have fourteen houses planted to stock plants and I can supply you with the right kind of cuttings.

	per 100	per 1000
S. A. Nutt Perkins, Buchner, Doyle	$1.25	$12.50
Viaud, Jaulin, Poitevine, L. Francis	1.50	15.00
Ricard, Castellane, Trego	1.50	15.00
Peter Henderson	2.00	20.00
Fleuve Blanc (White Poitevine)	5.00	50.00

These cuttings are carefully grown and will make a better plant than the average pot plant.

FIELD PLANTS

GERANIUMS

S. A. NUTT, CASTELLANE and RICARD ready for 3-inch pots, $2.00 per 100.

ALBERT M. HERR, Lancaster, Pa.

Mention the Florists' Exchange when writing.

GERANIUMS

Rooted cuttings, transplanted in soil, best varieties, mixed, to close out on account of removal. $10.00 per 1000.

CARNATION SUPPORTS, round, some new, some slightly used, $5.00 per 1000; $40.00 per 10,000. Cash with order.

G. F. NEIPP, Aqueduct, L. I., N. Y.

Mention The Florists' Exchange when writing.

Geraniums

S. A. NUTT, CASTELLANE and RICARD ready for 3-inch pots at $2.00 per 100.

ALBERT M. HERR, Lancaster, Pa.

Mention The Florists' Exchange when writing.

Field Grown Carnation Plants

ALL THE STANDARD VARIETIES

List and prices on application.

Rose plants 1000 Liberty 3 in. pots	$5.00	per 100
1000 " 2¼ " "	4.00	" 100

THE LEO NIESSEN COMPANY, 1217 Arch St. Philadelphia, Pa.

Mention The Florists' Exchange when writing.

CARNATIONS

Crisis Scarlet	$5.00 per 100	Cardinal	$7.00 per 100
Fiancee	5.00 "	Estelle	5.00 "
Joost	5.00 "	Queen	5.00 "
B. Market	5.00 "	Harlowarden	5.00 "

Second size $2.00 per 100 less. Cash with order.

SMITH & GANNETT, Geneva, N. Y.

Mention The Florists' Exchange when writing.

MABELLE--New Pink Carnation for 1907

Color.—A peculiar shade of lovely pink, with a faint yellowish cast; several shades lighter than the Lawson. Unlike most pinks, the brightest sun does not injure the color. **Size.**—Three to four inches in diameter when established. **Odor.**—Pleasing, but not strong. **Stems.**—Invariably strong, but always graceful, ranging from 12 to 30 inches during the season. **Habit, etc.**—A very quick active grower, making specimen plants in a short time, even from late cuttings. On account of its rapid growth, requires supporting very soon after benching. Gets away rapidly, blooms early and gives long stems right from the start. **Productiveness.**—Prodigious is the best word we know of to use here. It is the most incessant bloomer early and late, we have ever grown. Stock limited. Delivery Jan. 5th to 10th and later. Price, $12.00 per 100, $100.00 per 1000.

THE H. WEBER & SONS CO., OAKLAND, MD.

Mention The Florists' Exchange when writing.

ABUNDANCE

Healthy, stocky, field grown plants. First size. $12.00 per 100; $100.00 per 1000. Second size, $10.00 per 100; $75.00 per 1000; 250 at a 1000 rates. Delivery 15th of August.

CASH WITH ORDER.

RUDOLPH FISCHER, Great Neck, L.I., N.Y.

Mention The Florists' Exchange when writing.

Field Grown Carnations

Crane, Fair Maid, Gov. Wolcott, Roosevelt, Marquis. 6 inch pans **Boston Ferns,** $4.00 per doz. 2 in. **Standard Geraniums,** $2.00 per 100; $18.00 per 1000.

THE NATIONAL PLANT CO. Dayton, O.

Mention The Florists' Exchange when writing.

CARNATIONS

Let us have your order now for the coming new Carnations: January delivery. **Aristocrat, Windsor, White Enchantress, Helen M. Gould, Beacon and Rose Pink Enchantress.**

WM. SWAYNE, Box 226, Kennett Square, Pa.

Mention The Florists' Exchange when writing.

S. J. GODDARD

Framingham, Mass.

Rooted Carnation Cuttings a Specialty.

Correspondence Solicited.

Mention The Florists' Exchange when writing.

5000 FAIRMAID

Fine Field-Grown Plants

$5.00 per 100.

2000 Strong Field Grown **HYDRANGEAS,** $10.00 per 100

CHAS. EVANS
WATERTOWN - MASS.

Mention The Florists' Exchange when writing.

FIELD GROWN Carnations

Write for prices.

J. W. HOWARD, Woburn, Mass.

Mention The Florists' Exchange when writing.

CARNATION PLANTS

Fine, healthy Stock.

1500 WHITE LAWSON	$60.00	per 1000
250 ESTELLE	4.00	" 100
1400 DOROTHY	35.00	" 1000

Stock grown and shipped from Toledo, Ohio.

S. S. Skidelsky,
824 No. 24th St., PHILADELPHIA, PA.

Mention The Florists' Exchange when writing.

FIELD GROWN CARNATIONS

	Per 100		Per 100
Roosevelt	$4.00	Prosperity	$5.00
Hill Sport	4.00	Flamingo	5.00
Manley	5.00	Enchantress	6.00
Scarlet Seedling	6.00	Cash with order.	

Chas. T. Darling, Stony Brook, L. I., N.Y.

Mention The Florists' Exchange when writing.

2000 CHRYSANTHEMUMS

"THE BABY"

Fine for Thanksgiving Day. Field-grown plants to pot up. For 7 in. pots, 15c.; 6 in. 12c.; 5 in., 10c.; 4 in., 8c. each. Cash.

HENRY EICHHOLZ, Waynesboro, Pa.

Mention The Florists' Exchange when writing.

THE AMERICAN CARNATION

Price $3.50

A. T. DE LA MARE PTG. & PUB. CO. LTD., 2 to 8 Duane St., New York

Mention The Florists' Exchange when writing.

Commercial Violet Culture

Price, $1.50

The Florists' Exchange, 2-8 Duane St., New York

CARNATIONS

	Per 100	Per 1000
FIANCEE	$6 00	
LAWSON	6 00	$50 00
NELSON FISHER	7 00	60 00
GUARDIAN ANGEL	4 00	35 00
MORNING GLORY	$4 00	$35 00
LIEUT. PEARY	8 00	75 00
FRED BURKI	7 00	60 00
BOSTON MARKET	5 00	45 00
FLORA HILL	$5 00	$45 00
WHITE CLOUD	5 00	45 00
CHICAGO (Red Bradt)	5 00	45 00
HARLOWARDEN	6 00	50 00

WIETOR BROS., 51 Wabash Ave., CHICAGO

Mention The Florists' Exchange when writing.

CARNATIONS

STRONG, HEALTHY, FIELD GROWN PLANTS

PINK	100	1000
LAWSON	$5.00	$40.00
NELSON FISHER	7.00	60.00
NELSON	3.00	25.00
GUARDIAN ANGEL	3.00	25.00
ENCHANTRESS	7.00	60.00
MORNING GLORY	4.00	30.00
HIGINBOTHAM	3.00	25.00

WHITE	100	1000
BOSTON MARKET	$4.00	$35.
FLORA HILL	3.00	25
QUEEN LOUISE	3.00	25.00
WHITE CLOUD	3.00	25.00
VARIEGATED		
MRS. PATTEN	6.00	50.00
ARMAZINDY	3.00	25.00
RED		
ESTELLE	5.00	40.00
MRS. INE	3.00	25.00

ROSE PLANTS

	100	1000
LIBERTY 3 in. pots	$3.00	$25.00
CHATENAY 2½ in. pots	2.50	22.50

PETER REINBERG, 51 Wabash Ave., CHICAGO

Mention The Florists' Exchange when writing

CARNATIONS | FIELD PLANTS

	Per 100
.ENDALE	$10.00
)BT. CRAIG	12.00
)UNTIFUL	8.00
)ROTHY WHITNEY	8.00
LLE	7.00
AMINGO	7.00
ANCEE	7.00

	Per 100
BOSTON MARKET	$6.00
WHITE CLOUD	6.00
MRS. PATTEN	6.00
NELSON	5.00
ESTELLE	3rd size, 3.50

ROSES, 200 4 in. **Maids,** 150 4 in. **Brides,** $6.00 per 100. 500 2½ in. **Gates,** 300 2½ in. **Brides,**) 2½ in. **Perles,** $2.50 per 100. **Richmond Roses** own roots, fine 3 in. $5.00; 2 in. $4.00 per 100.
ASPARAGUS PLUMOSUS, 2 in., $2.00 per 100. **SPRENGERII,** 3 in., $6.00 per 100. Cash or C. O. D.

V. J. & M. S. VESEY, Fort Wayne, Ind.

Mention The Florists' Exchange when writing.

Field Grown CARNATIONS

Flamingo, Roosevelt, Crisis, Harlowarden
Price, $ 6.00 per 100.

E. A. Nelson, Flora Hill, Wm. Scott, Portia, Eldorado, Crocker, Queen Louise
Price, $5.00 per 100; $4.50 per 1000.

J. L. DILLON, Bloomsburg, Pa.

Mention The Florists' Exchange when writing.

FIELD GROWN Carnations

Extra fine healthy plants

	100	1000
QUEEN	$5.00	$45.00
FAIR MAID	5.00	45.00
FLORIANA	5.00	

50 Field-grown Jerusalem Cherries, stocky plants, $5.00 per 100.

CASH WITH ORDER

W. A. DAWSON, Willimantic, Conn.

Mention The Florists' Exchange when writing.

CARNATIONS

Strong Field Grown Plants

Crimson Glow (new variety) $12.00 per 100

Cash or references with order.

DAILLEDOUZE BROTHERS
Flatbush, Brooklyn, N. Y.

Mention The Florists' Exchange when writing.

CARNATION PLANTS

FIELD GROWN

	100	1000
Crusader, red	$5.00	$40.00
Lawson, pink	4.00	30.00
Flamingo, red	5.00	40.00
Mrs. Patten, variegated	5.00	45.00
Boston Market, white	4.00	30.00
Queen Louise, white	4.00	35.00
White Cloud, white	4.00	35.00
Liberty Rose planth, 1 year old	4.00	30.00

George Reinberg
35 Randolph Street, - CHICAGO, ILL.

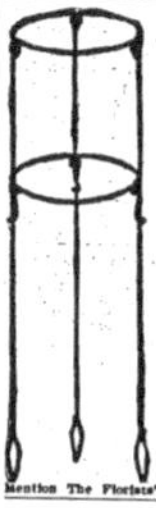

The Model EXTENSION
CARNATION SUPPORT

Endorsed by all the leading carnation growers as the best support on the market. Made with 2 or 3 circles. Write for prices and circulars.

We have special low prices to offer and can save you money on

Galvanized Wire ROSE STAKES

Write us for prices before ordering elsewhere. Prompt shipment guaranteed.

IGOE BROS.
226 North 9th Street
BROOKLYN, N. Y.

Mention The Florists' Exchange when writing.

MRS. JOOST

Still the best pink carnation for the average florist to grow.

Extra large plants, clean, healthy, and absolutely free from stem rot, $5.00 per 100.

Queen Louise, the finest plants I have ever offered, $5.00 per 100.

R. G. HANFORD, Norwalk, Conn.

Mention The Florists' Exchange when writing.

FIELD GROWN CARNATIONS

Strong, healthy plants. 2000 Hill, $5.00 per 100; $45.00 per 1000; 1000 McGowan, $3.50 per 100; $30.00 per 1000. Cash with order.

E. R. SHERWOOD, Norwalk, Conn.

Mention The Florists' Exchange when writing.

FIELD GROWN
Carnation Plants

5000 Enchantress, 6c. each; $50.00 per 1000
Queen, 5c. each; $40.00 per 1000.
Lawson, white, 2nd size, $4.00 per 100.
" variegated, 2nd size, $5.00 per 100.
" pink, 2nd size, $3.50 per 100.
Lady Bountiful, 2nd size, $5.00 per 100.
Glacier, 2nd size, $3.50 per 100.

CASH

GOVE BROS., Biddeford, Me.

Mention The Florists' Exchange when writing.

CARNATIONS

PLANTS FROM FIELD

Fair Maid, Queen, $5.00 per 100; $45.00 per 1000. Strong and healthy. Satisfaction guaranteed. Cash with Order.

HUGH CHESNEY, Farmington, Ct.

Mention The Florists' Exchange when writing.

Jensen & Dekema

CARNATION SPECIALISTS

674 W. Foster Ave., CHICAGO.

Mention The Florists' Exchange when writing.

CARNATIONS

ENCHANTRESS	$50.00	per 1,000
QUEEN LOUISE	40.00	" "
LAWSON	40.00	" "

Good, strong, healthy plants. Cash with order.

HENRY KRUSCHKA
616 Cookman Ave., Asbury Park, N. J.

Mention The Florists' Exchange when writing.

FIELD GROWN CARNATIONS

VICTORY, JOHN J. HAINES, $2.00 per doz.; $15.00 per 100.
FIANCEE, G. LORD, GOV. ROOSEVELT, $6.00 per 100.

CHARLES H. TOTTY
MADISON, N. J.

Mention The Florists' Exchange when writing.

CARNATIONS

F. DORNER & SONS CO.
LA FAYETTE, IND.

Mention The Florists' Exchange when writing.

40,000 extra fine field-grown Carnation plants. For particulars see under Stock for Sale.

M. J. SCHAAF
DANSVILLE, N. Y.

Mention the Florists' Exchange when writing.

CLASSIFIED ADVERTISEMENTS

CASH WITH ORDER.

The columns under this heading are reserved for advertisements of Stock for Sale, Stock Wanted, Help Wanted, Situations Wanted or other Wants; also of Greenhouse, Land, Second-Hand Materials, etc., For Sale or Rent.

Our charge is 10 cts. per line (7 words to the line), set solid, without display. No advt. accepted for less than thirty cents.

Display advertisements in these columns, 15 cents per line; count 12 lines agate to the inch.

[If replies to Help Wanted, Situation Wanted, or other advertisements are to be addressed care of this office, advertisers add 10 cents to cover expense of forwarding.]

Copy must reach New York office 12 o'clock Wednesday to secure insertion in issue of following Saturday.

Advertisers in the Western States desiring to advertise under initials, may save time by having their answer directed care our Chicago office at 127 E. Berwyn Ave.

SITUATIONS WANTED

SITUATION WANTED—By head gardener; understands his business. Call or write. C. F. G., 302 W. 28th street, New York City.

SITUATION WANTED—By middle aged American with long experience in general greenhouse work. Private place preferred. Address, E. R. Florist, Madison, N. J.

SITUATION WANTED—Salesman and designer, city experience. Wishes position in first-class store. F. W. Pettit, Box 898, Schenectady, N. Y.

SITUATION WANTED—Swede, 30 years old, single, as assistant in commercial or private place. 8 years in the last place. Address, Carl Anderson, 168th st & Broadway, N. Y. City.

SITUATION WANTED—By a thoroughly competent plantsman and grower to travel. Varied experience, and best of references. Address N. E., care The Florists' Exchange.

SITUATION WANTED—Grower, aged 31, 17 years experience in palms, roses, violets, carnations, mums and general stock. Address, D. H., 27 Sister street, Port Chester, N. Y.

SITUATION WANTED—As working foreman. 15 years experience in landscape and nursery work, ferns, palms, vegetables, etc. Best American and European references. Address, R. A., care The Florists' Exchange.

SITUATION WANTED—By a young man of good character, education, and experience as foreman of Eastern rose growing establishment. References on application. Address, O. C., care The Florists' Exchange.

SITUATION WANTED—By experienced gardener, well up in bedding plants, carnations, landscape work and nursery stock. Aged 29. Please state wages. Address, R. B., care The Florists' Exchange.

SITUATION WANTED—Florist, 37 years of age, single, good grower of roses, carnations, mums and general stock wishes position, private or commercial. References. Address, O. X., care The Florists' Exchange.

SITUATION WANTED—As section man on first-class place to grow roses or carnations. Married man; please state particulars in first letter. Satisfactory references. Address, A. B. C., care The Florists' Exchange.

SITUATION WANTED—By florist, 28, reliable. 10 years experience in Europe and this country. Good potter and caretaker of ferns and stove plants. Private or commercial place. State wages. Address, O. U., care The Florists' Exchange.

SITUATION WANTED—Young Swedish man wishes position at once as assistant in general greenhouse work. One and a half years in this coutry. First-class references from present employer. Address, Anton Ljungquist, Pine Bush, N. Y.

SITUATION WANTED—Gardener, first-class cultivator, with knowledge of in and outside work will change position as foreman on commercial or private place. If interested, please ask for ability and references. Address, R. C., care The Florists' Exchange.

SITUATION WANTED As superintendent or gardener by a thoroughly competent and practical man; experienced in all branches of horticulture, private and commercial, nursery and landscape work. Married, small family.

Address, O. Q., care THE FLORISTS' EXCHANGE

Mention The Florists' Exchange when writing.

SITUATIONS WANTED

SITUATION WANTED—As foreman on private place with greenhouses. Twelve years experience in up-to-date places; five years at present place. Aged 32, married, no children. Good references as to character and ability. State wages. Address, O. Y., care The Florists' Exchange.

SITUATION WANTED—As assistant on a first-class private place with glass, where fruit, orchids and other first-class stock is grown. By young man, with seven years experience indoors and out. No. 1 references. State wages. Alex. Michael, Box 78, Millbrook, N. Y.

HELP WANTED

WANTED—Florist, near Boston. German preferred. State wages with board and room. Address, O. Z., care The Florists' Exchange.

WANTED—At $35 per month, assistant in rose houses, give full particulars in first letter. Address Permanent, care The Florists' Exchange.

WANTED—Foreman manager for a large commercial place where cut flowers only are grown. Apply with references. The Gasser Co., Cleveland, Ohio.

WANTED—Gardener. If Matthew ? who worked for me a short time in 1898 desires a situation, he can address, C. B. Lawson, Mott av., & 146th st., N. Y. City.

WANTED—An expert orchid grower. Must be practical and thoroughly experienced. No amateur or experimenter need apply. Louis Burk, Girard av. & Third st., Philadelphia.

WANTED—Night fireman for commercial carnation range; one who is experienced in packing blooms and propagating carnations. Reply stating wages and references. J. D. Cockcroft, Northport, N. Y.

WANTED—A thoroughly competent man to take charge of a section of Beauties. Apply Frank Dolan, care of John Young Company, Bedford Station, New York.

WANTED—A first-class designer and decorator, one who understands handling first-class trade. State wages, and how soon can come, in first letter. Honaker, The Florist, 162 W. Main st., Lexington, Ky.

WANTED—A first-class man for retail florist in Chicago; no greenhouse work. Must be a good salesman and designer. State wages. References. Address, M. D., care The Florists' Exchange.

WANTED—An energetic young man to assist in landscape work; fair knowledge of stock, trimming, etc., essential. Dutch or German preferred. State wages expected with references. A. Van Leeuwen, Jr., Worcester, Mass.

WANTED—At once, a good grower of all kinds of cut flowers, Easter and Christmas stock, and general bedding plants, to take charge. Wages, $75.00 per month, with house rent free. Address, O. T., care The Florists' Exchange.

WANTED—September 1, young or midde aged man of experience in general nursery work. Must be able to take charge of shipping and propagating. State wages wanted, age, nationality and references. C. R. Fish & Company, West Side Nurseries, Worcester, Mass.

WANTED—Salesman, one who is a hustler, and understands all about nursery stock, and a fair knowledge of landscape work. To travel. Must have a good record. Steady employment and good pay. Address with references, P. A. Keene, The Morris Nursery Company, 1 Madison avenue, New York.

WANTED—An experienced man to work in one of the leading flower stores in Hartford, Conn. Must be a good designer and decorator and know how to wait on the best class of trade. Applicant please state age, single or married, wages expected and also give references. Address, O. W., care The Florists' Exchange.

WANTED—Man for store, must have had wide experience in designing and decorating, accustomed to waiting upon high class trade and come well recommended. Steady position and good salary to the right person. Give full particulars with application and state salary expected. Address, Randolph & McClements, Highland av. & Baum st., Pittsburg, Pa.

MISCELLANEOUS WANTS

WANTED—Partner with $2,000 to $3,000 capital to start wholesale business. Address, O. J., care The Florists' Exchange.

WANTED—5,000 Acer Saccharinum, 1 to 3 feet. State price and size. V. A. Vanicek, The Rhode Island Nurseries, Newport, R. I.

WANTED TO BUY—Greenhouses to be taken down. State full particulars of same when writing. Address, F. W., care The Florists' Exchange.

Thirty cents is the minimum charge for advertisements on this page.

FOR SALE OR RENT

FOR SALE or will rent to a responsible party, a fine greenhouse property, 13,000 feet of glass. Fine residence. Address, Silas C. Howell, Lock Box 14, Pine Bush, New York.

FOR SALE—Florist's business, corner lot, nearly 7 acres, 26 miles from Philadelphia, 3 hot houses, frame house, barn, outbuildings, on trolley, and near station. For particulars, address, O. M., care The Florists' Exchange.

FOR SALE—Greenhouses comprising over 8,000 square feet of glass, situated in Northern New Jersey. Including all stock, horse, wagons, harness, etc. Doing good retail business. Address, B., care The Florists' Exchange.

FOR RENT—In Montclair, N. J., 4 greenhouses stocked with carnations, roses, chrysanthemums, etc. Dwelling house if required. This is a spendid opportunity; good market for everything grown. Trolley car passes the door. Apply Mrs. Robert MacInnes, 676 Valley Road, Upper Montclair, N. J.

FOR RENT—On account of bad health, 2 greenhouses 42x16; 3 greenhouses 96x16; 1 greenhouse 87x16; with store connections. Established 23 years; all heated by steam; southern exposure, with dwelling. Will give lease; 2 minutes to trolleys in city of Philadelphia. Good place for right man. Address, O. V., care The Florists' Exchange.

FOR SALE—Owing to the ill health of the principal owner, it has become advisable to offer for sale the entire stock of the best known florist establishment in southern California. A long time lease hold on the grounds may be obtained. A fine opportunity to step into an established business, incorporated. For particulars, write to Box 94, Ventura, Cal.

FOR SALE—At a bargain on account of removal and having two places, I will sell four greenhouses, two houses 16 x 80, other two 22 x 80. Boiler house, 16 x 20, with one large boiler to heat the place and another in reserve. Both boilers can burn buckwheat coal at a small cost. Only three or four years in use. Price only $1500. Hill Top Greenhouses, 15-18 Gray avenue, Utica, New York.

FOR SALE—Owing to failing health, I will sell my florist establishment, beautifully situated between Larchmont Manor and Mamaroneck, Westchester Co., New York, near railroad station; trolley lines within one minute walk. First class opportunity for the right man. Plenty of landscape and jobbing work. The place contains four acres, 2 greenhouses, 104 feet long and lots of sash; well stocked with trees and shrubs, etc.; horse, wagon and tools. Address, Box 44, Larchmont, New York.

STOCK FOR SALE

IMPERIAL VIOLET plants from cold frame, $2.50 per 100; $20 per 1,000. Sample sent for 15c. Paul Thomson, West Hartford, Conn.

FOR SALE—Queen Louise and C. A. Dana carnations, fine stock, $5.00 per 100; $25.00 per 1000. Fox & Rosen, Parkerford, Pa.

JERUSALEM CHERRIES, full of fruit, for 5 and 6 in. pots, $7.50 per doz. Smaller in bloom, $1.00 per doz. Ellis Bros., Keene, N. H.

Asparagus Sprengerii and Plumosus, 2 1-2 in., extra fine stock, ready for 4 in., $3.00 per 100. Cash. William Hoffman, 673 East avenue, Pawtucket, R. I.

CARNATIONS, extra fine, field-grown, Harlowarden, Estelle, Queen Louise, Lawson, White Lawson, Fred Burki, $6.00 per 100; $50.00 per 1000. Buts Bros., New Castle, Pa.

GIANT PANSIES, mixed; double daisies and forget-me-nots, blue, 50c. per 100 mailed; $2.50 per 1000 express. Cash. Shippensburg Floral Co., Shippensburg, Pa.

15,000 strong, healthy, field-grown violet plants of Farquhar, Lady Campbell, La France and California, $5 per 100; $45 per 1000. Chard [illegible] N. Y.

BABY RAMBLER roses, fine dormant stock, $25 per 100. 2 1-2 inch pot plants, extra well rooted $7 per 100, $65 per 1000. Orders booked for delivery now or any time up to late Spring. Samples free. Brown Brothers Co., Rochester, N. Y.

STOCK FOR SALE

CARNATIONS—Extra fine, field-grown plan[ts] Enchantress, Mrs. T. W. Lawson, $6.00 [per] 100; $50.00 per 1000. Joost, New Daybrea[k], Prosperity, Wolcott, $5.00 per 100; $40.00 [per] 1000. Terms cash. M. J. Schaaf, Dansvil[le], N. Y.

2,000 Brides, 3,000 Bridesmaids, 1,000 Meteo[rs], 1,000 Beauties, out of 4 in. pots. No bett[er] plants grown. Packed and delivered at [ex]press office. Maids and Brides, 5c.; Meteo[rs], 4c.; Beauties, 12c. each. Louis M. No[...], Madison, N. J.

Field-Grown carnation plants, strong [and] healthy; 100 Queen Louise; 150 Gov. W[ol]cott; 175 Boston Market; 50 White Laws[on]; 50 Thos. Lawson; 40 Prosperity; 50 Mrs. P[at]ten; 40 Flamingo; 100 Dahelm; 50 Crane; [...] Estelle; 40 Floriana; 40 Marquis at $4.00 [per] 100. The whole lot for $30.00. Cash. Hen[ry] Hansen, Catskill, N. Y.

FOR SALE

FOR SALE—Good hot water boilers for [flo]rists' use, cheap. Address, Box 966, W[il]mington, Del.

FOR SALE—Greenhouses; a great bargain; [...] houses, four boilers about 1,250 ft. 2 [in.] pipe, same of 4 in., to be removed. W[ill] be sold at once to highest bidder. Inqui[re] E. Morris, 64 Ann St., Newark, N. J.

FOR SALE—12 Hitchings hot water expans[ion] tanks for 3 1-2 in. pipe, in good conditio[n], cleaned, ready to set up. 1-3 price of ne[w]. Also horse lawn mower, easy running, $20.0[0]. Address, K. D., care The Florists' Exchang[e].

BOILERS, BOILERS, BOILERS.

SEVERAL good second hand boilers on han[d], also new No. 16 Hitchings at reduced co[st]. Write for list. Wm. H. Lutton, West Si[de] Avenue Station, C. R. R. of N. J., Jersey Ci[ty], N. J.

FOR SALE

BOILERS Second hand, guaranteed to be in go[od] condition, 2 No. 17 Hitchings at $104. and $125.00. 1 No. 16 Weathered $75.00. 1—4 se[c]tion Cambridge $75.00. 2—5 section No. 11, 37 [in.] grates, J. L. Mott, will heat 12,750 sq. ft. glass $175.00. 1—10 H. P. steam, $25.00. 1 NEW 6 secti[on] 24 in. grate Novelty boiler, will heat 4,100 sq. [ft.] glass, $140.00. New Henderson at low prices.

PIPE Good serviceable second hand. No Jun[k] with new threads. 2in. 7c.; 1¼in. 5½c.; 1 in. 4c.; 1 in. 3c.; 2½ in. 10c.; 3in. 14c.; 4 in. 18c. in. cast iron greenhouse 14c. 2 in. NEW, standa[rd] full lengths, 8½c. ft. All kinds of fittings for 4 i[n.] cast iron and all sizes wrought iron.

STOCKS AND DIES NEW ECONOMY, EAS[Y] WORKING. Complete s[et] to thread ½ in. to 1 in. pipe, $3.00; 1¼ in. to 2 i[n.] pipe, $4.00.

PIPE CUTTERS NEW SAUNDERS PATTER[N]. Size No. 1 cuts ⅛ in. to 1 in. pi[pe] $ .75; Size No. 2 cuts 1 in. to 2 in. pipe, $1.10.

STILLSON WRENCHES NEW, NO IMITATIO[N]. Size 18 in., grips ¼ [in.] to 2 in. pipe, $1.20. Size 24 in., grips ¼ in. to 2½ [in.] pipe $1.60. Size 36 in., grips ½ in. to 3½ in. pipe $4.[..]

PIPE VISES NEW, REED MAKE, NO IMIT[A]TION. Size No. 1 grips ⅛ in. to [...] in. pipe $1.50.

GARDEN HOSE NEW, 50 ft. lengths ¾ in. gu[ar]anteed 100 lbs. pressure 7½c. NEW, 50 ft. lengths ¾ in. not guaranteed 4¾c. ft.

BRASS HOSE VALVES New; not faucet[s]; something new, [...] in. at 65c.

HOT-BED SASH New; Gulf Cypress, 3 ft. x 6 [ft.] 75c.; glazed complete $1.60 u[p]. VENTILATORS; all sizes made to order. Seco[nd] hand sash glazed $1.00 and $1.25, good condition.

GLASS New American, 50 ft. to the bo[x]. 10x12 single at $1.75. 10x12, 12x[...] 10x15 B double $2.55. 12x14 to [...] 20 and 14x14 to 14x20 B double $2.70. 16x16 and 16x[...] B double $2.90. 16x24 B double $3.15. 16x20 and [...] x22 $3.00. 6x8, 7x9, 8x10 old, single $1.50. 8x14 o[ld], double $1.65; 10x14 old, double $1.75.

LINSEED OIL Strictly pure; barrel lots, 42c. gallon.

CARNATION SUPPORTS second hand, 50c. hundred.

VENTILATING APPARATUS second ha[nd] Hitchings ma[ke] arms, 25c.; hangers, 10c.; machines, $3.50; c[ol]lars, 5c.

SCREWS all sizes; mixed wood, from 1 in. t[o] [...] in., in boxes, 25 and 50 lbs, at 5c. lb.

PUMPS hot air; well pumps and force pum[ps]; all repairs.

Get our prices on second hand wood mater[ial]. We can furnish everything in new material to er[ect] any size house. Get our prices.

METROPOLITAN MATERIAL CO.

Greenhouse Wreckers

1398-1408 Metropolitan Avenue, BROOKLYN, [N. Y.]

Mention The Florists' Exchange when writ[ing].

ANNOUNCEMENT

HJALMAR HARTMANN of the firm of HJALMAR HARTMANN & C[O.], COPENHAGEN, DENMARK, wholesale growers and specialists in Danish CAU[LI]FLOWER and CABBAGE SEED, begs to inform the seed trade that he is now on [his] annual visit to the States and invites correspondence. Address 31 BARCLAY S[T.], NEW YORK.

Mention The Florists' Exchange when writing.

St. Louis.

The Week's News.

J. Schloss, representing Schloss Brothers, New York, called on the trade the past week.

Mrs. Ellison and daughter, who were away all Summer up north, have returned home; Harry Ellison had charge of the store during their absence.

Carl and Mrs. Beyer have returned from their two weeks' Eastern trip.

George Kalish and wife, who were in the East buying stock, are home again, much pleased with the trip.

Joseph Hauser, at Webster Groves, Mo., reports that he will make a specialty of Enchantress carnations and California violets this Winter; he made a great success of them last year.

George Waldbart is making in his windows a fine display of dahlias, cut from his large farm at Clayton.

John Connon, vice-president-elect of the Florists' Club, reports that he has housed all his carnations; the plants are very fine, and he expects a big cut.

J. S. Dierkes & Company have moved from their old location to Union avenue, which will give them much needed room.

W. C. Smith & Company have booked a number of large orders for our growers.

A. G. Griener is making an extraordinarily fine display of cactus plants in front of his place on Natural Bridge road. Mr. Griener makes a specialty of these plants and has worked up quite a shipping trade.

A. C. Canfield, of Springfield, is sending some fine asters and American Beauty to Kuehn.

L. A. Gieger is now with Mrs. M. M. Ayers, Grand avenue; for the past two years he was with Grim & Gorley, Cass avenue.

It is said that the St. Clair Floral Company, Belleville, Ill., will this Fall open a large retail store in East St. Louis.

J. F. Ammann, President of the Illinois State Florists' Association, was in Springfield, Ill., on Labor Day, consulting with Robert O. Dwyer, superintendent of floriculture of the State Fair, regarding the floral exhibits. Mr. Ammann and Albert T. Hey, Springfield, were appointed a committee at a meeting of the executive committee during the Dayton convention. Mr. Ammann says that all florists throughout Missouri should interest themselves in this fair, and make displays; he would be pleased to meet visiting florists from other states.

Local florists experienced one of the biggest days this year caused by the opening of a large department store, The Grand Leader. Several hundred floral designs of all descriptions were made; the downtown florists had the bulk of the work. The designs made by C. Young & Sons, J. J. Beneke, Miss T. Badderacco, Alex. Siegel, Riessen Floral Company, and Grim & Gorley were large and tastefully arranged. Ostertag Brothers had the American Beauty rose decorations. It is said that nearly $3,000 worth of decorations in cut flowers and plants were used.

ST. PATRICK.

Buffalo.

News Items.

The local florists and greenhouse men made a very creditable display in the Labor Day parade, showing a fine float decorated with palms, ferns, etc.

E. A. Slattery has left for his annual vacation.

Mae Pendergast of Palmer's is back at her desk after a very enjoyable vacation.

Arthur Beyer has returned from his trip through the Erie Canal and down the Hudson as far as New York City.

Past-President of the S. A. F., Wm F. Kasting is showing his hosts of friends and admirers the handsome chest of silverware presented to him at the convention.

Joseph Streit, foreman at S. A. Anderson's greenhouses, has lost his father-in-law, Mr. Rosenkranz, by death.

W. H. G.

Wholesale Prices of Cut Flowers, New York, Sept. 13, 1906

Prices quoted are by the hundred unless otherwise noted

Roses—A. Beauty, fancy—special	8.00 to	15.00
" extra	5.00 to	6.00
" No. 1	4.00 to	5.00
" No. 2	3.00 to	4.00
" No. 3	1.00 to	1.50
Bride, Maid, fancy—spe'l	2.00 to	3.00
" extra	1.00 to	2.00
" No. 1	...... to	1.00
" No. 2	...... to	.50
Golden Gate	...... to	......
Liberty	...... to	......
Mme. Abel Chatenay	...... to	......
Adiantum	.50 to	.75
Crowsanum	.50 to	1.00
Asparagus	25.00 to	50.00
" Plumosus, bunches	8.00 to	15.00
" Sprengerii, bunches	8.00 to	15.00
Asters	.25 to	3.00
Cattleyas	50.00 to	60.00
Daisies	...... to	......
Gladiolus	.50 to	1.00

Carnations—Inf'r grades, all colors	.50 to	1.00
Standard Varieties—White	1.00 to	2.00
Pink	1.00 to	2.00
Red	1.00 to	2.00
Yel. & Var.	...... to	......
*Fancy— (*The highest grades of standard var.)—White	...... to	......
Pink	...... to	......
Red	...... to	......
Yel. & Var.	...... to	......
Novelties	...... to	......
Dahlias, per bunch	.05 to	.15
Lilies	6.00 to	8.00
Lily of the Valley	1.00 to	3.00
Mignonette	...... to	......
Smilax	8.00 to	10.00

Wholesale Prices of Cut Flowers—Per 100

Boston Sept. 10, 1906	Buffalo Sept. 10, 1906	Detroit Sept. 11, 1906	Cincinnati Sept. 8, 1906	Baltimore Sept. 8, 1906	NAMES AND VARIETIES	Milwaukee Sept. 11, 1906	Phil'delphia Sept. 11, 1906	Pittsburg Sept. 10, 1906	St. Louis Sept. 10, 1906
10.00 to 20.00	20.00 to 25.00	10.00 to 35.00	to 30.00	to	ROSES: A. BEAUTY, fancy—special	to 25.00	15.00 to 20.00	20.00 to 25.00	20.00 to 25.00
6.00 to 10.00	12.00 to 20.00	to	20.00 to 25.00	to	" extra	15.00 to 18.00	10.00 to 15.00	12.50 to 18.00	12.50 to 15.00
2.00 to 6.00	6.00 to 12.00	to	10.00 to 15.00	to	" No. 1	10.00 to 12.50	5.00 to 7.00	8.00 to 10.00	6.00 to 10.00
to	3.00 to 6.00	to	4.00 to 6.00	to	" Culls and ordinary	4.00 to 6.00	1.00 to 4.00	5.00 to 6.00	3.00 to 5.00
to	5.00 to 6.00	3.00 to 6.00	to 5.00	to	BRIDE, 'MAID, fancy-special	to 6.00	to	to	4.00 to 5.00
6.00 to 8.00	4.00 to 5.00	to	2.00 to 4.00	to 4.00	" extra	to 5.00	6.00 to 8.00	to 6.00	2.00 to 3.00
4.00 to 6.00	3.00 to 4.00	to	1.00 to 3.00	to 3.00	" No. 1	to 4.00	4.00 to 5.00	to 4.00	to 1.00
1.00 to 4.00	2.00 to 3.00	to	to 2.00	to 2.00	" No. 2	to 2.00	2.00 to 3.00	to 2.00	to
to	to	4.00 to 8.00	to	2.00 to 4.00	GOLDEN GATE	4.00 to 6.00	4.00 to 8.00	to	2.00 to 4.00
1.00 to 6.00	3.00 to 7.00	to	to	2.00 to 4.00	K. A. VICTORIA	4.00 to 8.00	4.00 to 6.00	4.00 to 12.00	2.00 to 6.00
1.00 to 8.00	3.00 to 7.00	to	to	2.00 to 3.00	LIBERTY	4.00 to 6.00	8.00 to 6.00	to	to
to	3.00 to 6.00	4.00 to 10.00	to	to	METEOR	to	to	to	to
to	3.00 to 5.00	4.00 to 10.00	to	2.00 to 3.00	PERLE	4.00 to 6.00	to	to	2.00 to 4.00
to	to	to 50.00	to	to	ORCHIDS—Cattleyas	to	to 50.00	to	to
to	.50 to 1.00	to	to	.50 to .75	CARNATIONS: Inferior grades, all colors	to 1.00	.75 to 1.00	1.00 to 1.25	.50 to .75
to	1.00 to 1.25	to 1.00	to 1.50	to 1.00	Standard Varieties: White	to 1.00	.75 to 1.00	1.00 to 1.25	.50 to .75
to	1.00 to 1.25	to	to 1.50	to 1.00	Pink	to 1.00	.75 to 1.00	1.00 to 1.25	.50 to .75
to	1.00 to 1.25	to	to 1.50	to 1.00	Red	to 1.00	.75 to 1.00	1.00 to 1.25	.50 to .75
to	to	to 3.00	to 1.50	to	Yellow and var.	to 1.00	.75 to 1.00	1.00 to 1.25	to
1.00 to 2.00	1.50 to 2.00	to	to	to	Fancy Varieties: White	1.50 to 2.00	2.00 to 2.50	1.00 to 1.25	1.00 to 1.50
1.00 to 2.00	1.50 to 2.00	to	to	to	Pink	1.50 to 2.00	2.00 to 2.50	1.00 to 1.25	1.00 to 1.50
1.00 to 2.00	1.50 to 2.00	to	to	to	Red	1.50 to 2.00	2.00 to 2.50	1.00 to 1.25	1.00 to 1.50
1.00 to 2.00	1.50 to 2.00	to 1.50	to	to	Yellow and var	1.50 to 2.00	2.00 to 2.50	1.00 to 1.25	1.00 to 1.50
to	to	to	to	to	Novelties	to	to	to	to
.75 to 1.00	.50 to 1.00	to 2.00	to 1.00	to 1.00	ADIANTUM	to 1.00	to 1.00	1.25 to 1.50	to 1.00
to 50.00	to	25.00 to 60.00	to 50.00	25.00 to 50.00	ASPARAGUS, Plum. and Ten	20.00 to 30.00	25.00 to 35.00	30.00 to 50.00	25.00 to 50.00
to	to	20.00 to 30.00	to 35.00	25.00 to 50.00	" Sprengeri, bunches	20.00 to 30.00	25.00 to 35.00	20.00 to 30.00	25.00 to 75.00
.35 to 1.50	.50 to 2.00	to	to	to	ASTERS	.50 to 1.00	to	.50 to 2.00	.50 to 3.00
to	8.00 to 10.00	to 10.00	to	6.00 to 8.00	CALLAS	to	to	to	to
to	to	.75 to 1.50	to	to	DAISIES	to .40	3.00 to 4.00	to	to
3.00 to 6.00	1.00 to 3.00	8.00 to 10.00	to 2.00	2.00 to 3.00	GLADIOLUS	to	8.00 to 12.00	1.00 to 4.00	to 2.00
to	to	to	to	to 10.00	LILIES, Harrisii	to 12.50	to	to	to
to	12.00 to 15.00	to	to 15.00	to	" Longiflorum	to 12.50	2.00 to 4.00	15.00 to 18.00	to
2.00 to 4.00	3.00 to 4.00	3.00 to 4.00	to 4.00	to	LILY OF THE VALLEY	to	1.00 to 2.00	3.00 to 4.00	3.00 to 4.00
to	to	to	to	to	MIGNONETTE, ordinary	to	to	to	to
to	to	to	to	to	" fancy	to	to	to	to
to	to	4.00 to 8.00	to	to	PEONIES	to	15.00 to 20.00	to	to
10.00 to 12.50	to 15.00	12.50 to 15.00	to 15.00	12.50 to 20.00	SMILAX	to 15.00	to	12.50 to 15.00	to 12.50
to	to	to	to	to	VIOLETS, ordinary	to	to	to	to
to	to	to	to	to	" fancy	to	to	to	to
to	to	to	to	to	NARCISSUS	to	to	to	to
.25 to .35	.15 to .25	.50 to .75	to	to	SWEET PEAS	.25 to .50	to .50	to	to
to	to	to	to	to		to	to	to	to
to	to	to	to	to		to	to	to	to

Washington, D. C.

The past season has been rather severe on out of door stock on account of so much rain; nevertheless there is plenty of everything to meet the growing demand from now on. Dahlias, asters and other plants of that class have made too much rank growth and few flowers in some localities; but, as a whole, there is any quantity of flowering stock among our local growers. Roses are plentiful; Bride, Bridesmaid, Richmond, Killarney, Kaiserin Augusta Victoria are all of good size for this time of the year. Gude Brothers are cutting fine American Beauty, also John Cook's new rose, Enchanter, which Mr. Gude classes as the best pink rose he has handled. He finds one fault with it, and that is, it is shy on strong wood; but that may be overcome.

Theodore Diedrich of Congress Heights is growing on his favorite Primula veris superba for the coming season. Another specialty is violets, with Farquhar and Princess of Wales as favorites; Dorsett's single and Governor Herrick are also grown. The beauty spot at Mr. Diedrich's place at present is a large bed of Baby Rambler; this rose is a continuous bloomer from early Spring until late in the Fall.

J. H. Small has returned from his vacation which he spent in Maine. His firm has built an addition of two houses, which will be devoted to stove plants and Adiantum Farleyense.

George H. Brown is at present engaged in laying out the grounds around the State Capitol in Richmond, Va.

At the last monthly meeting of the florists' club, President Peter Bisset was awarded two first class certificates by the committee on awards, Z. D. Blackistone, chairman, for his two new nymphæas—Bissetii, a beautiful pink, and dentata magnifica, a large white. On invitation of the club, Professor Norton of the Agricultural Department staff will give an informal talk on the hybridization of carnations along the lines of Mendel's law. An invitation was read from R. Vincent, Jr. of White Marsh, Md., to the members of the club, to visit his dahlia farm on September 19; quite a number have signified their intention of going.

George Field donated ten dollars to be given in three different prizes for the best geraniums grown by amateurs and to be exhibited at the next Spring show. A smoker will be tendered in the near future to the club's bowling team which captured the second prize at the Dayton convention. JOSEPH A. GAUGES.

PORTLAND, ME.—The Sunday Times (September 2) contains an illustrated write-up of the establishment of Albert Dirwanger, florist, along with a portrait of that gentleman. The Times says Mr. Dirwanger is a successful grower of Acacia pubescens, for which he finds a large demand. He came to America from Bavaria in 1856, and has been located at Portland for the past 46 years. His greenhouses now cover an acre of ground.

Wholesale Prices of Cut Flowers, Chicago, Sept. 11, 1906

Prices quoted are by the hundred unless otherwise noted

ROSES — American Beauty		
36-inch stems ....per doz.	....	4.0
30-inch stems .... "	....	3.0
24-inch stems .... "	....	2.5
20-inch stems .... "	....	2.0
18-inch stems .... "	....	1.50
12-inch stems .... "	....	1.00
8-inch stems and shorts "	.50	.75
Bride Maid, fancy special	5.00	6.00
" extra	4.00	5.00
" No. 1	2.00	3.00
" No. 2	.50	1.00
Golden Gate	2.00	6.00
Carnot	2.00	6.00
Uncle John	2.00	8.00
Liberty	2.00	8.00
Richmond	2.00	8.00
Kaiserins	2.00	8.00
Killarney	3.00	8.00
Perle	2.00	6.00
Chatenay	2.00	6.00
Orchids—Cattleyas	50.00	75.00
Smilax	8.00	12.00
Lily of the Valley	2.00 to	4.00
Dahlias	2.00 to	3.00

CARNATIONS			
Inferior grades all colors	.25	to	.50
Standard Varieties — White	.75	to	1.00
Standard Varieties — Pink	.75	to	1.00
Standard Varieties — Red	.75	to	1.00
Standard Varieties — Yellow & var.	.75	to	1.00
*Fancy (The highest grades of Sta'd var) — White	1.50	to	2.00
*Fancy — Pink	1.50	to	2.00
*Fancy — Red	1.50	to	2.00
*Fancy — Yellow & var.	1.50	to	2.00
Novelties	....	to	....
Adiantum	.50	to	1.00
Asparagus, Plum. & Ten.	.35	to	.50
" Sprengeri, bunches	.35	to	.50
Gladiolus	2.00	to	6.00
Lilies, Longiflorum	8.00	to	12.00
Harrisii	8.00	to	12.00
Auratum	6.00	to	8.00
Nymphaea	....	to	1.00
Mignonette, ordinary	1.00	to	2.00
Tuberoses, Spikes	4.00	to	8.00
....	....	to	....
....	....	to	....
Hardy Ferns per 1000	1.00	to	1.50
Galax "	1.00	to	1.25
Asters	.50	to	2.50

Chicago.

Week's News.

Kruchten & Johnson are making ...ensive improvements in their head...rters at 51 Wabash avenue, in...ding the installation of a large ice ...st. They open their first season ...h every reason to anticipate a fair ...re of consignments and a good ...rket, as both members of the new ...cern are well known to both the ...al and the shipping trade.

...A. Henderson, floor manager at ...ughan's Seed Store, is studying up ...e tables, cable ciphers, etc., pre...atory to a ten weeks' trip to his ...ive heath in Bonnie Scotland. ...ch pleasure and a happy return.

...The floral arrangements for the ...yan dinner at the Auditorium, given ...the Jefferson Club, would have ...n conspicuous by their absence had ...not been for the generosity of a ...al concern. From a daily paper ...quote that the only flowers in evi...nce were a profusion of Mrs. Mar...ll Field roses, lavishly strewn upon ...tables, and contributed to the ...asion by our fellow craftsman, Pe... Reinberg.

...At the afternoon reception given to ...lliam J. Bryan at the Iroquois Club, ...e Central Floral Company had charge of the floral work and appropriately made a special feature of golden rod, the State flower of Nebraska.

A. Lange, one of our best known and most popular retailers accompanied by Mrs. Lange, has returned from a vacation trip which extended to Omaha, Neb., and the encomiums which they freely express make one think that the Western section must be a terrestrial paradise.

Cliff Pruner of the Winterson force, in charge of the supply department, has been seriously ill with typhoid fever, but we are pleased to state that he is now on the read to recovery and will soon be on duty again.

A new retail concern has entered the field under the name of the Forty-eighth Avenue Floral Company with headquarters at 1 South Forty-eighth avenue. The proprietors are Hoeckner & Vogt, the former having been for a number of years a well known employee of the Peter Reinberg salesroom at 51 Wabash avenue.

C. L. Washburn returned on Friday of last week from his Northern hunting and fishing trip which extended one hundred miles into Canada, and which he asserts could not have been more delightful.

The Geo. Wittbold Company have nearly completed the reconstruction of their Buckingham Place houses and by the time this notice is in type the establishment will be thoroughly prepared for the approaching cold weather. The concern this season is especially well stocked with small ferns, which as will be seen in our advertising columns are being offered at a bargain rate to make room.

L. H. Winterson and Mrs. Winterson returned last Saturday from their Dayton and Eastern tour, the latter part of which included, Buffalo, Niagara Falls, Albany, the Hudson River, New York, Coney Island, Philadelphia, Atlantic City, and a return trip over nearly the same course.

Mr. Lynch of the E. H. Hunt Company, although on duty again after his recent recovery from an attack of typhoid pneumonia, is not yet fully recuperated having lost nearly thirty pounds of his avoirdupois during his indisposition.

A. T. Phyfer, for a number of years the bookkeeper and confidential assistant of manager James Hartshorne of the Chicago Carnation Company, has been appointed as his successor in the management of the company's affairs at Joliet.

William Hartshorne of Joliet spent Friday, Saturday, and Sunday last in Chicago visiting friends and various points of interest about the city and suburbs.

The latest returns from the Poehlmann Brothers Company's greenhouses at Morton Grove are to the effect that the stock was never in better condition.

The first shipment of Japanese longiflorum bulbs arrived this week.

A trip through the Peter Reinberg ranges, or at least part of them, as it is impossible to cover them all in one day, shows that Foreman Collins has not forgotten how roses should be handled.

A call at the Jensen & DeKema establishment on Foster avenue early this week found their 50,000 feet of glass, entirely devoted to carnations, giving evidence of a crop up to the high standard which this firm's flowers have attained.

Wietor Brothers point with just pride to the present line of goods which is being shipped twice daily from their houses to the city office at 51 Wabash avenue.

There is a fair prospect of a new carnation concern at Joliet.

A. H. Budlong is back at his home in Bowmanville after his Summer vacation.

The Jewish holidays which occur this month on the 18th and 28th are looked forward to by quite a large number of the retail dealers as the opening of the season's business.

E. E. Pieser of the Kennicott Brothers Company returned this week from Canada, where Mrs. Pieser is still rusticating and to which point Mr. Pieser extended his tour from Dayton.

A. L. Vaughan returned from his Michigan tour on Friday of last week and reports a delightful and successful trip.

Miss Starrett, stenographer and bookkeeper for the Chicago Rose Company, is enjoying a two weeks' vacation.

Miss Tonner, who has made a tour of Europe in the interest of the supply department of the A. L. Randall Company, has returned and claims that she found no place in her travels which she prefers to home.

Bassett & Washburn's stock is constantly improving both in quality and quantity. Foreman Benson had to return from Dayton on the third day of the convention and as a result of the excessive heat was confined to his bed for a day or two after reaching home, but has fully recovered.

E. H. Hunt Company received their first consignment of chrysanthemums on Saturday last. They were handsome specimens of Monrovia and sold readily at $4 per dozen.

Henry Goetz of the concern of J. B. Goetz's Sons of Saginaw, Mich., has been spending two weeks in town and left the first of the week for home.

Frank Williams, the well known Randolph street retailer, has been taking a vacation at Muskegon, Mich.

Peter Reinberg returned on Thursday of last week from his duck hunting trip to Minnesota.

Zech & Mann report the quality of the stock consigned to them as steadily improving and a constant increase in the demand.

William Walker of Louisville, Ky., and his son were among our recent visitors.

J. B. O'Neil of the Vaughan Seed Store staff, after a business tour succeeding his trip to Dayton, has returned to Chicago.

WILLIAM K. WOOD.

DALLAS, TEX.—E. H. R. Green has completed a range of nine houses, containing nearly 60,000 sq. ft. of glass.

Wholesale Prices of Cut Flowers—Per 100

Boston Sept. 10, 1906	Buffalo Sept. 10, 1906	Detroit Sept. 11, 1906	Cincinnati Sept. 8, 1906	Baltimore Sept. 3, 1906	NAMES AND VARIETIES	Milwaukee Sept. 11, 1906	Phil'delphia Sept. 11, 1906	Pittsburg Sept. 10, 1906	St. Louis Sept. 10, 1906
10.00 to 20.00	20.00 to 25.00	10.00 to 35.00	to 30.00		ROSES — A. BEAUTY, fancy—special	to 25.00	15.00 to 20.00	20.00 to 25.00	20.00 to 25.00
6.00 to 10.00	12.00 to 20.00		20.00 to 25.00		" extra	15.00 to 18.00	10.00 to 15.00	12.50 to 18.00	12.50 to 15.00
2.00 to 6.00	6.00 to 12.00		10.00 to 15.00		" No. 1	10.00 to 12.50	5.00 to 7.00	8.00 to 10.00	6.00 to 10.00
	3.00 to 6.00		4.00 to 6.00		" Culls and ordinary	4.00 to 6.00	1.00 to 4.00	5.00 to 6.00	3.00 to 5.00
	5.00 to 8.00	3.00 to 6.00	to 5.00		BRIDE, 'MAID, fancy-special	to 6.00			4.00 to 5.00
6.00 to 8.00	4.00 to 5.00		2.00 to 4.00	to 4.00	" extra	to 5.00	6.00 to 8.00	to 6.00	2.00 to 3.00
4.00 to 6.00	3.00 to 4.00		1.00 to 3.00	to 3.00	" No. 1	to 4.00	4.00 to 5.00	to 4.00	to 1.00
1.00 to 4.00	2.00 to 3.00		to 2.00	to 2.00	" No. 2	to 2.00	2.00 to 3.00	to 2.00	
		4.00 to 8.00		2.00 to 4.00	GOLDEN GATE	4.00 to 6.00	4.00 to 8.00		2.00 to 4.00
1.00 to 6.00	3.00 to 7.00			2.00 to 4.00	K. A. VICTORIA	4.00 to 8.00	4.00 to 6.00	4.00 to 12.00	2.00 to 6.00
1.00 to 8.00	2.00 to 7.00			2.00 to 3.00	LIBERTY	4.00 to 6.00	3.00 to 6.00		
	3.00 to 6.00	4.00 to 10.00			METEOR				
	3.00 to 5.00	4.00 to 10.00		2.00 to 3.00	PERLE	4.00 to 6.00			2.00 to 4.00
		to 50.00			ORCHIDS—Cattleyas		to 50.00		
	.50 to 1.00			.60 to .75	CARNATIONS — Inferior grades, all colors	to 1.00	.75 to 1.00	1.00 to 1.25	.50 to .75
	1.00 to 1.25	to 1.00	to 1.50	to 1.00	Standard Varieties — White	to 1.00	.75 to 1.00	1.00 to 1.25	.50 to .75
	1.00 to 1.25		to 1.50	to 1.00	Standard Varieties — Pink	to 1.00	.75 to 1.00	1.00 to 1.25	.50 to .75
	1.00 to 1.25		to 1.50	to 1.00	Standard Varieties — Red	to 1.00	.75 to 1.00	1.00 to 1.25	.50 to .75
		to 3.00	to 1.50		Standard Varieties — Yellow and var.	to 1.00	.75 to 1.00	1.00 to 1.25	
1.00 to 2.00	1.50 to 2.00				Fancy Varieties — White	1.50 to 2.00	2.00 to 2.50	1.00 to 1.25	1.00 to 1.50
1.00 to 2.00	1.50 to 2.00				Fancy Varieties — Pink	1.50 to 2.00	2.00 to 2.50	1.00 to 1.25	1.00 to 1.50
1.00 to 2.00	1.50 to 2.00				Fancy Varieties — Red	1.50 to 2.00	2.00 to 2.50	1.00 to 1.25	1.00 to 1.50
1.00 to 2.00	1.50 to 2.00	to 1.50			Fancy Varieties — Yellow and var.	1.50 to 2.00	2.00 to 2.50	1.00 to 1.25	1.00 to 1.50
					Novelties				
.75 to 1.00	.50 to 1.00	to 2.00	to 1.00	to 1.00	ADIANTUM	to 1.00	to 1.00	1.25 to 1.50	to 1.00
to 50.00		25.00 to 60.00	to 50.00	25.00 to 50.00	ASPARAGUS, Plum. and Ten.	20.00 to 30.00	25.00 to 35.00	30.00 to 50.00	25.00 to 50.00
		20.00 to 30.00	to 35.00	25.00 to 50.00	" Sprengeri, bunches	20.00 to 30.00	25.00 to 35.00	20.00 to 30.00	25.00 to 75.00
.35 to 1.50	.50 to 2.00				ASTERS	.50 to 1.00		.50 to 2.00	.50 to 3.00
	8.00 to 10.00	to 10.00		6.00 to 8.00	CALLAS				
		.75 to 1.50			DAISIES	to .40	3.00 to 4.00		
3.00 to 6.00	1.00 to 3.00	8.00 to 10.00	to 2.00	2.00 to 3.00	GLADIOLUS		8.00 to 12.00	1.00 to 4.00	to 2.00
				to 10.00	LILIES, Harrisii	to 12.50			
	12.00 to 15.00		to 15.00		" Longiflorum	to 12.50	2.00 to 4.00	15.00 to 18.00	
2.00 to 4.00	3.00 to 4.00	3.00 to 4.00	to 4.00		LILY OF THE VALLEY		1.00 to 2.00	2.00 to 4.00	3.00 to 4.00
					MIGNONETTE, ordinary				
					" fancy				
		1.00 to 8.00			PEONIES		15.00 to 20.00		
10.00 to 12.50	to 15.00	12.50 to 15.00	to 15.00	12.50 to 20.00	SMILAX	to 15.00		12.50 to 15.00	to 12.50
					VIOLETS, ordinary				
					" fancy				
					NARCISSUS				
.25 to .35	.15 to .25	.50 to .75			SWEET PEAS	.25 to .50	to .50		

Washington, D. C.

The past season has been rather severe on out of door stock on account of so much rain; nevertheless there is plenty of everything to meet the growing demand from now on. Dahlias, asters and other plants of that class have made too much rank growth and few flowers in some localities; but, as a whole, there is any quantity of flowering stock among our local growers. Roses are plentiful; Bride, Bridesmaid, Richmond, Killarney, Kaiserin Augusta Victoria are all of good size for this time of the year. Gude Brothers are cutting fine American Beauty, also John Cook's new rose, Enchanter, which Mr. Gude classes as the best pink rose he has handled. He finds one fault with it, and that is, it is shy on strong wood; but that may be overcome.

Theodore Diedrich of Congress Heights is growing on his favorite Primula veris superba for the coming season. Another specialty is violets, with Farquhar and Princess of Wales as favorites; Dorsett's single and Governor Herrick are also grown. The beauty spot at Mr. Diedrich's place at present is a large bed of Baby Rambler; this rose is a continuous bloomer from early Spring until late in the Fall.

J. H. Small has returned from his vacation which he spent in Maine. His firm has built an addition of two houses, which will be devoted to stove plants and Adiantum Farleyense.

George H. Brown is at present engaged in laying out the grounds around the State Capitol in Richmond, Va.

At the last monthly meeting of the florists' club, President Peter Bisset was awarded two first class certificates by the committee on awards, Z. D. Blackistone, chairman, for his two new nymphæas—Bissetii, a beautiful pink, and dentata magnifica, a large white. On invitation of the club, Professor Norton of the Agricultural Department staff will give an informal talk on the hybridization of carnations along the lines of Mendel's law. An invitation was read from R. Vincent, Jr. of White Marsh, Md., to the members of the club, to visit his dahlia farm on September 19; quite a number have signified their intention of going.

George Field donated ten dollars to be given in three different prizes for the best geraniums grown by amateurs and to be exhibited at the next Spring show. A smoker will be tendered in the near future to the club's bowling team which captured the second prize at the Dayton convention. JOSEPH A. GAUGES.

PORTLAND, ME.—The Sunday Times (September 2) contains an illustrated write-up of the establishment of Albert Dirwanger, florist, along with a portrait of that gentleman. The Times says Mr. Dirwanger is a successful grower of Acacia pubescens, for which he finds a large demand. He came to America from Bavaria in 1856, and has been located at Portland for the past 46 years. His greenhouses now cover an acre of ground.

Wholesale Prices of Cut Flowers, Chicago, Sept. 11, 1906

Prices quoted are by the hundred unless otherwise noted

ROSES — American Beauty		
36-inch stems.........per doz.	.... to	4.00
30-inch stems .... "	.... to	3.00
24-inch stems.......... "	.... to	2.50
20-inch stems.......... "	.... to	2.00
18-inch stems.......... "	.... to	1.50
12-inch stems.......... "	.... to	1.00
8-inch stems and shorts "	.50 to	.75
Bride Maid, fancy special......	5.00 to	6.00
" extra..............	4.00 to	5.00
" No. 1..............	2.00 to	3.00
" No. 2..............	.50 to	1.00
Golden Gate..........................	2.00 to	6.00
Carnot	2.00 to	6.00
Uncle John............................	2.00 to	8.00
Liberty...................................	2.00 to	8.00
Richmond	2.00 to	8.00
Kaiserins..............................	2.00 to	8.00
Killarney.............................	3.00 to	8.00
Perle.....................................	2.00 to	6.00
Chatenay	2.00 to	6.00
Orchids—Cattleyas.	50.00 to	75.00
SMILAX	8.00 to	12.00
LILY OF THE VALLEY............	2.00 to	4.00
DAHLIAS................................	2.00 to	3.00

CARNATIONS		
Inferior grades all colors	.25 to	.50
STANDARD VARIETIES — White........	.75 to	1.00
STANDARD VARIETIES — Pink...........	.75 to	1.00
STANDARD VARIETIES — Red..............	.75 to	1.00
STANDARD VARIETIES — Yellow & var....	.75 to	1.00
*FANCY (The highest grades of Sta'd var) — White.........	1.50 to	2.00
*FANCY — Pink.............	1.50 to	2.00
*FANCY — Red..............	1.50 to	2.00
*FANCY — Yellow & var	1.50 to	2.00
NOVELTIES	.... to	....
ADIANTUM................................	.50 to	1.00
ASPARAGUS, Plum. & Ten........	.35 to	.50
" Sprengeri, bunches.	.35 to	.50
GLADIOLUS..............................	2.00 to	6.00
LILIES, Longiflorum..........	8.00 to	12.00
HARRISII..............................	8.00 to	12.00
AURATUM.............................	6.00 to	8.00
NYMPHAEA............................	.... to	1.00
MIGNONETTE, ordinary	1.00 to	2.00
TUBEROSES, SPIKES............	4.00 to	8.00
....	.... to	....
....	.... to	....
HARDY FERNS per 1000	1.00 to	1.50
GALAX "	1.00 to	1.25
ASTERS...................................	.50 to	2.50

Chicago.

The Week's News.

Kruchten & Johnson are making extensive improvements in their headquarters at 51 Wabash avenue, including the installation of a large ice chest. They open their first season with every reason to anticipate a fair share of consignments and a good market, as both members of the new concern are well known to both the local and the shipping trade.

A. Henderson, floor manager at Vaughan's Seed Store, is studying up time tables, cable ciphers, etc., preparatory to a ten weeks' trip to his native heath in Bonnie Scotland. Much pleasure and a happy return.

The floral arrangements for the Bryan dinner at the Auditorium, given by the Jefferson Club, would have been conspicuous by their absence had it not been for the generosity of a local concern. From a daily paper we quote that the only flowers in evidence were a profusion of Mrs. Marshall Field roses, lavishly strewn upon the tables, and contributed to the occasion by our fellow craftsman, Peter Reinberg.

At the afternoon reception given to William J. Bryan at the Iroquois Club, The Central Floral Company had charge of the floral work and appropriately made a special feature of golden rod, the State flower of Nebraska.

A. Lange, one of our best known and most popular retailers accompanied by Mrs. Lange, has returned from a vacation trip which extended to Omaha, Neb., and the encomiums which they freely express make one think that the Western section must be a terrestrial paradise.

Cliff Pruner of the Winterson force, in charge of the supply department, has been seriously ill with typhoid fever, but we are pleased to state that he is now on the read to recovery and will soon be on duty again.

A new retail concern has entered the field under the name of the Forty-eighth Avenue Floral Company with headquarters at 1 South Forty-eighth avenue. The proprietors are Hoeckner & Vogt, the former having been for a number of years a well known employée of the Peter Reinberg salesroom at 51 Wabash avenue.

C. L. Washburn returned on Friday of last week from his Northern hunting and fishing trip which extended one hundred miles into Canada, and which he asserts could not have been more delightful.

The Geo. Wittbold Company have nearly completed the reconstruction of their Buckingham Place houses and by the time this notice is in type the establishment will be thoroughly prepared for the approaching cold weather. The concern this season is especially well stocked with small ferns, which as will be seen in our advertising columns are being offered at a bargain rate to make room.

L. H. Winterson and Mrs. Winterson returned last Saturday from their Dayton and Eastern tour, the latter part of which included, Buffalo, Niagara Falls, Albany, the Hudson River, New York, Coney Island, Philadelphia, Atlantic City, and a return trip over nearly the same course.

Mr. Lynch of the E. H. Hunt Company, although on duty again after his recent recovery from an attack of typhoid pneumonia; is not yet fully recuperated having lost nearly thirty pounds of his avoirdupois during his indisposition.

A. T. Phyfer, for a number of years the bookkeeper and confidential assistant of manager James Hartshorne of the Chicago Carnation Company, has been appointed as his successor in the management of the company's affairs at Joliet.

William Hartshorne of Joliet spent Friday, Saturday, and Sunday last in Chicago visiting friends and various points of interest about the city and suburbs.

The latest returns from the Poehlmann Brothers Company's greenhouses at Morton Grove are to the effect that the stock was never in better condition.

The first shipment of Japanese longiflorum bulbs arrived this week.

A trip through the Peter Reinberg ranges, or at least part of them, as it is impossible to cover them all in one day, shows that Foreman Collins has not forgotten how roses should be handled.

A call at the Jensen & DeKema establishment on Foster avenue early this week found their 50,000 feet of glass, entirely devoted to carnations, giving evidence of a crop up to the high standard which this firm's flowers have attained.

Wietor Brothers point with just pride to the present line of goods which is being shipped twice daily from their houses to the city office at 51 Wabash avenue.

There is a fair prospect of a new carnation concern at Joliet.

A. H. Budlong is back at his home in Bowmanville after his Summer vacation.

The Jewish holidays which occur this month on the 18th and 28th are looked forward to by quite a large number of the retail dealers as the opening of the season's business.

E. E. Pieser of the Kennicott Brothers Company returned this week from Canada where Mrs. Pieser is still rusticating and to which point Mr. Pieser extended his tour from Dayton.

A. L. Vaughan returned from his Michigan tour on Friday of last week and reports a delightful and successful trip.

Miss Starrett, stenographer and bookkeeper for the Chicago Rose Company, is enjoying a two weeks' vacation.

Miss Tonner, who has made a tour of Europe in the interest of the supply department of the A. L. Randall Company, has returned and claims that she found no place in her travels which she prefers to home.

Bassett & Washburn's stock is constantly improving both in quality and quantity. Foreman Benson had to return from Dayton on the third day of the convention and as a result of the excessive heat was confined to his bed for a day or two after reaching home, but has fully recovered.

E. H. Hunt Company received their first consignment of chrysanthemums on Saturday last. They were handsome specimens of Monrovia and sold readily at $4 per dozen.

Henry Goetz of the concern of J. B. Goetz's Sons of Saginaw, Mich., has been spending two weeks in town and left the first of the week for home.

Frank Williams, the well known Randolph street retailer, has been taking a vacation at Muskegon, Mich.

Peter Reinberg returned on Thursday of last week from his duck hunting trip to Minnesota.

Zech & Mann report the quality of the stock consigned to them as steadily improving and a constant increase in the demand.

William Walker of Louisville, Ky., and his son were among our recent visitors.

J. B. O'Neil of the Vaughan Seed Store staff, after a business tour succeeding his trip to Dayton, has returned to Chicago.

WILLIAM K. WOOD.

DALLAS, TEX.—E. H. R. Green has completed a range of nine houses, containing nearly 60,000 sq. ft. of glass.

MERIDEN, CONN.—Adolph Greenbacker, the florist has bought from Arthur E. Owens the latter's farm on Murdock avenue. The property comprises 110 acres of land and a fine house and barns. The place is considered one of the finest farms in this vicinity. One of Mr. Greenbacker's sons will take full charge of the farm.

AVERYVILLE, ILL.—B. Juergens is making improvements on his greenhouse in Birket's Hollow. Mr. Juergens' business has been exceptionally good this Summer and in order to take care of the trade in better shape he is putting up a 26x50 cement block display room.

COBBSKILL, N. Y.—Lewis S. Holmes has purchased the greenhouses and house occupied by A. Goldring and belonging to the Lane estate, for $3,300.

COLORADO SPRINGS, COL.—A hailstorm on the 30th of August broke some glass for Frank F. Crump and John W. Smith. Both were insured.

Baltimore.

News Notes.

Business is rather quiet at present, but "Jubilee Week" is being ushered in with a great hurrah. Already thousands of visitors are pouring into the city to help celebrate the rejuvenation and upbuilding of the greater and new Baltimore from the disastrous fire of several years ago; consequently business will likely be brisk the present week. Home product shows, trade exhibitions, parades, illuminations, and decorations on a lavish scale are in order, and the city is in holiday attire. The firemen of Baltimore and other cities, together with Uncle Sam's warships and sailors with the soldiers from the forts, will take part in the parades.

The Baltimore Florists' Club will visit the establishment of R. Vincent, Jr. & Son, White Marsh, Md., in a body on September 19, to inspect the thirty-acre dahlia field, which will be a sight to behold. Mr. Vincent expects a number of florists from Washington, Philadelphia, and other points.

The club meeting on Monday was enlivened by reports of the Dayton convention.

The long spell of wet and rainy weather during August has subsided just in time to save the carnations from destruction; field-rot, however, has wiped out thousands, especially in flat and poorly drained places.

From present indications there will be a celery famine in Baltimore, for celery plants can not be had for love or money. CHAS. L. SEYBOLD.

Indianapolis.

News Jottings.

Mr. Little, of the Morehead Manufacturing Company, finds this city a satisfactory territory for the sale of the firm's steam trap; he is installing several here.

Herman Junge, of the Smith & Young Company, has a new invention which, although it will not make him rank with Edison, is one of value to his brother florists. Heretofore Mr. Junge and his employees have been digging for grubs in violet pots. The grubs would immediately retire to their dens, usually directly beneath the heart of the plant. The new idea is for a grower to use a pitcher of water and a pair of shears, the water forcing the grub to the surface, his head being then severed by the shears.

The downtown stores have beautiful window displays for the Indiana State Fair visitors. A number of local and out-of-town florists will compete for the premiums which are not, however, as attractive as formerly. A. Wiegand & Sons have their window well arranged with fancy foliage plants. An interurban car bearing the inscription "State Fair Special" is the attraction in the window of Bertermann Brothers Company.

Thomas Hart has completed a new greenhouse.

Visitors: H. Freund, Milwaukee; Fred Weber, St. Louis; Mr. DeGraw, Denver; Mr. Fancourt, Philadelphia.
I. B.

Oceanic, N. J.

The meeting of the Monmouth County Horticultural Society took place September 7. The reading of Wm. Turner's paper on "Fruit Culture Under Glass" was postponed until the next meeting, September 21. The final premium list for the chrysanthemum show was ordered printed. Mr. Turner had on exhibition some beautiful Pitmaston pears averaging 1¼ pounds, and scoring 98 points. He also showed the Thomas Rivers peach, these scoring 95 points. This fruit was grown under glass. B.

WEADLEYTOWN, PA.—Julius Snyder has purchased several acres of ground adjoining his property, and intends to engage in business on a more extensive scale.

Cincinnati.

The Fall Festival Exhibit.

This exhibit was staged on Thursday, September 6, by W. K. Partridge, the Fall Festival Association paying $700 for the same. The show was made in the foyer of Music Hall, under direction of Fred. Belmer, and for artistic arrangement and fine quality of goods used, never was surpassed in this city. Three large oval shaped tables were situated in the center of the foyer; table No. 1 consisting of cut orchids and plants, baskets of roses, lilies and ferns, principally adiantum. Table No. 2, a vase in center containing one hundred long stemmed American Beauty roses, Wittboldi ferns and adiantum cuneatum; fancy leaved caladiums, well grouped, finished the base. Table No. 3 consisted of palms, anthuriums, crotons, araucarias and adiantum, the massing producing a gorgeous effect.

On six large pillars, standing twelve feet high, were huge vases of hydrangeas in bloom, while smaller vases carried chrysanthemums, Monrovia, yellow, one dozen, and Willowbrook, white. I believe the yellow were grown by The E. G. Hill Company, the white by H. Weber's Sons. Other vases contained gladioli, dahlias, roses, etc.; several vases of fine auratum lilies made a handsome showing. In a secluded nook, a large pan, five to six feet in diameter and fourteen inches deep, contained a miniature pond of lilies and aquatics; adiantum and Eulalia zebrina forming a very realistic effect for a background. Eight or ten window boxes were filled with hydrangea and gladiolus blooms, with ferns and palms scattered throughout, making a very pleasing effect. The balcony was draped with wild smilax and gladioli in bunches dispersed throughout with hanging baskets of Boston ferns in profusion. At either end of the foyer, worked out to a nicety, were two flags, one, Old Glory, the other an emblem of the Fall Festival, while the word "Partridge," done in immortelles, hung in full view.

Five hundred dollars will be divided up in the competition which takes place on September 20, of table decorations, wreaths, bridal bouquets, and baskets. We would like to see some outside talent here; this competition is open to all.

Business for September is starting out better than last year, and stock is commencing to come in. American Beauty roses are good, and sell at $1 per foot per dozen; asters, $1 to $1.50, with white scarce. Carnations are not worth much as yet, but what few do come in, are purchased quickly. Bride and Bridesmaid roses are fair, but small, and not in great demand. Chrysanthemums, the advent of which we always welcome, will be coming in soon.

E. G. GILLETT.

Cleveland.

With the cool nights and mornings which this month brings, a decided change can be noted in various cut-flower stocks; roses, for instance, are larger, color better, and a good length of stem, but mildew has the leaf, and at this time of year it is hard to fight. Field grown carnations look nice, and those which have been transferred to the houses are looking fine.

Bulb time is close at hand, and freesia, paper whites, Romans, callas, and Chinese lilies are in.

Gladioli are the Summer flower, and the quantities that are brought into the market are surprising; they are deservedly popular, and can be seen used in many ways, baskets, funeral designs, bouquets, etc.

Boston ferns are just coming in; plants look particularly fine. S. N. Pentecost has one large house filled with them and they are first class. He is building again this year, two new houses, 20x100 ft.

Milton Parks, the Citizens' "Lobby" florist, has a knock-down stand at Luna Park, three balls for a nickel, and he disposes of lots and lots of flowers in that way and makes money besides.

The Charlesworth's civil war badges in carpet bedding at the Public Square never looked better than this year.

William Brinker and Tilton & Son, seedsmen, report good Fall business.

There was a gladiolus show held out at Euclid Beach recently; it was quite a success. O. G.

Dayton, O.

On Thursday, August 30, a report of the recent S. A. F. convention was submitted, and showed that the financial end will come out about even.

MARION, IND.—Gunnar Teilmann has returned from a two months' trip to Europe. He has had chrysanthemum Monrovia in bloom since September 1. The flowers are shipped to Chicago.

FINDLAY, O.—J. J. Wanland, the florist, will erect an office at the Barnd-Karg greenhouse, recently purchased by the former and his associates from the latter.

THE FLORISTS' EXCHANGE

We are a straight shoot and aim to grow into a vigorou...

A WEEKLY MEDIUM OF INTERCHANGE FOR FLORISTS, NURSERYMEN, SEEDSMEN AND THE TRADE IN GENERAL

Vol. XXII. No. 12 — NEW YORK AND CHICAGO, SEPTEMBER 22, 1906 — One Dollar Per Year

O E Stone
Hatch Expt Sta
'07

NOW READY

Narcissus Paper White Grandiflora
---and---
White Roman Hyacinths

We offer the finest bulbs for immediate delivery, as follows:

Narcissus Paper White Grandiflora, finest quality bulbs, 13 c/m and up, 1,250 bulbs to the case, $11.25 per case; less quantities at $1.00 per 100.

Paper White Grandiflora Narcissus is always a money-maker. Plant at once for earliest crop, which is the most profitable.

White Roman Hyacinths, finest quality bulbs, 12 to 15 c/m, about 1,800 bulbs to the case, $2.50 per 100, $23.00 per 1,000.

Freesia Refracta Alba. Finest Bermuda-grown bulbs, ½ inch up, $7.50 per 1,000.

Bermuda Buttercup Oxalis. $1.00 per 100, $7.50 per $1,000.

Callas. Selected bulbs, 1½ to 1¾ in. in diameter, $6.00 per 100; mammoth bulbs, 1¾ to 2 in. in diameter, $8.00 per 100; exhibition bulbs, 2 to 2½ in. in diameter, $10.00 per 100.

F. R. PIERSON CO., Tarrytown-on-Hudson, N. Y.

Mention The Florists' Exchange when writing.

Hyacinths—Tulips,

Narcissus, etc., Ready Now

We quote below a few kinds Narcissus. Before buying send for our FALL BOOK FOR FLORISTS, or send us your list for pricing.

		100	1000
Narcissus,	Paper White True Grandiflora, 13 ctm.	$0.90	$ 8.50
"	Trumpet Major French, for Xmas forcing	1.25	10.00
"	Trumpet Major Dutch Selected	1.10	9.00
"	Empress	2.25	20.00
"	Emperor	1.80	16.00
"	Princeps	.85	7.00
"	Golden Spur	1.75	15.25
"	Double Von Sion, fancy select	1.45	12.00
"	" " " Double Nosed XXX	2.25	19.00
"	" " " Jumbo, Mother Bulbs	3.50	28.00

Write for Prices—HYACINTHS, TULIPS, FREESIA, OXALIS, CHINESE LILIES, JAPAN LONGIFLORUM etc., etc.

Vaughan's Seed Store

14 BARCLAY ST.
NEW YORK
CHICAGO, 84-86 Randolph Street, Greenhouses, Western Springs, Ill.

Mention The Florists' Exchange when writing.

Asparagus Plumosus Nanus

Cut strings, 50 cts. each

W. H. ELLIOTT

Brighton, Mass.

Mention The Florists' Exchange when writing.

HYDRANGEA OTAKSA

(York State strong field-grown plants.)

3 to 4 Heads, $1.50 per 12, $12.00 per 100; 4 to 5 Heads, $2.00 per 12, $15.00 per 100; 5 to 6 Heads, $2.50 per 12, $18.00 per 100; 6 to 7 Heads, $2.75 per 12, $20.00 per 100.

ASPARAGUS PLUMOSUS NANUS

Seedlings Grown in Flats. $2.00 per 100, $15.00 per 1000. Flat containing about 500 plants, $7.50.

FERNS IN FLATS, leading varieties or assorted, $2.50 per flat.

Write for Bulb Catalogue and Special Prices on Quantities of Bulbs.

ARTHUR T. BODDINGTON

342 West 14th Street . . . New York City

Mention The Florists' Exchange when writing.

CONTENTS AND INDEX TO ADVERTISERS, PAGE 343

Seed Trade Report.

AMERICAN SEED TRADE ASSOCIATION

Henry W. Wood, Richmond, Va., president; C. S. Burge, Toledo, O., first vice-president; G. B. McVay, Birmingham, Ala., second vice-president; C. E. Kendel, Cleveland, O., secretary and treasurer; J. H. Ford, Ravenna, O., assistant secretary.

The value of the imports of seeds for the year ended June 30, 1906 was $5,388,043 as against $3,457,619 in 1905.

OKLAHOMA CITY, OKLA. — The W. O. Church Seed Company has been incorporated with a capital stock of $5,000. The incorporators are W. O. Church, Jeamsey Church and W. O. Kneck.

NEW YORK.—Chr. Hansen, secretary and traveling representative of A. Hansen, cauliflower specialist of Copenhagen, Denmark, sailed for home on Thursday, September 20, after a successful trip, during which he visited the larger cities of the United States.

Alfred Emerich, representing Messrs. Vilmorin, Andrieux & Company, Paris, France, is expected in New York about September 22, to make his usual business trip through the United States and Canada. He was recently presented with a gold medal, as collaborator with his firm, at the St. Louis Exposition. His New York address will be care of H. Frank Darrow, 26 Barclay street.

CHICAGO.—J. E. Northrup of Northrup, King & Company, Minneapolis, Minn., has been quite ill in Chicago for the past two weeks, having undergone a surgical operation at the Presbyterian hospital. The latest reports are favorable.

C. C. Massie of the same firm was in town this week and passed on to Detroit.

BOSTON.—The H. E. Fiske Seed Company opened up their spacious store for business this week in the new building on the old W. W. Rawson site in Faneuil Hall Square. The whole store is new throughout and is elegant in its arrangement. The show windows are an improvement over those formerly in this location, and are unquestionably the best of any store in this line in the city. The offices occupy a prominent elevation in the rear of the store, and the vegetable, flower seeds and supplies alike occupy ample space in the main part of the store. The upper floors are used for the handling of seeds in large quantities, and there is ample storage room for an extensive business. D.

ORANGE, CONN.—Messrs. S. D. Woodruff & Sons, write as under September 17.—We are having the best possible weather for ripening up the sweet corn crops, and a fair crop of fine quality is practically now assured, although the acreage has been materially reduced, and the quantity therefore not up to that of the past two years. Most of the other seed crops have now been secured. The onion yield will be disappointing, although little of it is as yet threshed and cleaned up. The beet seed yield is good, with very light quantities in growers' hands, however, still unsold. Kale seed is a good crop, but practically all sold out. Carrot, parsnip and turnip have given only moderate yields. There is a slight demand for turnip; the call for almost all other seeds being extra good.

SEED CROPS ON LONG ISLAND.—The seed crops of 1906 are mostly cleaned up, and the returns, in many instances, are disappointing; in a few they are surprising. Many growers who have almost invariably had from good to extraordinary crops have this year fallen below the average, while those that, in previous years, have had but poor success, have had more than an average crop.

Cabbage.—From the acreage set the yield is below the average, and the sample, owing to the excessive rains during the harvest, will not be as bright as usual; but the seeds are large and plump. A peculiar condition as to the yield of the various varieties is noticeable; the "why" no one can understand. Take, for instance, the Mammoth Rock Red, which is usually a shy seeder. It would this year have given an enormous crop had it not been for the loss of the seed during harvest. This variety is usually grown in a section by itself to avoid cross fertilization Here the storms were more severe than in other parts of the Island, and a large quantity of seed was lost in the fields. As a rule, the Wakefields have done better than the flat-headed types, which is exceptional.

Brussels Sprouts.—This crop is the most uncertain of any of the Brassicas. This year the yield is surprising—more than three times as much as the average. This fact is wholly due to the past mild Winter. We find it a difficult matter to Winter over the crop; it will not stand putting away in trenches, like the cabbage, and will not endure an extreme low temperature unprotected. The present year's crop will be sufficient for the next three years.

Rutabagas have turned out very well, and a satisfactory crop of a fine sample has been secured. The same is true with the Purple Top Globe turnip, which is a specialty at the westerly end of Long Island.

Scotch kale did much better than usual, and all orders will be filled completely; the same is true with the slow-seeding and the ordinary Siberian types.

Spinach is no longer a Long Island industry, as the price paid the farmer is not sufficient to make it a paying crop. Many of the reports as to the large crops grown the past season are romantic.

What is the outlook for the crop of 1907? is the important question with the growers. It is a little early to form an opinion, and we can only say, the plants were set on time, but suffered from the heat and drought of the past month. The recent rains have come to the rescue, and a rapid growth is now being made.

GRASS SEED—Yellow Trefoil. In the protests of Benjamin Dusenbury against the assessment of duty by the collector of customs at the port of New York, before Board 3, General Appraisers; September 5, 1906. The merchandise was described as consisting of the seed of the yellow trefoil or black medic (Medicago lupulina), which was classified under the provision in paragraph 254, tariff act of 1897 for seeds not specially provided for, and was claimed to be free of duty under paragraph 656 as grass seed. Protests sustained. Opinion by Waite, General Appraiser: "It is invoiced as clover seed, which the Board has hitherto classed as grass seed for tariff purposes, G. A. 2442 (T. D. 14720). While Medicago lupulina is probably not clover in a botanical sense, which would seem to include only plants of the genus trifolium, it has the appearance of clover, is closely allied to that plant, and is classified as a clover in the catalogues of seed dealers if not in common speech. But whether to be regarded as clover or not, the plant in question is shown by the evidence to be a forage plant such as would fall in the category of the so-called "artificial grasses," and is, therefore, entitled to free entry under paragraph 656 in accordance with the principle applied in Board decision In re Willett Drug Company, G. A. 6350 (T. D. 27306).

European Notes.

The hot spell has burned itself out at last and abundant rains have fallen in most of the districts where seeds are grown. With the thermometer as high as 97 degrees in the shade in the southeast of England, it must be admitted that the conditions have been quite abnormal and that some unusual results may be expected later on. The crops most affected at present are those for 1907. The plants of the whole Brassica family have been standing in the seed beds, and are so stunted and drawn that it is hardly worth while to transplant them, for, in the case of the late cabbages especially, it is hardly possible for them to run next year. The earlier varieties may do better, but cannot possibly produce more than half a crop.

Beets and mangels may grow large enough if mild weather continues, for us to distinguish their true character; and as small plants of both these articles sometimes produce the heavient crops of seed, the outlook for them is more hopeful.

Turnip and rutabaga cause us the greatest anxiety both on account of the drought and the flea, which at a time like this is very abundant. Where the plants are still alive, especially in the southern districts, they may yet be saved; but as the work of transplanting should begin in about four weeks' time they have need of all the help we can give them.

Onions have ripened up very small; this will raise the value of the bulbs for market purposes and check the output, so that the surplus which we shall carry over this year will be very helpful.

As regards the present season's crops the rain is hardly welcome. Growers were busy clearing up the tail end of the parsnip crop and had started harvesting radish and parsley. For both these good weather is necessary, and we devoutly hope that the rainy spell will be of short duration.

Our German growers report that the wet weather they experienced in August has so seriously damaged the pea crop, and in some cases so seriously affected the samples, that there will be a waste of fully 50 per cent in the picking. The yield of the spinach crop has also turned out much smaller than was anticipated, and already an advance of several shillings per 100 kilos has taken place. Up to the present the crops of onion, leek, radish, beans, both the pole and dwarf varieties, have not suffered to any great extent, but lettuce and scorzonera have been seriously injured. The latter will be dear.

In flower seeds, sweet peas have done badly; this will help out last year's surplus. The dwarf asters in the Quedlinburg district are mostly destroyed. Common annuals, especially balsams, stand well, and pansies may possibly produce one-fourth of a crop if the brighter weather continues.

In Italy the cauliflower crop is a pleasant surprise; and broad and dwarf beans and lettuces are also good. Leek is only middling. Egg plants, peppers and tomatoes are a long way behind, but may give good crops. The Cucurbitaceæ (cucumbers and melons chiefly) are an entire failure.

The ashes of Vesuvius have done great damage to the crops of torenias, begonias and other delicate sorts of flower seeds, but zinnias, balsams, dahlias and the scarlet sages are doing well.

In market seeds the drought has caused a strong demand for crimson clover with a consequent rise in price; but the chief interest centers in rape. Owing to the low prices which have ruled the past three years the acreage in England was very small, while in Holland the culture has been supplanted where possible by sugar beet. A rise of fully 25 per cent. has already taken place, and the top-notch has not yet been reached.

EUROPEAN SEEDS.

NOTES FROM FRANCE.—The shipping time for French bulbs has come to a close. This year may be considered as one of the busiest that has ever been seen in this line of commerce. The number of bulbs exported is at least 60 per cent. greater than that of last year. We noted especially a large demand from America, probably owing to the low prices at which the bulbs have been offered. Several orders have been taken at so low a rate that the exporters will have a good deal of difficulty to make any profit on the transaction. The forwarding of the goods has been about a fortnight earlier than last year. The season has been marked by one very unlucky incident in the stranding of the "Brooklyn." Coming from Genoa, she called on her way to New York at the Azores Islands. Just at the entrance of the harbor of St. Michel she ran on the rocks and stuck there. All efforts to float her have been in vain so far. In the cargo were from 1,500 to 2,000 cases of French bulbs. It seems that a goodly part of the cargo has been damaged by the seawater. It is not known if the bulbs have been reforwarded or not. B.

EVERLASTINGS.—We learn from Berlin, says the Horticultural Trade Journal, that the harvest of these flowers has been a poor one, especially of flowers of the best quality, the prices ranging from 7 mk. to 10 mk. per kilo, and colored flowers 8.50 mk.; for natural yellow colored flowers, 7 mk. per 10 bundles, and for artificially colored, 8.50 mk.

NOTES FROM HOLLAND.—From prices which are now being offered for nearly all the best varieties of tulips it would make one think that the old tulip mania was again approaching. The fact is, however, that the present craze for starting new tulip cultures in the north of this country has caused an unusual demand for all sorts of tulips to be planted out, and more especially the varieties that have proven to be the best for market as cut flowers. This, combined with a very brisk demand for the American markets, has made prices go up by leaps and bounds, and this has also caused other varieties to advance and has considerably affected the ordinary export trade. At the present moment mixed tulips are at a premium and hard to get, while many of the cheaper sorts of tulips have been cleared off the market entirely. It may be said that all the red and scarlet sorts are scarcer than ever before, both in single and double tulips.

Hyacinths have also cleared off well so far, and of the cheaper grades nothing is left on the hands of the growers. As was already expected early in the season, crocus are very short and priced nearly double those of last year, notwithstanding that the crop has been very good. Narcissus are also, with the exception of a few sorts, clearing off well and such as Emperor are even at present in very good demand.

Shipments are now in full swing, and will be finished in another week's time, when preparations will be made again for the planting of stocks.—Horticultural Trade Journal.

Lily of the Valley Crops in Europe.

The lily of the valley in the growing districts of Germany are looking in every way satisfactory, according to latest reports, and it is now fairly certain above an average quantity of first quality pips will be harvested. The weather generally throughout the season has been very favorable, and growth has been vigorous resulting in good, solid pips likely to form first quality spikes. Owing to the recent hot weather the maturing is progressing very satisfactorily, and if dry weather continues the lifting and curing will be got through also in a very satisfactory manner. A larger variety of samples will be suitable for more general purposes, and there will be less distinction between a very early forcing sample and a late retarding sample, although there will of course still be the dividing line between heavy clay land and light sandy land grown samples. No amount of favorable weather can make the former a first-class early forcing sample, nor the latter a really first-class late retarding sample. There will probably be fewer of the black peat samples on offer than in previous years, at least for the English trade, growers in the United Kingdom avoiding these samples more and more. The American buyer, however, according to my experience, is not nearly so particular as the European customer. Samples this season will according to reports be very free from the swelled pip or black and prematurely grown bell trouble; and samples containing any swelled buds will be the exception and not the rule. Prices may be expected to be much higher this year and from 32s. to 40s. for first-class samples will probably be the general run. The demand in England, as well as in other parts of Europe is much larger and is rapidly increasing, probably also in America. Then again, owing to an exceptionally poor crop last year much less stock was planted, consequently prices will no doubt be up to the highest figures, and no drop may be expected.

ENGLISH CORRESPONDENT.

NURSERY DEPARTMENT.

Conducted by Joseph Meehan.

AMERICAN ASSOCIATION OF NURSERYMEN. Orlando Harrison, Berlin, Md., president; J. W. Hill, Des Moines, Ia., vice-president; George C. Seager, Rochester, N. Y., secretary; C. L. Yates, Rochester, N. Y., treasurer.

TESTS OF SPRAYS FOR SAN JOSE SCALE.—The West Virginia University Agricultural Experiment Station at Morgantown, has issued a bulletin (No. 107) showing the results of tests made with different sprays for the San Jose scale. The experiments demonstrate that Target Brand Scale Destroyer, gave apparently, the best results; and that Kil-o-Scale was about equal to it, there being practically no difference between them. The former material is manufactured by the American Distributing Company, Martinsburg, W. Va.

Seasonable Notes.

Clerodendron trichotomum is a hardy shrub which will be much more evident in collections in years to come than it is now. It flowers in late August, when flowering shrubs are rare; and the odor of its blossoms is very agreeable.

The dwarf evergreen, Skimmia japonica, which on account of its clusters of bright red berries sells so well for Christmas use, is also a valuable hardy evergreen. Were this made known to purchasers at Christmas it should add to its sales.

Tritonia aurea was a well known herbaceous plant to the gardeners of a generation ago. It has gone under many names since, montbretia among them. It is now called Crocosma aurea. All other montbretias are now put back to tritonias. One of them, T. crocosmiflora, is a handsome one, a hybrid between Pottsii and aurea. The flowers are orange scarlet, and are produced for many weeks in late Summer.

Tradescantia virginica and its varieties are recognized as Spring flowering plants, which they are, but in seasons of good Summer growth they flower again in September, often as profusely as they do in Spring.

Euonymus Sieboldianus is a good evergreen when it does not have to endure the extreme of our Northern Winters. In partly sheltered spots it holds its foliage well. Its foliage appears as between that of the E. Europæus and E. japonicus. It forms a handsome bush without any pruning.

The Caucasian walnut, Pterocarya fraxinifolia, is being called for from the Pacific Coast, apparently for the value of its nuts.

Rosa rugosa is valued almost as much for its beautiful red fruit as for its flowers. When grown almost standard form, which it can be if desired, the display its fruit makes is greatly admired. The size of the fruit on vigorous specimens is equal to that of red Siberian crab apples.

The use of golden rods in ornamental planting is now quite general. The tall growing, bushy species are greatly admired. A smaller growing one, Solidago nemoralis, is noted for the deep yellow color of its flowers. It is common in dry fields.

Those who tire of seeing so many hedges of the California privet are using the Ligustrum Regelianum. It is of less formal appearance, as the branches have an almost horizontal growth. In Philadelphia it is less evergreen than the Californian, but far more graceful. There is need of both kinds.

Preservation of Seeds.

From September on seeds of trees and shrubs ripen rapidly and those who wish to obtain them for sowing need to watch the ripening so as to secure and preserve them in good condition. Of the various kinds required for nursery purposes, the greater number can be sown in Autumn, all, in fact, excepting the coniferous sorts. On the other hand, it must not be forgotten, that where impracticable or undesirable to sow in Autumn the seeds can be preserved and sown in Spring.

Taking maples, ash, tulip, poplar, linden and all similar sorts, to have them do their best they must not be kept in a dry state too long. Maples soon suffer if allowed to become dry; linden and tulip will keep a longer time without moisture. Magnolia seeds soon become worthless if allowed to dry. The safest way is to prepare the seed beds in early October, and then sow all the seeds when they ripen and fall from the tree. A week or two's delay in sowing them does not hurt them, but a longer period is very apt to do so. When impossible to sow in the Fall, the seeds should be kept in a slightly moist state and in a temperature that is low all Winter. It is not essential that they be mixed with soil if the air is moist, but the conditions mentioned are better attained when in soil, and then it is not necessary that the air of the building be damp. It is quite essential that nut seeds be damp all Winter. These do just as well sown in Spring as in Autumn if well preserved in damp material, as they but require to absorb a certain quantity of moisture to cause the shells to part.

A great deal regarding the care of seeds has to be learned by practice. Taking the case of maples, for example, while as a rule they will not grow if kept dry all Winter and sown in Spring, there is a notable exception in the one from Oregon, Acer macrophyllum. The seeds of this tree will grow well when not kept damp, the only case of all that is known.

Fall sowing, followed by a good Winter mulching of forest leaves, is the safest of all plans to follow.

Syringa Pekinensis Pendula.

The syringa of our notes, S. pekinensis pendula, is what is known in the trade as the weeping lilac. There are two sections of syringas. In the first are the old-fashioned lilacs of our gardens, familiar to us all. In the second are those with not much resemblance to the others, having flower heads like those of privets but much larger, which at one time were known under the distinct generic name Ligustrina. The one we illustrate belongs to the latter class, and in former days it would have been called Ligustrina pekinensis. Now, however, that all are merged in Syringa, it is as we have it above. It was because of the failure of those who first sent it out to properly describe it that there was some dissatisfaction expressed by purchasers of it, who believed they were getting a weeping form of the old common lilac.

But this lilac, in its true botanical place, is a very good thing, as those know who have it and others will believe when they look on the picture herewith shown. The specimen illustrated stands on a lawn which is some eight feet higher than the sidewalk of the public avenue it faces. This elevated position affords an excellent view of the plant and when it was in its prime of flowering it was greatly admired by all who passed by.

While of a drooping habit, it is not so much so as to come under the head of a weeping tree as many understand this term. All the branches are rather above horizontal when first formed, but become below it in time, and in a more pronounced way when weighted with their foliage and flowers. The specimen before us has its first branches several feet above ground, yet, as will be seen, some of them sweep the ground.

The value of the weeping lilac is much enhanced because of the frequency of its flowering. Its chief efforts at blooming are made in June, then off and on other flowers appear in Summer, and it is not uncommon for it to make a good display in the last days of Autumn.

JOSEPH MEEHAN.

Syringa Pekinensis Pendula—Weeping Lilac.

A Trip Among Oregon Nurserymen.

A business trip a few days since took the writer to the Capital of Oregon—beautiful Salem on the Willamette river. The streets here are 100 feet wide with 15 foot sidewalks, while most of the stores are built on the same broad plan. The town was founded way back in the "fifties," and during the half century of its existence has gathered together about 15,000 souls. With a little more artistic spirit and a little of the Windy City push infused into it, it might become the city beautiful.

From a point near the river gradually sloping back for nearly a mile a parkway is maintained in which are located the court house, the post office and the State Capitol, all pretentious buildings for a city of this size. This parkway has been laid out in a hit and miss fashion, but the grounds surrounding the State building are quite attractive in spite of bad taste displayed.

Nearly every tree and shrub indigenous to the Pacific coast is found here, as well as many of the old time favorites seen in the East. Lawson's cypress, with its regular lacelike foliage and pyramidal habit of growth, is very fine. The globe headed and Chinese Arbor vitaes also furnish attractive specimens. Japanese maples in several charming varieties are very ornamental. But of all the trees grown on this coast none can surpass the Oregon maple for beauty and utility. The silver ash-leaved maple, Acer argentea, is a clean growing shrubby tree which is very ornamental and attractive. The European holly and the variegated member of hte species are also seen here. Then the different firs, pines, yews, cypress and retinisporas all lend their grace and beauty, while tree box and the odd monkey's puzzle are equally at home in this luxurious paradise of Nature. Magnolias, tulip trees, figs, chestnuts, walnuts, locust and many other fine and beautiful specimens, not common in the East or West, are also growing here. The effect is good, although the order of planting is poor.

C. F. Lansing, located about 2 miles from the city on the Garden road, came here from the East about 15 years ago. He was a tree agent but, full of the vim and energy of the Pennsylvania Dutch from which stock he sprung, he established a small nursery of his own. To-day he has 50 acres of growing stock consisting of a general line of fruit and ornamental trees and shrubbery. Everything is clean smooth and thrifty, and Mr. Lansing enjoys a nice trade.

The Oregon Nursery Company, established in 1867, passed into the hands of the present proprietors about 11 years since. M. McDonald is president and A. McGill secretary of this enterprising concern. Their plantings cover nearly 400 acres and their methods of cultivation and propagation are strictly up-to-date. More than 500,000 apples are budded each season, besides large numbers of pears, plums, cherries, prunes, peaches, apricots, nut trees, ornamentals, shrubs, hedging currants, raspberries, black berries, gooseberries, etc. They have acquired the stock of Burbank's new pitless plum and have appropriately named it "The Miracle." Everything here is spick and span. One year old trees here attain a height of 5 to 6 feet, and will caliper nearly as large as two year olds grown in the East. The soil is a deep, clayey loam and requires no fertilizing, though nursery stock is generally rotated with crops of grain and clover.

This firm has purchased 700 acres of land in Washington county, 12 miles west of Portland, where they expect to lay out a town and to which point they will remove their entire business within the next two years. In addition to their large interests here, they maintain a branch nursery in Chico, California and have recently planted a nursery in British Columbia to take care of their increasing business in that section of the country. Both Mr. McDonald and Mr. McGill are old time nurserymen, born in Canada and coming to the coast about 15 years ago. Affable, courteous, energetic, pushing, well acquainted with the business in all its branches, they well deserve the success which has been achieved.

VERITAS.

LIST OF ADVERTISERS

INDEX TO STOCK ADVERTISED

Contents.

REVIEW OF THE MARKET

NEW YORK.—The weather has turned quite warm again, and the cut flower business has received another set back. On the one or two cool days during the latter part of last week trade started up fairly well, but the spurt seems to have lasted only as long as the cool days remained with us.

Roses of all varieties and grades are much too plentiful for the demand, and prices are anything but firm. Carnations are few in number as yet; and the supply of asters is gradually diminishing, much to the satisfaction of those who are trying to push indoor grown flowers. Gladioli are but few and far between, and now that they are in shorter supply it is possible to get a little better prices for them than has been the rule for some weeks past. Dahlias are getting quite numerous, and judging from the supply seen of the variety Countess of Lonsdale it is evident that this is considered a favorite sort by most of the growers.

A few violets have already appeared in the market, but the weather is much too warm for them to be of any value as yet. The first chrysanthemums of the season appeared Saturday September 15, at J. K. Allen's, 106 West Twenty-eighth street. The shipment consisted of but two or three dozen, of the varieties Glory of the Pacific and H. W. Rieman. It is expected by to-day, Saturday, that fairly large quantities of chrysanthemums of the varieties Mme. Gastellier and Monrovia will be shipped into the market.

Orchids, lily of the valley and Harrisii lilies are in steady supply, but it cannot be said that there is any regular demand for any of these, and prices are not of a stable nature.

CHICAGO.—The recent weather has not been conducive to the most favorable results to the market; however, it is safe to say that conditions are steadily improving, but not as rapidly as the trade desires. Stock is constantly improving in quality. Roses, and especially American Beauty, were probably never better if as good at this season as they are now. Carnations are about in normal supply and of seasonable quality.

Outdoor stock begins to show the signs of a declining Summer although there is still a fair supply of asters which are of a grade that compares favorably with the general supply which the market here has received during the Summer.

Smilax and asparagus are in good condition and are in from fair to good demand. The opening of the Fall business season in millinery and dry and dress goods lines creates a good call for this stock, as well as for Southern smilax and other decorative materials.

W. K. W.

PHILADELPHIA.—Business this week has been much better; there is considerably more demand for all kinds of flowers. American Beauty are in stronger call with prices unchanged from those of last week. All tea roses are going better, and prices are on a slight advance. Killarney is being asked for much more than formerly. Carnations are moving better; some flowers from new stock inside are now coming in. Prices range from $1 to $2 per 100. Dahlias are arriving in large quantities, there is not much demand for the bulk of this stock. Some of the fancy cactus varieties are selling at $3 and $4 per 100, but most of the other varieties go at $1 per 100. Asters are now falling off in supply; choice flowers still bring $1 per 100. There has been a good demand for smilax; good strings sell at 20c. Asparagus plumosus and Sprengeri are both in good demand this week. The same may be said of lily of the valley, at from $3 to $5 per 100.

DAVID RUST.

ST. LOUIS.—The market shows sign of awakening, though from the reports of the retailers there are yet too many dull days in the week; were it not for funeral work business would be quiet. Stock is not of the best, and but few fancy grade flowers are seen, though of the poorer grades plenty is to be had which sell cheap in thousand lots. It is hard to quote prices correctly the way things go nowadays, but the following is what the wholesalers were asking for stock Monday morning: American Beauty, special, $4; next grade, $3; medium, $2; short from 50c. to $1 per dozen. Bride and Bridesmaid, special, $5; firsts, $3; seconds, $1 and $2 per 100. Souvenir du President Carnot, $3 to $5. Perle des Jardins, $2 to $4. Richmond and Killarney, $3 to $5 per 100. Carnations: best Enchantress may be had for $1.50; Mrs. T. W. Lawson, $1, and white from 50c. to $1 per 100. Asters are not so plentiful; good white are going at from $2 down to 50c.; other colors, 50c. to $1.50 per 100. Tuberose stalks are not over plentiful just now at $3 per 100. Dahlias, all colors, very fine don't bring over $1 to $1.50 per 100. Greens at usual prices are plentiful.

ST. PATRICK.

INDIANAPOLIS.—With cool weather comes a resumption of society and counter trade; at times there are flurries of business suggestive of the storm which will come later on. Seasonable flowers—dahlias, asters, gladiolus and hydrangeas find many buyers. Dahlias are of fine quality and retail at 75c. to $1 a dozen; asters wholesale at 50c. to $1 per 100, retailing at 25c. to 30c. a dozen. Many gladioli are shipped in at $1 to $1.50. A few chrysanthemums are seen now and then. Short-stemmed carnations are brought to market in masses at 60c. to 75c.; ten to twelve inch ones bring $1.50 to $2 per 100. Roses, with the exception of American Beauty, are hardly up to standard; mildewed Bridesmaid and Bride sell at $3 to $4 per 100; good Kaiserin Augusta Victoria from Chicago, bring $5 to $6 per 100.

I. B.

BOSTON.—The past week has had little life to it in the cut flower line. With the exception of American Beauty roses all kinds of stock seemed to pile up and flavor of a glut. American Beauty are good for this season, and they are the best selling of any of the roses. Wellesley is good and Bride and Bridesmaid are both improving. Carnations are very plentiful, and the prices have not held up to what they averaged a week ago. Lily of the valley and lilies are both fairly in demand. Asters still continue to pour in; the quality is good. Gladioli are plentiful enough, and tuberoses are seen in limited numbers. Violets have made their appearance, and although of dubious quality bring 75c. per bunch.

J. W. D.

CHANGES IN BUSINESS.

WESTVILLE, CONN.—Sigfred Henderson will engage in the florist business here.

FINDLAY, O.—Barnd Karg & Company will continue in the business at the old stand, 123 East Front street.

NEW ORLEANS, LA.—The Metairie Ridge Nursery Company will open a store on one of the prominent streets of the city. It will be stocked from the firm's growing establishment.

WINCHENDON, MASS.—Henry J. Whittemore has leased his buildings and sold his plants, bulbs, and miscellaneous stock to William Wallace Rhuland. Mr. Rhuland has for the past four years had charge of the greenhouses and growing stock of George W. Sutherland at Athol, and previous to that has worked in other places, including an apprenticeship at the Waban Rose Conservatories at Natick.

PLANT FOR NAME.—G. J. H., New Jersey—In the absence of flowers and foliage it is not possible to say precisely what this specimen is, but it has a great resemblance to Solanum nigrum, commonly called hound's berry. This solanum is of but annual growth, making a height of from one to two feet. The berries are not considered edible. As you state the plant you send is put up for Winter use, it can hardly be what we make it out to be, yet it appears to fit Solanum nigrum. J. M.

—V. B. Sons, New York.—The specimen you send is the wax myrtle, Myrica cerifera, a pretty evergreen shrub. The fertile plants bear berries covered with a wax-like substance. It has no botanical relationship to Laurus nobilis. This laurus is a native of Southern Europe. The myrica forms a handsome bush, and is often found in great masses near the sea coast, where it helps hold the drifting sand. J. M.

The Sun Scalds Roses.

(48) I have a house of roses and send you a few leaves which are spotted. Would you kindly let me know the name of the disease and a remedy? J. O. P.
Quebec.

—The leaves sent for examination do not seem to be affected with any disease, but are scalded or burned either through flaws in the glass, or from drops of water standing on the leaves, thus forming a lens through which the sun's rays do the damage.

Water Bugs in Carnation Benches.

(49) Will you kindly inform me what is the best way to rid carnation benches of water bugs? They are under the mulching in such large numbers that they are damaging the plants alarmingly. I have tried Paris Green and sugar, also Peterman's Roach Food, but it has little effect.
Ohio. J. H.

—If the water bugs (woodlice) are so numerous that the poisons mentioned as having been used are of no benefit we would clear off the mulch, clean all the wood work around the edges of the benches, then apply Hammond's Slug Shot next to the wood work and in every crevice. We would then put on a fresh mulch, being sure that it was absolutely free of vermin.

Tomato and Cucumber Troubles.

(50) Please inform me as to the cause and remedy for tomatoes dying: some say it is blight; others an insect that bores the stem, causing them to die. Also for cucumbers that are troubled with the blight.
SUBSCRIBER.

—I should imagine the trouble with the tomato plants is blight, climatic conditions being the primary cause. Extreme temperature and too much moisture seem to breed this disease rapidly. In the case of any tomato patch that is badly affected, it is simply a waste of time to try to get the plants back to health again. This disease spreads so fast that there is little use in trying to save the plants. Another season I certainly should not plant where I had experienced this trouble, but on fresh ground. Also, as a preventive, keep the vines sprayed with Bordeaux mixture, or any other fungicide. The safest and most successful way of using all fungicides is to commence spraying before any disease appears on the vines. To wait until the blight starts, it is then a difficult proposition to eradicate the pest.

Spray the cucumbers with Bordeaux mixture unless the foliage is badly affected; if such be the case Bordeaux mixture will not save them.
WM. TURNER.

To Make a Reservoir.

(51) Kindly let me know how to make a reservoir or basin to hold 1000 barrels of water. Our springs are all lower than our greenhouses. I thought I could make a basin below to hold the water from the springs, then pump it into a tank or another basin on a hill. How should I make the basin? Of what size to hold 1000 barrels? How many rows of brick would it take? The ground is of a hard loam or clay. Would you make the reservoir like the rough drawing herewith?

McK.

Penna.

—Figuring on the barrel of 31½ gallons, this will call for a tank of sufficient capacity to hold 31,500 gallons of water, or a tank of 4,200 cubic feet. A tank 21 feet long, 20 feet wide, and 10 feet deep will hold the quantity stated. A tank built of concrete will be the best, as it can be constructed at less cost than one of stone or brick. A hole should be dug a foot deeper, wider and longer than the foregoing figures, being careful to get a solid foundation for the walls to rest on, or they will crack, causing endless trouble later with leaks. After the excavation is completed, upright posts, 4 by 4 inches, should be set around the hole, about 4 feet apart, the lower ends being set firmly in holes dug in the soil on the bottom, the tops of sufficient length to reach to the surface of the bank. These posts should be firmly braced in position to prevent them from yielding when the concrete is being rammed. Rough 2 by 12 inch boards are set on edge against the upright posts all around the excavation, thus giving a space of twelve inches between them and the bank, to be filled with concrete. The boards will be more easily removed when all is finished if no nails are driven into the 2 by 12; they can be held in position by pieces of wood, 12 inches long, set between the boards and the bank. The concrete can be made of one part Portland cement, three parts sand, four parts broken stone (the stone can be broken in pieces from 4 inches down) and three parts of gravel or fine stone. This should be from the size of a hickory nut down to that of a pea. The ingredients should be carefully turned until all are thoroughly incorporated, when sufficient water should be added to make the concrete of the consistency of putty. Care should be taken not to use too much water or the concrete will be weakened by the loss of cement carried away by the water. When the batch is ready it can be wheeled to the excavation, and shoveled into place, tamping it tight as it is put in. When the first board is filled up, another is set on top of it, and so on until all is finished. The boards should remain in position for a week to allow the concrete to harden before being removed. While the concrete is drying the whole should be sprayed several times a day to prevent too rapid drying, as the slower the concrete sets the stronger it will be. After the boards are removed the bottom should receive 12 inches of the concrete rammed the same way as for the walls. The whole when finished in the rough should receive a finishing coating of cement and sand, put on with a smoothing trowel and composed of one part Portland cement to three parts of sand mixed with sufficient water. After the tank is sufficiently dried out, it should be thoroughly washed, to remove any acid adhering to it from the cement, before it is filled with water. If a pipe with a valve attached should be laid in the bottom of the tank, before the concrete is put in, and the same carried to some convenient emptying place, it will be found of great service when it is desired to clean out the tank.

If your correspondent prefers to build a brick tank, the walls should be 12¾ inches thick, or the thickness of one and one half bricks. Allowing for the usual waste and breakage 21 bricks will be required for every square foot, a total of 26,040 bricks to complete the tank. Hard arch brick should be used, laid in a mortar composed of one part Portland cement to three parts of sand, the walls and bottom to receive a coating of the same mortar applied with the smoothing trowel when finished.

The reservoir should have straight sides, not dished as per McK's drawin.

PETER BISSET.

Dahlias Not Blooming.

(52) I send you some cactus dahlias, leaves and buds. Will you please let me know what is wrong with them. The plants were all right before, but last year they only bloomed half, and this year they do not bloom at all. The roots seem good; the leaves are clean, but as soon as the buds appear they do not develop. The soil is good. I shall be pleased if you can tell me what to do for them; or if I have to get new roots for next year, and whether I can plant them in the same bed. J. H.

—We cannot give the scientific explanation of this trouble, but have never considered it a disease, rather a deformity, to which some varieties seem more subject than others, and to be the result of over propagation, or a tendency to degenerate, prevailing more in wet weather when the conditions are more favorable to bring about such results, and then developing more fully in each successive generation until the whole plant becomes afflicted. We have never attempted a cure, considering such a course almost useless, but always pull up the plants and throw them away. We would suggest that the roots be destroyed and that new, healthy stock be secured; and as a preventive of contagion and the new stock becoming affected, that the ground be well worked, left in a rough condition during the Winter, a heavy dressing of lime given, and that dahlias be not planted there for a season.

R. A. VINCENT.

White Marsh, Md.

OUR LITTLE PET

From Aschmann in Philadelphia I bought
An Araucaria, a pet for our little girl;
Now we have two pets, the pride of our thought:
The little girl so sweet, a head full of curls,
And the Araucaria with its everlasting green,
A more joyful home you never have seen.

FOUNDED IN 1888

THE FLORISTS' EXCHANGE

A Weekly Medium of Interchange for Florists, Nurserymen Seedsmen and the Trade in general

Exclusively a Trade Paper.

Entered at New York Post Office as Second Class Matter

Published EVERY SATURDAY by

A. T. DE LA MARE PTG. AND PUB. CO. LTD.

2, 4, 6 and 8 Duane Street,

P. O. Box 1697.
Telephone 3765 John. NEW YORK.

CHICAGO OFFICE: 127 East Berwyn Avenue.

ILLUSTRATIONS.

Electrotypes of the illustrations used in this paper can usually be supplied by the publishers. Price on application.

YEARLY SUBSCRIPTIONS.

United States, Canada, and Mexico, $1.00. Foreign countries in postal union, $2.50. Payable in advance. Remit by Express Money Order Draft on New York. Post Office Money Order or Registered Letter.

The address label indicates the date when subscription expires and is our only receipt therefore.

REGISTERED CABLE ADDRESS:
Florex, New York.

Mrs. Theodosia B. Shepherd.

The passing away of Mrs. Theodosia B. Shepherd of Ventura-by-the-Sea, Cal., whose death on September 6, 1906, is recorded in our obituary column this week, removes from the horticultural world a woman of many and varied attainments, one who was a credit to her sex, one whose example many other women might, with advantage, profitably pattern after. Never at any time possessed of a robust constitution, this plucky little woman, while occupied with the cares of her household and the rearing of her family, at first in order to counteract the forces of adversity from which her home, with those of many others at that time suffered, subsequently as a commercial venture, engaged in the business of seed and plant raising and hybridizatien, in both of which fields she was eminently successful.

It was one of the many generous traits that characterized the late Peter Henderson of New York, to give salutary advice, often accompanied with hopeful encouragement, to all who sought it; and it was owing to words of cheer and optimism received from Mr. Henderson that Mrs. Shepherd was prompted to engage in what afterward formed her life work. The prediction made over thirty years ago by that far-seeing man, that "before fifty years, California will become the great seed and bulb growing country of the world," has even now been fulfilled. Mrs. Shepherd was the pioneer in that industry; and although her output was small in comparison with that of many of the firms who have since entered the field, yet she is deserving of highest commendation for the superior character of her work, undertaken at the outset without experience, and at all times carried on under comparatively adverse circumstances.

Our deceased friend never failed to tender that help and encouragement of which she in her first essay had been the grateful recipient, to others of her sex, several of whom, inspired by her success and cheered on by her always available advice, have followed in her footsteps in the cultivation and breeding of plants. By her pen and voice she was ever ready to give of her experience and to promote and further the interests of horticulture generally. To her sorrowing family she leaves a priceless heritage—the record of work well done, and the inspiration that springs from a noble example; and they as well as every one engaged in the cultivation of flowers and plants in America owe to that unassuming, painstaking, self-reliant laborer in the vineyard, a large debt of gratitude. She rests from her labors and her works do follow her.

Special Societies.

From reports appearing in our own columns and those of our contemporaries the list of special societies is to be added to by the formation of a Dahlia Society, the initial meeting having been held in Boston, Mass., last week, when temporary officers were elected, and a committee appointed to arrange for another meeting to perfect details and place the organization on a permanent footing. The interest in the proposed association is demonstrated by the statement of the secretary pro tem, to the effect that he expects to have one hundred members before the society is fairly launched.

The aim, it is said, is not to have this society regarded as a purely commercial one, everybody interested in the dahlia being available for membership.

There is no society of this character, so far as we know, that is exclusive, as to its membership, yet somehow or other the erroneous conception of exclusiveness has gone abroad, to the disadvantage of these various bodies. Probably the restricting idea has arisen because, in the case of some societies, the work connected therewith has been conducted largely by tradesmen; and, perhaps, because no great effort has been put forth to secure what may be termed an amateur clientage.

With the possible exception of The American Carnation Society, but little progress in the way of obtaining a large membership has been made, and this chiefly if not wholly among trade representatives of the carnation cult. The reason of this has often been explained, and need not be here repeated.

The Late Mrs. Theodosia B. Shepherd.

In the case of the Rose society, considering the work doing in America along the lines of rose hybridization, the splendid exhibitions staged by this organization, the good that could be accomplished on behalf of the rose were the membership larger, the necessity of the work of the Rose Society, the apathy of a large majority of those most vitally concerned is incomprehensible. The same is true as regards the Chrysanthemum Society.

We believe, from the experience of the past, that societies devoted to special plants whose period of flowering is of limited duration, will have to seek the largest portion of their clientage from among the non-professional or amateur class. This may even be the case as regards the Rose Society.

But before progress along the line of increased membership can be expected, publicity must be given to the aims, objects and work of each special organization, in media that reach the people whom it is intended to interest. In this respect we in this country are hampered by the lack of periodicals devoted to horticultural matters in an amateur way, that care to exploit material of this kind. Therefore, it is necessary to resort to advertisement, circularizing and such like means to accomplish the end sought.

There is a great awakening in gardening matters at the present time, which would seem an opportune one for the various special societies to push their claims for recognition and support. And when this is done in a persistent, systematic manner, the membership of each organization will, we feel sure, be greatly augmented, and more representative of the interest taken in the plants for which these special societies stand sponsor, than is now the case.

We wish the proposed Dahlia Society every success and believe it is starting out along right lines with respect to its membership.

OUR READERS' VIEWS

Campbell's Sulphur Vaporizer.

Editor Florists' Exchange:

In your issue of the 15th inst., you print a paper read by John H. Dunlop, Toronto, before the Canadian Horticultural Association in which he speaks of "Campbell's Sulphur Vaporizer" being on the market. Can you give us any information as to where this Vaporizer can be bought? We would like to try it. STOCKTON & HOWE.

Princeton, N. J.

[Perhaps Mr. Dunlop will kindly supply us with this information, which no doubt will be of benefit to our readers generally. Ed. F. E.]

Carnations Drying Up.

Editor Florists' Exchange:

In your issue of September 8, John Stanley describes a carnation disease which has been baffling us in Texas this season. As misery loves company, it was some satisfaction to learn that others have been troubled in the same way. We have a house of white, pink and red Lawson, all affected with this disease, and may be obliged to throw them out. We have attributed the cause to excessive rains and too much cow manure before benching, but should be glad to hear other opinions on the subject. A. M.

Texas.

Growers and Flower Shows.

Editor Florists' Exchange:

Every man outside of the penitentiary and other kindred institutions of learning and correction enjoys the privilege granted ages ago of the freedom of his own will. If a grower feels like exhibiting anything at a flower show he is usually at liberty to do so and if he feels the other way, he is of course at liberty to keep his property on his own premises. But it has often struck me that growers might with advantage to themselves do more to encourage exhibitions of plants and flowers in towns throughout the country than they do.

If florists who are specialists in the growing of certain kinds of plants would exhibit specimens as samples of what they grow, thereby bringing such things to the attention of thousands, many of whom probably would never see them in any other way, I think the gain to themselves either directly or indirectly would more than pay them for their trouble. The feeling that the possession of plants and flowers is a part of the civilization of our day may come over every individual having the means to gratify the wish for such things without prompting from outside sources, but education is a powerful weapon in every good cause; and in the popularizing of plants and flowers it is as effectual as in any other.

The exhibition of plants that are new or of recent introduction seems to me almost a necessity, and the showing of such plants invariably, and very often speedily, is the means of bringing plant buyers to the buying point. These few will in time so leaven the whole lump that the indirect gain will be considerable.

This word for flower shows does not intend in the slightest degree to belittle the advantages of advertising; the one form of publicity has nothing to do with the other, unless it be that the one would be an aid to the other. Many who would see something new to admire at a flower show might never open a horticultural paper; but if many would have their interest thus awakened, horticultural advertising would be advantageous on a larger scale because of the fact that the increased interest created would make advanced methods of growing a necessity in such neighborhoods.

This is a great country; a country as yet only in part developed. The room for the further development of the horticultural business is as great as that of any other industry, and it would seem that one agency for such a development is the local exhibition. B.

Greenhouse Glass—The Import Duty as It Affects Florists.

Editor Florists' Exchange:

At the S. A. F. O. H. convention held at Dayton, O., President Kasting's address brought out matters which led to a discussion on the high cost of greenhouse glass, and that the tariff thereon had a marked effect in keeping up the very high cost.

How many millions of square feet of glass are used by the florists of the United States, I am unable to say, but all men who have greenhouses or cold frame plants, are greatly interested in the cost of this important commodity.

In the discussion which ensued at the time, it was stated that if there was to be anything done in the modification of the present tax on glass, some action must be taken, otherwise nothing would ever be accomplished. The matter, after debate, was referred to a committee of which the writer is a member, and to give a correct status of the present rate on glass, application was made to the Commissioner of Commerce and Labor.

Prior to the Spanish war (so-called), the rate on glass used by the greenhouse men was as follows:

On all sizes not exceeding 10 x 15 in. sq., the import duty was 1c. per pound; on sizes above 10 x 15 in. sq., and not exceeding 16 x 24 in. sq., 1¼c. per pound; above 16 x 24 in. sq., and not exceeding 24 x 36 in. sq., 1⅜c. per pound.

It will be noted that the tariff is not placed upon the square foot, nor is it an ad valorem rate, the valuation being placed at the net weight of glass in boxes, which are 50 feet, or as near as may be, and glass will approximate 50 to 80 pounds net in a box, according to thickness. Such was the rate in existence in 1896.

In 1897 the tariff was changed, and it is under this tariff that the glass now used in the United States is protected. The paragraph which governs that duty is as follows:

"Glass not exceeding 10 x 15 in. sq. at 1⅜c. per pound; above that and not exceeding 16 x 24 in. sq. at 1⅞c. per pound, and not exceeding 24 x 30 in. sq. at 2⅜c. per pound."

Provided, that the duties shall be according to the actual weight of the glass. The reader will see at a glance the substantial increase in the cost of each box of glass, which this protection gives over and above 1896 and previous. In 1896 the volume imported of the cylinder, crown and common window glass was $34,189,854.13 and for 1905 it was $17,933,028.50.

The question before the greenhouse men of the country is, whether it is worth while to make an effort to procure less duty on glass, to bring before the proper authorities the sense that the time is ripe and should be carried into effect of modifying for the general good the high rates of the present duties?

Of course, this matter affects not only greenhouse people, but every builder and sash maker in the land.

It was suggested at the Dayton convention that the florists of the United States should make known their interest in the matter by direct statement. The committee to whom this matter was referred would be glad to hear of the public expression, looking to a proper presentation of the matter in such shape that it will command the attention of the proper Congressional committees.

BENJAMIN HAMMOND

Fishkill on Hudson, N. Y.

CLUB AND SOCIETY DOINGS.

THE ST. LOUIS FLORISTS' CLUB held its first regular monthly meeting, since the S. A. F. convention, on Thursday afternoon, September 13, in Strausberger's Hall, Grand avenue. President Ammann occupied the chair. There was a very good attendance, including many visitors. Seven applications for membership were received—Edwin Denker, O. H. Huetterman, F. W. Alves, D. H. Pring, Chas. Fulgraf, William C. Young and Frank Vennemann. It was suggested that Article 5 Section 2 of the by-laws be amended to read, that no application can be withdrawn when once presented to the club for membership.

The installation of the newly elected officers then took place, President Ammann having appointed John Steidle and Frank Fillmore to assist him. President-elect H. C. Irish first took the oath of office, followed by Vice-President Connon, Secretary Beneke, Treasurer Bentzen and Trustee Smith. The retiring officers were given a vote of thanks for their faithful work, especially Ex-Secretary Schray, who had held the office for fifteen years.

The discussion which was to have been led by E. W. Guy and Emil Schray was postponed until next meeting, when F. C. Weber will also lead a discussion on "The Best and Most Attractive Way to Conduct a Retail Store," and George B. Windler, one on "Growing Pot Chrysanthemums for Exhibitions." These should draw a big attendance. Discussion followed on a Fall flower show. The meeting then adjourned until Thursday, 2 p. m., October 11 next.

ST. PATRICK.

CHICAGO FLORISTS' CLUB.—The monthly meeting of the Chicago Florists' Club was held at Handel Hall on Thursday evening of last week with a small attendance, even a number of the regulars being counted among the absentees. President Hauswirth and Financial Secretary Asmus had not returned from their Buffalo trip, so after the meeting was called to order, Secretary L. H. Winterson carried through the requisite formalities, previous to which, however, he entertained the party with a most interesting and entertaining account of his recent Eastern trip on which he met many nationally well-known members of the fraternity.

It may be well to state that there will be but one more regular meeting, October 11, before the Fall show. All members will be duly notified but it is well perhaps to put a blue mark on your calendar for that date so that you may not make any other arrangements.

WILLIAM K. WOOD.

COLUMBUS (O.) FLORISTS' CLUB.—During the past two months it has been so terrifically hot that as if by mutual consent very little business of importance has been transacted at the club. Our members turned out in goodly numbers for the Dayton convention, and all enjoyed the trip and proceedings to the utmost. We had intended to have had a bowling team there; but at the last moment, we decided to give it up for this year, as we did not consider that our team had had sufficient practice for that strenuous competition. Last Tuesday evening our first regular meeting of the Fall was held at Iroquois Hall, with vice-president Curry in the chair. The most important subject on hand was the question of the chrysanthemum show. Several weeks ago a committee consisting of Messrs. Faxon, Stephens, Woodrow, Knopf, and McKellar, was chosen to fully investigate this matter and report their findings to the club. This committee recommended that the show be postponed to, or rather the date set for November, 1907. The club endorsed this view of the matter and voted that the same committee serve in charge of this exhibition for next season. At this meeting it was also voted, on the motion of M. B. Faxon, that a large laurel wreath be sent by the club, as a tribute to the memory of our late president, to the unveiling of the McKinley Memorial Monument, by Mrs. Nicholas Longworth. These ceremonies took place Friday, September 14, and it has been estimated that some eighty thousand persons attended.

F. W.

BOSTON GARDENERS AND FLORISTS' CLUB.—About 125 members were present at the opening meeting of the season. President Wheeler occupied the chair and after the reading of the minutes, reports were made by the picnic committee on the picnic which was held during the Summer. Eighteen new members were elected. There was a spirited discussion on various topics pertaining to the recent convention of the S. A. F. O. H., which occupied the greater part of the evening. The speakers were Messrs. Palmer, Elliott, Welch, Orpet and Craig.

There was quite a number of exhibits on the table including Shirley and Mexican poppies from W. N. Craig; the latter he recommended strongly for cutting purposes; grasses from A. Poetsch; asters in variety and aconitum from the Blue Hills Nurseries, Buddleia variabilis Veitchiana from the Boston Park Department and celery from W. Heustis.

J. W. DUNCAN.

THE MORRIS COUNTY (N. J.) GARDENERS AND FLORISTS' SOCIETY held its regular meeting on September 12. Twenty-six members were present. The monthly exhibit, while not large, was of good quality. J. Heeremans showed onions, Ailsa Craig and Magnum Bonum. He was awarded a cultural certificate. He also put up four vases of asters, Hohenzollen in variety; all fine; honorable mention. E. Reagan staged several vases of Celosia Thompson's magnifica and dahlia Mrs. Theo. Roosevelt; award, honorable mention. Flower show discussion took up most of the time, and James Smith and Alex. J. Guttman, New York, entertained us with a description of the recent S. A. F. convention. At the next meeting President Heeremans is to tell us of his trip to "Old England."

E. R.

ELBERON (N. J.) HORTICULTURAL SOCIETY.—A very enthusiastic meeting of this society was held on September 10, President W. D. Robertson in the chair. Three new members were elected and two more proposed. It was decided to have a dahlia show at the meeting in October. Many prizes were donated by the members present and the outlook is bright for a good display of this popular flower. Some nice exhibits were staged, notably a vase of Maman Cochet rose by A. Bauer; a vase of Clematis vitalba by W. D. Robertson; a vase of dahlias by J. Kennedy and a dish of beans by A. Greib.

G. M.

LENOX (MASS.) HORTICULTURAL SOCIETY.—The regular meeting of this society was held Saturday, September 15, President S. Carlquist in the chair. Letters were read from the following firms offering premiums for our chrysanthemum show: Messrs. Howard & Morrow, Julius Roehrs Company, C. H. Totty, J. H. Harris and Bay State Nurseries. Votes of thanks were passed for the above. Everything promises well for a good exhibition, as the chrysanthemums in this section are looking particularly good.

G. F.

Turf and Manure.

Vice-Consul C. Kurminski, of Seville, writes concerning the effect of turf upon ordinary manure, as follows:

Director Immendorff, of the agricultural test station at Jena (Germany), advocates the use of turf as a means of preserving manure. Results obtained through experiments in and about Jena demonstrate that the use of turf is far more efficient in preventing loss of nitrogen, while fermentation is in progress, than is sulphate of lime, phosphate of lime, sulphuric acid, etc. Turf permits the escape of but very little nitrogen, while the application of the above-named chemicals is most deficient in result and expensive. The discovery of Professor Immendorff merely corroborates experiments of a similar nature conducted by Italian agriculturists.

Society of American Florists and Ornamental Horticulturists.

Department of Plant Registration.

Central Park Nursery, Topeka, Kansas, submits for registration the following cannas:

SUNBURST, a seedling of Souvenir d' Antoine Crozy; identical in foliage and habit with its parent; bloom differs in that there is no yellow edging but large yellow blotches on the under side. The flower is large, bright crimson in color, and truss is rigidly upright.

TOPEKA, a seedling of Charles Henderson; foliage very heavy and glaucous, habit extremely sturdy, compact and robust, bloom larger than that of Henderson; color rich crimson with distinct bright yellow shading along the lower edge of staminodia.

WM. J. STEWART, Secretary.

The Florists' Exchange is in receipt of an attractive book mark sent by Benjamin Hammond, Fishkill-on-Hudson, N. Y., secretary of The American Rose society, being a reminder that the society wishes every recipient well, and asking them to join the organization.

Obituary

Mrs. Theodosia B. Shepherd.

Mrs. Theodosia B. Shepherd of Ventura-by-the-sea, Cal., widely known as a seed and plant grower, died at her home there on Thursday, September 6, after a lingering illness. She was 61 years of age.

The story of Mrs. Shepherd's career has formed the theme of numerous newspaper and magazine articles, and probably no one engaged in California horticulture, outside of Burbank himself, was better or more favorably known both personally and by reputation, throughout the civilized world.

Mrs. Shepherd was born in Keosauqua, Iowa. She was the daughter of Augustus Hall, one of Iowa's most brilliant lawyers in early days, and afterwards Chief Justice of Nebraska. Her sister, Mrs. Ella H. Enderlien, is prominent in newspaper work in Los Angeles and is one of the leading lights among the progressive women of that city. She has one brother, R. S. Hall, a prominent and successful lawyer of Omaha. She was married to W. E. Shepherd, of Oskaloosa, Iowa, September 9, 1866. A son and daughter were born to them in Iowa, and two daughters in Ventura. They went to California for Mrs. Shepherd's health in 1873.

Several years after their arrival in Ventura, a dry year, added to the then general financial depression, made itself felt in the Shepherd home as well as all others. Instead of crushing, it acted as a stimulant upon the plucky woman. The many curios, such as sea mosses, shells, birds, the varied and beautiful California woods, etc., which she had collected for the love of them, and with which her home was beautified, began to have a commercial value. She commenced to exchange them for such articles as pictures, plaques, needlework, plants and curios from different States. In 1881 she sent a package of curiosities to Peter Henderson, seedsman, of New York, among them being a few choice flower seeds; at the same time informing him of the rare flowers that grow and flourish in Ventura in the open air. In a letter of thanks Mr. Henderson wrote: "I am certain that California, before fifty years, will be the great seed and bulb growing country of the world. You have the exact conditions necessary to grow seeds, and I would advise you to go to work systematically at once." That prophecy made a great impression upon this enthusiast, but it was a year or two before she could begin, and for the first few years she grew but little for sale.

She had no idea in those early days of establishing an industry, but more of having a beautiful home, and collecting rare plants without having to count the cost, when the piece of ground purchased by her husband was turned over to her for her experiments, and experiments they were at first, as she drifted along. The country was new and she had everything to learn. With no capital, she was constantly cramped for means with which to carry out her ideas and desires and thus she built from the ground up, patiently and hopefully—with no money to use except as she made it. Not so far seeing as she, her friends often discouraged her, especially when letters from eastern seedsmen would come, saying "We purchase our seeds in Europe; we do not know anything about California seeds." Not in the least discouraged, she would say: "I can and will sell them seeds; they do want California seeds, but they don't know it. It is only a question of time; all I have to do is to convince them, and I'll do it." And she did convince them.

It was slow work at first, for with no adviser, no knowledge of business, or of the work of seed growing except as an amateur, all had to be learned by experience alone. Endowed with a love of flowers and all things beautiful and helpful, and a strong will inherited from her talented father, this delicate-looking, gentle-mannered woman overcame all obstacles and achieved success where others would have failed. Thus did Mrs. Shepherd built up a business of which not only Ventura, but all California, is proud. She may justly be termed the pioneer seed-grower of the State and became a recognized grower of seeds, bulbs and plants for the trade and for some years had issued a retail catalogue and two wholesale lists, yearly.

In 1902 the business was incorporated with a capital stock of $30,000, the stockholders being members of her own family, namely, Mrs. Myrtle Shepherd Lloyd, Mrs. Margaret Shepherd Oaks, and Mrs. Edith Shepherd Kelsey. Two daughters and one son survive her.

Mrs. Shepherd did considerable hybridizing work, particularly among cosmos, cannas, nasturtiums and fibrous begonias. By her writings and lectures on plant life, and especially by her scientific attainments in a field of activity in which she was the pioneer woman worker in America, she did much to create an interest in the art she loved so well. She was a woman of noble and generous impulses, and labored to elevate all with whom she came in contact, both intellectually and morally.

The funeral was held September 8, the body, after cremation, being interred in Rosedale Cemetery, Los Angeles, Cal.

HARDY PLANT NOTES

Oriental Poppies.

Those who were fortunate enough to sow a good batch of oriental poppy seed last Spring will now find this a very good and seasonable time to get the strongest plants into pots as soon as possible, for if they have not already commenced to make their Fall growth they very soon will do so, especially where favorable rains have fallen. I have always found that just as soon as, or shortly after they commence to make their new Fall growth is the best time to pot, for either Spring or Fall sales, as it then takes but a few weeks for the plants to fully establish themselves in three and four-inch pots if liberally supplied with moisture. I have also found that seedlings raised from seed sown in very early Spring, in good soil, have produced sufficient growth to fill pots of the above named sizes by Fall, provided they have not been sown too thickly, kept free from weeds and well cultivated; and even then some have been too large to get into pots without breaking them. This, though, is easily overcome by leaving the plants out in the sun for a while, where they will soon wilt and become supple enough to pot. But care should be taken not to let them lie out too long, or long enough to dry up.

There is some prejudice about the safe removal or transplanting of these poppies, even among commercial men, but I may say I have never had the slightest difficulty in handling them, neither in Fall nor Spring; and while I recommend their being handled in pots for trade purposes, they will succeed just as well without being potted if properly handled either in Fall or very early Spring.

I think late Spring is when the conditions are most disastrous to them in removal, and this is where good pot plants come in, as then they can be handled for a much longer period, which is quite an advantage to both planter and dealer; especially is this so if the dealer has a very cold spot where he can place a few hundred for late comers.

After potting up I generally place the plants in a cold frame, in a good high and dry position, or where water won't be likely to stand or accumulate during the Winter months. Here the pots are plunged, and as soon as real cold weather sets in they are covered with ashes two or three inches deep. This gives them all the protection they need and also keeps them from heaving out of the pots during Winter. Or they may be covered with dry leaves just as soon as real severe wintry weather sets in; and in this place, a sash or even pine branches will keep the leaves in place, but with a sash they may be got at much earlier for early orders. Don't fail to raise the sash and ventilate very freely during the brightest days of Winter, as the covering under glass helps to retain heat which so readily agitates and starts plants into growth; so it is better to keep on the safe side and ventilate freely.

The smaller plants may be placed back into nursery rows, from two to three inches apart, where they readily establish themselves and make extra strong plants by the following Fall. But on the approach of cold weather they must be covered with loose litter or some other light material, which will give them protection during the thawings and freezings of Winter. Being very slender, straight-rooted plants when young they very readily heave out of the ground during Winter, and I know of nothing more detrimental to oriental poppies than constant freezings and thawings after being newly transplanted in Fall.

Spray of New Rose Anny Müller
(Pink Baby Rambler)

Old plants of very desirable kinds or colors may also be safely removed and if it is wished to numerously increase the stock, each individual eye may be taken with a piece of the root longitudinally slit down four or five inches, with the eye attached, and potted or planted as desired. The surplus roots should also be saved, as this is the only safely true method of increasing any desired color if grown in proximity to others. Seedlings are not to be depended upon to come true to color, although thousands of seedlings are annually raised and sold to name or color without ever being flowered to prove them. Only a very small percentage bloom the first year from seed, and these only under very favorable conditions.

The roots of the above may be cut up into smaller or larger lengths, according to the quantity desired, and each piece will soon form a series of eyes from the upper end, while the lower part will emit roots if placed in a box in rather sandy soil in a cool greenhouse; or they may be kept in a very cool cellar and brought into a greenhouse to start in Spring. If kept too warm they will start even in a cellar. From the box they may be potted at will as soon as they have made a nice top growth, but they should not be allowed to stand too long, as they soon overcrowd each other and thus suffer. From pots they may be transferred to the open ground, being previously hardened off somewhat by being placed in a cold frame for a short period and as soon as possible in Spring.

Many and numerous are the named varieties now offered by various firms, but none seems so taking to the American public, as far as my experience goes, as the old dark-flowered form of orientale. There are many and various shades of this type, but the deep dark scarlet seems to be the one most in demand, with P. bracteatum a good second.

Some years ago I saw a flower of P. o. var. Mrs. Marsh very distinctly feathered and blotched with white on each petal on a rich crimson scarlet ground. On securing plants from the same source and flowering them for three successive years they turned out each time nothing but good types of P. bracteatum; and yet I was assured last Summer, in England, by one of the foremost growers of hardy plants, that the true type was to be had, but often the first year it did not show its real character.

Papaver orientale var. Mahony, raised in Holland, is a very deep mahogany colored flower, of good size and substance, and as free flowering as the type; and where a distinct change of color is wanted this can be highly recommended as a really good and meritorious variety, if such stock has been propagated from root-cuttings or divisions.

P. o. Princess Louise Victoria, as seen growing last Summer, is also a very decided acquisition, very free and late flowering, perhaps not so large flowered as some; but its freedom of bloom and its beautiful rose-colored flowers make it both attractive and desirable.

Another very distinct form which impressed me very much, was P. o. Lady Roscoe, with attractive orange or terra cotta colored flowers; a very decided and attractive break in color and one which with the one above mentioned will be much appreciated and sought after when better known.

The ever increasing love for these gorgeous flowers should lead to a good, impartial trial of varieties, and the selections of the best and most distinct sorts should be made known, instead of a legion of confusing names and descriptions, with only a few varying shades of color. HERBERT GREENSMITH.

Boltonia Asteroides.

In this plant we have a hardy perennial that all lovers of the garden should possess or at least get acquainted with. It should be known far better than it is at present. Boltonias are plants closely allied to the wild asters or Michaelmas daisies, and, like them, form splendid material for massing in shrubberies or in the old-fashioned flower garden. They are of the easiest cultivation, calling for little attention, and when once established, will take care of themselves. B. asteriodes, sometimes known as B. glastifolia, grows to the height of six feet or more, with the flower rays varying from white to violet, seemingly adhering, however, more often to the white.

JOHN F. JOHNSTON.

Glen Cove, L. I.

New Rose Anny Muller (Pink Baby Rambler.)

Messrs. Ottolander & Hooftman, nurserymen, Boskoop, Holland, send us a picture of a spray of this new rose (herewith reproduced), along with the subjoined description:

"This excellent novelty is the result of a cross between Crimson Rambler and George Pernet. The freely branching plants attain a height of 1½ feet. The growth of this rose is similar to that of Mme. N. Levavasseur. The shining brilliant-rose flowers are produced in great profusion in large clusters from June until late in the Fall. Each individual flower measures about 2 inches in diameter; the petals are sometimes twisted. Like all polyantha roses, Anny Müller is immensely valuable for pots and open ground culture."

Boltonia Asteroides

Photo by J. F. Johnston

California Plant Notes.

Nicholson gives the height of Plumbago capensis as two feet. Here it grows to twenty feet or more; indeed, it is only limited by the height of the support given it. If watered freely it runs to wood and does not bloom as well as if kept on the dry side the entire Summer. It is one of the freest blooming plants we grow, being covered from early Spring until late into the Winter with its large spikes of azure colored flowers.

P. Larpentæ, or to be correct, Certatostigma plumbaginoides, is a valuable plant for borders. Its dark blue flowers make a fine effect with white flowering plants. It stands the warm dry atmosphere of the interior valleys to perfection, as well as the frosts of Winter.

Cestrum Parqui now fills the atmosphere at night with its odor, which is not agreeable to every person who inhales it. This plant grows to be a very large sized shrub, 10 to 20 feet on the higher levels in Southern California, but is too tender to stand the frost in the lower ones.

Cestrum aurantiacum is hardier, and one of our most attractive shrubs. It blooms profusely twice during the Summer. The flowers are of a beautiful orange color, and glisten in the sunlight as though frosted. To keep it within bounds on a small place it needs to be severely pruned every year.

Cestrum elegans is another member of this family of plants that is very showy throughout our long Summers, from April to December blooming continuously. The bright red flowers are followed by brilliant colored fruit in profusion. It is also known by the name of Habrothamnus elegans. It is the only member of the species that is hardy in the interior valleys, and seems to do better there than in this part of the State.

The Iochromas, of which there are two varieties grown here—fuchsiodes and lanceolata, are beautiful subjects for either large or small places. Severe pruning will keep them within bounds of small ones and not diminish the bloom; while if given room to develop they will grow twenty feet high and ten feet in diameter. They are covered all the warmer part of the year with their tube-shaped flowers—orange scarlet on the one, dark blue on the other, borne in clusters of fifteen or more in the axils of the leaves. All these shrubs are easily propagated from hard wood cuttings planted in March or April.

Ipomœa Learii is one of the most wonderful climbers in this state. A native of Ceylon and its humid atmosphere, one would reasonably suppose that it would not fit into a dry climate, yet in the interior valleys of the state it will, if given plenty of water, make more than one hundred feet of growth in one Summer. The frosts of Winter will kill the tops, but not injure the roots; and if not removed every Spring the new growth will again cover these dead vines with a mass of luxuriant foliage and dark blue flowers. The writer has seen at least a ton of dead vines, mixed with cobwebs and dust on a careless rancher's house, covering the entire building except the doorway and windows. Most houses in the interior sections of the state are known by the name of "California," for the reason that they are neither lathed nor plastered and many without a chimney. The boards, which are stood upright in building, are covered with muslin on the inside which is tacked on to them and on to this the paper is pasted. The cracks on the outside are covered with two inch strips. In the drying process of the lumber, cracks will occur which are never closed, and into these fissures the ipomœa vine finds its way, festooning pictures and statuary and otherwise decorating the room, according to the fancy of the housekeeper. Growing thus in the shade, the foliage is not so dark and dense as on the outside, yet if windows and doors are left open, which they usually are, enough of the brilliant sunlight enters to give a color to both leaf and flower that would astonish an Easterner. The roots in a few years become such a formidable bed that an axe is necessary to cut them out in chunks before they can be removed. Along the coast where nights are cooler, and the temperature never gets so high, the plant does not make this prodigious growth, yet covers buildings two stories high.

Jatropha integerrima is one of our beautiful foliage plants which is not as extensively grown as it should be where sub-tropical effects are desired in landscape work. The flowers are dark red, though not attractive, yet interesting in their construction; but the foliage and new growth are very pretty, and will stand a great deal of drought and some frost.

P. D. BARNHART.

FOR THE RETAILER

Brian Boru's Harp.

The illustration herewith shown is as near as possible an exact reproduction in size and shape of the musical instrument made famous by the illustrious Irish King, Brian Boru. Since the battle of Clontarf it has been adopted as Ireland's national emblem, and in all climes and under all circumstances is the one design that appeals most strongly to the Irish race. This is the first time, we believe, that it has ever been reproduced in flowers. It was made and presented by us as a prize for Gaelic singing at a recent musical festival held in New York city. It stands thirty-one inches in height, as does the original harp at present in Trinity's Museum, Dublin.

Facsimile of Brian Boru's Harp.
Artist, J. Ivera Donlan.

The larger portion of the frame is of green immortelles, with yellow and a line of white immortelles on the front of the sounding board. The 22 wires are wrapped in gold, silver and bronze tinsel ribbons, with a garland wreath of green silk shamrocks among the strings, and on the sounding board and base. The keys are of white, chenille covered wires. The harp stands upright; both sides are treated alike, the wires being attached to the keys on the left side. The small wreath at the bottom is of gilded leucothöe leaves.

We take particular pride in being able to show readers of The Florists Exchange the difference between Ireland's beautiful national design and the awful libels in the shape of harps too often seen at funerals.

J. IVERA DONLAN.

A Wreath for McKinley Monument.

The beautiful wreath of laurel, cycas leaves, and dark purple asters herewith shown, was the offering of The Columbus (O.) Florists' Club, as a tribute to the memory of our late president, at the unveiling of the McKinley Memorial monument by Mrs. Nicholas Longworth. These ceremonies took place at Columbus, O., Friday, September 14, 1906. The committee from the club in charge of the matter was composed of Messrs. Albert Knopf, Guy H. Woodrow, and M. B. Faxon.

Western Impressions of Eastern Men.

A few items of pleasant memories incident to a hurried but a very profitable outing of a couple of busy florists are here given, our objective point being Red Mountain, Colorado, which is some 14,000 feet above the sea level, where snow and ice abound every day in the year. Although with a special party in private cars and on pleasure bent, the flowers were too interesting to eliminate them entirely.

We left Washington, D. C., August 11, a. m., and arrived in Denver, Col. early in the morning of August 14. The writer naturally fell in with that genial, whole-souled president of the Park Floral Co., J. A. Valentine, who promptly asked for a few hours of our time, and we, having time to spend, were willing subjects. I might say that while in Mr. Valentine's place of business we were shown some dahlias the like of which we had never seen before on this side (or the other side) of the Atlantic. We were naturally interested to know where these dahlias grew, and a few minutes afterwards we were in an automobile being taken through a most interesting section of the city of Denver, and five miles northwest through some of the most fertile fields that it was ever our pleasure to behold.

In a short while we were on the grounds of Mr. W. W. Wilmore, a resident of Laurel, Md., many years ago. Here, at Mr. Wilmore's place, the beauty and perfection of all the flowers that he cultivates are simply unexcelled, but particularly so is his dahlia industry, which, from our observation, seemed to be perfection itself. The following are varieties particularly worthy of mention.

Bon Ton he considers the best dark red, and Lyndhurst an excellent red or scarlet. In white, Snow and Gloire de Lyon are both good. He considers Kriemhilde a most desirable pink. Cactus, and the old deep pink A. D. Livoni, are still general favorites, but he predicts that both of these will have to take a back seat when Mme. von Dael is fairly before the public; this he considers the grandest thing yet sent out in pink, but the stock has been too scarce for it to become generally known. It should have a slight shading in this climate to bring the flowers to perfection. Queen of Yellow and Miss Dodd are both good yellows. Twentieth Century has proven to be a valuable and striking variety for florists' use, but it is about the only single that is much in demand here. Mrs. Winters is a magnificent white for the garden, but wilts easily and on that account is not a valuable florists' flower.

He mentions two other new varieties which he confidently predicts have come to stay. Navajo, a very dark red, of decorative form, too dark for florists' purposes but just right for others; and Umatilla, a red with very long stem and fine flowers. A green freak noticed is named Verdiflora and is as perfect a formed green flower as we have ever beheld in any other color.

It might be well to state that these beautiful fertile acres were a barren waste before Mr. Wilmore took hold of them, but through the introduction and perfect control of an irrigation system, Mr. Wilmore has converted it into a model, commercial, floral and fruit farm, for the flavor of those juicy apples, dished out to us in the form of a liquid, was as pleasing to the taste as the beauty to the eye. In all, the home of Wilmore, with his sturdy family, his welcome, whole-souled greeting, his kind hospitality, and his heartfelt "come again," makes one feel proud to be a florist, and that such men as W. W. Wilmore are in the business to grow flowers to such perfection as we saw them here.

Leaving Mr. Wilmore's place, laden with arms full of his choice flowers, we stopped at the Union Depot to leave them in our cars. The members of our party were all Eastern people and they declared that they had never seen such specimens.

We next drove through the principal streets of the city, where we were shown lawns and window boxes to perfection, then to the Park Floral greenhouses, where everything that we saw was up-to-date and in fine condition, then through the extensive city park system, with its zoological park, boulevards, lakes and drives, second to none in the point of beauty and artistic arrangement. Reaching the far end of the park we suddenly discovered that it was nearly time for our train to leave, and had to beat a hurried retreat for the Union Depot to join our party to go farther West, after spending one of the most pleasant and profitable of days.

Having always been in favor of our national convention reaching out, I feel now more than ever that one of the best moves the society could make

would be to hold a convention in Denver, Col., in the near future.

In the midst of the Rocky Mountains we were again impressed by the clear color and wonderful beauty of the columbine, which grows wild in great profusion on the mountain tops, also the forget-me-not, with its vivid blue, growing in the highest altitude far above the timber line. At Colorado Springs and Manitou, we also noticed that the Western people put forth more effort in producing beautiful lawns and gardens than do our Eastern people.

ADOLPHUS GUDE.
Washington, D. C. WM. F. GUDE.

Wreath sent by Columbus, (O.) Florists' Club to Unveiling of McKinley Memorial Monument.

A Visit to White Marsh, Md.

Wednesday, September 19, will be a day long remembered by Richard Vincent, Jr., and his family, and the many visitors from Washington, Baltimore, Philadelphia and New York, who accepted his invitation to visit his establishment at White Marsh, Md.

Mr. Vincent has achieved a national reputation in several special lines, and it was with a great deal of pleasure that we accepted the invitation to view his dahlias while at the height of their flowering season.

Reaching Cowenton, the nearest railroad point to White Marsh, a short drive brought us to Mr. Vincent's establishment, and here we found that over 125 ladies and gentlemen, most of them from Baltimore and Washington, had preceded us, and were enjoying a bountiful luncheon served in the mammoth bulb and storage house recently erected.

The exhibit of cut dahlias arranged on the same floor of the building mentioned was very attractive indeed, but the lunch table seemed to be in need of immediate attention, so we of the New York and Philadelphia visitors first went through the bill of fare, from oysters to ice cream and enjoyed everything hugely.

Getting back to the exhibit of dahlias, we must say that these were most excellently arranged and presented a magnificent sight as a whole. The floor space utilized comprised 210 by 30 feet, and stages were used along each side, together with two rows of tables through the center. On the staging at one side single flowers in their respective classes were shown. For instance, here was the cactus class, one flower of each variety, next the show class, one flower of each, and so on through the various classes. On the other side of the room the different classes were staged in groups; thus there would be a group of the decorative class in variety, then a group of the cactus class in variety, following on with the remainder of the different classes. On the center tables the varieties were shown in clusters of one variety each, thus the visitors were enabled to see each variety as an individual, with a cluster of its own kind and as one in a collection of varieties belonging to its own particular class—a very comprehensive method of exhibiting dahlias, and one certainly appreciated by all who saw the flowers.

Many newly imported varieties were placed on exhibition, but as their suitability to the needs and requirements of the American trade, together with the climate, cannot be estimated in a single season, we will only mention here such sorts as have been found fully up to the requirements necessary for trade purposes.

Taking the single section first: while there are several finely colored varieties in this class, the Century collection is so far ahead in size, length of stem, etc., that it would seem unnecessary to grow any but these in their respective colors. There are now crimson, white, lavender, scarlet and the Twentieth Century, and they cannot be beaten among singles.

In the decorative class Professor Mansfield is a beautiful flower, showing yellow at the base of the petals, the tips pink, slightly touched with crimson, a very pleasing combination of color. Souv. de Gustave Douzon, is a rich crimson flower 10 inches across, perfect in its coloring, and the largest dahlia seen. Jean Charmot, is one of the novelties that has made good; a soft shade of lilac and a fine all-round sort. Mme. Van den Dael is a good one for light pink; and Princess Louise Victoria is a splendid sort for a deeper or rose-pink. Mrs. Roosevelt is also one of the best pink varieties in this class.

Among the cactus sorts the following are considered the cream of the collection: J. H. Jackson, crimson; Aegar, red; Mrs. H. J. Jones, scarlet with white tips; Gen. Buller, crimson with white tips; Volker, yellow; Nero, white; Blush Queen, something after the order of Kriemhilde, but thought to be superior to that variety. Innocence, cream yellow; and Country Girl, a novelty, a bronze colored variety having a yellow center.

Among the show varieties the following are considered in the lead: Bon Ton, crimson; Gettysburg, scarlet; John Walker, white; Lucy Fawcet, white speckled; M. D. Hallock, yellow; Queen Victoria, yellow; Camelliæflora, white; and Ruby Queen.

Some 40 varieties of pompons were on exhibition including almost every color.

In the above list of varieties we have endeavored to mention only such kinds as are of a free growing habit, and that will produce flowers on stems sufficiently long for all commercial purposes.

The collarette section was also represented by several varieties.

In going through the dahlia fields, which by the way cover some 40 or 50 acres, one is impressed with the general heavy and strong growth seen, also with the remarkable abundance of flowers produced. It might be well to mention that every plant set out in the fields was originally a rooted cutting; no dry tubers are planted outdoors here.

That Mr. Vincent is up-to-date in his methods and equipment is exemplified in the storage building recently erected. This is a three story and basement structure covering 210 x 30 feet. In the basement is ample storage room for roots; while in one end is an immense dynamo, run by a 80 h. p. engine, which furnishes a full supply of electric light for the whole establishment. On the first floor are the offices, and the second and third floors are equipped for the storing of bulbs, etc.

The greenhouses on the place cover a considerable area; one block, which covers exactly one acre, is at present almost filled with geraniums that are being grown for stock purposes. All the newest varieties are here, of both American and European origin, but this is no season of the year to discuss new sorts of geraniums that are being grown for stock purposes.

In addition to the glass mentioned there are six houses each 165 x 22 feet; six houses 228 x 28 feet; and two houses, each 100 x 20 feet; all heated by steam from a battery of six Furman boilers. The total area of the farm is 200 acres; it is favorably surrounded by woodland, and is all of it under cultivation in some crop or other.

It might perhaps not be out of place here to say a word or two about Mr. Vincent upbuilding his Maryland home. He located here in 1868 and built his first greenhouse in 1870; a modest structure, 10 x 15 feet in dimensions. He did a little in the nursery business, but soon left that and took up the raising of vegetable plants. And to give an idea of the volume of the vegetable plant business at the present time, we may say that this year twenty million plants were disposed of, 900,000 tomato plants alone being filled in one order. Dahlias, chrysanthemums and geraniums were also taken up in turn by Mr. Vincent; and it can in all truth be asserted, that he is one of the foremost specialists of the land in these flowers and plants.

Associated with Mr. Vincent are his three sons, all of whom are married and live on the estate. The eldest is Richard A. Vincent, who is the proud father of five girls. Thomas A. Vincent, the next son, who is just recovering from a serious illness, has one daughter and two sons. The youngest son, John S. Vincent, has two children also, so that it will be seen that the name of Vincent is likely to be perpetuated for some time yet in "My Maryland."

Mr. and Mrs. Vincent did all in their power to make their many guests happy during the afternoon, and when the little impromptu meeting was called after the luncheon, in order to express thanks and appreciations to the host and hostess, Mr. Vincent said that his earnest wish was for everybody to make himself at home.

Among the visitors present were three ex-persidents of the S. A. F. O. H. viz: Edwin Lonsdale, Patrick O'Mara and W. F. Gude. Professor H. J. Patterson, director of the Maryland Experiment Station, Professor Symons, entomologist; Dr. H. B. McDonnell, professor of chemistry, and Messrs. White and Ballard, assistant horticulturists, all of the Maryland Experiment Station. All of these gentlemen made short speeches at the meeting held, and voiced the sentiments of the entire gathering in expressing their thanks to Vincent & Sons for the pleasant day spent at White Marsh. Governor Warfield of the State of Maryland had intended to be at the gathering, but owing to that day being set for turning the first sod in preparation for the coming Jamestown Exposition, at which ceremony he had to officiate, he was unavoidably absent.

Richard Vincent, Jr.

Philadelphia.

The Week's News.

Most of the retail stores show a more healthy appearance this week, and several of them report good orders coming in for October weddings. The prospects for the coming season are very good for the florist trade. This city will have the best social season it has had for many years; the number of balls, receptions, etc., will far outnumber anything in the past six years.

S. S. Pennock is back from his vacation, or rather back from his attempt to escape hay fever. He tried the sea shore, but on account of the continued prevalence of land breezes, he had to take to the ocean, and took steamer to Jacksonville and return.

John McIntire will start in the wholesale commission business at the Flower Market, 1235 Filbert street, October 1. He is well known in the trade here, having had good experience in the retail business, and for the past four years in the wholesale business in which he has been very successful as a salesman.

C. B. Tustin, who has a very good retail business at 1537 W. Passayunk avenue, has been advised by his physician to give up the business and take up something less confining. He desires to sell out. This is probably the best stand in the city for funeral work, and has been so for years, all orders coming in unsolicited.

A meeting of the stockholders of the Flower Market has been called for the 25th, with the idea of liquidating. This is brought about by Chas. E. Meehan, who controls most of the stock, forming an amalgamation with S. S. Pennock. DAVID RUST.

Chicago.

News Items.

Flint Kennicott has received a letter from Mrs. Wells of Helena, Montana, requesting the address of John Bohanan, a well known grower in Chicago nearly a generation ago. If any of our readers can furnish the address the information will be most acceptable.

The supply department at The E. F. Winterson Company's headquarters, is receiving a thorough overhauling, and numerous improvements which will aid in the transaction of business are being installed.

A. L. Vaughan left on Monday for Buffalo, New York and other points in the East on a business trip.

Vaughan & Sperry have engaged the services of a new bookkeeper, Mortimer Speer.

The chrysanthemum season is opening especially early this year. Among the unusual features in this line may be mentioned the white, October Frost, and the yellow, Monrovia, which are coming in from Wietor Brothers' houses. They are certainly remarkable productions for mid-September.

Miss Starrett on Monday of this week entered the George Reinberg force as bookkeeper and stenographer.

The incoming crop of American Beauty from the new range at J. A. Budlong's, is certainly a floral feature of Chicago to-day.

A recent call at 1639 Belmont avenue found Edgar Sanders sitting on the front porch, enjoying to the full extent the beauties of a perfect September morning. It is hardly necessary to mention that "Pop," as he is most affectionately called by all the members of the profession in this vicinity, was profoundly interested in every detail in connection with the Dayton convention, and inquired personally as to the health and appearance of all of the old-timers with whom he has spent so many happy hours at conventions in various sections of the country.

WILLIAM K. WOOD.

St. Louis.

News Notes.

The landscape firm of Bourdet & Roehr of 1732 S. Vandeventer avenue, has dissolved partnership. Jules Bourdet, who laid out the French garden at the World's Fair, will continue the business at the same location.

Siegel & Burk, doing a retail business at 609 Locust street, also have dissolved partnership, John Burk continuing on at the old stand, while Alex. Siegel will be found at his old store, Sixth and Washington avenues.

James W. North, formerly with the North Floral Company, is in town visiting old friends. He is now with D. B. Honaker, Lexington, Ky., and says the new store which Mr. Honaker will open next week will be as fine as any retail store in the West.

Fred C. Weber has plans for a new residence to be built on Watterman avenue. Fred Jr. also contemplates building a flat.

George B. Windler, Delor street, will have a fine lot of extra pot chrysanthemums; his brother, Robert, who has a store on Grand avenue, will handle them.

On Saturday last the first chrysanthemums made their appearance at Kuehn's, having come from A. C. Canfield, Springfield. By the end of the week no doubt a supply will also be seen at the stores of Berning, Ellis and Augermuller. Shipping trade is again active, and Eddie Gerlach, Otto Bruning, Will Osic and Fred Alves, first assistants at these establishments, will be busy from now on.

ST. PATRICK.

ASPARAGUS

	per 100
Plumosus Nanus, 2¼ in. pots	$2.00
Plumosus Seedlings,	1.00
Sprengeril, 2½ in. pots	2.00
Vinca variegated from field, Oct.	5.00

PRIMROSES

	per 10
Obconica Alba, and Roses	2.00
Cannas, 5 var., field, clump	15.00

PANSY PLANTS, $8.00 per 1000; 50c. per 100.

CASH PLEASE.

JOS. H. CUNNINGHAM, Delaware, O.

Mention The Florists' Exchange when writing.

DRACAENA TERMINALIS Matured canes always ready for shipment. Delivered to any part of the United States for 10 cents a foot. Send cash for a trial order.

PORTO RICO PINEAPPLE CO., RIO PIEDRAS, PORTO RICO.

Mention The Florists' Exchange when writing.

A NEW REMARKABLE CAROLINA-MOUNTAIN PLANT

STENANTHIUM ROBUSTUM or MOUNTAIN FEATHER FLEECE

This remarkable hardy perennial is, without doubt, one of our best new introductions, and may be classed with the showiest of all herbaceous plants. As the buds begin to unfold in early August they are quite upright, and a light green tinge, gradually becoming whiter until at last they burst forth into a veritable snowbank of drooping, fleecy bloom of purest white, the panicles often 2 to 3 feet long. In September the flowers, as they ripen, turn to shades of pink and purple. It is a vigorous perennial, attaining a height of from 5 to 8 feet when well established, and is absolutely hardy throughout the United States and Canada.

The Mountain Feather Fleece is of easy cultivation, and if given plenty of food, makes a wonderful show equalled by few plants of any description.

The illustration gives some idea of the wonderful effect of Stenanthium when in full bloom, but inadequately conveys the beauty of the delicate, feathered, drooping flowers. When known, will be planted by thousands.

Prices, postpaid	Size 1.	Largest size	Each 60 cents; per 10, $5.00
	Size 2.	Heavier plants	Each 40 cents; per 10, $3.00
	Size 3.	Small Strong Plants	Each 25 cents; per 10, $2.00
By Express, not paid	Size 1.	Largest size	Per 10, $3.00; per 100, $25.00
	Size 2.	Heavier plants	Per 10, $2.25; per 100, $16.00
	Size 3.	Strong Plants	Per 10, $1.25; per 100, $10.00

Highlands Nursery, 100 acres, 3,800 feet elevation in the Carolina Mountains, and Salem Branch, Salem, Mass., "The Home of hardy Native Rhododendrons, Azaleas, Kalmias and Rare Carolina Mountain Flowers." Beautifully illustrated Catalog. Address

HARLAN P. KELSEY, Owner, - SALEM, MASS.

Mention The Florists' Exchange when writing.

FERNS and CARNATIONS

SPEAK QUICK

10,000 Healthy Field Grown Carnations, best commercial sorts, including **ELBON,** a fine, true red. **Send for list as they must be sold.**

1,000 **PIERSONI FERNS,** for 4 in., 15c.
1,000 " " for 3 in., 10c.
1,000 **BOSTON** " 3 in. ready for 4 in., 10c.
SCOTTII FERNS, 4 in., 20c.; 3 in., 10c.
ANNA FOSTER, 2½ in., 4c.
1,000 **ASPARAGUS PLUMOSUS NANUS,** 3½ in., 6c.; 2½ in., $2.50 per 100.
200 **ASPARAGUS SPRENGERII,** 3½ in., 6c.
1,000 **HYDRANGEA OTAKSA,** 2½ in., $2.50 per 100.
1,000 **VINCA MAJOR** var., 2½ in., $2.50 per 100.
All A No. 1 Stock. Cash please.

BENJ. CONNELL
WEST GROVE, PA.

Mention The Florists' Exchange when writing.

Ferns From Bench

BOSTON, PIERSONI, 3 in. 5c., 4 in. 10c. 5 in. 12½c. Boston 6 in. 15 cts.
TARRYTOWN, 3 in., 10c.; 4 in., 15c.; 5 in., 25c. Runners $20.00 per 1000.
SCOTTII, 3 in., 8c.; 4 in., 12½c.

CHINESE PRIMROSES

White, fine plants, 1½ cts.
Primula Obconica, Hybrid Alba Rosea, 2 in., 2 cts.
Floribunda Primroses, 2 in., 2 cts.
Pansy Plants, Giants, $3.00 per 100.
Daisies, double Snowball, Longfellow, Delicata, $2.50 per 1000.
Asparagus Sprengerii, 2 in., 2 cts.
Jerusalem Cherries, field grown, ready for 4 in., 3 cts.
Flowering Begonias, 8 kinds, 2 in., 2½ cts.
Begonia Rex, 2 in., 4 cts.
Alyssum Giant, White double, 2 in. 2c.

Cash or C. O. D.

BYER BROS., Chambersburg, Pa.

Mention The Florists' Exchange when writing.

ORCHIDS

Largest Importers, Exporters, Growers and Hybridists in the world.

Sander, St. Albans, England
and
235 Broadway, Room 1, New York City

Mention The Florists' Exchange when writing.

ORCHIDS

Arrived in superb condition **Cattleya Dowiana, C. Gigas, C. Mossiae, C. Percivaliana, C. Speciosissima, C. Eldorado, C. Superba, C. Labiata, C. Leopoldii** and many more.

Write for Prices.

LAGER & HURRELL, Summit, N. J.
Growers and Importers

Mention The Florists' Exchange when writing.

1,000 **Smilax,** 2½ in., strong, cut back, per 100, $1.50; the lot for $17.50.
200 **Asparagus Plumosus,** $2.50 per 100.
1,000 **Asparagus Sprengerii,** 2½ in., $2.00 per 100 the lot for $17.00. This is strong and ready for a shift.

J. S. BLOOM,
RIEGELSVILLE, PA.

Mention The Florists' Exchange when writing

ROBERT CRAIG & CO.

ROSES, PALMS, CROTONS

CARNATIONS and Novelties in DECORATIVE PLANTS

Market and 49th Sts. PHILADELPHIA, PA.

COCOS PALMS.

Strong 2½ inch at $1.50 per dozen. Write for lowest prices on **Kentias.**

Jas. F. Barclay. R. I. GREENHOUSES Pawtucket, R. I.

ASPARAGUS

Plumosus, 2½ and 3 in. strong plants, $25.00 per 1000.

Senecio Macroglossus, ever-blooming German Ivy; flowers, cream colored, large as a silver dollar, $3.00 per doz.

P. D. BARNHART,
573 S. Boyle Ave., Los Angeles, Cal.

Mention The Florists' Exchange when writing.

EMERSON C. McFADDEN

Wholesale Grower

Asparagus Plumosus Nanus, Etc.

Short Hills, N. J.
Tel. 28 A.

Mention The Florists' Exchange when writing.

Asparagus Sprengerii

We have a large stock of strong plants in 4 in. and 5 in. pots and will close them out at $4.50 per 100.

CASH WITH ORDER.

F. E. ALLEN & CO.
BROCKTON, MASS.

Mention the Florists' Exchange when writing.

SMILAX PLANTS

Strong, Bushy Plants, many times cut back and ready for shift.

2 in. pots ..... $1.00 per 100, $9.00 per 1000.
Seedlings from flats ..... $4.00 "

We have grown Smilax Plants for the trade 18 years, and never had finer stock.

Send for Samples.

R. KILBOURN, CLINTON, N. Y.

Mention The Florists' Exchange when writing.

ROOTED CUTTINGS

COLEUS, 20 kinds, 60c. per 100; $5.00 per 1000. **ALTERNANTHERA,** 3 kinds, $1.00 per 100; $8.00 per 1000. **LANTANA,** 8 kinds, $1.00 per 100. **AGERATUM,** 3 kinds, $1.00 per 100. **SALVIA,** 3 kinds, $1.00 per 100. Field Grown **PRINCE OF WALES VIOLETS,** Scotch Pink, $4.00 per 100. 2 in. **GERANIUM,** 20c. per 100.

THE NATIONAL PLANT CO., DAYTON, OHIO

Mention the Florists' Exchange when writing.

SURPLUS STOCK—CHEAP

We have a fine lot of **Jerusalem Cherries** for sale from 2-in. pots. In order to make room immediately we will close them out at $1.00 per 100; they are worth $5.00. 1500 **Smilax,** strong, 2 in. pots, $1.00 per 100; $9.00 per 1000. Also a big stock of **Geraniums,** S. A. Nutt and others, also assorted from sand, $1.00 per 100; from 2 in. pots, $1.75 per 100; from 3 in. pots, $4.00 per 100. Write for prices on other stock; we can save you money.

E. I. RAWLINGS, QUAKERTOWN, PA.

Mention the Florists' Exchange when writing.

PLANT HERBACEOUS PERENNIALS

this month and save the rush of Spring work. We offer the following list of field grown stock

	Per doz.	Per 100
Achillea, the Pearl	$ .75	$6.00
Agrostemma, Coronaria	.75	6.00
Anthemis, Tinctoria Kelwayii	.75	6.00
Aquilegia, Coerulea Canadensis	.75	6.00
Artemesia Abrotanum Purshiana Stelleriana	.75	6.00
Arabis, Alpina	.75	5.00
Boltonia, Asteroides, Latisquama	.75	6.00
Campanula, Grosseki, Punctata, Rapunculus	.75	6.00
Caryopteris, Mastacanthus	.75	6.00
Clematis, Davidiana	.75	6.00
Coreopsis, Rosea	.75	6.00
Delphinium, Chinensis	.75	6.00
Digitalis Gloxinaeflora, White, Purple, Rose. Extra large field grown clumps	.75	6.00
Eupatorium, Ageratoides, Coelestinum	.75	6.00

	Per doz.	Per 100
Funkia, Coerulea	.75	6.00
Helianthus, Multiflorus Maximus	.75	6.00
Heliopsis, Scaber Major	1.00	8.00
Hibiscus, Moscheutos, Crimson Eye	.75	6.00
Hollyhocks, Double White, Pink, Yellow, Single, Mixed and Allegheny Fringed	1.00	8.00
Hypericum Moserianum	.75	6.00
Liatris, Pycnostachya	.90	7.00
Mentha, Piperita	.60	4.00
Myosotis, Palustris Semperflorens	.60	4.00
Pardanthus, Sinensis	.90	7.00
Physostegia, Virginica	.75	6.00
Phlox, 10 varieties true to name	1.00	8.00
Rudbeckia, Golden Glow, Newmanii	.75	6.00
Salvia, Azurea Grandiflora	.90	7.00
Sedum, Acre	.75	6.00
Stokesia, Cyanea	.75	6.00
Tritoma, Pfitzeri	1.00	8.00

EDWARD J. TAYLOR - - Southport, Conn.

Mention The Florists' Exchange when writing.

WE ARE HEADQUARTERS FOR

Princess Violet Stock

Orders booked for September delivery. Strong field-grown plants, $50.00 per 1000.

WILLIAM SIM, Cliftondale, Mass.

Mention The Florists' Exchange when writing.

VIOLETS

MARIE LOUISE Violets, clean and healthy in every particular, ready August 15th. 3 in. pots, $5.00 per 100.

CASH WITH ORDER.

WM. J. CHINNICK,
TRENTON, N. J.

Mention The Florists' Exchange when writing.

HEADQUARTERS FOR

Choice Plants

English Ivy, Anthericums, Kentias Forsteriana and Belmoreana, Phoenix Canariensis, Araucarias, Bay Trees and Boxwood Pyramids, Asparagus Plumosus, Bird's Nest, Scottii Elegantissima, Piersoni Boston and Johnsoni Ferns, Cattleya Trianae Rubbers Dracaenas Terminalis and Fragrans, Pandanus Veitchii, Gardenia Veitchii, Cycas Revoluta, Cibotium Schiedei Livistonii Sinensis, Areca Lutescens, Crotons, Aspidistras, Lygodium Scandens, Primula Obconica, Begonia Rex, Daisies, Fern Balls, Lily of the Valley, Cut Flowers, Leaf Mold, Orchid Peat, etc. Write for prices.

Anton Schultheis 19th St. and 4th Ave. College Point, L. I., N. Y.

Mention The Florists' Exchange when writing.

A BARGAIN FOR YOU IN NICE PLANTS

2000 **Achillea,** The Pearl $2.00 per 100, 1500 **German Iris** 8 Varieties $2.00 per 100, 8900 **Iris sibirica** Blue and White $2.00 per 100, 1000 **Helianthus Divaricata,** $2.00 per 100, 1000 **Heliopsis Pitcheriana,** $2.00 per 100, 1000 **Digitalis,** Foxglove, $2.00 per 100, 500 **Crimson Eye,** Hibiscus $3.00 per 100, 400 **Peonies,** 3-5 eyes asstd. $8.00 per 100, 500 **Arundo Donax** Grass $5.00 per 100, 200 **Funkia Coerulea,** $4.00 per 100, 1500 **Trumpet Vines,** 2-3 ft. tr. 2c., 300 **Wistaria Multijuga** racemes of blooms 2-3 ft. long, 10c. each. Cash with Order please.

Ellsworth Brown & Co., Seabrook, N. H.

Mention The Florists' Exchange when writing.

To Clear the Land We Shall Sell For the Next 60 Days

	Per 1000
Berberis Thunbergii, 18 to 24 in., bushy plants	$40.00
Berberis Thunbergii, 24 to 30 in., bushy plants	50.00
Rosa Lucida, 3 years, twice transplanted, fine	40.00
Viburnum Dentatum, 24 to 30 in.	40.00
" " 30 to 36 in.	50.00

We also have some Viburnum cassinoides and Prunus maritima.

Littlefield & Wyman
North Abington, Mass.

Mention The Florists' Exchange when writing.

VIOLETS

Campbell, field-grown plants, fine, $4.00 per 100; $35.00 per 1000
California, out of 2½ in., $2.00 per 100; $17.00 per 1000
Alyssum, double Giant, for winter flowering, 2½ in., $1.50 per 100
Dracena Indivisa, large field-grown plants, ready for 6 in., $7.00 per 100; $1.00 per doz.
Hydrangeas, for forcing, 5 to 9 flowering crowns, $7.00 per 100
Parsley, moss curled, large field-grown plants, $2.50 per 1000

J. C. SCHMIDT CO.
BRISTOL, PA.

Mention The Florists' Exchange when writing.

VIOLETS

FINE FIELD GROWN PLANTS

Marie Louise and Princess of Wales, $4.50 per 100; $40.00 per 1000

Carnations

Enchantress and **Flamingo,** $6.00 per 100; $50.00 per 1000

Queen Louise, $4.50 per 100; $40.00 per 1000

THE BOOL FLORAL CO.,
ITHACA, N. Y.

Mention The Florists' Exchange when writing.

CARNATIONS

	Per 100	Per 1000		Per 100	Per 1000		Per 100	Per 1000
FIANCEE	$6 00		MORNING GLORY	$4 00	$35 00	FLORA HILL	$5 00	$45 00
LAWSON	6 00	$50 00	LIEUT. PEARY	8 00	75 00	WHITE CLOUD	5 00	45 00
NELSON FISHER	7 00	60 00	FRED BURKI	7 00	60 00	CHICAGO (Red Bradt)	5 00	45 00
GUARDIAN ANGEL	4 00	35 00	BOSTON MARKET	5 00	45 00	HARLOWARDEN	6 00	50 00
NCHANTRESS	7 00	60 00						

WIETOR BROS., 51 Wabash Ave., CHICAGO

Mention The Florists' Exchange when writing.

CARNATIONS

STRONG, HEALTHY, FIELD GROWN PLANTS

PINK	100	1000	WHITE	100	1000
LAWSON	$5.00	$40.00	BOSTON MARKET	$4.00	$35.00
NELSON	3.00	25.00	FLORA HILL	3.00	25.00
GUARDIAN ANGEL	3.00	25.00	QUEEN LOUISE	3.00	25.00
ENCHANTRESS	7.00	60.00	WHITE CLOUD	3.00	25.00
MORNING GLORY	4.00	30.00	VARIEGATED		
HIGINBOTHAM	3.00	25.00	ARMAZINDY	3.00	25.00
			RED		
			ESTELLE	5.00	40.00
			MRS. INE	3.00	25.00

ROSE PLANTS

	100	1000
LIBERTY 3 in. pots	$3.00	$25.00
CHATENAY 2½ in. pots	2.50	22.50

PETER REINBERG, 51 Wabash Ave., CHICAGO

Mention The Florists' Exchange when writing.

CARNATIONS | FIELD PLANTS

	Per 100		Per 100
GLENDALE	$10.00	BOSTON MARKET	$5.00
ROBT. CRAIG	12.00	WHITE CLOUD	6.00
BOUNTIFUL	8.00	MRS. PATTEN	6.00
DOROTHY WHITNEY	8.00	NELSON	5.00
BELLE	7.00	ESTELLE	3rd size, 3.50
FLAMINGO	7.00		
FIANCEE	7.00		

ROSES, 200 4 in. Maids, 150 4 in. Brides, $6.00 per 100. 500 2½ in. Gates, 300 2½ in. Brides, 150 2½ in. Perles, $2.50 per 100. Richmond Roses own roots, fine 3 in. $5.00; 2 in. $4.00 per 100.
ASPARAGUS PLUMOSUS, 2 in., $2.00 per 100. SPRENGERI, 3 in. $6.00 per 100. Cash or C. O. D.

W. J. & M. S. VESEY, Fort Wayne, Ind.

Mention The Florists' Exchange when writing.

CARNATIONS

Crisis Scarlet,	$5.00	per 100	Cardinal	$7.00	per 100
Fiancee	5.00	"	Estelle,	5.00	"
Joost	5.00	"	Queen	5.00	"
B. Market	5.00	"	Harlowarden	5.00	"

Second size $2.00 per 100 less. Cash with order.

SMITH & GANNETT, Geneva, N. Y.

Mention The Florists' Exchange when writing.

CARNATION PLANTS

Medium size. No stem rot.

500 Mag Naylor (white), 600 Queen, 200 Fair Maid, 50 GeneVieve Lord 50 Scott.

Second size; 150 Enchantress, 150 Lawson, 50 White Lawson, 50 Patten, 125 Joost, 75 Prosperity.

$8.00 per 100. Cash with order please.

H. M. WOUNDY, New Caanan, Conn.

Mention The Florists' Exchange when writing.

FIELD GROWN CARNATION PLANTS

Boston Market, large, $6.00 per 100. Mrs. T. W. Lawson, medium, $4.00 per 100. Manley, $4.00 per 100. Enchantress, $4.00 per 100. Asparagus Plumosus Nanus, fine plants, from 4 in. pots, $8.00 per 100. Asparagus Sprengeri, 4 in., strong, $8.00 per 100. Smilax, strong, 3 in., $3.00 per 100. Cash with order.

WENDEL BIEAR, Palmer Av., YONKERS, N. Y.

Mention The Florists' Exchange when writing.

CARNATIONS

Field Grown plants for August 27 and later delivery.

THE H. WEBER & SONS CO.,
OAKLAND, MD.

Mention The Florists' Exchange when writing.

FIELD GROWN CARNATIONS

	Per 100		Per 100
Roosevelt	$4.00	Prosperity	$5.00
Hill Sport	4.00	Flamingo	5.00
Manley	5.00	Enchantress	6.00
Scarlet Seedling	6.00	Cash with order.	

Chas. T. Darling, Stony Brook, L. I., N. Y.

Mention The Florists' Exchange when writing.

The Model EXTENSION

CARNATION SUPPORT

Endorsed by all the leading carnation growers as the best support on the market. Made with 2 or 3 circles. Write for prices and circulars.

We have special low prices to offer and can save you money on

Galvanized Wire ROSE STAKES

Write us for prices before ordering elsewhere. Prompt shipment guaranteed.

IGOE BROS.
226 North 9th Street
BROOKLYN, N. Y.

Mention The Florists' Exchange when writing.

FIELD GROWN

Carnation Plants

5000 Enchantress, 6c. each; $50.00 per 1000
Queen, 5c. each; $40.00 per 1000.
Lawson, white, 2nd size, $4.00 per 100.
" variegated, 2nd size, $5.00 per 100.
" pink, 2nd size, $3.50 per 100.
Lady Bountiful, 2nd size, $5.00 per 100.
Glacier, 2nd size, $3.50 per 100.

CASH

GOVE BROS., Biddeford, Me.

Mention The Florists' Exchange when writing.

CARNATIONS

Strong Field Grown Plants

Crimson Glow (new variety) $12.00 per 100

Cash or references with order.

DAILLEDOUZE BROTHERS
Flatbush, Brooklyn, N. Y.

Mention The Florists' Exchange when writing.

S. J. GODDARD

Framingham, Mass.

Rooted Carnation Cuttings a Specialty.

Correspondence Solicited.

Mention The Florists' Exchange when writing.

PANSIES

Brown's Extra Select Superb Giar Prize Pansies. Awarded Silver Meda St. Louis Exposition, 1904.

PLANTS, mixed colors, in any quantit $3.00 per 1000.

CASH WITH ORDER.

PETER BROWN, Lancaster, Pa

Mention The Florists' Exchange when writin

MABELLE--New Pink Carna tion for 1907

Color.—A peculiar shade of lovely pink, with a fai yellowish cast; several shades lighter than the Lawso Unlike most pinks, the brightest sun does not injure t color. Size.—Three to four inches in diameter when e tablished. Odor.—Pleasing, but not strong. Stems. Invariably strong, but always graceful, ranging fro 12 to 30 inches during the season. Habit, etc.—A ve quick active grower, making specimen plants in a sho time, even from late cuttings. On account of its rap growth, requires supporting very soon after benchi Gets away rapidly, blooms early and gives long ster right from the start. Productiveness.—Prodigious the best word we know of to use here. It is the mo incessant bloomer early and late, we have ever grow Stock limited. Delivery Jan. 5th to 10th and lat Price, $12.00 per 100, $100.00 per 1000.

THE H. WEBER & SONS CO., OAKLAND, MI

Mention The Florists' Exchange when writin

ABUNDANCE

Healthy, stocky, field grown plants. First sk $12.00 per 100; $100.00 per 1000. Second size, $10 per 100; $75.00 per 1000; 250 at a 1000 rates. I livery 15th of August.

CASH WITH ORDER.

RUDOLPH FISCHER, Great Neck, L.I., N.

Mention The Florists' Exchange when writin

CARNATION PLANTS

Fine, healthy Stock.

1500 WHITE LAWSON	$60.00	per 1
250 ESTELLE	4.00	"
1500 DOROTHY	35.00	" 1

Stock grown and shipped from Toledo, Ohio

S. S. Skidelsky,
824 No. 24th St., - - PHILADELPHIA,

Mention The Florists' Exchange when writi

Field Grown Carnation Plant

Only a few left. Write for list of variety and prices.

CHICAGO CARNATION CO.
JOLIET, Ill.

Mention the Florists' Exchange when writ

A. B. DAVIS & SON, In

PURCELLVILLE, VA.

WHOLESALE GROWERS OI CARNATIONS

Mention The Florists' Exchange when writ

CARNATION

Let us have your order now for the coo new Carnations: January delivery. Ari crat, Windsor, White Enchantr Helen M. Gould, Beacon and R Pink Enchantress.

WM. SWAYNE, Box 226, Kennett Square

Mention The Florists' Exchange when wri

HEATING.

Growers' Problems Solved by U. G. Scollay.

I want to heat two houses, 15x35 feet each, short roof connected style, one to 50 degrees, the other to 60 degrees; temperature outside, 20 degrees above zero. I will use 2-in. flows and can use 1½ or 1¼-in. returns. Bottom of the boiler will be about 10 ft. below floor of houses, and the expansion tanks will be in the houses. How much pipe will be needed and what sizes? If 2-in. pipe is used for flow and returned by leader through 1½ or 1¼-in. pipe, can I then run through another header not 2 in. at the end of the houses to carry back to the boiler? How high will expansion tanks need to be above floor of houses and what size? J. H.

California.

—In your 50-degree house, place 7 lines of 1½-in. pipe, four on the outer side, and three on the partition side. In the 60-degree house place ten lines of 1½-in. pipe, five on each side. If you have 1¼-in. pipe, and must use it, you will require eight lines in the 50-degree house, and twelve lines in the other, making two coils of four pipes each in the one, and two coils of six pipes each in the other. In running from the boiler to the coils, you must use the same size return main as in the flow main. Taking it from your letter that you do not wish to use anything larger than 2-inch in your mains, I would advise two sets of 2-inch mains from the boiler, a separate set for each house. If you could use a larger size, one set of 2½-inch would carry both houses nicely. Run your mains, in either case, diagonally from boiler to one end of the nearest house, the lowest end, of course, being preferred, provided one end is lower than the other. This will simplify your piping work. The headers supplied for such work by the jobbing concerns, whether for 1½ or 1¼-in. branches, are usually tapped 2-in. in the run, so that you will not be likely to experience any trouble in arranging whatever size connections to your coils you prefer.

I would not use smaller than 1½-in. flow or return to any one of the coils. If you use the two sets of mains, 2-in., you may find it easier to run your two flows diagonally to the upper end of your houses through a separate trench, flowing through the coils to the other end, thence back to the boiler with the two returns through another trench. I presume you understand that you must turn across one end of the houses with your coils, so as to provide for expansion of the piping. In your case I would advise that you use one expansion tank, having a capacity of not less than ten gallons. Place this tank at as high a point in the houses as possible, at the same time placing it where it will be in no danger of freezing. This should be connected to the system with not less than, say, 1-in. pipe. You can procure a tank specially made for the purpose, from any heating supply house. If your boiler-house is as high, or nearly as high, as the greenhouses, that is a good place to set it, connecting to the return main near the boiler. In either case, it will be necessary to place air vents on each coil. A good way to do this is at the highest header of each coil, using the tapping of same that is not connected with the mains; place 2-in. nipple and elbow, then a perpendicular piece of 2-in. pipe about one foot long with cap on top; into this cap fit a ⅛-in. pet cock, or hot water air valve. This gives you an air pocket for each coil, which will allow for accumulation of air, without in any way interfering with the circulation of water. These vents should be tried daily. If you still prefer the standpipe style of expansion tank, I would advise something larger than 2-in. pipe, as it does not hold enough for your case. These pipes should stand about four feet higher than the coils, that is, the top of them should be four feet above the coils, and they should aggregate about ten gallons in capacity.

U. G. SCOLLAY.

Kindly advise me through The Florists' Exchange how many lines of 2-in. pipe I will need in an even span house 16x50 feet, to keep a temperature of 55 degrees in zero weather; also in a three-quarter span house to have a temperature of 65 degrees? I have one of the old sectional boilers, with front and back sections out of business, but six sections between these in good condition, 26 in. x 44 in. grate surface. How will this boiler heat the houses and how many more could I put on? Would run 3 and 4-in. mains to end of houses and there branch off with 2-in. pipes. I give you here a rough sketch of how I expect to build and would appreciate your advice very much.

JULIUS RECK.

In the 55-degree house place nine lines of 2-in. pipe, and in the 65-degree house, 13 lines of 2-in. pipe. This will approximate about 750 sq. feet of radiating surface in the two houses. In the three-quarter span house, on exposed side, place five lines of pipe; under each of the two middle benches place two lines, and on the partition side four lines. In the south house, place three lines under the partition bench, two lines under center bench and four lines under remaining bench. The boiler you mention should certainly take care of the above amount of radiation, but how much more would be hard to say with any degree of positiveness, when the front and back sections are, as you say, "out of commission." However, as it is an eight-section boiler, I would say that the remaining sections should give you a capacity of 1,600 sq. ft. The original rating must have been about 2,300 sq. ft. If you will study the construction of your boiler, you will see that the front and back sections act as connecting links between the return headers, that is, they allow for free circulation between the two sides of the boiler. To put it still more clearly, supposing all your returns from your coils were collected together into one main return at the boiler, as many jobs are done nowadays, and that one return main connected into one of the return headers of your boiler, the water in the water legs on the other side of your firebox, not having a chance to circulate, would probably make steam, and be forced out of these water legs, with the result that the sections would crack or burn out at these points. The way to overcome this is to connect both headers with the main return. If there are tappings at the rear ends of the return headers, connect the two there, as that is really the best place. If none are there, you can easily connect in some other way, by means of the return mains. Your scheme of mains, as shown, is all right. The plugged tees, anticipating further extension, are O. K. Remember that even though you may have separate returns connected into each header, you should still arrange so that both sides of boiler will circulate.

U. G. SCOLLAY.

I am forwarding with this a plan of two houses we have just erected, and would like some information about heating them.

I am trying to adhere to the rules set down in Mr. Scollay's answer to Ind. Terr. in your issue of May 26. Each house is 21 ft. 3 in. by 100 ft., with 24-in. stationary glass on sides, glass in one end; location of boiler you will see on floor plan. The greenhouses and potting shed are on the same level, but floor of boiler room is 6 feet lower. We expect to use a trap for the return. There are two doors in each house, one at each end. The chimney stack is 2 feet in diameter and 40 feet high from top of boiler. House marked No. 3 is for carnations, No. 2 for geraniums, and a general line of plants; we expect to add another house to the east of those already up, is marked on the plan, and we wish to use steam heat.

N. E. W.

—The requirements for your two houses will be as follows: In No. 3 nine lines of 1¼-in. pipe; No. 2, eight lines, same size. The new house will need about the same surface as in No. 3. In No. 3 run four lines on exposed side of house, two lines on side of, or under center bench, and three lines on partition wall. In No. 2 house run three lines under each of the side benches, and one under each of the two center benches. Start from boiler with 4-in. steam main, at center of house No. 3, reduce to 3½-in., taking a 2½-in. overhead branch main into No. 3, running same to far end, there branching into the various coils of that house. Extend steam main to house No. 2 with 3½-in., taking a 2½-in. steam branch main into this house, in same way as described for No. 3. You can make the unused end of the tee on main at this point, 3 or 3½-inch, as you wish. I always advise, not only looking ahead, but looking "far" ahead. You have here ample capacity for still further extension of main, beyond the one extra house, and it costs you nothing more to make this opening 3½-in. than 3-in. It is good policy to avail yourself of such opportunity. In connecting coils in No. 3, use 1½-in. steam and 1¼ return on the four-pipe coil; 1½ steam and 1-in. return on the three-pipe coil, and 1¼ steam and 1-in. return on the two-pipe coil. In No. 2, use 1½ steam and 1-in. return for the two side coils, and 1¼-in. steam and 1-in. return for the two single lines. Your return main should start from house No. 2, with 2½-in., leaving a 2-in. plugged opening for the future house; continue the 2½-in. back to the boiler room, connecting, of course, No. 3 house into it, with 1½-in. return. In boiler room you can reduce your return main or otherwise, as the makers of your trap require. In steam heating, in addition to the valves on steam and return connections to each coil, it is well to put valves on the pipes, in such way that any number of lines in each coil may be shut off. Many growers using steam do this, claiming the results justify the expense. In a four-pipe coil, you would need but three pipes valved, as the remaining one can be controlled by shutting off the valves on steam and return connections to the coil. Your chimney is ample in size and height for your needs, both present and future, as laid down in your letter. U. G. SCOLLAY.

How many lines of 4-inch pipe will it take to heat by hot water a rose house 72 feet long, 25 feet wide, 15 feet high, three-quarter span; temperature 58 to 62 degrees. J. W.

Penna.

—To maintain a temperature of 58 to 62 degrees inside with the thermometer at zero outside, I would suggest that you put in twelve lines of 4-inch cast iron pipe. This calculation is based on an average temperature of the water in the pipes at about 160 to 170 degrees. U. G. SCOLLAY.

CARNATIONS

	Per 100	Per 1000		Per 100	Per 1000		Per 100	Per 1000
FIANCEE	$6 00		MORNING GLORY	$4 00	$35 00	FLORA HILL	$5 00	$45 00
LAWSON	6 00	$50 00	LIEUT. PEARY	8 00	75 00	WHITE CLOUD	5 00	45 00
NELSON FISHER	7 00	60 00	FRED BURKI	7 00	60 00	CHICAGO (Red Bradt)	5 00	45 00
GUARDIAN ANGEL	4 00	35 00	BOSTON MARKET	5 00	45 00	HARLOWARDEN	6 00	50 00
NCHANTRESS	7 00	60 00						

WIETOR BROS., 51 Wabash Ave., CHICAGO

Mention The Florists' Exchange when writing.

CARNATIONS

STRONG, HEALTHY, FIELD GROWN PLANTS

PINK	100	1000	WHITE	100	1000
LAWSON	$5.00	$40.00	BOSTON MARKET	$4.00	$35.00
NELSON	3.00	25.00	FLORA HILL	3.00	25.00
GUARDIAN ANGEL	3.00	25.00	QUEEN LOUISE	3.00	25.00
ENCHANTRESS	7.00	60.00	WHITE CLOUD	3.00	25.00
MORNING GLORY	4.00	30.00	VARIEGATED		
HIGINBOTHAM	3.00	25.00	ARMAZINDY	3.00	25.00
			RED		
			ESTELLE	5.00	40.00
			MRS. INE	3.00	25.00

ROSE PLANTS

	100	1000
LIBERTY 3 in. pots	$3.00	$25.00
CHATENAY 2½ in. pots	2.50	22.50

PETER REINBERG, 51 Wabash Ave., CHICAGO

Mention The Florists' Exchange when writing.

CARNATIONS FIELD PLANTS

	Per 100
GLENDALE	$10.00
ROBT. CRAIG	12.00
BOUNTIFUL	8.00
DOROTHY WHITNEY	8.00
BELLE	7.00
FLAMINGO	7.00
FIANCEE	7.00

	Per 100
BOSTON MARKET	$6.00
WHITE CLOUD	6.00
MRS. PATTEN	6.00
NELSON	5.00
ESTELLE	3rd size. 3.50

ROSES, 200 4 in. **Maids**, 150 4 in. **Brides**, $6.00 per 100. 500 2½ in. **Gates**, 300 2½ in. **Brides**, 150 2½ in. **Perles**, $2.50 per 100. **Richmond Roses** own roots, fine 3 in. $5.00; 2 in. $4.00 per 100.
ASPARAGUS PLUMOSUS, 2 in., $2.00 per 100. **SPRENGERI**, 3 in., $6.00 per 100. Cash or C. O. D.

W. J. & M. S. VESEY, Fort Wayne, Ind.

Mention The Florists' Exchange when writing.

CARNATIONS

Crisis Scarlet	$5.00	per 100
Fiancee	5.00	"
Joost	5.00	"
B. Market	5.00	"
Cardinal	$7.00	per 100
Estelle	5.00	"
Queen	5.00	"
Harlowarden	5.00	"

Second size $2.00 per 100 less. Cash with order.

SMITH & GANNETT, Geneva, N. Y.

Mention The Florists' Exchange when writing.

CARNATION PLANTS

Medium size. No stem rot.

600 May Naylor (white), 600 Queen, 200 Fair Maid, 60 Genevieve Lord, 50 Scott.

Second size; 150 Enchantress, 150 Lawson, 50 White Lawson, 50 Patten, 150 Joost, 75 Prosperity.

$3.00 per 100. Cash with order please.

H. M. WOUNDY, New Caanan, Conn.

Mention The Florists' Exchange when writing.

FIELD GROWN CARNATION PLANTS

Boston Market, large, $6.00 per 100. **Mrs. T. W. Lawson**, medium, $4.00 per 100. **Manley**, $4.00 per 100. **Enchantress**, $4.00 per 100. **Asparagus Plumosus Nanus**, fine plants, from 4 in. pots, $8.00 per 100. **Asparagus Sprengeri**, 4 in., strong, $8.00 per 100. **Smilax**, strong, 3 in., $3.00 per 100. Cash with order.

WENDEL BIEAR, Palmer Av., YONKERS, N. Y.

Mention The Florists' Exchange when writing.

CARNATIONS

Field Grown plants for August 27 and later delivery.

THE H. WEBER & SONS CO., OAKLAND, MD.

Mention The Florists' Exchange when writing.

FIELD GROWN CARNATIONS

	Per 100		Per 100
Roosevelt	$4.00	Prosperity	$5.00
Hill Sport	4.00	Flamingo	5.00
Manley	5.00	Enchantress	6.00
Scarlet Seedling	5.00	Cash with order.	

Chas. T. Darling, Stony Brook, L. I., N. Y.

Mention The Florists' Exchange when writing.

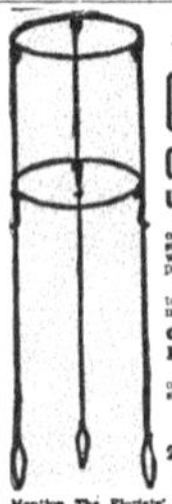

The Model EXTENSION

CARNATION SUPPORT

Endorsed by all the leading carnation growers as the best support on the market. Made with 2 or 3 circles. Write for prices and circulars.

We have special low prices to offer and can save you money on

Galvanized Wire ROSE STAKES

Write us for prices before ordering elsewhere. Prompt shipment guaranteed.

IGOE BROS.
226 North 9th Street
BROOKLYN, N. Y.

Mention The Florists' Exchange when writing.

FIELD GROWN

Carnation Plants

5000 **Enchantress**, 6c. each; $50.00 per 1000
Queen, 5c. each; $40.00 per 1000.
Lawson, white, 2nd size, $4.00 per 100.
" variegated, 2nd size, $5.00 per 100.
" pink, 2nd size, $3.50 per 100.
Lady Bountiful, 2nd size, $5.00 per 100.
Glacier, 2nd size, $3.50 per 100.

CASH

GOVE BROS., Biddeford, Me.

Mention The Florists' Exchange when writing.

CARNATIONS

Strong Field Grown Plants

Crimson Glow (new variety) $12.00 per 100

Cash or references with order.

DAILLEDOUZE BROTHERS
Flatbush, Brooklyn, N. Y.

Mention The Florists' Exchange when writing.

S. J. GODDARD

Framingham, Mass.

Rooted Carnation Cuttings a Specialty.

Correspondence Solicited.

Mention The Florists' Exchange when writing.

PANSIES

Brown's Extra Select Superb Giant Prize Pansies. Awarded Silver Medal, St. Louis Exposition, 1904.

PLANTS, mixed colors, in any quantity $3.00 per 1000.

CASH WITH ORDER.

PETER BROWN, Lancaster, Pa.

Mention The Florists' Exchange when writing.

MABELLE--New Pink Carnation for 1907

Color.—A peculiar shade of lovely pink, with a faint yellowish cast; several shades lighter than the Lawson. Unlike most pinks, the brightest sun does not injure the color. **Size.**—Three to four inches in diameter when established. **Odor.**—Pleasing, but not strong. **Stems.**—Invariably strong, but always graceful, ranging from 12 to 30 inches during the season. **Habit, etc.**—A very quick active grower, making specimen plants in a short time, even from late cuttings. On account of its rapid growth, requires supporting very soon after benching. Gets away rapidly, blooms early and gives long stems right from the start. **Productiveness.**—Prodigious is the best word we know of to use here. It is the most incessant bloomer early and late, we have ever grown. Stock limited. Delivery Jan. 5th to 10th and later. Price, $12.00 per 100, $100.00 per 1000.

THE H. WEBER & SONS CO., OAKLAND, MD.

Mention The Florists' Exchange when writing.

ABUNDANCE

Healthy, stocky, field grown plants. First size $12.00 per 100; $100.00 per 1000. Second size, $10.00 per 100; $75.00 per 1000; 250 at a 1000 rates. Delivery 15th of August.

CASH WITH ORDER.

RUDOLPH FISCHER, Great Neck, L. I., N. Y.

Mention The Florists' Exchange when writing.

CARNATION PLANTS

Fine, healthy Stock.

1600	WHITE LAWSON	$80.00	per 1000
250	ESTELLE	4.00	" 100
1500	DOROTHY	35.00	" 1000

Stock grown and shipped from Toledo, Ohio.

S. S. Skidelsky,
824 No. 24th St., - - PHILADELPHIA, PA.

Mention The Florists' Exchange when writing.

Field Grown Carnation Plants

Only a few left. Write for list of variety and prices.

CHICAGO CARNATION CO.
JOLIET, ILL.

Mention the Florists' Exchange when writing.

A. B. DAVIS & SON, Inc.

PURCELLVILLE, VA.

WHOLESALE GROWERS OF CARNATIONS

Mention The Florists' Exchange when writing.

CARNATIONS

Let us have your order now for the coming new Carnations: January delivery. **Aristocrat, Windsor, White Enchantress, Helen M. Gould, Beacon and Rose Pink Enchantress.**

WM. SWAYNE, Box 226, Kennett Square, Pa.

Mention The Florists' Exchange when writing.

HEATING.

Growers' Problems Solved by U. G. Scollay.

I want to heat two houses, 15x35 feet each, short roof connected style, one to 50 degrees, the other to 60 degrees; temperature outside, 20 degrees above zero. I will use 2-in. flows and can use 1½ or 1¼-in. returns. Bottom of the boiler will be about 10 ft. below floor of houses, and the expansion tanks will be in the houses. How much pipe will be needed and what sizes? If 2-in. pipe is used for flow and returned by leader through 1½ or 1¼-in. pipe, can I then run through another header not 2 in. at the end of the houses to carry back to the boiler? How high will expansion tanks need to be above floor of houses and what size? J. H.

California.

—In your 50-degree house, place 7 lines of 1½-in. pipe, four on the outer side, and three on the partition side. In the 60-degree house place ten lines of 1½-in. pipe, five on each side. If you have 1¼-in. pipe, and must use it, you will require eight lines in the 50-degree house, and twelve lines in the other, making two coils of four pipes each in the one, and two coils of six pipes each in the other. In running from the boiler to the coils, you must use the same size return main as in the flow main. Taking it from your letter that you do not wish to use anything larger than 2-inch in your mains, I would advise two sets of 2-inch mains from the boiler, a separate set for each house. If you could use a larger size, one set of 2½-inch would carry both houses nicely. Run your mains, in either case, diagonally from boiler to one end of the nearest house, the lowest end, of course, being preferred, provided one end is lower than the other. This will simplify your piping work. The headers supplied for such work by the jobbing concerns, whether for 1½ or 1¼-in. branches, are usually tapped 2-in. in the run, so that you will not be likely to experience any trouble in arranging whatever size connections to your coils you prefer.

I would not use smaller than 1½-in. flow or return to any one of the coils. If you use the two sets of mains, 2-in., you may find it easier to run your two flows diagonally to the upper end of your houses through a separate trench, flowing through the coils to the other end, thence back to the boiler with the two returns through another trench. I presume you understand that you must turn across one end of the houses with your coils, so as to provide for expansion of the piping. In your case I would advise that you use one expansion tank, having a capacity of not less than ten gallons. Place this tank at as high a point in the houses as possible, at the same time placing it where it will be in no danger of freezing. This should be connected to the system with not less than, say, 1-in. pipe. You can procure a tank specially made for the purpose, from any heating supply house. If your boiler-house is as high, or nearly as high, as the greenhouses, that is a good place to set it, connecting to the return main near the boiler. In either case, it will be necessary to place air vents on each coil. A good way to do this is at the highest header of each coil, using the tapping of same that is not connected with the mains; place 2-in. nipple and elbow, then a perpendicular piece of 2-in. pipe about one foot long with cap on top; into this cap fit a ⅛-in. pet cock, or hot water air valve. This gives you an air pocket for each coil, which will allow for accumulation of air, without in any way interfering with the circulation of water. These vents should be tried daily. If you still prefer the standpipe style of expansion tank, I would advise something larger than 2-in. pipe, as it does not hold enough for your case. These pipes should stand about four feet higher than the coils, that is, the top of them should be four feet above the coils, and they should aggregate about ten gallons in capacity.

U. G. SCOLLAY.

Kindly advise me through The Florists' Exchange how many lines of 2-in. pipe I will need in an even span house 16x50 feet, to keep a temperature of 55 degrees in zero weather; also in a three-quarter span house to have a temperature of 65 degrees? I have one of the old sectional boilers, with front and back sections out of business, but six sections between these in good condition, 26 in. x 44 in. grate surface. How will this boiler heat the houses and how many more could I put on? Would run 3 and 4-in. mains to end of houses and there branch off with 2-in. pipes. I give you here a rough sketch of how I expect to build and would appreciate your advice very much.

JULIUS RECK.

In the 55-degree house place nine lines of 2-in. pipe, and in the 65-degree house, 13 lines of 2-in. pipe. This will approximate about 750 sq. feet of radiating surface in the two houses. In the three-quarter span house, on exposed side, place five lines of pipe; under each of the two middle benches place two lines, and on the partition side four lines. In the south house, place three lines under the partition bench, two lines under center bench and four lines under remaining bench. The boiler you mention should certainly take care of the above amount of radiation, but how much more would be hard to say with any degree of positiveness, when the front and back sections are, as you say, "out of commission." However, as it is an eight-section boiler, I would say that the remaining sections should give you a capacity of 1,600 sq. ft. The original rating must have been about 2,300 sq. ft. If you will study the construction of your boiler, you will see that the front and back sections act as connecting links between the return headers, that is, they allow for free circulation between the two sides of the boiler. To put it still more clearly, supposing all your returns from your coils were collected together into one main return at the boiler, as many jobs are done nowadays, and that one return main connected into one of the return headers of your boiler, the water in the water legs on the other side of your firebox, not having a chance to circulate, would probably make steam, and be forced out of these water legs, with the result that the sections would crack or burn out at these points. The way to overcome this is to connect both headers with the main return. If there are tappings at the rear ends of the return headers, connect the two there, as that is really the best place. If none are there, you can easily connect in some other way, by means of the return mains. Your scheme of mains, as shown, is all right. The plugged tees, anticipating further extension, are O. K. Remember that even though you may have separate returns connected into each header, you should still arrange so that both sides of boiler will circulate.

U. G. SCOLLAY.

I am forwarding with this a plan of two houses we have just erected, and would like some information about heating them.

I am trying to adhere to the rules set down in Mr. Scollay's answer to Ind. Terr. in your issue of May 26. Each house is 21 ft. 3 in. by 100 ft., with 24-in. stationary glass on sides, glass in one end; location of boiler you will see on floor plan. The greenhouses and potting shed are on the same level, but floor of boiler room is 6 feet lower. We expect to use a trap for the return. There are two doors in each house, one at each end. The chimney stack is 2 feet in diameter and 40 feet high from top of boiler. House marked No. 3 is for carnations, No. 2 for geraniums, and a general line of plants; we expect to add another house to the east of those already up, is marked on the plan, and we wish to use steam heat.

N. E. W.

—The requirements for your two houses will be as follows: In No. 3 nine lines of 1¼-in. pipe; No. 2, eight lines, same size. The new house will need about the same surface as in No. 3. In No. 3 run four lines on exposed side of house, two lines on side of, or under center bench, and three lines on partition wall. In No. 2 house run three lines under each of the side benches, and one under each of the two center benches. Start from boiler with 4-in. steam main, at center of house No. 3, reduce to 3½-in., taking a 2½-in. overhead branch main into No. 3, running same to far end, there branching into the various coils of that house. Extend steam main to house No. 2 with 3½-in., taking a 2½-in. steam branch main into this house, in same way as described for No. 3. You can make the unused end of the tee on main at this point, 3 or 3½-inch, as you wish. I always advise, not only looking ahead, but looking "far" ahead. You have here ample capacity for still further extension of main, beyond the one extra house, and it costs you nothing more to make this opening 3½-in. than 3-in. It is good policy to avail yourself of such opportunity. In connecting coils in No. 3, use 1½-in. steam and 1¼ return on the four-pipe coil; 1½ steam and 1-in. return on the three-pipe coil, and 1¼ steam and 1-in. return on the two-pipe coil. In No. 2, use 1½ steam and 1-in. return for the two side coils, and 1¼-in. steam and 1-in. return for the two single lines. Your return main should start from house No. 2, with 2½-in., leaving a 2-in. plugged opening for the future house; continue the 2½-in. back to the boiler room, connecting, of course, No. 3 house into it, with 1½-in. return. In boiler room you can reduce your return main or otherwise, as the makers of your trap require. In steam heating, in addition to the valves on steam and return connections to each coil, it is well to put valves on the pipes, in such way that any number of lines in each coil may be shut off. Many growers using steam do this, claiming the results justify the expense. In a four-pipe coil, you would need but three pipes valved, as the remaining one can be controlled by shutting off the valves on steam and return connections to the coil. Your chimney is ample in size and height for your needs, both present and future, as laid down in your letter. U. G. SCOLLAY.

How many lines of 4-inch pipe will it take to heat by hot water a rose house 72 feet long, 25 feet wide, 15 feet high, three-quarter span; temperature 58 to 62 degrees. J. W.

Penna.

—To maintain a temperature of 58 to 62 degrees inside with the thermometer at zero outside, I would suggest that you put in twelve lines of 4-inch cast iron pipe. This calculation is based on an average temperature of the water in the pipes at about 160 to 170 degrees. U. G. SCOLLAY.

CLASSIFIED ADVERTISEMENTS

CASH WITH ORDER.

The columns under this heading are reserved for advertisements of Stock for Sale, Stock Wanted, Help Wanted, Situations Wanted or other Wants; also of Greenhouse, Land, Second-Hand Materials, etc., For Sale or Rent.

Our charge is 10 cts. per line (7 words to the line), set solid, without display. No advt. accepted for less than thirty cents.

Display advertisements in these columns, 15 cents per line; count 12 lines agate to the inch.

[If replies to Help Wanted, Situation Wanted, or other advertisements are to be addressed care of this office, advertisers add 10 cents to cover expense of forwarding.]

Copy must reach New York office 12 o'clock Wednesday to secure insertion in issue of following Saturday.

Advertisers in the Western States desiring to advertise under initials, may save time by having their answer directed care our Chicago office at 127 E. Berwyn Ave.

SITUATIONS WANTED

SITUATION WANTED as stockman. Not afraid of work, in high class shop only. Address R. V. care The Florists' Exchange.

SITUATION WANTED in a first-class flower store as salesman. City experience, hustler, sober. Address R. U. care of The Florists' Exchange.

SITUATION WANTED—Florist, decorator, gardener and salesman. Well up in all branches. Can handle fine trade. Sober and steady. Address, R. F., care The Florists' Exchange.

SITUATION WANTED—In retail store by young man, 24, good experience, first-class designer, etc. No bad habits. R. K., care The Florists' Exchange.

SITUATION WANTED—By young Englishman, aged 24, 2½ years in U. S. Philadelphia or New York. Address, Florist, 523 Rockland St., Philadelphia, Pa.

SITUATION WANTED—Young married man wishes position as gardener on private estate. Experienced in all branches under glass and outside. Well recommended. Address, R. G., care The Florists' Exchange.

SITUATION WANTED.—A young man thoroughly experienced in general greenhouse work wishes position in first class establishment. Strictly sober and honest. References. Married. Address R. Q. care of The Florists' Exchange.

SITUATION WANTED—By German, good gardener and florist. A good grower of roses, carnations, violets, palms, mums and all kinds of spring stock. First-class recommendation on private place. Address, R. E., care The Florists' Exchange.

SITUATION WANTED—As grower or foreman by single man of 29. 14 years' experience in roses, carnations, mums, palms, ferns, etc. Wages, $15.00 per week. O. K. references. R. O., care The Florists' Exchange.

SITUATION WANTED.—By a young single man, Austrian, 26 years of age, 15 months in this country, as assistant in private place, or in commercial place where roses and carnations are grown, in city or country. Adds. R. S. care The Florists' Exchange.

SITUATION WANTED—Florist and gardener wishes a position. Good carnation grower; 18 years in one place, 5 years in charge of the present establishment. Single, honest, sober and steady. Address, R. J., care The Florists' Exchange.

SITUATION WANTED.—A young married man, up to date in growing first class cut flowers, and plants. Wishes position as foreman, manager or caretaker of commercial place. A No. 1 references. Experience in making-up and designing and good salesman. Address R. R. care of The Florists' Exchange.

SITUATION WANTED—As foreman by first-class rose grower; have been several years with one of the largest rose growers. A No. 1 references, aged 30, single; wages expected, $100.00 per month. Only a first-class place wanted. Address, A. B., care The Florists' Exchange.

SITUATION WANTED—As foreman by first-class gardener and florist. Single; aged 30; 12 years' experience, American Beauty roses, carnations, potted plants; general management of private estate. References private and commercial. Address, R. M., care The Florists' Exchange.

SITUATION WANTED—Florist, German, with 19 years experience. Competent to take charge, honest and willing worker for employers. Wishes position, commercial or private. Please state particulars and wages when writing. Address, R. D., care The Florists' Exchange.

SITUATION WANTED—By a young man, 21 years of age, having worked two years in the florist business. Wants a position where roses, carnations and bedding stock are grown, and where he can learn to make up designs. New York State preferred. First-class habits. Please give full particulars with wages in first letter. Address, Hall Simons, Fairport, N. Y.

SITUATIONS WANTED

SITUATION WANTED—By gardener and florist, 20 years practical experience in landscape work, greenhouses, cut flowers under glass and outdoors, palms, ferns, and general bedding stock. Competent to take charge of private or commercial place. German, 37, married, small family. Address O. O., care The Florists' Exchange.

SITUATION WANTED—Gardener and florist, German, 38 years, single, a first-class workman, very neat, 24 years experience on private and commercial places, under glass and outdoors. Good grower of roses, carnations, mums and general stock. Some experience in decorating and designing. Wishes position, private or commercial. First-class references. Please state wages and particulars in first letter. Address B. C., care Mr. Sambraus, 169 Morningside Ave., New York City.

SITUATION WANTED As superintendent or gardener by a thoroughly competent and practical man; experienced in all branches of horticulture, private and commercial, nursery and landscape work. Married, small family.

Address, O. Q., care THE FLORISTS' EXCHANGE

Mention The Florists' Exchange when writing.

HELP WANTED

WANTED—First-class salesman and maker-up; none but thoroughly experienced need apply. L. Hart, 1000 Madison avenue, N. Y. City.

WANTED—An expert orchid grower. Must be practical and thoroughly experienced. No amateur or experimenter need apply. Louis Burk, Girard av. & Third st., Philadelphia.

WANTED—A thoroughly competent man to take charge of a section of Beauties. Apply Frank Dolan, care of John Young Company, Bedford Station, New York.

WANTED—A good florist, single, for a gentleman's place. Wages, $30.00 per month and board. Apply at Michell's Seed House, 1018 Market Street, Philadelphia, Pa.

WANTED—An experienced and capable young man to manage a wholesale business within 100 miles of Philadelphia. Address, F. E., care The Florists' Exchange.

WANTED—Young man as greenhouse assistant on large private place. Wages, $40.00 per month. Address, R. P., care The Florists' Exchange.

WANTED—Two thoroughly experienced men for watering in greenhouses. Wages, $12.00 per week. Apply to Peter Henderson & Co., 230 Arlington avenue, Jersey City, N. J.

WANTED.—Designer and salesman for retail store. Steady employment, must have references from last employer. Call or write to Chas. Kroonbach, 189 25th street, Brooklyn.

WANTED—Night fireman for commercial place; steam boilers, steady position for a competent man. Please furnish references and state wages. The Livingston Seed Co., Columbus, O.

WANTED—A good man with experience in growing roses, carnations and all cut flowers for the retail trade. State wages and experience. Hugh Scales, Birmingham, Ala.

WANTED—A first-class man for retail florist in Chicago; no greenhouse work. Must be a good salesman and designer. State wages. References. Address, M. D., care The Florists' Exchange.

WANTED—Bright, attractive, experienced lady to take charge of floral store in Kalamazoo, Mich. Must be able to do decorating and first-class funeral designs. Apply by letter with references to Lock Box 855, Kalamazoo, Mich.

WANTED—September 1, young or midde aged man of experience in general nursery work. Must be able to take charge of shipping and propagating. State wages wanted, age, nationality and references. C. R. Fish & Company, West Side Nurseries, Worcester, Mass.

WANTED—Good, all-around greenhouse man to work under foreman, to care for section of houses where plants are grown for catalogue and retail trade. Steady position. Please furnish references and state wages. The Livingston Seed Co., Columbus, O.

WANTED—An all-around florist as foreman who understands growing of bedding plants, bulbs and Easter stock, also carnations. Steady employment. Must have recommendation from last employer. Call or write to C. K., 189 25th Street, Brooklyn, N. Y.

WANTED—At $35 per month, assistant in rose houses; give full particulars in first letter. Address Permanent, care The Florists' Exchange.

MISCELLANEOUS WANTS

FOR SALE OR EXCHANGE—Extra double thick glass, 12x14, $2.00 per box. Take roses or carnations. Wm. P. Kastee, Walden, N. Y.

FOR EXCHANGE—Gardenia Florida—35—1 year old, A No. 1, in soil and 18 old stock plants in pots; would like to exchange for foliage plants to grow in a house 50-65 degrees. Make an offer. Frank Foley, Lawrence, L. I.

MISCELLANEOUS WANTS

WANTED—5,000 Acer Saccharinum, 1 to 3 feet. State price and size. V. A. Vanicek, The Rhode Island Nurseries, Newport, R. I.

WANTED TO BUY—Greenhouses to be taken down. State full particulars of same when writing. Address, F. W., care The Florists' Exchange.

WANTED TO LEASE—Would like to lease in some town inhabited by wealthy people, greenhouses in perfect running condition and stocked. Address, R. L., care The Florists' Exchange.

FOR SALE OR RENT

FOR SALE—Florist's store business, in a growing city near N. Y. of over 85,000 inhabitants; for price of stock and fixtures address Store, care The Florists' Exchange.

FOR SALE—Pots—1400 2 in., 4000 2½ in., 200 3 in., 550 4 in., 200 5 in., 100 6 in., and about 100 of larger sizes up to 12 in., mostly new. The first $15.00 check takes the lot. J. V. Cutler, Wassaic, N. Y.

FOR SALE—Florist's business, corner lot, nearly 7 acres, 26 miles from Philadelphia, 3 hothouses, frame house, barn, outbuildings, on trolley, and near station. For particulars, address, O. M., care The Florists' Exchange.

FOR RENT—In Montclair, N. J., 4 greenhouses stocked with carnations, roses, chrysanthemums, etc. Dwelling house if required. This is a spendid opportunity; good market for everything grown. Trolley car passes the door. Apply Mrs. Robert MacInnes, 676 Valley Road, Upper Montclair, N. J.

FOR SALE—Stock, good will, and fixtures of a well paying retail business. Four houses, three of them 17x70, the other 16x55 feet. Lease of piece of ground adjoining included in sale. The best stand in city for funeral work, all without soliciting. Owner wishes to sell on account of health. C. B. Tustin, 1337-39-41 West Passayunk Avenue, Philadelphia, Pa.

TO LEASE—Corner store, 25x100, at junction of three main thoroughfares, with small stocked greenhouse attached, heated by hot water. Owner has carried on business for past fortytwo years, but wishes to retire on account of age. Exceptional opportunity for right party. Address, Mrs. T. Clark, 96 Ft. Greene Place, Brooklyn, N. Y.

FOR SALE—Owing to the ill health of the principal owner, it has become advisable to offer for sale the entire stock of the best known florist establishment in southern California. A long time lease hold on the grounds may be obtained. A fine opportunity to step into an established business, incorporated. For particulars, write to Box 94, Ventura, Cal.

FOR SALE

On account of other business—4 greenhouses, barn and dwellinghouse and lot 200 x 300 on College Avenue, near Vassar College. Trade and location for trade with Vassar students unsurpassed.

JOHN E. MACK, Poughkeepsie, N. Y.

Mention The Florists' Exchange when writing.

FOR SALE—Owing to failing health, I will sell my florist establishment, beautifully situated between Larchmont Manor and Mamaroneck, Westchester Co., New York, near railroad station; trolley lines within one minute walk. First class opportunity for the right man. Plenty of landscape and jobbing work. The place contains four acres, 2 greenhouses, 104 feet long and lots of sash; well stocked with trees and shrubs, etc.; horse, wagon and tools. Address, Box 44, Larchmont, New York.

STOCK FOR SALE

QUEEN LOUISE and C. A. DANA carnations, fine stock, $5.00 per 100; $35.00 per 1000. Fox & Rosen, Parkerford, Pa.

IMPERIAL VIOLET plants from cold frame, $2.50 per 100; $20 per 1,000. Sample sent for 15c. Paul Thomson, West Hartford, Conn.

GIANT PANSIES, mixed; double daisies and forget-me-nots, blue, 50c. per 100 mailed; $2.50 per 1000 express. Cash. Shippensburg Floral Co., Shippensburg, Pa.

BEAUTY OF NICE stock, seed from selected home-grown flowers, fresh, double, $1.00 large trade pkt. Address, Waverly Greenhouses, Tuckahoe, N. Y.

ASPARAGUS SPRENGERII, field grown, 2 year-old plants, full of cutting growths. Best express or freight. Dozen, $2.40; per 100, $18.00. Cash. W. G. Gomersall, Nyack, N. Y.

FOR SALE—25 large plants of azalea alba, for cutting, 8 4-inch gate valves for hot water heating, $4 each. 100 large Adiantum cuneatum, grown in bed, 25c. each. J. Geist, Melrose, Mass.

BABY RAMBLER roses, fine dormant stock, $25 per 100. 2 1-2 inch pot plants, extra well rooted $7 per 100, $65 per 1000. Orders booked for delivery now or any time up to late Spring. Samples free. Brown Brothers Co., Rochester, N. Y.

STOCK FOR SALE

15,000 STRONG, healthy, field-grown violet plants of Farquhar, Lady Campbell, La France and California, $5.00 per 100; $45.00 per 1000. Richard Langle, North Street, White Plains, N. Y.

500 QUEEN LOUISE, white; 500 May Naylor, white; 500 Prosperity, var.; 200 Roosevelt, red. Fieldgrown plants; healthy. Will sell lot for $50.00. Not firstclass, but very good. G. E. S., 65 Bayview Avenue, Jersey City, N. J.

CARNATIONS—Extra fine, field-grown plants: Enchantress, Mrs. T. W. Lawson, $6.00 per 100; $50.00 per 1000. Joost, New Daybreak, Prosperity, Wolcott, $5.00 per 100; $40.00 per 1000. Terms cash. M. J. Schaaf, Dansville, N. Y.

2,000 Brides, 3,000 Bridesmaids, 1,000 Meteors, 1,000 Beauties, out of 4 in. pots. No better plants grown. Packed and delivered at express office. Maids and Brides, 5c.; Meteors, 4c.; Beauties, 12c. each. Louis M. Noe, Madison, N. J.

FOR SALE

FOR SALE—12 Hitchings hot water expansion tanks for 3 1-2 in. pipe, in good condition, cleaned, ready to set up. 1-3 price of new. Also horse lawn mower, easy running, $20.00. Address, K. D., care The Florists' Exchange.

BOILERS, BOILERS, BOILERS.

SEVERAL good second hand boilers on hand, also new No. 16 Hitchings at reduced cost. Write for list. Wm. H. Lutton, West Side Avenue Station, C. R. R. of N. J., Jersey City, N. J.

FOR SALE

Greenhouse Material milled from Gulf Cypress, to any detail furnished, or our own patterns as desired, cut and spliced ready for erection. Estimates for complete constructions furnished.

V. E. REICH, Brooklyn, N. Y.

1429-1437 Metropolitan Ave.

Mention The Florists' Exchange when writing.

FOR SALE

BOILERS Second hand, guaranteed to be in good condition. 2 No. 17 Hitchings at $100.00 and $125.00. 1 No. 16 Weathered $75.00. 1—4 section Cambridge $75.00. 2—8 section No. 11, 37x41 grates, J. L. Mott, will heat 12,750 sq. ft. glass at $175.00. 1—10 H. P. steam, $35.00. 1 NEW 6 section 24 in. grate Novelty boiler, will heat 4,100 sq. ft. glass, $140.00. New Henderson at low prices.

PIPE Good serviceable second hand. No Junk, with new threads. 2 in. 7c.; 1½ in. 5½c.; 1¼ in. 4c.; 1 in. 3c.; 2½ in. 10c.; 3 in. 14c.; 4 in. 19c. 4 in. cast iron greenhouse 14c. 2 in. NEW, standard, full lengths, 8½c. ft. All kinds of fittings for 4 in. cast iron and all sizes wrought iron.

STOCKS AND DIES NEW ECONOMY, EASY WORKING. Complete set to thread ⅜ in. to 1 in. pipe, $3.00; 1¼ in. to 2 in. pipe, $4.00.

PIPE CUTTERS NEW SAUNDERS PATTERN. Size No. 1 cuts ⅛ in. to 1 in. pipe $ .75; Size No. 2 cuts 1 in. to 2 in. pipe, $1.10.

STILLSON WRENCHES NEW, NO IMITATION. Size 18 in., grips ¼ in. to 2 in. pipe, $1.20. Size 24 in., grips ¼ in. to 2½ in. pipe $1.80. Size 36 in., grips ½ in. to 3½ in. pipe $4.50.

PIPE VISES NEW, REED MAKE, NO IMITATION. Size No. 1 grips ⅛ in. to 2 in. pipe $1.50.

GARDEN HOSE NEW, 50 ft. lengths ¾ in. guaranteed 100 lbs. pressure 7½c. ft. NEW, 50 ft. lengths ¾ in. not guaranteed 4½c. ft.

BRASS HOSE VALVES New; not faucets; something new, ¾ in. at 65c.

HOT-BED SASH New; Gulf Cypress, 3 ft. x 6 ft., 75c.; glazed complete $1.60 up. VENTILATORS; all sizes made to order. Second hand sash glazed $1.00 and $1.25, good condition.

GLASS New American, 50 ft. to the box, 10x12 single at $1.75. 10x12, 12x12, 10x15 B double $2.55. 12x14 to 12x20 and 14x14 to 14x20 B double $2.70. 16x16 and 16x18 B double $2.90. 16x24 B double $3.15. 16x20 and 16x22 $3.00. 8x8, 7x9, 8x10 old, single $1.50. 8x14 old, double $1.65; 10x14 old, double $1.75.

LINSEED OIL Strictly pure; barrel lots, 42c. gallon.

CARNATION SUPPORTS second hand, 50c. hundred.

VENTILATING APPARATUS second hand, Hitchings make, arms, 25c.; hangers, 10c.; machines, $3.50; collars, 8c.

SCREWS all sizes; mixed wood, from 1 in. to 3 in., in boxes, 25 and 50 lbs. at 5c. lb.

PUMPS hot air; well pumps and force pumps; all repairs.

Get our prices on second hand wood material. We can furnish everything in new material to erect any size house. Get our prices.

METROPOLITAN MATERIAL CO.

Greenhouse Wreckers

1398-1408 Metropolitan Avenue, BROOKLYN, N. Y.

Mention The Florists' Exchange when writing.

Thirty cents is the minimum charge for advertisements on this page.

UNITED STATES PATENT OFFICE.

BENJAMIN HAMMOND, of FISHKILL LANDING, NEW YORK.

TRADE-MARK FOR FUNGICIDE.

Statement and Declaration Registered Aug. 21, 1906.

Application filed July 3, 1905. Serial No. 9,799.

TRADE-MARK
No. 55,632.

STATEMENT.

To all whom it may concern :

Be it known that I, Benjamin Hammond, a citizen of the United States, residing at Fishkill Landing, Dutchess County, New York, and doing business at the northeast corner of the Long Dock, in said village, have adopted for my use the trade-mark shown in the accompanying drawing.

The class of merchandise to which the trade-mark is appropriated is Class 6, Chemicals not otherwise specified, and the particular description of goods comprised in said class upon which I use said trade-mark is a fungicide.

The trade-mark has been continuously used in my business since 1886 and is displayed on the packages containing the goods by placing thereon a printed label on which the same is shown.

BENJAMIN HAMMOND.

DECLARATION.

State of New York, County of Dutchess, ss:

Benjamin Hammond, being duly sworn, deposes and says that he is the applicant named in the foregoing statement; that he believes the foregoing statement is true; that he believes himself to be the owner of the trade-mark sought to be registered; that no other person, firm, corporation, or association, to the best of his knowledge and belief, has the right to use said trade-mark, either in the identical form or in any such near resemblance thereto as may be calculated to deceive; that said trade-mark is used by him in commerce among several States of the United States and between foreign nations and particularly with Canada; and that the description, drawing, and specimens presented truly represent the trade-mark sought to be registered.

BENJAMIN HAMMOND.

Subscribed and sworn to before me, a notary public, this 11th day of April, 1906.

M. E. CURTIS,
Notary Public.

Mention The Florists' Exchange when writing.

PEONIES

FOR EARLY FALL PLANTING. Choice selection of named sorts. Young plants of three to five eyes. Apply for rates per thousand.

Planted now they make root fibre and save nearly a year over next spring planting.

Beresford. Delicate rose. Creamy petaloids Tipped carmine. Large. Doz., $2.50; hun., $15.00.
Delicatissima. Blush rose with circle of buff under guard petals. Very large and full to center. Strong, robust habit. Doz., $4.50.
Eclatante. Cherry rose to center. Full, strong bloom. Early. Doz., $2.00; hund., $12.00.
Festiva Alba. Pure waxy white flaked with carmine at center. Large, full flower. Doz., $3.50. hund., $25.00.
Festiva Maxima. Snow white, flaked carmine at center. A grand, large bloom and very strong grower. Per doz., $5.00; per 100, $35.00.
Floral Treasure. Clear, brilliant pink. Very double; perfect form; Doz., $4.50; hund., $30.00.
Globosa. Incurved form. Brilliant rose with salmon center. Doz., $1.60; hund., $10.00.
Golden Harvest. Nearest approach to a yellow. Blush guard petals. Doz., $4.50; hund., $30.00.
Grandiflora Rubra. Extra large, perfect balls blood red. Late. Doz., $4.00; hund., $20.00.
Humei. Clear solid pink. Late. Doz., $1.50; hund., $10.00.
La Tulipe. Blush white. Outer petals flaked red. Distinct and fine. Doz., $5.00; hund., $35.00.
Marie Le Moine. Delicate flesh, fading to white. Very full; perfect form. Doz., $4.00; hund., $25.00.
Ne Plus Ultra. Solid shade of brilliant rose. A grand full petaled flower. Doz., $2.00; hund., $12.00.
Officinalis Rubra Plena. Deep crimson. Very early. Doz., $1.50; hund., $8.00; thous., $75.00.
Queen Victoria. Guard petals blush white. Flesh tinted center. A grand full flower. Very full and strong. Doz., $2.50; hund., $15.00.
Rosamond. Bright clear pink tipped pale rose. Very large. Doz., $2.50; hund., $15.00.
Rubra Triumphans. Brilliant deep crimson. Fine contrasting color. Doz., $2.00, hund., $12.00.
Somerset. Pale rose with carmine tint and circle of buff. Very large. Doz., $3.00; hund., $20.00.
Washington. Solid shade of delicate pink. Full bloom. Early. Doz., $2.50; hund., $15.00.
Mixed Pink Varieties. Hund., $8.00; thou., $75.00.

PHONE 312 **JAMES KING NURSERY, Elmhurst, Ill.**

Mention The Florists' Exchange when writing.

DRACAENA INDIVISA

	Per 100
Fine, strong, 6in. pots	$25 00
Asparagus Sprengerii, 3 in., strong	4 00
" 2 in	1.50
Asparagus Plumosus Nanus, 2 in	2.00
Primula Obconica Grandi flora Alba, Rosea and Hybrida, 2 in	2.00
" Buttercup, yellow, 2 in.	2.00
Paris Daisy, white and yellow, 3 in.	3.00
Shasta Daisy, 3 in.	3.00
Smilax, strong 2 in. to close out	.75
Vinca Variegated, field-grown	4.00
Swainsonia Galegifolia Alba, 3 and 4 in. $3.00 and	5.00
Jerusalem Cherries, 4 in., will sell with berries	8.00

Cash with order please.

GEO. J. HUGHES, BERLIN, N. J.

Mention The Florists' Exchange when writing.

Gardenia Veitchii

4½ inch, $35.00 per 100; 5 inch, $50.00 per 100; strong, bushy plants. Cash with order.

J. M. KELLER CO.
5th Ave., & 65th St.
BROOKLYN, N. Y.

Mention the Florists' Exchange when writing.

PANSY PLANTS

My Giant Pansy Plants, finest in the market in size and color. Taken from the Bugnot, Masterpiece, Perret, Parisian and other varieties. From my own home grown seeds. Ready now, $2.50 per 1000; 50c. per 100, postpaid. Send for prices on 5,000 lots. Cash with order.

E. A BLINN, CROMWELL, CONN.

Mention The Florists' Exchange when writing.

PEONIES

$6.00 to $10.00 per 100

EDWARD SWAYNE
WEST CHESTER, PA.

Mention the Florists' Exchange when writing.

A RECORD TO BE PROUD OF

The Florists' Hail Association has paid 950 losses amounting to $96,000.00

For particulars address

JOHN G. ESLER, Saddle River, N. J.

Mention the Florists' Exchange when writing.

Sphagnum Moss and Cedar Poles

Moss, 5 barrel bale, $1.25; 2 bales, $2.25; 5 bales, $5.00; 10 bales, $9.50. Poles, 2 in. butt, 8 ft. long, $16.00 per 1000; 2½ in. butt, 10 to 12 feet long, $22.50 per 1000.

H. R. AKERS, Chatsworth, N. J.

Mention The Florists' Exchange when writing.

Adiantum Farleyense

I can quote splendid stock at from $2.00 per dozen up to $24.00 per dozen, in 2-inch to 8-inch pots. If you are looking for Farleyense, better write me about it.

CHARLES H. TOTTY,
Madison, N. J.

Mention The Florists' Exchange when writing.

THIS WON'T APPEAR AGAIN

For Cash Only, 2000 Whittmanii Ferns at $15.00 per 100

F. H. KRAMER, 916 F Street, N. W., Washington, D. C.

PHONE Main 3987

Mention The Florists' Exchange when writing.

DREER'S SPECIALS IN FERNS

Nephrolepis Scottii

Nephrolepis Scottii

We have a grand lot of compact dwarf bushy specimens in 6 inch pots, 50 cents each; 8 inch pans, $1.00 each; 12 inch pans, $2.00 each; 2¼ inch pots, $4.00 per 100; $35.00 per 1000.

Adiantum Cuneatum

A fine lot of 6 inch pots, $3.50 per dozen; $25.00 per 100; 2¼ inch pots, $3.50 per 100; $30.00 per 1000.

Adiantum Farleyense

A grand lot of specimen plants in seven inch pots at $1.50 each. This is bushy stock with grand foliage, of excellent value. Also a fine lot of clean vigorous 3 inch pots for growing on, $2.00 per dozen, $15.00 per 100.

Nephrolepis Whitmani

The most distinct and desirable of the crested forms of the Boston Fern, its great points of merit are that it never reverts or shows any plain fronds or parts of fronds, it naturally makes a shapely compact plant, it is more graceful than any of the other sorts and is a quick grower. We offer strong
2¼ inch pots, $3.50 per dozen, $25.00 per 100.
3 " " 4.00 " " 30.00 " "
and fine plants in 6 inch pots at $1.00 each.

Pteris Wilsoni and Pteris Wimsetti Multiceps

are both useful varieties, perhaps the prettiest of the Pteris for growing into larger sizes for decorative plants, we have a fine lot of 6 inch pans, just right for table decoration, pretty plants at $3 50 per dozen; $25.00 per 100. In smaller sizes we can supply 2¼ inch pots, $3.50 per 100; $30.00 per 1000.
3 " " 6.00 " " 50.00 " "
4 " " 1.50 " doz. 10.00 " 100

Aspidium Tsussemense

Of this most useful of all Dish Ferns we still have a fine lot of seedlings in flats, which if potted up now will still make salable stock for this winter, about 200 plants to a flat at $2.00 per flat.

Mixed Ferns

Our usual superior assortment of varieties:
2¼ inch pots, $3.50 per 100; $30.00 per 1000.
3 " " 6.00 " " 50.00 " "

For a full line of Seasonable Stock, Decorative Plants, Palms, Ferns, Araucarias, Pandanus, Hardy Perennials, Bulbs, Seeds, etc., etc., see our quarterly Wholesale List.

HENRY A. DREER,
714 Chestnut St., PHILADELPHIA, PA.

Mention The Florists' Exchange when writing.

ASSORTED FERNS FOR FERNERIES
IN BEST VARIETIES

We have an exceptionally fine stock of these goods and to make room will fill immediate orders at $20.00 per 1000.

Let us have your order to-day.

WRITE FOR PRICE LIST OF GENERAL STOCK.

THE GEO. WITTBOLD COMPANY
No. 1657 BUCKINGHAM PLACE, CHICAGO

Mention The Florists' Exchange when writing.

NEPH. PIERSONI

Finest Stock we ever had
Strictly true to name

From 3 in. pots $6.00
" 3½ in. " 8.00
" 4 in. " 12.00

SEE LAST ADVERTISEMENT

NATHAN SMITH & SON
ADRIAN, MICH.

Mention The Florists' Exchange when writing.

FERNS. NEPHROLEPIS BARROWSII

2½ inch, $6.00 per 100.

HUGH GRAHAM CO.,
Logan Nurseries, York Road and Louden Street, PHILADELPHIA, PA.

Mention The Florists' Exchange when writing.

NEPHROLEPIS

Whitmani, 2¼ in., $25.00 per 100.
Barrowsii, $10.00 per 100.

Henry H. Barrows & Son, Whitman, Mass.

Mention The Florists' Exchange when writing.

BOSTON FERNS

Taken from bench, $10.00 and $20.00 per 100.
5 and 6 inch **Pot Ferns**, from $3.00 per doz. up
Extra fine stock.
Geraniums, 3½ inch stock, $4.00 per 100.

BOCK, THE FLORIST,
2394 MASS AVENUE NORTH CAMBRIDGE, MASS.

Mention The Florists' Exchange when writing.

FERNS

	Doz.	100
SCOTTII, 2½ inch	$0.75	$5.00
BARROWSII, 2½ inch	1.25	8.00

THE CONARD & JONES CO.
WEST GROVE, PA.

Mention The Florists' Exchange when writing.

FERNS

Several hundred Tarrytown Ferns.
N. PIERSONI ELEGANTISSIMA, from 2½ in. pots, $10.00 per 100; extra nice and strong Stock.

R. ENGELMAN & SON
PITTSFIELD, MASS.

Mention The Florists' Exchange when writing.

NEPHROLEPIS SCOTTII

Small plants from the benches, $5.00 per 100; $50.00 per 1000. Plants large enough for 6 in. pots, $25.00 per 100. Plants large enough to go in 7 and 8 in. pots, $50.00 per 100.

Asparagus Plumosus Nanus, 2½ in., fine plants, $3.00 per 100.

JOHN SCOTT,
Rutland Road and East 45th Street,
BROOKLYN, N. Y.
Telephone 2890 Bedford.

Mention The Florists' Exchange when writing.

FERNS OUR SPECIALTY

Cibotium Schiedei: We have a grand stock of this magnificent tree fern in all sizes, 3 in. pots, $25.00 per 100; 4 in. pots, $45.00 per 100; 5 in. pots, $70.00 per 100; 7 in. pots, $1.70 each; 8 in. pots, $2.50 each.
Assorted Ferns, from 2¼ in. pots, all the best market varieties, $3.00 per 100, or $25.00 per 1000; 4 inch pots, $12.00 per 100. **Fern Seedlings**, from flats, $1.00 per 100 plants, or $8.50 per 1000. If by mail add 10c. each 100 plants.
Adiantum Cuneatum, 2 in. pots, $3.50 per 100
" " 4 in. pots, 12.00 " "
" **Rhodophyllum** 4 in. pots $25.00 per 100
" **Lathomii**, 4 in. pots, $20.00 per 100
" **Regina**, 4 in. pots, $40.00 per 100
Fern Spores gathered from our own stock plants 35c. per trade package or $4.00 per doz. packages.

ANDERSON & CHRISTENSEN,
SHORT HILLS, N. J.

Mention The Florists' Exchange when writing.

FERNS

Are now in fine shape. A good variety and nice bushy stock, 2½ in., $3.00 per 100; $25.00 per 1000.
Kentia Belmoreana, 4 in., clean and bushy, 25c. 5 in. 50c.; 6 in. 75c.
Boston Ferns, Piersoni and **Scottii**, from bench, 25c. each.
Cocos Weddeliana, 10c.

H. WESTON, HEMPSTEAD, N. Y.

Mention The Florists' Exchange when writing.

Fern Seedlings

From flats, ten of the best varieties, at $1.00 per 100; $8.50 per 1000; if by mail add 10c. per 100. Ferns for dishes, good stocky plants from 2¼ in. pots, $3.00 per 100; $25.00 per 1000; 250 plants at 1000 rate.
Adiantum Cuneatum, 5 in. pots, $20.00 per 100.

FRANK N. ESKESEN, MADISON, N. J.

Mention The Florists' Exchange when writing.

Boston Ferns from Bench

10 to 20c. each **Asparagus Sprengerii**, 2¼ in. pots, $2.00 per 100. Good value in both the above.

Cohanzie Carnation Greenhouses,
New London, Conn.

Mention The Florists' Exchange when writing.

WM. STARKE
Wholesale Florist and Plantsman

Tel. No. 4582 Madison Sq. **52 W. 29th St.**
Between Broadway and 6th Ave., **New York**

Shipments of Plants made to any part of the country. A trial order solicited.

SATISFACTION GUARANTEED.

Mention The Florists' Exchange when writing.

N. LECAKES & CO.
53 W. 28th St., NEW YORK

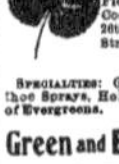

Tel. No. 1214
Madison Square

Stands at Cut Flower Exchange Coogan Bldg., W. 26th Street & 34th Street Cut Flower Market.

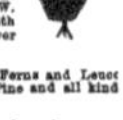

Specialties: Galax Leaves, Ferns and Leucothoe Sprays, Holly, Princess Pine and all kind of Evergreens.

Green and Bronze Galax Leaves

Mention the Florists' Exchange when writing

Wholesale Prices of Cut Flowers, New York, Sept. 20, 1906
Prices quoted are by the hundred unless otherwise noted

Roses	A. Beauty, fancy—special	8.00 to 15.00
Roses	" extra	5.00 to 6.00
Roses	" No. 1	4.00 to 5.00
Roses	" No. 2	3.00 to 4.00
Roses	" No. 3	1.00 to 1.50
Roses	Bride, Maid, fancy—spe'l	2.00 to 3.00
Roses	" extra	1.00 to 2.00
Roses	" No. 1	.50 to 1.00
Roses	" No. 2	.25 to .50
Roses	Golden Gate	to
Roses	Liberty	to
Roses	Mme. Abel Chatenay	to
Adiantum		.50 to .75
Adiantum	Croweanum	.50 to 1.00
Asparagus		25.00 to 50.00
Asparagus	" Plumosus, bunches	8.00 to 15.00
Asparagus	" Sprengerii, bunches	8.00 to 15.00
Asters		.25 to 3.00
Cattleyas		50.00 to 60.00
Daisies		to
Gladiolus		.50 to 1.25
		to

Carnations	Inf'r grades, all colors		.50 to 1.00
Carnations	Standard Varieties	White	1.00 to 2.00
Carnations	Standard Varieties	Pink	1.00 to 2.00
Carnations	Standard Varieties	Red	1.00 to 2.00
Carnations	Standard Varieties	Yel. & Var.	to
Carnations	*Fancy— (*The highest grades of standard var.)	White	to
Carnations	*Fancy—	Pink	to
Carnations	*Fancy—	Red	to
Carnations	*Fancy—	Yel. & Var.	to
Carnations	Novelties		to
Dahlias, per bunch			.05 to .15
Lilies			6.00 to 8.00
Lily of the Valley			1.00 to 3.00
Mignonette			to
Smilax			8.00 to 10.00
			to
			to
			to
			to
			to

Wholesale Prices of Cut Flowers—Per 100

Boston Sept. 17, 1906	Buffalo Sept. 17, 1906	Detroit Sept. 11, 1906	Cincinnati Sept. 16, 1906	Baltimore Sept. 3, 1906	NAMES AND VARIETIES	Milwaukee Sept. 11, 1906	Phil'delphia Sept. 11, 1906	Pittsburg Sept. 10, 1906	St. Louis Sept. 17, 1906
20.00 to 35.00	20.00 to 25.00	10.00 to 35.00	to 30.00	to	ROSES — A. BEAUTY, fancy—special	to 25.00	15.00 to 20.00	20.00 to 25.00	20.00 to 25.00
10.00 to 20.00	12.00 to 20.00	to	20.00 to 25.00	to	" extra	15.00 to 18.00	10.00 to 15.00	12.50 to 18.00	12.50 to 15.00
4.00 to 10.00	6.00 to 12.00	to	12.50 to 15.00	to	" No. 1	10.00 to 12.50	5.00 to 7.00	8.00 to 10.00	8.00 to 10.00
2.00 to 4.00	3.00 to 6.00	to	4.00 to 6.00	to	" Culls and ordinary	4.00 to 6.00	1.00 to 4.00	5.00 to 6.00	3.00 to 6.00
to	5.00 to 8.00	3.00 to 6.00	4.00 to 6.00	to	BRIDE, 'MAID, fancy-special	to 6.00	to	to	4.00 to 5.00
4.00 to 6.00	4.00 to 5.00	to	to 3.00	to 4.00	" extra	to 5.00	6.00 to 8.00	to 6.00	2.00 to 3.00
2.00 to 4.00	3.00 to 4.00	to	to 2.00	to 3.00	" No. 1	to 4.00	4.00 to 5.00	to 4.00	to
.50 to 2.00	2.00 to 3.00	to	1.00 to 1.50	to 2.00	" No. 2	to 2.00	2.00 to 3.00	to 2.00	to
2.00 to 4.00	to	4.00 to 8.00	to	2.00 to 4.00	GOLDEN GATE	4.00 to 6.00	4.00 to 8.00	to	2.00 to 4.00
2.00 to 8.00	3.00 to 7.00	to	to	2.00 to 4.00	K. A. VICTORIA	4.00 to 8.00	4.00 to 6.00	4.00 to 12.00	2.00 to 8.00
2.00 to 6.00	3.00 to 7.00	to	to	2.00 to 3.00	LIBERTY	4.00 to 6.00	3.00 to 6.00	to	to
to	3.00 to 6.00	4.00 to 10.00	to	to	METEOR	to	to	to	to
to	3.00 to 5.00	4.00 to 10.00	to	2.00 to 3.00	PERLE	4.00 to 6.00	to	to	2.00 to 5.00
to	to	to 50.00	to	to	ORCHIDS—Cattleyas	to	to 50.00	to	to
to	.50 to 1.00	to	to	.50 to .75	CARNATIONS — Inferior grades, all colors	to 1.00	.75 to 1.00	1.00 to 1.25	to .75
to	1.00 to 1.25	to 1.00	to 1.00	to 1.00	Standard Varieties — White	to 1.00	.75 to 1.00	1.00 to 1.25	to .75
to	1.00 to 1.25	to	to 1.00	to 1.00	Standard Varieties — Pink	to 1.00	.75 to 1.00	1.00 to 1.25	to .75
to	1.00 to 1.25	to	to 1.00	to 1.00	Standard Varieties — Red	to 1.00	.75 to 1.00	1.00 to 1.25	to .75
to	to	to 3.00	to 1.00	to	Standard Varieties — Yellow and var.	to 1.00	.75 to 1.00	1.00 to 1.25	to .75
.50 to 1.50	1.50 to 2.00	to	to	to	Fancy Varieties — White	1.50 to 2.00	2.00 to 2.50	1.00 to 1.25	1.00 to 1.50
.50 to 2.00	1.50 to 2.00	to	to	to	Fancy Varieties — Pink	1.50 to 2.00	2.00 to 2.50	1.00 to 1.25	1.00 to 1.50
.50 to 2.00	1.50 to 2.00	to	to	to	Fancy Varieties — Red	1.50 to 2.00	2.00 to 2.50	1.00 to 1.25	1.00 to 1.50
.50 to 2.00	1.50 to 2.00	to 1.50	to	to	Fancy Varieties — Yellow and var.	1.50 to 2.00	2.00 to 2.50	1.00 to 1.25	1.00 to 1.50
to	to	to	to	to	Novelties	to	to	to	to
.75 to 1.00	.50 to 1.00	to 2.00	to 1.00	to 1.00	ADIANTUM	to 1.00	to 1.00	1.25 to 1.50	to 1.00
to 50.00	to	25.00 to 60.00	to 50.00	25.00 to 50.00	ASPARAGUS, Plum. and Ten.	20.00 to 30.00	25.00 to 35.00	30.00 to 50.00	25.00 to 50.00
to	to	20.00 to 30.00	to 35.00	25.00 to 50.00	" Sprengeri, bunches	20.00 to 30.00	25.00 to 35.00	20.00 to 30.00	25.00 to 50.00
.25 to 1.50	.50 to 2.00	to	.50 to 1.50	to	ASTERS	.50 to 1.00	to	.50 to 2.00	1.00 to 3.00
to	8.00 to 10.00	to 10.00	to	6.00 to 8.00	CALLAS	to	to	to	to
to	to	.75 to 1.50	to	to	DAISIES	to .40	3.00 to 4.00	to	to
4.00 to 6.00	1.00 to 3.00	8.00 to 10.00	to 2.00	2.00 to 3.00	GLADIOLUS	to	8.00 to 12.00	1.00 to 4.00	to
to	to	to	to 15.00	to 10.00	LILIES, Harrisii	to 12.50	to	to	to
6.00 to 8.00	12.00 to 15.00	to	to	to	" Longiflorum	to 12.50	2.00 to 4.00	15.00 to 18.00	to
2.00 to 4.00	3.00 to 4.00	3.00 to 4.00	to 4.00	to	LILY OF THE VALLEY	to	1.00 to 2.00	2.00 to 4.00	to
to	to	to	to	to	MIGNONETTE, ordinary	to	to	to	to
to	to	to	to	to	" fancy	to	to	to	to
to	to	4.00 to 8.00	to	to	PEONIES	to	15.00 to 20.00	to	to
10.00 to 12.50	to 15.00	12.50 to 15.00	to 15.00	12.50 to 20.00	SMILAX	to 15.00	to	12.50 to 15.00	to 12.50
to	to	to	to	to	VIOLETS, ordinary	to	to	to	to
to	to	to	to	to	" fancy	to	to	to	to
to	to	to	to	to	NARCISSUS	to	to	to	to
.25 to .35	.15 to .25	.50 to .75	to	to	SWEET PEAS	.25 to .50	to .50	to	to
to	to	to	to	to		to	to	to	to
to	to	to	to	to		to	to	to	to

CANADIAN NEWS

LONDON, ONT.—Business is very good in wedding arrangements and funeral designs; outside of these there is little doing. Stock under glass is doing well. Chrysanthemums are coming along in good shape. Gammage & Son's stock of poinsettias, cyclamen, Begonia Gloire de Lorraine, palms, Boston ferns, etc., is in nice condition for the Fall trade.

Fred Dicks is remodeling his heating plant. F. C.

TORONTO.—Business is picking up and there is every indication of a very lively season. The last two weeks have brought large numbers of visitors into town; the weather has been favorable, and most of the craft have had a share of the trade agoing. Stock coming in is improving in quality. Albert Houle, of the Bedford Park Floral Company, is cutting some nice roses and the plants are looking splendid. Some good carnations are arriving from Mr. Jennings, of Brampton. Walter Muston, of the Toronto Floral Company, is sending in good roses. Most of the growers have their carnations housed, and generally the plants are doing well. Violets in the field are looking fairly good. Many glass structures are going up around our city, several being for early vegetables.

Arrangements for the Fruit and Chrysanthemum Show, in November, are in a forward condition. A celebrated band has been secured for the week; a cheap railway rate from all over Ontario is promised.

Archie Jennings, who was manager of the floral department of the T. Eaton Company, is opening a store on King street, which he expects to be ready for business this week. The Eaton Company have cut down their floral department very much, and say in future they will confine themselves more to cut flowers.

THOS. MANTON.

A Medium that Reaches Buyers.

The sale of begonias has far exceeded our expectations, we having sold out our stock completely. It is a pleasure to advertise in a medium through which we are sure to reach the people who are buyers, and we have certainly had success through yours. E. A. BUTLER & SON.
New York.

Wholesale Prices of Cut Flowers, Chicago, Sept. 18, 1906

Prices quoted are by the hundred unless otherwise noted

ROSES — American Beauty		
36-inch stems..........per doz.	3.00 to	4.00
30-inch stems.......... "	2.50 to	3.00
24-inch stems.......... "	2.00 to	2.50
20-inch stems.......... "	1.00 to	2.00
18-inch stems.......... "	.... to	1.50
12-inch stems.......... "	.... to	1.00
8-inch stems and shorts "	.50 to	.75
Bride Maid, fancy special......	5.00 to	6.00
" extra..........	4.00 to	5.00
" No. 1..........	2.00 to	3.00
" No. 2..........	.50 to	1.00
Golden Gate..........	2.00 to	6.00
Carnot..........	2.00 to	6.00
Uncle John..........	2.00 to	6.00
Liberty..........	2.00 to	6.00
Richmond..........	2.00 to	8.00
Kaiserine..........	2.00 to	8.00
Killarney..........	3.00 to	6.00
Perle..........	2.00 to	6.00
Chatenay..........	2.00 to	6.00
Orchids—Cattleyas..........	50.00 to	75.00
Smilax..........	8.00 to	12.00
Lily of the Valley..........	2.00 to	4.00
Dahlias..........	2.00 to	3.00

CARNATIONS		
Inferior grades all colors	.25 to	.50
Standard Varieties — White..........	.75 to	1.00
Standard Varieties — Pink..........	.75 to	1.00
Standard Varieties — Red..........	.75 to	1.00
Standard Varieties — Yellow & var....	.75 to	1.00
*Fancy (The highest grades of Sta'd var) — White..........	1.50 to	2.00
*Fancy — Pink..........	1.50 to	2.00
*Fancy — Red..........	1.50 to	2.00
*Fancy — Yellow & var....	1.50 to	2.00
Novelties..........	.... to	....
Adiantum..........	.50 to	1.00
Asparagus, Plum. & Ten..........	.35 to	.50
" Sprengeri, bunches	.35 to	.50
Gladiolus..........	2.00 to	6.00
Lilies, Longiflorum..........	8.00 to	12.00
Harrisii..........	8.00 to	12.00
Auratum..........	6.00 to	8.00
Nymphaea..........	.... to	1.00
Mignonette, ordinary..........	1.00 to	2.00
Tuberoses, Spikes..........	4.00 to	8.00
....	.... to	....
....	.... to	....
Hardy Ferns per 1000..........	1.00 to	1.50
Galax "	1.00 to	1.25
Asters..........	.50 to	2.50

New York.

News of the Week.

The weather continues too warm for the good of the retail business, and although we are now past the middle of September, there is as yet very little doing in that branch excepting funeral work.

Siebrecht & Sons, who have been occupying the corner store in the Siebrecht building, Thirty-eighth street and Fifth avenue, are moving their business around the corner on the Thirty-eighth street side, having rented the store they originally occupied to the Union Trust Company of New York.

Meyer, the florist of Fifty-eighth street and Madison avenue, is having an entirely new front put in his store; and is also making extensive interior alterations in order to meet his increasing trade.

Walter Mott, who for several years has been located in Jamestown, N. Y., will, on October 1, enter the services of the H. H. Berger & Company, 47 Barclay street, N. Y.

John J. Boschard, formerly with George F. Dominick, Greenwich, Conn., has returned from a two months' visit to Europe.

C. B. Weathered, the popular treasurer of the New York Florists' Club, will celebrate his silver wedding on October 1.

On Wednesday evening, September 12, the cook house adjoining the pavilion at Witzel's Point View Grove, College Point, was struck by lightning and suffered some damage. This is the pavilion in which the members of the New York Florists' Club have had their dinner on several occasions at the annual outing.

The Lord & Burnham Company have secured the contract for the erection of the iron and glass work of the conservatory which is to be built in Humboldt Park, Buffalo, N. Y. Their bid for the work was $8,215.

John H. Taylor of Bayside, L. I., has returned from his Summer's sojourn in Europe.

Clarence Saltford, who is associated with his father, George Saltford, wholesale florist at 46 West Twenty-ninth street, was married to Miss Bertha Lawson on Wednesday, September 12, at the Methodist Episcopal Church, One hundred and Fourth street, this city. The newly wedded pair will make their home here, and have the congratulations of the trade.

The wholesale dealers are now keeping their stores open each day until 5 p. m.

The Parker-Bruen Manufacturing Company, 1133 Broadway, inform us that Erle D. Parker, who was formerly superintendent of the firm's factory at Harrison, N. J., is no longer in its employ.

W. C. Duckham, president of the C. S. A., was a visitor this week, and advises us that he will shortly announce the committees for certificating the new chrysanthemums for the coming season.

Wm. Elliott & Sons, Fulton street, report a very satisfactory opening auction sale on Tuesday last. Messrs. Elliott will sell on Tuesday, October 2, the G. N. Montgomery collection of orchids, which, it is belived, is one of the best and most extensive in the neighborhood of New York. Some very rare and choice varieties will be offered.

Boston.

News of the Week.

Samuel Neil of Dorchester is rebuilding his store at his greenhouses on Washington street.

The first violets of the season made their appearance this week, E. E. Doran, Brookline, being the grower.

Charles Boyle and Wm. Goode, both with Galvin's Back Bay store, have severed their connections therewith and are considering starting in business on their own account with a location on Boylston street, thus adding one more to the number of Back Bay flower stores.

Houghton & Clark have remodelled their store on Boylston street greatly improving its appearance.

G. A. Sutherland returned this week from a three months' sojourn in Maine feeling much improved in health.

Wm. Nicholson writes that he will sail for home this week having had a very enjoyable trip in England.

John Pritchet of W. H. Elliott's New Hampshire establishment spent a few days in town this week. He reports a very favorable outlook for a mammoth cutting of roses at the Madbury place.

John Riley of Galvin's has gone to New York and Philadelphia for a week or two.

James Delay expects to open a fine new store at the corner of Boylston and Dartmouth streets, one of the finest locations in the Back Bay district.

Jas. D. Rough is now with Galvin at his Back Bay store.

The exhibition of products of children's gardens at Horticultural Hall on Saturday was undoubtedly the largest of its kind ever held in Boston, if not in America. The lecture hall was filled to overflowing, and the committee of the Massachusetts Horticultural Society who had the matter in charge are to be congratulated on their work. Sixteen schools were represented in the exhibit for schools, and individually there were exhibits from 16 boys and 8 girls. The quality of the exhibits was very good indeed, and in many cases would have done credit to professionals. It was noticeable that girls grew mostly flowers and boys mostly vegetables, though in many cases they had both.

J. W. D.

Buffalo.

News Items.

Charles Sandiford and Captain Braik were judging exhibits at the St. Catherine's show the past week.

All the large department stores having their Fall opening in the one week has called for large quantities of gladiolus, palms and laurel roping, and incidentally a lot of hustling on the part of the florists.

Carl Humphrey, who has been in the employ of W. J. Palmer & Son for the past few years, has left to enter on the life of a gentleman farmer. Miss Florence McNiece, also of the same firm, has left for the home of her parents, New York city, where she will rest and recuperate from her arduous duties as saleslady.

Emil Brucker is back at his stand in Wm. F. Kasting's, after spending his vacation visiting all his relatives in the vicinity.

W. H. G.

Cleveland.

News Notes.

On October 1 The Gasser Company will open a new wholesale cut flower house on Prospect avenue, in the Osborn block. They have secured a very desirable commodious store and basement, and as the building runs through to Huron road it gives them a double frontage and plenty of light. Heretofore the wholesale and retail business has been carried on in their store on Euclid avenue, but their wholesale department has increased so rapidly in late years that they have been compelled to open a separate store to better accommodate their many customers.

San Francisco.

News Jottings.

The inquiry comes from every quarter, "What is San Francisco doing for herself?" Reports for August show a prosperous state of affairs in this city. Former residents who were compelled to seek living quarters elsewhere as a result of the earthquake-fire are rapidly returning and the population, which was reduced from 485,000 to less than 200,000, is now 370,000. The receipts from import duties for the last thirty days aggregate $1,500,000. August building permits issued, 1,176; value $6,333,363. Real estate transfers recorded, 170; value, $1,429,114. Bank clearings, $180,844,594.73; for August, 1905, $155,841,918.86. Tonnage of Port of San Francisco, 157,370. Permanent buildings under construction, 711. Value of buildings on which work is being done, $50,000,000. Number of men doing construction work, 30,000. Average number of cars of debris removed daily, 125.

When this is printed is will be lacking only three days of five months since walking was good in San Francisco, yet for the last two weeks, owing to a grand stand made by street-car union labor employees for increased wages and decreased working hours, San Francisco has been a city of pedestrians, and 'buses and wagons are carrying passengers to and from the ferry and railroad stations. Market street, the main thoroughfare of the city, is a jumble of autos, motorcycles and vehicles of every description. Rapid passage is impossible, but the great majority are glad to go along even at a snail's pace, if their feet are spared the cobbles. The supply of vehicles is, of course, inadequate to accommodate those desiring transportation. More than this, the fee charged, twenty-five cents, makes a trip on wheels prohibitive to a large number.

Later—The street car men's strike has been declared off, and transportation is now as usual, a fact for which the flower trade is thankful.

California has developed the past week a man who claims he has out-Burbanked Burbank. His name is J. L. von Hoffman, owner of a plantation near Pasadeña, and he claims to have discovered a method by which he can produce by inoculation—charging the soil with a secret substance—roses, lilies and other flowers of any description desired and fix the color. He claims to have produced four jet black roses last year and to have lost them in the San Francisco fire. He also claims to be able to produce a carnation that will excel the famous Lawson, and says he can make green marigolds, red, white and blue shamrocks, and other wonders.

The most surprising news since last week's report is the dissolution of co-partnership that has existed so long between Sievers & Boland. Each of the partners has decided to go it alone, and a result of their business separation will be two flower stores instead of one. Mr. Sievers' new store is already opened, and a fine one it is, at 1660 California street, only a few doors from Van Ness avenue in the very bull's eye of the city's choicest retail trade.

The retiring partner, Mr. Boland, expects to be in ship-shape order by the first of October. He has a force of structural mechanics at work at 45-47 Geary street, the center of the burnt district, tranforming the two storerooms into one, which he is quite sure will be the prettiest flower store in the city.

Another floral beauty store, located this week in the Van Ness avenue trade center, at 1345-47 Sutter street, is an exemplification of the faith of the proprietors, Messrs. Pelicano & Rossi. This is their No. 2 store since the earthquake-fire, and both are doing well. ALVIN.

Los Angeles, Cal.

News Items.

The regular monthly meeting of the Horticultural Society was held in Symphony Hall, Monday evening, September 3. There was a good attendance. Belle Summer Anglers, a talented young woman, a recent editorial writer on The Times, read an interesting and instructive paper on "Floriculture and its Beneficent Influence on Home Life." Walter Raymond exhibited a bouquet of the rose Richmond, grown under glass. The color is a most beautiful shade of red. The buds are on the style of those of Cecil Brunner. A. D. Peterson made a fine display of double flowers of tuberous begonias, grown in the open. Miss Reese showed a bunch of bloom of Polygonium Baldschuanicum—the first flowers of this interesting and beautiful climber seen in this locality. The writer had a few spikes of the beautiful Hedychium coronarium, which were the first of this interesting, fragrant flower exhibited here. These, too, were from the open. Once its culture is thoroughly understood by growers in Southern California, it will be a valuable addition to our list of cut flowers for decorative purposes.

Henry Turner, superintendent of The Whittelsey flower gardens, made his first cut of Enchantress carnation August 15, which sold readily for $1.50 per hundred, while field grown stock found slow sale at 50c. This is the establishment which grows its carnations under muslin covers. These covers are rolled up or let down as the condition of the weather may require. The houses, ten in number, are heated with hot water during cool nights, and the products are equal to the best the writer has ever seen produced under glass.

A fungous disease has appeared among the semperflorens and Vernon types of begonias which has ruined some beds of plants. It attacks the tops first and finally kills the plant. Whether it is due to climatic or soil conditions is a question yet unsolved.

The product of the 160-acre field of sweet peas referred to in these notes July 14 is 100 tons of clean seed—certainly enough to make the gardens of the United States beautiful and fragrant the coming season.

E. D. Sturtevant has gone East to visit his old home and friends. In his absence, A. D. Peterson, gardener for Mr. John Singleton, will make his exhibit of aquatics at the coming flower show.

P. D. BARNHART.

SALEM, ORE.—On September 7 F. M. McElfresh, superintendent of the large Wallace orchard near this city, committed suicide by shooting himself in the head with a shotgun. Temporary insanity is the only possible explanation of his act. McElfresh was one of the best-known and highly esteemed fruit men in this part of the valley. He was a graduate of the University of Illinois and from 1898 to 1901 was professor of botany and entomology at the Oregon Agricultural College. In the Fall of 1901 he took the superintendency of the Wallace orchard and filled it with entire satisfaction to the owners.

Mr. McElfresh was a conscientious man and worried greatly whenever the work of the big orchard did not proceed to the best interests of his employers. He was just finishing the harvest of a 300-ton crop of pears, but in the last few days many pickers left to go to the hop fields and he worried over that.

McElfresh was a native of Illinois and was about 35 years of age. He was married in February, 1905, to Miss Gertrude Ewing, of Oswego, Ore. There are no children.

GREENWICH, CONN.—John G. Fleuti, manager for Alexander Mead & Son, 349 Lake avenue, sailed on September 15, per steamer La Bretagne on a two months' visit to his native country—Switzerland. The most important item in Mr. Fleuti's trip is the bringing back to this country of his bride, Miss Augsburger, also of Switzerland.

BIRMINGHAM, MICH.—H. J. Corfield, landscape architect, who is carrying out the work on the estate of G. G. Booth, "Cranbrook," Birmingham, Mich., has placed an order with the Elizabeth Nursery Company, New Jersey, for 1,000 Crimson Rambler roses, 3 to 4 ft. These are to be planted in one solid mass.

Cincinnati.

News of the Week.

The event of the week was the marriage of Benjamin Dulaney, the very popular traveling salesman of J. Charles McCullough, to Miss Katherine Stevens Whiteley of Bonaparte, Iowa. Their cards say, "Will be at home at 1325 Chase avenue." The many friends of Ben, both florists, Knights Templar and Shriners, as well as seedsmen, will join with me in extending warmest congratulations.

It is with much regret that I announce the very serious illness of Charles Evans, brother of our esteemed friend John A. Evans of Richmond, Ind. Charles was employed by his brother, but being taken ill, he went to Columbus, O., to his home where he underwent an operation, but without any apparent success. John Evans was in Cincinnati early this week consulting an eminent specialist, and from there he went to Columbus.

Mrs. Coates and a young lady friend, both employed by W. S. Bell, Lexington, Ky., were callers Friday. Mr. Thomas, with Bertermann Brothers, Indianapolis, was a caller Saturday morning; all here doing the Fall Festival.

Business is not bad, though not good. American Beauty roses of better quality are more in demand, and could be disposed of at good prices. Tea roses are improving somewhat, but a few more weeks will vastly improve them in quantity as well as quality.

Carnations, short stems, are now coming in and sell fairly well. Asters, good stock, sell well, while hundreds and hundreds of seconds and thirds will not fetch enough to pay express charges. Chrysanthemums will arrive this week, and we trust will start the ball rolling.

The floral exhibit, consisting of table decorations, baskets, bridal bouquets and wreaths, which should have taken place September 20, has been declared off by the directors of the Fall Festival Association, they claiming that not enough entries were made to justify the exhibit. I understand the board has again employed W. K. Partridge to provide another display similar to the one given on the sixth, which was such a success. Five hundred dollars will be paid for this coming exhibit to be held on the 20th. This makes twelve hundred dollars for Mr. Partridge, which is a nice business, besides a good advertisement.

The new Jewish temple in Avondale, one of the handsomest religious structures in the West, was dedicated September 14, Julius Baer having the decorations.

E. G. GILLETT.

AURORA, ILL.—On September 7 a small fire broke out in the greenhouses of J. Smely; fortunately, not much damage was done. It is thought that lime caused the fire.

IT'S NOT SO LONG AGO

when all greenhouses were constructed with heavy wooden sash bars, rafters and supports, and glazed with narrow glass—then came the iron frame house—but

U-Bar Greenhouses

Are the Best

Greenhouses Built

because they are just as far ahead of the iron frame house as the iron frame is ahead of the sash bar—no house is as light—as enduring.

Pierson U-Bar Co.

Designers and Builders
U-Bar Greenhouses
Metropolitan Building

4th Ave. & 23d St., New York

ntion The Florists' Exchange when writing.

UMMER IN WINTER

BY USING

Standard Greenhouse Boilers

One cent gets our Catalog

IBLIN & CO., UTICA, N. Y.

ntion The Florists' Exchange when writing.

THE

REENHOUSE COMPANY

2-228 Kearney Ave., JERSEY CITY, N. J.

Greenhouse Designers, Builders and Heating Engineers ❦ ❦ ❦

ntion The Florists' Exchange when writing.

Insure an Even Temperature In your Greenhouse

A Morehead Trap Will Do It

Write for Particulars

MOREHEAD MFG. CO.

1049 Grand River Ave., DETROIT, MICH.

Mention The Florists' Exchange when writing.

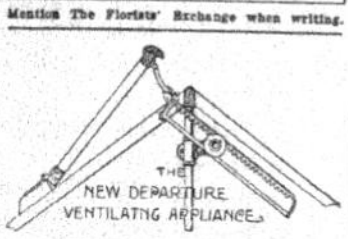

CHEAPEST and BEST

If you doubt it try them and be convinced.
Send for descriptive Price Circular.

J. D. Carmody, Evansville, Ind.

Mention The Florists' Exchange when writing.

Evans Improved Challenge

Roller bearing, self-oiling device automatic stop, solid link chain make the IMPROVED CHALLENGE the most perfect apparatus in the market.
Write for catalogue and prices before placing your orders elsewhere.

QUAKER CITY MACHINE CO.
RICHMOND, IND.

The Knowledge and Experience

embodied in our line of Pumping Engines cost us a good deal of time and money. Free to you for the asking.

The Standard Pump & Engine Co.
CLEVELAND, O.

Mention The Florists' Exchange when writing.

FREE HOSE

trial. We send our "Florist" hose on 60 days trial; if not satisfactory return and we pay charges both ways. Wrought iron pipe lasts longer than steel. Get our prices on Guaranteed wrought iron pipe. Send for Free catalogue "Kay" Boilers, Ventilating apparatus, Tools, Valves and Fittings.

WILLIAM H. KAY COMPANY,
244 Fulton Street, - - New York City.

Dealers in Boilers get best results when they advertise here.

The Test of Quality

Cypress is conceded by all authorities to be the best wood for greenhouse construction and quite a little has been said about the "right kind of cypress." What way have you of knowing the "right kind of cypress?" Can you tell by looking at a cypress plank just where the sap lies and what kind it is?

One way to be sure that you get the "right kind" of cypress is to place your order with a firm that makes a test of every piece before shipping and employs an expert to detect cypress defects. Send for "Why Use Cypress" and "The Mummy's Case."

Next Week, "THE TEST OF WORKMANSHIP."

John C. Moninger Co., Chicago

115 E. BLACKHAWK STREET

Mention The Florists' Exchange when writing.

SCOLLAY BOILERS

ARE BEST

For Green House heating. Standard Cast Iron Green House Pipe and fittings

We are Headquarters for all sizes Wrought Iron Pipe and Fittings.

It will pay you to get our special quotations. We also contract for, and erect **Steam** and **Hot Water Heating** apparatus in all parts of the country.

Illustrated catalogues free on application.

JOHN A. SCOLLAY,
74-76 MYRTLE AVE.,
BOROUGH OF BROOKLYN,
NEW YORK CITY.
Telephones 1492-1493 Main.
U. G. SCOLLAY, Manager.

GREENHOUSE LUMBER

BUILD WELL

There is a pleasant sense of satisfaction in knowing that when your order for Cypress is placed with us you will receive material upon which you can absolutely rely, and that shipment will be promptly made.

ESTIMATES AND PLANS

Furnished without charge. Let us hear from you if you contemplate building.

HOT BED SASH

CEDAR POSTS, IRON FITTINGS, ETC., ETC.

LOCKLAND LUMBER CO.
LOCKLAND, O.

GREENHOUSE MATERIAL

FREE FROM SAP AND MILLED TO FIT SNUG IS WHAT WE MANUFACTURE AT OUR OWN MILLS.

WE FURNISH EVERYTHING TO COMPLETE YOUR HOUSES INCLUDING GLASS, BOILERS AND PIPE.

CATALOGUE ON APPLICATION. GET OUR PRICES.

S. JACOBS & SONS,

GREENHOUSE CONSTRUCTION MATERIAL.

365-79 Flushing Ave., BROOKLYN, N. Y.

Mention The Florists' Exchange when writing.

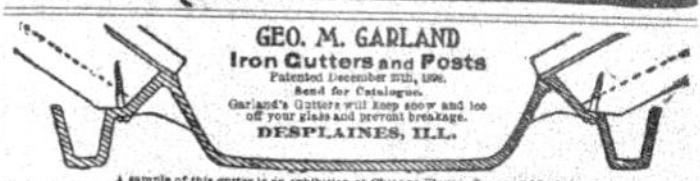

GEO. M. GARLAND
Iron Gutters and Posts
Patented December 27th, 1898.
Send for Catalogue.
Garland's Gutters will keep snow and ice off your glass and prevent breakage.
DESPLAINES, ILL.

A sample of this gutter is on exhibition at Chicago Flower Growers' Market.

Mention The Florists' Exchange when writing.

TILE DRAINED LAND IS MORE PRODUCTIVE

Earliest and easiest worked. Carries off surplus water; admits air to the soil. Increases the value. Acres of swampy land reclaimed and made fertile. Jackson's Round Drain Tile meets every requirement. We also make Sewer Pipe, Red and Fire Brick, Chimney Tops, Encaustic Side Walk Tile, etc. Write for what you want and prices. JOHN H. JACKSON, 90 Third Ave., Albany, N. Y.

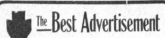

THE FLORISTS' EXCHANGE

We are a straight shoot and aim to grow into a vigorous plant

A WEEKLY MEDIUM OF INTERCHANGE FOR FLORISTS, NURSERYMEN, SEEDSMEN AND THE TRADE IN GENERAL

Vol XXII. No. 13 — NEW YORK AND CHICAGO, SEPTEMBER 29, 1906 — One Dollar Per Year

IF AT THE POINT

of buying refer you to our first consignment of

Virgin Mushroom Spawn, 10 lbs. 75c, $7.00 100

JUST RECEIVED.	Per 100	Per 1000
Narcissus Paper White grandiflora, largest size	$1.25	$9.00
Narcissus Von Sion, extra selected	1.35	11.50
Narcissus Von Sion, mammoth double nosed	2.00	18.50
Lilium Candidum, first grade forcing bulbs	6.00	50.00
Lilium Longiflorum (Japan) 6 to 8 in.	3.00	24.00
Lilium Longiflorum (Japan) 7 to 9 in.	4.50	40.00
Lilium Longiflorum Multiflorum, 6 to 8 in.	3.50	30.00
Freesias, selected French	.75	6.00
White Roman Hyacinths, 12 to 15 cmt.	2.50	22.00
Canes, Stakes, 6 to 9 ft.		6.00

Cineraria, choice mixed, Williams, tr. pkt. 50c.
Calceolaria, choice mixed, Williams, tr. pkt. 50c.
Pansy Rainbow, blended, tr. pkt. $1.00.
Primula Sinensis, ⅛ tr. pkt. 50c.
Stock, "Cut and Come Again," pure white, tr. pkt. 25c.

WM. ELLIOTT & SONS, 201 FULTON ST., NEW YORK

Mention The Florists' Exchange when writing.

C. C. MORSE & CO.

SEED GROWERS

171-173 Clay St., San Francisco, California

OUR SPECIALTIES

ONION LETTUCE SWEET PEAS

Also Carrot, Celery, Celeriac, Cucumber, Endive, Leek, Mustard, Parsley, Parsnip, Radish, Salsify, Spinach, Tomato and

FLOWER SEEDS

Growers for the trade on contract. Warehouses at Santa Clara; Farms and Farm headquarters Carnadero, near Gilroy.

Registered Cable Address: MORSEED, SAN FRANCISCO.

Mention The Florists' Exchange when writing.

Rawson's World-Renowned Cyclamen

FRESH CROP SEEDS NOW READY FOR DELIVERY

RAWSON'S ROYAL STRAIN

Unrivalled for Size, Beauty, Colors and Foliage. Has been awarded First Prize whenever exhibited.

We Offer

Deep Red, Purest White, Mauve, White with Claret Base, Bright Christmas Red, Delicate Salmon Pink, Delicate Pink and an exquisite mixture of all shades at $1.00 per 100 Seeds; $8.00 per 1000 Seeds.

RAWSON'S CONTINENTAL STRAIN

New — Our Own Introduction

Specially valuable on account of its early flowering habit. Will be in full bloom in September and October.

We Offer Pure White, Pink, White with Claret Base, Deep Red at 50c. per 100 Seeds, $4.00 per 1000 Seeds. Also Salmon Pink at $2.00 per 100 Seeds, $15.00 per 1000 Seeds. Superb mixture of all shades at 40c. per 100, $3.50 per 1000 Seeds.

A TRIAL WILL CONVINCE

W. W. RAWSON & CO.

5 UNION STREET, BOSTON, MASS.

Mention The Florists' Exchange when writing

PACIFIC SEED GROWERS' CO.
109 MARKET STREET
SAN FRANCISCO, CAL.
Specialties:
Onion, Carrot, Lettuce, Sweet Peas

Mention The Florists' Exchange when writing.

PRIMROSES

Improved Chinese: Finest grown, named or mixed. Strong 2 inch, $2.00 per 100. X X X Strong 3 inch, $5.00 per 100.

XXX SEEDS

CHINESE PRIMROSE

Finest grown, mixed, 500 seeds, $1.00; ½ pkt., 50c.

Cineraria: Finest large flowering dwarf, mixed, 1000 seeds 50c.

Cyclamen Giganteum: Finest Giant mixed, 200 seeds $1.00; ½ pkt., 50c.

DAISY: Double Giant mixed, 1000 seeds 25c.

GIANT PANSY. The best large flowering varieties, critically selected, 5000 seeds, $1.00; half pkt., 50c.; 500 seeds of Giant Mme. Perret, pansy seed added to every $1.00 pkt. of Giant Pansy. Cash. Liberal extra count of seeds in all packets.

JOHN F. RUPP, Shiremanstown, Pa.

The Home of Primroses

Mention the Florists' Exchange when writing.

Catalog Engravings

and ILLUSTRATIONS

that print EASILY. That's the kind we make — have been since '78

JAS. M. BRYANT, Horticultural Engraving and Printing

706 Chestnut Street, PHILADELPHIA, PA.

Write for our Catalogue of Stock Engravings

Mention the Florists' Exchange when writing.

SEEDS

Pansy, new crop, $1.00 per packet; $4.00 per oz.; $12.00 per ¼ lb. **Pansy Plants**, $4.00 per 1000. Cash.

B. SOLTAU,

199 Grant Ave., JERSEY CITY, N. J.

Mention The Florists' Exchange when writing.

S. & W. CO.'S BULB

	100	1000	10,000
Narcissus Paper White Grandiflora,	$1.00	$ 9.00	$ 80.00
Roman Hyacinths, 13/15 ctm.	3.00	27.00	260.00
" " 11/15 "	2.50	23.00	200.00

Chinese Sacred Lilies, per basket 30 bulbs, $1.30; per bale 120 bulbs,

Stumpp & Walter Co

50 Barclay St., New York

Mention The Florists' Exchange when writing.

CINERARIA

Large Flowering Prize, Splendid Mixed T. P. $0.50

Large Flowering, Semi Dwarf Prize, Splendid Mixed, T. P. $0.50

PANSY, Superb Mixed.

oz. $4.50. ¼ oz. $1.15 ⅛ oz. $0.60

W. C. BECKERT,

Allegheny, Pa.

Mention the Florists' Exchange when writing.

SEEDS

Christmas Flowering Sweet Pea Seed.

Christmas Pink. Florence Denzer, pure white, small quantity still on hand, price, ¼ lb., 75c.; 1 lb., $2.00.

New Christmas Carmine Red, Mrs. Eddie Wild, 1 oz., $1.00; 5 oz., $4.00.

New Christmas Hybrids, all sold.

ANT. C. ZVOLANEK

ORIGINATOR,

BOUND BROOK, N. J.

Mention The Florists' Exchange when writing.

MY GIANT CYCLAMEN

Are Ahead in Growth and Flowers

Bloodred, Carmine, Pink, Pure White, White with Carmine Eye.
Each color separate. Tr. pkt., $1.00, 1000 seeds, $6.00. An even mixture of the above 5 colors, tr. pkt., 75c.; 1000 seeds, $5.00.

Silver Leaved New Hybrids.
With semi-double flowers. Tr. pkt., $1.10; 1000 seeds, $10.00.

Snowball.
New, the real pure white and largest in existence. Tr. pkt., $1.00, 1000 seeds, $15.00.

For larger quantities, special quotations.

O. V. ZANGEN, Seedsman, **HOBOKEN, N. J.**

Mention The Florists' Exchange when writing.

SEED PANSY PLANTS

THE JENNINGS STRAIN

50,000 plants now ready. From finest selected stock, large flowering, fancy colors, in great variety. Stock is first-class in every respect. 100 by mail, 60c.; by express, 500, $2.00; 1000 $4.00; 2000, $7.00; 3000, $10.00. Seed, $1.00 per pkt. of 4000; 1 oz., $5.00; 2 oz., $9.00; 3 oz., $12.00. Cash with order.

E. B. JENNINGS,

Lock Box 254 **Southport, Conn.**

Grower of the Finest Pansies

Mention The Florists' Exchange when writing.

DAHLIAS

Now is the time to place your order for Bulbs which will insure you getting named varieties in any quantity; delivery to be made this fall or early spring.

DAVID HERBERT & SON,

Successors to L. K. PEACOCK, Inc.

ATCO, N. J.

Mention The Florists' Exchange when writing.

Thorburn Bul

HYACINTHS, TULIPS, NARCISSI
CROCUS, LILIES and all oth
BULBS for FLORISTS

Send for our Wholesale Flor
Bulb List Now Ready.

J. M. THORBURN & (

33 BARCLAY ST., through to 32 PARK

NEW YORK

Mention The Florists' Exchange when

VICK'S BULB

are now ready for distribution.

HYACINTHS, TULIP
NARCISSUS, CROCU
LILIES, CALLA
FREESIAS.

All of the best quality.

Send for our Wholesale
Bulb Catalogue.

JAMES VICK'S SON

ROCHESTER, N. Y.

Mention The Florists' Exchange when

BULBS FOR FLORI

Lilium Harrisii, Roman Hyacint Paper White Narcissus, Freesi
Send for special prices.
New Crop **Mushroom Spawn—En lish and Pure Culture.**

WEEBER & DON, Seed Mer and Grow

114 Chambers Street, NEW YOR

Mention The Florists' Exchange when

JOHN SCHEEPERS &

**DEALERS AND IMPORTE
OF BULBS AND PLANT**

2, 4 and 6 OLD SL

NEW YORK CITY

Mention The Florists' Exchange when

BURPEE'S SEE

PHILADELPHIA

Blue List of Wholesale P
mailed only to those wh
plant for profit.

Mention The Florists' Exchange when

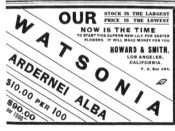

Seed Trade Report.

AMERICAN SEED TRADE ASSOCIATION

Henry W. Wood, Richmond, Va., president; C. S. Burge, Toledo, O., first vice-president; G. B. McVay, Birmingham, Ala., second vice-president; C. E. Kendel, Cleveland, O., secretary and treasurer; J. H. Ford, Ravenna, O., assistant secretary.

ST. PAUL, MINN.—S. D. Dysinger, formerly with L. L. May & Company in their seed department, and later of Chicago, has returned to this city. Mr. Dysinger recently made a trip to the Pacific Coast.

COLUMBUS, O.—The seedsmen have had a good business, and now that the Holland bulbs have arrived things are brisk. It even looks thus early as if bulbs would go out as scarce this Fall as they did last Autumn. Tulips and crocuses are much better in quality than hyacinths and narcissus. The first hard frost will make things very lively. F. W.

The manager of a large canning establishment says that the tomato crop of the West suffered severely from excessive wet weather, and the output of the pack is uncertain. As to western corn, he says the pack will naturally be much smaller this season, as the acreage was reduced fully 50 per cent. A large quantity of corn was carried over last year. The low prices that have been made in certain sections, he says, has been done to get rid of the stock carried over before the national pure-food law goes into effect on January 1. After that date much of this carried-over stock could not be disposed of, as it was not put up in accordance with requirements of that law.

TRADE IN SEEDS WITH NON-CONTIGUOUS POSSESSIONS.—During the year ending June 30, 1905, the trade in seeds with our noncontiguous possessions was as follows: The value of seeds exported to Alaska was $1,110; Hawaii, $5,790; Porto Rico, $1,883; Philippine Islands, $778. From Alaska were received seeds to the value of $241; from Hawaii, $5,069; from Porto Rico, $6,195; and from the Philippine Islands, $8.

EXPORTS OF SEEDS.—During the year ending June 30, 1905, there were exported from the United States 10,657,365 pounds of clover seed, valued at $1,114,015; 16,141,269 pounds of timothy, value $584,618; grass seeds not elsewhere specified to the value of $303,989; other seeds not elsewhere specified, $317,554. The following table shows the comparative value of all classes of seeds, and the principal countries to which the goods were sent, for the three years ending June 30, 1903, 1904 and 1905:

	1903.	1904.	1905.
Belgium ..$	869,858	$124,828	$41,980
Br. Austral.	78,233	57,332	45,872
Canada ...	999,218	572,869	418,692
Denmark .	202,382	101,068	86,451
France ...	341,801	53,448	28,891
Germany .	1,898,524	516,877	1,213,727
Italy	65,290	1,323	4,005
Mexico ...	63,391	38,701	88,024
Netherlands	2,192,116	274,353	141,649
Russia, E..	15,288	3,947	7,017
Sweden ...	29,543	22,431	6,524
Switzerl'd	19,000	60	81
U. King...	2,580,686	771,283	416,541
Other coun	99,953	44,815	58,293
Total ..	$9,455,283	$2,583,325	$2,557,747

European Notes.

Coming events cast their shadows before; and the fact that the record high temperature of September 1 has been followed by a severe frost on the night of the 11th may justly be taken as a sign of a severe Winter ahead. In spite of the rains which have followed the frost until the closing of the mail, and the fact that the long delayed planting of cabbage, etc., can now be rushed forward, we are badly prepared to meet a severe (if early) Winter.

Beets and mangels will be too small to be lifted and stored; Winter radishes are only now being sown; cabbages and other Brassicas can hardly obtain a good hold of the ground; and turnips and rutabagas must rest in the seed beds until the early Spring.

Surely, after such a scarcity as seems probable for next season, there will be a chance of clearing out stocks to such an extent that even those extraordinary surpluses which have a happy knack of turning up when least expected, may at last disappear.

Quite an excitement has been manifested in the market for rape, and one large dealer has been able to realize a handsome profit by selling the seed back to the original vendor. The European demand is good as a result of the drought, and, if the sugar beet factories pursue their present tactics next season in Holland the rise will be permanent for some time to come.

All the rape and Thousandhead kale sown in England will be needed for feeding purposes; and even with these the farmers and graziers will have great difficulty to feed their flocks and herds, for roots of mangels and rutabagas are poorly developed, and pastures are in many cases burned up beyond recovery.

EUROPEAN SEEDS.

TULIP PRICES.—Reports from Holland show that there has been an extraordinary rise in prices since the commencement of the season. We therefore strongly advise caution in making quotations, as it is now impossible to procure stock of the leading sorts at ordinary figures, so that all quotations should be marked "as far as unsold," or subject to fluctuation of the market. We hope that this rise may be taken as a sign that commercial horticulture is about to partake of the improvement in trade which is making itself felt in other industries.—Horticultural Advertiser.

ERFURT SEED CROPS.—I should like to supplement my last remarks by saying that although reports have been coming in from all sides about great heat and drought, we have had moist and cool weather all the time, so that the ground lost earliar in the season has not been made up.

Peas, especially wrinkled ones, will want a good deal of picking, and some disease has appeared among the lettuce. Mangels are also unsatisfactory, but onions, leeks, cabbages, swedes, etc., are good, and carrots very good. Beans are much behind, but look all right up to date.

As regards flower seeds, the situation has not altered much relatively. Our hopes for a warm August were not fulfilled, and so the later flowering annuals have to be marked with a note of interrogation. It is too late for sweet peas to recover, as if they fail to set at tha right time, they won't do it afterwards. Asters are thin in places but a warm Autumn will help the crop considerably. We have now had a few sunny days so that our hopes rise with the thermometer.

A good many visitors, both from America and England have been round of late, mostly on the lookout for novelties. Of these there will be a good selection this season. —Horticultural Trade Journal.

EUROPEAN AND TRANSATLANTIC GRASS AND CLOVER SEEDS CROP, 1906.—Concerning grass seeds the result in Europe may on an average be called pretty satisfactory, so that prices for most of them will probably not rule higher than last year. The reports from America, however, are with the exception of cockfoot, not at all favorable, and higher prices than last year are generally expected.

Of Agrostis capillaris (red top) the acreage is said to be reduced, for on account of the low prices during the last few years, farmers have used their land for better paying seeds, and, besides, cold dry weather in Spring seems to have had a bad effect on the plant's development, so that the crop is estimated much smaller than last year and higher prices are sure to rule.

A good crop is, however, to be expected of Agrostis stolonifera (genuine German florin grass), provided that the weather will be further favorable.

Alopecurus pratensis (meadow foxtail). The weather in Finland, the principal district of production of this sort, seems to have been favorable to the growth of this plant, for all indications point to a large yield. As to quality and prices nothing definite can be said as yet; to judge from several samples submitted so far, some lots seem to be filled heavily with larvæ, which of course reduces the quality. Contracts could not be concluded, for some speculators have paid prices recently to farmers which are unreasonable considering the large crop, and which will not be maintained. We shall see normal prices soon again; of course the business in the article will consequently be somewhat late.

Anthoxantum odoratum (sweet vernal true) is gathered also this year in very small quantities only, and will cost again more than last season. Qualities are very different, and really fine seed is scarce and much asked for. Anthoxantum puelli yielded well and will be obtainable in good qualities at last year's prices.

Avena elatior (tall oat grass) is reported from France to have suffered in some districts by continual drought, a good medium crop seems, however, to be expected all the same. Some of the samples submitted so far show very fine qualities, for which prices have opened somewhat higher than last season. Of Austrian and Silesian seed, which as a rule is inferior to the French produce, offers are also at hand; these districts are complaining of small yields.

Regarding Avena flavescens (yellowish oat grass, true), nothing definite can be said before next month. Bromus mollis (brome) has likely given a good result again, but Bromus inermis (awnless bromegrass) has apparently suffered by unfavorable weather. Anything reliable cannot be said, however, before next month; the same is the case with Bromus pratensis (meadow brome).

Cynosurus cristatus (crested dogstail) promises a satisfactory crop. Some centers of production give reports already on the probable result, but it all depends upon the weather yet during the next fortnight how the crop, especially as to quality, will turn out.

Dactylis glomerata (cocksfoot). New Zealand no doubt has had as to quantity a good result; qualities, although of heavy bushelweight do not show, however, or seldom only, the bright color of this produce to which we are accustomed.

Reports of an excellent crop in America have weakened the prices for New Zealand seed. Samples received so far from America show a fine color, but are poorly dressed and contain a good deal of shelled grains. The larger part of the American crop is reported by American shippers to be unsuitable for export, and really fine, well cleaned qualities will apparently not be offered. New Zealand produce, therefore, seems to be preferable to American seed. The German cocksfoot, which has had a good result too, shows very seldom a really pure sample, most of the lots contain sorrel and other weeds, also much ryegrass, which to take out, causes a good deal of work, and makes the seed too dear. Farmers got pretty high prices all the same, and it remains to be seen if the trade will take up the seed at the respective figures. The crop in Austria is reported well, France is said to have a small yield on account of drought, and Scandinavia speaks about a good crop concerning quality.

Festuca ovina and Festuca duriuscula (sheeps and hard fescue). Owing to the low prices the acreage of these two varieties has been considerably reduced. On the whole the crop turned out pretty well, but the quality is not always as it should be, so that for nice pure lots free from weeds, higher prices are allowed. Many lots are of light weight and contain a good deal of sorrel and other weeds, which causes that the loss in cleaning is rather large and prices for fancy seeds must consequently be higher in proportion.

Festuca ovina angustifolia (fine leaved fescue) no doubt yielded a medium crop as to quantity, but the qualities differ greatly. Good heavy seed is in brisk demand and will maintain its price. Festuca heterophylla (various leaved fescue) and Festuca rubra (red fescue), of genuine German growth, are harvested only in smallest quantities. Qualities are fair, and prices will be about same as last year. New Zealand produce is quoted at very high figures, and a perfect failure is reported.

Festuca pratensis (meadow fescue). Owing to a reduced acreage and to dry, cold weather the crop is said to be 60 per cent. smaller than last year. The purchasing of new seed will have its difficulties, as large stocks of old seed, some of them with a poor growth, are left over in America. Prices for new seed are not fixed yet.

Phleum pratense (timothy). Speculators have early in the season already made the prices rise, pretending a short crop on account of a reduced acreage and enormous drought; we shall see, if this was entitled. In Germany it looks as if the result is going to be a good one, and in such case, and if the prices are not too high, no doubt German seed will be preferred to American.

Poa memoralis (wood meadow grass). A medium crop; qualities turn out very different, so that good heavy seed is not obtainable much below last year's prices. Under such circumstances the purchasing is rather difficult, and it is probable that this favorite grass, cleaned up to the different grades, cannot be sold below last year's prices.

Of Poa pratensis (red top) this year's crop in America is late, and anything positive not known yet, although I am in constant cable communication with the most reliable and leading exporters. According to their reports the yield is about the same as last year. Prices will open higher than 1905, and it remains to be seen, if the American shippers will be able to maintain them, or if the ring, which dictated the prices already last year will break.

Poa trivialis (rough stalked meadow grass) has given in the north a good yield, both as to quality and quantity, and prices for this valued grass will not be higher than last year.

Agricultural Seeds and Clover.—Trifolium pratense (red clover). Reports on the European crop are conflicting, but in face of the fact that stocks are perfectly cleared out, very low prices cannot be expected, even if the crops will turn out satisfactory. Trifolium repens (white clover) a good yield as to quantity, but the quality could often be better. Market is very quiet owing to buyers holding back, and prices will rule lower yet than last year.

Trifolium hybridum (alsike) has done well both in America and in the European centers of production, and is quoted cheaper than last year. Qualities are good. Trifolium incarnatum (crimson clover). Both France and the Austrian and German districts had a large yield, so that the high opening prices could not be maintained, but had to be reduced before any important transactions were concluded. French grown seed was generally preferred, because it was not materially dearer, but much better than Austrian seed.

Lotus villosus and corniculatus (small and coarse grained bird's foot trefoil) a medium crop.

Medicago impulina (trefoil) a good result, and prices lower than last year.

Medicago sativa (lucerne) promises well in Italy, but it is said to have suffered in France considerably from drought, so that the Provence will only have a weak, medium crop. Nothing can be said as yet about quality.

Anthyllis vulneraria (kidney vetch) is offered already in quantities from Austria. No information can be had yet from France.

Hedysarum onobrychis (sainfoin) was saved under very unfavorable conditions; samples received so far show a dark color. An average yield is expected. Prospects for Hedysarum bifera (sainfoin, 2 cuts) are reported from France to be rather bad; considerable drought has damaged the plant's growth.—CONRAD APPEL, in The Horticultural Advertiser.

CATALOGUES RECEIVED.

WOOD BROTHERS, Fishkill, N. Y.—Trade List of Plants and Rooted Cuttings.

SIEGEL COOPER COMPANY, New York.—Catalogue of Bulbs, Roots and Plants.

AMOS PERRY, Winchmore Hill, London, England.—New Catalogue of Bulbs and Tubers.

A. T. BODDINGTON, New York.—Illustrated Catalogue of Quality Bulbs, Seeds, and Plants.

MOHICAN PEONY GARDENS, (Wm. W. Kline), Sinking Springs, Pa.—Descriptive List of Peonies.

HENRY A. DREER, Philadelphia. Autumn Catalogue of Bulbs, Seeds, Plants, etc. Illustrated.

GILES COUNTY NURSERY COMPANY, Pulaski, Tenn.—Price List of Fruit and Ornamental Trees.

JOHN LEWIS CHILDS, Floral Park, N. Y.—Trade Price List of Gladioli, Lilies, Iris and other Bulbs and Plants.

HENRY F. MICHELL COMPANY, Philadelphia, Pa.—Catalogues of Bulbs, Flower Seeds, Plants, Supplies, etc. Illustrated.

T. R. WATSON, Plymouth, Mass.—Trade List of Deciduous Trees and Shrubs, Roses, Vines, Climbers, Fruit Trees, etc.

CHICKASAW NURSERY AND SEED COMPANY, Duncan, Okla.—Price List of Fruit and Shade Trees, Grapes, Roses, etc.

BOBBINK & ATKINS, Rutherford, N. J.—Catalogue of Bulbs, Peonies, Evergreens, Flowering Shrubs, etc. Profusely Illustrated.

W. W. RAWSON & COMPANY, Union street, Boston, Mass.—Illustrated Catalogue of Bulbs for Fall Planting, Hardy Perennials, Roses, etc.

STUMPP & WALTER COMPANY, New York.—Catalogue of Strawberry, Celery, Cauliflower, and Cabbage Plants, Implements, Insecticides, etc.

WM. ELLIOTT & SONS, New York.—Catalogue of Bulbs, Plants, Seeds, and Sundries, with an attractive caver design of Daffodils in color. Illustrated.

SHATEMUC NURSERIES, Barrytown' N. Y.—Illustrated Catalogue of Plants for the Garden Border; also, list of Native Perennials for the Wild Garden.

STUMPP & WALTER COMPANY, New York.—Fall Catalogue of Bulbs, Plants, Seeds, Fertilizers, etc. Illustrated, with a Handsome front cover Lily Design.

P. J. BERCKMANS COMPANY, Augusta, Ga.—Illustrated Catalogue of Fruit Trees, Small Fruits, Ornamental Shrubs, Roses, etc. This is the Semi-Centennial anniversary of this well-known Southern firm.

PETER HENDERSON & COMPANY, New York.—Catalogue of Bulbs, Plants, Shrubs, Vegetables, Etc.; profusely illustrated, and containing colored plates of Tulips and Daffodils. Also catalogue of Agricultural Seeds for Fall sowing.

GOOSSENS & HELLEMONS, Oudenbosch, Holland.—Catalogue of Hardy Ornamental and Forest Trees, Evergreens, Shrubs, and other Nursery Stock. August Rölker & Sons, New York are the American agents of this firm.

NURSERY DEPARTMENT.

Conducted by Joseph Meehan.

AMERICAN ASSOCIATION OF NURSERYMEN, Orlando Harrison, Berlin, Md., president; J. W. Hill, Des Moines, Ia., vice-president; George C. Seager, Rochester, N. Y., secretary; C. L. Yates, Rochester, N. Y., treasurer.

The total value of the nursery stock imported into the United States for the year ending June 30, 1906, was $1,600,683 as against $1,512,566 in 1905.

ROCHESTER, N. Y.—Ellwanger & Barry were awarded 72 first prizes for their fruit exhibit at the New York State fair recently held in Syracuse. They also received fifty other prizes, making a grand total of 122 for the season of 1906.

TRADE WITH NONCONTIGUOUS POSSESSIONS.—During the year ending June 30, 1905, the value of nursery stock exported to our noncontiguous possessions was as follows: Alaska, $264; Hawaii, $1,931; Porto Rico, $1,387; Philippine Islands, $89; Tutuila, $8. The values of our imports were: From Hawaii, $78; Philippine Islands, $2,044.

EXPORTS OF NURSERY STOCK.—The subjoined statement shows the comparative value of the nursery stock exported from the United States, and the principal countries to which the goods were sent, during the years ending June 30, 1903, 1904 and 1905:

	1903.	1904.	1905.
Canada	$51,890	$71,062	$69,143
Cuba	24,651	36,653	62,881
Germany	14,074	9,060	14,700
Mexico	8,960	15,573	19,771
Netherlands	19,812	12,576	10,697
United Kingdom	28,372	120,730	23,930
Other countries	11,200	22,226	18,101
Total	$158,959	$287,880	$219,223

AMERICAN ASSOCIATION OF NURSERYMEN.—President Orlando Harrison has appointed the following committees:

Executive Committee—E. Albertson, Bridgeport, Ind.; J. H. Dayton, Painesville, Ohio; F. H. Stannard, Ottawa, Kan.

Committee on Transportation—W. C. Reed, Vincennes, Ind.; James McHutchinson, New York; J. C. Miller, Rome, Ga.; Howard Davis, Baltimore; E. S. Welch, Shenandoah, Iowa.

Committee on Tariff—J. C. Hale, Winchester, Tenn.; E. Runyon, Elizabeth, N. J.; William H. Moon, Morrisville, Pa.; J. H. Skinner, Topeka, Kan.; Fred Green, Ferry, Ohio.

Committee on Ways and Means—J. W. Hill, Des Moines, Iowa; Thomas B. Meehan, Dreshertown, Pa.; J. H. Dayton, Painesville, Ohio; F. H. Stannard, Ottawa, Kan.; J. Horace McFarland, Harrisburg, Pa.

Committee on Legislation—R. C. Berckmans, Augusta, Ga.; William Pitkin, Rochester, N. Y.; Hon. N. W. Hale, Knoxville, Tenn.; Peter Youngers, Geneva, Neb.; W. T. Hood, Richmond, Va.; Prof. John Craig, Ithaca, N. Y.; J. W. Hill, Des Moines, Iowa.

Special Committee on Uniform Inspection—R. C. Berckmans, Augusta, Ga.; Peter Youngers, Geneva, Neb.; Prof. John Craig, Ithaca, N. Y.

Committee on Program—Judge Eugene Stark, Louisiana, Mo.; Charles J. Brown, Rochester, N. Y.; Herbert Chase, Huntsville, Ala.

Committee on Publicity—J. M. Irvine, St. Joseph, Mo.; John C. Chase, Derry, N. H.; H. D. Simpson, Vincennes, Ind.

Committee on Exhibits—Thomas Meehan, Dreshertown, Pa.; H. P. Kelsey, Boston, Mass.; E. P. Bernardin, Parsons, Kan.; J. Woodward Manning, Reading, Mass.; Henry Chase, Huntsville, Ala.

National Council of Horticulture—Charles J. Maloy, Rochester, N. Y.; Charles T. Smith, Concord, Ga.

Committee on Arrangements—Charles Ilgenfritz, Monroe, Mich.; Charles Greening, Monroe, Mich.; Geo. S. Josselyn, Fredonia, N. Y.; Nelson Bogue, Batavia, N. Y.; John Morey, Dansville, N. Y.

Committee on Editing Reports—J. Horace McFarland, Harrisburg, Pa.; O. G. Chase, Geneva, N. Y.; George C. Seager, Rochester, N. Y.

Cedrela Sinensis.

Editor Nursery Department:

Allow me to give James King and other nurserymen in or near Chicago the advice not to invest in Cedrela sinensis. There is a specimen of that tree in Humboldt park, Chicago, which was planted there five to six years ago, and which has regularly frozen to the ground every Winter.

J. P. PEDERSEN.

[Our thanks are due to Mr. Pedersen for his information. Can he tell us how the ailanthus behaves in similar situations? J. M.]

Horticultural Notes.

Aster novæ angliæ and its variety, rosea are among the handsomest of the many beautiful asters we have. During September they are particularly handsome. These are native sorts, as are nearly all the kinds that are hardy.

Those who tried Scalecide on their fruit trees for the killing of San Jose scale report better success than with the lime-sulphur wash. In the writer's garden a peach tree badly injured by scale was made entirely free by its use. Not a scale was left alive.

The everlasting rains of the Summer and Autumn have given way to several weeks of hot, dry weather. If evergreens are moved now they must have drenchings of water for a few days after. Cool days will soon be along, and then with warm soil roots form quickly.

Professor Massey states that he once measured the trunk of a crape myrtle at the old Johnson place, Edenton, N. C., which girthed eight feet at two feet from the ground. The white flowered one, he adds, never makes the large size the others do, being merely a large shrub at best.

Golden leaved California privet is deemed hard to keep in its golden habit, because of the green shoots it will make. If these green shoots are persistently cut away as soon as they form there is no trouble in keeping the shrub to its desired character; and it is highly ornamental.

Objection to Golden Glow Rudbeckia is sometimes made because of the top heaviness of the flower heads. The double helianthus, multiflorus plenus,

Abies (Tsuga) Williamsoni

is free from this objection but it blooms later in the season than Golden Glow. It is a good thing, though.

Pinus resinosa, our red pine, is one of the handsomest trees in cultivation, and far too rare at the present time. It is of heavy growth, like the Austrian pine, but unlike it its needles are soft and drooping; a great recommendation.

Cephalotaxus is not a yew, though sometimes called Japanese yew, and it approaches the yew in appearance and relationship. It forms a small tree of spreading habit, and one very much admired when in vigorous growth. It is an evergreen that sells well.

Preservation of Acorns.

There is such a demand springing up for oaks that nurserymen are now exerting themselves to keep on hand a stock of good varieties, for whatever they raise is fairly sure to sell. In addition to the common species, such as the black, red, scarlet, pin and white sorts every one knows because found in most all woods, there are others in many ways just as valuable as those named. Take the chestnut oak, the Spanish, so called, the black jack, post, burr and others; the only reason why they are not common in collections is because nurserymen are not able to supply them. They should be able to do so, for the acorns can be supplied if asked for. Considering the great variety of oaks native to our country, coming generations will wonder why more use had not been made of them in plantings.

It will be but a few months now before acorns ripen. The white and the chestnut ripen toward the close of September; others of the North in October and November. The white and the chestnut start to grow as soon as they fall from the trees and reach moisture. For this season they are best treated when sown at once, but it is possible to keep them until Spring. If entirely free from moisture absorbed from the soil, pack them away, mixed with quite dry soil in a tight box, nailing the cover tight. Placed then in a cool situation they will be in good condition when Spring arrives. If to be shipped to a distant customer it would doubtless be just as good if they were packed in fine sawdust. The whole object is to keep the acorns in a dormant state, which will be accomplished if they neither gain nor lose moisture. They need packing as near air tight as possible, then they will be in condition for sowing when Spring comes.

Magnolia Seedlings.

Many a one fails to secure a stand of magnolia seedlings because of neglecting to properly prepare the seed. This is the season to secure the seed. It requires gathering as soon as ripe, a condition shown by the parting of the pods, displaying the seeds. To have success, no drying of the seeds must be permitted. As soon as freed of pulp, which can be accomplished by washing the seeds, they need mixing with soil or sand at once. A good way to get the pulp in a state to part readily from the seed is to first of all place them in sifted sand, well mixed, so that mould will not run through the mass. Allowed to remain in this state for a week or two the pulp will be so decayed that it will pass away readily when washed. After this the clean seeds should be placed again in sifted soil or sand, slightly moist, and put in some cool place until sown.

Outdoors the seeds can be sown either in Fall or Spring. Sown in Fall, the beds should be covered with forest leaves as soon as the seeds are sown, the leaves kept on with twigs of trees or anything else that suggests itself. The same covering does as well when Spring sowing is adopted.

When seeds are but few they are easily raised in a greenhouse. Prepare them in the same way, and when February, or even January arrives sow them in boxes. Cover the boxes with glass, with paper over it, until the seedlings appear, when both should be removed. The seedlings should be potted as soon as they are well above ground, and are just as well grown indoors the first Summer, as taller plants result than when they grow outside.

The secret of success is to sow the seeds of magnolias before they become dry, or in plainer words, never permit the seeds to become dry.

Those who procure and sell these seeds find they keep fresh longer when preserved with pulp on, but those who sow them should see that they are freed of pulp before going into the ground.

Abies (Tsuga) Williamsoni.

There are many more of our Pacific Coast evergreens that would flourish here than is supposed, were a little care taken in starting them. The illustration herewith is of the California hemlock, Abies Williamsoni, which stands unprotected in the vicinity of Philadelphia. It is the same with the Lawson express, the Thujopsis borealis and many pines. More of them could be grown here than is believed.

The Abies Williamsoni is called the California hemlock because of some resemblance to our common one, canadensis. There is, it is true, some resemblance to our hemlock, more to it than to any other one evergreen, and yet it is distinct. It is more pyramidal for one thing; its twigs and foliage are less pliable and growth shorter jointed. It is described as being found in the Sierra Nevada mountains, where it makes a tree over 100 feet high, while its trunk is but 2 to 3 feet through. It is frequently called A. Pattoniana, in fact, this name is thought to have claim to being the correct one.

The tree illustrated is on the southern slope of a hill, where all the northern winds are kept from it; and not far away from it is a creek of considerable width, both of which are in favor of trees in the Winter season.

Trees of doubtful hardiness are best set where there is no encouragement to late growth. To have wood well ripened is a great help toward wintering well. Soil not over deep and well drained is the best for this. Then if the planting can be where the cold wind is broken, it is another great help. There is still another thing—to keep the sun off in Winter. The tree photographed has all these advantages. Although on the slope of the hill, the hill is a long one. The fall is rapid and there is ample hill behind it to protect from wind; a long slope below it to give drainage; a wood in its rear to still further protect it, and as its face is rather southeast than south, the sun does not strike but a few hours in the morning in Winter time.

In addition to the common names mentioned as belonging to this tree it also claims alpine hemlock and weeping hemlock, as well as Williamson spruce. This spruce, as well as Mertensiana, bears a general resemblance to our common hemlock, although quite distinct. Locality often changes general character, as is shown in the case of the common northern hemlock and the one from the North Carolina mountains. Although both practically the same, close observers can separate one from the other.

JOSEPH MEEHAN.

700
Hardy Herbaceous Perennials

Strong, field grown clumps in over 700 varieties. Catalogue for the asking.

HIRAM T. JONES,
Union County Nurseries, Elizabeth, N. J.

Mention the Florists' Exchange when writing.

CALIFORNIA PRIVET

Fine well-graded, two year plants, well packed as follows: 15 to 20 inches, 3 or more branches, $1.50 per 100; $8.00 per 1000, this grade gives good satisfaction.

20 to 30 inches, 5 or more branches, $2.00 per 100; $12.50 per 1000, nice.

2½ to 3 ft., 7 or more branches, $3.00 per 100; $17.50 per 1000, very strong.

3 to 4 ft., strong selected, $4.00 per 100; $25.00 per 1000

CHAS. BLACK - Hightstown, N. J.

Mention The Florists' Exchange when writing.

HERBACEOUS PERENNIALS

for Summer and Autumn Planting. We offer NINE HUNDRED and SIXTY-SEVEN VARIETIES of STRONG FIELD-GROWN PLANTS. Send for Catalog and Trade List.

BAY STATE NURSERIES, NORTH ABINGTON, MASS.

Mention the Florists' Exchange when writing.

F. & F. NURSERIES

SPRINGFIELD NEW JERSEY

Wholesale Growers — TREES AND PLANTS in full assortment. — Trade Catalogue Free

Mention The Florists' Exchange when writing.

AMERICAN **TREE SEEDS** AND PLANTS

Our Descriptive Catalogue of American Seeds and Plants is ready for mailing. Ask for it.

OTTO KATZENSTEIN & CO.
Tree Seeds and Plants Specialists, ATLANTA, GA

Mention The Florists' Exchange when writing.

THE SHREWSBURY NURSERIES
EATONTOWN, N. J.

Offer a good line of well-grown NURSERY STOCK, Large, well developed Shrubs a specialty. SEND FOR WHOLESALE LIST

Mention The Florists' Exchange when writing.

HYDRANGEAS for FORCING

Otaksa and Thos. Hogg, with 7 to 12 Flowering Crowns, $12.00 per 100; with 5 to 6 Flowering Clowns, $9.00 per 100; with 4 Flowering Crowns, $7.00 per 100.

Japonica Rosea, (new), with 7 to 12 Flowering Crowns, $20.00 per 100; with 5 to 6 Flowering Crowns, $13.00 per 100; with 4 Flowering Crowns, $10.00 per 100.

We especially recommend the new Japonica Rosea; color, fine, rich pink, about the shade of Gloire de Lorraine Begonia; coloring is even, and does not show the white or washed-out shadings sometimes seen in Otaksa; foliage, uniform deep green, and does not streak nor yellow. Has taken medals in Europe and is a distinct acquisition.

Our plants are grown **outdoors** in beds and slat-houses; will be taken inside before frost and available for delivery next month, when wanted.

ROSES, field-grown, well-rooted, **especially suited for Forcing.** Write for prices. Full line of Ornamentals, Shrubs, Shades, Vines, etc.

JACKSON & PERKINS CO.
WHOLESALE NURSERYMEN AND FLORISTS
NEWARK, WAYNE CO., NEW YORK

Mention The Florists' Exchange when writing.

To Clear the Land We Shall Sell For the Next 60 Days

	Per 1000
Berberis Thunbergii, 18 to 24 in., bushy plants	$40.00
Berberis Thunbergii, 24 to 30 in., bushy plants	50.00
Rosa Lucida, 3 years, twice transplanted, fine	40.00
Viburnum Dentatum, 24 to 30 in.	40.00
" " 30 to 36 in.	50.00

We also have some Viburnum cassinoides and Prunus maritima.

Littlefield & Wyman
North Abington, Mass.

Mention The Florists' Exchange when writing.

P. OUWERKERK
216 Jane Street
WEEHAWKEN HEIGHTS, N. J.
P. O. No. 1, Hoboken, N. J.

JUST RECEIVED FROM OUR HOLLAND NURSERIES

Rhododendrons, Azaleas, Spiræa Japonica, Lilium Speciosum, Peonies, Bleeding Heart, Pot-Grown Lilacs, Hydrangea in sorts, Clematis and H. P. Roses in the best sorts.

PRICES MODERATE

Mention The Florists' Exchange when writing.

MUSHROOMS

From Tissue Culture, Pure Spawn

Last winter I sold over $200 worth of mushrooms from under benches of greenhouse, 14 ft. by 42 ft. My mushrooms sold for 20c. per pound more than my neighbors, who raised from other spawn. Try some of it and see for yourself. Three varieties on hand. Buy at home and save time and expense. Send for book free for the asking.

Pure Dried Sheep Manure in large or small lots at the lowest price.

2000 Geraniums, mostly red, in 4 in. pots. left over, $4.00 per 100.

F. A. BOLLES
CONEY ISLAND AV. & AV. L.
BROOKLYN, N. Y.

Mention The Florists' Exchange when writing.

Trees and Shrubs

We make specially low prices on nursery stock to **Parks, Cemeteries**, etc.

Wholesale price list on application.

We carry immense quantities of the finest named varieties of peonies.

PETERSON NURSERY
505 W. PETERSON AVE., CHICAGO, ILL

Mention The Florists' Exchange when writing.

CANNAS

250,000 roots for Fall delivery in 100 leading kinds, $8.00 to $20.00 per 1000. Write for our list. Send in your orders early.

SHELLROAD GREENHOUSES
Largest Canna Growers — Grange, Baltimore, Md.

Mention The Florists' Exchange when writing.

THE AMERICAN CARNATION
Price $3.50. Send for Sample Pages
A. T. DELAMARE PTG. & PUB. CO., Ltd. 2-8 DUANE STREET, NEW YORK

Large Assortment **PEONIES** Very best Varieties

LOW PRICES
THE KIND THAT FLORISTS LIKE

"We make a specialty of growing stocky transplanted shrubbery and trees"

FULL ASSORTMENT OF Ornamentals, Fruits, Roses, Clematis, and Herbaceous Plants. Write for our fall wholesale trade list.

W. & T. SMITH CO., GENEVA, N. Y.

Mention The Florists' Exchange when writing.

Viburnum Plicatum Japan Snowball

18 to 24 in.	$10.00 per 100
2 to 2½ ft.	12.00 "
2½ to 3 ft.	15.00 "
3 to 4 ft.	20.00 "
4 to 5 ft.	25.00 "

DOUBLE ALTHEAS

Jeanne D'Arc, pure white flowers fine for cutting. Banner—White striped crimson. Red—Rich ruby red flowered.

	per 100
Bushy Plants 18 to 24 in.	$6.00
2 to 2½ ft.	7.00
2½ to 3 ft.	8.00
3 to 4 ft.	10.00

BERBERRY THUNBERGII, Splendid for Hedges

Our plants are prown from Cuttings and are very bushy.

	per 100	per 1000
12 to 18 in.	$5.00	$45.00
18 to 24 in.	7.00	60.00
2 ft. to 2½ ft.	10.00	95.00

HYDRANGEA PAN. GRAND.
2 to 3 ft. $7.00 per 100, $60.00 per 1000

DEUTZIA LEMOINEI, Fine for Forcing
2 to 2½ ft. $7.00 per 100

DEUTZIA GRACILIS, 12 to 18 in. 4.50 "

SPIRAEA VAN HOUTTEI

		per 100	per 1000
" "	3 ft.	$6.00	$45.00
" "	3 to 4 ft.	8.00	60.00
" Blue, caryopteris	15 to 20 in.	5.00	45.00
" "	2 to 2½ ft.	7.00	65.00
" A. Waterer	12 to 18 in.	5.50	50.00
" "	2 to 2½ ft.	8.00	75.00
" "	2½ to 3 ft.	9.00	85.00

HONEYSUCKLE HECKROTTII, 1 year $6.00 per 100, 2 years, $10.00 per 100.

PLATYCODON LEICHTLINII, Dwarf, Bushy and very free flowering, 2 years, $8.50 per 100.

THE CONARD & JONES CO.
WEST GROVE, PA.

SEND TO
THE MOON COMPANY
For Your { TREES, SHRUBS, VINES and SMALL FRUITS
Descriptive Illustrated Catalogue Free
THE WM. H. MOON CO.
Morrisville, Pa.

Mention the Florists' Exchange when writing.

Holland Nursery Stock

Ask for Our Catalogue. It will interest you.

ENDTZ, VAN NES & CO. BOSKOOP, HOLLAND

Mention The Florists' Exchange when writing.

KOSTER & CO.
Hollandia Nurseries BOSKOOP, HOLLAND

Hardy Azaleas, Box Trees, Clematis, Conifers, Hydrangeas, Peonies.
Pot-Grown Plants for Forcing.
RHODODENDRONS, H. P. ROSES, Etc.
Catalogue free on demand.

Mention The Florists' Exchange when writing.

H. DEN OUDEN & SON,
BOSKOOP, HOLLAND.

Wholesale growers of nursery stock for the American trade. Catalogue free on demand. Also views in our nurseries.

Mention The Florists' Exchange when writing.

PEONIES
$6.00 to $10.00 per 100
EDWARD SWAYNE
WEST CHESTER, PA.

Mention the Florists' Exchange when writing.

LARGE TREES
OAKS AND MAPLES
PINES AND HEMLOCKS
ANDORRA NURSERIES
WM. WARNER HARPER, PROPRIETOR
Chestnut Hill, Philadelphia, Pa.

Plants Produced from 100 Dahlia Roots.

(53) How many plants, salable stock ready for delivery June 1, could be produced from 100 dahlia roots?

New York. P. A. T.

—P. A. T. should have stated something about the size of the roots he proposes to use, as a great deal depends on that, and also on the variety, some sorts producing much more prolificly than others. The general calculation is 10 to one, but they will nearly always run ahead of that number. If he has the regulation size of imported root, and gets 5 to one he will be doing well; while, on the other hand, if he has good whole field clumps, he can depend on getting at least 20 good cuttings from most varieties. R. A. VINCENT.

White Marsh, Md.

Easter Lilies in Solid Beds.

(54) Please inform us if it would be profitable to grow Easter lilies in solid beds for cut flowers for the New York wholesale market? About what time should the bulbs be started, and how far apart should they be planted? J. E. C.

Conn.

—It would not be profitable to grow lilies in solid beds for several reasons. The flowers would come in scattering crops; the plants would be difficult to keep free from aphis; and it would be next to impossible to give them the right temperature and moisture conditions, as some of the bulbs would be sure to come into flower much earlier than others. Grow the lilies in pots; then they can be moved from one house to another should conditions arise that the plants need to be either hurried along or retarded.

A BARGAIN FOR YOU IN NICE PLANTS

2000 Achillea, The Pearl $2.00 per 100, 1500 German Iris 8 varieties $2.00 per 100, 5000 Iris Siberica Blue and White $1.00 per 100, 1000 Hellanthus Divaricarta, $2.00 per 100, 1000 Heliopsis Pitcheriana, $2.00 per 100, 1000 Digitalis, Foxglove, $2.00 per 100, 600 Crimson Eye, Hibiscus, $3.00 per 100, 400 Peonies, 3-5 eyes asstd. $8.00 per 100, 500 Arundo Donax Grass $6.00 per 100, 300 Funkia Coerulea, $4.00 per 100, 1500 Trumpet Vines, 2-3 ft. tr. 2c., 300 Wistaria Multijuga racemes of blooms 2-3 ft. long, 10c. each. Cash with Order please.

Ellsworth Brown & Co., Seabrook, N. H.

Mention The Florists' Exchange when writing.

COMING EXHIBITIONS.

[Secretaries of other Societies will oblige by forwarding the schedules of their respective shows. Ed. F. E.]

OCTOBER 31 and NOVEMBER 1, 1906, Monmouth County (N. J.) Horticultural Society, ninth annual exhibition, Town Hall, Red Bank, N. J. H. A. Kettel, secretary.

OCTOBER 24 and 25, 1906.—Lenox (Mass.) Horticultural Society, annual chrysanthemum exhibition. G. Foulsham, secretary.

OCTOBER 30, 31 and November 1, 1906.—Tarrytown (N. Y.) Horticultural Society, eighth annual exhibition, Music Hall. E. W. Neubrand, secretary.

NOVEMBER 1 and 2, Morris County (N. J.) Gardeners and Florists' Society, Assembly Rooms, Madison, N. J. E. Reagan, secretary.

NOVEMBER 6-12, 1906. — Chicago Horticultural Society. W. N. Rudd, secretary.

NOVEMBER 6-8, 1906, New Haven County Horticultural Society. Thomas Pettit, 90 Prospect street, New Haven, Conn., secretary.

NOVEMBER 7, 8 and 9, American Institute, New York, annual chrysanthemum show, etc. Berkeley Lyceum Building. Leonard Barron, New York, secretary Horticultural Section.

NOVEMBER 8, 1906.—Worcester County (Mass.) Horticultural Society, annual exhibition of chrysanthemums.

NOVEMBER 9-10, 1906, Rhode Island Horticultural Society, C. W. Smith, 27-29 Exchange street, Providence, R. I., secretary.

ROSES

The past few weeks have been very trying ones for the rose grower; the weather has been anything but seasonable in the vicinity of New York; and prices have necessarily ruled very low. But frost can be expected at any time now, which will cut off the outdoor flowers, and at the same time help improve the quality of the rose product.

Very few growers have started firing as yet, and as long as the temperature of the houses does not drop below 56 degrees with the ventilators open a couple of inches, the plants are much better off. Of course, the foliage must he dry at such times. Where steam is used, the early Fall and late Spring firing is an easy matter; but where hot water only is employed, as is the case on nearly all the smaller establishments, heating is a more difficult problem. Once the fires are started the temperature in the houses should never go below 60 degrees nights at this time of the year. Never close up the ventilators early in the afternoon, with the idea of retaining the sun's heat, and save starting fires early, as this causes heavy condensation, bringing on mildew, black spot, etc. Keep at all times a pure, sweet atmosphere. The flows should be valved so that one or two pipes can be used as required. On these paint a little sulphur; start up a little fire, as soon as the temperature in the houses begins to fall; lower the ventilators gradually, leaving on at least two to four inches of air for the night; and if other conditions are right, mildew, etc., will not trouble you. On large establishments this work is down to a science, and that is why they have apparently no trouble. The plants, if they are to produce good stock next Winter, must be gradually accustomed to artificial heat.

As the days become shorter less water will be required, especially if the plants have just produced a heavy crop, and over watering at this period is dangerous.

Black Spot.

This disease is still quite troublesome and hard to eradicate in the case of some growers. It is caused principally by overwatering, though a check of any kind will bring it on. When the plants have been forced too much during the Summer, they make a rank, soft, sappy growth, which is a great deal more liable to be attacked than the slower and stronger growth. Fortunately, it is not all varieties of roses that are affected by this pest; only those like American Beauty, Richmond, Liberty, etc. This fungus consists of fine threads which feed on the tissues of a leaf, starting at a given point from a spore that has been brought through the air, or in water from a mature spot. It spreads in diverging lines until it gets to be the size of a dime. Each spot contains hundreds of spores, which under the microscope resemble tiny hits of horse hair. To prevent black spot, and prevention is better and easier than cure, pick off all the leaves that come in contact with the soil, and two or three inches above it; keep the atmosphere dry; avoid over watering and too sudden changes of temperature; and once a week spray lightly with the following solution: One quart of ammonia, six ounces of copper carbonate thoroughly dissolved, added to a barrel of water. Bordeaux mixture can also be used, but, best of all, Hammond's copper solution. Go over the benches at least twice a week, and pick off any leaves that may be affected; try not to miss a single spot. This is most important.

In spite of all these precautions, should spot secure a foothold, syringing should be dispensed with entirely for the time being, all spots removed, being careful to pick off only affected leaves, as if too many leaves are removed, the plants are weakened too much. Spray twice a week with the copper solution, and give special care to ventilators, at the same time keep the soil in as even a condition as possible. Avoid having it too wet or too dry; this can only be done by carefully examining the benches every day. The plants should soon recover, and start a clean growth, when more liberal treatment can be accorded them. But it should be borne in mind that houses once affected must be watched very carefully, or the trouble will start afresh in a much aggravated form.

PENN.

LIST OF ADVERTISERS

INDEX TO STOCK ADVERTISED

Contents.

REVIEW OF THE MARKET

NEW YORK.—With the arrival of seasonable Autumn weather the cut flower business is in a rather healthier condition. The demand for certain lines of roses, particularly American Beauty and Bride, has increased very much within the last few days, and prices are quite a little firmer than has been the rule for some time. For pink roses the call is not so good, and prices rule somewhat lower. There is an abundance of the variety Richmond coming in, mostly short-stemmed and inclined to open up singly in the course of a few hours after being received. It seems to be impossible to realize any satisfactory prices on this variety at present.

The supply of chrysanthemums has not increased to any extent yet. A few bunches of the variety Mme. Gastellier constituted the consignments that arrived last Saturday. It is supposed that it will be a matter of ten days or so before regular shipments of such varieties as Polly Rose and Glory of the Pacific are made.

Carnations are beginning to show up in fair quality now, the variety Enchantress seemingly having the best of all other sorts for the present in regard to size of flower and length of stem. The supply of lilies is constant, and 8c. each seems to be the ruling figure for the best of them. There is much comment just now among growers as to this 8c. figure, that seems to be the high mark for these early lilies, and it is a question whether it pays to bother with them at all when they have to be sold at such a price. The flowers are cut from bulbs that have been kept in cold storage, which bulbs only average about two flowers each.

There is a fairly good supply of Cattleya labiata arriving, and prices rule anywhere from 25c. to 40c. each, according to size and grade. There is also a moderate supply of oncidiums coming into the market regularly. Lily of the valley is in fair demand, and prices remain moderately firm. Asters are getting poorer in quality every day, and judging from present conditions, it would not seem that these flowers are to last over so as to come in competition with early chrysanthemums, as has been the case for the past few years. The gladiolus supply is almost over, very few of these flowers now being obtainable. Dahlias are coming in heavier every day, and the variety Countess of Lonsdale, is without a question, still in the lead of all others for cut flower purposes, and sells the readiest.

CHICAGO.—There seems to be little new to offer in the line of market pointers. Every dealer, wholesale and retail says tomorrow or next week it will surely be stronger, and the days go by and the weeks pass on with apparently no variation in conditions. The retailer upon whom the wholesaler depends is looking for the return from abroad, the East, or their Summer homes in neighboring states of the patrons who furnish the oil to keep the machinery running. The grower is looking for a killing frost. Further than this little can be said. There is no change in prices but greenhouse stock is generally improving in quality. W. K. W.

PHILADELPHIA.—American Beauty are reported scarce this week; prices have not gone higher than $3, but there is a stiffer tone. Good carnations are being sought. The demand is not strong, but a few of better quality could be used; $2 per 100 is the best price so far. The best Liberty and Kaiserin Augusta Victoria roses are bringing $8 per 100; for Killarney, $6 is the best price. The general stock of teas brings from $2 to $4.

A few chrysanthemums are around; $4 per dozen is being asked, but the buyers are few as yet. Large quantities of dahlias are now coming in. The stores are buying better and pay $3 and $4 per 100 for some of the fancy cactus and single varieties; but the bulk of the stock goes to the street men at prices best not quoted. Asparagus, bunched, is in good demand at 50c. and 75c. per bunch. Some asters are yet coming in, but the call for them is apparently over. DAVID RUST.

ST. LOUIS.—Business the past week consisted of a few small wedding decorations, an occasional box of flowers, and some funeral work. The opening, on Monday, of the Isenstadt wholesale jewelry firm, in its new quarters in the Star Building, called for a number of large and fine floral designs; Grim & Gorley had the decorations of plants and a number of the designs. Stock is not very plentiful especially in fancy grades of roses and carnations. American Beauty are limited in all grades and show some improvement in quality, size and color. Fancy long bring $4 per dozen; others, 75c. up to $2.50 per dozen. Smaller roses, fancy grades, run from $8; firsts, $4 to $5, seconds $2 and $3 per 100. These also show improvement in length of stem and color. Carnations are in great demand; the price for extra fancy Enchantress is $2 per 100; of course the extra fancy at present are not the fancy that will appear next month. Just a few asters are coming in. Some good lily of the valley may be had; a few chrysanthemums and some extra fine dahlias which bring as high as $5 per 100. All kinds of greens are in plenty. ST. PATRICK.

BOSTON.—Trade is somewhat improved this week Severe rain storms the end of last week destroyed many of the outdoor flowers, such as asters, and a general shortening up and better prices have been the result. Roses are very plentiful with but little demand for the shorter grades which sell very cheaply. American Beauty still have a good demand and some of them of very fine quality are now to be had at $2 to $3 per dozen. Carnations are improving daily, selling generally at $1 and $2. Asters of good quality bring $1 per 100 although the most that come in are cheaper grades. Lilies bring $10 and $12; lily of the valley sells well at from $3 to $5. Gladiolus realize $4 to $6; tuberoses $3 and $4. Violets are coming in in moderate quantities, selling at 50c. Smilax and other green goods have a steady demand, and there is an exceptionally fine grade on the market at the present time. J. W. D.

COLUMBUS, O.—The Summer is surely behind us, and trade at last has taken on signs of briskness that is very pleasing to the craft, and betokens a fine season ahead. Every year the demand for flowers is increasing in Columbus, and the present one has so far shown a most gratifying increase in this regard. As to stock, it has gradually been getting much better in quality the past few weeks which is a great relief to all, as certainly during the past Summer some pretty hard lots have been forced upon us. As always roses are in good demand, American Beauty bring $1.50 to $5 a dozen; Bride, Kaiserin Augusta Victoria and Bridesmaid, from $1 to $2 according to quality. Carnations hold at 50c., with a few fine Enchantress at 75c. a dozen. Asters still hold on, but it is about the last of them; at times asters have been such a glut that good ones have gone begging at 5c. a dozen, the normal rate has been 25c. to 35c a dozen. Gladiolus go at 50c. to 75c., and lily of the valley 75c. to $1 the dozen.

Plant Notes.

VINCAS. — Although vincas are very easily grown the poor quality of some offered for sale would indicate that little attention is given them, much less in fact, than the increasing demand for good strong plants warrants. Good growers of vincas have the young plants all Summer planted out in open frames where the soil is very rich. Grown in this way the plants during the season make a growth two feet long, occasionally exceeding that. These plants should be left in the frames as long as possible; when it begins to get too cold for them to be uncovered sashes should be placed over them and the frames closed at night, admitting air freely during the day. When it becomes necessary to remove the plants to a greenhouse, instead of mutilating the roots in order to get them into small pots they should be potted into 4-inch pots at once. In that size of pot if they are carefully watered all through the Winter and occasionally given some manure water, they will not only subsist but will increase their growth to three feet, and then the grower has plants that will sell quickly at from 15c. to 25c. each.

LILIUM PHILIPPINENSE.—A lily that can be forced into bloom in nine weeks, as is said of Lilium philippinense, is surely worthy of notice. I saw exhibited a vase of these lilies a little over a year ago, when an award of a silver medal was made to the exhibitor. As the award would indicate, the blooms, with their peculiar foliage, made a very favorable impression on those present. Again this year I came across a batch of this lily, grown evidently under different conditions from those under which the silver medal flowers were grown. The flowers I saw this year were quite satisfactory, but the foliage (all there was of it) was poor and limp, which gave me the impression that unless well furnished with foliage it is not much of a pot plant. But when this lily is well grown and used in considerable numbers for decorative purposes in the cut state, it produces an effect altogether unlike that produced by another lily. The foliage is long and narrow and of a character suited to florists' ideas of gracefulness in making up. The rapidity of growth of this lily will commend it to many.

CINERARIAS although easil[y] grown are also easily ruined; th[e] least neglect of their simple requirements often works injury that cann[ot] be remedied no matter how caref[ul] the treatment afterwards may b[e]. Cinerarias should not be allowed [to] get pot-bound until they are in the[ir] flowering pots. They require ve[ry] careful watering at all stages of the[ir] growth. They like a cool temper[a]ture, but in a week or two it will [be] the safer plan to bring the plants i[n]to a greenhouse than to leave the[m] in frames where they would be liab[le] to injury by dampness. Greenfly a[t]tacks cinerarias persistently, and [in] order to combat it the house shou[ld] be frequently fumigated.

PRIMULAS right through requi[re] much the same treatment as ciner[ar]ias except perhaps, that the form[er] do not stand strong sunlight as w[ell] as the latter; for that reason it [is] advisable to protect them with [a] movable shading until they get har[d]ened. Primulas and cinerarias [last] much longer in bloom when kept co[ol]. When the plants are shifted in[to] their flowering pots, in addition [to] good loam, leaf mold and sand, a [lib]eral portion of well rotted cow m[an]ure should be added to the pott[ing] compost.

ANTHURIUMS.—There are many kinds of plants but little grown by florists that nevertheless would be found very useful to them if they once got into the way of growing them. Among these I may mention anthuriums, the flowers of which are eagerly picked up when they come under the eyes of wide awake decorators. Beginners with anthuriums should at first procure established plants rather than attempt their propagation from either suckers or seed; although there is usually little difficulty experienced in propagating them if a high enough temperature is available. At all stages in the growth of anthuriums they thrive best in a rather high temperature and a humid atmosphere. They are usually potted in a compost of fibrous peat, broken crocks and charcoal; and in potting the material should be heaped above the rim of the pot with a layer of sphagnum moss. Good drainage is an absolute necessity in their cultivation. When anthuriums are intended to be grown exclusively for their flowers they can be planted in benches in a compost much the same as for pot culture, with the surface of the material raised in the same way and drainage afforded, also in the same proportion.

GLOXINIAS.—Although gloxinias have in the past been grown principally by private gardeners, they are receiving attention from florists and commercial growers because of the uses to which they can be put and the ease with which they can be successfully grown. Gloxinias when used with Adiantum cuneatum or with Adiantum Farleyense are very effective. The foliage of the gloxinias is a little stiff, but the use of either variety of adiantum along with them will eliminate that stiffness entirely. At the season of the year when Gloxinias are in bloom (which by the way can be considerably prolonged), there are few plants equal to them for brightening the greenhouse or the windows of florists' stores. It is always necessary that they be slightly shaded, especially while growing. Gloxinias are propagated from seed, which if sown in January will produce plants in bloom in July or August following. The seeds are very small and require very little covering when sown. When the seed is obtained, before sowing half fill a seed pan with broken crocks and over these place a light covering of sphagnum or pieces of turfy loam, then fill the pan with sifted leaf mold and fine sand, which should be pressed down firmly and the surface made very smooth and perfectly level. Then scatter the seeds evenly over the surface and cover them very lightly with finely sifted leafmold and sand. Water carefully with a fine rose. After watering plunge the pan in the propagating bed and cover it with glass. The seed germinates very quickly, and when very small the seedlings are liable to damp off. To avoid damping the glass should be removed occasionally and kept off for half an hour; and before replacing it it should be wiped with a dry cloth. When the soil in the pan appears dry it ought to be watered by immersing the pan in a tub of water. In doing so the pan should be plunged to within an inch of the top and let down easily so that the force of the water will not disturb the seed in course of germination. When the seedlings are large enough to handle they should be pricked off into pans or pots, and when they show signs of crowding there they should be potted into 3 or 3½ inch pots using a compost much the same as for the seed; but when subsequent potting is being done a portion of good fibrous loam should be added. It will also be beneficial if a little well rotted cow manure is mixed with the whole. Gloxinias like moisture, but the foliage should not be syringed; instead the atmosphere should be kept moist. Shade from the full light of the sun must always be provided, and care exercised in order that the plants never suffer for want of water. After gloxinias have flowered in Winter they should not be allowed to get dust dry; neither should they be exposed to a temperature much below 50 degrees while at rest, otherwise many will perish.

M. I.

(These notes were written for issue of September 22.)

FOUNDED IN 1888

FLORISTS' EXCHANGE

A Weekly Medium of Interchange for Florists, Nurserymen Seedsmen and the Trade in general

Exclusively a Trade Paper.

Entered at New York Post Office as Second Class Matter

Published EVERY SATURDAY by

A. T. DE LA MARE PTG. AND PUB. CO. LTD.

2, 4, 6 and 8 Duane Street,

P. O. Box 1697. Telephone 3765 John. NEW YORK.

CHICAGO OFFICE: 127 East Berwyn Avenue.

ILLUSTRATIONS.

Electrotypes of the illustrations used in this paper can usually be supplied by the publishers. Price on application.

YEARLY SUBSCRIPTIONS.

United States, Canada, and Mexico, $1.00. Foreign countries in postal union, $2.50. Payable in advance. Remit by Express Money Order Draft on New York. Post Office Money Order or Registered Letter.

The address label indicates the date when subscription expires and is our only receipt therefore.

REGISTERED CABLE ADDRESS:

Florex, New York.

ADVERTISING RATES.

One-half inch, 75c.; ¾-inch, $1.00; 1-inch, $1.25, special positions extra. Send for Rate Card showing discount of 10c., 15c., 25c., or 35c., per inch on continuous advertising. For rates on Wants, etc., see column for Classified Advertisements.

Copy must reach this office 12 o'clock Wednesday to secure insertion in issue of following Saturday.

Orders from unknown parties must be accompanied with cash or satisfactory references.

Chrysanthemum Society of America.

President Duckham has announced the committees to examine seedlings and sports on dates as follows: October 6, 13, 20 and 27, November 3, 10, 17 and 24, 1906.

Exhibits to receive attention form the committees must in all cases be prepaid to destination, and the entry fee of $2 should be forwarded to the secretary not later than Tuesday of the week preceding examination, or may accompany the blooms. Special attention is called to the rule requiring that sports, to receive a certificate, must pass three committees.

NEW YORK.—Eugene Dailledouze, chairman, care of New York Cut Flower Company, 55-57 Twenty-sixth street; William Turner, Thomas Head.

PHILADELPHIA, PA.—A. B. Cartledge, chairman, 1514 Chestnut street; John Westcott, Wm. K. Harris. Ship flowers in care of the chairman.

BOSTON, MASS.—E. A. Wood, chairman; Wm. Nicholson, James Wheeler. Ship to Boston Flower Market, care of the chairman.

CINCINNATI, O.—R. Witterstaetter, chairman; James Allen, Wm. Jackson. Ship to Jabez Elliott Flower Market, care of janitor.

CHICAGO, ILL.—J. S. Wilson, chairman; J. B. Deamud and George Wienhoeber. Ship care of J. B. Deamud, 51 Wabash avenue.

The official scales of the C. S. A. are as follows:

For Commercial Purposes		For Exhibition Purposes	
Color	20	Color	10
Form	15	Stem	5
Fullness	10	Foliage	5
Stem	15	Fullness	15
Foliage	15	Form	15
Substance	15	Depth	15
Size	10	Size	35
Total	100	Total	100

DAVID FRASER, Secretary.

Pittsburg, Pa.

American Carnation Society.

Variety Registered.

By Dailledouze Bros., Flatbush, N. Y.

WELCOME, a pink sport of Mrs. T. W. Lawson, the color of a Bridesmaid rose. Identical with its parent excepting in color and calyx, which seldom bursts. Color and habit permanently fixed; now in its fourth year.

N. B. This variety is registered provisionally, and subject to the approval of the judges at the show in Toronto, Can., next January.

ALBERT M. HERR, Secretary.

Express Rates.

Fred'k W. Kelsey, the well-known nurseryman of New York, who has been giving considerable attention to the subject of a parcels post, had the following to say on the express rate question:

"The reference in The Florists' Exchange and other horticultural papers to the attitude of the express companies in not showing any disposition to relieve the nursery, florist trade and other shippers of the apparently excessive and onerous express charges, especially for local service, should attract wide attention, and call for effective action by every man having his own affairs as well as the business of the country at heart.

"While competition is forcing planting material and its products to closer prices, the express companies, now in a position of overbearing monopoly, demand and collect these burdensome and increased charges, with a result, that while the prices of the nurserymen and florists are being forced down, the stocks and securities of the express companies, based on the enormously increased earnings, are advancing by leaps and bounds.

"The recent contest between the management and the minority stockholders of the Wells Fargo Company demanding an increase in the dividend to 12 or 16 per cent., and bringing out in this discussion the fact as to the enormous surplus of millions of dollars already accumulated by the express company over and above the 8 per cent. dividends heretofore paid on a largely inflated or watered capital, indicates the need of action by the public to protect itself from the excessive charges noted.

"The condition was perhaps well described in a statement accredited to John Wanamaker, based upon his practical experience as Postmaster-General, viz: that 'there are four reasons why the demand of the people for postal reform and a proper reduction in the parcel postal rates on third and fourth class mail matter have not been complied with. The first reason is the Adams Express Company; the second reason is the American Express Company; the third reason is the United States Express Company; and the fourth reason is the Wells Fargo Express Company.

"This quotation may not be exact, but it gives in substance the view acredited to former Postmaster-General Wanamaker.

"In the present awakening for better civic and legislative conditions, if every nurseryman and florist would, on the assembling of Congress, see or write a forceful letter to his representative in Congress and to the Senator from his State—and this plan should be generally followed—there would soon be relief, notwithstanding the opposition of the interested corporations."

The Adulteration of Seeds and its Exploitation.

It is quite evident that, in the case of some dealers, the publication by the Department of Agriculture, to the effect that it has been supplied by them with grass seeds containing adulterants, is of little avail as a complete deterrent against the practice of adulteration being continued by these firms, one or more of which have been listed several times by the Department. Probably some penalty, in addition to publication, might have a more salutary effect, and better accomplish the object sought.

There is no question of the great harm being done the seed trade in general by the announcement emanating from the Department that adulterated seeds are being sold by some American seedsmen, for few, if any, of the daily papers publish the names of the offending firms, and because of that fact the whole trade is laid under suspicion on account of the faults of a small minority of those engaged in the business of selling seeds. This condition, in justice to reputable tradesmen, should be put right; and the haling of the offenders before the Government authorities, publicity thereof being fully given, would, we think, have a tendency to show to the buyers of seed throughout the country just who the parties are who are transgressing the Congressional law. The present practice adopted by the Department, of distributing the particulars connected with seed adulteration by means of circulars, the full text of which is seldom or never reproduced in the daily press, although the fact of the adulteration is always generally exploited, is certainly doing more harm than good; and, in addition to failing of its object, apparently, is, as we have said, working irreparable and uncalled for injury on a body of men, whose reputations in general will measure up to those of men engaged in any other industry. A more just and fair method of exploitation is needed, and should be put in operation at once by the Department.

Advance in Prices of Seeds.

In view of the exceedingly short crops of onions and cucumber seed, and a deficiency in the supply of melon seeds, the Board of Directors of the Wholesale Seedsmen's League has issued a circular suggesting the probable values at this date in lots of ten pounds, with a decided possibility of further enhancement. It is announced that the seed supplies of beet, egg plant, spinach, French radish, and carrot are short, and the different varieties of all these will be increased in value to a marked degree.

Obituary

Mrs. Emil C. Metzmaier.

Mrs. Emil C. Metzmaier died Thursday, September 20, at her home, 1382 South Fourth street, Columbus, O. Mrs. Metzmaier had for many years been a great sufferer from rheumatism, although she was confined to her bed only the past six weeks. She is survived by her husband and six children. The deceased was born in Freiburg, Germany, 46 years ago, and came to Columbus with her family in 1884. Mr. Metzmaier is a prominent member of the florist's trade, and one of the charter members of the Columbus Florists' Club. Mrs. Metzmaier was greatly esteemed by all who knew her; and the club sent a beautiful wreath of laurel, bronze galax leaves, and white carnations. The interment was at Greenlawn.

F. W.

Paul R. B. Pierson.

Friends of the trade will be pained to hear of the death of Paul R. B. Pierson, of Tarrytown, N. Y., the respected father of F. R., P. M. and L. B. Pierson. Mr. Pierson was 78 years of age at the time of his death, which occurred on Tuesday, September 25, at his residence, College avenue, Tarrytown; the interment taking place on Friday, the 28th, at 2 p. m.

Mr. Pierson was an expert engraver, and executed some of the finest work for such magazines as Harper's and Scribner's. Later he was associated with the historian Lossing and illustrated that writer's works on the history of New York State. When at last Mr. Pierson's eyesight prohibited him from continuing the engraver's trade, some 20 years ago, he took up the hybridization of cannas, and some of his varieties were introduced to the florist trade by the F. R. Pierson Company, Tarrytown, N. Y.

Mr. Pierson leaves a widow and three daughters besides the three sons above mentioned.

Nephrolepis Exaltata Var. Canaliculata.

This is a recent "sport" introduced by H. B. May which recently received an award of merit from the Floral Committee of the Royal Horticultural Society. It is quite distinct from the numerous other varieties of the species which have originated of late years, the fronds being not merely furcate or cristate, as in previous forms, but they are also symmetrically narrowed. The pinnæ are incurved, bearing somewhat congested and curly multifid tassels, and the frond a much larger, rather corymbiferous one, the whole having a peculiarly neat appearance. The term canaliculata has been applied owing to the frond forming a kind of half tube, or channel, due to the inward curvature of the side divisions; and the fronds narrow at its base. The variety is a noteworthy addition to the many extraordinary sports which have quite suddenly characterized this species in the last few years after decades of cultivation on perfectly constant lines. It has been Mr. May's good fortune to introduce the majority of these as sports originating in his own nursery. The abundance of these varieties occurring within so short a period suggests that Professor De Vries' theory of the occasional occurrence of periods of mutation or sudden change in specific forms is not without foundation.—The Gardeners' Chronicle, London.

Campbell's Sulphur Vaporizer.

Editor Florists' Exchange:

We offer Campbell's Sulphur Vaporizer that Stockton & Howe inquire for on page 346 of last week's issue of The Florists' Exchange.

New York. VAUGHAN'S SEED STORE.

THE MASSACHUSETTS HORTICULTURAL SOCIETY'S annual exhibition of fruits and vegetables will be held at Horticultural Hall, Boston, Wednesday and Thursday, October 10 and 11. Much interest is being shown in this exhibition as it is the first exclusive fruit and vegetable show that has been held for some years, and the committee in charge propose to make it a grand success. The fruit schedule offers 68 classes of from one to five prizes each, amounting to $450, in addition to medals. Besides the prizes for the standard varieties of fruits, two offers are made under the Benjamin H. Pierce fund for a new seedling apple and pear.

For vegetables 39 classes are open with three to five prizes each, aggregating $400. Of special interest in this department will be the decorative displays for which large prizes are offered, there being several of these ranging from $5 up to $50.

All persons interested in fruit and vegetable culture are invited to send their best specimens to this exhibition and to attend themselves. It will be an educational opportunity, and will excite enthusiasm and stimulate interest in these two great departments of the society's work. The admission will be free.

Copies of the schedule of prizes can be had on application to William P. Rich, secretary, Horticultural Hall, Boston.

The Outlook Among Decorative Plants.

For several seasons past a more or less pessimistic state of opinion has prevailed in the minds of many growers of this class of plants, the result being that some of those growers disposed of the stock of palms that they had on hand, and decided to devote their glass to other crops that promised a quicker return.

This state of mind was undoubtedly based upon certain facts, among which was the comparatively long period of time occupied in the development of a crop of palms, and also the low prices at which much of the stock of this character was sold. It may truly be said that first class stock seldom failed to find a market, but yet the margin of profit remained too small to encourage the grower with only limited resources.

Then there has also been the importation of European grown plants to contend with, and although these perishable articles seldom arrive in a condition equal to good home grown plants, yet the appearance of a large quantity of such stock upon the market naturally has a depressing effect upon the home grown article.

Be that as it may, there will be plants imported in greater or less numbers just as long as a market is found for them in this country, and such a market will be found until a sufficient supply for all purposes is produced at home.

But the tide turns in due season, and this year has brought just a tinge of optimism to cheer the hearts and minds of the handlers of decorative plants, and the trade conditions are better and more promising than they have been for several seasons past.

The demand began earlier than usual, much stock being bought in July and early August, and reserved for future shipment, and by the beginning of September the scarcity of certain popular sizes of palms in particular was being felt and buyers who were not in the habit of ordering before September began to meet with some disappointments.

These conditions were not entirely unexpected by observant growers, and consequently the Summer price lists of the wholesalers in most cases showed some advances, though in justice to the growers it should be said that advances were not made all along the line, and that no disposition to hold up or squeeze the trade unfairly has been shown. It is a fair business proposition, however, that the demand should rule the price, consequently a small percentage of profit has been added to the price of some sizes of palms, but not enough to cause any serious loss of sleep among the retail men. The sizes that are in poor supply at the present time are among those that are most popular, for example; kentias in 7 and 8-inch pots, and also strong plants in 6-inch pots; while of the large and extra large sizes that are more used for decorating than for retailing, there may be enough to go around, an over supply of the latter in Europe during the past two years having caused very low prices for these large plants, consequently large exportations to this country.

A scare regarding the kentia seed supply has also had some effect in stiffening the holders of small plants, for the question arose as to whether such a corner of the seed product might not result in monopolistic prices for the necessary seed for next year.

But, in the meantime, it may be said that the seed of this season's crop is of good quality, and we will continue to hope that enough plants will be produced to obviate a serious shortage for a year or two anyway.

As to species and styles among the palms, there does not seem to be any radical changes in the demand of the present season over its predecessors.

In the compound or bush plants of the kentias there is a strong demand for K. Forsteriana, but this is rather a return to first principles than a new streak of thought, for K. Forsteriana was the original made-up kentia and is really better adapted for such a method of culturo than the shorter stemmed and more compact K. Belmoreana, the latter developing its full beauty as a well grown single plant. But well-balanced, made-up K. Belmoreana in 8-inch to 10-inch pots are also ready sellers, though possibly less profitable to the grower than the other variety.

Areca lutescens seems to be in slightly better demand than for a year or two, possibly owing to there being less of this palm grown lately.

Latania borbonica still sells in many portions of this wide country, and good plants in 6 and 8-inch pots find a fair market, the latter size not being over plentiful.

Larger latanias than these are not very profitable to the grower, and are only handled in small quantities.

Phœnix canariensis is still imported by some dealers and used by the large decorators with good effect, but phœnix generally are but little grown in this country, with the exception of California and the South, where they are used to advantage outdoors.

No serious shortage has appeared in Cocos Weddeliana, and so far as one may guess at the present time there will be enough to supply the demand, and at about the usual prices.

Araucarias must be produced at low cost in Europe, judging by the prices at which they are sold here, and there are large numbers of them sold, too, but in the smaller sizes chiefly, there being but little demand for large araucarias.

Dracænas of the fragrans and terminalis types are feeling the influence of prosperity in a reasonably good demand, though with probably little change in prices, there being little call for the ordinary D. fragrans, but more inquiry for its variegated form, D. Massangeana.

Of the making of new ferns there is no end, and we shall soon need a handbook for the sports from the Boston fern, and as each one is the best ever, it keeps the growers busy testing them as they come out. In the meantime, the original Boston fern is still in demand, though frequently sold at too low a price, as witness an offering of 3,000 Bostons at 35c each, plants in 5 or 6-inch pots, by a large department store in Philadelphia this week. This is not the fault of the department store, but rather should be blamed on a weak-kneed or over-loaded grower, who was badly in need of space or money, or both.

Small ferns for ferneries having sold well last season will probably be found in good supply this Winter, and there is no particular change in prices or in species, this having gotten down to a sort of standard, though a rather low one.

To sum up briefly, the prosperity of the plant trade, (and we sincerely hope it will last for the season) is not due to any artificial boom, but rather is partly owing to the general prosperity of business throughout the country, and in part to a slight shortage of stock, and though there may not be millions in it, we trust there may be a living in it for the trade.

W. H. TAPLIN.

Field of Conway & Company's New White Aster.

Craven House, Kingsway, London, England, where branch office of Yokohama Nursery Co., A. Dimmock, agent, is located.

Yokohama Nursery Co.'s London Office

Our illustration, kindly sent us by Alfred Dimmock, London agent of the Yokohama Nursery Company of Japan, shows the Craven House, located on Kingsway, one of the thoroughfares recently opened in the English metropolis. The office of the concern is on the fourth floor, at the left of the picture. The building is but three minutes' walk from the Covent Garden market, and in a letter sending the illustration Mr. Dimmock says:

"I have an opportunity of seeing the stock sold there from time to time. But there are no American Beauty, Bride or Bridesmaid roses. There is greater variety of garden (outdoor) flowers used than is done on your side. The trade in Chrysanthemum frutescens is very large, the flowers being utilized most extensively for table and window box decoration. Thousands of them are sold every morning during July and August.

"I note they are calling Ficus pandurata a new plant in Amreica: What constitutes a 'new plant?' I sold this in America for Sander & Sons some five years ago.

"Very sorry to see that Roger O'Mara has passed away; he was such a genial fellow."

A Tree for the Sea Coast.

Near the sea coast where the soil is sand to a great depth, it is difficult to get trees to thrive, unless of a few species. If started in fresh soil they do better, as it affords food for them until they get a good foothold. One tree at least can be named which does well in such a sandy place—osage orange. The reason for this is, no doubt, that it makes roots that penetrate to a great depth, and then sustain the tree, as there are better conditions met with far down than near the surface. This orange is not unknown as a good shade tree. It is not a tall grower, but makes a rounded head, good for shade, but not for shading tall buildings. It is thorny, we know, but this is not objectionable after it has attained a height above one's reach; and with age the thorns disappear from the older shoots, and could be made to do so at any time.

Conway's New White Aster.

The illustration shows a field of the new white aster, recently referred to in these columns, at the establishment of F. Conway & Company, Indianapolis, Ind. This aster is of unusual size, is of fine form and seldom shows an exposed center. The firm will place the seed on the market next season.

I. B.

AMONG THE GROWERS

The Metairie Ridge Nursery of New Orleans, La.

The Metairie Ridge Nursery Company, Limited, of New Orleans, organized a little over a year ago, with H. Papworth as its president, put up a fine range of greenhouses, with all the latest improvements, shortly after.

It may be considered the best equipped and most up-to-date establishment in the South. The six new greenhouses, the frame of which was furnished by the J. C. Moninger Company of Chicago, are 225 feet in length and 21 feet wide each, built of Louisiana cypress, and the roof is supported by one and two-inch iron pipes.

On the material as furnished by the Moninger Company there was nothing missing, even to a screw, and nothing was left over when the houses were completed; everything fitted nicely in its place, and no saw was used in putting up the framework. The lumber furnished was of the best, free from all defects.

The entire range of new houses, as well as the older ones on the place are heated by steam, for which purpose a 100-horsepower Stirling water tube boiler has been installed. The Stirling has given entire satisfaction and for heating a large range of houses we believe there is nothing like it.

The piping under the benches was done according to plans furnished by the American Engineering Specialty Company of Chicago by Mathis, Celestin & Company, heating engineers of New Orleans.

The Webster vacuum system, which is used in these houses, was found to be the most economical heating system, and a great fuel saver. The main and return pipes are all underground; therefore there is no obstruction in the walks of the houses.

In painting the houses only the best material was used, the Acme brand, furnished by the David Bernhardt Paint Company, gave the most satisfaction. The Bernhardt Company also furnished a large part of the glass.

To insure a plentiful supply of water, a water tower, 40 feet in height, with a tank of 12,500 gallons capacity, has been built, and the water is pumped by means of a six-horse power Fairbanks gasolene engine and pump, direct-connected from the Metairie Bayou, which runs through the place. The gasolene engine and pump have been running now almost a year and a half, day by day, and have during that time never missed, and no breakdown has occurred. The running expenses are next to nothing, 1⅛ cents per hour, and no attention is necessary. This beats electricity all hollow.

Attached to the house is a large potting and packing house, 165 feet in length and 30 feet wide, which communicates with all the houses. The office is situated in that building.

As during the Summer months palms, ferns, etc., are grown out of doors, and as they require some protection against the sun, a palm shed, 75 feet in length and 60 feet wide, has been erected.

The ventilators, on top and on the sides of the houses, are lifted by means of the Evans Challenge ventilating apparatus, which was found to be best and easiest working; others were tried before. This apparatus is made by the Quaker City Machine Company of Richmond, Ind. Considering the length of the house and the ease with which it works, using the new century arm, the apparatus does all and more than is claimed for it.

Metairie Ridge Nursery, New Orleans, La. Side View of New Houses, with Potting Shed and Packing House; Also Part of Small Range of Houses.

The nursery proper consists of 200 acres of the richest alluvial soil, 30 of which are at present under cultivation in palms, roses, shrubbery and shade trees of all kinds suitable for the South.

Noteworthy are several thousands of Areca lutescens, growing in full sun, which are very thrifty and of fine color.

S.

May Flowering Tulips.

I have many times noticed how little the May flowering section of tulips is used by American florists, being hardly ever spoken of in the American trade press. This cannot be because the section is not considered a useful or sufficiently valuable one for cut blooms and decorative work, but rather because it is little known, and its merits have never properly been placed before the American flower buying public, as during the month of May there is nothing so fine for cutting or so useful to make a fine effect for bedding and general border decoration. Probably no class of tulip is so easy to grow; in fact, it is perhaps because of their very simple cultivation and that they will bloom year after year, that greatly helps to make them so popular in Europe.

The Three Sections.

The May flowering varieties may be placed in three distinct sections—Cottage Garden or Species, Darwin, and Parrot tulips.

The first section is the most important commercially, comprising as it does all the varieties which can be bought in large quantities at sufficiently low prices to be profitable to grow for market work, such as Bouton D'Or (Golden Button), which is probably the finest commercial variety grown, the bloom lasting the longest and the bulb growing and increasing vigorously year after year. This section also includes nearly the whole of the useful cutting varieties, when the cost of procuring the bulbs is considered along with the ease with which they can be cultivated and increased afterward. In Lincolnshire and Cambridgeshire also in the Channel Islands these tulips are grown by the acre, especially Bouton D'Or, Macrophylla, Picotee, etc.

In the Darwin section is included probably some of the most lovely Spring flowers ever seen. There are about one hundred distinct named varieties in this section, all more or less distinct. The flowers are of magnificent perfect round form and immense size, borne on stiff stems, sometimes nearly three feet long. The colors are most intense and lovely, and nothing quite so handsome is seen in any other Spring flower. The only way to fully appreciate them is to see a field in full bloom.

The Parrot section is not of much value commercially, their greatest drawback being that if the very largest selected bulbs possible are secured never more than 60 to 80 per cent. will throw a flower. The bulbs grow and increase fast enough in any good ordinary fairly light garden soil. The flowers are very large, curiously splashed, marked and bordered with practically all colors except blue, and the edges of the petals are frilled and cut. Some people regard them as exceedingly handsome, while others say they are very ugly.

For the purpose of this article it is the cottage garden varieties which are of most concern, being the finest and most profitable commercially, whether for cutting, bedding, or for ordinary extensive garden, park or shrubbery decoration. More especially do I wish to draw attention to their cultivation in the open field by the acre for cutting for market work, at the same time making an extra profit in the sale of surplus bulbs. It may therefore be of considerable interest and value to American florists to give a few details of the methods employed in cultivation by the largest European growers.

The Best Soil.

To begin with, it must be thoroughly understood that tulips will not grow in just any soil, probably their greatest aversion being heavy clay or very heavy loam although the May flowering section is not nearly so particular as to soil as the early flowering section of forcing tulips. But the very best soil for growing tulips, and in fact, for all other sorts of bulbs, is a rich, previously heavily manured sandy loam, sand predominating, although many other sorts of soil grow bulbs with the best success. The bulb fields of Holland are, as is well known, mainly sand enriched with manure, watered from below, and at all times of the year water may be found a few feet below the surface. So that in choosing a situation it is necessary, provided the surface soil is sufficiently light and porous, to select a spot lying very low so that it is very close to the natural level of water, or "sock," as it is called in England. The districts selected for bulb growing in Ireland are almost identical with the Dutch soils. In Lincolnshire and other parts of the eastern counties of England the greatest success is attained on what are called light silt lands. These are usually found in low lying districts, which were previously marshes, and, in some cases, many years ago the seas washed over the spot. In the midlands of England some fine bulb growing spots are found in the river valleys which are formed of alluvium deposits.

Many bulbs, including tulips, but perhaps more particularly iris are somewhat aquatic in their habits, and from the time root action commences in the early Autumn until after they flower and are ready to stop growth and mature, they prefer and thrive better with a soil that is moist; in fact, nearly wet, for the roots to work in, the upper surface or soil lying around and above the actual bulb being dry, a climate that is moist and mild, of a regular equable temperature, at least from October to May, when the bulk of the growth is made. Such conditions as these prevail to the fullest extent in Holland, and in a lesser degree in Ireland and to some small extent in England.

Metairie Ridge Nursery, New Orleans, La. Water Tower and Pump House.

Of course, it will be understood that the above advice as to choosing the soil and locality would be quite suitable for undertaking general bulb culture on a large commercial scale, and may be perhaps getting away somewhat from the subject of this article. There is no doubt that most nursery grounds have a plot which is more or less suitable for bulb culture (especially May flowering tulips for producing a quantity of cheap cut bloom), with the addition of a little lime, some heavy animal manure, basic slag, or bone meal to make it as much as possible light and porous, and at the same time retaining a certain amount of moisture.

Cultivation.

As to actual cultivation the late tulips do not require much attention, if the soil and situation are fairly right. October and November are the best planting months. A mistake is often made by planting too early. Tulips are not like narcissus, that root as soon as ever planted from July onward; but if tulips are put in as early as July, they still do not commence to root until October or November, and the bulb, lying dormant in the damp soil, is very liable to rot more or less. It is therefore much safer to leave them in the dry store room until the time mentioned. Plant about four or five inches deep and about three apart from bulb to bulb and from six to nine inches apart from row to row, on beds raised about six inches. After that little more need be done beyond keeping down weeds with the hoe; and to save, as far as possible, the trouble of hoeing and hand weeding while the growth is above ground, the flats should be top flat-spitted over to the depth of about two inches. This is best done with a flat tined, flat-shaped, four-pronged fork, the operation being performed by keeping the tines and handle almost parallel with the ground so that the top end of the handle is not more than twelve inches above the soil when taking the spit to turn it over. Just before the growth is coming through in Spring the surface should be hoed and raked level, and during the time the bulbs are resting and there are no growths to injure, say, during August, September and October, the surface should be vigorously hoed. If no weeds are allowed to appear in these three months, there won't be many weeds to trouble a grower the whole remaining nine months.

The foliage and stems should never be cut off, but allowed to die down until they can be easily raked up. It is a great mistake to cut off the tops soon after the bloom has been severed. Many growers do this principally because they can so much easier get rid of the weeds, but it weakens the bulbs and stops their growth entirely for that season, and in some cases causes the bulbs to rot away.

During the Winter and Spring a surface dressing of soot, lime, basic slag, bone meal or similar material is very beneficial and will many times repay the cost in larger and better colored blooms and increase in quantity.

Tulips also require, during the late Autumn, a dressing of well rotted cow dung or other heavy farmyard manure; and in cold localities where Spring frosts are troublesome a covering of straw, reeds or similar material will be required during Winter and Spring, being taken off sufficiently early to prevent injury to the early growths.

Treated as above the May flowering section may remain undisturbed for two or three years, and when they get too thick, they should be lifted at about the time the foliage will just hang on to the bulb, dried in the shade to prevent the skins cracking, cleaned, and the largest taken out and either sold or planted again, separately, on a prepared piece of ground, very close together, for one year. After lifting again they will be found to have made fine perfectly round-shaped, solid bulbs with a good even salable appearance.

Some Good Sorts.

As to varieties, the "Cottage" section is the most useful and the following are the finest commercial selections. Bouton d'Or, orange or golden yellow; Spathulata, crimson scarlet, base of the flower dark blue; Golden Crown, golden, splashed red; Macrophylla, crimson scarlet, yellow base, very sweetly scented; Picotee, pure white, edged pink like a picotee, recurved petals; Retroflexa, canary yellow, recurved petals; White Swan, pure white, perfect egg-shaped blooms.

In the Darwin section it is difficult to give a selection as all the sorts are good for cutting. Perhaps a selection of unnamed separate colors would be the most useful, but the following are a few of the best: Clara Butt, salmon; Hecla, crimson maroon; Farncombe Saunders, bright red; White Queen, white; Mme. Krelage, rose pink; Yellow Perfection, yellow, edged golden.

In the Parrot section the mixed unnamed sorts are useful, but the best named are Admiral von Constantinople, orange and scarlet; Lutea major, yellow, green stripes; Mark Graff, golden striped with scarlet; Perfection, clear yellow.

ENGLISH CORRESPONDENT.

Partial View of Palm Shed of Metairie Ridge Nursery, New Orleans, La.

An Original Method of Cultivating Carnations.

During the season of frequent and heavy rains in the early Summer, noted, we are sure, by all growers, it has been impossible to cultivate our field of 75,000 carnations because of the soaked condition of the soil, and our superintendent, Mr. Taylor, realized that the case required some improvement over the methods heretofore employed for gtting rid of the weeds. Being of an ingenious turn of mind, he decided to make use of the boys' donkey to lighten the labor. He hitched the animal to an old whiffle-tree, to each end of which was attached a hand cultivator, one far enough in advance of the other to prevent their interfering with each other. He guiding one cultivator between two rows of plants, an assistant guiding the other between the two adjoining rows, and a third man leading the donkey, they proceeded back and forth across the field, as shown in the photograph, accomplishing their task in one-fifth of the time it would have taken the three men to do it in the old way, and much more satisfactorily. After the first heavy crop of weeds was thus disposed of, it required only two and a half hours of similar trouble once a week to keep the field clear of weeds, and as a result, our plants have never been finer when we took them up to plant in the houses than this year.

JAMES D. COCKCROFT.

Northport, L. I.

Cultivating Carnations in field of J. D. Cockcroft, Northport, L. I.

Tobacco Dust as a Fertilizer and Insecticide.

The waste product of all the American tobacco factories, in the form of stems stripped from the leaves in the manufacture of tobacco, is saved and finely ground, and forms a valuable by-product in the shape of a fertilizer and insecticide. Good unsoaked stems contain 2 to 3 per cent. of nitrogen and 6 to 10 per cent. of potash, and only a trace of phosphoric acid; the nitrogen exists in both the nitrate and organic forms. The stalks are richer in nitrogen than the stems, ranging from 3 to 4 per cent. nitrogen, but are considered poorer in potash. Tobacco is an exhausting crop, and the dust would prove an excellent fertilizer to apply to tobacco fields. A ton of good tobacco stems should contain nitrogen equivalent to 500 pounds of nitrate of soda, and potash equivalent to the amount contained in 200 pounds of sulphate of potash. I have used hundreds of tons of tobacco dust in the past twenty years, and my faith in its fertilising properties is unshaken, and could I procure it in any quantity in Jamaica, I would take all offering; but it is unprofitable to use unless finely ground, because, being so bulky in the form of stems, it becomes too expensive to haul and handle. Tobacco dust is especially valuable as a fertilizer and insecticide for pineapples.—Jamaica Agricultural Bulletin.

An Effectual Cure.

A farmer who was much troubled during the nutting season by trespassers in a wood bordering the roadside, ascertained from a botanical friend the scientific name of the hazel, and caused the following notice to be put up in the wood:

Trespassers Take Warning!
All Persons entering this wood do so at their own risk, for the
Corylus avellana
abounds here in company with more or less poisonous snakes!

The wood is now shunned by everybody, and the farmer is so pleased with the success of his ruse that he thinks of seeing his botanical friend again to find out the Latin name of the common edible field mushroom!—Exchange.

NATIONAL NUT GROWERS' ASSOCIATION.—The fifth annual convention of this association will be held at Scranton, Miss., October 31 to November 2, 1906. Members and all interested in the industry are cordially invited to attend. The prominent railroads offer a special rate of one and one-third fare for the round trip. Scranton will supplement the program by entertainments and excursions, which will include trips to nut orchards, boat rides and a clambake on the Gulf coast. The program, badge book and special notices of hotel rates will be issued about October 15. In order that the local committee can make complete arrangements for accommodating all who attend, it is desired that all who expect to be present notify the secretary.

E. W. KIRKPATRICK, President.
J. F. WILSON, Secretary.

FOR THE RETAILER

[All questions relating to the Retail Trade will be cheerfully answered in this column. We solicit good, sharp photographs of made-up work, decorations, store interiors, etc., for reproduction here.—Ed. F. E.]

Clean Up the Store.

The present is the time when the annual cleaning up of the store should be finished and everything in spick and span shape for the coming season, which promises to be exceptionally good. There is nothing better to start with than a freshly painted store. It is due to yourself, if not your customers, to show tokens of prosperity even if the facts do not justify your efforts. A dirty, slovenly kept store only tends to displease, no matter how indifferent you imagine your established trade is, and surely drives away any acquisition.

There are unlimited opportunities for individual ideas in color schemes of decoration, but white is the most economical and the best assimilator; and no matter if it be only whitewash so long as it is clean it will be better for stock, more pleasing to people and better for trade.

The present commendable and popular style of interior flower store furnishing dispenses with, as far as possible, the dust and eyesore accumulators in the way of shelves. A neat pedestal supporting a vase of flowers or a plant makes a more pleasing and enticing feature than the old and unclean, unsalable stock that too often but represents money lost.

At the present time the majority of stores are displaying a nice assortment of small, well-grown ferns, palms and foliage plants. Cleaner pots should be the rule. There is no excuse because young America dislikes the job of pot-washing. It is an insult—an evidence of inexcusable ignorance—to send a dirty pot or plant to any home. A few minutes more time spent in the packing or potting shed in the country would benefit the sender and receiver.

Outside Displays.

The weather just now permits outside displays and in the majority of cases it pays to have a good intelligent plantsman outside the door, who can busy himself cleaning, arranging, advising and selling; and with every plant a neat one-sheet card of practical house culture instructions should be given. Such can be printed on the back of your tag or business card, and the small outlay required is recompensed a hundred fold by the pleasure and confidence it brings forth. These short cultural instructions for such as ferns, palms, the different foliage or commonest plants, should be concise. Many an otherwise indifferent passerby may be attracted by a man handling a plant, and their resultant curiosity often ends in a purchase and lasting friendship. We despise fakeism in every sense. The 29½-cent method is not necessary in the florist's business, and should be discouraged. Well grown and seasoned stock deserves and can bring fair prices. The plant trade is growing tremendously, and we can all add our share of the glory by fair treatment; therefore, it is high time every effort was put forth to capture your share of the early Fall plant trade. There is no telling to what or where even the smallest sale may lead to; and great efforts must be used in the care of your own stock. It must be remembered that plants are brought to salable condition by up-to-date and the quickest possible methods by the grower. Much of the stock is accustomed to treatment and surroundings impossible in the average store. Sudden checks or indifferent watering soon tells, and depreciation in value means loss of trade besides loss of money.

Plant Boarders.

Every effort should be made to get rid of plant boarders as soon as possible, for no matter how well they may look, their proximity injures new stock. So polish them up and return them as soon as you can. This boarding of plants is a very troublesome feature of the business. In some cases they can neither be refused nor charged for at a remunerative figure, and the utmost diplomacy must be used in all cases. It is one of the phases of human nature that is unexplainable, except in the manner of general cussedness, that a poor, starved and nigh asphyxiated plant, after enduring all its torture serving to diffuse pleasure in an impossible atmosphere for many months, should be at length brought back to the florist with the full expectation of a complete recovery in a short period of time. Here in New York a stolid determination is invariably the rule not to take boarders; or if it is judicious then to charge at the rate of fifty cents per month and upwards for each plant. This often at the end of the season assumes a formidable figure, and many times new plants can be had for a less figure; and, indeed, as is often the case, new plants are substituted in order to face the music or derive good results. A manly explanation to the customer at the start would, unless in the case of an old pet plant, result in the sending of the most of plant cripples to the cause of sweet charity. The hospitals or various charitable institutions so numerous in all parts would at all times bless the florist for his steering to them the sick and the weary in plant life.

The Dahlia in Decorative Work.

Volumes could be written on the dahlia as a decorative flower, and a visit to any of the shows, or grounds, where they are being extensively shown or grown dazzles one with brilliancies of color unobtainable in any other class of plants. The present classification of the different types, or rather the name given to them is, to say the least, ridiculous, and should for the sake of present day intelligence be at once rectified. There is not the slightest justification in dubbing the most beautiful type as "cactus," as if it were related to some monstrosity of the desert; or that another should have the title "decorative." If we are to have a Dahlia Society, it is to be hoped a different and more correct if not prettier appellation will be given these beautiful flowers, and that our "follow the leader" catalogue and schedule compilers will quickly adopt that which will most appeal to the buyer and flower lover.

Unfortunately, the foliage of the dahlia does not add to its beauty when used for decorative purposes; therefore, in the vast majority of cases, particularly in table decoration, their own foliage must be substituted by fern or asparagus. Many of the flowers, nearly all of some of the prettiest varieties, will need wiring. Invisible wiring can be neatly done with the aid of any fine greenery. We do not advocate the

Milwaukee Florists on an Outing.

wiring of all the blooms, just enough to control their awkwardness and give a design a finished appearance. The type erroneously styled "cactus" dahlias are by far the most suitable for the retailer's work or sales, and these flowers are destined to be better known and appreciated. In naming a few varieties of these we do so merely to designate the type and color of flower most suitable; yet with one or two exceptions they can be considered the best for all around purposes; and in naming their colors we merely take the general effect. Marie Schwartz, old rose and plum; Master Carl, orange and apricot; Galliard, rich crimson; Mary Service, old rose; J. H. Jackson, very dark crimson maroon; Mrs. Seagrave, claret or burgundy; Radium, rosy pink tinged with orange; Mrs. Mortimer, orange red; Imperator, claret red; A. F. Perkins, white; Floradora, deep damask maroon; Jean Charmant, lavender and white; and Mrs. Manley, yellow. These with one or two exceptions represent the best of the quilled flowers, and the most attractive colors.

A table properly decorated, we mean in formal or elaborate style, with any of the above would far exceed in color effect any other material available at any time of the year, because such brilliant intermediate or soft tones are not in any other flowers, except perhaps cannas. The idea of their being common or of a repugnant odor cannot be said of them, for they are neither; and if you desire to make a hit, and the people are ever ready to permit you to attempt it, you cannot do better than use the fine colors in cactus dahlias.

The ways and methods of constructing decorative work are numerous and more or less confined to materials at hand. There is not a floral artist who does not despise the blunt cut offness of any green stock. Particularly does this occur in the case of Asparagus plumosus, and unless for filling in purposes such had better be avoided. Shallow bowls or flat baskets filled with damp moss, or greenery, are best; and regularity in arrangement of the flowers will do much to spoil the art effect. Flowers such as dahlias need massing at least in one particular part of the work; there is ample opportunity to taper off into gracefulness in the garlanding or outer work on most designs, be it in bowl or basket work. Stiff flowers need light arranging but the cactus dahlias are adaptable to all manner of work and sprays of adiantum furnish them with a most becoming dress. J. IVERA DONLAN.

A Milwaukee Picnic.

The picnic given by the C. C. Pollworth Company, to the florist trade of Milwaukee, Wis., was largely attended. The weather was ideal for such an affair and all enjoyed themselves. There were numerous prizes donated for the various events of which a list follows.

Men's Race (C. Dallwig's prizes)—A. Peterson, first; C. Dettman, second.
Ladies' Race (Holton & Hunkel's prizes)—Miss Kennedy, first; Miss Hunkel, second.
Girls' Race (W. A. Kennedy's prizes)—Miss Kennedy, first; Miss Husslein, second.
Girls' Race, under twelve (F. Pollworth's prizes)—G. Baumgarten, first; Hilda Menger, second.
Boys' Race (Hunkel's Seed Store prizes)—J. Klokner, first; A. Menger, second.
Three legged Race (Holton & Hunkel's prizes)—Kuhl and G. Manke, first; Welke and W. Manke, second.
Sack Race (Chas. Menger's prizes)—A. Rice, first; H. Welke, second.
Hurdle Race (Holton & Hunkel's prize)—G. Ruesch, first; W. Kuhl, second.
Potato Race (C. C. Pollworth's prizes)—Mrs. Wolf, first; Miss Hunkel, second.
Peanut Race (Nic Zweifel's prizes) First, Miss Potswald.
Tug of War [Prize donated by John C. Heitman—The team captained by A. Klokner easily defeated the team captained by F. Kaiser, although the latter team was by far the heavier. P.

The Commercial Club of Topeka, Kan., is seriously considering the matter of inviting the S. A. F. O. H. to hold its annual meeting and convention in that city. If an invitation is sent it will probably be for 1909 or 1910 so that any new ideas absorbed by the Topeka people may be put in beautifying the city for the semi-centennial.

The value of the cut flowers exported from the United States during the year ending June 30, 1905, was $4,522 as compared with $5,076 in 1904.

New York.

The Week's News.

The Autumn exhibition and dahlia show of the American Institute was held this week, Tuesday, Wednesday and Thursday, in the Berkeley Lyceum, 19 and 21 West West Forty-fourth street. Richard Vincent, Jr., & Sons, White Marsh, Md., made a representative showing of their many varieties of dahlias; as also did H. F. Burt, Taunton, Mass., and W. P. Lothrop of E. Bridgewater, Mass. John L. Childs, Floral Park, N. Y., made quite an exhibit of various flowers, including gladiolus, tuberous rooted begonias, montbretias and tritomas. A. J. Manda, superintendent of the Pratt estate, Brooklyn, staged a very choice collection of stove and greenhouse plants, among which were several well grown nepenthes and platyceriums. George Hale, superintendent for Mr. E. D. Adams, Seabright, N. J., showed a large collection of dahlias; as also did James Dowlan, gardener to Mr. H. Terrill, Oceanic, N. J., and J. T. Lovett, Little Silver, N. J. Lager & Hurrell of Summit, N. J., staged a nice exhibit of orchids. Among the exhibits of fruit there was a large and varied collection from Ellwanger & Barry, Rochester, N. Y. A collection of dahlias, including a large number of pompon varieties, was shown by F. R. Pierson Company, Tarrytown, N. Y.

The Huntington Horticultural and Agricultural Society held its annual show September 20 at Huntington, L. I. Among the prize winners for flowers and plants were H. T. and A. H. Funnell, August Hechscher, Joseph Mercier, W. O'Hara, Huntington Nursery Company, A. J. Matheson, T. S. Williams, Peter Mee and John McCulloch.

The exhibits at the County Fair, Staten Island, were this year under the management of A. C. Nellis. Among the prize winners were Chris. Boehe, Castleton Corners; Charles Boehe, Tompkinsville; John Nickel, Stapleton; August Spies, New Springville; Charles Hunt, Port Richmond; Charles Ruff, West New Brighton; Fred G. Hawkins, Stapleton; A. J. Scott, West New Brighton; and H. F. Burt of Taunton, Mass., with a display of seventy-five distinct varieties of dahlia blooms.

At the recent dahlia and aster show held in New London, Conn., R. J. Irwin, one of the traveling salesmen for Vaughan's Seed Store, acted as judge of plants and flowers.

Wm. Elliott & Sons are receiving regular consignments of palms and other decorative plants, and are now holding their auction sales twice a week, Tuesday and Friday. The collection of orchids of the late G. L. Montgomery, Staten Island, will be sold at auction by this firm on Tuesday, October 2, beginning at 11:30 a. m.

Louis Schmutz, the veteran Flatbush florist, is home again after a five weeks' sojourn in France.

Phil. Kessler reached home on Wednesday, September 19, from a trip to Germany, and reports having had a splendid time. Since reaching home he has added considerable space to his cut flower rooms in the Coogan building, and has now about double the area he formerly had. This move was made necessary on account of his increasing business.

Benjamin Hammond, Fishkill-on-Hudson, N. Y., presided at a political meeting in his home town on Saturday, September 15, and was reappointed a member of the District Committee. Mr. Hammond is a staunch Republican.

The Pierson U-Bar manufacturers struck a right chord with florists who grow and retail their own products, in designing greenhouses specially for show purposes. As soon as their advertisement of this line of business had appeared, they received many orders for that style of show house. This would indicate that florists generally are in a prosperous condition, and are ready to have their establishments make a pretentious showing when the right idea comes along.

The Cottage Gardens Company, Queens, L. I., are now making regular shipments of carnations to John Young, 51 West Twenty-eighth street.

Rev. A. Scott, brother of the popular president of the Florists' Club John Scott, was married on Wednesday, September 26, in Jersey City.

John Scott will add two more houses, each 85 x 18 feet, to his already large plant.

CANADIAN NEWS

OTTAWA.—We are having grand weather; the 19th of September, and coleus not touched by frost. But it is very dry. All crops are pretty well planted, Wright of Aylmer being the only one to have carnations out. A visit to this place showed some great beds of American Beauty; Toronto and Brampton will have to look to their laurels.

The Central Canada exhibition was held recently. The horticultural part was ahead of former years, the display of cut flowers being very good. Having been judge of flowers at Toronto, I had a good chance to compare the two exhibits. In plants, of course, Toronto was away ahead, having many civic and government establishments to draw from; but in cut flowers Toronto was not in it. Asters, sweet peas, gladiolus, phlox, etc., were away ahead here, and in exhibits we had three times the number. The plant prizes were principally divided among the Parliament greenhouses, Scrim and the Government house; McCann, the well-known superintendent, being ahead in geraniums, fuschias and coleus. The cut flower awards were well divided, although our farmer friends took most of the prizes on asters and the like. Scrim took first on carnations, roses and bouquets, the only made-up work on exhibition. The Wright Floral Company made a pretty exhibit of palms, and a dinner table not for competition. The judges were: J. Bennett on plants, G. Tressell on flowers, both of Montreal. There was quite a delegation from Montreal: Messrs. Tressell, Bennett, McKenna (2), McHugh (2), Wilshire, Barrows, Walsh, Dupuy and Smith, and as it was the first visit of some, they enjoyed it.

The Wright Floral Company is opening a retail store in Montreal which will be under the charge of Max Nischki, who has done good work for them in Ottawa.

Graham Brothers have moved into their new store, and it is a grand one, the envy of us all. The available space is 33 by 100 feet. The fitting up is tasteful, useful and rich. The ice box is built in the wall; mirrors abound, with marble slabs at their base. The counters are neat, as are the office, cloak rooms and other conveniences. The tinting of the store is very pleasing, and the two large windows with tile bottoms are great. With a hardwood floor, the whole makes the finest store in Canada, in my opinion.

E.

Louisville, Ky.

State Fair Show.

The State Fair, held here during the past week was a decided success even though the weather and some disappointed competitors tried to make it a failure. The time to make the necessary arrangements was very short, only two months elapsing since Louisville was selected as the permanent home for the Fair. On this account the exhibitors in the floricultural department were not as numerous as might have been. In another year, the Kentucky Society of Florists expects to make this department a feature of the fair. This year Mrs. M. D. Reimers and Nanz & Neuner were the principal exhibitors and carried away the prizes. Mrs. C. B. Thompson made an exhibit of cut flowers that attracted much attention.

The Kentucky Society of Florists will hold its monthly meeting on Tuesday evening, October 2; every member should be present.

The florist bowlers held their annual prize contest last Tuesday evening. It was a handicap affair, A. R. Baumer being "scratch" man. You can tell how well Fred Schulz handicapped the boys when you learn that the three high average men were the lowest in the contest. There was a prize for every member, the high man having first choice and so on down the list, as follows: Ross Walker, Jos. Wettle, Louis Kirch, Will Walker, Jacob Schulz, Anders Rasmussen, George Rasmussen, Henry Fuchs, A. R. Baumer, Fred Schulz, and George E. Schulz. These games were bowled on foreign soil as we, on invitation of A. Rasmussen, visited him at his place in New Albany, Ind. After an examination of his well kept place we sat down to a most excellent supper. We all ate more than athletes should, consequently the scores do not show as they otherwise would, and I will not publish them.

Society Banquet.

The annual banquet of the Kentucky Society of Florists was held Tuesday evening, September 11, with a representative number of the members gathered around the festive board. While no elaborate entertainment was attempted, a royal good time was spent in the exchange of ideas and a few short speeches. August R. Baumer acted as toastmaster. President Rasmussen spoke in behalf of the society urging upon the members to better attend the monthly meetings. Kentucky Vice-President of the S. A. F., Fred L. Schulz, spoke for the national society. Jacob Schulz, in a grandfatherly manner, gave us some up-to-date, modern ideas regarding the relationship of the members, one with another, and of the harmony that should exist in our family. "The Ladies" was assigned to J. E. Marrett who did full justice to his subject. Bowling was the subject allotted to Louis Kirch, our most enthusiasic bowler; he claimed he was no speaker but was willing to demonstrate the pleasures to be derived from the sport, so he and several congenial spirits retired to the alleys and spent the balance of the evening bowling.

A. R. B.

Utica, N. Y.

News Items.

Mr. and Mrs. George H. Benedict of Yorkville gave a reception on September 19 to their florist friends and others in honor of the twenty-fifth anniversary of the establishment of their business, one of the most prosperous enterprises of the village. There were 125 present, among them many Utica florists. Mr. and Mrs. Benedict received the guests, assisted by members of the Utica Florists' Club. The greenhouses, to the number of 24, were inspected and everything was found in first-class condition. A very enjoyable afternoon was spent by all. There were on exhibition the account book kept 25 years ago, and the old boiler then used. Mr. Benedict was the recipient of a handsome leather, mahogany chair, the gift of the Utica florists. May he live to enjoy it 25 years more is the wish of all those who were present.

The florists from out of town included Mr. and Mrs. E. J. Byam, Rome; Mr. and Mrs. Seward Hakes, Ilion; Mr. and Mrs. J. R. Auld, New Hartford; Mr. and Mrs. J. Owen, Whitesboro; Mr. and Mrs. Schesch, Ilion; Mr. Cokeley of the Scranton Supply Company.

Wm. Mathews & Sons have about 5,000 orchids, each one of which Mr. Mathews can name without referring to the label. His carnations, roses and chrysanthemums are looking splendid. Mr. Mathews still grows one house of violets; he says he cannot give them up, even if he does fail with them every year.

C. F. Baker & Son's carnations, planted in all Summer, are in fine condition. Chrysanthemums and poinsettias are also done well here.

I called on Mr. and Mrs. Wm. Wagner, of Cooperstown, while on my trip to the lake. Mr. Wagner has a fine place and is doing a very nice business, being ably assisted by his good wife.

J. C. Spencer and family have returned from their camp at Otsego Lake, after being away two weeks.

The next meeting of the Utica Florists' Club will be held at the store of Spencer & Martin on October 2. A full house is hoped for.

Henry Brant has recovered from his sickness after having been in the hospital about one month.

QUIZ.

Nassau County (N. Y.) Horticultural Society Outing.

The Nassau County Horticultural Society held its first annual outing and dinner on Thursday, August 30, at Karatsonyi & Kemet's GlenWood hotel. The occasion was a grand success and was well attended by the members with their families and their friends.

A series of athletic sports, arranged for in a nearby field, were the interesting features of the afternoon. The results were as follows:

100 yards race for fat men over 180 lbs.—First, Thos. Harrison, prize, a pipe; second, Wm. Rickards, tobacco pouch; third, V. Cleris, match box. 100 yards race for married men—First, A. J. Rickards, pipe; second, J. Kennedy, tobacco pouch; third, A. Mackenzie, match box. 100 yards race for single men—First, F. G. Boulon, brass wedding ring; second, F. Siler, lady's picture; third, F. Demack, doll. 50 yards race for ladies—First, Mrs. S. J. Trepass, umbrella; second, Mrs. J. Everitt, box handkerchiefs; third, Mrs. C. F. Bertanzel, pocketbook. 50 yards race for boys—First, Donald Mackenzie, base ball glove; second, Lascal Drombrousky, base ball bat; third, Lockland Mackenzie, base ball. 50 yards race for girls under seven—First, Miss V. Bertanzel, doll; second, Miss E. Everitt, doll carriage; third, Miss Albertta Johnson, box of candies. 50 yards race for girls under 14—First, Miss Ruth Trepass, work box; second, Miss Nellis Mogford, post card album; third, Miss M. Mackenzie, box of candies. 100 yards sack race—First, J. Kennedy, stein; second, E. J. Brown, long pipe; third, Alex. Mackenzie, box of candies.

Three-legged race, 60 yards—First, V. Cleris and H. Matz, pipes; second, Thos. Harrison and J. Kennedy, knives; third, C. F. Bertanzel and F. Bracker, match boxes.

High jump—First, J. Kennedy, box cigars; second, Alex. Mackenzie, tobacco pouch; third, A. J. Rickards, pipe. Broad jump—First, Alex. Mackenzie, box cigars; second, A. J. Rickards, tobacco pouch; third, J. Kennedy, pipe. Ladies' bowling match—First, Mrs. Mogford, brush and comb; second, Miss Mense, hand mirror; third, Mrs. Thos. Harrison, bottle perfume; fourth, Mrs. E. J. Brown, pin cushion. Bowling match for men—First, F. Dumack, stein with cover; second, F. Mense, pipe with case; third, S. Drombrousky, pouch; fourth, S. J. Trepass, box cigars. Booby prize, Jas. Duthie.

After the sports all adjourned to the dining hall where an excellent dinner was served.

The committee of arrangement to whom credit is due for the success of the outing was composed of J. W. Everitt, S. Drombrousky, A. Johnson, C. F. Bertanzel and F. G. Boulon.

F. G. B.

Ferns From the Bench

BOSTON, PIERSONI, 3 in. 5c., 4 in. 10c. 5 in. 12½c. Boston 6 in. 15 cts.
TARRYTOWN, 3 in., 10c.; 4 in., 15c.; 5 in., 25c. Runners $20.00 per 1000.
SCOTTII, 3 in., 8c.; 4 in., 12½c.

CHINESE PRIMROSES
White, fine plants, 1½ cts.
Primula Obconica, Hybrid Alba Rosea, 2 in., 2 cts.
Floribunda Primroses, 2 in., 2 cts.
Pansy Plants, Giants, $3.00 per 100.
Daisies, double Snowball, Longfellow, Delicata, $2.50 per 1000.
Asparagus Sprengerii, 2 in., 2 cts.
Jerusalem Cherries, field grown, ready for 4 in., 3 cts.
Flowering Begonias, 8 kinds, 2 in., 2½ cts.
Begonia Rex, 2 in., 4 cts.
Alyssum Giant, White double, 2 in. 2c.
Rubbers, top grown, 4 to 5 in. 15 to 25 cts.
Forgetmenots, $2.50 per 1000
Stevia Serrata, field-grown, 4 cts.
Cash or C. O. D.

BYER BROS., Chambersburg, Pa.

Mention The Florists' Exchange when writing.

FERNS *and* CARNATIONS

SPEAK QUICK

10,000 Healthy Field Grown Carnations, best commercial sorts, including **ELBON,** a fine, true red. **Send for list as they must be sold.**
1,000 **PIERSONI FERNS,** for 4 in., 15c.
1,000 " " for 3 in., 10c.
1,000 **BOSTON** " 3 in. ready for 4 in., 10c.
SCOTTII FERNS, 4 in., 20c.; 3 in., 10c.
ANNA FOSTER, 2½ in., 4c.
1,000 **ASPARAGUS PLUMOSUS NANUS,** 3½ in., 6c., 2½ in., $2.50 per 100.
200 **ASPARAGUS SPRENGERII,** 3½ in., 6c.
1,000 **HYDRANGEA OTAKSA,** 2½ in., $2.50 per 100.
1,000 **VINCA MAJOR** var., 2½ in., $2.50 per 100.
All A No. 1 Stock. Cash please.

BENJ. CONNELL
WEST GROVE, PA.

Mention The Florists' Exchange when writing.

Adiantum Farleyense

I can quote splendid stock at from $2.00 per dozen up to $24.00 per dozen, in 2-inch to 6-inch pots. If you are looking or Farleyense, better write me about it.

CHARLES H. TOTTY,
Madison, N. J.

Mention The Florists' Exchange when writing.

NEPHROLEPIS SCOTTII

Small plants from the benches, $5.00 per 100; $50.00 per 1000. Plants large enough for 6 in. pots, $25.00 per 100. Plants large enough to go in 7 and 8 in. pots, $50.00 per 100.
Asparagus Plumosus Nanus, 2¼ in., fine plants, $30.00 per 100.

JOHN SCOTT,
Rutland Road & E. 45th St., BROOKLYN, N. Y
Telephone 2890 Bedford.

Mention The Florists' Exchange when writing.

Boston Ferns from Bench

10 to 20c. each **Asparagus Sprengerii** 2¼ in. pots, $2.00 per 100. Good value in both the above.

Cohanzie Carnation Greenhouses,
New London, Conn.

Mention The Florists' Exchange when writing.

Fern Seedlings

From flats, ten of the best varieties, at $1.00 per 100; $8.50 per 1000; if by mail add 10c. per 100. **Ferns** for dishes, good stocky plants from 2¼ in. pots, $3.00 per 100; $25.00 per 1000; 250 plants at 1000 rate.
Adiantum Cuneatum, 5 in pots, $20.00 per 100

FRANK N. ESKESEN, MADISON, N. J.

Mention The Florists' Exchange when writing.

DREER'S SPECIALS IN FERNS

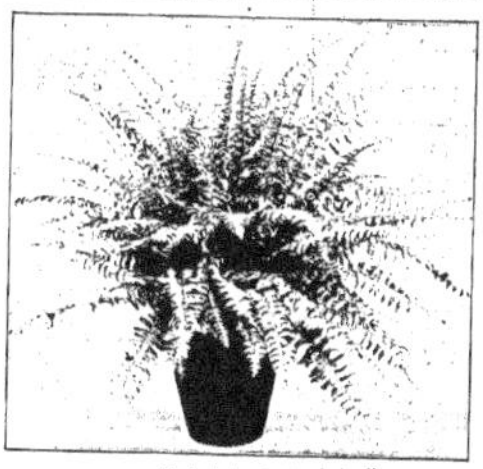

Nephrolepis Scottii

Nephrolepis Scottii

We have a grand lot of compact dwarf bushy specimens in 6 inch pots, 50 cents each; 8 inch pans, $1.00 each; 12 inch pans, $2.00 each; 2¼ inch pots, $4.00 per 100; $35.00 per 1000.

Adiantum Cuneatum

A fine lot of 6 inch pots, $3.50 per dozen; $25.00 per 100; 2¼ inch pots, $3.50 per 100; $30.00 per 1000.

Adiantum Farleyense

A grand lot of specimen plants in seven inch pots at $1.50 each. This is bushy stock with grand foliage, of excellent value. Also a fine lot of clean vigorous 3 inch pots for growing on, $2.00 per dozen, $15.00 per 100.

Nephrolepis Whitmani

The most distinct and desirable of the crested forms of the Boston Fern, its great points of merit are that it never reverts or shows any plain fronds or parts of fronds, it naturally makes a shapely compact plant, it is more graceful than any of the other sorts and is a quick grower. We offer strong
2¼ inch pots, $3.50 per dozen, $25.00 per 100.
3 " " 4.00 " " 30.00 " "
and fine plants in 6 inch pots at $1.00 each.

Pteris Wilsoni and Pteris Wimsetti Multiceps

are both useful varieties, perhaps the prettiest of the Pteris for growing into larger sizes for decorative plants, we have a fine lot of 6 inch pans, just right for table decoration, pretty plants at $3 50 per dozen; $25.00 per 100. In smaller sizes we can supply 2¼ inch pots, $3.50 per 100; $30.00 per 1000.
3 " " 6.00 " " 50.00 " "
4 " " 1.50 " doz. 10.00 " 100

Aspidium Tsussemense

Of this most useful of all Dish Ferns we still have a fine lot of seedlings in flats, which if potted up now will still make salable stock for this winter, about 200 plants to a flat at $2.00 per flat.

Mixed Ferns

Our usual superior assortment of varieties:
2¼ inch pots, $3.50 per 100; $30.00 per 1000.
3 " " 6.00 " " 50.00 " "

For a full line of Seasonable Stock, Decorative Plants, Palms, Ferns, Araucarias, Pandanus, Hardy Perennials, Bulbs, Seeds, etc., etc., see our quarterly Wholesale List.

HENRY A. DREER,
714 Chestnut St., PHILADELPHIA, PA.

Mention The Florists' Exchange when writing.

FERNS OUR SPECIALTY

Cibotium Schiedei: We have a grand stock of this magnificent tree fern in all sizes. 3 in. pots, $25.00 per 100; 4 in. pots, $45.00 per 100; 5 in. pots, $70.00 per 100; 7 in. pots, $1.70 each; 8 in. pots, $2.50 each.
Assorted Ferns, from 2¼ in. pots, all the best market varieties, $3.00 per 100, or $26.00 per 1000; 4 inch pots, $12.00 per 100.
If by mail add 10c. each 100 plants.
Adiantum Cuneatum, 2 in. pots, $3.50 per 100
" " 4 in. pots, 12.00 " "
" **Rhodophyllum** 4 in. pots $25.00 per 100
" **Lathomii,** 4 in. pots, $20.00 per 100
" **Regina,** 4 in. pots, $40.00 per 100
Fern Spores gathered from our own stock plants 35c. per trade package or $4.00 per doz. packages

ANDERSON & CHRISTENSEN,
SHORT HILLS, N. J.

Mention the Florists' Exchange when writing.

HOLLY FERNS

Finest stock we ever offered in 3 inch pots, $6.00 per 100.

R. G. HANFORD.
NORWALK, CONN.

Mention the Florists' Exchange when writing.

Nephrolepis Scottii

Plants ready for 6 in. pots at 20c.; 7 in. at 40c. Grown in full sun, stocky compact plants. For lots of 25 and upwards. Cash with order.

J. CONDON, 734-5th Ave., Brooklyn, N. Y.

Mention The Florists' Exchange when writing.

ASSORTED FERNS FOR FERNERIES

IN BEST VARIETIES

We have an exceptionally fine stock of these goods and to make room will fill immediate orders at $20.00 per 1000.

Let us have your order to-day.

WRITE FOR PRICE LIST OF GENERAL STOCK.

THE GEO. WITTBOLD COMPANY
No. 1657 BUCKINGHAM PLACE, CHICAGO

Mention The Florists' Exchange when writing.

FERNS. NEPHROLEPIS BARROWSII

2¼ inch, $6.00 per 100.

HUGH GRAHAM CO.,
Logan Nurseries, York Road and Louden Street, PHILADELPHIA, PA

Mention The Florists' Exchange when writing.

NEPHROLEPIS

Whitmani, 2¼ in., $25.00 per 100.
Barrowsii, $10.00 per 100.

Henry H. Barrows & Son, Whitman, Mass.

Mention The Florists' Exchange when writing.

FERNS

For jardinieres, etc., 2¼ inch, $3.00 per 100.
Kentia Belmoreana, clean and bushy, 5 in. 50c.
Boston Ferns, Piersoni and **Scottii,** from bench, 10c. to 25c. each, 4 in. pot grown, 15c.
Cocos Weddeliana, 2¼ in. 10c.
Asparagus Plumosus, 2¼ in. $3.00 per 100.

H. WESTON, HEMPSTEAD, N. Y.

Mention The Florists' Exchange when writing.

CLASSIFIED ADVERTISEMENTS

CASH WITH ORDER.

The columns under this heading are reserved for advertisements of Stock for Sale, Stock Wanted, Help Wanted, Situations Wanted or other Wants; also of Greenhouse, Land, Second-Hand Materials, etc., For Sale or Rent.

Our charge is 10 cts. per line (7 words to the line), set solid, without display. No advt. accepted for less than thirty cents.

Display advertisements in these columns, 15 cents per line; count 12 lines agate to the inch.

[If replies to Help Wanted, Situation Wanted, or other advertisements are to be addressed care of this office, advertisers add 10 cents to cover expense of forwarding.]

Copy must reach New York office 12 o'clock Wednesday to secure insertion in issue of following Saturday.

Advertisers in the Western States desiring to advertise under initials, may save time by having their answer directed care our Chicago office at 127 E. Berwyn Ave.

SITUATIONS WANTED

SITUATION WANTED—By young lady in up-to-date retail store. Address, S. K., care The Florists' Exchange.

SITUATION WANTED—By a young man, good decorator and maker-up. Address, F. Winters, Newtown, L. I.

SITUATION WANTED—By young German gardener, 20, as assistant in greenhouse or flower store. Address, S. A., care The Florists' Exchange.

SITUATION WANTED—As assistant gardener in first-class private place; thirty, single, American references. Address, S. J., care The Florists' Exchange.

SITUATION WANTED—In retail store by young man, 24, good experience, first-class designer, etc. No bad habits. R. K., care The Florists' Exchange.

SITUATION WANTED—By a first-class grower of cut flowers, also a competent nursery man; commercial or private. Address, R. W., care The Florists' Exchange.

SITUATION WANTED—German florist, all around hand in greenhouses. Strictly sober, best of references, wishes position. L. Geh, 150 Central Av., Brooklyn, N. Y.

SITUATION WANTED—Good grower of commercial stock wants position. Wholesale or retail. Long experience in charge. First-class references. N. E. preferred. Address S. F., care The Florists' Exchange.

SITUATION WANTED — Intelligent young man, German, 24, wants position in retail flower store in New York City. Single, reliable, well recommended. Address, R. X., care The Florists' Exchange.

SITUATION WANTED—On private or commercial place, experienced in carnations, mums and bedding plants. 28 years of age, single. Abraham Appledorn, E. Bridgewater, Mass.

SITUATION WANTED—By middle aged, single man, 15 years experience; grower of carnations, roses, mums and general stock. Good references. Bettak, 285 Avenue A., New York City.

SITUATION WANTED—By German, 37 years old, single; good grower of roses, carnations and general stock; also good maker-up. Wages, $15.00 per week. Address, S. H., care The Florists' Exchange.

SITUATION WANTED—Florist, single, 37 years old, well up in growing roses, carnations, mums and general stock. Able to take charge. References. Address, S. I., care The Florists' Exchange.

SITUATION WANTED—Young man would like a situation as assistant gardener on private or commercial place. P. J. T., care of Brawn & Frideman, Flatbush, Holy Cross Cemetery, Brooklyn, N. Y.

SITUATION WANTED—Young married man wishes position as gardener on private estate. Experienced in all branches under glass and outside. Well recommended. Address, R. G., care The Florists' Exchange.

SITUATION WANTED—Specialist in orchids, stove plants, palms, ferns, farleyense, filmy, etc. Wishes situation commercial or private. Good designer and decorator, 24 years experience both in Europe and this country. Address, Specialist, care The Florists' Exchange.

SITUATION WANTED—As assistant park and cemetery superintendent. Theoretical training and long practical experience. American, 35, single. Good references. Address, Edward Raymond, Back Bay P. O., Boston, Mass.

SITUATION WANTED—Gardener and florist, German, 38 years, single, a first-class workman, very neat, 24 years experience on private and commercial places, under glass and outdoors. Good grower of roses, carnations, mums and general stock. Some experience in decorating and designing. Wishes position, private or commercial. First-class references. Please state wages and particulars in first letter. Address B. C., care Mr. Sambraus, 189 Morningside Ave., New York City.

SITUATIONS WANTED

SITUATION WANTED—Position in a retail store; have had extensive experience in all branches, including landscape work. Competent to take entire charge. Nothing but first-class and steady position considered. Address, E. Z., care The Florists' Exchange.

SITUATION WANTED—In Florida, as working foreman in nursery or landscape department. Can handle men. 13 years American and European experience. Best references from all employers. Send particulars and wages offered in first letter. Address, S. D., care The Florists' Exchange.

SITUATION WANTED—As superintendent on private place by a thoroughly competent man. 18 years experience in all branches of the business. Married, one child. Address, F. J., 560 Maple st., Flatbush, Brooklyn, N. Y.

SITUATION WANTED—American, 30 years old, 10 years experience in greenhouses and stores, designing and decorating, bedding out, etc. Strictly temperate, good references; willing to go West or South, at once. Address, C. Gray, Sta. A., G. D., Boston, Mass.

SITUATION WANTED—By gardener and florist, German, single man, well up in Christmas, Easter and bulb stock, palms, bedding plants, carnations, mums. Private or commercial. Address, S. B., care The Florists' Exchange.

SITUATION WANTED—Gardener, first-class cultivator, 37 years of age, single, 24 years experience, with knowledge of in and outside work; will change position as foreman on commercial or private place. If interested, please ask for ability and references. Address, B. C., care The Florists' Exchange.

SITUATION WANTED—As foreman by first-class gardener and florist. Single; aged 30; 12 years' experience. American Beauty roses, carnations, potted plants; general management of private estate. References private and commercial. Address, R. M., care The Florists' Exchange.

SITUATION WANTED—As foreman in an up-to-date place. Eastern states preferred. 23 years practical experience in Europe and this country in growing cut flowers and hot house plants. Single man, aged 39; please state full particulars in first letter. Address, S. H., care The Florists' Exchange.

SITUATION WANTED—Head gardener, German, married, no children, competent in all branches of gardening, expert grower of roses, carnations and chrysanthemums, seeks position on gentleman's private place. Ten years experience. Please state wages. Address, Gardener, care of Chas. Frank, 144 Palisade Av., Yonkers, N. Y.

SITUATION WANTED—As foreman on private place, 38, married, one child, 21 years experience in landscape gardening and greenhouse management. Palms, ferns, carnations, mums, violets and general bedding stock. Wife can cook for helper. State full particulars. Address, Joseph Crozat, Flintstone, Ga.

SITUATION WANTED

As superintendent or gardener on a private place. German, 31 years of age, married, no children, over 16 years' experience in all branches of horticulture, nursery and landscape work.

E H., 45 E. 2nd St., Brooklyn, N. Y.

Mention The Florists' Exchange when writing.

HELP WANTED

WANTED—At once, good grower of carnations, mums and bedding stock. Wages, $35 room and board. T. Malbranc, Johnstown, Pa.

WANTED—A good sober and industrious man for general greenhouse work. Apply to J. Horan & Son, Florists, Bridgeport, Conn.

WANTED—Thoroughly competent man for growing general greenhouse stock. Address, stating experience, references and wages desired, Iowa Seed Company, Des Moines, Ia.

WANTED—First-class store man and decorator. Must be up-to-date on high grade table work. Good salary to first-class man only. At once, address S. C., care The Florists' Exchange.

WANTED—One good carnation grower, also one thoroughly experienced man for watering and other greenhouse work. Please state wages expected and references in first letter. Evendon Bros., Williamsport, Pa.

WANTED—A first-class man for retail florist in Chicago; no greenhouse work. Must be a good salesman and designer. State wages, References. Address, M. D., care The Florists' Exchange.

WANTED—Thoroughly experienced greenhouse assistant for private place. One who understands roses and carnations especially. Wages, $35.00 per month. Apply S. E., care The Florists' Exchange.

HELP WANTED

WANTED—Bright, attractive, experienced lady to take charge of floral store in Kalamazoo, Mich. Must be able to do decorating and first-class funeral designs. Apply by letter with references to Lock Box 855, Kalamazoo, Mich.

WANTED—Section man for roses and one for carnations; married or single. $15.00 per week to men with references as to capability and soberness. Pittsburgh Rose and Carnation Co., Crystal Farm, Gibsonia, Pa.

WANTED—September 1, young or middle aged man of experience in general nursery work. Must be able to take charge of shipping and propagating. State wages wanted, age, nationality and references. C. R. Fish & Company, West Side Nurseries, Worcester, Mass.

WANTED—A foreman to grow roses, carnations and a general line of greenhouse stock. Place situated in New York State. Wages, $15.00 per week to commence. C. D., care Arthur T. Boddington, 342 West 14th street, New York.

WANTED—A single man as second gardener, experienced in greenhouses and the general run of a private establishment. Wages, $30.00 per month and board. Apply to Philip Bovington, Sandanona Gardens, Millbrook, N. Y.

WANTED—Florist, for commercial place, with experience in growing choice pot plants. Wages, $50.00 per month to start. Send copy of references and particulars in first letter. Address, O. K., care The Florists' Exchange.

WANTED—An A No. 1 grower of roses and carnations, also potted plants. Must be a first-class designer; have about 15,000 feet of glass, mostly new houses, steam heat. Party will have under his charge two assistants; place pays $15.00 per week, laundry and room. Best day board can be had at $3.00 per week. No transportation furnished. Apply at once with references for a steady situation. T. L. Metcalfe, Hopkinsville, Ky.

WANTED—A florist, must be first-class grower, propagator and designer. Address E., Canonsburg, Pa.

Mention The Florists' Exchange when writing.

WANTED.

2 young men on carnation place as helpers. $12.00 per week.

HESSION,

Clarkson St., Flatbush, BROOKLYN, N.Y.

Mention The Florists' Exchange when writing.

WANTED

Section man for rose houses. State wages.

EDW. J. TAYLOR,
Southport, Conn.

Mention The Florists' Exchange when writing.

WANTED.

A thoroughly competent rose grower to take charge of section. Wages, $15.00 per week; to the right man a chance to work himself up to high wages.

Address,

EXPERT, CARE THE FLORISTS' EXCHANGE.

Mention The Florists' Exchange when writing.

MISCELLANEOUS WANTS

WANTED TO BUY—Greenhouses to be taken down. State full particulars of same when writing. Address, F. W., care The Florists' Exchange.

WANTED—Correspondence with nurserymen who have trees, oaks and elms, suitable for street planting. Address, The Tree and Park Commission, 1317 Sumter street, Columbia, S. C.

WANTED TO RENT—With privilege of buying, one or two greenhouses with some land. Near Buffalo or Northern part of New York State preferred. Address, A. D., care The Florists' Exchange.

FOR SALE OR RENT

FOR RENT—The Lindley Graperies, Frankford, Philadelphia, Pa., with house, also conveniences and stable. Apply to Robert T. Corson, Attorney for Estate of George Lindley, 4629 Frankford Av., Philadelphia, Pa.

FOR SALE—Florist's business, corner lot, nearly 7 acres, 26 miles from Philadelphia, 3 hothouses, frame house, barn, outbuildings, on trolley, and near station. For particulars, address, O. M., care The Florists' Exchange.

TO LEASE—Corner store, 25x100, at junction of three main thoroughfares, with small stocked greenhouse attached, heated by hot water. Owner has carried on business for past fortytwo years, but wishes to retire on account of age. Exceptional opportunity for right party. Address, Mrs. T. Clark, 90 Ft. Greene Place, Brooklyn, N. Y.

FOR SALE OR RENT

FOR SALE—Owing to failing health, I will sell my florist establishment, beautifully situated between Larchmont Manor and Mamaroneck, Westchester Co., New York, near railroad station; trolley lines within one minute walk. First class opportunity for the right man. Plenty of landscape and jobbing work. The place contains four acres, 2 greenhouses, 104 feet long and lots of sash; well stocked with trees and shrubs, etc.; horse, wagon and tools. Address, Box 44, Larchmont, New York.

FOR SALE

A well equipped place, consisting of seven greenhouses, over 30,000 feet of glass, a nine roomed house, barn, stock, etc., and eight acres of land. This is a decided bargain and a rare opportunity. For particulars address

S. S. SKIDELSKY,

824 N. 24th St., Philadelphia, Pa.

Mention The Florists' Exchange when writing.

TO LET

Florist Establishment consisting of nine greenhouses, heated by hot water, containing about 10,000 square feet of glass; sheds, barn and dwelling, in Long Island City, within one hour's drive of the wholesale markets of the City of New York. For further particulars address **Box R. Y., Florists' Exchange**

Mention The Florists' Exchange when writing.

STOCK FOR SALE

QUEEN LOUISE and C. A. DANA carnations, fine stock, $5.00 per 100; $35.00 per 1000. For & Rosen, Parkerford, Pa.

BEAUTY OF NICE stock, seed from selected home-grown flowers, fresh, double, $1.00 large trade pkt. Address, Waverly Greenhouses, Tuckahoe, N. Y.

CARNATIONS—Extra fine field-grown plants; Joost, New Daybreak, Prosperity, Wolcott, $5 per 100; $40 per 1,000. Terms cash. M. J. Schaaf, Dansville, N. Y.

GIANT PANSIES, mixed; double daisies and forget-me-nots, blue, 50c. per 100 mailed; $2.50 per 1000 express. Cash. Shippensburg Floral Co., Shippensburg, Pa.

FOR SALE.—25 large plants of azalea alba, for cutting, 8 4-inch gate valves for hot water heating, $4 each. 100 large Adiantum cuneatum, grown in bed, 25c. each. J. Geist, Melrose, Mass.

15,000 STRONG, healthy, field-grown violet plants of Farquhar, Lady Campbell, La France and California, $5.00 per 100; $45.00 per 1000. Richard Langle, North Street, White Plains, N. Y.

500 QUEEN LOUISE, white; 500 May Naylor, white; 500 Prosperity, var.; 200 Roosevelt, red. Fieldgrown plants; healthy. Will sell lot for $50.00. Not firstclass, but very good. G. B. S., 65 Bayview Avenue, Jersey City, N. J.

BABY RAMBLER roses, fine dormant stock, $25 per 100. 2 1-2 inch pot plants, extra well rooted $7 per 100, $65 per 1000. Orders booked for delivery now or any time up to late Spring. Samples free. Brown Brothers Co., Rochester, N. Y.

2,000 Brides, 3,000 Bridesmaids, 1,000 Meteors, 1,000 Beauties, out of 4 in. pots. No better plants grown. Packed and delivered at express office. Maids and Brides, 5c.; Meteors, 4c.; Beauties, 12c. each. Louis M. Noe, Madison, N. J.

CAMPBELL VIOLETS, fine, large, field-grown clumps, also Princess of Wales, the same, at $5.00 per 100. Dracaena indivisa, extra heavy, fine, sturdy, field-grown, 18 to 26 in. above ground, 20c. to 25c. each; per dozen, $2.50. W. G. Kroeber, New Bedford, Mass.

PANSIES, 50c. per 100; $3.50 per 1,000. Daisies (Bellis), 50c. per 100; $2.50 per 1000. Alex Haeseler, Meshanticut, R. I.

FOR SALE

FOR SALE—4 Hitchings hot water expansion tanks. No. 2 high tank Fig. E. of catalogue. All in good condition. F. O. B., $2.00 each. Address, K. D., care The Florists' Exchange.

FOR SALE

Greenhouse Material milled from Gulf Cypress, to any detail furnished, or our own patterns as desired, cut and spliced ready for erection. Estimates for complete constructions furnished.

V. E. REICH, Brooklyn, N. Y.

1429-1437 Metropolitan Ave.

Mention The Florists' Exchange when writing.

CHANGES IN BUSINESS.

ADAMS, MASS.—A. J. Boothman is having a large addition built to his greenhouse.

SCARBORO, ILL.—The address of J. L. Lutz, Sr., is now Scarboro, Lee County, Ill.

AMHERST, MASS.—Morris B. Kingman has reopened his florist store on Amity street.

NEWTON CENTER, MASS.—H. J. McGrady has reopened the flower store at 67 Union street.

GOSHEN, IND.—E. N. Burt has bought the A. J. Santschi greenhouse located on South Eighth street.

FULTON, ILL.—The firm of Hills & Mackenzie has been changed to Hills Brothers, Mr. Mackenzie having sold his interest to the new firm.

ANNAPOLIS, MD.—George Fox, formerly florist for Rudolph Kaiser, has resigned his position and has opened a flower store of his own on Maryland avenue.

BLOOMINGTON, ILL.—The Phoenix Nursery Company has opened a floral establishment at 314 North Main street. Fred H. Rowe, formerly of Chicago, is manager.

NORTHAMPTON, MASS. — The address of Thomas Foulds will be as follows: "Office of Home Culture Clubs, Nursery Department, 10 Jewett street, Northampton, Mass.," to be known as Northampton Nurseries. This company has lately acquired the property of Charles W. Loomis, florist of this city, for the purpose of enlarging its facilities for the benefit of its members and patrons. Catalogs will be thankfully received.

Chicago.

News Notes.

The latest addition to our local houses was opened last week under the name of the Gem Floral Company (not incorporated) wholesale and retail florists, 2023 West Madison street, opposite the Garfield Park Bank. A. R. Ratsch is in charge of the new establishment.

F. W. Timme was seen last week at his home, 2459 West Forty-second court and found in perfect physical condition after his return from a European trip during which he visited Bremen, Hamburg, the heather region of Northern Germany which was in a full blaze of beauty, Hanover, Brunswick, Berlin, Magdeburg, Erfurt, Quedlinburg, The Harz Mountains, up the Rhine, Interlaken, Zurich, Berne, Tyrol, Munich and Nuemberg. In his tour Mr. Timme had planned to visit Scotland and England, but cut out this part of his itinerary with the intention of going over again next season accompanied by his wife and daughter and visiting the interesting points of the British Isles. There was one point of interest to commercial horticulturists which was especially noted on the trip and that was the entire absence of nephrolepis in any of its numerous forms so familiar to the American florist, except a few specimen plants in public parks or the greenhouses connected with them.

Miss Wolf, bookkeeper for the J. A. Budlong concern, left last week for Colorado where she expects to put in her two weeks' vacation.

Otto Goerisch, for many years a well known and trusted employee of the A. L. Randall Company, is receiving the congratulations of his many friends in the trade on the event of his having become a benedict. He was married last week to Miss Giggel at the residence of the bride's parents, 2953 Quinn street.

Cliff Pruner, who has been suffering from an attack of typhoid, returned to his desk at the Winterson Company supply department on Monday of this week.

After the severe storm on Friday afternoon of last week, C. Paasch was exceedingly surprised at the delivery of an automobile in his basement which in turning out for a street car skidded over the slippery pavement, jumped the sidewalk and deposited itself under the florist establishment.

Marriages are generally admitted to be a sure sign of prosperity in any line of business or in any community so it is with pleasure that we continue to note the increasing number of members of the craft who are entering the marital state. One of the latest was Henry Vent of the J. A. Budlong city store, who last week married Miss Garretson, of De Kalb, Ill.

On Monday afternoon last the executive committee of the Horticultural Society of Chicago met in the Auditorium Annex and laid their plans for the coming flower show which will be held the second week in November. In the absence of President Uihlein who is abroad, J. C. Vaughan occupied the chair and a list of committees for the coming exhibition was appointed and general plan of proceedure adopted. As everything points to the coming show being the greatest ever held in Chicago, if not in the country, the plans are being very carefully perfected.

WM. K. WOOD.

Pittsburg.

News Notes.

The month of September was a fair one in regard to business, particularly the last week, when considerable funeral work as well as wedding orders caused a good demand for stock. The outlook for October so far is quite good, a few prominent weddings having been announced to take place. There is yet considerable stock of all sorts on hand, particularly asters, which are very plentiful and low in price. The first chrysanthemums have been seen for a week or more, but it will be several weeks yet before many are cut around home. Gladiolus are shortening up. Quite a few lilies are on hand, but not in much demand.

Bulb trade is yet slow; not much is expected until frost appears. The quality of bulbs this Fall is good, but they are not quite as large as last season.

The Pittsburg Florists' Exchange has laid in a stock of all sorts of florists' supplies the past month; also opened up a shop for the manufacture of all kinds of wire work in their present store.

The cool weather is keeping the growers busy getting things indoors, as frost may be expected any time from now on.

The next meeting of the Florists' Club takes place Tuesday, October 2, at 8 p. m. Quite an interesting program is expected, and every one should come.

E. C. REINEMAN.

Boston.

The News.

Welch Brothers are busy moving this week from their old location on Province street, which they have occupied so long, to their commodious new store at 226 Devonshire street, which they have fitted up in splendid shape for the quick handling of their business.

Charles Boyle and Wm. Goode will not embark in business as reported last week, but are both back at their old positions with Thos. F. Galvin.

Ernest Stickels is now salesman for the Montrose Greenhouses in the Park street flower market.

Peter Murray of Fairhaven, who is Eastern agent for F. R. Pierson Company for their new carnation Winsor, reports a good sale for this variety, the color of which will prove its popularity as it becomes known.

W. Grady of Newtonville is on the road these days with a fine, new trotter.

J. W. D.

New Bedford, Mass.

Carnations are about all planted in the houses in this section. We have had no frost as yet, but expect it any night now. Some of the growers have commenced to fire in their rose houses, the nights being damp and cool.

From all appearances there will be plenty of chrysanthemums here this Fall; the plants are looking fine and healthy.

H. A. Jahn has some interesting seedling carnations. One of them which he exhibited at the dahlia show last week, is a grand crimson; this he will put on the market the coming Spring. He is working up a big stock of his new white seedling.

On Friday, the 14th inst., James Garthley, gardener to Mr. H. H. Rogers of Fairhaven, Mass., received a cablegram from Scotland informing him of his wife's sudden illness. Mr. Garthley started on the 15th for Scotland. Monday, the 17th another cablegram was received here saying that Mrs. Garthley had passed away. Mr. Garthley has the heartfelt sympathy of the craft in his sudden bereavement. The deceased leaves a husband, one son and one daughter to mourn her loss.

HORTICO.

Philadelphia.

Trade Notes

A better tone prevails all along the line as to trade. The retailers are booking wedding orders for October, and indications point to some good business in that line. Habermehl's Sons and the William Graham Company have both been very busy with department store decorations; some of these were on an elaborate scale.

The Flower Market.

A meeting of the flower market stockholders was held on Tuesday when it was decided to go into liquidation and wind up the corporation by July 1, 1907, or before if the directors could dispose of the lease on the building. The finances are in such good shape that the stockholders will receive all they paid in. There was a disposition on the part of those growers who have used the market to make some arrangements to continue, but it seems impossible in this city to get the support of all the growers. Some of the principal retailers held out and would not go to the market; this compelled the growers to continue to carry their flowers to the stores. The growers who rented stalls at the market were well pleased. As the stall feature did not take, the market has been doing a commission business; this, last year, amounted to over $50,000, and had been worked up by the manager, Charles E. Meehan; and as he has now consolidated with S. S. Pennock there is nothing to do but close up the market.

Club News.

The Florists' Club meets on Tuesday next when a discussion will be invited as to plans for the S. A. F. convention next year. The question most prominent just now, is, Where shall the convention be held? Nearly everyone thinks of Horticultural Hall, on Broad street, which is the home of the club. Some say it is not large enough, while others say, Have the exhibit in the hall and the meetings in Broad street theater opposite the hall. Then again there are some who desire to continue the outdoor exhibit of plants, and they wish to go to the Exposition Buildings at Thirty-fourth and South street, where ground is available for an outdoor display. So come to the meeting next Tuesday. This is an important question, and the club should be well represented to get everyone's views.

Jottings.

John McIntyre has rented a store at 1601 Ranstead street for his commission business.

Edward Reid is making extensive improvements at his wholesale commission place.

The first chrysanthemums of this season arrived on September 11; the variety was Opah and came from Weber & Sons, Oakland, Md.

Arthur F. Mac Iver, who is in the Wm. Graham Company store, was married recently to Miss Ethel V. Whitman. The bride was the president of a bachelor girls' club, so that the event caused quite a flurry in down town circles, as the girls were supposed to be banded together against the male sex. This made the wedding a prominent affair. The couple are now back from their honeymoon tour and are living in West Philadelphia.

DAVID RUST.

FIRMS WHO ARE BUILDING.

OTTUMWA, IOWA.—Fred Schaub is building a new greenhouse 100 x 20 feet.

BOUND BROOK, N. J.—A. Bidwell has erected another greenhouse, 100 x 20 ft.

SIDNEY, N. Y.—Harry Thorndycraft has added a large new greenhouse to his plant.

RAHWAY, N. J.—C. E. Baumann has built one house 100 x 30 ft. for cut flower growing.

B.

MERIDEN, CONN.—R. W. Barrow is adding 25,000 square feet of glass to his establishment.

FRANKLIN, MASS.—Kelley Bros. are adding a greenhouse, 22 by 70 feet to their Prospect street place.

TERRE HAUTE, IND.—The Terre Haute Rose & Carnation Company has added a house 150 x 30 feet.

ST. PAUL, MINN.—Holm & Olsen have built five new houses containing about 9,000 square feet of glass.

SHERMAN, TEXAS. — The Texas Nursery Company has added about 11,000 square feet of glass to its plant.

ROSELLE, N. J.—A. Fink has built one house 100 x 30 ft., and one 100 x 20 ft., for cut flowers and bedding plants.

KANSAS CITY, MO. — Augustus Blankenfeld has torn down his greenhouses and is erecting a new range at Rosedale, Kan.

SILVERDALE, PA.—George K. Kester has rebuilt his greenhouse using entirely double strength glass. His new house is 158 x 28 feet.

A Paying Investment.

My advertisement of Calla Bulbs in The Florists' Exchange brought in $2,152.25. Thanks. A. MITTING.

Santa Cruz, Cal.

Mr. Mitting's advertisement of Calla Bulbs occupied a 2-inch double column space, and was inserted as a separate advertisement four times in The Florists' Exchange, being included in a mixed advertisement six times, making ten insertions, altogether, at a total cost of $44.—Ed. F. E.

St. Louis.

The Week's News.

Visitors last week included J. J. Kierns, representing H. A. Dreer, Inc., Philadelphia, who reported a successful trade; C. Brown, of Springfield, Ill.; who called at the wholesale district; he is sending in some fine stock to this market; and Charles Ford, the man who sells everything in the florist line.

George Waldbart, Jr. son of Alex. Waldbart, was married recently to Miss Emma R. Hoyle. The happy couple will reside on Horton place.

Louis A. Gieger, on September 26, married Miss Marie Hirshfield. He is with the Ayers Floral Company on Grand avenue.

Henry Berning has the appointment as judge of flowers at the Centralia, Ill., and Sedalia, Mo. fairs; the former fair occurs this week; the latter, next week.

Mrs. F. M. Ellis is expecting daily the return of her husband who has been looking after business interests at Panama, where he has been the past eight months.

Harry Braun, manager for A. Jablonsky's big range of glass, has resigned. No better man to grow roses and carnations can be found than Harry Braun.

Charles Schoenle, J. J. Beneke, Robert Beyer, A. Meyer, Sr., Chas. Juengel and Wm. Young, have been selected as judges and clerks for the coming Fall election.

Eddie Gerlach has quit bowling for a while at least. Can it be that Eddie, like so many of the trade, has the matrimonial bee buzzing in his bonnet?

Councilman Rolfes has introduced a bill into Council prohibiting the ringing of door bells and soliciting orders of any kind whatsoever. Should this bill go through (and it will if the local club can aid any) it would sound a death knell to the many crepe pullers; this infamous practice is becoming more general every day and should be stopped. The bill states a fine for each offence of not less than $5 and not more than $100.

The bowling season is about to open and it is to be regretted that most of the local florist bowlers have lost interest in the game; the effort to organize a florist league has failed. Those who will join different leagues are C. A. Kuehn, J. J. Beneke, Carl Beyer and A. Y. Ellison.

ST. PATRICK.

Washington, D. C.

At the last meeting of the Florists' Club, the following resolution was offered by Z. D. Blackistone: "Whereas, the Washington Florists' Club has noted with approbation the efforts of the Jobbers' and Shippers' Association in the furtherance of the development of Greater Washington. Therefore, be it resolved, that the said Florists' Club does hereby extend to the said Jobbers' and Shippers' Association its congratulations and good wishes in this laudable project; and furthermore begs to assure the association of its hearty co-opcration and support." The resolution was supplemented by an order to the treasurer to send ten dollars as initiation fee.

A very pretty wedding took place at the home of Mr. and Mrs. William E. Thorne, New Glatz, Md., September 5, when their eldest daughter, Lilias Watson, was married to Mr. Ernest Kletsch of the Department of Agriculture. The long avenue leading to the residence, lined with trees and boxwood hedges, was brilliantly lighted with lanterns. The large reception room was profusely decorated with boughs of oak bordered with golden rod; the mantels were banked with wild ferns, red sumach and golden rod, with bunches of white roses. The work was done by August Mayer of the Department of Agriculture, a friend of the groom.

A portion of the Government reservation, known as Potomac Park, was transferred to the District by Robert Shaw Oliver, acting Secretary of War. This transfer was made at the request of the commissioners so as to establish definite lines of demarcation.

There are miles of public roads in the District of Columbia and Maryland practically lined with thickets of poison ivy, or which have the stone walls overgrown with it. There should be a law enacted compelling authorities in local communities to abate the nuisance. When we see our friends returning to town from their country sojourn with faces red and sore, it is convincing proof that this detestable weed should be extirpated.

Cromwell, Conn.

The Pierson Plant.

The Hartford (Conn.) Courant of Wednesday, September 12, contains an illustrated write-up of the large greenhouse plant of A. N. Pierson. He has now 600,000 square feet of glass. To heat the greenhouses and other buildings requires a battery of eleven boilers, two of them being of eighty horsepower and nine of 125 each or more. Some of these are kept in service day and night throughout the year. To keep the plant warm men yearly shovel 6,000 tons of coal into the furnaces, the coal being a mixture composed of one-fifth bituminous and the rest anthracite of the size known as buckwheat. The coal is brought to Cromwell by the barge load and a stock sufficient for two years is kept on hand. Water is used almost as lavishly as coal and his yearly bill from the local company amounts to $1,600.

In addition to the other items of expense connected with the greenhouses are the care of twenty-five horses used on the farm, big, sleek fellows all of them, and a herd of 100 cows, whose milk is a by-product that pays for the herd which is really kept for the purpose of furnishing fertilizer for the plant. Besides what manure the farm can supply Mr. Pierson buys all that is for sale in Middletown and also brings it in by the carload from outside the county. It's a pretty big business that Mr. Pierson carries on in the town of Cromwell.

If Mr. Pierson is asked where he learned his trade he is apt to say that he has not learned it and that he never expects to finish his apprenticeship. He was born near Lund, a city in Sweden, fifty-six years ago and worked in greenhouses there until 18 years old. He came to this country in 1868 and to Portland in 1871. The next year he hired Charles O. Post of Cromwell and built one greenhouse about fifty feet long. A year or two later he married Miss Allison of Middletown and occupied an unpretentious house near his greenhouses. Each year has seen one or more new greenhouses, one just finished this year being 60 by 408 feet, and the limit seems as far off as ever. Mr. Post, his original workman, is still in his employ and is likely to be as long as he works for any one. Four children have been born to Mr. and Mrs. Pierson, one dying in infancy, one, Representative Frank Pierson, dying last year, and two are living, Wallace R. Pierson, who is associated in business with his father, and a daughter, the youngest of the family.

Primula Obconica Grandiflora Compacta.

My Unsurpassed Strain OF THE New Primula Obconica Hybrids,

is ready now in 2½ in. pots. Fine plants.

Carmine, Pink, Purple, Violet, White, all giant flowered.

Each color separate	per 100,	$ 4.00
The same mixed	" "	3.50
Compacta, a fine potter	" "	5.00
Triumph, latest novelty	" "	10.00

P. S.—Do not sell less than 25 of each color.

O. V. ZANGEN, Seedsman, **Hoboken, N. J.**

Mention The Florists' Exchange when writing.

HEADQUARTERS FOR

Choice Plants

English Ivy, Anthericums, Kentias Forsteriana and Belmoreana, Phoenix Canariensis, Araucarias, Bay Trees and Boxwood Pyramids, Asparagus Plumosus, Bird's Nest, Scottii Elegantissima, Piersoni Boston and Johnsoni Ferns, Cattleya Trianae Rubbers Dracaenas Terminalis and Fragrans, Pandanus Veitchii, Gardenia Veitchii, Cycas Revoluta, Cibotium Schiedei Livistona Sinensis, Areca Lutescens, Crotons, Aspidistras, Lygodium Scandens, Primula Obconica, Begonia Rex, Daisies, Fern Balls, Lily of the Valley, Cut Flowers, Leaf Mold, Orchid Peat, etc. Write for prices.

Anton Schultheis 19th St. and 4th Ave, College Point, L. I., N. Y.

Mention The Florists' Exchange when writing.

CYCLAMEN

SPLENDENS GIGANTEUM HYBRIDS

This strain has no equal or better. Perfect flowers of Giant type in five true colors, well grown plants from 4 in. pots $15.00 per 100, from 5 in. pots $2.50 per doz. $20.00 per 100.

PRIMULA SINENSIS FIMBRIATA

Only fringed varieties Giant flowers in the best market sorts, all colors from 2½ in. pots $3.00 per 100.

PRIMULA OBCONICA GRANDIFLORA

The celebrated Ronsdorfer and Lattmans Hybrids in the most beautiful colors from 2½ in. pots $3.00, from 3½ in. pots $10.00 per 100.

BEGONIA REX

In 12 choice market varieties, extra well grown plants from 5 in. pots $2.00 per doz. Rooted cuttings labeled $2.00 equally mixed $1.50 per 100.

Asparagus Plumosus Nanus

Special offer for first class grown stock from 2½ in. pots $2.50 per 100, $20.00 per 1000.

CINERARIAS HYBRIDA MAXIMA GRANDIFLORA

No better strain from 2½ in. pots $2.50 per 100.

PAUL MADER, EAST STROUDSBURG, PA.

CYCLAMEN PRIMULAS

Cyclamen. Giganteum Splendens, in fine colors, including **Rococo, Low's Pioneers, Butterfly, Fringed, Lilac Salmon,** all that is best, 3 in. ready for 5 in., per 100 $6.00.

Primula, Obconica Grandiflora Fimbriata, rose, carmine, new giants, all the best, 2½ in. ready for 4 in., $3.50 per 100.

Chinese, Vaughan's International, New Giants, two best English strains, 3 in. ready for 4 in., per 100 $5.00.

J. SYLVESTER,
FLORIST,
OCONTO, WIS.

Cyclamen Giganteum

Extra fine plants, large flowering, 3-inch, $5.00 per 100; 4 inch $10.00 per 100; 5 inch $15.00 per 100. **Primulas,** Chinese and Obconica 2½ inch, $2.00 per 100; 3 inch $3.00 per 100; 4 inch $6.00 per 100.

Asparagus Sprengeri, 3½-inch, $5.00 per 100. Asparagus Plumosus Nanus, 3½-inch, $6.00 per 100.

SAMUEL WHITTON, 15-16 Gray Ave., Utica, N. Y.

Mention The Florists' Exchange when writing.

Decorative Plants

Latania Borbonica, 2¼ in. pots, $3.00; 3 in. $8.00; 4 in., $15.00 per 100. Large specimen plants from $2.00 to $5.00 each.

Kentia Belmoreana and Forsteriana, 2¼ in. pots, $8.00; 3 in., $15.00; 4 in., $26.00 per 100; 5 in., $60.00 per 100; 6 in., $15.00 per doz.; 7 in. and upward, $1.75 to $36.00 each.

Areca Lutescens, 3 in. $10.00; 4 in. $20.00 per 100; 6 in., $1.00 each and upward.

Pandanus Utilis, 2 in. pots, $3.00; 4 in., $20.00 per 100.

Phoenix Reclinata, 5 in. pots, $35.00 per 100.

Phoenix Canariensis, fine specimen plants, from $2.00 to $35.00 each.

Araucaria Excelsa, 5 in. pots, $65.00 per 100.

Assorted Ferns, 2¼ in. pots, $3.00 per 100.

Nephrolepis Compacta, 3 in. pots, $8.00; 4 in., $15.00 per 100.

Plants in Fine Condition.

JOHN BADER, Troy Hill, Allegheny, Pa.

Mention The Florists' Exchange when writing.

POINSETTIAS

2½ in. pots, $5.00 per 100; $40.00 per 1000, Cash with order.

S. N. PENTECOST,
1790-1810 East 101 St., CLEVELAND, O.

Mention The Florists' Exchange when writing.

Primula Obconica Grandiflora

2 1-2 in., $2.50 per 100. Ask for list (seedlings of hardy plants)

BAUDISCH & CO.,
537 Fulton Street UNION HILL, N. J.

Mention The Florists' Exchange when writing.

ROOTED CUTTINGS

COLEUS, 20 kinds, 60c. per 100; $6.00 per 1000. **ALTERNANTHERA,** 3 kinds, $1.00 per 100; $8.00 per 1000. **LANTANA,** 8 kinds, $1.00 per 100. **AGERATUM,** 3 kinds, $1.00 per 100. **SALVIA,** 3 kinds, $1.00 per 100. **Field Grown PRINCE OF WALES VIOLETS,** Scotch Pink, $4.00 per 100. 2 in. **GERANIUM,** 20c. per 100.

THE NATIONAL PLANT CO., DAYTON, OHIO

Mention the Florists' Exchange when writing.

STUDER OFFERS

Palms, Latanias, Phoenix, from 4 to 7 in. pots; Kentia and Chamerops Excelsa, 4 and 6 in.

Ferns, Bostons, 4, 5, 6 and 7 in. size; Adiantums, 3 and 4 in.; Asparagus Plumosus Nanus, 3 in.; Maranta Zebrina, 3 in.

Begonia Vernon and Erfordi, 4 in. in bloom. **Aucuba Japonica,** 4 and 5 in. pots, for window boxes. **Roses,** pot grown, 3, 4, 5 and 6 in. pots; also rooted rose cuttings. All cheap for cash, or 2 to 3 months negotiable notes.

N. STUDER, FLORIST, ANACOSTIA, D. C.

Mention The Florists' Exchange when writing.

SURPLUS STOCK—CHEAP

We have a fine lot of **Jerusalem Cherries** for sale from 2 in. pots. In order to make room immediately we will close them out at $1.00 per 100; they are worth $5.00. Also **Smilax,** strong, 2 in. pots, $1.00 per 100; $9.00 per 1000. Also a big stock of **Geraniums, S. A. Nutt** and others, also assorted from sand, $1.00 per 100; from 2 in. pots, $1.75 per 100; from 3 in. pots, $4.00 per 100. Write for prices on other stock; we can save you money.

E. I. RAWLINGS, QUAKERTOWN, PA.

Mention the Florists' Exchange when writing.

Commercial Violet Culture

PRICE, $1.50

The FLORISTS' EXCHANGE, 2-8 Duane St., New York

OUR LITTLE PET

From Aschmann in Philadelphia I bought
An Araucaria, a pet for our little girl;
Now we have two pets, the pride of our thought:
The little girl so sweet, a head full of curls,
And the Araucaria with its everlasting green,
A more joyful home you never have seen.

Watch us Grow!!

ARAUCARIA EXCELSA, the best of all decorative plants nature produces: a specialty. Every man in business life, to be successful, must adopt one thing as his specialty, and that specialty, whatever he may select, and of whatever nature it may be, he must guard, study and push to such an extent, that it not only benefits himself, but he must conduct it so, that every one who seeks his aid, service or his articles, whatever he advertises or practices, will **share a slice** of his **activity** and **prosperity.** I made the importation and cultivation of Araucaria as a special study in my life. The following figures will show you my success in business: In the first year I began with an import of 250; in the eleventh year (now 1906) my importation has grown up to 6,000 (come and see it). On account of the Araucaria growing yearly in favor as a much admired decorative plant for the arbor, bed room, dining and sitting rooms, stores, hotels, lawns and porches by the plant-consuming peoples all over the country, the **outlook** will be of an importation of at least 8,000 to 10,000 in the Spring of 1907. To secure this vast amount for 1907, I am now in Belgium making contracts for next year. I shall also at the same time bring over with me a large lot of choice Azalea Indica, Palms, etc. for Christmas and Easter forcing. No money will be spared in obtaining for my customers the cream of the Belgium greenhouses.

Please note lowest price now going for September:

ARAUCARIA EXCELSA

12 to 14 in. 5½ in. pots, 3 to 4 tiers, 2-yr. old, 50c. 14 to 16 in., 5½ in. pots, 3 to 4 tiers, 2-yr. old, 60c. 16 to 18 in. 5½ to 6 in. pots, 4 to 5 tiers, 3-yr. old, 75c. 18 to 20 in., 6 in. pots, 5 to 6 tiers, 4-yr. old, $1.00. 20 to 24 in. 6 in. to 7 in. pots, 5 to 6 tiers, 4-yr. old, $1.25. 36-40 to 50 in. 7 in. pots, specimen plants from $2.50 to $8.00 each.

ARAUCARIA COMPACTA ROBUSTA—have several thousand of them; can supply all wants. These plants were never so fine in shape and condition as this year. The set of the greenhouse, as broad as long, 12 to 20 in. in height, 3 to 4 perfect tiers, 20 to 30 inches across, 3-4-5 year old, 6 to 7 in. pots, $1.25, $1.50, $1.75, $2.00, $2.50 to $3.00 each.

ARAUCARIA EXCELSA GLAUCA—This variety on account of its beautiful Green-Bluish tiers, dwarf habit, fine compact shape, gives it a striking appearance, and anybody seeing them, must undoubtedly fall in love with them at sight. Plants, 6-7 inch pots, 3-4-5 perfect tiers, 3-4 year old, 15 to 25 inch high, from 15 to 30 in. across, $1.25, $1.50, $1.75, $2.00 to $2.50 each.

KENTIA BELMOREANA, 5½ to 6 in. pots, bushy, fine plants, from 75 cts. to $1.00 to $1.25 each.

KENTIA FORSTERIANA, 7 in. pots, made-up plants, 1 large in center, 3 smaller sizes, 22 to 25 in. high around, gives them a good appearance, $2.00 each. 6 in. pots, single plants, 35 to 40 in. high, 5 to 6 good leaves, 4 year old, $1.25 to $1.50 each; 6 in. pots, 30 to 35 in. high, 4 year old, 5 good leaves, $1.00; 5½ in. pots, 3 year old, 25 to 30 in. high, 5 good leaves, 75c. made-up plants, 3 and 4 in. pots, 18 to 20 in. high, 25 cts. to 30 cts. each.

ARECA LUTESCENS, made-up, 25 cts.

COCOS WEDDELIANA, 15 cts.

NEPHROLEPIS BARROWSII, 5 in. pots, strong, ready for 7-8 in., 50c. 4 in. pots, ready for 6-7 in., 25c.

NEPHROLEPIS SCOTTII, 6 in. pots, large, ready for 6-7 in. 50c.; 5½ in. pots, 40c.; 5 in. 35c.; 4 in. 20c. to 25c.

BOSTON FERNS, 4 in., 20c. to 25c. I have them by the thousand. 5 in.; 30c. to 35c.

FERNS for dishes, a fine assortment, 2½ in., $5.00 per 100; 3 in., $6.00 per 100.

FICUS ELASTICA, 6 in., 50c.

ASPARAGUS PLUMOSUS NANUS, 3 in., 6c.; 4 in., 10c.

PRIMULA SINENSIS, in 4 in., pots ready to shift; will bloom for Christmas. $10.00 per 100.

CASH WITH ORDER

When ordering, say whether the plants should be shipped in the pots or not

GODFREY ASCHMANN

Importer and Wholesale Grower of Pot Plants

1012 Ontario Street, - - PHILADELPHIA, PA.

DRACAENA INDIVISA

	Per 100
Fine, strong, 6 in. pots	$25.00
Asparagus Sprengeri, 3 in., strong	4.00
" 2 in.	1.50
Asparagus Plumosus Nanus, 2 in.	2.00
Primula Obconica Grandiflora Alba, Rosea and Hybrida, 2 in.	2.00
" **Buttercup** yellow, 2 in.	2.00
Paris Daisy, white and yellow, 3 in.	3.00
Shasta Daisy, 3 in.	3.00
Smilax, strong 2 in. to close out	.75
Vinca Variegated, field-grown	4.00
Swainsona Galegifolia Alba, 3 and 4 in.	$3.00 and 5.00
Jerusalem Cherries, 4 in., will sell with berries	8.00

Rooted Cuttings by Mail.

Heliotrope, dark, from soil	1.00
Lantanas, dwarf 6 var., from soil	1.25

Cash with order please.

GEO. J. HUGHES, BERLIN, N. J.

DIFFERENT STOCK

Genistas, fine healthy pot grown plants, 3 in., 8c., 4 in., 10c., 5 in., 15c.

Asparagus Plumosus, strong, 2½ in., 3c.; 4 in., 8c.

Asparagus Sprengerii, 2½ in., 2c.

Ferns for Jardinieres, 2½ in., 3c.; **Boston,** 5 x 6 in., 25c.; **Tarrytown ferns,** 6 in., 50c.

Smilax, strong, 2½ in., $1.50 per 100.

Parsley Plants, large, $2.00 per 1000.

Rex Begonia, 4 in., 12c. Cash Please.

F. B. RINE, Lewisburg, Pa.

Mention The Florists' Exchange when writing.

A Few Good Things YOU WANT

Dracaena Indivisa, 4 and 6 in., $10.00 and $25.00 per 100.

Asparagus Sprengeri, 2 in., $2.50 per 100.

Geraniums, S. A. Nutt, Castellane, John Doyle, Perkins, Double Gen. Grant, Poitevine, Mme. Salleroi, 2 in. pots, $2.00 per 100; 3 in. pots $4.00 per 100. Rooted Cuttings, $1.00 per 100.

Rex Begonia, nice plants, 2 and 2½ in., $5.00 per 100.

Asparagus Plumosus, 2 in. $3.00 per 100.

Boston Fern 5 in. 20c each.

Pierson Fern 6 in. 50c each.

GEO. M. EMMANS, Newton, N. J.

Mention The Florists' Exchange when writing.

PRIMROSES

Obconica Alba and Rosea, $18.00 per 1000; $2.00 per 100.

ASPARAGUS

Plumosus, 2¼ in. pots $18.00 per 1000; $2.00 per 100.

Vinca, var. from field, $5.00 per 100.

Cannas, 5 var. field grown Clumps $15.00 per 100.

Pansy Plants, large flowering, $3.00 per 1000; 50c. per 100. Cash.

JOS. H. CUNNINGHAM, Delaware, O.

Mention The Florists' Exchange when writing.

Portland, Ore.

Its Stores and Greenhouses.

Portland, the rose city, is a good city for the florists, if we are to judge by the number of floral establishments in and about it. This will no doubt be a surprising statement to the majority of your readers as it is to me. Vegetation of all kinds flourishes in this climate. Everything grows and blossoms and keeps on growing and blossoming. Roses, I am told, bloom every month in the year in the open. Pansies may be picked as freely in December as in May. To be sure, the trees shed their leaves and have their period of rest, as in the East: but warm periods in Midwinter are likely to start the buds swelling and the roses into blossom. Roman hyacinths often bloom in the open ground in November and December. Uninterrupted growth continues for at least eight months in the year. Notwithstanding this generosity of Dame Nature and her lavish display of flowers, artificial flower raising is profitable.

Portland boasts of a population approximating 200,000 souls, and supports four as fine flower stores as could be found west of the Mississippi, while greenhouses and suburban places are counted by the scores.

Clarke Brothers have a very neat and attractive store on Morrison street, in one of the best locations in the city. Their windows are always attractive and their trade the best.

A few blocks distant Tonseth & Company, who opened up a year ago, have a neat and tasty store, and are rapidly acquiring their share of the business.

One block north of Tonseth's place is to be seen the up-to-date store of L. G. Pfunder, the pioneer of the trade in the city. This store is always bright with seasonable stock.

A block or so away on Washington street, Martin & Forbes have one of the best stores and enjoy a rapidly increasing business. This firm is strictly wideawake and up-to-date and is hustling for business at all seasons.

So much for the best stores. In my short stay here I have only visited a few of the growers. On a recent bright morning I walked out to Tonseth Brothers' plant near Mount Tabor. Here I found two modern ranges containing about 18,000 square feet of glass, heated by hot water and planted with a general line of flowering stock. In roses Golden Gate, Ivory, Bridesmaid and Bride are cultivated, with one bench of Kaiserin Augusta Victoria in another house for Summer cutting. Owing to the cool nights heat is necessary, and even with the utmost caution mildew is bound to appear. This and the cloudy weather during a large portion of the Winter, renders rose growing in this climate an uncertain venture at the best, although one large grower here has devoted nearly a whole range to roses.

Two houses and part of a third are planted to carnations. The favorites are Enchantress, Mrs. Lawson and Lady Bountiful. Owing to an unusually dry Summer, stock made but poor growth in the field and is backward in the benches. Chrysanthemums of all the leading late varieties are cultivated here. The demand for these is best at Thanksgiving time. Early varieties are not grown, as asters take the place of them up till October 15 or later. Violets at this place were looking fine. Princess of Wales for single and Imperial for double are grown. The first blooms are picked about September 20. These are also grown in open frames during the Winter with sash protection afforded during December and January. The best blooms from these come in a little later than the bench grown, thus prolonging the season.

Asparagus and ferns are also propagated here. Bulbous stock is likewise grown, and the entire output is disposed of at the firm's retail store. This firm has been established here five years and has been eminently successful.

A short distance from Tonseth's range of houses is the establishment of L. G. Pfunder. He came to Portland 35 years ago, building a small place in what is now the down town business section. Twenty-six years ago he built on Washington street, where he maintained a store in connection with his greenhouses until a year ago. Realizing that sooner or later he would have to move from Washington street, and also on on account of his rapidly expanding business, he bought a tract of land 14 years ago, out in the country, as he thought, and commenced building the nucleus of his present plant, which contains upward of 40,000 square feet of glass. Here he grows a general line of stock, which is disposed of at his retail store. In roses he has Kaiserin Augusta Victoria, Bride, Bridesmaid, Perle des Jardins and a few American Beauty and Liberty. A single row of La France in solid beds, where they have been planted for many years, reminded us of that almost forgotten leader of 20 years ago.

In carnations here as elsewhere Enchantress leads them all. Mrs. Lawson is a good producer, but is a poor keeper and shipper. Alaska seems to do well as a commercial white. We also noted Governor Roosevelt and Robert Craig as good reds.

Several houses were filled with chrysanthemums just showing their buds. Violets are also extensively cultivated. One house of smilax with heavy 8-foot strings showed good care and attention.

Mr. Pfunder also has a good collection of orchids, some of which were imported from Sander & Sons 25 years ago. Not the least showy of his many ornamental plants are the elegantissima ferns, which thrive here as nowhere else. We also noted Nephrolepis exaltata, an old-time friend now much neglected by many, as well as a bench of bouvardia. It would require hours to describe the many beautiful things seen at this place. Mr. Pfunder at 65 years of age, is still as active as most men at 30 and possesses that rare faculty of being an instructive entertainer, and one could have spent hours in his company but time forbade.

VERITAS.

San Francisco.

The News.

The "Letts-Love Flower Store" is the most affectionate trade name I have met with in this part of the country. It's no honeymoon affair either; they've been at it for years. Messrs. H. J. Letts and S. K. Love have, as proprietors of the Piedmont Floral and Seed Company of Oakland, in which city they relocated this month at 60 San Pablo avenue, opposite the City Hall, a prettier store than their old one on Broadway.

The estimate is that eight thousand Native Sons went last week from San Francisco and the cities about the bay to Santa Cruz to attend the annual celebration of California's Admission day, admission as a State of the Union. The daily papers published many portraits of the "natives," one of the larger being that of Angelo J. Rossi of the florist firm, Pelicano & Rossi, whose two stores re-established since the fire are at, respectively, 1343 Sutter street, near Van Ness avenue, and 1944 Post street, near Fillmore.

A local grower for the cut flower trade returned this week from a business trip to Portland, Oregon, and was prodigal in good words relating to the Sibson Rose Nursery, a 25-acre two-year-old enterprise, largely devoted to popular varieties of roses with the Richmond and Kate Moulton as latest additions. It is scarcely two years since Mr. Sibson made this location, and now he has four 100-foot and three 200-foot houses and a propagating house, an altogether range of glass second to none in Portland. Additional to this Mr. Sibson conducts a cut flower stand in Portland at 1180 Milwaukee avenue. Alfred Woodington, a graduate from several large nurseries roundabout Chicago, is the efficient foreman of the Sibson Rose Nursery.

The "Young American Florists," E. Rosaia & Co., in business many years before the earthquake-fire extinguished their place at 63 Fourth street, reopened in the trade last week at 3008 Mission street.

ALVIN.

Spokane, Wash.

Hundreds of professional and amateur growers from various parts of the Inland Empire, which takes in parts of Washington, Oregon, Idaho, Montana and southern British Columbia, have entered for the eighth annual aster show by the Spokane Floral Association, to be held in connection with the Spokane Interstate fair, September 24 to October 6. There will be classes for children, with four prizes for girls and boys, while for other floral exhibits there will be nearly a score of awards for competition. Mrs. R. Well of Spokane, who gave away 10,000 packets of seeds to the children of the Spokane district last Spring, will also give special cash prizes to the amount of $100 for the best exhibits by the children.

The Spokane Floral Association is doing everything in its power to encourage the growing of flowers by the children as well as adults, and as a result Spokane has some of the finest gardens in this part of the Northwest.

The eighteenth annual rose fair at Natatorium Park by the women of All Saints cathedral of Spokane was such a success that the managers are already planning for the coming year, when it is expected to secure the grounds of the Spokane Country Club for exhibition purposes.

SPENCER, IND.—E. T. Barnes, florist, carried off first prize, at the recent State Fair, on an exhibit of dahlias.

Hint to Contributors.

If you're writing for the Press,
Boil it down;
Better say a little less,
Boil it down.
Periphrastic methods wear
On the readers everywhere;
Don't be long in getting there—
Boil it down.

You've a message for mankind?
Boil it down;
Do not be to mercy blind,
Boil it down;
If you think you have a great
And important truth to state,
Do not circumambulate—
Boil it down.

Do not loiter by the way,
Boil it down;
Say the thing you want to say,
Boil it down.
Wasting language is a sin,
Screeds too long and weak won't win,
So, before you send stuff in,
Boil it down.

Be it praise or cold retort,
Boil it down;
Earnest thought or said in sport,
Boil it down;
Crack the nut you'd have us eat,
Keep the shell, produce the meat,
This your motto—"Short and sweet"—
Boil it down.

—Scottish American.

J. K. ALLEN

Wholesale Commission Dealer in **Cut Flowers**

106 West 28th St., NEW YORK

Open at 6 a. m. every day.
Telephone, 167 Madison Square.
Consignments Solicited.

Mention The Florists' Exchange when writing.

Wm. Stuart Allen Co.

Commission Merchants in CUT FLOWERS
ORCHIDS AT ALL SEASONS
53 WEST 28th STREET, NEW YORK
Telephone 356 Madison Square

Mention the Florists' Exchange when writing.

C. BONNET G. H. BLAKE

BONNET & BLAKE

Wholesale Florists
06 Livingston Street, BROOKLYN, N. Y.
Telephone: 4638 Main.
Consignments solicited. Out-of-town orders carefully attended to. Give us a trial.

Mention The Florists' Exchange when writing.

CUT FLOWER EXCHANGE

Sixth Ave. and 26th St.
Coogan Building, NEW YORK
Open every Morning at Six o'clock for the Sale of Cut Flowers.
Wall Space for advertising purposes to Rent.
V. S. DORVAL, Jr., Secretary.

Mention the Florists' Exchange when writing

Joseph S. Fenrich

...Wholesale Florist...
—THE RELIABLE HOUSE—
110 West 28th Street
Telephone 324-325 Madison Square,

Mention The Florists' Exchange when writing.

FORD BROS.

Wholesale Florists
48 WEST 28th ST., NEW YORK
Telephone, 3870-3871 Madison Square

Mention The Florists' Exchange when writing.

GROWERS, ATTENTION!
Always Ready to Receive Fine Stock

GUNTHER BROTHERS

50 West 29th Street
Phone, 551 Madison Square. NEW YORK
Violets, Roses, Carnations, Orchids
Established 1888.

Mention the Florists' Exchange when writing.

ALEX. J. GUTTMAN

The Wholesale Florist of New York
43 WEST 28th STREET
Phones 1664-1665 Madison Square

Mention The Florists' Exchange when writing

A. M. HENSHAW

..Wholesale Florist..
52 West 28th Street, NEW YORK
First class Roses and Carnations a specialty.
Consignments Solicited. Tel. 5583 Madison Sq.

Mention The Florists' Exchange when writing.

HICKS & CRAWBUCK, Inc.

Wholesale Florists
And Dealers in FLORISTS' SUPPLIES
76-78 Court Street
Phone. 3660-3661 Main BROOKLYN, N. Y.

Mention The Florists' Exchange when writing

HEADQUARTERS FOR NOVELTIES

ORCHIDS A SPECIALTY

THE HIGHEST GRADE OF **VALLEY** ALWAYS ON HAND
CARDENIAS, DAISIES, ROSES, CARNATIONS.
JAMES McMANUS, Telephone 759 Mad. Sq. 42 W. 28th St., New York.

PHILIP F. KESSLER

Wholesale Florist
55-57 W. 26th St., NEW YORK.
Telephone, 2921-5243 Madison Square.

Mention the Florists' Exchange when writing.

JULIUS LANG

Wholesale Florist
53 WEST 30th STREET
NEW YORK
Consignments Solicited. Telephone: 280 Madison Sq.

Mention the Florists' Exchange when writing

WILLIAM H. KUEBLER

Wholesale Commission Dealer in
CUT FLOWERS
28 Willoughby St.,
Telephone, 4591 Main. BROOKLYN, N. Y.

Mention the Florists' Exchange when writing

FRANK MILLANG

Wholesale Commission Dealer in
CUT FLOWERS
55-57 West 26th Street, New York
Telephone Call: 299 Madison Square.

Mention the Florists' Exchange when writing

ALFRED H. LANGJAHR

55 WEST 28th STREET, NEW YORK
Telephone, 4626-4627 Madison Square Established 1891
SPECIAL VALLEY AND TOP GRADE ASPARAGUS
Consignments of First Class Stock Solicited.

Horace E. Froment

SUCCESSOR TO

W. GHORMLEY

WHOLESALE COMMISSION FLORIST
Receiver and Shipper of all varieties of Cut Flowers
Telephones. 2200 and 2201 Madison Square 57 West 28th St., NEW YORK

Wholesale Prices of Cut Flowers, New York, Sept. 27, 1906

Prices quoted are by the hundred unless otherwise noted

Roses: A. Beauty, fancy—specia	12.00	to	25.00
" extra	5.00	to	10.00
" No. 1	4.00	to	5.00
" No. 2	3.00	to	4.00
" No. 3	1.00	to	1.50
Bride, Maid, fancy—spe'l	2.00	to	4.00
" extra	1.50	to	2.00
" No. 1	1.00	to	1.50
" No. 2	.50	to	.75
Golden Gate	......	to	......
Liberty	......	to	......
Mme. Abel Chatenay	......	to	......
Adiantum	.50	to	.75
Croweanum	.50	to	1.00
Asparagus	25.00	to	50.00
" Plumosus, bunches	8.00	to	15.00
" Sprengerii, bunches	8.00	to	15.00
Asters	.25	to	1.00
Cattleyas	25.00	to	40.00
Daisies	......	to	......
......	......	to	......
......	......	to	......

Carnations: Inf'r grades, all colors	.50	to	1.00
Standard Varieties: White	1.00	to	2.00
Standard Varieties: Pink	1.00	to	2.00
Standard Varieties: Red	1.00	to	2.00
Standard Varieties: Yel. & Var.	......	to	......
*Fancy— (*The highest grades of standard var.): White	......	to	......
*Fancy: Pink	......	to	......
*Fancy: Red	......	to	......
*Fancy: Yel. & Var.	......	to	......
Novelties	......	to	......
Dahlias, per bunch	.05	to	.15
Lilies	6.00	to	8.00
Lily of the Valley	1.00	to	3.00
Mignonette	......	to	......
Smilax	8.00	to	10.00
......	......	to	......
......	......	to	......
......	......	to	......
......	......	to	......
......	......	to	......

WALTER F. SHERIDAN

Wholesale Florist
Telephone, 902 Madison Square 39 WEST 28TH ST., NEW YORK
ALL VARIETIES OF CUT FLOWERS IN SEASON

TOP GRADE FOR SHIPPING

American Beauty, Bridesmaid, Bride, Liberty, Meteor, Lily of the Valley, Carnations
Telephone, 1998 Madison Square JOHN I. RAYNOR, 49 West 28th St., NEW YORK

Edw. C. Horan

55 West 28th St., NEW YORK
TELEPHONE, 1462-1463 MADISON SQUARE
CUT FLOWERS AT WHOLESALE

Mention The Florists' Exchange when writing.

JOHN YOUNG

Wholesale Florist
51 W. 28th St., NEW YORK
TELEPHONE: 4463-4464 MADISON SQUARE

Mention the Florists' Exchange when writing.

A. MOLTZ

Wholesale Florist
55-57 West 26th St., NEW YORK
1st Floor. Telephone, 2921-5243 Madison Sq.

Mention The Florists' Exchange when writing.

MOORE, HENTZ & NASH
WHOLESALE
GROWER AGENT
COMMISSION FLORISTS
55 West 26th St., New York

Telephone Call, 756 Madison Square

Mention The Florists' Exchange when writing.

GEORGE SALTFORD

Wholesale Florist
CONSIGNMENTS SOLICITED
46 West 29th Street, New York
TELEPHONE: 3393 MADISON SQUARE

Mention The Florists' Exchange when writing.

J. Seligman Joseph J. Levy

JOHN SELIGMAN & COMPANY

Wholesale Florists
56 West 26th Street,
Tel. 4878 Madison New York
Opposite New York Cut Flower Company

Mention The Florists' Exchange when writing.

B. S. SLINN, JR.

Wholesale Florist
55 and 57 West 26th Street, NEW YORK
SPECIALTIES—Violets, Carnations and Roses.
Shipping orders receive prompt attention. Consignment Solicited.
Telephone: 3864 Madison Square

Mention the Florists' Exchange when writing.

FRANK H. TRAENDLY CHARLES SCHENCK

TRAENDLY & SCHENCK

Wholesale Florists
44 WEST 28th STREET, NEW YORK
and CUT FLOWER EXCHANGE
Telephones: 798 and 799 MADISON SQUARE
— CONSIGNMENTS SOLICITED

Mention the Florists' Exchange when writing.

A. L. YOUNG & CO.

WHOLESALE FLORISTS
54 West 28th St., NEW YORK
Telephone 3559 Madison Square.
Consignments of choice cut flowers solicited.
Prompt payments. Give us a trial.

Mention The Florists' Exchange when writing.

THOMAS YOUNG

Wholesale Florist
43 West 28th Street, NEW YORK
Telephone, 4850 Madison Square
Consignments of Choice Flowers solicited

Mention The Florists' Exchange when writing.

Wholesale Prices of Cut Flowers—Per 100

Boston Sept. 25, 1906	Buffalo Sept. 25, 1906	Detroit Sept. 11, 1906	Cincinnati Sept 16, 1906	Baltimore Sept. 3, 1906	NAMES AND VARIETIES	Milwaukee Sept. 11, 1906	Phil'delphia Sept. 11, 1906	Pittsburg Sept. 26, 1906	St. Louis Sept. 17, 1906
20.00 to 35.00	20.00 to 25.00	10.00 to 35.00	25.00 to 30.00	— to —	ROSES A. BEAUTY, fancy—special	— to 25.00	15.00 to 20.00	20.00 to 25.00	20.00 to 25.00
10.00 to 20.00	12.00 to 20.00	— to —	— to 20.00	— to —	" extra	15.00 to 18.00	10.00 to 15.00	15.00 to 18.00	12.50 to 15.00
4.00 to 10.00	6.00 to 12.00	— to —	10.00 to 15.00	— to —	" No. 1	10.00 to 12.50	5.00 to 7.00	6.00 to 10.00	8.00 to 10.00
1.00 to 4.00	3.00 to 6.00	— to —	4.00 to 6.00	— to —	" Culls and ordinary	4.00 to 6.00	1.00 to 4.00	— to —	3.00 to 6.00
— to —	5.00 to 6.00	3.00 to 6.00	4.00 to 6.00	— to —	BRIDE, 'MAID, fancy-special	— to 6.00	— to —	— to 6.00	4.00 to 5.00
3.00 to 4.00	4.00 to 5.00	— to —	— to 3.00	— to 4.00	" extra	— to 5.00	5.00 to 8.00	— to 4.00	2.00 to 3.00
1.00 to 8.00	3.00 to 4.00	— to —	— to 2.00	— to 3.00	" No. 1	— to 4.00	4.00 to 5.00	2.00 to 3.00	— to —
— to .50	2.00 to 3.00	— to —	— to 1.00	— to 2.00	" No. 2	— to 2.00	2.00 to 3.00	— to 1.50	— to —
— to —	— to —	4.00 to 8.00	— to 4.00	2.00 to 4.00	GOLDEN GATE	4.00 to 6.00	4.00 to 8.00	— to —	2.00 to 4.00
3.00 to 6.00	3.00 to 7.00	— to —	— to —	2.00 to 4.00	K. A. VICTORIA	4.00 to 8.00	4.00 to 6.00	3.00 to 10.00	2.00 to 8.00
3.00 to 6.00	3.00 to 7.00	— to —	— to —	2.00 to 3.00	LIBERTY	4.00 to 6.00	3.00 to 6.00	— to —	— to —
— to —	3.00 to 6.00	4.00 to 10.00	— to —	— to —	METEOR	— to —	— to —	— to —	— to —
— to —	3.00 to 5.00	4.00 to 10.00	— to —	2.00 to 3.00	PERLE	4.00 to 6.00	— to —	— to —	2.00 to 5.00
— to —	— to —	— to 50.00	— to —	— to —	ORCHIDS—Cattleyas	— to —	— to 50.00	— to —	— to —
— to —	.50 to 1.00	— to —	— to .50	.50 to .75	CARNATIONS Inferior grades, all colors	— to 1.00	.75 to 1.00	.75 to 1.00	— to .75
— to —	1.00 to 1.25	— to 1.00	— to 1.00	— to 1.00	Standard Varieties White	— to 1.00	.75 to 1.00	— to 1.50	— to .75
— to —	1.00 to 1.25	— to —	— to 1.50	— to 1.00	Standard Varieties Pink	— to 1.00	.75 to 1.00	— to 1.50	— to .75
— to —	1.00 to 1.25	— to —	— to —	— to 1.00	Standard Varieties Red	— to 1.50	.75 to 1.00	— to 1.50	— to .75
— to —	— to —	— to 3.00	— to —	— to —	Standard Varieties Yellow and var.	— to 1.00	.75 to 1.00	— to 1.50	— to .75
1.00 to 2.00	1.50 to 2.00	— to —	— to —	— to —	Fancy Varieties White	1.50 to 2.00	2.00 to 2.50	— to 2.00	1.00 to 1.50
1.00 to 2.00	1.50 to 2.00	— to —	— to —	— to —	Fancy Varieties Pink	1.50 to 2.00	2.00 to 2.50	— to 2.00	1.00 to 1.50
1.00 to 2.00	1.50 to 2.00	— to —	— to —	— to —	Fancy Varieties Red	1.50 to 2.00	2.00 to 2.50	— to 2.00	1.00 to 1.50
1.00 to 2.00	1.50 to 2.00	— to 1.50	— to —	— to —	Fancy Varieties Yellow and var	1.50 to 2.00	2.00 to 2.50	— to 2.00	1.00 to 1.50
— to —	— to —	— to —	— to —	— to —	Novelties	— to —	— to —	— to —	— to —
.75 to 1.00	.50 to 1.00	— to 2.00	— to 1.00	— to 1.00	ADIANTUM	— to 1.00	— to 1.00	1.25 to 1.50	— to 1.00
— to 50.00	— to —	25.00 to 60.00	35.00 to 50.00	25.00 to 50.00	ASPARAGUS, Plum. and Ten	20.00 to 30.00	25.00 to 35.00	20.00 to 50.00	25.00 to 50.00
— to —	— to —	20.00 to 30.00	— to 35.00	25.00 to 50.00	" Sprengeri, bunches	20.00 to 30.00	25.00 to 35.00	20.00 to 40.00	25.00 to 50.00
.50 to 1.00	.50 to 2.00	— to —	.50 to 1.50	— to —	ASTERS	.50 to 1.00	— to —	.50 to 2.00	1.00 to 3.00
— to —	8.00 to 10.00	— to 10.00	— to —	6.00 to 8.00	CALLAS	— to —	— to —	— to —	— to —
— to —	— to —	— to —	— to —	— to —	CHRYSANTHEMUMS	— to —	— to —	— to —	— to —
— to —	1.50 to 2.50	.75 to 1.50	— to —	— to —	DAISIES	— to .40	3.00 to 4.00	— to —	— to —
— to —	— to —	— to —	— to —	— to —	GALAX LEAVES	— to —	— to —	— to —	— to —
4.00 to 6.00	12.00 to 15.00	8.00 to 10.00	— to 3.00	2.00 to 3.00	GLADIOLUS	— to —	8.00 to 12.00	3.00 to 4.00	— to —
— to —	3.00 to 4.00	— to —	— to —	— to 10.00	LILIES, Harrisii	— to 12.50	— to —	— to —	— to —
10.00 to 12.00	— to —	— to —	— to 15.00	— to —	" Longiflorum	— to 12.50	2.00 to 4.00	15.00 to 18.00	— to —
3.00 to 5.00	— to —	3.00 to 4.00	3.00 to 4.00	— to —	LILY OF THE VALLEY	— to —	1.00 to 2.00	2.00 to 4.00	— to —
— to —	— to —	— to —	— to —	— to —	MIGNONETTE, ordinary	— to —	— to —	— to —	— to —
— to —	12.00 to 15.00	— to —	— to —	— to —	" fancy	— to —	— to —	— to —	— to —
— to —	— to —	4.00 to 8.00	— to —	— to —	PEONIES	— to —	15.00 to 20.00	— to —	— to —
10.00 to 12.50	— to —	12.50 to 15.00	— to 15.00	12.50 to 20.00	SMILAX	— to 15.00	— to —	— to 15.00	— to 12.50
— to .50	— to —	— to —	— to —	— to —	VIOLETS, ordinary	— to —	— to —	— to —	— to —
— to —	.15 to .25	— to —	— to —	— to —	" fancy	— to —	— to —	— to —	— to —
— to —	— to —	— to —	— to —	— to —	NARCISSUS	— to —	— to —	— to —	— to —
— to —	— to —	.50 to .75	— to —	— to —	SWEET PEAS	.25 to .50	— to .50	— to —	— to —

Grand Rapids.

News Items.

We have lately experienced not only the hottest spell of weather ever known in September, but it has been a great many years since even a July month has been as warm. There has been no rain for over four weeks; everything is parched and drying up; and dust is inches thick on the roads. Cut flowers are having their trouble; it is hard to keep them in good condition even for a day. The quality of the carnations is much impaired by the excessive heat; and roses open quickly and are soft in texture. Bride roses seem to stand the weather better than either Kaiserin Augusta Victoria or Bridesmaid. Asters and other outdoor flowers are about over, dried up; but as chrysanthemums will soon be in full sway, their going will not be felt. The aster beetle was a serious pest this season; and the grasshoppers are still in their glory, and are eating the carnations and smilax.

While business is good, it could be lots better, if cooler weather would only set in. When we do get a change we expect to have a hard frost very quickly; in the meantime everybody is praying for rain.

Carnations are all benched; they took hold better this season than last, and while there are signs of stem rot it is trifling as compared with last year. Roses have grown finely and promise a good crop for Winter. Violets are cleaner and freer from disease this year than for several seasons past, which will assure a crop of better quality blooms than usual.

The West Michigan State Fair held at Grand Rapids, September 10 to 14, was a pronounced success, ideal weather prevailing during the entire week. Horticultural building was devoted to fruits and flowers and was filled to its entire capacity.

The Grand Rapids Floral Company and Crabb & Hunter were the principal exhibitors in both plants and cut flowers. Eli Cross entered for the design, and also carnations, getting first on each; Charles Chadwick entered for design and cut flowers, getting third on design, first on display of roses, second on American Beauty; Grand Rapids Floral Company was first on Beauty on account of length of stem, first on basket of asters, and second on carnations. Crabb & Hunter, on account of the sudden sickness of Mr. Crabb, were two hours late in putting up their design and flowers, and although the judges said the design was the best, it was barred, the flowers also, from getting first. Their awards were: Second for American Beauty, third for carnations, second for display of roses, first on display of asters, theirs being the only entry.

In my last report I mentioned the fact that Henry Steneman was to be manager for the Manistee Floral Company. It has transpired that the negotiations fell through, and instead it turned out to be Charles Siegh, formerly of Wilcox's, Joliet, Ill., who secured the position.

GEO. F. CRABB.

BANGOR, ME.—Carl Beers, writing from Paris, France, on September 16, 1906, says he will return to America about October 1, to reside in this city. Mr. Beers has been abroad about a year.

Wholesale Prices of Cut Flowers, Chicago, Sept. 25, 1906

Prices quoted are by the hundred unless otherwise noted

ROSES — American Beauty		
36-inch stems..........per doz.	3.00 to	4.00
30-inch stems.......... "	2.50 to	3.00
24-inch stems.......... "	2.00 to	2.50
20-inch stems.......... "	1.00 to	2.00
18-inch stems.......... "	.... to	1.50
12-inch stems.......... "	.... to	1.00
8-inch stems and shorts "	.50 to	.75
Bride Maid, fancy special......	5.00 to	6.00
" extra..........	4.00 to	5.00
" No. 1..........	2.00 to	3.00
" No. 2..........	.50 to	1.00
Golden Gate..........	2.00 to	6.00
Carnot..........	2.00 to	6.00
Uncle John..........	2.00 to	6.00
Liberty..........	2.00 to	6.00
Richmond..........	2.00 to	8.00
Kaiserina..........	2.00 to	8.00
Killarney..........	3.00 to	6.00
Perle..........	2.00 to	6.00
Chatenay..........	2.00 to	6.00
Orchids—Cattleyas..........	50.00 to	75.00
SMILAX..........	8.00 to	12.00
LILY OF THE VALLEY..........	2.00 to	4.00
DAHLIAS..........	2.00 to	3.00

CARNATIONS			
Inferior grades all colors		.25 to	.50
STANDARD VARIETIES	White..........	.75 to	1.00
	Pink..........	.75 to	1.00
	Red..........	.75 to	1.00
	Yellow & var....	.75 to	1.00
*FANCY (The highest grades of Sta'd var)	White..........	1.50 to	2.00
	Pink..........	1.50 to	2.00
	Red..........	1.50 to	2.00
	Yellow & var....	1.50 to	2.00
NOVELTIES..........		.... to	....
ADIANTUM..........		.50 to	1.00
ASPARAGUS, Plum. & Ten..........		.35 to	.50
" Sprengeri, bunches.		.35 to	.50
GLADIOLUS..........		2.00 to	6.00
LILIES, Longiflorum..........		8.00 to	12.00
HARISU..........		8.00 to	12.00
....		.... to	....
....		.... to	....
....		.... to	....
....		.... to	....
....		.... to	....
HARDY FERNS per 1000..........		1.00 to	1.50
GALAX "		1.00 to	1.25
ASTERS..........		.50 to	2.00
CHRYSANTHEMUMS..........		25.00 to	35.00

Baltimore.

ɛws Notes.

The great jubilee week is over, nd business was very brisk; large uantities of cut flowers, greens, etc., ʼere used in the different parades nd processions, and the end of the ʼeek found everything pretty well ɩeaned up.

The last regular meeting of the ardeners' Club was very well at- ɜnded and a number of interesting uestions were discussed.

The inspection trip to the Vincent ahlia farm was a decided success. ɩore than 250 persons availed them- ɜlves of the opportunity to visit ɩessrs. Vincent & Sons' establishment. he large packing building was trans- ɔrmed into an exhibition hall. ɩvery variety was labeled and very astefully arranged for the more con- enient inspection by the visitors resent. Over 10,000 cut blooms, all pecimen flowers, and many novelties ʼere shown. The outdoor display was most remarkable exhibit of grow- ŋg dahlias, comprising over 40 acres f blooming plants, with over 265 arieties. The visitors present were ʼithout exception florists and horti- ulturists, all of them having words f praise for the Messrs. Vincent.

The establishment was brightly illuminated at night by many hundreds of electric bulbs from a plant which Messrs. Vincent recently installed; and in the evening the display in the packing hall was open to the neighbors and all comers.

The Baltimore Florists' and Gardeners' Club, knowing what was in store for them, attended in a body, more than 150 members and ladies being present. But it was especially pleasing to have so many prominent florists from Washington, Philadelphia, New York and Boston present. The Washington Florists' Club, together with the Agricultural Department, were represented by 30 visitors, headed by Messrs. Gude and Bisset. After a sumptuous repast speeches were made by Messrs. Bisset, Gude, O'Mara, Lonsdale, Perry, Seybold, H. A. Patterson, Professor T. B. Symons and others. Messrs. Amos and Symons extended a general invitation to the guests to attend the Maryland State Horticultural meeting, December 5 and 6, which will be held in the Fifth Regiment armory building, with a floor space greater than Madison Square Garden, New York. Everybody is invited to bring an exhibit.

A rising vote of thanks was given to Mrs. Vincent and daughters for the splendid repast, after neat speeches by Miss Mildred J. Campbell and Mrs. MacRichmond of Baltimore. The party returned home on an evening train loaded down with flowers.

C. L. S.

Cincinnati.

Trade News.

Jewish New Year always creates a demand for good flowers, and of course American Beauty roses had the call. Tea roses are improving slowly, but will be in good shape by the time they are badly needed. The writer had two hundred chrysanthemums in on the 19th—Opah and Marquis de Montmort. They are early, and that's about all you can say for them. They were grown by Henry Weber & Sons, Oakland, Md. Carnations are beginning to put in an appearance, but I can't say much for quality as yet.

Thursday was "Flower Day" again at The Fall Festival, and as there were not enough entries to make a suitable display, the directors of the Fall Festival turned the exhibition over to W. K. Partridge, giving him five hundred dollars to make the exhibit. Table No. 1 was devoted principally to filled baskets, orchid display, roses, tritoma, Farleyense ferns, lily of the valley, and an ocean greyhound worked out in purple and white asters. The center of the foyer contained an aquatic pond, in which a fine collection of lilies from Henry A. Dreer was shown. At each corner was a pedestal with a vase containing 100 American Beauty roses, the four vases making a beautiful show. Window boxes filled with hydrangeas and cannas made an attractive appearance. Ficus pandurata was an attractive plant seen here, and it certainly looks like a good decorator. Tritoma is very showy, and attracted much attention. At another point was a lunch table decorated with cattleyas. The hangings from the balcony were the same as at the former exhibit, consisting of wild smilax, hanging baskets of Boston ferns, gladiolus, etc., creating a very pretty effect, and certainly affording a fine lot of advertising to W. K. Partridge.

E. G. GILLETT.

Indianapolis.

News Notes.

A visit to the chrysanthemum houses in this vicinity is most gratifying, as the growers have tried to outdo the flower records, judging from the quality of the stock seen. No large flower show is to be held this year, but with the general prosperity no trouble should be experienced in disposing of all the chrysanthemums at satisfactory prices.

Much comment has been made on the small flower display at the Indiana State Fair this year. Prizes were smaller than usual; many of the exhibitors found that it did not pay to exhibit for the amounts offered, and it is believed that the State Board of Agriculture now realize that the florists cannot be drawn by the small premiums heretofore offered, and will make a decided change next year. W. W. Coles, Kokomo, made a creditable display of cut flowers and roses. E. T. Barnes, Spencer, Ind., with whom dahlia growing is a hobby, exhibited a fine collection of these. There were also numerous amateur exhibits.

F. A. Conway & Company are growing a seedling aster which promises well, several florists who are handling it pronouncing it the best white aster yet produced.

Wilfred Emmons, formerly manager of the Cedar Rapids Floral Company, Iowa, has accepted a position with Bertermann Brothers Company.

B. F. Hensley, proprietor of the West View Greenhouses, Knightstown, Ind., has added 20,000 feet of glass to his business this Summer; the new range is located about a mile from the old establishment, and is devoted to roses and carnations. Mr. Hensley ships almost all his products to Indianapolis.

W. K. Partridge's undertakings at the Cincinnati Fall Festival are most favorably commented upon here. We understand that his first exhibition was a most successful one. If one man can make such a showing, what might not the combined forces of that city accomplish?

H. W. Rieman has about completed the improvements at his establishment in South East street.

The Smith & Young Company and John Grande are to supply the Indianapolis market with violets this year. Both firms have unusually fine plants.

Clarence Thomas visited the Cincinnati retailers last week.

Visitors: Fred Dorner, Jr., LaFayette; J. Murdoch, Pittsburg; W. A. Rieman, Vincennes, and M. Abrahamson, Chicago.

I. B.

DETROIT, MICH.—We are sorry to learn of the illness, from typhoid fever, of our esteemed correspondent, Harry A. Rackham, son of the well known grower of this city, George A. Rackham.

Minneapolis.

State Fair Awards.

At the recent State fair the following trade firms were among the prize winners. The judge was A. Swanson, St. Paul:

Collection of Foliage and Decorative Plants—First, Minneapolis Floral Company, Minneapolis; second, E. Nagel & Son, Minneapolis; third, John Vasatka, 3356 Chicago avenue, Minneapolis.

Collection Greenhouse Plants—First, Minneapolis Floral Company; second, E. Nagel & Son; third, John Vasatka.

Collection of Five Hanging Baskets—First, E. Nagel & Son; second, John Vasatka; third, Minneapolis Floral Company.

Collection of Coleus—First, E. Nagel & Son; second, John Vasatka; third, Minneapolis Floral Company.

Collection of Palms in Pots—First, E. Nagel & Son; second, Minneapolis Floral Company; third, John Vasatka.

Single Specimen Palm, One in Pot—First, John Vasatka; second, Minneapolis Floral Company; third, E. Nagel & Son.

Single Specimen Fern, One in Pot—First, E. Nagel & Son; second, J. Vasatka; third, Minneapolis Floral Company.

Collection of Geraniums in Bloom—First, E. Nagel & Son; second John Vasatka; third, Minneapolis Floral Company.

Collection of Carnations in Bloom.—First, E. Nagel & Son; second, Minneapolis Floral Company; no third prize.

Vase Filled with Plants—First, E. Nagel & Son; second, Minneapolis Floral Company; third, John Vasatka.

Best Collection of Cut Flowers, not less than 15 Varieties—First, Minneapolis Floral Company; second, E. Nagel & Son; third, John Vasatka.

Collection of Dahlias—First, George E. Gerston; second, John Vasatka.

Collection of Sweet Peas—First, E. Nagel & Son; second, John Vasatka.

Collection of Asters—First, E. Nagel & Son; second, Mary Murphy, Stillwater; third, John Vasatka.

Collection of Carnations—First, Minneapolis Floral Company; second, John Vasatka; third, E. Nagel & Son.

Collection of Roses—First, Minneapolis Floral Company; second, John Vasatna; third, E. Nagel & Son.

Collection of Gladioli—First, George E. Kerston; second, E. Nagel & Son; third, John Vasatka.

Table Decorations—First, Minneapolis Floral Company; second, R. A. Latham; third, E. Nagel & Son; fourth, John Vasatka.

Twelve-Inch Basket of Flowers—First, Minneapolis Floral Company; second, E. Nagel & Son; third, John Vasatka.

Table Bouquet—First, Minneapolis Floral Company; second, E. Nagel & Son; third, Charles Krause; fourth, John Vasatka.

Hand Bouquet—First, Minneapolis Floral Company; second, E. Nagel & Son; third, John Vasatka.

Bridal Bouquet (white flowers)—First, Minneapolis Floral Company; second, John Vasatka; third, E. Nagel & Son.

News Notes.

Oscar Amundson, formerly of the Rosary, and Ashton Kerschner, formerly of the State Nursery, Helena, Mont., have formed a copartnership, under the name of Amundson & Kerschner, and have opened a very attractive store on Hennepin avenue, between Fourth and Fifth streets. They have a good location, and as Mr. Amundson has been in the business for years here, they will no doubt do a nice trade.

The Donaldson Glass Block is putting up possibly one of the finest ice boxes in any cut flower department. It is to be between 50 and 60 feet long, made of cement, and small mosaic blocks.

Whitted has one of the finest stores in the city; a great many new mahogany fixtures have been added and the place has an oriental effect which is indeed very pleasing. A number of Turkish rugs are on the floor, which adds greatly to the appearance of the store.

The Minneapolis Floral Company has made a great many improvements in its range of houses, having added some and changed others. New boilers have also been installed and the firm is in better shape than ever to help supply the demand during Winter.

PAUL.

Syracuse, N. Y.

State Fair Flower and Fruit Show.

The New York State Fair held here from September 10 to 15, was favored with glorious weather. The attendance was a record-breaking one; over 200.000 paid the admission fee which is only twenty-five cents. It is safe to say that the horticultural and floricultural departments have never been better filled than this year. The immense pavilion devoted to this section being inadequate, it is proposed to make a larger building for next year's show. P. R. Quinlan, as usual stood in the foremost rank; among his plants calling for special mention were palms, ferns, begonias, fuchsias and cannas. His collection of cut flowers was superb and his floral design was a masterpiece.

Meneilly & Sons were also large exhibitors, and staged a very creditable lot of palms, ferns, begonias and geraniums. They also had a large collection of cut flowers.

In the cut flower section Arthur Cowee, Berlin, N. Y., was a giant among the exhibitors; his collection of gladioli was most gorgeous and worth going a long way to see. It is marvelous to note the great strides that are making in the improvement of this beautiful flower; it seems there is no limit to the colors that can be produced. The enormous crowds always around this exhibit, demonstrated how much the public was interested in the flower.

James Vick's Sons, Rochester, N. Y., staged a magnificent collection of asters, and were awarded the first prize They also had collections of other flowers grown from their own seed, as supplied to their customers. Beckstedt, of Oswego, N. Y., was, as usual, a large exhibitor of cut flowers and floral designs. Mrs. W. A. Syron, Clyde, N. Y., staged a very fine collection of cut dahlias, which were greatly admired and received first prize. I should judge from the way she was booking orders that she was well repaid for her trouble. Park Superintendent D. A. Campbell was in charge of this department. The duty of judging was carried out by W. Hewson, Buffalo, and F. Vick, Rochester.

The fruit department is always one of the strongest drawing cards at this fair, and it never seems to make any difference how short the general crop may be, one will always find a magnificent collection staged. Messrs. Ellwanger & Barry, Rochester, N. Y., contributed very largely to the success of the fruit department, their exhibit being most complete and their specimens magnificent.

F. H. Ebeling, seedsman, had a most attractive exhibit in a large tent of his own. Mr. Ebeling is the largest dealer in bulbs, holly and Christmas greens in this part of the State.

The grounds of the State Fair reflect the highest credit on Superintendent Smith, who has spared no pains to make them most attractive. his carpet bedding evinces considerable taste.

H. Y.

DAVENPORT, IA.—The Tri-City Florists' Society held a regular meeting on September 13 with Henry Gaethje of South Rock Island. "The Forcing of Bulbs" was the topic for consideration, and as nearly every member of the society was present an excellent discussion resulted. After the meeting refreshments were served and the members enjoyed a social session. The next meeting will be with Julius Staack of Moline, who has recently completed a range of greenhouses. The State convention of Iowa florists will be held in Dubuque October 17. John Temple and Theo. Ewoldt of Davenport expect to attend. Mr. Ewoldt is vice-president and Mr. Temple is ex-president of the Iowa State Association.

MECHANICSBURG, PA.—H. R. Gronbeck lost about 700 square feet of glass by a hail storm on the 11th inst. He was insured in the F. H. A.

TIFFIN, O.—The Schoen Floral Company, of Toledo, has been incorporated, with a capital stock of $10,000. Lewis Ullrich and Edmund Ullrich of this city are the principal stockholders of the company. The store will be on the corner of Adams and St. Clair streets. This will be the Toledo market for Ullrich's greenhouse products. At a recent meeting of the company, Edmund Ullrich was elected a director.

UNITED STATES PATENT OFFICE.

BENJAMIN HAMMOND, of FISHKILL LANDING, NEW YORK.

TRADE-MARK FOR FUNGICIDE.

Statement and Declaration Registered Aug. 21, 1906.

Application filed July 3, 1905. Serial No. 9,799.

No. 55,632.

STATEMENT.

To all whom it may concern:

Be it known that I, Benjamin Hammond, a citizen of the United States, residing at Fishkill Landing, Dutchess County, New York, and doing business at the northeast corner of the Long Dock, in said village, have adopted for my use the trade-mark shown in the accompanying drawing.

The class of merchandise to which the trade-mark is appropriated is Class 6, Chemicals not otherwise specified, and the particular description of goods comprised in said class upon which I use said trade-mark is a fungicide.

The trade-mark has been continuously used in my business since 1886 and is displayed on the packages containing the goods by placing thereon a printed label on which the same is shown.

BENJAMIN HAMMOND.

DECLARATION.

State of New York, County of Dutchess, ss:

Benjamin Hammond, being duly sworn, deposes and says that he is the applicant named in the foregoing statement; that he believes the foregoing statement is true; that he believes himself to be the owner of the trade-mark sought to be registered; that no other person firm, corporation, or association, to the best of his knowledge and belief, has the right to use said trade-mark, either in the identical form or in any such near resemblance thereto as may be calculated to deceive; that said trade-mark is used by him in commerce among several States of the United States and between foreign nations and particularly with Canada; and that the description, drawing, and specimens presented truly represent the trade-mark sought to be registered.

BENJAMIN HAMMOND.

Subscribed and sworn to before me, a notary public, this 11th day of April, 1906.

M. E. CURTIS,
Notary Public.

THE FLORISTS' EXCHANGE

We are a straight shoot and aim to grow into a vigorous plant

A WEEKLY MEDIUM OF INTERCHANGE FOR FLORISTS, NURSERYMEN, SEEDSMEN AND THE TRADE IN GENERAL

Vol. XXII. No. 14 — NEW YORK AND CHICAGO, OCTOBER 6, 1906 — One Dollar Per Year

NOW READY EASTER LILIES

Should be potted at once, as Easter is early this year.

Japan stocks are now arriving, and are in first-class shape.

Japan Longiflorum,	7 to 9 in. bulbs, case of 300 bulbs		$14.25
" "	9 to 10 " " " " 200 "		15.00
" " Multiflorum,	7 to 9 " " " " 300 "		15.00
" " "	9 to 10 " " " " 200 "		17.00
" " Giganteum,	7 to 9 " " " " 300 "		18.75
" " "	9 to 10 " " " " 200 "		21.00

Lilium Candidum, selected bulbs, $5.00 per 100.

A Few of the Leading Narcissus.

Paper White Grandiflora, 13-15 c/m, fine bulbs, case of 1250 bulbs	$11.25
Double Von Sion, first size	$ 9.00 per 1000
" " " extra size	12.00 " "
" " " mammoth double nosed, or top-root	20.00 " "
Princeps, early, single, fine bulbs	7.00 " "
Golden Spur, the favorite single yellow	19.00 " "
Empress, a grand bicolor	20.00 " "
Alba Plena Odorata	6.00 " "
Barri Conspicuus	8.00 " "
Poeticus	4.50 " "
Poeticus Ornatus	7.00 " "

White Roman Hyacinths, 12-15 c/m	$23.00 per 1000
" " " 13-15 "	28.00 " "
Freesia Refracta Alba, finest Bermuda bulbs	7.50 " "
Bermuda Buttercup Oxalis	7.50 " "
Spanish Iris, four best sorts	5.00 " "
" " mixed	2.50 " "

For other bulbs and for smaller quantities, see our Wholesale Price List, in which will be found a full assortment of all kinds of bulbs for winter and spring flowering. Send for list if you have not already received one.

F. R. PIERSON CO., Tarrytown-on-Hudson, N. Y.

Mention The Florists' Exchange when writing.

Asparagus Plumosus Nanus

Cut strings, 50 cts. each

W. H. ELLIOTT

Brighton, Mass.

Mention The Florists' Exchange when writing.

LILIUM LONGIFLORUM

Now Ready, Fine Stock

	100	1000
Lilium Longiflorum, 7-9 in.	$4 50	$40 00
" " 9-10 in.	7 50	67 50
" " Early flowering Multiflorum, much superior to the ordinary type, flowers very like L. Harrisii, 7-9 in.	5 00	45 00
9-10 in.	9 00	80 00
Lilium Longiflorum Giganteum, dark stem, very fine, 7-9 in.	6 50	60 00
9-10 in.	10 00	90 00

TULIPS, Forcing and Bedding

	100	1000
Single Artus Red	1 25	11 00
" **Belle Alliance,** scarlet	2 15	19 00
" **Couleur Cardinal,** forcer	3 00	28 00
" **Chrysolora,** yellow	0 90	7 50
" **Cottage Maid,** pink	1 10	9 00
" **Dusart,** red, forcer	2 15	19 50
" **La Reine,** fancy bulbs	0 95	8 00
" **Vermilion,** brilliant best scarlet	3 00	28 00
" **Yellow Prince**	0 95	8 50

	100	1000
Double Murillo, forcer	$2 10	$19 00
" **Imperator Rubrorum**	2 75	25 50
" **Tournesol,** red and yellow	1 65	15 00
" **Rex Rubrorum**	1 50	14 00
" **La Candeur**	1 25	11 50
" **Yellow Rose**	0 85	7 50

TULIP MIXTURES

Our mixtures are made up from large flowering bright colors, they bloom at same time and will give good satisfaction.

	100	1000
Single, Early, extra fine mixed	$0 90	$7 50
" " fine mixed	75	6 00
Double, Early, extra fine mixed	1 10	9 00
" " fine mixed	90	7 50
Double, Late, extra fine mixed	1 00	8 50
Single, " extra fine mixed	95	8 00

Send for our book for Florists. **Write for Prices.**

All Fall Bulbs

Vaughan's Seed Store

14 BARCLAY ST. NEW YORK

CHICAGO, 84-86 Randolph Street. Greenhouses, Western Springs, Ill.

Mention The Florists' Exchange when writing.

FLORISTS' BULBS

ALL our HOLLAND BULBS have arrived in excellent condition--our Tulips are FIRST SIZE FLOWERING BULBS only, Hyacinths STRAIGHT, 1st and 2nd sizes.

SINGLE TULIPS

	100	1000
Artus, dark scarlet	$1.15	$10.75
Belle Alliance, scarlet	2.00	19.00
Chrysolora, pure yellow	.95	7.50
Cottage Maid, rosy pink	.85	8.00
Keizerskroon, red and yellow	1.50	14.50
La Reine, white	1.00	8.00
Pottebakker, scarlet	1.60	15.00
Yellow Prince, yellow	.90	8.00

DOUBLE TULIPS

	100	1000
Couronne d'Or, yellow	$2.75	$24.50
Gloria Solis, bronze red	1.25	12.00
Imperator Rubrorum, scarlet	2.75	24.00
Murillo, blush white	2.00	18.50
Rex Rubrorum, scarlet	1.50	14.00
Tournesol, red and yellow	1.75	15.00
Tournesol, yellow	2.25	20.00
La Candeur, white	1.25	11.50

HYACINTHS

	Per 12	100	1000
Extra Selected Strictly First Size Named Dutch Hyacinths, in a General Selection	$1.00	$7.50	$70.00
Extra Selected Strictly Second Size Named Dutch Hyacinths, in a General Selection	.75	5.50	50.00
Boddington's Quality Named Bedding or Fancy Hyacinths	.50	4.00	35.00
Boddington's Special Mixed Hyacinths for Bedding or Forcing—To Color	.35	2.25	22.00
DUTCH ROMANS or MINIATURE HYACINTHS to name	.35	2.25	20.00

FREESIAS, ½ to ¾ inch (surplus to close), 75c. per 100, $6.00 per 1000.

ARTHUR T. BODDINGTON

342 W. 14th ST., - - NEW YORK CITY

Mention The Florists' Exchange when writing.

LILY OF THE VALLEY

Perfection pips for Dec. forcing, $1.50 100; $14.00 1000; case 2000 $26.00.
Selected 3 yr. Hamburg, for late forcing, $1.25 100; $10.00 1000.

New Mushroom Spawn, $7.00 100 lbs.

	100	1000
Lilium Longiflorum (Japan) 6 to 8 in.	$3.00	$24.00
Lilium Longiflorum (Japan) 7 to 9 in.	4.50	40.00
Lilium Longiflorum Multiflorum, 6 to 8 in.	3.50	30.00
Freesias, selected French	.75	6.00
Narcissus Paper White grandiflora, largest size	1.25	9.00
Narcissus Von Sion, extra selected	1.35	11.50
Narcissus Von Sion, mammoth double nosed	2.00	18.50

Narcissus or Sacred Lilies, basket 30 bulbs, $1.30; mats of four baskets, $4.75.

Sterilized Sheep Manure, $20.00 a Ton

CANE STAKES, 6 TO 9 FT., 1000 $6.00.

WM. ELLIOTT & SONS, 201 FULTON ST., NEW YORK

Mention The Florists' Exchange when writing.

C. C. MORSE & CO.

SEED GROWERS

171-173 Clay St., San Francisco, California

OUR SPECIALTIES

ONION LETTUCE SWEET PEAS

Also Carrot, Celery, Celeriac, Cucumber, Endive, Leek, Mustard, Parsley, Parsnip, Radish, Salsify, Spinach, Tomato and

FLOWER SEEDS

Growers for the trade on contract. Warehouses at Santa Clara; Farms and Farm headquarters Carnadero, near Gilroy.

Registered Cable Address: MORSEED, SAN FRANCISCO.

Mention The Florists' Exchange when writing.

Rawson's World-Renowned Cyclamen

FRESH CROP SEEDS NOW READY FOR DELIVERY

RAWSON'S ROYAL STRAIN

Unrivalled for Size, Beauty, Colors and Foliage. Has been awarded First Prize whenever exhibited.

We Offer

Deep Red, Purest White, Mauve, White with Claret Base, Bright Christmas Red, Delicate Salmon Pink, Delicate Pink and an exquisite mixture of all shades at $1.00 per 100 Seeds; $9.00 per 1000 Seeds.

RAWSON'S CONTINENTAL STRAIN

New Our Own Introduction

Specially valuable on account of its early flowering habit. Will be in full bloom in September and October.

We Offer Pure White, Pink, White with Claret Base, Deep Red at 50c. per 100 Seeds, $4.00 per 1000 Seeds. Also Salmon Pink at $2.00 per 100 Seeds, $15.00 per 1000 Seeds. Superb mixture of all shades at 40c. per 100, $3.50 per 1000 Seeds.

A TRIAL WILL CONVINCE

W. W. RAWSON & CO.

5 UNION STREET, BOSTON, MASS.

Mention The Florists' Exchange when writing

PACIFIC SEED GROWERS' CO.

109 MARKET STREET

SAN FRANCISCO, CAL.

Specialties:

Onion, Carrot, Lettuce, Sweet Peas

Mention The Florists' Exchange when writing.

PRIMROSES

Improved Chinese: Finest grown, named or mixed. Strong 2 inch, $2.00 per 100. X X X Strong 3 inch, $5.00 per 100.

XXX SEEDS

CHINESE PRIMROSE

Finest grown, mixed, 500 seeds, $1.00; ½ pkt., 50c.

Cineraria: Finest large flowering dwarf, mixed, 1000 seeds 50c.

Cyclamen Giganteum: Finest Giant mixed, 200 seeds $1.00; ½ pkt., 50c.

DAISY: Double Giant mixed, 1000 seeds 25c.

GIANT PANSY. The best large flowering varieties, critically selected, 5000 seeds, $1.00; half pkt., 50c.; 500 seeds of Giant Mme. Perret, pansy seed added to every $1.00 pkt. of Giant Pansy. Cash. Liberal extra count of seeds in all packets.

JOHN F. RUPP, Shiremanstown, Pa.

The Home of Primroses

Mention the Florists' Exchange when writing.

SEEDS

Pansy, new crop, $1.00 per packet; $4.00 per oz.; $12.00 per ¼ lb. **Pansy Plants**, $4.00 per 1000. Cash.

B. SOLTAU,

199 Grant Ave., JERSEY CITY, N. J.

Mention The Florists' Exchange when writing.

Catalog Engravings

and ILLUSTRATIONS

that print EASILY. That's the kind we make—have been since '73

JAS. M. BRYANT, Horticultural Engraving and Printing

706 Chestnut Street, PHILADELPHIA, PA.

Write for our Catalogue of Stock Engravings

Mention the Florists' Exchange when writing.

S. & W. CO.'S BULBS

	100	1000	10,000
Narcissus Paper White Grandiflora,	$1.00	$9.00	$80.00
Roman Hyacinths, 13/15 ctm.	3.00	27.00	260.00
" " 11/15 "	2.50	23.00	200.00

Chinese Sacred Lilies, per basket 30 bulbs, $1.30; per bale 120 bulbs, $4.8

Stumpp & Walter Co.

50 Barclay St., New York

Mention The Florists' Exchange when writing.

STOKES STANDARD SEEDS

ARE MONEY MAKERS

Write me your wants.

STOKES SEED STORE

219 Market Street

Philadelphia

Mention The Florists' Exchange when writing.

CINERARIA

Large Flowering Prize, Splendid Mixed T. P. $0.50

Large Flowering, Semi Dwarf Prize, Splendid Mixed, T. P. $0.50

PANSY, Superb Mixed.

oz. $4.50. ¼ oz. $1.15 ⅛ oz. $0.60

W. C. BECKERT,

Allegheny, Pa.

Mention the Florists' Exchange when writing.

SEEDS

Christmas Flowering Sweet Pea Seed.

Christmas Pink. Florence Denzer, pure white, small quantity still on hand, price, ¼ lb., 75c.; 1 lb., $2.00.

New Christmas Carmine Red, Mrs. Eddie Wild, 1 oz., $1.00; 5 oz., $4.00.

New Christmas Hybrids, all sold.

ANT. C. ZVOLANEK

ORIGINATOR,

BOUND BROOK, N. J.

Mention The Florists' Exchange when writing.

RAISE YOUR OWN

TREES & SHRUBS

from SEED.

Send to-day for our new

TRADE SEED LIST

and also for our *Descriptive Catalog*, which is replete with valuable information.

OTTO KATZENSTEIN & CO.

WHOLESALE DEPT.

ATLANTA, GA.

Mention The Florists' Exchange when writing.

BURPEE'S SEEDS

PHILADELPHIA

Blue List of Wholesale Prices mailed only to those who plant for profit.

Mention The Florists' Exchange when writing

MY GIANT CYCLAMEN

Are Ahead in Growth and Flowers

Bloodred, Carmine, Pink, Pure White, White with Carmine Eye.

Each color separate. Tr pkt., $1.00, 1000 seeds, $6.00. An even mixture of the above 5 colors, tr. pkt., 75c.; 1000 seeds, $5.00.

For larger quantities, special quotations.

O. V. ZANGEN, Seedsman, HOBOKEN, N. J.

Mention The Florists' Exchange when writ

BULBS FOR FLORISTS

Lilium Harrisii, Roman Hyacinths Paper White Narcissus, Freesias

Send for special prices.

New Crop Mushroom Spawn—English and Pure Culture.

WEEBER & DON, Seed Merchants and Growers

114 Chambers Street, NEW YORK

Mention The Florists' Exchange when writ

Thorburn's Bulbs

HYACINTHS, TULIPS, NARCISSUS, CROCUS, LILIES and all other BULBS for FLORISTS

Send for our Wholesale Florists' Bulb List Now Ready.

J. M. THORBURN & CO.

33 BARCLAY ST., through to 32 PARK PL.

NEW YORK

Mention The Florists' Exchange when wri

Seed Trade Report.

AMERICAN SEED TRADE ASSOCIATION

Henry W. Wood, Richmond, Va., president; C. S. Burge, Toledo, O., first vice-president; G. B. McVay, Birmingham, Ala., second vice-president; C. E. Kendel, Cleveland, O., secretary and treasurer; J. H. Ford, Ravenna, O., assistant secretary.

The Canary Islands sold $46,613 worth of onion seed to the United States in 1905, an increase of nearly 300 per cent. over 1904.

During the year ending June 30, 1905, the quantity and value of the beans and dried peas imported into the United States were 472,572 bushels, worth $628,775. Canada sent the largest quantity, followed by Mexico, Germany, France, Italy, the Netherlands, United Kingdom, and other countries.

IMPORTS OF SEEDS.—During the year ending June 30, 1905, the total value of the seeds, other than flaxseed or linseed, imported into the United States, was $3,138,932, as against $3,386,245 in 1904, and $2,637,255 in 1903. The countries, and values from which the goods were consigned were as under:

	1903	1904	1905
Africa, n. e. s.	$6,256	$10,820	$5,689
Argentina	64		40,806
Austria-H'g'ry	13,933	14,544	7,990
Belgium	13,610	10,136	12,972
Brazil	67,441	68,314	27,508
Br. Australasia	32,377	44,606	13,150
Canada	133,049	423,219	237,051
Denmark	27,395	37,389	36,118
France	367,209	400,023	450,186
Germany	827,250	1,012,052	949,553
Italy	45,346	114,870	137,551
Netherlands ..	290,428	263,203	286,630
Russia, Eur.	29,182	33,600	15,101
Spain	4,601	15,850	18,829
Turkey, As...	6,358	3,037	25,924
Turkey, Eur...	30,231	70,871	26,796
U. Kingdom...	709,130	824,584	803,738
Other c'ntries.	33,405	89,117	43,340

NEW YORK.—S. B. Dicks of Cooper Taber & Company, London, will sail for home on the Caronia on Tuesday, October 9, after a very successful trip.

ST. PAUL, MINN.—Seed sales through traveling men are about the same as last year; selling is becoming harder every day on account of the territory being pretty well covered. Southern trade has been somewhat better, but in the Middle and Northern States about the same number of orders has been booked for Spring delivery.

P.

ORIENT, L. I.—All late crops on the east end of the north fork of Long Island from Mattituck down, such as Brussels sprouts, cauliflower and turnips, are threatened with complete destruction by the cabbage worm and a worm which the farmers designate as the "looper," which has come upon the crops mentioned in large numbers and is eating them up. The farmers at Orient say that it is already too late to save some of the crops of cauliflower and sprouts, but they are all trying to find a solution which can be used as a spray to kill the worms. Many farmers have already sprayed with Paris green and Bordeaux mixture, but it has had no effect on the worms so far, and at present the farmers seem practically helpless before the ravages of these pests.—Brooklyn (N. Y.) Eagle.

SHEBOYGAN, WIS.—The John H. Allen Seed Company, under date of September 29, 1906, write as follows: "Regarding the pea crop in Wisconsin, our crop is about half in, and we can have a very fair forecast of the result. In this section of the State, which stands dry weather better than wet, the crops average well; while in the northern portion of the State, around Sturgeon Bay, they are coming in far short of a good crop, and, indeed, not nearly up to field estimates, as the hot, dry weather succeeding the roguing time—when estimates were made—prevented the pods from filling. This shortage is so serious that the outlook is quite different from that of a month ago, and it now seems probable that there will be no more peas of desirable sorts than will be wanted; and there is a distinctly firmer feeling in the atmosphere.

"Very few beans have come in yet, but these, as well as peas, are unusually bright and sound, although the deliveries are less than field estimates."

European Notes.

The damage inflicted by the persistent drought on the plants of biennial crops is beginning to affect the values of stocks now being harvested, especially rutabagas and turnips (field varieties), both of which have advanced fully 25 per cent. during the past seven days. One reason of this is the extraordinary demand in Eastern Europe, and the willingness with which the increased prices are paid. There will not be any difficulty in maintaining the increased values if even only a moderate demand should continue.

German growers report an unfavorable change in the weather which has reduced the later crops of spinach fully 50 per cent. Choice carnations are a very poor crop; dwarf Vienna are a little better. Nasturtiums are very fair; Phloxes are good; Chinese pinks are not grand. Asters, what there is left standing, are doing very well and a fair crop may be expected. Sweet peas in the Erfurt district are reported to be a complete failure.

EUROPEAN SEEDS.

Italian vs. German Seeds.

In the Italian seed growing business the German trade is receiving very severe competition. Of late years the business of the leading Italian export firms has considerably increased, and this increase is going steadily on year by year. These remarks, of course, principally apply to flower seeds, more especially asters, stocks, etc. The difference in price of asters quoted by Italian export houses from that quoted by German growers is very marked, causing considerable surprise to retail seedsmen. On an average Italy quotes asters at less than one third the price of Germany, and the very lowness of price causes many would-be buyers to avoid purchasing, they thinking because the price is so low the quality is likely to be even lower; consequently they still give from 40s. to 60s. per pound to German growers for the same thing that can be bought in Italy for 17s. 6d. per pound.

That the quality of Italian seeds is fully equal if not superior to German products is amply proved by the tests recently made in England, and by the steady growth of the business; also by the continually increasing number of orders from the largest English firms—a plain proof that the seeds can stand the test, both in germination, purity, and selection of strain, as the leading English houses with a big retail or even wholesale reputation to keep up, are hardly likely to buy a second and third year an article that proved a failure in previous years. But perhaps the greatest and most conclusive test of all is the fact that German export firms are big buyers of seeds from Italy. Especially does this apply to asters and other flower seeds.

The seedsmen in England who have for some time past regularly bought seeds from Italy will state that the quality is equal to that obtained from Germany, and, during the last year, even superior. Much complaint has been heard of the more or less satisfactory blooming of German asters this year, principally on account of mildew being so prevalent, and it is a very significant fact that in the case of asters produced from Italian seeds no complaint whatever has been made, showing that in prevalence of mildew the latter country enjoys a great immunity over the German seed.

In vegetables the difference in price is almost as marked. In cauliflower, for instance, the variety Snowball is offered in Italy at 16s. per pound against about 3s. per ounce in Germany; and, of course, it is now a well known fact that Italy can produce cauliflower seed second to none in the world. Probably the bulk of the cauliflower seed used throughout Europe is produced in Italy, one firm with whom I am acquainted cultivating no fewer than 85 acres this year for seed.

It may be of interest to mention here that the cauliflower crops in Italy this year are very light and the large firms are not offering any seed at all except at full catalogue price. The eruption of Vesuvius, followed by terrific hail storms, completed the destruction of many cultures. The same remarks apply to onion seed, the bulk of this article being produced in Italy; and many acres are often cultivated by one grower. Of course, it is well known this article is, in quality, far superior to that grown in any other country, and no other cultures can compete in price with those of sunny Italy.

The same remarks as to the condition of the onion crops apply to cauliflower. The destruction by Vesuvius was terrific, almost ruining some of the small onion and cauliflower growers; the hail following in terrific storms, the destruction of many fields was complete. One of the largest growers is not, this season, offering any seed of all colored sorts as a result. In many, in fact, most of the lighter vegetable seeds this country is able to compete, to their own considerable advantage, with any other culture in Europe.

Many buyers express wonder why the seeds can be grown so much cheaper in Italy. I imagine the principal cause is the climate, which is almost perfect in ordinary seasons, and no better conditions than are usually found there, particularly those experienced during ripening and harvesting, can be desired. In the growing of the majority of seeds success and failure principally depend on suitable weather prevailing during harvesting and ripening. I am told California is almost identical with Italy in climate in every particular. Be that as it may, from my own experience with the seeds produced in the two countries I imagine the Italian climate and its seed products are Californian, considerably improved, perhaps, more particularly in the strength of the resulting growths.

ENGLISH CORRESPONDENT.

CATALOGUES RECEIVED.

FRANK E. RUE, Peoria, Ill.—Catalogue of Bulbs, Plants, Seeds, Supplies, etc.

ERNST BENARY, Erfurt, Germany.—Illustrated List of Novelties for 1906-7; always an interesting list.

PITTSPURG FLORISTS' EXCHANGE, Pittsburg, Pa.—Price List of Wire Designs and other Florists' Supplies.

THE UNITED STATES NURSERY COMPANY, Rich, Miss.—Catalogue of Field Grown Roses, Iris, Peonies, etc.

THE FRASER NURSERY, Huntsville, Ala.—Wholesale Price List of Fruit Trees, Roses, Magnolias, etc.

F. E. CONINE NURSERY COMPANY, Stratford, Conn.—General Catalogue of Nursery Stock. Illustrated.

NATHAN SMITH & SON, Adrian, Mich.—Wholesale Fall List of Seasonable Stock—Phlox, Carnations, Cannas, Ferns, etc.

TEXAS SEED & FLORAL COMPANY, Dallas, Texas.—Illustrated Catalogue of Bulbs for Fall Planting. An attractive publication giving practical advice on the making of a bulb garden.

ALCOHOL FROM CORNCOBS.—The Department of Agriculture is developing a new industry in the production of alcohol from corncobs, which, the Department says, promises to be of much commercial value. Investigations are being made at Hoopeston, Ill., and have proved that the large quantities of corncobs which every year go to waste can be made to produce alcohol in sufficient quantities to justify the erection of a distilling plant in connection with a corn cannery.

NURSERY DEPARTMENT.

Conducted by Joseph Meehan.

AMERICAN ASSOCIATION OF NURSERYMEN, Orlando Harrison, Berlin, Md., president; J. W. Hill, Des Moines, Ia., vice-president; George C. Seager, Rochester, N. Y., secretary; C. L. Yates, Rochester, N. Y., treasurer.

Nurserymen interested will find much valuable information in Bulletin 154, September, 1906, of the Connecticut Agricultural Experiment Station, New Haven, on the subject of "Chestnut in Connecticut and The Improvement of the Woodlot," written by Austin F. Hawes, M. F., State and Station Forester.

SUDDEN DEATH OF A NURSERYMAN.—Albert Wyckoff, vice-president of the Albaugh Nursery Company, Cincinnati, O., died suddenly on September 25, while traveling on a train near Buffalo, N. Y. He was 60 years of age, served through the Civil War and escaped twice from Andersonville prison. He was formerly postmaster of Jacksonville, Ill., and was a prominent horticulturist.

IMPORTS OF NURSERY STOCK.—The following table shows the comparative value of nursery stock imported into the United States during the years ending June 30, 1903, 1904 and 1905, and the countries from which received:

	1903.	1904.	1905.
Belgium	$289,637	$228,666	$223,181
Bermuda	49,726	32,954	35,424
France	261,777	283,787	297,850
Germany	93,139	111,871	98,901
Japan	61,255	68,584	71,222
Netherlands	535,442	644,059	642,859
United Kingdom.	99,847	95,513	106,326
Other countries..	32,375	35,993	36,303
Total	$1,373,198	$1,496,427	$1,512,066

Seasonable Topics.

In some nursery lists Viburnum Sieboldi is said to have berries of a bluish black color when ripe. This is a mistake. When ripe they are of a bright red, on carmine colored stalks, the whole forming a beautiful display backed with the large green leaves of this large growing shurb.

When recommending the Irish yew to customers do not forget that in addition to its pyramidal growth and lovely green foliage there is to be considered its profusion of red berries in Autumn. When well studded with these, as they usually are, the plants are greatly admired.

The past season has just suited the althæas. They like heat and moisture, and this is what they had. It made them grow vigorously and the more growth the more flowers. These beautiful shrubs are easily raised from hardwood cuttings, set out in Spring.

Scalecide, which was tried last Spring on trees here, completely killed all the San Jose scale it reached. Many trees that were full of scale had not a single one left alive after the spraying.

Among florists the name myrtle is applied to the periwinkle, Vinca minor. The true myrtle is Myrtus communis, a shrub of southern Europe which will stand but a few degrees of frost, hence exists here only as a greenhouse plant.

Florists find in the Hydrangea paniculata grandiflora flowers something useful not only when in their perfected state, but when the flowers commence to fade as well. Their pink color then renders them serviceable.

Those who may have the climbing Clothilde Soupert rose and find it does not flower, should bud it with some other sort. Gloire de Dijon is a good one where hardy as it is here, and it blooms from June until November.

Every one recognizes the value of the hardy asters at this season of the year. One of the good, yet rather uncommon, ones is the A. formosissima. Its flowers are of a deep lilac, and the whole habit of the plant is bushy, yet erect.

Reference has been made before to the value of the buddleia for late Summer blooming. One of the best, B. intermedia, has been in bloom for nearly two months, and it will continue so until frost stops it, from present appearance of the bushes.

Trees stricken with scale of any kind may be let go now until the leaves are off. Then one spraying may be given as soon as the leaves fall; another just before the buds expand in Spring. Often the one towards the close of Winter is sufficient.

Figs Outdoors.

The fruit of the fig is so delicious that it is surprising more of the bushes are not seen in gardens. In the vicinity of Philadelphia several private gardens have them. In some of them they have been grown for years, and a good crop is produced annually. A few persons are found who do not relish the taste of fresh figs, but by almost everyone the fruit is esteemed for its delicious flavor. In the South the fig ripens one crop after the other, making a succession of fruit the season through. In the North two crops are ripened. The very small figs barely discernible, when Fall ends, are those that give the first crop. These ripen in early August. The second crop, the last one in the North, ripens throughout September.

It is interesting to watch the ripening of the figs. The fruit grows to about half its size. It then appears to rest a little while, and at this stage some may drop, from imperfect fertilization or other causes, something that cannot be avoided. After what appears to be a short rest the fruit begins to swell rapidly, becoming of twice the size it was in a few weeks, and taking on whatever its colors are—black, brown, yellow, etc.—as it ripens.

Winter protection in the North consists of burying the branches six inches below ground. This can be done by digging out the soil on one side, throwing the bushes over on the other; or digging them up completely, burying them where they grew or elsewhere. The latter plan is followed by the writer. The loss of roots in digging is rather a gain, checking a too strong growth and tending toward free fruiting.

Useful Hardy Vines.

Nurserymen are usually asked to make a selection of vines for customers when an assortment is desired. When the collection is to be of self climbing varieties the following list will be found satisfactory: Ampelopsis Veitchii, A. virginica, Bignonia radicans, B. grandiflora, Decumaria barbara, Euonymus radicans, English ivy, and Hydrangea scandens. These will cling fast to brick-work or any like surface, and are all good vines. The Decumaria barbara is a southern

Hydrangea Arborescens.

vine, and may not prove hardy north of New York city. Although the above list comprises the self climbers, so-called, they are not really the only climbers, for all vines, if planted to a trellis, tree or the like, will in time gain the top of the support. Here is a list of such as are fast growers: Akebia quinata, Celastrus scandens, clematis, loniceras, flowering grape, wistarias, and Dolichos japonicus.

By one means or another these vines cling to their supports, some of them quickly reaching the top. The akebia, wistaria, lonicera and others will bind their shoots around a supporting branch or stick so tightly that they cannot be unfastened. The clematis attaches itself by a twist of its leaf stalk, so that, as said, in one way or another all find a way to climb. The Celastrus scandens and Lycium chinense are famed for their scarlet fruit in the Fall, a feature that often causes their planting. The celastrus has scarlet pods, the lycium scarlet berries, and both are handsome long after Winter sets in.

Pruning Rhododendrons.

A correspondent, R. S. Scott, asks me if it is right to prune rhododendrons, and when. He has some large bushes, too large for the position they occupy, and would prune them, but has been informed that these bushes will not submit to pruning. There is an opinion prevailing that rhododendrons should not be pruned, but it is an error to think this cannot be done. If a part of a bush only be pruned the rest unpruned, the pruned portion rarely breaks afresh in a satisfactory way, but prune away the whole top and it starts again very well. This should be added, however; that when rhododendrons are very old and are cut back severely they do not always break again in a way desired. But those of a height of from three to four feet may be cut back to two feet and would make a nice, fresh growth.

As to the preferred time to prune, Spring is the best, as soon as Winter passes. Usually shrubs or trees with such hard wood do not break well, but rhododendrons will. In the case of pines it is commonly agreed that they do not stand pruning back to hard wood very well, yet those accustomed to traveling where pines grow wild will have noticed how the P. rigida will sprout, even from the trunk, when cut back severely; but not so the P. inops, P. mitis or P. strobus.

Hydrangea Arborescens.

One of our native hydrangeas, H. arborescens, has been in collections of cultivated shrubs for many years, and not unworthily so, for when in good soil and where it has room afforded it, it is well worthy of cultivation. Our illustration of it will bear us out in this assertion, we think. Certainly the plant as we saw it made a display calling for the attention of all who came near it.

There is found great variation in the plants as regards their flowering. Many of them produce blooms almost wholly perfect. These are the small ones seen in the center of the flower heads in the illustration. Others have blossoms almost altogether sterile. Our own specimen, the one before us, has a sufficient number of the large sterile flowers to make it attractive, and when a bush is as handsome as is the one pictured, the effect of the whole mass of flowers is very pleasing.

The older botanical works gave as its home, "the Middle and Western states," but it extends as well into the South, growing freely in North Carolina, along streams and on its mountain and hill sides; and it is common in the Southwestern states as well.

Mentioning its variations in the way of flowering, there is now an uncommonly handsome one on the market, or about to be put there, which has all its flowers sterile, giving a head of bloom the appearance of a "snowball." It has been proposed to call it the "snowball hydrangea," an appropriate name, we think. An illustration of it appeared in The Florists' Exchange last July. We agree with the writer of the notes that accompanied the illustration referred to that the plant will prove of great value to the florist and to the amateur. Imagine the one of our illustration to be full of "snowball" heads instead of those it has, and an idea will be had of the great beauty of the newcomer!

Hydrangea arborescens and its varieties are easily raised. The typical one can be increased by dividing the plant, by cuttings and by seeds. It seeds freely, and the seeds vegetate well. The snowball one has few or no perfect flowers so is out of the list of those that can be raised from seeds.

Another native hydrangea is H. radiata, sometimes called H. nivea. Its radical difference is in the color of the under sides of its leaves, they being of a silvery white, looking like down.

JOSEPH MEEHAN.

You have a valuable paper.

Berlin, Md. J. G. HARRISON & SON.

700
Hardy Herbaceous Perennials

Strong, field grown clumps in over 700 varieties. Catalogue for the asking.

HIRAM T. JONES,
Union County Nurseries, Elizabeth, N. J.

Mention the Florists' Exchange when writing.

Holland Nursery Stock

Ask for Our Catalogue. It will interest you.

ENDTZ, VAN NES & CO. BOSKOOP, HOLLAND

Mention The Florists' Exchange when writing.

HERBACEOUS PERENNIALS

for Summer and Autumn Planting. We offer NINE HUNDRED and SIXTY-SEVEN VARIETIES of STRONG FIELD-GROWN PLANTS. Send for Catalog and Trade List.

BAY STATE NURSERIES, NORTH ABINGTON, MASS.

Mention the Florists' Exchange when writing.

F. & F. NURSERIES

SPRINGFIELD NEW JERSEY

Wholesale Growers — **TREES AND PLANTS** in full assortment. — Trade Catalogue Free

Mention The Florists' Exchange when writing.

THE SHREWSBURY NURSERIES
EATONTOWN, N. J.

Offer a good line of well-grown NURSERY STOCK, Large, well developed Shrubs a specialty. SEND FOR WHOLESALE LIST

Mention The Florists' Exchange when writing.

To Clear the Land We Shall Sell For the Next 60 Days

	Per 1000
Berberis Thunbergii, 18 to 24 in., bushy plants	$40.00
Berberis Thunbergii, 24 to 30 in., bushy plants	50.00
Rosa Lucida, 3 years, twice transplanted, fine	40.00
Viburnum Dentatum, 24 to 30 in.	40.00
" " 30 to 36 in.	50.00

We also have some Viburnum cassinoides and Prunus maritima.

Littlefield & Wyman
North Abington, Mass.

Mention The Florists' Exchange when writing.

P. OUWERKERK
216 Jane Street
WEEHAWKEN HEIGHTS, N. J.

P. O. No. 1, Hoboken, N. J.

JUST RECEIVED FROM OUR HOLLAND NURSERIES

Rhododendrons, Azaleas, Spiræa Japonica, Lilium Speciosum, Peonies, Bleeding Heart, Pot-Grown Lilacs, Hydrangea in sorts, Clematis and H. P. Roses in the best sorts.

PRICES MODERATE

Mention The Florists' Exchange when writing.

KOSTER & CO.

Hollandia Nurseries **BOSKOOP, HOLLAND**

Hardy Azaleas, Box Trees, Clematis, Conifers, Hydrangeas, Peonies.
Pot-Grown Plants for Forcing.
RHODODENDRONS, H. P. ROSES, Etc.
Catalogue free on demand.

Mention The Florists' Exchange when writing.

CALIFORNIA PRIVET

Fine well-graded, two year plants, well packed as follows: 15 to 20 inches, 3 or more branches, $1.50 per 100; $8.00 per 1000, this grade gives good satisfaction.
20 to 30 inches, 5 or more branches, $2.00 per 100; $13.50 per 1000, nice.
2½ to 3 ft., 7 or more branches, $3.00 per 100; $17.50 per 1000, very strong.
3 to 4 ft., strong selected, $4.00 per 100; $25.00 per 1000.

CHAS. BLACK, Hightstown, N. J.

Mention the Florists' Exchange when writing.

CANNAS

300,000 roots for Fall delivery in 100 leading kinds, $8.00 to $20.00 per 1000. Write for our list. Send in your orders early.

SHELLROAD GREENHOUSES
Largest Canna Growers — Grange, Baltimore, Md.

Mention The Florists' Exchange when writing.

H. DEN OUDEN & SON,
BOSKOOP, HOLLAND.

Wholesale growers of nursery stock for the American trade. Catalogue free on demand. Also views in our nurseries.

Mention The Florists' Exchange when writing.

LARGE TREES
OAKS AND MAPLES
PINES AND HEMLOCKS

ANDORRA NURSERIES
WM. WARNER HARPER, PROPRIETOR
Chestnut Hill, Philadelphia, Pa.

Mention the Florists' Exchange when writing.

SEND TO
THE MOON COMPANY

For Your { TREES, SHRUBS, VINES and SMALL FRUITS

Descriptive Illustrated Catalogue Free
THE WM. H. MOON CO.
Morrisville, Pa.

Mention the Florists' Exchange when writing.

Trees and Shrubs

We make specially low prices on nursery stock to **Parks, Cemeteries**, etc.
Wholesale price list on application.
We carry immense quantities of the finest named varieties of peonies.

PETERSON NURSERY
505 W. PETERSON AVE., CHICAGO, ILL

Mention The Florists' Exchange when writing.

PEONIES

We still have quite a block of **No Plus Ultra**, and need the ground. While they last we offer them at $7.50 per 100; $60.00 per 1000. Send for list.

EDWARD SWAYNE
WEST CHESTER, PA.

Mention the Florists' Exchange when writing.

BABY RAMBLER ROSES

Strong plants from 2¼ in. pots, April propagation. Per doz., 60c.; 100, $3.50; 1000, $30.00.

VICK & HILL CO.
P. O. Box 613, Rochester, N. Y.

Mention The Florists' Exchange when writing.

Commercial Violet Culture

Price, $1.50
The Florists' Exchange, 2-8 Duane St., New York

Mention The Florists' Exchange when writing.

Large Assortment **PEONIES** Very best Varieties

LOW PRICES
THE KIND THAT FLORISTS LIKE

"We make a specialty of growing stocky transplanted shrubbery and trees"

FULL ASSORTMENT OF Ornamentals, Fruits, Roses, Clematis, and Herbaceous Plants. Write for our fall wholesale trade list.

W. & T. SMITH CO., GENEVA, N. Y.

Mention The Florists' Exchange when writing.

Viburnum Plicatum Japan Snowball

18 to 24 in.	$10.00	per 100
2 to 2½ ft.	12.00	"
2½ to 3 ft.	15.00	"
3 to 4 ft.	20.00	"
4 to 5 ft.	25.00	"

DOUBLE ALTHEAS

Jeanne D'Arc, pure white flowers fine for cutting. Banner—White striped crimson. Red—Rich ruby red flowered.

	per 100
Bushy Plants 18 to 24 in.	$6.00
2 to 2½ ft.	7.00
2½ to 3 ft.	8.00
3 to 4 ft.	10.00

BERBERRY THUNBERGII, Splendid for Hedges

Our plants are grown from Cuttings and are very bushy.

	per 100	per 1000
12 to 18 in.	$5.00	$45.00
18 to 24 in.	7.00	60.00
2 ft. to 2½ ft.	10.00	90.00

HYDRANGEA PAN. GRAND.
2 to 3 ft. $7.00 per 100, $60.00 per 1000

DEUTZIA LEMOINEI, Fine for Forcing
2 to 2½ ft. $7.00 per 100

DEUTZIA GRACILIS, 12 to 18 in 4.50 "

SPIRAEA VAN HOUTTEI

		per 100	per 1000
" "	3 ft.	$5.00	$45.00
" "	3 to 4 ft.	6.00	50.00
" Blue, caryopteris,	15 to 20 in.	5.00	45.00
" " "	2 to 2½ ft.	7.00	65.00
" A. Waterer	12 to 18 in.	5.50	50.00
" "	2 to 2½ ft.	8.00	75.00
" "	2½ to 3 ft.	9.00	85.00

HONEYSUCKLE HECKROTTII, 1 year $6.00 per 100, 2 years, $10.00 per 100.

PLATYCODON LEICHTLINII, Dwarf, Bushy and very free flowering, 2 years, $6.00 per 100.

THE CONARD & JONES CO.
WEST GROVE, PA.

HYDRANGEAS for FORCING

Otaksa and Thos. Hogg, with 7 to 12 Flowering Crowns, $12.00 per 100; with 5 to 6 Flowering Clowns, $9.00 per 100; with 4 Flowering Crowns, $7.00 per 100.

Japonica Rosea, (new), with 7 to 12 Flowering Crowns, $20.00 per 100; with 5 to 6 Flowering Crowns, $13.00 per 100; with 4 Flowering Crowns, $10.00 per 100.

We especially recommend the new Japonica Rosea; color, fine, rich pinke about the shade of Gloire de Lorraine Begonia; coloring is even, and does not show the white or washed-out shadings sometimes seen in Otaksa; foliage, uniform deep green, and does not streak nor yellow. Has taken medals in Europe and is a distinct acquisition.

Our plants are grown **outdoors** in beds and slat-houses; will be taken inside before frost and available for delivery next month, when wanted.

ROSES, field-grown, well-rooted, **especially suited for Forcing.** Write for prices. Full line of Ornamentals, Shrubs, Shades, Vines, etc.

JACKSON & PERKINS CO.
WHOLESALE NURSERYMEN AND FLORISTS
NEWARK, WAYNE CO., NEW YORK

Mention The Florists' Exchange when writing.

YOUR
Spring Catalogue

We have been printing Trade Catalogues for the past sixteen years; have been accumulating stock cuts and photographs for the past sixteen years, and, equally important, perhaps most important of all, have been steadily improving in our knowledge as to what is required in the way of style, workmanship and finish in order to produce a catalogue that

Will Be Effective

Send in full specifications and we will promptly give you an estimate. We have several hundred illustrative stock cuts free to our customers.

A. T. DE LA MARE PTG. & PUB. CO. Ltd.
2 to 8 Duane Street, New York City.

COMING EXHIBITIONS.

[Secretaries of other Societies will oblige by forwarding the schedules of their respective shows. Ed. F. E.]

OCTOBER 24 and 25, 1906.—Lenox (Mass.) Horticultural Society, annual chrysanthemum exhibition. G. Foulsham, secretary.

OCTOBER 25, 26 and 27, 1906.—United Bay Shore Horticultural Society, Fifth Annual Exhibition, Carleton Opera House, Bay Shore, N. Y. Manager, John Tobin, Box 635, Bay Shore, N. Y.

OCTOBER 30, 31 and November 1, 1906.—Tarrytown (N. Y.) Horticultural Society, eighth annual exhibition, Music Hall. E. W. Neubrand, secretary.

OCTOBER 31 and NOVEMBER 1, 1906, Monmouth County (N. J.) Horticultural Society, ninth annual exhibition, Town Hall, Red Bank, N. J. H. A. Kettel, secretary.

NOVEMBER 1 and 2, Morris County (N. J.) Gardeners and Florists' Society, Assembly Rooms, Madison, N. J. E. Reagan, secretary.

NOVEMBER 6-12, 1906. — Chicago Horticultural Society. W. N. Rudd, secretary.

NOVEMBER 6-8, 1906, New Haven County Horticultural Society. Thomas Pettit, 90 Prospect street, New Haven, Conn., secretary.

NOVEMBER 7, 8 and 9, American Institute, New York, annual chrysanthemum show, etc., Berkeley Lyceum Building. Leonard Barron, New York, secretary Horticultural Section.

NOVEMBER 8, 1906.—Worcester County (Mass.) Horticultural Society, annual exhibition of chrysanthemums, Adin A. Hixon, secretary.

NOVEMBER 9-10, 1906, Rhode Island Horticultural Society. C. W. Smith, 27-29 Exchange street, Providence, R. I., secretary.

NOVEMBER 13, 14 and 15, Faith Home Association, Thirteenth Annual Chrysanthemum Show, Houston, Texas, Mrs. F. A. Reichardt, secretary.

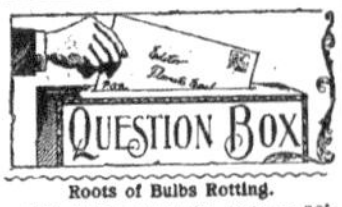

Roots of Bulbs Rotting.

(55) What causes the roots on potted bulbs to die and rot before the bulbs are brought into the greenhouse? I have this trouble of dead and rotten roots every year. For example, this year I potted up Paper White narcissus bulbs in 6-inch fern pots and set them under the benches, covering them with a little swale hay. The root growth was fine, but later when I examined them I found the roots all dead and rotten. This happens every year wth my bulbs of all kinds. Sometimes I bury them out of doors; sometimes I put them in a frost-proof root cellar, sometimes under the greenhouse benches, but the result is always the same. What is the remedy? B.

New York.

—The trouble with this grower's bulbs is quite evidently due to the treatment they receive between the time when the pots get filled with roots and the time they are taken into the greenhouse. If the bulbs are kept under benches where water can drip on them, and keep them in a sodden state, they will rot every time; but why they should decay when buried outdoors seems strange, unless the land is extremely wet. Using green manure in the soil for potting bulbs will also cause the roots to wither after a short time, but if inquirer will give an exact description of his methods of treating the bulbs, from start to finish, we would be in a better position to suggest a remedy for the trouble of which he complains.

Hydrangeas.

(56) I have 25 hydrangeas; four are beautiful tub specimens, which hitherto have had 80 and 100 full blooms. This Spring the stems were tall and yellow, also the leaves, and had very few blooms. Will you kindly tell me if they need close pruning, also what temperature they require? T. F. D.

—Hydrangeas should only be cut back as a means to keep the plants of a desired size, or of getting them to branch out, when they are young; for whenever a growth is shortened back a flower is lost for that season, as the flower always comes on the tip of the growth that is made the previous season. The plants in question are no doubt in need of more nourishment than is afforded them in their present quarters. This can best be remedied by taking them out of the tubs, and replacing the old soil with new, adding a goodly proportion of well rotted manure to the new soil. We would also cut down all the longest of the stems two-thirds of their length; the shorter stems we would leave uncut, to provide flowers for next season. A temperature anywhere between freezing point and 45 degrees will keep the plants nicely through the Winter, and little or no water will be required for them while they are in their Winter quarters.

Hastening Blooming of Stocks.

(57) I sowed seed of stocks (gillyflower) in the open, August 10; and transplanted to greenhouse. In a week's time the plants were growing as well as ever. I had hoped to cut before November 1 as the bench is wanted then. Kindly tell me when I may expect to cut; and if there is any way of hastening the blooming.

Mass. S. E. B.

—If the stocks are not already showing their flower stalks, there is certainly not much chance of the crop being gathered by November 1. The only thing that would hasten flowering would be to provide more heat; but if the plants are not thoroughly established in the benches, such a course would no doubt ruin them entirely. We cannot tell exactly when the stocks may be expected to flower, as the transfer from the open ground might help to make their growing season a longer one, and they might not flower until December or January.

Treatment of Giant Marguerite.

(58) Would it be profitable to sow the seed of Giant marguerite and plant out early in the Spring for Summer and Fall blooms? Or would it pay to root the side shoots that come with the flowers during November and December? Or is there any other plan you would advise for Summer and Fall flowers? N. & J.

S. Dakota.

—We presume that by the Giant marguerite, the Paris daisy, Chrysanthemum frutescens, is referred to, and would advise as the best way for producing flowering plants to propagate from the side shoots during November and December.

PLANTS FOR NAME.—P. B. Brooklyn, N. Y.—No. 1 Kerria Japonica, variegata; No. 2, Pachysandra terminalis; No. 3, Physostegia denticulata; No. 4, Mullein pink (agrostemma); cannot say what variety from specimen; No. 5, Aster tataricus; No. 6, Clematis Davidiana; No. 7, Caryopteris mastacanthus; No. 8, Helianthus Maximilliana; No. 9, Possibly Pityrospermum acerinum.

LIST OF ADVERTISERS

INDEX TO STOCK ADVERTISED

Contents.

REVIEW OF THE MARKET

NEW YORK.—There has been such a shortening up in the supply of flowers of nearly every kind that prices along all lines have taken a jump upward. The weather has been quite cool for several days past, and the diminishing of the supply is probably more due to that than to anything else.

American Beauty roses of the best grade are very scarce indeed, and at times $4 per dozen has been realized for the best of them. Special grades of Bride and Bridesmaid are also very scarce, and there have been occasions when 10c. each has been realized, though 8c. has been the predominating figure.

Carnations also have felt the benefit of the upward tendency, and for such varieties as Enchantress, $4 per 100 has been obtained. With orchids it is the same; prices have advanced considerably, and dahlias are not far behind, many of the latter bringing $3 per 100 easily. We do not believe that dahlias have sold so well for several years as they are doing at present. Of course, the absence of good asters, together with chrysanthemums not showing up in any considerable quantity, has helped the dahlia demand very much. Lilies have also advanced materially since our last quotations; 12c. each is now the ruling figure for good flowers.

A few fancy chrysanthemums appeared on the market last Saturday, and brought $6 per dozen. Regular shipments are not arriving as yet, however, but we presume that by another week regular supplies will be on hand. A few violets are coming in intermittently, but there is no regular demand for these as yet. If the cool weather continues, we shall perhaps see them in daily supply within the next few days.

As an offset to the increase all around in the prices of flowers, we might say that the demand for asparagus, smilax and adiantum continues very poor indeed, and prices are anything but firm.

BOSTON.—There seems to be a marked improvement all along the line. Stock is better and prices have advanced. The weather is cooler, consquently better for the flower trade. American Beauty roses continue to be the leader in selling, and prices have advanced somewhat, $4 per dozen now being the figure for the best grades. Other grades of American Beauty sell wll. Kaiserin Augusta Victoria is the only white variety of good quality. Bride and Bridesmaid continue to improve, however, but there is a raft of the smaller grades of these flowers on the markt. Carnations are selling well; there are no large flowers yet and stems are rather short, but prices are better. Asters continue to come in in quantities, but the quality now is not so good as it has been. Violets are getting more plentiful. Dahlias have been selling well of late. Gladioli are still in large supply. Lily of the valley is selling well. Lilies are not so plentiful as they were. Candytuft is abundant. There is a good demand for green goods of all kinds.

J. W. D.

NEW BEDFORD, MASS.—Trade continues quite active here, with plenty of flowers to supply the demand. Asters are about done, though a few short stemmed flowers are still to be seen. Carnations are coming in of very fine quality. The stems are very short as yet; 35c. per dozen retail is asked. Roses are doing very nicely; the market seems to be pretty well supplied with them at present; $1.50 per dozen is the price they realize. A few short stem-equipped with a Kroeschell heating appearance, bringing $1 per hundred. Everything outdoors is in full bloom, no frost as yet appearing in this section. The propagation of geraniums is now being pushed, also other bedding stock.

HORTICO.

CINCINNATI.—September business was fair, and probably all we could expect. Two causes may be given why it was not better; first, the stock was not to be had, and, second, the flower buying public were not home and settled from their Summer vacations. October will no doubt be a busy month, many large wedding orders now being booked. The inquiries for good American Beauty roses and chrysanthemums are many. American Beauty is undoubtedly the popular rose, take it the season through, and when other flowers are lying dormant, American Beauty generally sells at some price. At this writing this rose is bringing 50c., 75c., $1, $1.25, $1.50, $1.75, $2, $2.50 and $3 per dozen, while Bridesmaid and Bride fetch 2c. to 3c. and 4c. to 5c. Carnations are still scarce; $1 to $1.50 is obtained for what comes in. Lily of the valley realizes 4c.; asters, 50c. to $1 per 100; dahlias, 1c. to 1½c. each. chrysanthemums, 15c. to 25c. each. Greens of all kinds are at usual prices.

E. G. G.

ST. LOUIS.—The cut flower trade is improving and prices on all first-class stock are stiffening, with a good demand. The cool weather has given a better color to most of the stock, and florists' windows in the West End show fine displays of cut flowers. This is home coming week, something doing every day, and we hope it will do our business some good. Some of our largest retailers report orders booked ahead for weddings, receptions, and dinner parties this month. The Veiled Prophets' ball, Tuesday night, should sell much extra choice stock of all kinds. To-day, Monday morning, stock is scarce. American Beauty have been and are in big demand, with long fancy grades at $4; 30-inch stems, $3, 24-inch stems, $2.50, and shorts, 75c. per dozen Of the smaller roses, fancies are up as high as $8 per 100. Just now 5c. and 6c. roses sell best. Carnations are improving in quality every day, and fancy sell at $2 per 100. Enchantress are fine; and Mrs. T. W. Lawson have better color. Prime lily of the valley sell at $4 per 100. Cosmos is coming in, but only in small lots. A few asters and tuberoses help to make up the daily market supply.

ST. PATRICK.

INDIANAPOLIS.—Heavy frosts are predicted soon which will make florists lose an important source of supply in dahlias, snapdragon, cosmos, etc. September business with the majority of our retailers shows a substantial increase over the corresponding month last year. Funeral work is plentiful, but counter trade is lacking at present. There is little demand for the chrysanthemums now in the market, at $3 a dozen. American Beauty roses continue to outsell all others, at $5 to $25 a 100; $1 to $6 a dozen is the customary retail figure. Bride, Bridesmaid and Golden Gate roses have improved in quality very much, and sell at $3 to $5 per 100. Short-stemmed Killarney bring $3. Carnations are plentiful enough, but short stems make them difficult to sell. A few callas and Harrisii lilies bring $10 per 100. Lily of the valley is shipped in at $4. Asparagus and adiantum are scarce. Smilax is plentiful at 12½c. per string.

A prominent department store manager says the number of styles designed for plant receptacles this season is wonderful, and judging from the number of such filled so far, this line should prove satisfactory for the florist.

I. B.

ST. PAUL.—Trade is apparently much improved, as all of the retailers report good business, particularly in loose flowers. The demand for roses and carnations is much heavier, but stock in colored roses is indeed scarce. There is considerable medium grade stock on the market, but first-class flowers are hard to get. A great many Richmond roses are being grown, but very few first grade flowers are seen. Bridesmaid are also very small. Bride are coming in much better than other varieties; the consequence is there is considerable white stock on the market. Out door flowers, such as asters and dahlias, are gone; the demand for them has been transferred to carnations, which are also very scarce and inferior. Enchantress is about the only variety that any where near approaches the standard of good stock in the carnations. The past week we received the first shipment of new violets, and they were fine; but as they come in in only limited numbers it is hard to fill a very large order. The demand for violets has not been very heavy, and we cannot expect it to be such for some time. American Beauty are very good and while not plentiful there is a fair lot coming in, about equal to the demand. Chrysanthemums have not made their appearance as yet, but judging by the looks of the plants in the different greenhouses, it will only be a matter of a week or two before we will have a number of the early varieties. Prices are very fair. Roses range from $1 to $2.50 per dozen for standard sorts; Beauties form $3 to $6 per dozen; carnations, 50c. a dozen.

PAUL.

FORT ATKINSON, WIS.—Louis Prochaska's greenhouses were hit by a hail storm on the 21st September. The loss was small.

Plant Notes.

GARDENIAS.—There is no apparent reason why gardenias should not prove a paying crop if the plants are properly grown. For Winter blooming the plants should now be in the benches; if they are not, the sooner the work is attended to the better. A great deal of the success or failure in gardenia growing depends on how the benches are prepared, the depth of soil in the benches, and the drainage. Before beginning planting a good layer of broken bricks, or crocks, should be laid evenly over the bottom of the bench, reserving the smallest particles of the material for the surface of the drainage system. Over all a covering of sod, with the grass side down, should be placed. When the important part of drainage is satisfactorily settled, the benches will require filling with soil, which should be composed of good fibrous loam two thirds and one third well rotted cow manure with a good sprinkling of charcoal intermixed. The depth of the soil in the bench ought not to exceed three and a half inches. A greater depth of soil may be disadvantageous in several ways; in one way, the action of the heat from the pipes underneath the benches, which is absolutely indispensable in the successful cultivation of gardenias, will be much slower and in like manner the plants slower to respond when too much soil envelops the roots. In another way, the plants are likely to make too much wood, other conditions being favorable, if an excess of soil is put in for them to feed and grow rank on. And although a reasonable growth is necessary, yet abnormal growth is not only unnecessary, but it is to be rigidly guarded against, because when it exists the absence of flowers is invariably noticeable for reasons known to every grower familiar with the forcing of flowering plants. After a time and when the roots have penetrated all the soil in the bench, in the event of the plants showing signs of exhaustion through want of nourishment, the benches should be top dressed with good loam and bone meal and the process repeated as often as necessary while the plants remain in the benches.

Gardenias require a night temperature not much less than 70 degrees and a humid atmosphere continually. The plants should be syringed regularly, in order to be kept in good growing and in a clean condition. Gardenias are greatly pestered with mealy bug, and from the start this pest should be kept away. Frequent sproying with kerosene emulsion will keep it at a safe distance.

For Summer flowering gardeni[as] cuttings should be started now, an[d] when rooted potted and repotted un[til] they are in 3½ or 4 inch pots. These are the sizes of pots in whic[h] gardenias should be planted fo[r] either flowering period.

ADIANTUMS.—Large plants [of] Adiantum cuneatum that have sup[plied] fronds through the Summe[r] may now be laid away to rest for [a] season, and water almost entirel[y] withheld from them until they ar[e] started into growth again in th[e] Spring. This disposition of th[e] plants will obviate the necessity [of] giving them larger pots at any tim[e] which they would need if grown [on] continuously. Some growers may [be] inclined to discard old plants en[tirely], but sometimes it has happen[ed] that those that were kept over in th[e] manner indicated here came in ve[ry] handy for certain purposes. Youn[g] plants of Adiantum cuneatum shou[ld] be kept growing unchecked rig[ht] along.

It is as yet perhaps too early f[or] the convenience and purpose of ma[ny] growers to break up Adiantum Fa[r]leyense for increase of stock, but [in] choosing plants for this purpose [it] may be well to remark that com[paratively] young stock is much pr[e]ferable to old stock for propagatin[g]; therefore, a supply of that kind [of] material should be reserved for th[at] purpose. Plants grown in pans a[re] also much better for dividing th[an] those that were grown in deep po[ts] because a large number of wh[ite] roots can be secured with the crow[ns] when breaking up the plants. This variety of adiantum is yearly gaining in popularity, and the price obtained for it, both for the cut fronds and the plants in pots, should make it quite profitable to grow despite the somewhat exacting nature of its requirements.

Now that the time is drawing near when growers of plants for house decoration will realize on their product and reap a harvest commensurate with that which they should, there are several points that in the eagerness and hurry incidental to the conduct of many growers' establishments are lost sight of, but which if kept in mind might add considerably to the returns ultimately. Many growers of plants are so eager to excel in volume of production that quality suffers in consequence; or I should say, the quality of the stock grown suffers with the consequence that much of it remains in the hands of the growers. To instance this, I will take the case of a man who grew 2000 Nephrolepis Scottii in 6 inch pots on a bench, never moving the plants after placing them closely together on the bench. At the height of the season, when the demand was the briskest and the plants began to move, they were found to be poor specimens, spare and mean, all from overcrowding. The result was that almost the entire stock had to be sold at a depreciation, whereas if only two-thirds of the number stated had been placed on that bench, and the plants turned and moved occasionally, all would not only have sold at the standard figure but the grower's reputation as a grower would have been sustained.

Another point worth noticing, is the inclination of some growers to unduly prolong the life of a novelty, as such, long after it has ceased to be a novelty, whereas it would seem that it might be more profitable to them to allow the "novelties" that are things of the past to go the way of all such, and then continue it if possible as a standard article, getting ready to push another novelty on its appearance whether of their own origin or that of others. In the case of a novelty that is not likely ever to become a standard article, the sooner after it has lost general interest it is discarded the better.

Reputation goes a long way in the business of growing plants as in most other lines of industry, but retail florists usually take the trouble to find out whether or not they are paying too high a price for some one else's reputation. The man who was scarcely known a year or two ago as a grower, by means of advertising his product has placed himself and his goods just as directly in view of the purchasing florist as the man who boasts of a score or more years of business activity. The point in this is, that nowadays uniform prices count for more than they did formerly, and that energetic beginners, if they make known through the trade papers what they have, need not fear being neglected. Their reputations will quickly be found out and rewarded according to merit.

M. I.

FOUNDED IN 1888

THE FLORISTS' EXCHANGE

A Weekly Medium of Interchange for Florists, Nurserymen Seedsmen and the Trade in general

Exclusively a Trade Paper.

Entered at New York Post Office as Second Class Matter

Published EVERY SATURDAY by

A. T. DE LA MARE PTG. AND PUB. CO. LTD.

2, 4, 6 and 8 Duane Street,

P. O. Box 1697. Telephone 3765 John. NEW YORK.

CHICAGO OFFICE: 127 East Berwyn Avenue.

ILLUSTRATIONS.

Electrotypes of the illustrations used in this paper can usually be supplied by the publishers. Price on application.

YEARLY SUBSCRIPTIONS.

United States, Canada, and Mexico, $1.00. Foreign countries in postal union, $2.50. Payable in advance. Remit by Express Money Order Draft on New York. Post Office Money Order or Registered Letter.

The address label indicates the date when subscription expires and is our only receipt therefore.

REGISTERED CABLE ADDRESS:
Florex, New York.

ADVERTISING RATES.

One-half inch, 75c.; ¾-inch, $1.00; 1-inch, $1.25, special positions extra. Send for Rate Card showing discount of 10c., 15c., 25c., or 35c., per inch on continuous advertising. For rates on Wants, etc., see column for Classified Advertisements.

Copy must reach this office 12 o'clock Wednesday to secure insertion in issue of following Saturday.

Orders from unknown parties must be accompanied with cash or satisfactory references.

The S. A. F. Funeral Design.

In another column of this week's issue appears an illustration of the floral design at one time sent by the S. A. F. to the funerals of its deceased members—a very appropriate and commendable practice, unfortunately now abolished. We quite agree with the correspondent, who sends us the picture and its description, that the society should re-adopt this method of expressing the sense of loss it has sustained in the death of its members, as well as its sympathy and condolence with the bereaved families. No such costly tribute as that originally sent is necessary; a simple, inexpensive token being all that is required.

It seems somewhat inexplicable that the S. A. F. which is regarded as an exemplar for all our florist organizations, should among these be one that fails in the performance of a duty to its dead along this and other lines; for there are few, if any, of the florists' clubs that, on the passing away of a member, neglect to adopt suitable resolutions, or to send a floral tribute to the funeral. Our national society, on the other hand, now seems to consider the simple record of demise in its minutes, and the reading thereof, all sufficient. This, we submit, displays a heartless indifference that cannot be condoned under any circumstance, and we are heartily in favor of a return to former usage, when the society recognized by resolution the worth of its departed members, and demonstrated its fraternal sorrow and sympathy through the mute but expressive funeral floral tribute.

To Our Readers.

Is any reader in position to oblige us with photographs of an amateur's water garden? We would be pleased to receive clear pictures showing aquatics growing in tubs, or small pools, or in specially constructed water basins. Examples of this year's work preferred. With each photograph please send a few lines of descriptive matter giving names of plants used and results accomplished. Accepted photographs will be promptly paid for.

Notice.

Our readers are hereby informed that Henri Beaulieu, Woodhaven, N. Y., is no longer authorized to solicit subscriptions and advertisements for The Florists' Exchange.

A CARNATION SPORT.—I send today a box of cut blooms of carnation sport. Do you think the color would be desirable for a profitable market flower? R. T. COOKINGHAM.

—The color of the carnation is a very pretty shade of pink, and one that will no doubt be very desirable for commercial purposes. If the variety is up to the standard in every other respect, and the flowers have lasting qualities, it should, we think, prove a good sort for any market.

The Wholesale Cut Flower Industry.

The various changes recorded in this week's issue of The Florists' Exchange connected with Philadelphia and Boston wholesale cut flower houses, tend to force upon us more strongly than ever the fact of the importance and magnitude which this branch of the florist industry has assumed. Scarcely more than thirty years old, its advancement has been phenomenal, and it is but a reflex of the progress making in other lines of the industry during that period.

The wholesale cut flower trade is one the demands of which are exacting to a degree not experienced in any other branch of the business; and it is gratifying to note that it has drawn and is drawing to it a class of men capable of coping with its strenuous requirements. If we search into the history of those who are making the greatest success in the wholesale cut flower line we shall find that they are men who have endeavored and are endeavoring to devise the best methods by which their business can be put on a basis tending to the satisfaction of all concerned; men whose integrity and honesty are above suspicion; men with whom "the square deal" is paramount in all their transactions. For, lacking these qualities, no merchant was ever able to build up a stable trade, or remain any length of time in business.

So it is all the more creditable to the wholesale cut flower dealers as a class, and to the individuals of whom the story is told, that the Boston house referred to has been in active operation for twenty-nine years, and that some of its consignors have been shipping stock to it continuously for a quarter of a century. Such a record is enviable.

It must also be gratifying to these tradesmen that their personal worth is becoming more and more recognized by their fellows. From among them have been chosen presidents of local florists' clubs; the present year saw a wholesale commission man fill the chair of the S. A. F. O. H. with credit to himself and acceptably to the organization; and more than one representative has served on the society's executive board.

The part played by the commission man in the development of the cut flower industry has often been exploited and need only be referred to now. Of criticism, too, he has had his share, full and overflowing. Yet withal, the immense strides he has made and is making, and the great business enterprises he is building up are proof positive of the indispensable character of the helpful and satisfactory service he gives, rendered under conditions many times the most trying and never without drawbacks seldom, if ever, encountered by those whose every desire in a business way he is doing his best to satisfy.

Suggested Reform in Floral Funeral Designs.

It is because we believe in congruity in all matters connected with the carrying out of the customs of our country that we are inclined to characterize as needless the agitation by a contemporary for reform in the appearance of the present day floral funeral designs, so far as these taking on an aspect less funereal than they do to-day is concerned. To be consistent everything associated with the sad event of losing a friend or relative by death, should partake more of "cheer to the living than a memorial to the dead." As well advocate changing the sombre habiliments of the mourner to those that will create a more joyful feeling; abolish the funeral dirge and in its place substitute the quickstep or something equally lively; remove the nodding plumes and the gloomy drapings of the hearse, and in exchange therefor supply a gaudily painted and decorated conveyance; clothe the parson in evening dress, or such as would indicate mirth instead of mourning; and bring about many other reforms of that kind.

There are some philosophers who would have us believe that death is an occasion for joy, because the departed has left for ever this vale of tears, and gone to a sphere where, it is said, "the wicked cease from troubling and the weary are at rest," also that a birth should be an event accompanied with dolefulness and depression because the infant making its advent into the world, has before it all the cares, sorrows, troubles and other evils that attend human kind. But the majority of mankind has decreed that just the reverse should rule, and to this decree florists as well as others must conform.

So far as the sending of flowers to funerals is concerned, we cannot see that the degree of comfort and sympathy derived by the living is any the less, whether the gift take on the form of a design or a loose bunch of flowers. It is the spirit that actuates the sender that is deserving of the greatest consideration. And it must not be forgotten that floral designs have been in vogue from time immemorial, each having its own symbolical significance, whether it be a wreath, an anchor, a cross or a pillow. Were an attempt made to reform the custom, it would, we think, be a difficult matter to determine just what form, different from the present, floral funeral designs should assume; for no matter their nature, we cannot dissociate from their presence in the home the fact of bereavement, nor can we sever them from connection with an "evidence of tender fellow feeling and affection."

The statement of our contemporary that certain people take an aversion to certain flowers, fragrant ones especially, because such flowers are seen at funerals, is far fetched; and there is no ground for any other belief, than that the same people would have the same adverse feeling toward the same fragrant flowers, were these flowers seen at a wedding, a christening, or even in the horseshoe or standing wreath sent to a Tammany politician.

What we do protest against, however, is the fabrication of abortions occasionally seen, travesties of art, repulsive to good taste, such as the floral ox for the butcher, the badge for the policeman, the hat for the fireman, the brick for the bricklayer, ship for the sailor, shears for the tailor, and such like floral monstrosities that are supposed by the vulgar to have a certain degree of compatibility with the funerals of the dead. All such reflect adversely on the artistic taste of the florist who makes them.

But so long as custom has decreed that all things associated with death shall partake of solemnity, sombreness, sorrow and sadness, the florist will be his own best friend who conforms to these conditions, and allows his customer free choice in the selection of the floral tokens that manifest the feelings created within him by the loss which death has occasioned. And so long as he keeps within the confines of good taste in the making of these tokens, there is little fault to find with him because such designs are in keeping with all that is connected with the occasion for which they are intended.

OUR READERS' VIEWS

Do We Need a National Canna Growers' Association?

Editor Florists' Exchange:

We wish that every grower of and dealer in cannas would consider the above question carefully and then express, either through the trade papers, or to us personally by letter, their own candid opinion of it. If such an association could be formed, and include in its membership the thousands of small florists all over the country who handle from a few dozen to a few hundred cannas each year, and awaken an interest in each to take hold and push literature regarding the beauties of the canna as a plant for growing in small home gardens as well as for planting in parks and public gardens, into the hands of the general public, and keep up the campaign of education by donations to city parks of some of the best and most showy varieties, not necessarily of anyone's high priced novelties, but something new in the community, that would attract attention, there could, by united action, be such an interest worked up for cannas that the demand would be doubled in less than three years.

We see no reason why such an association could not be mutually helpful to every one in the trade; but expect that a few would be jealous for fear that they would not be recognized as the great and only canna growers.

Let the association have a fee of one dollar per year, and reach out for members not only among florists and dealers, but among amateur growers and gardeners everywhere.

There are hundreds, yes, thousands of growers who could be induced to become members of such a society that would not think of joining the S. A. F., with its much larger membership fee. Many of them, however, after being brought in closer contact with other growers in such an association, would no doubt in a few years become deeper interested in floriculture generally and would then likely become members of the S. A. F.

There is a great chance to do educational work along floricultural lines, and no one should try to discourage any movement along such lines even though it be in the nature of kindergarten work. Let us reach out and take hold of the work, and educate the general public up to a better understanding of the beauties of floriculture.

New Varieties and Registration.

Now, a word about new varieties and the registration of same. We note that our new varieties have stirred up considerable discussion, and although two or three self styled experts condemned them as worthless, hundreds of others have declared them very fine. We are willing to trust the public as judges of the quality of our novelties; and if these do not compare favorably with the products of other growers they will, of course, have to take a back seat.

One great trouble with many dealers in this country is that they don't want to handle over 10 to 20 kinds, and those mostly of the commonest sorts, such as President Carnot, Robusta, Grand Rouge, etc. This old type of foliage cannas forms 15 to 20 per cent. of our entire sales and we could dispose of even more if we grew enough of them to supply the demand, as we always have to turn down lots of orders for them after our stock is exhausted. This is one reason we have named and introduced several new varieties of this type, believing that the people admire the foliage type and will appreciate some new forms of that class. We believe that the dealer needs educating as well as the general public and see no reason why any list should be considered complete with only 10 to 20 kinds of cannas when the same list probably contains 40 to 50 kinds of roses and, comparatively, as long a list of many other species of plants. Some of the European firms offer over 300 varieties of cannas, which makes a rather cumbersome list; but there are over sixty varieties that are in general use and are found in many of the leading catalogues.

We were greatly surprised to find so many of inferior types growing in the small home gardens of Dayton, in a city which in other lines of floriculture is far in the lead of most other cities. But we predict that there will be an interest awakened in that city for cannas this season that will last for years to come. Our display in the city parks, of nearly 200 varieties, has been an object lesson that will be seen by thousands, and will bear much fruit. It will not only bring orders to us, but to the local tradesmen and to scores of other dealers in all parts of the country. In fact, it will be a step along the road of educating the public to plant more and better cannas than they have been planting; and many dealers will get returns from this display of ours, and we are willing that they should. We do not expect to corner the market, nor do we want to do so. We would not have the stock to supply the demand. We are, however, in the canna business to stay, and if we should step on anybody's toes, we shall not do so out of spite, but through stepping lively in order to get what we consider our share of the business.

In regard to registration, we have never considered that there was any implied recommendation, or acknowledged merits, attributed to such varieties as are offered for registration by the S. A. F.; only the notice that a certain name has been given to a certain variety, and the brief description given it is simply a help to identify it in future if it should come into general cultivation. We believe that the present system of registration is the only one that can be carried out without friction by any society. It is certain that no committee can pass on the merits of flowers so fragile as those of the canna in a satisfactory manner without seeing several plants of each variety growing and watch their growth for several weeks; and this would mean a vast amount of work for a committee, provided that there were several hundred new applicants for their favorable mention. Then if those composing the committee should live in widely separated parts of the country, and each member had to be supplied with samples for growing, it would mean quite an expense to the originator.

The question of certificating varieties for merit should be another question altogether.

Some months ago a new pink canna was registered under the name of Venus. This name was given to a variety of a yellowish white color, in 1900, so there are now two distinct varieties on the market with that appellation. Persons naming new kinds should be careful not to repeat names of varieties already in commerce.

Another thing that should be condemned is the changing, even in a minor way, of the name of a plant after once given, for this makes but more confusion. We saw on the fair grounds at Dayton a bed of cannas labeled "Imperial Gardener Hoppe." This should have been "Hofgartner Hoppe." The two names mean the same, but there is no excuse for trying to substitute the one for the other, as it but makes more confusion and places the same kind on the market under two different names.

Fruitdale, Ala. L. H. READ.

Hardiness of Ailanthus at Chicago.

Editor Florists' Exchange:

In reference to the inquiry in your columns relative to the hardiness and, perhaps, growth, of the ailanthus, or tree of heaven, I would say that it is hardy enough to stand all but our extreme Winters here, that every few years come along, and has for twenty-five years had its place on the lawn seen from where I write.

The first young shoot was planted something like twenty-five years ago, right in front of the window, on what happened to be a rather sandy knoll, which undoubtedly just suited it; for it stood and grew till it is now quite a comely tree, with spreading branches. At first it had quite long and beautiful leaves, but as it grew older, as is usual with the tree, it became smaller and its leaves more like those of a thrifty sumac, that is plentiful hereabouts.

Some ten or a dozen of Winters ago, I forget how many just now, we had one of the old timers, and as I remember a dry one, always bad; and lo and behold! the following Spring the showy tree failed to leaf out, and was indeed gone. But it had become rather straggly, and not so sightly as in the younger state, so its condition was not so greatly regretted, more particularly as from suckers my son-in-law had others jogging along, although on another part of the ground. There were four of these, now only three, the fourth having died, not from frost, but happening not to be in just the right position, it was taken up and transplanted, which is not easily done. It struggled on weakly a couple of years and finally was blown down in a windstorm, from the lack of good rootage, and gave up the ghost. The remaining ones are flourishing, although getting a little spready; and I think from the lower situation of the ground, although not more than twenty-five feet from the first position, I always considered these later ones did not seem quite as much at home as the first one planted.

Now, the ailanthus is quite an attractive tree, and particularly so in its young state. Many stop to inquire what it is, and if they could see a young plant in a good position, cut down each year to produce the strong growth of shoots and leaves that it will produce, they would admire the tree more. Although not by any means a really scarce tree hereabout, from some cause or other it is not plentiful.

Those of us who lived fifty or sixty years back recollect the cry of the late A. J. Downing in the old Horticulturist, "Down with the ailanthus." This was for special reasons. Its flowers, or at least the female ones, I think, had a very offensive odor. I am inclined to the belief that in certain places, if this flowering is plentiful and as the tree gets quite old, in favorable locations, it might be a nuisance. The trees of which I am speaking have flowered but little. The first one spoken of, before its demise, had a few panicles of flowers (no beauty to them), and I thought I occasionally got a waft of odor that was not very pleasant; but certainly nothing to prevent planting, thus obtaining the years of beauty they have given. The last planted three as yet show no signs of flowering.

As to suckering, in the case of those on a lawn, with the lawn mower at work every week, a sucker is a thing that rarely shows itself; but no doubt,

The Late Paul R. B. Pierson
(See Obituary, Issue of Sept. 29, 1906)

as the tree grows so freely from pieces of roots under favorable conditions, it will sucker. But according to my idea neither objection should stand, to prevent its planting and use as a young tree, easily grown, or as an object plant, cut down with annual growth only. Hence, you see, even where the tree is not hardy as a tree, if cut down each year it would be a pretty tough Winter in localities where it could not be grown at all.

EDGAR SANDERS.

Chicago.

Editor Florists' Exchange:

Information about the ailanthus is hardly necessary for those whom I meant to warn against the cedrela, the ailanthus having been used in plantations in and around Chicago for many years. In the exceptionally severe Winter of 1898-99 several large specimens of that tree were killed in the Chicago parks. But so were catalpas, and, if I am not much mistaken, even gleditschias. Young plants of ailanthus may freeze back, or even get killed, in ordinary Winters, if transplanted in the Fall and left unprotected, but with a good cover of litter on the ground, or, still better, Spring planting, there is no danger, and we Chicagoans regard the tree as "perfectly hardy." J. P. PEDERSEN.

Chicago.

Campbell's Sulphur Vaporizer.

In a recent issue of The Florists' Exchange I observe an inquiry about Campbell's Sulphur Vaporizer. I wish to state that this material can be bought of Peter Henderson & Company, 35-7 Cortlandt street, New York City. I had occasion to use the vaporizer last Winter in a low rose house heated by hot water, and I have to admit that the results against mildew were very satisfactory. Instructions are given with the vaporizer when purchased.

WM. J. KAULBACH.

Obituary

Harry Turner, Slough, Eng.

Our English exchanges announce the death of Harry Turner of the Royal Nurseries, Slough, England on September 14, 1906. Mr. Turner was about 58 years of age. He was a most successful rose grower, his name being closely associated with the dissemination of the favorite Crimson Rambler and other varieties of roses. Mr. Turner was a Victorian medallist of Horticulture.

The Journal of Horticulture, London, commenting on Mr. Turner's death, gives the following particulars concerning the origin and introduction of the Crimson Rambler rose into England.

"The story goes that Mr. Turner acquired the plant of this rose from Mr. Gilbert, of Dyke, by Bourne, in Lincolnshire, some fourteen years ago. Mr. Gilbert had received it from the then president of the Edinburgh Botanical Society in 1890, who owed it to the grateful recognition of an engineer engaged in the Japanese trade whom he had befriended. Mr. Turner having hopes of his trouvaille from Japan, proceeded to propagate it, and put out the first plants under the appropriate name of 'The Crimson Rambler.' Its wild beauty and luxuriance at once caught the fancy of the public, and for the last twelve years the British Isles have grown more beautiful in each succeeding Summer with the crimson festoons of this lovely wildling, which blooms in the garden of the palace as in that of the cottage, and is adding another beauty to the antique walls and church towers of our rural home-land. It and the Ampelopsis Veitchii will some day effect more than a metamorphosis of Ovid for our native land."

Charles W. Turnley.

Charles W. Turnley, proprietor of the Haddon Nurseries, Haddonfield, N. J., with a store in Camden, N. J., died last week.

Mr. Turnley was born in London, England, eighty years ago, and came to this country when a boy. He taught school for twenty years, going to Haddonfield more than forty years ago, thirty-two of which he spent in the florist business.

Mr. Turnley was probably the oldest florist in America actively engaged in business. He was a member of the Society of American Florists for many years, and regularly attended the annual conventions, never missing a meeting, and was present this year at Dayton, when he was just recovering from a long illness. Mr. Turnley was opposed to the addition to the society's title of "Ornamental Horticulturists," and his humorous description of that imaginary individual created much merriment at the time the altered title was adopted. He was State vice-president of the S. A. F. for New Jersey last year.

The funeral was held on Friday of last week, the services being conducted at his late residence by the Rev. John W. Lyall, pastor of the First Baptist Church of Camden, of which Mr. Turnley was for many years a member, and the pall-bearers were of the deacons and trustees of the Baptist Church, Haddonfield. Interment was in Harleigh cemetery.

Patrick J. Donahue.

Patrick J. Donahue, one of the best known among the many gardeners at Lenox, Mass., died on Friday, September 28, 1906, at the age of 60 years. He was superintendent of Morris K. Jessup's estate, Belvoir Terrace, for 16 years.

Mr. Donahue was born in Galway, Ireland, and served his apprenticeship under his father, who was a noted gardener. He came to America in 1864, and did much creditable landscape work at Lenox, Newport, and other places. He was a member of the Lenox Horticultural Society, Catholic Benevolent League, Yokun Council, Royal Arcanum and Berkshire Hills Council, Knights of Columbus. He is survived by two daughters, and a son, John J. A brother, Fred., conducted a retail store in New York city for many years.

The funeral was held on Saturday, September 29.

The Free Seed Humbug.

Those who are conducting the anti-free seed campaign, to break down the custom that has grown up in Congress of appropriating large sums yearly to distribute common garden and flower seeds, have received a powerful object lesson from Brooklyn, N. Y. A short time ago a bonfire was made of more than ten thousand packages of the free seeds that had been sent out, but for which no use could be found by the recipient. He was burning them to get them out of his way. Before they were all destroyed a bushel or more of the packages were taken to a seed dealer in New York. He became interested in looking up the history of the varieties represented, as, under the act of Congress, they were classed as "new, rare and valuable seeds." A searching of seed catalogues developed that one variety of parsnip, two of lettuce, three of turnip, one of tomato, one of onion and two of radish had been catalogued as long ago as 1879. One of lettuce, one of tomato and one muskmelon came into use in 1884. Five other varieties of lettuce were introduced between 1875 and 1890. The newest variety of seed was an onion first introduced in 1899, while the oldest was traced back thirty years, and its first introduction is lost in antiquity. Not one variety was found that was either "new," "rare," or "valuable." Most of them had long since been abandoned by dealers to give place for improved varieties.

CLUB AND SOCIETY DOINGS.

THE COLUMBUS (O.) FLORISTS' CLUB held its regular meeting on Tuesday evening; President Stephens in the chair. The attendance was good. M. B. Faxon and Guy H. Woodrow addressed the club at length on some economic questions of management, especially in regard to increasing the annual dues of membership; our club is growing so fast that our financial end requires more and more attention. After a long discussion of this subject, Messrs. Woodrow, Faxon, and Wedemeyer were appointed a committee to investigate this matter of dues and report at next meeting. The question of better and more central quarters for our club rooms was also given attention. While this matter has been agitated from time to time, our members now insist on new rooms, and Messrs. McKellar and Faxon were empowered to act for the club in the matter. Miss Cook, for the committee on school gardens, notified the club that five or six of the best gardens had been selected from all the entries as worthy of prizes; and requested that a delegate from the club be appointed to award the prizes. Our vice-president, Mr. Curry, was named by the club for this work. President Stephens reminded the members that at the next meeting, on October 2, nominations for the election of officers would be in order, as the annual meeting takes place the last of next month. At this meeting, Edward Helfrich, the florist and gardener at the Columbus Imbecile Institution, was elected an active member. It has been proposed to hold exhibitions of seasonable flowers once a month, when suitable prizes will be awarded; no doubt the first of these shows will be held in November, with chrysanthemums. Our next meeting will be October 2. F. W.

AMERICAN POMOLOGICAL SOCIETY.—The Kansas City meeting of this great national society was one of the most notable in its history. It was held in the heart of the rapidly developing Middle West, and was attended by a representative gathering of noted pomologists from all parts of the country. It follows that an interesting and valuable report is the result. This report was distributed to all members in good standing by Secretary John Craig, of Ithaca, N. Y., early in September. It is available to all who become members of the organization. It is made up of three principal divisions. First, a record of the papers presented and discussions which followed during the three days' sessions. Second, a valuable chapter giving the horticultural history of six of the States of the Southwest—absolutely new historical data. Third, the reports of the standing committees of the society, including one on inspection of apples; one on score-card judging; and the exceedingly comprehensive report of the general fruit committee which authoritatively depicts the condition of the fruit industry in all its phases in every State in the Union as well as the newer dependencies and the provinces of Canada. Membership in this national society is open to amateur and professional fruit growers alike. The president is L. A. Goodman, Kansas City, Mo.; treasurer, L. R. Taft, Agricultural College, Mich.; secretary, John Craig, Ithaca, N. Y.

Interior of new house recently built by W. W. Coles, Kokomo, Ind. The house is of the King Construction type, and is 31 x 300 ft.

DAHLIA SOCIETY.—The executive committee of the Dahlia Society will meet in Boston, Mass., to-day (Saturday, October 6). Some good results are expected from this meeting. Applications for membership in the society are quite numerous, and M. Fuld, secretary pro tem., predicts a prosperous organization.

American Carnation Society.

Varieties Registered.

By F. Dorner & Sons Company, Lafayette, Ind.

RED CHIEF, an even clear shade of scarlet, very early and exceptionally free.

BONNIE MAID, edged white and shaded to a pink center.

WINONA, a clear medium pink.

Lancaster, Pa. ALBERT M. HERR, secretary.

NEWPORT (R. I.) HORTICULTURAL SOCIETY.—Tuesday evening, September 24 this society held the most interesting and in every way the most profitable meeting of the year; in fact it was more of an exhibition than a meeting, the hall being uncomfortably filled with plants and flowers. Although no schedule was prepared judges were appointed and did their work in the same manner and to the same end as at a regular show. In cut flowers dahlias predominated and there was certainly a fine showing of them. Of the local growers James Robertson was the largest exhibitor and took the principal prizes, while William F. Turner, of New Bedford, put up a fine exhibit of the best new varieties of cactus sorts. Richard Gardner staged a mixed lot of orchids including Oncidium varicosum; Cattleya gigas and C. labiata; they were all well grown and received the highest award of the evening. David McIntosh staged dracænas for which he was given the next highest award. Colin Robertson showed some exceedingly well grown crotons; John Marshall, orchids and gladioli. There were many other creditable exhibits all of which shared in the $125 appropriated for the evening. The judges were: Bruce Butterton, Stewart Ritchie and David Smith of Stranraer, Scotland, who was visiting in Newport at the time. Mc.

Chrysanthemum Society of America.

President Duckham has announced the committees to examine seedlings and sports on dates as follows: October 6, 13, 20 and 27, November 3, 10, 17 and 24, 1906.

Exhibits to receive attention from the committees must in all cases be prepaid to destination, and the entry fee of $2 should be forwarded to the secretary not later than Tuesday of the week preceding examination, or may accompany the blooms. Special attention is called to the rule requiring that sports, to receive a certificate, must pass three committees.

NEW YORK.—Eugene Dailledouze, chairman, care of New York Cut Flower Company, 55-57 Twenty-sixth street; William Turner, Thomas Head.

PHILADELPHIA, PA.—A. B. Cartledge, chairman, 1514 Chestnut street; John Westcott, Wm. K. Harris. Ship flowers in care of the chairman.

BOSTON, MASS.—E. A. Wood, chairman; Wm. Nicholson, James Wheeler. Ship to Boston Flower Market, care of the chairman.

CINCINNATI, O.—R. Witterstaetter, chairman; James Allen, Wm. Jackson. Ship to Jabez Elliott Flower Market, care of janitor.

CHICAGO, ILL.—J. S. Wilson, chairman; J. B. Deamud and George Wienhoeber. Ship care of J. B. Deamud, 51 Wabash avenue.

The official scales of the C. S. A. are as follows:

For Commercial Purposes		For Exhibition Purposes	
Color	20	Color	10
Form	15	Stem	5
Fullness	10	Foliage	5
Stem	15	Fullness	15
Foliage	15	Form	15
Substance	15	Depth	15
Size	10	Size	35
Total	100	Total	100

DAVID FRASER, Secretary.

Pittsburg, Pa.

The annual exhibition of the C. S. A. will be held in connection with the show of the Horticultural Society of Chicago, November 6 to 12, 1906. The following is a list of the special prizes to date:

Special Prize List.

C. S. A. prize, silver cup, for best flowers, one variety.

Prizes of $50, $25 and $10 are offered for twelve blooms on 24-inch stems, for the best seedling or sport not yet in commerce. The color to be white, pink, or yellow; the name to be given by the donor of the prize.

W. Wells of Merstham, Surrey, England, offers gold, silver gilt and silver medals for six varieties of chrysanthemums, two of each on 12-inch stems. The following varieties are eligible in this competition: Mrs. H. Partidge, Mrs. D. Willis James, Merstham Crimson, Mary Aun Pockett, Beatrice May, T. Richardson, Mrs. Heaume, E. J. Brooks, Mrs. F. F. Thompson, Mrs. Wm. Knox, Mrs. J. E. Dunn and Miss May Siddon.

Charles H. Totty offers prizes of $12, $8 and $5 for twelve blooms in twelve varieties, stems not over 12 inches long, introductions of 1906. Open to all.

F. R. Pierson offers a silver cup for 36 chrysanthemums, six varieties, six blooms of each, introduced in America in 1905 and 1906.

Nathan Smith & Son offer $25 for best 24 blooms of American origin, introductions of 1904, 1905 and 1906; three varieties—white, pink, and yellow, eight blooms of each, shown in separate vases.

Vaughan's Seed Store offers a silver cup, value $15, for the best specimen bush chrysanthmum plant, which has not rceived any other award. Open to private gardeners only.

The E. G. Hill Company offers a special prize of $15 for the best twenty-five blooms of chrysanthemum Mary Mann and $10 for the best fifteen blooms of any introduction of 1906.

Aster Incisus (Calimeris Incisa)

Aster Incisus (Calimeris Incisa).

As a hardy perennial the Aster incisus is greatly prized by those interested in such plants. It is not alone that it is a beautiful flowering plant; it is also one of a very few asters that bloom in early Summer. Hardly another aster does this. It is the leader of a long procession of asters that flower from July until the close of October.

The plant photographed was in perfection of bloom in late June, being in a sunny position, and having received good care. In other situations plants flower in July, and by the time they finish their bloom the regular Fall flowering ones come; and last of all the A. tataricus appears. It happens that both the first and the last to flower—the incisus and the tataricus—are Asiatic species.

Those who see the Aster incisus growing in rows in a nursery or in clumps in a bed, will not see such a fine plant among them as is the one we illustrate. It is evidence of what good care will produce; for good care is what it had.

The clor of this aster flower is a light violet, fading to almost white when in perfection; but at all times there is to it a deeper color than white.

The name of this plant has seen some changes. It is known under both names, aster and calimeris. It came to Philadelphia collections under the name of calimeris, and some botanies still retain this name for it. JOSEPH MEEHAN.

Exported English Garden.

In one respect, at least, America cannot compete with this "effete old country," and that is the beauty of the old British garden. A graceful compliment is being paid us at the present moment by Mrs. Whitelaw Reid, who, according to the American Press, is having an old-fashioned English garden laid out at her Ophir Farm in Purchase, New York, modelled on that of the Queen's at Windsor. Flowers, shrubs, and trees are being exported to America by Mrs. Reid's orders to adorn her proposed beauty-spot at Purchase. Fuchsias, coral honeysuckle, and hawthorn are to make the hedges radiant, as well as some eighteen or twenty varieties of old-fashioned flowers which the Queen especially admires.

According to one authority, Mrs. Whitelaw Reid may have to spend anything from £5,000 to £10,000 on her whim.

Several Americans have come over lately to England and spent far more time in the study of English gardens than on their old hobby, the cathedrals. The craze for the past few years has been for the old-fashioned type of garden.

In one respect, however, Mrs. Reid cannot hope to see her garden perfect, and that is in possessing a perfect English grass-lawn. It will be remembered that an American millionaire once offered an Oxford college gardener a fabulous amount for the recipe for producing the emerald-velvet carpets that abound in the University town. "Easy enough," said the man. "You plants your grass seed, and you rolls it and you cuts it, and you cuts it and you rolls it for three hundred years, and there you are."—Guernsey Evening Press.

Coles' New Greenhouse.

The accompanying illustration is a photograph of a house built this year by W. W. Coles, Kokomo, Ind. It is 300 by 31 feet, of the King construction type. The roof is entirely supported by truss rods instead of columns. The sash bars are spaced 24 inches apart; and the ventilators are iron framed so that there is the greatest amount of light possible in a greenhouse. There is a concrete wall three feet high, and four feet of glass all around the house. The photograph was taken before the benches or side glass were put in. The house is now planted to carnations, about one-half Mrs. T. W. Lawson and most of the other half with the rest of the Lawson tribe. Ample provision has been made for heating, as the house is intended for roses, probably American Beauty, next year.

New Bedford (Mass.) Horticultural Society's Show

Last year a visit was made to the exhibition of the New Bedford, (Mass.) Horticultural Society with such pleasure attending it that this year it was determined to go there again. Very often outsiders get a totally different impression of things than that received by persons more directly interested in, and familiar with those things, for this reason a few notes taken by an outsider while viewing the exhibits at the New Bedford show may be of some interest.

When the great dahlia craze was making its way along the Atlantic Coast Newport was, I think, the first place it struck with such violence that at least two-thirds of the inhabitants suffered some more and some less. Our visit last year to New Bedford convinced us that this craze in its triumphant madness switched off from the straight course it had hitherto pursued and made for New Bedford, where the grandsons and great grandsons of hardy old whalers received it with open arms and took advantage of it in the same degree as their forefathers took, of things more formidable in their day.

To-day there are more commercial dahlia growers in and around New Bedford than anywhere else in New England; and what is more they grow as good if not better dahlias there than are grown in any other section of New England.

At the exhibition recently held in Newport there were no local commercial growers exhibiting; on the other hand, at the exhibition in New Bedford not only did the trade growers exhibit, but they also carried away the bulk of the premiums with blooms that were far ahead of any we had seen hitherto.

Now, if this dahlia craze had done nothing else of good than what it accomplished in New Bedford, its coming was amply justified, because without dahlias that city would not have had an exhibition, that is an exhibition worth going very far to see, although the improvement in other lines of exhibits since last year was so marked that doubtless in a few more years dahlias will cease to be the main feature of the shows.

Excepting dahlias cut flowers were conspicuously absent. Plants in single specimens were shown fairly well. Groups of palms and foliage plants were much better than last year; Mr. Garthey's in particular. This took first, while Mr. Peckham, a commercial grower, was a good second. Mr. Keith, the president of the society, had a neat group in another class with which he took first.

What impressed us very much at this exhibition was the prominence of exhibits for competition and otherwise from commercial growers, and the extreme good nature of the rivalry between them and the gardeners on private estates. Unless there are many growers around that city as well as in it, whom we never heard of, nearly every one had something at the show.

Perhaps the most pretentious exhibit from a trade grower was that put up by Peter Murray, the raiser of the Winsor carnation. Next came that of Mr. Woodhouse, who showed among other good things a well grown lot of medium size Nephrolepis elegantissima. By the way, this fern seemed to be shown by everybody and in all stages of growth. Mr. Garthley showed Nephrolepis Mayii, but in such a small size that a description of the plant would not perhaps be justifiable. The same grower had a collection of Pteris Childsii which shows how quickly good things are picked up. Apart from his group Mr. Murray had a collection of well grown foliage plants of medium size.

James J. Rooney, gardener for Mrs. Frederick Grinnell, had on exhibition among other things some seedling carnations. E. H. Weber, an amateur dahlia grower showed some of the finest blooms we ever had the pleasure of seeing. Among the most noticeable exhibits from commercial growers were those of Messrs. Jahn, Fish, Turner, Woodhouse, Peckham and Forbes.

Mr. Garthley staged some superb blooms of tuberous begonias for which he was awarded the society's silver medal.

D. M.

California Plant Notes.

The Bignonia family of plants is one of great diversity of habit of growth, color of flowers and character of foliage. The different members of the family are equally at home in this climate, no matter whether they are brought from the Atlantic States and West Indies, or the high elevations of Mexico. Some are shrubs; others climbers; some are deciduous; others evergreen. At this season of the year Tecoma jasminoides, with its dark green foliage and white flowers, one variety having a dark pink throat, is one of the most beautiful vines we have in cultivation. Some seasons it is severely injured by frost, on the low lands. A native of Australia, it luxuriates in our warm dry atmosphere.

The most brilliant flowering variety, which is now in bloom, too is T. capensis. A specimen growing at Hollenbeck Home has a trunk eighteen inches in diameter at the base. It is a Winter bloomer.

Tecoma Smithii is a beautiful shrub, with small pinnate foliage. The flowers are borne in clusters, of a light yellow color, tipped with dark orange. It will be in bloom from now until next May.

Bignonia Cherere, a native of Mexico, is a rapid growing vine, producing large trumpet-shaped flowers, dark red outside, yellow within.

The Acacia family is another, of which several members make beautiful our landscape at all seasons of the year. A. Farnesiana has begun to flower, and will continue to do so until next May. The flowers are large, solitary, and dark orange colored. They are delightfully fragrant, the most so of any variety the writer knows anything about. It is a variety too little known in California. It is not adapted to street planting, growing low and spreading instead of upright, and very thorny.

The crop of alligator pears, Persea gratissima, is not as large as last season. In localities where this tree will live it should be extensively planted. The fruit is delicious and healthful. At present it commands a fabulous price in our markets—$6 to $9 per dozen fruits. The fruit of one tree sold last year for over $150. It would be well for people of Southern California to experiment with this tree and fin out the degree of frost it will stand. There is one variety growing here which has small, seedless fruits, borne in clusters. The tree is evergreen, free from insect pests and fungous diseases.

P. D. BARNHART.

Samuel S. Pennock

Charles E. Meehan

Our London Letter.

BY A. HEMSLEY.

THE NATIONAL ROSE SOCIETY'S AUTUMN SHOW was held at the Royal Horticultural Society's hall on September 19. Several failed to fill the classes entered for, owing to the dry weather we have had; but there was a very good exhibition, the Scotch and Irish growers being the most prominent. In new varieties Hugh Dickson, Belfast, was awarded a gold medal for Mrs. Stewart Clark, a very fine hybrid tea, color red with a cerise shade, large full globular flowers with good petals. Messrs. Alex. Dickson, Newtownards, also secured a gold medal for tea rose Dorothy Page Roberts, a fine variety, salmon rose, with a shade of amber at base, large petals of good substance, and ought to make a good market rose. The most prominent rose in the show was Frau Karl Druschki. This was good in all exhibits, and in some of the groups it was shown in large numbers. Mrs. John Laing was also very prominent. J. B. Clark, the gold medal sort of last year, fully maintains its good points, and secured the first prize for a bunch of twelve blooms (any variety). Hugh Dickson was brighter in color, and is one of the best red roses we have. Liberty was well shown; and if not so large it is a most useful rose. Maman Cochet and its white variety were very good. Madame Joseph Combet is a fine hybrid tea, and secured a silver medal for being the best of the class. Other silver medal roses were Maman Cochet, Mrs. J. Laing (the best h. p.).

Among single roses used for floral arrangements was Irish Elegance, a most effective rose, which was much admired.

DAHLIAS are much to the front just now. The London Dahlia Union had a most successful show at the Royal Botanic Society's Gardens on September 18 and 19. We continue to get improved varieties, the cactus kinds being the most prominent. Daisy Staples, a fine shade of pink, is one of the best I have seen. Dr. G. G. Gray, scarlet, should prove valuable. Ruby Grinstead, Rev. Arthur Hall, Gazelle, Meteor, and Hamlet are among those I have noted. Other sections are also receiving attention. S. Mortimer has raised some good show varieties. J. T. West is looking after the pompons. Messrs. Cheal & Sons have the singles in most perfect form and varied colors. The peony-flowered varieties first introduced by Messrs. H. Copjin & Sons, Utrecht, Holland, are likely to become popular, but want a little improvement.

CHRYSANTHEMUMS in new sorts are already to the front. Mrs. Arthur Beech, Mercedes, and White Countess, which I have seen in the market, are likely to become leading kinds. Clara, a deep yellow, is also a promising variety. These have recently received first class certificates from the Chrysanthemum Society as decorative sorts. The blooms are only of medium size, but they are more appreciated by florists than the very large sorts are. We have been rather overdone with good blooms in the market already.

The children's competition inaugurated by the Evening News proprietors was a success. About 1,700 children sent plants; these were not very showy, but many of the market growers put up good collections and some of the leading florists showed good designs. Of the sorts noted Etoile Blanche, Miss B. Miller, La Pactole, Carrie, Champ de Neige, Perle Rose (a fine pink), Crimson Pride and La Vestal were among the good ones.

WINTER FLOWERING CARNATIONS.—The society recently formed has arranged for a show to be held at the Royal Botanic Gardens on December 4, when it is expected there will be a grand display. Prizes are offered for each separate color, all blooms to be shown without any support in vases. There are classes for vases of 36 blooms and others for 18 of each color; also for large collections, but except in the case of those arranged in bouquets, etc., no supports can be used.

S. S. Pennock—Meehan Company.

We have pleasure in presenting to our readers this week, reproductions of the portraits of Samuel S. Pennock and Charles E. Meehan, members of the new firm of S. S. Pennock-Meehan Company, Philadelphia, Pa., which began business, under the new style, on October 1, 1906. A brief sketch of the interesting and progressive careers of these two well-known representatives of the cut flower industry of Philadelphia has already appeared in our columns. Matters leading up to the combination now perfected have also been previously dealt with; and in this connection it may be of benefit to all interested to state that a complete history of the amalgamation, the aims and objects of the new concern, is very fully set forth in a tastefully gotten up illustrated pamphlet just issued by the Pennock-Meehan Company. From that document we quote as follows: "The new house will give better service than heretofore because of concentrated action and a united responsibility and interest, as well as better material facilities to be found in a larger and greatly improved building, offices, equipment, working force, floor space, etc. These last named features, properly taken advantage of, will make for the benefit of every one of our growers and customers."

The illustrations in the pamphlet referred to show an exterior view of the firm's building at 1608-18 Ludlow street, Philadelphia; the general office, shipping department, general views of store before and after business hours, ribbon department, and storage rooms on first floor, and cellar of building. A cordial invitation is extended to all to pay the new concern a visit.

FOR THE RETAILER

[All questions relating to the Retail Trade will be cheerfully answered in this column. We solicit good, sharp photographs of made-up work, decorations, store interiors, etc., for reproduction here.—Ed. F. E.]

The Use of Herbaceous Flowers.

Even at this late date the herbaceous garden is extremely interesting to the observant retailer, for though the majority of the most gaudy blooms have long since faded, there still remain, and yearly pleading in vain for better recognition, many lovely and useful flowers. To the florist with a local trade many delicate flowers are available which are seldom if ever seen by the city florists, and among the leaders of these are cannas. Many of these gorgeous flowers are obtainable now, and glorious they look in table decoration in conjunction with any light feathery greens. Their being easily damaged should not prevent their more general use; and, as in the case of orchids, density should be avoided. Many and beautiful are the boltonias, asters, Michaelmas daisies or whatever other name the doctors of botany may yet decide to call these flowers; and most of them are native and are to be had in abundance, even out in the woods. Aster novæ angliæ (why it should be christened that is not apparent to us) is a beautiful violet colored flower, splendid for solid wreath work, for edging or fringing a wreath, or for bases or festooning. Its color makes it especially good for funeral work, or even a loose bunch backed with greens. Aster multiflorus has very small white flowers, but in densely covered racemes, that make it extremely valuable for fringing wreaths, or for semi-groundwork instead of greens. A. cordifolius, mauvish white, grows in great masses and is elegant. A. ericoides is a pretty miniature white flower grown in such masses that it is nicknamed "the white heather aster." A. puniceus, mauvish white; A. paniculata, white; and A. salicifolius, white, are all grand, worthy of general cultivation because they are valuable for vase work and especially for almost all kinds and values in funeral designs and to put in cut flower boxes instead of so much greens. Wherever there is need of filling in, making a good showing, or giving a light, feathery appearance to otherwise stiff designs, the above mentioned flowers are splendid. Use them; grow them, or if you market them bunch them right.

In yellow flowers there are the beautiful Helenium autumnale, Helianthus tuberosa, Rudbeckia subtomentosa and the fine white, daisy-like blooms of Chrysanthemum uliginosum; all of which are queens, defying the oncoming army of celestial chrysanthemums. Gerbera Jamesoni, the orange red "Transvaal daisy," is capable of superb effects. It is gloriously offering itself now; use it for entire table designs, or for vase work, separate or to lend its color; and if any occasion occurs where those present have been out to South Africa, you can make a big hit by its use. Although the foliage is of no use in decorative work the blooms are elegant. We advise its cultivation under glass during Winter; you cannot have too much of it. There is at all times a demand for something odd or choice. This gerbera fills that want. Use a little select fern with it; and don't put it near dahlias or chrysanthemums.

When we see bunches of the dull and dirty white weed, Eupatorium ageratoides, sold for good prices, too, on the New York market, it makes us sorry for the ignoring of the many more beautiful and serviceable flowers at present abundant in the vales and woods, which should be in the gardens also. Solidago cæsia, the wreath golden rod, is very pretty just now, and its long spike-like torches of rich yellow flowers give a unique effect to a vase of mixed blooms. Golden rod has ceased to be the flower pre-eminent for Autumn decorations. Years ago it was more popular, and its use was urged by the majority of florists. The introduction of more, larger and brighter varieties of flowers has, in the larger cities at least, pushed aside the golden rod and it is good, and very often necessary, too, for sentimental reasons to suggest the use of such a flower, but the growing-up and know-all American of to-day, even to yourself, undervalues that which is overplentiful or is easy to obtain. Consequently, any of you who are fortunate enough to be able to contract for Autumn wedding decorations in town or country, had better consider well the people and opportunities before specializing golden rod. The sentimental part of it is the real thing. You can go the limit with it perhaps with the old folks, where they are consulted, or with the ethereal young bride-to-be; but the Lord help your chances if you advocate its sole use to the bizarre tape-watcher.

He who is fortunate enough to have a batch of tuberous begonias in bloom has the material for extra elegant table decoration. Either mixed or in separate colors, they can be made the decoration par excellence. Don't scatter colors; group them or use one. Often the whole plant can be employed, either as a specimen pot plant or massed in a shallow receptacle. If, as is often the case in the city, refined and light effects are demanded in order to conform to the service used, which mostly on all occasions is costly, then the begonia blooms and fern such as Adiantum cuneatum alone is permissible. The reverse sides of begonia petals are of such a rich color that it is not necessary to have every bloom staring full face upright, for that creates a too apparent studied arrangement. A little intentional semi-carelessness will often add to the beauty of flower as well as work. Whenever, as is often the case, begonia flowers fall off their stems, they can be easily and neatly wired on to a spray of Asparagus Sprengeri and kept low; or else use the floret on the cloth. One or two broken flowers used judiciously will not injure anything.

There is many a bed of glowing salvia flowers asking for a chance to adorn some green or yellow furnished room, or to catch the admiration of the jovial around the festive board. You may consider them common because Madame Coleus surrounds them; but oh, my! strip their leaves and mass the unmatchable red spikes among Asparagus Sprengeri, and you'll have a table to remember.

There is a long season before you where it will be roses and carnations and carnations and roses, with chrysanthemums for a time as an ever ready change; so if only for a last chance at a "something different" if you can, give the outside flowers, such as those mentioned and the dahlias, a show.

J. IVERA DONLAN.

An Historic Funeral Design.

The illustration herewith shown is reproduced from a photograph of the last official funeral design of the Society of American Florists, now the S. A. F. O. H. Contemplating it will no doubt stir up many memories of the long ago in the minds and hearts of the old members. Only three of these

The Original S. A. F. Funeral Design.

designs were made. The first was for the funeral of William F. Bennett, who was the first member of the society to depart this life, and the last was for James Y. Murkland.

We remember (we think the year was 1884 or 1885) that one day a committee, headed by John Thorpe, came into the store of Adolphe Le Moult at 172 Bowery, New York. They wanted a design to represent all that was glorious in floriculture, and it was intended that the one selected would be sent as the official token of esteem to the funeral of every member of the S. A. F. After a great deal of consideration, the design shown in the picture was adopted. It was a 3 foot high scroll on a 5 foot square table, which stood 3 feet in height. The first design, if we remember aright, cost $125; the last one $75, and, on account of scarcity of cut bloom, it had to be made mostly of Cape flowers, which were a novelty at that time. For the first design we remember having to send messengers on all night excursions to the wilds of Bayside, L. I., to the late Frank Millang's (father of the present Millang Brothers) place for a few Lamarque roses and for La Purite carnations, to Boll's at Jamaica for Hinze's white carnations, and to distant Flatbush and Secaucus for scraps in roses, stocks, sweet alyssum or whatever there was in white flowers. The whole State was scoured for carnations and Niphetos roses.

Very few, no doubt, of those at present engaged in American floricultural pursuits know that the society had an official funeral design; and to us it seems strange that with the present over-abundance of materials the society, whose very existence depends on and whose main and professed aims are to encourage floriculture, and in this particular branch, too, should itself ignore the principles of and fail to see any use or beauty in the custom of sending flowers to a funeral. If only for consistency, we are of the opinion that the S. A. F. O. H. should send a token, if only a simple wreath or spray of flowers, to the funerals of its deceased members. Simply reading the record of a member's death at the annual meeting is poor recognition for one who, perhaps, has spent many long years in hard work for the society and its ambitions.

J. IVERA DONLAN.

Retail Trade Notes.

NEW YORK.—Myer, the florist at Fifty-eighth street and Madison avenue, recently executed some very fine work for the funeral of a prominent doctor. Among the designs were a casket cover made entirely of roses and cattleyas; a ten foot high standing wreath composed of Richmond roses and lily of the valley; a wreath of Kaiserin Augusta Victoria roses, and a wreath of white asters with a cluster of Killarney roses. Also a bunch of American Beauty roses containing one hundred flowers made in the form of a sheaf, and a large pillow of lilies and Adiantum Farleyense. The interment of the doctor was in Catskill, N. Y., and the designs were forwarded there in care of two special messengers.

The total value of the cut flowers imported into the United States during the year ending June 30, 1905, was $29,080, as against $42,612 in 1904, and $31,577 in 1903. The principal countries from which they were received were Canada, France, Germany, and others.

THE OPEN COURT PUBLISHING COMPANY of Chicago, publishers of Professor De Vries's interesting book "Species and Varieties," inform us that a second edition of the work has been published this year; also that a translation from the German of a larger work by the same author, entitled "The Mutation Theory" will be issued in three volumes.

Welch Brothers, Boston, Mass.

The opening on Monday of this week of the new wholesale flower market of Welch Brothers, at 226 Devonshire street, Boston, Mass., marks a radical change in the flower trade of Boston and New England generally. This store, which contains over 12,000 square feet of floor space, is in the midst of the wholesale business district of the city, within one block of three large express companies, near telegraph stations and conveniently located to railroad transportation, so that flowers have only a short distance to travel in coming into or leaving the city.

On the tenth of the present month the firm of Welch Brothers will have rounded out twenty-nine years of active work in the wholesale cut flower business. It was in a modest way that P. Welch first started as a commission florist, in the rear of 165 Tremont street, but after a short time the firm of Welch Brothers was formed by the three brothers—Patrick, Edward and David—and more commodious quarters were secured at the corner of Tremont and West streets. Their increasing business, however, soon outgrew that location and they moved to Beacon and Tremont streets, where they remained five years; but some eight years ago they again sought larger quarters and moved to 15 Province street. Here again it was soon found that their quarters were entirely too inadequate for the efficient handling of their immense trade, and for some time past an eye has been kept open for a good location, which has now presented itself.

Patrick

Edward

David

WELCH BROTHERS, WHOLESALE CUT FLOWER COMMISSION MERCHANTS, BOSTON, MASS.

The firm has at all times given strict personal attention to all details of the business and has from time to time improved its methods of conducting its operations. It was the first to send out weekly price lists in order that purchasers for the retail trade would know how to buy, and it was also the first to induce the American Express Company to allow the exclusive use of two teams for the handling of the Christmas and Easter trade. Welch Brothers also adopted a plan of attaching letters to each consignor's flowers, so that confusion as to the different growers could be avoided.

When the business was in its infancy much difficulty was experienced through flowers being shipped just as they were cut, without any reference as to difference in quality; but now this has been simplified by every grower grading his stock before he packs it. The flowers are graded by the grower and marked extra, A 1, number 2 and number 3; and the price being regulated by the quality, nobody is disappointed. The retailer knows what to order, and the grower knows that he will get the highest price for the best articles, while the inferior stock will not remain unsold but will be disposed of at its proper value to suit the requirements of the vendor who supplies the public.

Welch Brothers sell flowers only on commission, and they have a large list of customers in all the towns and cities of the North and East, and ship a vast quantity of stock into Canada and the provinces. They make it a point to send out flowers every day, only putting in cold storage those that it will be found of advantage to place there, it being conceded that flowers keep better and carry farther when treated in this manner.

Welch Brothers sell the flowers of nearly a hundred growers, including some of the largest and best cultivators in New England, and specialties are made of such as American Beauty, Killarney and Queen of Edgeley roses, lily of the valley, etc. Many of these growers have been shipping to this firm continuously for over twenty-five years, and others having tried elsewhere for a short time have again returned.

The regular working staff of Welch Brothers, numbers 18, which is increased to 25 during holiday seasons.

On entering the new store one is surprised at the very complete arrangements. On the right is the cashier's office presided over by the genial and smiling David Welch, while immediately back of this is the private office of the senior partner, Patrick. On the right is situated the department of Edward, and the telephone booths where three long-distance 'phones are almost continuously in use. The middle and main part of the store is devoted to the receiving and handling of flowers, many tables being in use for the purpose. On the extreme right is situated one of the cold storage vaults, 45 x 12 feet, while another occupies the whole farther end and is 55 x 15 feet in dimensions. These two vaults alone occupy almost as much floor space as was formerly occupied by the firm. The whole is lighted by electricity, and in the basement has been placed an electric motor which runs the cold storage plant. But the basement of the store is by no means the least important. It contains some 6,338 square feet of floor space, and it is here that the wire workers, and florists' supplies of all kinds, may be found. This latter branch of the firm's business has reached enormous proportions recently, so that every article pertaining to the florist trade can be supplied.

J. W. D.

Immortelle Culture in France.

The trade in immortelles in France is rapidly increasing. At present the time for shipping has just started. The harvest falls in the month of June.

Toward the end of August the cuttings for new plants are prepared. The cuttings have but little foliage and from two to four buds. The culture is the most simple imaginable. It is best to consider the plants as weeds, and let them go their own way. The soil is not of the slightest importance; they thrive sometimes in half gravel; if they have a somewhat sheltered position they will certainly do well. The watering depends exclusively on rain fall, as no water is ever carried to the plants. No manure is needed, but the ground has to be kept clean of other plants. The cuttings are put in about two feet apart; only very few die. The first year the plants come into bloom the yield is not worth much; the second, third and fourth years the harvest can be considered the strongest. Very old plants obtain a circumference of 10 feet, and in the season are covered with flowers.

In June, in the early morning before the sun throws its full light, men and women are fully occupied picking the blooms, in which the center is just appearing—a little black spot. At home the under leaves are cleaned off, and bundles of about two pounds are made. The dyers, at the same time exporters, buy the flowers by weight. The prices run from 30c. to 35c. per kilo. (about two pounds) according to quality. After bleaching (the natural color is yellow) the dyeing process begins. The very fine colors are prepared of ingredients of which the mixing proportions are a secret of the firm. The ordinary colors (red and violet) have often been written about.

After drying in the open air and full sunshine, they are tied into bunches and shipped in cases which contain one hundred and twenty-five bunches each. The women, in their leisure time at home or on the place of the exporter, during the whole work day, manufacture wreaths, which consist of single flowers tied on rings of straw or other material. The American demand is for red more than any other color. Lately a new kond of wreath has been put in the trade; it is made of little bunches instead of single flowers, giving it a rather striking appearance. Crosses and other designs are also made.

B.

Catalpa Speciosa as a Street Tree.

A writer in Gardening Illustrated, mentioning trees both good and bad for city planting, places among the good ones the catalpa. The good word for this tree is merited. There are a few set out along the sidewalk of one of Philadelphia's streets, and they thrive very well. These, however, are of the bignonioides species, and are not as good as the speciosa would be. The latter is of more tree-like habit, much better adapted for street planting than the other. It makes usually a straight leader, which is what a street tree should do until it has gained height sufficient that it will shade the upper stories of buildings. Another advantage is, that so far as the C. speciosa has behaved in these parts it does not produce seed pods nearly as freely as does C. bignonioides. Why this is an advantage is explained by stating that the bignonioides is a great seed producer. The seeds are in pods of over 18 inches in length, many of them, and they hang on the trees all Winter, falling with the making of new leaves in Spring. These pods may not be thought objectionable by many; in fact, some look on them with interest. But as C. speciosa does not produce as many pods, it will be generally preferred.

The Catalpa speciosa gets to be a tall tree, compared with the other species, but not too tall for street planting. It does not form a thicket of branches, nor is there need of its doing so, as its very large leaves afford all the shade required. It is a tree that can be safely recommended for city streets.

Besides the catalpa the English writer referred to mentions as suitable for planting in smoky cities the plane, yellow locust, ailanthus, sycamore and Norway maples and the tulip tree. The only one condemned is the linden, but in many city plantings here the European linden does very well; not so the native one. The yellow locust is too much subject to borer attacks to permit of its use here.

J. M.

Delphiniums (Larkspurs)—What of Them?

Truly this is the genus of heavenly blues. There is not a shade either in the skies, or on the earth, or under the earth, where a blue of any shade is known, but its actual color counterpart is to be found in this genus. The blues in the plumage of birds; the blues in sapphires, or lapis-lazuli; and the cœrulean blues of the Italian skies are all seen among these larkspurs. But blues are not the only colors these plants so extravagantly display; there are all shades of bronzes on blue; all shades of pink on blue; shades of red on blue, and of pearl and brown, as brilliant and as iridescent as the rainbow. Then, there are some with pure red tone; others nearly pure yellow, and several pure white. What a wealth of color!

Then, too, they are hardy beyond question. When in flower and seen at a distance, they are as pillars to the sky; every individual flower is more artistic than that displayed in the finest workmanship as seen in the finer metals and precious stones. They are superb for large decorations in upright classical vases; and they are as easily grown as any other garden plants. Much more could be said in their favor. This and what I say further on should, however, be sufficient to awake further interest in this responsive and easily taken care of family.

My earliest recollections of delphiniums are when as back row blue flowers in herbaceous borders there was the bee larkspur, tall and telling, 6 to 7 feet, and an occasional plant of the then rare double Barlowi, which had been raised by Mr. Barlow of Manchester, about 1834. It was a gem, but so very vagarious. Sometimes it would make a growth 6 feet high, with a two-foot spike. Then it would break up in the Spring and give nothing but sprays, some with four flowers, others with twelve or more. Then, for second rows, we had Meseleucum grandiflorum and sinense. I am reminded that two other blue flowers were the monkshoods, Aconitum autumnale and napellus, and its varieties. This was before D. formosum, as either in 1856 or 1857, from the Wellington Nurseries, St. John's Wood, London, came in May. The usual sets of verbenas, fuchsias and dahlias—also five plants of D. formosum each, in two pots, one a thumb, the other a fifty-four size. Some of us remember how these new, very small plants used to arrive, carefully wrapped and woven and securely tied for fear of their being lost or disturbed—these five plants cost a guinea—single plants, price 5s. each. And I remember these plants were not two inches high and the lot would not weigh five ounces, pots and all. I had charge of these. By September they all flowered, with what delight to me is still fresh in my memory.

Clematis Stans Var

The French hybridists, who have always been foremost in the good work of changing, were then sending us some varieties of D. elatum—some double and some single, with changed color tones. In 1861, a superb deep blue flower was shown at the Botanic Gardens, London, named alopecuroides, which caused much comment. Donald Beaton said they ought to call it "fox's tail," as that is what it meant. In 1856 T. S. Ware, a king among hardy plants, was shown at Kensington and Triomphe de Pontoise, with most beautiful double sky blue flowers, on spikes two feet long. What a gem!

Since then many thousands of beautiful varieties have been raised, double and single and of every shade, which unfortunately are not known or seen as frequently as they deserve to be.

Now, has not the delphinium as much beauty to give up as the rose, the peony or the phlox? Let us hope so.

The great number of varieties now catalogued affords opportunity to make distinct and beautiful collections at moderate cost. However beautiful D. formosum is, it is only the initial—which should not be the only one of the family to be found, as it now is, in so many gardens.

Of the species most desirable for gardens, which cannot fail to be of general interest, the following list embraces nearly all those which have been instrumental in delphinium culture. They are all perennial except three species, which see.

The two annual species, ajacis and consolida, should not be forgotten or neglected, as they are daintily beautiful in their prim habits and many colors. They, however, need good living and room to bring out their beauty.

Delphinium Species.

Azureum, flowers deepest sky blue, individual florets large, upper petals bearded, lower ones densely covered with a very fine villose texture; spikes upright, dense and of good size; leaves three to five-parted; height 3 feet; May to July. Native of America.

Azureum album, flowers creamy white borne in long wand-like racemes; leaves deeply lobed. A very distinct species. Height 3 to 4 feet. May to July. America.

Bruonianum, flowers light blue with purple margins, center black; large; lower leaves kidney-shaped, upper ones trilobed; 6 to 18 inches. A fine dwarf plant, having the odor of musk. June to July. Thibet, 1864.

Cardinale, flowers brightest scarlet shaded golden yellow, of good size, disposed in rather lax spikes; leaves resembling those of the hepatica; height 3 or more feet. August. A gem of gems, worthy of careful selection. It must be grown in well-drained, high positions to go safely through the Winter. Fine for rockeries. California. Biennial.

Cardiopetalon, flowers deepest violet blue, borne on long racemes densely crowded; leaves smooth, much divided, somewhat branching in habit.

Cashmerianum, flowers from one to two inches across, with broad sepals of a rich pale blue color, in rather loose heads; leaves tufted, on long stalks, divided palm-like four or more inches across, deep green, slightly hairy; one to two feet. July. Kashmir, 1875.

Cashmerianum Walkeri, flowers 1½ in. in diameter, sepals pale blue striped with darker blue, petals yellow tipped with brown; singly on stems 5 to 6 inches long; leaves circular, distinctly lobed; 10 to 18 inches. July. A fine rockery plant. Kashmir, 1885.

Cheilanthum, flowers intense, dark blue, petals shorter than the sepals, two lower ones obliquely depressed; borne in branchy loose spikes; leaves five-parted, much divided; two to three feet. June to September. Dahuria, 1819.

Dasycarpum, flowers deep cobalt blue, two-thirds of the petals marked deep brown, large, racemes loose and spreading; leaves five-lobed, deeply toothed. Height 4 to 6 feet. Caucasus, 1819.

Exaltatum—elatum—(bee larkspur), flowers from blue to white, of medium size, borne in graceful spikes of 20 or more flowers on each, with several branches from the base of main spike; spurs straight and long; leaves large, flat, much divided; 3 to 7 feet. June to September. America.

Formosum, flowers sky blue shaded indigo; spur long and divided, of a violet hue; sepals longer than the petals; spikes from 18 inches to 3 feet, branching; leaves dark green, lobed and divided; 2 to 4 feet. All Summer. Orient, 1855.

Grandiflorum, flowers blue and all intermediate shades to white, occurring both in the double and single forms, large; petals shorter than calyx, two lower ones quite rounded; borne in rather loose spreading spikes; leaves diversely divided. Height 1 to 3 feet. June. Siberia, 1816.

Hybridum, flowers light blue, the two lower petals white and bearded, the spur much longer than the flowers are wide; leaves many times divided. Height 3 to 5 feet. June to August. Tauria, 1794.

Hybridum ochroleucum, flowers yellowish white, smooth on the outside; spur straight, long and blunt; spikes long and crowded; leaves many parted; 3 to 4 feet. June to August. Armenia, 1823.

Laxiflorum, flowers deep blue, borne in loose racemes much branched; leaves large and variously divided. June to August. Siberia, 1819.

Mesoleucum, flowers blue with pale yellow center, of good size; in graceful spikes; leaves of medium size, deeply lobed; 4 feet. June. Siberia, 1816.

Nudicaule, flowers deep red, lower petals yellow, spatulate, two cleft and fringed; spur twice the length of the calyx; racemes loose; lower leaves round, divided into four or more lobes, upper ones entire; height 1 to 2 feet. California. A beautiful plant for rockeries or high, dry, deep soils. It requires covering in Winter.

Sinense (Northern China and Siberia); by some this is classed as a form of grandiflorum, but in my experience it is distinct, in its always dwarfer stature and its more decidedly spreading habit. In my early days grandiflorum and sinense were companions, and I think now, as I thought then, they are distinct, though Dr. Lindley once said that he had raised two or three species (so called) from one pod of seed, which never was proved. The very best specimens of any of the sinense varieties I have grown or seen did not exceed 2 feet 6 inches. There are double and single, and blue to white flowers, as in grandiflorum; but, in my opinion, they are distinct enough to be separated. Introduced previous to 1820 as an annual.

Tricorne, flowers most beautiful blue, petals shorter than the calyx; a distinctly formed, interesting dwarf species suitable for the most select collection of rock plants. Height 9 to 12 inches. May. America.

Triste, flowers dark brown suffused with red at the edge of the sepals and petals; spur violet blue, interior of corolla tinted yellow; racemes loose. Height 2 feet. Siberia, 1819. In this species are all the shades of color known in the genus—a very interesting fact for hybridizers.

Zalil, flowers pale yellow, more than an inch in diameter, borne in long, loose racemes; leaves dark green, finely divided; stems numerous and branching; 12 to 20 inches. Afghanistan, 1887. This species also affords a new field for the hybridist. Annual or biennial.

The Growing of Delphiniums.

It is no use trying to grow delphiniums in poor, shallow soil; better forget than thus abuse them. The soil must be deep (three or more feet; six feet is better), rich and well drained. Manure heavily with rich stable manure, commercial fertilizer, bone dust or any other material capable of making the best and most available food for the plants. The strong growing species and varieties require lots of room—4 by 3 feet; 5 by 4 feet will be none too much for each plant after the first year. When they grow from 6 to 9 feet high, they need room in proportion. Mulch the spaces between the plants with manure, leaves, grass clippings, or anything to prevent the burning of the surface roots, whether in beds by themselves or in borders mixed with other plants. The less robust kinds do not require as much room, but they need the same care. Water should be given in sufficient quantities to thoroughly soak the ground.

When needed, liquid manure, nitrate of soda, or guano, or any other stimulant will be beneficial when growth is being rapidly made. It is necessary to early stake and carefully tie all the tall kinds, not forgetting to thin out the growth in its early stages—4 or 5 at most in 2-year-old plants; 9 to 12, in 3-year-old, and 13 to 18 in 4-year-old plants is about the average growth to leave. After four years it is time to get a new place for them. If the growths are taken 2 or 3 inches in length, they make fine cuttings for propagation.

Delphiniums have not many enemies, the worst being white mildew and some black potato-like destroying fungus, which are easily destroyed by the use of a weak solution of Bordeaux or other copperas mixture. Slug Shot will keep the few caterpillars in check.

The propagation of delphiniums is as readily, as easily, and as cheaply done as is that of chrysanthemums—by cuttings, at any season when they are to be had; by divisions in Spring or Fall and by seed in Spring, raised in frames or under glass, as are the general run of Summer-flowering plants.

Chicago. JOHN THORPE.

Clematis Stans Var.

The subject of this sketch is a chance seedling that originated in the garden of E. F. Dwyer, Lynn, Mass. It is a remarkably strong grower and a very showy vine, coming into bloom in Midsummer when few other plants of its class have any showiness. The flowers, which are borne in great profusion, are white shading to a delicate blue at the edge of the petals. The foliage, like that of others of the heracleifolia class, is clean and imposing, and the plant should prove popular and useful for Midsummer ornamentation. The variety, which as yet has not been named, was recently awarded a first-class certificate by the Massachusetts Horticultural Society.

J. W. D.

Kalamazoo, Mich.

: Notes.

At last the long expected im-
ement in trade here is noted, and
business of the past week or so
vs a steady increase of sales in
ines. After a Summer of intense
: and drought, during which the
flower business dwindled to al-
t nothing, the change to cool Fall
ther and increasing business seems
bly welcome this year.

› far as my observation extends
ng the growers here, stock of all
ls is in excellent shape, indeed;
risingly so after the exceptional
ther experienced this season.
es have been a trifle soft, as might
expected, but are rapidly harden-
up now; while carnations stood
splanting remarkably well, and
to date very few losses from any
e are reported. The earlier plant-
carnations are yielding quite ser-
able flowers. Chrysanthemums
e not yet made their appearance,
soon will, and, I think, in larger
hers than usual.

he Central Nursery Company have
nice house of chrysanthemums
ch will be followed by the Zvo-
k strain of sweet peas planted
n 4-inch pots into the benches as
become empty. I notice here a
rn to the raised bench system
r a trial of the solid beds for
s. Regarding the latter system
eems to me cement walls for sides
upy too much space to be profit-
. The above company is now un-
new management, L. P. Thurs-
being general manager, with Ra-
h Wells greenhouse foreman.
se gentlemen intend to introduce
e reforms which will eventually
e the company on a strong basis.

he Dunkley Floral Company has
been busy remodeling its plant
is introducing the Wittbold wa-
ng system in one house for trial.
Cook is getting things in good
pe now, although planting was de-
d on account of work being un-
hed.

Meyers, the East side florist, has
his place in good order for the
ter's business, and his stock looks
edingly well just now. The stork
ted his dwelling recently with a
y girl. Mrs. Meyers is a daughter
Mr. Coles, the well known florist
Kokomo, Ind.

understand the firm of Fisher
Rocklin has dissolved, Mr. Fisher
tinning the business and Mr. Rock-
returning to Chicago.

red Marker has completed his new
se for bedding plants. He has
n on the sick list; but is getting
und again to visit his old friends.

S. B.

ELMHURST, N. Y.—Louis Boelser, formerly a grower of vegetables, has built three greenhouses and will engage in the cultivation of cut flowers for the New York market. B.

MASPETH, N. Y.—A. Sauenwald has completed his two new houses and dwelling; he is busy planting in carnations.

John Lappe has sown 30 pounds of pansy seed. B.

Bulk that Bluffs.

When we hear of a trade paper inserting advertisements free, doubling space ordered without authority, and adopting other fake methods to bring about bulk, we are reminded of the toad that insisted on being inflated, that it might be mistaken for an ox. Don't be deceived by the bulk that bluffs. Wind is often responsible for largeness.

Chicago.

The Week's News.

Louis Coatsworth left on Friday of last week for Romney, Ont., from which point he expects to return this week accompanied by his family, the members of which have been rusticating in that section since the recent family reunion.

Winnipeg, Manitoba, has presented the latest sensation to the Chicago market in the retail line, by the announcement of a perfectly up-to-date establishment under the management of H. E. Philpot. The plans as laid out are to do a general retail cut flower and plant business under the firm name of the Chicago Floral Company, and as the manager is so well known here, as in fact, he is all over the country, there is no question as to the result of the venture.

Miss Anna Ziska has taken charge of the books and clerical work in the office of the Chicago Rose Company as the assistant of her brother, John, the secretary-manager, who controls the general run of affairs on the lower floor, with the exception of the cut flower department, over which John Starrett holds his banner.

At this writing there is no available information, but it seems only a fair presumption that, as a result of the recent hurricane which in its course included the States which furnish the Southern smilax for this market, there is liable to be a scarcity in that decorative green for the present.

The friends of Capt. A. S. Simmons that include the entire "troop" of the Chicago florists are congratulating him on his recent appointment to a position of "A. D. C." on the Governor's staff.

The Union Floral Company established by the efforts of former president Louis Heidtmann of the Gardeners and Florists' Union No. 10615, with headquarters at 467 Ogden avenue, held a meeting and initiation at the store on Wednesday evening of last week, which was enlivened by refreshments and speeches. Although the store has been opened only about a month, a very satisfactory business is being carried on, and the prospects for the future are very encouraging.

The rearrangement and remodeling of the E. F. Winterson Company's establishment has certainly produced a transformation at their headquarters, 45 Wabash avenue. There has also been quite a change in department management and a large line of up-to-date supplies is now being received. John P. Degnan is back with the concern in his former position, and Cliff Pruner has returned to his duties after his recent illness.

At J. A. Budlong's special pride is enjoyed in displaying the present cut of American Beauty roses from the new range of houses, and the flowers are surely worthy of all the good words that can be said about them.

It matters not what the world says, it is results that count. A year ago the Horticultural Society of Chicago, at a thirty days' notice launched out on the experiment of holding a flower show in the Coliseum, and when all hands pulled together the result was, if not the best, certainly one of the best floral exhibitions ever held in this country. Not only artistically and botanically was the show a remarkable success, but financially it netted several thousand dollars, which obviates the necessity of procuring a guarantee fund for the coming show to be held in the Coliseum, November 6 to 12 inclusive. Indications point to the fact that the next month will see the greatest flower show ever held in the country, if not in the world. On behalf of the society the executive committee extended an invitation to the parties most interested to attend an informal supper at the Union Restaurant on Monday evening last and have "a good talk," to which about one hundred of the leading members of the craft from Chicago and its environs responded. After the disposition of the edibles, Secretary W. N. Rudd opened the post-prandial exercises with a few appropriate remarks and introduced J. C. Vaughan as toastmaster, who in his usual forcible style stated the object of "getting together" and what could be accomplished with a long pull, a strong and a pull all together. Ben Hammond of Fishkill on Hu N. Y., Secretary of the Ame Rose Society, was then called and gave a very interesting sto his recent experiences in this cit freely admitted that Chicago is as large as it thinks it is, and as good as it can be. Chairman dett of the press committee, Ma George Asmus, Phil. J. Haus Carl Cropp and a number of members of the local craft made gestions and Mr. Keeley, editor o Tribune, Chicago's leading daily, introduced with loud acclaim a the few minutes at his disposal what the papers would do and they ought to do to advance th terests of the show and hortic in all lines.

The fact that the Chrysanthe Society of America will hold it nual exhibition in conjunction the local society, gives addition terest to the prospects, and if th thusiasm displayed at the M Evening Meeting is a fair ind what is to take place, the c flower show in Chicago will equ not excel anything of this nature held in America.

Benjamin Hammond of Fishki Hudson, N. Y., secretary of the A ican Rose Society has been tak tour through this section, whe says he has met with some de ful surprises. He left this wee Ontario, Canada, to investigate mineral property in which he interested.

C. L. Ford, representing A. mann of New York, has just ret from the West, reporting a pleasant and successful trip.

Miss Ruth Eaton of the E. H. force was married last Saturda Chester Eaton.

William Dingle, the popular of the Adams Express Compan well known in every wholesale in Chicago, resigned last week left for his old home in Denver.

Michael Rocklin, formerly wit E. H. Hunt Company of this cit later of the retail concern of & Rocklin, Kalamazoo, Mich., ha turned to Chicago and asso himself with the Bassett & Was force.

C. W. McKellar's rooms have on a wonderfully improved ap ance since the recent house cle painting and general all-roun novating.

Among our recent visitors was Ruston of Evansville, Ind.

WILLIAM K. WO

CANADIAN NEW

MONTREAL.—The Fall bu has opened up very well, but wh cool weather sets in trade will in this city; at least we hope so retail trade is all agog ove Wright Floral Company of C opening up a first-class store ri the busiest uptown district. N pense is being spared in fitting place, and when completed it the most handsomely furnished store in the city.

Mrs. Cairns reports business good, and would like to get mo lets, having a great demand for flowers.

Harris & Hopton are putting enormous lot of bulbs this Their new houses are complete are already filled with general Wikhue Brothers are cutting lot of late asters. They ha completed and planted a new 20 x 100 feet.

Messrs McKenna & Son hav pleted extensive alterations i store. W. C

TORONTO.—At a meeting Toronto Gardeners' and Floris sociation held in St. George' on September 18, 1906, a co was appointed to arrange for t vention of the American Ca Society, which will be held in t in January, 1907. Thomas ton read an instructive paper chids."

CLASSIFIED ADVERTISEMENTS

CASH WITH ORDER.

The columns under this heading are reserved t advertisements of Stock for Sale, Stock anted, Help Wanted, Situations Wanted or ber Wants; also of Greenhouse, Land, Sec-d-Hand Materials, etc., For Sale or Rent.

Our charge is 10 cts. per line (7 words to the ie), set solid, without display. No advt. cepted for less than thirty cents.

Display advertisements in these columns, 15 nts per line; count 12 lines agate to the inch.

[If replies to Help Wanted, Situation Want-, or other advertisements are to be addressed re of this office, advertisers add 10 cents to ver expense of forwarding.]

Copy must reach New York office 12 o'clock ednesday to secure insertion in issue of fol-wing Saturday.

Advertisers in the Western States desiring to ivertise under initials, may save time by hav-g their answer directed care our Chicago office 127 E. Berwyn Ave.

SITUATIONS WANTED

TUATION WANTED—By gardener, 30 years of age, German; good grower, deco-tor and designer. Address, W. P., care e Florists' Exchange.

TUATION WANTED—First-class orchid grower and gardener; fully up-to-date; first-ss references. Apply, S. M., care The lorists' Exchange.

TUATION WANTED—As assistant gardener in first-class private place; thirty, single, merican references. Address, S. J., care be Florists' Exchange.

TUATION WANTED—By a Swede, single, 35 years experience in roses. Wishes posi-on commercial or private. No. 1 references. ddress, S. L., care The Florists' Exchange.

TUATION WANTED.—Young man wants position in first-class florist store as sales-an, etc. Sober and industrious. Experi-ced. Address, S. U. care The Florists' Ex-ange.

TUATION WANTED—As section man in car-nations and roses, or working foreman on nall place. 11 years experience. 26 years d, married. Can furnish references. Ad-ress, S. Q., care The Florists' Exchange.

TUATION WANTED—As superintendent on private place by a thoroughly competent an. 18 years experience in all branches of e business. Married, one child. Address, J., 560 Maple st., Flatbush, Brooklyn, N.

TUATION WANTED—By German, 37 years old, single; good grower of roses, carnations nd general stock; also good maker-up. Vages, $15.00 per week. Address, S. H., are The Florists' Exchange.

TUATION WANTED—An assistant park or cemetery superintendent. Theoretical train-g and long practical experience. American, 5, single. Good references. Address, Ed-ard Raymond, Back Bay P. O., Boston, lass.

TUATION WANTED—By single, competent grower of roses, carnations and chrysan-hemums. Take charge 50,000 feet glass. 36.00 and board. Florist, 201 East 34th treet, New York.

TUATION WANTED—By horticulturist and florist, 30 years of age, 18 years exper-ence, speaks Russian, would like to have some uitable position. Fine workman, knows bed-ing thoroughly. Inquire, V. Kosubof, River-iew, Md.

TUATION WANTED—Thoroughly learned gardener, 25 years of age, German, single, vants a steady position; good grower of oses, carnations and bedding plants; able to ake charge, private or commercial. Refer-nces. Address, S. P., care The Florists' Exchange.

TUATION WANTED—Carnation grower of ighest abilities, open for situation. Grower f as fine stock as can be seen in the East. ood wages expected. References from last mployer as to abilities and as hard, brainy worker. Address, S. R., care The Florists' Exchange.

TUATION WANTED—As foreman in an up-to-date place. Eastern states preferred. 23 ears practical experience in Europe and this ountry in growing cut flowers and hot house lants. Single man, aged 39; please state ull particulars in first letter. Address, S. L., care The Florists' Exchange.

TUATION WANTED—Head gardener, Ger-man, married, no children, competent in all ranches of gardening, expert grower of roses, arnations and chrysanthemums, seeks posi-ion on gentleman's private place. Ten years' eference. Please state wages. Address, ardener, care of Chas. Frank, 144 Palisade venue, Yonkers, N. Y.

Thirty cents is the mini-num charge for advertise-nents on this page.

SITUATIONS WANTED

SITUATION WANTED—by single German, age 45, on private place. Good Rose and Carnation grower, also Vegetables indoors and outside. References, honest, sober and industrious. Address S. T., Florists' Exchange.

HELP WANTED

WANTED—General utility man for carnation plant. Steady, single; middle aged man pre-ferred. Lebanon Greenhouses, Lebanon, Pa.

WANTED—A night fireman, soft coal. $12.00 per week. References required. John Reck & Son, Bridgeport, Conn.

WANTED—At once, good grower of carnations, mums and bedding stock. Wages, $35 room and board. T. Malbrane, Johnstown, Pa.

WANTED—Young man for the store; one with experience to wait on trade and make-up. John C. Gracey, 2034 Columbia av., Phila-delphia, Pa.

WANTED—A rose grower to take charge of a section; must be sober and reliable; state references and wages. C. C. Pollworth Co., Milwaukee, Wis.

WANTED—Two thoroughly experienced men for watering in greenhouses. Wages, $12.00 per week. Apply to Peter Henderson & Co., 390 Arlington avenue, Jersey City, N. J.

WANTED—First-class store man and decora-tor. Must be up-to-date on high grade table work. Good salary to first-class man only. At once, address S. C., care The Flor-ists' Exchange.

WANTED—A first-class man for retail florist in Chicago; no greenhouse work. Must be a good salesman and designer. State wages. References. Address, M. D., care The Florists' Exchange.

WANTED—Section man for roses and one for carnations; married or single. $15.00 per week to men with references as to cap-ability and soberness. Pittsburgh Rose and Carnation Co., Crystal Farm, Gibsonia, Pa.

WANTED.—Two experienced men to assist in landscape, nursery and general greenhouse work. Steady position. German preferred. J. H. Small & Sons, cor. 14th & G sts., Wash-ington, D. C.

WANTED—One good carnation grower, also one thoroughly experienced man for water-ing and other greenhouse work. Please state wages expected and references in first let-ter. Evenden Bros., Williamsport, Pa.

WANTED.

A thoroughly competent rose grower to take charge of section. Wages, $15.00 per week; to the right man a chance to work himself up to high wages.

Address,

EXPERT, CARE THE FLORISTS' EXCHANGE.

Mention The Florists' Exchange when writing.

WANTED—Thoroughly competent and sober man for growing carnations, mums and general greenhouse stock—capable of taking charge if necessary. Married man preferred; permanent place for the right man. Address

A. V. D. SNYDER, Ridgewood, New Jersey.

Mention The Florists' Exchange when writing.

MISCELLANEOUS WANTS

WANTED TO BUY—Greenhouses to be taken down. State full particulars of same when writing. Address, F. W., care The Florists' Exchange.

WANTED—Correspondence with nurserymen who have trees, oaks and elms, suitable for street planting. Address, The Tree and Park Commission, 1317 Sumter street, Colum-bia, S. C.

FOR SALE OR RENT

FOR SALE—Owing to failing health, I will sell my florist establishment, beautifully situated between Larchmont Manor and Mama-roneck, Westchester Co., New York, near railroad station; trolley lines within one min-ute walk. First class opportunity for the right man. Plenty of landscape and jobbing work. The place contains four acres, 2 green-houses, 104 feet long and lots of sash; well stocked with trees and shrubs, etc.; horse, wagon and tools. Address, Box 44, Larch-mont, New York.

FOR SALE OR RENT

FOR RENT, cheap to responsible party, an old established florist business, six greenhouses and grounds. Apply at once to E. E. Morris, 64 Ann street, Newark, N. J.

FOR SALE

A well equipped place, consisting of seven greenhouses, over 30,000 feet of glass, a nine roomed house, barn, stock, etc., and eight acres of land. This is a decided bargain and a rare opportunity. For particulars address

S. S. SKIDELSKY,

824 N. 24th St., Philadelphia, Pa.

Mention The Florists' Exchange when writing.

TO LET

Florist Establishment consisting of nine greenhouses, heated by hot water, containing about 10,000 square feet of glass; sheds, barn and dwelling, in Long Island City, within one hour's drive of the wholesale markets of the City of New York. For further particu-lars address **Box R. Y., Florists' Exchange**

Mention The Florists' Exchange when writing.

STOCK FOR SALE

WE STILL HAVE 1000 QUEEN LOUISE; last ca . 3 1-2c. each. Fox & Rosen, Parkerford, Pa. ll

DRACAENA INDIVISA, 4 in. pots, $10.00 per 100. Stocky plants. Cash with order. Mrs. B. K. Eggert, New Britain, Conn.

PANSIES, 50c. per 100; $3.50 per 1,000. Daisies (Bellis), 50c. per 100; $2.50 per 1000. Alex Haeseler, Meshanticut, R. I.

CARNATION PLANTS, extra fine, field-grown, no better plants anywhere. Joost, Wolcott, Pond, Prosperity and 100 White Lawson, per 100, $5.00. Terms: Cash. M. J. Schaaf, Dans-ville, N. Y.

15,000 STRONG, healthy, field-grown violet plants of Farquhar, Lady Campbell, La France and California, $5.00 per 100; $45.00 per 1000. Richard Langle, North Street, White Plains, N. Y.

BABY RAMBLER roses, fine dormant stock, $25 per 100. 2 1-2 inch pot plants, extra well rooted $7 per 100, $65 per 1000. Orders booked for delivery now or any time up to late Spring. Samples free. Brown Brothers Co., Rochester, N. Y.

FOR SALE—Ten acres of fine nursery stock; must be sold at sacrifice prices as lease of land expires next Spring. 15,000 Ligistrum Ibota, 18 in. to 2 ft. at $30.00 per 1000; 5,000 Ligistrum Ibota, 2 1-2 to 3 ft. at $45.00 per 1000; Aralia pentaphylla, Spirea Von Houteii, Viburnum tomentosum, Kerria Japonicum fl. pl., Rhodotypus Kerrioides, and 60,000 other shrubs. Write for particulars and prices to Rhode Island Nurseries, New-port, R. I.

FOR SALE—10 **Latania Borbonica** from 10 to 12 feet high. 1 **Phoenix Rupi, cola**, 10 to 12 feet high 1 **Kentia Bel-moriana**, 14 to 16 feet high. All plants in first-class condition; can be had at reasonable price.

Address, S. O., care The Florists' Exchange.

Mention The Florists' Exchange when writing.

FOR SALE

FOR SALE—Glass, second hand, a few boxes, double thick, 12 x 14 left, $2.00 per box. Wm. P. Kesteloo, Walden, N. Y.

BARGAIN IN BOILERS—Two five foot hori-zontal tubular boilers, complete. High test; good as new. Price, $500, on cars. One boiler, $300. G. S. Ramsburg, Somers-worth, N. H.

BOILERS, BOILERS, BOILERS.

SEVERAL good second hand boilers on hand, also new No. 16 Hitchings at reduced cost. Write for list. Wm. H. Lutton, West Side Avenue Station, C. R. R. of N. J., Jersey City, N. J.

FOR SALE—4 Hitchings hot water expan-sion tanks. No. 2 high tank Fig. B. of cat-alogue. All in good condition. F. O. B., $2.00 each. Address, E. D., care The Flor-ists' Exchange.

BOILERS

One **No. 4 Weathered** with shaking grate $40.00.
One **No. 4 Weathered** with dumping grate $37.50.

Both in good condition. Price includes delivery to cars.

R. G. HANFORD

NORWALK, : : CONN.

Mention The Florists' Exchange when writing.

FOR SALE

FOR SALE—One No. 5 Lord & Burnham boiler; been in use two seasons; 1,000 feet of four inch cast iron pipe, four valves, two expansion tanks, and one platform spring top wagon. In good condition. Apply to C. M., 209 Boyd Av., Jersey City, N. J.

FOR SALE

Greenhouse Material milled from Gulf Cypress, to any detail furnished, or our own patterns as desired, cut and spliced ready for erection. Estimates for com-plete constructions furnished.

V. E. REICH, Brooklyn, N. Y.

1429-1437 Metropolitan Ave.

Mention The Florists' Exchange when writing.

FOR SALE

BOILERS Hitchings, No. 17 at $110.00. No. 6 Weathered, round, $70.00. 4 section round Cambridge steam boiler $75.00. 8 section No. 11, J. L. Mott boiler will heat 12,760 ft. glass, $175.00. 10 H. P. upright steam, $25.00. 6 section new Novelty boiler, will heat 4,100 ft. glass, $140.00. New Henderson boilers; send for price on size wanted.

PIPE Good serviceable second hand. No Junk, with new threads. 2 in. 7c.; 1½ in. 5½c.; 1¼ in. 4c.; 1 in. 3c.; 2½ in. 10c.; 3in. 14c.; 4 in. 19c. 4 in. cast iron greenhouse 14c. 2 in. NEW, standard, full lengths, 8½c. ft. All kinds of fittings for 4 in. cast iron and all sizes wrought iron.

STOCKS AND DIES New Economy, easy work-ing, No. 1 cuts ½-¾-1 in. $3.00; No. 2 cuts 1¼-1½-2 ins. $4.00; Armstrong Adjustable No. 2 cuts ¾-1 in. $4.00; No. 3 cuts 1¼-1½-2 ins. $6.60.

PIPE CUTTERS Saunders, No. 1 cuts to 1 in. $1.00; No. 2 cuts to 2 in. $1.30; No. 3 cuts to 3 in. $3.00; No. 4 cuts to 4 in. $4.60.

STILLSON WRENCHES Guaranteed. 12 in., grips 1½ in. $1.10; 18 in. grips 2 in. $1.60; 24 in., grips 2½ in. $2.25; 36 in., grips 3½ in. $4.50.

PIPE VISES Reed's Best Hinged Vise, No. 1 grips 2 in. $1.75; No. 2 grips 4 in. $3.50.

GARDEN HOSE 50 ft. lengths ¾ in. not guar-anteed; 4½ guaranteed for light work; 7½, guaranteed for heavy work, 10c. ft.

BRASS HOSE VALVES New; not faucets; ¾ in. 65c.; 1 in. 95c.

HOT-BED SASH New; Gulf Cypress, 3 ft.x6 ft. 75c.; glazed complete $1.60 up. VENTILATORS; all sizes made to order. Second hand sash glazed $1.00 and $1.25, good condition.

GLASS New American, 50 ft. to the box. 10x12 single at $1.75. 10x12, 12x12 10x15 B double $2.55. 12x14 to 12x20 and 14x14 to 14x20 B double $2.70. 16x16 and 16x18 B double $2.90. 16x24 B double $3.15. 18x20 and 16x22 $3.00. 9x8, 7x9, 8x10 old, single $1.50. 8x14 old, double $1.65; 10x14 old, double $1.75.

LINSEED OIL Strictly pure; barrel lots, 42c. gallon.

CARNATION SUPPORTS second hand, 50c. hundred.

VENTILATING APPARATUS second hand, Hitchings make, arms, 25c.; hangers, 10c.; machines, $3.50; col-lars, 3c.

SCREWS all sizes; mixed wood, from 1 in. to 3 in., in boxes, 25 and 50 lbs. at 6c. lb.

PUMPS hot air; well pumps and force pumps; all repairs.

Get our prices on second hand wood material. We can furnish everything in new material to erect any size house. Get our prices.

METROPOLITAN MATERIAL CO.

Greenhouse Wreckers

1398-1408 Metropolitan Avenue, BROOKLYN, N.Y.

NIKOTEEN APHIS PUNK

THE ORIGINAL AND GENUINE

NICOTINE FUMIGANT

STRONGEST AND MOST UNIFORM

PRICE 60¢ PER BOX OF 12 LONG SHEETS

$6.50 PER CASE OF 12 BOXES

NIKOTEEN

LIQUID

FOR SPRAYING OR VAPORIZING

PRICE $1.50 PER PINT BOTTLE

$13.92 PER CASE OF 10 PINT BOTTLES

NICOTINE MFG. CO. ST. LOUIS MO.

Mention The Florists' Exchange when writing.

VIOLET CULTURE

Price, $1.50 Postpaid

A. T. De La Mare Ptg. & Pub. Co. Ltd., New York

OUR LITTLE PET

From Aschmann in Philadelphia I bought
An Araucaria, a pet for our little girl;
Now we have two pets, the pride of our thought:
The little girl so sweet, a head full of curls,
And the Araucaria with its everlasting green,
A more joyful home you never have seen.

Watch us Grow!!

ARAUCARIA EXCELSA, the best of all decorative plants nature produces: a specialty. Every man in business life, to be successful, must adopt one thing as his specialty, and that specialty, whatever he may select, and of whatever nature it may be, he must guard, study and push to such an extent, that it not only benefits himself, but he must conduct it so, that every one who seeks his aid, service or his articles, whatever he advertises or practices, will **share a slice of his activity and prosperity.** I made the importation and cultivation of Araucaria as a special study in my life. The following figures will show you my success in business: In the first year I began with an import of 250; in the eleventh year (now 1906) my importation has grown up to 6,000 (come and see it). On account of the Araucaria growing yearly in favor as a much admired decorative plant for the arbor, bed room, dining and sitting rooms, stores, hotels, lawns and porches by the plant-consuming peoples all over the country, the outlook will be of an importation of at least 8,000 to 10,000 in the Spring of 1907. To secure this vast amount for 1907, I am now in Belgium making contracts for next year. I shall also at the same time bring over with me a large lot of choice Azalea Indica, Palms, etc. for Christmas and Easter forcing. No money will be spared in obtaining for my customers the cream of the Belgium greenhouses.

Please note lowest price now going for September:

ARAUCARIA EXCELSA

12 to 14 in. 5½ in. pots, 3 to 4 tiers, 2-yr. old, 50c. 14 to 16 in., 5½ in. pots, 3 to 4 tiers, 2-yr. old, 60c. 16 to 18 in. 5½ to 6 in. pots, 4 to 5 tiers, 3-yr. old, 75c. 18 to 20 in., 6 in. pots, 5 to 6 tiers, 4-yr. old, $1.00. 20 to 24 in. 6 in. to 7 in. pots, 5 to 6 tiers, 4-yr. old, $1.25. 36-40 to 50 in. 7 in. pots, specimen plants from $2.50 to $3.00 each.

ARAUCARIA COMPACTA ROBUSTA — have several thousand of them: can supply all wants. These plants were never so fine in shape and condition as this year. The set of the greenhouse, as broad as long, 12 to 20 in., in height, 3 to 4 perfect tiers, 20 to 30 inches across, 3-4-5 year old, 6 to 7 in. pots, $1.25, $1.50, $1.75, $2.00, $2.50 to $3.00 each.

ARAUCARIA EXCELSA GLAUCA — This variety on account of its beautiful Green-Bluish tiers, dwarf habit, fine compact shape, gives it a striking appearance, and anybody seeing them, must undoubtedly fall in love with them at sight. Plants, 6-7 inch pots, 3-4-5 perfect tiers, 3-4 year old, 15 to 25 inch high, from 15 to 30 in. across, $1.25, $1.50, $1.75, $2.00 to $2.50 each.

KENTIA BELMOREANA, 5½ to 6 in. pots, bushy, fine plants, from 75 cts. to $1.00 to $1.25 each.

KENTIA FORSTERIANA, 7 in. pots, made-up plants, 1 large in center, 3 smaller sizes, 22 to 25 in. high around, gives them a good appearance, $2.00 each. 6 in. pots, single plants, 35 to 40 in. high, 5 to 6 good leaves, 4 year old, $1.25 to $1.50 each; 6 in. pots, 30 to 35 in. high, 4 year old, 5 good leaves, $1.00; 5½ in. pots, 3 year old, 25 to 30 in. high, 5 good leaves, 75c. made-up plants, 3 and 4 in. pots, 18 to 20 in high, 25 cts. to 30 cts. each.

ARECA LUTESCENS, made-up, 25 cts.

COCOS WEDDELIANA, 15 cts.

NEPHROLEPIS BARROWSII, 6 in. pots, strong, ready for 7-8 in., 50c. 4 in. pots, ready for 6-7 in., 25c.

NEPHROLEPIS SCOTTII, 6 in. pots, large, ready for 6-7 in. 50c.; 5½ in. pots, 40c.; 5 in. 35c.; 4 in. 20c. to 25c.

BOSTON FERNS, 4 in., 20c. to 25c. I have them by the thousand. 5 in.: 30c. to 35c.

FERNS for dishes, a fine assortment, 2½ in., $5.00 per 100; 3 in., $6.00 per 100.

FICUS ELASTICA, 6 in., 50c.

ASPARAGUS PLUMOSUS NANUS, 3 in., 6c.; 4 in., 10c.

PRIMULA SINENSIS, in 4 in., pots ready to shift: will bloom for Christmas. $10.00 per 100.

CASH WITH ORDER

When ordering, say whether the plants should be shipped in the pots or not

GODFREY ASCHMANN

Importer and Wholesale Grower of Pot Plants

1012 Ontario Street, - - PHILADELPHIA, PA.

Mention The Florists' Exchange when writing.

GERANIUMS

Named standard varieties in all the leading colors, double **White, D. Pink, D. Scarlet, Nutt,** good stock plants, 4 in. pots, not from open ground, $5.00 per 100. Same varieties from 2 in. pots, $1.50 per 100; $14.00 per 1000. **Pansies,** largest flowers and finest colors, ready to transplant in cold frames, $2.50 per 1000 by express; 50c. per 100 by mail. **Hydrangeas,** all sizes, all from pots; 4 in., $8.00 per 100. Larger plants up to 10 in. pots, nice, young stock, $2.50 per 100. Stock is offered cheap for cash and to make room.

E. FRYER, Johnstown, Pa.

Mention The Florists' Exchange when writing.

Geraniums Geraniums

4 in. pots at $6.00 per 100.
3 in. pots at $4.00 per 100.
Heliotrope, 4 in. $4.00 per 100.
" 2 in. $3.00 per 100.
Lobelia, 2 in. $2.00 per 100.
Coleus, in variety, 2½ in. pots, $2.00 per 100.

Don't get left, but get your order in. Cash must accompany same.

J. E. FELTHOUSEN,

154 VAN VRANKEN AVE., SCHENECTADY, N. Y.

Mention The Florists' Exchange when writing.

GERANIUMS

ROOTED CUTTINGS

Orders booked for delivery Dec. 1st and after. I will have fourteen houses planted to stock plants and I can supply you with the right kind of cuttings.

	Per 100	Per 1000
S. A. Nutt, Perkins, Buchner, Doyle	$1.25	$12.50
Viaud, Jaulin, Poitevine, L. Francis	1.50	15.00
Ricard, Castellane, Trego	1.50	15.00
Peter Henderson	2.00	20.00
Fleuve Blanc (White Poitevine)	5.00	50.00

These cuttings are carefully grown and will make a better plant than the average pot plant.

ALBERT M. HERR, Lancaster, Pa.

Mention The Florists' Exchange when writing.

GERANIUMS

Double Grant and **Bruanti,** large, healthy, 2 in. $1.50 per 100; $14.00 per 1000; ready now. 12 other varieties ready November and December, $16.00 to $20.00 per 1000. Special price in large quantities. **ARDISIA CRENULATA,** well berried, from bench, ready for 5-6 in. $9.00 per doz. Cash please.

WM. S. HERZOG, MORRIS PLAINS, N. J.

Mention The Florists' Exchange when writing.

CYCLAMEN

SPLENDENS GIGANTEUM HYBRIDS

This strain has no equal or better. Perfect flowers of Giant type in five true colors, well grown plants from 4 in. pots $15.00 per 100, from 5 in. pots $2.50 per doz. $20.00 per 100.

PRIMULA SINENSIS FIMBRIATA

Only fringed varieties Giant flowers in the best market sorts, all colors from 2½ in. pots $3.00 per 100.

PRIMULA OBCONICA GRANDIFLORA

The celebrated Ronsdorfer and Lattmann Hybrids in the most beautiful colors from 2½ in. pots $3.00, from 3½ in. pots $10.00 per 100.

BEGONIA REX

In 12 choice market varieties, extra well grown plants from 5 in. pots $2.00 per doz. Rooted cuttings labeled $2.00 equally mixed $1.50 per 100.

Asparagus Plumosus Nanus

Special offer for first class grown stock from 2½ in. pots $2.50 per 100, $20.00 per 1000.

CINERARIAS

HYBRIDA MAXIMA GRANDIFLORA

No better strain from 2½ in. pots $2.50 per 100.

PAUL MADER, EAST STROUDSBURG, PA.

Cyclamen Giganteum

Extra fine plants, large flowering, 3-inch, $5.00 per 100; 4 inch $10.00 per 100; 5 inch $15.00 per 100. **Primulas,** Chinese and Obconica 2½ inch, $2.00 per 100; 3 inch $3.00 per 100; 4 inch $6.00 per 100.

Asparagus Sprengeri, 3½-inch, $5.00 per 100.
Asparagus Plumosus Nanus, 3½-inch, $6.00 per 100.
Cinerarias, 2¼ inch, $2.00 per 100; 300 for $5.00.

SAMUEL WHITTON, 15-16 Gray Ave., Utica, N. Y.

Mention The Florists' Exchange when writing.

Primula Obconica Grandiflora

2 1-2 in., $2.50 per 100. Ask for list (seedlings of hardy plants)

BAUDISCH & CO.,

537 Fulton Street UNION HILL, N. J.

Mention The Florists' Exchange when writing.

GERANIUMS

From 2 in. pots ready for immediate delivery

Alliance, Lemoine 1905. Hybrid, Ivy and Zonal, semi-double, lilac, white, upper petals feathered and blotched crimson maroon, 25c. each; $2.00 per doz. **Fleuve Blanc,** the semi-double Bruant, that promises to become the standard white, flowers and foliage equal to Alph. Ricard. $1.50 per doz.; $10.00 per 100. **Cactus Geraniums,** four varieties, petals curled and twisted similar to the Cactus Dahlia. $2.00 per doz.; $15.00 per 100. **Double Drydon,** $1.00 per doz.; $5.00 per 100. **S. A. Nutt, La Pilote, Beaute Poitevine, Mme. Barney, Centaur, Miss Kendell, Mme. Jaulin, Jean Viaud, Mme. Charrotte,** 40c. per doz.; $2.00 per 100; $18.00 per 1000. **Ville Poitiers, Marquise de Castellane, Berthe de Presilly, M. Jeli de Bammeville, Thomas Meehan,** 50c. per doz.; $3.00 per 100; $25.00 per 1000. Send for Geranium catalogue, let us figure on your future supply. **Alternantheras,** red and yellow, $2.00 per 100; $15.00 per 1000. **Hardy English Ivy,** $2.00 per 100; $15.00 per 1000. **Smilax,** $2.00 per 100; $15.00 per 1000. **Rubbers,** good stock from 4 in. pots, $2.00 per doz., $15.00 per 100.

Coleus, Lemon Verbenas 40cts. doz. $2.00 per 100.

Ageratum, "Inimitable." Giant blue. $1.25 per doz., $8.00 per 100.

VEGETABLE PLANTS

Cabbage: — Early Jersey and Charleston Wakefield. Succession and Early Summer, $1.00 per 1000. $8.50 per 10,000.

Lettuce. Grand Rapids, Big Boston and Boston Market. $1.00 per 1000, $8.10 per 10,000.

Parsley, Moss curled. $1.25 per 1000.

A cordial invitation is extended to all interested in Horticulture to visit us. Cowenton Station, Philadelphia division, B. & O. R. R., 12 miles north of Baltimore.

R. VINCENT Jr. & SON,

WHITE MARSH, MD.

GERANIUMS.

Rooted Cuttings ready Nov. 1. **Nutt** and **Buchner,** $1.00 per 100; $10.00 per 1000.

Viaud, Ricard, Poitevine, Doyle, Pasteur, Herett **Perkins, Castellane,** $1.25 per 100; $12.00 per 1000. Cash with order.

ERNEST HARRIS, Delanson, N. Y.

Mention The Florists' Exchange when writing.

ABUNDANCE

Healthy, stocky, field grown plants. First size $12.00 per 100; $100.00 per 1000. Second size, $10.00 per 100; $75.00 per 1000; 250 at a 1000 rates. Delivery 15th of August.

CASH WITH ORDER.

RUDOLPH FISCHER, Great Neck, L.I., N.Y.

Mention The Florists' Exchange when writing.

FIELD GROWN CARNATIONS

Strong, healthy plants. 2000 **Hill,** $5.00 per 100; $45.00 per 1000; 1000 **McGowan,** $3.50 per 100; $30.00 per 1000. Cash with order.

E. R. SHERWOOD, Norwalk, Conn.

Mention The Florists' Exchange when writing.

TO CLOSE

2000 **QUEENS,** good, clean, healthy, field-grown plants, $3.50 per 100; $30.00 per 1000.

CASH

GOVE BROS., Biddeford, Me.

Mention The Florists' Exchange when writing.

CARNATIONS

	100
Crisis Scarlet	$5.00
Fiancee	6.00
B. Market	5.00
Cardinal	7.00
Estelle	6.00
Queen	5.00

Cash with order.

SMITH & GANNETT, GENEVA, N. Y.

Mention The Florists' Exchange when writing.

CHRYSANTHEMUMS

Fine extra large, budded, in all colors, 7 and 8 in pots. $25.00 per 100.

F. K. LAMEREAUX

PORT JERVIS, N. Y.

Mention The Florists' Exchange when writing.

2000 CHRYSANTHEMUMS

"THE BABY"

Fine for Thanksgiving Day. Field-grown plants to pot up. For 7 in. pots, 15c.; 6 in. 12c.; 5 in., 10c.; 4 in., 8c. each. Cash.

HENRY EICHHOLZ, Waynesboro, Pa.

Mention The Florists' Exchange when writing.

Gardenia Veitchii

4½ inch, $35.00 per 100; 5 inch, $50.00 per 100; strong bushy plants. Cash with order.

J. M. KELLER CO.

5th Ave., & 65th St.

BROOKLYN, N. Y.

Mention the Florists' Exchange when writing.

Geraniums

Big lot of **S. A. Nutt, J. Doyle, Mme. Buchner,** rooted cuttings ready, $10.00 per 1000. Other varieties will be ready later. Cash with order.

PETER BROWN,

LANCASTER, PA.

Mention The Florists' Exchange when writing.

THE AMERICAN CARNATION

Price, $3.50

A. T. DE LA MARE PTG. & PUB. CO. LTD.

2-8 Duane Street, New York

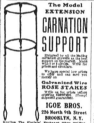

New York.

The Week's News.

On Monday evening, October 8, the monthly meeting of the New York Florists' Club will take place in the Grand Opera House, corner of Twenty-third street and Eighth avenue. Dahlias are in the order of exhibition, and it is expected that a nice showing will be made.

The retail business throughout the city is gradually improving, and funeral work seems to be quite plentiful just now.

Dr. Britton left for Jamaica on August 25, accompanied by Mrs. Britton and Dr. Underwood. Professor Evans, of Yale University, joined the expedition at Kingston. Collections will be made at high elevations on the mountains about Cinchona, where the tropical laboratory of the Garden is located, and also in the lower and more arid regions of the island, suited to the growth of palms and cacti.

Samuel Decker, florist of Nyack, N. Y., has gained quite a reputation as a collector of Indian relics. Among his most valuable curios is an Indian head dress, which is composed of twigs braided together, and ornamented with birds' feathers and shells cut in many beautiful shapes. This is conceded to be one of the finest pieces of Indian workmanship in the country.

Daniel Haas, Portchester, N. Y., has taken a three years' lease of the greenhouses of Mrs. Robert McInnes, Upper Montclair, N. J.

The body of Frederick Stephans, a young man 18 years of age, who had been employed for some time by E. C. Matthies, florist of Woodside, L. I., was found in a vacant lot in the rear of the greenhouses on Monday morning last. The young man had been missing for five weeks, and from all indications it was apparent that he had committed suicide, as a 38-calibre revolver was found underneath the body. Stephans come from a wealthy and aristocratic family in Hamburg, Germany. Several years ago he ran away from home, and shipped as a sailor on a German ship which plies between Bremen and New York. Last July he broke his leg, and was sent to a hospital in Manhattan. When he was discharged the ship had sailed away, and he was given a home with Matthies in exchange for labor until the boat returned. It is believed that Stephans had written home for forgiveness, and lately he had made many trips to Hoboken for a letter which never came, and he became very despondent.

Wm. Tricker, who recently accepted a position at Oyster Bay, has had to return to his home at Lansdowne, Pa., on account of serious illness in his family.

The opening meeting for the Winter session of the Horticultural Society of New York will be held on Wednesday, October 10, in the Museum Building of the N. Y. Botanical Garden. In connection with the meeting, there will be an exhibition of hardy flowers, etc., which will be continued on the Thursday. Specimens of interest are solicited. The exhibition not being of a competitive character, the awards will be made on the merits of the individual exhibits. Further application can be made to the secretary, Leonard Barron, 133 East Sixteenth street, New York city.

Emil Zeller, son of the late Charles Zeller, has opened a flower store on Flatbush avenue, in the Flatbush district.

C. Coleas, florist, Fifth avenue, near Union street, Brooklyn, died suddenly in his store on Tuesday, September 25. Heart trouble was the cause of death. He was 23 years of age, and had been in the business five years. A brother of the deceased operates a flower store on Seventh avenue, Brooklyn.

Sealed bids or estimates will be received by the Park Board at the office of the Department of Parks until 3 o'clock p. m. on Thursday, October 11, 1906, Borough of Manhattan, for furnishing all the labor and materials required for the erection and completion of greenhouses to be situated in Central Park, opposite One Hundred and Fourth street and Fifth avenue.

On Wednesday last, Judge Waite handed down a decision in behalf of the Board of General Appraisers, in which it was held that several thousand dollars' worth of plants imported by the Missouri Botanical Garden of St. Louis are entitled to free entry, in view of the fact that the plants are to form part of a permanent public exhibit. The action of the Surveyor of Customs in exacting duty is reversed.

Philadelphia.

The Week's News.

The principal event this week is the consolidation of the S. S. Pennock and Charles E. Meehan businesses. The new firm started on Monday morning under the title of the S. S. Pennock-Meehan Company. The entire force under Charles E. Meehan at the Flower Market went with him to the S. S. Pennock building on Ludlow street, where both the principals in this business change were kept busy all day Monday receiving the congratulations of the trade.

The recent improvements at the S. S. Pennock building have made much more floor space available, so that a larger number of packing and grading tables have been put in to handle the extra consignments of cut flowers brought in by the consolidation. All the various departments have been strengthened; more telephones installed and the whole establishment equipped to handle more business in such a way as to insure prompt service and satisfaction to customers.

An assertion was recently made in the trade papers that 7-inch kentias were scarce around here. The Henry A. Dreer people are glad to deny this, as they have at present three houses of this size plants in fine condition.

William McKissick has the sympathy of the trade in the loss of his father, who died on Tuesday last.

We are very sorry to learn of the death of C. W. Turnley, of Haddonfield, N. J., which occurred one week ago. He never became a member of our club but always went with our delegations to the conventions.

At the Florists' Club meeting on Tuesday night S. S. Pennock was elected president, F. Hahman, vice-president, Edwin Lonsdale secretary and J. W. Colflesh treasurer. Each of these officers made appropriate remarks on being elected. Convention matters formed the topic of discussion and many suggestions were made in regard to the best place to hold the meetings and exhibitions, but no definite action was taken, as the committee will be appointed when the new officers take their places next meeting.

The directors of the Flower Market have proceeded with the liquidation of that concern and have ordered 50 per cent. of the amount received for capital stock to be paid back to stockholders; as soon as the Real Estate Trust Company's affairs are straightened out the remainder will be paid. DAVID RUST.

The latest news received from Godfrey Aschmann was to the effect that he had been enjoying the International Exposition in Italy, where on September 23, they planted a bed of coleus around the building, he says. Mr. Aschmann is remembering his customers by sending them souvenir postal cards, 1000 of which he has forwarded to date. He will sail from Rotterdam for home on the steamer New Amsterdam, arriving in New York October 15 or 16.

FIRMS WHO ARE BUILDING.

ELMWOOD, CONN.—W. S. Andrews is making extensive improvements at his greenhouses.

LISBON FALLS, Me.—H. W. Blethen is getting ready to build an addition of 150 feet to his greenhouse plant.

CLINTON, MASS.—C. P. Lodes has completed a new greenhouse. He will raise flowers only.

FINDLAY, O.—S. J. McMichael has about completed two houses, each 24 x 186 feet, for the growing of vegetable plants, and expects to be able to fill all orders for 1907.

SAGINAW, MICH.—The Wm. Roethke Floral Company proposes erecting a building on the lot recently purchased by it, corner of Michigan avenue and Adams street, in which a downtown flower store will be established. The company has just completed several new large greenhouses.

STREATOR, ILL.—George A. Whitcomb and his son, George G., are building eight greenhouses here, each 15x300 feet; also a packing shed, 20x64 feet, and a boiler room capable of accommodating three 80 horse-power boilers, two of which will be installed this Fall.

RANDOLPH, VT.—H. W. Totman has completed a greenhouse, 221 x 23 feet, for carnations. The plant is being equipped by a Kroeschell heating apparatus on the down hill system. An office and potting room are also being constructed.

DES MOINES, IA.—The Iowa Seed Company has just completed the erection of two new greenhouses, and is building five more on the big flower-growing tract at Thirtieth and Kingman boulevard. The company is also constructing an immense seed warehouse at Altoona adjoining the interurban railway for the storing of grain raised there. The new warehouse will have a storage capacity of 25,000 bushels. The company owns a large farm near Altoona and also rents some land, so that altogether about 800 acres of land are used.

All Alive.

Every advertisement appearing in The Florists' Exchange is ALIVE, hence the excellent results obtained. Our advertisers, as well as ourselves, cut out all dead wood; it is worthless, and wasteful of money.

CHANGES IN BUSINESS.

DENVER, COL.—The Braidwood Floral Company has been incorporated with a capital stock of $25,000; incorporators, John B. Braidwood, C. A. Braidwood and William Williamson, of Denver.

DENISON, TEX.—Will B. Munson has rebuilt and remodeled his greenhouses, using double thick glass in their construction.

CHAMBERSBURG, PA.—D. E. Zearfoss has added to his plant a new greenhouse containing 1100 square feet of glass.

SPRINGFIELD, MO.—The Pioneer Floral Company has been incorporated, capital $5,000. Incorporators—L. H. Murray, R. R. Ricketts, W. D. Murray and others.

GLOVERSVILLE, N. Y.—F. W. Wilson, who formerly conducted a business at Scranton, Pa., under the name of The Reliable Seed Company, has opened a flower store in this city.

PONCHATOULA, LA.—Mrs. Annie H. Parks, formerly of Chicago, has built three greenhouses, and will add more, for the cultivation of vegetables for market.

SALEM, VA.—J. J. Curran, formerly of Chicago and of the United States Cut Flower Company, Elmira, N. Y., has purchased of J. Schartzer his old established and well known greenhouses. Mr. Schartzer started here some 17 years ago on a small scale, and by skill and industry had built up what is now one of the largest and best equipped plants in the State. Owing to advancing years and failing health he felt compelled to retire from active business. Mr. Curran's intention is to grow roses, carnations, lilies and a general supply of other flowers in their season and cultivate a wholesale and retail trade. His son-in-law, J. E. Simpson, (a nephew of Robert Simpson of Clifton, N. J.) has taken a position with him as rose grower.

J. K. ALLEN

Wholesale Commission Dealer in **Cut Flowers**

106 West 28th St., NEW YORK

Open at 6 a. m. every day.
Telephone. 167 Madison Square.
Consignments Solicited.

Mention The Florists' Exchange when writing.

Wm. Stuart Allen Co.

Commission Merchants in CUT FLOWERS

ORCHIDS AT ALL SEASONS

53 WEST 28th STREET, NEW YORK

Telephone 356 Madison Square

Mention the Florists' Exchange when writing.

C. BONNET — G. H. BLAKE

BONNET & BLAKE

Wholesale Florists

106 Livingston Street, BROOKLYN, N. Y.

Telephone: 4638 Main.

Consignments solicited. Out-of-town orders carefully attended to. Give us a trial.

Mention The Florists' Exchange when writing.

CUT FLOWER EXCHANGE

Sixth Ave. and 26th St.

Coogan Building, NEW YORK

Open every Morning at Six o'clock for the Sale of Cut Flowers,

Wall Space for advertising purposes to Rent.

V. S. DORVAL, Jr., Secretary.

Mention the Florists' Exchange when writing

Joseph S. Fenrich

...Wholesale Florist...

—THE RELIABLE HOUSE—

110 West 28th Street

Telephone 324-325 Madison Square.

Mention The Florists' Exchange when writing.

FORD BROS.

Wholesale Florists

48 WEST 28th ST., NEW YORK

Telephone, 3870-3871 Madison Square

Mention The Florists' Exchange when writing.

GROWERS, ATTENTION!

Always Ready to Receive Fine Stock

GUNTHER BROTHERS

30 West 29th Street

'Phone, 551 Madison Square. NEW YORK

Violets, Roses, Carnations, Orchids

Established 1888.

Mention the Florists' Exchange when writing

ALEX. J. GUTTMAN

The Wholesale Florist of New York

43 WEST 28th STREET

Phones 1664-1665 Madison Square

Mention The Florists' Exchange when writing

A. M. HENSHAW

..Wholesale Florist..

52 West 28th Street, NEW YORK

First class Roses and Carnations a specialty.

Consignments Solicited. Tel. 5583 Madison Sq.

Mention The Florists' Exchange when writing.

HICKS & CRAWBUCK, Inc.

Wholesale Florists

And Dealers in FLORISTS' SUPPLIES

76-78 Court Street

Phone. 3660-3661 Main BROOKLYN, N. Y.

Mention The Florists' Exchange when writing.

HEADQUARTERS FOR NOVELTIES

ORCHIDS A SPECIALTY

THE HIGHEST GRADE OF **VALLEY** ALWAYS ON HAND

CARDENIAS, DAISIES, ROSES, CARNATIONS.

JAMES McMANUS, Telephone 759 Mad. Sq. 42 W. 28th St., New York.

PHILIP F. KESSLER

Wholesale Florist

55-57 W. 26th St., NEW YORK.

Telephone, 2921-5243 Madison Square.

Mention the Florists' Exchange when writing.

WILLIAM H. KUEBLER

Wholesale Commission Dealer in

CUT FLOWERS

28 Willoughby St.,

Telephone, 4591 Main. BROOKLYN, N. Y.

Mention the Florists' Exchange when writing.

JULIUS LANG

Wholesale Florist

53 WEST 30th STREET

NEW YORK

Consignments Solicited. Telephone: 280 Madison Sq.

Mention the Florists' Exchange when writing

FRANK MILLANG

Wholesale Commission Dealer in

CUT FLOWERS

55-57 West 26th Street, New York

Telephone Call: 299 Madison Square.

Mention the Florists' Exchange when writing

ALFRED H. LANGJAHR

55 WEST 28th STREET, NEW YORK

Telephone, 4626-4627 Madison Square — Established 1891

SPECIAL VALLEY AND TOP GRADE ASPARAGUS

Consignments of First Class Stock Solicited.

Horace E. Froment

SUCCESSOR TO

W. GHORMLEY WHOLESALE COMMISSION FLORIST

Receiver and Shipper of all varieties of Cut Flowers

Telephones, 2200 and 2201 Madison Square. 157 West 28th St., NEW YORK

Wholesale Prices of Cut Flowers, New York, Oct. 4, 1906

Prices quoted are by the hundred unless otherwise noted

Roses — A. Beauty, fancy—special	20.00	to	30.00
" extra	10.00	to	15.00
" No. 1	8.00	to	10.00
" No. 2	4.00	to	6.00
" No. 3	3.00	to	4.00
Bride, Maid, fancy—spe'l	6.00	to	8.00
" extra	4.00	to	5.00
" No. 1	3.00	to	4.00
" No. 2	1.50	to	2.00
Golden Gate	......	to	......
......	......	to	......
Mme. Abel Chatenay	......	to	......
Adiantum	.50	to	.75
Croweanum	.50	to	1.00
Asparagus	25.00	to	50.00
" Plumosus, bunches	8.00	to	15.00
" Sprengeri, bunches	8.00	to	15.00
......	......	to	......
Cattleyas	40.00	to	50.00
Daisies	......	to	......
......	......	to	......
......	......	to	......

Carnations — Inf'r grades, all colors	1.00	to	1.50
Standard Varieties — White	1.50	to	2.50
Standard Varieties — Pink	1.50	to	2.50
Standard Varieties — Red	1.50	to	2.50
Standard Varieties — Yel. & Var.	1.50	to	2.50
*Fancy— (*The highest grades of standard var.) — White	3.00	to	4.00
*Fancy — Pink	3.00	to	4.00
*Fancy — Red	3.00	to	4.00
*Fancy — Yel. & Var.	3.00	to	4.00
Novelties	......	to	......
Dahlias	2.00	to	3.00
Lilies	10.00	to	12.00
Lily of the Valley	3.00	to	4.00
Mignonette	......	to	......
Smilax	8.00	to	10.00
......	......	to	......
......	......	to	......
......	......	to	......
......	......	to	......
......	......	to	......

WALTER F. SHERIDAN

Wholesale Florist

Telephone, 1902 Madison Square — 39 WEST 28TH ST., NEW YORK

ALL VARIETIES OF CUT FLOWERS IN SEASON

TOP GRADE FOR SHIPPING

American Beauty, Bridesmaid, Bride, Liberty, Meteor, Lily of the Valley, Carnations

Telephone, 1998 Madison Square — JOHN I. RAYNOR, 49 West 28th St., NEW YORK

Edw. C. Horan

55 West 28th St., NEW YORK

TELEPHONE, 1462-1463 MADISON SQUARE

CUT FLOWERS AT WHOLESALE

Mention The Florists' Exchange when writing.

JOHN YOUNG

Wholesale Florist

51 W. 28th St., NEW YORK

Telephone: 4463-4464 MADISON SQUARE

Mention the Florists' Exchange when writing.

A. MOLTZ

Wholesale Florist

55-57 West 26th St., NEW YORK

1st Floor. Telephone, 2921-5243 Madison Sq.

Mention The Florists' Exchange when writing.

MOORE, HENTZ & NASH
WHOLESALE
GROWER — AGENT
COMMISSION FLORISTS
55 West 26th St., New York

Telephone Call, 756 Madison Square

Mention The Florists' Exchange when writing.

GEORGE SALTFORD

Wholesale Florist

CONSIGNMENTS SOLICITED

46 West 29th Street, New York

Telephone: 3393 Madison Square

Mention The Florists' Exchange when writing.

J. Seligman — Joseph J. Levy

JOHN SELIGMAN & COMPANY

Wholesale Florists

56 West 26th Street,

Tel. 4878 Madison — New York

Opposite New York Cut Flower Company

Mention The Florists' Exchange when writing.

B. S. SLINN, JR.

Wholesale Florist

55 and 57 West 26th Street, NEW YORK

SPECIALTIES—Violets, Carnations and Roses

Shipping orders receive prompt attention. Consignments Solicited.

Telephone: 3864 Madison Square

Mention the Florists' Exchange when writing.

WM. STARKE

Wholesale Florist and Plantsman

Tel. No. 4582 Madison Sq. — 52 W. 29th St.

Between Broadway and 6th Ave., New York

Shipments of Plants made to any part of the country. A trial order solicited.

SATISFACTION GUARANTEED.

Mention The Florists' Exchange when writing.

Frank H. Traendly — Charles Schenck

TRAENDLY & SCHENCK

Wholesale Florists

44 WEST 28th STREET, NEW YORK

and CUT FLOWER EXCHANGE

Telephones: 798 and 799 MADISON SQUARE

Consignments Solicited

Mention the Florists' Exchange when writing.

THOMAS YOUNG

Wholesale Florist

43 West 28th Street, NEW YORK

Telephone, 4850 Madison Square

Consignments of Choice Flowers solicited

Mention The Florists' Exchange when writing.

Wholesale Prices of Cut Flowers—Per 100

Boston Oct. 1, 1906	Buffalo Oct. 1, 1906	Detroit Sept. 11, 1906	Cincinnati Oct. 1, 1906	Baltimore Oct. 1, 1906	NAMES AND VARIETIES	Milwaukee Sept. 11, 1906	Phil'delphia Sept. 11, 1906	Pittsburg Oct. 1, 1906	St. Louis Oct. 1, 1906
25.00 to 50.00	20.00 to 25.00	10.00 to 35.00	30.00 to 40.00	to	ROSES A. BEAUTY, fancy—special	to 25.00	15.00 to 20.00	20.00 to 25.00	25.00 to 30.00
10.00 to 25.00	15.00 to 20.00	to	20.00 to 30.00	20.00 to 25.00	" extra	16.00 to 18.00	10.00 to 15.00	15.00 to 18.00	15.00 to 20.00
4.00 to 10.00	10.00 to 15.00	to	10.00 to 15.00	12.50 to 15.00	" No. 1	10.00 to 12.50	5.00 to 7.00	8.00 to 12.00	6.00 to 10.00
1.00 to 4.00	8.00 to 10.00	to	4.00 to 6.00	5.00 to 10.00	" Culls and ordinary	4.00 to 6.00	1.00 to 4.00	to	4.00 to 8.00
to	6.00 to 8.00	3.00 to 6.00	4.00 to 5.00	to	BRIDE, 'MAID, fancy-special	to 6.00	to	to 6.00	4.00 to 5.00
4.00 to 6.00	5.00 to 6.00	to	to 3.00	4.00 to 5.00	" extra	to 5.00	6.00 to 8.00	to 4.00	2.00 to 3.00
1.00 to 4.00	4.00 to 5.00	to	to 2.00	3.00 to 4.00	" No. 1	to 4.00	4.00 to 5.00	to 3.00	to
.50 to 1.00	3.00 to 4.00	to	to 1.00	2.00 to 3.00	" No. 2	to 2.00	2.00 to 3.00	to 2.00	to
to	3.00 to 6.00	4.00 to 8.00	to 8.00	2.00 to 5.00	GOLDEN GATE	4.00 to 6.00	4.00 to 8.00	to	2.00 to 5.00
1.00 to 8.00	3.00 to 7.00	to	3.00 to 4.00	3.00 to 5.00	K. A. VICTORIA	4.00 to 8.00	4.00 to 6.00	4.00 to 10.00	2.00 to 8.00
1.00 to 8.00	3.00 to 8.00	to	to	3.00 to 5.00	LIBERTY	4.00 to 6.00	3.00 to 6.00	to	to
to	3.00 to 6.00	4.00 to 10.00	to	2.00 to 4.00	METEOR	to	to	to	to
to	2.00 to 5.00	4.00 to 10.00	to	2.00 to 4.00	PERLE	4.00 to 6.00	to	4.00 to 6.00	2.00 to 5.00
to	to	to 50.00	to	to	ORCHIDS—Cattleyas	to	to 50.00	to	to
to	1.00 to 1.25	to	to .50	to .75	CARNATIONS Inferior grades, all colors	to 1.00	.75 to 1.00	to	to 1.00
to	1.25 to 1.50	to 1.00	1.00 to 1.50	1.00 to 1.50	Standard Varieties White	to 1.00	.75 to 1.00	to 1.50	to 1.00
to	1.25 to 1.5	to	1.00 to 1.50	1.00 to 1.50	Pink	to 1.00	.75 to 1.00	to 1.50	to 1.00
to	1.25 to 1.50	to	1.00 to 1.50	1.00 to 1.50	Red	to 1.00	.75 to 1.00	to 1.50	to 1.00
to	to	to 3.00	to	1.00 to 1.50	Yellow and var.	to 1.00	.75 to 1.00	to 1.50	to 1.00
1.00 to 2.00	2.00 to 2.50	to	to	to	Fancy Varieties White	1.50 to 2.00	2.00 to 2.50	to 2.00	1.50 to 2.00
1.00 to 2.00	2.00 to 2.50	to	to	to	Pink	1.50 to 2.00	2.00 to 2.50	2.00 to 3.00	1.50 to 2.00
1.00 to 2.00	2.00 to 2.50	to	to	to	Red	1.50 to 2.00	2.00 to 2.50	to 2.00	1.50 to 2.00
1.00 to 2.00	2.00 to 2.50	to 1.50	to	to	Yellow and var	1.50 to 2.00	2.00 to 2.50	to 2.00	1.50 to 2.00
to 2.50	to	to	to	to	Novelties	to	to	to	to
.75 to 1.00	.50 to 1.00	to 2.00	to 1.00	to 1.00	ADIANTUM	to 1.00	to 1.00	.75 to 1.50	to 1.00
to 50.00	15.00 to 20.00	25.00 to 60.00	to 50.00	25.00 to 50.00	ASPARAGUS, Plum. and Ten.	20.00 to 30.00	25.00 to 35.00	25.00 to 35.00	25.00 to 50.00
to	15.00 to 20.00	20.00 to 30.00	to 35.00	25.00 to 50.00	" Sprengeri, bunches	20.00 to 30.00	25.00 to 35.00	20.00 to 30.00	25.00 to 75.00
.75 to 1.00	to	to	.50 to 1.00	to	ASTERS	.50 to 1.00	to	.50 to 2.00	1.00 to 3.00
to	8.00 to 10.00	to 10.00	to 10.00	6.00 to 8.00	CALLAS	to	to	to	to
to	to	to	10.00 to 15.00	5.00 to 10.00	CHRYSANTHEMUMS, ordinary	to	to	4.00 to 6.00	to
to	1.50 to 2.50	.75 to 1.50	to	to	DAISIES	to .40	3.00 to 4.00	to	to
to	to	to	to	to	GALAX LEAVES	to	to	to	to
3.00 to 4.00	to	to	to 4.00	to 3.00	GLADIOLUS	to	to	to	to
to	to	to	to	10.00 to 12.50	LILIES, Harrisii	to 12.50	to	to	to
6.00 to 10.00	12.50 to 15.00	to	to 16.00	to	" Longiflorum	to 12.50	to	to	to
2.00 to 5.00	3.00 to 4.00	3.00 to 4.00	to 4.00	to	LILY OF THE VALLEY	to	1.00 to 2.00	2.00 to 4.00	3.00 to 4.00
to	to	to	to	to	MIGNONETTE, ordinary	to	to	to	to
to	to	to	to	to	" fancy	to	to	to	to
to	to	4.00 to 8.00	to	to	PEONIES	to	to	to	to
to 12.50	12.00 to 15.00	12.50 to 15.00	to 15.00	to	SMILAX	to 15.00	to	12.50 to 15.00	to 12.50
to .50	to	to	to	.35 to .50	VIOLETS, ordinary	to	to	to	to
to	.15 to .25	to	to	to	" fancy	to	to	to	to
to	to	to	to	to	NARCISSUS	to	to	to	to
to	to	.50 to .75	to	to	SWEET PEAS	.25 to .50	to .50	to	to

Washington, D. C.

A Dahlia Exhibition.

The Dahlia show, which was held at the rooms of the Florists' Club on October 2, was a complete success, over one hundred varieties being on exhibition. W. R. Gray of Oakton, Fairfax County, Va., one of the exhibitors, staged some fine blooms of Mrs. Roosevelt, large pink, and Cuban Giant, large red; Lemon Giant, yellow with thirty other varieties in bunches of from ten to twenty-five blooms in each vase. Richard Vincent, Jr. & Son, White Marsh, Md., had on exhibition some extra fine blooms of white Century, Frank Smith, Souvenir de Gustave Douzan, large scarlet, and Oban, Bridesmaid pink. Their collection consisted of one hundred varieties, each one in a separate vase.

Notes.

George W. Oliver has returned from his Summer vacation, part of which he spent at Harper's Ferry, W. Va.

H. Holtzapfel of Hagerstown, Md., and C. W. Ward, Queens, N. Y., were visitors at the Capitol lately.

Wm. Furnage, rose grower at the Propagating gardens, met with a painful accident on Monday, October 1. He slipped from some staging in one of the houses, breaking three ribs.

J. A. G.

WOONSOCKET, R. I.—H. E. Redfern, florist, was married on September 26 to Miss Theo Byrl Crosby, at the home of the bride's parents.

CHARLES CITY, IA.—The Sherman Nursery Company has installed two new boilers, one 75, the other 8 horse power.

The Best.

Your paper is the best there is.

Ilion, N. Y. THEO. H. SCHESCH

Wholesale Prices of Cut Flowers, Chicago, Oct. 2, 1906

Prices quoted are by the hundred unless otherwise noted

ROSES — American Beauty		
36-inch stems.........per doz.	3.00 to	4.00
30-inch stems .... "	2.50 to	3.00
24-inch stems.......... "	2.00 to	2.50
20-inch stems.......... "	1.00 to	2.00
18-inch stems.......... "	.... to	1.50
12-inch stems.......... "	.... to	1.00
8-inch stems and shorts "	.50 to	.75
Bride Maid, fancy special......	5.00 to	6.00
" extra............	4.00 to	5.00
" No. 1............	2.00 to	3.00
" No. 2............	.50 to	1.00
Golden Gate..................	2.00 to	6.00
Carnot.......................	3.00 to	6.00
Uncle John...................	2.00 to	6.00
Liberty......................	2.00 to	6.00
Richmond.....................	2.00 to	8.00
Kaiserina....................	2.00 to	8.00
Killarney....................	3.00 to	6.00
Perle........................	2.00 to	6.00
Chatenay.....................	2.00 to	6.00
Orchids—Cattleyas..........	50.00 to	75.00
SMILAX.......................	8.00 to	12.00
LILY OF THE VALLEY...........	2.00 to	4.00
DAHLIAS......................	2.00 to	3.00
VIOLETS......................	.50 to	1.00

CARNATIONS			
Inferior grades all colors		.25 to	.50
STANDARD VARIETIES	White..........	.75 to	1.00
	Pink..........	.75 to	1.00
	Red..........	.75 to	1.00
	Yellow & var....	.75 to	1.00
*FANCY (The highest grades of Sta'd var)	White..........	2.00 to	3.00
	Pink..........	2.00 to	3.00
	Red..........	2.00 to	3.00
	Yellow & var....	2.00 to	3.00
NOVELTIES..................		.... to	....
ADIANTUM...................		.50 to	1.00
ASPARAGUS, Plum. & Ten......		.35 to	.50
" Sprengeri, bunches.		.35 to	.50
GLADIOLUS..................		2.00 to	6.00
LILIES, Longiflorum........		8.00 to	12.00
Harisii....................		8.00 to	12.00
....		.... to	....
....		.... to	....
....		.... to	....
....		.... to	....
....		.... to	....
HARDY FERNS per 1000.......		1.00 to	1.50
GALAX "		1.00 to	1.25
ASTERS.....................		.50 to	2.00
CHRYSANTHEMUMS.............		25.00 to	35.00

St. Louis.

News Notes.

Charles Ford, of A. Hermann, New York, left here Friday night for Chicago well pleased with the trade he got.

J. F. Ammann, of Edwardsville, and A. S. Halsted, of Belleville, were visitors last week. Mr. Ammann was booming the Springfield Fair while Doctor Halsted was talking Syracuse geranium to the boys at the commission houses.

F. W. Bruening will this coming Spring build a range of glass at his place across the river, near Columbia, Ill. Mr. Bruening grew all his Summer stock this year at his place.

C. Young & Son Company will this year again decorate the hall for the ball of the Veiled Prophets, which takes place in the Merchant's Exchange. This is a large job, generally taking two or three days to complete.

The club meeting, which occurs next Thursday afternoon, will be a very interesting one, and should attract a large attendance. President Irish and Secretary Beneke are putting forth every effort to make things interesting for the members. Chairman Smith of the trustees has something up his sleeve for the young folk, which he will spring at this meeting; so if you come you will spend a pleasant afternoon.

The annual horse show begins October 8, and the big Coliseum in Exposition Building is being handsomely decorated for the event by the Shuermann Floral Company.

A. G. Bentzen has fine cyclamen; A. Jablonsky, Begonia Gloire de Lorraine; George Windler and Henry Fetter, pot chrysanthemums. Beyer Brothers and C. C. Sanders, are also in line with fine blooming plants for the holiday season.

Fred Foster, of the Foster Floral Company, has entered his string of horses for prizes at the horse show next week.

Vincent Gorly, of Grim & Gorly, reports heavy orders for funeral work.

George Waldbart is showing finely grown out-door stock in his big show windows, and his show house is packed with nice palms and ferns and other decorative plants.

ST. PATRICK.

CANTON, O.—The local newspapers speak highly of the display made by the Brown Floral Company at the county fair here. Conspicuous in the exhibit was a floral piece designated "heaven's portals."

TOLEDO, O.—Frank J. Schoen, formerly with Murdoch of Pittsburg, Pa., is manager of the Schoen Floral Company's store, recently opened here.

St. Paul.

News Notes.

L. L. May & Company's roses are looking splendid; heavy cuts are made daily. The plants are almost perfect. Their rose houses are possibly the best in this section. Killarney are grown extensively for pink and the demand for it is indeed heavy. Richmond are also grown in large numbers. Much credit is due to L. Anderson, the foreman, for the appearance and good results already realized from their new stock.

E. F. Lemke has made a great many improvements this Summer; his Snelling avenue place is now his principal source of supply. Mr. Lemke says trade is very fair and all that can be expected at this time of the season.

C. F. Vogt has had considerable funeral work the past week, but reports the demand for flowers for social occasions very light.

F. W. Ramaley, of the Ramaley Floral Company will spend the Winter in California.

The demand for flowers for Fall weddings has been very light; there have only been one or two weddings during the past month, at which any large amount of stock was used. Funeral work for the victims of the railroad wreck which occurred on the M. & St. L. R. R. Monday was heavy, and all of the florists had something to do, the unfortunate victims being all well known here.

L. L. May & Company have a force of 150 men busy with their Fall planting of nursery stock, which is unusually heavy this season. Mayfield, where their nurseries are located, is indeed a busy place these days; the recent frost has put things in fine shape. Their stock of trees and hardy shrubs never looked better. PAUL.

Boston.

News of the Week.

At the next regular meeting of the Gardeners and Florists' Club, which will be held on the evening of the 16th inst., J. B. Velie of the Lord & Burnham Company will read a paper on "Greenhouse Construction." As this is a very pertinent subject there is every assurance of a large attendance for the October meeting, at which by the way the president will appoint a nominating committee for the selection of officers for the coming year.

A. S. Quint & Company have moved from their old location at 99 Warren street to a larger and more up-to-date store at 111 Warren street in the new Broxmouth building.

Henry M. Robinson & Company have secured the store just vacated by Welch Brothers at 15 Province street and 9 Chapman place. The increasing business of this firm necessitated their obtaining more floor space and now they will have three stores all near together—8, 11 and 15 Province street.

J. Newman & Sons have moved into a fine new store at 24 Tremont street in the Kimball building, just across the street from their old location.

Thomas Pegler has made his appearance in the market with double violets.

The stall holders in the Music Hall market took their new locations in the floor above that which they have occupied the past year.

The executive committee of the proposed Dahlia Society will hold a meeting on Saturday next at 2 p. m. at the office of W. W. Rawson & Company for the purpose of arranging plans of a meeting for the regular formation of the society.

Maurice Fuld has returned from a week spent in Pennsylvania and New York.

A. M. Davenport of Watertown has secured a stall in the Park street market which he will use for his plant trade, he being one of the plantsmen of this neighborhood, making a specialty of such as cyclamen and primroses.

The Houghton Horticultural Society of Lynn held its annual exhibition on Wednesday and Thursday of last week. Children's garden exhibits formed one of the principal features this year. They wound up the exhibition this year with a banquet on Thursday evening at which there was an attendance of some four or five hundred.

Welch Brothers are handling a fine lot of Adiantum Croweanum, for which they are the Boston agents.

J. W. DUNCAN.

Columbus, O.

Trade Conditions.

Trade is improving every week, and the general opinion is that the coming season will be one of the best in years. Stock of all kinds is getting much better in quality, which helps a great deal. Funeral work is of very large proportions.

Club News.

Our club will meet Tuesday evening, when the question of larger and more convenient quarters will be discussed. The question of giving Holland bulbs as prizes for the childrens' gardens will also be in order. A goodly attendance is expected.

The Ohio State Fair.

The State exhibition recently held here was a great success. The horticultural department was especially fine. The Livingston Seed Company had, as usual, the largest and best exhibit. The gross receipts were $61,000 and the net profits $12,000.

News Notes.

James McKellar has been confined to his home for a week, and it was feared a fever would result; he is more comfortable at this writing. Mr. McKellar is with Graff Brothers.

The Bell Pottery Company is in the hands of a receiver at its own request. It is reported the firm will be solvent when matters are straightened out. When the plant is running at its fullest capacity, some fifty men are employed.

The Livingston Seed Company opened the chrysanthemum season here last week, by offering some very fine Monrovia at $8 a dozen.

Gustave Drobisch's youngest daughter, Hulda, was married on October 3 to Walter Jones. Mr. Drobisch is the oldest established florist in Columbus.

There has been an unusual demand for fancy evergreens lately; it is very pleasing to the trade that a permanent market for these and fine shrubbery is developing here. F. W.

FLINT, MASS.—Mr. and Mrs. John Lambert, the former the well-known florist of 72 Jepson street, celebrated their fifteenth wedding anniversary last Saturday evening. About 75 of their friends were present and a very enjoyable evening was passed. A bountiful supper was served. Mr. and Mrs. Lambert received many presents, including silverware, cut glass, china, table linen and many other useful as well as handsome gifts, for which they extended their thanks to their friends and donors.

WEST GROVE, PA.—Louis Wintzer, florist, in the employ of the Conard & Jones Company, was suddenly taken ill a few days ago with symptoms of appendicitis and was hurried to the Pennsylvania Hospital, Philadelphia, where an operation disclosed the fact that he was suffering from rupture of the bowels. He is now recovering, the prompt surgical work no doubt saving his life.

Newport, R. I.

News and Trade Notes.

Newport is at its best now so far as weather and other conditions are concerned, and many Summer residents think likewise and will prolong their stay indefinitely, but there are many others who possess country residences in other parts, who are leaving Newport to spend the Autumn months as they have done in past years. Consequently things are a little easier in business circles.

The season for large entertainments has just closed, and from now on florists will find plenty of time to attend to all orders coming in for cut flowers and for the decorations for numerous small, but select dinner parties that are customarily given during the few quiet weeks succeeding the exciting times of more strenuous entertaining.

One large estate and several smaller ones have changed hands, and it is the intention of the purchaser of "Friedheim," Mr. Pembroke Jones, to thoroughly remodel the grounds, which by reason of their extent will give scope to whoever may be entrusted with the work to show good results.

There are a few lawns in Newport almost perfect, both as regards their unvarying condition and their absolute freedom from weeds. It is a pleasure to look at those lawns, and I suppose were it not for the expense of keeping them in that condition there would be many more like them. The expense is considerable and as far as freeing the grass from weeds is concerned, it consists in the cost of an annual weeding which is absolutely necessary to secure a lawn clear of weeds. On those places where such perfect lawns are seen, the most critical time was considered to be the Summer after renovation when every weed was taken out.

Fully as important as a good lawn and considered by some even more so for the appearance of a place are fine trees properly taken care of. There are many places in Newport and the number is perhaps increasing where every facility is given to those in charge to look after the trees in a way that will in a few years result in many beautiful places made such by fine specimen trees. There are other places, however, where little attention is given the trees, with the result that if they have grown better than the care given them warranted they are overcrowded and shapeless.

The demand for hothouse fruit has eased considerably, a condition in no way alarming to local growers because most of them are sold out. James McLeish, the largest commercial grower of grapes and nectarines, reports a better market than that of last year. In August of this year he sold eighteen hundred pounds of grapes. Nectarines in supply were at no time equal to the demand. Ferretti, the largest retailer in Newport, had on several occasions to send out of town for fruit, whereas in other years he frequently shipped fruit to other Summer places.

For several years white grapes (Muscat of Alexandria) were in greater demand than black, but this year there was no marked tendency in the favor of white.

For the first time in a number of years the foliage of outdoor grown melons was unaffected by blight, with the result that the fruit finished well. Mr. McLeish sold his crop at $6 per dozen, which is considered a good price even for selected fruit.

Outdoor grown peaches were almost a total failure with most growers; the weather was responsible for this.

John S. Cox was a visitor in Newport last week. Mr. Cox now represents F. R. Pierson Company of Tarrytown, N. Y., and says the establishment is now better stocked than ever before. Extensive improvements recently made and others now under way make it in equipment and capacity far ahead of what it was. Mr. Cox spoke of the two mammoth carnation houses just about completed; these houses will turn out a large number of plants and flowers without doubt.

V. A. Vanicek of the Rhode Island Nurseries is now busily engaged preparing his recently purchased farm for the reception of nursery stock.

Island potatoes have always been considered the best in the market and commanded a better price than the product of other localities, but this year the weather during the several critical periods of their growth was so unfavorable that not only is the crop short by at least a half, but the quality is much inferior to that of former years. For these reasons it is consoling to know that in Maine potatoes have yielded abnormally.

E. R. Thomas, Bellevue avenue, contemplates the erection of a large palm house and is considering the advisability of adding another plant house.

Oscar Schultz is erecting a large store house, and is also moving the greenhouses that stood on the Wells estate to his own place.

Dahlias are still alive in Newport as evidenced by the fact that two men have recently announced their intention of growing them commercially. One of these parties has gone so far as to issue an elaborate catalogue.

Carl Jurgens is receiving large consignments of bulbs from Europe.

Henry Hass reports having had a very good season, August being especially a good month with him. All the other dealers permanently located here likewise express their satisfaction with the season as a whole, although they say they have experienced better in their time. It was always thus, and it always will be.

At the sale of the Caswell greenhouses a week ago several growers were in attendance, but although some of the houses offered and sold were in fair condition only one grower was a purchaser. Carl Jurgens bought one house to use the glass in the construction of a large house under way on his place. Oscar Schultz purchased some boilers and ventilating apparatus. Everything sold at very reasonable figures. It may be of interest to some branches of the trade to know that some bought houses and no boilers, consequently they will need these later. Joseph Peckham, Middletown, bought one house and John Howland, Jamestown, another. D. M.

San Francisco.

News Notes.

The east side of the bay fl informed me this week that more funeral work has come their way the middle of September; that th cation people are returning to homes and patronizing flower st that many hundreds of pretty h have been built in Oakland this mer and are being moved int former residents of San Francisc are proving a good factor in th proving business of flower store chants; that this side of the which they claim is the choice f production section San Francisc rists have always looked to for is just now, owing to the hot we spell prevailing and in vogue for eral weeks, short of quality flo What surprised me most of all the information vouchsafed tha of San Francisco's well known fl made propositions last week to two of Oakland's prominent f stands.

E. Gill and his eldest son, have gone on a business trip to gon, Washington, and British C bia. When the parent started c the nursery business in Oakland, forty years ago, a boy could sta either end or side of the groun throw a stone across it, but no well-tilled plantation at Ber Cal., widely known throughou Pacific Coast as "Gill's Nursery," ers hundreds of acres, and its cious cultivation has made Mr one of the very wealthy of Califo residents. He is also propriet "Gill's Floral Depot" in Oaklan of the popular cut flower, see bulb stores of the east side of th

John Young, who shortly afte Francisco's disaster, sold his D Way Nurseries in Berkeley, where he made an envious nam himself as a grower of Am Beauty roses of magnificent p tions, returned this week from a months' camping out recreation foot of Mount Shasta.

I found in Oakland H. H. Lill well known to San Francisco gr and florists. He left the metr months before the earthquake, abandoned his flower-paper pu tion business. He is now a pro socialistic speaker and worker f cause in Oakland, though rank the Oakland directory as a lan gardener.

Fifty thousand dollars made flower business is being investe new building under constructi Greater San Francisco. J. W. S han, proprietor for many ye Shanahan's Floral Depot" on street, is the gentleman who is ing on a 100x160 foot lot on H street, between Eighth and Nin

Incorporation papers were file urday for the Sievers Floral Com with a capital stock of $25,000. incorporators are Frederick J. J. George Ils and John R. S son of John H. Sievers, the nu man.

AL

ROCHESTER, N. Y.—A. H. S formerly of Madison, N. J., i with the firm of J. B. Keller's this city.

IN THE U-BAR CONSTRUCTION

we encase the wooden sash bar with a galvanized steel U shaped bar: the combined member being no larger than the smallest sash bar used in other constructions.

U-Bar Greenhouses Are the Best Greenhouses Built

because they eliminate all heavy iron rafters, many lateral supports, place the bars farther apart, while still giving a house of wonderful rigidity and durability

Pierson U-Bar Co.

Designers and Builders
U-Bar Greenhouses
Metropolitan Building

4th Ave. & 23d St., New York

Mention The Florists' Exchange when writing.

KROESCHELL BROS. CO.

IMPROVED

Greenhouse Boiler

33 ERIE STREET, CHICAGO

Boilers made of the best of material, shell firebox sheets and heads of steel, water space all around front, sides and back). Write for information.

Mention The Florists' Exchange when writing.

WEATHERED COMPANY.

Builders of Iron and Cypress Greenhouses, Greenhouse Heating and Ventilating Apparatus.

P. O. Address, Box 789,
New York City.

Mention The Florists' Exchange when writing.

PLANT CULTURE

PRICE, $1.00.

The best book for the plant grower.

A. T. DE LA MARE PTG. & PUB. CO. LTD.

THE TEST OF PRODUCTS.

Here is a test that every florist and grower can make for himself as the construction of your house vitally affects the stock you grow. If your houses are not built right you cannot expect to turn out perfect plants.

Does your house produce the amount of stock and the kind of stock it should? Let us furnish you the material for your next house and then make a test—we only ask for a trial order.

Our catalogue will tell you more.

Next Week, "The Test of Construction."

John C. Moninger Co., Chicago

115 E. BLACKHAWK STREET

Mention The Florists' Exchange when writing.

GREENHOUSE LUMBER

BUILD WELL

There is a pleasant sense of satisfaction in knowing that when your order for Cypress is placed with us you will receive material upon which you can absolutely rely, and that shipment will be promptly made.

ESTIMATES AND PLANS

Furnished without charge. Let us hear from you if you contemplate building.

HOT BED SASH

CEDAR POSTS, IRON FITTINGS, ETC., ETC.

LOCKLAND LUMBER Co. LOCKLAND, O.

Mention The Florists' Exchange when writing.

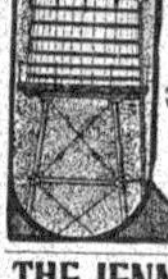

"Always Safe and Reliable. Ask Your Friends."

No one is so far away that a

Caldwell Tank and Tower

cannot be shipped him advantageously. They combine lightness with strength, enabling them to be shipped compactly and at the minimum freight rate.

It don't take an expert mechanic to put up the Caldwell tower as in other styles. They are so simple an ordinary workman can easily and quickly erect them from our detailed plans sent with each outfit.

The Caldwell outfit is the personification of strength and stability, lightness and gracefulness. Wherever you are it will pay you to get the Caldwell as it is always a permanent fixture. Ask for our illustrated catalogue and book of fac-simile letters.

W. E. CALDWELL CO., Louisville, Ky.

Tanks {Steel-Wood / Galvanized} Towers

Wind Mills—Pumps—Gas Engines

THE JENNINGS IMPROVED IRON GUTTER

PATENT IRON BENCH FITTINGS AND ROOF SUPPORTS. VENTILATING APPARATUS. IMPROVED VAPORIZING PANS for Tobacco Extracts, Etc.

SEND FOR CIRCULARS

DILLER, CASKEY & CO.

Successors to JENNINGS BROS

S. W. CORNER SIXTH AND BERK STS., PHILADELPHIA, PA.

Mention The Florists' Exchange when writing.

GEO. M. GARLAND

Iron Gutters and Posts

Patented December 27th, 1898.

Send for Catalogue.

Garland's Gutters will keep snow and ice off your glass and prevent breakage.

DESPLAINES, ILL.

A sample of this gutter is on exhibition at Chicago Flower Growers' Market.

WHAT YOU LOSE

Because of poor heating this winter will be felt for several seasons. The best Boilers, the best pipe, and the most careful attention to installation will pay in the end.

"Perfect" Water Boiler Great Fire and Water Surfaces

"PIERCE" Boilers are made in the most modern of plants, perfected by 30 years of experience. Every Boiler carefully tested and conservatively rated. They do what they are said to do.

Greenhouse Pipe and Fittings also carried in stock.

Blank form, catalogs and prices on request.

PIERCE, BUTLER & PIERCE MFG. CO.

Dept. 11. SYRACUSE, N. Y.

Pierce Mark Boston, New York, Philadelphia.

Mention The Florists' Exchange when writing.

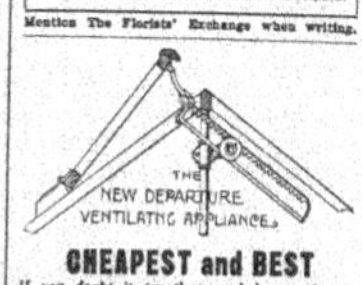

CHEAPEST and BEST

If you doubt it try them and be convinced.
Send for descriptive Price Circular.

J. D. Carmody, Evansville, Ind.

Mention The Florists' Exchange when writing.

The STANDARD VENTILATING MACHINERY

The original machine with self oiling cups: the most powerful, least complicated, very compact, with ease of operation.

The New Duplex Gutter over six miles in use and highly recommended; the only **drip proof** gutter in the market.

The Standard Return Steam Trap has no equal for simplicity or its workings. Catalogue free.

E. HIPPARD, Youngstown, O.

Mention The Florists' Exchange when writing.

Evans Improved Challenge

Roller bearing, self-oiling device automatic stop, solid link chain make the IMPROVED CHALLENGE the most perfect apparatus in the market.

Write for catalogue and prices before placing your orders elsewhere.

QUAKER CITY MACHINE CO.
RICHMOND, IND.

Mention The Florists' Exchange when writing.

Standard Pumping Engines

are for PUMPING WATER for the use of Florists and Gardeners. They will help you improve your facilities for WATERING. Wouldn't you like to know how?

The Standard Pump & Engine Co.
CLEVELAND, O.

Mention The Florists' Exchange when writing.

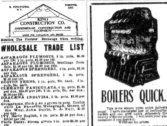

THE FLORISTS' EXCHANGE

We are a straight shoot and aim to grow into a vigorous plant

A WEEKLY MEDIUM OF INTERCHANGE FOR FLORISTS, NURSERYMEN, SEEDSMEN AND THE TRADE IN GENERAL

ol. XXII. No. 15 — NEW YORK AND CHICAGO, OCTOBER 13, 1906 — One Dollar Per Year

CONTENTS AND INDEX TO ADVERTISERS, PAGE 435

Seed Trade Report.

AMERICAN SEED TRADE ASSOCIATION

Henry W. Wood, Richmond, Va., president; C. S. Burge, Toledo, O., first vice-president; G. B. McVay, Birmingham, Ala., second vice-president; C. E. Kendel, Cleveland, O., secretary and treasurer; J. H. Ford, Ravenna, O., assistant secretary.

A large crop of field beans has been harvested in Michigan, dealers estimating the yield as high as 5,000,000 bushels. However, there is always a disposition on the part of buyers to be somewhat generous in estimating crop yields. Prices for bulk pea beans at Michigan shipping stations have ranged around $1.20 to $1.25 per bushel.—Farm and Home.

HARRISVILLE, MICH.—E. W. Conklin & Son's seed house is now in active operation.

CHARLEVOIX, MICH. — The Ferry Seed Company began "picking" peas in the warehouse Monday, October 1, and the force of pickers will be busy from now until some time in March. While the crop of peas is short, there will be as much work for the pickers, as the same quantity of peas will be picked over in the warehouse here as if the yield had been larger.

CHAUMONT, N. Y. — Rogers Brothers write as follows: October 6: "We have begun to receive in store our crop of peas, but deliveries are quite disappointing, not coming up to our earlier estimates, and if the balance of crops yet to be delivered do not pan out better than those that have already been received, we shall be short on all varieties—both early and late. We have had ideal harvest weather for beans, but as yet we have not begun to receive any in store."

CHICAGO.—The new onion warehouse of Knud Gundestrup & Company presents a busy and interesting sight just at present. It is located near their store on the line of the railroad with a side track, offering every facility for the transaction of their large and constantly growing business. Just at present there are 12,000 bushels of onion sets of the different sorts therein undergoing the process of drying and winnowing, this quantity representing one-half of the crop the concern will handle this year. Another season a large addition to the warehouse facilities is contemplated.

It is stated on good authority that Sears, Roebuck & Company, the large mail order house of Chicago, are about to abandon the department devoted to seeds and bulbs, the reason given being that even with the 40 acres of floor space in their immense new structure they are so crowded in many of the older and more thoroughly established departments that the newer one must be deserted.

PUMPKIN SEED — ASPARAGUS SEED—DRUGS—In the protests of J. L. Hopkins & Co. against the assessment of duty by the Collector of Customs at the port of New York, before Board 3, General Appraisers, September 26, 1906, the following opinion was rendered by Waite, General Appraiser: "After reading the testimony of the single witness for the importers in this case, the board finds itself unable to rule that pumpkin seed and asparagus seed are 'aromatic seeds' or 'seeds of morbid growth,' or that they have a medicinal use of sufficient magnitude to warrant their classification as 'drugs' within the meaning of paragraph 548 of the tariff act of 1897. Some stress is laid upon the fact that the United States Dispensatory refers to asparagus as having reputed medicinal qualities and to pumpkin seed as furnishing a remedy for tapeworm, but this can not be the test. Many table vegetables, or the plants or seeds producing them, contain medicinal principles and are mentioned in the Dispensatory, such as lettuce (18 ed., p. 772), celery (p. 1569), pbtatoes (p. 487), tomatoes (p. 488), beans (p. 1764). It would be opposed to common knowledge and sound construction to class such articles as drugs unless the particular substance imported was of such variety, quality, condition, or stage of growth as to be unfit for its common use and to be adapted to the uses of the drug trade. This was true of the celery seed held to be a drug in Clay vs. Magone (40 Fed. Rep., 230), which was not in such condition that it could be sold for planting purposes. We conceive that it might also be true of lettuce after it had reached the period of inflorescence, when it is unfit for food and yields the drug known as lactucarium (U. S. Disp., 18 ed., p. 772). We understand the importers to concede that the asparagus and pumpkin seed in controversy are of the common garden kind, and it is nowhere suggested that it would be impracticable to put the 15 bags of seed imported upon the market and sell them for agricultural purposes. Upon such a record the board has no alternative but to affirm the collector's assessment of the seed at 30 per cent., under paragraph 254, as seeds not specially provided for." The protests were overruled.

European Notes.

The spell of poor luck which has dogged the steps of the Erfurt seed growers culminated about the middle of the month in what can only be described as a regular flood. As a consequence, valuable time has been entirely lost and wasted, both for general work and for setting and maturing of seed. The extent of the injury is not yet fully apparent, and if the favorable change in the weather, which has since taken place, proves somewhat permanent, no harm may result; but the harvesting of these valuable crops has been still further delayed.

It is now quite certain that the German crop of pansy seed will be very short, the hoped-for revival of the plants not having taken place.

Scorzonera must now be added to the list of failures; this will hardly affect the trade on your side to the same extent as salsify. The practically total failure of the latter artiele is a serious matter for us all.

Following upon the report of the failure of the German sweet pea crop, the English growers are making very small deliveries. Judging by the numerous requests for quotations of this article recently received from your side, there must be a shortage even in California, in which case, much higher prices will easily be obtained. Another poor delivery from the Golden shore will shake the faith of European buyers in its reliability, and the trade will drift East once more. Unfortunately our French growers do not take kindly to this culture, although it would be quite as profitable as hemp, or radish, and does not involve so much labor.

EUROPEAN SEEDS.

Narcissus Princeps Maximus.

It is noticeable in England how little the Narcissus Princeps are used for forcing, considering how cheap they are and what a valuable forcing bulb they make. But each year less and less are used here, growers mostly finding that they are not profitable, often producing little more than 70 per cent. of blooms even when the largest bulbs are procured. Our growers say the plants are of very little more service than to produce an immense quantity of strong foliage by the new year, which is useful for utilizing with other early bulb bloom where foliage is scarce.

Probably this unsatisfactory blooming is the result of ignorance on the part of the growers, both as to variety and the type of bulb to force. Very few know there are two distinct sorts of Princeps. There is Ajax Princeps and Ajax Princeps Maximus. The former is a useless, smaller bloomed strain, some bulbs of which hardly ever flower at all; do little else than give immense leaves, and produce offsets; while the maximus type is a much larger and bolder bloom, and much deeper in color. If the true type is obtained, it will force from first-class selected bulbs at least 150 to 200 per cent. blooms of best grade, and with careful treatment they may easily be had in flower by Christmas week or soon after. The bloom is in every way as stiff, and has as much substance as that of Golden Spur, and will make as much money on the market. At the same time, the plants may be had in bloom several days before those of Golden Spur with the same treatment.

True it is that when a grower is ordering the bulbs of Princeps from the Dutch, Guernsey or English growers, they will tell him in response to a qestion that they are selling only the true maximus giant strain. In reply to this the buyer should demand a guarantee of, say, 150 blooms per cent., and he will find this is not forthcoming, as a general rule. There are no Dutch growers and, probably, no Guernsey growers but know full well the difference between the two types; and where they are in possession of the common sort, these are usually offered at ridiculously low figures that tempt the market man to buy. I have known tons of this worthless sort bought in Guernsey and sold to Holland for as low as 100s. per ton; and for a time enormous quantities were exported, but since the Dutch growers know the different strains few will stock up with the inferior sort at any price.

Another frequent cause of failure is the badly selected bulbs. Probably few bulb exporters know (or, at any rate, they don't act upon their knowledge), and probably still fewer growers of forcing stock are aware of the proper type of bulb to select. Most people think if the bulbs are only large, firm and humpy, with two or three necks, or one very thick, coarse neck, they are the best, sure to force well, and produce fine bloom. According to my experience this is not so. These heavy mother bulbs are just the thing for planting outside to produce stock and an immense quantity of foliage; but when forced they still only produce one bloom, and, in most cases, this is of poor quality, owing to the strength of the bulb being exhausted producing foliage and maturing of the numerous off sets, which even if not actually clinging to the outside are just as much in evidence in the skin of the original bulb.

An ideal forcing Princeps should be perfectly round, the larger the better, with one neck, and the thinner this is in comparison to the size of the bulb the better. A thin neck is a proof there is only one center to the bulb, which is the main and most important item of success. If such a bulb is cut open it will be found that all the layers of flesh are in a perfect, unbroken circle, without a sign of an offset forming.

If growers always take care to obtain the true maximus strain, and in addition always select the round bulbs as herein described, complaints of this variety being unprofitable to force would soon cease. In fact, I estimate it would be one of the most profitable and popular sorts we have of the trumpet section of narcissus.

ENGLISH CORRESPONDENT.

CATALOGUES RECEIVED.

EASTERN NURSERIES, M. M. Dawson, manager, Jamaica Plain, Mass.—Price List of Clematis mongolica, new.

T. C. THURLOW & COMPANY, West Newbury, Mass.—Catalogue of Trees, Shrubs, Vines, Herbaceous Plants, Small Fruits, etc.

NURSERY DEPARTMENT.

Conducted by Joseph Meehan.

AMERICAN ASSOCIATION OF NURSERYMEN, Orlando Harrison, Berlin, Md., president; J. W. Hill, Des Moines, Ia., vice-president; George C. Seager, Rochester, N. Y., secretary; C. L. Yates, Rochester, N. Y., treasurer.

SMITHVILLE, TENN.—Messrs. Moore & Hicks, proprietors of the Smithville Nurseries, have purchased another farm and will make preparations at once to put part of it in nursery stock.

Sambucus Aurea—Golden-Leaved Elder.

Golden-leaved trees and shrubs are of much use to planters. Of late years there is more display made on grounds by the massing of trees or shrubs together. This is done with shrubs to a great extent; in the case of some for their flowers, with others for their ornamental fruit; or, as in the case of the golden elder, for their beautiful foliage.

The leaves of the golden elder, Sambucus aurea, are very large. They change from their deepest yellow color to a lighter shade as the Summer declines, but there is no time when they are not of a good yellow color.

This golden-leaved elder is a variety of the Sambucus nigra, a European species, abundant in England and other parts of Europe. It differs materially from our common elderberry, S. canadensis. One great difference is that our species is a shrub, while the European one, S. nigra, is a small tree. The one of our notes S. nigra aurea, it will be seen has the bold foliage of the type, as well as the sturdier growth of branches. Allowed to grow on without pruning, it would become a small tree, but with a little attention to pruning, as the specimen illustrated shows, a shapely ornamental bush results.

We do not recall just now any other golden-leaved bush of similar character that could be used in situations that this one fills so well. It is a moisture-loving shrub, as are all the elderberries. The one pictured is at almost the base of a steep hill; just below it is a small lake, so that a better situation for it could not be found.

Although this shrub will come fairly true to color from seeds, nurserymen propagate it from cuttings. It roots readily, and when so raised the color is assured.

The fine bush illustrated is on the grounds of Mr. John T. Morris, Chestnut Hill, Philadelphia—grounds made beautiful through the generosity and love of gardening of Mr. Morris and the enthusiasm of his esteemed gardener, Frank Gould.

Seasonable Topics.

It is strange that lindens, horse chestnuts, and many other big trees "are nearly leafless in England the first week in September," as a writer in Gardening says they are. Our trees of these and almost all others hold their foliage until the close of October. At this date, October 10, all are in the best of condition.

Aspidistra lurida is very nearly hardy in Philadelphia. In fact it has lived out uninjured when in the shelter of a building, growing close to the eastern side of it.

Standard hydrangeas are as useful in their way as those of bush shape. They are formed by cutting to the ground some strong plants, allowing but one strong shoot to each plant to grow when the new ones push. The shoots are topped near the end of their growth to permit heads to form.

The verbena shrub, caryopteris, makes a handsome display of its blue flowers in late September and October. It is not over hardy, and a plant in a pot in a greenhouse, to give cuttings in early Spring, will be found useful. The cuttings root easily.

When a white birch is asked for, supply your customer with the canoe, or paper birch, Betula papyracea, the best of all the white barked birches.

This is the month for the flowering of Aster tataricus, the violet flowered one, which sends its spikes of bloom to a height of from five to six feet, and is nearly or quite the last aster to flower.

Nyssa multiflora, the sour gum, prefers a damp situation. It is one of the first of all trees to change its bright green leaves to a scarlet color in Autumn, after which change they quickly drop from the tree.

Echinacea purpurea, the purple cone flower, as it is called, is a welcome subject to those who look for September and October blooming perennials. The cone is brownish purple, but the ray flowers are rosy pink with purple shade. It is a native of the Western States, and is much sought for by those who know its worth.

When in an open, sunny place the flowers of Hydrangea paniculata grandiflora become of a bright pink color when they are quite mature, and are then in demand by florists as "pink hydrangeas."

Shrubs and vines with beautiful berries are the charm of Autumn. Planters should set out such shrubs as Callicarpa purpurea, Pyrus arbutifolia, Berberis Thunbergii, and the vines, Celastrus scandens, Lycium chinensis and Vitis variegata.

Prunus Davidiana, Cornus Mas, Cornus officinalis and Lonicera fragrantissima are the first shrubs to flower in Spring. Though frosts sometimes catch their early blooms, this does not happen often; and all want early flowers.

Pussy willow is Salix caprea. When in flower in early Spring it is as pretty as any other flowering tree or shrub, especially when its anthers are well developed. Plant it in Fall, if possible.

Plant Saxifraga crassifolia to have an early flowering perennial you will like. The frost is hardly out of the ground before its showy pink blossoms appear; and its leaves are large, handsome and evergreen.

Pines when transplanted can have their needles shortened back one half to advantage, and Arbor vitaes, retinisporas and the like, their latest growth shortened back somewhat; but pruning back to hard wood is not good practice.

The Virginia creeper, permitted to overspread some half dead tree or shrub, forms a pretty object, a delight to behold in Autumn when its foliage becomes of a scarlet color. Wild grape vines are useful in the same way, but do not take on handsome Fall colors.

Propagation of Oaks.

The older planters of trees notice a great difference in the character of what are planted now and what used to be planted. In no class of trees is this more apparent than in oaks. On all old estates the oak trees that were planted are nearly all of the English species, Quercus Robur. On grounds showing modern planting the species are almost entirely of our own sorts, and the number planted is increasing every day. There is good reason for this, for even in the Northern States there are a dozen or more grand looking species hardy enough to withstand the cold, and this number can be increased largely when the plantings are from Virginia southward.

This is the time to procure acorns looking to the getting of a crop of seedlings. The first acorns to fall are those of the white oak section. With us they fall in October. The alba, Prinus, prinoides and castanea all fall at about this time, and as they make root at once on reaching damp ground and will not keep in sound condition but a week or two when out of the ground, it is necessary to be on the alert to secure them.

The other oaks do not call for such a hurried sowing. In fact, they need not be sown until Spring if kept in moist sand or soil all Winter; and many prefer this way as entailing less trouble than Fall sowing.

Several of the oaks are planted for their lovely Autumn foliage, but there is one that calls for planting because of its beautiful burrs. This is the Quercus macrocarpa, also known as mossy cup and burr oak. The acorns are very large, and at the edge of the cups is a fringe-like growth, sometime quite enveloping the acorn, forming in all a pretty object.

Sambucus Aurea—Golden-Leaved Elder.

Chinese Cork Tree.

When the Phellodendron amurense was introduced to cultivation it brought with it the common name of Chinese cork tree. As the trees grew in size and no semblance of cork whatever appeared, it was difficult to understand how the name came to be applied. Later on another species appeared in cultivation, going under the name of P. Regeliana, and this proves to be the one entitled to the common name cork tree. The bark is corky in a most pronounced way. It is not only corky, as is the mossy cup oak, many of the elms and euonymus, but it is of a soft, spongy nature, giving to pressure, which cannot be said of some of the other so-called cork-barked trees.

It must be said with regret that there is but a very small number of this tree in cultivation. There are no seed bearing trees of it here that there is any knowledge of. But as the other species, amurense, seeds freely, it is probable that this could be used as a stock on which to graft the cork tree, in which case a stock of it could soon be secured. A good, hardy cork tree would be desired by all lovers of trees.

The merits of this tree are not ended with its corky bark. It makes a handsome round-headed tree, having pinnate leaves; and in early Fall the foliage changes to a deep yellow color, making the tree conspicuous at a great distance.

Mulberries for Stocks.

Nurserymen know the difficulty of getting good straight stocks of mulberry for the grafting on of the weeping variety. This weeper is a variety of the Morus tatarica, known as the Russian mulberry; and this one, really, is a fair stock for it when grown on in rich soil, so as to stimulate it to make a strong, straight growth. The weeping form is desired as a grafted plant of about 6 feet in height; and to obtain straight stocks to cut off at this height and be grafted is not always easily accomplished. Good, straight stocks can generally be had by stimulating a row of plants the whole season through. Then when Spring approaches cut them to a few inches above ground. The Summer following they should make a growth of ample length to fit them for grafting.

There are two mulberries of much stronger growth than those named which would make excellent stocks for grafting, provided they proved a suitable one to the scion. These two are the Morus rubra and M. multicaulis. Young plants when cut down to the ground will make a single straight shoot of from 6 to 8 feet in a season. Both of these have proved good stocks for the everbearing kinds, and I have no doubt they would be equally as valuable for the weeping one. Morus rubra is our native red mulberry, while M. multicaulis is claimed by China. The latter is a very distinct species, and it is the one that had much to do with the silkworm industry fever which swept over the country some 50 years ago. The leaves are very large, the growth strong; and as it roots freely from cuttings, it would make an ideal stock for Teas' weeping mulberry, if the latter kind has no objections to it.

JOSEPH MEEHAN.

700 Hardy Herbaceous Perennials

Strong, field grown clumps in over 700 varieties. Catalogue for the asking.

HIRAM T. JONES,
Union County Nurseries, Elizabeth, N. J.

Mention the Florists' Exchange when writing.

SEND TO

THE MOON COMPANY

For Your { TREES, SHRUBS, VINES and SMALL FRUITS

Descriptive Illustrated Catalogue Free

THE WM. H. MOON CO.
Morrisville, Pa.

Mention the Florists' Exchange when writing.

HERBACEOUS PERENNIALS

for Summer and Autumn Planting. We offer NINE HUNDRED and SIXTY-SEVEN VARIETIES of STRONG FIELD-GROWN PLANTS. Send for Catalog and Trade List.

BAY STATE NURSERIES, NORTH ABINGTON, MASS.

Mention the Florists' Exchange when writing.

F. & F. NURSERIES

SPRINGFIELD NEW JERSEY

Wholesale Growers — TREES AND PLANTS in full assortment. — Trade Catalogue Free

Mention The Florists' Exchange when writing.

THE SHREWSBURY NURSERIES

EATONTOWN, N. J.

Offer a good line of well-grown NURSERY STOCK, Large, well developed Shrubs a specialty. SEND FOR WHOLESALE LIST

Mention The Florists' Exchange when writing.

Viburnum Plicatum Japan Snowball

18 to 24 in.	$10.00 per 100
2 to 2½ ft.	12.00 "
2½ to 3 ft.	15.00 "
3 to 4 ft.	20.00 "
4 to 5 ft.	25.00 "

DOUBLE ALTHEAS

Joanne D'Arc, pure white flowers fine for cutting. Banner—White striped crimson. Red—Rich ruby red flowered.

	per 100
Bushy Plants 18 to 24 in.	$6.00
2 to 2½ ft.	7.00
2½ to 3 ft.	8.00
3 to 4 ft.	10.00

BERBERRY THUNBERGII, Splendid for Hedges

Our plants are grown from Cuttings and are very bushy.

	per 100	per 1000
12 to 18 in.	$5.00	$45.00
18 to 24 in.	7.00	60.00
2 ft. to 2½ ft.	10.00	90.00

HYDRANGEA PAN. GRAND.
2 to 3 ft. $7.00 per 100, $60.00 per 1000

DEUTZIA LEMOINEI, Fine for Forcing
2 to 2½ ft. $7.00 per 100

DEUTZIA GRACILIS, 12 to 18 in. 4.50 "

SPIRAEA VAN HOUTTEI

		per 100	per 1000
" "	3 ft.	$6.00	$45.00
" "	3 to 4 ft.	6.00	50.00
" Blue, caryopteris,	15 to 20 in.	5.00	45.00
" "	2 to 2½ ft.	7.00	65.00
" A. Waterer	12 to 18 in.	5.50	50.00
" "	2 to 2½ ft.	8.00	75.00
" "	2½ to 3 ft.	9.00	85.00

HONEYSUCKLE HECKROTTII, 1 year $6.00 per 100, 2 years, $10.00 per 100.

PLATYCODON LEICHTLINII, Dwarf; Bushy and very free flowering, 2 years, $6.00 per 100.

THE CONARD & JONES CO.
WEST GROVE, PA.

Mention The Florists' Exchange when writing.

SEASONABLE STOCK FOR FLORISTS

HYDRANGEAS for forcing { OTAKSA and THOS. HOGG { With 7-12 flowering crowns, $12.00 per 100.
" 4-6 " " 9.00 "
" 4 " " 7.00 "

From 6-inch pots and open beds; all out-door grown.

ROSES, Strong, two-years, field-grown, selected for forcing.

HYBRID PERPETUALS	$10.00 and $12.00 per 100.
CRIMSON RAMBLER	9.00 "
DOROTHY PERKINS	7.00 "

and

LADY GAY, a new hardy climbing Rose of exceptional merit; ready now from 2¼ inch pots only. Write for prices.

JACKSON & PERKINS CO.
WHOLESALE NURSERYMEN AND FLORISTS
NEWARK, WAYNE CO., NEW YORK

Mention The Florists' Exchange when writing.

To Clear the Land We Shall Sell For the Next 60 Days

	Per 1000
Berberis Thunbergii, 18 to 24 in., bushy plants	$40.00
Berberis Thunbergii, 24 to 30 in., bushy plants	50.00
Rosa Lucida, 3 years, twice transplanted, fine	40.00
Viburnum Dentatum, 24 to 30 in.	40.00
" " 30 to 36 in.	50.00

We also have some Viburnum cassinoides and Prunus maritima.

Littlefield & Wyman
North Abington, Mass.

Mention The Florists' Exchange when writing.

P. OUWERKERK

216 Jane Street
WEEHAWKEN HEIGHTS, N. J.
P. O. No. 1, Hoboken, N. J.

JUST RECEIVED FROM OUR HOLLAND NURSERIES

Rhododendrons, Azaleas, Spiraea Japonica, Lilium Speciosum, Peonies, Bleeding Heart, Pot-Grown Lilacs, Hydrangea in sorts, Clematis and H. P. Roses in the best sorts.

PRICES MODERATE

Mention The Florists' Exchange when writing.

Large Assortment **PEONIES** Very best Varieties

LOW PRICES
THE KIND THAT FLORISTS LIKE

"We make a specialty of growing stocky transplanted shrubbery and trees"

FULL ASSORTMENT OF Ornamentals, Fruits, Roses, Clematis, and Herbaceous Plants. Write for our fall wholesale trade list.

W. & T. SMITH CO., GENEVA, N. Y.

Mention The Florists' Exchange when writing.

A Reminder

I WILL HAVE THIS FALL FOR SALE

- 100,000 California Privet, 2 to 4 feet, bushy.
- 500 California Privet Stauter, 5 feet, large heads.
- 500 California Privet Stauter, bush and sheared, fine for lawn.
- 2,000 American Elm, 10 to 12 feet, fine trees.
- 500 Horse Chestnut, 8 to 12 feet, fine heads and stocky.
- 1,000 Deutzia Gracilis, 2 to 3 years, good for forcing.
- 1,000 Roses, Clothilde Soupert.
- 2,000 Double Hollyhocks, 2 years, red, pink, white and yellow.
- 5,000 Dahlia Roots, all fine colors.
- 1,000 Althaeas, double, variegated, 2 to 4 feet.
- 500 Yucca Filamentosa, large blooming plants. Send for prices to

CARLMAN RIBSAM
31 Wall St., TRENTON, N. J.

Mention The Florists' Exchange when writing

A BARGAIN FOR YOU IN NICE PLANTS

2000 Achillea, The Pearl $2.00 per 100, 1500 German Iris 3 varieties $2.00 per 100, 8000 Iris Sibirica Blue and White $2.00 per 100, 100 Helianthus Divaricarta, $2.00 per 100, 1000 Heliopsis Pitcheriana, $2.00 per 100, 1000 Digitalis, Foxglove, $2.00 per 100, 500 Crimson Eye, Hibiscus, $3.00 per 100, 400 Peonies, 3-5 eyes asstd. $6.00 per 100, 500 Arundo Donax Grass $5.00 per 100, 200 Funkia Coerulea, $4.00 per 100, 1500 Trumpet Vines, 2-3 ft. tr. 2c., 300 Wisteria Multijuga racemes of blooms 2-3 ft. long, 10c. each. Cash with Order please.

Ellsworth Brown & Co. Seabrook, N. H.

Mention The Florists' Exchange when writing.

CALIFORNIA PRIVET

Fine well-graded, two year plants, well packed as follows: 15 to 20 inches, 3 or more branches, $1.50 per 100; $8.00 per 1000, this grade gives good satisfaction.

20 to 30 inches, 5 or more branches, $2.00 per 100; $12.50 per 1000, nice.

2½ to 3 ft., 7 or more branches, $3.00 per 100; $17.50 per 1000, very strong.

3 to 4 ft., strong selected, $4.00 per 100; $25.00 per 1000.

CHAS. BLACK, Hightstown, N. J.

Mention the Florists' Exchange when writing.

KOSTER & CO.

Hollandia Nurseries BOSKOOP, HOLLAND

Hardy Azaleas, Box Trees, Clematis, Conifers, Hydrangeas, Peonies.
Pot-Grown Plants for Forcing.
RHODODENDRONS, H. P. ROSES, Etc.
Catalogue free on demand.

Mention The Florists' Exchange when writing.

CHOICE CALIFORNIA PRIVET

2000 4 year old, well branched, 6 to 8 feet, $10.00 per 100; very fine plants.

	100	1000
3 year, 3 to 4 feet	$3.00	$20.00
2 year, 2 to 3 feet	2.00	15.00

2 year, 15 to 20 in., $10.00 per 1000; 600 plants at 1000 rate. Terms: Cash with order; packing free; prompt shipment.

ATLANTIC COAST NURSERIES,
OFFICE: 606 4th Ave., Asbury Park, N. J.

Mention The Florists' Exchange when writing.

Trees and Shrubs

We make specially low prices on nursery stock to Parks, Cemeteries, etc.

Wholesale price list on application.

We carry immense quantities of the finest named varieties of peonies.

PETERSON NURSERY
505 W. PETERSON AVE., CHICAGO, ILL

Mention The Florists' Exchange when writing.

H. DEN OUDEN & SON,

BOSKOOP, HOLLAND.

Wholesale growers of nursery stock for the American trade. Catalogue free on demand. Also views in our nurseries.

Mention The Florists' Exchange when writing.

Holland Nursery Stock

Ask for Our Catalogue. It will interest you.

ENDTZ, VAN NES & CO. BOSKOOP, HOLLAND

Mention The Florists' Exchange when writing.

PEONIES

We still have quite a block of No Plus Ultra, and need the ground. While they last we offer them at $7.50 per 100; $60.00 per 1000. Send for list.

EDWARD SWAYNE
WEST CHESTER, PA.

Mention the Florists' Exchange when writing.

10,000 VINCA

Strong, From Field, 3c. 4c.

English Ivy, 2 in. pots, 18 to 24 in., 2c.
" " 2½ in. pots, 18 to 24 in., 2½c.
English Ivy, 4 in., 8c.
Primula Obconica, 2½ in., strong, 3c.
" " 3 in., strong, 4c.
" Chinese, 2 in., 2c.
Rex Begonia, 4 in., 10c.
Hydrangea P. G., 2 feet, 6c.

J. H. DANN & SON,
WESTFIELD, N. Y.

Mention The Florists' Exchange when writing.

VINCA

Variegated, strong, field clumps, $3.50 per 100; $15.00 per 500. Pansies, stocky, field plants, my own giant strain, and Roemer's supurb, prize giants, $4.00 per 1000. Cash.

W. J. ENGLE,
R. D. No. 8, DAYTON, O.

Mention The Florists' Exchange when writing.

VINCA VARIEGATED

Field clumps, fit for 4 in., $4.00 per 100. Rooted Tips, strong, $1.00; $9.00 per 1000. Vinca Minor, 3 in., $4.00 per 100. Pansies of superior strain, $3.00 per 1000. Dracaena Indivisa, 4 in., $10.00; 2½ in., $3.00 per 100. Cash. Write for samples.

C. F. MAHAN, R. D. No. 8, Dayton, O.

Mention The Florists' Exchange when writing.

HOLLYHOCKS

Large field-grown plants, double, in 6 separate colors, $7.00 per 100; $60.00 per 1000. Send for samples. Cash with order, please.

GEO. F. KIMBEL, JR., Flourtown, Pa.

Mention The Florists' Exchange when writing.

HARDY ENGLISH IVY

Good, strong plants, field grown, over 3 ft. long, $5.00 per 100; $45.00 per 1000.

John Gilkinson & Sons,
HOLLIS, L. I.

CANNAS

300,000 roots for Fall delivery in 100 leading kinds, $8.00 to $20.00 per 1000. Write for our list. Send in your orders early.

SHELLROAD GREENHOUSES
Largest Canna Growers Grange, Baltimore, Md.

Mention The Florists' Exchange when writing.

Commercial Violet Culture

Price, $1.50

he Florists' Exchange, 2-8 Duane St., New York

Mention The Florists' Exchange when writing.

LIST OF ADVERTISERS

INDEX TO STOCK ADVERTISED

Contents.

REVIEW OF THE MARKET

NEW YORK.—The cut flower business continues in a satisfactory condition so far as the disposal of stock is concerned. Supplies along all lines are somewhat limited, and this fact chiefly is what tends to keep up the prices of everything. With the exception of dahlias, outdoor flowers can be said to be at an end now, and even these are not near such a factor in the market as they have been for several weeks past. American Beauty roses are still holding up to our quoted prices, and there are occasional sales of small lots when these figures are even exceeded to a slight extent. With Bride and Bridesmaid conditions remain practically the same; prices are unchanged; special grade lots are anything but plentiful, and growers who are fortunate enough to be cutting at the present time are receiving better returns, considering the season of the year, than has been possible for several years. Carnations are scarcely equal to the demand, and prices, if anything, are slightly firmer than one week ago; and with the improvement in the quality of some of the fancy varieties it has been possible to realize 5c. each occasionally. What has been said about roses and carnations is equally true about cattleyas. These are bringing figures that are almost double what could be obtained for the same kind of flowers at this time in 1905. The demand for lily of the valley, while somewhat erratic, is still such as to keep the prices up to our last week's quotations. Lilies continue to sell out at good figures compared with what has been the rule all Summer, and the supply at no time has been much in excess of the demand.

Chrysanthemums are coming in in rather limited quantities as yet. John Young has had one or two shipments of such varieties as Polly Rose, Glory of the Pacific and Monrovia, the two former varieties bringing 20c. each, Monrovia fetching $5 per dozen.

With smilax, asparagus and maidenhair fern conditions have not yet arisen where it has been possible to increase values, and we presume so long as Autumn foliage can be used with such telling effects the greenhouse materials will not have much of a place in the retailers' work.

CHICAGO.—At last, although the retail trade is still more or less spasmodic, the wholesalers begin to feel a much stronger and steady pulse in the life of trade. Although no frosts have been reported in this section, out-of-door stock, with the possible exception of cosmos, has practically exhausted itself, and the much cooler weather has greatly improved the quality of, as well as the demand for, greenhouse goods.

The shipping trade, though still not absolutely settled, is on the whole perfectly satisfactory, and the fact that it has become a frequent occurrence to see a representative of a concern scurrying around through the various establishments of his neighbors looking for enough of this or that to make out his order is ocular evidence that business has once more returned to life.

Monday of this week opened with less force, but with the prospect quietly pronounced that the dropping of the curtain on Saturday would excel the preceding week. W. K. W.

PHILADELPHIA.—All the wholesale houses present quite a busy appearance this week, there being a good demand for all kinds of stock. American Beauty roses have reached the $4 mark for the choicest flowers, the bulk of the stock going at $2.50 and $3 per dozen. The choicest grades of other roses are Kaiserin Augusta Victoria, Bridesmaid and Wellesley, at $8; Killarney, Richmond and Liberty $6.00 per 100. Gardenias are selling this week at $5 per 100; Cattleyas at 50c. and 60c. per flower.

Many more chrysanthemums are arriving this week; $4 is the top price per dozen. Polly Rose, Glory of the Pacific and Monrovia are the varieties now seen.

Carnations are improving in quality very fast; $3.00 per 100 has been obtained for some choice Enchantress and Beacon, the majority of the other stock going at $2.00 and $2.50. Dahlias are in brisk demand; some choice flowers of Grand Duke Alexis have been disposed of at $5 per 100. Kriemhilde and Perle d'Or have also sold very well.

There is rather too much asparagus on the market this week; this applies to bunches. Strings are not yet in much demand. Lily of the valley still has a brisk call at $3 to $6.

There are still considerable quantities of flowers from hardy plants on sale. Cosmos is selling well, and the demand for tritomas has been very good; these have been used largely for window decorations. DAVID RUST.

INDIANAPOLIS.—Cooler weather has been accompanied with a general increase in the various lines of business. Counter trade is much improved; funeral work was heavy all last week and at times stock was difficult to obtain; decorations are numerous, but not large. Monrovia and Polly Rose chrysanthemums are in the market at $1.50 to $2 a dozen. Excellent dahlias continue to be shipped in at $1.50 to $3 per 100. A downtown firm displayed two hundred varieties in its window; all were labeled and attracted much attention. Cosmos wholesale well at 50c. per 100; the crop is so late that the major part will be nipped by frost. Carnations are much improved in quality, selling well at $1 to $1.50 per 100; 35c. to 50c. a dozen is the retail figure. The first single violets appeared this week, and many retail inquiries are made for them. Lily of the valley is plentiful at $4. The rose market lately has been most satisfactory; Bridesmaid have improved in color and sell at $3 to $4, as also do Bride and Golden Gate. Red roses are selling better; Richmond and Liberty bring $3 to $7 per 100. The retail demand for American Beauty makes them scarce sometimes, at $5 to $25 a 100.

Tomlinson Hall market reports a good business; all good stock brought there is wholesaled early in the day. I. B.

ST. LOUIS.—A general improvement in the cut flower business is noted throughout the city, the downtown florists particularly reporting good over-the-counter trade. While the days are warm, the cool nights have good effect on roses and carnations. A brisk call was experienced for fancy American Beauty, with the top price at $4 per dozen; other grades, $3 to $1 per dozen. Bride, Bridesmaid, Richmond, Ivory and Perle des Jardins are of much better quality, and $8 per 100 is asked for fancies; other grades, $2 to $5.

As the season advances, carnations are of better quality, and fancy Enchantress bring as high as $3 per 100; other varieties like Boston Market, Lady Bountiful, Mrs. T. W. Lawson, and Mrs. Frances Joost, $1.50 to $2. Some extra fine lily of the valley is now to be had at $4 per 100. Cosmos is also coming along fine, selling at 50c. and 75c. per 100. Chrysanthemums are as yet scarce, being limited to a few hundred in this market; yellow and white bring $1.50 to $2 per dozen. Violets continue small in size, and not many are received, though the cool nights will help the size and color; at present violets don't bring over 25c. per 100.

The market is well supplied with greens of all kinds. ST. PATRICK.

PITTSBURG.—Business the past few weeks has been fair. The month of October is always a good one for wedding orders, of which there have been quite a number so far. The change in weather has caused a shortage in various stocks of outdoor growth, and carnations and roses must be counted on to fill up, but they are not over plentiful. Chrysanthemums are coming a little better, yet they are too high priced for general use. Dahlias still hold out and are in good demand; $1 and better is asked for good ones. A good many cactus varieties were handled this season which found a ready demand and were much used for work. Asters and gladiolus are about done. The flowers of a beautiful species of gentian, blue in color, were noticed in the Allegheny market a few weeks ago. It is a useful flower not often seen in florists' stores, although it is quite common in some parts of the State and worthy of cultivation. E. C. R.

BOSTON.—Prices are a little firmer than a week ago, although business is quiet except in American Beauty roses, which seem to have a lively demand. Other roses are still small and in large quantities, with a very slight increase in price for the better grades. Carnations have advanced somewhat; blooms are yet small and stems are not long. Chrysanthemums are becoming quite plentiful for early sorts, selling at $1.50 and $2 per dozen. Violets are improving. Tuberoses remain about the same. Cosmos is quite plentiful and dahlias have been used quite extensively recently. Other stock remains at practically the same prices as last week.

J. W. D.

WHITE MARSH, MD.—We regret exceedingly to learn that the condition of Thomas Vincent, son of Richard Vincent, Jr., does not improve any. On the 8th inst. he passed a very bad night.

TEWKSBURY, MASS.—Mr. Kenefick, florist from Halifax, N. S., was a visitor at Patten & Company's place last week one day. Mr. Kenefick is visiting with his relatives in Lowell and Lynn.

THE WEEK'S WORK.

Timme's Timely Teachings.

Peonies.

Although the planting of herbaceous peonies may safely be undertaken quite late in the Fall, may even be deferred until the last moment just before Winter puts a stop to all outdoor operations, it is better for plants and planter to attend to this important part of Autumn work earlier in the season, unless good reasons for the delay exist. The month of October is rightly considered the best time for the lifting, dividing and replanting of peonies. The then thoroughly matured plants are eager for a fresh start, already showing well defined new growth, not yet too far advanced to be easily broken off in handling, but far enough to enable a practiced hand to unerringly divide the roots into smooth, nicely crowned, well proportioned pieces without the excessive use of the knife.

In the making of entirely new plantations, when the stock must be purchased, it also is to the advantage of the prospective grower to have the work of planting over with in good season, to order early while stock in the leading commercial varieties is offered and available in quantity, to plant as soon as received, while the weather is the finest, the land in the best condition, and yet plenty of time to do the work thoroughly. In the buying of peonies, more than in that of other florist's stock, the most reliable firms should be dealt with.

Lifting Peonies.

A good workman, knowing how to use a spade and what he is about, will begin his trench around an old, large-sized peony at a respectful distance from its center, throw out the soil, lay bare the outlying roots, lift and loosen the clump and then remove as much of the old soil in and about the roots, working his way toward the center, as is possible with spade, trowel and fingers. Very large and heavy clumps, those having grown in clayey ground, should not be much handled and thrown about before being cleaned and divided, lest many of the fleshy, very crisp tail ends and out runners of roots will be broken off by the weight of the adhering soil. The best and quickest means of freeing the roots of this tightly sticking old earth is a forceful stream of water from a hose attached to a high pressure system. In order to lessen the loss occasioned by the snapping in two of the sappy roots in repeated handling, or in the packing for shipment, recourse is often had to a somewhat heroic measure. The dug up clumps, after being cleaned of the old soil and before being cut up into divisions, are exposed to a full day's wind and sunshine, allowing them to become quite wilted. They are then pliable and less easily broken. I am not in a haste to recommend this way of preparing valuable stock for replanting. It may do no harm, as is averred; but it has the appearance of something that had better be left out of the program.

Dividing Peonies.

As regards the multiplication of peonies by division of the roots, I will say this, that if I were to draw the stock for a new plantation from a certain number of old clumps and had the dividing of them, I would rather make the new field somewhat smaller and the root divisions considerably larger than to spread the material at hand in the form of single crowned small pieces over a large area of ground, as is usually done. The planter's hope of effectually increasing the output of peonies by a resetting must rest in the multiplication and betterment of their product by a removal from old, exhausted ground to a new and fertile field, rather than in the making of a great number of individual plants. I know from actual experience that there is considerably more money in planting fifty good-sized divisions, each one showing a crown of half a dozen or more plump, roseate shoots, than in planting two hundred small, one-eyed pieces, obtained by the all too free use of the knife. It is true, they all will grow into great bushes in time, even those showing no crowns at all at the time of planting, but one has to wait a long while for tangible results—too long for this rapidly striding age of ours. Pieces that can be detached from the main root without using the knife, even if a trifle too large, hold out a fairer promise of good returns in a near future than those of the usual marketable size; or, to make my meaning fully clear, there will be more and better flowers, coming sooner, too, from the entire bulk of an old clump divided sparingly, than if the same clump had been cut up into a great number of much smaller divisions. Such large, multi-crowned divisions, if ever offered for sale, should, of course, bring more than double the price of those sent out by most peony specialists; but I for one would not hesitate to pay the higher figure, knowing that I would still be considerably ahead in the transaction. All this applies to the well-known, abundantly available, commercially profitable varieties, raised in quantity for the cut flower market. When rare and scarce sorts come to be considered, close propagation alone will result in the rapid increase of the stock; this, for the time being, must be the chief aim.

Planting Peonies.

The first thought in planning for an extensive growing of peonies for profit must be given to site and soil. In all gardening operations, when the grower had to deal with plants exceptionally modest in their requirements, unusual and often unlooked for results were obtained by extraordinary culture, care and treatment. In the case of peonies the clear gain in their culture has been doubled and trebled by ignoring the fact that they will thrive and bloom almost anywhere and in any kind of soil, and by giving them instead a most favored situation, nicely prepared ground and the best of treatment. Deep digging or plowing, indeed trenching or subsoiling, and the intermixture of the so loosened soil with large quantities of rich barnyard manure, should not be deemed too great an expense or too laborious a task, when it is borne in mind that peonies form one of the most prominent of profit-yielding outdoor crops, and that they will occupy the so prepared bit of ground for many years to come; in fact, will only be at their best when they require the least of culture.

Four feet each way, rather more than less, is about the right distance between newly set roots. The crown or top of the root should not be less than three inches below the leveled surface of the ground. The soil in the depression on which the root is to be set should first be well firmed by the feet of the planter, but after the root is in position the feet should take no part in firming the plant, lest more harm than good be done. In the planting of large fields it is best to grade the root sets into several sizes, planting the large as well as the small ones by themselves; at the same time taking care not to mix varieties. If in future the field is well cultivated, kept free of weeds, receiving a top dressing of manure now and then, it will do no harm to raise a crop of something else the first and perhaps second year after planting between the rows of peonies. Later on this should be discontinued, as also deep top cultivation.

Peonies planted late in the Fall should not be suffered to pass through their first Winter without a good mulch of straw, hay, or coarse manure overhead. This will prevent Jack Frost in his playful tricks from lifting and loosening the newly set roots.

Other Hardy Perennials.

Of other hardy herbaceous perennials none can claim so important a place as is enjoyed by the peony. But some of them are most useful as producers of a fine and welcome kind of cut material, while all of them with few exceptions are good sellers nearly all the year around. While a border of hardy herbaceous plants is admittedly a ready source of easily earned income and considerable profit on any place where the raising and selling of bedding plants is the mainstay of the concern, I cannot help seeing and saying that on most places of this kind the most dejected and neglected feature of the establishment is invariably the hardy plant border. This should not be so. The bed should at least be kept clean of weeds. So also should the fact that these plants stand a deal of neglect not furnish an excuse for letting them grow up to an unwieldy size and into unsalable proportions, crowding one another for room. If in early Spring, when most late flowering sorts should properly be divided and replanted, time is scarce and too precious to attend to anything willing to wait, as is invariably the case, then a lifting, cleaning and resetting of such stock at this time, or even later, should take place. Such sorts as rudbeckias, phloxes, pyrethrums, lobelias, gypsophila, iberis, helenium, asters, digitalis, coreopsis and many others do not suffer in the least by being divided and transplanted in late Fall. October and early November is a good time for this kind of work. After the planting is done and the new bed is neatly leveled, a heavy layer of manure should be spread over it and on this six or eight inches of dry tree leaves to prevent heaving of the plants by frost.

FRED. W. TIMME.

erns From Bench

STON, PIERSONI, 3 in. 5c., 4 in. 10c, in. 12½c. Boston, 6 in. 15 cts.
RRYTOWN, 2½ in., 4c.; 3 in., 10c.; in., 15c.; 5 in., 25c. Runners $20.00 per 00.
OTTII, 3 in., 8c.; 4 in., 12½c.

CHINESE PRIMROSES

hite, fine plants, 1½ cts.
sy Plants, Giants, $3.00 per 100.
sies, double Snowball, Longfellow, llcats, $2.50 per 1000.
aragus Sprengeri, 2 in., 2 cts.
wering Begonias, 3 kinds, 2 in., 2½ cts.
seum Giant, White double, 2 in., 2c.
bers, top grown, 4 to 6 in., 15 to 25 cts.
getmenots, $2.50 per 1000
lyhocks, double, 4 kinds, 1 year old, 3cts.
dy Pinks, 3 kinds, field plants, 3½cts.
rdy Carnations, nice young plants from ses, $2.00 per 100.

Cash or C. O. D.

ER BROS., Chambersburg, Pa.

tion The Florists' Exchange when writing.

HITMANI FERN

rge stock of strong plants, 2¼ inch pots, 00 per 100.

TARRYTOWN FERN

	100
h pots....................................	$10.00

SCOTTII

inch pots..............................	$ 5.00
h pots..................................	15.00

t grown Ampelopsis, staked, strong ts, $10.00 per 100.
o order for less than 10 plants accepted.

CHAS. H. CAMPBELL,
GERMANTOWN AVE., PHILA., PA
ion The Florists' Exchange when writing.

ERNS OUR SPECIALTY

otium Schiedei: We have a grand stock of magnificent tree fern in all sizes. 3 in. pots, .00 per 100; 4 in. pots, $45.00 per 100; 5 in. pots, .00 per 100; 7 in. pots, $1.70 each; 8 in. pots, 0 each.
orted Ferns, from 2¼ in. pots, all the best rket varieties, $3.00 per 100, or $25.00 per 1000; ch pots, $12.00 per 100.
by mail add 10c. each 100 plants.
antum Cuneatum, 2 in. pots, $3.50 per 100
" " 4 in. pots, 12.00 " "
" Rhodophyllum 4 in. pots $35.00 per 100
" Lathomii, 4 in. pots, $30.00 per 100
" Regina, 4 in. pots, $35.00 per 100
n Spores gathered from our own stock plants . per trade package or $4.00 per doz. packages

DERSON & CHRISTENSEN,
SHORT HILLS, N. J.
ion the Florists' Exchange when writing.

EPHROLEPIS

hitmani, 2¼ in., $25.00 per 100.
arrowsii, $10.00 per 100.

y H. Barrows & Son, Whitman, Mass.
ion The Florists' Exchange when writing.

diantum Farleyense

can quote splendid stock at from $2.00 dozen up to $24.00 per dozen, in 2-inch -inch pots. If you are looking for Farse, better write me about it.

ARLES H. TOTTY, Madison, N. J.

ERNS

Jardinieres, etc., 2¼ inch, $3.00 per 100.
ntia Belmoreana, clean and bushy, 5 in.
ston Ferns, Piersoni and Scottii, from h, 10c. to 25c. each; 4 in. pot grown, 16c.
coe Weddeliana, 2¼ in. 10c.
paragus Plumosus, 2¼ in. $3.00 per 100.

WESTON, HEMPSTEAD, N. Y.
tion The Florists' Exchange when writing.

BARGAIN
TO MAKE ROOM

N. Piersoni Elegantissima Ferns, from n. pots, $8.00 per 100. A No. 1 stock; ready l and 5 in. pots. Cash with order, please.

. ENGELMAN & SON
PITTSFIELD, MASS.
tion The Florists' Exchange when writing.

DREER'S SPECIALS IN FERNS

Nephrolepis Scottii

Adiantum Farleyense

A grand lot of specimen plants in seven inch pots at $1.50 each. This is bushy stock with grand foliage, of excellent value. Also a fine lot of clean vigorous 3 inch pots for growing on, $2.00 per dozen, $15.00 per 100.

Nephrolepis Whitmani

The most distinct and desirable of the crested forms of the Boston Fern, its great points of merit are that it never reverts or shows any plain fronds or parts of fronds, it naturally makes a shapely compact plant, it is more graceful than any of the other sorts and is a quick grower. We offer strong
2¼ inch pots, $3.50 per dozen, $25.00 per 100.
3 " " 4.00 " " 30.00 " "
and fine plants in 6 inch pots at $1.00 each.

Pteris Wilsoni and Pteris Wimsetti Multiceps

are both useful varieties, perhaps the prettiest of the Pteris for growing into larger sizes for decorative plants, we have a fine lot of 6 inch pans, just right for table decoration, pretty plants at $3.50 per dozen; $25.00 per 100. In smaller sizes we can supply 2¼ inch pots, $3.50 per 100; $30.00 per 1000.
3 " " 6.00 " " 50.00 " "
4 " " 1.50 " doz. 10.00 " 100

Nephrolepis Scottii

We have a grand lot of compact dwarf bushy specimens in 6 inch pots, 50 cents each; 8 inch pans, $1.00 each; 12 inch pans, $2.00 each; 2¼ inch pots, $4.00 per 100; $35.00 per 1000.

Adiantum Cuneatum

A fine lot of 6 inch pots, $3.50 per dozen; $25.00 per 100; 2¼ inch pots, $3.50 per 100; $30.00 per 1000.

Aspidium Tsussemense

Of this most useful of all Dish Ferns we still have a fine lot of seedlings in flats, which if potted up now will still make salable stock for this winter, about 200 plants to a flat at $2.00 per flat.

Mixed Ferns

Our usual superior assortment of varieties:
2¼ inch pots, $3.50 per 100; $30.00 per 1000.
3 " " 6.00 " " 50.00 " "

For a full line of Seasonable Stock, Decorative Plants, Palms, Ferns, Araucarias, Pandanus, Hardy Perennials, Bulbs, Seeds, etc., etc., see our quarterly Wholesale List.

HENRY A. DREER,
714 Chestnut St., PHILADELPHIA, PA.

Mention The Florists' Exchange when writing.

FERNS AND ASPARAGUS

Fine stock; pot grown.

Piersoni, 6 in. 35c.; 5 in. 25c.; 4 in. 15c
Bostons, 5 in. 25c.; 4 in. 15c.
Scottii, 4 in. 20c.; 3 in. 15c.
Anna Foster, 2½ in. 4c.
Asparagus Plumosus and **Sprengeri**, 3½ in. fine, 6c. **Plumosus Nanus**, 2½ in., extra, $2.50 per 100. **Vinca Major**, field stock, long tops, $5.00 per 100. **Vinca Major**, variegated, and **Hydrangea Otaksa**, 2½ in. $2.50 per 100. **Hydrangea Grandiflora** and **Spirea** Anthony Waterer, 3 year old bushes, 8c. 50,000 **Shrubs, Vines, Cannas**, etc., low; these must be sold. List free. Cash please.

BENJ. CONNELL
WEST GROVE, PA.
Mention The Florists' Exchange when writing.

FERNS

Boston, Barrowsii and Scottii, 6 in., $4.00 per doz.
Boston and Scottii, 3 in., $6.00 per 100. 4 in., $8.00 per 100.

Larchmont Nurseries
Larchmont, N. Y.

ASSORTED FERNS FOR FERNERIES
IN BEST VARIETIES

We have an exceptionally fine stock of these goods and to make room will fill immediate orders at $20.00 per 1000.

Let us have your order to-day.

WRITE FOR PRICE LIST OF GENERAL STOCK.

THE GEO. WITTBOLD COMPANY
No. 1657 BUCKINGHAM PLACE, CHICAGO
Mention The Florists' Exchange when writing.

FERNS. NEPHROLEPIS BARROWSII

2½ inch, $6.00 per 100.

HUGH GRAHAM CO.,
Logan Nurseries, York Road and Louden Street, PHILADELPHIA, PA
Mention The Florists' Exchange when writing.

Nephrolepis Scottii

Plants ready for 6 in. pots at 20c.; 7 in., at 40c. Grown in full sun, stocky compact plants. For lots of 25 and upwards. Cash with order.

J. CONDON, 734-5th Ave., Brooklyn, N. Y.
Mention The Florists' Exchange when writing.

FERNS

Assorted, for jardinieres strong, healthy plants, from 2¼ in. pots, $3.00 per 100; $25.00 per 1000; 250 at 1000 rate; 4 in., $12.00 per 100.
ADIANTUM CUNEATUM, 5 in. pots, $20.00 per 100; 4 in. pots, $12.00 per 100.

FRANK N. ESKESEN, MADISON, N. J.
Mention The Florists' Exchange when writing.

FOUNDED IN 1888

FLORISTS' EXCHANGE

A Weekly Medium of Interchange for Florists, Nurserymen Seedsmen and the Trade in general

Exclusively a Trade Paper.

Entered at New York Post Office as Second Class Matter

Published EVERY SATURDAY by

A. T. DE LA MARE PTG. AND PUB. CO. LTD.

2, 4, 6 and 8 Duane Street,

P. O. Box 1697. Telephone 3765 John. NEW YORK.

CHICAGO OFFICE: 127 East Berwyn Avenue.

ILLUSTRATIONS.

Electrotypes of the illustrations used in this paper can usually be supplied by the publishers. Price on application.

YEARLY SUBSCRIPTIONS.

United States, Canada, and Mexico, $1.00. Foreign countries in postal union, $2.50. Payable in advance. Remit by Express Money Order Draft on New York. Post Office Money Order or Registered Letter.

The address label indicates the date when subscription expires and is our only receipt therefore.

REGISTERED CABLE ADDRESS:

Florex, New York.

ADVERTISING RATES.

One-half inch, 75c.; ¾-inch, $1.00; 1-inch, $1.25, special positions extra. Send for Rate Card showing discount of 10c., 15c., 25c., or 35c., per inch on continuous advertising. For rates on Wants, etc., see column for Classified Advertisements.

Copy must reach this office 12 o'clock Wednesday to secure insertion in issue of following Saturday.

Orders from unknown parties must be accompanied with cash or satisfactory references.

Obituary

Nels Pierson.

Nels Pierson died on Friday evening, October 5, at the home of his son, A. N. Pierson, of Cromwell, Ct., in the 85th year of his age. He was born in Gladsax, Sweden, and came to this country with his family in 1869. As a young man Mr. Pierson learned the cabinet-maker's trade, afterward attending a seminary and fitting himself for a teacher, which profession he followed for 13 years before coming to America. He located in Plainville, Conn., where he resided until the death of his wife, which occurred in 1900. He then moved to Cromwell and made his home with his son until his death. He leaves six sons, three of whom reside in Cromwell, two in Florida and one in Chicago. Funeral services were held at the house and at the Swedish church last Sunday afternoon. The burial was in Cromwell.

H.

CHRYSANTHEMUM RUST.—W. W. Wells, the English chrysanthemum specialist, uses the following remedy for rust: "Half-pound each of sulphur, soft soap, soot and lime. The lot should be boiled for half an hour in one gallon of water, a half pint of paraffin should then be added, and the mixture allowed to simmer for a minute or so, care being taken to prevent it from boiling over. The dressing should be allowed to stand until it gets clear, and may be kept in bottles. A quarter of a pint of the dressing may be used to a gallon of water. If, however, the fungus is very bad, and has obtained a hold of the plant, double the strength can be used without injuring the chrysanthemum.

"The solution should be applied by a syringe with a spray nozzle, and so that the under side of the foliage is thoroughly wetted with the finest possible film, repeating at fortnightly intervals. Mr. Wells advises treatment to commence from July 1, so as to prevent the stage of the disease when the most abundant crop of spores is produced, or from August onward, and also to prevent infection by spores when the cuttings are rooting, the spores no doubt having fallen from the old leaves on to the cuttings below."

Our esteemed contributor, Fred. W. Timme, this week resumes his "Timely Teachings," which have been so highly eulogized by many of our readers for the practical and serviceable instruction which the notes convey. Correspondence arising out of these weekly letters should be sent to the office of The Florists' Exchange direct and not to the author.

To Stamp Out the Stove Plant.

The New York Florists' Club had before it on Monday night last the perplexing problem, Is a Stove Plant a Greenhouse Plant in America? This is the same inquiry which was submitted to the S. A. F. O. H. for solution at the Dayton (O.) convention, and which, after several expressions of opinion had been given, was ultimately laid on the table as being too fine a point for definite and authoritative settlement by that august body.

The New Yorkers, however, disposed of the question in the most simple manner. They did not attempt to decide it, but considered that the interests of American horticulture, so far as they were concerned, would be best served by the elimination of the word "stove" from all exhibition schedules of the club, using only the words "greenhouse plants," the conditions surrounding the cultivation and employment of plants regarded as stove plants in countries where the designation and specific use of such stock may fit the term, not applying in the United States, with its extensive territory and widely varying climate. This abolition of the use of the word "stove" from flower show schedules by other horticultural bodies in America is also suggested by the New York Club.

In disposing of this ticklish matter along the line of least resistance, the New Yorkers displayed commendable sagacity; and their desire to unfetter themselves from the conventionalities and antiquated attachments that at times clog horticultural progress in other bodies is again made manifest.

Since the question seems to be an intermittent one, which like Banquo's ghost will not down, it might be well to present here the views of accepted authorities, both lay and technical, on the subject.

The Century Dictionary says, while the word "stove" is obsolete in the main, yet it is still in use specifically in some cases. Among these is Horticulture, and the following is the Century's definition of a stove house: "A closed and artificially heated building for the culture of tender plants; the same as a greenhouse or hothouse except that the stove maintains a higher temperature—not lower than 60 degrees F."

A hothouse, according to the same authority, is "a structure kept artificially heated for the growth of tender exotic plants or sub-tropical plants, or for the production of native fruits, flowers, etc., out of season. In degree of temperature, strictly, the hothouse stands between the greenhouse and the stove or orchid house."

The following information on the subject is given in Bailey's Cyclopedia of American Horticulture, the latest work of its class:

"In America the word greenhouse is used generleally for any glass building in which plants are grown, with the exception of cold frames and hotbeds. Originally, and etymologically, however, it means a house in which plants are kept alive or green; in the greenhouse plants are placed for Winter protection, and it is not expected that they shall grow. . . . . The old or original conception of a greenhouse as a place for protecting and storing plants is practically extinct, at least in America.

'Other types of plant houses are the conservatory, in which plants are kept for display; the forcing-house, in which plants are forced to grow at other times than their normal season; the stove or warmhouse; the propagating pit. Originally the warmest part of the planthouse, that part in which tropical plants were grown, was heated by a stove made of brick, and the house itself came to be called a stove. This use of the word stove to designate the warmest part or room of the range is universal in England, but in America we prefer the word warmhouse (and this word is used in this Cyclopedia). Originally, hothouse was practically equivalent to stove, but this term is little used in this country, and when used is mostly applied generically in the sense of greenhouse.

"It will thus be seen that there is no one word which is properly generic for all glass plant houses. The word glasshouse has been suggested, and it is often used in this work; but there are other glass houses than those used for plants. It seems best, therefore, to use the word greenhouse for all glass buildings in which plants are grown; and usage favors this conclusion."

The latter paragraph quoted from Bailey is significant, and seems to justify the step the New York Florists' Club has taken. It is self-evident that any other appellative method than that now decided upon by the New Yorkers, in view of the complex character of the question, can only continue to be creative of confusion, complaint, and dissatisfaction. In the designating of classes in our flower show schedules, as in everything else connected with horticulture in America, we must conform to American conditions and requirements, if we would seek the best welfare and contentment of all concerned. Classes for "stove and greenhouse plants" should therefore, we think, cease to be included in these schedules; and while the designation "greenhouse plants" may not fully meet the case, it comes nearer doing so than anything else yet presented, for the particular class of stock which the term is intended to cover; i.e., tender as against purely hardy plants.

The subject is an important one to exhibitors, and it would, we believe, greatly simplify matters if the S. A. F. O. H., instead of summarily disposing of it, would either officially endorse the action taken by the New York Florists' Club, recommending that action for general acceptance, or evolve a classification, or specification, that would more completely and adequately cover the case in point. A change of some kind, along the lines mentioned, is necessary, as against compelling schedule makers to specify separately every plant eligible under the heading "stove and greenhouse plants," which is now all but imperative in order that a just decision may be rendered; and an individual or promiscuous conception or definition by judges of that term and what is embodied in it, is neither sensible nor satisfying.

At all events, we believe American conditions demand a reform in the use and application of the term "stove," in the case under consideration, even to the extent of its complete elimination from our horticultural vocabulary.

After the U. S. Express Company.

According to the daily press, the S. A. F. O. H. has filed a complaint, regarding the excessive rates charged by the United States Express Company for cut flowers from points in New Jersey and Pennsylvania to New York, with the Inter-State Commerce Commission. It is stated the complaint sets forth that the high price of flowers in New York is due in part to these excessive express charges. The petition asks the commission to fix a just and reasonable rate for the transportation of flowers by express.

We hope the society may succeed in its endeavor and feel that its present action may well be regarded as a rebuke to those who unthinkingly advance the assertion that the national society does but little for the trade at any time, and nothing in the interval between the annual meetings. It is to be hoped also, that those whose cause the organization is now more directly championing will show their appreciation of its endeavor in their behalf by swelling the membership list.

OUR READERS' VIEWS

The Original S. A. F. Funeral Design.

Editor Florists' Exchange:

Our good friend, J. Ivera Donlan, has done well in calling attention to the beautiful emblem that was used at the funerals of three of the first members of the S. A. F. How dear and yet how full of sadness it is to me, who at this moment can so vividly remember the events! The death of William Bennett occurred in March, 1884, on the Monday after the great and glorious show of C. H. Klunder (who, also, is no more) held in the Metropolitan. Mr. Bennett was a king in horticulture in every branch, and a prince otherwise. Henry Sackersdorff was just making his mark—young, ambitious, and a worker. My heart to-day goes out to John H. Taylor (for whom Mr. Sackersdorff was foreman) for the manner in which he cared for the widow and the children. Some people called him "young John Taylor." May he never grow old! The third, one of the most brilliant, capable, studious, alert, winning and confident of all of my acquaintances in the broader lines of horticulture—how I loved him—was the only James Young Murkland.

So far, seemingly, the S. A. F., the society of all societies, ought to have an acknowledged emblem, one that shall redound to the society—as it is to me the one society that should have something which wherever it is seen shall be beyond question artistic, beautiful and commemorative.

In a Western city a year ago, in the company of a score or more members of several organizations such as Masons, Elks, Oddfellows, Knights, Royal Arcanums and others, the conversation drifted from one thing to another to memorial emblems of the various representative orders. When it came my turn I was asked, "What is the S. A. F.'s emblem?" I replied, "Originally it was a roll of honor." Is it a case of blacksmiths' horses and shoemakers' wives, or what?

JOHN THORPE.

National Council of Horticulture.

Arrangements have been made for a meeting of the National Council of Horticulture, at Chicago, Friday, November 9, at 10 o'clock a. m. Delegates are requested to meet at the flower store of Mr. P. J. Hauswirth, 227 Michigan avenue, and from there will go to a room in the Auditorium Annex, where the sessions will be held.

Details for the press bureau work for the coming year will be considered and acted upon, together with the matter of holding a National Congress of Horticulture and Horticultural Exhibition at the Jamestown Exposition, in 1907. It is expected that a report will be made by Robert Craig, who is making a personal visit to the Jamestown Exposition Company for the purpose of investigating the practicability of holding a congress and exhibition. Other matters which should be brought before the congress will be considered at this time.

Those having thoughts or suggestions for the consideration of the Council are asked to correspond with the secretary, or if possible to be present at the meeting of the Council and present their veiws.

H. C. IRISH, Secretary.

CLUB AND SOCIETY DOINGS.

NEW YORK FLORISTS' CLUB.—The regular nthly meeting of this club was held in the Grand era House building, corner of Eighth avenue and enty-third street, on Monday evening, October 1906. President John Scott occupied the chair, d there was a large attendance. Mr. Wheeler, the outing committee, reported that after all penses had been paid connected with the last ting, a balance of $4.40 remained to the credit of e club. The committee was discharged with anks, Mr. O'Mara characterizing it as one of the rdest-working bodies of the club. Resolutions re read on the deaths of Roger O'Mara, Joseph rsyth Johnson and James Weir, Jr., by Messrs. allace, Wheeler and Birnie, respectively. The folwing new members were elected: Anton Zvonek, L. C. Lovett and H. Turner. L. Boelson and drew Wilson were proposed for membership. ree resignations were tendered, among them that Mr. Samuel L. Thorne of Millbrook, N. Y. In ew of the eminent services rendered to horticulre by Mr. Thorne, and his liberality in furthering e art, the club voted to elect him an honorary ember.

The following committee was appointed to nomite officers for the ensuing year: Messrs. A. Wal-e, Chas. Lenker, Geo. A. Skene, Jas. T. Scott, hn Donaldson, Walter F. Sheridan and Wm. ckham.

President Scott appointed as a committee to draft solutions on the death of the mother of the Burtt Brothers, seedsmen, Messrs. L. W. Wheeler, W. Marshall and Wm. Rickards. A committee was so appointed, consisting of Messrs. Wallace and ller, to perform a similar service in the case of e late Paul R. B. Pierson of Tarrytown, N. Y.

President Scott urged the members to make more tensive use of the "Question Box," in which also uld be placed for the consideration of the club, ggestions tending to its betterment and progress.

An animated discussion, originated by A. Jænicke, the subject of, "Is a Stove Plant a Greenhouse ant in America?" then took place. The question s one which had been previously considered by the ciety of American Florists and Ornamental Horulturists at Dayton, and had been there laid on the ble, the point of difference having been considered fine for definite settlement. It was brought out the discussion that plants considered stove plants England were used in this country as sub-tropical dding plants, for instance: crotons, fancy-leaved ladiums, etc. After the subject had been thorghly discussed by Messrs. Butterfield, O'Mara, heeler, Lenker, Birnie, Wallace, Beaulieu, Turner, gent and others, the following motion, presented Mr. O'Mara, was carried, namely: "That the esent designation of stove and greenhouse plants changed in all exhibitions of this club to read eenhouse plants;' further that we suggest to horticultural bodies the advisability of conformg to this action by this club." President Scott cated the chair, and took the floor against a too sty settlement of the matter. He stated that all rdeners recognize a distinction between stove and eenhouse plants, and that the subject should be ferred to a competent committee for full considation before the motion was adopted. This view put into the form of an amendment, which was st. Mr. Weathered, while agreeing that the plan oposed was the easiest way out of the difficulty, ated that when called on to carry out heating rk connected with stove houses, the temperature such a house was always supposed to be 75 deees or over. Mr. O'Mara thought the word tove" was obsolete, and had its origin back in the riods of antiquity when greenhouses were heated stoves. This view was also held by Mr. Wheeler. r. Birnie stated that in Scotland, when serving his prenticeship as a gardener, stove plants were rerded as those requiring fire heat all the year und. It was pointed out that the Massachusetts orticultural Society adopted the classification of ove and greenhouse plants in its schedules, thus owing that the term "stove plants" was recogzed in this country as well as in England. The scussion ended, as stated, in the adoption of Mr Mara's motion.

The exhibition committee was instructed to make strenuous endeavor to have a representative showg of seasonable stock at the November meeting.

The exhibits of the evening were neither numers nor varied. O. V. Zangen, Hoboken, N. J., owed very fine blooms of the Barberton daisy, rbera Jamesoni. The stems were approximately o feet in length, and Mr. Zangen informs us that e flowers had been cut from plants grown from ed, sown in the late Summer of 1905, the plants naining outdoors all Winter, being afforded some otection with salt hay. This is certainly an easy y to grow the gerbera, and now it is up to somedy to get this plant so that it will flower undantly at Christmas time, a matter which Mr. ngen says can be very easily done if suitable eenhouse conditions are afforded.

Fred Hollander of Ozone Park, N. Y., showed a se of mixed dahlias; and Henri Beaulieu of Woodlven, N. Y., several vases, among which was the riety Gros Pappe. Chas. H. Totty of Madison, J., exhibited a few flowers of the chrysanthemum, s. P. R. Fothergill, a variety that seems more apted for exhibition than commercial purposes. drew Wilson, Summit, N. J., had samples of his nt oil.

THE COLUMBUS (OHIO) FLORISTS' CLUB held its first regular meeting last Tuesday evening, with President Stephens in the chair. Owing to the sickness of our secretary, M. B. Faxon took charge of the records for the evening. It was decided some time ago that our club give no public exhibition of chrysanthemums this Fall; but at this meeting arrangements were made for a display of plants and cut-blooms at one of the November evening meetings for the enjoyment of the members and their friends. While this show will be in a way informal, nevertheless many fine exhibits will be made, as practically every member of the craft here has this season been growing chrysanthemums more extensively than ever before. To take charge of this chrysanthemum display, a committee consisting of Messrs. Albert M. Hills, John H. Williams, and Edward Helfrich was appointed. In regard to the children's school gardens, Vice-President Curry reported that in a few days the sweepstake prizes of $5 and $3 would be awarded. These prizes are in addition to the many already given out by the school committee. The club voted $20 to buy bulbs for distribution to the public school children; this matter also to be in charge of Mr. Curry. P. F. Hemer was elected a member. The committee appointed at the last meeting, consisting of Messrs. Stephens, McKellar, and Faxon, reported that new quarters for our club's headquarters had been secured in the Brent building, and that the rooms were very desirable. The matter of raising the annual dues again came up for discussion, but the committee on this matter was not ready to report; so the subject went over to the next meeting. The club empowered the committee on the chrysanthemum show to be held at the club rooms in November to use a reasonable amount of money for prizes. The topic of discussion was the one started at the last meeting—the question of economic financial management. Messrs. Faxon, Stephens, Curry, Hemer and others took part in this talk. The next meeting, which is the annual one, will be held Tuesday evening, October 16. Much interest is already manifested in the forthcoming election of officers, and a very large attendance is expected.

F. W.

The Late C. W. Turnley.

Chrysanthemum Gossip for 1906.

With most florists who grow roses, carnations and chrysanthemums, first place and choicest position are always given the rose; the second best is accorded the carnation, while the chrysanthemum is relegated to "any old place," only provided that there be tolerably fair head room for it. Plants are much like people. Let a person insist on having a certain place or on being accorded a certain consideration, and let him resent in a spirited manner any disregard of his expressed wishes and he is pretty sure to get what he wants, whether granted cheerfully or not. In this way the rose has secured for herself the upper seats in every establishment where she is grown, or failing this, she retaliates by a shower of mildew or black spot, which quickly brings her manager to time. The carnation, while less given to open resentment, has means of keeping her grower in wholesome awe of her; but it is only of late years, and with the most ambitious exhibitors that the chrysanthemum has received much consideration as to her blooming quarters; but as the old style greenhouse passes, and the new up-to-date structures replace it, the chrysanthemum is being counted in, and will be found growing in high, broad houses, where the pure air is in free circulation carrying life and vigor into every leaf.

Two of our 400 foot houses are 18 feet high at the ridge, and we had several times reconsidered and decided that they probably contained a good many cubic feet of wasted space; but this year in a rearrangement of stock with the new place, they somehow got planted to chrysanthemums, with an apology to ourselves for giving up such valuable space to this tribe from the East, who are supposed to care little where their tents may be pitched, if only the man with the knife will make no mistake in selecting their buds. But—on tile benches, with plenty of room overhead, and free air coursing in every direction, these chrysanthemums have developed heavier stems and more perfect foliage than we have ever before seen on our place, and we feel sure that the big houses are largely responsible. Good sanitary conditions bring out the best in plant or man.

The most interesting thing in chrysanthemums to date has been Monrovia, of which we cut our first half dozen on September 4—big exhibition blooms—while on October 4 the bench is cleared. Monrovia leads the procession, sure, and is drum major at that. On October 1, we cut some nice Opah, though not comparable in size to Monrovia, but very graceful and pure in color. Then there will be nothing doing in standard varieties till Polly Rose comes in. Every grower of this grand early white has been surprised and delighted at the quickness with which it spreads into a broad disc of white from a very small and unpromising bud. It is grand for its date, and would be even more valuable, if it could be brought in with selected Monrovia stock in September.

And still there is no good early pink. Glory of the Pacific is so persistently faded in tone, that it is little grown at present. Among the newer sorts, we have been watching with interest the early pink Rosiere, which is showing good habit and foliage and a bright lilac color on October 5, though it will not be finished for another week.

October Frost looks to be an unusually valuable early white, finishing nicely by October 8, pure in color, of fine form, a decided improvement on its parent, Opah.

Clementine Touset is living up to its record, a nice straight stiff grower, with dainty, firm foliage that allows close planting, and develops its buds very rapidly after showing the first touch of color.

Early varieties with big flowers that are easy doers are good property these days. Talk about chrysanthemums not being popular! The regular flower buyer is absolutely hungry for them as a change from the rose and carnation of the early crops, and before these staples are in the full glory of their Winter perfection. Any florist who caters to the cutflower trade will do well to watch for the really fine things among the new earlies.

M. Nonin in France and several of the large growers in England make a specialty of sets of earlies, but so far as tested they do not meet American demands, as they approach the pompon class too closely in size of bloom and shortness of stem, though many of them have a beauty of their own, and, worst of all, too many of them fail to bloom to date and coming later, have to compete for place with the big Japs against which they have no show at all. So many points need consideration in the testing of a new chrysanthemum and there are so many ways in which one may miss bringing out its best points, that we are very glad indeed to have the experience of T. D. Hatfield to corroborate our own, his one exception being the yellow Henri Martin, which he has found to be a good early.

This matter of date of blooming seems as unaccountable as some of the other queer habits of the chrysanthemum family; yet it is far from being an erratic plant, and if we only knew the combination in full, we should be able to figure out results exactly I am sure. But several varieties with well established dates on one side of the water may come with a very different one on the other side.

Among the novelties on trial the present year, some half dozen sorts have already shown finished blooms, which is a remarkable thing for October 8.

One of these is Dubuisson-Foubert, a big golden yellow, 4 feet, with splendid foliage and habit. The first bloom, an early crown, was finished October 1; both form and size are fine.

Sargeant Lovy on September 28, had three very large, deep blooms finished. One of the very best of the year apparently; color, deep yellow, petals, broad and heavy with incurving center and of splendid substance.

President Loubet is one of the very largest varieties extant; approaching the Colosse Grenoble in type. It had finished nearly all its blooms by October 6. It may prove a trifle soft for reshipping, but any florist growing for his own city trade could not fail to find it a grand drawing card. The color is white lightly tinted pearl; habit and foliage all right. This is a wonder among earlies.

Director Gerard and Souv. Scalarandis are two other magnificent early yellows. Both are dwarf growers, with beautiful foliage and large, finely formed flowers. Until these are seen they cannot be appreciated.

Another very fine early white is a sport from Mlle. Suzanne Gauthier, 4 feet, pure white, very large and full and perfecting bloom by October 1.

Miss Roosevelt is one of the prettiest growers on the place, and we are confidently expecting it to prove one of the best of the year. The short joints, good stiff leaves, and plump buds certainly show wonderful promise, and the admiration in which the Roosevelt family is held abroad assures a fine variety to grace the name.

S. A. HILL.

Richmond, Ind.

NEW PLANTS

Stenanthium robustum.

Through the courtesy of Harlan P. Kelsey, nurseryman, Salem, Mass., we present a picture of Stenanthium robustum (mountain feather fleece), from a photograph taken at Mr. Kelsey's Highlands Nursery, North Carolina, which comprises 100 acres and stands at an elevation of 3,800 feet in the Carolina mountains.

The following description of this new plant is also furnished by Mr. Kelsey: "This remarkable hardy perennial is, without doubt, one of our best new introductions, and may be classed with the showiest of all herbaceous plants. As the buds begin to unfold in early August they are quite upright, and of a light green tinge, gradually becoming whiter until at last they burst forth into a veritable snowbank of drooping, fleecy bloom of purest white, the panicles often 2 to 3 feet long. In September the flowers, as they ripen, turn to shades of pink and purple. It is a vigorous perennial, attaining a height of from 5 to 8 feet when well established, and is absolutely hardy throughout the United States and Canada.

"The mountain feather fleece is of easy cultivation, and, if given plenty of food, makes a wonderful show equaled by few plants of any description.

"The illustration gives some idea of the wonderful effect of stenanthium when in full bloom, but inadequately conveys the beauty of the delicate, feathered, drooping flowers.

"The plant will do well in either a quite sunny border, or with some shade, but likes a warm location, with plenty of food. It does not show its best results until well established, say, the second or third season after setting out the smaller plants."

Mr. Kelsey adds that he has shipped many thousands of this plant to points in this country as well as abroad.

A Novelty in Antirrhinums.

Editor Florists' Exchange:

We have a decided novelty in antirrhinums of which the following is a description:

"The plant has a variegated leaf, the color of the leaves being about the same as those of Madame Salleroi geranium. The flower resembles that of the Queen of the North antirrhinum. This plant makes an ideal border plant, as it can be kept at any height desired. It is also useful as a specimen pot plant, besides being a novelty in cut flowers. About a year ago it appeared as a little side shoot among a batch of thousands of small potted antirrhinums, and after careful selection of cuttings it has now come to perfection. It has not been named yet; possibly it will be called Antirrhinum variegatum.

"Just now my stock consists of fifty plants, and it will not be offered to the trade before next Spring."

E. I. RAWLINGS.

Quakertown, Pa.

The Newer Gladiolus.

In the issue of the Rural New Yorker for October 6, 1906, Dr. Van Fleet describes some of the newest sorts of gladiolus that have come under his observation. The doctor has given considerable study to the gladiolus, has himself produced some excellent varieties, and his comments are therefore all the more valuable and interesting.

A Good-sized Gladiolus.—An attractive new gladiolus has been bred on the Rural Grounds from the now well-known G. Princeps. The parentage is Princeps, pollenized by Lord Fairfax, a vigorous direct hybrid between Gladiolus purpureo-auratus and G. Saundersii, bearing many large, drooping, crimson and yellow bell-shaped flowers. The new variety, which has not yet been named, is a straight and sturdy grower, tall enough when in bloom to look a six-foot man squarely in the face, and a picture of good health throughout the whole growing season. The coloring is bright, deep crimson lightened in the throat with creamy white. The bloom spike is usually about two feet long, bearing 16 to 20 large flowers, of which four to six open at the same time. It appears highly desirable for the garden on account of its vigor and soldier-like uprightness of growth as well as for the brilliancy and large size of the blooms, and is equally valuable for cutting, overtopping all other kinds when arranged in a vase. This new variety blooms normally in August, and has very large and solid corms, keeping well over Winter. It is not likely the stock will increase enough for dissemination before the Autumn of 1908.

Gladiolus Novelties.—Thousands of gladiolus varieties have been named and introduced to cultivation during the last 50 years. The standard has been raised so high that it is difficult to excel the efforts of earlier growers, yet a considerable number of new kinds are yearly offered here and abroad. They are the best efforts of industrious breeders devoted to this magnificent flowering plant. Some of the newcomers are good and distinct—others are apparently mere "fillers" to the lists, to be tested by well-to-do amateurs and soon consigned to oblivion. The following have been grown in sufficient quantity fairly to judge their merits.

America, of the hybrid Saundersii or Childsii group, originated in Ohio, the very fine blooms being sold in the Buffalo market for a season or two previous to its introduction under another name. It is a good, thrifty grower and produces a fine spike of large well-opened blooms of a pleasing shade of lavender-pink, a color much liked by florists and decorators. It was used last year to the exclusion of other kinds on the occasion of the first meeting of the Japanese and Russian peace envoys. Many flowers open at the same time, making it especially desirable for cutting. As a garden plant it is not particularly striking, the floral effect being rather fleeting.

Klondyke.—This and the following are of western origin, but we have not been informed just where they were produced. Klondyke is a purpureo-auratus hybrid of the Lemoinei section, and is offered as the best new yellow-flowered kind. As grown here it is not yellow at all, but barely cream white in tinge, with a deep crimson blotch in the center. It is strong in growth, and has fine thick-petaled rounded blooms of good size. While a good type of its class it is misleading to offer it as yellow.

Mrs. Francis King.—A plant of wonderful vigor, producing long, branching spikes of very large, light scarlet flowers. The shade is not pleasing to all observers, but shows up well under artificial light. A good variety for florists, and decorative in the garden.

Prophetess.—Sent from England as a fine new white variety. It is an offshoot of the Lemoinei section, and bears large round blooms, pearly white, but with a conspicuous crimson throat. A healthy grower and early bloomer. The red blotching is too conspicuous for this gladiolus to be termed white. The best true white we know is White Lady, of German origin.

Spray of Clematis Stans Var.

(See page 414 issue of Oct. 6, 1906

French Varieties.—The following were sent out by V. Lemoine et Fils, Nancy, France, two or three seasons ago, and are the best of their respective colors so far tested on the Rural Grounds. They have not yet been offered in this country.

President McKinley.—A tall variety of the Nanceianus section, i. e., a purpureo-auratus hybrid crossed with Saundersii. The large well-opened flowers are a striking shade of maroon-crimson with faint markings, the color being in effect nearly self or uniform. The plant has considerable vigor and seems adapted to cultivation in this country.

Feyen Perrin.—An enormous salmon-colored flower, borne in fine spikes, and relieved by conspicuous maroon blotches. Plant vigorous and sturdy.

Ferdinand Passay.—This is just what Klondyke turns out not to be—a good sulphur yellow purpureo-auratus hybrid. The habit and bloom are about the same and the crimson blotches are quite similar, but the main coloring is light, clear yellow, varying in shade in different individuals. It is a fine grower and profuse bloomer.

Chrysanthemum Society of America.

President Duckham has announced the committees to examine seedlings and sports on dates as follows: October 6, 13, 20 and 27, November 3, 10, 17 and 24, 1906.

Exhibits to receive attention from the committees must in all cases be prepaid to destination, and the entry fee of $2 should be forwarded to the secretary not later than Tuesday of the week preceding examination, or may accompany the blooms. Special attention is called to the rule requiring that sports, to receive a certificate, must pass three committees.

NEW YORK.—Eugene Dailledouze, chairman, care of New York Cut Flower Company, 55-57 Twenty-sixth street; William Turner, Thomas Head.

PHILADELPHIA, PA.—A. B. Cartledge, chairman, 1514 Chestnut street; John Westcott, Wm. K. Harris. Ship flowers in care of the chairman.

BOSTON, MASS.—E. A. Wood, chairman; Wm. Nicholson, James Wheeler. Ship to Boston Flower Market, care of the chairman.

CINCINNATI, O.—R. Witterstaetter, chairman; James Allen, Wm. Jackson. Ship to Jabez Elliott Flower Market, care of janitor.

CHICAGO, ILL.—J. S. Wilson, chairman; J. B. Deamud and George Wienhoeber. Ship care of J. B. Deamud, 51 Wabash avenue.

The official scales of the C. S. A. are as follows:

For Commercial Purposes		For Exhibition Purposes	
Color	20	Color	20
Form	15	Stem	5
Fullness	10	Foliage	5
Stem	15	Fullness	15
Foliage	15	Form	15
Substance	15	Depth	15
Size	10	Size	25
Total	100	Total	100

DAVID FRASER, Secretary.

Pittsburg, Pa.

Stenanthium robustum

Courtesy of Harlan P. Kelsey, Salem, Mass

The House of Thorburn, New Yurk—An Interesting History.

The business was established by Grant Thorburn in 1802 at 20 Nassau street, New York. Grant Thorburn was born in Dalkeith near Edinburgh, Scotland, February, 1773. Business was carried on at 20 Nassau street, and in 1808 by a miracle escaped total destruction by a fire which commenced in a soap and candle factory adjoining the store.

In 1814 the business was totally prostrated by the proprietor "expending his whole capital, and more, in fruitless preparations and attempts to raise seeds, etc., which could not be imported during the war." This notice appeared as an advertisement on back cover of G. Thorburn & Son's catalogue of 1827.

On the back cover of 1822 catalogue appeared the following advertisement:

"G. Thorburn & Son take the liberty of informing their friends and the public that they are constantly supplied at their warehouse, No. 20 Nassau street, New York, with a general assortment of Garden Seeds suitable for cultivation in the U. S. and West Indies; Grass seeds of every important and valuable kind; Hawthorn Quicks for Live Fences or Hedging, a great variety of flower seeds and roots, procured from various parts of the world; Spades, Shovels, Rakes, Hoes, Hand Ploughs etc., etc. Bird Seed of every kind; English split and whole peas for boiling; American and Scotch Oatmeal; English Grifts, etc., etc. A constant supply of Garden Seeds put up by the Society of Shakers at Lebanon, also their compressed Medicinal and Culinary Herbs!

"The more effectually to accommodate their customers they have connected with the seed trade a Botanical and Agricultural Book Store, where a great variety of the most valuable publications on subjects, especially the modern works of merit, may now be had, including the Agricultural Almanacs of the States of New York, Pennsylvania, and Connecticut, to be had every year as soon as published."

In 1816 Grant Thorburn recovered from the prostration of his business as recorded in 1814, and "with the help of $500 advanced by a friend" he commenced anew, "having for nine years past stood the attacks of several powerful opponents, and among the last though not the least, was the great Ruta Baga of Botley, the famous Wm. Cobbett, of political memory."

In 1822 catalogue we notice the following interesting quotations under the heading "Wholesale prices of Seeds For the information of those who sell again."

Asparagus	per lb.	$1 00
Beet	"	1 50
Ey. York Cabbage	"	2 50
Carrot	"	1 50
Corn Salad	"	1 50
White Spine Cucumber	"	4 00
Mangel Wurzel	"	1 60
Nasturtium	"	2 00
Spinach	"	1 00
Turnip	"	75 to 1 00
Fine Mixed Tulips	per doz.	2 00
Crocus	"	75
Hyacinths Mixed	"	2 60

In 1826 Grant Thorburn & Son purchased the Friends' meeting house in Liberty street. The house had been occupied by the Society of Friends (Quakers) "as a place of burial, school and meeting house for upwards of 140 years." This house is described in the Thorburn catalogue of 1827 as "a commodious two-story brick building, 40x60 feet, lighted with 20 windows."

This "commodious" building contained as well as a large assortment of seeds and bulbs a valuable assortment of song birds; "to the inspection of our whole collection, the public is welcome, every lawful day from sunrise to sunset."

The catalogues of the firm between 1827 and 1844 were destroyed by mice.

In 1844 we find the firm "James M. Thorburn & Company, at 15 John street, near Broadway; Garden and Greenhouses at Astoria, L. I., six miles from New York on the banks of the East River near Hurigate." Stages to Astoria at that time ran several times daily "from Chatham street opposite the City Hall," and prospective customers were given at the end of catalogues precise directions (of which above is an extract) as to how to get to the greenhouses with the assurance that the precise plants selected would be sent "carefully packed, to any part of the U. S. or West Indies." Up to this time the Thorburn catalogue was a small volume indeed, measuring only 7½ inches long and 4½ inches wide, and containing only 60 pages. Yet the assortment of seed of all kinds, including tree and shrub seeds, which has continued to be a specialty with the firm, was quite large, and cultural directions were given quite exhaustively.

In 1865 we notice the price of Daniel O'Rourke peas at $14 per bushel; Advancer, $1 per quart; Champion of England, $13 per bushel.

In 1864 the firm introduced the popular "New White Peach Blow" potato, a variety which in its day represented the highest achievement in the improvement of the potato.

In 1865 they listed for the first time Carter's First Crop peas at $2 per quart; and in 1866 McLean's Little Gem, at $45 per bushel. We also notice Yorkshire Hero priced at $20 per bushel, McLean's Advancer, $20 per bushel; Champion of England, $9 per bushel.

In 1867 the firm began to specialize particularly grass seeds and its catalogue of that year gave very comprehensive instructions for the formation of lawns from seed. The varieties of grasses listed as far back as 1865 included about 35. Since then special attention has been given this subject, and the grass seed end of the firm's business is ever on the increase.

In 1870 was first listed a collection of "Novelties," etc., under which head we find Conover Colossal asparagus, New Egyptian Blood Turnip beet, Crosby sweet corn and Alpha peas.

In 1871 hand lawn mowers were quoted and appeared in the catalogue for the first time—14 inch at $25; 18 inch at $30. In 1872 was introduced "Thorburn's Late Rose" potato, an unrivaled Winter sort of that day.

We have not spoken of flower seeds the firm having issued special catalogues of these only up to 1878 when their catalogue embraced seeds for all purposes.

In 1878 was introduced by Thorburn & Company the ever popular potato "Beauty of Hebron," and in the same year "Thorburn's First and Best" peas. In 1881 came the "White Elephant" potato, also this firm's own introduction. In 1882 the Challenger lima bean first appeared: it commanded a price quite high—$1 per quart; $25 per bushel.

In 1867 the firm listed for the first time "Trimble '5 Sugar Corn" which was carried along for a number of years until 1882, when it took its new and better known name "Ne Plus Ultra." The Country Gentleman variety, now so well known, was first catalogued by this firm in 1893, so that this popular late variety is Thorburn's introduction.

In 1886 "The Thorburn" potato was introduced, and in 1887 "Oemler's Triumph" water melon. In 1882 Thorburn Extra Early Refugee bean was first brought to light, and the same year the firm introduced its Market Gardener private stock lettuce. In 1889 appeared Thorburn's Pride of Newton beans, Thorburn's Improved Stonehead Heavy Red Dutch cabbage, Thorburn's Market Gardener private stock, Large Late Flat Dutch cabbage, and in the same year the firm introduced the still popular seedling potato "Rural New Yorker No. 2."

In 1890 we find the following introductions of the firm's:—Refugee wax beans, Extra Early Flat Turnip beet, New Everbearing Cucumber, Coldframe White Cabbage lettuce. In 1892, Thorburn Commercial pickle cucumber; and Thorburn Long Keeper tomato. In 1893, the first dwarf lima bean ever introduced was placed on sale by J. M. Thorburn & Company (their own introduction). In the same year were introduced two new tomatoes, viz:—Lemon Blush (Thorburn's) and Terra Cotta (Thorburn's). In 1894 came the world famous Carman No. 1 potato introduced by this firm and in the following year Carman No. 3 also introduced by them. Thorburn & Company have probably done more for the improvement of the potato than any other concern, and when the announcement came in 1905 of the new potato "Noroton Beauty," the greatest of them all, it was received with much acclaim and met with almost unprecedented sale.

We might go on noting the firm's own new introductions ad libitum if space and time would permit.

J. M. Thorburn & Company was incorporated in 1895 with F. W. Bruggerhof as president, Mr. Bruggerhof having been connected with the business and associated in its earlier days with Jas. M. Thorburn, for over 50 years. He is still actively engaged and is conversant with everything going on, himself superintending everything.

In the Fall of 1898 the concern was obliged to vacate the building occupied by it for upwards of 60 years at 15 John street, the property there having been condemned. It has been since then located at 36 Cortlandt street from which it has again been compelled to move owing to the condemnation of the building and many others in the same block for tunnel and railroad purposes.

The new warehouse at 33 Barclay streeet is a model one, and had just been completely remodelled. It is five stories high and has in addition to the basement a sub-cellar. Some idea of the floor space can be had when the depth of the building is considered. It extends through to 38 Park place, is 160 feet deep, and has a frontage of 25 feet on both Barclay street and Park place.

The Park place entrance will be used for shipping and receiving goods. A new elevator has been installed at Park place and the structure is therefore decidedly modern and up-to-date.

The path of advancement of the firm has certainly been very marked, and it is interesting to note for the sake of comparison the dimensions of the "large and commodious" building at 67 Liberty street of 1827 and the new, modern twentieth century structure now occupied by the firm. No expense has been spared to make this probably the finest seed store in America.

There is 28,000 square feet of floor space, over 1,200 drawers and closets for vegetable seeds; about 150 bins for vegetable seeds in bulk, about 2,000 flower seed drawers, over 250 receptacles for tree and shrub seeds alone, and over 40 bins for grass seeds.

Thorburn & Company have been in the city for about 104 years, and have almost from the beginning conducted both a wholesale and retail trade.

J. M. Thorburn & Co.'s New Store.

F. W. Bruggerhof of J. M. Thorburn & Company.

THE MONMOUTH COUNTY (N. J.) HORTICULTURAL SOCIETY held its monthly meeting on October 5. Final arrangements were made for the chrysanthemum show, and the premium lists were distributed by the secretary. From all appearances this will be the best exhibition the society ever had. Wm. Turner exhibited some of his seedling greenhouse melons; they averaged 7 3-4 pounds and received 98 points. They are the best flavored and the prettiest melons we have ever seen. George Hale staged as fine a collection of dahlias as can be seen anywhere; they scored 95 points.

This society will hold its fourth bowling match on the Sheridan alleys, with the Elberon Society. B.

FOR THE RETAILER

[All questions relating to the Retail Trade will be cheerfully answered in this column. We solicit good, sharp photographs of made-up work, decorations, store interiors, etc., for reproduction here.—Ed. F. E.]

Although the weather in New York is at this writing treacherous, we still urge as a last request, take care of and appreciate the dahlia. Any one who has batches of Dahlia camelliæflora, watch Jack Frost; pick them and save them, for they and spikes of the gladiolus you have put away in the cool cellar or room are wanted for what more expensive flowers cannot do.

We have noticed that for a great many seasons there is an early and extensive demand for high-colored foliage plants, so much so that toward Christmas there is very little of this desirable stock on hand. We are of the opinion that a large number of these expensive plants are wasted, for they are used to serve no other purpose than to make window displays. The cold nights will chill many of these plants, and care must be used in watering and otherwise attending to them. We suggest to the growers the keeping of a good reserve of such plants as Pandanus Veitchii, Dracæna terminalis, and high-colored crotons, for they will be badly needed later on in the season.

This is the time of year when there is a tremendous hotel trade, with the great on-rush of the traveling public and the wealthy citizens coming in to attend the opening of city residences. Sending flowers in a nice box is perhaps an easy way of doing things, but where they are sent to particular customers the putting of a cheap vase in the box, or sending the flowers in a vase, is more satisfactory to the recipient and shows thoughtful consideration on your part. There are very few hotels that supply guests with flower vases, and often fine flowers are put in the water pitcher or wash basin. Money expended in a judicious selection of cheap vases is a good investment, for not only are they continuously required, but they add much to the appearance of a store. Many bargains can be picked up in cheap glass vases at this time of the year. Have a few on the counter, with some dainty flower arrangement. They can but create a desire to purchase. Occasions occur when you can deliver many orders arranged thus, or have the artist arrange them for the people. Wealth is not an indication of excessive taste, and many an otherwise lovely cluster of flowers is spoiled by poor or faulty arrangement.

An Ideal Laurel Wreath.

The illustration is from a photograph of a wreath we made some years ago for the funeral of an officer of the "Rough Rider Regiment." The occasion called for a design commensurate with the deeds and events and feelings of the time when the pulse of the Nation beat high and the hearts of the people were alternately surged in sorrows and the pleasures of victory. We had often contemplated the making of such a design as is shown, but the occasion was shy in presenting itself; however, when it did occur it had our entire sympathy. And let me tell you, sympathy has a lot to do with the artistic makeup or finish of most work.

We used a 24-inch semi-crescent wreath, mossed it carefully round and on both sides with select and well-dampened sphagnum, and then covered the whole with green sheet moss. We stripped a couple of deformed bay trees of their leaves and washed the leaves thoroughly. We used twenty-five hundred of these leaves on this wreath, and each one was wired separately—the first set on wires and the selected top set on toothpicks. Both sides of the wreath were finished alike with the laurel leaves. When complete a piece of cotton dipped in a very few drops of olive oil was touched over the leaves to lend them a bright appearance.

The cycas leaves, one slightly shorter than the other, were pushed through the wreath at the stems and the tops tied to the wreath to keep them in position. A silk 18-inch American flag with a piece of crepe in its folds was attached.

The wreath was built on classical outlines, and being solid, made a most beautiful design, one we were and are very proud of, and it is still remembered by all who saw it.

It seems pleasantly reminiscent to look back at the days when the ivy and the laurel were the only green wreaths seen at funerals; and there was a time when the late Charles Zeller of Flatbush was the only one about New York who had a few bushes of Laurus nobilis, and we were willing and often paid fifty cents a hundred for the leaves. At that time there were soldiers, scholars and artists who knew and demanded the right material and work. Meaningless foliage was not recognized.

In the case where you are called upon to make a wreath symbolic of Fame, Victory or a Nation's or Society's esteem for its dead soldier, statesman or man of arts, or where you are called upon to furnish a funeral design to be shipped abroad or a long distance, we recommend this design. The flag of any country the occasion may require can be used, or in its stead a bow of royal purple ribbon. The two palm leaves represent Victory. The Laurus nobilis, the true bays and laurels of historic Greece and Rome, with the wreath represent everlasting fame. From $25 to $50 can be obtained for such a design. JAMES IVERA DONLAN.

AMONG THE GROWERS

F. R. Pierson Co., Tarrytown, N. Y.

The F. R. Pierson Company of Tarrytown and Scarboro, N. Y., has just completed the erection of two mammoth greenhouses at the latter mentioned place, and has them planted with carnations. This latest addition gives Mr. Pierson three houses devoted to carnations, covering an area of about 54,000 square feet. Of the two houses built this Summer, one is 350 by 56 feet, the other, 325 by 56 feet. These were built by Lord & Burnham Company, the style of construction of the first large house which Mr. Pierson built some two years ago being of the U-Bar type. The houses run east and west, and are what they term a three-fifth span, that is, there is a short span on the north side of two-fifths, and a longer span to the south side of three-fifths. Hot water will be employed for heating, and an immense boiler pit is in course of construction. Some idea of its size may be gathered from the fact that 75,000 square yards of soil had to be excavated. The heating will be done by two large locomotive boilers, and is being installed by the Johnson Heating Company of New York.

Owing to some delay, the houses were late in being finished, and planting in was somewhat late; still the stock is all in very good condition. One house is filled throughout with carnation Winsor. This is a

An Ideal Laurel Wreath.
Artist J. Ivera Donlan.

variety which has often been described in our columns, and which is to be disseminated the coming season. Mr. Pierson informs us that a very large number has been sold in advance, and it is evident from the condition of the stock that there will be no trouble in filling all orders, as Winsor is certainly in the pink of condition for propagating purposes. The varieties planted in the two other houses are White Enchantress, a novelty that Mr. Pierson will introduce; Helen Gould, a variegated variety also to be introduced; Red Lawson, Mrs. Thos. W. Lawson, Enchantress, Melody, which is a flower about the color of Enchantress, probably a little brighter, with the habit of Mrs. Lawson; and White Lawson.

Importations of azaleas have begun to arrive, and the stock received is in very fine condition this year, every plant being well budded, and bound to give satisfaction to the grower.

At the Tarrytown greenhouses of Mr. Pierson, there is another sport of nephrolepis that is being worked up into quantities, which will probably be introduced into the trade in 1908. This sport has a much more complicated form of frond than any other commercial form of the nephrolepis, and is a most difficult one to describe. From each of the pinnæ there seems to spring a new frond, perfect in its outline and character, which gives it a very full and massive effect. In addition to this sub-division of the fronds, the variety is distinct in its coloring. It has a rich, dark green shade, darker than any other variety of the nephrolepis we have ever seen, and this alone, together with its unique habit and compact form, will place it in a class by itself among decorative ferns. No name has yet been given to the newcomer, but we presume in the near future it will be named and placed before the trade at some prominent exhibition.

PITTSBURG (PA.) FLORISTS' CLUB.—The October meeting of the club was unusually well attended, considering that most growers are very busy at this time of the year. Fred Burki of the Bakerstown Rose & Carnation Company showed samples of diseased carnation plants. Stem rot seems to be the worst trouble in our vicinity, and the opinion of those present was that too much moisture was the main cause of the trouble. Mr. Crall of Monongahela City stated that his first planted were much affected and the late ones hardly any. Several other growers have lost many plants, causing somewhat of a shortage around the city. R. W. Smith, the Sixth avenue florist, showed some of the best varieties of dahlias used at present, which were grown at their farm in Ohio, about five acres being under cultivation. The cactus kinds seem to be in good demand, also the single flowers. Mr. Smith thought that the latter were more used than ever before, being most useful florist flowers. He also spoke of window decoration in florists' stores, stating what could be used advantageously and how it should be done. The decorations should not be disturbed, no flowers taken away for sale, and no old blooms permitted to remain. Frequent changes should be made, whether flowers or plants are used.

Wm. Loew, who carves "flowers" out of all sorts of vegetables, showed samples of his handiwork. He is quite an artist in this line. From the Phipps conservatories, Schenley Park, came a good collection of decorative plants, and cut material from outdoors. Among the plants were splendid crotons, dracænas, Pandanus Veitchii, aralias, ficus and others. The cut flowers consisted of Symphoricarpus racemosus, the snowberry, Viburnum opulus in fruit, with its bright red berries, Lycium vulgare, better known as the matrimony vine, very showy for decorations, and fruiting branches of Ligustrum vulgare variegatum, the Privet.

T. P. Langhans commented upon a window decoration made of dahlias and ferns, in one of our largest department stores; the effect was beautiful and most artistic, the rich colored blooms harmonizing with the surrounding colors of the goods displayed.

A motion was made instructing the secretary of the club to send a letter to the firm, expressing the club's appreciation of the display. One new member was elected. The next meeting in November will be Chrysanthemum night. E. C. REINEMAN.

Philadelphia.

News Notes.

The first sign of frost came on Sunday night; the ground was white Monday morning, and the thermometer stood at 34 degrees. From some of the dahlia fields in New Jersey reports come that frost injured some open flowers, but at other places no damage was done. Atco was affected, as but few flowers came from there Tuesday morn, although from Williamstown, three miles away, the usual shipment arrived. Already we hear that too many red roses are coming in, so that later on a glut of these may be looked for.

The new building into which on its completion the Leo Niessen Company will move, is being constructed of reinforced concrete. Three stories are already up.

The Hugh Graham Company have just received a very large consignment of plants from Europe, mostly of araucarias and palms of the best commercial sizes. These are what Victor Groshens bought on his recent trip abroad.

Godfrey Aschmann was in Milan, Italy, September 27. He will sail for home from Genoa.

The L. K. Peacock Company is shipping some very choice dahlias to Leo Niessen Company. The Grand Duke Alexis flowers were 3½ inches in diameter, on long disbudded stems. Mr. Niessen is very enthusiastic over the prospects of the coming season; he will be very strong on American Beauty and other roses and has a very large supply of cattleyas to draw upon. The carnation consignments, too, will be even better than last year.

John F. Sullivan of Detroit was here last week on a visit to relatives in West Grove. He says that the trade in Detroit is against the proposed change of holding the S. A. F. convention in November in 1908. There have been many like comments made in this city. DAVID RUST.

Rochester, N. Y.

News Notes.

The market in this place, has begun to take on its Fall aspect, and cut flower and plant trade is in full swing. Although to date no killing frost has visited us, still its very lateness has caused outdoor stock to be on the wane. Owing to heavy rains the last few days Fall digging has been set back, and as soon as possible outside work will be rushed in anticipation of severe weather later on.

Several new and decided advantageous changes have occurred this Fall, both in store and greenhouse, and from present conditions, a good season is looked forward to. A pleasant change is the moving of our commission florist, George Hart to more commodious quarters, also the fact that he now carries a full line of florists' supplies, the convenience of which is attested to by the frequent visits of florists in need of same. Only occasionally he receives visits from others than tradesmen, in the persons of Masonic fraternity who cleared his place of rakes, used by the local Masons to "rake in" the visitors to the annual convention of Shriners held here last week.

Referring to the cut flower trade, the market is good at present, a decided shortage being noticed in the roses of medium and better grades, for which there is a good demand at prices from $3 to $5 and higher for best assorted stock. Carnations are only fair, and bring from $1 to $2 per 100.

Difficulty has been experienced here in securing regular shipments from out of town of lily of the valley flowers, and while just now, perhaps, not so much in demand, a good price could be obtained for same if offered for sale, as few growers here care to bother about forcing this stock.

Reports from the seed houses are very satisfactory, and considerable has been accomplished in the sale of bulbs for outdoor planting, the grand showing yearly made in our parks by bulbous stock being largely responsible for this. COCKNEY.

Utica, N. Y.

News of the Week.

The Utica Florists' Club held a very largely attended meeting on October 2. The members were the guests of Spencer & Martin. After the meeting refreshments were served and a good time generally was had. The club has now invitations enough to last it through nearly all Winter. We find this a very pleasant plan, bringing out always a larger attendance. The next meeting will be with Wm. P. Pfifer, on November 6, at his residence 608 Whitesboro street.

Chas. Seitzer has his place in fine shape. He is growing mostly carnations this year, and they are some of the best. He is cutting extra good Enchantress. He has also a fine house of mignonette that bids fair to be grand, and a large bed of freesia.

Frank McGowan has also a good lot of carnations and chrysanthemums. He has repiped his place and made some changes at the entrance to his office, to great advantage.

Wm. Pfifer has about 9,000 carnations planted; he has a bench of Boston Market that is grand, and a fine lot of Enchantress and Mrs. Lawson.

Your scribe made a flying visit to Syracuse last week. P. R. Quinlan has been building a large house for American Beauty. The old plants are fine and the young ones will shortly be giving a good account of themselves. Richmond is well thought of. Chrysanthemums are extra good; they have two big houses of them. Mr. Quinlan has also extended his carnation houses 50 feet each, making six houses, each 200 feet long.

At Marquisee's place carnations are in good shape. Enchantress is as good in color and of nearly the size one gets them in Winter. One large house is devoted to seedlings. Some very promising crimsons were seen. Of his new white he has about 800 plants. It is the best I ever saw; and every one attending the Carnation Society's convention next year will have the privilege, I think, of seeing one of the best whites ever brought out. He has not yet named it.

Will Day is salesman and manager at Quinlan's Salina street store. He says business is good. Mr. Quinlan has another store at the corner of Railroad and Warren streets, looked after by his daughter.

Mr. Wheadon was busy with a big decoration; he also reports business good, extra so all Summer.

Joseph Trandt of Canajoharie was in Utica a few days ago showing some flowers of his seedling double petunia named the Queen. Its color is a crimson and white; some of the flowers are nearly all white on the surface with a tint of crimson deep in the flower, making it very pleasing. He says the plant is a very free bloomer. We shall probably hear more about it later on.

Peter Crowe has his plant completed now. He has been rebuilding some six houses this Summer, all for Adiantum Croweanum. He has taken out a 40 horse power and installed another 80 horse power boiler besides one he had before. Croweanum is extra good now. Peter says he will never build any more; he's got enough, he thinks, to last him the rest of his life.

Bulbs are moving somewhat. The quality is very good. Carnations are good and sell the best of all flowers now. Roses are improving in quality every day. No chrysanthemums have appeared here yet. QUIZ.

NEW BEDFORD, MASS.—We are now having cooler weather, and as a result trade has been very good, with a fair supply of flowers. Carnations are coming in of very good quality, though the stems are a little short as yet; 85c. per dozen retail is the price they bring. Roses are quite plentiful, selling at $1.50 per dozen retail. Most of the growers have commenced to fire their rose houses, the nights being very cool, but without any frost. Violets of very fair quality are arriving. $1 per hundred is asked. Chrysanthemums will be in bloom in a few days. Estelle and Polly Rose are the early ones grown here.

The Horticultural Society held its monthly meeting on Monday evening, October 8. Reports of the flower show were read and accepted. HORTICO.

FIRMS WHO ARE BUILDING.

MONTICELLO, IA.—C. L. Van Meter is building a new greenhouse.

BURLINGTON, IA.—J. W. Fye is erecting a greenhouse here.

WELLSVILLE, N. Y.—A. E. Boyce is building a greenhouse, 50 x 150 feet.

SOUTH RUMFORD, ME.—E. B. Dowie has built a greenhouse for carnations.

LINCOLN, ILL.—Otto Hembreiker is making additions to his greenhouse plant.

BRATTLEBORO, VT.—C. E. Allen is making improvements at his greenhouses, also adding an ell to his residence.

IOWA CITY, IA.—The board of regents has set aside $3,000 to be used in the construction of a greenhouse for the department of botany of Iowa university. The building will be 18 x 60 feet, and half will be used for a greenhouse, and half for a laboratory.

CHANGES IN BUSINESS.

MAYWOOD, ILL.—F. R. Hills has opened a new flower store at 503 Lake street.

CLINTON, MASS.—John A. Kittredge will open a flower store here in connection with a Boston house.

VENTURA, CAL.—The business of the late Mrs. Theodosia B. Shepherd will be conducted by her son-in-law, W. H. Francis.

HADDONFIELD, N. J.—The business of the late C. W. Turnley will be continued by his son, Albert L. Turnley, who has had charge of the greenhouse plant here for the past 20 years.

SPRINGFIELD, O.—P. J. Agnew has leased his greenhouses on Johnson avenue to William Campbell, and moved to Dayton, O., where he has assumed charge of a large greenhouse plant on Floral avenue.

MURRAY, UTAH.—Oliver F. Bunch and John and E. L. Post have formed a copartnership under the title of Bunch & Post Brothers. Their chief business is the growing of fruit trees on contract. They planted 300,000 grafts and stocks for budding last year, also about 80 bushels of peach pits; and expect to plant as many, probably more, the coming Spring.

KENILWORTH, N. J.—Charles Frost, the veteran vegetable grower under glass, is improving his greenhouses and will raise flowers for the New York market. At present he has a fine lot of Semple's asters. B.

HAMILTON, ONT.—F. H. Lamb, assignee for The Webster Floral Company, has disposed of the stock-in-trade to a new company, composed of several of Hamilton's influential merchants, which has been formed to carry on the business on a more extensive scale as wholesale and retail florists. In addition to maintaining the greenhouses and nursery on Wentworth street north, the new company is completing arrangements for a centrally located retail store, which will be fitted up in an attractive manner and should fill a much-needed want in Hamilton. The management of the new company will be under J. Connon, for several years with the late Robert Evans, and at present manager of The Steele Briggs Seed Company, and associated with him is George Davidson, who has gained a varied experience in some of the best greenhouses in Ontario. The directors will be well-known Hamilton men with the exception of W. W. Gammage, of London.

Euonymus Scale.

(59) I have been raising euonymus for the last eight years, and I never was aware of the existence of such a disease as I have noticed since last year. I have used strong tobacco water on the plants and kept them out in cold frames all last Winter. The disease clings to leaf and stem, and leaves a barren bush, like enclosed sample. Kindly inform me of this disease, and a possible cure, so that I may save my young stock and rooted cuttings now in sand.

H. Y. Z.

—The scale insects which you send with your letter of September 29 prove to be the euonymus scale (Chionaspis euonymi Comst.). This scale insect was described by Professor Comstock in the Agricultural Report for the year 1880, and was then recorded as being a serious pest on euonymus throughout Virginia. For the control of this insect we recommend the use of 20 to 25 per cent. kerosene emulsion made according to directions given in Circular No. 42, enclosed.

F. H. CHITTENDEN,

Acting Chief of Bureau of Entomology, Washington.

It is made after the following formula:

Petroleum ....gallons 2
Whale-oil soap (or 1 quart soft soap).....pound ½
Water (soft) ....gallon 1

The soap, first finely divided, is dissolved in the water by boiling and immediately added boiling hot, away from the fire, to the oil. The whole mixture is then agitated violently while hot by being pumped back upon itself with a force pump and direct discharge nozzle throwing a strong stream, preferably one-eighth inch in diameter. After from three to five minutes' pumping the emulsion should be perfect, and the mixture will have increased from one-third to one-half in bulk and assumed the consistency of cream. Well made, the emulsion will keep indefinitely and should be diluted only as wanted for use.

In limestone regions, or where the water is very hard, some of the soap will combine with the lime or magnesia in the water, and more or less of the oil will be freed, especially when the emulsion is diluted. Before use, such water should be broken with lye, or rain water should be employed.

Spots on Chrysanthemums.

(60) I am enclosing some leaves of chrysanthemum Colonel D. Appleton which are attacked with some kind of a spot. Could you please tell me what is is, and give me a remedy for it? I have been syringing rather heavily on account of red spider, and so have the roots more wet than usual.

C. S. B.

Ohio.

—The leaves of the chrysanthemum seem to be suffering only from too much dampness. This is probably caused by the warm nights, and the best remedy for the same is to have a little fire on, and a little ventilation also all through the night.

Mignonette.

(61) This Summer we planted a bed of mignonette seed. The seed was bought from a New York seed firm, we paying $4 per ounce for it. It was supposed to be Allan's Defiance. The plants are now 30 to 36 inches high, and some of them show bud. What we would like to know is whether the seed is true to name, as we have seen Allen's Defiance in bloom, and the plants were only 18 to 20 inches high. Our seed is planted in very rich soil; the spikes on the stems of the plants are the size of a lead pencil.

X. Y. Z.

New York.

—If there is any doubt about the seed being true, the proper place to apply would be to the merchants who supplied the seed.

Shavings as a Mulch.

(62) I mulched my Shasta daisies with shavings from the planing mill. After a year's trial it appears to be a success. But I am told if continued it will make the soil sour. Lately I see now and then a toadstool that comes up in a night. Is that a bad sign? Another person tells me that spading in the shavings is valuable in loosening a heavy soil. It looks reasonable. What would be the effect?

J. S.

Cal.

—It is a great mistake to incorporate shavings, sawdust or any green material in the soil, or to use it as a mulch; and the practice if persisted in will soon make the soil sour, and fill it with woodlice, ants and other vermin.

Propagating Clematis.

(63) How is clematis propagated? From three plantings of seed from a 10 cent package procured from an Eastern firm I did not get a single plant. Will it grow from cuttings, layers or slips?

JOSEPH SINTON.

—Clematis can be successfully grown from seed. Of course there are times when seed does not germinate, and a good plan would be to try again. Clematis can also be propagated from side shoots and layers.

Bordeaux Mixture for Tomatoes and Cucumbers.

(64) How strong should Bordeaux mixture be used for tomatoes and cucumbers; and how is it prepared?

Conn. R. D. M.

—To prepare Bordeaux mixture, take copper sulfate 6 pounds, unslacked lime 5 pounds. The lime should be slacked in just enough water to cover the lime. This formula is enough for 60 gallons of water. Suspend the sulfate in a bag just below the surface of the water; when dissolved the material is ready for use. Bordeaux should be used fresh—or, say, if spraying with Bordeaux, prepare the material the night previous to using it.

Another formula that is very effective for all fungicides is the ammoniacal copper solution. Take copper carbonate 5 ounces, ammonia 3 pints, water 45 gallons. Make a paste of the copper carbonate with a little water; dilute the ammonia with 7 or 8 quarts of water, add the copper carbonate to the ammonia and water and stir until thoroughly dissolved. This also is best used soon after being made. The advantage in using copper solution is that it does about the same work as Bordeaux, but will not disfigure the foliage, or, at least, it can be noticed only slightly.

WM. TURNER.

FERN FOR NAME.—W. C. H., Montreal.—The fern enclosed is a pellæa nearly allied to our common cliff-brake (Pellæa atropurpurea) and to various other species common to the West and Southwest. It would be practically impossible to give its specific name without more data than the two parts of fronds afford. Can you not tell me the character of the scales on the root stock and from what country it comes? The pellæas are often so much alike that their habitat aids in identification. If you will give me this data, I have no doubt that the exact specific name can be sent.

WILLARD N. CLUTE.

We Feel Flattered.

Imitation is the sincerest flattery; so says the sage. Bu[t] plays an awful lack of ori[ginality] "The Men We Meet" column i[n] teemed contemporary is a point.

Plant Notes.

LABELING AND STORING.—The Winter storage of cannas, dahlias, etc., will now occupy a considerable part of the time and attention of many growers. It is of the utmost importance, especially to those who sell the plants dormant or otherwise, that everything be true to name. Occasionally names get mixed in spite of all precautions, but very often this happens because of insufficient care, not to say carelessness. The growing importance of the dahlia and the numberless varieties cultivated make it necessary to guard against disappointments, by seeing to it that every plant before it is cut has a label securely fastened to it with the proper name of the variety written on the label. It should not be enough to label one of each variety, because the label on that one might in some way get detached from the tuber, causing annoyance and perhaps loss; better take the little extra trouble necessary and be surely right.

Although cannas are not as numerous in variety as dahlias, still it is better to label them also.

BEGONIAS.—Tuberous begonias should be lifted from the open ground whenever the foliage get nipped with the fall in temperature. A sufficient number of plants of fibrous-rooted begonias should be lifted and potted from which cuttings can be obtained later on. Begonias occasionally come true from the seed purchased or saved, and again at times they do not. When the latter is the case it is very bothersome, besides tending to have foreigners mixed with what is wanted in a batch of begonias from seed. I think cuttings are preferable, because stockier plants result from that method of propagation.

HYDRANGEAS.—In some localities from now on hydrangeas require that a sharp eye be kept on the weather. Small and medium-sized plants should be lifted and stored in a cellar or some other place where little if any frost can reach them. Large specimen plants will, if properly covered, be safe outdoors all Winter. Small and medium-sized plants would also be just as safe, but the method of covering for protection is so cumbersome that in their case it is more expeditious to remove them indoors on the first appearance of frost, or the unmistakable signs of it. The preliminary steps in the protection of hydrangeas to remain outdoors should be taken by removing all the foliage, leaving the plants thus denuded for a few days if the weather warrants it. Then, if a number of plants are together, the wood should be bent down and securely fastened; the wood of the first plant to a stake in the ground, the wood of the next to that previously tied down, and so on until all are secure. Afterward either cover the wood with green sods, which are preferable, or cover entirely with dry soil to a depth of at least 8 inches. Large specimen plants standing alone can be protected by the erection over them of a case made of cheap lumber, leaving space all round the plant for about 6 inches of soil, which can be thrown in from the top, an opening being left for that purpose. The wood of these specimens should also be tied tightly in bringing the top to a point. M. I.

New York.

The Week's News.

The warm Autumn weather has been the means of causing the chrysanthemum crop to be later than usual. This might seem strange, but it is a fact nevertheless, the warmer the weather during September the later will be the early crop of chrysanthemums. Such blooms as have arrived thus far have sold extremely well, and it is only to be hoped that this good beginning will continue right through the season.

G. F. Neipp, formerly of Aqueduct, L. I., has removed to Chatham, N. J., and is operating the establishment he purchased there under the name of the Floral Hill Gardens. As was mentioned in a previous issue, Mr. Neipp's Long Island property was purchased by the water commissioners for the city of Brooklyn.

W. F. Sheridan, 39 West Twenty-eighth street, has had a telephone switchboard established in his office, and his telephone numbers have been changed to 3532 and 3533 Madison Square.

Thomas Young, Jr., has secured additional space for his wholesale department by adding the store on the second floor of 41 West Twenty-eighth street.

Perkins & Schumann, wholesale florists, move this week from Twenty-eighth street to the Coogan building, corner Twenty-sixth street and Sixth avenue.

An unoccupied cottage and the adjacent greenhouses owned by Mr. Sloder, and formerly occupied by W. G. Gomersall, at Grand View, N. Y., were burned to the ground at 1:50 o'clock Monday morning. The origin of the blaze is a mystery. The loss amounts to about $4,000.

Chas. Robinson, who is with the F. R. Pierson Company, Tarrytown, N. Y., has been spending a vacation in Peekskill, N. Y., and while there took the opportunity to marry an estimable young lady of that village. Congratulations are in order.

Benjamin Hammond, Fishkill-on-Hudson, N. Y., writing from Port Arthur, Ont., says the city contains elevators storing millions of bushels of wheat.

The marriage of Miss Adele A. Taylor, daughter of John H. Taylor, of Bayside, L. I., to John P. Manning, of this city, will take place November 15 at The Oaks, the country place of the bride's parents in Bayside, L. I.

Miss Belle H. Kidd, a daughter of J. B. Kidd, of this city, died on Thursday, October 4, at St. Helena, Cal., aged 29 years. Miss Kidd had been ill ever since the earthquake and fire in San Francisco. During those troublous times she with her mother and sisters were encamped in a cemetery, and the strain experienced there brought on an illness from which she never recovered. The sympathy of the trade will go out to Mr. Kidd in his sad bereavement.

Minneapolis.

News Notes.

The Minneapolis Floral Company has made the most improvements among the growers with the possible exception of Will & Son, who built a large number of houses. But the Floral Company has expended fully $20,000 on new boilers and a boiler room which is up-to-date. The concern has also added three large houses to its plant. John Munson, the proprietor, reports a prosperous past season's trade and was forced to make the additions in order to meet the heavy demand. He has in all 45,000 carnations planted, besides vast quantities of bulbous stock which he expects to have in for the Christmas trade.

PAUL.

CLASSIFIED ADVERTISEMENTS

CASH WITH ORDER.

The columns under this heading are reserved for advertisements of Stock for Sale, Stock Wanted, Help Wanted, Situations Wanted or other Wants; also of Greenhouse, Land, Second-Hand Materials, etc., For Sale or Rent.

Our charge is 10 cts. per line (7 words to the line), set solid, without display. No advt. accepted for less than thirty cents.

Display advertisements in these columns, 15 cents per line; count 12 lines agate to the inch.

[If replies to Help Wanted, Situation Wanted, or other advertisements are to be addressed care of this office, advertisers add 10 cents to cover expense of forwarding.]

Copy must reach New York office 12 o'clock Wednesday to secure insertion in issue of following Saturday.

Advertisers in the Western States desiring to advertise under initials, may save time by having their answer directed care our Chicago office at 127 E. Berwyn Ave.

SITUATIONS WANTED

SITUATION WANTED—As foreman by a first-class grower of roses and carnations. 15 years experience; married. Address, T. D., care The Florists' Exchange.

SITUATION WANTED—By single young man as assistant in greenhouses on private place. Please state wages. Address, S. Y., care The Florists' Exchange.

SITUATION WANTED—By a thoroughly competent grower, experienced in both private and commercial work. John Fabian, 2158 West Kinzie street, Chicago, Ill.

SITUATION WANTED—Single working foreman. A No. 1 grower of roses and carnations. Take charge 50,000 feet of glass. Address, Florist, care Rich, 111 East 9th street, New York.

SITUATION WANTED—Young man wants position in first-class commercial or private place; 14 years' experience; first-class recommendations. Address, T. F., care The Florists' Exchange.

SITUATION WANTED—Florist and gardener, married, thorough and practical worker, wishes position with florist or on private place. Gardener, care Muller, 40 Charles st., New Rochelle, N. Y.

SITUATION WANTED—As manager and foreman, well up in cut flowers, especially roses. Strictly sober, competent to manage any sized place; can furnish best of references; answer with full particulars; mention wages. Address, T. B., care The Florists' Exchange.

SITUATION WANTED—As superintendent on private place by a thoroughly competent man. 18 years experience in all branches of the business. Married, one child. Address, F. J., 560 Maple st., Flatbush, Brooklyn, N. Y.

SITUATION WANTED—In greenhouse by Irish-American, single, aged 25, good habits, 2 years' experience inside and out. Am willing to work and take an interest in same. Have good references. Thomas Houlihan, Uxbridge, Mass.

SITUATION WANTED—At once, by first-class gardener, to take full charge of a private place, only where a learned and practical gardener is wanted. Married, no children, 31 years old. Can furnish best of references. Please state full particulars in first letter. Address, S. Z., care The Florists' Exchange.

SITUATION WANTED—By a nurseryman, 30 years of age, lifetime experience in one of the most prosperous nursery centers. State particulars and wages in first letter. Address, L. I. Rauber, 47 Chestnut street, Dansville, N. Y.

SITUATION WANTED—Young man, 20 years of age, having some experience, wishes a position in first-class flower store where he can learn to make up, decorate, etc., or in greenhouse with shipper of cut flowers and who does some design work. In or near New York City preferred. State wages. Address, T. A., care The Florists' Exchange.

SITUATION WANTED

By German florist, as a first-class designer and decorator, aged 35 years. Have been employed by some of the largest establishments in Europe. One year in America. Boston or New York preferred. EDWARD WEIFS, 14 Franklin Street, Norwich, Conn.

Mention The Florists' Exchange when writing.

Thirty cents is the minimum charge for advertisements on this page.

HELP WANTED

WANTED—Man for general greenhouse work; a good potter. German preferred. Address, T. R., care The Florists' Exchange.

WANTED—At once, good grower of carnations, mums and bedding stock. Wages, $35 room and board. T. Malbranc, Johnstown, Pa.

WANTED—General utility man for carnation plant. Steady, single; middle aged man preferred. Lebanon Greenhouses, Lebanon, Pa.

WANTED—Young man for plants and to assist in retail flower store. The Fernery, 14 West 33d street, New York City.

WANTED—Young man with good experience as greenhouse assistant on large private place. Wages $45.00 per month. Apply, Carl Lindroth, Narberth, Pa.

WANTED—Young man for the store; one with experience preferred, to wait on trade and make up. Munro, Florist, 974 Chapel St., New Haven, Conn.

WANTED—Experienced man to grow carnations, mums and bedding stock. Steady work. Apply, D. Y. Mellis, Holy Cross Cemetery, Flatbush, Brooklyn.

WANTED—Experienced night fireman for commercial place; steady work both Winter and Summer. Wages, $50.00 per month. J. D. Cockcroft, Northport, L. I., N. Y.

WANTED—A seedsman who is capable of taking full and complete charge of a retail mail order department in a well established seed house. Address, S. X., care The Florists' Exchange.

WANTED—A first-class man for retail florist in Chicago; no greenhouse work. Must be a good salesman and designer. State wages. References. Address, M. D., care The Florists' Exchange.

WANTED—An experienced foreman, capable of handling men and taking charge of a retail and commercial place. For further particulars address, J. J. McMannon, 8 Prescott St., Lowell, Mass.

WANTED—Young, single man to work in rose house and general greenhouse work. Wages to commence with $30.00 per month. Apply to Wm. A. White, gardener to R. T. Wilson, Jr., Palmetto Bluff, Bluffton, S. C.

WANTED—Section man for carnations; married or single. $15.00 per week to man with references as to capability and soberness. South View Floral Co., Room 36, Shannon Bldg., 326 Fourth Ave., Pittsburg, Pa.

WANTED—Competent young man to assist in the growing of pot plants; good potter and transplanter preferred. Permanent place. Address, stating experience, references, and wages desired. Paul Mader, East Stroudsburg, Pa.

WANTED—At once, experienced grower to take charge of a commercial place. Must be a first-class grower of roses and carnations, and be able to grow bedding and bulbous stock well. Answer with references and state wages desired. E. W. W., 50 W. Chippewa st., Buffalo, N. Y.

WANTED—Reliable grower of roses, carnations, mums and general stock on a place of 10,000 feet of glass. Must be sober and well recommended. Location, Western Pennsylvania. Give full particulars of references and wages wanted in first letter. Address, Box 690, Beaver, Beaver Co., Pa.

WANTED.

A thoroughly competent rose grower to take charge of section. Wages, $15.00 per week; to the right man a chance to work himself up to high wages.

Address,

EXPERT, CARE THE FLORISTS' EXCHANGE.

Mention The Florists' Exchange when writing.

WANTED

SEEDSMAN, capable of taking charge and developing retail department of an established house in a large Eastern city. A good opportunity for a bright up-to-date man. State age, experience, salary required. All comunications confidential. Address,

SEEDS, care The Florists' Exchange.

Mention the Florists' Exchange when writing.

MISCELLANEOUS WANTS

WANTED TO BUY—Greenhouses to be taken down. State full particulars of same when writing. Address, F. W., care The Florists' Exchange.

WANTED TO RENT—Commercial place of 10,000 to 25,000 feet of glass; must be in good running order near New York. Give full particulars. Address, T. C., care The Florists' Exchange.

WANTED—Correspondence with nurserymen who have trees, oaks and elms, suitable for street planting. Address, The Tree and Park Commission, 1317 Sumter street, Columbia, S. C.

FOR SALE OR RENT

FOR SALE—Established retail florists' business in Cleveland, O. For particulars address A. B., care The Florists' Exchange.

FOR SALE—Old established retail florist store. For particulars write to F. K., 700 N. 5th street, Philadelphia. Reason for selling: going West.

FOR RENT, cheap to responsible party, an old established florist business, six greenhouses and grounds. Apply at once to E. E. Morris, 64 Ann street, Newark, N. J.

FOR SALE—To a first-class florist only, stock and good will of a well-established retail place; "Fifth Avenue Trade" in New York City. Address, care Kervan Company, 20 West 27th street.

FOR SALE

A well equipped place, consisting of seven greenhouses, over 30,000 feet of glass, a nine roomed house, barn, stock, etc., and eight acres of land. This is a decided bargain and a rare opportunity. For particulars address

S. S. SKIDELSKY,
824 N. 24th St., Philadelphia, Pa.

Mention The Florists' Exchange when writing.

TO LET

Florist Establishment consisting of nine greenhouses, heated by hot water, containing about 10,000 square feet of glass; sheds, barn and dwelling, in Long Island City, within one hour's drive of the wholesale markets of the City of New York. For further particulars address Box R. Y., Florists' Exchange

Mention The Florists' Exchange when writing.

SEED BUSINESS FOR SALE

Established over twenty years. Located in large and prosperous city. Doing a business of about One Hundred Thousand Dollars per year. Splendid mail order business. Large counter and Market Gardener's trade. Best proposition in the United States to any one desirous of engaging in the Seed trade. Present owners wish to go exclusively in the Wholesale Growing business. This offer is unequaled as the House is thoroughly equipped in all departments with the best of Fixtures, Office Furniture, Cleaners, Electrotypes, etc., and can be purchased on favorable terms and at a cost many thousands of dollars less than the actual value. Address S. V., care The Florists' Exchange.

Mention The Florists' Exchange when writing.

STOCK FOR SALE

WE STILL HAVE 1000 QUEEN LOUISE; last call, 3 1-2c. each. Fox & Rosen, Parkerford, Pa.

PANSIES, 50c. per 100; $3.50 per 1,000. Daisies (Bellis), 60c. per 100; $2.50 per 1000. Alex Haeseler, Meshanticut, R. I.

200 CROTONS, 6 to 18 in. high, planted in field. 10c. each. F. W. Bornemann & Co., Lansdowne, Pa.

CARNATIONS—Strong, healthy, field-grown plants, extra large, Ethel Crocker and Flora Hill, $5.00 per 100. Cash with order. W. C. Pray & Co., Kinkora, N. J.

DOUBLE CAMPBELL VIOLETS, field-grown clumps, healthy, $5.00 per 100. Large Dracaenas, field-grown, $15.00 per 100. W. G. Kroeber, New Bedford, Mass.

ERICA GRACILIS — Beautiful pot-grown plants for forcing; delivery about October 20th. Price, $37.50, $45.00 and $55.00 per 100 according to size. 100 plants in each case. H. Frank Darrow, 26 Barclay St., New York City.

CARNATION PLANTS, extra fine, field-grown, no better plants anywhere. Joost, Wolcott, Pond, Prosperity and 100 White Lawson, per 100, $5.00. Terms: Cash. M. J. Schaaf, Dansville, N. Y.

BABY RAMBLER roses, fine dormant stock, $25 per 100. 2 1-2 inch-pot plants, extra well rooted $7 per 100, $65 per 1000. Orders booked for delivery now or any time up to late Spring. Samples free. Brown Brothers Co., Rochester, N. Y.

STRONG FIELD-GROWN CARNATIONS — About 500 Queen Louise, white, 500 May Naylor, white, 500 Prosperity, white, $3.50 per 100. No reasonable offer refused. Assorted stock geraniums, 1,000 best kinds, cheap, or will exchange all for pink cuttings next Spring. G. Stone, 64 Bay View Avenue, Jersey City, N. J.

PANSIES

None better, $3.00 per 1000. Daisies, Forget-Me-Nots, 50c. per 100. Foxglove, $1.00 per 100.

A. WENISCH,
Duncombe Ave., Williamsbridge, New York City.

Mention The Florists' Exchange when writing.

FOR SALE

600 Norway Maples, 12 to 16 feet, 2½ in. to 4 in. diameter, twice transplanted. 30 Elms, 4 in. or more in diameter. 2000 Evergreens, 2 to 5 feet, Blue Spruce, Norway Spruce, etc.

A. L. GILBERT, 40 Homer St., Springfield, Mass.

Mention The Florists' Exchange when writing.

FOR SALE—Ten acres of fine nursery stock; must be sold at sacrifice prices as lease of land expires next Spring. 15,000 Ligistrum Ibota, 18 in. to 2 ft. at $30.00 per 1000; 5,000 Ligistrum Ibota, 2 1-2 to 3 ft. at $45.00 per 1000; Aralia pentaphylla, Spirea Von Houteii, Viburnum tomentosum, Kerria Japonicum fl. pl., Rhodotypus Kerrioides, and 60,000 other shrubs. Write for particulars and prices to Rhode Island Nurseries, Newport, R. I.

FOR SALE

BARGAIN IN BOILERS—Two five foot horizontal tubular boilers, complete. High test; good as new. Price, $500, on cars. One boiler, $300. G. S. Ramsburg, Somersworth, N. H.

FOR SALE—4 Hitchings hot water expansion tanks. No. 2 high tank Fig. B. of catalogue. All in good condition. F. O. B., $2.00 each. Address, K. D., care The Florists' Exchange.

BOILERS, BOILERS, BOILERS.
SEVERAL good second hand boilers on hand, also new No. 16 Hitchings at reduced cost. Write for list. Wm. H. Lutton, West Side Avenue Station, C. R. R. of N. J., Jersey City, N. J.

FOR SALE.—One No. 26 Perfect Hot Water Boiler, made by Pierce, Butler and Pierce Mfg. Company, Syracuse, N. Y., having a capacity of 1200 square feet, in good condition, delivered F. O. B. New York, price $50.00. John A. Scollay, 74-76 Myrtle Avenue, Brooklyn, N. Y.

FOR SALE

Greenhouse Material milled from Gulf Cypress, to any detail furnished, or our own patterns as desired, cut and spliced ready for erection. Estimates for complete constructions furnished.

V. E. REICH, Brooklyn, N. Y.
1429-1437 Metropolitan Ave.

Mention The Florists' Exchange when writing.

FOR SALE

BOILERS Hitchings, No. 17 at $110.00. No. 6 Weathered, round, $70.00. 4 section round Cambridge steam boiler $75.00. 8 section No. 11, J. L. Mott boiler will heat 12,760 ft. glass, $175.00. 10 H. P. upright steam, $25.00. 6 section new Novelty boiler, will heat 4,100 ft. glass, $140.00. New Henderson boilers; send for price on size wanted.

PIPE Good serviceable second hand. No Junk, with new threads, 2 in. 7c.; 1½ in. 5½c.; 1¼ in. 4c.; 1 in. 3c.; 2½ in. 10c.; 3 in. 14c.; 4 in. 18c. 4 in. cast iron greenhouse 14c. 2 in. NEW, standard, full lengths, 8½c. ft. All kinds of fittings for 4 in. cast iron and all sizes wrought iron.

STOCKS AND DIES New Economy, easy working, No. 1 cuts ½-¾-1 in. $3.00; No. 2 cuts 1¼-1½-2 ins. $4.00; Armstrong Adjustable No. 2 cuts ¾-1 in. $4.00; No. 3 cuts 1¼-1½-2 ins. $6.50.

PIPE CUTTERS Saunders, No. 1 cuts to 1 in. $1.00; No. 2 cuts to 2 in. $1.30; No. 3 cuts to 3 in. $3.00; No. 4 cuts to 4 in. $4.50.

STILLSON WRENCHES Guaranteed. 12 in. grips 1½ in. $1.10; 18 in. grips 2 in. $1.50; 24 in. grips 2½ in. $2.25; 36 in. grips 3½ in. $4.50.

PIPE VISES Reed's Best Hinged Vise, No. 1 grips 2 in. $1.75; No. 2 grips 4 in. $3.50.

GARDEN HOSE 50 ft. lengths ¾ in. not guaranteed: 4½; guaranteed for light work; 7½, guaranteed for heavy work, 10c. ft.

BRASS HOSE VALVES New: not faucets; ¾ in. 85c.; 1 in 95c.

HOT-BED SASH New; Gulf Cypress, 3 ft. x 6 ft. 75c.; glazed complete $1.60 up. VENTILATORS; all sizes made to order. Second hand sash glazed $1.00 and $1.25, good condition.

GLASS New American, 50 ft. to the box, 10x12 single at $1.75. 10x12, 12x12 10x15 B double $2.55. 12x14 to 12x20 and 14x14 to 14x20 B double $2.70. 16x16 and 16x18 B double $2.90. 16x24 B double $3.15. 16x20 and 16x22 $3.00. 6x8, 7x9, 8x10 old, single $1.50. 8x14 old, double $1.65; 10x14 old, double $1.75.

LINSEED OIL Strictly pure; barrel lots, 42c. gallon.

CARNATION SUPPORTS second hand, 50c. hundred.

VENTILATING APPARATUS second hand, Hitchings make, arms, 25c.; hangers, 10c.; machines, $3.50; collars, 5c.

SCREWS all sizes; mixed wood, from 1 in. to 3 in., in boxes, 25 and 50 lbs. at 5c. lb.

PUMPS hot air; well pumps and force pumps; all repairs.

Get our prices on second hand wood material. We can furnish everything in new material to erect any size house. Get our prices.

METROPOLITAN MATERIAL CO.
Greenhouse Wreckers
1398-1408 Metropolitan Avenue, BROOKLYN, N.Y.

San Francisco.

News Notes.

The handsomest bouquet that can be formulated with the picturesque and fantastical flowers that will show their colors the last week in this month in the experimental gardens of Luther Burbank, is what he has in mind to construct. It is to be a contribution to the adornment of the home of the Wicksons on Bancroft Way, Berkeley, Cal., where the wedding will occur—the wedding of Miss Edna Wickson, daughter of E. J. Wickson, Dean of the College of Horticulture and Agriculture of the University of California, and one of Mr. Burbank's closest friends and stanchest defenders.

The better Chinese are reported to have a strong feeling against the enormous extension of the growth of the poppy throughout the empire. A San Francisco paper has a Pekin correspondent who writes: "China has asked India to consent to an annual reduction in the import of opium to China, which would have the effect of extinguishing the trade in ten years, and as an evidence of good faith has issued an imperial edict condemning the use of opium and forbidding the employment in the Government service of any opium eater, and has ordered an annual reduction in poppy cultivation leading to its extinction in ten years."

Like the airy structures built to adorn the great expositions of the world, the two-story temporary City Hall of San Francisco will rival in beauty of design and grace many of the more substantial public buildings. The authorities decided this week to proceed with its construction at once, the location to be the block of ground bounded by Van Ness avenue, Linden avenue and Franklin and Hayes streets, the site for forty years before the earthquake-fire of the Hayes Valley nursery and flower gardens conducted by F. A. Miller, president of the State Floral Society.

A personal check for $5,000 for the earthquake-fire refugees yet living here in tents was received last week by the relief committee from William J. Dingee, a floriculturist for the personal pleasure he finds in it, and an enthusiastic member of the Golden Gate Park commission.

ALVIN.

PATERSON, N. J.—No evidence of negligence could be found in the case of Conrad Fehter, the florist, against Simon Phillips, which was tried in District Court here, consequently, Judge Lewis granted a nonsuit after the defence had presented its testimony. Fehter maintains a store at 428 Main street, and Phillips lives above it. Some time ago a vessel, containing dirty water, was upset in Phillips' apartment and the water trickled through the ceiling to the store. It was distributed over natural and artificial flowers and also over a pair of pants, a straw hat and other wearing apparel. Damage to the amount of about $30 was due and suit was started in District Court for the recovery of that amount.

Lawyer David Bilder asked for a nonsuit, which was opposed by Lawyer Geyer on the opposite side. Judge Lewis in giving decision said that if a person were carrying a pail of water in rooms on the second floor of a building, were seized with a paralytic stroke, so that the water pail would drop to the floor and the water run through the cracks to the floor below, there would be no cause for sign of negligence in that. As the plaintiff failed to show how the water in this case was upset he had the right to presume it was an accident. No negligence was proved, so there was nothing left to do but to grant the nonsuit.

PASSAIC, N. J.—Fred Hansen, who is on a visit to relatives in Denmark, is expected home about October 10.

Wholesale Prices of Cut Flowers, New York, Oct. 11, 1906

Prices quoted are by the hundred unless otherwise noted

Roses	A. Beauty, fancy—special	20.00 to	30.00
	" extra	10.00 to	15.00
	" No. 1	8.00 to	10.00
	" No. 2	4.00 to	6.00
	" No. 3	3.00 to	4.00
	Bride, Maid, fancy—spe'l	6.00 to	8.00
	" extra	4.00 to	5.00
	" No. 1	3.00 to	4.00
	" No. 2	1.50 to	2.00
	Golden Gate	1.50 to	5.00
	Richmond	1.50 to	5.00
	Mme. Abel Chatenay	1.50 to	5.00
Adiantum		.50 to	.75
	Croweanum	.50 to	1.00
Asparagus		25.00 to	50.00
	" Plumosus, bunches	8.00 to	15.00
	" Sprengerii, bunches	8.00 to	15.00
		to	
Cattleyas		40.00 to	50.00
Daisies		to	
		to	
		to	

Carnations	Inf'r grades, all colors	1.00 to	1.50
	Standard Varieties — White	1.50 to	2.50
	Standard Varieties — Pink	1.50 to	2.50
	Standard Varieties — Red	1.50 to	2.50
	Standard Varieties — Yel. & Var.	1.50 to	2.50
	*Fancy— (*The highest grades of standard var.) — White	3.00 to	4.00
	*Fancy — Pink	3.00 to	4.00
	*Fancy — Red	3.00 to	4.00
	*Fancy — Yel. & Var.	3.00 to	4.00
	Novelties	3.00 to	5.00
Dahlias		2.00 to	3.00
Lilies		10.00 to	12.00
Lily of the Valley		3.00 to	4.00
Mignonette		to	
Smilax		8.00 to	10.00
Violets		.25 to	.50
		to	
		to	
		to	
		to	

Wholesale Prices of Cut Flowers—Per 100

Boston Oct. 8, 1906	Buffalo Oct. 8, 1906	Detroit Sept. 11, 1906	Cincinnati Oct. 6, 1906	Baltimore Oct. 1, 1906	NAMES AND VARIETIES	Milwaukee Sept. 11, 1906	Phil'delphia Sept. 11, 1906	Pittsburg Oct. 9, 1906	St. Louis Oct. 8, 1906
25.00 to 50.00	20.00 to 25.00	10.00 to 35.00	30.00 to 40.00	to	ROSES A. BEAUTY, fancy—special	to 25.00	15.00 to 20.00	25.00 to 35.00	20.00 to 25.00
10.00 to 25.00	15.00 to 20.00	to	20.00 to 25.00	20.00 to 25.00	" extra	15.00 to 18.00	10.00 to 15.00	18.00 to 20.00	12.50 to 15.00
6.00 to 10.00	10.00 to 15.00	to	10.00 to 15.00	12.50 to 15.00	" No. 1	10.00 to 12.50	5.00 to 7.00	10.00 to 12.00	6.00 to 10.00
2.00 to 6.00	3.00 to 10.00	to	4.00 to 6.00	5.00 to 10.00	" Culls and ordinary	4.00 to 6.00	1.00 to 4.00	3.00 to 6.00	3.00 to 5.00
to	6.00 to 8.00	3.00 to 6.00	to 5.00	to	BRIDE, 'MAID, fancy-special	to 6.00	to	to 6.00	5.00 to 6.00
4.00 to 6.00	5.00 to 6.00	to	to 4.00	4.00 to 5.00	" extra	to 5.00	6.00 to 8.00	to 5.00	3.00 to 4.00
2.00 to 4.00	4.00 to 5.00	to	to 3.00	3.00 to 4.00	" No. 1	to 4.00	4.00 to 5.00	3.00 to 4.00	to 2.00
1.00 to 2.00	3.00 to 4.00	to	to 2.00	2.00 to 3.00	" No. 2	to 2.00	2.00 to 3.00	to 2.00	to
to	3.00 to 6.00	4.00 to 8.00	2.00 to 6.00	2.00 to 5.00	GOLDEN GATE	4.00 to 6.00	4.00 to 8.00	to	2.00 to 5.00
2.00 to 8.00	3.00 to 7.00	to	3.00 to 4.00	3.00 to 5.00	K. A. VICTORIA	4.00 to 8.00	4.00 to 6.00	4.00 to 12.00	2.00 to 8.00
2.00 to 8.00	3.00 to 8.00	to	to	3.00 to 5.00	LIBERTY	4.00 to 6.00	3.00 to 6.00	4.00 to 6.00	to
to	3.00 to 6.00	4.00 to 10.00	to	2.00 to 4.00	METEOR	to	to	to	to
to	2.00 to 5.00	4.00 to 10.00	to	2.00 to 4.00	PERLE	4.00 to 6.00	to	2.00 to 6.00	2.00 to 4.00
to	to	to 50.00	to	to	ORCHIDS—Cattleyas	to	to 50.00	to	to
to	1.00 to 1.25	to	to 1.00	to .75	CARNATIONS Inferior grades, all colors	to 1.00	.75 to 1.00	to 1.00	to 1.00
to	1.25 to 1.50	to 1.00	1.00 to 1.50	1.00 to 1.50	Standard Varieties White	to 1.00	.75 to 1.00	1.50 to 2.00	to 1.00
to	1.25 to 1.5	to	1.00 to 1.50	1.00 to 1.50	Standard Varieties Pink	to 1.00	.75 to 1.00	1.50 to 2.00	to 1.00
to	1.25 to 1.50	to	1.00 to 1.50	1.00 to 1.50	Standard Varieties Red	to 1.00	.75 to 1.00	1.50 to 2.00	to 1.00
to	to	to 3.00	to	1.00 to 1.50	Standard Varieties Yellow and var.	to 1.00	.75 to 1.00	1.50 to 2.00	to 1.00
1.00 to 2.50	2.00 to 2.50	to	to	to	Fancy Varieties White	1.50 to 2.00	2.00 to 2.50	to 3.00	1.50 to 2.50
1.00 to 2.50	2.00 to 2.50	to	to	to	Fancy Varieties Pink	1.50 to 2.00	2.00 to 2.50	2.00 to 3.00	1.50 to 2.50
1.00 to 2.50	2.00 to 2.50	to	to	to	Fancy Varieties Red	1.50 to 2.00	2.00 to 2.50	to 3.00	1.50 to 2.50
1.00 to 2.50	2.00 to 2.50	to 1.50	to	to	Fancy Varieties Yellow and var.	1.50 to 2.00	2.00 to 2.50	to 3.00	1.50 to 2.50
to	to	to	to	to	Novelties	to	to	to	to
.75 to 1.00	.50 to 1.00	to 2.00	to 1.00	to 1.00	ADIANTUM	to 1.00	to 1.00	.75 to 1.00	to 1.00
to 50.00	15.00 to 20.00	25.00 to 50.00	35.00 to 50.00	25.00 to 50.00	ASPARAGUS, Plum. and Ten.	20.00 to 30.00	25.00 to 35.00	25.00 to 35.00	25.00 to 50.00
to	15.00 to 20.00	20.00 to 30.00	25.00 to 35.00	25.00 to 50.00	" Sprengeri, bunches	20.00 to 30.00	25.00 to 35.00	15.00 to 20.00	25.00 to 75.00
.50 to 1.00	to	to	.50 to 1.00	to	ASTERS	.50 to 1.00	to	.50 to 2.00	to
to	8.00 to 10.00	to 10.00	to 10.00	6.00 to 8.00	CALLAS	to	to	to	to
6.00 to 8.00	to	to	10.00 to 15.00	5.00 to 10.00	CHRYSANTHEMUMS, ordinary	to	to	20.00 to 40.00	to
to	1.50 to 2.50	.75 to 1.50	to	to	DAISIES	to .40	3.00 to 4.00	to	to
to	to	to	to .15	to	GALAX LEAVES	to	to	to	to
3.00 to 4.00	to	to	to 4.00	to 3.00	GLADIOLUS	to	to	to 4.00	to
to	to	to	to 15.00	10.00 to 12.50	LILIES, Harrisii	to 12.50	to	18.00 to 20.00	to
8.00 to 10.00	12.50 to 15.00	to	to	to	" Longiflorum	to 12.50	to	to	to
2.00 to 5.00	3.00 to 4.00	3.00 to 4.00	to 4.00	to	LILY OF THE VALLEY	to	1.00 to 2.00	2.00 to 4.00	3.00 to 4.00
to	to	to	to	to	MIGNONETTE, ordinary	to	to	to	to
to	to	to	to	to	" fancy	to	to	to	to
to	to	4.00 to 8.00	to	to	PEONIES	to	to	to	to
to 12.50	12.00 to 15.00	12.50 to 15.00	to 15.00	to	SMILAX	to 15.00	to	12.50 to 15.00	to 12.50
.50 to .75	to	to	to	.35 to .50	VIOLETS, ordinary	to	to	to	.25 to .40
to	.15 to .25	to	to	to	" fancy	to	to	to	to
to	to	to	to	to	NARCISSUS	to	to	to	to
to	to	.50 to .75	to	to	SWEET PEAS	.25 to .50	to .50	to	to

Pittsburg.

The Week's News.

George D. Blind has taken unto himself a wife, Miss Lillian M. Born the daughter of Jacob Born. The marriage ceremony was performed in the presence of relatives and intimate friends of the two families. Mr. and Mrs. Blind left for an eastern trip and expect to be home by the end of the month.

The Botanical Society of Western Pennsylvania will celebrate its twentieth anniversary by a banquet which will be held in the Hotel Schenley, Saturday evening, October 20 at 7 o'clock. The society has accomplished a great deal during the twenty years of its existence. It has accumulated an extensive herbarium, particularly of the flora of Allegheny county, which is in the keeping of the botanical department of the Carnegie Institute, and always available for examination and study. The society owns a valuable library on botanical subjects, housed in bookcases in the same institute, and accessible to members. In season field outings into country districts where the flora is varied are held, also public exhibitions of plants and flowers; and the indoor meetings once a month bring together people who are interested in flowers and plants. The membership is over 100.

E. C. REINEMAN.

Indianapolis.

News Items.

Mr. Hitz, formerly in the florist business at Madison, Ind., has purchased a tract of ground near Ashland avenue and Twenty-fifth street. A range comprising eight large houses is to be erected here in the near future. The plant formerly owned by Mr. Hitz was purchased by the State of Indiana last year for a public institution. He intends catering to both the wholesale and retail trades.

John Rieman has been unusually busy with funeral orders for customers in the Gas Belt cities.

Bertermann Brothers Company are cutting a quantity of Monrovia chrysanthemums at their Washington street place.

W. Stuart of Stuart & Haugh, Anderson, Ind., was in town in the interest of large wedding orders. This firm always keeps up-to-date.

A reunion, or at least it seemed so to the writer, of local florists occurred last week at the Customs House, when getting plants, bulbs, etc., out of bond.

A. Wiegand & Sons have had several store openings to keep them busy.

Mr. Petitt has finished a large greenhouse on Mayer's road. I. B.

Wholesale Prices of Cut Flowers, Chicago, Oct. 9, 1906

Prices quoted are by the hundred unless otherwise noted

ROSES

American Beauty		
36-inch stems.......per doz.	3.00 to	4.00
30-inch stems......... "	2.50 to	3.00
24-inch stems......... "	2.00 to	2.50
20-inch stems......... "	1.00 to	2.00
18-inch stems......... "	...... to	1.50
12-inch stems......... "	...... to	1.00
8-inch stems and shorts "	.50 to	.75
Bride Maid, fancy special......	5.00 to	6.00
" extra............	4.00 to	5.00
" No. 1............	2.00 to	3.00
" No. 2............	...... to	1.00
Golden Gate............	2.00 to	6.00
Carnot............	2.00 to	6.00
Uncle John............	2.00 to	6.00
Liberty............	2.00 to	6.00
Richmond............	2.00 to	8.00
Kaiserina............	2.00 to	8.00
Killarney............	8.00 to	6.00
Perle............	2.00 to	6.00
Chatenay............	2.00 to	6.00
Orchids—Cattleyas............	50.00 to	75.00
SMILAX............	8.00 to	12.00
LILY OF THE VALLEY............	2.00 to	4.00
DAHLIAS............	2.00 to	3.00
VIOLETS............	.50 to	1.00

CARNATIONS

Inferior grades all colors	...... to	......
STANDARD VARIETIES White......	1.00 to	1.50
Pink......	1.00 to	1.50
Red......	1.00 to	1.50
Yellow & var......	1.00 to	1.50
*FANCY (The highest grades of Sta'd var) White......	2.00 to	3.00
Pink......	2.00 to	3.00
Red......	2.00 to	3.00
Yellow & var......	2.00 to	3.00
NOVELTIES......	...... to	......
ADIANTUM......	.50 to	1.00
ASPARAGUS, Plum. & Ten......	.35 to	.50
" Sprengeri, bunches.	.35 to	.50
......	...... to	......
LILIES, Longiflorum......	12.00 to	18.00
HARRISII......	12.00 to	18.00
......	...... to	......
......	...... to	......
......	...... to	......
......	...... to	......
......	...... to	......
HARDY FERNS per 1000......	1.00 to	1.50
GALAX "	1.00 to	1.20
......	...... to	......
CHRYSANTHEMUMS per doz	2.00 to	4.00

Chicago.

The Week's News.

The State Fair which closed at Springfield, Ill., on Friday of last week was decidedly the most successful ever held. Notwithstanding the rain on the last day, "Springfield day," there was an attendance of 25,000.

It is announced that Garfield park is to become the flower center of the West Side park system by the erection of conservatories to cost $250,000, for which, by direction of the West park board, designs are now being prepared by Hitchings & Company.

Very extensive improvements were brought to light by a recent visit to the establishment of Knud Gundestrup & Co., 4273 Milwaukee ave. The former wooden building has been demolished and a substantial brick structure is being erected in its stead, the basement of which will be devoted to the culture of mushrooms, the ground floor to the business of the concern, and the second floor will be finished off as a hall with lodge room accommodations.

The usual Fall openings, which are carried out in this city to a degree hardly approached elsewhere in the country, are beginning to have their evidence felt in the trade.

Mr. Smith of the Chicago Carnation Company of Joliet was a recent visitor.

"The Busiest House in Chicago," is the trade mark recently adopted by the J. B. Deamud Company, and it must be admitted that there is certainly a very catchy and attractive sound to the phrase.

Louis Coatsworth returned from Canada last week, but owing to the quite serious illness of one of his children, afflicted with typhoid, his family was compelled to remain for the present in Canada. The little one is improving.

The Fall bulb business is rushing, and the employees of this department in the seed houses are working overtime.

Paul Berkowitz of Philadelphia was in town for a few days last week.

J. A. Peterson of Cincinnati, Ohio, and Mr. Kezer of Rockford, Ill., were among members of the craft registered here last week.

At J. A. Budlong's their early chrysanthemums are of high order, and a call at the houses gives ground for the belief that the season will be a long and continuous one and that the lofty quality will be maintained throughout.

Charles L. Hutchinson, a director of the Horticultural Society who has been abroad for a number of months, before his departure was authorized to procure a design for a medal to be known as the "Medal of the Horticultural Society of Chicago." The design has been developed, a print of which was recently sent here, and soon the dies will be made and the medals cast, and the awards made at the last show, about which there has been some worry, will be delivered.

The finding of an alligator by one of A. Lange's decorators in a case of smilax last week recalls the occasion during the holidays last Winter when E. E. Pieser of Kennicott Brothers Company sold a case of smilax that contained an opossum to a fruit dealer. Evidently the smilax shippers of the Southern States do not realize that Chicago is now in possession of one of the most complete zoological collections in the country.

A number of the wholesale associates have formed an organization to be known as "The Wholesale Florists Employee's Social Club," and have made arrangements to hold their first annual ball at Columbia hall on the evening of October 31. It is the intention of the interested parties to make this a permanent organization.

If the Mrs. Marshall Field rose attains a national popularity equal to that which it has achieved in this vicinity, and if the growers of the country meet success in cultivating it equal to that of Foreman Collins at the Peter Reinberg establishment, a wonderful future is in store for this variety when it is disseminated.

John Zech on Saturday last acted as clerk in his precinct during the registration of voters. There are a number of Chicago florists who take an active interest in politics.

August Poehlmann returned from the State fair at Springfield justifiably proud of the long list of blue ribbons won by the productions of the Morton Grove establishment as they captured nearly all the honors in the lines of roses and carnations where they entered.

Bassett & Washburn have issued a type written letter to the trade which says in opening. "We have a range of glass containing 800,000 square feet now completely rounded out and producing the finest flowers coming into this market. We cut our flowers especially to suit the shipping trade and watch the weather conditions closely. We bring the stock in from the greenhouses twice each day. In this manner the flowers are always fresh." Then follows a description of the present and prospective crops.

To paraphrase Shakespeare, "The show's the thing," and now all endeavors are being concentrated on the success of the coming exhibition. A tour of the greenhouses gives ample proof that the exhibitors, owing to the very fortunate early publication of the coming competition, have taken advantage of the fore-knowledge, and it seems probable, if not absolutely positive, that Chicago will receive a remarkable awakening from a horticultural standpoint between the 6th and 12th of the coming month. The executive committee and several subcommittees are actively at work.

Max Wilhelmi of the Barteldes Seed Company of Lawrence, Kan., spent last week in the city.

C. A. Urbach of Toronto, Canada, has been in town visiting his old friend Sam Pearce.

F. H. Kramer of Washington, D. C., passed through Chicago this week on his return from a trip through Mexico, and accompanied by his friend Mr. Hall was entertained by a party of the local florists at the Kunz Remmler on Monday evening just before their departure.

Vaughan & Sperry are at work on improvements in connection with their establishment, which includes the installation of one of the most complete refrigerators in the city.

John Bruckner has sold out his retail store at 35 Monroe street.

During the extension of the Auditorium Annex, P. J. Hauswirth has been offered temporary accommodations on the north side of the building at 13 Congress street. Spacious arrangements are being made by the architect for the Auditorium florist when the addition is completed.

Mrs. Vande Sande has opened a retail store in the corridor of the building at 209 State street.

Miss Luffmann, who is well acquainted with all the members of the S. A. F., having assisted Secretary Stewart at many conventions, passed through Chicago the first of the week.

Fred Schmeling of Wauwatosa, a suburb of Milwaukee, was in the city last Saturday. WM. K. WOOD.

WEST CHESTER, PA.—An addition has been built to the packing sheds of Hoopes, Bro. & Thomas at their nurseries.

Boston.

New England Dahlia Society.

On September 5, 1906, about twenty-five enthusiastic dahlia growers (amateurs and professionals) held a meeting at Horticultral Hall Boston, for the purpose of organizing a dahlia society. At that meeting a temporary president and secretary were elected, viz., F. H. Burt of Taunton, Mass., and Maurice Fuld of Boston, Mass., respectively; also an executive committee of five consisting of N. Allen Lindsey, Marblehead Mass.; J. H. Flint, Salem, Mass.; Mrs. H. A. Jahn, New Bedford Mass.; A. E. Johnson, Montello, Mass.; and W. P. Lothrop, East Bridgewater, Mass.; for the purpose of meeting and planning all necessary details to start a permanent organization. The executive committee held its first session October 6. After lengthy consideration the committee suggests the following: That the new society be called the "New England Dahlia Socity," that the object of the society is to promote the culture and development of the dahlia, to accurately determine the several classes thereof, to disseminate information and to secure uniformity in awarding prizes at the various flower shows, to establish a standard nomenclature and to award recognition to new varieties of sterling merit. Any person interested in dahlias is eligible to membership; fee $1 per year.

An annual meeting will be held in connection with and on the first day of the annual dahlia show of the Massachusetts Horticultural Society and at such other times as the Board of Directors may determine.

The first meeting of the proposed Dahlia Society will be held in the library rooms at Horticultural Hall, Friday, November 6, at 8 p. m. sharp. The purpose of the meeting is to effect a permanent organization and to act upon a plan suggested by the temporary executive committee. The day of the meeting is the first day of the chrysanthemum show.

This new society should start with at least one hundred members, and if you will only try to assist them in this effort they can not only accomplish it, but do better.

If you are aware of any one interested in dahlias, kindly send their names to the secretary, who will furnish further particulars. The secretary's address is Maurice Fuld, 6 Union street, Boston.

News Items.

The next meeting of the Gardeners and Florists' Club on Tuesday evening will be extremely interesting. Not only will there be a fine paper by Mr. Velie on "Greenhouse Construction," but the committee in charge of the work of classes for landscape gardening will announce their plans, and those wishing to join can enroll on the membership list.

H. M. Robinson & Company are planning branching out their business into a wholesale cut flower trade as soon as they get their new location at 15 Province street fitted up.

John Clark of the Botanical Gardens, Washington, D. C., is visiting in town this week.

Jos. J. Fee, manager of the Park street flower market, is happy over the arrival of a son at his home on Saturday last.

J. W. D.

Cincinnati.

News of the Week.

S. G. Cobb, one of the old time florists of Covington, Ky., died on Thursday of last week, aged 7[illegible] years. Mr. Cobb had been associated with the florist business for many years.

On Wednesday, quite an accident occurred at the Price Hill Incline Plane, on the freight side, when the cable broke and the car made a swift descent of 825 feet, the incline being 315 feet high. This elevator is used by all the florists living on Price Hill, of which there are many but fortunately none of the craft was aboard. On the elevator at the time of the accident were two wagons, four horses, and two men. The men were not badly injured but the horses were killed, and the cars and wagons were reduced to kindling wood.

E. G. GILLETT.

Baltimore.

News Notes.

The Gardeners' Club has decided to hold its annual chrysanthemum show at the new Florists' Exchange Hall, the assurance having been given by the builders and directors of the Exchange that the new building will be ready by the second week in November.

Trade conditions are favorable at this time, and from present indications Jack Frost is close at hand.

J. D. Blackistone, brother of the prominent Washington florist, has acquired "The Fernery," at 1421 North Charles street this city. The extensive floor space was sufficiently large for a small dahlia show, which was held during the past week. Over 200 varieties of dahlias were on exhibition, and the flowers were banked on all sides of the room in a very artistic manner.

The Park Board of Baltimore has decided to switch its four district superintendents from one park district to another. The change was made in the interest of the future development of the greatly enlarged park system as mapped out by the Olmsted plans. A considerable area of unfinished park lands is in the Carroll district recently purchased. The beautiful valley of the Quinn's Falls, between Carroll and Druid Hill parks, will be connected, forming a part of the chain which will encircle the city. It is expected that in the near future the necessary land will be acquired to continue the gigantic parking scheme from Druid Hill to Clifton and Patterson parks. The various superintendents have been assigned as follows: C. L. Seybold from Patterson to Carroll; N. F. Flitton from Clifton to Patterson; J. F. Wessler from Carroll to Druid Hill; and James Boone from Druid Hill to Clifton Park. C. L. S.

The Park Board has decided to reestablish the flower shows. The first large one will be held in the Fall of 1907. After that they will be given twice a year. Because of the abuses that existed in connection with the shows, they were abandoned several years ago by the board. In a number of cases it was found flowers were given away without being on exhibition, and, because of their high cost, the board decided to stop them. During that time small chrysanthemum shows have been given at the different conservatories and have attracted large crowds.

St. Louis.

News Notes.

Paul Berkowitz, of H. Bayersdorfer & Company, Philadelphia, reports business done here in supplies of all kinds as excellent.

Among the floats in the Label Parade, which occurred last Thursday, were those of The Bentzen Floral Company and Grim & Gorley. Both floats were very handsome, attracting much attention.

Charles Kuehn took in the Springfield Fair, and was greatly interested in the floral display, which he said were very fine and a credit to the florists of Springfield. George Augermuller also attended the Fair.

Will Smith, chairman of the trustees of the club, reports that he will call a meeting of that body some time this week to arrange matters concerning the entertainment of members at the meetings of the club this Winter. Mr. Smith is this early talking flower show for next year; he is a great hustler.

The Riessen Floral Company had plenty to do last week in decorative and design work. Alex. Siegel, John Burke, and the Foster Floral Company, the extreme downtown florists, report trade in all branches opening up nicely. Fred H. Weber, on Boyle avenue, has his fine place in good shape for a big season's business. Harry Rieman, manager for the Michel Plant & Bulb Company, Maryland avenue, had the decoration for Statue, St. Louis, on Thursday last. Mr. Rieman reports a good store trade since the opening up of the Fall business.

Henry Braun, until recently foreman for A. Jablonsky, is now with Alex. Johnson, Easton avenue.

ST. PATRICK.

Palm Beach, Fla.

Andrew Henderson, a member of the one-time firm of E. G. Henderson & Son, of the old Wellington Nursery, St. John's Wood, London, Eng., died here on August 31 last, aged 83 years. His widow survives him. Some 16 years ago Mr. Henderson came to Florida from England with the intention of growing pineapples for market. A succession of cold Winters rendered his project inadvisable, and he turned his attention to forcing lily of the valley and other flowers for sale, continuing the business with a moderate degree of success until his death. He had a great knowledge of plants, and in the flourishing days of the Wellington Nursery sent out many new ones.

CRESTON, IA.—While William Dittmer, proprietor of a greenhouse plant at Grinnell, was at the express office after some flowers last week, some person broke into his house and carried off jewelry and other valuables amounting to about $15.

MORRISVILLE, ILL. — Davis Brothers are completing a show room, to be lighted by electricity.

HEATING.

Growers' Problems Solved by U. G. Scollay.

We are building a greenhouse 100 feet long, 25 feet wide, 9 feet high in peak, 2½ feet high at sides. We have one tubular boiler, with 30 tubes 1½ inches and 8 feet long; fire-pot, 3 feet x 2 feet 3 inches; diameter of boiler, 3 feet. Could you give us the heating capacity of this boiler and will it heat this house to 70 degrees with hot water or steam? How much pipe will it take with hot water and with steam? What size pipe would you recommend?

Mass. D. N. CO.

—The ordinary greenhouse for commercial purposes is never heated to 70 degrees except in very rare cases. Of course, you will understand I am now referring to zero weather. However, since you ask for 70 degrees I will give you what is required on that basis. The boiler you have has a maximum capacity of 1,000 square feet of steam and 1,600 square feet of hot water radiation. It is about large enough to heat the house described, with reasonable reserve power left over. I would suggest that you place 12 lines of 4-inch cast iron standard greenhouse pipe, or its equivalent, for hot water; or about 14 lines of 1 1-4 inch wrought iron pipe for steam. In the case of hot water do not use smaller than 2-inch wrought iron pipe.

U. G. SCOLLAY.

Please inform me how many feet of 2-inch pipe to put in a coil boiler, the size fire-box, and a plan of making same to heat 1,400 square feet of glass. C. L. S.

Ohio.

—It would not only be difficult, but dangerous, to reply to this letter offhand. Pipe boilers rely greatly on their "form" for their efficiency; in other words, they must be so made that their surfaces are properly distributed, so that the fire gets in its work. Many good pipe boilers are made. I have both seen them and made them, but I never saw one made for small work, excepting in the spiral form, that was worth considering. Pipe boilers are made in such a way that the tubes form a part at least of the fire-box, allowing the hot fuel to come into contact with them. I am speaking now entirely of "efficient" pipe boilers. In order to construct such a boiler, and otherwise distribute surfaces so as to secure any decent results from the fuel burned, one must use up at least 250 feet of pipe, say, 1½-inch in size. There are so many ways and shapes into which this can be worked up, it is hard to describe anything intelligently without drawings. In your case from 50 to 55 feet of 2-inch pipe would do the work if placed so that the fire came in contact with a portion of it. Frankly, I think you will waste both time and substance in supplying or attempting to supply heat from such a source. The size of your fire-box will be governed pretty much by the shape of your boiler, as you build it in brick-work, I presume. A grate 24 x 24 should be large enough.

U. G. SCOLLAY.

Enclosed find a rude sketch of my greenhouse. I have been growing chrysanthemums for four years, leaving them in the benches just as they grew until Spring, then making cuttings. In extreme weather I find it hard work to keep out the frost. I want to put in more pipes and to know how many more and how to do it to maintain a temperature of 50 or 60 degrees if I want it. My boiler is in the cellar of the dwelling, about 4 feet lower than the level of the house. At east end the ridge is 6 feet higher than the remainder. The expansion tank is in this part at or near the top of the ridge.

J. H. L.

—I would suggest that you put [in] your house at least four additional lines of 2-inch pipe. The capacity [of] your boiler is equal to 350 square fee[t]. This will do for the temperature r[e]quired, but you will need to fire prett[y] hard. According to catalogue you[r] boiler is tapped 3-inch flow and retur[n]; if this is so, why do you reduce it [to] 1 1-2-inch flow and return? That w[ill] certainly interfere with the result[s] and, besides, it is entirely inadequat[e]. When you install the additional pip[e] I would advise running from the boi[l]er into the house with at least 2 1[-2] inch flow and return main. Divide th[e] heating surface into two coils—one [of] five pipes on the north side, and fi[ve] pipes on the south. Why did you n[ot] locate the expansion tank in you[r] dwelling? It could have been plac[ed] there instead of making the speci[al] compartment in the greenhouse. Wh[en] you make the changes see that you[r] tank is connected to the return pi[pe] and not on the flow, as you have [it]. It would seem from your sketch [as] though the flow pipe made a "dip". If this is so, see that you get rid [of] it; and in making the new connectio[ns] from boiler to coils, have all the co[n]nections give a rise from boiler [to] coils. If the boiler pit in your dwel[l]ing is not deep enough to allow of thi[s] I think it would be a good investme[nt] to deepen it a little. In the new a[r]rangement be sure and place air ven[ts] at the highest point at the west end [of] the coils.

U. G. SCOLLAY.

Mention The Florists' Exchange when writing.

WHOLESALE TRADE LIST

ASPARAGUS PLUMOSUS, 3 in. pots, $6.00 per 100; 2 in. pots, $2.00 per 100.
ASPARAGUS PLUMOSUS, Seedlings from flats, $1.00 per 100, $8.00 per 1000.
ASPARAGUS SPRENGERI, 5 in. pots, $3.00 per doz.
ASPARAGUS SPRENGERI, 2 in. pots, $2.00 per 100.
BOSTON FERNS, 4 in. pots, 20c. each. 5 in. pots, 75c. each.
CLEMATIS PANICULATA, 4 in. pots, $1.50 per doz., $10.00 per 100; 3 in. pots, 75c. per doz.; $5.00 per 100.
DRACAENA INDIVISA, 5 in. pots, $2.00 per doz.
GERANIUMS, Stock plants grown in pots. Double white La Favorite, Telegraph, Queen of the West, John Doyle, S. A. Nutt, $1.00 per doz.
HYDRANGEAS, Otaksa and Thos. Hogg, fine field grown plants, $10.00 per 100.
IVY, Hardy English, 4 in. pots, $1.50 per doz.; $10.00 per 100.
Paris Daisy, Strong plants 3 in. pots $6.00 per 100.
SANSEVIERA, (Zebra plant) 4 in. pots, strong $1.50 per doz.; 3 in. pots, $1.00 per doz.

C. EISELE, 11th & Roy Streets, PHILADELPHIA, PA.

Mention The Florists' Exchange when writing.

The STANDARD VENTILATING MACHINERY

The original machine with self oiling cups; the most powerful, least complicated very compact, with ease of operation.
The New Duplex Gutter over six miles in use and highly recommended; the only **drip proof** gutter in the market.
The standard Return Steam Trap has no equal for simplicity or its workings. Catalogue free.

E. HIPPARD, Youngstown, O.

Mention The Florists' Exchange when writing.

SUMMER IN WINTER

BY USING

Standard Greenhouse Boilers

One cent gets our Catalog

GIBLIN & CO., UTICA, N. Y.

Mention The Florists' Exchange when writing.

"THE BEST INVESTMENT I EVER MADE"

is the verdict of one of the largest rose growers who placed two of these **GREENHOUSE BOILERS** instead of two others of well known make.
Estimates furnished for heating plants erected complete, or for material only.

JOHN A. PAYNE
Horticultural Architect and Builder.

33 Clendenny Ave., Jersey City, N. J.

Sash opening apparatus and all kinds of greenhouse structural material.

Mention The Florists' Exchange when writing.

CYPRESS
IS FAR MORE DURABLE THAN PINE.
CYPRESS
SASH BARS
UP TO 32 FEET OR LONGER.
GREENHOUSE
AND OTHER BUILDING MATERIAL,
MEN FURNISHED TO SUPERINTEND
ERECTION WHEN DESIRED.
Send for our Circulars.
THE A. T. Stearns Lumber Co.,
NEPONSET, BOSTON, MASS.

PLANT CULTURE

PRICE, $1.00.

The best book for the plant grower.

A. T. DE LA MARE PTG. & PUB. CO. LTD.

WE DON'T ASK YOU TO MAKE A "TEST" OF OUR MATERIALS OR PRODUCTS

NOW, the word "test" has another meaning, it's virtually a case of experiment. It costs money to experiment—you don't want to spend your money that way. We'll make all the "tests" at our expense, and when you buy materials from us you get proven facts, for if the practicalness, the economy hadn't already been tested and proven we would not sell you those materials.

Well, perhaps our materials may cost a shade more than the "make your own test kind"—but what's the test going to cost you? —there's where the actual real difference comes in.

Lord & Burnham Co.

Greenhouse Designers and Manufacturers.

1133 Broadway, corner 26th St., NEW YORK.

BOSTON BRANCH, 819 Tremont Building.

Mention The Florists' Exchange when writing.

"The test of years is the real test."

Scollay Boilers
ARE BEST

See our advertisement in next issue.
Catalogues sent on application.

JOHN A. SCOLLAY,
74-76 MYRTLE AVE.,
BOROUGH OF BROOKLYN,
NEW YORK CITY.
Telephones 1492-1493 Main.
U. G. SCOLLAY, Manager.

Mention The Florists' Exchange when writing.

WEATHERED COMPANY.

Builders of Iron and Cypress Greenhouses, Greenhouse Heating and Ventilating Apparatus.

P. O. Address, Box 789,
New York City.

Mention The Florists' Exchange when writing.

Evans Improved Cha

Roller bearing, self-oil... vice automatic stop, so... chain make the IMP... CHALLENGE the most ... apparatus in the market.
Write for catalogue an... before placing your ord... where.

QUAKER CITY MACHI...
RICHMOND, IND

THE JENNINGS IMPROVED IRON GUTT

PATENT IRON BENCH FITTINGS AND ROOF SUPPORTS. VENTILATIN... APPARATUS. IMPROVED VAPORIZING PANS for Tobacco Extracts, Et...

SEND FOR CIRCULARS

DILLER, CASKEY & CO.

Successo... JENNINGS

S. W. CORNER SIXTH AND BERK STS., PHILADELPHIA, PA.

Mention The Florists' Exchange when writing.

A. HERRMANN
Manufacturer of Floral Metal Designs

IMPORTER AND DEALER IN FLORISTS' SUPPLIES

FACTORY: 709 FIRST AVENUE, BETWEEN 40th AND 41st STREETS, NEW YORK

OFFICE AND WAREROOMS: 404, 406, 408, 410, 412 East 34th St.

WRITE FOR NEW CATALOGUE

Mention The Florists' Exchange when writing.

THE FLORISTS' SUPPLY HOUSE OF AMER
Now is the time to buy goods
Before we move

SEND FOR CATALOGUE.

H. BAYERSDORFER & CO., 50, 52, 54, 56 North Four... PHILADELPHIA, PA

Mention The Florists' Exchange when writing.

THE FLORISTS' EXCHANGE

We are a straight shoot and aim to grow into a vigorous plant

A WEEKLY MEDIUM OF INTERCHANGE FOR FLORISTS, NURSERYMEN, SEEDSMEN AND THE TRADE IN GENERAL

Vol. XXII. No. 16 — NEW YORK AND CHICAGO, OCTOBER 20, 1906 — One Dollar Per Year

CONTENTS AND INDEX TO ADVERTISERS, PAGE 465

Seed Trade Report.

AMERICAN SEED TRADE ASSOCIATION

Henry W. Wood, Richmond, Va., president; C. S. Burge, Toledo, O., first vice-president; G. B. McVay, Birmingham, Ala., second vice-president; C. E. Kendel, Cleveland, O., secretary and treasurer; J. H. Ford, Ravenna, O., assistant secretary.

LOUISVILLE, KY.—Onion sets are getting somewhat stiffer in price; and the Fall trade on grass seeds has been about the same as usual.

ZANESVILLE, O.—Howard Broomhall has opened a seed and cut flower store on North Fifth street. Mr. Broomhall was formerly in the employ of J. D. Imlay.

SEDALIA, MO. — Archias' Seed Store won first premium on display of seeds at the recent State Fair here. This is the fifth year that this firm has held this honor.

CHICAGO. — Charles Hollenback has returned from his several weeks' honeymoon tour and is again in harness after the most pleasant vacation of his life. The concern is now in the midst of the onion set rush, and they have a fine stock of the several varieties. It may be mentioned incidentally that the Chicago onion set crop this year, though short, is of a quality that was never excelled anywhere.

"WILD RICE."—This is the title of an illustrated monograph being distributed by Messrs. Northrup, King & Company, seedsmen, Minneapolis, Minn. The utilitarian uses of this product are interestingly set forth, recipes being given for its preparation as a food. Full particulars concerning the cultivation and behavior of the plants are also furnished.

FREMONT, NEB.—On October 8, 1906, the Western Seed & Irrigation Company write as follows: "There has been no material change for the better in the crop prospects for vine seeds. The growers are now harvesting their cucumber and melon crops; and the recent frosts killed the vines to such an extent that it is now easier to estimate the pumpkin and squash crops to better advantage.

"We have devoted the largest part of the last month to field inspection of our growing crops, and have not only inspected our own crops, but have seen a great many others and talked with growers generally throughout the West, and to the best of our judgment, we believe the crops will make an average yield about as follows, namely:

Name.	Yield per acre, about lbs.
Cucumber, Short Green vars.	100 to 150
Cucumber, White Spine vars.	100 to 150
Cucumber, Long Green vars.	60 to 75
Musk Melon	75 to 100
Water Melon	100 to 150
Pumpkin	100 to 150
Squash	100 to 150

"We have made the above figures on a basis of general field estimates, and in some instances the crops will yield somewhat better, while in quite a number of cases they will yield considerably less. The sweet and field corn crops, as far as quality is concerned, are better than we have had for the past few years. The acreage of the sweet corn, however, is considerably smaller this year than for several years, and we therefore do not look for any large surplus stocks of sweet corn.

"We therefore believe that what few surplus crops are in sight this year will be rapidly taken, and that the carried-over surplus from last year's crops will be required before Spring."

European Notes.

The spell of wet weather, from which such great things was expected, has ceased, and the ground two inches below the surface is just as hard as a brick. Transplanting biennials for 1907 has come to a standstill once more. In Germany the rains are too abundant, in the Erfurt district especially, and as a consequence grave fears are entertained for the aster crop, both in quantity and germinating qualities. Kidney beans have also suffered badly, and the growers of both are quite pessimistic, especially as there are indications of early frosts.

On the other hand, the English growers are reporting very heavy crops of peas; in many instances as many as 40 bushels per acre have been harvested, and, as is usual with good crops, the loss in picking is not very great.

Owing to the extraordinary heat the crops of tomatoes and musk melons have been very fine, and the flavor of the latter article as good as any one could desire.

EUROPEAN SEEDS.

Some Continental Novelties.

FREDERICK ROEMER, Erfurt, Germany, this year lists among others the following novelties:

Gladiolus Præcox, the annual gladiolus, seedlings of which bloom the first season from seeds sown early in Spring. The variety of colors is said to be very rich, all those known in the older types being found in the new class.

Double hybrid everblooming fringed hollyhocks, in colors black and brilliant crimson rose. The "black," it is stated, will be found most valuable for funeral decorations, because "there are only few flowers that show such a deep, fine, black color." Also in the same class of plants, cherry-red, and mauve.

Asters dwarf Comet, Perfection, crimson, azure-blue and dark blue; extra early Hohenzollern, azure-blue; July ray, salmon-rose; cinnabar-carmine; Christmas Tree Comet, reddish-lilac; Lady, white changing to azure-blue; Giant Comet, amethyst; Ostrich Feather, rose with white center, and light blue with white center; Branching, chamoise-rose.

F. C. HEINEMANN, Erfurt, Germany, lists Begonia hybrida gigantea Crown Princess; flowers have the edges of a brilliant carmine, turning toward the center to a pure white.

Dianthus laciniatus punctatus "Princess Pinks;" the flowers, quite independent from their original colors, are intensely dotted and lined, "rather leoparded and tigered."

Cyclamen persicum giganteum marginatum Victoria. "The vigorous habit, floriferousness and the most elegant appearance of the gracefully marginated and fringed flowers" are the prominent features of this new introduction. The coloration of the margin always corresponds with that at the base of the flower.

Myosotis alpestris stricta grandiflora alba, white forget-me-not.

Also new hybrids of Nicotiana affinis, having a "sweet fragrance."

CATALOGUES RECEIVED.

GLENN CLIFF NURSERY, Winchester, Tenn.—Surplus List of Fruit Trees, etc.

CARL SONDEREGGER, Beatrice, Neb.—Surplus List of Nursery Stock; also Price List of Tree Seeds.

LUDVIG MOSBAEK, Onarga, Ill.—Descriptive List of Cannas; also, Surplus List of Hardy Perennial Plants and Hardy Flowering Shrubs.

WATKINS & SIMPSON, London, England. Illustrated Catalogue of Novelties and Specialties for 1907. Among the former are Chrysanthemum Coronarium, Tom Thumb, "Golden Gem," Cineraria hybrida compacta, "Starfish;" variegated leaved Nasturtiums "Queen of Tom Thumb" and "Queen of the Tall;" Sweet Peas, Nora Unwin, white; Mrs. Alfred Watkins, pink, of Gladys Unwin type; Frank Dolby, pale blue; E. J. Castle, rich carmine rose, with salmon shading in the standard; Wallflower (Kewensis) "Bronze King," a cross between Cheiranthus kewensis and Wallflower Eastern King, flowers a reddish bronze and very early.

NURSERY DEPARTMENT.

Conducted by Joseph Meehan.

AMERICAN ASSOCIATION OF NURSERYMEN, Orlando Harrison, Berlin, Md., president; J. W. Hill, Des Moines, Ia., vice-president; George C. Seager, Rochester, N. Y., secretary; C. L. Yates, Rochester, N. Y., treasurer.

The Iowa State Railway Commission will adopt the western classification as it applies to the nursery business. This will effect a material saving to the nurserymen of Iowa.

POMONA, N. C.—J. Van Lindley Nursery Company has erected a storage house, 190x200 feet, greatly adding to its stock-handling facilities.

Professor N. E. Hansen, the horticulturist at the South Dakota experiment station, is making his third trip to Europe to collect hardy fruits and incidentally anything else he may run across of value to this country. He will work principally in the Scandinavian Peninsula and northern Russia, though his field of investigation is not strictly confined to these countries. Professor Hansen's two previous visits to Russia and Siberia for a similar purpose will make it easier for him to accomplish what he is undertaking to do in this visit.

COMMITTEE ON TARIFF.—As I am one of the members on the committee on tariff, I would like all nurserymen who are interested in the tariff, express or freight rates, east of Syracuse and the New England States, including New Jersey, to write me; and those of western New York and Pennsylvania to write W. H. Moon of Morrisville, Pa. We hope to call a meeting in New York about December 1, and would like the views of all the nurserymen before that time, so that we may get our reports ready.

E. RUNYAN.

Elizabeth, N. J.

AMERICAN ASSOCIATION OF NURSERYMEN.—The report of the proceedings of the Dallas (Tex.) meeting, June 13, 14 and 15, 1906, has now been issued by Secretary Seager. The delay in the appearance of the report is laid to the tardiness of the official stenographer. We think the labor of that very necessary functionary at annual conventions could be greatly lessened were all such superfluous matter as the routine language used in putting the motion, etc., expunged. It is of no value to the report, which it only encumbers. An account of the actual "work" done is the greatest essential. The papers read, with the discussions thereon, the exhibits shown, list of members, copy of Nurserymen's Telegraphic Code are included in the pamphlet, which is up to the usual standard in the interesting character of the material presented.

Seasonable Notes.

Cornus florida rubra, the pink dogwood, is one of the grandest of early Spring flowering shrubs. It is better planted in Spring than late Fall. It rarely makes much growth the first year after planting; on the other hand, it seldom fails to live. This and all its fellow varieties flower regularly every Spring.

Exochorda grandiflora is a tall growing shrub, bearing lovely clusters of white flowers in May. It is not over abundant in collections. When not in flower it is not over attractive merely as a shrub, which may account for this. Its flowers make up for it all; and it grows easily from seed.

Horse chestnuts are unsuited for street planting in cities. The heat of the pavements and other disadvantages cause the foliage to burn badly. When on a lawn, where soil is deep, the burning of the foliage does not occur, and then the horse chestnut is one of the handsomest of trees.

Staphylea colchica is used for forcing by English florists. It is an Asiatic species; the flowers are not unlike those of a white lilac, and they are sweet scented. It is not used by our florists that we know of. Perhaps what they do force answers as well.

Among desirable pines the Himalayan, P. excelsa, is not the least of the number. Its silver colored foliage and long, soft needles, together with a vigorous habit, make it an object of beauty wherever planted; and then it is easily transplanted.

Where Winters are no more severe than they are in Philadelphia, the Ligustrum japonicum, a true evergreen, will be found a valuable addition to the now meager list of broad-leaved evergreens.

The beautiful and sweet-scented Magnolia stellata is seen occasionally in a pot as an indoor plant in Winter. Plants lifted now, with care to have a ball of earth with the roots, would be in good condition for forcing. Flower buds are visible now.

Beautiful as many of the sumach family are when their Fall display of Autumn foliage is on, there are two native species poisonous to the touch of those who are susceptible to their poison. These are Rhus radicans and R. venenata. The former is the well-known poison vine; the latter, a small tree. There is a Japanese small tree, R. succedanea, equally as poisonous as the R. venenata.

Pontederia cordata, the pickerel weed so called, is well worthy of a place in fountains and ponds. It is a native plant, conspicuous in Summer and Autumn, when it displays its spikes of sky-blue flowers well above the water.

The white birch scourge, which caused the death of so many of the English and our poplar birches, appears to have run its course. Trees that escaped, and others set out within a year or two past, are growing unmolested.

Rhododendrons and all plants with surface spreading roots should have a thick covering over them of forest leaves before hard freezings set in. It is a great help to such plants, keeping back the freezings and thawings that so injure them, and as well keeps the soil moist.

Hardiness of Cedrela and Ailanthus.

Edgar Sanders's notes on the hardiness of ailanthus in Chicago are very interesting, and it is gathered from them that the tree may be considered available for planting there. It is the male flowers, however, that give off the offensive odor. If the seed-bearing ones possess it, it is in a much smaller degree; and some there are who claim the seed-bearing trees to be quite free of any odor.

Regarding suckering, I quite agree with Mr. Sanders that when the tree is on a lawn the suckering amounts to nothing. This I have mentioned before in connection with the sassafras. Both are terrible fellows to sucker when undisturbed above ground and when their roots are cut or injured underground, wherever hurt there arises a thicket of shoots. On a lawn the growth is cut off as fast as it appears, and this kills the ambitious shoots in a short time. I have seen large ailanthus and sassafras on lawns with not a sucker showing anywhere.

Mr. Pederson thinks it hardly necessary for those he warned against the cedrela to have information about the ailanthus, but I think it has a close bearing on the subject. The two trees are closely allied botanically, and both are from Northern China. This being the case it is fair to suppose they would not differ much in hardiness, hence my inquiry as to the hardiness of the ailanthus; and I would suggest further trials of the cedrela.

Mr. Pederson mentions that in the severe Winter of 1898-99 catalpas were killed in Chicago. May I ask him if these were bignonioides or speciosa? My reason for asking is that it has been said that C. bignonioides will not survive ordinary Chicago Winters.

Returning to the cedrela tree, it will be in favor where it will be hardy as, while possessing all the virtues of the ailanthus, there is no odor whatever in the flowers, nor does the tree sucker to the same extent.

Spiræa Anthony Waterer.

Lycium Chinense.

Whether to call the Lycium chinense a shrub or a vine, I do not know. It can be used for either purpose, just as the Jasminum nudiflorum can be, and in horticultural works it is called a shrub by some, a vine by others. Set out as a shrub it forms a mass of drooping branches, shrub-like in appearance, and when used as a vine for covering porches, arbors, and the like, there is no question of its utility for the purpose. Of one thing I am sure, it is not used nearly to the extent it should be. It makes a thick, close growth; the foliage is neat; its purplish flowers are pretty, and following the flowers there are abundant berries which late in Summer become of an orange scarlet color, and are extremely ornamental. It is sometimes excellently well placed on a sloping bank, where its drooping branches closely cover the ground about it. And where a retaining wall has been built alongside a bank, the lycium placed there, planted in the bank and permitted to droop over the top of the wall, will prove as good a plant as can be used for the purpose.

The lycium possesses the additional merit of proving a good seaside shrub, or vine. It does well near the shore, and for the matter of that it is not particular as to position. It is often found in the yards of dwellings where it would be thought neither soil nor position would suit it.

Spiraea Anthony Waterer.

Our gardens would lack much of their attractiveness in Summer were we without spiræas. The first days of Spring usher in such sorts as Thunbergii, Reevesii, Van Houttei, etc. Others follow them, and toward the close of June we get the one of our notes, the S. Anthony Waterer. This spiræa is a variety of S. Bumalda, which originated in the grounds of the late Anthony Waterer, the well-known nurseryman of Knap Hill, England. As an ornamental shrub it is more useful than any other spiræa. It flowers, as said, in the latter part of June, and lasts then quite a while, as all the flower heads do not expand at once. When all have finished a new growth ensues, from which later on a fresh crop of flowers appears, and still later a third succession will follow; so that should the Autumn prove favorable for growth, there will be a nice display of blossoms when freezing weather comes. The abundance of flowers depends on the growth the bush makes. Every new shoot will bear a flower head. It is a great help to go over this spiræa as soon as flowering of the first crop is over and cut off all decaying heads. Cut them off well down the shoots, that the operation may partake of the nature of a pruning. This encourages strong shoots to form, and good-sized flower heads follow. This cutting away of the old flower heads must go on all through the season; flowers are sure to follow until growth stops for the year.

The blooms of this spiræa are of an almost crimson color, perhaps quite so when just expanded. Like the type, the flowers fade somewhat as they age, but at all times the color is deeper than that of its parent, S. Bumalda. And this, too, in face of the statement in Nicholson that in this variety—the A. Waterer—the flowers are paler than those of the type.

Most excellent Fall flowering plants of this spiræa are had from cuttings made in Summer from green wood. These potted, and planted out in Spring, make a strong growth, and when late Fall comes are usually a mass of flowers.

JOSEPH MEEHAN.

700 Hardy Herbaceous Perennials

Strong, field grown clumps in over 700 varieties. Catalogue for the asking.

HIRAM T. JONES,

Union County Nurseries, Elizabeth, N. J.

Mention the Florists' Exchange when writing.

SEND TO

THE MOON COMPANY

For Your { TREES, SHRUBS, VINES and SMALL FRUITS

Descriptive Illustrated Catalogue Free

THE WM. H. MOON CO.

Morrisville, Pa.

Mention the Florists' Exchange when writing.

HERBACEOUS PERENNIALS

for Summer and Autumn Planting. We offer NINE HUNDRED and SIXTY-SEVEN VARIETIES of STRONG FIELD-GROWN PLANTS. Send for Catalog and Trade List.

BAY STATE NURSERIES, NORTH ABINGTON, MASS

Mention the Florists' Exchange when writing.

F. & F. NURSERIES

SPRINGFIELD NEW JERSEY

Wholesale Growers

TREES AND PLANTS in full assortment.

Trade Catalogue Free

Mention the Florists' Exchange when writing.

THE SHREWSBURY NURSERIES

EATONTOWN, N. J.

Offer a good line of well-grown NURSERY STOCK, Large, well developed Shrubs a specialty. SEND FOR WHOLESALE LIST

Mention the Florists' Exchange when writing.

Viburnum Plicatum Japan Snowball

18 to 24 in.	$10.00	per 100
2 to 2½ ft.	13.00	"
2½ to 3 ft.	15.00	"
3 to 4 ft.	20.00	"
4 to 5 ft.	25.00	"

DOUBLE ALTHEAS

Jeanne D'Arc, pure white flowers fine for cutting. Banner—White striped crimson. Red—Rich ruby red flowered.

	per 100
Bushy Plants 18 to 24 in.	$6.00
2 to 2½ ft.	7.00
2½ to 3 ft.	8.00
3 to 4 ft.	10.00

BERBERRY THUNBERGII, Splendid for Hedges

Our plants are grown from Cuttings and are very bushy.

	per 100	per 1000
12 to 18 in.	$5.00	$45.00
18 to 24 in.	7.00	60.00
2 ft. to 2½ ft.	10.00	90.00

HYDRANGEA PAN. GRAND.

2 to 3 ft. $7.00 per 100, $60.00 per 1000

DEUTZIA LEMOINEI, Fine for Forcing

2 to 2½ ft. $7.00 per 100

DEUTZIA GRACILIS, 12 to 18 in 4.50 "

SPIRAEA VAN HOUTTEI

		per 100	per 1000
" "	3 ft.	$5.00	$45.00
" "	3 to 4 ft.	6.00	50.00
" Blue, caryopteris,	16 to 20 in.	5.00	45.00
" "	2 to 2½ ft.	7.00	65.00
" A. Waterer	12 to 18 in.	6.50	60.00
" "	2 to 2½ ft.	8.00	75.00
" "	2½ to 3 ft.	9.00	85.00

HONEYSUCKLE HECKROTTII, 1 year $8.00 per 100, 2 years, $10.00 per 100.

PLATYCODON LEICHTLINII, Dwarf, Bushy and very free flowering, 2 years, $8.50 per 100.

THE CONARD & JONES CO.

WEST GROVE, PA.

Mention the Florists' Exchange when writing.

To Clear the Land We Shall Sell For the Next 60 Days

	Per 1000
Berberis Thunbergii, 18 to 24 in., bushy plants	$40.00
Berberis Thunbergii, 24 to 30 in., bushy plants	50.00
Rosa Lucida, 3 years, twice transplanted, fine	40.00
Viburnum Dentatum, 24 to 30 in.	40.00
" " 30 to 36 in.	50.00

We also have some Viburnum cassinoides and Prunus maritima.

Littlefield & Wyman

North Abington, Mass.

Mention the Florists' Exchange when writing.

P. OUWERKERK

216 Jane Street

WEEHAWKEN HEIGHTS, N. J.

P. O. No. 1, Hoboken, N. J.

JUST RECEIVED FROM OUR HOLLAND NURSERIES

Rhododendrons, Azaleas, Spiræa Japonica, Lilium Speciosum, Peonies, Bleeding Heart, Pot-Grown Lilacs, Hydrangea in sorts, Clematis and H. P. Roses in the best sorts.

PRICES MODERATE

Mention the Florists' Exchange when writing.

CHOICE CALIFORNIA PRIVET

2000 4 year old, well branched, 6 to 8 feet, $10.00 per 100; very fine plants.

	100	1000
3 year, 3 to 4 feet	$3.00	$20.00
2 year, 2 to 3 feet	2.00	15.00

2 year, 16 to 20 in., $10.00 per 1000; 500 plants at 1000 rate. Terms: Cash with order; packing free; prompt shipment.

ATLANTIC COAST NURSERIES,

OFFICE: 606 4th Ave., Asbury Park, N. J.

Mention the Florists' Exchange when writing.

Veronica Longifolia Subsessilis

Good, field-grown plants, $6.00 per 100. Strong clumps, $7.50 per 100.

SALVIA AZUREA GRANDIFLORA, $5.50 per 100.

HARDY PHLOX, strong clumps, $6.00 per 100.

HOLLYHOCKS, double mixed, $4.00 per 100. Separate colors, $6.00 per 100.

Cash with order. Samples free.

CHAS. W. SCHNEIDER

LITTLE SILVER, N. J.

Mention the Florists' Exchange when writing.

CANNAS

300,000 roots for Fall delivery in 100 leading kinds, $8.00 to $20.00 per 1000. Write for our list. Send in your orders early.

SHELLROAD GREENHOUSES

Largest Canna Growers Grange, Baltimore, Md.

Mention the Florists' Exchange when writing.

Large Assortment

PEONIES

Very best Varie

LOW PRICES

THE KIND THAT FLORISTS LIKE

"We make a specialty of growing stocky transplanted shrubbery and trees"

FULL ASSORTMENT OF Ornamentals, Fruits, Roses, Clematis, and Herbaceous I

Write for our fall wholesale trade list.

W. & T. SMITH CO., GENEVA, N.

Mention the Florists' Exchange when writing.

SEASONABLE STOCK FOR FLORIS

HYDRANGEAS for forcing { OTAKSA and THOS. HOGG } With 7-12 flowering crowns, $12.00 p; " 5-6 " " 9.00; " 4 " " 7.00

From 6-inch pots and open beds; all out-door grown.

ROSES, Strong, two-years, field-grown, selected for forcing.

HYBRID PERPETUALS	$10.00 and $12.00 p
CRIMSON RAMBLER	9.00
DOROTHY PERKINS	7.00

and

LADY GAY, a new hardy climbing Rose of exceptional merit; ready now fr inch pots only. Write for prices.

JACKSON & PERKINS C

WHOLESALE NURSERYMEN AND FLORISTS

NEWARK, WAYNE CO., NEW YORK

Mention the Florists' Exchange when writing.

PLANT HERBACEOUS PERENNIALS

this month and save the rush of Spring work. We offer the following list of field grown

	Per doz.	Per 100
Achillea, the Pearl	$ .75	$6.00
Agrostemma, Coronaria	.75	6.00
Anthemis, Tinctoria Kelwayii	.75	6.00
Aquilegia, Coerulea Canadensis	.75	6.00
Artemesia Abrotanum Purshiana, Stelleriana	.75	6.00
Arabis, Alpina	.75	5.00
Campanula, Grosseki, Punctata, Rapunculus	.75	6.00
Caryopteris, Mastacanthus	.75	6.00
Clematis, Davidiana	.75	6.00
Coreopsis, Rosea	.75	6.00
Delphinium, Chinensis	.75	6.00
Digitalis Gloxinaeflora White, Purple, Rose. Extra large field grown clumps	.75	6.00
Eupatorium, Ageratoides, Coelestinum	.75	6.00

	Per doz.
Funkia, Coerulea	.75
Helianthus, Multiflorus Maximus	.75
Heliopsis, Scaber Major	1.00
Hibiscus, Moscheutos, Crimson Eye	.75
Hollyhocks, Double White, Pink, Yellow, Single, Mixed and Allegheny Fringed	1.00
Hypericum Moserianum	.75
Liatris, Pycnostachya	.90
Mentha, Piperita	.60
Myosotis, Palustris Semperflorens	.60
Pardanthus, Sinensis	.90
Physostegia, Virginica	.75
Phlox, 10 varieties true to name	1.00
Rudbeckia, Golden Glow, Newmanii	.75
Salvia, Azurea Grandiflora	.90
Sedum, Acre	.75
Stokesia, Cyanea	.75
Tritoma, Pfitzeri	1.00

EDWARD J. TAYLOR - - Southport, Co

Mention The Florists' Exchange when writing.

A Reminder

I WILL HAVE THIS FALL FOR SALE

100,000 California Privet, 2 to 4 feet, bushy.
500 California Privet Stanter, 5 feet, large heads.
500 California Privet Stanter, bush and sheared, fine for lawn.
2,000 American Elm, 10 to 12 feet, fine trees.
500 Horse Chestnut, 8 to 12 feet, fine heads and stocky.
1,000 Deutzia Gracilis, 2 to 3 years, good for forcing.
1,000 Roses, Clothilde Soupert.
2,000 Double Hollyhocks, 2 years, red, pink, white and yellow.
5,000 Dahlia Roots, all fine colors.
1,000 Altheas, double, variegated, 2 to 4 feet.
500 Yucca Filamentosa, large blooming plants. Send for prices to

CARLMAN RIBSAM

31 Wall St., TRENTON, N. J.

Mention the Florists' Exchange when writing.

Trees and Shrubs

We make specially low prices on nursery stock to Parks, Cemeteries, etc.

Wholesale price list on application.

We carry immense quantities of the finest named varieties of peonies.

PETERSON NURSERY

506 W. PETERSON AVE., CHICAGO, ILL

Mention the Florists' Exchange when writing.

H. DEN OUDEN & SON,

BOSKOOP, HOLLAND.

Wholesale growers of nursery stock for the American trade. Catalogue free on demand. Also views in our nurseries.

Mention the Florists' Exchange when writing.

KOSTER & C

Hollandia Nurseries BOSKOOP, HOLLA

Hardy Azaleas, Box Trees, Clematis, Co Hydrangeas, Peonies.

Pot-Grown Plants for Forcing.

RHODODENDRONS, H. P. ROSES,

Catalogue free on demand.

Mention the Florists' Exchange when

EBBINGE & VAN GR

Formerly THE HORTICULTURAL C

BOSKOOP, HOLLA

Hardy Nursery Stock, such as H. P. Rhododendrons, Azaleas, Clemati us, Choice Evergreens, Peonies, etc

Ask for Catalogue.

Mention the Florists' Exchange when

Holland Nursery St

Ask for Our Catalogue. It interest you.

ENDTZ, VAN NES & CO.

Mention the Florists' Exchange when

CALIFORN PRIVET

Branched, $8.00 and $10.00 p

Samples Free

HENRY EICHHOLZ, Waynesbo

Mention the Florists' Exchange whe

PLANT CULT

Price, - - - $1.0

A. T. De La Mare Ptg. & Pu

2-8 Duane St., New Yo

THE WEEK'S WORK.

Timme's Timely Teachings.

Hydrangeas.

As a desirable Easter plant and as a most attractive subject for open air effects during the early part of Summer, Hydrangea hortensis and its varieties, Thomas Hogg, Otaksa, etc., still holds its own. Plants grown in pots and kept outdoors all Summer should now be at the close of their growing season, beginning to drop some of their leaves. These, if properly handled, will, when forced into bloom next Spring, be the most compact, freest flowering and altogether best appearing of hydrangeas, offered in conjunction with other stock. Plants yet in the field should now be potted up, using heavy, liberally enriched loam and ample-sized pots or wooden tubs, in which hydrangeas do better.

Hydrangeas of this class are much hardier than is generally supposed. Ordinary light frosts, causing their foliage to drop, will not injure them, are rather an aid in ripening their wood and thus preparing the plants for the needful rest during the first half of Winter. Hydrangeas, being in pots and handily placed for quick removal to safer quarters, should therefore remain out of doors until this removal becomes really necessary. When hard frosts threaten, which might destroy the tips of the branches and with these the best part of next season's bloom, it is time to store away the plants for Winter. In a cool, frost-proof cellar, shed or greenhouse they will do well for two or three months, needing but little water until again started into growth in early Spring

Cannas.

There is no valid reason for believing that the improvement in cannas, so enthusiastically begun years ago and resulting in such astonishing achievements at the very start, had ceased then and there The first decided steps in this direction which brought cannas to the fore as worthy of extended cultivation by florists and amateurs, since then led to the production of still finer varieties, and the end is not yet. The best of these newer sorts, listed in all catalogues, deservedly rank among the grandest and most effective plants employed in Summer outdoor plantings. Strange, too, we here can grow them far better than they can in Europe, where most of the finer first varieties originated, as I had ample occasion to notice.

We have now such excellent kinds of cannas, so great a number of superb varieties to choose from, that to still persist in the cultivation of comparatively old and inferior sorts must seem utter folly. Yet many of the florists who do a flourishing plant business carry the same stock to-day that they started with years ago, when the Frenchman's first labors in canna improvement had swept the antiquated Indian shot out of existence. I advise the laying off and discarding of such old stock. This is most radically done by allowing the roots to perish by frost this Fall. As long as the roots are considered stock worth saving, inferior varieties will multiply and replenish the earth. Good varieties of superior merit, on the other hand, should not be suffered to be killed down to the ground before lifting and housing their roots. These will winter best when dug up right after the first light frosts have shriveled the foliage. The plants are then cut down, and the clumps of roots lifted and safely stored away.

Dahlias.

Here we come to a Summer-flowering plant that, as far as I can judge, shows up better in Europe than it does here, and is there most extensively used in all kinds of decorative work. I never before saw fields of cactus dahlias so large and their flowers so perfect and produced in such bewildering abundance. On this side of the Atlantic it is a trifle difficult to hit on a variety that throws flowers in profusion which sell well and also keep well. A grower here may try scores of the best varieties recommended for florists' use every year and still not find one that will take to his peculiar soil, or in his particular market.

Dahlia flowers of whatever type, if blemishless in color and form, would sell readily, if once buyers were assured of their durability. Until the presence of this all-important requisite in the flowers of any one variety possessing it has ceased to be a doubtful point, purchases will be considered a risky investment. At just this time, when asters are out of the way and the rushing in of chrysanthemums still a few weeks off, good dahlia flowers with reasonably well established lasting qua l should prove most desirable stock. l ty

Dahlias of all kinds, grown in small pots from cuttings, have been found to be quite profitable when handled in the Spring in connection with other kinds of bedding plants. The providing of good and sufficient stock for this trade should therefore not be lost sight of. The first step in this direction is the saving of roots from good kinds yet in the field. As with the roots of cannas, so will those of dahlias be in better condition next Spring when lifted after the first slight frosts, than when left in the ground until the plants are entirely cut down by frost.

Storing Roots and Tubers.

Clumps of canna roots, lifted from the ground with most of the soil left clinging to them, the stalks being sharply cut down to within stumps of six or eight inches, may at once go to their Winter quarters. Any frost-free, cool place with a bed of dry earth underneath but not too dry an atmosphere will do. Most varieties keep well under a bench in any cool greenhouse, where the stock growing therein requires but little sprinkling during the Winter.

Dahlia roots, dug up and freed of top growth and adhering soil, are first dried off in an airy but shady place, then stored away with finely sifted earth under, between and over them. They may thus be packed in boxes, tubs or barrels, these to be placed where the roots will not be injured by frost or too great heat, or by an excess in either dryness or moisture. Any place where potatoes winter well is also a good place for dahlia roots.

Gladioli, tigridias and such like corms, as also those of Caladium esculentum, may be treated as advised for dahlias, with this difference, that they should not be cleaned of top growth and roots before being thoroughly dried and cured. Sawdust instead of sifted earth may then be used in packing them away.

The roots, corms or bulbs of fancy caladiums, amaryllis, zephyranthes, ismene, sprekelia, achimenes, tuberoses, gesnerias, gloxinias, vallota and tuberous rooted begonias should be allowed to ripen off in their pots before taking them out and storing them away. All of these want warm Winter quarters, not below 50 degrees. Some of them require but a short rest and may again be started right after New Year.

Primulas.

Whatever additional benefit to primulas may accrue by leaving them in outdoor frames much longer after this week is hardly worth the extra labor involved in their caretaking from now on. An almost daily opening, closing and perhaps covering of the frames will soon become necessary, and the attendant must be on a constant outlook for the danger signals of approaching Winter. All this botheration at the eleventh hour adds little or nothing to the value of the stock. Primulas sinensis, obconica and Forbesi, unlike other nearly hardy but frost-shunning stock, such as cinerarias and calceolarias, gain nothing in the way of vigor or durability by a late sojourn out of doors, and therefore had better be transferred now at any time to a cool well-ventilated greenhouse, where they will finish up nicely and with less trouble to the grower. They should now be almost full grown, requiring much bench room, more than is usually granted. Should there be some yet needing a transplanting, this last shift should now be given without further delay. Four and five-inch plants, as also neatly made-up pans and fancy dishes and baskets, sell fastest and prove most profitable. Should the grower, in transplanting a great deal of this stock, run out of the regularly prescribed and carefully prepared brand of primula soil, he may fearlessly and safely use any other good kind of light and fairly rich potting soil, setting the plants deep enough to secure a straight and rigid stand, but not so deep as to cause the speedy decay of the crowns. Moderation in the matter of watering is advisable.

Cyclamens.

Frame-grown cyclamens should, by this time, have undergone their last shifting and be safely housed. Of those grown in the free soil of a greenhouse bench many will now be ready for the final potting up. A rather high bench, or a shelf near the glass, with plenty of room between the plants, will now be of advantage in the farther development of cyclamens. From now on they can bear the full sunlight, and all shading contrivances have lost their value for the time being. Placing each specimen plant on an inverted pot or pedestal of some kind is a way of doing which has lost none of its good points by age; neither has that of spreading a layer of tobacco stems between the pots. But in effectually keeping down aphis, which surely will make their appearance at the advent of fire heat, light fumigation at regular intervals must be resorted to, until the flowers open, when no more tobacco fumes should touch them. A steady heat of about 60 degrees will bring well-established, vigorous cyclamens, soon beginning to send up buds, into bloom by Christmas. A somewhat lower temperature will best suit those that are yet behind in their development but holding out fair promise of becoming good stock for later sales. From now on there is more danger from too little than too much water at the roots, and a thoughtless, forgetful workman should not be intrusted with the care of an exceptionally fine batch of cyclamens. The open flowers should never be wetted, but a daily spraying of the foliage does much in keeping this bright and healthy. Flowering cyclamens for next year's Christmas may easily be had by sowing the seeds now and not disturbing the seedlings until early Spring.

Boston Ferns.

There are several good reasons why Boston ferns grown in pots all along are finer stock than those raised in benches and potted up in the Fall. The principal reason, the one considered of least significance by many growers, is that pot-raised ferns can with greater confidence be depended upon to give entire satisfaction as subjects for hall, parlor or store window, and this mainly because they are more firmly established in their pots than those bench-grown, potted up quite late and offered as salable stock immediately after. An early potting up of Summer benched Boston ferns should therefore be made the rule, so as to minimize as far as possible their shortcoming on this score and in order to give them time to overcome, to a certain extent, another, by attaining length of fronds and graceful form.

All Boston ferns of salable size, hopefully relied upon by their grower as bringers of good returns at the season, now close at hand, should have his full attention. Those newly potted are easily overwatered. A yellowing of the fronds quickly shows it. Pot-bound specimens, on the other hand, rapidly dry out. The regular round of hose or can may not entirely meet their wants. It is here where watching and working mate excellently. If at any time, the full light and sunshine should now be afforded Boston ferns, the original as well as newer types. Plants raised on inverted pots above the bench with plenty of room between them, turned occasionally and sprinkled regularly, are sure to become nice specimens.

Hardy Ferns.

Bay trees, hollies, aucubas, boxwood, etc., together with the nobler kinds of decorative subjects, such as palms, ficus, dracænas, crotons, ferns and many other good things from our hothouses, are now largely used for the exterior adornment of many business houses, in halls, anterooms and approaches to stores, hotels, restaurants, clubhouses and theaters. Of equal value for similar purposes, and serviceable at all seasons and under the most trying conditions, are hardy, pot-grown evergreen trees and shrubs. The demand for anything in this class, shapely plants of a densely set, compact growth, manageable size and pleasing appearance, well established in pots or tubs, is great and is, as yet, never fully met. Here is an opening lying within easy reach of the florist, who should not consider it out of his line. The handling of potted hardy evergreens, regarded as a side line to almost any general plant business, must, everything considered, prove fairly profitable, and, in my opinion, even deserves to be made a specialty by anyone favorably located near a large city. In making a start it is necessary to procure from any well appointed nursery judiciously selected stock suitable for the purpose, varying in variety, size and character. There are many hardy evergreens to choose from, each one furnishing suitable specimens in plenty. Spruces, junipers, cypress, Arbor vitæ and retinispora are some of them. This is a good time for the lifting and potting of the plants. A somewhat heavy soil rather than a sandy mixture, and one but sparingly enriched, should be used for this special kind of work.

FRED W. TIMME.

LIST OF ADVERTISERS

INDEX TO STOCK ADVERTISED

Contents.

PLANTS FOR NAME.—I am sending you specimens for identification. The variegated leaved plant is hardy, creeping, and grows about one foot high, blooming in June, I think, with small white blossoms, something like those of caraway. It is a pretty plant, and I hope you will be able to identify it. O. J. R.

West, Vermont.

—The name of the variegated leaved plant is Ægopodium podograria variegata; and the other plant, the fragrant one, is Santolina incana.

Boston.

The meeting of the Gardeners and Florists' Club on Tuesday evening was one of the best ever held in its history. About 150 members attended to hear the able paper on "Greenhouse Construction," by J. H. Velie of the Lord & Burnham Company. Mr. Velie's paper, which appears in another column, created a lively discussion when the following points were brought out. In answer to a question by Mr. Wheeler, Mr. Velie said the truss greenhouse had some advantages, mainly the elimination of inside posts, that for foundations cement was the best if properly constructed. Replying to a question from Mr. Iliffe, Mr. Velie said that for commercial purposes in heating with hot water 2-inch pipe was better than the larger size, but for private greenhouses 3½-inch pipe was preferable. If a night fireman was kept, steam would always be found the most satisfactory.

Mr. Patten asked if any difference had been found in heating an iron constructed house from a wooden one, as he had found on his establishment that the latter kind of house was easier to heat. Mr. Velie said that was the first time he had heard of any difference.

Mr. Patten said that wooden houses had more breakage of glass than iron ones. In answer to a question by Mr. Finlayson as to the best width for a house Mr. Velie said that 40 feet was wide enough, and had proved as satisfactory as any. Regarding length, he said it was immaterial; and Mr. Montgomery said the length depended upon the length of the field the house was built on. Mr. Montgomery gave some interesting statistics regarding heating, which showed in favor of large houses. Replying to a question he said that he had found little difference in the breakage of glass if 16x24 glass was set the wide way; in fact, the advantage of more light was so great that if he were to build again he would set the glass the wide way. In reply to a question on ventilating, Mr. Montgomery said in small houses ventilators were better opened from the ridge, that less mildew would be the result.

On the exhibition tables were three well-grown geranium plants for the prizes offered last Spring. The grower, an under gardener, was W. D. Nickerson, and he was awarded both first and second prizes. The first prize plant was of the variety S. A. Nutt and carried an immense lot of blooms, being exceptionally well grown.

The H. A. Stevens Company exhibited some promising seedling carnations, including a white variety and a form of the Pink Lawson, both of which received an award of honorable mention. Duncan Finlayson was awarded a report of superior merit for very finely grown plants of Dendrobium Phalaenopsis.

J. A. Pettigrew reported for the committee in charge of landscape gardening classes, and said that these classes would start about November 1. A competent teacher had been secured, and a prospectus would be sent each member within a day or two, so that those wishing to join the classes might do so.

It was voted that the club offer three prizes—$6, $4 and $2—at the September meeting next year for the geranium plants grown by under gardeners or florists' assistants.

Ammendments were made to the by-laws raising the annual dues to $2.50. The president appointed Robert Cameron, Julius Heurlin and E. O. Orpet a nominating committee to bring in lists of officers to be elected at the November meeting to serve for the coming year.

The nominating committee of the Massachusetts Horticultural Society for the present year make the following report for the annual election of officers, November 17 next: President, Stephen M. Weld of Dedham; vice-president (for two years), Charles S. Sargent of Brookline; trustees (for three years), William N. Craig of North Easton; Arthur F. Estabrook, John K. M. L. Farquhar, and Arthur D. Hill of Boston; nominating committee, Arthur F. Estabrook of Boston; Warren H. Heustis of Belmont; William Nicholson of Framingham; Loring Underwood of Belmont and Edward B. Wilder of Boston.

J. W. DUNCAN.

Philadelphia.

News Notes.

The retail stores have all been very busy with wedding orders; and now orders are already coming in for debutante teas. These promise to make some good trade the coming season.

Phil. Breitmeyer of Detroit was a visitor here on Tuesday.

Godfrey Aschmann arrived home on Monday from his European trip.

George Samtmann has started in this week with the S. S. Pennock-Meehan Company. His position is to grade roses, in which he has had a large experience.

Chas. E. Meehan says that the sun still sets in the west; and it is difficult to get all orders off even by that time.

H. R. Martin, who has a retail store on Columbia avenue, has bought the C. H. Tustin place on Passyunk avenue.

The Chrysanthemum Show this year will close on Friday night instead of Saturday night, the dates now being November 5 to 9 inclusive.

Among the Growers.

The establishment of Godfrey Aschmann at 1012 Ontario street, Philadelphia, has become so well known of late years, as the proprietor is such a persistent advertiser, that a description of the stock at the opening of the season is in proper order. Mr. Aschmann has been in Europe for the past two months and comes home and finds his place and stock in such good order that it is a great credit to his three sons, in whose care he left the place. In the first house we saw the center bed filled with kentias in 6 and 7 inch pots, also some made-up plants in 7 inch.; on the side benches were Araucaria excelsa in 6 inch pots, good, stocky plants. A nice batch of Nephrolepis Scottii in 8 inch pots, and a block of cocos in 3 inch pots, were also observed. In house number two the center bench is occupied with Araucaria excelsa in 5, 6 and 7 inch sizes; one side bench is filled with Nephrolepis Barrowsii in 4 inch pots, the other side bench with assorted ferns in 2 and 3 inch sizes for fern dishes. In house number three the center table is occupied with Nephrolepis Barrowsii in 5, 6 and 7 inch pots; this is very desirable stock. On one side is a block of Boston ferns in 4 inch, the other side containing Primula chinensis in 5 inch. These are being grown on for the Christmas trade.

The fourth house has in the center bench a grand lot of Nephrolepis Scottii in 8-inch, very well grown stocky plants, the side benches being occupied with an assortment, such as flowering begonias, small ferns, etc. One flowering begonia seen here, of the Vernon type, with a dark red flower, looks very good. The stock came from Germany two years ago. It makes a very stocky plant and is very free flowering. These are being grown on for Christmas. The next house was occupied with Nephrolepis Barrowsii and N. bostoniensis in the center, with Araucaria excelsa in 5-inch and Asparagus plumosus in 4-inch pots on the sides. In the sixth house we find a good lot of Araucaria compacta and glauca in 6 and 7-inch pots, Primula chinensis in 4-inch pots; cinerarias in 3-inch for Spring trade, a block of over two thousand. It was here remarked that cineraria seed for some reason was very poor this past season. Seed though bought from four different sources was poor in germination.

The next house was filled entirely with newly imported azaleas, there being about 5,000 in all. These were in good condition, well budded, and nice stocky plants. In the eighth house was a nice lot of Araucarias compacta and glauca in 7-inch pots; the side benches were filled with Begonia Gloire de Lorraine in 6-inch pots, and solanums in 7-inch, the latter all nice bushy plants well berried. Outside in frames were more azaleas, also a large batch of hydrangeas, while in the shed were seen several cases of bulbs ready to pot up and several cases of Lilium longiflorum. The packing shed was full of plants just picked out for orders.

DAVID RUST.

Indianapolis.

News of the Week.

John Hartje has sold his property on N. Illinois street, at a good figure; the land in that vicinity became very valuable for residence property, so he decided to sell and rebuild on a suburban site.

B. F. Hensley, of Knightstown, as usual is in the market with quantities of early chrysanthemums.

Herman Junge, of Smith & Young Company, narrowly escaped with his life in an exciting runaway last Monday; an employee, who was riding with Mr. Junge, suffered dangerous injuries. The horse, a spirited one, became frightened on account of a broken shaft. An ambulance sent to their relief was wrecked on the way by an automobile.

All lines of stock are scarce, consequently Tomlinson Hall Market presents a deserted appearance. The chrysanthemums brought there by growers were immediately bought by market retailers.

The cold snap did quite a little damage at Aug. Hoerger's place; an accident to the chimney prevented the heating of his houses.

J. A. E. Haugh, of Anderson, Ind., stopped here, homeward bound from a pleasant fortnight's vacation.

Anthony Wiegand, travelling in the Hawaii Islands, writes that he enjoys immensely the scenery and plant life there.

Thomas Knipe, of Marion, Ind., who started in business this summer, is sending in violets. J. B.

Plant Culture

By GEORGE W. OLIVER

OF THE BUREAU OF PLANT INDUSTRY, UNITED STATES DEPARTMENT OF AGRICULTURE. LATE PROPAGATOR TO THE UNITED STATES BOTANIC GARDEN, WASHINGTON, D. C., AND THE ROYAL BOTANIC GARDEN, EDINBURGH

A Standard Work Written by Request of the Publishers of the Florists' Exchange

WORKING hand-book of every day practice for the Florist and Gardener, and those who intend to grow plants and flowers, in the greenhouse or garden, as a means of obtaining a livelihood. Each and every article is written in :ise, simple language, and embodies wholly and solely the experience of the er.

The plants dealt with comprise those which are commercially handled by ists, Gardeners and Nurserymen, and include Florists' Flowers, Stove and enhouse Plants, Hardy Herbaceous Plants, Annuals, Shrubs, Hardy and Tender s, and a chapter on miscellaneous subjects in connection with the above.

This reliable cultural book has been gotten up for use not ornament, there- the price has been fixed at a figure within the reach of all, while it contains e real practical information for those for whom it is intended than is found :uch more pretentious works costing five, ten and twenty times as much ey. Cloth; strongly bound to stand rough handling and plenty of it. Price,), by mail, postpaid. Send for sample pages, free.

A. T. DE LA MARE PRINTING AND PUBLISHING CO., Ltd.

:es, 2 to 8 Duane Street, N. Y. Address P. O. Box 1697, New York City

:ULTURAL DIRECTIONS

Specially written for the use of your amateur customers. Send Twenty- e cents for complete sample set, which amount will be deducted from order first thousand.

The universal favor in which these Directions are held, as shown by the iny orders received therefor, encourages us in the belief that these Leaflets : just the neat little factor to help promote business and establish better re- ions between the dealer and his customer.

TRY SOME!

BIG BUSINESS ASSISTANT

TO SAVE TIME, QUICKEN SALES, AND AID YOU PLEASE YOUR CUSTOMER, WE HAVE PREPARED

Cultural Directions

COVERING A NUMBER OF THOSE PLANTS AND BULBS MOST LARGELY IN DEMAND

THE "CULTURALS" have been written by experts; they are fuller, and contain more detailed directions than it is possible to embrace in a catalogue. Equipped with these, just hand one out with each sale, and save yourself nsiderable present and future trouble, as the customer will then be able to con- lt the directions, grow his plants, seeds or bulbs intelligently, and so receive tisfactory results, without having to continually resort to you for advice.

The following "Culturals" are now ready:

MARYLLIS (Hippeastrum)
NNUALS FROM SEED
SPARAGUS
STERS
EGONIA, TUBEROUS
ULBS
ABBAGE and CAULIFLOWER
ANNA
ARNATIONS, MONTHLY
ELERY
HINESE SACRED LILY
HRYSANTHEMUM
LIMBING PLANTS, Hardy
OLEUS, and other bedders
CROCUS, Snowdrop and Scilla Sibirica
DAHLIA
FERNS
FREESIA
GERANIUM
GLADIOLUS
GLOXINIA
HOT BEDS and FRAMES
HOUSE PLANTS, Care of
HYACINTHS, Dutch and Roman
IRIS AND TRITOMA
LAWNS
LILY CULTURE for House and Garden
MUSHROOM CULTURE
ONIONS
PALMS, House Culture of
PANSY
PEONIES
PERENNIALS, Hardy
PRIMULA
ROSE CULTURE
SWEET PEA, The
TOMATOES
TUBEROSE
TULIP
VEGETABLES
VIOLETS
WATER GARDEN, How to make and Manage a

PRICE LIST

500 Cultural Directions for $1.50
,000 - - - - - - 2.50
Printed on white paper, clear type, size 6 x 9½ inches, in an assortment, your selection of not less than 100 of each, delivered carriage paid.

Sufficient space will be left at the bottom of each leaflet for your name, address, etc. If you sire this imprint (3 lines) we will put same on for you at 50 cents for 500, 75 cents for 1000. ecial quotations will be made on quantities of 2500 "CULTURALS" or over.

A. T. De La Mare Ptg. and Pub. Co. Ltd.

ubs. The Florists' Exchange. P. O. Box, 1697, NEW YORK

'ERNS

orted, for jardinieres, strong, healthy , from 2¼ in. pots, $3.00 per 100; $25.00 per 250 at 1000 rate; 4 in., $12.00 per 100.

ANTUM CUNEATUM, 5 in. pots, $20.00 ; 4 in. pots, $12.00 per 100.

IK N. ESKESEN, MADISON, N. J.

n The Florists' Exchange when writing.

BARGAIN
TO MAKE ROOM

1,000 N. Piersoni Elegantissima Ferns, from 2¼ in. pots, $8.00 per 100. A No. 1 stock; ready for 4 and 5 in. pots. Cash with order, please.

R. ENGELMAN & SON
PITTSFIELD, MASS.

Mention The Florists' Exchange when writing.

FERNS. NEPHROLEPIS BARROWSII

2¼ inch, $6.00 per 100.

HUGH GRAHAM CO.,

Logan Nurseries, York Road and Louden Street, PHILADELPHIA, PA

Mention The Florists' Exchange when writing.

Ferns From Bench

BOSTON, PIERSONI, 3 in. 5c., 4 in. 10c. 5 in. 12½c. Boston, 6 in. 15 cts.
TARRYTOWN, 2½ in., 4c.; 3 in., 10c.; 4 in., 15c.; 5 in., 25c. Runners $20.00 per 1000.
SCOTTII, 3 in., 8c.; 4 in., 12½c.

CHINESE PRIMROSES

White, fine plants, 1½ cts.
Pansy Plants, Giants, $3.00 per 100.
Daisies, double Snowball, Longfellow, Delicata, $2.50 per 1000.
Asparagus Sprengeri, 2 in., 2 cts.
Flowering Begonias, 8 kinds, 2 in., 2½ cts.
Alyssum Giant, White double, 2 in., 2c.
Rubbers, top grown, 4 to 6 in. 15 to 25 cts.
Forgetmenots, $2.50 per 1000.
Hollyhocks, double, 4 kinds, 1 year old, 3cts.
Hardy Pinks, 3 kinds, field plants, 3½cts.
Hardy Carnations, nice young plants from frames, $2.00 per 100.

Cash or C. O. D.

BYER BROS., Chambersburg, Pa.

Mention The Florists' Exchange when writing.

FERNS OUR SPECIALTY

Cibotium Schiedei: We have a grand stock of this magnificent tree fern in all sizes. 3 in. pots, $25.00 per 100; 4 in. pots, $45.00 per 100; 5 in. pots, $70.00 per 100; 7 in. pots, $1.70 each; 8 in. pots, $2.50 each.
Assorted Ferns, from 2¼ in. pots, all the best market varieties, $3.00 per 100; or $25.00 per 1000; 4 inch pots, $12.00 per 100.
If by mail add 10c. each 100 plants.
Adiantum Cuneatum, 3 in. pots, $3.50 per 100
" " 4 in. pots, 12.00 " "
" **Rhodophyllum** 4 in. pots $25.00 per 100
" **Lathomii**, 4 in. pots, $20.00 per 100
" **Regina**, 4 in. pots, $35.00 per 100
Fern Spores gathered from our own stock plants 35c. per trade package or $4.00 per doz. packages

ANDERSON & CHRISTENSEN,
SHORT HILLS, N. J.

Mention The Florists' Exchange when writing.

WHITMANI FERN

Large stock of strong plants, 2¼ inch pots, $20.00 per 100.

TARRYTOWN FERN

	100
3 inch pots	$10.00

SCOTTII

2¼ inch pots	$ 5.00
4 inch pots	15.00

Pot grown Ampelopsis, staked, strong plants, $10.00 per 100.

No order for less than 10 plants accepted.

CHAS. H. CAMPBELL,
3601 GERMANTOWN AVE., PHILA., PA

Mention The Florists' Exchange when writing.

FERNS

For jardinieres, etc., 2¼ inch, $3.00 per 100.
Kentia Belmoreana, clean and bushy, 5 in. 50c.
Boston Ferns, Piersoni and Scottii, from bench, 10c. to 25c. each, 4 in. pot grown, 15c.
Cocos Weddeliana, 2¼ in. 10c.
Asparagus Plumosus, 2¼ in. $3.00 per 100.

H. WESTON, HEMPSTEAD, N. Y.

Mention The Florists' Exchange when writing.

NEPHROLEPIS

Whitmani, 2¼ in., $25.00 per 100.
Barrowsii, $10.00 per 100.

Henry H. Barrows & Son, Whitman, Mass.

Mention The Florists' Exchange when writing.

Adiantum Farleyense

I can quote splendid stock at from $2.00 per dozen up to $24.00 per dozen, in 2-inch to 6-inch pots. If you are looking for Farleyense, better write me about it.

CHARLES H. TOTTY, Madison, N. J.

Mention The Florists' Exchange when writing.

FERNS AND ASPARAGUS

Fine stock; pot grown.

Piersoni, 6 in. 35c.; 5 in. 25c.; 4 in. 15c
Bostons, 5 in. 25c.; 4 in. 15c.
Scottii, 4 in. 20c.; 3 in. 15c.
Anna Foster, 2½ in. 4c.
Asparagus Plumosus and **Sprengeri**, 3½ in. fine, 6c. **Plumosus Nanus**, 2½ in., extra, $2.50 per 100. **Vinca Major**, field stock, long tops, $5.00 per 100. **Vinca Major**, variegated, and **Hydrangea Otaksa**, 2½ in. $2.50 per 100, **Hydrangea Grandiflora** and **Spirea** Anthony Waterer, 3 year old bushes, 8c. 50,000 **Shrubs, Vines, Cannas**, etc., low; these must be sold. List free. Cash please.

BENJ. CONNELL
WEST GROVE, PA.

Mention the Florists' Exchange when writing.

FERNS

Boston, Barrowsii and Scottii, 6 in., $4.00 per doz.

Boston and Scottii, 3 in., $6.00 per 100. 4 in., $8.00 per 100.

Larchmont Nurseries
Larchmont, N. Y.

Mention The Florists' Exchange when writing.

Scottii Ferns

For 4 in., $10.00; 5 in., $15.00; 6 in., $20.00.

Boston Ferns, 6 in., $25.00.

English Ivy, 3 to 4 feet, bushy, $5.00 per 100.

CHAS. IFFINGER,
Ozone Park, L. I.

Mention The Florists' Exchange when writing.

To Close Out

4 in. **BOSTON FERNS** . . 15c.
5 in. " " . . 20c.

Good value for money.

JOHN WOLF
SAVANNAH, GA.

Mention the Florists' Exchange when writing.

Grower of Palms, Ferns and other Decorative Stock.

Nephrolepis Scottii all the year round

JOHN SCOTT

Rutland Road & E. 45th St., BROOKLYN, N. Y

Telephone 2890 Bedford.

Mention The Florists' Exchange when writing.

FOUNDED IN 1888

FLORISTS' EXCHANGE

A Weekly Medium of Interchange for Florists, Nurserymen Seedsmen and the Trade in general

Exclusively a Trade Paper.

Entered at New York Post Office as Second Class Matter

Published EVERY SATURDAY by

A. T. DE LA MARE PTG. AND PUB. CO. LTD.

2, 4, 6 and 8 Duane Street,

P. O. Box 1697. NEW YORK.
Telephone 3765 John.

CHICAGO OFFICE: 127 East Berwyn Avenue.

ILLUSTRATIONS.

Electrotypes of the illustrations used in this paper can usually be supplied by the publishers. Price on application.

YEARLY SUBSCRIPTIONS.

United States, Canada, and Mexico, $1.00. Foreign countries in postal union, $2.50. Payable in advance. Remit by Express Money Order Draft on New York. Post Office Money Order or Registered Letter.

The address label indicates the date when subscription expires and is our only receipt therefore.

REGISTERED CABLE ADDRESS:
Florex, New York.

ADVERTISING RATES.

One-half inch, 75c.; ¾-inch, $1.00; 1-inch, $1.25, special positions extra. Send for Rate Card showing discount of 10c., 15c., 25c., or 35c., per inch on continuous advertising. For rates on Wants, etc., see column for Classified Advertisements.

Copy must reach this office 12 o'clock Wednesday to secure insertion in issue of following Saturday.

Orders from unknown parties must be accompanied with cash or satisfactory references.

Chrysanthemum Society of America.

President Duckham has announced the committees to examine seedlings and sports on dates as follows: October 20 and 27, November 3, 10, 17 and 24, 1906.

Exhibits to receive attention from the committees must in all cases be prepaid to destination, and the entry fee of $2 should be forwarded to the secretary not later than Tuesday of the week preceding examination, or may accompany the blooms. Special attention is called to the rule requiring that sports, to receive a certificate, must pass three committees.

NEW YORK.—Eugene Dailledouze, chairman, care of New York Cut Flower Company, 55-57 Twenty-sixth street; William Turner, Thomas Head.

PHILADELPHIA, PA.—A. B. Cartledge, chairman, 1514 Chestnut street; John Westcott, Wm. K. Harris. Ship flowers in care of the chairman.

BOSTON, MASS.—E. A. Wood, chairman; Wm. Nicholson, James Wheeler. Ship to Boston Flower Market, care of the chairman.

CINCINNATI, O.—R. Witterstaetter, chairman; James Allen, Wm. Jackson. Ship to Jabez Elliott Flower Market, care of janitor.

CHICAGO, ILL.—J. S. Wilson, chairman; J. B. Deamud and George Wienhoeber. Ship care of J. B. Deamud, 51 Wabash avenue.

The official scales of the C. S. A. are as follows:

For Commercial Purposes		For Exhibition Purposes	
Color	20	Color	10
Form	15	Stem	5
Fullness	10	Foliage	5
Stem	15	Fullness	15
Foliage	15	Form	15
Substance	15	Depth	15
Size	10	Size	35
Total	100	Total	100

DAVID FRASER, Secretary.

Pittsburg, Pa.

A Western contemporary is endeavoring to make capital for itself through its efforts to show how big it is. Appearances certainly do tend to produce impressions, especially on the outsider, but the effect is considerably discounted when the conditions under which the bulk is secured are known. To date, however, the mere grossness of our contemporary's advertising columns has not affected the substantial patronage accorded The Florists' Exchange by its advertisers; the reason therefor being that advertising in The Florists' Exchange pays, something which the meanest kind of competition cannot counteract.

Society of American Florists and Ornamental Horticulturists.

Department of Plant Registration.

The Conard & Jones Company, West Grove, Pa., submit for registration the following:

ROSA RUGOSA MAGNIFICA (Rugosa X Victor Hugo). Habit vigorous; flowers 5 inches in diameter, double; color bright crimson; foliage resembles that of rugosa.

CANNA METEOR; foliage green; flowers large, deep crimson, in enormous trusses; height 5 feet.

CANNA NEW YORK, seedling No. 1549, flower true orchid form, unusually thick petals; foliage veined and splashed with bronze; height, 6 to 7 feet.

C. G. Roebling, Trenton, N. J., submits for registration Laelio-Cattleya Washington A. Roebling 2nd, (Laelia harpophylla × Cattleya granulosa). Flower bright yellow, with pink on lip, bulbs slender, ten inches long, double-leaved; leaves one and one-half inches broad and eight inches long.

WM. J. STEWART, Secretary.

The Secret of Burbank's Success.

Speaking before the Minnesota State Horticultural Society recently on the subject of "Two Hours with Luther Burbank," Professor Hansen of the South Dakota experiment station said: "His (Burbank's) secret, as I see it, is the application of the law laid down by Darwin in regard to the variation of plants: 'Excess of food causes variation.' He has three or four acres around his house, and this made up into beds, and the soil is filled as full of commercial fertilizers and plant food in general as it is possible to get it. This 'excess of food causes variation.' * * * Burbank's success lies in his ability to determine initial variation at an early stage of the work. He can induce variation to a marvelous degree by high feeding. Furthermore he is very skillful; his mechanical execution of the work is perfect. He showed me a small knife, with a very thin blade, with which he removes the stamens before the flowers open. The stamens are not always removed. Burbank said there is no need of it if the stigmas are closely watched as they become receptive, and with the pollen applied at the right time there will be no self-pollination."

American Horticultural Nomenclature.

Professor L. C. Corbett, horticulturist, Bureau of Plant Industry, Department of Agriculture, Washington, D. C., in a very able paper read before the recent meeting of the Society for Horticultural Science at New Orleans, La., makes the recommendation that American horticulturists, especially writers and those issuing catalogues, should follow the nomenclature used in Bailey's Cyclopedia of American Horticulture. "This work," he says, "has the advantage of being new and up-to-date, and purely American."

We fully endorse Professor Corbett's suggestion; and it is evident in some catalogues that their makers are already doing just what he recommends.

Some thirteen years ago the S. A. F. adopted rules regulating nomenclature, specifying that natural species and varieties of plants shall bear the Latin names assigned to them in Nicholson's Dictionary of Gardening, so far as they are named, except that where differences exist between the dictionary and Kew Index, the name adopted by the latter shall be chosen.

Nicholson's dictionary adopts what appears to us to be an incongruity in the use of the capital letter in the case of certain specific and varietal plant names, something we cannot understand. For instance, varieties named in compliment to persons, whether the originators or others, are capitalized, such as Veitchii, Sanderi, etc. In the case of applying a geographical name to a plant the lower case initial letter is used, e. g., brasiliensis, zanzibarensis, canadensis, americana, etc. In Bailey's cyclopedia the capital letter is employed always, in instances of the kind cited.

The Florists' Exchange has always endeavored to follow Nicholson's style along orthographic lines—and many catalogue men do likewise—since it may be regarded as the one authorized and endorsed by the S. A. F. But there was no Cyclopedia of American Horticulture when the rule was adopted by the national society; and for the sake of general uniformity in plant nomenclature throughout the United States, and for the reason, as already stated, that the Bailey system of spelling is now being adopted by some American catalogue men, we are heartily in favor of the Cyclopedia of American Horticulture being taken as a guide by the horticulturists of the United States along the lines referred to, and should like to see the S. A. F. O. H. so recommend officially. Professor Corbett has given some excellent reasons for this being done, not the least potent of which is that the work in question is up-to-date, and, further, that it is American. With all due respect to the English works cited, we are of the opinion that American horticulturists and botanists have reached that stage when it is unnecessary to follow alien systems, whether in nomenclature or otherwise, and when all things pertaining to their profession should be strictly American, and universally regarded as such.

OUR READERS' VIEWS

Stove vs. Greenhouse Plants.

Editor Florists' Exchange:

I have not considered this as a burning que
The word "greenhouse" in this country seems to
come to be a generic one applied to all glass s
tures used for growing plants. On the other hand
words "stove plants" still convey a very distinct
definite idea to me and, I think, to most garden

W. N. RU

Editor Florists' Exchange:

In my opinion a stove plant is a greenhouse
The name stove house is only found in the En
language. Greenhouse, as it is called here, h
equivalent in German, "Treibhaus," which m
warm house, and includes also the cool and
mediate house. It is the same in France; there
have warm, intermediate and cool houses.

I think that stove house plants should be c
fied as greenhouse plants; and that other hor
tural societies should take the same view o
matter as the New York Florists' Club has
and abolish the term "stove house plants."

N. BUTTERBA

Editor Florists' Exchange:

The question of "stove plants," which app
in your editorial columns, issue of 13th inst.,
438, is one of importance to the trade gene
And the action of the New York Florists' Cl
disposing of the question as they did, by dro
entirely the word "stove" and adopting i
"greenhouse plants" in their vocabulary, see
be the part of wisdom. To my mind, the
"stove" as applied to plants is an importation
does not fit here, and may be dropped withou
to anyone.

ALEXANDER MACLELL

Newport, R. I.

Editor Florists' Exchange:

While the action of the New York Florists'
in deciding by a vote of the members tha
designation "stove and greenhouse plants
changed in all exhibitions of the club to "
house plants" may be the most sensible that
have been taken from a purely commercial
of view, it is nevertheless questionable if fr
broader horticultural view it will prove alto
beneficial. To a young gardener a "stove"
a house where he might expect to find plant
required a warmer temperature, and other
tions different from those in what was known
"greenhouse"; and he was by means of th
ference in designation, although perhaps in
direct way, made familiar in a shorter time
he otherwise would with the requirements
different kinds of plants. The statement th
this country plants called stove plants in E
are used in sub-tropical bedding is no argum
all in favor of doing away with the distinctio
tween stove and greenhouse plants, because
although used for the purpose stated, such
when stored for the Winter, will not be kep
house where the temperature would suit cyc
geraniums, cinerarias, primulas, and many
things known as "greenhouse plants."

The different terms were applied to plants
directly to distinguish one from the other for
ment when grown under glass, not merely to
cate which could stand the lower temperatur
many good gardeners ascribe at least a port
their knowledge of the needs of plants to th
that during their apprenticeship days, "stove
were kept by themselves, and "greenhouse
the same. It may be said that the same kno
could be gained if plants requiring a highe
perature than others were simply kept in a v
house without the word "stove" being men
but I think that the word and all it implied
an impression more lasting than would hav
the case had the term not been in established

A great deal of the agitation in favor of
away with the different designations has
from the fact that in this country there is
difference of opinion regarding the temperat
which plants thrive best. There is no doub
are growers in the United States who very s
fully treat what were known as "stove pla
England much the same as "greenhouse
were treated there in regard to temperatu
well as light.

In the foregoing I have defended the p
of the different terms under discussion mor
I have attempted the justification of its conti
especially in this country, where the com
branch of horticulture in magnitude greatly
the private branch; and it must be allowe
for the most important to lead. Many flo
this country do not know what is meant by a
plant" when they see the term used in a sc
Such ignorance is no discredit, and if it h
still is the means of confusing them to the
of preventing them from exhibiting, or of hi
to them in any way, it is but right that
should be simplified in order that all may be
on an equality. At the same time let the
gardener still have his "stove and greenhouse
if he wishes.

I

tor Florists' Exchange:

'e read with much interest the discussion which k place on October 8 at the meeting of the v York Florists' Club on the question of "Stove Greenhouse Plants," also your comments on the ie. We cannot but think the club and yourself a little hasty in suggesting the obliteration of word "stove" from our horticultural calendar. are well aware that climatic conditions differ erially here as compared with those of Europe. Summers are much warmer and our Winters ier—at least over a large area of our country— we fail to see any satisfactory solution by drop- the word "stove" and retaining "greenhouse." ne speaker says the word "stove" is antiquated obsolete. Is "greenhouse" any more modern? word "greenhouse" was used to designate the earliest glass structures erected in Great Brit- in the seventeenth century or earlier. "Stoves" e unknown until about the beginning of the teenth century. A "greenhouse" may mean a cture where a minimum temperature of 40, 50, or 70 degrees is maintained, if the new definition ccepted. The plant stove we have always taken mean a structure devoted to such plants as are ves of warm or tropical climates; the tempera- is necessarily high, a Winter minimum being 55 degrees, and the plants need much humidity. he fact that caladiums and crotons, to say hing of other species, can be bedded out here in mmer does not make out any case for the drop- of the word "stove," any more than because e same plants may be grown in "greenhouses" a part of the year in Europe. For at least six ths in the year they must have what is now wn as "stove" culture; they will exist in an nary greenhouse or even a dwelling house where temperature does not run too low, but to be wn well they need tropical warmth.

seems to us if the word "stove" is to be pped some other must be substituted which is vague than "greenhouse." In some parts of land the term "tropical house" is used instead "stove," but the latter word is the more popular more generally accepted. We do not believe any action the S. A. F. O. H. or any club may toward the abolition of the word "stove" from horticultural vocabulary will meet with general ptance; it certainly will not from private gar- ers. The words "greenhouse," "hot house" and ss house" to-day mean about anything with a s roof on for the growth of plants; the "stove" se is in reality the only one the temperature of ch every practical gardener at least knows, or ld know.

'e fail to see any reason for dropping the word ve" from the schedule of any horticultural society ch retains it, unless some word like "tropical" l displace it.

W. N. CRAIG.

(Other Letters will appear next week.)

The Lagerstroemia Indica.

tor Florists' Exchange:

is remarkable how very easily this shrub is ed from seed, at least here in China. There is ly a shrub that will grow quicker and with r results. We have thousands of seedlings, from sown Spring, 1905, which were just a mass of m about a month ago. The plants are quite 4 feet high. I like this shrub pruned back to w inches every year so that it forms a round of young shoots all bearing flowers.

'e could supply rather a large quantity of seeds plants, and, if any nurseryman is interested, should like to hear from him. However, seed ld ripen well in the South, and could probably ecured from there.

THEO. ECKARDT, of L. Boehmer & Co. anghai.

Obituary

Paul Goebel.

aul Goebel, a florist of Grand Rapids, Mich., on Tuesday, October 9, 1906, aged 73 years. was born in Germany and had lived in Grand ids 22 years. Mr. Goebel was an honorary nber of the Arbeiter Society. He is survived by Goebel and four sons. One of the sons, Eu- e, is superintendent of the city cemeteries.

Rudolph Ulrich.

udolph Ulrich, the well-known landscape gar- er, died on Monday, October 15, 1906, at Santiago, where he had been for a year superintending laying out of Chateau Kearney Park, Fresno, He was superintendent of Prospect Park, Brook- under Mayor Schieren. He was superintendent the grounds of the Chicago, Buffalo, and Omaha ibitions, and designed the gardens of many es- s.

r. Ulrich was born in Weimar, Germany, in 1841, had been for many years in this country. His dence was at 398 Macdonough street, Brooklyn. is survived by a widow, two daughters, and two s, J. L. Ulrich and William G. Ulrich.

CLUB AND SOCIETY DOINGS.

THE CHICAGO FLORISTS' CLUB held its regular monthly meeting in Handel hall on Thursday evening, October 11, with all the officers of the club in their chairs, and the largest attendance of members since the meeting preceding the flower show a year ago. The regular routine of business was carried through and the following officers were placed in nomination for the ensuing year: President, H. N. Bruns; vice-president, Leonard Kill; secretary, L. H. Winterson; treasurer, Edgar Sanders; financial secretary, Henry E. Klunder; trustees, F. F. Benthey, Carl Cropp, J. F. Klimmer, John Reardon and W. L. Palinsky.

It was voted to hold a banquet on the Thursday evening of flower show week, November 8, and Messrs. Rudd, Samuelson and Simmons were appointed a committee to make the necessary arrangements.

Booths were tendered by the Horticultural Society of Chicago in which flowers are to be sold for the benefit of the heirs of the late James Hartshorne, which were accepted with the thanks of the club and the following resolutions were unanimously adopted:

WHEREAS, in the death of James Hartshorne, our late companion and associate, we feel that we have lost one of our most valuable members. Be it

RESOLVED that the Chicago Florists' Club realizes to the full extent the loss, not only from a personal standpoint, but in full measure the loss to the horticulturists of the country, of whom the deceased had been a sincere and faithful supporter. And be it further

RESOLVED that the sympathy of the club be extended to the family of our departed friend; that a copy of these resolutions be spread upon our records, and a copy be engrossed and forwarded to Mrs. Hartshorne.

GEORGE ASMUS,
L. H. WINTERSON,
WILLIAM K. WOOD,
Committee.

A general talk was then indulged in regarding the coming show by a number of members, and the meeting adjourned subject to a special call, as it is probable that it will be found expedient to hold more than one special meeting between this date and show week.

W. K. W.

ST. LOUIS FLORISTS' CLUB.—The meeting held last Thursday afternoon was well attended. Professor H. C. Irish, the newly elected president, occupied the chair; all the other officers were also present. The president, after disposing of the regular routine business, referred to an article in one of the trade papers, regarding a bill in the council to stop crepe pulling, which subject was thoroughly discussed and will be brought up again at our next meeting.

James W. Dunford spoke about the holding of flower shows, and from his talk and plans, the club will at its next meeting bring up the subject, and start in at once to prepare to hold a big show next year in November.

It was decided by full vote to invite the press and the trade in general to our meetings when anything special is to come up.

On motion and by full vote, it was decided that the club hold a chrysanthemum show in its meeting rooms; prizes to be $50 divided into three lots, white, pink and yellow. The trustees will have full charge of this show and will send out in due time a circular with full particulars.

Only one of the gentlemen who were to lead discussions, on four subjects being present, these were consequently not heard, and instead we had one by Henry Braun, on "Growing bulbs, as it is done in Holland"; this was very interesting. The others were: "Are Asters grown for Cut Flowers Around the City?" "Are Dahlias grown for Cut Flowers Around the City?" "Does it Pay to Grow High Grade Flowers for the Market?" All the members took part in these discussions, and many good points were brought out.

By full vote, the club opposed the holding of the S. A. F. Convention in the Fall of the year.

The trustees assigned two discussions for next meeting, one to Harry Young on "Growing Poinsettias for Pans and Cut Flowers;" the other, to A. J. Bentzen on "Growing Cyclamen Plants."

The attending members said this had been one of the most interesting meetings yet held by our club. The next session will be held on Thursday afternoon, November 8, at 2 o'clock, in the regular meeting hall.

ST. PATRICK.

MORRIS COUNTY (N. J.) GARDENERS AND FLORISTS' SOCIETY.—Final arrangements for the coming flower show took up most of the time of the 26 members present at last meeting. The show will be held November 1 and 2. Each member took his quota of tickets to sell and a bundle of posters to put up. It looks now as if we would have the goods on hand to show, and we are determined to bring the people here to see them.

Two members were elected and four new names proposed. Our judges come from Lenox, Mass., this year.

E. R.

NASSUA COUNTY (N. Y.) HORTICULTURAL SOCIETY held its regular monthly meeting at the usual place on Wednesday, October 10. The attendance was unusually large. President Harrison occupied the chair. Six new members were elected to active membership and one nominated. The show room looked a blaze of color with the monthly exhibits of flowers. In the points class H. F. Meyer scored 93 2-3 with carnations and fruits; J. F. Johnston, 86 2-3 with a vase of Countess of Lonsdale dahlia; F. Mense, 81 2-3 with a bunch of single violets; S. Trepass, 81 1-3 with a vase of single dahlias. H. F. Meyer was awarded the box of cigars for the best collection of out of door flowers. The fountain pen prize for the best collection of outdoor flowers, six varieties, was won by S. Trepass. Other members showing in this class were H. Matz, and Adolph Jænecke, Floral Park, N. Y.

This was the last meeting before the society's annual flower show, to be held on October 31 and November 1, so that the chief business was the preparation for the exhibition. Special prizes are coming in. Stumpp & Walter Company give $10 for 100 single and 100 double violets; Rickard Brothers, $10 for table of foliage plants 12x3 feet, pots not to exceed 6 inches; Society's prize, $15, for best collection of carnations for commercial members. Certificates of merit will be awarded for meritorious seedlings. Mrs. Paul Dana gives books for best ten chrysanthemums, distinct varieties.

JOHN F. JOHNSTON.

NEW JERSEY FLORICULTURAL SOCIETY.—Dahlia night was observed by the society upon the 5th inst. with a large exhibition and a full house. Premiums were offered for the best 24 in six varieties, the best 12 in three varieties, and the best 25 in variety. William Runkle (D. Kindsgrab, gardener) received first for 24 in six sorts, and A. B. Jenkins, second. Walter M. Gray, of Maplewood, took the prize for the best 12 in three varieties, and A. C. von Gaasbeck (William Bennett, gardener) for the best vase of 25 varieties. Of special note was the large and varied exhibit of J. C. Williams, of Montclair, comprising most of the newer single and cactus sorts. Herbert Bradley (Robert Carruthers, gardener) of the same place, staged thirty-two varieties. John Crosby Brown (Peter Duff, gardener) had a magnificent vase of Cuban Giant and Grand Duke Alexis. Exhibits were also made by A. T. Gillespie, (George Oakley, gardener), Mrs. Stewart, H. Hartshorne (A. T. Caparn, gardener), S. and A. Colgate, (William Reid, gardener), Chas. Hathaway (Max Schneider, gardener), and Col. H. A. Potter (William Phillips, gardener).

In the general competitive exhibit, Lager & Hurrell staged Odontoglossum grande, Cattleyas chrysodoxa, and labiata; William Barr (Arthur W. Bodwell, gardener), Cattleya labiata, Oncidium varicosum, and Epidendrum vitellinum majus.

Two new members, Andrew Wilson, of Summit, and Orson A. Miller, of East Orange, were elected.

Announcement was made that through the generosity of one of the patrons of the society, the new hall of the Woman's Club of the Oranges had been placed at its disposal for the Fall exhibition on November 5 and 6, afternoon and evening. Joseph A. Manda has been appointed general manager.

J. B. D.

THE ELBERON (N. J.) HORTICULTURAL SOCIETY held a very successful dahlia show on Monday evening, October 1. The exhibits of cactus, decorative, and single dahlias were certainly fine. Among the out-of-town exhibitors were F. R. Pierson Company, Tarrytown, N. Y., who were awarded a certificate of merit for a display of new dahlias. G. H. Hale, superintendent for Mr. E. D. Adams, and James Dowlen, superintendent for Mr. H. L. Terrell, Seabright, were each awarded certificates of merit for fine collections of cactus dahlias. A. Strohmenger, superintendent for Mrs. Chatalong, Seabright, was awarded a diploma for a vase of celosias. Among the members of the society the principle prize-winners were J. Kennedy for collection of cactus dahlias; E. O'Rourke, collection of dahlias; W. D. Robertson, vase of dahlias; J. Kennedy, collection of single dahlias; W. D. Robertson, collection of outdoor flowers; F. Dettlinger, bunch of violets; J. Kennedy, collection of outdoor roses; A. Bauer, dish of fruit; A. Greib, collection of vegetables; E. O'Rourke, best single rose. A fine exbibit of Cattleya labiata was staged by Peter Murray.

G. M.

A GOOD SWEET POTATO.—Through the courtesy of H. Austin, specialist in sweet potatoes, Felton, Del., we have been favored with a basket of his new sweet potato, Early Golden. After sampling this variety, we are free to admit it is one of the best, if not the best, sweet potato we have ever tasted, and should easily become a favorite. The name "Early Golden" is well applied, as the tuber is of a rich golden color, being very large and early. Mr. Austin speaks with great confidence of this variety, and says that it will produce more marketable tubers than any other yellow sweet potato in cultivation on that peninsula.

Godfrey Aschmann's Trip Abroad.

Godfrey Aschmann, the well known Philadelphia florist, returned from his trip abroad on Monday morning, October 15, 1906. Mr. Aschmann had been absent since August 15, and during the interval had visited several European towns and cities on business and pleasure bent. On his arrival in New York he called at the office of The Florists' Exchange, and very kindly granted an interview regarding his trip. He said: "It was Saturday, August 25, during a terrible wind and rain storm, rough and cold enough for a heavy overcoat, when I struck the beautiful green meadows of Holland. I visited the principal bulb growers of Sassenheim, including the establishments of Van Leeuwen & Son, and Beorhorst & Son. They were busy packing and shipping American orders, some of which had already been forwarded. I was shown the process of propagating hyacinths in the large houses used for that purpose, which are heated by hot water, and have been specially erected. The mother bulbs are hollowed in the center, one by one, and placed on wooden racks made of laths about eighteen inches apart, right from floor to ceiling, one tier above the other. After about three weeks, the small bulbs will form around the mother bulbs, being separated when big enough, then planted in the open ground which has previously been well prepared and fertilized. It takes from three to four years to obtain bulbs large enough for market.

Godfrey Aschmann.

"I visited Ghent, the great world center for the growing of azaleas, palms, and other decorative plants; in all, there are about 800 large florist establishments there. The azalea crop this year is very fine, the large sizes and good varieties, well shaped plants, are in demand, and are bringing good prices. Kentias Forsteriana and Belmoreana are very scarce, and prices are high. Some establishments are declining to take any more orders for this stock. Other decorative plants are plentiful, going at moderate prices.

"It is a great sight to see the many acres of tuberous rooted begonias, both single and double, in all colors; millions of them are planted here, and there is a big market for them all over Europe.

"After visiting the botanical gardens and other places in Brussels, I went to Paris, France. I was charmed with the beautiful carpet beds seen around the public buildings and villas, many thousands of plants being used for this purpose. The flower markets in the public squares all over Paris are quite interesting spots for the florist; there one can find large collections of all kinds of plants as well as bouquets, which are disposed of at moderate prices. From Paris I sent to some of my customers 300 souvenir postal cards to give them an idea of the beauty spots of the noted French capital.

"From Paris I went to Zurich, Switzerland, the home of my birth. Much credit is due to the people of Switzerland for the manner in which they utilize to advantage every foot of ground in their beautiful gardens. These gardens are generally divided into four parts: the lawn, which is planted with shrubbery, perennials, etc.; the vegetable garden, the fruit garden planted with dwarf fruit trees, such as pears, apples, peaches, apricots, etc., trained in various forms—pyramidal, espalier, on houses, fences, and on wires around the walks. These trees were loaded with the finest table fruit, that brings excellent prices to the growers. Blackberries, raspberries, and other small fruits are also cultivated. The flower gardens are composed of various forms of beds containing blooming plants similar to those found in America. The dark red and Vernon as well as Erfordii begonias are pretty plants, and nearly every garden has a few of these. All these beds are prettily bordered with boxwood, or cement edging surrounded with gravel walks. Bohnhoffstrasse, in Zurich, is one of the finest avenues there, extending from the lake to the main railroad station. Florists, farmers and truckers have the privilege from the city of using both sides of the pavement on Tuesday and Friday for the sale of their products, which are exhibited on their hand-wagons. It is a sight worth seeing to watch these from four hundred to five hundred produce dealers from all parts of the Canton of Zurich; all seem to make out pretty well. At 11 o'clock in the morning the street is vacated, swept, and in a very short time afterward looks as clean as a parlor. Switzerland has enjoyed a very large crop of fruit this year, and the best is being stored; the common used for cider. The raising of the grape vine for the making of wine is carried on there with great success. As is well known, the people of Switzerland are very industrious, and their industries of silk, watchmaking, musical instruments, laces, woodcarvings, etc., not to forget the Swiss cheese of Emethal and Berne are world famous. The country is visited by travelers from all over the globe. Its lake and mountain scenery are unsurpassed anywhere. It is difficult at times to secure accommodations in the hotels there.

"From Zurich, I went to Lucerne; no pen can describe the beauty of this little town; it is like a paradise on earth.

"The next stage of my journey was to Milan in Italy. I visited the international exposition which opened there in April, and will close in November. In going from Lucerne to Milan the traveler has to pass through thirty-five tunnels, the longest of these being the St. Gothard, which took a fast train twenty minutes to go through. Milan is a fine city. The exposition buildings are very tastefully erected, containing samples of almost every industry of the globe, many being in process of manufacture. Around the exposition buildings were interesting exhibits from the large Belgian florists, Ghent being especially well represented with a full line of decorative plants, and carrying off many prizes. The French growers also exhibited there beds of standard and dwarf roses, mostly all new varieties, which were very much admired.

"To give you an idea of the mild climate of Milan, I may state that I saw florists there planting on September 21 a bed of one thousand coleus. Other decorative plants were at that time being set out around the buildings.

"From every city visited by me I sent souvenir postal cards, 1100 in all, to my customers. These I feel sure will be appreciated and kept as a slight token of remembrance of my trip."

AMONG THE GROWERS

Dailledouze Brothers, Flatbush, N. Y.

The range of glass owned and personally operated by these eminent carnation growers never presented more interesting and educational features than it does this season. We recently had the privilege of spending a half day with the three brothers Dailledouze; and although familiar with the excellent quality of stock usually produced at their establishment, we must say the general condition of their carnations at the present time surpasses all previous efforts, and the whole range of glass from one end to the other presents a picture that is worthy of a few hours of observation and study by anyone interested in plant growing under glass.

With the exception of a few weeks, including the latter part of August and the beginning of September, which were rather too warm and humid, weather conditions this season have been very favorable for carnation culture. Stock planted in the fields grew remarkably well all through, and disease and insects were conspicuous by their absence. It is the custom of this firm to plant the houses as early as is convenient. The plan of growing indoors all through the Summer has not yet been adopted to any extent, at the present time there being but a few benches of plants that have had inside cultivation right through the season.

Bloom of Chrysanthemum October Frost.
Courtesy Nathan Smith & Son.

In view of the fact that the number of varieties of carnations on the market in these days is so large, one is very much impressed by the seemingly few kinds that are cultivated here. Many people make the mistake of trying to grow too many varieties, but such is not the case with the Dailledouze Brothers, who seem to have got the selection of kinds to grow down to an extremely fine point. Their list this season includes a smaller number of sorts than we have ever before known them to have under cultivation. For instance; in white varieties, the main supply comes from two kinds only—Lieutenant Peary and The Queen. The latter variety is planted in large numbers, and not only is it remarkable for its coming into flower early, but it continues all through the season to be a first-class white in every respect. That it is considered the best in its class is plainly evidenced by the numbers in which it has been planted.

Another variety that is on trial, of which but a small quantity is planted, however, is White Perfection, raised by F. Dorner & Sons Company, Lafayette, Ind. It is yet too early to say much about it. For scarlet, two varieties are grown, one a seedling of the firm's, of bright color, which is planted largely, and has been found very satisfactory. The other variety is Victory, introduced last season by Guttman & Weber. For crimson there is only one variety grown—Crimson Glow, one of their own seedlings, which was disseminated by them at the beginning of this year. In variegated sorts, Mrs. M. A. Patten and Prosperity are the only varieties grown in quantity. Prosperity continues to be a leader in its class, and meets with just as much favor from the retail trade as it did the first year it was introduced, which is doing pretty well for a variegated carnation. Mrs. Patten, which is considered the best of its type, is all that is desired in size, length of stem and free-flowering qualities. For cerise pink, Mrs. Thos. W. Lawson is still grown in quantity; and in the other shades of pink there are Enchantress, a pink seedling of the concern's own, Genevieve Lord and Welcome. The latter variety is a pink sport of Mrs. Thos. W. Lawson, and is a clear pink in its coloring. It has been registered provisionally with the American Carnation Society, and is to be disseminated the coming year. Of the several sports that have come from Mrs. Thos. Lawson, this pink one, Welcome, is sure to find favor with carnation growers who do the Lawson varieties well. There has been a white Lawson introduced that has proved a marked success, and owing to the pleasing shade of Welcome, we have no hesitation in saying that this variety, when disseminated, will give as good general satisfaction as has been obtained from the other sports occurring in this family.

In addition to carnations, at the present time chrysanthemums are very much in evidence with these growers. Cutting has hardly commenced yet, a few dozen a day being about the total output just now; but by the time these notes are read, cutting in quantity will be on in earnest. As an indication of what the Dailledouze Brothers grow in chrysanthemums, we may mention the following varieties, which are considered to be standard with them: Intensity, crimson; J. K. Shaw, pink; Alice Byron, considered one of the best all-around whites; Timothy Eaton, white; Colonel D. Appleton, yellow; Polly Rose, white; Glory of the Pacific, pink; Maud Dean, pink; and Nagoya, yellow. Among the varieties that are more in an experimental stage than otherwise are Thornycroft, a bronze yellow; Merstham, yellow; Beatrice May, white; Rosiere, a lilac pink that seems to be a good one, though hardly filled up well enough in the center as yet to be assured of a place in the first rank; Jeannie Nonin, white; Mrs. Duckham, yellow; and a very late crimson variety called General Maceo.

John Scott, Flatbush, N. Y.

A recent visit to the establishment of John Scott, at Flatbush, Brooklyn, N. Y., found that gentleman busy supervising the laying of the foundations for the three houses which he is to erect on the property he recently acquired, adjoining his own place. Although it seems rather late in the season to commence building operations, Mr. Scott informs us that he will have the roofs on the houses and the boilers installed in the course of a week or ten days.

Mr. Scott is still growing enormous numbers of Nephrolepis Scottii, which is to be seen in all sizes almost, and fills one entire range of glass. One of the finest things at this establishment this year is a house of gardenias. We have never before seen gardenias in such a healthy and floriferous condition. The plants are grown on raised benches, and are showing buds from every shoot, many of them with stems 18 inches in length. Without a doubt, this house will net a handsome profit when the returns are all in, as gardenias in the New York market always fetch a good price through the Winter months.

Begonia Gloire de Lorraine is also being grown extensively, and by Thanksgiving handsome plants of a good marketable size will be ready for shipment. Of Dracænas Massangeana and Lindeni, together with Pandanus Veitchii and araucarias, there is a good stock of marketable sized plants on hand. Crotons are also being grown in quantity; and a stock of that coming decorative plant, Ficus pandurata, is being worked up for future trade.

Mr. Scott is this year also growing several houses of chrysanthemums for cut flowers; and has quite a stock of the new marguerite, Queen Alexandra, which will be grown on for next season. Cibotium Schiedii is also being grown in some quantities here, for which fern there is always a ready market.

Chrysanthemum October Frost.

Editor Florists' Exchange:

During the last few weeks there have been several complimentary comments regarding the new early chrysanthemum, October Frost. This variety, we believe, is destined to meet popular favor, being early, white, and producing a large flower. They come best from early buds, being then larger and more double.

NATHAN SMITH & SON.

Adrian, Mich.

(A photograph of a flower is shown herewith.)

HARDY PLANT NOTES

Hardy Ferns.

With the increasing popularity of hardy plants there has also sprung up a demand for hardy ferns; and considering the adaptability and usefulness of these plants, this is not to be wondered at. In Europe they have long been used, and no list of any consequence seems complete without them. Many and varied are the forms to be had; in fact, one well-known writer, and a great specialist in these ferns, ridicules the use of our common forms, declaring that the varieties raised from them are of much superior grace, adaptability and habit.

However that may be, our American ferns are very desirable, and there is variety, beauty and form enough in them to satisfy most admirers for the present; and as a knowledge of them and of their uses for the decoration or adornment of the waste places and shady nooks in our gardens, etc., are more appreciated, or they become better known, there will not be wanting the sources from which new and superior forms will come forth.

Few of these newer varieties have as yet made their appearance in the American trade, but there are one or two especially worthy of mention, viz., Asplenium filix-fœmina var. Victoria, an exceed-

Asplenium Filix-Fœmina Var. Victoria
Courtesy Henry A. Dreer.

ingly pleasing form or variety of our native lady fern, which words fail to describe adequately or accurately. The long, graceful fronds, with the beautiful cut pinnæ laid crosswise over each other, are exceedingly pretty, and to get a proper conception of their real beauty one must needs see them. This fern is as easy of cultivation as the native form, A. filix-fœmina, of our woods, pastures, and roadsides, but, of course, pays much better for more liberal treatment and can be very readily moved at almost any season of the year. It is perfectly hardy, having stood the rigors of our last six Winters unharmed. Often the plants receive no other protection than what their foliage affords, being, on several occasions, in a very open spot. They are readily increased by division, and, to the enthusiast, by spores.

Another beautiful form and equally as hardy is Scolopendrium crispum, a very beautiful crested form of the hart's tongue fern, worthy of a place in any garden and always bright, neat, and attractive. The original hart's tongue fern is also worth growing, and wherever seen is admired. By many it is only considered a greenhouse fern; this is a mistake, for it is found growing wild in New York State.

Our native form, Asplenium filix-fœmina, also lends itself very readily to cultivation and can with care be removed at any time. Once established, it is not very fastidious as to position. I have successfully grown it on the shady side of a rockery, and consider it one of the most attractive of the group. For other positions in which to grow it, we need only go to nature to discover these. As I have previously mentioned, it is found growing in woodland shade, in rocky, open pastures, swamps, and by the roadside, which would indicate that it will grow almost anywhere.

A. thelypteroides is very good for wet, shady places, and I have seen it growing nicely in the open.

Asplenium ebeneum is a graceful fern when seen at its best. I have frequently found it growing in New Jersey on gravelly banks, and even among blackberry bushes, in dense shade, and in a dry, sandy soil; but if removed from these positions I always think it seems to lose its beauty somewhat. Although it will grow year after year, I have never been very successful with it; but I sometimes think I have not just adapted it to its natural home surroundings. I find that it is not one that will yield very readily to the ordinary method of cultivation; it seems to insist on some adaptation to its natural habitat.

A. trichomanes is a very diminutive species compared with the others, being of a somewhat similar nature. To be successful with it it must have a somewhat rocky situation. I have been able to establish it in pots, the plants grown in a cool, shady place during the Summer months, plunged in peat; and I find that this is about the only presentable way of sending established pot plants of these small ferns to a customer.

The walking fern (Camptosorus rhizophyllus) and Lygodium palmatum, the various cheilanthes and pellæas, ought to be similarly established, as, when coming direct from the collectors, some of them are so small and others so straggly and dry looking in appearance, that they do not create a very favorable impression upon an unaccustomed purchaser. Other varieties called for by the retail trade generally, which, when well established in pots, present a more favorable impression upon the purchaser, are Aspidium novarborescens (the New York shield fern), botrychiums in variety, Cystopteris bulbifera and C. fragilis, Dicksonia pilosiuscula (the bowlder fern), and perhaps the most lovely of the dwarfer species and one of the easiest to establish; the phegopteris, the woodsias and rock polypodys. The last named seven species are among the most beautiful and easy to cultivate. They readily establish themselves even when directly received from the collector's hands; but when grown on one year in 3-inch pots, placed in a cool, shady spot, notably under a hedgerow, plunged in peat or peaty soil, and attention occasionally given to watering them, they make a fine growth, fill the pots with roots, and form a good presentable solid clump, fit to send to the most fastidious customer.

Adiantum pedatum can be dug from the woods, with a large flat mass of fibrous roots attached; but upon close examination the roots will be found to belong to surrounding vegetation. Nevertheless, this makes them good presentable clumps; but I think them more so when grown for one year in a three or four-inch pot. This is a lovely fern, and it seems a great pity it is so much overlooked. It is always admired when seen, and it lends itself so very readily to cultivation, its chief requirements being shade, or partial shade, with good drainage and a fairly rich soil.

The aspidiums are probably among the most showy and useful of our ferns, and these again readily yield themselves to cultivation. Probably the most common and best known of this species are A. acrostichoides (the Christmas fern) and A. marginale, evergreen varieties. Both are in great demand for their cut fronds, and are stored and used by all our florists during the Winter season. There are many and varied forms of this species in cultivation, and deservedly so, on account of their beautiful characters, and all are worthy of a place where room, space and time in their care can be afforded them.

Onoclea sensibilis is found growing almost everywhere in sun or shade, wet or dry places, on rocks and in dry, sandy soils. Especially does it seem to delight in spots where it can get an occasional flooding of water. In such situations, in semi-shade, I have found it growing five feet high. Its commonness almost excludes it from the list of cultivated forms.

The ostrich fern, Onoclea struthiopteris, is the best member of this genus, and I think most beautiful of the whole fern family. It grows exceedingly well in a moist position, in open sunlight or in semi-shade, and has graceful, spreading fronds, from 6 to 10 inches in width and 1 to 5 feet high, yet it is but little known.

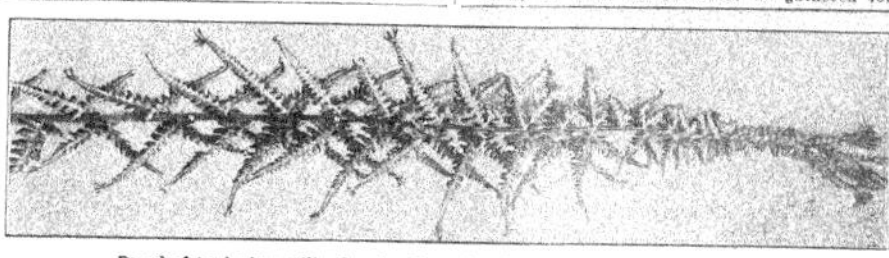

Frond of Asplenium Filix-Fœmina Var. Victoria. Courtesy Henry A. Dreer.

Three other of our native ferns which can be grown in sun or shade, all beautiful objects and among the largest and most graceful, as well as the most easy to cultivate, are the osmundas—O. regalis, the royal fern, found growing abundantly

Osmunda Cinnamomea.

in dense clumps in swamps and marshy places from which it is readily dug and transplanted successfully. But for best results it should be planted where it can secure plenty of moisture, as it is often found flourishing with its crown from a few inches to a foot out of still water.

O. cinnamomea, the cinnamon fern, is often found growing in close proximity to the last named, and is especially fond of wet, mucky soil. Although it will grow on upland soils, it is never so happy as when in the former state. It flourishes in both sun and shade.

O. Claytoniana, the interrupted fern, although sometimes found growing in wet places, is more often seen under more adverse circumstancs and will be found quite a useful fern for the rougher or drier positions than the other two members of this genus.

The woodwardias are also useful subjects for cultivation, but I think they are never so handsome and never do so well as when in their native haunts. They grow in wet bogs or by the side of running streams. W. virginica is at home here, and where it can be given a similar situation it is well worthy of all the pains and care that may be bestowed upon it.

In the planting of ferns many seem to defer the work until Spring, when the plants are almost in full leaf. This, I think, is a serious mistake; for although many of them will grow when thus transplanted, the tender fronds at this period are so very easily damaged that very often a new transplantation looks indeed a very sorry sight for the whole year. If planted in the Fall this could be avoided, and much better results obtained, as the plants would then be in a position to re-establish themselves as soon as they commenced to make their Spring growth, and would not resent the removal to their new quarters nearly so much as they do if moved in the Spring or early Summer. Besides they would give a more pleasing effect the first season after planting.

Many of those named could be gathered locally now, but collectors would gladly furnish them very cheaply at this season, and this is the best time to secure them.

The foregoing list embraces most of the best of our native forms, and among them will be found ferns suitable for any and all outside positions. All, with the noted exceptions, are of easiest cultivation; and if these are successfully grown, doubtless their culture will instil inspiration and love for other both useful and beautiful forms.

HERBERT GREENSMITH.

Asplenium Filix-foemina, Lady Fern.

Among deciduous hardy ferns the lady fern holds a prominent place. It is such a one to accommodate itself to its position and to thrive wherever other ferns will grow, that it is usually found where collections of ferns exist. It is one, too, that will quickly spread, forming in time a large mass of green. As ferns are known to love shade, these masses of green are greatly desired in many instances. Our photograph shows a good sized clump of this fern, yet it is but the half of what is there, all spread from one small plant set out a few years ago.

This fern possesses more varieties perhaps than any other hardy sort, it being so prone to vary. There are over two dozen striking varieties of it in some of the European nurseries, many of the crested forms being particularly beautiful.

The lady fern is one of many others that grow in different countries distant from one another. It is a native here, as well as over a wide portion of Europe. The position of the one illustrated is in a line with a row of ferns planted on the northeast side of a building and having in their front shrubs and trees. It is a good position for ferns; and it does not require great space to contain one each of all the hardy sorts. On one side of this asplenium may be seen the king fern, Osmunda regalis, and on the other, the left hand one, of Aspidium Goldianum.

When setting out a row of ferns, an evergreen one should be set here and there. It affords a showing of green until snows cover the fronds, and all Winter long where Winters are mild. This asplenium and nearly all others have been called athyrium in their time, but present botanists stand by the old name—asplenium.

Osmunda Cinnamomea, Cinnamon Fern.

In the whole list of ferns there are none more useful than the osmundas, and in this genus perhaps the most useful of all is the one we illustrate, O. cinnamomea. Why we say this is because O. cinnamomea makes such a tall, broad, handsome frond, and that it is in the class of what are called flowering ferns, as are, in fact, all the osmundas. Why these are called flowering ferns is that, unlike the greater number of ferns, they produce both fertile and infertile fronds. The fertile one springs up like a spike of flowers, as is shown in the plant illustrated, which, as will be seen, has some half dozen of such "spikes." These fertile fronds when they reach perfection, which they soon do, become of a deep cinnamon color, very prettily ensconced in the circular arranged green fronds surrounding them.

This fern is classed as always having fronds either wholly fertile or wholly infertile, and to find any variation from this is a great curiosity. Nevertheless the very plants pictured—for there are two of them—have a case of the other kind. The plant on the right has a frond the upper half only fertile, as will be noticed. This is such a rare occurrence that it is the first instance of it the writer has met with.

There are two other osmundas valued for their usefulness, the O. Claytoniana and O. regalis. The first of these has fronds fertile in their centers: the other, O. regalis, has the fertile portion at the upper part of the frond. This fern is a native of Great Britain as well as of this country, as are other ferns.

The tuft of fronds at the base of the osmundas in the illustration is of the Onoclea sensibilis, and all are part of a row which occupies the northeast side of a wall. It is an ideal spot for them. The sun ceases to shine on them after 11 a. m., and the ground is cool and moist always. Where space admits of it, it affords a chance to have an assortment of hardy kinds; and such a collection is of great interest.

JOSEPH MEEHAN.

Horticultural Nomenclature.

Horticultural nomenclature has become endlessly mixed because many of the horticulturists are not systematic botanists and because some horticulturists, for commercial or other reasons, wishing to provide high-sounding and catching names for plants in order to sell them, have taken the botanical names and tacked on such prefixes and endings as "florabunda," "floraplena," etc., for the purpose of distinguishing some form of superior merit, with the result that it is difficult to determine, in many

Scolopendrium Crispum
Courtesy Henry A. Dreer

instances, just what particular plant was under consideration when the names were given. Then, too, the unsettled condition of botanic nomenclature itself has placed the horticulturist, with his limited knowledge of botany, in a very awkward position. It not unfrequently happens that we find the same plant described by different authors under two or three different names. This is very confusing and leads to distrust on the part of the purchaser. For instance, I may be an admirer of shrubs, and I purchase a shrub from A under one name, from B under another, and from C under still another, supposing that I am paying for three different plants. When these come into bloom and I find they are all identical, I am at once impressed with the dishonesty of the dealers in sending out the same thing under three distinct names. Each one of these introducers or disseminators may be absolutely honest and sincere in his work, and yet because the authority which he has used in naming his plants is different from the authority used by another, the catalogues give the appearance of dishonesty. Here is then a point upon which there is an opportunity for doing some work of actual value. If all horticultural writers will decide to follow some standard work upon horticultural subjects, such a multiplicity of names for a single object will be avoided. While I have no authority to bring before this meeting any work which should be taken as a model, it is my belief that in general we would be safe in following the nomenclature adopted in Bailey's Cyclopedia of American Horticulture. This work has the advantage of being new and up-to-date, and purely American. True, it does not go into details in all cases to the extent that it is frequently desirable for students of cultivated plants to carry their studies, but when it comes to the consideration of varieties, if one will take the trouble to search out the introducer and determine the name under which any variety was introduced, this will form a safe basis for the study of all cultural varieties. For the avoidance of future complications from duplication of names, the renaming of old sorts, and various unnecessary and undesirable complications of this character, I wish at this time to call attention to a paper which I prepared in 1897, and which was presented at the Minneapolis meeting of the Association of American Agricultural Colleges and Experiment Stations. This was a report of a committee appointed to consider the feasibility of establishing a bureau of plant registration, the object of which should be:

First—To discourage the duplication of names and the renaming of old sorts for commercial purposes.

Second.—To form a national herbarium of economic plants, which shall be made up largely of type specimens.

Third.—To simplify the matter of nomenclature.

Fourth.—To aid the student of varieties as well as of variation of plants under culture.

Fifth.—To secure the originator of a truly valuable variety some reward for his labor, the same as is now accorded the inventor.

The idea set forth in this paper was that in the case of the use of like names by different originators, before they were published and became common property they would first be submitted to the bureau where the plants would be registered and preserved, and where any such duplication would be detected. The originator's attention would thus be called to the necessity for modifying the name because of the fact that it had already been employed for the purpose of distinguishing or designating a variety belonging to the same family or group. I have not yet abandoned the hope that at some time there may be connected with the horticultural work of the U. S. Department of Agriculture an office which shall carry out in more or less detail the ideas proposed for this bureau of plant registration. There are at the present time a number of factors in the work of the department, which, if properly co-ordinated, would make it a comparatively easy matter to accomplish this work, provided we could secure the active co-operation of those engaged in plant production and dissemination.

The importance of uniformity in plant names is greater at the present time than ever before, because of the great demand for plants to use in the decoration of home surroundings. There is an ever increasing demand for the simple, old-fashioned plants of our grandmothers' gardens, and an increasing demand for plants indigenous to the region. Many of our nurserymen are alive to this movement and are providing themselves with large stocks of our native trees and shrubs, and they should pay special attention to the naming of these sorts as they are put upon the market in order that confusion in the future may not arise.

Another important and gratifying sign of the times is that common names are being largely replaced by scientific or botanic names of a binomial nature. In cases where botanists are in dispute over the correct authority, it would, in my judgment, be wise to follow the precedent established by Bailey in his cyclopedia, and use both names, so that no matter what the final decision of the botanists may be the book or writing will stand the test of the decision. It is unfortunate that this is necessary, but so long as two schools of botany exist with opposing viewpoints it will be necessary for the botanic artisan to recognize both names in order to prevent confusion and deception.—Professor L. C. Corbett, Horticulturist, Bureau of Plant Industry, Department of Agriculture, Washington, before Society for Horticultural Science at New Orleans, La.

Asplenium Filix-Fœmina, Lady Fern

Florist's Dream Is Blasted.

A Grand Rapids florist sought to cheat his plants out their night's rest by installing an electric plant and making the plants believe the sun was shining, so they would grow every hour in the 24. The scheme worked well for a few nights, when a plague of lightning bugs infested his greenhouses and ate up the tender leaves, while the sturdier branches began to grow electric currants. Discouraged by the failure of what he thought a utopian scheme for florists, he turned the lights off, and the young plants have been shedding all their watery secretions because they are compelled to go to bed in the dark.—Detroit Journal.

FOR THE RETAILER

[All questions relating to the Retail Trade will be cheerfully answered in this column. We solicit good, sharp photographs of made-up work, decorations, store interiors, etc., for reproduction here.—Ed. F. E.]

The Exhibitions.

The end of this month will see flower shows held throughout the country. It has long been common complaint that the retailers do not support these shows. Much that is unpleasant can be said on both sides. Schedules are defective and pecunious. Judges are deficient in judgment, and so on; and the fact, alas, is only too apparent that there is an absence of enthusiasm, and the consequent failures or semi-failures for almost all our exhibitions. This should not be the case, for the flower show is a commercial show, and like all such is intended to bring material under the eyes of the people. So show a little spirit. Get a schedule, or make your mind up to exhibit something even in the non-competitive class, for it is the best possible medium of advertising your goods and ability. Write us for hints or pointers. Tell us the stock you have or intend to use, and we'll gladly and promptly do our best to help you out.

The Chrysanthemum.

Next week we will discuss show designs. Madame Chrysanthemum and her regal retinue have arrived. No extensive decoration, especially for weddings, is complete without the use of these flowers from now on. Get acquainted with the varieties and the quantities obtainable at any date in order to be able to estimate on work. There may be a lot of imperialism about a large flower, but there is quite a lot of beauty in the small one. Never mind about the grower's craze for the abnormal in size and shape of bloom. The general public want flowers, and their pockets only hold enough of cash to purchase the medium sized or the small one. People do not treat the florist's store as they do the other stores if they get overcharged for a flower. They remember it all their lives, and it is a vindictive memory, too; so it doesn't pay in the end to carry an overload of high-priced chrysanthemums. There is more money and satisfaction in the general utility kind.

Use of Autumn Leaves.

Window displays and most kinds of work show extensive use of Autumn leaves. Out along the water front and among the swamps you will find the brightest colored leaves, but your greens man, or even your wholesale florists (who this year have gone into this branch as well as selling flowers) can supply you with Autumn foliage. The cut-leaved oak and the red or sugar maples are the best. Many sentimental people consider Autumn leaves with a tinge of sadness and shudder at their use at wedding decorations. Be careful of such. The foliage is distinctly appropriate for funeral work, and you can never hurt intelligence by its use in wreath or other design; besides it provides the most enhancing background for most flowers and light greenery. For particular table decorative work care should be taken not to use ill-smelling or rough Autumn leaves; instead use a few well-colored tips of Ampelopsis Veitchii, which can be had from the nurseries or from the walls where they are grown.

Ferns.

At this time of the year, when there seem to be loads of small ferns, most effective wreaths can be made of these ferns. Take, for instance, a 26 or 30-inch round frame, 75 or 100 Adiantum cuneatum from 2½ inch pots; cover bottom and sides of wreath with green sheet moss or any greens, and secure them. Then start arranging your fern plants, and pack with moss as you proceed, securing them and the moss with wire here and there to the frame. When finished you should have a well-rounded green fern wreath, no framework in sight. A cluster of roses or orchids at one side, and you will have not only a most beautiful design but one that will last a long time.

Where it is of necessity or advisable to use different kinds of ferns, don't mix them; cluster them, they look better. Wreaths of growing ferns recommend themselves to many people for their lasting quality and economy. The grower with a local trade having small plants may often use them in design work.

Sending Flowers to Europe.

I have just received a pleasant letter from Cork, Ireland, which informs me that the dozen American Beauty roses (which I obtained from Walter F. Sheridan) were not only used every day on the steamer going over, but remained in excellent condition four days in Cork. We have often sent roses over to Paris and London in the days of slow steamers. Why don't our wholesalers, or growers, dispose of the over-supply of elegant stock here during the Winter by sending them to the roseless markets and shops of Europe? Imagine, if you can, 500 6-foot-long stemmed American Beauty or 1,000 3-foot stemmed carnations in Covent Garden any day during the Winter. Why, Germany and France would send their delegations to see them. But this is not idle chatter; it is not dreaming either, but what will surely and regularly happen. At the present time don't forget to suggest to your customers that Americans on the Continent of Europe or their friends can be supplied with American grown rose blooms. Reliable florists in New York city should be able to guarantee their arrival in good condition.

A Good White Flower.

The choicest white flower outside of lily of the valley or orchids and gardenias, in New York this Summer and Autumn, was Bouvardia Humboldtii corymbiflora. Only one or two growers seem to be able to manage the cultivation of this flower successfully, and they have made money on it. It is true that it is not a flower for general purposes, and the demand for it in consequence will always be limited, but there is nothing prettier for a box of white flowers, or to alternate with a bunch of valley where variety is wanted. Separately, the flower is not much to behold, but in a cluster it is all convincing. It is a good keeper and sweet.

Wreath Made of Outdoor Grown Flowers in July, 1906.

A. Le Moult, Artist

About Ribbons.

Ribbon cases need looking over and filling up. Now we find that most of those who cater to supplying florists with ribbon require touching up. They are too frequently of the opinion that anything chaotic in colors, any creation of erroneous judgment, is good enough for the florists. Such is not the case, however, for flowers being in themselves the very essence of refinement in color and the harmonies thereof, demand that whatever adornment man puts on or near them should be the nearest imitation in color man is capable of producing. All colors, be they in paint or ribbon, are supposed to be the reflections of flowers; but, alas! for the dyer's skill! All we will say now is, don't throw money away on useless frills. The coming season will demand boldness and richness, with little of the stripes, plaids, or gauze left over from past seasons or at present in the hands of jobbers.

Violets.

Violets are as yet poor, but have commenced to be worn at church. It is the only flower, one might add, that properly belongs to Sunday church parades. They must somehow be given to the people in a sweeter condition. The growers and wholesalers must help the retailer to accomplish this, or woe betide the violet trade this season! It is the most sensitive and receptive of all flowers in the way of odors. The box they are shipped or kept in should be odorless.

A Ghoulish Practice.

One important thing we wish to speak about and ask the support of all decent florists and dealers is the repainting and re-using of cemetery used wire designs. Wire manufacturers inform us that their trade is being demoralised by the fakirs and grafters who like ghouls go out and rob the graves in the cemeteries of the wire designs sent there by sorrowing relatives and friends, repaint them and peddle them at one-fourth price among the florists. Now this contemptible thing must be stopped, and the cemetery authorities who profit by it must be taught a lesson.

Suppose, for instance, it became known through sensational journalism that florists bought and used over again wire designs taken from graves? Why, it would ruin the funeral design trade for ever! Suppose your own customers were told that your store was full of designs stolen from graves, what would happen? For the sake of morality, if not the law itself, this ghoulish outrage should be stopped, and we respectfully first submit the matter to every right-thinking florist and their societies.

A Beautiful Wreath.

The wreath illustrated this week was made by Adolphe Le Moult, New York city. A similar wreath is yearly made by that artist for a young Cuban's grave. It shows what can be done with the most simple flowers in the month of July. Small cycas leaves among which are arranged in clusters these flowers, as you see, constitute a very beautiful design. There is not a greenhouse grown flower in the design.

It is a splendid example of what could be done in an emergency or by many a small country florist had he the artistic fingers of a Le Moult. Not even a wire frame would be necessary for this design. We specially recommend it, because apart from its beauty it illustrates the uses of simple materials. The price was $40.

J. IVERA DONLAN.

Greenhouse Construction.

Paper read by J. B. Velie of Lord & Burnham Company, before the Gardeners and Florists' Club of Boston, Mass., Tuesday evening, October 16, 1906.

Greenhouse construction may be divided into two distinct classes, private and commercial. In the former class appearance enters more largely into the design and construction than in the latter, but the object in both is to secure the most durable construction combined with one that will admit the greatest amount of light, the element of expense nearly always being a factor to be considered.

For private use where it is assumed the owner is not compelled to sacrifice durability or appearance because of a lack of capital, the almost uniform construction is an iron frame greenhouse on masoury walls. This has been proven by years of experience to more nearly meet the requirements than any other construction.

Commercial Houses.

The person desiring to build commercially, who to be successful, must closely count expenditures, cannot usually afford to place a large amount of money in expensive masonry walls. To this person a choice of several distinct forms of construction is offered; first, the iron frame greenhouse on cast iron foot pieces; second, the wood frame or so-called sash bar house, having angle iron plate and posts with cast iron foot pieces; third, trussed roof house having angle iron plate and posts and cast iron foot pieces; fourth, an all wood house of sash bar construction having wood plate and wood posts; and fifth, an all wood sash bar house having wood plate and wood sill on concrete walls.

For one starting in the florists' business or adding to their present range, the question is, which construction will pay the greatest dividends in the business? This point rests on the amount of light admitted, the durability of construction, and the probable cost of repairs.

From the standpoint of light, assuming that all of the constructions have 16x24 glass placed the 16-inch way, the iron frame house has a considerable advantage. The size of the standard sash bar in this construction is 15-16x1⅞ inches and the wood cap for rafter is 1⅞ inches each way. The size of the standard bar for sash bar construction is 1⅜ inches wide by 2½ inches deep. In an iron frame house 100 feet long, provided the sun shines at right angles to the length of the house, you would have 6 feet 6¾ inches of shade against 8 feet 3 inches in a sash bar house, which makes a difference in favor of the iron frame house of 1 foot 8¼ inches of solid shade. It has been argued that because of the depth of the iron rafters, when the sun shines from the direction of the gable of the house, there is more shade with the iron frame construction than in the sash bar. This is not so. There is about 15 per cent. more shade in the sash bar house if the sun shines from the direction of gable than in the iron frame house with 3 inch iron rafters. Furthermore, in one construction the iron frame supports the house, while in the other the sash bars only give strength to the roof. This allows the bars to be omitted under the ventilating sash in the iron frame house, while they have to be run to the ridge in the sash bar house, making additional shade at that point in the latter construction by having two rows of bars, one above the other at the ridge sash.

It may seem to some that these figures show so small a difference in light between one method of construction and that of the other, that it would not pay in dollars and cents, as far as light goes, to invest any greater amount of money in one construction than in the other. I think, however, if you will go into a house of sash bar construction and then into one of iron frame construction, you will at once notice a difference in the amount of light in the houses; and I also think you will admit that if this is easily discernible to the eye, better results will be obtained in the lighter houses, provided all other conditions are the same, than in the one having more shade.

Strength of Structures Compared.

As for strength of construction, the iron frame house is decidedly the strongest, especially in a wide house. But for a house not over 33 feet 4 inches wide of usual pitch, which allows for five benches each about 4 feet 4 inches wide, with usual walks, the sash bar construction with angle iron posts and plate offers an excellent solution for a person who has not the capital to invest in an iron frame structure. Although many sash bar houses are built wider, in my opinion, to secure an element of safety and strength without undue supports and trussing, the iron frame house should be used in wider structures than that of about 33 feet. This sash bar construction, as previously stated, has some disadvantages as regards the amount of light admitted, but compares favorably in durability to the iron frame structure. The same general form of cast iron foot piece and angle iron plate is used in both constructions.

The trussed roof house of sash bar construction, having angle iron posts and plate and cast iron foot pieces, has the advantage of doing away with supporting columns in a house not over 29 feet wide.

The all wood house of sash bar construction, having wood plate and posts has the redeeming feature of being the least expensive construction that one can erect, considering first cost only. The sash bar house having wood plate and wood sills on concrete walls is a construction more expensive than a house having angle iron plate, angle iron posts with cast iron foot pieces, double boarding of cypress below glass, and removable base board, while it has the disadvantage of not being as durable because of the liability of the wood plate and the wood sill on the masonry wall to decay in a short time. Especially is the wood sill on the masonry wall a weak member in greenhouse construction.

Comparative Cost.

Let us compare the cost of a house 100 feet long, having angle iron plate, angle iron posts and cast iron foot pieces, with the all wood house, having wood plates and wood posts. The cost of the angle iron plate for both eaves together with angle iron posts and cast iron foot pieces spaced every six lights of glass, would be about $120. The cost of the wood plate and cypress posts spaced every three lights of glass, which is the usual spacing for this construction, would be approximately $60. This makes a difference of $60 in the cost of one house over the other.

Assuming that you build a house 100 feet long, with wood posts and plate, superstructure costing $1,500 complete, you will see that the additional cost of $60 for iron plate and posts is 4 per cent. of the total cost of the superstructure of the all wood house. The heating and benches would be the same in either case. Let us further assume that the all wood house would last 15 years. If you add the same percentage, 4 per cent. to the life of the all wood house, the house with iron plate and posts would have to last you only between seven and eight months longer than the all wood house. However, by investing $60 more, you lose the interest on this except as it is earned in the length of life of your building. If this $60 otherwise invested should double itself in 15 years, you would have to figure 8 per cent. increase in the length of life of the iron and wood house over the all wood in order that your investment on either one may pay you equally well. This 8 per cent. added would mean that the iron and wood house would have to last about one year and three months longer than the all wood. The actual increase of length of life of house, because of the iron posts and plate, would be many times the one year and three months. If the house with iron plate and posts lasts twenty-two and one-half years, or half as long again as the all wood house, which it is reasonable to suppose, on a basis of the figures just given your cost per year for superstructure of house would be between $69 and $70 for the iron and wood construction against $100 for the all wood, or a saving of nearly a third of your cost per year for superstructure of greenhouses by using iron plate and posts.

Design of Houses Important.

The design of a greenhouse is fully as important as the construction to be used, in order to cover the ground at the least expense, secure the best circulation of air, and heat to the best advantage. One can readily see that no matter what the width of the house, the expense of the side walls is the same, consequently the wider the house, provided one keep within reasonable limits, the smaller the cost per square foot covered so far as superstructure goes. The circulation of air is much better in a wide house than in a narrow one, and the wide house is more easily heated in proportion to the surface covered than a narrow one. An example of this can be seen at Waban Conservatories, Natick, where in a house 21 feet wide, with ridge about 14 feet high, there are twelve 1¼-inch pipes, and in a house 40 feet wide with ridge about 21 feet high, there are twenty 1¼-inch pipes, and I understand that a higher and more even temperature can be maintained in this wide house than in the narrow one.

These ridge and furrow houses, while in almost universal use through the West, are not extensively built in New England. These houses present the advantage of being more economical than the detached house, because of the elimination of several sides in a block of houses, but they have the disadvantage of casting more or less shade from the gutters, and more breakage of glass is caused by ice and snow than in the detached house. There seems to be a growing tendency, however, toward this construction.

The even span house is the cheapest and in a large majority of cases is the style built. Where houses run east and west, which is conceded by the majority of growers to be the most desirable way of locating them, several of the best growers have the roof on the north side of a steeper pitch than that on the south, both eaves being of the same height. This throws the ridge north of the center, and is done to avoid shade from the ridge on the rear bench or bed. In Boston on the twenty-second day of December the sun shines at an angle of 23 degrees, while on the twenty-second of June at 71 degrees. This makes a rise of the sun 8 degrees per month. With an eve span house running east and west, having the ro 32 degrees pitch, you will see that you will get i shade from the ridge on the rear bench until abo the first of February, or until the sun gets high than the pitch of roof on the north side. If tl north side of the house has a pitch of 45 degree with the house running east and west, you will get i shade on the rear bench until about March 20. Tl steeper the pitch of the roof the more surface in and a proportionate increase in cost.

It is a question of opinion as to whether the savi of shade on the north bench compensates for the a ditional cost. If the house is placed facing a few d grees to the east in order to obtain the morni sun more directly, the shade from the ridge on tl north bench is varied. This facing of the hou slightly to the east of south seems the ideal arrang ment to secure the benefits of the morning su There is but little difference the year through b tween the amount of sunshine in the morning ar that in the afternoon. Boston weather reports f five years show an average of twenty-four mo hours sunshine each year in the morning than in tl afternoon.

Ordinarily the pitch of roof giving the best resul is 33 degrees, or a rise of 7½ inches to a foot. Thi however, is varied occasionally for various reason In the even span ridge and furrow houses runni east and west, a pitch of about 27 degrees is oft used with good results. With this arrangement tl roof of one house shades the other less than wou be the case if the pitch were steeper.

Other Important Details.

The spacing of 16x24 inch glass in the roof the inch way is quite often done with very desirab results as far as the amount of light in the hou is concerned, but this is usually at the sacrifice more or less glass, as the breakage is usually great in the house constructed in this manner.

Continuous ventilation on both sides of the rid gives the best results. If one places top ventilato one light apart, there is more space for air be admitted than if the sashes were continuous, b there is also more liability of a draught. Side ve tilation, while desirable for violets or cool plants, in decreasing demand for use in carnation growin

The durability of the wood work in a greenhou depends on the wood, the method and thoroughne of drying, the manner of applying the first coat paint, the manner in which paints are made, and tl thoroughness with which it is kept painted after ere tion. Red Gulf Cypress from the swampy Southe States stands the test of durability in greenhou construction better than any other wood. This, how ever, must be free from sap and should be thorough air-dried. To insure the best results the first coat paint should be applied to the wood work by dippin rather than by painting it with a brush, for in tl dripping process the wood absorbs several times tl amount of oil that is retained in the grain by tl other process. This gives a durability and a found tion for future coats of paint that cannot be secur in any other way. Milling and construction shou be such that there will be as little chance of wat lodging at the joints as possible.

The purchasing of glass, putty and white lead f paint to be used after the priming coat, are matte to be as carefully looked into as any other part the construction. If a poor grade of any of these used, it may materially affect the dividends of tl florist's business.

There is no class of building construction expos to more trying conditions than a greenhouse, cons quently there is every reason for making the stru ture as durable as possible consistent with a reaso able outlay. The majority of successful florists, they have not previously built of a durable constru tion, are fast learning that a small additional cost f durable members in the construction pays them very large percentage on their investment. I ha seen many florists kept from deserved advanceme because of the constant outlay for repairs on buil ings erected in what at the time seemed an ine pensive manner.

I appreciate the honor of having been requested address this Club, and if I have been able to s anything that will induce any person to build mo substantially than he otherwise would, I shall co sider that something has been gained.

CONCRETE SLABS FOR GREENHOU BENCHES.—Some florists have been using a fram work of iron pipe for the support of wood benches, and these iron frames are now being us to carry concrete slabs in place of the wood boards, a cement edging being formed on the t of the slabs after they are in place. This work done quite readily by ordinary laborers with a l tle practice and oversight, the manufacture of t slabs being as follows: A sufficient space of ha ground is leveled off, and on this is laid a ser of molds of the size for the required slabs, a fran work of scantling answering for the molds. A pi of heavy paper is then laid upon the ground in ea mold, this giving a smooth face to the bottom the slab. The mold is then half filled with the p pared concrete, and before the latter sets a pi of strong screen wire of either inch or half-in mesh is laid upon the concrete, and the mold th filled to the required thickness, thus giving a enforcement of wire in the center of the sl Such slabs soon dry enough to stand handling, a may then be removed from the molds and the l ter used over again.—W. H. Taplin in Rural N Yorker.

Luther Burbank.

A Short Review of His Work in Plant Hybridizatiou and Brief Comparison with Other Hybridizers.

By Patrick O'Mara, Jersey City, N. J.

Following my visit to Santa Rosa, California, and a short trip on the Pacific Coast, in the Summer of 1905, I very briefly alluded to the work of Mr. Luther Burbank as a plant breeder before a meeting of the New York Florists' Club, taking the ground that his achievements in that line did not warrant the fulsome and extravagant praises bestowed on him by certain writers in the magazines and current newspapers. The few remarks I made were generally sustained by writers in the horticultural press in the United States and abroad. At the request of many who are interested in the subject I have undertaken to amplify what I said then and incorporate some of what has been written on the subject since that time.

As a fair start, so to speak, be it remembered, that the climatic conditions existing on the Pacific Slope are diametrically opposite to those encountered here. Many plants which succeed there fail here. A plant that will thrive here is in all likelihood going to thrive there. A notable example is the European grape vine, which does admirably on the Pacifii Slope and will not thrive here. As a further example I would cite fuchsias and ivy geraniums; they will not flourish here as they do on the Pacific Coast.

Practical men have therefore looked for many years with some suspicion on varieties which occur on the Pacific Slope, and when they come heralded with all manner of praise—such praise as only the Golden West can bestow upon its products—we do not accept them with all the praise that the Golden West puts upon them. We go cautiously. We say we will try them here first. Many of the plants that have come out of the Golden West have been sad failures in the Leaden East, if I may so dub it. I have a very distinct recollection when the Oregon ever-bearing strawberry was launched upon an unsuspecting public. I pricked up my ears and said to the man who urged it upon me, "I am rather inclined to believe that we require the soil and particularly the climate of the Pacific Coast to get out of that variety all that you get out of it there." What I feared was the result. The Oregon ever-bearing strawberry was tried extensively in the East, and it failed and disappeared completely.

Some time after this the name of Burbank loomed up on the horticultural horizon, and it came to us in a very peculiar way, through a very modest little booklet, his catalogue, modest in appearance but not very modest in its title. It found its way East and it was dubbed "The Creations of Mr. Burbank." Many are rather inclined to believe that there is only one Creator and once a week at least we bend in reverence to Him. The position which I took in relation to that title when I made my first public utterance upon it has been questioned by very good friends of mine. I still believe that when Luther Burbank assumed the title of a "creator" of new plants, he filed a presumptuous claim, and that he has no more right to claim the title of "creator" of new plants than he has to apply it to the bee that flits from flower to flower and carries the pollen; that he has no more right to claim it than the insects, or the winds. However, it gave an index as to what might be expected from such a source, and many were very wary of everything emanating from it. That wariness, up to the present time, has been fully justified by the results. I will not go over the entire list of "creations," but will begin with the potato which Mr. Burbank "created" in Massachusetts, and which was a "volunteer" seedling of the Early Rose not hybridized by him. It was a good potato, but it has outlived its usefulness in the East at all events. It is still, I understand, cultivated in the West; and it is said to be peculiarly adapted to the climate of the Pacific Coast, where there is a considerable precipitation of rain.

But there have been other men working on the potato, such as Mr. E. L. Coy, who has raised many good potatoes, and I want to say that the Early Rose, which the Burbank was supposed to supersede, is still grown here, while the Burbank has almost disappeared. Mr. Coy also raised the various Hebron varieties, the Beauty of Hebron and so forth. Mr. E. F. Carman, late editor of The Rural New Yorker, is also responsible for several excellent varieties of the various "Rural" potatoes, such as the Rural New Yorker, Rural Blush, Carman Nos. 1, 2, and 3; they are all potatoes which have superseded and outlived the Burbank. So much for that particular part of Mr. Burbank's achievements.

There are three views of Mr. Burbank at the present time; one is the view of the magazine writer, although I can hardly class Mr. Wickson of the University of California in that category, notwithstanding he has written for the Sunset Magazine—contributing splendid articles in relation to Mr. Burbank and his work. These articles were subsequently issued in book form under the title: "Luther Burbank, An Appreciation." Many friends and admirers of Mr. Burbank contend that he is not responsible for the extravagant claims made for him in that publication; but it is well to bear in mind that he helped to circulate it and therefore gave a semblance of sanction to its contents.

When I visited Mr. Burbank's gardens at Santa Rosa, I did not see anything startling in the place, and I want to say it fearlessly and candidly and without prejudice, to warrant the reputation given to Mr. Burbank in the magazines, either by Mr. Wickson or Mr. Harwood. When I returned to New York I was interviewed by the editor of The Florists' Exchange as to my trip. I didn't intend to initiate a controversy, but dropped the remark that I did not see anything on the place to show me that Mr. Burbank was entitled to the reputation he had received from the magazines. That remark called for the reply by Mr. Burpee of Philadelphia, trying to show me the light, but I could not see the light, and at a subsequent meeting of the New York Florists' Club, I enlarged on the subject, and thus my name became connected with "Burbankitis," as it is called.

am rather inclined to think his (Mr. Burbank's) science is somewhat of the Mary Baker Eddy or Helen Wilmans order.

The next quotation is: "Plant development is one of the phases of civilization, and it makes new conquests as they are needed in the onward rush of mankind. We are now at the beginning of an epoch of accelerated motion in this direction. Burbank is the prophet of this epoch. Obeying the command of the Infinite, he is carrying the gates developed. We call him a great horticulturist. He of Gaza. Let not the Delilah of modern organization shear him of his God-given strength and make him like other men."

Then he reaches out and gets the $100,000.

The other day we had Professor Ostwald of Leipsic lecturing at Columbia University. I do not believe the Professor ever met Mr. Burbank, and therefore he must have drawn his inspiration from the published accounts. He believes "that science is able to produce a piece of protoplasm and command it in the first step of evolution; that man has control of vegetable life, taking it out of the slow hands of nature and hastening its evolution from one form to another. The man Burbank, for instance, has so assisted nature in this work that she is almost out of a job. By combination and evolution, he produces new forms at will, and endows them with economic values that nature left un-

Exhibit of J. Gammage & Sons at Western Fair, London, Ont.

Mr. Burbank unquestionably says things very well; at least I think so. He has a happy knack of saying things. A good many of them are somewhat involved, but nevertheless, a thing that one cannot quite understand appeals to us sometimes as being very wise. But he says some things that appear easy to understand, and one of them is this: "Heredity is the sum of all past environment." Now if heredity is the sum of all past environment, it is a foregone conclusion that a plant produced in the climate of California and raised in that climate will have to dissociate itself from its environment when it is brought East, and therefore it is heavily handicapped before it can achieve distinction in commerce in this section of the country. This is from "An Appreciation," by Mr. Wickson: "For such a gifted seer neither weird altar fires nor incense cloud nor ecstatic state could add to insight. He could hear the 'still small voice' without preparatory earthquake or whirlwind. Like David of old, he could do his work with smooth pebbles from the brook, and he cast aside the elaborate armament of his scientific brethren lest it should impede his movements."

There is a desperate attempt being made to make a scientific man out of Mr. Burbank; that is, to put him amongst the scientists, or rather, to make him first among equals, or even to put him above the scientist; in fact above the men whom we florists have come to regard as scientists, such as the men in charge of experiment stations and the United States Department of Agriculture.

I want to remark parenthetically, from having read what Mr. Burbank has written, and from Mr. Harwood in the magazines—also from what I have gleaned from his little books of "creations," that I

is one of the greatest biologists in the use of existing forms to produce others that nature did not make until shown the way."

The great poet said: "The art itself is nature."

In Burbank's "Creations" for 1901, his foreword in the little booklet reads as follows: "Education and selection are the two greatest forces used in the production of all these fruits and flowers. Not knowing the facts, and because some of them happen to be crossed, people often jump to the conclusion that they are summarily produced by crossing, and with about as little science or ceremony as a wizard would appear to do it with his magic wand."

Cross fertilization is the only process that will produce new varieites, except mutations from buds; these are the only ways in which new varieties are produced. When anyone speaks about "educating" a plant to be a new variety, I think he is mistaken, and that is why I thought that Mr. Burbank's science was of the Mary Baker Eddy or Helen Wilmans order. Others have boldly come out and said that by mental processes exercised on a certain plant they can change its character.

Mr. Burbank says about "educating" a plant: "We do not fill this catalogue with testimonials of the value of these new fruits and flowers, though we have enough to fill one twenty times as large. The best way to judge of the value of any novelty is to look to its source, and the fruits and flowers which have been bred and educated on Burbank's Experimental Farms and are now growing all around the world are the very best testimony which can be given."

(To be continued.)

REVIEW OF THE MARKET

NEW YORK.—Chrysanthemums are beginning to be the main factor in this market, and, as a consequence, the prices of roses, particularly American Beauty, have a downward tendency. For the last three weeks roses of every description almost have been scarce, and the values maintained through that period have been almost phenomenal. Now, however, just as supplies are beginning to get heavier every day, the chrysanthemum is beginning to assert itself, and, no doubt, for some time will dominate the market to a large extent. Of the varieties coming in, Polly Rose and Glory of the Pacific are as yet the main supply, though Monrovia, October Sunshine and Omega are arriving regularly in limited numbers. So far as prices go, the season has started in fairly well, for while small or half-opened flowers (and there are many sent in in that condition) are disposed of at 75c. per dozen, there is a fairly good call for the better class of flowers, for which anywhere from 15c. to 30c. each can be obtained, according to size and quality.

The greatest drop in the price of roses has occurred in the case of American Beauty. Where it was possible to get 30c. last week without much effort, it is now hard to realize 20c. each, and a great many are offered much below that figure. Not only that, but the stock is accumulating in the hands of the dealers. With the other varieties, such as Bride, Bridesmaid, Mme. Abel Chatenay and Killarney, not only are the daily receipts heavier, but prices have a downward tendency.

Cattleyas are becoming more plentiful daily, and prices are not quite so firm. The shipments of carnations are also on the increase, and although values are not quite so firm as last week, there has been no radical reduction. Of lily of the valley the supply is ample for all demands, and we notice a cheapening in the better grade. Outdoor flowers, such as dahlias, cosmos and anemones, are now out of the market for the season. The frosts the latter part of last week seem to have wound up the supply altogether. Violets, while coming in regularly, are not at all plentiful; whether this is because the growers do not want to flood the market so early, or that crops are not ready for cutting, we are unable to say.

CHICAGO.—The market in the Western cities is daily becoming stronger and assuming what may be termed normal conditions. There is very little strengthening in prices, but the demand is strong enough from all points to hold values as quoted in our table. Chrysanthemums are now making their appearance in good form; and the general line of carnations and roses has noticeably improved within the past few days during which we have had some good cold weather, the thermometer having dropped to ten degrees below the freezing point.

W. K. W.

BOSTON.—Business has been good the past week, and many kinds of stock have been scarce. There has been a brisk demand for white flowers; such as white carnations have advanced in price and readily bring $3. Carnations generally are scarce. Roses are selling better, and have improved in quality. American Beauty of the best grades bring $4 per dozen, while the best Killarney and Wellesley realize $1.50. Chrysanthemums are not so plentiful yet as expected and sell at from $1 to $2.50 per dozen. Violets are not plentiful. Gladiolus are nearly all gone. Lilies bring $1.50 and $2 per dozen. Candytuft and feverfew sell for 25 cents per bunch. Cosmos brings $1 per 100; tuberoses, 75 cents; lily of the valley $2 to $5. All kinds of greens are without change. J. W. D.

PHILADELPHIA.—There is a very good demand for flowers this week. Roses are becoming more plentiful with the exception of American Beauty, the supply of which is not yet quite up to the demand, and $4 per dozen is obtained for the first quality. Nearly all tea roses are plentiful, and prices are not quite so stiff; $8 per 100 is top figure with good value given at that. Chrysanthemums are now arriving in larger quantities and can be bought for from $2 to $4 per dozen. Carnations are in brisk demand; the number of good flowers is yet small and $3 per 100 is asked for the best, more of which could be used. Cattleyas are somewhat stiffer in price this week, at 50c. to 60c each. There has been a very strong demand for lily of the valley; the price ranges from $3 to $5 per 100. So far not many double violets are arriving; all growers report these later in blooming this year. The increase in out of town orders is very noticeable around the commission houses. DAVID RUST.

ST. LOUIS.—The local retailers have had a busy week, though not much society work is going on, just small affairs. The weather has been cool, and is considered seasonable for chrysanthemums and violets, but to date both these flowers are very scarce. The Horse Show helped business somewhat, though not so much as in former years when chrysanthemums were more plentiful. Only a few Monrovia, Glory of the Pacific, and Mme. F. Bergmann are coming in, hardly enough to go round; $2 per dozen is the average price; a few extra long-stemmed flowers bringing $3. At present carnations are the scarcest flowers in the market; something is not right, for usually at this time of year carnations are very plentiful. This, Monday morning, none sold under $1.50, with $4 the top price for fancy Enchantress. The poorer grades of roses found little demand last week, and even the choicest brought low values; best long American Beauty bring $3 a dozen, with fair demand; these are not scarce by any means. The medium-stemmed stock sells better and is plentiful at $1 to $2 a dozen; shorts, $3 to $5 a 100. Smaller roses are of fine quality. There are plenty of fancy Kaiserin Augusta Victoria, Richmond, Souvenir du President Carnot, Perle des Jardins, Bride and Bridesmaid; also a fine lot of Killarney. The best of these bring $6 to $8 per 100; first and seconds, $3 to $4 per 100; common short stock, $1 to $2 per 100.

Lily of the valley is fine, but not over plentiful, at $3 and $4 per 100. Violets are getting better in quality, though they are still scarce and short-stemmed, at 25c. to 35c. per 100.

There are plenty good smilax, asparagus, fancy and common ferns, at usual prices. ST. PATRICK.

COLUMBUS.—We had our first frost the past week and with it our first snow, temperature dropping suddenly to 27 degrees. Trade is very brisk, this week especially so, on account of the exhibition of the American Street and Interurban Railway Association, which is being held here. Almost all the exhibitors have very elaborately decorated their booths, which has used up large quantities of palms, ferns, and other foliage plants, as well as numbers of roses and carnations. One dealer's orders for carnations amounted to over ten thousand, and it has been no easy matter to get them. Flowers when wanted in quantity seem much more difficult to obtain than for many seasons. In addition to these special orders, there has been good over-the-counter trade, and many funeral orders.

Since the colder weather has come, trade in chrysanthemums has started off quite briskly. As yet the varieties offered have been mostly Monrovia, Glory of the Pacific, and Polly Rose. A few especially fine ones have brought $6 a dozen, but most of them went for $2.50 to $4. Roses are gradually working higher; some small and short stemmed sorts bring $1 but anything really good commands $1.50 to $2 a dozen. American Beauty are very fine for so early in the season, the color being remarkably good; the best quality bring $6 a dozen. Lily of the valley sells at 75c. to $1 a dozen; carnations, 50c. for regular, and 75c. for Enchantress; asters and gladioli are gone; in fact, since the frost outdoor stock has about stopped coming in. Both Marie Louise, and Princess of Wales violets are in the market, but the color is not yet what it should be; these sell in bunches to suit the customer at $2 to $3 per hundred. Green goods are in plenty and at the usual rates.

F. W.

NEW BEDFORD, MASS.—We have had slight frosts in this section; all outdoor stock has been killed, and, as a consequence, cut flowers from the greenhouse are more in demand. Carnations are looking fine and healthy; prices for good stock are 50 cents per dozen retail. Roses are coming in very freely; these bring $1.50 per dozen. From all appearances there will be plenty of violets the coming Winter; prices for these now are $1 per hundred. The single variety Princess of Wales is most extensively grown in this section.

E. H. Chamberlin has Christmas sweet pea in bud now; he has also a fine batch of cyclamen which will be all right for the holidays.

Peter Murray of Fairhaven, eastern agent for Winsor carnation and originator of same, reports a heavy demand for stock of this variety. There promises to be a big demand for the cut flowers this season.

Most of the growers here are putting in their forcing bulbs just now. The rooting of geranium cuttings is being rushed with all speed. We are all looking forward to a prosperous season.

HORTICO.

PITTSBURG.—The first frost in our vicinity was decidedly a killing one, as everything in outdoor flowers is ruined, consequently a scarcity of stock is much felt, except in roses, which seem to be abundant. Dahlias were in their glory and in strong demand at $1 to $1.50 per dozen, retail, and only a few were cut before frost killed them, so not many are to be had. Roses are of fair quality and are quoted at 2c. up American Beauty are choice and plentiful. Carnations are rather scarce, from $1.50 up; good ones bring $2.50 to $3 per 100. Chrysanthemums are coming in more plentifully, yet are too high priced for general use, from 15c. up being the figure asked. A few gladioli are sold at $5 per 100.

E. C. R.

INDIANAPOLIS.—A decided advance was made in business last week. Numerous funeral and small decoration orders kept trade lively. The flower market lacks variety, as the severe freeze, not frost, last week put an end to outdoor stock, and dahlias and cosmos particularly are missed. Chrysanthemums are being cut in larger quantities every day, and henceforth the supply should be ample for all needs; $1 to $3 a dozen is the usual wholesale price, and $1.50 to $5 the retail. Indianapolis planted many more chrysanthemums than ever before, and should be able to ship some fine stock in a few days. Carnations have been very scarce, at $1.50 to $2 per 100, and at times orders are refused for them. Roses are much improved in quality, and sell well. No. 1 Bride, Bridesmaid and Golden Gate bring $4 to $5 per 100 wholesale, and $1 to $1.50 per dozen retail. Good Richmond are received at $4 to $6 per 100. American Beauty continue to lead, and $5 to $35 a 100 is asked. Lily of the valley is much used for weddings at $4 per 100. A limited number of cattleyas is offered at $25 per 100.

The green goods market has recovered and it is now possible to obtain anything in that line. I. B.

ST. PAUL.—Trade continues good and great difficulty is experienced in getting sufficient stock of some sorts, particularly carnations, with which to supply the demand. Roses are plentiful, although the grade is not as good as we expect a few weeks later on. Some very fine American Beauty are shipped in. Prices are fair, roses commanding $1.50 per dozen, while the carnations are not worth more than 50c. to 75c. a dozen. Chyrsanthemums have started to come in, and some fine blooms of the early varieties are seen. The demand, however, is light as yet. Decorations for different social occasions have started up nicely. Funeral work has also been particularly heavy the past week. Sunday mroning orders are heavy; some of the leading dealers are doing more than almost any morning during the week. PAUL.

MINNEAPOLIS.—Business the past week has shown a marked improvement over the preceding two or three weeks, and the majority report a fair trade. Heavy frosts have killed all outdoor flowers, except those heavily covered. Roses are in big demand, especially first grade stock; there is an abundance of seconds of the different varieties. Some very fine Richmond are shipped in, but the local stock, speaking particularly of the best, is very scarce. Bride and Bridesmaid are plentiful, especially the former variety; the demand, however, is not equal to the supply; all dealers apparently have an overstock of white. Carnations are poor and small; Enchantress is really the only variety that is good at present. At most of the greenhouses, large numbers are planted, but very few blooms are cut. The prospects for good carnations about a month from now appear very bright, but the cut at the present time is so limited that it is hardly worth mentioning. Violets are coming along nicely; many of the growers who have experimented with new varieties are back to the old standby, Marie Louise, which from all reports gives good results in this locality. Chrysanthemum plants are looking very good. While but very few of the early varieties have been on the market, the prospects are the trade will be well supplied within the next two weeks. From an observation of the greenhouses, there are very few chrysanthemums grown in pots for the plant trade here. Some of the cheaper varieties are raised, but only in small numbers. Prices are kept up nicely, and the retailers are getting as much for good roses as they will at any time during the Winter, outside of the holiday season, and, of course, American Beauty excepted.

PAUL.

CLASSIFIED ADVERTISEMENTS

CASH WITH ORDER.

The columns under this heading are reserved for advertisements of Stock for Sale, Stock Wanted, Help Wanted, Situations Wanted or other Wants; also of Greenhouse, Land, Second-Hand Materials, etc., For Sale or Rent.

Our charge is 10 cts. per line (7 words to the line), set solid, without display. No advt. accepted for less than thirty cents.

Display advertisements in these columns, 15 cents per line; count 12 lines agate to the inch.

[If replies to Help Wanted, Situation Wanted, or other advertisements are to be addressed care of this office, advertisers add 10 cents to cover expense of forwarding.]

Copy must reach New York office 12 o'clock Wednesday to secure insertion in issue of following Saturday.

Advertisers in the Western States desiring to advertise under initials, may save time by having their answer directed care our Chicago office at 127 E. Berwyn Ave.

SITUATIONS WANTED

SITUATION WANTED—By a carnation and violet grower, also good grower of bedding stock. Ira P. Hersey, 29 So. Main St., Attleboro, Mass.

SITUATION WANTED—By man with sixteen years' experience in seeds, bulbs and plants, both mail order and counter trade. Address, T. J., care The Florists' Exchange.

SITUATION WANTED—As foreman by a first-class grower of roses and carnations. 15 years experience; married. Address, T. D., care The Florists' Exchange.

SITUATION WANTED—By first-class salesman and decorator, 12 years' experience. Can give first-class references. 10 years in one place. Joseph J. Werrick, Box 19, Ridgway, Ont., Canada.

SITUATION WANTED—Single working foreman. A No. 1 grower of roses and carnations. Take charge 50,000 feet of glass. Address, Florist, care Rich, 111 East 9th street, New York.

SITUATION WANTED—As foreman or to take charge. English, age 32, 18 years' experience 15 years in this country. Practical all-around grower, A No. 1 references. Good wages expected. Address, T. I., care The Florists' Exchange.

SITUATION WANTED—As superintendent on private place by a thoroughly competent man. 18 years experience in all branches of the business. Married, one child. Address, F. J., 560 Maple st., Flatbush, Brooklyn, N. Y.

SITUATION WANTED — Thoroughly learned gardener, 25 years of age, German, single, wants a steady position by November 1. Good grower of carnations, 'mums and bedding plants. Private or Commercial. References. Address, T. G., care The Florists' Exchange.

SITUATION WANTED—As working foreman; A No. 1 grower of carnations, roses, Easter plants, bedding stock, palms and ferns. Quick worker, first-class references, 19 years experience, married, no children. Address, J. 356, Midwood Street, Flatbush, Brooklyn, N. Y.

SITUATION WANTED—As manager and foreman, well up in cut flowers, especially roses. Strictly sober, competent to manage any sized place; can furnish best of references; answer with full particulars; mention wages. Address, T. B., care The Florists' Exchange.

SITUATION WANTED—Man of thirty wishes to make a change, twelve years' experience, private and commercial. Seven years in one situation. Have been with present employers (one of the largest firms in the country) nearly three years. Can refer to employers, whose name will be given on application. Kindly give particulars and state wages when writing. Address, T. K., care The Florists' Exchange.

HELP WANTED

WANTED—General utility man for carnation plant. Steady, single; middle aged man preferred. Lebanon Greenhouses, Lebanon, Pa.

WANTED—Experienced man to grow carnations, mums and bedding stock. Steady work. Apply, D. Y. Mellis, Holy Cross Cemetery, Flatbush, Brooklyn.

SEEDSMAN

capable of taking charge and developing retail department of an established house in a large Eastern city. A good opportunity for a bright up-to-date man. State age, experience, salary required. All communications confidential. Address,

SEEDS, care The Florists' Exchange.

Mention the Florists' Exchange when writing.

HELP WANTED

WANTED—Single man for general greenhouse work. Must understand propagating and growing of cut flowers. Apply, Chas. L. Stanley, Plainfield, N. J.

WANTED—A young man for general greenhouse work, wages, $20.00 per month with board and room. Address, Mrs. Flora T. Howell, Pine Bush, N. Y.

WANTED—Young man to pack and ship cut flowers and help around greenhouses. State experience, wages, etc. W. K. Partridge, 148 E. Fourth Street, Cincinnati, O.

WANTED—Young man to assist in high-class retail flower store. Must be of good appearance and have good references. State wages, etc. W. K. Partridge, 148 E. Fourth Street, Cincinnati, O.

WANTED—Night fireman, accustomed to firing large steam boilers in commercial greenhouses, near Philadelphia. Apply, The Floral Exchange, 335 North Sixth Street, Philadelphia, Pa.

WANTED—Night fireman who understands steam boilers, etc. Steady position. State experience, salary wanted and give references. W. K. Partridge, 148 E. Fourth Street, Cincinnati, Ohio.

WANTED—A first-class man for retail florist in Chicago; no greenhouse work. Must be a good salesman and designer. State wages. References. Address, M. D., care The Florists' Exchange.

WANTED—At once, good grower of carnations, mums and violets, also bedding stock. Sober and willing worker. Address, stating wages with references and nationality. Converse Greenhouses, Webster, Mass.

WANTED—A first-class plant man; one who understands forcing bulbs and store stock. State wages, and how soon can come. Permanent place to capable man. Honaker, The Florist, Lexington, Ky.

WANTED—Section man for carnations. Married man preferred, who would be willing to board one or two men. Have five roomed house on place. State wages, etc. W. K. Partridge, 148 E. Fourth Street, Cincinnati, O.

WANTED—A seedsman who is capable of taking full and complete charge of a retail mail order department in a well established seed house. Address, S. X., care The Florists' Exchange.

MISCELLANEOUS WANTS

WANTED TO BUY—Greenhouses to be taken down. State full particulars of same when writing. Address, F. W., care The Florists' Exchange.

WANTED TO RENT—Commercial place of 10,000 to 25,000 feet of glass; must be in good running order near New York. Give full particulars. Address, T. C., care The Florists' Exchange.

WANTED—Correspondence with nurserymen who have trees, oaks and elms, suitable for street planting. Address, The Tree and Park Commission, 1317 Sumter street, Columbia, S. C.

FOR SALE OR RENT

FOR SALE—Old established retail florist store. For particulars write to F. K., 700 N. 5th street, Philadelphia. Reason for selling: going West.

FOR SALE—To a first-class florist only, stock and good will of a well-established retail place; "Fifth Avenue Trade" in New York City. Address, care Kervan Company, 20 West 27th street.

FOR SALE—Greenhouses, consisting of 26,000 sq. ft., up to date, all covered with 16x24 in. glass, 3 acres of ground, house 9 rooms, and barn. 14 miles from New York. Address, T. H., care The Florists' Exchange.

FOR SALE

A well equipped place, consisting of seven greenhouses, over 30,000 feet of glass, a nine roomed house, barn, stock, etc., and eight acres of land. This is a decided bargain and a rare opportunity. For particulars address

S. S. SKIDELSKY,
824 N. 24th St., Philadelphia, Pa.

Mention the Florists' Exchange when writing.

TO LET

Florist Establishment consisting of nine greenhouses, heated by hot water, containing about 10,000 square feet of glass; sheds, barn and dwelling, in Long Island City, within one hour's drive of the wholesale markets of the City of New York. For further particulars address **Box R. Y., Florists' Exchange**

Mention the Florists' Exchange when writing.

STOCK FOR SALE

PANSIES, 50c. per 100; $3.50 per 1,000. Daisies (Bellis), 50c. per 100; $2.50 per 1000. Alex Haeseler, Meshanticut, R. I.

CARNATIONS—Strong, healthy, field-grown plants, extra large, Ethel Crocker and Flora Hill, $5.00 per 100. Cash with order. W. C. Pray & Co., Kinkora, N. J.

PRINCESS VIOLETS—5,000 strong, healthy, field-grown plants, $4.00 per 100. Cash with order. J. K. Zeininger, 58 Cutter Street, Melrose, Mass.

ENGLISH PRIZE PANSY PLANTS—I have 10,000 fine plants more than I need. For sale at $3.00 per 1000, cash. Some very odd and beautiful markings among them. Reuben Powell, Florist, White Plains, N. Y.

BABY RAMBLER roses, fine dormant stock, $25 per 100. 2 1-2 inch pot plants, extra well rooted $7 per 100, $65 per 1000. Orders booked for delivery now or any time up to late Spring. Samples free. Brown Brothers Co., Rochester, N. Y.

FOR SALE—Ten acres of fine nursery stock; must be sold at sacrifice prices as lease of land expires next Spring. 15,000 Ligistrum Ibota, 18 in. to 2 ft. at $30.00 per 1000; 5,000 Ligistrum Ibota, 2 1-2 to 3 ft. at $45.00 per 1000; Aralia pentaphylla, Spirea Von Houteii, Viburnum tomentosum, Kerria Japonicum fl. pl., Rhodotypus Kerrioides, and 60,000 other shrubs. Write for particulars and prices to Rhode Island Nurseries, Newport, R. I.

FOR SALE

FOR SALE—4 Hitchings hot water expansion tanks. No. 2 high tank Fig. E. of catalogue. All in good condition. F. O. B., $2.00 each. Address, K. D., care The Florists' Exchange.

BOILERS. BOILERS. BOILERS.
SEVERAL good second hand boilers on hand, also new No. 16 Hitchings at reduced cost. Write for list. Wm. H. Lutton, West Side Avenue Station, C. R. R. of N. J., Jersey City, N. J.

FOR SALE.—One No. 26 Perfect Hot Water Boiler, made by Pierce, Butler, and Pierce Mfg. Company, Syracuse, N. Y., having a capacity of 1200 square feet, in good condition, delivered F. O. B. New York, price $50.00. John A. Scollay, 74-76 Myrtle Avenue, Brooklyn, N. Y.

FOR SALE

BOILERS Hitchings, No. 17 at $110.00. No. 6 Weathered, round, $70.00. 4 section round Cambridge steam boiler $75.00. 8 section No. 11, J. L. Mott boiler will heat 12,750 ft. glass $175.00. 10 H. P. upright steam, $25.00. 6 section new Novelty boiler, will heat 4,100 ft. glass, $140.00. New Henderson boilers; send for price on size wanted.

PIPE Good serviceable second hand. No Junk, with new threads. 2 in. 7c.; 1½ in. 5½c.; 1¼ in. 4c.; 1 in. 3c.; 2½ in. 10c.; 3 in. 14c.; 4 in. 19c. 4 in. cast iron greenhouse 14c. 2 in. NEW, standard, full lengths, 8½c. ft. All kinds of fittings for 4 in. cast iron and all sizes wrought iron.

STOCKS AND DIES New Economy, easy working, No. 1 cuts ⅜-¾-1 in. $3.00; No. 2 cuts 1¼-1½-2 ins. $4.00; Armstrong Adjustable No. 2 cuts ¾-1 in. $4.00; No. 3 cuts 1¼-1½-2 ins. $6.50.

PIPE CUTTERS Saunders, No. 1 cuts to 1 in. $1.00; No. 2 cuts to 2 in. $1.30; No. 3 cuts to 3 in. $3.00; No. 4 cuts to 4 in. $4.50.

STILLSON WRENCHES Guaranteed, 12 in., grips 1¼ in. $1.10; 18 in. grips 2 in. $1.60; 24 in., grips 2½ in. $2.25; 36 in., grips 3½ in. $4.60.

PIPE VISES Reed's Best Hinged Vise, No. 1 grips 2 in. $1.75; No. 2 grips 4 in. $3.50.

GARDEN HOSE 50 ft. lengths ¾ in. not guaranteed; 4¾, guaranteed for light work; 7½, guaranteed for heavy work, 10c. ft.

BRASS HOSE VALVES New; not faucets; ¾ in. 85c.; 1 in. 95c.

HOT-BED SASH New; Gulf Cypress, 3 ft.x6 ft. 75c.; glazed complete $1.60 up. VENTILATORS; all sizes made to order. Second hand sash glazed $1.00 and $1.26, good condition.

GLASS New American, 50 ft. to the box. 10x12 single at $1.75. 10x12, 12x12 10x15 B double $2.55. 12x14 to 12x20 and 14x14 to 14x20 B double $2.70. 16x16 and 16x18 B double $2.90. 16x24 B double $3.15. 16x20 and 16x22 $3.00. 6x8, 7x9, 8x10 old, single $1.50. 8x14 old, double $1.65; 10x14 old, double $1.75.

LINSEED OIL Strictly pure; barrel lots, 42c. gallon.

CARNATION SUPPORTS second hand, 50c. hundred.

VENTILATING APPARATUS second hand, Hitchings make, arms, 25c.; hangers, 10c.; machines, $3.50; collars, 8c.

SCREWS all sizes; mixed wood, from 1 in. to 3 in., in boxes, 25 and 50 lbs. at 5c. lb.

PUMPS hot air; well pumps and force pumps; all repairs.

Get our prices on second hand wood material. We can furnish everything in new material to erect any size house. Get our prices.

METROPOLITAN MATERIAL CO.
Greenhouse Wreckers
1398-1408 Metropolitan Avenue, BROOKLYN, N. Y

Thirty cents is the minimum charge for advertisements on this page.

COMING EXHIBITIONS.

[Secretaries of other Societies will oblige by forwarding the schedules of their respective shows. Ed. F. E.]

OCTOBER 24 and 25, 1906.—Lenox (Mass.) Horticultural Society, annual chrysanthemum exhibition. G. Foulsham, secretary.

OCTOBER 25, 26 and 27, 1906.—United Bay Shore Horticultural Society, Fifth Annual Exhibition, Carleton Opera House, Bay Shore, N. Y. Manager, John Tobin, Box 635, Bay Shore, N. Y.

OCTOBER 30, 31 and November 1, 1906.—Tarrytown (N. Y.) Horticultural Society, eighth annual exhibition, Music Hall. E. W. Neubrand, secretary.

OCTOBER 31 and NOVEMBER 1, 1906, Monmouth County (N. J.) Horticultural Society, ninth annual exhibition, Town Hall, Red Bank, N. J. H. A. Kettel, secretary.

OCTOBER 31 AND NOVEMBER 1, 1906, Nassau County (N. Y.) Horticultural Society, Pembroke Hall, Glen Cove, N. Y. Alexander Mackenzie, secretary.

NOVEMBER 1 and 2, Morris County (N. J.) Gardeners and Florists' Society, Assembly Rooms, Madison, N. J. E. Reagan, secretary.

NOVEMBER 2-4, 1906.—Massachusetts Horticultural Society, Horticultural Hall, Boston. Wm. P. Rich, secretary.

NOVEMBER 5 and 6, 1906., Twelfth Annual Flower Show of New Jersey Floricultural Society, Hall of Woman's Club, East Orange, N. J. Joseph A. Manda, Orange, N. J. Manager.

NOVEMBER 6-8, 1906, New Haven County Horticultural Society. Thomas Pettit, 90 Prospect street, New Haven, Conn., secretary.

NOVEMBER 6 to 8, 1906, Pennsylvania Horticultural Society, Horticultural Hall, Broad street, Philadelphia, Pa. David Rust, secretary.

NOVEMBER 6-12, 1906. — Chicago Horticultural Society. W. N. Rudd, secretary.

NOVEMBER 7, 8 and 9, American Institute, New York, annual chrysanthemum show, etc., Berkeley Lyceum Building. Leonard Barron, New York, secretary Horticultural Section.

NOVEMBER 8, 1906.—Worcester County (Mass.) Horticultural Society, annual exhibition of chrysanthemums. Adin A. Hixon, secretary.

NOVEMBER 8, 9, 10, 1906, Denison Tex.: Flower Show under auspices of Denison Civic Improvement League. Secretary, T. W. Larkin.

NOVEMBER 9-10, 1906, Rhode Island Horticultural Society. C. W. Smith, 27-29 Exchange street, Providence, R. I., secretary.

NOVEMBER—10, Third Annual Ontario Exhibition, Massey Music Hall, Toronto. Secretary, H. B. Cowan, Toronto.

NOVEMBER 13, 14 and 15, Faith Home Association, Thirteenth Annual Chrysanthemum Show, Houston, Texas, Mrs. F. A. Reichardt, secretary.

FOR SALE

Greenhouse Material milled from Gulf Cypress, to any detail furnished, or our own patterns as desired, cut and spliced ready for erection. Estimates for complete constructions furnished.

V. E. REICH, Brooklyn, N. Y.
1429-1437 Metropolitan Ave.

Mention the Florists' Exchange when writing.

SEED BUSINESS FOR SALE

Established over twenty years. Located in large and prosperous city. Doing a business of about One Hundred Thousand Dollars per year. Splendid mail order business. Large counter and Market Gardener's trade. Best proposition in the United States to any one desirous of engaging in the Seed trade. Present owners wish to go exclusively in the Wholesale Growing business. This offer is unequaled as the House is thoroughly equipped in all departments with the best of Fixtures, Office Furniture, Cleaners, Electrotypes, etc., and can be purchased on favorable terms and at a cost many thousands of dollars less than the actual value. Address S. V., care The Florists' Exchange.

Mention the Florists' Exchange when writing.

NEWPORT, R. I.—Quietness prevails in the cut flower market. Stock has not up to the end of the week been anything to boast of. Roses were of fair quality on Saturday, however, with carnations also a trifle better. Asters are still coming in and are used for funeral work; they are poor enough for any kind of work. Violets have not made their appearance here yet; in fact, last week there was very little variety in the stock offered in the market. Dahlias are still very good in quality and are selling fully as well as they were last year. Plants are selling principally in the lines of small to medium kentias and Nephrolepis Scottii and N. Piersoni elegantissima. D. M.

CANADIAN NEWS

TORONTO.—Business is rapidly improving. Stock of good quality is by no means plentiful, but there is enough inferior grade material to go round. More orchids are to be seen than I have ever before heard of here, Oncidium varicosum being rather in over-supply. Cattleyas are cheap and many are used; most of the larger stores this week have orchid displays. Cattleyas of the labiata type are not plentiful, and bring fairly good prices. Quite a number of chrysanthemums are to be had and realize good figures, but as yet the flowers are not of a high grade. Carnations are coming in freely—short stems and fair blooms, generally. American Beauty roses, really good ones, do not stay long in hand. Dunlop is sending in fine Kaiserin Augusta Victoria, and the Toronto Floral Company, fine Bride. Richmond and Killarney both do well here, and good crops of both are in sight. In this neighborhood, dahlias have been almost a failure, though a few fairly good flowers are coming in now. We have not yet had a frost severe enough to cut off tender plants, and fine beds of musas, cannas, etc., in full glory, are seen; but this state of things cannot last much longer. Large quantities of bulbs are handled, and as soon as the other flowers are cut off, no doubt there will be a great rush for bulbs of all kinds.

Arrangements for the Ontario Horticultural Exhibition, to be held on November 6 to 11, are progressing. The Black Dyke Band, a famous English organization, has been engaged to play at the show. More money than ever before will be spent on advertising. The railway companies have agreed to give an excursion rate of a single fare for the first two days of the show, from all over the province, and a single fare on the certificate plan for the other days, and as well have promised to advertise the show. A city press agent has been engaged, and already our daily papers are publishing notices of the show. We have been promised several exhibits, and we also hope to have many visitors from the United States.

Arrangements are making for the meeting of the American Carnation Society here in January, and all who come are sure of a hearty welcome and an interesting meeting. We expect to have an ideal hall for the exhibition, with a temperature just right for the flowers; also splendid light. THOS. MANTON.

LONDON, ONT.—Now that the outside flowers are about over, business is getting a great deal better for carnations, roses etc. Trade has been very brisk in design work the last few days: several large weddings have also helped to use up the better quality of flowers.

Some very fine carnations and roses are cut at Gammage & Son's place. This firm is installing an acetylene gas plant, for lighting its offices, potting-shed, boiler room, etc.

The Western fair held in this city during September, was the largest and best in the history of the exhibition. The exhibit of plants was not as large as usual, but of better quality. There was a fine display of cut flowers, made-up work and fruit. J. Gammage & Son had a large showing of florists' supplies, gold fish and aquaria, also fancy vases, baskets, etc. F. C.

EDMONTON, ALBERTA.—Everard Heim Groos, operating the Alexandra Nurseries here, has suddenly left for parts unknown, leaving business matters in a very tangled condition. The nurseries and greenhouses are in charge of the sheriff. Part of the stock was to have been sold on October 6, but the sale was postponed owing to some legal difficulty. From present appearances creditors will receive little or nothing. F. B.

St. Paul.

rs Notes.

The first killing frost of the son occurred a few nights since l put an effectual quietus on out- r stock, although pyrethrums and er perennial flowers are still being . Asters are all gone, and the in reliance of the store men is on es and carnations. Trade has been ly good, several large store open- s and an unusual amount of fune- work contributing quite largely the volume of sales.

. L. May & Company are display- a window of Dutch bulbs which y find very profitable as a side .

he Swanson Floral Company has usual window display of decora- plants.

Iolm & Olson are busy preparing move but report trade very good.

he Clinton Falls Nursery Com- y is sending in some extra fine hmond roses with stems of good gth and blooms of large size and d substance.

. Clausen of Albert Lea is shipping d single and double violets—the t seen on the market here.

. D. Ramsley has gone to Cali- nia.

. J. Olson recently bagged 94 ks in two days' hunt. While he was ng this his wife gave birth to a healthy boy. Rather a joke on f, but he is passing around ducks cigars together to his many nds.

. D. Dysinger is now located with m & Olson.

. W. Scott of Vaughan's Seed re, Chicago, was a recent visitor.

VERITAS.

---

ohn A. May, of L. L. May & Com- y, met with an accident the fore of the week by falling down- rs, which laid him up for the week a partial dislocation of the hip.

he Hoyt Plant & Seed Company e rented part of the Ramaley ral Company store for the sale hrubs, etc., for the Fall trade.

he Swanson Floral Company re- ts a good trade and a heavy de- d for the new rose, Minnehaha, ch seems to sell well, in some s taking the place of American uty. The color is somewhat lighter that of the latter rose, but in r respects the variety is very ilar to Beauty.

Holm & Olson contemplate getting into their new store this coming week; their fixtures, including a mammoth ice box, are all made of pure mahogany.

PAUL.

Buffalo.

News Items.

The department store flower stands in the Wm. Hengerer and Sweeney Company establishment report a very good business in palms and Boston ferns.

Wm. Hewson of the Wm. Scott Co. was judge of the floral exhibits at the recent New York State Fair at Syracuse.

Mr. and Mrs. R. E. Boettger last week celebrated their silver wedding at their home in Eggertsville, and were the recipients of many handsome presents from their friends.

George McClure has returned from Europe, highly pleased with his trip.

W. H. G.

MEMPHIS, TENN.—On October 8 the Idlewild Greenhouses had a grand opening of their new and beautiful store. The decorations were very elaborate, and were viewed by thousands of people from 9 a. m. to 9 p. m. Otto Schwill is proprietor of the store; and the decorations were the work of his assistant W. H. Englehart, who has been in Mr. Schwill's employ for seven years, and a proficient corps of young ladies.

New York.

The Week's News.

The first frost of the season around this city and vicinity occurred on the morning of October 4, and although the drop below freezing point was but slight, it was sufficient to touch the tender plants in gardens, and cut off the supply of outdoor flowers which find their way to this market from nearby territory.

The dahlia season of 1906 has, we believe, been a record-breaker so far as prices obtained goes, among growers who supply the New York market. Unfortunately for some of the Long Island growers, the growing season was so dry at times that dahlias did not begin to produce the number of blooms they usually do. There is no doubt that the fact of asters being of so poor quality this season tended to help the sale of dahlias. Added to that, chrysanthemums have been quite a little later in coming in than usual, consequently every condition has been favorable for the sale of dahlias; and as we said before, growers who have been fortunate enough to have a good supply, have reaped a good harvest this year.

We have been informed by a large dealer in Southern greens that there has been no advance in express rates over the Southern railroads as yet. We mention this fact, as it seems that express rates have been advanced on this class of material when shipped from the South to other citites.

If some one would invent a method whereby express companies could be made or taught to handle boxes of flowers a little more carefully, they would be conferring a great benefit on all receivers and shippers of cut flowers. We recently saw two large boxes of orchids sent to a wholesale house in this city; one a box of Dendrobium formosum, the other a box of cattleyas. The latter flowers were fastened to the bottom of the box with double pointed tacks, each flower stem being so held that it could not get loose; the former flowers were fastened by strips of cloth and tacks to the bottom of the box. With ordinary care these should have traveled without being disturbed in the slightest manner, and should have reached their destination without a petal being broken. On the contrary, they had been handled so carelessly that in the case of the cattleyas there was scarcely a flower that did not have some parts of it broken, while the dendrobiums had been shaken loose, and many of them scattered about the inside of the box. It would seem that after taking every precaution in packing these flowers and marking the box so that those who handle it would be careful of it, the express companies would be able to deliver them in a perfect condition, but evidently they throw these receptacles about like so many trunks, and take no interest whatever in trying to carry delicate and perishable flowers as they ought to be carried.

The eleventh annual flower show of the Morris County Gardeners and Florists' Society will be held on Thursday and Friday, November 1 and 2, in the Assembly rooms at Madison, N. J.

Steam was turned on in the conservatories of the New York Botanical Garden, Bronx Park, for the first time this season on September 24. This was eleven days later that heat had to be applied than in any previous year in the history of the Garden. In 1903 it was necessary to apply heat to the conservatories as early as August 28.

Thos. Stock of Dorchester, Mass., was in town recently to confer with his wholesale dealer, Alfred H. Langjahr. Lewis Acheson, Pittsfield, Mass., was also a visitor this week.

Godfrey Aschmann, the well known plant importer and dealer of Philadelphia, Pa., who has been spending the Summer in Europe buying and inspecting stock, returned on Monday morning and spent a few hours in this cty before proceeding to his home in Philadelphia. Mr. Aschmann reports having had a splendid time while abroad, and having thoroughly enjoyed his combined business and pleasure trip.

Pittsburg.

News Notes.

Several new florist stands were opened up the past week, one of them in the Allegheny Market by Erhardt & Swartz, of which Charles Erhardt is well known, having conducted a florist business in Cleveland, Ohio, and for a few years past he was with E. C. Ludwig, in the Allegheny Market. Mr. Erhardt is pretty well acquainted and he has a thorough knowledge of the florist business, so the firm should succeed.

Alfred McCoyd took charge of the stand in the Arcade on Fifth avenue, a very prominent place for display. Mr. McCoyd had been with Blind Brothers, Fifth street, and he expects to do a nice business in the Arcade.

P. Demas, of the Pittsburg Florists' Exchange, has been in the East for the past week looking up stock and new shippers. Edward McCallum, of the same firm, hurt his right hand so that he will not be able to use it for some time; cause, football.

Philip Breitmeyer of Detroit spent a day in the city. Jas. F. Smith, of Wm. Boas & Company, paper box manufacturers of Philadelphia, was in town and reports trade very satisfactory.

Warren H. Manning of Boston, delivered an address in Sewickley last week, after having spent some time in looking over the borough and drawing plans of improvements which he suggested. Sewickley is about ten or twelve miles from this city, where some of our wealthy people have homes; it is a beauty spot, having been much improved within the last ten years or more by some of the best landscape architects in the country.

The park conservatories of the two cities are getting things in shape for the annual chrysanthemum shows which will be ready soon for the public and promise to excel last year's displays in size and number of sorts.

E. C. REINEMAN.

Syracuse, N. Y.

News Items.

Despite the fact that at the present time of writing, October 3, we have had no killing frosts, trade holds remarkably good. The death recently of one of the city's most prominent physicians called for the largest quantity of flowers seen at a funeral for many years.

Park Superintendent Campbell has just cause to feel proud of the display he has made this year, in all our parks, which now number fifty-two, and the citizens are so pleased with the results that it is intended to greatly extend them, and to make boulevards around the city. George E. Kessler of Kansas City has been engaged for three years to formulate plans for carrying out the work.

In my notes of the State fair I inadvertently omitted to mention the splendid exhibit made by the Herald Gardening Club, which is composed of thousands of our school children who are supplied with flower seeds by this enterprising paper, and I should be lacking in honesty and fairness if I did not accord to the Herald a large share of the credit for the great improvement in the appearance of the gardens of our city. Before the paper took up the idea of encouraging the poor children to cultivate flowers, many of our wealthy citizens had to give up having flower beds around their houses, in quence of the constant depre made by the children. Now t all changed, and I have not a single complaint this year. I there are some florists who loo ance at a newspaper selling seeds to children at one cent a age, but results are the thin must look at; and right here w abundant proof of its wisdom.

J. K. ALLEN
Wholesale Commission Dealer in **Cut Flowers**
106 West 28th St., NEW YORK
Open at 6 a. m. every day.
Telephone, 167 Madison Square.
Consignments Solicited.
Mention the Florists' Exchange when writing.

Wm. Stuart Allen Co.
Commission Merchan's in CUT FLOWERS
ORCHIDS AT ALL SEASONS
53 WEST 28th STREET, NEW YORK
Telephone 356 Madison Square
Mention the Florists' Exchange when writing.

C. BONNET G. H. BLAKE
BONNET & BLAKE
Wholesale Florists
106 Livingston Street, BROOKLYN, N. Y.
Telephone: 4638 Main.
Consignments solicited. Out-of-town orders carefully attended to. Give us a trial.
Mention the Florists' Exchange when writing.

CUT FLOWER EXCHANGE
Sixth Ave. and 26th St.
Coogan Building, NEW YORK
Open every Morning at Six o'clock for the Sale of Cut Flowers.
Wall Space for advertising purposes to Rent.
V. S. DORVAL, Jr., Secretary.
Mention the Florists' Exchange when writing.

Joseph S. Fenrich
...Wholesale Florist...
—THE RELIABLE HOUSE—
110 West 28th Street
Telephone 324-325 Madison Square.
Mention the Florists' Exchange when writing.

FORD BROS.
Wholesale Florists
48 WEST 28th ST., NEW YORK
Telephone, 3870-3871 Madison Square
Mention the Florists' Exchange when writing.

GROWERS, ATTENTION!
Always Ready to Receive Fine Stock
GUNTHER BROTHERS
30 West 29th Street
Phone, 551 Madison Square. NEW YORK
Violets, Roses, Carnations, Orchids
Established 1888.
Mention the Florists' Exchange when writing.

ALEX. J. GUTTMAN
The Wholesale Florist of New York
43 WEST 28th STREET
Phones 1664-1665 Madison Square
Mention the Florists' Exchange when writing.

A. M. HENSHAW
..Wholesale Florist..
52 West 28th Street, NEW YORK
First class Roses and Carnations a specialty.
Consignments Solicited. Tel. 5583 Madison Sq.
Mention the Florists' Exchange when writing.

HICKS & CRAWBUCK, Inc.
Wholesale Florists
And Dealers in FLORISTS' SUPPLIES
76-78 Court Street
Phone. 3660-3661 Main BROOKLYN, N. Y.
Mention the Florists' Exchange when writing.

HEADQUARTERS FOR NOVELTIES
ORCHIDS A SPECIALTY
THE HIGHEST GRADE OF VALLEY ALWAYS ON HAND
GARDENIAS, DAISIES, ROSES, CARNATIONS.
JAMES McMANUS, Telephone 759 Mad. Sq. 42 W. 28th St., New York.

PHILIP F. KESSLER
Wholesale Florist
55-57 W. 26th St., NEW YORK.
Telephone, 2921-5243 Madison Square.
Mention the Florists' Exchange when writing.

WILLIAM H. KUEBLER
Wholesale Commission Dealer in
CUT FLOWERS
28 Willoughby St.,
Telephone 4591 Main BROOKLYN, N. Y.
Mention the Florists' Exchange when writing.

JULIUS LANG
Wholesale Florist
53 WEST 30th STREET
NEW YORK
Consignments Solicited. Telephone: 280 Madison Sq
Mention the Florists' Exchange when writing.

FRANK MILLANG
Wholesale Commission Dealer in
CUT FLOWERS
55-57 West 26th Street, New York
Telephone Call: 299 Madison Square.
Mention the Florists' Exchange when writing.

ALFRED H. LANGJAHR
55 WEST 28th STREET, NEW YORK
Telephone, 4626-4627 Madison Square Established 1891
SPECIAL VALLEY AND TOP GRADE ASPARAGUS
Consignments of First Class Stock Solicited.

Horace E. Froment
SUCCESSOR TO
W. GHORMLEY WHOLESALE COMMISSION FLORIST
Receiver and Shipper of all varieties of Cut Flowers
Telephones, 2200 and 2201 Madison Square. 57 West 28th St., NEW YORK

Wholesale Prices of Cut Flowers, New York, Oct. 18, 1906
Prices quoted are by the hundred unless otherwise noted

Roses — A. Beauty, fancy—special	12.00 to	20.00
" extra	8.00 to	10.00
" No. 1	6.00 to	8.00
" No. 2	3.00 to	6.00
" No. 3	2.00 to	3.00
Bride, Maid, fancy—spe'l	5.00 to	6.00
" extra	4.00 to	5.00
" No. 1	2.00 to	4.00
" No. 2	1.00 to	1.50
Golden Gate	1.50 to	5.00
Richmond	1.50 to	5.00
Mme. Abel Chatenay	1.50 to	5.00
Adiantum	.50 to	.75
Croweanum	.50 to	1.00
Asparagus	25.00 to	50.00
" Plumosus, bunches	8.00 to	15.00
" Sprengerii, bunches	8.00 to	15.00
	...... to	......
Cattleyas	40.00 to	50.00
Daisies	...... to	......

Carnations — Inf'r grades, all colors	1.00 to	1.50
Standard Varieties — White	1.50 to	2.50
Standard Varieties — Pink	1.50 to	2.50
Standard Varieties — Red	1.50 to	2.50
Standard Varieties — Yel. & Var.	1.50 to	2.50
*Fancy— (*The highest grades of standard var.) — White	3.00 to	4.00
*Fancy — Pink	3.00 to	4.00
*Fancy — Red	3.00 to	4.00
*Fancy — Yel. & Var.	3.00 to	4.00
Novelties	3.00 to	5.00
Chrysanthemums	6.00 to	12.00
" Fancy	15.00 to	30.00
Lilies	10.00 to	12.00
Lily of the Valley	2.00 to	3.00
Mignonette	...... to	......
Smilax	8.00 to	10.00
Violets	.35 to	.60
	...... to	......
	...... to	......
	...... to	......
	...... to	......

WALTER F. SHERIDAN
Wholesale Florist
Tel. 3532-3533 Mad. Sq. 39 WEST 28TH ST., NEW YORK
ALL VARIETIES OF CUT FLOWERS IN SEASON

TOP GRADE FOR SHIPPING
American Beauty, Bridesmaid, Bride, Liberty, Lilies, Lily of the Valley, Carnations
Telephone, 1998 Madison Square JOHN I. RAYNOR, 49 West 28th St., NEW YORK

Edw. C. Horan
55 West 28th St., NEW YORK
TELEPHONE, 1462-1463 MADISON SQUARE
CUT FLOWERS AT WHOLESALE
Mention The Florists' Exchange when writing.

JOHN YOUNG
Wholesale Florist
51 W. 28th St., NEW YORK
Telephone: 4463-4464 MADISON SQUARE
Mention the Florists' Exchange when writing.

A. MOLTZ
Wholesale Florist
55-57 West 26th St., NEW YORK
1st Floor. Telephone, 2921-5243 Madison Sq.
Mention the Florists' Exchange when writing.

MOORE, HENTZ & NASH
WHOLESALE
GROWER AGENT
COMMISSION FLORISTS
55 West 26th St. New York
Telephone Call, 756 Madison Square
Mention the Florists' Exchange when writing.

GEORGE SALTFORD
Wholesale Florist
CONSIGNMENTS SOLICITED
46 West 29th Street, New York
Telephone: 3393 Madison Square
Mention the Florists' Exchange when writing.

J. Seligman Joseph J. Levy
JOHN SELIGMAN & COMPANY
Wholesale Florists
56 West 26th Street,
Tel. 4878 Madison New York
Opposite New York Cut Flower Company
Mention the Florists' Exchange when writing.

B. S. SLINN, JR.
Wholesale Florist
55 and 57 West 26th Street, NEW YORK
SPECIALTIES—Violets, Carnations and Roses
Shipping orders receive prompt attention. Consignment Solicited.
Telephone: 3864 Madison Square
Mention the Florists' Exchange when writing.

WM. STARKE
Wholesale Florist and Plantsman
Tel. No. 4582 Madison Sq. 52 W. 29th St.
Between Broadway and 6th Ave., New York
Shipments of Plants made to any part of the country. A trial order solicited.
SATISFACTION GUARANTEED.
Mention the Florists' Exchange when writing.

Frank H. Traendly Charles Schenck
TRAENDLY & SCHENCK
Wholesale Florists
44 WEST 28th STREET, NEW YORK
and CUT FLOWER EXCHANGE
Telephones: 798 and 799 MADISON SQUARE
Consignments Solicited
Mention the Florists' Exchange when writing.

THOMAS YOUNG Jr.
Wholesale Florist
43 West 28th Street, NEW YORK
Telephone, 4850 Madison Square
Consignments of Choice Flowers solicited
Mention the Florists' Exchange when writing.

Wholesale Prices of Cut Flowers—Per 100

Boston Oct. 15, 1906	Buffalo Oct. 15, 1906	Detroit Oct. 11, 1906	Cincinnati Oct. 15, 1906	Baltimore Oct. 1, 1906	NAMES AND VARIETIES	Milwaukee Oct. 11, 1906	Phil'delphia Oct. 11, 1906	Pittsburg Oct. 15, 1906	St. Louis Oct. 15, 1906
30.00 to 50.00	20.00 to 25.00	10.00 to 35.00	... to 40.00	... to ...	ROSES — A. BEAUTY, fancy—special	... to 25.00	20.00 to 40.00	30.00 to 35.00	20.00 to 25.00
20.00 to 30.00	15.00 to 20.00	... to ...	... to 30.00	20.00 to 25.00	" extra	15.00 to 18.00	... to ...	15.00 to 20.00	12.50 to 15.00
10.00 to 20.00	10.00 to 15.00	... to ...	20.00 to 25.00	12.50 to 15.00	" No. 1	10.00 to 12.50	... to ...	10.00 to 12.50	6.00 to 10.00
4.00 to 10.00	8.00 to 10.00	... to ...	7.50 to 15.00	5.00 to 10.00	" Culls and ordinary	4.00 to 6.00	... to ...	... to 6.00	3.00 to 5.00
5.00 to 10.00	6.00 to 8.00	3.00 to 6.00	... to 6.00	... to ...	BRIDE, 'MAID, fancy-special	... to 6.00	... to ...	... to 6.00	5.00 to 6.00
6.00 to 8.00	5.00 to 6.00	... to ...	4.00 to 5.00	4.00 to 5.00	" extra	... to 5.00	... to ...	... to 5.00	3.00 to 4.00
2.00 to 6.00	4.00 to 5.00	... to ...	... to 4.00	3.00 to 4.00	" No. 1	... to 4.00	... to ...	3.00 to 4.00	... to 2.00
1.00 to 2.00	3.00 to 4.00	... to ...	... to 3.00	2.00 to 3.00	" No. 2	... to 2.00	... to ...	... to 2.00	... to ...
... to ...	3.00 to 6.00	4.00 to 8.00	3.00 to 6.00	2.00 to 5.00	GOLDEN GATE	4.00 to 6.00	2.00 to 6.00	... to ...	2.00 to 5.00
2.00 to 10.00	3.00 to 7.00	... to ...	3.00 to 4.00	3.00 to 5.00	K. A. VICTORIA	4.00 to 8.00	2.00 to 8.00	4.00 to 12.00	3.00 to 8.00
2.00 to 10.00	3.00 to 8.00	... to ...	... to ...	3.00 to 5.00	LIBERTY	4.00 to 6.00	4.00 to 8.00	4.00 to 8.00	... to ...
... to ...	3.00 to 6.00	4.00 to 10.00	... to ...	2.00 to 4.00	METEOR	... to ...	... to ...	... to ...	... to ...
... to ...	2.00 to 5.00	4.00 to 10.00	... to ...	2.00 to 4.00	PERLE	4.00 to 6.00	... to ...	2.00 to 6.00	2.00 to 5.00
... to ...	... to ...	... to 50.00	... to ...	... to ...	ORCHIDS—Cattleyas	... to ...	... to 40.00	... to ...	... to ...
... to ...	1.00 to 1.25	... to ...	... to 1.00	... to .75	CARNATIONS — Inferior grades, all colors	... to 1.00	... to 2.50	.75 to 1.50	1.00 to 1.50
... to ...	1.25 to 1.50	... to 1.00	1.00 to 2.00	1.00 to 1.50	Standard Varieties — White	... to 1.00	... to 2.50	2.00 to 3.00	1.00 to 1.50
... to ...	1.25 to 1.50	... to ...	1.00 to 2.00	1.00 to 1.50	Standard Varieties — Pink	... to 1.00	... to 2.50	2.00 to 3.00	1.00 to 1.50
... to ...	1.25 to 1.50	... to ...	1.00 to 2.00	1.00 to 1.50	Standard Varieties — Red	... to 1.00	... to 2.50	2.00 to 3.00	1.00 to 1.50
... to ...	... to ...	... to 3.00	... to ...	1.00 to 1.50	Standard Varieties — Yellow and var.	... to 1.00	... to 2.50	... to ...	1.00 to 1.50
2.00 to 3.00	2.00 to 2.50	... to ...	... to ...	... to ...	Fancy Varieties — White	1.50 to 2.00	... to 3.00	... to ...	2.00 to 3.00
2.00 to 3.00	2.00 to 2.50	... to ...	... to ...	... to ...	Fancy Varieties — Pink	1.50 to 2.00	... to 3.00	... to ...	2.00 to 3.00
2.00 to 3.00	2.00 to 2.50	... to ...	... to ...	... to ...	Fancy Varieties — Red	1.50 to 2.00	... to 3.00	... to ...	2.00 to 3.00
2.00 to 3.00	2.00 to 2.50	... to 1.50	... to ...	... to ...	Fancy Varieties — Yellow and var	1.50 to 2.00	... to 3.00	... to ...	2.00 to 3.00
... to ...	... to ...	... to ...	... to ...	... to ...	Novelties	... to ...	... to ...	... to ...	... to ...
.75 to 1.00	.50 to 1.00	... to 2.00	... to 1.00	... to 1.00	ADIANTUM	... to 1.00	... to 1.00	.75 to 1.00	... to 1.00
... to 50.00	15.00 to 20.00	25.00 to 60.00	... to 50.00	25.00 to 50.00	ASPARAGUS, Plum. and Ten	20.00 to 30.00	50.00 to 75.00	25.00 to 50.00	25.00 to 50.00
... to ...	15.00 to 20.00	20.00 to 30.00	... to 35.00	25.00 to 50.00	" Sprengeri, bunches	20.00 to 30.00	... to 50.00	20.00 to 30.00	25.00 to 75.00
... to ...	8.00 to 10.00	... to 10.00	... to 10.00	6.00 to 8.00	CALLAS	... to ...	... to ...	... to ...	... to ...
10.00 to 20.00	20.00 to 25.00	... to ...	10.00 to 15.00	5.00 to 10.00	CHRYSANTHEMUMS	... to ...	... to 40.00	10.00 to 25.00	3.00 to 8.00
... to ...	1.50 to 2.50	.75 to 1.50	... to ...	... to ...	DAISIES	... to .40	... to 1.00	... to ...	... to ...
8.00 to 10.00	... to ...	... to ...	... to 12.50	10.00 to 12.50	LILIES	... to 12.50	... to ...	18.00 to 20.00	... to ...
2.00 to 5.00	3.00 to 4.00	3.00 to 4.00	... to 4.00	... to ...	LILY OF THE VALLEY	... to ...	3.00 to 5.00	2.00 to 4.00	3.00 to 4.00
... to ...	... to ...	... to ...	... to ...	... to ...	MIGNONETTE, ordinary	... to ...	... to ...	... to ...	... to ...
... to ...	... to ...	... to ...	... to ...	... to ...	" fancy	... to ...	... to ...	... to ...	... to ...
... to 12.50	12.00 to 16.00	12.50 to 15.00	12.50 to 15.00	... to ...	SMILAX	... to 15.00	... to ...	12.50 to 15.00	... to 12.50
.50 to .75	... to ...	... to ...	.75 to 1.00	.35 to .50	VIOLETS, ordinary	... to ...	... to ...	.50 to .75	... to ...
... to ...	.15 to .25	... to ...	... to ...	... to ...	" fancy	... to ...	... to ...	... to ...	... to ...
... to ...	... to ...	... to ...	... to .15	... to ...	GALAX LEAVES	... to ...	... to .15	... to ...	... to .15

Newport, R. I.

A Silver Wedding.

Last Saturday evening Mr. and Mrs. Henry J. Hass celebrated their silver wedding. The guests, to the number of nearly six hundred, could not be accommodated in the house. Mr. Hass had a preconceived idea of this, so he had his carriage house decorated and in other ways put in order for their reception. Many of those present last Saturday evening knew Mr. and Mrs. Hass's liberality as host and hostess, but on this occasion both excelled themselves. The presents of silver were numerous, and many of them beautiful and costly. Both Mr. and Mrs. Hass are very popular among all classes in the community, and the esteem in which both are held prompted many of those who attended more than a desire for their own enjoyment. But once there, under Mr. Hass's roof, their enjoyment was the main consideration under discussion and allowed.

Estimates are being asked for a large nectarine and peach house for Mrs. Astor at "Beechwood." D. M.

Wholesale Prices of Cut Flowers, Chicago, Oct. 16, 1906

Prices quoted are by the hundred unless otherwise noted

ROSES — American Beauty		
36-inch stems......per doz.	3.00 to	4.00
30-inch stems...... "	2.50 to	3.00
24-inch stems...... "	2.00 to	2.50
20-inch stems...... "	1.00 to	2.00
18-inch stems...... "	...... to	1.50
12-inch stems...... "	...... to	1.00
8-inch stems and shorts "	.50 to	.75
Bride Maid, fancy special......	5.00 to	6.00
" extra......	4.00 to	5.00
" No. 1......	2.00 to	3.00
" No. 2......	...... to	1.00
Golden Gate......	2.00 to	6.00
Carnot......	2.00 to	6.00
Uncle John......	2.00 to	6.00
Liberty......	2.00 to	6.00
Richmond......	2.00 to	8.00
Kaiserins......	2.00 to	8.00
Killarney......	3.00 to	6.00
Perle......	2.00 to	6.00
Chatenay......	2.00 to	6.00
Orchids—Cattleyas......	50.00 to	75.00
SMILAX......	8.00 to	12.00
LILY OF THE VALLEY......	2.00 to	4.00
DAHLIAS......	2.00 to	3.00
VIOLETS......	.50 to	1.00

CARNATIONS			
STANDARD VARIETIES	White......	1.50 to	2.00
	Pink......	1.50 to	2.00
	Red......	1.50 to	2.00
	Yellow & var......	1.50 to	2.00
*FANCY (The highest grades of Sta'd var)	White......	3.00 to	4.00
	Pink......	3.00 to	4.00
	Red......	3.00 to	4.00
	Yellow & var......	3.00 to	4.00
NOVELTIES......		...... to	......
ADIANTUM......		.75 to	1.00
ASPARAGUS, Plum. & Ten......		.35 to	.50
" Sprengeri, bunches.		.35 to	.50
......		...... to	......
LILIES, Longiflorum......		15.00 to	18.00
HARRISII......		15.00 to	18.00
......		...... to	......
......		...... to	......
......		...... to	......
......		...... to	......
......		...... to	......
HARDY FERNS per 1000......		...... to	1.50
GALAX "		1.00 to	1.25
......		...... to	......
CHRYSANTHEMUMS per doz		2.00 to	4.00

Chicago.

Show Notes.

The flower show committees are well settled to their work and daily progress is reported. A meeting of the chairmen of committees was held on Thursday evening of last week prior to the Florists' Club meeting, and matters pertaining to the grand coming event were talked over and a general exchange of ideas indulged in. Following is a list of the chairmen of committees, nearly all of whom were present:

Manager, George Asmus; press, J. H. Burdette; examination of plants, J. F. Klimmer; examination of cut flowers, H. E. Klunder; inside decorations, C. A. Samuelson; exterior decorations, W. H. Kidwell; music committee, A. I. Simmons; admissions, P. J. Hauswirth; privileges, J. B. Deamud; floral arrangements, F. F. Benthey; committee on special features, H. Hasselbring; general advertising, Aug. Lange; postal cards and trade tickets, Ed. F. Winterson; poster and souvenir cards, J. C. Vaughan; printing, E. A. Kanst; program, W. N. Rudd; private gardeners' exhibits, John Reardon; reception at show, C. L. Washburn; reception of out-of-town florists, C. W. Scott; appropriations, Philip C. Schupp; finance committee, C. L. Hutchinson; information bureau, Fritz Bahr; benefit flower sales, W. P. Kyle.

The executive committee is composed of J. C. Vaughan, George Asmus, P. J. Hauswirth, Edwin A. Kanst, Leonard Kill, N. P. Miller, Edgar Sanders and R. H. Warder by election, and ex-officio Edward G. Uihlein, president, Harry G. Selfridge, Ernst Wienhoeber and William A. Peterson, vice-presidents, and Willis N. Rudd, secretary-treasurer.

T. Hopkington, manager of the Downer's Grove Floral Company, Downer's Grove, Ill., was a visitor last week.

Wm. Abrahamson of the E. H. Hunt supply department recently returned from an extended Southern business trip on which he started after the close of the convention at Dayton.

Among our recent visitors, we note Arthur Bryant of Bryant & Son's Nursery, Princeton, Ill.

E. Francis, manager of the new headquarters of Scheiden & Schoos in the Flower Growers' Market, reports that, up to date, business has exceeded their most sanguine expectations.

The Foley Manufacturing Company have broken ground for their new factory and expect to have the roof on the four-story structure by the first day of the coming year. According to the plans the facilities for production of greenhouse material will be doubled within a few months.

Stephen N. Raisek of 442 West Twelfth street has been making extensive alterations and improvements, including the erection of a two-story building and a conservatory.

Simpson, 1585 Ogden avenue, presents a very attractive store after recent renovation.

J. Sanstrom of Momence, Ill., has sold out the interest in his local business to Chicago parties.

Bob Fitzsimmons figured to a certain extent in the Chicago flower market last week. On Friday evening the two lower boxes at the Bijou, where he was playing the star part in his play, "A Fight for Love," were occupied by a dozen or more prominent members of the craft, and on Saturday morning he returned the call by taking a trip through the flower market.

The John C. Moninger Company have already made plans and contracts for the erection of a large addition to their plant, which will practically double their present output.

"Pop" Sanders, the most popular man in the profession, a unique character because everyone who ever met him has nothing but kindness to lay at his feet, celebrated the anniversary of his birth on Wednesday of last week, the tenth of October. Threescore and ten, plus nine; and in heart and spirit as young as ever.

A Dietsch, who is recuperating in Colorado, reports a delightful tour and that physical progress is all that could be expected.

To any one interested in orchids a trip out to the exhibition houses at Lincoln Park at the present time would prove a treat. There is a beautiful assortment of cattleyas and an extensive collection of cypripediums, epidendrums and other members of this most interesting family now in the zenith of their glory.

The reputation of a large concern is seldom built on one structure, but probably there is nothing that has done more to furnish the superstructrue for the well-established reputation of Peter Reinberg's house than the perfect form and style in which they produce red roses. A tour through some thirty odd acres of glass the first of this week found the American Beauty, Richmond, and Liberty fully up to the standard which has always been maintained at the Robey street houses.

Wietor Brothers are now furnishing the market with an excellent line of roses and carnations and some early chrysanthemums, which are certainly a credit to Foreman Pscnicka.

Chas. W. McKellar is offering a fine line of Cattleya labiata and other seasonable orchids, including Dendrobium formosum, all of which are arriving in perfect condition.

Zech & Mann are doing an excellent business, and with liberal shipments of roses, carnations and chrysanthemums, are prepared to fill all orders which land at their office at 51 Wabash avenue.

At E. F. Winterson Company's may be found some of the best stock coming into the city, especially in the line of carnations and chrysanthemums.

Is the Killarney rose all it's cracked up to be? That is the question. Some say yes, others say no.

WM. K. WOOD

ROCHESTER, N. Y.—The storm which swept over western New York last week destroyed many thousands of dollars worth of fruit trees. The peach trees suffered the most, and many peach and quince orchards in Monroe county are ruined.

AVERYVILLE, ILL.—The new building of B. Juergens, is now completely furnished. It is an imposing structure, built completely of cement blocks, and is a beautiful landmark on the cemetery drive. Mr. Juergens reports business in a flourishing condition, and this new, large display room was furnished none too soon to accommodate his trade.

Kalamazoo, Mich.

News of the Week.

In common with the rest of the country Kalamazoo experienced the recent cold snap, the thermometer going as low as 18 degrees on the night of the 10th. However, no damage to speak of was experienced by the florists here, as all had their work sufficiently forward to be out of danger of frost. This was not the case with the celery growers who have suffered severely, it being estimated by the daily papers that their losses will perhaps reach $100,000, as the entire late crop is nearly ruined.

The cold snap seemed to put life into the cut flower business, and inquiries from outside towns were numerous. As all the outside flowers were cut down and the chrysanthemums not yet in, a scarcity of cut flowers at present prevails, and for the next week or two there certainly will be no surplus in this department. Prices have accordingly stiffened.

Chrysanthemums are a little later here than usual, but I notice Van Bochove have a large house at the Third street place nearly ready to cut and the flowers will be very fine when fully developed. This firm also has quite a variety of pot plants here in fine shape for store trade. Carnations are also being cut of good quality. Roses are grown entirely on the new plant at the Rose Hill addition and from what I see at the store, the plants must be in good shape.

James Fraser at Mountain Home has, as usual, his place in the best of condition and says his business has been good all the season. Recently a deputation from the local Eastern Star Lodge waited upon him and presented him with a very handsome diamond ring in recognition of his services for the good of that order.

At the recent Republican county convention held here three of our local florists served as delegates from their respective districts.

S. B.

San Francisco.

On October 11, a Republican paper had an editorial entitled "Give Burbank a Rest," as follows:

"A stormy remonstrance compiled of equal parts of pleading and indignation is on distribution by a sort of volunteer organization described by its members as 'the friends and relatives of Luther Burbank.' It seems that Mr. Burbank is harvesting a full crop of the penalties of greatness, and its garnering leaves no time to pay attention to the eccentric tomato of his choice or the boneless cactus that he would embrace were not so many curious idiots looking. Now, Mr. Burbank's volunteer 'friends and relatives' desire to protect him from the intrusive sightseers who regard him as the keeper of a museum in which he is himself the chief exhibit. Further, they, the 'friends and relatives,' seek to answer by circular some of the ten thousand questions with which they say, in a strange and interesting confusion of metaphors, 'the mail bags continually boil and seethe.'"

The tale of woe has for further specifications these:

"Over 6,000 visitors were received on Mr. Burbank's grounds last month. All the important experimental work was delayed beyond recall, grounds overrun with crowds from daylight to 10 o'clock at night, no rest even on Sundays or holidays. Business destroyed, rare plants died from want of care. Attention constantly drawn from legitimate matters, letters neglected, telegrams delayed. Meals taken standing, sleep disturbed, health at the point of destruction, visitors calling at all hours without any regard to Mr. Burbank's convenience, each one being under the fixed and unalterable impression that he or she was the one particular one who should be admitted. This was too much. The question arose, should he continue his valuable researches undisturbed, or should he be murdered piecemeal as a showman?

"Once upon a time, when San Francisco had a big hotel, the survivor remembers how all the little great men of California gathered in a gilded chamber and banqueted and wined this simple-minded genius and thereafter slobbered all over him clumsy compliments, born neither of knowledge nor discretion. It was, on the whole, a rather painful exhibition, although they meant well. The habit of hero worship has certain drawbacks. We made fools of Dewey and Hobson.

"Give Burbank a rest. Let him pursue in peace the daisy and the peach and the jim dandy, be the official dry nurse of the blameless potato and the foster-father of the hot and rebellious pepper. 'Tis a fine, confused family."

Saturday evening last, October 6, the Pacific Coast Horticultural Society held the best meeting it has had since the April fire scattered its members. The well-attended meeting was held in the picturesque ivy-covered Park Lodge of Golden Gate Park, and although the discussion relating to the holding of the regular November exhibition was not very spirited, the conclusion being that any time for a show this year would not be auspicious, the matter was deferred till next Spring. The meeting then resolved itself into an election campaign and a spirited time ensued, the result being the following selection of officers for the ensuing year: President, J. W. Bagge, reelected; vice-president, F. Sultz; recording secretary, T. F. Taylor; financial secretary, J. H. Atkinson; treasurer, F. Cleis; librarian, John Thiergasten; usher, H. Plath. Succeeding the election Superintendent John McLaren of the park escorted the members to his park residence, a few steps distant, and regaled all with a repast.

ALVIN.

Cleveland, O.

Owing to the recent cold snap here the supply of outside flowers has been cut off, making a large demand for roses and carnations. Chrysanthemums have not come in yet. All stock is scarce.

The Cleveland Cut Flower Company has been receiving large shipments of very fine dahlias, but the early frosts (unknown here for twenty years before) have cut off that supply.

F. J. Piggot, Meyers avenue, is adding two new houses, with all up-to-date apparatus, to his large plant.

Fred Moritz has finished building his new range of houses; they are also well stocked.

Albert Hart, brother of Herman Hart, has built some new greenhouses on Lake avenue.

Ogden Gaul, formerly with Wm. Brinker, seedsman, has resigned, and accepted the position of traveling salesman for the Cleveland Cut Flower Company. O. G.

Cincinnati.

The News.

Business is booming, and stock is scarce. Last Wednesday night the thermometer dropped to 34 degrees, consequently dahlias and cosmos are no more. Chrysanthemums Polly Rose and Glory of the Pacific are fetching 20c. each, while medium yellow bring 12½c. to 20c.

In roses, American Beauty is a quick seller at $1 per foot per dozen; Bride and Bridesmaid are improving in quality, selling in grades at from 3c. to 6c. each. Carnations are very scarce, and from what I have seen it looks to me as though it will be January 1, 1907, before the plants give a good crop of flowers.

Weddings and openings, receptions and funerals, are consuming all flowers in sight, and prices remain firm.

Paul Berkowitz, Philadelphia, Pa., was a caller on Saturday.

George Murphy, brother of William Murphy, is quite ill with typhoid fever.

Charles Dieterich, Mayville, Ky., was in town Monday, and reported all outdoor stock frozen; he said the ground there was covered with snow on the 10th inst.

Stock never was scarcer than on Sunday and Monday, and prices, of course, stiffened. Chrysanthemums are commencing to come in, and from now on will be more plentiful.

E. G. GILLETT.

Boston.

Fruit and Vegetable Show.

The annual fruit and vegetable show of the Massachusetts Horticultural Sociey, which was held at Horticultural hall on Wednesday and Thursday, 10th and 11th inst., proved interesting, although there were only a few special exhibits of flowers on exhibition. There were over a hundred exhibitors of fruits. Exceptionally fine displays came from the experiment stations of Maine, Massachusetts and Rhode Island, as well as from the State Board of Agriculture of North Carolina. The vegetable classes were extensively represented and altogether it was the finest exhibition of its kind held in the present hall. In the flower displays, Towle's Dahlia Gardens made a showing of dahlias; the Blue Hills Nurseries, one of herbaceous flowers being awarded a first-class certificate for Aconitum Fisherii and honorable mention for Actæa japonica. A first-class certificate was awarded to J. C. Forbes for seedling dahlias Ruth Forbes and Newport.

News Notes.

H. H. Barrows & Son, of Whitman, Mass., have just completed two houses, each 100 feet, which have been filled with their specialty Nephrolepis Whitmanii.

Welch Brothers announce that they have placed in the windows of their new store, cases for the purpose of exhibiting novelties in the way of plants and flowers, and growers from a distance anxious to show the Boston trade any new variety of carnation, rose or chrysanthemum will find it to their advantage to accept of this opportunity.

Harry Kelly for a number of years with J. Newman & Sons, has opened a retail store in Pemberton square. His brother Frank, who has had charge of the floral stands of J. R. Whipple & Company, will be associated with him.

Joseph Fay is now buyer for both Galvin's Tremont street and Back Bay stores.

James Farquhar has a new sash bar which is likely to materially change greenhouse construction. It is a steel bar, and asbestos is used between the metal and glass. Mr. Farquhar has been at work on this for a number of years and has given his method several years' test. He has secured patents on the article.

The Waban Rose Conservatories have been improving their salesroom until it is now neatness throughout. They are cutting some extra fine Killarney and Wellesley roses, and their American Beauty are also very fine.

Andrew Christensen is cutting some of the finest white carnations seen in this market. The variety is Queen. Mr. Christensen will make his appearance in person at the Park street market hereafter.

The Worcester conservatories are cutting exceptionally fine Kaiserin Augusta Victoria roses; and they have have also a fine lot of Helen Goddard and Harry Fenn carnations.

John Farquhar sailed for home on the Ivernia on Tuesday last.

J. W. DUNCAN.

New Orleans.

News Notes.

After several weeks of continued rain and some unusually severe storms. which fortunately damaged the florists' places but little, good, seasonable weather is now with us. Chrysanthemums form the interesting topic now; the majority of them seem to be doing well and ready for our great Decoration Day (All Saints' Day) November 1. In a few localities the flowers were damaged by too much rain. Roses are improving in quality; and the demand for all kinds of flowers and plants is on the increase. the society people returning from their travels.

The Metairie Ridge Nursery has opened a retail store at 141 Carondelet street, a very centrally located place.

Henry Ziegler opened a small place on St. Charles street near Polymnia.

Richard Eichling, formerly with Rehn, is now with the Jos. Schindler Company, who have opened a branch store on Canal street.

P. A.

Los Angeles, Cal.

News Items.

George Wharton James, who has spent years of time studying plant life of Colorado, Arizona, and California, gave an interesting lecture before the Southern California Horticultural Society at its regular monthly meeting on Saturday evening, October 6. About two hundred were present. A preliminary schedule of exhibits for the flower show of the society, which is to be held November 1 to 3, was distributed to the audience.

Fred Howard has returned from his trip to Europe and says that he has brought some new things along of which we shall hear more in the future.

Edward H. Rust, who for years had his sale yards on Broadway, has moved to the corner of Eleventh and Flower streets, where he has more room and better facilities for meeting the requirements of his rapidly increasing trade. The country is filling up at an amazing rate, and the demand for ornamental stock keeps our nurserymen on the jump to supply the wants of planters.

P. D. H.

THE FLORISTS' EXCHANGE

We are a straight shoot and aim to grow into a vigorous plant

A WEEKLY MEDIUM OF INTERCHANGE FOR FLORISTS, NURSERYMEN, SEEDSMEN AND THE TRADE IN GENERAL

Vol. XXII. No. 17 — NEW YORK AND CHICAGO, OCTOBER 27, 1906 — One Dollar Per Year

CONTENTS AND INDEX TO ADVERTISERS, PAGE 497

Seed Trade Report.

AMERICAN SEED TRADE ASSOCIATION

Henry W. Wood, Richmond, Va., president; C. S. Burge, Toledo, O., first vice-president; G. B. McVay, Birmingham, Ala., second vice-president; C. E. Kendel, Cleveland, O., secretary and treasurer; J. H. Ford, Ravenna, O., assistant secretary.

From Michigan a report comes that wrinkled peas will be 25 per cent. short of the usual crop owing to adverse weather conditions.

All interested in the subject of irrigation will find much valuable information thereon in Farmers' Bulletin No. 263 U. S. Department of Agriculture.

France imported from the United States during the year 1905, seeds for sowing, including lucerne and clover, to the value of 159,000 francs, as against 225,000 francs in 1904.

PROVIDENCE, R. I.—A. M. Rennie, of the seed firm of Rennie & Pino, has sold his interests in the concern to Mr. Pino, who will continue the business.

CHICAGO.—C. J. Hess was unfortunate in the loss by fire of 5,000 bushels of onion sets, that valuable commodity of the present season.

Alfred J. Brown of Grand Rapids, Mich., was in town a few days ago.

RAVENNA, O.—Crops in this locality have been, as a rule, good. Cucumbers, however, were poor, on account of blight. Tomatoes produced a heavy crop with us. Our new Nectar sweet corn has pleased us greatly; one small patch of ¾-acre produced over 100 bushels of husked ears. It is early and bears a large ear, like Evergreen. The Glory cabbage surely covered itself with glory. In our trial grounds every plant produced a head as hard as rock and of excellent quality. These two novelties we will introduce the coming year.

FORD SEED COMPANY.

Floral Park, L. I.

Ex-Senator John Lewis Childs has bought 365 acres of fine, rolling land, with fertile soil, in a good state of cultivation, on the Port Jefferson branch of the Long Island Railroad, between St. James and Stony Brook. The tract comprises what is known as the Brennan, Corbin and Charles Powell farms, and is on both sides of the railroad, mainly on the north side, and adjacent to the tracks. The reported price is from $200 to $250 per acre.

Mr. Childs expected to start there a large seed and bulb farm, similar to his extensive gardens at Floral Park, and to build up a village, with seed houses, hotel, private dwellings and Post Office, similar to that at Floral Park. He is now considering dropping the whole project and offering the land for sale, for the reason, as he says, that the Long Island Railroad Company has declined to accede to his request to establish a depot at the location of the proposed seed and bulb farm and village. He says it would be impracticable to locate his establishment far from any railroad depot.

The distance between the two stations of St. James and Stony Brook is three miles, and as every effort is now being made to reduce the time on the Wading River branch, this accounts for the reluctance of the company to establish another station between two so short a distance apart in such a sparsely settled country. In view of the fact that Mr. Childs proposes to spend several hundred thousand dollars in the course of a few years, it is thought the company may reconsider its decision and establish a station at which a few trains may be stopped daily.—Brooklyn Eagle.

MITCHELL, S. D.—Professor W. A. Wheeler of the State agricultural college was in this city recently in conference with a few of the leading business men relative to the establishment of a seed house in Mitchell. The industry will consist of the raising of seeds of every variety grown in South Dakota and the establishment of a wholesale house for their distribution. The proposition of Professor Wheeler was enthusiastically received and it is quite probable that sufficient stock will be sold to warrant the establishment of such an industry.

COPENHAGEN.—The harvest in Denmark of cauliflower and cabbage seed is now safe, and the result is, considering the hot and dry weather we have had, very good. The favorable weather conditions in the Fall have allowed the seed to get quite ripe, so that the germination and the appearance are first-class, and the quantity will very likely be sufficient to cover usual orders.

A. HANSEN.

NOTES FROM HOLLAND.—Continued fine and unusual warm weather marked the month of September and growers have been able to push the planting of bulbs with all possible speed. By this time many millions of bulbs are in the ground, and no doubt as many will have to be planted still. Shipments of bulbs have now come to an end and soon preparations will be made for the lifting of the late ripening crops such as gladioli, spiræa and lilium, and although liliums have suffered in many localities very much from the effects of the long dry spell, gladioli and spiræa crops are expected to turn out fairly good. Of Gladioli Colvillei the crops have now been lifted and in many sections stocks are so badly infected by disease that good healthy bulbs are really scarce and command good prices. Too heavy manuring seems to play havoc with Gladioli Colvillei, and is generally supposed to be the cause of the many diseased stocks.—Horticultural Trade Journal.

EUROPEAN AND CONTINENTAL GRASS AND CLOVER SEEDS.—L. C. Nungesser, seedsman, Griesheim near Darmstadt (Germany), under date September 5, 1906, sends us the following report:

The European crop of all grasses can be defined as satisfactory, so that prices are not higher, taken all round, than last year. American crops, however, are stated to have turned out less favorably, excepting orchard grass, cocksfoot, which was cropped in good condition. Australia yields also a medium crop in the latter kind.

Agrostis stolonifera, German creeping bent grass, has a good crop of apparently good quality, prices ranging as last year. The accounts from America generally are not as favorable as for years, and the prices quoted as yet are fairly high.

Aira caespitosa, tufted hair grass, and Aira flexuosa, knotted hair grass, yield good medium crops pricing accordingly.

Avena elatior, tall meadow oat grass, also came in well, prices remaining the same.

Anthoxantum odoratum, true sweet vernal, yields only a short crop, prices being higher than last season's.

Anthoxantum ödoratum puelii, annual sweet vernal, yielded well and is very cheap.

Avena flavescens, true golden oat grass, cannot yet be truly estimated.

Alopecurus pratensis, meadow foxtail, has not cropped up to expectations and prices are exceptionally high, such as only a very short crop would warrant. Time will show whether prices can be maintained, the probability being disputed in many quarters.

Bromus inermis, awnless brome grass, and Bromus pratensis, meadow brome, also crop well and are moderate-priced.

Ceratochla australis, Schrader's brome grass (prairie grass), is reported a small crop.

Cynosurus cristatus, crested dog's tail, is stated to have yielded well, as is evidenced by the fine qualities hitherto offered and it is to be assumed that this first-class grass will be more extensively sown.

Dactylis glomerata, orchard grass, cocksfoot. As already stated America has a good crop and is in a position, for the first time in years, to export. Only a small percentage, however, is fit for export to Europe, as the qualities generally are not sufficiently clean, although the color is bright. New Zealand seed on the contrary is perfect in respect of color and purity, but the percentage of germination is somewhat below that of former years. The European crop cannot compete with the above produces, being too insignificant in quantity and quality.

Festuca ovina, sheep's fescue, and Festuca duriuscula, hard fescue, crop lighter than last year, still there will be sufficient for the demand. Qualities of many parcels do not tempt and are mixed with trefoil, etc., so that first-class qualities will at least command the same values as last season.

Festuca ovina angustifolia, small-leaved fescue, crops fairly satisfactory, but not free from other seeds, so much so that well cleaned qualities will not be much cheaper than last year.

Festuca rubra, red fescue, and Festuca heterophilla, various-leaved fescue, are however rare and rather dear.

Festuca pratensis, meadow fescue, is stated to have yielded poorly in America and high prices are asked. As considerable stock is left over from last year, buyers will do well to be cautious.

The crop of Festuca elatior (arundinacea), tall fescue, that excellent grass so much in request, is reported to be plentiful and good from the grounds in question and prices will doubtless range lower than last season. Up to date no sales have been registered.

Holcus lanatus, woolly soft grass, a good crop.

Poa pratensis, smooth stalked meadow grass, has cropped very poorly as far as can be gathered from the reports to date and quotations are most unusually high. It remains to be seen whether buyers will not hold back in the face of such high prices, especially as the seed is 1 lb. per bushel lighter than in 1905.

Poa nemoralis, wood meadow grass, has only a medium crop of not tempting quality. First-class samples will hardly come cheaper than last year in consequence of the loss in cleaning and dressing.

Poa trivialis, rough stalked meadow grass, has become so necessary for certain soils that it has maintained its price easily for years and it is not likely that values will waive much this year in spite of the reported good yield.

Phleum pratense, timothy, is stated to be a short crop and opening prices are much higher than usual in former years. It remains to be seen whether they can be kept up.

Phalaris arundinacea, reed canary grass, a small crop.

It is too early to report definitely concerning clovers generally, particularly is this the case with red clover and alsike. The development takes place in September, but the prospects in Europe are excellent for all sorts.

Bad accounts have just come to hand concerning the results of the crops of Medicago sativa, alfalfa. The yield is said to have turned out very poor, so that at the best the same prices as last year may be expected.

Those cropped up to date, such as Medicago lupulina, yellow trefoil, which yields well in choice quality, Hedysarum onobrychis, simple sainfoin, which is far behind last year's quality and short in crop, and Trifolium repens, white clover, yielding a full crop of prime quality, will not be offered in bulk for some weeks.

Trifolium incarnatum, crimson clover, also yields well, but prices do not coincide, being fairly high, and I am of opinion that more favorable quotations will rule during the Winter.

Lotus villosus, greater bird's foot trefoil, and Lotus corniculatus, common bird's foot trefoil, yield about the same as last year and prices are expected to range equally favorable.

Rye grasses yield satisfactorily and qualities are choice.

THE BLIGHTING OF FIELD AND GARDEN PEAS, chiefly due to seed infection and Powdery Mildew of the Pea, are treated upon in Bulletin 173 of the Ohio Agricultural Experiment Station, Wooster, O. The prevention of the blight, it is said, has been found especially difficult. Any seed treatment which destroyed the indwelling fungus likewise destroyed the seed peas. Prevention must therefore begin with the growth of the seed peas themselves; promising results have been obtained in the prevention of seed infection by supporting the vines and by spraying the plants with Bordeaux mixture. The importance of this initial work in growing healthy seed will bear special emphasis, as will the necessity of crop rotation in field operations. Powdery mildew, while generally prevalent on late plantings of peas, is easily prevented by the use of Bordeaux mixture. The information contained in the bulletin should be of aid to seedsmen in producing healthy seed, as well as to canners in their pea growing.

CATALOGUES RECEIVED.

W. C. KENNEDY, St. Joseph, Mo.—Catalogue and Price List of Fall Bulbs.

A. HANSEN, Copenhagen, Denmark.—Price List of Cauliflower and Cabbage Seed. Illustrated.

JOHN SCHEEPERS & COMPANY, 2-6 Old Slip, New York.—Wholesale Plant and Bulb catalogue.

C. VAN KLEEF & COMPANY, Boskoop, Holland.—Catalogue of Hardy Ornamental Trees and Shrubs, Conifers, Herbaceous Plants, etc.

NURSERY DEPARTMENT.

Conducted by Joseph Meehan.

AMERICAN ASSOCIATION OF NURSERYMEN, Orlando Harrison, Berlin, Md., president; J. W. Hill, Des Moines, Ia., vice-president; George C. Seager, Rochester, N. Y., secretary; C. L. Yates, Rochester, N. Y., treasurer.

France exported to the United States, during 1905, plants and shrubs to the value of 545,000 francs, as against 459,000 francs in 1904.

THE BROWN-TAIL MOTH AND HOW TO CONTROL IT.—This is the subject of Farmers' Bulletin No. 264 (illustrated), United States Department of Agriculture, Washington, D. C., written by Professor L. O. Howard, government entomologist. In addition to an enumeration of the natural enemies and parasites of this pest, the former including such birds as the yellow-billed and black-billed cuckoos, the Baltimore oriole, the yellow-throated vireo, the bluejay and English sparrow, also bats and toads; the parasites including the Fall webworm and the tussock moth, the following information is furnished as to remedies:

The most obvious means of controlling the brown-tail moth, and the easiest one, is the collection and destruction of the Winter nests after the leaves have fallen. These webs, elsewhere described, are conspicuous from October to April. Many of them are within reach, and as each contains 200 caterpillars or more, each one capable of destroying a number of buds in the Spring, the value of this work is at once evident. The webs should be removed before the first part of April. In Massachusetts, on the larger trees, are used long ladders and climbing irons, and some men make a business of destroying these nests upon private estates. The twigs carrying the nests are clipped off with one of the ordinary tree pruners and the collected nests are burned.

After the leaves come out in Spring the nests remaining on the trees will be empty, and it is no longer worth while to make an effort to collect them. Practically the only remedy after this date is spraying with an arsenical mixture. When they are young the larvæ may be effectively destroyed by spraying with arsenate of lead. They may also be destroyed by a Paris-green spray, in the proportion of one pound to 100 or even 150 gallons of water. A stronger mixture will burn the foliage. Arsenate of lead, however, may be applied much stronger, and this substance should be used when the caterpillars are larger. Mr. Sanderson, as the result of an experiment in New Hampshire, recommends five pounds of arsenate of lead to a barrel of water when the caterpillars are large.

Organized efforts have been made in many villages and towns, under the auspices of local associations, to secure the collection and destruction of the nests in the Winter. In some cases the services of school children and others have been enlisted by the payment of a small bounty, and very many thousands of nests have been collected and destroyed in this way. Massachusetts is now working under a good State law (a summary of which is given in the bulletin). Other states already infested or liable to infestation in the near future should pass similar laws.

Seasonable Notes.

Aralias are among the most ornamental of Summer blooming small trees. The foliage is of a pinnate nature and handsome, and its large heads of white flowers followed by dark red berries are strikingly distinct. Some species flower earlier than others, lengthening the display.

All nurserymen have difficulty in finding the proper relationship of many of the junipers. The one long in cultivation of strong, spreading concave habit of growth, is certainly a form of J. communis. So is the Douglas's golden juniper.

Polygonum cuspidatum is a hardy perennial, growing from 5 to 6 feet in height, bearing creamy white flowers in feathery panicles, in August and September. As it is a plant increasing wonderfully from stolons, or underground shoots, it must be planted only where a mass of it is unobjectionable, for when once planted and allowed to grow for some years, it takes time to exterminate it, should such be desired.

An exceedingly early flowering iris is pumila, a quite dwarf sort, bearing its purple flowers in a few weeks after Spring opens. It is not more than three or four inches high when it commences to bloom.

Cercis japonica is the prettier of the two Judas trees; its flowers are larger and a deeper pink. Canadensis makes the larger tree. The European one, siliquastrum, is not hardy north of Virginia.

Azalea indica alba is the one florists often use as a hardy shrub in Philadelphia gardens. Its single white flowers make it much sought for.

The drooping golden bell is Forsythia suspensa. Let grow at will, it forms a bush in shape much as the yellow jasmine does, round-headed, the branches drooping to the ground.

English ivy is generally used where a hardy evergreen is wanted for covering a dead tree. The evergreen euonymus can be used as well where a close growing vine is desired. A third vine is the cross vine, Begonia capreolata. All are of different habit of growth, and evergreen.

A writer in an English magazine recommends the ailanthus as a good street tree, at the same time condemning the linden. The ailanthus is all right for growth, but it had to be banished here because of its suckering.

As the larch and the willow are so impatient to start growth in Spring and do not succeed well planted after they have pushed, it is the rule with nurserymen to plant them in Autumn whenever it is possible. The trees are then in condition to push as soon as they wish to.

Pyrus Parkmanni is one of the most salable of Spring blooming trees. It has pink blossoms, deeper pink when in the bud, with leaves of a lustrous green. It is considered prettier in the bud than when its flowers are expanded.

Menispermum Canadense, Moon Seed Vine

Wier's Weeping Maple.

While the foliage of the Wier's cut-leaved weeping maple is fresh and green, as it is at this season of the year, there are few more desirable trees to be met with on a lawn. As usually listed by nurserymen, it is called Wier's cut-leaved maple, but it should also be called weeping, for it is as true a one as many others sold under that name. It is well fitted for an avenue tree or for a single specimen on a lawn. When grounds are large it can be let grow at will, but even then a little pruning, when young, to bring it into shape, is to the advantage of the tree; and when a tree not over large is desired such a pruning brings about the wished for result and adds to a good shape as well.

The common silver maple, Acer dasycarpum, will often produce seedlings of a quite drooping habit. Wier's cut-leaved weeping is known to be a variety of this, and it has the drooping habit referred to in a marked degree.

This maple, as well as many other varieties of trees, will produce seedlings many of them true to character, but the method to increase them universally adopted is that of budding them on the common silver maple stock before growth has ceased for the Summer.

Hollies for Christmas.

As this is the season for the ordering of hollies for Christmas sales, it will be well to keep in mind that the English holly, the one usually sold for this, is hardy from Philadelphia southward. This fact presented to the attention of a customer would be an incentive to purchase, apart from the use of the plant for Christmas.

There is another thing to remember when getting in a stock of hollies. Although all may have berries on, all may not be perfect flowering kinds. There are male flowering hollies, female sorts, and others bearing perfect flowers. When plants are set by themselves with no others near them, there will be no fruit unless they are perfect flowering sorts. Knowing this it may sometimes be possible to get from the growers such plants as are known to be of the sort desired. There are numbers sold of those full of berries that have fruited through artificial fertilization, and these, of course, would not bear berries when planted out far from any other.

The English holly stands our Winters best when it is on high ground and yet is well sheltered from the wind. The wood gets thoroughly well ripened then, enabling it to stand more cold than it would if its growth were poorly ripened; and this is true of all plants of which there are doubts of their hardiness. There is a variegated form of this holly which, it is claimed, will stand our Winter better than the green one.

Fruit bearing hollies are general favorites, and no nurseryman has ever found he had enough plants of them for sale. Our common holly could be had in its wild state in fruit, and these plants pruned back severely and all foliage cut off, usually live. Whether offered afterward for sale, in tubs or from the open ground, there is no question of a great demand for them.

Two Choice Magnolias.

Those who have extensive grounds should have one or more of every sort of magnolia, for all are beautiful when in flower, not one being without special merit. But in the species M. tripetala there is one of the very best of all those that make trees. It has smooth, clean bark, large, handsome green leaves, large white flowers, and in late Summer and through Autumn it is adorned with its lovely carmine colored pods of seeds. Passing through a collection of trees in late Summer there is not one the equal in beauty of the Magnolia tripetala, and mainly so because of the colored pods of seeds it bears. The foliage is handsome the whole season, keeping up its bright green color until late in October.

In late September or early October the seeds are loosened from the pods and this is the time to collect them for sowing purposes. The pulp should be washed from them and the seeds sown shortly afterward, or be kept in moist sand until Spring and then be sown.

Among other magnolias one of the very best is Soulangeana. It is the first of the showy flowered ones to greet us in Spring, and its foliage is handsome the whole season through. This variety does not seed freely, but it is easily raised from layers. Good, strong plants should be cut down almost to the ground in late Winter. The shoots it will make when Spring comes are the ones to make layers of. Put down early, they root well in one year, and are fit to cut free of the parent stock in Spring and be planted out by themselves, first cutting them back to half their lengths. JOSEPH MEEHAN.

Menispermum Canadense, Moon Seed.

One of our native vines, too seldom seen in cultivation, is the moon seed vine, Menispermum canadense. It extends through many States, from Canada to Carolina and west to the Mississippi, but is not abundant in any one position, or, at least, collectors so report. It may be that it is often not observed, as unless it finds a support it likes, it trails the ground, and in this way it may be unobserved. To have it do its best it needs to be given a stake to cling to, such as was afforded the specimen illustrated, but a branch stake would be still better, for this vine, as in the case of all vines, grows better when there is ample support for it. Almost all vines appear to make extra growth efforts when there are supports for all the shoots they may make.

To see this vine trailing on the ground and then to see one growing on a support, is a lesson that teaches to support them all. There is little or no display of flowers when the plant is on the ground, while the fine showing it makes when staked, the photograph demonstrates. It is an exceedingly handsome flowered vine. The flowers are light yellow in color, and hang in lengthy clusters, as shown; very graceful and beautiful. After the blossoms, berries form in the fertile vines. These are black, resembling Clinton grapes, and ornament the vine late in the Fall.

The name moon seed vine is given the plant because of the seed when divested of its pulp resembling a half moon. The vine dies to the ground every Fall, but reappears every Spring, gaining strength as time goes on, in this way being of interest every year. What properties the berries may have we do not know, but the bitter principle in the roots is the basis of a valuable tonic.

JOSEPH MEEHAN.

THE WEEK'S WORK.

Timme's Timely Teachings.

Bulbs.

We are now in the midst of a season when bulbs claim priority of place in the discussion of timely subjects. The quantities of bulbous stock now handled by nearly every one engaged in floricultural pursuits are much in excess of anything attempted in this line some few years ago. Vast numbers of various species, and in hundreds of varieties, annually pass through the deftly working fingers of florists, and whatever profits are realized in their culture must amount to a pretty good sized sum. While almost all of the early received kinds are now in the ground, some of this stock already well forward in growth, very much in the way of planting has yet to be done, and a great deal of the grower's attention will be required in the caretaking of this particular kind of stock, in the mastering of the more important details in its culture, on which a satisfactory finish chiefly depends.

Lilies.

There is now hardly any period in all the year when lilies appear out of season. Varieties now foremost as florists' forcing sorts, closely follow one another, and their season of flowering is, by the aid of fire heat and cold storage, made to extend from one end of the year to the other. Intermissions between crops, if there are any at all, are brief. At present the early started Lilium Harrisii, in closely graded lots, occupies considerable bench room in many greenhouse establishments, all intended for the early Winter and holiday trade. Most of this stock will be out of the way by the beginning of the new year, a great part of it much sooner. Meanwhile watchful care is necessary. At this season with its occasional over-heated bright days necessitating excessive ventilation, followed by pretty cold nights and hard firing, it becomes wellnigh impossible to maintain that degree of immutable steadiness in temperature which is one of the chief essentials in lily forcing. The heat for this early stock should not fall below 60 nor rise much above 65 degrees. Any great deviation or excess in either direction greatly favors an exhibition of all the bad traits hidden in the bulbs of Bermuda lilies. It also augments the trouble with greenfly, usually called forth by the first fire heat. The use of nicotine, tobacco dust or stems in regular fumigation, and of tobacco tea for spots not touched by the fumes, will alleviate the nuisance. These early forced lilies care little for a feeding with liquid fertilizer of any kind, but in the matter of watering and sprinkling they require close watching in order to be just right as to their exact requirements.

The later arrivals in lily bulbs make an immediate planting necessary, if wanted for a Midwinter and early Spring trade. They can all remain in outdoor frames until some visible headway in root formation has been made. Under a covering of several inches of soil or decayed manure, with the frames closed and protected against hard freezing, should this become needful, they will do better there than in any greenhouse. The forcing of Lilium longiflorum and L. candidum, intended for this season's Easter, should not begin later than December 15. Lilium auratum, L. speciosum and such sorts are planted at any time from February until late in the Spring.

French Bulbs.

Many other good things for florists in the bulb line besides Roman hyacinths and Paper White narcissi come from the bulb fields of France and Italy. But these two varieties take a prominent place among bulbs extensively forced, easy of culture and rapidly converted into ready cash. It takes barely twelve weeks from the time Roman hyacinths are planted until their flowers are ready for marketing and it is only one third of this time, three or four weeks, when they require bench room and fire heat. Their culture as forcing stock is a smooth-running, sure-going affair. There are no diseases or insects to fight. In late seasons the flowers have sold fairly well, at prices which meant a little more than the doubling of the money expended for the bulbs. The same may be said of the Paper White narcissi. Though it may take a little longer to bring their flower spikes to a perfect finish by a prolonged stand in a cool and well-lighted greenhouse, this is fully made good by the higher price obtainable for such stock.

All bulbs of this class that were boxed and buried as soon as received, if not already housed should now be taken in. They will, by this time, be well rooted, showing advancing top growth and the low nestling embryo flowers. If in that condition, forcing may begin at any time, shielding for a day or two this waxy white crown growth against the direct rays of a bright Autumn sun, until it has turned to a natural green. Roman hyacinths force well in a warm atmosphere and on a darkened bench with a brisk and steady bottom heat, requiring lots of water for the roots and overhead. Narcissi produce finer spikes under a less severe course of forcing.

Dutch Bulbs.

The planting of Holland grown bulbs is now in full swing. Their number, as annually imported and made use of for forcing, for ordinary pot culture and for outdoor plantings, is astonishingly great. It is this class of bulbs more than any other which suffers least by being kept in a dry state and out of ground for a considerable length of time, some varieties even gaining in value by thus attaining complete maturity. The experience of observant growers confirms the truth of this statement. Very often it happens that a portion of the main bulk in Dutch hyacinths, or tulips intended for the Spring trade, cannot for the lack of time or other reasons be attended to by the planter until a time in late Fall which seemed hopelessly beyond the proper period when these bulbs should be planted. But in most cases of this kind they proved the best and most easily managed lot. So also will hardy bulbs of all kinds, planted in open beds and borders quite late in the Fall, make a finer show in the Spring than those planted much earlier. All this goes to show that there is yet plenty of time for the potting up, boxing and outdoor planting of Dutch bulbs.

Hyacinths, daffodils and other suitable varieties of narcissi, tulips, snowdrops, crocus, anemones, scillas and some other things of minor importance but good for pots or shallow dishes, should be planted in the richest of thoroughly composted earth, while tulips and the various kinds of bulbs intended for forcing in early Spring, and usually grown in trays or boxes for their flowers alone, will do fairly well in any good grade of potting soil. Thoroughly watered after being planted, buried under four inches of fresh soil, protected against a solid freezing up, they can remain out of doors until rooted and wanted for forcing.

Bulb Forcing as a Specialty.

There are now many growers who devote a larg part of their time, space and attention to the forcing of bulbs, some of them doing little else. They handle bulbs of all kinds and in incredible quantities, carloads of them, and just at this season they are the busiest people on earth. The unpacking, assorting and planting of so many thousands of bulbs of one or the other species, this and that variety, is no small matter, and it may well be believed that thoughtful foresight in the planning, thorough and timely preparations and system, order and dispatch in coping with the amount of work involved, are expedients as reliably serviceable, in this as in any other branch of gardening conducted on a large scale. The soil used in potting or boxing the many different kinds of bulbs usually all taken from one great pile is a nice friable loam, liberally enriched with old, thoroughly decomposed stable manure. It has undergone careful preparation some time before it is used, and on some places it is piled up under some shed-like, airy structure while other large bulb growers do all their planting in the open air with the compost heap at their elbow. A goodly number of spacious cold frames are conveniently near, but most of the stock, after being planted, is heeled in where the garden land has been cleared for the purpose. A set of greenhouses especially fitted up for the growing d forcing of bulbs is sometimes a aspicuous feature on places devoted this specialty, but more often any range of glass structures is made to swer the purpose Although green-uses, to be suitable for this work, ed not be of the most improved dern designing, they must neverthe-s be equipped with ample means for ntilation and an efficient, reliable ating apparatus, the system so ar-nged as to enable the grower under conditions of weather to maintain proper degree of temperature for differing kinds under forcing in any rt of the range. Well-working cold rage facilities, forming a part of ch an establishment, would then me very near to making the outfit mplete.

As to the profits in the mass culture bulbous flowers and flowering plants cannot speak from actual experience. have done my rightful share in the owing and forcing of bulbs, but, as t, have never made this a sweeping, -absorbing industry. While the av-age carnationist or rose grower is spected of being much given to either mplaining or boasting whenever pro-s are discussed, the bulbist, or the lbarian, whichever may be right, re-ains calm and serenely quiet when this bject is broached, and is very reluc-nt in holding forth graspable figures. t it is tolerably certain that the net ofits realized in working this parti-ar field of commercial floriculture mpare favorably with the clear earn-gs from other lines. It is evident at on the finding of outlets for the ished product, of means and ways to spose of it most profitably, and on ving it ready when the demand is eatest success in great part depends. a wisest circumspection in the plan-ng for a coming season's activity in is peculiar line does not prevent an casional loss, a portion of the stock ing to ruin now and then, or being sposed of at prices leaving no ap-eciable profit; but such losses are ually fully made good by some grand t with this or that variety, and the m total of returns furnishes little use for discouragement.

Bulbs for Outdoor Effects.

Taking orders for the laying out and aking of bulb beds is a line of busi-ss which shoould be more pushed by rists. It is a business very far om being overdone. There is, as yet, competition to fight and no necessity r the cutting of prices. It is now ne to plant the bulbs. Most of the ople who want bulb beds made have eir own ideas as to what kind would ove most effective and what sort of a sign would best fit their particular se and place. Very often they evince better taste in these matters than any a gardener; sometimes they don't. either case, I have found it is wis-to let them have their way, as long the varieties determined upon can be d. It is quite another thing—much ore to the liking of the good gardener when the designing and formulating a bed is left entirely to him. It is en when the opportunity is his to ow what can be done with hardy bulbs outdoor plantings, the difference be-reen possible real effect with care-lly selected varieties and imagined possible splendors with a lot of in-ngruous sorts. When planning these ds, or when offering hints and sug-estions to people who need and ask r advice, it is well to bear in mind at several small beds of simple form ill always make a better showing an one unusually large one; that beds borders of intricate and elaborate sign often fail to come up to expec-tions; that with a few well chosen rieties finer, more pleasing effects e obtained than with many; that rong contrasts in color should be but aringly employed; and that all the rieties made use of in carrying out y one design should be very near one ight and should flower simultane-usly.

FRED W. TIMME.

Hydrangea Otaksa.

(65) I have in the ground 200 Hydrangea otaksa, with two to eight branches. I propose to winter them in a cool cellar, ground floor. Ought the leaves to fall before I take them in? Will a frost causing the leaves to drop injure flowering buds? Will they need water crowded close on cellar floor? Please answer through the indispensable Florists' Exchange—the best in the world. J. B. T.
N. J.

—We would take the hydrangeas into the cellar before they got touched with frost, if possible, although they should be left outdoors just as long as can be done without injury. But do not wait until a frost comes sufficiently hard to make them drop their leaves. Through the Winter they should be looked over occasionally, and as the leaves fall, these should be cleared away. While they should not need any water while stored in the cellar, at the same time, if the cellar happens to be a very dry one and it was seen during the Winter that some of the plants were getting dry enough so that the wood was shriveling, it would be advisable in such a case to give a little water occasionally. Should the cellar have a dirt floor, we do not think it would be necessary to give the plants any water from the time they are put in until they are taken out in the Spring.

Sow Bugs.

(66) Kindly tell me what I can do to exterminate the sow bug that is in my violets and maidenhair fern. This bug seems to get down into the heart of the plant and eat it out. It is a small grey creature that rolls up in a ball upon being disturbed.
Virginia. L. G. B.

—To exterminate the sow bug, we would first suggest that all the decayed woodwork throughout the benches be taken out and replaced with new, and that every part of the greenhouse, both under the benches and along the side walls, have a thorough cleaning. After a thorough clean-up has been given, commence systematically to poison the sow bugs, either by sprinkling Slug Shot all over the benches, or by mixing arsenic with bran and laying little heaps here and there all over the surface of the benches, cleaning away the bran and renewing with fresh every few days. If this practice is continued faithfully, the sow bugs can be gotten rid of, provided, of course, the house is kept perfectly clean otherwise.

Gall Fly on Violets.

(67) Can you give me any information that will help me get rid of gall fly on violets? I have used hydrocyanic acid gas, also smoking with tobacco, but without any success.
New Jersey. W. C. P.

—Professor Galloway, in his book on Commercial Violet Culture, suggests the following remedy: "Air-slacked lime thrown into the crown will be found beneficial. It should be thrown into the plant with considerable force and plenty should be allowed to reach the soil. Following this practice and giving the best cultural conditions possible, such as allowing plenty of air and stirring the soil, is about all that can be suggested in the line of treatment."

Roses Refusing to Grow.

(68) We have taken the liberty of sending you by express to-day a sample of rose plants and a small quantity of soil in which these plants have been grown. These roses have acted so queerly that our grower is unable to tell why they refuse to grow, and we are curious to ascertain the reason. You have always been good enough to answer your correspondents with reference to matters of this kind, and we shall appreciate it if you investigate the sample of soil and rose plants carefully and diagnose the case if possible. The house in which these roses are planted is 400x20 feet. The four benches have all had the same soil put in them at the same time. Probably half the roses in the house located at different positions have done very well, yet the other half, or approximately so, have not done anything at all. When first put out these plants were healthy and began to grow, but in a very short time the leaves would get crisp and finally the plant would die. Some few of them did not grow at all, but the roots remained just as they were planted in the beds. In so far as we know, the roses have been properly treated, but somehow they do not grow. Any information that you can give us will be very much appreciated. N. L.

—The rose plants sent for examination show plainly that they are being slowly starved to death for want of food; and after closely examining the soil in which it is being attempted to grow them, we are at a loss to understand why some of the plants in the house are doing very well, as the letter states. It is only a question of a short time, however, when those that are seemingly doing well will succumb for want of food, as the soil in which they are planted will never grow roses, neither under glass nor out of doors. It does not require a chemical analysis to see that the soil is utterly unadapted for roses; it seems to be composed entirely of red clay and old garden soil, with not a particle of fibre in it, and roses will not push their roots into such a combination of material. The only remedy we could suggest at this time would be to procure fresh soil from the top of some old pasture, first paring off a thin sod, and refill the house, transplanting such plants into the new soil as seem to be so far in good health. If suitable young stock could not be procured so late in the season for filling in the vacant space, we would plant it to some other crop.

CROTONS FOR NAME.—J. R. Nahant.—We herewith give names of all of the crotons submitted by you, excepting No. 2, which we are unable to identify. It is, however, with the long list of crotons that we now grow, difficult to name positively the variety from a single leaf, and we should not like to say definitely that the names given are correct. The Robert Craig Company of Philadelphia have made a specialty of crotons for some years, and we would suggest that you submit a set of the foliage to them. We believe that they are more competent to identify this plant than we are. The names follow: (1), Baron J. H. Rothschild; (2), do not know; (3), Queen Victoria; (4), Undulatum; (5), Fascination; (6), Mortii; (7), Charmer.

HENRY A. DREER, INC.

Guayule.

Please ask our horticultural brethren for either generic name (Latin), photo, drawing, or any other details about "guayule." This is a hardy bush, which grows in the Mexican State of Coahuila (capital Saltillo). It will only grow where cactus or yucca grows. By accident it has been found that this weed can be used in the manufacture of rubber, hence its commercial value which is $80 per ton. Possibly it may grow in this country—South Africa.

INQUIRER.

Powderette.

We have an inquiry for manure Powderette. Can anyone inform us who is the manufacturer of same? No one seems to offer it, therefore we think it is not on the market any more.

B. BROS.

"C" is respectfully reminded that no attention is paid by The Florists' Exchange to anonymous inquiries. The name and address of our correspondents should be forwarded with all questions, not necessarily for publication, but as an evidence of good faith.

LIST OF ADVERTISERS

INDEX TO STOCK ADVERTISED

Contents.

New York.

News of the Week.

H. Bradbury, South Orange, N. J., spent a few hours in town one day this week. Mr. Bradbury in spite of his eighty-six years, was hale and hearty and a most interesting conversationalist. Coming from England fifty-four years ago he established his nursery and greenhouses at South Orange, and is still personally interested in their management. Before coming to the United States, Mr. Bradbury was gardener to the Mayor of Sheffield, Yorkshire, England, and has many interesting reminiscences of the gardeners' profession as it was conducted at that time.

The auction sales of William Elliott & Sons, Fulton street, are proving of much interest to local buyers these days, the demand for ferns and decorative plants being gradually on the increase.

Robert Angus, who several years ago was gardener for Major Hopkins, Tarrytown, N. Y., and later held a gardening position in Connecticut, is again in the Tarrytown district, commencing the first of the month as superintendent of the Jos. Eastman estate, lately made vacant by the resignation of Wm. Scott, who with his brother, J. T. Scott, has joined the commercial ranks as florists and nurserymen at Elmsford, N. Y.

Wm. Griffen, who for some time has been with Alex McConnell, retail florist, the Arcade building, Fifth avenue, will, on November 1 take charge of the estate of George Gould at Lakewood, N. J., as superintendent.

A. L. Marshall, recently with J. D. Crimmins, Noroton, Conn., has gone to Katonah, N. Y., to take charge of the Jay farm. Mr. Marshall assumed his new position on the 16th inst.

The fifth annual exhibition of the United Bay Shore Horticultural Society will be held at the Carlton Opera House, Bay Shore, L. I., on Thursday, Friday and Saturday, November 1, 2 and 3. It is a pleasure to note that the Bay Shore and Suffolk County Horticultural Associations have been united under the above title, and the combination is sure to result in a fine exhibition, one that it will no doubt be a pleasure to visit, as the membership of these combined societies practically includes all of the gardeners employed on the estates between Patchogue and Babylon, L. I.

The Bronx Arboretum and Rosarium, with office and show grounds at 967 East One hundred and sixty-sixth street, is a new horticultural establishment. It is the intention of the society to have an exhibition of the products of American and European growers of hardy plants. The management, with F. Von Hoffman, landscape architect, St. James building, as chairman, intend to hold a rose and peony exhibition in the Spring of 1908, at which time they expect that the plants already set out in their pots will have reached sufficient development for show purposes.

A. E. Covell, of Hampton Meadows, R. I., together with Mrs. Covell, were visitors in town this week. John Walker, Youngstown, O., was also a visitor.

Malcolm McRorie of Orange, N. J., with Mrs. McRorie, have just returned from a two month's pleasure trip spent in Scotland.

The J. M. Hodgson Company of Fifty-sixth street and Fifth avenue, we are informed, has discontinued its retail flower business.

William R. Smith, superintendent of the Botanic Gardens, Washington, D. C., was likewise a visitor this week. He was accompanied by Mr. Thomson, of Edinburgh, assistant librarian of the Carnegie system of libraries in Scotland, who was on his way home after a stay of several weeks in Washington, during which time he was engaged in cataloguing Mr. Smith's collection of Burnsiana, probably now the largest in the world. This catalogue will be printed and will form a most interesting document.

Benjamin Hammond, Fishkill-on-Hudson, N. Y., is contributing interesting letters to a local newspaper, giving an account of his Canadian trip. He mentions having spent a pleasant day examining the Detroit park and boulevard system, accompanied by Park Commissioner Breitmeyer, Superintendent Dilger and City Forester Hunter of that city.

On and after December 1, 1906, John Scheepers will be permanently located at 2-6 Old Slip. Mr. Scheepers will continue to travel, and will also be assisted by two salesmen, both Hollanders, well acquainted with the bulb business. We regret to state that Mrs. Scheepers is at present in the hospital, where she has just undergone a very painful operation.

P.T. Devoy, Poughkeepsie, N. Y., has taken over the property of his late father, and will continue the business under the title Thomas Devoy's Son.

Rochester, N. Y

News and Trade Items.

The cut flower market here is very encouraging, everything available being used up. There is a decided shortage in the better grade of roses, prices for which are from $6 to 8 for top grades, others according to quality, and variety. Carnations are good, and in fair demand, although perhaps now, and for the next few weeks, the Autumn Queen will take first place in supplying the demand. Good shipments of chrysanthemums of varieties Glory of the Pacific, Pink and White Ivory, have been received, the best of which bring 15 cents for single stem flowers. Carnations realize $2 to $3 a 100.

Among the growers all is activity preparing for Winter; several of them are anticipating the letting of contracts for new additions next Spring.

The firm of E. H. Rueston Company have a scarlet seedling, which as viewed by your scribe, has all the qualifications necessary for a fine marketable carnation. At this place may be seen a nice bench of Enchantress, the same being old plants kept over from last year. Regular fertilizing is given; and red spider kept in check with the aid of a spraying machine, used at frequent periods, and liquid applied by means of compressed air. This is very effective, as was evident by the absence of that pest.

The new greenhouse of Ed. Bausch, being constructed by the Lord & Burnham Company is nearing completion, as are also the alterations to the houses of Hiram Sibley.

That it pays to get out and see what other men in the business are doing, is a fact that Geo. Hart can speak of; he having just returned from a visit to New York, after spending three days among the commission men of that city. Cordiality on every hand is expressed, and business methods are found to be ahead of anything ever attempted here. COCKNEY.

Notes on Decorative Foliage Plants.

DRACÆNAS are not in such con- ant demand as Pandanus Veitchii r various reasons, chief among em being the fact that they are not enduring as pandanus; and per- ps a secondary reason is, that for- erly dracænas were scarcer, espe- ally the choice varieties of high lor, because of the supposed diffi- ilty attending their propagation and ter culture. When it is considered w profitable a batch of well colored racæna terminalis of Dracæna Lord 'olseley would be to a grower around hristmas, and that he might have own them had he known there was othing exceptionally difficult in the dertaking, I may be doing some one service by stating that from experi- ice I have found dracænas of the rieties mentioned exceedingly easy culture and multiplication.

Plants can be grown to a size fit- ng 6-inch pots and ready for mar- t in about fifteen months from cut- ngs taken from portions of canes, aced in sand, leaf mold or moss, er heat; or from cuttings made om the fleshy portion of the roots old plants. In either case, when e eyes have sprouted and grown to height of 3½ or 4 inches, these owths should be taken off with a arp knife and immediately insert- in sand in the propagating bench, here they will root freely. Very ten when at work taking these cut- ngs off it will be noticed that roots uld be taken with them, and if e growths are short and have aves formed, they may be potted ithout resorting to rerooting. But r the bulk of the stock it will be und more satisfactory to sever em from the old stems, or roots, d put them in sand to root. After e cuttings are rooted they should potted into small pots, in a com- st of fibrous loam two-thirds, and e other third between leaf mold d sand. Subsequent pottings, ich should take place whenever e plants have filled the pots with ots, will require to be done from compost having in it less leaf mold d sand, and in place thereof well- tted manure and a little bone meal. e latter ingredient is especially de- able for the last potting. When e plants are growing rapidly they e of necessity soft and, in conse- ence, should not be exposed to the ll light of the sun; but in order bring out all they are capable of the matter of color they will have be brought into light gradually. A culiar point about the culture of acænas is, that no matter how high e temperature can be kept in the use where they are, they will not ow luxuriantly without bottom at; whereas if there is bottom heat e temperature of the house can ll as low as 50 degrees without jury to the plants. However, they rive much better in a temperature 65 to 70 degrees along with bottom at. The atmosphere should be pt very moist and the plants sy- nged frequently with a very fine ray; the syringing should be done om underneath the foliage.

Old plants remaining unsold will kely lose their bottom leaves but ll retain the makings of good ants; in case larger specimens are anted it may pay to moss some of ese, pursuing the same methods th them as with rubber plants, hen the same results are desired.

Dracæna Godseffiana is distinctly fferent from all the other varieties they are grown with us, in that is hard-wooded and branching, re- mbling somewhat a well colored ucuba japonica, but much more aceful and attractive. This variety easily propagated from cuttings of ther hard or half ripened wood. nall plants of this variety are very eful and ornamental for filling shes, while large plants are very fective as specimens for house or nservatory decorations.

PHYLLANTHUS VAR. ROSEA ICTA is a plant that seems to be serving of more attention from owers and florists than it has here- fore received. Considering that it ill thrive well outdoors in Summer, may be described as a half-hardy rub, of a loose graceful habit, with aves beautifully mottled with pink, d, white, and green, and when ven a little extra care and nourishment five and sometimes eight inches of every growth in their entirety are a brilliant combination of red and pink. The plants are propagated easily from almost any part of the wood. They require good rich soil and abundance of water. When plants of this variety of phyllanthus have attained a height of three feet or more they are invaluable to florists for mixing in with palms when something is needed to give color to the decoration without detracting from its gracefulness. The phyllanthus instead of detracting will by its use add a considerable degree of gracefulness to any kind of decoration where grouping is resorted to. This is also one of the most ornamental shrubs for conservatory or greenhouse decoration. It is of easy culture and very enduring.

PANDANUS VEITCHII.—In the eyes of those who purchase plants for the ornamentation of their homes there is no species more popular nor more deserving of popularity than Pandanus Veitchii, with the possible exception of palms. The uses to which Pandanus Veitchii are put are almost innumerable, and wherever used they are bright and attractive. Small plants are more in demand than those in what is known as the specimen stage, because during the Winter there is a constant call for baskets and other kinds of receptacles to be filled in great part with Pandanus Veitchii out of small pots. In growing a stock for medium size plants care should be taken to select short cuttings that have leaves formed at the base, in appearance much the same as those on a fully developed plant, because plants from such cuttings will when rooted and potted look like little specimens, whereas, on the other hand, if those lanky suckers are used as cuttings for stock it will be a much longer time before they are in any way shapely. In fact, I hardly think they ever make stocky plants with properly formed leaves down to the rim of the pot. Whenever bottom heat is available the small suckers may be severed from the old plants and placed in sand where they will root quickly. After they are rooted they should be potted in as small pots as will be found practicable; good fibrous loam, broken up (not sifted), with a little well-rotted manure mixed in it, answers their requirements. Pandanus require a temperature ranging from 60 to 70 degrees, and when growing vigorously need a good deal of water, especially in Summer; but in Winter great care has to be exercised in watering, because overwatering causes the foliage to lose color, and sometimes when the plants are persistently overwatered they collapse entirely—a common occurrence in the experience of purchasers very soon after the plants come into their possession. With reference to that matter I think it is the duty of dealers to caution customers not to overwater such plants, believing as I do that it would eventually be to their interests that the plants should live at least for a reasonable time after leaving their hands. Pandanus stand much more sunlight and thrive better in consequence of its effect than many growers permit them to have. Pandanus Veitchii in pots from 3½ to 6 inches are seldom found overstocking the market, and it pays to grow them well.

D. M.

FOUNDED IN 1888

THE FLORISTS' EXCHANGE

A Weekly Medium of Interchange for Florists, Nurserymen Seedsmen and the Trade in general

Exclusively a Trade Paper.

Entered at New York Post Office as Second Class Matter

Published EVERY SATURDAY by

A. T. DE LA MARE PTG. AND PUB. CO. LTD.

2, 4, 6 and 8 Duane Street,

P. O. Box 1697. Telephone 3765 John. NEW YORK.

CHICAGO OFFICE: 127 East Berwyn Avenue.

ILLUSTRATIONS.

Electrotypes of the illustrations used in this paper can usually be supplied by the publishers. Price on application.

YEARLY SUBSCRIPTIONS.

United States, Canada, and Mexico, $1.00. Foreign countries in postal union, $2.50. Payable in advance. Remit by Express Money Order Draft on New York. Post Office Money Order or Registered Letter.

The address label indicates the date when subscription expires and is our only receipt therefore.

REGISTERED CABLE ADDRESS:
Florex, New York.

ADVERTISING RATES.

One-half inch, 75c.; ¾-inch, $1.00; 1-inch, $1.25, special positions extra. Send for Rate Card showing discount of 10c., 15c., 25c., or 35c., per inch on continuous advertising. For rates on Wants, etc., see column for Classified Advertisements.

Copy must reach this office 12 o'clock Wednesday to secure insertion in issue of following Saturday.

Orders from unknown parties must be accompanied with cash or satisfactory references.

The Century Plant and Some other Plants of the Dry Country.

The third lecture in the popular Fall course offered by the Field Museum of Natural History was delivered last Saturday in Fullerton Memorial Hall at the Art Institute, Chicago, by Professor William Trelease, whose subject was "The Century Plant, and Some other Plants of the Dry Country." Dr Trelease, who is director of the Missouri Botanical Garden, at St. Louis, has long been engaged in a study of agave and its relatives, and in addition to having under his charge one of the largest and best existing collections of these plants, he has repeatedly visited the principal gardens of Italy and other European countries where they are grown, and has traveled extensively in the mountains of Mexico and Central America, where they are at home, for the special purpose of studying them. His lecture was illustrated by a large series of pictures taken in the course of his travels, supplemented by copies of the first pictures of the century plant, which were published in 1576 and 1588, and other views, among which were shown some of the beautiful plants that have been popular in gardens.

The agaves, he said, range all the way from the queer little Agave pumila, known only as a pot-grown plant with leaves about an inch long, to the giant pulque maguey that weighs several tons and has leaves stiff enough to bear a man's weight.

The lecture was popular rather than technical, though there was a logical thread of botanical information running through it; and the economic value of the plants for the production of the usual fermented drink of the Mexicans (pulque) and their principal distilled liquor (mezcal or tequila), and as a source of the great Mexican fiber industries in the production of sisal grass or henequen and Tampico fiber or ixtle, was treated at greater length than any other topic of the subject, as being most closely connected with the purposes of the museum.

Perhaps the most striking statements made were that the "bamboo" of the Bahamas, which is an agave that must have been seen by the discoverers of the New World in 1492, is still without a published scientific description or a tenable botanical name; and that the real century plant, Agave americana, which is the best known of all the agaves and might be supposed to be one of the commonest Mexican plants, is not known to-day as a wild plant anywhere except around the Mediterranean, where it is extensively established as an introduced plant, and as an evident local escape from cultivation in a few other localities.

Enthusiasm of Exhibitors at Boston Shows Declining.

For many years the exhibitions of the Massachusetts Horticultural Society, Boston, Mass., have taken a justly foremost place among the shows held in the United States. The gardeners of the locality have vied with each other in the production of plants and flowers, with the result that probably nowhere else in America has the standard of perfection stood so high as at Boston. It is therefore with some surprise and a tinge of regret that we read the report of Chairman Arthur H. Fewkes of the Committe on Plants and Flowers of the Massachusetts Horticultural Society for the year 1905, appearing in Part II of the Transactions of that body for the year named, recently issued. In that report Mr. Fewkes says:

"It must be admitted that the enthusiasm displayed some years ago has been steadily declining, this being particularly noticeable at the large exhibitions in the classes calling for displays of decorative plants. In this connection great credit should be given the Harvard Botanic Garden for the magnificent displays made at different times by Robert Cameron, the superintendent, not only for the excellence of the specimens shown but also for the interest manifested in the success of our exhibitions. In fact if we had not been favored with these displays several of our shows would have been failures, almost, through lack of competition.

"The decline of interest has been, perhaps, most apparent in the displays of trained chrysanthemum plants; one by one the prominent growers have dropped out after reaching the goal of first prize, until those who still keep up the race are few indeed.

"There seems to be a popular demand for plants grown in a more natural way, having in view the great artistic decorative capabilities of the plant, but it is seldom indeed that the grower develops the artistic sense to the same degree that he does the ability to grow his plants well, and it is extremely doubtful if satisfactory results will be attained in this direction unless some extraordinary means are adopted to secure them.

"The chrysanthemum is unique in the position it holds and it practically has no rivals at the time it is at its best. The before mentioned decline of interest in it, from the point of view of the public, is largely due to rebellion against a mistaken conception on the part of the grower of what goes to make up a beautiful plant. With this should be recognized the fact that the public is annually satiated by the almost overwhelming displays of chrysanthemum flowers of the finest quality seen on every hand in store windows and on street corners during the chrysanthemum season.

"When some genius arises endowed with the necessary artistic skill for arrangement, coupled with the ability to grow the plants in a suitable manner for the purpose, and backed by ample means or sure prospect of very liberal prizes, then we shall have chrysanthemum shows which will be a revelation and stop the cry of monotony and sameness so often heard in connection with these shows.

"Here is an opportunity for some individual or individuals, abundantly supplied with this world's goods, to come forward and offer, fully a year in advance, one or more prizes sufficiently large to make it an object for growers to seriously consider the artistic side of the matter and break away from the stereotyped character of these shows as seen today.

"With restrictions sufficient to secure the object sought, it would make our chrysanthemum exhibitions educational as well as a paying proposition for the society.

"While there is a decrease of interest in the direction indicated there is an increase in others, notably the carnation, the peony, and the dahlia. Hardy roses barely hold their own although the introduction of the new Rambler class is doing much to keep up the interest. These with the hybrid teas and rugosa hybrids should be given careful attention, for the most important improvements in the rose are being made in these classes.

"The February show of carnations has become a very important one both to the grower and the public, for it is at this season that the finest exhibits can be made and at a time when the public is most interested in them.

"At the March show the interest seems to be changing considerably and where a few years ago the Dutch bulbs formed the center of attraction, they are now secondary and have given place to such things as orchids, cyclamens, cinerarias, roses, and plants grown for Easter decorations.

"The sweet pea has increased in popularity from year to year and has now reached a point where a special exhibition is necessary to do it justice.

"The peony and dahlia, both old-time favorites, but for many years almost forgotten, have through their inherent beauty and worth forced themselves to the front, until our peony shows have eclipsed the rose shows and the dahlia has attained a new beauty which entitles it to the first place in our Autumn exhibitions.

"A wise course to follow, it seems to us, would be to exploit these flowers to their fullest extent. They are the flowers in which the general public is most interested and which are attracting a corresponding commercial interest. We would include the rose in this category, for although the interest in it seems not to be as pronounced as it was a few years ago, it is only dormant and needs but little to arouse it to its old-time life and energy."

The tenor of the remarks of Mr. Fewkes tends to create the thought that the commercial spirit is largely dominating the Boston shows; that the displays of classes of stock which can be sold in large numbers to the public either as plants or cut flowers, are the most successful, while on the other hand, as in the cases of decorative plants and trained chrysanthemum plants, and to some extent roses of certain kinds, the enthusiasm of exhibitors is gradually but surely waning. It would seem, therefore, that the society, in order to counteract this decline of interest, must make it an object, more so than is now presented, in the way of premiums to bring out displays that are being neglected; and Mr. Fewkes does well in calling attention to the necessity of offering more liberal prizes for these exhibits.

There is also food for thought presented in the report of Mr. Fewkes regarding the artistic, or rather the inartistic side of the trained chrysanthemum plant. Our exhibitions in this respect annually present a most monotonous appearance, and, in many cases, the stakes used in the training process of the plants, obtruding themselves so pronouncedly on the examining visitor, add anything but a charm to the completed creation. That "breaks" from the conventional exhibit of trained chrysanthemum plants create interest and comment has been made manifest at several shows where such subjects as the chrysanthemum Shower of Gold, with its telling shower effect, has been placed on view. We feel sure a little more brain work on the part of our plantsmen is only needed to bring forth new ideas in chrysanthemum plant training; and to that end sufficient inducement in the way of prizes should be held forth by flower show managers.

Not only is improvement necessary in the artistic character of the plants themselves, but also in their arrangement in the exhibition hall. The very sameness in the appearance of the tout ensemble at a flower show, year after year, is palling on the visitor, and anything but conducive to increased attendance. Our style of exhibiting seems to have got into a rut, that speaks not too well for the originality of those in charge, and needs emendation. Probably this remedy might be brought about were our retail florists to take a hand, more than they do now, in the lay out and arrangement. Or, perhaps, some trained landscape gardener in charge of such work could introduce reforms or innovations that would tend to betterment all round. And it might here be added that natural as against spectacular effects are always the most desirable.

There is a passage in Mr. Fewkes's report that is particularly discouraging. He says, touching on the displays of trained chrysanthemum plants: "One by one the prominent growers have dropped out after reaching the goal of first prize, until those who still keep up the race are few indeed." We are sorry to read these words. While we are aware that the cultivation of plants of the character named, to their highest perfection, requires lots of greenhouse space and a considerable degree of skill, if the gardener's employer presents no objection to a continuation of the culture, the craftsman should not, for the sake of the exhibition itself, if for nothing else, be satisfied to rest on his laurels and cease to compete. Such a spirit displays an indifference—and conceit—anything but commendable. One never knows what will happen the next time at a flower show, and he proves himself the true sportsman who is willing at all times to enter the arena against any and all comers to defend his claim to the championship, and who never lies down under defeat.

It is unfortunate, too, we think that the old-time rivalry for the mere sake of winning laurels is passing away, not only in Boston but in other cities as well; and that the dollar and not the honor that accompanies award, and pride in one's products are the modern dominating factors in the matter of exhibiting at flower shows. But this spirit is in consonance with that of the age in which we live, and must be tolerated, nay even catered to, until such times as resulting glory will displace present greed, and an honest pride in his profession and the satisfaction that springs from a public display of its grand achievements, shall be the forces impelling the flower show exhibitor. Hasten that day.

The Chicago Flower Show.

The final list of premiums offered by the Chrysanthemum Society of America and the Horticultural Society of Chicago at the forthcoming show, to be held in the Coliseum Building, Chicago, November 6 to 11, inclusive, has ben issued. The first day of the exhibition will be devoted to displays of cut flowers of chrysanthemums with prizes, in the respective classes, ranging from $3 to $50, the latter for 100 blooms in the various specified colors; also to chrysanthemum plants, for which premiums of from $5 to $50 will be awarded, and miscellaneous plants, which are likewise well cared for in the way of prizes.

On the second day orchids and roses will be the features, liberal premiums being offered. For best 100 American Beauty, $100, $75, $50, and $25 are to be given. Silver cups, valued at $25, $15, and $10, are to be awarded for 12 blooms of a new rose never exhibited in this country previous to this season.

The third day will be carnation day, and premiums of $5 and $3 are offered for 50 blooms of the varieties enumerated in white, red, crimson, pink, striped or stained, yellow and new sorts. Special prizes of $12, $7 and $4 are to be given in the 100 classes. Violets, lily of the valley, and floral arrangements will also be shown on this day.

The fourth day will be given up to exhibits by private gardeners; also to cut roses, and seedlings and sports of carnations and chrysanthemums, the usual premiums, including a sweepstakes prize (a silver cup, value $25) being offered for best seedling carnation and best seedling chrysanthemum respectively.

On the fifth day there will be more floral arrangements; and a competition for prizes of $15 and $10, offered by Benjamin Hammond, secretary of The American Rose Society, for the exhibit of cut flowers presenting the best appearance throughout the exhibition, the exhibitor to be permitted to renew and rearrange his flowers daily.

Copies of the premium list may be obtained by addressing W. N. Rudd, secretary, 1411 First National Bank Building, Chicago.

OUR READERS' VIEWS

Stove vs. Greenhouse Plants.

Editor Florists' Exchange:

I am pleased to see the question of "stove plants" is still very much alive to discussion, and I should like to see gardeners and others interested in the growing of these beautiful plants express their views thereon through the columns of this paper.

At the last convention of the S. A. F. O. H. in Dayton, O., at which were present such prominent men and plantsmen as Robert Craig, E. V. Hallock, Professor Irish, W. J. Stewart, C. W. Turnley and A. Wintzer, this important question was discussed, and after pondering over it for some considerable time it was laid over as being a subject of too delicate a nature to settle without having more time for consideration.

This same question was submitted for discussion at the October meeting of the New York Florists' Club and was disposed of after a short time in a business-like manner. The club has proposed to drop the word "stove" and substitute the word "greenhouse" for all plants grown under glass.

Of course, this may be all right from a commercial, but not from a horticultural point of view. It may suit the dealer in florists' supplies, the seedsmen, the wholesale commission men or the storekeepers, for it matters not to them what they sell, whether it is a plant or a flower grown in an ordinary greenhouse or in a hot-house with a temperature of 80 degrees or over, or whether it comes from the north pole, as long as they can sell it and make a profit. But to a bona-fide gardener, a horticulturist, a lover of plants and nature, and to horticultural societies, it is a question of great importance.

Long before our time the term "stove plants" was in existence and was used all through the European countries; designating, as far as my knowledge goes, plants that are grown in a greenhouse intended for them, with a high temperature of 75 degrees or over, and with plenty of moisture; or, in other words, it is a greenhouse specialty constructed to imitate as near as possible the climatic conditions of tropical countries. In these the plants are grown and developed in their natural beauty, the same as we find them in their native haunts, which cannot be accomplished in an ordinary greenhouse temperature.

It is true, as has been suggested, that crotons, caladiums and other tropical plants can be bedded out here in the Summer with much satisfaction. This is on account of our tropical-like Summer. Nevertheless, when the sun has turned his face from us and looks over the other side of the globe, and when the days are getting short and cold, these plants will have to be taken up, and in order to be able to preserve their natural beauty during Winter and Spring, we must give them the "stove" house temperature, otherwise they will make a poor looking showing. They are therefore "stove" plants and not bedding nor ordinary greenhouse plants; the fact that they are grown outside during Summer does not change their nature. I myself use Pandanus Veitchii, which is a "stove" plant, for planting out in large vases in the Summer (instead of Dracæna indivisa) with satisfactory results.

Now, we must have, without any question, such houses with a high temperature, in which to grow and maintain the different tropical ornamental foliage and flowering plants in their natural condition, and such houses must or should be distinguished from others by some name. If the present appellation of "stove" is objectionable to our American horticulturists, they must find another name to take its place; and I would suggest "tropical" as being the nearest and most suitable name. As for calling all tender plants "greenhouse" plants and making no distinction, I think that would be absolutely ridiculous.

I would further suggest that a committee of practical and interested gardeners be appointed by any well organized horticultural society or club, who would take this matter in hand and specify in detail what constitute "stove plants," giving a full list of plants requiring such temperature and treatment. Further, that this matter, with lists, be laid before the S. A. F. O. H. at its next convention, and if approved by that body, that the lists be printed in small booklet form and distributed to the different horticultural societies and clubs from whom it would be obtainable by any intending exhibitor in these particular classes, by which he could govern himself. In my opinion this would save a lot of difficulty, confusion and unpleasantness to the exhibitors, the judges, and the societies, through which this discussion has originated.

Brooklyn, N. Y. A. J. MANDA.

Editor Florists' Exchange:

As to the use of the term "stove plant" by gardeners and others, I would say that the term is obsolete, as the brick stoves, or flues, gave meaning to the term originally. There is no excuse today for its retention in prize schedules or in the vernacular even. The present day horticulturist needs something more definite, and we do well always to cut out all ambiguous terms that can be spared, for there are enough hard names to learn without these.

It seems strange that the S. A. F. O. H. declined to consider the matter in detail, and render at least a tentative opinion; and it may be that in this instance it is a repetition of the "fool stepping in," etc. But to the writer, and indeed to anyone who has read the history of the introduction of exotic plants, the "stove house" has been the death of more fine things that arrived alive, but were stewed or broiled as the case might be, directly they saw or experienced the light of cultivation. The difference was only in the amount of moisture used during the process—the amount of stove heat prescribed was the same, identically.

Now, it is a recognized principle that one should not tear down or destroy unless prepared to replace with something equivalent, or better, and one can easily anticipate the request for a term, if such must be used, in place of that of stove plant. In American horticulture to-day there are but two classes of plants grown under glass, that is to say, in Winter. There are others, such as bay trees, etc., which are merely stored, that do not figure in this connection; they are under cover for protection from the severest weather, or, possibly, from fluctuation of temperature, their growth being made at the normal period, in Summer.

Of the two classes named, one is essentially a warm house section that needs a minimum of 60 degrees Fahr. in Winter to make the occupants feel comfortable and grow. In this section we may class the palms, crotons, and most of the ferns. It might even be called the tropical section, for this minimum of 60 degrees will winter any plant introduced from the tropics. There are few orchids that need this amount of heat in Winter, a few cypripediums and the phalænopsis comprising the whole.

The cool house may be described as a structure kept 10 degrees lower in Winter, and this will include the balance of cultivated plants under glass.

Physiologically, it is well known that growth ceases under glass when the temperature goes below 45 degrees. This may be partly due to the lack of light during the depth of Winter; but the plants must be kept in a receptive mood by heat, that they may avail themselves of the light available during the short days, the growth being made during the night and the light putting life into the growth by day.

A temperature of 50 degrees will care for anything that is not of tropical origin and will answer to the term "greenhouse" used in contradistinction to "stove house"; and we have so used the term greenhouse in American horticulture that it has a generic meaning; hence the term "cool house" would seem fitting to the needs in contradistinction to that suggested of warm house, and these two will include easily all cultivated plants found under glass in America.

In British horticultural journals and books we find several other terms used, such as intermediate house, East Indian house, orangery, etc., and the use of these terms is a puzzle to the novice oftentimes; but we must bear in mind that the sun here in Summer fixes it so that temperatures are out of our control for about four months, and during this time almost all growth is made, it only remaining for the cultivator to keep the plants in good health the remainder of the year.

It may safely be borne in mind that it is a waste of coal to keep higher temperatures than 60 degrees at night in Winter, and a waste of labor and money to attempt to run one much less than 50 degrees Fahr.

In the compiling of schedules it may be desirable to be explicit, and the use of the phrase "warm house" may be too comprehensive. We have still "tropical plants" to fall back on; but no matter how carefully worded, there is room always for a difference of opinion, and this must be left to the discretion of the judges for decision, as in the past.

E. O. ORPET.

Notes on Current Comment.

Cedrela and Ailanthus.

Editor Florists' Exchange:

I have been interested in the discussion about cedrela and ailanthus in The Florists' Exchange. I believe that it is now generally conceded by botanists that cedrela is properly Ailanthus lutea. I have grown both trees. Cedrela is the prettier of the two and without disagreeable odor. I have had the pistillate form of Ailanthus glandulosa and never found that it had any disagreeable odor either. It is the staminate form that smells bad. Then, too, I noticed that the pistillate form, for some reason or other, though right alongside of cultivated land, did not sucker like the male form, though these were in sod. I know of no good reason for this, but simply note the fact in my experience. Trees of cedrela that I planted in an avenue at the North Carolina College of Agriculture fifteen years ago, have never suckered to my knowledge though on the edge of cultivated land. As to the hardiness of the trees, I have never had the cedrela in a cold climate, but in January, 1880, we had in the hills of Northern Maryland a temperature of 18 degrees below zero, and not a shoot of the ailanthus was injured; and I imagine that it will seldom get colder than that in Chicago.

Stoves and Stove Plants.

Now as to the use of the term "stove" and "stove plants," I think that the term comes in very handily to indicate the house and plants needing the highest temperature. To say that a certain structure is a greenhouse, or that a certain plant is a greenhouse plant, does not give the amateur any idea of how the temperature must be regulated, or how much cold the plant will endure. Certain plants, like the gardenia, that are greenhouse plants here, are hardy enough to endure the Winter as far north as North Carolina. A greenhouse is properly a structure where plants are merely kept green and dormant in Winter, like the old-fashioned orangeries, the oldest one of which in this country I formerly had in charge, and, strictly speaking, in a large part of our country there is no such thing as a greenhouse without fire heat. Our houses are all warm or hot houses, and certain terms to distinguish a temperate, warm and hot house are needed. Anyone will understand that a stove is a place for the most tender of the tropical vegetation.

Lagerstroemia Indica.

Your Shanghai correspondent mentions the ease with which the crape myrtle (Lagerstroemia indica) is grown from seed. I once grew a large number of these from seed that had been hand-pollenized by W. R. Smith at the Botanic Gardens, Washington, and white and colored ones crossed. The seeds were sown in the greenhouse in early Winter and transplanted to thumb pots. In these they got rather pot-bound before the time to set outside, and to my surprise some of the little plants bloomed that Summer when less than a foot high. I got a great variety of shades, from white, pale flesh color, lilac, pink, to deep purple. I agree with Mr. Eckardt in preferring to prune crape myrtles to a bush form instead of the tree-like habit so common in the South. In the fine old terraced gardens of the Richmond Club in Richmond, Va., there are two specimens about 15 feet high that are branched from the ground and are perfectly globular in form. When in bloom they are simply big bouquets of flowers.

Bulb Growing in the South.

As is generally known, I spent some years and a great deal of effort in trying to get our people in the South Atlantic coast states interested in bulb culture. My efforts were badly handicapped by the fact that those in control of the station work could see nothing of value in anything beyond cotton and corn, and most of my work was done at my own expense, aided by friends in the trade who sent me stock for trial. After vainly endeavoring to get the proper soil and location for the work I abandoned the effort. But gradually the seed sown is taking root. Narcissus bulbs are now grown by several in Virginia, and the tuberose growers of North Carolina are branching out into the culture of other bulbs. Recently I have had some correspondence with an English grower who was seeking a location for bulb growing. A few days ago I received a letter from him stating that he has located near Portsmouth, Va., has built a 100-foot greenhouse and has planted 30 tons of bulbs that he brought over with him. Another man is growing bulbs on Roanoke Island, N. C., and I believe that in a few years the bulk of the bulbs now imported will be produced in the South Atlantic states, especially Roman and Italian hyacinths and narcissus.

W. F. MASSEY.

Philadelphia, Pa.

Our Question Box.

It is gratifying to us that this valuable feature of The Florists' Exchange is so widely taken advantage of, and that by means of it we are afforded the pleasure of helping our subscribers over difficulties which they encounter in the conduct of their business. A careful comparison will reveal the fact that more real assistance is rendered readers by The Florists' Exchange than by any one of its contemporaries, through this medium—a convincing proof of the merit of the responses given to the several inquiries submitted. These answers are all practical, written by men experienced in the respective lines on which the questions treat, are not one-man knowledge or advice.

Numerous as are the problems presented to us for solution, we would welcome more of them, all we ask being that the name and address of the party seeking the information be furnished, not necessarily for publication, but as an evidence of good faith. For we are of the opinion expressed by the late Dean Hole, to the effect that, "Of all the prides since Lucifer's attaint there is not one more disastrous to progress and success than that which will never acknowledge ignorance, and would rather remain in darkness than ask a neighbor for a light."

So don't be backward in asking us questions. Your difficulty may be that of some others engaged in the same branch of the business as yourself, and in that way the Question Box may become a source of widespread assistance.

Obituary

A. D. Webb.

A. D. Webb, of Bowling Green, Ky., died October 14, 1906, at the home of his son-in-law, Lucien Minor, in Nashville, as the result of a fall received some time ago. Mr. Webb was a well-known horticulturist and always took a prominent part in the State Horticultural meetings. He originated a number of fine varieties of strawberries, among them the Warren, Longfellow, and Rural, which have been extensively grown throughout the United States. Mr. Webb was eighty-eight years of age and leaves three daughters and one son, Joe P. Webb.

AMONG THE GROWERS

Holm & Olson, St. Paul.

A recent visit to Holm & Olson's greenhouses opened our eyes to the large amount of choice stock being grown at this comparatively new establishment. The only cut flowers raised here are chrysanthemums and bulbous stock. The houses were built for growing plants and everything in this line is certainly done to perfection. Several houses are devoted to ferns aggregating in the total about 20,000 plants. Elegantissima nephrolepis is shown to perfection and is certainly far ahead of its parent stocks. Large numbers of Boston ferns are also grown and find a ready market. Asparagus plumosus and Sprengeri are in fine shape.

In blooming plants nothing can surpass the cyclamen which are worth going many miles to see. Begonia Gloire de Lorraine is in splendid condition. A few hundred poinsettias in pans, three to six plants to a pan, will, of course, help to swell the holiday business. Not the least of their beautiful Christmas plants is a bench of several hundred well-berried Solanum capsicastrum, which are easily grown, form nice, bushy heads, and with their loads of well-reddened fruit tempt the buyers of moderate means. Palms, rubber plants and araucarias by the thousands are also seen. Three greenhouses were erected the past Summer, making a total glass area of 30,000 square feet. A bulb storage shed has just been completed, with a total capacity of 1,000,000 bulbs more than 500,000 are now forced annually, while the firm's rapidly increasing trade will soon tax this shed to its limit. The greenhouses are ably superintended by C. Christensen.

L. L. May & Company.

At L. L. May & Company's greenhouses on Como avenue we found everything spick and span under the management of Ludvig Anderson. Roses are very fine here. Richmond, though a little late, is just coming into full crop with long, stiff stems and large buds. This place has always enjoyed a local reputation for producing excellent Bridesmaid roses, but in the opinion of Mr. Anderson these are totally eclipsed by Killarney. As grown here it certainly bids fair to distance its rival and be classed with American Beauty for length of stem, size of bloom and fragrance. Chrysanthemums here, as in all other places I have visited, are late, though the first cuttings will be made soon. Several benches of Boston fern reflect the good care and attention which has been bestowed upon them.

Clinton Falls Nursery Company.

The picture herewith is that of the Clinton Falls Nursery Company greenhouses, located at Owatonna, Minn. Although I have never visited the place I have been reliably informed that it is strictly up-to-date in every particular. Roses are the principal stock grown here, though some carnations and smilax are cultivated. Mr. Chapman, formerly of Chicago, is superintendent, and is sending in the finest Richmond roses ever seen on the Minneapolis market.

VERITAS.

Greenhouses and Grounds of Clinton Falls Nursery Company, Owatonna, Minn.

Anton Schultheis, College Point, N. Y.

With each succeeding year some new additions are made to his glass area by Anton Schultheis, until now one can safely say that he has in operation the largest range of glass on Long Island devoted to flowering and decorative plants for commercial purposes. In addition to the yearly increase in the glass area, Mr. Schultheis is gaining a national reputation for the excellent quality of the stock he is distributing, and he is kept busy every day filling and shipping orders for plants to all parts of the country.

The greenhouses at this time of the year are replete with seasonable stock of both decorative and flowering plants. The numerous sheds contain collections of bay trees and boxwood shrubs in marketable sizes and forms. Outdoors are thousands of sash frames filled with ericas, hydrangeas, orange plants, solanums, etc., while the thousands of roses that are to be forced for Easter are yet resting outdoors in their pots, all staked and tied and ready to be taken in at a moment's notice when the time arrives.

Mr. Schultheis has been located here some twelve or thirteen years, and in the art of producing plants for commercial purposes he has become a past master. Growing as he does thousands of plants for special purposes—that is getting them ready for certain dates—he has got his business systematised to the point of perfection.

His oldest son, Anton, recently graduated from high school, is taking much interest in the establishment, and besides having charge of the office work, including all correspondence, he is rapidly becoming familiar with the management of the place, and gives great promise of relieving Mr. Schultheis of many of the details connected with the conduct of his large establishment.

Among the flowering plants which are a feature just now, chrysanthemums of course are in the lead. Many thousands of pot plants of these are grown, comprising both late and early varieties, and to say that they are in excellent condition, but poorly expresses the general state of all of this line of stock. In addition to the usual run of plants in bush form, there are many that have been grown to standard shape, and these, no doubt, will find much favor among the retail trade of New York. There are also in pot plants a large number of pompon chrysanthemums, including six of the best varieties. No disbudding has been attempted with these, and they will make perfect masses of blossom when fully developed. This batch of stock should be particularly desirable for store work. There are also several benches of chrysanthemums grown for cut flowers, from which daily cuttings are being made. The varieties for this purpose include such as Mrs. Jerome Jones, John E. Lager, Mrs. Henry Robinson, Mrs. Coombes, pink; A. J. Balfour, pink; Ben Wells, Clementine Touset, Colonel Appleton, and others.

Other flowering plants which are coming in bloom now are cyclamens, Primula obconica, gardenias, camellias and Erica Wilmoreana. There are several other varieties of ericas grown here in quantity. Mr. Schultheis has always made a specialty of this class of plants, and grows them to perfection every year. Most of them, however, are still in the frames outdoors. Of Erica Cavendishii and E. melanthera there is a goodly stock on hand in various sizes. There is also a nice collection of orange plants, well covered with fruit, all of which will be ripened and in nice shape for the holidays. Ponderosa lemon is also represented in fairly large numbers, many of them carrying several fruits almost as large as a cocoanut. This is a decorative plant that is not grown very largely around New York.

For cut flowers a house is devoted to lily of the valley, from which daily shipments are made to New York. There is also a house of gardenias planted on raised benches, which are throwing off a regular supply of cut blooms. Marguerites of both varieties—that is, the old Paris daisy and the new Queen Alexandra—occupy two houses, and cutting from these will be on in full in the near future. That Easter plant, Boronia elatior, is grown in fair quantity, as also are acacias and genistas. There is coming along for Christmas purposes a heavy supply of the Jerusalem cherry (Solanum capsicastrum). These are as yet in the frames, and are covered with ripening fruit, and will be in grand shape for the holiday business.

A house of Begonia Gloire de Lorraine, in various sizes, shows careful cultivation, and by Thanksgiving time good sized plants of this favorite begonia will be ready for market.

The stock of ferns grown is quite extensive, and among the varieties are to be seen Nephrolepis Piersoni, N. bostoniensis, N. Whitmani, N. Scottii and Cibotium Schiedei, also fern balls and limited quantities of the bird's nest fern, Asplenium nidus. In the general line of decorative plants, palms of all commercial varieties, and in many sizes, are on hand, also dracænas in variety, Pandanus Veitchii, cycas, livistonas and aspidistras. Another plant that has been gone into heavily by Mr. Schultheis is the orchid, one house, 150 feet long, being entirely filled with cattleyas of this year's collecting, which have already been potted up and are becoming established in good order.

Azaleas have ben imported in extremely large numbers; houses are being filled with the earlier blooming varieties, and by Christmas time many hundreds of these plants will be in bloom. Among the varieties represented are Deutsche Perle, Simon Mardner, Mme. Van der Cruyssen, Vervæneana, Mme. Petrick, Empress of India, De Schryveriana, Niobe and Mme. Marie Planchon. Some of these are in pyramid form, others in bush shape, and quite a number are in the large specimen sizes, more of these specimen plants having been imported than ever before.

PAMPHLETS RECEIVED.

TRANSACTIONS OF THE MASSACHUSETTS HORTICULTURAL SOCIETY, for 1905, Part II. Secretary Wm. P. Rich, Boston, Mass.

ANNUAL REPORT OF THE PARK DEPARTMENT, City of Cincinnati, O.—Through the courtesy of J. W. Rodgers, superintendent. The report says that 1905 has been a banner year for park improvements and extensions in Cincinnati. The city has acquired a considerable amount of park area. The report is freely illustrated, and reflects much credit on Mr. Rodgers.

Le Jardin, in a recent issue, contains an interesting illustrated account of the methods employed in carnation culture in America, written by L. Maillard, who was for a time in the employment of the Cottage Gardens Company, Queens, N. Y.

CARNATIONS

Stem Rot as It Is.

Among diseases of cultivated plants stem rot, in bold defiance, persistently holds its place as the most unconquerable of fell destroyers. For years this arch enemy to flourishing plant life has given cause for widespread complaint and considerable discussion. All sorts of cures and remedies were suggested and eagerly tried with a hope of ultimate victory, but all of them, even ridicule, failed to rout the enemy. This season the great loss of valuable stock through this cause alone has been most discouraging to growers in all sections of the country. The disease has thinned out promising crops to an alarming extent, and is still at it.

That there are at least two kinds of stem rot is now generally admitted. There can be no doubt on this point. While each of them is equally suregoing in its death dealing on march, there still is a great difference between the two as to character, cause, prevalence and possibility of cure.

DRY ROT is a form of the disease which has puzzled all interested in plant pathology more than any other known malady. It is met with on nearly all plants under high cultivation, occasionally attacking roses, ericas, lilies, mignonette, even shrubs and fruit trees, always showing a decided predilection for anything foreign, insufficiently acclimated or transferred from distant localities to uncongenial soils and environments. However, it is only since the disease has selected carnations for its favorite prey, caused some varieties to become most risky stock and others to be entirely swept out of existence, that this particular form of stem rot became the object of deeply felt apprehension, serious discussion and diligent inquiry.

Dry rot is a malady for which, as yet, neither cause nor cure has been found. It is a disease most insidious, giving no warning, stealthily making its entry, steadily pursuing its deathly course, gnawing off a branch here, another there, spreading corrosive destruction in its path, but hardly ever attacking the main stem or felling its victim with one stroke.

Some varieties of carnations are more susceptible to dry rot than others; some never show a trace of it. Varieties of a dense, bushy growth, amply furnished with a healthy grass-like foliage and numerous young side shoots from smooth barked, slender branches, are hardly ever attacked by true dry rot, and when attacked, suffer least. Carnations of a sturdy, rigid growth with coarse, thick leaves, sparingly distributed along the upper half or two-thirds of stout, roughly surfaced, hard wooded branches, few in number and bare of foliage, where they join the main stem, and markedly disinclined to make new side-breaks, are the sorts that most readily yield to dry rot.

Predisposed varieties, while yet in the open field, often fall victims to dry rot at a very dry period of the season, immediately following a spell of continued warm rains and the best of growing weather. So also does the trouble start quickly on such varieties immediately after being removed from the field to the benches of a well ventilated greenhouse at a time when they were making their best and most rapid growth.

It would then seem that one cause of dry rot may be found in the disproportion between roots and foliage, and another in the check of rapid growth at any time when large, elongated cells have formed elastic, soft tissue, this still depending for proper assimilation of sap on a continuance of this rapid growth. An entire lack of or a mere stop in properly adjusted circulation may thus be regarded as the first and probably main cause of a disease, hard to account for otherwise. But although the premises seem correct and are upheld by facts, the conclusion arrived at may, after all, be faulty. Dry rot is too sly an enemy to allow of being so easily found out by ordinary observation and reasoning, and I fear that nothing but eternal vigilance and the prompt destruction of diseased stock will lead to the final extermination of the scourge. Dry rot in its worst form is, indeed, a hopelessly bad disease, but it is by no means so widespread, so formidable, so devastating a plant destroyer as the ordinary stem rot.

COMMON STEM ROT, or stem rot proper, attacks the main stem or lower branches of half hardy plants in any and all stages of their growth, neither sparing the little seedling or cutting nor the fully developed specimen, but mostly confining its ravages to the kinds whose bushy growth is supported by a stem of semi-woody nature, encased in a thin, sappy cuticle or outer skin. The rotting off of this tender covering alone causes the death of the plant. But very often decay enters on one side only, then gradually eats its way into the heart of the hardened stem, until at last all that part forming the crown of the roots, or base of the stem, is turned into a slimy mass of decaying pulp. This explains why plants so attacked wither and die off on one side first, show a wilting, shriveling shoot or two, the ruin rapidly spreading until the entire plant is gone.

Ordinary stem rot is responsible for more loss of valuable stock than all other plant diseases combined. The toppling over of cuttings, the damping off of seedlings, the dying out of perennials, the rotting off among outdoor and indoor crops, lucidly exemplified by calceolarias, bouvardias, asters and carnations, must all be laid to common stem rot.

But while this is the most destructive of the several forms of stem rot, it is also the one of which we know the causes, each one suggestive of a proper remedy. It may be caused by over watering, by a too slowly dispersed accumulation of moisture in some form at or about the base of the plant. The presence of abrasions on the bark, or punctures made by tools or insects, augments the danger. Very often a minute worm (sometimes a whole colony of them) makes its way into the lower part of the stem, causing a wholesale rotting off in fields and in houses overrun with these particular kinds of larvæ. The fungus from cutting or seed bed, faulty planting, sour or too highly enriched soil, lack of drainage, over feeding, careless cultivation with clumsy tools, needless sprinkling, all may be set down as direct or indirect causes of stem rot, to which may be added the lack of fresh circulating air and the maintenance of too great a heat combined with an atmosphere heavily charged with stagnant moisture during the time when outdoor stock is housed.

Where the cause is known, the searching for the right remedy should not be regarded as desperately hopeless. I advise moderation in the use of fertilizers and a more extensive use of lime, as also a careful avoidance of anything in the way of treatment that might invite or favor the onset and spread of stem rot.

FRED. W. TIMME.

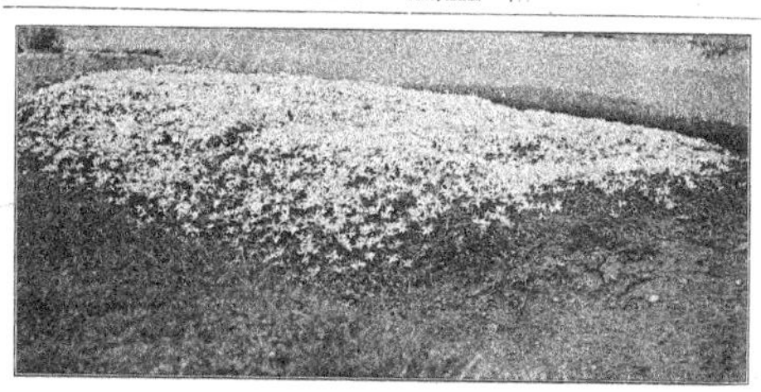

Photo by W. H. Waite

Pratia Angulata

Bacteriosis on Mrs. Thomas W. Lawson.

Editor Florists' Exchange:

To the successful novice, flushed with the outcome of his work, the extreme caution with which the older and more experienced florist speaks of his enterprises is usually a great surprise. That this conservatism pays, one who has been "up against it" can testify. Until this year we would have been willing to stake almost any sum that the carnation Mrs. Thos. W. Lawson was the thing and no trouble to grow. Our reasons for thinking so were, that for five years we have had them first-class. That "dumb luck" was in a measure responsible for our success has been proven by the fact that this year, having treated the stock in every respect in the same manner as in previous years, the only decent Mrs. Lawson we have on the place are a few which have never been outside. Our field-grown plants all went to pieces. The disease, which seems to be an aggravated form of "bacteriosis," shows itself by the appearance of a small patch on the foliage which looks as though it may have been scalded, and is about the size of a globule of dew or water, often seen upon the plants. In many cases the infection is at the junction of the leaf and stem, and the "scalded" (for want of a better word) stem cuts off most of the supply from below, preventing further growth of the terminal shoots. Indeed, in many cases, the infection strikes right through and the shoot topples over dead. Invariably growths appear from below, very weak and debilitated, however, in appearance. Occasionally a plant dies, but generally stands with foliage all dried up, and only some appearance of life at the extreme tips of such shoots as have not been infected in the stem. With several varieties in the field, Mrs. Lawson and White Lawson seem to be the only ones that have been put out of business; some of the others show a few "scalded" spots, but are not badly infected.

It is our first experience with the disease, but we hear of it a few miles out of Baltimore city; in fact, we saw it at one place, where they have had it before. There the grower gets ahead of it by cultivating the plants under glass. I think, if I remember right, it is claimed that it is worse with the firm in question this year than ever before, and if Mrs. Lawson is continued to be grown, the plants will be kept always under glass.

This firm showed us some fine stock which had been grown along in pots until the preceding crop was ready to go out. The plants were large and well branched and in fine condition. At another place, on the other side of the city, we were shown a small house of field-grown Mrs. Lawson in fine condition, and apparently free from disease.

Our Summer has been wet, extremely wet, but we have been having wet Summers for several years. Wishing to increase our stock, we bought in, last Spring, one hundred rooted cuttings of several varieties. They were a sickly looking lot upon arrival—pale strawy in color and weak looking, as though they had been standing weeks too long in the sand bed of a warm house. Not much improvement had been made at planting time, but we put them out. The following weeks were dry and nearly all of the plants died; Mrs. Lawson perished to the last plant. All stock of our own propagation started off well. Question—If the disease which finally ruined our whole stock of Mrs. Lawson is a bacterial disease, and it evidently is, did not we inoculate the patch by introducing the bacterium on this new stock? We think so and hereafter all new stock will be kept and planted out in a different location, far apart, until it is proven healthy.

My advice to all growers would be, if your Mrs. Lawson stock is healthy, do not get any new stock of that variety from the outside, but stick to your own; and if new varieties are bought quarantine them for a season.

THOS. H. WHITE.

Maryland.

BLUE GLADIOLI.—Blue coloring is not often found in wild gladiolus species, nor in strict verity in garden hybrids. There are several northern purple species and one South African form, G. papilio, which is mainly reddish brown, but with an undertinge of blue-red. By hybridizing this species with light colored Lemoinei seedlings a profuse progeny has been reared, the blooms embracing may shades of purple, lavender and heliotrope, but thus far true light blue has appeared very scantily, if at all. The "blue" section, so-called for convenience, is now an extensive one, but there is much similarity among the varieties, all being rather small flowered in imitation of the parent species. They are, however, desirable for their novel color effects. We have grown and raised from seed many "blue" varieties, but value most Baron Joseph Hulot and Timbuctou, both products of the French Lemoine nurseries. The former has a comparatively large flower, bright heliotrope, with reddish throat, while the latter is rich blue-purple, nearly self colored. Blue Jay, sent out this season by an American grower, appears very similar to Timbuctou.—Dr. Van Fleet in Rural New Yorker.

Pratia Angulata (Syn. Lobelia Littoralis).

This is a pretty creeping lobelia from New Zealand and keeps flat on the surface of the ground, each little shoot rooting into the soil almost at every node. The flowers, which are pure white, are produced in great profusion in Summer on very short pedicels scarcely rising above the foliage, and they are followed in Fall by red berries. Where hardy it is a splendid subject for rock work, but it is not hardy in the vicinity of New York. It is of the easiest possible cultivation, and where not hardy it may be grown in large pans, with the protection in Winter of a cool greenhouse.

W. H. WAITE.

CLUB AND SOCIETY DOINGS.

Chrysanthemum Society of America.

President Duckham has announced the committees to examine seedlings and sports on dates as follows: October 20 and 27, November 3, 10, 17 and 24, 1906.

Exhibits to receive attention from the committees must in all cases be prepaid to destination, and the entry fee of $2 should be forwarded to the secretary not later than Tuesday of the week preceding examination, or may accompany the blooms. Special attention is called to the rule requiring that sports, to receive a certificate, must pass three committees.

NEW YORK.—Eugene Dailledouze, chairman, care of New York Cut Flower Company, 55-57 Twenty-sixth street; William Turner, Thomas Head.

PHILADELPHIA, PA.—A. B. Cartledge, chairman, 1514 Chestnut street; John Westcott, Wm. K. Harris. Ship flowers in care of the chairman.

BOSTON, MASS.—E. A. Wood, chairman; Wm. Nicholson, James Wheeler. Ship to Boston Flower Market, care of the chairman.

CINCINNATI, O.—R. Witterstaetter, chairman; James Allen, Wm. Jackson. Ship to Jabez Elliott Flower Market, care of janitor.

CHICAGO, ILL.—J. S. Wilson, chairman; J. B. Deamud and George Wienhoeber. Ship care of J. B. Deamud, 51 Wabash avenue.

The official scales of the C. S. A. are as follows:

For Commercial Purposes		For Exhibition Purposes	
Color	20	Color	10
Form	15	Stem	5
Fullness	10	Foliage	5
Stem	15	Fullness	15
Foliage	15	Form	15
Substance	15	Depth	15
Size	10	Size	35
Total	100	Total	100

DAVID FRASER, Secretary.

Pittsburg, Pa.

Work of the Committees.

CHICAGO, October 13.—Chrysanthemum President Loubet, creamy white, exhibited by the E. G. Hill Company, Richmond, Ind.; scored 86 points, exhibition scale.

CINCINNATI, October 20.—Chrysanthemum Director Gerard, yellow Japanese reflexed; exhibited by the E. G. Hill Company, Richmond, Ind.; scored 87 points; commercial scale.

Fusee, light yellow, Japanese; exhibited by the E. G. Hill Company; scored 85 points, commercial scale.

Comoleta, clear bright yellow; exhibited by Nathan Smith & Son, Adrian, Mich.; scored 88 points, commercial scale.

NEW YORK, October, 20. — Chrysanthemum President Loubet, creamy white, exhibited by the E. G. Hill Company, Richmond, Ind.; scored 90 points, exhibition scale.

Mary Godfrey, yellow, Japanese incurved; exhibited by C. H. Totty, Madison, N. J.; scored 85 points, commercial scale.

Mrs. A. T. Miller, Japanese, pure white; exhibited by C. H. Totty, Madison, N. J.; scored 87 points, commercial scale. DAVID FRASER, secretary.

THE COLUMBUS (OHIO) FLORISTS' CLUB held its annual meeting last Tuesday evening, with a very large number of members present. President Stephens was in the chair. It was a most harmonious gathering; and the following officers were unanimously elected for the ensuing year: President Sherman F. Stephens; vice-president, Robert A. Currie; recording secretary, James McKellar; treasurer, Jacob Reichart; sergeant-at-arms, John H. Williams; and a board of five trustees as follows—Messrs. Albert Knopf, Gustave Drobisch, Guy H. Woodrow, George Bauman, and John Brust. The matter of the chrysanthemum show came up for consideration. The committee in charge submitted recommendations as regards a list of prizes, and the same was approved and ordered printed and distributed to the members. The judges of the show were then chosen—Messrs. M. B. Faxon, William Graff and Richard Sinclair. Special prizes were offered by Messrs. M. B. Faxon, and Graff Brothers. Robert A. Currie was appointed manager of the exhibition. On or before November 10, intending exhibitors are requested to notify the secretary of this club in what classes they intend to compete. The show will take place Tuesday evening, November 13, in our new rooms in the Brent building. These new rooms are more central, and have many conveniences which were lacking in the old quarters; the committee have also had added a piano, in order that social entertainments may be held. As all members of the trade have already promised to make displays at the show, we hope to have a very attractive exhibition. Vice-president Currie, acting for the club in the matter of the children's gardens, reported that he had visited and examined all the gardens entered, and had found the entire eight gardens of such attractiveness, that he had deemed it advisable to award four prizes instead of two as at first planned. He also reported that a good assortment of hyacinths, tulips, narcissus, and crocuses had been distributed, as directed by the club at its last meeting, to ten of the public schools. It was voted at this meeting, after considerable discussion, to change the regular meeting night from the first and third to the second and fourth Tuesday in each month. The meeting then adjourned till Tuesday evening, November 13.

F. W.

ELBERON (N. J.) HORTICULTURAL SOCIETY.—A meeting of this society was held on October 15. Two new members were admitted. The following officers were elected to serve for the ensuing year: President, W. D. Robertson (re-elected); vice-president, Henry Wood; treasurer, James Kennedy (re-elected); secretary, George Masson (re-elected); assistant secretary, Fred Dettlinger. An interesting discussion took place on the advisability of leaving the foliage of asparagus on the plant until Spring. The majority of the members were in favor of cutting it down in November or December. It was decided to experiment on the matter. Among the exhibits was a fine vase of Richmond roses, shown by Peter Murray. This is certainly one of the best roses of recent introduction. A vase of carnations, good for this season of the year, was shown by A. Bauer. W. D. Robertson exhibited a dish of sweet potatoes, variety Yellow Yam; and A. Greib a nice vase of cosmos. The newly elected officers will be installed at the first annual general meeting on November 5. G. M.

Chrysanthemum Comoleta, Certificated by C. S. A. Growers, Nathan Smith & Son, Adrian, Mich.

Our London Letter.

BY A. HEMSLEY.

CHRYSANTHEMUMS.—The market is now well supplied both with cut blooms and plants. There is no better yellow either for pots or cut flowers than Miss B. Miller. It is good with all growers. Carrie is another good yellow for pots. La Pactole is one of the best bronzes; it makes a splendid pot plant, and stands well when cut. Crimson Pride takes the lead among dark varieties. Goacher's Crimson is good for pots, but we want a brighter variety. Kathleen Thompson, which comes in a little later, has a better color. In whites we have so many that it is difficult to say which are the best. Of the earlies Lady Fitzwygram is one of the best, and selected stock of Madame Desgranges is still largely grown. Market White comes in a little later, and Tapis de Neige, as recently shown by H. J. Jones, is likely to prove valuable. A first-class certificate was awarded it by the Chrysanthemum Society. J. W. Scott, as grown by J. Lowe, is a splendid white for cut flowers; it somewhat resembles Western King, but is much earlier. The finest early large Japanese white is Mrs. A. T. Mitter. I recently saw a cross made of this; only eight blooms were used, with a green base. The flowers were of immense size and of a beautiful clear ivory white. This design was made by H. J. Jones, who introduced the variety. The best large yellow I have seen is Messrs. Wells & Company's Mrs. W. Knox. This variety is a pale yellow, of great substance and size. A newer variety from the same firm is Dorothy Goldsmith; it has deep flowers with very long drooping florets. Mrs. W. Wells, deep golden yellow with a very slight bronze shade, is another new large Japanese of great promise. Mrs. Wingfield is one of the best pink varieties for pots. Pearl Rose, which is also known as Charles Jolly, is another fine pink; and one which comes from J. Lowe under the name of Litz is a fine thing. Nina Blick, is a fine chestnut red of medium size. I have only seen a few blooms of Moneymaker yet, but at Mr. Jones' nursery I noticed a fine lot of plants which will shortly be in flower, and they are quite equal in habit to Soliel d'Octobre, which is one of the finest varieties we have for pots. Nellie Blake is a good bronzy red. Mytchett Beauty is another good dark red, or crimson.

CARNATIONS.—Messrs Cutbush & Sons were recently given an award of merit for a fine white variety named Mrs. R. Norman. As compared with Lady Bountiful it certainly appeared a much better variety. At the same meeting Messrs. H. Low & Company had a good white named White Perfection, but this, though a good thing, failed to get an award. One of the best of the American scarlets I have yet seen is Cardinal. Robert Craig and Victory have been shown, but as yet they may not have been seen in their best form; neither is equal to Britannia. I think I have previously referred to this variety, but I may add that blooms now coming into the market are very fine indeed, and the raiser, A. Smith, is also sending in Progress, a very fine pink carnation, which has large flowers, on long stiff stems. Nelson Fisher is a favorite in the market, but no other variety yet takes so well as Enchantress. We have this good all the year, though Fair Maid is a prettier shade of color and, at its best, is a very fine variety, but it is not quite so free.

An English View of S. A. F. O. H.

Under the caption of "Ideas for Trade Conventions" the Horticultural Advertiser has the following to say:

The recent successful meeting of the Horticultural Trades Association in Edinburgh, followed very closely on those organized by our brethren in Canada and the United States. As the reports of these meetings appeared almost simultaneously, we read them with much interest, not only for their general information, but with a view of noting wherein the gatherings over the water differed from our own, and if they afforded any hints whereby our meetings here might be made still more attractive and useful.

The most prominent point of difference in our judgment is the admission of the fair sex. So far, the ladies have not been invited to our gatherings, while at the S. A. F. they appear to form a very considerable proportion of those attending the annual meetings. There is much to be said for the wisdom of either course, and the subject having been mooted by several members this season, will very likely come up for discussion and possible revision in the near future. No one will dispute that the admission of "friends, wives, and sweethearts," would brighten our meetings, and that some members who now stay at home would be with us, if they could bring the lady members of the family with them and make an annual holiday of it. On the other hand it is equally clear that the presence of the ladies would alter the tone and character of everything, excepting the formal business meetings in the evenings. Many members feel that the most valuable side of a trade gathering is the opportunities for quiet business chat which occur while walking round the nurseries or driving from place to place. At these times, not only are fresh acquaintances made, but notes are compared as to abundance or poverty of various stocks, probable values, etc. They say that the entrance of the ladies would mean the exit of business, and that instead of "2 yr. 1 yr." and similar subjects, the conversation would range on frocks, art, games, the weather, or anything but business.

Then there is the question of sports, bowling, shooting, and so on, which seem to claim a largish share of convention time and interest with our cousins. Here we feel on more solid ground and have no hesitation in registering an emphatic negative against their introduction. The average American man of business seems bent on solving the problem of how many hours' work a day he can put in without actually killing himself, and with many in the florists' section, Sunday is not much more of a rest day than the other six; under which circumstances we can easily understand the protest against all work and no play, when away from home on convention. With us, however, sport enters pretty fairly into the general routine—at any rate with the younger members—and sa far from relaxation of this kind being a welcome introduction to our program, we believe it would be repudiated by a large majority as an absolute waste of time.

The subject of an annual exhibition of sundries, novelties, etc., such as forms a regular and important feature at the American gathering, has not yet even been mooted with us, but we think it is worthy of the most careful consideration. Keen business men on an outing of this kind are more than ever on the watch for novelties suited to their trade, and only need to have a good thing put before them to begin to feel for their pocket book. We would suggest, that before any steps are taken to organize a regular show, a small test should be made by placing a table in the meeting room, so that any member having a good novelty in plant, fruit, or flowers, could place a vase, dish, or plant upon it for the inspection of members present. We fancy this would prove a good means of making a novelty known to the leading members of the trade, and that once started, the thing would grow and become a feature of great interest in our annual gatherings.

Our association has not been able to follow the lead set in the acquisition of a paid secretary and staff, with a special vote of $200 to cover expenses of attending shows and canvassing members. This, however, is merely a question of funds, there being no doubt as to the advantages of having affairs upon a strict business footing. Until we reach this point we must do what we can by voluntary effort; and meanwhile we commend the example of one of the members who brought in four recruits on his last journey. If this were generally followed we should soon include in the ranks all those still outside who are worth having, and make such an increase in numbers as would cause the association to be a real power in the land.

Seed of Red Clover and Its Impurities.

A very valuable bulletin (Farmers' No. 260) to seedsmen and planters, prepared by Edgar Brown, botanist in charge of seed laboratory, and F. H. Hillman, assistant botanist, Bureau of Plant Industry, Department of Agriculture, Washington, D. C., has just been issued by the Department. From that document we make the following extracts:

Importance of Red Clover.

Red clover is the principal leguminous crop of the United States, although the cultivation of alfalfa is increasing rapidly. At the time of the last census there were approximately four million acres in red clover and two million acres in alfalfa. Red clover, appearing as it does in rotation at intervals of three to five years on the greater part of the best agricultural land of this country, plays a most important part in the maintenance of successful agriculture, and consequently special attention should be given to the quality of seed used.

The Seed.

QUALITY.—Red clover seed of good quality is of large size, dark colored, has a decided luster, and is practically free from weed seeds. Red clover and timothy seed are sold in more grades than any other seeds, all of the large dealers offering from five to ten qualities at a time. Among these grades will be found seed that is practically free from weeds and dirt, germinating 96 to 98 per cent., as well as screenings made up of small, light-colored or shriveled brown seed with a large percentage of weed seeds, including dodder and many other noxious weeds. These extremes are well represented by the analyses of the two following samples:

Sample No.	Price paid per 100 pounds.	Percentage of weed seeds.	Percentage of dirt, sticks and stones.	Percentage of red clover seed.	Percentage of red clover seed that germinated.	Number of weed seeds per pound.	Actual cost per 100 lbs. of red clover seed that germinated.
1	$5.20	25.78	26.16	48.06	18.26	130,727	$28.48
2	15.00	.09	1.08	98.83	95.86	150	15.65

Sample No. 1, imported at 5 1-5 cents per pound, contained about 18¼ per cent. of red clover seed that would grow and most of this was small, light seed that would not produce vigorous plants. Large quantities of seed of this grade are constantly being imported. The quality of such seed is so poor that it is not often sold alone; neither is it recleaned, as the good seed it contains actually costs more than the best quality of seed. None of this poor seed is imported to be wasted, but it is mixed in varying proportions with better seed and sold to the farmer.

Sample No. 2 contained more than 95 per cent. of red clover seed that would grow, and was practically free from weed seeds. In order to sow the same amount of good seed from these samples, it would be necessary to sow 5¼ pounds of the poor sample to one pound of the other. Every time 150 weed seeds were sown with the good sample, 783,567 weed seeds would be sown with the poor one.

SIZE.—Red clover seed varies greatly in size, this being to a large extent a good indication of quality. In average seed grown in the United States there are about 800,000 seeds to the pound. English seed is somewhat larger, having about 220,000 seeds to the pound, while Chilean seed is much larger, having only 190,000 seeds to the pound. There are frequently imported large lots of screenings similar to sample No. 1 referred to above, which are made up of light-colored clover seed, very small in size, there often being as many as 480,000 seeds to the pound.

Improved Standard Germinating Chamber.

Reproduced from Circular No. 34 U. S. Dept. of Agriculture.

Imported Seed.

The United States is a large exporter of clover seed, our annual sales ranging from 5,000,000 to 30,000,000 pounds per annum. At the same time we are importing relatively smaller quantities of seed of lower quality. In most European countries there is some sort of seed control, either voluntary or otherwise, by means of which the people have been educated to the use of seed of good quality. This leaves a large bulk of poor seed that cannot be sold there, which, being offered for export at low prices, is sent to the United States and either sold as low-grade seed or, in case it is especially bad, mixed with other better seed in the so-called grading-down process before being put on the market.

A very stringent seed law has recently been enacted in Canada, prohibiting the sale there of seed containing more than a very small number of weed seeds. It contains the following clause:

The provisions contained in this act shall not apply to seed marked "not absolutely clean," and held or sold for export only.

While the provisions of this law prevent the local sale of screenings or seeds containing weeds in quantity, it encourages the exportation of such seed from Canada.

As a result of the conditions in Canada and Europe the United States, where quality is not considered as carefully as it should be and where there are no restrictions on sale of poor seeds, becomes a ready market for low-grade seed.

That this low-grade seed is not imported for the purpose of recleaning is shown by the fact that in samples like No. 1 previously referred to the red clover seed which will grow costs nearly twice as much as the best clover seed offered on the market, notwithstanding the fact that this sample was imported at 5 1-5 cents per pound.

CHILEAN RED CLOVER.—Last year about 275,000 pounds of Chilean red clover seed were imported. This is especially fine-looking seed on account of its dark color and extremely large size. It has not been given a thorough trial in the United States, and it is not certain how successful it will prove. It should, however, be carefully examined, as all of this seed which has been imported has been found to contain large quantities of a large-seeded dodder, which may prove to be a destructive clover parasite in the United States.

(To be continued.)

Apparatus for Testing Seeds for Germination.

Your letter of October 19, inclosing a card from G. H. P., of Albany, N. Y., making inquiry relative to a small apparatus for testing seed for germination, is received. In reply I would say that all of our testing is done in incubators, either between folds of blue blotting paper or cotton flannel cloths; the paper being used for the smaller seed and the cloth for the large seed. This method of testing can be adapted on either a large or small scale and seems to be the most satisfactory of any we have tried.

Under separate cover we are sending you a copy of Circular No. 34, Revised, Office of Experiment Stations, which gives the apparatus and methods of testing now used by this laboratory.

E. BROWN,

Dept. of Agriculture.

Botanist in Charge.

The following descriptions and illustrations of germinating chambers are taken from the circular referred to:

Improved Standard Germinating Chamber

This chamber is essentially the same as the one designed by the late Gilbert H. Hicks, and described in Circular No. 34 of the Office of Experiment Stations. The principal changes that have been made are as follows: A solid door has been substituted for the glass one, it having been found that the light admitted through the glass door does not in any way affect germinations under ordinary conditions. Air-cell asbestos has been substituted for felt, the asbestos making a satisfactory lagging and being much more durable than felt. An ice box has been added on top. This was found necessary in order to maintain the low temperatures required for certain seeds during warm weather. By means of low-temperature thermostat this chamber can be regulated very accurately, and it is recommended for use when work is being done on methods of germination.

It is made of 20-ounce corrugated sheet copper, the 2 inch space between the double walls serving as a water jacket. Outside the water jacket is a 1-inch covering of air cell asbestos on all sides except the bottom. The ice box is an extension of the water jacket and opens into the latter through the perforated bottom. It is fitted with a cover which can be removed to put in ice or to fill the water jacket. The door is made of 20-ounce plain sheet copper with air cell asbestos the same as the sides of the chamber.

There is a felt-lined groove around the door, which fits over a flange on the chamber. There are two openings into the top of the chamber, which serve as ventilators and through which thermometers may be inserted. The six small openings into the chamber under the door, which may be closed by a copper slide, serve for ventilation and the escape of CO_2. A Rouux or other slow thermostat can be inserted in the water jacket through the opening in the top. The cock in the bottom of the water jacket serves to draw off the water when desired. The overflow pipe serves as a drain for the water from the melting ice when the ice box is being used. The opening through the side of the chamber is for the insertion of a self-registering thermometer. The trays are made of nineteen strands of No. 12 brass wire bound with copper strips and are supported by ledges on the sides of the chamber. The copper water pan rests on the bottom of the chamber, and the evaporation from it serves to keep the air in the chamber moist. The base is made of heavy galvanized sheet iron provided with ventilators at top and bottom to supply fresh air to the lamp or gas burner, which can be inserted through the door.

Sempers Germinating Chamber.

This germinating chamber is modeled after one designed and used by Mr. Frank W. Sempers, of Blythedale, Md. While the temperature can not be kept as uniform in this as in the standard chamber, it gives excellent results for regular work. On account of its simple construction it can be made at a low cost by any good carpenter with the aid of a tinsmith.

It is essentially a tight, wooden box, with doors on the front, ledges on the sides and in the middle to carry the trays, and an open water tank let through the bottom. This differs from other forms of germinating chambers in that the heat is applied directly underneath the water tank, which opens into the chamber. The water vapor furnishes the necessary heat and keeps the germinating seeds and substratum moist. A small space (h) is left between the two tiers of trays in which a thermometer and thermostat can be inserted. The water tank (d) is copper with a 1-inch flange (f) around the top by which it is fastened to the bottom of the chamber. The sides of the tank extend 2½ inches below the bottom (e) to partially confine the heat from the lamp or gas burner underneath. The doors shut against wide cleats all around so that shrinking and swelling will not prevent their opening and shutting easily.

Working drawings of the Sempers germinating chambers are shown herewith.

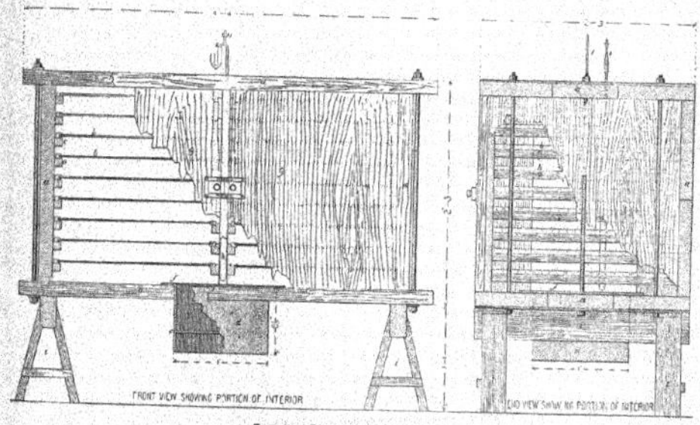

Sempers Germinating Chamber.

Reproduced from Circular No. 34 U. S. Department of Agriculture.

FOR THE RETAILER

[All questions relating to the Retail Trade will be cheerfully answered in this column. We solicit good, sharp photographs of made-up work, decorations, store interiors, etc., for reproduction here.—Ed. F. E.]

Flower Shows Again.

Again on the eve of an annual flower show, we consider it opportune and of the utmost importance to urge a more general or all-round effort to make them successful—not alone financially, but artistically and in the varied forms of interest resultant in general good. As we previously stated, flower shows are of great importance; directly and indirectly they help all engaged in growing or selling. They who stand aloof and criticise the efforts of others are benefited, despite their pettiness. Only a broader understanding can bring forth a brighter spirit, so get into the push, and if you go into competition comply with the wording of the schedule (which is often at variance with the intent). You can most often, however, derive greater results from showing your individuality in work, not always provided for in schedules, and such need not require much expenditure in money or time. The design is the thing; its finish the prize.

At the average small exhibition, or for that matter the large ones, too, some very funny pancaky-like table centerpieces are shown. Often very nice material is spoiled by a too studied compactness in arrangement; and if there is anything more out of place, or very wrong, it is the mud-pie form of a centerpiece. Table decorations should be of a quality to sharpen not dull the appetite. The eye as well as the mouth has an important function in the matter. The setting up of a centerpiece for exhibition means the best that is in your thought or materials at hand.

Where certain flowers are called for, care must be taken to conform, but otherwise the field is unlimited. In the matter of chrysanthemums, we have always found the incurved varieties far superior to the reflexed; and pink and yellow are the two safest colors. Without in anyway reflecting on the merits of varieties or forms, we merely mention one or two to illustrate our preference. In the yellow class it is hard to beat a good Major Bonnaffon and in the pink Helen Bloodgood or Harry Balsley. There are many colors in chrysanthemums unsuited for the entire table decoration, and incongruity in shape or size of bloom is generally a deterring factor. Femininity naturally prefers effeteness; Masculinity inclines more to the bizarre. This is one of the technicalities to consider when thinking of the official judges only.

Always select the round table or centerpiece, for they provide you the best opportunity to display, and over-crowding must be avoided. It is entirely wrong to imagine that flowers or foliage are the only things room should be made for on a dining table. They are merely intended as an adornment—an appetizing picture as it were—not to interfere with, but to add to the pleasures of the festive board. From eighteen inches to two feet should be reserved for service and be clear of all flower or foliage; and this doesn't by any means insinuate formality of arrangement.

There are, we are sorry to say, only one or two flower shows in the United States where the prize list would justify the setting up of a formal dinner decoration; were we to consider the actual monetary side of the case there is not one, for at least $250 would be required to set up and keep in condition a really fine table. But there are other reasons besides the money side of the question why the wealthy or progressive retailer should come forward and do his best at the flower show. There are very few waiters who know how to set up a table, and the many books touching on the subject are, to say the least, amusing. Better avoid displaying service or napkins that jar with or constitute a dominant part of the decorations. Harmony is everything; obstruction means annoyance. Therefore, be careful about the height of your arrangements, and good flowers or foliage will dispense with the use of ribbons. There are some who consider it almost advisable to tie a bow of ribbon on the knife, fork or spoon; they are ribbon-mad and dangerous to American floricultural art.

In the matter of foliage though Autumn leaves are more or less associated with chrysanthemums, they should not be permitted to dominate. They should be used on the table merely to add a light touch of color to bring out the contrasting beauty of green fern on vine. A few select sprays of Japanese maple or Ampelopsis Veitchii will suffice.

Although the custom of wearing flowers has almost disappeared, it might be well to keep the suggestion alive; therefore your offering in the way of corsage or buttonhole bouquet should be dainty—not the cabbage bunch usually seen, which not only tends to injure clothes, but produces disgust and justifies general abhorrence. Overdoing is but a form of overfeeding; both are alike in results. One fine flower is in this sense worth more than twenty poor ones.

We have in our mind's eye a table decorated with single, pompon or anemone chrysanthemums, with the flowers to wear composed of the same as those used for decoration. To be sure they have not the brazen richness shown by the big fellows, but there is a lightness, a daintiness, added to their beauty which endears them to many hearts, old and young; and if only in the manner of showing how the simple or outdoor flowers can be used to advantage, or merely as a contrast to the surroundings at the exhibition, no mistake can be made in their proper display.

The small grower, retailer or gardener need not hesitate on paucity of materials, for really very little is required to make a very presentable centerpiece; and where they are arranged on benches, it is always wise to use a white cloth or even white paper in order to bring out the full beauty of your work. While we do not wish to injure the basket trade, rather the reverse is intended, you need not worry about baskets in the matter of a centerpiece. Anything flat—a saucer, the lid of a barrel anything at all round and flat—can be mossed and covered most carefully with ferns or light greens. Taper off with a few sprays of any light vine, then arrange the blooms, not in checker-board regularity, but exercise your mind in the proper heights and distances between flowers.

Where roses are used some of the newer or scarce varieties may bring you more success. The eye is always attracted by the unusual. The same may be said in the case of carnations; where as in the matter of chrysanthemum shows where there is apt to be a surfeit of these flowers, anything in the way of variety attracts, if it does not otherwise succeed.

Apart from table decoration there are numerous other forms of decorative work that should be displayed. In order to make flower shows more educational and of increasing interest to the general public, we would like to see practical demonstrations given, not only in the arranging of cut flowers, but in the care of house plants.

J. IVERA DONLAN.

A Floral Horse Shoe
Artists, Underwood Bros., Columbus, O.

Preventing Ice or Frost on Show Windows.

Editor Florists' Exchange:

Have double windows by all means, with a space of four or five inches between the sash. Make a set of oblong holes at the top of the outside sash, 2 inches in length and ¾-inch wide, about 2 inches apart. Have one hole on the bottom end of the inside window, or sash, large enough to take in a 3-inch water conductor pipe, said hole to be next to the wall or partition. Take a piece of water conductor pipe 3 inches in diameter, with an elbow on same to go through the hole before described. Bore holes in this pipe about the diameter of an eightpenny wire nail, about 2 inches apart; putting the holes so that they will face the outside window on an angle of 45 degrees. Have the pipe long enough to reach across between the windows, stop up one end of the conductor; put the elbow through said hole, connect with the conductor; stop up all air spaces on the inside window; leave the end of the elbow sticking out on the outside of the inside window. Take a piece of conductor pipe of the same size long enough to reach to a place where there is heat of some kind; elevate the end to near the top of said heated place, connect with the elbow at the window, having the conductor as straight as possible. Procure an electric fan of the kind blacksmiths use, only smaller. Connect it with the water conductor; turn on the power, and you will not have any ice, frost or mist on your show windows, no matter how cold it is outside. Do not run the fan very fast, as this will not be necessary except on very cold mornings. After you have run it a few days, you will understand it better. "We shall know each other better when the mists have rolled away."

The above described device has been in use twelve Winters, only we used a water motor the first seven Winters. Should any one wish to know more about it, make your wants known to The Florists' Exchange. It is the best device I have seen for the purpose intended.

E. D.

A Unique Floral Horseshoe.

The accompanying illustration of a floral horseshoe shows a very unique and artistic design, worked out in white roses, carnations, and asters—a white and green effect. This beautiful tribute was presented by the Hartman Hotel to the veteran driver, Edward Geers, at the recent races at Columbus, O., when Ardelle, the famous trotter, won the $5,000 Hartman Hotel stake. The design was executed by Underwood Brothers of Columbus, O.

F. W.

Boston.

News of the Week.

The annual meeting of the Boston Co-operative Flower Growers Association will be held Saturday, 27th inst., at Young's Hotel.

J. J. McCormack has re-opened his store on Somerset street for the sale of plants, flowers, etc.

Kidder Brothers are cutting exceptionally fine single violets at the present time.

Joseph McCarthy, who has been with Grimmer Brothers for several years past, has now charge of the flower department of J. R. Whipple & Company, at their different hotels.

G. Nicholson, with the E. G. Hill Company, Richmond, Ind., was in town the past week, having come home to attend the wedding of his sister at their father's home in Framingham.

The Waban bowling team played the McCarthy team on Tuesday evening.

Frank Fallon is now with N. F. McCarthy & Co.

Last week was a prosperous one among the florists. Burt Peirce is happy over the arrival of a son; William Chase of a daughter, and B. T. McCarthy of twin daughters, while the genial George Cartwright smiles to think the boys may again call him grandpa.

Carl Jurgens is shipping to Welch Brothers, some of the finest American Beauty roses ever seen in Boston.

William Sim is much pleased with the new violet, Governor Herrick, of which he has a large stock. Mr. Sim's entire establishment is planted with violets this year. J. W. DUNCAN.

The annual chrysanthemum exhibition of the Massachusetts Horticultural Society will be held at Horticultural Hall, 300 Massachusetts avenue, Boston, on Friday, Saturday, and Sunday, November 2, 3 and 4. This is the society's greatest show of the year and it is expected that the display of this Queen of Autumn on this occasion will surpass in magnificence any previous exhibition. In addition to chrysanthemums there will be a fine showing of other flowering plants, orchids, fruits, and vegetables, from many noted gardens and greenhouses in the vicinity of Boston. A special feature will be the competition for decorated dinner tables for which three large prizes are offered. Band concerts will be given every afternoon and evening from 3 to 5 and 7.30 to 9.30. The exhibition will open Friday at 2 o'clock, continuing Saturday and Sunday from 10 a. m. to 10 p. m.

Buffalo.

The News.

Walter Boettger has left for his annual vacation to the North Woods of Michigan on a hunting trip.

Albert W. Reichert, formerly at the flower stand of the Wm. Hengerer Company, has accepted a position with W. J. Palmer & Son.

The death of Daniel O'Day, who formerly resided in Buffalo, called for a whole lot of funeral work from the local as well as the out-of-town florists, W. A. Adams of the S. A. Anderson Company having the bulk of the work locally, while Thorley sent Jack Curry to place a casket cover of violets on green velvet, which was one of the pieces mostly admired at the funeral. Smith of Pittsburg also sent a man with many fine designs.

On Wednesday, the 17th, W. J. Palmer & Son had the Bissel-Warren wedding, which was one of the most elaborate affairs of the month.

The large board fence which has inclosed the McKinley monument has been taken down, which will give the Park Board the chance to beautify the square. W. H. GREVER.

BAY SHORE, N. Y.—On account of our growers not being able to finish the bloom of their chrysanthemums on time for the flower show of our society, which was to be held on October 25, 26 and 27, the dates have been postponed to November 1, 2, and 3.

ZANESVILLE, O.—John D. Imlay addressed the local horticultural society recently on the subject of bulb growing and planting.

COMING EXHIBITIONS.

[Secretaries of other Societies will oblige by forwarding the schedules of their respective shows. Ed. F. E.]

OCTOBER 30, 31 and November 1, 1906.—Tarrytown (N. Y.) Horticultural Society, eighth annual exhibition, Music Hall. E. W. Neubrand, secretary.

OCTOBER 31 and NOVEMBER 1, 1906, Monmouth County (N. J.) Horticultural Society, ninth annual exhibition, Town Hall, Red Bank, N. J. H. A. Kettel, secretary.

OCTOBER 31 AND NOVEMBER 1, 1906, Nassau County (N. Y.) Horticultural Society, Pembroke Hall, Glen Cove, N. Y. Alexander Mackenzie, secretary.

NOVEMBER 1 and 2, Morris County (N. J.) Gardeners and Florists' Society, Assembly Rooms, Madison, N. J. E. Reagan, secretary.

NOVEMBER, 2-4, 1906.—Massachusetts Horticultural Society, Horticultural Hall, Boston. Wm. P. Rich, secretary.

NOVEMBER 5 and 6, 1906., Twelfth Annual Flower Show of New Jersey Floricultural Society, Hall of Woman's Club, East Orange, N. J. Joseph A. Manda, Orange, N. J. Manager.

NOVEMBER 6-8, 1906, New Haven County Horticultural Society. Thomas Pettit, 90 Prospect street, New Haven, Conn., secretary.

NOVEMBER 6 to 9, 1906, Pennsylvania Horticultural Society, Horticultural Hall, Broad street, Philadelphia, Pa. David Rust, secretary.

NOVEMBER 6-12, 1906. — Chicago Horticultural Society. W. N. Rudd, secretary.

NOVEMBER 7, 8 and 9, American Institute, New York, annual chrysanthemum show, etc., Berkeley Lyceum Building. Leonard Barron, New York, secretary Horticultural Section.

NOVEMBER 8, 1906.—Worcester County (Mass.) Horticultural Society, annual exhibition of chrysanthemums, Adin A. Hixon, secretary.

NOVEMBER 8, 9, 10, 1906, Denison Tex.; Flower Show under auspices of Denison Civic Improvement League. Secretary, T. W. Larkin.

NOVEMBER 9-10, 1906, Rhode Island Horticultural Society. C. W. Smith, 27-29 Exchange street, Providence, R. I., secretary.

NOVEMBER—10, Third Annual Ontario Exhibition, Massey Music Hall, Toronto. Secretary, H. B. Cowan, Toronto.

NOVEMBER 13, 14 and 15, Faith Home Association, Thirteenth Annual Chrysanthemum Show, Houston, Texas, Mrs. F. A. Reichardt, secretary.

NOVEMBER 13, 14, 15 and 16, 1906.—Gardeners' Club of Baltimore, Md., in Florists' Exchange new building, St. Paul and Franklin streets. J. J. Perry, 505 North Eutaw street, Baltimore, Secretary of Show Committee.

CHANGES IN BUSINESS.

PIQUA, O.—Herman G. Hershey has opened a flower store in Main street.

WARREN, O.—Mrs. George W. Gaskill has sold her greenhouse plant to D. P. Nelson of Chicago.

CAMBRIDGE, MASS. — Davis has opened a branch store at 508 Massachusetts avenue, to be known as "The Rosary."

MONTANDON, PA.—W. O. Smith and brother have purchased the greenhouses wrecked by fire, formerly belonging to J. C. Wenzel, and will fix them up as soon as possible.

WARREN, MICH.—Harvey Brown, proprietor of the Hartland Nurseries, has consolidated his business with that of the White Elm Nursery, of Oconomowoc and Watertown. Mr. Brown will continue to reside here and devote his time to the interests of the company.

FIRMS WHO ARE BUILDING.

WEILERSVILLE, O.—John S. Yoder is building a greenhouse.

PAW PAW, MICH.—Roy Tuttle is building a large greenhouse.

CHAMPAIGN, ILL.—Frank has added a carnation house to his plant.

DES PLAINES, ILL.—Nick Dahm, Sharp Corner, has erected an additional greenhouse 20x150 feet.

BALTIMORE, MD.—Halliday Brothers have obtained a permit to build a two-story conservatory to cost $200.

DE KALB, ILL.—J. Leonard Johnson has begun the excavations for his greenhouse plant east of town.

BARTLESVILLE, I. T.—J. R. and J. M. Pendroy have opened a flower store here; George W. Myhard is the florist.

FALL RIVER, MASS.—Frank Spooner's new greenhouse is nearing completion. He will make a specialty of mushrooms.

WHEATON, ILL.—J. F. Kidwell, Chicago, has purchased a farm here and will, it is said, erect a dozen greenhouses thereon.

MORRISVILLE, PA.—William H. Moon Company, Glenwood Nurseries, are erecting two large greenhouses to be used for the propagation of nursery stock.

BLOOMINGTON, ILL.—The Phœnix Nursery Company is erecting three greenhouses, each 225 feet in length, also a boiler house, and is installing a water system.

EAST BERWICK, PA.—D. W. Davis is erecting three greenhouses, one 160x25 feet; one, 140x10 feet, and one 22x28 feet. He will also add in the near future another rose house.

NORFOLK, VA.—Lloyd G. Blick has added two more greenhouses to his plant; each house is about 150 feet long. This makes twelve houses on Mr. Blick's place, the new ones being devoted to growing pink and white roses.

CLASSIFIED ADVERTISEMENTS

CASH WITH ORDER.

The columns under this heading are reserved for advertisements of Stock for Sale, Stock Wanted, Help Wanted, Situations Wanted or other Wants; also of Greenhouse, Land, Second-Hand Materials, etc., For Sale or Rent.

Our charge is 10 cts. per line (7 words to the line), set solid, without display. No advt. accepted for less than thirty cents.

Display advertisements in these columns, 15 cents per line; count 12 lines agate to the inch.

[If replies to Help Wanted, Situation Wanted, or other advertisements are to be addressed care of this office, advertisers add 10 cents to cover expense of forwarding.]

Copy must reach New York office 12 o'clock Wednesday to secure insertion in issue of following Saturday.

Advertisers in the Western States desiring to advertise under initials, may save time by having their answer directed care our Chicago office at 127 E. Berwyn Ave.

SITUATIONS WANTED

SITUATION WANTED—By young experienced gardener. Please state particulars. Address, T. N., care The Florists' Exchange.

SITUATION WANTED—As foreman by a first-class grower of roses and carnations. 15 years experience; married. Address, T. D., care The Florists' Exchange.

SITUATION WANTED—By two young Germans, on commercial or private place. Not long in this country; reliable. Address, T. P., care The Florists' Exchange.

SITUATION WANTED—By single young man on private place as assistant. Have considerable experience in greenhouses. Address, W. Mc A., P. O. Box 312, Millbrook, N. Y.

SITUATION WANTED—Assistant gardener wishes position on private place. Has knowledge of general greenhouse work. Single; aged 34. Address, J. Meally, Box C., Locust Valley, L. I.

SITUATION WANTED—By alpine and hardy plant grower. German, aged 26, single, good propagator; English and German experience. First-class references. Address, T. M., care The Florists' Exchange.

SITUATION WANTED—As working foreman or section man in commercial or private place. 26 years' practical experience; good grower in all cut flowers, pot plants and vegetables; also good landscape gardener. German, 40 years of age, married, best references. Please state particulars in first letter. Address, E., 413 Breckenridge street, Lexington, Ky.

SITUATION WANTED—By German, 6 years in this country, married, one child, to take charge of a private place, or as foreman in nursery. 15 years experience in all branches. Must be steady place. Best references can be furnished upon request. Address, J. B., P. O. Box 203, Riverside, Burlington Co., N. J.

SITUATION WANTED—As manager of large commercial place by young man with all-around experience as a florist, nurseryman and landscape architect. Prefer to manage a place for one who has lots of money to invest, and would pay salary and part of the profits. Good references. Address, Horticulturist, care The Florists' Exchange.

SITUATION WANTED—As working foreman, growing roses, carnations, chrysanthemums and pot plants in general. Life experience with trade in Europe and this country. Please state full particulars in first letter. Single man, aged 39. Address, T. U., care The Florists' Exchange.

POSITION WANTED

By expert decorator in retail store where ability [to handle the most select trade will be appreciated.

State wages and particulars.

Address: T. S.
The Florists' Exchange.

HELP WANTED

WANTED—Young man to pack and ship, cut flowers and help around greenhouses. State experience, wages, etc. W. K. Partridge, 148 E. Fourth Street, Cincinnati, O.

SEEDSMAN

capable of taking charge and developing retail department of an established house in a large Eastern city. A good opportunity for a bright up-to-date man. State age, experience, salary required. All communications confidential. Address,

SEEDS, care The Florists' Exchange.

Mention the Florists' Exchange when writing.

HELP WANTED

WANTED—Married man for rose section. State wages wanted, also experience had. Steady position. Address, T. L., care The Florists' Exchange.

WANTED—An all-around florist for 10,000 ft. commercial glass in general stock. Permanent place for reliable man. C. L. Dole, Lockport, N. Y.

FOR SALE—To a first-class florist only, stock and good will of a well-established retail place; "Fifth Avenue Trade" in New York City. Address, care Kervan Company, 20 West 27th street.

WANTED—Young man to assist in high-class retail flower store. Must be of good appearance and have good references. State wages, etc. W. K. Partridge, 148 E. Fourth Street, Cincinnati, O.

WANTED—Thoroughly competent rose grower for section of houses to grow Tea roses. State wages wanted, copy of references should be sent with application. Edw. J. Taylor, Southport, Conn.

WANTED—Night fireman, accustomed to firing large steam boilers in commercial greenhouses, near Philadelphia. Apply, The Floral Exchange, 335 North Sixth Street, Philadelphia, Pa.

WANTED—Section man for carnations. Married man preferred, who would be willing to board one or two men. Have five roomed house on place. State wages, etc. W. K. Partridge, 148 E. Fourth Street, Cincinnati, O.

WANTED—A seedsman who is capable of taking full and complete charge of a retail mail order department in a well established seed house. Address, S. X., care The Florists' Exchange.

WANTED at once a good grower of carnations, chrysanthemums, also bedding stock, as asistant. (25,000 square foot glass.) $35 per month, room and board. German preferred. T. Malbranc, Johnstown, Pa.

WANTED—Nurseryman and landscape gardener, with general knowledge of pruning and the care of fruit and ornamental stock. State experience and salary expected. The Continental Nurseries, Franklin, Mass.

WANTED—An assistant in seed store, New York City. Good wages to the right man. Have also an opening for a bright young man to learn the seed trade, to be quickly advanced if ability shows. Address, T. Q., care The Florists' Exchange.

WANTED

General manager and superintendent of large commercial place situated in Ohio—where Cut Flowers are a feature. Prefer a man of some means and sterling worth, who would be able to buy an interest in the place after twelve months employment and he has proved his ability to grow first-class stock. Address

"INVESTMENT," care Florists' Exchange, New York, N. Y

Mention the Florists' Exchange when writing.

SEEDSMAN

A large Eastern Seedhouse desires to engage a competent and well experienced stock clerk who can take charge of the entire stock, and is capable of filling bulk orders. Good wages to the right party. Applications must give full experience, age, salary expected, and should be addressed to

T. O., care Florists' Exchange.

Mention the Florists' Exchange when writing.

MISCELLANEOUS WANTS

WANTED TO BUY—Greenhouses to be taken down. State full particulars of same when writing. Address, F. W., care The Florists' Exchange.

WANTED—Correspondence with nurserymen who have trees, oaks and elms, suitable for street planting. Address, The Tree and Park Commission, 1317 Sumter street, Columbia, S. C.

WANTED.—Special prices on the following: 3,000 mixed sweet peas, 3,000 mixed tall nasturtiums, 3,000 mixed dwarf nasturtiums. I also want large quantities of all kinds of garden and flower seed. What have you to offer and what is your best price? Write at once to William D. Burt, Dalton, N. Y.

WANTED

MARECHAL NIEL ROSES, 2 plants, 2 or 3 years old, large and healthy. Address
FRANKLIN D. BOWEN, Woodstock, Conn

Mention the Florists' Exchange when writing.

Thirty cents is the minimum charge for advertisements on this page.

FOR SALE OR RENT

FOR SALE—Seed business, established 40 years and at present enjoying a fine retail and wholesale trade. Interested parties will address The Batchelor Seed Store, 28 Liberty St., Utica, N. Y.

FOR SALE—Greenhouses consisting of 20,000 sq. ft., up to date, all covered with 16x24 in. glass, 3 acres of ground, house 9 rooms, and barn. 14 miles from New York. Address, T. H., care The Florists' Exchange.

FOR RENT—Or to lease at Babylon, L. I., three violet houses, 130 ft. long by 11 ft.; in good repair; also dwelling house, eight rooms, barn, 1 1-4 acre good land, 5,500 violet plants in good condition. An assortment of pots and hot bed sash. A splendid chance for a young man at jobbing and landscape gardening. 10 minutes walk from depot. City water in greenhouses. Application can be made to O. H. House on premises or W. Wincott, Box 500, Babylon, L. I., N. Y.

TO LET

Florist Establishment consisting of nine greenhouses, heated by hot water, containing about 10,000 square feet of glass; sheds, barn and dwelling, in Long Island City, within one hour's drive of the wholesale markets of the City of New York. For further particulars address Box R. Y., Florists' Exchange

Mention the Florists' Exchange when writing.

FOR SALE

A well equipped place, consisting of seven greenhouses, over 30,000 feet of glass, a nine roomed house, barn, stock, etc., and eight acres of land. This is a decided bargain and a rare opportunity. For particulars address

S. S. SKIDELSKY,
824 N. 24th St., Philadelphia, Pa.

Mention the Florists' Exchange when writing.

STOCK FOR SALE

PANSIES, 50c. per 100; $3.50 per 1,000. Daisies (Bellis), 50c. per 100; $2.50 per 1000. Alex Hasseler, Meshanticut, R. I.

CARNATIONS—Strong, healthy, field-grown plants, extra large, Ethel Crocker and Flora Hill, $5.00 per 100. Cash with order. W. C. Pray & Co., Kinkora, N. J.

PRINCESS VIOLETS—5,000 strong, healthy, field-grown plants, $4.00 per 100. Cash with order. J. K. Zeisinger, 56 Cutter Street, Melrose, Mass.

ENGLISH PRIZE PANSY PLANTS—I have 10,000 fine plants more than I need. For sale at $3.00 per 1000, cash. Some very odd and beautiful markings among them. Reuben Powell, Florist, White Plains, N. Y.

BABY RAMBLER roses, fine dormant stock, $25 per 100. 2 1-2 inch pot plants, extra well rooted $7 per 100, $65 per 1000. Orders booked for delivery now or any time up to late Spring. Samples free. Brown Brothers Co., Rochester, N. Y.

FOR SALE—Ten acres of fine nursery stock; must be sold at sacrifice prices as lease of land expires next Spring. 15,000 Ligistrum Ibota, 18 in. to 2 ft. at $30.00 per 1000; 5,000 Ligistrum Ibota, 2 1-2 to 3 ft. at $45.00 per 1000; Aralia pentaphylla, Spirea Von Houttei, Viburnum tomentosum, Kerria Japonicum fl. pl., Rhodotypus Kerrioides, and 60,000 other shrubs. Write for particulars and prices to Rhode Island Nurseries, Newport, R. I.

FOR SALE

FOR SALE—4 Hitchings hot water expansion tanks. No. 2 high tank Fig. E. of catalogue. All in good condition. F. O. B., $2.00 each. Address, K. D., care The Florists' Exchange.

BOILERS, BOILERS, BOILERS.
SEVERAL good second hand boilers on hand, also new No. 16 Hitchings at reduced cost. Write for list. Wm. H. Lutton, West Side Avenue Station, C. R. R. of N. J., Jersey City, N. J.

FOR SALE

Greenhouse Material milled from Gulf Cypress, to any detail furnished, or our own patterns as desired, cut and spliced ready for erection. Estimates for complete constructions furnished.

V. E. REICH, Brooklyn, N. Y.
1429-1437 Metropolitan Ave.

Mention the Florists' Exchange when writing.

Newport, R. I.

News and Trade Notes.

Usually Fall planting of trees and shrubs began on private estates in October and continued with some forced interruptions right through the Winter. This season the weather has been so exceedingly pleasant that many owners of places disliked to disturb anything so long as these conditions permitted the enjoyment of a prolonged season in the country. Consequently planting is just getting under way now. In small sized trees of most every kind up to the present the demand pretty nearly equaled the supply but in medium and large sized specimens of many kinds there is a scarcity, resulting from an abnormal demand during three successive seasons for spruce and Norway maples in particular. Large specimen and medium sized spruce are scarce for planting on estates for immediate effect. Norway maples of the same sizes are scarcer still, with very good prices offered for any that are for sale. Lindens are also in good demand.

The estate of Mr. W. S. Wells, on Bellevue avenue, is again undergoing what will perhaps be for many years a final transformation. Mr. Meikle, the gardener is in search of dozens of fine specimen maples and lindens.

Confidence in the commercial future of dahlias by Newport men can be well explained by noting the fact that this Fall two new men have announced their entry into the lists of commercial growers. One of these, W. S. Sisson, has by his recent purchase of the entire stock, comprising the superb collection of cactus varieties, owned by Mr. Wefer of New Bedford, become the possessor of one of the largest and most select collections of cactus dahlias in this section. The other new grower, George S. Stoddard, is to start with more modest proportions, but he himself is imbued with enthusiasm for his new calling sufficient to make up for what he lacks in stock.

John Gibson of Gibson Brothers left Newport last week for an extended trip through Canada. He was accompanied by George Proud, cashier of the Island Savings Bank. D. M.

FOR SALE

BOILERS Hitchings, No. 17 at $110.00. No. 6 Weathered, round, $70.00. 4 section round Cambridge steam boiler $75.00. 8 section No. 11, J. L. Mott boiler, will heat 12,750 ft. glass, $175.00. 10 H. P. upright steam, $35.00. 6 section new Novelty boiler, will heat 4,100 ft. glass, $140.00. New Henderson boilers; send for price on size wanted.

PIPE Good serviceable second hand. No Junk, with new threads. 2 in. 7c.; 1½ in. 5½c.; 1¼ in. 4c.; 1 in. 3c.; 2½ in. 10c.; 3 in. 14c.; 4 in. 19c. 4 in. cast iron greenhouse 14c. 2 in. NEW, standard, full lengths, 8½c. ft. All kinds of fittings for 4 in. cast iron and all sizes wrought iron.

STOCKS AND DIES New Economy, easy working, No. 1 cuts ¼-¾-1 in. $3.00; No. 2 cuts 1¼-1½-2 ins. $4.00; Armstrong Adjustable No. 2 cuts ¾-1 in. $4.00; No. 3 cuts 1¼-1½-2 ins. $6.60.

PIPE CUTTERS Saunders, No. 1 cuts to 1 in. $1.00; No. 2 cuts to 2 in. $1.30; No. 3 cuts to 3 in. $3.00; No. 4 cuts to 4 in. $4.60.

STILLSON WRENCHES Guaranteed. 12 in., grips 1½ in. $1.10; 18 in., grips 2 in. $1.50; 24 in., grips 2½ in. $2.25; 36 in., grips 3½ in. $4.50.

PIPE VISES Reed's Best Hinged Vise, No. 1 grips 2 in. $1.75; No. 2 grips 4 in. $3.50.

GARDEN HOSE 50 ft. lengths ¾ in. not guaranteed; 4½c. guaranteed for light work; 7½c. guaranteed for heavy work, 10c ft.

BRASS HOSE VALVES New; not faucets; ¾ in. 65c; 1 in. 95c.

HOT-BED SASH New; Gulf Cypress. 3 ft. x 6 ft. 75c.; glazed complete $1.60 up. VENTILATORS; all sizes made to order. Second hand sash glazed $1.00 and $1.25, good condition.

GLASS New American, 50 ft. to the box, 10x12 single at $1.75. 10x12, 12x12 10x16 B double $2.55. 12x14 to 12x20 and 14x14 to 14x20 B double $2.70. 10x16 and 10x18 B double $2.90. 18x24 B double $3.15. 16x20 and 16x22 $3.00. 6x8, 7x9, 8x10 old, single $1.50. 8x14 old, double $1.65; 10x14 old, double $1.75.

LINSEED OIL Strictly pure; barrel lots, 42c. gallon.

VENTILATING APPARATUS second hand, Hitchings make, arms, 20c.; hangers, 10c.; machines, $3.50; collars, 8c.

SCREWS all sizes; mixed wood, from 1 in. to 3 in., in boxes, 25 and 50 lbs. at 5c. lb.

PUMPS hot air; well pumps and force pumps; all repairs.

Get our prices on second hand wood material. We can furnish everything in new material to erect any size house. Get our prices.

METROPOLITAN MATERIAL CO.
Greenhouse Wreckers
1398-1408 Metropolitan Avenue, BROOKLYN, N. Y

Providence, R. I.

News Notes.

The firm of Rennie & Pino, seedsmen and dealers in florists' supplies, Washington and Eddy streets, have dissolved partnership. Mr. Pino will continue the business.

The crape-puller has about exhausted himself here. I don't think there is more than one concern doing business here in that way; seven months ago there were at least eight. It was a common thing for two or three of those pullers to meet on a car all going to the house of some bereaved family looking for the same order.

James Lavery, with J. B. Canning, while doing a large decoration with some extra heavy palms, sprained his back quite severely, and was laid up for a week. He has returned to duty.

John A. Macrae's place never looked better. Especially fine are his carnations, chrysanthemums and violets. He has the finest yellow seedling chrysanthemum of his own growing, Number 49, shown in New England last Fall, and expects to have rooted cuttings for the trade by January 1, 1907. E. G. Hill Company of Richmond, Ind., will introduce it.

T. J. Johnston has renovated his store in first-class shape, put in a large new modern tiled refrigerator, redecorated the walls, ceiling, etc. He has got an extension of 10 years on his last lease.

Frank Maxfield of Barrington has sold out to Walter Nichols of the same place. Mr. Maxfield is engaged now with patent appliances for staking carnation plants; also one to put on the calyx of those that burst. The latter is a very good thing, as you can take it off after picking the flowers. It can be used a long time, being made of metal.

Our city fathers are talking of putting in a city forester here, something that is needed very much. We don't expect anything done until after election. I understand Major Alexander Johnson is aspiring to the position. He would make a very good man for it, as he understands the business thoroughly.

Flowers of all kinds are extremely plentiful, that is, seasonable flowers, and business is very quiet. The weather is warm here and very little is going on in society. William Hay is cutting a very fine crop of roses.

G. J.

WALDEN, N. Y.—William C. Hart, a farmer owning one hundred acres of land, has three acres in dahlias. He has secured several promising seedlings among them Mrs. Frank Hulf, Mrs. Harry Lydecker, and the Marjorie.

St. Louis.

News Notes.

Martin Reukauf, traveler for H. Bayersdorfer & Company, Philadelphia, Pa., is calling this week. He has been out on the Coast the past month, and reports a good business trip.

Henry Ostertag made a flying trip to Chicago on Friday of last week to buy stock for his big order for the Faust funeral, which takes place on Saturday of this week. He says this is one of the largest funeral orders he has ever filled, there being no limit to the price on the designs.

The Bankers' Convention the past week used up a lot of American Beauty, as all the large banks were beautifully decorated with these flowers every day.

Fred H. Weber, the Boyle avenue florist, had a swell decoration of chrysanthemums at the Jefferson Hotel. The work was very artistic and nicely handled.

Adolph Brix, St. Louis avenue, has leased the Klockenkemper place in North St. Louis. Mr. Brix reports that he has engaged Henry Braun, formerly foreman for A. Jablonsky.

M. M. Ayers, George Walbart, Miss Neuman and F. C. Weber all had a busy week with work for the Bankers' Convention; American Beauty and chrysanthemums were mostly used.

Our wholesalers, Messrs. Kuehn, Berning, Ellis and Augermuller, report a heavy trade in almost everything, especially American Beauty and fancy chrysanthemums.

Frank Ellis has returned from Panama where he spent the past eight months on his banana plantation. He reports that there is a bright future for him, and the chances are that he will return in the near future after settling his business affairs here.

W. C. Smith & Company, brokers, have a car-load of wild smilax in cold storage for the trade. They have had a big run on small ferns, palms, sheet moss and florists' supplies.

Beyer furnished one of the largest decorations he ever had (and that is saying a good deal) for the Bankers in Art Hall, at the old World's Fair grounds; those who saw it say it was the most artistic decoration ever displayed in this city.

The annual free chrysanthemum show for the public, will take place at Shaw's Garden on November 12, at which time fine specimen blooms will be shown.

President H. C. Irish, Vice-president John Connon, Secretary Beneke, Treasurer A. J. Bentzen and Trustees Carl Beyer, H. C. Smith and Frank Weber, of the St. Louis Florists' Club, held a special officers' session last week, to discuss plans for entertaining the club members at the meetings to be held this Winter; also to perfect arrangements for the chrysanthemum exhibition to be given in the club rooms, November 8, at 2 o'clock, p. m. The discussion also led to the holding of a large flower show next Fall, which will be taken up at the next meeting of the club. No doubt the Florists' Club will have a successful season. ST. PATRICK.

Cincinnati.

News Notes.

On Saturday evening there was a meeting of the Cincinnati Florists' Society, and the principal business transacted was not to hold any flower shows in the club rooms during the coming season.

The Chrysanthemum Society committee had three seedlings before it; two from the E. G. Hill Company and one from Nathan Smith & Son. Blooms were fair, but no special improvement over existing kinds. Director Gerard, from the Hill Company, was probably the best.

E. G. Hill was a visitor Saturday.

E. G. GILLETT.

Indianapolis.

News Notes.

Miss Millie Dorner of La Fayette visited here last week. She mentioned that the customary lot of fine seedling carnations produced by F. Dorner & Sons are not lacking the coming season.

J. D. Carmody of Evansville, Ind., was here on business for a few days. Our friend looks better and younger than ever, and will be with you at Chicago next month, boys.

Huntington & Page are removing to 237 North Delaware street. Their object is to gain much needed room for business, as the new site contains two stories and is one-third larger. Three prominent seed houses may now be found in one block on Delaware street.

Charles Ealand has taken a position at E. Hitz's new place.

F. Harrett has purchased fifteen acres southeast of the city for nursery purposes. He is doing quite a business in this line, having just completed a thousand dollar contract for F. Van Camp, of pork and bean fame.

Elegant windows of chrysanthemums are displayed by the downtown florists; those of John Rieman, Wm. Billingsley, A. Wiegand & Sons and Bertermann Brothers Company never showed to better advantage.

Tomlinson Hall Market is well stocked these days. Sales, particularly retail, are reported as satisfactory.

The building of the Coliseum is not to affect the florists' department in any way.

Bertermann Brothers Company are preparing to hold a flower show in a small way, and an opening at their store about November 7.

Wm. Dow has completed a remodelling of the heating plant at his Broad Ripple greenhouses. I. B.

DETROIT, MICH.—Gustav Knoch, the florist at No. 2463 Fort st. west, won a lawsuit against the Detroit Gas Light & Coke Co. in the Circuit court, securing a verdict for $800. The florist was raising the water hyacinth and claimed that his plants were killed by the gas company letting foul and poisonous water into a ditch in which he was cultivating the flowers.

HAZELTON, PA.—On Monday, October 15, 1906 fire in McGuire's greenhouses did $300 damage. It is thought the fire was of incendiary origin. No insurance was carried.

REVIEW OF THE MARKET

NEW YORK.—The cut flower business is falling off a little in volume, and prices are anything but firm. Business began to decline during the latter part of last week through some cause or other, and the fact that some lines had been bringing pretty stiff values for several weeks, tended to make the present conditions seem rather out of joint.

Chrysanthemums are, of course, becoming more numerous, and the heavy supplies of such early varieties as Polly Rose and Glory of the Pacific—many of which are sent in both short of stem and undersized—have tended probably to push down the prices of chrysanthemums; but as this early crop will soon be a thing of the past, it is believed that the mid-season and later sorts will not come in insufficiently large numbers to bear values to any great extent; at least it is hoped so by the more optimistic flower handlers. Of the high grade blooms of chrysanthemums arriving at the present time, such varieties as Mrs. Henry Robinson, Clementine Touset and Monrovia are bringing the top figures.

American Beauty roses are realizing about the same prices as quoted last week and they do not clear out very readily, although the supply of special grades is diminishing. In the general line of tea roses there has been a gradual decrease in values, even for the best stock; and for such as are mildewed (and there is yet a fair supply of mildewed stock coming in) such a thing as a fixed price is out of the question. The dealer has to get rid of mildewed stock the best way he can, which is usually at a great sacrifice below quoted prices.

While the values of carnations have diminished but slightly the demand is not at all brisk; the supply coming in is probably better than has ever been seen before at this season of the year. Lily of the valley continues in good demand on certain days, and for the better grades $3 and $4 per 100 are the ruling figures.

Smilax is accumulating to quite an extent in the hands of the dealers, and as a consequence prices had to be cut. A little curtailing of the shipments of this product for the next week or two would seem to be a desirable thing.

Gardenias are a regular feature in this market, and we shall, no doubt, see a constant supply from now until next April.

Violets are not cutting much of a figure yet; the supply is not heavy by any means, still there are enough to meet all demands and quite a few to spare; consequently, if a few hundred are sold at the top quoted figures, the averages are brought down materially when the remnants have to be disposed of to the speculators at almost anything they wish to offer.

CHICAGO.—The market continues in a satisfactory and perfectly healthy condition. Though there have been some fluctuations from day to day they have on the whole been of minor importance. It is a safe assertion that the first three weeks of October never saw a stronger market at as high prices, especially on carnations, chrysanthemums, and longiflorum lilies, as has been witnessed this month. The latter part of last week showed an increasing supply of the smaller varieties of early chrysanthemums, and although they cleaned up nicely the effect on the early fancies and on roses showed immediately on prices. Carnations, so far, seem to have been unaffected, having held their own against all comers; but if the present perfectly favorable weather conditions continue it is hardly safe to prognosticate what a few days or even what one day may bring forth.

The quality of stock in all lines is good, and the more recent introductions of early chrysanthemums certainly mark an epoch in the cultivation of the Autumn favorite.

New York violets are arriving in all necessary quantities, and for this early season may be said to be of color and size rather better than might be expected.

The above notes were written at the close of business last Saturday, but Monday of this week presents a different view. Without any announced change in market prices there is a remarkable difference in local conditions, as chrysanthemums are coming in from all directions and the weather has forced everything to the front. Probably the special feature is the excess production of the American Beauty roses, which, judging from shipments and telegraphic reports, extends far beyond the Middle West. Carnation receipts and reports are much easier. W. K. W.

PHILADELPHIA.—The tone of the market here this week is very healthy; all kinds of flowers are moving well. A good demand exists for first-class stock. While the influx of chrysanthemums has curtailed the demand for roses to some extent, it is not so noticeable as reported from other cities; our flower buyers never drop American Beauty roses altogether for chrysanthemums. Choice American Beauty are still selling at $4 per dozen; certainly not so many are sold at that figure, the bulk of general stock going at $3. All tea roses are a trifle easier in price; the principal reason being that all are off color and weak in stem from the effects of six days of cloudy rainy weather. Killarney are selling at $10 per 100, for the choicest stock; Liberty and Richmond at $8; Bride, Bridesmaid, and Kaiserin Augusta Victoria at $6 to $8.

For chrysanthemums the top price recorded this week has been $5 per dozen for a few extra large flowers; others bring $2 to $4 per dozen, while such varieties as Polly Rose and Mme. F. Bergmann are going at $6 to $8 per 100.

Carnations are still not in sufficient supply of choice flowers; some very good Enchantress and a few Mrs. Lawson have sold at $4 per 100, but most of the stock goes at $2 to $3 per 100.

Some choice antirrhinums are arriving in white, yellow, and red, and sell at from $4 to $5 per 100. Double violets, so far, are not extra as to quality; the best sell at 75c. and $1, while the large singles bring 40c. to 50c. per 100. Double violets are later this year; the season has been unfavorable to the growth of the plants and they have not yet taken hold of the soil well.

Orchids are in much better demand; Oncidium varicosum sells at 2 1-2c., Dendrobium Phalænopsis at 8c., and Cattleya labiata at 50c. to 60c. per flower. Bouvardia is coming more freely and brings 50c. to 75c. per bunch of 25. Cut fronds of some of the later varieties of nephrolepis realize $5 per 100. Smilax is selling at $12 and $15 per 100; Asparagus plumosus $35 to $50 per 100 bunches. DAVID RUST.

INDIANAPOLIS.—As soon as the flower market was reinforced by heavier cuts of chrysanthemums, the brisk business of the week preceding diminished instead of increasing as was hoped. At this time quantities of seasonable flowers are on hand, and prices are much easier. Funeral work is light, but counter trade is encouraging. Little decorating is doing at present.

Carnations, which were so eagerly taken ten days ago, are no longer such desirable property, and probably will not be until the chrysanthemum season has passed; $2 to $2.50 per 100 buys the best varieties in the market. Enchantress invariably stands above as a seller at this early date.

The market for roses is much lighter, and there are indications of a drop in prices. Select Bridesmaid, Bride and Golden Gate are bringing $5 to $6 per 100. Fine Kaiserin Augusta Victoria are sold at $4 to $7 per 100. American Beauty retail better than other roses at $2 to $9 per dozen; $6 to $35 per 100 is the growers' price for them.

Indianapolis will certainly have her share of chrysanthemums this season. The cut now is heavy, and it will take hustling to get rid of the flowers later on; $1.50 to $2 per dozen is the average price. Well shaped plants, in 6-inch to 9-inch pots, sell at 60c. each. A few cattleyas retail well at $9 per dozen. Harrisii lilies and callas are offered at $1.50 per dozen, but there is little demand for them. I. B.

ST. LOUIS.—Trade is improving steadily. The past week found most of us very busy with work of all kinds. The Bankers' Convention held here last week tried to corner the American Beauty market, as one could see displays of these flowers in all of the banks and hotels. Society work, too, was quite plentiful among the West End florists. Among the North and South St. Louis florists considerable funeral work was done.

Roses are holding up well, considering that chrysanthemums are much in evidence, but will sooner or later have to give way to the latter, as is the case every year, unless this be an exceptional one. American Beauty are in plenty in all grades and sell well; fancy long bring $4, extra $3, medium $2 per dozen, and shorts from 75c. to $1 per dozen. In the smaller sorts Bride and Bridesmaid realize from $3 to $6 per 100, Richmond and Killarney from $3 to $6, Souvenir du President Carnot, $4 to $8, Perle des Jardins, $3 to $4; some fine Kaiserin Augusta Victoria bring $6 to $8 per 100.

Chrysanthemums are selling in large numbers, and are coming in much improved in quality; extra fancy bring $3 per dozen in yellow and white; very fine pink are also arriving. Other grades run from $1 to $2 per dozen.

Carnations are as scarce as ever, and the wholesalers have little trouble to clean up at $2 and $3 per 100. Some very good Nelson Fisher and Enchantress are coming in; whites are very scarce.

Violets bring a better price this week, owing to better color and quality; choice are at 50c. per 100. Lily of the valley is selling well at $4 per 100.

Jack Frost has completely wiped out outdoor stock. With green material the market is well supplied.

ST. PATRICK.

BOSTON.—The past week has seen quite a change in the flower trade. While prices have not been greatly reduced, still there is a tendency to a downward movement, and stock is much more plentiful. Chrysanthemums especially are beginning to get very abundant, of such varieties as Polly Rose, Glory of the Pacific, Mme. F. Bergmann. Not many fancy varieties have yet made their appearance. Prices are from $6 to $12 for the general run, while fancies bring $2 and $2.50 per dozen. In roses American Beauty still have a brisk demand and are of fine quality; Richmond is doing well and Killarney is popular, as is Wellesley. Carnations are getting very plentiful and there is a great improvement in quality; prices range from $1.50 to $2 for general stock, while fancies bring $3. Lily of the valley remains the same. Lilies are also without change. J. W. D.

NEW BEDFORD, MASS.—Trade is very good at present, with flowers none too plentiful, the past week having been cloudy. We have not had any very cold weather as yet; no heavy firing has been done. Prices for flowers are: carnations, retail 50c. per dozen, roses $1.50 to $2.00 per dozen. Violets are coming in of very fair quality; these bring $1 per hundred. Sweet peas will be in bloom here by Thanksgiving.

E. H. Chamberlin has a few thousand geraniums potted up already; these are Fall cuttings. R. H. Woodhouse, is cutting some fine Boston Market and Queen carnations. Mr. Woodhouse is trying out most of this year's novelties. Chrysanthemums are now in the market, and will hold sway for the next month or so.

Wm. Mosher's place on North street is in excellent shape for the Winter; he has a nice batch of young hydrangeas. HORTICO.

CINCINNATI.—Chrysanthemums have full sway at this writing, with American Beauty a close second. The varieties of chrysanthemums coming in are Willowbrook, Monrovia, Estelle, Glory of the Pacific, Polly Rose and Mme. F. Bergmann, and they bring $1.50 to $2 per dozen, all going off rapidly. Bride and Bridesmaid roses are selling well at $3 and $6; American Beauty, $1 and $4 per dozen. Carnations!—well you must have a search warrant to find any, they are just that scarce; but with the bright clear weather we are having the plants will harden up, the soft growth will gradually disappear and flowering shoots will begin to assert themselves, so that by Christmas we should have carnations.

The first part of last week saw this market cleaned up every day, but on Wednesday it commenced to lag, and continued to do so until Saturday, when it took a brisk turn, and by Sunday noon stock was all cleaned up. E. G. G.

EATON, O.—S. J. Galloway has torn down some old houses and erected a new one, 16x50 feet.

J. K. ALLEN
Wholesale Commission Dealer in **Cut Flowers**
106 West 28th St., NEW YORK
Open at 6 a. m. every day.
Telephone, 167 Madison Square.
Consignments Solicited.
Mention the Florists' Exchange when writing.

Wm. Stuart Allen Co.
Commission Merchan's in CUT FLOWERS
ORCHIDS AT ALL SEASONS
53 WEST 28th STREET, NEW YORK
Telephone 356 Madison Square
Mention the Florists' Exchange when writing.

C. BONNET G. H. BLAKE
BONNET & BLAKE
Wholesale Florists
106 Livingston Street, BROOKLYN, N. Y.
Telephone: 4638 Main.
Consignments solicited. Out-of-town orders carefully attended to. Give us a trial.
Mention the Florists' Exchange when writing.

CUT FLOWER EXCHANGE
Sixth Ave. and 26th St.
Coogan Building, NEW YORK
Open every Morning at Six o'clock for the Sale of Cut Flowers.
Wall Space for advertising purposes to Rent.
V. S. DORVAL, Jr., Secretary.
Mention the Florists' Exchange when writing.

Joseph S. Fenrich
...Wholesale Florist...
—THE RELIABLE HOUSE—
110 West 28th Street
Telephone 324-325 Madison Square.
Mention the Florists' Exchange when writing.

FORD BROS.
Wholesale Florists
48 WEST 28th ST., NEW YORK
Telephone, 3870-3871 Madison Square
Mention the Florists' Exchange when writing.

GROWERS, ATTENTION!
Always Ready to Receive Fine Stock
GUNTHER BROTHERS
30 West 29th Street
Phone, 551 Madison Square. NEW YORK
Violets, Roses, Carnations, Orchids
Established 1888.
Mention the Florists' Exchange when writing.

ALEX. J. GUTTMAN
The Wholesale Florist of New York
43 WEST 28th STREET
Phones 1664-1665 Madison Square
Mention the Florists' Exchange when writing.

A. M. HENSHAW
Wholesale Commission Florist.
Consignments of first class stock solicited.
Prompt returns.
THE SQUARE DEAL
Guaranteed to all who trade here.
52 West 28th Street,
TEL. 5583 Madison Square, NEW YORK
Mention the Florists' Exchange when writing.

HICKS & CRAWBUCK, Inc.
Wholesale Florists
And Dealers in FLORISTS' SUPPLIES
76-78 Court Street
Phone, 3660-3661 Main BROOKLYN, N. Y.
Mention the Florists' Exchange when writing.

HEADQUARTERS FOR NOVELTIES
ORCHIDS A SPECIALTY
THE HIGHEST GRADE OF VALLEY ALWAYS ON HAND
GARDENIAS, DAISIES, ROSES, CARNATIONS.
JAMES McMANUS, Telephone 759 Mad. Sq. 42 W. 28th St., New York.

PHILIP F. KESSLER
Wholesale Florist
55-57 W. 26th St., NEW YORK.
Telephone, 2921-5243 Madison Square.
Mention the Florists' Exchange when writing.

JULIUS LANG
Wholesale Florist
53 WEST 30th STREET
NEW YORK
Consignments Solicited. Telephone: 280 Madison Sq.
Mention the Florists' Exchange when writing.

WILLIAM H. KUEBLER
Wholesale Commission Dealer in
CUT FLOWERS
28 Willoughby St.,
Telephone 4591 Main BROOKLYN, N. Y.
Mention the Florists' Exchange when writing.

FRANK MILLANG
Wholesale Commission Dealer in
CUT FLOWERS
55-57 West 26th Street, New York
Telephone Call: 299 Madison Square.
Mention the Florists' Exchange when writing.

ALFRED H. LANGJAHR
55 WEST 28th STREET, NEW YORK
Telephone, 4626-4627 Madison Square Established 1891
SPECIAL VALLEY AND TOP GRADE ASPARAGUS
Consignments of First Class Stock Solicited.

Horace E. Froment
SUCCESSOR TO
W. GHORMLEY WHOLESALE COMMISSION FLORIST
Receiver and Shipper of all varieties of Cut Flowers
Telephones, 2200 and 2201 Madison Square. 157 West 28th St., NEW YORK

Wholesale Prices of Cut Flowers, New York, Oct. 24, 1906
Prices quoted are by the hundred unless otherwise noted

Roses	A. BEAUTY, fancy—special	12.00 to	20.00
	" extra	8.00 to	10.00
	" No. 1	6.00 to	8.00
	" No. 2	3.00 to	6.00
	" No. 3	2.00 to	3.00
	Bride, Maid, fancy—spe'l	4.00 to	5.00
	" extra	3.00 to	4.00
	" No. 1	1.00 to	2.00
	" No. 2	.50 to	.75
	Golden Gate	.75 to	5.00
	RICHMOND	.75 to	5.00
	Mme. Abel Chatenay	.75 to	5.00
ADIANTUM		.50 to	.75
	CROWEANUM	.50 to	1.00
ASPARAGUS		25.00 to	50.00
	" Plumosus, bunches	8.00 to	15.00
	" Sprengerii, bunches	8.00 to	15.00
		...... to	......
CATTLEYAS		30.00 to	40.00
DAISIES		...... to	......

Carnations	Inf'r grades, all colors		1.00 to	1.50
	STANDARD VARIETIES	White	1.50 to	2.00
		Pink	1.50 to	2.00
		Red	1.50 to	2.00
		Yel. & Var.	1.50 to	2.00
	*FANCY— (*The highest grades of standard var.)	White	2.50 to	4.00
		Pink	2.50 to	4.00
		Red	2.50 to	4.00
		Yel. & Var.	2.50 to	4.00
	NOVELTIES		4.00 to	6.00
CHRYSANTHEMUMS			4.00 to	8.00
"		Fancy	12.00 to	30.00
GARDENIAS, per doz.			2.00 to	3.00
LILIES			10.00 to	12.00
LILY OF THE VALLEY			1.00 to	4.00
MIGNONETTE			...... to	......
SMILAX			5.00 to	8.00
VIOLETS			.35 to	.60
			...... to	......
			...... to	......
			...... to	......
			...... to	......

WALTER F. SHERIDAN
Wholesale Florist
Tel. 3532-3533 Mad. Sq. 39 WEST 28TH ST., NEW YORK
ALL VARIETIES OF CUT FLOWERS IN SEASON

TOP GRADE FOR SHIPPING
American Beauty, Bridesmaid, Bride, Liberty, Lilies, Lily of the Valley, Carnations
Telephone, 1998 Madison Square JOHN I. RAYNOR, 49 West 28th St., NEW YORK

Edw. C. Horan
55 West 28th St., NEW YORK
TELEPHONE, 1462-1463 MADISON SQUARE
CUT FLOWERS AT WHOLESALE
Mention The Florists' Exchange when writing.

JOHN YOUNG
Wholesale Florist
51 W. 28th St., NEW YORK
TELEPHONE: 4463-4464 MADISON SQUARE
Mention the Florists' Exchange when writing.

A. MOLTZ
Wholesale Florist
55-57 West 26th St., NEW YORK
1st Floor. Telephone, 2921-5243 Madison Sq.
Mention the Florists' Exchange when writing.

MOORE, HENTZ & NASH
WHOLESALE
GROWER AGENT
COMMISSION FLORISTS
55 West 26th St., New York
Telephone Call, 756 Madison Square
Mention the Florists' Exchange when writing.

GEORGE SALTFORD
Wholesale Florist
CONSIGNMENTS SOLICITED
46 West 29th Street, New York
TELEPHONE: 3393 MADISON SQUARE
Mention the Florists' Exchange when writing.

J. Seligman Joseph J. Levy
JOHN SELIGMAN & COMPANY
Wholesale Florists
56 West 26th Street,
Tel. 4878 Madison New York
Opposite New York Cut Flower Company
Mention the Florists' Exchange when writing.

B. S. SLINN, JR.
Wholesale Florist
55 and 57 West 26th Street, NEW YORK
SPECIALTIES—Violets, Carnations and Roses
Shipping orders receive prompt attention. Consignment Solicited.
Telephone: 3864 Madison Square
Mention the Florists' Exchange when writing.

WM. STARKE
Wholesale Florist and Plantsman
Tel. No. 4532 Madison Sq. 52 W. 29th St.
Between Broadway and 6th Ave., New York
Shipments of Plants made to any part of the country. A trial order solicited.
SATISFACTION GUARANTEED.
Mention the Florists' Exchange when writing.

FRANK H. TRAENDLY CHARLES SCHENCK
TRAENDLY & SCHENCK
Wholesale Florists
44 WEST 28th STREET, NEW YORK
and CUT FLOWER EXCHANGE
Telephones: 798 and 799 MADISON SQUARE
CONSIGNMENTS SOLICITED
Mention the Florists' Exchange when writing.

THOMAS YOUNG Jr.
Wholesale Florist
43 West 28th Street, NEW YORK
Telephone, 4850 Madison Square
Consignments of Choice Flowers solicited
Mention the Florists' Exchange when writing.

Wholesale Prices of Cut Flowers—Per 100

Boston Oct. 22, 1906	Buffalo Oct. 22, 1906	Detroit Oct. 11, 1906	Cincinnati Oct. 22, 1906	Baltimore Oct. 1, 1906	NAMES AND VARIETIES	Milwaukee Oct. 11, 1906	Phil'delphia Oct. 11, 1906	Pittsburg Oct. 24, 1906	St. Louis Oct. 22, 1906
30.00 to 50.00	20.00 to 25.00	10.00 to 35.00	... to 40.00	... to ...	ROSES — A. BEAUTY, fancy—special	... to 25.00	20.00 to 40.00	20.00 to 25.00	25.00 to 30.00
10.00 to 30.00	15.00 to 20.00	... to ...	25.00 to 30.00	20.00 to 25.00	" extra	15.00 to 18.00	... to ...	15.00 to 18.00	15.00 to 20.00
6.00 to 10.00	10.00 to 15.00	... to ...	15.00 to 20.00	12.50 to 15.00	" No. 1	10.00 to 12.50	... to ...	10.00 to 12.00	8.00 to 12.50
2.00 to 6.00	8.00 to 10.00	... to ...	6.00 to 8.00	5.00 to 10.00	" Culls and ordinary	4.00 to 6.00	... to ...	3.00 to 6.00	4.00 to 6.00
6.00 to 8.00	6.00 to 8.00	3.00 to 6.00	... to 6.00	... to ...	BRIDE, 'MAID, fancy-special	... to 6.00	... to ...	... to 6.00	5.00 to 6.00
4.00 to 6.00	5.00 to 6.00	... to ...	... to 5.00	4.00 to 5.00	" extra	... to 5.00	... to ...	... to 5.00	3.00 to 4.00
2.00 to 4.00	4.00 to 5.00	... to ...	... to 4.00	3.00 to 4.00	" No. 1	... to 4.00	... to ...	3.00 to 4.00	... to 2.00
1.00 to 2.00	3.00 to 4.00	... to ...	... to 3.00	2.00 to 3.00	" No. 2	... to 2.00	... to ...	... to 3.00	... to ...
... to ...	3.00 to 6.00	4.00 to 8.00	2.00 to 6.00	2.00 to 5.00	GOLDEN GATE	4.00 to 6.00	2.00 to 6.00	3.00 to 6.00	2.00 to 5.00
2.00 to 10.00	3.00 to 7.00	... to ...	2.00 to 6.00	3.00 to 5.00	K. A. VICTORIA	4.00 to 8.00	2.00 to 8.00	3.00 to 6.00	3.00 to 8.00
4.00 to 12.00	3.00 to 8.00	... to ...	... to ...	3.00 to 5.00	LIBERTY	4.00 to 6.00	4.00 to 5.00	3.00 to 5.00	... to ...
... to ...	3.00 to 6.00	4.00 to 10.00	... to ...	2.00 to 4.00	METEOR	... to ...	... to ...	... to ...	... to ...
... to ...	2.00 to 5.00	4.00 to 10.00	... to ...	2.00 to 4.00	PERLE	4.00 to 6.00	... to ...	3.00 to 6.00	2.00 to 5.00
... to ...	... to ...	... to 50.00	... to ...	... to ...	ORCHIDS—Cattleyas	... to ...	... to 40.00	... to ...	... to ...
... to ...	... to ...	... to ...	... to ...	... to .75	CARNATIONS — Inferior grades, all colors	... to 1.00	... to 2.50	.75 to 1.00	1.00 to 1.50
1.50 to 2.00	1.50 to 2.00	... to 1.00	... to 2.00	1.00 to 1.50	Standard Varieties — White	... to 1.00	... to 2.50	2.00 to 3.00	1.00 to 1.50
1.50 to 2.00	1.50 to 2.00	... to ...	... to 2.00	1.00 to 1.50	Standard Varieties — Pink	... to 1.00	... to 2.50	2.00 to 3.00	1.00 to 1.50
1.50 to 2.00	1.50 to 2.00	... to ...	... to 2.00	1.00 to 1.50	Standard Varieties — Red	... to 1.00	... to 2.50	2.00 to 3.00	1.00 to 1.50
1.50 to 2.00	... to ...	... to 3.00	... to ...	1.00 to 1.50	Standard Varieties — Yellow and var.	... to 1.00	... to 2.50	2.00 to 3.00	1.00 to 1.50
2.00 to 3.00	2.00 to 3.00	... to ...	... to ...	... to ...	Fancy Varieties — White	1.50 to 2.00	... to 3.00	... to 4.00	2.00 to 4.00
2.00 to 3.00	2.00 to 3.00	... to ...	... to ...	... to ...	Fancy Varieties — Pink	1.50 to 2.00	... to 3.00	... to 4.00	2.00 to 4.00
2.00 to 3.00	2.00 to 3.00	... to ...	... to ...	... to ...	Fancy Varieties — Red	1.50 to 2.00	... to 3.00	... to 4.00	2.00 to 4.00
2.00 to 3.00	... to ...	... to 1.50	... to ...	... to ...	Fancy Varieties — Yellow and var.	1.50 to 2.00	... to 3.00	... to 4.00	2.00 to 4.00
... to ...	... to ...	... to ...	... to ...	... to ...	Novelties	... to ...	... to ...	... to ...	... to ...
.75 to 1.00	.50 to 1.00	... to 2.00	... to 1.00	... to 1.00	ADIANTUM	... to 1.00	... to 1.00	.75 to 1.00	... to 1.00
... to 50.00	15.00 to 20.00	25.00 to 60.00	... to 50.00	25.00 to 50.00	ASPARAGUS, Plum. and Ten.	20.00 to 30.00	50.00 to 75.00	30.00 to 50.00	25.00 to 50.00
... to ...	15.00 to 20.00	20.00 to 30.00	... to 35.00	25.00 to 50.00	" Sprengeri, bunches	20.00 to 30.00	... to 50.00	20.00 to 30.00	25.00 to 50.00
... to ...	8.00 to 10.00	... to 10.00	... to ...	8.00 to 8.00	CALLAS	... to ...	... to ...	6.00 to 12.00	... to ...
6.00 to 20.00	6.00 to 25.00	... to ...	10.00 to 30.00	5.00 to 10.00	CHRYSANTHEMUMS	... to ...	... to 40.00	6.00 to 30.00	... to ...
... to ...	1.50 to 2.50	.75 to 1.50	... to ...	... to ...	DAISIES	... to .40	... to 1.00	... to ...	... to ...
8.00 to 10.00	... to ...	... to ...	... to ...	10.00 to 12.50	LILIES	... to 12.50	... to ...	18.00 to 20.00	... to ...
2.00 to 5.00	3.00 to 4.00	3.00 to 4.00	... to 4.00	... to ...	LILY OF THE VALLEY	... to ...	3.00 to 5.00	2.00 to 4.00	3.00 to 4.00
... to ...	... to ...	... to ...	... to ...	... to ...	MIGNONETTE, ordinary	... to ...	... to ...	... to ...	... to ...
... to ...	... to ...	... to ...	... to ...	... to ...	" fancy	... to ...	... to ...	... to ...	... to ...
12.50 to 15.00	12.00 to 15.00	12.50 to 15.00	... to 15.00	... to ...	SMILAX	... to 15.00	... to ...	12.50 to 15.00	... to 12.50
... to .50	.50 to .60	... to ...	... to 1.00	.35 to .50	VIOLETS, ordinary	... to ...	... to ...	.75 to 1.00	.25 to .35
... to .75	.60 to .75	... to ...	... to ...	... to ...	" fancy	... to ...	... to ...	... to 1.25	... to ...
... to ...	... to ...	... to ...	... to .15	... to ...	GALAX LEAVES	... to ...	... to .15	... to ...	... to .15

Philadelphia.

News Notes.

The retail stores present a very active appearance this week; wedding orders are still keeping up, and the use of baskets of flowers has been noticeably on the increase this season. Habermehl's Sons report some very good business at the Bellevue-Stratford Hotel; every day there are several small dinner tables to decorate. This concern has had a very good demand for cattleya sprays for use as corsage bouquets.

Edward A. Stroud brought in on Tuesday from his Overbrook place a very good seedling chrysanthemum. It is a yellow, with very stiff stem, and foliage right up to the flower, and will no doubt be much sought after. It matures by October 10, and has been named Mrs. Westray Ladd (Appleton × Cinna).

Edward Linvill, who looks after the retail store trade for Wm. K. Harris, has the sympathy of the craft in the loss of his wife, who was buried on Monday last.

Invitations are out for the marriage of Godfrey Aschmann's daughter, Flora Emma, to Peter J. Ott on October 31.

Wm. R. Smith, of Washington, was in town this week.

A Pointer on Valley Forcing.

This is the age of percentages in business. A grower of lily of the valley recently told the writer of his results from pips purchased from Henry A. Dreer, Inc. In placing the order he asked this firm as to what results they could guarantee, and was told that no guarantee could be given; but that from the pips forced before any were put in cold storage, the result should be about 95 per cent., and from cold storage pips the result should be 75 per cent. to 80 per cent. The grower reports a result of 97½ per cent. on the first lot, and 82 per cent. on the cold storage pips. This information no doubt will be useful to other growers.

H. Bayersdorfer & Company are very busy; in fact, they cannot get goods in fast enough. One steamer the Menominee, has just arrived, and there are three others now coming over with goods for this firm.

DAVID RUST.

DUBUQUE, IA.—The Society of Iowa Florists met here on Wednesday, October 17, 1906. Among the papers discussed were:

Greenhouse heating and care of boilers, John T. Temple, Davenport, P. S. Larson, Fort Dodge.

Greenhouse gutters and posts—Judson Kramer, Cedar Rapids, M. K. Zimmer, Woodbine.

Best special quick crop for cut flowers—W. E. Kemble, Oskaloosa, E. C. Keck, Washington, T. L. Ewoldt, Davenport.

Best Shrubs to Force for Retail Trade—J. F. Wilcox, Council Bluffs, Wm. Trillow, Des Moines.

Best Shrubs for Park and Lawn—Peter Lambert, Des Moines, Herman Martin, Mt. Ayr.

Wholesale Prices of Cut Flowers, Chicago, Oct. 23, 1906

Prices quoted are by the hundred unless otherwise noted

ROSES	
American Beauty	
36-inch stems.........per doz.	.... to 8.00
30-inch stems........ "	2.50 to 3.00
24-inch stems........ "	2.00 to 2.50
20-inch stems........ "	1.00 to 2.00
18-inch stems........ "	.... to 1.50
12-inch stems........ "	.... to 1.00
8-inch stems and shorts "	.50 to .75
Bride Maid, fancy special	5.00 to 6.00
" extra	4.00 to 5.00
" No. 1	2.00 to 3.00
" No. 2	.... to 1.00
Golden Gate	2.00 to 6.00
Carnot	2.00 to 6.00
Uncle John	2.00 to 6.00
Liberty	2.00 to 6.00
Richmond	2.00 to 8.00
Kaiserine	2.00 to 8.00
Killarney	3.00 to 6.00
Perle	2.00 to 6.00
Chatenay	2.00 to 6.00
Orchids—Cattleyas	..... to 50.00
SMILAX	8.00 to 12.00
LILY OF THE VALLEY	2.00 to 4.00
V.OLETS	.50 to 1.00

CARNATIONS		
STANDARD VARIETIES	White	1.50 to 2.00
	Pink	1.50 to 2.00
	Red	1.50 to 2.00
	Yellow & var.	1.50 to 2.00
*FANCY (The highest grades of Sta'd var.)	White	2.50 to 3.00
	Pink	2.50 to 3.00
	Red	2.50 to 3.00
	Yellow & var.	2.50 to 3.00
NOVELTIES		.... to ....
ADIANTUM		.75 to 1.00
ASPARAGUS, Plum. & Ten.		.35 to .50
" Sprengeri, bunches		.35 to .50
		.... to ....
LILIES, Longiflorum		15.00 to 18.00
HARRISII		15.00 to 18.00
		.... to ....
		.... to ....
		.... to ....
		.... to ....
		.... to ....
HARDY FERNS per 1000		.... to 1.50
GALAX "		1.00 to 1.25
		.... to ....
CHRYSANTHEMUMS per doz		1.00 to 4.00

Chicago.

News of the Week.

From all sources most favorable reports are made regarding the probable success of the dance to be given in Columbia hall, North avenue and North Clark street, on Wednesday evening next. There can be no question of the advantageous results to the trade of the getting together in a social way of the members thereof, and it is to be regretted that such affairs are not more frequent, not only in Chicago but in other sections of the country.

As one tours the growing establishments of Chicago it becomes evident that that most gorgeous of all holiday floral offerings, the Poinsettia pulcherrima (Euphorbia pulcherrima), is yearly becoming much more extensively and successfully cultivated.

Monrovia, October Frost, and Rosiere may be mentioned as the early chrysanthemums which have proved to be the best of the early sorts and have found a splendid market here.

The E. F. Winterson Company reports a favorable advance in daily business transactions both in cut flowers and supplies, and has been fortunate in closing a contract for three car loads of holly with the party who has supplied them for the past two years with such general satisfaction to the trade.

Mr. Simonds of the Ogden Floral Company has been in a quarrel with one of the hardest enemies to overcome—rheumatism.

J. B. Deamud of the "Busiest house in Chicago," returned on Saturday from a business trip to Michigan.

Last Saturday morning's Chicago Tribune produced an imprint of the "poster" of the coming flower show. These lithographs have always been a prominent feature in the advertising department of the annual exhibition of the Horticultural Society of Chicago, and this year's production promises to be one of the handsomest in the list. The attractive features of the young lady which appear among the chrysanthemums bear a striking resemblance to those of one of the best known and most popular book-keepers in the Chicago wholesale district.

At J. A. Budlong's carnations and roses are reported to be moving well and the Bride and Bridesmaid, from their Bowmanville houses, are certainly above the average market receipts. In chrysanthemums last week the choicest cuts were Omega and Mme. Clementine Touset, the best of which brought $3.00 and $5.00 per dozen, respectively.

Mrs. Ziska, mother of Joseph Ziska of the Chicago Rose Company, died on Saturday morning last, aged 77 years, after a sickness extending over seven weeks, the first serious illness of her life. This is the second death in the family within a few weeks.

Fred. Ostertag of Ostertag Brothers, St. Louis, Mo., was in town on Saturday last.

Miss Nellie Moore, of N. C. Moore & Company, has returned to her city position at the Flower market after three months at the Morton Grove range superintending the renovation and planting of the houses, and reports everything in readiness for the Winter's business.

Vaughan & Sperry are busy at their stand in the market, selling out daily everything consigned to them, and report an excellent business last week, the sale of violets, of which they are making a specialty, having been unprecedented at such an early date.

A. L. Randall Company's catalogue will be published and mailed to-day (Saturday) and will certainly reflect credit on the exertions of that energetic young lady, Miss Tonner, who has toured Europe in the interest of the concern.

J. P. Brooks of Morton Grove is a sincere believer in following up a successful trail. Last season the carnation Queen proved absolutely all that its name implies under his treatment, and as a result, his twelve houses are practically all devoted to this beautiful white variety this season.

Kirscht & Co., of Morton Grove, are making a specialty of carnations Boston Market, Enchantress, Nelson Fisher, and Mrs. Lawson, all of which appear at present in the most promising condition.

All Saints' Day, November 1, and All Soul's Day, November 2, both of which are important religious festivals in New Orleans, have already cast their shadows before, as several orders have been received for delivery on these dates.

There has been no surplus of lily of the valley in this market at any time this Fall, but for the past week or more, good valley or even second grade stock has been more than in active demand.

W. W. Randall returned last Friday from his outing at West Baden, thoroughly recuperated and more than delighted with his experience at this popular resort.

American Beauty roses were never seen in the great central market at this season of the year in better condition than at present, and the crops coming in from the Peter Reinberg ranges are fully up to the highest standard.

Wietor Brothers, who claim with just pride to be the largest growers of chrysanthemums in this section, are offering this season a line of these flowers which has never been excelled. This week they offer in their prime, Mrs. Buch, Viola, J. H. Doyle, Chas. Cronin, M. Wanamaker, Timothy Eaton, Yellow Eaton, Colonel Appleton, Major Bonnaffon, White and Pink Ivory, Oakland, Wm. Duckham, M. F. Plant, Mrs. Partridge, White and Yellow Mayflower, and a number of other seasonable varieties.

The executive board of the S. A. F. O. H., will meet in this city on November 8, 1906, to consider the question of the proposed National Flower Show for the Fall of 1908.

C. W. McKellar's specialty of cattleyas is receiving just appreciation, and the beautiful display of upwards of three hundred blossoms laid out on his counter Monday morning was an attractive sight.

The daily delivery of American Beauty, Richmond and other tea roses arriving at the Randolph street store from the George Reinberg range of glass is proof positive that foreman Arnold has started out this season to keep up with, if not to excel, the excellent work he has accomplished within the past two or three years.

WM. K. WOOD.

The Best He Ever Came Across.

Yours is the best paper I ever came across, and will recommend it to all who are interested in the florist trade. W. VAN BREEMEN.
Passaic, N. J.

San Francisco.

News Notes.

Another flower store has opened, under the title of "The Geary Street Florists." The location is 1136 Geary street, a few doors from Van Ness avenue. Prominent in this enterprise is E. Rosaia, who is the head of the "Young American Florists," established two months ago at 3098 Mission street, a trade name he made popular in connection with the Fourth street store he conducted many years before the April disturbance. With him in the proprietorship of the new store is E. Matraia, formerly with the Art Floral Company, and G. Rosaia, who formerly conducted a flower store at 31 Geary street.

I took a trip yesterday, October 17, to Stanford University to hear Luther Burbank make a speech. He was received with a whirlwind of enthusiasm by the appreciative students. The much discussed horticulturist told in his speech of the best way to regard inventions and discoveries and advised the students to be generous with their ideas. "If you happen to get a new idea," he said, "don't build a barbed wire fence around it and label it yours. By giving your best thoughts freely others will come to you so freely that you will soon never think of fencing them in. Thoughts refuse to climb barbed wire fences to reach anybody." Of his most recent developments he exhibited apples unlike any he has produced before, and gave two bites to each of the students to convince them that one half is sour and the other half is sweet. One side of this new fruit is a brilliant russet and the other yellow.

The Japanese on the east side of San Francisco bay have formed a Gardeners' and Floriculturists' Union. The growers' employees have been getting $1.50 a day, and the Union immediately advanced the scale to $2 a day.

Floriculturists and landscape gardeners of California have plenty of time to brew ideas of surpassing grandeur for the Pacific Ocean Exposition in San Francisco in 1913. It's bound to be held, says the California Promotion Committee. This week this committee received a telegram from Rufus P. Jennings, chairman, now in the East, saying that Harlow N. Higinbotham, president of the Columbian Exposition of Chicago, is heartily in sympathy with the movement to hold a Pacific Ocean Exposition at the time named. Mr. Higinbotham says now is the proper time to launch the proposition. He thinks there will be a world-wide attendance, and that exhibitors will be greatly interested. By the time the exposition is held San Francisco will have fully recovered from the effects of the recent fire and will in itself be an object lesson to the world of the way things are done in this part of the country.

ALVIN.

RALEIGH, N. C.—The hardest freeze ever known in this section at such an early date came on October 10, 11 and 12. The temperature dropped to 26 and 27 degrees above zero. Everything was killed, including the buds of azaleas and camellias that stood out. Magnolia grandiflora were scorched brown; they rarely suffer from frost even in Mid-winter.

J. L. O'Quinn & Company are building one house, 20x80 feet. They have just overhauled their heating plant, dropping the boilers three feet lower, hoping to get better results.

O'Q.

RICHMOND, IND.—E. G. Hill Company will occupy the new west side greenhouses this week. The entire plant of the company will be gradually moved from east of the city. It required more than 100,000 feet of glass in the construction of the west side houses.

LOS ANGELES, CAL.—The salary of W. J. Gowans, foreman in the conservatories of Eastlake Park, has been raised from $100 to $110 a month, because "he is recognized as one of the best plant propagation experts in the country."

Grand Rapids, Mich.

News Notes.

The weather has been ideal since the heavy frost of the 8th and 9th, which simply annihilated all outdoor flowers of every description, and seems to have given business an impetus that is gratifying. Carnations are very scarce, so much so that out of town purchasers have been fortunate indeed if they received 50 to 60 per cent. of the quantity ordered. Roses are in heavy crop, but with both growers and shippers, no more than enough to meet the increased demand caused by the scarcity of carnations, and good cleanups are reported of even short and poor grade stock. Chrysanthemums have been on the market for three weeks; and the full crop of early varieties, such as Polly Rose, Mme. F. Bergmann, October Sunshine and Willowbrook, is now on, with Mrs. Henry Robinson following close behind. Violets are slowly showing up at the different establishments, but are, as yet small and of poor quality, the weather being too warm for good flowers. L. longiflorum bulbs are arriving daily. The number planted will be large. Crabb & Hunter and Eli Cross will each plant about 7,000, while Smith and the Floral Company plant from 2,000 to 3,000 each.

George Peiser of Kennicott Brothers Company, Chicago was a recent visitor.

Paul Goebel was buried October 8 from his home, 1090 Hall street. Twenty-two years ago he started in business alongside Fulton street cemetery, then removed to his late location adjoining Oak Hill and Valley City cemeteries. He built up a fine trade and was respected by all who knew him. He is survived by his widow and four sons. Eugene is superintendent of Oak Hill and Valley City cemeteries; Frank has a greenhouse plant at Warsaw, Ind., while Max and Charles live at home.

There was one noticeable feature about the heavy freeze of Monday night. All verdure was in full vigor; trees were in full leaf, and such a hard frost in early October has not occurred before in twenty years. At Kalamazoo the growers were caught with their celery not yet banked up and it froze, entailing a loss reported to be $250,000. G. F. C.

Baltimore.

Trade Notes.

There is a daily improvement in the cut flower maket. Outdoor stock is practically wiped out; and the supply of indoor flowers has been rather short, especially in roses and carnations. Numerous weddings and other functions have increased the demand for select roses.

Early chrysanthemums have made their appearance at the Exchange, and some few exceptionally good ones have been received from William Weber, Oakland, and others.

The sale of American Beauty roses seems very brisk and the quality is improving; but few are being grown in this locality. C. L. S.

PROVIDENCE, R. I.—The jury has returned a verdict for the defendant in the trespass and ejectment case brought by the J. B. Barnaby Company against John J. Johnston, the florist. The case went to the Superior Court on the defendant's appeal from the decision of the Sixth District Court. The plaintiff gave the defendant notice to vacate the premises on the supposition that the letting was a month to month tenancy, but the defendant contended that he occupied the place at 202 Westminster street under a yearly tenancy. If the later contention was correct the notice given was not legal, and this was the view taken by the jury.

BUCYRUS, O.—Early in the morning of October 15, a fire in an adjoining property extended to and damaged the greenhouse plant of F. J. Norton, causing a loss of between $900 and $1,000, partially covered by insurance. Mr. Norton will postpone his Texas trip for a week or more. He feels very thankful that the weather was mild or he would have suffered a much more severe loss.

On Thursday evening, October 18, a very important pre-arranged bowling match took place between a select team of New York seedsmen and a team of florists and gardeners of Madison, N. J. The match was played on the alleys of the Madison boys, and being on their own grounds they naturally rubbed it in pretty hard to the New York seedsmen. A return match will be played on some alleys in New York, not yet selected, on Saturday, December 1, when it is expected the seedsmen will turn the tables on the Madison growers. The individual scores of the recent match were as follows:

MADISON GROWERS	
A. Herrington	136-210-171
Chas. H. Totty	147-123-146
Robt. Schultz	127-119-184
Keating	186-147-176
W. Duckham	166-145-209
Total	762-744-886

NEW YORK SEEDSMEN	
W. Proters	166-168-146
W. Rickards	117-103-150
L. W. Wheeler	100-125-121
A. Rickards	198-182-139
Chadwick	174-154-184
Total	755-741-740

U-BAR

THE wooden core bars are used to prevent the injurious expansion and contraction of the house, and consequently glass breakage—the method of imbedding the glass insures strength—long life. U-Bar Greenhouses are the Best Greenhouses Built because none are so thoroughly fortified against expansion and contraction—none have so sure and enduring a putty bed. Pierson U-Bar Co., Designers and Builders of U-Bar Greenhouses, Metropolitan Building, 4th Avenue and 23d Street, New York

This is a Money Saver

…HE

…MOREHEAD TRAP

Will Reduce the Cost of Operating your STEAM PLANT

— Write us for information —

…MOREHEAD MFG. CO.

…049 Grand River Ave., Detroit, Mich.

…PLANT CULTURE

PRICE, $1.00.

The best book for the plant grower.

…T. DE LA MARE PTG. & PUB. CO. LTD

GREENHOUSE LUMBER

BUILD WELL

There is a pleasant sense of satisfaction in knowing that when your order for Cypress is placed with us you will receive material upon which you can absolutely rely, and that shipment will be promptly made.

ESTIMATES AND PLANS

Furnished without charge. Let us hear from you if you contemplate building.

HOT BED SASH

CEDAR POSTS, IRON FITTINGS, ETC., ETC.

LOCKLAND LUMBER Co.
LOCKLAND, O.

GREENHOUSE MATERIAL

FREE FROM SAP AND MILLED TO FIT SNUG IS WHAT WE MANUFACTURE AT OUR OWN MILLS.

WE FURNISH EVERYTHING TO COMPLETE YOUR HOUSES INCLUDING GLASS, BOILERS AND PIPE.

CATALOGUE ON APPLICATION. GET OUR PRICES.

S. JACOBS & SONS,

GREENHOUSE CONSTRUCTION MATERIAL.

1365-79 Flushing Ave., BROOKLYN, N. Y.

Greenhouse Material of Louisiana Cypress and

Hot Bed Sash Washington Red Cedar

Greenhouse Hardware and Post. Patent V and U Gutters.

OUR GRADE INVARIABLY THE BEST, OUR PRICES RIGHT.

Write for Catalogue and Estimate when figuring on your new houses.

A. DIETSCH CO., 615 to 621 Sheffield Avenue, CHICAGO, ILL.

THE TEST OF DURABILITY

Durability in greenhouse material is of first importance. It is expensive and tiresome to be constantly re-building and repairing, trying to patch up houses built of poor material.

If you want lasting houses get material that stands the test. Our cypress material will stand the most critical examination or comparison. "Time waits for no man." Send for Catalogue and estimate to-day.

Next Week,
"THE TEST OF QUALITY."

John C. Moninger Co.
CHICAGO
115 E. Blackhawk Street

Plant Experiment

Is more satisfactory when you have a temperature easily controlled. "Pierce" Boilers are noted for their ease of control with use of any fuel.

"Ontario" Steam or Water Boilers with any fuel An Even Temperature

A boiler with a capacious fire-pot, large fuel-door, deep grate is appreciated where any fuel is burned.

We have a Boiler that will please you. Send today for catalogue and prices. We also carry Greenhouse Pipe and Fittings.

PIERCE, BUTLER & PIERCE MFG. CO.
Dept. 15 SYRACUSE, N. Y.
Pierce Mark Boston, New York, Philadelphia

Standard Pumping Engines

have been on the market for years. Write for a list of Florists who have them in daily use.

The Standard Pump & Engine Co.
CLEVELAND, O.

FURMAN BOILERS FOR GREENHOUSE HEATING

Valuable Catalogue on Modern Steam and Hot-Water Heating, mailed free upon request. Address

THE HERENDEEN MANUFACTURING CO.
Dept. F, GENEVA, N. Y.
…98 Pearl Street, NEW YORK OKLAHOMA CITY, O. T.

Furman Boilers have been awarded the Certificate of Merit at Five different Florists' Conventions. Have a record of 20 years. Over 25,000 in use.

SELLING AGENTS:
EDW. S. DEAN, Bloomington, Ill. E. K. BARR, La Crosse, Wis.

Mention the Florists' Exchange when writing.

WHOLESALE TRADE LIST

ASPARAGUS PLUMOSUS, 3 in. pots, $6.00 per 100; 2 in. pots, $2.00 per 100.
ASPARAGUS PLUMOSUS, Seedlings from flats, $1.00 per 100, $8.00 per 1000.
ASPARAGUS SPRENGERI, 5 in. pots, $2.00 per doz.
ASPARAGUS SPRENGERI, 2 in. pots, $2.00 per 100.
BOSTON FERNS, 4 in. pots, 20c. each. 5 in. pots, 35c. each.
CLEMATIS PANICULATA, 4 in. pots, $1.50 per doz., $10.00 per 100; 3 in. pots, 75c. per doz.; $6.00 per 100.
DRACÆNA INDIVISA, 5 in. pots, $2.00 per doz.
GERANIUMS, Stock plants grown in pots. Double white La Favorite, Telegraph, Queen of the West, John Doyle, S. A. Nutt, $1.00 per doz.
HYDRANGEAS, Otaksa and Thos. Hogg, fine field grown plants, $10.00 per 100.
IVY, Hardy English, 4 in. pots, $1.50 per doz.; $10.00 per 100.
Paris Daisy, Strong plants 3 in. pots $6.00 per 100.
SANSEVIERA, (Zebra plant) 4 in. pots, strong $1.50 per doz.; 3 in. pots, $1.00 per doz.

C. EISELE, 11th & Roy Streets, PHILADELPHIA, PA.

Mention the Florists' Exchange when writing.

The STANDARD VENTILATING MACHINERY

The original machine with self oiling cups; the most powerful, least complicated very compact, with ease of operation.
The New Duplex Gutter over six miles in use and highly recommended; the only **drip proof** gutter in the market.
The Standard Return Steam Trap has no equal for simplicity or its workings. Catalogue free.

E. HIPPARD, Youngstown, O.

Mention the Florists' Exchange when writing.

WEATHERED COMPANY.

Builders of Iron and Cypress Greenhouses, Greenhouse Heating and Ventilating Apparatus.

P. O. Address, Box 789,
New York City.

Mention the Florists' Exchange when writing.

BOILERS QUICK.

This is the season when quick deliveries count. I have the largest line of horticultural boilers and can give quick shipments from twenty different points. I will erect your plant complete if you desire it.
Write me for prices.

JOHN A. PAYNE
Horticultural Architect and Builder
33 CLENDENNY AVE., JERSEY CITY
Sash Opening Apparatus.
All kinds of Greenhouse Structural and Heating Material.

Mention the Florists' Exchange when writing.

CYPRESS
IS FAR MORE DURABLE THAN PINE
CYPRESS
SASH BARS
UP TO 32 FEET OR LONGER.
GREENHOUSE
AND OTHER BUILDING MATERIAL,
MEN FURNISHED TO SUPERINTEND ERECTION WHEN DESIRED.
Send for our Circulars.
The A. T. Stearns Lumber Co.,
NEPONSET, BOSTON, MASS.

Mention the Florists' Exchange when writing.

GEO. M. GARLAND
Iron Gutters and Posts
Patented December 27th, 1898.
Send for Catalogue.
Garland's Gutters will keep snow and ice off your glass and prevent breakage.
DESPLAINES, ILL.

A sample of this gutter is on exhibition at Chicago Flower Growers' Market.

Mention the Florists' Exchange when writing.

ARE YOU GOING TO BUILD

Assure yourself of **HONEST COMPETITION** figures by obtaining an estimate from me on Iron **Frame** or **Sash bar** greenhouses. My prices are the lowest for the best class of **work.**

FRANK VAN ASSCHE
(FORMERLY SUPT. FOR WEATHERED)
FACTORY: Fulton and Rose Ave., Jersey City, N. J.

Mention The Florists' Exchange when writing.

A. HERRMANN
Manufacturer of Floral Metal Designs

IMPORTER AND DEALER IN FLORISTS' SUPPLIES
FACTORY: 709 FIRST AVENUE, BETWEEN 40th AND 41st STREETS, NEW YORK
OFFICE AND WAREROOMS: 404, 406, 408, 410, 412 East 34th St.
WRITE FOR NEW CATALOGUE

Mention the Florists' Exchange when writing.

WHERE COMMON SENSE COMES IN.

Isn't it a common sense proposition that the firm who simply makes materials and does not erect greenhouses is on the wrong side of the question to see vital faults in their materials? To the firm who erects their own greenhouses the faults show up—they see at once where improvements should be made—and make them. Of course, we do not erect all our houses, but we erect enough of them to keep the improvements away ahead of the other concerns.

There are plenty of firms who adopt improvements in construction, but there are improvements in materials as well to be considered—from putty to Cypress, there's but one L & B kind—it's the kind that makes the stay put house.

Lord & Burnham Co.

Greenhouse Designers and Manufacturers.

1133 Broadway, corner 26th St., NEW YORK.
BOSTON BRANCH, 819 Tremont Building.

Mention The Florists' Exchange when writing.

"The test of years is the real test."

Scollay Boilers
ARE BEST

See our advertisement in next issue.
Catalogues sent on application.

JOHN A. SCOLLAY
74-76 MYRTLE AVE.,
BOROUGH OF BROOKLYN,
NEW YORK CITY.
Telephones 1492-1493 Main.
U. G. SCOLLAY, Manager.

Mention The Florists' Exchange when writing.

THE FLORISTS' SUPPLY HOUSE OF AMERICA
Now is the time to buy goods
Before we move

SEND FOR CATALOGUE.

H. BAYERSDORFER & CO., 50, 52, 54, 56 North Fourth St., PHILADELPHIA, PA.

Mention the Florists' Exchange when writing.

THE FLORISTS' EXCHANGE

We are a straight shoot and aim to grow into a vigorous plant

A WEEKLY MEDIUM OF INTERCHANGE FOR FLORISTS, NURSERYMEN, SEEDSMEN AND THE TRADE IN GENERAL

Vol XXII. No. 18 — NEW YORK AND CHICAGO, NOVEMBER 3, 1906 — One Dollar Per Year

NOW READY EASTER LILIES

Should be potted at once, as Easter is early this year.

Japan stocks are now arriving, and are in first-class shape.

Japan Longiflorum,	9 to 10 in. bulbs, case of 200 bulbs	$15.00
" " **Multiflorum**,	7 to 9 " " " " 300 "	15.00
" " "	9 to 10 " " " " 200 "	17.00
" " **Giganteum**,	7 to 9 " " " " 300 "	18.75
" " "	9 to 10 " " " " 200 "	21.00

Lilium Candidum, selected bulbs, $5.00 per 100.

A Few of the Leading Narcissus.

Paper White Grandiflora, 13-15 c/m, fine bulbs, case of 1250 bulbs	$11.25
Double Von Sion, first size	$ 9.00 per 1000
" " " extra size	12.00 " "
" " " mammoth double nosed, or top-root	20.00 " "
Princeps, early, single, fine bulbs	7.00 " "
Golden Spur, the favorite single yellow	18.00 " "
Empress, a grand bicolor	20.00 " "
Alba Plena Odorata	6.00 " "
Barri Conspicuus	8.00 " "
Poeticus	4.50 " "
Poeticus Ornatus	7.00 " "

White Roman Hyacinths, 12-15 c/m	$23.00 per 1000
" " " 13-15 "	28.00 " "
Freesia Refracta Alba, finest Bermuda bulbs	7.50 " "
Callas, Exhibition Bulbs, 2 inch-2½ inch in diameter	10.00 " 100
Bermuda Buttercup Oxalis	7.50 " 1000
Spanish Iris, mixed	2.50 " "

For other bulbs and for smaller quantities, see our Wholesale Price List, in which will be found a full assortment of all kinds of bulbs for winter and spring flowering. Send for list if you have not already received one.

F. R. PIERSON CO., TARRYTOWN-ON-HUDSON NEW YORK

Mention the Florists' Exchange when writing.

Asparagus Plumosus Nanus

Cut strings, 8 feet long, 50 cts. each.

W. H. ELLIOTT

Brighton, Mass.

Mention the Florists' Exchange when writing.

Gladiolus For Winter Forcing

Colvillei Alba (The Bride). Per 100, 80c.; per 1000, $6.50.

Colvillei Rubra, red. Per 100, 75c.; per 1000, $6.00

Blushing Bride (or Delicatissima). New variety of decided merit; splendid forcer, coming into bloom six weeks before Colvillei Alba. Flowers are large, pure white with pink spots, all opening at the same time, thus making a better cut-flower than any other Gladiolus. Can be had in bloom for Easter. Per 100, $1.25; per 1000, $10.00.

Peach Blossom. Same class as Blushing Bride but of a beautiful shade of pink, excellent cut-flower; very large. Per 100, $2.00; Per 1000, $18.00.

SPIRAEA

We are very careful to import Spiraea clumps which have large plump eyes, as these are the only kind that will give satisfaction.

Astilboides Floribunda.—New, strong and more developed than the common Astilboides, from which it is a sport. Produces large, pure white plumes and is unquestionably one of the best Spiraeas. Per doz., 85c.; per 100, $4.25.

Astilboides Superbe.—A splendid new variety which makes a beautiful shaped plant with abundant flowers (20 to 30 on a good plant). Per doz., 85c.; per 100, $5.00.

Blondin.—One of the best varieties for Easter. Per doz., $1.00; per 100, $5 00.

Compacta Multiflora.—This new variety, which has foliage of rich green color, grows from 8 to 10 inches in height, and produces larger and finer blossoms than Japonica. It is about two weeks earlier. Per doz., 75c.; per 100, $4.25.

Gladstone.—Without question one of the choicest Spiraeas in market, and "up to date" Florists cannot afford to be without it. Per doz., $1.25; per 100, $6.75.

Japonica.—Extra strong clumps. Per doz., 75c.; per 100, $4.00.

F. O. B.: N. Y. add $1.00 per 100 if shipped from Chicago.

Vaughan's Seed Store

14 BARCLAY ST. NEW YORK

CHICAGO, 84-86 Randolph Street. Greenhouses, Western Springs, Ill.

Mention The Florists' Exchange when writing.

FLORISTS' BULBS

SINGLE TULIPS

	100	1000
Coleur Cardinal, crimson scarlet	$3.00	$25.00
Cottage Maid, rosy pink	.85	8 00
Keizerskroon, red and yellow	1.50	14.50
La Reine, white	1.00	8.00
Pottebakker, scarlet	1.60	15.00
Princess Marianna, white	1.00	9.00
Proserpine, silky rose	2.75	25.00
Rosa Mundi Huykman	.85	8 00
Van Gooyen, rosy pink	1.25	12.00
Yellow Prince, yellow	.90	8.00
Superfine Mixture	.75	7.50
Fine Mixture	.60	5.50

DOUBLE TULIPS

	100	1000
Alba Maxima	$1.25	$11.00
Duc Van Thuyll, red and yellow	.75	6.50
Duke of York, red, white edge	1.00	9.00
Gloria Solis, red and yellow	1.25	12.00
Imperator Rubrorum, scarlet	2.75	24.00
La Candeur, white	1.25	11.50
Murillo, blush white	2.00	18.50
Rosine, beautiful rose	1.50	14.50
Salvator Rosa, deep rose	3.00	27.00
Yellow Rose, yellow	.80	7.00
Superfine double mixed	1.00	8.00
Fine double mixed	.75	7.00

LILIUM MULTIFLORUM

Boddington's Early or Easter Flowering Type

	Per 100	1000
7 to 9 inch bulbs, 300 in a case	$5.00	$45.00
9 to 10 inch bulbs, 200 in a case	8.50	80.00

Also **Lilium Giganteum** and all other bulbs. Send for special prices and catalogue.

DUTCH ROMANS or MINIATURE HYACINTHS

	Per 12	100	1000
All colors to name	$.30	$2.25	$18.00

ARTHUR T. BODDINGTON

342 W. 14th ST., - - NEW YORK CITY

Mention the Florists' Exchange when writing.

CONTENTS AND INDEX TO ADVERTISERS, PAGE 529

FALL IN BULBS

	100
TULIPS, double superfine mixed	$ .85
" Single Artus	1.25
" Belle Alliance	2.00
" Yellow Prince	.90
" La Reine	.80
" Gesneriana Scarlet	1.35
CROCUS, Blue, White, Striped and Yellow	.50
NARCISSUS, Emperor	.90
" Double Incomparable	.85
" Von Sion, mam. double rose	2.00
LILIUM LONGIFLORUM, limited quantity, 5 to 7	2.00
" " MULTIFLORUM, 5 to 7	2.75

COLD FRAME MATS

	Each	Dozen
Straw Mats, best for hot beds	$1.25	$14.00
Burlap Mats, extra serviceable	1.25	14.00

Sterilized Sheep Manure, $1.25 100 lbs, $20.00 a Ton.

WM. ELLIOTT & SONS, 201 Fulton Street, NEW YORK.

Mention the Florists' Exchange when writing.

TRUE IRISH SHAMROCK SEED

NEW CROP SEED JUST RECEIVED

Plant soon if you wish good strong plants by MARCH 17

Price 1/8 oz. (About 5000 Seeds) 50c.

W. W. RAWSON & CO.

5 UNION STREET, BOSTON, MASS.

C. C. MORSE & CO.

SEED GROWERS

171-173 Clay St., San Francisco, California

OUR SPECIALTIES

ONION LETTUCE SWEET PEAS

Also Carrot, Celery, Celeriac, Cucumber, Endive, Leek, Mustard, Parsley, Parsnip, Radish, Salsify, Spinach, Tomato and

FLOWER SEEDS

Growers for the trade on contract. Warehouses at Santa Clara; Farms and Farm headquarters Carnadero, near Gilroy.

Registered Cable Address: MORSEED, SAN FRANCISCO.

Mention the Florists' Exchange when writing.

PACIFIC SEED GROWERS' CO.

109 MARKET STREET

SAN FRANCISCO, CAL.

Specialties:

Onion, Carrot, Lettuce, Sweet Peas

Mention The Florists' Exchange when writing.

BURPEE'S SEEDS

PHILADELPHIA

Blue List of Wholesale Prices mailed only to those who plant for profit.

Mention the Florists' Exchange when writing.

MY GIANT CYCLAMEN

Are Ahead in Growth and Flowers

Bloodred, Carmine, Pink, Pure White, White Carmine Eyed.

Each color separate. Tr. pkt., $1.00; 1000 seeds, $6.00. An even mixture of the above 5 colors, tr. pkt., 75c.; 1000 seeds, $5.00.

For larger quantities, special quotations.

O. V. ZANGEN, Seedsman, HOBOKEN, N. J.

Mention the Florists' Exchange when writing.

Catalog Engravings

and ILLUSTRATIONS

that print EASILY. That's the kind we make—have been since '73

JAS. M. BRYANT, Horticultural Engraving and Printing

706 Chestnut Street, PHILADELPHIA, PA.

Write for our Catalogue of Stock Engravings

Mention the Florists' Exchange when writing.

W. & D.'s Specialties for Forcing

Mignonette "New York Market"

Sweet Peas "True" Christmas Flowering (Pink and White)

Tomato "The Don" Tomato "Stirling Castle"

Mushroom Spawn "English" and "Pure Culture"

Special prices on application

WEEBER & DON, Seed Merchants and Growers

114 Chambers Street, NEW YORK

Mention The Florists' Exchange when writing.

NEW CROP SWEET PEAS

SEND FOR LIST OF THE NEW

GIANT FLOWERING VARIETIES

STUMPP & WALTER CO., 50 Barclay Street NEW YORK

Mention the Florists' Exchange when writing.

BELATED SHIPMENT

PAPER WHITE NARCISSUS

Choice, sound, 13-15 cm. Bulbs, 1300 to the case, at $7.00 per M. in full case lots only; in less quantity at $8.00 per M.

Stokes Seed Store

219 Market Street, Philadelphia.

Mention the Florists' Exchange when writing.

AT THE S. A. F. O. H. CONVENTION AT DAYTON, OHIO

AMERICA

was conceded to be the very best Gladiolus on the market. Strong bulbs for delivery after Dec. 1, 1906. $10.00 per 100; $75.00 per 1000.

JOHN LEWIS CHILDS, Floral Park, L. I., N. Y.

ARTHUR COWEE, GLADIOLUS SPECIALIST

MEADOWVALE FARM, BERLIN, N. Y.

United States Representative and Grower of GROFF'S HYBRIDS, MIXTURES and COLLECTIONS to color. Fine Mixtures of all colors. Named Novelties of rare beauty. WRITE FOR CATALOG.

Mention the Florists' Exchange when writing.

Thorburn's Bulbs

Lilium Longiflorum

7 to 9-in. $5.00 per 100; $45.00 per 1000

8 to 10-in. 7.00 per 100; 68.00 per 1000

Also many of the leading sorts of Hyacinths, Tulips and Narcissus.

PANDANUS UTILIS

Fresh seed just received, $6.00 per 1000 seeds.

Send for Trade List.

J. M. THORBURN & CO.

33 Barclay St., through to 38 Park Place, NEW YORK.

Mention the Florists' Exchange when writing.

GROW YOUR OWN

TREES

and SHRUBS from

SEED.

TREE AND SHRUB SEEDS ROOTS BULBS KATZENSTEIN

Send today for our

TRADE SEED LIST

and also for our *Descriptive Catalog*, which is replete with valuable information.

OTTO KATZENSTEIN & CO.

Wholesale Dept. ATLANTA, GA.

Mention The Florists' Exchange when writing.

CINERARIA

Large Flowering Prize, Splendid Mixed, T. P. $0.50

Large Flowering, Semi Dwarf Prize, Splendid Mixed, T. P. $0.50

PANSY, Superb Mixed.

oz. $4.50. 1/4 oz. $1.15 1/8 oz. $0.6

W. C. BECKERT

Allegheny, Pa.

Mention The Florists' Exchange when writin

FORCING BULBS

Let us quote you prices

PERENNIAL GARDENS CO., - TOLEDO,

Mention the Florists' Exchange when writin

BOOKS

GARDENER'S ASSISTANT, $15.0

Write for Prospectus

VIOLET CULTURE,	1.5
THE HEATHER,	1.5
AMERICAN CARNATION,	3.5
PLANT CULTURE,	1.0
HOUSE PLANTS, cloth	1.0
" " paper	.5
RESIDENTIAL SITES,	2.5
TELEGRAPH CODE,	2.5

A. T. De La Mare Ptg. and Pub. Co. Ltd., N.

Your Money is well spent when you advertise in
THE FLORISTS' EXCHANGE

Seed Trade Report.

AMERICAN SEED TRADE ASSOCIATION

Henry W. Wood, Richmond, Va., president; C. S. Burge, Toledo, O., first vice-president; G. B. McVay, Birmingham, Ala., second vice-president; C. E. Kendel, Cleveland, O., secretary and treasurer; J. H. Ford, Ravenna, O., assistant secretary.

The 1906 crop of potatoes, according to American Agriculturist's final report, is estimated at 277,000,000 bushels, compared with 253,000,000 bushels in 1905, and 289,000,000 bushels in 1904.

COLUMBUS, O.—The seedsmen have been having a very brisk bulb season; all kinds have sold well, especially tulips and narcissus. There is no question, but that all Holland stock will be practically cleaned up before the ground closes for the Winter.

F. W.

CLEVELAND, O.—The Home Gardening Association will this year give to the public schools 130,000 bulbs. Twenty thousand of this number will be given as prizes for creditable flower shows. In addition, 18,000 will be given to workers on vacant lots, where the gardens have been under the direction of the Association.

CINCINNATI, O.—The Pure Culture Spawn Company has established a branch with main offices at 609 West Fourth street, this city, where C. H. Winkler is manager. The move was necessary in order to handle properly the firm's Eastern trade. The Western branch at Pacific, Mo., will be maintained, and all trade west of St. Louis will be handled from Pacific.

CONRAD APPEL, the wholesale seed grower of Darmstadt, Germany, whose house was established in 1789, was lately awarded at this year's international exhibition, Milan, Italy, for his beautiful ornamental lawn, second prize, the "prize of honor;" and for a fine show case containing all kinds of cleaned grass, clover and agricultural seeds, deciduous and evergreen tree seeds, grass seed mixtures, and his complete collection of rare conifer cones, the highest award—the "grand prize."

PROVIDENCE, R. I.—Rennie & Thomson is the name of a new firm just about to embark in the business. The store at 135 and 137 Washington street has been leased by the firm and operations started in fitting it up for opening with a full line of seeds, bulbs and sundries at an early date. Mr. Rennie has been a member of the firm of Rennie & Pino, from which he recently retired, and is well known in this city. Mr. Thomson has had a wide business experience both in Chicago and in the East, having for a number of years been manager for R. & J. Farquhar & Company, Boston, and more recently with Vaughan's Seed Store, New York. J. W. D.

European Notes.

An unusually mild Autumn is doing its very utmost to compensate for a prolonged and exceptionally hot Summer, with the result that the work of harvesting and cleaning up our crops and preparing the land for next season's work has never been more advanced than at present. Of the crops the less said the better, for while these notes have prepared your readers for very great shortages in early beets and forcing radish, the worst has not yet been told.

In your issue of October 6 just to hand appears an article on Italian vs. German seeds from an "English Correspondent." The article will no doubt call forth replies from the German seed growers who are interested, but the writer would like to point out that the story about the destruction of all the colored onions by hail storms was reported in these notes early in August. In this connection the following extract from a letter from one of the most responsible and reliable Italian seed growers will doubtless be read with interest. "It is true that in some districts the crop of onion seeds has been damaged somewhat by hail, but this is not the chief reason of the shortage of the red skinned onions. Two or three years ago there was a large surplus of these varieties and everyone kept back from cultivating them again, so last year there has been very few planted of all red onions."

The statement that probably the bulk of the cauliflower seed used throughout Europe is grown in Italy will cause a smile to appear on the faces of many readers of the article. It is, of course, quite true of the Italian varieties. The firm whose interests the whole article is intended to boom are to be congratulated on the free advertisement they have secured.

S. B. Dicks is back in London.

EUROPEAN SEEDS.

Italian vs. German Seeds.

Editor Florists' Exchange:

In reading your issue of October 6, I notice on page 400, in an article headed "Italian vs. German Seeds," some statements which are calculated to mislead American horticulturists and to prejudice the German seed growing industry in their eyes. I beg therefore you will kindly give space in your columns to the following reply.

It is true that seed merchants here, as elsewhere, depend on Italy and other southern countries for certain articles. For instance, among vegetables some southerly sorts of cauliflower and the Tripoli class of onions; but Tripoli onions form but a small part of the onion seed trade as a whole, and your correspondent errs greatly if he thinks that the bulk of the European crop of onion seed is raised in Italy. The same remark applies to cauliflowers. We also look to the South for various kinds of flower seeds, especially of the half hardy section, such as ricinus, solanum and a good many others, and we sometimes divide our cultures by placing there a part of our requirements in such articles as are apt to fail in unfavorable seasons in Germany.

With respect to asters, however, as far as Erfurt is concerned I must emphatically protest against the statement that we buy from Italy. Certanly nine-tenths, if not all of the aster seed sent from Erfurt is raised in the district; our frequent American visitors can testify as to the immense scale on which we grow it, and our reputation for quality never stood higher than it does at present. As regards the quality of the cheap Italian aster seed, we must leave it to the public to try it if they wish, and to judge if it suits their purpose.

We need nearly every country to get certain seeds from, the same as we send seeds to nearly every country, and no doubt there is competition between growing districts, but we think your readers ought to know that when buying asters from Erfurt they are buying genuine German-grown seed, which we consider the best in the world.

AN ERFURT SEED GROWER.

CATALOGUES RECEIVED.

PAPE & BERGMAN, Quedlinburg, Germany.—List of Novelties in Flowers and Vegetables.

C. F. BRAINARD, Thompsonville, Conn.—Price List of Trees, Shrubs, Plants and Bulbs.

SLUIS & GROOT, Enkhuizen, Holland.—Price List of Vegetable, Flower, and Agricultural Seeds.

G. BERNARD, Olivet-Orleans, France.—Catalogue of Forest and Ornamental Trees, Conifers, Shrubs, etc.

OTTO KATZENSTEIN & COMPANY, Atlanta, Ga., and New York.—Catalogue of Tree and Shrub Seeds, Roots, Bulbs, etc.

NURSERY DEPARTMENT.

Conducted by Joseph Meehan.

AMERICAN ASSOCIATION OF NURSERYMEN, Orlando Harrison, Berlin, Md., president; J. W. Hill, Des Moines, Ia., vice-president; George C. Seager, Rochester, N. Y., secretary; C. L. Yates, Rochester, N. Y., treasurer.

AUSTIN, TEX.—On October 22 Insurance Commissioner Clay gave out a statement showing 227 nurseries in the State, to which certificates will be issued. It is estimated the value of all nurseries is $725,000. The general condition of the nurseries throughout the State is fully fifty per cent. better than this time last year.

SHRUB FOR NAME.—A. E. C., Providence, R. I. —The shrub appears to be some rubus, either R. odoratus or R. phœnicolasius. J. M.

TREE FOR NAME.—Kindly tell me the name of the tree of which I send a leaf. The branches are covered with a small pink flower before the leaf growth starts in Spring. H. B. McK.
New Jersey.

—The leaf, coupled with your description, is sufficient to make it safe to say your shrub is the Judas tree. Cercis japonica is the Japanese species and Cercis canadensis the native one. I think yours is the Japanese, especially if it is a bushy grower, with bright rosy pink flowers.

Send specimens of anything whenever you wish to know what they are. J. M.

SALE OF NURSERY LAND.—A deal has just been consummated whereby a portion of the ground of the nursery of Thomas Meehan & Sons, Germantown, Philadelphia, has been sold for building purposes, probably about one-third of the whole. There was no wish to dispose of the ground, but the offer for it was a tempting one, which could hardly be resisted. Those acquainted with the nursery will know the portion sold when mentioned that it is that which extends from the railroad to Stenton avenue. Ample time was asked and accorded to transplant the stock to other ground; and as the larger portion of the nursery is still retained the business will be pushed with the old time vigor.

This, the Germantown nursery, represents the retail department of Thos. Meehan & Sons nurseries; the wholesale department is at Dreshertown, but a few miles away, and it consists of several hundred acres.

Seasonable Notes.

On page 493, issue of October 27, under this heading, in second last paragraph, read Bignonia capreolata, and not Begonia, as previously printed.

The cat brier, Smilax rotundifolia, is sometimes planted when a prickly, rampant-growing vine is desired—a place, for instance, where it is desired to keep out intruders. In late Autumn the foliage of this vine changes to a bright red, when it is quite ornamental.

Until real freezing weather comes the clusters of scarlet berries of Viburnum Wrightii remain in perfect condition, as do its leaves. The leaves do not change, but keep deep green to the last. It is a valuable new shrub.

At this date, October 26, the showiest herbaceous plant in flower is Helianthus Maximiliani. Its tall spikes are full of its yellow flowers, and they are not fading, but in their prime as well expanded flowers. There is no other perennial of like character that could take its place.

Among old style "berry" shrubs, set out for their bright red fruits in Autumn, the high bush cranberry, Viburnum opulus, or V. oxycoccos, as many call it, still holds its place. It is now in fine display and will continue so until Spring.

Sweet gum, liquidambar, is not often mentioned as a tree conspicuous for its Autumn foliage, yet in some years its leafage rivals in splendor that of any other tree. It is to be preferred to the sour gum all the time. Although classed as a Southern tree it is wild in Southern Pennsylvania and along the coast to Connecticut.

The red-stemmed dogwood is greatly valued because of the blood-red color of its shoots in the Winter season. There is now a variety of it having yellow-colored shoots, and it proves a valuable sort. When these cornuses are planted in groups they give beds of color through the Winter season.

The two passion vines preferred for the use of their fruit are Passiflora quadrangularis and P. edulis. The fruit of the former is known as granadilla and is to be found in its season in market in the South. The fruit of the P. incarnata, known as May pops, can be eaten, but is in little demand.

Suckers from fruit trees should not be used as stocks on which to graft fruits. The suckering habit becomes fixed by doing so, the suckers proving a great nuisance.

The light pink flowers of Pyrus coronaria, the sweet-scented crab, are greatly admired. The odor from them is very agreeable, and then its "apples" are nicely perfumed as well. There is no trouble in increasing it. By seeds, grafting and budding are all available ways.

Acalypha Sanderi, with its long strings of scarlet flowers, is not only a lovely pot plant, but it has also proved useful as an outdoor subject. Beds of it have made an attractive appearance, plants having been set out when the warm weather of June came.

Potting Evergreens for Christmas.

Every year those who sell small evergreens in pots for Christmas report an increased call for them. An evergreen seems always in place when used in a decorative way; especially is this true at Christmas time, for in all countries houses and churches are decorated with green for this festival. There is probably but little thought given to the practicability of using the plants afterward; it is the best plant possible for the joyful time that is in the minds of all to a great extent, yet it will be of interest to many to know that the plants they are using for the holidays are available afterward for planting outdoors.

The different positions the plants are to fill call for different styles of growth—some globe-shaped, some of pyramidal growth and others of normal habit. One who sells great numbers of such evergreens finds, he says, that it makes little difference what he selects from the nursery, so that he gets an assortment of all sizes available for placing in pots. The many varieties of retinisporas, Arbor vitæs, junipers and spruce he finds the most useful. The junipers and yews give the best choice among the pyramidal-shaped sorts, although the common American and the common Chinese Arbor vitæ are of the same class. Retinisporas are very useful and always good sellers, the best two being R. plumosa and plumosa aurea. When the Lawson cypress can be had it and its variety, stricta viridis, are greatly in demand, not only for their beautiful growth but for the deep green of their foliage as well; and in this respect the Chinese Arbor vitæ is on an equal footing with them.

When it comes to something on which presents may be hung such as are desired for small children, the common Norway spruce, the hemlock spruce and the silver fir are in great demand. The silver fir is good; its branches are of horizontal growth and its needles are not so stiff as to irritate the hand that touches them.

For globe-shaped evergreens there are several varieties of the common Arbor vitæ, known as globe pumila, Hoveyi and others, and in the Chinese class the Golden Rollinson's, Berckmans' Golden and aurea nana are all of that outline to a greater or less extent.

This is the time to pot the stock. Potted now it can be set under cover outdoors in some sections of the country, to remain there for some time; and all being hardy there is no call to give them heat at all. But it is better that they be in a greenhouse free from freezing until sold, as the foliage is of better color then, and the plants make some root growth before they are sold.

Waiting for the Leaves to Fall.

In former days it was the practice of nurserymen to wait until the leaves fell from tree and shrub before attempting to transplant them; but this is no longer the rule. Planting starts now in early October, and with many nurserymen fully one-half of their orders are shipped before the leaves fall naturally. This is extra expense, as in the case of trees and large shrubs the leaves have to be hand-picked. Smaller bushes can be buried in sand for a few days, which will take off the foliage. But the extra expense referred to is more than compensated for in the satisfaction resulting from successful planting. Such early planted stock is sure to live, while that late planted is not so sure.

It is a great help to newly set trees and shrubs to have them secured tightly in their positions, and well mulched with leaves, or litter, to keep out frost. Nothing is better for mulching than leaves applied to a depth of 6 inches when pressed down. Quite large trees are easily kept from swaying by having soil heaped around them for the Winter, close to the trunk, to be removed when Spring comes; and this mound acts in keeping frost out of the ground as well.

Spiraea Regeliana.

We look on the early Summer flowering spiræas with a good deal of interest. Their flowering is not until after the great rush of Spring blooming subjects is over, and yet they flower before the close of July, a time that sees so many of their owners absent on their vacations. Spiræa Regeliana comes into bloom about the close of June and lasts well through July; and then with a favorable growing season later blossoms may be looked for to some extent through August and September. Especially is this the case if a fair pruning back of the branches be given when the first crop of flowers fade. The blossoms are of a light pink, and, as the photograph will show, they are borne in clustered panicles, differing from many other pink ones which bear their blossoms in a finger-like spike.

Spiraea Regeliana.

There are several other spiræas bearing pink flowers on elongated heads as S. Regeliana does. Just now we think of Billardi, Douglasi, and tomentosa as of the same character, and then there are many more with pink flowers but borne in flat corymbs.

The illustration is reproduced from a photograph of a bush on the estate of John T. Morris, Chestnut Hill, near Philadelphia, Pa., and it is an example of the care every shrub on the place is receiving. Every shrub and tree in the botanical quarters has room to grow, and has its botanical name placed in front of it, forming the most instructive collection in Philadelphia. The collection is young yet, and every year is adding to its interest.

Chinese Allspice, Chimonanthus.

When not too far North and in sheltered places the Chinese allspice, Chimonanthus fragrans, thrives out of doors. In the vicinity of New York city and on Long Island and along the coast of the Sound it is hardy. But as this shrub is impatient to flower it pushes forth its small yellow sweet scented blossoms in Winter if a week of mild weather occurs, and so it happens that its flowers are rarely enjoyed in the North. It follows that the plan many adopt of growing it in a pot, or tub, for indoor use is a good one, and were the nurseryman or florist to recommend the plant for this purpose, many a specimen of it could be sold. There are parties having collections of plants in greenhouses who would be glad to know of the allspice. It is not the sight of the flowers, but the delicious odor emanating from them that recommends this shrub. One flower alone when expanded will fill a room with delicious fragrance; and one flower after another is expanding for some time. As the flowers are produced from shoots made the previous season it places this shrub in the class of those that need a good pruning in Spring when flowering is over, to bring forth a good lot of young shoots.

Because its flowers are not enjoyed outdoors where hard freezings occur the chimonanthus is not in all nurseries outside of southern ones, but it is much valued by nurserymen of the South, who find a ready sale for it there, which its free seeding enables them to meet. JOSEPH MEEHAN.

BOXWOOD

By the Car Load.

3 feet Pyramids .... $1.50 each
5 feet " .... 4.00 each

Other sizes at proportionate prices. Every plant a specimen.

HIRAM T. JONES, Union County Nurseries, Elizabeth, N. J.

Mention the Florists' Exchange when writing.

KOSTER & CO.

Hollandia Nurseries BOSKOOP, HOLLAND

Hardy Azaleas, Box Trees, Clematis, Conifers, Hydrangeas, Peonies.

Pot-Grown Plants for Forcing.

RHODODENDRONS, H. P. ROSES, Etc.

Catalogue free on demand.

Mention the Florists' Exchange when writing.

HERBACEOUS PERENNIALS

for Summer and Autumn Planting. We offer NINE HUNDRED and SIXTY-SEVEN VARIETIES of STRONG FIELD-GROWN PLANTS. Send for Catalog and Trade List.

BAY STATE NURSERIES, NORTH ABINGTON, MASS

Mention the Florists' Exchange when writing.

F. & F. NURSERIES

SPRINGFIELD NEW JERSEY

Wholesale Growers

TREES AND PLANTS in full assortment.

Trade Catalogue Free

Mention the Florists' Exchange when writing.

SEASONABLE STOCK FOR FLORISTS

HYDRANGEAS for forcing | OTAKSA and THOS. HOGG | With 7-12 flowering crowns, $12.00 per 100.
" 4-6 " " 9.00 "
" 4 " " 7.00 "

From 6-inch pots and open beds, all out-door grown.

ROSES, Strong, two-years, field-grown, selected for forcing.

HYBRID PERPETUALS .... $10.00 and $12.00 per 100.
CRIMSON RAMBLER .... 9.00 "
DOROTHY PERKINS .... 7.00 "

and

LADY GAY, a new hardy climbing Rose of exceptional merit; ready now from 3¼ inch pots only. Write for prices.

JACKSON & PERKINS CO.

WHOLESALE NURSERYMEN AND FLORISTS

NEWARK, WAYNE CO., NEW YORK

Mention the Florists' Exchange when writing.

Viburnum Plicatum Japan Snowball

18 to 24 in. .... $10.00 per 100
2 to 2½ ft. .... 12.00 "
2½ to 3 ft. .... 15.00 "
3 to 4 ft. .... 20.00 "
4 to 5 ft. .... 25.00 "

DOUBLE ALTHEAS

Jeanne D'Arc, pure white flowers fine for cutting. Banner—White striped crimson. Red—Rich ruby red flowered.

per 100

Bushy Plants 18 to 24 in. $6.00
2 to 2½ ft. 7.00
2½ to 3 ft. 8.00
3 to 4 ft. 10.00

BERBERRY THUNBERGII, Splendid for Hedges

Our plants are grown from Cuttings and are very bushy.

	per 100	per 1000
12 to 18 in.	$5.00	$45.00
18 to 24 in.	7.00	60.00
2 ft. to 2½ ft.	10.00	90.00

HYDRANGEA PAN. GRAND.

2 to 3 ft. .... $7.00 per 100, $60.00 per 1000

DEUTZIA LEMOINEI, Fine for Forcing

2 to 2½ ft. .... $7.00 per 100

DEUTZIA GRACILIS, 12 to 18 in 4.50 "

SPIRAEA VAN HOUTTEI

		per 100	per 1000
"	2 ft.	$5.00	$45.00
" "	3 to 4 ft.	6.00	50.00
" Blue, caryopteris	15 to 20 in.	5.00	45.00
" "	2 to 2½ ft.	7.00	65.00
" A. Waterer	12 to 18 in.	6.50	60.00
" "	2 to 2½ ft.	8.00	75.00
" "	2½ to 3 ft.	9.00	85.00

HONEYSUCKLE HECKROTTII, 1 year $6.00 per 100, 2 years, $10.00 per 100.

PLATYCODON LEICHTLINII, Dwarf, Bushy and very free flowering, 2 years, $8.50 per 100.

THE CONARD & JONES CO.

WEST GROVE, PA.

Mention the Florists' Exchange when writing.

EBBINGE & VAN GROOS

Formerly THE HORTICULTURAL CO.

BOSKOOP, HOLLAND

Hardy Nursery Stock, such as H. P. Roses, Rhododendrons, Azaleas, Clematis, Buxus, Choice Evergreens, Peonies, etc.

Ask for Catalogue.

Mention the Florists' Exchange when writing.

Holland Nursery Stock

Ask for Our Catalogue. It will interest you.

ENDTZ, VAN NES & CO. BOSKOOP, HOLLAND

Mention the Florists' Exchange when writing.

Specimen Nursery Stock

DECIDUOUS TREES and SHRUBS, EVERGREENS, RHODODENDRONS, AZALEAS, over one hundred (100) acres of the choicest varieties. Send for price list.

COTTAGE GARDENS COMPANY

QUEENS, LONG ISLAND, N. Y.

Mention the Florists' Exchange when writing.

PEONIES

We still have quite a block of Ne Plus Ultra, and need the ground. While they last we offer them at $7.50 per 100; $60.00 per 1000. Send for list.

EDWARD SWAYNE

WEST CHESTER, PA.

Mention the Florists' Exchange when writing.

Queen Beatrice Rose

Four to one shot. Four times as many flowers as Maid.

F. H. KRAMER, 916 F St., Washington, D. C.

Mention The Florists' Exchange when writing.

Leedle grown Roses are now Big

FLORAL COMP'Y	H. P.'s, H. T.'s, T.'s,	values for
Springfield, O.	R.'s, Cl.'s, B., etc.	the buyer.
Expert Growers	101 best sorts.	Send your
Send for price list	On own roots.	want list.

Mention the Florists' Exchange when writing.

Large Assortment PEONIES Very best Varieti

LOW PRICES

THE KIND THAT FLORISTS LIKE

"We make a specialty of growing stocky transplanted shrubbery and trees"

FULL ASSORTMENT OF Ornamentals, Fruits, Roses, Clematis, and Herbaceous Pla
Write for our fall wholesale trade list.

W. & T. SMITH CO., GENEVA, N.

Mention the Florists' Exchange when writing.

ROSES

Climbing Clothilde Soupert, Marie Pavie, Crimson Rambler and Dorothy Perkins . . .

Grafted Oranges and Kin Kans, Palms, Biota Aurea Nana, Conifers and Other Stock for Florists and Nurserymen

IN IMMENSE QUANTITIES

400 ACRES IN NURSERIES 60,000 FEET OF GLA

CATALOG ON APPLICATION

P. J. BERCKMANS CO. (Inc.)

FRUITLAND NURSERIES

Established 1856. AUGUSTA,

Mention The Florists' Exchange when writing.

PEONIES

Queen Victoria (the cold storage flower) $9.00 per 100. Festiva Maxima, $30.00 per 100. Fragrans (late Rose) $6.00 per 100. For 1000 rates or other varieties, write,

Large stock of M. L. Rhubarb and Lucretia Dewberry Plants. Write for pri

GILBERT H. WILD, SARCOXIE, M

Mention the Florists' Exchange when writing.

FERNS and Crimson Rambler ROSES

10,000 Ferns, in fine shape, low stocky plants, not drawn, grown in full light, and as they were pot plants, lifts with fine balls.

Bostons, for 6 in., $30.00 per 100; for 5 in. $16.00.

Piersoni, for 6 in., $25.00 per 100; for 5 in. $20.00.

Scottii, for 5 in., $20.00 per 100; for 4 in., $15.00.

2,000 Crimson Ramblers, for Easter forcing, 2 year old, 3 to 4 ft., several canes well ripened and good roots, $2.00 per doz.; $15.00 per 100.

Asparagus Plumosus Nanus, 2½ in., fine, $2.50 per 100.

Sprengeri and Plumosus Nanus, 4 in., $1.00 per doz.

5,000 Vinca Major, variegated, field stock, extra fine, $5.00 per 100; $45.00 per 1000

Vinca Major, variegated, and Hydrangea Otaksa, 2¼ in., pot plants, $2.50 per 100. Hydrangea Paniculata Grandiflora, Spirea, Anthony Waterer, and Spirea Van Houtti, 3 year old, large bushes, $1.00 per dozen or $7.00 per 100.

50,000 Shrubs, Vines, Cannas, etc. These must be sold low. List free.

Cash please.

BENJ. CONNELL

WEST GROVE, PA.

Mention the Florists' Exchange when writing.

GRAFTED ROSES

Fine Stock from 3-in. pots.

Richmond, $2.50 per doz., $15.00 per 100, $125.00 per 1000.

Killarney, $2.00 per doz., $15.00 per 100.

Etoile de France, $3.00 per doz., $18.00 per 100.

Kaiserin, Carnot, Uncle John, Chatenay, $2.00 per doz., $15.00 per 100.

Bride, Bridesmaid, Golden Gate, Wootton, $2.00 per doz., $12.00 per 100.

ROSES OWN ROOTS

Fine Stock from 3-in. pots.

Richmond, $10.00 per 100; $90.00 per 1000.

Etoile de France, $12.00 per 100.

Sunrise, Perle, Sunset, Chatenay, $8.00 per 100.

Bride, Bridesmaid, Golden Gate, $7.00 per 100.

RUBBER PLANTS

Fine stock 3 feet high, 60c. each; $6.00 a doz.; 2½ to 3 feet high, 60c. each; $6.00 a doz.

Asparagus Plumosus Nanus from 3-inch pots, $8.00 per 100; Sprengeri from 3-inch pots, $8.00 per 100.

Stevia Compacta, strong field plants, $10.00 per 100. Send for Catalogue.

WOOD BROS., Fishkill, N. Y.

Mention The Florists' Exchange when writing.

Commercial Violet Culture

PRICE, $1.50

The FLORISTS' EXCHANGE, 2-8 Duane St., New York

New Pink Rose

Miss Kate Moultc

Is the QUEEN of all Pink Roses

Write us about it

Minneapolis Floral Co., - Minneapolis,

Mention the Florists' Exchange when wri

Rose Baby Rambl

X X X

Our plants are last year's propagation and had a full season's growth. Extra fine b- $12.00 per 100. Special price in quantities

NATHAN SMITH & SON, Adrian,

Mention the Florists' Exchange when w

Grafted Roses

Edw. J. Ta
Southpor
Connectic

Mention the Florists' Exchange when w

Chrysanthemum

STOCK PLANTS

Testout, Nonin, White Shaw, The Baby per doz., $10.00 per 100.

Ivory, Bonnaffon, Jones, white and y Kalb, Mrs. Duckham, Robinson, An Smith, Helen Frick, Am. Beauty, C Godwin, crimson, Appleton, White naffon, 75c. per doz., $5.00 per 100.

CASH

HENRY EICHHOLZ, Waynesboro,

Mention the Florists' Exchange when w

A BARGAIN FOR YOU IN NICE PLAN

2000 Achillea, The Pearl $2.00 per 100, 150 man Iris 6 varieties $2.00 per 100, 6000 Iri irica Blue and White $2.00 per 100, 100 H thus Divaricarta, $2.00 per 100, 1000 Hel Pitcheriana, $2.00 per 100, 1000 Digitalis, glove, $2.00 per 100, 500 Crimson Eye, Hi $3.00 per 100, 400 Peonies, 3-5 eyes asstd. $ 100, 500 Arundo Donax Grass $5.00 per Funkia Coerulea, $4.00 per 100, 1500 Tr Vines, 2-3 ft. tr. 2c., 500 Wisteria Mult racemes of blooms 2-3 ft. long, 10c. each, with Order please.

Ellsworth Brown & Co. Seabrook

Mention the Florists' Exchange when w

ROSES

The past two weeks have been very trying ones for the growers in the vicinity of New York, there being scarcely any sunshine; and while we had little rain, the weather continued warm and muggy. Under these conditions the plants become soft, and the flowers lose color and substance. As suggested in last notes, the only thing to do under these circumstances is to leave the ventilators open an inch or so and keep on a little heat in the pipes, allowing the benches to remain a little on the dry side. When the sun does come out the temperature must not be permitted to run up too high or the tender growth will burn. At the same time, the ventilators must be raised gradually, or the plants, not being accustomed to the air, will get chilled and a bad dose of mildew result.

Green fly multiply very rapidly in muggy weather, and should never be permitted to gain much headway. Fumigating with tobacco stems is not permissible so late in the season, so punk or paper should be employed instead. Where steam is used for heating, a little nicotine put on the pipes will prove very effective; but it must be borne in mind that light doses, frequently applied, are much more economical and effective than stronger ones at longer intervals.

It is to be regretted that rose growers take so little interest in the flower shows. The variety of roses grown for cut flowers is small, nevertheless a vase of well grown roses, no matter the kind, is always admired, and an object lesson to possible flower buyers. The cost or value of the flowers is small at this time of the year, and all growers should make an effort to send a few of their best blooms to the exhibition.

Preparations should now be made for next year by storing some potting soil; not under the greenhouse benches, but in some dry place where it can be reached easily. Some sand for propagating should also be procured before heavy frosts set in. Another important thing is to prepare the compost heaps for next season. As has often been stated in these notes, the best is none too good, for upon the quality of the soil our success or failure greatly depends. Sod taken from an old pasture, put up in heaps at the rate of five parts sod to one of fresh cow manure, is an ideal compost. Bear in mind that American Beauty does best in a light soil, while Bride, Richmond, Killarney and nearly all other roses do best in a little heavier soil.

PENN.

Caroline Testout and Her Descendants.

The rose Caroline Testout was obtained by Pernet in 1891 and was the issue of Madame Tartas and Mary Fitzwilliam. In 1901 appeared the climbing Caroline Testout. The original variety has been used in crossing at times as seed bearer, at other times as the pollen parent, and up to 1904 some 35 varieties have been obtained as the result of these crosses. From 1891 to 1896 no descendant of Testout appeared; in 1897, one; in 1898, one; in 1899, four; in 1900, five; in 1901, six; in 1902, six; in 1903, five, and in 1904, six. Among the best are: Edmée et Roger (obtained by Ketten Brothers in 1903); Grossherzogin Victoria Melita (P. Lambert, in 1897); Mme. J. P. Soupert (Soupert & Notting, in 1900); Marguerite Guillot (Guillot); Souvenir d'Anne-Marie (Ketten Brothers, in 1903); Conrad Strassheim (Soupert (Soupert & Notting, in 1900); Meta (same firm, in 1900); Frau Peter Lambert (Lambert); and Helene Walter.

Crosses with Caroline Testout have been effected successfully with Mme. Hoste, Mme. Chidane-Guinoisseau, Safrano (four times), Alice Furon, Antoinette Durien, Victor Verdier, Charles Darwin, Bell Siebrecht (twice), Ferdinand Jamin, Souvenir du President Carnot, Kaiserin Augusta Victoria (twice), Mme. Jules Grolez, Reine Emma des Pays-Bas, Mme. Lombard (twice), Marquise Litta de Breteuil, Mme. Abel Chatenay, American Beauty, W. F. Bennett, Xavier Olibo, Marie Baumann, Bridesmaid, Princesse Alice de Monaco, Liberty (twice), and Catherine Mermet.—From Revue Horticole.

Home Again From Europe

BARGAINS—Room Wanted—BARGAINS

to place the big importation of plants I bought in Belgium and Holland. Prices greatly reduced, for a short time only. Buy now while the weather is warm enough for shipping, and while prices are low.

PLEASE NOTE LOWEST PRICE GOING FOR NOVEMBER:

OUR SPECIALTY—ARAUCARIA EXCELSA—OUR SPECIALTY

We are one of the largest importers of this beautiful plant, the **Araucaria**. Can sell cheaper than any other house in America.

Take Notice: Sizes given below are taken three months ago, and are now fully 3 to 5 inches larger than stated here.

12 to 14 in. 5½ in. pots, 3 to 4 tiers, 2-yr. old, 50c. 14 to 16 in., 5½ in. pots, 3 to 4 tiers, 2-yr. old, 60c. 16 to 18 in. 5½ to 6 in. pots, 4 to 5 tiers, 3-yr. old, 75c. 18 to 20 in., 6 in. pots, 5 to 6 tiers, 4-yr. old, $1.00. 20 to 24 in. 6 in. to 7 in. pots, 5 to 6 tiers, 4-yr. old, $1.25. 36-40 to 50 in. 7 in. pots, specimen plants from $2.50 to $3.00 each.

ARAUCARIA COMPACTA ROBUSTA—have several thousand of them; can supply all wants. These plants were never so fine in shape and condition as this year. The pet of the greenhouse, as broad as long. 20 to 25 in., in height, 3 to 4 perfect tiers. 20 to 25 inches across, 3-4-5 year old, 6 to 7 in. pots, $1.25, $1.50, $1.75, $2.00, $2.50 to $3.00 each.

ARAUCARIA EXCELSA GLAUCA—This variety on account of its beautiful Green-Bluish tiers, dwarf habit, fine compact shape, gives it a striking appearance, and anybody seeing them, must undoubtedly fall in love with them at sight. Plants, 6-7 inch pots, 3-4-5 perfect tiers, 3-4 year old, 20 to 30 inch high, from 20 to 30 in. across. $1.25, $1.50, $1.75, $2.00 to $2.50 each.

KENTIA BELMOREANA, 5 1-2 to 6 in. pots, bushy, fine plants, from $1.00 to $1.25 each.

KENTIA FORSTERIANA, 7 in. pots, made-up plants, 1 large in center, 3 smaller sizes, 22 to 26 in. high around, gives them a good appearance, $2.00 each, 6 in. pots, single plants, 36 to 40 in. high, 5 to 6 good leaves, 4 year old, $1.25 to $1.50 each; 6 in. pots, 30 to 35 in. high, 4 year old, 5 good leaves, $1.00; 5 1-2 in. pots, 3 year old, 25 to 30 in. high, 5 good leaves, 75c, made-up plants, 3 and 4 in. pots, 18 to 20 in. high, 25 cts. to 30 cts. each.

FICUS ELASTICA, 6 in., 40c. and 50c.

ARECA LUTESCENS, 5 in. pots, 24 in. high, made-up with 3 plants, 35c. 4 in. pots, 20 to 24 in. high, made up with 3 plants, 25c.

ARECA SAPIDA, just imported from Belgium, something new, looks like a Kentia palm about 25 in. high. Look! only 50c. each worth $1.00 this is a bargain seldom offered.

ASPARAGUS PLUMOSUS NANUS, 4 in. pots, large, bushy, 10 to 12c.

ASPARAGUS SPRENGERI, 4 in. pots, 10c.

FERNS, all raised in pots and not on benches as follows:

NEPHROLEPIS BARROWSII, 7 in. pots, as big as a bushel basket, 75c. to $1.00 each. 6 in. pots, large, ready for 7 in., 50c.; 5 1-2 in., 40c.; 5 in., 35c.; 4 in., 25c.

NEPHROLEPIS SCOTTII, 8 in., as big as a washtub, worth $2.00, now $1.25; 7 in., as big as a bushel basket, worth $1.25, now 75c.; 6 in., 50c.; 5 1-2 in., 40c.; 4 in., 20c.

NEPHROLEPIS ELEGANTISSIMA, 5 in. pots, 30c.

BOSTON FERNS, 7 in., very bushy, only 75c.; 6 in., 50c. or $5.00 per doz.; 5 in., 30c. to 35c.; 4 in., 20c.

AZALEA INDICA, just arrived, selected by myself on my recent trip to Belgium. Have all leading varieties such as Deutsche Perle, Simon Mardner, and Vervæneana. These three sorts are good for Christmas forcing. Later varieties: Empress of India, Oroff, Wolters, Niobe, Bernard Andrew Alba, Mad. Van der Cruyssen, and many others, price as follows: 35c., 40c., 50c., 60c., 75c., $1.00, $1.25 to $1.50 each.

BEGONIA, new improved **ERFORDI** fine bloomer for Christmas and all through the Winter, pinkish flowers, 4 in. pots, 20c.

BEGONIA FLAMBEAU, good seller, large, 4 in., fit for 6 in., 20c.

BEGONIA GLOIRE DE LORRAINE, 6 in. pots, bushy, in full bloom, in December, all showing buds now, 50c. each; 3 in., 20c.

COCOS WEDDELIANA, 3 in., strong, 15c.

CYCLAMEN, will bloom for Christmas, 5 in. pots, 20c.; 4 in. pots, 12c.

DRACAENA BRUANTI (imported), 30 in. high, 6 in., pots, 50c., $5.00 per doz.

FERNS for dishes, best varieties, 2½ in., 5c.; 3 in., very strong, 6c.

HYDRANGEA OTAKSA, only pot grown is offered, sure success for Easter forcing, 6 in. pots, 25c.; 7 to 8 in., 50c.

JERUSALEM CHERRIES (or Solanum), 6 in., pots, very bushy, full of berries, from $3.00 to $6.00 per doz.

PRIMULA OBCONICA, best strain, 4 in. pots, 10c.; 5 1-4 in., $2 per dozen.

PRIMULA SINENSIS, 4 in., strong; John Rupp, best strain, for Christmas blooming, 10c.; 5 in., $2 per doz.

CASH WITH ORDER

When ordering, say whether the plants should be shipped in the pots or not

GODFREY ASCHMANN

Importer and Wholesale Grower of Pot Plants

1012 Ontario Street, - - PHILADELPHIA, PA.

Mention the Florists' Exchange when writing.

PLANT CULTURE

PRICE $1.00.

THE BEST BOOK FOR THE PLANT GROWER.

A. T. DE LA MARE PTG. & PUB. CO. LTD., 2-8 DUANE STREET, NEW YORK

DRACAENA TERMINALIS Matured canes always ready for shipment. Delivered to any part of the United States for 10 cents a foot. Send cash for a trial order.

PORTO RICO PINEAPPLE CO., RIO PIEDRAS, PORTO RICO.

Mention The Florists' Exchange when writing.

GOOD BARGAINS IN

DRACAENA INDIVISA

Must sell; must have room.	Per 100
6 in. pots, 2½ to 3 ft. high	$20.00
2 to 2½ ft.	12.00
4 in., 18 in. to 2 ft.	10.00
Asparagus Sprengeri, 2 in.	1.50
Asparagus Plumosus Nanus, 2 in.	2.00
Cinerarias, Michelle Giant Prize, 2 in.	2.00
Primula Obconica Grandiflora Alba, Rosea and Hybrida, 2 in.	2.00
Paris Daisy, white and yellow, 3 in.	3.00
Shasta Daisy, 3 in.	3.00
ROOTED CUTTINGS BY MAIL	
Abutilon, French Dwarf, 6 var.	1.50
Cuphea, (Cigar Plant)	.75
Heliotrope, dark, from soil	1.00
Lantanas, dwarf 6 var., from soil	1.25

Cash with order please.

GEO. J. HUGHES, BERLIN, N. J.

Mention the Florists' Exchange when writing.

GOOD STOCK AT REDUCED PRICE

TO MAKE ROOM

VINCA, strong field plants	4c.
" No. 2	3c.
ENGLISH IVY, 2 in.	1½c.
" " 2½ in.	2c.
" " 4 in.	5c.
PRIMULA OBCONICA, 2½ in.	3c.
" " strong, 3 in.	4c.
" CHINESE, 2 in.	1½c.
REX BEGONIA, 4 in.	4 in.
HYDRANGEA P. G., 2 ft.	6c.

J. H. DANN & SON,
WESTFIELD, N. Y.

Mention the Florists' Exchange when writing.

PRIMROSES

BIG BARGAIN TO MAKE ROOM

IMPROVED CHINESE, finest grown, all varieties, mixed, single and double.

X X 2 in., $1.50 per 100.
X X X 3 in., $4.00 per 100.
X X X X 4 in., $6.00 per 100.

CINERARIAS, large flowering, dwarf, 2 in., $2.00 per 100. Cash. Order at once. Only a few thousand left. Extras added liberally.

JOHN F. RUPP, Shiremanstown, Pa.

The Home of Primroses

Mention the Florists' Exchange when writing.

CYCLAMEN

SPLENDENS GIGANTEUM HYBRIDS

This strain has no equal or better. Perfect flowers of Giant type in five true colors, well grown plants from 4 in. pots $15.00 per 100, from 5 in. pots $2.50 per doz., $20.00 per 100.

PRIMULA SINENSIS FIMBRIATA

Only fringed varieties Giant flowers in the best market sorts, all colors, from 2½ in. pots $3.00 per 100.

PRIMULA OBCONICA GRANDIFLORA

The celebrated Ronsdorfer and Lattmans Hybrids in the most beautiful colors from 3½ in. pots $10.00 per 100.

BEGONIA REX

In 12 choice market varieties, extra well grown plants from 5 in. pots $2.00 per doz. Rooted cuttings equally mixed $1.50 per 100.

Asparagus Plumosus Nanus

Special offer for first-class grown stock from 2½ in. pots $2.50 per 100, $20.00 per 1000.

PAUL MADER, EAST STROUDSBURG, PA.

Mention the Florists' Exchange when writing.

POINSETTIAS

Best stock, 3½ in. pots, $6.00 per 100; $55.00 per 1000.

Begonia Gloire de Lorraine, best stock, 2½ in. pots, $10.00 per 100.

P. R. QUINLAN, SYRACUSE, N. Y.

Mention the Florists' Exchange when writing.

POINSETTIAS

2½ in. pots, $5.00 per 100; $40.00 per 1000, Cash with order.

S. N. PENTECOST,
1790-1810 East 101 St., CLEVELAND, O.

Mention The Florists' Exchange when writing.

PRIMROSES

Obconica Alba and Rosea, $1.50 per 100; $12.00 per 1000.

ASPARAGUS

Plumosus, 2¼ in. pots $18.00 per 1000; $2.00 per 100.

Vinca, var. from field, $5.00 per 100.

Cannas, 5 var. field grown Clumps $10.00 per 100.

Pansy Plants, large flowering, $3.00 per 1000; 50c. per 100. Cash.

JOS. H. CUNNINGHAM, Delaware, O.

Mention The Florists' Exchange when writing.

Primula Obconica Grandiflora

Mixed, strong, 5 in., $12.00 per 100.

JERUSALEM CHERRIES, dwarf, strong, 5 in. specimens, $15.00; $20.00 and $25.00 per 100, loaded with berries.

GERANIUMS, 12 best varieties, extra fine, large 2 in., $17.00 per 1000.

Double G. Grant, healthy, large, 2 in., $14.00 per 1000. Cash.

WM. S. HERZOG, MORRIS PLAINS, N. J.

Mention the Florists' Exchange when writing.

Primula Obconica Grandiflora

2 1-2 in., $2.50 per 100. Ask for list (seedlings of hardy plants)

BAUDISCH & CO.,
537 Fulton Street UNION HILL, N. J.

Mention The Florists' Exchange when writing.

Different Stock

Genistas, fine healthy pot grown plants, 3 in., 8c., 4 in., 10c., 5 in., 15c.

Boston Ferns, 5x6 in., 25c.; Tarrytown ferns, 6 in., 50c.

Parsley Plants, large, $2.00 per 1000.

Cash Please.

F. B. RINE, Lewisburg, Pa.

Mention The Florists' Exchange when writing.

500,000

VERBENAS

60 Finest named varieties; **rooted cuttings**, 75c. per 100; $6.00 per 1000.

Plants, $2.50 per 100; $20.00 per 1000.

Our list is the choicest from millions of seedlings. Order early.

J. L. DILLON, Bloomsburg, Pa.

Mention the Florists' Exchange when writing.

CYCLAMEN GIGANTEUM

Extra fine plants, large flowering, 3-inch, $5.00 per 100; 4-inch $10.00 per 100; 5-inch $15.00 per 100. **Primulas**, Chinese and Obconica, 2½ inch, $2.00 per 100; 3-inch $3.00 per 100; 4-inch $6.00 per 100.

Asparagus Sprengeri, 3½-inch, $5.00 per 100.

Asparagus Plumosus Nanus, 3½-inch, $6.00 per 100.

Cinerarias, 2¼-inch $2.00 per 100, 300 for $5.00. 3-inch $3.00 per 100.

SAMUEL WHITTON, 15-16 Gray Av., Utica, N.Y.

Mention The Florists' Exchange when writing.

Mention The Florists' Exchange when writing.

LIST OF ADVERTISERS

INDEX TO STOCK ADVERTISED

Contents.

Chicago.

News Notes.

By request of Fritz Bahr we did not mention the samples of his beautiful new white carnation which he exhibited at the committee meeting last week. Having turned the stock over to the J. D. Thompson Carnation Company of Joliet, Mr. Bahr asked us not to say a word about his pet until it was entered in the show.

Word just received from Louis Coatsworth reports his family entirely recovered and on the return to Chicago next week.

If you are interested in your business call on Ed. Winterson and get a few hundred flower show postal cards.

Ed. Washburn of the concern of A. Washburn & Sons, Bloomington, Ill., accompanied by Mrs. Washburn, spent a few days in Chicago last week.

The E. F. Winterson Company employes have been busy the past week unpacking importations of immortelles, Christmas bells, Cape flowers, and other holiday supplies. Cliff Pruner of this house is now on the road and meeting with very flattering success.

At the J. A. Budlong houses the specialty this week is along the line of tea roses, Bride and Bridesmaid being far above par.

John Burton of Philadelphia, Professor Cowell of Buffalo, N. Y., and John T. Temple of Davenport, Iowa, will be welcome guests at the flower show, where as judges they will have an opportunity to express their opinion on the quality of the exhibits placed before them.

Captain A. I. Simmons of the Governor's staff has returned from his trip to Vicksburg, Miss., where the Illinois monument was dedicated on the battlefield.

B. L Van Acken of Coldwater, Mich., was in town the first of the week and if reports are true, he placed a beautiful seedling chrysanthemum to good advantage.

All preparations are practically complete for the show which opens at the Coliseum on Tuesday next. The various committees have finished their work and are prepared to "make good" on the promise for the advertisement of the "World's Greatest Flower Show."

Percy Jones, the manager of the Flower Market, is happy in the belief that the Garland contributors to his bench are delivering some of the best goods coming to Chicago.

Chicago will miss Charles Johnson, The Limits Florist, who has bought the Butler property at Chillicothe, O., where he will soon be located.

The horticultural friends of Alderman Thomas M. Hunter are exerting themselves to aid his election to the position of chief bailiff of the Municipal Court. Regardless of political affiliations all voters seem to be working to the same end.

The leading exponents and successful cultivators of the Killarney rose take exceptions to a note recently printed in this column, and place the blame on those who are dissatisfied with results to the lack of having found out the special requirements in the cutivation of their favorite. With some of our growers Killarney has certainly proved to be a marvellous success, and an inquiry among the retailers gives more, much more, than a satisfactory report of the flower on the market.

Albert T. Hey, of Springfield, Illinois, was a recent visitor.

Word has reached Chicago that A. Henderson of Vaughan's Seed Store on his recent trip across the water was one day late in the object of his voyage, as his brother, who was on the verge of the great unknown, passed away a few hours before our friend reached the European shore.

A. L. Barnett, representing Reed & Keller of New York, spent a few days in Chicago last week on his way West and reports an excellent business in all the sections he has visited.

Among our recent callers was Martin Reukauf of the H. A. Bayersdorfer Philadelphia house, who was on his return from the Pacific Coast.

WM. K. WOOD.

CANADIAN NEWS

TORONTO.—Business has been good, and is improving. Chrysanthemums are coming in freely and are being used as fast as they arrive. All colers are seen, good pink is rather scarce, Glory of the Pacific offered not being a bright enough color. Eepecially good roses are offered, extra fine American Beauty being seen. More orchids are in the market this season than ever before; cattleyas have been plentiful but will be scarce in a few days; C. labiata is the variety offered. Oncidium varicosum also has been plentiful. Large quantities of good ferns move along nicely. Bulbous stock sells well; many varieties of tulips are about sold out. The weather being fine, bulb planting is in full swing.

There are some fine chrysanthemums around, and the chrysanthemum show next month is likely to be by far the best we have yet had. Arrangements are in a progressive way; the general committee meets every Monday evening and appears to have plenty of business to keep it going for two hours. The Black Dyke Band will bé a great attraction, without any doubt, and tickets are selling freely. Our expenses will be more than twice as large as in other years, but we expect to make this up in extra attendance. The railway rate of single fare will help, and our friends from all over the Province of Ontario can secure this rate by asking for a standard certificate; on the first two days of the show all can get this rate without a certificate by asking for the special excursion ticket.

I am very sorry to report that W. C. Day, one of our most popular Yonge st. florists, while getting off a street car last week was thrown to the ground and taken home unconscious. Slight hopes are held out for his recovery. The family have the sympathy of the whole trade. We hope that youth and a fine constitution may yet pull him through.

THOS. MANTON.

MONTREAL.—Not for many years have we had such remarkably fine weather. It is much too warm for business. Only yesterday (October 29) I came across a fine bed of castor oil plants which were not in the least damaged by any little frost we have had.

Miss Murray has the decorations in hand for the opening of the new Mount Royal Club.

Wilshires arranged the floral work for the May wedding last week.

C. Campbell is cutting fine stock at his place at Rockfield.

There are rumors in the air of another retail store opening up in this city, also of another wholesale place.

Wm. Wilshire will judge the chrysanthemums at Toronto, I understand. Jos. Bennett, George Robinson, George Pascoe and others will go up to Toronto also.

J. D. Sinclair was in town on Sunday. He is well pleased with the business done so far at his branch here.

W. C. H.

LONDON, ONT.—Chrysanthemums are coming in in splendid shape and find a ready sale, retail, at $1 to $2 a dozen for medium size. In the market good chrysanthemums can be had at 25c. to 75c. a dozen.

Bulbs are being handled here in large numbers. With J. Gammage & Sons and Darch & Hunter the retail demand is much better than last year. Prices are fairly good considering that one of the five and ten cent stores is selling bulbs cheaper at retail than the florists can buy them from the growers. Carnations are coming in of very good quality, but not in sufficient numbers to meet the demand. Roses are being used up as fast as they come in. There is quite a steady run of funeral work, also quite a number of small weddings.

Azaleas that Gammage & Sons should have received about the first of October, from Belgium, have not yet arrived.

F. C.

Araucaria Excelsa, 5 in. pot, 50c. and 75c. each, three to four tiers; 5½ in. to 6 in. $1.00, $1.25, 4 to 5 tiers; 7 in. pots, $1.50, $2.00 and $2.50; 8 in. pots, 3½ ft. tall, $3.00 to $3.50.
Asparagus Plumosus, 4 in. pots, $1.50 per doz.; 4½ in. pots, $2.00 per doz.; extra large in 4½ in. pots, $3.00 per doz.
Asparagus Sprengeri, $5.00 per 100.
Bay Tree Pyramids, 50-60 in. high from top of tub, $14.00 per pair. 65-70 in. high from top of tub, $16.00 to $18.00 per pair.
Begonia Gloire de Lorraine, $6.00 $9.00, $12.00 and $18.00 per doz. Also some larger plants.
Cyclamen Persicum, $9.00 and $12.00 per doz.
Superb Boxwood, just arrived, perfectly shaped.
Bushes for window boxes, 12 to 20 ins. high from top of root ball, 75c. a pair; 24 ins. high, $1 a pair.
Pyramids, 3 foot high, $2.50 and $3 a pair; 4 foot high, $3 and $4 a pair; 4 foot 6 inches high, $5 a pair; 5 foot high, $7 a pair.
Chrysanthemums, pot plants in bloom. One flower to each stem. Fine and bushy, 7 and 8 inch pots, $6.00, $9.00 and $12.00 per doz. Also Standards with about 3 ft. stem, $1.00, $1.50 and $2.00 each.
Cibotium Schiedei, 6½ and 7 in. pots, $2.00 and $2.50 each.
Cycas Revoluta, 5½, 6, 7 and 8 in. pots, 50c. to $1.50 each.
Dracæna Fragrans, 6 in. pots, $6.00 per doz.; 7 in. pots, $9.00 per doz.; 8 in. pots, $15.00 per doz.
Dracæna Lindeni, 6 in. pots, $9.00 per doz.; 7 in. pots, $18.00 per doz.;
Dracæna Indivisa, 4 in. pots, $10.00 per 100; 5½ in. pots, $20.00 per 100.
Dracæna Terminalis, 5 in. pots, $4.00 per doz.; 5½ in. pots, $5.00 per doz.; 7 in. pots, $15.00 per doz.
Boston Ferns, 5 in. pots, $3.00 per doz.; 6 in. pots, $5.00 per doz.; 6½ in. pots, $9.00 per doz.; 8 in. pots, $15.00 per doz.; 11 in. pots, $2.50 and $3.00 each. Specimens in 12 inch pots $5.00, $6.00 and $7.00 each. 14 inch pots, $15.00 per pair.

Cash or satisfactory New York references.

For Christmas: Fruited Ardisias and Oranges.
Grafted Baby Ramblers on Manetti, nice bushy plants in 3½ and 4-inch pots; prepared for early forcing. $15.00 per 100.
Hydrangea Otaksa pink fine field-grown plants, well budded and bushy, $15.00 per 100; selected plants $20.00 per 100.
Scottii Fern, 5½ in. pots, $3.00 per doz.; 6 in. pots, $6.00 per doz.; 7 and 8 in. pots, $12.00 per doz.
N. Elegantissima, 5½ in. pots, $5.00 per doz.
N. Whitmani, 4½ in. pots, $6.00 per doz.
N. Piersoni, 5 in. pots, $4.00 per doz.; 6 in. pots, $6.00 per doz.; 6½ in. pots, $9.00 per doz.; 7 in. pots, $12.00 per doz.
English Ivy, 4½ in. pots, $2.00 per doz.; $15.00 per 100, 3 to 4 feet high.
Jerusalem Cherries, $6.00 per doz.
Kentia Forsteriana, combinations 3 and 4 plants in 8 in. pots, $1.50 to $3.00. 10 in. pots, $6.00 each. 14 in. pots, $15.00 to $20.00 each. Single plants 50c. to $2.00 each.
Kentia Belmoreana and Forsteriana, all sizes, single and combinations, from $1.00 to $20.00 each. Give us a trial.
Livistona Sinensis, superior to Latania Borbonica, 5 and 5½ in. pots, $5.00 per doz.; 6½ in. pots, $9.00 per doz.; 7 in. pots, $12.00 per doz.
Pandanus Veitchii, 5 in. pots, $4.00 per doz.; 6 in. pots, $6.00 per doz.; 6½ in pots, $9.00 per doz.; 7 in. pots, $18.00 per doz.; 8 in. pots, $2.00 each.
Primula Obconica, $2.00 per doz.
Rubbers, 6 in. pots, $6.00 per doz.; 6½ in. branched, $9.00 per doz.; 6½ in. pots, single stem, $8.00 per doz.; 7 in. pots, branched, $9.00 per doz.; 10 in. pots, 3 in a pot, $2.00 to $2.50 each.
Surplus of Ardisia Crenulata for next year, fruiting very fine, branched, 4 in. pots, 1 ft. tall; spread 8 to 10 inches, $40.00 per 100; 4½ in. pots, $50.00 per 100.

Cash or satisfactory New York references.

ANTON SCHULTHEIS. 19th Street & 4th Avenue COLLEGE POINT, N. Y.

Mention the Florists' Exchange when writing.

ASPARAGUS PLUMOSUS NANUS

2 in. pots, $3.00 per 100; $25.00 per 1,000.
2½ in. pots, $4.50 per 100; $40.00 per 1,000.
3 in. pots, $7.00 per 100; $65.00 per 1,000.
4 in. pots, $10.00 to $12.00 per 100.

ASPARAGUS SPRENGERI

2 in. pots, $3.00 per 100; $25.00 per 1,000.
2½ in. pots, $4.50 per 100; $40.00 per 1,000.
3 in. pots, $7.00 per 100; $65.00 per 1,000.

SMILAX

2¼ in. pots, $2.50 per 100; $20.00 per 1,000.

GARDENIAS

3 in. pots, $12.00 per 100, 4 in. pots, $20.00 per 100.
5 in. pots, $35.00 per 100; 6 in. pots, $60.00 per 100.
10 in. pots, $3.00 each.

A. N. PIERSON
Cromwell, Conn.

Mention the Florists' Exchange when writing.

COCOS WEDDELIANA

Nice Plants in 3 in. pots, per 100 $15.00

KENTIA BELMOREANA

Fine clean stock in 3 in. pots, about 15 in. high, per 100 $15.00; about 20 in. high, per 100, $20.00

ADIANTUM CUNEATUM

Fine Plants, 2½ in. pots, per 100 $5.00

O. V. ZANGEN
SEEDSMAN, BOX 114, HOBOKEN, N. J.

Mention the Florists' Exchange when writing.

VIOLET CULTURE
Price, $1 50 Postpaid
A. T. De La Mare Ptg. & Co. Ltd., New York

EMERSON C. McFADDEN

Wholesale Grower
Asparagus Plumosus Nanus, Etc.
Short Hills, N. J.
Tel. 28 A.

Mention the Florists' Exchange when writing.

ROBERT CRAIG & CO.

ROSES, PALMS, CROTONS

CARNATIONS and Novelties in DECORATIVE PLANTS

Market and 49th Sts. PHILADELPHIA, PA.

Mention The Florists' Exchange when writing.

SMILAX PLANTS

Strong, bushy growing stock. From 3 in. pots, $2.00 per 100, $18.00 per 1000. 2 in. pots, $1.00 per 100; $9.00 per 1000. Seedlings from flats, large, summered out of doors, $4.00 per 1000. Send for samples.

R. KILBOURN, CLINTON, N. Y.

Mention the Florists' Exchange when writing.

NEPHROLEPIS

Whitmani, 2¼ in., $25.00 per 100.
Barrowsii, $10.00 per 100.

Henry H. Barrows & Son, Whitman, Mass.

Mention The Florists' Exchange when writing.

COCOS PALMS.

Strong 2¼ inch at $1.60 per dozen. Write for lowest prices on Kentias.

Jas. F. Barclay R. I. GREENHOUSES, Pawtucket, R. I.

Mention The Florists' Exchange when writing.

Adiantum Farleyens

Good thrifty stock, 3 inch pots . . . $20.00 pe

THORN HEDGE GREENHOUSES, Newtown Square,

Mention the Florists' Exchange when writing.

FERNS. NEPHROLEPIS BARRO

2½ inch, $6.00 per 100.

HUGH GRAHAM CO.,
Logan Nurseries, York Road and Londen Street, PHILADELPHI

Mention The Florists' Exchange when writing.

To Close Out

4 in. BOSTON FERNS . . 15c.
5 in. " " . . 20c.

Good value for money.

JOHN WOLF
SAVANNAH, GA.

Mention the Florists' Exchange when writing.

FERNS

Boston, Barrowsii and Scottii, 6 in., $4.00 per doz.; 5 in., $2.50 per doz.
Boston and Scottii, 3 in., $6.00 per 100. 4 in., $8.00 per 100.
Strong runners of **Whitmani** $15.00 per 100.

Larchmont Nurseries
Larchmont, N. Y.

Mention The Florists' Exchange when writing.

WHITMANI FERN

Large stock of strong plants, 2¼ inch pots, $20.00 per 100.

TARRYTOWN FERN

	100
3 inch pots	$10.00

SCOTTII

2¼ inch pots	$ 5.00
4 inch pots	15.00

Pot grown **Ampelopsis,** staked, strong plants, $10.00 per 100.
No order for less than 10 plants accepted.

CHAS. H. CAMPBELL,
3601 GERMANTOWN AVE., PHILA., PA

Mention The Florists' Exchange when writing.

BARGAIN
TO MAKE ROOM

1,000 **N. Piersoni Elegantissima Ferns,** from 2½ in. pots, $8.00 per 100. A No. 1 stock; ready for 4 and 5 in. pots. Cash with order, please.

R. ENGELMAN & SON
PITTSFIELD, MASS.

Mention The Florists' Exchange when writing.

FERNS

For jardinieres, etc., 2½ inch, $3.00 per 100.
Kentia Belmoreana, clean and bushy, 5 in. 50c.
Boston Ferns, Piersoni ,and Scottii, from bench, 10c. to 25c. each, 4 in. pot grown, 15c.
Cocos Weddeliana, 2½ in. 10c.
Asparagus Plumosus, 2½ in. $3.00 per 100.

H. WESTON, HEMPSTEAD, N. Y.

Mention The Florists' Exchange when writing.

The American Carnation Price, $3.50
A. T. De La Mare Ptg. & Pub. Co., 2 Duane St., New York

FERNS OUR SPECIAL

Cibotium Schiedei: We have a grand s this magnificent tree fern in all sizes, 3 $25.00 per 100; 4 in. pots, $45.00 per 100; 6 $70.00 per 100; 7 in. pots, $1.70 each; 8 $2.50 each.
Assorted Ferns, from 2¼ in. pots, all market varieties, $3.00 per 100, or $25.00 p 4 inch pots, $12.00 per 100.
If by mail add 10c. each 100 plants.
Adiantum Cuneatum, 2 in. pots, $3.50
" " 4 in. pots, 12.00
" **Rhodophyllum** 4 in. pots $25.
" **Lathomii,** 4 in. pots, $30.00
" **Regina,** 4 in. pots, $35.00
Fern Spores gathered from our own stoc 25c. per trade package or $4.00 per doz. p

ANDERSON & CHRISTEN
SHORT HILLS, N. J.

Mention The Florists' Exchange when

ASPIDIUM TSUSSEMI

Extra large bushy plants in 3-inch $6.00 per 100.

CYRTOMIUM FALCATUM

Large, full plants, 3-inch pots, the stock we have ever offered, 6c.; 2 pots, 3c.

ASSORTED FERNS

Fine bushy plants, 2-inch pots,

Two No. 4-Weathered boilers in good c at a bargain

R. G. HANFORD, - NORWALK,

Mention the Florists' Exchange when

FERNS FROM BE

BOSTON, PIERSONI, 4 in. 10c.
TARRYTOWN, 2½ in., 4c.; 4 i 5 in., 25c. Runners $20.00 per 1000
SCOTTII, 4 in., 12½c.
Pansy Plants, Giants, $3.00 per 100.
Daisies, double Longfellow, D $2.50 per 1000.
Asparagus Sprengeri, 2 in., 2 cts.
Flowering Begonias, 8 kinds, 2 in., 2½
Forgetmenots, $2 50 per 1000.
Hollyhocks, double, 4 kinds, 1 year ol
Hardy Pinks, 3 kinds, field plants, 3½
Hardy Carnations, nice young pla frames, $2.00 per 100.

Cash or C. O. D.

BYER BROS., Chambersbur

Mention The Florists' Exchange when

Adiantum Farleyer

I can quote splendid stock at fr per dozen up to $24.00 per dozen, to 6-inch pots. If you are looking eyense, better write me about it.

CHARLES H. TOTTY, Madison,

Mention The Florists' Exchange when

FERN

Assorted, for jardinieres, strong plants, from 2½ in. pots, $3.00 per 100; 1000; 250 at 1000 rate; 4 in., $12.00 per 10
ADIANTUM CUNEATUM, 5 in. po per 100; 4 in. pots, $12.00 per 100.

FRANK N. ESKESEN, MADISON,

Grower of Palms, Ferns and Decorative Stock.

Nephrolepis Scottii all the yea

JOHN SCOTT
Rutland Road & E. 45th St., BROOKL
Telephone 2890 Bedford.

Carnation Growing in New Jersey.

(69) "A" bets that very few commercial carnations are grown in the neighborhood of Short Hills, Summit and Madison, N. J., because of climatic conditions; while "B" bets that the climate and soil will produce just as good commercial carnations as are grown on Long Island. Why is it that no commercial carnations are grown through that part of New Jersey? Please answer through your valued paper. SUBSCRIBER.
Hoboken, N. J.

—According to our judgment, "B" is right, as there is no doubt whatever that just as good carnations can be grown, have been grown, and doubtless are being grown at the present time in the vicinity of Madison and Summit, N. J., as can be produced in any part of Long Island. We have in mind the good carnations grown by John N. May of Summit, N. J., and by Wm. Duckham of Madison, N. J. We do not think there is anything in the climatic conditions of the places mentioned that is detrimental to the growing of good carnations, provided the grower wants to interest himself in them. That few commercial carnations are produced in that part of New Jersey is no doubt because of the fact that commercial growers there are more interested in roses, the district at one time having had quite a reputation for producing these flowers; and most of the glass constructed there has been with the object of raising roses only.

Field-Grown Hydrangeas and Spiraeas

(70) Please give the treatment for hydrangeas and Spiræa japonica, field-grown. I have the hydrangeas lifted and potted in a house 50-52 degrees. I would like to have these plants in for Easter, 1907.
Penna. SUBSCRIBER.

—The hydrangeas will be just as well off if they are kept under the benches, and partially dried, until the latter part of December, at which time it would be advisable to place them in full light and start them growing, giving them a night temperature of 52 to 55 degrees as soon as growth commences, keeping them going at that temperature right through the Winter. Easter, 1907, is very early, March 31, and the hydrangeas must not have any check whatever, if they are to be in flower on time.

The spiræas should be potted as soon as received, and after giving them a good watering they may be placed under the benches in a cool house and remain there until the middle of January. Then it will be necessary to give them full light, and a good growing temperature similar to that afforded the hydrangeas.

Hydrangeas for Easter.

(71) Please give treatment or culture of hydrangeas, field-grown clumps, to be in bloom for Easter, 1907. P. & P.
Ohio.

—The field-grown hydrangeas should be potted up by this time, and before frost comes they should be placed in some shed or cool greenhouse. Give them enough water to keep them from getting dust dry only, and there let them remain until the latter part of December, at which time they should be placed in the greenhouse, first removing all dead leaves, if any, but not cutting back any of the growths. Give them water and a light syringing occasionally, and as soon as it is seen that growth is commencing, apply a little more heat—say, a temperature of 55 degrees at night. This temperature should be maintained right along for five or six weeks, and if the flower buds do not show by that time, afford more heat to hurry the plants along; but if the buds can be seen, say, by the middle of February, no change in the temperature will be necessary. Keep them well supplied with water at all times; and at the first appearance of green fly, fumigate, as this pest must be kept down if nice, salable stock is to be had for Easter. Bear in mind that Easter, 1907, comes on March 31, and it takes four or five weeks to finish up the plants nicely after the flower buds appear.

Carnation Leaves Diseased.

(72) Answer to J. L. O. Q. & Co., North Carolina. — The carnation leaves show that the plants are suffering from a bacterial disease. If the disease has not progressed too far it may be checked by carefully cutting away all diseased leaves and stems and burning what is removed. Then spray with a solution of commercial formaldehyde, one part to five-hundred parts of water. This should be done in the forenoon, so that the plants may dry before night. Give them plenty of light and air, and keep the foliage comparatively dry.—A. F. W.

Wire for Carnation Supports.

(73) Kindly advise me whether whole gauge wire is the best for wiring carnations, and give me the address of a good firm from whom it can be obtained. Also whether (my carnations being planted 10 x 12 inches, 10 inches across and 12 inches the long way) one strand of wire between the rows will be sufficient, or whether I should have two wires for each plant? X. Z.
N. Y.

—For wiring carnations, No. 18 gauge will be found to answer the purpose as well as any other, and we would not use more than one strand each way of the benches. The wire can, no doubt, be procured from the firm of Igoe Brothers, 226 North Ninth street, Brooklyn, N. Y.

PLANTS FOR NAME.—P. B., Brooklyn, N. Y.—(10) Forsythia; but whether suspensa or Fortunei, it is difficult to say from the meager information supplied. Either form is good; the former is the more slender growing. (11) Symphoricarpus fructo-rubra; (13) Aster tataricus.

When sending specimens for identification it would greatly facilitate our work if readers would also furnish some pertinent facts, such as flowering period, approximate height, and some data as to the habits of the plants submitted. H. G.

FOUNDED IN 1888

FLORISTS' EXCHANGE

A Weekly Medium of Interchange for Florists, Nurserymen Seedsmen and the Trade in general

Exclusively a Trade Paper.

Entered at New York Post Office as Second Class Matter

Published EVERY SATURDAY by

A. T. DE LA MARE PTG. AND PUB. CO. LTD.

2, 4, 6 and 8 Duane Street,

P. O. Box 1697. Telephone 3765 John. **NEW YORK.**

CHICAGO OFFICE: 127 East Berwyn Avenue.

ILLUSTRATIONS.

Electrotypes of the illustrations used in this paper can usually be supplied by the publishers. Price on application.

YEARLY SUBSCRIPTIONS.

United States, Canada, and Mexico, $1.00. Foreign countries in postal union, $2.50. Payable in advance. Remit by Express Money Order Draft on New York. Post Office Money Order or Registered Letter.

The address label indicates the date when subscription expires and is our only receipt therefore.

REGISTERED CABLE ADDRESS:
Florex, New York.

ADVERTISING RATES..

One-half inch, 75c.; ¾-inch, $1.00; 1-inch, $1.25, special positions extra. Send for Rate Card showing discount of 10c., 15c., 25c., or 35c., per inch on continuous advertising. For rates on Wants, etc., see column for Classified Advertisements.

Copy must reach this office 12 o'clock Wednesday to secure insertion in issue of following Saturday.

Orders from unknown parties must be accompanied with cash or satisfactory references.

Chrysanthemum Society of America.

President Duckham has announced the committees to examine seedlings and sports on dates as follows: November 3, 10, 17 and 24, 1906.

Exhibits to receive attention from the committees must in all cases be prepaid to destination, and the entry fee of $2 should be forwarded to the secretary not later than Tuesday of the week preceding examination, or may accompany the blooms. Special attention is called to the rule requiring that sports, to receive a certificate, must pass three committees.

NEW YORK.—Eugene Dailledouze, chairman, care of New York Cut Flower Company, 55-57 Twenty-sixth street: William Turner, Thomas Head.

PHILADELPHIA, PA.—A. B. Cartledge, chairman, 1514 Chestnut street; John Westcott, Wm. K. Harris. Ship flowers in care of the chairman.

BOSTON, MASS.—E. A. Wood, chairman; Wm. Nicholson, James Wheeler. Ship to Boston Flower Market, care of the chairman.

CINCINNATI, O.—R. Witterstaetter, chairman; James Allen, Wm. Jackson. Ship to Jabez Elliott Flower Market, care of janitor.

CHICAGO, ILL.—J. S. Wilson, chairman; J. B. Deamud and George Wienhoeber. Ship care of J. B. Deamud, 51 Wabash avenue.

The official scales of the C. S. A. are as follows:

For Commercial Purposes		For Exhibition Purposes	
Color	20	Color	10
Form	15	Stem	5
Fullness	10	Foliage	5
Stem	15	Fullness	15
Foliage	15	Form	15
Substance	15	Depth	15
Size	10	Size	35
Total	100	Total	100

DAVID FRASER, Secretary.

Pittsburg, Pa.

Work of Committees.

PHILADELPHIA, October 27.—Mrs. G. A. Lotz (creamy white); exhibited by Gustav A. Lotz, Glen Burnie, Md.; scored 90 points, commercial scale, and 89 points, exhibition scale.

Mrs. Westray Ladd, yellow, Japanese incurved; exhibited by Edward A. Stroud, Overbrook, Philadelphia; scored 87 points, commercial scale.

NEW YORK, Oct. 27.—White sport of Wm. Duckham (white blush tint); exhibited by C. H. Totty, Madison, N. J.; scored 90 points, commercial scale, and 90 points, exhibition scale.

Mlle. L. H. Cochet, pink, Japanese incurved; exhibited by the E. G. Hill Company, Richmond, Ind.; scored 85 points, exhibition scale.

DAVID FRASER, secretary.

BOOKS RECEIVED.

HOW TO MAKE A FRUIT GARDEN. By S. W. Fletcher. Publishers, Doubleday, Page & Company, New York.

This volume forms part of the Library of Country Life in America, and the subject matter, original and compiled, occupies some 283 pages. The work seems all comprehensive, but brevity or conciseness forms no part of its make up. However, quite a good deal of very useful and instructive information is to be gleaned from its numerous pages, which are well illustrated.

In these days of plethoric experiment station bulletins devoted to the cultivation of orchard as well as other fruits, with their lists of varieties, etc., it would seem that the interested reading public was well supplied with literature of that class; yet to have the best of this fugitive material agoing, as well as the experiences of one who has given considerable study to the matter dealt with, combined in one handy volume, cannot be otherwise than of benefit. Such subjects as selection of site, drainage, and the study of zones in which certain classes of fruit are known to do well are treated on elaborately, also the arrangement of the fruit garden; and instructions are given how to plant for permanent bearing, where to buy young fruit trees, and a warning against the tree agent, who, it is said, has "injured more homes than he has blessed." In speaking of novelties, it is stated that the value of a new variety is obtained in inverse ratio to the length of its description, and the buyer should not be misled by a glib tongue or a rainbow picture. The author advises the planter to plant such varieties as he likes best, as then they are sure to have better care. There is appended a list of varieties of fruit for certain districts—a feature that will be of real helpfulness to the maker of a new fruit garden.

Among planting instructions some good information is furnished as to how far apart certain trees should be set; and the measuring of distances is also well explained. Much attention is paid to the pruning of various trees, both as regards root pruning, and the annual pruning that should follow. The chapters on the tillage of orchards will be found valuable, as also those on saving and adding fertilizer. In advising as to the pruning of peach trees, the author could have been more explicit, we think. For instance, he recommends the annual heading in for the peach, saying that the fruit is "borne only on new wood." Some readers will gather from that statement that the fruit is borne on the wood to be made the season following the pruning. As is well known, the peach bears its fruit on the wood made the previous year, and it would require quite a stretch of the imagination to call the last year's wood the "new wood," although that is evidently the author's intention.

In the chapter treating on strawberries much stress appears to be laid upon how these plants should be trained in order to secure the best results. It might be all right for an amateur to try to train strawberry runners around the parent plant in the form of spokes of a wheel, but to any one who has ever grown strawberries, this chapter on training will appear amusing, to say the least, for it certainly cannot avail an amateur strawberry grower very much to spend time in training runners in any particular direction.

A very great drawback, considering the mass of matter (much of which is immaterial) presented in the volume, is that no index is provided.

Specific Names.

At the Botanical Congress held in Vienna last year the following "recommendation" was made: that all specific names should be written with a small initial letter, except those derived from the names of men or women (whether used as substantives or as adjectives), or those which represent the names of old genera (substantives or adjectives), thus: Ficus indica, Brassica Napus (Napus being a name of an old genus), Phyteuma Halleri, Malva Tournefortiana. In this way the confusion engendered by the recent practice of spelling words derived from the names of persons in two ways, according as they are used as substantives or as adjectives, is abolished, and all personal names, whether substantives or adjectives, should be spelt with a capital letter, thus: Rosa Hookeri or Rosa Hookeriana. It is generally understood that the substantive form implies that the person whose name is connected with a species has been connected with its discovery, its description, or in some other way; whilst the adjective form anus, or, in the feminine, ana, is merely complimentary.—The Gardeners' Chronicle.

American Carnation Society.

Variety Registered.

By Malachi Tieney, Gardener to Robert Hartshorne, Highlands, N. J.

MRS. ROBERT HARTSHORNE, a cross between General Maceo and Mrs. T. W. Lawson; color bright scarlet; size three to three and one-half inches, with a good strong calyx that does not burst; strong, stiff stems, two to three feet in length. An exceptional keeper, flowers having kept fresh from twelve to fifteen days; has a strong clove odor. A good clean grower producing an abundance of bloom.

ALBERT M. HERR,
Secretary.

OUR READERS' VIEWS

Peony Nematode—A Senseless Scare.

Editor Florists' Exchange:

There is something of a panic among peon growers on account of the nematodes which ar sometimes formed in the roots of the plants. Le us get at the facts. There are two classes of thes insects; one works on the tiny rootlets, and yo often find these filled with nodules. These ar everywhere. Every grower has them to a greate or less extent. They originate in America; prot ably no field is exempt from them. These ar perfectly harmless. They are peculiar in thei work. They will often select one of the most vigoi ous types, and the whole row will be infested wit them. They will not appear on another row besid them of another variety.

A grower hears about nematodes, and digs up h plants, and says, "I've got 'em;" and he is fille with consternation. I have watched this thin closely for a good many years. The other day dug up a row of late Rose—the most vigorous them all. The roots were enormous; the tops fres and green, and they had bloomed beautifully. Bu the rootlets were all filled with nodules.

I have sometimes thought it was with peonies with the nodules on the alfalfa. It is well know that this clover does not come to its best until th ground is filled with bacteria and the roots are fil ed with nodules. Be that as it may, this branch the nematode family is harmless, and if you wa to destroy the insects you can very easily do One of our best entomologists tells me that har wood ashes, muriate and sulphate of potash, plent fully applied, is a sure cure for them. These ca be readily used if one wishes.

The real trouble is with a different branch of th family, and these are imported with stock fro Europe, though not always. I have received plan from France, Holland and England, and never ha this type among them. Unfortunately most, if n all, of the importations from a noted French prop gator are full of them. How they first get in th roots is as hard a problem as the origin of s Probably the ground is filled with them, and th enter through the cuts in the roots; but once they stay there. You can easily tell of their pre ence. Some of your readers have doubtless seen th roots of the apple trees affected by what is term the "root louse." The roots are clubby, knotte gnarled and sadly deformed. Peony roots of i fected plants have a similar appearance. They a fearfully deformed and have an uncanny loo When once these pests get in, they don't let g You may cut up the roots and replant on the ric est soil, and the little fiends stay right there. Th is a disease which never cures itself. Your plan will get worse instead of better.

Years ago I got some Humei alba from one our leading growers. The matter had not th been agitated, and I planted them in a row themselves. After two years I divided them, a had quite a row of them. Two weeks ago I d them up, and they were just awful. Profess Bruner says that while ashes may kill the surfa nematodes, he does not know how to reach th encased in the roots. I thought I would try. I p a can of concentrated lye in two pails of wat left the roots exposed to the sun and air two da until they were well wilted and thirsty. I th packed a wash-tub full of the roots, and poured the lye, then let them soak three days. No whether this will kill or cure I don't know. I do care a great deal. If they can't be cured, they to the brush pile.

It is said the insects cannot stand a great deg of cold. Mine stood thirty degrees below zero. have sent plants to Minnesota to be planted on top of the bleakest hill, to leave them at the me of 40 degrees below, to see what they will do.

Now, here are the bare facts deduced from most careful observation: First—The number affected plants is very small.

Second—They may stand side by side with ot plants in adjoining rows for years, and yet th do not cross over to affect their neighbors.

Third—The best entomologists in the Uni States are at work on them, but it will take ti perhaps years, to solve the problem. Individu should try every possible means of cure, if th have any diseased plants.

Fourth—If any such affected plants are recei they should be put by themselves through fear infesting the ground. Peonies should not be plan after peonies.

Fifth—Then be sensible and discriminating. dealer who sent out roots affected with fore nematodes writes, "Everybody has them in Eur and America." Now here is where the scare co in. People who know the deadly work of the f eign nematodes will say, "Why! they are all o the country, and it isn't safe for us to buy plant;" and so the whole business gets a black

Sixth—Those having foreign plants known to affected ought not to sell them. It is too much selling San Jose scale—not so bad of course, cause they do not spread to other plants.

Seventh—Isn't it about time to stop these miscuous importations and run the risk of get diseased plants? I have bought hundreds peonies of American origin and never had among them all thus affected. Some of the imported ones of the very best type are absolutely worthless: however, they are doomed.

In conclusion, let me say to florists, Keep cool! Don't get up a smallpox scare over a little thing like this. Only an infinitesimal number are affected, and these can be kept until killed or cured. And if perchance you receive any (and you can readily tell them), put them by themselves. A man may buy tens of thousands and not get a diseased one. Don't say, "Everybody has them," and so get up a panic, for some people know that a few are badly affected. Let the condemnation fall on those death-struck, which are few indeed; and don't condemn them all.

C. S. HARRISON.

York, Neb.

Dictionary Definition of "Creations."

Editor Florists' Exchange:

I desire to confess to the fact that many years ago when I saw the first of Mr. Burbank's announcements bearing the title "New Creations" I felt a little of the shock which has apparently affected very seriously some recent writers, because of the impression that the use of the word was presumptuous if not actually impious. I remember very distinctly that I was cured of the impression by recourse to the dictionaries and careful consideration of what the word "creations" really means. It may help some of your readers to escape misplaced qualms of reverence if they will also consider the word in the light of the dictionary makers, viz: Webster says "Create is to effect by the agency and under the laws of causation; to be the occasion of; to cause; to produce; to form or fashion; to renew." The Imperial Dictionary says: "To make or form by investing with a new character; to constitute; to be the occasion of; to cause; to produce; to generate; to bring forth." The Century Dictionary says: "To bring into being; cause to exist; to make or produce from crude or scattered materials; bring into form; embody; to beget; generate; originate; engage in originative action." The Standard Dictionary says: "To cause to be or to come into existence; to produce as a new construction out of existing material; to make a new form out of pre-existing substance." Worcester says: "To cause to exist by the force of original power by the agency of deputed power; to bring into being; to originate; to be the occasion of; to produce; to cause; to invest with any new character; to make."

Are both Burbank and the makers of all the dictionaries wrong in using the term "New Creations" as he has used it, or are some of his critics unacquainted with the meaning of the word "creations?"

California. E. J. WICKSON.

The Sweet and Sour Apple.

Editor Florists' Exchange:

Here is another from Mr. Burbank, the author of the Marvelous in Creation, particularly along the lines of plant breeding. "Burbank, the wizard, has produced an apple red and sweet on one side, and yellow and sour on the other."

This wonderful production is, at least, one hundred and fifty years old. The writer, 70 years ago, and for several years thereafter, gathered from a tree in the Winegar orchard in Union Springs, N. Y., apples, one side of which was sweet and the other sour. The two characters were distinctly marked by a line running from stem to calyx, as is generally a feature with Tallman's Sweeting. The same variety is now to be found in an old orchard of H. C. Anthony's at Portsmouth, R. I.

The only information we could ever get regarding the origin of this apple was found in Loudon's Magazine of Gardening, London, 1830, page 596, as follows:

Sweet and Sour Apples. Mr. Brady in his Treatise on Gardening, mentions an apple which was sweet and boiled soft on one side, and sour and boiled hard on the other side; and the late John Jay of New York notices another sweet on one side and sour on the other. I can relate a third case of a similar nature. The late Levi Hollingsworth, merchant, who resided for more than sixty years in Philadelphia, and was a man of the highest integrity, informed me, several years since, that when he was a boy, living in Elkton in Maryland, there was a full grown apple-tree, the fruit of which was sweet on one side, and sour on the other; on the same limbs there grew apples quite insipid, others sweet and others sour. He mentioned the fact as of his own knowledge to a club of literary gentlemen, who met at a public-house once a week to discuss useful subjects, in the year 1762, in Philadelphia, but the doctrine of the marriage of plants was not familiar to them, and the fact was doubted. This so mortified him, that he went down to Elkton, in company with the late Samuel Nichols, who was a respectable citizen, and brought away several apples to the club. Mr. Hollingsworth assured me the tree had never been grafted.

J. M.

Philadelphia, Sept. 7, 1869.

Floral Park, N. Y. C. L. ALLEN.

Poudrette.

Editor Florists' Exchange:

Replying to the inquiry signed B. Brothers in October 27 issue of The Florists' Exchange, we would say that our firm has handled quite extensively Poudrette manure for some years, and shall be pleased to forward any information to the inquirer regarding same.

Philadelphia, Pa. HENRY F. MICHELL CO.

Editor Florists' Exchange:

Poudrette can be obtained from the Quaker City Poudrette Manufacturing Company, Hugh McAnany, 19 North Juniper street, Philadelphia, Pa. We use it quite freely, and like it real well.

Mount Holly, N. J. J. & J. ELBERTSON.

Packing Orchid Flowers for Shipment.

The tender, delicate flowers, especially cattleyas, require careful methods of handling and packing. The merciless methods of handling express matter must be taken into consideration and means adopted to counteract the difficulty and obviate result-

The Late J. L. Dillon

ant loss. The open formation and frail character of the flowers prevent close packing.

Delivery by hand by special messenger may at first glance appear like a costly method, but it will pay in the end if within reasonable distance. The value of fifty flowers per month saved by hand delivery will more than compensate for the extra cost, and there is the further saving from less care required and time expended in packing. For hand delivery, ordinary pasteboard boxes twenty-three inches long, twelve inches wide and four inches deep are sufficient. They cost about four cents each. They can be packed to contain fifty cattleya flowers, and from one to six boxes can be easily handled at one time by a messenger.

A reasonably safe packing method for express shipment, however, had to be devised for orders to distant points, and the following method was finally adopted after much experimentation. The boxes used are of second quality, three-eighths inch pine, thirty inches long, eleven inches wide and five inches deep, costing about twenty-two cents each for material cut to size and ready to nail together. Such boxes can be packed to contain about fifty flowers. They are lined with tissue paper. Each spray of flowers has a small square of the same paper partially wrapped around it to prevent the blossoms rubbing against each other. The sprays are laid in rows across the box, and on the completion of the row a strip of manila or other stiff wrapping paper is folded three or four times into a band and tacked to the bottom of the box at the ends and between the main stems of the sprays of flowers, thus holding them in position. If this is followed with every row, when packed complete the box may be turned upside down without a flower moving from its position. For long distance shipments it is most desirable that the flowers be cut and placed in water for at least twelve hours previous to packing. The best test of this method was a shipment sent from Madison, N. J., to New Orleans, which arrived in perfect condition, and after a few hours in water, the flowers freshened up as though just cut.—A. Herrington, in Country Life in America.

Obituary

R. J. Mendenhall.

R. J. Mendenhall of Minneapolis, Minn., the pioneer florist of the Northwest, died at his home on Friday morning, October 19. His greenhouse business, which was started about forty years ago, was at one time very successful. In later years he rented the plant, and it finally was sold, he himself retiring from the business. He was prominent in city affairs, having been one of the trustees of the Lakewood Cemetery, city treasurer and president of the State Bank of Minneapolis, and secretary and treasurer of the Board of Education. He was at one time a member of the S. A. F. O. H. and the Minnesota Horticultural Society.

Mr. Mendenhall was a Quaker, and funeral services were held on Sunday, October 21, in the church with which he had long been identified.

John L. Dillon.

John L. Dillon, florist and greenhouse builder, Bloomsburg, Pa., met with a fatal accident at 9:30 o'clock Tuesday morning, October 30, 1906. Mr. Dillon was directing the work of unloading coal from a car at East Bloomsburg. The car had to be moved a few feet in order to get it in a position to unload the coal in a bin. After giving directions to his men, Mr. Dillon stepped in front of the car just as it was got in motion. No one knows how it occurred, but in some way he stumbled or slipped and fell under the moving car, which, being on a down grade, was not easily stopped. The wheels ran over Mr. Dillon's legs, and a bolt caught in his collar, dragging him about five or six feet on his face. It took about seventeen minutes to release him, and when this was done he expired in a few moments. Mr. Dillon had been troubled with rheumatism in his legs and feet for some time, and this may have been the cause of his being unable to move quickly enough to get out of the way of the car.

The sad occurrence is doubly sad for Mrs. Dillon, as her father, Mr. Hutchinson, of Kingston, Pa., died in Philadelphia the day preceding.

Mr. Dillon was 55 years old, and leaves a widow, three sons and one daughter, the latter the wife of Boyd Firman, who has managed the Dillon greenhouses for some time. The eldest son is in college. The funeral services, which were Masonic, were held on Friday afternoon at 2 o'clock.

Mr. Dillon had been in business as a florist for many years, and was a successful grower of roses, carnations, and verbenas. He was an extensive advertiser and built up a very considerable trade. Among the new varieties of carnations which he originated were Queen Louise and Crisis, both lately introduced.

He was for many years a member of the Society of American Florists, seldom missing a meeting. He was also a member of the American Carnation Society. In late years he had engaged in greenhouse building, and was interested in greenhouse material, composition posts, etc.

Mr. Dillon was a quiet, unassuming man, and built up his business on strictly business principles. He had hosts of friends in the trade, who will be grieved to learn of his untimely and sad death.

NEWPORT, (R. I.) HORTICULTURAL SOCIETY.—A meeting of this society was held last Tuesday evening, President MacLellan in the chair. There was a fair attendance. Andrew Pow, gardener for Mrs. Cornelius Vanderbilt, had on exhibition a very large and well grown lot of nerines for which the committee, consisting of Messrs. James Robertson, Joseph Gibson and Colin Robertson, recommended an award of $10, which recommendation was adopted by the society. W. J. Watson, gardener for Miss Keteltas, exhibited a very good seedling cactus dahlia, for which a suitable award was given; he was requested to name the variety and show it again.

The question of stove and greenhouse plants came up rather late for extended discussion, but from what took place it was noted that opinion is divided. Before long, however, we may expect that the subject will be revived, and receive the attention it deserves from the society. D. M.

AMONG THE GROWERS

Henry A. Dreer, Inc., Riverton, N. J.

Azaleas and Rhododendrons.

Forty thousand azaleas all in sight as one steps into the range of short span houses on this establishment. That was the first impression the writer got the other day; and never before was such a grand lot of azaleas seen at one time. No picking out is required in filling orders, all the plants being good. They were all arranged in lots, by size and variety, and among them were some very good specimen plants. These latter are becoming scarcer each year.

In the same houses was a fine lot of rhododendrons for forcing—all healthy, well-budded plants.

We then started on a tour, after learning that 30 men were working until 10 o'clock the previous night to get orders packed that were left over at 6 p. m.

Decorative Stock.

Of araucarias there are three houses filled with excelsa compacta and glauca from 4-inch sizes up. The excelsa in 6-inch pots were equally as good as we have often seen A. compacta. The writer does not remember ever before seeing such a grand lot of compact plants of Araucaria excelsa. All other varieties were also very good.

A bench of Asplenium nidus-avis was seen in another house—nice plants for growing on, now in 3-inch pots. Of Dracæna terminalis a fine lot of young plants in 1½-inch pots was noticed. Pandanus Veitchii has a whole house devoted to it, in from 2 to 6-inch pots, of good value. Caryota urens occupies a whole bench, young plants, in 2½-inch pots. Some will query, Why so many of this palm? Because it does well, is liked and a demand is found for it.

Impatiens Holstii was seen in five new varieties, all to go out next Spring. The flowers are far superior to those now in existence, and of more desirable shades of color. Also in this house was noticed ivy-leaved geranium Alliance, practically new; flowers very much like those of a pelargonium, and certainly very desirable.

Probably nowhere else can such a quantity of Dracæna Godseffiana be seen, all well grown and very desirable plants. The method of propagation and getting up of a good stock of marantas has been mastered here, and now the retail florists are awakening to the fact that a few of these plants are very desirable in the store. For florists' use the best two are imperialis and rosea lineata, both erect growers, with nicely colored foliage, and both stand well.

Of Phœnix Roebelinii we observed a large batch in 6 and 7-inch pots; also a big lot in 3-inch pots, all good, sturdy, healthy plants, very graceful and in brisk demand. In kentias in tubs a large number of plants were seen, very desirable for the decorator, in all sizes up to 10 and 12 feet tall. Then around this range were observed thousands of both K. Belmoreana and K. Forsteriana in 5, 6 and 7-inch pots, all well done, stocky plants. Several blocks of latanias were also noticed. While many establishments have given up these palms they are yet in good demand here. Areca lutescens are in quantity; nice plants in 6 and 7-inch pots. The demand for these keeps up, but there is not much call for the very large plants. Several center benches were filled with cocos in 3-inch pots, all very healthy and compact plants. Some are set aside to grow on to 5-inch pots.

Of bay trees a very large importation has recently arrived in all desirable sizes and shapes—pyramids of several sizes, standards from 10-inch tubs up to large specimens. A new form has the appearance of the head of a standard stuck in a tub, no stem being seen.

Ferns.

It would take a whole page to tell of the ferns alone, hence we can dwell only on a few. This firm has finally got Adiantum Farleyense to perfection, and a grand lot of plants in 6 and 7-inch pots were seen. They occupy a house by themselves, which is heated by hot water. A little heat has been kept on all season to control the moisture; and certainly perfection has been gained, as a most perfect lot of plants has resulted. There are also two side benches filled with smaller plants, all in good shape; those in 4 and 5-inch pots will all make desirable stock for the holidays. Adiantum Lathami, in 6-inch pots, is a very desirable fern, and by many is considered as good as A. Farleyense. All the varieties of nephrolepis are seen here. Scottii is very dwarf and in all the sizes, very well done. The cream of all is a house of N. Whitmanii; in 5 and 6-inch pots, all exceedingly well done; and in a block of 5,000 plants only four fronds of the old Boston type have been found. The feeling here is, stop at N. Whitmanii; don't bother about another variety, this one is good enough for all. Pteris Wilsonii, in 6-inch pans, is not only a very pretty plant, but very desirable as a jardinere subject.

In other houses and out in the frames are millions of small ferns in all stages and sizes to meet the endless demand made on this establishment.

Perennials.

We now take a glimpse at a part of this department. At this late season were noticed a large block of poppies, Papaver nudicale, in full bloom, while farther over were observed the last of the flowers of the white stokesia, a larger bloom and evidently a stronger grower than the blue variety. All over this department order clerks were busy picking out plants, as at this season of the year orders are getting more numerous for this stock, and the system of growing here has been developed to such an extent that good results can always be obtained, for any plant that cannot stand being dug up at any time is grown in a pot, and will go right ahead.

The Packing Shed.

In the packing shed were seen all kinds and sizes of stock, choice exotic plants side by side with pæony roots. On one table a collection of perennials; on another bundles of one-year-old phlox, grand plants, with really two-year roots, some of them actually in flower.

The bins for storing dahlias are being cleaned out, as this week the roots will be dug and drought in. Much attention has been given the past season to getting the dahlias true to name, and those about which there was any doubt have been destroyed. Similar precaution marks this vast establishment, and the increased orders received each year demonstrate that customers are getting satisfaction.

DAVID RUST.

At Vaughan's Nurseries, Western Springs, Ill., in 1905. See next page.

Vaughan's Greenhouses, Western Springs, Ill.

Among the most interesting points in and aroun Chicago there is one paramount from a horticu tural point of view which attracts the attention visitors to this section because it is complete; is ideal; it is unique; and it is absolutely perfe in management, detail and production. Vaughan Seed Store is too well known throughout the Cen tral West to require any encomiums for their wor or their productions from the Randolph street stor but a trip to Western Springs, the source of sup plies, is a treat to the visitor long to be remem bered.

Passing up to the greenhouses before the rece freeze I walked through the trial field where hun dreds of varieties of annuals, perennials and vege tables were passing or trying to pass the examina tion which will allow them to be listed in the cat log of the concern for the ensuing year. This most assuredly an interesting department and or where the few hours at our disposal could hav been spent advantageously without further invest gation, but directly ahead after looking over th numerous beds of cannas of the best of late intr ductions, also on trial, are the greenhouses.

An acre, more or less, of cold frames filled wit herbaceous and other commercial plants and vine and then the office, a model of the up-to-date bus ness requirements. Manager J. S. Wilson greets th visitor and escorts him through house after hou of as perfect stock as ever grew under glass, in cluding pandanus in its different forms, palms all the favorite commercial varieties, one house Celestial peppers, Araucarias, excelsa, glauca an robusta compacta, nephrolepis in variety, Bal Rambler roses, ficus, a house of Begonia Gloire Lorraine, caladiums and many other commerci plants and all in the pink of perfection.

One is perhaps more impressed by what Chicag ians can do in a short time by a visit to the nu sery about a mile distant where this enterprisin house purchased in 1905 a tract of land embraci 40 acres encumbered by a shack and absolute devoid of embellishment. In one short year und the careful direction of H. J. Stockmans, the lan scape gardener of the concern, a transformation h been wrought. The house has been remodeled, th grounds artistically laid out and a well stock nursery is now under thorough cultivation, amo the specialties being a choice collection of peoni and a desirable assortment of ornamental shru The accompanying illustrations will give but a fai idea of the year's improvements.

W. K. W.

A. L. Thorne, Flushing, N. Y.

A recent visit to this plant found everything splendid order. A. L. Thorne, the genial propriet who evinces great interest in the business, to pains to pilot the writer through the entire pla which, though built some ten years since, is ke in such excellent shape that all seems new. Th houses were built by the Pierson-Sefton Compa and are heated by six Hitchings No. 57 and one N 58 boilers, which do the work of heating 60,0 square feet of glass entirely satisfactorily. Ros and carnations are the chief items grown; Ric mond, Wellesley, and Bride being a trio of ro hard to beat. Robert Craig, Prosperity, Lieutena Peary, Mrs. M. A. Patten, The President, Encha tress and Mrs. Lawson are leaders among carn tions and find a ready market through John I. Ra nor, 49 West Twenty-eighth street, New York, w has always handled the product of this up-to-da establishment.

M.

A Progressive Pittsburg Wholesale Hous

The Pittsburg Cut Flower Company, Ltd., has cured new quarters at 222 Oliver avenue, Pittsbu a very central location right in the retail flor district, and in close proximity to the railroad d pots and express offices. This building has 10,0 square feet of floor space, with 4,000 square f of basement room, and will be used entirely for t handling and selling of cut flowers and florists' su plies. It is fitted up with the latest and most mo ern equipments for the handling of cut flow quickly and carefully, enabling the concern take the best care of local and out-of-town tra with great dispatch, and in this way insuri promptness of delivery, so important a factor in t cut flower business.

The growth and development of the Pittsbu Cut Flower Company has been phenomenal. F several years previous to 1898 the founding of wholesale cut flower commission house in Pit burg was discussed, but the suggestion was disco aged by the growers and retailers who have sin profited most by a local establishment. In 18 Fred Burki, one of the best known and most su cessful growers in the locality, Wm. A. Clarke, o of the oldest Pittsburg men employed in the ret cut flower business, and Theodore P. Langhans, young man with several years' experience in t retail trade coupled with a practical business tra ing in commercial lines, organized the Pittsburg C Flower Company, the first house of its kind betw the East and the Middle West. Though the vent was regarded by some as dubious, it has, throu the pluck, energy, patience and perseverance of t originators, proved an unqualified success. Th first opened on September 1, 1898, at 705 Penn avenue, the floor space measuring only 540 square feet, with 700 feet of basement. After a year it was found that these quarters were inadequate, and others were secured at 504 Liberty avenue containing a larger floor space and basement area. This has also been found too small for the company's increasing business, and, as stated, a further move has been found necessary.

The Pittsburg Cut Flower Company represents over 144 growers of cut flowers, and handles the products of several millions of feet of glass. Though only established a little over eight years, it now does a most extensive trade, built up on strictly business principles, courteous and fair dealing with customers; attending promptly to all orders, and returning to growers exactly what their stock is worth based on the production and market price; and last, but not least, the meeting of all financial obligations with the utmost promptness.

Chrysanthemum Gossip for 1906.

As to Clementine Touset, among early whites this outdistances every other variety. Anyone who has grown it the past year, we are sure, will agree with us when he counts the shekels it has brought him. It well deserves the name of "Early Chadwick." It was certificated on October 8, but came some four days later this year, and for October 12 it is still the grandest white to be had. The stem is stiff, of good medium length, with crisp, small foliage that allows close planting. It is the easiest possible "doer" provided the right bud is taken, when it will perfect every bloom. I heard Mr. Lemon discussing its buds the other day. He says that our bench shows early started plants and also late struck cuttings of this variety. The first bud (early crown) taken on the late struck plants, came n the earliest by over a week, with smooth well-'ormed, large pure white flowers. The same bud on the older plants is bringing a white flower crowded with petals and finishing a full two weeks ater; while the terminal buds are prefecting at the same date beautiful smooth flowers of shell pink with a luster like satin. There are still mysteries in he chrysanthemum that are far from being fathomed, and each variety must be studied and its habits earned separately. It is very evident that the date of the taking of the bud is of quite as much importance as the type of bud taken, and it is evident hat this information will have to be furnished by ntroducers so far as possible in order to avoid loss o growers. The fact that buds of the different lates must be tested on seedlings and importations nakes it quite difficult, often, to secure the six blooms required for the examininng committees of he C. S. A. on any given date, for one must be ready to show six of any of the three buds taken—earlies, seconds or terminals—which means a considerable planting of a rare variety. To conclude as to Touset—never take the bud before August 1.

Here, in Indiana, Beatrice May is finishing up nagnificently, the grandest white imaginable, perfect in every point save foliage. The form is grand, broad and deep; size, mammoth; finish, smooth and elegant. Very few whites could stand against it on he exhibition table, and as a super-fancy commercial it would be found satisfactory, for it keeps and carries well. It is a very easy doer, but will require selection to keep the foliage in good condition, and the variety is well worth the trouble required. The blooms are at their best October 20 and later this year, but could be cut earlier.

For pure commercial cutting October 20 sees few iner whites than Alice Byron. In purity of color, finish, form, texture, stem and foliage, as well as general tractability, it has no superior. Mrs. Henry Robinson is equally good with us, though with many growers the stems lack strength.

We are just now revelling in some magnificent pinks after a long wait for this color. M. Loiseau-Rousseau (October 20) is one of the biggest, an enormous incurved variety with beautiful stem and foliage, fine enough to bear company with Beatrice May, and maturing about the same time. Another beautiful pink is the soft seashell variety, Mme. Guinard, a big rosette in form, every petal set, apparently, with an eye to perfect symmetry in form, shorter center petals shading to creamy pink, a base of them having an indescribably beautiful effect above the perfect foliage.

Then there is Mme. L. H. Cochet, which might best be characterized as an "Early Viviand-Morel;" very similar in shade to that variety, of the same form, perfect in stem and foliage, a grand grower, of very easy management. We expect this to prove a permanent addition to our lists, and of the greatest value in October pinks.

Mrs. M. F. Plant is showing an exquisite color, a fine grower, stem and foliage excellent, but it remains to be seen if our Indiana soil will give it full size as the days go by.

Mary Mann is the brightest, highest shade of pink that we have yet seen in a chrysanthemum. The form is a perfect Japanese incurve, big and round, with petals so loosely arranged as to show the brilliant inside color to perfection. A Liger seedling, it has all the best qualities of that fine sort, with the addition of brilliance in tint. The finish very refined, and the variety is the easiest possible grow; for October 18 and later it is without peer.

We had hoped much from Marjorie Shields in this color, but it burns badly and does not perfect its blooms in large enough proportion to be profitable.

Norman Davis is a very big loose flower of showy color—a brassy red and reddish copper, but lacking sadly in petals. J. G. Shrimpton and Connie Jamison are both of general Chinese type for which we seem to have no liking in this country.

Chas. Weeks is a large, flat reflexing variety, of pretty shade of old rose and Autumn leaf tint, a nice color, but not popular here as yet. It is odd how as one works with chrysanthemums we fall in love with these "off colors" and are a little impatient with the general public who have not yet become "cultured" enough to enjoy them, though flower buyers generally take quite kindly to the bronzes where high tints predominate; and while they may not often select them when ordering unaided, they are delighted with results when these grand colors are properly arranged in their decorations.

One of the finest new sorts of the year is Director Gerard, already noted as an early golden yellow (certificated October 20 by a score of 87 points, commercial), yet the second bud on this variety brings an unusually fine shade of orange bronze, or what I always carry in my own mind as the "Source d'Or color" and which I always recall with a deep sense of pure pleasure.

Incandescent is an enormous brassy-red, finely formed and full, a splendid addition to the exhibition bronzes, while the queen of them all in this color is Mme. L. Roussel, round as a ball, and big as a football—an improved and enlarged Henry the II.

As I close these notes one of the most interesting varieties on the place is just pushing out its petals and showing a brilliant golden shade. We are extremely anxious to see it develop, for we have pinned a great deal of faith to it from the descriptions given of it by competent judges. The variety is now known as "J. A. Macrae's Golden Eaton." It is a grand shade of yellow for an opening bud, and the foliage while differing enough from Timothy Eaton to be noticeably distinct, still shows its kin to the parent and is every whit as beautiful. The bloom is said to have the form of Major Bonnaffon and the variety will not be named finally until after the Chicago show! This variety was fully described on page 760 issue of December 16, 1905 of The Florists' Exchange.

S. A. HILL.

Richmond, Ind.

Profits in Orchid Growing.

Writing to Country Life in America, A. Herrington, Florham Farms, Madison, N. J., who superintends the commercial plant of W. H. McK. Twombley, says that orchid culture for profit will never appeal to wealthy men as a glittering business opportunity, because it is hard to make more than 8 per cent. profit out of it, which is too small for most financiers to consider. Mr. Herrington believes that the smallest scale of operations on which orchid culture could be profitably undertaken involves a capital of $50,000. Orchids must be grown in quantity in order to cut from 100 to 500 flowers at a time, or you cannot realize upon the product to the best advantage. If the number of plants is below a desirable quota it may happen that there are few or no flowers available during a particular week when prices are high; and, moreover, a steady continuous supply of each kind in season insures a regular market.

In a tabulated statement, the results of actual experience, Mr. Herrington shows that on an investment of $50,000 in eight 100 foot houses and 9,000 plants—6,000 cattleyas, 2,000 cypripediums, 1,000 oncidiums—the net profits for a year were $1,620. The Florham Farms orchid department is still in operation.

At Vaughan's Nurseries, Western Springs, Ill., 1906.

EXHIBITIONS

Lenox, Mass.

The annual show of the Lenox (Mass.) Horticultural Society was held in the Town Hall on October 24-25, 1906. Owing to the lateness of the season the cut blooms of chrysanthemums were not up to the Lenox standard; in only one or two cases were the flowers shown in perfect condition. Most of them lacked finish, but this was the fault of the season rather than that of the grower. The quality showed in the flower if it had had time to develop.

All of last year's novelties were prominently to the front. The most conspicuous of all was undoubtedly Beatrice May. This is a grand chrysanthemum and will be one of the standard sorts for both commercial and private purposes. On the early crown bud it comes pure white; on a late bud it is tinged with pink; but even this latter color is also beautiful. It seems to be a first-class grower in every respect. Morton F. Plant also showed up in good condition; this variety was not finished and would have required at least another week to have been in perfect condition. Mrs. F. F. Thompson, contrary to expectation, was exhibited in wonderful condition. Its beautiful flower is not altogether pure white, but has a delicate pink shade running through it. It has, of course, that objectionable long neck, but as done at Lenox proves that it is a very good chrysanthemum—and there is lots of room for it.

Mrs. E. G. Brooks, T. Richardson, W. Wells, Mrs. Heaume, Montigny, Mrs. Henry Partridge, Glenview, and Dorothy Oliver, were all shown in good condition, being in most of the winning stands. Mrs. A. J. Miller, Mrs. Duckham, and Wm. Duckham were also exhibited in very good form. A white sport of Wm. Duckham was staged; the flower was far from being fully developed to do it justice, but it may be said that this is a pure white variety with all the good characteristics of the parent, and will undoubtedly be an acquisition to the white class. There is still room for it; it fills in a place between Beatrice May and D. V. West, and will be found a very beautiful chrysanthemum for private or commercial purposes. We predict a great future for it.

The classes were not very well contested, in many cases only one exhibitor being entered. The F. R. Pierson Company cup went to E. Jenkins, gardener to Mr. Geraud Foster, his flowers being very good; they consisted of the following varieties: Beatrice May, Montigny, Mrs. F. F. Thompson, D. V. West, Mrs. Heaume, and Morton F. Plant.

The great feature of the show was the first prize group of plants exhibited by F. Heeremans, gardener to Mr. W. D. Sloan. It was probably one of the prettiest groups ever put up in this country, being carefully and lightly arranged. Standing in front of it one could see every plant, and each was so placed that its individuality was evident. It contained many rare specimens of palms, besides large numbers of orchids and lily of the valley, color being added by beautiful crotons. It was indeed a revelation to the ordinary gardener, and it would be well if the average exhibitor could pay a visit to Lenox on one of these occasions and see how a group of plants ought to be staged. If this were done, certainly we would have fewer of the "haycock" character at our shows.

The second prize group, exhibited by E. Jenkins, was a magnificent collection, also of well grown plants. It had fewer flowering plants in it, and on the whole was rather more compactly arranged than the prize-winning group. Mr. Jenkins's collection contained some very fine specimen plants of crotons, but lacked that loose, easy style which won the honors for Mr. Heeremans.

A. T. Boddington's prize was also won by E. Jenkins for twenty-four blooms, distinct varieties. Chas. H. Totty's prizes for six blooms of Beatrice May on long stems were won by E. Jenkins, first; Thos. Proctor, second; and S. Carlquist, third. Howard & Morrow's prizes for vase of thirty-six blooms went to R. Spiers, first; A. H. Wingett, second; and E. Jenkins, third. The premiums in the other chrysanthemum classes were won by E. Jenkins, Robert Spiers, A. H. Wingett, S. Carlquist, A. J. Loveless, Thos. Proctor, J. J. Donahue, D. Dunn and F. Heeremans. Bay State Nursery prizes for three specimen plant and one specimen plant were won by E. Jenkins and R. Spiers.

F. Heeremans put up a good group of orchids on a round table in the middle of the hall.

Roses were well shown; Thos. Proctor's Richmond were excellent, the principal winners in these classes were Thos. Proctor, E. Jenkins, F. Heeremans, Thos. Page, J. J. Donahue, R. Spiers, A. H. Wingett, Thos. Dixon, and D. Dunn.

The carnation benches were where the judges found a hard proposition, competition being very close. The winners were those named above, with E. Dolby, H. P. Workey and L. Wacheson added. In E. Dolby's vase of fifty blooms was an excellent white seedling of his own raising which promises fair to become a winner.

Vaughan's Seed Store prize for collection of eighteen varieties of vegetables was won by E. Jenkins.

Lager & Hurrell, Summit, N. J., staged a nice group of orchids and were awarded a first class certificate, as also was F. I. Drake of Pittsfield for a bunch of Gov. Herrick violet. Jas. Crawshaw of Olneyville, R. I., was also awarded a first class certificate for his new Asparagus plumosus Crawshawii.

Mr. Curtis, of the Curtis Hotel, exhibited some very fine plants in pots of the new cosmos, Lady Lenox, a beautiful pink; the flowers are large, but its principal quality seems to lie in its color and the breadth of the petals. A. T. Boddington, of New York, is putting it on the market.

C. Carlquist staged a nice exhibit of the Lilium Philippinense. These were potted up from bulbs received after September, and showed how early this lily can be brought into flower.

Fruit and vegetables were also well shown and in large numbers. Ailsa Craig onions, staged by several exhibitors, were monsters, and would easily weigh about two pounds each. The vegetable classes were keenly contested, and the decisions were close. Some very fine carrots were staged by Walter Angus, Chapinville, Conn.

The judges were C. H. Totty, A. Herrington, Wm. Duckham, and G. H. Hale. J. T. SCOTT.

Tarrytown, N. Y.

The eighth annual Fall exhibition of the Tarrytown (N. Y.) Horticultural Society, held in the Music hall on October 30, 31 and November 1, was all through quite up to the usual high standard of former years. Chrysanthemums in this section are a little late, about a week being still necessary to finish the majority of the blooms; consequently they were hardly at their best. Nevertheless some magnificent flowers were staged.

In the plant classes, Mrs. J. B. Trevor, Yonkers, N. Y. (Howard Nichols, gardener) was the most extensive and successful exhibitor, carrying off the first prizes for the group of decorative plants, specimen ferns, Adiantum Farleyense, etc. E. Berolzheimer, Tarrytown, N. Y. (D. McFarlane, gardener) was first for the table of decorative plants, showing some beautiful, clean-grown stock.

In chrysanthemum plants the principal exhibitors were Wm. Rockefeller, Tarrytown (George Middletown, gardener), and Fred Potter, Ossining, N. Y. (Wm. Roberts, gardener). The principal prize in this section was a silver cup donated by Mrs. George Lewis. The competition was very close, Mr. Rockefeller winning out with two well-grown plants, Fred Potter being second.

In the cut bloom classes another tight hold occurred for the cup offered by F. R. Pierson Company for the twelve best blooms of Glenview. Wm. Rockefeller again won out, with E. Berolzheimer second. Giraud Foster, Lenox, Mass. (E. Jenkins, gardener) was first in the class calling for twenty-five blooms distinct; also for twelve blooms distinct, showing some magnificent flowers. Among his best varieties were Beatrice May, Mrs. F. F. Thompson, T. S. Richardson, Emily Mileham, May Siddon, Mrs. H. Partridge, Morton F. Plant, Mrs. Miller, Mme. Herrwich, W. W. Wells and Montigny. In both the last named classes Wm. Rockefeller took second place; some of his best flowers were H. J. Jones, Lady Hopetoun, Mrs. Partridge, Mrs. Miller, Morton F. Plant, Mrs. Wm. Knox, Beatrice May, F. S. Vallis and Mme. Marc de Mons. E. Berolzheimer was first for thirty-six blooms, six varieties, six of each, showing among others a beautiful vase of Lady Hopetoun.

In the rose classes, Mrs. George Lewis, Tarrytown, N. Y. (J. Ballantyne, gardener) was well to the front, carrying off two cups, one given by Mrs. H. Fairchild Osborne for the best twelve Richmond and the other for twelve Killarney.

The carnation classes were well filled, and fine flowers were staged. The only new one exhibited was Winsor by F. R. Pierson Company, a fine vase of fifty blooms of this variety being awarded the first prize in a class open to commercial growers only.

For the best new decorative plant, not now in commerce, Scott Brothers, Elmsford Nurseries, were awarded a silver medal for a seedling from Dracæna Godseffiana. In this the habit of growth is the same as the parent, but the variegation is much prettier and more distinct.

The table decorations, judged by ladies on the second day of the show, brought out eight competitors. After much deliberation the judges awarded first prize to James Ballantyne. His was a beautiful arrangement of orchids. A certificate of merit was awarded to David McFarlane, his table being done with crimson chrysanthemums and Autumn leaves. WM. SCOTT.

Luther Burbank.

A Short Review of His Work in Plant Hybridization and Brief Comparison with Other Hybridizers.

By Patrick O'Mara, Jersey City, N. J.

(Continued from page 475.)

Further on in the same book he says: "During the past few years when Shasta daisies were being bred and educated up to their state." I wish to say, and make it as emphatic as possible, that in my opinion no exercise of the human mind by way of suggestive thought directed upon a plant can change one cell or filament of it.

Now, let me say a word about the Shasta daisy. When the magazines and the daily newspapers issued side by side pictures of an ordinary daisy and of a Shasta daisy, my suspicions were allayed at once. I said, "If anybody can produce from an ordinary daisy growing in that climate a flower of this size it will not deteriorate in the East." Therefore, I thought we were safe in taking that. We obtained some Shasta daisy seed. We raised enough plants to fill two frames, and when they bloomed, we sent a man up there with a hoe and he hoed them all out and threw them over the fence, because they were hardly any better than the ordinary field daisy which grows in the fields of the East. It is only fair to say that I believe the Shasta daisy has been very much improved since that time and is now generally recognized as an acquisition.

On the front of the catalogue for 1901 of the "Creations" of Burbank, there is a picture of a plum tree known as the Burbank plum. The Burbank plum is an importation pure and simple; he got it from Japan and he never produced it at all. In Burbank's catalogue for that year occurs the following, copied from the Santa Rosa "Republican". The first line says: "The Creation of the Horticultural Wizard are so wonderful that even science has to be convinced."

A great many of his friends say that he does not want to be called a wizard, and that what is said of him is said without his knowledge and consent, but in this particular matter that somewhat offensive word occurs. The article continues:

"An amusing incident in the visit of the Associated Agricultural Colleges and Experiment Stations of America to the Sebastopol grounds gives a fair illustration. When the party had traversed but a small portion of the grounds and tested but a few of the fruits therein, one of the professors called a halt, requesting from his brethren their brief attention. Calling upon Mr. Burbank to step forward so that all might better view him, the producer of the wonders, he delivered the following: 'Gentlemen, in the presence of you all I wish to make known that one of my objects in coming to this Coast was to expose Mr. Burbank's fraud. I have read that man's catalogue annually and I have long considered him about the biggest liar in the United States. I now retract all that and declare that Mr. Burbank has never told one-half the marvels that he might. Gentlemen, hats off to the wizard before you.' The motion needed no second.

This needs no comment from me.

This I quote from Mr. Harwood. Mr. Burbank is supposed to say:

"We say to Miss Golden Cup, or Miss Eschscholtzia as the bon-ton call her, this beautiful dress of bright golden hue which you have always worn on all occasions is very becoming to you, and exceedingly appropriate to this land of perpetual sunshine, but, Miss Queen Golden Cup, if you will sometimes adorn yourself with a dress of white, pale cream, pink or crimson we could love you still better than we do. Now, Miss Eschscholtzia, though having her family tastes and characteristics very thoroughly fixed, still belongs to the great Papaver race, which has often shown itself willing to adapt itself to the discipline of new conditions, even at first distasteful in the extreme. So, taking Miss Golden Cup into our gardens and constantly making these suggestions to her, she hesitatingly consents to don a dress a shade lighter in color, and then lighter still, until now we have her not only in dresses of gold but in deepest orange, light and dark shades of cream, purest snowy white, or all these combined, and by constant selection and various educational influence in this line, she will adorn herself in a dress of almost any color which may be desirable and at the same time seems to take the greatest pleasure in improving herself in every grace of form and feature."

This particular flower, as is well known, is the flower of California which grows all over the fields making them golden. In Mr. Harwood's book he tells very touchingly of how Mr. Burbank going over a field one evening, noticed a delicate stain of red in one of the flowers. His eagle glance caught it and he saved that particular plant. After four or five years, I have forgotten which, he was able to put upon the market a beautiful crimson eschscholtzia, which is offered by a Philadelphia seed house this year. That is an achievement in itself without question. But look at another side of it. Over in England twenty years ago Carter of London who had been devoting some attention to Miss Eschscholtzia or Golden Cup, produced the variety "Mandarin," a distinct break from the yellow, an orange colored one. About seven years ago or thereabouts they produced the Rose Cardinal, a rose colored one. This year they offer the Crimson King. I have not seen the variety, but the color plate, contrasted with Burbank's shows that Carter's variety is by all odds the better of the two. I merely mention this to show that without any great flourish of trumpets, but simply by the ordinary processes of fertilization, selection and propagation, as to this particular flower, others are accomplishing what is said to be a marvellous achievement by Mr. Burbank.

The English people, particularly the Kew authorities, attracted by the noise and furor in the magazines, and seeing that the American people were not sufficiently appreciative of Burbank and that the great catalogue houses were rather chary of offering these wonders, and thinking that perhaps it was the old story of the prophet without honor in his own country, wrote to Burbank and asked him if he would sell or exchange some of these various marvels which he was supposed to have. I quote his letter in reply:

May 8, 1905.

My dear sir:—Your esteemed note of April 10th received. I am sorry to say that the Press has gotten hold of my work a little too soon. I have a great number of hybrid thornless cactus, but it takes time and thought to select the ones which are to be winners, and I have been obliged to make an invariable rule never to send out anything until it is properly finished."

(Then I thought of the Shasta daisies that we hoed out.)

"The perpetual poppy and fragrant Dahlia will probably be sent out by a Chicago firm next season. The 'Pomato' will not be ready for a year or two."

(This "Pomato" is a cross between the potato and the tomato, they belong to the same family and so will cross; it has been done before; I think it is just sixteen years ago last Summer since E. S. Carman, in a paper read before the Society of American Florists in Boston, told how he had effected this cross. It was of no particular use. Of course, Mr. Burbank may make use of it, but as an achievement it is nothing.)

"The coreless-apple fraud is none of my work; I must add that it is no doubt worthless; though I have known it for forty years.

"I shall be pleased to exchange with you when I have these ready for introduction."

My object in injecting this letter is to show that while these things are probably in existence, yet as far as being of any economic value or being on the market, as most of us were led to believe, they were not available at that particular time.

The cactus is mentioned there. If there is any one plant attributed to Mr. Burbank that has seemed to catch the popular fancy more than another, it is the spineless cactus. I think I have heard more of that than anything else—to think that a man could by manipulation take that miserable thing, that you could not even look at without feeling hurt, and breed all those thorns off of it, so that you might sit down on it if you wanted to. I never crossed the desert myself except on a railroad train, but I can imagine that if a man is crossing the desert and wants to sit down, how handy it would be to have one of these thornless cacti handy. I want to say in all seriousness that so far as I know, the original plant which Burbank had was given to him right straight out of the Department of Agriculture. Harwood in these magazine articles distinctly credits Burbank with having "created" it, and during the months which intervened between the publication of these articles in the Century Magazine and the publication of Harwood's book, that statement was never contradicted by Burbank. I realize that he is a very busy man; but it does seem to me that in a matter of that kind somebody representing him at all events should issue a statement saying: "No, I did not 'create' that, but I am breeding from it and I expect to improve it." That's a fair statement. Now, there is hardly a botanical garden in the world that you cannot go in to-day and find a thornless cactus. In an exhibition that we had down at Herald Square Hall, here in New York, given by the American Institute, they exhibited three of these thornless cacti, just to show that such things could be had outside of Santa Rosa. And yet Harwood goes on to say that this is the plant that is going to turn arid deserts into populous plains, and that it will be in a certain sense the vine and fig tree of the desert. Bulletin No. 74, Dept. of Agriculture, is devoted exclusively to cacti as food for stock. It relates in detail how they are utilized at present and states further: "In this connection it may be remarked that were it not for the spines on this class of plants they would probably have been exterminated long ago," and there is some doubt whether there would be any use for spineless forms in the future. One poet sung of Mr. Burbank as follows:

"He touched the spiculed desert—cacti cursed—
And turned its thorns to figs; its thistles fruit.
He nodded to the daisy half immersed
In dwarfing dust, and lo! a lily mute
Rose from the weeds—a perfume with a flute."

That's the way it affects the poet. They say when a poet gets after a man he is done for. Here is another "poem" that occurs to me. This man was a florist, and he is supposed to be one of the "knockers":

"O, Mr. Burbank, won't you try and do some things
for me?
A wizard clever as you are can do them easily.
A man who turns a cactus plant into a feather bed
Should have no trouble putting brains into a cabbage
head."

(To be continued.)

FOR THE RETAILER

[All questions relating to the Retail Trade will be cheerfully answered in this column. We solicit good, sharp photographs of made-up work, decorations, store interiors, etc., for reproduction here.—Ed. F. E.]

Among the Vines.

We were out among the vines the other day, and need not dwell upon their individual beauties here, only to remind the designer that nothing can add more finish to his work in design, bunch, basket, vase or box of loose flowers, than a few tips of Rosé Wichuraiana or its numerous types. These can be had in abundance of your grower or nurseryman almost for the asking. Try them in your fine work.

Chrysanthemums in Decorative Work.

The all-absorbing question of the hour is how to most profitably use the great quantity of chrysanthemums at present on the market. This is an annual quandary and much aggravation is created in some quarters over this flower. There are never, can never, be too many flowers grown. The only trouble is too much, yes, nigh the impossible, is expected for them or from them. What are called "gluts" on the market could often be obviated were a little more generosity shown.

Now when chrysanthemums are so plentiful it would be well to acquaint every hotel or restuarant keeper in your section how cheaply he could decorate his tables. Very many of the new hotel dining rooms are resplendent with flowers, just a few in a vase on each table. This custom can be made general.

Then again, there are the theaters. Many a manager would present a flower to his lady matineeists at times, did he know at what little cost he could do it. The same could be said of the many lines of business. The green stamp, souvenir or gratuity offered by them could be in the more acceptable form of natural flowers.

A diplomatic and timely suggestion, to go half way in presenting schools, hospitals or institutions where girls are with flowers, might often result in great good all around; at least, the attempt to do good seldom hurts anyone. The question of the hour is how to best reach the flower-buying public, and individual methods must be employed to make opportunities and satisfy them.

Chrysanthemums are the most imposing flowers to use for decorative purposes, and for the many weddings and other festivities they are pre-eminently appropriate. In the most elaborate forms of work mass them. We are continually urging our readers to mass or concentrate their material where possible. Decorators often spoil their work and material by scattering it, or pursuing wrong formations. To tie large chrysanthemum blooms on vine strings, or in semi-curtain style, is entirely devoid of art. To plaster bunches of blooms flat against any background whatever is to show a lack of appreciativeness. Wherever it is possible in large decorations try and arrange your blooms in groups as if they were growing where you put them, loose, graceful and natural-like. To create the impression that they are growing, and are permanent, is not only more pleasing, but the attempt really displays your stock and work to the best advantage.

As often is the case, a great amount of space must be covered at little cost. Cheaper greens or other foliage can be introduced. Save your flowers for the most prominent places where the eye will be attracted and the senses gratified.

Wherever a mirror can be utilized or introduced on wall space, or to create grotto effects, seize the opportunity to lend distance and charm to your design. Many an intensely attractive and interesting exhibit can be cheaply put up at the principal shows next week. Try a wedding arbor or arch, one side palms and foliage plants; the other a tall handsome vase and group of chrysanthemums or roses. Don't use any set frame, just the imposing and natural. Mirror and mantel decorations are usually too stiff and overdone. We could beat all the troublesome formal carpentered and chiseled work with our simple forms. Just a few strong wires, plenty of rose foliage, and the roses arranged as if growing, here and there an intensified cluster. No ribbons.

New Ribbons.

There are many designs which require ribbons, and the exhibition is the place for the richest of ribbon procurable. The broadest and finest ribbon ever made is on the market at present. It is flowered, and the different flowers are remarkably well done. Almost any commercial flower can be had on these ribbons, and the broadest, twelve to fourteen inches wide, costs all the way up to $5 per yard. They are worth it, when one considers the exhibition and your reputation; and these ribbons need not be spoiled in tying. Just use the loop bow, with strings or small ribbon ties.

Evergreens for Winter Use.

Never before in the history of the trade have there been so many boxwoods imported into this country. New York city is fairly flooded with them, and from their great numbers one would imagine that all there were in Holland and Belgium must have been sent over. They are being used for almost all kinds of exterior and semi-exterior decorative work. Now boxwood is no doubt a very effective evergreen for tub, vase, or window box uses, but these imported plants will not, the first year, stand the severe Winters we generally get here, and some care should be exercised in not depending on their hardiness too much. They do doubt constitute a very effective and clean shrub for the purposes mentioned, but there are others and hardier ones too claiming recognition. It is one of the pleasing signs of the times that modern architecture demands plant adornment, and to such an extent that there is a tremendous and increasing trade being done in this line. It is up to our nurserymen to provide the material. There is just as much beauty in a collection of shrubs as there is in a collection of flowers when viewed from the right standpoint: The beauty is more permanent in the former. There is a sad scarcity of suitable material in the shrubs offered in the vicinity of New York; at least, if or where there is material, it is most bashful in offering itself, hence the ready acceptance by the retailer of anything offered by importers. The whole efforts of plantsmen seem to be concentrated on landscape work: and while not wishing to divert this commendable energy, we claim that the city decorative part of the business is most important, and should be attended to.

The work of filling window boxes, etc., with hardy evergreens is well under way, and where possible the ivy used during the Summer should not be disturbed. All Winter there will be calls for small or medium good clean and bright biotas, retinisporas and abies, and the local nurserymen will do well to lift and shed a fair supply of these. The magnificent hotels and private homes of to-day, in many cases, demand the beauties of the Winter gardens, and it behooves us to be up and in advance of the times. There is a great future for the evergreen trade here. It should be intelligently catered to, and variety sustains many efforts.

J. IVERA DONLAN.

A Knights of Columbus Floral Banner
Artist Staples, Woonsocket, R. I.

Growers and Retailers.

Large growers, especially those making specialties of certain things either in plants or flowers, may be expected, as they usually are, to turn out these things in better shape than growers who also combine with growing the sale of plants and cut flowers at retail. These men, I notice, are sometimes at a disadvantage when in the same locality they have as competitors in the retail branch men who buy their supplies from specialists, while those who do not grow their own stock are but very slightly, if in any way, handicapped by having to do so, because invariably stock can be purchased at a less expense than would be incurred in growing it.

As I consider this condition is somewhat of a difficulty to the combination dealers, I may be allowed to suggest two ways out of it. One is for them to pay more attention to quality than to quantity (large growers have seen the force of this long ago); the other is to have always on hand plants and flowers, though it be in limited quantity, of a quality fully equal to that offered by competitors, that in the event of customers insisting on the best, the best is on hand to give them. The other grades need not as a consequence be lost; they can easily be worked in by those who are wide-awake.

D. M.

A Beautiful Banner.

I send you a photograph of a floral banner (herewith reproduced) designed by us for our local lodge of Knights of Columbus and carried in Providence, R. I., on October 20, at the annual State parade.

The banner was a full-sized one, measuring, when finished, 5 feet high and 4 feet in width. The emblem in the center was 18 inches in diameter, made of the usual material. The shield was formed of Mrs. Lawson carnations surrounded by chrysanthemums, roses, and carnations. The upper corners were tied with beautiful red, white, blue, and purple ribbon, with streamers, carried by men in the rear. It took three strong men to carry the banner.

Woonsocket, R. I. JAMES A. STAPLES.

THE WEEK'S WORK.

Timme's Timely Teachings.

Poinsettias.

Among the various kinds of stock now in training for a glorious Christmas array, poinsettias deservedly hold a most prominent place. Few things in the holiday plant line more fully meet the requirements of the occasion than this showiest of Winter flowering exotics. They are therefore an important feature wherever Christmas stock is grown, but they very often fail to finish up in a way to just suit either buyer or grower. Poinsettias have a knack of their own to either grow into exquisitely fine stock or into such hardly worth raising. To bring about complete success it is necessary to faithfully observe two or three important points in their culture, which just at this time call out the growers' attention. Poinsettias to be fine must have heat, not lower than 60 degrees at night and as high as 75 degrees or more during bright days. Nobody can raise really good poinsettias in an ordinary cool greenhouse with a temperature that occasionally drops down to a point below 50 degrees.

The roots of poinsettias should be as little disturbed as ever possible; it is nearly always followed by a yellowing and loss of leaves. Any transplanting or much shifting after this date is pretty sure to lessen the market value of the stock. Small plants from late rooted cuttings had now better remain in 2 1-2 or 3-inch pots until shortly before Christmas, when they will produce better effects in the filling of pans than now.

Poinsettias to be in exceptionally fine trim for the holidays need feeding. Liquid manure, regularly applied, does much in giving size, substance, durability and lustre to bracts and foliage.

Begonias.

It is to be regretted that commercial florists are losing interest in begonias, are losing sight of the fact that besides the great Gloire de Lorraine there are so many splendid varieties that well deserve to be included in any of the stock grown for an all season's plant trade. Though still a most important class of plants with the private gardener, who fully appreciates their value and is slow in slighting merit where it exists, this grand and beautiful genus, embracing in its many greatly diversified forms and types all that is admirable in foliage and flowering plants, is but sparingly represented in collections now seen in commercial establishments. Why this should be so is hard to understand. Begonias are now, as they have always been, great favorites with the plant-loving and plant-buying public, and there is nothing in their culture that could be considered either expensive, laborious or difficult. Their propagation is simple, and stock at almost any time may be worked up and increased rapidly with ordinary means at hand.

At this season nearly all of the well known sorts have come to a standstill in their growth. Those of the flowering, half-shrubby or fibrous rooted section should be induced to take a good rest until after the holidays—some few varieties until nearly Spring—by a withholding of water and a stand on some out-of-the-way place in a moderately warm house. Rex begonias also appreciate a short rest, but can be kept in active vegetation right along if so desired. All begonias at any time resent over-watering, and all of them require a pretty high temperature, never below that of a rose house.

Begonia Gloire de Lorraine.

We have now several distinctly differing forms of Begonia Gloire de Lorraine, Turnford Hall, the white one, and one or two lighter in color than the original type, all of them valuable acquisitions, no doubt; but, in my opinion, none of these newer sorts comes any nearer to being a capital all around Christmas plant than their illustrious forerunner. It is now when this begonia makes its fastest growth, when much may be gained by giving it special care and attention. Thrifty plants in 5, 6 or 7-inch pots now need light and room for perfect development. This demand must be met by doing away with any sort of shading, by bringing or raising the plants closer to the glass, and by affording sufficient room between them for the unhampered spread of pendant branches, respacing and turning them from time to time. Very fine specimens may be grown on shelves. This is also a good place for the smaller stock intended for the filling of hampers, baskets and pans. Gloire de Lorraine begonias require for the accommodation of their roots only pots and pans of moderate size, a point in their culture very often lost sight of. Many a well promising specimen missed its way to final excellence by being over-potted. Six-inch begonia pots are plenty large enough for most well grown single plants, many of which will finish up to perfection in the 5-inch size. All these should now be beyond their last shift, fairly well established and some of them showing buds and blossoms. If so, it is time to begin feeding with liquid manure of moderate strength, which sustains vigor and imparts brightness to bloom.

Violets.

From now until January I consider the most critical period in the growing of violets. It is the time when black spot lies in wait ready to seize its prey at the slightest encouragement held out by inadvertent or faulty treatment of the stock. Over-watering, close quarters, the absence of fresh air and instead the presence of an over-moist, stagnant, clammy atmosphere, all of these factors bunched into one form the most frequent cause of black spot and discouraging results in violet culture. Fresh air is the remedy and preventive cure. Fresh air, whenever the weather permits making a free use of it, blowing breezily through a violet house, sweeps away all stagnant impurities and is the greatest aid in upholding the vigor of the plants and in keeping away disease. Without this ever ready and efficient helpmate the grower cannot hope to make this culture a gratifying venture. It is well to keep in mind the full import of the warning.

Heavy watering from now on should be discontinued, reducing the quantity to a point just absolutely necessary to keep the stock from showing a lack of it. A rather dry state of things should prevail. To this end ample ventilation on bright days and fire heat in cloudy damp weather must be called into play. The temperature for Marie Louise, Imperial, Farquhar and most dark flowering varieties should be held at from 38 to 44 degrees, while Swanley White, Lady Hume Campbell and single flowering sorts require from five to eight degrees higher for the perfect opening of their buds. The soil in the beds should be stirred occasionally, and the plants kept free of dead leaves and superfluous runners.

Chicago Flower Show Poster.

The "Furman Girl."

Courtesy Herendeen Manufacturing Co., Geneva, N. Y.

Stocks and Wallflowers.

Fragrance is an attribute in flowers and flowering plants which by a certain class of people is prized above all other qualities. It is the sweet odor of the violet which has made it popular, not its modest, unobtrusive beauty, free of all ostentation and less gaudy than many of the meanest weeds on the roadside. A plant widely differing in character from the violet is the wallflower; but it also depends for its being considered at all among flowering plants solely on its peculiarly sweet fragrance. It is difficult, aside from this, to detect any beauty in the best grown wallflower other than what is to be found in shape and vigor. The same might be said of stocks, the Ten Week as well as the biennial varieties, though we have now sorts, extensively grown too, that show but little of the rigidly stiff character so objectionable in the older types. Wallflowers and stocks, however, possess two or three other good qualities besides fragrance, which should go far in lending weight to anything said in their favor. They are excellent house plants, long lasting and profusely free in their bloom, and as easily raised as few other plants.

The best double wallflowers are raised from cuttings, but can also be grown from seeds. These and the seeds of Brompton stocks are sown in March, planted in the field in April or June, and are by this time large bushes, plainly showing which are double and which are single flowered. The latter are thrown away; the others potted up and held cool throughout the Winter. In February and March they begin to flower, continuing for months. Ten Week stocks and French single wallflowers bloom in the Winter and are fine for cutting, bringing a good price. They may be planted into the free soil of cleared chrysanthemum benches.

Carnations for Pots.

The time has come or is very near when it must be considered queer business policy to conduct a retail plant concern and not include in the stock carried a good assortment of potted carnations and roses. The latter have already gained a place of some consequence among potted plants, but, as yet, the supply still falls short of the demand; while potted carnations are but rarely seen, and, where seen, are usually so few and far from being nice, presentable stock, that it would seem no better plan to discourage buyers, to ward off a good line of trade, could be adopted. The call for border carnations and for the home garden during the Summer is steadily on the increase. Hardy pinks, Marguerite carnations, feathered and Chinese pinks do not entirely fill the bill, and something better in carnations must be provided; and growers of bedding stock and flowering potted plants, will act wisely in trying to meet this demand.

Most suitable varieties for the purpose are Dwarf Vienna and Grenadin, both of them quite hardy, but not flowering, when raised from seeds, until the second year. They are most easily raised. The seeds are sown in March or April and appear above ground in a few days. In May they are planted in the field. By the middle of November they are good sized, sturdy, compact bushes, just finding room in 4 and 5-inch pots. After being potted up they are stowed away in frames, and later on are covered with leaves or dry, loose litter of some kind. In early

Spring they are freed of the protecting covering and may then either be brought into the greenhouse or be left in the frames, where they will soon be a mass of bright large-sized flowers.

Where no special efforts have been made to provide good material for pot-culture, enough plants for a decent start may be found among those considered not good enough for benching and forcing. It should not be hard to discover nice, sturdy little bushes here and there among the leavings and rejected plants dotting the fields where the forcing carnations were grown last Summer, too good to be plowed under and just right to be potted up, placed under some cool greenhouse bench and pinched back and started into active growth any time before Spring sets in.

Hardy Perennials.

Nicely established cuttings and seedlings of hardy herbaceous varieties, that were started some months ago, should not now be disturbed, and any transplanting, even if badly needed, should be deferred until Spring. Under a light covering of tree leaves they will winter safely where they are. Those sown or rooted, early in the season are now fine sturdy plants, if pricked off or transplanted at the proper time. Many varieties of hardy perennials can be grown to advantage in pots. People prefer to buy such stock, already started into a good growth and coming out of pots with a firm ball of roots, to anything dug up in the garden; and it pays the grower to have it for them. All such, therefore, that is of suitable size, either young stock raised from seeds, divisions or cuttings, or that to be had by dividing old clumps now, should at this time be potted up and stored away where a too severe freezing cannot crack the pots. They are best started into growth in frames about April first.

Hardy Ferns.

In a recent issue (October 20) I advised florists to make a more extensive use of potted evergreen shrubs for decorative purposes. The paragraph containing this advice appeared under the heading "Hardy Ferns" when it should have been "Hardy Evergreens." I don't know whose fault it was, and am not greatly distressed over it; but the misplaced headline most opportunely reminded me of work in my own garden that should be attended to now, and also that I had intended to write a few lines on this very subject.

I have several batches of hardy ferns on my place which badly need overhauling. Ugly bare spots here and there, where customers made us dig up plants for them, do not improve the looks of a fern border much. Then there are some varieties, fast spreading bushes, intermingling with others less obtrusive, that need thinning out. The potting up of such, that will make fine specimens in that form for Spring sales, should also now be attended to. This is the very best time for doing this work. Hardy ferns allow of pretty late planting in the Fall, and all dividing, resetting and making of new beds had better be done then than at any other period of the season, if there is a choice.

I am of the opinion that hardy ferns are good things to have about any florist's establishment. They are much in favor with all classes of plant-buyers, sell readily and their culture is an easy and inexpensive affair. They also furnish a most desirable decorative green for Summer cutting and home use. The best varieties are listed in nearly all plant catalogues and there is therefore no need of hunting for hardy ferns in the woods. FRED W. TIMME.

Decorative Foliage Plants.

CROTONS.—Crotons are beautiful plants when well grown, and since the demand for choice foliage plants has increased more attention has been given crotons. To obtain perfect plants crotons require to be grown uninterruptedly from start to finish, and although they do pretty well outdoors during the Summer, it is not advisable to plant out stock to be offered for sale during the Winter, because stock planted out usually shows many imperfections resulting from winds and other causes. Crotons besides having great variation of color are so varied in form of leaf and plant that the species comprise varieties suitable for numerous forms of decoration. For instance, few plants can compare with a well finished specimen of Croton Andreanum or C. fasciatum for house decoration, used in conjunction with and to give some life to palms when employed in large numbers. There are many other large leaved varieties, some of which are of greater beauty still, but the two mentioned can be grown into large perfect specimens in less time than any of the others. When decorative foliage plants are needed in medium size very few things can beat well grown, well furnished plants of croton Queen Victoria. This variety has, in addition to being comparatively easily grown, the important point in its favor of attaining perfect form and developing its variations of color in its small state. It can easily be grown to a suitable specimen for table decoration in a 6-inch pot.

For the purposes of filling dishes and baskets there are many good varieties suitable, but one of the best, if not the best, is Interruptum. The leaves of this variety are long and graceful, besides being twisted and also interrupted, as the name implies. One plant or more of this variety, with as many as may be required to fill the basket or dish of Croton Weismanii in addition, makes a pretty effect. The last named variety is somewhat upright in habit, necessitating, perhaps, something of a more drooping habit for the edge, but the color—green and golden blotched—is ideal in its pleasing contrast to the crimson and red of Interruptum.

There are almost numberless varieties of crotons, every one of which possesses one or more beautiful or peculiarly interesting characteristics, and although during their time of growth they require a rather high temperature, they are in the hands of competent growers hardened so as to make them moderately durable and safe for retailing.

Croton cuttings can be rooted at any time, but from the first of November to the first of May is the most suitable time to propagate. It has often been said that cuttings from any old kind of a plant will root; so they will, but further than that it may be well to remark that just the same kind of plants will result from propagating from that kind of stock. In taking cuttings, clean healthy wood should be chosen. These should be put in sand in the propagating bench, well watered and kept moist until rooted. If a sash can be placed over the section where the cuttings are, so much the better; but they should be aired frequently before taking them out of the sand to prevent a check after potting. When rooted they should be potted into very small pots, repotting them when they have well filled their first pots with roots, aiming at all stages of their growth to keep the foliage on the plants down to the rims of the pots, otherwise half the beauty of the plants is gone. When the plants are making luxuriant and rapid growth the direct light of the sun may seem to injuriously affect them, but if they are closely watched and never allowed to get dry at the roots, it will be found that the sunlight will be more agreeable to them than otherwise.

Large, healthy specimen crotons that have outlived their usefulness as such can from now on be mossed after the stem where the roots are desired has been cut fully half through and an upward incision made. It may be advisable to place a stake in the pot for the support of the wounded plant, tying it firmly. Fresh clean moss should be packed tightly in the incision made, then the stem where the wound is tied with raffia or any kind of string. Until roots have made their appearance, the moss should be kept continually moist; at the same time the roots of the plant in the pot should receive only water in sufficient quantity to keep it alive. When the tops are cut off and potted, care should be taken to keep them shaded for a few days, otherwise they are liable to drop some of their bottom leaves. A frequent moistening will aid them in holding their leaves until they get established.

Crotons crowded together never grow into shapely specimens; and when it is considered that one perfect plant is worth more than two poor ones, it is a wonder they are not given more consideration in that respect than they usually receive.

PHOENIX ROEBELENII is of comparatively recent introduction and may still be called a novelty and an interesting one at that. It is distinctly different from the other varieties of phœnix, having the marked peculiarities of being both compact and graceful. The plant in its small and medium size stages of growth is compact, while the leaves are almost as graceful as those of a cocos. Before the advent of this variety phœnix were not much in favor with retail florists, but in this variety they find something well suited for many purposes.

There is one peculiarity (it may be cultural) in the condition of this variety that struck me on the several occasions on which I saw it offered for sale, which seemed to me in a measure against it in the eyes of retail purchasers, and that was, the apparent overpotting of the plant. Everyone knows that a small plant in a large pot is undesirable from any point of view, and a small palm in a large pot is an especially undesirable subject. Therefore it would appear incumbent on growers of Phœnix Roebelinii, for their own interests as well as in the interests of the plant itself, to give this matter attention with the view of remedying the defect, as a defect it surely is. D. M.

BRIDGEPORT, CONN.—Hans Beck, a florist, after a quarrel with his sweetheart, committed suicide, on October 27, on the steps of her home by drinking carbolic acid.

SCRANTON, PA.—The Thomson Seed Company last week consigned a package of ginseng roots to a firm in New South Wales. The package was sent through the mails and the postage on it was 12 cents a pound.

Hustling Bostonians.

Henry M. Robinson & Co.

The opening of a wholesale cut flower department this week marks a new departure in the enterprise of the firm of Henry M. Robinson & Co., Boston. It is only eight years ago since this firm started in the cut evergreen business in a very modest way at 3 Court square. After some three years at this location it was found that the place was entirely too small and the store at 11 Province street was secured; but after only two years the business had grown enormously and larger quarters were obtained at 8 Province street. A new branch was here added to the business in the way of florists' supplies of all kinds. Hitherto the firm had dealt exclusively in hardy cut ferns and evergreens. This branch of their business soon proved as successful as the others, so that now the large store at 15 Province street, running through to 9 Chapman Place, has been secured, a large new ice-box installed, and the other necessary fixtures put in for the quick handling of a wholesale florist's business.

The members of the firm are Henry M. Robinson, Joseph Margolis and Charles Robinson, and they have earned the estimable reputation which they justly deserve by their strict personal attention to all details of the business, no order being shipped out without the supervision of one member of the firm.

Besides their stores on Province street they have a storehouse on Bowker street and cold storage space in Quincy market, in addition to having stalls in the Music Hall market and a counter in the Park street market. Their regular employees number twelve, but this number has to be increased during the holiday season.

When the first year's business had been done the firm was well pleased to find that its sales had amounted to one million hardy cut ferns; now their annual sales exceed fifteen million with an equal number of galax. Cut holly, box wood, laurel, wild smilax and other seasonable greens are handled in large quantities, and all are goods of the finest procurable grades.

That the wholesale business is increasing in Boston is shown by this firm's action; and it already has a regular trade in its former lines as far West as Chicago and as far South as New Orleans, while much is shipped to all parts of New England and Eastern States. J. W. D.

Henry M. Robinson — Charles Robinson — Joseph Margolis

Members of the Firm of H. M. Robinson & Company, Boston, Mass.

An Attractive Advertisement.

The accompanying illustration of the "Furman Girl" is reproduced from a placard being distributed by the Herendeen Manufacturing Company of Geneva, N. Y. A full line of the firm's well known heaters is shown on the card; and no one will, we think, question the attractiveness of the young lady who smilingly surveys the interesting collection.

New York.

The Week's News.

The next meeting of the New York Florists' Club, which takes place on Monday, November 12, should be the banner one of the season. There will be an exhibition of chrysanthemums; and as this will also be ladies' night, special entertainment will be furnished on that account. The chairman of the house committee, John B. Nugent, Jr., is making extensive preparations for the event, and in addition to his culinary masterpieces, there will be, no doubt, musical attractions. The nominating committee will report at this meeting, and this of itself is enough to warrant a large attendance.

In the beginning of the year there will be a new orchid firm somewhere in the neighborhood of this city under the name of "Ordenez De Nave & Company." The firm is composed of Paul de Nave, and Manuel and Antonio Ordenez. The two latter gentlemen are collectors of orchids, and Mr. de Nave has been with the firm of Lager & Hurrell of Summit, N. J., as an employe in the greenhouses during the last four years.

Walter Mott, who for several weeks has been with H. H. Berger & Company, has accepted a position as traveling salesman with Bobbink & Atkins of Rutherford, N. J. Mr. Mott commenced his duties with that firm on Monday, October 29.

Phil. Kessler, wholesale florist at 55 West Twenty-sixth street, had an increase in his family on Monday morning. The newcomer was a daughter, and mother and baby are doing well.

Chas. H. Totty, Madison, N. J., will attend the Chrysanthemum Society's annual meeting at Chicago, Ill., to be held at the time of the Chicago Horticultural Society's annual exhibition, November 6 to 12.

John P. Cleary has taken over the business of the Cleary Horticultural Hall, and is now running the same in his own name—John P. Cleary, auctioneer.

Dobbs Ferry Horticultural Society has postponed the dates of its annual chrysanthemum show, on account of the flowers coming in later this season, until November 9 and 10, when the exhibition will be held in the Dobbs Ferry town hall with Wm. Scott and D. MacFarlane of Tarrytown acting as judges.

The annual exhibition of the Morris County (N. J.) Gardeners and Florists' Society held its annual exhibition in the Assembly Rooms, Madison, N. J., on Thursday and Friday, this week.

The annual exhibition of the American Institute takes place next Wednesday, Thursday and Friday, November 7, 8 and 9, in the rooms at the Berkeley Lyceum, West Forty-fourth street.

Phil. Breitmeyer, Detroit, Mich., was a recent visitor.

A rare and beautiful orchid, together with over 5,000 specimens of tropical flora, including other orchids, numerous kinds of cacti, palms, bromeliads, etc., has been added to the already rich collection of the New York Botanical Garden, as the result of a trip of exploration and observation in Jamaica, from which Dr. Nathaniel Lord Britton, the Director in Chief of the garden, has just returned.

The rare orchid is a yellow and purple Schomburkia Thompsoniana. The species was first described in 1887, after it had been exhibited in flower at a meeting of the Liverpool Horticultural Society, by W. J. Thompson of St. Helen's, Lancashire. At that time its origin was unknown. In 1901 the Hon. William Fawcett, Director of Public Gardens and Plantations of Jamaica, discovered that it grew wild on the Cayman Islands. The specimen brought back by Dr. Britton was presented to him by Sir Alexander Swettenham, the Governor of Jamaica, who obtained it in the course of a tour of inspection in the Caymans.

Most of the 5,000 specimens were gathered from mountain top and forest at the cost of arduous and sometimes perilous effort. They comprise some species not hitherto known to scientists. Others were obtained from the public gardens of the island through the courtesy of William Harris, Superintendent of Public Gardens and Plantations, who accompanied Dr. Britton and his party on several of their exploring trips from the New York institution's tropical laboratory at Cinchona. Dr. Britton had with him his wife, Miss Celia Marble and Prof. L. M. Underwood. The women insisted on going with the explorers, and they shared with them the discomforts and risks of their travels.

The J. M. Hodgson Company, retail florists at Fifty-sixth street and Fifth avenue, and Newport, R. I., have not closed their New York store as we intimated in our notes last week. Mr. Spalding, one of the members of the firm, arrived from Newport on Tuesday of this week, and the Fifth avenue store is being conducted as usual.

The second annual convention of the National Association of Gardeners will be held in his city early in January.

Wm. Elliott & Sons are in receipt of their first consignments of roses and conifers, which they will offer at auction on Friday, November 9. Owing to next Tuesday being Election day, no auction sale will be held.

A pure white Cattleya Eldorado is at present in bloom at John Lewis Childs' private greenhouses, Floral Park. This plant was found among six, which were bought of Messrs. Lager & Hurrell, Summit, N. J., of which orchid they imported a large number recently. The specimen in question is large and healthy, with three sheaths; therefore, the plant will be in bloom for another two weeks. The flowers are unusually large—6 inches across. The whole flower is pure white, with the exception of the under lip, which is pale yellow.

Wm. H. Waite has resigned his position as superintendent of the estate of Senator Dryden, and returned to his old place as superintendent for Mr. Samuel Untermyer, Greystone, Yonkers, N. Y., on November 1.

David Dean, who for two years has represented A. T. Boddington, seedsman, in the Eastern States, has resigned from that position and has entered the employ of W. W. Rawson & Company, seedsmen, Boston, Mass.

New Orleans.

Trade Notes.

A trip among the chrysanthemum growers showed immense quantities of well grown flowers in readiness for "All Saints' Day." Perhaps there is no other city of its size in America where such an abundance of flowers is used on this day as in New Orleans, and some idea can be gathered of what is required from the figures supplied by some of the growers visited. Dubois, of Carrollton, estimated that he would cut 45,000; these are all disbudded flowers, although not of the largest size, and must have entailed an enormous amount of time and patience to grow them. The plants were grown in the open, but as the buds began to show color a light frame-work was built over them, covered with sheeting to protect the plants from the heavy dews and hot sun.

Newsham had about 5,000 Mrs. Henry Robinson which would be hard to beat; these have a temporary covering of sashes.

At the Metairie Nursery Company place there were about 12,000 magnificent flowers which grower Lockerbie ought to feel proud of. In addition to Mrs. Robinson they had a fine lot of Clementine Touset with which Harry Papworth is very much impressed as an early variety. Some nice Col. D. Appleton and Mrs. Coombes were also seen, which with other growers are rather late this year. They are also cutting a fine lot of American Beauty roses daily, which sell well at the magnificent store which this firm recently fitted up in the business section of the cty.

Abele Brothers have a fine display of Mrs. Robinson, as have Ziegeler & Werner.

Wm. Nelson at Nine Mile Point had 2,000 well finished blooms of Mrs. Robinson which were grown entirely under glass. Menard also has a fine display of this variety as has Holst.

CRESCENT CITY.

CLASSIFIED ADVERTISEMENTS

CASH WITH ORDER.

The columns under this heading are reserved for advertisements of Stock for Sale, Stock Wanted, Help Wanted, Situations Wanted or other Wants; also of Greenhouse, Land, Second-Hand Materials, etc., For Sale or Rent.

Our charge is 10 cts. per line (7 words to the line), set solid, without display. No advt. accepted for less than thirty cents.

Display advertisements in these columns, 15 cents per line; count 12 lines agate to the inch.

[If replies to Help Wanted, Situation Wanted, or other advertisements are to be addressed care of this office, advertisers add 10 cents to cover expense of forwarding.]

Copy must reach New York office 12 o'clock Wednesday to secure insertion in issue of following Saturday.

Advertisers in the Western States desiring to advertise under initials, may save time by having their answer directed care our Chicago office at 127 E. Berwyn Ave.

SITUATIONS WANTED

SITUATION WANTED—By a young gardener and florist. German, single; in greenhouse or private place. Address, W. H., care The Florists' Exchange.

SITUATION WANTED—By man with sixteen years' experience in seeds, bulbs, and plants, both mail order and counter trade. Address, T. J., care The Florists' Exchange.

SITUATION WANTED—By young man, 21 years old; steady, sober and industrious; can give good references. Address, W. B., care The Florists' Exchange.

SITUATION WANTED—Assistant gardener wishes position on private place. Has knowledge of general greenhouse work. Single; aged 34. Address, J. Meelly, Box C., Locust Valley, L. I.

SITUATION WANTED—Single, competent grower; roses, carnations; take charge 50,000 ft. glass; $35.00 board. Address, Florist, care Rich, 111 East 9th street, New York City.

SITUATION WANTED—By German, aged 30, single, 16 years' practical experience in all branches; also good decorator. Please state full particulars in first letter. Address, C. D., 1346 Franklin St., Brookland, D. C.

SITUATION WANTED—By German, 37 years old, single, good grower of roses, carnations and general stock. Also good maker-up. Wages, $15.00 per week. Address, W. G., care The Florists' Exchange.

SITUATION WANTED—By alpine and hardy plant grower. German, aged 26, single, good propagator; English and German experience. First-class references. Address, T. M., care The Florists' Exchange.

SITUATION WANTED—By experienced grower of roses, carnations, chrysanthemums and all kinds of pot plants. Married man, 38, no children. 23 years' experience. Foreman's position only. Fair wages and decent treatment. Address, J. G. F., 58 Dey St., New York.

SITUATION WANTED—As manager or foreman; private or commercial place where roses are grown and first-class results wanted. Able to take charge of any sized place; also well up in all lines of cut flowers and pot plants. Best of references. State particulars with wages in first letter. Address, W. C., care The Florists' Exchange.

POSITION WANTED

As foreman or manager on up-to-date commercial or private place by first-class florist, designer, landscape gardener and nurseryman. Single, 28 years of age, 15 years good practical experience in all branches of gardening in Germany, England, France, Austria and this country. Best of references. Salary expected, $85.00 per month. Please state particulars in first letter. Address W. A., care The Florists' Exchange.

Mention the Florists' Exchange when writing.

POSITION WANTED

By expert decorator in retail store where ability to handle the most select trade will be appreciated.

State wages and particulars.

Address: T. S.
The Florists' Exchange.

HELP WANTED

SEEDSMAN

capable of taking charge and developing retail department of an established house in a large Eastern city. A good opportunity for a bright up-to-date man. State age, experience, salary required. All communications confidential. Address,

SEEDS, care The Florists' Exchange.

Mention the Florists' Exchange when writing.

HELP WANTED

WANTED—At once, seedsman for retail house. State experience and salary expected in own handwriting. Address, T. Z., care The Florists' Exchange.

WANTED—Young man experienced in florists' supply business. State particulars; address T. V., care The Florists' Exchange.

WANTED—Immediately, man to care for plants and help in retail store. Call at The Fernery, 14 West 33d street, New York City.

WANTED—Willing young man as assistant in retail florist store. Steady position for the right person. M. Hendberg, 411 Washington St., Hoboken, N. J.

WANTED—An all-around florist for 10,000 ft. commercial glass in general stock. Permanent place for reliable man. C. L. Dole, Lockport, N. Y.

WANTED—Married man for rose section. State wages wanted, also experience had. Steady position. Address, T. L., care The Florists' Exchange.

WANTED—Single man as assistant in greenhouse. One who has had some experience in roses preferred. Frederick E. Schweinfurth, Ridgewood, N. J.

WANTED—Young man to pack and ship, cut flowers and help around greenhouses. State experience, wages, etc. W. K. Partridge, 148 E. Fourth Street, Cincinnati, O.

WANTED—Night fireman who understands steam boilers, etc. Steady position. State experience, salary wanted, and give references, W. K. Partridge, 148 E. Fourth street, Cincinnati, O.

WANTED—An assistant on commercial florist's place; one who has had some previous experience in the business. Apply, A. N. Towell, West 200th St. & Ft. Washington Ave., New York City.

WANTED at once a good grower of carnations, chrysanthemums, also bedding stock, as assistant. (25,000 square foot glass.) $35 per month, room and board. German preferred. T. Malbranc, Johnstown, Pa.

WANTED—Section man for carnations. Married man preferred, who would be willing to board one or two men. Have five roomed house on place. State wages, etc. W. K. Partridge, 148 E. Fourth Street, Cincinnati, O.

WANTED—Young man to assist in high-class retail flower store. Must be of good appearance and have good references. State wages, etc. W. K. Partridge, 148 E. Fourth Street, Cincinnati, O.

WANTED—A seedsman who is capable of taking full and complete charge of a retail mail order department in a well established seed house. Address, S. X., care The Florists' Exchange.

WANTED—An assistant experienced florist in carnations, violets and general assortment of plants in a new range of greenhouses. Wages $10.50 per week, without board. References required. Apply, P. O. Box 694, Newburgh, N. Y.

WANTED—Nurseryman and landscape gardener, with general knowledge of pruning and the care of fruit and ornamental stock. State experience and salary expected. The Continental Nurseries, Franklin, Mass.

WANTED—An assistant in seed store, New York City. Good wages to the right man. Have also an opening for a bright young man to learn the seed trade, to be quickly advanced if ability shows. Address, T. Q., care The Florists' Exchange.

WANTED

Florist; working foreman. Must understand roses, carnations, bulbs, ferns, etc. A good place for the right man. Apply

MICHELL'S SEED HOUSE,
1018 Market St., Phila.

Mention the Florists' Exchange when writing.

WANTED

In each large city, agent to sell our bulbs and plants to the florists at a commission. Must be reliable party, florist preferred.

JOHN SCHEEPERS,
2, 4, 6 OLD SLIP, NEW YORK.

See our ad., page 528 this paper.

Mention the Florists' Exchange when writing.

WE WANT

a first-class young travelling man acquainted with bulb, seed and plant business, one who is willing to start at bottom. Will pay right party salary, expenses and commission. Without first class references it is unnecessary to apply. State age, experience and salary wanted. Address **RELIABLE**, care Florists' Exchange.

Mention the Florists' Exchange when writing.

VIOLET CULTURE

Price, $1 50 Postpaid

A T. De La Mare Ptg. & Pub. Co. Ltd., New York

WANTED

A young man between 25 and 35 years of age who has had some experience on an Ornamental Nursery and who is interested in the work. Applicants must be of sober habits, industrious, not afraid of work, and possess executive ability. A German, Hollander or Swede preferred, but any hustler will be considered. For the right party this will be a very good position, on one of the largest Ornamental Nurseries in the country. Location 60 miles from New York, 30 miles from Philadelphia. One mile from a city of 65,000 inhabitants. Reference required.

Apply at once, stating nationality and religion, and whether married or single, last employer and wages expected. Address

T. W., care Florists' Exchange.

Mention the Florists' Exchange when writing.

MISCELLANEOUS WANTS

WANTED TO BUY—Greenhouses to be taken down. State full particulars of same when writing. Address, F. W., care The Florists' Exchange.

WANTED—To rent, with privilege of buying, about 15,000 sq. ft. modern glass, suitable for roses, with a few acres of sod land. New England or New York preferred. Address, W. D., care The Florists' Exchange.

WANTED.—Special prices on the following: 3,000 lbs. mixed sweet peas, 3,000 lbs. mixed tall nasturtiums, 3,000 lbs. mixed dwarf nasturtiums. I also want large quantities of all kinds of garden and flower seed. What have you to offer and what is your best price? Write at once to William D. Burt, Dalton, N. Y.

FOR SALE OR RENT

FOR SALE—Florist store on one of the best avenues in Brooklyn. Established over 10 years; will have to sell. Reasons given to intended purchaser only. Address, W. F., care The Florists' Exchange.

FOR SALE.—5,500 ft. of glass, well stocked with roses, carnations, chrysanthemums, callas, bedding plants, etc. Can sell more stock than grow. Land, 108 x 288 in good town, Southern Ohio. Price for all $2,700, if sold soon. Address, W. E., care The Florists' Exchange.

FOR SALE—A profitable seed and plant catalogue business, with full equipment and everything needful to carry on the business. A well established trade, which owing to pressure of other business we are willing to sacrifice for much less than its actual value. A moderate amount of capital is all that is necessary. Address, T. X., care The Florists' Exchange.

FOR SALE—A well established florist business, with dwelling houses. Also plenty of outdoor ground in up-to-date condition. Greenhouses are well filled with foliage plants, and the place is in a most desirable location to reach the wholesale New York City trade within a drive of about 30 minutes. It must be seen. Reason for selling; ill health. For particulars communicate with O. V. Zangen, Seedsman, Hoboken, N. J.

FOR SALE, CHEAP:

Four small greenhouses, with dwelling house, all in first-class condition. An elegant opportunity for an enterprising florist. Apply to

S. L. ARMOUR, 411 Concord Ave., Chester, Pa. **or** **MICHELL'S SEED HOUSE,** 1018 Market St., Philadelphia, Pa.

Mention the Florists' Exchange when writing.

FOR RENT—Or to lease at Babylon, L. I., three violet houses, 130 ft. long by 11 ft.; in good repair; also dwelling house, eight rooms, barn, 1 1-4 acre good land, 5,500 violet plants in good condition. An assortment of pots and hot bed sash. A splendid chance for a young man at jobbing and landscape gardening. 10 minutes walk from depot. City water in greenhouses. Application can be made to O. H. House on premises or W. Wincott, Box 500, Babylon, L. I., N. Y.

TO LET

Florist Establishment consisting of nine greenhouses, heated by hot water, containing about 10,000 square feet of glass; sheds, barn and dwelling, in Long Island City, within one hour's drive of the wholesale markets of the City of New York. For further particulars address **Box R. Y., Florists' Exchange**

Mention the Florists' Exchange when writing.

Thirty cents is the minimum charge for advertisements on this page.

FOR SALE

A well equipped place, consisting of seven greenhouses, over 30,000 feet of glass, a nine roomed house, barn, stock, etc., and eight acres of land. This is a decided bargain and a rare opportunity. For particulars address

S. S. SKIDELSKY,
824 N. 24th St., Philadelphia, Pa.

Mention the Florists' Exchange when writing.

STOCK FOR SALE

PRINCESS VIOLETS—5,000 strong, healthy, field-grown plants, $4.00 per 100. Cash with order. J. K. Zeininger, 58 Cutter Street, Melrose, Mass.

CARNATIONS—Strong, healthy, field-grown plants, extra large, Ethel Crocker and Flora Hill, $5.00 per 100. Cash with order. W. C. Pray & Co., Kinkora, N. J.

ENGLISH PRIZE PANSY PLANTS—I have 10,000 fine plants more than I need. For sale at $3.00 per 1000, cash. Some very odd and beautiful markings among them. Reuben Powell, Florist, White Plains, N. Y.

Asparagus Plumosus, strong, bushy plants, ready for shifting. We need the room. $1.75 per 100; $15.00 per 1,000. Sprengeri, $1.25 per 100; $10.00 per 1000. Monadnock Greenhouses, Keene, N. H.

BABY RAMBLER roses, fine dormant stock, $25 per 100. 2 1-2 inch pot plants, extra well rooted $7 per 100, $65 per 1000. Orders booked for delivery now or any time up to late Spring. Samples free. Brown Brothers Co., Rochester, N. Y.

Althea, double, red and white, 3 to 4 ft., 4c.; Berberis Thunbergii, 18 to 20 in., 3c.; 24 to 30 in., 5c.; Clethra Alnifolia, fine, 2 to 3 ft., 5c., Forsythia Viridissima, 2 to 3 ft., 3c.; 3 to 4 ft., 5c.; Tamarix Africana, 4 to 5 ft., 4c.; 5 to 6 ft., 5c.; Privet, 4 to 5 ft., 4c.; 5 to 6 ft., 5c., Virginia Creeper, strong, 3 year, 2c.; Yucca, strong, 2 and 3 years, 4c. Packed free for cash with order. James McColgan, Red Bank, N. J.

FOR SALE

BOILERS, BOILERS, BOILERS.

SEVERAL good second hand boilers on hand, also new No. 16 Hitchings at reduced cost. Write for list. Wm. H. Lutton, West Side Avenue Station, C. R. R. of N. J., Jersey City, N. J.

FOR SALE—4 Hitchings hot water expansion tanks. No. 2 high tank Fig. E. of catalogue. All in good condition. F. O. B., $2.00 each. Address, K. D., care The Florists' Exchange.

FOR SALE

BOILERS Hitchings, No. 17 at $110.00. No. 6 Weathered, round, $70.00. 4 section round Cambridge steam boiler $75.00. 8 section No. 11, J. L. Mott boiler, will heat 12,750 ft. glass, $175.00. 16 H. P. upright steam, $35.00. 6 section new Novelty boiler, will heat 4,100 ft. glass, $140.00. Newt Henderson boilers; send for price on size wanted.

PIPE Good serviceable second hand. No Junk, with new threads. 2 in. 7c.; 1½ in. 5½c.; 1¼ in. 4c.; 1 in. 3c.; 2½ in. 10c.; 3 in. 14c.; 4 in. 19c. 4 in. cast iron greenhouse 14c. 2 in. NEW, standard, full lengths, 8½c. ft. All kinds of fittings for 4 in. cast iron and all sizes wrought iron.

STOCKS AND DIES New Economy, easy working, No. 1 cuts ¼-¾-1 in. $3.00; No. 2 cuts 1¼-1½-2 ins. $4.00; Armstrong Adjustable No. 2 cuts ½-1 in. $4.00; No. 3 cuts 1¼-1½-2 ins. $6.50.

PIPE CUTTERS Saunders, No. 1 cuts to 1 in. $1.00; No. 2 cuts to 2 in. $1.30; No. 3 cuts to 3 in. $3.00; No. 4 cuts to 4 in. $4.50.

STILLSON WRENCHES Guaranteed. 12 in. grips 1½ in. $1.10; 18 in., grips 2 in. $1.60; 24 in., grips 2½ in. $2.25; 36 in., grips 3½ in. $4.50.

PIPE VISES Reed's Best Hinged Vise, No. 1 grips 2 in. $1.75; No. 2 grips 4 in. $3.50.

GARDEN HOSE 50 ft. lengths ¾ in. not guaranteed; 4½c. guaranteed for light work; 7½c. guaranteed for heavy work, 10c. ft.

BRASS HOSE VALVES New; not faucets; ¾ in. 65c.; 1 in. 90c.

HOT-BED SASH New; Gulf Cypress, 3 ft x 6 ft. 75c.; glazed complete $1.60 up.

VENTILATORS; all sizes made to order. Second hand sash glazed $1.00 and $1.25, good condition.

GLASS New American, 50 ft. to the box, 10x12 single at $1.75. 10x12, 12x12 10x15 B double $2.65. 12x14 to 12x20 and 14x14 to 14x20 B double $2.70. 16x16 and 16x18 B double $2.90. 16x24 B double $3.15. 16x20 and 16x22 $3.00. 6x8, 7x9, 8x10 old, single $1.50. 8x14 old, double $1.65; 10x14 old, double $1.75.

LINSEED OIL Strictly pure; barrel lots, 42c. gallon.

VENTILATING APPARATUS second hand, Hitchings make, arms, 25c.; hangers, 10c.; machines, $3.50; collars, 8c.

SCREWS all sizes; mixed wood, from 1 in. to 3 in., in boxes, 25 and 50 lbs. at 5c. lb.

PUMPS hot air; well pumps and force pumps; all repairs.

Get our prices on second hand wood material. We can furnish everything in new material to erect any size house. Get our prices.

METROPOLITAN MATERIAL CO.
Greenhouse Wreckers
1398-1408 Metropolitan Avenue, BROOKLYN, N.Y

The Best Either to Buy or Sell

It has been my desire for some time past to inform you of a recent sale of greenhouse property. The property in question is that formerly owned by John Dingwall, purchased by R. W. Zobel.

Mr. Dingwall, over a year, tried to sell his property, and placed such in the hands of every real estate agent in this city; but they all reported their inability to find a purchaser. Being a personal friend of Dingwall, I interested myself in his affairs, and hence suggested that if he would insert an advertisement in The Florists' Exchange, he would surely get a purchaser before the Summer of 1906. Advertisement was written up and signed "Graveline," forwarded to The Florists' Exchange, and in less than one month the property was sold, and the purchaser is well satisfied, and would not sell for 50 per cent. more than the purchase price.

My object in writing to you is to set forth the great value of your paper as the best advertising medium from a florist's standpoint.

Personally, I have procured good bargains through your paper. Pardon this lengthy letter; the sale was too good to keep down.

J. H. VOGEL.

Albany, N. Y.

P. S.—In a recent purchase of glass, I procured such of the Metropolitan Material Company of Brooklyn at $1 less per box than of local houses. Again it shows the necessity of careful perusal of the advertisements as noted in The Exchange.

Indianapolis.

News Items.

Mr. Athlee, gardener at Mr. Wm. Churchman's, has had a new carnation house completed; he is cutting fine stock for this market.

M. Braendlein is cutting a fine crop of Ivory chrysanthemums.

Edward Schmidt has taken a position with John Rieman.

Highly colored Autumn foliage is sadly missed this year; the early severe weather darkened the leaves or caused them to fall, and bright yellow or red ones are scarce.

In anticipation of the customary demand for chrysanthemums on "All Souls' Day," great quantities of these flowers were brought to Tomlinson Hall Market on Saturday, but adverse weather spoiled sales, and by evening the blooms were offered at wholesale rates with a liberal discount.

Visitors: E. G. Barnett of Reed & Keller, New York; W. W. Coles, Kokomo, Indiana. I. B.

New Bedford, Mass.

News Items.

A. H. Ashley has bought a place on Palmer street where he may erect greenhouses later on.

Napoleon Le Mair, at his place on Hillman street is cutting some fine carnations; he has about 5,000 plants benched.

R. H. Woodhouse has a house of chrysanthemums in bloom which is a grand sight.

J. C. Forbes captured two prizes at the Massachusetts Horticultural Society's exhibition last week for his two seedling dahlias. HORTICO.

Pittsburg.

News of the Week.

Trade last week was satisfactory. Plenty of stock is on hand, with the exception of good carnations which are scarce. Quantities of chrysanthemums are in the market; from 4c. up is the present figure, and a fairly good market is found. Roses are abundant: prices unchanged. Plenty of American Beauty are in. More violets are received, and there is a good demand.

The sale of bulbs for bedding purposes has been very good since the last frost; people are appreciating early Spring flowers more from year to year.

Chrysanthemum shows are in full blast; besides the public exhibitions, in the Phipps conservatories in the two cities, the private houses of Henry Frick and A. Peacock are open to the public and well worthy of a visit.

John Bader continues to receive plants and bulbs from abroad, all arriving in good shape.

W. C. Beckert, the Allegheny seedsman, reports trade excellent; this fact can be easily realized after a visit to the establishment, as they can hardly keep up with orders. Mr. Frischkorn, who has charge of the seed and bulb departments, says they have had the best bulb trade ever experienced by them, and although they imported more than in previous years they ran out of some sorts and were compelled to buy in the open market. Mr. Beckert has for years furnished the bulbs and seeds for the public parks of both cities, and they are of the best quality, as the flower shows prove.

The new firm of Erhardt & Swartz, in Allegheny Market, have completed alterations on their stand, which makes a good appearance and is well adapted for their purpose. Mr. Erhardt is well satisfied with trade since the opening.

E. C. Ludwig introduced what was to us a novel advertising scheme, though it may not be new to other cities. It was a good-sized feather, of various colors, with his card printed thereon. At the end of the quill was a burr, the seed of the burdock, slightly weighted with lead, and when thrown at anyone it would adhere to the clothing. It was very amusing, and he used about ten thousand in a few days.

J. W. Ludwig was chairman of the committee on decorations for the Turners' Fair last week in Allegheny; the decorations were unique and the best of the kind ever seen here, consisting of live plants, Autumn foliage, and colored papers.

Visitors last week included: J. A. Peterson, Cincinnati; N. M. Bassinger, treasurer of the Templin Company, Calla, O. Mr. Bassinger conducts the store in Youngstown, formerly E. Hippard's.

E. C. REINEMAN.

Boston.

News of the Week.

The Boston Co-operative Flower Growers' Association, held its annual dinner and meeting on Saturday evening last, at Young's Hotel. The trade press was represented by W. N. Craig and J. W. Duncan. After a sumptuous repast, speeches were in order, and wit and good humor prevailed. The first speaker was Mr. Craig, who talked of horticultural topics generally, touching on the prosperity of the Florists' Club and the coming chrysanthemum show. He spoke of the correspondence going on at present in The Florists' Exchange and said that he was afraid that one writer, "Job," was asleep.

J. W. Duncan called attention to the fact that many of the horticulturists in the locality were not taking the interest they should in public matters, and referred to the editorial in The Florists' Exchange of last week on the Boston shows. He assured his hearers that "Job" was not asleep, but only waiting to give some of these other writers a chance to air their views when he would no doubt make his appearance and give some of these stove plant men a roaster.

Andrew Christensen gave a brief talk on his recent trip to Europe, but said that where he had visited, horticulture could not compare with what was seen in Boston and New England. W. H. Elliott gave an amusing account of horticultural progress in Cuba from his point of view; and Fred. R. Matheson gave an extended talk on his trip to the Pacific slope last Spring. The presiding officer was W. C. Stickel, and he introduced the speakers with his usual jocular ability.

At the business meeting, which was held before the party broke up, the following officers were elected for next year: President, W. C. Stickel; vice-president, Wm. Nicholson; secretary and Treasurer, George Cartwright; directors, Alex Montgomery, W. W. Edgar, E. Sutermeister, E. Allan Peirce, Lester W. Mann and A. Christensen.

A misunderstanding in conversation with Wm. Sim last week made me mention the new violet he was growing as Governor Herrick. Mr. Sim does not grow that variety nor has he any plants of it. The variety Mr. Sim grows is entirely distinct, having been raised by James Wheeler of Brookline some two or three years ago.

Welch Brothers have now got settled in their new quarters and already a considerable increase of business is the result. Alex. McKay is now shipping his products to this firm.

Frank White of Holbrook is cutting quantities of antirrhinum at the present time.

The wholesaler bowling team is C. Donovan, captain; Fallon, Reynolds, Campbell and Fee, the Waban team is composed of P. Donohue, captain; Cartwright, Lamey, Hannon and White. Tuesday evening is their regular meeting night.

Henry M. Robinson & Company, have got their new quarters at 15 Province street in full running order. They had a formal opening on Monday evening, when cigars and other good things were passed around among the boys.

Robert E. Berry, representing H. Frank Darrow, New York, was in town this week looking up old friends and telling many interesting reminiscences of the Old Guard of twenty-five or thirty years ago.

J. W. Howard of Somersville has a new carnation of a fine shade of pink, which he has named Debutante, and has been showing some blooms in Welch Brothers' store the past week.

J. W. DUNCAN.

Columbus, O.

News and Trade Notes.

The Livingston Seed Company is cutting, in large quantities, some superbly grown chrysanthemums, among which were especially noted Mrs. O. P. Bassett and Lord Hopetoun.

W. R. Meeks has as usual been making his Autumn canvass of the city and suburbs, booking nursery stock orders for immediate and Spring delivery.

A. Pharo-Gagge, the New York landscape architect, has so many contracts booked in this city that he has closed his offices in the former city, and established his headquarters in the Outlook building here.

S. N. Kiner & Son are making a specialty this Fall of supplying and setting large street trees. The sizes most in demand are from $3 to $8 for the completed work.

The Franklin Park Floral Company, among other work, arranged with palms, bay trees, and wild smilax, the stage of the new Franklin Memorial Hall for the Republican political meetings.

Superintendent Underwood of Franklin Park, has unsuccessfully tried to stop the vandalism and pilferings of flowers and valuable plants from the grounds; especially on Sunday afternoons.

The department stores have killed the sales of the Chinese sacred lilies here; they have cut the price to 2 1-2 cents each.

W. L. Clark of Leamington, Ontario, was a visitor recently; he reports business in seeds in his section in a most prosperous condition.

The Fifth Avenue Floral Company has been disposing of a lot of potted stock, at its stand on the Central market.

Graff Brothers have been having a violet sale this week, disposing of a large quantity in small bunches, at 25 cents.

Professor Selby, of the Agricultural College at Wooster, Ohio, was a recent visitor.

F. W.

REVIEW OF THE MARKET

NEW YORK.—The cut flower business just now seems to be running more to chrysanthemums than anything else. The supply is fairly heavy, and the quality is superior; in fact, there is a death of short-stemmed and inferior stock of these flowers just now. Among the varieties coming in in quantity are Adelaide, J. K. Shaw, Ivory, Col. D. Appleton, Ben Wells, Merstham Yellow; Mrs. Henry Robinson, Mrs. Coombes, Robert Halliday and Major Bonnaffon. The most popular sizes are those that can be sold at from $1.50 to $2 per dozen; $3 per dozen seems rather a hard figure to get, although some are sold at that price. Some fancy blooms, of which there is a supply at times, fetch as high as $6 per dozen; and one day recently a dozen mammoth blooms were disposed of at $1 each, wholesale.

The supply of American Beauty roses is not nearly so heavy as formerly, yet prices remain about the same. Of tea roses there is a slight increase in the supply, and they are somewhat difficult to clear out; in fact, we hardly think the averages will come up to our quoted prices.

There is little change in carnation conditions; the supplies are not heavy, and the demand is such that prices are slightly weaker, if anything, than they were a week ago.

There seem to be plenty of cattleyas around just now, and the demand is not so brisk as it ought to be for these beautiful blooms. Consignments of antirrhinums are arriving regularly. Lily of the valley is not going quite so fast as it was and longiflorum lilies are coming in every day. Evidently we shall see no break this season in the supply of the latter. Violets are a regular feature, though so far this season they do not seem to have asserted themselves to the extent that they have in former years. While there is an occasional sale made at 75c. per 100, the majority of the better class of flowers can be purchased at 60c. per 100.

Smilax and asparagus are both very plentiful, and prices are anything but firm. A slight advance is noted in Adiantum Croweanum, but for the ordinary maidenhair fern prices remain about the same.

CHICAGO.—The market, which has more than held its own for the territory to which it contributes its output, took a frisky fall last week and as a result of the large shipments of chrysanthemums, which came in from all directions, the prices took a tumble, although the high grades of stock have held their prices fairly well. Although we have had a very satisfactory week, all that could be expected at this season, it was not all that might be desired. The quality of stock is constantly on the mend, and though the grade bears an important factor prices have been more or less declining. While fancy chrysanthemums are fully holding their own, the smaller grades are selling at a discount; and roses and carnations have taken the seasonable drop. It is a safe and conservative statement to place all stock in a normal condition for the beginning of November. Lilies, longiflorum or Harrisii, are hard to procure even at listed prices. Lily of the valley is somewhat easier than it was a week ago. Violets of good size and excellent color are in plentiful supply both from local and Eastern sources. All sorts of greens are in good demand and in ample supply. W. K. W.

BOSTON.—The market is overstocked. Chrysanthemums have been coming in in quantities, especially of the smaller grades. Roses, too, are very plentiful, but the quality is better. Some extra fine American Beauty are arriving. Bride and Bridesmaid are both better in size of flower and stem. Carnations have improved a great deal; many fine flowers are now to be seen. Lilies are not very plentiful. Violets are fine, especially singles. Lily of the valley is good. There are a few sweet peas, and snapdragons have made their appearance. Candytuft and feverfew are still being brought in, but the quality is not so good, and there is little call for them. J. W. D.

CINCINNATI.—Cold weather is stimulating trade, and stock cleans up nicely every day. Chrysanthemums are, of course, the leaders, and sell well at fair prices. Tea roses are lagging a little, but American Beauty are still holding their own, and sell out clean nearly every day. E. G. G.

PHILADELPHIA.—While there is some good business going on in cut flowers this week, yet stock is not moving quite as freely as last week. Chrysanthemums are arriving in large quantities daily; $5 per dozen is yet being obtained for the best: Yellow Eaton and Florence Harris are both bringing this price. The bulk of the chrysanthemums are selling at from $10 per 100 up to $3 per dozen. American Beauty roses are not moving quite so freely; $4 per dozen is asked for specials, while the majority of this rose are sold at $2 to $3 per dozen. In tea roses the choicest stock of Bridesmaid, Bride, Richmond, Killarney, etc., is selling at $8 per 100. All roses are better in color this week, but most varieties are weak in stem.

Carnations are much more plentiful this week, and while $4 per 100 is obtained for the choicest flowers $2 to $3 per 100 is the best prices for most of the stock. Lily of the valley has been in good demand, the best still going at $5 per 100; most of this stock has been rather weak. Violets remain scarce, except the large singles, which are becoming more plentiful. Asparagus is selling at 50c. per bunch. DAVID RUST.

ST. LOUIS.—The cut flower market was in splendid condition the past week. The commission men had nearly everything wanted in plenty, excepting carnations, which continue scarce, though this week a much larger supply is anticipated. Local retailers have little complaint regarding last week's business, as there was work for weddings, socials, dinners, receptions, and seemingly plenty of funeral calls for large designs. Every one seems satisfied over the trade done during October. A number of the uptown florists have orders this week for weddings of good size, which should use up fancy stock. A large supply of fine chrysanthemums is coming in, including exhibition blooms; this fancy stock sells for $4 per dozen, among which are Col. D. Appleton, Timothy Eaton, and Mrs. Henry Robinson. Other stock runs from $3 to $1 a dozen. Notwithstanding the heavy increase in the supply of chrysanthemums, roses hold their own, and extra fancy American Beauty bring $3 to $4 per dozen. Others bring prices according to the length of stem, from $2 per dozen down to 75c. for shorts. The carnation market is very stiff; $4 per 100 is asked for extra fancy Enchantress. Mrs. T. W. Lawson are becoming of better quality and bring $3 for the best. Any kind of white carnation sells well, and nothing at less than $2.50 per 100 can be bought. Lily of the valley has a fair demand, with very little fancy stock in, going at $4 per 100. California violets are of better quality this week; the best bring 50c. per 100.

Asparagus, smilax, galax leaves, common and fancy ferns are in plenty at usual prices. ST. PATRICK.

INDIANAPOLIS.—Since the middle of last week business has been heavier and much stock is used up. More funeral orders are now received than at any time this Fall. Numerous weddings, though most calling for small decorations, keep the plantsmen busy. The market is firmer than last week, but no great change in prices is noticed. Chrysanthemums are more reasonable than in former seasons; good average stock of Monrovia, Col. D. Appleton and Polly Rose may be had at from $1 to $2 a dozen; fine pink and white Ivory are received at $1 per dozen. The demand for chrysanthemums has been everything the retailer could expect. The anticipated slump in carnations has not taken place, and all that reach this market are sold at $2 to $2.50 per 100. As a seller, Enchantress leads.

Highly colored Bridesmaid roses are bringing $5 to $6 per 100 wholesale, $1.50 to $2 per dozen retail. A few Killarney are received at $3 to $4 per 100; Richmond sell more easily as the season advances, at $4 to $7 per 100. The heavy sale of American Beauty has been lessened by the fine selection of chrysanthemums.

Violets are received in quantity at 50c. to 60c. per 100. Cattleyas retail unusually well at $9 to $10 a dozen. Much lily of the valley is used for shower bouquets, at $3 to $4. Well-shaped six and eight-inch chrysanthemum plants find ready customers at 50c. to 75c. each. I. B.

ST. PAUL.—Business the past week has been exceptionally good, the demand for loose flowers being very strong. Stock has been somewhat scarce, especially carnations; in fact, we have not had any good carnations so far this season with the possible exception of a few Enchantress. Roses with some of the growers are in crop, while with some of the largest growers they are off crop, and it has been very difficult for the retailer to get sufficient good stock. Killarney seems to be the favorite in pink roses, and when good stock of this variety is shown it is hard to dispose of others, especially Bridesmaid. Mme. Abel Chatenay are not far behind Killarney, but they have not as yet reached prefection. Richmond are coming in fairly well and seem to have forced out other varieties of red roses. While there are a few Liberty on the market, the percentage is so small that it is hardly worth while mentioning them. American Beauty all come from outside points, very few being grown here. Early varieties of chrysanthemums have just started to come in, and the demand is heavy; some very fine blooms are sold at retail at $3 per dozen. Some good Monrovia are in and seem to command a ready sale. Violets are only fair; few have been furnished by the local growers, the main supply coming from the East. PAUL.

COLUMBUS, O.—We have had a most excellent business the past fortnight; funeral orders, wedding decorations, and over-the-counter trade in good volume have all helped, but the orders which have so greatly added to the regular business were from the exhibitors at the convention of the American Street and Interurban Railway Association, whose annual meeting lasted a week. The chrysanthemum season is now fairly under way, and the prospects are certainly very bright for a great run. The early sorts are about gone, and this week our growers are bringing in such elegant ones as Clementine Touset, Ethel Fitzroy, Mrs. O. P. Bassett, S. T. Wright, and Col. D. Appleton. As regards prices, the very best brought $7 a dozen, and from that down to $2. Carnations bring 50c. to 75c. a dozen, a few very nice Enchantress commanding $1; and have not been over plentiful lately. Roses are of especially fine quality for the season, and in good supply; the best American Beauty bring $5 a dozen, other varieties $1 to $2. Violets, while in fair quantity, are not as yet in general demand, and will not be until after chrysanthemums have passed; $1.50 to $2 per 100 is the price. Lily of the valley is at 75c. to $1 a dozen. Green goods are plentiful and good. F. W.

PROVIDENCE, R. I.—There has been a decided change in the business during the past week. There was a great demand for funeral designs, also wedding decorations, and an abundance of first class stock. Chrysanthemums are very plentiful, and the great supply of such varieties as Polly Rose, Glory of the Pacific, Mme. F. Bergmann, etc., are at the height of their season; they bring from $1 to $2 per dozen wholesale. Not many of the late and choice varieties have come in yet, the growers preferring to work off the early and cheaper kinds first. In roses Bride, Bridesmaid, Liberty, Richmond and Kaiserin Augusta Victoria are very plentiful and bring from $3 to $8 per 100 according to grade. American Beauty are not seen here in numbers, as there is a limited quantity grown about Providence, not over three houses in all. Violets are arriving in an abundance, especially the single varieties, and are bringing from 50c. to 75c. per 100. The double varieties have not shown up very plentifully yet, and not so many of these are grown about here, as in late years; they are not so prolific or profitable as the single sorts. I believe the trade is beginning to give the single kinds the preference, as they are of better color and have longer stems. Carnations are coming in better now and of very good quality; the prices are governed by the varieties and grades. Good flowers bring from $1.50 to $2 per 100.

All kinds of greens are plentiful. Callas have just shown up here for the first time this season. G. J.

KANSAS CITY, MO.—The store of the Alpha Floral Company was robbed last week, $194.30 being secured by the thieves. The money was contained in a safe, which had been opened without the use of explosives. The robbers apparently knew the combination.

CHANGES IN BUSINESS.

WHITMAN, MASS.—George Cook has opened a flower store in the Beckford building.

TRINIDAD, COL.—The Trinidad Floral Company formally opened its downtown store on October 17.

BALTIMORE, MD.—Edwin A. Seidewitz has leased the entire first floor of 323 North Charles street for a flower store.

ALVIN, TEX.—Theo. De Vries of Holland, who recently purchased a farm near here, is building a large barn and outbuilding and is preparing to start a nursery.

ROCHESTER, N. Y.—Grover Nursery Company has been incorporated to deal in nursery stock and seeds; capital $2,000. Incorporators: F. E. Grover, J. H. Welch and F. A. Parmenter, all of Rochester.

NEW ROCHELLE, N. Y.—Anthon S. Petersen has started in business here under the name of the "Fifth Avenue Nurseries," and will grow hardy nursery stock, especially adapted for landscape work. Mr. Petersen solicits catalogues.

FIRMS WHO ARE BUILDING.

NEWTON HIGHLANDS, MASS.—A. H. Fewkes is building another greenhouse.

BOONE, IA.—J. Lohrer is erecting a large new greenhouse on Monona street.

Wholesale Prices of Cut Flowers, New York, Oct. 31, 1906

Prices quoted are by the hundred unless otherwise noted

Roses: A. Beauty, fancy—special	12.00 to	25.00
" extra	8.00 to	10.00
" No. 1	6.00 to	8.00
" No. 2	3.00 to	6.00
" No. 3	2.00 to	3.00
Bride, Maid, fancy—spe'l	4.00 to	5.00
" extra	3.00 to	4.00
" No. 1	1.00 to	2.00
" No. 2	.50 to	.75
Golden Gate	.75 to	5.00
Richmond	.75 to	5.00
Mme. Abel Chatenay	.75 to	5.00
Adiantum	.50 to	.75
Croweanum	1.00 to	1.25
Asparagus	25.00 to	50.00
" Plumosus, bunches	8.00 to	15.00
" Sprengeri, bunches	8.00 to	15.00
	to	
Cattleyas	30.00 to	40.00
Daisies	to	

Carnations: Inf'r grades, all colors	1.00 to	1.50
Standard Varieties: White	1.50 to	2.00
Standard Varieties: Pink	1.50 to	2.00
Standard Varieties: Red	1.50 to	2.00
Standard Varieties: Yel. & Var.	1.50 to	2.00
*Fancy— (*The highest grades of standard var.): White	2.50 to	4.00
Pink	2.50 to	4.00
Red	2.50 to	4.00
Yel. & Var.	2.50 to	4.00
Novelties	4.00 to	5.00
Chrysanthemums	6.00 to	8.00
" Fancy	12.00 to	25.00
Gardenias, per doz	2.00 to	8.00
Lilies	10.00 to	12.00
Lily of the Valley	1.00 to	4.00
Mignonette	to	
Smilax	5.00 to	8.00
Violets	.35 to	.75
	to	
	to	
	to	
	to	

Wholesale Prices of Cut Flowers—Per 100

Boston Oct. 29, 1906	Buffalo Oct. 22, 1906	Detroit Oct. 29, 1906	Cincinnati Oct. 29, 1906	Baltimore Oct. 29, 1906	NAMES AND VARIETIES	Milwaukee Oct. 25, 1906	Phil'delphia Oct. 25, 1906	Pittsburg Oct. 30, 1906	St. Louis Oct. 22, 1906
30.00 to 50.00	20.00 to 25.00	10.00 to 35.00	... to 40.00	... to ...	ROSES: A. BEAUTY, fancy—special	... to 25.00	20.00 to 40.00	20.00 to 25.00	25.00 to 30.00
15.00 to 30.00	15.00 to 20.00	... to ...	... to 30.00	20.00 to 25.00	" extra	15.00 to 18.00	... to ...	15.00 to 18.00	15.0 to 20.00
6.00 to 15.00	10.00 to 15.00	... to ...	20.00 to 25.00	12.50 to 15.00	" No. 1	10.00 to 12.50	... to ...	10.00 to 12.50	8.00 to 12.50
2.00 to 6.00	8.00 to 10.00	... to ...	6.00 to 8.00	5.00 to 10.00	" Culls and ordinary	4.00 to 6.00	... to ...	4.00 to 6.00	4.00 to 6.00
6.00 to 8.00	6.00 to 8.00	3.00 to 6.00	4.00 to 6.00	... to ...	BRIDE, 'MAID, fancy-special	... to 6.00	... to ...	... to 8.00	5.00 to 6.00
4.00 to 6.00	5.00 to 6.00	... to ...	3.00 to 5.00	4.00 to 5.00	" extra	... to 5.00	... to ...	... to 6.00	3.00 to 4.00
2.00 to 4.00	4.00 to 5.00	... to ...	2.00 to 4.00	3.00 to 4.00	" No. 1	... to 4.00	... to ...	... to 4.00	... to 2.00
1.00 to 2.00	3.00 to 4.00	... to ...	2.00 to 3.00	2.00 to 3.00	" No. 2	... to 2.00	... to ...	... to 3.00	... to ...
... to ...	3.00 to 6.00	4.00 to 8.00	2.00 to 6.00	2.00 to 5.00	GOLDEN GATE	4.00 to 6.00	2.00 to 6.00	4.00 to 6.00	2.00 to 5.00
2.00 to 8.00	3.00 to 7.00	... to ...	2.00 to 4.00	3.00 to 5.00	K. A. VICTORIA	4.00 to 8.00	2.00 to 8.00	4.00 to 10.00	3.00 to 8.00
2.00 to 16.00	3.00 to 8.00	... to ...	... to ...	3.00 to 5.00	LIBERTY	4.00 to 6.00	4.00 to 8.00	4.00 to 8.00	... to ...
... to ...	3.00 to 6.00	4.00 to 10.00	2.00 to 6.00	2.00 to 4.00	METEOR	... to ...	... to ...	... to ...	... to ...
... to ...	2.00 to 5.00	4.00 to 10.00	... to ...	2.00 to 4.00	PERLE	4.00 to 6.00	... to ...	4.00 to 6.00	2.00 to 5.00
... to ...	... to ...	... to 50.00	... to ...	... to ...	ORCHIDS—Cattleyas	... to ...	... to 40.00	... to ...	... to ...
... to ...	... to ...	... to ...	... to 1.00	... to .75	CARNATIONS: Inferior grades, all colors	... to 1.00	... to 2.50	... to 1.00	1.00 to 1.50
1.00 to 2.00	1.50 to 2.00	... to 1.00	... to 2.00	1.00 to 1.50	Standard Varieties: White	... to 1.00	... to 2.50	... to 2.00	1.00 to 1.50
1.00 to 2.00	1.50 to 2.00	... to ...	... to 2.00	1.00 to 1.50	Pink	... to 1.00	... to 2.50	... to 2.00	1.00 to 1.50
1.00 to 2.00	1.50 to 2.00	... to ...	... to 2.00	1.00 to 1.50	Red	... to 1.00	... to 2.50	... to 2.00	1.00 to 1.50
1.00 to 2.00	... to ...	... to 3.00	... to ...	1.00 to 1.50	Yellow and var.	... to 1.00	... to 2.50	... to 2.00	1.00 to 1.50
2.00 to 3.00	2.00 to 3.00	... to ...	... to ...	... to ...	Fancy Varieties: White	1.50 to 2.00	... to 3.00	3.00 to 4.00	2.00 to 4.00
2.00 to 3.00	2.00 to 3.00	... to ...	... to 3.00	... to ...	Pink	1.50 to 2.00	... to 3.00	... to 3.00	2.00 to 4.00
2.00 to 3.00	2.00 to 3.00	... to ...	... to ...	... to ...	Red	1.50 to 2.00	... to 3.00	... to 3.00	2.00 to 4.00
2.00 to 3.00	... to ...	... to 1.50	... to ...	... to ...	Yellow and var	1.50 to 2.00	... to 3.00	... to 3.00	2.00 to 4.00
3.00 to 4.00	... to ...	... to ...	... to ...	... to ...	Novelties	... to ...	... to ...	... to 3.00	... to ...
.75 to 1.00	.50 to 1.00	... to 2.00	... to 1.00	... to 1.00	ADIANTUM	... to 1.00	... to 1.00	.75 to 1.00	... to 1.00
... to 50.00	15.00 to 20.00	25.00 to 60.00	35.00 to 50.00	25.00 to 50.00	ASPARAGUS, Plum. and Ten	20.00 to 30.00	50.00 to 75.00	30.00 to 50.00	25.00 to 50.00
... to ...	15.00 to 30.00	20.00 to 30.00	25.00 to 35.00	25.00 to 50.00	" Sprengeri, bunches	20.00 to 30.00	... to 50.00	20.00 to 40.00	25.00 to 50.00
10.00 to 12.00	8.00 to 10.00	... to 10.00	... to ...	6.00 to 8.00	CALLAS	... to ...	... to ...	8.00 to 12.00	... to ...
... to ...	6.00 to 25.00	... to ...	10.00 to 25.00	5.00 to 10.00	CHRYSANTHEMUMS	... to ...	... to 40.00	6.00 to 20.00	... to ...
... to ...	1.50 to 2.50	.75 to 1.50	... to ...	... to ...	DAISIES	... to .40	... to 1.00	1.00 to 2.00	... to ...
10.00 to 12.00	... to ...	... to ...	... to 15.00	10.00 to 12.50	LILIES	... to 12.50	... to ...	12.50 to 15.00	... to ...
3.00 to 5.00	3.00 to 4.00	3.00 to 4.00	... to 4.00	... to ...	LILY OF THE VALLEY	... to ...	3.00 to 5.00	2.00 to 4.00	3.00 to 4.00
... to ...	... to ...	... to ...	... to ...	... to ...	MIGNONETTE, ordinary	... to ...	... to ...	... to ...	... to ...
... to ...	... to ...	... to ...	... to ...	... to ...	" fancy	... to ...	... to ...	... to ...	... to ...
... to 12.50	12.00 to 15.00	12.50 to 15.00	... to 15.00	... to ...	SMILAX	... to 15.00	... to ...	12.50 to 15.00	... to 12.50
.35 to .50	.50 to .60	... to ...	... to .50	.35 to .50	VIOLETS, ordinary	... to ...	... to ...	.50 to .75	.25 to .35
.60 to .75	.60 to .75	... to ...	... to 1.00	... to ...	" fancy	... to ...	... to ...	... to 1.00	... to ...
... to ...	... to ...	... to ...	... to .15	... to ...	GALAX LEAVES	... to ...	... to .15	... to ...	... to .15

Kalamazoo, Mich.

Trade Notes.

The Indian Summer we are now enjoying, while of immense benefit to our plants, does not advance the demand for cut flowers, as business is reported rather slow at present. Indeed, it would appear as if our people needed inducements to make them buy, as I note roses have been offered the last two weeks by various concerns as low as 50 cents per dozen. Chrysanthemums are also offered in bargain lots; still, on the whole, really good stock fetches fair prices.

Van Bochove & Brother are at present cutting lots of fancy chrysanthemums, which although not of the very largest size are well colored and finished, and sell readily at from $2.50 to $3 per dozen, which is about as high as our people care to go for chrysanthemums. Good roses can be bought at from $1 to $1.50 per dozen while carnations, which are somewhat scarce, command anywhere from 40 to 60 cents.

Considerable business is being done with bulbs, which steadily gain in popularity; yet the florists here do not push this line, or seeds, very hard.

Our nurserymen are busily engaged packing and filling their Fall orders and all seem to have plenty to do and express satisfaction with the business prospects.

At Grofvert & De Smit's, the stock is looking well, especially carnations. I noticed Vesper, a white which has been somewhat unfavorably commented on, doing well with them, and looking quite a money maker. Two reds, Elbon and Flamingo were also conspicuous among a lot of well grown stock.

S. B.

Wholesale Prices of Cut Flowers, Chicago, Oct. 30, 1906

Prices quoted are by the hundred unless otherwise noted

ROSES American Beauty		
36-inch stems.......per doz.		3.00
30-inch stems "	2.5	3.00
24-inch stems "	2.00	2.50
20-inch stems "	1.00 to	2.00
18-inch stems "	to	1.50
12-inch stems "	to	1.00
8-inch stems and shorts "	.50 to	.75
Bride Maid, fancy special	6.0	8.00
" extra	4.00	5.00
" No. 1	2.00	3.00
" No. 2		1.00
Golden Gate	2.00	6.00
Carnot	2.00	6.00
Uncle John	2.00	6.00
Liberty	2.00	6.00
Richmond	2.00	8.00
Kaiserine	2.00	8.00
Killarney	2.00	6.00
" extra	8.00	10.00
Perle	2.00 to	6.00
Chatenay	2.00 to	6.00
	to	
	to	

CARNATIONS			
STANDARD VARIETIES	White	1.50 to	2.00
	Pink	1.50 to	2.00
	Red	1.50 to	2.00
	Yellow & var.	1.50 to	2.00
*FANCY (The highest grades of Sta'd var)	White	2.50 to	3.00
	Pink	2.50 to	3.00
	Red	2.50 to	3.00
	Yellow & var.	2.50 to	3.00
NOVELTIES		to	
ADIANTUM		.75 to	1.00
ASPARAGUS, Plum. & Ten.		.35 to	.50
" Sprengeri, bunches		.35 to	.50
		to	
LILIES, Longiflorum		15.00 to	18.00
HARRISII		15.00 to	18.00
Orchids—Cattleyas		to	50.00
SMILAX		8.00 to	12.00
LILY OF THE VALLEY		2.00 to	4.00
VIOLETS		.50 to	1.00
HARDY FERNS per 1000		to	1.50
GALAX "		1.00 to	1.25
		to	
CHRYSANTHEMUMS per doz		1.00 to	4.00

NEW BEDFORD, MASS.—The cut flower trade is fairly good here, with plenty of flowers to supply the demand. All outdoor stock is in full bloom yet, as we have not had any killing frost. Chrysanthemums are now in their glory and will have full sway a month or so. The prices they bring are from $1 to $2 for the best. There seem to be plenty of carnations on the market, the recent warm spell helping to bring them out quickly; they realize 50c. per dozen. Roses are of good quality at $1.50 to $2.00 per dozen, violets bring $1 per hundred.

St. Louis.

News of the Week.

The regular monthly meeting of the Florists' Club will be held next Thursday afternoon, at 2 o'clock. A big chrysanthemum exhibit will be seen, cut blooms and plants, and $50 in prizes are offered, as follows: For the best 12 blooms, white, $7.50 for first; $5 second, $2 third. For the best 12 blooms, pink, $7.50 for first; $5 second, $2.50 third. Best 12 blooms, yellow, $7.50 for first; $5 second, $2.50 for third. Any one variety—For the best specimen plant; $5 for first, any color. In addition to the show attraction, two splendid discussions will take place: A. J. Bentzen and Harry Young will lead. "Shall we have a Flower Show next Fall?"; a vote will be taken on this question. The question of the day, "Does it pay to advertise?" will be answered by Frank A. Weber. The next discussion will be: "Have we any axes to grind?" A vote will also be taken on changing the By-laws. This meeting of the club will be an open one, and President Irish extends a personal invitation to all the florists in and around our city to be present.

J. F. Johnson, who conducts a floral establishment at Fort Smith, Ark., was a caller last week.

Alex. S. Halsted, president of the St. Clair Floral Company, Belleville, Ill., was also a visitor and reported his new range of glass completed—one of the largest plants now in Belleville. Mr. Halsted will be in Chicago next week, he said, to see the beauties of the big show there.

Wm. Edlefsen, of Milwaukee, an uncle of Willie Smith, is in town; he came to attend the celebration of his mother's 92d birthday; she makes her home with Mr. Smith.

Fred. Meinhardt has been busy with Fall planting. He will go to Chicago next week to attend the opening of the Flower Show.

Wm. C. Smith & Company received a large shipment of kentias from Calla, O., Monday morning. The palms were received in bad condition owing to poor packing.

James North has opened an office at 1305 Pine street, and will do a shipping order business in floral designs for surrounding towns.

"Billy" Smith gave a little dinner to a few friends at the Hotel Peabody last week. American Beauty roses were the decorations.

Gus Eggeling, of the Eggeling Floral Company, reports that he has a new variety of chrysanthemum. Show it to us, Gus, at the next club meeting, and we will pass judgment on it.

Henry Braun wishes his friends to know that he is now located at the Klockenkemper place, on Mead avenue, and is in the employ of Adolph Brix who leased this place.

John Steidle, at Central, is having great success with roses, of which he is cutting a fine crop. His carnations, too, are looking fine.

Henry Lohrens still has the bowling fever, and every Monday night may be found at the Palace alleys. As soon as the new De Soto alleys are finished, the Florists' Club will start its Winter bowling meetings, every Monday night. The alleys are located downtown at Seventh and Pine streets. Two teams, composed of wholesale and retail florists, will be formed.

ST. PATRICK.

OKLAHOMA, OKL.—A rumor is current that there is a deal on foot between the owners of the Belle Isle addition to the city and the Stiles Floral Company which includes the removal of the greenhouses from their present location to that addition. It is proable that if the arrangements are perfected the floral company would take charge of the landscape improvements in the addition, including the laying out of several parks.

SPRINGFIELD, ILL.—W. T. Buckley has purchased the interest of his mother, Mrs. Ella Buckley, and his brother, Harry T. Buckley, in the greenhouse business heretofore operated by the W. T. Buckley Plant Company, and has taken possession as sole proprietor.

COMING EXHIBITIONS.

[Secretaries of other Societies will oblige by forwarding the schedules of their respective shows. Ed. F. E.]

NOVEMBER, 2-4, 1906.—Massachusetts Horticultural Society, Horticultural Hall, Boston. Wm. P. Rich, secretary.

NOVEMBER 5 and 6, 1906., Twelfth Annual Flower Show of New Jersey Floricultural Society, Hall of Woman's Club, East Orange, N. J. Joseph A. Manda, Orange, N. J. Manager.

NOVEMBER 6-8, 1906, New Haven County Horticultural Society. Thomas Pettit, 90 Prospect street, New Haven, Conn., secretary.

NOVEMBER 6 to 9, 1906, Pennsylvania Horticultural Society, Horticultural Hall, Broad street, Philadelphia, P. David Rust, secretary.

NOVEMBER 6-12, 1906, — Chicago Horticultural Society. W. N. Rudd, secretary.

NOVEMBER 7, 8 and 9, American Institute, New York, annual chrysanthemum show, etc., Berkeley Lyceum Building. Leonard Barron, New York, secretary Horticultural Section.

NOVEMBER 8, 1906.—Worcester County (Mass.) Horticultural Society, annual exhibition of chrysanthemums, Adin A. Hixon, secretary.

NOVEMBER 8, 9, 10, 1906, Denison Tex.; Flower Show under auspices of Denison Civic Improvement League. Secretary, T. W. Larkin.

NOVEMBER 13-14, 1906, Rhode Island Horticultural Society. C. W. Smith, 27-29 Exchange street, Providence, R. I., secretary.

NOVEMBER—10, Third Annual Ontario Exhibition, Massey Music Hall, Toronto. Secretary, H. B. Cowan, Toronto.

NOVEMBER 13, 14 and 15, Faith Home Association, Thirteenth Annual Chrysanthemum Show, Houston, Texas, Mrs. F. A. Reichardt, secretary.

NOVEMBER 13, 14, 15 and 16, 1906.—Gardeners' Club of Baltimore, Md., in Florists' Exchange new building, St. Paul and Franklin streets. J. J. Perry, 805 North Eutaw street, Baltimore, Secretary of Show Committee.

SPRINGFIELD, ILL. — David Wirth was painfully injured recently through a wagon which he was driving colliding with a trolley car. Mr. Wirth was thrown to the ground and received two deep gashes in his head.

Newport, R. I.

Some time ago in notes similar to these for The Florists' Exchange, I intimated that fruit growing, especially peach growing, was increasing on the Island and that on account of the ready market near at hand for good fruit the near future would see a greater increase still. By way of a corroboration of the foregoing I state now that the peach season is about over that the men who recently planted orchards, express themselves well satisfied with this year's returns.

Notwithstanding the common understanding that this was to be an apple year, apples are very high in price which ranges at retail from $2.75 to $5 per barrel. Pears have been a good crop and are cheaper in proportion.

Newport like most other sections of New England, and other sections too for that matter, hails with satisfaction the news that a very good crop of cranberries has been safely harvested in Cape Cod. Some years one-half to two-thirds of a barrel from a rod of bog was considered a fair crop; this season the owners of several of the good bogs gathered a barrel from a rod. At this time of the year cranberries sell in Boston at from $5 to $6 per barrel wholesale. Around Thanksgiving and up to Christmas a much higher figure is often obtained, but the net returns are not in proportion because of the fact that the berries have to be gone over again, a shrinkage resulting. From one bog 3,000 barrels were gathered this Fall.

Chrysanthemums are not very extensively grown in Newport now and when it is considered how growers, private and commercial, are taxed for space in which to grow material for use during the time the demand is briskest, an excuse will be found for the apparent neglect of the chrysanthemum. Still I think there is a slight reaction in their favor. A recent visit I paid to the greenhouses of Mrs. Cornelius Vanderbilt, where A. J. Pow is gardener, made me wonder that reaction was not more pronounced than it is. Here the plants are still grown and grown well. My attention was particularly attracted to a batch of that superb white, Polly Rose, magnificently grown and finished in 6 in. pots.

D. M.

BURLINGTON, IA.—Peter Nies, the old florist, whose yodle still wakes the echoes on the hills, and who does not seem to have aged in the last quarter of a century, celebrated the 83d anniversary of his birth on October 22, 1906. He is perhaps the youngest old man in the city, and he believes that keeping close to the soil and keeping out of doors has kept him hale and strong. And he promises to yodle for many years to come.

CLARKSVILLE, TENN., will have a chrysanthemum show. James Morton has arranged with the ladies of the Methodist Church for a display. The show will open November 20 and continue four days. The railroads have been asked to grant reduced rates, and the show promises to be largely attended.

St. Paul.

News Notes.

The trade was shocked to learn of the death of John Nelson, who has been in the midst of us for a number of years, until a few years ago when he accepted a position with the State Reformatory at St. Cloud. Mr. Nelson was a man of sterling qualities, being very conservative and honest in all his dealings. His death was so sudden that but very few were aware of it, and he passed away in the hands of strangers. He was never married and was known to have possessed a fair amount of means. Friends are now endeavoring to find out full particulars.

L. L. May & Company have added greatly to the beauty of their retail department by installing a handsome fountain and aquarium in a prominent place.

Frank Gustafson, proprietor of the St. Paul Floral Company, has been cutting some very fine Bride and Bridesmaid roses. His four new houses have been built with all the latest improvements.

E. F. Lemke has been cutting some very nice Mme. F. Bergmann chrysanthemums. He has not been able to offer any at wholesale as yet, as the cut will not warrant it.

PAUL.

Cincinnati.

News Notes.

Henry Youell from Syracuse, N. Y., passed through this city on his way to Knoxville, Tenn., where he has accepted a position with Crouch, the florist. Mr. Youell gives quite an interesting account of two years spent in his native country, England, but says he came back more Americanized than ever.

Eli Cross, of Grand Rapids, has been shipping the writer some fine Mme. Clementine Touset chrysanthemums; that seems to be the variety to grow.

Dr. Frank E. Howald of Atlanta, Ga., states that the recent freeze down there injured the outdoor chrysanthemums somewhat. This concern grows about two acres. He also reports his carnations acting badly.

George & Allan have had to replace Mrs. Lawson in one house, all having vanished with stem rot. This variety is behaving very badly in all sections that I have heard of this season.

The florists in the Jabez Elliott Flower Market are installing oil stoves at the various stands; this will help keep out the frost.

E. G. GILLETT.

Providence, R. I.

Building and News Notes.

Thomas Curley has just completed a new house 100 x 25 feet.

William Hay has built a large house for roses, 220 x 35 feet. He also has 25,000 violets housed.

E. J. Johnston has put up a house 100 x 25 feet.

T. J. Johnston is about to break ground for a new modern 12 room cottage on Cypress street.

T. O'Connor has added another house 200 x 35 feet to be devoted to carnations.

Owing to an extraordinary rush of funeral work and wedding decorations James B. Canning had to postpone his annual trip through Connecticut and southern Massachusetts. Mr. Canning takes a trip of this kind every Fall.

William Chappell has been nominated for alderman from his ward.

GEO. A. JOHNSTON.

Minneapolis.

Death of R. J. Mendenhall.

The trade will be grieved to hear of the death of R. J. Mendenhall, the pioneer florist of the Northwest. Mr. Mendenhall had until a few years ago the largest plant in this section. He was at one time a very wealthy man, owning considerable real estate here, but misfortune overtook him. The last few years he had not been active in business. He was a man of sterling qualities and a thorough Christian.

PAUL.

Philadelphia.

News Items.

From present indications most of the gardeners who are growing large plants of chrysanthemums for the show of next week, will have difficulty to get them in full bloom by Tuesday next. Plants are more backward than the cut flowers.

My friend Phil has had trouble with his appendix and underwent an operation on Saturday last. On Tuesday he was reported as doing well.

John B. Cella has bought the store and business of Miss Knapper at Fifth and Fairmount avenue.

DAVID RUST.

HEATING.

Growers' Problems Solved by U. G. Scollay

I wish to know the number of feet of 2-inch pipe to heat the house shown in the enclosed sketch to 60-70 degrees in zero weather. Solid beds are used. Please tell me what will be the best way (as well as the amount of pipe) to place the pipes for the most satisfactory results. A. F. D.

—Ordinarily the temperatures you mention are not required for such a house; however, assuming that you want the extreme temperature, I would advise placing at least eighteen lines of 2-inch pipe in this house. From the sketch submitted it seems the only way to place the pipe would be five on each of the side walls, and two on each side of the two outer benches. As you simply desire to know the amount of pipe required, and how to place it, I will not go into details as to a layout.

U. G. SCOLLAY.

The Morehead Steam Trap.

The Morehead Manufacturing Company, Detroit, Mich., report that they have recently sold return steam traps, for returning the water of condensation in greenhouse heating systems, to firms representing a glass area of over 2,000,000 square feet. The following are some of the recent purchasers: Herman H. Ritter, Dayton, O., 40,000 square feet glass surface; J. A. Oldham, Rochester, Ind.; Wm. Roethke Floral Company, Saginaw, Mich.; Wietor Brothers, Chicago, Ill., 500,000 square feet of glass surface; Bertermann Brothers Company, Indianapolis, Ind., 40,000 square feet glass surface; John Boehman, Frank Kuntz, and W. J. Engle, all of Dayton, O., and the Park Floral Company, Denver, Col.

DUBUQUE, IA.—At its recent meeting here the society of Iowa florists elected the following officers: President, Theodore Ewold, Davenport; vice-president, Judson Kramer, Cedar Rapids; secretary, Wesley Green, Des Moines; treasurer, Wil Harkett, Dubuque. The board of directors was named as follows: W. S. Kemble of Oskaloosa; J. F. Wilcox, Council Bluffs; Ben Adams, Manchester.

At the conclusion of the business session, the florists enjoyed a pleasant launch ride upon the Mississippi.

Des Moines was chosen as the meeting place for 1907, the gathering to be held during the time the State Fair is in progress.

LANSING, MICH.—Fire occurred in the greenhouse plant of John A. Bessinger on October 21, but was extinguished before doing much damage.

THE FLORISTS' EXCHANGE

We are a straight shoot and aim to grow into a vigorous plant

A WEEKLY MEDIUM OF INTERCHANGE FOR FLORISTS, NURSERYMEN, SEEDSMEN AND THE TRADE IN GENERAL

ol XXII. No. 19 — NEW YORK AND CHICAGO, NOVEMBER 10, 1906 — One Dollar Per Year

CONTENTS AND INDEX TO ADVERTISERS PAGE 561

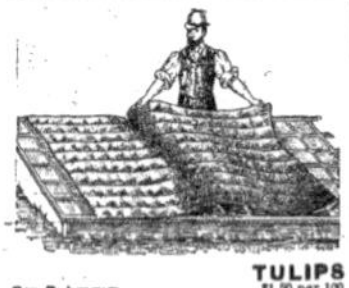

Mats of Burlap or Straw

which will cover two cold frames

$1.25 Each; $14.00 Dozen

TULIPS SINGLE

	100		100
Superfine mix	$ .85	Single Artus	$1.25
Belle Alliance	2.00	Yellow Prince	.90
La Reine	.80	Chrysoliora	.90
Duchess de Parma	1.00	Duke Van Thol, yel	2.00
Keizerkroon	1.75	Queen Vic	.80
Yellow Prince	.90	Fine Mix	.75

TULIPS DOUBLE

Rex Rubrorum .... $1.50 per 100 Fine Mixed .... 85c per 100

TULIPS LATE

Gesneriana .... $1.35 per 100 Parrot .... 85c per 100

DAFFODILS DOUBLE

Incomparable .... 85c per 100 Von Sion, double nose .... $2.00 per 100

DAFFODILS SINGLE

Emperor .... $1.75 per 100 Poeticus .... 45c per 100

Sterilized Sheep Manure, $1.25 100 lbs, $20.00 a Ton.

WM. ELLIOTT & SONS, 201 Fulton Street, NEW YORK.

Mention the Florists' Exchange when writing.

C. C. MORSE & CO.

SEED GROWERS

171-173 Clay St., San Francisco, California

OUR SPECIALTIES

ONION LETTUCE SWEET PEAS

Also Carrot, Celery, Celeriac, Cucumber, Endive, Leek, Mustard, Parsley, Parsnip, Radish, Salsify, Spinach, Tomato and

FLOWER SEEDS

Growers for the trade on contract. Warehouses at Santa Clara; Farms and Farm headquarters Carnadero, near Gilroy.

Registered Cable Address: MORSEED, SAN FRANCISCO.

Mention the Florists' Exchange when writing.

TRUE IRISH SHAMROCK SEED

NEW CROP SEED JUST RECEIVED

Plant soon if you wish good strong plants by MARCH 17

Price 1/8 oz. (About 5000 Seeds) 50c.

W. W. RAWSON & CO.

5 UNION STREET, BOSTON, MASS.

Mention the Florists' Exchange when writing.

PACIFIC SEED GROWERS' CO.

109 MARKET STREET

SAN FRANCISCO, CAL.

Specialties:

Onion, Carrot, Lettuce, Sweet Peas

Mention The Florists' Exchange when writing.

GROW YOUR OWN

TREES

and SHRUBS from

SEED.

TREE AND SHRUB SEEDS ROOTS BULBS KATZENSTEIN & CO.

Send today for our

TRADE SEED LIST

and also for our *Descriptive Catalog*, which is replete with valuable information.

OTTO KATZENSTEIN & CO.

Wholesale Dept. ATLANTA, GA.

Mention The Florists' Exchange when writing.

MY GIANT CYCLAMEN

Are Ahead in Growth and Flowers

Bloodred, Carmine, Pink, Pure White, White Carmine Eyed.

Each color separate. Tr. pkt., $1.00; 1000 seeds, $6.00. An even mixture of the above 5 colors, tr. pkt., 75c.; 1000 seeds, $5.00.

For larger quantities, special quotations.

O. V. ZANGEN, Seedsman, HOBOKEN, N. J.

QUALITY SEEDS BULBS PLANTS

SEND FOR CATALOGUE.

ARTHUR T. BODDINGTON

342 West 14th St., New York.

Mention the Florists' Exchange when writing.

NEW CROP SWEET PEA

SEND FOR LIST OF THE NEW

GIANT FLOWERING VARIETIES

STUMPP & WALTER CO., 50 Barclay St NEW YORK

Mention the Florists' Exchange when writing.

BELATED SHIPMENT

PAPER WHITE NARCISSUS

Choice, sound, 13-15 cm. Bulbs, 1300 to the case, at $7.00 per M. in full case lots only; in less quantity at $8.00 per M.

Stokes Seed Stor

219 Market Street, Philadelphia.

Mention the Florists' Exchange when writing.

Thorburn's Bulbs

Lilium Longiflorum

7 to 9-in........$5.00 per 100; $45.00 per 1000
8 to 10-in........ 7.00 per 100; 68.00 per 1000

Also many of the leading sorts of **Hyacinths, Tulips and Narcissus.**

PANDANUS UTILIS

Fresh seed just received, $6.00 per 1000 seeds.

Send for Trade List.

J. M. THORBURN & CO.

33 Barclay St., through to 38 Park Place, NEW YORK.

Mention the Florists' Exchange when writing.

Catalog Engravin

and ILLUSTRATION

that print EASILY. That's the kin we make — have been since '7

JAS. M. BRYANT, Horticultu Engraving and

706 Chestnut Street, PHILADELPHIA,

Write for our Catalogue of Stock Engr

Mention the Florists' Exchange when

BURPEE'S SEE

PHILADELPHIA

Blue List of Wholesale Pr mailed only to those wh plant for profit.

Mention the Florists' Exchange when

W. & D.'s Specialties for For

Mignonette "New York Market"

Sweet Peas "True" Christmas Flow ing (Pink and White)

Tomato "The Don" Tomato "Stirling Ca

Mushroom Spawn "English" and "Pure Cul

Special prices on application

WEEBER & DON, Seed Mer and Growe

114 Chambers Street, NEW YOR

Mention The Florists' Exchange when

VICK'S BULBS

are now ready for distribution.

HYACINTHS, TULIPS, NARCISSUS, CROCUS, LILIES, CALLAS, FREESIAS.

All of the best quality.

Send for our Wholesale Bulb Catalogue.

JAMES VICK'S SONS

ROCHESTER, N. Y.

Mention The Florists' Exchange when writing.

Brocton Dahlia Farm

Has the largest and finest collection of Dahlias in the United States, with prices that will suit the trade.

SEND FOR PRICE LIST

W. P. LOTHROP, Prop., East Bridgewater, Mass

Mention the Florists' Exchange when writing.

FORCIN BULBS

Let us quote you prices

PERENNIAL GARDENS CO., - TOL

Mention the Florists' Exchange when

DAHLIAS

Now is the time to place your o Bulbs which will insure you getting varieties in any quantity; deliver made this fall or early spring.

DAVID HERBERT &

Successors to L. K. PEACOCK,

ATCO, N. J.

Mention the Florists' Exchange when

ARTHUR COWEE, GLADIOLUS SPECIAL

MEADOWVALE FARM, BERLIN, N. Y.

United States Representative and Grower of GROFF'S HYBRIDS, MIXTURES and COLLECTIONS to color. Fine Mixtures of all colors. Named Novelties of rare beauty. WRITE FOR CATALOG.

Mention the Florists' Exchange when writing.

Seed Trade Report.

AMERICAN SEED TRADE ASSOCIATION

Henry W. Wood, Richmond, Va., president; C. S. Burge, Toledo, O., first vice-president; G. B. McVay, Birmingham, Ala., second vice-president; C. E. Kendel, Cleveland, O., secretary and treasurer; J. H. Ford, Ravenna, O., assistant secretary.

ST. PAUL, MINN.—Alfred Emerich of Vilmorin Andrieux & Company, Paris, France, was a caller this week.

CHICAGO.—The present high price of onion sets, has called for such quantities of onion seed that leading varieties are becoming very scarce; and the fact that the quality of sets from this section this year is superior may and probably has greatly increased the demand.

Present reports from crop centers of supply evidence an ample and early delivery of all requirements for practically all varieties of pea and bean seed.

From present indications, from the wholesale point of view where large orders are now being placed, the trade expects to exceed in 1907 the successful season of 1906. W. K. W.

ALBERT LEA, MINN.—The annual meeting of the stockholders of the Thompson Seed Company, was held at the offices of the company last week. The following gentlemen were elected directors: O. C. Thompson, W. A. Morin, M. M. Jones, Clarence Wedge and C. L. Hill. Mr. Wedge was elected to fill the vacancy caused by the resignation of A. W. Larson. Mr. Larson will retain his stock in the company, but will not give his time to the work, as he plans on going West, where he will locate if he finds a desirable opening.

ALFILARIA, also known as alfilerilla, filaree, pin clover, etc., is so well adapted to the prevailing climatic conditions in the Southwest, particularly in Arizona, and has proved of such great value as a range plant, that it is considered as ranking first in merit among introduced plants. Full particulars concerning alfilaria are given in Arizona station bulletin 52. About three pounds of seed are considered sufficient to sow an acre. The seed sells for $1 a pound, but it is estimated that in a good alfilaria region two men can collect from 40 to 50 bushels of reasonably clean seed in four days. The station observed that seeds stored in sacks in buildings during the Summer months are very low in germination, and it is advised to sow them in favorable areas as soon as convenient after collecting.

Long Island Seed Notes.

MATTITUCK, L. I.—The farmers who are interested in seed growing are now getting all things in readiness to put away their cabbage and root crops. The Autumn has been unfavorable for a large growth of plant, and there are but few fields that are up to the usual standard as regards size. But nearly every field shows health and vigor. Should the present growing weather continue for two weeks, as is usually the case, nearly every piece will be sufficiently grown to insure good plants for the Spring setting.

As last year, the newly introduced Russian variety, the Volga, has made fine large and solid heads, and has again shown itself the quickest growing late cabbage in cultivation. One field of three acres, from seed sown at the same time as the Wakefield, has heads fit for market, while the pieces of the Wakefield are not half size.

Brussels sprouts have made a fine growth and are heading nicely, considering the drought, which ruined a large share of the cauliflower crop, as well as injuring the cabbage.

Kale is looking fine, and we look for a good crop of seed.

The seed of all the Brassicas cleaned up badly. Much was discolored, which gave it an unattractive appearance, but, so far as we know, germination was not materially injured.

C. L. Allen has moved his crop to Floral Park, where it is all being re-cleaned by a new method, which is a very great improvement on old methods.

The Long Island Seed Company reports a good season's business, and will make an aggressive canvass for trade the coming season.

KENTUCKY FARMERS AGAINST FREE SEEDS.—The Kentucky State Grange and the Farmers' Institute last week unanimously adopted resolutions condemning the present method of free seed distribution and calling upon Congress to give the money now appropriated for that purpose "toward the upbuilding of our agricultural colleges and experimental stations, the development of important crops and the advancement in education pertaining to agriculture."

When this matter was before Congress last year several members of the Kentucky delegation said on the floor of the House that the farmers of Kentucky insisted on receiving free peas, beans and turnip seeds, and gave the attitude of Kentucky farmers as the reason why they voted for this appropriation. The action of the State Grange and the Farmers' Institute should conclusively prove to their representatives in Congress that they were mistaken and that the farmers do not want five cents packages of well-known and common varieties of garden seeds, but do want the money advantageously expended. The action of the Kentucky farmers is in line with that of the National Grange and the National Farmers' Congress and hundreds of other State and local bodies. It is in line with the recommendations of Secretary Wilson, of the Department of Agriculture. At the last session of Congress Representatives Bennett, Hopkins, James, Rhinock, Richardson, Stanley, and Trimble, all of Kentucky, voted for free seeds. Representatives Stanley and Trimble were especially active in behalf of the appropriation. What they will do now in view of the action of their constituents remains to be seen.

Two-cent letter postage for each half ounce went into effect between New Zealand and the United States on November 1. This arrangement will no doubt bring the two countries into closer business relationship.

THE PRICKLY PEAR AS A FARM AND RANGE PLANT.—This subject is treated upon in bulletin No. 91 of the Bureau of Animal Industry, Department of Agriculture, by Dr. David Griffiths of the Bureau of Plant Industry. In his letter of submittal Dr. Galloway says: "The results indicate that six pounds of fresh cactus are equivalent in feeding value to one pound of dry sorghum hay" . . . "Stockmen are justified in making use of cactus as an efficient and cheap source of nutriment for cattle."

John Scheepers & Company, New York.

John Scheepers & Company will open new headquarters at 2-4-6 Old Slip, New York City, on December 1 next. Mr. Scheepers for about ten years travelled through the United States as salesman for a Holland bulb grower, as well as for Belgian and Dutch plant growers, always with more or less success according to the firms he represented. He extended his travels from New York to British Columbia and the Pacific Coast, and from New Orleans to Winnipeg, Man. While in Europe Mr. Scheepers purchased the goods required by his American customers in the countries where the stocks were grown for the firms he reprensented, and in this way became thoroughly familiar with the best sources of supply.

John Scheepers

After building up a considerable solid and reliable trade in Amerca, he began business on his own account in 1905, which is increasing very satisfactorily. In June, 1906, his business was properly financed, a partner taken in, the firm of John Scheepers & Company established, and an agency for the packing of bulbs and plants started in Arnhem, Holland. The increasing trade of the young firm has made it necessary for Mr. Scheepers to remain in charge of the offices in New York, and two competent Holland traveling men will be placed on the road by the firm next month.

Mr. Scheepers has made a study of lily of the valley, and his sales of this article are very gratifying. Such growers as Siebrecht, Jurgens, Pennock, Roehrs and others are among his satisfied customers. He is making a specialty of lily of the valley "Excellenta," which is conveniently put up in cases of 500 extra pips.

Mr. Scheepers will continue to go to Europe annually, and personally supervise the packing of his goods.

THE "CORRUPTION" BILL.—We hear that there is a feeling among some members of the horticultural trade that a discount of 5 per cent., payable to the gardener, should be treated as a recognized legitimate custom, and not be deemed "corrupt." Of course, if the master who pays the bill is aware of the practice, and raises no objection, the odious word corruption would have no place. The master in this case knows that it is he who in some way or another pays the tax, though why he should be called on to do so is not apparent. A much better plan would be for the master to pay a fair price for his purchases, give higher wages and not expose his servant to the temptation of receiving "unearned increment." We believe the solution of this matter rests with the traders themselves. If they would co-operate and agree to take no further unfair advantage of their neighbor we should not hear so much of discounts bribes, commissions, or "grafts." To say that a gratuity, by whatever name it be called, is of necessity "corrupt," and to enact that it shall cease forthwith is to use vain words. We cannot in every case define where "corrupton" comes in. In most instances we must leave that to the consciences of the persons concerned; all we can do is to quicken the conscience both of giver and receiver—especially of the giver, and to plead for such a rate of remuneration as shall render the offer or the receipt of secret discounts, commissions, presents, or whatever they may be called, an offence against morality.—The Gardeners' Chronicle, London, Eng.

[We believe the soundness of our esteemed contemporary's comments on the pernicious system of giving commissions to gardeners will strongly appeal to merchants in the United States as well as in England. Adequate remuneration for services rendered, and a higher moral plane among both workmen and traders will go a long way toward abolishing "graft."

Ed.—F. E.]

THE NATIONAL FARMERS' CONGRESS in session at Rock Island, Ill., last week, passed a unanimous resolution condemning the free distribution of seeds by the government. The congress recommended that the money so spent be devoted to investigate agricultural methods in foreign lands, and introducing them here through agricultural schools.

CATALOGUES RECEIVED.

THE LEEDLE FLORAL COMPANY, Springfield, O.—Wholesale Price List of Own Root Roses. This firm grows 101 varieties of roses, and has increased its facilities 75 per cent.

SOUPERT & NOTTING, Luxemburg, Germany.—Price List of New Roses, including Bar-le-Duc, a climbing variety, and tea roses, Marichu Zayas, Mme. J. W. Budde and Mme. Pol. Varin Bernier, the "golden Richmond."

NURSERY DEPARTMENT.

Conducted by Joseph Meehan.

AMERICAN ASSOCIATION OF NURSERYMEN, Orlando Harrison, Berlin, Md., president; J. W. Hill, Des Moines, Ia., vice-president; George C. Seager, Rochester, N. Y., secretary; C. L. Yates, Rochester, N. Y., treasurer.

SHIPPERS' TABLE.—E. Albertson, Bridgeport, Ind., special representative of The American Association of Nurserymen, is distributing a "Nurseryman's Shippers' Table," giving valuable information as to freight classifications, import freight rates, etc.—a most useful document.

Seasonable Notes.

The delicious odor of the flowers of the Daphne cneorum creates a demand for the plants from those who know of its value. It should be tried as a pot plant for selling purposes. Those who propagate the plants indoors find they flower freely in the early days of Spring.

It is a pity the Gordonia pubescens is not found in more nurseries than it is. Its beautiful white sweet-scented flowers are produced from August until November. A bush in view as this is written, October 31, has still three unexpanded blossoms on it.

Cryptomeria japonica is often met with on old estates, but too rarely on those recent date. It needs planting where the wood will ripen well before Winter sets in. It is then quite hardy as far as New York city, perhaps farther.

Box bushes are greatly benefited by having a good dressing of manure at this season of the year. They need good food to bring forth the rich green foliage which every one desires to see.

The downward tendency of the branches of the pin oak, Quercus palustris, gives it a character distinct from any other species. The native beech, Fagus ferruginea, is another example. Its branches have such a downward growth that trees in woods have often been mistaken for real weepers.

When lawns are bare of grass owing to the ravages of "Fall grass," rake away the remains of the latter and sow good grass and clover seeds. If these latter kinds make a good, strong growth through the Summer, the "Fall grass" is unable to completely smother them out.

Catalpa Bungei, as the trade knows the round-headed catalpa, is sometimes disfigured by a storm breaking a branch or two, destroying the tree's regularity of outline. In all such cases cut back the whole head to beyond the point of the injury when Winter comes. At the end of the next Summer there will be a head more beautiful than before.

Of the many shrubs valued for their Autumn foliage, Itea virginica is greatly overlooked. Through October and until freezing weather comes its foliage is of the deepest crimson. There are very few shrubs approaching it in beauty then; and in Spring its finger-like spikes of flowers add to its value.

Flowering of Yucca Gloriosa.

The behavior of the Yucca gloriosa in its time of flowering in this country and in England has surprised and interested many persons here. While with us it does not flower until late in September, sometimes so late that freezings catch the blooms before they expand, in England it flowers in July and August, as letters from correspondents to their horticultural magazines show, and as many of us recollect. As this yucca is native here and our Summers are so much hotter than those of England, it is singular that its flowering there should precede ours by a month or two. Can it be that in a cooler climate the flowers our plants make in September and October would not appear until July of the next year? This may be the true explanation. The writer knows of a case where a Yucca recurva was grown in a given greenhouse room in Winter and when planted out in April, it flowered in May, considerably in advance of those wintered outside. Another point of difference in these yuccas as seen in the two countries is the height to which they attain. In England it grows for 20 to 30 years without flowering in many instances, allowing it to attain a height of 10 feet or more. Here it blooms much earlier, and as its flowering ends the growth of the branch that bore the panicles, the height ends and a low, bushy growth results instead of a tall one. In the Northern States in which it is hardy, it is seldom seen taller than two to three feet.

Osage Orange, a Seaside Tree.

In these days when so many persons are owning seaside residences and are looking for suitable trees to plant about them, it would be well for them to consider the osage orange as an available subject. Here and there along the coast this tree has been set out as a hedge plant. In many cases the hedge has been permitted to grow at will, and in those cases trees have resulted which have pleased all who behold them, because of their vigor and the deep green of their foliage. The reason of their doing well is that the osage orange is a free-rooting tree, and when let grow at will without the pruning it gets as a hedge, the roots penetrate to a great depth, in this way finding sustenance in the seacoast soil they could not obtain were they growing near the surface. The thorny trunk of the tree is an objection, but there is no trouble in ridding the trunks of these thorns as far up as one can reach, as is often done with the honey locust.

The osage orange, whenever seen as a tree, is of pleasing appearance. It forms a round-headed specimen, not unlike an apple tree in shape, affording ample shade for the placing of seats under it, but not of tall enough growth for the shading of the upper stories of buildings. Let those who have difficulty in securing suitable seaside trees try the osage orange.

Washington Thorn, Crataegus Cordata.

Whether or not the name Washington thorn is but a local Philadelphia one for the Cratægus cordata, I do not know, but for half a century I have known it under this common name. It is a hawthorn that was found on many old estates about Philadelphia, especially in the vicinity of Germantown; but "improvements" have removed the most of them now.

Rubus odoratus, Flowering Raspberry

This hawthorn has the general merits of all other ones regarding foliage and flowers, but what makes it more valuable than some other species is the late display created by its bright scarlet berries. Other species, Crus-galli and the like, maintain their berries on the trees until quite late, but the color of most of them, notably Crus-galli, is not nearly as handsome a scarlet as are those of C. cordata, the Washington thorn. The berries of the latter are small, in clusters, and are well set off by the bright green foliage, for the leaves are green when those of many other species are turning brown for their ending for the season. The various good points this hawthorn possesses make it one of the most desirable of lawn specimens. The full and annual bearing of berries makes the propagation of this hawthorn an easy matter; and the same may be said of all the species. When gathered, the berries should be placed in sifted sand for a while, that the pulp may decay. Later, the seeds should be washed free of pulp. They should then be again mixed with sand, placed in a box and kept in a cool place for a year, when they should be sown outdoors. They could, of course, be sown at once when washed free of pulp, but that would mean a watching and a cleaning of the bed a whole season—something the keeping in a box obviates.

Unfair Competition.

It has not come to pass that the Government of Australia has adopted "free seed distribution" as yet, but under the head of Unfair Competition the Australian nurserymen complain of their Metropolitan Board of Works. At a meeting held to protest against the actions of the officials of that board a Mr. Brunning said: "The Metropolitan Board of Works were growing thousands of sugar gums. They were selling them at 15s. per 100 (in pots), about 3½ feet high. About 4,000 of sugar gums had been sold to Mr. Chirnside. The board would be growing fruit trees and selling them in competition with nurserymen. They were now raising sheep and wool, and before long they would be cultivating trees of all descriptions. When he supplied Mr. Chirnside with sugar gums he sold them at 30s. per hundred, but it seemed that the gums could be obtained from the Metropolitan Board of Works for 15s. per hundred. The same principle would likely be applied to fruit trees."

Competition of this kind is wrong and ought not to be permitted. We have nothing here just like it. Objections are made to our Government distributing free seeds, and no doubt it is wrong in principle and should be stopped. Objections have been raised to cemetery companies selling flowers; but these companies are formed for business and profit, and if flowers are sold in a fair way it would seem as unobjectionable as the selling of lots. In the case of the Australian officials the extract shows not only that they are selling trees, but that they sell them at half price.

Douglas Golden Juniper.

Douglas golden juniper is one of the varieties of the common wild juniper, J. communis. The common form varies greatly. In some localities, the vicinity of Philadelphia for one, when in its wild state, it is of upright conical growth, not unlike that of the Swedish juniper. In the New England and Northwestern States it forms a low-growing, spreading bush, usually of concave shape; this form is what is commonly called prostrata. The golden-leaved one sent out by the late Robert Douglas and now known as Douglas's golden juniper, is this one, prostrata. It is an evergreen of great value, there being so many situations an evergreen of this character can fill to advantage. Like all junipers it makes but few roots; and to have success when transplanting it, it should be moved often when young. Besides this, it is with other evergreens in this, that if the roots become dried when out of the ground, it is almost sure to die.

The forms of juniper that trail over the ground, or nearly so, appear to be varieties of the red cedar. There are a great many varieties of it, some of which are listed by nurserymen as belonging to J. sabina, which is a mistake. The two varieties of "Waukegan junipers," one of which grows close to the ground, appear to be forms of Juniperus virginiana.

Magnolia Seedlings.

Many of those who obtain magnolia seeds to sow fail to raise seedlings from them, and the chief reason is, usually, that the seeds are permitted to become too dry before sown. When they fall from their pods, a little delay in sowing does not hurt them, because the pulp on them prevents actual drying out; but it is not safe to let them lie out of the ground more than a few weeks. The sooner they are mixed with soil the better. A good way is to place the seeds in a box of sifted sand as soon as they are gathered, mixing them well. Let the sand be damp, and allow the seeds to remain in it for about two weeks, when the pulp will have sufficiently decayed when the sand should be sifted out and the seeds washed clean of pulp. Should the weather permit of sowing before the ground freezes, it may be done then, covering the beds with some litter, both to keep the soil moist and to pervent the freezing and thawing that takes place when not so covered. But the seeds do just as well kept in a cool place under cover and sown early in Spring. In this case, remix the seeds with sand or soil, and see that it is a trifle damp all Winter, and there will be, or should be, a good crop of seedlings resulting from the operation.

Rubus Odoratus, Flowering Raspberry.

Our illustration represents a beautiful flowering shrub of our country, the Rubus odoratus, well known as the flowering raspberry. It is not misnamed, for it is a true raspberry; it not only has handsome purplish rose colored flowers, but bears fruit as well. This fruit, however, though sweet to the taste, consists nearly altogether of seeds, hence its value is in its fine display of flowers. These are nearly two inches in diameter, and are not unlike those of many single roses, excepting that their stamens are whitish. The plant is found wild in Fairmount Park, Philadelphia, as well as in upland woods, even into Canada, although not usually abundant in any one spot.

The bush makes a height of from three to four feet, of an open spreading head, the flowers appearing in June. As with others of the Rubus family it increases from canes it makes from year to year, though not to a very great extent, but it is well to plant it where its increasing itself is desirable.

Following the line other raspberries require, a good pruning out of old wood in Spring is an advantage to it, as this causes young canes to form; these give the flowers the following year.

JOSEPH MEEHAN.

BOXWOOD

By the Car Load.

3 feet Pyramids .... $1.50 each
5 feet " .... 4.00 each

Other sizes at proportionate prices. Every plant a specimen.

HIRAM T. JONES, Union County Nurseries, Elizabeth, N. J.

Mention the Florists' Exchange when writing.

Specimen Nursery Stock

DECIDUOUS TREES and SHRUBS, EVERGREENS, RHODODENDRONS, AZALEAS, over one hundred (100) acres of the choicest varieties. Send for price list.

COTTAGE GARDENS COMPANY
QUEENS, LONG ISLAND, N. Y.

Mention the Florists' Exchange when writing.

HERBACEOUS PERENNIALS

for Summer and Autumn Planting. We offer NINE HUNDRED and SIXTY-SEVEN VARIETIES of STRONG FIELD-GROWN PLANTS. Send for Catalog and Trade List.

BAY STATE NURSERIES, NORTH ABINGTON, MASS

Mention the Florists' Exchange when writing.

F. & F. NURSERIES

SPRINGFIELD NEW JERSEY

Wholesale Growers — TREES AND PLANTS in full assortment. — Trade Catalogue Free

Mention the Florists' Exchange when writing.

SEASONABLE STOCK FOR FLORISTS

HYDRANGEAS for forcing { OTAKSA and THOS. HOGG }
With 7-12 flowering crowns, $12.00 per 100.
" 5-6 " " 9.00 "
" 4 " " 7.00 "

From 6-inch pots and open beds; all out-door grown.

ROSES, Strong, two-years, field-grown, selected for forcing.
HYBRID PERPETUALS .... $10.00 and $12.00 per 100.
CRIMSON RAMBLER .... 9.00 "
DOROTHY PERKINS .... 7.00 "
and
LADY GAY, a new hardy climbing Rose of exceptional merit; ready now from 2¼ inch pots only. Write for prices.

JACKSON & PERKINS CO.
WHOLESALE NURSERYMEN AND FLORISTS
NEWARK, WAYNE CO., NEW YORK

Mention the Florists' Exchange when writing.

PEONIES

Queen Victoria (the cold storage flower) $9.00 per 100. Festiva Maxima, $30.00 per 100. Fragrans (late Rose) $6.00 per 100. For 1000 rates or other varieties, write,

Large stock of M. L. Rhubarb and Lucretia Dewberry Plants. Write for prices

GILBERT H. WILD, SARCOXIE, MO.

Mention the Florists' Exchange when writing.

NOW IS THE TIME TO PLANT

Herbaceous Perennials

We have a very large stock of PHLOX, IRIS, PINKS, etc.

Send for Price List.

VICK & HILL CO., P. O. Box 613, ROCHESTER, N. Y.

Mention The Florists' Exchange when writing.

PEONIES

We still have quite a block of Ne Plus Ultra, and need the ground. While they last we offer them at $7.50 per 100; $60.00 per 1000. Send for list.

EDWARD SWAYNE
WEST CHESTER, PA.

Mention the Florists' Exchange when writing.

KOSTER & CO.

Hollandia Nurseries BOSKOOP, HOLLAND

Hardy Azaleas, Box Trees, Clematis, Conifers, Hydrangeas, Peonies.
Pot-Grown Plants for Forcing.
RHODODENDRONS, H. P. ROSES, Etc.
Catalogue free on demand.

Mention the Florists' Exchange when writing.

BULBS
Fancy Selected

LET US QUOTE YOU PRICES

S. G. Harris, Tarrytown, N. Y.

Mention the Florists' Exchange when writing.

Sphagnum Moss and Cedar Poles

Moss, 5 barrel bale, $1.25; 2 bales, $2.25; 5 bales, $5.00; 10 bales, $9.50. Poles, 2 in. butt, 8 ft. long, $15.00 per 1000; 2½ in. butt, 10 to 12 feet long, $22.50 per 1000.

R. H. AKERS, Chatsworth, N. J.

Mention The Florists' Exchange when writing.

A BARGAIN FOR YOU IN NICE PLANTS

2000 Achillea, The Pearl $2.00 per 100, 1500 German Iris 8 varieties $2.00 per 100, 8000 Iris Sibirica Blue and White $2.00 per 100, 100 Helianthus Divaricatus $3.00 per 100, 1000 Heliopsis Pitcheriana, $2.00 per 100, 1000 Digitalis, Foxglove, $2.00 per 100, 500 Crimson Eye, Hibiscus, $3.00 per 100, 400 Peonies, 3-6 eyes asstd. $8.00 per 100, 500 Arundo Donax Grass $6.00 per 100, 200 Funkia Coerulea, $4.00 per 100, 1500 Trumpet Vines, 2-3 ft. tr. 3c., 300 Wisteria Multijuga racemes of blooms 2-3 ft. long, 10c. each. Cash with Order please.

Ellsworth Brown & Co. Seabrook, N. H.

Mention the Florists' Exchange when writing.

Holland Nursery Stock

Ask for Our Catalogue. It will interest you.

ENDTZ, VAN NES & CO. BOSKOOP, HOLLAND

Mention the Florists' Exchange when writing.

GRAFTED ROSES

Fine Stock from 3-in. pots.

Richmond, $2.50 per doz., $15.00 per 100, $125.00 per 1000.

Killarney, $2.00 per doz., $15.00 per 100.

Etoile de France, $3.00 per doz., $18.00 per 100.

Kaiserin, Carnot, Uncle John, Chatenay, $2.00 per doz., $15.00 per 100.

Bridesmaid, Golden Gate, Wootton, $2.00 per doz., $12.00 per 100.

ROSES OWN ROOTS

Fine Stock from 3-in. pots.

Richmond, $10.00 per 100; $90.00 per 1000.

Etoile de France, $12.00 per 100.

Sunrise, Perle, Sunset, Chatenay, $8.00 per 100.

Bridesmaid, Golden Gate, $7.00 per 100.

Asparagus Plumosus Nanus from 3-inch pots, $8.00 per 100; Sprengeri from 3-inch pots, $6.00 per 100.

Send for Catalogue.

WOOD BROS., Fishkill, N. Y.

Mention The Florists' Exchange when writing.

Large Assortment **PEONIES** Very best Varieties

LOW PRICES
THE KIND THAT FLORISTS LIKE

"We make a specialty of growing stocky transplanted shrubbery and trees"

FULL ASSORTMENT OF Ornamentals, Fruits, Roses, Clematis, and Herbaceous Plants. Write for our fall wholesale trade list.

W. & T. SMITH CO., GENEVA, N. Y.

Mention the Florists' Exchange when writing.

ROSES

Climbing Clothilde Soupert, Marie Pavie, Crimson Rambler and Dorothy Perkins . . .

Grafted Oranges and Kin Kans, Palms, Biota "Aurea Nana, Conifers and Other Stock for Florists and Nurserymen

IN IMMENSE QUANTITIES

400 ACRES IN NURSERIES — 60,000 FEET OF GLASS

CATALOG ON APPLICATION

P. J. BERCKMANS CO. (Inc.)
FRUITLAND NURSERIES
Established 1856. AUGUSTA, GA.

Mention The Florists' Exchange when writing.

Leedle grown Roses are now Big

FLORAL COMP'Y Springfield, O. Expert Growers Send for price list	H. P.'s, H. T.'s, T.'s, R.'s, Cl.'s, B., etc. 101 best sorts. On own roots.	values for the buyer. Send your want list.

Mention the Florists' Exchange when writing.

Queen Beatrice Rose

Four to one shot. Four times as many flowers as Maid.

F. H. KRAMER, 916 F St., Washington, D. C.

Mention The Florists' Exchange when writing.

New Pink Rose

Miss Kate Moulton

Is the QUEEN of all Pink Roses
Write us about it

Minneapolis Floral Co., - Minneapolis, Minn.

Mention the Florists' Exchange when writing.

Grafted Roses

Edw. J. Taylor, Southport, Connecticut

Mention the Florists' Exchange when writing.

Rose Baby Rambler

X X X

Our plants are last year's propagation and have had a full season's growth. Extra fine bushy. $12.00 per 100. Special price in quantities.

NATHAN SMITH & SON, Adrian, Mich.

Mention the Florists' Exchange when writing.

PINK AND WHITE COCHET ROSE PLANTS

Field grown, $8.00 per 100; $70.00 per 1000.

GEORGE M. COOK - Arlington, Md.

Mention the Florists' Exchange when writing.

VIOLETS

CAMPBELL, from 3 in. pots, well established $3.00 per 100.
CALIFORNIA, strong, field-grown plants $2.50 per 100.
field-grown CAMPBELL, all sold. Securely packed to carry safely.

CHAS. BLACK
HIGHTSTOWN N. J.

Mention the Florists' Exchange when writing.

FERNS and Crimson Rambler ROSES

10,000 Ferns, in fine shape, low stocky plants, not drawn, grown in full light, and as they were pot plants, lifts with fine balls.
Bostons, for 6 in., $20.00 per 100; for 5 in. $15.00.
Piersoni, for 6 in., $25.00 per 100; for 5 in. $20.00.
Scottii, for 5 in., $20.00 per 100; for 4 in., $15.00.
2,000 Crimson Ramblers, for Easter forcing, 1 year old, 3 to 4 ft., several canes well ripened and good roots, $2.00 per doz.; $15.00 per 100.
Asparagus Plumosus Nanus, 2½ in., fine, $3.50 per 100.
Sprengeri and Plumosus Nanus, 4 in., $1.00 per doz.
5,500 Vinca Major, variegated, field stock, extra fine, $5.00 per 100; $45.00 per 1000
Vinca Major, variegated, and Hydrangea Otaksa, 2½ in., pot plants, $2.50 per 100. Hydrangea Paniculata Grandiflora, Spirea, Anthony Waterer, and Spirea Van Houtti, 3 year old, large bushes, $1.00 per dozen or $7.00 per 100.
50,000 Shrubs, Vines, Cannas, etc. These must be sold low. List free.
Cash please.

BENJ. CONNELL
WEST GROVE, PA.

Mention the Florists' Exchange when writing.

POINSETTIAS

To close, 2½ in., $4.00 per 100.
HYDRANGEAS, 2½ in., $3.00 per 100.
" 4 in., pot grown, $8.00 and $10.00 per 100.
" 5 in., pot grown $20.00 per 100.
BEGONIA SANDERSONII, 2½ in., $8.00 per 100.

MUM STOCK PLANTS

C. Touset, Early White, $1.50 per doz. Pink—Glory of the Pacific, A. J. Balfour, Wm. Duckham, Viviand-Morel, Maude Dean, White—Alice Byron, Polly Rose, Ivory; Yellow—Robt. Halliday, Col. Appleton, Mrs. Wm. Duckham, Yellow Jones, $1.00 per doz.; $6.00 per 100.

S. N. PENTECOST,
1790-1810 East 101 St., CLEVELAND, O.

PRIMROSES

BIG BARGAIN TO MAKE ROOM

IMPROVED CHINESE, finest grown, all varieties, mixed, single and double.
X X 2 in., $1.50 per 100.
X X X 3 in., $4.00 per 100.
Cash. Order at once. Only a few thousand left.
Extras added liberally.

JOHN F. RUPP, Shiremanstown, Pa.
The Home of Primroses

Mention the Florists' Exchange when writing.

Different Stock

Genistas, fine healthy pot grown plants, 3 in., 8c., 4 in., 10c., 5 in., 15c
Boston Ferns, 5x6 in., 25c.; Tarrytown ferns, 6 in., 50c.
Parsley Plants, large, $2.00 per 1000.
Cash Please.

F. B. RINE, Lewisburg, Pa.

Mention The Florists' Exchange when writing.

Decorative Foliage Plants.

PALMS — KENTIAS. — Within the past two or three years the demand for specimen kentias has greatly increased, while in the same period the call for Latania borbonica has dwindled to very small proportions, until to-day, large plants of the latter can hardly be given away. These conditions should prompt buyers possessing greenhouses to realize as soon as possible on latanias, and to bear in mind that there is but little likelihood of there being much call in the future for these plants in the larger sizes. On the other hand, kentias are always good stock in all stages. As an investment it will pay country dealers especially (I mean, of course, those with greenhouses), to purchase a fairly large supply of kentias in small size pots, growing them on until they are marketable, which they will soon be, provided they are given reasonable care. Kentias, after they are established in 5-inch pots, gain rapidly in value, while many of the smaller size can be profitably used up to make room for the growing specimens, these specimens themselves to be disposed of whenever customers appear. Only be sure always to keep on hand a large number of all sizes, replenishing the stock at frequent intervals with young plants from the wholesale grower, who can produce them much cheaper from seed or by importation, than the average retail dealer and grower can do.

PANDANUS SANDERI.—At the time Pandanus Sanderi was introduced into commerce in this country, it was predicted that before very long it would rival, if not outstrip, Pandanus Veitchii for commercial purposes as a decorative foliage plant. While it can hardly be said now by the actual standing of the plant that the prediction then made is verified, still the plant has many points to commend it to the attention of commercial growers. In form, especially in its smaller stages, it is decidedly inferior to P. Veitchii; but when it is grown into a large specimen and its peculiarities understood, its graceful appearance, made more striking by the intense coloring of the foliage, makes up for what it lacked in form at an earlier stage. Pandanus Veitchii is very resentful of overwatering, but colors well in partial shade. In the case of Pandanus Sanderi I have found that it colors much better when given less water than is invariably given the other variety, and that if grown in the shade, the foliage turns and grows almost green in color. From that it may be concluded that it thrives best in a light situation. I have also found that Pandanus Sanderi stands much more rough usage and a lower temperature than P. Veitchii. The new variety suckers very freely and grows more rapidly than the older one.

MARANTAS.—Although the marantas individually are perhaps not in very great demand, they are nevertheless very useful to florists for various purposes, such as filling dishes and baskets. Well grown plants are also admirably adapted for table decoration when plants are exclusively used. The foliage on many of the easiest grown varieties droops gracefully over the pot or pan in which they are grown, leaving nothing to be desired in the way of well furnished specimens for this kind of work. Marantas are also very serviceable for the decoration of store windows in the way of groundwork for taller plants; in fact, there are endless ways in which these charming little plants may be utilized. I said little; by that meaning those kinds that creep, and the smaller growing varieties. Others, like Maranta zebrina, are very handsome and many of them are used in some of the large florists' stores for decorative effect, also by decorators in their work; but these kinds are principally grown for greenhouse decoration where there are collections of choice foliage plants.

There are two ways of propagating marantas—a different method to suit the requirements of the two distinctly different forms of construction in the plants. Those making secondary growths are propagated from cuttings of these growths. The method attended by the most success is to place these cuttings in very small pots that have been provided with liberal drainage and sand, placing the pots with the cuttings in the propagating bed over a gentle heat. When the cuttings are well rooted they should be repotted into larger pots, in a soil composed of good fibrous loam, leaf mold, fibrous peat, and clean sand, in about equal proportions. In mixing the materials to form the compost, it will be more satisfactory if they are left as lumpy as possible. In the subsequent shifting of the plants, pans will be found to answer their requirements and the purposes to which later they will be put, better than deep pots.

Marantas thrive in a rather warm temperature (about 60° minimum) and a moist atmosphere. In the matter of space on benches, after they are established they are not very exacting. A palm house, or the warmest parts of one, will do very well. The plants may be set on inverted pots, or temporary shelves underneath the shade of the palms. They like partial shade. The early Spring is the best time to propagate marantas.

The other kinds, or I might perhaps and more correctly say species, of marantas or calatheas, do not make secondary growths, and these are propagated by division of the crowns. After dividing, pot them into small pots, placing them over bottom heat until established. When they have made leaves anew, they require abundance of water and frequent syringings and protection from the direct rays of the sun. D. M.

FALL SPECIALTIES:

DRACAENA INDIVISA. (Field grown.) 5 inch pot size, $15.00 per 100. 6 inch pot size, $25.00 per 100.
PEONY—DORCHESTER. 3 to 6 eye divisions—Latest and best paying clear pink, about shade of Daybreak Carnation. $25.00 per 100
PEONY—QUEEN VICTORIA. Best cut flower white, 3 to 6 eye divisions. $10.00 per 100, $90.00 per 1000.
BOUGAINVILLEA GLABRA SANDERIANA. Beautiful plants, bushy and nicely rounded, 4 in. pot plants, $20.00 per 100.
HYBRID ROSES. Extra size Magna Charta, best possible condition for winter forcing in pots, strong, 2 yr. field grown, $12.00 per 100.
NARCISSUS VON SION, $1.00 per 100.
NARCISSUS TRUMPET MAJOR, 75c. per 100.
NARCISSUS IMCOMPARABLE, 80c. per 100.
ROMAN HYACINTHS. 12 to 15, $2.20 per 100.

Write for prices on large lots.

Send for Catalogue No. 5 for full list of Bulbs, Seeds and Plants.

The STORRS & HARRISON CO.,
PAINESVILLE, OHIO.

Mention The Florists' Exchange when writing.

ASPARAGUS

ASPARAGUS PLUMOSUS, 2 in. at $2.00, 4 in. at $10.00, 5 in. at $15.00, 6 in. at $25.00 per 100.
ASPARAGUS SPRENGERI, 3 in. at $5.00, 4 inch at $8.00, 5 in. at $15.00 per 100.
PIERSONI FERN, 5 in. at 30c., 6 in. at 40c. each.
FICUS, 5 in. at 35c., 6 in. at 40c. each.

Chrysanthemum Stock Plants

Opah, Monrovia, Omega, Lady Harriett, Viviand-Morel, Duckham, Alice Byron, Pearson, Halliday, Robinson, Appleton, Et. Bonnefond, Dalskov, Ivory, Dr. Enguehard, Timothy Eaton, Yellow Eaton, White Bonnaffon, Major Bonnaffon, $5.00 per 100.

Cash or C. O. D.

W. J. & M. S. VESEY, Fort Wayne, Ind.

Mention the Florists' Exchange when writing.

Practical Books for the Trade Published and Controlled exclusively by A. T. DeLaMare Ptg. and Pub. Co., Ltd.

WATER GARDENING $2.50
By Peter Bisset. A grand book in every particular, profusely illustrated. Ready February, 1907.

PRACTICAL VIOLET CULTURE 1.50
By Prof. B. T. Galloway. Second edition, revised. Fully illustrated.

THE AMERICAN CARNATION... 3.50
By C. W. Ward. The only practical book on the subject, and most valuable for the professional as well as for the learner. Profusely illustrated.

PRACTICAL PLANT CULTURE.. 1.00
By G. W. Oliver. The very best book on the subject, well written, covering all plants cultivated by commercial men for profit; with cultural methods and propagating directions, complete.

SUCCESS WITH HOUSE PLANTS
Cloth 1.00
Paper .... .50
By Lizzie Page Hillhouse. The best book on the market for florists to sell, or to give to their customers. Many thousands sold.

ARNOLD'S TELEGRAPH CODE.. 2.50
By E. A. Arnold. The most valuable and complete code on the market; thoroughly intelligible; covers every need of the florist, seedsman, and nurseryman.

Every one of these eminently practical books, written specially for the trade, should be in your library. We will deliver the six books above listed, carriage paid, on receipt of $10.50.

THE GARDENER'S ASSISTANT
(2 volumes) 15.00
The Standard Encyclopedia on practical and scientific horticulture.

Prospectus of Any of the Above Books Will Be Sent Free on Application.

Offices—

2 to 8 Duane St., NEW YORK CITY

Address P. O. Box 1697

Cineraria Benary, Cannell and Sutton's Prize Strains; dwarf or semi-dwarf, large flowers, all shades and colors, mixed 2¼ in., $1.50 per 100. Cash please.
SHELLROAD GREENHOUSES, Grange, Baltimore, Md.

Mention the Florists' Exchange when writing.

COCOS WEDDELIANA

Nice Plants in 3 in. pots, per 100 $15.00

KENTIA BELMOREANA

Fine clean stock in 5 in. pots, about 15 in. high, per 100 $15.00; about 20 in. high, per 100, $20.00

ADIANTUM CUNEATUM

Fine Plants, 2½ in. pots, per 100 $5.00

O. V. ZANGEN
SEEDSMAN, BOX 114, HOBOKEN, N. J.

Mention the Florists' Exchange when writing.

COCOS PALMS.

Strong 2¼ inch at $1.50 per dozen. Write for lowest prices on Kentias.

Jas. F. Barclay R. I. GREENHOUSES Pawtucket, R. I.

Mention The Florists' Exchange when writing.

ROBERT CRAIG & CO.

ROSES, PALMS, CROTONS

CARNATIONS and Novelties in DECORATIVE PLANTS

Market and 49th Sts. PHILADELPHIA, PA.

Mention The Florists' Exchange when writing.

SMILAX PLANTS

Strong, bushy growing stock. From 3 in. pots, $2.00 per 100, $18.00 per 1000. 2 in. pots, $1.00 per 100; $9.00 per 1000. **Seedlings** from flats, large, summered out of doors, $4.00 per 1000. Send for samples.

R. KILBOURN, CLINTON, N. Y.

Mention the Florists' Exchange when writing.

EMERSON C. McFADDEN

Wholesale Grower

Asparagus Plumosus Nanus, Etc.

Short Hills, N. J.

Tel. 28 A.

Mention the Florists' Exchange when writing.

PRIMROSES

Obconica Alba and Rosea, $1.50 per 100; $12.00 per 1000.

ASPARAGUS

Plumosus, 2¼ in. pots $18.00 per 1000; $2.00 per 100.
Pansy Plants, large flowering, $3.00 per 1000; 50c. per 100. Cash.

JOS. H. CUNNINGHAM, Delaware, O.

Mention The Florists' Exchange when writing.

FERNS. NEPHROLEPIS BARROWSII

2¼ inch, $6.00 per 100.

HUGH GRAHAM CO.,
Logan Nurseries, York Road and Louden Street, PHILADELPHIA, PA

Mention The Florists' Exchange when writing.

Adiantum Farleyense

Good thrifty stock, 3 inch pots . . . $20.00 per 100

THORN HEDGE GREENHOUSES, Newtown Square, Pa.

Mention the Florists' Exchange when writing.

WHITMANI FERN

Large stock of strong plants, 2¼ inch pots, $12.00 per 100. 4 inch pots $25.00 per 100.

TARRYTOWN FERN 100
3 inch pots $8.00

SCOTTII
2¼ inch pots $5.00
4 inch pots 12.00

KENTIA FORSTERIANA
4 inch pots, made up, strong and bushy $25.00
5 inch pots, made up, strong and bushy 50.00

No order for less than 10 plants accepted.

CHAS. H. CAMPBELL,
3601 GERMANTOWN AVE., PHILA., PA

Mention The Florists' Exchange when writing.

FERNS FROM BENCH

BOSTON, 4 in. 10c.; 5 in., 12½c.
TARRYTOWN, 2½ in., 4c.; 3 in., 10c.; 4 in., 15c.; 5 in., 25c. Runners $20.00 per 1000.
SCOTTII, 3 in., 8c.; 4 in., 12½c.
Pansy Plants, Giants $3.00 per 100.
Daisies, double **Longfellow, Delicata,** $2.50 per 1000.
Asparagus Sprengeri, 2 in., 2 cts.
Flowering Begonias, 8 kinds, 2 in., 2½ cts.
Forgetmenots, $2.50 per 1000.
Hollyhocks, double, 4 kinds, 1 year old, 3 cts.
Hardy Pinks, 3 kinds, field plants, 3½ cts.
Hardy Carnations, nice young plants from frames, $2.00 per 100.

Cash or C. O. D.

BYER BROS., Chambersburg, Pa

Mention The Florists' Exchange when writing.

FERNS OUR SPECIALTY

Cibotium Schiedei: We have a grand stock of this magnificent tree fern in all sizes, 3 in. pots, $35.00 per 100; 4 in. pots, $45.00 per 100; 5 in. pots, $70.00 per 100; 7 in. pots, $1.70 each; 8 in. pots, $2.50 each.
Assorted Ferns, from 2¼ in. pots, all the best market varieties, $3.00 per 100, or $35.00 per 1000; 4 inch pots, $12.00 per 100.
If by mail add 10c. each 100 plants.
Adiantum Cuneatum, 2 in. pots, $3.50 per 100
" " 4 in. pots, 12.00 " "
" **Rhodophyllum** 4 in. pots, $25.00 per 100
" **Lathamii,** 4 in. pots, $20.00 per 100
" **Regina,** 4 in. pots, $35.00 per 100
Fern Spores gathered from our own stock plants 35c. per trade package or $4.00 per doz. packages

ANDERSON & CHRISTENSEN,
SHORT HILLS, N. J.

Mention The Florists' Exchange when writing.

ASPIDIUM TSUSSEMENSE

Extra large bushy plants in 3-inch pots, $6.00 per 100.

CYRTOMIUM FALCATUM

Large, full plants, 3-inch pots, the best stock we have ever offered, 6c.; 2 inch pots, 3c.

ASSORTED FERNS

Fine bushy plants, 2-inch pots, 3c.

Two No. 4 Weathered boilers in good condition at a bargain

R. G. HANFORD, · NORWALK, CONN.

Mention the Florists' Exchange when writing.

FIELD-GROWN

VINCA VARIEGATED, $4.00 per 100.
PANSY plants, strong and stocky; flowers immense size, all colors, rich and rare, from strain second to none.
DAHLIA clumps, named, $5.00 per 100.
2-in. **GERANIUMS,** standard varieties, all colors, $2.00 per 100; $18.00 per 1000.

THE NATIONAL PLANT CO., Dayton, Ohio.

Mention the Florists' Exchange when writing.

FERNS

Boston, Barrowsii and Scottii, 6 in., $4.00 per doz.; 5 in., $2.50 per doz.
Boston and Scottii, 3 in., $6.00 per 100. 4 in., $8.00 per 100.
Strong runners of **Whitmani** $15.00 per 100.

Larchmont Nurseries
Larchmont, N. Y.

Mention The Florists' Exchange when writing

FERNS

For Jardinieres, etc., 2½ inch, $3.00 per 100.
Kentia Belmoreana, clean and bushy, 5 in 50c.
Boston Ferns, Piersoni and Scottii, from bench, 10c. to 25c. each, 4 in. pot grown, 15c.
Cocos Weddeliana, 2½ in. 10c.
Asparagus Plumosus, 2½ in. $3.00 per 100.

H. WESTON, HEMPSTEAD, N. Y.

Mention The Florists' Exchange when writing

Fine Ferns from Bench

400 **Bostons,** 5 to 6 in. 200 **Scottii,** 5 to 6 in. 10 **Piersoni,** 5 to 6 in. 100 **Barrowsii,** 4 to 5 in. 10 **Tarrytown,** 4 to 5 inch. Any of the above varieties at $20.00 per 100. Nice clean stock and grown in full sunlight. Also 200 of the above varieties from 8 in. pans at $1.00 each. Cash with order.

DEAN & PARSE
Summit, N. J.

Mention the Florists' Exchange when writing

BARGAIN

TO MAKE ROOM

1,000 **N. Piersoni Elegantissima Ferns,** from 2½ in. pots, $8.00 per 100. A No. 1 stock; ready for 4 and 5 in. pots. Cash with order, please.

R. ENGELMAN & SON
PITTSFIELD, MASS.

Mention The Florists' Exchange when writing

NEPHROLEPIS

Whitmani, 2¼ in., $25.00 per 100.
Barrowsii, $10.00 per 100.

Henry H. Barrows & Son, Whitman, Mass

Mention The Florists' Exchange when writing

Adiantum Farleyense

I can quote splendid stock at from $2. per dozen up to $24.00 per dozen, in 2-inch to 8-inch pots. If you are looking for Farleyense, better write me about it.

CHARLES H. TOTTY, Madison, N. J

Mention The Florists' Exchange when writing

Grower of Palms, Ferns and other Decorative Stock.

Nephrolepis Scottii all the year round

JOHN SCOTT
Rutland Road & E. 45th St., BROOKLYN, N.
Telephone 2890 Bedford.

Mention the Florists' Exchange when writing

LIST OF ADVERTISERS

INDEX TO STOCK ADVERTISED

Contents.

PAGE

THE WEEK'S WORK.

Timme's Timely Teachings.

The Tail End of Outdoor Work.

There is still much to do in field and garden that should not be deferred until Winter is upon us in real earnest. Anything yet in the field, grown for indoor culture, should now be lifted, and either be potted up or heeled in where it can be covered in case of need. Deutzias, lilacs, prunus, Azaleas mollis, amœna and pontica, raised on the premises and intended for forcing, together with some other good things in the line of hardy shrubs suitable for a like purpose, should now be dug up and placed in frames, some in pots, before the ground freezes up solid. Free exposure of their top growth for several weeks yet is necessary to secure full maturity of the wood, on which success in forcing depends.

Roses raised in the field and intended for pot culture can now be lifted and potted up at any time before hard feezings render the task less agreeable. In potting, a rather stiff but highly enriched soil should be used. These also should remain out of doors a good while yet after being potted up. There is time for the pruning of these roses until shortly before they are to be started into growth later on.

This is also a good time for the planting of deciduous trees and shrubs, or for the moving of any found to be out of place or in the way. While early Spring may be a better time for the work, it is not for the gardener, and, with proper care, it can be done now fully as well, and the long planned and often postponed job is over with. For the transplanting of evergreens, however, it is now too late.

It would also be a good idea, worthy to be acted upon at once, to install one or several tastefully designed, fitly placed and carefully executed bulb beds, where they are sure to be seen by all passers by next Spring. There is nothing among early flowering things more interestingly attractive on a florist's front lawn, and nothing more capable of bringing trade than these. It is like planting money that is sure to sprout. Then there is other work, less playful perhaps, but certainly fully as important, that should now be done.

Plowing and Digging.

Land plowed in the Fall instead of in the Spring thereby gains considerably in texture, fertility, ease of cultivation and general character. Heavy clay soils specially are greatly improved by being turned over at the approach of Winter, and at the same time given a liberal dressing of coarse barnyard manure. It is about the only means of bringing such soils into proper condition for early planting the following season. Fresh manures, plowed under in the Spring, are of doubtful value the first year, are only of service mechanically by imparting looseness to heavy soils. But even this benefit is often turned into a harmful factor by Spring plowing, inasmuch as it renders the ground too spongy and springy—a condition but partly overcome by the use of heavy rollers. All this is averted by Fall plowing or digging. The ground in field, garden and flower beds will be in fine growing condition when Spring opens, will be nicely settled during the Winter, freed of all acidity and sogginess, finely pulverized by freezing and thawing, needing nothing in the way of final preparation for early tillage and planting but a leveling of the surface with harrow or rake.

Lawn Making.

New residences usually near completion in the Fall, and for that matter many old homesteads also necessitate the laying out and bringing into pleasing shape of the remaining ground space, befitting a well designed and often costly home. Florists are often called upon to carry out the plans determined upon by the owner, the services of a landscape gardener being required only in rare cases of this kind. Unfortunately, all is frequently deferred until Spring, when there is no better time for having the roughest part of the work done than just at this season. And it is necessary to do it now to have the ground in readiness for sowing, sodding and planting at a time in Spring, early enough to assure success. The job in most cases amounts to no more than the making of a good bit of front lawn, and the all around florist does wisely in securing as many orders for this line of work as ever possible, forthere is money in it, provided the right kind of laborers can also be obtained. If anything of this kind is now on the order book, no time should be lost in giving it immediate attention. The work sometimes involves a deal of filling in, which can now be done better and with less expense than in the Spring. More often, however, the plot to be fixed up is a jumble of all sorts of refuse building material, debris and odds and ends usually found strewn about newly finished buildings. Some of this could well be dug under, but the greater part of it must be got out of the way by complete removal. The depth of good soil, covering rubbish, dead clay or coarse gravel, as thrown from cellar or basement, should not be less than a good foot for dense, thrifty grass growth.

Fundamental Requisites.

It is now time to make sure of being well provided as to compost, potting soils, fertilizers, propagating sand and anything that may come under this head. Most of this can now be had at less expense and with less exertion than at any other season, and time is never so pressing just now but what some of it could well be spared and profitably employed in storing up goodly quantities of such materials that must be regarded as of first and foremost importance in all gardening pursuits. Most growers and greenhouse establishments experience little trouble in procuring all they need in this line at any time, and at a reasonable price too, but there is quite a number less favorably placed.

Good, richly-fibered sods from fertile fields or pastures, leaf-mold in proper condition, even a fair grade of loam or common black earth have, in many localities, become scarce and high-priced commodities, must be hauled long distances and, in many instances, can only then be had by inducing teamsters and laborers to forego high wages for still higher ones. Florists so situated, therefore, wisely seize upon every opportunity that offers to lay in a good supply of anything that by composting and proper preparation might be worked into good bench or potting soil. Thus sods for florists' use are dug and hauled at any time during the entire season, when the months of May and November should be chosen for the work, because it is only then when fresh sods are really good for composting. In May, of course, florists find little time to attend to this matter. November, therefore, finds nearly all of them busily at work preparing soils for the ensuing season's needs.

Bench of Poinsettias

Grower, J. J. Hellenthal, Columbus, O.

Compost.

There is no need of preparing a great variety of soils. For an all around use in commercial establishments there is nothing superior to the soil resulting from the composting of freshly cut sods and green barnyard manure in the proportion of three parts of the sods to two of the manure. Of these the manure will lose in bulk more than half during the process of decomposition, while the sods will barely lose one-third. Both ingredients will work up better into nice, friable soil by being at once piled up in alternate layers and allowed to gradually merge into proper condition, than when mixed together just before using, even if each part by itself has undergone decomposition to the proper extent. The material, beginning with a layer of sods and ending with one of manure, should be piled up in rather high heaps, not finished off with a rounded top, but leaving a flat and level surface. After this compost has stood from five to eight months, having been worked over several times during that time, it is in its prime as a soil for nearly all kinds of cultivated plants, but will rapidly lose in value thereafter, finally being no better than ordinary garden soil. This compost when used while at its best is the soil that gives entire satisfaction in almost all cultures. Where special cultures call for the use of special soil, its character may be modified to suit the case by adding sand, leaf-mold, more loam or more fertilizing matter, as may be deemed necessary, these additional components to be intermixed when preparing the compost for immediate use.

Potting Soils.

While composted sods as the elementary base of all soil mixtures is most to be relied upon as giving best cultural results, it is also the most expensive of soils for the growing of ordinary florist's stock. On a place where potted and bedding plants are raised exclusively the item of soil is one of considerable magnitude in the long list of expenditures. There are now numerous florist concerns where a good grade of sod soil comes very near being a high-priced luxury, not obtainable in quantity sufficient for the entire needs of the place. In such cases common black loam is made to do as the main part in all soil preparations.

This black soil can be had easily enough at times from farmers, building contractors and others who regularly supply the smaller florists, always preferring to haul it in late Fall. But they need close watching while they are at it, or they will go down too deep in digging it, bringing even the dead ground from low excavations, anything as long as it is black in color, and bring the stipulated price as per load. Soil, taken from the surface of a field, garden or even from the roadside and along fences, emitting a peculiarly sweet, pleasant odor, as all unfertilized fresh top soil does when purified by long exposure to the elements, is a pretty good substitute for sod-soil. When enriched with well-decayed manure, made lighter by the addition of some sand if need be, broken up and worked into proper condition, it is fit for immediate use. Sufficiently large quantities of potting soil ready for use should always be at hand; some of it should now be placed under shelter.

The main bulk of the soil, large quantities for Spring work, should remain out of doors, the very best storage magazine during Winter. Nicely piled up in rounded heaps, exposed to alternate freezings and thawings, but kept clear of snow, it will remain in better condition than when stored in moist and warm potting sheds, and can usually be had in such quantities as needed for immediate use.

Special Soils.

There is a great diversity in soils as found in the widely separated sections of the country, or even in those of a township. Florists are located everywhere, and must freely make use of the soil as they find it. It stands to reason that the stock grown in these differing soils must also differ, and this is a fact not doubted by any one frequently receiving stock from variously located growers. That plants of any and all kinds can be grown equally well in any and all kinds of earth is far from being true, though statements which seem to convey that idea are often made. We must take the soil as we find it; that is plain and cannot be helped. But we can do much in making it come as near to meeting the requirements of certain kinds of stock, known to be quite exacting in their wants in this particular point, as is possible, by intermixture and preparation. I do not believe in the necessity of following to a dot the old school precepts for the compounding of soils—a different formula for every kind of stock. But while there is no need of being over-nice as to the various components in soil-preparations, it is well to bear in mind facts, established by every-day experience, plainly demonstrating that in certain soils certain crops thrive better and can more profitably be raised.

Manures.

Florists in their labors are in constant need of fertilizing material. They all agree in giving a good grade of well-decayed barnyard manure first place among fertilizers for general use, but all experience the same difficulty in procuring it in a condition sufficiently decomposed to render it fit for immediate use. They must therefore lay in fresh manure, which at this time of year is not hard to obtain, pile it up and give it time to decay. In doing this it must be remembered that the shrinkage in bulk through decomposition is considerable, and that in laying up a supply for the entire coming season due allowance must be made on this score. It is best to build up the raw material into long, low, flat heaps, instead of giving it the usual high piled conical form. For the sake of appearance these flat-topped heaps should then be covered with a thinly spread layer of fresh soil. This also will, to some extent, prevent the escape of valuable gases, and the piles of hoarded treasure are less like-

Carnation House of J. J. Hellenthal, Columbus, O.

ly to be considered a public nuisance by the neighbors. Forked over once or twice during the process of decomposition, it will be in proper condition for use next Spring.

Horse manure, if not stirred up frequently, burns quickly and is then of little value. It should always be kept in a soaked condition by letting the hose have a play on it occasionally, should no rains fall. Refuse or spent brewers' hops quickly but somewhat fiercely pass through the stage of fermentation and need no forking over. Manure from horned cattle is usually overrun with all sorts of worms and the larvæ of bugs and bettles. By freely exposing it to the action of heat and frost, the trouble is greatly lessened.

FRED. W. TIMME.

The Future of Dutch Bulbs.

I think very few of us have realized to any extent the enormous increase in the consumption of what are known as "Dutch bulbs" that has taken place in this country during the past decade, and especially in the last two or three years. Most careful investigation of this subject convinces me, that so steady and regular have been the increasing sales of hyacinths, tulips, narcissus, and crocuses, year by year, that many of us have lost sight of this gradual broadening of consumers' demands, attributing our own larger sales to the natural increase of our own business, and not stopping to consider that every other dealer in bulbs was repeating our experience. But last Autumn the trade awoke to the fact that certain varieties of Holland bulbs could not be had; and this happened some weeks before the ending of the season. I will say here, that every indication at this writing is for just such another shortage of stock this year. The real state of the case is, that imperceptibly the bulb trade of the United States has increased to enormous proportions—and last Fall the trade was caught napping, sufficient quantities to supply the demand for the planting of the Autumn of 1905 had not been imported. There could only be one result—many customers had their money returned, and the past Spring missed many displays of flowers from bulbous stock, that had been planned.

Some of you may feel that I have unduly emphasized the bulb shortage of last Autumn; it is a fact, nevertheless, that the Fall bulb trade of America is no longer a side issue; it is an enormous and steadily growing element of business, and has a most wonderful future yet to be devoloped.

Why Bulbs are in Such Demand.

In the first place, an incalculable amount of publicity has been bestowed upon Dutch bulbs, during the last half dozen years especially, by the better class of horticultural publications, magazines, and the daily press as well. This wonderful advertising is having its effect. There never was a time when everything hardy, was in such enormous demand; and this being the case, it goes without saying that such subjects as hyacinths, tulips, daffodils, and crocuses, with their glorious past, should be used in larger numbers than ever before.

Influence of the Department Stores.

Again I am convinced that it is a case of the more places any goods are offered for sale, the more each individual firm offering them for sale can dispose of. What I mean is this. Go back with me ten years, yes twenty years, to the time when what are now known as the department stores, and general mail order houses of this country first began to sell seeds and other horticultural goods, including, incidentally, a few tulips and crocuses. At first the department stores started with those bulbs that could be sold for a few cents at the most; it took some years to work up to the more expensive varieties, such as hyacinths. In those days (say from 1880 to 1885) a few hundred tulips, a few baskets of Chinese sacred lilies, and some crocuses, were considered, and were quite an order from one of these stores. But I must not stray from my subject, although at some other time I will trace the seed business back through the past three decades for you. To continue. Stop and think what has happened in the last twenty-five years as regards Fall bulbs; it seems almost incredible to those of us who handled them then and now, the increase in sale totals that have taken place. A seedsman who imported ten cases did quite a business. How is it to-day? A customer of those same seedsmen who buys ten cases is not considered an especially large consumer.

To return to the department stores, and general mail order houses—these same stores now carry complete stocks of seeds and bulbs, and issue enormous editions of catalogues devoted to this special branch of their trade. The writer has seen the Dutch bulb business in the United States, from the little side-issue it was twenty-five years ago, expand until it has reached the enormous magnitude we all know to-day. The present condition has been reached so gradually, and by such solid and healthy slight increases in sales each year, that there is no chance for any backward step. The way has been gradually paving itself, for the enormous sales of bulbs that are being made this Autumn, and the end is by no means yet; we have only just begun to develop this branch of horticultural trade in this country.

Continually Increasing Sales of Stock.

Now what about the enormous quantities of bulbs and seeds, that the department stores and general mail order houses dispose of annually? The cry was at first that what we know as the regular seed stores would be ruined—you all know what did happen, and is happening every day—a market such as no country in the world ever dreamed possible has been created by horticultural education, until now our people as a whole buy seeds and bulbs, yes and plants, in such quantities as has never been the case before since horticultural goods have been for sale. In fact, the exact contra of what the pessimists prophesied has happened, and the fundamental theory that "the more everybody sells, the more each individual can sell" has again been verified. Hundreds of thousands of women, and men also, have purchased seeds, bulbs, and plants, at the department stores, simply because they happened to see them, and they looked cheap. Then what followed? The seeds, bulbs, or plants were taken home; and, as they had cost money; it matters little how little, they must be used. And so a garden was started. And then what happened? They became interested in their garden; and in some way, probably by seeing some seedsman's advertisement or catalogue, they learned that there were other people in the world besides the department stores who sold seeds, bulbs and plants. You can follow this natural story in your mind, as well as I can write it—gradually a garden was a yearly feature, and meant a good order every Spring and Autumn for some seedsman who never in the world would have had this customer had not his interest first been awakened as a result of his purchases at the department stores.

The Seedsman's Great Opportunity.

You may think that I have accorded too much value to the services of the department stores as introductory distributors, so to speak, but my conclusions have been reached after many years of the most careful observation. Once enlist the average person's interest in garden work, and an ever-developing enthusiasm for things horticultural follows. The very first step of all, was the putting in the hands of "the great public" what was practically paid-for samples of seeds, bulbs and plants—the rest followed naturally—just as soon as these numberless thousands of gardens reached beyond the infant stage, these interested amateur gardeners sought and became regular customers of the legitimate seedsman. And never, without the department store, would this universal gardening have been so thoroughly accomplished.

It matters not where the first supplies for a start in gardening are obtained; for just as soon as the least headway is made, headquarters are sought, consulted, and ever after patronized. The owner of a garden of any pretensions at all trades with the seedsman.

M. B. FAXON.

COLUMBUS, O.—The greenhouses of J. R. Hellenthal, are, as usual, in prime condition. Roses are exceptionally fine, and promise a heavy cut this Winter. Chrysanthemums are also good, and a bench of poinsettias is in the best of condition, making fine growth, also a lot in pans. The new carnation house, 140 x 30 feet, is planted with Enchantress, Flamingo, Estelle, Queen, Lady Bountiful, White and Pink Lawson and Ethel Ward, all varieties making a heavy growth.

Our illustrations show the poinsettias and carnations.

C. M. J.

COMING EXHIBITIONS.

[Secretaries of other Societies will oblige by forwarding the schedules of their respective shows. Ed. F. E.]

NOVEMBER 13-14, 1906, Rhode Island Horticultural Society. C. W. Smith, 27-29 Exchange street, Providence, R. I., secretary.

NOVEMBER—10, Third Annual Ontario Exhibition, Massey Music Hall, Toronto. Secretary, H. B. Cowan, Toronto.

NOVEMBER 13, 14 and 15, Faith Home Association, Thirteenth Annual Chrysanthemum Show, Houston, Texas, Mrs. F. A. Reichardt, secretary.

NOVEMBER 13, 14, 15 and 16, 1906.—Gardeners' Club of Baltimore, Md., in Florists' Exchange new building, St. Paul and Franklin streets. J. J. Perry, 805 North Eutaw street, Baltimore, Secretary of Show Committee.

A Tip on Botany.

William C. Whitney, Jr., who has spent a year in Indian Territory learning practical mining at Quapaw, described at a dinner party in New York a Quapaw restaurant.

"At this restaurant one evening," he said at his description's end, "two miners near me got into a botanical argument about the pineapple, one claiming that it was a fruit and the other that it was a vegetable.

"In the midst of their argument the waiter entered in his shirtsleeves and looked about to see what was the cause of the loud talking.

"The miners decided to let the waiter settle their argument, and accordingly one of them said:

"'Pete, what is a pineapple? Is it a fruit or a vegetable?'

"The waiter, flicking the ash from his cigar, smiled at the two men with pity.

"'It's neither, gents,' he said. 'It's an extra.'"—N. Y. Tribune.

Chicago.

The Week's News.

The John C. Moninger Company report a continuance of orders for construction, those for two large extensions and one new establishment having been recently received from California. Rush of work and weather conditions have somewhat delayed their building extensions.

The local papers are doing their utmost to aid the flower show, not only by hundreds of dollars worth of free advertising, but by the additions of columns of news matter and editorials.

E. F. Winterson Company have had a busy week in their wire design manufacturing department, and have recently added a number of assistants to fulfil the requirements of this new line in their business.

"The Busiest House in Chicago" is as usual, as busy as can be. If you doubt it, go and see.

At Peter Reinberg's the strong feature, as usual, is roses of their own production with reds and Mrs. Marshall Field as favorites.

At the Flower Growers' Market, 60 Wabash avenue, where some of our best growers are represented from neighboring sections, business has taken on a rush and the local representatives have enjoyed a more than comfortable trade, in some cases about all that could be handled.

WM. K. WOOD.

ADAMS, MASS.—Boothman is adding another greenhouse and fitting it up with electric lights.

FOUNDED IN 1888

FLORISTS' EXCHANGE

A Weekly Medium of Interchange for Florists, Nurserymen Seedsmen and the Trade in general

Exclusively a Trade Paper.

Entered at New York Post Office as Second Class Matter

Published EVERY SATURDAY by

A. T. DE LA MARE PTG. AND PUB. CO. LTD.

2, 4, 6 and 8 Duane Street,

P. O. Box 1697. Telephone 3765 John. **NEW YORK.**

CHICAGO OFFICE: 127 East Berwyn Avenue.

ILLUSTRATIONS.

Electrotypes of the illustrations used in this paper can usually be supplied by the publishers. Price on application.

YEARLY SUBSCRIPTIONS.

United States, Canada, and Mexico, $1.00. Foreign countries in postal union, $2.50. Payable in advance. Remit by Express Money Order Draft on New York. Post Office Money Order or Registered Letter.

The address label indicates the date when subscription expires and is our only receipt therefore.

REGISTERED CABLE ADDRESS:

Florex, New York.

ADVERTISING RATES.

One-half inch, 75c.; ¾-inch, $1.00; 1-inch, $1.25, special positions extra. Send for Rate Card showing discount of 10c., 15c., 25c., or 35c., per inch on continuous advertising. For rates on Wants, etc., see column for Classified Advertisements.

Copy must reach this office 12 o'clock Wednesday to secure insertion in issue of following Saturday.

Orders from unknown parties must be accompanied with cash or satisfactory references.

The Marketing of Plants and Flowers.

We print elsewhere in this issue the first prize essay in the S. A. F. O. H. competition on the subject of "The Best Method of Marketing the Product of the Plant and Flower Growers." The author of the prize winning paper advocates as the "best" method of marketing plants, the traveling salesman or "drummer." The fallacy of this proposition, viewed in the light of its general applicability, will be at once apparent to all who give the matter any serious thought. But comparatively few establishments can or do afford the services or expense of a traveling representative; and we presume the object of President Kasting, in offering the prizes in this contest, was to bring out suggestions on methods, not generally in vogué at present, that would bring about the greatest good to the greatest number.

So far as the marketing of cut flowers is concerned, the wholesale commission agent is recommended—not new nor without wisdom; and the recommendations are clothed with a lot of platitudes.

Taken as a whole, the first prize essay may be regarded as a failure in evolving anything new or tending to the enlightenment of the trade on a most important subject.

S. A. F. O. H. Ladies' Auxiliary.

While at the late S. A. F. O. H. convention at Dayton, a few ladies seeing so many with whom they were not acquainted, took it upon themselves to call a meeting on Friday, August 24, to consider the subject of a pin for identification. Mrs. W. J. Vesey of Fort Wayne, Ind., was chosen chairman, and four ladies to confer with her—Mrs. E. A. Scribner, Detroit; Miss Tillie Meinhardt, St. Louis; Mrs. John Sibson, Philadelphia; Mrs. Charles H. Maynard, Detroit—and it was voted to leave the selection of the pin with them.

On September 11 another meeting was held at the home of Mrs. Vesey when the auxiliary question was put in charge of the same committee. Mrs. Scribner was appointed treasurer, Mrs. Maynard, secretary. It was voted to call a meeting at Philadelphia next Summer at the date of the S. A. F. convention.

In the meantime we wish to get as many ladies as possible to join as charter members before January 1 next. The fee for joining, including pin, is $3; annual dues thereafter $1. First year to end January, 1908.

We wish your hearty co-operation in forming a society of our own, where we can get to know each other socially and educationally. We have quite a list of members as a start, and prospects are good for a large society. Applications for membership and pin may be sent to the secretary—Mrs. Charles H. Maynard, 219 Horton avenue, Detroit, Mich.

OUR READERS' VIEWS

Stove vs. Greenhouse Plants.

Editor Florists' Exchange:

I notice the action of the New York Florists' Club at a recent meeting eliminating from its flower show schedules the term "stove and greenhouse plants." I most heartily endorse this action. Other committees will doubtless do as their wisdom dictates, but there is little doubt that the sensible action of the New York men will be adopted by all horticultural and florist societies on this continent. I may be pardoned for saying that in all my feeble contributions to the floricultural press I have never used the term "stove house" or "stove plant," always preferring to speak of a plant as tropical or needing a tropical atmosphere.

The description "stove plant" is doubtless British, where climatic conditions are widely different from ours; where there is the year round a very distinct difference between a greenhouse and a hothouse plant; where the show pelargoniums, Indian azaleas and camellias may be taken as a type of greenhouse plants, and allamanda, stephanotis and maranta are known as stove plants. There is a separation of the two classes of plants the year round. In this country there is no such distinction. From May to October our greenhouse plants have to endure what in Western Europe would be called a "stove temperature." Therefore, I consider the words "stove plant" meaningless, crude and obsolete, entirely misunderstood by our patrons, the public.

Dropping the word "stove" is excellent, but it leaves a vacuum that is not quite filled by the simple word "greenhouse." Greenhouse flowering and greenhouse foliage would help somewhat; but by all means cut out that crude word "stove."

You have a very bright man in your club, and his name is Pat.

WM. SCOTT.

Buffalo.

Dictionary Definition of "Creations"

Editor Florists' Exchange:

As Mr. Wickson, in his communication, page 533 of your issue of November 3, has started us to look into our dictionaries—I have only one, and that is Webster's—let us have the entire lesson as he, Webster gives it. "The truth, the whole truth, and nothing but the truth," on Mr. Burbank's "New Creations" is what many of us have been seeking for some time.

The definitions of the word "create" as given by Webster are:

"1. To bring into being; to form out of nothing; to cause to exist."

To further strengthen this basic definition he gives a quotation as follows:

"In the beginning God created the heaven and the earth."—Gen. 1, 1.

"2. To effect by the agency and under the laws of causation; to be the occasion of; to produce."

To further elucidate that definition he quotes as follows:

"Your eye, in Scotland,
Would create soldiers, and make women fight."
—Shak.

"3. To invest with a new form, office, or character; to constitute; to appoint; to make."

To explain that definition he gives other quotations as follows:

"Arise my knights of the battle, I create you
Companions to our person." —Shak.

"O, rather gracious sir,
Create me to this glory." —Ford.

Of the word "creation" he says:

"1. The act of creating, causing to exist, or constituting; especially the act of bringing the universe or this world into existence."

Then he quotes, to amplify the meaning, as follows:

"Chaos heard his voice; him all his train
Followed in bright succession to behold
Creation and the wonders of the night."
—Milton.

He gives two other subsidiary definitions similar to those used in defining the word create.

The question, then, is in what sense did Mr. Burbank use the words "New Creations" in advertising the plants produced through cross-breeding; and in what sense did his eulogists use them in dilating on his work? Let him answer for himself. As to his eulogists, the extravagant tone of their writings conveys the impression that the highest sense was the one intended.

To my mind, it is beneath the dignity of his work to use the word in any of its collateral meanings; as it is manifestly improper to employ it in its primal sense. He is dealing with natural forces, very largely uncontrollable, and to speak of the products of nature, no matter how assisted by man, in the same sense that a milliner, a tailor, a dressmaker, or any craftsman, speaks of the result of combining dull and senseless material, is to lower the tone of his work. Neither can he, in the eternal fitness of things, speak of it in the sense of a king creating a knight, an official a new office, or a hysterical person creating a scene.

The general impression created by him, and I believe it was his deliberate intention, in his use of the word, is that it was intended to convey the first meaning as given by Webster.

Mr. Wickson's comunication impelled me to look farther into Webster's dictionary, and I came to the word "sophist," which he defines as follows:

"1. One of a class of men who taught eloquence, philosophy and politics in ancient Greece, and who, by their fallacious but plausible reasoning, puzzled inquirers after truth, weakened the faith of the people and drew upon themselves general hatred and contempt."

"2. Hence, a captious or fallacious reasoner."

PATRICK O'MARA.

Jersey City, N. J.

Owing to illness, James H. Veitch of the well-known English firm of that name has relinquished active work. Harry J. Veitch has again resumed the position of managing director of the concern.

In 1905 there were 31 failures among British florists, gardeners and nurserymen, with liabilities amounting to £27,065.

Obituary

William Doogue.

William Doogue, for many years Superintendent of Public Grounds of the City of Boston, Mass., died at his home in Dorchester, Mass., on Friday, November 2, 1906, aged 78 years. Last Spring he was taken down with pneumonia, which, for a man of his years, was a severe tax upon his constitution. His anxiety for the welfare of his department was so great that he did not allow himself sufficient time to become fully restored to health before he again took upon him personal and active management of its affairs. His last illness dated back about three months and was the result of a general breaking up.

The deceased came to this country from Ireland in 1840 in company with his parents, three brothers and four sisters, the family settling in Middletown, Conn., where Mr. Doogue was graduated from the high school in 1843. He was then apprenticed to the firm of George Affleck & Co., of Hartford, who at that time maintained the only greenhouses and nurseries outside of New York and Boston. This nursery contained over fifty acres, a very large establishment for those days. After his term of apprenticeship was over, the old concern passed out of existence, and a new firm was established under the style of Whitmore & Company, into which Mr. Doogue was taken on equal terms on a five years' contract. For a number of years he applied himself also to the study of botany under the celebrated Professor Comstock, of Trinity College, Hartford.

In 1856 Mr. Doogue went to Boston and assumed charge of the estate of the late Charles Copeland, Esq., of Melrose, where he remained some years. Later he established the "Floral Place Greenhouses," and it was here that the florist trade of Boston, now grown to such wonderful proportions, received its first impetus.

In 1876, at the Centennial Exposition in Philadelphia, he laid out the grounds for the Pacific Guano Company, making such a grand display of tropical and sub-tropical plants that the Centennial Commissioners awarded him four medals of bronze, silver and gold.

Two years later, in 1878, Mr. Doogue was appointed to the position of Superintendent of Public Grounds, and it was to his wonderful transformation and development of this department that he largely owes his national and even world-wide reputation. His training and experience had prepared him thoroughly, and when the opportunity was granted the effect was almost magical, and in his twenty-eight years of stewardship he lifted the department from a state of simple nonentity to one of perfection probably unequalled in any part of this broad land.

Mr. Doogue had served as City Forester under 13 mayoralty administrations. From the first year of his superintendence the flower exhibits upon the public garden and in other parts of Boston have surpassed the most beautiful municipal displays in the country. Visitors to the city have been unstinted in their praise of these flower shows. Especially did Mr. Doogue display his fine taste and his skill in special decorations made in compliment to visiting bodies, such as the Masons, the Odd Fellows, the Christian Endeavor Society and the Grand Army of the Republic.

Mr. Doogue was a man whom it was more than a pleasure for any horticulturist to meet, and he was never so busy, notwithstanding the innumerable duties pertaining to his important position, but that he had a minute to spare to discuss any topic relating to floriculture, and was always happy to share his extensive knowledge of the subject by enlightening anyone who saw fit to apply for information.

From his youth up he was closely affiliated with the leading social, beneficial and patriotic Irish societies, and by word and purse furthered their objects. He was liberal, but quiet, even to secretiveness, in his contributions for religious charitable works.

His five surviving children are Mrs. Timothy Mc-

Carthy, Mrs. D. H. Sullivan, Mrs. John O'Connell and Luke J. and William J. Doogue.

The funeral was held on Monday, November 5. A solemn high mass of requiem was celebrated in the Church of the Immaculate Conception, and was attended by an assemblage which filled that great edifice almost to overflowing. Many prominent persons were present. The floral tributes were many and beautiful. The body was taken to Middletown, Conn., where it was interred in St. John's Cemetery, where Mr. Doogue's wife and parents were also buried.

Lewis Ullrich.

Lewis Ullrich, florist, Tiffin, O., died at his home on Monday, October 29, 1906. Death was caused by

The Late William Doogue.

heart disease which first manifested itself about one year ago. About three months ago his serious condition became apparent and everything was done within the scope of medical science to retard the progress of the fatal malady. Seven weeks ago, accompanied by his wife, he went to a sanitarium at Rome City, Ind., in hope of finding relief, but so rapidly grew worse that he was brought home, soon after which he was compelled to take to his bed.

Mr. Ullrich was born at Kerweiler, Bavaria, in 1848, coming to this country in 1850 with his father and mother. They moved backward and forward from New York to Monroeville, O., twice, and finally after leaving New York for the third time, settled in Tiffin, O., in 1862. Here Mr. Ullrich attended the public school, graduating in 1866, and the following year, by an extra effort taking the studies of the junior and senior classes in one year, he succeeded in graduating in 1867 from Heidelberg University, standing second in the class. He then served an apprenticeship in a drug store and afterward practiced as a druggist for 16 years. Mr. Ullrich married in 1871 and raised a family of eight children, four boys and four girls, most of whom were associated with their late father in business.

In 1874 Mr. Ullrich built his first greenhouse, a lean-to, 15x20 feet, adding thereto as the increase of trade demanded, until the Fall of 1882, when he purchased a few acres of land in the suburbs of the city, building thereon a dwelling and two greenhouses, one 25x50 feet, the other 12x50 feet; two years later he built another of the latter size, his establishment at his death comprising 60,000 feet of glass, in which he grew a general line of plants which he sold locally at wholesale. The new Geranium Tiffin, now being introduced to the trade, originated with him.

Mr. Ullrich took an active interest in municipal and county affars. In 1886 he was elected clerk of the courts of Seneca County, O., being re-elected in 1889. After serving in this capacity six years he was appointed by the County Commissioners for a further term of six months. He was also elected to represent his ward as a member of the City Council, and served in this capacity for a number of years.

From boyhood up he was a student of nature, fond of botany, entomology and zoology. At one time he had quite an extensive herbarium, having analysed and classified many hundreds of plants indigenous to Seneca County, O. He also collected about 800 birds and animals, which he himself prepared and stuffed, being a practical taxidermist. He likewise collected, named and classified many thousand specimens of butterflies from all parts of the world.

Mr. Ullrich was a member of several fraternities, among them the Knights of Columbus. He had been actively associated with the Society of American Florists for many years, having been a regular attendant at the meetings. He was also a member of the American Carnation Society. Mr. Ullrich was a candidate for the presidency of the S. A. F. O. H., at the recent St. Louis and Washington conventions, but was unsuccessful on both occasions. He was a man of many parts: a gifted speaker, and was in requisition as a post-prandial orator on florists' festive occasions. He possessed high musical attainments, and was for years leader of St. Joseph's choir, of which church he was a member. For several years he was also leader of St. Mary's choir. He was also one of the most enthusiastic members of the Bruderbund, one of Tiffin's prominent musical societies composed of prominent Germans of the city.

The funeral was held on Friday, November 2, 1906, and was largely attended.

The Late J. L. Dillon.

The post-mortem examination conducted on the body of J. L. Dillon, whose untimely and sad calling away was announced in our columns last week, disclosed that death had been caused by the shock and accident. Mr. Dillon had been in poor health for the last few years, and that undoubtedly was largely responsible for the accident resulting in death. The condition of his health made it desirable that a postmortem be held. It was found he had lost but very little blood, not in any quantity that would have endangered his life.

Mr. Dillon was the son of Patrick and Mary Emerson Dillon and was born in Bloomsburg, July 7, 1851. His father, after being a clerk for the Bloomsburg Irondale Company for 18 years, bought the Dimm farm of 20 acres north of the Normal School, where he engaged in farming and trucking, his son, J. L. Dillon, becoming a partner in the business at the age of 21 years, after attending the public schools of Bloomsburg and the Bloomsburg Literary Institute. Three years later he started in business for himself, building a greenhouse 20x60 feet, the first to be built in Bloomsburg. In 1879 he directed his entire attention to the cultivation of flowers, his business extending to every corner of the United States. His greenhouses now contain about 150,000 feet of glass.

Mr. Dillon's business interests were varied. He became interested in copper mining and was president and owned the controlling interest in the Keystone Bromide Copper Company with mines in Rio Arriba County, New Mexico, 1,000 acres in all. He was sole owner of the Dillon Greenhouse Construction Company, manufacturers of concrete greenhouses, in which a considerable number of men are employed. He was a stockholder of the Bloomsburg National Bank, a director of the Bloomsburg Land Improvement Company, and was actively interested in a number of other business projects.

He always took an active interest in Masonry and was a member of Washington Lodge No. 265, F. & A. M.; Bloomsburg Chapter No. 218, R. A. M.; Mt. Moriah Council No. 10, R and S. Masters, Crusade Commandery No. 12, K. T., and Enoch Grand Lodge of Perfection; Zerubbabel Council P. of J.; Evergreen Chapter of Rose Croix of Caldwell Consistory S. P. R. S. He was also a member of Irem Temple A. O. M. S.

The funeral was held on Friday afternoon, November 2, and the services at the grave, in charge of Washington Lodge 265, with 78 members in attendance, were characterized by all the impressiveness of the Masonic burial ritual. Hundreds of people gathered at the grave to pay their last tribute. The pall-bearers were employees of Mr. Dillon and were: Frank Bundy, Winthrop Bryfogle, George Waver, Frank Zeigler, George Dreisbach and Michael Eyerly The floral tributes were many and beautiful. The employees sent a beautful pillow upon which was the word "Employees." Handsome designs were sent by the Shriners and the Masonic bodies of town. Davis Brothers and a number of out-of-town florists, while many floral tributes came from other friends. The funeral was marked by the presence of a large number of out-of-town florists.

The business will be continued under Mr. Dillon's name by his executors, Louis H. Dillon and Alice D. Furman.

The Late Lewis Ullrich.

The Late R. J. Mendenhall.

The ancestors of the late R. J. Mendenhall emigrated from England with William Penn and lived for many years in Philadelphia. Richard Mendenhall, Mr. Mendenhall's father, was an extensive tanner at Jamestown, N. C., and his mother was a descendant of an old Welsh family which settled in America at an early period.

The Late R. J. Mendenhall.

Richard J. Mendenhall was born in Jamestown, N. C., November 25, 1828. While a boy he acquired a familiarity with farm life and took special delight in the culture of flowers and fruit. The greenhouses with which Mr. Mendenhall afterwards built up such an extensive business were first erected to gratify his love for flowers.

After leaving school Mr. Mendenhall engaged in railroad work in Ohio and North Carolina and his experience in this profession led him to come west. After a year of surveying in Iowa he went to Minneapolis when twenty-eight years old. A New England friend, Cyrus Beede, followed a year later and they became associated in the land, loaning and banking business, under the firm name of Beede & Mendenhall.

In November, 1862, Mr. Mendenhall, became president of the State Bank of Minnesota. This was afterwards merged into the State National Bank of Minnesota, of which Mr. Mendenhall also became president, continuing in this position until 1871. He was also president of the state Savings association, which was forced to suspend in the panic of 1873.

At much personal sacrifice Mr. Mendenhall satisfied nearly all the claims growing out of this failure. In 1862 he was town treasurer and for several years secretary and treasurer of the board of education.

Mr. Mendenhall was married in 1858 to Miss Abby G. Swift, a daughter of Captain Silas Swift of West Falmouth, Mass. Mrs. Mendenhall died six years ago.

About 30 years ago, he entered the florist business in a commercial way, the pioneer in this branch in Minneapolis. His trade grew rapidly and for many years the Mendenhall greenhouses were the leaders, not only in Minneapolis but in the entire Northwest. A large and profitable trade was maintained and some of the finest decorations ever seen in this section were furnished by Mendenhall. His older houses were very expensive and were models of their kind at the time of building. In later years however they became a constant source of expense and in time rotted down and were unprofitable. Orchids, palms and ferns were an especial hobby, and some splendid specimens were grown. A modern range of rose houses was erected and some very choice flowers grown under the direction of able foremen.

Poor health, the death of his estimable wife and the enormous taxes which he had to pay on the property, which had become valuable, induced him to sell the entire greenhouse property including his homestead some 2½ years ago, and the entire place was dismantled and torn down.

He built a house on vacant property across the street and with his wife's faithful sister as housekeeper spent the past two years, gradually growing weaker until the end, which came peacefully.

He was always the kind and courteous gentleman, the quiet, unobtrusive Christian spirit.

C. W. Clark.

Charles Webster Clark, a florist who was born in Brooklyn, May 9, 1861, died Saturday, November 3, 1906, at his home, 62 Rogers avenue, after a month's illness. He was a member of the New York Avenue M. E. Church. He leaves a widow, a son and two daughters.

Awards of S. A. F. Committee on Prize Essays.

Subject: "The Best Method of Marketing the Product of the Plant and Flower Growers."

Judges: C. T. Guenther, F. C. Weber, E. F. Winterson.

First Prize: Author J. Austin Shaw.

This subject presents for our consideration two distinct sections of the wholesale florist business. First, the best method of marketing the product of the wholesale plant growers. To market the plants profitably, they must be well grown, for to "market" means to sell quickly and advantageously. Therefore, the selling of surplus or inferior plants by any plan is hardly worthy of the name "marketing," in its highest sense. Granted then that the plants to be offered are perfect, it will, I think, be conceded that the best method adopted, up to the present, is to dispose of them through the agency of the commercial representatives. Advertising in the trade papers constantly and intelligently is of great advantage. Personal letters to one's customers are very effective; established reputation and a long record of square dealing are of vast importance; but the gentlemanly, persistent, magnetic "drummer" is irresistible. His supreme value is demonstrated by the fact that every successful grower of this country and Europe, in every department of the plant industry, has his accredited representative, whose yearly, or monthly, or weekly visits keep his firm constantly in touch with his clientage.

Much might be said here of the man required for this important work—of his personality, his habits, his character. All these have to do with his efficiency. And more might be said of the firm he represents—its ability to produce perfect products, its careful filling of orders received, its generous recognition of patronage, its quick correction of errors, its tact, its propmtness, its indisputable honesty. But all these must be conceded to arrive at the fulfillment of our contention, that the best method of marketing the product of the wholesale plant grower is through the agency of the commercial traveler.

Here, too, it would not be out of place, the fact being conceded, to consider what manner of man the salesman should be, that he may be best competent to market the goods his grower has to offer. But this subject has been fully covered in the essays of 1905 on the "Ideal Salesman."

Secondly: The marketing of the product of the wholesale flower grower is an entirely different proposition. Here we have to consider a perishable commodity, and at once, we must admit the necessity of rapid disposal as of paramount importance. Ice box preservation is uncertain, restricted and preservative but for a day. Shipments from the grower direct to the retailer have seldom proven profitable because of the retailers' frequent inability to dispose of all the product daily of a greenhouse plant of any dimensions, or from the limit of the supply. Personal soliciting by the grower leaves him subject to the needs or whims of the retailer, and prices fluctuate downward as the day advances and the handling of the flowers deteriorates their quality. I think there is but one opinion possible as to the best method of disposing of or marketing cut flowers, and that is through the medium of the wholesale florist.

For over a quarter of a century the advantages of this system, now so universally popular, have been thoroughly established. Here, centralization of the market facilities for purchase is at once apparent, and a depot is established for shipments, accessible at any hour of the day or night.

The grower, therefore, having assured himself of the honesty and ability as a salesman of his wholesale agent, can add, as prosperity makes it wise, house after house to his base of supply, conscious that there will never come a time when a fair recompense will not reward him for every flower that reaches the market.

The wholesaler is always in touch with his customers by telephone and is ready early and late to wait upon the demands of the great retail public. It is to his interest to maintain honest values, to dispose of his stock as rapidly as he can to the mutual advantage of his grower and himself, and to make such returns as have actually been received, promptly and honestly.

The subject confines one to the finding of "the best method" only. Having demonstrated this, what more can be added, except to advise the grower to exercise business acumen in the selection of his representative, and having decided upon the best wholesaler, to trust him implicitly; and until a better method is discovered or a better wholesaler discovered, stand by both loyally, ship the entire product of his greenhouses daily, avoiding absolutely the dishonesty of "pickled flowers," and so build up the reputation of flowers and method on such a basis that success and permanent prosperity may be assured.

It having been admitted then that the grower may best dispose of his product through the wholesaler, there remains only for our consideration the best methods whereby the wholesaler may complete the expectations of the grower to his profit and satisfaction. The wholesaler must establish a reputation for honesty. He must have the facilities for handling carefully any quantity of stock that reaches him and be prepared for any possible emergency. His ice box must be capacious, his room for display ample, his employees reliable, his personal attention to every detail persistent, his reputation must be unsullied, his returns prompt and absolutely correct, his shipping conveniences abundant. He must not only be ready to meet the local demand but by judicious advertising must induce the confidences of the best trade in adjacent cities and towns. He must create a demand for out-of-town shipments by personal solicitation and correspondence. He must as rapidly as possible in his own city secure orders for a regular daily allotment to be assorted and delivered promptly on arrival, and must hold his trade by every legitimate method, making the satisfaction of these regular customers his first consideration.

Granting all this, the complete "marketing" of the product of the wholesale flower grower is a foregone conclusion and in no other way can the certainty of complete disposal be assured.

The second prize was won by Charles Ingram, and the third by M. B. Faxon. Their papers will appear later.

The Common Sense Carnation Support.

This is a new carnation support which will shortly be put on the market by C. C. Pollworth Company, Milwaukee, Wis. The accompanying illustration shows the character of the support very clearly. It will be observed that the support is formed of a single stake which is grooved at intervals, preventing the rings, which are detachable, from slipping. The anchor at the base holds it firm in the ground, preventing the support from hanging over or turning around when the grower is cultivating the plants on the bench. The manufacturers say that the simplicity of construction, with the least amount of material, will enable them to put the support on the market at a very low figure.

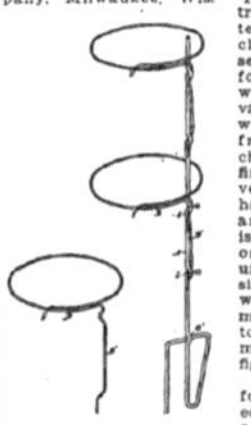

A New Carnation Support.

Messrs. Pollworth inform us that they obtained a patent for this support on February 20, 1906, and are in communication with several manufacturers in regard to the output. The capacity of the machinery at present in operation is about 1,000 a day, but as soon as the machine has been perfected the firm expects to turn out about 10,000 supports daily.

Our readers are requested to bear in mind that the firm is not yet ready to distribute this article, which Messrs. Pollworth believe is an improvement on the supports now generally in use among carnation growers.

Greenhouse Gutters and Posts.

(Read by Judson A. Kramer, Cedar Rapids, Ia., before the Society of Iowa Florists.)

The stability of any structure depends first on the foundation. Posts, the true foundation in greenhouse construction, should have the elements of strength and durability.

Wood is the most common, and I might say, the most unsatisfactory material used, owing to decay caused by excessive changes of heat and moisture. The lasting qualities may be improved by a coating of tar, paint or oil; or, better still, set the post in concrete, care being taken to have same extend a few inches above the soil and rounded off so that water will not accumulate around the posts. Of the different kinds of wood used, red cedar is found to be the most satisfactory. Another objection to wood is large size, which reduces the amount of light.

To meet the increasing demand for better material, iron was introduced and has proven very satisfactory, so much so that iron posts are now almost exclusively used in modern, up-to-date constructions. The posts should always be set in concrete, the same as recommended for wood. A cast iron base may be used, though it is not necessary if care is taken in setting the posts as recommended.

Another material used for posts is cement. This so far as lasting qualities is concerned cannot be excelled. Strength can also be obtained by re-enforcing with iron; but why add cement to the iron above ground at the expense of light?

Gutters in connected houses are an absolute necessity, but for various reasons I would not recommend their use in disconnected, or on the outside walls of connected houses. They may be made of either wood, iron or cement. Wood is the most common, in fact the only material used until recent years. The constant expansion and contraction caused by the changing conditions of heat and moisture soon start decay, loosen the joints and render the gutter unfit for one of the uses for which it was made. Thorough painting is beneficial but not lasting. Again, wood being a nonconductor of heat does not absorb sufficient heat from within the house to keep the gutter free from snow and ice during cold weather.

In connected houses gutters usually serve a three-fold purpose. They are used as a conductor of water, and as a walk in which to work in making repairs, and for sills or the framework on which to build the roof. Great strength is therefore required, as in all methods of construction with one or two exceptions, the gutter is compelled to carry the entire weight and strain of the roof and in order to do this, with the use of wood, large dimensions are required, which is at the expense of light.

In order to overcome the objections made to wood, iron is now largely used and with great success; it being a conductor of heat absorbs sufficient from within the houses to keep the gutter free from snow and ice in the coldest weather. An objection is made to iron on account of the condensation which forms on the inside; this, however, is overcome by the use of an auxiliary gutter, or what might be called a drip conductor, which is placed beneath the gutter proper.

For strength we have in iron either for posts or gutters the maximum with the minimum size part for part, which admits of more light than any other construction. There are many styles or makes of iron gutters, all of which have more or less good points. Where strength is not needed for the support of the roof, a very thin galvanized sheet iron may be used. In this case all that is necessary is iron of sufficient strength to use for a walk in making repairs.

In constructions of this kind brackets are used on the posts. A connecting purlin running a few inches from and parallel with the gutter, forms the framework of which are attached the bars of roof. The gutter is attached to the bars, as in other constructions but does not in any way carry any of the weight or strain of the building.

The use of cement for gutters is comparatively limited. Lasting quality is about its only redeeming feature.

CEMENT BENCHES FOR GREENHOUSES.—Some years ago I erected some concrete or cemen benches as an experiment. I put up temporar wooden benches, using wire mesh the full width o the bench, and put in two inches of concrete, put ting up also wooden forms for posts or upright and running the cement in these forms to suppo the bench. We left cracks or openings in the concret for drainage. We used iron pipe bearers ever four feet, these resting on the cement uprights o posts. The benches are very substantial and du able, lasting for years without needing any repair The only trouble is that if great care and judgme are not used, the plants standing on the bench are easily over-watered or get soggy, and they a not considered as good for planting out stock are the wooden benches or the terra cotta or ti tables. However, a great many cement or concre benches are now being constructed throughout th West, more so than in the East. I have just learne of one large range of glass, six houses, 500 feet lo each, having concrete benches. These are co structed in much the same manner; temporar wooden forms are put up with a false bottom, an light steel frames used, the cement or concrete bein cast or made in slabs or large pieces; three pos are constructed of cement, one on the back edg one in front and one in the middle, thus making very substantial construction. For ordinary width table, say three to 3 1-3 feet, 1½ inch thickness w be plenty, but for the wider tables, two inches thic ness is preferable. This construction of bench ne not necessarily interfere with any piping unde neath the tables. As lumber is getting scarcer a higher in price from year to year, either concre or tile and other material of light endurance w necessarily have to be used, and no doubt a nu ber of inventions will be brought out by the nece city.—H. A. Siebrecht, in Rural New Yorker.

NEW JERSEY FLORICULTURAL SOCIETY.—Orchids and chrysanthemums were the promine features at the monthly meeting of this society the second instant. Of the first, Lager & Hurr staged a table of cypripediums and cattleyas, a John N. May some of his specialties of pompo The Fall show was the topic of the evening a the reports from various sources promised a m successful and interesting exhibition in the new h of the Woman's Club at East Orange. While tra ed chrysanthemum plants and big blooms will there, the pumpkin contest, for the prize given a local dealer, bids fair to furnish the most amu ment. Additional prizes were announced from Pe Henderson & Company, J. M. Thorburn & Co pany, Vaughan's Seed Store, Charles H. Totty, F. Kelsey and George Smith. J. B. D.

EXHIBITIONS

Boston, Mass.

The chrysanthemum show of the Massachusetts Horticultural Society, which was held on Friday, Saturday, and Sunday last although a fine exhibition and well arranged was not nearly equal to the former shows of like kind given by the society. That there is a lack of interest in growing chrysanthemums for exhibition purposes is evident, for although there were many blooms at this exhibition the majority of them were of a rather common grade of flowers, and hardly what would have been worth while bringing into an exhibition hall a few years ago. That the season was against the growers was very evident, especially in the plant exhibits, for there was not a plant in the hall but would have shown better a week hence. The exhibition was a very successful one, however, and called forth a large attendance, especially on Sunday.

Plants.

As usual, the main hall was devoted to the plant exhibits and the lecture hall to the cut blooms. Among the most noticeable tables in the hall was a large collection of single varieties of chrysanthemums exhibited by John Ash, gardener to Miss E. J. Clark, Pomfret, Conn. This collection was awarded a silver medal and was considered the most attractive feature in the hall. Some of the finer varieties in the collection were Kitty Bourne, Miss A. Holden, Florence Robinson, Sir George Bullough, a very striking yellow, Miss Mary Anderson of fine apple blossom shade, Stella, a pure white, and Edith Pagham, a fine dark pink.

Cut Blooms.

William A. Riggs was awarded a first class certificate of merit for arrangement of a magnificent vase of over fifty large blooms of chrysanthemums. A first class certificate was awarded to Chas. H. Totty, Madison, N. J., for new white sport from Mrs. Duckham.

Honorable mentions were given to H. A. Jahn for carnations No. 1 and No. 2; to William Sim, for vase of new violet, sport from Princess of Wales; to F. R. Pierson Company, for new fern; to Peter B. Robb, for seedling Cattleya Louise; to F. W. Fletcher & Company, for Ficus altissima; to E. O. Orpet, for seedling cattleyas and lælias; to Julius Roehrs Company for Tillandsia Duvalliana, and for new Begonia rex The Marquis.

Fine vases of Wellesley roses were exhibited by the Waban Rose Conservatories and by W. H. Elliott. Mr. Elliott also had a magnificent vase of Richmond and the Waban Conservatories a vase of American Beauty.

F. R. Pierson Company exhibited two fine vases of Winsor carnation one of which had been on exhibition for the three previous days at the Tarrytown show. This carnation showed up well, and was admired by all. Peter Fisher exhibited a vase of carnation Beacon, one of Evangeline, and one of White Perfection.

Chrysanthemum Mrs. Westray Ladd.
Grower, E. A. Stroud, Overbrook, Pa. Certificated by C. S. A.

Fine displays of dahlias were made by George H. Walker, Wm. C. Winter, and N. Allen Lindsay. Displays of plants were made by Edward McMulkin, R. & J. Farquhar & Company, Lager & Hurrell, Summit, N. J.; Julius Roehrs Company, Rutherford, N. J.; and by C. D. Sias, the latter showing Begonia Gloire de Lorraine in excellent shape.

A display of hardy conifers in tubs was made by R. & J. Farquhar & Company.

In the competition classes for chrysanthemum plants the exhibitors were J. S. Bailey (J. Nilen, gardener) who captured five first prizes; E. J. Mitton (J. Lawson, gardener), who won seconds; Geo. F. Fabyan (Jas. Stuart, gardener), who captured one first; Mrs. Lester Leland, who had one first and W. H. Elliott who succeeded in winning several second, third and fourth prizes.

In the groups of flowering and foliage plants Wm. Whitman (M. Sullivan, gardener), was first; Edward McMulkin, second; and Sidney Hoffman, third. In the display of orchids arranged for effect Mrs. J. L. Gardner (Wm. Thatcher, gardener), was first, and Edward McMulkin, second.

In the cut bloom classes for twenty-five flowers an excellent lot was exhibited by Thos. Proctor, gardener to R. W. Paterson, which captured first prize; Peter B. Robb being second, and Wm. Whitman third.

The dinner table decorations, which were a new feature at this show, called out quite a competition there being in all seven exhibitors. The judges were three society ladies and more or less criticism was heard on their decisions. The prize winners were first, Sidney Hoffman; second, J. J. Casey; third, Houghton & Clark; while the exhibit of G. A. Severy & Company was highly commended.

J. W. DUNCAN.

Madison, N. J.

The eleventh annual flower show of the Morris County Gardeners and Florists' Society was held on Thursday and Friday, November 1 and 2, in the Assembly Rooms, Madison, N. J. This was a very pretty exhibition, though not so large in specimen cut flowers of chrysanthemums as has been the rule for several years past. The fact of A. Herrington, superintendent for Mr. H. McK. Twombley, and Wm. Duckham, superintendent for Mr. D. Willis James, not entering in the classes for cut blooms, left out two of the largest exhibitors at this annual show, and the absence of their flowers from the exhibition tables was very apparent. It seems rather unfortunate that these two well-known growers had to refrain from exhibiting at their local show, but we presume there are good and sufficient reasons why this was done.

The arrangement of the exhibits throughout the hall was very creditable, the center space being occupied by a group of miscellaneous foliage plants and single chrysanthemums, while on the stage were a group of ferns and foliage plants, with specimen blooms of chrysanthemums freely interspersed. These two groups were put up by Mr. Duckham and Mr. Herrington, respectively, for exhibition purposes only.

Chas. H. Totty staged a number of cut blooms of chrysanthemums, varieties to be introduced in 1907. Besides receiving a certificate of merit for the collection, six of the varieties were each awarded a special certificate. These were W. Duckham, white; Miss Miriam Hankey, a beautiful pink variety; Mrs. Henry Barnes, a large, bronze-gold flower; Mrs. George Hunt, Mrs. A. T. Miller, white; and A. L. Stevens, yellow.

In the competition for specimen cut flowers the principal varieties seen among the prize winners were Beatrice May, white; W. Duckham, pink; F. S. Vallis, Major Bonnaffon, yellow; Merza, white. In the classes where flowers were staged with short stems the varieties most conspicuous were Glenview, bronze; Ch. Montigny, yellow; Mrs. F. F. Thompson, blush white; Valerie Greenham, rose pink; Mrs. W. Duckham, yellow; Merstham Crimson, Mme. G. Rivol, yellow; Nellie Pockett, white; Lady Hopetoun, pink; Donald McLeod, bronze; Harrison Dick, bronze yellow; General Hutton, yellow; and Viola, pink. It will be seen that the novelties of 1906 have not superseded to any extent varieties introduced in previous years.

The judges of the exhibition were F. Heeremans, A. H. Wingett and A. J. Loveless, all of Lenox, Mass. Their decisions were as follows:

Chrysanthemum Cut Blooms.

For 36 flowers in 6 varieties, R. Vince, gardener to Mr. R. O. Foote, first, no second being awarded. For 18 blooms in 6 varieties, James Fraser, gardener to Mr. O. H. Kahn, first with Cheltoni, F. A. Cobbold, Mrs. C. B. Page, a blush white, F. S. Vallis, Merza, and a large bronze variety; John Downing, gardener to Brooklawn Farms, second. For 12 blooms, dissimilar, R. Vince, first; James Fraser, second. Ten blooms any yellow variety, F. L. Moore, Chatham, N. J., was the winner with Major Bonnaffon.

The Stumpp & Walter prizes for 10 flowers any pink variety went to R. Vince and James Fraser, respectively. Mr. Vince also capeured the prize for 24 blooms in 24 distinct varieties. Mr. Fraser was first for 12 flowers, dissimilar, also for 6 flowers, any pink variety, and second for a vase of flowers with foliage arranged for effect. J. Downing was second for 12 varieties. H. Vyse took first for 6 flowers, dissimilar, J. Heeremans, gardener to Mr. A. H. Whitney, being second. Mr. Heeremans was also second for 6 flowers pink, and first for 6 flowers white, the second going to A. R. Kennedy. H. B. Vyse won first for 6 yellow, A. L. Caparn, gardener to Dr. Leslie Ward, second. A. R. Kennedy was first for 6 flowers any color but pink, H. B. Vyse being second.

Chrysanthemum Ongawa.
Growers, Nathan Smith & Son. Certificated by C. S. A.

The special prize offered by F. R. Pierson Company, Tarrytown, N. Y. for 6 blooms of the variety Glenview, was won by R. Vince; J. Heeremans, second. Mr. Vince also was first for 6 blooms 1905 introductions, and 6 blooms of 1906 introductions, Peter Duff, Orange, N. J., being second. E. Regan, gardener to Mr. L. A. Thebaud, was the winner for a vase of blooms with foliage arranged for effect. John N. May, Summit, N. J., captured first prize for display of pompom chrysanthemums; C. H. Totty second. For 10 blooms any white variety, Mr. Totty, first; Wm. Muhlmichel, second.

Roses.

The rose classes were better filled than has been the rule for several years past, and the general quality of the flowers exhibited was of a superior order. For the best vase of 25 blooms Richmond, C. H. Totty captured the first prize; M. Muhlmichel, second; L. B. Coddington, third. Best 18 American Beauty, L. A. Noe first; L. M. Noe, second; Henry Hentz, third. Twenty-five Bridesmaid, H. A. Neuner, first; Henry Hentz, Jr., second; D. Falconer, third. Twenty-five Bride L. A. Noe, first; D. Falconer, second; W. G. Badgley, third. Twelve Bride E. C. McDaniel, grower to J. H. Wagner, first; L. V. Badgley, second. Six Bridesmaid, C. H. Totty first. Six Bride, J. Heeremans, first; C. H. Totty second.

The W. E. Marshall & Company's prizes offered for American Beauty were won by A. R. Kennedy and Wm. Duckham in the order named; and the same firm's prizes for tea roses by A. R. Kennedy and A. Brown, gardener to Mr. G. McMiller, respectively.

Carnations.

Th silver cup offered by R. & J. Farquhar & Co., Boston, Mass., for two vases of carnations each containing 25 blooms, was captured by Wm. Duckham with a vase each of Robert Craig and White Lawson; R. Vince taking second honors. Mr. Vince won the Vaughan's Seed Store prize for 25 blooms of carnations, mixed varieties. A. H. Secker prizes for 25 carnations were captured by John N. May and R. H. Schultz, respectively. R. Vince was first for 3 vases any 3 varieties, with Robert Craig, Fiancee and Enchantress. For the best vase of 12 blooms any one variety, John Fraser took first; R. Vince, second; and C. H. Totty, third, the winning variety being Robert Craig. For best vase of carnation Victory, prizes offered by Guttman & Weber, C. H. Totty was first, and Heeremans second.

Peter Duff was first for the best bunch of single violets; R. Vince second.

Plants.

The Pierson U-Bar Company's prizes, offered for the best group of chrysanthemums with foliage plants, on a space not more than 50 feet, were won by J. Heeremans, J. Downing and H. B. Vyse, respectively; R. Vince also receiving a special prize in this class. For specimen chrysanthemum in flower, P. Duff took first, he also capturing the first prize for 3 specimen plants in pots not larger than 12 inches, and for 12 plants in flower, in 12 varieties, R. Vince being second in the latter class. J. Heeremans was first for 6 varities, no second being awarded.

Vegetables and Fruits.

In the class for vegetable and fruits, the A. T. Boddington prize was won by W. Duckham. Peter Henderson & Company's prizes were won by J. Heeremans and A. F. Caparn. The prize offered by Weeber & Don was captured by H. B. Vyse. W. Duckham was first for 6 heads of celery, R. Vince being second, and E. Reagan receiving the special prize.

Certificates Awarded.

Lager & Hurrell of Summit, N. J., staged a beautiful collection of orchids, for which they received a certificate of merit, also special certificate of merit for Cattleyo labiata alba and Oncidium alba. A certificate of merit was granted to W. Duckham for his arrangement of decorative plants, and for a specimen plant of a Pandanus Sanderi. C. H. Totty also received a certificate of merit for single chrysanthemums as a general collection, and special certificates of merit for the following varieties: Linton, Nancy Perkins, Crown Jewel, Belle of Weybridge and Amber Queen. A certificate of merit was awarded Henry Hentz, Jr. for a vase of Killarney roses, a similar award being given to L. M. Noe for a vase of Meteor; and to R. Vince for a specimen plant of Adiantum Farleyense. For specimen Boston fern Frank Esheran got a certificate of merit; as did A. T. Boddington ,seedsman, New York, for cosmos Lady Lenox.

F. R. Pierson Company of Tarrytown, N. Y., staged a vase of their carnation, Windsor ,not for competition, which was very much admired.

H. Weber & Sons Company, Oakland, Md., showed a bunch of their new pink carnation Mabelle, which attracted much attention.

Philadelphia.

The annual exhibition of the Pennsylvania Horticultural Society has been holding this week in Horticultural Hall, Philadelphia. The doors were opened to the public at 6 p. m. Tuesday evening, the exhibition continuing until to-day, Saturday. The many and varied exhibits seen at this show this year fully verified the fact that the interest in plants, particularly chrysanthemums, is not waning in this city. Secretary David Rust, with his corps of assistants, arranged the material very tastefully, and deviated somewhat from the style of arrangement seen here in former years. The center of the main hall was occupied by six magnificent specimen ferns, some of them measuring six to seven feet across, and around these were grouped the specimen plants of chrysanthemums shown for competition. The stage was occupied entirely by an exhibit of new and choice decorative plants from Henry A. Dreer. Among this collection were noticed a choice lot of marantas in variety; Ficus Parcelli, variegated; Adiantum album striatum, a very pretty fern with white variegation; aralias in many varieties; alocasias, heliconias and Asplenium nidus albus.

Lager & Hurrell of Summit, N. J., and Julius Roehrs Company of Carlton Hill both made exhibits of orchids, but not so extensive as we have previously seen from these firms at the Philadelphia exhibition. The foyer was made very attractive with specimen bay trees and ferns; especially noticeable was a plant each of Cibotium Schiedei and Gleichenia dichotoma. The staircase leading to the main hall was lined on each side with large vases of chrysanthemums, cut blooms, these being such as were entered in classes calling for 12 and 20 flowers to the vase.

First Prize Chrysanthemum Mizpah, Boston Show. Grower, James Stuart.

Miscellaneous Exhibits.

In the lower hall Richard Vincent, Jr., & Son, White Marsh, Md., and Thos. Meehan & Sons had each a display of hardy chrysanthemums. The H. F. Michell Company made a magnificent showing of everything pertaining to the trade. Their exhibits seemed to cover every requisite that a florist, market gardener or private gardener would require, and were very tastefully arranged. Henry A. Dreer also had a large exhibit on this floor, showing not only everything required for the trade in the way of seeds, bulbs, mushroom spawn, etc., but also a full line of implements and tools. Henry Waterer, seedsman, was likewise an exhibitor here. Among the plant exhibitors on this floor were W. K. Harris, who showed Bougainvillea W. K. Harris, the variegated one; Saintpaulias in full bloom, Begonia Gloire de Lorraine, and Begonia hybrida Winter Cheer. This begonia has somewhat the habit of B. Gloire de Lorraine, only it is much heavier and stronger; the flowers are red, measure about 1½ inches across, and seem to be produced freely. Robert Craig & Sons showed some well grown oranges, ferns, cyclamen, and some nicely branched plants of Ficus pandurata.

Chrysanthemum Plants.

It is to the chrysanthemum, however, that the most interest is supposed to be directed at an exhibition at this time of the year. To return to the exhibits of chrysanthemum plants, we noted that for plants in 14-inch pots, 6 varieties, the winning kinds were G. W. Childs, Minerva, Morton F. Plant, Georgiana Pitcher, Mrs. H. Weeks and W. Duckham. These were grown by J. Hurley, gardener to Mr. J. W. Paul, the second prize going to Gordon Smirl, gardener to Mr. J. F. Sinnot, and third to J. McCleary, gardener to Mrs. Walker. For the best two plants, two varieties, in not over 10-inch pots, J. Hurley again was first, with the varieties Wm. Duckham and Mutual Friend, the second prize going to S. Batchelor, gardener to Mr. C. B. Newbold. Gordon Smirl captured the first prize for a specimen plant, white, with the variety Honesty, J. Hurley being second. Mr. Hurley was also the winner for the best yellow, with Minerva; and second in the class for specimen plant, any other color, S. Batchelor taking the first with the variety Wm. Duckman. For 6 plants, yellow, in not over six inch pots, J. McCleary was first with Col. Appleton; S. Batchelor, second. For six plants, red, the winning variety was Merstham, grown by S. Batchelor; J. T. Whittaker, gardener to Robert Le Boutillier, second. For the best 6 plants, white, one variety, Merza was the winner. These were exhibited by T. J. Holland, gardener to Mr. H. B. Rosegarten; J. T. Whittaker being second. S. Batchelor was first for 6 plants, pink, with the variety Wm. Duckham; Wm. Kleinheinz, gardener to Mr. P. A. B. Widener, second. S. Batchelor was also first for 12 plants in 2 varieties with Cheltoni and Beatrice May, and first for 6 plants, any color, with Colonel D. Appleton, also first for 12 plants, 12 varieties, the second prize going to Mr. Whittaker and Mr. Kleinhens. J. Hurley was first for 4 plants, Japanese, with the varieties G. W. Childs, Mrs. H. Weeks, Dr. Enguehard and Golden Age; Mr. Smirl being second. Mr. Hurley also won first for 3 plants, 3 varieties, with Viviand-Morel, Dr. Enguehard and Wm. Duckham; Mr. Smirl second. Mr. Hurley was also first for specimen of Mrs. Frank Thomson; J. McCleary second; he also winning for 4 plants, any 4 varieties; G. Smirl second. The exhibits of plants were very fine throughout, and the judges had quite a task in selecting the winners, as the competition was in many cases very close indeed.

Chrysanthemum Cut Blooms.

In the cut flower chrysanthemum classes the competition was also very keen, and it was remarkable to note how well the older varieties are keeping up with the standard of the new ones. There does not seem to have been much change among the prize winning varieties this year over last. In the class for 60 blooms of 12 distinct varieties the winning kinds were Lady Hopetoun, Mrs. G. Beech, W. R. Church, Viola, W. Duckham, Rivol, J. H. Silsbury, a large yellow; Merza, Mrs. F. F. Thompson, Viviand-Morel, Mrs. Henry Robinson and Col. D. Appleton shown by J. McCleary. For 36 blooms in 6 varieties the same exhibitor won with Dr. Enguehard, General Hutton, S. T. Wright, Valerie Greenham, Timothy Eaton and Colonel Appleton. For 12 blooms, one variety, any color, W. Kleinheinz was first with Gen. Hutton, E. G. Hill, second. Mr. Kleinheinz also captured the first for 12 blooms, 12 distinct varieties, T. J. Holland being second. For the best variety not disseminated, E. e. Hill was first with Mlle. E. Chebanne, a large pink flower of a pleasing shade, but rather open in the center. Chas. Hickey, gardener to Mr. H. W. Martin, was first for 6 blooms, white, with Timothy Eaton; J. McCleary second for 6 blooms of Mrs. Frank Thomson, the second first with the variety May Seddon; J. McCleary, second. For 6 blooms, yellow, A. G. Williams, gardener to M. S. T. Bodine, took first with F. S. Vallis. For 6 blooms, yellow, J. Coleman, gardener to Mr. W. Lippincott, was first with Colonel D. Appleton; Thos. Gaynor second. W. Kleinheinz was first for 6 blooms of Mrs. Frank Thomson, the second going to J. McCleary. Among the other prize winners in these classes were S. Batchelor, C. Hickey and A. Morrison.

Decorative Plants.

The competition in the decorative plant classes was quite keen, many beautiful specimens being exhibited. J. Hobson, gardener to Mr. E. A. Schmidt, was the winner in the class for six foliage plants, palms not admissible, with very well grown specimens of Anthurium crystallinum, Phormium variegata, Phyllanthus vivosum, Croton Dayspring, Panax Victoria and Dieffenbachia picta. For 6 foliage plants, 6 species, J. Thatcher was the winner with fine plants of Dracæna Godseffiana, Maranta virginalis major, Carludovica humilis, Adiantum decorum and Croton superba; Wm. Robertson, gardener to Mr. J. W. Pepper, taking second. For the best specimen plant John Thatcher was first with Dracæna Godseffiana. Thos. Long, gardener to G. W. Childs Drexel, was first, as usual, for specimen ferns. Other winners for palms and decorative plants were J. Hurley, S. Batchelor, J. Hobson and J. McCleary.

The judges on plants were J. W. Colflesh, James Verner, Chester Davis and Wm. Graham; on flowers, A. B. Cartledge, A. B. Scott, S. S. Pennock, C. Eisele and H. B. Surman; on fruits, John G. Gardner, P. Pedersen and Wm. Warner Harper; and on vegetables, W. Atlee Burpee, Wm. F. Dreer, Rich. C. Kaighn, John Hobson and J. Cheston Morris, M. D.

The remainder of the report will appear in next week's issue.

Bay Shore, N. Y.

The flower show of the United Horticultural Societies, held here November 1 and 2, was a great success. The display of chrysanthemums was as usual the center of attraction. The finest came from the country seat of S. T. Peters, of which William McCullom is gardener. Another fine exhibit from the Peters place was a fine collection of stove and greenhouse plants. Mr. Peters' place was the heaviest winner, taking thirty-six awards. The Bossert-Timmerman-Wagstaff places also made a fine showing. The Central Islip Hospital exhibit of vegetables was as usual a feature.

The Boddington prize for collection of vegetables was won by McCollum; as were the Totty prize for six blooms chrysanthemums, and the Stumpp & Walter prize, for 12 blooms of chrysanthemums.

The Peter Henderson & Company prize, for largest collection of vegetables, was also won by Mr. Peters.

The star exhibit was a grand specimen trained chrysanthemum, Mrs. Tranter; it measured 5 feet high and 7 feet in diameter, showing 350 well-opened flowers. It was awarded a certificate of merit, and was exhibited by Mr. Edwin Thorne, gardener John Tobin. In the class for 12 blooms the silver cup was won by S. T. Peters with a dozen Peter Kay. The largest bloom in the show was Beatrice May, shown by Mr. Peters. For 6 white blooms, L. Bossert was first with Mrs. Tranter; S. T. Peters, second, with Mrs. Henry Robinson. For 6 pink S. T. Peters, first; L. Bossert second, both showing W. Duckham. Six yellow, first, S. T. Harbeck, second, S. T. Peters, both with Colonel D. Appleton. Six crimson, first, S. T. Peters, with Mrs. Partridge; second, Louis Bossert, with H. J. Jones. Six any other color, first, S. T. Peters; second, Louis Bossert. Six Glenview, first, Col. A. Wagstaff, second, S. T. Peters. Six Mrs. Dunne, first, S. T. Peters.

The carnation classes were well filled, Victory

beating Robert Craig. Mr. Kalbfleisch, gardener R. Camerson, showed some fine roses, winning with La France, Bride, Richmond, and Killarney.

A certificate of merit was awarded to C. H. Totty for a white sport of W. Duckham.

S. T. Peters was the largest winner with 24 firsts and 15 seconds; L. Bossert, 18 firsts and 10 seconds; E. Thorne, 8 firsts and 1 second; E. P. Strong, 8 firsts and 2 seconds; Col. A. Wagstaff, 7 firsts and 10 seconds; J. E. Timmerman, 8 firsts and 6 seconds; C. A. Schieren, 5 firsts and 1 second.

Chicago.

The show is the success of the day. Although the weather conditions on the opening day were not perfect, the arduous duties performed by all the contributory elements were amply rewarded by a most beautiful presentation of horticultural attractions and encouraged by a generous attendance. It was unfortunate that there was not more time between the closing of the horse show and the opening of the flower show, which from a society view are fast becoming close rivals in Chicago. In the short time, however, between Sunday morning and Tuesday noon a wonderful transformation was wrought. The following is a list of the early prize winners.

Chrysanthemums—Cut Flowers.

ONE HUNDRED BLOOMS.

White.—First, Nathan Smith & Son, Adrian, Mich.; second, E. G. Hill Company, Richmond, Ind.; third, Bassett & Washburn, Chicago.

Pink.—First, E. G. Hill Company; second, N. Smith & Son; third, Poehlmann Brothers, Chicago.

Yellow.—First, Poehlmann Brothers; second, Bassett & Washburn; third, E. G. Hill Company.

Any other color.—Wietor Brothers, Chicago.

SIX BLOOMS, ONE VARIETY.

White.—First, Mr. D. Willis James (Wm. Duckham, gardener); second, E. G. Hill Company; third, Nathan Smith & Son.

Yellow, not darker than Major Bonnaffon.—First, D. Willis James; second, E. G. Hill Company; third, N. Smith & Son.

Yellow, darker than Major Bonnaffon.—First, Poehlmann Brothers; second, Smith & Son; third, D. Willis James.

Pink, lighter than Viviand-Morel.—First, D. Willis James; second, Hill Company; third, Smith & Son.

Pink, not lighter than Viviand-Morel.—First, D. Willis James; second, Smith & Son; third, H. Schmidt, Oxford, O.

Red.—First, Hill Company; second; Smith & Son.

Bronze.—First, D. Willis James; second, Smith & Son; third, R. H. Allerton.

Any other color.—First, D. Willis James; second, Smith & Son; third, Hill Company.

Twelve Blooms, 12 varieties.—First, R. D. Foote, Morristown, N. J.; second, Smith & Son; third, R. H. Allerton.

Collection, named varieties, one bloom each, 40 varieties.—First, C. H. Totty, Madison, N. J.; second, Hill Company; third, Smith & Son.

Collection, named varieties, one bloom each, 40 varieties, shown on mossed boards.—First, D. Willis James; second, Hill Company; third, Smith & Son.

Collection, 12 varieties, shown on mossed boards.—First, R. D. Foote; second, Hill Company; third, Smith & Son.

Display of Pompons.—E. G. Hill Company.

Plants—Chrysanthemums.

Specimen white.—First, John J. Mitchell; second, Vaughan's Seed Store; third, M. A. Ryerson.

Specimen yellow.—First, M. A. Ryerson; second; Vaughan's Seed Store.

Specimen pink.—First, John J. Mitchell; second, Vaughan's Seed Store; third, M. A. Ryerson.

Specimen, any other color.—First, Vaughan's Seed Store; second, John J. Mitchell; third, M. A. Ryerson.

Specimen single.—First, Vaughan's Seed Store; second, Martin A. Ryerson.

Specimen anemone.—Vaughan's Seed Store.

Three Standards.—First, Vaughan's Seed Store; second, A. S. Trude.

Five Standards, 5 varieties.—First, Vaughan's Seed Store; second, A. S. Trude.

Five specimen, 5 varieties.—First, Vaughan's Seed Store; second, A. S. Trude; third, M. A. Ryerson.

Five specimen, single varieties.—Second, Vaughan's Seed Store.

Five specimen pompons.—Vaughan's Seed Store.

Twenty-five grown to single stem.—Vaughan's Seed Store.

Plants—Miscellaneous.

Most interesting grafted specimen plant of any kind.—Vaughan's Seed Store.

Ten Palms.—George Wittbold Company.

One Palm.—George Wittbold Company.

Boston Fern or Sports.—First, C. A. Samuelson; second, Vaughan's Seed Store.

Basket Asparagus Sprengeri.—First, Anton Then; second, Vaughan's Seed Store.

Ten Araucarias.—First, Vaughan's Seed Store; second, A. McAdams.

Ten Begonia Gloire de Lorraine.—J. A. Peterson, Cincinnati, O.

Best Flowering plant, chrysanthemums excluded.—Second, J. A. Peterson, Cincinnati.

Six Boston ferns or sports.—First, C. A. Samuelson; second, Vaughan's Seed Store.

Group of foliage plants, 50 square feet.—First, Vaughan's Seed Store; second, John J. Mitchell.

Group of palms and decorative plants, 100 square feet.—First, George Wittbold Company; second, E. G. Uihlein.

Five plants flowering tobacco.—Second, M. A. Ryerson.

Best filled fern dish.—First, E. G. Uihlein; second, C. Frauenfelder Company.

Best basket or hamper of plants.—First, Frauenfelder Company; second, A. McAdams.

Display of cut greens.—First, Albert Amling; second, Poehlmann Brothers.

Best orchid plant in bloom.—E. G. Uihlein.

Orchids.

Collection cut blooms.—E. G. Uihlein.

Roses.

25 American Beauty.—First, Poehlmann Brothers; second, Bassett & Washburn; third, Peter Reinberg.

FORTY BLOOMS.

Liberty or Richmond.—First, Peter Reinberg; second, Poehlmann Brothers; third, Bassett & Washburn.

Golden Gate or Uncle John.—Poehlmann Brothers.

Mme. Abel Chatenay.—First, Poehlmann Brothers; second, Peter Reinberg.

Bride.—First, Bassett & Washburn; second, Poehlmann Brothers.

Bridesmaid.—Poehlmann Brothers.

Killarney.—Poehlmann Brothers.

Any other variety.—First, Poehlmann Brothers; second, Peter Reinberg.

100 BLOOMS.

American Beauty.—First, Poehlmann Brothers; second, Bassett & Washburn; third, Peter Reinberg; fourth, Wm. Dittman, New Castle, Ind.

Liberty or Richmond.—First, Peter Reinberg; second, Poehlmann Brothers; third, Wietor Brothers.

Golden Gate or Uncle John.—First, Poehlmann Brothers; second, Wietor Brothers.

Bride.—First, Poehlmann Brothers; second, Benthey-Coatsworth Company; third, Wietor Brothers.

Bridesmaid.—First, Benthey-Coatsworth Company; second; Poehlmann Brothers.

Mme. Abel Chatenay.—First, Peter Reinberg; second, Poehlmann Brothers; third, Wietor Brothers.

Any other variety.—First, Benthey-Coatsworth Company; second, Poehlmann Brothers; third, Peter Reinberg.

Twelve blooms, new rose never exhibited in this country previous to this season.—First, Poehlmann Brothers; second, E. G. Hill Company; third, Bassett & Washburn.

Twenty-five blooms, any variety not in commerce.—E. G. Hill Company.

(Balance of report next week.)

New York.

The annual chrysanthemum show of the American Institute was held in Berkeley Lyceum on November 7, 8 and 9. The first impression of the show was a keen disappointment, but a closer examination brought out much that was of great interest, and lack of room no doubt prevented competition in many of the classes, particularly in foliage and flowering plants, the absence of which deprived the cut flowers of their appropriate setting.

Chrysanthemums—Cut Blooms.

The schedule was generous, and there was keen competition in some of the classes. There were two entries in the class for 50 blooms, one variety. Ernest Ashley, Allentown, Pa. won first with Major Bonnaffon, the E. G. Hill Company, Richmond, Ind., being second with a pink variety. The prizes offered were $30 and $20. The blooms in competition were below the average. There were three competitors in the class calling for 30 varieties, one bloom of each: John J. McNicoll, of Glen Cove, N. Y., won first with a superb lot of blooms; Wm. Turner, Oceanic, N. J., was second, in which lot was the largest flower in the show, an immense yellow, F. S. Vallis. There were three entries in the class for 20 varieties, one of each: Alex. Mackenzie captured first; John J. McNicoll, second. Eight clever growers tried to win in the class calling for 10 varieties, one of each, and a grand exhibit was seen. Wm. Turner landed first prize with Nellie Pockett, Mrs. Henry Partridge, Montigny, Wm. Duckham, Mrs. George Heaume, Mrs. J. Dunne, Godfrey's Pride, Merza, Mary Ann Pockett and Cheltoni; Alex. Mackenzie was awarded second prize. For ten blooms, any one variety, Wm. Hastings was first, with Beatrice May; N. Butterbach, second. For ten yellow, one variety, Wm. Turner took first with Cheltoni; Alex. Mackenzie, second. Ten bronze, one variety, Alex. Mackenzie, first with Brutus; Thos. Aitchison, second. In the class for 10 pink, Wm. Hastings won second. For 10 blooms, any variety in commerce, Chas. H. Totty, second. For 10 varieties, one of each, R. Vince was first; J. S. Howarth, second. Eighteen in six varieties, Wm. Turner captured first with Cheltoni, Nellie Pockett, M. F. Plant, Ben Wells, Mrs. J. Dunne, and Guy Hamilton; John McNicoll was second.

Chas. H. Totty, Madison, N. J., made an interesting display of novelties in chrysanthemums, among which are some very promising sorts, Winter Cheer being the most artistic. In the class for 6 blooms, white, any new variety, Mr. Totty landed first with White Duckham; and in the class calling for 6 pink, any new variety, George Hale was first with immense blooms of an unnamed variety, a seedling of his own raising which promises to be in all collections of the future. Some very good blooms were put up in the classes calling for 6 of one variety. Wm. Turner was first in the class for crimson with Mersham Red; the same exhibitor won first in bronze with Ethel Fitzroy; Alex. Mackenzie, second. For six white named, Wm. Turner was first with Merza; George Hale, second. For six yellow, Wm. Turner, first with Col. D. Appleton. J. S. Howarth also won a first prize with the same kind. In the class for six blooms, white, Wm. Turner was first with Nellie Pockett; Alex. Mackenzie, second. For six pink, Wm. Turner, first, with Wm. Duckman; Chas. H. Totty, second. For six yellow, any variety, Wm. Turner was again first with Colonel Appleton; Mackenzie, second. For six reflexed yellow, John McNicoll was first; Wm. Hastings, second. The latter exhibitor won first for six white reflexed; and George Hale won first prize for five blooms, any variety in commerce with Cheltoni. For six anemone bronze and six anemone pink, John McNicoll won out. N. Butterbach's six splendid Garza captured first for white. In the class for six incurved pink Wm. Turner was first with Wm. Duckman; George Hale, second. Six bronze, George Hale, first; with Kate Bromhead. Six reflexed crimson, Hale was again first with H. J. Jones. In the class for six reflexed pink John McNicoll took first with Leila Filkins; George Hale, second.

Thomas Meehan & Sons, Philadelphia, were awarded a special prize for hardy chrysanthemums. John N. May, Summit, N. J., took first for a grand collection of lovely pompons. Chas. H. Rice captured first for collection of chrysanthemums grown in the open, and the soil on the Palisades certainly deserves praise for this lot of beautiful flowers. C. H. Totty won first for a vase of elegant single chrysanthemums; R. Vince being second. Oscar Carlson, Fairfield, Conn., was awarded second for collection of pompons.

Chrysanthemum Plants.

The best features of the show were the remargably well grown specimen plants exhibited by Peter Duff, Orange, N. J. His plant of Lady Lydia bore 265 elegant flowers and was one of the best specimens seen in New York City for some years. It easily won first in the class for white. Mr. Duff was also first for bush yellow with Mrs. Hooper Pearson; for standard yellow with Cheltoni; for bush anemone with Garza, for bush pink with A. J. Balfour; for standard white and special prize for standard anemone Garza; for bronze with Brutus. He was also first for 6 singles in 6-inch pots with elegant Merza. They were a grand lot and ought to revive this almost lost art. Alex. Mackenzie won seconds in almost all the foregoing classes, and first for bush plants as grown for marketing and for 12 plants grown to single stem. John McNicoll captured seconds in the above two classes, also for bush plants white, pink, and yellow.

Carnations.

C. W. Ward, of the Cottage Gardens Company, Queens, exhibited some magnificent blooms of that grand white, Alma Ward, on 2½ foot stems; Mrs. C. W. Ward, a most impressive shade of pink on sturdy long stems; Mrs. Tom Harvey and Beacon, intensified reds. Each of these four varieties was awarded a certificate. Mr. Ward also displayed vases of well grown Lieutenant Peary, Evangeline, Aurora, and Robert Craig.

The F. R. Pierson Company, Tarrytown, N. Y., staged a vase of well grown blooms of their new pink variety Winsor.

In the classes calling for three varieties, 25 of each, R. Vince, Morristown, N. J, took first with Robert Craig, Fiancee, and Enchantress. G. T. Schuneman, Baldwins, L. I., won second.

Miscellaneous.

Messrs Lager & Hurrell, Summit, N. J, arranged an interesting group of orchids in flower among which were some fine dark Cattleya labiata, and C. labiata alba. Fred Varden, gardener to Mr. Seth A. Borden, Fall River, Mass.; was awarded a special prize for 12 sprays of Cattleya labiata containing 44 immense blooms.

G. T. Schundman took first for 100 violets; and R. Vince first for 100 single violets. The latter exhibitor also showed 3 vases of well grown sweet peas.

Thos. Aitchison had a group of begonia Gloire de Lorraine. A. J. Manda captured first with a fine specimen Rhapis humilis, and J. P. Sorenson, Stamford, Conn., showed a well trained Cissus discolor.

Roses.

In the rose classes, L. A. Noe, Madison, N. J, took first for 25 Bride, 25 Perle des Jardins, 25 Bridesmaid, 25 Lberty, 12 American Beauty, and second for 25 Killarney. R. Vince was first for a dozen Perle, second for 25 Richmond, N. Butterbach won second for 25 Bridesmaid. The latter exhibitor also showed some well grown Golden Gate. John N. May, was awarded first for 25 Wellesley.

The judges were: L. A. Martin, Peter Duff, Jas. Ballantyne, and John Heeremans. There was quite a gathering of noted gardeners from the surrounding villages and towns, and it seems inexplicable that here in the greatest city on earth we cannot among other things also have the greatest flower show on earth.

J. IVERA DONLAN.

American Carnation Society.

Variety Registered.

By Stevenson Bros., Govanstown, Md.

DEBUTANTE, a cross between Mrs. T. W. Lawson and Queen Louise. The color is a soft pink, similar to that of Mrs. Frances Joost but brighter; very fragrant and most prolific. A very early variety and a grand keeper. The flowers are borne on stiff yet graceful stems, and have a calyx that allows the full expansion of the flower without bursting.

ALBERT M. HERR, Secretary.

Red Bank, N. J.

The ninth annual exhibition of the Monmouth County (N. J.) Horticultural Society was held at Red Bank, October 31 and November 1, and was a great success. The blooms shown by Wm. Turner were enormous. That exhibitor was successful in the class calling for twenty-five varieties, among his best flowers being T. Carrington, Henry Barnes, Salter, Merstham Red, Montigny, Mrs. Duckham, D. Willis James, Merza, Donald McLeod, Col. D. Appleton, Mme. G. Heaume, Cheltoni, Ethel Fitzroy, Mrs. H. Partridge, Ben Wells, Mrs. J. E. Dunne, Wm. Duckham, F. S. Vallis, Beatrice May, F. Cobbold, Loveliness, Nelly Pockett, Mrs. W. Knox, H. J. Jones, and Morton F. Plant. H. A. Kettel was second in this class.

Mr. Turner was again the winner in the class for thirty-six varieties. For twelve blooms, twelve varieties, Geo. H. Hale, superintendent of the E. D. Adams estate, was first, Anton Bauer second. Mr. Hale also captured the first prize in the class for eighteen blooms, six varieties, N. Butterbach being second. Wm. Turner was the winner in the classes for six blooms of yellow, white, pink, crimson, bronze and any other color, Geo. Hale being second. The latter exhibitor was also the winner for the best twenty-five blooms arranged for effect, Turner second.

In the chrysanthemum groups A. Bauer was first, Butterbach, second; and for three specimen bush plants Hale was first, Kettel, second. Hale was also the winner for one bush plant, Wm. Dowlen, second. In the class for anemone varieties, Hale was first, followed by Kettel. The last named exhibitor won on group of foliage plants, Butterbach being second. Mr. Butterbach was also successful in the class for specimen palms. Turner won on foliage plants, Hale, second, and Butterbach beat Hale on six specimen ferns, distinct varieties.

In the rose classes Kennedy won on American Beauty, Hale, second. The other prizes for roses were won by Butterbach and Kennedy. Turner, Kettel, Kennedy and Tierney divided the carnation prizes. There were, as usual, fine exhibits of fruits and vegetables.

W. W. Kennedy showed a fine seedling chrysanthemum, Garza X T. Carrington, which will also be exhibited at Chicago this week.

Charles H. Totty, Madison, N. J., exhibited some very fine blooms of the white sport of William Duckham, which received the society's certificate of merit.

Lager & Hurrell, Summit, N. J., had a grand display of orchids; they also received a certificate of merit, as did William Kennedy for his new seedling chrysanthemum.

Glen Cove, L. I.

The second annual exhibition of the Nassau County (N. Y.) Horticultural Society, which opened October 31, more than duplicated the success of the first show, given a year ago. The number of exhibits was larger and the varieties as fine or finer. Exhibits were entered from as far away as Lenox, Mass., the Lenox exhibits taking a number of prizes. There was a wonderful display of orchids exhibited, not for competition, by Lager & Hurrell, of Summit, N. J. Another "not for competition" exhibit was made by James Hollaway, gardener for the Pratt estate.

The judges found it no easy task to decide on the merits of the universally excellent exhibits. The special prizes were awarded as follows:

The "Troy" cup, presented for the best collection of outdoor roses, was awarded to L. I. Forbes, gardener for R. J. Preston, of Jericho. This cup must be won three times to be held. Mr. Forbes won it from Mr. Hollaway, the winner of last year.

The Ladew silver cup presented by Mrs. L. B. W. Ladew, went to Mr. Harrison, superintendent at Elsinore. W. Eccles, gardener for Mortimer Schiff, won the Mrs. Percy Chubb cup for the best collection of carnations. The special prizes presented by Vaughan's Seed Store for the best six celery plants went to J. Hennessey, G. H. Morgan, of Lenox, Mass., and to J. F. Johnston, gardener at the Dana estate. Mrs. Paul Dana's special prizes went to Alexander Mackenzie, the Chubb gardener, and to J. F. Johnston. The Weeber & Don prize for the six best varieties of chrysanthemums went to Mr. Mackenzie. Mrs. J. K. O. Sherwood's special prize of $10 went to Felix Mense for violets.

Rickards Brothers' special prizes for best foliage plants went to Mrs. Ladew's and J. R. Maxwell's exhibits. The F. R. Pierson special prize for best twelve Glenview chrysanthemums went to A. Mackenzie.

C. F. Bertanzel won the special prize for the best collection of carnations shown by a commercial grower. Mr. Bertanzel also won first prize for the best floral design, the second going to F. G. Boulon. Mr. Boulon got the first prize for a bridal bouquet.

In the regular classes A. Mackenzie, the Chubb gardener, swept several of the classes, especially in the chrysanthemums. J. F. Johnston, was a winner in a number of classes in both flowers and vegetables. Peters & Son, of Hempstead, won in a number of the carnation and some other classes. The commercial exhibits which won the most prizes were shown by F. Boulon & Son, Peters & Son, J. Hennessey, and Jacob Bracher, of East Williston.

CHRYSANTHEMUM SOCIETY OF AMERICA.

The annual meeting of the society was held in Chicago this week in connection with the joint exhibition of this organization and the Horticultural Society of Chicago. There was a large attendance. President William Duckham occupied the chair and presented the following address:

President Duckham's Address.

Gentlemen and Fellow Members of the Chrysanthemum Society of America:

It affords me great pleasure to greet you and bid you welcome. When last you assembled in annual session I had gone across the ocean and had to leave a written word to represent me in my absence. It is now my pleasure and privilege to meet with you, to see your interest and join in your enthusiasm, to counsel with you as to the future, and to take record of the past, with its trials and triumphs.

I must begin my adress by a very sincere expression of thanks for the honor you have done me in a re-election to the office of president. I wish I might count myself worthy of this endorsement. There are perhaps few pleasures in life superior to that of a kind recognition from the men who work with one in the business of life. I fear that I must reckon to friendliness, kindliness and generosity rather than to judgment the honors you have been pleased to confer on me.

Chicago's Horticultural Development.

And now when I come to such message as I have to deliver let me begin by expressing my sincere pleasure that we are meeting in this magnificent city, abounding in vigorous, developing life. I deem it truly an ideal city for our exhibition and meeting. Nowhere else in America, I may truly say, are there such quantities of material on which to draw. We who hail from the eastern part of the country are amazed at the strides and progress made in horticulture in and about Chicago; and no little of this success is due the members of the Horticultural Society of Chicago. We are happy, thrice happy, to meet in such an atmosphere of success. It is good to be among people who are doing things, who are going ahead by leaps and bounds. But great as is your progress, I must own it is not great enough in some ways. The ultimate basis, in America at least, of all great progress must be the commercial basis; you have that basis magnificently laid.

Four years have passed since we last met in Chicago, and the commercial progress hereabout since then is perfectly staggering. I had an opportunity of viewing some of it at the time of the St. Louis Fair, for I passed through your great city at that time. There seems no end to your development, to the founding of new firms and to the enlargement of old ones.

But I am not quite sure that the development of a higher culture of the chrysanthemum has quite kept step with the commercial development. We have seen a fine development in culture undoubtedly, but whether it is as large as it ought to be is not quite clear in my mind. We must do better, or in a real sense we are not doing all that might be done.

A Good Suggestion.

However that may be, it is perfectly certain that the growth of the society in membership is disappointing. I suggested in my message last year that personal solicitation was the surest method of increasing membership. I am still of that opinion. There are far too many growers, both amateur and professional, who are not in this society. We need a little more judicious "buttonholing." Will you let me make another suggestion? Would it not be possible for us to impose on our admirable committees at Chicago, Cincinnati, Philadelphia, New York and Boston the slight additional burden of increasing our membership list? I hope you will not consider the suggestion indelicate.

Well, we are here, and perhaps our chief business after all is to take an account of stock and ask where we stand in relation to the real progress —the development of newer varieties. The newer ones are obviously a great improvement on their predecessors. We are going forward, every one of you will concede; especially does this apply to exhibition varieties. But we are still too much dependent upon Europe and Australia. Furthermore, it seems to me that private gardeners are too much dependent on their commercial friends, and are indifferent, more or less, where or how the newer varieties are obtained. Yet each year how eagerly some of us are looking for striking novelties over those of the preceding year.

Progress in America.

Our progress in America, as far as new varieties is concerned, is almost wholly made by these great houses who have laid such broad and deep commercial foundations. Such men as Smith, Hill, May, and, in the last few years, Totty, have all done much to raise the standard and create a love for the flower we at this time represent.

It is fully time for the private gardeners to have a bit bigger try at hybridizing and raising new varieties. It is the most fascinating of all works, and once entered upon is sure to be an increasing delight and a practical enterprise. Somebody may smile and point at me and ask me to take my own medicine. Well, perhaps I may have a try. Meantime I commend and urge this upon others who may have better opportunities in some ways than are mine.

Seen in Scotland.

In the message sent you last year I ventured to say that perhaps during my absence I might see something worthy of comment this year. I had the great pleasure of attending the Edinburgh (Scotland) show, and I must confess I was completely overwhelmed by it, both by the magnificent blooms shown and the attendance. There were over 70,000 paid admissions in three days. Think of that, and be humble! Nay, think of that, and lay plans day and night to rouse our people to a similar interest! What could we accomplish if we had a constituency like that?

Perhaps I may say a word about the varieties that reigned supreme at Edinburgh. They were Elsie Fulton, Mrs. Barclay, J. A. Silsbury, Mrs. T. W. Vallis. Are you not surprised? The finest flower I have ever seen was a Mrs. T. W. Vallis. You know how poor a performer it is here. I saw also the variety Lady Conyers, which, as you know, is small and hard under our conditions, and after several unsuccessful trials many have discarded it. But this same variety at Edinburgh was wonderful in size, delicate in color and with long trailing petals. It seems impossible, but it is true, that the Scotch climate appears to suit the flower, for many varieties that with us are usually dull and unattractive were brilliant, showing at once that climatic conditions play no small or unimportant part in the culture of the chrysanthemum.

What Germany and France are Doing.

One word more and I shall cease to tax your patience. The Germans and French have both gone into the growing of the chrysanthemum with great energy, especially the latter; and many fine varieties can be traced to the handiwork of the French hybridist. Therefore, it behooves us to be up and doing. Nay, I would say it is our duty to see to it that we raise such varieties as we can give to the world.

That our society is very grateful to the Horticultural Society of Chicago for the courteous and generous treatment received you will all agree, and I feel sure I voice the sentiments of all members of the National Society in expressing our thanks and appreciation for the privilege and honor of meeting here.

I thank you, gentlemen, for your kind attention and I wish you increasing success.

Work of Committees.

CHICAGO, October 27.—Wm. Loisseau Rosseau, pink, exhibited by the E. G. Hill Company, Richmond, Ind., scored 82 points, exhibition scale.

CINCINNATI, November 3.—Ongawa, bronze, Japanese incurved, exhibited by Nathan Smith & Son, Adrian, Mich.; scored 88 points, exhibition scale. DAVID FRASER, Secretary.

Chrysanthemum Mrs. Westray Ladd.

The new seedling yellow chrysanthemum Mrs. Westray Ladd, of which an illustration is herewith given, originated at Overbrook Gardens (E. A. Stroud proprietor), Overbrook, Pa., season of 1905. Parentage, Cinna × Colonel D. Appleton. The first bloom was cut October 15, 1906, from first crown bud.

This chrysanthemum was certificated by the Philadelphia committee of the C. S. A., on Saturday October 37, 1906, scoring 87 points, commercial scale.

Chrysanthemum Ongawa.

The accompanying illustration shows a bloom of Nathan Smith & Son's new seedling chrysanthemum Ongawa. The firm says the variety is "a dwarf grower, not exceeding two feet in height; very similar in form to the seed parent, W. R. Church, and in color is intermediate between this variety and General Hutton, the pollen parent, being a golden chamois."

The variety was shown before the Cincinnati committee of the C. S. A. , on Saturday, November 3, and was certificated, scoring 88 points, exhibition scale.

(See Illustrations page 567.)

FOR THE RETAILER

[All questions relating to the Retail Trade will be cheerfully answered in this column. We solicit good, sharp photographs of made-up work, decorations, store interiors, etc., for reproduction here.—Ed. F. E.]

Funeral Designs.

Most wonderful achievements have been made by plant and flower growers in some lines of culture during the past few years, but we appear to be living in an age when even wonders seem to be looked upon as part of the day's work and pass unnoticed. There was a time, and not many years ago, when such flowers as Lilium Harrisii could only be had at one time of the year; when, in fact, it was well nigh impossible to procure any kind of flower suitable for the loose flat bunch. Now L. Harrisii can be had almost any day in the year, and can readily be considered the most valuable flower to keep in stock where there is a funeral flower trade.

It often occurs that time is an important factor in the making of a design, and that many people would order a floral tribute did they know at what short notice it could be obtained. In an emergency from five to ten minutes is all that is required to arrange a presentable bunch of lilies or chrysanthemums. And never hesitate to chop up a dollar fern if by doing so you add many times its value to your work or your trade.

There is in some quarters a disposition to substitute loose flowers for designs at funerals, and while the sending of flowers in any manner is a most commendable characteristic of human thought and consideration, still loose flowers are more or less a troublesome feature at funerals, and the sender's intent loses itself in general aggravation. On the other hand, the loose bunch can be made one of the most beautiful features, in fact, next to the wreath it is the most appropriate and the prettiest design. With an abundance of splendid materials at present procurable there is ample opportunity for fine work in this line, and the justly increasing aversion to set or incongruous designs obviated or overcome. There is still in many quarters a feeling of dislike for colored flowers at funerals, yet, on the other hand, vast quantities of American Beauty roses are sent by the most prominent stores and when, as is often the case, a cluster of white chrysanthemums or lilies is added to the roses, they constitute a most impressive effect.

Standing Wreath
Artist, J. J. Foley, New York

In the making of a loose bunch of such flowers as chrysanthemums or Lilium Harrisii the greens used should be such as will materially add to the formation as well as the beauty of the design. In this way large quantities of defective palms can be cut up and employed most profitably. There is too much stiffness and the general appearance of artificiality about the average leaves of Cycas revoluta to use them in conjunction with palms; but there is a great deal of graceful beauty about the leaves of Areca lutescens, Cocas Weddeliana or palms of that class. We don't wish to be understood as recommending the unnecessary and injudicious cutting up of good salable stock, but there is an unreasonable aversion to thus using up deformed or unsalable plants, which not alone injures the sale of plants in general, but becomes an all-round burden.

If as is often the case a pair or three palm leaves are wanted, try a few tips of small leaved ivy, in a reversible cluster, at the ribbon bow. In the matter of many wreaths seen nowadays there is a woeful lack of formation. The desire to make them appear large and loose results only in their losing all semblance to wreaths; they appear more like flat placques. Often a 30-inch frame is made up in a way that not six inches of an open center is left. This is particularly the case in galax wreaths. Such work only gives expression to a most ridiculous idea of what constitutes this most classical of all designs.

At a time like the present when roses can be had comparatively cheap, it is best for your future and to the greatest satisfaction of your customers to recommend wreaths of roses. Very fine wreaths can be made with two or three hundred roses (we hope to be able to show one next week) and we consider it good policy to once in a while give customers the full benefit of the market. Very seldom the occasion presents itself as it does just now, and it is an opportune time to encourage trade for the forthcoming season by the exercise of a little generosity.

The design illustrated this week is one made by our old friend, John J. Foley, New York. It was ordered by the Letter Carriers' Association of New York City for the funeral of their late postmaster. It was photographed under extreme difficulties, consequently little justice was done the design in that respect. It was an immense wreath on a stand, and its imposing size, the material and manner of arrangement, gave the greatest satisfaction to a large humber. This design, the so-called standing wreath, has for many years been a popular one in New York in cases where large and showy effects are desired. Considering it from the classical standpoint, it is somewhat troublesome and meaningless; nevertheless it is very far superior to the vacant chair, clock, gates ajar, or cradle style of things, and where as in the case of the association or "chipped in" for tribute, when it is necessary to make an impressive display, this design is one of the best to recommend. J. IVERA DONLAN.

Crepe Paper for Florists' Use.

1. A heavily sized crepe paper used largely by florists for wrapping around pots of flowers on account of its waterproof quality, being in fact crepe paper and known as such among dealers in manufacturers of crepe paper, held to be dutiable under the specific provision therefor in paragraph 397, tariff act of 1897.

2. An eo nomine provision in the tariff law applies to any article that falls properly under such designation, even if the article were not introduced into commerce until after the passage of the tariff law.—Pickhardt v. Merritt (132 U. S., 257) and G. A. 5535 (T. D. 24905) cited and followed.

In the matter of protests of Wm. Fiegel et al. against the assessment of duty by the collector of customs at the port of New York, October 30, 1906, before Board 2, General Appraisers.

Opinion by Fischer, General Appraiser: The merchandise here in question is paper, which was returned by the appraising officer as crepe paper, and upon which duty was assessed at the rate of 5 cents per pound and 15 per cent. ad valorem under the specific provision therefor in paragraph 397 of the tariff act of 1897. It is claimed to be dutiable properly at 25 per cent. under paragraph 402 of said act as paper not specially provided for.

At the hearings on protest 186641 much testimony was taken on behalf both of the Government and the importers, but after a full consideration of the same we are unable to reach a conclusion favorable to the contention which the importers have endeavored to maintain. In the first place, the paper is undoubtedly a crepe paper in the ordinary acceptation of the term—that is, it has the crinkled surface peculiar to the fabric from which it takes its name. This is shown in the record and by the sample admitted in evidence. (Exhibit 1.) The only apparent difference is that the paper under protest is the heavier of the two, but the testimony of some of the Government witnesses that crepe paper is made from stock of different weights, and that it is not always made from tissue renders this circumstance immaterial. It was furthermore shown that this paper had been offered for sale in this country under the name "Krep-Papier," the German equivalent for crepe paper, and all the Government witnesses, who are manufacturers of and dealers in crepe paper and eminently well qualified to say, agreed that the article is undoubtedly a crepe paper.

Briefly, the argument is importer's that it should not be classified as crepe paper, because it was not on the market at the time of the passage of the tariff act of 1897, and because it is waterproof and is so invoiced to him. These circumstances are not decisive. Even if crepe paper be a commercial designation, a point which the importer utterly failed to prove, then this article is clearly dutiable as such, notwithstanding that it was not introduced into commerce until after the passage of the present law. As was said in G. A. 5535 (T. D. 24905)—

It is, now, however, well settled that a tariff provision for an article designating it by a particular name operates upon any goods imported which are commercially known by that name, although said designation had originally a much narrower signification. * * *

Again, it was held in Pickhardt vs. Merritt (132 U. S., 257) that—

The fact that at the date of an act imposing duties goods of a certain kind had not been manufactured, does not withdraw them from the clause to which they belong when the language of the statute clearly and fairly includes them, but it is sufficient if it so includes them according to commercial understanding.

If, on the other hand, crepe as a term applied to paper is merely a descriptive word, then this article is crepe paper beyond a doubt. The testimony indicated above and an inspection of the samples are conclusive as to this point.

The importer attempted to distinguish between his paper and an illustrative exhibit of a crepe paper which he put in evidence by saying that the "fluffy effect" was the distinctive feature of crepe paper and that his paper did not possess it, while the other did, but a glance at the exhibits is sufficient to show the falsity of this assertion. Another claim of the importer is that the paper is waterproof and is so known; and to substantiate this he called a witness, who testified that the paper is used to wrap around pots of flowers, and that it is known as waterproof crepe paper. He also stated that if an order for waterproof paper came to him he would furnish the paper here in question. He likewise admitted that that was the only kind of waterproof paper he had.

Waterproof, as applied to paper, is certainly a descriptive term, for this Board has had before it protests covering many different varieties of paper all of which were waterproof, and the fact that the paper in question has more sizing than usual, thus adding to its water-resisting qualities, gives the importer no right to arrogate to his product as a commercial designation the word "waterproof."

We find that the mercandise in question is crepe paper and we hold that it is dutiable properly as assessed. Protests 186641 and 204105, 205,924, and 205980, which were submitted for decision on the same testimony, are overruled and the decision of the collector affirmed in each case.

New York.

The Week's News.

Reed & Keller of 122 West Twenty-fifth street are putting a new device on the market that will be greeted with much satisfaction by all retail florists. This device, which is patented, is one of Mr. Reed's inventions, and is made for the purpose of holding together cycas leaves when being made into a bunch for funeral or other purposes. All florists who have ever had to tie together two or three cycas leaves for this purpose know the difficulty there is in getting the leaves fastened so that they will stay; but this little arrangement, which is made of wire, simplifies the operation to such an extent that two or three leaves can be put together in an instant. The process is done by simply laying the leaves, with their stems, in a little groove, and pulling over a wire clasp. They are fixed in place firmly, yet without breaking the tissue of the stem, and no amount of handling can make the leaves come loose. We predict for this little device an enormous sale as soon as the florists of the country are made aware of its usefulness.

Mr. Reed is also working on another device which is intended for the hanging of pot plants. By its use plants can be hung at any desired angle, or in any position. As this pot hanger is not yet complete, we cannot at this time give any details about it, but we are assured when it is ready for market it will be found a great improvement over all other similar devices for displaying pot plants.

Lambros Mulinus, 301 Columbus avenue, has opened a branch store at 503 Fifth avenue, the store known as number 5 in that building, which is at the corner of Forty-second street and Fifth avenue. Mr. Mulinus is one of the progressive Greek florists of the city. He is known in the wholesale district as one of the largest buyers, and also as one who always wants the best there is on the market, and never fails to get it.

The express companies have seemingly got it in for the cut flower growers, and do not care how much they harass them. The American Express Company has issued an order to its agents in the violet growing sections that no shipping is to be done on Sundays, so that from now on, no violets will come down the river between 6 p. m. on Saturday evening and 11 a. m. on Monday morning. Any special orders to be filled on Sunday will have to be brought down by a messenger in the future. This is a very costly method of getting violets into the city.

Julius Lang, who for many years conducted a wholesale store at 53 West Thirtieth street, has retired from business.

A. J. Guttman, left on Wednesday night for Chicago, to attend the chrysanthemum show there.

During the night following the close of the exhibition of the Nassau County Horticultural Society held at Glen Cove, L. I., last week, thieves broke into the hall and stole many of the flowers, fruits and plants. A watchman had been provided to look after the exhibits through the night; but he could give no explanation as to how the thieves had got away with the booty. The officers of the society are conducting a strict investigation.

Fred Schruver, recently foreman for Poehlmann Brothers, Morton Grove, Ill., has taken a position as manager for Komitsch & Junge, Secaucus, N. J., at their newly acquired property, which has been rented from Wiegand Brothers, and which contains 50,000 feet of glass.

The annual chrysanthemum show of the American Institute was held this week in the Berkeley Lyceum building, West Forty-fourth street.

A. L. Young & Company, 54 West Twenty-eighth street, have recently added considerable floor space to their store, and are receiving regularly a nice line of all seasonable cut flowers.

The sympathy of the trade will go out to August Millang, florist, Long Island City, whose wife died this week, the interment being on Tuesday, November 6.

John G. Fleuti, formerly with A. Mead, Greenwich, Conn., has just returned from a vacation spent in Europe.

J. F. Huss, Hartford, Conn., was a visitor in town this week.

William Tricker is now located at Lyndonville, Vt., with Theo. N. Vail.

Peters & Sons, carnation growers, Hempstead, L. I., won six prizes in the carnation classes at the recent exhibition of the Nassau County Horticultural Society, held at Glen Cove, L. I., last week.

The next meeting of the New York Florists' Club will be held Monday evening, November 12 in the club's rooms, corner Twenty-third street and Eighth avenue. This is to be a ladies' night, and special preparations for their entertainment are being made by Mr. Nugent, chairman of the house committee. Among the musical talent provided is a glee club of twenty-five members from a prominent Scotch Society in Brooklyn. The nominating committee will report at this meeting, and there will be an exhibit of chrysanthemums. Let every member attend and make this the largest meeting in the history of the club.

ORANGE, CONN.—Watson S. Woodruff, of S. D. Woodruff & Sons, was elected on November 6 to represent his town in the General Assembly by one of the largest majorities ever given a candidate. His vote in his own district was one of the most remarkable, from the fact that out of a total vote cast in the district of 155 he received all but four.

BELLEVILLE, ILL.—Mrs. Susanna Kaiser, wife of Joseph Kaiser, a florist, died Friday, October 26, 1906, at her home, 721 East Seventh street, aged about 50 years. She is survived by her husband and several sons and daughters.

CLASSIFIED ADVERTISEMENTS

CASH WITH ORDER.

The columns under this heading are reserved for advertisements of Stock for Sale, Stock Wanted, Help Wanted, Situations Wanted or other Wants; also of Greenhouse, Land, Second-Hand Materials, etc., For Sale or Rent.

Our charge is 10 cts. per line (7 words to the line), set solid, without display. No advt. accepted for less than thirty cents.

Display advertisements in these columns, 15 cents per line; count 12 lines agate to the inch.

[If replies to Help Wanted, Situation Wanted, or other advertisements are to be addressed care of this office, advertisers add 10 cents to cover expense of forwarding.]

Copy must reach New York office 12 o'clock Wednesday to secure insertion in issue of following Saturday.

Advertisers in the Western States desiring to advertise under initials, may save time by having their answer directed care our Chicago office at 127 E. Berwyn Ave.

SITUATIONS WANTED

SITUATION WANTED—By a young man, 19 years old; steady, sober and industrious; can give good references. Address, W. B., care The Florists' Exchange.

SITUATION WANTED—By landscape gardener and florist, single man, 16 years' experience; references. Address, W. M., care The Florists' Exchange.

SITUATION WANTED—By florist, single, 30 years of age. German, good designer and grower, also landscape gardener. Address, W. care The Florists' Exchange.

SITUATION WANTED—By industrious man, experienced in general greenhouse work. Please state particulars. Address, W. L., care The Florists' Exchange.

SITUATION WANTED—As assistant on private place. American, single, aged 30 years. References. State particulars in letter. Address, W. J., care The Florists' Exchange.

SITUATION WANTED—Single, competent grower of roses, carnations and chrysanthemums. Take charge 60,000 ft. glass. Address, Florist, 21 University Place, New York City.

SITUATION WANTED—By all-around grower of general florist stock and landscape gardener. 20 years' experience, good references, 11 years in last place. Private place preferred. Address, W. N., care The Florists' Exchange.

SITUATION WANTED—As assistant park or cemetery superintendent by experienced engineer and landscape gardener with long practical experience; aged 30. Address, W. K., care The Florists' Exchange.

SITUATION WANTED—By good grower and propagator of roses, carnations, mums and general stock. 15 years' experience; good references. State full particulars. Address Buckeye State, care The Florists' Exchange.

SITUATION WANTED—Gardener, single, 32, reliable, speaks French and German, has first-class European references, seeks position on gentleman's place. Address, E. Hanzel, 170 East 80th street, New York City.

SITUATION WANTED—As foreman, by up-to-date, experienced, all-around florist; 38 years of age, 23 years' experience; fair wages expected. References. Address, J. G. F., 18 Dey St., New York City.

SITUATION WANTED—By German, 37 years old, single, good grower of roses, carnations and general stock. Also good maker-up. Wages, $15.00 per week. Address, W. R., care The Florists' Exchange.

POSITION WANTED

By expert decorator in retail store where ability to handle the most select trade will be appreciated.

State wages and particulars.

Address: T. S.
The Florists' Exchange.

POSITION WANTED

As foreman or manager on up-to-date commercial or private place by first-class florist, designer, landscape gardener and nurseryman. Single, 28 years of age, 15 years good practical experience in all branches of gardening in Germany, England, France, Austria and this country. Best of references. Salary expected, $65.00 per month. Please state particulars in first letter. Address W. A., care The Florists' Exchange.

Mention the Florists' Exchange when writing.

HELP WANTED

WANTED—To take charge of Florist's store, young lady or man, must understand bouquet and design work, also assist with the books, 20 miles from New York City. Good wages to competent person. Address Store, care The Florists' Exchange.

WANTED—At once, night fire-man; Hitching's boilers. Komitsch & Junge, Secaucus, N. J., near Hackensack River.

WANTED—Man for fern, palm and orchid section. Apply to Mr. Bloy, care The Gasser Company, Cleveland, O.

WANTED—Young man experienced in florists' supply business. State particulars; address T. V., care The Florists' Exchange.

WANTED—Man for rose section, references, and salary wanted, in first letter. Apply, Mr. M. Bloy, care The Gasser Company, Cleveland, O.

WANTED—An assistant on commercial florist's place; must understand firing. Apply, A. N. Kinney, West 200th st. & Ft. Washington ave., New York City.

WANTED—An all-around florist for 10,000 ft. commercial glass in general stock. Permanent place for reliable man. C. L. Dole, Lockport, N. Y.

WANTED—Driver, married, German preferred, who can help in greenhouses. For good sober man a steady position. Address, Whitestone, care The Florists' Exchange.

WANTED—Young man to pack and ship, cut flowers and help around greenhouses. State experience, wages, etc. W. K. Partridge, 148 E. Fourth Street, Cincinnati, O.

WANTED—Competent sober man for grafting roses and general greenhouse propagating. Mention references, wages, etc. Steady work. Address, Jackson & Perkins Co., Newark, N. Y.

WANTED—Night fireman who understands steam boilers, etc. Steady position. State experience, salary wanted, and give references. W. K. Partridge, 148 E. Fourth street, Cincinnati, O.

WANTED—Bright young man, aged 25-35, for established florist business. Good position for right man. State experience and salary expected. Chas. H. Fox, 21st & Columbia Avenue, Philadelphia, Pa.

WANTED—Nurseryman and landscape gardener, with general knowledge of pruning and the care of fruit and ornamental stock. State experience and salary expected. The Continental Nurseries, Franklin, Mass.

WANTED—Young man to assist in high-class retail flower store. Must be of good appearance and have good references. State wages, etc. W. K. Partridge, 148 E. Fourth Street, Cincinnati, O.

WANTED—Section man for carnations. Married man preferred, who would be willing to board one or two men. Have five roomed house on place. State wages, etc. W. K. Partridge, 148 E. Fourth Street, Cincinnati, O.

WANTED—General manager with good business ability and a general knowledge of plant and flower production, indoors and out. Some knowledge of nursery and ornamental stock no disadvantage. Working force, 20 to 30 men. A live commercial place in Central Ohio. Good dwelling house. A good position for the right man; middle-aged preferred. Give detailed experience, references and salary wanted in first letter. Address, W. L., care The Florists' Exchange.

SEEDSMAN

capable of taking charge and developing retail department of an established house in a large Eastern city. A good opportunity for a bright up-to-date man. State age, experience, salary required. All communications confidential. Address,

SEEDS, care The Florists' Exchange.

Mention the Florists' Exchange when writing.

WANTED Young man for store work, must be up-to-date in general store work, good maker-up and decorator. Permanent position to sober hustling young man. State age, last position, references and salary expected. Address,

W. R., care Florists' Exchange.

WANTED Young lady in florist's store, must be well up in the business, neat appearance, come well recommended, near New York. Steady place to the right party; can start at once. Address,

W. J., care Florists' Exchange.

GROW MUSHROOMS

If you do not know how, procure that simple but complete and practical book called "How to Grow Mushrooms." The price is ten cents and it can be secured from this office. Special rates will be made to the trade who wish to supply their customers.

THE FLORISTS' EXCHANGE
2 Duane St., New York

Mention the Florists' Exchange when writing.

MISCELLANEOUS WANTS

WANTED TO BUY—Greenhouses to be taken down. State full particulars of same when writing. Address, F. W., care The Florists' Exchange.

WANTED—Tenant, to develop market garden, 26 acres, 5 roomed house, barn, water, trolley, school. Chance for competent man of small means. Floribel Greenhouse, Indiana, Pa.

WANTED—To make arrangement direct with grower, by retail florist, near Washington, D. C., to furnish (500) five hundred pink carnations or more twice a week. Address, M. B., care The Florists' Exchange.

FOR SALE OR RENT

FOR RENT—Florist's store and greenhouse, old established business; 16 x 150; central part Atlantic City, N. J.; hot water heat supplied by city. Address, W. P., care The Florists' Exchange.

FOR SALE—A profitable seed and plant catalogue business, with full equipment and everything needful to carry on the business. A well established trade, which owing to pressure of other business we are willing to sacrifice for much less than its actual value. A moderate amount of capital is all that is necessary. Address, T. X., care The Florists' Exchange.

FOR SALE—A well established florist business, with dwelling houses. Also plenty of outdoor ground in up-to-date condition. Greenhouses are well filled with foliage plants, and the place is in a most desirable location to reach the wholesale New York City trade within a drive of about 30 minutes. It must be seen. Reason for selling: ill health. For particulars communicate with O. V. Zangen, Seedsman, Hoboken, N. J.

FOR RENT—Or to lease at Babylon, L. I., three violet houses, 130 ft. long by 11 ft.; in good repair; also dwelling house, eight rooms, barn, 1 1-4 acre good land, 5,500 violet plants in good condition. An assortment of pots and hot bed sash. A splendid chance for a young man at jobbing and landscape gardening. 10 minutes walk from depot. City water in greenhouses. Application can be made to O. H. House on premises or W. Wincott, Box 500, Babylon, L. I., N. Y.

TO LET

Florist Establishment consisting of nine greenhouses, heated by hot water, containing about 10,000 square feet of glass; sheds, barn and dwelling, in Long Island City, within one hour's drive of the wholesale markets of the City of New York. For further particulars address **Box R. Y., Florists' Exchange**

Mention the Florists' Exchange when writing.

FOR SALE

A well equipped place, consisting of seven greenhouses, over 30,000 feet of glass, a nine roomed house, barn, stock, etc., and eight acres of land. This is a decided bargain and a rare opportunity. For particulars address

S. S. SKIDELSKY,
824 N. 24th St., Philadelphia, Pa.

Mention the Florists' Exchange when writing.

For Sale; Price Reasonable

IT WILL PAY YOU TO INVESTIGATE

Only green-house in city of 3500, Southern Wisconsin. Six houses. One acre of beautifully situated land on Rock River; near business center; 300 feet river front, boat house.

Good House and Barn; good supply carnations, roses, chrysanthemums, ferns, palms fruits, etc. Coal House with 70 ton coal. Owner too old. Splendid business worked up for young man; rigid investigation desired. Address at once,

A. M. WEBB, Fort Atkinson, Wis.

STOCK FOR SALE

ASPARAGUS PLUMOSUS, strong plants, 2 1-4 in. ready for 3 in., $1.50 per 100, $14.00 per 1000. Cash. Toug & Weeks, Ashtabula, O.

BRENCHLEYENSIS GLADIOLUS, 1st. size, $10.00 per 1000; 2d. size, $8.00 per 1000. Cash with order. Est. Louis Siebrecht, Floral Park, N. Y.

CHRYSANTHEMUMS, stock plants, Polly Rose, Glory of Pacific, Halliday, and Intensity, fine, 50c. per doz.; $3.50 per 100. F. P. Sawyer, Clinton, Mass.

CARNATIONS—Strong, healthy, field-grown plants, extra large, Ethel Crocker and Flora Hill, $5.00 per 100. Cash with order. W. C. Pray & Co., Kinkora, N. J.

ENGLISH PRIZE PANSY PLANTS—I have 10,000 fine plants more than I need. For sale at $3.00 per 1000, cash. Some very odd and beautiful markings among them. Reuben Powell, Florist, White Plains, N. Y.

STOCK FOR SALE

Asparagus Plumosus, strong, bushy plants, ready for shifting. We need the room. $1.75 per 100; $15.00 per 1,000. Sprengeri, $1.25 per 100; $10.00 per 1000. Monadnock Greenhouses, Keene, N. H.

BABY RAMBLER roses, fine dormant stock, $25 per 100. 2 1-2 inch pot plants, extra well rooted $7 per 100, $65 per 1000. Orders booked for delivery now or any time up to late Spring. Samples free. Brown Brothers Co., Rochester, N. Y.

Althea, double, red and white, 3 to 4 ft., 4c.; Berberis Thunbergii, 18 to 20 in., 3c.; 24 to 30 in., 5c.; Clethra Alnifolia, fine, 2 to 3 ft., 5c., Forsythia Viridissima, 2 to 3 ft., 3c.; 3 to 4 ft., 5c.; Tamarix Africana, 4 to 5 ft., 4c.; 5 to 6 ft., 5c.; Privet, 4 to 5 ft., 4c.; 5 to 6 ft., 5c., Virginia Creeper, strong, 3 year, 2c.; Yucca, strong, 2 and 3 years, 4c. Packed free for cash with order. James McColgan, Red Bank, N. J.

FOR SALE

FOR SALE—4 Hitchings hot water expansion tanks. No. 2 high tank Fig. B. of catalogue. All in good condition. F. O. B., $2.00 each. Address, K. D., care The Florists' Exchange.

BOILERS, BOILERS, BOILERS.

SEVERAL good second hand boilers on hand, also new No. 16 Hitchings at reduced cost. Write for list. Wm. H. Lutton, West Side Avenue Station, C. R. R. of N. J., Jersey City, N. J.

FOR SALE

Greenhouse Material milled from Gulf Cypress, to any detail furnished, or our own patterns as desired, cut and spliced ready for erection. Estimates for complete constructions furnished.

V. E. REICH, Brooklyn, N. Y.
1429-1437 Metropolitan Ave.

FOR SALE

BOILERS No. 6 Weathered, round, $60.00. One 11 section Sunray hot water sectional boiler, grate 3 by 3. Price $150.00. 6 Section new Novelty boiler, will heat 100 ft. glass. $140.00. New Henderson boilers; send for price on size wanted.

PIPE Good serviceable second hand. No Junk, with new threads: 2in. 7c.; 1½ in. 6½c.; 1¼ in. 4c.; 1 in. 3c.; 2½ in. 10c.; 3in. 14c.; 4 in. 18c. 4 in. cast iron greenhouse 14c. 3 in. NEW, standard, full lengths 8½c. ft. All kinds of fittings for 4 in. cast iron and all sizes wrought iron.

STOCKS AND DIES New Economy, easy working. No. 1 cuts ¼-¾-1 in. $3.00; No. 2 cuts 1¼-1½-2 ins. $4.00; Armstrong Adjustable No. 2 cuts ¼-1 in. $4.00; No. 3 cuts 1¼-1½-2 ins. $6.50.

PIPE CUTTERS Saunders, No. 1 cuts to 1 in. $1.00; No. 2 cuts to 2 in. $1.30; No. 3 cuts to 3 in. $3.00; No. 4 cuts to 4 in. $4.50.

STILLSON WRENCHES Guaranteed. 12 in., grips 1½ in. $1.10; 18 in. grips 2 in. $1.50; 24 in., grips 2½ in. $2.25; 36 in., grips 3½ in. $4.50.

PIPE VISES Reed's Best Hinged Vise, No. 1 grips 2 in. $1.75; No. 2 grips 4 in. $3.50.

GARDEN HOSE 50 ft. lengths ¾ in. not guaranteed; 4½ guaranteed for light work; 7½, guaranteed for heavy work, 10c. ft.

HOT-BED SASH New; Gulf Cypress, 3 ft x 6 ft. 75c.; glazed complete $1.60 up. VENTILATORS; all sizes made to order. Second hand sash glazed $1.00 and $1.25, good condition.

GLASS New American, 50 ft. to the box. 10x12 single at $1.75, 10x12, 12x12, 10x16 B double $2.55, 12x14 to 12x20 and 14x14 to 14x20 B double $2.70, 16x16 and 16x18 B double $2.90, 16x24 B double $3.16, 16x20 and 16x22 $3.00, 6x8, 7x9, 8x10 old, single $1.50, 8x14 old, double $1.65; 10x14 old, double $1.75.

Get our prices on second hand wood material. We can furnish everything in new material to erect any size house. Get our prices.

METROPOLITAN MATERIAL CO.
Greenhouse Wreckers
1398-1408 Metropolitan Avenue, BROOKLYN, N. Y.

Mention the Florists' Exchange when writing.

PLANT CULTURE

PRICE $1.00

A. T. DE LA MARE PTG. & PUB. CO.,
2 Duane Street, New York

Mention the Florists' Exchange when writing.

Thirty cents is the minimum charge for advertisements on this page.

As a matter of course you are looking for the best and most profitable Pink Carnation. What shall it be? Our answer is: Invest in th

ROSE PINK ENCHANTRESS

TO still further satisfy you that we make no groundless claims, we call upon the hundred and odd growers in various sections of the coun among whom we disseminated during the past season about 50,000 rooted cuttings (all we had), to bear witness to our assertion, namely: That our **ROSE PINK ENCHANTRESS** is the **BEST** and the **FINEST** sport of them all. And so, "lest you forget," we say again: **Don't hesitate,** don't doubt, don't delay mailing your order. The **ROSE PINK ENCHANTRESS** is an ideal variety viewed from whatever standpoint.

Price for strong rooted cuttings, January and latter delivery, **$7.00 per 100; $60.00 per 1000**

A letter from J. Breitmeyer's Sons: We are pleased to infor that the stock of Rose Pink Enchantress furnished by you last was of a high character; the plants are producing blooms super its parent (Enchantress) from which it sported. We believe it far superior; its shade of pink is a color long sought after. W sure it is one of the best acquisitions in carnations we have had long time. Wishing you success.

Yours truly,
J. BREITMEYER'S

Our Rose Pink Enchantress are simply grand and we shall no any cuttings, but reserve for ourselves.
GEO. E. BUXTON, Nashua

ADDRESS ALL CORRESPONDENCE TO:

S. S. SKIDELSKY,
824 N. 24th Street, - - - Philadelphia

B. SCHROETER,
59 Broadway, - - - - Detroit, Mi

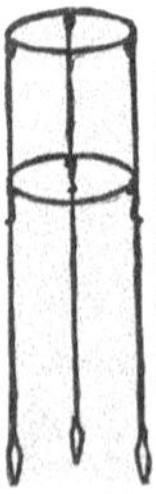

The Model EXTENSION

CARNATION SUPPORT

Endorsed by all the leading carnation growers as the best support on the market. Made with 2 or 3 circles. Write for prices and circulars.

We have special low prices to offer and can save you money on

Galvanized Wire ROSE STAKES

Write us for prices before ordering elsewhere. Prompt shipment guaranteed.

IGOE BROS.
226 North 9th Street
BROOKLYN, N. Y.

Mention the Florists' Exchange when writing.

IMPERIAL

THE NEW PINK VARIEGATED CARNATION

This novelty has been exhibited extensively and has received 10 Certificates of Merit and several Diplomas. It is a free and continuous bloomer and always comes in long stems.

PINK IMPERIAL

This is of a pleasing pink color, and cannot fail to become a favorite with every grower. It is a sport from Imperial, and has all the good qualities of that variety; its color is magnificent.

These two varieties are my own origination.

Prices: Selected cuttings, delivery commencing in December, 1906.
$2.50 per doz., $12.00 per 100, $100.00 per 1000
50 at 100 rates, 250 at 1000 rates.
5% discount for cash with order

PLACE YOUR ORDER AT ONCE.

JOHN E. HAINES, Bethlehem, Pa.
Mention the Florists' Exchange when writing.

Jensen & Dekema

CARNATION SPECIALISTS

674 W. Foster Ave., CHICAGO.
Mention the Florists' Exchange when writing.

CHICAGO CARNATION CO.

JOLIET, ILL.

We have the leaders in Carnations for 1907

Mention the Florists' Exchange when writing.

MABELLE-- New Pink Carnation for 1907

Color.—A peculiar shade of lovely pink, with a faint yellowish cast; several shades lighter than the Lawson. Unlike most pinks, the brightest sun does not injure the color. Size.—Three to four inches in diameter when established. Odor.—Pleasing, but not strong. Stems.—Invariably strong, but always graceful, ranging from 12 to 30 inches during the season. Habit, etc.—A very quick active grower, making specimen plants in a short time, even from late cuttings. On account of its rapid growth, requires supporting very soon after benching. Gets away rapidly, blooms early and gives long stems right from the start. Productiveness.—Prodigious is the best word we know of to use here. It is the most incessant bloomer early and late, we have ever grown. Stock limited. Delivery Jan. 5th to 10th and later. Price, $12.00 per 100, $100.00 per 1000.

THE H. WEBER & SONS CO., OAKLAND, MD.
Mention the Florists' Exchange when writing.

ABUNDANCE

Carnation plants from the field all sold. Rooted cuttings of this variety will be ready about January.

RUDOLPH FISCHER, Great Neck, L.I., N.Y.
Mention the Florists' Exchange when writing.

S. J. GODDARD

Framingham, Mass.
Rooted Carnation Cuttings a Specialty
Correspondence Solicited.
Mention the Florists' Exchange when writing.

CARNATIONS

F. DORNER & SONS CO.
LA FAYETTE, IND.
Mention the Florists' Exchange when writing.

A. B. DAVIS & SON, Inc.

PURCELLVILLE, VA.

Place your orders now for Red Sport cuttings, the best red carnation grown. $3.50 per 100; $30.00 per 1000.

Mention the Florists' Exchange when writing.

CARNATIONS

SMITH & GANNETT
GENEVA, N. Y.
Mention the Florists' Exchange when writing.

1906 Florists' Directory

THE AMERICAN FLORIST Directory for 1906 is now ready for distribution. It contains 475 pages, including complete lists of the **Florists, Seedsmen** and **Nurserymen** of the United States and Canada, arranged both by states and towns and all names alphabetically. Also lists of Foreign Merchants, Firms which issue catalogues, Horticultural Supply Concerns, Parks, Cemeteries, Landscape Architects, Experiment Station Horticulturists, Botanical Gardens and other invaluable trade information.

Price, $2.00 Postpaid

Address
A. T. DeLaMare Ptg. & Pub. Co. Limited
2 to 8 Duane Street, New York

GERANIUMS

Transplanted stock **S. A. Nutt, Mme. Buchner, Grant,** double, $15.00 per 1000.

Rooted Cuttings, S. A. Nutt, Grant, double, **Buchner, Doyle, Castellane** (Gervais rose pink) $10.00 per 1000. Cash with order.

PETER BROWN,
LANCASTER, PA.
Mention the Florists' Exchange when writing.

GERANIUMS.

Rooted Cuttings ready Nov. 1. **Nutt and Buchner,** $1.00 per 100; $10.00 per 1000.

Viaud, Ricard, Poitevine, Doyle, Pasteur, Brett, Perkins, Castellane, $1.25 per 100; $12.00 per 1000. Cash with order.

ERNEST HARRIS, Delanson, N. Y.
Mention the Florists' Exchange when writing.

Geraniums Geraniu

4 in. pots at $6.00 per 100.
3 in. pots at $4.00 per 100.
Heliotrope, 4 in. $4.00 per 100.
" 2 in. $3.00 per 100.
Lobelia, 2 in. $2.00 per 100.
Coleus, in variety, 2¼ in. pots, $ per 100.

Don't get left, but get your order Cash must accompany same.

J. E. FELTHOUSEN,
154 VAN VRANKEN AVE., SCHENECTADY,
Mention The Florists' Exchange when wri

ROOTED CUTTING GERANIUMS AND CARNATIO

Send a list of what you want and how man each variety and I will be pleased to quot ures on your complete order.

ALBERT M. HERR, LANCASTER,
Mention the Florists' Exchange when wri

GERANIUMS

Rooted, replan No cutt Shipped set from sand. **Nutt, Doyle, Bruantii and B ner,** $14.00 per 1000. **Ricard, Castellane, P vine, Perkins, Viaud,** etc., $16.00 per 1000. 100 at 1000 rates. Cash. **Coleus, Gladiol** any details please write

DANIEL K. HERR, Lancaster,
Mention the Florists' Exchange when wri

GERANIUMS

In good vari 2½ in. pots, r March 1 1907,

WM. J. CHINNICK, Trenton, N
Mention the Florists' Exchange when wri

SURPLUS STOCK—CHEA

We have a fine lot of **Jerusalem Cherries** sale from 2 in. pots. In order to make room mediately we will close them out at $1.00 per they are worth $5.00. 1500 **Smilax,** strong, 2 pots, $1.00 per 100; $9.00 per 1000. Also a big s of **Geraniums,** S. A. Nutt and others, also asso from sand, $1.00 per 100; from 2 in. pots, $1.75 100; from 3 in. pots, $8.00 per 100. Write for pr on other stock; we can save you money.

C. I. RAWLINGS, QUAKERTOWN,
Mention the Florists' Exchange when wr

JERUSALEM CHERRIES

dwarf, fine, full of fruit, 4-5-6 in. pots, $5.00, and $15.00 per 100.

Boston-Piersoni and Scottii, Fern plants, pots, 4-5-6-8-10 in. pans, 10c., 15c., 75c., and $1.00 each.

Primroses, 4 in., $6.00 per 100.

J. S. BLOOM,
RIEGELSVILLE, PA.
Mention The Florists' Exchange when wr

VICTORY

strong healthy field grown plants, now ready. First size, $15.00 per 100; Second size, $12.00 per 100; Third size, $10.00 per 100. A discount for cash with order. GUTTMAN & WEBBER, 43 West 28th St.

Among New York Wholesale Houses.

Wm. Starke, wholesale dealer in ants, 52 West Twenty-ninth street, rries at all times a full line of lms, ferns and decorative plants, ɔich is a great convenience to the tailers of this city.

John Young, 51 West Twenty-eighth reet, is handling American Beauty ses from his Bedford place, which e among the finest coming into the y at the present time. Mr. Young also handling the entire output of rnations from the Cottage Gardens mpany, Queens, N. Y., and a steady pply of gardenias from the estabhment of John Scott, Flatbush, ooklyn, N. Y., and a line of excelıt chrysanthemums.

Walter F. Sheridan, 49 West venty-eighth street, is one of the rgest handlers of American Beauty ses in the city, and also carries a e line of carnations, violets and her seasonable stock.

E. C. Horan, 55 West Twenty-eighth reet, is showing an immense lot of rysanthemums these days in addin to his consignments of Bride and idesmaid roses and violets.

John I. Raynor, 49 West Twentyghth street, is handling Adiantum oweanum from the originator of at fern, Peter Crowe, Utica, N. Y.; so the output of many of the best se growers in this vicinity. His supy of lilies and lily of the valley is gular, a fact which makes this store adquarters at all times for these oducts.

H. E. Froment, 57 West Twentyghth street, is receiving large supies of chrysanthemums, violets and chmond roses, also a fine line of nerican Beauty and tea roses.

A. H. Langjahr, 55 West West venty-eighth street, is carrying a ll line of chrysanthemums, carnaıns and violets; he also makes a ecialty of asparagus, smilax and liantum fern.

George Saltford, 46 West Twentynth street, in addition to specializing violets, has many growers of rysanthemums, roses and carnations ho are making him regular consignents just now.

Traendly & Schenck, 44 West wenty-eighth street, besides handıg the famous roses from Clifton, J., are carrying heavy supplies of ırysanthemums and carnations.

Ford Brothers, 48 West Twentyghth street, are receiving heavy ipments of chrysanthemums,Ameran Beauty and other roses, also rnations and violets.

J. S. Fenrich, 110 West Twentyghth street, is handling chrysanthe-ums from Chas. H. Totty of Madin, N. J., also chrysanthemums, lily the valley and gardenias from An-n Schultheis, College Point, L. I.

Wm. Stuart Allen Company, 53 'est Twenty-eighth street, is handng the orchids from the Julius oehrs Company of Carlton Hill, and ie well-known lily of the valley from N. Pierson, grower, Cromwell, onn.; together with consignments of rnations and chrysanthemums from her well-known growers.

J. K. Allen, 106 West Twenty-eighth reet, who, by the way, opens at o'clock every morning, is busy these ays with his immense consignments chrysanthemums, carnations, etc. nd is also handling a fine lot of viots just now.

Moore, Hentz & Nash, 55 West wenty-sixth street, handle roses from ie establishments of F. L. Moore, enry Hentz, Jr., and The Floral Exange, Edgely, Pa., in addition to any other growers of roses, carnaons and green material.

B. S. Slinn, Jr., 55 West Twenty-sixth street, is as usual making a special line of violets, though he carries a nice line of carnations and other stock as well.

Gunther Brothers, 30 West Twenty-ninth street, are carrying a full line of seasonable flowers, and as in former years, are making a specialty of violets.

James McManus, 42 West Twenty-eighth street, has built up an enormous trade in his special line, orchids. It must not be understood, however, that Mr. McManus is in the orchid business only, for he is receiving daily consignments of all other varieties of cut flowers.

Alex J. Guttman, 43 West Twenty-eighth street, is handling a nice line of roses from his own greenhouses at Summit, N. J., also chrysanthemums, violets and carnations from his many consignors.

Phil. F. Kessler, 55 West Twenty-sixth street, does not go in for many roses, but his store is filled to overflowing every morning with heavy shipments of carnations, chrysanthemums and other seasonable flowers.

Thomas Young, Jr., 43 West Twenty-eighth street, has a completely equipped wholesale store in the building he occupies and is receiving daily much choice cut flower stock.

A. M. Henshaw, 52 West Twenty-eighth street, besides handling a general line of cut flowers, receives regularly the output of roses from Henshaw Brothers' greenhouses, Short Hills, N. J.

REVIEW OF THE MARKET

NEW YORK.—Business in cut flowers is waning a little as the week progresses. American Beauty roses are being offered at figures quite a little lower than they were a week ago, and a similar weakening of prices among chrysanthemums is noticed. Carnations are becoming more plentiful, and at times accumulate somewhat in the hands of the dealers. Bride and Bridesmaid roses, while not showing much change in quoted figures, are not firm by any means.

Lily of the valley and lilies remain about the same as quoted last week. Violets are, if anything, a little more in demand, and prices remain fairly firm; some of the best are bringing as high as 75c. per 100. The condition of the market for green material is unchanged. Tuesday being Election Day, there was very little business done.

CHICAGO.—It is owing probably more to the several days of severe wintry weather, with snow, clouds and rain, and a total absence of sun, more than any direct cause of demand, that stock has been shorter for the past few days. The horse show, the flower show, etc., may have and do have a most pronounced effect unquestionably, but when one stops to consider the result on fifteen to twenty million feet of glass which daily place their products within gunshot of Randolph street and Wabash avenue, it is hardly necessary to say that one day's sunshine is worth more than a good many thousand tons of coal, or a dozen society shows—provided it comes at the right time.

The market the early part of the week had more than recovered in demand, without a great deal of variation in prices, and the particular feature to occasion comment, and one which is seldom seen in any market, "the fancy goods were going begging," while the cheaper grades were in demand. Consequently, cheap stock became high and the best grade waited for a purchaser at a still higher price. Recently in this market fancy stock has held its own, while the cheaper grades, though more in demand, have failed to break to any extent the prices of the best stock. There are some local grown violets of excellent quality now appearing which with their full fragrance are quite attractive and holding well at somewhat above the price the imported stock is bringing. W. K. W.

BOSTON.—The past week has seen quite a surplus of most kinds of stock, although toward the end of the week the market was cleaning up better. Chrysanthemums, of course, are the most plentiful of all flowers and they vary much in price. For the fancy blooms from $6 to $10 per 100 up to $2 and $3 per dozen for the extra large long stemmed blooms is obtained. There are many of the poorer grades selling in bunches at 35c. and 50c. per bunch. Roses remain at about the same prices as a week gao, although the demand is somewhat better, especially for the fancy sorts like Killarney. Wellesley and Richmond There is an exceptionally fine grade of the latter to be seen at present. Carnations are gradually improving in quality, bringing from $1 to $3. Lilies realizes $8 and $10; violets, 35c. and 50c.; sweet peas, $1, and lily of the valley $3 to $5.

J. W. D.

KANSAS CITY, MO.—The cut flower market is holding up well, the only trouble being the scarcity of stock. There is a good steady demand, and it is impossible to get enough flowers to supply it. What stock is coming in is of exceptionally good quality. The chrysanthemum season is on in full blast and some fine blooms are being cut. There is as yet a scarcity of good carnations, but the prospects are good for an abundant supply in the near fucut. Roses are cleaned up on sight. There has been a large amount of funeral work lately, and it has kept the trade busy trying to secure enough stock to fill their orders. The outlook for the coming season in this city is very bright. D. L.

LOUISVILLE, KY.—Stock of all kinds has been short and cut very close. All the chrysanthemums in the local market have been cut before they were half developed, and the prices received so far this season have been in advance of those of any previous year. Carnations are also in very short supply. Retail prices received are American Beauty, $2 to $6; other roses, $1 to $2; carnations, 75c. to $1 per dozen; violets, 50c. to $2 per 100; chrysanthemums, $1 to $6 per dozen.

A. R. B.

MINNEAPOLIS.—Business has been very good the past week. Stock is looking much better. The chances are that, with the aid of the present bright weather, we will have more roses, which have been badly needed for some time. Even the largest of the growers have been cutting but a mere handful of stock. Kate Moulton roses appear to be the favorites with the best stores, and they always bring a much better price than other pink roses. The selects of this variety are easily sold at $2.50 and $3 per dozen; seconds, however, do not command much better than $1 per dozen.

Early varieties of chrysanthemums are on the market, principally Monrovia, Glory of the Pacific, Polly Rose, and Mme. Bergmann. The demand is heavy. The higher priced roses will undoubtedly suffer through the chrysanthemums. Carnations are few and far between; a year ago at this time they were in abundance and the blooms were perfect. It would be a hard matter to obtain about 100 choice carnations in the city at this writing. Violets are offered, but only in limited numbers. Lily of the valley is good, but the cut is so light that very few have any at all in stock. PAUL.

ST. PAUL.—A decided advance was noticeable in trade the past week. Chrysanthemums have relieved the market to a larger extent. Roses with the majority of the growers are off crop, and Monrovia and Robert Halliday are the best chrysanthemums we have had so far, although some dealers have been showing some good October Frost. American Beauty roses find slow sales. Richmond are not up to grade yet and very few are cut, although the prospects look bright for heavy cuts within the next few weeks. Killarney seems to be the favorite pink. The Bridesmaid grown here are not in the same class with the Killarney and Mme. Abel Chatenay. Kaiserin Augusta Victoria are also much better in quality than Bride. Perle des Jardins appear to be more plentiful this season, and the demand is also heavier. It is quite evident that the florists' stock was not complete without a yellow rose, and it appears that the Perle will stay with us until something better is originated.

Carnations up to the present date have been a dead issue from the growers' standpoint, as not one this season has been cutting enough to supply his own demand. The only carnations to speak about are shipped in and are of an inferior grade. Violets are hardly perfect as yet, and the demand is only moderate. PAUL.

ST. LOUIS.—The past two weeks we have had fine weather, and this meant much to trade in general. However, business for the first week of November was not so good as it should have been. Chrysanthemums have an immense call, and florists' windows show beautiful displays of this flower. Prices range from $4 for extra fancy in white and yellow to $1 per dozen. Pink are not good sellers and, of course, go at cheaper rates. Carnation bring $4 per 100 for extra fancy, but the bulk sell for $3 with $1.50 to $2 for the poorer grades; Mrs. T. W. Lawson are of poor quality. Lady Bountiful and Boston Market are fine; Enchantress is the best seller, and these are by no means plentiful, the wholesalers selling out almost every day. In roses, American Beauty have a good call, fancy long bringing $3 to $4 per dozen, and from this down to $1 per dozen for shorts. Other roses don't bring over $5 per 100 for extra fancy, and considering the big demand for chrysanthemums roses hold up in price well. Cooler nights have brought out the color of violets, and the price is up to 50c. per 100 for fancy California. A good call is reported for smilax and other greens. Adiantums are scarce; everything else is plentiful.

ST. PATRICK.

FIRMS WHO ARE BUILDING.

LIVERMORE FALLS, ME.—George H. Fuller is building a greenhouse.

WHITMAN, MASS.—W. B. Bowen has commenced work on a new greenhouse. Further additions will be made in the Spring.

MOBERLY, MO.—H. V. Estill is erecting a large greenhouse, and will grow flowers for the store conducted by his wife.

ROCKFORD, ILL.—J. J. Soper has added three new greenhouses, each 25 x 80 feet. Frank P. Zimmerman, formerly of Chicago, has charge of the plant.

HEATING.

Growers' Problems Solved by U. G. Scollay.

I am changing from steam to hot water heating and want to use all my old material, rebuilding on some other place. Please let me know how large the main and return from boiler to greenhouses have to be? Distance is about 60 feet. I would like to use the system shown on enclosed cut, if same can be recommended. The two houses, 34 x 80 each inside, have rock walls three feet high, banked up on outside; ridge pole is 11 feet from the ground. How many 1 1-4-inch pipe will it take for each house? Of what size should the feed pipe for each house be to heat to 55 degrees at zero? What is a heat circulator? Will a tubular boiler 9 feet long and 3 feet wide, with 26 3-inch flues, be large enough for the above two houses? If not, will it be half large enough? R. G. R.

—Each house will require about 900 feet of 4-inch cast iron greenhouse pipe or its equivalent. I would not advise using any of the 1 1-4-inch pipe for your heating work, as it is small for the purpose. You could easily use up a lot of your pipe of that size for columns when rebuilding. If you feed with one overhead main in each house, as per plan submitted with your letter, I would suggest not less than 4-inch for each. Using a heat circulator, such as I am familiar with, you could get along with smaller mains, but it is always well to provide for such things getting out of order, and in that case your small mains would throw your job out of commission, or practically so. I am not familiar with the circulator mentioned on your sketch. I know of one made in the East that works on the principle of the Archimedean screw in conjunction with an electric motor. It does splendid work.

The boiler you have will be about large enough for the two houses. It has a maximum capacity of 2,500 feet of 4-inch cast iron pipe for hot water.

U. G. SCOLLAY.

CHANGES IN BUSINESS.

TERRE HAUTE, IND.—Harry Richmond, who for years has been connected with J. G. Heinl & Son, has opened a greenhouse of his own on Chestnut street.

HUNTINGTON, L. I.—Walter Shaw, formerly a private gardener, has embarked in business, purchased in this vicinity eight acres of land, on which nursery stock will be grown, and built a greenhouse, 135 x 30 feet, to be devoted to carnations and sweet peas.

PLAINVILLE, CONN.—The Woodford greenhouses on Whiting street have been purchased by Harry and Daniel Tompkins, who will conduct them under the firm of Tompkins Brothers.

Wholesale Prices of Cut Flowers, New York, Nov. 7, 1906

Prices quoted are by the hundred unless otherwise noted

Roses — A. Beauty, fancy—special	10.00 to	20.00	Carnations — Inf'r grades, all colors	1.00 to	1.50
" extra	8.00 to	10.00	Standard Varieties — White	1.50 to	2.00
" No. 1	6.00 to	8.00	Pink	1.50 to	2.00
" No. 2	3.00 to	6.00	Red	1.50 to	2.00
" No. 3	2.00 to	3.00	Yel. & Var.	1.50 to	2.00
Bride, Maid, fancy—spe'l	4.00 to	5.00	*Fancy— (*The highest grades of standard var.) White	2.50 to	4.00
" extra	3.00 to	4.00	Pink	2.50 to	4.00
" No. 1	1.00 to	2.00	Red	2.50 to	4.00
" No. 2	.50 to	.75	Yel. & Var.	2.50 to	4.00
Golden Gate	.75 to	5.00	Novelties	4.00 to	5.00
Richmond	.75 to	5.00	Chrysanthemums	6.00 to	8.00
Mme. Abel Chatenay	.75 to	5.00	" Fancy	10.00 to	20.00
Adiantum	.50 to	.75	Gardenias, per doz.	2.00 to	3.00
Croweanum	1.00 to	1.25	Lilies	10.00 to	12.00
Asparagus	25.00 to	50.00	Lily of the Valley	1.00 to	4.00
" Plumosus, bunches	8.00 to	15.00	Mignonette	...... to	......
" Sprengerii, bunches	8.00 to	15.00	Smilax	5.00 to	8.00
......	...... to	......	Violets	.35 to	.75
Cattleyas	30.06 to	40.00	......	...... to	......
Daisies	...... to	......	......	...... to	......

Wholesale Prices of Cut Flowers—Per 100

Boston Nov. 5, 1906	Buffalo Nov. 5, 1906	Detroit Oct. 29, 1906	Cincinnati Oct. 29, 1906	Baltimore Nov. 5, 1906	NAMES AND VARIETIES	Milwaukee Oct. 25, 1906	Phil'delphia Oct. 25, 1906	Pittsburg Nov. 7, 1906	St. Louis Oct. 22, 1906
20.00 to 50.00	20.00 to 25.00	10.00 to 35.00	— to 40.00	— to —	ROSES A. BEAUTY, fancy—special	— to 25.00	20.00 to 40.00	— to 25.00	25.00 to 30.00
10.00 to 20.00	15.00 to 20.00	— to —	— to 30.00	— to 25.00	" extra	15.00 to 18.00	— to —	— to 20.00	15.00 to 20.00
4.00 to 10.00	10.00 to 18.00	— to —	20.00 to 25.00	12.50 to 20.00	" No. 1	10.00 to 12.50	— to —	12.00 to 15.00	8.00 to 12.50
2.00 to 4.00	3.00 to 10.00	— to —	6.00 to 8.00	5.00 to 8.00	" Culls and ordinary	4.00 to 6.00	— to —	— to 6.00	4.00 to 6.00
6.00 to 10.00	6.00 to 8.00	3.00 to 6.00	4.00 to 6.00	— to 5.00	BRIDE, 'MAID, fancy-special	— to 6.00	— to —	— to 8.00	5.00 to 6.00
4.00 to 6.00	5.00 to 6.00	— to —	3.00 to 5.00	— to 4.00	" extra	— to 5.00	— to —	— to 6.00	3.00 to 4.00
2.00 to 4.00	4.00 to 5.00	— to —	2.00 to 4.00	— to 3.00	" No. 1	— to 4.00	— to —	— to 4.00	— to 2.00
1.00 to 2.00	3.00 to 4.00	— to —	2.00 to 3.00	— to 2.00	" No. 2	— to 2.00	— to —	— to 2.00	— to —
— to —	3.00 to 6.00	4.00 to 5.00	2.00 to 6.00	2.00 to 5.00	GOLDEN GATE	4.00 to 5.00	2.00 to 6.00	4.00 to 6.00	2.00 to 5.00
— to —	3.00 to 7.00	— to —	2.00 to 4.00	3.00 to 5.00	K. A. VICTORIA	4.00 to 8.00	2.00 to 5.00	4.00 to 8.00	3.00 to 5.00
4.00 to 20.00	3.00 to 8.00	— to —	— to —	3.00 to 5.00	LIBERTY	4.00 to 6.00	4.00 to 5.00	4.00 to 5.00	— to —
— to —	3.00 to 6.00	4.00 to 10.00	2.00 to 6.00	3.00 to 5.00	METEOR	— to —	— to —	— to —	— to —
— to —	2.00 to 5.00	4.00 to 10.00	— to —	2.00 to 4.00	PERLE	4.00 to 6.00	— to —	4.00 to 6.00	2.00 to 5.00
— to —	— to —	— to 50.00	— to —	— to —	ORCHIDS—Cattleyas	— to —	— to 40.00	— to —	— to —
— to —	1.00 to 1.50	— to —	— to 1.00	1.00 to 1.25	CARNATIONS Inferior grades, all colors	— to 1.00	— to 2.50	1.00 to 1.50	1.00 to 1.50
1.00 to 2.00	1.50 to 2.50	— to 1.00	— to 2.00	1.50 to 2.00	Standard Varieties White	— to 1.00	— to 2.50	— to 2.00	1.00 to 1.50
1.00 to 2.00	1.50 to 2.50	— to —	— to 2.00	1.50 to 2.00	Standard Varieties Pink	— to 1.00	— to 2.50	— to 2.00	1.00 to 1.50
1.00 to 2.00	1.50 to 2.50	— to —	— to 2.00	1.50 to 2.00	Standard Varieties Red	— to 1.00	— to 2.50	— to 2.00	1.00 to 1.50
1.00 to 2.00	— to —	— to 3.00	— to —	1.50 to 2.00	Standard Varieties Yellow and var	— to 1.00	— to 2.50	— to —	1.00 to 1.50
2.00 to 3.00	2.00 to 3.50	— to —	— to —	2.50 to 3.00	Fancy Varieties White	1.50 to 2.00	— to 3.00	2.50 to 3.50	2.00 to 4.00
2.00 to 3.00	2.00 to 3.50	— to —	— to 3.00	2.50 to 3.00	Fancy Varieties Pink	1.50 to 2.00	— to 3.00	2.50 to 3.50	2.00 to 4.00
2.00 to 3.00	2.00 to 3.50	— to —	— to —	2.50 to 3.00	Fancy Varieties Red	1.50 to 2.00	— to 3.00	2.50 to 3.50	2.00 to 4.00
2.00 to 3.00	— to —	— to 1.50	— to —	2.50 to 3.00	Fancy Varieties Yellow and var	1.50 to 2.00	— to 3.00	2.50 to 3.50	2.00 to 4.00
3.00 to 4.00	— to —	— to —	— to —	— to —	Novelties	— to —	— to —	2.50 to 3.50	— to —
.75 to 1.00	.50 to 1.00	— to 2.00	— to 1.00	— to 1.00	ADIANTUM	— to 1.00	— to 1.00	.75 to 1.00	— to 1.00
— to 50.00	15.00 to 20.00	25.00 to 60.00	35.00 to 50.00	25.00 to 50.00	ASPARAGUS, Plum. and Ten	20.00 to 30.00	50.00 to 75.00	30.00 to 50.00	25.00 to 50.00
— to —	15.00 to 20.00	20.00 to 30.00	25.00 to 35.00	25.00 to 50.00	" Sprengeri, bunches	20.00 to 30.00	— to 50.00	20.00 to 30.00	25.00 to 50.00
8.00 to 10.00	8.00 to 10.00	— to 10.00	— to —	6.00 to 10.00	CALLAS	— to —	— to —	10.00 to 12.00	— to —
6.00 to 20.00	6.00 to 25.00	— to —	16.00 to 25.00	4.00 to 25.00	CHRYSANTHEMUMS	— to —	— to 40.00	4.00 to 25.00	— to —
— to —	1.50 to 2.50	.75 to 1.50	— to —	— to —	DAISIES	— to .40	— to 1.00	— to 1.50	— to —
[illegible] to 10.00	— to —	— to —	— to 15.00	— to 12.50	LILIES	— to 12.50	— to —	15.00 to 20.00	— to —
3.00 to 5.00	3.00 to 4.00	3.00 to 4.00	— to 4.00	— to 4.00	LILY OF THE VALLEY	— to —	3.00 to 5.00	2.00 to 4.00	3.00 to 4.00
— to —	— to —	— to —	— to —	— to —	MIGNONETTE, ordinary	— to —	— to —	— to —	— to —
— to —	— to —	— to —	— to —	— to —	" fancy	— to —	— to —	— to —	— to —
— to 12.50	12.00 to 15.00	12.50 to 15.00	— to 15.00	— to 20.00	SMILAX	— to 15.00	— to —	12.50 to 15.00	— to 12.50
— to .35	.60 to .75	— to —	— to .50	— to .50	VIOLETS, ordinary	— to —	— to —	.50 to .75	.25 to .35
.50 to .75	— to 1.00	— to —	— to 1.00	— to .60	" fancy	— to —	— to —	1.00 to 1.25	— to —
— to —	— to —	— to —	— to .15	— to —	GALAX LEAVES	— to —	— to .15	— to —	— to .15

Kansas City, Mo.

Trade Notes.

The White House Greenhouse presents a handsome appearance since Max Ellers of the People's Floral Company has taken charge of it.

Our commission man, Wm. A. Bastian, reports business good, but stock very scarce. Mr. Bastian has embarked in the manufacture of a new plant food that he is now placing on the market.

H. Humfeld is cutting some fine chrysanthemums this Fall. Everything is looking well at his place.

The W. L. Rock Flower Company is displaying some handsome chrysanthemums. Charles Helte has charge of the greenhouses and the stock he grows is not surpassed by any seen on the market.

W. J. Barnes is making an enviable reputation as a decorator and is building up a splendid business in this line. Mr. Barnes handled some of the largest society decorations last year, and he seems to be keeping up the gait this season. D. I.

SALT LAKE CITY, UTAH.—The B. C. Morris Floral Company, of which Councilman Thomas Hobday is manager, suffered a heavy loss in the recent wind storm. Two of the greenhouses at Tenth East and Fifth South streets were greatly damaged and the plants in them were totally destroyed. Mr. Hobday estimates that the damage to the houses is about $2,500 and the damage to plants is fully $3,000.

DETROIT, MICH.—John Breitmeyer's Sons will give a chrysanthemum exhibition at their store, corner Gratiot avenue and Broadway, November 13-17 inclusive.

BAY CITY, MICH. — Bohnhoff Brothers are building a large addition to their office.

Wholesale Prices of Cut Flowers, Chicago, Nov. 6, 1906

Prices quoted are by the hundred unless otherwise noted

ROSES American Beauty		
36-inch stems.........per doz.	.... to	3.00
30-inch stems .... "	2.50 to	3.00
24-inch stems.......... "	2.00 to	2.50
20-inch stems.......... "	1.00 to	2.00
18-inch stems.......... "	.... to	1.50
12-inch stems.......... "	.... to	1.00
8-inch stems and shorts "	.50 to	.75
Bride Maid, fancy special......	6.00 to	8.00
" extra..............	4.00 to	5.00
" No. 1..............	2.00 to	3.00
" No. 2..............	.... to	1.00
Golden Gate..................	2.00 to	6.00
Carnot.......................	2.00 to	6.00
Uncle John...................	2.00 to	6.00
Liberty......................	2.00 to	8.00
Richmond.....................	2.00 to	8.00
Kaiserine....................	2.00 to	8.00
Killarney....................	2.00 to	6.00
" extra..............	8.00 to	10.00
Perle........................	2.00 to	6.00
Chatenay.....................	2.00 to	6.00
....	.... to	....
....	.... to	....

CARNATIONS			
STANDARD VARIETIES	White..............	1.5 to	2.00
	Pink...............	1.5 to	2.00
	Red................	1.5 to	2.00
	Yellow & var.......	1.5 to	2.00
*FANCY (The highest grades of Sta'd var.)	White..............	2.5 to	3.00
	Pink...............	2.5 to	3.00
	Red................	2.50 to	3.00
	Yellow & var.......	2.50 to	3.00
NOVELTIES		.... to	....
ADIANTUM		.75 to	1.00
ASPARAGUS, Plum. & Ten.		.35 to	.50
" Sprengeri, bunches		.35 to	.50
....		.... to	
LILIES, Longiflorum		15.00 to	18.00
Harrisii		15.00 to	18.00
Orchids—Cattleyas		.... to	50.00
SMILAX		8.00 to	12.00
LILY OF THE VALLEY		2.00 to	4.00
VIOLETS		.25 to	1.00
HARDY FERNS per 1000		.... to	1.50
GALAX "		1.00 to	1.25
....		.... to	....
CHRYSANTHEMUMS per doz		1.00 to	4.00

Buffalo.

News Notes.

Trade has increased considerably lately. Flowers are coming in more plentifully. Good varieties of chrysanthemums are arriving daily, also American Beauty roses, which have not been selling so well since the chrysanthemums arrived.

S. S. Skidelsky of Philadelphia was in town looking up a new novelty flower pot cover, which he intends to show in the West, and which will be introduced as the "Palmer Flower Pot Cover." It has made an instantaneous hit wherever shown.

The local florists' show windows were handsomely decorated with corn on the cob, corn stalks and pumpkins for Hallowe'en. W. J. Palmer's upper store used the old-fashioned fence rail which was one of the most admired decorations. W. A. Anderson also exhibited a good window of corn stalks and pumpkins, which were arranged in a way that showed much artistic ability.

Professor Cowell of South Park conservatory is showing some fine chrysanthemums in his annual exhibition of specimen flowers and plants.

Reichert's have completed their range of greenhouses, which will be devoted to a general line of stock. They also had one house built expressly for palms, of which they have over 600, for renting purposes exclusively.

W. H. GREVER.

Baltimore.

News Items.

Cut flower business and general market conditions are exceptionally good. Roses and carnations continue somewhat scarce.

Several houses of poinsettias at Halliday Brothers are the finest ever seen in this locality.

I. H. Moss has his new houses in full operation; everything working to perfection.

Our bowling team is now affiliated with the regular Baltimore Bowling League. All our members are practicing diligently; two games out of three were recently won from the strong Maryland team, by the following scores:

FLORISTS			
Richmond	161	209	182
Moss	141	148	157
Boone	148	183	165
Kramer	176	169	175
Seybold	203	179	195
Totals	829	888	874

MARYLAND			
Kaiser	187	157	181
Lautenberg	137	158	153
Russell	143	149	161
Schaefer	191	171	170
Rossell	185	169	188
Totals	843	804	853

The new Florists' Exchange building is practically completed and everything is ready for the Chrysanthemum Show next week.

C. L. S.

New Orleans, La.

News Notes.

Edward Baker, who for the last seven years, has been superintendent of Audubon Park, has tendered his resignation to the Board of Park Commissioners, and will branch out as a landscape gardener and architect on his own account. The commissioners were very anxious for Mr. Baker to reconsider his resignation; this he refused to do. He has the best wishes of the local craftsmen (among whom he is very popular) in his new venture. Jules Fonta, a former superintendent, has been offered the position and will undoubtedly be appointed. Mr. Fonta is a very capable gardener and gave great satisfaction when he formerly held the position, which he resigned to spend a year or two at his old home in France.

On a recent visit to the establishment of M. Cook's Sons, everything was found in first-class order. This firm is composed of the two sons of that veteran Southern florist, Matthew Cook, who think it is time their father took a rest; he was found, however, still helping the boys. The whole place had to be remodeled on account of some of the land having been sold for building purposes. They had one large house of well grown chrysanthemums, principally Mrs. Henry Robinson, and Colonel D. Appleton, for All Saints' Day; also some later varieties.

All Saints' Day, as usual, kept everyone busy. A rushing business was done, mainly on large chrysanthemum flowers, although a good many were left over, a fact accounted for by the exceptionally large number grown this year.

Chas. Eble had a few sweet pea flowers in his store November 3, the first of this year's outdoor crop.

There died on October 22, Chas. White, aged 84 years, an old time gardener of this city, one of the original members of the New Orleans Horticultural Society, and a veteran of two wars. Mr. White was a native of Germany and a bachelor.

CRESCENT CITY.

WILMINGTON, DEL.—Greenhouses of the local florists are suffering from the raids of a strange yellow bug that is destroying the chrysanthemums. The insects attack the leaves and the flowers wither and die. Florists have lost hundreds of dollars' worth of valuable flowers from the pest.

Boston.

The New England Dahlia Society.

Dahlia growers, to the number of about twenty, met at Horticultural Hall on Friday, November 2 and formed the New England Dahlia Society, having adopted the recommendations of the committee as published in a recent issue of The Florists' Exchange. The following officers were elected: President, H. F. Burt, Taunton; vice-president, W. F. Turner, New Bedford; secretary, M. Fuld, Boston; treasurer, H. A. Lindsay, Marblehead; executive committee: H. W. Kendall, Newton; H. E. Johnson, Brockton; W. Moon, Lynn; Geo. H. Walker, North Dighton; and L. M. Bates, Brockton. It was voted to ask the Massachusetts Horticultural Society to change its schedule, so as to dscard the classes of eighteen blooms and include instead classes of twenty-four blooms, and to create if possible a class of fifty blooms. It is the purpose of the society to publish pamphlets, etc., diffusing knowledge on the cultivation of the dahlia. The first paper to be issued will be written by H. F. Burt and will be a simple tale of his experience in dahlia growing.

H. F. Burt, the president of the society was born and brought up in Taunton. He was a school teacher until about sixteen years ago, when his love for the dahlia caused him to give up his vocation and devote his whole time to the cultivation of his favorite flower. His knowledge of the dahlia is wonderful, he having read and studied every book on the subject, and he can relate the history of every variety known in cultivation.

M. Fuld, the secretary, has an experience with dahlias back to his European apprenticeship days with Dippe Brothers, Quedlinburg, Germany, and later with Huber Brothers, in France. He is at present manager for W. W. Rawson & Company, seed merchants, having also had experience in that line with August Rölker & Sons and Peter Henderson & Company, New York, and R. & J. Farquhar & Company, Boston.

News Notes.

Thos. Benwell, the popular salesman for A. H. Hews & Company, flower pot manufacturers, rounded out his fortieth year with that firm this week.

Thomas Roland of Nahant has a new auto truck, which this week made its first trip to Boston laden with plants and flowers.

J. D. Twombley of Winchester is happy over the arrival of a son at his home.

Alfred Poetsch, recently in charge of the propagating houses of the Public Grounds Department, is now with W. W. Rawson & Company. Mr. Poetsch had a wide experience in horticulture in Germany before coming to this country several years ago.

Visitors the past week included Julius Roehrs and G. Struck, Rutherford, N. J.; Thos. Knight, Summit, N. J.; J. R. Fotheringham, Tarrytown, N. Y.; and C. B. Weathered, N. Y.

The Park Street Market bowling team beat the Joseph Breck team at their weekly meeting, the scores being Park street, 1305; Brecks, 1161.

The delegation to the Chicago flo show from here included: W. H. llott, Alex. Montgomery and Wm Stewart.

Mr. Campbell has resigned his p tion with N. F. McCarthy & Co.

Besides the nominees for officer the Massachusetts Horticultural ciety already published the name W. W. Rawson has been put up, there is likely to be a lively con for the honorable office.

John K. M. L. Farquhar has to New York for a few days.

J. W. DUNCA

Newport, R. I.

Trade Notes.

Nursery stock is moving rap now. Business is unusually brisk the Rhode Island Nurseries. Var kinds of shrubs are in good dema that class of stock Mr. Vanicek in large quantities wholesale. week several very large orders also filled for herbaceous plants, order alone being for 3,000 plants.

Business in decorative plants is proving with the approach of co weather. Zeigler received an exc ingly fine lot of Nephrolepis Sc last week, of which he is at pre making a specialty. Palms at r are a little higher in price than year. Kentias in the varieties moreana and Forsteriana are the sellers. In cut flowers, dahlias and other outdoor material are thing the past for a season, conseque more costly and choicer flowers benefitting. Roses are coming i much better condition. Carna also show marked improvement. lets are as yet scarce and of inf quality, although these also are proving. Some recent inquiries that there will be quite a numbe violets here this Winter after al

D.

Cleveland, O.

Illness of J. M. Gasser.

J. M. Gasser, the well-k florist, has broken down under too close application of business constant worry over labor trou which he greatly magnified, and sequently brought on such a sta mental depression bordering on a collapse, that his friends interp and at the suggestion of se physicians he has been prevailed to take a complete rest as the hope of restoring him to health left last Saturday for a p sanatarium at Walnut Hills, Ci nati, where a complete chang scene and surroundings, it is h will restore him to health in months, when he will either retu active work for the Easter seas pay a long visit to relatives in T

St. Paul.

News Items.

Bulb sales appear to be o wane, and judging from the number left on hand at the dif places, sales have been very go

Holm & Olson have got move their new quarters. They rep good business. Their new ice b certainly a beauty, being solid m any with marble flooring and French mirrors.

Wm. Desmond, formerly wit Minneapolis Floral Company, is with Holm & Olson.

PA

St. Louis.

News Notes.

Quite a number of the trade are visiting Chicago this week, including F. C. Weber, Theo. Miller, F. H. Meinhardt, Harry Young and O. G. Koenig. Those from the east side are J. F. Ammann, of Edwardsville, and A. T. Halsteadt, of Belleville. On account of so many leaving the city we regret it makes it impossible for them to attend the club metting on Thursday afternoon, when we hold our annual chrysanthemum show. Most of the above mentioned gentlemen are identified with a new local organization to be known as the St. Louis Horticultural Society, of which Harry Young is president; Fred C. Weber, treasurer, and O. G. Koenig, secretary. No doubt pointers will be obtained as to how the horticultural society in Chicago is run.

On Tuesday many of our florists had a day off, acting as judges, clerks, etc., of election; among them were Charles Juengel, Robert Beyer, A. Meyer, Sr., G. Kalish, Will Young, J. J. Beneke, and George Windler.

Henry Felter, C. C. Sanders, and Charles Beyer will exhibit specimen chrysanthemum plants at the club meeting on Thursday.

After making the rounds of the trade, Wm. Edlefsen, of Milwaukee, has returned home.

The free chrysanthemum exhibition will open at the Missouri Botanical Garden next week, beginning November 12 and lasting throughout the week. Some elegant plants of old and new varieties will be shown to the public. This exhibition always draws a very large attendance.

ST. PATRICK.

Pittsburg.

News of the Week.

The display of chrysanthemums at the Phipps conservatories at Schenley Park was visited last Sunday by about 25,000 people: from 8 a. m. until closing time, particularly in the afternoon, there were so many people that the line extended out into the park for quite a distance. The exhibit is the best ever made in these conservatories; about 20,000 blooms in 200 varities are to be seen to best advantage. The blending of colors and effective massing are perfect and reflect great credit upon superintendent Burke and foreman Jones. The best blooms were among the older sorts, while among about a dozen of the newer varieties very few, if any, came up to the former. The blooms were as good as any grown by commercial florists. The Klondike cosmos, seen in one of the houses, is something comparatively new for many, and should be valuable as a commercial flower. The color is a fine orange yellow and the plant seems to be an easy grower. The show will last until the end of the month and should be visited by everybody.

The exhibition at the Allegheny Park conservatories was also well patronized; although not nearly as large as the one at Schenley Park, a fine exhibit is seen.

Chrysanthemums sold well last week; they are very plentiful, and prices have dropped somewhat. Roses also are reasonable in price; but carnations are in good demand at fair figures. The commission houses are all stocked up, but are not complaining about trade.

The Pittsburg Cut Flower Company moved into its new store room last week and now has as fine a building for its purpose as any in the country. The locality is very central, right among the dealers. Several new ice boxes have been installed, and the storage capacity of the firm is far greater than formerly. The floor space also is ample for the trade in supplies, which has much increased the last year.

The Botanical Society's November meeting will be an interesting one; the subject, "Mosses" will be presented by O. E. Jennings and Dr. Wm. Hamilton, and will be illustrated by specimens and in other ways.

E. C. REINEMAN.

Kalamazoo, Mich.

James Frazer Honored.

James Frazer has been elected by a large majority, associate patron of the Michigan Order of the Eastern Star. Mr. Fraser is a thirty-second degree Mason and has held many offices in the local orders. During 1901 and 1902 he was worshipful master of Kalamazoo lodge, No. 22, F. & A. M. In 1898, 1899 and 1900 he was high priest in Kalamazoo chapter, No. 13, R. A. M. He was thrice illustrious master of Kalamazoo council, R. & S. M. During the years 1904 and 1905 he was eminent commander of Peninsular commandery, Knights Templar. At present he is worthy patron of Corinthian chapter, No. 123, O. E. S. He also held this office during the years 1903, '04 and '05.

Besides holding office in these orders Mr. Frazer was a member of Dewitt Clinton consistory, A. A. S. R., and Saladin temple, A. A. N. M. S.

NEW BEDFORD, MASS.—With the advent of cooler weather here, the past week saw an increase of trade; also a shortened supply of flowers; prices remain as usual. Chrysanthemums are now in all their glory; selling at from 75c. to $2 per dozen according to size.

The gardeners are now busy putting in bulbs before very severe weather comes. Most of the lily bulbs have been started for next Easter's crop. The bulbs this year are not as good as last year's. A large number are forced here; these have been potted up and stored away until such time as they will be wanted. E. G. Davis on Shawmut avenue has his stock in fine shape; his carnations are looking good, and he is cutting heavily of asparagus. Mr. Davis does a big gardening business.

There will not be a chrysanthemum show here this year. HORTICO.

MINNEAPOLIS, MINN.—James Souden, of the Donaldson Glass Block, Oscar Carlson of Carlson & Sandberg, and Ralph Latham attended the flower show at Chicago this week.

PAUL.

Providence, R. I.

News Items.

The suit of John J. Keller, father of Thomas Keller, florist, against the Rhode Island Company was placed on trial Wednesday in the superior court before Judge Baker and a jury. It was claimed that Mr. Keller was riding on a car, September 23, 1905, when flames burst forth from the controller box, causing the car to stop suddenly, and throwing Mr. Keller to the ground. Several of his ribs were broken and other injuries inflicted by the accident. A settlement was made by agreement between counsel before the trial proceeded far. Mr. Keller claimed $10,000 damages.

Callers on the trade the past week included Mr. Friedstead of Welch Brothers, Boston, Mass.; Mr. Green of Bayersdofer, Philadelphia; Mr. Williams of A. Herrmann, New York.

J. Kopiman, proprietor of the flower stand in Union station, has opened a wholesale cut flower room in the Flatiron building better known as Butts Block, Dorrance and Washington streets.

A large quantity of flowers was sent to the opening of the store of Hall & Lyons, apothecaries, etc. This store is situated in the Providence Journal Company Building; it is rumored the firm is to put in a cut flower department. Several hundred chrysanthemums were given away on opening day.

T. J. Johnston has been confined to the house the past two weeks with rheumatism. G. A. J.

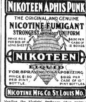

Los Angeles, Cal.

News Notes.

Albert Knapper, an old time fl ist of Frankford, Pa., after reading plant notes from Southern Califor for several months in The Florists' I change, decided to come and see himself the subjects written abo He arrived in Los Angeles about tober 1, and is so pleased with appearance of our city, which is pr tically a great park, with hor among palms and other semi-tropi plants and trees, that he has deci to stay, and has bought a home Fifty-sixth street near Figueroa str His sister, Mrs. Louisa Fleck, ca with him; and as soon as his far can close up their business affairs the East they will come to Los A geles, too, and go into the seed, pla and cut flower trade.

"One of our enterprising seed hou has a large bed of artificial tulips d played in its show window, that pr pective buyers of the bulbs may what they may expect when they b and plant the bulbs. It is a beauti theory, but does not work out practice. The writer has yet to see bed of tulips in bloom in South California. Climatic conditions do favor their growth. All Eastern peo who locate here think that they m have beds of tulips as they grew th in the East; and after repeated tri at great expense, abandon the i and devote their time and energ to Cape bulbs, which grow to perf tion in this warm, dry climate.

The weather this month has b very severe on vegetation, native humid climates. Beginning with S tember 30, when the temperature w was reached October 20, when hum ity was as low as 7 per cent. was reached October 20, when the midity was as low as 7 per cent, the temperature 86, wth the w blowing 20 miles per hour. The midity for several days has been half as much at 5 a. m. as at 5 p. I give these figures that East growers may understand what Patr O'Mara means when he says in a cent article in The Florists' Exchan "Climatic conditions existing on Pacific Slope are diametrically op site to those encountered here."

David Hewes of Orange, Cal., pioneer of the State now four sc and four years of age, is at work a park of fifty acres which is to typical of California scenery and pl life. Located on an elevation of hundred feet above the valley, it fords a commanding view of mo tains, valley and sea.

P. D. BARNHAR

SAN FRANCISCO, CAL.—Botan experts at the University of Califor are engaged in classifying and ca loguing the Brandegee collect which recently was given to the stitution. The gift of the herbari places in possession of the univers the most complete collection of Pac Coast flora now extant. This is garded important by the college thorities, as it will bring many mous men to the State University the purpose of study. ALVI

FOR a greenhouse for general purposes, there's no type of house that equals the U-Bar even-span. It combines in a practical, economical way the ornamental and the productive. U-Bar Greenhouses are the best Greenhouses built, because no other house meets so thoroughly all the demands of private estates or parks—none so attractive and productive. Pierson U-Bar Co., Designers and Builders of U-Bar Greenhouses, Metropolitan Building, 4th Avenue and 23d Street, New York.

Heating Fuels

"Tell us what fuel you have and we will give you the name of a Boiler that will give you the best results."

Sectional Boiler

Some "Pierce" Boilers are designed for different fuels; others are designed to burn soft or hard coal, gas coke or wood.

Send for catalogue and prices. We also carry Pipe and Fittings.

PIERCE, BUTLER & PIERCE MFG. CO.
Dept. 15. SYRACUSE, N. Y.
Pierce Mark Boston, New York, Philadelphia.

THE AMERICAN CARNATION
Price $3.50
A. T. DE LA MARE PTG & PUB CO. LTD
2-8 Duane Street, New York.

GREENHOUSE MATERIAL

FREE FROM SAP AND MILLED TO FIT SNUG IS WHAT WE MANUFACTURE AT OUR OWN MILLS.

WE FURNISH EVERYTHING TO COMPLETE YOUR HOUSES INCLUDING GLASS, BOILERS AND PIPE.

CATALOGUE ON APPLICATION. GET OUR PRICES.

S. JACOBS & SONS,
GREENHOUSE CONSTRUCTION MATERIAL.
1365-79 Flushing Ave., BROOKLYN, N. Y.

Mention The Florists' Exchange when writing.

GREENHOUSE LUMBER

BUILD WELL

There is a pleasant sense of satisfaction in knowing that when your order for Cypress is placed with us you will receive material upon which you can absolutely rely, and that shipment will be promptly made.

ESTIMATES AND PLANS

Furnished without charge. Let us hear from you if you contemplate building.

HOT BED SASH
CEDAR POSTS, IRON FITTINGS, ETC., ETC.

LOCKLAND LUMBER Co.
LOCKLAND, O.

Mention The Florists' Exchange when writing.

Greenhouse Materia **Hot Bed Sash**
of Louisiana Cypress and Washington Red Cedar
Greenhouse Hardware and Post Patent V and U Gutters.
OUR GRADE INVARIABLY THE BEST, OUR PRICES RIGHT.
Write for Catalogue and Estimate when figuring on your new houses.
A. DIETSCH CO., 615 to 621 Sheffield Avenue, CHICAGO, ILL.

Mention The Florists' Exchange when writing.

The Test of Workmanship

No greenhouse is a perfect house unless all the materials which enter into its construction are properly made by experienced workmen. All of our material is made by men who know that perfect material is needed to make a perfect house, and you can't grow the best stock without a perfect house. Well made material costs less than the inferior kind—less repairing to be done.

Our workmanship will stand the most critical test—how about making a comparison with the houses you have? Write for catalogue.

Next Week,
"The Test of Products."

John C. Moninger Co.
CHICAGO
115 E. Blackhawk Street

Mention the Florists' Exchange when writing.

KROESCHELL BROS. CO.
IMPROVED
Greenhouse Boiler
33 ERIE STREET, CHICAGO

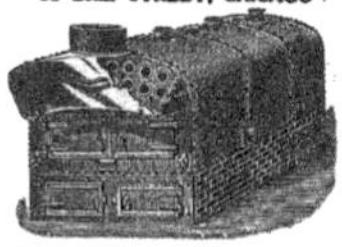

Boilers made of Steel Boiler Plate, shell firebox (sheets and heads of steel, water space all around front, sides and back). Write for information.

Mention the Florists' Exchange when writing.

FURMAN BOILERS FOR GREENHOUSE HEATING

Valuable Catalogue on Modern Steam and Hot Water Heating, mailed free upon request. Address
THE HERENDEEN MANUFACTURING CO.
620 Pearl Street, NEW YORK. Dept. F. GENEVA, N. Y.

Furman Boilers have been awarded the Certificate of Merit at Five different Florists' Conventions. Have a record of 20 years. Over 25,000 in use.
SELLING AGENT: EDW. S. DEAN, Bloomington, Ill.

Mention The Florists' Exchange when writing.

THE FLORISTS' EXCHANGE

We are a straight shoot and aim to grow into a vigorous plant

A WEEKLY MEDIUM OF INTERCHANGE FOR FLORISTS, NURSERYMEN, SEEDSMEN AND THE TRADE IN GENERAL

Vol. XXII. No. 20 | NEW YORK AND CHICAGO, NOVEMBER 17, 1906 | One Dollar Per Year

CONTENTS AND INDEX TO ADVERTISERS, PAGE 593

Mats of Burlap or Straw

which will cover two cold frames

$1.25 Each; $14.00 Dozen

TULIPS SINGLE

	100		100
Superfine mix	$ .85	Single Artus	$1.25
La Reine	.80	Chrysolora	.90
Duchess de Parma	1.00	Duc Van Thol, yel	2.00
Yellow Prince	.90		

TULIPS DOUBLE

Rex Rubrorum .... $1.50 per 100
Fine Mixed .... 85c per 100

TULIPS LATE

Gesneriana .... $1.85 per 100
Parrot .... 85c per 100

DAFFODILS DOUBLE

Incomparable .... 85c per 100
Von Sion, double nose .... $2.00 per 100

DAFFODILS SINGLE

Poeticus .... 45c per 100

Spirea Japonica, $4.00 per 100; $38.00 per 1000.
Compacta Multiflora, $5.00 per 100; $42.00 per 1000.
Astilboides Floribunda, $6.00 per 100; $45.00 per 1000.
Lily of the Valley, selected 3 year old, $10.00 per 1000; $24.00 per case of 2500.
Lilium Auratum, 9 to 11, $8.00 per 100.

Sterilized Sheep Manure, $1.25 100 lbs, $20.00 a Ton.

WM. ELLIOTT & SONS, 201 Fulton Street, NEW YORK.

Mention the Florists' Exchange when writing.

C. C. MORSE & CO.

SEED GROWERS

171-173 Clay St., San Francisco, California

OUR SPECIALTIES

ONION LETTUCE SWEET PEAS

Also Carrot, Celery, Celeriac, Cucumber, Endive, Leek, Mustard, Parsley, Parsnip, Radish, Salsify, Spinach, Tomato and

FLOWER SEEDS

Growers for the trade on contract. Warehouses at Santa Clara; Farms and Farm headquarters Carnadero, near Gilroy.

Registered Cable Address: MORSEED, SAN FRANCISCO.

Mention the Florists' Exchange when writing.

TRUE IRISH SHAMROCK SEED

NEW CROP SEED JUST RECEIVED

Plant soon if you wish good strong plants by MARCH 17

Price 1/8 oz. (About 5000 Seeds) 30c.

W. W. RAWSON & CO.

5 UNION STREET, BOSTON, MASS.

Mention the Florists' Exchange when writing.

PACIFIC SEED GROWERS' CO.

109 MARKET STREET
SAN FRANCISCO, CAL.
Specialties:
Onion, Carrot, Lettuce, Sweet Peas

Mention The Florists' Exchange when writing.

GROW YOUR OWN **TREES** and SHRUBS from **SEED.**

Send today for our

TRADE SEED LIST

and also for our *Descriptive Catalog*, which is replete with valuable information.

OTTO KATZENSTEIN & CO.

Wholesale Dept. ATLANTA, GA.

Mention The Florists' Exchange when writing.

MY GIANT CYCLAMEN

Are Ahead in Growth and Flowers
Bloodred, Carmine, Pink, Pure White, White Carmine Eyed.

Each color separate. Tr. pkt., $1.00; 1000 seeds, $6.00. An even mixture of the above 5 colors, tr. pkt., 75c.; 1000 seeds, $5.00.

For larger quantities, special quotations.

O. V. ZANGEN, Seedsman, HOBOKEN, N. J.

BURPEE'S SEEDS

PHILADELPHIA

Blue List of Wholesale Prices mailed only to those who plant for profit.

Mention the Florists' Exchange when writing.

NEW CROP SWEET PEA[S]

SEND FOR LIST OF THE NEW
GIANT FLOWERING VARIETIES

STUMPP & WALTER CO., 50 Barclay Str[eet] NEW YORK

Mention the Florists' Exchange when writing.

STOKES STANDARD SEEDS

ARE MONEY MAKERS

Write me your wants

STOKES SEED STORE

219 Market Street
Philadelphia

Mention the Florists' Exchange when writing.

ARTHUR COWEE, GLADIOLUS SPECIALIS[T]

MEADOWVALE FARM, BERLIN, N. Y.

United States Representative and Grower of GROFF'S HYBRIDS, MIXTURES and COLLECTIONS to color. Fine Mixtures of all colors. Named Novelties of rare beauty. WRITE FOR CATALOG.

Mention the Florists' Exchange when writing.

VICK'S BULBS

are now ready for distribution.

HYACINTHS, TULIPS, NARCISSUS, CROCUS, LILIES, CALLAS, FREESIAS.

All of the best quality.

Send for our Wholesale Bulb Catalogue.

JAMES VICK'S SONS

ROCHESTER, N. Y.

Mention The Florists' Exchange when writing.

SURPLUS BULBS

Special Price to Close Out

TULIPS

Fancy Selected. Twenty best bedding and forcing varieties.

NARCISSUS

Von Sion, Double Nose XXX, Trumpet Major, Golden Spur and Trumpet, Trumpet Maximus, Emperor, etc.

HYACINTHS

Bedding and Forcing. Czar Peter, La Grandesse, Baron Van Thuyll, pink; Madam Van der Hoop, Baron Van Thuyll, blue; Queen of Blues, and others.

S. G. HARRIS, TARRYTOWN, N. Y

Mention the Florists' Exchange when writing.

Catalog Engravings

and ILLUSTRATIONS

that print EASILY. That's the kind we make—have been since '73

JAS. M. BRYANT, Horticultural Engraving and Printing

706 Chestnut Street, PHILADELPHIA, PA.

Write for our Catalogue of Stock Engravings

Mention the Florists' Exchange when writing.

Thorburn's Bulb[s]

SPIRAEA per 10[0]

Japonica—Extra strong clumps .... $3 5[0]
Astilboides Floribunda .... 4 0[0]
Compacta Multiflora .... 4 5[0]
Gladstone .... 6 5[0]

LILIUM LONGIFLORUM

	per 1000	per 10[0]
6 to 8 inches	$27 00	$3 0[0]
7 to 9 "	45 00	5 0[0]
Multiflorum, 6 to 8 inches	28 00	3 0[0]
7 to 9 "	50 00	5 5[0]

PANDANUS utilis

Fresh Seeds just received $8.00 per 100 Seeds. Send for Trade List.

J. M. THORBURN & CO.,

33 Barclay St., through to 38 Park Place, NEW YORK.

Mention the Florists' Exchange when wr[iting].

Brocton Dahlia Far[m]

Has the largest and finest collection [of] Dahlias in the United States, with pri[ces] that will suit the trade.

SEND FOR PRICE LIST

W. P. LOTHROP, Prop., East Bridge[water], Mass.

Mention the Florists' Exchange when wr[iting].

JOHN SCHEEPERS & C[O.]

2, 4 and 6 OLD SLI[P]

NEW YORK CITY.

Finest Valley in cases of 500 p[ips]

See our ad. in last week's paper.

W. & D.'s Specialties for Forc[ing]

Mignonette "New York Market"
Sweet Peas "True" Christmas Flowe[r]ing (Pink and White)
Tomato "The Don" Tomato "Stirling Cas[tle]"
Mushroom Spawn "English" and "Pure Cultu[re]"
Special prices on application

WEEBER & DON, Seed Merch[ants] and Grower[s]

114 Chambers Street, NEW YORK

Mention the Florists' Exchange when w[riting].

Seed Trade Report.

AMERICAN SEED TRADE ASSOCIATION

Henry W. Wood, Richmond, Va., president; C. S. Burge, Toledo, O., first vice-president; G. B. McVay, Birmingham, Ala., second vice-president; C. E. Kendel, Cleveland, O., secretary and treasurer; J. H. Ford, Ravenna, O., assistant secretary.

PHILADELPHIA.—W. Atlee Burpee & Company were quite alarmed on Tuesday last, as a fire broke out next door to their warehouses. The only damage they sustained, however, was the flooding of their bulb storage cellar, and as there was not much stock on hand the loss was trifling.

D. R.

BERLIN, N. Y.—A fitting climax to the end of the gladiolus bulb harvest at Meadowvale Farm was a dinner given to the employes by Arthur Cowee its proprietor, at the Berlin House. The tables were beautifully decorated with chrysanthemums and roses, and smilax was tastefully festooned about the room. The harvest this year consisted of about 15,000 bushels.

DES MOINES, IA.—The Iowa Seed Company, on November 10 and 11, held an opening and flower show in their new store, which was quite a success. The firm gave away souvenirs in the form of a pamphlet setting forth the history of the concern, which was established in 1870, and containing illustrations of some of its buildings and portraits of the officers and heads of departments. M. Kurtz and Charles N. Page, general manager.

CONNECTICUT SEED NOTES.—The final round-up of Connecticut products in seeds would indicate nothing in surplus, with the possible exception of a little turnip. Sweet corn has cured perfectly, and will be fine stock and sample, but the quantity, on account of a much reduced acreage, is very much less than for the past two or three years. Onion has developed shorter than the lowest estimates, and is altogether a very disappointing crop. Prices for Connecticut grown seeds must be advanced to the wholesale seed trade for contract orders, or it will be impossible to produce quantities wanted by the trade.

CATALOGUES RECEIVED.

Remy de Provence, France.—Catalogue of Seeds.

M. HERB, Naples, Italy.—List of Novelties for 1907.

SNEED & WOOD, Tyler, Tex.—Price List of Yellow Swan and Augbert Peaches.

F. C. HEINEMANN, Erfurt, Germany.—Special Trade List of Novelties for 1907; also Colored Plate.

IMPERIAL SEED AND PLANT COMPANY, Baltimore, Md.—Trade Price List of Bulbs, Plants, etc.

NORTHAMPTON NURSERIES, Northampton, Mass.—Catalogue of Nursery Stock, Hardy Perennials, Roses, etc.

European Notes.

The phenomenal Summer of 1906 is ended at last, and the rains necessary for our Fall plantings of turnips and rutabagas which have survived the drought are now fairly abundant. While in the face of the present condition of the market for these articles the inevitable shortage may not cause any immediate alarm, it may well be borne in mind when prices are being fixed for next season's trade.

To such of the British farmers as grow red clover the drought has been a blessing in disguise, for instead of having a second cut, a big crop of seed has been secured which is readily sold at very good prices. It is reported that considerable quantities of this seed are being exported to your side. Rape still keeps very high and will probably go higher still, although it is reported that some of the large dealers in Holland are holding back heavy stocks in anticipation of a big demand in the Spring. It is reported that some of the more important buyers on your side have not yet placed their orders, and as some of them are reported to have cut prices very badly in the past, the legitimate trader should now have a chance to make a profit on his early sales.

As regards garden seeds, the conditions are very discouraging, as every crop delivered only emphasizes the loss occasioned by the drought.

Flower seeds, with the exception of sweet peas, make a better showing, and even asters promise to be good in quality, although there can hardly be an average crop.

EUROPEAN SEED.

FOREIGN TARIFF SCHEDULES.—The Department of Commerce and Labor, through its Bureau of Manufactures, has compiled from the tariff schedules of all countries rates of duty imposed on agricultural products of every description. Following are rates affecting the seed trade on imports into Austria-Hungary.

(A Kilogram is 2.2046 pounds; Krone, $0.203).

	Unit of Quantity	Rate of Duty General	Conventional
	Kilos	Kronen	Kronen
Beans, Peas, Lentils	100	4.50	2.40
Rape seed and Colza seed, also hedge mustard seed and oleaginour radish seed	"	3.50	3.00
Poppy seed	"	14.00	3.00
Linseed and hemp seed, oil seed not otherwise specified	"	Free	Free
Mustard seed (also ground mustard in casks)	"	3.00	...
Mustard seed (not ground in casks)	"	3.00	Free
Clover seed			
(a) esparcet seed	"	10.00	8.00
(b) other	"	30.00	8.00
Grass seed	"	30.00	Free

Under the heading of vegetables and vegetable substances not specially mentioned, live trees and plants, seeds, and flower bulbs are admitted into Belgium duty free.

Seeds other than medicinal, and especially colza and all other oleaginous seeds, are admitted duty free into Denmark.

The French tariff admits oleaginous fruits and seeds duty free. On seeds for planting (including vetch) the maximum and minimum rate of duty per 100 kilos is 3 francs; on beet-root seed, 30 francs; and on alfalfa and clover seeds the maximum rate is 30 francs and the minimum 25 francs.

NURSERY DEPARTMENT.

Conducted by Joseph Meehan.

AMERICAN ASSOCIATION OF NURSERYMEN, Orlando Harrison, Berlin, Md., president; J. W. Hill, Des Moines, Ia., vice-president; George C. Seager, Rochester, N. Y., secretary; C. L. Yates, Rochester, N. Y., treasurer.

THE VERMONT HORTICULTURAL SOCIETY will hold its annual meeting in Armory Hall, Burlington, on December 5 and 6. An interesting program has been arranged; among the speakers will be J. H. Hale, South Glastonbury, Conn., and S. D. Willard, Geneva, N. Y. Full particulars can be obtained of Secretary Wm. Stuart, Burlington, Vt.

Seasonable Notes.

There is no end to the demand for Rosa rugosa—for single planting, grouping and all purposes for which it is used. It is such a hardy subject and stands well wherever planted, that it is no wonder it is continually called for.

Only those who have tried it know what a help to plants in Winter is a good litter of leaves placed around the roots. Many plants are hardy, but the heaving out by freezings and thawings causes their death. When leaves are placed around them it keeps out hard freezings—a great help to plants transplanted in Autumn.

Even the hardiest rhododendrons are much the better for a covering of forest leaves, such as they usually get in their wild state. The foliage has a better appearance when Spring comes when this is done. Shade, too, is what they desire and what the leaves give them.

The golden and bronze leaved varieties of Arbor vitæ are of their brightest color when growing in the full sun. Those who have them in pots for selling should remember this. When shaded by crowding or from other causes, there is but little change from the green color.

A Pottstown (Pa.) correspondent asks which is the most profitable market pear to plant—Kieffer or Lawrence. Lawrence is by far the better quality pear, but the Kieffer is the better shipper. Both are in demand, and it may prove well to set out an equal number of each.

When tree seeds are sown in the Autumn they will do better if covered with sand or sandy loam rather than with stiff soil. Sand settles about the seeds completely, and this close contact is most beneficial. Besides this, when Spring comes there is easy work for the seedlings to come through the covering.

Where space for spreading is limited and an evergreen to grow tall is required for protection or for screening, there is nothing better than American Arbor vitæ. It is often used in this way to hide objectionable objects, and sometimes for a Winter shelter.

The partly evergreen character of the California privet is well displayed in early Winter. When surrounding bushes are bare of leaves the deep green of those of the privet are a cheering sight. It is worth planting for this alone.

Ribes sanguineum, a native of Washington and Oregon, does not thrive very well in the Eastern States. One called Gordonianum, of a light red color, does much better. The climate of England just suits the R. sanguineum.

Globe Arbor Vitaes.

As the season for making cuttings of Arbor vitæs and other evergreens will soon be here, a word or two concerning globe Arbor vitæs will be in order. In nurseries globe Arbor vitæs stand for those of the variety of American Arbor vitæ known as Thuja globosa. This is the most globe-shaped grower of all the varieties, but it has the objection of having foliage of a dull brown color. There are two other fairly globe-shaped ones to be had in nurseries, one is Hoveyi, another pumila. Hoveyi is of a pleasing green color all the time; so is pumila, and where it is but a question of a dwarf Arbor vitæ of globe growth, both of these are to be preferred to the common globosa when one of a deep green is required.

Cuttings of these may be made at any time now. The sooner they are made the better rooted they will be before Spring, but very nice plants result from cuttings made by New Year's and placed in a warm greenhouse.

There is a miniature Arbor vitæ called Little Gem, which grows but about three inches a year. It is an interesting sort, but it is really too dwarf to be very serviceable.

A Red Snowberry Tangle.

At this season of the year, early November, one of the pleasing sights on many a lawn are the groups of the red snowberry, Symphoricarpos vulgaris. This is a bush which left to itself forms a graceful, drooping habit, in itself very pleasing. The greenish white flowers of Spring make no display, but in Autumn its branches are weighted down with clusters of small red berries, the clusters so close together that the berries cover the whole length of the shoots. This is when its Autumn display is at its best. When growing in one place for a few years there spring up about it numerous suckers, forming in time large clumps, and it is these large clumps that produce such a display of color when the Autumn season comes.

On account of the suckering referred to, as well as to its low growth, the red snowberry has been named as a very desirable shrub for planting on sloping ground liable to wash in stormy weather; and it is an excellent shrub for the purpose, its underground shoots holding the ground well.

The name snowberry is probably applied to the symphoricarpos because of the white berries of one of them, the S. racemosus, though as the berries of all the species are in good condition when Winter sets in, it may come from this fact and not because of the color of the fruit. Whether the red or the white berried one be used, a tangle of them, where such a mass of plants is fitting, would be sure to give pleasure when the display of berries is at its height in Autumn. Occasionally this shrub is seen as a pot plant, and the wonder is that it is not more grown in this way, since it holds its berries long after Christmas, and there is such a demand for red-berried plants for that occasion.

Getting Roots to Hickory Trees.

Every nurseryman and every planter knows the difficulty of getting hickories to live when transplanted. Unless some means have been taken to induce a formation of roots there is little success following the transplanting of trees over a year or two old.

The late A. S. Fuller, a good authority on such matters, because he spoke from his own experience, contended that by sowing the hickory nuts in sandy soil the seedlings would be fairly fibrous, while sown in deep soil the opposite would be the result. In nursery sowings good soil is usually sought out for the seed of all kinds, and as a result the hickories are found with but one root and it a tap root of some length. Transplanted when but a year or two old such seedlings do well, but how much better it would be had the seedlings the fibrous roots the sandy soil is said to produce!

Hickory seedlings should be transplanted when two years old, and at that time the end of the root cut off. Then when reset they may stand two or three years longer, when another transplanting should be given them, after which they would be tolerably safe to be sold with but little risk of their being lost in transplanting. As it is to-day, it is the hardest work possible to get these trees from nurseries, whereas the sales of them would be good, if they could be had as other trees are. It is this uncalled-for scarcity of hickories in nurseries that makes the presence of one of them in newly planted collections a rare sight, thus ignoring one of the most useful of our native forest trees. Almost all the trees found in grounds are of natural growth.

This is the time to sow the nuts, now or in early Spring. If sown now, cover with about four inches of soil, and after this afford a covering of forest leaves or corn stalks for the Winter. Should Spring sowing be preferred, keep the nuts in a cool place mixed with damp sand or soil, and sow as early in Spring as can be done. It is always quite late in Spring before the seedlings appear.

JOSEPH MEEHAN.

AMONG THE GROWERS

L. E. Marquisee, Syracuse, N. Y.

An afternoon can be profitably spent at any season of the year in the company of that enthusiastic member of the fraternity, L. E. Marquisee, whom we fortunately found at home at time of our visit last week. We discussed the merits and demerits of a house of seedling carnations as we passed through until reaching a house of Flamingo, which was a grand sight, being in full crop, and will continue so until Christmas. Here is a carnation that will yet prove its value as a commercial variety. Next was a house of Dorner's White Perfection, which grown in a temperature of 58 degrees does well. Following was a house of Enchantress, and undoubtedly it would be impossible to see a grander sight than what we looked upon. "It is the best money-maker yet introduced," said Mr. Marquisee. "We commenced cutting September 1, and there has been no let-up since that date."

The Marchioness is said here to be the grandest white yet discovered. It is a gem of the first water, being of translucent whiteness, a perfect ball, reminding one of a double hollyhock, excepting that the petals are deeper; finely serrated, borne on long stem, does not burst, very fragrant and free. It is now in full crop, although pinched back twice; otherwise it would have been in crop by October 1. We counted 19 flowering shoots on a plant of average size. As this is its third season, and it has proved so satisfactory thus far, there is little reason to doubt a great future for this grand flower. Its parents are two of our best standard kinds.

A companion seedling is a fine crimson, also a gem, just the color needed—light shading to dark, without a trace of purple or black. In habit and floriferousness it leaves nothing to be desired.

Passing to chrysanthemums we saw some excellent varieties. In white, for succession, are grown in the flowering order: October Frost, Opah, G. S. Kalb, and Ivory. Amorita is the earliest pink, followed by Dr. Enguehard. Harry Sinclair is a fine yellow and should be more largely grown. Later kinds are Wm. H. Lincoln, Major Bonnaffon, and Timothy Eaton.

We noted an adiantum which has been grown here for several years and has not been identified. It looks like an improved decorum. Firm of texture, and deep in color, it is a valuable variety.

M.

A Field of Kudzu Vines.

The accompanying illustration shows a field of kudzu vines at the nursery of John C. Teas, near Carthage, Mo. The immense leaves, sometimes more than half a yard across, were waist deep, and had completely enveloped everything within their reach, including a large old elm and a group of Rhus cotinoides, and other large trees. Visitors very appropriately named it "an ocean of bean vines."

The kudzu vine was brought to this country by the Japanese for their exhibit at the centennial exhibition in Philadelphia in 1876. John C. Teas secured plants soon afterward, and the original vines were planted near the foreground (as shown in the picture) more than 25 years ago.

Field of Kudzu Vine at Nurseries of John C. Teas, Carthage, Mo.

BOXWOOD

By the Car Load.

8 feet Pyramids .... $1.50 each
5 feet " .... 4.00 each

Other sizes at proportionate prices. Every plant a specimen.

HIRAM T. JONES, Union County Nurseries, Elizabeth, N. J.

Mention the Florists' Exchange when writing.

H. DEN OUDEN & SON,

BOSKOOP, HOLLAND.

Wholesale growers of nursery stock for the American trade. Catalogue free on demand. Also views in our nurseries.

Mention the Florists' Exchange when writing.

HERBACEOUS PERENNIALS

for Summer and Autumn Planting. We offer NINE HUNDRED and SIXTY-SEVEN VARIETIES of STRONG FIELD-GROWN PLANTS. Send for Catalog and Trade List.

BAY STATE NURSERIES, NORTH ABINGTON, MASS

Mention the Florists' Exchange when writing.

F. & F. NURSERIES

SPRINGFIELD NEW JERSEY

Wholesale Growers — TREES AND PLANTS in full assortment. Trade Catalogue Free

Mention the Florists' Exchange when writing.

SEASONABLE STOCK FOR FLORISTS

HYDRANGEAS for forcing { OTAKSA and THOS. HOGG } With 7-12 flowering crowns, $12.00 per 100.
" 5-6 " " 9.00 "
" 4 " " 7.00 "

From 6-inch pots and open beds, all out-door grown.

ROSES, Strong, two-years, field-grown, selected for forcing.

HYBRID PERPETUALS .... $10.00 and $12.00 per 100.
CRIMSON RAMBLER .... 9.00 "
DOROTHY PERKINS .... 7.00 "

and

LADY GAY, a new hardy climbing Rose of exceptional merit; ready now from 2¼ inch pots only. Write for prices.

JACKSON & PERKINS CO.

WHOLESALE NURSERYMEN AND FLORISTS

NEWARK, WAYNE CO., NEW YORK

Mention the Florists' Exchange when writing.

CALIFORNIA PRIVET

Branched, $8.00 and $10.00 per 1000. Samples Free

HENRY EICHHOLZ, Waynesboro, Pa.

Mention the Florists' Exchange when writing.

CALIFORNIA PRIVET

Fine well-graded, two year plants, well packed as follows: 15 to 20 inches, 3 or more branches, $1.50 per 100; $8.00 per 1000, this grade gives good satisfaction.

20 to 30 inches, 5 or more branches, $2.00 per 100; $13.50 per 1000, nice.

2½ to 3 ft., 7 or more branches, $3.00 per 100; $17.50 per 1000, very strong.

3 to 4 ft., strong selected, $4.00 per 100; $25.00 per 1000.

CHAS. BLACK, Hightstown, N. J.

Mention the Florists' Exchange when writing.

Trees and Shrubs

We make specially low prices on nursery stock to Parks, Cemeteries, etc.

Wholesale price list on application.

We carry immense quantities of the finest named varieties of peonies.

PETERSON NURSERY

508 W. PETERSON AVE. CHICAGO, ILL

Mention the Florists' Exchange when writing.

Specimen Nursery Stock

DECIDUOUS TREES and SHRUBS, EVERGREENS, RHODODENDRONS, AZALEAS, over one hundred (100) acres of the choicest varieties. Send for price list.

COTTAGE GARDENS COMPANY

QUEENS, LONG ISLAND, N. Y.

Mention the Florists' Exchange when writing.

KOSTER & CO.

Hollandia Nurseries BOSKOOP, HOLLAND

Hardy Azaleas, Box Trees, Clematis, Conifers, Hydrangeas, Peonies.

Pot-Grown Plants for Forcing.

RHODODENDRONS, H. P. ROSES, Etc.

Catalogue free on demand.

Mention the Florists' Exchange when writing.

Commercial Violet Culture

PRICE, $1.50

The FLORISTS' EXCHANGE, 2-8 Duane St., New York

Holland Nursery Stock

Ask for Our Catalogue. It will interest you.

ENDTZ, VAN NES & CO. BOSKOOP, HOLLAND

Mention the Florists' Exchange when writing.

FERNS and Crimson Rambler ROSES

10,000 Ferns, in fine shape, low stocky plants, not drawn, grown in full light, and as they were pot plants, lifts with fine balls.

Bostons, for 6 in., $20.00 per 100; for 5 in., $15.00.
Piersoni, for 6 in., $25.00 per 100; for 5 in., $20.00.
Scottii, for 5 in., $20.00 per 100; for 4 in., $15.00.

1,000 Crimson Ramblers, for Easter forcing, 2 year old, 3 to 4 ft., several canes well ripened and good roots, $2.00 per doz.; $15.00 per 100.

Asparagus Plumosus Nanus, 2½ in., fine, $2.50 per 100.

Sprengeri and Plumosus Nanus, 4 in., $1.00 per doz.

5,000 Vinca Major, variegated, field stock, extra fine, $5.00 per 100; $45.00 per 1000

Vinca Major, variegated, and Hydrangea Otaksa, 2½ in., pot plants, $2.50 per 100. Hydrangea Paniculata Grandiflora, Spirea Anthony Waterer, and Spirea Van Houtti, 3 year old, large bushes, $1.00 per dozen or $7.00 per 100.

50,000 Shrubs, Vines, Cannas, etc. These must be sold low. List free.

Cash please.

BENJ. CONNELL

WEST GROVE, PA.

Mention the Florists' Exchange when writing.

New Pink Rose

Miss Kate Moulton

Is the QUEEN of all Pink Roses

Write us about it

Minneapolis Floral Co., - Minneapolis, Minn.

Mention the Florists' Exchange when writing.

Grafted Roses

Edw. J. Taylor Southport, Connecticut

Mention the Florists' Exchange when writing.

Large Assortment PEONIES Very best Varieties

LOW PRICES

THE KIND THAT FLORISTS LIKE

"We make a specialty of growing stocky transplanted shrubbery and trees"

FULL ASSORTMENT OF Ornamentals, Fruits, Roses, Clematis, and Herbaceous Plants

Write for our fall wholesale trade list.

W. & T. SMITH CO., GENEVA, N. Y

Mention the Florists' Exchange when writing.

ROSES

Climbing Clothilde Soupert, Marie Pavie, Crimson Rambler and Dorothy Perkins . . .

Grafted Oranges and Kin Kans, Palms, Biota Aurea Nana, Conifers and Other Stock for Florists and Nurserymen

IN IMMENSE QUANTITIES

400 ACRES IN NURSERIES 60,000 FEET OF GLASS

CATALOG ON APPLICATION

P. J. BERCKMANS CO. (Inc.)

FRUITLAND NURSERIES

Established 1856. AUGUSTA, GA

Mention The Florists' Exchange when writing.

GRAFTED ROSES

Fine Stock from 3-in. pots.

Richmond, $2.50 per doz., $15.00 per 100, $125.00 per 1000.

Killarney, $2.00 per doz., $15.00 per 100.

Etoile de France, $3.00 per doz., $18.00 per 100.

Kaiserin, Carnot, Uncle John, Chatenay, $2.00 per doz., $15.00 per 100.

Bridesmaid, Golden Gate, Wootton, $2.00 per doz., $12.00 per 100.

ROSES OWN ROOTS

Fine Stock from 3-in. pots.

Richmond, $10.00 per 100; $90.00 per 1000.

Etoile de France, $12.00 per 100.

Sunrise, Perle, Sunset, Chatenay, $8.00 per 100.

Bridesmaid, Golden Gate, $7.00 per 100.

Asparagus Plumosus Nanus from 3-inch pots, $8.00 per 100; Sprengeri from 3-inch pots, $6.00 per 100.

Send for Catalogue.

WOOD BROS., Fishkill, N. Y.

Mention The Florists' Exchange when writing.

Rose Baby Rambler

X X X

Our plants are last year's propagation and have had a full season's growth. Extra fine bushy. $12.00 per 100. Special price in quantities.

NATHAN SMITH & SON, Adrian, Mich.

Mention the Florists' Exchange when writing.

ROSES

EXTRA HEAVY IMPORTED HYBRID PERPETUALS

in all leading varieties, per 10 $1.50, per 100 $12.50
CRIMSON RAMBLER .... " 15.00
BABY RAMBLER .... " 17.50

PERENNIAL GARDENS CO., - TOLEDO, O.

Mention the Florists' Exchange when writing.

Queen Beatrice Rose

Four to one shot. Four times as many flowers as Maid.

F. H. KRAMER, 916 F St. Washington, D. C.

Mention The Florists' Exchange when writing.

PANSIES

Brown's Extra Select Superb Giant Prize Pansies. Awarded Silver Medal, St. Louis Exposition, 1904.

PLANTS, mixed colors, in any quantity, $3.00 per 1000.

CASH WITH ORDER.

PETER BROWN, Lancaster, Pa.

Mention The Florists' Exchange when writing.

SEED PANSY PLANT

THE JENNINGS STRAIN

50,000 plants now ready. From finest selecte[d] stock, large flowering, fancy colors, in gre[at] variety. Stock is first-class in every respe[ct]. 100 by mail, 60c.; by express, 500, $2.00; 1000 $4.[00]; 2000, $7.00; 3000, $10.00. Seed, $1.00 per pkt. [of] 4000; 1 oz., $5.00; 2 oz., $9.00; 3 oz., $12.00. Cash with order.

PANSIES in bud and bloom, fine plants for winter blooming, $1.00 per 100; $7.50 per 1000.

E. B. JENNINGS

Lock Box 254 Southport, Conn.

Grower of the Finest Pansies

Mention the Florists' Exchange when writin[g].

PANSY PLANTS

The best strain on the market; none better, fi[ne] plants, 40c. per 100; $2.50 per 1000.

DAISIES (Bellis), 35c. per 100; $2.00 per 1000.

FORGET-ME-NOTS, 50c. per 100; $3.00 [per] 1000.

SWEET ALYSSUM, double Giant, for win[ter] flowering, 2½ in., $1.50 per 100.

SMILAX, bushy plants, 2½ in., $1.00 per 100.

CINERARIAS, 2½ in., $2.00 per 100; 4 in., $[...] per 1000.

GERANIUMS, 100,000 ready in 2½ in., best va[ri]eties, $15.00 per 1000. Send for list.

J. C. SCHMIDT CO., BRISTOL, P[A].

Mention the Florists' Exchange when writ[ing].

VEGETABLE PLANT[S]

CABBAGE New Early and Successi[on] $1.25 per 1000

LETTUCE Grand Rapids, Big Boston, B[os]ton Market and Tennis B[all] $1.00 per 1000.

PARSLEY Moss Curled, $1.25 per 1000.

TOMATOES Lorillard and Mayflower [...] cts. per doz., $2.00 per 100.

R. VINCENT, Jr. & SON, White Marsh, M[d].

Mention the Florists' Exchange when writ[ing].

Leedle grown Roses are now Bi[g]

FLORAL COMP'Y Springfield, O. Expert Growers Send for price list	H. P.'s, H. T.'s, T.'s, R.'s, Cl.'s, B., etc. 101 best sorts, on own roots from 2½ and 4 in pots.	values the bu[...] Send [...] want [...]

Mention the Florists' Exchange when writ[ing].

AMERICAN BEAUTIE[S]

We have them. You want them. We [are] booking orders for early delivery. Fine st[ock]. Write us for price.

ALDRICH FLORAL COMPANY, 26 E. High SPRINGFIELD

Mention the Florists' Exchange when writ[ing].

Decorative Plant Notes.

COCOS WEDDELIANA.—For various forms of decoration there is no plant grown that combines so many serviceable qualities as Cocos Weddeliana. In its small state it is used by itself in filling dishes, and along with ferns and other small decorative plants. It is also used frequently for dinner table decoration either in the form of a center-piece made of a number of plants, or when occasion calls for more elaborate display, small or medium size well grown plants are used with graceful effect in the scheme of decoration.

When the decoration of rooms calls for material in keeping with the delicate character of the interior furnishings and other embellishments, cocos falls right in line for this kind of work. Plants in sizes of pots from 3-inch to 6-inch are best suited.

The cultivation of Cocos Weddeliana differ in one or two essential points from that of most other palms in that the former require a slightly higher temperature, and that they take less kindly to syringing overhead. Instead of planting several cocos seeds in one deep pot, as is sometimes done, with the perplexing result that in potting singly there arises the difficulty of getting the long tap root in a pot of the desired size, the better way is to put one seed only in a thumb pot, thereby reducing to a minimum the danger of breaking the tap root, essential for the growth of the plant. The compost for the seed pots should be leaf mold and peat. Over potting should be especially avoided with cocos; and as heavy syringing is injurious in order to sustain the plants as long as is consistent with safety to their development, the bench on which they stand should be kept as damp as possible and the path also frequently sprinkled with water.

I am of the opinion that for various obvious reasons every species of plant thrives best when given a house for its own exclusive occupancy, and I think it will pay to keep this in mind in the cultivation of cocos especially. But if, as is often the case, such accommodation is out of the question, a bench at least should be given to it. For the repotting of cocos a good compost is made out of leaf mold, peat, a third of each, and the other part of fibrous loam and sand. Cocos should not be potted with the persistent ramming usually adopted in potting palms; easier and looser potting suits them better.

D. M.

Forcing Rhubarb.

There are very few things that respond to forcing so easily as rhubarb, and there are also but few things requiring so little care and attention during the period of forcing as it does. Now when the ground outdoors begins to harden by the action of frost, rhubarb should, when intended for forcing, be taken up in the quantity desired for the season and placed in some easily accessible corner ready for operations. A slight rest is beneficial, and after that has been given the plants or roots may be placed under a greenhouse bench, or in any other place where light can be excluded and the temperature does not fall below 45 degrees. Horse manure may and doubtless will to most persons be objectionable in a greenhouse, but anywhere else a layer of horse manure laid on the ground and the roots placed thereon will hasten results. For covering, any kind of soil will do, but leaf mold suits better than anything else. For greenhouse forcing under benches use for a bottom leaf mold, covering the roots with the same material. A thorough watering should be given after the roots are covered, and water occasionally afforded afterward, as their condition may indicate. Two to four year old roots answer the purposes of forcing better than younger stock.

D. M.

Adiantum Farleyense

Good thrifty stock, 3 inch pots . . . $20.00 per 100

THORN HEDGE GREENHOUSES, Newtown Square, Pa.

Mention the Florists' Exchange when writing.

FERNS. NEPHROLEPIS BARROWSII

2¼ inch, $6.00 per 100.

HUGH GRAHAM CO.,

Logan Nurseries, York Road and Louden Street, PHILADELPHIA, PA

Mention The Florists' Exchange when writing.

FERNS OUR SPECIALTY

Cibotium Schiedei: We have a grand stock of this magnificent tree fern in all sizes, 3 in. pots, $35.00 per 100; 4 in. pots, $45.00 per 100; 6 in. pots, $70.00 per 100; 7 in. pots, $1.70 each; 8 in. pots, $2.50 each.

Assorted Ferns, from 2¼ in. pots, all the best market varieties, $3.00 per 100, or $25.00 per 1000; 4 inch pots, $12.00 per 100.
If by mail add 10c. each 100 plants.

Adiantum Cuneatum, 3 in. pots, $3.50 per 100
" " 4 in. pots, 12.00 " "
" **Rhodophyllum** 4 in. pots, $25.00 per 100
" **Lathamii,** 4 in. pots, $20.00 per 100
" **Regina,** 4 in. pots, $35.00 per 100

Fern Spores gathered from our own stock plants 35c. per trade package or $4.00 per doz. packages

ANDERSON & CHRISTENSEN,
SHORT HILLS, N. J.

Mention The Florists' Exchange when writing.

FERNS FROM BENCH

BOSTON, 4 in. 10c.; 5 in., 12½c.
TARRYTOWN, 2½ in., 4c.; 3 in., 10c.; 4 in., 15c.; 5 in., 25c. Runners $20.00 per 1000.
SCOTTII, 3 in., 8c.; 4 in., 12½c.
Pansy Plants, Giants, $3.00 per 1000.
Daisies, double Longfellow, Delicata, $2.50 per 1000.
Asparagus sprengeri, 2 in., 2cts.
Flowering Begonias, 8 kinds, 2 in., 2½ cts.
Forgetmenots, $2.50 per 1000.
Hollyhocks, double, 4 kinds, 1 year old, 8 cts.
Hardy Pinks, 3 kinds, field plants, 3½ cts.
Hardy Carnations, nice young plants from frames, $2.00 per 100.

Cash or C. O. D.

BYER BROS., Chambersburg, Pa

Mention The Florists' Exchange when writing.

ASPIDIUM TSUSSEMENSE

Extra large bushy plants in 3-inch pots, $6.00 per 100.

CYRTOMIUM FALCATUM

Large, full plants, 3-inch pots, the best stock we have ever offered, 6c.; 2 inch pots, 3c.

ASSORTED FERNS

Fine bushy plants, 2-inch pots, 3c.

Two No. 4-Weathered boilers in good condition at a bargain

R. G. HANFORD, - NORWALK, CONN.

Mention the Florists' Exchange when writing.

FERNS

Boston, Barrowsii and Scottii, 6 in., $4.00 per doz.; 5 in., $2.50 per doz.

Boston and Scottii, 3 in., $6.00 per 100. 4 in., $8.00 per 100.

Strong runners of **Whitmani** $15.00 per 100.

Larchmont Nurseries

Larchmont, N. Y.

Mention The Florists' Exchange when writing.

COCOS PALMS.

Strong 2¼ inch at $1.50 per dozen. Write for lowest prices on Kentias.

Jas. F. Barclay R. I. GREENHOUSES Pawtucket, R. I.

Mention The Florists' Exchange when writing.

WHITMANI FERN

Large stock of strong plants, 2¼ inch pots, $12.00 per 100. 4 inch pots $25.00 per 100.

TARRYTOWN FERN 1.00

3 inch pots.....$8.00

SCOTTII

2¼ inch pots.....$ 5.00
4 inch pots..... 12.00

KENTIA FORSTERIANA

4 inch pots, made up, strong and bushy.....$25.00
5 inch pots, made up, strong and bushy..... 50.00

No order for less than 10 plants accepted.

CHAS. H. CAMPBELL,

3601 GERMANTOWN AVE., PHILA., PA

Mention The Florists' Exchange when writing.

Grower of Palms, Ferns and other Decorative Stock.

Nephrolepis Scottii all the year round

JOHN SCOTT

Rutland Road & E. 45th St., BROOKLYN, N. Y

Telephone 1890 Bedford.

Mention the Florists' Exchange when writing.

Adiantum Farleyense

I can quote splendid stock at from $2.00 per dozen up to $24.00 per dozen, in 2-inch to 6-inch pots. If you are looking for Far eyense, better write me about it.

CHARLES H. TOTTY, Madison, N. J.

Mention The Florists' Exchange when writing.

NEPHROLEPIS

Whitmani, 2¼ in., $25.00 per 100.
Barrowsii, $10.00 per 100.

Henry H. Barrows & Son, Whitman, Mass.

Mention The Florists' Exchange when writing.

BARGAIN TO MAKE ROOM

1,000 **N. Piersoni Elegantissima Ferns,** from 2½ in. pots, $8.00 per 100. A No. 1 stock: ready for 4 and 5 in. pots. Cash with order, please.

R. ENGELMAN & SON
PITTSFIELD, MASS.

Mention The Florists' Exchange when writing.

FERNS

For jardinieres, etc., 2½ inch, $3.00 per 100.
Kentia Belmoreana, clean and bushy, 5 in. 50c.
Boston Ferns, Piersoni and Scottii, from bench, 10c. to 25c. each, 4 in. pot grown, 15c.
Cocos Weddeliana, 2½ in. 10c.
Asparagus Plumosus, 2½ in. $3.00 per 100.

H. WESTON, HEMPSTEAD, N. Y.

Mention The Florists' Exchange when writing.

ROBERT CRAIG & CO.

ROSES, PALMS, CROTONS

CARNATIONS and Novelties in DECORATIVE PLANTS

Market and 49th Sts. PHILADELPHIA, PA.

Mention The Florists' Exchange when writing.

OPEN YOUR EYES

PREPARE FOR THANKSGIVING and the HOLIDAYS

Watch Prosperity Look

Election is now over, the country settled, the outlook is good. Great prosperity is now in sight for us all. Why not for you? A little fortune lies now before your door; why not grab it while there is a chance open for you? Look at others, see how successful they are. How is that? Because they are wide awake; they are on the lookout and watch the market, and take advantage when bargains can be had. A big demand is in sight for now and for the coming holidays, for **Araucaria, Excelsa, Araucaria Excelsa Glauca,** and **Araucaria Compacta Robusta. THE PET OF ALL DECORATIVE PLANTS.** What do you think: where will you buy them? Surely from a man who makes a specialty of ARAUCARIAS, and who can offer you bargains. Godfrey Aschmann is the man who has the reputation for the last 10 years as the great Araucaria Importer and Cultivator of America. Prices are now slaughtered down one-half of their usual valuation; never have they been so low in the history of **araucaria** cultivation. You ask, how is that? Just for the simple reason we want the room to cultivate our immense stock for Easter.

We plant 5,000 **Araucarias,** together with an immense stock of **Boston, Scottii, Barrowsii fern, Kentia Forsteriana,** Arecas, Gloire de Lorraine Begonias, and many thousands of other plants must be sold by Christmas; numerous prices.

ARAUCARIA EXCELSA. Only Spring importation is offered. Well rooted and stand shipping well. 5 1-2 in. pots, 15 to 18 in. high, 4 to 5 tiers, 3 years old, 60c., 5 1-2 to 6 in. pots, 18 to 23 in. high, 5 to 6 tiers, 4 years old, 75c. 6 in. pots, 23 to 25 in. high, 5, 6, 7 tiers, 4 years old, $1.00. 6 to 7 in. pots, 25 to 30 in. high, 5, 6, 7 tiers, 4 years old, $1.25. 7 in. specimen plants from $1.50 to $2.00.

ARAUCARIA COMPACTA ROBUSTA—Have several thousand of them; can supply all wants. These plants were never so fine in shape and condition as this year. The pet of the greenhouse, as broad as long, 6 in. pots, 3 tiers, 12-14-18 ins. high, same across, 3 years old, $1.00 to $1.25. 6 to 7 in. pots, 4 to 5 tiers, 18-20-22-25 ins. high, same across, 4 years old, $1.50 to $1.75. 7 in. pots, specimens, 6 to 7 tiers, 25 to 30 in. high, same across, 5 years old, $2.00 to $2.50.

ARAUCARIA EXCELSA GLAUCA—This variety on account of its beautiful Green-Bluish tiers, dwarf habit, fine compact shape, gives it a striking appearance, and anybody seeing them, must undoubtedly fall in love with them at sight. Plants, 6 in. pots, 3 tiers, 14 to 20 in. high, same across, 3 years old, $1.00 to $1.25. 6 to 7 in. pots, 4 to 5 tiers, 20-25 to 30 in. high, same across, 4 years old, $1.50 to $1.75. 7 in. pots, specimens, 5 tiers, 30 to 35 in. high, as broad as long, the finest you ever have seen, $2.00 to $2.50.

KENTIA BELMOREANA, 5 1-2 to 6 in. pots, bushy, fine plants, from $1.00 to $1.25 each.

KENTIA FORSTERIANA, 7 in. pots, made up, 1 large size, about 45 to 45 in. high in the center, and 3 smaller size shoots 25 to 30 in. high around, which gives them a fine appearance, price, $2.00 to $2.50 each. 6 in. pots, single plants, 36 to 45 in. high, 5 to 6 good leaves, 4 years old, $1.25-$1.50-$1.75 each. 6 in. pots, 32 to 36 in. high, 5 to 6 good leaves $1.00 each. 5 1-2 to 6 in. pots, 30 in. high, 5 good leaves, 4 years old, 75c. to 85c. each. 4 in. made up, with 3 plants to the pot, 18-20-25 in. high, 25c., 30c., 35c. each

FICUS ELASTICA, 6 in., 40c. and 50c.

ARECA LUTESCENS, 5 in. pots, 24 in. high, made-up with 3 plants, 35c. 4 in. pots, 20 to 24 in. high, made up with 3 plants, 25c.

ARECA SAPIDA, just imported from Belgium, something new, looks like a Kentia palm, about 25 in. high. Look! only 50c. each, worth $1.00. This is a bargain seldom offered.

ASPARAGUS PLUMOSUS NANUS, 4 in. pots, large, bushy, 10c to 12c.

ASPARAGUS SPRENGERI, 4 in. pots, 10c.

FERNS, all raised in pots and not on benches as follows:

NEPHROLEPIS BARROWSII, 7 in. pots, as big as a bushel basket, 75c. to $1.00 each. 6 in. pots, large, ready for 7 in., 50c.; 5 1-2 in., 40c.; 5 in., 35c.; 4 in., 25c.

NEPHROLEPIS SCOTTII, 8 in., as big as a washtub, worth $2.00, now $1.25; 7 in., as big as a bushel basket, worth $1.25, now 75c.; 6 in., 50c.; 5 1-2 in., 40c.; 4 in., 20c.

NEPHROLEPIS ELEGANTISSIMA, 5 in. pots, 30c.

BOSTON FERNS, 7 in., very bushy, only 75c.; 6 in., 50c. or $5.00 per doz.; 5 in., 30c. to 35c.; 4 in., 20c.

AZALEA INDICA, just arrived, selected by myself on my recent trip to Belgium. Have all leading varieties such as Deutsche Perle, Simon Mardner, and Vervæneana. These three sorts are good for Christmas forcing. Later varieties: Empress of India, Oroff, Wolters, Niobe, Bernard Andrew Alba, Mad. Van der Cruyssen, and many others, price as follows: 35c., 40c., 50c., 60c., 75c., $1.00, $1.25 to $1.50 each.

BEGONIA, new improved **ERFORDI,** fine bloomer for Christmas and all through the Winter, pinkish flowers, 4 in. pots, 20c.

BEGONIA FLAMBEAU, good seller, large, 4 in., fit for 6 in., 20c.

BEGONIA GLOIRE DE LORRAINE, 6 in. pots, bushy, in full bloom, in December, all showing buds now, 50c. each; 3 in., 20c.

COCOS WEDDELIANA, 3 in., strong, 15c.

CYCLAMEN, will bloom for Christmas, 5 in. pots, 20c.; 4 in. pots, 12c.

DRACAENA BRUANTI (imported), 30 in. high, 6 in., pots, 60c., $5.00 per doz.

FERNS for dishes, best varieties, 2½ in., 5c.; 3 in., very strong, 6c.

HYDRANGEA OTAKSA, only pot grown is offered, sure success for Easter forcing, 6 in. pots, 25c.; 7 to 8 in., 50c.

JERUSALEM CHERRIES (or Solanum), 6 in. pots, very bushy, full of berries, from $3.00 to $6.00 per doz.

PRIMULA OBCONICA, best strain, 4 in. pots, 10c.; 5 1-4 in., $2 per dozen.

PRIMULA SINENSIS, 4 in., strong; John Rupp, best strain, for Christmas blooming, 10c.; 5 in., $2 per doz.

CASH WITH ORDER

When ordering, say whether the plants should be shipped in the pots or not

GODFREY ASCHMANN

Importer and Wholesale Grower of Pot Plants

1012 Ontario Street, - - PHILADELPHIA, PA.

PLANT CULTURE

PRICE $1.00.

THE BEST BOOK FOR THE PLANT GROWER.

A. T. DE LA MARE PTG. & PUB. CO. LTD., 2-8 DUANE STREET, NEW YORK

LIST OF ADVERTISERS

INDEX TO STOCK ADVERTISED

Contents.

THE WEEK'S WORK.

Timme's Timely Teachings.

Heaths.

There is nothing half so gratifying to a good gardener as to be able to show his professional colleagues among his stock of the everyday class a batch of exceptionally well done plants, rare and choice in kind but avowedly hard to grow. Ericas have this reputation. The number of American plantsmen who may justly pride themselves on their achievements in erica culture is not great, but is increasing from year to year. Unfavorable climatic conditions, an unusually slow growth and the need of great care in treatment are some of the reasons why heaths are not cultivated here as extensively as they deserve to be. Indiscriminate and over-expeditious broadcast methods of culture as practiced in rearing the common run of commercial stock, of course, are not what ericas will readily submit to. But the bestowal of an extra amount of care and skill, called for in their culture, has always been adequately repaid.

There are a great many varieties of cultivated heaths, none without merit, all highly prized by European gardeners. They may, with some degree of accuracy, be divided into two distinct sections—the hard-wooded, shrub-like class, and those of a soft and comparatively rapid growth. The former are the most difficult to grow, even in Europe; but since most of these flower only in the Summer and are of small value to commercial florists in this country, I will confine my remarks to heaths of the latter class and only to such varieties in this class as bloom in the Fall and Winter and are of comparatively easy culture. Such varieties—nearly every one again being subdivided into several kinds as to color of bloom—are Erica nivalis, E. grandinosa, E. hyemalis, E. Wilmoreana, E. colerans, E. densa, E. gracilis, E. floribunda and E. incarnata. These are most suitable sorts for the American florist, very attractive when well finished and the least difficult to manage of Winter-flowering heaths.

We are now at a time of year when many of these varieties are slowly coming into bloom, or are nearing final development. It is just at this, stage, and in giving perfect finish, when growers experience the greatest difficulty and often fail at the very last moment, when up to that point all went smoothly and promised well. Two diseases peculiar to heaths most to be feared and to be guarded against at this season and at this stage in their growth are stem rot and a sort of mildew, only seen on heaths. Over watering, deep planting, too high a temperature, close or crowded quarters, restricted ventilation and a moisture-laden atmosphere are sure to result in a disastrous ending to the grower's labors.

The fact alone that these ericas are natives of the Cape of Good Hope suggests the need of abundant ventilation, a cool stand, care in watering and a dry, buoyant atmosphere in their culture. The plants now should be afforded an elevated position near the glass, where the light is clearest and the air freshest. A thorough drying out of the soil at any time is followed by as fatal results as would over-watering. Fire heat is antagonistic to the welfare of heaths and should only be resorted to when absolutely necessary in their first stages of growth, to keep up the temperature at a point eight or ten degrees above freezing. When they show buds they can stand more fire heat, even to the extent of being slowly forced into full bloom, but 45 degrees should be considered the normal. There must be no spraying of foliage, wetting of walks or staging from now on; and air whenever possible must be freely admitted and the plants so placed that they get the full benefit of it. Sweeping currents are the best safeguard against stem rot, but favor the onset of mildew; ventilation, therefore, should be so adjusted as to steer clear of either disease. Liquid stimulants, though quite a help in giving superb finish to some varieties, had better be used with greatest caution, for it is very easy to go beyond the safety limit. Flowers of sulphur, blown through the foliage, check the spread of mildew, when first noticed, but it is better to prevent the appearance of the disease by a faultless treatment of the plants. In potting ericas a peat-like, turfy, fibrous soil should be used. This should be strictly sweet and fresh, and in preparing it, sharp, clean sand or coarse gravel should be added, to form about one-fifth of the entire mass. A sieve must never be used in mixing s[oil] for ericas.

The fact that stunted plants of eric[as] flower most freely should not give ri[se] to the idea that these are the best spe[c]imens, not any more than that cuttin[gs] from half-gone, dying plants, althou[gh] rooting most readily, should be tak[en] for propagation. It is the vigorou[s] healthy plant, by skilful treatment i[n]duced to set buds freely, that carri[es] off the prize as the finest of floweri[ng] specimens.

Epacris.

Among New Holland plants none mo[re] fully deserves a place in greenhouse [or] conservatory than epacris. There [are] several varieties, most of them flo[w]ering profusely in the Winter, and [all] of them are good. They much resembl[e] heaths as to their cultural requiremen[ts] but are less exacting in their wan[ts], need less petting, are more robust a[nd] do not yield quite so readily to the [de]structive or enfeebling ills peculiar [to] ericas. Cool quarters and plenty [of] clear light and fresh air are the pr[in]cipal points to be observed in their c[ul]ture. Success with epacris is an eas[ily] earned reward where judicious care-t[ak]ing of all other greenhouse stock [is] considered needful and a paying pra[c]tice. Epacris are easily raised fr[om] cuttings, and now is the time to p[ut] them in the sand. Sturdy side sho[ots] are taken for the purpose, with a [bit] of a heel from the older wood at [the] butt end. Unlike erica cuttings, the[y] grow rapidly into flowering size wh[en] once fairly well started. Older plan[ts] remaining unsold should be cut do[wn] to within three or four inches of [the] pot; this to be done right after th[ey] have finished flowering in the Spri[ng]. This is necessary to keep the plan[ts] within shapely bounds. During [the] Summer old and young plants of ep[a]cris are plunged outdoors in so[me] loose, non-fermenting material, sele[ct]ing a place for them that affords p[ar]tial shade in the brightest hours of [the] Midsummer days. If they need tra[ns]planting, it should be done right af[ter] the flowers begin to wilt away and [a] few weeks before the plants are tak[en] outdoors. A too early transfer fr[om] greenhouse to garden often causes yellowing of the growth, hard to ov[er]come by the best of subsequent tre[at]ment.

Azaleas.

The first thing to do when unpack[ing] azaleas is to sort out the early from [the] late flowering kinds. The best variet[ies] for early forcing, easily to be had [in] bloom by Christmas, are Simon Ma[rd]ner, Apollo, Duetsche Perle, Paul Mardner and Vervæneana. These sho[uld] at once be potted up; while those [in]tended for later forcing might, for [the] present, be plunged in the loose soil [of] a deep frame until time for pott[ing] them could be spared. Most specim[ens] of the medium or commercial si[zes] when received, need root trimming. [The] ball of roots is cut down all aro[und] with a sharp knife until it is reduce[d in] size to a degree consistent with pro[por]tionate shape and good looks w[hen] potted up. After this a dipping of [the] ball of roots for a minute or two [in a] tub of water should not be omi[tted]. This gives full assurance of their b[eing] thoroughly wetted clear through be[fore] they go into the pots. A dried-out [ball] of roots, especially if embedded in [Eu]ropean peat soil, will hardly ever [take up] moisture after being surrounded [by a] thin shell of fresh soil in potting; [and] in the ordinary way in which plants [are] watered. All imported plants, cor[ning] with compactly formed root-balls sh[ould] be treated to a good dipping right a[fter] arrival, or at least before being po[tted] up. But I have witnessed cases w[here] the core of the roots eventually d[ried] out in spite of this precautionary m[eas]ure and no matter how plentifully [the] plants were watered or how wet [they] appeared. The great difference [be]tween old and new soil may have s[ome]thing to do with this, but I think [bad] potting must be held responsible [for] trouble of this kind in most cases. [A] grower not understanding why [his] plants should act so queerly and d[o so] poorly, instead of attributing the [mis]chief to other, often most unli[kely] causes, should examine the roots, [and] if he finds the innermost solidly pa[cked] part dry, he has found the root of [the] evil. The remedy is dipping the po[t] to the rim into water and holdin[g it] there until air bubbles cease to dis[turb] the surface of the water.

For the usual sizes of azaleas, from six to eight inches will be pl[enty] large enough. For these any grade of potting soil may be used, [the] point being of less importance than [firm] planting. After those preliminary [es]sentials have been attended to, [the] plants are placed in pots just [large] enough to leave room between pot [and] root-ball for the free play of a flatt[ened] stick or the handle of a small ham[mer] which is used in solidly firming fresh soil around the ball of roots, [fin]ishing off with a layer of rich [com]post at the top.

Those varieties wanted for ea[rly] forcing must then go into heat [imme]diately after having stood in a [cool] and shaded place for a few day[s]. [A] temperature of 60 degrees will be right for most of them, but a gr heat—up to 70 degrees if necessary—may safely be afforded in bringing slow and backward azaleas out in time for the holidays. While under forcing they need water in ample quantities, both at the roots and in the form of sprinkling; also plenty of room and light. In some houses a turning of the plants now and then is necessary to bring about a uniformly distributed opening of the flowers. When at that stage it is time to remove the plants to a house several degrees cooler, so as to have them sufficiently hardened off for handling.

Heliotropes.

A too high temperature and too close an atmosphere at this season are most to blame for the lack of bloom on Winter-flowering heliotropes, and this too at a time when well done plants of this universal favorite, displaying their fragrant racemes, would be a gladly welcomed addition to the season's offerings in flowering plants and decorative material. Young stock of the Fall and Winter-blooming varieties, propagated in November or December, grown into some size by May or June, summered in frames and again housed in the first week of September, should by that time be large, freely branched bushes in 5-inch pots, getting ready to bloom and never failing to do so if placed in a cool, airy and sunny house. A heat of not over 50 degrees at that stage is high enough for them. With the fullest light and direct sunshine overhead and plenty of fresh air, keeping the atmosphere cool and buoyant, root-bound heliotropes will exert all their energies in forming buds. If at that time they are shifted into larger pots, a need suggested by their size and root-bound condition and therefore deemed necessary by the less experienced grower, they will simply keep on growing in size and luxuriance of foliage, but at the expense of bloom. The same will happen when the plants are placed in the warm and over-humid quarters. Another point to be observed in the growing of this most desirable class of greenhouse plants is the damaging consequence of cold draughts and sudden falls of temperature, causing leaves to drop and flowers to damp off. Heliotropes at all times need good watering and frequent spraying before the flowers open. This is a good time to put in cuttings of the best varieties, bearing in mind that light shades and pure whites flower most freely, while those of a deep purple and dark colored bloom emit a stronger fragrance and their flowers also last longer. Cuttings root within a week if put in the warmest part of the propagating bed. They should be potted up before the roots reach the length of an inch, and be grown on in a temperature of not less than 60 degrees, repotting them before they become root-bound.

Fuchsias.

Some few varieties of fuchsias can be had in bloom in the very depth of Winter and are then a most pleasing and attractive sight. Of the several kinds in this class that I have tried none is more reliable and less disappointing than Fuchsia speciosa, the steadfast standby of the fuchsia grower. It needs the temperature, ventilation and moisture of a rose house, wants room and light, but cares little for bright sunshine. If so placed it will bloom in profusion right along for months, its flowers daintily arrayed in the merry Yuletide colors. Its very fast growth, however, is rather a fault than a merit, for it becomes a baffling factor in an effort to impart compact, nicely rounded form of growth—the prime requisite in most other kinds of potted plants. In this respect some other varieties of Winter flowering fuchsias surpass it, but its unfailing readiness to bloom in the dead of the season and the great ease with which it can be grown into the flowering size, fully atone for this its only shortcoming. All the varieties of Summer-blooming fuchsias should now be placed under benches and allowed to gain maturity of wood. Cut down to hardened wood in February and started into growth, they will come in right time for Spring sales. FRED W. TIMME.

FOUNDED IN 1888

THE FLORISTS' EXCHANGE

A Weekly Medium of Interchange for Florists, Nurserymen Seedsmen and the Trade in General

Exclusively a Trade Paper.

Entered at New York Post Office as Second Class Matter

Published EVERY SATURDAY by

A. T. DE LA MARE PTG. AND PUB. CO. LTD.

2, 4, 6 and 8 Duane Street,

P. O. Box 1697. Telephone 3765 John. NEW YORK.

CHICAGO OFFICE: 127 East Berwyn Avenue.

ILLUSTRATIONS.

Electrotypes of the illustrations used in this paper can usually be supplied by the publishers. Price on application.

YEARLY SUBSCRIPTIONS.

United States, Canada, and Mexico, $1.00. Foreign countries in postal union, $2.50. Payable in advance. Remit by Express Money Order Draft on New York. Post Office Money Order or Registered Letter.

The address label indicates the date when subscription expires and is our only receipt therefore.

REGISTERED CABLE ADDRESS:

Florex, New York.

ADVERTISING RATES.

One-half inch, 75c.; ¾-inch, $1.00; 1-inch, $1.25, special positions extra. Send for Rate Card showing discount of 10c., 15c., 25c., or 35c., per inch on continuous advertising. For rates on Wants, etc., see column for Classified Advertisements.

Copy must reach this office 12 o'clock Wednesday to secure insertion in issue of following Saturday.

Orders from unknown parties must be accompanied with cash or satisfactory references.

Obituary

Richard Harrison.

Richard Harrison, president and treasurer of the Harrison Yarn and Dye Company and founder of The Rhode Island Greenhouses, died at his residence at Pawtucket, R. I., Monday, November 5, in his 80th year. Death was due to a succession of shocks covering a period of two years, which kept Mr. Harrison in his home almost that entire time. Mr. Harrison was best known to cloth manufacturers, as he was one of the first to dye worsted braids in this country. He was born at Huddersfield, England, March 29, 1827. The greenhouse business was only a side line with him, as he had a great liking for flowers. Mr. Harrison is survived by a son and two daughters. G. A. J.

William S. Wilson.

William S. Wilson, one of the large rose growers in the vicinity of Boston, Mass., died at his home in Wellesley, on November 8, of pneumonia, after an illness of only five days. Mr. Wilson was born at Ayr, Scotland, forty-eight years ago. At the age of seventeen he commenced to serve his apprenticeship as a gardener at Partick, near Glasgow, subsequently going to Helensburgh, where he remained two years. He decided to come to America and found employment at New London, Conn., with the late John Spalding, a pioneer New England florist. He remained with Mr. Spalding for about eight years and went to Norwich, Conn., where he took charge of the Blackstone estate. After two years on this place he started in business on his own account and removed to Concord, N. H., where he was located for ten years. About six years ago he acquired the Burnside Conservatories at Wellesley and started growing roses for the wholesale Boston market. He grew mostly Bride and Bridesmaid although at times he made specialties of Mme. Abel Chatenay and other varieties. He is survived by a widow, two daughters and a son, the latter a student at the Institute of Technology, Boston.

J. W. D.

ST. PAUL.—L. L. May & Company are erecting a large storage and packing plant at their Mayfield Nurseries, Lakeland, Minn. It is 200 feet long by 150 wide. The idea is to use it to store their nursery stock. They report sales very good, the past Fall delivery being about double that of a year ago. PAUL.

Scientific Aspects of Luther Burbank's Work.

The practical side of Burbank's work has received considerable attention of late from practical men who have studied the result of that work from the utilitarian or æsthetic point of view, and the opinions expressed thereon have not, in the main, been altogether eulogistic or encouraging. Now the scientific aspect is being inquired into, and the latest effusion on the subject which has come under our observation is an article by Vernon L. Kellogg, professor of entomology at the Stanford University, California, appearing in the Popular Science Monthly for October, 1906, which has just been issued in pamphlet form, a copy of same having been kindly forwarded us. It may interest our readers to be informed of some of the professor's conclusions—the views of one engaged in the study of insect life on the work of a man devoting his time and attention to plant life. Professor Kellogg says:

"Mr. Burbank has so far not formulated any new or additional laws of species-change, nor do his observations and results justify any such formulation, and we may rest in the belief that he has no new fundamental laws to reveal. He has indeed the right to formulate, if he cares to, some valuable and significant special conclusions touching certain already recognized evolution factors, in particular the influence on variability of the two long-known variation-producing factors of hybridization and modification of environment. His reliance on the marked increase in

Luther Burbank—From His Latest Portrait

variability to be got after a crossing in the second and third generations over that obvious in the first will come as a surprise to most men first getting acquainted with his work. He has got more starts for his new things from these generations than in any other way. He is wholly clear and convinced in his own mind as to the inheritance of acquired characters; 'acquired characters are inherited or I know nothing of plant life,' he says; and also convinced that the only unit in organic nature is the individual, not the species; that the so-called species are wholly mutable and dependent for their apparent fixity solely on the length of time through which their so-called phyletic characters have been ontogenetically repeated. He does not agree at all with De Vries that mutations in plants occur only at certain periodic times in the history of the species, but rather that, if they occur at all, they do so whenever the special stimulus derived from unusual nutrition or general environment can be brought to bear on them. He finds in his breeding work no prepotency of either sex as such in inheritance, though any character or group of characters may be prepotent in either sex. He believes that no sharp line can be drawn between the fluctuating or so-called Darwinian variations and those less usual, large, discontinuous ones called sports. Ordinary fluctuation variation goes on under ordinary conditions of nutrition, but with extraordinary environmental conditions come about extraordinary variation results, namely discontinuous, sport or mutational variation. These variations are the effects of past environment also, having remained latent until opportunity for their development occurs. Starvation causes reversions, but reversions can also be produced by unusually rich nutrition. New variations are developed most often, as far as environmental influences go, by rich soil and generally favorable conditions. So-called new qualities are usually, if not always (the fact may sometimes not be obvious) simply new combinations of old qualities, both latent and obvious. To get a new and pleasing odor it may often be sufficient simply to lose one bad element in an old odor. So one might go on for some pages with specific conclusions or deductions reached by Burbank on a basis of experience. But it is true that he has at his command the knowledge of no new fundamental scientific principles to give him advantage over us. And yet none of us has done what Burbank has been able to do, although many of us have tried. What then is it that Burbank brings to his work of modifying organisms swiftly and extremely and definitely that others do not?

"To answer this it will be advisable to analyze, in general terms, at least, the various processes which either singly, or in combinations of two or three, or all together, are used by Mr. Burbank in his work. We may roughly classify these processes and means. First, there is the importation from foreign countries, through many correspondents, of a host of various kinds of plants, some of economic value in their native land and some not, any of which grown under different conditions here may prove specially vigorous or prolific or hardy, or show other desirable changes or new qualities. Among these importations are often special kinds particularly sought for by Burbank to use in his multiple hybridizations; kinds closely related to our native or to already cultivated races which, despite many worthless characteristics, may possess one or more particular, valuable ones needed to be added to a race already useful to make it more useful. Such an addition makes a new race.

"Second, the production of variations, abundant and extreme, by various methods, as (a) the growing under new and, usually, more favorable environment (food supply, water, temperature, light, space, etc.) of various wild or cultivated forms, and (b) by hybridizations between forms closely related, less closely related and, finally, as dissimilar as may be (not producing sterility), this hybridizing being often immensely complicated by multiplying crosses, i. e., the offspring from one cross being immediately crossed with a third form, and the offspring of this with still another form, and so on. These hybridizations are made sometimes with very little reference to the actual useful or non-useful characteristics of the crossed parents, with the primary intention of producing an unsettling or instability in the heredity, of causing, as Burbank sometimes says, 'perturbations' in the plants, so as to get just as wide and as large variation as possible.

"Third, there is always immediately following the unusual production of variations the recognition of desirable modifications and the intelligent and effective selection of them, i. e., the saving of those plants to produce seed or cuttings which show the desirable variations and the discarding of all the others. In Burbank's gardens the few tenderly cared for little potted plants or carefully grafted seedlings represent the surviving fittest, and the great bonfires of scores of thousands of uprooted others, the unfit, in this close mimicry of Darwin and Spencer's struggle and survival in nature.

"It is precisely in this double process of the recognition and selection of desirable variations that Burbank's genius comes into particular play. Right here he brings something to bear on his work that few other men have been able to do. It is the extraordinary keenness of perception, the delicacy of recognition of desirable variations in their (usually) small and to most men imperceptible beginnings.

"Now this recognition, this knowledge of correlations in plant structure, born of the exercise of a genius for perceiving through thirty years of opportunity for testing and perfecting it, is perhaps the most important single thing which Burbank brings to his work that other men do not (at least in such unusual degree of reliability). Enormous industry, utter concentration and single-mindedness, deftness in manipulation, fertility in practical resource, has Burbank—and so have numerous other breeders and experimenters. But in his perception of variability in its forming, his recognition of its possibilities of outcome, and in his scientific knowledge of correlations, a knowledge that is real, for it is one that is relied on and built on, and is at the very foundation of his success, Burbank has an advantage of true scientific character over his fellow workers, and in it he makes a genuine contribution to scientific knowledge of plant biology, albeit this knowledge is so far only proved to be attainable and to exist. It is not yet exposed in its details and may never be, however unselfish be the owner of it. For the going to oblivion of scientific data of an extent and value equivalent, I may estimate roughly, to those now issuing from any half dozen experimental laboratories of variation and heredity, is the crying regret of all evolution students acquainted with the situation. The recently assumed relations of Mr. Burbank to the Carnegie Institution are our present chief hope for at least a lessening of this loss. * * *

"Another of Burbank's open secrets of success is the great range of his experimentation—nothing is too bold for him to attempt, the chances of failure are never too great to frighten him. And another secret is the great extent, as regards material used, of each experiment. His beds of seedlings contain hundreds, often thousands, of individuals where other men are content with hundreds. Another element in his work is his prodigality of time. Experiments begun twenty years ago are actually still under way.

"Let us, in a paragraph, simply sum up the essential things in the scientific aspects of Burbank's work. No new revelations to science of an overturning character; but the revelation of the possibilities of accomplishment, based on general principles already known, by an unusual man. No new laws of evolution, but new facts, new data, new canons for special cases. No new principle or process to substitute for selection, but a new proof of the possibilities of the effectiveness of the old principle. No new categories of variations, but an illuminating demonstration of the possibilities of stimulating variability and of the reality of this general variability as the fundamental and transforming factor. No new evidence either to help the Darwinian factors to their death-bed or to strengthen their lease on life; for the 'man' factor in all the selecting phenomena in Burbank's gardens excludes all 'natural' factors.

"Finally, in any summation of the scientific aspects of Burbank's work must be mentioned the hosts of immensely valuable data regarding the inheritance of characteristics, the influence of epigenetic factors in development, the possibilities of plant variability, and what not else important to evolution students, mostly going unrecorded, except as they are added in mass to the already too heavy burden carried by the master of the laboratory, and as they are summed up in those actual results which the world gratefully knows as Burbank's 'new creations.'"

OUR READERS' VIEWS

Look Out for Him.

Editor Florists' Exchange:

I wish to warn the gardening fraternity of a base impostor who is going the rounds at the present time. He is a tall, stout, middle-aged man, with moustache which is mixed with gray. To all appearances he would weigh about 200 pounds. His modus operandi is as follows: He finds out the names of his intended victims in some manner, and comes to them and usually says he is of the same name. If the victim is Scotch, the fellow says he a Scotsman newly over, and pretends to be very broad. He tells a story about bringing over some horses from Scotland, says he has a draft on a bank but has nobody to identify him, and then puts up quite a pathetic tale about being penniless and cannot get his horses away from the dock; and if he could only get enough money to take him to his brother in Schenectady, he would return it in a few days, with a good present for the accommodation. He also offers his watch as security.

Now he is one of the basest impostors under the sun. He was operating two years ago, as I know some whom he swindled then. He was in the vicinity of Glen Cove, L. I., last week, but got scared away. I hope this note may be seen and put the craft on the outlook for him; and if he comes their way it would be well to detain him and call in a policeman.

W. H. WAITE.

An Open Letter to Job.

Editor Florists' Exchange:

Where ever art thou, Job? With all the beautiful opportunity "created" for you by O'Mara and others hammering and defending Mr. Burbank, I cannot see how you can keep quiet. Mr. O'Mara's latest effusion, wherein he defines "creation" is an example of what a prejudiced mind can insist on not seeing. Any late up-to-date dictionary bears out the remarks of Mr. Wickson. Note definition 2 below; also 3, clause 2.

Funk & Wagnalls Standard Dictionary defines "creation" as follows:

1. The act of creating; production out of nothing; especially, the act of God in bringing the world or universe into existence.

"Apersonal volition in the proceedings of creation is as necessary to make the world in Darwin's way as in that of Agassiz." John Weiss Immortal Life, chapter 1, page 18. (L. B. & Co. '81.)

2. An act of construction, physical or mental; the combining or organizing of existing materials into new form; as, the "creation" of an empire.

"That in the creation of the United States the world had reached one of the turning points in its history seems at the time to have entered into the thought of not a single European Statesman." Green History of English People, vol. IV, book IX, chapter 3, page 272. (Macm. '80).

3. That which is created, in any sense. Specifically: (1) The product of God's creative power; the universe; as, the whole creation testifies to his goodness.

"Creation sleeps. 'Tis as the gen'ral pulse
Of life stood still, and nature made a pause."
Young Night Thoughts 1, 1.23.

(2) Any remarkable product of the power of scientific, artistic, or practical construction; as, the creations of genius; the creations of Shakespeare

"All Goethe's feminine creations grow; but usually it is the growth of affection only."
Hutton Essays, Goethe in vol. 11, p. 39. (Macm. '80).

4. The act of investing with a new rank or character or of placing in a new office; as, the creation of two additional judges.

"Nobles by the right of an earlier creation, and priests by the imposition of a mightier hand.
Macaulay Essays, Milton, page 16. (P. S. & Co. '54).

It seems hard that we must not only suffer from "Burbankitis," but in addition have an epidemic of "Mal-de-O'Mara." Wish you would ask Pat to consult his dictionary further. Would suggest he look up "Ostentatiousness."

A FELLOW SUFFERER.

The C. S. A. and Its Work.

Editor Florists' Exchange:

I read with much interest Wm. Duckham's address before the convention of the Chrysanthemum Society of America in Chicago, and I noticed particularly what he had to say in reference to the slow growth of the organization, also his suggestion for the members to do a little judicious "buttonholing" to help swell the membership. His suggestion is very good, but I don't think that the members need to be very aggressive in this line. I know of plenty of good men, mostly private gardeners, who grow chrysanthemums for exhibition and who are interested in the work of the C. S. A., but who have never joined the society simply because they were never approached on the subject.

Another suggestion I would like to make (although not a member of the C. S. A., but would be glad to join it if I knew the fees, address of secretary, etc.); would it not be a good plan to print in our trade papers a heading in the society news, giving the name of the society, its objects, initiation fee, dues, address of secretary and such other information as a person is desirous of knowing before joining a society?

Would it not be possible to hold a convention of the C. S. A. some time during the early Summer, have delegates attend from all the horticultural societies which hold an annual chrysanthemum show, fix the dates for all these various exhibitions, and not have them all jam in on top of each other? I know the time for exhibition is short, but I think matters could be much better regulated by a head body composed of delegates from the different societies than by each society selecting its own dates. The scaling could also be attended to at this convention. Have the C. S. A. scale of points universal throughout the country; have it printed in full in all the schedules of the different societies. I also think it would not be amiss, if the C. S. A. could carry through some plan of this kind, to have a delegate appointed by the C. S. A. attend all the shows possible, he to act as one of the judges at the various exhibitions. In that way it would seem as if all the horticultural societies had a tie connecting them with the national organization.

Of course all this depends upon the attitude of the different horticultural societies, which plan, however, need not interfere in any way with any of the plans or workings of the societies, only in reference to the annual exhibitions which most societies hold in the Fall and which practically might be termed chrysanthemum shows.

I think if something of this kind could be accomplished it would build up the C. S. A. and promote more friendship and good feeling among the lovers of the chrysanthemum.

W. McCOLLOM.

[The address of the secretary is David Fraser, Penn and Homewood avenues, Pittsburg, Pa., from whom all particulars relative to membership, etc., in the C. S. A. can be obtained. Ed.]

Alfred J. Loveless, President-Elect, C. S. A.

Postal Rates.

Editor Florists' Exchange:

I have just noticed the item in your last issue regarding the postal rates in New Zealand. If you will kindly look up postal regulations you will see it stated in the November postal supplement that this reduced rate is from New Zealand to the United States and does not apply from the United States until after October 1, 1907. The foreigners always have the advantage over the citizens of the United States.

While the people of this country are accustomed to look with pride on our postal system, still, as the writer has previously stated, there is scarcely a civilized country in the world where the postal facilities are not better than those of the United States.

At the last election many new congressmen were elected, and we most devoutly hope that there will be more who are willing to think and act for the benefit of the people instead of making laws for the benefit of the railroad and express companies. Germany, England, France, Canada, Australia and, in fact, most other countries have lower rates and better facilities than the United States. The railroads are receiving about ten times more from the Government for mail matter carried than the express companies pay. The rural route carriers average only about eighteen pounds of mail matter per day, when they could just as well carry ten times that amount and thus add to the income of that part of the service.

The various associations of country merchants are acting as "catspaws" for the express companies in trying to keep out the parcels post system which would be of such inestimable benefit to the farmers and in fact to everyone in the country; but I believe the sentiment is constantly growing in favor of parcels post and I hope that some favorable action will be taken in Congress at the next session. If the florists of this country would write to their congressmen favoring the parcels post system it might help along the good work.

Des Moines, Ia. CHAS. N. PAGE.

CHRYSANTHEMUM SOCIETY OF AMERICA.

The Chrysanthemum Society of America held its annual meeting in Chicago, on Wednesday afternoon, November 7, 1906. A fairly representative attendance was present, including some of the largest chrysanthemum growers of the country. President Duckham read his address, which was published in last week's issue, page 570, the reading of which was followed by the reports of Secretary Fraser and Treasurer John N. May.

The society decided to issue an annual report. Elmer D. Smith, of Adrian, Mich., volunteered to give the members all available information in regard to dates, origin, etc., of varieties introduced and imported. Mr. Smith asked that chrysanthemum growers favor him with full particulars of new varieties for the purpose of having this record complete.

The election of officers resulted as follows: President, Alfred J. Loveless, Lenox, Mass.; vice-president, William Kleinheinz, Ogontz, Pa.; treasurer, John N. May, Summit, N. J.; secretary, David Fraser, Pittsburg, Pa.; the three latter gentlemen having been re-elected.

Invitations were received, to hold the next annual meeting, from Jamestown, Va.; Indianapolis, Ind., and St. Louis, Mo., the selection being left to the officers.

A paper prepared by E. G. Hill on the "Influence of Climatic Conditions on Chrysanthemum Culture" was read, and an interesting discussion ensued, participated in by Messrs. Smith, Totty, Herrington and Wallace R. Pierson.

Work of Committees.

CHICAGO, November 3.—Claremont, yellow; exhibited by Adam Wolnewicz, Chicago, Ill.; scored 80 points, commercial scale.

BOSTON, November 3.—White sport of William Duckham, Japanese incurved; exhibited by C. H. Totty, Madison, N. J.; scored 86 points, commercial scale, and 88 points, exhibition scale.

PHILADELPHIA, November 6.—Mlle. E. Chabanne, light pink, loose incurved; exhibited by the E. G. Hill Company, Richmond, Ind.; scored 87 points commercial scale, and 87 points, exhibition scale.

CINCINNATI, November 10.—Charles Ragee, ivory white, incurved, exhibited by John Fries, Newport, Ky.; scored 86 points, commercial scale.

No. 74-4-05: pink Japanese incurved; exhibited by Nathan Smith & Son, Adrian, Mich.; scored 83 points, commercial scale.

No. 55-4-05, bronze Japanese reflexed, exhibited by Nathan Smith & Son, Adrian, Mich.; scored 80 points, exhibition scale.

DAVID FRASER, Secretary.

President-Elect Alfred J. Loveless.

Alfred J. Loveless, president-elect of the Chrysanthemum Society of America, was born Septem- 26, 1866, at Langford, Somerset, England. After completing his common school education, he started to work at the age of 12 years at Langford House Gardens, and at 19 years of age was appointed head gardener, not of his own will, but through force of circumstances and the entire confidence of his employer, Mr. Sidney Hill, in his ability to take charge. After serving two years in that capacity, he left to take charge of the flower gardens and pleasure grounds of Killarney House, Killarney, the seat of the Earl and Countess of Kenmare. Here he came in contact with the finest collection of herbaceous plants and shrubs that he has ever met with. On reaching his majority, he resigned his position to take charge of the gardens of Strathallan Hall, Douglas, Isle of Man, where he remained for two years, sailing on March 9, 1889, for New York City, arriving on St. Patrick's Day. His first position in this country was on the estate of W. B. Dinsmore, Staatsburgh, N. Y., where he had charge of the stove plants, ferns, and palms. Owing to poor health he resigned and later was engaged as gardener to Senator Robbins, of Wethersfield, Conn. Here he remained three years, then went to England on a vacation. On his return to America he acted as assistant in the greenhouses of Mr. James B. Colgate, Yonkers, N. Y., subsequenty going to Lenox as foreman under J. F. Huss, at Ventford Hall, being latterly engaged as superintendent for Mr. John Sloane at Wyndhurst Gardens, a position he has held for the past eleven years.

Mr. Loveless is Master of Evening Star Lodge F. and A. M.; member of Berkshire Commandery Knights Templar, member of Melha Temple A. A. O. N. M. S., and an ex-president of the Lenox Horticultural Society.

He is an all around successful plantsman, and is particularly interested in the chrysanthemum.

AMERICAN BREEDERS' ASSOCIATION.—The proceedings of the meeting of this association held at Lincoln, Neb., January 17-19, 1906, have been issued in book form, and distributed by Secretary W. M. Hays. An immense amount of most valuable information regarding the breeding of plants and animals is contained in the volume.

It is gratifying to observe that the membership of the organization is steadily increasing, showing that there is need of the association and that its work is being appreciated.

S. A. F. O. H. Prize Essay Contest.

Marketing Plants and Cut Flowers.

Second Prize Paper, Charles Ingram, Author.

The methods of disposing to the retailer by growers have passed through almort as many stages of evolution within the last twenty years as have the construction of greenhouses, varieties grown, size of structures, etc. The methods that were fully competent to take care of the market end of the growers' cares up to a very short time ago would now prove totally inadequate to handle the ever-increasing supply; "and the end is not yet."

To my way of thinking there is no one method at present in vogue that would apply equally to all growers, for the simple reason that all growers are not equally favorably situated as regards location of plant. To be more explicit, the grower that is in close proximity to a large center of distribution can handle a "rush order" with greater facility than one at some distance from said center, where shipping facilities may be limited to a certain number of expresses a day. Where the former can bring into use anything from a horse and wagon to an auto, the latter is handicapped by distance, etc., although undoubtedly he is better off as regards taxation and several other important items. There are other vast differences between growers that will be referred to later on.

The very largest growers, who produce stock enough to enable them to run a shipping department of their own, on practically the same lines as a wholesale commission house, have, it would seem, almost reached the climax of perfection; but with many growers this method of disposing of their goods would be totally impractical, so we may safely eliminate the former from the subject and confine our remarks to the case of those growers whose conditions and surroundings do not justify this mode of procedure.

To answer the question at issue according to our views on the subject, a further classification is necessary, and to simplify the matter we will divide them thus:

Class A.—Growers who are close to a city or cities.

Class B.—Growers too "far out," and who are only able to ship say twice a day.

Class C.—Specialists.

Class A.

In those cities where a combination of growers have formed a flower market, it will invariably be found the best medium for the larger growers to dispose of their goods, but we have always thought that the smaller grower would do far better by consigning to a reputable commission house. But again there are cities where there is neither market nor commission house; to growers thus situated we would advise them to get into line as soon as possible. Before going any further a few words of explanation as to recommending the smaller growers to patronize the commission house, in preference to the market: Many men are good growers, but indifferent salesmen; the commission man will do it more satisfactorily than most men you could hire to do it for you, with infinitely less worry to yourself, and invariably succeed in getting better returns, if all items are faithfully figured in. Several other reasons might be given in favor of the commission house, but simply to state the fact that, in our opinion, it is the best method for the smaller growers to follow, is all that is necessary here.

The Boston Show—View in Main Hall

Class B.

Where growers are restricted as to shipping accommodation, and many both large and small are so situated, we would again name the commission house as the best medium for disposing of their stock. Many growers in years past have consigned goods to commission men at times when they had no other outlet, and because the returns were not satisfactory have held a strong prejudice against them on that account; but it must be remembered that the methods now practiced by these gentlemen have advanced the same as all other lines of horticulture, until to-day their system is perfected to such an extent that it would seem almost impossible to improve on it. In fact, in most cases where "misunderstandings" occur it is more often the fault of the grower than the consignee. We allude to such instances as where the grower at holiday times disposes of quantities of his goods to retailers; some may think this mode of procedure all right, but look at both sides of the question. Any commission man at all up in his business knows pretty nearly the amount of stock to expect from his growers, and figures the effect that inclement weather and other adverse conditions will have on the development of the stock, and makes his calculations accordingly. Is it right, we ask, when, after expending considerable cash for advertising, and otherwise obtaining orders for goods he honestly expects to handle, he is not only disappointed himself but has to disappoint others depending on him, possibly having the effect of losing their patronage and thereby indirectly damaging the grower himself? Again, although it must be admitted the practice is not nowadays nearly as prevalent as it was a few years ago, think of the pernicious habit of "holding up" large quantities of stock and landing it on the commission man too late for him to handle to advantage, and quite often in such condition as to be absolutely worthless, which no reputable dealer would ship, or retailer receive! We crave pardon for inserting a quotation from Kipling's "Mandalay," but the lines always suggest themselves to us when we run across a consignment in such condition.

"Ship me somewheres east of Sues,
Where the best is like the worst,
Where there ain't no 'Ten Commandments,'
And a man can raise a thirst."

Another vitally important detail is packing the stock so that it receives the least possible damage in transit. It must always be borne in mind that quite a percentage of these goods have to be reshipped. Right here we would offer a suggestion, which we feel sure is bound to be generally adopted in the near future, viz: to have light receptacles capable of holding twenty-five, fifty and one hundred flowers that could be handled in that manner, such as violets, carnations, certain roses (of course it would be impractical in the case of extra American Beauty, etc.), most bulb stock and several other subjects. This method of displaying "the goods" has been followed in Covent Garden, London, for years, and we have often wondered why it has not been adopted here. We feel sure, however, that American ingenuity will contrive receptacles that will fill the bill.

These remarks about "shipping" would be incomplete if we failed to mention two other important items, viz: cleanliness of all paper, etc., used, and grading. We are all aware how liable one is, if he be a few short of an even number of "firsts," to put in the required number of good "seconds;" but it should also be borne in mind that the prospective buyer will almost always "spot" those very ones, frequently with the effect of declining the deal, or else standing out for a reduction in price.

Class C.

The specialist is in a distinct class by himself, not alone as regards the goods he handles, but in the enviable position he enjoys with respect to the disposal of the same. Specialists as a rule are so well known, not only in their neighborhood but further afield, that the judicial use of the advertising columns of the horticultural papers, in their case, is all that is necessary. These remarks only apply to the "bona-fides," as many call themselves in this class that have no earthly reason for so doing. I once heard a witty son of the Green Isle, in answer to the question of, "What is a specialist?" reply, "A man that thinks he is one, blows his own trumpet, but the 'raal thing,' why, other people blow it for him."

The majority of the foregoing remarks have dealt principally with the cut-flower trade. In regard to the plant business, very few cities are large enough to warrant a plant market, and it seems to us that the methods at present in vogue by the gentlemen engaged in this line are as practical as any that can be recommended. But we cannot miss this opportunity of paying tribute to the vast improvement of the last few years in regard to the methods of packing plants. When one looks back a few years and remembers the condition in which one received a shipment of plants he cannot fail to highly appreciate the great improvements that have taken place. The only people who have lost by these improvements are the express companies.

In conclusion, we would state that in this paper we did not start out with any idea of enjoying a new mode of procedure, but have tried to offer a few suggestions that might improve existing conditions, which seem to answer their purpose satisfactorily.

The Greenhouse White Fly.

The white fly of greenhouses, or greenhouse aleurodes (Aleurodes vaporariorum) has long been recognized as a serious pest of greenhouse crops. In Connecticut the pest has been exceedingly injurious to tomatoes and cucumbers under glass. Fumigating with tobacco was found not to be an effective remedy. Hydrocyanic-acid gas, when used at the rate of 2½ ounces potassium cyanid per each 1,000 cubic feet of space, killed the insects but also injured tomato plants. A cheap and effective remedy was found in spraying the under surfaces of the leaves with common laundry soap dissolved in water at the rate of 1 pound in 8 gallons of water. In order to prevent all injury from soap it should be washed from the leaves occasionally with water, with frequent applications of the insecticide when necessary. At the Maine Station fumigation with hydrocyanic-acid gas was the most successful remedy tried. When fumigation was done early in the afternoon, the tomato plants were somewhat injured by the application of 1 ounce of cyanid per 1,000 cubic feet of space. The same amount of cyanid, however, caused no injury when the fumigation was done in the evening. It is recommended that no fumigation be done while the sun is shining or while the temperature is above 60 degrees F. In Massachusetts it was found possible in some instances to prevent serious injury from this pest by mere cultural measures. Spraying tomato plants in greenhouses is not recommended. Hydrocyanic-acid was found to be the cheapest and most effective remedy for greenhouse aleurodes. It is recommended that this be used at the rate bf 0.1 dram of potassium cyanid per cubic foot of space and that the plants be exposed after sunset. This will destroy all of the insects except the eggs and a few pupæ and will not injure tomato plants. In New Hampshire the greenhouse white fly was easily destroyed by spraying with a 5 per cent. mechanical mixture of kerosene. For this purpose a knapsack sprayer was used. In spraying, it is recommended that the operator begin at the top of the plants and work down. The same method was used out of doors with good results. The most successful and satisfactory treatment, however, was fumigation. A greenhouse was fumigated in July at 10 o'clock in the forenoon of a clear day, the period of fumigation being fifteen minutes. At the end of this time all of the flies were dead and the plants of the greenhouse were uninjured, except the leaves of a lily. Similar treatment applied in the afternoon was also successful and without injury to the plants.—From Report of Office of Experiment Stations.

EXHIBITIONS

Poughkeepsie, N. Y.

The twelfth annual flower show of the Dutchess County (N. Y.) Horticultural Society opened in the State armory on Wednesday of last week, and was a successful affair. The hall was tastefully decorated, and the disposition of the exhibits most attractive. One of the features of the show was the pavilion in the center of the floor, decorated by W. G. Saltford, florist. Most of the prizes were won by local gardeners, although some exhibitors from Lenox carried off a few of the honors.

In the carnation classes W. G. Saltford was first for 25 red, 25 variegated, 25 white, and second for 25 dark pink. A. W. Williams, Highland, N. Y., was second for 25 red and 25 crimson. Adam Laub, Hughsonville, N. Y., was awarded a certificate of merit for a seedling carnation.

The Mayor Hine prize, for 200 double blue violets, was captured by George A. Saltford, Rhinebeck, N. Y. The Mitchell premium, for 100 double blue violets, was won by Benjamin Willig.

John Bahret and C. F. Bahret were successful in the vegetable classes.

In the dinner table competition F. Heeremans was first; he used orchids. Chauncey Marshall took second with a table of Winsor carnations.

The judges were William Turner, Oceanic, N. J.; Thos. Harrison, Glen Cove, L. I.; R. W. Allen, Hudson.

Los Angeles.

The Autumn exhibition of the Southern California Horticultural Society was given in Blanchard Hall, October 31 to November 3. It was a great success. The display of chrysanthemums was very fine. Considering the high temperature and low relative humidity of the latter part of September and the first half of October in this part of the State, the size and beauty of this flower as shown were wonderful.

W. W. Marugg, who located in North Pomona two years ago, beginning as an amateur the cultivation of the Queen of Autumn, has achieved remarkable success, and is now a full-fledged professional, issuing a handsome catalog of his fine blooms. He took first prize for best twelve blooms of one variety in each color of yellow, pink, red, white and bronze; also first for best exhibit of 25 varieties, 6 blooms of each.

Mrs. G. W. Bowers and A. S. Burrage (W. C. Collett, gardener) of Redlands had fine exhibits. Her Glory of the Pacific, and his Good Gracious were exceptionally fine. Bernard Whitehead of Pasadena showed some fine Mary Ingalls. Alex. Urquhart, gardener to D. R. Cameron of Altadena, showed large collection of beutiful blooms; chief among them were General Hutton and Black Hawk.

The display of carnation, both field and cover grown, was very fine. The Oceanside Floral Company, E. S. Langford, manager, staged field-grown flowers of White Perfection, Nelson Fisher, Fair Maid, Harry Fenn and Enchantress that proved conclusively that good stock can be grown in the open if properly cared for. They were awarded first for their exhibit of fourteen varieties, twelve blooms of each.

C. P. Meyer of Burlingame showed several new varieties originating with him—one a very dark crimson, of immense size and good form, as yet unnamed. A companion to this was an immense white variety, which he has been pleased to name in compliment to his wife.

Howard & Smith took first for best collection of flowering plants, also for best display of dahlias, fifty blooms in twelve varieties.

E. H. Rust was first for best collection of ornamental plants. Dieterich & Huston, took five blue ribbons—best collection of palms, foliage plants, specimen Kentia Forsteriana; K. Belmoreana, and Piersonii fern.

The Signal Hill Floral Company, E. R. Meserve, manager, made a fine exhibit of Mount Blanc and Earliest of All, sweet peas, also of two plants of Asparagus plumosus with thoroughly furnished strings fourteen feet in length, which were sufficient to decorate one side of the hall.

L. H. Wright was first for best exhibit of roses grown under glass. Outdoor stock was not in evidence because of the peculiar climatic conditions, referred to before, that have prevailed here this Fall. C. P. Meyer of Burlingame took first for American Beauty. The sensation of the show in roses was a large vase of Richmond, grown under glass by Mr. Laclede, gardener to Mr. Walter Raymond. If this rose is adapted to outdoor conditions on this coast, it will be a great acquisition to our rose collection. From this same place came a fine vase of Clianthus Dampieri; indeed, this exhibitor seems to be the only one in these parts who can grow this dazzling beauty to perfection.

Miss Session of San Diego exhibited a basket of the ornamental berried solanum, the specific name of which the writer has not yet learned. Experiments with it about town this year will decide the question of its adaptibility to our section of the State. If it proves to be hardy, and will mature clusters of its scarlet colored berries here as it does at San Diego, it will be a valuable acquisition to our list of ornamental shrubs.

From the small but well kept greenhouse of Mrs. E. H. Childs came a fine lot of orchids—odontoglossums, oncidiums, and cypripediums—which were gracefully set amid a lot of well grown Adiantum cuneatum. C. P. Taft of Orange, the Burbank of this end of the State, sent in some fine Japan persimmons, Carissa arduina and several branches of Feijoa Sellowiana well set with fruit. This last is yet in its experimental stage, while the carissa is so well adapted to our climate that it is destined to become one of our leading ornamental, as well as economic shrubs.

The botanic collection of ninety-five exotics, as they grow here, proved to be interesting to many of the visitors. The exhibit contained subjects, representing every part of the temperate and torrid zones.

A unique feature of the show was a cup offered by the society for the exhibit getting the largest number of votes. A coupon attached to every ticket of admission entitled the holder of the ticket to a vote, on which he or she recorded the number of the exhibit which pleased the most. The idea was a good one; nevertheless, several of the exhibitors were very industrious during the show soliciting votes, which was, in the very nature of the case, contrary to the spirit in which the cup was offered, and can hardly be called a fair test as to the nature of a flower show desired by the public.

Howard & Smith demonstrated what may be done in decorative work with poles of the giant bamboo. Their pergola was original in design, graceful in appearance, and a fit frame-work for their large and varied exhibit.

P. D. BARNHART.

Exhibited by Martin Sullivan. First Prize Group of Plants at Boston Show

New Haven, Conn.

The annual Fall exhibition of the New Haven County Horticultural Society was held in the Music Hall, New Haven, on Tuesday, Wednesday and Thursday, November 6, 7 and 8. This year's exhibition was made more of a chrysanthemum show than formerly, and this made it necessary to reduce somewhat the space that in other years was given to groups of plants. Chrysanthemums in consequence were the main feature and attraction of the exhibition, and on the whole they were well shown. With but one notable exception exhibitors were local men, and their exhibits showed that the gardeners of New Haven and vicinity know how to grow plants and cut flowers. The exception referred to was Edwin Jenkins from Lenox, and considering the reputation he had already established as a grower it belittled in no way the local growers that he was able to take several firsts. Mr. Jenkins was first in nearly all the larger classes with superb blooms. Among the most successful local exhibitors of chrysanthemums were Walter Angus, David Kydd, Oscar Carlson, Robert Patton, Henry Cliff and J. P. Sorenson.

Roses were of very good quality but not numerous. Carnations were very well staged and the competition was close. The winner of the prize for the best seedling carnation very much resembled Enchantress, being fully as large as the average bloom of that variety, with color, when compared side by side, if anything in favor of the seedling. Violets were in point of quality and size superior to any I have seen in a long time.

The prize for the best group of plants and cut flowers arranged for general effect, not to exceed one hundred square feet, was won by Frank S. Platt Company. The same exhibitors won out in the class for display of seeds, bulbs, tools, and garden fixtures. Robert Paton and David Kydd were large winners in the plant classes, as were Carrol and Breitschneider.

In the classes for chrysanthemum plants Walter Angus won on 12 in 6 varieties, and 6 in 6 varieties. Carrol had best specimen, and A. J. Thomson was first for 25 in 6 or more varieties. H. Cliff captured the premium for pompons.

The Elm City Nursery Company prize, for best collection of fruited branches of trees, shrubs, and vines, was won by D. Kydd, Jr.

In the classes for cut blooms of chrysanthemums, Cliff, Carlson, Jenkins and Angus carried off most of the honors.

The prizes for roses were won by J. P. Stevenson, A. J. Long, Carlson and Sorenson. Carlson and Cliff were also leaders in the carnation classes.

John Slocombe took first for 400 double violets.

Groups of plants were not up to what might be expected of gardeners able to produce such creditable exhibits in other lines. Specimen plants were fairly well shown in numbers and quality. Nephrolepis elegantissima predominated wherever possible in classes for ferns and decorative plants without restriction. N. Scottii were rather short at this show. In the class for orchids two very good exhibits were staged, but that of Henry Cliff was in point of superiority of bloom and greater variety so much in advance of the other that the judges had no trouble reaching a decision. Vegetables were exhibited both as regards quality and arrangement in a way that made me wish Arthur T. Boddington could see them. Everything in the collections was of superior quality and they were arranged in an orderly and tasteful manner. Walter Angus took first and Oscar Carlson second.

An object of much comment and interest in the hall was a vase of Winsor carnation exhibited by the introducers, F. R. Pierson Company. Although the blooms here displayed were cut ten days previously they showed few if any signs of fading. This carnation was greatly admired by both private gardeners and commercial growers.

The displays of plants and other material pertaining to the trade by local growers and dealers were not very numerous, but those seen were very creditable to the exhibitors, especially those of Frank S. Platt & Company and Mrs. Woodworth. The Elm City Nursery Company had a large number of specimen bay trees, more for the decoration of the hall than anything else. Mr. Murray, superintendent of the grounds of Yale College, exhibited a group of plants some of which were of more than passing interest.

Taking this exhibition all through, it did credit to the exhibitors and to the society, but what struck me most about it was the disinterestedness of its promoters as shown by the wide range of classes and in certain other matters which went to show that the aim of the society and its officers is the advancement of horticulture and not personal gain or gratification.

The judges at the exhibition were: Edwin Jenkins, Lenox, Mass.; William Scott, Tarrytown, N. Y.; and David McIntosh, Newport, R. I. VISITOR.

Providence, R. I.

The chrysanthemum and carnation show of the Rhode Island Horticultural Society, held on Tuesday and Wednesday, November 13 and 14, was not as largely attended as some former exhibitions of this society. The public here, as well as the growers, seem to be losing interest. The judges were A. H. Hixon, Worcester, Mass. and James Burns, gardener for Mr. J. A. Forster, Warwick, R. I.

In the classes for chrysanthemum plants in pots, F. A. Sayles, Pawtucket, R. I., took the majority of the prizes.

For 25 blooms of Col. D. Appleton, S. A. Borden, Fall River was first. For 25 A. J. Balfour, John Macrae, won first; F. A. Sayles, second. Mr. Sayles also took first for 25 Dr. Enguehard; John Macrae, second. The latter exhibitor captured first for 25 Timothy Eaton, and also for 50 bottles of not less than 10 varieties. For 12 cut blooms, distinct varieties, Mr. Sayles was first; S. A. Borden, second. The same exhibitors in the same order were the winners in the class for 6 blooms distinct varieties. E. J. Johnston took first for vase of 50, and Mr. Borden first for best single flower of any variety, best single yellow, Mr. Sayles being first for best single pink and best single white; John Macrae, second. Mr. Macrae took the three prizes for best 6 vases of 10 blooms each in distinct sorts.

Carnations.

For 50 blooms Enchantress, J. A. Cushing, Quidnick, R. I. captured first; John Macrae, second. For 6 varieties, Cushing was again first, and for 25 blooms crimson, John Macrae won out, S. J. Goddard, Framingham, Mass., second. Mr. Macrae also captured the first prizes for 25 dark pink and 25 light pink; S. J. Goddard, second. Mr. Goddard was first for 25 scarlet; Mr. Macrae, second. John G. Girard, Bristol, Pa., won out for 25 yellow. Mr. Macrae was first for 20 blooms of new seedling introduction of 1906; Mr. Goddard, second.

Wm. Hill took first and second for collection of Begonia Gloire de Lorraine, and second on orchids, Mr. Borden being first for the latter.

One of the best chrysanthemums on exhibition was John Macrae's new Yellow Eaton. Many of the visiting florists said it was the finest yellow chrysanthemum ever shown in New England. It is certainly a grand thing, a well-shaped flower, color bright yellow, stem strong, with the best of foliage. It is an excellent keeper, having stood cut for two weeks in a temperature of 60 degrees. The E. G. Hill Company, of Richmond, Ind., will introduce this new variety in February, 1907.

G. A. J.

Toronto.

The horticultural exhibition held here last week was a fine show, and a winner in every way, but financially, and even in that important factor I think we will not be far behind. The weather was good, while the plants were being taken to and from the show, thereby avoiding freezing and in most cases much wrapping.

The general show was not quite up to the average, but the display of orchids was very fine. The Dale Estate sent in an exhibit of Cattleya labiata and Oncidium varicosum, which were a credit to their grower, Mr. Hansen; a number of the cattleyas in 6-inch pots had from 14 to 20 flowers, the oncidiums had fine sprays of large flowers. Exhibition Park had a large quantity of cattleyas and several other orchids. Thomas Manton and the Allan Gardens also had nice exhibits.

Plants.

The groups of palms, ferns and chrysanthemums were all of good quality. Exhibition Park took first prize, thereby winning the Hallam cup for the third time. Sir Henry Pellatt, J. McVittie, gardener, took second place with a fine group; the Allan Gardens and T. Manton won third and fourth. These groups were placed at the back of the stage and produced a fine effect. The Begonia Gloire de Lorraine were fine, D. Robertson taking first prize, Sir H. Pellatt, second; Allan Gardens, third. The bush plants were not nearly developed, the blooms being scarcely half opened. The prizes went to Exhibition Park and the Allan Gardens. The single stemmed plants were good, all of them, and competition keen; Allan Gardens, Exhibition Park, D. Robertson, and the Steele Briggs Company, J. Stephens, gardener to F. B. Fudger, being the exhibitors. There was only one exhibit of cyclamen, from Jay & Son; two lots of callas, from Sir H. Pellatt and Jay & Son. A good exhibit of ferns in specimen sizes came from Sir H. Pellatt, Exhibition Park, the Allan Gardens, and the Steele Briggs Seed Company.

Chrysanthemums—Cut Blooms.

The display of cut chrysanthemums was fine, although many of the best varieties were not ready to cut, all the later varieties being just half opened. The best blooms again came from Montreal, though Sir H. Pellatt ran very close, and considering that Mr. McVittie has not been over from Europe more than twelve months he put up a fine exhibit. The Dale Estate, D. Robertson, J. H. Dunlop and R. Cameron all had good flowers. Thos. McHugh again won the prize for the largest bloom in the show.

Carnations.

The carnations were not up to our usual standard either in quantity or quality. The cup for blooms of a new variety not in commerce brought out two exhibitors, and was awarded to the Dale Estate for a dark variety of Enchantress. The other variety was Winsor, exhibited by F. R. Pierson Company, Tarrytown, N. Y. The judges' decision was protested, as it was claimed that the other sport had occurred in the States and had been sold last Spring. The committee has about decided to have this point settled at the carnation meeting to be held here next January, when we hope to have all the experts with us.

Roses.

There was a splendid exhibit of roses, the Dale Estate taking the largest number of first prizes. The Toronto Floral Company, J. H. Dunlop, and the Bedford Park Floral Company all put up fine flowers in several classes. W. Allen and G. D. Manton each staged some good American Beauty.

Design Work.

For standing funeral design, J. H. Dunlop was first with a very fine piece; T. Manton, second, J. Simmons, third, this design not being up to Mr. Simmons's standard, being very closely packed and out of proportion. The premiums for other made-up work were about evenly divided between Dunlop and Simmons.

There were four decorated dinner tables which were judged by nine society ladies with Mrs. M. Clark, wife of the Lieutenant Governor, as president. Simmons was awarded first prize for a very elaborate decoration of Cattleya labiata and lily of the valley; A. Jennings, second, with a center-piece made of a good plant of Phœnix Roebelenii and Adiantum Lathami, in which were placed some long sprays of Oncidium varicosum. T. Manton was third with a center-piece made up of Adiantum Farleyense, in which were placed long sprays of well-colored Bougainvillea Sanderiana and lily of the valley. Dunlop's table was fourth and was quite distinct from all the others; it was a fine example of the use of millinery in combination with flowers and electric lights for decoration. Many thought it was the finest of the lot, while others thought it much overdone. Personally, I have an old gardener's dislike to millinery effects, so am not in position to say who is right, but the judges decided against this style of decoration.

Wm. Wilshire of Montreal judged the plants and cut chrysanthemums; E. I. Mepsted, of Ottawa the designs and other cut flowers. Their decisions gave general satisfaction; I did not hear many complaints.

Lager & Hurrell, Summit, N. J. sent a fine exhibit of orchids, not for competition. Mr. Gilchrist, of Toronto, sent a nice exhibit of ferns. T. Manton showed a vase of yellow G. S. Kalb chrysanthemum, which were rather past their best, having been held for some time. Mr. Simmons staged an elaborate made-up piece as an extra entry.

The tickets prove that over ten thousand people visited the show. We had many out-of-town people, among them being George Struck, of Summit, J. Fotheringham, representing F. R. Pierson Company, T. McHugh, T. McHugh, Jr., J. Bennett, J. McKenna, A. Ferguson of Montreal; E. I. Mepsted, Ottawa; Wm. Taylor and Louis Vair, Barrie; Wm. Hayes, Brantford; A. Jennings, Ed. Dale, and about seventy others from Brampton; A. Jansen also others from Berlin; and A. H. Ewing, from Woodstock. There were a great many others at the show to whom we hardly had a chance to speak; when taking an active part one gets little chance to say much to old friends. The secretary of the floral department, E. Collins, did an immense amount of work; he was on deck all the time, and always at the right time. George Mills was superintendent again, and carried out all arrangements in good order.

THOS. MANTON.

Chicago, Ill.

The Horticultural Society of Chicago held its fifteenth annual exhibition at the Coliseum last week, and it is most assuredly not saying too much to state that it goes down into history as one of the most successful flower shows ever held. The advertising department made a point of the catchy headline "The World's Greatest Flower Show," which was thoroughly heralded throughout the city by signs and through the medium of the daily papers; and although that is a broad statement, and the writer must confess that he has not seen all the horticultural exhibitions in the world, there is no hesitancy in saying that it was a marvelous aggregation of the finest products and most artistic arrangement by an exceeding expert class of the members of the profession, and if the effect as a whole was ever excelled, it would be difficult to locate the location.

This was the second year of the show having been held in the Coliseum, and the general arrangement showed a vast improvement over last year. The management is entitled to a great deal of credit for the perfect manner in which every detail was handled, and though the attendance fell off slightly from that at the preceding show, this was due probably more to incidental conditions than to a lack of interest. Tuesday, the opening day, was also election day, which undoubtedly detracted largely from the attendance; and Saturday, usually the best day of the week, was so disagreeable meteorologically that again a noticeable falling off of the visitors resulted.

The general arrangement of the retailers' booths, which nearly surrounded the hall, could not be objected to by the most severe critic; while the special features, many of which were positively unique, were so numerous that they became almost bewildering. Probably the one that attracted the most attention was the beautiful specimen chrysanthemum plant of the variety Mrs. J. R. Tranter, which Arthur Herrington, Madison, N. J., shipped so carefully, and, with its five hundred blooms, arrived, and as it stood directly in front of the entrance, looked as perfect in condition as it could have done in the house where it was grown.

On the opening day, the following chrysanthemums were the most noticeable: Beatrice May, General Hutton, Colonel D. Appleton, Miss Marion Hankey and W. Duckham, all well finished blooms. In the class for 100 blooms, white, Nathan Smith & Sons won with Fidelity; E. G. Hill Co., second with Alice Byron, and Bassett & Washburn third with the same variety. E. G. Hill Co. took first for 100 pink, with Mary Mann; Nathan Smith & Son following with Mayor Weaver, and Poehlmann Brothers third with Dr. Enguehard. Colonel Appleton was the prize winning variety in 100 blooms, yellow, being shown by all three prize-takers. Wietor Brothers won out on 100 blooms, any color, with Mrs. J. E. Dunne.

John Thorpe's List of Best Varieties.

John Thorpe, who is recognized as an authority on chrysanthemums, named the following varieties as being the best shown at the Chicago show, and advises that those he mentions be included in every grower's collection: British Empire, Mme. Russell, Amateur Consiel, Suzanne Gauthier, Joe Roacher, Loisseau Rosseau, Mrs. W. H. Barnes, Miss M. Hankey, Mrs. H. Partridge, May Seddon, Mayor Weaver, Fidelity, White Duckham, Ongawa, Mlle. Chabanne, Mme. Pechon, Leroux, M. L. Dupuy, General Hutton, Norman Davis, M. F. Plant, Mary Mann, Sans Souci and Lady Hopetoun.

Special Features.

J. A. Peterson of Cincinnati, O., made an impression with his new begonia, Agatha, the result of a cross between Moonlight and Socrotana. This begonia was introduced by Veitch of London, and resembles the well known Gloire de Lorraine, its habit being more robust, the foliage stronger, and it flowers earlier. It is also of easier culture; the color of the flowers being a more delicate shade of pink.

The Selfridge collection of orchids, which was recently turned over to the care of Superintendent Frey of Lincoln Park, made a most attractive display, some particularly well developed specimens of cattleyas, oncidiums and cypripediums being presented.

Robert Craig & Son of Philadelphia made a beautiful display of decorative plants, among which the following were the most noticeable: Ficus pandurata, Otaheite oranges, crotons, dracænas, Nephrolepis elegantissima and N. Whitmani.

J. K. Andrews of Elgin, Ill., made a good display of his specialties, including flower pots, hanging baskets and parlor urns, the latter being a very successful patent which overcomes the so well known difficulty with decorative house plants by obviating the souring of the soil.

The Dundee Nurseries of Dundee, Ill., made an excellent showing of their stock wherein conifers were a very strong point.

At the south end of the building the unique display made by the Vaughan's Seed Store was very interesting and attracted much attention, being surrounded by a new variety of privet recently imported from Northern China, of a dwarf habit not unlike some of the box hedges with which we are all familiar. Within the enclosure was a carefully selected collection of garden plans, mostly annuals, such as marigold, asters, Phlox Drummondi, salvias, antirrhinums, cosmos and nicotianas, all of which had been pot-grown for this occasion. The effect was beautiful and reflects great credit on Messrs. Cropp and Wilson.

One of the exhibits which proved of unusual interest was the miniature greenhouse shown by the John C. Moninger Company. The model was staged on a base of green moss and surrounded by bay trees and various plants, the inside having small potted plants arranged in benches filled with sand. This miniature house was complete in every detail, being fitted with roof and side sash and ventilating apparatus for operating them. The house showed lapped and butted glass, bottom and top ventilation, also plain ridge and ridge with cap. This model was made almost entirely by hand and finished with white enamel. It was decorated with small electric lights and attracted much attention on account of its completeness and its originality.

Special C. S. A. Awards.

In the competition for the Chrysanthemum Society's silver cup for the best ten flowers, one variety, there were six entries, Poehlmann Bros. winning with Colonel Appleton.

In the class for 12 blooms for the best seedling or sport not yet in commerce, there were five entries. The first prize was given to C. H. Totty with a white sport from William Duckham, renamed Helen Clay Frick; the second going to E. G. Hill Co. for a pink seedling.

The Totty prizes for 12 blooms of 12 varieties were won by R. D. Foote, first, who showed Mme. G. Rivol, Mrs. D. Willis James, Beatrice May, G. J. Brooks, Morton F. Plant, Mrs. F. F. Thompson, Mrs. George Heaume, W. Wells, Mrs. John E. Dunne, Mrs. Henry Partridge and Merstham Crimson; E. G. Hill Co. winning the second prize.

The Pierson silver cup for 36 chrysanthemums, 6 varieties, 6 blooms of each, introductions of 1905 and 1906, was awarded to R. D. Foote, who showed Morton F. Plant, Beatrice May, Mrs. William Duckham, Professor Galloway, Sunburst and Mrs. E. D. West.

Nathan Smith & Son's prize, for 24 blooms of

American origin, introductions of 1904, 1905 and 1906, three varieties, white, pink and yellow, 8 blooms of each, was won by the donor of the prize, with the varieties Fidelity, Sunburst and Mayor Weaver. There were only two entries in this competition.

For the E. G. Hill prize, for the best 25 blooms of Mary Mann, there were three entries, the B. K. and B. Floral Co., Richmond, Ind., being the winners.

The Vaughan silver cup for the best specimen bush chrysanthemum plant was won by Martin A. Ryerson.

Carnations.

FIFTY WHITE.

White Lawson.—First, Anton Then, Chicago; second, Poehlmann Brothers; third, Peter Reinberg.

White Cloud.—Bassett & Washburn.

Boston Market.—Peter Reinberg.

Lady Bountiful.—First, Anton Then; second, Poehlmann Brothers.

Lieutenant Peary.—Poehlmann Brothers.

Any other White.—First, The Chicago Carnation Company, Joliet, Ill.; second, Gunnar Tielmann, Marion, Ind.

FIFTY RED.

Cardinal.—Anton Then.

Red Lawson.—First, Poehlmann Brothers; second, H. W. Buckbee, Rockford, Ill.

Any other red.—First, Chicago Carnation Company, with an unnamed seedling; second, Poehlmann Brothers, with Victory.

FIFTY CRIMSON.

Harlowarden.—First, Bassett & Washburn; second, Anton Then.

FIFTY PINK.

Enchantress.—First, The Chicago Carnation Company; second, Poehlmann Brothers.

Mrs. Thos. W. Lawson.—First, Bassett & Washburn; second, Poehlmann Brothers.

Fiancee.—First, The Chicago Carnation Company; second, Anton Then.

Nelson Fisher.—A. C. Brown.

Any other pink, Daybreak class.—First, The W. C. Hill Floral Company, with Melody; second, Poehlmann Brothers, with Phyllis.

Any other pink, Scott class.—First, The Chicago Carnation Company; second, E. H. Blameuser, Niles Center, Ill., both with Pink Enchantress.

Any other pink, Lawson class.—First, The Chicago Carnation Company; second, the J. D. Thompson Carnation Company, Joliet, Ill.

FIFTY STRIPED OR STAINED.

Mrs. Patten.—First, Sol. Garland; second, Poehlmann Brothers.

Prosperity.—First, Poehlmann Brothers; second, H. W. Buckbee.

NEW VARIETIES—FIFTY BLOOMS. INTRODUCTION OF 1906.

White.—First, The Chicago Carnation Company; second, Bassett & Washburn, with White Perfection.

Pink, Scott class.—First, The Chicago Carnation Company, with Rose Pink Enchantress; second, J. C. Ahrenfeld.

Pink, Lawson class.—First, Gunnar Tielmann.

Red.—First, Sol. Garland, with Robert Craig; second, J. D. Thompson Carnation Company, with same variety.

Any other color.—Poehlmann Brothers, with Glendale.

ONE HUNDRED BLOOMS.

White.—First, The Chicago Carnation Company; second, Poehlmann Brothers, with Governor Wolcott.

Pink, Daybreak class.—First, The Chicago Carnation Company; second, Poehlmann Brothers, with Enchantress.

Pink, Scott class.—First, The Chicago Carnation Company, with Rose Pink Enchantress.

Pink, Lawson class.—First, The Chicago Carnation Company, with Aristocrat; second, Poehlmann Brothers, with Pink Lawson.

Red.—First, The Chicago Carnation Co., with seedling 49; second, Poehlmann Brothers, with Victory.

Any other color.—Poehlmann Brothers, with Prosperity.

Miscellaneous.

Violets, not less than 800 blooms.—First, the Eaton Floral Co., 86 Jackson boulevard, Chicago.

Lily of the valley, not less than 500 blooms.—First, A. Jurgens, Chicago.

Bride's and bridesmaid's bouquets.—First, Henry E. Klunder; second, R. Jahn; third, Eaton Floral Store.

Dinner table decoration for 12 covers.—First, C. Frauenfelder & Co.; second, John Mangel; third, Henry E. Klunder.

Floral Arrangements.

Basket of roses—First, C. Frauenfelder & Co., Chicago; second, Butler Floral Company, Chicago.

Basket of carnations—First, Eaton's flower shop, Chicago; second, C. A. Samuelson, Chicago.

Basket of chrysanthemums—First, C. A. Samuelson, Chicago; second, Anton Then, Chicago.

Best arrangement for bridal party roses, original design—First, Butler Floral Company, Chicago; second, C. A. Samuelson, Chicago; third, E. G. Uihlein, Chicago.

Exhibit of cut flowers presenting the best appearance throughout the exhibition; exhibitor allowed to renew and rearrange flowers daily—First, Peter Reinberg, Chicago; second, John May, Summit, N. J.

On Saturday the school children were admitted to the exhibition.

During the existence of the show several lectures were delivered, one by Miss Sipe of Washington, D. C., on "School Gardening for Teachers."

The Banquet.

It is doubtful if a more successful banquet has ever been enjoyed by a meeting of florists in the country than was participated in on Thursday evening of last week. The unusual large representation of out-of-town members of the craft made the affair one of remarkable enjoyment to the local fraternity. Every important floricultural center was represented, and it is no exaggeration to state that the party encompassed a very large proportion of the ablest members of the profession of the United States. President Hauswirth of the local club, in a few well chosen remarks of welcome to the visitors closed by introducing J. C. Vaughan as the toastmaster of the evening. Mr. Vaughan facilitated matters in unquestionable form, and not only exhausted the wits of the guest table, but drew largely from the contributing element on the floor. On the whole it may be said to have been "a perfect success." Among the speakers were: President Kasting of the S. A. F. O. H., President Duckham of the C. S. A., Secretary Stewart of the S. A. F. O. H., John N. May, John Burton, J. T. Temple, J. D. Carmody, E. V. Hallock, Professor Cowell, J. A. Valentine, P. J. Hauswirth, George Asmus, J. F. Ammann, J. F. Klimmer and others.

Influence of Climate.

(*A paper by E. G. Hill, Richmond, Ind., read before the Chrysanthemum Society of American at the Chicago meeting, November 7, 1906.*)

The responsibility of writing a paper on the subject of chrysanthemums, or any branch pertaining thereto, is no small one. Since the beginning of the chrysanthemum era much has been written on the subject; so much, indeed, has been written and printed, and so much of value withal, that it smacks of pure presumption for me to undertake to speak entertainingly upon any branch of chrysanthemum culture.

Chrysanthemum Literature.

Would you know how to take care of your stock plants? Would you inquire as to the best time to take cuttings, or the best kind of cuttings to take? Would you ask as to the ideal soil, as to the best methods of shipping and marketing, or a complete set of rules for growing, staging and exhibiting chrysanthemums at the annual exhibitions? If so, you will naturally turn to the able and excellent book published by our ex-president, Arthur Herrington, or the older but no less valuable work published by Elmer D. Smith, that old-time expert of Adrian, Mich.

Then look at our cultural notes in the trade papers. What volumes these notes would make if brought together into book form! In justice to the judgment and ability of the writers for these papers, I believe that a compiler of these notes would find it hard to cut anything out, for they are of universal value. With all these facts staring me in the face, it becomes a hard problem to select a branch of this subject on which I may say anything other than repetitions and quotations from abler men.

However, facing the necessity of fulfilling a promise made without the full realization of its responsibility, I have decided to make a few remarks along the line of the influence of climatic conditions upon the culture of chrysanthemums.

When Humidity Influences.

No doubt many of the members present have read the valuable work from the hands of W. Wells, the famous chrysanthemum expert of England. In this book Mr. Wells endeavors to describe the methods which have won him so many prizes and so much honor before the National Chrysanthemum Society of England, yet after a study of this book, with my mind entirely open to conviction and with a desire to learn from him, it is exceedingly hard to find any point of value in our part of the country.

Some of the most able chrysanthemum notes which have been published in the United States in years are coming from time to time from the pen of our honored member, Mr. Totty, yet there are points in his notes which will scarcely fit the ultra-dry atmospheric conditions facing us in the central states.

Mr. Wells very carefully directs his reader to avoid overwatering as one would avoid a serpent. In Indiana it is extremely difficult to overwater chrysanthemums when they are growing vigorously during the hot summer months. Our greatest trouble lies in our benches drying out at the bottom while we are carefully watering on top, so we find that to succeed in producing fine flowers we must daily go to the bottom of our benches to discover whether the water is penetrating the depth of the bench. Mr. Wells grows his magnificent exhibition blooms in pots, sitting upon cement ledges out-of-doors. On the other hand, we of Indiana plant our chrysanthemums in a bench constructed with a view to "keeping their feet cold."

We have become firmly convinced that benches with too thorough drainage are not the best benches for chrysanthemum growing. Of course, we must always avoid letting our soil become water-logged, but it is difficult in our section of the country, where the air in the summer is intensely hot and dry, and where evaporation from foliage is extremely rapid, it is almost impossible, we think, to overwater chrysanthemums.

Selection of Buds.

The influence of climate upon the selection of buds for obtaining the best results with different varieties is a subject of the utmost interest. It is certain that chrysanthemums do not act in this country, at least in our section, in the same manner as they do in England, or even along our eastern coast. We are convinced that it is much more difficult to properly develop first crown buds in our section of the country than in a locality where the atmosphere is somewhat more humid.

On the other hand, we have less excuse for losing flowers from damping. The English writers tell of their methods of timing the buds. We have repeatedly attempted to accomplish something of this kind, but find that it is utterly impossible to change the date of any particular variety to any considerable extent. The reason we assign is the subject of this paper.

When Control is Greatest.

To explain more fully our views: Where the weather is cool and much of the time cloudy, the conditions for growing chrysanthemums are far more fully under the control of the grower, and he may, by studying individual varieties, control his results. Where the atmosphere is dry and evaporation from the foliage is rapid, chrysanthemums grow and develop more in accordance with nature's laws and are less under control of the operator.

France and the United States Alike.

How often we have followed the directions given by our English friends, regarding first crown buds, only to see the result of our year's work a great, abnormal flower commonly known as bullhead, instead of the beautiful bloom as described in the catalogue.

It is generally understood that the French growers are unable to produce flowers of size or color to compare with those grown by many experts in England. Also, in spite of the wonderful blooms produced by prominent members of this society in the east, we have understood that they are somewhat behind our English friends.

Now, is it not entirely feasible that conditions in France and the United States, which we know are somewhat alike as to climate, may prove the stumbling block?

It has always seemed peculiar to us that the varieties originating in France are frequently beautiful upon the terminal bud, while varieties which come from England, as a class, are worthless on this bud. It is certain that we get by far the most beautiful color on our terminals, while in England the use of a terminal bud is the exception rather than the rule.

I am loath to believe that the growers in this country are behind our English friends in ability; also, I would not do credit to the west did I not say that the men of the west are as well able to grow fine flowers as those in the east. It comes down to a question of local conditions, and I am firmly convinced that the climate is the most potent factor of all.

Partial View of Exhibition of New Jersey Floricultural Society.

Orange, N. J.

The twelfth annual flower show of the New Jersey Floricultural Society was held in the new hall of the Woman's Club in East Orange, November 5 and 6. Cash prizes to the amount of $160 were awarded, and twenty certificates of merit were given for exhibits not for competition. An area of 3,500 square feet gave ample opportunity for five groups and many decorative efforts, besides specimen plants. The cut flowers, fruits and vegetables were placed around the walls. The stage was filled by the orchid display of Wm. Barr, set off by palms and ferns, this display numbering five hundred plants alone.

The principal prize winners were J. Crosby Brown, Peter Duff, gardener, who took first for best twelve chrysanthemum plants, best six chrysanthemum plants, bush plant, best flowering plant other than chrysanthefum, specimen fern, twelve cut chrysanthemums, six white, six bronze, best fifty double violets, and best fifty single violets. Wm. Barr, A. W. Bodwell gardener, was first for display of orchids, capturing the George Smith prize. He was also first for the best orchid in flower. The Peter Henderson & Company prize, for the best dozen roses, one or more varieties, was won by A. B. Jenkins. The J. M. Thorburn & Company prize, for best exhibit of vegetables, was won by Peter Duff; and the Totty prize, for best six flowers of chrysanthemum Morton F. Plant, was captured by the same exhibitor. Hale, the florist, won the society's prize for the best arrangement of flowers. The Kelsey prize for the best display of fruit was captured by A. T. Gillespie. John N. May, Summit, N. J., took first for the best display of pompon chrysanthemums.

Certificates of merit were awarded to Lager & Hurrell, Summit, N. J., for an exhibit of orchids; to Chas. H. Totty, Madison, N. J., for six magnificent blooms of the white sport of Wm. Duckham; to F. R. Pierson Company, Tarrytown, N. Y., for carnation Winsor; to John Riemels, Woodhaven, L. I., for carnation, Winsome; to Popkin & Collins, Orange, N. J., for a group of chrysanthemums and table of pompons; to J. Hansen for group of decorative plants; to H. C. Potter, William Phillips, gardener, for vase of chrysanthemum Colonel D. Appleton and seedling carnations; to Charles Hathaway, Max Schneider, gardener, for vase of rose Killarney; and to T. A. Gillespie, George Oakley, gardener, for vase of pompon chrysanthemums.

J. B. D.

International Conference on Plant Hardiness and Acclimatization.

New York, 1907.

The responses to the preliminary letter of inquiry issued in the early part of this year have proved so encouraging that the Council of the Horticultural Society of New York, at the meeting held on October 10, decided to proceed with the project, and is arranging to hold the conference in New York City about the end of September, 1907.

From all parts of the United States, from several European countries, and from South America and Canada, as well as the West Indian Islands, active interest has been expressed, and at this early date a number of papers and contributions have been promised. The conference has the endorsement of the United States Department of Agriculture, and the majority of the directors and horticulturists of the State experiment stations have signified their intention of contributing information, or sending delegates.

Theg reat importance of the subjects to be discussed in their relationship to practical horticulture, fruit growing and the nursery trade is evident to every one, and the council of the Horticultural Society of New York, in soliciting your further support, thanks you for any attention in the past.

A special committee of the society in charge of the arrangements for the conference was appointed as follows: James Wood, N. L. Britton, P. O'Mara, H. A. Siebrecht and Leonard Barron. Communications from those interested should be addressed to the office of the society, Roof 60, Bryant Building 55 Liberty Street, N. Y. City.

LEONARD BARRON, Secretary.

English Firms Renaming American Carnations.

Our English friends seem to be renaming American varieties of carnations. A correspondent of the Gardeners' Chronicle points out that at the October 23 meeting of the Royal Horticultural Society an award of merit was given for a variety called St. Louis, "which I am firmly of the opinion is none other than the new American variety Victory, it being identical in color and general build. On one of the stands I noticed a variety labeled Mr. W. I. Omwake; this, I believe, is Rose Enchantress, and sent out in America as such."

The Englishman's vaunted claim for fair play in all things should remedy this evil.

Campbell's Sulphur Vaporizer.

Editor Florists' Exchange:

I see some inquiries have been made in your paper about "Campbell's Sulphur vaporiser." From the experience I have had with it I cannot praise it too highly. There is nothing to equal it in destroying mildew and red spider, and at a very small cost. When more known, I am sure no grower will be without it.

JOHN ROBSON.

Altrincham, Eng.

CLUB AND SOCIETY DOINGS.

NEW YORK FLORISTS' CLUB.—The attendance at the meeting on Monday evening, November 12, was the largest in the club's history. It was Ladies' Night, and the fine entertainment provided by the house committee, headed by Chairman Nugent, was most thoroughly enjoyed. President John Scott, although present, was unable to officiate, owing to severe lameness, the result of a previous accident to his right leg, so the chair was occupied by Patrick O'Mara, who put through the business with characteristic celerity. Resolutions on the death of Paul R. B. Pierson, father of Frank R. and Paul M. Pierson, Tarrytown and Scarborough, N. Y., were read by Alex. Wallace, and those on the demise of the mother of the Burnett Brothers, seedsmen, by L. W. Wheeler.

The nominating committee presented the following as its selection of officers for the ensuing year: For president, Charles H. Totty and John B. Nugent, Jr.; vice-president, Harry O. May and Anthony J. Manda; secretary, John Young and Alexander J. Guttman; treasurer, Charles B. Weathered and L. W. Wheeler; trustees, John Scott, Walter F. Sheridan, Julius Roehrs, Jr., E. V. Hallock, John Donaldson, and Charles Lenker.

Chrysanthemum Miss Alice Roosevelt.

Growers, E. G. Hill Company.

Andrew Wilson and L. Boelson were elected members and the following proposed: Emil Savoie, B. De Meyer, C. Sierens, H. D. Darlington, and Paul Niehoff.

Secretary Young read a letter from Samuel Thorne, Milbrook, N. Y., expressing appreciation of his election as an honorary member of the club.

The chair appointed as a committee to draw up resolutions on the death of the father of Philip Kessler, Messrs. Pepper, Sheridan and Traendly.

The remainder of the evening was devoted to entertainment, which included songs, recitations, violin and piano solos, terpsichorean stunts, bagpipe playing and the rendering of several concerted pieces in fine style by the Glee Club of Clan Macdonald, Brooklyn, N. Y., under the able leadership of Clansman Ritchie. Among others who contributed to the evening's amusement were Andrew Wilson (violin playing and buck and wing dance); highland dancing by Misses Annie and Jeanie Birnie, Piper William Cameron officiating on the Scottish national instrument; Miss Barnett, (recitation); Rickard Brothers (songs); Miss Pollock, Miss Boujay and Mr. Kelly (vocal solos and piano), and others. Special refreshments were served to the ladies and "ladies' men," the wants of the male members in this respect being also well looked after. The affair, which was "maistly Scotch," broke up at a late hour, and was voted the best among the many given by the club.

The exhibits of the evening consisted of three vases of chrysanthemums from H. Turner, superintendent at Castle Gould, L. I., of the varieties Mrs. Henry Partridge, Morton F. Plant and Colonel D. Appleton, for which a cultural certificate was awarded. A vase of the new scarlet carnation, Beacon, from Peter Fisher, Ellis, Mass., which scored 87 points and was awarded a preliminary certificate. A collection of chrysanthemums from A. A. McDonald, Somerville, N. J., including Mersa, Mrs. Thirkell, Colonel D. Appleton, Mrs. A. J. Miller, Morton F. Plant, T. Richardson, Dr. Enguehard, T. Carrington, Nellie Pockett, Beatrice May, Cheltoni, Valerie Greenham, General Hutton, Mrs. D. V. West, Mrs. Swinburn, W. R. Church, Brighthurst and W. Duckham. Most of these flowers were cut from plants grown in 6 inch pots, and were excedingly well done; they were awarded a cultural certificate.

H. H. Barrows & Son, Whitman, Mass., showed two 8 inch pans of their new fern. As this fern N. Whitmani, has previously been awarded the club's certificate, no further award was given. C. W. Ward, of the Cottage Gardens, Queens, L. I., exhibited a magnificent bunch of carnations, among which were many beautiful sorts not known to the trade and for which he was accorded a vote of thanks.

Charles H. Totty, Madison, N. J., showed a dozen blooms of the new chrysanthemum, White Duckham, a variety that seems destined to become a standard commercial sort, and which has been named Helen Clay Frick. A preliminary certificate was granted. Guttman & Weber showed vases of Victory and Rose Pink Enchantress carnations for which they received a vote of thanks. Paul Niehoff, Lehighton, Pa., exhibited a nice vase of his new rose Aurora. This variety had been previously before the club, but at an unfavorable time of the year. As shown now it attracted much favorable comment, and the committee awarded it a preliminary certificate.

THE ST. LOUIS FLORISTS' CLUB held a very fine exhibit of chrysanthemums on Thursday afternoon of last week. The regular monthly meeting was held at the same time, 35 members and as many visitors being present. Had it not been show week elsewhere our exhibit would have been larger; however, the local growers put up a creditable lot of cut blooms. The exhibitors were: Himmers Brothers, of Meramec Highlands, who showed a vase each of Colonel D. Appleton, Major Bonnaffon, and Timothy Eaton. James W. Dunford of Clayton, Mo., exhibited Dr. Enguehard, Timothy Eaton, Florence Vaughan and Colonel D. Appleton. The Bentzen Floral Co. staged St. Louis—a fine white, Alice Bryon, also Mrs. Buckbee, Mrs. Perrin and A. J. Balfour. Edwin Denker, St. Charles, Mo., a vase of fine Yellow Eaton. Nathan Smith & Son, Adrian, Mich., sent a vase of magnificent varieties which caught the eye of growers, who selected as the best in the lot, Sunburst and Theodore Roosevelt. The judges, Messrs. Young, Goebel and Pring, awarded the prizes as follows:

Best 12 cut blooms, white—Himmers Bros., with Timothy Eaton; J. W. Dunford, second, with same variety; Bentzen Floral Company, third, with Alice Bryon. Twelve yellow—Himmers Bros., first, with Major Bonnaffon; they also took second prize with Colonel D. Appleton; J. W. Dunford, third, with same variety. Twelve pink—Bentzen Floral Company, first with A. J. Balfour, this firm also capturing second with Mrs. Perrin; J. W. Dunford, third, with Dr. Enguehard. The collection sent by Nathan Smith & Son was not for competition, but all voted the blooms very fine and worthy to be included in any chrysanthemum collection.

The meeting opened late, with President Irish in thec hair. W. C. Young, State Vice-president of the S. A. F. O. H., stated he had been notified by the railroads that he should ask for rates for the next convention early in December. A discussion took place on providing a new meeting room, the present hall being too far out of the way for some of the members. It was finally voted to vacate the present quarters by the first of the new year, the trustees being instructed to secure another meeting hall and report at the next meeting. All the members took part in the discussion as to whether we should have a flower show next year; a final vote was taken, and it was decided we shall hold show next November. A committee of three was appointed—Frank A. Weber, A. J. Bentzen, and W. C. Smith—to raise a fund of $10,000 among business men, including the Shaw prizes amounting to $500, which we get yearly. Frank Weber's essay on "Does it Pay to Advertise?" enthused the members more than ever that a successful flower show can be held with the right kind of advertising and management.

Gustave Eggeling, of the Eggeling Floral Company, made application for membership.

At the next meeting H. G. Pring, who has charge of the orchid houses at Shaw's Garden, will read a paper on "Growing orchids and Other Varieties of Choice Plants."

W. C. Smith auctioned off the prize-winning blooms, and all brought good prices.

The next meeting will be held on Thursday, December 13, at 2 p. m.

ST. PATRICK.

THE DETROIT FLORISTS' CLUB met Wednesday November 7, 1906, and decided to make the annual pilgrimage to Mt. Clemens on Friday, November 9. The members assembled at the store of John Breitmeyer's Sons, whence they took the rapid car to their destination. About 60 were in the party. In former years the florists enjoyed the primitive sport of riding from place to place on hay wagons, but this year they assumed a college spirit and indulged in a cross-country trot. They visited the greenhouses of Leopold Maliast and found his carnations exceptional for the season. His violets also are in the pink of condition; while those of others did not appear so well. At Breitmeyer's the stock was found in good shape; chrysanthemums being fine as usual. Here a substantial lunch was enjoyed. Thence they visited other growers including Robert Klagge, Stevens, John Carey, James Taylor, and finally wound up at August von Boeslager's place. Generally stock was in fine shape and an excellent Christmas supply is anticipated. Everywhere they received the hearty reception for which Mt. Clemens florists have established a record.

HARRY.

FOR THE RETAILER

[All questions relating to the Retail Trade will be heerfully answered in this column. We solicit good. harp photographs of made-up work, decorations, store nteriors. etc., for reproduction here.—Ed. F. E.]

A Liliputian Flower Store.

Our illustration shows, perhaps, the smallest flower tore proper in the United States, if not in the world. he measurement of the entire building is 5x30 feet he store, occupying 5x15 feet, with a greenhouse of imilar dimensions, is located at Virginia avenue and oardwalk, Atlantic City, N. J., and was opened on une 1, 1904, by Littman, the florist; here he is uilding up a lucrative business.

A Seed Incubator, Propagator and Plant Stand.

The Templin Crockett Company of Cleveland, O., introducing what they consider a simple and in- xpensive device whereby anybody may successfully st all kinds of seeds, grow early vegetable and ower plants from seed, propagates flower plants rom slips or cuttings and care for blooming plants the house during the Winter months.

The device consists of two shallow pans made of alvanized iron and a detachable glass case. The wer pan is 12 by 28 inches and 3 inches deep, and provided with divisions in the bottom which are onnected with a small boiler beneath the center such a manner that when filled with water and a mp placed beneath the boiler, a perfect circula- ng warm water system is obtained, insuring a uni- rm even temperature throughout the entire sur- ice of the pan. The warm water flows from the p of the boiler along the outside channels to the rthest corners of the pan, returning back through e middle of the pan and entering the boiler the bottom, thereby ensuring a perfect circulating stem. The upper pan or propagating tray 2 inches deep and rests on the divisions in the wer pan. It is perforated in the bottom for drain- ge, and is proveded with detachable corner posts ving grooves for holding glass in position, form- g a closed glass case. By filling the propagating ay with soil or sand, inserting a thermometer which the firm supplies) and regulating the flame the lamp, one can maintain the temperature at y desired degree. A moist even bottom heat and umid temperature are provided, exactly like the ofessional florist maintains in his propagating ouse.

The inventor, R. L. Templin, has had thirty years practical experience in the seed and plant busi- ess, and in all that experience never had better ccess in germinating and successfully growing the ost delicate varieties of flowers than "we had last pring in the first incubator that we built."

Some New York Decorations.

Last week some very artistic wedding decora- ons were executed by Myer, 609-11 Madison ave- e, a description of which will prove interesting our readers.

For the marriage of Miss Eliz. Stobo to Philip yman James, of Chicago, a nephew of the late arshall Field, at the "Heavenly Rest" a very rge and fashionable affair. In the church impos- g bowers of exotic palms, on each side of the altar, ere used with four large torches of white chrys- nthemums in each one. Large specimen palms ere placed on each side of the center aisle, form- g arches under which the bridal party passed. very other pew had on it a large bunch of white rysanthemums tied with white ribbon. Over a ousand of these blooms were used. At the resi- ence, 343 West 55th street, a large bower of palms as formed where the bridal party received. Un- erneath it and behind them was arranged a Paris- n canopy made of lattice work covered with as- aragus interspersed with large bunches of white rysanthemums tied with white ribbon—one of e prettiest effects imaginable. The dining room as decorated with vases of Bridesmaid roses. The aircase, from first floor to third, was one mass of nk chrysanthemums tied with ribbon to match. hese decorations were under the able management Maurice Kleiman, one of Myer's lieutenants.

For the wedding of Miss Ethel Howell, daughter the late Geo. R. Howell, to George Willis Peters, ., at St. Thomas' Church. The decorations at the urch were somewhat similar to those at the Heavenly Rest" but more imposing and plentiful, eing a carte blanche order. At the residence, 26 Fifty-fourth street, the main hall had the walls overed with oak foliage. From the ceiling were uspended wire rods containing 300 cornucopia glass- filled with pink chrysanthemums. The stair rail ading to the third story was covered with oak foli- ge and large bunches of pink chrysanthemums stened with pink ribbon. The first floor had in e several rooms 31 cut glass vases filled with ecimen pink and white chrysanthemums. The rlor, where the bridal party received, had a large wer of palms, in the center of which was a large escent suspended from the ceiling containing 21 asses filled with white chrysanthemums. The ectric light shining on this was too lovely for scription. The decorator was ably assisted in is work by Mr. Blauvelt formerly of the N. Y. ut Flower Company. The bridal bouquets con- sted of white orchids and lily of the valley, in ower style; the bridesmaids' bouquets, one of yel- w chrysanthemums tied with ribbon to match, the other. Killarney roses with similar ribbon made to hang on the arm, were finely executed by Henry Luhrs and gave great satisfaction. Altogether over 4000 chrysanthemums were used.

The American Rose Society.

The executive committee held a meeting at the Hotel Martinique, New York City, November 9, 1906. All members reported in person or by letter. The arrangements for the Spring show, in connection with the Washington Florists' Club, to be held in March, 1907, were reported to be perfected, the agreement having been signed by Peter Bissett and Chas. E. McCauley, on behalf of the Washington Florists' Club, and Robert Simpson, President of the American Rose Society. The secretary reported that when at Chicago last month he attended the Cook County Horticultural Society's meeting, and was introduced there on behalf of the American Rose Society, receiving from the association courteous consideration, and that he had urged the Western people, as far as he could, to join hands earnestly to make the Rose Society a great popular educating association, to bring in the era of "A rose for every home and a bush for every garden," which to the commercial grower meant a standing and expanding interest in outdoor floral decorations of all kinds.

Littman's Liliputian Flower Store, Atlantic City, N. J.

Letters were read from P. J. Lynch, West Grove, Pa.; Jas. J. Curran, Salem, Va.; and Patrick Welch of Boston, Mass., encouraging the best efforts possible to make the show at the Capitol a great success.

Since the committee meeting in August last, S. S. Pennock of Philadelphia has sent in an application for life membership with the full fee of $50.

A special prize of $10 was reported for an exhibit of three good roses, suitable for door-yard planting, that held the foliage to the best advantage. Robert Simpson, Clifton, N. J., offered a silver cup valued at $50 for the best collection of crimson roses. H. O. May, Summit, N. J., offered a silver cup valued at $25 for American seedling roses not yet introduced. F. R. Pierson, Tarrytown, N. Y., offered a silver cup valued at $25 for the best collection of hybrid Wichuraiana, and Ex-president W. C. Barry advised that his firm would be pleased to offer a suitable prize to be designated later.

It was moved by Mr. May, and seconded by Mr. Farenwald, that the chair appoint a committee to prepare a synopsis of the organization and doings of the American Rose Society up to the present time. The secretary and vice-president, with Mr. Pierson, were appointed as such committee.

BENJAMIN HAMMOND,
Secretary.

A State Plant Breeders' Association.

As an outcome of the efforts of the American Breeders' Association, a meeting was called at New Haven, Conn., on November 3, 1906, to organize a state plant breeders' association. Everyone interested in this work is invited to join the association, and its objects are well stated in the call signed by George A. Hopson:

(1) A study of methods of plant breeding in present use, and the possibilities of their improvement; (2) the actual improvement in yield and quality of the important farm crops, and the adaptation of strains suited to local peculiarities of soil and climate by the use of such methods; (3) the adoption of a system of registration of plant breeding work, whereby members conducting such work suitable for record may receive certificates to that effect, and thus be helped to command a price for improved seed that will be a suitable compensation for their work.

A Large Contract.

The heaviest individual order for concrete machines in the world was negotiated recently by the Ideal Concrete Machinery Company, of South Bend, Ind., with a large Eastern concern which deals extensively in concrete machine and construction supplies, the order amounting to the magnificent sum of $250,000.

The figures tend to show the wonderful sentiment that is developing throughout the country in favor of concrete as a building material. The recent disasters at Buffalo, N. Y., and at San Francisco have contributed largely to the movement in this direction, as in both instances the buildings of concrete were the only ones to resist the ravages of the destructive elements.

Th Ideal Concrete Machinery Company has made rapid strides since its location in South Bend about two years. The company is doing an extensive business in foreign countries. The United States government has constructed the Provincial building at Zamboango, P. I., of "Ideal" blocks, and the engineer reports very favorably on the appearance. Other big contracts have been received for export shipments.

NEW SINGLE VIOLET BARONNE DE ROTHSCHILD.—An English firm (R. H. Bath, Ltd., of Wisbech) has a good word for the new single violet Baronne de Rothschild, which they consider one of the best introduced. "Its chief qualities are earliness of flowering and the fact that it will produce double the number of blooms produced by Princess of Wales." The perfume is much more pronounced than in other varieties. The plant is "exceedingly vigorous in growth, and resists attacks of red spider much better than any other singles."

Pittsburg.

Club News.

The November meeting of the Florists' Club was one of the best attended of the year. Having been held election day perhaps helped the attendance, as many were anxious to hear the early returns and came to the city. It was chrysanthemum night, and I doubt if we ever before had a better exhibition of blooms, particularly of large flowers. Quite a few growers from a distance sent exhibits, and all arrived in fine condition.

The following firms made displays: E. G. Hill Company, Richmond, Ind., fine flowers of Mrs. Geo. Beech, Mrs. Geo. Truffaut, Dubuisson Foubert, M. Pechon, Detroyat, a very large flower, 11 inches across, 15 inches overhead; Bois de Boulogne, Mme. L. Roussel, Mme. G. Rivol, pink; Mme. Suzanne Gauthier, Beatrice May, Marie Vieillermet, white.

Chas. H. Totty, of Madison, N. J., showed a half-dozen blooms of a fine white, which unfortunately was not labeled, or the label was lost, as many were anxious to know what it was (probably White Duckham.—Ed.). R. Vincent, Jr. & Son, White Marsh, Md., and Thomas Meehan & Sons, Philadelphia, sent hardy varieties, which were much admired—about 50 sorts, all labeled, some particularly good ones among them. The only trouble with these flowers in our vicinity is, that they get too dirty when grown outdoors, and it hardly pays to grow them under glass, as they are sold too cheaply. C. Peterson, of East Liverpool, Ohio, showed Yellow Queen; Godwin Brothers, Bridgeville, Pa., Pearl Queen, Major Bonnaffon, Mrs. Henry Robinson, Niveus, Adelia and Dr. Enguehard. McCrea & Jenkinson showed Golden Wedding, Cheltoni, Timothy Eaton, Colonel D. Appleton and Mrs. Wm. Duckham. Blind Brothers exhibited some Wm. Duckham, Robert Halliday, Maud Dean, Timothy Eaton and Ivory. Mr. Westhoff, of De Haven, Pa., staged Viviand-Morel, Ivory, A. J. Balfour, white and yellow Bonnaffon, Silver Wedding, and a fine bunch of Mrs. Lawson and Lady Bountiful carnations. Mr. Westhoff is a new beginner in the business and grows as good stock as comes into this market.

The Pittsburg Cut Flower Company made a good display of Col. D. Appleton, Major Bonnaffon, Wm. Duckham, A. J. Balfour, Alliance, Mary Mann, Mrs. Wm. Duckham, Beatrice May, Mrs. H. W. Buckbee, Mrs. Henry Robinson and Fidelity.

The Pittsburg Florists' Exchange showed Viviand-Morel, Dr. Enguehard Col. D. Appleton and Mrs. Robinson.

From A. Peacock's private conservatory the following fine blooms were exhibited: M. F. Plant, Mrs. G. Heaume, S. T. Wright, Viviand-Morel, Leila Filkins, Mrs. J. H. Tranter, Mrs. T. W. Pockett, Wm. Duckham, Mrs. A. J. Miller, also good blooms of pink and red Lawson, Nelson Fisher, and Enchantress carnations. The Phipps Conservatories, of Schenley Park, sent in a fine lot of flowers, of Mrs. G. Heaume, F. S. Vallis, a large bloom measuring 11 inches across and 18 inches overhead, Mrs. Wm. Duckham, Col. D. Appleton, Viviand-Morel, Wm. Duckham, Mary Ann Pockett, Etherington and Mrs. Wright.

At our December meeting it was decided to have a half-dozen members of the club give short talks about Christmas plants, how to grow them properly, and put them on the market for sale.

Trade is moving along satisfactorily; plenty of good stock is coming in; prices about the same as last week. Chrysanthemums are plentiful, selling fairly well, the smaller blooms being in most demand. Carnations are yet scarce. 3c. and better is asked for good blooms.

Joseph Heacock, of Wyncote, Pa., spent several days in the city taking orders for plants.

The weather is somewhat wintry, a few inches of snow covering the ground. E. C. REINEMAN.

Last week an automobile ran down a florist wagon belonging to the Randolph-Clements Company, at Baum street and South Highland avenue. The driver of the wagon, Gilbert Wheeler was thrown to the pavement, and received a serious scalp wound and bruises on the body.

Providence, R. I.

News Notes.

It was with the deepest sorrow the many friends of the late William Doogue, city forester, Boston, learned the sad news of his death, although we were aware of his dangerous illness for some time. Mr. Doogue was very well known about here as he was a regular visitor to his son-in-law, Timothy McCarthy, the popular superintendent of Swan Point Cemetery.

John F. Wood is still doing business at the same store. Although he had made all the necessary arrangements, except the selling out of his store and stock, to locate in Seattle, Wash., he has now made up his mind to stay with us another season. He has added a bookkeeper and designer to his help the past week. G. A. J.

New York.

News of the Week.

The meeting of the New York Florists' Club on Monday night was a success in every particular. The only trouble with these meetings, it seems to us, is the fact that the nights are too short to give all the talent assembled a fair show. Mr. Nugent could, no doubt, have kept the program going until four or five o'clock in the morning without exhausting the repertoire of the many excellent musicians he had collected together for this event.

Frederick Kessler, father of Phil. Kessler, wholesale florist at No. 55 West Twenty-sixth street, died on Wednesday, October 31, at his home in Woodside, L. I., aged 62 years. Mr. Kessler had been ill for some time, first suffering a paralytic stroke and then other troubles, so that his death was not unexpected. The interment took place on Saturday, November 3, in St. Michael's Cemetery, Woodside.

Next week is Horse Show week in this city, and while this event in former years was looked upon by florists as a sure-thing business-bringer, no anticipations of that kind are now entertained by the craft, as, with the exception of a little extra demand for corsage bouquets, the horse show season brings little grist to the florist. Time was when violets only were considered the proper thing for ladies to wear at this social event, but the increase in the supply of cattleyas and gardenias, and the popularity which these flowers have gained for wearing purposes, will, no doubt, reduce to a certain extent the number of violets required for the coming week.

Charles Ebermann, who for some time had charge of the Siegel-Cooper plant department, has leased a store at No. 53 West Thirtieth street, and is conducting a wholesale plant business there.

The annual chrysanthemum show in the Prospect Park greenhouses, Brooklyn, is now at its best; the collection includes upwards of one hundred and thirty varieties, among them being several of the best novelties of late introduction.

The chrysanthemum show at the Central Park greenhouses, which opened last Monday, is attracting great crowds of people, 30,000 being in attendance on the opening day. Some two hundred and fifty varieties are in bloom, the collection numbering six thousand plants altogether, fifty kinds being new and never before grown at the Park greenhouses.

Dr. N. L. Britton of the New York Botanical Garden attended a dinner of the Staten Island Association of Arts and Sciences at Castleton, S. I., Monday, November 12. This Society was incorporated in 1885. The association has thousands of specimens illustrative of the botany, mineralogy, geology, zoology and archæology of the island. The act of incorporation gives the city power to afford the society such a home as it desires, and also an annual appropriation of $10,000 for its maintenance.

Visitors in town: William H. Elliott, Brighton, Mass.; M. A. Patten, Tewksbury, Mass.; Peter Fisher, Ellis, Mass., and A. J. Cowee, Berlin, N. Y.

The auction sales of plants at Wm. Elliott & Sons, 201 Fulton street, are being extremely well attended by buyers every Tuesday and Friday. Prices obtained are quite satisfactory, and the present season bids fair to be the banner one in plant auction records.

Braun & Friedman, florists, Canarsie avenue, Brooklyn, dissolved partnership by mutual agreement on November 7. The business will be continued at the same place by Louis Braun.

New Orleans, La.

News Notes.

As predicted in my notes last week, Jules Fonta was appointed to the superintendency of Audubon Park to succeed Ed. Baker, resigned. Mr. Fonta has stated his intention of retaining the services of head gardener Weller and all the other park employes.

Charles Eble is building a large palm house. He finds this necessary to winter his fine stock of palms, ferns, etc., which he uses for decorating.

New Orleans is sadly in need of rain, none having fallen in this neighborhood for the last six weeks. Vegetation is suffering accordingly. Such long droughts are a strain on gardeners not within reach of the city's water mains.

Many growers are cutting fine chrysanthemums of the mid-season varieties; some well grown flowers are to be seen. Unfortunately New Orleans is not holding any chrysanthemum show this Fall.

CRESCENT CITY.

Washington, D. C.

A New Rose.

At a recent smoker, given by the Washington Florists' Club, the table was decorated with a superb bunch of W. S. Clark's seedling rose No. 1. As this was the first time this rose has been publicly exhibited, it created a sensation among the assembled brethren, its intensely bright pink color showing up splendidly under the gaslight. The unanimous opinion of the boys was that Clark has got a winner.

A Chrysanthemum Show.

The annual chrysanthemum show of the Bureau of Plant Industry of the Department of Agriculture was officially opened Thursday, November 8. Thousands of Washingtonians and visitors to the city have taken advantage of the opportunity to view the display. The method of growing these plants is different from that at the Propagating Gardens, where they are grown on benches under glass and to single stems, on the commercial plan; whereas at the Department of Agriculture they are grown on in pots, until they reach 12-inch pots and are left out of doors all Summer, until they show flower buds; then they are brought in, which is about the first of September. The number of plants generally grown for this purpose is in the neighborhood of one thousand, bearing from fifteen to seventy-five flowers to a plant, according to variety. Some of the most admired are the following:

Pompons—Bohemia, Blenheim, Cerise Queen, Daybreak, Delicatissima, Ethel, Empress, Hestor, Lyndhurst, Prince of Wales, Queen of Whites, Ruby Queen, The Czar, King Philip and Mamie.

Small-flowered or button varieties—Blushing Bride, Anna Marie, Austin, Dawn, Dundee, Edna, Eleganta, Erminie, Fred Peel, Golden Pheasant, James Boon, Little Pet and Tennyson.

Anemone-flowered—Blanche, Furnessia, Nantucket, Kershaw, Lady Olivia.

Single varieties—Aaron, Clara, Northumberland, Princess of Thule, Providence, Rosy Morn, and Wallie.

New French large flowering—Mosaka, Senegambia, Libreville and Aubaughe.

Of the fifty large flowering kinds, the following are most conspicuous: Prefet Tillier, Lanona, Belle Gasconne, President Roosevelt, Merstham Crimson, Mrs. F. F. Thompson, Nara, Sappho, Leslie P. Ward, Mme. Cecil Andre, Sans Souci, Le Grand Precoce, M. P. Lachman, M. Emile David, Reine Wilhelmina and Mrs. Roosevelt.

Of the one hundred seedlings of 1906, one has been named Mrs. Donald McLean, in honor of the president general of the Daughters of the Revolution. It is a beautiful white, large and full.

A feature, aside from the chrysanthemums, which should be of great interest, is a lot of Poinsettia pulcherrima hybrids. The seed was sown in May, and now the plants are in flower, with stems averaging from three to four feet in height.

J. A. G.

CLASSIFIED ADVERTISEMENTS

CASH WITH ORDER.

The columns under this heading are reserved r advertisements of Stock for Sale, Stock anted, Help Wanted, Situations Wanted or er Wants; also of Greenhouse, Land, Sec-l-Hand Materials, etc., For Sale or Rent.

ur charge is 10 cts. per line (7 words to the), set solid, without display. No advt. epted for less than thirty cents.

Display advertisements in these columns, 15 ts per line; count 12 lines agate to the inch.

If replies to Help Wanted, Situation Want- or other advertisements are to be addressed e of this office, advertisers add 10 cents to er expense of forwarding.]

Copy must reach New York office 12 o'clock dnesday to secure insertion in issue of fol-ing Saturday.

Advertisers in the Western States desiring to vertise under initials, may save time by hav- their answer directed care our Chicago office 127 E. Berwyn Ave.

ED—As assistant gardener tical young man, 11 years' rofession. Address W. U., Exchange.

NTED—By a good general English; 23 years of age, 9 good references. T. Goldney, Portchester, New York.

TED—As foreman on up-to- place; best references from and others in Chicago trade. are The Florists' Exchange.

ITED—Young man, 24, Ger- with good recommendation, i first-class retail store in ss W. T., care The Florists'

ITUATION WANTED—Single; life experience growing roses, carnations; competent worker; take charge 50,000 ft. glass; $35.00 board. Address Florist, 270 7th Avenue, New York City.

SITUATION WANTED—German florist, 24 years of age, one year in this country, wants steady position in greenhouses. References. Address Anton Moser, 1106 18th Stret, N. W., Washington, D. C.

SITUATION WANTED—By single young man after December 1st, on private or commercial place. Experienced in carnations, chrysanthemums and general stock. Address X. B., care The Florists' Exchange.

SITUATION WANTED—By all-around grower of general florist stock and landscape gardener. 20 years' experience, good references, 8 years in last place. Private place preferred. Address, W. N., care The Florists' Exchange.

SITUATION WANTED—Young, single man, aged 27, American, wants position on private or commercial place. Massachusetts or Eastern States preferred. Four years' experience. Recommendation; good wages expected. Address W. S., care The Florists' Exchange.

SITUATION WANTED—By Englishman, twenty-three years of age, as assistant in greenhouses in large commercial or private place. Excellent references. Please state particulars and wages paid. Address S. Swatton, Pine Bush, N. Y.

HELP WANTED

WANTED—Man for general greenhouse work, one that knows how to work Hitchings Boilers. A steady place and fair wages to good man. George Darsley, cor. Jackson & Claremont ave., Jersey City, N. J.

WANTED—Assistant florist for commercial place; middle West. Wages $30.00 per month and board. Send copy of references in first letter. Address W. Z., care The Florists' Exchange.

WANTED—Driver, married, German preferred, who can help in greenhouses. For good sober man a steady position. Address, Whitestone, care The Florists' Exchange.

WANTED—Young man to pack and ship cut flowers and help around greenhouses. State experience, wages, etc. W. K. Partridge, 148 E. Fourth Street, Cincinnati, O.

SEEDSMAN

capable of taking charge and developing retail department of an established house in a large Eastern city. A good opportunity for a bright up-to-date man. State age, experience, salary required. All communications confidential. Address,

SEEDS, care The Florists' Exchange.

Mention the Florists' Exchange when writing.

HELP WANTED

WANTED—Man experienced in greenhouse work, neat and active. Good wages paid if satisfaction is obtained. Apply at once, personally, to Louis Dupuy, Whitestone (via. 34th street ferry), L. I., N. Y.

WANTED—Night fireman who understands steam boilers, etc. Steady position. State experience, salary wanted, and give references. W. K. Partridge, 148 E. Fourth street, Cincinnati, O.

WANTED—Young man to assist in high-class retail flower store. Must be of good appearance and have good references. State wages, etc. W. K. Partridge, 148 E. Fourth Street, Cincinnati, O.

WANTED—Section man for carnations. Married man preferred, who would be willing to board one or two men. Have five roomed house on place. State wages, etc. W. K. Partridge, 148 E. Fourth Street, Cincinnati, O.

WANTED—Nurseryman and landscape gardener, with general knowledge of pruning and the care of fruit and ornamental stock. State experience and salary expected. The Continental Nurseries, Franklin, Mass.

WANTED—Two reliable sober young men for rose houses, to work under the direction of foreman, wages $50.00 per month, reference in first letter. Address X. C. care Florists' Exchange.

WANTED—A bright young man, aged 22 to 35, for an established florist business. Good position to right man. State experience and salary expected. Chas. Henry Fox, 21st Street and Columbia Avenue, Philadelphia, Pa.

WANTED—Experienced working foreman to take charge 30,000 feet glass, roses and carnations. Only those who can give results need apply. State references and wages expected. Address, W. care manager, Music Hall Market, Boston.

WANTED—On January 1st, a salesman familiar with plants, bulbs and seeds, who controls trade in New York and vicinity. Unusual opportunity to earnest worker. State experience, references and salary expected. Address W. V., care The Florists' Exchange.

WANTED—Young man who understands the care of palms, ferns; also to grow Dutch bulbs and do general work around retail florist establishment. Good wages to a hustler. State particulars in first letter. Address W. W., care The Florists' Exchange.

WANTED—December 1st, two men. An assistant, competent to take charge in owner's absence; wages $30.00 per month, board and room; must understand firing. Also a young man, experience not necessary, to do general greenhouse work; wages $20.00 per month, board and room. Address Flora T. Howell, Pine Bush, N. Y.

WANTED—Salesman and canvasser; greater New York and vicinity. Single, energetic young horticulturist, with some experience in ornamental stock, who is willing to identify himself permanently with new horticultural establishment. Salary and commission. Give full particulars. Address W. T. care The Florists' Exchange.

WANTED

At once, a first-class grower of roses, to take charge of rose section, a man that has business ability, not afraid of work. Must have first-class reference, sober and steady. State salary and experience, also reference in first letter. If you can't fill above bill don't answer, if satisfactory must be ready to come at once.—F. H. KRAMER 916 F St. N. W., Washington, D. C.

Mention the Florists' Exchange when writing.

MISCELLANEOUS WANTS

WANTED TO BUY—Greenhouses to be taken down. State full particulars of same when writing. Address, F. W., care The Florists' Exchange.

WANTED—Tenant, to develop market garden, 26 acres, 5 roomed house, barn, water, trolley, school. Chance for competent man of small means. Floribel Greenhouse, Indiana, Pa.

WANTED—At once, (4,000) four thousand each Genevieve Lord and Queen Louise carnation cuttings, either rooted or unrooted. State price. Mann & Brown, Richmond, Va.

WANTED—Special prices on the following: 3,000 lbs. mixed sweet peas, 3,000 lbs. mixed tall nasturtiums, 3,000 lbs. mixed dwarf nasturtiums. I also want large quantities of all kinds of garden and flower seed. What have you to offer and what is your best price? Write at once to William D. Burt, Dalton, N. Y.

FOR SALE OR RENT

FOR RENT—Florist's store and greenhouse, old established business; 18 x 150; central part Atlantic City, N. J.; hot water heat supplied by city. Address, W. P., care The Florists' Exchange.

FOR SALE OR RENT

TO LET

Florist Establishment consisting of nine greenhouses, heated by hot water, containing about 10,000 square feet of glass; sheds, barn and dwelling, in Long Island City, within one hour's drive of the wholesale markets of the City of New York. For further particulars address Box R. Y., Florists' Exchange

Mention the Florists' Exchange when writing.

FOR SALE—Garden and seven greenhouses, 10,000 sq. ft. of glass, and a nine roomed dwelling on the premises. In a neighborhood where you can do business and save money. For particulars write to Arthur H. Lanser, Wayne, Del. Co., Pa.

FOR SALE—A well established florist business, with dwelling houses. Also plenty of outdoor ground in up-to-date condition. Greenhouses are well filled with foliage plants, and the place is in a most desirable location to reach the wholesale New York City trade within a drive of about 30 minutes. It must be seen. Reason for selling: ill health. For particulars communicate with O. V. Zangen, Seedsman, Hoboken, N. J.

FOR RENT—Owing to continued ill health, I am compelled to give up business for a while, and want a thoroughly reliable and competent man, well up on growing roses and other stock, to rent my place (10,000 feet glass). Will sell to the proper party; good business can be done. This is a fine opportunity for a man with small capital to secure an established trade. References exchanged. Terms reasonable. Possession at once or in Spring. Don't answer unless you can fill the bill. For particulars address Opportunity, care The Florists' Exchange.

FOR SALE

A well equipped place, consisting of seven greenhouses, over 30,000 feet of glass, a nine roomed house, barn, stock, etc., and eight acres of land. This is a decided bargain and a rare opportunity. For particulars address

S. S. SKIDELSKY,

824 N. 24th St., Philadelphia, Pa.

Mention the Florists' Exchange when writing.

FOR SALE—Opportunity of a life-time, in Baltimore, five greenhouses, 70 feet long, about 8,000 sq. feet of glass, room for more. Lot 200x150; two Hitchings' No. 17 hot water boilers, together with well stocked houses of palms, ferns, roses, plants, flowers, bulbs, etc. Office and potting house, all connected with a nice eight roomed dwelling, heated by a Hitchings' Upright hot water boiler; bath and toilet room, porches, etc. Cold frames, stable, wagon house, chicken houses, etc. Two spring wagons, one cart and one horse. Also one stall in the greatest market house in the world. Have a large exclusive non-competitive suburban custom in adjoining neighborhood. This is a well-established profitable business. Have sufficient income for balance of life, reason for selling. Price, $8,000; cost $12,000. Part can remain on mortgage. J. W. Linton, 848 Equitable Building, Baltimore, Md.

STOCK FOR SALE

CARNATIONS—Strong, healthy, field-grown plants, extra large, Ethel Crocker, $5.00 per 100. Cash with order. W. C. Pray & Co., Kinkora, N. J.

BRENCHLEYENSIS GLADIOLUS, 1st. size, $10.00 per 1000; 2d. size, $8.00 per 1000. Cash with order. Est. Louis Siebrecht, Floral Park, N. Y.

CHRYSANTHEMUMS, stock plants, Polly Rose, Glory of Pacific, Halliday and Intensity, fine, 50c. per doz.; $3.50 per 100. F. P. Sawyer, Clinton, Mass.

ENGLISH PRIZE PANSY PLANTS—I have 10,000 fine plants more than I need. For sale at $3.00 per 1000, cash. Some very odd and beautiful markings among them. Reuben Powell, Florist, White Plains, N. Y.

BABY RAMBLER roses, fine dormant stock, $25 per 100. 2 1-2 inch pot plants, extra well rooted $7 per 100, $65 per 1000. Orders booked for delivery now or any time up to late Spring. Samples free. Brown Brothers Co., Rochester, N. Y.

CHRYSANTHEMUMS, stock plants—Nevins, Mrs. Coombes, J. H. Troy, Minnie Wanamaker, Robert Halliday, Col. D. Appleton, Polly Rose, White Coombes, Mrs. Robinson, October Sunshine, Alice Byron, Ivory, Pink Ivory, Wm. Duckham, A. J. Balfour, Dr. Enguehard, 75c. per doz.; $5.00 per 100. Cash please. Henry Hansen, Catskill, N. Y.

THE AMERICAN CARNATION

Price, $3.50

A. T. DE LA MARE PTG. & PUB. CO. LTD.

2-8 Duane Street, New York

Mention the Florists' Exchange when writing.

FOR SALE

FOR SALE—Four brand new volumes of Prof. Bailey's Encyclopedia of American Horticulture, cost $20.00; will sell for $15.00. Address, P. J. Cunniff, 181 Northampton St., Boston, Mass.

FOR SALE—4 Hitchings hot water expansion tanks. No. 2 high tank Fig. E. of catalogue. All in good condition. F. O. B., $2.00 each. Address, K. D., care The Florists' Exchange.

BOILERS. BOILERS. BOILERS.

SEVERAL good second hand boilers on hand, also new No. 16 Hitchings at reduced cost. Write for list. Wm. H. Lutton, West Side Avenue Station, C. R. R. of N. J., Jersey City, N. J.

FOR SALE—One No. 16 boiler, $70.00; one No. 5 Weathered, $56.00; one Kay boiler, $40.00. All boilers with shaking grates and in good condition. J. H. Flesser, Hamilton avenue, near Hudson Boulevard, P. O. Weehawken, N. J.

FOR SALE

Greenhouse Material milled from Gulf Cypress, to any detail furnished, or our own patterns as desired, cut and spliced ready for erection. Estimates for complete constructions furnished.

V. E. REICH, Brooklyn, N. Y.

1429-1437 Metropolitan Ave.

FOR SALE

BOILERS No. 6 Weathered, round, $80.00. One 11 section Sunray hot water sectional boiler, grate 3 by 3. Price $160.00. 6 Section new Novelty boiler, will heat 100 ft. glass $140.00 New Henderson boilers; send for price on size wanted.

PIPE Good serviceable second hand. No Junk, with new threads. 2 in. 7c.; 1½ in. 5½c.; 1¼ in. 4c.; 1 in. 3c.; 2½ in. 10c.; 3 in. 14c.; 4 in. 19c. 4 in. cast iron greenhouse 14c. 3 in. NEW standard, full lengths 8½c. ft. All kinds of fittings for 4 in. cast iron and all sizes wrought iron.

STOCKS AND DIES New Economy, easy working, No. 1 cuts ¼-¾-1 in. $3.00; No. 2 cuts 1¼-1½-2 ins. $4.00; Armstrong Adjustable No. 3 cuts ¼-1 in. $4.00; No. 3 cuts 1¼-1½-2 ins. $6.50.

PIPE CUTTERS Saunders, No. 1 cuts to 1 in. $1.00; No. 2 cuts to 2 in. $1.30; No. 3 cuts to 3 in. $3.00; No. 4 cuts to 4 in. $4.60.

STILLSON WRENCHES Guaranteed. 12 in., grips 1½ in. $1.10; 18 in. grips 2 in. $1.50; 24 in., grips 2½ in. $2.25; 36 in., grips 3½ in. $4.50.

PIPE VISES Reed's Best Hinged Vise, No. 1 grips 3 in. $1.75; No. 2 grips 4 in. $3.50.

GARDEN HOSE 50 ft. lengths ¾ in. not guaranteed; 4½, guaranteed for light work; 7½, guaranteed for heavy work, 10c. ft.

HOT-BED SASH New; Gulf Cypress, 3 ft. x 6 ft. 75c.; glazed complete $1.60 up. VENTILATORS; all sizes made to order. Second hand sash glazed $1.00 and $1.25, good condition.

GLASS New American, 50 ft. to the box. 10x12 single at $1.75. 10x12; 12x12 10x15 B double $2.55. 12x14 to 12x20 and 14x14 to 14x20 B double $2.70. 16x16 and 16x18 B double $2.90. 16x24 B double $3.15. 16x20 and 18x22 $3.00. 6x8, 7x9, 8x10 old, single $1.50. 8x14 old, double $1.65; 10x14 old, double $1.75.

Get our prices on second hand wood material. We can furnish everything in new material to erect any size house. Get our prices.

METROPOLITAN MATERIAL CO.

Greenhouse Wreckers

1398-1408 Metropolitan Avenue, BROOKLYN, N.Y

Mention the Florists' Exchange when writing.

ANNOUNCEMENT

BRAUN & FRIEDMANN.

Notice is hereby given that the copartnership of the above name, formed by the undersigned Louis Braun and Charles Friedmann, doing business as florists at Canarsie Avenue, Brooklyn, New York City, has this day been dissolved by mutual consent of the partners. The business will be continued by the said Louis Braun who has assumed all the firms liabilities.

Dated, November 7, 1906.

Signed—LOUIS BRAUN.
—CHARLES FRIEDMAN.

GROW MUSHROOMS

If you do not know how, procure that simple but complete and practical book called "How to Grow Mushrooms." The price is ten cents and it can be secured from this office

Special rates will be made to the trade who wish to supply their customers.

THE FLORISTS' EXCHANGE

2 Duane St., New York

Mention the Florists' Exchange when writing.

Affected Violet Leaves.

(74) Having long been a subscriber to your valuable paper, and having noticed the excellent information contained in the Question Box every week, I send you two violet leaves, affected, and trust you will be able to furnish a cure for the trouble. One leaf is affected with aphis, which I have tried all ways to get rid of. The other is affected with a spot, a whole house being similarly attacked. The leaf does not get dry, but rots. I have the plants in solid beds; they have done nicely since I planted them, which was August 20.

Conn. D. & T.

—The violet leaves are very badly infested with black fly, and while fumigating with tobacco will usually destroy these pests on most plants, it has been found that for violets there is no better remedy than fumigating with hydrocyanic acid gas. Full instructions as to how to use this will be found in the answer to H. A. S.

Carnation Troubles.

(75) Can you give me an effective remedy for rust on carnations; also a successful method for propagating carnations so as not to lose many in striking? Which are the best months? X. Y. Z.

London, England.

—Carnation rust is not considered a dangerous disease any more. If the affected leaves are kept picked off, and the plants are kept dry—that is, the foliage not being kept wet from syringing—the disease will soon run itself out, and cause no further trouble. If it is desired, however, to spray the plants with some mixture, we would recommend that salt water only be used—a 6-inch potful of salt to every 6 gallons of water—letting the solution remain on the plants two or three days before washing it off with clear water.

In regard to propagation, the best method is to have a propagating bench on the north side of a house where the temperature is the same as that in which the carnations have been growing, and where a bottom heat can be obtained 5 to 8 degrees higher. The best time for propagating carnations is from the middle of January to the middle of March. If a north side bench is not available, it will be necessary to shade the cuttings every day during sunshine until they are rooted.

I enclose you some leaves of Mrs. Lawson carnation. I have picked off the leaves until there is practically nothing left but stems. They were large healthy plants when I placed them in the greenhouse in early September, but they have steadily gone to pieces, and now I notice the same trouble on a bench of Queen Louise. Please tell me what it is, and if I can do anything to check it.

Va. F. T. C.

—The carnations are suffering from what is called "dry rot," for which, so far, there has been no cure discovered. The best thing to do would be to pull out all the affected plants, transplanting all the good ones to one end of the house, and use the vacant space for some other crop.

Enclosed find some carnation foliage. The lower leaves are all dry, and the upper ones have little spots on them. Kindly tell me if there is any cure for this disease. I sprinkled air-slacked lime over them, but with little result. Is it rust, or what do you call this disease? M. B.

New Jersey.

—It is not rust that is troubling the plants, but it seems to be a general dying off of the lower leaves, which frequently happens to carnations that have had some check or other after being planted in the house. We think that if all of the diseased leaves are picked off and the plants kept perfectly clean, strict attention being paid to their wants in regard to watering, etc., no serious trouble will result. It is all right to dust air-slacked lime on the plants occasionally, and after picking away all of the dead leaves, we would afford a dressing of the lime all over the surface of the soil.

I send you a top of carnation Mrs. Lawson, the same having a yellow stripe. Kindly tell me what the trouble is. A. B.

Mass.

—The only trouble with the carnations is that they have been attacked with thrips, which pest may be kept in check by frequent syringing with some good tobacco extract.

I send some leaves of carnations for inspection; also soil. Kindly tell me what is the trouble with the plants and the remedy. A. B.

New Jersey.

—The soil sent in for inspection is quite sour and full of minute insects. We would recommend that a good watering with lime water be given, repeated in the course of ten days or two weeks. This will sweeten the soil and destroy the worms.

The carnation leaves are badly affected with what is called "carnation spot." This is supposed to be the result of improper treatment and uncongenial soil. To cure the leaf spot we would recommend that the plants be syringed thoroughly with a mixture of salt and water in the proportion of a 6-inch potful of salt to six gallons of water. Give the foliage a thorough syringing, stirring up the liquid repeatedly during the operation, and letting the solution remain on the plants two or three days; then washing it off with clear water, repeating the process in about two weeks.

We send you some leaves from our carnation plants, covered in places with a blister-like breaking out and a black smut-like substance. Adonis are troubled most, but an occasional leaf like the ones sent is found on other varieties. The health of the plants so far does not seem to be injured, but we should like to know what is the trouble, if there is danger of it hurting the plants seriously, and if so what to do for it. We noticed a few similar leaves last year, but the disease got no worse and gave u no serious trouble. K. & S.

Mo.

—The carnation leaves are badl affected with rust. To get rid of thi trouble keep every diseased leaf pick ed off; go over the plants every day and where it is seen that rust has ap peared, pick off the leaf. Avoid al syringing, give the plants carefu treatment otherwise, and the diseas will soon run itself out.

Roses; Flowers for Designs.

(76) My Bride, Bridesmaid an Papa Gontier roses are growing nice ly, but the flowers are small—onl

about half as large as I want them. I have been using liquid cow manure about twice a week. Should I use any other kind of fertilizer? Or do you think the flowers are small because the plants are small so far? I planted out the rooted cuttings in June.

Please give the names of some flowers for the greenhouse that would be suitable for cut flowers for designs.

N. C. R. E. G.

—No uneasiness need be felt at this time owing to the flowers of the roses coming small. The next crop will, no doubt, be much better, and we would not recommend feeding too hard yet, as the soil in which they are planted cannot be exhausted by this time. If we had a supply of liquid cow manure, we would not try to find any other fertilizer, as there is nothing to equal the former for growing roses.

As to flowers to be grown indoors through the Winter, suitable for designs we would suggest carnations, stocks, sweet peas, double sweet alyssum, tulips, hyacinths, and narcissus in variety.

Cyaniding Violets.

(77) We wish to know how much cyanide to use to fumigate a violet house 100 x 25 feet, and the best plan for using it. H. A. S.

New York.

—In order to ascertain how much cyanide to use for fumigating violets, it is first necessary to determine how many cubic feet of space the house contains. This we could not do in the present case, as inquirer does not give the height of the ridge and side walls of the house. Professor Galloway in his book on "Violet Culture," on the subject of fumigating recommends the following method:

"The gas is made by combining potassium cyanide (ninety-eight per cent. pure) and commercial sulphuric acid. It has been found by experiment that for violets 0.15 of a gram (one gram equals fifteen and a half avoirdupois) of ninety-eight per cent cyanide of potassium will be required for each cubic foot of space in the house, and from these data it is easy to figure out the exact amount of cyanide of potassium wanted for a given amount of greenhouse room. When the cubic contents have been determined and 0.15 of a gram of the cyanide of potassium has been weighed out for each cubic foot, the next step is to crush all the large lumps and place the cyanide in paper bags so as to have it ready for use in the house. We usually use two bags, one within the other, for the purpose, in order to insure perfect safety. For a house one hundred feet long and twelve feet wide there should be provided two ordinary earthenware jars, each holding about two gallons. These jars should be placed in the walk, about equal distances apart and equal distances from each end of the house. As soon as the proper quantities have been put in the bags, the latter are taken to the jars and then a string is arranged so that each jar will have suspended directly over it one of the bags containing the cyanide. The end of the string is then run out to the door and can be easily tied so as to hold the bags in position just above the jars. The string can be easily run through screw eyes fastened to the sash bars or by some other method which will readily suggest itself to the operator. Everything being in readiness, pour enough cold water into the jars to about cover the amount of potash in the bags. As soon as the water is poured in bring the acid forward and slowly add this to the water until steam begins to rise. When the steam commences to show stop pouring in the acid and arrange the next jar in the same way. While doing this it is best to have the bags of cyanide rest on the ground. The water and acid now being ready re-adjust the bags in their proper places so that they will drop directly into the jars when the string holding them is loosened. The operator now goes to the door and by taking hold of the string allows the bags to drop directly into the jars. The door is then closed and in about a minute (sometimes less) the violent action of the chemical changes can be heard."

No attempt whatever must be made to enter the house at this time, for by doing so death would result in a few seconds.

From the time the gas begins to generate it should be allowed to remain 20 minutes in the house, then the doors and ventilators should be opened from the outside being careful not to breathe any of the gas. The house should not be entered under any circumstances for half an hour, for it will take at least that time for the fumes to be driven out.

Cyaniding a Greenhouse.

(78) I am tired fighting aphides, etc., and I would like to use hydrocyanic acid gas; I used it some years ago when I was an assistant. It was given to me in proper quantity for a tomato house, and used with very good results. I read some time ago in a periodical, in regard to tomatoes, to use:

1 oz. cyanide of potassium, 98 per cent strength.

2 oz. sulphuric acid, 66 per cent strength.

4 oz. of water.

This for 1,000 cubic feet of house space. The water and acid to be combined, the cyanide to be weighed and dropped into this, and the operator to walk briskly away. It has occurred to me, why could not this be used for killing black fly on chrysanthemums, green fly, etc., on roses, carnations and violets? How many cubic feet of space in a 3-4 span house 50 x 20, 5 feet high on one side, 9 feet high on back and 12 feet 10 inches high in center, and how can that be figured out to get the exact dimensions? I have tried every way, but I am not sure how to get a result that is correct. The answer to this would, no doubt, be greatly appreciated by many more fellow craftsmen who look to The Florists' Exchange for answers to little kinks, as well as to ONE INTERESTED.

New York.

—For full information regarding fumigating with hydrocyanic acid gas see answer to H. A. S.

To ascertain the cubic measurement of a 3-4 span house, 13 feet high at ridge, 9 feet high back wall, 5 feet high front wall, 20 feet wide and 50 feet long, draw an imaginary line from the ridge to the ground; this will give two imaginary houses, one 15 feet wide, 13 feet high at the back and 5 feet high at the front; the other will be 5 feet wide, 9 feet high on one side and 13 feet high on the other. To measure the first one multiply the width by the height of the front wall, plus half the number of feet there is difference between the height of the front wall and the height of the ridge—which in this case would be a total of 9 feet; then multiply the answer by the length of the house in feet; this would give 15 x 9 x 50. Treat the other part of the house in the same way, which would give 5 x 11 x 50; then add the totals, which would give 9,500 cubic feet.

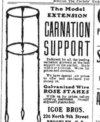

REVIEW OF THE MARKET

NEW YORK.—This week sees the cut flower market just about deluged with chrysanthemums. While a great many are of the finest quality, there are also some that seem to have been held too long, which present a rather weary appearance. It is unfortunate that the retail business is not in a more flourishing condition than it is just at present. There seems to be very little doing in a retail way, consequently a great many more chrysanthemums, as well as other flowers are coming in than can be moved at satisfactory figures. Among the varieties seen in quantity are Wm. Duckham, Mrs. Coombes, Soleil d'Octobre, Major Bonnaffon ,pink and white Ivory, Maud Dean, Mrs. Jerome Jones and Dr. Enguehard. There are also some supplies of white Bonnaffon, J. R. Shrimpton and W. H. Chadwick. Many of the blooms are of superfine quality and ought to bring $4 or $5 per dozen, but such prices are altogether out of the question at this time; in fact, on some days clearances have to be made at any figure the speculators will offer.

The rose situation has undergone no change this week. Prices remain about the same, and the supply keeps a little too much in excess of the demand. Carnations are about holding their own in values, though it is difficult at times to clear out without making sacrifices. There has appeared lately a supply of mignonette and antirrhinum (snapdragon), but there is absolutely no chance of selling either of these two commodities. The retailers semingly will not touch them, and the dealers who are receiving them have no amount of trouble on their hands to get rid of them.

Gardenias are in pretty fair demand. Cattleyas are not clearing out as well as could be desired. Violets have shown evidence of better appreciation the last few days, and the best have reached the dollar mark. Callas are a regular feature, but there is no particular rush for them as yet. Paper White narcissus have begun to arrive regularly, and the supply of lilies and lily of the valley keeps about an even pace with the demand, with no change in prices

BOSTON.—Business has been dull the past week. The market is overstocked, especially with chrysanthemums, although roses and carnations are almost equally plentiful. Saturday saw quite a clearing out of colored chrysanthemums, especially reds. It was the day of the Carlisle-Harvard football game, and the latter's colors were much in demand; $3 per dozen was the general price for red blooms. During the week extra flowers sold at from $2 to $4 per dozen, but the general run went at from $4 to $6 per 100.

American Beauty roses are in fine shape and have a good demand. Richmond are also very satisfactory, as are Wellesley and Killarney. Bride and Bridesmaid are of good quality, but very plentiful; prices generally run from $1 to $8. Carnations are beginning to show good stems, the flowers also are larger. They bring from $1 to $4. Violets are of first class quality both in doubles and singles. Sweet peas are good, selling at $1. Lilies are not very plentiful, though there is quite a supply of callas. Paper White narcissus have made their appearance, but only in small quantities. J. W. D.

PROVIDENCE, R. I.—Business has not been so good as it was the two weeks previous, still it cannot be called dull, by any means. Social decorations and funeral work are very fair and the stores report a good transient trade. Chrysanthemums are at their height now with most of the growers and are very plentiful. I saw good medium sized flowers sold the past week for $6 per hundred. The finer varieties and the first class flowers bring from $1.50 to $2 per dozen wholesale. These varieties are not moving very fast, but it is only two weeks to Thanksgiving and there is always a great demand for first class chrysanthemums at that time. Carnations are plentiful and bring $1.50 to $2.50, according to grade and varieties. Roses remain the same as in the first part of the month; teas of all kind bring from $3 to $8 per hundred. Violets are plentiful and of good qualty, at from 50c. to 75c. per hundred. G. A. J.

NEW BEDFORD, MASS.—The past week has been a very poor one for the flower trade. The market went to pieces, and stock sold at prices unheard of. All the florists report the same dullness; ice boxes are filled to overflowing, and there is a regular glut. HORTICO.

ST. LOUIS.—Business last week was not good in all parts of the city, according to reports; very few orders were received for society events and funerals. At the wholesale houses all stock in season was overplentiful, especially chrysanthemums. The varieties noticed at the commission houses were, Timothy Eaton, Mrs. Henry Robinson, Major Bonnaffon, Colonel D. Appleton, A. J. Balfour, Alice Byron, White and Pink Ivory, Yellow Eaton, and Dr. Enguehard. The best brought not over $3 a dozen, the $2 grade selling best, with plenty of the smaller kinds going at $1 to $1.50 a dozen. The buyers wanted chrysanthemums, so other flowers went begging, and prices therefore were cut in half, including roses and carnations. The glut in roses is on, the wholesalers selling them in lots of 1,000 at $5 to $10, according to length of stem, extra fancy grades of course excepted, they holding up to $5 per 100, among these latter being short American Beauty. Extra long fancy American Beauty are down to $3 per dozen, other grades $1.50 per dozen. The best carnations can be bought for $1.50 to $2 a 100; common at $1. Enchantress, always a good seller, was very slow the past week.

Violets are in fair demand; stock is very good in California, and 40c. to 60c. per 100 is obtained for the best. Paper White narcissus and some callas have made their appearance. Orchids are becoming a factor in this market, and will be more so as the season advances.

Of smilax we have more than enough, also of other greens. ST. PATRICK.

INDIANAPOLIS. — Large quantities of chrysanthemums, roses, and carnations are being received. Decorations are larger and as numerous as in October; one leading retailer had ten in one week, all fair sized. The designer should now be, if ever, in his glory, as funeral orders are plentiful and material on hand never better for turning out elegant work. Immense stocks of finely grown chrysanthemums help beautify the florists' stores. The general retail price is $1 to $6 per dozen; $3 is the average. The wholesale price is $1.50 to $4 a dozen. A few fancies, such as Col. D. Appleton and Timothy Eaton bring as high as $9 a dozen. Well shaped 6 to 9-inch pot plants sell rapidly; plants which cost 75c. to $2 find the best sale. Carnation growers manage to dispose of their stock at fairly good prices, but the market suffers on account of the quantity of chrysanthemums for sale. High grade carnations bring $2 to $2.50 per 100. Complaints are heard regarding sleepy carnations, this condition being attributed to the bright warm weather.

Excellent Bridesmaid and Bride roses are wholesaling at $4 to $6 a 100. Richmond and Liberty are in prime condition at $5 to $8. A few Killarney are received at $6; these find ready sale. The demand for American Beauty has decreased somewhat; $5 to $25 a 100 is the price.

Cattleyas are generally handled by retailers, at 75c. per flower. Some of the flowers are home-grown; others shipped from the East. Lily of the valley move well at $4 per 100. The local supply of violets is not sufficient at 60c. a 100. Harrisii lilies and callas are plentiful at $1.50 a dozen, but at times it is difficult to dispose of them.

KALAMAZOO, MICH.—Business continues quite lively owing to a number of weddings, receptions, etc., which added to a fair amount of funeral work use up the available crop of flowers. Carnations are now being cut of good quality and length of stem, consequently prices have advanced slightly, 40c., 50c., 60c., 75c., per dozen being the figures asked. Chrysanthemums are selling well; medium at $1.50 to $2 perhaps in the lead. Tea roses are in good supply at $1 to $1.50 per dozen; American Beauty are worth anywhere from $2 to $6 per dozen, according to quality. Pot grown chrysanthemums are in abundance and sell fairly well. Violets seem to be rather scarce at 25c. per bunch.

DETROIT, MICH.—Chrysanthemums are coming in more plentifully and are moving fairly well with the exception of yellow; there is but little sale for these. Carnations are steadily growing better both in quality and quantity, and are selling very well, bringing 3c. for choice stock. Roses are not doing so well, and a great many of them in the commission houses show mildew on the foliage, owing to the very damp and cold weather the past month. A very few violets are being sent in now, and are meeting with a ready sale.

COLUMBUS.—Our market for the past two weeks has been, and until after Thanksgiving will be, entirely dominated by the chrysanthemum. As regards varieties, those that can be retailed for from $2 to $3 a dozen are in most general demand; and at present no sorts are more popular than white and pink Ivory and small Major Bonnaffon. The top price obtained this year has been by Livingston; they have been getting for their most elegant Mrs. O. P. Bassett, Lord Hopetoun, Col. Appleton, and Ethel Fitzroy, 75 cents each. Notwithstanding the enormous quantity of chrysanthemums daily brought to our market, the prices at retail have remained on a most profitable basis the whole season thus far, and the approach of Thanksgiving will keep them so to the end of the season. Other stock has suffered and will be only in steady demand until the chrysanthemums have passed their height. There has been an especially good number of funeral and decorative orders which have used up large quantities of roses, carnations and some violets. Ross are very fine in quality and color, and range from $1 to the top rate of $6 per dozen for the very best American Beauty. In regard to carnations while they are in better supply than for some time the quality is still below par, and for this reason more than any other the whole market has been held back from going on a Winter basis of prices. Carnations are still ranging from 35c. to 60c. a dozen. Green goods are in plenty and good. Trade altogether is very satisfactory. F. W.

ST. PAUL.—Trade in general started out very poorly but along to the end of the week it took a brace and the last few days found all of the dealers doing about all they could conveniently handle. Funeral work was especally active. The call for flowers for social occasions, has not as yet settled down to a steady basis, and it will in all probability be a matter of thirty or sixty days before we can expect a heavy business for social functions. Stock is equal to the demand, with the possible exception of carnations, which are far from being up to grade. The carnations shipped in are not equal to the home-grown stock. Some of the growers are having very good success with Mrs. Lawson and the flowers appear to be much better in quality, consequently command a ready sale. Chrysanthemums appear to have a hold on the market which makes the sale of roses very limited, and has had a very depressing effect particularly on the American Beauty which can hardly be disposed of to good advantage. In nearly every store one can see a number of this variety, which cannot be sold, gradually finding their way to the dump pile. Violets while not plentiful are coming in nicely, the supply being about equaing the demand. Plant sales are active, especially in small palms and ferns. Boston and elegantissima seem to lead. PAUL.

ROCHESTER, N. Y.—The market report here cannot be said to be encouraging. The unsettled weather has no doubt had a good deal to do with this, and although no material has gone to waste, the prices realized have not been so satisfactory. The plant trade so far has been very good, especially in Boston ferns and palms; and now that chrysanthemums are in the stores, potted plants of these of all sizes are in good demand at fairly good prices.

Cut flower prices as follows: Carnations, $1.50 to $2.50 per 100; roses, $5 to $8 and higher for the better grades; chrysanthemums, $5 to $12, according to variety. Ferns, especially A. Croweanum, sell very well. COCKNEY.

CINCINNATI.—November is starting out fairly well, and stock is plentiful for all orders as a general thing, but trade runs more in spots than it used to. Perhaps for two or three days in the week everything in sight goes, then business will drop like a hot potato, and for two or three days it will be very quiet. E. G. G.

In a Luther Burbank Garden.

White are the coreless apple buds,
As your hand in mine I clasp,
And we wander through the eyeless spude
And the raspberries, sans rasp.

You plucked a blackberry, dazzling white,
As we chanted a tuneless rune,
And I took a luscious soulful bite
Of a pitless, skinless prune.

The cactus plant ne'er cackles now,
As its teeth have all been drawn,
And calm there falls upon your brow
The light of a sunless dawn.

In this dear place I would live for aye,
Discussing the whyless how,
And speeding the minuteless hours by,
From the path of the pastless now.

—Denver Republican.

FIRMS WHO ARE BUILDING.

LAWRENCE, KAN.—Mrs. S. E. Luther has added a new house to her range of glass.

NEWBURYPORT, MASS.—George E. Tessimond, Highlands, has greatly enlarged his greenhouse plant.

CHANGES IN BUSINESS.

MOUNDSVILLE, VA.—G. W. Miller has opened a flower store on Lafayette avenue.

PATERSON, N. J.—William Thurston has moved into commodious quarters, several doors nearer Main street than where he was formerly located. His business has increased so as to demand much more room.

NEW YORK.—The Specimen Tree Transplanting & Construction Company has been incorporated to cultivate, remove and deal in trees, shrubs, etc.; cap., $10,000. Incorporators: J. L. Lockwood, Jr., Manhattan; H. B. Pettit, Brooklyn; E. S. Hopper, Paterson, N. J.

ALVIN, TEX.—The Rio Grande Nursery Company, of Brownsville, has been incorporated; capital stock, $10,000. Incorporators: Norman G. Kittrell of Houston, H. G. Stilwell, J. C. Fernandez, Parker Longworth of Brownsville, and Arthur A. Parkhurst of Colorado Springs, Colo.

Philadelphia.

News Notes.

It is very noticeable this week that business has not had the same snap to it as during the past two week. Roses and carnations are selling fairly well, but chrysanthemums have not been in such good demand.

In spite of the very favorable weather of last week the annual show of the Pennsylvania Horticultural Society was not a success financially. Every day of the exhibition was warm and clear, and the local papers gave very good accounts and illustrations. On Wednesday and Thursday the public attended fairly well, but the attendance fell off very considerably on Friday.

The classes for roses and carnations on Wednesday did not bring out much competition. F. R. Pierson Company, Tarrytown, N. Y., and the Cottage Gardens Company, Queens, N. Y., were the only out-of-town exhibitors who competed for carnation prizes; while the special prize offered by Lord & Burnham Company for American Beauty roses did not bring out any competition, growers saying they were only cutting sufficient stock to fill orders with.

The Cottage Gardens Company captured the Craig cup for 25 blooms best American seedling, never disseminated, with the variety Mrs. C. W. Ward.

George Burton, Wyndmoor, was first in fifty blooms, American Beauty roses (Lord & Burnham Special).

Certificates of merit were awarded to William K. Harris for hybrid begonias; Henry A. Dreer for collection of new and rare plants.

The following exhibitors received special mention: William K. Harris for a collection of new and rare plants; Robert Craig & Son for a collection of plants; Henry A. Dreer for bay trees and palms; Hugh Graham & Co. for bay trees; Lager & Hurrell and Julius Roehrs Company, each for a collection of orchids; E. G. Hill Company, Richmond, Ind., for a vase of chrysanthemums, Hon. Robert Forderer.

Honorable mention was given to John E. Haines, Bethlehem, Pa., for carnation Imperial.

A. Foster of Westerly, R. I., was a visitor here this week.

Wm. J. Stewart stopped off here on his way home from Chicago to talk over convention matters with the officers of our club.

DAVID RUST.

GRAND RAPIDS, MICH.—The Sunday Herald of November 4 had an illustrated "flower section," in which the establishments of several local growers were pictured and described, and practical cultural instructions written by some of the craft here. All this should prove of benefit to business.

J. K. ALLEN
Wholesale Commission Dealer in **Cut Flowers**
106 West 28th St., NEW YORK
Open at 6 a. m. every day.
Telephone, 167 Madison Square.
Consignments Solicited.
Mention the Florists' Exchange when writing.

Wm. Stuart Allen Co.
Commission Merchants in CUT FLOWERS
ORCHIDS AT ALL SEASONS
53 WEST 28th STREET, NEW YORK
Telephone 356 Madison Square
Mention the Florists' Exchange when writing.

C. BONNET G. H. BLAKE
BONNET & BLAKE
Wholesale Florists
106 Livingston Street, BROOKLYN, N. Y.
Telephone: 4638 Main.
Consignments solicited. Out-of-town orders carefully attended to. Give us a trial.
Mention the Florists' Exchange when writing.

CUT FLOWER EXCHANGE
Sixth Ave. and 26th St.
Coogan Building, NEW YORK
Open every Morning at Six o'clock for the Sale of Cut Flowers.
Wall Space for advertising purposes to Rent.
V. S. DORVAL, Jr., Secretary.
Mention the Florists' Exchange when writing.

Joseph S. Fenrich
...Wholesale Florist...
—THE RELIABLE HOUSE—
110 West 28th Street
Telephone 324-325 Madison Square.
Mention the Florists' Exchange when writing.

FORD BROS.
Wholesale Florists
48 WEST 28th ST., NEW YORK
Telephone, 3870-3871 Madison Square
Mention the Florists' Exchange when writing.

GROWERS, ATTENTION!
Always Ready to Receive Fine Stock
GUNTHER BROTHERS
30 West 29th Street
Phone, 551 Madison Square. NEW YORK
Violets, Roses, Carnations, Orchids
Established 1888.
Mention the Florists' Exchange when writing.

ALEX. J. GUTTMAN
The Wholesale Florist of New York
43 WEST 28th STREET
Phones 1664-1665 Madison Square
Mention the Florists' Exchange when writing.

A. M. HENSHAW
Wholesale Commission Florist.
Consignments of first class stock solicited. Prompt returns.
THE SQUARE DEAL
Guaranteed to all who trade here.
52 West 28th Street, NEW YORK
Tel. 5583 Madison Square,
Mention the Florists' Exchange when writing.

HICKS & CRAWBUCK, Inc.
Wholesale Florists
And Dealers in FLORISTS' SUPPLIES
76-78 Court Street
Phone, 3660-3661 Main BROOKLYN, N. Y.
Mention the Florists' Exchange when writing.

HEADQUARTERS FOR NOVELTIES
ORCHIDS A SPECIALTY
THE HIGHEST GRADE OF VALLEY ALWAYS ON HAND
GARDENIAS, DAISIES, ROSES, CARNATIONS.
JAMES McMANUS, Telephone 759 Mad. Sq. 42 W. 28th St., New York.

PHILIP F. KESSLER
Wholesale Florist
55-57 W. 26th St., NEW YORK.
Telephone, 2921-5243 Madison Square.
Mention the Florists' Exchange when writing.

A. MOLTZ
Wholesale Florist
55-57 West 26th St., NEW YORK
1st Floor. Telephone, 2921-5243 Madison Sq.
Mention the Florists' Exchange when writing.

WILLIAM H. KUEBLER
Wholesale Commission Dealer in
CUT FLOWERS
28 Willoughby St.,
Telephone 4591 Main BROOKLYN, N. Y.
Mention the Florists' Exchange when writing.

FRANK MILLANG
Wholesale Commission Dealer in
CUT FLOWERS
55-57 West 26th Street, New York
Telephone Call; 299 Madison Square.
Mention the Florists' Exchange when writing.

ALFRED H. LANGJAHR
55 WEST 28th STREET, NEW YORK
Telephone, 4626-4627 Madison Square Established 1891
SPECIAL VALLEY AND TOP GRADE ASPARAGUS
Consignments of First Class Stock Solicited.

Horace E. Froment
SUCCESSOR TO
W. GHORMLEY WHOLESALE COMMISSION FLORIST
Receiver and Shipper of all varieties of Cut Flowers
Telephones, 2200 and 2201 Madison Square. 57 West 28th St., NEW YORK

Wholesale Prices of Cut Flowers, New York, Nov. 14, 1906
Prices quoted are by the hundred unless otherwise noted

Roses	A. Beauty, fancy—special	10.00 to	20.00
	" extra	8.00 to	10.00
	" No. 1	6.00 to	8.00
	" No. 2	3.00 to	6.00
	" No. 3	2.00 to	3.00
	Bride, Maid, fancy—spe'l	4.00 to	5.00
	" extra	3.00 to	4.00
	" No. 1	1.00 to	2.00
	" No. 2	.50 to	.75
	Golden Gate	.75 to	5.00
	Richmond	.75 to	5.00
	Mme. Abel Chatenay	.75 to	5.00
Adiantum		.50 to	.75
	Croweanum	1.00 to	1.25
Asparagus		25.00 to	50.00
	" Plumosus, bunches	8.00 to	15.00
	" Sprengeri, bunches	8.00 to	15.00
		...... to	......
Callas		10.00 to	12.00
Cattleyas		30.00 to	40.00
Cypripediums		...... to	12.50
Daisies		...... to	......

Carnations	Inf'r grades, all colors	1.00 to	1.50
	Standard Varieties — White	1.50 to	2.00
	Standard Varieties — Pink	1.50 to	2.00
	Standard Varieties — Red	1.50 to	2.00
	Standard Varieties — Yel. & Var.	1.50 to	2.00
	*Fancy— (*The highest grades of standard var.) — White	2.50 to	4.00
	*Fancy — Pink	2.50 to	4.00
	*Fancy — Red	2.50 to	4.00
	*Fancy — Yel. & Var.	2.50 to	4.00
	Novelties	4.00 to	5.00
Chrysanthemums		3.00 to	6.00
	" Fancy	10.00 to	15.00
Gardenias, per doz.		3.00 to	5.00
Lilies		10.00 to	12.00
Lily of the Valley		1.00 to	4.00
Mignonette		...... to	......
Narcissus, Paper White		2.00 to	3.00
Smilax		5.00 to	8.00
Violets		.50 to	1.00

WALTER F. SHERIDAN
Wholesale Florist
Tel. 3532-3533 Mad. Sq. 39 WEST 28TH ST., NEW YORK
ALL VARIETIES OF CUT FLOWERS IN SEASON

TOP GRADE FOR SHIPPING
American Beauty, Bridesmaid, Bride, Liberty, Lilies, Lily of the Valley, Carnations
Telephone, 1998 Madison Square JOHN I. RAYNOR, 49 West 28th St., NEW YORK

Edw. C. Horan
55 West 28th St., NEW YORK
TELEPHONE, 1462-1463 MADISON SQUARE
CUT FLOWERS AT WHOLESALE
Mention The Florists' Exchange when writing.

JOHN YOUNG
Wholesale Florist
51 W. 28th St., NEW YORK
Telephone: 4463-4464 MADISON SQUARE
Mention the Florists' Exchange when writing.

MOORE, HENTZ & NASH
WHOLESALE
GROWER AGENT
COMMISSION FLORISTS
55 West 26th St. New York
Telephone Call, 756 Madison Square
Mention the Florists' Exchange when writing.

GEORGE SALTFORD
Wholesale Florist
CONSIGNMENTS SOLICITED
46 West 29th Street, New York
Telephone: 3393 Madison Square
Mention the Florists' Exchange when writing.

J. Seligman Joseph J. Levy
JOHN SELIGMAN & COMPANY
Wholesale Florists
56 West 26th Street,
Tel. 4878 Madison New York
Opposite New York Cut Flower Company
Mention the Florists' Exchange when writing.

B. S. SLINN, JR.
Wholesale Florist
55 and 57 West 26th Street, NEW YORK
SPECIALTIES—Violets, Carnations and Roses
Shipping orders receive prompt attention. Consignment Solicited.
Telephone: 3864 Madison Square
Mention the Florists' Exchange when writing.

WM. STARKE
Wholesale Florist and Plantsman
Tel. No. 4582 Madison Sq. 52 W. 29th St.
Between Broadway and 6th Ave., New York
Shipments of Plants made to any part of the country. A trial order solicited.
SATISFACTION GUARANTEED.
Mention the Florists' Exchange when writing.

Frank H. Traendly Charles Schenck
TRAENDLY & SCHENCK
Wholesale Florists
44 WEST 28th STREET, NEW YORK
and CUT FLOWER EXCHANGE
Telephones: 798 and 799 MADISON SQUARE
Consignments Solicited
Mention the Florists' Exchange when writing.

THOMAS YOUNG Jr.
Wholesale Florist
43 West 28th Street, NEW YORK
Telephone, 4850 Madison Square
Consignments of Choice Flowers solicited
Mention the Florists' Exchange when writing.

PLANT CULTURE
PRICE, $1.00.
The best book for the plant grower.
A. T. DE LA MARE PTG. & PUB. CO. LTD.
Mention the Florists' Exchange when writing.

Wholesale Prices of Cut Flowers–Per 100

Boston Nov. 12, 1906	Buffalo Nov. 2, 1906	Detroit Nov. 11, 1906	Cincinnati Nov. 12, 1906	Baltimore Nov. 5, 1906	NAMES AND VARIETIES	Milwaukee Oct. 25, 1906	Phil'delphia Oct. 25, 1906	Pittsburg Nov. 12, 1906	St. Louis Nov. 12, 1906
30.00 to 50.00	20.00 to 25.00	... to 50.00	... to 40.00	... to ...	ROSES — A. BEAUTY, fancy—special	... to 25.00	20.00 to 40.00	... to 25.00	20.00 to 25.00
20.00 to 30.00	15.00 to 20.00	... to 25.00	20.00 to 30.00	... to 25.00	" extra	15.00 to 18.00	... to ...	... to 15.00	12.50 to 15.00
10.00 to 20.00	10.00 to 15.00	... to 15.00	15.00 to 17.50	12.50 to 20.00	" No. 1	10.00 to 12.50	... to ...	... to 10.00	8.00 to 10.00
2.00 to 10.00	3.00 to 10.00	... to 12.00	4.00 to 6.00	5.00 to 8.00	" Culls and ordinary	4.00 to 6.00	... to ...	4.00 to 6.00	4.00 to 6.00
6.00 to 8.00	6.00 to 8.00	3.00 to 6.00	6.00 to 8.00	... to 5.00	BRIDE, 'MAID, fancy-special	... to 6.00	... to ...	... to 10.00	5.00 to 6.00
4.00 to 6.00	5.00 to 6.00	... to ...	6.00 to 7.00	... to 4.00	" extra	... to 5.00	... to ...	... to 8.00	3.00 to 4.00
1.00 to 4.00	4.00 to 5.00	... to ...	4.00 to 5.00	... to 3.00	" No. 1	... to 4.00	... to ...	4.00 to 6.00	... to 2.00
1.00 to 2.00	3.00 to 4.00	... to ...	2.00 to 3.00	... to 2.00	" No. 2	... to 2.00	... to ...	... to 2.00	... to ...
... to ...	3.00 to 6.00	4.00 to 8.00	2.00 to 8.00	2.00 to 5.00	GOLDEN GATE	4.00 to 6.00	2.00 to 6.00	2.00 to 6.00	2.00 to 5.00
1.00 to 8.00	3.00 to 7.00	... to ...	... to ...	3.00 to 5.00	K. A. VICTORIA	4.00 to 8.00	2.00 to 8.00	2.00 to 8.00	2.00 to 8.00
1.00 to 16.00	3.00 to 8.00	... to ...	... to ...	3.00 to 5.00	LIBERTY	4.00 to 6.00	4.00 to 8.00	4.00 to 8.00	... to ...
... to ...	3.00 to 6.00	3.00 to 8.00	... to ...	3.00 to 5.00	METEOR	... to ...	... to ...	... to ...	... to ...
... to ...	2.00 to 5.00	4.00 to 10.00	... to ...	2.00 to 4.00	PERLE	4.00 to 6.00	... to ...	4.00 to 8.00	2.00 to 5.00
... to ...	... to ...	... to 50.00	... to ...	... to ...	ORCHIDS—Cattleyas	... to ...	... to 40.00	... to ...	... to ...
... to ...	1.00 to 1.50	... to ...	... to ...	1.00 to 1.25	CARNATIONS — Inferior grades, all colors	... to 1.00	... to 2.50	1.00 to 1.50	... to 1.50
1.00 to 2.00	1.50 to 2.50	1.50 to 3.00	1.50 to 2.00	1.50 to 2.00	Standard Varieties — White	... to 1.00	... to 2.50	... to 2.00	... to 1.50
1.00 to 2.00	1.50 to 2.50	... to ...	1.50 to 2.00	1.50 to 2.00	Pink	... to 1.00	... to 2.50	... to 2.00	... to 1.50
1.00 to 2.00	1.50 to 2.50	... to ...	1.50 to 2.00	1.50 to 2.00	Red	... to 1.00	... to 2.50	... to 2.00	... to 1.50
1.00 to 2.00	... to ...	... to ...	... to ...	1.50 to 2.00	Yellow and var.	... to 1.00	... to 2.50	... to 2.00	1.00 to 1.50
2.00 to 3.00	2.00 to 3.50	... to ...	2.00 to 3.00	2.50 to 3.00	Fancy Varieties — White	1.50 to 2.00	... to 3.00	... to 3.00	2.00 to 3.00
2.00 to 3.00	2.00 to 3.50	... to ...	2.00 to 3.00	2.50 to 3.00	Pink	1.50 to 2.00	... to 3.00	... to 3.00	2.00 to 3.00
2.00 to 3.00	2.00 to 3.50	... to ...	2.00 to 3.00	2.50 to 3.00	Red	1.50 to 2.00	... to 3.00	... to 3.00	2.00 to 3.00
2.00 to 3.00	... to ...	... to ...	... to ...	2.50 to 3.00	Yellow and var.	1.50 to 2.00	... to 3.00	... to 3.00	2.00 to 3.00
3.00 to 4.00	... to ...	... to ...	... to ...	... to ...	Novelties	... to ...	... to ...	... to ...	... to ...
.75 to 1.00	.50 to 1.00	... to 2.00	1.00 to 1.50	... to 1.00	ADIANTUM	... to 1.00	... to 1.00	.75 to 1.00	1.00 to 1.50
... to 50.00	15.00 to 20.00	25.00 to 60.00	... to 50.00	25.00 to 50.00	ASPARAGUS, Plum. and Ten.	20.00 to 30.00	50.00 to 75.00	40.00 to 50.00	25.00 to 50.00
... to ...	15.00 to 20.00	20.00 to 30.00	25.00 to 35.00	25.00 to 50.00	" Sprengeri, bunches	20.00 to 30.00	... to 50.00	20.00 to 40.00	25.00 to 50.00
8.00 to 10.00	8.00 to 10.00	... to 10.00	... to ...	6.00 to 10.00	CALLAS	... to ...	... to ...	... to 8.00	... to ...
4.00 to 16.00	5.00 to 20.00	4.00 to 20.00	5.00 to 30.00	4.00 to 25.00	CHRYSANTHEMUMS	... to ...	... to 40.00	4.00 to 20.00	5.00 to 40.00
... to ...	1.50 to 2.50	... to ...	... to ...	... to ...	DAISIES	... to .40	... to 1.00	1.00 to 2.50	... to ...
8.00 to 10.00	... to ...	... to 15.00	... to 12.50	... to 12.50	LILIES	... to 12.50	... to ...	15.00 to 18.00	... to ...
3.00 to 5.00	3.00 to 4.00	3.00 to 4.00	... to 4.00	... to 4.00	LILY OF THE VALLEY	... to ...	3.00 to 5.00	2.00 to 4.00	3.00 to 4.00
... to ...	... to ...	... to ...	... to ...	... to ...	MIGNONETTE, ordinary	... to ...	... to ...	... to ...	... to ...
... to ...	... to ...	... to ...	... to ...	... to ...	" fancy	... to ...	... to ...	... to ...	... to ...
... to 12.50	12.00 to 15.00	4.00 to 6.00	... to 15.00	... to 20.00	SMILAX	... to 15.00	... to ...	10.00 to 15.00	... to 12.50
.35 to .50	.50 to .75	.50 to .75	... to .35	... to .50	VIOLETS, ordinary	... to ...	... to ...	.50 to .75	.40 to .50
.60 to .75	... to 1.00	... to ...	.50 to .75	... to .60	" fancy	... to ...	... to ...	1.00 to 1.25	... to ...
... to ...	... to ...	... to ...	... to .15	... to ...	GALAX LEAVES	... to ...	... to .15	... to ...	... to ...

Indianapolis.

News Notes.

One of the features of the week was the flower show and opening held by Bertermann Brothers Company, at their Massachusetts avenue store, on Thursday and Friday and at times the number of visitors became so great that admittance had to be temporarily stopped. All the features of a large flower show were carried out in detail. A table decoration of roses, with a vase of Madame Abel Chatenay as a center-piece, attracted much attention. A wedding decoration of candles, wedding gates, palms, etc., took well with the public. An orchid exhibit, arranged with miniature lights and fancy foliage plants, backed by a large mirror, was designed as the principal feature of the show. The window display consisted of arrangements of American Beauty, Mlle. Liger and Robert Halliday, chrysanthemums, the latter blooms being arranged in a $500 vase loaned for the occasion by a downtown firm. In the conservatory were seen a hedge of chrysanthemum plants about 150 feet in length; a number of well grown cyclamen and begonias, banked with masses of foliage plants; numerous ferneries and baskets.

The unanimous verdict concerning the Chicago show is "the best and largest." Henry Rieman, Homer and George Wiegand and John Bertermann attended.

Tomlinson Hall Market is heavily stocked these days, but business is remarkably good; hundreds of high grade blooms are wholesaled early in the day. More pot plants are disposed of at this market than at all the stores combined.

The Smith & Young Company are cutting an excellent crop of cattleyas.

Mrs. William Billingsley, who has been alarmingly ill, is on the road to recovery.

I. B.

Wholesale Prices of Cut Flowers, Chicago, Nov. 13, 1906

Prices quoted are by the hundred unless otherwise noted

ROSES — American Beauty			
36-inch stems........per doz.	....		8. 0
30-inch stems........ "	2.		8. 0
24-inch stems........ "	2.50		2. 0
20-inch stems........ "	1.00		2.00
18-inch stems........ "	....		1.80
12-inch stems........ "	....		1.00
8-inch stems and shorts "	.50		.75
Bride Maid, fancy special....	6.00		8.00
" extra..........	4.00		5.00
" No. 1..........	2.00		3.00
" No. 2..........	....		1.00
Golden Gate............	2.00		6.00
Carnot............	2.00		6.00
Uncle John............	2.00		6.00
Liberty............	2.00		8.00
Richmond............	2.00		8.00
Kaiserine............	2.00		8.00
Killarney............	2.00		6.00
" extra............	8.00		10.00
Perle............	2.00	to	6.00
Chatenay............	2.00	to	6.00
....	....	to	....
....	....	to	....

CARNATIONS				
STANDARD VARIETIES	White..........	1.50	to	2.00
	Pink..........	1.50	to	2.00
	Red..........	1.50	to	2.00
	Yellow & var....	1.50	to	2.00
*FANCY (The highest grades of Sta'd var)	White..........	2.50	to	3.00
	Pink..........	2.50	to	3.00
	Red..........	2.50	to	3.00
	Yellow & var....	2.50	to	3.00
NOVELTIES..........		....	to	....
ADIANTUM..........		.75	to	1.00
ASPARAGUS, Plum. & Ten....		.35	to	.50
" Sprengeri, bunches.		.35	to	.50
....		....	to	....
LILIES, Longiflorum..........		15.00	to	18.00
Harrisii..........		15.00	to	18.00
Orchids—Cattleyas..........		....	to	50.00
SMILAX..........		8.00	to	12.00
LILY OF THE VALLEY..........		2.00	to	4.00
VIOLETS..........		.25	to	1.00
HARDY FERNS per 1000..........		....	to	1.50
GALAX "		1.00	to	1.25
....		....	to	....
CHRYSANTHEMUMS per doz		1.00	to	4.00

WESTVILLE, CONN.—Fire in the greenhouses of Mr. Schroto, on November 4, did damage to the extent of $800. It is thought the fire started in the boiler room from live coals falling on the floor.

FAIRHAVEN, MASS. — A very mysterious fire occurred Monday morning, November 5, at S. S. Peckham's place, when the barn, well stocked with hay, carriage house and tool shed were completely demolished. Fortunately the live stock was not in the barn at the time of the fire. Mr. Peckham estimates his loss at about $1,800, and carried an insurance of only $500.

Kansas City, Mo.

Dullness in Trade.

The continued warm weather is having a most depressing influence on business. Good home-grown stock is rather scarce, but the demand the past week has been very light. The one exception has been chrysanthemums, which are selling better than for several years. Some Southern violets are being shipped in, but are a drug on the market.

One of our florists ascribes the poor business of the past week to the fact that it was election time.

It is the humble opinion of the writer that the florists of Kansas City made a great mistake in not holding another flower show this Winter. The flower show in the past has given the business a great stimulus and has been the means of developing a love of flowers that would never have been accomplished in any other way. If we cannot have a show, national in its scope as the others were, let the local florists get together and give an exhibition, anyway.

Al. Murray, who has been with James Hayes at Topeka, Kans., for some time, has returned to Kansas City and accepted a position with his brother, Sam. Murray.

Heinz of Leavenworth, Kans., was a visitor one day last week.

One of the 10 cent stores here has added a cut flower department. We noticed a couple of jars of very forlorn looking roses with a sign attached to them reading "3 for a dime."

L.

Columbus, O.

News and Trade Notes.

The Livingston Seed Company will hold their annual chrysanthemum show at their North High street store from November 13 to 17. This has now become with them a yearly feature, and they prepare for it months ahead, growing large quantities of such splendid exhibition varieties as Mrs. O. P. Bassett, Major Bonnaffon, Col. Appleton, Lord Hopetoun, S. T. Wright, and many others equally grand. This show brings thousands of visitors to the store.

The Florists' Club holds its chrysanthemum show this week, which will also be the first meeting in the new rooms in the Brent Building. A very large gathering is expected Tuesday evening, when a good musical program has been arranged by the committee in charge.

The show at Chicago has created much interest among the craft here. William Graff and A. M. Hills attended the exhibition from here.

Gustave Ackerman is adding another house to his already extensive establishment; his other greenhouses are also being repaired and painted. Chrysanthemums and lettuce are the specialties at this plant.

The Chinese Sacred Lily has this season sold slowly and indifferently here; even low prices do not seem to move them at retail in any quantity.

John Peter Menger, who died in this city the past week at the good old age of eighty-six years, was in his younger days one of the head-gardeners to the Emperor of Germany.

A special Winter course in Agriculture has been inaugurated at the Ohio State University; the course will begin January 7 and last ten weeks.

The Columbus Pottery Company was visited by a most disastrous fire last Friday morning. The main building was constructed three years ago, and was 400 feet long by 54 feet in width; it was about half destroyed. The site, buildings and equipment cost $131,000, and about 200 people were steadily employed. The plant was partially insured, the exact amount is not known at this writing. The loss is estimated to be about $50,000; that is on both stock and buildings. The fire started on the outside of the plant in a new kiln.

Professor W. R. Lazenby last Friday evening delivered an address at the Y. M. C. A. on "Fruits and Their Value"; the lecture being illustrated by charts and pictures. Mr. Lazenby is a professor at the Ohio State University, and a life member of the American Pomological Society.

F. W.

RIDGEWOOD, N. J.—Wm. Barkham has been overrun during the past week with funeral work and wedding decorations.

San Francisco.

An Outing

The members of the Pacific Coast Horticultural Society, on November 3, had a very pleasant outing at the Tevis estate, Burlingame, over a hundred being present. The grounds were thrown open to the visitors, and refreshments were served. The numerous conservatories, the orchards and expansive grounds, the grand specimen trees especially called forth enthusiastic praise from the delighted gardeners and florists. The araucarias were particularly fine, President Bagge venturing the opinion that they could hardly be duplicated in California.

At the November 3 meeting in Park Lodge, Golden Gate Park, a resolution of thanks to Mr. Tevis was ordered spread on the minutes. At this meeting Superintendent McLaren showed the blue-print plans of Architect Burnham of Chicago for the beautifying with parks and boulevards of Greater San Francisco. These plans were drawn and are being submitted for suggestions by the city aldermen. A committee of landscape gardeners was appointed by the meeting to take the plans and submit suggestions. At this meeting a new seedling pear, originated by the late John Rock of the California Nursery Company of Niles, called "the Winter Bartlett," was tasted and voted a certificate of merit. The Niles company will place it on the market very shortly. The sense of the meting was that for quality, size and flavor this pear is not excelled.

ALVIN.

Cincinnati.

News Items.

Dr. F. E. Howald of Atlanta, Ga., was in the city for a few hours during the week. The doctor is the proprietor of the Atlanta Floral Company.

It was with much regret that we learned of the deaths of Lewis Ullrich and J. L. Dillon. How true is the saying, in Mr. Dillon's case, "In the midst of life we are in death."

J. A. Peterson and R. Witterstaetter were the only members of the craft who attended the Chicago show, which from all accounts must have been a dandy. Cincinnati will have nothing of the kind this year; not even a little one.

Theodore Bock, or "Judge" as we call him, was up to see us last week. He states that his business keeps him pretty much at home. He grows good stock, and retails every bit of it at good, fair prices.

E. G. GILLETT.

ALEXANDRIA, VA.—A damage suit that is attracting considerable attention is that of J. Louis Loose, florist, against the Southern Railway Company, in which the plaintiff seeks to recover damages in the sum of $20,000 for injuries alleged to have been done his plants and greenhouses by smoke and cinders from the defendant company's engines and roundhouse. The case has been in progress in the Circuit Court, Judge C. E. Nicol presiding, for several days. A witness from Chicago has been summoned to testify in behalf of the railway company.

Boston.

News of the Week.

The meeting of the Gardeners and Florists' Club on Tuesday next promises to be an interesting one. It is the annual meeting for the election of officers and a large attendance is looked for. The prospectus for the landscape gardening classes has been issued, and the classes will start on an early date.

A recent call at the establishment of A. Leuthy & Company found these greenhouses finely stocked with a large lot of plants for the Christmas trade. Some three thousand azaleas were looking well and were an even lot of plants. A new fern, which Mr. Leuthy thinks will be very useful for pan work, was doing finely; it is a crested form of Aspidium tsussemense which made its appearance here in a chance lot of seedlings several years ago.

J. S. Manter has resigned as salesman for Anderson & Williams in the Park street market, and William Aylward has taken the position.

Wm. Hastings, with A. H. Hews & Company, has returned from a very successful Southern trip.

E. Sutermeister has gone to Portland for a few days.

H. M. Vose was the first to bring in Paper White narcissus this season.

W. S. Wilson of Wellesley, one of the large rose growers of that locality, died Thursday after an illness of only four days.

At the weekly meeting of the bowling teams on Thursday the wholesalers had everything their own way, the Wabans having failed to show up.

Mrs. Geo. Cartwright is visiting her daughter in Philadelphia.

Wm. Nisbet has taken the rear of J. J. McCormack's store and will start again in the wholesale hardy fern and evergreen business.

Welch Brothers are handling an exceptionally fine grade of American Beauty at the present time, the grower being Carl Jurgens of Newport, R. I.

Thos. Pegler, who recently started in the violet growing business at Wollaston, is bringing in well grown blooms of the variety Lady Hume Campbell.

J. W. D.

Kalamazoo, Mich.

News Items.

G. Van Bochove was present at the show in Chicago looking up novelties, etc., for next season's planting.

H. Heithouse has built a frame house, 70 x 14 feet, on the west side and intends to grow mainly bedding and vegetable plants as a beginning.

I am in receipt of the first annual floral number of the Grand Rapids Herald. The florists of that town are to be congratulated on the result, as it is a very good piece of work, in which its readers are given in an interesting and intelligent manner many items regarding the business. This must prove beneficial to the trade of that town, and is a first class example of collective advertising which could well be copied in many other places.

S. B.

CHESTER, PA.—Since the sale of the effects of the Delahunt estate, located at Twenty-first street and Edgemont avenue, the purchasers have begun to remove the greenhouses. The glass, woodwork and the whole outfit are being taken apart and will be removed. This is the last of what once was a very prosperous business while the owner was alive.

NORTH ABINGTON, MASS.—An addition is being built to the new greenhouse of the Bay State Nursery Company on Adams street.

Utica, N. Y.

News Notes.

On November 6 the Utica Flo ists' Club met at the establishme of Wm. P. Pfeifer, No. 608 White boro street. About twenty were in a tendance, and it was a very spirit meeting. A great many questio were discussed, one of the most in portant being that we hold a cl flower show and banquet on Nover ber 22, in the Elks' Hall. An e cellent dinner was provided by M Pfeifer, and after giving our host a hostess a hearty vote of thanks, left for home about midnight.

Mr. Pfeifer's carnations are in fi condition, especially a house of Bo ton Market which are particular grand for this time of the year.

S. Ritchie, of Newport, R. I., in town calling on the trade. main object, however, was to Adiantum Croweanum at home, he went away perfectly satisfied. J Cokely, of the Scranton Supply C pany, was also a visitor, and busy selling Winsor and White chantress, meeting with much succ He was proposed as a member our club; any one who happens to at one of our meetings we are sure get. S. S. Skidelsky was likew calling on the trade booming R Pink Enchantress, for which he cured quite a number of orders.

Your scribe visited the recent fl er show at Poughkeepsie, N. Y., was cordially received. He was ta in hand by George Saltford, of Rh beck. The show was very credita a fine lot of chrysanthemums be on view. Violets were in extra c dition for this time of the year made a number of calls on the vi growers and found the plants ge ally looking well. I do not th Poughkeepsie has lost any of its time popularity for the cultivatio this favorite flower.

I next made a call on F. R. P. M. Pierson, at Scarboro. place has been much improved s my last visit two years ago. The has just finished two more ho each 350 by 60 feet, making t now covering one and one-half a One house contained 26,000, ano 20,000, and still another 18,000 nation plants. The house of Wi was a little short of flowers, as Pierson said he had forwa blooms a few days before to flower shows, but a grand crop in sight. A new propagating ho with something like 30,000 cutt now in, mostly all Winsor, wa grand sight. This variety seem have great commercial value, an is worth any one's time to pa visit to this establishment to see of stock in sight.

It is the wish of the secretary our Florists' Club that every m ber be present at the show and b quet, and bring something along make the exhibition a success.

QUI

N. TONAWANDA, N. Y. — TORONTO, ONT.

KING CONSTRUCTION CO.
GREENHOUSE CONSTRUCTION AND EQUIPMENT
WRITE FOR CATALOGUE AND PRICES

Mention the Florists' Exchange when writing.

WHOLESALE TRADE LIST

ASPARAGUS PLUMOSUS, 3 in. pots, $6.00 per 100; 2 in. pots, $3.00 per 100.

ASPARAGUS PLUMOSUS, Seedlings from flats, $1.00 per 100, $8.00 per 1000.

ASPARAGUS SPRENGERI, 3 in. pots, $2.00 per 100.

BOSTON FERNS, 4 in. pots, 20c. each. 5 in. pots, 25c. each.

CLEMATIS PANICULATA, 4 in. pots, $1.50 per oz., $10.00 per 100; 3 in. pots, 75c. per doz.; $6.00 per 100.

DRACÆNA INDIVISA, 5 in. pots, $2.00 per doz.

GERANIUMS, Stock plants grown in pots. Double white La Favorite, Telegraph, Queen of the West, John Doyle, S. A. Nutt, $1.00 per doz.

HYDRANGEAS, Otaksa and Thos. Hogg, fine field grown plants, $10.00 per 100.

IVY, Hardy English, 4 in. pots, $1.50 per doz.; $10.00 per 100.

Paris Daisy, Strong plants 3 in. pots $4.00 per 100.

YELLOW DAISY (Etoile d'Or), 3 in. pots, $6.00 per 100.

SANSEVIERA, (Zebra plant) 4 in. pots, strong $1.50 per doz.; 3 in. pots, $1.00 per doz.

O. EISELE, 11th & Roy Streets, PHILADELPHIA, PA.

Mention the Florists' Exchange when writing.

SUMMER IN WINTER

BY USING

Standard Greenhouse Boilers

One cent gets our catalog.

GIBLIN & CO., UTICA, N. Y.

Mention the Florists' Exchange when writing.

A Standard Pumping Engine

just like this cut is saving one of our customers $496.00 a year in wages. Write for a copy of his letter.

The Standard Pump & Engine Co.
CLEVELAND, O.

Mention the Florists' Exchange when writing.

BOILERS QUICK.

This is the season when quick deliveries count. I have the largest line of horticultural boilers and can give quick shipments from twenty different points. I will erect your plant complete if you desire it. Write for prices.

JOHN A. PAYNE
Horticultural Architect and Builder
33 CLENDENNY AVE., JERSEY CITY
Sash Opening Apparatus.
All kinds of Greenhouse Structural and Heating Material.

GREENHOUSES.
MATERIAL FURNISHED AND MEN TO SUPERINTEND ERECTION IF DESIRED.
CYPRESS SASH BARS
ANY LENGTH UP TO 32 FT OR LONGER.
THE A. T. Stearns Lumber Co.,
NEPONSET, BOSTON, MASS.

Mention the Florists' Exchange when writing.

WE MADE A SUGGESTION

last week that you give a little hard sensed thought to the comparative lasting qualities of the Iron Frame House—against the wooden house, with its everlasting repair bill—we only mentioned the endurance side then, but now want to suggest a few things to think about on the shade question.

¶The wooden house requires a sash bar 1⅜" x 2⅛"

¶The Iron Frame sash bars are only $^{15}/_{16}$" x 1⅞"

¶Wooden houses require numerous heavy purlins and supportin members.

¶The Iron Frame House simply requires a truss rod from rafter to rafter across the peak; or even in a 40 foot house, two small columns are all that are necessary.

¶The wooden house carries the sash bars from eave to ridge, which in connection with the bars of ventilating sash just about doubles the shade at that point.

¶The Iron Frame sash bars are carried to the header only—giving one-half the shade.

"The man who looks ahead is the man who gets ahead."
The man who has the lightest house grows the best plants—gets the best prices.
The man whose repair bills are way down, has profits way up.
Send for our Iron Frame Circular.

Lord & Burnham Co.

Greenhouse Designers and Manufacturers.

1133 Broadway, corner 26th St., NEW YORK.

BOSTON BRANCH, 819 Tremont Building.

Mention The Florists' Exchange when writing.

Are You Now Deciding

on the details of your new houses?

Write us for Sketches and Suggestions, they will be of interest to you.

A. DIETSCH CO.

Louisiana Cypress and Washington Red Cedar GREENHOUSE MATERIAL

619 Sheffield Ave., Chicago, Ill.

Mention The Florists' Exchange when writing.

SCOLLAY BOILERS

ARE BEST

For Green House heating. Standard Cast Iron Green House Pipe and Fittings.

We are Headquarters for all sizes wrought iron pipe and fittings.

It will pay you to get our special quotation. We also contract for and erect **Steam and Hot Water Heating** apparatus in all parts of the country.

Illustrated catalogues free on application.

JOHN A. SCOLLAY,
74-76 MYRTLE AVE.,
BOROUGH OF BROOKLYN,
NEW YORK CITY.
Telephones 1492-1493 Main.
U. G. SCOLLAY, Manager.

Mention The Florists' Exchange when writing.

A. HERRMANN

Manufacturer of Floral Metal Designs

IMPORTER AND DEALER IN FLORISTS' SUPPLIES

FACTORY: 709 FIRST AVENUE, BETWEEN 40th AND 41st STREETS, NEW YORK

OFFICE AND WAREROOMS: 404, 406, 408, 410, 412 East 34th St.

WRITE FOR NEW CATALOGUE

Mention the Florists' Exchange when writing.

THE FLORISTS' SUPPLY HOUSE OF AMERICA

Now is the time to buy goods

Before we move

SEND FOR CATALOGUE.

H. BAYERSDORFER & CO., 50, 52, 54, 56 North Fourth St., PHILADELPHIA, PA.

Mention the Florists' Exchange when writing.

THE FLORISTS' EXCHANGE

We are a straight shoot and aim to grow into a vigorous plant

A WEEKLY MEDIUM OF INTERCHANGE FOR FLORISTS, NURSERYMEN, SEEDSMEN AND THE TRADE IN GENERAL

XXII. No. 21 NEW YORK AND CHICAGO, NOVEMBER 24, 1906 One Dollar Per Year

CONTENTS AND INDEX TO ADVERTISERS, PAGE 625

Mats of Burlap or Straw

which will cover two cold frames

$1.25 Each; $14.00 Dozen

TULIPS SINGLE

	100		100
Superfine mix	$ .85	Single Artus	$1.25
La Reine	.80	Chrysolora	.90
Duchess de Parma	1.00	Duc Van Thol, yel	2.00
Yellow Prince	.90		

TULIPS DOUBLE

Rex Rubrorum .... $1.50 per 100
Fine Mixed .... 85c per 100

TULIPS LATE

Gesneriana .... $1.35 per 100
Parrot .... 80c per 100

DAFFODILS DOUBLE

Incomparable .... 85c per 100
Von Sion, double nose .... $2.00 per 100

DAFFODILS SINGLE

Poeticus .... 45c per 100

Spirea Japonica, $4.00 per 100; $88.00 per 1000.
Compacta Multiflora, $5.00 per 100; $42.00 per 1000.
Astilboides Floribunda, $6.00 per 100; $45.00 per 1000.
Lily of the Valley, selected 3 year old, $10.00 per 1000; $24.00 per case of 2500.
Lilium Auratum, 9 to 11, $8.00 per 100.

Sterilized Sheep Manure, $1.25 100 lbs, $20.00 a Ton.

WM. ELLIOTT & SONS, 201 Fulton Street, NEW YORK.

Mention the Florists' Exchange when writing.

C. C. MORSE & CO.

SEED GROWERS

171-173 Clay St., San Francisco, California

OUR SPECIALTIES

ONION LETTUCE SWEET PEAS

Also Carrot, Celery, Celeriac, Cucumber, Endive, Leek, Mustard, Parsley, Parsnip, Radish, Salsify, Spinach, Tomato and

FLOWER SEEDS

Growers for the trade on contract. Warehouses at Santa Clara; Farms and Farm headquarters Carnadero, near Gilroy.

Registered Cable Address: MORSEED, SAN FRANCISCO.

Mention the Florists' Exchange when writing.

EXCEPTIONAL OFFER

To save storage we offer for immediate shipment the following roots at remarkably low prices.

SPIREA JAPONICA (170 clumps in a case) per case........ $3.50
SPIREA COMPACTA MULTIFLORA (250 in a case) per case........ 6.50
SPIREA ASTILBOIDES FLORIBUNDA (175 in a case) per case........ 4.25

Subject to being unsold on receipt of order. Cash must accompany every order.

W. W. RAWSON & CO.

5 UNION STREET, BOSTON, MASS.

Mention the Florists' Exchange when writing.

PACIFIC SEED GROWERS' CO.
109 MARKET STREET
SAN FRANCISCO, CAL.
Specialties:
Onion, Carrot, Lettuce, Sweet Peas

Mention The Florists' Exchange when writing.

GROW YOUR OWN TREES and SHRUBS from SEED.

Send today for our

TRADE SEED LIST

and also for our *Descriptive Catalog*, which is replete with valuable information.

OTTO KATZENSTEIN & CO.
Wholesale Dept. ATLANTA, GA.

Mention The Florists' Exchange when writing.

MY GIANT CYCLAMEN

Are Ahead in Growth and Flowers
Bloodred, Carmine, Pink, Pure White, White Carmine Eyed.

Each color separate. Tr. pkt., $1.00; 1000 seeds, $6.00. An even mixture of the above 5 colors, tr. pkt., 75c.; 1000 seeds, $5.00.

For larger quantities, special quotations.

O. V. ZANGEN, Seedsman, HOBOKEN, N. J.

QUALITY SEEDS BULBS PLANTS
SEND FOR CATALOGUE
ARTHUR T. BODDINGTON
342 West 14th St., New York.

SURPLUS

BULBS. SEND FOR LIST.

STUMPP & WALTER CO., 50 Barclay St NEW YORK

Mention the Florists' Exchange when writing.

STOKES STANDARD SEEDS ARE MONEY MAKERS
Write me your wants.
STOKES SEED STORE
219 Market Street
Philadelphia

Mention the Florists' Exchange when writing.

SEEDS If you are in need of any of the following, write us for Beets, Cabbage, Cannon Ball and Rocky Ford Melon, Southern grown Water Melon, Bermud other Onion seed, Okra, Mustard, French and ornia grown Radish, Tomato, Mexican June Corn, Kaffir Corn, German Millet, D Yellow Milo Maize, Sugar Cane, Winter Barley, Red Rust Proof Oats, Cotton seed, W poorwill and White Black-eyed Field Peas, Spanish Peanuts, Johnson and Ber Grass.

TEXAS SEED & FLORAL CO. DALLAS, TE

Mention the Florists' Exchange when writing.

ARTHUR COWEE, GLADIOLUS SPECIALI

MEADOWVALE FARM, BERLIN, N. Y.

United States Representative and Grower of GROFF'S HYBRIDS, MIXTURES and COLLECTIONS to color. Fine Mixtures of all colors. Named Novelties of rare beauty. WRITE FOR CATALOG.

Mention the Florists' Exchange when writing.

ESTABLISHED 1894

Bridgeman's Seed Warehouse
Rickards Bros., Props.
IMPORTERS AND GROWERS OF HIGH GRADE
Seeds, Bulbs, Plants, Etc.
37 EAST 19TH ST. Near Broadway NEW YORK CITY
Telephone: 4235 Gramercy

Mention the Florists' Exchange when writing.

W. & D.'s Specialties for Forcing
Mignonette "New York Market"
Sweet Peas "True" Christmas Flowering (Pink and White)
Tomato "The Don" Tomato "Stirling Castle"
Mushroom Spawn "English" and "Pure Culture"
Special prices on application
WEEBER & DON, Seed Merchants and Growers
114 Chambers Street, NEW YORK

Mention the Florists' Exchange when writing.

BURPEE'S SEEDS
PHILADELPHIA
Blue List of Wholesale Prices mailed only to those who plant for profit.

Mention the Florists' Exchange when writing.

Catalog Engravings
and ILLUSTRATIONS
that print EASILY. That's the kind we make—have been since '73
JAS. M. BRYANT, Horticultural Engraving and Printing
706 Chestnut Street, PHILADELPHIA, PA.
Write for our Catalogue of Stock Engravings

Mention the Florists' Exchange when writing.

SPIRAEA pe
Japonica—Extra strong clumps 4
Astilboides Floribundi ....
Compacta Multiflora ....
Gladstone ....

LILIUM LONGIFLORU

	per 1000	pe
6 to 8 inches	$27 00	$
7 to 9 "	45 00	
Multiflorum, 6 to 8 inches	28 00	
" 7 to 9 "	50 00	

PANDANUS utilis
Fresh Seeds just received $6.00 per Seeds. Send for Trade List.

J. M. THORBURN & C
33 Barclay St., through to 3
Park Place, NEW YORK.

THE CHRISTMAS N of The Florists' Exc will be issued Sat December 8, 1906. That issu appear at an opportune time advertisers will make no m in placing therein a liberal d of their offerings for the hol Copy of advertisement should us at the very latest by 12 Wednesday, December 5.

Mention The Florists' Exchange when

Seed Trade Report.

AMERICAN SEED TRADE ASSOCIATION.

Henry W. Wood, Richmond, Va., president; C. S. Burge, Toledo, O., first vice-president; G. B. McVay, Birmingham, Ala., second vice-president; C. E. Kendel, Cleveland, O., secretary and treasurer; J. H. Ford, Ravenna, O., assistant secretary.

The 1906 bean crop of Michigan is commercially estimated at 5,000,000 bushels.

SEDALIA, MO.—The Archias Seed Company have just placed the order for printing their forthcoming Spring catalogue, which will be beautifully illustrated, somewhat larger than any of the former issues, and several thousand more copies will be printed.

ST. PAUL.—Some anxiety is felt among the trade here on account of the condition of lycopodium or Christmas green. The supply is but limited, and from present prosjects the price will be very high. The pickers have only been able to get a small quantity, and are holding it at a premium. P.

PHILADELPHIA.—There is quite a lot of dissatisfaction among the seed trade here this Fall on account of the Holland bulb growers doing so much substituting. Some of this has always been done, but never to such an extent as this season. The practice has been most common in the case of tulips. Artus has been sent for Belle Alliance, and Duchesse de Parma for Keizerskroon. Substitution has also been done in the case of other varieties, but with the two mentioned it has been very general. This is a far-reaching abuse. In some cases the substitution was detected, but no doubt lots of complaints will come in from customers later on; then woe to the bulb man when he comes around in 1907! D. R.

Burnet Landreth recently read an instructive and interesting paper on "The New Agriculture" before the Philadelphia Philosophical Society.

ROGERS BROTHERS of Chaumont, Jefferson County, N. Y., the past few years have been gradually transferring their business of seed growing (beans and peas) to Alpena, Mich., growing their stock of peas in Northern Michigan and their beans in Central Michigan and Western New York. They have recently sold their seed house at Chaumont to a milling company that handles feed, flour, hay and farm produce. The Jefferson county section was once a favorable location for growing peas and beans, but the bugs became so thick and other conditions so unfavorable to the growing of peas that the firm, with others in its line, was forced elsewhere to grow stock.

Seeds, with the exception of those which are oleaginous, are admitted into Italy duty free.

The German tariff imposes the following duties on seeds imported into that country: Rape, colza, oil-radish, dodder, mustard and hedge mustard seed, per 100 kilos, 5 marks general rate, and 2 marks conventional; poppy and sunflower seeds, 2 marks conventional and general; red clover, white clover, and other clover seed 5 marks general, conventional free; grass seed of all kinds, 2 marks general, conventional free; common beet and sugar beet seeds, 1 mark general and conventional; other field-root seeds, carrot, chicory, vegetable seeds, flower seeds, and other seeds for agriculture not separately mentioned, free. Dill seed and tobacco seed free. One mark equals $0.238.

The duty on plants and seeds for agricultural purposes imposed by the Portuguese tariff is 3 reis per kilo. (1,000 reis equal $1.08.)

Vegetable, garden, forest, and fodder seeds, other than those specially mentioned; also tobacco seed going to Roumania are subject to a duty, general, of .20 lei per 100 kilo. (Leu equals $0.193.)

The Spanish tariff imposes a maximum and minimum rate of duty on seeds not elsewhere specified of 1.60 pesetas per 100 kilos. The value of a peseta is $0.193.

Under the Swedish tariff the duty on seeds per kilo is as follows: Canary, 10 kroner; pine, 4.00 kroner; fir, 1.50 kroner; timothy, .05 kroner; other seeds, not mentioned elsewhere, free. The value of a krone is $0.268.

Seeds are among the agricultural products admitted into the United Kingdom free of duty.

The Canadian tariff on seeds is as follows: Garden, field and other seeds for agricultural or other purposes, n. o. p., sunflower, canary, hemp, and millet seed, when in bulk or in large parcels, 10 per cent. ad valorem; when put up in small papers or parcels, 25 per cent. ad valorem. Beans are subject to a duty of 15c. per bushel; and peas, n. e. s. to one of 10c. per bushel.

W. W. Rawson & Co., Boston.

This enterprising firm, which has become famed all over the country for its selected varieties of vegetable and flower seeds, was established by Warren W. Rawson in 1884, when he bought out the seed house of Everett & Gleason at 34 South Market street, Boston. The business was continued

W. W. Rawson

at this location till 1897, and Mr. Gleason remained for some years with the new firm. B. K. Bliss, of American Wonder and other peas fame, was also for several years with the firm, which devoted its attention particularly to the market garden and florist trade. In the Fall of 1897 the business having outgrown the quarters occupied at 34 South Market street, the firm secured a lease of the whole of the building at 13 Faneuil Hall square, the main store being on the ground floor, a new departure for Boston seed houses. This was the historic building occupied by Wm. Read & Sons during the Civil War, where were enacted exciting scenes during the draft riots. The firm remained here until the disastrous fire on March 23, 1906, when all stock was completely destroyed.

Some idea of Mr. Rawson's enterprise may be gained, however, when it is said that inside of eight days he had the lower floor of the building again open for business, using strawberry baskets in place of seed drawers, which had all been destroyed. The confidence of the public in this firm was shown by the fact that notwithstanding its being handicapped by the fire the total business for the year was equal to that of the previous one.

A change in ownership of the property caused the firm to find a new location, and so the present store at No. 5 Union street was secured. Here four floors are occupied, the salesrooms being on the main and second floors of the building. The new store is unique in its arrangements, with a nice waiting room where customers may enjoy the privileges of an extensive horticultural library. The entire attention of the firm is devoted to seeds, plants, and bulbs, the handling of tools and sundries having been discontinued.

Some of the introductions sent out by this firm are Rawson's hothouse lettuce, Rawson's crumpled-leaf lettuce, and Rawson's hothouse cucumber.

The other enterprises of the concern, besides the seed store, are 100 acres in vegetable growing and 11 acres under glass for vegetable and plant growing at Arlington, Mass.; 400 acres for seed growing at Newton, N. H., and a special dahlia farm at Marblehead, Mass.

Warren W. Rawson, the founder of the firm, was born at Arlington, January 23, 1847, the son of the late Warren Rawson, a prominent agriculturist of that beautiful progressive and historical town. After receiving his education in the Arlington schools and the academy, he entered upon a business course at a well known commercial college, subsequently, receiving instruction in music and elocution and becoming a well-versed parliamentarian by reason of close attention to the study of parlimentary law.

Early in life he succeeded his father in the market garden business with increasingly pronounced and advanced efforts, until now he is considered one of the leading men in his line in the country. That he is held in high esteem by his business associates is evident by the many positions he has held in the council of their affairs, and in the many high positions he has filled as president of several organizations in the horticultural field.

As a citizen of Arlington his reputation is equally noteworthy, having been moderator for a number of years, a member of the school board for many years, of the sewerage commission of the town for a long period and in various other capacities where he has had abundant opportunity to display his honesty, ability, broad mindednes, and interest in the affairs of his native town.

Notwithstanding the fact that Mr. Rawson is a very busy man, he has found time and inclination to unite his interests with those of others in a fraternal way, and he is associated with Masonic and Odd Fellows' organizations in the highest degrees of those eminent orders. He is also a member of the well known Middlesex and Home Market clubs, besides very many other organizations, numbering at least 25 in all.

Mr. Rawson's home life surpasses in importance to him all other interests, and his fine estate is a monument to his love of home and nature; he is one of the heaviest taxpayers in the town. Mr. Rawson's family consists of a wife and three children, a son, Herbert W., now associated with him in business, being a graduate of Cornell University. J. W D.

HOLLAND NOTES.—The trade in hyacinths, tulips and narcissus has been a very uncommon one this season. Every one knew beforehand that the quantity was very limited, and in consequence of the ever increasing demand, prices were continually advancing. Those on most of the varieties of tulips fluctuated from 10 to 20 per cent. above last year's, and real first-sized hyacinths, of pure white, good red and good light blue, from 15 to 20 per cent. Of narcissus the stock was sufficient for the demand, hence a little decline on last year's prices; however, those on crocus jumped from 25 to 50 per cent.

Most growers are planting for cultivation considerably less, especially of mother bulbs, than last year. About all bulbs are planted, and the growers are busily occupied covering them with reeds in order to protect them from frost.

Next year there will be an exhibition of flowering bulbs in the open air at Sassenheim. J. B.

CATALOGUES RECEIVED.

RIVOIRE PERE ET FILS, Lyon, France—Catalogue of Seeds, including Novelties.

AMOS PERRY, Enfield, England.—Catalogue of Border and Rock Plants; also catalogue of Trees and Shrubs.

THOMAS IMMERSCHITT, Aschaffenburg, Bavaria.—Price List of Fruit Tree, Ornamental Shrub, Forest and Palm Seeds.

EASTERN NURSERIES (M. M. Dawson, manager), Jamaica Plain, Mass.—"Everything for the Hardy Garden;" handsomely illustrated.

W. W. Rawson & Co.'s New Store—Flower Seed Department.

W. W. Rawson & Co.'s New Store—General Seed Department

EPARTMENT.

Joseph Meehan.

ON OF NURSERYMEN; Md., president; J. W. Hill, esident; George C. Seager, ry; C. L. Yates, Rochester,

EVERGREENS FOR NAME.—I enclose four speciens of retinisporas, which I would like to have entified. I have quite a number of them, which propagated a few years ago from instructions reived from your notes in The Florists' Exchange. o. 2 and No. 3 are similar in coloring, but appear differ in habit; however you will know whether ey are the same or not. C. C.
Mass.

—No. 1 is Retinispora plumosa; No. 2, R. plumosa urea; Nos. 3 and 4, R. squarrosa. J. M.

San Jose Scale.

Is California privet subject to San Jose scale and o what extent?

Are chestnut trees (the ordinary varieties) subect to this pest? QUAKER.

—The San Jose scale does not confine itself alogether to fruit trées, but we have never heard f its attacking the California privet. Nor do we hink chestnut trees are ever attacked by the scale. Ve think you may plant either or both of these ithout any fear of this pest. J. M.

Seasonable Notes.

Both gooseberries and currants are favorite bushes f the San Jose scale. As the presence of this scale now so widespread, the bushes mentioned should looked over every Winter, and if scale be deected a spraying of Scalecide will be in order.

In Europe the myrobolan plum, the one so much sed here for stocks, is a favorite hedge plant. It ould be as much in favor here, were it not that it one of the scale's favorites, and this would realt in the necessity of its being sprayed—someing everyone wishes to avoid as much as possible.

The Japanese maple, Acer rufinerve, is the counterart of our native one, A. striatum, excepting that its Autumn coloring of foliage it is far better than urs. The leaves are large, and are of a deep orange ed. This color appears for some time before the eaves fall; and the tree is not bare of foliage until fter freezing weather comes.

When planting with a view of having a tree with andsome Fall foliage, be sure to include the double lowering Japanese cherry, Cerasus Sieboldi. There re but few trees that equal it in this respect; and n beauty of flowers in Spring it has no superior.

Where a heavy looking pine is required, plant our ed pine, Pinus resinosa, or the Pinus ponderosa of Colorado. The red pine is preferred by many, its eedles being less rigid than those of P. ponderosa. Formerly Pinus austriaca was much used for the urpose, and it is still a good one.

One of our Texan clematises, C. coccinea, having carlet flowers, is not as prominent in collections as t should be. It is herbaceous in the North, whatever t may be in Texas; but strong plants will make hoots 10 feet in length in Summer, and these shoots lower freely.

Pseudo-Larix Kæmpferi is a beautiful deciduous onifer. The foliage becomes of a golden yellow in Autumn. The leaves have more substance than those f the larch; and its deciduous cones provide another way of distinguishing it from the latter. It is oo seldom seen in collections.

Ash trees do best in moderately damp ground. The Western green ash, viridis, does not make as large tree as the alba, or americana, but it is a nice tree where a medium sized ash is required. The common white ash, alba, retains its leaves until quite late in Autumn.

Hawthorns are great favorites, both for their own merits and for having been the theme of so many writers. The following list flower in the order named: Cratægus coccinea, oxycantha, Crus-galli and cordata. The colored and the double-flowered sorts are all varieties of oxycantha. These are increased by budding or grafting them on some other stock, either oxycantha or some other common sort.

Robinia hispida, the rose acacia, when left to itself forms a rather straggling bush. To get it of good height European nurserymen graft it on the yellow locust, R. pseud-acacia. It is so beautiful when its flowers are expanded that it is a good selling shrub.

Evergreen Cuttings.

Many nurserymen are still busy in their selling departments, the open weather of the early part of November being favorable for planting. Although early for the making of evergreen cuttings, there is no question that those made now make by far the best plants. Rooting better than those made later, they are in superior condition for planting out when the Spring season opens.

The best cuttings are made from strong, well-matured shoots of the present season. There is no exact limit to length; it depends on what the evergreen is that is being handled. Some sorts make a more lengthy growth than others, and these admit of the cuttings being made longer than those that make but a few inches of growth. As a rule, a four inch cutting is a good one, and this length may be borne in mind for the making of all.

The best way is to use shallow boxes for cuttings. A size easily lifted is preferred, say, 20 by 20 inches, having a depth of 4 or 4 1-2 inches. Clean, pure sand should be used for filling. When the boxes are filled with cuttings they should be placed in a fairly warm greenhouse, kept shaded and well moistened daily. The shade may be obtained by newspapers or sheets of muslin placed over them. This is better than whitewashing the glass, as there are cloudy days when no shading is required, on which days the light is to be desired rather than kept out.

After the cuttings have been in the greenhouse for a month, rather more heat may be given them; and when later on they show roots, which can be ascertained by lifting a few, the shading should be discontinued.

Fruiting of Lonicera Morrowi

When fairly rooted there are two plans to select from for further treatment. The little plants can be transplanted or potted, or allowed to remain in the boxes until Spring. The best plants follow potting, but this means that much space will be required for them. It pays when stock is scarce and plants valuable. In the case of the general run of nursery stock the plants may remain in boxes until Spring and then be transplanted into open frames or into the nursery. When poorly rooted by Spring, it is unwise to set them out in the nursery; the Summer tries them too much. But cuttings made early are usually so well rooted by Spring that they may be set out in nursery rows if got out the very first nice days of Spring. These would require a mulching in Summer, probably, and they should have one the first Winter.

In the list of evergreens that root very well from Winter made cuttings are the following: Azalea amœna; Biota orientalis and varieties; Buxus in variety; calluna and heaths of all kinds; cephalotaxus; cryptomeria; Chamæcyparis Lawsoniana; euonymus, all the evergreen sorts; juniperus in variety; libocedrus; retinisporas; taxus, in sorts; thuja, in variety, and Thujopsis borealis. The various abies, piceas and pinus will root, but not in the satisfactory way the other evergreens do, and their propagation by grafting, by seeds, and in other ways than cuttings, will be found preferable.

The Salisburia as a Street Tree.

When the stock of salisburias had to be imported from abroad the use of the tree for street or avenue planting was but little mentioned; but since the seeds are now easily had from trees growing here, and seedlings are plentiful in nurseries, there is more talk of this tree as one available for avenue planting, as it surely is. In the vicinity of the older cities here there are many trees bearing seeds, and these large trees, as well as others of good size, are examples of the style of growth of the tree when of mature size. The natural growth of the salisburia is pyramidal. This suggests that it would be well placed along wide avenues where its pyramidal growth would be in keeping with the surroundings. While a tall pyramidal growth is its natural one, there is ample evidence that it can be changed to a more spreading one if desired. A young tree of it of, say, 12 feet in height, has branches of perhaps a foot but are at an angle not varying much from the perpendicular. But cut off the leader of such a tree and at once there is a partial change in the character of it. It begins to be more spreading, and ends in being a very satisfactory spreading tree.

There is a great deal in the salisburia to recommend it. Its pretty leaves, like those of the maidenhair fern in shape, its freedom from all insect attacks, the bright green of its foliage until late in Autumn, when the leaves change to a clear yellow, and the ease with which it can be transplanted, are all in its favor. Altogether the tree is one that can well be called to the attention of prospective customers.

Fruit of Lonicera Morrowi.

Shrubs bearing bright colored berries are much valued by those who have the planting of grounds, there is such a call from the owners of places to or two in length; these are not of horizontal growth, set shrubs that will produce fruit of an ornamental character in late Summer and Autumn. Midsummer displays are not so much valued, as it is so common for everyone to travel at that season.

The call for such shrubs as named is not for ones or twos, as it used to be, but for dozens and hundreds of a kind. These lots are planted all in groups, to produce a great display of the color desired. Among the many shrubs in the list of favorites is the Lonicera Morrowi, one of the bush honeysuckles. Inasmuch as concerns the flowers of this plant, these do not differ greatly from those of some other species of loniceras, but the berries are beautiful, and a shrub when well studded with them, and the berries ripe, is a great attraction. The flowers are yellowish white, the berries red; and how thickly they are often set along the branches is shown in the illustration of a branch of ripe fruit herewith presented.

The berries commence to assume their red color in early Summer, and carry it in good condition until the close of Autumn.

As this and all similar loniceras flower and fruit on shoots of the same season, it is to their benefit to give them a good pruning in the Winter, cutting out old shoots and leaving those of the previous season, from which the flowering ones will some.

Lonicera Morrowi is from Japan. It is a thoroughly hardy shrub, and one that is readily propagated from cuttings of hard wood set out in Spring.

Tamarix Hedges.

The foliage of the tamarix is so small that the shrub makes little display when standing alone and allowed to grow as it will. But it is of a different appearance when pruned in year after year as it is when grown as a border or hedge plant. It is then a pleasing looking plant, the mass of green foliage being particularly refreshing. As seen in the sandy soil of many of our sea coasts its appearance proves its adaptability to these situations. It does not really need the sand. It will grow in any soil, even that of a clayey nature; but that it will thrive in sand is much in its favor. Better than all, though, is the fact of its not objecting to the sea air, as the list of shrubs that will thrive near the coast is no larger than it should be. As a single specimen, or as a hedge, it can be safely recommended to those asking for seashore plants.

Many of the species are so nearly alike that they can hardly be distinguished apart. Time was when the period of flowering enabled one to be fairly sure of the correctness of names, some being Spring blooming and others Autumn flowering, but at the present day, from some mixture of stock, a pp a r-ently, there seems confusion in collections in this respect.

But keep in mind the tamarix when making up a list of seashore shrubs. JOSEPH MEEHAN

BOXWOOD

By the Car Load.

3 feet Pyramids........$1.50 each
5 feet " ....4.00 each
Other sizes at proportionate prices. Every plant a specimen.

HIRAM T. JONES, Union County Nurseries Elizabeth, N. J.

Mention the Florists' Exchange when writing.

LILAC BUSHES

Large blooming, white, fine for cutting: plants from 4-6 ft. high: about 150 of them. This lot will sell cheap on account of removal. Also, a few hundred Peony Roots, large clumps. Write for prices.

RUDOLPH FISCHER, Great Neck, L.I., N.Y.

Mention the Florists' Exchange when writing.

HERBACEOUS PERENNIALS

for Summer and Autumn Planting. We offer NINE HUNDRED and SIXTY-SEVEN VARIETIES of STRONG FIELD-GROWN PLANTS. Send for Catalog and Trade List.

BAY STATE NURSERIES, NORTH ABINGTON, MASS

Mention the Florists' Exchange when writing.

F. & F. NURSERIES

SPRINGFIELD NEW JERSEY

Wholesale Growers

TREES AND PLANTS in full assortment.

Trade Catalogue Free

Mention the Florists' Exchange when writing.

SEASONABLE STOCK FOR FLORISTS

HYDRANGEAS for forcing { OTAKSA and THOS. HOGG } With 7-12 flowering crowns, $12.00 per 100.
" 5-6 " " 9.00 "
" 4 " " 7.00 "

From 6-inch pots and open beds; all out-door grown.

ROSES, Strong, two-years, field-grown, selected for forcing.
HYBRID PERPETUALS........$10.00 and $12.00 per 100.
CRIMSON RAMBLER........9.00 "
DOROTHY PERKINS........7.00 "
and
LADY GAY, a new hardy climbing Rose of exceptional merit; ready now from 2¼ inch pots only. Write for prices.

JACKSON & PERKINS CO.

WHOLESALE NURSERYMEN AND FLORISTS

NEWARK, WAYNE CO., NEW YORK

Mention the Florists' Exchange when writing.

P. OUWERKERK

216 Jane Street

WEEHAWKEN HEIGHTS, N.J.

P. O. No. 1, Hoboken, N. J.

JUST RECEIVED FROM OUR HOLLAND NURSERIES

Rhododendrons, Azaleas, Spiræa Japonica, Lilium Speciosum, Peonies, Bleeding Heart, Pot-Grown Lilacs, Hydrangea in sorts, Clematis and H. P. Roses in the best sorts.

PRICES MODERATE

Mention the Florists' Exchange when writing.

LARGE TREES

OAKS AND MAPLES
PINES AND HEMLOCKS

ANDORRA NURSERIES
WM. WARNER HARPER, PROPRIETOR
Chestnut Hill, Philadelphia, Pa.

Mention the Florists' Exchange when writing.

CALIFORNIA PRIVET

Fine well-graded, two year plants, well packed as follows: 15 to 20 inches, 3 or more branches, $1.50 per 100; $8.00 per 1000, this grade gives good satisfaction.

20 to 30 inches, 6 or more branches, $2.00 per 100; $13.50 per 1000, nice.

1½ to 3 ft., 7 or more branches, $3.00 per 100; $17.50 per 1000, very strong.

3 to 4 ft., strong selected, $4.00 per 100; $35.00 per 1000.

CHAS. BLACK, Hightstown, N. J.

Mention the Florists' Exchange when writing.

Holland Nursery Stock

Ask for Our Catalogue. It will interest you.

ENDTZ, VAN NES & CO. BOSKOOP, HOLLAND

Mention the Florists' Exchange when writing.

Sphagnum Moss and Cedar Poles

Moss, 5 barrel bale, $1.25; 3 bales, $3.25; 5 bales, $5.00; 10 bales, $9.50. Poles, 2 in. butt, 8 ft. long, $16.00 per 1000; 2½ in. butt, 10 to 12 feet long, $22.50 per 1000.

H. H. AKERS, Chatsworth, N. J.

Mention The Florists' Exchange when writing.

Trees and Shrubs

We make specially low prices on nursery stock to Parks, Cemeteries, etc.

Wholesale price list on application.

We carry immense quantities of the finest named varieties of peonies.

PETERSON NURSERY
505 W. PETERSON AVE. CHICAGO, ILL

Mention the Florists' Exchange when writing.

SEND TO
THE MOON COMPANY

For Your { TREES, SHRUBS, VINES and SMALL FRUITS

Descriptive Illustrated Catalogue Free

THE WM. H. MOON CO.
Morrisville, Pa.

Mention the Florists' Exchange when writing.

CHOICE CALIFORNIA PRIVET

4 year; 7 to 8 ft., well branched, $7.00 per 100; 5 to 7 ft., $6.00; 4 to 5 ft., $4.00.

3 year, 3 to 4 ft., $3.00 per 100; $20.00 per 1000; lighter grade, 2 to 3 ft. $10.00 per 1000.

2 year, 2½ to 3 ft., $1.50 per 100; $12.50 per 1000; 1½ to 2½ ft., $1.00 per 100; $8.00 per 1000.

25 at 100 and 250 at 1000 rate. Packing Free.

Cash with order.

ATLANTIC COAST NURSERIES,
OFFICE: 606 4th Ave., Asbury Park, N. J.

Mention the Florists' Exchange when writing.

Specimen Nursery Stock

DECIDUOUS TREES and SHRUBS, EVERGREENS, RHODODENDRONS, AZALEAS, over one hundred (100) acres of the choicest varieties.

Send for price list.

COTTAGE GARDENS COMPANY
QUEENS, LONG ISLAND, N. Y.

Mention the Florists' Exchange when writing.

H. DEN OUDEN & SON,

BOSKOOP, HOLLAND.

Wholesale growers of nursery stock for the American trade. Catalogue free on demand. Also views in our nurseries.

Mention the Florists' Exchange when writing.

VIOLET CULTURE

Price, $1 50 Postpaid

A. T. De La Mare Ptg. & Co. Ltd., New York

Large Assortment **PEONIES** Very best Varieti

LOW PRICES

THE KIND THAT FLORISTS LIKE

"We make a specialty of growing stocky transplanted shrubbery and trees"

FULL ASSORTMENT OF Ornamentals, Fruits, Roses, Clematis, and Herbaceous Plan

Write for our fall wholesale trade list.

W. & T. SMITH CO., GENEVA, N. Y

Mention the Florists' Exchange when writing.

Climbing Clothilde Soupert, Marie Pavie, Crimson Rambler and Dorothy Perkins - - - **ROSES**

Grafted Oranges and Kin Kans, Palms, Biota Aurea Nana, Conifers and Other Stock for Florists and Nurserymen

IN IMMENSE QUANTITIES

400 ACRES IN NURSERIES 60,000 FEET OF GLA

CATALOG ON APPLICATION

P. J. BERCKMANS CO. (Inc.)
FRUITLAND NURSERIES

Established 1856. AUGUSTA, G

Mention The Florists' Exchange when writing.

NEW DEPARTURE
IN
GRAFTING ROSES

SCIONS TO BE FURNISHED BY THE CUSTOMER.

If you are planning to use any quantity of Roses the coming season, write to us for prices. cannot get enough wood from our plants for all of our orders, but our facilities for grafting first-class. Write for prices.

EDW. J. TAYLOR, Southport, Con

Mention the Florists' Exchange when writing.

GRAFTED ROSES

Fine Stock from 3-in. pots.

Richmond, $2.50 per doz., $15.00 per 100, $125.00 per 1000.

Killarney, $2.00 per doz., $15.00 per 100.

Etoile de France, $3.00 per doz., $18.00 per 100.

Kaiserin, Carnot, Uncle John, Chatenay, $2.00 per doz., $15.00 per 100.

Bridesmaid, Golden Gate, Wootton, $2.00 per doz., $12.00 per 100.

ROSES OWN ROOTS

Fine Stock from 3-in. pots.

Richmond, $10.00 per 100; $90.00 per 1000.

Etoile de France, $12.00 per 100.

Sunrise, Perle, Sunset, Chatenay, $8.00 per 100.

Bridesmaid, Golden Gate, $7.00 per 100.

Asparagus Plumosus Nanus from 3-inch pots, $6.00 per 100; Sprengeri from 3-inch pots, $6.00 per 100.

Send for Catalogue.

WOOD BROS., Fishkill, N. Y.

Mention The Florists' Exchange when writing.

ROSES

EXTRA HEAVY IMPORTED HYBRID PERPETUALS

in all leading varieties, per 10 $1.50, per 100 $12.50
CRIMSON RAMBLER........ " 15.00
BABY RAMBLER........ " 17.50

PERENNIAL GARDENS CO., - TOLEDO, O.

Mention the Florists' Exchange when writing.

Queen Beatrice Rose

Four to one shot. Four times as many flowers as Maid.

F. H. KRAMER, 916 F St. Washington, D. C.

Mention The Florists' Exchange when writing.

KOSTER & CO.

Hollandia Nurseries BOSKOOP, HOLLAND

Hardy Azaleas, Box Trees, Clematis, Conifers, Hydrangeas, Peonies.

Pot-Grown Plants for Forcing.

RHODODENDRONS, H. P. ROSES, Etc.

Catalogue free on demand.

Mention the Florists' Exchange when writing.

New Pink Rose
Miss Kate Moulto

Is the QUEEN of all Pink Roses

Write us about it

Minneapolis Floral Co., - Minneapolis, M

Mention the Florists' Exchange when wri

Leedle grown Roses are now B

FLORAL COMP'Y Springfield, O. Expert Growers Send for price list	H. P.'s, H. T.'s, T.'s, R.'s, Cl.'s, B., etc. 101 best sorts, on own roots from 2½ and 4 in pots.	valu the Send wan

Mention the Florists' Exchange when wr

American Beauti

We have them. You want them. W booking orders for early delivery. Fine Write us for price.

ALDRICH FLORAL COMPANY, 26 E. High SPRINGFIE

Mention the Florists' Exchange when wr

DAHLIAS

Now is the time to place your ord Bulbs which will insure you getting n varieties in any quantity; delivery made this fall or early spring.

DAVID HERBERT & S
Successors to L. K. PEACOCK, Inc.
ATCO, N. J.

Mention the Florists' Exchange when wr

CANNA

200,000 STRONG ROOTS

Including the very choicest varieties. Se Price List.

THE CONARD & JONES CO., West Grove

Mention the Florists' Exchange when wr

European Notes.

ain falling incessantly for 56 rs has put a stop to all outdoor rations and enabled the laggard wer to push on his deliveries of s that have been lying in barns ting for a favorable opportunity to them cleaned up. Many of these never seem to realize that their s are needed until the day before ing time, and as they feel that r shooting and Autumn plowing t not be neglected the seed mer- nt has to wait the farmer's con- ence. The fact that there will not much money to take when the s are delivered doubtless has e effect with the grower; in the ntime shipments are delayed.

he damage done to the Italian s of cauliflower by the eruption Vesuvius in April last has caused rgely increased demand for vari- s grown in other countries. As prices for the latter had sunk so during the past two years as to uite unprofitable, and good heads e readily sold at very high prices he Northern markets during the Spring, a very much smaller age was allowed to stand for . The drought has still further uced the crop so that such vari- s as Early London, Early Paris, f Early Paris and Walcheren are ly sold to-day for more than dou- last season's prices. The rise in later and larger Italian varieties not been so great, mainly be- se the merchants have found it essary to prove the strain before ng the seed and thus hold a mod- e quantity of last year's seed. It atisfactory to know that the crop Danish grown seed is very good fairly abundant. Danish cabbage is sufficiently plentiful to satisfy probable requirements.

he death is announced of Mons. Forgeot of Paris whose checkered er is well known to many on your . His attempts to boom Laberger- Solanum Commersonii Violette ld have no doubt been a success for the unfortunate resemblance he tuber to a well known variety S. tuberosum hailing originally n Germany.

EUROPEAN SEEDS.

No attention is paid to inquiries unless accompanied with the names and adresses of senders.

Trouble with Rubber Plants.

(79) My rubber plants were very healthy; suddenly some brown spots appeared on them and in about two weeks the leaves were yellow and falling off. Kindly inform me of the cause and cure if possible. I have always had very good success with ficus before. I enclose some of the diseased leaves. B. R. T.

New York.

—We do not believe the ficus is suffering from any disease at all; the leaves show every indication of having been injured through being subjected to too low a temperature.

Pink Sport of Mrs. M. A. Patten.

(80) We have a pink sport of Mrs. M. A. Patten carnation; same habit and growth as the type; color of Mrs. Lawson. Is there another pink sport of Patten already introduced? C. A. B.

Penna.

—While we believe that the carnation Mrs. M. A. Patten has sported pink at one or two places, we do not think any one of these sports has been as yet introduced to the trade.

Temperature for Bays and Box.

(81) How low a temperature will bays and box in tubs stand with safety? VIRIDIS.

New York.

—Box trees, when well established in the open ground, are perfectly hardy. If they are grown in pots or tubs, they require slight protection to carry them through the Winter. Bay trees should be stored in a shed where the temperature does not go below 38 or 40 degrees; anything lower than 38 degrees is likely to injure them.

Stocks.

(82) Can one grow a second crop of blooms on Ten Week stocks and have them as "fancy" as the first cutting, due care being given to disbudding and to fertilizing? S. E. B.

Mass.

—With careful treatment the stocks will grow a second crop of flowers; and with the help of liquid manure occasionally there is no reason why the later blooms should not be as good as the first crop.

"Little Gem" Heater.

(83) What number of the "Little Gem" hot water heater would heat one-third of the space heated by a number 16 of same make? S. E. B.

Mass.

—Inquire of the manufacturers of the heater named.

LIST OF ADVERTISERS

INDEX TO STOCK ADVERTISED

Contents.

OUR ENDEAVOR

is to place THE FLORISTS' EXCHANGE in the hands of every reader within 1000 miles on Saturday of each week.

In order to effect this even distribution, which makes for the benefit of our advertisers, it is necessary that all advertising copy for current issue should reach us by

12 noon, on Wednesday.

Mention the Florists' Exchange when writing.

THE WEEK'S WORK.

Timme's Timely Teachings.

Begonia Gloire de Lorraine.

It is none too early to begin th propagation of begonias. Exceptional fine stock of Gloire de Lorraine for ne year must spring from early struck le cuttings. There can be no doubt as the superiority of early started plan over those propagated later by rootin side shoots in the usual way, thoug the latter have their uses and are pro ably as valuable as anything express raised for a holiday trade. But whe ever there is a ready market for larg superbly done specimen plants, and effort is to be made to creditably me this demand, recourse must be had early propagation from leaves. This a propitious season for the rooting leaf sets. Steady fire heat from now can be depended upon and exceeding fine material for propagation can had in plenty.

Well-matured leaves, but still of healthy, spotless green, are taken fro the most vigorous plants in such a ma ner as to cause no disfigurement the same. Cutting away the stubby e of the leaf stalk, about half an in below the leaf, is all the trimmi needed. This lower end when insert in the sand, will just bring the base the leaf in close contact with the su face of the sand bed, and when w firmed holds the leaf in a position ve nearly erect, allowing room for quite number of cuttings in a small space.

A steady heat of not less than degrees in the sand with a few degre lower overhead, a somewhat close a moderately humid atmosphere, freque sprinkling and the exclusion of brig sunshine by portable shades, insure good start and healthy headway in ro formation. A muggy atmospher charged with stagnant moisture, ho ever, would soon result in great lo of cuttings by decay, and the vivifyi element of fresh air must therefo never be entirely excluded. It is w to cover the bed with sashes while t house is ventilated, so as to ward draughts or excessive changes in te perature. Such sashes, making the b a regular propagating case, are a gre aid in holding the required degree heat and moisture, if properly manag so as not to forego the benefit of lig and ventilation. Where careful atte tion to these details is not withheld t percentage of loss will be small, a nicely rooted little plants in good numbers will be ready for being pott up in from six to eight weeks. For t first shift small pots and a very lig soil, preferably sandy leaf mold, shou be used, and the plants, after bei potted up, should be placed over botto heat and in a pretty warm house, un well established. A close air at th stage is of little advantage, but a sha ing on bright days should never omitted, being most needful in ear Spring.

While thus providing for a time y far ahead, we must not neglect t duties connected with preparations f the holidays, now close at hand. Mu of the small stock of Begonia Gloire Lorraine, intended for the filling of sorts of plain and fanciful receptacle is now so thoroughly root bound th nothing but a speedy repotting will ke it in proper shape. Such stock, inste of giving it another shift into larg pots, might as well be made up at on into the various styles and forms holiday offerings, even better now th later. It will give the plants time outgrow the effects of the operatio and another step toward having thin ready for Christmas has been made.

Smilax.

It pays to grow smilax, pays be to grow it well; and it is then when requires more in th way of daily atte tion than many other crops we gro If the bed chosen for the purpose deep, richly fertilized piece of solid round in a house easily held at 60 or degrees day and night, and it was ocked with thrifty young plants jas ummer and properly attended to since, one of the preliminary essentials to ccessful smilax culture are wanting. here should now be a fair yield of ood strings, a daily cut right along, the bed is a large one.

Favorable elementary conditions ever fail to promote luxurious rowth, but after it has been called rth, yes, before it ever gains any apreciable headway, it needs the guiding and of the cultivator, needs it at the ery start in the case of smilax. A elay of but a few days in the stringing a smilax bed results in a mass of enngled vines, hard to straighten out d of questionable value for cutting. nd there is really no let-up in the roviding of strings as long as a smilax d is productive and the daily cut of e marketable output encourages vigorus new growth. Heavy trails of wellathered, finely colored smilax are the oods that bring the high price, and ese can only be raised by constant d careful attention to stringing and aining. Vines losing their hold and raying away from their strings must omptly be put back to prevent any tertwining with neighboring vines. All eak and yellowish growth is cut out herever seen. By nipping off the upermost tip of a strong leader, after has reached the desired height, it is ade to push forth delicate side shoots om every joint along the main vine. ntil this has been accomplished the rings of smilax can not be considered eavyweight or first grade. Nor should ey be cut before they have attained at degree of hardiness and durability hich alone renders them fit for shiping and handling.

Smilax is a greedy feeder, and addional nourishment in some form must e held out to sustain vigor and productiveness, even for years if so anned. At this season there is nothing etter in the way of feeding than a ulch of rich compost spread between e plants, this to be repeated from me to time during the Winter. Conderable quantities of water at the ots are needed, but too much of it uses vines and leaves to turn yellow d the latter to drop off. Syringing on right days keeps the air properly arged with healthful humidity and e foliage clean and lustrous, but for bstance in texture and durability of liage the grower must depend mainly judicious ventilation.

Adiantum Cuneatum.

Bench-grown maidenhair ferns selom fail to furnish an abundant crop of e fronds for the increased demand the holidays, if in any way properly anaged. The exercise of ordinary good dgment is especially of value in the rn house at this time of the year. ny bench of Adiantum cuneatum, havg produced up to date an abundant op of cut fronds, must now appear ite bare and well stripped. But if all right and the stock is in a healthful ndition, a closely following new owth should now be in full evidence over the bench. If this is the case, e course of treatment followed until w is only modified by exercising a tle more care in watering for the me being and by the entire removal all shading contrivances. Should the ants, however, be less forward in the aking of a new growth, although arly denuded of mature foliage by nstant close cutting, it is time to put halt to the regular cultural proceedgs. Carrying adiantums safely rough this critical stage at this sean amounts to a bit of skillful maeuvring. Allowing them time for a ort recuperative rest usually sets ings right. At this period, the inrval between two main crops, water ust be given sparingly, though it ould never be entirely withheld. So so should atmospheric moisture be duced to a minimum. The surface il should be allowed to become fairly y by giving it a good stirring or allow hand hoeing, while enough oisture must be present about the ots to maintain crisp sprightliness the plants. Abundant air, light and en sunshine will and in calling forth vigorous new growth. In a very ort time new fronds will be seen ishing upward from all around the d stools. For a while yet sprinkling ill afford all the moisture needed, and t until most of the new growth atins shape and spread should water given in the usual quantities, these accord with the wants of the stock all times. Marketable fronds, should ere still be any on the plants from e preceding crop, should not be cut ntil the new growth has made apeciable headway. New fronds, yet in eir initial stage, are easily ruined by migation. In fern culture it is safest fight disease and insects with flows of sulphur and liquid insecticides.

Sweet Peas.

Benches, cleared of chrysanthemums, not wanted for other stock badly needing the room, might profitably be utilized in the raising of sweet peas for a bounteous crop of flowers in early Spring. It is then when sweet peas under glass are least liable to disappoint the grower. A fine and long lasting crop of flowers at that time may nearly always be looked for with certainty, and in figuring on quick sales and fair prices for the output the grower is seldom mistaken.

The culture of sweet peas in the open during their natural season, or in the greenhouse for an early cut in Winter, is never entirely free of harassing drawbacks, often making it a profitless endeavor. There is no doubt that good flowers would sell at any time and at good prices, but to overcome the difficulties met with in late years in outdoor culture, or to produce the flowers in paying quantities in Midwinter, is no easy task. The only chance in the entire year to make money by growing sweet peas is to sow the seeds now so that they will be in full bearing from early March until May. Very early varieties would begin to flower sooner, but their season is too short, and for a sowing at this time they are not the sorts to choose. The increasing sun heat under glass in early Spring soon discolors or scorches the flowers of these earliest varieties, or they are in so great a haste to form seed pods that the grower can hardly keep pace in picking them off.

In preparing cleared-off chrysanthemum benches for sweet peas it is only necessary to stir the old soil well and to let it dry out once thoroughly. A great depth of soil is not required, would only bring forth an endless, unmanageable luxuriance of flowerless vines, and that is not wanted. Nor should new manure be added to the old soil in which chrysanthemums were grown. If these were of good growth and fairly up in quality, the soil will contain enough latent fertilizing matter to fully meet the requirements of the sweet peas. The house should be kept at about 50 degrees at first, rather lower than higher, to bring about a sturdy vigor in the first stages of growth, assisted by ample ventilation and the clearest light overhead. Much of the hoped for success depends on this. When buds have formed an increase in heat up to 60 degrees is necessary to prevent buds from coming blind and to meet the increase of sun heat during the days of early Spring. From that time until the end of the flowering season the plants use up incredible quantities of water, but must have it to prevent wilting, the least sign of which announces the speedy end of the performance. If ventilation is not too gingerly attended to, but with sufficient care to prevent cold draughts and icy air from ever touching the vines, there will be no trouble from insects, not on sweet peas sown now. Fumigation in light doses, if greenfly is to be routed, will not harm the vines, but it will discolor open flowers and destroy their odor. Heavy tobacco fumes will scorch and shrivel the foliage—a damage very closely approaching total ruin. Insecticides, nicotine or tobacco preparations, applied in liquid form, are less apt to do harm and are fully as effective.

FRED W. TIMME.

W. W. Rawson & Co.'s New Store—Show and Reading Room.

(See Page 620.)

FOUNDED IN 1888

FLORISTS' EXCHANGE

A Weekly Medium of Interchange for Florists, Nurserymen Seedsmen and the Trade in general

Exclusively a Trade Paper.

Entered at New York Post Office as Second Class Matter

Published EVERY SATURDAY by

A. T. DE LA MARE PTG. AND PUB. CO. LTD.

2, 4, 6 and 8 Duane Street,

P. O. Box 1697.
Telephone 3765 John. NEW YORK.

CHICAGO OFFICE: 127 East Berwyn Avenue.

ILLUSTRATIONS.

Electrotypes of the illustrations used in this paper can usually be supplied by the publishers. Price on application.

YEARLY SUBSCRIPTIONS.

United States, Canada, and Mexico, $1.00. Foreign countries in postal union, $2.50. Payable in advance. Remit by Express Money Order Draft on New York. Post Office Money Order or Registered Letter.

The address label indicates the date when subscription expires and is our only receipt therefore.

REGISTERED CABLE ADDRESS:
Florex, New York.

ADVERTISING RATES.

One-half inch, 75c.; ¾-inch, $1.00; 1-inch, $1.25, special positions extra. Send for Rate Card showing discount of 10c., 15c., 25c., or 35c., per inch on continuous advertising. For rates on Wants, etc., see column for Classified Advertisements.

Copy must reach this office 12 o'clock Wednesday to secure insertion in issue of following Saturday.

Orders from unknown parties must be accompanied with cash or satisfactory references.

Obituary

Joseph Baehler.

Joseph Baehler, one of the old-time gardeners of Pittsburg, Pa., died last week in his 78th year. He was born in Laupheim, Wurtemburg, Germany, and came to this country in 1852, locating in Allegheny city where he had lived ever since. He was a grower of bedding plants and stood in the Pittsburg market for many years, and later had a stand in Allegheny market, but retired a few years ago. He is survived by his widow, one daughter, and a step-son.

E. C. R.

Society of American Florists and Ornamental Horticulturists.

Department of Plant Registration.

The H. Weber & Sons Co., Oakland, Md., submit for registration the following:

CARNATION TOREADOR, white, overlaid with deep pink, after the style of Prosperity, but showing more and deeper color, particularly the inner portion of the flower, bounded on the outer edge of petals by a distinct white zone. Flowers fully as large as Prosperity at its best. A strong grower, stems long and extra strong.

CHRYSANTHEMUM, WEBER'S CHADWICK, a yellow sport of Golden Chadwick, much deeper in color than its parent, and several shades deeper than Major Bonnaffon.

WM. J. STEWART,
Secretary.

The National Flower Show.

At a special meeting of the Board of Directors of the S. A. F. O. H., called to consider ways and means for the purpose of the proposed national flower show to be held at Chicago in November 1908, a general committee of fifty was appointed to take charge of the work, under the supervision of the Board, and to undertake the duty of securing the necessary guarantee fund of $10,000. About one-half of this amount has already been subscribed. It is not expected that more than one-half the amount subscribed in each case will be called for, and it is hoped that the show will be made so successful financially that all the amount advanced by subscribers may be returned to them. The general committee has been divided into local sections for special work.

We invite special attention to this excellent movement, which should be liberally supported. The guarantors' risk seems a small one at most; and the general benefit sure to accrue from the exhibition is well worth the hazard.

Chrysanthemum Society of America.

Although interest in this useful organization and its work seems to be increasing annually, still it must, we think, be admitted that such interest has not yet nearly reached the standard which the great service rendered by the society to American chrysanthemum growers merits and should command. The institution of committees for judging seedlings at various points throughout the country has been of incalculable value not only to seedling raisers but to the trade and chrysanthemum devotees generally; for from the decisions of these committees, as they are published from time to time, can be gleaned a good idea of the worth of the novelties submitted for inspection. In fact, in such high esteem are the C. S. A. judgments held by originators of new chrysanthemums in the United States, that seldom, if ever, is a variety introduced into commerce that fails to win the coveted certificate. Such service, if nothing else were done by the organization, entitles it to the support of all who grow chrysanthemums.

It is gratifying to note that the society is to publish an annual report. This should form an additional incentive to growers and others interested to join the association. The important data concerning the origin, introduction, etc., of new varieties, proffered by Mr. Elmer D. Smith, together with the papers read (more of which we hope to see forthcoming at future conventions), brought together in pamphlet form, and distributed to the members, will be worth many times the amount of the annual dues paid in necessary to be the recipient of the document.

We believe with President Duckham that "judicious buttonholing" would result in an increased membership. The various judging committees, as he suggests, might do very effective work along this line at the exhibitions held in their respective centers, at the time when interest in the chrysanthemum is at its height, but there are many other points where shows take place when good service in securing new members could be rendered by those already affiliated with the organization, and who desire to see it progress. Especially should private gardeners and amateur growers be canvassed. The private gardener seems to be taking a very active part in the work of the society, and his endeavor is being recognized and rewarded with presidential honors and election to the most important offices in the C. S. A. This fact should be sufficient to dissociate the society, its objects and work, from the commercialism bogey which has to some extent (but without foundation) militated against representative membership in this as well as in other similar bodies, and should be the means of strengthening the society's ranks from that particular class of chrysanthemum growers.

We hope, too, the time is not far distant when, in addition to the very liberal prizes offered by the C. S. A. at its own annual exhibition, the society will be in a position to donate its medals to be competed for at the principal shows held throughout the country, thus promoting and furthering interest in the special work common to itself and other horticultural organizations, and binding these latter closer to the national society. For this purpose, however, funds are required; and here again increased membership would prove helpful.

Finally, the C. S. A. is doing an important work for American floriculture, a work which, we regret, is not appreciated to its fullest extent by those most benefiting under the society's operations. We have, however, full confidence that by well directed effort the C. S. A. will ultimately "get there;" and our hope in that consummation being reached is not at all lessened because the conduct of the society's affairs has largely passed from the hands of the commercial grower into those of the private gardener—although, we admit, just why this has happened has piqued our curiosity to some extent.

A Fine Point.

What is the proper interpretation of "this season," as applied to the introduction of a carnation or other flower for that matter? Does it mean the year 1906, or does it mean the Fall of 1906; or if placed in a schedule next Spring would it mean the Fall of 1906 and the Spring of 1907 or only the Spring of 1907?

This question came up at the recent show in Chicago. Under the heading "Seedlings and Sports" were offered seven prizes as follows: for best white, red, pink (Daybreak class), pink (Scott class), pink (Lawson class), yellow, and any other color, 20 blooms each. Then, class 134 sweepstakes; best seedling carnation entered in these classes, excluding such varieties as have been exhibited previous to this season, a silver cup. The committee whose duty it was to examine the contributions as to number, etc., and o. k. those that were found correct performed the duties and the judges proceeded with theirs. The sweepstakes cup and first prize in this class were awarded to F. R. Pierson Company's Winsor; and some hours later it was brought to the attention of the executive committee that the Winsor was shown at the meeting of the American Carnation Society in Boston last Spring and so far as the cup is concerned the Winsor was consequently disqualified.

The opinion of exhibitors who have been consulted is that, "this season," in this case would refer to the year 1906; however, that decision is by no means unanimous.

OUR READERS' VIEWS

Stem Rot in Carnations.

Editor Florists' Exchange:

In one of your October numbers I read with great interest Mr. Timme's article on stem rot, and perhaps you may be pleased to hear of a little experience I had lately.

I took charge of this place on July 1, and among other things found some carnations, imported from France last Spring, in a very bad condition. On looking closely, I found they had been planted too deep, so the first thing I did was to repot them properly. But in doing so I was quite surprised to find a whole colony of small worms inside the lower part of the stems. I first washed the roots in lime water, and with a little brush gave the whole stem a good washing with strong tobacco water, planted them in rather light soil, in 6-inch pots. These placed in front of the greenhouse, syringed them carefully every morning, but kept the soil rather dry. Once a week I dusted them over with tobacco. I lost only two plants, and those living have since made a wonderful growth, some having very thick healthy stems, while at the base there is only a bi[t] of bark, as you might say, to feed the plant.

I think that by keeping the soil rather dry, with vigorous syringing every bright day, careful planting, giving the plants plenty of room, along with proper ventilation, they will not be troubled much by disease.

OSCAR E. ADDOR.

"Creations."

Editor Florists' Exchange:

Common people have always thought there is only one Supreme Creator, and leaving oceans of word[s] and quotations from dictionaries aside, they are still inclined to think that. To create means to "produc[e] something out of nothing." Of course, commo[n] people always differ from the more enlightened ones the theoretical and the practical very seldom agre[e]. It is just like scientific horticulture and commo[n] horse sense gardening.

The spade Father Adam used in the Garden o[f] Eden was not up-to-date and much inferior to th[e] ones we have to-day, but both of them are spade[s] pure and simple. I haven't seen a shingle yet read[ing]: "Spade Creating Company," but they surel[y] are entitled to it, as this useful tool couldn't b[e] made any better. But of a good many creations th[e] less said the better; many times I could smell sul[phuric] language from "innocents" who made in[vestments] in them.

What's the matter with Job? Is he dead? If no[t] perhaps he could settle the hash!

Cal. B. FLOSSMANN.

Editor Florists' Exchange:

A joke in sad earnest has been perpetrated upo[n] us. Driven to an anonymous communication, one [of] the few remaining victims of "Burbankitis," in [a] clumsy attempt at disguise, makes a feeble appe[al] for help. Maybe the joke is on him. He may u[n]wittingly have helped to lay bare a secret. He a[p]peals to "Job," and the silence of that caustic cri[tic] "creates" the horrible suspicion that O'Mara may [be] "Job." But isn't "A Fellow Sufferer" absurd? E[...] light-headedness is too natural to be assumed [...] sporadic. No wonder his head swam lately at t[he] spectacle of his friend, the "ustabe" great "creato[r]" being lampooned on all sides. Cheer up, old ma[n], the worst is yet to come.

But we are much obliged to you for putting [us] wise. We are glad to know that it was Burban[k's] "personal volition in the proceedings of creatio[n]" which made this world in Darwin's way. Ple[ase] relieve the suspense and let us know if that inclu[des] the sun, moon and stars?

It is an immense relief to know that "creat[ion] sleeps," i. e., the Burbank brand. May its sleep [be] long and profound! Since O'Mara and the ho[rti]cultural press got "on the job" it has apparen[tly] gone into a deep slumber.

If "A Fellow Sufferer" wants Burbank in the cl[ass] he designates as "three, clause two," he must sh[ow] cause. What scientific, artistic or practical constr[uc]tion has Burbank put together to allow him [to] enter that class?

DICK SHINARY

Editor Florists' Exchange:

This endemic outbreak of "Mal-de-O'Mara" [a]parently so virulent, is not necessarily to be cons[id]ered contagious; indeed the local nature of its o[ri]gin suggests that an application of some suita[ble] emollient at the right time might even have p[re]vented the attack.

There is a peculiar reverse side to it all in [the] fact, which is a matter of record very easily ve[ri]fied, that for many years the Burbank potato w[as] the salvation of parts of Ireland from famine, being the best disease-resister known until th[ey] adopted the use now so general there, of the B[or]deaux Mixture. Would it not be possible that so[me] of Patrick's kith and kin may owe a measure [of] their prosperity to the originator of the Burba[nk] potato?

It has unfortunately been true in the past t[hat] Burbank has been in need of salvation from [his] friends, but his dignified bearing now would [not] indicate that there is any present stress.

E. O. ORPET

Stove vs. Greenhouse Plants.

ditor Florists' Exchange:

I do not think that any decision of the Society ' American Florists in regard to settlement of .e stove and greenhouse plant question will make uch impression on the private gardener, who, in .e majority of cases, is an imported product. Nat- 'ally the terms applied to the different glass ructures are also imported. In England, where .e normal temperature during the Summer aver- ;es from 15 to 20 degrees lower than here, and here many plants have to be grown with artificial at for the greater part of the year, there is more ed for the various terms applied to glass struc- res. However, if the term "stove" is objectionable the American trade, they have the right to dis- rd it if they think that necessary. In the for- ation of schedules where more minute classifica- on of plants is essential, it seems to me that the bject is one which can be treated to better ad- ntage locally. WM. R. THORNHILL.

Influence of Climate in Chrysanthemum Culture.

ditor Florists' Exchange:

I fully agree with Mr. Hill that climate and eather conditions play a powerful part in the de- lopment of the chrysanthemum or any other plant flower. But we do not have to go to England or ance to prove this. For example, Timothy Eaton as not developed enough to be shown or win any izes at shows up to October 15, this season, while former years, this variety was king at every show. e wet, cloudy, retarding season was the cause this. In some sections, where Major Bonnaffon d Col. D. Appleton formerly grew like weeds, ack spot or some fungus destroyed not only the liage, but attacked the buds also. The wet sea- n was the cause.

Weber & Sons, Oakland, Md., are sending all vari- ies a week or two ahead of any other grower into e city markets. The high dry mountain atmos- ere hastens the development.

Convince yourself by planting a batch of Septem- r flowering varieties such as Goacher's Crimson, rrie, Mme. F. Bergmann, etc., outside and another tch inside. The outdoor plants will bloom two eeks and more ahead of the indoor grown, prov- g that the natural, cool outside atmosphere has- ns, and the damp, warm, inside air retards, de- lopment. The grower that puts just a little steam to hasten the early varieties into bloom is tting the opposite result; while one or two degrees frost will open the flowers quicker, without the ast injury to them.

As to selection of buds, I again indorse Mr. Hill's ew; the terminal bud is the safest and will pro- ce the best color on nearly all varieties, with few ceptions. HENRY EICHHOLZ.

ditor Florists' Exchange:

I must say that the results of my observations and perience give me the same opinion as has Mr. ill, pointing out that the date of cutting the first rysanthemum blooms is set by the weather condi- ons which prevail during the month of September. ake for instance the extreme heat which we had om the 10th to the 25th of September of this ar in the vicinity of New York City, which re- rded the opening of the blooms. During the past e years I have received from Europe over fifty rieties, early flowering, not novelties, but old va- eties, which are grown in quantity by market owers and which bloom in the vicinity of Paris early as August 25, always from first crown buds ken in July. These same varieties I have grown pots, in benches, outside and inside, but have ver been able to get a fine bloom before October, d by that time the market is usually supplied with uch better varieties.

The above proves that these failures were due to imatic conditions. L. DUPUY.

ditor Florists' Exchange:

I fully agree with all that E. Gurney Hill has said his very instructive and interesting paper read fore the Chrysanthemum Society of America at its nual meeting recently held in Chicago. Only the esent season I saw some pot plants that had en grown outdoors the past Summer, not from oice, nor because the grower did not know any tter, but because, owing to the rebuilding of me of the greenhouses under his charge there was place for the plants to grow under glass, and, in nsequence of which, many of the flowers were ipples. No matter how carefully and conscienti- sly the man behind the hose administers to the ants of his plants, the same climatic conditions sur- unding them cannot be produced that exist in me parts of Europe and in less degree along the aboard in the United States.

Chrysanthemum culture is making rapid strides this side of the ocean and the end is not yet.

So far as I know a light flimsy material on rollers, at may be rolled up and down at will, to shade e plants during the very hottest part of the day as not yet been used in Amerca. Such a device ght to conserve moisture in the atmosphere to me extent, and surely modify the fierce rays of the n when the atmosphere is clear outside. On a rge area of glass this seems like a big under- king, but I believe it is worthy of a trial. I don't ke lime-wash or anything of a like character that is not under complete control, especially for the sun-loving chrysanthemum.

The properly constructed solid bed has its advantages over benches with some varieties, because a more uniform condition of moisture at the root may be maintained. EDWIN LONSDALE.

Philadelphia.

Renaming American Carnations in England.

Editor Florists' Exchange:

You are doing the Englishman an injustice in claiming that Mrs. W. T. Omwake is a renamed Rose-Pink Enchantress. We introduced our sport of Enchantress through your columns only, under the name of Mrs. W. T. Omwake and sold some stock in England. Our sport is not the dark rose-pink one, but is of a color between those of Enchantress and the rose-pink sport. It is at its best the color which Enchantress should be, as Enchantress in Spring and Fall is too pale. Unfortunately, the past wet season had its influence on our sport, as well as on other sports, so that the color does not come alike, some flowers shading darker, some lighter, which is also the habit of the parent itself; but by careful propagation the shades may be separated.

But England was not guilty of renaming an American variety, in this case, as was claimed on page 602, issue of November 17.

HENRY EICHHOLZ.

Better Packing Methods Needed.

Editor Florists' Exchange:

Perhaps a few words in your valuable aid to florists might be of interest and benefit to shippers of cut flowers. No matter in what town I have been, the cry seems to be always the same concerning poorly shipped or packed flowers. Is it the want of thought, cheap labor, lack of time, or poor growing methods, that stock, especially roses, reaches its destination in such a bruised condition? Only last week our commission man received a box of roses, first and second grades, containing 950, the box being of the same size as one in which a few days previous a shipment of 450 roses, same grade, had been received. What was the outcome? The contents of the first box sold at sight, while the second shipment was literally out of sight, the outer petals of all having turned spotted from sweating and bruising.

This is only one instance. Thousands could be cited, not only in cut flowers, but in plants and rooted cuttings, as every florist can testify, who has to depend on what he buys to supply his trade. Who is the loser? That is plainly seen; but apart from the loss a bad feeling is soon apparent, and discouragement is uppermost, so we buy from here and there in the hope that soon a reliable party may be found to fill all orders satisfactorily.

Bear in mind that I speak after years of practical experience. There are, of course, occasionally a few exceptions to the general rule.

What then is the remedy? A thorough knowledge of the requirements of what is being shipped, in what condition it should be before being packed, and an idea as to how far goods are to go.

First: See that at the final disposition of goods a competent man sees to it that goods are in fit condition to pack; second, that where plants are being shipped, air holes are made in crates, to prevent any heating; third, that where cut flowers are concerned, enough paper should be placed among the blooms to prevent jolting and bruising, and that flowers have enough water in stem to keep them in good condition until unpacked.

Perhaps a few cents extra in the cost of expressage may be necessary; but show me the buyer who would not be willing to pay the difference if he could sell stock when received, rather than send his whole financial outlay to the rubbish heap.

I have no prejudice against any particular party, but consider that as the packing and shipping season is at hand, a word in this manner may be a fitting rebuke to those who, perhaps not aware of the fact, are doing themselves more harm than good. AMBROSE H. SECKER.

American Carnation Society.

Varieties Registered.

By the Chicago Carnation Co., Joliet, Ill.

RED RIDING HOOD, in color, a bright scarlet; in form, a well-built flower, nicely fringed and a well-filled center, with a large calyx that does not burst. Stem long and strong, perfectly straight. In substance, the keeping qualities are of the best; in productiveness, it is early, free and always in crop; in habit, it has strong, clean growth, with wide, heavy grass, establishing itself readily and making a rapid advance.

By The H. Weber & Sons Company, Oakland, Md.

TOREADOR, white overlaid with pink, after the style of Prosperity but showing more and deeper color, particularly the inner portion of the flower, bounded on the outer side of the petals with a distinct white zone. Flowers fully as large as those of Prosperity at its best. A strong, vigorous grower, with no surplus grass, and will stand close planting. Stems long and extra strong. August 1 planting will give first class blooms by October 1.

By J. D. Thompson Carnation Co., Joliet, Ill.

LUCILLE, a large white bloom overlaid with pink, with a long stiff stem.

ALBERT M. HERR, Secretary.

Reflections on Current Topics.

MR. EDITOR:—If the worth of a man's opinions be demonstrated by the demand for such opinions, then may I regard those of myself as having merit—or something else—seeing that I have recently been called "to arms" on several occasions by your readers.

I observe in your columns that I have been the subject of post-prandial particularization at Boston, where one speaker is said to have expressed his belief that I am in a state of innocuous somniferousness. I admit that such a condition has been mine, brought on by a too strenuous and earnest endeavor to read through the proceedings of the recent Dayton convention of the S. A. F. O. H. When I reached the discussion on stove and greenhouse plants, I was completely overcome by Morpheus. Just fancy men like George Watson, an authority on everything horticultural from crab-grass to sparrows, and others equally enlightened, displaying an ignorance on the stove plant subject which the merest tyro who ever donned a greenhouse apron would be ashamed of. Of course, there are stove and greenhouse plants; and "hot air" men, like W. N. Craig and myself, can never be otherwise convinced. The fellows who wouldn't know a stove plant when they see it are always ready to welcome changes or "reforms" in line with the limitations of their knowledge. The true test of a judge's ability is when a so-called difficulty like the one in question confronts him, and the real gardener will never balk when called upon to decide as between stove and greenhouse plants, any more than he would as between carrots and caladiums. As a means of elevating and maintaining the standard of horticultural knowledge, I am in favor of the term "stove plants" being retained in schedules, and would suggest, further, that practical men only be employed as judges at exhibitions.

As to the "O'Mara vs. Burbank" matter, to which a correspondent directs my attention, the only important information disclosed by this almost one-sided controversy is the pietism of Pat O'Mara, and the fact that several of your correspondents occasionally consult the dictionary—an institution that often proves a friend in need. The quibble over the word "creations," while perhaps edifying to sticklers for correct diction, is of but little import generally so long as the "goods" are there. And so far as the learned disquisitions disclose there does not, I think, seem to be much the matter with it as applied by Burbank. Were we certain John Birnie could create the number of geraniums he claims to be able to do, no one would, I imagine, begrudge him the title of geranium creator, and certainly only the most reverent and pious would conclude that John desired to usurp the position of the Almighty who is not a plant propagator. All of us are "creators;" it being only a question of degree as to the position on this mundane sphere we are entitled to assume in this respect. From the number of "creations" discarded by Burbank, he can, I think, be well dubbed the Boss Plant Creator. Where O'Mara comes in here, I have not yet learned.

It seems to me unfair, without a knowledge of the actual facts, to criticise Burbank for having been the creator of the matter that has brought out O'Mara's denunciation and derision. The Californian, still a poor man, I believe, in spite of publicity and pious criticism, shows great wisdom, I think, by remaining silent. Life is too short, and his time, I fancy, too precious, to waste on chasing "the wind;" and I firmly believe that when Pat O'Mara looks into that thoughtful, sensitive face, as pictured in your last week's issue, he, too, will be convinced of the truth of the saw that "silence is golden," when to speak would be of but little avail or valueless.

I have been much interested in the S. A. F. O. H. prize essay contest; and regret, with yourself, that President Kasting's good money should have been all but wasted. There is one point in the first prize paper that, I think, needs elucidation in justice to the wholesale commission cut flower dealer. The essayist, J. Austin Shaw, says the wholesaler should "make such returns (for stock sold) as have actually been received, promptly and honestly." Again, "the wholesaler must establish a reputation for honesty;" "his reputation must be unsullied; his returns prompt and absolutely correct." This harping on "reputation" and "honesty" is apt to create the suspicion that there are "rogues" among the commission dealers, or why keep dinning into those concerned the need of such qualifications as the essayist points out? Does he know of any commission dealer who conducts his business contrary to this preacher's preachments?

In your Boston contemporary's report of the last meeting of the New York Florists' Club, I notice that John Birnie has become a full-fledged piper. That shows that John's "wind" is still intact; but again I express my sympathy with the New Yorkers who suffered, willingly or unwillingly, Birnie's bagpipe infliction. The sufferers are to be complimented on their nerve which stands the strain.

I notice that all the offices, worth having, in the Chrysanthemum Society of America, are now filled by private gardeners—with the exception of that of treasurer, which that efficient official John N. May retains. The trade may well paraphrase Fletcher of Saltoun in this wise: "We care not who run the minor affairs of the C. S. A., so long as we handle its funds." What's the matter with the commercial chrysanthemum grower, these days? Is he down and out as regards the operations of this organization? It looks that way to JOB.

S. A. F. O. H. Prize Essay Contest.

Marketing Plants and Cut Flowers.

Third Prize Paper. M. B. Faxon, Author.

This is a vital question, and on its rational solution depends not only the business success of the large wholesale growers, but also the very existence of the little men with their one, or at the most half a dozen greenhouses. In considering this matter we must have clearly in our minds this fact, that whether a man has one small greenhouse or one hundred large ones, he is a wholesale grower if he sells his product to another man to sell again. In other words, quantity has nothing whatever to do with determining the grade of trade a man is in—it is what he does with his product that settles the question. Growing a vast quantity of stock no more makes a florist a wholesale grower than a man limited to the output of one small greenhouse is a retail dealer. I have tried to give you a clear definition of what I understand the word "wholesale" to mean: otherwise I am afraid what is to follow would have had a mixed meaning to you. The tendeney of the times is toward large establishments, toward consolidation of interests; but whether this is practical, as applied to the subject under discussion, I am very much in doubt. In fact, I think it is not beyond a reasonable limit.

M. B. Faxon

OUR LIMITATIONS.

There is one essential and vital point of difference between an establishment where plants or flowers are produced and a manufacturing business of almost any kind, and it is this—the larger the manufacturing plant, the better should be the product; but as an establishment for growing flowers or raising plants becomes larger and larger, as a rule the product turned out suffers in quality. I fully understand that there are brilliant exceptions to all rules, but that only goes to prove my statement, which I think no practical florist or plant grower will deny. On the other hand, we are all acquainted with some little growers who produce such superb stock that they have established a name for their product that insures its sale the moment it appears in any market, and at the very top price. The point I wish to emphasize here is, that large establishments in our line, if they are large enough, put a limit to quality; while the little grower still imparts to his plants and flowers that individuality which reveals the guidance of the master hand, and gives to his product the hall mark of superb quality. I wish forcibly here to maintain that the little wholesale grower, has, in these years of greenhouse expansion, an opportunity for his quality product to find a lucrative market as never before. This question of amount of stock produced and its quality has a most intimate connection with finding a market for it.

SELLING TERRITORY.

Plants and flowers, owing to their perishable nature, have a limit of territory in which they can be sold and give satisfaction to the buyer. This may be a five hundred mile limit, or it may be much greater; but be it more or less, there is a limit. We have by long custom become so used to this limitation of selling territory that we imperceptibly do our daily business without thinking much, if any, about it. Nevertheless, we have a serious handicap in this respect that dealers in goods not perishable do not have to take into consideration. Now, it being a fact that we have a limited territory in which to secure customers, it most certainly behooves us to study well the needs and requirements of our territory for trade, and cater judiciously to our market, remembering always that ours is a business in which, granting quality and price equal, the retailer will, as a rule, purchase from the nearest grower. It certainly takes business acumen and vigilance of the never-give-up kind to hold what should be the legitimate customers of a grower's territory.

ADVERTISING.

As a business builder for large wholesale plant and flower growers, those of us who are large enough to maintain a selling headquarters and produce an almost unlimited amount of seasonable stock for every day in the year, there is nothing equal to systematic, persistent advertising in the standard trade papers devoted to our business. Advertising is cumulative in its effects; any given amount spent steadily increases your business more and more every year that passes. But it must be supported by honesty and fulfillment of promises. Now in order to be justified in building a business by advertising, especially in cut flowers, a large establishment must be behind the advertising, as otherwise you will sooner or later be receiving continuous daily orders that cannot be filled. And here again is where this business differs from almost all others—you are limited to your own productions. Once sold out you cannot replace like other lines of trade.

WHOLESALE COMMISSION FLORISTS.

A grower who daily has large quantities of cut flowers to find a market for, and yet does not wish to maintain a selling establishment of his own, cannot do better than to entrust a wholesale commission florist with the entire selling of his stock. Now if you expect good returns from your flowers, you must give your commission florist a chance to represent you properly and get you good returns; and the only way to accomplish this is to send all your stock every day in the year to him. Then you will be one of the instrumental elements that go to make his business a success; and if his business is to continue prosperous he must for self-preservation return to you a good price (the market price) for your stock. "You cannot have your cake and eat it, too"—you cannot sell all you can anywhere and to anybody who will pay you a good price, and then send the leavings and culls to your commission man, expecting any return. You will fare by him just as well as you treat him, and no better. Wholesale all your stock through him, and he will make it his business that you receive the fullest measure of value for every flower you grow.

THE SMALL GROWER.

The small wholesale grower of plants and flowers will, on the other hand, do much better to find one or more retail dealers who will handle his product. Especially, if he be a grower of the "superb quality stock," will he encounter no trouble in finding dealers with whom he can contract his entire cut by the year. I have a case in mind where a grower of carnations, with only two small greenhouses and a cut not exceeding a few hundreds a day, has done well and made money by contracting the entire product of his houses by the year. Being a grower of superb stock he can do this without the least trouble, and the extra price obtained always insures a handsome profit. The same method of disposal applies with equal force to the plant product of a small grower—there are always plenty of retail dealers only too willing and ready to purchase well-grown, seasonable plants.

MARKETING THE PRODUCT.

I believe that the best method of marketing our product depends wholly upon the size of the establishment we wish to maintain, and the volume of trade it is our purpose to do. For those of us whose desires are to build a business of the very largest magnitude; that is, one of the mammoth establishments of the present day, there is no way equal to legitimate trade paper advertising. Proper advertising, regularly and persistently followed, will dispose of all the plants and flowers any establishment can produce. For the large grower of cut flowers, who does not wish to maintain an establishment of his own for selling his product, there is no better outlet than through the agency of the wholesale commission florist, as fully explained. Do not think I have forgotten the little grower, for such is very far from the case. I am sure, from personal experience, that in no way can he begin to realize the substantial profits from his labors as by contracting his entire product, both plants and flowers, to some good retailer who has a trade that demands goods of the best quality. For the little grower has no excuse for turning out anything else. Even the larger grower of plants will always find plenty of nearby retail dealers ready to take them. In closing, allow me one word of advice—the best advertising sign a wholesale grower ever puts up in his greenhouses contains these words—"No Goods At Retail."

AMONG THE GROWERS

S. J. Reuter, Westerly, R. I.

A visit to S. J. Reuter's place at Westerly, R. I., is interesting at any time of the year; but as good luck would have it my visit was made last week, and from what I saw there I do not think I could have hit upon a better time. The range of greenhouses is extensive, comprising in all forty houses devoted to roses, carnations, violets, chrysanthemums, ferns and lilies principally, while other stock is also grown in limited quantity. The establishment in its running and equipment is thoroughly up-to-date in every particular, and Mr. Reuter is just the type of grower whom it does a person a world of good to talk and listen to. His place and everything on it are a credit to his industry and to his skill; his enthusiasm in his work is unbounded, and this could not be better illustrated than by quoting his own words in answer to the question as to when he thought he would fill his place with greenhouses. His answer was, "It depends on how long I live. I believe in going ahead. I don't believe there is such a condition as standing still in business; you must either go back or go ahead, and I don't want to go back."

This question, as well as the answer, was called forth when in our tour of inspection we came to the new house recently built. This house is 500 feet long and 35 feet wide, and in connection with it Mr. Reuter's only regret is that he did not make it ten feet wider. Preparations are now well under way for the erection of several mammoth houses like the one mentioned, but instead of being 35 feet they will be 45 feet wide.

The large house is planted with roses, Bride and Bridesmaid exclusively; and the plants from one end of the house to the other were in excellent condition. The flowers seen were also good; especially fine roses are cut from a section where the plants are three years old, but they were replanted this year.

In addition to the house referred to there are a number more planted with roses, and in every one the stock looked clean and thrifty, without a sign of mildew anywhere. The varieties of roses grown are Bride, Bridesmaid, Killarney, Kaiserin Augusta Victoria and Richmond. The latter rose seems to do exceptionally well here.

Mr. Reuter plants nearly all grafted stock, grafting on the manetti, the supply of which he imports from John Palmer & Sons, Annan, Dumfriesshire, Scotland. He does not grow American Beauty, being of the opinion evidently that the other varieties pay better.

While Mr. Reuter's roses, as seen in the hands of the packer, and the appearance of the plants without exception, left nothing to be desired, still I think, on the whole, that carnations were even better. There are seven houses planted exclusively with Mrs. Lawson. These houses are the oldest in the range, consequently not so light as the others. Mr. Reuter finds Mrs. Lawson more satisfactory than any other variety when planted in houses of that character. In one house, 200 feet long, Enchantress were especially fine; blooms with stems over twenty inches long were being cut. The varieties of carnations principally grown are Mrs. Lawson, White Lawson, Queen, Queen Louise, Enchantress, Victory, Harlowarden and Fiancee. Of the latter variety Mr. Reuter said that for quite a while it behaved very well with him, but latterly it began to give evidence of the failing common to it, a fact that he regretted exceedingly, because otherwise he considered it a good carnation. Of Winsor Mr. Reuter has great hopes, in proof of which he informed me that on his recent visit to the F. R. Pierson Company place at Tarrytown, N. Y., he purchased one thousand plants of this variety.

Chrysanthemum Dakoma

Growers, Nathan Smith & Son.

Of chrysanthemums Mr. Reuter grows a very large number, both for cutting and for plants for sale in pots. One house was devoted entirely to chrysanthemum plants in 6-inch pots, all good serviceable stock.

One house, 200 feet long, had the center bench filled with Lilium Harrisii in pots, looking well and at a stage that leads Mr. Reuter to expect to be cutting and shipping before Christmas. Several houses are in part given up to nephrolepis in variety. I noticed in particular a wide bench in one house planted with N. Whitmanii, and every plant was perfect and in condition for a 6-inch pot. Mr. Reuter is very much taken with this variety, because of his expressed belief that there is "money in it." Nephrolepis elegantissima is also grown largely.

In a house of smilax and Asparagus plumosus I observed that along the edges of the benches on both sides, the entire length of the house, callas in pots were placed and doing exceedingly well. Princess of Wales violets promised well. Sweet peas looked quite natural and at home in a house close by; the Christmas flowering variety is grown exclusively. Mignonette was in good condition for use. Primulas in another house looked fairly well.

A recent addition to the equipment of the establishment is a cool store-house. Here among other things were a thrifty lot of azaleas lately purchased.

Mr. Reuter markets his product in Boston, New York and Philadelphia.

D. M.

Rawson & Company's Novelties.

. W. Rawson & Company, Boston, Mass., are devoting much time to the introduction of speties such as new gladiolus and dahlias. Some the exclusive introductions for the coming season : GLADIOLUS HARVARD, of a rich maroon or, giant size, measuring 6 and 7 inches across, m 6 to 8 flowers on a spike which grows to a ght of four feet. The flowers are gracefully arged along a slender waving stem.

HOW DAHLIA GOVERNOR GUILD; snowy te, without even the least suggestion of any other de either at base of petal or center of flower. flower is full and round, built loosely of most uisitely fluted petals. The spread of the flowers ive inches.

HOW DAHLIA EDWARD LE FAVOUR; deep shading to a most pleasing pink. The flowers perfectly globe-shaped, measure four inches and r, and are produced in great abundance on bushy nts four feet high.

ECORATIVE DAHLIA FIREBURST; probably largest decorative dahlia extant. It is a seedling Le Colosse, has broader and longer petals, is more ly built, but of a far more intense scarlet, slightshaded orange, and produces specimens which asure eight inches and over.

ECORATVE DAHLIA THE NORTH SHORE; of dium size; petals broad at base but taper to a y sharp point; flowers five inches across, rich roon tipped scarlet—a distinct new color. Excelt for cutting.

ECORATIVE DAHLIA MRS. STUYVESANT SH; rich deep amber. The first decorative dahlia this color. The flower is often seven inches in meter, perfect in formation, very double; petals medium broad and gracefully curved. The nts grow four feet high and with fair treatment duce masses of flowers quite early in the season.

ECORATIVE DAHLIA W. W. RAWSON. Conering the formation of this flower, it appears be a cross between Grand Duke Alexis and s. Roosevelt and is superior to both. It has own off the stiff formation of the first, retained more flatly fluted petal of the latter, but imved the appearance by being more compact, as it tains more petals to the individual flower. The om is well built up, perfectly round and double. measures six to seven inches in diameter. The or is white overlaid with amethyst blue; each al of the flower being completely colored gives the ole bloom the appearance of a most fascinating ender.

FANCY DAHLIA MRS. GORDON ABBOTT; a giant size, and distinct in coloring, several specimens t Fall measuring from tip to tip five and a half hes. The color is brightest golden, mottled, ckled and striped intense scarlet. The flowers are ll formed, very full and double.

Chrysanthemums at Shaw's Garden.

For the fortnight ending with the 24th there has en in St. Louis a rather novel chrysanthemum ow, differing in a number of respects from the ual exhibition known by this name all over the untry.

"Shaw's Garden," or the Missouri Botanical Garn as it is properly called, is very well known as scientific establishment of international reputation d a place worth seeing by every visitor to St. uis. It has also won recognition as a place to ich florists may turn for information or carry eir professional troubles with the certainty of getg willing help. But comparatively few people tside of St. Louis know that for several years st it has vied with the florists' clubs and hortiltural societies of other large citites in staging rysanthemums on a large scale. In 1904, without pairing its own exhibit, the garden easily won the st prize for chrysanthemums in number and variy at the national flower show that was held in e horticultural building of the World's Fair, even e Japanese exhibit falling behind it.

These Botanical Garden exhibitions differ from ornary chrysanthemum shows in several respects. e plants are all grown by the garden itself; they e not confined to commercially profitable varies; they are arranged so as to represent the varis chrysanthemum types instructively, and as cut wers are not used, their arrangement is made ghly artistic. Perhaps the greatest difference lies the fact that they are absolutely free to the blic.

This year the chrysanthemums were displayed in large circular tent, nearly a hundred feet in diamer, covering a large part of the parterre or sunk- garden just within the main entrance, and the ants were plunged in the beds that a little later ll be planted to tulips for Spring blooming. This rangement in turf-bordered beds, separated by m well-drained walks, has made seeing them a light to visitors, who have thronged the tent notthstanding unprecedentedly inclement weather. r a part of the first week a dense blanket of oke hung over the city, and offices and even street cars were kept lighted for a good part of the day. To meet this emergency, which reduced all of the flowers to a uniform cherry color, electric lights were installed, and the directors of the garden took advantage of this circumstance to throw the tent open to the public during the evenings—a concession which has never before been made in the history of the garden, and which has enabled a very large number of busy men and women to see the flowers when they could not have done so during the daytime.

Everyone who has had to stage chrysanthemums knows how hopeless the first plant—or the first half dozen plants, even—looks when it is moved into place bly named and all worked into as great harmony of color as the entire gamut of chrysanthemum color allows. The primitive yellow Chrysanthemum Indicum and the very similar but later blooming "Golden Chain" variety have attracted a good deal of interest in contrast with the mammoth heads of the best trade varieties in all shades of white, yellow and red. As usual, a grafted plant occupied a prominent place, and attracted the attention of curiosity hunters; and in a sense this was justified by the plant itself, for it had been surrounded by potted plants of the 25 varieties to be grafted on it, and these were allowed to grow on their own roots until the inarching was completed, so that their

W. W. Rawson — Mrs. Stuyvesant Fish

Fireburst — Governor Guild

W. W. RAWSON & COMPANY'S NEW DAHLIAS.

in a hall. It was the same when the first specimens were set in the big tent, though they were large enough to make it necessary to take off roof sections of the houses they had been grown in, in order to get them out; but for all this, the tent has been full to overflowing with superb, single-head, bush and standard grown specimens, to the number of over 3,000 and representing over 300 varieties, each legi- flowers, instead of being starved as grafted flowers often are, were of normal size and perfection.

One good effect of the botanical exhibition is that the florists of the city have begun hustling for a fine flower show next year, and are talking of a $10,000 guarantee fund, to be raised in the course of the Winter, so as to ensure an unusually good exhibit next Fall.

EXHIBITIONS

Baltimore, Md.

The annual chrysanthemum show and horticultural exhibition of the Gardeners' Club of Baltimore was held at the new building of the Florists' Exchange on November 13, 14, 15 and 16, the first and second floors of the building being utilized. The judges were William F. Gude, Peter Bisset, and Otto Bauer, of Washington, D. C. On Tuesday, November 13, a banquet was given in honor of the visitors and judges at the Academy Hotel, the visitors praising the exhibition and complimenting the Florists' Exchange on its beautiful new building.

The display of foliage and exotic plants in conjunction with the chrysanthemums, roses and carnations was very effective. Mrs. T. Harrison Garrett, Mrs. Henry Barton Jacobs, Halliday Brothers, and I. H. Moss sent many decorative plants which materially aided in bringing out the effect produced.

Notable features of the show were a complete collection of large sized fancy-leaved caladiums exhibited by Mrs. T. Harrisson Garrett, Chas. Uffler, gardener; an immense specimen of Begonia Haageana in full bloom, by George Morrison, gardener to Mrs. H. B. Jacobs; the standard and single stem chrysanthemums in pots exhibited by Mr. C. R. Diffenderfer, C. M. Wagner, gardener, and the exquisite designs made by F. G. Burger.

Three new unnamed roses were shown by John Cook; these give great promise. Henry Fischer had on exhibition fine specimens of Nephrolepsis Whitmanii. R. Vincent, Jr. & Son displayed a choice collection of pompon chrysanthemums which were much admired. Roses were well shown by Stevenson Brothers, A. Anderson, George Morrison, John Cook, Wm. Madsen and I. H. Moss.

The carnation exhibit was also very good. Stevenson Brothers, Govanstown, Md., exhibited their new seedling Debutante, which shows up exceptionally well under artificial light; in color it is a shade between those of Mrs. Frances Joost and Mrs. T. W. Lawson.

Mr. Hannigan, gardener to Mr. Jas. A. Gary, G. A. Lotz, George Morrison, Edwin Bishop, Ed. Herrmann, F. C. Bauer, I. H. Moss, Halliday Brothers, and Feast & Sons exhibited chrysanthemums.

Among the prize winners were G. A. Lotz, who took the Franklin Davis Nursery Company premium for 25 chrysanthemums, 5 varieties; also the Waterer prize for 12 blooms, and the Michell prize for 12 Dr. Enguehard. Ed. Herrmann and C. M. Wagner were also winners in these classes. In the 12 classes, George Morrison, Ed. Bishop, F. C. Bauer, and I. H. Moss took most of the premiums, and in the 6 classes George Morrison, I. H. Moss and John Cook were successful. G. A. Lotz took the prize for 25 blooms in 25 varieties; also for the sixes of white and yellow seedlings. R. Vincent, Jr. & Son captured the Ferguson prize for pompons.

For roses, Stevenson Brothers were first for Richmond, also for 25 pink. Andrew Anderson and William Madsen were first for 25 white and 25 Golden Gate, respectively.

In the carnation classes, D. B. Welsh, George Morrison and Stevenson Brothers were the winners.

The prize for 50 blooms, pink, one variety, was won by F. R. Pierson Company, Tarrytown, N. Y.; also for 12 blooms pink.

F. C. Burger was the winner of all the premiums for designs.

Columbus, O.

The second annual chrysanthemum show of the Columbus Florists' Club was held Tuesday afternoon and evening, November 13. While the exhibition was held later than had been intended, owing to the club's moving its headquarters, it turned out to be the very best date that could possibly have been selected, as all the chrysanthemums in this section are unusually late in finishing this year. Our exhibition was an unqualified success; the exhibits were all of the finest quality, and better still there was a large attendance of members and their friends to see them. Besides being our chrysanthemum show, last Tuesday evening was also our house-warming in our new rooms in the Brent Building; and in honor of the occasion the committee of arrangements had arranged a musical program also for the evening.

The first prize for six exhibition blooms, in three varieties, was awarded to the Fifth Avenue Floral Company, for Timothy Eaton, W. H. Chadwick, and Golden Wedding; all these blooms were perfectly finished and of very superior quality. In this same class E. Metzmaier was second with Alice Byron, Golden Chadwick, and W. H. Chadwick; John H. Williams with Major Bonnaffon, Modesta, and Philadelphia, came third. These three fine yellows were much admired. In the next class the highest award, for three cut blooms in three varieties, went to E. P. Torrey for Miss May Seddon, Souvenir de Montbrun, and Merza; three better blooms were not

Chrysanthemum Mrs. G. A. Lotze

Grower, G. A. Lotze.

in our show. Miss May Seddon is the daintiest of pure whites, with narrow bevel or slightly reflexing petals; in fact, it is of the general type of Nellie Pockett. Souvenir de Montbrun is a most beautiful incurved cream-yellow, with just a line edge of purplish-red. Merza is grand; all the craft here are enthused over its beautiful finish and dainty form. The second prize for three blooms went to the Fifth Avenue Floral Company, for Timothy Eaton, W. H. Chadwick, and Yellow Eaton.

Of cut blooms, to be judged by the commercial scale, there were four classes. The first class was for six blooms, cut from three plants; in this class John H. Williams was first with Major Bonnaffon, and for commercial purposes this splendid yellow is unsurpassed. The scond prize went to E. Metzmaier for Golden and W. H. Chadwick; and W. H. Chadwick secured the third award for the Fifth Avenue Floral Company. This variety fully repays the extra trouble required to grow it, for it is by no means an easy doer; its size and color are both magnificent. The next commercial class was for two blooms cut from one plant, and the Franklin Park Floral Company, with two elegant W. H. Chadwick, was first; the second prize going to the Fifth Ave-

Chrysanthemum 34-3-05

Growers, Nathan Smith & Son.

nue Floral Company for the same variety. The third commercial class was for nine blooms cut from three plants, and with Golden and W. H. Chadwick, E. Metzmaier was first; the second prize went to John H. Williams with Major Bonnaffon. The last class to be judged by the commercial scale was for three blooms cut from one plant, and again the beautiful W. H. Chadwick secured both the prizes; Sherman Stephens taking first, and the Fifth Avenue Floral Company the second award.

The special prizes offered by Graff Brothers and M. B. Faxon brought out the very keenest competition. Graff Brothers' prize was for the best dozen blooms in the show, to be judged by the commercial scale. The committee awarded this prize to the Franklin Park Floral Company for six Golden Chadwick and six W. H. Chadwick.

The M. B. Faxon prize was for the best vase of five cut blooms of any variety, to be judged by the commercial scale; to decide who was entitled to this award was no easy task, as all the entries were of the most splendid quality and finish. The award was made to the Fifth Avenue Floral Company, for five superb W. H. Chadwick.

The Livingston Seed Company received honorable mention for a splendid collection of cut blooms; among this collection the following sorts attracted special attention: Lord Hopetoun, Merza, Alice Byron, Major Bonnaffon, W. H. Chadwick, Golden Chadwick, Yellow Eaton, Dr. Enguehard, Timothy Eaton, Golden Wedding, and a number of other fine varieties; all the blooms in this collection were perfectly finished. C. A. Roth also staged a very large number of cut blooms, which included some elegant Golden and W. H. Chadwick, Yellow and Timothy Eaton; honorable mention was the award. Sherman Stephens also was given honorable mention for his splendid vase of exhibition flowers; he arranged them especially artistically, and they attracted much favorable notice. The committee wishing to particularly call attention to the superb Dr. Enguehard blooms staged by the Franklin Park Floral Company, attached highly commended to them.

The committee on awards was composed of M. B. Faxon, Samuel Graff, and T. A. Sexton, A. M. Hills, John H. Williams, and Edward Helfrich arranged the show in all its details; and R. A. Currie was manager of the exhibits. The show was a credit to the Columbus Florists' Club and the exhibitors.

F. W.

Houston, Tex.

The Faith Home Association of Houston, Texas, held its thirteenth annual chrysanthemum show at Turner Hall, November 13, 14 and 15. There were quite a number of new exhibitors this year; while on the other hand, some of the out-of-State growers who had made elegant displays in former years did not materialize on this occasion. The largest and most successful exhibitors were J. W. Vestal & Son of Little Rock, Ark., and as they had but little competition they carried off all the prizes for which they entered. Their displays were exclusively in cut blooms, which were of a very high order, embracing some of the new and popular varieties as follows: T. Richardson, Matchless, Antonio Marmonet, Mrs. Swinburn, Souvenir de Countess Reville, Helen Bloodgood Madam Delitze, G. Talbert, Wm. Duckham, O. P. Bassett S. T. Wright, Col. D. Appleton, Dr. Enguehard, Silver Wedding and a few others of the older varieties.

Among the new exhibitors was W. A. Hawkins of Houston Heights, who did not enter for competition. Among other good blooms displayed by him was noticed especially the old variety, Julia Scaramanza, which seems to be very little grown of late, though it is certainly, in the opinion of the writer, as good or better in the bronze or old gold class than any similar variety yet advanced since its time. It is unfortunate that this splendid artistic old favorite should be so sparsely cultivated at the present time.

Mrs. S. E. Byers, one of Houston's pioneer florists, gave valuable assistance in an artistically arranged collection of palms, ferns, crotons and other foliage plants for which first prize was awarded. In the class for Texas growers only, Chas. Ehlers, florist, won easily in each of ten blooms, white, yellow, pink and the best bloom any color. He displayed some white Timothy Eaton and Dr. Enguehard that were equal to any in the hall. Mrs. H. Kaden of Gainsville, Tex., was another successful exhibitor who had not shown in Houston before, and won one of the prizes in the cut bloom competition. Wm. Kutchbach and Robert Leupke, florists, Houston, each made a very creditable display, but did not enter for competition. Mr. Kutchbach's Col. D. Appleton, bush plant in bloom, was one of the finest types of plant culture ever exhibited here, and was a source of much pleasure to all visitors. Mr. Ehlers's display of palms, ferns, and other foliage plants was exceptionally well done and there was no trouble in giving it first prize.

The exhibits in the cut bloom class were very artistically displayed on white covered tables arranged to form a Greek cross reaching near to the entire extremities of the hall, and made a very pretty effect as the center piece of the decoration as a whole. The exhibits were so systematically arranged that the work of judging was reduced to a minimum, and Mr. Preussner of Galveston, who placed the awards, seemed to give entire satisfaction.

The attendance on the show was at times most gratifying though there were many counter attractions in the city during the time, it being carnival week when all of South Texas assemble for a gala time.

S. J. MITCHELL.

Dobbs Ferry, N. Y.

The sixth annual flower show of the Dobbs Ferry Gardeners' Association was held November 11 and 12. The net proceeds of this exhibition are always donated to the local hospital, and this year some $300 was realized for this purpose.

In addition to the displays made by the local gardeners, the Cottage Gardens, Queens, N. Y., sent a fine showing of seedling carnations. Scott Brothers, of Elmsford, N. Y., and F. R. Pierson Company, Tarrytown, N. Y., were also exhibitors. Among the prize winners were S. Bradley, J. Bradley, H. Kastberg, Thomas Lee, R. Boreham, Mr. Macrea, J. Howorth, J. Hogleson, H. Kieling, A. Kneifel, and others. The judges were Messrs. Scott of Elmsford and McFarland of Tarrytown. Their decisions gave entire satisfaction. The committee of arrangements comprised C. Wilson, manager, H. Kastberg, secretary; J. Dunbar, treasurer.

Chrysanthemum Society of America.

President Duckham has announced the committees to examine seedlings and sports on dates as follows: November 24, 1906.

Exhibits to receive attention from the committees must in all cases be prepaid to destination, and the entry fee of $2 should be forwarded to the secretary not later than Tuesday of the week preceding examination, or may accompany the blooms. Special attention is called to the rule requiring that sports, to receive a certificate, must pass three committees.

NEW YORK.—Eugene Dailledouze, chairman, care of New York Cut Flower Company, 55-57 Twenty-sixth street; William Turner, Thomas Head.

PHILADELPHIA, PA.—A. B. Cartledge, chairman, 1514 Chestnut street; John Westcott, Wm. K. Harris. Ship flowers in care of the chairman.

BOSTON, MASS.—E. A. Wood, chairman; Wm. Nicholson, James Wheeler. Ship to Boston Flower Market, care of the chairman.

CINCINNATI, O.—R. Witterstaetter, chairman; James Allen, Wm. Jackson. Ship to Jabez Elliott Flower Market, care of janitor.

CHICAGO, ILL.—J. S. Wilson, chairman; J. B. Deamud and George Wienhoeber. Ship care of J. B. Deamud, 51 Wabash avenue.

The official scales of the C. S. A. are as follows:

For Commercial Purposes		For Exhibition Purposes	
Color	20	Color	10
Form	15	Stem	5
Fullness	10	Foliage	5
Stem	15	Fullness	15
Foliage	15	Form	15
Substance	15	Depth	15
Size	10	Size	35
Total	100	Total	100

DAVID FRASER, Secretary.

Pittsburg, Pa.

Fancy Dahlia Mrs. Gordon Abbott
Introducers, W. W. Rawson & Co., Boston.

Work of Committees.

CHICAGO, November 10.—Miss Clay Frick (white sport of William Duckham) exhibited by C. H. Totty, Madison, N. J., scored 91 points, commercial scale.

Mlle. E. Chabanne, pink; exhibited by E. G. Hill Company; scored 89 points, commerical scale.

Incandescent, bronze and gold; exhibited by E. G. Hill Company; scored 86 points, commercial scale.

Mlle. Semon Jossier, cream white, incurved; exhibited by E. G. Hill Company; scored 89 points, commercial scale.

Dubuisson Foubert, light yellow, reflexed; exhibited by E. G. Hill Company; scored 87 points, exhibition scale.

Alice Roosevelt, cream white; exhibited by E. G. Hill Company; scored 89 points, commercial scale.

Detroyat, silvery pink, reflexed; exhibited by the E. G. Hill Company; scored 89 points, exhibition scale.

NEW YORK, November 10.—General Pecquart, lilac silver reverse, Japanese incurved; exhibited by Howard Nichols, Yonkers, N. Y.; scored 85 points, commercial, and 85 points, exhibition scale.

PHILADELPHIA, November 12.—Sadie May Stremler (sport of Queen) light yellow; exhibited by J. S. Stremler, Princeton, Ky.; scored 84 points, commercial scale.

PHILADELPHIA, November 17.—Golden Dome (sport of Yellow Eaton) yellow, Japanese incurved; exhibited by John A. Macrae, Providence, R. I.; scored 89 points commercial, and 86 points exhibition scale.

NEW YORK, November 17.—Golden Dome (sport of Yellow Eaton) a decided improvement on parent both in color and form; exhibited by John A. Macrae, Providence, R. I.; scored 89 points, commercial scale.

CINCINNATI, November 17.—No. 34-3-05, Daybreak pink, Japanese incurved; exhibited by Nathan Smith & Son, Adrian, Mich.; scored 83 points, commercial scale.

DAVID FRASER, Secretary.

New Chrysanthemums.

At the regular monthly meeting of the Pittsburg and Allegheny Florists and Gardeners' Club, Tuesday evening, November 6, there was a very beautiful display of chrysanthemum flowers, both from home and distant growers. Prominent among all stood forth a group of new varieties, magnificent blossoms, from the E. G. Hill Company, Richmond, Ind. So strikingly fine were these that a special committee was appointed to report on them. John W. Jones, the president of the club, being chairman of it; the other members were: P. S. Randolph, Robt. Chive and William Falconer.

Grandest of all the blooms was Detroyat, a clear pale pink; lights up beautifully in night light; very large. Mr. Randolph declared it is the best pink chrysanthemum he ever saw. Others were: Mme. L. Roussel, incurved golden bronze, very large and full; one of the finest of its color. Mme. G. Rivol, bronzy pink, large, full, solid; a good commercial flower. M. Pechon, golden yellow, full, open flower; good for private growers. Mrs. George Beech, incurved golden yellow, very full and fine, reminding one of Major Bonnaffon. M. Georges Truffaut, clear yellow, incurved, very full, fine commercial or otherwise; paler in color but style of Bonnaffon. Marie Viullermet, clear, pure white, somewhat flat, suggestive of Silver Wedding but larger. Dubuisson Foubert, warm yellow, very large, very full of petals, paler than but suggestive of Golden Wedding. Fine for private growers. Mlle. Suzanne Gauthier, very white, reflexed narrow petals but globular-shaped head, later than the others. Beatrice May, pure white, very large and full, fine stem and good foliage. Amateur Consiel, a very fine bold, velvety crimson, full headed flower, with excellent stem.

Chrysanthemum Dakoma.

Our illustration shows a single bloom of bronze Chrysanthemum Dakoma, originated by Nathan Smith & Son, Adrian, Mich., which, although not certificated, that firm has decided to disseminate on the variety's merits. They say "its strong stem, large, high, rounded flower, and its decided bronzy color will make it very useful in the vase classes of 25 blooms and over."

THE GLADIOLUS AS AN ANNUAL.—Commencing on the Præcox strain of gladiolus announced by a German firm as flowering the same season from seed, Dr. Van Fleet says, in the Rural New Yorker: "Most raisers of gladioli find precocious individuals among their seedlings, but it is the usual experience that they are of little decorative value as compared with those coming on the second and third years. Varieties of the Lemoinei section, the offspring of Gladiolus purpureo-auratus, are more disposed to bloom quickly from seeds than the descendants of other species, and we are informed the Præcox strain is largely made up of such sorts. We have for many years secured blooms within a year of sowing from seedlings of the most diverse parentage, by planting under glass in October, drying off the little corms the succeeding March, and planting outside in May. Abundant blooms follow, usually beginning in July, but this method imitates nature in that there are two periods of growth, with a resting period of several weeks between while the new German kind is supposed to grow continuously until it flowers and seeds."

New Gladiolus Harvard
Introducers, W. W. Rawson & Co., Boston

The New President of Mass. Hort. Society.

Stephen M. Weld, the newly elected president of the Massachusetts Horticultural Society, is a well known cotton merchant, lives on a fine estate in Dedham and is very fond of horticulture, and has been interested in the society for many years and a frequent exhibitor at its flower shows. He has never held office in the society before.

Born in Jamaica Plain on January 4, 1842, Mr. Weld received his education at Harvard. After graduating, he enlisted as a soldier and early in the rebellion became an aide on the staff of General Horatio G. Wright, serving later on the staffs of Generals Reynolds and Newton. In January, 1862, he was made second lieutenant of the 18th Massachusetts, and in 1863 lieutenant-colonel of the 56th Massachusetts, his appointment as colonel coming in May, 1864. He fought at Hilton Head, Port Royal, was at Petersburg, and went through the campaigns of the Wilderness and of the Army of the Potomac. Captured twice by the rebels, at Gaines Mills and at the mines, he ended his service in 1865 with the brevet of brigadier-general, having made one of the most brilliant records of the rebellion. After his return from the war, General Weld amassed a fortune in the woollen and cotton industry.

Plant Breeding.

Among the standing committees of the American Breeders' Association is one on carnations, composed of Chas. W. Ward, Queens, N. Y., chairman; Peter Fisher, Ellis, Mass.; Fred. Dorner, Lafayette, Ind., and Richard Witterstaetter, Cincinnati, O. The duties of this committee are (1) to investigate and report on methods and technique of improving carnations by breeding; and (2) to encourage the production of new carnations.

There is also a committee on breeding roses, composed of E. G. Hill, Richmond, Ind., chairman; M. H. Walsh, Woods Holl, Mass.; Luther Burbank, Santa Rosa, Cal.; and Fred. Dorner, Lafayette, Ind. The duties of this committee are (1) to investigate and report on methods and technique of improving roses by breeding, and (2) to encourage the production of varieties of roses to meet the many conditions of climate, soil and greenhouse, or fashion and market.

Chrysanthemum Mrs. G. A. Lotze.

Our illustration shows a bloom of the new white chrysanthemum Mrs. G. A. Lotze, originated by G. A. Lotze, Glen Burnie, Baltimore, Md. The new variety is the result of a cross between Alice Byron and Nellie Pockett. It has been certificated by the C. S. A., scoring 90 points. It has also been awarded premiums at Madison, N. J., and Baltimore shows, at the former for best seedling, and at the latter in the class for best six white.

New York.

The Week's News.

This is horse show week in New York, and there is a most creditable absence of boots and saddles and borrowed plumes in the retail show windows. It would seem that the time has passed when retailers make special displays for this annual event. It is believed, however, that there will be many social affairs following the show that will create a demand for elaborate floral decorations.

Rickards Brothers, 37 East Nineteenth street, since taking over the store and business of the Bridgeman Company, have remodeled the entire premises and have met with unqualified success.

Frank Millang, wholesale florist of 55 West Twenty-sixth street, had the misfortune to sprain his ankle and break one of the small bones in his foot several days ago. He is progressing favorably towards recovery, and will be able to attend to business shortly. In the meantime the business is being carefully looked after in all details by his efficient force of help.

The retail business conducted by Josephine Joslin at 2603 Broadway has been sold to one of the pushing Greek florists of the city.

A special meeting of the stockholders of the Cut Flower Exchange will be held in the offices on the third floor of the Coogan building, corner Sixth avenue and Twenty-sixth street on Saturday, December 1, at 9 a. m., for the purpose of making some amendments to the by-laws of the organization. There will also be a meeting of the Board of Directors the same morning at the same place.

In our report of the chrysanthemum show of the Morris County (N. J.) Gardeners and Florists' Club, held at Madison, N. J., on Thursday and Friday, November 1 and 2, we made an error in crediting the winning in the class for twelve chrysanthemums in twelve distinct varieties, stem not to exceed twelve inches, to James Fraser. We should have stated that J. Downing, superintendent of the Brooklawn Farms, Madison, N. J., won the first prize in this class, J. Fraser being second.

Charles H. Totty, who after attending the chrysanthemum show at Chicago journeyed to Denver, Colo., returned to his home in Madison, N. J., last Sunday.

C. B. Weathered is in Rochester this week on a business trip.

The Hodgson Company, florists at Fifty-sixth stret and Fifth avenue, had an elaborate decoration at the home of Mrs. H. Weatherby on the 15th inst., the occasion being the coming out of a daughter of Mrs. Weatherby.

Mr. and Mrs. M. A. Merin of Rye, N. Y., celebrated their silver wedding on Thursday, November 15. Mr. Merin is a landscape architect, and previous to his establishing himself in Rye he was employed in the park department of New York City.

There must be all-powerful thorns on Pittsburg roses. Monday's papers relate that an operatic singer foiled a desperate highwayman with the thorns on her bunch of roses.

Thanksgiving Day comes next Thursday, and from present indications there will be an ample supply of everything in the cut flower line.

David D. Howells, formerly superintendent at Windyhoul, Beaver County, Pa., has been appointed general superintendent at Laurelton Hall, Long Island, the estate of L. C. Tiffany, Esq.

Paul and Henry Dailledouze, of the firm of Dailledouze Brothers, Flatbush, Brooklyn, visited the recent flower show in Chicago, and then took a trip to Denver, Colo. The brothers Dailledouze are now on their homeward journey. A call was made at the Dorner establishment, Lafayette, Ind.; and on Wednesday they were visiting the craft in Cincinnati, O., and are expected home in a day or two.

The New York Sun printed a paragraph on Wednesday, stating that Paul and Henry Dailledouze had purchased the new carnation Winona from Dorner & Son, at a price believed to be more than $15,000; but inquiry at the Dailledouze establishment failed to get corroboration of the report.

Providence, R. I.

News Items.

The Rhode Island Horticultural Society awarded John A. Macrae a $50 gold medal as a gratuity for the best seedling chrysanthemum ever raised in Rhode Island. The variety has been named Golden Dome.

A. N. Pierson, of Cromwell, Conn., called on the trade here last Saturday. Mr. Barnscroft from the Pennock-Meehan Company, of Philadelphia, was also in town the past week.

J. L. Reynolds has resigned his position with T. J. Johnston. He is to enter the jewelry business, which is booming here.

John A. Macrae attended the meetings of the Chrysanthemum Society committees at New York and Philadelphia, during the past week, and exhibited his new chrysanthemum Golden Dome.

The Rhode Island Florists Club held its monthly meeting Monday evening November 19. The only business of importance done was the nomination of officers as follows: Alexander Macrae, president; Charles MacNair, vice-president; William Chappell, secretary; Alexander Rennie, treasurer. Election next month.

It was John Gerrard, Bristol, R. I., who was the winner in the carnation competition at last week's show, and not John H. Girard, Bristol, Pa., as printed. Mr. Gerrard won second prize with 25 blooms of Prosperity.

G. A. J.

FOR THE RETAILER

[All questions relating to the Retail Trade will be cheerfully answered in this column. We solicit good, sharp photographs of made-up work, decorations, store interiors, etc., for reproduction here.—Ed. F. E.]

Finger Bowl Flowers.

We have received an inquiry anent the finger bowl flower, and in answer will state that the average decorator, or for that matter a person in any capacity whatsoever, seems to be either unaware or entirely disregardful of the uses of the finger bowl. Not that there is much harm in reality done by this condition of affairs; but since this foible of the table is an established feature at most functions, and is a consideration in all or at least most table decorations, it is best to understand its full significance. It is wrong to make the finger bowl appear like an individual guest's bowl of flowers; it is a mere adjunct to, and not a part of the table's "make-up." It is a modernized form of a very ancient custom, its sole purpose being to divest the fingers of any possible trace of food. The flower or leaf put into the bowl is intended to be bruised between the fingers to impart its fragrance to them. These flowers should never be tied or appear like a boutoniere, and should consist of a small spray of such as lemon verbena, rose geranium, orange leaf or similar foliage, or three sprays of lily of the valley, three or four violets, a couple of pansies, a spray of star jasmine, Bouvardia Humboldtii corymbiflora, a few sweet peas, etc. Flowers such as hyacinths, or anything of a sticky nature, should not be used unless under extreme pressure. The simpler the flowers, the better. Arrange them on the side of the bowl and not swimming in water.

Flower Combinations.

Some very pretty features can cheaply be maintained in your window or on your counter, and their arranging need not disqualify the stock for sale. A loving cup, or low bowl, is most often used as a centerpiece at informal table decorations, and very often, in fact daily, suggestions can be made as to the proper method of arrangement and the most suitable and seasonable flowers. Lily of the valley left in the original bunches but loosened up, and a cluster of crimson or pink roses, always is attractive. Lily of the valley or Roman hyacinths and clusters of Bon Silene roses, daisies, and bouvardia or carnations, cypripediums and mignonette. A bowl of Uncle John, Killarney, Sunset, Liberty or Richmond, Mme. Abel Chatenay, Perle des Jardins, Sunrise, or any such roses, and betimes, and also to disturb the monotony, a few of some contrasting color or flower can be introduced, say a few Killarney with the Liberty, Perle with Sunrise or Richmond; Richmond and Perle, or Perle with Bride, or K. A. Victoria; numerous combinations can be made, but a dominant color should prevail; that is, only a few, say, about six in a cluster, of the contrasting rose should be used.

The intent in all combinations in decorative art is to intensify the beauty of each in a frame of harmony. Some grand cattleyas are on hand; the full beauty of these flowers is often interfered with by placing them in close proximity to the vulgar or bizarre. Such a flower as lily of the valley will harmonize, almost enhance, but hyacinths or narcissus will jar with and depreciate the value of orchids except in the case of cypripediums; they and the former flower have long been companions in cool-house, on table and in bouquet. Some of the lightest cypripediums, such as C. Spicerianum, C. insigne, the very lightest colored varieties, and again the very dark ones of the C. Harrisianum type, are beautiful in combination with crimson roses and mignonette.

Try a very loose bunch of single violets, with any small white flower. A light green adiantum goes with all these. A cluster of light-colored pansies will always attract. The wideawake buyer is always on the lookout for something out of the regular run, and it is advisable, where one has some particular customers to humor, to hide away anything you think they would like. We don't believe in displaying some rarity or special flower intended for a certain customer and telling inquirers or would-be purchasers that such a flower is sold, for that is only aggravating and causes resentment and pique. On the other hand, you secure the goodwill and feed the conceit of the fussy or particular by drawing forth from its hiding any special specimen or flower.

Violets.

Violets are almost in full cry and demand the most careful consideration. Open up and air well the boxes you intend delivering them in or else they will absorb that pasty or gluey smell of the boxmaker's bench. For some years past very small green galax leaves have been used to reinforce the foliage of violets, and it is well, too, to have these galax leaves clean and ordorless. A few days ago we saw a box of violets just arrived from the grower; the flowers must have been bunched in the kitchen, for instead of having the violet fragrance there was an unmistakable smell of fried bacon about them. If you can possibly do so, try and have your violets put up for you specially by the grower. Show him how you would like to have them bunched. Have them put in a box specially for you, and when they arrive keep as many as you don't need for orders or display in that box. Even your richest customer will be pleased to think he is getting his violets fresh from the grower's box—and in addition we find it the best way to preserve the sweetness of that vicarious though lovable flower.

Cut Flower Boxes.

There is not so much of the wallpaper or savagery seen about cut flower boxes this year. The common sense and good taste of the plain white box seem to be general. There is a little commendable individualism shown about tags though; and while some of them are elephantine, others show progressive spirit. To our way of thinking the worst feature about the delivery of flowers, and one which borders on the abominable, is the all too prevalent custom of cutting out the ends of boxes. This is frequently done without the slightest necessity, and apart from the sure possibility of injury to the flowers there is a decided meanness in appearance of the package which intensifies its very cumbersomeness. Try to leave the box intact by reversing a few of the flowers.

A Use for Chrysanthemums.

At a time like the present when there is an ever attendant army of veteran white and sickly pink chrysanthemums, it is well to be on the lookout for the chance to use them up in funeral work; the very poorest as well as the best of them can be made to do duty in outlining crosses, wreaths, etc. It is the only profitable method of using them up.

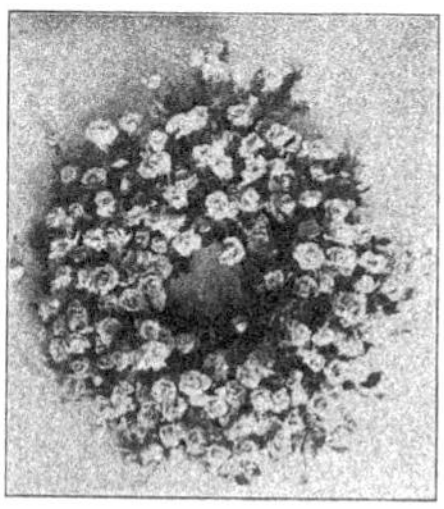

A Wreath of Roses, With Their Own Foliage Only.

Artist, James Ivera Donlan.

A Hint for Table Decoration.

Wherever you have a chance at club banquets, or large society affairs, and the price will permit it, try the effect of alternate low and very tall table decorations. Tall glass vases filled with long-stemmed American Beauty roses or chrysanthemums interspersed with low vases or baskets of flowers have a most imposing effect; as a rule, most of these events are too flat. Introduce the rose garden or bower of roses idea; it is sure to please the most exacting or fastidious, and be a certain winner with the great majority.

A Wreath of Roses.

The wreath illustrated was made of Bride roses and at a time of the year when the flowers could be bought for less than one dollar per hundred. Almost three hundred roses were used in this design. The frame was 30 inches in diameter. There was not a bit of green employed other than the rose foliage and there was no ribbon. The whole cost of material was somewhat less than five dollars, and twenty-five dollars was gladly given for the wreath. We do not mention these prices to create false ideas of enormous profits in the retail business—for there is not, and competition is decreasing profit every year—but merely to show that there are times, when the market is low, that good clean work can be turned out at small cost and when it is neither necessary nor wise to count or begrudge the material. The photograph was taken by a small kodak and in consequence is not sharply defined; but despite this drawback we submit it as our idea of a wreath of roses—loose yet conforming to design. The flowers are in every degree of development from the tightest bud to the open bloom, each arranged to bring out the best effect; and the leaves so often trampled under foot or otherwise ignored are here recognized as the very finest material and take their proper places. This is not merely mentioned from an economical point of view, but to show the thread in all our writings and the nature study in the arranging of flowers.

Dyed Chrysanthemums.

The other night when walking along Broadway we observed, in a prominent florist's window, chrysanthemums dyed the exact color of salmonized codfish. Try and imagine that color, ye hybridizers. Make a note of it on the same page where lie the green carnation and purple rose. Verily 'tis a queer brand of comedy to see florists attempting to "paint the lily." Some of our enterprising retailers are exhibiting "black" chrysanthemums almost the exact shade of undertakers' gloves. This is high art for the purpose of being in harmony with the horses and hearse. Then, again, during the past week we have seen "blue" chrysanthemums shown in two prominent windows. In one there was a label exploiting the fact that they were "blue chrysanthemums." One of these attempts came near being the shade of that lead-bluish clay seen on mountain sides; the other was more like the blue of a bloodless nose on a frosty morning! Now, ye hybridizers and specialists, take notice of what some people are attempting. If you cannot satisfy them, then schedulize the dyed flowers; it will surely please at least the foot-light set.

J. IVERA DONLAN.

St. Louis.

The Week's News.

We had a number of visitors last week, including S. S. Skidelsky, of Philadelphia, selling Rose-Pink Enchantress; W. W. Abrahamson, who represents E. H. Hunt, of Chicago; and B. Eschner of M. Rice & Company, Philadelphia.

John Himmer of Himmer Brothers, Meramec Highlands, has the sympathy of the trade in the loss of his wife, who died last week leaving a large family.

At the next meeting of the Florists' Club two very important discussions will take place, the trustees having asked Theo. Miller to tell the members "How to Decorate a Retail Store for the Christmas Holidays," and H. G. Pring, an able young man from Shaw's Gardens, to present a paper on "Growing Orchids and other Choice Plants of Different varieties." Another of those pleasant officers' meetings will be called next week by President Irish for the purpose of laying out a program for the next club meeting, so that all members will be well repaid for their attendance. The committee to raise the big flower show fund is progressing, and the officers can help the work at this special meeting.

George Augermuller was reported very ill Monday morning; he had a fainting spell on Saturday. His brother Fred is in charge of the business and expects George to be about in a few days.

Mary Ostertag's old establishment on Grand avenue is again open under new management.

George Ostertag, superintendent of Public Parks, and John Ratchford, keeper of Forest Park, were agreeably surprised on Saturday night last by 125 employees of the Park Department, when each of the gentlemen named was presented with a fine gold watch richly engraved. Keeper H. Vembregreen, of O'Fallen Park, made the presentation speech. The gifts were well deserved as both men have done excellent work since they were appointed to office. Two additions have recently been made to the Forest Park greenhouses.

ST. PATRICK.

New Orleans, La.

News of the Week.

The first heavy frost of the season appeared on the morning of November 13, but seemingly did not do much damage as one still sees pandanus, coleus, etc., but very slightly touched. Alternanthera appears to have taken on brighter colors since the advent of cool weather. The day following the frost we had some good heavy showers, the first rain since the latter part of September, consequently vegetation has taken on a much fresher look.

The last meeting of the Horticultural Society was chrysanthemum night, and the flowers shown were very fine indeed, the exhibitors including Newsham, Metairie Nursery Company, Cook & Sons, Abele Brothers, and Wichers & Son, of Gretna. Especially fine were chrysanthemums General Hutton, Col. Appleton, Convention Hall, and a number of last year's novelties.

The E. G. Hill Company of Richmond, Ind., sent some magnificent well finished blooms. The Metairie Nursery Company in addition to their display of chrysanthemums, staged a lot of roses, their Golden Gate being worthy of particular notice. Such a fine display of flowers raised the enthusiasm of the members to such an extent that a committee was appointed to make arrangements for holding a chrysanthemum show in 1907.

J. A. Newsham, of the Nashville avenue Rose Gardens, who is an ardent orchidist, has arranged to send his man Guillot to Central America on an orchid collecting expedition. This is not the first trip Mr. Guillot has made in quest of orchids.

The New Orleans Horticultural Society is trying to inaugurate a series of lectures on botany—a laudable endeavor worthy of encouragement.

Jules Fonta, who has entered upon his new duties as superintendent of Audubon Park, has sold his entire stock of plants to Dubois, of Carrollton.

CRESCENT CITY.

Washington, D. C.

News Items.

At the recent chrysanthemum show at the U. S. Propagating Gardens on November 8, when the entire establishment was open to the public, some of the most conspicuous varieties seen were: Reine de Italie (large yellow); A. J. Balfour (pink); Lord Alverton (maroon and gold); Edgar Sanders (light chocolate); Baden Powell (rosy pink), Donald McLeod (yellow and bronze); Ethel Fitzroy (yellow); Black Hawk (dark crimson); Mrs. J. A. Miller (buff); Henry Sinclair (sulphur yellow); Brutus, (terra cotta); Mrs. T. Richardson (shell pink); General Hutton (golden yellow); Brighthurst (pink with silver tips); Beatrice May (white). These and many other varieties were bench grown to single stems. Also worthy of mention was a house of crotons which comprises some of the newest sorts. The rose houses are filled with American Beauty, Killarney, Richmond, Golden Gate and Bride. In the carnation houses may be seen Enchantress, Flamingo, and white and pink Lawson. All this stock which is first-class, is grown for the exclusive use of decorating the White House. I may state that the former White House greenhouses have been merged with those of the Propagating Gardens and are practically under the same management, the officer in charge of Public Buildings and Grounds, superintendent by the landscape gardener, G. H. Brown, under whose able guidance the gardens have been for years. It is from here that the city parks are supplied with a general collection of bedding stock, reaching into hundreds of thousands.

J. R. Freeman is showing some fine plants of azalea Deutsche Perle in his store. He has several hundred of these plants many of which will be in bloom by Thanksgiving Day.

Business is fair this week, with a good demand for violets, especially double, which are scarce.

J. A. G.

Indianapolis.

News Notes.

Tomlinson Hall Market looked like a flower show last week; at no other time have so many blooms been displayed. Potted plants found many customers and were on hand by the hundreds; cut flowers did not sell well and late in the day were offered at half the customary wholesale figure.

The outlook is promising for Thanksgiving business, and as trade of late years has steadily increased, preparations are making accordingly. There will likely be enough chrysanthemums to meet all demands; violets will be scarce unless Eastern stock is resorted to. Roses and carnations are usually plentiful for Thanksgiving trade, and a similar condition is likely this year.

George B. Wiegand is investing in north side real estate.

Extensive improvements at the establishment of Henry Rieman are completed, and on Saturday evening a number of his friends celebrated the fact.

Bertermann Brothers Company have completed a large propagating house for carnations; it is their intention to grow a number of carnations in the field for Summer cuttings.

I. B.

Buffalo.

News Notes.

Business is picking up daily; better stock is arriving and better prices prevailing. Enchantress carnations are particularly fine.

S. A. Anderson held his usual chrysanthemum show, which is always very popular.

Chas. Keltsch is making some alterations in his store.

Wm. F. Kasting, Wm. Scott and Prof. John F. Cowell have returned from the Chicago show and report it the "best ever."

E. A. Slattery of W. J. Palmer & Son had a handsome table of oncidiums and violets at the Ramsdall reception, which made one of the biggest hits of the season.

W. H. G.

CANADIAN NEWS

MONTREAL.—Florists here ar busy. The large number of wedding tea and dinner decorations, which ar now in full swing, use up a lot o flowers. There has been a great cal for all kinds of stock, and as th weather has been very fine to date the supply has been heavy, and goo quality flowers have always cleare up.

Messrs. McKenna & Son are now occupying their re-arranged store The new refrigerator is a model o perfection; it is beautifully finishe with mirrors and a tile floor. An iro table with marble top occupies th center of the store for display pur poses. The offices are located at th rear. A stairway leads from the stor to a very neat conservatory overhea where all the potted stock is kept. A new delivery wagon has also been pu in commission which will, no doubt give the public a good impression o how the firm turns out its orders.

Montreal gardeners are much elat ed over T. McHugh winning the cu for the second time at Toronto, fo the best twelve chrysanthemums.

The committee appointed by th club to look into the matter of hold ing a show in November of next yea will report at the next meeting i favor of having an exhibition. It wi probably take place at the Arena.

Bertie Graves has recovered fro his recent illness, and is back again.

Harris & Hopton are the Montrea "mushroom kings." One hundre pounds were cut last week and sol at retail as fast as cut.

W. C. H.

LANCASTER, O.—W. E. Gravet gave a chrysanthemum exhibitio here last week. The blooms show were of fine quality reflecting muc credit on Walter Day, the grower who is a graduate from the establishment of John N. May, Summit N. J.

CLASSIFIED ADVERTISEMENTS

CASH WITH ORDER.

The columns under this heading are reserved for advertisements of Stock for Sale, Stock Wanted, Help Wanted, Situations Wanted or other Wants; also of Greenhouse, Land, Second-Hand Materials, etc., For Sale or Rent.

Our charge is 10 cts. per line (7 words to the line), set solid, without display. No advt. accepted for less than thirty cents.

Display advertisements in these columns, 15 cents per line; count 12 lines agate to the inch.

[If replies to Help Wanted, Situation Wanted, or other advertisements are to be addressed care of this office, advertisers add 10 cents to cover expense of forwarding.]

Copy must reach New York office 12 o'clock Wednesday to secure insertion in issue of following Saturday.

Advertisers in the Western States desiring to advertise under initials, may save time by having their answer directed care our Chicago office at 127 E. Berwyn Ave.

SITUATIONS WANTED

SITUATION WANTED—By experienced men in rose houses; private or commercial. Good references. Address X. G., care The Florists' Exchange.

SITUATION WANTED—Single, competent grower, roses and carnations; take charge 50,000 ft. glass; $35.00 and board. Address Florist, 270 Seventh Avenue, New York.

SITUATION WANTED—By a married German, in good commercial or private place around New York; good worker; good references. State wages. Address, H. J., care The Florists' Exchange.

SITUATION WANTED—By competent man in retail florist store, aged 40, married, German-American, good maker-up, A No. 1 references. Address X. M., care The Florists' Exchange.

SITUATION WANTED—By single young man after December 1st, on private or commercial place. Experienced in carnations, chrysanthemums and general stock. Address X. B., care The Florists' Exchange.

SITUATION WANTED—By competent greenhouse man and fireman; married, German, aged 28, thoroughly capable. Can give good reference from last employer. Address, Edward Schultz, 2339 Bathgate Avenue, Bronx, New York City.

SITUATION WANTED—As assistant on small commercial place where only one assistant is employed and which does a retail business. Ten years' experience. Single, American, trustworthy. Can come immediately. Address X. I., care The Florists' Exchange.

SITUATION WANTED—By grower of roses, carnations and general stock. Neat, quick worker and hustler. Open for engagement at once. Good references. State full particulars with salary. Address, Buckeye State, care The Florists' Exchange.

SITUATION WANTED—As foreman, grower of cut flowers and general pot plants for retail trade. State of Massachusetts preferred. Life experience in the trade in Germany and this country. Aged 39, single, honest and sober. Please state full particulars in first letter. Address X. K., care The Florists' Exchange.

SITUATION WANTED—As manager or foreman, private or commercial place where roses are grown. Able to take charge of any size place, also well up in all lines of cut flowers and pot plants. Best of references. State particulars with wages in first letter. Address X. J., care The Florists' Exchange.

SITUATION WANTED—By expert grower of roses, carnations, chrysanthemums and all kinds of pot plants. Also decorator and maker-up. Married man, 38, no children, 23 years' experience. State particulars and wages in first letter. Address, John G. Fleutl, 58 Dey Street, New York City.

HELP WANTED

WANTED—Competent rose grower to take charge of section of six houses. Unless you are a good grower do not apply. Address X. L., care The Florists' Exchange.

WANTED—At once, seedsman for retail house. State experience and salary expected in own handwriting. Address X. F., care The Florists' Exchange.

WANTED—Reliable sober man who understands growing carnations, chrysanthemums and general bedding stock. Able to take charge of 18,000 sq. ft. of glass. Steam heat. Wages, $15.00 per week. Apply giving references and experience. Geo. R. Geiger Estate, Nazareth, Pa.

HELP WANTED

WANTED—A florist, good designer and decorator, reliable and sober. Apply by mail stating wages and experience to H. H. J., 128 Broadway, Brooklyn, N. Y.

WANTED—Fireman, experienced in greenhouse firing. Must come well recommended. Strictly temperate. Call or address, Elizabeth Nursery Company, Elizabeth, N. J.

WANTED—Day fireman for steam boilers. Married man preferred. State wages required, experience and references. Address, Rowayton Greenhouses, Rowayton, Conn.

WANTED—Young man to pack and ship cut flowers and help around greenhouses. State experience, wages, etc. W. K. Partridge, 148 E. Fourth Street, Cincinnati, O.

WANTED—Night fireman who understands steam boilers, etc. Steady position. State experience, salary wanted, and give references. W. K. Partridge, 148 E. Fourth street, Cincinnati, O.

WANTED—Young man to assist in up-to-date flower store. Must be decorator, of good appearance and able to wait on select trade. Address X. D., care The Florists' Exchange.

WANTED—Young man with some experience in greenhouses, as assistant in roses and carnations. $9.00 per week. Must give good reference as to character. Address X. H., care The Florists' Exchange.

WANTED—Man for general greenhouse work, one that knows how to work Hitchings Boilers. A steady place and fair wages to good man. George Darsley, cor. Jackson & Claremont ave., Jersey City, N. J.

WANTED—Nurseryman and landscape gardener, with general knowledge of pruning and the care of fruit and ornamental stock. State experience and salary expected. The Continental Nurseries, Franklin, Mass.

WANTED—Man experienced in greenhouse work, neat and active. Good wages paid if satisfaction is obtained. Apply at once, personally, to Louis Dupuy, Whitestone (via 34th street ferry), L. I., N. Y.

WANTED—Young man to assist in high-class retail flower store. Must be of good appearance and have good references. State wages, etc. W. K. Partridge, 148 E. Fourth Street, Cincinnati, O.

WANTED—Section man for carnations. Married man preferred, who would be willing to board one or two men. Have five roomed house on place. State wages, etc. W. K. Partridge, 148 E. Fourth Street, Cincinnati, O.

WANTED—Salesman and canvasser; greater New York and vicinity. Single, energetic young horticulturist, with some experience in ornamental stock, who is willing to identify himself permanently with new horticultural establishment. Salary and commission. Give full particulars. Address W. T. care The Florists' Exchange.

WANTED—December 1st, two men. An assistant, competent to take charge in owner's absence; wages $30.00 per month, board and room; must understand firing. Also a young man, experience not necessary, to do general greenhouse work; wages $20.00 per month, board and room. Address Flora T. Howell, Pine Bush, N. Y.

MISCELLANEOUS WANTS

WANTED—Scott's Manual for Florists and Ward's Carnation Culture; second-hand. State price. Address Z. Akerson, 481 East Oak street, Portland, Ore.

WANTED TO BUY—Greenhouses to be taken down. State full particulars of same when writing. Address, F. W., care The Florists' Exchange.

WANTED TO BUY—About 12,000 ft. of glass, in good condition, near R. R. Station, with few acres of ground preferred. State terms and particulars. Address E. T., care The Florists' Exchange.

AN established nursery and greenhouse business, with retail flower and landscape departments, located in the far East, desires the services of a young man possessing a general knowledge of gardening. Applicant should have a pleasing address and a fairly good education. Whilst capital is not an absolute essential, there will exist every opportunity to become a partner in this business, therefore, preference will be given to those who, if satisfied with the outlook, would be in a position to invest up to about $10,000. To a person with a desire to go abroad (China and Japan) this advertisement offers peculiar opportunities. Address with fullest particulars, T. E., care The Florists' Exchange.

FOR SALE OR RENT

FOR SALE—Garden and seven greenhouses, 10,000 sq. ft. of glass, and a nine roomed dwelling on the premises. In a neighborhood where you can do business and save money. For particulars write to Arthur H. Lanser, Wayne, Del. Co., Pa.

TO RENT—Two greenhouses in a reliable location; good business can be done; everything in good shape for any one who wants to start for the Spring trade. A good Hitchings boiler. Can reach New York in 30 minutes. Address Mrs. M. Palumbo, Greenleaf Avenue, West New Brighton, S. I.

FOR SALE At a price that is bound to sell. 7600 ft. glass, stocked with carnations, violets and other stock. Boilers worth $430.00. Memorial Day trade amounts to $[illegible].00. The chance of a life-time. Address STAR, care The Florists' Exchange.

Mention the Florists' Exchange when writing.

FOR SALE—A well established florist business, with dwelling houses. Also plenty of outdoor ground in up-to-date condition. Greenhouses are well filled with foliage plants, and the place is in a most desirable location to reach the wholesale New York City trade within a drive of about 30 minutes. It must be seen. Reason for selling: ill health. For particulars communicate with O. V. Zangen, Seedsman, Hoboken, N. J.

A SNAP IF TAKEN AT ONCE—Greenhouses and Dwelling house newly remodelled, well stocked with carnations, roses, bedding plants and vegetables. No competition, only place in town of 3,000 inhabitants, no other house nearer than twenty miles, plenty of ground, and patients at Keeley Institute insuring steady paying trade. Owner has other business. Price $4,000, including Winter supply of fuel. J. C. Nelson, Proprietor, Dwight, Ill.

FOR SALE—Opportunity of a life-time, in Baltimore, five greenhouses, 70 feet long, about 8,000 sq. feet of glass, room for more. Lot 200x160; two Hitchings' No. 17 hot water boilers, together with well stocked houses of palms, ferns, roses, plants, flowers, bulbs, etc. Office and potting house, all connected with a nice eight roomed dwelling, heated by a Hitchings' Upright hot water boiler; bath and toilet room, porches, etc. Cold frames, stable, wagon house, chicken houses, etc. Two spring wagons, one cart and one horse. Also one stall in the greatest market house in the world. Have a large exclusive non-competitive suburban custom in adjoining neighborhood. This is a well-established profitable business. Have sufficient income for balance of life, reason for selling. Price, $8,000; cost $12,000. Part can remain on mortgage. J. W. Linton, 848 Equitable Building, Baltimore, Md.

STOCK FOR SALE

BRENCHLEYENSIS GLADIOLUS, 1st. size, $10.00 per 1000; 2d. size, $8.00 per 1000. Cash with order. Est. Louis Siebrecht, Floral Park, N. Y.

CHRYSANTHEMUMS, stock plants, Polly Rose and Glory of the Pacific, $2.50 per 100. Cash with order please. G. E. S., 64 Bay View Avenue, Jersey City, N. J.

CARNATIONS—Strong, healthy, field-grown plants, extra large, Ethel Crocker, $5.00 per 100. Cash with order. W. C. Pray & Co., Kinkora, N. J.

CHRYSANTHEMUMS, stock plants, Polly Rose, Glory of Pacific, Halliday, October Sunshine and Intensity, fine, 50c. per doz.; $3.50 per 100. F. P. Sawyer, Clinton, Mass.

ENGLISH PRIZE PANSY PLANTS—I have 10,000 fine plants more than I need. For sale at $3.00 per 1000, cash. Some very odd and beautiful markings among them. Reuben Powell, Florist, White Plains, N. Y.

BABY RAMBLER roses, fine dormant stock, $25 per 100. 2 1-2 inch pot plants, extra well rooted $7 per 100, $65 per 1000. Orders booked for delivery now or any time up to late Spring. Samples free. Brown Brothers Co., Rochester, N. Y.

CHRYSANTHEMUMS, stock plants—Nevins, Mrs. Coombes, J. H. Troy, Minnie Wanamaker, Robert Halliday, Col. D. Appleton, Polly Rose, White Coombes, Mrs. Robinson, October Sunshine, Alice Byron, Ivory, Pink Ivory, Wm. Duckham, A. J. Balfour, Dr. Enguehard, 75c. per doz.; $5.00 per 100. Cash please. Henry Hansen, Catskill, N. Y.

CALLIOPSIS, California Sunbeams, Golden Fleece; Dahlia Monarch, mixed; Eschscholtzia, Golden West; Freesia; Geranium, Good Venture; Heliotrope, Lemoines; Ipomea, Heavenly Blue, White Tassel; Nasturtium, Butterfly, Jupiter, Saturn, mixed; Poppy, Fayal, Irresistible, Maid of the Mist; Tacsonia Buchananii. Write for prices. Theodosia B. Shepherd Co., W. H. Francis, Manager, Ventura, Cal.

FOR SALE

FOR SALE OR EXCHANGE—Glass, 2nd hand, double thick, 12x14, $2.00 per box, or will exchange for stock suitable for retail trade. W. P. Kesteloo, Walden, N. Y.

FOR SALE—One No. 4 Weathered boiler in good condition, rated to heat 2,300 sq. ft. of glass to 60 degrees in zero weather, $35.00 cash, F. O. B., cars or boat. R. G. Hanford, Norwalk, Conn.

BOILERS, BOILERS, BOILERS.
SEVERAL good second hand boilers on hand, also new No. 16 Hitchings at reduced cost. Write for list. Wm. H. Lutton, West Side Avenue Station, C. R. R. of N. J., Jersey City, N. J.

THE CHRISTMAS NUMBER of The Florists' Exchange will be issued Saturday, December 8, 1906. That issue will appear at an opportune time, and advertisers will make no mistake in placing therein a liberal display of their offerings for the holidays. Copy of advertisement should reach us at the very latest by 12 noon, Wednesday, December 5.

Boston.

Annual Meeting of M. H. S.

The annual meeting of the Massachusetts Horticultural Society was the most exciting held for several years, there being a spirited contest for the presidency between Stephen M. Weld and Warren W. Rawson. The meeting was called to order by President Arthur F. Estebrook, and it was voted to appropriate the sum of $5,500 for prizes and gratuities for the ensuing year. Hon. Aaron Low read a memorial in honor of the late Benjamin P. Ware, for forty-one years an active member of the society and for several years its vice-president. The following were elected corresponding members of the society: Dr. Henry L. Ridley, director Botanic Garden, Singapore; Lieut. Col. David Prain, director Royal Gardens, Kew, England; Señor Don Salvador Izquierdo, Santiago, Chili; Miss E. Willmott, Essex, England. The president appointed E. P. Wilder, J. Allen Crosby, and W. P. Rich tellers when the polls were declared open at 12 o'clock. They remained open for four hours, the result being for President, Stephen M. Weld 136 votes; W. W. Rawson 66; vice-president for two years, C. S. Sargent; trustees for three years, W. N. Craig, A. F. Estebrook, John K. M. L. Farquhar and Arthur D. Hill; for nominating committee A. F. Estebrook, W. H. Heustis, William Nicholson, Loring Underwood and Edward P. Wilder.

News Notes.

D. Henry Sullivan, for years assistant superintendent of the Public Grounds Department, has been appointed superintendent to succeed the late William Doogue.

Charles Algren, buyer for J. Newman & Sons, sustained rather severe injuries on Summer street the other day.

Mathews, the florist, has opened a store at 1496 Dorchester avenue, with a full line of seasonable plants and flowers.

Club Meeting.

There was a rousing meeting of the Gardeners and Florists' Club on Tuesday evening, over 150 members being present. President Wheeler occupied the chair. Fine displays of various kinds were on the tables. A collection of single Zonale geraniums from W. N. Craig were exceptionally well done, receiving a report of merit. The same exhibitor also had some fine seedling single chrysanthemums. C. H. Totty of Madison, N. J., sent a nice collection of some 25 varieties of pompon and single chrysanthemums; and Duncan Finlayson exhibited two dozen varieties of chrysanthemums and a fine plant Calanthe lutea oculata carrying some excellent spikes of bloom. It received a report of superior merit. S. J. Goddard staged carnations. The Ideal, Cardinal, Victory and a vase of seedlings. Other exhibitors were W. H. Heustis & Son, Ilex glabra; F. W. Fletcher Company, Auburndale, Ficus altissima; M. A. Patten & Company, seedling carnations; H. A. Stevens, seedling carnations; William Sim, Cliftondale, Mass., violets.

Sixteen new members were elected. The following officers were elected for the ensuing year: President, Thos. H. Westwood; vice-president, F. E. Palmer; secretary, W. N. Craig; treasurer, Edward Hatch; executive committee, Robert Cameron, James Wheeler, Thos. J. Grey and Wm. Nicholson.

It was announced that at next meeting of the club W. H. Wyman of the Bay State Nurseries would be the essayist of the evening. Mr. Howard, who is to have charge of the club's landscape gardening classes, gave a brief outline of the work to be done; forty-five members agreed to join the classes.

The meeting adjourned at a late hour.

J. W. DUNCAN.

The annual exhibition of the Amer-

THE CHRISTMAS NUMB of The Florists' Exchan will be issued Saturd December 8, 1906. That issue w appear at an opportune time, a advertisers will make no mista in placing therein a liberal displ of their offerings for the holida Copy of advertisement should rea us at the very latest by 12 noo Wednesday, December 5.

CHRYSANTHEMUM NOVELTIES

THIS YEAR I have to offer once more a splendid lot of new varieties. Among them will be found in whites:

MISS CLAY FRICK, the white sport of Wm. Duckham, winner of the Frick prize at Chicago. The best new variety of the year.

Mrs. A. T. Miller, Moneymaker, Kathleen Stoop.

IN PINKS—Miss Mariam Hankey, Mrs. Walter Jenks, etc.

IN YELLOW – Mary Godfrey, Mrs. Geo. Hunt, Norman Davis, Buttercup, Etc.

Also J. W. Moreman, Mrs. Henry Barnes, W. J. Crossley and many others shown at the different exhibitions.

I offer young stock for delivery early in the new year. 50 new varieties of Singles, the latest craze. Send for my complete list issued Dec. 1.

CHARLES H. TOTTY, Madison, N. J.

CHRYSANTHEMUM NOVELTIES

For 1907

Are you wanting some grand, big, early mums to grow with **Monrovia** and **Touset** for next year?

President Loubet was completely finished on October 8th, and is the largest of all the October varieties: traveled in fine style to New York and scored 90 points before the C. S. A. 4 ft.; color, mother of pearl; stiff stem; foliage perfect.

Dubuisson-Foubert, a grand yellow, new in form, full, with twisted petals, a glorious shade, of the largest size. 4 ft.; splendid stem and foliage; first flowers cut September 30, and lasting up to November 1.

Mme. S. H. Cochet, an early V. Morel; October 20 and later; a beautiful shade of pink, bright and deep, as fine as a good Morel.

Mlle. E. Chabanne, a very large, pure pink; in form and size a nice companion for Beatrice May.

Director Gerard, pure commercial, of Gen. Hutton shade of yellow; ready October 1; large and deep.

Mme. L. Roussel, a perfectly formed Jap. incurve; the best pure bronze to date; an improvement on Henri the II.

Sergeant Lovy, large, golden yellow; cut on September 20; splendid substance.

Miss Alice Roosevelt, white as snow, round as a ball; looks as though carved from marble.

On Seedling Day at the Chicago Show, our novelty entries took every First Premium:—For white, **Miss Alice Roosevelt**; pink **Mlle. E. Chabanne**; yellow, **Dubuisson-Foubert**; bronze, **Incandescent**; "other color," **Mme. Armand Detroyat.**

We also have from Mr. W. Wells: **Miss Miriam Hankey,** a sensational pink; **Mrs. H. Barnes,** a reddish bronze; and the **White Sport,** from Wm. Duckham, besides a number of other prize winners, all grand in their color. Strengthen your lists.

We can also supply full sets of last year's novelties, many of which are very strong varieties for exhibition: **E. J. Brooks, Mary Ann Pockett, May Seddon, Mrs. F. F. Thompson, Mrs. H. Partridge, Mrs. West, Mrs. Mason, Mrs. Beech, Mrs. Mrs. Morton F. Plant;** and don't forget **May Mann,** the winner of the prize for 100 pink at Chicago; high-colored, round, an easy doer with perfect stem.

Very early in the year we can supply cuttings of the standard varieties that you need most: **Monrovia, Touset, Opah, October Frost, Beatrice May, Rosiere,** the two **Chadwicks,** the two **Eatons, etc.**

A complete set of charming **Pompons** in reds, yellows, whites and all shades of pink.

Another set of **Well's** finest singles, for sprays or pots; they are both beautiful and lasting.

Send for novelty list now in press.

STOCK PLANTS, ready now
$1.00 per dozen.

Alice Byron	Lord Hopetoun
C. Tousel	Monrovia
Col. D. Appleton	Matchless
Dr. Enguehard	Mrs. Robinson
Dr. Galloway	Mrs. Coombes
Ethel Fitzroy	Opah
Geo. W. Childs	Polly Rose
Ivory	Roi D' Italia
Jeannie Nonin	T. Eaton

Yellow Eaton

The globular commercial pink **Mary Mann** } $2.00 per dozen.

Mrs. Geo. Buch, the golden sport from **Mrs. Swinburne** } $2.00 per dozen.

THE E. G. HILL CO.,
RICHMOND, - - - IND.

Mention the Florists' Exchange when writing.

CHRYSANTHEMUMS

STOCK PLANTS

WHITE

Early—George S. Kalb, Polly Rose, Willowbrook.
Mid-Season—Miss Minnie Wanamaker, Ivory, Mrs. H. Robinson, Niveus, Queen, Alice Bryon, Eureka.
Late—Mrs. McArthur, Timothy Eaton, W. H. Chadwick.

PINK

Early—Glory of the Pacific.
Mid-Season—Pink Ivory, J. K. Shaw, Adela, Mrs. Perrin, Ethelyn, A. J. Balfour, Wm. H. Duckham, Dr. Enguehard, Marion Newell.
Late—Maud Dean, Lavendar Queen, The Harriott.

YELLOW

Early—Monrovia.
Mid-Season—G. Pitcher, Col. D. Appleton, Golden Gate.
Late—Major Bonnaffon, Mrs. Trenor L. Park, H. W. Reiman.

RED

Cullingfordii, Matchless.

BRONZE

Kate Broomhead, Mrs. Duckham.

Guaranteed to be strong, healthy plants, $1.00 per doz., $6.00 per 100.

A. N. PIERSON, CROMWELL, CONN.

Mention the Florists' Exchange when writing.

HELP WANTED TO SUCCESSFULLY GROW CHRYSANTHEMUMS?

If this is your cry REMEMBER

SMITH'S REVISED CHRYSANTHEMUM MANUAL

NOW OUT.

IS A RELIABLE HELPER

Written by ELMER D. SMITH, the Noted Chrysanthemum Specialist.

Many of the important chapters have been revised and enlarged, giving more complete details, with additional Illustrations. New and up-to-date. Price within reach of all.

CLOTH BINDING, 100 PAGES, ONLY 40c. POSTPAID.

NATHAN SMITH & SON, Adrian, Mich.

Mention the Florists' Exchange when writing.

1000 Jeannie Nonin Mums

The very finest late white. Stock plants, $7,00 per 100. Cash with order.

WM. KEIR, Pikesville, Md.

Chrysanthemum growers who have a surplus of stock plants should advertise them in THE FLORISTS' EXCHANGE.

REVIEW OF THE MARKET

NEW YORK.—The horse show in Madison Square Garden is in full swing this week, yet there is no perceptible advantage to the cut flower business coming from this social event. The weather has been unusually warm and has had a very bad effect upon flowers, roses and chrysanthemums probably suffering more than any others.

American Beauty roses are plentiful enough for all demands, although it seems rather difficult to pick out strictly special grade stock, so that at times when these have been obtainable, prices have reached as high as 40c. each in some few instances. For Bride and Bridesmaid and other tea roses there has been an occasional 8c. each obtained for limited numbers that have been of exceptional good quality, but this is by no means the ruling figure for the general run of special grade stock. The lower grades, on account of their coming in soft and decidedly off color, have had to be sacrificed at times in order to make clearances.

The carnation situation seemed to improve at the beginning of the week, but this was not of long duration, as by Tuesday prices had dropped very materially, and stock was being offered at figures below those of our last week's quotations.

Cattleyas are anything but plentiful just now; a fair supply of dendrobiums is coming in, for which there does not seem to be any special demand just at this time. The supply of lily of the valley is ample for all calls and prices remain about the same. Paper White narcissus are now arriving regularly; and Roman hyacinths are reaching the market every day in limited numbers. The supply of gardenias, while regular, is anything but heavy, consequently prices remain moderately firm. Lilies are clearing out fairly well, and there is a disposition to advance the values of these among the dealers.

Chrysanthemums are clearing out very unsatisfactorily: there are so many of them, and mostly of good quality, that even the cutting of prices does not appear to move them as one would expect. With the exception of a very few of special quality, which fetch anywhere from $4 to $6 per dozen, the general run of prices remains about the same.

The supply of violets has been limited, on one or two mornings, and $2 per 100 has been realized on some shipments of extra stock.

PHILADELPHIA.—Somewhat of an unsteady condition has prevailed in the cut flower market for a week past. Business showed an improvement on Monday afternoon, but this was mostly on account of out-of-town orders. The very best American Beauty roses are selling at $4.00 per dozen. In tea roses the stock is generally soft and not of usual quality; most varieties are selling at from $6 to $8 per 100, a few bringing $10. Carnations move very slowly; prices are quoted at from $1.50 to $3, $4 being obtained for a few fancy Enchantress. Chrysanthemums are very numerous; values start at $8 per 100 up to $3 per dozen for the general stock. Some William H. Chadwick from Edward A. Stroud sold at $6 per dozen; they were exceptionally fine. Double violets are not yet plentiful; $1.50 per 100 is asked for the best stock. The large singles are selling at 75c. to $1. There has been a very good demand for lily of the valley, which ranges from $3 to $5 per 100. Bouvardia is selling very well at $3 per 100. Gardenias are not yet very plentiful; they bring $6 per dozen. Sweet peas are selling for $1 to $1.50, the latter price for good white. The flowers are good, but the stems rather short yet. Smilax is quoted at 15c. per string; Asparagus plumosus and A. Sprengeri at 50c. per bunch, but not moving well. A. plumosus strings are being asked for.

D. R.

CHICAGO.—The demand which fell to a point indicating a glut on show week was followed last week by an identical report, owing doubtless, to some extent, to the extremely dubious weather which prevailed throughout the week. Cold winds, rain and an entire absence of sun were continuous and have, so far as roses and carnations are concerned, retarded development; but consignments have been heavy and the week closed with the heaviest stock of chrysanthemums on hand yet left over. All sizes and all seasonable varieties are to be had in unlimited numbers, and as usual the poorer grades are the greatest sufferers.

But what is Thanksgiving going to bring to the trade? Optimistic in general are the prophesies, and by the time these lines are in type in all probability a more distinct shadow of coming events may be outlined. But one important fact may be stated, and that is, that the stock in this market is all around in excellent shape.

It does not appear at this writing, Tuesday, that any very marked advance over our quoted prices will occur along general lines. There is at present plenty of everything to go around. Beyond the glut in the poorer grades of chrysanthemums, and possibly in some cases carnations, there is not much to offer. Lily of the valley and violets are in good demand and are of good quality. There is plenty of green stock of all kinds, though hardy ferns are running in many cases somewhat to the bad; however, boxwood is abundant and of excellent quality and seems destined to receive its full appreciation here. Pompon chrysanthemums appear to be regaining their former popularity.

W. K. W.

INDIANAPOLIS.—The flower market lacked spirit last week. Bright warm weather caused hundreds of blooms to be offered at low prices. Funeral work is heavy and aids in disposing of surplus stock. In carnations, the common grades are plentiful at $2 per 100; fancies, such as Enchantress, are not always to be obtained at $2.50 to $3 per 100. Chrysanthemums, any color, any size, any quantity, are offered at reasonable prices. The retail demand has been fairly good, but the production in this vicinity is so large it takes very brisk business to keep from selling the blooms at unprofitable rates; the customary wholesale figure is $1 to $2 a dozen; at times very select bring $3 to $4.

The local retailers could not use the immense supply of roses, so many were shipped to neighboring cities. Select Bride and Bridesmaid bring $5 to $6; Madame Abel Chatenay, $5; American Beauty outsell these at $25 per 100.

Violets are the only scarce article and 50c. to 60c. per 100 is paid for medium grades. A few Blanche Ferry sweet peas are offered at $2 per 100. Lily of the valley finds ready sale at $4.

Quite a number of orchids are grown here; little trouble is experienced in disposing of them and they seem to sell better each year.

I. B.

ST. LOUIS.—Only a slight improvement in business was noticeable last week; transient trade was poor, and but few orders were received for weddings and large funerals. Chrysanthemums are plentiful, the fancy sorts selling well. A large number of pink varieties move slowly; white and yellow have the call. Fine Golden Wedding are seen. Prices range from $2 to $3 per dozen for the best to $1.50 and 60c. per dozen for other grades.

Plenty of roses of fine quality are in the market; American Beauty are in demand and not overplentiful in all grades; $3 to $4 is the price for long fancy, for others according to length of stem. Bride, Golden Gate, Ivory, Richmond, Bridesmaid and Killarney are in largest supply, and the wholesaler has a hard time to regulate the price for them.

Violets are of good quality, but there are not enough for the demand; 60c. for the best California is the price. There are no doubles in the market. Lily of the valley is again coming in fine at from 20c. to 30c. for the best

The West End establishments, especially those which have show houses, are selling many blooming plants.

ST. PATRICK.

BOSTON.—There has been little activity in business the past week. Prices have not changed a great deal and all kinds of stock are plentiful enough. Chrysanthemums are right in the height of their season. Many fine blooms are on the market, although there is most demand for the smaller or medium sized blooms like Ivory and Major Bonnaffon. Prices for chrysanthemums vary a good deal; can be bought at from 2c each up to $4 per dozen for the choicest large blooms. Roses run from $1 to $8 and there are lots of them available. American Beauty are fine at from 20c. to 50c. for the best grades. Carnations are a little better in price, ranging from $1 to $3, while some of the better grades of darks bring $4. There are quite a few lilies and callas now at $10 and $12.50. Violets bring 50c. and 75c. for the best grades. Some fine bouvardia is bringing 25c. and 50c. a bunch. Lily of the valley sells at from $3 to $5; snapdragon 4c. No change in prices of ferns and other green goods.

J. W. D.

PITTSBURG.—Trade seems to be generally satisfactory. Society affairs are rather numerous; the horse show and football games caused a good demand, particularly for chrysanthemums. A good stock of cut flowers is handled by the commission houses and they have been kept busy the past week. Chrysanthemums are in their glory; prices are perhaps not what they should be, but the flowers must be sold and at times low prices prevail. The retailers are not complaining, for they always realize a fair figure for chrysanthemums—from $1 per dozen upwards—but the grower must at times be satisfied with less than half of that. Roses seem abundant, and prices are a little higher; some nice Killarney are offered at from 8c. up. American Beauty are choice and prices reasonable. Carnations are coming in slightly better as to quantity and quality, but complaints are heard about their keeping qualities. Very few hardy chrysanthemums are seen this year; they would sell readily. Violets are in fair demand. The window displays in some of the florist stores are very attractive; chrysanthemums, and plenty of them, are used for the purpose.

The weather has been good for plant trade, the demand being principally for large ferns and decorative plants.

E. C. REINEMAN.

FIRMS WHO ARE BUILDING.

ROCKY HILL, CONN.—L. C. Austin will build another greenhouse, 100x21 feet.

WAXAHACHIE, TEXAS.—Bird Forrest has added 4,000 square feet of glass to his plant.

CHANGES IN BUSINESS.

SIOUX CITY, IA.—The Queen City Nursery Company, with a stock of $500, has been incorporated by A. E. Betts, A. L. Betts and W. H. Betts.

WALLINGFORD, CONN.—The estate of G. H. Rowden will now be known under the style of the Rowden & Mitchell Company. Mr. Mitchell was in the employ of the late Mr. Rowden for 16 years, and with the administrator, Wm. G. Rowden, forms the new concern.

Wholesale Prices of Cut Flowers, New York, Nov. 21, 1906
Prices quoted are by the hundred unless otherwise noted

Roses	A. Beauty, fancy—special	15.00 to 30.00
	" extra	8.00 to 15.00
	" No. 1	6.00 to 8.00
	" No. 2	3.00 to 6.00
	" No. 3	2.00 to 3.00
	Bride, Maid, fancy—spe'l	4.00 to 6.00
	" extra	3.00 to 4.00
	" No. 1	1.00 to 2.00
	" No. 2	.75 to 1.00
	Golden Gate	1.00 to 6.00
	Richmond	1.00 to 6.00
	Mme. Abel Chatenay	1.00 to 6.00
Adiantum		.50 to .75
	Croweanum	1.00 to 1.25
Asparagus		25.00 to 50.00
	" Plumosus, bunches	8.00 to 15.00
	" Sprengerii, bunches	8.00 to 15.00
		to
Callas		10.00 to 12.00
Cattleyas		30.00 to 40.00
Cypripediums		to 12.50
Daisies		to

Carnations	Inf'r grades, all colors		.75 to 1.00
	Standard Varieties	White	1.50 to 2.00
		Pink	1.50 to 2.00
		Red	1.50 to 2.00
		Yel. & Var.	1.50 to 2.00
	*Fancy— (*The highest grades of standard var.)	White	2.50 to 4.00
		Pink	2.50 to 4.00
		Red	2.50 to 4.00
		Yel. & Var.	2.50 to 4.00
	Novelties		4.00 to 5.00
Chrysanthemums			3.00 to 8.00
	" Fancy		10.00 to 15.00
Gardenias, per doz.			3.00 to 5.00
Lilies			10.00 to 12.00
Lily of the Valley			1.00 to 4.00
Mignonette			to
Narcissus, Paper White			to 2.00
Roman Hyacinths			2.00 to 3.00
Smilax			5.00 to 8.00
Violets			.75 to 1.50
			to
			to
			to
			to

Wholesale Prices of Cut Flowers—Per 100

Boston Nov. 19, 1906	Buffalo Nov. 19, 1906	Detroit Nov. 11, 1906	Cincinnati Nov. 12, 1906	Baltimore Nov. 5, 1906	NAMES AND VARIETIES	Milwaukee Nov. 19, 1906	Phil'delphia Oct. 25, 1906	Pittsburg Nov. 20, 1906	St. Louis Nov. 19, 1906
20.00 to 30.00	30.00 to 40.00	... to 50.00	... to 40.00	... to ...	ROSES — A. BEAUTY, fancy—special	... to 25.00	20.00 to 40.00	25.00 to 35.00	... to 25.00
10.00 to 20.00	20.00 to 30.00	... to 25.00	20.00 to 30.00	... to 25.00	" extra	... to 20.00	... to ...	15.00 to 20.00	15.00 to 20.00
6.00 to 10.00	15.00 to 20.00	... to 15.00	15.00 to 17.50	12.50 to 20.00	" No. 1	... to 18.00	... to ...	10.00 to 12.00	10.00 to 12.50
2.00 to 6.00	5.00 to 15.00	... to 12.00	4.00 to 6.00	5.00 to 8.00	" Culls and ordinary	... to 12.00	... to ...	6.00 to 8.00	4.00 to 8.00
6.00 to 8.00	6.00 to 8.00	3.00 to 6.00	6.00 to 8.00	... to 5.00	BRIDE, 'MAID, fancy-special	... to 6.00	... to ...	6.00 to 8.00	5.00 to 6.00
4.00 to 6.00	5.00 to 6.00	... to ...	6.00 to 7.00	... to 4.00	" extra	... to 5.00	... to ...	... to ...	3.00 to 4.00
2.00 to 4.00	4.00 to 5.00	... to ...	4.00 to 5.00	... to 3.00	" No. 1	... to 4.00	... to ...	... to 4.00	... to 2.00
1.00 to 2.00	3.00 to 4.00	... to ...	2.00 to 3.00	... to 2.00	" No. 2	... to 3.00	... to ...	... to ...	... to ...
... to ...	3.00 to 6.00	4.00 to 8.00	2.00 to 8.00	2.00 to 6.00	GOLDEN GATE	3.00 to 6.00	2.00 to 6.00	... to ...	2.00 to 5.00
1.00 to 8.	3.00 to 7.00	... to ...	... to ...	3.00 to 5.00	K. A. VICTORIA	3.00 to 6.00	2.00 to 8.00	... to ...	2.00 to 8.00
2.00 to 16.00	8.00 to 8.00	... to ...	... to ...	3.00 to 5.00	LIBERTY	3.00 to 8.00	4.00 to 8.00	6.00 to 8.00	... to ...
... to ...	3.00 to 6.00	3.00 to 8.00	... to ...	3.00 to 5.00	METEOR	... to ...	... to ...	... to ...	... to ...
... to ...	2.00 to 5.00	4.00 to 10.00	... to ...	2.00 to 4.00	PERLE	3.00 to 6.00	... to ...	... to ...	2.00 to 5.00
... to ...	... to ...	... to 50.00	... to ...	... to ...	ORCHIDS—Cattleyas	... to ...	... to 40.00	... to ...	... to ...
... to ...	1.00 to 1.50	... to ...	... to ...	1.00 to 1.25	CARNATIONS — Inferior grades, all colors	2.00 to 4.00	... to 2.50	... to ...	1.00 to 1.50
1.00 to 2.00	1.50 to 2.50	1.50 to 3.00	1.50 to 2.00	1.50 to 2.00	Standard Varieties — White	... to ...	... to 2.50	... to 1.00	1.00 to 1.50
1.00 to 2.00	1.50 to 2.50	... to ...	1.50 to 2.00	1.50 to 2.00	Pink	... to ...	... to 2.50	... to ...	1.00 to 1.50
1.00 to 2.00	1.50 to 2.50	... to ...	1.50 to 2.00	1.50 to 2.00	Red	... to ...	... to 2.50	... to ...	1.00 to 1.50
1.00 to 2.00	... to ...	... to ...	... to ...	1.50 to 2.00	Yellow and var.	... to ...	... to 2.50	... to ...	1.00 to 1.50
2.00 to 3.00	2.00 to 3.50	... to ...	2.00 to 3.00	2.50 to 3.00	Fancy Varieties — White	... to ...	... to 3.00	2.00 to 3.00	2.00 to 3.00
2.00 to 3.00	2.00 to 3.50	... to ...	2.00 to 3.00	2.50 to 3.00	Pink	... to ...	... to 3.00	... to ...	2.00 to 3.00
2.00 to 3.00	2.00 to 3.50	... to ...	2.00 to 3.00	2.50 to 3.00	Red	... to ...	... to 3.00	... to ...	2.00 to 3.00
2.00 to 3.00	... to ...	... to ...	... to ...	2.50 to 3.00	Yellow and var	... to ...	... to 3.00	... to ...	2.00 to 3.00
3.00 to 4.00	... to ...	... to ...	... to ...	... to ...	Novelties	... to ...	... to ...	... to ...	... to ...
.75 to 1.00	.50 to 1.00	... to 2.00	1.00 to 1.50	... to 1.00	ADIANTUM	... to ...	... to 1.00	1.25 to 1.50	1.00 to 1.50
... to 50.00	15.00 to 20.00	25.00 to 60.00	... to 50.00	25.00 to 50.00	ASPARAGUS, Plum. and Ten	25.00 to 50.00	50.00 to 75.00	30.00 to 50.00	25.00 to 40.00
... to ...	15.00 to 20.00	20.00 to 50.00	25.00 to 35.00	25.00 to 50.00	" Sprengeri, bunches	25.00 to 50.00	... to 50.00	25.00 to 40.00	10.00 to 30.00
10.00 to 12.00	8.00 to 10.00	... to 10.00	... to ...	6.00 to 10.00	CALLAS	12.00 to 15.00	... to ...	... to ...	... to ...
2.00 to 20.00	5.00 to 20.00	4.00 to 20.00	5.00 to 30.00	4.00 to 25.00	CHRYSANTHEMUMS	8.00 to 30.00	... to 40.00	3.00 to 20.00	3.00 to 25.00
... to ...	1.50 to 2.50	... to ...	... to ...	... to ...	DAISIES	... to ...	... to 1.00	... to 1.00	... to ...
... to 12.50	... to ...	... to 15.00	... to 12.50	... to 12.50	LILIES	... to ...	... to ...	15.00 to 18.00	... to ...
2.00 to 5.00	3.00 to 4.00	3.00 to 4.00	... to 4.00	... to 4.00	LILY OF THE VALLEY	3.00 to 4.00	3.00 to 5.00	3.00 to 4.00	3.00 to 4.00
... to ...	... to ...	... to ...	... to ...	... to ...	MIGNONETTE, ordinary	... to ...	... to ...	... to ...	2.00 to 3.00
... to ...	... to ...	... to ...	... to ...	... to ...	" fancy	... to ...	... to ...	... to ...	... to ...
... to 12.50	12.00 to 15.00	4.00 to 6.00	... to 15.00	... to 20.00	SMILAX	... to ...	... to ...	10.00 to 15.00	12.50 to 15.00
.35 to .50	.75 to 1.00	.50 to .75	... to .35	... to .50	VIOLETS, ordinary	... to ...	... to ...	... to ...	.25 to .40
.50 to .75	1.00 to 1.25	... to ...	.50 to .75	... to .60	" fancy	... to ...	... to ...	1.00 to 1.50	... to .50
... to ...	... to ...	... to ...	... to .15	... to ...	GALAX LEAVES	... to ...	... to .15	... to ...	.12½ to .15

Des Moines, Ia.

News Jottings.

The Des Moines Florists' Club which was organized last Winter, and held regular meetings until the busy season came, seems to have gone to sleep, and there is not much inclination among its members to awaken.

Al. Lozier has gone to Southern Texas to look after his cotton farm, and incidentally to recover his health. The business will be ably managed by his brother Harvey until he returns.

The Iowa Floral Co. have been more than busy with funeral work of late, and their shipping business is steadily increasing. They have started quite an innovation in the shipping of cut flowers by mail, and have improvised a mailing tube, whereby a bunch of violets, a dozen roses or carnations may be safely sent by mail without being crushed. They have also issued a very attractive catalogue, several thousands of which will be mailed to the flower buying public of Iowa and adjoining States.

T.

New Haven, Conn.

In New Haven where is situated Yale College, where hundreds are trained for the world's work, one might reasonably expect to come across a few well-appointed retail florists' stores. Being in that city the other day I visited two of the principal ones, and I found them up-to-date in every way. Mr. Munro's store is a spacious one and the stock displayed was of a quality to convince the observer that a high class trade is conducted. Mr. Munro grows a part of the stock he sells. He showed us some very fine chrysanthemums of his own growing. A large part of his supply, however, comes from Welch Brothers of Boston.

John N. Champion's store is admirably located, just opposite the college, and the interior is in keeping with the surroundings. The stock displayed is proof that the best class of business is done. I noticed some very fine Enchantress carnations. Roses also looked much better than my recollections were of those I had lately seen in my own town. The violets would do credit to Rhinebeck growers; perhaps the flowers come from there. Students are very fond of violets, and doubtless the best are procured for them.

D. M.

Wholesale Prices of Cut Flowers, Chicago, Nov. 20, 1906

Prices quoted are by the hundred unless otherwise noted

ROSES American Beauty		
36-inch stems..........per doz.	4.00 to	5.00
30-inch stems .... "	2.50 to	3.00
24-inch stems........ "	2.00 to	2.50
20-inch stems........ "	1.00 to	2.00
18-inch stems........ "	.... to	1.50
12-inch stems........ "	.... to	1.00
8-inch stems and shorts "	.50 to	.75
Bride Maid, fancy special......	6.00 to	8.00
" extra..........	4.00 to	5.00
" No. 1..........	2.00 to	3.00
" No. 2..........	.... to	1.00
Golden Gate..................	3.00 to	6.00
Carnot......................	3.00 to	6.00
Uncle John..................	3.00 to	6.00
Liberty......................	3.00 to	10.00
Richmond....................	3.00 to	10.00
Kaiserins....................	3.00 to	8.00
Killarney....................	3.00 to	6.00
" extra	8.00 to	10.00
Perle........................	3.00 to	6.00
Chatenay	3.00 to	6.00
Callas......................	.... to	16.00
....	.... to	....

CARNATIONS			
STANDARD VARIETIES	White..........	1.50 to	2.00
	Pink..........	1.50 to	2.00
	Red..........	1.50 to	2.00
	Yellow & var....	1.50 to	2.00
*FANCY (The highest grades of Sta'd var)	White..........	3.00 to	4.00
	Pink..........	3.00 to	4.00
	Red..........	3.00 to	4.00
	Yellow & var	3.00 to	4.00
NOVELTIES..................		.... to	....
ADIANTUM..................		.75 to	1.00
ASPARAGUS, Plum. & Ten......		.35 to	.50
" Sprengeri, bunches.		.35 to	.50
LILIES, Longiflorum........		15.00 to	18.00
HARRISII..................		15.00 to	18.00
Orchids—Cattleyas.		...... to	50.00
SMILAX....................		8.00 to	12.00
LILY OF THE VALLEY..........		2.00 to	5.00
VIOLETS		.75 to	1.25
" single		.50 to	1.00
HARDY FERNS per 1000........		.... to	1.50
GALAX "		1.00 to	1.25
NARCISSUS, Paper White........		.... to	4.00
CHRYSANTHEMUMS per doz		.50 to	3.00

St. Paul.

News Notes.

Holm & Olson have not got anywhere near settled in their new store They are now tiling their windows and from present prospects it will be some time before they will be finally straightened out. One the 21st, J. J. Hill's daughter will be married. It is understood that the work has been divided between two of our florists. PAUL.

PITTSBURG.—The Pittsburg Cut Flower Company, Limited, has issued a neat little catalogue setting forth its offerings for Christmas decorations.

Philadelphia.

Bayersdorfer's New Quarters.

The principal event of this week has been the removal of H. Bayersdorfer & Company from Fourth street to 1129 Arch street. The first sale in the new building was made on Monday morning, Robert Kift being the customer. The new building is 35 feet front and 135 feet deep to an alley. On entering from Arch street to the right on the first floor are the offices; all along the wall to the left are wall show cases for metallic wreaths, fancy vases, etc. Down the center of the room and on the right wall are cases containing staple articles that are in constant demand. At the back of the first floor is the receiving room, and an electric freight elevator. The basement is filled with cases of goods, and in the rear is the shipping room. The second floor is occupied almost entirely with baskets, all now arranged that the entire stock can be seen. The third floor is for general stock, and the rear part for full cases of immortelles, Cape flowers, waterproof paper, etc. The fourth floor is devoted to the factory; the workshop is in the front part, while the rear is devoted to cases of goods used in manufacturing Now we still climb higher to the roof, which is a flat slag roof; here this firm has erected a paint shop. The roof has been floored over, and this will be used for drying manufactured goods.

When all the goods are properly arranged, this firm will have a grand store, and be able to wait on customers with more despatch and fill shipping orders better in every respect.

Three steamers—the Acillia, Manitou and Amerika—are now in with lots of goods for this concern, consisting of moss wreaths, immortelle wreaths, and other things for the holiday trade.

News Notes.

The football game on Saturday last made good business for violets; doubles were difficult to get. Edw. Reid got in 6,000 Marie Louise which sold at $1.50. Alf. Campbell got 3,000 doubles on Saturday, and got $2 per 100 for them.

The S. S. Pennock-Meehan Company received the first shipment of new crop bronze galax this week.

Alphonse Pericat came in on Monday with the first lot of Cattleya Trianæ flowers this season.

John Welsh Young was taken home end of last week from the hospital and is reported as doing nicely.

P. Vervæcke, a new grower of large single violets at Wallingford, Pa., is erecting two new houses each 20 x 150 feet. One is finished and the other well under way.

Joseph Whittman, a jobbing gardener was electrocuted on Tuesday afternoon last at Oak Lane, a suburb of this city. He was trimming a tree and came in contact with a live electric wire.

At the Pennsylvania Horticultural Society's meeting on Tuesday the present officers were renominated for 1907, viz.: President, James W. Paul, Jr.; vice-presidents, James M. Rhodes, Edward Le Boutillier, Rudolph Ellis, and Henry F. Michell; treasurer, S. W. Keith; secretary, David Rust.

Mrs. John A. Shellem was injured in a trolley car collision at Eighteenth and Market streets Tuesday evening.

DAVID RUST.

Baltimore, Md.

The exhibition of the Gardeners' Club, which has just closed, has been a success in almost every particular, and would have turned out better financially had it not been for an extremely wet, snowy and sloppy Thursday which kept hundreds from attending. The quality of the flowers, was of an exceptionally high order; the local growers without exception are encouraged and are looking forward to continue and improve in their future efforts and exhibitions.

Trade in general is very satisfactory, but warm, foggy and cloudy weather has followed clear and cool days, and if these conditions continue their effect will be shown on roses, carnations, etc.

On account of the scarcity of bulb for spring display the Department of Parks is negotiating with several firms for large quanities of pansies.

C. M. Ricker a florist and gardener died suddenly on Tuesday last of heart failure. C. L. S.

THE CHRISTMAS NUMBER of The Florists' Exchange will be issued Saturday, December 8, 1906. That issue will appear at an opportune time, and advertisers will make no mistake in placing therein a liberal display of their offerings for the holidays. Copy of advertisement should reach us at the very latest by 12 noon. Wednesday, December 5.

San Francisco.

News Notes.

"Artistic Floral Designs for [illegible] Occasions" is the way the new s[illegible] erected this week reads, and ab[illegible] it all the store trade name, "R[illegible] Florists." It location is 1765 Ge[illegible] street, near Filmore.

A local paper tells its readers [illegible] Professor L. O. Howard, of the U[illegible] Department of Agriculture, is in [illegible] State studying the "bug vs. b[illegible] method of exterminating fruit [illegible] pests, and concludes its observa[illegible] with the announcement that nurse[illegible] men throughout all the coast re[illegible] the Fall trade much better than [illegible] year's good trade, and that a [illegible] demand for all classes of stand[illegible] nursery stock continues. I find [illegible] report corroborated by the Cox S[illegible] Company, nursery superintend[illegible] Charles Abraham, proprietor of [illegible] Western Nurseries, the Califo[illegible] Nursery Co., of Niles and Man[illegible] Lynch of the M. Lyrick Nurse[illegible] Menlo Park.

For forty years Thomas Woo[illegible] was a well-known gardener in O[illegible] land, Cal., and his death this w[illegible] is generally spoken of by the t[illegible] with regret. Most of the time he [illegible] gardener of the Convent of the [illegible] cred Heart, but later served simil[illegible] for State Senator E. J. Lukens. [illegible] left an estate valued at $10,000, [illegible] vised to his only brother and s[illegible] stating that he knew they would [illegible] vide for their aged mother. All [illegible] devisies live in Hereford, England.

Fancy roses have come to the t[illegible] for years from the Redwood [illegible] growers, Angus & Murray, and d[illegible] ers are pleased with the informa[illegible] that their dissolution of co-part[illegible] ship last week, will not end the u[illegible] supplies. Mr. Murray is the fi[illegible] successor, and as a rose specialist [illegible] continue the business. ALVI[illegible]

CINCINNATI.—We regret to [illegible] nounce the death of the mothe[illegible] our esteemed correspondent, E[illegible] Gillett, which occurred at the h[illegible] of her son on Sunday, Novembe[illegible] Mrs. Gillett was in her eightieth [illegible] and was one of the pioneer w[illegible] of Clark Company. She was bo[illegible] Springfield, O., on December 28, [illegible] The funeral took place on Tue[illegible] November 20, interment being in [illegible] family lot at Ferncliff Ceme[illegible] Springfield, O. We extend our [illegible] pathy to Mr. Gillett in his irrepa[illegible] loss.

DOVER, N. H.—On Novembe[illegible] Charles A. Davis, florist, was ma[illegible] to Miss Ella Gertrude Libby a[illegible] home of the bride's parents. [illegible] newly wedded pair were made [illegible] recipients of many beautiful and [illegible] ful presents, and followed by the [illegible] wishes of their many friends [illegible] bridal pair left amid showers o[illegible] on a late train to enjoy their h[illegible] moon. On their return they wi[illegible] side on Washington street.

ALBION, MICH.—The Dy[illegible] Sisters have completed their [illegible] greenhouse; it is equipped with [illegible] tricity, and is up-to-date in [illegible] other particular.

Chicago.

News Jottings.

It is reported by one of the best known wholesalers that there will be a number of new retail stores opened before the holidays.

The E. F. Winterson Company are making a specialty in the supply department of artificial poinsettias for the holidays.

Kroeschell Brothers are pushing matters, and with a supply of their specialties on hand are prepared and in daily practice are filling orders on immediate notice.

H. N. Bruns reports an excellent crop of lily of the valley coming in and the demand generally is reported good.

The Foley Manufacturing Company are making continual progress in their extensive new establishment, which when finished will be one of the most complete of its kind extant.

It is all speculation now as to Thanksgiving business, but the general tenor of prediction is of a very sanguine nature.

It was a happy suggestion, the sales booth at the show, and it was with pronounced generosity that the growers contributed of their choicest cuts, and it was with unalloyed enthusiasm that W. P. Kyle and his assistants transformed them into ducats to a handsome amount for the benefit of Mrs. James Hartshorne and family.

The extensive range of Anton Then is filled with a choice assortment of plants and flowers in excellent condition, of varieties most available for use in his two retail establishments, little of the product finding its way into the general market.

In the continuation of our report of the show in last week's issue the awards in the seedling classes were inadvertently omitted. They were as follows: In the carnation classes, calling for twenty flowers each, the first premium for white went to the B. K. & B. Floral Company, with Sarah Hill. For red the Chicago Carnation Company was first with a seedling numbered 49. The same firm won out in the Daybreak pink class with J. A. Valentine. F. R. Pierson Company, Tarrytown, N. Y., captured first in the Scott pink class with Winsor. The B. K. & B. Floral Company was again the winner in the Lawson pink class with Superior.

In the seedling chrysanthemum classes the E. G. Hill Company won all the premiums. Six flowers were called for, the winning varieties being in white, Miss Alice Roosevelt (pictured in last week's issue, page 602); light yellow, Dubuisson Foubert; light pink, Detroyat; dark pink, Mlle. E. Chabanne; any other color, Incandescent. Messrs. Hill Company also captured the sweepstakes prize in this class, for best six in the competition, with Mlle. E. Chabanne.

Vaughan & Sperry are making a great success of Hudson River violets of which they are receiving increased daily consignments. They also report Thanksgiving orders somewhat in advance and of larger proportions than those of last year.

T. V. Brown is the latest addition to the E. H. Hunt force. He is well known to the trade in this city.

Peter Reinberg returned the first of the week from a successful quail hunting trip to Southern Illinois.

At Zech & Mann's on Monday we noted among an excellent line of stock some Maud Dean chrysanthemums which were of the prize winning grade.

John R. Fotheringham representing the F. R. Pierson Company, Tarrytown, N. Y., spent nearly two weeks in this vicinity taking orders for the Winsor carnation which has created a very favorable impression here. After a successful visit he left for home this week.

Wietor Brothers have been congratulating themselves and others have been congratulating them on the sale on Saturday last of ten thousand chrysanthemums in one order to the Boston store which retailed the flowers at the purchasing price, a nickle each. Though the price may seem a little low, there were no restrictions on color and many odd and mixed lots were disposed of; and as an advertisement for the store the plan was a huge success.

The J. B. Deamud Company is having a successful run on boxwood of which this firm is handling large quantities.

For the present the Chicago Rose Company, which has been entirely absorbed by the Ziska interests, will retain their city headquarters at 58 Wabash avenue.

One of the pleasant features of Wednesday forenoon of show week was the presence of Edgar Sanders, who made his annual pilgrimage hither, accompanied by his daughter.

At Peter Reinberg's they are showing Mrs. Marshall Field roses with beautiful heads surmounting 36 inch stems which readily find a market at $25 a hundred. Among the other especially fine products at present time are Liberty and Uncle John roses which were never better.

Gardenias and orchids are the tidbits among the general assortment offered by Charles W. McKellar.

George Samter of Marengo, Ill., died last week. He was a brother of Mrs. Pieser, who was one of the active organizers of the present corporation of Kennicott Bros. Company.

A. L. Randall Company is already preparing for Easter and is now showing in the supply department some beautiful and unique samples of offerings for that festival in the form of eggs, rabbits, etc.

The E. F. Winterson Company is shipping bouquet green in large quantities and booking Christmas orders for bells, wreaths, and holly in very satisfactory amounts.

Kruchten & Johnson, though among the youngest concerns in the Chicago wholesale district, are procuring their share of patronage.

One of the oldest and most experienced growers in this vicinity predicts a scarcity of carnations during the Winter months. As the party grows roses exclusively he is not trying the old scheme of a secret boom.

It is seldom that such a deluge of floral offerings is brought together as on the occasion of the funeral of Mrs. Richard Howe on Monday last.

WILLIAM K. WOOD.

Correction.

In the advertisement of J. E. Felthousen, page 606 of our last week's issue, the price of geraniums was made to read $8 per 1,000 and should have been $18 per 1,000.

NEW BEDFORD, MASS.—Trade improved wonderfully the past we The supply of stock is about equal the demand. Prices remain about same as usual. Chrysanthemums still the leading factors; there will plenty of these flowers for Than giving. Jeannie Nonin is just com into bloom; as an all around flower this variety has no equal. C nations are looking fine. Some L Bountiful, grown by Woodho measured 3½ inches; it is a gr white but not productive enough h Fairmaid has completely surpa Enchantress in this section. Bo Market is considered the best wh

Thousands of people visited chrysanthemum show given by H. Rogers, the oil man, James Garth gardener, it was a sight well wo seeing.

Peter Murray of Fairhaven has Winsor stock in fine condition. ports put this variety down as a w ner; Mr. Murray is the originator

E. H. Chamberlin, and E. Y. Pi are cutting Christmas sweet p also good violets. HORTIC

RIDGEWOOD, N. J.—Wm. Jo son, formerly foreman for And Snyder, has taken charge of grounds of Ex-U. S. Attorney Gen John W. Griggs of Paterson, N.

HERE is what Thomas Proctor, Superintendent for R. W. Paterson, Lenox, Mass., says about U-Bar houses. "So far as the style of construction is concerned, I believe that the U-Bar type is as much superior to the very best type of the ordinary iron frame construction as the iron frame houses are to the old wooden sash bar houses." Send for new catalog and know why they are so "much superior." **Pierson U-Bar Co., Designers and Builders of U-Bar Greenhouses,** Metropolitan Building, 4th Avenue and 23d St., New York.

Mention the Florists' Exchange when writing.

The Test of Products

Here is a test that every florist and grower can make for himself, as the construction of your house vitally affects the stock you grow. If your houses are not built right you cannot expect to turn out perfect plants.

Does your house produce the amount of stock and the kind of stock it should? Let us furnish you the material for your next house and then make a test—we only ask for a trial order.

Our catalogue will tell you more.

Next Week,
"The Test of Construction."

John C. Moninger Co.
CHICAGO
115 E. Blackhawk Street

Mention the Florists' Exchange when writing.

Your Money is well spent when you advertise in
THE FLORISTS' EXCHANGE

TELEGRAPH ORDERS—Can Ship Any Size at Once

Ask For Our Catalogue And Prices

Order Now

KROESCHELL BROS. CO., 33 Erie Street, CHICAGO

Mention the Florists' Exchange when writing.

GREENHOUSE LUMBER

BUILD WELL

There is a pleasant sense of satisfaction in knowing that when your order for Cypress is placed with us you will receive material upon which you can absolutely rely, and that shipment will be promptly made.

ESTIMATES AND PLANS

Furnished without charge. Let us hear from you if you contemplate building.

HOT BED SASH

CEDAR POSTS, IRON FITTINGS, ETC., ETC.

LOCKLAND LUMBER Co.
LOCKLAND, O.

Mention The Florists' Exchange when writing.

Greenhouse Materia of Louisiana Cypress and

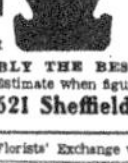

Hot Bed Sash Washington Red Cedar

Greenhouse Hardware and Post — Patent V and U Gutters.

OUR GRADE INVARIABLY THE BEST, OUR PRICES RIGHT.

Write for Catalogue and Estimate when figuring on your new houses.

A. DIETSCH CO., 615 to 621 Sheffield Avenue, CHICAGO, ILL.

Mention The Florists' Exchange when writing.

ARE YOU GOING TO BUILD

Assure yourself of **HONEST COMPETITION** figures by obtaining an estimate from me on **Iron Frame** or **Sash bar** greenhouses. My prices are the lowest for the best class of work.

FRANK VAN ASSCHE
(FORMERLY SUPT. FOR WEATHERED)
FACTORY: Fulton and Rose Ave., Jersey City, N. J.

Mention The Florists' Exchange when writing.

If you are having delay in getting your roof material, send your orders to us and don't be in trouble. We will handle any order in the time agreed. Try us.

FOLEY MANUFACTURING COMPANY
471 W. 22nd St., Chicago

Mention the Florists' Exchange when writing.

Commercial Violet Culture
PRICE, $1.50
The FLORISTS' EXCHANGE, 2-8 Duane St., New York

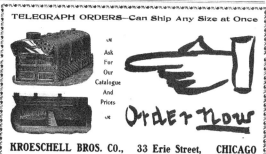

Mention the Florists' Exchange when writing.

WHOLESALE TRADE LIST

ASPARAGUS PLUMOSUS, 3 in. pots, $5.00 per 100; 2 in. pots, $2.00 per 100.

ASPARAGUS PLUMOSUS, Seedlings from flats, $1.00 per 100, $8.00 per 1000.

ASPARAGUS SPRENGERI, 2 in. pots, $2.00 per 100.

BOSTON FERNS, 4 in. pots, 20c. each. 5 in. pots, 35c. each.

CLEMATIS PANICULATA, 4 in. pots, $1.60 per doz., $10.00 per 100; 3 in. pots, 75c. per doz.; $6.00 per 100.

DRACÆNA INDIVISA, 5 in. pots, $2.00 per doz.

GERANIUMS, Stock plants grown in pots. Double white **La Favorite**, **Queen of the West**, **John Doyle**, **S. A. Nutt**, $1.00 per doz.

HYDRANGEA Otaksa and **Thos. Hogg**, 4-6 flowering branches, $10.00 per 100; larger plants for tubs, 35c. each.

IVY, Hardy English, 4 in. pots, $1.50 per doz.; $10.00 per 100.

YELLOW DAISY (Etoile d'Or), 3 in. pots, $5.00 per 100.

SANSEVIERA, (Zebra plant) 4 in. pots, strong $1.50 per doz.; 3 in. pots $1.00 per doz.

C. EISELE, 11th & Roy Streets, PHILADELPHIA, PA.

Mention the Florists' Exchange when writing.

SUMMER IN WINTER

BY USING

Standard Greenhouse Boilers

One cent gets our catalog.

GIBLIN & CO., UTICA, N. Y.

Mention the Florists' Exchange when writing.

A Standard Pumping Engine

is not a difficult thing to install or operate. You can do it yourself.

The Standard Pump & Engine Co.
CLEVELAND, O.

Mention the Florists' Exchange when writing.

"THE BEST INVESTMENT I EVER MADE"

is the verdict of one of the largest rose growers who placed two of these **GREENHOUSE BOILERS** instead of two others of well known make.

Estimates furnished for heating plants erected complete, or for material only.

JOHN A. PAYNE

Horticultural Architect and Builder.

33 Clendenny Ave., Jersey City, N. J.

Sash opening apparatus and all kinds of greenhouse structural material.

C[illegible]S
IS FAR MO[illegible]THAN PINE
C[illegible]
S[illegible]S
UP T[illegible]GER.
G[illegible]E
AND OTH[illegible]TERIAL,
MEN FUR[illegible]ERINTEND
EREC[illegible]DESIRED.
S[illegible]S.
THE A[illegible] CO.,
NEP[illegible]ASS.

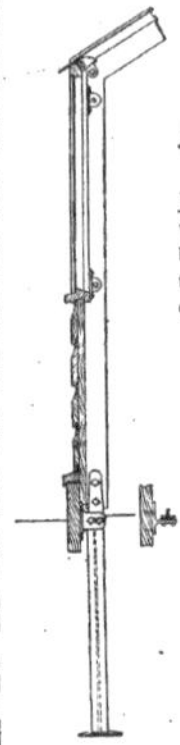

AS IT ACTUALLY IS

Just as it looks—cast iron foot piece, galvanized angle iron, eave plate and all—a combination of iron, wood and brains that goes to make the strongest, lightest and the longest to last of any greenhouse construction.

And Here's Why:

Cast Iron Foot Pieces last for ever. Wood or wrought iron are soon eaten away at grade line.

Base board is detachable for replacing.

Rafter is bolted directly to foot piece, is bent at the eave and continues in one solid piece to the ridge.

The eave plate and sash bar clasp make a lasting joint and give tremendous strength to the entire house.

Every part is perfectly accessible for repairs.

Send for Iron Frame Circular for the rest.

Lord & Burnham Co.

Greenhouse Designers and Manufacturers.

1133 Broadway, corner 26th St., NEW YORK.

BOSTON BRANCH, 819 Tremont Building.

GREENHOUSE MATERIAL

FREE FROM SAP AND MILLED TO FIT SNUG IS WHAT WE MANUFACTURE AT OUR OWN MILLS.

WE FURNISH EVERYTHING TO COMPLETE YOUR HOUSES INCLUDING GLASS, BOILERS AND PIPE.

CATALOGUE ON APPLICATION. GET OUR PRICES.

S. JACOBS & SONS,

GREENHOUSE CONSTRUCTION MATERIAL.

1365-79 Flushing Ave., BROOKLYN, N. Y.

Mention The Florists' Exchange when writing.

PROMPTNESS AND GOOD WORKMANSHIP

The above combined with personal attention to all work, and the fact that I have in my employ men especially selected for their proficiency in green-house heating assures you of the best results possible for the amount of money expended.

Private gardeners and commercial florists in all parts of the country for whom I have installed work will verify the above (send for list).

IS YOUR HEATING PLANT IN ORDER FOR THE COMING WINTER?
IF NOT CAN SEND YOU COMPETENT MECHANICS AT ONCE.

Everything for Heating and Ventilating, Grates, Smoke Boxes, Etc.

WILLIAM H. LUTTON

West Side Ave. Station, JERSEY CITY, N. J.

Tel. 412 R. Bergen. Eastern Agent Furman Boilers, write for prices.

A. HERRMANN

Manufacturer of Floral Metal Designs

IMPORTER AND DEALER IN FLORISTS' SUPPLIES

FACTORY: 709 FIRST AVENUE, BETWEEN 40th AND 41st STREETS, NEW YORK

OFFICE AND WAREROOMS: 404, 406, 408, 410, 412 East 34th St.

WRITE FOR NEW CATALOGUE

Mention the Florists' Exchange when writing.

GEO. M. GARLAND

Iron Gutters and Posts

Patented December 27th, 1898.

Send for Catalogue.

Garland's Gutters will keep snow and ice off your glass and prevent breakage.

DESPLAINES, ILL.

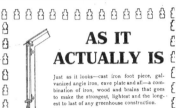

THE FLORISTS' EXCHANGE

We are a straight shoot and aim to grow into a vigorous plant

A WEEKLY MEDIUM OF INTERCHANGE FOR FLORISTS, NURSERYMEN, SEEDSMEN AND THE TRADE IN GENERAL

[Vo]l XXII. No. 22 NEW YORK AND CHICAGO, DECEMBER 1, 1906 One Dollar Per Year

CONTENTS AND INDEX TO ADVERTISERS, PAGE 657

THE CHRISTMAS NUM... of The Florists' Exch... will be issued Next Satu... December 8, 1906. That issu... appear at an opportune time... advertisers will make no m... in placing therein a liberal di... of their offerings for the holi... Copy of advertisement should ... us at the very latest by 12 ... Wednesday, December 5.

CLEARING :: SALE ::

SURPLUS BULBS

FOR POT CULTURE AND FORCING

	Per 100	Per 1000
Single Dutch Hyacinths. Named Sorts. Comprising such varieties as Roi des Belges, L'Innocence, Mad. Van der Hoop, Grand Maitre, Gigantea, Chas. Dickens, blue; Chas. Dickens, rose, Czar Peter, Robert Steiger, etc.	$3.50	
White Roman Hyacinths (French) 12-15 cm	2.25	$21.00
Narcissus, Giant Princeps and Double Incomparable, fine for forcing	.75	6.00
Narcissus, Single Incomparabilis, Cynosure and Albus Stella	.60	5.00
Narcissus, Bicolor Grandee, large flower, similar to Empress	.90	8.00
Narcissus, Single Trumpets, choice mixed exceptional value	.60	5.00

Write for prices of Tulips, Chinese Lilies, Peonies, Lily of the Valley, Begonias, Gloxinias, Fern Balls, etc.

JOHNSON SEED CO., 217 Market Street, Philadelphia, Pa.

Herbert W. Johnson, of the late firm of Johnson & Stokes, Pres.

Going -- Going -- Gone

Just a few left overs, good stock, fine, but we must have room and **Sell below cost** as long as stock lasts.

	100	1000
Double or Single **Tulips,** mixed, finest sorts	$0 60	$4 50
Late **Tulips,** Byards	0 60	5 00
" " Bybloemen, rose or violet	0 60	5 00
NARCISSUS		
Empress, extra large bulbs	1 25	12 00
Stella Incomparabile, single	0 40	3 00
Sulphur Phoenix	1 00	8 00
Orange Phoenix	0 50	4 00
Obvallaris	0 60	5 00
Paper White Grandiflora	0 80	7 50
Golden Spur	1 10	10 00
Jonquils, Rugulosus	0 50	4 00
" double	0 60	5 00
Ixias, finest mixture	0 20	1 75
Spanish Iris "	0 20	1 75
English	1 00	

For price of Spiraeas, etc., see page 619, issue of Nov. 24

H. H. BERGER & Co., 47 BARCLAY ST., NEW YORK

RENNIE & THOMPSON

SEED, BULB and PLANT GROWERS and MERCHANTS

FLORISTS' SUPPLIES

135 & 137 Washington Street, - - PROVIDENCE, R. I.

Opening Announcement

WE desire to announce that we have opened extensive modern rooms at the above address for the purpose of conducting a high grade Seed, Bulb and Plant Business.

The members of our firm are well-known, Mr. Rennie having been identified with the trade in this locality for the past 20 years, and Mr. Thompson for a like period, with leading houses in this country, more recently for eight years with R. & J. Farquhar & Co. of Boston. Our combined experience and intimate knowledge of the best sources of supply place us in the position of being able to serve you in an acceptable manner.

QUALITY. The first and foremost consideration in the purchase of seeds is quality. It represents satisfaction or dissappointment. We will establish a store that shall be known as headquarters in Providence, if not in the East, for quality and fair dealing. We, therefore, hope by careful attention to business to merit your confidence and enjoy a liberal share of your patronage.

Our Catalogue for 1907 will be issued in January, but meanwhile when you are in need of anything in our line, please favor us. Orders will be filled carefully and promptly at lowest prices.

RENNIE & THOMPSON

ARTHUR COWEE, GLADIOLUS SPECIALIST

MEADOWVALE FARM, BERLIN, N. Y.

United States Representative and Grower of GROFF'S HYBRIDS, MIXTURES and COLLECTIONS to color. Fine Mixtures of all colors. Named Novelties of rare beauty. WRITE FOR CATALOG.

A BED OF MUSHROOMS

Raised from our Spawn, will **bear longer and yield better** than from any other variety of Spawn. This is proven by facts. Full particulars and information how to succeed in mushroom raising free. We warrant you if using our method of growing mushrooms that all will go well.

KNUD GUNDESTRUP & CO., MUSHROOM SPECIALISTS, 4273 Milwaukee Ave., CHICAGO

Lambert's Pure Culture Mushroom Spawn. Produced by new grafting process from selected and prolific specimens, thoroughly acclimatized.

Has never failed to run. Sold by Leading Seedsmen. Practical instructions on "Mushroom Culture" mailed free on application.

American Spawn Co., St. Paul, Minn.

Mention the Florists' Exchange when writing.

JOHN SCHEEPERS & CO.

2, 4 and 6 OLD SLIP, NEW YORK CITY.

Finest Valley in cases of 500 pips.

See our ad. in last week's paper.

Mention the Florists' Exchange when writing.

LAST CALL

SPECIAL LOW PRICES ON BULBS

FRENCH ROMAN HYACINTHS

	per 100	per 1000
White, 13-15	$3.00	$28.00
Light Blue, 12-15	2.15	19.00
WHITE ITALIAN ROMAN HYACINTHS Will bloom later than the French	2.25	22.00
NARCISSUS Paper White Grandiflora	1.00	9.00
LILIUM CANDIDUM Extra Selected Bulbs	3.75	35.00
LILIUM LONG. MULTIFLORUM 7-9 in. 300 bulbs in case	5.00	45.00
LILIUM LONG. GIGANTEUM 6-8 in. 400 bulbs in case	5.25	47.50
7-9 in. 300 bulbs in case	6.25	60.00

Send for our Wholesale Catalogue of Bulbs, Seeds and Supplies.

HENRY F. MICHELL CO.

1018 Market St., Philadelphia, Pa.

Mention the Florists' Exchange when writing.

LAST OFFER

Superfine Single Mixed

TULIPS

$ .60 - - per 100

4.50 - - " 1000

Single Mixed Hyacinths. Freesias

Paper White Narcissus

PRICES ON APPLICATION

JAMES VICK'S SONS

ROCHESTER, N. Y.

Mention The Florists' Exchange when writing.

Thorburn's Bulbs

LILY OF THE VALLEY PIPS

Just arrived and are, as usual, the finest imported into this market **no matter under what name. Send for prices.**

SPIRAEA

	per 100
Japonica—Extra strong clumps	$3 50
Astilboides Floribunda	4 00
Compacta Multiflora	4 00
Gladstone	6 50

LILIUM LONGIFLORUM

	per 1000	per 100
6 to 8 inches	$27 00	$3 00
7 to 9 "	45 00	5 00
Multiflorum, 6 to 8 inches	28 00	3 00
" 7 to 9 "	50 00	5 50

J. M. THORBURN & CO.

33 Barclay St., through to 38 Park Place, NEW YORK.

Mention the Florists' Exchange when writing.

Pure Culture Mushroom Spawn

Per 10 bricks $1.50. Per 25 bricks $3.50

Per 50 bricks $6.50. Per 100 bricks $12.00

Fresh Tobacco Stems

In bales of 300 lbs. $1.50.

W. C. BECKERT,

Allegheny, Pa.

Advertisement Correction.

In the advertisement of H. H. Berger & Co., page 619 of our issue of November 24, the price of Empress Brand Lily of the Valley, per 1,000, should have read $13.00, instead of $18.00.

Large Privet

From 2 ft. to 8 ft. Prices on application. **Creeping or Trailing Roses.** Write for wholesale list.

ELIZABETH NURSERY CO., ELIZABETH, N. J.

Mention the Florists' Exchange when writing.

SURPLUS STOCK

SPIRAEA AND LILY-OF-THE-VALLEY

We wish to close out this stock at once and offer it at prices below value to move it out. We have no room to hold it, subject to being unsold when order received.

SPIRÆA

	Per 100		Per 100
125 Japonica	$3.00	200 Superba	$4.00
500 Floribunda	3.50	220 Washington	4.00
400 Compacta	3.75	125 Gladstone	6.00

LILY-OF-THE-VALLEY

5,000 Strong Berlin Pips for less than 500, price $1.15 per 100, or $11.00 per 1000. The above stock is strictly 1st class. Terms Cash or Reference, 2% discount for cash with order.

We carry full Line Vegetable & Flower Seeds at lowest wholesale prices, quality guaranteed.

J. M. PHILIPS' SONS, Wholesale Seedsmen

646 GRANT ST., PITTSBURGH, PA.

Mention the Florists' Exchange when writing.

S. M. ISBELL & CO.

JACKSON, MICH.

Seed Growers for the Trade

BEANS, CUCUMBER, TOMATO, Radish, Peas, Muskmelon, Squash, Watermelon, Sweet Corn.

CORRESPONDENCE SOLICITED

Write for Prices on Surplus Stocks for Immediate Shipment.

Mention the Florists' Exchange when writing.

Seed Trade Report.

AMERICAN SEED TRADE ASSOCIATION

Henry W. Wood, Richmond, Va., president; C. S. Burge, Toledo, O., first vice-president; G. B. McVay, Birmingham, Ala., second vice-president; C. E. Kendel, Cleveland, O., secretary and treasurer; J. H. Ford, Ravenna, O., assistant secretary.

There is a duty of 5 per cent. ad valorem on seeds entering British India.

The following are the duties imposed by the Japanese tariff on the articles mentioned: Beans—soja, per 100 kin, .43 yen; red or white, small, .45 yen; Vicia faba, .37 yen; green, small, .44 yen; peas, .38 yen; rape seed, .51 yen; cotton seed, .20 yen; all other grains and seeds, 15 per cent. ad valorem. The value of a yen is $0.498; a kin equals 1.32277 pounds.

SOUTH AFRICAN DUTY ON CATALOGUES.—The trouble caused by the catalogue tax in South Africa has been ameliorated to some extent by Lord Selborne's announcement that the catalogues of oversea firms are to be relieved of the impost, though the South African Export Gazette says that the duty is still apparently enforced on packages weighing over 8 ounces, affecting expensively produced and often heavy catalogues of engineering firms and bulky sample books of soft goods houses. There is one way, a clumsy one, out of the difficulty. Catalogues may be dispatched in bulk to a clearing house in South Africa, duty paid on them there, then stamps affixed and posted, but few manufacturers are in a position to go to all that trouble and expense, as it requires the assistance of agents in Africa. It is said that the South African governments are anxious to get rid of this obnoxious tax, though they will do so only by degrees.

SHIPPING SEED CORN.—On account of remonstrances by seed corn breeders' and growers' associations, backed by representative farm journals, the Official Classification Committee has rescinded the order instructing railroads not to receive seed corn in crates for shipment. The committee in addition has entered seed corn in crates as sixth class freight, instead of fourth, as it has heretofore been classed.

MITCHELL, S. D.—The Dakota Improved Seed Company has been established here. The company has a limited capital of $100,000, of which $25,000 is paid up. Of this amount $10,000 is held by Mitchell business men, and $15,000 by outside people. The following officers have been elected: President, L. R. Erskine of Highmore; vice-president, T. J. Morrow, Mitchell; secretary and manager, W. A. Wheeler, Brookings; treasurer, S. E. Morris. Professor Wheeler, who has been selected as the manager of the seed house, will return to the city March 1 to assume charge of the affairs of the company at that time, when it will commence doing business. Professor Wheeler is connected with the faculty of the State Agricultural College at Brookings as botanist, and is in charge of the State experiment station at Highmore. Before coming to South Dakota Professor Wheeler was associated with the Minnesota experiment station for ten years, and has made pure seed a study throughout all these years. Last year he accompanied the seed special trains over the Milwaukee and the Northwestern roads and visited 75 towns in the State. In his line of work Professor Wheeler is an exceptionally capable gentleman and he will make a most thorough and efficient manager for the company. The directors of the concern are L. R. Erskine, J. H. Morrow, and I. W. Seaman. The object of the company is to grow and sell the highest grade of seed that can be produced.

THE CLEVELAND SEED COMPANY of Avon, N. Y., writes under date of November 26, 1906, as follows: Our pea crops in Canada are pretty well gathered in; what are out at this time probably will not show up very favorable deliveries, therefore we are in a position to know to a certainty what we can depend upon. It has developed that dwarf wrinkled peas are only about one-half of an average yield, while round hard sorts such as Alaska, First and Best, proved to be a fairly average yield. Second earlies and medium sorts, such as Advancer, Market Garden, Telephone and Stratagem, are on the light side, probably 50 to 60 per cent. of an average yield. The severe drought that struck them during the filling season did the business.

Beans, which we are growing in the Genesee Valley district, are all very nice samples this year, shrinkage being much lighter than it has been for many seasons. Dwarf wax varieties are on the light side, and probably will not be sufficient to satisfy the demands. The dwarf green pods are turning out quite satisfactorily; a much better yield than last season. Growers have been backward in making deliveries on account of excessive rains during the month of October, and so far this month there has only been an occasional bright day. Farmers have been very much embarrassed in gathering their cabbage and potatoes. It has been impossible to get on to the ground to harvest on account of excessive rains; but they are catching up now, so that they will probably gather all without being caught by the frost.

If you hear of anyone wanting to locate a canning factory in a desirable section, let them communicate with the undersigned. A good opening is here, one of the finest agricultural districts in New York State. Peas, beans, sweet corn, cabbage and tomatoes can be grown here to perfection.

S. M. PEASE.

ONIONS AND ONION SEED.—I cannot recall any season within my experience when the blasting of the crop of onion seed has extended over so large an area of the United States. The great crop of California was ruined in its largest per cent., and in New England it played sad havoc among the largest growers. The natural result is that California raised seed will be retailed the coming season at a price near to or the same as that raised for the more carefully selected New England stock. Last season in some sections of California the onion crop itself was a bad failure; we know of one firm that came East and purchased several carloads of nice stock in Chicago and transported it to the Golden State for seed growing. It is obvious that if the blight to which the onion and the seed stalks are so liable East have located themselves on the Pacific slope, seed cannot be raised there in the future at the old low rates.

J. J. H. GREGORY.

LONG ISLAND SEED CROPS.—The cabbage seed crops on Long Island are all cleaned up, as previously stated, but the results are not as favorable as at first reported. The seed is there, but very much of it is of low germination, which is due to the rainy weather and humidity at the time of harvest. The effect of this is the germs started while the seed was yet in the pods; while not noticeable when the seeds were cleaned, in the trial beds they show very plainly. In some instances germination is not 25 per cent.; this is particularly true with the late growing sorts, as they did not ripen as early as the Wakefield, Early Spring, and the Volga, all of which germinate from 90 to 98 per cent. Most of the seed is of a large size and of a dark color, which makes a poor looking sample; even though the germination is satisfactory its appearance excites suspicion.

The stocks for crop of 1907 are all entrenched, and in a healthy condition. The size of the heads is not quite as large as desirable for a heavy seed crop, but sufficiently large to show the types, and, with a moderate Winter, strong enough to give a full yield. Contracts are already being placed for 1907 crops of cabbage, kale and ruta baga, but with difficulty. The high price of potatoes, with the large yield of the past three years, has made the potato the crop, and the farmers indifferent to all others.

John Lewis Childs, Floral Park, reports the best Fall trade in many years, the bulb trade showing a very considerable gain. The gladiolus crop is much larger than ever before, and the bulbs are of good size and in healthy condition. Active preparation is now making to fill foreign orders; fully two thousand barrels will be shipped.

European Notes.

The President of the Water Trust, fearful of the next move of His Excellency Theodore, has capitulated, and the result is that we are fairly deluged with supplies that could not be bought at any price during the Summer that is past. All over Europe such heavy rains have fallen that the annual average to date is exceeded, and all our water courses are full once more. In this connection the proposal to provide Paris with electricity generated by the rapid Rhone is likely to affect the water supplies of the south of France seed growers, whose irrigation works are supplied from the Durance, a tributary of the Rhone. During the past Summer this supply practically gave out, and the damming up of the Rhone, which will be necessary for a continuity of the service, will add to the difficulties already in existence.

Great efforts are making in France just now to utilize the rivers as means of transit in opposition to the privately owned railways, and any hindrance to the flow of a river so important as the Rhone is certain to be very strongly resented.

The trade between Europe and American via the English ports and New York is so great that it is almost impossible to obtain room for even moderate consignments unless the goods are at the docks fully seven days before the steamer sails. The exposure to a humid atmosphere, which this entails, is hardly beneficial to seeds. The special treasury spies of the United States are getting busy once more with designs on the patience and purses of American importers. It is simply inconceivable to us "poor, down-trodden, helpless slaves" that our brethren in "The Land of the Free" should for one moment tolerate such an iniquitous system. What with Government spies and free seeds, the wonder to us is that they do not go in for politics or life insurance, and thus secure a share of the spoils.

Coming nearer home, the sweet pea trade in England is simply phenomenal. This is especially true of the better varieties. The cheap offers of worn-out varieties are practically neglected. The National Sweet Pea Society is mainly responsible for this good work, and it is a pleasure to learn from the genial and energetic secretary that the society's operations during the past year have been an unqualified success. The income has been more than £350, and the treasurer has a balance in hand. The annual exhibition next year will be held in the Horticultural Hall at Westminster on July 16. Intending visitors please carefully note the date. A most important feature of the society's work will be a complete and impartial test of all the best and newest varieties, which will be made in the grounds of University College, Reading, Eng., under the able superintendence of Charles Foster, head of the horticultural department. Any of our American friends who are wishful to have their novelties tested and brought before the notice of an interested public should send samples to Mr. Foster forthwith.

EUROPEAN SEEDS.

NOTES FROM HOLLAND.—Fortunately no surplus of hyacinths or crocus is to be disposed of this season, as they are all completely sold out here, and many late orders for them had even to be left unfilled. Spiræa have moved slowly this season, but gladioli have been making up for this, and especially Brenchleyensis in first size bulbs have been extremely scarce, as the crop turned out very poor, and many orders could not be filled at any price. Only the early gladioli of the nanus type have proved a drug in the market, principally caused by their not being known.—Horticultural Trade Journal.

CATALOGUES RECEIVED.

J. H. ROGERS & Sons, Woodlawn, Ark.—Price List of Nursery Stock.

J. M. THORBURN & COMPANY, New York.—Preliminary Trade List of Seeds.

W. ATLEE BURPEE & COMPANY, Philadelphia.—Advance Wholesale Price List of Seeds.

ARCHIAS SEED STORE, Sedalia, Mo.—Price List of Bulbs, Seeds, Gold Fish, Birds, and Supplies.

CHICO NURSERY COMPANY, Chico, Cal.—Descriptive Catalogue of Hardy Fruits and Ornamentals, Illustrated.

NURSERY DEPARTMENT.

Conducted by Joseph Meehan.

AMERICAN ASSOCIATION OF NURSERYMEN. Orlando Harrison, Berlin, Md., president; J. W. Hill, Des Moines, Ia., vice-president; George C. Seager, Rochester, N. Y., secretary; C. L. Yates, Rochester, N. Y., treasurer.

NORMAL, ILL.—The Phœnix Nursery Company have abandoned their greenhouses at Bloomington, Ill., and constructed others at this place.

DES MOINES, IA.—Fire destroyed one of the large stock buildings at the C. L. Watrous nursery on South Ninth and Park avenue on November 16. The loss will reach $2,000 at least. The origin of the fire is unknown.

GENEVA, N. Y.—The reports appearing in the daily press concerning the affairs of the R. G. Chase Company are greatly exaggerated. We hope to give the correct details in next week's issue.

MONROE, MICH.—The Ilgenfritz Nursery Company has installed a complete electric lighting system throughout its cellars and buildings. The company is experiencing the best season in the tree business, requiring it to do considerable shipping at night.

Seasonable Notes.

Sequoia gigantea, the big tree of California, is quite hardy in the Middle States. It is not seen on many grounds because it is attacked by a fungus, but this fungus can be controlled by sprayings with Bordeaux mixture.

Unless paulownias have well-developed heads it is a good plan to cut them to the ground when planting them. A strong, straight shoot results, forming the basis of a good tree.

Melia Azederach, the China tree, lives outdoors in Winter in the vicinity of Philadelphia, but unless in mild Winters it gets partly killed back. It needs planting on high ground where its growth will ripen well before the Summer season ends.

The long-leaved pine of the South, Pinus palustris, has been tried North several times, and while appearing hardy has died out in a year or two. Probably if given a sandy soil, the plants to come from its extreme Northern range, it would succeed. Are there any specimens outdoors north of Baltimore or Washington?

Buddleia globosa, known as the orange ball tree, will endure a temperature of 20 degrees, but not more, hence is unfitted for planting except in the far Southern States. The buddleias that survive the cold of our Northern Winters are such as the curviflora, intermedia and the like, the flowers of which are borne in rather drooping racemes.

Newspaper writers are again lauding the eucalyptus trees as suitable for growing in our country. One of them says: "The fact that several of our Western railroads have planted large tracts of land with red and iron-bark gum trees, to cut down and use as railroad ties, has drawn some attention to this valuable tree." No one should be misled by such writers. The "Western railroads" must have planted where there is practically no frost, for in no other place can the useful eucalyptus tree be grown.

Yucca glauca, better known as Y. angustifolia, is the first of the genus to flower in Spring. It is not usually classed as an arborescent species, but it does make a little height of trunk in time. Its leaves are very narrow, much more so than those of any other species.

Seeds of maples should be sown before Winter sets in. Excepting the Oregon maple, Acer macrophyllum, maple seeds will not grow in Spring unless kept moist over Winter. Better mix them in damp sand over Winter if not ready to sow them.

Pinus flexilis is one of the hardiest and handsomest pines of our country. It seems strange it should be so scarce in all nurseries. Although a native, no doubt the large European nurseries have a good stock of it.

Sterility of Some Composite Plants.

Gardening Illustrated has pointed out more than once that single plants of Gerbera Jamesoni are sterile, and that in order to get seeds two or more plants should grow together. In a recent reference to this subject it says:

It is a mistake to suppose that seeds are not easily produced, but it is essential that pollen should come from another plant, for single plants of gerbera are sterile. This is frequently the case among the Compositæ; indeed, self-sterility throughout the vegetable kingdom is far more common than is supposed, and the failure to obtain seed from plants is often due to the need of pollen from another individual. In crossing gerbera, take the pollen from the anthers by squeezing gently between the thumb-nails, and convey it to the stigmas in flowers that have just opened.

This accounts for the fact that when choice asters are grown singly, with no others near, it is difficult to find them with any perfect seeds, when by setting two of the same kind near each other good seeds would be produced.

Hollies from Seed

A correspondent asks if hollies can be raised from cuttings. They can, but the cuttings root very slowly, and hardly any grower follows this way of increasing them. Choice sorts are propagated by budding or grafting; the common sorts by seeds. As there will be an abundance of seed in florists' stores in a short time with the advent of Christmas, a supply should be collected by those who wish to sow them. If both the native one of the North, Ilex opaca, and the English species I. aquifolium there are usually a lot of berries in the boxes in which the supplies reach the florists' stores.

Holly seeds do not germinate under a year or more. The way to proceed with the seeds is to mix them with sand in a box as soon as they are ripe or in early Winter. The box may be kept in a shed or building through the Winter; when Spring comes the mass should be washed out that the seeds be freed of pulp, as if allowed to remain as they were, the pulp is apt to cause fungus to form, to the detriment of the seeds. After the seeds are cleaned they are to receive another mixture of fresh clean sand and again be placed in a box, there to remain until Autumn, when they should be sown. The seedlings may be expected in late Spring.

It is better to treat the seeds as recommended than to sow them as soon as ripe as some do. Such sowings render a bed useless a whole season, and, worse, it requires weeding and care, which preserving in a box for a season obviates.

Celastrus Scandens.

Those who frequent the woods or thickets in the Fall of the year where the Celastrus scandens is wild are well rewarded by viewing the rich display the vine makes when loaded with its scarlet fruit.

In favorable situations the vine reaches a great height, often 30 feet or more, and when its growth is well overhead there is a fine view of the red fruit. The flowers are borne in small racemes, greenish white, of no value for display. The fruit is borne in three-angled pods, the pods when they burst displaying the seeds; and both pods and seeds are of a scarlet color.

This vine is useful in many ways. Any position calling for a fast growing vine may be supplied with it. Let it be for roaming at will over a tree or shrub, or for covering a bank or setting on the top of a bank to clothe its sides, it is at home in any one of them. In our illustration it is on the top of a terrace, clothing the walls that support steps leading to a higher elevation. The vines are fairly full of fruit, but not so full as they would be when they are older and become more fruitful, and as the photograph was taken in Summer the fruit was not ripe then. The mass of white which appears at the base of the century plant on the far side of the steps is composed of flowers of the Clematis paniculata, which was in full flower at the time.

There is now another celastrus common in our nurseries, the C. articulatus, from Japan. It is greatly admired for its prolific fruiting, which is thought to be in excess of ours, the C. scadens. As may be gathered from the appearance of the vine in the illustration its shoots are heavy. It climbs by its branches interlacing those of others and not by twining or clinging tightly, as some vines do.

Celastrus Scandens on Terrace.

Beauty of the Strawberry Tree.

One of our native shrubs that could be used oftener than it is is the strawberry tree, Euonymus atropurpureus, a native of our more open woods over a large extent of territory. It is as abundant in Illinois as it is in Pennsylvania; and wherever met with it delights all who see it in late Autumn and early Winter, for then it displays its scarlet fruit. It sheds its leaves with the approach of Winter, leaving to full view its scarlet fruit, which is usually produced in great abundance. This fruit hangs on the bushes in good condition until quite late in the season, some time after freezing weather sets in. It is generally seen as a shrub, but if desired it can be made to become a small tree by allowing but one strong shoot to grow. Another native euonymus is americana. This is entirely distinct from atropurpureus. It is often seen as a creeping form, in which case it is an evergreen, but now and again a shoot arises and forms an upright bush, as many other creeping plants will do. Late botanists have made two species of it, one creeping, the other the upright grower. The pods or fruit of E. americana are distinctly pretty. They are of a warty appearance, unlike those of any other euonymus, and in this respect characterizing it. The seeds are of a dull orange color, while those of atropurpureus are of a bright orange and much larger. Nurserymen find a great call for berried shrubs of all sorts, and these two euonymuses are not the least worthy of those of our woods. It does not take a great while to get a good stock of plants. Wash the seeds of pulp and sow them at once, and Spring should bring a good crop of seedlings.

An Action Against an Express Company.

In The National Nurseryman, Mr. W. Warner Harper has this to say of his experience in shipping trees from his Andorra nurseries to Germany:

In express we are equally fortunate, the only trouble now on hand being for a shipment sent this Spring to Germany by Adams Express. The shipment consisted of dogwoods, and three months after shipment left here, the express people presented an expense bill, covering expressage from Chestnut Hill to Germany on the shipment, and notifying us that as American nursery stock was not admitted into Germany, the shipment had been destroyed. Our reply was to refuse to honor their expense, and we made a claim for the value of the shipment, basing our claim on the grounds that the company should have known they could not get them in before they took the goods, and that if they could not get them in, the goods belong to us, and should have been returned and not destroyed. We have hopes of collecting this account.

It seems just to claim that the express company should not undertake to do that which it is generally known it could not do, for it has been the law in Germany for many years that plants from this country cannot be admitted there. In fact, hardly a single European country, excepting England, will so admit them; and as Mr. Harper rightly says, it is the business of an express company to know matters of this kind. Too add to the above, and for the information of nurserymen, it may be stated that even South Africa prohibits the importation of plants from the United States; and those who have orders from any other country for our plants should look up the laws carefully before shipping.

JOSEPH MEEHAN.

BOXWOOD

By the Car Load.

3 feet Pyramids .... $1.50 each
5 feet " .... 4.00 each

Other sizes at proportionate prices. Every plant a specimen.

HIRAM T. JONES, Union County Nurseries, Elizabeth, N. J.

Mention the Florists' Exchange when writing.

LILAC BUSHES

Large blooming, white, fine for cutting; plants from 4-6 ft. high; about 150 of them. This lot will sell cheap on account of removal. Also, a few hundred **Peony Roots,** large clumps. Write for prices.

RUDOLPH FISCHER, Great Neck, L.I., N.Y.

Mention the Florists' Exchange when writing.

HERBACEOUS PERENNIALS

for Summer and Autumn Planting. We offer NINE HUNDRED and SIXTY-SEVEN VARIETIES of STRONG FIELD-GROWN PLANTS. Send for Catalog and Trade List.

BAY STATE NURSERIES, NORTH ABINGTON, MASS

Mention the Florists' Exchange when writing.

F. & F. NURSERIES

SPRINGFIELD NEW JERSEY

Wholesale Growers

TREES AND PLANTS in full assortment.

Trade Catalogue Free

Mention the Florists' Exchange when writing.

SEASONABLE STOCK FOR FLORISTS

HYDRANGEAS for forcing { OTAKSA and THOS. HOGG } With 7-12 flowering crowns, $12.00 per 100
" 5-6 " " 9.00 "
" 4 " " 7.00 "

From 8-inch pots and open beds, all out-door grown.

ROSES, Strong, two-years, field-grown, selected for forcing.

HYBRID PERPETUALS .... $10.00 and $12.00 per 100.
CRIMSON RAMBLER .... 9.00 "
DOROTHY PERKINS .... 7.00 "

and

LADY GAY, a new hardy climbing Rose of exceptional merit; ready now from 2½ inch pots only. Write for prices.

JACKSON & PERKINS CO.

WHOLESALE NURSERYMEN AND FLORISTS

NEWARK, WAYNE CO., NEW YORK

Mention the Florists' Exchange when writing.

P. OUWERKERK

216 Jane Street

WEEHAWKEN HEIGHTS, N. J.

P. O. No. 1, Hoboken, N. J.

JUST RECEIVED FROM OUR HOLLAND NURSERIES

Rhododendrons, Azaleas, Spiræa Japonica, Lilium Speciosum, Peonies, Bleeding Heart, Pot-Grown Lilacs, Hydrangea in sorts, Clematis and H. P. Roses in the best sorts.

PRICES MODERATE

Mention the Florists' Exchange when writing.

KOSTER & CO.

Hollandia Nurseries BOSKOOP, HOLLAND

Hardy Azaleas, Box Trees, Clematis, Conifers, Hydrangeas, Peonies.

Pot-Grown Plants for Forcing.

RHODODENDRONS, H. P. ROSES, Etc.

Catalogue free on demand.

Mention the Florists' Exchange when writing.

EBBINGE & VAN GROOS

Formerly THE HORTICULTURAL CO.

BOSKOOP, HOLLAND

Hardy Nursery Stock, such as H. P. Roses, Rhododendrons, Azaleas, Clematis, Buxus, Choice Evergreens, Peonies, etc.

Ask for Catalogue.

Mention the Florists' Exchange when writing.

Trees and Shrubs

We make specially low prices on nursery stock to **Parks, Cemeteries,** etc.

Wholesale price list on application.

We carry immense quantities of the finest named varieties of peonies.

PETERSON NURSERY

505 W. PETERSON AVE. CHICAGO, ILL

Mention the Florists' Exchange when writing.

H. DEN OUDEN & SON,

BOSKOOP, HOLLAND.

Wholesale growers of nursery stock for the American trade. Catalogue free on demand. Also views in our nurseries.

Mention the Florists' Exchange when writing.

Specimen Nursery Stock

DECIDUOUS TREES and SHRUBS, EVERGREENS, RHODODENDRONS, AZALEAS, over one hundred (100) acres of the choicest varieties. Send for price list.

COTTAGE GARDENS COMPANY

QUEENS, LONG ISLAND, N. Y.

Mention the Florists' Exchange when writing.

SEND TO

THE MOON COMPANY

For Your { TREES, SHRUBS, VINES and SMALL FRUITS

Descriptive Illustrated Catalogue Free

THE WM. H. MOON CO. Morrisville, Pa.

Mention the Florists' Exchange when writing.

LARGE TREES

OAKS AND MAPLES
PINES AND HEMLOCKS

ANDORRA NURSERIES

WM. WARNER HARPER, PROPRIETOR

Chestnut Hill, Philadelphia, Pa.

Mention the Florists' Exchange when writing.

Holland Nursery Stock

Ask for Our Catalogue. It will interest you.

ENDTZ, VAN NES & CO. BOSKOOP, HOLLAND

Mention the Florists' Exchange when writing.

PLANT CULTURE

PRICE $1.00

THE BEST BOOK FOR THE PLANT GROWER

A. T. DE LA MARE PTG. & PUB. CO. LTD., 2-8 DUANE STREET, NEW YORK

Large Assortment **PEONIES** Very best Varieties

LOW PRICES

THE KIND THAT FLORISTS LIKE

"We make a specialty of growing stocky transplanted shrubbery and trees"

FULL ASSORTMENT OF Ornamentals, Fruits, Roses, Clematis, and Herbaceous Plants. Write for our fall wholesale trade list.

W. & T. SMITH CO., GENEVA, N. Y.

Mention the Florists' Exchange when writing.

SPECIAL OFFER

SOMETHING GOOD AND CHEAP FOR CATALOGUE MEN.

Per 100

1000 HIBISCUS PEACH BLOW, extra strong, 2 in. pots .... $ 3.50
1000 " " " very fine plants, 3 in. pots 5.00
1250 " DOUBLE CRIMSON, 4 in. pots 5.00
500 ABUTILON DUKE DE LONLAY, 2 in. pots 2.50
1500 " MAIDEN BLUSH, 2 in. pots 2.50
2000 GERANIUM ACHIEVEMENT, strong, 2½ in. pots, finest of all the hybrids, Ivy-zonale Section 3.00
1000 GERTRUDE PEARSON, extra fine, 3 in. pots 4.00
500 LONICERA SUPERBA GIGANTEA, Novelty, the grandest giant-flowered large-foliage Honeysuckle in existence 10.00
1200 BEGONIA ARGENTEA GUTTATA, strong, 2½ in. 3.00
2000 HYDRANGEA OTAKSA MONSTROSA, extra heavy stock, 3 in. pots 4.00
500 LANTANA TRAILING QUEEN, 2½ in pots 2.00
1150 CRIMSON RAMBLER ROSES, 2 year olds, extra fine canes—4 to 5 ft. high 15.00
1300 CLIMBING CLOTHILDE SOUPERT ROSES, 2-4 in. pots, 2 to 4 branches. Very fine stock, 4 to 5 ft. high 15.00

(Roses shipped without soil on the roots in dormant condition during December with perfect safety), f. o. b. Los Angeles. No less than 100 lots at 100 rate, on any of above.

The above are all extra fine stuff and cheap at the prices quoted. Cash with all orders.

HOWARD & SMITH, Inc.

NURSERYMEN, P. O. Box 484, LOS ANGELES, CALIFORNIA

Mention The Florists' Exchange when writing.

Climbing Clothilde Soupert, Marie Pavie, Crimson Rambler and Dorothy Perkins - - - **ROSES**

Grafted Oranges and Kin Kans, Palms, Biota Aurea Nana, Conifers and Other Stock for Florists and Nurserymen

IN IMMENSE QUANTITIES

400 ACRES IN NURSERIES 60,000 FEET OF GLASS

CATALOG ON APPLICATION

P. J. BERCKMANS CO. (Inc.)

FRUITLAND NURSERIES

Established 1856. AUGUSTA, GA.

NEW DEPARTURE IN

GRAFTING ROSES

SCIONS TO BE FURNISHED BY THE CUSTOMER.

If you are planning to use any quantity of Roses the coming season, write to us for prices. We cannot get enough wood from our plants for all of our orders, but our facilities for grafting are first-class. Write for prices.

EDW. J. TAYLOR, Southport, Conn.

Queen Beatrice Rose

Four to one shot. Four times as many flowers as Maid.

F. H. KRAMER, 916 F St., Washington, D. C.

Mention The Florists' Exchange when writing.

ROSES

EXTRA HEAVY IMPORTED HYBRID PERPETUALS

in all leading varieties, per 10 $1.50, per 100 $12.50
CRIMSON RAMBLER .... " 15.00
BABY RAMBLER .... " 17.50

PERENNIAL GARDENS CO., - TOLEDO, O.

Mention the Florists' Exchange when writing.

GRAFTED ROSES

Fine Stock from 3-in. pots.

Richmond, $2.50 per doz., $15.00 per 100, $125.00 per 1000.

Killarney, $2.00 per doz., $15.00 per 100.

Etoile de France, $3.00 per doz., $18.00 per 100.

Kaiserin, Carnot, Uncle John, Chatenay, $2.00 per doz., $15.00 per 100.

Bridesmaid, Golden Gate, Wootton, $2.00 per doz., $12.00 per 100.

ROSES OWN ROOTS

Fine Stock from 3-in. pots.

Richmond, $10.00 per 100; $90.00 per 1000.

Etoile de France, $12.00 per 100.

Sunrise, Perle, Sunset, Chatenay, $8.00 per 100.

Bridesmaid, Golden Gate, $7.00 per 100.

Asparagus Plumosus Nanus from 3-inch pots, $8.00 per 100; Sprengeri from 3-inch pots, $6.00 per 100.

Send for Catalogue.

WOOD BROS., Fishkill, N. Y.

Mention The Florists' Exchange when writing.

ROSES

The plants should now be well advanced in growth. Among the work of most importance tying comes first, if nice straight stems are to be secured. Some growers have an idea that if American Beauty is permitted to grow on till near the glass at this season of the year it will be more apt to set. This is a mistake, for if not kept tied, the plants will go blind entirely; on the other hand, it is not wise to tie down the long shoots with the idea that if bent well it will not be necessary to again tie for some time. Keep the shoots straight, as near the glass as possible, but never allow them to hang or lie over each other. In bending a good opportunity is thereby offered to distribute the canes on the wires, so that there is a free circulation of air on all sides of each shoot.

Where a weak plant is found it is a good plan to dust a little air-slacked lime around it; this will be a good guide in watering at the same time benefiting the plant. No matter how well the house may appear, there will always be a few of these plants, which if not nursed along will die.

Care should be taken in cutting so as not to deprive a plant of all its growth at one time. If the plants are vigorous a little liquid manure should be afforded them to sustain the growth, but let it be weak, and apply oftener.

It is not advisable to put on a heavy mulch at this time of the year, especially when we have any amount of cloudy weather as at present. With the extra heat now needed the benches will dry out at the bottom, while on top they appear moist, especially after syringing. If this condition prevails, the plants will lose the lower leaves and the growth become stunted and hard; therefore the soil should be kept as even as possible. A good grower will watch his plants while watering, and the strong ones he will soak while the weaker ones will receive less water, and some may be passed entirely.

The ventilators need a great deal of attention now, and with variable weather no set rule can be laid down; only bear in mind to give all the air possible avoiding draughts. Should the night be warm carry a little fire and leave the ventilators on a crack.

It seems strange, but it is true nevertheless, that after watching over his plants and growing good stock a grower is careless in cutting and taking care of his cut blooms. In the first place a sharp knife is necessary so that a clean cut can be made. When cutting place the heads of the flowers together: there is then no danger of the thorns on the longer flowers injuring the petals of the shorter stemmed ones. Do not pile too many on top of each other. As soon as the blooms are cut grade and put them in water. Never allow them to wilt. If graded as soon as cut an extra handling is saved and with roses the less they are handled the better. The jars that hold the flowers should always be fresh and clean, and never allowed to get slimy.

How roses should be packed was well described and illustrated in the columns of The Florists' Exchange some time ago; but it should be remembered that a rose should be at least two hours in water before going any great distance.

As the season for propagating approaches some clean sharp sand should be procured and put in a place where it can be kept clean if it cannot be put in the propagating bench at once.

PENN.

Climbing Rose, Rubin or Ruby (Rosa multiflora.)

In its issue for August 25, 1906, the Deutsche Gartner-Zeintung, Erfurt, publishes on page 414 a large illustration of the climbing rose "Rubin," originated by J. C. Schmidt, a horticulturist at Erfurt, Germany, and introduced in 1899. This climbing rose, which is very vigorous, is especially recommended for decorating pillars as well as for quickly covering arbors. It is simply an imporved variety of Crimson Rambler, with which it has much similarity; its flowers are a little larger and of a brighter red. These are the principal characteristics which distinguish it from Crimson Rambler.

This rose is the variety which was exhibited as a novelty in 1905, in the rose division of the French National Horticultural Society, by Messrs. Cayeux & Leclerc, seedsmen, Paris, under the erroneous name of "Ruby." Why change further the already badly mixed nomenclature of roses! The first name of this sort is the one which should be retained for this climbing rose, whose purchase and planting are to be particularly recommended in high and cold regions because of its hardiness. — Translated from the Journal des Roses, September, 1906.

FERNS. NEPHROLEPIS BARROWSII

2½ inch, $6.00 per 100.

HUGH GRAHAM CO.,

Logan Nurseries, York Road and Louden Street, PHILADELPHIA, PA

Mention The Florists' Exchange when writing.

DRACAENA TERMINALIS

Matured canes always ready for shipment. Delivered to any part of the United States for 10 cents a foot. Send cash for a trial order.

PORTO RICO PINEAPPLE CO., RIO PIEDRAS, PORTO RICO.

Mention The Florists' Exchange when writing.

FERNS

BOSTON, PIERSONI AND SCOTTII 4 in., 15c.; 5 in., 25c.; 6 in., 50c.; 7 in., 75c.; 8 in., $1.00; 10 in., $2.00 and 12 in., $3.00.

WHITMANI, 2¼ in., 12c.; 3 in., 25c.; 4 in., 50c. 5 in., 75c. and $1.00; 6 in., $1.00 and $1.25; and 7 in., $1.50 and $2.00.

50,000 ASSORTED FERNS, 3 in., for fern dishes, $3.00 per 100; $25.00 per 1000.

AZALEAS, 10 to 12 in. crowns and up, 35c to $2.75. My Azaleas arrived in fine condition and are good value.

ARAUCARIA EXCELSA, 4 in., 40c.; 5 in., 60c. and 80c.; 6 in., $1.00 and $1.25; 7 in., $1.25 and $1.50.

ARAUCARIA COMPACTA, specimen, $2.00 each.

BEGONIA GLOIRE DE LORRAINE, just right for Christmas. 3 in., 20c.; 4 in., 35c.; 5 in., 50c.; 6 in., 65c.

Palms and Decorative plants of all kinds Write for prices. The largest grower of palms and ferns in Western Pennsylvania.

JOHN BADER, Troy Hill, Allegheny, Pa.

Mention the Florists' Exchange when writing.

10,000 FERNS THAT MUST BE SOLD

10,000 Ferns, in fine shape, low stocky plants, not drawn, grown in full light, and as they were pot plants, lift with fine balls.

Bostons, for 6 in., $20.00 per 100; for 5 in. $15.00.

Piersoni, for 6 in., $25.00 per 100; for 5 in. $20.00.

Scottii, for 5 in., $20.00 per 100; for 4 in., $15.00.

1,000 Crimson Ramblers, for Easter forcing, 2 year old, 3 to 4 ft., several canes well ripened and good roots. $1.00 per doz.; $15.00 per 100.

Asparagus Plumosus Nanus, 2½ in., fine, $2.50 per 100.

Sprengeri and Plumosus Nanus, 4 in., $1.00 per doz.

6,000 Vinca Major, variegated, field stock, extra fine, $5.00 per 100; $45.00 per 1000

Vinca Major, variegated, and Hydrangea Otaksa, 2½ in., pot plants, $2.50 per 100. Hydrangea Paniculata Grandiflora, Spirea, Anthony Waterer, and Spirea Van Houttei, 3 year old, large bushes, $1.00 per dozen or $7.00 per 100.

50,000 Shrubs, Vines, Cannas, etc. These must be sold low. List free.

Cash please.

BENJ. CONNELL
WEST GROVE, PA.

Mention the Florists' Exchange when writing.

ORCHIDS

Arrived in fine condition. Cattleya Harrisoniae, C. Intermedia, C. Gigas, C. Trianae, Speciosissima, C. Leopoldii, Laelia Purpurata, Oncidium Varicosum Rogersii, O. Marshallianum, Phalaenopsis Amabilis and P. Schilleriana. Write for prices.

LAGER & HURRELL, Summit, N. J.
Growers and Importers

Mention The Florists' Exchange when writing.

ORCHIDS

In all stages. Amateurs and the trade please write.

STANLEY & CO.
SOUTHGATE, LONDON, N.

ORCHIDS

Largest Importers, Exporters, Growers and Hybridists in the world.

Sander, St. Albans, England
and
235 Broadway, Room 1, New York City

Mention The Florists' Exchange when writing.

Palms, Ferns, Etc.

WHOLESALE PRICE LIST.

Araucaria Excelsa, 6 in. 3 to 4 tiers, each. $1.00; doz., $12.00.

Asparagus Plumosus, 2 in., $3.00 per 100; 3 in., $6.00 per 100.

Asparagus Sprengeri, 2 in., $3.00 per 100; 3 in., $6.00 per 100; 4 in., $1.50 per doz.; 5 in., $2.00 per doz.

Asparagus Scandens Deflexus, a beautiful green for wedding and funeral work, 3 in. pots, at $1.50 per doz.

Boston Ferns, 5 in. pots, $3.00 per doz.; 6 in. pots, strong, $6.00 per doz.; 7 in pots, $9.00 per doz. Larger specimens, $1.50, $2.00 and $3.00 each.

ASSORTED FERNS FOR DISHES, $3.00 per 100; $25.00 per 1000. We have a large lot to offer in best varieties.

Aspidium Tsussemense, 3 in., $1.00 per doz.; $8.00 per 100.

Pteris Argyraea, 3 in., $1.00 per doz.; $8.00 per 100.

Pteris Wimsetti, 3 in. 75c. per doz.; $6.00 per 100.

Dracaena Fragrans, 5 in. pots, 50c. each; $5.00 per doz. 6 in pots, 75c. each; $9.00 per doz.; 7 in. $12.00 per doz.

Dracaena Indivisa, 2 inch pots, $2.50 per 100; 6 in. pots, 20 to 26 inches high, 50c. each; $5.00 per doz.; 7 in. pots, 30 to 34 inches high, 75c. each; $9.00 per doz.

Dracaena Terminalis, 2 in. Nicely colored, $1.25 per doz.; 3 in., $2.00 per doz.; 6 in., $9.00 per doz.

Pandanus Utilis,	3 in....per doz.,	1.50
" "	4 in....per doz.,	3.00
" "	5 in....per doz.,	6.00

Cocos, for dishes, 2½ in., $1.50 to $1.75 per doz.

Cocos Bonneti large specimens, $40.00 each.

	In.	Each	Per Doz
Kentia Belmoreana	3		$ 2.00
Kentia Forsteriana	....7x	2.50	
" "	....7xx	3.00	
" "	7	2.00	24.00

Phoenix Canariensis, 2 in...per doz., 1.00
" " fine bushy plants, 10 in. pots, $2.50 each. Large specimens.

Phoenix Reclinata, 3½ in. per doz., $2.00
" " 4 in. per doz., 3.00

Aucuba Japonica, 10 in. pots, 3 ft. high, $1.50 each.

Rhododendrons, 50c. and 75c. each.

Boxwoods, 1 ft. high, 35c. each.; $4.20 per doz.

Boxwoods, 1½ ft. high, 50c. each.

Boxwoods Bush Form in tubs, 4 ft., $5.00 each.

Boxwoods Pyramids in tubs, 3 ft., $4.00 each; 4 ft., $6.00 each.

HARDY PERENNIALS

Boltonia White and Pink, $1.00 to $5.00 per 100 clumps.

Golden Glow (Rudbeckia), $1.00 to $5.00 per 100 clumps.

German Iris, Asst. Colors, $1.00 to $5.00 per 100 clumps.

The Geo. Wittbold Co.

1657 BUCKINGHAM PLACE, **CHICAGO**

Mention the Florists' Exchange when writing.

FERNS OUR SPECIALTY

Cibotium Schiedei: We have a grand stock of this magnificent tree fern in all sizes. 3 in. pots, $25.00 per 100; 4 in. pots, $45.00 per 100; 5 in. pots, $70.00 per 100; 7 in. pots, $1.70 each; 8 in. pots, $3.50 each.

Assorted Ferns, from 2¼ in. pots, all the best market varieties, $3.00 per 100, or $25.00 per 1000; 4 inch pots, $12.00 per 100.

If by mail add 10c. each 100 plants.

Adiantum Cuneatum,	3 in. pots, $3.50	per 100
" "	4 in. pots, 12.00	" "
" **Rhodophyllum**	4 in. pots, $25.00	per 100
" **Lathamii,**	4 in. pots, $20.00	per 100
" **Regina,**	4 in. pots, $36.00	per 100

Fern Spores gathered from our own stock plants 30c. per trade package or $4.00 per doz. packages

ANDERSON & CHRISTENSEN,
SHORT HILLS, N. J.

Mention The Florists' Exchange when writing.

BARGAIN
TO MAKE ROOM

1,000 **N. Piersoni Elegantissima Ferns,** from 2¼ in. pots, $8.00 per 100. A No. 1 stock: ready for 4 and 5 in. pots. Cash with order, please.

R. ENGELMAN & SON
PITTSFIELD, MASS.

Mention The Florists' Exchange when writing.

NEPHROLEPIS

Whitmani, 2¼ in., $25.00 per 100.
Barrowsii, $10.00 per 100.

Henry H. Barrows & Son, Whitman, Mass.

Mention The Florists' Exchange when writing.

FERNS FOR JARDINIERES

Strong, healthy plants, from 2½ in. pots, $3.00 per 100; $25.00 per 1000; 250 at 1000 rate; 3 in., $6.00 per 100; 4 in., $12.00 per 100.

Adiantum Cuneatum, 3 in., $6.00 per 100; 4 in., $12.00 per 100.

FRANK N. ESKESEN, MADISON, N. J.

Mention the Florists' Exchange when writing.

Grower of Palms, Ferns and other Decorative Stock.

Nephrolepis Scottii all the year round

JOHN SCOTT

Rutland Road & E. 45th St., BROOKLYN, N. Y
Telephone 2890 Bedford.

Mention the Florists' Exchange when writing.

100 Scottii Ferns

Extremely fine, 6 in. for $25.00 cash

Larchmont Nurseries
Larchmont, N. Y.

Mention The Florists' Exchange when writing.

WHITMANI FERN

Large stock of strong plants, 2¼ inch pots, $12.00 per 100. 4 inch pots $25.00 per 100.

TARRYTOWN FERN

3 inch pots.......................$ 8.00

SCOTTII

2¼ inch pots.......................$ 5.00
4 inch pots....................... 12.00

KENTIA FORSTERIANA

4 inch pots, made up, strong and bushy.......$25.00
5 inch pots, made up, strong and bushy....... 50.00

No order for less than 10 plants accepted.

CHAS. H. CAMPBELL,
3601 GERMANTOWN AVE., PHILA., Pa

Mention The Florists' Exchange when writing.

Holly FERNS

Now is the time to buy for your Christmas trade. The plants can be shipped with perfect safety at this season, and you will have the first selection in a stock of over 16,000.

Fine bushy plants, 2 in., $3.00 per 100; 3 in., $4.00 per 100.

ASPIDIUM TSUSSEMENSE, one of the best and hardiest ferns for table ferneries, 3 in., bushy, 6c.; 2 in. 3c.

ASSORTED FERNS, fine bushy plants, the best varieties, including a good proportion of the **Holly Ferns,** $3.00 per 100.

Prompt Shipments: Careful Packing: Liberal Count.

R. G. HANFORD, · NORWALK, CONN.

Mention the Florists' Exchange when writing.

Adiantum Farleyense

I can quote splendid stock at from $2.00 per dozen up to $24.00 per dozen, in 2-inch to 6-inch pots. If you are looking for Farleyense, better write me about it.

CHARLES H. TOTTY, Madison, N. J.

Mention The Florists' Exchange when writing.

Phoenix Roebelenii

Beautiful—Graceful—Useful

	Each	10	100
7 in. pot plants	$4.00	$35.00	$300.00
4 in. pot plants	1.00	9.00	80.00

Well Rooted Seedlings

	100	1000	10,000
4 to 5 in. high.........	$5.00	$40.00	$300.00

JOHN LEWIS CHILDS, Floral Park, N. Y.

Mention the Florists' Exchange when writing.

Araucaria Excelsa

16 to 18 inches High, 4 to 5 Tiers, 50 cents each; $5.00 per dozen.

THE CONARD & JONES CO., West Grove, Pa.

KENTIA BELMOREANA

5 in., clean and bushy, 50c. and 75c. each. 2½ in., for center of fern dishes, 10c. each; $9.00 per 100.

SCOTTII FERNS, 6 in., 40c.
DRACAENA INDIVISA, 6 in., 35c.
FERNS FOR JARDINIERES, etc., $3.00 per 100

H. WESTON, HEMPSTEAD, N. Y.

COCOS PALMS.

Strong 2¼ inch at $1.50 per dozen. Write for lowest prices on Kentias.

Jas. F. Barclay R. I. GREENHOUSES Pawtucket, R. I.

Mention The Florists' Exchange when writing.

ROBERT CRAIG & CO.

ROSES, PALMS, CROTONS

CARNATIONS and Novelties in DECORATIVE PLANTS

Market and 49th Sts. PHILADELPHIA. PA.

Mention The Florists' Exchange when writing.

FERNS FOR FERNERIES

From 2¼ in. pots, $3.00 per 100; $25.00 per 1000.

Smilax, from 2½ in. pots, $2.00 per 100; $18.00 per 1000.

Asparagus Plumosus and **Sprengeri,** 2¼ in. pots, $2.50 per 100; $20.00 per 1000.

EVENDEN BROS., Williamsport, Pa.

Mention the Florists' Exchange when writing.

ASPARAGUS

ASPARAGUS PLUMOSUS, 2¼ in. at $2.50, 4 in. at $10.00, 6 in. at $25.00 per 100.

ASPARAGUS SPRENGERI, 3 in at $6.00, 4 inch at $8.00, 5 in. at $15.00 per 100.

PIERSONI FERN, 5 in. at 30c., 6 in. at 40c. each.

Chrysanthemum Stock Plants

Oneh, Monrovia, Omega, Lady Harriett, Viviand-Morel, Duckham, Alice Byron, Pearson, Halliday, Robinson, Appleton, Et. Bonnefond, Dalskov, Ivory, Dr. Enguehard, Timothy Eaton, Yellow Eaton, White Bonnaffon, Major Bonnaffon, $5.00 per 100. Cash or C. O. D.

W. J. & M. S. VESEY, Fort Wayne, Ind.

Mention the Florists' Exchange when writing.

SMILAX PLANTS

Strong, bushy growing stock. From 3 in. pots, $2.00 per 100, $18.00 per 1000. 2 in. pots, $1.00 per 100; $9.00 per 1000.

ASPARAGUS PLUMOSUS NANUS, fine thrifty, from 3 in pots $4.00 per 100.

R. KILBOURN, CLINTON, N. Y.

Mention the Florists' Exchange when writing.

LIST OF ADVERTISERS

INDEX TO STOCK ADVERTISED

Contents.

Newport, R. I.

News and Trade Notes.

Gardeners and others engaged in tree moving and planting are taking full advantage of the opportunity the present weather affords to push operations toward completion. There is every season more or less work done here in the way of changes of arrangement and renovation, and this year there seems to be more than usual of both under way.

Anyone who has been in the habit of visiting Newport at varying intervals during the last thirty or more years never failed to be struck with the imposing effect of the towering elm trees in front of the estate of E. J. Berwind on Bellevue avenue. I have not the slightest doubt but the greater number of those will regret to learn that on their next visit those elms will not be seen; last week they were all cut down. In case it may be supposed that the elm leaf beetle was responsible for their removal, I hasten to acquit these little rascals of the charge. The reason why these trees were sacrificed was that in the opinion of Mr. Berwind and his advisors the trees, by reason of their predominating majesty, detracted from the effect that was desired that the magnificent pile of masonry they overshadowed would produce. It has been decided to plant in place of the elms very choice specimen evergreens, a great number of which Mr. Butterton is now in search of for that purpose.

Early this year the city of Newport by vote of the tax payers adopted a new charter increasing the representation in the representative council nearly tenfold and otherwise changing things. One effect of this action is seen now in the entry into the political arena of a surprisingly large number of gardeners and horticulturists of another type side by side and in opposition to nearly as many millionaires. I am totally unable at this date to forecast how largely either class will be represented in the new representative council.

Notwithstanding that Newport experienced a rather indifferent season on the whole as regards Summer visitors, now in the beginning of Winter things look brighter than conditions indicated some time ago. Labor is fully employed and business good. Florists are especially pleased that such is the case because prosperity being general, means a great deal to them from now on. Most of the dealers are actively preparing for Thanksgiving.

The advance in wages which is now becoming general throughout the country is, to some extent at least, shared in by Newport gardeners; several individuals have recently received the welcome news of increased salary.

D. M.

San Francisco.

News Items.

It has been settled beyond a doubt that there is to be a social season in San Francisco, and many events are promised which would be hailed with delight in the gayest Winter San Francisco has had; nevertheless the society folk are grievously slow in beginning to entertain, but the city's marriageable daughters are going off for better or for worse like hot cakes on a zero morning.

Among those participating in the work for these occasions have been the Sievers Florist Company, Seulberger, and Boland.

San Franciscans since the earthquake, are scattering roundabout more than ever before, locating largely on the East Side of the bay. They have taken a notion of late to Piedmont Heights, an Oakland suburb, the site for a score of years or more of the greenhouses and extensive nurseries of H. M. Sanborn. So much has this site become admired by the city's business men who want to establish homes outside that Mr. Sanborn has received a handsome price for his Piedmont Heights location and is to remove his nursery stock and greenhouses very shortly. He has purchased grounds adjacent to the Oakland nursery of the Cox Seed Company in Glen Echo.

ALVIN.

Decorative Plants.

ARAUCARIAS.—On account of the extremely low cost of labor abroad, especially in Belgium where araucarias are grown in great numbers for export to the United States and to the principal cities of other European countries, these plants can be purchased at figures that have so far almost entirely prevented their cultivation being engaged in in this country. Araucarias are exceedingly popular during the time the holiday business lasts, and although it may be a little risky for retail florists to order a great many more than last season's sales warrant, still I have invariably noticed that fewer araucarias remained unsold than any other plants.

In addition to their unquestionable selling qualities araucarias properly displayed help in the decoration of stores to a degree unsurpassed by anything else; then by all means get a supply of araucarias from Aschmann or some other dealer.

GREVILLEA ROBUSTA, with its graceful foliage and diminutive tree appearance is by many florists considered indispensable, and certain it is that it will pay anyone to cultivate it. Seed sown now or in the near future will in the course of a year develop into plants that will be found in many ways serviceable. The seed should be sown in a pan or shallow flat, and when the seedlings are fit to handle they should be potted into thumb pots and thereafter shifted into larger ones whenever the condition of the roots require it. On no account should the plants be allowed to suffer in the pots until the desired size has been attained. The plants need careful watering, and to be kept in good condition should have frequent syringing.

ARDISIAS.—There are few plants offered to Christmas buyer's that give more general satisfaction than ardisias. This is not only because of the bright cheerful berries they bear in profusion, but because with ordinary care they remain in serviceable condition longer than most other plants.

A. crenulata, the red berried variety, is the one most extensively cultivated. Ardisias are propagated from seed and from cuttings of half ripened wood. Seed sown in early Spring will produce plants well furnished with foliage and berries the following year, and by Christmas the berries will be well-colored.

For the successful growing of ardisias careful watering in the Summer is an important requirement; if allowed to get too dry at the roots they will surely suffer permanent injury. Ardisias are very often injured by a too high temperature. A night temperature in the Winter to 50 degrees suits them very well.

Plants remaining unsold after being grown into specimens fit for the market will, after a time, most likely lose their bottom leaves rendering them unfit in that condition for further use, but it will be found practical as well as profitable to hold on to these old plants and transform them into specimens more shapely and more valuable than they were before. This can be accomplished by rooting the tops much in the same way as rubber plants are rooted, which is done by making an incision in the stem filling and covering the incision with clean moss, then tying the moss around the incision with raffia or soft string. In about five weeks the tips will have sufficient roots embedded in the moss to warrant severing them from the part of the stem underneath, and be potted. From the time of mossing until they are cut, the mossed parts should be kept constantly moist. By this method of propagation beautifully furnished specimens can be obtained with but little trouble.

Ardisias are invariably pestered with a brown scale; for the removal as well as the prevention of this pest the foliage and stems should be frequently sponged with tobacco water into which a bit of whale oil soap has been dropped to dissolve. D. M.

THE CHRISTMAS NUMBER of The Florists' Exchange will be issued Next Saturday, December 8, 1906. That issue will appear at an opportune time, and advertisers will make no mistake in placing therein a liberal display of their offerings for the holidays. Copy of advertisement should reach us at the very latest by 12 noon, Wednesday, December 5.

Baltimore, Md.

News Items.

The Gardeners' Club of Baltimore held its regular meeting last week. The show committee reported that the recent exhibition had been a financial success.

Elaborate preparations are making for the exhibition and annual meeting of the Maryland Horticultural Society which will be held in the Fifth Regiment Armory Hall, December 4, 5, 6, and 7. The banquet of the society, to which ladies will be invited, will be held on Thursday, December 6. Governor Warfield and Mayor Timanns will attend this function. The Gardeners' Club will take a prominent part in the exhibition, and over 35 of its members will be at the banquet.

The club meetings will in the near future beheld at the new Florists' Exchange hall, Franklin and St. Paul street.

The Park Board has purchased from Geo. W. Vanderbilt's Biltmore Estate Nurseries, N. C., a large number of trees, shrubs and plants which are to be used in the adornment of the parks and squares during the coming season. The landscape department of the Biltmore Estate agreed to furnish all that was needed for $3,250 and the offer was accepted.

CHAS. L. SEYBOLD.

FOUNDED IN 1888

THE FLORISTS' EXCHANGE

A Weekly Medium of Interchange for Florists, Nurserymen Seedsmen and the Trade in general

Exclusively a Trade Paper.

Entered at New York Post Office as Second Class Matter

Published EVERY SATURDAY by

A. T. DE LA MARE PTG. AND PUB. CO. LTD.

2, 4, 6 and 8 Duane Street,

P. O. Box 1697. Telephone 3765 John. NEW YORK.

CHICAGO OFFICE: 127 East Berwyn Avenue.

ILLUSTRATIONS.

Electrotypes of the illustrations used in this paper can usually be supplied by the publishers. Price on application.

YEARLY SUBSCRIPTIONS.

United States, Canada, and Mexico, $1.00. Foreign countries in postal union, $2.50. Payable in advance. Remit by Express Money Order Draft on New York. Post Office Money Order or Registered Letter.

The address label indicates the date when subscription expires and is our only receipt therefore.

REGISTERED CABLE ADDRESS: Florex, New York.

ADVERTISING RATES.

One-half inch, 75c.; ¾-inch, $1.00; 1-inch, $1.25, special positions extra. Send for Rate Card showing discount of 10c., 15c., 25c., or 35c., per inch on continuous advertising. For rates on Wants, etc., see column for Classified Advertisements.

Copy must reach this office 12 o'clock Wednesday to secure insertion in issue of following Saturday.

Orders from unknown parties must be accompanied with cash or satisfactory references.

National Council of Horticulture.

A meeting of the National Council of Horticulture was held at the Auditorium Annex, Chicago, November 9 and 10, 1906. There were present Messrs. J. C. Vaughan, C. E. Kendel, W. F. Kasting, Professor L. R. Taft, Professor W. W. Tracy, H. C. Irish, J. H. Burdett, E. V. Hallock and John N. May. Mr. Burdett gave an exhaustive report on the press bureau work as conducted during the past year, after which detailed plants for the continuation of the service were considered; it was voted to begin another series of articles early in the New Year. Reports were made of an unusual demand for certain seeds the cause of which had been traced direct to its exploitation through the press bureau last Spring.

A list of subjects to be written up for the coming year was presented by Mr. Kendel, and the secretary was instructed to correspond with nurserymen and florists for further subjects.

A report was read from Robert Craig on a visit to the Jamestown Exposition Company in the interests of a horticultural exhibition and congress. It showed that the Exposition Company was not in a position to offer cash premiums for a special horticultural exhibition, but in his opinion the project could be successfully carried out if the money was guaranteed by individuals. It was voted to arrange for a horticultural congress at Norfolk during the Exposition period, and Professor W. W. Tracy was appointed to draft a call to supplement the one which had been issued and to arrange a preliminary program.

H. C. IRISH, Secretary.

Chrysanthemum Society of America.

Work of Committees.

CHICAGO, November 17.—Sadie May Stremler. (Sport of Queen), exhibited by J. S. Stremler, Princeton, Ky., scored 81 points, commercial scale.

DAVID FRASER, Secretary.

Chrysanthemum Ialene.

This new chrysanthemum, pictured in our issue of November 24, page 632, under Number 34-3-05, is to be introduced by the raisers, Nathan Smith & Son, Adrian, Mich. It is a Japanese incurved: color a Daybreak pink. The illustration clearly shows its other good qualities.

Ladies' Auxiliary S. A. F. O. H.

Mrs. Chas. H. Maynard, secretary, reports that the ladies are sending in their fees to join the auxiliary to S. A. F. O. H. promptly, and with their checks come words of enthusiasm and hopes of its success. She writes: "Ladies, don't wait. Keep me busy, and we will meet at Philadelphia next Summer."

Report of Secretary of Agriculture, 1906.

The report of Hon. James Wilson, United States Secretary of Agriculture, for the year 1906, has just been issued. Among the features of the report of most direct interest to our readers are those coming under the head of the work of the Bureau of Plant Industry, from which we make the following extracts:

The search by agricultural explorers in foreign lands for new crops has been continued. A trained man has spent the last year in the cultivated fields and wild mountains of north China and Manchuria searching for new plants and seeds worthy to be transplanted to this country and for wild forms of our cultivated fruits and vegetables which may have characters of hardiness so unusual vigor that will make them useful for the plant breeders of the United States. Shipments of scions and seeds representing hundreds of interesting things have been sent in and are now growing in the trial gardens of the Department. Among the things secured are new hardy Pekin persimmon varieties, interesting varieties of the English walnut, the Chinese pistache, wild and cultivated apricots, the wild peach from its supposed original home, hardy apples and edible-fruited hawthorns, millets and field beans, a lawn sedge that is promising, and a very remarkable lot of Chinese grape varieties, not to mention a most unusually interesting collection of ornamental trees and shrubs suited to the climate of the Eastern and Middle States.

Thomas H. Westwood
President-Elect Boston Gardeners and Florists' Club

A new Siberian alfalfa, an excellent forage plant with yellow instead of the usual blue flowers, is announced This plant is native on the dry steppes of Siberia, where the mercury sometimes freezes without snow, thus proving the ability of the plant to withstand with no protection a temperature of about 40 degrees below zero.

The most distinct of any of the alfalfas is reported to be the newly introduced Arabian, which is proving of special value in the irrigated sections of California and the Southwest, though its lack of hardiness makes it unsuited to the colder parts of the country. A species of vetch, called the Tangier pea, has proved superior to all others in California n ts lururiance of growth, having yielded as high as nine tons of green feed per acre. A large quantity of seed is being grown so as to introduce it extensively next season. A most luxuriant sub-tropical grass, called the Para grass, has proved well adapted to the Gulf Coast region, Arizona, and California. A wilt-resistant melon, obtained by breeding the melon with the citron, has been secured—a heavy yielder, of excellent quality, and well adapted to shipping. Next season it will be propagated for distribution.

Under the heading of "Good Seed for the Farmer" appears the following:

"Several lines of work carried on during the year have for their object the improvement of the seed upon which the farmer must depend for his crops. The investigations of seed adulterations previously mentioned in these reports have been continued, and there is every evidence that the publication of the names of firms found to be selling adulterated seed has been the means of checking the evil. In all this work the Department has but one object, namely, to protect the farmer from unscrupulous dealers who make a practice of foisting bad seed upon him. The rank and file of American seedsmen do not follow any such practices and are as anxious as the Department to protect the farmer.

"The Seed Laboratory has tested for both seedsmen and farmers hundreds of samples of seeds during the past year, and in this way has greatly encouraged the propaganda for good seed. A feature of the work has been a campaign of education for better seed. Cheap seed is often the most expensive thing connected with a crop. A few cents saved on each pound of alfalfa or clover seed may cost the farmer all of his work in preparing and fertilizing the ground, besides the loss of an entire season in getting the crop started. The Bureau has also been actively engaged in encouraging the good-seed work through addresses at farmers' institutes and other meetings.

"Special work has been done during the past year in demonstrating the great importance of high-grade seed corn. The work was inaugurated to establish the great value of proper care of the ordinary seed as grown by the farmer. The main point at issue was the gain in yield due to the vitality of the seed. Actual field demonstrations have shown that, taking corn in the average—that is, corn from different parts of the United States as ordinarily saved for seed by farmers—the yield would be increased about 15 per cent. if the vitality were perfect. The Department has pointed out simple methods of testing vitality that any farmer can follow, and has shown in field practice that the adoption of such methods by the farmer may increase his yield from 10 to 15 per cent. Similar work has been conducted with a number of other crops."

Good results have attended work in securing high-grade strains of sugar-beet seed, and espcially satisfactory results have been secured in the development of the sugar-beet seed containing a single germ, which will eliminate a considerable portion of the work of thinning.

The Department grounds, consisting of 40 acres, are now in a well developed state. During the year all the roads have been improved, a special appropriation of $3,500 being used for the purpose. The glass houses on the grounds have been further improved and are now being used for many lines of work carried on by the Bureau.

At the Arlington Experimental Farm there are about 350 acres under cultivation. Many varied lines of work are being carried on, including the testing of foreign crops, variety tests of all seeds and plants sent out cover crops for orchards, variety orchard and other fruit tests, etc. The farm now has a well-equipped range of glass houses for experimental work and al the newer portions of the land are being brought into good tilth by the use of proper management and green manures.

Secretary Wilson has but little to say on "Congressional Seed Distribution:" his comments thereon follow:

"The Congressional seed work for the year has been conducted along practically the same lines as in the past. The number of packages of miscellaneous vegetable and flower seed sent out during the year was abou 7,000,000. There has been no change in this numbe during the past five years." An expression of hi views, setting forth his attitude toward this unjus and useless custom, would have rendered this part o his report much more interesting than it is.

Florists and the Smoke Nuisance.

The suit of J. L. Loosé of Alexandria, Va., whicl he brought against the Southern Railroad Compan for damages alleged to have been done to his stoc through smoke emitted from stacks recently built b the railroad company and adjoining Mr. Loosé greenhouse establishment, recalls the case of Ru dolph Asmus, rose grower, New Durham, N. J against a rubber company under circumstance somewhat similar to those which affected Mr. Loos In the case of Mr. Asmus a verdict was found for th defendant company, while as regards Mr. Loosé suit, the jury failed to agree. The defence in eac of the suits referred to was that smoke-emitting i stitutions were located in the neighborhood of t greenhouses other than those of the defendant and the judge's charge to the jury in each case w almost identical, being to the effect that no discrim nation could be made against any one of the co tributing causes of complaint; it would be necessa to trace the particular agency creating the dama to the one source before a just decision could rendered. It was also claimed by the defence Mr. Loosé's suit that the smoke from his own sta was a factor in the case.

Under conditions such as those referred to seems almost impossible for the florist to obtain r dress. The remedy appears to be, as we previous have stated, for those engaged in the growing plants and flowers to locate as far away from fa tories and railroads as they conveniently can, or, the case of those already established, to secure i junctions against parties who would build ne them institutions from which emissions of smoke a likely to proceed and prove a nuisance and a det ment. This latter course is fraught with many di ficulties, still it might be possible at least to comp factories and such like to install smoke-consumi appliances, which to some extent would mitigate evil that is a pernicious and expensive one to a plant grower who suffers from it.

Thomas H. Westwood.

Thos. H. Westwood, the newly elected president the Boston Gardeners and Florists' Club, was bo in Kirkcaldy, Scotland. The greater part of gardening life in America has been spent in the e ploy of the Forest Hills Cemetery Corporation, head gardener, he having held that position the past 16 years, succeeding such men as Timot McCarthy, superintendent of Swan Point Cemet and James Farquhar, of the firm of R. & J. Farqu & Company. Mr. Westwood believes in allowing work to speak for itself. He is one of the m members who take the deepest interest in the G deners and Florists' Club, and no doubt under leadership the organization will continue to show same marked and satisfactory progress which characterized it the past few years.

Obituary

Frank E. Hodgman.

Frank E. Hodgman, for more than thirty years in the florist business at Louisville, Ky., died November 19, at his residence, 1912 West Walnut street, of a complication of diseases. He had been in poor health for several weeks and his death was not unexpected.

Mr. Hodgman was seventy years of age and had been a resident of Louisville for thirty-two years. He was a native of New Hampshire. He established a place at 1914 West Walnut street, Louisville, and conducted it till his death. Mr. Hodgman is survived by his widow, and a step-son, John Besler, of Bullitt county. The funeral took place from the residence Wednesday afternoon, November 21, burial being in Cave Hill cemetery.

George Ellwanger.

George Ellwanger, of the firm of Ellwanger & Barry, Rochester, N. Y., died at his home on Monday, November 26, at the advanced age of ninety years.

Mr. Ellwanger was born on December 2, 1816, at Gross-Heppach, Wurtemberg, Germany, the son of a grape grower. He was educated in Europe at the Sorbonne and the University of Heidelberg. He came to America in 1835, and as he passed through New York State on his way to Tiffin, O., he was greatly impressed with the beauty of the Genessee country. He returned to Western New York and in partnership with Patrick Barry established the Mount Hope Nursery Company in 1839. Mr. Barry died on June 23, 1890.

Messrs. Ellwanger & Barry set out together to create and supply a demand for fruit. They selected their stock in Europe by personal visits to France and Germany, shipping the stock to this country in sailing vessels. The nursery comprised seven acres at first and was on the site of the present extensive establishment. Ellwanger & Barry also established large nurseries in Columbus, O., and Toronto, Canada, and subsequently sold them.

After producing a brisk trade in fruit trees the firm created a demand for ornamental stock which increased rapidly. From the pioneer days to the present time it has kept pace with the wonderful progress in fruit and ornamental tree culture, much of which has been the direct result of the firm's efforts. The Mount Hope Nurseries now comprise over 500 acres.

In 1846 Mr. Ellwanger married the daughter of General Micah Brooks, one of the pioneers of Western New York. Four sons were born of this marriage, who received the advantages of education afforded in the best schools and colleges of this country, and of extended study and travel in Europe. One son, the late H. B., was author of "The Rose," and another, George H., who died April 23 of this year, was the author of several books on outdoor and other subjects. Two sons surivve, Wm. D. being an active member of the nursery firm.

As a citizen Mr. Ellwanger exerted a beneficial influence upon the growth and material prosperity of the community, and was always prominently identified with every public enterprise of a helpful nature. For many years he was connected officially with the banking interests of Rochester, being successfully a director of the Union and Flour City banks and a trustee of the Monroe County Savings bank and the Rochester Trust and Safe Deposit Company. He also served as a director of the Rochester Gas Company, the Eastman Kodak Company, and the Rochester & Brighton Street Railway Company.

Mr. Ellwanger accomplished much in the business world, and his various enterprises were of such a character as to have benefited and advanced general prosperity while contributing to his success. A man of strong force of character, determined purpose and sound judgment, he possessed not only the ability to plan, but was able to execute large business interests, and through all the long years of a successful career he maintained an enviable reputation for honesty and square dealing. Beginning at the very bottom of the ladder, Mr. Ellwanger advanced steadily step by step until he occupied a position of prominence and trust reached but by few men, and throughout his long business career he was upheld as a model of honor and integrity, never making an engagement he did not fulfil. He stood as an example of what determination and force combined with the highest degree of business integrity can accomplish for a man of natural ability and strength of character. He was greatly respected by the community at large, and honored by his business associates. Mr. Ellwanger was president of the Ellwanger & Barry Nursery Company, and the Ellwanger & Barry Reality Company; first vice-president of the Reynolds Library and vice-president of the Powers Hotel Company. He was a life member of the American Pomological Society, the New York State Agricultural Society, and the Western New York Horticultural Society, and a corresponding member of the Massachusetts Horticultural Society. He was also a member of Pundit Club.

In 1900 Mr. Ellwanger donated eight acres of land including a large building on South avenue, which is now used as a Home for Aged Germans and to his firm the city is indebted for its gift of beautiful Highland Park. He was a lover of paintings and statuary, and in his home are many rare works of the sculptor's and painter's art. Two years ago a birthday celebration was given as a tribute to his character, by many prominent citizens. He was a member of St. Andrew's Episcopal Church.

OUR READERS' VIEWS

What is a Season?

Editor Florists' Exchange:

Being accustomed to use words and to spell them according to the dictates of my inner consciousness I haven't any dictionary, but I remember way back in my early school days how we used to chant in unison. "The year is divided into four seasons—Spring, Summer, Fall, and Winter." Then there was the obstinate lad who stoutly maintained that the four seasons were vinegar, salt, pepper, and mustard. I also seem vaguely to recall certain expressions appearing from time to time in the columns of The Florists' Exchange, such as, "The Christmas season," "the Lenten season," "the Spring planting season," "the dull season," "the growing season," "the fruiting season," "the chrysanthemum season," "the season of rest," "dry season," "wet season," "out of season," "in season," and especially "the present season."

I am not from Missouri, but I will have to be shown good and plenty how the word "season" can be made synonymous with the word "year." The

The Late George Ellwanger

throwing out of plants, the cleaning of houses and the replanting with new stock would seem to make a definite dividing line between seasons.

W. N. RUDD.

John Birnie on "Creations," Quotes Scripture.

Editor Florists' Exchange:

I see Job has had the gall to mix my name with that Burbank humbug and the word "create." Having been brought up under the refining influence of peat reek and stern Presbyterianism, I was taught that there is only one Creater, who is The Supreme Being. But now it seems that there is another, a poor imitation of the real.

The dictionary definition of the word "create" may be all right; but I think a better idea of what it really means—at any rate to the right thinking man—will be found in the first chapter of Genesis. It won't hurt to read the whole chapter, but we can take the eleventh verse for a sample. "Let the earth bring forth grass, the herb yielding seed, and the fruit tree yielding fruit after his kind, whose seed is in itself, upon the earth, and it was so." When creator number two can create in like manner, then and not till then can he be considered a creator.

I cannot understand how any human being can have the presumption to try to usurp the prerogative of the very being who created him.

JOHN BIRNIE.

Gladiolus Harvard.

Editor Florists' Exchange:

We note in your issue of November 24 an illustration of a new gladiolus called Harvard. We are always interested in new gladioli that are brought out, but it is unfortunate that the introducers have given this one a name that has been attached to a gladiolus for ten or twelve years, as it will be confusing to buyers in the years to come. Anyone referring to our old catalogue will find that we listed a variety called Harvard as far back as 1897. While this one that is being offered is a new one and it may be entirely distinct from the old Harvard, yet the names are bound to be more or less confusing.

JOHN LEWIS CHILDS.

Floral Park, N. Y.

The Glass Question as it Affects the Greenhouse Men.

Pursuant to the action taken by the S. A. F. O. H. at the Dayton (Ohio) convention in appointing a committee to consider what might be done with the glass tariff, the correspondence appearing below is of interest to everyone in the craft.

Fishkill-on-Hudson, N. Y., Nov. 20, 1906.

Hon. Sereno E. Payne, Auburn, N. Y.

Dear Sir:—I am constrained to address you upon a matter of considerable interest to a large craft of men who use window glass in their business to the amount of millions of square feet, and that is the florists of the United States.

At the annual convention of the Society of American Florits, held at Dayton, Ohio, one of the most important matters brought up was that o fthe duty now imposed upon window glass, which is an advance so much greater than existed prior to 1896, and which tariff raised the price of this commodity very materially per pound on every box of glass used.

With the knowledge of your standing in Congress and being a member of the committee appointed by the convention. I have for some time thought of laying this matter before you, and to ask that now election is over and we know how the drift of affairs will be the next two years, if the matter of reduction of tariff rates would stand any chance of receiving consideration at the approaching session of Congress, or if at the present stage of public opinion it would be labor lost to attempt to do anything directly without pronounced agitation.

The greenhouse men of the United States, which run into the thousands, all feel that the present high cost of this ncessary article is to them very largely enhanced by the existing excessive duty, and that if this duty could be brought down to the rate prior to the tariff of 1897 it would be an economib gain which would work no harm to producers, because many of us believe and think that the tariff as it exists today is overdone, and the party that should correct the matter is the Republican in control of the majority.

Our General Ketcham is dead, so we cannot go to the old gentleman for advice as to what we might gain if we went to Washington.

Enclosed is an article from a florist trade paper, which shows the interest by the florist craft.

We should be glad to hear from you upon this important subject. Yours respectfully,

BENJAMIN HAMMOND.

Committee on Ways and Means, House of Representatives, Washington, D. C.

Auburn, N. Y., Nov. 21, 1906.

Mr. Benjamin Hammond, Fishkill-on-Hudson, N. Y.

Dear Sir:—Yours of the 20th inst. received. Congress meets this year on the 3d of December, and the term of this Congress expires on the 4th of March, giving three months, with the exception of the holidays, for what work we have to do. The time is barely sufficient to give consideration to the appropriation bills which will come up. All would agree it would be entirely impossible to pass a tariff bill.

While you desire but one item of the tariff changed, this could not be considered without taking up the whole subject of tariff revision and considering all the claims for changes to be made to the different schedules. This, of course, is a matter that requires much time and deliberation.

I read with interest your statement in the weekly florists' paper. While we imported $54,000,000 of cylinder, crown and common window glass in 1896 and but $18,000,000 in round numbers in 1906, it would appear that our workmen had $36,000,000 worth more glass to manufacture at the latter date than in 1896. This means, of course, prosperity to the workmen in the glass manufacturing business.

You would readily admit that your business had been much better since 1897 than it was in the three years preceding that year undr the Wilson Tariff Act, and the year or two before that when the country was prostrated because of the uncertainty of what the Wilson people might do, for your business must be very dependent upon the general prosperity of the country. It would be well for you to take into consideration whether it is not better to have the country generally prosperous under the present act, which brings prosperity to yeor business, rather than to restore the glass business to its condition under the Wilson Tariff, thereby bringing your business back to the same condition of affairs. I only throw out this suggestion for your consideration, because when the subject of tariff revision is taken up, I shall hope to hear from the florists on this subject. Yours very truly,

SERENO E. PAYNE.

MORRIS COUNTY (N. J.) GARDENERS AND FLORISTS' SOCIETY.—The November meeting of this society was postponed one week to give the many members a chance to return from the various places where they had exhibited. Twenty members were present. Nomination of officers was the principal business transacted. Richard Vince and R. M. Schultz were nominated for president. Percy Herbert for vice-president; Wm. Charlton, our veteran treasurer, was reported ill, and desired to be relieved of the burden of office. Nominations for the office were, Wm. Charlton and Wm. Duckham; for secretary, E. Reagan. Mr. Vince had a vase of carnation White Perfection. It was grand and received a cultural certificate. Mr. Totty had a dozen of the new chrysanthemums. Miriam Hankey is the best of any pink that we have seen this year. By request Mr. Totty will tell us at our next meeting of the new chrysanthemums as they showed up at the different exhibitions. One new member was elected, three proposed.

E. REAGAN.

The Fumigation and Treatment of Nursery Stock.

There is a sentiment more or less prevalent among orchardists and nurserymen that stock is injured by fumigation with hydrocyanic acid gas, and some refuse to purchase stock which has been so treated, preferring to run the risk of obtaining scale-infested stock thereby. We cannot state that this sentiment is without foundation, because in many cases it is doubtless true that nursery stock has been injured by the treatment, but we have yet to learn of such injury where the work was properly and carefully done and where the stock was well ripened. At the meeting of the Official Horticultural Inspectors at Washington, D. C., November, 1905, the consensus of opinion was that no injury would result if the treatment was properly done. Trees should not be fumigated when wet, and they should not be fumigated longer than the prescribed period, half to three-quarters of an hour.

If the gas is started generating at night and the house not opened until morning, or if the trees are wet when put into the house, we may expect injury. It is well known that a weaker dose for a longer time than is prescribed is both less fatal to the scale and more injurious to the trees. Some injury, especially bruising, results from the extra handling of the trees when fumigated, but it seems probable that injuries of other kinds, such as drying of the roots, or freezing, are often attributed to fumigation.

Since the San Jose scale became such a pest in the Eastern States it has been the custom of many official inspectors to advise or compel nurserymen to fumigate certain kinds of nursery stock before sending it out, especially if any infested trees have been found in or near it.

The Fumigating House.

The house, if small, should be as nearly square as possible, with the generating basin at the bottom near the center, in order to insure the greatest possible uniformity in the distribution of the gas. The house should be gas-tight, with a door for transporting stock, and adequate ventilators manipulated from the outside. A house ten feet square will be found adequate in most nurseries of not more than one hundred acres, and if not large enough, it will often be more convenient to have two of this size than one larger. At any rate, a small house or box is absolutely necessary in any nursery to save the expense of chemicals in charging the large house when only a few trees or plants are to be treated.

A satisfactory house may be constructed of wood and double-boarded, with building paper between the boards. A slat floor raised a foot or more above the ground, with space for the generator beneath, ensures a more even distribution of the gas and also keeps the trees from contact with the moist earth. The accompanying diagram will give an idea of a good pattern of fumigating house.

Simple contrivances may be used for manipulating the ventilators from the outside and for removing the generating jar and replacing it, as well as for dropping the cyanide into it. All doors and ventilators should be arranged so that the house will be perfectly tight when closed.

Directions for Fumigating.

The space to be fumigated should first be measured carefully, the quantities of chemicals computed, and the figures posted in some place convenient for ready reference. The cyanide for charging the generator a number of times can be weighed out in advance, each lot being placed in a paper or cheese cloth bag ready to be dropped, bag and all, into the acid, but these should be kept dry in a tight tin box or glass jar until wanted.

Formula.

The following simple formula for preparing the gas was adopted by the Association of Official Horticultural Inspectors at a meeting in Washington in 1903:—

Quantity for each 100 cubic feet of space: 1 oz. (av.) Potassium cyanide 98-100 per cent. purity; 2 fluid ozs. high-grade sulphuric acid, 66 degrees B. test; 4 fluid ozs. water.

A house 10x10x8 feet, such as is shown in the diagram, contains 800 cubic feet, and for each charge requires ½ pound Potassium cyanide; 16 fluid ozs. (1 pint) Sulphuric acid; 32 fluid ozs. (1 quart) Water.

Caution! Potassium cyanide is one of the deadliest poisons. Do not let it come in contact with cuts or bruises, nor inhale the dust or fumes which rise from it when it is handled.

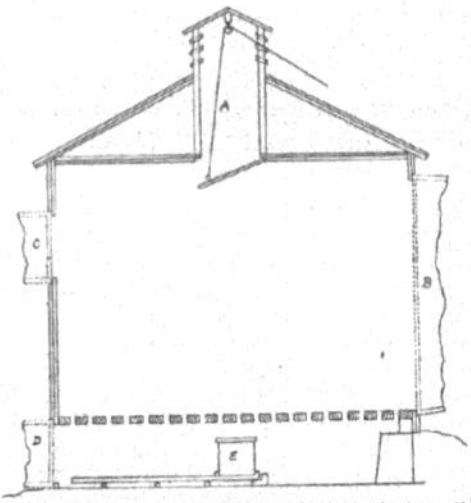

Fig. 1.—Diagram showing cross-section of a fumigating house 10 x 10 x 8 feet in size, with slat floor. A, ventilator that can be opened and closed from the outside; B, door where trees are carried in and out; C, small door opposite large one, for ventilation; D, small door for communicating with generator; E, jar for generating the gas.

Filling the House.

The trees should be placed horizontally upon the slat floor with the roots outside and the tops meeting in the center over the generating jar. Trees or plants may be tied together loosely in bunches, but should not be packed in bales for shipping, as the packing may prevent the gas from reaching the insects, and thus render the operation valueless.

Generating the Gas.

For a small house like that described, a single jar in the center will suffice. If much larger and square, four jars will insure a more even distribution of the gas. If the house is much longer than broad, it is well to have two jars, one under the center of each half of the house. Stone, glass, or earthenware should be used for generating jars. Metal is corroded by the acid, and wood is charred

After the nursery stock has been placed in the by it.

house and the ventilators and doors closed, all is in readiness to generate the gas. The water should first be placed in the jar and the acid poured into it in a thin stream with constant stirring in order to prevent too rapid generation of heat. The jar should then be put in place and the cyanide dropped into it. The house should remain closed for at least thirty and not more than forty-five minutes. The overhead ventilator should first be opened, and then the side ventilator and the door. Care must be taken not to breathe the gas, which is one of the most deadly of poisons. The house should be aired for at least ten minutes before allowing any one to enter or remove the trees.

The liquid and residue from the generating jars is poisonous, and should be buried, and not left where children or domestic animals can get at it.

Chemicals.

Much of the cyanide on the market contains, with other impurities, more or less sodium chloride, which decomposes a certain amount of the hydrocyanic acid gas, and is unsatisfactory for fumigating purposes. The Georgia State Board of Entomology collected a number of different brands of cyanide from various dealers and had them analyzed. Only two brands were sufficiently pure to be reliable for fumigating nursery stock, and nurserymen were recommended to buy these brands, which are: Merck & Co.'s "98-100 per cent." potassium cyanide; Baker & Adamson Chem. Co.'s "99 per cent." potassium cyanide.

Fig. 2—Fumigating House, Keney Park, Hartford, Conn. Reproduced from Bulletin 5., Conn. Agr. Exp. Stn.

Both kinds are prepared for chemical use, and may be ordered in advance from any wholesale druggist or dealer in chemicals. The nurseryman should insist on getting one of these brands in the original sealed packages, and not be supplied with something else "just as good." The Station has just purchased a five pound package of Merck's cyanide at 35 cents per pound.

A high grade commercial sulphuric acid (66 degrees B.) should be employed. In the large nurseries it will pay to buy acid in carboys, but small quantities can be had in bottles.

Fumigate Buds and Cions.

The most serious source of infestation of growing nursery stock is through the buds or cions. If slightly infested when set, the scales multiply sufficiently to mark the stock by the time it is inspected, or is large enough for sale, consequently much of it must be destroyed on account of scale. Where the scale is introduced on buds or cions, the lower portion of the trunk is the first to show the infestation, but if brought by animals, the scale is usually found in the tops of the trees. If allowed to remain untreated in either case, the tree soon becomes coated. All buds and cions should therefore be fumigated thoroughly before setting. A small box can be used, and the cost of materials will be much less than if the large fumigating house is charged.

Treatment of Growing Stock.

The foregoing directions are applicable only to such nursery stock as may be dug for sale or shipment. Of course, much of the stock cannot be so treated, because it is too small for sale, and if dug and replanted its growth will be greatly checked. Though possible to fumigate growing stock by covering it with gas-tight canvas, the expense is too great, and spraying must be relied upon to destroy any scale that may be on the trees. Official inspections commonly practised is sufficient to detect the infestation unless it be extremely slight, but it is practically impossible on account of the time and expense involved to examine the stock with such care that an absolute statement can be made that it is not infested. Too many nurserymen rely solely upon the official inspector for detecting the scale, and give no inspection themselves or treatment to hold the scale in check, if it be present. It often happens that a few specimens of scale may be overlooked during the annual September inspection, or perhaps may be brought to the trees after the inspection. These will multiply until December, and go on spreading the next season, becoming badly covered by Fall; and from this source birds, insects or other agencies carry the pest to surrounding stock, necessitating the destruction of a large quantity of it. The scale breeds from June 25th to December 1st in Connecticut, and during this time anything coming in contact with the bark of an infested tree is liable to carry away some of the new-born scales. From a badly infested tree the scales are certain to be distributed along the row by the men and horses in cultivating the field. The owner should inspect his own stock each year not later than July 1st. One tree destroyed then may save a dozen later in the season. The workmen should be familiar with the pest, and whenever an infested tree is discovered it should be taken out.

Spray Growing Nursery Trees.

Even though we guard against the introduction of the scale by means of buds or cions, it may be brought to the trees by birds and insects during the growing season, especially if in a region where scale is common and the environs are not under direct control of the nurseryman. By spraying the young trees, during the Winter or while dormant, with the lime and sulphur wash, "Scalecide," or some other "soluble oil," it is possible to keep the pest in check. "Scalecide" has given satisfactory results, and on account of ease of preparation it is preferable to lime and sulphur. It is especially adapted to nursery purposes, as it leaves no white coating on the trees. It forms no spots on painted buildings or fences, and is not unpleasant to handle. On the other hand, lime and sulphur possesses fungicidal properties not found in the "soluble oils."

The cost of this spraying should not be more than fifteen or twenty dollars per acre, and the work probably can best be done by men working separately, each fitted with a knapsack sprayer. The spraying should be done when there is no snow on the ground and on a still day—Professor W. E. Britton, State Entomologist, Connecticut Agricultural Experiment Station.

English Society's Points for Carnations.

The Winter-flowering Carnation Society (of England) have adopted the following standard. A variety must gain at least thirty points to entitle it to a first class certificate, and twenty-five points to entitle it to an award of merit.

Color	5 points
Size	5 points
Fragrance	5 points
Substance	5 points
Calyx	5 points
General appearance	5 points
Length and substance of stem	5 points
Habit of Plant	5 points

—The Journal of Horticulture.

Chrysanthemum Notes.

Now that the season is closing it is extrémely interesting to look over the field carefully and to plan the campaign for the coming year, for a year is none too long in which to lay plans either for exhibition or for market.

When it comes to exhibitions—the notes made on varieties at the various shows should be carefully gone over and elaborated and arranged for use early in the coming season. Where stock is weak in certain colors plan now to strengthen it; where an old favorite lacks finish and a new comer surpasses it in this important point, don't let sentiment stand in the way, but use the better one, and add the giants to your list, for size counts, no matter how the conservatives may protest.

And even more important is it that you profit by the season's lessons in the line of commercial and retailers' varieties. Look up your earlies carefully; decide the number that you will grow, and the kinds, and plan now for early propagation of the few sorts that need an early start; and don't propagate in February those that you ought to root in May. In short, profit by your Autumn's experience, and be sure and don't mislay your notes on the taking of your buds.

A grower has a variety of feelings in his mind when the last weeks of November come round. He recalls the pride that stirred him over those fancy early blooms that brought $3 and $4 per dozen. He has a leaf from his note book yet where he figured "so many plants to the bench, so many to the house at so much per dozen," and the total "looked good" to him; but now as he gazes at the dismantled houses, and remembers the varieties that failed to make their promise good, some by damping petals others by hollow centers, or long bare necks, or by bullheaded crowns, or weak stems, he turns back to that page and writes out a good big discount, and if he is wise, weeds out and reorganizes his varieties, so that his percentage of good blooms may be increased for another season. For every square foot of bench space must render adequate returns or it will speedily show on his ledger account.

Too many florists fail to plan ahead, and when planting time comes round they set in the bench whatever happens to be on hand at the moment until the space is filled, without much reference to last year's records. The sucessful grower early in the year decides on the space and the location that he will give his chrysanthemums for the coming year, estimates the number of early, midseason and late that he must have, then reduces this number into a certain quantity of each of the kinds that he considers most profitable, and holds fast to it. No plant grown for profit in a greenhouse requires such constant and careful reference to a note book in its culture as does the chrysanthemum; in fact the grower needs his book in his left hand while he works with his right; and at the same time there are a hundred points that evade the book and must be worked out by the closest observation and attention. The compelling charm of the chrysanthemum is that its mysteries are never quite fathomed; there is always one more problem to be figured out the next season.

Every Fall the novelties on trial must be scored up, if not by the national committee, certainly by the grower. The year has seen the usual number of immigrants, and in justice to the raisers it must be said that they are so fine a lot as a whole that it is embarrassing to make a selection. The imported early sorts have already been pretty well reviewed in this paper, and from them, half a dozen good commercial varieties will be added to the class of Monrovia and Clementine Touset; the midseason novelties fall naturally into either commercial or exhibition. In the former class is Mlle. E. Chabanne, which won a first prize at the Philadelphia show, scored 89 points, commercial scale, before the C. S. A., won first in its color among the seedling entries, besides taking the sweepstakes. This is a beauty in color, of splendid size and depth, with a good stem, and the tint only becomes prettier as it matures. It always reminds the writer of a pink Beatrice May.

Then there is Mme. Armand Detroyat, on which we unfortunately took a majority on the wrong bud. From the second bud the color is deeper than that of William Duckham, a lovely shade of pink, and the form is perfect while the size is grand. This was also a prize winner in the seedling class at Chicago, and scored 89 points before the national committee. It is a beautiful grower with perfect stem and foliage.

Mlle. Jeanne Rosette is a very late variety, coming in with Jeannie Nonin, is of the largest size, a big compact pink, as good a traveler as Timothy Eaton, and at this writing seems to have every qualification for a profitable late pink.

It is a noteworthy fact that every winner of the seedling prizes at Chicago this year is a French sort. For some reason the conditions in France and here seem to be quite similar, and since the French raisers have been sending us dwarf varieties with good foliage, our collections have been greatly enriched by their offerings, especially in the commercial class.

To our English and Australian friends we owe some of our grandest exhibition sorts, though it requires considerable skill to show them at their best before the second year. The most noteworthy English variety this year is the white sport from William Duckham named Miss Clay Frick, which needs no further description after saying that it won the C. S. A. prize as "best undisseminated variety at the Chicago show." Only one point below it in the scoring was Mr. Wells's enormous pink, since named by Mr. Fraser Mlle. Ogiz. This variety will have to be reckoned with as an exhibition entry.

British Empire, as beseems it when carrying such a name, is magnificence itself from the proper bud; burnished gold is the color, the size grand, and the form like exquisite carving.

Of American productions Golden Dome from John A. Macrae is one of the most valuable, for it is golden yellow with the pointed form of a Major Bonnaffon. It scored 89 points before both the New York and Philadelphia committees. As a consequence of its fine reputation made in the East it is being taken up in large quantity; it will doubtless rank high as a late commercial. S. A. HILL.

Richmond, Ind.

Chrysanthemums.

(Abstract of paper read by Herman Knope before the Detroit Florists' Club, Wednesday, November 21, 1906.)

In his preliminary remarks Mr. Knope referred to the great popularity of the chrysanthemum; the necessity of growers being perfectly familiar with varieties, the vagaries of public predilection and the value of flower shows and window displays. He believed that many chrysanthemum flowers were sold at too low a price, and that values commensurate with the work entailed in growing the blooms should be the object striven for. Proceeding to the cultural requirements of the chrysanthemum he said:

The Stock Plants.

In the first place we must have enough stock and plant it out in a good suitable place in order to secure good healthy cuttings. When the time comes to propagate we must be careful to select good strong, healthy wood. Here is where the growing of good chrysanthemums begins. I prefer planting stock plants in a bench. By this method I believe we can secure more and better cuttings.

One more good plan, if one has the frames and sash, is to plant stock out in frames and protect the plants from the frost with straw mats. I have noticed that the strongest and healthiest cuttings have been secured from such stock.

Antirrhinum—Snapdragon

Photo by J. F. Johnston

Propagation.

There are no two people who hold the same ideas regarding the propagating of chrysanthemums. I have had fairly good success planting out doors in frames; but if one has a good side bench, in an airy house I would prefer it to cold frames. We should use good clean sharp sand. Give plenty of water and protect the cuttings from the sun by shading. By following this method one will have no trouble in striking cuttings.

The time to begin propagating chrysanthemums will depend on the varieties one wishes to grow. If it is desired to grow the earliest ones, and good blooms are expected they should be propagated by April 1, and should be ready to plant the latter part of May. The midseason varieties should be propagated in May and planted the first part of June. The late ones can be planted as late as the middle of July, and if well cared for will produce good flowers. Chrysanthemums that are to be grown for exhibition purposes should all be propagated by the last week in March or the first week of April, and the best of wood must be taken. Plant the same the latter part of May.

The Number of Varieties to Grow.

The number of varieties one should grow is a matter of some importance. I believe that any grower of chrysanthemums, who cultivates for the wholesale market, should limit himself to not more than twelve or fifteen varieties. By so doing one will find it much less work. Out of the number of varieties we have to-day, one can hardly find more than the above given number for a wholesaler to grow.

Some of the Best Shipping Sorts.

For shipping I will name some of the varieties that I think are good for commercial use. In white I would suggest White Bonnaffon, Mrs. Jerome Jones, and W. H. Chadwick. Good pink ones are, Glory of the Pacific, J. K. Shaw, Ivory Rose, and Maud Dean. There are many good yellows, among which are Robert Halliday, Harry Hurrell, Major Bonnaffon, Nagoya, Yellow Jones, Golden Chadwick, and H. W. Rieman. In considering good whites we must not overlook White Ivory. It is by far the best selling chrysanthemum we have to-day. It requires less room than any other and will on the average net the grower more than the larger varieties.

Planting and Cultural Care.

The space to give chrysanthemums depends entirely on the varieties one plants. We all know from experience that we must allow more room for those that are clothed with heavy foliage than those that have small foliage.

The soil suitable for growing good chrysanthemums must be good stiff soil. I don't mean hard clay, but good stiff sod piled up and well manured in the Fall and turned over in the Spring.

The depth of soil in which to plant chrysanthemums is of great importance. Some plant in 4 or 5 inches of soil, others in from 6 to 8 inches. There is the greater advantage in planting in 4 or 5 inches of soil because the watering and feeding can be controlled more successfully.

In order to grow chrysanthemums in solid benches these must be well drained. Cinders or broken bricks make excellent drainage. It is also well to sprinkle the bottom of the bench with air-slacked lime to prevent the angle worms from working in the soil.

In order to have good success with chrysanthemums one should plant a house or a bench with varieties which are uniform as to their time of blooming.

After a bench of chrysanthemums has been planted about two weeks it is essential that the soil be firmed about them. Suckers and side shoots must be removed if one wishes success.

The next step is the disbudding; in this one cannot be too careful and thorough. Great care must be taken in removing buds, not to injure the terminal one.

The feeding of chrysanthemums is also an interesting study. Feeding should begin at the time the bud first shows, and should be discontinued when first the bud shows color. The color of the chrysanthemum has a great deal to do with the amount of food given. Pink varieties should be fed least, as they are most susceptible to fading. Yellows are not so delicate in this regard, while it is almost needless to say white chrysanthemums can be fed the heaviest. Liquid fertilizer has, I think, proved best for chrysanthemums.

Insects and Other Pests.

Last but not least of the growers troubles are those caused by insects. Every effort should be made to keep the plants clean. The black fly or aphis is the chrysanthemum's worst enemy and the hardest to kill. It can, however, be successfully fought and conquered by beginning early and spraying with nicoticide, nicotine or their equivalents. Then there are green fly and red spider, both of which are easier killed than the black fly.

Mildew can be easily avoided by painting the steam pipes with sulphur and linseed oil.

The watering of chrysanthemums is of no little importance. The plants can be watered every day during the Summer. When Autumn comes, sunny days must be used to the best advantage in watering, for by watering on cloudy days the foliage remains damp, causing rust and black spot. A good plan to follow is to have the steam pipes coated with sulphur when first you turn on your steam, thus purifying the air.

Antirrhinums (Snapdragons).

The popularity of the snapdragon seems to be increasing. It is well to note it, for the plant is deserving of all attention. Antirrhinums are really perennials, but they do best and produce better results when treated as annuals. Without a doubt they form grand material for cut flower purposes; their colors are so bright and varied. Also they make most effective displays in the flower garden, and how well they conform to greenhouse culture. These, when well grown, produce flower spikes from 4 to 5 feet long. A temperature as for carnations suits snapdragons well. Plants from Spring sown seed when planted in the garden will flower in July and continue to do so until frost cuts them down. As there are tall growing kinds so are there dwarf or Tom Thumb varieties, which also have their place in the flower garden.

Long Island. JOHN F. JOHNSTON.

Philadelphia.

News Notes.

The retail stores are very busy this week and most of them are decorating their windows very tastefully. White and yellow pompon chrysanthemums are being used quite extensively for this work. The yellow Baby pompon is seen around all the stores, and is very popular with flower buyers; it appears to go better as a cut flower than it did last year as a pot plant.

Alburger & Cascaden, at West Laurel Hill, have over 6,000 blooms of Dorothy Faust chrysanthemums which they are just commencing to cut.

Alex. B. Scott is out again after being confined to the house for three weeks with an acute attack of bronchitis.

Moore & Simon, seedsmen, are very busy now on vegetable seed orders from the Southern States; those from Florida are very heavy this season.

Ralph Faust, who has charge of the office force of the S. S. Pennock-Meehan Company and is also treasurer of the company, was married on November 21 to Miss Ida E. Keithan of Shenandoah, Penna.

W. E. McKissick is still receiving some very good consignments of pompon chrysanthemums and Paper White narcissus. He has found it necessary to rent another store this week in order to properly handle his large consignments of chrysanthemums for Thanksgiving. He is very strong on White Bonnaffon.

George Burton has given Lord & Burnham Company an order for material for three new houses each 20¼ by 150 feet. The plans embrace all the latest improvements and also iron posts and gutters.

Horace T. Dumont is making a specialty of Delaware holly and laurel wreathing this season, in connection with his regular commission business.

The Hugh Graham Company have just received a large shipment of evergreens and boxwood trees from Europe. These are all pot grown and are very choice stock.

Adolf Müller at Gwynedd, Pa., has a new asparagus which he imported from Germany; the name it came under is Marktbeherrscher (champion of the market). It is a very free grower, is a climber, and the foliage is very dense, the under part of the fronds being as good as the upper. It will no doubt be in strong demand when he has a stock to offer. This energetic young florist has five houses in roses Richmond, Miss Kate Moulton, Bride and Bridesmaid, which are all doing well. He is well pleased with Kate Moulton; it is very prolific and sells well. He also has a house of Adiantum hybridum and in addition has ten acres planted in young nursery stock, among which are some nice specimen evergreens.

Jacob Becker had a very disastrous fire at his Fiftieth and Chestnut street place on Sunday night. The boiler house was entirely destroyed, and a house of Killarney roses ruined.

DAVID RUST.

Detroit, Mich.

Club Notes.

The Detroit Florists' Club had an exhibit of chrysanthemums and other seasonable stock at the regular meeting, Wednesday, November 21, 1906. H. V. Pierce was elected a member. Among the most striking exhibits were some La Detroit and Richmond roses staged by Robert Klagge. Breitmeyer's chrysanthemums were also very fine. The Park and Boulevard Commission very kindly exhibited an elegant lot of tropical and ornamental plants. P. J. Lynch, representing Dingee & Conard, was present.

Mr. Lohengrin of the Chicago Carnation Company was in town last week.

Roses and carnations are selling well. Chrysanthemums are moving slightly better, but there is still a great glut in the market. Yellow seem to be a back number. There are but few good violets in the market, but a large demand for all that can be had. Lily of the valley brings a good price, but moves rather slowly.

HARRY.

Pittsburg.

News Notes.

Randolph & McClements, since acquiring the Siebert place, have now about the largest establishment in the city and two of the finest stores. The old place on Forbes street will be run for another year or more. It is an old landmark erected by the Murdochs quite a few years ago, and is now in bad shape. One of the boilers gave out recently causing a lot of trouble; fortunately the weather was warm at the time. Mr. Randolph is one of our oldest growers and takes great pride in choice and rare plants. He has a fine lot of Phœnix Roebelenii, a graceful palm, and his pandanus, of which he has the largest stock in our vicinity both of Veitchii and Sanderi, are in fine shape. The latter is grown here quite successfully, making as fine plants as P. Veitchii. Ferns are also extensively grown and sold at fancy prices. Mr. Randolph, who has charge of the greenhouses, has bought a fine residence on Stanton avenue near the Siebert place, which he will soon occupy.

Dan Mailley, well known in Allegheny, has taken an interest in the firm of Blaney & Company in the Allegheny market house. There are now five large florist stands in this market, besides about a dozen other stands where plants and cut flowers are sold. All are doing a fair trade.

Fred Burki of the Bakerstown Rose & Carnation Company returned from a two weeks' visit in Virginia.

Next Tuesday, December 4, is the date of the Florists' Club's last meeting of the year, and the subject for discussion will be "Christmas Materials." Five or six members will give short talks about Christmas plants, how to grow them and market them. Well-grown plants sell remarkably well in our city, commanding the best of prices.

E. C. REINEMAN.

Boston.

News Items.

John A. Macrae of Providence, R. I., exhibited a fine vase of his new chrysanthemum Golden Dome to the growers at the Park street market on Saturday. This variety is one of the finest of new sorts, and is a sport from Timothy Eaton. It scored 90 points at Boston last year, and 89 points both at Philadelphia and New York this year. It captured the gold medal of the Rhode Island Horticultural Society at its recent show, and will be put on the market this year. The E. G. Hill Company, Richmond, Ind., will disseminate it.

J. T. Butterworth of South Framingham is cutting excellent Cattleya labiata at the present time; they are some of the largest blooms ever seen in Boston.

Peter Fisher has a large stock of his new carnation Beacon for which he is now booking orders. This variety is proving one of the best yet sent out by Mr. Fisher, and that is saying a good deal.

Peter Miller of Breck's seed store sails to-day (Saturday) for a two months' trip to Europe.

Stephen Chase of Nashua, N. H., exhibited a vase of seedling carnations in Welch Brothers this week which is a decided improvement on Fair Maid.

Welch Brothers have found the enlarged accommodations in their new location of great advantage to them in handling their Thanksgiving trade, which has been the best in the history of the firm.

J. W. D.

PUEBLO, COL.—M. Domoto, of San Francisco, was in Bessemer recently on a visit to Charles Koike, leader of the Japanese colony in Pueblo. Domoto is the proprietor of an immense florist establishment in San Francisco and has made a fortune out of the business. He landed in the Golden Gate city fifteen years ago and opened a small flower store, making the Japanese chrysanthemum his specialty. He recently erected a large building which is the headquarters for football players during the season. He is known as an authority on the game and is always in attendance at the larger contests. When jiu jitsu was first spoken of in this country Domoto demonstrated its usefulness by putting down the center rush of one of the heaviest teams around the bay. Domoto and Koike were intimate friends in Japan, and while making a business trip to Salt Lake the former took occasion to come to Pueblo to visit his friend.—Chieftain.

CANADIAN NEWS

TORONTO. — Business continues good; stock quite plentiful. Chrysanthemums are coming in of fine quality. The Dale Estate are sending in some specimen blooms, also some good general stock; their roses are always fine. Dunlop is sending in good roses; the Toronto Floral Company, fine Bride and Bridesmaid. Plant stocks generally are good. Violets are scarce, but usually of good quality. Carnations as yet are not of first grade and are by no means plentiful. Large quantities of orchids have been used this Fall, but cattleyas are getting scarce. Lælia anceps will be in about next week. Lily of the valley is offered regularly and is of fine quality. The weather has been good and large numbers of tulips and hyacinths have been planted this Fall; the bulbs are nearly sold out.

The annual meeting of the Gardeners and Florists' Club was held on the 20th, President Wilshire in the chair; about twenty members were in attendance. Secretary Collins reported about eighty members in good standing, and several new members were nominated. The last year has been a successful one, several of the meetings being very good. The arrangements for the convention of the American Carnation Society next January were talked about, and general satisfaction was expressed at what has already been accomplished. The fine room in City Hall which has been secured for the show, will, we think, be found very satisfactory, as it will be cool and light. The meetings will be held in a room adjoining the exhibition hall, and one well away from noise. Everything will be done to give our visitors an enjoyable time. The treasurer reported the finances in good condition, all accounts paid, and a nice balance in hand. A hearty vote of thanks was tendered the treasurer for his services. The secretary also was tendered a like vote, accompanied with a check for $25 as a slight recognition of the work he has done for the association during the past year. The new officers elected are: President, Ed. Dale, Brampton; first vice-president, A. Houle, Bedford Park; second vice-president, E. Graham, Reservoir Park; treasurer, G. H. Mills, city; secretary, E. Collins, city; assistant secretary, J. Matthews, city. These were all elected by acclamation. The executive committee are: J. H. Dunlop, G. Douglass, Wm. Foord, Wm. Jay, D. McIntire, A. Jennings, W. Wilshire, and T. Manton. The representatives to the Industrial Exhibition are: J. H. Dunlop, and T. Manton; to the Ontario Horticultural Exhibition: Wm. Jay, Wm. Foord, W. Wilshire, and C. Collins.

I am pleased to report that Wm. Jay, Jr., is still improving and we have good hopes of his recovery.

THOS. MANTON.

OTTAWA.—No snow as yet; rather unusual in Ottawa, but if it comes before Christmas we will be satisfied. The usual holiday worry is being experienced; this year it is azaleas, as they seem to be slow in opening. Many of them will take 75 degrees to get there; Vervæneana seems to be the slowest. Plants generally are in good condition; cyclamen, cherries, poinsettias, primulas, and begonias are very good. The cut flower crop also promises fair. Carnations are well budded, and roses will be in crop. Violets will not be plentiful; what doubles are grown are poor, and singles will not be a heavy crop. Chrysanthemums have been good and have sold well, but there will not be a large quantity left for Christmas—some W. H. Chadwick, H. W. Rieman, Quito and Merry Christmas.

Last Saturday called for quantities of choice flowers, being The King's Drawing Room, the most important social function of the opening of parliament. The demand for bouquets was about as usual, and well divided among the three florists. Roses, carnations, lily of the valley, and violets were used principally, orchids not being procurable.

J. Graham, of Graham Brothers, has been obliged to go South for a long stay on account of ill health; he has engaged C. Craig, of Montreal, to take charge of his greenhouses during his absence.

Visitors included F. Darrow and Harry A. Bunyard, New York.

E. I. M.

EDMONTON, ALBERTA. — The long spells of fine mild, and bright weather broke November 1, and since then there have been three snow storms with—for this locality—the phenomenal fall of 18 inches. The first real cold for which the northland is celebrated arrived November 15, and for three days the thermometer has registered 25 below with no promise of a moderation in sight. The air is absolutely calm and dry, and not more radiation is required to heat the houses than under much milder conditions with the usual breeze stirring.

The Walter Ramsay establishment was completed in time for a formal opening on the Canadian Thanksgiving Day, October 17. At least 2,500 people took advantage of the invitation, including the Lieutenant-governor of the Province; the Provincial Premier, Mayor May, and the leading society in the city. The establishment, which is without doubt the most northerly greenhouse plant on the American continent, came in for much commendation.

Trade to the present has been moderate, and confined mostly to the higher officials and society leaders, with a few most gratifying inquiries from visitors from points as distant as Winnipeg and Vancouver, and is about equal to what was expected. It will undoubtedly take some time to overcome the prejudice against buying flowers that has been caused by the unsatisfactory condition of the "shipped" stock that has been sold to the present. About 1,000 chrysanthemums were grown, and although they were June struck cuttings and not planted until the beginning of August, they were a splendid success. Monrovia and George S. Kalb were in by October 15, Amorita, Alice Byron, and Viviand-Morel by November 1; Golden Wedding and Dr. Enguehard by November 10. These latter varieties were grown to single stem, were really magnificent, and would easily have stood comparison with any I have seen at any exhibition. Only a limited number were grown, but these were taken readily at $5 per dozen, while supposedly first grade flowers shipped in would not move at $2.50. Roses, although planted very late, have done remarkably well, Richmond easily taking the lead as regards quality of flowers. General MacArthur has done equally well, but the blooms seem to have a tendency to turn blue since the cold weather came. Bride, Bridesmaid and Canadian Queen are coming fine and sell for $2 to $2.50 per dozen. Richmond with 18 to 24 inch stems go freely at $4 per dozen. As this variety grows here there is no doubt in my mind that it has got American Beauty beaten to a standstill. Carnations are just coming into crop and bring $1; customers must, however, see the flowers picked. Sweet peas are just coming in. The rank growth of the Zvolanek hybrids seems to suggest the culinary article at present. Lettuce and tomatoes were planted very late, and are growing slowly. Fuel is scarce and rapidly rising in price, for although the country for thousands of miles is underlaid with coal the development of the immense territory is proceeding quicker than the mining development.

The Dominion landscape architect, Mr. Todd of Montreal, is in town in connection with the planning of the grounds around the new two million dollar parliament buildings that are just being started. The cities of Edmonton and Strathcona have also secured his services for plans for boulevards and parks on the banks of the Saskatchewan river.

Mr. Greenway has opened a store in the Opera House block on Jasper avenue.

FRED. BENNETT.

Rochester, N. Y.

Trade Notes.

Business in this section has been satisfactory to the grower and retailer, alike, and the oncoming of the holidays keeps us in anticipation of something better. The new feature here is the opening of a cut flower department in the large department store under the management of E. R. Fry. There is of course, the usual amount of faultfinding by some of the trade, on account of the low price of cut flowers. While this, of course, is to be regretted, we sincerely hope it may have its influence in creating a desire for flowers among those who visit such stores very often, and seldom enter a florist's establishment.

A very fine display of different varieties of pompon chrysanthemums was seen at the wholesale house this week, having been shipped in from the greenhouses of Vick & Hill Company, that firm having grown them under glass. These, when grown in such conditions find a ready market, and more of them could be used.

A real estate deal of interest is the purchase of the Furnam block on East Main street, by H. E. Wilson, florist, whose store is now on Main street. The building is one of the city's first brick buildings, put up nearly a century ago, and considered one of the oldest landmarks. Mr. Wilson will not now occupy it, as the present lease runs for three or four years more. It was bought partly as an investment, and partly to be sure of a Main street location for his store in case of removal from his present place.

A novelty seen at the greenhouses of Salter Bros., is a small fish globe filled with a green vine, Gaultheria nummularioides, having a profusion of red berries, which, as seen through the globe, present a very pleasing sight, and should sell when offered, very readily.

Present wholesale prices of cut flowers are: Roses, $4 to $8, according to quality; carnations, $2.50 to $3.50 per 100; chrysanthemum, $4 to $10 and a good market for them.

COCKNEY.

FOR THE RETAILER

[All questions relating to the Retail Trade will be cheerfully answered in this column. We solicit good, sharp photographs of made-up work, decorations, store interiors, etc., for reproduction here.—Ed. F. E.]

FUNERAL DESIGNS AT NEWPORT, R. I.—The funeral of Commodore Kane last Tuesday was notable because of the unusually large number of floral tributes sent by friends. On the grave was placed a cross nearly six feet long, composed entirely of violets. These flowers also entered into the make-up of several other beautiful pieces. There were several wreaths made of green and bronze galax leaves and cattleya flowers; two large and beautiful wreaths of Killarney roses, two of Liberty, one of Bride roses and cattleyas, one of White Lawson carnations and cypripediums. One wreath of green galax leaves and violets was especially noticeable. These were only the ones strikingly effective among ever so many more that were perhaps equally beautiful and effective in their way. The greater number of those pieces were made in New York. It was, considering that fact, surprising how unruffled and fresh every piece looked the day after the funeral. One feature connected with all these floral pieces was the beautiful effect produced by Princess of Wales violets composing one-third of the circle of a wreath, with the remainder of green galax leaves, the wreath being tied with a broad crimson ribbon.

D. M.

CLUB AND SOCIETY DOINGS.

THE UTICA (N. Y.) FLORISTS' CLUB held its fourth annual banquet and flower show on Thursday evening, November 22, 1906, in the Elks' hall. There were eighty in attendance including the ladies. Three long tables were well filled with choice flowers, including chrysanthemums, roses, carnations and violets. At 9:30 p. m. all sat down to a fine menu served by caterer Stockhauser, which was much enjoyed. Miss Clara Bach very skillfully played on the piano during the evening.

The largest exhibitor was the Lake View Rose Gardens, Jamestown, N. Y., showing the following chrysanthemums: Josephine, Nagoya, Mlle. Liger, Major Bonnaffon, Maud Dean, Mutual Friend, Dr. Enguehard, Minnie Wanamaker, and many others, all well done; a large vase of Bride, Bridesmaid, and Richmond roses, Mrs. Lawson, White Lawson, Enchantress, Fair Maid, Boston Market, White Enchantress and Rose-Pink Enchantress; all very fine; also Paper White narcissus.

John Haines, Bethlehem, Pa., sent Pink Imperial, Imperial and a seedling with extra long stems. Chas. H. Totty, Madison, N. J., showed a large variety of pompons. F. R. Pierson Company, Tarrytown, N. Y., had a vase of 50 flowers of carnation Winsor; it was surely grand and made a great many friends. Alex. J. Guttman, New York, staged a vase of Victory, as good as we saw it a year ago; it can't be beat.

Joe Trandt of Canajoharie staged some very fine plants of Begonia Gloire de Lorraine in two sizes; J. O. Graham, Little Falls, N. Y., carnations; E. J. Byam, Rome, carnations, both of excellent quality; Robert Train, Gloversville, N. Y., roses, carnations and pompon chrysanthemums; W. A. Rowlands, Pink Enchantress, fine; George H. Benedict, a large vase of mixed roses and a vase of Richmond; Spencer & Martin, American Beauty; Frank McGowan, chrysanthemums Nellie Pockett, Yellow Eaton, Sunburst, Alice Byron and others. Baker & Company had a fine vase of Bride and Bridesmaid; R. Kilbourn, Clinton, N. Y., smilax and Asparagus plumosus, extra good. The Cottage Carnation Comapny sent Red Riding Hood and Aristocrat carnations; the latter a bright cerise pink, grand in color and make-up.

Moonlight carnations were shown by Wm. P. Pfifer; it is an old variety but better than some of the so-called new ones.

After the banquet the flowers were sent to the hospitals. Among the speakers were F. R. Pierson, Tarrytown, N. Y.; A. J. Guttman, New York; P. R. Quinlan, Syracuse, N. Y. President Baker acted as toastmaster. Votes of thanks were passed to the committee in charge, also to the secretary. The committee was composed of J. C. Spencer, Wm. P. Pfifer and Frank McGowan. The officers of the club are F. J. Baker, president; Seward Hakes, vice-president; C. F. Seltzer, treasurer; J. C. Spencer, secretary. Members and guests from out-of-town were E. J. Byam and wife, Rome, N. Y.; J. O. Graham and wife, Little Falls, N. Y.; Joe Trandt, Canajoharie; Robert Train and wife, Gloversville; Seward Hakes and wife, Theo. Schesch, wife and son, Ilion; Dr. and Mrs. Rowlands, Whitesboro; Mr. and Mrs. Auld, New Hartford; Mr. and Mrs. Owens, Whitesboro; R. Kilbourn, Clinton, N. Y.; Jacob Fries, Ilion; F. R. Pierson, Tarrytown, N. Y.; P. R. Quinlan, Syracuse; Alex. J. Guttman, New York.

This banquet goes on record as the very best one the club has ever had. Mr. Pierson, Mr. Quinlan and Peter Crowe were so well pleased that they entered their names as members.

QUIZ.

ELBERON (N. J.) HORTICULTURAL SOCIETY.—A meeting of this society was held on November 19. President Robertson in the chair. There was a large attendance. Two new members were elected. A number of questions from the question box tending to the betterment and progress of the society were discussed. Some beautiful exhibits were staged. W. D. Robertson was awarded a certificate of merit for a magnificent specimen of Microlepia hirta cristata; A. Bauer showed a good vase of carnation Victory. J. Kennedy exhibited some hardy chrysanthemums. W. D. Robertson was awarded the gold medal presented by George Steele, Shrewsbury nurseries, for the member scoring the highest number of points during the past year for exhibits at the regular meetings.

GEORGE W. MASSON, Secretary.

John H. Dunlop's Prize Dinner Table Decoration at Ontario Horticultural Exhibition.

Waco, Tex.

The eleventh annual flower show of the Texas State Floral Society, held November 14, 15, and 16, was an unqualified success, despite the fact that the society was cramped for room, a condition that will no doubt be remedied another season. Much of the credit for the success of the show is due the president, Mrs. W. S. Plunkett, and her co-workers. H. F. Goode, Springfield, O., was again the judge and his awards gave general satisfaction.

In the classes for out-of-town growers, Nathan Smith & Son, Adrian, Mich., captured the following first premiums: For fifty blooms, four varieties; fifteen blooms, three varieties, white, pink and yellow, respectively; one bloom yellow, and one bloom red, and for best ten blooms staged singly; also for fifteen blooms, staged singly; twenty blooms, new variety, and best bloom, new variety.

Mrs. W. K. Rose, Cleburne, Texas, won out for best fifteen blooms in variety.

In the open classes for cut chrysanthemums Charles H. Mayer, J. M. Hickman, and Walter Reese were the principal prize-winners.

Mr. Reese was also successful in the rose classes as was Miss Annie Wolfe.

Mrs. J. Park won first for the most artistically decorated table, and for best arranged vase of cut flowers. In the design classes Miss Annie Wolfe and Charles H. Mayer were the winners. The former exhibitor was awarded a gold medal for the most unique exhibition display during the entire show. The design was dedicated to the Elks. It was a "grandfather's clock," which had stopped at 11, the symbolic number. The clock was surmounted with the head of an elk made in flowers.

THE WEEK'S WORK.

Timme's Timely Teachings.

Winter Protection.

Stock claimed to be entirely hardy should go unharmed through our Winters, even if not protected. To describe stock as perfectly hardy means little or nothing unless it is plainly stated how far north it has been found to safely endure the Winter without protection. To do this with new and untried stock would be of greatest importance, but is not possible in every case; and the distributor of a novelty, not being certain on this point, instead of saying so allows the purchaser to guess and find out for himself. Florists investing in new varieties of so-called hardy stock or in such that they have had no experience with before, or if so, in localities differing greatly as to climatic conditions from their present abode, will do well to first make sure as to its entire hardiness before going into it largely. Of late hardy roses, for instance, as also various species of herbaceous perennials in extensive plantations, have proved exceedingly profitable for Summer cutting. This fact, established by those who set the pace, has been a strong inducement to many others to follow the example set, and thus profitably utilize open ground space abundantly available at or near many of these establishments. Whether or not there is any likelihood of this line of floricultural industry ever being overdone, as has been predicted, we must let the future decide. My duty at present is to point out the necessity of selecting for this particular purpose only such stock as has been proven to be hardy enough to pass through any Winter without protection, if need be. Then the grower with any kind of experience at all in the culture of hardy stock would see his way clear at the approach of Winter. He would know that some of said stock, even if perfectly hardy, would be greatly benefited by protection, while many other kinds would not only fare better without it, but would be positively injured by anything that would probably protect them from frost, which, if they were entirely hardy, should not hurt them, but would cause them to perish by decay. He would act accordingly, and so far as he was enabled to prevent it there would be no loss of valuable stock.

In the last three or four years I have seen several costly outdoor plantations go to ruin from causes just alluded to. Entirely hardy perennials of a fleshy, soft growth, needing no Winter protection whatever but nevertheless covered with a heavy layer of fresh manure, perhaps long before the ground was touched by frost, were rotted down when uncovered in the Spring. A large border of Maman Cochet roses, properly protected by forest leaves, which, however, failed to protect in this case, were a sorry sight in the Spring and never during the following Summer did they fully outgrow the injuries inflicted by the first Winter. This teaches us that to attempt raising anything not absolutely hardy is an unwise undertaking, an expensive and risky affair. On the other hand, such things as we know are perfectly hardy should not be deliberately killed by an overdose of Winter protection. On private estates the carrying through the Winter of rare specimen plants by careful protection when they can only there be grown by taking this precaution, is entirely proper and in place, but stock extensively raised for profit on commercial places as an outdoor crop year after year should above all else be strictly hardy.

When and Where Winter Protection is Needed.

Florists of necessity must depend on proper protection for the safe keeping of much of their stock out of doors during all or a great part of Winter. Lilies and other bulbs in pots and boxes, hardy forcing shrubs and herbaceous plants, already potted up or merely heeled in, rooted cuttings of roses and other hardy things struck during the Summer, hollyhocks, pinks, daisies, pansies, lily of the valley and the like, all either growing or stored away in outdoor frames for the present, will soon be in need of protection against hard freezing. Most of these plants will not be greatly harmed by a few good frosts, some of them, as hardy shrubs for forcing and lily of the valley, will even be benefited thereby. But a solid freezing up must be prevented because it would injure azaleas, narcissi, lilies and many of the biennial bedding plants, and, besides, it would render almost impossible the bringing in of the forcing stock at the proper time. This stock, whether in closed frames or buried in the open garden, should now be covered with a layer of coarse manure or with hay, this layer to be increased in thickness should there be need of it before the plants can be brought in. Pansies, daisies and other hardy and half-hardy seedlings, as also the rooted and now firmly grounded rose and other cuttings of like nature, should be exposed to the open weather as long as ever possible without running any risk of seeing them come to harm. Only after a thin crust has formed at the surface of the soil by frost should a covering take place. A loosely spread layer of dry tree leaves between the plants will likely be sufficient protection for some time yet; altogether should good snowing set in and provide an all Winter's covering. But this is rarely the case, and growers must in their labors never rely on improbable possibilities when it is in their power to attend to the proper regulation of affairs themselves. Tightly closing the sashes later on and covering all with straw matting or a layer of hay or rough manure, when the cold reaches zero and below, is all sufficient to carry the stock safely through the Winter. During Midwinter spells of unseasonably warm and fine weather the outer covering is removed and the sashes are opened for the time being. If this is omitted or the covering stays on too long in early Spring, the plants will become drawn and spindly, while, on the other hand, a too early removal of all the covering in the Spring is likely to cause grower and plants to be caught by belated cold spells, severe enough to ruin the stock.

Beds of outdoor roses are best protected against Winter-killing by dry tree leaves strewn thickly among them after the ground is somewhat frozen. Farther north and in very severe Winters, rose beds and borders, stocked with plants not entirely hardy, should in addition to the covering with forest leaves be boxed in and then again covered with straw or manure.

Isolated plants or groups of anything not quite hardy, if their branches can be bent down to the ground, easy enough in the case of climbers, are perfectly safe under a covering of fresh earth. This also is done after frost has formed a crust and not until the plants have shed all of their foliage. Earth is the cleanest and altogether most reliable material for the covering of deciduous plants during Winter, and wherever it can be used it should be employed in preference to hay, manure, tan bark or sawdust. Even beds of the more tender sorts of everblooming roses may safely be carried through severe Winters under a cover of fresh earth. Freeing the wood of leaves and weighting down the strongest growth with lumps of the frozen ground is all that is needed in the way of preparing the bed for its Winter cover. Loose soil, taken from below the frozen crust, is shoveled in between and on the plants to a depth of from six to ten inches according to size and age of plants, leaving all the upper parts and tips of the branches uncovered. These are allowed to freeze and are cut away in the Spring when the plants are pruned after being cleared of the covering. All this is well enough when but a bed or two are to be wintered under a protecting cover, but this mode of covering is not practicable in the case of large rose plantations, and any other way of affording protection is either too expensive or too unreliable to be adopted in the growing of plants not entirely hardy on a somewhat large scale commercially.

Winter-Killing in Various Ways.

It is not always the direct action of a very low temperature with which we have to contend in trying to save outdoor plant life. Indirectly it may be responsible for all the mischief wrought, but agencies and conditions lending a helping hand in the work of destruction are many and varied. So, for instance, will the hardy kinds of evergreen species and also all hardy herbaceous plants of a soft growth, as well as the more hard-wooded of this class and even some of the half-hardy greenhouse stock, endure the greatest cold of our severest Winters under a good covering of snow, though the ground underneath may be solidly frozen to a depth of several feet. Many kinds, completely covered with earth or sawdust, would also come through unharmed, but under a cover of boards, manure, straw or such like material most of them would either be much damaged and disfigured or be killed outright. The hardy kinds would pull safely through a severe, dry cold without being covered at all, but let a warm spell set in, with alternate thawings in daytime and freezings at night, very few would survive the ordeal. Or let rain, freezing to ice as it falls, set in, and complete and speedy ruin would be the consequence. This I consider the surest going and most destructive of all factors in the Winter killing of outdoor vegetation, most frequent in mild Winters and responsible for most of the damage done to evergreens and soft-wooded stock. This can only be guarded against by completely covering the plants. Screens or a partial covering with some light, loose material will protect valuable specimens of evergreens, including hollies, rhododendrons and other shade-loving choice plants against the unwelcome rays of the Winter sun, more to be feared than any great cold. Where nearby trees provide a natural shade and shelter it is seldom necessary to resort to any other means of protecting these plants against the inroads of Winter casualties. A heavy layer of manure, widely spread over roots and base of the plants in cases like this is always beneficial.

Another efficient cause of outdoor stock failing to come safely through our Winters is lack of moisture at the roots. Evergreens of all kinds, as also many other plants, depend for a perfect wellbeing on a never-ceasing circulation of sap. Deprived of moisture at the roots, the incessant loss by evaporation from foliage and top growth cannot be replaced, and the plant must perish. In this way many of our evergreen trees and shrubs are killed. A severe Winter, solidifying the ground about the roots, is to blame, but more often an exceedingly dry Fall. Watering well before Winter sets in and afterward covering the ground around the plants with manure is the preventive.

This often prevents one form of Winter-killing and inaugurates another. A very dry Fall tends to bring about a general good ripening of wood on all things of a deciduous nature, preparing them for a start of new growth at the very first opportunity that offers. Any fairly long-lasting warm spell in Midwinter or early Spring, sure to be followed by more of the Winter's killing cold, excites them into renewed activity, causing a premature growth and inevitable death, or, at least, the total loss of a season's crop in fruit or flowers. There is nothing that might be put forward as a remedy in this case. But dormant stock, wintered in sash-covered frames, could well be prevented from being aroused too soon by a top covering of shutters, boards or hay. It is my opinion that much valuable stock in the florists' line is ruined every Spring, or its commercial value lessened considerably, by being started too early, and, I may add, much of florists' indoor stock also, by being exposed to outdoor conditions altogether too early for its welfare.

Still another cause of Winter-killing is the upheaval of newly-planted or loosely-rooted stock during the Winter, otherwise secure from damage in the coldest of seasons. By the united action of alternate freezings and thawings the plants are lifted, dry out and die, unless measures to counteract imminent loss are taken in time. Much money value, represented by stock thus hazardously placed, is annually sacrificed to the Winter's wily whims. There are a good many ways in which to prevent losses due to this cause. In the first place, rooted or root-established stock, especially that coming out of pots, should be planted early enough in late Summer or Fall to make sure of its taking a firm hold of the soil before the approach of Winter, which is certain to bring with it cessation of root activity. The planting should be firm, aided in making it so by the use of the feet if need be. This is a means of causing the plants to become more quickly established, but as a preventive measure against upheaval by frost it stands no show and acts quite contrary, playing into the hands of the destroyer. Loose planting, when this is done too late to expect stock to in any way become sufficiently well established before Winter sets in, is therefore more apt to save the plants than excessive firming of the soil, which latter way of doing the work properly should, however, be adopted when it is intended to cover the surface with an ample layer of manure to prevent a freezing of the soil to any great depth. This is the best protection of newly-planted stock of all kinds otherwise quite safe from injury during the Winter. Bulb beds should thus be covered, especially those being stocked with lilies, narcissi and hyacinths.

FRED. W. TIMME.

CLASSIFIED ADVERTISEMENTS

CASH WITH ORDER.

The columns under this heading are reserved for advertisements of Stock for Sale, Stock Wanted, Help Wanted, Situations Wanted or other Wants; also of Greenhouse, Land, Second-Hand Materials, etc., For Sale or Rent.

Our charge is 10 cts. per line (7 words to the line), set solid, without display. No advt. accepted for less than thirty cents.

Display advertisements in these columns, 15 cents per line; count 12 lines agate to the inch.

[If replies to Help Wanted, Situation Wanted, or other advertisements are to be addressed care of this office, advertisers add 10 cents to cover expense of forwarding.]

Copy must reach New York office 12 o'clock Wednesday to secure insertion in issue of following Saturday.

Advertisers in the Western States desiring to advertise under initials, may save time by having their answer directed care our Chicago office at 127 E. Berwyn Ave.

SITUATIONS WANTED

SITUATION WANTED—By single, competent grower, roses and carnations; can take charge 50,000 ft. glass; $35.00 and board. Address, Florists, 270 Seventh avenue, New York City.

SITUATION WANTED—Young man, 24 German, wants position in retail store in New York. Sober, reliable and well recommended. Address, X. R., care The Florists' Exchange.

SITUATION WANTED—Active young man wants steady position. Experienced in general greenhouse work. Please state particulars. Address, X. X., care The Florists' Exchange.

SITUATION WANTED—By single young man; has experience in rose and carnation houses. Private or commercial place. Have good references. State full particulars with salary. Address, X. S., care The Florists' Exchange.

SITUATION WANTED—At once, by first-class rose grower. Competent to take full charge; best of references, good wages expected. State full particulars in first letter. Address, F. G., General Delivery, Utica, N. Y.

SITUATION WANTED—By A No. 1 rose grower on private or commercial place. Best of references furnished on application. Only those who want a first-class man need apply. Address, X. W., care The Florists' Exchange.

SITUATION WANTED—By single man as first man on private place or on first-class commercial place. Experience in roses, chrysanthemums, carnations and bedding stock. Please state wages with or without board in first letter. Address, X. Q., care The Florists' Exchange.

SITUATION WANTED—As foreman, grower of cut flowers and general pot plants for retail trade. State of Massachusetts preferred. Life experience in the trade in Germany and this country. Aged 39, single, honest and sober. Please state full particulars in first letter. Address X. K., care The Florists' Exchange.

SITUATION WANTED—January 1st, by a young man, American, honest and strictly sober, with two year's experience as salesman and designer on commercial place of 100,000 sq. ft. Understands bookkeeping. Desire steady position. New England States preferred. Address, X. U., care The Florists' Exchange.

HELP WANTED

WANTED—Sober, intelligent man for rose section; one who understands the business. Send references to Wm. F. Kasting, Buffalo, N. Y.

WANTED—Man who understands potting and greenhouse work. Sober and industrious. Address, James Horan & Son, Florists, Bridgeport, Conn.

WANTED—Salesman in retail florist store; party must be wide awake, understanding the business. References required. P. O. Box 598, Troy, N. Y.

WANTED—Young man to assist in up-to-date flower store. Must be decorator, of good appearance and able to wait on select trade. Address X. D., care The Florists' Exchange.

WANTED—Young man to assist in high-class retail flower store. Must be of good appearance and have good references. State wages, etc. W. P. S., care The Florists' Exchange.

WANTED—Salesman in retail florist store position for capable young man. Give full particulars as to age, experience, etc. in first letter. William Donaldson & Co., Glass Block, Minneapolis, Minn.

WANTED—A good reliable man to rent or to run in partnership for business purposes a large greenhouse, containing large assortment of fruit trees. Also a section with roses, various kinds of carnations, stove and foliage plants, bedding plants, palms, ornamental trees, also grapery and hot water heated hot beds for vegetable and cold frames. All is new and in perfect order. The location is excellent, 40 minutes from New York City Hall. Address, X. Y., care The Florists' Exchange.

HELP WANTED

WANTED—Seed salesmen by the D. Landreth Seed Company, Bristol, Pa. Two experienced commercial travelers familiar with the Garden Seed trade in the Cotton States; engagement to commence first of February.

WANTED—Seed salesman by the D. Landreth Seed Co., Bristol, Pa. A seed salesman having a personal acquaintance and influence in Philadelphia City and adjacent counties with private or professional gardeners.

WANTED—Section man who understands bedding plants; ferns, palms, etc. One who is up in all varieties. To a capable man good pay and permanent place. State salary and experience in first letter. Honaker, The Florist, Lexington, Ky.

WANTED—Young man with experience in flower store as assistant in our flower department. Good position for capable young man. Give full particulars as to age, experience, etc. in first letter. William Donaldson & Co., Glass Block, Minneapolis, Minn.

WANTED—For a commercial place, young man with experience in growing choice plants; wages $30.00 per month and board. Copy of references must accompany first letter. Address, J. A. Peterson, McHenry ave., Westwood, Cincinnati, Ohio.

WANTED—At once, a first-class grower of roses, carnations, chrysanthemums, violets and potted plants. A man who has business ability and not afraid of work. Must have first-class references, sober and steady. State salary, experience and references in first letter. If you cannot fill above bill do not answer; if satisfactory, must be ready to come at once. Address, X. Z., care The Florists' Exchange.

WANTED SALESMEN

For Nursery stock. For Southern New York, Penna., New Jersey, and Conn. Men of experience, and having some knowledge of Landscape work. Must be hustlers and well recommended. For an old established Nursery. Good pay to those who are satisfactory. Address with particulars,

SALESMEN, care Florists' Exchange

Mention the Florists' Exchange when writing.

SEEDSMAN.

An up-to-date seedhouse in the East requires the services of a man who is well experienced in flower seeds and bulbs and who can give good references. Apply stating age, salary expected. X. O., care Florists' Exchange.

Mention the Florists' Exchange when writing.

SEEDSMEN WANTED

Several Men experienced in all branches of the business; capable of waiting upon Customers, but this experience not entirely essential. State full particulars and wages wanted. Applications considered up to Dec. 15th.

RENNIE & THOMSON
135-137 WASHINGTON ST., PROVIDENCE, R. I.

Mention the Florists' Exchange when writing.

WANTED

A young man between 25 and 35 years of age who has had some experience on an Ornamental Nursery and who is interested in the work. Applicants must be of sober habits, industrious, not afraid of work, and possess executive ability. A German, Hollander or Swede preferred, but any hustler will be considered. For the right party this will be a very good position on one of the largest Ornamental Nurseries in the country. Location 60 miles from New York, 30 miles from Philadelphia. One mile from a city of 85,000 inhabitants. Reference required. Apply at once, stating nationality and religion, and whether married or single, last employer and wages expected. Address

T. W., care Florists' Exchange.

Mention the Florists' Exchange when writing.

HOW TO GROW MUSHROOMS

Price, . . . 10 cents.

A. T. De La Mare Ptg. & Pub. Co.
2-8 Duane St. New York.

MISCELLANEOUS WANTS

WANTED—Small range of glass with some ground in New Jersey. State particulars, price, etc. Address X. N., care The Florists' Exchange.

WANTED TO BUY—Greenhouses to be taken down. State full particulars of same when writing. Address, F. W., care The Florists' Exchange.

WANTED—Special prices on the following: 3,000 lbs. mixed sweet peas, 3,000 lbs. mixed tall nasturtiums, 3,000 lbs. mixed dwarf nasturtiums. I also want large quantities of all kinds of garden and flower seed. What have you to offer and what is your best price? Write at once to William D. Burt, Dalton, N. Y.

AN established nursery and greenhouse business, with retail flower and landscape departments, located in the far East, desires the services of a young man possessing a general knowledge of gardening. Applicant should have a pleasing address and a fairly good education. Whilst capital is not an absolute essential, there will exist every opportunity to become a partner in this business, therefore, preference will be given to those who, if satisfied with the outlook, would be in a position to invest up to about $10,000. To a person with a desire to go abroad (China and Japan) this advertisement offers peculiar opportunities. Address with fullest particulars, T. E., care The Florists' Exchange.

FOR SALE OR RENT

FOR SALE—Well established retail florist store in near by town, inquire, Joseph J. Levy, 56 W 26th St., New York City.

FOR SALE—Five greenhouses with 7500 sq. ft. of glass and two boilers; stocked with commercial plants in city of over 25,000 inhabitants. Price, $2,250.00. Address, J. H. Lahm, Hazleton, Pa.

FOR SALE—A good paying retail establishment in Chicago. To be disposed of as the owner has other business which requires his attention. Address, X. P., care The Florists' Exchange.

FOR SALE—Garden and seven greenhouses, 10,000 sq. ft. of glass, and a nine roomed dwelling on the premises. In a neighborhood where you can do business and save money. For particulars write to Arthur H. Lanser, Wayne, Del. Co., Pa.

FOR RENT—A greenhouse establishment, several greenhouses and large plot of ground; all in good condition and partly stocked. Located in Central Pennsylvania coal region. Coal very cheap also natural gas. Can sell all that can be raised at good prices. Old age reason for wanting to rent. Address, X. T., care The Florists' Exchange.

TO LET Retail Florist Store situated at 98 Broad Street, Newark, N. J., with three greenhouses attached, good show room facilities. Address

THOS. ELSUM
243 Belleville Av., Newark, N. J.

Mention the Florists' Exchange when writing.

A SNAP IF TAKEN AT ONCE—Greenhouses and Dwelling house newly remodelled, well stocked with carnations, roses, bedding plants and vegetables. No competition, only place in town of 3,000 inhabitants, no other house nearer than twenty miles, plenty of ground, and patients at Keeley Institute insuring steady paying trade. Owner has other business. Price $4,000, including Winter supply of fuel. J. C. Nelson, Proprietor, Dwight, Ill.

FOR SALE—A well established florist business, with dwelling houses. Also plenty of outdoor ground in up-to-date condition. Greenhouses are well filled with foliage plants, and the place is in a most desirable location to reach the wholesale New York City trade within a drive of about 30 minutes. It must be seen. Reason for selling; ill health. For particulars communicate with O. V. Zangen, Seedsman, Hoboken, N. J.

FOR SALE

A well equipped place, consisting of seven greenhouses, over 30,000 feet of glass, a nine roomed house, barn, stock, etc., and eight acres of land. This is a decided bargain and a rare opportunity. For particulars address

S. S. SKIDELSKY,
824 N. 24th St., Philadelphia, Pa.

Mention the Florists' Exchange when writing.

FOR RENT—Owing to continued ill health, I am compelled to give up business, and want a thoroughly reliable and competent man, well up in growing roses in pots for wholesale trade, to rent my place (10,000 feet glass). Will sell to the proper party; good business can be done. This is a fine opportunity for a man with small capital to secure an established trade. References exchanged. Terms reasonable. Possession at once or in Spring. Don't answer unless you can fill the bill. For particulars address Opportunity, care The Florists' Exchange.

STOCK FOR SALE

CHRYSANTHEMUMS, stock plants, Polly Rose, Glory of Pacific, Halliday, October Sunshine and Intensity, fine, 50c. per doz.; $3.50 per 100. F. P. Sawyer, Clinton, Mass.

BRENCHLEYENSIS GLADIOLUS, 1st. size, $10.00 per 1000; 2d. size, $8.00 per 1000. Cash with order. Est. Louis Siebrecht, Floral Park, N. Y.

CYCLAMEN plants for Christmas sales, in 5 and 6 in. pots, $6.00 and $9.00 per doz. Selling fast, so place your orders early. Safe arrival guaranteed. Geo. A. Rackham, 880 Van Dyke Av., Detroit, Mich.

ENGLISH PRIZE PANSY PLANTS—I have 10,000 fine plants more than I need. For sale at $8.00 per 1000, cash. Some very odd and beautiful markings among them. Reuben Powell, Florist, White Plains, N. Y.

BABY RAMBLER ROSES, fine dormant stock, one year, $12.00 per 100; 2 1-4-in. pot plants, extra well rooted, $4.00 per 100; $30.00 per 1,000. Orders booked for delivery now or any time up to late Spring. Samples free. Brown Brothers Company, Rochester, N. Y.

100,000 greenhouse grown Asparagus Plumosus Nanus seed; ready about Dec. 15, $4.00 per 1,000. Joseph Wood, Spring Valley, N. Y.

WHITE AND YELLOW BONNAFFON, Black Hawk, Buguehard and Maud Dean chrysanthemums, 75c. per doz.; $5.00 per 100. A. D. Egolf, Lansdowne, Pa.

CALLIOPSIS, California Sunbeams, Golden Fleece; Dahlia Monarch, mixed; Eschscholtzia, Golden West; Freesia; Geranium, Good Venture; Heliotrope, Lemoines; Ipomea, Heavenly Blue, White Tassel; Nasturtium, Butterfly, Jupiter, Saturn, mixed; Poppy, Fayal, Irresistible, Maid of the Mist; Tacsonia Buchananii. Write for prices. Theodosia B. Shepherd Co., W. H. Francis, Manager, Ventura, Cal.

FOR SALE

FOR SALE—One No. 5 Lord & Burnham boiler, used very little, therefore practically new; price, $47.50. N. Gelb, 229 Livingston St., Newark, N. J.

FOR SALE—Greenhouse pipe, 4 in. boiler tubes second-hand, in fine condition. Absolutely free from scale and with ends cut square. Sample and prices on application. Kroeschell Bros. Co., 33 Erie St., Chicago, Ill.

BOILERS BOILERS, BOILERS.
SEVERAL good second-hand boilers on hand, also new No. 16 Hitchings at reduced cost. Write for list. Wm. H. Lutton, West Side Avenue Station, C. R. R. of N. J., Jersey City, N. J.

FOR SALE

BOILERS No. 6 Weathered, round, $60.00. One 11 section Sunray hot water sectional boiler, grate 3 by 3. Price $150.00. New Henderson boilers; send for price on size wanted. One No. 387 Lord & Burnham hot water boiler, 7 sections, 38 in. grate, heat 8,000 sq. ft. of glass, used one season, price $150.00, guaranteed.

PIPE Good serviceable second hand. No Junk, with new threads. 2in. 7c.; 1½ in. 5½c.; 1¼ in. 4c.; 1 in. 3c.; 2½ in. 10c.; 3in. 14c.; 4 in. 19c. 4 in. cast iron greenhouse 14c. 2 in. NEW, standard, full lengths, 9½c. ft. All kinds of fittings for 4 in. cast iron and all sizes wrought iron.

STOCKS AND DIES New Economy, easy working, No. 1 cuts ½-¾-1 in. $3.00; No. 2 cuts 1¼-1½-2 ins. $4.00; Armstrong Adjustable No. 2 cuts ½-1 in. $4.00; No. 3 cuts 1¼-1½-2 ins. $6.50.

PIPE CUTTERS Saunders, No. 1 cuts to 1 in. $1.00; No. 2 cuts to 2 in. $1.30; No. 3 cuts to 3 in. $3.00; No. 4 cuts to 4 in. $4.50.

STILLSON WRENCHES Guaranteed. 12 in. grips 1½ in. $1.10; 18 in., grips 2 in. $1.50; 24 in., grips 2½ in. $2.25; 36 in., grips 3½ in. $4.50.

PIPE VISES Reed's Best Hinged Vise, No. 1 grips 2 in. $1.75; No. 2 grips 4 in. $3.50.

GARDEN HOSE 50 ft. lengths ¾ in., guaranteed; 9c.; for heavy work, guaranteed; 12½c.

HOT-BED SASH New; Gulf Cypress, 3 ft. x 6ft. 75c.; glazed complete $1.60 up. Second hand sash glazed $1.00 and $1.25, good condition.

GLASS New American, 50 ft. to the box. 10x12 single at $1.90. 10x12, 12x1[illegible] 10x15 B double $2.65. 12x14 to 12x20 and 14x14 to 14x20 B double $2.85. 16x16 and 16x1[illegible] B double $2.95. 16x20 to 16 x 24 double $3.20 per bo[x]. 6x8, 7x9, 8x10 old, single $1.50. 8 x 10 and 8x14 old double $1.65. 12 x 14 old single $1.75.

Get our prices on second hand wood materia[l]. We can furnish everything in new material to ere[ct] any size house. Get our prices.

METROPOLITAN MATERIAL CO.
Greenhouse Wreckers
1398-1408 Metropolitan Avenue, BROOKLYN, N.

Mention the Florists' Exchange when writin[g]

Thirty cents is the minimum charge for advertisements on this page.

Buffalo.

News Notes.

S. S. Pennock, Philadelphia, called on the trade in this vicinity, and while in town made arrangements to handle in Philadelphia the "Ever Ready Pot Cover."

W. A. Adams of S. A. Anderson's made a short trip to Chatham, Canada, on a matter of business.

At the present writing it looks as if flowers will be plentiful for Thanksgiving, with the exception of carnations, which have been very scarce, owing to the dark weather. Of chrysanthemums there seems to be enough to supply the demand.

Violets find a ready sale. American Beauty roses seem to sell spasmodically. W. H. G.

New York.

News of the Week.

Probably never before was there such a goodly array of chrysanthemums for Thanksgiving as has been the case this year. Not only were they in quantity, but the quality also surpassed what is usually seen for this holiday. There is one variety, however, that seems to have been overdone a little this season, and that is Maud Dean. Through some cause or other—perhaps weather conditions—this chrysanthemum has not been up to its usual standard of quality, showing its center a little to much in many instances, and also being a little too much off color to please some of the fastidious buyers.

We notice there has been a supply of holly in the city for the Thanksgiving holiday, but it seems that this green material cannot be pushed to any extent until Christmas. Dealers have for several years endeavored to create a call for holly at Thanksgiving, but it cannot be said that their efforts have met with any particular success. The demand for holly at this time is indeed very limited.

James W. Begbie, well known in seed circles in this city, and lately with A. T. Boddington, 342 West Fourteenth street, has opened a seed store and florist business at Shreveport, La. The many friends of Mr. Begbie will wish him every success in his undertaking.

A. J. Pieters, Hollister, Cal., will shortly leave for the East on a business trip, and will call on the seed trade.

Rickards Brothers, proprietors of the Bridgeman Seed Warehouse, 37 East Nineteenth street, are sending out a barometer to their customers and friends that will, no doubt, prove a very useful souvenir. As the reading of a barometer is always a very complicated matter and requires long experience before one can prognosticate with any degree of certainty the weather that is to come, Rickards Brothers have sent out a barometer the utility of which is the verifying of the weather that is. This barometer is in the shape of a quadruped, better known in the Southern States than it is here, which has a tail very flowing, and flax-like in its composition. The barometer is not to be hung indoors, but must be placed outside, and attached to it are the following directions: "If the tail is dry, the weather is fair; if the tail is wet, rain; if the tail is swinging, it is windy; if the tail is wet and swinging, it is stormy; if the tail is frozen, it is cold." Such a barometer should be of real use to persons desiring to know what the weather has been, and, no doubt, Rickards Brothers will be glad to furnish samples free on application.

In the family of a prominent Hebrew florist of Brooklyn a christening ceremony was held last Sunday, and several of the New York wholesale dealers were in attendance. Those who could not attend sent congratulatory telegrams to the family.

Bonnet & Blake, wholesale florists at 106 Livingston street, Brooklyn, have inaugurated a wagon service to meet their consignments at the trains in the morning and for delivery purposes. Christian Bonnet of this firm has been confined to his house for seven weeks with a severe attack of rheumatism. This firm is now handling the entire carnation output of the John N. May establishment at Summit, N. J.

Plans have been filed with Buildings Superintendent Murphy for the enlargement of the horticultural gardens in Central Park by the addition of eight greenhouses, and also a palm house to be built alongside the conservatories opposite One Hundred and Fifth street. The greenhouses are to be 12½ feet wide and 65 feet long each. They will be arranged in two groups of four wings each on either side of the central palm house. They are to be of brick, trimmed with limestone and roofed with glass. The palm house will cost $14,675 and the greenhouses $23,600, making a total outlay of $38,275 for the imporvement. Michael and Mitchell Bernstein are the architects.

Fleischman, the florist, has leased for ten years stores in the arcade of the United States Express Company's building at Rector street and Trinity place.

Rudolph Fischer of Great Neck, L. I., originator of freesia Purity and carnation Abundance, will on the first of May next move to California and reside there. Mr. Fischer's wife and family are already established in their new Californian home, and have made extensive plantings of the Purity freesia.

Alexander J. Guttman again visited John E. Haines of Bethlehem, Pa., recently and is satisfied that the two carnations, Imperial and Pink Imperial, will prove to be valuable acquisitions, and has arranged with Mr. Haines to disseminate them this season.

Henry Hess of the staff of James McManus, orchid specialist, 42 West Twenty-eighth street, had an addition to his family on Monday of this week.

P. R. Quinlan of Syracuse, N. Y., was in town on Tuesday.

Chicago.

News of the Week.

The annual exhibition of chrysanthemums at Lincoln Park which has been open for the past two weeks or more has been fully up to the previously established standard of excellence an dhas as heretofore attracted through the days and evenings the usual large attendance of North side residents. The plants number many thousands, in every conceivable form of bush, single stem, and standards and embracing between 300 and 400 varieties including all classes and many, especially among the seedlings, which could not safely be placed in any recognized class. It was especially noticeable that a very large assortment of pompons was in the collection. The hanging baskets were also attractive but the most interesting feature of the show was the display of Lincoln Park seedlings which certainly bespeak wonders for Mr. Frey's genius as an hybridist. These were not remarkable for size but displayed some remarkably unique forms, some resembling clusters of Shasta daisies while others were not unlike cinerarias and still others were most peculiarly quilled, and the coloring was in many cases most fantastic and original, in some cases certainly never seen in chrysanthemums before.

Ernst Weber at his houses at 2300 Lincoln avenue, where he is running about 23,000 square feet of glass, has everything in good shape for the season. His chrysanthemums, of which he grows Timothy Eaton, Dr. Enguehard, Maud Dean, W. H. Chadwick, and Major Bonnaffon, are now all in and their space is occupied by 5,000 pots of Japanese longiflorum lilies. In carnations Mr. Weber devotes himself to Enchantress, Mrs. Nelson and Boston Market, and though the plants appear in perfect health; in common with nearly all the growers of this section the cut at present is light.

Fred Weber on the Bowmanville Road has met with unparalled success for the last two years in growing American Beauty roses, having made a great hit in bringing in a high grade Summer crop at a time when he had a practical monoply of first class stock. His success warrants an enlargement of his plant and he is preparing next Spring to erect two houses each 300 x 27½ feet—just doubling the glass area of his present establishment.

Sam Graff of Graff Bros., Columbus, O., was here until Sunday when he returned home to assist in attending to the Thanksgiving business. He says his house is prospering and that even during the Summer months a nice comfortable business was carried on throughout.

Fred Hinks of the Chicago Carnation Company of Joliet, when seen a few days since seemed to wear a much broader smile than of yore. It is the first one, and the young lady and Mrs. Hinks, a sister of the late James Hartshorne, are progressing nicely.

O. P. Bassett has planned to spend the Winter in Italy for which destination he is booked to sail on December 10.

Joe Trinz left on Sunday last for Milwaukee where he intended to spend a few days on business connected with a new theatre which he is erecting there, and which it is expected will be open for business by February 1.

The first of the week Weiland & Risch reported a very satisfactory advance prospect for Thanksgiving trade and a good stock of flowers coming in with Killarney as a leader.

The Retail Florists' Association has decided to renew activity after the holidays and plans are being perfected to hold a series of dances and entertainments and in other ways enliven the interests in the organization, to improve conditions and make the association stronger than it has heretofore shown itself.

J. A. Budlong included among their Thanksgiving week specialties a fine cut of chrysanthemums, Timothy Eaton, Yellow Eaton, W. H. Chadwick, and Golden Chadwick, and an especially choice line of Bride and Bridesmaid roses largely from the grafted stock which has proved to be a decided success with this concern. They are still cutting late varieties of chrysanthemums in good form.

Quite an extended tour among the growers within the past few days makes more emphatic the opinion recently expressed in this column that a scarcity of carnations in this market is evident; and with the chrysanthemums out of the way a few weeks hence will occasion a field to ponder on, as it appears from the present point of view that the stock-in-trade will be largely composed of roses, which fortunately are looking well in all the principal centers.

The E. F. Winterson Company has been busy the past week handling holiday green having been among the fortunate concerns that procured a stock in advance of the announcement of the short supply. The concern is making a specialty of wreathing, artificial poinsettias, Christmas bells and other holiday supplies.

Cliff Pruner returned Monday from a short trip into neighboring states and reports a remarkable life in all branches of the trade.

The Chicago Rose Company is delivering some fine stock from its Libertyville range, and John Sterratt, who handles the goods in the city, puts in a just claim that the buyer must go further to get it better.

Among our recent visitors we noted, W. W. Britz, of Danville, Ill., Martin Reukauf, going west; Gus. Fredrickson, Glen Lord, Mich.; and B. Eschner of Philadelphia representing M. Rice & Company.

George Reinberg closes out with this season his commercial interest in carnations, and in the future will devote his energy and space to roses, with a strong tendency to American Beauty.

Louis Coatesworth, the golf specialist of the Chicago florist trade, was honored last week by being elected president of the Ravenswood Golf Club.

The scarcity of holiday green, or more, correctly princess pine, has become an important factor in Chicago within the past few days. Owing to several causes the normal expectations of delivery are reduced to from 40 to 60 per cent., and the price for immediate or future delivery is now in the "gambling pit."

H. Schuenemann, representing the Northern Michigan Evergreen Nursery, reached his old stand at Clark street bridge on Saturday last, with a full equipment of greens for the holidays. WM. K. WOOD.

ALEXANDRIA, VA.—The jury in the case of J. Louis Loosé against the Southern Railroad Company failed to agree. Mr. Loosé entered suit to recover damages caused by a number of stacks erected at the machine shop coal elevators recently built by the Southern Railroad Company to the north of his place. All the evidence sustained his claim. The defence argued that part of the damage was caused by other stacks, his own included. The judge charged that if the jury found the injury complained of was done exclusively by the railroad company, a verdict for the complainant was in order; if they found that injury was caused not only by the railroad but that others were a party to same, no matter how little their share in the total, the jury was to render a verdict for the defendants, as they could not discriminate the damage caused by one from the damaged caused by the other. The jury stood 11 to 1 in favor of the complainant, and after 24 hours 7 to 5 in favor of the complainant. Finding it impossible to agree they asked to be discharged.

THE CHRISTMAS NUMBER of The Florists' Exchange will be issued next Saturday, December 8, 1906. That issue will appear at an opportune time, and advertisers will make no mistake in placing therein a liberal display of their offerings for the holidays. Copy of advertisement should reach us at the very latest by 12 noon, Wednesday, December 5.

A Hardy Gladiolus.

(84) I have a gladiolus which ha[s] stood outside, planted in betwee[n] roses, and getting the usual mulchin[g] of two to three inches of old stabl[e] manure in Winter. It withstood th[e] severe Winters of 1894, 1895 and als[o] last Winter without any other pro[-]tection. Is this anything unusual, o[r] may this gladiolus be the beginnin[g] of a new hardy race of this usefu[l] plant? The flowers are of the usua[l] size, white and lavender, violet stripe[d] or blotched; the spikes 5 feet high. Stock was wintered at Worcester, Mass. A. V. L.
Mass.

—There is nothing unusual abou[t] the gladiolus standing out all Winte[r] when protected as has been done i[n] the present case. Gladiolus will stan[d] quite some degrees of frost when i[n] the ground and receive no injur[y] therefrom.

Caring for House Plants.

(85) What is the best way to car[e] for inside window garden boxes palms and other plants—includin[g] flowering plants—in conservatorie[s] and other rooms in private houses? We have a number of plants (som[e] of them very large) rented out fo[r] the Winter season. These plants ar[e] subjected to great fluctuations of hea[t] and cold, except in the conservatorie[s] the temperature seldom rising abov[e] 60 degrees nor going below 50. Ou[r] man sees to the regulating of hea[t] in conservatories, except on speci[al] occasions, when entertainments tak[e] place, and then the lady of the hous[e] wants extra heat for the comfort [of] her guests. Many of the plants a[re] stood in vases in their pots, other[s] are planted in the vases, consequentl[y] have no drainage. Would lime wate[r] as advised in your columns for ca[r]nations, be beneficial? W. B.
New York.

—The best way to care for insid[e] window gardens and specimen plan[ts] that are rented out for decoratio[n] is to have a thoroughly compete[nt] gardener make regular visits to t[he] house where such things are car[ed] for. If there is to be any soci[al] gathering where tender plants a[re] used and where the temperature, f[or] certain varieties, would be injurio[us] to the plants, the only thing to [do] is to remove the plants to some sui[t]able room for the time being. A[ny] gardener who understands his bus[i]ness will not transplant palms [or] other expensive plants direct into [a] jardiniere, as such a thing will [be] sure death to plants thus treated, a[nd] the use of lime water or other pre[p]aration on such plants cannot be [of] any benefit to them.

Tulips and Hyacinths for Easter.

(86) Is it too late to plant tul[ip] and hyacinth bulbs to be forced in flowers for Easter? FLORIST.
New York.

—If the tulips and hyacinths a[re] wanted for Easter forcing, or late[r], it is not yet too late to plant t[he] bulbs.

Peonies for Cut Flowers.

(87). Please give a list of twent[y-]four varieties of the best peonies f[or] cut flower purposes. I have nev[er] grown such, and would like to kno[w] the names of some specialists whe[re] the roots can be had in quantities.
Ind. E. T. B.

—To obtain a list of the best vari[e]ties of peonies for cut flower pu[r]poses, the best thing to do wou[ld] be to correspond with some of t[he] dealers. In growing peonies for cut flowers we would certainly not recommend that such a large number be used; five or six kinds grown in quantity would be far better than twenty-four varieties, a few of each kind.

—We connot give a list of more than 14 varieties of peonies which we would recommend for cut flower purposes out of the list we are now growing. We have many varieties, but they have not been sufficiently tested as yet The list is as follows: Amabilis Grandiflora, white, very large, double, fringed petals, fine, very sweet; Caroline Mather, purple crimson, large, double and very dark; Delicatissima, rose, large, full, fine, sweet; Duchesse de Nemours, rose-pink, very large, double, sweet, one of the best; Elagans, outside petals dark pink, large salmon center, loose, fine sweet; Festiva Maxima, creamy white with small center of carmine, round, early, in clusters, sweet; Francis Ortegal, dark purple crimson, very large, fine, deep, double, and sweet; Fulgida, very dark crimson, good; Humei, rose, full, large, late, one of the best; La France, pink, outside petals with yellowish center, very fine; Perfection, outside petals rose lilac, inside salmon, sweet; Reine Hortense, pink, large, full, globular, fine, fragrant; Triumph du Nord, violet rose, lilac shade; Victoria, rose, center yellowish. W. & T. SMITH COMPANY.

Geneva, N. Y.

—Regarding a list of twenty-four varieties of peonies which we consider best for cut flower purposes, we are pleased to name you the following list: Achillea, blush white, early; Alba Sulphurea, white, late; Alexander Dumas, pink and salmon; Beaute Francaise, flesh pink; Charles Verdier, lilaceous pink; Couronne d'Or, white; Delachei, purple crimson; Duke of Wellington, sulphur white; Duchesse de Nemours (Calot), white; Duchesse de Nemours (Guerin), pink, early; Festiva, white, early; Festiva Maxima, white, early; Humei Carnea, pink, late; Louis Van Houtte, crimson, late; Mme. Breon, rosy flesh white, early; Mme. Forel, pink, late; Ne Plus Ultra, pink; Mme. Coste, tender rose and white; Queen Victoria, flesh white; Jennie Lind, pink, early; Lady Bramwell, pink; Officinalis rubra fl. pl., crimson, earliest; Officinalis rosea superba, rose pink, earliest; Rubra Triumphans, crimson, early.

COTTAGE GARDENS CO.

—We herewith submit a list of 24 varieties of peonies for cut flower purposes arranged in their several colors. We have taken into consideration the various times of blooming, keeping qualities, fragrance, size of flower, and strong stems in making this selection:

White—Festiva Maxima, Queen Victoria, M. Dupont, Couronne d'Or, Madam Crousse, La Tulipe, Madame de Verneville, Marie Lemoine, Duchess de Nemours.

Pink—Beaute Francaise, Delicatissima, Livingstone, Princess Beatrice, M. Jules Elie, Edulis Superba, Alexandrina.

Red—Adolph Rosseau, Souvenir de l'Exposition Universelle, Modeste Guerin, Delachei, Marechal de MacMahon, M. Krelage, Richardson's Rubra Superba, Felix Crousse.

PETERSON NURSERY.

Chicago

'Christmas Beauty"; Begonia Agath

(88) Can you give me any information concerning a plant belonging to the echeveria family sometimes called Christmas Beauty? A florist who has a plant for sale tells me that it is very rare and worth $25.00. There is nothing attractive about the plant, though he tells me the flowers cover the plant and are of a rose color in the blooming period, which is at Christmas time. Is the begonia Agatha, which was exhibited at the Chicago show recently by J. A. Peterson, Cincinnati, O., as mentioned in your paper of November 17, for sale by any florist?

Mass. GREEN HEYS.

—We know of no plant of the echeveria family that throws a rose-colored flower at Christmas time, but there is a plant called crassula that gives rose-pink flowers, which is closely related to the echeveria, and might be the one referred to, though it has no such value as stated.

The begonia Agatha which was exhibited at Chicago is of English introduction, though we are not aware that any growers on this side are as yet offering it to the trade. If stock of the same is required, we would suggest you enter into communication with J. A. Peterson, Cincinnati, O.

Maman Cochet Roses Off Color.

(89) My pink Maman Cochet roses when cut seem to lose all color and to become neither pink nor white; in fact, their color is not good even on the bench. What ought I to give them to remedy this?

Texas. E. E. S.

—It is not an unusual thing for a pink rose of any variety to be off color at this time of year, and if the plants are in good health otherwise, no uneasiness should be felt. We do not know of any special line of feeding that could be given them at this particular time to help the color.

Geraniums; Sweet Peas.

(90) What is the proper time to put geranium cuttings in sand to be in bloom for Decoration Day?

Also the time to plant sweet peas for the market and the best kinds. Could they be planted on a bench about 2½ feet from the glass, and what is the temperature they would require? W. BROS.

New Jersey.

—Geraniums that are wanted in flower for Decoration Day may be propagated any time up to February.

Sweet peas for Winter flowering should have been sown several weeks ago, but we would not advise attempting to grow these on any bench where there is only 2½ feet of head room. The best kinds of sweet peas for this purpose can be found in any seedman's catalogue, and for Winter forcing they should have a temperature ranging from 45 to 55 degrees.

Leaf Spot on Carnations.

(91) Kindly inform me what is the matter with the carnation foliage enclosed, also cause and cure.

New York. H. A.

—The carnation leaves are affected with what is called "leaf spot." To get rid of the disease we would suggest that all the worst leaves be picked off the plants, and a spraying of salt and water be given once in two weeks, using a six-inch potful of salt to every six gallons of water.

Fumigating Violets.

(92) What is the best fumigator for violet Princess of Wales? I have some tobacco stems; will they burn the leaves? H. B.

Penna.

—Tobacco stems can be used with safety for fumigating violets, and in the main are effectual in removing aphis.

Bone Meal for Carnations.

(93) Kindly give me some information on feeding carnations with bone meal. I fed some two days after they were watered. I scattered the fertilizer between the rows and then loosened the soil with a hoe. Mold has formed here and there over the bench. I gave no water till three days after. It was dull weather.

Mass. H. B.

—The bone meal spread between the rows of carnations is all right, but the soil needs to be kept stirred occasionally, so that the bone will dissolve and become assimilated by the soil. No apprehension need be had on account of the bone meal showing a moldy appearance; keep the soil loosened and that will soon disappear.

A Plant for Property Dividing Line.

(94) I am to plant a line between two parties, and wish something out of the usual line of shrubs or other plants that would give a reasonable amount of bloom during the season. Part of the line is now planted to Weigelia variegata and Spiræa Anthony Waterer. The position faces north and is partially shaded afternoons. Plants named must be hardy.

MAC.

—Suitable shrubs for such a hedge would be althæa or Rosa rugosa.

Corrugated Paper Shipping Boxes.

(95) Kindly give the name and address of the firm which makes corrugated paper shipping boxes. I think they are located in Indiana; also have a house in Chicago.

H. B.

The J. W. Sefton Mfg. Co., Chicago, Ill., and Anderson, Ind., is no doubt the firm to which you refer.

Protesting a Judge's Decision.

(96) I notice that you answer almost any kind of a question on horticultural subjects, so would like your opinion on the following: In the rules governing our chrysanthemum show one read: "Any exhibitor wishing to protest must submit the same in writing to the secretary." The result was that one exhibitor protested the judge's decision, claiming his blooms were not beaten, and would not be satisfied until other judges were appointed to rejudge the flowers. The committee's reason for drawing up that rule was not for the purpose of having exhibitors protest the judges' decision, but to have them comply strictly with the rules of the show. Supposing the second lot of judges upheld the protest, what would prevent the exhibitor who won on the former judges' decision from protesting against their (the second judges') decision? Can an exhibitor protest the judges' decision on such a very fine point?

COMMITTEE.

—With regard to the question of what is right and what is wrong in the matter of protests at exhibitions, there is absolutely nothing to be gained by the expression of personal opinions on the subject. When a schedule is made out for an exhibition, exhibitors can only follow such instructions as are laid down therein, and it is for the makers of these schedules to get them up in such a manner that there can be no difference of opinion as to their meaning afterward. In the meantime, exhibitors can only follow the rules, and abide by such decisions as are rendered.

REVIEW OF THE MARKET

NEW YORK.—The cut flower business seems to have taken a little spurt this week. Stock of all kinds is clearing out much more satisfactorily than has been the rule lately, and prices are advancing. Roses of any variety in special grades are not over plentiful; the same may be said of carnations. Chrysanthemums are very plentiful, and while fancy prices seem to be out of the question, there has been a good demand for that grade of blooms which can be sold at anywhere from $1 to $2 per dozen. Cattleyas are quite scarce, and there does not appear to be any hope for a heavy supply within the next few days. Lily of the valley has sold well; but lilies have become more plentiful and prices on these are much lower than they were.

Roman hyacinths and Paper White narcissus are in full supply; but the crop of gardenias does not seem to be any too heavy for the demand as yet.

Smilax is selling much beter than it was and is also bringing better prices.

Violets are becoming more plentiful and the best do not realize more than $1 per 100, some grades selling at much below that figure.

On Wednesday morning the supply of roses was rather light and quoted prices for that day were inclined to be firm. The supply of carnations was heavier than during the previous days of the week, and prices were not so firm.

Thursday.—Cut flower market conditions during Thanksgiving day and the evening before again demonstrate that the anticipated large and increased business for this national holiday are a delusion, and any efforts on the part of either dealers or growers to provide for extraordinary supplies for this occasion, are only so much wasted energy. Business in this city on Thursday was not equal in volume to that of any good ordinary Saturday during the Fall and Winter season. There were many chrysanthemums over and above what were required to meet all demands, and prices averaged lower than they had been during the early part of the week. Carnations came in in quantities beyond expectations, and large numbers remained unsold when the bauiness of the day was over. It was the opinion of some dealers experienced in the many fine details of a wholesale market, that if a better knowledge of the probable supply had been available, prices would have been started a little easier and the stock worked off cleaner, as it was, however, consignments increased tremendously at the eleventh hour, and, although prices were cut so that they averaged lower than those obtained on Monday and Tuesday, it was impossible to make a satifactory clearance.

The results with the violet consignments were exactly the same as with the carnations. On Wednesday evening 123 boxes arrived from the Hudson River district, and early on Thursday morning another cargo, almost as large, followed in its wake. Some were sold at $1.25 per 100, more went at $1.00; a great many were let go at 60c, and there were thousands still in the hands of the dealers at closing time, so what the average will be we have not the faintest idea.

There were even too many American Beauty roses on hand, 60c. each was obtained for some of the special grade, but many were sold at 50c, and there was a good supply left over. The shorter grades cleaned out better. Bride and Bridesmaid were actually scarce and realized good money from $10 per 100 down to $3 and $4 for the short grades.

Of cattleyas there were sufficient to meet all demands, and some to spare, though the supply is quite light just now.

As we said before, trade did not equal that of a good Saturday. The weather was beautiful and clear, so that no complaint on that score can be entertained; and it might just as well be admitted now, and be borne in mind in future years, that Thanksgiving time, with its loads of chrysanthemums always in full crop, cannot be made a special occasion for the disposal of other flowers in more than ordinary quantities, or for any material advance in values over ordinary prices.

CHICAGO. — Chrysanthemums are still in abundance, though there appears to be quite a welcome relief by the dropping off of the cheaper grades. The better quality stock is holding at good prices and unless that which is supposed to be in reserve materializes this week, there can be no question that the crop will clean up well at profitable prices.

Carnations have been coming in from outside sources in somewhat larger proportions than were anticipated, yet there seems hardly a possibility of enough to go around and at this writing, Monday evening, the prices are soaring even to five and six cents for first-class goods.

Roses, with the exception of American Beauty, are in greater supply than the present demand rquires; yet the best fancy stock of Bride and Bridesmaid finds a market at ten and twelve cents, and the prospect is that the week will clean up the poorer grades at a fair price. American Beauty, even with short stems if carrying good heads, are in demand and are commanding high prices.

Violets are in evidence in larger numbers, but are readily cared for, while lily of the valley has drawn back a little.

W. K. W.

Tuesday, Nov. 27.—The market in this city broke to-day on everything to a greater or less extent, with the exception of American Beauty roses, violets and lily of the valley in flowers, and holiday greens, which are daily increasing in price. A great surprise in the market is the abundance of carnations which has materialized within the past twenty-four hours, a field where the experts looked for a shortage. Large sales were made to-day at 2 cents and under for good stock.

PHILADELPHIA.—All the wholesale houses are doing an active business this week. Orders for Thanksgiving appear to be good; shipping to other cities has also been very brisk all week. American Beauty roses are selling at $5 per dozen for first-class stock, while some specials selected for shipping have brought $6 per doz. There does not appear to be a sufficient quantity of first-class tea roses to fill all demands. The strongest call is for Bridesmaid; $12 per 100 is obtained for the very best. All other tea roses are selling at from $6 to $10 per 100; most of them are yet off color and weaker in stem than usual at this time of year.

Carnations are improving in quality, but on Tuesday the supply of good stock was not up to the demand. Extra choice stock sold at $5 per 100, while other stock went at from $3 to $4. There are lots of flowers that will not bring these prices, but the quality is not such as good retail stores want.

Chrysanthemums are plentiful, probably more so than usual, and the demand is very good. The most popular are those at $2 and $3 a dozen. White Bonnaffon is a very quick seller and more of this variety could be used. Some extra choice W. H. Chadwick have sold at $6 per dozen. Gardenias are not in sufficient supply to meet all calls; they are still held at $6 per dozen. Double violets are scarce, and it is no trouble to sell all at $1.50 per 100. The large single violets are more plentiful, and bring 75c. to $1 per 100. A few bunches of the new variety Governor Herrick are seen; the bright color of this is liked very much. Lily of the valley is in brisk demand; prices remain unchanged at $3, $4 and $5 per 100, but there is more of the higher priced stock now being sold. Cattleyas are in good demand at 50c per flower; some choice blooms of C. Trianæ have sold at 60c. each.

DAVID RUST.

INDIANAPOLIS. — Good steady business has characterized the past week; all lines were kept active, but counter trade showed a decided improvement. Thanksgiving trade promises to be exceptionally heavy. Chrysanthemums, of course, have led the sales throughout the week; if anything the retail prices are a trifle lower than in other years; $2 to $4 a dozen is obtained by retailers for the bulk. A fine supply has been held in reserve for the present week, and an advance of about ten per cent. is asked. Carnations are in strong demand and not always obtainable, at $3 and $4 per 100; $1 per dozen is the retail figure. Roses are plentiful and of good quality; Bridesmaid, Bride, and Golden Gate bring $6 a 100; Liberty and Richmond sell well at $5 to $8; the sale of American Beauty lags at times at $8 to $35 a 100. Home-grown violets at $1 per 100 do not cover the demand, so Eastern violets are resorted to, and for some reason there is not only a lack of fragrance in these, but they have a repulsive odor; this has not been noticeable heretofore.

Lily of the valley sells briskly at $4 per 100. Harrisii and callas have a difficult time trying to displace chrysanthemums, at $12.50 a 100; Lilium rubrum are still in the market at $8.

Begonia Gloire de Lorraine, cyclamen, and chrysanthemums in 6 to 8 inch pots, find many customers.

The green market is well supplied at current prices.

Tomlinson Hall Market was heavily stocked last week; trade was reported quiet.

I. B.

ST. LOUIS.—The approach of Thanksgiving has put life into trade and good business is looked for from now on. A number of large sized orders for weddings, receptions, dinners and funerals, were executed last week. Over the counter sales are increasing with the downtown retailers. Commission men are kept busy all day long with shipping and local demands. Chrysanthemums, especially fancy grades which run up to $4 per dozen, are in good demand; other grades bring $3 down to $1 per dozen. Ivory realize $5 per 100, with extra good demand. California violets are up to $1 per 100, and by Thursday they say the price will be $1.50. Violets are not overplentiful by any means. Carnations are fine, and plenty of them, but the big demand cleans them out almost daily. Extra fancy Enchantress bring $4 per 100; white, $3; red are scarce as are Mrs. T. W. Lawson. American Beauty roses are selling well—$5 per dozen for fancy long. Other roses on the whole have been of good quality and prices low, but Monday values were up to $3 and $4 for first and second; for fancy, $6 and $8. These prices will hold for Thanksgiving sales. Our wholesalers are looking daily for Roman hyacinths and other bulbous stock. Extra long smilax brings $12.50 per 100. Asparagus plumosus and Sprengeri are in good demand; also other greens, which are plentiful.

ST. PATRICK.

ST. PAUL.—Trade conditions must be reported as very good indeed. All varieties of roses are coming in nicely; the quality is as good as we can expect at any time during the season. American Beauty with 18 inch stems seem to sell well at $4 and $5 per dozen; other varieties range from $1 to $1.50. Specimen stock is sold quite readily at $2 and $2.50 per dozen. Medium priced chrysanthemums have taken quite a brace and the market can be considered strong. A week ago we had what one might call a glut in chrysanthemums but the demand has greatly improved of late, thus moving medium priced stock to good advantage. Carnations are still an uncertain quantity; the stock is not any too good, and but small numbers are brought on the market. Prices consequently are kept high and stock of only medium grade is selling quite nicely at $1 and $1.50 per dozen. Some very nice blooms of Winsor were shown by one of our dealers, being sold at $1.50 per dozen. Violets are scarce; the crop in this section is very small and as the season is fast approaching when the demand will no doubt be heavy, dealers are in a bad way to know how they are to supply the demand.

PAUL.

BOSTON.—Business has been better generally; Thanksgiving week always makes more activity. Roses are still very plentiful; the quality now is good. American Beauty are quite plentiful and there are a good many Richmond and other colored roses coming in. Killarney and Wellesley, too, are in supply, while there are plenty of all grades of Bride and Bridesmaid.

Chrysanthemums are still in their glory, and there are a fine lot of sizeable Major Bonnaffon and Ivory in the market. There has been a good demand for the medium-sized flowers this year, and any grower who happened to have pompons that could be cut in sprays found a ready sale for them. Carnations are now of fine quality and there is a good call for the better grades. Paper White narcissus are plentiful. Lilies are abundant and so are callas. There are some very fine cattleyas at the present time lily of the valley is good, and has a steady demand. Stevia is being brought in. Violets command better prices than they have done this season.

J. W. D.

NEW BEDFORD, MASS.—The past two weeks have seen a big improvement in the cut flower trade. Flowers are none too plentiful, and the demand is about equal to the supply. Pretty fair prices for Thanksgiving will prevail—about 60c. and 75c. per dozen retail for carnations; roses, $3 per dozen; violets $1 per hundred. Some good chrysanthemums are still in the market, Jeannie Nonin being the best of all just now; $3 per dozen is the price asked for the big ones.

Charles Ames, a young man who has worked in several florist stores here, has opened a store on Purchase street.

HORTICO.

KALAMAZOO, MICH.—The contin ous rains with dismal weather redu the volume of the retail trade qui considerably, and the absence of funer work during the past week or two ad also to the depression. Consequent values have not risen, but on the co trary bargain sales in roses especiall have been advertised several Saturda in succession. This evidently has son effect in using up any surplus accum lated during the week, and the week u ually starts out with firm quotation Shipping trade is reported fair to goo and orders for Thanksgiving are sa to be reaching quite an encouragi standard and promise to exceed those last year. Prices at retail will rema as usual. American Beauty, $1.50 $5 per dozen; teas, 50c. to $1.50; carn tions 60c. to $1.; violets, 35c. p bunch; chrysanthemums 50c. to $3.

Pot plants, such as cyclamen, prim las, etc., while a trifle late will be sufficient supply and there are yet considerable number of pot chrysanth mums to be worked off.

S. A. B.

CINCINNATI, O.—Business is fa Chrysanthemums lead, but it looks though Thanksgiving trade would abo clean them up. They have sold ve well this season; Major Bonnaff white and yellow, have the greatest c and will so long as they are well do Carnations are scarce and will be un the first of the new year. Roses plentiful; quality good. American Bea will be scarce for Thanksgiving, wh should insure a good crop for Chr mas. Some complaints about busin are heard from the retailers, they thi ing they should be doing more.

E. G. GILLETT

PITTSBURG.—The last few weeks November showed a good improvem in the cut flower trade, particularly week before Thanksgiving day w stock commanded good prices and not over abundant. The prospect fo good Thanksgiving day trade are v bright. Chrysanthemums are still p tiful but prices have stiffened con erably. Roses have advanced slig with a good demand. Good carnati bring a fancy price; the supply is weak. The first Paper White narcis and Roman hyacinths are in the mar . G. & J. W. Ludwig had several de ations the past week at which they u artificial poinsettias very effectively.

E. C.

GENEVA, N. Y.—The Rochester (N. Union and Advertiser of November 22 s "There was a rumor afloat yesterday that R. G. Chase Company, one of the lar nursery concerns in the country, woul forced into the hands of a receiver as result of the alleged dishonesty of one o officers.

"According to a statement made by officer of the company, the facts of the are that Howard A. Chase, of Philadel treasurer of the company, had organiz separate company under the laws of Dela and was doing business under the nan 'The Chase Nurseries.' It is further all that this new company was planning to hold of the entire force of salesmen o R. G. Chase Company. Sweeping and manent injunctions are said to have obtained in the United States courts ag the new company. Howard A. Chase resigned as treasurer and his place has filled by the election of Orville G. Chas Geneva, who is also secretary of company."

CHANGES IN BUSINESS

SHREVEPORT, LA.—James W. ble has started in business here seedsman and florist at 511 M street.

ELMIRA, N. Y.—Louis Soldan o on December 1 a florist and seed at corner of West Water street College avenue.

Wholesale Prices of Cut Flowers, New York, Nov. 28, 1906

Prices quoted are by the hundred unless otherwise noted

Roses	A. Beauty, fancy—special	30.00 to	50.00	Carnations	Inf'r grades, all colors	1.50 to	2.00
	" extra	15.00 to	20.00		Standard Varieties White	2.00 to	3.00
	" No. 1	8.00 to	10.00		Pink	2.00 to	3.00
	" No. 2	6.00 to	8.00		Red	2.00 to	3.00
	" No. 3	5.00 to	6.00		Yel. & Var.	2.00 to	3.00
	Bride, Maid, fancy—spe'l	8.00 to	10.00		*Fancy— (*The highest grades of standard var.) White	3.00 to	4.00
	" extra	5.00 to	6.00		Pink	3.00 to	5.00
	" No. 1	3.00 to	5.00		Red	3.00 to	5.00
	" No. 2	1.50 to	2.50		Yel. & Var.	3.00 to	5.00
	Golden Gate	1.50 to	10.00		Novelties	5.00 to	8.00
	Richmond	1.50 to	10.00		Chrysanthemums	2.00 to	6.00
	Mme. Abel Chatenay	1.50 to	10.00		" Fancy	10.00 to	40.00
	Adiantum	.50 to	.75		Gardenias, per doz.	3.00 to	5.00
	Croweanum	1.00 to	1.25		Lilies	8.00 to	10.00
	Asparagus	25.00 to	50.00		Lily of the Valley	1.00 to	4.00
	" Plumosus, bunches	8.00 to	15.00		Mignonette	...... to	......
	" Sprengerii, bunches	8.00 to	15.00		Narcissus, Paper White	...... to	2.00
	......	...... to	......		Roman Hyacinths	2.00 to	3.00
	Callas	10.00 to	12.00		Smilax	8.00 to	12.00
	Cattleyas	40.00 to	75.00		Violets	.65 to	1.00
	Cypripediums	...... to	12.50		......	...... to	......
	Daisies	...... to	......		......	...... to	......
	......	......	......		......	...... to	......
	......	......	......		......	...... to	......

Wholesale Prices of Cut Flowers—Per 100

Boston Nov. 26, 1906	Buffalo Nov. 28, 1906	Detroit Nov. 26, 1906	Cincinnati Nov. 26 1906	Baltimore Nov. 62, 1906	NAMES AND VARIETIES	Milwaukee Nov. 19, 1906	Phil'delphia Nov. 26, 1906	Pittsburg Nov. 27, 1906	St. Louis Nov. 26, 1906
20.00 to 30.00	40.00 to 50.00	to 50.00	to	to	ROSES — A. BEAUTY, fancy—special	to 25.00	50.00 to 60.00	30.00 to 50.00	20.00 to 25.00
15.00 to 20.00	30.00 to 40.00	to 25.00	40.00 to 50.00	to 25.00	" extra	to 20.00	to	to 20.00	12.50 to 15.00
6.00 to 15.00	20.00 to 25.00	to 16.00	30.00 to 35.00	12.50 to 20.00	" No. 1	to 18.00	to	to 15.00	8.00 to 10.00
2.00 to 6.00	8.00 to 10.00	to 12.00	6.00 to 8.00	5.00 to 8.00	" Culls and ordinary	to 12.00	to	to	3.00 to 6.00
8.00 to 10.00	8.00 to 10.00	4.00 to 8.00	6.00 to 8.00	to 5.00	BRIDE, 'MAID, fancy-special	to 6.00	6.00 to 10.00	8.00 to 10.00	5.00 to 6.00
6.00 to 8.00	6.00 to 8.00	to	4.00 to 6.00	to 4.00	" extra	to 5.00	to	4.00 to 6.00	3.00 to 4.00
2.00 to 6.00	to	to	3.00 to 4.00	to 3.00	" No. 1	to 4.00	to	to 3.00	to 2.00
1.00 to 2.00	4.00 to 6.00	to	2.00 to 3.00	to 2.00	" No. 2	to 3.00	to	to	to
2.00 to 8.00	4.00 to 6.00	4.00 to 8.00	2.00 to 6.00	2.00 to 5.00	GOLDEN GATE	3.00 to 6.00	to	to	2.00 to 5.00
2.00 to 8.00	4.00 to 8.00	to	to	3.00 to 5.00	K. A. VICTORIA	3.00 to 6.00	to	to	2.00 to 6.00
2.00 to 12.00	4.00 to 10.00	to	2.00 to 8.00	3.00 to 5.00	LIBERTY	8.00 to 8.00	to	to	to
to	to	3.00 to 8.00	to	3.00 to 5.00	METEOR	to	to	to	to
to	4.00 to 8.00	4.00 to 10.00	to	2.00 to 4.00	PERLE	3.00 to 6.00	to	to 6.00	2.00 to 5.00
to	to	to 50.00	to	to	ORCHIDS—Cattleyas	to	to 60.00	to	to
to	to	2.00 to 4.00	to	1.00 to 1.25	CARNATIONS — Inferior grades, all colors	2.00 to 4.00	2.00 to 3.00	to	1.00 to 1.50
1.00 to 2.00	2.00 to 3.00	to	to 2.00	1.50 to 2.00	Standard Varieties — White	to	2.00 to 3.00	2.00 to 3.00	1.00 to 1.50
1.50 to 2.00	2.00 to 3.00	to	to 2.00	1.50 to 2.00	Pink	to	2.00 to 3.00	to	1.00 to 1.50
1.50 to 2.00	2.00 to 3.00	to	to 2.00	1.50 to 2.00	Red	to	2.00 to 3.00	to	1.00 to 1.50
1.50 to 2.00	to	to	to	1.50 to 2.00	Yellow and var	to	2.00 to 3.00	to	1.00 to 1.50
2.00 to 3.00	4.00 to 5.00	to	to	2.50 to 3.00	Fancy Varieties — White	to	4.00 to 5.00	4.00 to 6.00	2.00 to 3.00
2.00 to 3.00	4.00 to 5.00	to	3.00 to 4.00	2.50 to 3.00	Pink	to	4.00 to 5.00	to	2.00 to 3.00
2.00 to 3.00	4.00 to 5.00	to	3.00 to 4.00	2.50 to 3.00	Red	to	4.00 to 5.00	to	2.00 to 3.00
2.00 to 3.00	4.00 to 5.00	to	to	2.50 to 3.00	Yellow and var	to	4.00 to 5.00	to	2.00 to 3.00
3.00 to 4.00	to	to	to	to	Novelties	to	to	to	to
.75 to 1.00	.50 to 1.00	to 2.00	1.00 to 1.50	to 1.00	ADIANTUM	to	to 1.00	.75 to 1.50	1.00 to 1.50
to 50.00	15.00 to 20.00	25.00 to 60.00	35.00 to 50.00	25.00 to 50.00	ASPARAGUS, Plum. and Ten.	25.00 to 50.00	50.00 to 75.00	35.00 to 50.00	25.00 to 40.00
to	15.00 to 20.00	20.00 to 30.00	to 25.00	25.00 to 50.00	" Sprengeri, bunches	25.00 to 50.00	to 50.00	10.00 to 50.00	10.00 to 30.00
8.00 to 10.00	10.00 to 12.00	10.00 to 12.50	to	6.00 to 10.00	CALLAS	12.00 to 15.00	to	to	to 12.50
2.00 to 20.00	8.00 to 25.00	4.00 to 25.00	8.00 to 20.00	4.00 to 25.00	CHRYSANTHEMUMS	8.00 to 30.00	10.00 to 50.00	6.00 to 25.00	5.00 to 25.00
to	to	to	to	to	DAISIES	to	to	to	to
8.00 to 10.00	to	to	to	to 12.50	LILIES	to	to	to	to
3.00 to 5.00	to	3.00 to 4.00	to 4.00	to 4.00	LILY OF THE VALLEY	3.00 to 4.00	4.00 to 5.00	3.00 to 4.00	3.00 to 4.00
to	1.50 to 2.00	to	to	to	MIGNONETTE, ordinary	to	to	to	2.00 to 3.00
to	2.00 to 3.00	to	to	to	" fancy	to	to	to	4.00 to 5.00
to 12.50	to 15.00	12.50 to 15.00	to 15.00	to 20.00	SMILAX	to	to	12.50 to 15.00	12.50 to 15.00
.50 to .75	to 1.50	1.00 to 1.50	to .50	to .50	VIOLETS, ordinary	to	to	to 1.50	.40 to .50
to 1.00	to 2.00	to	to 1.00	to .00	" fancy	to	to 1.50	to 2.00	to
to	to .15	to 1.25	to .15	to	GALAX LEAVES	to	to	to	.12½ to .15

New Orleans, La.

News Notes.

Ed. Baker was presented with a gold watch and fob chain by the employes of Audubon Park on Friday, November 16. The fob bore the following inscription, "From the employes of Audubon Park, November 9, 1906," this being the date on which Superintendent Baker resigned his position. The presentation was a great surpise to Mr. Baker, who thoroughly appreciated the thoughtfulness of the men who had worked under him for the last seven years.

Henry Kraack, head gardener for Mr. Lawrence Fabacher, is just convalescing after a protracted spell of typhoid malaria.

Robert Reinecicke has completed a nice greenhouse for his specialty, maindenhair fern. He is very much impressed with Adiantum hybridum, of which he has a good stock; finding this variety the best for cutting on account of its good keeping qualities, long stems, and free growth. This fern is also a favorite with C. W. Eichling, who was the means of introducing it to the South. Eichling's stock of ferns, both adiantums and nephrolepis in variety, is in tip top condition.

At the opening of the French Opera the past week the local papers spoke of the large amount of flowers that were to be seen; American Beauty roses appeared the favorites.

CRESCENT CITY.

MINNEAPOLIS, MINN.—The Mendenhall greenhouse property was recently conveyed from Lawrence Donaldson to C. F. Haglin for $1,500.

Wholesale Prices of Cut Flowers, Chicago, Nov. 27, 1906

Prices quoted are by the hundred unless otherwise noted

ROSES — American Beauty		
36-inch stems........per doz.	5.00 to	6.00
30-inch stems......"	4.00 to	5.00
24-inch stems......"	3.00 to	4.00
20-inch stems......"	2.00 to	3.00
18-inch stems......"	.... to	....
12-inch stems......"	.... to	....
8-inch stems and shorts "	.... to	....
Bride Maid, fancy special	10.00 to	12.00
" extra	6.00 to	8.00
" No. 1	4.00 to	5.00
" No. 2	.... to	3.00
Golden Gate	3.00 to	6.00
Carnot	3.00 to	6.00
Uncle John	3.00 to	6.00
Liberty	3.00 to	12.00
Richmond	3.00 to	12.00
Kaiserina	3.00 to	8.00
Killarney	3.00 to	6.00
" extra	8.00 to	10.00
Perle	3.00 to	6.00
Chatenay	3.00 to	6.00
Callas	.... to	16.00
....	.... to	....

CARNATIONS			
STANDARD VARIETIES	White	3.00 to	4.00
	Pink	3.00 to	4.00
	Red	3.00 to	4.00
	Yellow & var.	3.00 to	4.00
*FANCY (The highest grades of Sta'd var.)	White	4.00 to	6.00
	Pink	4.00 to	6.00
	Red	4.00 to	6.00
	Yellow & var.	4.00 to	6.00
NOVELTIES		.... to	....
ADIANTUM		.75 to	1.00
ASPARAGUS, Plum. & Ten.		.35 to	.50
" Sprengeri, bunches		.35 to	.50
LILIES, Longiflorum		15.00 to	20.00
HARRISII		15.00 to	20.00
Orchids—Cattleyas		.... to	50.00
SMILAX		8.00 to	12.00
LILY OF THE VALLEY		2.00 to	5.00
VIOLETS		1.00 to	1.50
" single		.75 to	1.00
HARDY FERNS per 1000		.... to	1.50
GALAX "		1.00 to	1.25
NARCISSUS, Paper White		3.00 to	4.00
CHRYSANTHEMUMS per doz.		.50 to	4.00

KALAMAZOO, MICH.—A terrific storm raged around this locality on the 21 doing much damage. I am glad to note very little damage was done to florists; a few ventilators broken off and a small number of panes of glass blown off sums up the total. S. B.

BENTON HARBOR, MICH.—Charles Carlson, proprietor of the Morton Hill greenhouses, died on Sunday, November 18, 1906, aged 60 years. His wife died some years ago. He leaves one daughter, who is a florist in Chicago.

St. Louis.

News Notes.

Judge and Mrs. M. S. Vesey, of Fort Wayne, Ind., called on the trade on Friday of last week, Mrs. Vesey stopping a few days as the guest of Miss T. Meinhardt, the judge leaving the same evening for a two weeks' trip to Mexico, with a party of friends, in a special Pullman.

C. A. Kuehn had a very fine exhibition of carnations on Friday; all the prominent growers around St. Louis called to see the display. Among the new varieties were Bonnie Maid, Red Chief, White Perfection, Red Riding Hood, and Aristocrat. All the blooms arrived in fine condition and attracted a great deal of attention.

Chas. L. Connon, late of the Connon Floral Company has opened up a flower stand in one of the big department stores on Washington avenue.

George Augermuller has recovered from his illness and is again attending to business.

Henry Ostertag got back loaded down with game from a hunting trip.

President Irish and the other officials of the Florists' Club held a special officers' meeting on last Thursday night, at the Hotel Rozier, called for the purpose of discussing plans for the mammoth flower show next Fall. Messrs. F. A. Weber, A. J. Bentzen, and W. C. Smith, the committee, reported the progress making: $350 was subscribed by those present, who were, besides those already mentioned, J. J. Beneke, Carl Beyer, and John Connon.

Frank M. Ellis has sold his wholesale commission business to W. C. Smith & Company, who will continue at the old stand. Mr. Smith, the head of the firm, is just the man to make a success of it, as he has had much experience in that line, and no man has more friends in the trade than he.

All florists who wish to join the Winter bowling games are requested to meet at the new Desoto Bowling Alleys, 708 Pine street, third floor, where two alleys have been reserved. Captain Lohrenz will be on hand early to enter the names of those who wish to take part. ST. PATRICK.

Indianapolis.

News Jottings.

Robert Ellis, foreman at Bertermann Brothers Company's Cumberland plant, was married on Sunday, November 25, to Miss Morgan, bookkeeper for Stuart & Haugh, Anderson, Ind. A host of friends wish them a prosperous future.

E. G. Hill, E. B. George, and Irwin Bertermann have been named on the committee of fifty appointed by the Executive Committee of the S. A. F. O. H. to raise the $10,000 guarantee fund for the National Flower Show in 1908. The three named are to represent Ohio and Indiana. W. W. Coles, of Kokomo, and Robert McKeand, of Marion, attended.

Mr. Hyatt, foreman for Stuart & Haugh, visited the carnation growers in this section.

Adolph Baur and Edward Larsen were recently at Lafayette visiting the carnation houses of F. Dorner & Sons Company. Local newspapers recently printed a lengthy article describing the seedling carnations at Dorner's, and the visitors bear out the statement that a fine lot is seen there.

Mrs. Alvin Schreiber, who has been very ill, is convalescing.

Visitors included S. S. Skidelsky, and J. McHutchinson, New York.

I. B.

St. Paul.

News Notes.

The Swanson Floral Company's store was damaged to some extent by a fire in an adjoining shop. A number of plants were practically ruined and the store was pretty well water-soaked, necessitating a general clean up in the way of painting, etc.

The decorations for the Hill wedding were supplied by Holm & Olson and the bouquets by August S. Swanson. The latter were made of orchids and white violets.

E. F. Lemke, has been cutting as nice a lot of chrysanthemums as have been seen in this section. His carnations are also turning out exceptionally well. Mr. Lemke was favored with the Sanders wedding order which from observation was the most elaborate in this section this season. L. G. Venzke did the decorations at Christ Church. PAUL.

CHRISTMAS GREENS HEADQUARTERS

HOLLY, WILD SMILAX $3.50 and $7.00 per case. **GALAX** New Crop Bronze and Green, $1.00 per 1000, $7.50 per 10,000.

Boxwood $15.00 per 100 lbs. Laurel Wreaths, extra quality, $2.50 per doz. upwards. Ferns, Fancy and Dagger, $1.25 per 1000. Laurel Festooning, extra quality, 5c. and 6c. per yd. Branch Laurel, 50c. per bunch. Leucothoe Sprays, $1.00 per 100. Princess Pine Festooning, $6.00 per 100 yds. Bouquet Green. $7.00 per 100 lbs. Green and Spagnum Moss, $1.00 per bbl.

Headquarters for all Florists' Supplies, such as RED IMMORTELLES, Wire Designs, Cut Wire, Letters of all kinds, Immortelles, Cycas Leaves, Milkweeds, Sheaves of Wheat, Ribbons, Boxes, Folding, Blue Corrugated, &c.

THE HOUSE THAT CAN SUPPLY THE GOODS ON A MOMENT'S NOTICE.

HENRY M. ROBINSON & CO., 11-15 PROVINCE ST., 9 CHAPMAN PLACE, L. D. Tel., Main 2617-2618. **BOSTON, MASS**

Mention The Florists' Exchange when writing.

SOUTHERN WILD SMILAX

Now ready in any quantity

Book orders now for future delivery. **Beaven's Fadeless Sheet Moss,** $3.50 per bag, delivered. Send for samples. Also **Fancy Holly** for **Xmas** trade. Satisfaction guaranteed. Write for prices.

E. A. BEAVEN EVERGREEN, ALA.

Mention The Florists' Exchange when writing.

Fancy or Dagger Ferns

$1.00 per 1000

Galax, Bronze or Green, 75c. per 1000.

Boxwood, No. 1 Stock, 50 lb. cases, $8.50

Laurel Festooning, 4c., 5c. and 6c. per yard. Finest quality

Laurel Wreaths, $3.00 per doz. Cheaper grades if wanted

Southern Smilax, fancy stock, 50 lb. cases $5.50

Laurel Branches, 35c. per bundle

Send your orders for **LAUREL FESTOONING** in now for Christmas, as later we may be unable to fill them.

Telegraph Office: New Salem, Mass. Long distance telephone connections.

CROWL FERN CO., MILLINGTON, MASS.

Mention the Florists' Exchange when writing.

SOMETHING NEW IN **CHRISTMAS TREE STANDS**

NEAT, ABSOLUTELY SECURE, EASILY ADJUSTED

Simple in construction, light in weight, durable and cheap.

Will sell on sight during the Christmas season at a good profit.

$1.90 per doz; $15.00 per 100; $140.00 per 1000.

Price F. O. B. Bridgeport, Conn.

Send for illustrated circular with full description.

ELBRIDGE E. WHEELER

Seedsman, BRIDGEPORT, CONN.

Mention the Florists' Exchange when writing.

EXTRA FINE NEW CROP FANCY FERN

$1.25 per 1000. Discount on large orders. GALAX, per 1000, $1.25. Green Galax, $1.25 per 1000.

MICHIGAN CUT FLOWER EXCHANGE

WILLIAM DILGER, Manager.

Let us have your standing order for Ferns, we will make Price right all through the season.

38 & 40 Broadway. Formerly Miami Ave. **DETROIT, MICH.**

Send for our weekly price list on Cut Flowers.

Mention The Florists' Exchange when writing.

REED & KELLER 122 W. 25th STREET NEW YORK

Importers and Manufacturers of **FLORISTS' SUPPLIES** Galax Leaves and Decorative Greenery

New York Agents for Caldwell's, Monroe, Ala., Parlor Brand Smilax.

Mention the Florists' Exchange when writing.

HOLLY! HOLLY! HOLLY

Holly Wreaths, Lycopodium and Lycopodium Wreaths

My Man in the Woods with 12 years' experience in packing, can ship you direct, and thus save extra expense in freight. Choice Delaware Holly, well berried, at $3.00 per case. Wreaths $10.00 to $15.00 per 100. Cash with order.

H. T. DUMONT & CO. - 1305 Filbert St., Philadelphia, P

Mention the Florists' Exchange when writing.

HOLLY

CHOICE DELAWARE

STOCK

Dark green and well filled with bright red berries, solidly packed in standard cases. Freight prepaid, cash in advance with order, single case, $4.00; five cases or more, $3.50 per case. By express, C. O. D., $3.00 per case. Holly Wreaths, 14 in. in diameter, made from perfect green holly, with four large clusters of berries; by freight, prepaid, per 100, $10.00; by express, C. O. D., per 100, $9.00. Order early and can ship promptly on any date desired.

H. AUSTIN, Felton, Del.

Mention the Florists' Exchange when writing.

N. LECAKES & CO.

53 W. 28th St., NEW YORK

Tel. No. 1214 Madison Square

Stands at Cut Flower Exchange Coogan Bldg., W. 26th Street & 34th Street Cut Flower Market.

SPECIALTIES: Galax Leaves, Ferns and Leucothoe Sprays, Holly, Princess Pine and all kinds of Evergreens.

Green and Bronze Galax Leaves

Mention the Florists' Exchange when writing.

WHOLESALE

GALAX and LEUCOTHOE

Direct from the woods to the dealer.

Galax Green and Bronze .... 50c per 1000

Leucothoe Sprays (green only) .... $2.00 per 1000

Ferns (dagger and fancy) .... 70c. per 1000

Special prices on lots of 100,000 and up.

Terms strictly cash, F. O. B. Elk Park, N. C.

F. W. Richards & Co., Banners Elk, N.C.

Mention the Florists' Exchange when writing.

MISTLETOE

The best Mistletoe grows in New Mexico. Sprays all heavily berried. Samples free if desired. We are prepared to quote wholesale prices delivered to any express office in the U. S. or Canada.

F. C. BARKER & CO., Las Cruces, New Mexi

Southern Smilax

If you want **SMILAX**, and you want to get it when you want it, send your orders to

JAS. TOMLINSON - Newton, A

Mention the Florists' Exchange when writ

BRILLIANT

Galax and Leucothoe SPRAYS

Wholesale Trade Solicited

J. L. BANNER & CO., Montezuma, N.

Mention the Florists' Exchange when writ

HOLLY AND HOLLY WREATH

Dark Green and Well Berried

CHOICE DELAWARE, per case, $3.00, 2x2x4 ft.

CHOICE VIRGINIA, per case, $2.75, 2x2x4 ft.

HOLLY WREATHS, 10c and 12c.

LAUREL ROPING, 5c. yard.

Cash. Order early, and will ship on any date des

HARRY L. HUBBS, Commission Merchant, N. E. Cor. 34th & Cumberland, **Philadelphia, Pa**

Mention the Florists' Exchange when wri

WIRED TOOTHPICK

10,000, $1.50; 50,000, $6.25

MANUFACTURED BY

W. J. COWEE, BERLIN, N.

Samples free. For sale by dealers.

Mention the Florists' Exchange when wri

THE AMERICAN CARNATI

Price, $3.50

A. T. DE LA MARE PTG. & PUB. CO.

2-8 Duane Street, New York

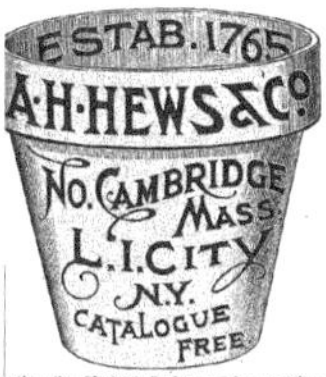

Kansas City, Mo.

News Items.

Business has been very fair the past week. Good stock as yet is none too plentiful, with the exception of chrysanthemums, which were never before of better quality, and there is a greater demand for them this season than there has been for several years. The yellow varieties seem to predominate; very few pink comparatively are seen. There is very little call for violets, which is perhaps fortunate, as the supply is limited and the quality mostly poor. W. A. Bastian is receiving some Southern violets, but reports no demand for them. We are having the first real snowstorm of the season, and this, coupled with the fact that a large number of important society events are scheduled for the next few weeks, will no doubt liven up trade.

Miss Jennie Murray has one of the handsomest window displays in the city; she is showing some unusually fine Colonel Appleton chrysanthemums.

There are rumors that one of our enterprising young florists is contemplating the opening of an up-to-date store in a prominent location on Walnut street.

We visited Samuel Murray's greenhouses one day last week and found everything as usual looking in the best of shape. His house of Begonia Gloire de Lorraine is worth a trip to see. There is probably no one in this country that can excel Mr. Murray in growing these plants, he has an entire house devoted to them. His display of Piersoni and elegantissima ferns is also second to none. He grows very few cut flowers, devoting most of his space to pot plants.

We dropped in at Charles Biederman's place on our way back. He was out, but we took a look around his plant and found everything in shipshape.

R. S. Brown & Sons are sending in some fine stock this year. Their chrysanthemums are very fine, and they are cutting some of the best carnations on this market.

If the growers of this vicinity would consign their cut flowers to a commission house here instead of peddling them around as is the method employed now, I think they would soon discover that they would realize better prices for their products than they do under the present system. There is too much competition now, and the result is that the dealer buys of the grower that offers stock the cheapest, whereas if all were consigned to the commission house the stock would be sold and a uniformly better price realized, and there would be no price-cutting as there is now.

The outlook for Easter lilies is splendid, and there is a much larger stock of them planted than usual.

L.

DAVENPORT, IA.—The monthly meeting of the Tri-City Florists' Club was held last week at the home of C. O. Boehm, superintendent at Central Park. Fifteen members assembled and partook of the supper which was served before the business meeting. A talk on roses, carnations and violets was the chief topic. The report of John Temple, who was one of the judges at the Chicago flower show, was heard with interest and Mr. Temple gave some very interesting descriptions. The next meeting will be held on the second Thursday in December at the home of Mr. Bills.

Columbus, O.

News and Trade Notes.

Every sign points to a great Thanksgiving trade; plenty of stock is coming in, and its quality is good. All the craft have made extensive preparations.

Alfred Emerich, representing Vilmorin-Andrieux & Company, of Paris, France, was a business visitor here the past week. Mr. Emerich, who is making his usual trip through the United States and Canada, expressed himself as well satisfied with business conditions.

John H. Williams having made special preparations to have a fine lot of Major Bonnaffon for Thanksgiving, is this week bringing in a very heavy cut.

The Livingston Seed Company had a special sale of cut flowers last Saturday, preparatory to starting the Thanksgiving prices; they disposed of quantities of carnations at 35c., roses at 50c., and chrysanthemums at $1 a dozen.

Jones, the wholesale grower at Lynden, is bringing in some especially good chrysanthemums this week.

Nursery stock orders have been very plentiful the last two weeks; in fact, much more so than early in the season. This is probably accounted for by the fine open weather we are having.

Samuel Graff of Graff Brothers has been in Chicago for some ten days past, making arrangements for his firm's supply of Thanksgiving stock.

The Fifth Avenue Floral Company has been doing a lot of chrysanthemum decorations lately; especially one for a fashionable wedding at the Lincoln apartments.

Watson S. Woodruff of S. D. Woodruff & Sons, Orange, Conn., was a visitor this week; as regards seed growing contracts for the future, he expects somewhat advancing prices to rule.

Owen Harbage has been appointed receiver for the Columbus Pottery Company; Judge M. G. Evans required a bond of $25,000. The suit against the company, which resulted from the fire of last week, was brought by Mr. Harbage and J. T. Gratigny.

The discussion of the status of Luther Burbank, which just at present is attracting such universal attention, is being followed with much interest by the craft here. The concensus of opinion seems to be that jealousy of Burbank is largely at the bottom of the matter.

Several dry-goods stores are having Thanksgiving sales and openings. The feature which interests our craft is that they give every visiting patron a chrysanthemum—this means still another good outlet for stock.

F. W.

SYRACUSE, N. Y.—The sympathy of the trade will go out to Robert Bard, florist, of this city, in the death of his wife, which occurred on Thursday, November 15. Mrs. Bard was well known to many of the traveling men and others engaged in the trade. It was her delight to have visitors stay at her home over night and relate their experiences.

Elmira, N. Y.

The United States Cut Flower Company is growing its entire stock of tea roses, both grafted and own roots, in cut-back plants, some houses two and others three years old. The first crop has been cut, while there is a grand prospect for a Christmas crop. Mme. Abel Chatenay, Ivory and Richmond prove satisfactory grown in this manner. American Beauty is coming along nicely; all the stock looks very healthy.

Four benches of Enchantress carnations are very fine, also the Pink Enchantress which Richard King, the able foreman, thinks superior to the parent variety. Harlowarden is the scarlet, but later than Flamingo. Lady Bountiful is preferred to White Lawson, being earlier and very free flowering.

Chrysanthemums are nearly over, a few good varieties being left for Thanksgiving trade, which from present indications will surpass that of previous years. It is intended to add to the present capacity next Spring.

M.

Louisville, Ky.

News Notes.

The next meeting of the Kentucky Society of Florists will be held at the store of August R. Baumer on Tuesday evening, December 4. Every member is urged to be present as it is the night of the annual election of officers; and for the good of the society every member should vote.

John Hettinger, who is Jacob Schulz's right hand man at the greenhouses, has been laid up for three weeks with a carbuncle but is now able to be out again.

A. R. B.

WILLIAMSPORT, PA.—Daniel E. Gorman was a recent visitor in Pittsburg.

LAST week we had to omit part of Thomas Proctor's letter about U-Bar houses because of lack of space, but here is his last clause: "The light we get is perfect and the growing capacity of the houses seems to me to be beyond anything I have ever experienced." You will recall that Mr. Proctor is Superintendent for R. W. Patterson, Lenox, Mass. Send for New Catalog. Pierson U-Bar Co., Designers and Builders of U-Bar Greenhouses, Metropolitan Building, 4th Avenue and 23d St., New York.

Mention the Florists' Exchange when writing.

The Test of Construction

Of what use is first-class workmanship and the best material if the construction of your house is antiquated and out of date? There is as much in the style of house as in the material of which it is built, and too much stress cannot be laid on the "right kind of construction."

There is a special house for each special condition, and the ordinary planing mill knows nothing of construction details. The first step towards "right construction" is to get our catalogue and estimate. Write now and start right—erect houses that will enable you to compete with the other fellow.

John C. Moninger Co.
CHICAGO
115 E. Blackhawk Street

Mention the Florists' Exchange when writing.

Your Money is well spent when you advertise in
THE FLORISTS' EXCHANGE

GREENHOUSE LUMBER

BUILD WELL

There is a pleasant sense of satisfaction in knowing that when your order for Cypress is placed with us you will receive material upon which you can absolutely rely, and that shipment will be promptly made.

ESTIMATES AND PLANS

Furnished without charge. Let us hear from you if you contemplate building.

HOT BED SASH
CEDAR POSTS, IRON FITTINGS, ETC., ETC.

LOCKLAND LUMBER CO.
LOCKLAND, O.

Mention The Florists' Exchange when writing.

Are You Now Deciding
on the details of your new houses?

Write us for Sketches and Suggestions, they will be of interest to you.

A. DIETSCH CO.
Louisiana Cypress and Washington Red Cedar GREENHOUSE MATERIAL
619 Sheffield Ave., Chicago, Ill.

Mention The Florists' Exchange when writing.

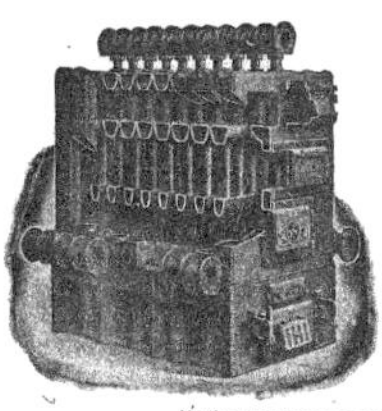

SCOLLAY BOILERS
ARE BEST

For Green House heating. Standard Cast Iron Green House Pipe and Fittings.

We are Headquarters for all sizes wrought iron pipe and fittings.

It will pay you to get our special quotation. We also contract for and erect **Steam and Hot Water Heating** apparatus in all parts of the country.

Illustrated catalogues free on application.

JOHN A. SCOLLAY,
74-76 MYRTLE AVE.,
BOROUGH OF BROOKLYN,
NEW YORK CITY.
Telephones 1492-1493 Main.
U. G. SCOLLAY, Manager.

Mention the Florists' Exchange when writing.

ARE YOU GOING TO BUILD

Assure yourself of **HONEST COMPETITION** figures by obtaining an estimate from me on **Iron Frame** or **Sash bar** greenhouses. My prices are the lowest for the best class of work.

FRANK VAN ASSCHE
(FORMERLY SUPT. FOR WEATHERED)
FACTORY: Fulton and Rose Ave., Jersey City, N. J.

Mention The Florists' Exchange when writing.

SUN DRIED CYPRESS
GREENHOUSE MATERIAL
IS THE BEST.
WRITE
FOLEY MFG. CO.
471 W. 22ND ST.
- CHICAGO -
FOR FREE CATALOGUE
VENTILATING APPARATUS, FITTINGS
HOT-BED SASH.
WE MAKE SKETCHES AND ESTIMATES-

If you are having delay in getting your roof material, send your orders to us and don't be in trouble. We will handle any order in the time agreed. Try us.

FOLEY MANUFACTURING COMPANY
471 W. 22nd St., Chicago

Mention the Florists' Exchange when writing.

The STANDARD VENTILATING MACHINERY

The original machine with self oiling cups; the most powerful, least complicated, very compact, with ease of operation.

The New Duplex Gutter over six miles in use and highly recommended; the only **drip proof** gutter in the market.

The Standard Return Steam Trap has no equal for simplicity or its workings. Catalogue free.

E. HIPPARD, Youngstown, O.

Mention the Florists' Exchange when writing.

SUMMER IN WINTER
BY USING
Standard Greenhouse Boilers
One cent gets our catalog.

GIBLIN & CO., UTICA, N. Y.

Mention the Florists' Exchange when writing.

CHRISTMAS NUMBER

The Florists' Exchange

We are a straight shoot and aim to grow into a vigorous plant

A WEEKLY MEDIUM OF INTERCHANGE FOR FLORISTS, NURSERYMEN, SEEDSMEN AND THE TRADE IN GENERAL

Vol XXII. No. 23 | NEW YORK AND CHICAGO, DECEMBER 8, 1906 | One Dollar Per Year

CONTENTS AND INDEX TO ADVERTISERS, PAGE 691

Red Berried Hollies

Fine decorative trees well berried $1.00 up.
Bouquet Green, choice Saratoga Co., $7.00 per 100.
Holly Bright, well berried, $5.00 case.
Immortelles, in best colors, $2.50 doz.
Cape Flowers, Mistletoe, Needle Pines, etc.

Lily of the Valley, selected 3 yr. old for Christmas forcing. $10.00, 1000; $24.00 case of 2500.

	Per 100	1000
Spirea Japonica	$4.00	$38.00
" Compacta	5.00	42.00
" Astilboides Floribunda	6.00	45.00
Bleeding Hearts, strong roots	7.00	
Lilium Speciosum Album, 8x9	8.00	
" " Rubrum, "	7.00	

WM. ELLIOTT & SONS
201 Fulton Street NEW YORK

Mention the Florists' Exchange when writing.

C. C. MORSE & CO.

SEED GROWERS
171-173 Clay St., San Francisco, California
OUR SPECIALTIES
ONION LETTUCE SWEET PEAS
Also Carrot, Celery, Celeriac, Cucumber, Endive, Leek, Mustard, Parsley, Parsnip, Radish, Salsify, Spinach, Tomato and
FLOWER SEEDS
Growers for the trade on contract. Warehouses at Santa Clara; Farms and Farm headquarters Carnadero, near Gilroy.
Registered Cable Address: MORSEED, SAN FRANCISCO.
Mention the Florists' Exchange when writing.

EXCEPTIONAL OFFER

To save storage we offer for immediate shipment the following roots at remarkably low prices.

SPIREA JAPONICA (170 clumps in a case) per case $5.00
SPIREA COMPACTA MULTIFLORA (250 in a case) per case 9.50
SPIREA ASTILBOIDES FLORIBUNDA (175 in a case) per case 5.50

Subject to being unsold on receipt of order. Cash must accompany every order.

W. W. RAWSON & CO.

5 UNION STREET, BOSTON, MASS.
Mention the Florists' Exchange when writing.

PACIFIC SEED GROWERS' CO.
109 MARKET STREET
SAN FRANCISCO, CAL.
Specialties:
Onion, Carrot, Lettuce, Sweet Peas
Mention The Florists' Exchange when writing.

GROW YOUR OWN
TREES
and SHRUBS from
SEED.
Send today for our
TRADE SEED LIST
and also for our *Descriptive Catalog*, which is replete with valuable information.
OTTO KATZENSTEIN & CO.
Wholesale Dept. ATLANTA, GA.
Mention The Florists' Exchange when writing.

MY GIANT CYCLAMEN
Are Ahead in Growth and Flowers
Bloodred, Carmine, Pink, Pure White, White Carmine Eyed.
Each color separate. Tr. pkt., $1.00; 1000 seeds, $6.00. An even mixture of the above 5 colors, tr. pkt., 75c.; 1000 seeds, $5.00.
For larger quantities, special quotations.
O. V. ZANGEN, Seedsman, HOBOKEN, N. J.

QUALITY SEEDS BULBS PLANTS
SEND FOR CATALOGUE
ARTHUR T. BODDINGTON
342 West 14th St., New York.

SPECIAL BULB OFFER

TO DISPOSE OF SURPLUS

TULIPS

	100	1000
Single Mixed	$ .65	$ 4.
Duc Van Thol, scarlet	1.25	12.50
La Immaculæ	.75	6.00
Pottebaker, scarlet	1.20	11.
Wouvermann	1.35	13
Yellow Prince	.75	7
Chicago, pink	.90	8.
Cramoisie Brilliant	2.00	16
Rose Grise de Lin	1.10	10
White Swan	1.00	9.
Mon Tresor	1.25	12
Double Agnes	1.00	9
" Blanche Hativa	2.00	17
" Rose Blanche	.75	7
" Count Leicester	.75	7.
" La Matador	1.75	16.
" La Blason	1.00	9.
" Murillo	1.60	15
" Salvator Rosa	2.50	22
" Titian	.90	8.
" Tournesol, yellow	1.75	16.
" red and yellow	1.25	12.00
" Mixed	.80	7.00

TULIPS

	100	100
Late Bouton d'Or	$ .60	$5.
" Golden Eagle	.50	4.
" Maiden's Blush	1.00	9.
" Byblooms	.50	4.
" Mixed	.75	6

NARCISSUS

Poeticus	$ 40	$3.
Ornatus, mother bulbs	.60	5.
Golden Spur, mother bulbs	2.25	20.
" Mammoth	1.75	16.
Alba Pleno Odorata	.40	3.
Empress	2.25	20.
Orange Phoenix	1.00	7
Silvar	2.00	17
Von Sion, Mammoth	1.25	11.

LILIUM MULTIFLORUM

6 x 8, 400 to case .... $12.50 per ca
7 x 9, 236 " .... 10.00 "
8 x 10, 225 " .... 13.50 "

LILIUM GIGANTEUM

6 x 8, 400 to case .... $20.00 per ca
7 x 9, 300 " .... 19.50 "
9 x 10, 180 " .... 22.00 "

STUMPP & WALTER CO

50 BARCLAY ST., NEW YORK
Mention the Florists' Exchange when writing.

FORCING RHUBARB

Under the Greenhouse, bench, or in any old cellar or mushroom house, is entirely practical and an easy proposition.

Send for my Special Florists' Circular on Rhubarb Forcing

It gives ample directions for successful culture

I have a good supply of large UNDIVIDED CLUMPS. Price $2.00 per dozen, 25 for $3.75; $12.00 per 100; $100 per 1000 (500 at 1000 rate)

Stokes Seed Store

219 MARKET ST., - - PHILADELPHIA, PA.
Mention The Florists' Exchange when writing.

We Sell More Flower Seeds Than Any Other Firm in the British Empire.

Send for Special List of our grand selections, and list of REAL NOVELTIES.

WATKINS & SIMPSON, Wholesale Seed Merchants.
12 Tavistock St., Covent Garden, LONDON, ENGLAND.
Mention the Florists' Exchange when writing.

SEEDS

If you are in need of any of the following, write us for pric Beets, Cabbage, Cannon Ball and Rocky Ford Mu Melon, Southern grown Water Melon, Bermuda a other Onion seed, Okra, Mustard, French and Ca ornia grown Radish, Tomato, Mexican June Corn, Kaffir Corn, German Millet, Dwa Yellow Milo Maize, Sugar Cane, Winter Barley, Red Rust Proof Oats, Cotton seed, Whi poorwill and White Black-eyed Field Peas, Spanish Peanuts, Johnson and Bermu Grass.

TEXAS SEED & FLORAL CO. DALLAS, TEXA
Mention the Florists' Exchange when writing.

Catalog Engravings

and ILLUSTRATIONS
that print EASILY. That's the kind we make — have been since '73
JAS. M. BRYANT, Horticultural Engraving and Printing
706 Chestnut Street, PHILADELPHIA, PA.
Write for our Catalogue of Stock Engravings
Mention the Florists' Exchange when writing.

BURPEE'S SEED

PHILADELPHIA
Blue List of Wholesale Price mailed only to those who plant for profit.
Mention the Florists' Exchange when writi

THE AMERICAN CARNATIO
Mention the Florists' Exchange when writi

Advertisement Correction.

In the advertisement of Wm. Elliott & Sons, on page 650 of our last week's issue, the price of double tulips, Rex Rubrorum, should have read $14 per 1000 instead of $11; and the price of La Candeur should have read $11 per 1000 instead of $17 per 1000.

Seed Trade Report.

AMERICAN SEED TRADE ASSOCIATION

Henry W. Wood, Richmond, Va., president; C. S. Burge, Toledo, O., first vice-president; G. B. McVay, Birmingham, Ala., second vice-president; C. E. Kendel, Cleveland, O., secretary and treasurer; J. H. Ford, Ravenna, O., assistant secretary.

The tariff on clover seed, gross weight, imported into Cuba from the United States is $3.60 per 100 kilos; on flaxseed, gross weight, $.82; on timothy seed, gross weight, $2.00; beans, gross weight, $1.144; peas, gross weight, $1.144. The importation of foreign tobacco seed into the island of Cuba is prohibited until further orders.

NEW YORK.—Horatio Nellis died suddenly at the residence of his son, A. C. Nellis, seedsman, November 13, in his eightieth year. Mr. Nellis was born and lived in the Mohawk Valley the greater part of his life, and at one time was prominently connected with the dairy interests of Montgomery and Herkimer counties.

CHRISTMAS GREEN.—An unprecedented shortage of princess pine has developed in Chicago within the past few weeks, said by experts to have produced the shortest crop in proportion to the demand that has occurred in the past fifteen years. This is attributed by different authorities to various causes. One of the largest handlers of this line of goods blames the government for having recently paid the Indians their pension money, and, as he stated, an Indian will not work when he has money in his belt. Another important factor in the trade lays the short crop to unfavorable weather and early snows in the Northern woods, which have made it impossible to gather green for the past three weeks—the season when a large proportion of the year's product is taken in. In connection with this subject the writer was last week shown through the establishment of the W. W. Barnard Company on Kinzie street where one hundred women have been engaged for the past month in tying festooning and making wreaths of bouquet green, and are just starting in on the holly wreaths. The crop of the latter, which is coming in from the Eastern States, is of an exceptionally fine quality, the foliage and berries both being very heavy. Twenty-five thousand yards of festooning per diem is the average output of this one house alone, and the yearly business in this line amounts to eighty freight carloads or two extra long freight trains. This year's crop is variously estimated at from 40 to 60 per cent. of the requirements, and within the past week the price has been steadily soaring.

W. K. W.

NEBRASKA SEED CROPS.—In the majority of instances the crops of cucumber and muskmelon have been disappointing, and as a rule have not equaled field estimates when delivered by the growers. We understand the same applies to the Waterloo growers. The watermelon, pumpkin and squash crops have turned out better, with a few exceptions. Sweet and field corn crops are fully equal to a good average, and we believe the quality will be better than for the past several years. The Fall, however, has not been quite as favorable as we hoped for, and the cloudy, stormy and cold weather has delayed the seeding and harvesting operations, so that the deliveries of the vine seeds are backward and considerably later than usual; and we understand this delay is causing some inconvenience with the dealers, who have Southern orders for early shipments, especially in the line of watermelons. Crops are now coming in from the growers faster than at any time previously this Fall, and we hope to have our vine seeds all in, cleaned and shipped within the next three or four weeks. We expect to commence receiving our sweet and field corn crops next week, and hope to make better progress in making same ready for shipment on account of the superior quality.

WESTERN SEED & IRRIGATION COMPANY.

GOVERNMENT SEED TESTING.—E. Brown, botanist in charge of the Seed Laboratory, U. S. Department of Agriculture, writes to the Rural New Yorker to the effect that the publication of the names and addresses of firms found to have offered for sale adulterated seed, together with the analyses of the samples found to be adulterated, has had "a very stimulating effect on the trade, if we are able to judge from the number of samples constantly being sent to the department by dealers for examination as to the presence of adulterants."

GOVERNMENT FREE SEEDS.—While it is not expected that the House of Representatives will devote a week to discussing the question whether the Government should continue distributing pumpkin and squash seeds as it did last session, the matter will no doubt again come before that body when the agricultural appropriation bill is considered. Last session the House Committee on Agriculture, which had considered the matter very carefully reached the conclusion that as the Government had been distributing the same varieties of seeds for many years and that all the seeds sent out have been on the market for from ten to fifty years and could be purchased at any seed store, the farmers had been well educated as to the characteristics of these seeds and it was a waste of money to spend $242,000 annually in distributing such common varieties of garden seeds. In order that those opposed to free seeds shall have an opportunity to present their case to the House Committee on Agriculture, that committee has granted them a hearing on December 12, at which the entire matter will be very carefully gone into. The anti-free seed movement has the support of the National Grange, National Farmers' Congress and other National and State organizations.

GOVERNMENT BULB EXPERIMENTS.—Thirty thousand bulbs have been received at the Government Experiment Station at Hillyard Orchard Heights and are now being set out. Ten thousand of these bulbs come direct from Holland. The farm lies east of Hillyard in volcanic ash at the base of the hill and is owned by John Mass. Associated with him is John Vander Bosch, who has had practical experience both in Holland and England in bulb culture. The bulbs are tulips, narcissus and hyacinths. They are furnished free by the government, but one-tenth of the first crop must be returned. Three of these farms have been established in Washington. One is at Tacoma, another at Bellingham and the other at Hillyard Orchard Heights. The farm which makes the best showing will be made a permanent experiment station.

Mr. Vander Bosch visited various parts of the State before locating his farm at Hillyard, which he says has some of the best soil for bulb culture he has seen. It is estimated by Mr. Vander Bosch that from 50,000 to 60,000 bulbs can be grown on a quarter acre. These are set out in the Fall, will bloom by Easter, and all the flowers, which are a by-product, go to the growers. The men expect a handsome profit. In addition to bulbs, cauliflower and other tender varieties of vegetables will be grown.—Spokane (Wash.) Spokesman-Review.

SEED TRADE CONDITIONS.—Change, which is the soul of nature, is as marked in the seed trade as in any other condition in life. While the seed trade in our country is constantly increasing, as it must do to supply the demands of an increasing population, the distribution of seeds is done in a very different way from former customs. Competition of the most aggressive character is manifest in every direction. The original seed grower, who had but few customers and grew but few varieties and of a given class, inspired by the spirit of trade has become an important factor in seed distribution. Seeing the marked differences in prices between the grower and the retailer, without the slightest knowledge of the cost of selling, which the retailer has to assume, the former seed-grower plunges in without the faintest knowledge of the business, other than of the few types he has formerly grown, and soon becomes an adventurer considerably to be dreaded by the legitimate trade.

The pioneers in the seed trade were all able, honorable, and most conservative men, could not and did not recognize the new aspirants for public favor as seedsmen, and, what was good business methods, did not reduce prices, as all other business houses found necessary to do, in order to meet legitimate competition, which their margin of profit would have warranted and would have been good business economy, as it would have resulted in keeping down competition, and in the keeping up to the highest possible standard the quality of the seeds sold.

On the other hand, the truckers or market gardeners, who are the largest consumers of seeds, began to feel the necessity of economy in the purchase of their supplies; seeds being an important factor, they turned their attention toward the base of supplies. As they paid the agents that handled their productions a given percentage for selling, they could not see why they could not pay the same percentage for buying their seeds as they did for their other supplies, as "it is a poor rule that will not work both ways." It would not appear to the owner of a few acres worth while to economize in the buying of seeds, and it would not be. Not so, however, with the owner of a five thousand acre farm, and there are such. There is one man near Charleston, S. C., who uses annually 1,500 pounds of cabbage seed. Another man, whose name and locality we are not permitted to give, buys annually more than 100 pounds of tomato seed, 40 pounds egg plant, 50 pounds of Ruby King tomato, and 1,000 pounds cucumber seed. To this may be added the fact of one New York agent who buys for these large truckers, who has now in store 6,000 pounds Teneriffe onion seed which will be used the coming season. Of course these facts do not materially affect the general seed trade, although the influence is felt. As a rule, trade prospects are very good. Business along all lines being highly prosperous, men of wealth are buying liberally for the vegetable and ornamental garden. The bulb trade has been exceptionally good, and so far as we have been able to learn, the trade generally has been well satisfied with the past year's business, and is making preparations for the coming year with every assurance of a good trade. The seed crops are all secured, and there is no danger of any great shortage along general lines; and what is more satisfactory, there will be no great surpluses, which are always an enemy to prosperous business. L.

European Notes.

The cold, wet weather which prevailed in Germany during the harvesting time for onion seed has caused a lot of seed to sprout, and the markets are consequently flooded with this article quoted at a price which cannot possibly repay the initial outlay for bulbs. The Holland crop of Brown Strasburg onion is also equally abundant and seed of fine quality is being practically given away. The heavy surplus in France has already been reported, but its full extent is only now being realized. If such varieties as Straw-colored (white) Spanish, Giant Zittau, Bedfordshire Champion or Brown Strasburg would do for our American friends the seed could be bought for a mere song.

Leek is also abundant and the quality good; the same is true of cabbage and kale. Beet is far worse than our worst estimate; Crosby's Egyptian and Detroit are especially short. The trade in peas is improving.

EUROPEAN SEEDS.

The HORTICULTURAL TRADES' ASSOCIATION of Great Britain and Ireland, at a recent meeting at which some seventy of the principal firms in the trade were represented, held to consider the position created by the Prevention of Corruption Act which comes into operation January 1 next year, resolved "to loyally accept the position as defined by the act, and to avoid anything which might in any way appear to transgress its provisions." The Journal of Horticulture says: "The general feeling, so far as we could discover, was that a five per cent. discount be adopted by nurserymen generally; and, if the discount is awarded openly, it ought in no way to infringe the Corruption Act, 1906. Will foreign nurserymen adhere to five per cent?"

SOUTH AFRICAN CATALOGUE TAX.—The catalogue tax imposed by the British colonies in South Africa brought forth very earnest protests from the exporters in the United Kingdom. A complaint sent to the British Government was answered by Lord Elgin with the statement that the high commissioner for South Africa had reported that it had been decided to relax the restrictions on the importation of catalogues and price lists to the following effect:

"Ordinary catalogues and price lists imported through the post, weighing less than eight ounces, will not be charged with duty, but in the case of South African firms sending large quantities of catalogues or advertisements through the post duty will be charged upon them even if weighing less than eight ounces. The Natal, Transvaal, and Orange River Colony Governments and administration of Southern Rhodesia have further agreed to forego the 6-penny delivery fee hitherto collected on catalogues or price lists imported through the post. The Cape Government has made a like decision with regard to similar articles imported by book or letter post."

The London Times says: "Compared with the original tax and the 'clearance fee' of 6d., the procedure which is sanctioned by this agreement seems fairly reasonable. It will be noted that the Cape still intends to exact duty on catalogues, etc., imported by parcels post. Why a line should be arbitrarily drawn between catalogues of eight ounces and those over that weight is not stated."

In addition to the abolition of the duty on catalogues weighing less than eight ounces the Natal, Transvaal, Orange River Colony, and Rhodesian Governments have agreed to forego the 6d. delivery fee hitherto collected on catalogues or price lists imported through the post, and the Cape Government has made a like decision with regard to similar articles imported by book or letter post. But the whole impost is still in force in respect to South African firms sending large quantities of catalogues or advertisements through the post.

CATALOGUES RECEIVED.

M. HERB, Naples, Italy.—Gener Catalogue of Seeds, Bulbs, Plants, e

COTTAGE GARDENS COMPAN Queens, N. Y.—Price list of Carnatior including the new variety, Beacon.

IOWA FLORAL COMPANY, D Moines, Ia.—A neat Catalogue of Flo al Designs, and other supplies for R tail Customers.

NATHAN SMITH & SON, Adria Mich.— Preliminary List of Chrysa themum Novelties for 1907 and Oth Seasonable Stock.

NURSERY DEPARTMENT.

Conducted by Joseph Meehan.

AMERICAN ASSOCIATION OF NURSERYMEN. Orlando Harrison, Berlin, Md., president; J. W. Hill, Des Moines, Ia., vice-president; George C. Seager, Rochester, N. Y., secretary; C. L. Yates, Rochester, N. Y., treasurer.

DUNDEE, ILL.—The Foley Manufacturing Company of Chicago are building the new greenhouse for the Dundee Nursery. The greenhouse will be used for propagating evergreens from cuttings.

Horticultural Notes.

Magnolia grandiflora grows so much faster when in pots in a greenhouse than when planted outdoors that they should be raised in this way, to say nothing of the safety of the plants when transplanted from pots. It is practicable to grow all sorts of magnolias in pots to some extent.

Hydrangea Hortensia should either be dug up and buried under ground or have a mound of sawdust, soil or ashes placed over them for the Winter. Heavy freezings kill the branches, in which case there are no flowers next season.

One may form an idea of the rapid disappearance of timber trees when noting the report of the United States Department of Agriculture that there were used by the various steam and electric roads of our country the past season ninety-one millions of ties. This accounts for the increased calls for seedlings of forest trees which nurserymen say are coming to them. Oak leads all; next pine.

The Carolina jasmine so called, Gelsemium sempervirens, the beautiful evergreen climber of the South, flowers freely when grown in pots and wintered in a greenhouse. The flowers are sweetly odoriferous and are of a golden yellow color.

Quercus tinctoria, Q. coccinea and Q. alba hold their leaves very late in Autumn after the foliage is dead. For this reason many value them, as they act as a screen while the leaves are on them. The alba, which is the common white oak, often holds its foliage until toward Spring. Young trees of all oaks hold their dead foliage a longer time than older ones.

Two of our sumachs, the Rhus typhina and Rhus glabra, are in greater demand than ever. Their compound leaves are attractive through the Summer and in Autumn both their seeds and their leaves are a blaze of scarlet. Set in groups they are very attractive.

Daphne Mezereum.

In many old gardens a specimen of the mezereon, as the Daphne Mezereum is called, is to be found, but it is not as often met with as its merits call for. It is not for its general appearance in Summer, for this is not striking; but it is its delightfully sweet-scented flowers in early Spring that count. As soon as Winter days are over and before many a person thinks of Spring flowers, the daphne surprises them by its sweet odor, which often is wafted to them before they know the shrub is in bloom.

There are two colors prominent in collections; one has white flowers, the other rosy-red, both being highly fragrant. While the flowers are not of a size that a great display is made, the mezereon is an excellent plant to have in a pot to place in a room or in a greenhouse for the gaining of the sweet odor of its flowers. One plant is sufficient for this, unless the room is a large one.

Standing alone the mezereon does not make much display as a shrub, but it has the advantage of enduring uninjured our severest Winters; and the berries that follow the flowers are quite ornamental, being bright red on the red flowered and yellow on the white flowered one. The seeds need to be sown as soon as ripe, in early Summer, when they quickly germinate.

Covering Small Stock for Winter.

One of the most profitable things a nurseryman can do at this season of the year is to cover his small stock with leaves or some other material to protect it in the Winter season. In the case of very small plants, especially evergreens, tops and all are better for a covering, but to place a protection about the roots is especially beneficial. Ever so small a covering is a help, but one that will keep out frost is better, as the plants are benefited in every way when their roots are free from frosts. Anyone having access to woods should secure loads of leaves, as they make the best of all coverings.

Many trees and shrubs planted within a year have their roots but a few inches under ground, and it is these that need a covering of leaves more than any others. A few inches, if no more, of covering will keep out many degrees of frost. Evergreens need it more than deciduous stock, because carrying their foliage all Winter more moisture is demanded, and when the soil is unfrozen the roots are free to convey it from the ground.

It has often been remarked how much better rhododendrons winter when their roots have the protection of a covering of leaves, and the reason for it is the ease of keeping the foliage supplied with moisture when so covered.

There is no necessity to apply the leaf-covering to the ground before hard freezings come; on the other hand, no harm is done by fixing it earlier, and if left till later snows may prevent the operation, were snows to remain on the ground all Winter, nothing more would be required, but this rarely happens in the milder portion of the Middle States, hence the wisdom of placing leaves for a covering.

Shade for the tops of evergreens is a great advantage, but it is impracticable to secure it on a large scale. Evergreens will endure cold far better when in the shade than when in the sun in Winter. It is well to keep this in mind, for there are many choice plants it may be possible to shade in some way when whole collections could not be so covered.

Pines in Pots for Christmas.

Years ago pine trees were in much demand for Christmas trees, and they are still called for by those who are fond of the pine tree odor which many of them emit. In this respect the Pinus rigida, the pitch pine of the Northern States, is unrivaled.

There is more demand to-day for pines in pots, not altogether for Christmas trees on which to hang presents, but for general Christmas effect, evergreens of this kind adding so much to the beautifying of dwellings for this occasion. Two pines that can be confidently recommended are the Swiss pine, cembra, and the white pine, strobus. There are several reasons for this. Both of these pines have soft needles very different from the stiff ones of many other sorts. Then they are known as being exceptionally easy to transplant safely. There is merit, too, in their natural shapeliness. The cembra makes a conical growth, which shape fits it for placing in situations where a spreading pine could not be used. The white pine is more spreading, but is not too much so; and then its silvery foliage adds to its merits.

When a pine is wanted the branches of which are stiff enough to hold presents of some weight, the Scotch answers very well, but this is one of those mentioned as having stiff, harsh needles.

Dug up carefully with all the roots intact, the pines first mentioned—the cembra and the white—will do more than last out the holidays; they will do this and can be used later to plant outdoors, or they may be kept in pots stored in some partly protected place through the Winter, should the weather or other reasons make the planting out at once undesirable.

Flower Day in Cemeteries.

The custom of having an annual "flower day" on which all lot holders are invited to decorate graves, has been noted as a popular one in several cemeteries. Park and Cemetery has this to say of it:

Oak Grove Cemetery, Springfield, Mass., adopted the idea in 1903, and Superintendent J. C. Sackett has found it to be growing in favor and productive of much interest in the cemetery. This general decoration day takes place every year the first Sunday after Labor Day, when a notice similar to the following is sent to new lot holders: "Third Annual Flower Sunday, Oak Grove Cemetery. Our third annual flower day will be Sunday, September 9, 1906, to be observed by all those who wish, as a day for a general remembrance and the bringing of flowers for the decoration of their lots." The quick response to the notices each year is an assurance that the experiment is passing into a custom which will stay bcause the people love it.

Accompanying the notes an illustration is given, showing the graves in the cemetery beautifully strewn with choice flowers. The work of placing the flowers and embellishing the lots is performed on the day preceding, Saturday, so that visitors may be at the cemetery as early in the morning of Sunday as they wish. In the case of Oak Grove Cemetery referred to, it is said on the last occasion of decorating the graves the cemetery was the centre of groups of people all day. The custom seems worthy of a general following. Aside from its being of value to florists in a business way—a view which all occasions bring to the front—it brings to those who use the flowers one of the gentlest influences of human experience.

Memorial Day, which the close of May brings every year, is the day many select for the embellishing of their lots with plants and flowers, but a "flower day" in September would see a greater assortment of blossoms used and a more beautiful display than is possible in the earlier month.

Erica Vagans Var. Capitata

Erica Vagans Capitata.

One of a few heaths that have proved hardy in the Middle States is the Erica vagans, var. capitata, the one of our illustration. It is a heath that thrives so well when given a good location that it gives us pleasure to present a picture of it, that others may see how well it can be grown and what a beautiful evergreen shrub it is. It is planted nearly at the summit of a hill which slopes to the south. It is growing in sod, the grass from which is cut regularly during the whole season from time to time, and as both the grass and the heath are well fed there is no necessity for one to rob the other of food. It is not uncommon to hear it said that heaths will not thrive here; but the lovely specimen figured proves they will, for a better one than this could not be desired.

This heath is a native of England and of Western Europe, and in the British Isles it is known as the Cornish heath, growing wild in Cornwall. We refer to the species vagans. Our specimen is in cultivation under the name of vagans capitata. Those familiar with both the species and our variety, capitata, think the flowers of the latter of not quite as deep a purple as those of the former.

There are a few other heaths that do well with us. Erica stricta, from Southwestern Europe, is one; E. carnea, from Germany, is another; E. ciliaris, from England, does well, and several others are known to thrive. Then we have the Scotch heather, Calluna vulgaris, to add to the list.

All heaths are of close, compact growth, and by good care and culture can be had of as beautiful an appearance as the one photographed. A light soil formed of sand, loam and leaf mold is what they delight in. JOSEPH MEEHAN.

BOXWOOD

By the Car Load.

3 feet Pyramids.......... $1.50 each
5 feet " .... 4.00 each

Other sizes at proportionate prices. Every plant a specimen.

HIRAM T. JONES, Union County Nurseries, Elizabeth, N. J.

Mention the Florists' Exchange when writing.

H. DEN OUDEN & SON,

BOSKOOP, HOLLAND.

Wholesale growers of nursery stock for the American trade. Catalogue free on demand. Also views in our nurseries.

Mention the Florists' Exchange when writing.

ROSES

CRIMSON RAMBLER, DOROTHY PERKINS, and other leading climbers. BABY RAMBLER, Hybrid Wichuraiana, Hybrid Sweet Briar, Hybrid Rugosa and Hybrid Perpetual. Large assortment of varieties, fine stock and reasonable prices. Send for catalog or trade list.

BAY STATE NURSERIES, North Abington, Mass.

Mention the Florists' Exchange when writing.

F. & F. NURSERIES

SPRINGFIELD NEW JERSEY

Wholesale Growers — TREES AND PLANTS in full assortment. — Trade Catalogue Free

Mention the Florists' Exchange when writing.

MANETTI STOCKS

Especially for Florists' use, Best French Grown.

Grafting Size, 3 to 5 m-m., per 1000.......... $7.00; per 10,000.......... $65.00
First Size, 5 to 10 m-m., per 1000.......... 9.00; per 10,000.......... 80.00

Newark prices. DUTY PAID. For prompt delivery, order now and avoid disappointment.

ROSES, two years, field-grown, well-rooted

DOROTHY PERKINS.......... per 100, $8.00
CRIMSON RAMBLER.......... per 100, 10.00
HYBRID PERPETUALS, in good assortment, per 100, $10.00 to $12.00.

Send for our Wholesale Price List of Roses, Clematis, Flowering Shrubs, Conifers, Etc.

JACKSON & PERKINS CO., NEWARK, NEW YORK. (Wayne County.)

Mention The Florists' Exchange when writing.

ROSES

Climbing Clothilde Soupert, Marie Pavie, Crimson Rambler and Dorothy Perkins . . .

Grafted Oranges and Kin Kans, Palms, Biota Aurea Nana, Conifers and Other Stock for Florists and Nurserymen

IN IMMENSE QUANTITIES

400 ACRES IN NURSERIES — 60,000 FEET OF GLASS

CATALOG ON APPLICATION

P. J. BERCKMANS CO. (Inc.)
FRUITLAND NURSERIES

Established 1856. AUGUSTA, GA.

Mention the Florists' Exchange when writing.

Not a bloomin' thing

but *roses* to offer you

101 best sorts. Own roots. 2 1-2 and 4 in.

Get our price-list. Send your want list.

THE LEEDLE FLORAL COMPANY, SPRINGFIELD-OHIO.

Mention the Florists' Exchange when writing.

American Beauties

We have them. You want them. We are booking orders for early delivery. Fine stock. Write us for price.

ALDRICH FLORAL COMPANY, 26 E. High St., SPRINGFIELD, O.

Mention the Florists' Exchange when writing.

New Pink Rose

Miss Kate Moulton

Is the QUEEN of all Pink Roses

Write us about it

Minneapolis Floral Co., - Minneapolis, Minn.

Mention the Florists' Exchange when writing.

GRAFTED ROSES

Fine Stock from 3-in. pots.

Richmond, $2.50 per doz., $15.00 per 100, $135.00 per 1000.
Killarney, $2.00 per doz., $15.00 per 100.
Etoile de France, $3.00 per doz., $18.00 per 100.
Kaiserin, Carnot, Uncle John, Chatenay, $2.00 per doz., $15.00 per 100.
Bridesmaid, Golden Gate, Wootton, $2.00 per doz., $12.00 per 100.

ROSES OWN ROOTS

Fine Stock from 3-in. pots.

Richmond, $10.00 per 100; $90.00 per 1000.
Etoile de France, $12.00 per 100.
Sunrise, Perle, Sunset, Chatenay, $8.00 per 100.
Bridesmaid, Golden Gate, $7.00 per 100.
Asparagus Plumosus Nanus from 3-inch pots, $8.00 per 100; Sprengeri from 3-inch pots, $6.00 per 100.

Send for Catalogue.

WOOD BROS., Fishkill, N. Y.

Mention The Florists' Exchange when writing.

Get Our Prices on

Galvanized Wire Rose Stakes and Tying Wire

IGOE BROTHERS,

Manufacturers of the Model Plant Supports for Carnations, Dahlias, Golden Glow, Peonies, Chrysanthemums and Tomatoes.

226 North 9th Street, Brooklyn, N. Y.

Mention the Florists' Exchange when writing.

Rooted ROSE Cuttings

AMERICAN BEAUTIES	per 100, $3.00;	per 1000, $25.00
KAISERIN	" 2.50	" 20.00
CARNOT	" 2.50	" 20.00
LA DETROIT	" 2.50	" 20.00

BASSETT & WASHBURN

Office, 76 Wabash Ave., Chicago — Greenhouses, Hinsdale, Ill.

Large Assortment **PEONIES** Very best Varieties

LOW PRICES

THE KIND THAT FLORISTS LIKE

"We make a specialty of growing stocky transplanted shrubbery and trees"

FULL ASSORTMENT OF Ornamentals, Fruits, Roses, Clematis, and Herbaceous Plants

Write for our fall wholesale trade list.

W. & T. SMITH CO., GENEVA, N. Y.

Mention the Florists' Exchange when writing.

Roses! Dahlias! Cannas! Violets!

Miscellaneous Plants!

Roses. We have in stock upwards of 1000 different varieties, consisting of the very latest European varieties, as well as all the leading varieties of American origin. Stock from 2½ and 4 and 5 inch pots, all on own roots. Ask for catalogue.

Dahlias. 25 leading varieties, all under name, guaranteed true, including the best sorts in cultivation, such as Admiral Dewey, Constancy, Gloriosa, Orange King, Prof. Baldwin, Maid of Kent, C. W. Bruton, and Uncertainty. Field clumps as dug, $5.00 per 100; $45.00 per 1000. Catherine Duer, field clumps, $8.00 per 100.

Cannas. 40 leading varieties. $10.00 per 1000 and upwards. Write for list and prices.

Violets. Lady Hume Campbell, Princess of Wales, Swanley White, Admiral Avellan and Luxonne, nice strong plants, from 2½ inch pots, $3.50 per 100; $30.00 per 1000.

Miscellaneous Plants

Ampelopsis Veitchii, nice strong two-year-old field-grown plants, per 100, $6.00, per 1000, $55.00.
Clematis Paniculata, two-year-old field-grown stock, strong plants, per 100, $7.00, per 1000, $65.00.
Cissus Discolor, nice plants, from 2½ inch pots, per 100, $4.00.
Cyperus Gracilis, from 2½ inch pots, per 100, $3.50.
Asparagus Sprengeri, from 2½ inch pots, per 100, $4.00.
Asparagus Plumosus, from 2¼ inch pots, per 100 $4.00.
Weeping Lantana, from 2½ inch pots, per 100, $3.50.
Viburnum Plicatum and a complete list of hardy shrubs, vines and miscellaneous plants of all kinds. Send us your list for prices. Ask for catalogue—it's free. Address.

The Dingee & Conard Co., Rose Growers, WEST GROVE, PA.

Established 1850 — 70 Greenhouses

SPECIAL OFFER

SOMETHING GOOD AND CHEAP FOR CATALOGUE MEN.

		Per 100
1000	HIBISCUS PEACH BLOW, extra strong, 2 in. pots	$ 3.50
1000	" " " very fine plants, 3 in. pots	5.00
1250	" DOUBLE CRIMSON, 4 in. pots	5.00
500	ABUTILON DUKE DE LONLAY, 2 in. pots	2.50
1500	" MAIDEN BLUSH, 2 in. pots	2.50
2000	GERANIUM ACHIEVEMENT, strong, 2½ in. pots, finest of all the hybrids, Ivy-zonale Section	3.00
1000	GERTRUDE PEARSON, extra fine, 3 in. pots	4.00
500	LONICERA SUPERBA GIGANTEA, Novelty, the grandest giant-flowered large-foliage Honeysuckle in existence	10.00
1200	BEGONIA ARGENTEA GUTTATA, strong, 2½ in.	3.00
2000	HYDRANGEA OTAKSA MONSTROSA, extra heavy stock, 3 in. pots	4.00
500	LANTANA TRAILING QUEEN, 2½ in. pots	2.00
1150	CRIMSON RAMBLER ROSES, 2 year olds, extra fine canes—4 to 5 ft. high	15.00
1300	CLIMBING CLOTHILDE SOUPERT ROSES, 2-4 in. pots, 2 to 4 branches. Very fine stock, 4 to 5 ft. high	15.00

(Roses shipped without soil on the roots in dormant condition during December with perfect safety), f. o. b. Los Angeles. No less than 100 lots at 100 rate, on any of above.

The above are all extra fine stuff and cheap at the prices quoted. Cash with all orders.

HOWARD & SMITH, Inc.

NURSERYMEN, P. O. Box 484, LOS ANGELES, CALIFORNIA

NEW DEPARTURE IN GRAFTING ROSES

SCIONS TO BE FURNISHED BY THE CUSTOMER.

If you are planning to use any quantity of Roses the coming season, write to us for prices. We cannot get enough wood from our plants for all of our orders, but our facilities for grafting are first-class. Write for prices.

EDW. J. TAYLOR, Southport, Conn.

Deutzias, Spireas, Lilacs and Roses for Easter

(97) When shall I bring deutzias, spiræas and lilacs, potted plants, into the house to have them for Easter? How long after potting up will it take Spiræas japonica and Gladstone to flower? I want them for Easter. I have just potted up mine and have them under a carnation bench. Also when should I bring in potted Crimson Rambler roses for Easter.

New Jersey. W. J. H.

—If the inquirer will carefully read the cultural directions that appear from week to week in The Florists' Exchange, he will find correct information about bringing in his various flowering plants for Easter. The deutzias do not need more than four or five weeks in the greenhouse. The spiræas require from ten to twelve weeks from the time of potting, and they can be left under the benches for the first three or four weeks. As these are already potted, we would leave them under the benches until eight or nine weeks before Easter, keeping them as cool as possible. The Crimson Rambler roses will need to be brought into the greenhouse right after New Year's, letting them stay in a rather cool house for the first two or three weeks.

Gathering and Preparing Fern Leaves.

(98) At what season and month of the year are fern leaves gathered, and how are they prepared?

Mich. C. M. S.

—The hardy ferns used for florist purposes during the Winter months may be gathered any time after October 1. No preparation of the ferns is necessary; simply lay them straight in bunches in some cool cellar where it is not too dry; give them a little covering of moss or other material to keep them from freezing hard, and they will keep through the Winter.

Asparagus, Ferns, Roses, Stevia.

(99) 1. Are there two kinds of Asparagus plumosus nanus? I have planted one house and the plant grows tall.

2. Which is better, Adiantum cuneatum or Farleyense for solid bench planting for cutting? When and how to plant? Will it pay just as good as asparagus?

3. Which are the best roses to plant solid in the field for Summer cut flowers—own roots Ulrich Brunner or grafted ones; if the latter, on what wild stock?

4. What is the variety of the common stevia—not stevia serrata. And how should it be grown not to have it so terribly long?

AN OLD TIMER.

—(1) We do not know that there are two varieties of Asparagus plumosus nanus. Evidently the plants used were two or three years old, and, of course, are sending out long strings—like any old plants of asparagus will.

(2) The best kind of adiantum for planting in solid beds or benches would be Adiantum Croweanum. A. cuneatum is the best if a small-fronded variety is desired. It would be useless to plant Adiantum Farleyense on either beds or benches, as this variety requires special treatment, and we would not advise growing it unless a special house could be devoted to it and the grower has had good experience among ferns.

(3)) Ulrich Brunner roses are considered to do best when grafted on manetti stock, whether for indoor or outdoor growing, and we would certainly recommend such stock for Summer cut flowers.

(4) There are two forms of the Stevia serrata, one of which is much more dwarf than the other, but they require exactly the same treatment. If the dwarf form is desired, we think it can be obtained through some of the wholesale plant dealers.

Peonies for Cut Flowers.

—Of course tastes differ. With me the two very best are Baroness Schroeder and Golden Harvest. In the West we need different kinds from those required in the East. Most of Kelway's are of little account out here; we need something strong and robust that will endure heat and drought. I might have mentioned some of Terry's, which are of especial merit on account of robustness, hardiness and beauty. His Elta, Victor, Morning Star, Prince of Wales, Bell Hough, Sada Evans and Cynthia stand well at the head. Here is my list of the best 24 varieties of peonies for cut flowers: Baroness Schroeder, Festiva Maxima, Golden Harvest, Madam de Verneville, Duke of Dorchester, Belle de Nancy, Mt. Blanc, Couronne d'Or, Pottsii Alba, Livingstone, M. Geissler, Madame Emil Lemoine, Floral Treasure, Richardson's Grandiflora, Richardson's Rubra Superba, La Tulipe, Marie Crousse, Modeste Guerin, Marie Lemoine, Mons. Dupont, Prince Imperial, Sunbeam, Louis Van Houtte, L'Esperance.

C. S. HARRISON.

—I herewith give a list of 19 varieties of peonies I consider best for cut flower purposes. I did not make out the 24, as there are so many varieties that are just about alike; another reason, one going into the cut flower business doesn't want too many varieties. I would cut it down to ten. The following is my list: White—Queen Victoria, Festiva Alba, Golden Harvest, Duc de Wellington, the late Marie Lemoine and Festiva Maxima.

Pink—Delicatissima (the genuine one called shell pink), Floral Treasure, Canisteo, L'Esperance, Lady Bramwell, Triumph de Paris and Early Rose; I think the correct name for this Duc d'Orleans; I call it pinkish-yellow.

Red—Richardson's Rubra Superba, Officinalis Rubra, Fragrans, Pottsii, Delachei and Louis Van Houtte.

GILBERT H. WILD.

—We would recommend the following peonies: Ambroise Verschaffelt, Charles Verdier, Mme. Geissler, Festiva Maxima, Mme. Victor Verdier, Modeste, Prince de Talindyke, Eugene Verdier, Solfaterre, Edulis, Jeanne d'Arc, Mme. Lemoine, Delicatissima, Triomphe de l'Exposition de Lille, Mme. Crousse, Constant Devred, Bernard Palissy, Fulgida, Louis Van Houtte, Daniel d'Albert Charles Binder, Mon. Boucharlat, Purpurea Superba, Rubra (Officinalis), Tenuifolia fl. pl. and Charlemagne.

ELLWANGER & BARRY.

Such a question should be modified. When one says the "best," the price is often too high, when price is taken into consideration. The following is my list. Richardson's Grandiflora, Officinalis Alba, O. Rosea, O. Rosea Superba, O. Rubra, Achillea, Delachei, Duchesse de Nemours (Calot), Duchesse de Nemours (Guerin), Festiva Maxima, Floral Treasure, Marie Lemoine, M. Boucharlat Aine, Mons. Jules Elie, Victor Hugo, Mme. Galle, Whittleyi, Delicatissima, Aug. Villaume, Gismonda, Avalanche, La France, Michelet, Jenny Lind, Mme. de Verneville.

C. BETSCHER.

HEATING.

Growers' Problems Solved by U. G. Scollay.

I am enclosing a sketch of nine houses containing about 18,000 square feet of glass. If one were to build new and required, say, four houses, containing about the same number of feet of glass, what would you suggest as the best arrangement and size of the houses?

New York. J. Y.

—The best arrangement for four greenhouses to contain about 18,000 square feet of exposed glass cannot accurately be determined without an intimate knowledge of all conditions. In a general way I would advise, if it is desired to build four houses, that each house be about 140 feet long by 26 feet wide. One end of each house may be connected to a workroom or to a glazed passage. If space permits, a more economical arrangement would be to have two houses, about 280 feet long by 26 feet wide, connected at the center to each other, and to a workroom built by glazed passages, each house divided into two compartments thus forming four houses. A good arrangement for the walks and benches for such houses would be: four benches, each 4 feet wide, and five walks, occupying in the aggregate 9 feet of space, the walks and benches measuring 25 feet which would be the inside measurement of the house, the two outside walks each to be 2 feet wide and the other three walks 1 foot 8 inches wide. The above house would be well adapted for growing almost any variety of plants raised by commercial florists. Each grower has his own ideas as to the width of the benches and walks, and as these dimensions control the width of the houses, you can easily see that the same would be varied according to the individual judgment of different growers; consequently it is impossible to state the width of the house best suited to the particular case in question without interviewing the manager and learning his ideas. As to whether the houses should be even span or ¾ span would also be determined by local conditions. I may, however, say in a general way, there are being built, I believe, fewer ¾ span, and more even span houses, regardless of the direction in which they extend.

U. G. SCOLLAY.

Azaleas for Forcing

We can still supply a fine lot of well budded plants at import prices for immediate delivery.

We offer a full assortment of standard varieties:

	Per doz.	Per 100
8 to 10 inch crowns	$ 3.25	$25.00
10 to 12 " "	4.50	35.00
12 to 14 " "	6.00	45.00
14 to 16 " "	7.00	55.00
16 to 18 " "	12.00	90.00

A fine lot of plants of exceptionally good value in the following varieties; 18 inches in diameter at $18.00 per doz.:

Deutsche Perle, Simon Mardner, Niobe, Empress of India, Mme. Van der Cruyssen, Apollo, Bernhard Andrea Alba, De Schryveriana, Empress of Brazil.

A nice lot of specimen plants 18 to 20 inches in diameter at $2.00 each:

Mme. Camille Van Langenhove, Empress of India, Simon Mardner, Niobe, Bernhard Andrea Alba, Mme. Van der Cruyssen

A grand lot of specimen plants of **Mme. Van der Cruyssen** 20 to 22 inches in diameter at $2.50 each.

Place your orders now, as we will not carry any Azaleas in stock after Jan. 1st.

Henry A. Dreer, 714 Chestnut Street PHILADELPHIA, PA.

Mention the Florists' Exchange when writing.

Araucaria Excelsa, 5 in. pot, 50c. and 75c. each, three to four tiers; 5½ in. to 6 in. $1.00, $1.25, 4 to 5 tiers; 7 in. pots, $1.50, $2.00 and $2.50; 8 in. pots, 3½ ft. tall, $3.00 to $3.50.

Ardisia Crenulata. Berries well colored $6.00, $9.00, $12.00, $15.00 and $18.00 per doz.

Asparagus Plumosus, 4 in. pots, $1.50 per doz.; 4½ in. pots, $2.00 per doz.; extra large in 4½ in. pots, $3.00 per doz.

Asparagus Sprengeri, $5.00 per 100.

Begonia Gloire de Lorraine, $6.00 $9.00, $12.00 and $18.00 per doz. Also some larger plants. Wire Hanging baskets, $2.00, $3.00 and $4.00 each. Can be planted to order.

Cyclamen Persicum, $4.00, $6.00, $9.00 and $12.00 per doz. A limited number of made-up pans, $1.50 and $2.00 each.

Superb Boxwood, just arrived, perfectly shaped bushes for window boxes, 12 to 20 in. high, 75c. a pair; 24 in. high, $1.00 to $1.50 a pair.

Pyramid Box, 3 ft. high, $2.50 to $3.00 a pair; 3½ ft. high, $4.00 a pair; 4 ft. high, $4.50 and $5.00 a pair; 4½ ft. high, $6.00 to $7.00 a pair; 5 feet, $8.00 a pair; 5½ and over, perfect specimens, $9.00, $10.00, $11.00 and $12.00 a pair, in tubs, without a blemish.

Dracæna Fragrans, 6 in. pots, $6.00 per doz.; 7 in. pots, $9.00 per doz.; 8 in. pots, $15.00 per doz.

Boston Ferns, 5 in. pots, $3.00 per doz.; 5½ in. pots, $9.00 per doz.; 8 in. pots, $15.00 per doz.; 11 in. pots, $2.50 and $3.00 each. Specimens in 12 in. pots $5.00, $6.00 and $7.00 each. 14 inch pots, $15.00 per pair.

Dracæna Indivisa, 4 in. pots, $10.00 per 100; 5½ in. pots, $20.00 per 100.

Cash or satisfactory New York references.

For Christmas: Fruited Oranges $1.00, $1.50, $2.00 and some at $5.00 each.

Scottii Fern, 5½ in. pots, $3.00 per doz.; 6 in. pots, $6.00 per doz.; 7 and 8 in. pots, $12.00 per doz.

N. Elegantissima, 5½ in. pots, $5.00 per doz.

N. Whitmani, 4½ in. pots, $5.00 per doz.

N. Piersoni, 5 in. pots, $4.00 per doz.; 6 in. pots, $6.00 per doz.; 6½ in. pots, $9.00 per doz.; 7 in. pots, $12.00 per doz.

English Ivy, 4½ in. pots, $2.00 per doz.; $15.00 per 100, 3 to 4 feet high.

Jerusalem Cherries, $4.00, $5.00 and $6.00 per doz.

Kentia Forsteriana, combinations 3 and 4 plants in 8 in. pots, $1.50 to $3.00. 10 in. pots, $6.00 each. 14 in. pots, $15.00 to $20.00 each. Single plants 50c. to $2.00 each.

Kentia Belmoreana and Forsteriana, all sizes, single and combinations, from $1.00 to $20.00 each. Give us a trial.

Livistona Sinensis, superior to Latania Borbonica, 5 in. pots, $5.00 per doz.; 6½ in. pots, $9.00 per doz.; 7 in. pots, $12.00 per doz.

Pandanus Veitchii, 5 in. pots, $4.00 per doz.; 6 in. pots, $9.00 per doz.

Primula Obconica, $2.00 per doz.

Rubbers, 6 in. pots, $5.00 per doz.; 6½ in. branched, $9.00 per doz.; 6½ in. pots, single stem, $8.00 per doz.; 7 in. pots, branched, $9.00 per doz.; 10 in. pots, 3 in a pot, $2.00 to $2.50 each.

Erica Fragrans, from $1.50 to $5.00 each.

Erica Regerminans, 75c., $1.00 and $1.50 each.

Azaleas, in bloom from 75c. to $20.00 each.

Roman Hyacinths, now in bloom, $2.50 per box.

Epacris, white, $3.00 per doz.; larger plants in 5½ in., $1.00 to $1.25 each.

Cash or satisfactory New York references.

When sending orders please state whether plants are to be shipped with or without pots.

ANTON SCHULTHEIS, 19th Street & 4th Avenue COLLEGE POINT, N. Y.

Mention the Florists' Exchange when writing.

A FEW GOOD THINGS YOU WANT

DRACAENA INDIVISA, 4 and 5 in., $10.00 and $25.00 per 100.
ASPARAGUS SPRENGERI, 2 in., $2.50 per 100.
GERANIUMS. S. A. Nutt, John Doyle, Perkins, Double Gen Grant, Poitevine, 2 in. pots, $2.00 per 100. Rooted cuttings $1.00 per 100.
GLADIOLUS, blooming bulbs, extra fine mixture to close out while they last, 60c. per 100; $5.00 per 1000.
VINCA, Var., 2 inch, $2.00 per 100.
PRIMULA OBCONICA, 2 inch, $2.00 per 100.
REX BEGONIA, nice plants, 2 and 2½ in., $5.00 per 100.
ASPARAGUS PLUMOSUS, 2 in. $3.00 per 100; 3 in. $5.00 per 100.
BOSTON FERN, 5 in. 30c. each.
PIERSON FERN, 6 in. 60c. each.

GEO. M. EMMANS, Newton, N. J.

Mention the Florists' Exchange when writing.

Primula Obconica Grandiflora

2 1-2 in., $2.50 per 100. Ask for list (seedlings of hardy plants)

BAUDISCH & CO.,
537 Fulton Street UNION HILL, N. J.

Mention The Florists' Exchange when writing.

CHRISTMAS CHERRIES

Extra fine shapely plants, heavily fruited, 20c., 25c., 35c.

Geraniums, S. A. Nutt, fine rooted cuttings, $10.00 per 1000.

L. E. MARQUISEE, Syracuse, N. Y.

Mention the Florists' Exchange when writing.

PRIMULA OBCONICA GRANDIFLORA

The celebrated **Ronsdorfer** and **Lattmans Hybrids** in bud and bloom from 5 inch pots $2.00 per doz.; $15.00 per 100, from 3½ in. pots $10.00 per 100.

Primula Chinensis (fringed varieties) all colors in bud from 4 in. pots $5.00 per 100.

Cinerarias Hybrida Maxima Grandiflora well grown plants from 3 in. pots $5.00 per 100

Geraniums in standard varieties true to name from 2½ in. pots, fine plants, $2.50 per 100, $22.50 per 1000.

Asparagus Plumosus Nanus 2½ in. pots $3.00, from 3 in. pots $5.00, from 3½ in. pots $8.00 per 100. Satisfaction Guaranteed.

PAUL MADER, EAST STROUDSBURG, PA.

Mention the Florists' Exchange when writing.

POINSETTIAS

To close, 2½ in., $4.00 per 100.
HYDRANGEAS, 2½ in., $8.00 per 100.
" 4 in., pot grown, $8.00 and $10.00 per 100.
" 5 in., pot grown $20.00 per 100.
BEGONIA SANDERSONII, 2½ in., $8.00 per 100.

MUM STOCK PLANTS

C. Touset, Early White, $1.00 per doz. Pink-Glory of the Pacific, A. J. Balfour, Wm. Duckham, Viviand-Morel, Maud Dean, White—Alice Byron, Polly Rose, Ivory; Yellow—Robt. Halliday, Col. Appleton, Mrs. Wm. Duckham, Yellow Jones, $1.00 per doz.; $6.00 per 100.

Cash with order.

S. N. PENTECOST,
1790-1810 East 101 St., CLEVELAND, O.

Mention the Florists' Exchange when writing.

ASPARAGUS

ASPARAGUS PLUMOSUS, 3 in. $6.00 per 100; 4 in. at $10.00, 6 in. at $25.00 per 100.
ASPARAGUS SPRENGERI, 3 in at $6.00, 4 inch at $8.00 per 100.
BOSTON FERNS, 8 in. at $1.25 each.
PIERSONI FERN, 6 in. at 40c. each.
ASPIDISTRA, green, 6-7 in., 6-12 leaves, at 5c. per leaf.

CHRYSANTHEMUM STOCK PLANTS

Opah, Monrovia, Omega, Lady Harriett, Viviand-Morel, Duckham, Alice Byron, Pearson, Halliday, Robinson, Appleton, M. Bonnefond, Dalskov, Ivory, Dr. Enguehard, Timothy Eaton, Yellow Eaton, White Bonnaffon, Major Bonnaffon, $6.00 per 100. Cash or C. O. D.

W. J. & M. S. VESEY, Fort Wayne, Ind.

Mention the Florists' Exchange when writing.

Primula Obconica Grandiflora

Mixed, strong, 5 in., $12.00 per 100.
JERUSALEM CHERRIES, dwarf, strong, 5 in. specimens, $20.00 and $25.00 per 100, loaded with berries.
GERANIUMS, 12 best varieties, extra fine, large 2 in., $17.50 per 1000.
GERANIUMS, double Grant and Bruant, unrooted cuttings, large healthy stock, $6.00 per 1000.

WM. S. HERZOG, MORRIS PLAINS, N. J.

Mention the Florists' Exchange when writing.

Palms, Ferns, Etc.

WHOLESALE PRICE LIST.

Asparagus Plumosus, 2 in., $3.00 per 100; 3 in., $6.00 per 100.

Asparagus Sprengeri, 2 in., $3.00 per 100; 3 in., $6.00 per 100; 4 in., $1.50 per doz.; 5 in., $2.00 per doz.

Asparagus Scandens Deflexus, a beautiful green for wedding and funeral work, 3 in. pots, at $1.50 per doz.

Boston Ferns, 5 in. pots, $3.00 per doz.; 6 in. pots, strong, $6.00 per doz.; 7 in pots, $9.00 per doz. Larger specimens, $1.50, $2.00 and $3.00 each.

ASSORTED FERNS FOR DISHES, $3.00 per 100; $25.00 per 1000. We have a large lot to offer in best varieties.

Aspidium Tsussemense, 3 in., $1.00 per doz.; $8.00 per 100.

Pteris Argyræa, 3 in., $1.00 per doz.; $8.00 per 100.

Pteris Wimsetti, 3 in, 75c. per doz.; $6.00 per 100.

Dracæna Fragrans, 5 in. pots, 50c. each; $6.00 per doz. 6 in pots, 75c. each; $9.00 per doz.; 7 in. $12.00 per doz.

Dracæna Indivisa, 2 inch pots, $2.50 per 100; 6 in. pots, 20 to 26 inches high, 50c. each; $5.00 per doz.; 7 in. pots, 30 to 34 inches high, 75c. each; $9.00 per doz.

Dracæna Terminalis, 2 in. Nicely colored, $1.25 per doz.; 3 in., $2.00 per doz.; 6 in., $9.00 per doz.

Pandanus Utilis,	3 in....per doz.,	1.50
" "	4 in....per doz.,	3.00
" "	5 in....per doz.,	6.00

Cocos, for dishes, 2½ in., $1.50 to $1.75 per doz.

Cocos Bonneti large specimens, $40.00 each.

	In.	Each	Per Doz
Kentia Belmoreana	3		$ 2.00
Kentia Forsteriana	....7x	2.50	
" "	....7xx	3.00	
" "	7	2.00	24.00

Phœnix Canariensis, 3 in...per doz., 1.00
" " fine bushy plants. 10 in. pots, $2.50 each. Large specimens.

Phœnix Reclinata, 3½ in. per doz., $2.00
" " 4 in. per doz., 3.00

Aucuba Japonica, 10 in. pots, 3 ft. high, $1.50 each.

Rhododendrons, 50c. and 75c. each.

Boxwoods, 1 ft. high, 35c. each.; $4.20 per doz.

Boxwoods, 1½ ft. high, 50c. each.

Boxwoods Bush Form in tubs, 4 ft., $5.00 each.

Boxwoods Pyramids in tubs, 3 ft., $4.00 each; 4 ft., $5.00 each.

HARDY PERENNIALS

Boltonia White and Pink, $1.00 to $5.00 per 100 clumps.

Golden Glow (Rudbeckia), $1.00 to $5.00 per 100 clumps.

German Iris, Asst. Colors, $1.00 to $5.00 per 100 clumps.

The Geo. Wittbold Co.
1657 BUCKINGHAM PLACE, CHICAGO

Mention the Florists' Exchange when writing.

WHOLESALE TRADE LIST

ASPARAGUS PLUMOSUS, 2¼ inch pots, $3.00 per 100.

ASPARAGUS PLUMOSUS, Seedlings from flats, $1.00 per 100, $8.00 per 1000.

ASPARAGUS SPRENGERI, 2 in. pots, $2.00 per 100.

BOSTON FERNS, 5 in. pots, 20c. 6 in. pots, 25c.

CLEMATIS PANICULATA, 4 in. pots, $1.50 per doz., $10.00 per 100; 3 in. pots, 75c. per doz.; $5.00 per 100.

DRACÆNA INDIVISA, 5 in. pots, $2.00 per doz.

FERNS, fine assortment, 2¼ inch pots, $3.00 per 100.

GERANIUMS, Stock plants grown in pots. Double white La Favorite, Queen of the West, John Doyle, S. A. Nutt, $1.00 per doz.

HYDRANGEA Otaksa and Thos. Hogg, 5-6 flowering branches, $10.00 per 100; larger plants for tubs, 25c. each.

IVY, Hardy English, 4 in. pots, $1.50 per doz.; $10.00 per 100.

NEW PARIS DAISY, Queen Alexandra, 3 in. pots, $5.00 per 100.

YELLOW DAISY (Etoile d'Or), 3 in. pots, $5.00 per 100.

SANSEVIERA (Zebra plant), 4 in. pots, strong $1.50 per doz.; 3 in. pots, $1.00 per doz.

C. EISELE, 11th & Roy Streets, PHILADELPHIA, PA.

Mention the Florists' Exchange when writing.

2½ in. **ASPARAGUS PLUMOSUS**, $3.00 per 100.
3 in. " **SPRENGERI**, $4.00 per 100.
2 in. **HIBISCUS**, in variety, $2.50 per 100.
2 in. Flowering **BEGONIA**, $2.50 per 100.
2 in. **BOSTON FERN**, $3.00 per 100.
2 in. **TARRYTOWN FERN**, $5.00 per 100.
2 in. **SCOTTII**, $4.00 per 100.
3 in. " $6.00 per 100.
4 in. " $10.00 per 100.

THE NATIONAL PLANT CO., Dayton, Ohio

Mention the Florists' Exchange when writing.

DRACAENA TERMINALIS

Matured canes always ready for shipment. Delivered to any part of the United States for 10 cents a foot. Send cash for a trial order.

PORTO RICO PINEAPPLE CO., RIO PIEDRAS, PORTO RICO.

Mention The Florists' Exchange when writing.

Practical Books for the Trade Published and Controlled exclusively by A. T. DeLaMare Ptg. and Pub. Co., Ltd., Publishers The Florists' Exchange.

WATER GARDENING $2.50
By Peter Bisset. A grand book in every particular, profusely illustrated. Ready February, 1907.

PRACTICAL VIOLET CULTURE 1.50
By Prof. B. T. Galloway. Second edition, revised. Fully illustrated.

THE AMERICAN CARNATION... 3.50
By C. W. Ward. The only practical book on the subject, and most valuable for the professional as well as for the learner. Profusely illustrated.

PRACTICAL PLANT CULTURE.. 1.00
By G. W. Oliver. The very best book on the subject, well written, covering all plants cultivated by commercial men for profit; with cultural methods and propagating directions, complete.

SUCCESS WITH HOUSE PLANTS
Cloth 1.00
Paper .... .50
By Lizzie Page Hillhouse. The best book on the market for florists to sell, or to give to their customers. Many thousands sold.

ARNOLD'S TELEGRAPH CODE.. 2.50
By E. A. Arnold. The most valuable and complete code on the market: thoroughly intelligible; covers every need of the florist, seedsman, and nurseryman.

Every one of these eminently practical books, written specially for the trade, should be in your library. We will deliver the six books above listed, carriage paid, on receipt of $10.50.

THE GARDENER'S ASSISTANT (2 volumes) 15.00
The Standard Encyclopedia on practical and scientific horticulture.

Prospectus of Any of the Above Books Will Be Sent Free on Application.

Offices—
2 to 8 Duane St., NEW YORK CITY
Address P. O. Box 1697

10,000 FERNS THAT MUST BE SOLD

10,000 Ferns, in fine shape, low stocky plants, not drawn, grown in full light, and as they were pot plants, lift with fine balls.
Bostons, for 6 in., $20.00 per 100; for 5 in. $15.00.
Piersoni, for 6 in., $25.00 per 100; for 5 in. $20.00.
Scottii, for 5 in., $20.00 per 100; for 4 in., $15.00.
1,000 Crimson Ramblers, for Easter forcing, 2 year old, 3 to 4 ft., several canes well ripened and good roots, $2.00 per doz.; $15.00 per 100.
Asparagus Plumosus Nanus, 2½ in., fine, $2.50 per 100.
Sprengeri and Plumosus Nanus, 4 in., $1.00 per doz.
5,000 Vinca Major, variegated, field stock, extra fine, $5.00 per 100; $45.00 per 1000.
Vinca Major, variegated, and Hydrangea Otaksa, 2½ in., pot plants, $2.50 per 100. Hydrangea Paniculata Grandiflora, Spirea, Anthony Waterer, and Spirea Van Houttei, 3 year old, large bushes, $1.00 per dozen or $7.00 per 100.
50,000 Shrubs, Vines, Cannas, etc. These must be sold low. List free.
Cash please.

BENJ. CONNELL
WEST GROVE, PA.
Mention the Florists' Exchange when writing.

BOSTON FERNS

From bed, growing in full sunlight; must be sold as in need of room; $15.00 per 100, ready for 8 inch pans.

DEAN & PARSE
2 Ashwood Avenue SUMMIT, N. J.
Mention the Florists' Exchange when writing.

Cineraria

Benary, Cannell and Sutton's Prize Strains; dwarf or semi-dwarf, large flowers, all shades and colors, mixed 2½ in., $2.50 per 100. Cash please.
SHELLROAD GREENHOUSES, Grange, Baltimore, Md.
Mention the Florists' Exchange when writing.

Phoenix Roebelenii

Beautiful—Graceful—Useful

	Each	10	100
7 in. pot plants	$4.00	$35.00	$300.00
4 in. pot plants	1.00	9.00	80.00

Well Rooted Seedlings

	100	1000	10,000
4 to 5 in. high........	$5.00	$40.00	$300.00

JOHN LEWIS CHILDS, Floral Park, N. Y.
Mention the Florists' Exchange when writing.

KENTIA BELMOREANA

5 in., clean and bushy, 50c. and 75c. each. 2½ in., for center of fern dishes, 10c. each; $9.00 per 100.
SCOTTII FERNS, 6 in., 40c.
DRACAENA INDIVISA, 6 in., 35c.
FERNS FOR JARDINIERES, etc., $3.00 per 100

H. WESTON, HEMPSTEAD, N. Y.
Mention the Florists' Exchange when writing.

COCOS PALMS.

Strong 2¼ inch at $1.50 per dozen. Write for lowest prices on Kentias.

Jas. F. Barclay R. I. GREENHOUSES Pawtucket, R. I.
Mention The Florists' Exchange when writing.

ROBERT CRAIG & CO.

ROSES, PALMS, CROTONS

CARNATIONS and Novelties in DECORATIVE PLANTS

Market and 49th Sts. PHILADELPHIA, PA.
Mention The Florists' Exchange when writing.

Araucaria Excelsa

16 to 18 inches High, 4 to 5 Tiers, 50 cents each; $5.00 per dozen.

THE CONARD & JONES CO., West Grove, Pa.
Mention the Florists' Exchange when writing.

SMILAX PLANTS

Strong, bushy growing stock. From 3 in. pots, $2.00 per 100, $18.00 per 1000. 2 in. pots, $1.00 per 100; $9.00 per 1000.
ASPARAGUS PLUMOSUS NANUS, fine thrifty, from 3 in pots $4.00 per 100.

R. KILBOURN, CLINTON, N. Y.
Mention the Florists' Exchange when writing.

ORCHIDS

Arrived in fine condition. **Cattleya Harrisoniae, C. Intermedia, C. Gigas, C. Trianae, Speciosissima, C. Leopoldii, Laelia Purpurata, Oncidium Varicosum Rogersii, O. Marshallianum, Phalaenopsis Amabilis** and **P. Schilleriana.** Write for prices.

LAGER & HURRELL, Summit, N. J.
Growers and Importers
Mention The Florists' Exchange when writing.

ORCHIDS

Largest Importers, Exporters, Growers and Hybridists in the world.

Sander, St. Albans, England
and
235 Broadway, Room 1, New York City

Mention The Florists' Exchange when writing.

SWEET PEAS, Christmas white and pink, best for forcing, 4 to 6 seeds to pot 2½ in., $3.00 per 100. **Chrysanthemum Stock Plants**, Willow Brook, Alice Byron, Ivory, Appleton, Bonnaffon, Maud Dean, Dr. Enguehard, Adella, 50c. per doz.

GEO. M. COOK -:- Arlington, Md.
Mention the Florists' Exchange when writing.

SPIRAEAS, AZALEAS, RHODODENDRONS, Etc.

Spiraea Japonica, ... $4.00 per 100. **Spiraea Ast. Floribunda**, $4.25 per 100.
Spiraea Nana Compacta, $4.00 per 100. **Spiraea Gladstone**, ... $6.50 per 100.
Azalea Indica, Fine list early and late varieties. Simon Mardner, Empress of India, Niobe, Prof. Walters, Mad. Vander Cruyssen, Helen Thielman.
10 to 12 in. crowns—$35.00 per 100.
12 to 14 in. crowns—$45.00 per 100.
14 to 16 in. crowns—$55.00 per 100.
16 to 18 in. crowns—$90.00 per 100.
Azalea Mollis, Bushy, well budded seedling
12 to 15 in. high—$25.00 per 100
15 to 18 in. high—$35.00 per 100
Rhododendrons, Bushy, perfect shaped plants of leading forcing varieties
18 to 20 in. high, full of buds, $9.00 per doz.
20 to 24 in. high, full of buds, $12.00 per doz.
Latania Borbonica, strong 4 in. .... $15.00 per 100.
Kentia Belmoreana, 5 in. Bushy .... 60.00 per 100.
Nephrolepis Elegantissima, 2½ in. pots .... 5.00 per 100.

The STORRS & HARRISON CO.,
PAINESVILLE, OHIO.

Mention The Florists' Exchange when writing.

DREER'S UNRIVALED STRAIN
—OF—

DOUBLE PETUNIAS

ROOTED CUTTINGS BY MAIL	100
White, pink, red and crimson varieties	$1.25
Petunia Grandiflora, single, 13 varieties..	1.25
Abutilon Savitzii	1.50
Cuphea (Cigar Plant)	.75
Ageratum, 4 varieties	.75
Strobilanthes Dyerianus	1.25
Gazania Splendens	1.50
Flowering Begonia, 4 varieties	1.50
Heliotrope, Dark, from soil	1.00
Lantanas, dwarf, 6 varieties, from soil	1.25
Lantanas, trailing	1.25
Ivy Geranium, 5 varieties	1.50
Scarlet Sage, tall and dwarf	1.00
Mme. Salleroi Geranium	2.00

PLANTS	
Dracaena Indivisa, 18 to 36 in. high, $10.00, $15.00 and	$20.00
Asparagus Sprengeri, 2 in.	1.50
Cinerarias, Michell's Giant Prize, 2 in...	2.00
Cinerarias, Stellata, Sutton's, 2 in.	3.00
Shasta Daisy, 3 in.	3.00
Rose and Oak Leaved Geraniums, 2 in.	2.00

Cash with order please.

GEO. J. HUGHES, BERLIN, N. J.
Mention the Florists' Exchange when writing.

SEED PANSY PLANTS

THE JENNINGS STRAIN

50,000 plants now ready. From finest selected stock, large flowering, fancy colors, in great variety. Stock is first-class in every respect. 100 by mail, 60c.; by express, 500, $2.00; 1000 $4.00; 2000, $7.00; 3000, $10.00. Seed, $1.00 per pkt. of 4000; 1 oz., $5.00; 2 oz., $9.00; 3 oz., $12.00. Cash with order.

PANSIES in bud and bloom, fine plants for winter blooming, $1.00 per 100; $7.50 per 1000.

E. B. JENNINGS,
Lock Box 254 Southport, Conn.
Grower of the Finest Pansies
Mention the Florists' Exchange when writing.

CYCLAMEN GIGANTEUM

Extra fine plants, large flowering, 3-inch, $5.00 per 100; 4-inch $10.00 per 100; 5-inch coming in bud, $15.00 per 100. **Primulas**, Chinese and Obconica, 3-inch, $3.00 per 100; 4-inch, $6.00 per 100.
PRIMULA, Chinese and Obconica, 4-in., in bud or bloom, $6.00 per 100. Asparagus Plumosus Nanus, 3-inch, $6.00 per 100. **Cinerarias**, 2½ inch $2.00 per 100; 300 for $5.00. 3-inch $3.00 per 100.

SAMUEL WHITTON, 15-16 Gray Av., Utica, N.Y.

VEGETABLE PLANTS

CABBAGE New Early and Succession $1.25 per 1000
LETTUCE Grand Rapids, Big Boston, Boston Market and Tennis Ball. $1.00 per 1000.
PARSLEY Moss Curled, $1.25 per 1000.
TOMATOES Lorillard and Mayflower, 40 cts. per doz., $2.00 per 100.

R. VINCENT, Jr. & SON, White Marsh, Md.
Mention the Florists' Exchange when writing.

500,000 VERBENAS

60 Finest named varieties: **rooted cuttings**, 75c. per 100; $6.00 per 1000.
Plants, $2.50 per 100; $20.00 per 1000.
Our list is the choicest from millions of seedlings. Order early.

J. L. DILLON, Bloomsburg, Pa.

The Floral and Plant Business of the late Mr. J. L. Dillon will be continued under his name by his executors.
Louise H. Dillon, Alice D. Furman, } Executors

TO CLEAR OUT

	100
3000 Vinca, strong field plants	$3.00
English Ivy, 2 in., vines 18 to 24 in.	1.50
" " 2½ in., vines 18 to 24 in	2.00
" " 4 in.	6.00
Primula Obconica, 2½ in.	3.00
" " 3 in.	4.00
" Chinese, 2 in.	1.00
Rex Begonia, 4 in.	8.00
" " 3 in.	3.00
Hydrangea, 1-2½ feet	6.00

J. H. DANN & SON, WESTFIELD, N. Y.

Brockton Dahlia Farm

Has the largest and finest collection of Dahlias in the United States, with prices that will suit the trade.

SEND FOR PRICE LIST

W. P. LOTHROP, Prop., East Bridgewater, Mass.

ROOTED CUTTINGS

HELIOTROPES (dark) 60c. per 100; $5.00 per 1000.
GERMAN IVY, 50c. per 100; $4.00 per 1000.
AGERATUM, P. PAULINE, 50c. per 100; $4.00 per 1000. Cash With Order.

J. P. CANNATA, MT. FREEDOM New Jersey.
Mention the Florists' Exchange when writing.

SURPLUS STOCK—CHEAP

We have a fine lot of **Jerusalem Cherries** for sale from 5 in. pots. In order to make room immediately we will close them out at $1.00 per 100; they are worth $4.00. 1500 **Smilax**, strong, 2 in. pots, $1.00 per 100; $9.00 per 1000. Also a big stock of **Geraniums**, S. A. Nutt and others, also assorted from sand, $1.00 per 100; from 2 in. pots, $1.75 per 100; from 3 in. pots, $4.00 per 100. Write for prices on other stock; we can save you money.

E. I. RAWLINGS, QUAKERTOWN, PA.

PRIMROSES

Obconica Alba and Rosea, $1.50 per 100; $12.00 per 1000.

ASPARAGUS

Plumosus, 2¼ in. pots $18.00 per 1000; $2.00 per 100.
Pansy Plants, large flowering, $3.00 per 1000; 50c. per 100. Cash.

JOS. H. CUNNINGHAM, Delaware, O.
Mention the Florists' Exchange when writing.

FOR CHRISTMAS

500 **Erica Melanthera**, 6-8 and 10 in. pots, good stock. Write for prices

H. ABEL, E. Rutherford, N. J.
Mention the Florists' Exchange when writing.

PLANT CULTURE

PRICE $1.00.

A. T. DE LA MARE PTG. & PUB. CO.
2 DUANE STREET, NEW YORK

CHRYSANTHEMUM NOVELTIES

THIS YEAR I have to offer once more a splendid lot of new varieties. Among them will be found in whites:

MISS CLAY FRICK, the white sport of Wm. Duckham, winner of the Frick prize at Chicago. The best new variety of the year.

Mrs. A. T. Miller, Moneymaker, Kathleen Stoop.

IN PINKS—Miss Mariam Hankey, Mrs. Walter Jenks, etc.

IN YELLOW — Mary Godfrey, Mrs. Geo. Hunt, Norman Davis, Buttercup, Etc.

Also J. W. Moreman, Mrs. Henry Barnes, W. J. Crossley and many others shown at the different exhibitions.

I offer young stock for delivery early in the new year. 50 new varieties of Singles, the latest craze. Send for my complete list issued Dec. 1.

CHARLES H. TOTTY, Madison, N. J.

1907 CHRYSANTHEMUMS 1907

OUR SPECIALTY

We can supply your needs in

New or Old, Exhibition or Commercial

Wells Pocket Set

Exhibition Wonders

Best of

CALVAT'S, NONIN'S, PINS'

And other French growers

Brunning & Son's Set

(Raisers of Beatrice May)

Also the

Cream of English Raisers

(Some XXX)

LAST BUT NOT LEAST

Our Novelties for 1907 and those of other American Breeders

Our Preliminary List Describes All, also quoted

BARGAIN PRICES on CANNAS, SEEDS, ETC.

SEND FOR A COPY **NATHAN SMITH & SONS, Adrian, Mich.**

MUMS

Extra large stock plants.

Robinson, Wanamaker, Ivory, Dekalb, Willowbrook, Estelle, Appleton, Bonnaffon, Halliday, Mrs. Coombes, 75c. per doz., $5.00 per 100. **Dr. Enguehard,** $1.00 per doz.; $7.00 per 100.

JENSEN & DEKEMA, 674 W. Foster Ave. **Chicago, Ill.**

Mention the Florists' Exchange when writing.

Chrysanthemum Stock Plants

Mary Mann, $3.00 per doz., **U. Tonset and Rio de Italia,** $1.25 per doz., $10.00 per 100. **Mrs. Kalb, Pacific, Estelle, Appleton, M. Bailey Enguehard, Maud Dean, Merstham, Yellow L. Eaton, White and Yellow Bonnaffon, Yellow Jones,** $1.00 per doz., $6.00 per 100. 5,000 **Ivory,** $4.00 per 100.

WM. SWAYNE, Box 226, Kennett Square, Pa.

Mention the Florists' Exchange when writing.

Chrysanthemum Stock Plants

Nellie Pockett, Glory of the Pacific, Halliday, White Ivory, Appleton, Bonnaffon, Niveus, Enguehard, Maud Dean and Timothy Eaton. Guaranteed to be strong, healthy plants, $4.00 per 100. CASH WITH ORDER.

Hike & Jones,

Cortland, N. Y.

Mention The Florists' Exchange when writing.

CHRYSANTHEMUM STOCK PLANTS

Now Ready

75c. per doz.; $6.00 per 100

COL. APPLETON—yellow	GLORY OF PACIFIC—pink
MAUD DEAN—pink	MAIOR BONNAFFON—yellow
YELLOW JONES—yellow	TIMOTHY EATON—white
JEROME JONES—white	GLORIOSA—white
WHITE IVORY—white	ROBERT HALLIDAY—yellow
PINK IVORY—pink	
DR. ENGUEHARD—pink	MRS. HENRY ROBINSON—white
POLLY ROSE—white	

B. F. BARR & CO.

Keystone Nurseries LANCASTER, PA.

Mention the Florists' Exchange when writing.

Chrysanthemums

STOCK PLANTS

Testout, Nonin, White Shaw, The Baby, $1.50 per doz., $10.00 per 100.

Ivory, Bonnaffon, Jones, white and yellow, **Kalb, Mrs. Duckham, Robinson, Amorita, Smith, Helen Frick, Am. Beauty, Carrie, Godwin,** crimson, **Appleton, White Bonnaffon,** 75c. per doz., $5.00 per 100.

CASH

HENRY EICHHOLZ, Waynesboro, Pa.

Mention the Florists' Exchange when writing.

DIFFERENT STOC

Chrysanthemum Stock, Strong and healt clumps. **Mrs. Robinson, George Kalb, Wan maker, Chamberlain, Col. Appleton, Bonnaffo** white and yellow, **Zimmerman's Early, J. Jone American Beauty, Maud Dean, Nonin, Mer Christmas, Florence Davis, Paisley,** pink, 5c clump; 50c. a dozen.

Begonia Gloire de Lorraine, 4-in. pots 30c.; 3- pots 20c.

Boston Ferns, 5x6 in., 25c.; **Tarrytow ferns,** 6 in., 50c.

Jerusalem Cherries, strong, very bushy, full fruit, 6-in. pots 15c.; 5-in. pots 10c.; 4-in. po 8c.

Cash Please

F. B. RINE, Lewisburg, P

Mention the Florists' Exchange when writi

We will exchange the following stock plants **MUMS** at $4.00 per 100; varieties, **Yanou Appleton, Cheltonii, T. W. Pockett, Pol Rose, Golden Wedding, Robinson, B Wells,** for the following plants: **AZALEA GLOIRE DE LORRAINE BEGONIA,** or 3 inch, **FERNS** (no Adiantum), **CYCL MEN, PRIMULAS** in bloom, **OBCONICA CHINENSIS.** Write us what you have to change.

EDWARDS FLORAL HALL CO.

104 S. Carolina Av. ATLANTIC CITY, N.

Mention the Florists' Exchange when writi

CHRYSANTHEMUMS STOC PLAN

Polly Rose, Glory of the Pacific, Geo. S. Kalb, Halliday, White Ivory, Pink Ivory, H. Robins Wm. Duckham, Black Hawk, 60c. per doz.; $ per 100. Dr. Enguehard, Col. Appleton, T. Ea J. Jones, 75c. per doz.; $5.00 per 100. Merza, Brooks, Autumn Glory, Mrs. Wm. Duckham, $ per doz.; $10.00 per 100. Cash with order.

ALFRED FUNKE, Baldwin Road, HEMPSTEAD, L

Mention the Florists' Exchange when writi

1000

Jeannie Nonin Mum

The very finest late white. Stock pla $7.00 per 100. Cash with order.

WM. KEIR, Pikesville, M

Mention the Florists' Exchange when writ

Commercial Violet Cultu

Price, $1.50

The Florists' Exchange, 2-8 Duane St., New Y

Mention the Florists' Exchange when writ

LIST OF ADVERTISERS

bel H 689
kers H B 684
ldrich Floral Co .686
llen J K 719
llen W S Co 719
merican Spawn Co 683
nderson & Christensen 697
ndorra Nurseries 684
schmann Godfrey 697
ader J 697
anner & Co J L ..723
arclay Jas F 689
arr & Co E F ..690
arrows H H & Son 697
assett & Washburn 686
audisch & Co 688
ay State Nurs ..686
ayersdorfer & Co 713-22
eaven E A 722
eckert W C 683
erckmans Co P J 686
erger & Co H H 683
erning H G 720
ishop E 698
oddington A T ..682
olles F A 683
onnet & Blake 717-19
reitmeyer's Sons J 692
rown Peter 698
ryant Jas M 682
udlong J A 721
urpee W A Co ..682
yer Bros 697
aldwell W E Co ..726
ampbell Chas H ..697
annata J P 689
hicago Car. Co. ..691
hicago Rose Co ..721
hilds J L 689
hinnick W J 697
onard & Jones 687-89
onnell B 689
ook Geo M 689
684
ottage Gardens Co 684
owee A 683
owee W J 722
owen's Sons N ..727
raig & Co Robt 689-718
rowl Fern Co 722
unningham J H ..689
ut Fl Exch 719
ann & Son J H ..689
arsley Geo 695
avis A B & Son ..696
eamud Co J B ...721
ean & Parse 689
enouden H & Son 686
ietsch & Co A ..727
iller Caskey & Co 726
illon J L 689
ingee & Conard Co 686
orner F & Sons Co 696
reer Hy A 688-96-727
umont & Co 722
berman C W 718
dwards Floral Hall Co 696
dwards Folding Box Co 722
ichholz Henry 690
isele C 688
lizabeth Nurs Co 683
lliott W H 681
lliott W & Sons 682
mmans Geo M 688
ndtz Van Nes & Co 684
ngleman & Son ..696
akesen F N 697
wenden Bros 697
elthousen J E ..697
enrich Jos E ...719
& F Nurseries 686
ischer Rudolph ..695
lower Gr Mkt ..721
oley Mfg Co 727
ord Bros 715-19
roment H E ..717-19
unke Alfred 690
arland G M 726
ublin & Co 727
oddard S J 696
raham Hugh Co .697
ude Bros 692
undestrup Knud & Co 683
unther Bros 719
uttman A J ...706-19
uttman & Haines 696
uttman & Weber 696-712
aines John E 696-712
anford R G 697
ardesty & Co ..692
arris E 696
enshaw A M 716-19
erbert & Son David 687
erendeen Mfg Co 726
err A M 696
err D K 697
errmann A 723
erzog Wm 688
ews A H & Co ..723
icks & Crawbuck 719
ike & Jones 690
ilfinger Bros 723
ill E G & Co ...721
ill Floral Co W C 712
ippard E 726
itchings & Co 726
oran E C 719
orneeker H 698
olton & Hunkel ..721
oward & Smith Inc 686
ubbs Harry L ...723
ughes G J 680
unt E H 723
gee Bros 686
sbell & Co S M 683
ackson & Perkins 686
acobs S & Son ...726
Jennings E B 689
Jensen & Dekema 690
Johnson Seed Co ..682
Jones H T 686
Kasting Wm F ..720
Katzenstein & Co 682
Kay Wm H Co ..723
Keir William 690
Kentucky Tobacco Product Co 723
Kessler P F ...706-19
Kilbourn R 689
King Con Co 727
Koster & Co 684
Krick W R 723
Kroeschell Bros ...725
Kuebler Wm H....719
Lager & Hurrell ..689
Langjahr A H ...719
Larchmont Nurs ..712
Lauritzen C 718
Leedle Co 686
Lehman Bros 725
Lord & Burnham Co 728
Lothrop W P 689
McMulkin Edw ...723
Mader P 688
Mansfield W C ...692
Marquisee L E 688
May & Co L L 721
McFadden E C....718
McKellar C W 721
McKissick Wm E ..720
McManus J ...704-5-19
Michell H F Co ..683
Mich Cut Fl Exch 722
Millang F 719
Minneapolis Floral Co 686
Moltz A 719
Moninger J C Co ..727
Moon Wm H Co....684
Moore Hentz & Nash 712-19
Morse C C & Co ..682
Mullinos Lambros ..692
Murray Samuel 692
Myer 692
Natl Florists Bd of Trade 722
Nat Plant Co 688
Nicotine Mfg Co ..723
Niehoff Paul 687
Niessen Leo Co 720
Northern Michigan Evergreen Nurs .722
Ouwerkerk P 684
Pacific Seed Growers Co 682
Palethorpe P R Co 723
Park Floral Co 692-721
Payne J A 726
Pennock-Meehan Co 712-20
Pentecost S N 688
Perennial Gardens Co 687
Peterson Nurs 684
Phila Cut Fl Co ..720
Pierson F R Co 681
Pierson U-Bar Co ..727
Pierson A N 697
Pieters Seed Co A J 683
Pittsburg Cut Fl Co 720
Pollworth C C Co 721-692
Porto Rico Pineapple Co 689
Quaker City Mach Co 726
Quidnick Ghouses .696
Randall Co A L ..721
Rawlings E I 689
Rawson & Co W W 682
Raynor J I 716-19
Reed & Keller 723
Reich V E 721
Reid Edward 720
Reinberg G 721
Reinberg P 721
Richards & Co F W 723
Richards Bros 683
Rine F B 690
Ripperger G 723
Robinson H M & Co 720-27
Roemer Fred 683
Rupp J F 683
Saltford Geo 719
Sander & Sons 680
Scheepers J & Co .683
Schmidt Co J C ..712
Schrader E 696
Schultheis Anton ..688
Schweinfurth F C ..698
Scollay J A 725
Scott John 718
Seligman & Co .718-19
Shellroad G'houses .680
Sheridan W F ..715-19
Shippensburg Floral Co 718
Simpson R 723
Sinner Bros 721
Skidelsky S S 711
Slinn B S Jr ..712-19
Smith N & Son 690
Smith W & T Co 686
Smith & Gannett ..696
Standard Pump & Engine Co 727
Starke Wm 716-19
Stearns A T Lum Co 726
Stokes Seed Store .682
Storrs & Harrison .689
Stumpp & Walter Co 682
Swayne Edw 687
Swayne William ..690
Syracuse Pottery Co .. 725
Taylor E J 686
Texas Seed & Floral Co 682
Thorburn J M & Co .. 683
Tomlinson James ..723
Totty C H 690-97
Traendly & Schenck .. 703-19
Treichler C F 714
Van Assche Frank 727
Vaughan's Seed Store 681-718
Vaughan & Sperry 721
Vesey W J & M S 688
Vick's Sons James 683
Vincent R Jr & Son 681-89
Watkins & Simpson 682
Weathered Co 727
Weber C S & Co ..727
Weber H & Sons Co 696
Weeber & Don 683
Welch Bros 720-24
Weston H 689
Wheeler E B 722
Whilldin Pottery Co 723
Whitton Samuel ...689
Wietor Bros 721
Wild G H 687
Winterson E F & Co 713-21
Wittbold Co The Geo 688
Wood Bros 686
Worcester Cons 720
Young A L & Co..715
Young J 703-19
Young Jr Thos ...719
Young & Nugent . 692
Zangen O V 682
Zech & Mann 721

INDEX TO STOCK ADVERTISED

Contents.

FOR THE RETAILER

[All questions relating to the Retail Trade will be cheerfully answered in this column. We solicit good, sharp photographs of made-up work, decorations, store interiors, etc., for reproduction here.—Ed. F. E.]

Suggestions for Christmas.

The many downtown stores with their loads of material prepared for Christmas shoppers make the florist begin to wonder if there is to be any room for his wares, which must be sold at the end of the buying season. His only encouragement is the fact that the articles to be found in the florist's shop can be duplicated at no other place, and that they are more natural and Christmas-like than any other presents. Holly, mistletoe, laurel, lycopodium and Winter berries all have a tendency to make the mind of the customer revert to the period when Christmas was really at its best. At any rate, the store man who will tax his ingenuity to the utmost to prepare plants and flowers in a manner which is far removed from the amateur, will have no trouble in obtaining his share of the business the coming season.

Bells.

Bells have lost much of their popularity because of their general use and of the poor quality of many, but their employment will never be entirely discontinued as they are almost indispensable in decorating. Only the better grade of immortelle bells should be carried by the florist, as the paper ones tend to cheapen finer grades of stock. Chimes with four to seven bells form a salable article, especially the small ones which appeal to the customer as being cute. The ordinary coathanger covered with ribbon, or a holly branch reft of leaves and twigs, forms an excellent groundwork.

Trees.

So many people in the larger cities are now making their homes in apartment houses and flats that room for the old-fashioned family tree is no longer found. Therefore, the florist of to-day is prepared with numerous small, well-shaped trees, twelve to fourteen inches in height. These are planted in square boxes of birch, finished with holly and Winter berries at the base, and ornamented with small bows or otherwise. These should be placed before the customers some time previous to Christmas or well advertised.

Table Decoration at the Chicago Show.

Artist, H. E. Klunder.

Of late years it has become more necessary for the florist to combine plants, ribbons, flowers and baskets in a manner to make them more attractive than they would be if handled in the natural state. That is, the combination of these various articles, also the manner in which they are prepared, must be the drawing card.

Wreaths and Crosses.

The history of the wreath and the many uses to which it has been put will, of course, always make this article take the lead at Yuletime. The ordinary, cheap holly wreath is no longer handled by the better class of florists. Wreaths eighteen to twenty-four inches in diameter, extra heavy and accompanied with bows, immortelles or other attractive decorations, and ranging in price from $1 to $2.50, are mostly used. Boxwood wreaths are very choice, but must be prepared at a late day, as they soon wither. Red immortelle wreaths with relief work, that is, wreaths with two or three tiers of immortelles, are strong favorites. The cover of a popular magazine recently pictured a wreath of statice, California pepper and ribbon, which would make an excellent Christmas article.

Crosses of holly or other material find favor with certain classes. A large bough of mistletoe, artfully constructed and bedecked with bows or red ribbon, helps very much to decorate a shop, and can often be used in emergency cases for decorations during the holidays. The branch or limb of any tree is taken and covered with cork bark. Branches of mistletoe are inserted in the various openings afterward. In this manner a bough of any size may be constructed.

Plant Combinations.

The poinsettia, ordained king of holiday flowers, is becoming a stronger favorite each year. Flat pots containing seven to eight blooms sell exceedingly well. These, of course, are much enhanced by pot covers of red, white or green Porto Rican matting. The pot tops must be covered with moss, or bear some other suggestive decoration.

Gloire de Lorraine begonia may now be considered the popular Christmas plant because of the wide range in price and its grand blooming qualities. Small plants in two to four-inch pots sell at 35c. to 75c. and are fine subjects, as they fill in a wide gap at this price, trouble being always experienced in obtaining a choice article which answers for a small present. Porto Rican matting undoubtedly makes the best pot cover for these. These covers may be prepared in advance and stored away. Twenty-five to fifty plants should be prepared and placed in a flat basket, in prominent view, and the writer promises that few of them will remain unsold. Bows of wood ribbon prepared by an experienced hand are found very useful, either on the pot cover or in the midst of the plant. Large specimen plants in seven to nine-inch pots readily bring $4 to $5 during the shopping period.

Ardisias and Jerusalem cherries, because of their red fruit, are always in demand, though the keeping qualities of the latter must be firmly impressed upon the customer because of its price.

Large French baskets filled with select Christmas plants, blooming and foliage, command good prices. The handles of the same should be covered with a few small red bells, suspended over the center. Long hampers of maidenhair or Farleyense ferns with small ribbon bows at either end are prime favorites. Ferneries planted with from one to five dozen lily of the valley and small ferns form an old and suitable holiday arrangement.

An enterprising florist last year filled his entire window with French handle baskets of red immortelles fitted in closely and tied with red bows or with sprigs of holly. They were all sold before Christmas at much better prices than the material itself would have brought.

Araucarias make an excellent combination of the Christmas tree and house plant. These should be prepared in a manner that suggests to the customer the use for which they are intended. Some are even bedecked with various fineries of the regular tree, but this, of course, is not always advisable for the florist.

Sleighs, a novelty of the present season, promise to find a wonderful sale. These are constructed of black twigs and should be well filled with small plants—baby primroses, lily of the valley, maidenhair fern, hyacinths, Gloire de Lorraine begonias, etc. Of course the small token suggestive of the holidays must accompany these.

Small mangers of birch or other bark, with a receptacle for cut flowers, are a novelty to be tried this year. It will be found that the smaller ones ranging in price from $1.50 to $5 will find the most buyers, Fifth avenue and similar shops barred.

Baskets of California peppers make a suitable centerpiece at Christmas time. A basket with a low handle is generally found the most useful.

The buyer with taste looking through the downtown stores can readily discover articles which, when properly filled or decorated, form novelties to be found with none of the other florists, and often lead to some which are used the succeeding year by the trade of the land. Let it be remembered that no matter what the arrangement may be, it must be prepared in a skillful and attractive manner. That is, it is always the neatly and tastefully arranged pieces which find the most ready sale.

Indoor window baskets of plain chip furnished by the supply houses, filled with holly, Winter berries, and mistletoe, are good for a background in the home. They may be offered at a low price as the materials are inexpensive.

It is generally wise to cater to the tastes of many, so that some of the specimen plants are arranged with pot covers, others without; a part have ribbons, and then again a bit of moss may prove attractive.

In the writer's mind, there is no fad in flowers. An artistically arranged hamper or plant is always in good taste, though of course care must be taken in the arrangement of the store so that the colors in the individual pieces do not clash, and that the general view of the establishment is one of harmony and good taste. IRWIN BERTERMANN.

CLUB AND SOCIETY DOINGS.

THE COLUMBUS (OHIO) FLORISTS' CLUB held its regular meeting for November on the 27th, President Stephens in the chair, with a very good attendance of members. This being the first meeting since our Chrysanthemum Show, the reports of the various committees of the exhibition were in order. Vice-president R. A. Currie, who was manager of the show, reported that the 10 per cent. of the first prize in the class entered, charged each exhibitor, while a very small tax on each individual competitor was a most beneficial help to the club, as the money so collected amounted to practically one-half the prize money paid out by the club. M. B. Faxon, chairman of the committee on awards, submitted the official list of prizes awarded, which was approved by the club, Mr. Faxon read an exhaustive report on the various varieties of chrysanthemums exhibited at the show, and congratulated the members on the splendid showing made. The question of raising the annual dues of the club then came up for discussion; started by Guy H. Woodrow, chairman of the committee on this matter. After a lengthy talk which Messrs. Hills, Faxon, Williams, McKellar, Currie, Stephens, Torrey, Wedemeyer, and others took part in, it was voted to leave the dues as they are for the present at least—$2 a year from employers, and $1 a year from employees. This is not income enough to run the club in good shape, but conservative opinion was against doing anything to disturb our continually growing membership. At this meeting three active members were admitted—Messrs. Charles Buehler, Wesley A. Hamm, and E. B. Milnor. Our club is certainly growing very rapidly; in fact, several more names are expected to be proposed before the new year.

After these various matters had been disposed of, the question of the proposed change of the S. A. F. O. H. convention from August to some time in the Autumn was brought up for discussion. After quite a debate it was unanimously voted "that The Columbus Florists' Club favors the holding of the annual convention of the S. A. F. O. H. in the month of August, as has been the custom for so many years." For some time many of our enthusiastic members have wished to have displays of plants and flowers at every meeting of the club; and gradually we have been nearing the point where this plan seemed feasible. To start these semi-monthly shows, M. B. Faxon offered a special prize for the most attractive and best grown plant exhibited at our next meeting. The topic of discussion for the evening was an explanation and various illustrations of the commercial and exhibition scales of judging chrysanthemums. A very interesting talk resulted, and the remaining hour of the evening was most profitably and enjoyably passed. Before adjourning to December 11, the club passed votes of thanks to the various committees and to all those whose earnest efforts made the recent chrysanthemum show such a marked success. F. W.

Gathering Christmas Holly.

Editor Florists' Exchange:

The accompanying illustration represents a party encamped, engaged in gathering evergreens for Christmas decorating, principal among which is holly.

Gathering holly for decorating purposes is quite a business especially in lower Delaware and a great many men, women and children are engaged in it for several weeks before the Christmas holidays. The men gather and pack the holly branches and the women and children make much of it into wreaths. There is no section that grows finer holly than Delaware and the adjoining Eastern shore of Maryland. The foliage is dark green and well berried. The quality is especially fine this season. While there is quite a quantity of holly in this section this year it is more expensive to gather, people having to go farther into the swamps where there is always plenty of moisture. H. AUSTIN.

Felton, Del.

Courtesy of H. Austin

Gathering Christmas Holly in Delaware

The Climate of California.

So much has been printed and spoken in regard to the climate of California by enthusiastic visitors and interested real estate men, that people who have no personal knowledge of it, acquired by several years' residence therein, arrive at wrong conclusions from what they read and hear in regard to it because some of the most important facts relative to the climate are never published.

California is a law unto itself, both from a climatic and agricultural point of view. In regard to these two characteristics it is impossible for any one who has not lived in the State for at least five years to understand wherein it differs in these respects from the Atlantic Coast States. The literature, as a rule, sent out over the world, descriptive of these two elements, is truthful, yet misleading to those who have no personal knowledge of them, acquired by years of experience and observation. Some years before coming to the State I read an illustrated circular descriptive of the climate, in which the statement was made and the section designated where the mean temperature for the year was 75 degrees Fahrenheit. To a florist and agriculturist such a land looked very attractive, but because the whole truth was not told in that circular I got erroneous impressions about it. There was nothing said about the high Summer temperature, when for weeks at a time the thermometer will register 100 to 110 and sometimes reach 115 degrees in the shade, while during the Winter months it is not often that the temperature will fall below 22 degrees although it does drop to 16 degrees sometimes. With a knowledge of these facts, the high mean temperature for the year is easily understood. Nor was there anything said about the daily range of temperature, from 20 to as much as 40 degrees.

The most important factor, however, in climatic conditions as they exist here was not even alluded to, namely, relative humidity and its influence on vegetation. The Southern half of the State at least may be divided into two sections on account of this one great distinguishing feature, high and low atmospheric humidity, which makes it so entirely different from that part of the United States east of the Mississippi river, namely, coast section and interior section, which are separated by the coast range of mountains. Within the limits of the first, where the atmosphere is tempered by the sea breeze, the temperature does not run so high during the Summer, nor does it drop so low during the Winter; consequently a greater range of plant life is possible within its bounds, and the physical comfort of animal life is greater than in that of the second, while the relative humidity never gets as low as it does in the interior section.

On account of the dry atmosphere the sunlight is not suspended as is the case on the Atlantic Coast, but comes to the earth with a directness and intensity unknown to an Easterner. Because of this condition there is no twilight morning and evening, but day breaks full as soon as the sun is above the horizon, and the shades of night soon settle over the earth after it sets.

Again, on account of this aridity life is more tolerable in a temperature of 100 or even 110 degrees than it is in the East at 85 degrees with its humid atmosphere. Without having an official record at hand for reference, I think I am safe in saying that the relative humidity during the Summer never gets above 16 per cent. August 29, 1905, the Los Angeles weather bureau report was: Temperature 101 degrees, relative humidity 20. For the same year during October the humidity was as low as 11 per cent. Such conditions must be experienced to be appreciated and understood.

There are trees and plants that will endure a low temperature, while a low relative humidity is fatal to them. Gooseberries and currants, rhododendrons and kalmias may be mentioned as subjects whose life goes out under such conditions, while the sorghum family of plants give the most satisfactory results under those same climatic influences, and alfalfa will grow one inch a day to maturity, making a crop of hay every thirty days during the Summer months.

California climate has an intrinsic or commercial value not easily estomated. For the curing of grapes, figs, apricots, peahes and prunes, which grow in the highest state of perfection in the interior section, the warm dry climate which prevails there takes the place of expensive drying plants necessary in humid regions for the same purpose, which makes it possible to turn out the finished product of the orchard and vineyard in a higher state of perfection and at less cost than it is possible to do by artificial means.

For the production of sugar beets, lima beans, sweet peas and corn the coast section, where fogs prevail during the night and part of the forenoon during the early Summer months, is pre-eminent, for the reason that up to this time these profitable crops have been and are produced without irrigation, rain or fertilizers.

Another peculiarity of the State is the different climatic conditions at different elevations in both divisions before named—a thing entirely unknown in the Eastern States. A difference in distance of two miles and an elevation of 100 feet will make a difference of forty days in earliness in favor of the higher level in maturing garden truck, and when late Spring frosts come, as they do some seasons, tender vegetation on the lower level will be damaged, while that growing on a higher will be unharmed.

Right here it may be proper to say that no part of California is absolutely free from frost, thereby correcting an error that has gotten beyond the boundaries of the State from statements made in advertising matter to that effect, and from others that would lead any one to that conclusion who is not familiar with the facts. P. D. BARNHART.

Los Angeles, Cal.

Queries.

The Ladies' Auxiliary looks like a winner. The ladies always get there, whether in chase of a new bonnet or a new society. Why not add a ladies' committee to help organize the big show in 1908?

Brother Rudd is always hot stuff. Why did he omit pepper sauce as one of the "seasons?"

The glass manufacturer should receive at least 10 per cent. per annum for wear and interest on his plant. The workman should receive better pay than the European glass blower. If there still remains a difference the S. A. F. O. H. should be prepared to show what it is when the tariff is re-adjusted. Why not put the facts in such lucid form that the Hon. Serene E. Payne cannot fail to understand them?

Enthusiasm in the large chrysanthemum blooms for exhibition purposes is evidently on the wane in England. The reason is, says E. Molyneux, the chrysanthemum expert, "that such huge blossoms are almost useless for decoration."

FOUNDED IN 1888

A Weekly Medium of Interchange for Florists, Nurserymen Seedsmen and the Trade in general

Exclusively a Trade Paper.

Entered at New York Post Office as Second Class Matter

Published EVERY SATURDAY by

A. T. DE LA MARE PTG. AND PUB. CO. LTD.

2, 4, 6 and 8 Duane Street,

P. O. Box 1697. Telephone 3765 John. NEW YORK.

CHICAGO OFFICE: 127 East Berwyn Avenue.

ILLUSTRATIONS.

Electrotypes of the illustrations used in this paper can usually be supplied by the publishers. Price on application.

YEARLY SUBSCRIPTIONS.

United States, Canada, and Mexico, $1.00. Foreign countries in postal union, $2.50. Payable in advance. Remit by Express Money Order Draft on New York. Post Office Money Order or Registered Letter.

The address label indicates the date when subscription expires and is our only receipt therefore.

REGISTERED CABLE ADDRESS:
Florex, New York.

ADVERTISING RATES.

One-half inch, 75c.; ¾-inch, $1.00; 1-inch, $1.25, special positions extra. Send for Rate Card showing discount of 10c., 15c., 25c., or 35c., per inch on continuous advertising. For rates on Wants, etc., see column for Classified Advertisements.

Copy must reach this office 12 o'clock Wednesday to secure insertion in issue of following Saturday.

Orders from unknown parties must be accompanied with cash or satisfactory references.

PUBLICATIONS RECEIVED.

MISSOURI BOTANICAL GARDEN, Seventeenth Report, 1906. Illustrated. The director, Dr. Wm. Trelease, says that last year about 37,500 plants were used in ornamental bedding in the Garden. Among the special greenhouse collections, the succulents, palms, cycads, and orchids have attracted particular attention, and each of these has received material enlargement. Out of doors, massed economic plants from the tropics, asters, pinks, and dahlias, were satisfactorily grown in more than usual number and variety. For the fortnight beginning November 13, a notable feature of the Garden was a collection of about 3,000 chrysanthemums, representing 211 varieties. These were viewed by about 25,000 people—one-fourth of the visitors for the entire year. As in earlier years, surplus bedding plants, together with many of those removed from the grounds at the end of the season, including duplicates of ferns, begonias, etc., not needed for the houses, have been given to charities and schools.

A number of scientific papers are given in the report, including one on the "Constriction of Twigs by the Bag Worm and Incident Evidence of Growth Pressure," by Professor Hermann Von Schrenk.

Chrysanthemum Society of America.

Work of Committees.

NEW YORK, December 1.—Mlle. Jeanne Rosette, rose-pink and silver reverse; Japanese incurved; exhibited by E. G. Hill Company; scored 90 points, commercial scale.

PHILADELPHIA, December 1.—Mlle. Jeanne Rosette, rose-pink; Japanese incurved; exhibited by E. G. Hill Company; scored 86 points, commercial, and 87 points, exhibition scale.

CINCINNATI, December 1.—Mlle. Jeanne Rosette, pink; Japanese incurved; exhibited by E. G. Hill Company; scored 90 points, commercial, and 91, exhibition scale.

PHILADELPHIA, November 26.—Sport of Timothy Eaton (white), exhibited by J. S. Stremler, Princeton, Ky.; scored 81 points, commercial scale.

In a note from A. B. Cartledge, chairman of the Philadelphia committee he states: "The variety shown was so entirely different from Timothy Eaton we wondered if the raiser could have been mistaken in any way. I wrote to Mr. Stremler, and in reply he says he found the variety in 1904 among his Eatons and does not know where it came from except it be a sport from that variety. He sent two blooms to the E. G. Hill Company who said they thought it was Mrs. Jerome Jones. Would the E. G. Hill Company please give their views on the matter?" DAVID FRASER, Secretary.

Registration of Plants.

It is gratifying to note that this subject is receiving considerable attention not only in the United States but also in Canada. And from the several discussions ensuing thereon something of a practical and workable nature is likely to proceed, more in keeping with the importance of the matter than the systems now prevalent, which at their best are faulty and of but little value.

Speaking on the subject of "Pedigree or Grade Breeding" recently before the Canadian Seed Growers' Association, Professor Herbert J. Webber, Physiologist, in charge of the Plant Breeding Laboratory of the United States Department of Agriculture, submitted the following views on the matter of plant registration:

"The writer believes that no line of breeding work presents greater possibilities or greater value than what he has termed pedigree or grade breeding, and he trusts that some means may shortly be provided so that growers may register pedigree stock in a manner similar to the methods used by animal breeders. He believes that such a registration is feasible and practicable, and that it would greatly stimulate careful methods of selection, and be a protection furthermore to the growers interested in breeding. He believes that this registration should be by private organizations similar to the various organizations among animal breeders maintaining herd-books. Here the societies are made up of the individuals to be benefited, and they make their own governing rules. If a member is not benefited he need not register his new strain or race, but if the societies' work is well done it will soon become important to register new things. Put a plan of registration in good working order and the writer believes that the now apparently insuperable difficulties would soon be overcome. Suppose that the American Breeders' Association should begin pedigree records of varieties of various plants, and for registration of a new race, strain or clan require that an affidavit of pedigree and performance record be filed with a good description of the strain registered, photographs, etc., such records to be published periodically from the fees charged for registration. Such records would, the writer believes, stimulate care and honesty. We now have too many varieties renamed to defraud the public into believing them new. A strong society by refusing registration to aggressors in this field has a strong whip to keep breeders, seedsmen and nurserymen in line and prevent dishonesty. Such a registration would tend to prevent the promiscuous renewing of sorts which is now a flagrant abuse of public confidence. If a man were to wilfully violate the rules of registration, he would soon be found out, and refused registration of his strains and new sorts. Such registration would soon result in the public buying only registered strains."

It will be seen that Professor Webber desires that registration shall mean something more than the mere safeguarding of nomenclature, which as now carried out, it has been asserted is its primary and only virtue; and his suggestion that registration represent something tangible, something of real permanent value regarding the claims made for a new plant by the originator or other party registering it, is in the line of practical wisdom, as is his suggested penalty, the refusal of further registration, to be inflicted on those found guilty of violating rules or of having otherwise transgressed in respect to any one or more of the points for which registration should stand.

American Carnation Society.

Varieties Registered.

By James D. Cockroft, Northport, N. Y. Long Island.

HARVARD, a cross between Prosperity and General Maceo; color glowing crimson, just the Harvard color; size 3¼ to 4 inches; calyx non-bursting; stiff stems averaging thirty inches in length from early Fall to Spring. Has an exceptionally clean habit and is a free bloomer.

GEORGIA, a cross between Prosperity and Morning Glory; color clear white; size 3½ to 4 inches; calyx does not burst; strong stems 24 to 30 inches in length. An exceptional keeper, with a growth where every shoot produces a flower which is very fragrant.

FAUST, a cross between General Maceo and Morning Glory; color bright scarlet; size 2½ to 3 inches; strong calyx which will not burst; strong, stiff stem two to three feet in length. A good, clean grower, producing flowers all the time.

Change in Carnation Registration.

About a month back Messrs. Stevenson Brothers, of Govanstown, Md., registered with this society a carnation under the name of Debutante. This registration was made early in the week, but in order that published registrations may appear in all of the trade papers simultaneously the secretary holds all registrations received during the week until Saturday, and they then appear the following week.

On account of this delay of one week another carnation appeared in print under the name of Debutante although it was not registered with any society. This of course gave this carnation precedence in print, and as the owner thereof would not consent to change the name, Messrs. Stevenson Brothers have kindly consented to change the name of theirs in order that there may be no confusion in the trade.

They now register their carnation under the name of Splendor, a very pretty shade of pink, large flower, good calyx, stiff stem, extremely prolific and a grand keeper. ALBERT M. HERR, Secretary.

Reflections on Current Topics.

MR. EDITOR.—It was a source of great delight to me to read the sound advice tendered by a contemporary to societies and clubs relative to the selection of their "standard bearers." I have at all times regarded this as a solemn duty on the part of horticultural organizations, and have looked upon the institution of nominating committees as a means toward helping bring about the end desired. Then we have the case of the office seeking the man, and not the reverse condition, which, to me, has always appeared as one demonstrating an overweening ambition, conceit, egotism and to a greater or less degree, ignorance.

That was a close contest for the presidency of the Boston club, and the vote polled is certainly an excellent tribute to the personal worth of the two gentlemen running for the office. I observe that the successful candidate, as well as the unsuccessful one, hails from the Land of the Thistle, which no doubt explains the result. It seems to be a characteristic of the Scotsman to show his doggedness in any contest or controversy, (see John Birnie on geraniums) especially in one with a "brither Scot."

Your New England contemporary says that President-elect Westwood of the Boston club is "a native of Kirkcaldy, Scotland—Peter Henderson's birthplace." History records that the little Scotch fishing town has produced some famous men, among them Adam Smith, the political economist; but it cannot lay claim to being the birthplace of America's "greatest gardener." Peter Henderson was born at Pathhead, not many miles from the Scottish capital, Edinburgh; at least, so says that excellent Memoir written by his late talented son, Alfred. Kirkcaldy, however, has perhaps a greater distinction than any heretofore referred to. An old ballad says it was there that His Satanic Majesty was buried. R. I. P.

I hope Mr. Westwood will not introduce into Boston the latest New York method of elevating horticulture—by blowing it up with bagpipes.

Quite a good deal has been said about the silence of Burbank in not disavowing as his the published statements which, according to some, have brought American horticulture and horticulturists into ridicule. It has from time immemorial been a trait of genius to treat criticism with contempt, and in Burbank's case history seems to be but repeating itself. One of the ancient poets—not a horticultural rhymer—thus answered his numerous critics:

"No mastiff minds a yawping cur;
A rock defies a frothy wave;
Nor will a lion raise his fur
Although a monkey misbehave."

The foregoing lines may not fit the present case, but as a crumb of comfort, I merely give them to Burbank's critics so that these parties may not feel slighted because he remains sphinx-like, nor take his silence too sorely to heart.

My authority for classifying Burbank as a genius is Professor L. H. Bailey, who has said: "He is all that he has ever been said to be, and more. He is a genius."

These seem to be the days of anomaly in the supplies of horticultural literature for the different periodicals. We have the youngest apologizing for the large number of left-over manuscripts it has on hand, while the oldest is padding its columns with details of what happened twenty years ago. I like the latter: they remind me of the interesting dead past facts appearing in the pages of the Old Farmer's Almanac, which has been a "welcome visitor" to my homestead for the last half century or more. The editor, whom a plethora of brain products has compelled to make an apology to his subscribers, shows, I think, great prudence in restricting his weekly literary feast—such as it is. Some of your bulky contemporaries always bring to mind the fable of the inflated toad, or the difficulties of the rotund policeman whose paunch "gets there" before the rest of his anatomy. A 49-day fast might improve both their appearance and healthfulness.

Speaking of health, I was sorry to read of the illness of "Phil," and am glad he is now all but recovered therefrom. The eating of sandwiches and smoking of pipes are sure in time to affect some part of the anatomy of those indulging in such luxuries, and the vermiform appendix is likely to be that part as well as any other. However, scientists say the latter is an unnecessary accessory of the human frame, and it is well the trouble landed in such a useless member in "Phil's" case. I would advise him to go in for a square meal and a good cigar from now on. We horticulturists can ill afford to be deprived of either "Phil's" philosophy or his poetry, even for the brief time it takes to remove his appendix. JOB.

GLASS EXPORTS FROM BELGIUM.—The exports of window glass from Belgium in 1905 amounted to 335,130,627 pounds, an increase of 213,522,981 pounds over 1904. The leading countries making purchases were, England, 104,930,166 pounds; Japan, 25,875,021 pounds; China, 25,541,996 pounds; United States, 21,745,852 pounds; Netherlands, 22,612,982 pounds; Canada, 21,218,274 pounds, and India 19,036,567 pounds.

OUR READERS' VIEWS

Carbonate of Lime Fertilization.

Editor Florists' Exchange:

Without doubt but few florists realize what great benefits in plant propagation are obtainable by a thorough understanding of the lime question and acting in accord with such knowledge, since even the technical agricultural authorities generally fail in comprehending it. Though some of these authorities, particularly in the United States Department of Agriculture and a few at State Experiment Stations are learning by culture tests that an understanding of agricultural use of lime is far more important than generally realized, and can as history and recent tests indicate revolutionize agriculture in some sections—which of course, concerns florists. There is much more to be learned than the usually well-known facts, that caustic lime corrects soil acidity, also improves the physical condition of heavy soils and thereby benefits plants to which these conditions are detrimental.

Additionally there is a physiological effect on plant growth by lime that is of utmost importance with many plants, and also the caustic form of lime—the only kind generally used or thought of—is not the form that ought to be used, since there is another that gives all the advantages and more, too, and without certain and often serious disadvantages of the caustic. This is the finely divided true carbonate of lime, as in calcareous marl (80 to 95 per cent, wood ashes about 35 per cent.), chalk (nearly pure), ground limestone or oyster shells—the former often carrying a large percentage of magnesia. This form of lime is the exact opposite of the caustic as to certain chemical actions, especially as to nitrogen.

So to state the question broadly, caustic lime is destructive to manurial elements, while the carbonate conserves them; and their respective use means the difference between injury and decided benefits for many plants.

There are about a score of technical reasons why it is better to use a true carbonate than caustic lime, but a number of pages would be required to fully explain them. Suffice it to say here, that florists should investigate the matter for themselves by some practical tests, since such can readily be done by pot culture.

The few plants that are native to and must have wet, mucky soil are likely to be hurt by lime, while those which must have a light soil are likely to be benefited by it, as also will many of the intermediary class of plants, though there are exceptions to such rule, and the plants benefited are greatly in the majority.

One advantage of using the carbonate is that rich manure can be used along with it and obtain remarkable benefits, getting more value from the manure than when used by itself. I have seen marvellous results from the use of night soil mixed with calcareous marl on ten acres of carnations, (80,000) on a run down light soil during a dry season. The same florist also found great benefits from this fertilizer on roses and geraniums. The peculiar feature was the extraordinary root growth, which with the hygroscopic power of the carbonate of lime made drought-proof fertilization. It also gave well-balanced plants, tops with roots, and produced what is invariably noticeable with this kind of fertilization—perfection of leaf coloring, flowering and fruition. The florist himself said that this application of fertilizer was worth about $1,500 to him, and that a florist could tell a mile or two away that the carnations had some remarkable favorable treatment.

The Rhode Island Agricultural Experiment Station has been making tests with lime for some years, but using caustic lime (partly re-carbonated) under the mistaken idea that it was the only form of lime readily obtainable by the farmers of that State; it was also used with and without each nitrate of soda and sulphate of ammonia, for better technical comparison for nitrogen, and on a soil of acid tendency.

The following are some of the results obtained on small plots and approximately proven by check tests, that will interest florists; and to fully comprehend the benefits they should be compared on a percentage basis:

Asparagus.	Pounds obtained.
Unlimed, sulphate of Ammonia	0.00
Limed, sulphate of Ammonia	5.87
Unlimed, nitrate of soda	1.01
Limed, nitrate of soda	9.62

Pansy	Number blossoms.
Unlimed, sulphate of Ammonia	9.75
Limed, sulphate of Ammonia	12.10
Unlimed, nitrate of soda	14.37
Limed, nitrate of soda	25.43

Poppy.	Blossoms.	lbs. of plant.
Unlimed, sulphate of Ammonia	0.00	0.00
Limed, sulphate of Ammonia	504.00	0.75
Unlimed, nitrate of soda	329.00	2.25
Limed, nitrate of soda	3143.00	4.50

Sweet Peas.	Blossoms.	lbs. of plant.
Unlimed, sulphate of Ammonia	780.00	12.70
Limed, sulphate of Ammonia	3433.00	19.05
Unlimed, nitrate of soda	2777.00	14.55
Limed, nitrate of soda	3591.00	19.40

Previous tests for lime advantages alone showed the number of times the crop was increased as follows: Lettuce, 77.9; spinach, 24.7; onion, 31.; celery, 27.7; sugar beet, 12.1; salsify, 9.5; parsnips, 6.9; carrot, 6.6; pumpkin, 5.3; muskmelon, 4.7; tobacco, 4.5; egg plant, 3.7; barley, 3.7; alfalfa, 3.6; with many other plants showing smaller increases, as well as some with slight injury.

The calcareous marl (fresh-water shell marl) is as favorable a source of carbonate of lime as any. At present the prepared supply is largely used for making Portland cement, but experts in that line say that eventually this material for producing cement will be outclassed by rock, so that these plants will be ready then to sell for agricultural use ample quantities of this marl at a low price.

FRANKLIN NOBLE.

Brooklyn, N. Y.

Nicotiana Sanderae.

Editor Florists' Exchange:

In your issue of February 24, 1906, page 249, Mr. Timme writes of his experience with Nicotiana Sanderæ. I will ask, through you, how he made out with the newer forms and hybrids? I also gave plants to some of my best customers last year, and was told that if all the Miller family were no better judges of tobacco than I they would have died in the poor house.

Is it not fortunate that Nicotiana Sanderæ was not one of Burbank's "creations?" As it is only one of our European introductions no criticism of it is made by Brother O'Mara and others.

I should be pleased to see Mr. Timme's portrait in The Florists' Exchange.

NATHAN A. MILLER.

Ed. Dale
Pres.-Elect Toronto Gardeners and Florists' Association

Carnation Pink Patten.

Editor Florists' Exchange:

In your issue of November 24 in the Question Box is an inquiry about a pink sport of Mrs. M. A. Patten carnation. As the person who answered the question seemed to be in doubt, we will refer you to your own paper of last season, in which Pink Patten was advertised for sale. It was exhibited by us in Chicago when the American Carnation Society held its last meeting there; also in Boston last season at the society's meeting, where it received the Schlegel & Fottler special prize for the best 100 dark pink. It received a first-class certificate from the Massachusetts Horticultural Society. It has also been exhibited before many florists' clubs. We have registered the name with the American Carnation Society.

Tewksbury, Mass. PATTEN & COMPANY.

Ed. Dale.

Ed. Dale, the newly elected president of the Toronto Gardeners and Florists' Association, was born in 1866 at Brampton, Ontario, on the estate where his firm's greenhouse plant now stands. He attended school until he was 12 years of age, then went to work for his father and brother, the late Harry Dale, who were engaged in market gardening. Several years later they dissolved partnership, and Mr. Dale then was employed by his brother until he was 18 years of age in the market gardening business in connection with the growing of a general line of pot and bedding plants, also a small quantity of cut flowers, the demand for cut flowers in Canada at that time being very limited. Mr. Dale made a trip to Europe, and on his return re-entered the employ of his brother for a year, leaving which he went to Chicago and was engaged there in growing a general line of plants and cut flowers. Here he remained for 1½ years, again returning to Brampton to the establishment of Harry Dale, who was at that time erecting his first houses for the growing of cut flowers, only one house 200 x 21 and one 100 x 10 feet. He remained here until the time of his brother's death, some seven years ago; since that date he has been superintendent of the estate. The plant now comprises 15 acres under glass.

Mr. Dale was elected vice-president of the local association last year, and this year became its president.

Tributes to the Late George Ellwanger.

The Rochester, (N. Y.) daily newspapers paid the following tributes, editorially, to the late George Ellwanger:

"His name long ago became known on two hemispheres; it stood everywhere for the highest ideals of the science in which Mr. Ellwanger had attained to eminence. As a citizen, Mr. Ellwanger was held in the highest esteem. He interested himself all his life in all that pertained to the welfare of this community. His benefactions were many and he was ever ready with helpful counsel and willing effort in behalf of every good work. From his labors and the influence of his example this city has gained much, both materially and morally, and has many reasons to bear him in grateful remembrance.—Union and Advertiser.

"The opportunities which lay round about him at the beginning multiplied with the development of the country, and so he won reputation and wealth for himself in forwarding the higher cultivation of the farms to purposes of use and beauty. He was happy in the choice of a partner, moreover, whose strong qualities supplemented and strengthened his own; so that the names of both, at home and abroad, became literally household words, as associated with the pleasant surroundings of countless homes.

"In the course of time, Mr. Ellwanger became identified in many ways with the growth of Rochester, took an active part in its business enterprises, aided in charitable work, was noted for his hospitalities, and developed into harmony with the multiplying responsibilities and opportunities of his environment. The simple German vine-dresser was transformed through the quickening influences of American life into a leading citizen of the community.

In the nursery grounds, fronting on Mount Hope avenue, there are two great trees, an American and a Belgian elm. The latter was planted by Mr. Ellwanger many years ago; and it has grown in hardy strength and graceful form, branching low, spreading wide, and rising high. There is something in it typical of the man who flourished so fairly under the kindly sky of a new world.

"No better praise need be given to him than that in Whittier's song in honor of those who create civilization out of the richness of the earth,—among whom he had a foremost place:

This day two hundred years ago,
  The wild grapes by the river's side
And tasteless groundnuts trailing low,
  The table of the woods supplied.

Unknown the apple's red and gold,
  The blushing tints of peach and pear;
The mirror of the river told
  No tale of orchards ripe and rare.

Wild as the fruits he scorned to till,
  These vales the idle Indian trod;
Nor knew the glad creative skill,
  The joy of him who toils with God.

O painter of the fruits and flowers!
  We thank thee for thy wise design,
Whereby these human hands of ours
  In Nature's garden work with thine.

Give fools their gold and knaves their power;
  Let fortune's bubbles rise and fall;
Who sows a seed, or trains a flower,
  Or plants a tree, is more than all.

For he who blesses most is blest:
  And God and man shall own his worth,
Who toils to leave as his bequest
  An added beauty to the earth.

—Post Express.

"If one were asked to name the citizen of Rochester whose influence had been greatest in contributing to the beauty of lawn, park and street in this city, he would truthfully say that this man was George Ellwanger. He would also say that the influence of this great horticulturist—in many respects the greatest of his time—was even more widely and permanently evident beyond the boundaries of Rochester than within them. Probably there is to be found hardly a single vineyard, orchard or rural dooryard east of the Mississippi River in which there is no trace of his genius and art. It is not too much to say that no other American—not even the famous Burbank—has done more to inspire the love of the flower, the tree and the vine than this modest and unpretending citizen of Rochester who, to the end of his life, never fully realized the extent or the value of his life's great work. * * * * It is the rule of human experience that one who loves every living thing is lovable in himself. George Ellwanger was a fine example of the truth of this principle. His private life was a constant radiation of the warmth and generosity of a kindly spirit. He bestowed happiness upon everyone who came within the circle of his association. Young and old, rich and poor, cultured and unlettered reveled in the joy of his companionship. And the pleasure that was had from contact with his life mellowed and became richer with his increasing age, like the wine on his generous table or the fruit of his cherished trees and vines."—Herald.

Los Angeles, Cal.

Trade Notes.

The magnitude on which horticultural operations may be carried on in California, because of favorable climatic conditions, is illustrated by what the Signal Hill Floral Company and The Oceanside Floral Company, the first named located twenty miles, the second eighty-four miles south of Los Angeles, are doing. At the first named place is one lath house, 60x250 feet, planted to Asparagus plumosus for cutting, and one 120x120 feet, 14 feet high, for the growing of seed. Last year there was gathered from this house one and a half million seeds. The estimated crop for this season will be double that quantity. On this place are also growing three and a half acres of Princess of Wales violets; 31,000 narcissus were planted during October for the cut flower trade. These bulbs were delivered here by English growers for six dollars pr thousand less than American growers bid on the lot. Climatic conditions are such at this location that egg plants live throug the Winter, checked in growth, to be sure, but ready for business when warm Spring days return. There is also growing on this place several acres of an unnamed blackberry, evidently a cross between a dewberry and high bush blackberry, which matures its crop of fruit before the earliest dewberries, yielding fabulous returns per acre. Cucumbers are here grown by the acre in early Spring, under muslin covers, which are rolled and unrolled as the weather may require. Operations at this establishment are under the directions of E. R. Meserve.

At Oceanside is grown in the open 48,500 carnations. It was from this field that the prize winning field-grown blooms were exhibited at our last flower show. The firm has about completed the planting of 150,000 young stock which will yield cut flowers the coming year. Whether this vast acreage will be disbudded, as has been done with the smaller planting, is a question yet to be decided by the ability of the management to get sufficient help.

This location seems to be especially adapted to the growth of early sweet peas. They began cutting October 15 from the two and a half acres of Blanche Ferry, Mont Blanc, and Earliest of All, for our local market and up to the present are about the only growers around here that have any of this class of stock for sale. From an acre of Centaurea imperialis they are bringing in fine large blooms in various shades of color.

This place is under the management of E. S. Langford. The two places belong to one company, which has a wholesale store at 349 S. Los Angeles street, and two retail stands, one at 344 the other at 400 S. Broadway.

The first rain of the season—.53 of an inch, fell November 22. The mountains to the northeast of the town are covered with snow which gleams in the sunlight like polished steel. And while we of the valleys have this sight of the Artic regions, we are surrounded with orange groves of ripening fruit; our gardens are bright with geraniums, bougainvilleas, Bignonia venusta, and the rich-colored foliage of Acalypha marginata.

P. D. BARNHART.

TORONTO, ONT.—R. O. King of the King Construction Company, Tonawanda, N. Y., and this city, is receiving the congratulations of his friends on the prominent part he took in the raising of the wrecked steamship, the Bavarian, one of the greatest feats of salvage ever accomplished. Mr. King and another party, both experts in the use of compressed air, had charge of the interior work in connection with the raising of the vessel. Mr. King is a graduate of McGill University in engineering, and afterward studied at Harvard. He is well known in the florist trade on account of his connection with the greenhouse construction and heating firm that bears his name.

LOCKLAND, O.—The Lockland Lumber Company contemplates withdrawing from the greenhouse building business.

The Christmas Trade of Fifty Years Ago

When one stops to consider the condition of the florist's Christmas trade of to-day and that of fifty years ago, it becomes a matter of startling significance. Not only in the city of Chicago, where at the

Edgar Sanders

time it had positively no existence, but even in the three great eastern cities—New York, Philadelphia and Boston—it had but little more than the color of a title as a florist's "harvest" day; while New Year's day, that is now but a glimmer, was then the day, thanks to the good old custom of New Year's calls, as being of some importance to the bouquet trade.

Old Santa Claus, and the German's Christmas tree, if we would but take time to consider a moment, are both factors that helped to work up the present status, being more in evidence in old times, and, directly, though cutting but a small figure to the average florist nowadays.

How few of the many things that go to make up the sum total of the products used now were then even known, or at least used for the purposes for which they are now employed! Since then whole races of plants have sprung into existence and are raised for cut flower purposes only.

The difference in high art in the fifties, and the twentieth century, is as great as that of the materials to work with then and now, each perhaps equally suitable for the surroundings and persons of the times. The accessories that Time has evolved may be said to have expanded and glorified the work, and he who hopes to be at the top must be forever progressive and awake for new or useful improvements all along the line.

The regal camelia fifty years ago was king indeed, and entered well into the formal type of made-up work that was then so much in vogue.

To transform Pope's lines of "Groves" in the formal parterre or garden, "Flower nodded to flower" at measured distances and as precise as a wall-paper pattern, that, I am afraid, "Ivera" would sadly condemn as an art product.

The queen, the rose, was apt to be of season flowering, like Lamarque, and not continuous as now, although good old Safrano was in evidence in the best places—veritable bushes and not of annual growth as now.

The florists' princess, the new style of carnation, was just then peering in the late Dailledouze & Zeller's introductions of President Degrauw, La Purite and some other forerunners of the brilliant galaxy of varieties in vogue to-day. Even the tools and conveniences of the maker-up were limited. He had no fine wire and many other things; and to fashion his wreath, whether for Christmas or funeral, he was apt to form its base with anything handy, as bending the willow twig. There was much more spoken about the bouquet maker, the stemmer, etc., than we hear at the present time. The pyramidal form of made-up flowers was used on the dining room table, if it was not some fanciful imitation of a pagoda fashioned by some artist of the period; although for some years the caterer had a cinch, mostly of the center-piece work in a candy contraption. The so-called flat or mantel bouquet, a teaser to make to all but the proficients, was then the go.

Fifty years ago lycopodium or Christmas green, so-called, I recollect, began to create something of a stir in New York; so much so, that in 1853, after some search in the pine woods west of Albany I found the article which was wanted at the time in a made-up Christmas tree, and I thought it, when finished, far superior to the natural one. It was not until 1866 that the first little box of the same article reached me from the woods of Wisconsin, from which time it dates its use here, afterward to be measured by hundreds of tons, and thousands of yards of wreathing almost in universal use, though this year the supply seems so scarce.

A year after, a little box of mistletoe reached me from South Pass, Ill.; and holly came in small quantities from the East, then in carloads—jolly Christmas, indeed, from an English ideal. Other red berried plants showed up later from time to time.

In Chicago at least the ready made-up stringed smilax did not appear till near the seventies; the chaste asparagus much later, while the exceedingly useful wild smilax, although growing in the Southern woods so plentifully, is of comparatively recent introduction.

Basket of Begonia Gloire de Lorraine
Grower, Samuel Murray, Kansas City

Where Chicago Stood Fifty Years Ago.

In August just a half century ago, according to a city census then taken, Chicago had a population of 84,113 inhabitants. But for being so new a country, it might be supposed to figure somewhat in a floral way, as older cities with fewer inhabitants were at that time known to do. In the city proper then, there was one florist, if we may call him such, as he had a fifty-foot greenhouse out on West Lake street, opposite what is now Union Park. Then there was another florist, to the manner born, with another fifty-

Viburnum Opulus (Oxycoccos) in Fruit

foot house in Hyde Park. The third was just over the city limits, in Lake View, the north part of which is now so noted as the growers' or wholesalers' home. Here good sized farms are covered with glass, and nearly all to supply Chicago's great central wholesale market with cut flowers to-day.

These three houses, fifty feet each, were glazed with 7x9 glass, heated by the old-fashioned brick flue, and filled with a mixed class of bedding out and window plants. Is it not safe to say that even a beginning of the florists' Christmas had no existence at that time?

My appearance on the scene was a few months later. I also commenced in a modest way, but was all the time advancing; and I find in a diary kept at that time that "by 1864" the Christmas trade had grown and was thought worthy of record." It was, all told, $50.40. Think of that, ye retail florists, who are counting on your coming Christmas trade, which with some of you reaches the thousands of dollars!

Fifty years ago, it is safe to say, from the greenhouses your predecessors did not take altogether to exceed one thousand dollars, during, not Christmas, but for the entire year, and that for plants and cut flowers combined. As compared with the present verily the world do move, and the florists keep up with the procession.

The cry of over-production is as old as my memory goes, and still the great work goes on. It is surely a far cry from 700 feet of glass to an establishment of one and a quarter million feet, all for cut flowers; from glass 6x8 or 7x9, to a pane of 16x24, making a house as light as day! Yet there are several hundred firms now with from five thousand feet of glass up to the previous figures named. What will the next half century see? Who can tell?

At the present day a new town springs up in the wilderness, and very shortly there is found room for and need of the materials in which the florist deals. If he cannot grow his own stock in sufficient quantity, the grower stands ready, the shipper and express company place the goods at his door for him to work with. He does not grow gradually, but jumps into it. The retail florist takes an order from his customer, to be delivered across the continent. The trick is done in a twinkling by another florist, who fills the order—not with flowers from the point of receipt, but with fresh flowers from the greenhouses at the point of delivery.

So we end by wishing A Merry Christmas to you all, and joy go with you. EDGAR SANDERS.

[The Editor has great pleasure in presenting the foregoing article from the pen of Mr. Sanders who is now in his eightieth year. The article shows that our venerable friend's mental faculties are still as alert as ever. We feel sure our readers will join with us in wishing the dean of the florist trade in America a very happy Christmas, and many of them.]

Berries and Berried Plants for Christmas

With the approach of Christmas the thoughts of the florist and the nurseryman run toward the holly and other berry-bearing plants, so closely are they associated with that great festival.

Of the hollies the two in most demand are our native one, Ilex opaca, and the English species, I. aquifolium. For uses where cut branches are required our native one is mostly employed, being near at hand and therefore cheaper. Yet the English species finds its way here, for one reason because it has far handsomer foliage, the glossy green of its leaves far surpassing that of our native sort. When it comes to tub plants, one sees the English holly only.

Besides those already given for the preference for the English holly, there exists the reason that it is grown especially for the purpose of using it as a tub specimen. The plants are prepared years in advance, by careful pruning and transplanting, and those bearing female flowers only are carefully fertilized, that they may become full of berries. The time may come when our own holly may be treated in the same way. Although, as said, it is not the equal in beauty of the English one it has the advantage of being hardy in the North, whereas the English sort cannot be depended on north of Philadelphia.

The deciduous holly, Prinos (Ilex) verticillatus, is considerably used now, though it is not known to be by those who buy it. In the wreaths and festoons so common along the streets at Christmas week the "holly berries" appearing among the foliage are often largely those of the prinos, sometimes entirely so. It makes no difference for they are just as pretty as those of the true holly.

The pretty dwarf evergreen, Skimmia japonica, is becoming a favorite as a pot plant. Its foliage is pretty, the leaves being of thick texture and of a bright green; the berries are scarlet and remain in good condition all Winter. And to add to its usefulness it is entirely hardy in the vicinity of New York. It could be more used for planting than it is.

Fruit of Ilex Cornuta

Aucuba japonica is well known as a useful pot plant and one that sells well. Besides its large, handsome foliage it becomes heavily berried when carefully fertilized.

Among climbing vines with red berries there is one which finds its way to the cities now in small quantities, and it is one that could be used a great deal more than it is. This is the Smilax Walteri. It is evergreen and has the advantage of having no spines, as so many smilax have.

In addition to the plants mentioned there are quite a number of others which it seems possible could be used and which are now rarely or never seen at Christmas. Here is a list of shrubs and vines bearing red berries which look well in pots, and which would keep their berries well until Christmas and after: Berberis Thunbergii, Callicarpa purpurea (violet-purple), Euonymus atropurpureus, Pyrus arbutifolia, Cratægus pyracantha, Symphoricarpos vulgaris, Ilex cornuta, Cotoneaster Simmondsi, Taxus hibernica, Celastrus scandens and Lycium chinense. And mention should be made of the Elæagnus umbellata, with its rosy flesh-colored fruit. Of these special mention may be made of Pyrus arbutifolia, Berberis Thunbergii, Callicarpa purpurea (violet-purple berries), symphoricarpos and cotoneaster because of their ease of culture and their fruitful character. The beauty of the callicarpa consists in its long, slender branches being full of violet-purple berries. There is just enough weight in the berries to cause the shoots to droop gracefully. The same may be said of symphoricarpos. The red berries are thickly set along the branches, and they, too, cause the branches to bend over. When in pots, all these plants are of pleasing appearance, and the wonder is that they are not sometimes seen in Christmas collections.

Fruit of Mountain Ash
(Pyrus Americana)

Besides the shrubs last mentioned, a few others could be added, all of which would admit of their branches being used for the sake of their berries, which are red, with the exception of those already named: Cornus florida, mountain ash, Cratægus cordata, Viburnum oxycoccos and Ilex cornuta. Taking the last first, it is a beautiful holly, coming from Japan. The berries are large, red, and are generally produced in great abundance. A photograph of a small spray of it taken from a fine bush, growing in North Carolina, which we herewith produce, will give an idea of its appearance. It is an uncommonly desirable holly, and one well suited to the South, for it is not hardy North of Philadelphia. Our Southern florists should grow it.

Many of the branches of the shrubs named could be cut before freezings mar the appearance of the berries and be preserved in jars of water in any place cool and free from frost, keeping in this way until Christmas. Mountain ash, Berberis Thunbergii, Elæagnus umbellata and Viburnum oxycoccos would all keep very well. Excepting the berries of the mountain ash, which birds have carried away, those of all the plants mentioned are still in fresh condition on the bushes, and the date of this writing is November 28.

Fruit of Elaegnus Umbellata
(Silver Thorn)

The symphoricarpos mentioned is the red snowberry—a plant wild in some places—which could be had probably in fair quantities; and when used in vases of water the sprays keep many weeks in as good condition as when gathered.

JOSEPH MEEHAN.

Fruit of Berberis Thunbergii

Philanthropy and Mr. Johnson

"When it comes to stackin' up agen wads of hard luck," began Johnson, dexterously manicuring a venerable calla, "any man in the retail business seems like old man Trouble's only son. What with coal bills, busted bilers, mildew and the general run of customers, about the only way a florist gets his livin' nowadays is by makin' it first in some other line of business.

"But when it comes to buckin' agen hoodoos, and just fairly drippin' with adversity, you take one of these cultivated stiffs that butts into the business, like that chap I worked for down in Indiana. He'd made a barrel of money writin' a book on 'How to Feed a Family of Six on $2 Per,' which is dead easy as long as the lumber trust don't raise the price of sawdust, and he goes into retail growin' because it brings him in touch with the beautiful things of Nature—which it did, includin' me.

"It was one of those graveyard hamlets, where the society gents takes lunch at a dog wagon by the depot, and the ladies swap rubber plants to decorate a real swell tea fight; the only time I ever got over 30 cents a dozen for carnations I had to give the customer knockout drops. They'd cough up a measly $2 for roses about Easter, and you could generally hit 'em with an ardisia in a red petticoat at Christmas, but it was tough sleddin' for the florist the rest of the year.

"Well, the boss learned all there was to the business in about six weeks, studyin' through a correspondence school, and then hired me and a couple of Skowhegians to do the hustlin.' We put in about seven days a week shorin' up the rafters with railroad ties and clothes-props, and the rest of the time doin' ambulance work around the boilers but things grew, somehow, and the boss was such a looloo at handin' out hot air that he'd sell wooden Romans to a Dutch bulb agent if he only got three minutes start. Pretty soon any society fairy that didn't have a bunch of greens in one of his bargain fern pans was a dead one, and the boss piled up enough scads to whitewash the pottin' shed. Then they made him one o' the trustees of the new orphan asylum and that's where old Mr Hard Luck was waitin' around the corner for him with a club. You'll notice when any kind of charity con game starts there's always a bunch of calico mixed in it. Whenever they hooked a come-on for the orphan asylum, it was his stunt to donate a day's profits for the poor orphans—run a benefit performance—savvy?

"Well, the boss run up agen a lady that wanted an orchid luncheon, with no expense spared, for about $4.98, and as the boss didn't see his way to bankin' the mantels, decoratin' the table, and sendin' to New York for favors without raisin' the ante, she just soaked him! 'Everyone's so generous at Christmas,' says she, 'what's one day's profits, when you think of them sufferin' orphans?' 'Ain't it a lovely idea,' says the rest of the bunch, 'buyin' those beautiful flowers to console the sick and sufferin' and knowin' that you're helpin' the fatherless orphan on the side!'

"The boss sees his finish and tries to sidetrack the scheme till after Christmas, but the rest of the trustees says 'Nay, nay, Pauline.' They'd all been initiated the same way, till it seemed like the orphans was the only outfit in town that could flash a wad of real money. Then the lady trust-buster, that started throwin' the hooks into the boss says how sweet it would be if a few of the society fairies would help him out by actin' as salesladies just for that one day! Say, you could have heard him holler a mile when he come into the pottin' shed to tell us about it. He tried hot-air treament on the committee, tellin' em the young ladies was such a basket of peaches that customers would forget to buy any flowers so long as they was around, but it didn't work, and he couldn't make a strong getaway without soundin' as though he was tryin' to knock down the profits and rob the poor-box.

1. Combination Christmas Basket

Artists, Bertermann Bros. Co., Indianapolis

"'Say, you should have seen the pottin' shed outfit make a break for the boiler pits when the ammytoor saleisladies broke in. I don't know just how they worked the customers, but it's straight goods that the only trust magnet in town met the boss on the street next day and struck him for the price of a shave. And the chief of the fire department up and died just so's he could ring in his funeral flowers for the benefit of them bloomin' orphans! All the dead swell who's-whoers in the county was there, givin' their Christmas orders on a bargain basis, while the boss shut himself up in the icebox and tore his hair out in chunks. By noontime the whole place looked like a Kansas ranch after a grasshopper lunch, and them good kind ladies was wonderin' whether to figure out profits with the boss, or whether they'd give him a meal ticket and freeze onto the rest.

2. Combination Christmas Basket

Artists, Bertermann Bros. Co., Indianapolis

"Well, there was nothin' doin' after that. Christmas trade was busted, and the society bunch went back to tissue paper and rubber trees for decorations. Seemed like folks quit dyin', too, to save funeral expenses, and when the boss started to put notes in my pay envelope I just quit; I thought he'd be offerin' me a share in the business if I didn't break away. But there—you can't tell me that Providence aint keepin' an eye on the florists. About six months after I quit, when the boss was ready to cadge for his meals at the orphan asylum, somebody struck an oil well right next door. The boss sold his place to the oil company, tellin' everybody how the pirates and vultures of modern finance ground down the toiler. Now he's goin' around with a wad you could choke a dog on, and they've named the orphan asylum after him. The oil well? I don't rightly know just what ailed it, but somehow it wouldn't cough up good and proper. Last I heard of it, the boss was workin' the oil company into some scheme for growin' mushrooms and pie plant in the holes.

"Moral? Well, I don't know as there is any— except that it aint always safe to bet on a sure thing."

HIS KNOWLEDGE OF HORTICULTURE.—When I joined the horticultural society about three years ago I knew about as much about the subject of horticulture as a certain Hebrew I heard of the other day knew about his anatomy. Isaac met a friend on the street and said, "Moses iss awful seek." "So? Vat iss de matter mit Moses?" "Oh, Moses haf got upendesitus." "Upendesitus, vat iss dot?" "Oh, dey are goin' to take hees upendix avay from heem." "Ach, Himmel! Vat a peety dot he didn't have it in his vife's name!" (Great laughter.) My knowledge of horticulture was equal to that Hebrew's knowledge, and for that matter it has not gone much beyond that stage, but your proceedings are so elevating that with your advice and encouragement I am not sure but what by and by I shall become a horticulturist.—HON. S. A. STOCKWELL to Minnesota State Horticultural Society.

Society of American Florists and Ornamental Horticulturists.

Department of Plant Registration.

The Conard & Jones Co., West Grove, Pa., submit for registration Canna New York, (C. & J. Seedling No. 1549); height, 6 to 7 feet, with broad bronze leaves and mammoth flowers of intense carmine.

W. J. STEWART,
Secretary.

The Legal Relations of the Nurseryman, His Agent and the Customer.

The subject assigned to me is so large that I can only touch upon a few points within the time allowed me. It involves the whole law of "sales," on which large text books have been written, the laws of agency, warranty and breach of contract and damages for the same. You will thus see that I can only make a few categorical statements of general principles, but for the law applying to any particular case I must refer you to your own lawyer.

The legal relation of the nurseryman to his agent is that of any principal to his agent; the rights and liabilities are the same, the duties of both are the same, the power of the agent to bind his principal is the same.

The legal relation of the nurseryman to his customer is in general the same as that of any manufacturer or merchant selling goods to a customer. There is no material difference between them except such as is involved in the kind of wares sold, grown or manufactured by each.

Buying Through an Agent.

The agent is bound at his peril to carry out the express orders of his principal and is responsible to him for failure to do so. As between them he has no right to warrant the goods sold or make representation as to their kind, quality or the condition of the plants sold beyond the express or implied authority conferred upon him. In the absence of orders to the contrary he is authorised to warrant the plants sold as good, marketable stock, fit for the purpose for which they are sold unless he is selling stock then in presence of the customer, for the nurseryman is presumed to sell good, marketable stock only unless the customer picks out his own plants; then if asked any question he must tell the truth.

The principal is not bound by any opinions expressed by the agent as differentiated from a warranty; nor has the customer, on the other hand, a right to rely upon them, except as opinions.

As between the customer and the agent, the customer has a right to rely upon any warranty, statement or material representation made by the agent, within the scope of his business as seller of nursery stock, as to its kind and quality and the ability of his principal to carry out his contracts and deliver the goods sold. If the customer wants to hold the principal to an express agreement as to what he can expect from the plants in the future, he should require a warranty, but the right to give such a warranty by the agent will depend upon the authority actually conferred upon the agent or existing in him by reason of his position with the principal. If a notice of lack of authority to warrant is brought home to the customer, he cannot hold the principal responsible for such warranty. This is often done by a printed notice in the sale blank or order blank or in the catalogues supplied to the agent for soliciting business, to the effect that no statement or representation not included in the written contract or differing from the catalogue shall bind the principal. And here it is to be noted that if a written contract is entered into for the sale of plants or any other article, no statement or representation varying or tending to vary the terms of the written contract is in general admissible in evidence. An oral warranty in such cases is not valid, as a rule.

It is important that the customer guard his rights by insisting that every warranty or representation or promise made shall be embodied in the written contract. The principal on the other hand has a right to rely upon such contract as a complete contract, subject to the right of recision or cancellation for fraud or misrepresentation.

Christmas Basket
Artist, C. A. Samuelson, Chicago

Buying by Catalogue or Sample.

A purchaser buying by catalogue or sample is entitled to expect good marketable stock, of the kind contracted for or according to the sample, but must inspect the plants delivered promptly upon the receipt of the shipment and either reject the whole shipment if not up to the standard or, if the orders are severable, reject the part not according to contract, or keep the shipment and deduct those delivered and the value of the plants as it would have been if according to contract.

There is a great difference between making a contract for future delivery of plants that you have not seen or that you have bought by sample or catalogue and the buying of plants that you yourself selected from the stock on hand. In the first case in the absence of express warranty or representation there is an implied warranty that the plants shipped are of the kind and quality contracted for and, within the terms of the contract, good marketable stock of the variety ordered. If you select your own plants there is no implied warranty that they are of good marketable stock or even the kind you wanted. The warranty if existing at all is an express warranty and must be proved as such.

Cancelling Orders.

The question is often asked: Suppose after a sale is made for future delivery an attempt is made to cancel the order. Can it be done legally? To this I answer the facts in each case must govern the decision, and you should always consult your attorney if you care to either insist on the order of a nurseryman or reject a shipment, which may be made notwithstanding a cancellation, or insist on a claim for damages by reason of loss of sale.

As a general proposition, an accepted contract of sale, legally made and otherwise valid, cannot be cancelled on the mere whim of either party, however much he may desire to do so, but, as a practical question, it usually costs so much to enforce such a contract, compared with the result obtainable and considering the delay of litigation, that it does not pay to enforce it. A contract can be cancelled or rescinded by reason of fraud in the making of the same, or false representation material thereto and relied upon by either party, by reason of which it was entered into; as, for instance, a positive statement as to the ability of the principal to perform the contract, his financial standing, his being a grower of plants instead of being merely a dealer in the same, or as to the kind or quality or other features of the plants sold.

Another reservation should also be made. If the contract is to be accepted by the principal before it becomes valid—and it must be accepted within a reasonable time—then before such acceptance it is a mere offer and subject to cancellation at the whim of the customer. This provision is very commonly inserted in the order blanks used by agents of large jobbers, where the principal wishes to reserve for himself the right to pass upon the desirability of the sale or the financial responsibility of the customer or for many other reasons.

If the plants delivered are not up to contract grade or kind or not delivered on time, if time is important, the contract can usually be rescinded and is always subject to rescission by the other party if either party refuses to perform. The customer must act promptly and positively. He cannot accept the goods and then after a few days send them back. He has, however, the right to open the shipment and examine the plants and then reject them if not according to contract. If he fails to reject promptly, his only remedy is to accept the shipment and recoup himself in damages on the ground of breach of warranty.

In this connection it may be worth while to say a word or two about the remedy of the nurseryman in case of unlawful cancellation. Even if the same be unlawfully cancelled, he has no right to make shipment notwithstanding the same, but can sue only for the actual damage suffered by him for the loss of his contract of sale. He is further obliged to reduce the damage as much as possible by trying to sell the plants to other persons, and, of course, if the goods are sold at the contract price he suffers no loss and can only collect nominal damages at the best. If he is obliged to sell for less than the contract price, he is entitled to hold the customer for the difference between the sale price and the contract price. If the plants have no market value, the contract price less the cost of shipment is the measure of damages.

From this you will see that, as a general rule, cancellation of contract even though illegal is usually effective and does not result in punishment to the customer by reason of the slight damages and the cost of recovering them.

Substitution.

Another question often arises in the mind of the nurseryman upon the receipt of an order for plants which he may be out of. It is this: Can I substitute another variety in place of the one ordered? The actual doing so is perhaps one of the sources of the greatest amount of friction between the nurseryman and his customer and may lead to expensive litigation. As a general proposition I answer "no" to the question, with the reservation that if the substituted plants or varieties are accepted by the customer with the knowledge of the substitution he must pay for them as a matter of course.

Christmas Basket
Artists Jos. Kift & Son, Philadelphia, Pa.

It may further be asked: Suppose in the catalogue or order sheets there is a printed clause reserving the right to substitute other varieties if out of those ordered. Even then I should say a substitution cannot be made without the express consent of the customer to the particular substitution, except in a very limited degree. If the plants shipped are a substantial performance of the order, so that the difference in grade, variety or plant is not a material one to the customer, then it can probably be made, but each case must depend upon its own facts and circumstances. If you cannot fill the order as given, the only safe thing to do is to notify the customer and ask him for orders as to the substitution. If without such orders you ship a substituted article, it is a mere offer to the customer to take the plants shipped instead of those ordered, which he is at liberty to reject at his pleasure, and if you cannot carry out the contract as made, or decline to do so, he may rescind or hold you for damages. He is not bound to take what he did not order but must act promptly in rejecting as soon as he becomes informed of the substitution.

I do not know that I can add anything further which will be of direct interest to your body, and I can only say that the questions applying to each particular case are so ramified and interwoven with other questions and legal principles that you can never rely upon any such book of legal lore as "Every Man His Own Lawyer" but must use common sense and honesty, tempered with good judgment and discretion and, perhaps, a little sound legal advice.—Wm. BABCOCK, in The Minnesota Horticulturist for December, 1906.

ATLANTIC, IA.—The Stark Brothers Nursery Company is to quit business in Atlantic, says the Democrat. This was the word received some days ago by I. N. Brown, local manager for the concern, in the shape of an order from the main office at St. Louis to ship teams, stock, etc., to them and wind up the business here. The reason of the decision on the part of the well-known nursery firm is not exactly known, but it is said that they have not found the local nursery a profitable one and that many of the local conditions are not auspicious. The company purchased the Wilson nursery business some years ago.

THE IOWA STATE HORTICULTURAL SOCIETY holds its forty-first annual convention in the horticultural room in the Capitol, Des Moines, December 11, 12, and 13. An interesting and varied program has been prepared. Wesley Greene, Davenport, Ia., is secretary of the organization.

CARNATIONS

There is great need of indefatigable perseverance in the raising of new carnations. A notable falling off in the production of new varieties would speedily be followed by an all around decrease in profitable carnation culture—a total cessation would bring our fine chariot of triumphant advancement to a standstill, probably turn it into a dump cart. In four or five years we would entirely run out of anything in carnations worth growing. The lucrative traffic in rooted cuttings would come to a sad and much deplored end. In less than a decade nothing visible in petaled garb would remain to memorize the present era of progressive carnation culture.

Some Facts.

The great improvement manifest in the flowers of the present day carnation is again well balanced by the loss of some of the plant's best attributes through constant inbreeding, high culture and processes tending to improve in one direction by sacrificing good points in others. Not the least to be regretted is the shortening of the carnation's life term, naturally limited in duration, a weak point in its constitution, incessantly levied upon in the present course of evolution.

The prototype of the florists' forcing carnation is the old-time garden flower, Dianthus caryophyllus, a native of Southern Europe, a true perennial. From it sprung the so-called remontant or tree carnation, D. c. semperflorens, finer in habit and bloom but less hardy or long-lived than its progenitor. By selection and cross-breeding the present race of carnations was obtained. In late years astounding improvements have been made in the carnation as well as in the methods of growing it under glass. But of the many excellent varieties called into existence none lives long enough to eliminate the pressing need of farther origination, or cause it to be less keenly felt.

Some of the new varieties, as distributed annually, are seen but once or twice in their full glory and are hardly recognized in their rapidly waning beauty ever afterward. Three out of every five new sorts are already past their prime when introduced, and are not any more heard of two or three years later.

Bridesmaid's Bouquet
Artist, H. E. Klunder, Chicago

A few novelties enjoy a longer run, an occasional prodigy sometimes even gaining in point of excellence for a few seasons after being first sent out. But all of them, nevertheless, are doomed to inevitable oblivion long before the average grower becomes able to pronounce their names correctly or the public becomes fully aware of their existence. The originator painstakingly spends three, four or five years in the raising of a new carnation, one out of thousands of seedlings grown along for companionship at considerable expense. Then at still more expense he sends it out, and in a couple of years more he sees it displaced by some newer paragon, just as short-lived. It seems hardly worth while.

The carnation, oldest and grandest of cultivated flowering plants, is, after all, but an evasive reality, forcefully demonstrating the instability of all things terrestrial. And yet in spite of its ephemeral term of existence there is no plant more worthy of tireless cultivation and ceaseless reproduction, more entitled to the grower's best endeavors in its behalf than the carnation.

Propagation by Cuttings.

In propagating carnations from cuttings as a means of increasing the number of plants and providing stock for a coming season, something more than this has been accomplished. In calling forth new roots on parts of the original stock some provision has been made for the upholding of its inherent vitality, so as to enable the original plant, represented by these detached parts, to run its full course of natural life under conditions most trying to its nature. But it must not be imagined that propagation by cuttings lengthens the life term of this plant or any rooted part of it. It will ever tend to shorten its naturally fixed term of productive life, though by this means it may be made to merely exist and eke out the remnant of waning life for an indefinite number of years, inspiring hope that is never realized.

A first year's seedling carnation, removed to a garden spot in some congenial climate—say Italy, Southern France, the Riviera—and there allowed to take its chances, unmolested by the propagator, would thrive and flower for five or six years, then exhibit signs of rapid decline in vital energy, and in a year or two more it would be ready to succumb to the first one of adverse conditions coming its way. A cutting taken from this carnation when still in its vigor would grow into a thrifty plant, but it would cease to be productive at the same time, when its parent gives out. Cuttings taken from either old or new plants when in their last stages of declining productiveness would amount to little, and soon yield to all the ills that beset old age. All efforts to arrest deterioration by increasing the number of individual plants and styling the lot a new variety, would fail to add a single season to the useful life of this new variety, which is merely the life of the original seedling.

New vs. Old Varieties.

It is not easy to convince the average carnation grower that the character of his stock has as much to do with the making or marring of success as culture. It is a fact, notwithstanding all protests to the contrary, that the growing of carnation blooms as a business, in spite of the adoption of modern appliances and improved cultural methods, has proved a profitless vocation in very many instances, especially at the medium-sized concerns where an extensive trade in rooted cuttings as a means of salvation does not exist. The air is full of complaints uttered in all the gamut from shout to whisper. The main and most frequent cause of failure to make it pay is the persistent culture of so-called old standbys. The growers are ever ready to install at great cost improved apparatus and to heed cultural advice, but are unbelievingly slow in finding out that flowerless, wornout varieties cannot be coaxed back into their former state of productiveness, no matter how fine their grass growth may appear or how much sturdy material for propagation they may hold forth. When the small grower depending for a living on the sale of the cut blooms alone finally decides to do away with some of his ungrateful old standbys and to buy newer sorts in their place, he has come to a juncture in his career offering the finest opportunities for the making of mistakes. The number of new carnations and those new to the grower is great. They also differ greatly one from the other, and their intrinsic characteristics are manifold and difficult to fathom.

The New Carnation.

It seems a deal of money that must be expended for new carnations every now and then. While large establishments cannot afford to do otherwise but invest in nearly all of the latest introductions, the grower with restricted means must confine his purchases to but a few kinds of the newer sorts. Acute judgment in choosing is all important. The grandest and most bewitching novelty, prize winner at all exhibitions, very seldom proves the most profitable one for the grower of marketable cut blooms. The vigorous plant, freely and abundantly producing flowers of medium size, bright, pure color and long

Bride's Bouquet
Artist, H. E. Klunder, Chicago

lasting quality, holds out a greater assurance of bringing adequate returns right along for a number of years. This is the small grower's reliable standby, and also that of many a large concern.

I think a little more of the speculative spirit manifest in other quarters would also be of service to the smaller grower in bettering the state of his affairs. Whenever he invests in new carnations he age to stock up with, and perhaps a dozen or two of some of the newest sorts. And, again, in four cases out of every five all those purchased at a low price turn out to be nearly as worthless and unprofitable as those they are to replace. The newer sorts, bought dozen-wise, will likely be also backnumbers by the time he has succeeded in working up a stock of some consequence. If a new carnation is worth buying by the dozen, twenty-five or fifty, it is worth risking by the five hundred or thousand. The risk in no instance amounts to a real loss of money in the transaction; in most cases proves highly profitable.

Going in deeply for a novelty of high repute and latest introduction, carefully weighing all chances, partakes less of the character of wild speculation than going into carnation culture for a living with a lot of old, unproductive varieties as is done every day. Stocking up anew with sorts introduced years ago and already giving out, just because the grower saw them in their prime here or there, and now they cost less, is a hopeless beginning in an effort to increase the profits in carnation culture.

The Raising of Seedlings.

In summing up the one point remains conspicuously clear—the necessity of constant reproduction by seeds. There is no immediate danger of running out of new varieties in the near future, nor need there be any fear of this line of horticultural industry ever being overdone, as has been predicted repeatedly. There is reason to believe that the raising of seedlings on a somewhat restricted scale as a side line to every good sized concern exclusively devoted to the growing of carnation blooms, would prove a profitable feature if rightly conducted. It would become the means of furnishing the establishment with vigorous new sorts as the older sorts gave out. The raising of fairly good commercial sorts worthy of extended cultivation would probably be the first result of any newly made attempt. Though such work would not entirely be in line with the progressive labors of the carnation hybridist, it would not go amiss in serving the purpose aimed at. Nor would it exclude the possibility of calling forth new sorts exceptionally fine. The first telling step in the raising of seedlings is the raising of seeds. A beginning made in December or January will enable the grower to start the seeds early in Spring—the most propitious time.

FRED. W. TIMME.

O'Mara on Burbank.

(Concluded from Page 536.)

One of the first new "creations" in flowers that rivetted the attention of the people of the East was the Burbank canna. That was produced probably by the same parentage as a similar variety produced in Italy. Unfortunately for Mr. Burbank, others were working along the same lines as he without his knowledge, and the year that he was ready to send out his canna we received from Europe two varieties, known as the Austria and the Italia. The Italia was such a glorious canna that it eclipses the Austria completely, and the Austria and the Burbank were identical. It It shows how, with the ocean between men working along the same lines, they will arrive at the same results. I could cite dozens of instances where that has occurred. The Austria had the priority of claim, and so it remains to-day the recognized variety. I cite this as showing what the plain, ordinary hybridizer over in Italy can do as against a wizard.

The White Blackberry. I take issue with Mr. Burbank again in this matter. The magazine writer undoubtedly leads the public to believe that Burbank was the first one to produce white blackberries. He said that it is a fruit which he "created;" he does not say that he had anything at all to work on, while for sixty years or more we have had white blackberries. Fifteen or twenty years ago the trade generally gave up selling them. They had their little day and they drifted out. The old Chrystal White was the last one that we offered, and when Jackson and Perkins, who have a California place, came to us and wanted us to push this "Iceberg" blackberry, we said, "Nonsense, people don't want a white blackberry; they want a black blackberry." But the phenomenal "Iceberg" was issued with a great flourish of trumpets—Wickson states that it is a feather in the cap of Burbank.

They say that with his psychological instinct he reaches out and gets two species together (the raspberry and blackberry) that had never been gotten together before, and he produced an absolutely new species, and nature was out of a job. This was achieved not only by Mr. Carman, but also by Professor Saunders of Canada about eighteen years ago. As to these gentlemen who exploit Burbank in this way, I think if they knew the truth they ought to tell it, and if they do not know they ought to ask somebody who does know.

The Aguilegia clematidea; that is a spurless aquilegia. Burbank it is alleged bred the spurs off the aquilegia and it is heralded as an achievement, but two hundred years ago there were spurless aquilegias. Henderson's Handbook of Plants shows aquilegias, some with spurs and some without. Now, the beauty of an aquilegia is really in its spurs. Without them the flower is characterless, and so the spurless aquilegia gradually drifted out altogether. Nobody cultivated them for years until Burbank produced or found them. There is also a variety in Japan, Aquilegia ecalcarata, which can be bought from European seedsmen, which, placed alongside the spurless aquilegia produced by Burbank proves to be exactly the same. The supposition is natural enough in some minds that possibly the seed came from Japan.

I want to call attention to the Bartlett pear plum. In the published matter relating to that it is stated that it is a plum with the flavor of a Bartlett pear, as showing how much can be accomplished by Burbank. It does not say whether that plum is as big or as heavy as a Bartlett pear, but by taste it is a pear; and Harwood tells a story of an expert, a man who had been all over the world. He was blindfolded and a plum was handed to him and he was told to bite it and tell what it was; he immediately pronounced it a pear, but it was a plum. It strikes many that the man who doesn't know a plum from a Bartlett pear when he takes it in his hand is not much of an expert.

The plumcot we have all heard of: it is a crossing of two species, which may or may not be of value.

Much is made of Mr. Burbank's lilies in magazine articles, but I only want to say that anyone who has ever done anything at all with lilies can get exactly the same results as shown in the published articles on Burbank's achievements in lilies. W. A. Manda is unquestionably a man of some attainments in horticulture, and he told me that he hybridized lilies extensively and got such results. That was confirmed by my own experience of twenty odd years ago.

The article states: "Lily growers from all over the world have stood dazed, intoxicated with the marvels of beauty and the perfumes of this acreage of new lilies in full bloom." Some of the dealers in the East have tried them. I asked one man, and he shook his head sadly and said that he would not try any more of them.

It is told in the magazines how one pleasant evening Burbank was walking along a field by some verbenas and he detected an odor which he traced back to the plant from which it emanated. He saved it and bred scented verbenas. When I was down in the seed fields of C. C. Morse & Compay at Gilroy, at the end of the Santa Clara Valley, California, I said to Mr. Landrum, the principal there, as we were driving along: "By the way, have you got any scented verbenas?" He said, "I don't know; I never bothered about them." I said, "In my young days the Sylph type was always fragrant in the whites; that I am certain of." We jumped out of the wagon, and we hadn't gone ten feet before I stooped down and picked up a white one. It had fragrance.

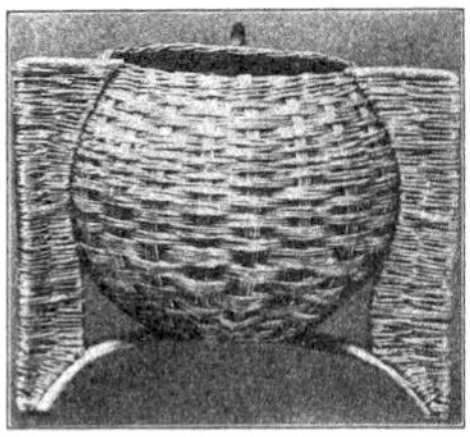

Willow Basket for Plants
Bayersdorfer & Co.

One other matter is about the blue rose. Now, if there is one thing that horticulturists have dreamed over for many years it is to obtain a blue rose. There is an axiom that there are three colors not found in varieties of one species, namely, a true blue, a true yellow and a true scarlet. You will get them to a certain extent in the asters, and to a certain extent in hyacinths, but nothing like a true scarlet, a blue or a yellow in varieties of any one species. We have yellow in the rose and a red that is nearly scarlet, so that all we want now to complete the trinity of colors is a blue. In one of these talks Harwood asks Burbank: "Did you ever consider the producing of a blue rose?" "Oh, yes," he said. "Do you think it is possible?" and he said: "Oh, it is a very simple matter, from what I have learned", —or words to that effect. From his investigations he thought it was a very simple matter, but he said: "My time has been taken up with more important matters, and I have not paid any attention to it." Now, judging from the output that has come from the garden at Santa Clara, I am certain that Burbank was engaged in matters somewhat trivial as compared with the production of a blue rose. If it is possible for him to do it, and if he wants to "square" himself with the florists, all he has to do is to produce a good blue rose and they will say: "Come back, everything is forgiven."

"The lost flower—the tragedy in plant life. A tiny pinkish white blossom upon a brilliant green vine. But one morning a workman discovered that in the night every plant had died. The flower could never be recovered because the conditions under which it had been created would never occur again."

There is a prophet; if he had said they never could occur again, it would show that he had some well grounded reason for it in his mind, but he said that they would never occur again, which is a very different thing as I view it. But the description recalls the Dolichos lignosus orAustralian pea vine, which is one of the most beautiful things in the California country. I think somebody must have been handing out a joke to Mr. Harwood and he didn't know it.

Another thing: "He took a French plum, unknown in America, and grafted it upon a Japanese plum. The graft bore no bloom, but the tree was recreated if you will; its seedlings took on a wholly new life and became hybrids, its vital essence was changed through the medium of the graft."

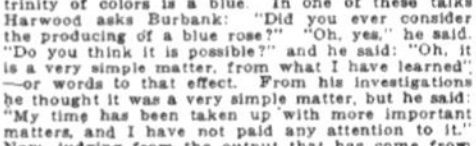

Chip and Fiber Baskets for Lily of the Valley and Roses
Bayersdorfer & Co.

I do not say that Mr. Burbank is responsible for this except by indirection. It is an old theory since men began to think of the influence of the graft upon the stock. It is useless to thresh it out here and I have no intentions of doing it, but I merely want to show the kind of mental pabulum that has been handed out from Santa Rosa to the body politic and the horticultural public at large.

It would not be fitting, I think, after all I have stated, to close without paying my tribute to Mr. Burbank, as far as I can honestly do it. I believe that Mr. Burbank is a sublime enthusiast. I believe that he has sacrificed much in his efforts to improve plant species. I want to say that I doubt if there is anyone who takes more comfort in the fact that he has been provided with the wherewithal to carry on his researches than I do. All that the professional florists ask is that the truth be known and nothing but the truth, and we say: "We are perfectly satisfied to have you go on as you are going, but don't let matters get out which are discrediting you and us, and which only result eventually in making American horticulture a laughing stock for everyone who stops to think of it." So much has been said about scientists that I am going to close by quoting a letter which I have received on the subject. It is but one of several which I have received from the Experimental Stations. I also want to say that from men in the trade, both in this country and abroad, since I lifted my voice in this matter I have received many complimentary letters, saying to me that they were glad I took the stand which I did and that they coincided with my views; so much has been said about the scientists and the ordinary rag-tag and bobtail of the florists that I will reproduce the following letter without disclosing who was the writer of it:

"I have just been reading your article in Florists' Exchange on Burbank, and I want to compliment you on your honest, temperate and straightforward statement of the case. The situation is fast becoming intolerable. The things that are claimed for Burbank are ridiculous—they go beyond hysteria and arrive at lunacy. If any man raises a word of protest the Burbank rooters immediately call him a sore head and say he is jealous of the marvelous achievements of the Master. We poor scientists, in particular (if I may class myself in that category) are discounted in advance. The public is told that the scientists have always been against Burbank and are all jealous of his achievements. The very opposite is true. To my personal knowledge every scientist who has ever said anything of Burbank has gone out of his way to pay him a compliment, and has nearly always rated him higher in print than his actual merits deserve.

"But the thing which most makes me want to fight is the vicious and false comparison always made or inferred between Burbank and other plant breeders. From the magazines you would think Burbank has done more than all the rest of the world put together, when the fact is that there are and have been hundreds of men who have done more for the improvement of economic plants than Burbank has ever done, or, in my opinion, ever will do.

"Any man who has the backbone to stand up and fight this infernal nonsense deserves public thanks, and for my part I want to assure you that you have struck a chord that will find more than one response among the horticulturists of America."

The fairest test of a man's ability is a comparison with others in the same sphere of work. One of Mr. Burbank's eulogists said: "Luther Burbank has done more for the human race than all other horticulturists." We florists and nurserymen do not endorse that statement; it is derided by every horticultural publication which has spoken on the subject. I even venture to say, from the test of comparison of products, that he is not the superior even of hybridizers in California. The Logan berry, introduced by Judge Logan, is better than any of his productions. The Phillips cling peach is of more value to California in my opinion than any fruit which he has produced, and sad to relate, the man who produced it is in the Yuba Co. almshouse, so announced in the Pacific Rural Press of Jan. 6th last.

The contributions to the fruits of the country by Mr. Burbank are not as valuable for instance as the Concord grape of Ephraim W. Bull, the Wealthy apple by Peter M. Gideon, the hybrid grapes by Rogers, Jacob Moore and T. V. Munson, not to mention others. In the realm of flowers he is hopelessly outclassed in this country by John Cook, E. G. Hill, Dr. W. Van Fleet and others in roses, and by Alex. Dickson, Notting, Lambert, Levavasseur and others in Europe. In carnations he is again outclassed, eclipsed I may say, by Fred Dorner, C. W. Ward, Peter Fisher and others. In cannas Antoine Wintzer outclasses him here, and in this connection I must pay a passing tribute to Mons. Crozy who was the originator of the present race of cannas. I also wish to mention the work of Mr. Groff in gladioli, superior to that of Mr. Burbank in its results. As a general improver of flowering plants he is again impressively behind Lemoine of France, whose work in shrubs and soft wooded plants actually borders on the marvelous. In sweet peas Henry Eckford of England stands supreme. But I will not give a catalogue of illustrious men in plant hybridization; sufficient has been said, I trust, to show the extravagant claims for the

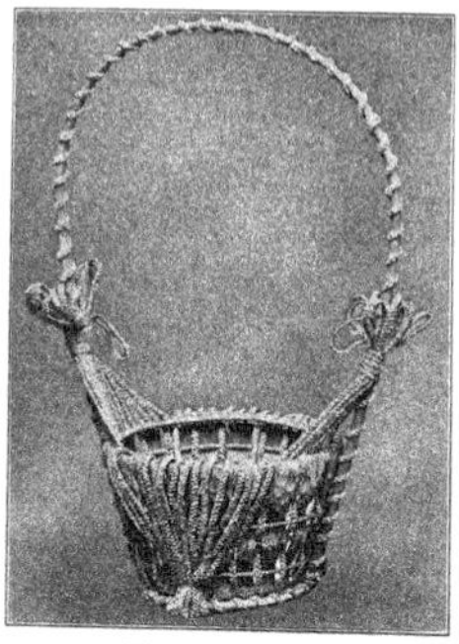

Willow Basket for Plants
Bayersdorfer & Co.

superiority of Mr. Burbank in his chosen field. It is further claimed for him as a great achievement in the cause of science that he produces and destroys acres of worthless plants. The really expert plant hybridizer does not do it and would hardly file a claim for fame on that score. Rather by close study of prospective results he aims at improvement by the most direct and least expensive method.

"Burbankitis."

Editor Florists' Exchange:

I am always interested in reading what is said about Burbank and his work. I noticed what E. O. Orpet said in your November 24 issue about the potato which bears Burbank's name. I did not know until then that this particular variety was such a great success and the one to be relied upon as a cropper of this excellent esculent in that country which some people seem to think is the "home of the potato.

The Burbank potato is looked upon by some conservative people as Burbank's greatest achievement, or "creation" as his ardent admirers prefer to call what he has done, and so far is his only claim to fame. However that may be, the potato referred to was Mr. Burbank's first new variety that, so far as I know, there is any record of, and this happened when Luther Burbank was a boy going to school. When crossing a potato patch he espied seed balls on one of the plants. Seed balls on potatoes in America are somewhat rare; they were more plentiful in England when I was a boy.

Every day when the boy was on his way from home to school, so the story goes, he would take a look at his discovery, when on one occasion it was missing; apparently it had been flicked off by a passer-by—unconsciously no doubt—with a cane or lighter switch. His young heart was full at what he believed to be his great loss, but after diligent search it was found and in due course the seed was sown and out of the numerous seedlings resulting the one bearing his name was selected, and in the course of human events it was disseminated, and is, it is supposed, in cultivation in some parts of the world today, though so far as I know it is not offered for sale in the Middle States. Whether because it has run its course and has been superceded by better kinds I do not know; certain it is that this potato episode is largely the cause of the fulsome praise we have been less or more regaled with for months past in magazines and newspapers, and it does go to show that the boy had an inquiring mind, and it was the cause, no doubt, of him turning his attention to the work he is now engaged in.

I read somewhere that the plum bearing his name was raised by him from seed received from China; others claim trees of this plum were imported direct from the Celestial Empire and with them the San Jose scale! The latter information appeared in the columns of the Rural New Yorker a few weeks ago, from one of its correspondents.

The Burbank rose I do not remember to have seen, but Wm. K. Harris, a Philadelphia plantsman and a keen observer, invested in some stock, but discarded it after careful trial as of no value for this critical clientage.

Burbank has no more insight into the mysteries of nature than any other practitioner, nor does he make use of any other process to produce seed than anybody else. He uses pollen from the stamens and applies it to the stigma of the pistils, just the same as had been done long before he was born and will he done long after he has been forgotten.

Where he differs from others in similar lines is—he is not satisfied to try to improve what we already have, but he does try by violent crosses to "create" something startling, odd or strange, regardless of whether it is likely to prove of value to humanity or not. His "plum-cot," a hybrid between a plum and an apricot, is a case in point and that is how he has mystified editors of magazines and newspapers and through them the public, and earned for himself the sobriquet of "The Wizard of Horticulture!"

His reputed efforts to produce a spineless cactus with the object in view of making the desert smile, so to speak, with a desirable cattle food, are exceptions to this rule, but even in this his misguided interviewers gave him more credit than he was entitled to. The original varieties of spineless cactus have been collected under the direction of the United States Department of Agriculture, and were sent to Mr. Burbank for him to experiment with same; but he was in no way responsible for the "crention" of the spineless cactus as is claimed for him by his exploiters, and goes to the public with his sanction and by his authority—so announce some of the magazines wherein appeared the gushing and over-drawn articles to which all those who have had some little experience with cross-fertilization of plants righteously and naturally object to.

It would never do for Mr. Burbank to deny any of the things that have been said about him, especially by those who have extolled his achievements so extravagantly; that would not be in accordance with the vain-glory of the situation.

One of Burbank's friends once said that he could produce a blue rose if he only felt so disposed and had the time. It would take time and a long time to eliminate all the red coloring matter there is in a crimson rose and leave nothing but sky-blue or forget-me-not blue! But why continue? We must all admit that the thoroughly practical improver of plants and flowers could never have attracted the attention in his hum-drum plodding way that our friend on the Pacific Coast has attracted, and we must give him that much credit for accomplishing that much. The public may be now in a condition to listen to what workers in plant improvement are attempting and accomplishing nearer home without the blare of trumpets made use of by the so-called Wizard of Horticulture. EDWIN LONSDALE.

P. S. Since writing the foregoing I have found the following in one of our daily papers:

SERIOUS POTATO FAMINE.

"Ireland is again threathened with her old-time woe. The potato crop, upon which a large majority of the peasantry rely for food, has utterly failed in some districts and is very short everywhere. The situation is really serious, as the supply will be entirely exhausted by January 1. The peasant farmers have no tubers for seed, and Irish members of Parliament will ask for Government aid to enable the people to start on another year."

It appears that even the Burbank potato is failing in Ireland! E. L.

Plant Baskets for Christmas.

The plant basket trade at holiday times is showing a continual annual increase in Chicago and some of the retailers, more especially in the districts lying outside of the mercantile center, are doing a very large business in this line. Baskets and hampers ranging in price from $5 to $10 were last season the most popular and found a ready sale, while more expensive creations moved slowly.

Charles A. Samuelson enjoys an extensive patronage in artistic plant combinations and decorated plants at his Michigan avenue establishment at Christmas time and last year the call for this line of goods was large. Azaleas, cyclamen, poinsettias, ericas, Begonia Gloire de Lorraine, Pandanus Veitchii, with the different nephrolepis and other ferns formed the leading features in the basket effects, while azaleas, ardisias, peppers, and araucarias appeared to be the favorites for individual adornment, the latter looking particularly bright, in quantity, with a diminutive scarlet bow attached to each branch and the pots dressed with various colored matting or crepe paper with ribbons.

The baskets shown in the pictures as the productions of Bertermann Brothers Company, Indianapolis, Ind., were made up of the following plants: In basket Number 1, cyperus, Asparagus Sprengeri and plumosus, white cyclamen, poinsettias and narcissus. Five red bells were fastened to the handles with red bows.

Number 2 was a zinc-lined basket of Adiantum Farleyense, Begonia Gloire de Lorraine, cypripediums and adiantum. The center plant was a highly-colored croton.

Some Bayersdorfer Novelties.

The illustrations herewith presented show some of the novelties in baskets and other designs being introduced by H. Bayersdorfer & Company, Philadelphia, Pa., and are reproduced from photographs kindly supplied by that concern. The fiber basket shown on page 708 is fitted with zinc pan, for ferns and small decorative plants. These baskets are made up natural, also in moss green color or in shaded effects. The chip baskets, also illustrated on page 708, can be used for violets, lily of the valley or roses. The designs on the lids and sides are hand painted.

The willow basket for plants (p. 708) can be supplied with zinc pans. The fiber ribbon plant basket in group, page 709, has zinc pan; the umbrella basket and the others are of willow, fitted with zinc pan, and can be used either for plants or cut flowers.

Willow Basket **Willow Umbrella Basket** **Fiber Ribbon Plant Basket**
H. Bayersdorfer & Co.

THE WEEK'S WORK.

Timme's Timely Teachings.

The Holiday Plant Trade.

The steady drift from cut flowers to potted plants, which strongly marked the character of the holiday business in recent years, has wrought manifold changes throughout the domain of present day floriculture. While there is sufficient evidence to prove a notable increase in the sale of cut flowers at all the principal holidays, this growth has not kept pace with that of the plant trade. The latter, in the hands of but a few some ten years ago, has become the leading feature of a great number of flourishing establishments, the mainstay of hundreds of progressive floricultural concerns. Entire ranges of houses are now given over to the growing and forcing of potted plants, the growers making it a chief point to be well stocked in this line for the holidays. But it is not enlargement in area alone which is worthy of note. More gratifying still must be the fact that most of the stock offered nowadays bears unmistakable evidence of having been well grown, plainly exhibiting the beneficent effects of careful attention to all the details of proper treatment in culture.

Christmas Stock.

The number of varieties in potted plants, easily to be had in perfect shape and profuse bloom at the Midwinter holidays, is not great. The material readily available and made the best possible use of for the occasion remains practically the same from year to year. But for all that there need be no cause for deeply felt regret on this account. Sufficient variety in what is put forth by florists at this season is not lacking, when it is borne in mind that every article purchased is destined to fulfill no other mission than that assigned to it as a Christmas gift. There is a fairly wide range of bright colors in foliage and flowers of the plants, and an endless diversity in embellishment and make-up to satisfy all tastes and fancies. Single specimen plants always prove the most profitable goods to handle at any one of the holidays, especially at Christmas. But it is only when exceptionally well grown that the larger sizes can readily be disposed of at prices figured upon by the grower. Well-shaped flowering plants, singly potted, displaying a crown of bright, freshly-opened bloom, are as good sellers as ever, be they of the high priced or common greenhouse species. The sale in well done foliage plants, as regards single specimens in the usual marketable sizes, is not very much larger at the holidays than at any time during the year. But Christmas trade offers one of the few opportunities to dispose of the larger plants in this class at prices not readily obtainable at most other times. There is little profit in carrying a stock of large sized palms, ficus, pandanus and the like, for either the holiday or general plant trade, and unless they are freely made use of in well paying decorative work all the year around, they should be speedily disposed of at the first opportunity that offers and at any seemingly fair price. Of small plants in this line, handily sized for all the various forms of artistic plant arrangements now so much in favor by all classes of buyers, there will never be too many. It is only by providing long ahead of time that sufficient supplies must be secured for the purpose.

Flowering Plants.

There is, after all, nothing in all the florist's line that so appropriately meets the prevailing Christmas demand as flowering plants. The stock grown for the purpose this year does not fall short either in quantity or quality of what was raised last year, and the probability is that demand and supply will be nearly even, resulting in a more thorough clean-up at the close of the festival season. In recalling the experiences of last year and in sizing up this year's stock, one is easily led to place Begonia Gloire de Lorraine at the head of the list in flowering plants as far as fitness, sales and profit are concerned. Most observers assign first place to azaleas, and no doubt where the trade is such that they can be disposed of readily at the higher price and in considerable numbers, they are the greatest yielders of clear profit, considering the short period of time required in bringing them into marketable condition.

Heaths and a few other rare things always find favor with the more refined class of people, whether well-to-do or humbly placed. But this class of plants, however keenly they may be desired, enter so sparingly into the general Christmas trade as to leave but a dim impression of their ever having played any part at all.

The Easter lily seems out of place at Christmas, but loses little thereby in prestige, since it enjoys a good and steady run right along regardless of holidays. Cyclamens are the connecting link between the high-priced and less costly flowering plants raised for the Christmas trade. They are disposed of in great numbers, but the price at which they are offered does not win them a place among profitable stock. Although the cyclamen is one of the best living room subjects, and therefore most satisfactory to buyers, it also is, in my opinion, one of the many things grown by florists out of the culture of which the grower extracts more genuine pleasure than clear profit. It never adequately repays him for the extraordinary care, the great amount of time, space and labor required in the long course of its raising. Far more profitable are such things as bulbs, primulas and the many other plants brought forward from the most common stock for the greater class of Christmas patrons.

Combination Christmas Basket

Artists, Joseph Kift & Son, Philadelphia

Berried Plants.

Hollies and oranges, well fruited, are the aristocrats among a type of plants that have found great favor with many searchers for something suggestively appropriate for Christmas in the plant line. In growing either of these two it is wise to make use of freshly imported stock and to start it in early Spring, giving it plenty of time to become pot-bound and to set fruit under favoring conditions. Specimen plants of this sort with bright foliage and unimpaired health, even if showing fruit but sparsely, are readily disposed of at good figures. Nicely proportioned but not over-large bushes of ardisias, quite thickly hung with fruit, are the finest of the more common kinds of berried plants. They never present that cheap and shabby appearance, when somewhat below the recognized standard of excellence, that neglected Jerusalem cherries and celestial peppers do. These latter, in fact, require a lot of artful trickery in their culture to bring them to a state of perfection. In most cases little in the way of careful attention in the raising of these highly serviceable plants is deemed at all necessary, and the outcome is stock of questionable value.

Plant Arrangements.

A noteworthy feature of the holiday plant trade is the increase in the sales of made-up combinations in all conceivable forms and styles. This line of the business offers a wide scope for the exertion of inventive genius, artistic discernment and executive ability. The proof of advancement in this direction is not wanting. But if a clearer understanding of what is desired and of what can be accomplished in work of this kind has gained any great pace, there is yet little circumstantial evidence to back up the fact. There are yet to be seen at every holiday season quite a number of clumsily done samples, hurriedly thrown together, it would seem, built up in a manner plainly showing that the hands did not work under the guidance of a sense for beauty and an eye to symmetry and pleasing outline. Incongruity in shape and colors, the use of too many plants, needlessly crowded and closely packed, a clear waste of good material, are to blame in nearly all such cases; very seldom the lack of suitable material or form and color of receptacle.

The demand for pleasing arrangements of flowering and foliage plants in boxes, jardinieres, hampers, pans, baskets and dishes of fanciful design, light and airy, dainty and graceful, is increasing in so marked a degree that it seems well worthy of receiving the earnest attention of all the growers of holiday stock. It should prove a strong incentive to raise suitable material for this particular purpose in ample quantities, to master the art of constructing truly beautiful pieces without wasting stock, or impairing the lasting qualities of the finished article. There is yet plenty of room for improvement in this line.

Embellishment.

The stock in holiday plants as now offered everywhere is so far ahead in quality of that grown for the purpose in former years that little in the way of artificial embellishment is needed. The beauty of a well grown, perfect plant cannot be enhanced by any sort of drapery, but as a holiday offering it greatly gains in attractive charm by a single bright ribbon of gauze or other airy and delicate fabric, tastefully adjusted. In trimming a single specimen plant properly, much more refined taste and judgment are required than in the adornment of hampers and baskets. Some persons never err in the proper trimming and finishing off of orders, do it amazingly quick and to everybody's satisfaction. Such help is invaluable and good to have around a busy place at the holidays. Plants or make-ups with scant or blemished foliage are improved in appearance by judicial trimming, serving to hide the defects. The term "dressing" here has its full meaning. An overdone bedecking of living plant beauty with ribbons and frills, attached without aim or object, is a senseless waste of time and material and not likely to attract custom. A stroll through the large retail stores at the busy time of Christmas would prove of great benefit to those new in the business.

Cultural Hints.

With Christmas yet two weeks away, much may be accomplished in properly preparing the stock for the occasion. Two weeks of hard forcing may bring lilies, azaleas and bulbous stock to a timely finish. Azaleas, Roman hyacinths and Harrisii lilies stand a deal of high pressure forcing and willingly respond to extreme measures in bringing them out in time, unless too far behind to justify any such hope. The buds of lilies must be well forward in final development now in order to be forced into full expansion by Christmas; so should the buds of azaleas, Deutsche Perle and Simon Mardner, if showing the least sign of color now, will need little in the way of hastening to be in fine form for Christmas. Lilies showing one or two open blooms and several buds that have turned from green to white, some five or six days before Christmas trade begins, should then go into cool quarters, not necessarily well lighted, where they will finish up nicely and be better in every respect when sent out than if left in heat to the last. The anthers in fully expanded lily flowers must be cut out before they scatter the pollen all over the petals. Liquid feeding must be discontinued when flowers begin to open, as also tobacco fumigation and overhead sprinkling.

Another despoiler of beauty is the yellowing, tip-drying and dropping of foliage, caused in several ways. Over-watering, lack of drainage in the pot, cold draughts, disturbance of potbound roots, feeding with liquid fertilizer of too great strength, sun-scorching, any one of these may be held responsible for the trouble, and there are several other causes that might be added. But, I trust, the observant grower will not be slow in rightly tracing the cause in his own particular case, should he be so troubled. This dropping of leaves, even when yet green, is especially bad and calling for prompt attention as soon as noticed, when it occurs on heaths, dwarf oranges, fuchsias, azaleas and poinsettias. Small plants of the latter, to be used in the filling of pans and dishes, should not be disturbed any more than necessary. If root-bound, the making up into effectively grouped masses should be deferred until a day or two before these are needed for display.

On the other hand, any filling of pans, baskets and receptacles of various design with plants other than poinsettias or bulbous stock should be done now or as soon as the busy grower can get at it. The plants to be used in filling, usually firmly root-bound, should be well watered through or dipped before being made up. Lily of the valley, Roman hyacinths, etc., must be set as closely as it is possible to do, even in the construction of mixed combinations, while a single four- or five-inch plant of Begonia Gloire de Lorraine, cyclamen or primula, bushy and well spread, will produce a finer effect in jardiniere, basket or hamper than several of smaller size. Small plants of ferns as a fringe are hardly ever out of place, and should therefore be used less stingily than is commonly the case. Fern dishes, unless ordered otherwise, should contain a number of distinctly differing varieties, even including a few plants of Asparagus plumosus. Somewhat more taste and skill are required in arrangements entirely to be made up of foliage plants of varying kinds. Here also ferns will do much in giving delicate and graceful finish. Most foliage plants will gain in freshness and appearance by a good sponging off, some needing it badly.

FRED. W. TIMME.

The Gardener.

The gardener in his old brown hands
  Turns over the brown earth,
As if he loves and understands
  The flowers before their birth.
The fragile childish strands
  He buries in the earth.

Like pious children, one by one,
  He sets them head by head,
And draws the clothes, when all is done,
  Closely about each bed,
And leaves his children to sleep on
  In the one quiet bed.

—[The Gardening World.

CLASSIFIED ADVERTISEMENTS

CASH WITH ORDER.

The columns under this heading are reserved for advertisements of Stock for Sale, Stock Wanted, Help Wanted, Situations Wanted or other Wants; also of Greenhouse, Land, Second-Hand Materials, etc., For Sale or Rent.

Our charge is 10 cts. per line (7 words to the line), set solid, without display. No advt. accepted for less than thirty cents.

Display advertisements in these columns, 15 cents per line; count 12 lines agate to the inch.

[If replies to Help Wanted, Situation Wanted, or other advertisements are to be addressed care of this office, advertisers add 10 cents to cover expense of forwarding.]

Copy must reach New York office 12 o'clock Wednesday to secure insertion in issue of following Saturday.

Advertisers in the Western States desiring to advertise under initials, may save time by having their answer directed care our Chicago office at 127 E. Berwyn Ave.

SITUATIONS WANTED

SITUATION WANTED—By experienced young man, 19 years old; good references. Address, A. W., care The Florists' Exchange.

SITUATION WANTED—As working foreman by first-class all-around florist. Good Beauty grower. Single; state wages. Address, A. H., care The Florists' Exchange.

SITUATION WANTED—Young man would like a situation as assistant gardener on private or commercial place. Address, A. X., care The Florists' Exchange.

SITUATION WANTED.—At once by married man, good grower of carnations and all around stock. Address, A. G., care The Florists' Exchange.

SITUATION WANTED—As greenhouse assistant in first-class private place. Swede, aged 26 years, good experience. Address, F. L., 1535 Euclid Av., Philadelphia, Pa.

SITUATION WANTED—Young man wants work in greenhouse. No experience. Will work at anything to start. Address, Theo. J. Gunderson, Gladbrook, Iowa.

SITUATION WANTED—By single, competent grower; roses and carnations; can take charge of 50,000 ft. of glass; $35.00 and board. References. Address, Florist, 270 Seventh Avenue, New York.

SITUATION WANTED—By hustling, energetic, well-educated young man of 28, with up-to-date firm in some central western city, to learn decorating, designing and store work. Have had some experience. Address, A. P., care The Florists' Exchange.

NURSERY FOREMAN

Will be open for engagement after January 1st. Has thorough ornamental nursery training, including herbaceous plants. References. Address A. Z., care The Florists' Exchange.

Mention the Florists' Exchange when writing.

SITUATION WANTED—By January 1st, as foreman or grower. I have had 20 years' experience in growing roses, carnations, violets, chrysanthemums, palms, ferns, bedding plants, etc. Not afraid of work. German aged 34, married. Can furnish A No. 1 references as to my ability and character. State salary with full particulars in first letter. Address, A. B. C., L. B. 120, West Mentor, O.

HELP WANTED

WANTED—Sober, intelligent man for rose section; one who understands the business. Send references to Wm. F. Kasting, Buffalo, N. Y.

WANTED—Seed salesman by the D. Landreth Seed Co., Bristol, Pa. A seed salesman having a personal acquaintance and influence in Philadelphia City and adjacent counties with private or professional gardeners.

WANTED—First class night fireman thoroughly familiar with high pressure steam boilers, who has had experience with the vacuum system, to work at large greenhouse plant. Pay good salary. Write, Green Floral & Nursery Co., Dallas, Texas.

A young man of good address and fair education, with strong recommendations for honesty and business ability, is herewith offered an exceptional opportunity to advance in life. Applicants to be noticed must give in detail their experience with and knowledge of bulbs, imported plants and commercial stocks generally. Experience as a traveling salesman preferred but not absolutely necessary. Before selecting a person to fill this position ample time will be given for answers from any part of the United States. State salary desired. Address A. Y., care Florists' Exchange.

HELP WANTED

WANTED—Single man as assistant in rose houses. Steady position. Frederick C. Schweinfurth, Ridgewood, N. J.

WANTED—A good rose and carnation grower; must be well recommended as such; wages $50.00 per month and house. Geo. Stewart, Tuxedo, N. Y.

WANTED—Two men for greenhouses in the South. Roses, carnations and general stock. $10.00 per week. Address, A. N., care The Florists' Exchange.

WANTED—Young man to assist in up-to-date flower store. Must be decorater, of good appearance and able to wait on select trade. Address X. D., care The Florists' Exchange.

WANTED—Seed salesmen by the D. Landreth Seed Company, Bristol, Pa. Two experienced commercial travelers familiar with the Garden Seed trade in the Cotton States; engagement to commence first of February.

WANTED—By importing house on January 1st a salesman familiar with plants, bulbs and seeds, who controls trade in New York and vicinity. To a willing worker opportunity to manage department. Salary and commission. State experience, references and expectations. Address, Onward, care The Florists' Exchange.

WANTED—At once, an able-bodied, intelligent young man of good character to learn the florist business. An excellent opportunity of advancement for the right man. Carnations, violets and bedding plants. Must be able to drive and care for one horse. $20.00 per month, room and board, to start. Send references in first letter. P. O. Box 108, Berwyn, Chester Co., Pa.

WANTED—Working foreman or head gardener; experienced carnation cut flower grower, to go to Germany and take charge of place where American carnations are grown; only thoroughly experienced and steady men need apply. Give full particulars of yourself, age, references and salary expected. Address, Theodore Wiest, Feudenheim, Mannheim, Germany.

WANTED—A good, reliable man to rent or to run in partnership for business purposes, a large greenhouse, containing assortment of fruit trees. Also section with roses, carnations, stove and foliage plants, bedding plants, palms, ornamental trees, grapery, and hot water heated hot beds for vegetables and cold frames. All is new and in perfect order. Dwelling house and out buildings on the place. The location is excellent, 40 minutes from New York City Hall. Address, X. Y., care The Florists' Exchange.

WANTED SALESMEN

For Nursery stock. For Southern New York, Penna., New Jersey, and Conn. Men of experience, and having some knowledge of Landscape work. Must be hustlers and well recommended. For an old established Nursery. Good pay to those who are satisfactory. Address with particulars,

SALESMEN, care Florists' Exchange

Mention the Florists' Exchange when writing.

AN established nursery and greenhouse business, with retail flower and landscape departments, located in the far East, desires the services of a young man possessing a general knowledge of gardening. Applicant should have a pleasing address and a fairly good education. Whilst capital is not an absolute essential, there will exist every opportunity to become a partner in this business, therefore, preference will be given to those who, if satisfied with the outlook, would be in a position to invest up to about $10,000. To a person with a desire to go abroad (China and Japan) this advertisement offers peculiar opportunities. Address with fullest particulars, T. B., care The Florists' Exchange.

SEEDSMEN WANTED

Several Men experienced in all branches of the business; capable of waiting upon Customers, but this experience not entirely essential. State full particulars and wages wanted. Applications considered up to Dec. 15th.

RENNIE & THOMSON

135-137 WASHINGTON ST., PROVIDENCE, R. I.

Mention the Florists' Exchange when writing.

MISCELLANEOUS WANTS

WANTED TO BUY—Greenhouses to be taken down. State full particulars of same when writing. Address, F. W., care The Florists' Exchange.

FOR SALE OR RENT

FOR SALE—An established retail business, located in Jersey City. Reason for selling, wish to leave the city. For full particulars address, A. T., care The Florists' Exchange.

FOR SALE—Five greenhouses with 7500 sq. ft. of glass and two boilers; stocked with commercial plants in city of over 25,000 inhabitants. Price, $2,250.00. Address, J. H. Lahm, Hazleton, Pa.

FOR SALE—Garden and seven greenhouses, 10,000 sq. ft. of glass, and a nine roomed dwelling on the premises. In a neighborhood where you can do business and save money. For particulars write to Arthur H. Larser, Wayne, Del. Co., Pa.

FOR RENT—A greenhouse establishment, several greenhouses and large plot of ground; all in good condition and partly stocked. Located in Central Pennsylvania coal region. Coal very cheap also natural gas. Can sell all that can be raised at good prices. Old age reason for wanting to rent. Address, X. T., care The Florists' Exchange.

FOR SALE—A well established florist business, with dwelling houses. Also plenty of outdoor ground in up-to-date condition. Greenhouses are well filled with foliage plants, and the place is in a most desirable location to reach the wholesale New York City trade within a drive of about 30 minutes. It must be seen. Reason for selling; ill health. For particulars communicate with O. V. Zangen, Seedsmen, Hoboken, N. J.

A SNAP IF TAKEN AT ONCE—Greenhouses and Dwelling house newly remodelled, well stocked with carnations, roses, bedding plants and vegetables. No competition, only place in town of 3,000 inhabitants, no other house nearer than twenty miles, plenty of ground, and patients at Keeley Institute insuring steady paying trade. Owner has other business. Price $4,000, including Winter supply of fuel. J. C. Nelson, Proprietor, Dwight, Ill.

FOR SALE

Des Moines, Iowa, wholesale and retail greenhouse establishment, 29,000 feet of glass, three acres of ground, well located, all in good order, with good wholesale and retail trade. Price, about $8,400; terms reasonable.

VAUGHAN'S SEED STORE

CHICAGO

Mention the Florists' Exchange when writing.

FOR SALE

A well equipped place, consisting of seven greenhouses, over 30,000 feet of glass, a nine roomed house, barn, stock, etc., and eight acres of land. This is a decided bargain and a rare opportunity. For particulars address

S. S. SKIDELSKY,

824 N. 24th St., Philadelphia, Pa.

Mention the Florists' Exchange when writing.

STOCK FOR SALE

100,000 greenhouse grown Asparagus Plumosus Nanus seed; ready about Dec. 15, $4.00 per 1,000. Joseph Wood, Spring Valley, N. Y.

WHITE AND YELLOW BONNAFFON, Black Hawk, Enguehard and Maud Dean chrysanthemums. 75c. per doz.; $5.00 per 100. A. D. Egolf, Lansdowne, Pa.

CYCLAMEN plants for Christmas sales, in 5 and 6 in. pots, $6.00 and $9.00 per doz. Selling fast, so place your orders early. Safe arrival guaranteed. Geo. A. Rackham, 880 Van Dyke Av., Detroit, Mich.

ENGLISH PRIZE PANSY PLANTS—I have 10,000 fine plants more than I need. For sale at $3.00 per 1000, cash. Some very odd and beautiful markings among them. Reuben Powell, Florist, White Plains, N. Y.

BABY RAMBLER ROSES, fine dormant stock, one year, $12.00 per 100; 2 1-4-in. pot plants, extra well rooted, $4.00 per 100; $30.00 per 1,000. Orders booked for delivery now or any time up to late Spring. Samples free. Brown Brothers Company, Rochester, N. Y.

SURPLUS STOCK OF SEEDS—Calliopsis, (California Sunbeams), Golden Fleece; Dahlia Monarch, mixed; Eschscholtzia, Golden West; Freesia, Geranium, Good Venture; Heliotrope, Lemoines'; Ipomea, Heavenly Blue, White Tassel; Nasturtium, Butterfly, Jupiter, Saturn, mixed; Poppy, Fayal, Irresistible, Maid of the Mist; Tacsonia Buchananii. Write for prices. Theodosia B. Shepherd Co., W. H. Francis, Mgr., Ventura, Cal.

HOW TO GROW MUSHROOMS

Price, . . . 10 cents.

A. T. De La Mare Ptg. & Pub. Co.

2-8 Duane St. New York.

Thirty cents is the minimum charge for advertisements on this page.

FOR SALE

FOR SALE—Second-hand, four-inch, cast-iron pipe, hubs cleaned and in good order. Address, Wm. G. Grimm, Cedar Lane, Woodhaven, L. I.

FOR SALE—One No. 5 Lord & Burnham boiler, used very little, therefore practically new; price, $47.50. N. Gelb, 220 Livingston St., Newark, N. J.

BOILERS BOILERS BOILERS.

SEVERAL good second-hand boilers on hand, also new No. 16 Hitchings at reduced cost. Write for list. Wm. H. Lutton, West Side Avenue Station, C. R. R. of N. J., Jersey City, N. J.

FOR SALE GREENHOUSE PIPE

4-inch boiler tubes, second hand, in fine condition, absolutely free from scale and with ends cut square. Sample and prices on application.

KROESCHELL BROS. CO., 33 Erie St. Chicago.

Mention the Florists' Exchange when writing.

NOTICE

To be sold immediately at great sacrifice, florists' delivery outfit, consisting of two top wagons, three open wagons, two horses with harness, one rubber-tired surrey; all in fine condition. An exceptional opportunity. Apply,

EDWARD HIGGINGS

1 West 28th St. - N. Y. CITY

Mention the Florists' Exchange when writing.

FOR SALE

BOILERS No. 6 Weathered, round, $80.00. One 11 section Sunray hot water sectional boiler, grate 3 by 3. Price $160.00. New Henderson boilers; send for price on size wanted. One No. 867 Lord & Burnham hot water boiler, 7 sections, 38 in. grate, heat 8,000 sq. ft. of glass, used one season, price $150.00, guaranteed.

PIPE Good serviceable second hand. No Junk, with new threads. 2 in. 7c.; 1½ in. 5½c.; 1¼ in. 4c.; 1 in. 3c.; 2½ in. 10c.; 3 in. 14c.; 4 in. 18c. 4 in. cast iron greenhouse 14c. 2 in. NEW, standard, full lengths, 9½c. ft. All kinds of fittings for 4 in. cast iron and all sizes wrought iron.

STOCKS AND DIES New Economy, easy working. No. 1 cuts ¼-¾-1 in. $3.00; No. 2 cuts 1¼-1½-2 ins. $4.00; Armstrong Adjustable No. 2 cuts ¼-1 in. $4.00; No. 3 cuts 1¼-1½-2 ins. $6.50.

PIPE CUTTERS Saunders, No. 1 cuts to 1 in. $1.00; No. 2 cuts to 2 in. $1.30; No. 3 cuts to 3 in. $2.00; No. 4 cuts to 4 in. $4.50.

STILLSON WRENCHES Guaranteed. 12 in., grips 1½ in. $1.10; 18 in., grips 2 in. $1.50; 24 in., grips 2½ in. $2.25; 36 in., grips 3½ in. $4.50.

PIPE VISES Reed's Best Hinged Vise, No. 1 grips 2 in. $1.75; No. 2 grips 4 in. $3.00.

GARDEN HOSE 50 ft. lengths ¾ in., guaranteed; 8c.; for heavy work, guaranteed; 12½c.

HOT-BED SASH New; Gulf Cypress, 3 ft x 6 ft. 80c.; glazed complete $1.60 up. Second hand sash glazed $1.00 and $1.36, good condition.

GLASS New American, 50 ft. to the box. 10x12 single at $1.90. 10x12, 12x12 10x15 B double $2.65. 12x14 to 12x20 and 14x14 to 14x20 B double $2.85. 16x16 and 16x18 B double $2.95. 16x20 to 16 x 24 double $3.20 per box 6x8, 7x9, 8x10 old, single $1.50. 8 x 10 and 8x14 old, double $1.85. 12 x 14 old single $1.75.

PLATE GLASS MIRROR with white enameled frame 3x7, price $12.00.

Get our prices on second hand wood material. We can furnish everything in new material to erect any size house. Get our prices.

METROPOLITAN MATERIAL CO.

Greenhouse Wreckers

1398-1408 Metropolitan Avenue, BROOKLYN, N.Y

Mention the Florists' Exchange when writing.

THE CHRYSANTHEMUM

Arthur Herrington's New Book

The most complete and comprehensive work on the cultivation of the Chrysanthemum that has as yet been published in America. Handsomely illustrated, 168 pages, 5 x 7 inches. Price only 50 cents, postpaid.

SEND YOUR ORDER FOR A COPY NOW.

A. T. De La Mare Ptg. & Pub. Co., Ltd.

J. SELIGMAN **JOSEPH J. LEVY**

When we review the past year, we feel like covering this space with CHRISTMAS GREETINGS to our fellow-craftsmen. It has been a prosperous and an eventful year, yet it is only the shadow of what we hope and expect to accomplish

During the Next Twelve Months

We Have Lots of Room for More Growers

We Can Sell to YOUR ADVANTAGE

Everything You Grow

TRY US AND BE CONVINCED

Remember the Address—DIRECTLY OPPOSITE THE NEW YORK CUT FLOWER COMPANY

JOHN SELIGMAN & CO.

56 West 26th Street, NEW YORK

Telephone—4878 Madison Square

The most convenient Cut Flower Headquarters in NEW YORK

Open every day in the year at 6 A. M.

POINSETTIAS

FOR THE HOLIDAYS

WE HAVE a reputation for supplying the **Choicest Poinsettias** shipped out of the Chicago market. Our grower is **"Right in Line"** again this year. **Place your order now.** $2.00, $3.00 and $4.00 per doz. We also anticipate having a good supply of all kinds of **Christmas Cutflowers**—get in touch with us now. It will pay you.

Headquarters for **Bouquet Green, Evergreen Wreathing, Holly Wreaths, Fancy Holly, Artificial Poinsettias,** (sample mailed for 25c).

COMPLETE HOLIDAY CIRCULAR MAILED FREE

E. F. WINTERSON CO.

45-47-49 Wabash Ave. **CHICAGO, ILL.**

The

Florists' Supply House of America

can take care of all your wants for the holiday trade and make prompt shipment.

Red Immortelle Wreaths. **Ruscus Wreaths.**

Statice Wreaths. There will be a large demand for these, as The Ladies' Home Journal devoted their first cover page to an illustration of this wreath.

Magnolia Wreaths. With or without flowers.

Loose Laurel and **Magnolia Leaves** in original baskets, to make up your own designs.

Waterproof Crepe Paper. All colors.

Pleated Waterproof Crepe Paper. In all shades.

Folding Paper Christmas Bells. We have a large stock; our sizes, 6, 9 and 12 in.

We have better facilities and can give prompt attention to all orders. Send for catalogue.

H. Bayersdorfer & Co.,

1129 Arch Street, Philadelphia, Pa.

REVIEW OF THE MARKET

NEW YORK.—Supplies of roses of all varieties are anything but heavy this week, and prices are moderately firm all around. Carnations are clearing out fairly well, with little change in values from last week's quotations. There has been a decided decrease in the consignments of chrysanthemums, and it is generally conceded that the season of these flowers this year has been a fairly good one so far as prices go.

Paper White narcissus and Roman hyacinths are getting more plentiful every day, as also are lilies and callas. Lily of the valley is rather short at times, and there have been occasions when $5 per 100 has been realized.

Gardenias are scarce, and prices are a trifle higher. The extreme cold weather has harmed the violet sales very much, and although the supply cannot be called heavy, prices have a downward tendency.

CHICAGO.—Thanksgiving has come and gone and it has left regrets to both the grower and wholesaler. The past scarcity of carnations having caused dealers to put up the price to such an extent that many growers, and most of those who keep in touch with quotations in trade papers, went through the old practice of "pickling," and as a result there was a hard fall in prices and some of the "pickles" were to be seen on tables as late as Monday of this week. Tea roses were in crop with most growers about Chicago, consequently there was a tendency toward a glut, although good stock moved off with a little shading of prices. Violets were extremely shy in supply up to two days before Thanksgiving, when large arrivals required forced sales to move them, some dealers reporting the lowest prices of the season, and even these did not clean up stocks. American Beauty roses were in abundance, but the demand was good and fair prices were obtained. Chrysanthemums were plentiful, but sold well; however, the prices generally obtained were not up to the mark for holiday time by any means. Plenty of greens abounded, with an especially healthy call for boxwood, which is coming into more popular favor daily. W. K. W.

PHILADELPHIA.—The market has been decidedly in favor of the grower the past week; but the grower has not had sufficient stock to fill all orders, as a consequence prices are firmer. American Beauty roses are not in supply to meet all demands; $6 per dozen is obtained for the best stock. All varieties of tea roses are in short supply; $12.00 per 100 is asked for the best. A few specials have sold at $15. Quite a lot of inferior stock is offered. The greatest demand has been for white this week. Carnations are getting better in quality every week; the very best Enchantress are selling at $6 per 100, with $3 to $5 for other stock. Double violets are still scarce, and the commission men have to divide up their consignments among regular buyers; $1.50 per 100 is the regular price. The large singles are selling well at 75c. and $1 per 100.

Bouvardia is being used much more freely than in former years; white sells at $4 per 100 and pink at $3. Cattleyas are in strong demand and the supply does not quite meet it; 60c. per flower is obtained. A few Dendrobium formosum and D. Phalænopsis are coming in. Paper White narcissus and Roman hyacinths are both more plentiful, selling at $3 to $4 per 100.
DAVID RUST.

BOSTON.—With cooler weather business has increased. Thanksgiving trade all around was the best ever known in this city. A stormy day preceding the holiday somewhat spoiled the near-by trade; but all kinds of stock were cleaned up. Colored flowers went better than white; especially was this so in the case of carnations. Prices advanced somewhat and they have continued fairly firm. American Beauty of the better grades bring from $1.50 to $6 per dozen; other roses $2 to $8 per 100. Some fancy varieties like Richmond, Killarney, Wellesley, Mrs. Pierpont Morgan and Mrs. Oliver Ames realize $2 per dozen. Colored carnations bring from $3 to $5; white go slowly at $2 and $3. Chrysanthemums realize from $2 to $12, with some fancy sorts at $2 per dozen. Major Bonnaffon has been in most demand for a yellow. Mignonette sells at $2, $3 and $4 with some fancy still higher. Lily of the valley brings $3 to $5. Sweet peas are plentiful at $1. Violets sell well at 75c. and $1; lilies, $1.50 and $2 per dozen. Paper White narcissus are plentiful at $2. J. W. D.

INDIANAPOLIS.—Not much enthusiasm is displayed regarding Thanksgiving trade, as if anything business was not up to last year's. The pleasant unseasonable weather of Wednesday and Thursday is held accountable for the decrease; sales were numerous, but large orders were scarce. Most customers were contented with a dozen carnations, a half-dozen roses, or three or four large chrysanthemums. Prices on Wednesday were much lower than the week previous. The poor sale of violets surprised every one; many hundreds were left on the retailers' hands. The retail price of $3 per 100 seemed prohibitive for the quality of the stock offered; $2 per 100 wholesale was the general quotation. Carnations while they outsold all other flowers did not meet expectations; $4 per 100 was the highest price paid for home-grown stock, so it will be readily realized that not many were brought from Chicago and other large centers where the price was as high as $6 per 100 for fancy and $4 per 100 for medium. One dollar per dozen was generally asked by the retailers. Chrysanthemums found many buyers at $2 to $3 a dozen, but as stated sales were more often made by the flower than by the dozen. In roses, Bridesmaid, Richmond and American Beauty led; the latter rose brought $3 to $9; Richmond and Liberty, $2 to $3, and Bride and Bridesmaid, $1.50 to $2 a dozen. Lily of the valley was on hand by hundreds, but little demnd for it was experienced. A few poinsettias sold well; this date is rather early for them. A limited number of Paper White narcissus and Roman hyacinths wholesaled at $4 per 100.

Plants, with the exception of small chrysanthemums, did not go as they should have done. Fine Begonia Gloire de Lorraine, cyclamen, and other plants were on hand but did not sell well.

Since Thursday, business has been exceptionally brisk, in fact some days more trade is done than when great preparations have been made. I. B.

ST. LOUIS.—Thanksgiving trade was good this year; everybody seems satisfied with it. The only complaint heard is that stock was too high priced. There was some pickling done, but this stock was set aside until the other was disposed of, and then it brought very little. Our four wholesalers had plenty of flowers in all grades, and were well cleaned out after the local and shipping orders had been filled. Most of the chrysanthemums are over, except a few late varieties, of which there are some good bloms which bring $3 per dozen. Carnations are in full crop, and the demand all that can be expected; Mrs. T. W. Lawson is not so good this season, and the best do not bring over $4. The best seller is Enchantress, fancy bringing as high as $5 per 100. Extra good red are scarce; Robert Craig are limited in number. All white varieties are plentiful. The average price this week is about $3 per 100. The market is well supplied with the lesser grades of roses; extra fancy are not so plentiful. Bride and Bridesmaid fetch $2 to $4; extra fancy $5 and $6; same prices for Richmond, Souvenir du President Carnot, Killarney and Perle des Jardins. American Beauty, long fancy, bring $4 to $5 a dozen; $2 to $3 for medium, and shorts 50c. to $1; of these latter there are none too many.

Bulbous stock is coming in more freely; Roman hyacinths and Paper White narcissus are as yet limited at $3 and $4 per 100. Lily of the valley realizes $4 and $5 for extra fine; stevia, $1 per 100.

Greens are in good supply in everything except common ferns, which have advanced to 20c. per 100.
ST. PATRICK.

BUFFALO.—Business last week was exceedingly satisfactory. All the local florists report trade very good for Thanksgiving. Chrysanthemums have been selling well this season, especially for Thanksgiving, retailing at from $2 to $7.50 per dozen. Carnations still remain very scarce. Enchantress, Red Lawson are the best varieties arriving in the market. Carnations are retailing at $1 per dozen. Roses are not any too plentiful, and the quality is not up to standard. Bride, Bridesmaid and Souvenir du President Carnot bring from $1 to $2 retail. Liberty and Richmond range from $1 to $3. American Beauty still sell spasmodically bringing anywhere from $2 to $9 retail. Violets sell well at $2 to $3 per hundred retail. Cattleyas find a ready sale, retailing at $1 per flower. Lily of the valley goes briskly at $1 to $2 per bunch of 25 at retail. W. H. G.

COLUMBUS, O.—While our great preparations for the Thanksgiving business did not result in the enormous volume of trade many of us had hoped for, still we did a large trade and disposed, at good prices, of a lot of stock. The general verdict seems to be that our holiday trade was about a good average one. This the writer feels was good under the circumstances of not very propitious Thanksgiving weather. It did not storm, but it was cold, raw, and overcast the whole week. Chrysanthemums never before were in such demand; they ruled the market. Even our best American Beauty roses were overshadowed by them. The chrysanthemums in best form were Golden Wedding, W. H. Chadwick, Major Bonnaffon, and Jeannie Nonin. Just a word about this last-named sort. For Thanksgiving certainly it has no superior. Of the largest size, perfectly globular, finely finished, and such a fine keeper and shipper, this variety is surely queen of the commercial whites. Its color is very pure, in fact, from every point of view it is hard to beat. The best stock of these and other chrysanthemums brought $4 to $5 per dozen; a very few special flowers were noted that sold up to 75c. each. On the other hand, large quantities of chrysanthemums were sold to over the counter trade at from $2 to $3 a dozen. American Beauty roses always sell, but this year there was no great boom in them; they went to customers at $4, $5, $6, and $8 per dozen for 20, 24, 30, and 36-inch stems respectively. Other roses realized $1.50 to $2 a dozen for white and pink varieties; red roses brought $2 to $2.50 the dozen. Carnations did not sell with the rush of past years; they were too high in price to catch the crowd. When we pay up to $6 a hundred for them, it always means slow sales. When we can sell carnations at not exceeding 75c. a dozen they go fast; this year $1 was the going price. Violets sold at $1 a 50 bunch for Marie Louise, and $1.25 for Princess of Wales. Both kinds found good sales. Other stock brought good holiday prices.

In regard to plants, a goodly number were sold; but Thanksgiving is not an especially active time for plant sales. Most of the trade kept open until noon on Thanksgiving Day filling orders, and with a few it was evening before the last customer had been given attention. F. W.

CINCINNATI.—Thanksgiving trade was equal to last year's, which was the best had for that day. Stock, with the exception of roses, moved nicely. When I say roses I mean Bride and Bridesmaid; Richmond, American Beauty and some Bridesmaid did well, but white were not wanted in roses for Thanksgiving. The sale of white carnations had to be forced. Chrysanthemums sold out clean; they are in great demand now, with but few coming into the market, and these sell at sight. Carnations are not plentiful by any means. Paper White narcissus are making their appearance and will be good stock from now on. Violets are scarce and many more could be used; 50c., 75c. and $1 per 100 is the price they fetch. The best American Beauty roses sell at $5 per dozen; shorter grades in proportion.

Nothing new to report in the way of news. J. A. Peterson has a grand lot of Begonia Gloire de Lorraine in full bloom for Christmas. I am afraid that stock will be scarce, but we trust our growers will tell us what we may expect. If they would only do this, it would be dollars and cents in their pockets. E. G. G.

KALAMAZOO, MICH.—Thanksgiving business proved to be very satisfactory to all concerned. There was plenty of stock of all grades. Roses and chrysanthemums of a very fair grade were offered as low as 50c. per dozen; and a similar quality of carnations at 40c. per dozen, which prices certainly gave the buyers full value for their money and possibly also established a record for low values at this season in this city. Chrysanthemums in pots were offered as low as 25c. However inquiries indicate that the bulk of business done was in the better grades, and satisfaction is generally expressed at the volume of trade done at medium and higher prices. The cheap lots cleared up the stocks nicely, and from now on prices should rule better. Chrysanthemums here are about all out. This season the quality has been above the average and the flowers have proved good sellers though at moderate prices, and I doubt if they have been as profitable as they ought. Roses suffered considerably in value during the chrysanthemum season, much more so than carnations, which owing to light cuts were held at good prices right along, and these conditions are likely to prevail for some time, as the varieties now grown do not produce like the old-timers we used to grow, though I regret to say prices have not advanced in accordance. Indeed, as a large grower recently remarked, we must get more for them or soon we will be losing money growing carnations. Personal experience endorses this opinion.

As usual at this season the soft coal burners are experiencing difficulty in obtaining supplies with any degree of promptness. S. B.

MINNEAPOLIS.—Business has been very good the past week. Thanksgivnig Day it was exceptionally good, not only in the city, but a vast improvement was also evident in country business. Stock supplies have kept up remarkably well; we could use a great many home-grown roses, but it appears that nearly all varieties are off crop. Chrysanthemums come in nicely and in a great many instances are sold in preference to roses. It is noticeable, however, that the growers are not bringing in anywhere near as many as they did a week ago. American Beauty roses have sold a great deal better, and at a good price.

Some very fine Richmond and Killarney have been shipped in which went readily at $2 and $2.50 per dozen, while ordinary stock could not command more than $1.50 per dozen. Carnations are much improved in quality, some very nice Enchantress and Lady Bountiful coming in. No violets to speak of are grown in this vicinity this year, consequently the dealers are all using Eastern stock, which it seems loses its fragrance before it reaches us. PAUL.

PROVIDENCE, R. I.—Not in several years have the florists here been so thoroughly cleaned out of flowers as they were the first part of this week. There could not be bought $20 worth of first-class stock in all the flower stores Monday evening, owing to the extraordinary business done at Thanksgiving and the funeral of our late Mayor Elisha Dyer. Several society events also occurred Monday which gave the stores such a thorough cleaning out that they are not liable to recover from it until after New Year's. For Thanksgiving there was an abundance of all kinds of seasonable flowers except carnations. Chrysanthemums were very much the leading flower and brought from $3 to $6 retail per dozen. First-class carnations were very scarce, bringing at retail from $1 to $2 per dozen; the cheapest carnations sold for 75c. per dozen. Violets were plentiful and of very good quality, averaging $1 per hundred wholesale. Tea roses of about all the good kinds were abundant and brought from $8 to $12 wholesale. Paper White narcissus were very plentiful at from $2 to $3 per 100. Lily of the valley fetched $4 per 100. G. A. J.

FIRMS WHO ARE BUILDING

MONROE, N. Y.—Jonah R. Brooke is building a greenhouse, 100x16 feet.

HASTINGS, NEB.—C. W. Sidles has completed another greenhouse and installed a new steam heating plant.

JUNCTION CITY, KAN.—W P. Ranson has completed a house containing 1000 square feet of glass.

OAKTON, VA.—W. R. Gray has recently built a 16 by 100 foot greenhouse.

The second bowling match between the Morris County Gardeners and Florists' Society and the seedsmen of New York was played on the allays of the Press Club in this city on Saturday, December 1. The individual scores were as follows:

NEW YORK SEEDSMEN.

Al. Rickards	141	205	180
W. Rickards	112	141	164
L. W. Wheeler	146	131	86
A. Protin	182	161	167
B. Chadwick	169	193	189
Total	750	831	786

MADISON GROWERS.

Herrington	141	206	180
Totty	109	121	109
Schulz	94	165	124
Kating	223	148	145
Duckham	189	219	181
Total	756	858	739

The third game will be played in New Jersey some time in the near future.

It is worth a great deal to you to know that your orders will be filled with carefully selected stock, properly packed

You can have this assurance by dealing with

WALTER F. SHERIDAN

WHOLESALE DEALER IN

CUT FLOWERS

39 West 28th Street, New York

TELEPHONE—3532 3533 MADISON SQUARE

Telephone 3559 Madison Sq.

We do business on the level and act on the square

NOTICE!

A. L. YOUNG & CO.

Wholesale Florists, 54 West 28th Street,
Receivers and Shippers of Choice Cut Flowers.

New York, Dec 8, 1906

To Growers :—

We need a greater quantity of stock to supply the demands of our increasing trade and desire to communicate with growers of good stock and will make very favorable terms to you. We are wholesale Florists: goods contracted for, bought for cash or sold on commission, by the thousand or ten thousand. Write us what you have, and make us a shipment, and we will write you at once highest market value.

We have ample accommodations for large shipments and have everything conveniently arranged for receiving and handling goods with facility and dispatch and selling same promptly and satisfactorily. Our location is unsurpassed.

Are you looking for a place where there is a real outlet for your goods? Where they will be sold quickly and for your best advantage? Where you will get your returns at once and in full and where care and attention will be paid to all details? Then we are the people, for we can assure you that is our constant aim.

Let us hear from you at once.

Yours very truly,

A. L. Young & Co.

WE are receiving and *can ship* the best **Carnations, Roses, Beauties** and **Violets** in *New York Market.* We have **Lilies, Asparagus, Poinsettias** and **Lily of the Valley** from the best growers who ship to this city. We can furnish **Carnations** and **Violets** that cannot be equaled in any market.

FORD BROS.,

Wholesale

COMMISSION FLORISTS,

48 West 28th Street,
NEW YORK.

Telephones—3870-3871 Madison Square

New Orleans, La.

News Notes.

U. J. Virgin, who is moving his greenhouse establishment from St. Charles avenue to Canal street, is just putting the finishing touches to his six houses, each 150 feet long, of various widths. These houses are built on a concrete foundation, the first Southern establishment to use this method of construction. Mr. Virgin has installed a Kroeschell boiler with which he is well pleased. In spite of the fact of the greenhouses having to be torn down and moved such a distance and rebuilt, his plants look in the pink of perfection. He has an excellent stock of palms and other plants for decorative purposes. One large house is devoted entirely to Asparagus plumosus; another to Harrisii lilies and callas, and the balance to an assortment of stock which he uses at his store.

M. M. Lapouyade, who is located on Bienville street, has a fine stock which he grows for the market. His specialty is outdoor roses which he propagates by the Southern style of layering. From the appearance of his plants his soil must be well adapted for rose culture. He also has a nice stock of a long-leaved variety of Adiantum capillus veneris, which the writer considers to be the A. c. v. magnificum of Nicholson. It is certainly a fine thing for this climate. He also has a fine bench of carnations which he has carried over the Summer—an unusual thing for this latitude.

That old established florist, J. H. Menard, is also stocked up well for the Winter. Mr. Menard does a fine market trade, and also retails from the home establishment. He has a nice bed of Asparagus plumosus growing in the open ground. He says it would be hard to realize the number of sprays this bed has given, and it still looks so well that he is going to cover it with glass to protect it from the cold, which usually does not reach us until the beginning of the year.

CRESCENT CITY.

Boston.

News of the Week.

The committee on children's gardens of the Massachusetts Horticultural Society announce a school garden conference on Saturday afternoon, December 15 at 2 o'clock. Addresses will be made by Geo. H. Martin on the "Educational Value of School Gardens;" by F. A. Waugh on "Horticultural Education for School Garden Teachers;" by W. A. Baldwin on "School Gardens and Normal Schools;" and by Frank M. Marsh on "Children's Gardens and the Public."

At the next meeting of the Gardeners and Florists' Club December 18, Winsor H. Wyman of the Bay State Nurseries will speak on "Craft and the Craftsman."

Robert Cameron of the Harvard Botanical Gardens will deliver an illustrated lecture on "A Winter Trip through the West Indies" at the quarterly meeting of the New England Cemetery Association, to be held at the New American House, Monday, December 10.

Henry M. Robinson & Company are doing quite a trade in the wholesale cut flower line, which they recently added to their business. They have a large supply of Christmas evergreens on hand for the holiday trade.

J. W. D.

J. K. ALLEN
holesale Commission Dealer in **Cut Flowers**
106 West 28th St., NEW YORK
pen at 6 a. m. every day.
Telephone, 167 Madison Square.
Consignments Solicited.
ntion the Florists' Exchange when writing.

Wm. Stuart Allen Co.
ommission Merchan's in CUT FLOWERS
ORCHIDS AT ALL SEASONS
3 WEST 28th STREET, NEW YORK
Telephone 356 Madison Square
ntion the Florists' Exchange when writing.

C. BONNET G. H. BLAKE
BONNET & BLAKE
Wholesale Florists
6 Livingston Street, BROOKLYN, N. Y.
Telephone: 4638 Main.
Consignments solicited. Out-of-town orders carefully attended to. Give us a trial.
ntion the Florists' Exchange when writing.

UT FLOWER EXCHANGE
Sixth Ave. and 26th St.
oogan Building, NEW YORK
Open every Morning at Six o'clock for the Sale of Cut Flowers.
Wall Space for advertising purposes to Rent.
V. S. DORVAL, Jr., Secretary.
ntion the Florists' Exchange when writing.

Joseph S. Fenrich
...Wholesale Florist...
—THE RELIABLE HOUSE—
10 West 28th Street
Telephone 324-325 Madison Square.
ntion the Florists' Exchange when writing.

FORD BROS.
Wholesale Florists
48 WEST 28th ST., NEW YORK
Telephone, 3870-3871 Madison Square
ention the Florists' Exchange when writing.

GROWERS, ATTENTION!
Always Ready to Receive Fine Stock
GUNTHER BROTHERS
30 West 29th Street
hone, 551 Madison Square. NEW YORK
iolets, Roses, Carnations, Orchids
Established 1888.
ention the Florists' Exchange when writing.

A. M. HENSHAW
Wholesale Commission Florist.
onsignments of first class stock solicited. Prompt returns.
THE SQUARE DEAL
Guaranteed to all who trade here.
52 West 28th Street, NEW YORK
el. 5583 Madison Square.
ention the Florists' Exchange when writing.

HICKS & CRAWBUCK, Inc.
Wholesale Florists
And Dealers in FLORISTS' SUPPLIES
76-78 Court Street
Phone 3660-3661 Main BROOKLYN, N. Y.
ention the Florists' Exchange when writing.

PHILIP F. KESSLER
Wholesale Florist
55-57 W. 26th St., NEW YORK.
Telephone, 2921-5243 Madison Square.
ention the Florists' Exchange when writing.

HEADQUARTERS FOR NOVELTIES
ORCHIDS A SPECIALTY
THE HIGHEST GRADE OF **VALLEY** ALWAYS ON HAND
GARDENIAS, DAISIES, ROSES, CARNATIONS.
JAMES McMANUS, Telephone 759 Mad. Sq. 42 W. 28th St., New York.

WILLIAM H. KUEBLER
Wholesale Commission Dealer in
CUT FLOWERS
28 Willoughby St.,
Telephone 4591 Main BROOKLYN, N. Y.
Mention the Florists' Exchange when writing.

FRANK MILLANG
Wholesale Commission Dealer in
CUT FLOWERS
55-57 West 26th Street, New York
Telephone Call: 299 Madison Square.
Mention the Florists' Exchange when writing.

Alexander J. Guttman
THE WHOLESALE FLORIST OF NEW YORK
43 WEST 28th STREET
PHONES, 1664--1665 MADISON SQUARE
ENOUGH SAID

ALFRED H. LANGJAHR
55 WEST 28th STREET, NEW YORK
Telephone, 4626-4627 Madison Square Established 1891
SPECIAL VALLEY AND TOP GRADE ASPARAGUS
Consignments of First Class Stock Solicited.

Horace E. Froment
SUCCESSOR TO
W. GHORMLEY WHOLESALE COMMISSION FLORIST
Receiver and Shipper of all varieties of Cut Flowers
Telephones, 2200 and 2201 Madison Square. 57 West 28th St., NEW YORK

Wholesale Prices of Cut Flowers, New York, Dec. 5, 1906

Prices quoted are by the hundred unless otherwise noted

Roses: A Beauty, fancy—special	40.00 to 60.00
" extra	20.00 to 25.00
" No. 1	12.00 to 15.00
" No. 2	6.00 to 8.00
" No. 3	5.00 to 6.00
Bride, Maid, fancy—spe'l	8.00 to 12.00
" extra	6.00 to 8.00
" No. 1	5.00 to 6.00
" No. 2	3.00 to 4.00
Golden Gate	3.00 to 12.00
Richmond	3.00 to 12.00
Mme. Abel Chatenay	3.00 to 12.00
Adiantum	.50 to .75
Croweanum	1.00 to 1.25
Asparagus	25.00 to 50.00
" Plumosus, bunches	6.00 to 15.00
" Sprengerii, bunches	8.00 to 15.00
......	...... to ......
Callas	10.00 to 12.00
Cattleyas	40.00 to 75.00
Cypripediums	...... to 12.50
Daisies	...... to ......

Carnations: Inf'r grades, all colors	2.00 to 2.50
Standard Varieties: White	2.50 to 3.00
Pink	2.50 to 3.00
Red	2.50 to 3.00
Yel. & Var.	2.50 to 3.00
*Fancy— (*The highest grades of standard var.) White	3.00 to 4.00
Pink	3.00 to 5.00
Red	3.00 to 5.00
Yel. & Var.	3.00 to 5.00
Novelties	5.00 to 8.00
Chrysanthemums	2.00 to 6.00
" Fancy	10.00 to 35.00
Gardenias, per doz.	3.00 to 6.00
Lilies	8.00 to 12.00
Lily of the Valley	2.00 to 4.00
Mignonette	...... to ......
Narcissus, Paper White	...... to 2.00
Roman Hyacinths	2.00 to 3.00
Smilax	8.00 to 12.00
Violets	.60 to 1.00

WALTER F. SHERIDAN
Wholesale Florist
Tel. 3532-3533 Mad. Sq. 39 WEST 28TH ST., NEW YORK
ALL VARIETIES OF CUT FLOWERS IN SEASON

TOP GRADE FOR SHIPPING
American Beauty, Bridesmaid, Bride, Liberty, Lilies, Lily of the Valley, Carnations
Telephone, 1998 Madison Square JOHN I. RAYNOR, 49 West 28th St., NEW YORK

Edw. C. Horan
55 West 28th St., NEW YORK
TELEPHONE, 1462-1463 MADISON SQUARE
CUT FLOWERS AT WHOLESALE
Mention The Florists' Exchange when writing.

JOHN YOUNG
Wholesale Florist
51 W. 28th St., NEW YORK
Telephone: 4463-4464 Madison Square
Mention the Florists' Exchange when writing.

MOORE, HENTZ & NASH
WHOLESALE
GROWER AGENT
COMMISSION FLORISTS
55 West 26th St., New York
Telephone Call, 756 Madison Square
Mention the Florists' Exchange when writing.

A. MOLTZ
Wholesale Florist
55-57 West 26th St., NEW YORK
1st Floor. Telephone, 2921-5243 Madison Sq.
Mention the Florists' Exchange when writing.

GEORGE SALTFORD
Wholesale Florist
CONSIGNMENTS SOLICITED
46 West 29th Street, New York
Telephone: [illegible] Madison Square
Mention the Florists' Exchange when writing.

J. Seligman Joseph J. Levy
JOHN SELIGMAN & COMPANY
Wholesale Florists
56 West 26th Street.
Tel. 4878 Madison Square, N. Y.
Opposite New York Cut Flower Company
Mention the Florists' Exchange when writing.

B. S. SLINN, JR.
Wholesale Florist
55 and 57 West 26th Street, NEW YORK
SPECIALTIES—Violets, Carnations and Roses
Shipping orders receive prompt attention. Consignment Solicited.
Telephone: 3864 Madison Square
Mention the Florists' Exchange when writing.

WM. STARKE
Wholesale Florist and Plantsman
Tel. No. 4582 Madison Sq. 52 W. 29th St.
Between Broadway and 6th Ave., New York
Shipments of Plants made to any part of the country. A trial order solicited.
SATISFACTION GUARANTEED.
Mention the Florists' Exchange when writing.

Frank H. Traendly Charles Schenck
TRAENDLY & SCHENCK
Wholesale Florists
44 WEST 28th STREET, NEW YORK
and CUT FLOWER EXCHANGE
Telephones: 798 and 799 MADISON SQUARE
Consignments Solicited
Mention the Florists' Exchange when writing.

THOMAS YOUNG Jr.
Wholesale Florist
43 West 28th Street, NEW YORK
Telephone, 4850 Madison Square
Consignments of Choice Flowers solicited
Mention the Florists' Exchange when writing.

Wholesale Prices of Cut Flowers—Per 100

Boston Dec. 3, 1906	Buffalo Dec. 3, 1906	Detroit Nov. 25, 1906	Cincinnati Dec. 3, 1906	Baltimore Nov. 82, 1906	NAMES AND VARIETIES	Milwaukee Nov. 19, 1906	Phil'delphia Nov. 26, 1906	Pittsburg Dec. 3, 1906	St. Louis Dec. 3, 1906
30.00 to 50.00	40.00 to 50.00	to 50.00	to 60.00	to	ROSES A. BEAUTY, fancy—special	to 25.00	50.00 to 60.00	to 40.00	25.00 to 35.00
20.00 to 30.00	30.00 to 40.00	to 25.00	40.00 to 50.00	to 25.00	" extra	to 20.00	to	25.00 to 30.00	15.00 to 20.00
10.00 to 20.00	20.00 to 25.00	to 16.00	20.00 to 30.00	12.50 to 20.00	" No. 1	to 18.00	to	to 6.00	10.00 to 12.50
2.00 to 10.00	8.00 to 10.00	to 12.00	10.00 to 15.00	5.00 to 8.00	" Culls and ordinary	to 12.00	to	1.00 to 3.00	3.00 to 8.00
6.00 to 8.00	8.00 to 10.00	4.00 to 8.00	8.00 to 10.00	to 5.00	BRIDE, 'MAID, fancy-special	to 6.00	6.00 to 10.00	3.00 to 8.00	6.00 to 8.00
4.00 to 6.00	6.00 to 8.00	to	to 6.00	to 4.00	" extra	to 5.00	to	to 6.00	4.00 to 5.00
2.00 to 4.00	to	to	to 5.00	to 3.00	" No. 1	to 4.00	to	to 4.00	2.00 to 3.00
1.00 to 2.00	4.00 to 6.00	to	to 3.00	to 2.00	" No. 2	to 3.00	to	to 3.00	to
to	4.00 to 6.00	4.00 to 8.00	2.00 to 6.00	2.00 to 5.00	GOLDEN GATE	2.00 to 6.00	to	2.00 to 6.00	2.00 to 6.00
to	4.00 to 8.00	to	to	2.00 to 5.00	K. A. VICTORIA	3.00 to 6.00	to	to 8.00	2.00 to 8.00
3.00 to 10.00	4.00 to 10.00	to	to	3.00 to 5.00	LIBERTY	3.00 to 8.00	to	4.00 to 10.00	to
to	to	3.00 to 8.00	to	3.00 to 5.00	METEOR	to	to	3.00 to 8.00	to
to	4.00 to 8.00	4.00 to 10.00	to	2.00 to 4.00	PERLE	3.00 to 6.00	to	2.00 to 6.00	2.00 to 6.00
to	to	to 50.00	to	to	ORCHIDS—Cattleyas	to	to 60.00	to	to
to	to	2.00 to 4.00	to	1.00 to 1.25	CARNATIONS Inferior grades, all colors	2.00 to 4.00	2.00 to 3.00	1.00 to 1.50	1.50 to 2.50
1.50 to 2.00	2.00 to 3.00	to	2.00 to 3.00	1.50 to 2.00	Standard Varieties White	to	2.00 to 3.00	2.00 to 3.00	1.50 to 2.50
2.00 to 3.00	2.00 to 3.00	to	2.00 to 3.00	1.50 to 2.00	Standard Varieties Pink	to	2.00 to 3.00	3.00 to 4.00	1.50 to 2.50
2.00 to 3.00	2.00 to 3.00	to	2.00 to 3.00	1.50 to 2.00	Standard Varieties Red	to	2.00 to 3.00	3.(0 to 4.00	1.50 to 2.50
2.00 to 3.00	to	to	to	1.50 to 2.00	Standard Varieties Yellow and var.	to	2.00 to 3.00	to 3.00	1.50 to 2.50
2.00 to 4.00	4.00 to 5.00	to	to	2.50 to 3.00	Fancy Varieties White	to	4.00 to 5.00	to 4.00	3.00 to 4.00
3.00 to 4.00	4.00 to 6.00	to	2.00 to 4.00	2.50 to 3.00	Fancy Varieties Pink	to	4.00 to 5.00	to 5.00	3.00 to 4.00
3.00 to 4.00	4.00 to 5.00	to	3.00 to 4.00	2.50 to 3.00	Fancy Varieties Red	to	4.00 to 5.00	to 5.00	3.00 to 4.00
3.00 to 4.00	4.00 to 6.00	to	3.00 to 4.00	2.50 to 3.00	Fancy Varieties Yellow and var	to	4.00 to 5.00	to 4.00	3.00 to 4.00
5.00 to 6.00	to	to	3.00 to 4.00	to	Novelties	to	to	to	to
.75 to 1.00	.50 to 1.00	to 2.00	1.00 to 1.50	to 1.00	ADIANTUM	to	to 1.00	to 1.00	1.00 to 1.50
to 50.00	15.00 to 20.00	25.00 to 60.00	35.00 to 50.00	25.00 to 50.00	ASPARAGUS, Plum. and Ten	25.00 to 50.00	50.00 to 75.00	to 20.00	25.00 to 50.00
to	15.00 to 20.00	20.00 to 30.00	to 35.00	25.00 to 50.00	" Sprengeri, bunches	25.00 to 50.00	to 50.00	to 20.00	25.00 to 75.00
10.00 to 12.00	10.00 to 17.00	10.00 to 12.50	to	6.00 to 10.00	CALLAS	12.00 to 15.00	to	to 12.50	12.50 to 15.00
2.00 to 16.00	8.00 to 25.00	4.00 to 25.00	to 12.50	4.00 to 25.00	CHRYSANTHEMUMS	8.00 to 30.00	10.00 to 50.00	12.50 to 20.00	5.00 to 25.00
to	to	to	to	to	DAISIES	to	to	to	to
to 12.50	to	to	to	to 12.50	LILIES	to	to	12.50 to 15.00	to
3.00 to 4.00	to	3.00 to 4.00	to 4.00	to 4.00	LILY OF THE VALLEY	3.00 to 4.00	4.00 to 5.00	3.00 to 4.00	3.00 to 4.00
2.00 to 4.00	1.50 to 2.00	to	to	to	MIGNONETTE, ordinary	to	to	to	3.00 to 4.00
5.00 to 6.00	2.00 to 3.00	to	to	to	" fancy	to	to	to	to 5.00
12.50 to 15.00	to 15.00	12.50 to 15.00	to 15.00	to 20.00	SMILAX	to	to	to 15.00	12.50 to 15.00
.50 to .60	to 1.00	1.00 to 1.50	to .50	to .50	VIOLETS, ordinary	to	to	to 1.00	.40 to .50
.75 to 1.00	1.25 to 1.50	to	to 1.00	to .60	" fancy	to	to 1.50	to 1.25	.60 to .75
to	to .15	to 1.25	to .15	to	GALAX LEAVES	to	to	to	to .15

St. Louis.

News Notes.

Martin Reukauf, of H. Bayersdorfer & Company, Philadelphia, is showing us Christmas novelties this week. H. McFarland of Litchfield, Ill., spent Sunday with the Kirkwood growers; in his city he reports a good Thanksgiving trade.

Louis A. Giger is no longer connected with the Ayers Floral Company, Grand avenue.

Wm. C. Smith & Company, our new wholesalers, on Monday unloaded two carloads of pots for local growers. They had a good Thanksgiving trade.

Chas. Beyer, Schray Brothers, George Windler, Bentzen, and Jablonsky all have fine stock of blooming plants for holiday trade. Henry Berning had an unusually big Thanksgiving business, both local and shipping. Charles Kuehn was long on carnations for Thanksgiving; he had a fine stock of roses and chrysanthemums.

Fred. C. Weber showed quite a novel window display of decorated pumpkins which was very attractive.

George Augermuller disposed of a big lot of fancy long American Beauty from the South Park Floral Company; also fancy chrysanthemum blooms.

President Irish requests the members of the Florists' Club to attend the meeting, which will be held on Thursday afternoon next. This will be our last meeting in the present hall. The flower show committee's report will interest every member, as will the two discussions which will be held. This meeting will be of importance to growers who have holiday plants to sell.

ST. PATRICK.

Wholesale Prices of Cut Flowers, Chicago, Dec. 4, 1906

Prices quoted are by the hundred unless otherwise noted

ROSES — American Beauty		
36-inch stems.......per doz.	5.00 to	6.00
30-inch stems .... "	4.00 to	5.00
24-inch stems....... "	3.00 to	4.00
20-inch stems....... "	2.00 to	3.00
18-inch stems....... "	1.50 to	2.00
12-inch stems....... "	...... to	1.50
8-inch stems and shorts "	...... to	1.00
Bride Maid, fancy special......	10.00 to	12.00
" extra............	6.00 to	8.00
" No. 1............	4.00 to	5.00
" No. 2............	...... to	3.00
Golden Gate............	3.00 to	6.00
Carnot............	3.00 to	6.00
Uncle John............	3.00 to	6.00
Liberty............	3.00 to	12.00
Richmond............	3.00 to	12.00
Kaiserina............	3.00 to	8.00
Killarney............	3.00 to	6.00
" extra............	8.00 to	10.00
Perle............	3.00 to	6.00
Chatenay............	3.00 to	6.00
Callas............	...... to	16.00
....	...... to	......

CARNATIONS			
STANDARD VARIETIES	White............	2.00 to	3.00
	Pink............	2.00 to	3.00
	Red............	2.00 to	3.00
	Yellow & var....	2.00 to	8.00
*FANCY (*The highest grades of Sta'd var)	White............	3.00 to	4.00
	Pink............	3.00 to	4.00
	Red............	3.00 to	4.00
	Yellow & var....	3.00 to	4.00
NOVELTIES............		...... to	......
ADIANTUM............		.75 to	1.00
ASPARAGUS, Plum. & Ten........		.35 to	.50
" Sprengeri, bunches.		.35 to	.50
LILIES, Longiflorum........		15.00 to	20.00
Harrisii........		15.00 to	26.00
Orchids—Cattleyas, ...		50.00 to	75.00
SMILAX		8.00 to	12.00
LILY OF THE VALLEY........		2.00 to	4.00
VIOLETS		1.00 to	1.50
" single		.75 to	1.00
HARDY FERNS per 1000........		...... to	1.50
GALAX "		1.00 to	1.25
NARCISSUS, Paper White........		3.00 to	4.00
CHRYSANTHEMUMS per doz		8.00 to	20.00

CLEVELAND, O. — The Circuit Court has issued a writ of habeas corpus for the release of J. M. Gasser from a Cincinnati sanitarium and to grant a rehearing in his case. The action for his release has been brought by his aged sister, Mrs. Magdeline Kaltenmayer, who says Mr. Gasser is perfectly sane and capable of taking care of himself. In the action that has been filed, Mrs. Gasser, the Cincinnati sanitarium, and John C. Sheets, its president, are made defendants. Mr. Gasser is about 65 years of age, and his estate is estimated at about $500,000.

BARABOO, WIS.—William Toole, the pansy specialist, will read a paper on "Pansies" before the Iowa State Horticultural Society on December 12 at Des Moines, Ia.

GOVANSTOWN, MD.—M. Thaw is now manager of the Fernery Greenhouses, Bellona avenue, and would like price lists.

New York.

The Week's News.

On Monday evening next the December meeting of the New York Florists' Club will be held in the rooms, corner of Twenty-third street and Eighth avenue. The principal business will be the election of officers for the ensuing year, and as this is always an interesting event, a very large attendance is assured.

The third annual meeting of the Horticultural Society of New York for the season of 1906-7, will be held in the rooms of the American Institute, 19-21 West Forty-fourth street, on Wednesday, December 12. A public meeting under the auspices of the society will also be held in the same rooms at 4:30 p. m. on that date, and a lecture on "Sports" will be given by Patrick O'Mara.

The National Plant, Flower and Fruit Guild, through its New York city branch, has recently distributed twenty-three first prizes for window boxes in this city. These window boxes were given out early in the season, about eight hundred of them in all, to dwellers in the tenement districts, and the prizes have been awarded to those who had been most successful in taking care of the plants.

The annual ball of the Wholesale Florists' Employees' Association will be held on Saturday, January 5, in the Manhattan Casino, One hundred and fifty-fifth street and Eighth avenue. As will be remembered, this association held a ball last January, which was a decided success in every particular, and it is hoped to have one equally successful this year.

It seems that with each succeeding Christmas there is a growing demand for artificial poinsettias, and to a grower who is making efforts to have a supply of this beautiful plant for the holidays this fact must be rather discouraging. While there can be no gainsaying that the artificial poinsettia is well gotten up, the same thing can be said of artificial roses and other flowers; and it seems poor policy for retail stores, who are otherwise catering to the best trade, to be furnishing artificial poinsettias in mixed baskets of plants. The use of artificial material, whether for flowers or plants, is, no doubt, all right in its place, and that is in the cemetery, where something is wanted that will stand all kinds of weather for a reasonable period without having to be renewed every day or two; but an up-to-date retail florist store is certainly not the place where customers would expect to have either artificial plants or flowers sold to them over the counter.

The weather on one or two days this week has been extremely cold. On Tuesday morning the thermometer went down to 10 degrees, and some flowers reached the city in a frozen condition. These extremes of weather always have a quieting effect on the retail business. It seems to be the same, whether it is heat or cold; the effect is similar whenever one of the extremes is reached.

On Wednesday, December 5, Thorley opened his fourth branch store in this city, at the southeast corner of Eighty-sixth street and Columbus avenue.

Friends of David A. Rose of Montclair, N. J., will be glad to hear of his recovery from a recent serious illness.

Maurice Fuld of W. W. Rawson & Company, Boston, secretary of the New England Dahlia Society, was in town this week. Mr. Fuld says that interest in the Dahlia Society is increasing, and a large membership seems assured. Julius Heurlein of the Blue Hills Nurseries, Mass., was also a visitor.

Christmas Greens Headquarters

Holly

Boxwood - - - $15.00 per 100 lbs.
Laurel Festooning, extra quality, 5c and 6c. per yd.
Princess Pine Festooning, $6.00 per 100 yards.

Wild Smilax $3.50 and $7.00 per case.

Laurel Wreaths, extra quality, $2.50 per doz. upwards.
Branch Laurel, - - 50c. per bunch.
Bouquet Green - $7.00 per 100 lbs.

Galax New Crop Bronze and Green, $1.00 per 1000, $7.50 per 10,000.

Ferns, Fancy and Dagger, $1.25 per .000
Leucothoe Sprays, - - $1.00 per 100
Green and Sphagnum Moss, $1.00 per bbl.

Headquarters for all Florists' Supplies, such as **RED IMMORTELLES**, Wire Designs, Cut Wire, Letters of all kinds, Immortelles, Cycas Leaves, Milkweeds, Sheaves of Wheat, Ribbons, Boxes, Folding, Blue Corrugated, &c. **THE HOUSE THAT CAN SUPPLY THE GOODS ON A MOMENT'S NOTICE.**

HENRY M. ROBINSON & CO., 11-15 PROVINCE ST., 9 CHAPMAN PLACE, BOSTON, MASS.

L. D. Tel., Main 2617-2618.

Mention The Florists' Exchange when writing.

SOUTHERN WILD SMILAX

Now ready in any quantity

Book orders now for future delivery. **Beaven's Fadeless Sheet Moss**, $3.50 per bag, delivered. Send for samples. Also **Fancy Holly** for Xmas trade. Satisfaction guaranteed. Write for prices.

E. A. BEAVEN EVERGREEN, ALA.

Mention The Florists' Exchange when writing.

SOMETHING NEW IN CHRISTMAS TREE STANDS

NEAT, ABSOLUTELY SECURE, EASILY ADJUSTED

Simple in construction, light in weight, durable and cheap.

Will sell on sight during the Christmas season at a good profit.

$1.90 per doz; $15.00 per 100; $140.00 per 1000.

Price F. O. B. Bridgeport, Conn.

Send for illustrated circu'ar with full description.

ELBRIDGE E. WHEELER

Seedsman, BRIDGEPORT, CONN.

Mention the Florists' Exchange when writing.

REMOVAL NOTICE!

H. Bayersdorfer & Co., Philadelphia

THE FLORISTS' SUPPLY HOUSE OF AMERICA

Beg to announce to their patrons and the trade their removal into new spacious and up-to-date quarters, occupying the entire building at

1129 ARCH STREET

where with most modern facilities and increased working force, they will endeavor to still further improve their already well established record for promptness and reliability.

When in Philadelphia, step in. Make the new centrally located store your headquarters.

ALWAYS WELCOME

Mention the Florists' Exchange when writing.

Fancy or Dagger Ferns

$1.00 per 1000

Galax, Bronze or Green, 75c. per 1000.

Boxwood, No. 1 Stock, 50 lb. cases, $8.50

Laurel Festooning, 4c., 5c. and 6c. per yard. Finest quality

Laurel Wreaths, $3.00 per doz. Cheaper grades if wanted

Southern Smilax, fancy stock, 50 lb. cases $6.50

Laurel Branches, 35c. per bundle

Send your orders for **LAUREL FESTOONING** in now for Christmas, as later we may be unable to fill them.

Telegraph Office: New Salem, Mass. Long distance telephone connections.

CROWL FERN CO., MILLINGTON, MASS.

Mention the Florists' Exchange when writing.

EXTRA FINE NEW CROP FANCY FERN

$1.25 per 1000. Discount on large orders. GALAX, per 1000, $1.25. Green Galax, $1.25 per 1000.

MICHIGAN CUT FLOWER EXCHANGE

WILLIAM DILGER, Manager.

Let us have your standing order for Ferns, we will make Price right all through the season.

38 & 40 Broadway. Formerly Miami Ave. **DETROIT, MICH.**

Send for our weekly price list on Cut Flowers.

Mention The Florists' Exchange when writing.

WIRED TOOTHPICKS

10,000, $1.50; 50,000, $6.25

MANUFACTURED BY

W. J. COWEE, BERLIN, N. Y.

Samples free. For sale by dealers.

Mention the Florists' Exchange when writing.

BOUQUET GREEN

Best quality at **lowest rates**. We gather our own **Greens** and bring by our own boat direct.

Also **CHRISTMAS TREES**

Northern Michigan Evergreen Nursery.

SCHOONER GEO. L. WRENN, S. W. cor. Clark St. Bridge, **CHICAGO**. H. Schuenemann, Capt.

Mention the Florists' Exchange when writing.

HOLLY! HOLLY! HOLLY!

Holly Wreaths, Lycopodium and Lycopodium Wreaths

My Man in the Woods with 12 years' experience in packing, can ship you direct, and thus save extra expense in freight. Choice Delaware Holly, well berried, at $3.00 per case. Wreaths $10.00 to $15.00 per 100. Cash with order.

H. T. DUMONT & CO. - 1305 Filbert St., Philadelphia, Pa

Mention the Florists' Exchange when writing.

THE BEST WAY

to collect an account is to place it with the

National Florists' Board of Trade

56 Pine St., New York

WHY? Because many debtors will pay the Board fearing otherwise a bad rating in our Credit List. Full information as to methods and rates given on application.

Mention the Florists' Exchange when writing.

CUT FLOWER BOXES

EDWARDS FOLDING BOX CO

MANUFACTURERS

PHILADELPHIA, PA.

Mention the Florists' Exchange when writing.

REED & KELLER 122 W. 25th STREET NEW YORK

Importers and Manufacturers of **FLORISTS' SUPPLIES** Galax Leaves and Decorative Greenery

New York Agents for Caldwell's, Monroe, Ala., Parlor Brand Smilax.

Mention the Florists' Exchange when writing.

PLANT CULTURE

PRICE $1.00.

THE BEST BOOK FOR THE PLANT GROWER.

A. T. DE LA MARE PTG. & PUB. CO. LTD., 2-8 DUANE STREET, NEW YORK

San Francisco.

News Notes.

The pioneer florist and nurseryman of this city, state and coast, F. A. Miller, who had the only nursery in the burned district, and lost by the fire many valuable plants and much select nursery stock, and several good rent-producing residences he had on the nursery plot, has not enjoyed his usual health since the severe shakeup he experienced the 18th of last April. At the first meeting of the California State Floral Society, which was organized by Mr. Miller in the early fifties, held since the April disturbance, among the important business was the resignation of Mr. Miller as president, regretfully presented because of enfeebled health. The meeting was largely attended and a splendid paper was contributed and read by Mrs. A. R. Gunnison, on "The Floriculture of San Francisco, Past and Present."

Benicia, the original capital town of California, is to have an original industry of the State of interest to the trade. The first concern in California to manufacture a chemical spray for fruit trees and all horticultural and floricultural purposes will very shortly erect a plant in Benicia. It is said that the Earl Fruit Company of Suisun, Cal., has placed an order with the manufacturers for fifty carloads of the spray.

ALVIN.

AURORA, ILL.—The big greenhouses operated by the C., B. & Q. Railway here have been torn down to make more room for the locomotive blacksmith shop. The novel undertaking—for a railroad—will now be abandoned, and hereafter flowers will be purchased of professional growers. The greenhouses cost $12,000 and were built to supply cut flowers for the road's dining cars and potted plants for ornamenting depot grounds along the line.

Chicago.

The Glass Situation.

The glass market here has been in a very unsteady and precarious condition of late, the instability of prices causing one of the largest houses in Chicago to refuse an order last week for twenty-five carloads at a price which was accepted by another concern who, as the proprietor of the first mentioned establishment put it, was willing to take all kinds of chances.

Change in Charter.

The city's municipal charter was revised last week by the Chicago charter convention, one of the four most important changes being the abolition of the present form of government of the park systems, and the management of the parks to become a department of the city government.

A Sad Fatality.

After spending the night in terpsichorean pastimes at Glen View two employees of the Poehlmann Brothers' Company were returning, on the railroad track, to their home at Morton Grove early Thanksgiving morning when, owing to a dense fog which pervailed at the time, they failed to observe the head-light of an approaching freight train of the Chicago, Milwaukee and St. Paul line until they were struck by the locomotive. Ferdinand Kading, a flower packer, was instantly killed, his body being terribly mutilated; and Robert Hand, a rose foreman, who has been in the employ of the concern for the past eight years, sustained injuries which though of a serious nature are not expected to prove fatal. A third member of the party, also of the Poehlmann force, escaped uninjured.

Here and There.

At Peter Reinberg's salesroom the receipts on Monday were double in amount the total of previous receipts. The stock in hand was very heavy and of fine quality, a fair estimate placing the cut for the Thanksgiving holiday at twice the amount cut for the same occasion last year.

George Reinberg has been for the past few weeks cutting a very even crop, there being but a slight variation from day to day; and the prospect for the Christmas crop, especially on American Beauty roses, is very promising. The concern is planning to desert the carnation business next year.

Wietor Brothers are more than holding their own during the dull weather that has prevailed in this vicinity of late, American Beauty and Richmond roses being particularly noticeable, followed by a fine line of chrysanthemums, carnations and tea roses.

It is reported that H. F. Holly of West Madison street will open a retail establishment on the north side at an early date.

Vaughan & Sperry are receiving daily consignments of Hudson River violets, which arrive in good condition and find a ready market.

The A. L. Randall Company are, in addition to their regular line of cut flowers, showing an interesting and attractive line of supplies, which Miss Tonner selected during her European trip last Summer.

Bassett & Washburn were kept busy last week with large shipping orders. In addition to the ordinary fine cut of roses a particularly nice line of fancy carnations and chrysanthemums has been delivered daily at the Wabash avenue office from the Hinsdale houses.

Alex Henderson, floor manager at Vaughan's Seed Store, returned this week from his trip to his native heath in Scotland. Just for a sample, Vaughan's Seed Store opened up three carloads of holly and two carloads of princess pine last week, with an absolute assurance of an ample supply on the road. Other items of interest to the trade, learned from the Randolph street headquarters, were that the two carloads of lily of the valley pips received last week were more than half sold; and that large orders for Christmas greens are being filled for the Pacific Coast.

Wieland & Risch, after a careful study of their books, report an increase of from 40 to 70 per cent. over the returns of the preceding season, the largest percentage coming from their specialty, Killarney rose.

Charles A. Johnson, who was known for many years as the Limits Florist of Chicago and who recently establihed a range of houses in Chillicothe, Ohio, was around the first of the week and claims that growing is much more successful than retailing.

The J. B. Deamud Company have been adding to their reputation of late by handling in connection with their regular lines, a large lot of fine single violets of local production.

Zech & Mann were proud last week of having doubled their Thanksgiving business of a year ago, this having exceeded their expectations on the second year of the existence of the concern.

With gardenias, lily of the valley and Dendrobium formosum as leading cards, C. W. McKellar stood in the front rank in ability to supply his customers last week.

C. H. Grant has entered the employ of Frank Williams at the State street headquarters.

Among the younger concerns who are making a good showing, especially on carnations, may be mentioned Scheiden & Schoos, who have recently established a plant at South Evanston, where they are meeting with unqualified success. E. F. Francis manages their salesrooms in the Fower Growers' Market.

For the past three years the E. F. Winterson Company has made a specialty of poinsettias, natural growth, for the holidays, taking each year the entire output of a specialist, who grows them in larger numbers and to perfection. This year the firm is again in line with a larger supply than ever before and numerous orders are already booked.

On Western avenue between Twenty-fifth and Twenty-sixth streets, the Foley Manufacturing Company is rapidly completing its structure which with adjoining land and side tracks and adjacent property belonging to the concern will cover between eight and ten acres. Everything is expected to be running in first-class order by the second month of the coming year.

Among the recent deaths is that of an old timer, Swiss born, but Yankee raised, C. F. Imoberstag, who came from the Alps at twenty-one, and who had by close application to business made a success of it in the Western hemisphere. He leaves a large family. The business will be continued by the widow and sons under the concern name of Mrs. C. F. Imoberstag & Sons.

When all is said and done, it looks to the close observer as if the Fall business, at least up to Thanksgiving and the incoming of December, was hardly up to expectations with the grower, the commission man, the wholesaler, and the retailer. The Thanksgiving trade was on the whole a great disappointment in this market. The prices kept breaking on all regular lines until Thursday, when it could be safely said that nothing in the field had absolutely held its price except American Beauty roses, high grade lily of the valley and best quality of violets. Owing to the short drop of Christmas greens the regular lines of green goods are holding well up in price.

WILLIAM K. WOOD.

Indianapolis.

News Jottings.

Would it not be best for the wholesalers to issue a telegraphic price list about two days preceding a holiday? The advance price lists generally act as a scarecrow for the prices immediately before one.

E. T. Barnes, Spencer, Ind., visited the florists here this week. It is his intention next year to plant and dispose of an enormous lot of dahlias.

Carl Sonnenschmidt, of the Smith & Young Company, visited the St. Louis wholesalers the past week.

Thomas Knipe of Kokomo is in the city buying for his Christmas trade.

Tomlinson Hall Market business has been slow; the same conditions prevailed there on Thanksgiving as with the store men; sales were numerous but very small.

The seed houses are making elaborate preparations for the green goods business; they are situated within a block and competition is keen.

Irwin Bertermann has disposed of his residence in East Washington street at a good figure. I. B.

Philadelphia.

The Week's News.

All the retail stores report a very good Thanksgiving business. The demand for cut flowers was strong, and many of the wholesale houses kept open late to get stock in to fill orders. On Friday and Saturday the business kept up, occasioned no doubt by the great numbers of people that came in for the Army and Navy football game, which made lots of work in dinner decorations. Everyone who had chrysanthemums sold them readily, until nothing but late white varieties were left.

On Monday the social season opened with Mrs. Frederick Thurston Mason's dancing class at Horticultural Hall. The dance was preceded by a large number of dinners and receptions which kept the retailers busy. Corsage bouquets were also more in demand than in previous years.

At the dinner of the St. Andrew's Society held at the Bellevue-Sratford on Monday, the table decorations were done by the Robert Craig Company. A feature of the decoration were plants of Otaheite oranges in fruit.

Visitors this week included Miss Ritter, Fitchburg, Mass.; and George Siedel, Hazleton, Pa.

Bayersdorfer & Company have three steamers—the Vaderland, Pallanza, and Menomince—in with goods this week; and although the firm has a larger force on, it is compelled to work overtime.

William P. Craig has been successful in obtaining half of the stock of the new fern Nephrolepis Amerpohlii. He has brought it outright, without any restriction, and it will be grown under contract by the Robert Craig Company.

Florists' Club Meeting.

The regular meeting was held on Tuesday night. P. J. Lynch was to have read an essay, but on account of the death of his mother he sent his regrets. At the January meeting S. S. Skidelsky will read a paper on our "Credit System; Its Use and Abuse."

Among Growers.

At the establishment of Robert Scott & Son, all roses are in good condition, considering the dull and warm weather. With clear and colder days a very large cut should be the result of the next three months. Both Killarney and Richmond are doing well here; the plants are in solid beds and making nice growth. The prospect for American Beauty at Christmas is very good. In roses the most interesting house just now is the one containing the latest introductions from Hugh Dickson & Sons of Belfast, Ireland. Of the 1905 introductions there are now several good ones in flower. The yellow rose spoken of last Spring continues to improve; then there is another good one, blush pink in the center of the flower shading to almost white on the outer edge of the petals. Apparently this is a good grower, and has very attractive foliage. A good white, like a K. A. Victoria, in July, is also very noticeable and deserves taking care of. But the most interesting thing on this place is a grand lot of gardenias. At last it looks like plenty of these flowers in December and January; for here is one house filled with very healthy thrifty plants, many of them having from 25 to 40 buds and no buds are dropping. Alex. Scott has tried hard for this result; and we sincerely hope no setback will come to mar the achievement of his ambition.

The establishment of the Robert Craig Company is now in good condition. They have a very fine lot of stock on hand. In their Christmas specialties they have a grand lot of Otaheite oranges, all well fruited—the best we have seen for some time. Poinsettias in made-up pans, both oval and round, with small asparagus plants intermixed, form another feature and are selling well.

The chief attraction here is the house planted with the new fern, Nephrolepis Amerpohlii. This is attracting many people, and among those who had not seen it before it causing much comment. It certainly is a great acquisition. The full developed frond is like a piece of lace, and the fern will no doubt find a ready market for cut fronds for floral work. One entire house on this place is devoted to Ficus pandurata. This plant is becoming more popular every week. The plants, five and six feet tall, in tubs, are grand specimens and very decorative. A large number of azaleas are coming along for Christmas. In addition to the usual varieties we noticed a lot of Jeanne Peters, a bright red, and a few plants of Pharilda Mathilda a new one, variegated, a sport from Vervæneana, but with larger and much more delicate flowers. We also saw some nice specimens of Pandanus pacificus, in 6-inch pots, very desirable plants. Another house contained a nice lot of Dracæna terminalis in 4 and 5-inch pots, all well colored. In the Boston ferns they have all the varieties in good shape: best of all was a batch of elegantissima; these are very well done and should sell on first sight. They are in 6 and 7-inch pots.

The new late chrysanthemum Jeannie Nonin fills one house. This is the best late white yet seen, very full, just like a ball when finished, clear white and large. The blooms can be held for Christmas very easily. We also saw several benches of poinsettias for cutting, also a bench of Euphorbia Jacquiniæflora, an old time favorite and very desirable for the holiday trade.

DAVID RUST.

LENOX, MASS.—The annual meeting of the Lenox Horticultural Society was held December 1, 1906, President S. Carlquist in the chair. The following members were unanimously elected officers for the ensuing year: F. Heeremans, president; W. Jack, vice-president; Robert Speirs, treasurer; Geo. Foulsham, secretary; Jos. Tansey, assistant secretary. After the business had been despatched, refreshments were served, and several of the members gave an exemplification of their vocal and instrumental abilities. A very enjoyable evening was spent.

G. F.

H AND Co

ONE MAN IDEA

You can't carry your hobbies into your business and make the dollars roll up—the other chap's point of view, his reasons for having that view, are what you want to get a line on. Our construction, our materials, are not one man's idea—they represent the growth, the successful meeting of problems resulting from the conclusions of the best experts in greenhouse building. That's why our houses are the very acme of up-to-date construction. Get a line on our houses. Get to know us.

HITCHINGS & COMPANY

GREENHOUSE DESIGNERS AND BUILDERS

Manufacturers of Heating and Ventilating Apparatus

1170 BROADWAY, - NEW YORK

H AND Co

Mention the Florists' Exchange when writing.

FURMAN BOILERS FOR GREENHOUSE HEATING

Valuable Catalogue on Modern Steam and Hot-Water Heating, mailed free upon request. Address

THE HERENDEEN MANUFACTURING CO.

629 Pearl Street, NEW YORK. Dept. F. GENEVA, N. Y.

Furman Boilers have been awarded the Certificate of Merit at Five different Florists' Conventions. Have a record of 20 years. Over 25,000 in use.

SELLING AGENT: EDW. S. DEAN, Bloomington, Ill.

Mention The Florists' Exchange when writing.

"Always Safe and Reliable. Ask Your Friends."

You can settle the question of water supply for your greenhouse for all time by installing a

CALDWELL TANK and TOWER

which stores abundant water and delivers same at high pressure to any part of your premises. The tank material and hooping are so durable and strong there is no chance for a leak to develop, for a hoop to burst, or repairs to become necessary. The stability and strength of the steel towers have been tested by a hundred fierce storms, many of them cyclones, and not found wanting in a single instance.

Ask for references, and illustrated catalogue"

W. E. CALDWELL CO., Louisville, Ky

Tanks (Steel-Wood / Galvanized) Towers

Wind Mills—Pumps—Gas Engines

Mention the Florists' Exchange when writing.

SAVE TIME AND MONEY

OUR GREENHOUSE MATERIAL

CUT AND SPLICED REQUIRE NO MECHANICS

LET US ESTIMATE ON YOUR HEATING VENTILATING APPARATUS HOT BED SASH

Putty **GREENHOUSE GLASS** Points

S. JACOBS & SONS,

1365-79 Flushing Ave., BROOKLYN, N. Y.

Mention The Florists' Exchange when writing.

BOILERS QUICK.

This is the season when quick deliveries count. I have the largest line of horticultural boilers and can give quick shipment from twenty different points. I will erect your plant complete if you desire it.

Write for prices.

JOHN A. PAYNE

Horticultural Architect and Builder

33 CLENDENNY AVE., JERSEY CITY

Sash Opening Apparatus.

All kinds of Greenhouse Structural and Heating Material.

Mention the Florists' Exchange when writing.

C...S - IS FAR MO... THAN PINE

C...S

S... BARS

UP T... LONGER.

GREENHOUSE

AND OTH... MATERIAL,

MEN FUR... SUPERINTEND

ERECTION... DESIRED.

S... S.

THE ... Co.,

NEPONSET, BOSTON, MASS.

M... writing.

GEO. M. GARLAND

Iron Gutters and Posts

Patented December 27th, 1898.

Send for Catalogue.

Garland's Gutters will keep snow and ice off your glass and prevent breakage.

DESPLAINES, ILL.

A sample of this gutter is on exhibition at Chicago Flower Growers' Market.

Mention The Florists' Exchange when writing.

THE JENNINGS IMPROVED IRON GUTTER

PATENT IRON BENCH FITTINGS AND ROOF SUPPORTS. VENTILATING APPARATUS. IMPROVED VAPORIZING PANS for Tobacco Extracts, Etc.

SEND FOR CIRCULARS — DILLER, CASKEY & CO. — Successors to JENNINGS BROS

S. W. CORNER SIXTH AND BERK STS., PHILADELPHIA, PA.

Mention the Florists' Exchange when writing.

The STANDARD VENTILATING MACHINERY

The original machine with self oiling cups; the most powerful, least complicated, very compact, with ease of operation.

The New Duplex Gutter over six miles in use and highly recommended; the only drip proof gutter in the market.

The Standard Return Steam Trap has no equal for simplicity or its workings. Catalogue free.

E. HIPPARD, Youngstown, O.

Mention the Florists' Exchange when writing.

Evans Improved Challenge

Roller bearing, self-oiling device automatic stop, solid link chain make the IMPROVED CHALLENGE the most perfect apparatus in the market.

Write for catalogue and prices before placing your orders elsewhere.

QUAKER CITY MACHINE CO.

RICHMOND, IND.

Mention the Florists' Exchange when writing.

VIOLET CULTURE

Price, $1 50 Postpaid

A T. De La Mare Ptg. & Pub. Co. Ltd., New York

Buffalo.

News Items.

Joseph Sangster has returned to Buffalo after spending a couple of years in the East, and will again accept his old position at S. A. Anderson's.

Jacob Wiese has gone East on a business trip looking for novelties for his Christmas trade.

Walter Stroh of Batavia, N. Y., has accepted a position with W. J. Palmer & Son.

J. Benson Stafford made a decided hit in a play, written by himself at Concert Hall, Friday night, November 30.

W. H. G.

Providence, R. I.

News Notes.

Floral designs were numerous at the funeral of our late mayor, Gen. Elisha Dyer. O'Connor had the greatest number of pieces, and it is said he used 60,000 violets as well as a great many expensive orchids.

December has started in with all the indications of being an extraordinary busy month. The weather is cold and bright, and everything has been picked very close, owing to the active business here the first few days of the month.

Our florists are making arrangements for a big Christmas business. Everything now points to a great trade in evergreens, which is always very extensive here. I think a good boxwood wreath for cemetery, office, or house decoration is the most satisfactory.

G. A. J.

APPLETON, WIS.—A party consisting of M. Crawford of the M. Crawford Company of Cuyahoga Falls, Ohio, George Bridge of Elgin, Ill., F. A. Bridge of Chicago, and N. V. S. Mallory, secretary of the Shiocton Garden Land Company, with headquarters at Shiocton, held a conference here last week. The significance of the trip is the visit of M. Crawford to make a final inspection of the swamp lands of Bovina township before conferring finally with the other members of his firm in regard to the transfer of the business of the company from the present location at Cuyahoga Falls to the fertile tract of about 4,000 acres owned by the Shiocton Garden Land Company in Bovina township.

Mr. Crawford gave a list of the products he thought the land adapted to and what will probably be raised, these including gladiolus bulbs, strawberry plants, asparagus, onions, cabbage, celery, sugar beets, cauliflower, cucumbers, and musk melons.

The annual exhibition of the Amer-

THE FLORISTS' EXCHANGE

We are a straight shoot and aim to grow into a vigorous plant

A WEEKLY MEDIUM OF INTERCHANGE FOR FLORISTS, NURSERYMEN, SEEDSMEN AND THE TRADE IN GENERAL

. XXII. No. 24 — NEW YORK AND CHICAGO, DECEMBER 15, 1906 — One Dollar Per Year

CONTENTS AND INDEX TO ADVERTISERS, PAGE 737

Seed Trade Report.

AMERICAN SEED TRADE ASSOCIATION

Henry W. Wood, Richmond, Va., president; C. S. Burge, Toledo, O., first vice-president; G. B. McVay, Birmingham, Ala., second vice-president; C. E. Kendel, Cleveland, O., secretary and treasurer; J. H. Ford, Ravenna, O., assistant secretary.

Seeds of flowers, vegetables and others not specified are admitted into Guatemala duty free.

The Costa Rican tariff imposes a duty of 0.02 colon per kilo on seeds for vegetables, flowers, and plants. The value of a colon is $0.465.

Some of the daily papers are exploiting the fact that the farmers of Iowa are finding the raising of pumpkins for the seed a profitable industry. The yield per acre is said to be from $5 to $6, and the average price paid 5 cents per pound.

On Wednesday, December 5, Senator Brandegee, of Connecticut, presented a memorial of Rippowan Grange, Patrons of Husbandry, of Stamford, Conn., remonstrating against the enactment of legislation providing for the free distribution of seeds; which was referred to the Committee on Agriculture and Forestry.

SANTA ROSA, CAL.—Luther Burbank's fine new residence in Santa Rosa avenue is nearing completion, and will be very attractive. In the new residence Mr. Burbank will have a laboratory, seed room and many other conveniences for the carrying on of his work that are not available in the old cottage.

STURGEON BAY, WIS.—The Allan Seed Company have finished picking over peas, and last week made their last shipment for this season. Last year the crop was much better and the pickers were kept at work several weeks longer. The W. W. Barnard Co. will keep their picking crew at work until the first of the year.

ALBERT LEA, MINN.—At the meeting of the stockholders of the Thompson Seed Company, held at the offices of the company Saturday afternoon, December 1, 1906, it was decided by an almost unanimous vote to ratify the action of the board of directors for the appointment of a trustee who will take charge of the business of the corporation and dispose of it at once. D. R. P. Hibbs was chosen by the board as trustee, and he will sell the entire stock, fixtures, plant and other assets as soon as possible and turn the proceeds over to the board of directors, who will settle all debts of the concern; if anything remains after that is done, distribute it pro rata, among the stockholders.

Mr. Thompson, the president and manager, has not fully determined what he will do in the future. He will assist the trustee in closing out the business, and after this work is done will go to Minneapolis with the expectation of locating there if he can find a desirable opening.—Tribune.

European Notes.

Whatever benefits the Morgan steamship combine may have brought to the promoters it certainly has not benefited the general public, whose interests and requirements are entirely disregarded, and services are suspender at a few days' notice and without any apparent cause. Take the present week as an example. The London boat to New York has been taken off and all the traffic turned over to a Boston boat. Owing to the heavy shipments now being made, all the available space was appropriated before the steamer reached port and, as a consequence, many tons of seeds, that are badly needed on your side, are lying at the wharves until the shipping companies condescend to remove them. This, together with the irritating hindrances caused by the continuously wet weather, has a somewhat unhappy effect upon the sweetly angelic tempers of the European shippers; at the same time it accounts for delays.

Contrary to expectation the Giant peppers are yielding very poor crops of seed this season. The Ruby King and Square Chinese are especially short. Tomatoes on the other hand are very abundant, especially the early, dwarf-growing varieties; prices for these rule low.

As regards flower seeds, the crop of the cheap mixtures grown in the south of France is very large, while in Germany the crop of all varieties is poor. Sweet peas are causing a lot of trouble and anxiety and some unkind things are being said about some of the growers on your side, whose deliveries are extremely disappointing. Nasturtiums come to hand very slowly, but there will probably be enough to go round.

The Sweet Pea Society has secured Sir George Cooper for president and Leonard W. Sutton for chairman of committees. As regards the tests of novelties to be made next year at Reading, I am requested to state that 20 seeds of any one variety will be sufficient.

Two new retail seedsmen have commenced business in the London area—John McKerchar, for many years representative of B. S. Williams & Son, and H. J. Wright, late secretary to the National Sweet Pea Society. As they are both capable, energetic and popular men they are certain to succeed.

The writer has been particularly requested to state for the information of the mailing departments in U. S. A. seed stores that the rate of postage to Europe is 5 cents for every half ounce, and that double rates are charged for any deficiency. Also that letters insufficiently prepaid are delayed several hours in delivery. Verb. sap. sat. EUROPEAN SEEDS.

CATALOGUES RECEIVED.

WM. H. HILL, San Juan, Porto Rico.—Price List of Dracæna terminalis canes.

HENRY NUNGESSER & COMPANY, New York.—Wholesale Price List of Grass and Clover Seeds.

H. F. MICHELL COMPANY, Philadelphia, Pa.—Price List of Flower Seeds, Supplies, etc.; also of Christmas greens.

German Lily of the Valley Trade.

The lily of the valley trade for the season of 1906 is now about at an end with the German exporting houses; and in looking back upon the year's business one cannot help being struck with the great success of the season's trade and the satisfactory business done, viewing it from the German merchant's standpoint. On the other hand, looking at the year's trade from the English market grower's point of view, probably a more unsatisfactory year has never before been passed through. Prices for cut spikes have never been smaller on the markets; there has never been a worse glut of second rate quality, and prices paid for the pips, both fresh and retarded, have probably never been higher. The quality of retarded deliveries on the whole also has been poor, some bulk quantities absolutely useless, with the exception of the deliveries of some of the few larger and more expert firms in Germany who are thoroughly experienced in the art of retarding.

From the large number of bulk quantities I have seen, which have been delivered, many are a total or partial failure. It is more than ever apparent to me that just any sample will not retard, and out of the score or so of different types of samples of crowns offered to the growers there are generally only one or two samples absolutely certain to retard quite successfully. It requires an expert at the business to pick these out, and unless a grower who undertakes to retard his own is an expert, it is far safer to leave the selection of the sample in the hands of the German exporter, providing the grower knows full well that said exporter can be absolutely relied upon.

There are quite a number of smaller firms who take up the lily of the valley exporting trade almost as a side line; they have had no experience of the growing and sampling and probably know absolutely nothing about what a retarding sample should be. They buy a lot of crowns as cheap as they possibly can without regard to their suitability for any particular purpose; they sell all they can in England and America, to be used as fresh forcing crowns, and what are left are delivered to firms who wish to retard their own; or the dealers put the balance in some public cold stores and sell them later as retarded with the result that in nine cases out of ten they are a failure. Evidences of these statements have been numerous on the English cut flower markets this year, where the second rate quality has always been in great excess of the demand; and these second rate spikes, by their appearance and the constant supply, were the produce of samples unsuitable for retarding. They are now, however, getting a list of large firms who handle lily of the valley of all samples and forms in huge quantities, making a special study of it and touching practically nothing else, catering to the English and American trade. With offices probably situated in Hamburg, they will have an expert buyer down in the growing districts from July onward, who will know the growth, strain, characteristics, age, soil grown on and everything there is to be known about any bulk quantity they buy. When these are offered in England and America this buyer will give the firm's seller a detailed description of each particular sample. In many cases also a duplicate sample will be retained in Hamburg, or wherever the headquarters are situated, which will be tested in growth, the firm perhaps running some glass houses for testing all samples. All lots retarded will be bloomed by sample in this way before being sent out, and if any lot turns out very fine, or any customer reports he is particularly pleased with the result of any particular lot, the firm will secure the stock of that particular batch and have it grown by a system of contract on a selected piece of land which is well known to their representative in the growing districts. Such firms as these, in addition to years of experience, collect further experience as they go along, all of which is duly entered in a sort of stock book. These firms require an immense capital, and could not probably spare either cash or time for any other trade.

One of the lessons of the past year's out lily of the valley business is to deal only with firms who thoroughly understand the many ins and outs of the trade, who can satisfy the buyers that their deliveries will be in every way a success.

ENGLISH CORRESPONDENT.

NURSERY DEPARTMENT.

Conducted by Joseph Meehan.

AMERICAN ASSOCIATION OF NURSERYMEN.
Orlando Harrison, Berlin, Md., president; J. W. Hill, Des Moines, Ia., vice-president; George C. Seager, Rochester, N. Y., secretary; C. L. Yates, Rochester, N. Y., treasurer.

SAC CITY, IA.—Wayne & Butler have given up their nursery business here.

HOUGHTON, MICH.—Ira E. Randall will establish a nursery here, and will grow stock suitable for a northern climate.

PRUNING PEACH TREES.—I have about fifty peach trees from one year to three years old. Kindly tell me if it would hurt them to prune them back, the same as young apple trees; and the best time to prune them, and oblige. W. A.

—You could not do better than prune the peach trees, doing it towards the close of Winter. When let alone the peach has a tendency to make long limbs with but few branches near the ground, and this is an evil which pruning prevents. A pinching back of the ends of growing shoots in Midsummer also helps make the trees bushy. J. M.

Horticultural Topics.

It has been claimed that the pink-flowered dogwood was discovered in South Carolina. While a pink one was found there by James Macpherson, the one in cultivation was discovered in the Virginia forests, and was sent out by the firm of Parsons & Sons, of Flushing, N. Y.

Pyrus Parkmanni, as imported from Europe last Spring, was not the Parkmanni of our nurseries. It was not as beautiful, appearing like some other kind of Japanese pyrus. The true Parkmanni is a beautiful small tree, rosy pink in bud, lighter when expanded—a most attractive subject. It can be increased by budding or grafting on the common apple stock.

The best honeysuckle of an evergreen character is the one known as Lonicera brachypoda, the Japanese evergreen. There is another one from Japan, partly evergreen, called Halleana, but it is not as good as brachypoda, the leaves suffering when heavy freezings come. Evergreen honeysuckles are cheering to look upon when Winter finds so many trees, shrubs and vines bare of foliage.

Correspondents in Europe who are not familiar with our oaks are often confused on account of our common names. This is the case with Quercus nigra and Q. tinctoria. The nigra is black jack oak, the tinctoria black oak. The latter is the better known, and when wanted is often asked for under the name of nigra. The black jack oak, by the way, is a tree with beautiful foliage, and should be planted much oftener than it is.

If seeds of Clematis paniculata are sown in February in a greenhouse, nice plants are obtained by Spring, which may be grown in pots or planted outdoors when Spring opens. Its late and profuse flowering makes it in great demand.

Wistaria sinensis, the Chinese species, is too heavy-wooded a climber for some situations. As its branches soon thicken and become almost tree-like it almost sustains itself, requiring but slight tying to keep it in position. Its racemes of flowers are one of the glories of Spring.

For the grafting of the various beautiful Japanese maples the common one of Japan, polymorphum, is used. It is better to purchase stocks of these than the seeds, as the latter will not grow unless kept moist from the time they are gathered; and they are rarely to be had in growing condition.

Those interested in catalpa growing for forestry purposes assert that the two species, bignonioides and speciosa, hybridize freely, and that these hybrids are of no use for forestry purposes. While perhaps not the equal in all respects of speciosa, to say they are of no use is questionable. The wood of the common C. bignonioides is known to be very durable, and it would be but in hardiness that the hybrids might not equal C. speciosa.

Hollies After Christmas Use.

Hollies for Christmas use are being called for every year to a greater extent. Those used are the European species, Ilex aquifolium, and its varieties. The plants are imported direct from Europe every season, save a few that have been kept over from the preceding year. These hollies are grown for the purpose, one of the aims being to have a ball of fibrous roots to insure their living when transplanted. More care is exercised in this respect than would be were the transplanting to be to some spot outdoors. The plants have to be potted and have to endure the ordeal of being in dwellings for two weeks or so at Christmas, and unless well-rooted they will not stand the treatment.

Just what to do with the plants after the festival days of Christmas are over puzzles many purchasers. Though the weather may permit it, the change from the heated dwelling to outdoors is not good for the plants. Customers should be instructed to place them in a closed shed, stable or like place, or in a cold greenhouse, for the Winter, free from sunlight, if possible. It will greatly add to their chances of living if after their use for Christmas every leaf be cut off, and the branches pruned back one half, and keep them well watered and sprinkled with water all Winter.

An Evergreen View.

When grounds are laid out and planted the landscape gardener always has a difficult task before him. It is not always practicable to obtain trees of large size when large ones are required, and then there are places where a large tree is not wanted at any time, and one that will keep dwarf for all time is not always obtainable. Then, to wait years for the trees to grow to a proper size to make the picture the design calls for, is something the owner of the grounds is not prepared to do in many cases. All these things result in the planting of more trees than will be desirable in after years, and this it seems to us is the most sensible way of working.

We do not know what the thought was when the group of evergreens we illustrate was planted, but, as a glance reveals, hardly any but the small ones on the outer row could have been let grow as they would. By the close pruning every year which all but those in the rear have received, none has had to be cut out, and, really, as a picture the arrangement is very good, those in the rear being of natural growth, forming a well-arranged background to the pruned-in ones in front.

Allowing for a difference in taste, and for reasons calling for a closely trimmed evergreen, our own thoughts are that a few of the trimmed-up ones on the left of the group would be better removed, especially if duplicates of others, which they appear to be. This would allow those remaining to grow more at will, presenting a more natural appearance. What we would prefer is to see the whole looking as do the evergreens on the right—the end one being Picea cephalonica, and the one next it Abies orientalis. The cuttings down or transplanting is what should be done when trees crowd each other; and it is what the landscape gardener often has in mind when the first plantings are made.

The center trees in the planting pictured are mainly Retinispora plumosa and R. plumosa aurea, two of the best of the genus for general planting, and when R. pesifera is added there are three of the best. Interspersed are some R. compacta, Buxus arborescens, Thuja gigantea, Taxus baccata and its golden variety, and at the extreme end on the left there is an exceedingly nice specimen of the Cephalotaxus Fortunei, in prime health and vigor.

The photograph of this group was taken soon after the evergreens had received their annual clipping. The proper time for this is while the trees are still growing, as then it permits of further growth before the season ends, relieving a too formal look, which closely pruned evergreens so often present. JOSEPH MEEHAN.

A Charming Disposition of Evergreens

Forcing Rhubarb.

(100) Some time ago you published an article on the growin[g] of rhubarb in cellars or other dar[k] places, from plants grown from see[d] the same year. If so, would you b[e] so kind as to republish it? K. N.

—In regard to the forcing of rhubarb, we would refer the questione[r] to page 591 of the issue of The Florists' Exchange for November 17. A[s] rhubarb roots have to get to a considerable size before they produ[ce] stalks large enough for culinary purposes, it would simply be impossibl[e] to have roots large enough to forc[e] the first year from seed.

Agaricus Subrufescens.

(101) A few years ago quite a li[t]tle stir was made over a supposedl[y] new mushroom, viz.: Agaricus subrufescens. I purchased second lots o[f] spawn, and finally got a large be[d] well run and a few mushrooms, whe[n] the building was burned. Since the[n] I have tried to obtain some spaw[n] of it to experiment with, but hav[e] not succeeded. I am sure it is n[ot] advertised, but possibly some o[ne] grows it for home use. Any assis[t]ance you may be able to render w[ill] be most thankfully received by

A SUBSCRIBER.

—Perhaps some reader can supp[ly] the desired information. This mus[h]room was introduced into the tra[de] by the late F. Boulon, Sea Cliff, N.

Remedy for Ants.

(102) Will you please tell me ho[w] to rid my greenhouse of small ant[s]. They are very numerous, especial[ly] in the propagating bed.

Ky. J. A. T.

—A very good remedy for ants [is] to make a mixture consisting of on[e] third Fowler's solution, arsenic a[nd] two-thirds common sugar syru[p;] scatter a few drops about near t[he] ants' runways. This is a sure remedy without danger.

Supply Catalogues Wanted.

(103) Will you kindly give the names of manufacturers of ja[r]dinieres, fern dishes, etc., as I wou[ld] like to receive one of their catalogue[s]. I noticed a manufacturer's name [in] The Florists' Exchange not long a[go] dealing in the new green color[ed] ware, but cannot recall it. I wou[ld] like to have one of their catalogu[es], also one from a concern that h[as] the China cornucopia hangings f[or] cut flowers.

New Jersey. L.

—While we have not the names [of] manufacturers of the florist supp les desired, we would refer the irer to the advertisements in our mns of the various florist supply es, who no doubt can furnish all materials required.

Unsatisfactory Mushrooms.

04) Please let me know what ies mushrooms to come up so l and spindly. Temperature was at from 55 to 60 degrees.

1. E. D. E.

The mushroom grower does not whether it is the beginning or last of the crop. We presume, ever, that it must be the last of crop, and if so we would advise ng a mulch of equal parts of a soil and fresh stable manure from straw, about one inch in h.

Plants for Easter.

05) Kindly let us know whether son Rambler roses should be ed now in a night temperature ·2 degrees to be in flower next :er. Also if it is too soon to : Spiræa japonica. Can well ed Lilium longiflorum be forced that date? Can Lilium Harrisii, ches high, be held in a cool temture for Easter?

SUBSCRIBER.

For information regarding the :ing of Crimson Rambler roses spiræa for Easter flowering, we ld refer the inquirer to the an-' to W. J. H., on page 687 of our week's issue. Started Lilium iflorum should come in all right Easter, but they will need to be growing right along. The Lili-Harrisii, which are now 6 inches , can be had for Easter, and ld come along with a night temture of about 50 degrees.

intum Hybridum vs. A. Croweanum

06) Kindly tell us the differ-between Adiantum hybridum A. Croweanum, if any. Where A. hybridum be obtained?

C. J. L. O'Q.

This question has been raised ral times, and the introducers of se two ferns agreed to submit cimens to the Society of American rists to determine whether there s any difference or not between m. The plants were given to bert Cameron, curator of the Har-d Botanical Garden, Cambridge, s., for examination, and the fol-ing is his report on the subject.

After growing Adiantum Crowean-and Adiantum hybridum for one r I find they are quite distinct. antum Croweanum has longer nds, grows more upright and has ller pinnules than A. hybridum. antum hybridum does not grow te as tall as A. Croweanum; the nds are not quite as straight or ight as those of A. Croweanum l are of a darker shade of green. pinnules are much larger than in Croweanum.

'Dr. Benjamin Robinson of the y Herbarium examined the plants said they are quite distinct."

diantum Croweanum originated h Peter Crowe, Utica, N. Y.; and hybridum with the late John H. ', Washington, D. C.

Nitrate of Soda for Lettuce.

107) How, under what conditions when should nitrate of soda be lied to lettuce? In what quantity every hundred square feet of ch? K. N.

–I have always found, in using ni-e of soda, that a great deal de-ds on the condition of the crop. netimes lettuce will make a quick wth without the use of nitrate; on other hand, ofttimes the crop will benefited by its use. The safest hod in regard to feeding is for h grower to experiment on a small te; this will give him a line to work better than anyone else can advise, the simple reason that soils vary much in different localities. How-r, I would recommend using ni-e of soda dissolved in water, say, ablespoonful to a three gallon can water, affording enough to give the a fair watering. Keep the water the foliage as much as possible. best time to use this fertilizer is er the plants are established in ir permanent quarters when mak-their growth before heading.

W. TURNER.

Victory Has Made Good

Place your orders early for rooted cuttings. Prices $6.00 per 100. $50.00 per 1000.

Guttman & Weber, 43 W. 28th St. NEW YORK — Grower, LYNBROOK, L. I.

Mention the Florists' Exchange when writing.

RED RIDING HOOD, New Scarlet for 1907

If you want to be in line get your order in early. This is the scarlet you will pay your coal bill with.

Strong, healthy, well rooted cuttings ready Jan. 1st, 1907. This speaks for the healthy condition of our stock winning first prizes on every vase of carnations exhibited at the Chicago Flower Show, 15 in all.

We also have **ARISTOCRAT, WHITE PERFECTION, DAY BREAK LAWSON** a grand variety of the Lawson family in some respects superior to Enchantress, and many others of the best varieties.

SEND FOR COMPLETE LIST AND PRIZES

CHICAGO CARNATION CO. A. T. PYFER, Mgr. JOLIET, ILL.

Mention the Florists' Exchange when writing.

ROOTED CUTTINGS

	Per 100	Per 1000
WHITE—Queen	$1.50	$12.50
Lady Bountiful	2.50	20.00
White Lawson	2.00	17.50
Perfection	6.00	
PINK—Enchantress	2.00	15.00
Rose Pink Enchantress	6.00	
Lawson	1.50	12.50
Pink Patten	4.00	
Helen Goddard	4.00	
Ethel Ward	2.00	15.00
RED—Red Lawson	2.00	17.50
Robert Craig	5.00	
Victory	5.00	
Harry Fenn	2.00	15.00
VARIEGATED—Mrs. Patten	2.50	20.00

QUIDNICK GREENHOUSES J. H. CUSHING, Prop., QUIDNICK, ANTHONY P. O., R. I.

Mention The Florists' Exchange when writing.

MABELLE--New Pink Carnation for 1907

Color.—A peculiar shade of lovely pink, with a faint yellowish cast; several shades lighter than the Lawson. Unlike most pinks, the brightest sun does not injure the color. Size.—Three to four inches in diameter when established. Odor.—Pleasing, but not strong. Stems.—Invariably strong, but always graceful, ranging from 12 to 30 inches during the season. Habit, etc.—A very quick active grower, making specimen plants in a short time, even from late cuttings. On account of its rapid growth, requires supporting very soon after benching. Gets away rapidly, blooms early and gives long stems right from the start. Productiveness.—Prodigious is the best word we know of to use here. It is the most incessant bloomer early and late, we have ever grown. Stock limited. Delivery Jan. 5th to 10th and later. Price, $12.00 per 100, $100.00 per 1000.

THE H. WEBER & SONS CO., OAKLAND, MD.

UNROOTED CARNATION CUTTINGS

ENCHANTRESS, QUEEN, FAIR MAID, RED SPORT, HARLOWARDEN, pink, white and variegated LAWSON, $10.00 per 1000. WHITE PERFECTION and VICTORY, $30.00 per 1000.
LADY BOUNTIFUL, $12.00 per 1000.
LIEUTENANT PEARY, $15.00 per 1000.
SCOTTII FERNS, 6 in., $25.00 per 100.
COLEUS Verschaffeltii and Golden Bedder, 2 in., $18.00 per 1000.

Larchmont Nurseries

Larchmont, N. Y.

Mention The Florists' Exchange when writing.

White Enchantress

white sport of Enchantress, rooted cuttings $12.00 per 100; $100.00 per 1000.

E. SCHRADER, NEW SPRINGVILLE
Richmond Borough, N. Y.

Mention the Florists' Exchange when writing.

CARNATIONS

No. 1 stock rooted cuttings these prices for Dec. and Jan. delivery only.

	Per 1000		Per 1000
Enchantress	$20 00	B. Market	$15 00
L. Bountiful	15 00	Lawson	15 00
Cardinal	25 00	Harlowarden	15 00

100 at thousand rates. Cash with order.

SMITH & GANNETT, Geneva, N. Y.

Mention the Florists' Exchange when writing.

ROOTED CARNATION CUTTINGS

Good, clean, healthy stock, free from all disease. Enchantress, best light pink; Robert Craig, fine red; Nelson Fisher, best dark pink; M. A. Patten, excellent variegated; Lady Bountiful, white; Queen, white. Orders taken now will be ready for January delivery. Write for prices.

VALLEY VIEW GREENHOUSES,
YELIE Bros., Props. MARLBOROUGH, N. Y.

Mention the Florists' Exchange when writing.

CARNATIONS

F. DORNER & SONS CO.
LA FAYETTE, IND.

Mention the Florists' Exchange when writing.

ABUNDANCE

Rooted cuttings of the most prolific white carnation will be ready for delivery in January. Price, $6 00 per 100; $40.00 per 1000; 250 at 1000 rate; 5 per cent. discount for cash with order.

RUDOLPH FISCHER, Great Neck, L.I., N.Y.

Mention the Florists' Exchange when writing.

CARNATIONS

Rooted cuttings ready January 1. Victory, $6.00 per 100; $50.00 per 1000; Enchantress, Bountiful, White Lawson, Var. Lawson, Patten, $3.00 per 100; $25.00 per 1000; Pink Lawson, Boston Market, Queen, H. Fenn, and Fair Maid, $2 00 per 100; $15.00 per 1000. 5 per cent. for cash with order.

R. ENGELMAN & SON, Pittsfield, Mass.

Mention the Florists' Exchange when writing.

S. J. GODDARD

Framingham, Mass.

Rooted Carnation Cuttings a Specialty.

Correspondence Solicited.

Mention the Florists' Exchange when writing.

JOHN E. HAINES

The leading scarlet, brilliant color, fine stem, the most productive ever introduced, blooms early until thrown out in July no extra grass, all shoots make flowers. Watch the papers and see what growers say about it. None but well-rooted healthy cuttings leave the place. Rooted Cuttings ready December 15, 1906. Price, $6.00 per 100; $50.00 per 1000.

JOHN E. HAINES, Bethlehem, Pa.

A. B. DAVIS & SON, Inc.

PURCELLVILLE, VA.

Place your orders now for Red Sport cuttings, the best red carnation grown. $3.50 per 100; $30.00 per 1000.

Mention the Florists' Exchange when writing.

The American Carnation

Mention The Florists' Exchange when writing.

A BED OF MUSHROOMS

Raised from our Spawn, will **bear longer and yield better** than from any other variety of Spawn. This is proven by facts. Full particulars and information how to succeed in mushroom raising free. We warrant you if using our method of growing mushrooms that all will go well.

KNUD GUNDESTRUP & CO., MUSHROOM SPECIALISTS, 4273 Milwaukee Ave., CHICAGO

Rip Van Winkle

Has finally got awake, and finds that he has at least 125,000 Geraniums in 2 in. pots and in fine condition, and will sell at $18.00 per 1000; composed of the following varieties: Poitevine, La Favorite, F. Perkins, Viaud, Doyle, D. Grant, Bruantii, Pasteur, Brett, Nutt and several other varieties. This is to make room "Get a move on you," and get some fine stock.

Cash with order.

J. E. FELTHOUSEN,
154 VAN VRANKEN AVE., SCHENECTADY, N. Y.

Mention the Florists' Exchange when writing.

GERANIUMS

Ricard, Doyle, Buchner, Nutt, Poitevine, Brett, 2 in. pots, ready in January. Orders booked now at $20.00 per 1000.

ROOTED CUTTINGS BELOW READY NOW

	100
Fuchsias, best varieties	$1.50
Double Petunias	1.50
Heliotropes	1.00
Ageratum	.75

ERNEST HARRIS, DELANSON, N. Y.

Mention the Florists' Exchange when writing.

GERANIUMS

Rooted Cuttings, S. A. Nutt, Buchner, Grant, double, $10.00 per 1000. Alphonse Ricard, $15.00 per 1000. Cash with order.

PETER BROWN,
LANCASTER, PA.

Mention the Florists' Exchange when writing.

GERANIUMS

Rooted, then replanted. Good plants which will start readily. Nutt, Doyle, Bruantii and Buchner, $14.00 per 1000. Ricard, Castellane, Poitevine, Perkins, Viaud, etc., $16.00 per 1000. Any 100 at 1000 rates. Plenty of Nutt and Doyle. Coleus, Red and yellow, 60c. Fancy, 50c. per 100. Gladioli, Groff's mixed, 500 for $3.00. Cash or C. O. D.

DANIEL K. HERR, Lancaster, Pa.

Mention the Florists' Exchange when writing.

GERANIUMS

in good varieties 2½ in. pots, ready March 1 1907.

WM. J. CHINNICK, Trenton, N. J.

Mention the Florists' Exchange when writing.

ROOTED CUTTINGS GERANIUMS AND CARNATIONS

Send a list of what you want and how many of each variety and I will be pleased to quote figures on your complete order.

ALBERT M. HERR, LANCASTER, PA.

Mention the Florists' Exchange when writing.

GERANIUMS

Rooted cuttings of S. A. Nutt, at $10 00 per 1000; Beaute de Poitevine, $12.00 per 1000; well rooted and packed right.

C. F. TREICHLER, SANBORN, N. Y.

Mention the Florists' Exchange when writing.

A FEW GOOD THINGS YOU WANT

DRACAENA INDIVISA, 4 and 5 in., $10.00 and $25.00 per 100.
ASPARAGUS SPRENGERI, 2 in., $2.50 per 100.
GERANIUMS. S. A. Nutt, John Doyle, Perkins, Double Gen Grant, Poitevine, 2 in. pots, $2.00 per 100. Rooted cuttings $1.00 per 100.
GLADIOLUS, blooming bulbs, extra fine mixture, to close out while they last, 60c. per 100; $5.00 per 1000.
VINCA, Var., 2 inch, $2.00 per 100.
PRIMULA OBCONICA, 2 inch, $2.00 per 100.
REX BEGONIA, nice plants, 2 and 2½ in., $5.00 per 100.
ASPARAGUS PLUMOSUS, 2 in. $3.00 per 100; 3 in. $5.00 per 100.
BOSTON FERN, 5 in. 30c. each.
PIERSON FERN, 6 in. 50c. each.

GEO. M. EMMANS, Newton, N. J.

Mention the Florists' Exchange when writing.

CINERARIAS

Fine, large flowering, dwarf Prize Strain, 4 in. $6.00 per 100.

AGERATUM (Inimitable): It is the finest Ageratum in cultivation. R. C., $1.50 per 100; 2 in., $3.00 per 100.

GERANIUMS, out of 1½ in. pots, best varieties $15.00 per 1000. Send for list.

J. C. SCHMIDT CO., BRISTOL, PA.

Mention the Florists' Exchange when writing.

FOR CHRISTMAS

500 Erica Melanthera, 6-8 and 10 in. pots, good stock. Write for prices

H. ABEL, E. Rutherford, N. J.

Mention the Florists' Exchange when writing.

LIST OF ADVERTISERS

INDEX TO STOCK ADVERTISED

Contents.

ROSES

During the Winter, and especially now when prices are a little higher and every inch of stem means more money, it is a great temptation for the grower to cut his plants back to hard wood, thus getting much longer stems; but the difference in the increased value of the blooms is lost later on, for plants thus treated will break much slower, and generally come weak. Therefore, always leave at least two good eyes for a future crop where the shoot is strong, and one if weak. Cutting should only be entrusted to experienced help, as it is one of the most important parts of our work. The best profit from our plants comes during the Winter months, therefore we should strive to have the plants at their best. Do not try to hurry a crop for the holidays. The result is always disastrous, for in the first place the plants get weak, and though more flowers may be cut the quality will be poorer, consequently a lower figure will be realized for them. In days gone by a rose was a rose, but to-day only the fancy stock commands good prices and a ready sale. If, however, the plants are in fine shape, and it is desired to have a few extra blooms for the holidays, the temperature can be raised one or two degrees on sunny days, giving the plants a light spray, thus causing the flowers to develop more rapidly; but no undue forcing should be attempted.

I am glad to note that each year there is less pickled stock dumped on the market the day before Christmas.

As steady firing has now commenced red spider will again begin to assert itself in corners and around supports where it is not always handy to get at. Care should be taken therefore to syringe thoroughly just such places, remembering that this pest is on the under side of the leaves. We are often asked for a remedy for these mites; there is nothing so good as a hose in the hands of a careful man. Before syringing, especially after a few cloudy days, make sure the soil in the benches is not too dry, or the plants will scald badly. Spray only on clear days; then the plants should be well shaken, so that the foliage will dry off by night if possible. Also start the fires a little earlier, so that air can be left on a little longer, and the pipes being warm there is less danger of the plants being chilled. If the night is but moderately cold leave on a crack of air all night, keeping the houses a couple of degrees warmer. This will not require much more fuel and will greatly benefit the plants.

PENN.

ST. LOUIS.—Since last report trade conditions have changed. Retail business is not as good as it should be at this time of year; society is not giving many entertainments and dinners just before the holidays, and wedding orders are few as are calls for funeral work. Monday morning stock at the wholesale houses was scarce, even roses, which had been very plentiful last week. Richmond and Killarney are in good demand, with the top price at $6 per 100. Bride and Bridesmaid are very plentiful, at $5 for the best. Ivory, fancy, $8; Souvenir du President Carnot, $8. Perle des Jardins have little call, only for special orders; $5 is obtained for the best fancy. American Beauty are scarce in fancy grades, which run at $5 per dozen; other grades are more plentiful. Roman hyacinths are in the market and with Paper White narcissus bring $4 per 100 for fancy; other grades, $2 and $3. Lily of the valley is coming in fine, at $4 for choice, $3 other grades. While carnations are plentiful they are not in sufficient supply for the demand and are cleaned out early in the morning for orders ahead; late buyers generally get left. Extra fancy Enchantress, Robert Craig, White Perfection, and Mrs. T. W. Lawson bring as high as $5 per 100. California violets are coming in in goodly numbers, and with seasonable weather should be very plentiful during the next two weeks; 35c. and 50c. is the price this week. Smilax is having a good call at $12.50 per 100 strings. All other greens are in demand. Ground pine is scarce; holly very plentiful.

ST. PATRICK.

Decorative Plants.

SCIRPUS CERNUUS.—Although the advent into commerce within the last few years of several grasses choicer in character and more ornamental in make-up than Scirpus cernuus, or as it is more commonly known Isolepis gracilis, it is questionable if for many purposes there is even now anything to equal this accommodating little favorite. There is certainly nothing to surpass it in gracefulness and for the soothing effect it produces when used in bordering groups of stiffer plants put together for decoration. Again, it is a charming little plant for small dishes, as well as for finishing off around the edges of baskets or pans made up in the main of erect growing plants. About the only thing that Isolepis gracilis insists on having without stint is water, and that it must have in abundance to live either in the store window or in the greenhouse.

Isolepis gracilis is most conveniently propagated by division, and this is accomplished by tearing apart old plants and potting the divided portions into the smallest size pots, then when these are filled with roots the plants can be potted into three or three and a half inch pots, the latter size being large enough for the purposes to which the plants will in all likelihood be eventually put. But if larger specimens are required they can easily be had by shifting the plants either into larger pots or pans. When growing, the plants will develop their characteristics more advantageously if they are placed so that they can droop unhindered.

REX BEGONIAS.—Rex begonias are exceedingly useful plants, and since their propagation and culture are so easy every grower of miscellaneous stock should raise them in quantity, especially as it appears that recently the demand for them has increased considerably. Hitherto it has been noticeable that many growers of these plants contented themselves with the cultivation of the old and commoner varieties to the entire exclusion of the many beautiful kinds that have for some time been offered at quite reasonable prices. These choice sorts, once a stock of them is obtained, are just as easily propagated and grown as the commoner kinds.

There are several ways of propagating rex begonias, but on the whole I think the most expeditious method is that of cutting the nerves or ribs on the under side of healthy and perfect leaves and then laying the leaves on clean sand in the propagating bench. It will be necessary to peg down the leaves to keep them in place and close to the sand. The leaves, in course of propagation, will require to be shaded, and it may be as well to keep them shaded until roots have emitted and young leaves formed directly above where each cut was made. When that stage has been reached they may be potted into small pots. While in these pots as well as when they were in the sand they require to be kept moist. For the first potting well sifted soil should be used, and for subsequent potting a compost of good fibrous loam two-thirds and one-third of well rotted manure, leaf mold and sand.

SWAINSONA.—There are but few flowering plants that invariably give so much satisfaction for an indefinite period as swainsonas. The swainsonas are grown in variety, but the white one is of the greatest value to florists. They thrive equally well when planted in a bench or in pots; they flower readily when young, in small pots, and if the plants are kept growing and in good form, they make very acceptable subjects in six-inch pots. Swainsona is easily rooted from cuttings, and from now on these should be put in sand to root. The cuttings will require shading from the time they are put in the sand until they begin to make roots. When rooted well the little plants should be potted into small pots, and these also kept shaded for a few days until they get in a measure established. Whenever swainsona plants get potbound they show flower and thereafter almost exhaust themselves with a persistency of blooming; to avoid this they should be shifted as occasion requires it until the desired size has been attained. Any good potting material will suit the plants, but if strong growth and extra bloom in size and substance are desired, good rich soil is necessary. When plants are required for cutting from permanently, plants out of three-inch pots should be planted in a part of a bench in a rose house or anywhere where a like temperature is maintained. For Summer bloom the best method is to plant a sufficient number in a frame outdoors, where they will bloom freely all through the season.

PROPAGATION OF CROTONS.—There are many growers of crotons who defer the propagation of these plants until after Christmas, and there are others who put off the work still later for reasons that are apparent. The two methods of propagating crotons are by cuttings and mossing the tops of plants that are rendered useless for any other purpose by reason of being denuded of foliage at their base. It makes no difference which method is practiced in regard to the time when the operation should begin. There is no question but it pays to moss all the good tops available, and the sooner a beginning is made the better. Anyone who has been in the habit of rooting rubber plants can make a success with crotons by this method, the main requisite being to keep the moss continually moist right into where the incision has been made in the stem. It will hasten the process of root making in the stem if the roots of the stock plants are kept on the dry side. When the plants, the tops of which have been operated on and mossed as suggested, are scattered here and there among others on which this operation is not to be performed, there is usually some difficulty experienced in keeping the former uniformly and sufficiently moist. To obviate this difficulty, as well as for convenience in other matters, it will be well to place all the plants with mossed tops on a bench or benches devoted exclusively to themselves, and as conditions are favorable, three or at most four weeks only will elapse before they are sufficiently rooted for potting. They can be placed quite close to each other on the bench without fear of spoiling the shape of the plants. When roots are seen peeping out through the moss it will then be safe to sever the tops from the stock plants. The period immediately following this procedure is usually the most critical in the life of the plant, and if the requirements of the case are not well understood and adopted failure to obtain well furnished specimen plants will result. When the tops are potted they should be placed over a gentle bottom heat (if they can be closed in by a frame so much the better) and kept continually moist at the roots and on the foliage. The roots should by no means be soaked with water, only extreme care should be exercised that they do not get dry. They also require to be shaded for a week or more from the sunlight, the sole purpose being to keep the plants newly severed and potted as much as possible from realising what they went through and suffered during the process of transformation. When it is seen that the foliage is in no way limp and the plants generally have the appearance of being able to look out for themselves to a certain extent, they can be taken out of their close quarters and placed a little apart on another bench to make room for another batch of newly potted tops.

The other method of propagation consists of the making of cuttings of young healthy wood and the placing of these in the propagating bench, taking care to have the sand very firm around the cuttings. What was said about moisture in relation to the other method is fully as applicable to cuttings, which should never be allowed to get dry. It is also much better with cuttings if they can be covered over and kept close by having a sash put over the propagating bench. It is very important for the successful rooting of any hard-wooded cutting, and especially so with crotons, that they be left undisturbed in the sand until they are rooted; and the time necessary usually is not more than three weeks, varying of course according to the intensity or the reverse of the bottom heat available. In order that the cuttings should not be disturbed, watering with force should be carefully avoided and instead a gentle spray should only be used. Some growers put a small batch of cuttings in at one time, using the remaining available room in the propagating bench for something else, and the something very often needs radically different treatment from that necessary for crotons. It is much the better plan, I think, for crotons, as well as for many other things, not to make two bites of a cherry, but to put in as many as can be had at once; this will save many little annoyances in the routine of the work.

When the cuttings are rooted they should be potted very carefully into small pots and then placed where they can be shaded and kept close and moist until they get established, after which it is very plain sailing. In putting in crotons cuttings I have found it a very satisfactory plan, especially with strong growing varieties, to tie a little clean moss around each cutting before putting it into the sand.

D. M.

FOUNDED IN 1888

THE FLORISTS' EXCHANGE

A Week [Medium] of Interchange for Florists, Nurserymen Seedsmen and the Trade in General

Exclusively a Trade Paper.

Entered at New York Post Office as Second Class Matter

Published EVERY SATURDAY by

A. T. DE LA MARE PTG. AND PUB. CO. LTD.

2, 4, 6 and 8 Duane Street,

P. O. Box 1697.
Telephone 3765-6 Beekman. NEW YORK.

CHICAGO OFFICE: 127 East Berwyn Avenue.

ILLUSTRATIONS.

Electrotypes of the illustrations used in this paper can usually be supplied by the publishers. Price on application.

YEARLY SUBSCRIPTIONS.

United States, Canada, and Mexico, $1.00. Foreign countries in postal union, $2.50. Payable in advance. Remit by Express Money Order Draft on New York, Post Office Money Order or Registered Letter.

The address label indicates the date when subscription expires and is our only receipt therefor.

REGISTERED CABLE ADDRESS:

Florex, New York.

ADVERTISING RATES.

One-half inch, 75c.; ¾-inch, $1.00; 1-inch, $1.25, special positions extra. Send for Rate Card showing discount of 10c., 15c., 25c., or 35c., per inch on continuous advertising. For rates on Wants, etc., see column for Classified Advertisements.

Copy must reach this office by 12 noon Wednesday to secure insertion in issue of following Saturday.

Orders from unknown parties must be accompanied with cash or satisfactory references.

Chrysanthemum Society of America.

Work of Committees.

CHICAGO, December 1.—Mlle. Jeanne Rosette, pink; exhibited by the E. G. Hill Company; scored 91 points, commercial scale. DAVID FRASER, Secretary.

American Rose Society.

More Prizes.

The President of the Washington Florists' Club, Peter Bisset, notifies us that Mrs. S. C. Briggs offers a cash prize of $10 for six or more blooms of any new rose never before exhibited. This prize is given especially to encourage private gardeners, who would be likely to exhibit six blooms, but would not be able, owing to limited space, to show a greater number.

Messrs. H. F. Michell Company of Philadelphia offer a cup valued at $25 for a vase of 50 Richmond roses to be exhibited next March; and Miss M. I. Hammond of Fishkill-on-Hudson, N. Y., offers a $5 gold piece for the prettiest exhibit in the hall, to be decided by some three Washington ladies visiting the exhibition.

BENJAMIN HAMMOND, Secretary.
Fishkill-on-Hudson, N. Y.

Some Nature Books.

REAL THINGS IN NATURE, by E. S. Holden. Publishers, The Macmillan Company, New York.—This is a reading book of science for American boys and girls. Among other things on which it treats is the subject of botany. The teachings are useful and instructive and numerous illustrations are given descriptive of the text. An excellent work for the purpose for which it is intended.

THE HEART OF NATURE, by Mabel Osgood Wright. Publishers, The Macmillan Company, New York.

Another of the Standard School Library books published by this well known house. It is written in Mrs. Wright's most fascinating style, is profusely illustrated, and cannot fail to interest young readers and draw them closer to the heart of Nature.

We have on hand several interesting articles which are unavoidably crowded out of this week's issue. Among them is a paper on "Orchid Culture," by G. H. Pring, of Shaw's Garden, recently read before the St. Louis Florists' Club.

The carnation is the favorite flower of Queen Alexandra of England, and is in a fair way to become the Winter fashionable flower in that country.

Well-Merited Recognition.

The New York Florists' Club has an honorary membership, an honor which it bestows only for superior service rendered in some form to the interests of horticulture. On its list are included the names of the late Dean Hole, Wm. R. Smith, W. Bayard Cutting, John H. Starin and Samuel Thorne, all of whom, each in his own way, have contributed to the advancement of the art for which the club stands sponsor.

At the meeting on Monday evening last the club added two more names to this list, viz., those of John N. May and Charles H. Allen, both ex-presidents of the organisation, who from unavoidable causes have resigned from active membership.

The honor bestowed was well merited, particularly in the case of Mr. May, who was one of the founders of the club, its first president, an office he held for two successive terms; and who is one of the hardest and most earnest workers on behalf not only of the New York Florists' Club, but for the cause of the craft generally. To devote twenty years of one's life, unselfishly, to the welfare of any horticultural association speaks volumes for the loyalty of the worker in our common cause, and we are very glad that the New York Florists' Club has taken this method of rewarding efficient service on its behalf. Mr. May's health has not been of the best for some time, and that is the principal cause preventing him from further active participation in the club's affairs. That he may be long spared to enjoy the honor now conferred upon him is, we feel sure, the hearty wish of his confrères as it is of ourselves.

Mr. Allen, who was for years most active in club matters, and who also served as its president for two successive terms, has been compelled to sever his affiliation with the organisation on account of his business demanding all his time. His resignation as well as that of Mr. May was received with regret. It is a pleasure, indeed, that because of honorary membership the advice and counsel of two of the club's ablest adherents will still be available.

Plant Registration.

The paragraph appearing in our last week's issue (page 694) from the secretary of The American Carnation Society, with regard to the renaming of a new carnation rendered necessary through delay in publishing timeously the original registration of the new variety, a similar name having in the meantime appeared in print, presents a condition for which there seems to be no legitimate excuse. The explanation of the delay in publication given by Mr. Herr is to the effect that he desired simultaneous appearance of the registration in all the trade papers. This may or may not be a laudable policy to pursue; but it is a question whether it is of sufficient value to offset the inconvenience and injustice to those registering new varieties with the Carnation Society that the method entails, as is evidenced by the case in point. The convenience of the trade papers is of secondary importance to the rights of the registrars of new plants, and the duty of those responsible for such registration seems clear, namely, to forward at the earliest possible moment to the different media through which publication of registration is effected the names which it is desired to place on record, as safeguarding these names to the originators or introducers. Then will the society accepting the registration, and its official, be held blameless in the premises. It might be well, too, to furnish for publication, in case of delay, the date on which registration was sought from the secretary of the society, although this cannot altogether counteract priority of publication of a similar name without registration.

The present case emphasizes what we have already asserted, that societies registering new plants cannot control publication. It also demonstrates the need of all introducers or originators conforming to some practical plan of registration which shall work no injustice to anyone concerned; and this, at the present time, seems to be through recognized organizations—when the work of publication is attended to promptly and properly. And for the best welfare of all, as well as tending to completeness of record, we would strongly urge upon those naming new varieties the adoption of this plan.

While on this subject it may be well to call attention to the inexcusably lax methods existing in connection with registration in the S. A. F. O. H. The October 20, 1906, issue of this paper contains a registration notice of Canna New York; a duplicate registration of the same canna by the same society and the same originators, is announced in our issue of last week, December 8, 1906 without comment.

Of what practical value is a registration plan which permits of a happening of this kind within the short period of a month or two?

THE VILLAGE is the name of a new monthly publication, the first number (December, 1906) of which has just reached us. The new periodical proposes "to be an earnest attempt to reflect and interpret the actual life in American villages—and something more." The work of village improvement societies will receive considerable attention. The newcomer promises well; we wish it the greatest success.

Obituary

Thomas Hefling.

Thomas Hefling, a retired florist of Milwaukee, Wis., died at his residence, 547 Thirty-fourth street, on Sunday night, December 2, aged 80 years. Mr. Hefling came to Milwaukee at an early day and was for a number of years employed by the late S. S. Merrill, general manager of the Milwaukee road, as a gardener. He is survived by his widow and seven children, three sons and four daughters.

Ernest Huckreide.

Indianapolis has lost one of her pioneer florists—Ernest Huckreide, who for the past eighteen years has conducted his business in South State street. Mr. Huckreide was born in Westphalia, Germany, on August 23, 1835. Soon after his arrival in Indianapolis he took a position with the Vandalia Railroad Company, but during his spare time he cultivated flowers, and his interest along this line soon induced him to adopt the vocation of florist. He is survived by one son, Fred, his partner in business. He leaves a host of friends. I. B.

William C. Elliott.

William C. Elliott, an old time Newport gardener passed away November 28, after a long illness. Mr. Elliott came to Newport from the north of Ireland, more than thirty years ago. He was for the greater part of that time and until a few years ago gardener on the Wm. Brenton Greene estate. Mr. Elliott was a great enthusiast in the work of improving sweet corn, so much so in fact, that he devoted the most of his time during the last four years of his life to this work, with the result that he at least improved old varieties materially, in flavor and otherwise. He was a man of sterling character and honest convictions. D. M.

George R. Moore.

George R. Moore, president of the village of Fredonia, N. Y., died December 2 at the home of Dr. Nash, a relative. A fortnight ago he had started for Buffalo for medical treatment, but became so ill en route that he had to leave his train at Irving and go to Dr. Nash's home in that village.

Mr. Moore was 55 years old and one of the most popular and most generally liked men of the village. He had been village president for several terms, was president of the Chautauqua & Erie Grape Company, a co-operative organization of grape-growers, and had extensive farm and vineyard interests. He accumulated a considerable fortune. Mr. Moore was also well known as a horticulturist.

About a year ago Mr. Moore fell through a trap-door in a firehouse in Dunkirk, sustaining a compound fracture of the left leg. He never recovered from this injury.

Mr. Moore is survived by a widow, and a son, William.

PUBLICATIONS RECEIVED.

SECRETS OF MUSHROOM GROWING SIMPLY EXPLAINED, by A. V. Jackson, Chicago, Ill.—There is a host of practical advice contained in this pamphlet, which tells how to carry out every step from the preparation of material and making the beds to picking the crop and sending it to market. Mr. Jackson has had ten years' experience in growing mushrooms, and claims to be the largest grower of this esculent in America.

A Handsome Geranium Catalogue.

That the common but popular geranium should have devoted to itself a catalogue of the charming character of that just issued by R. Vincent, Jr., & Son, White Marsh, Md., would never occur to those unfamiliar with the extent of the geranium industry in the United States. Here, however, we have a publication of 32 pages, 9x7 inches, devoted to an enumeration and descriptions, with accompanying illustrations, of hundreds of varieties of geraniums, standard sorts, as well as novelties, in the different sections into which this class of plants has been divided, grown and for sale by this well-known enterprising firm.

In addition to its great value from a horticultural standpoint, the catalogue is one of the handsomest that has come to our desk, reflecting the highest credit on the distributing concern as well as on the printers. The front cover design shows Berthe de Presilly, the back cover a truss of E. H. Trego, geraniums, both printed in their natural color as near as the art of the printer can approach.

All the inside illustrations are from duograph plates printed in black and green on white enamel paper; these soften the tone and impart great realistic appearance to the finished product. The booklet is not only a catalogue, and that the finest of its kind ever issued, it is as well representative of the energy and broad liberal character of the house of R. Vincent, Jr. & Son.

OUR READERS' VIEWS

O'Mara and Burbank.

Editor Florists' Exchange:

In your last one or two issues I read a part of Mr. O'Mara's "amplification" of his criticism of Luther Burbank and his work; the remaining part I waded through the best way I could. In the beginning, Mr. O'Mara tells the world that in 1905 he visited the Pacific Coast, and he dropped in, no doubt, to have a social chat with the "Wizard." Mr. O'Mara does not say that he gave Mr. Burbank advance notice of his coming, that in consequence of such notice he expected to have miracles performed in honor of his presence, and that as an additional mark of favor, he might be urged to carry to the "leaden East" with him some token or tokens to convince those by whom he was sent that his mission was successful. Alas for the "Wizard!" He failed to do any stunts for the gratification of the great critic of the East; he let escape the opportunity of his lifetime. If he had only known the momentous consequences, one way or the other, of his reception of the great man from the East, he would not to-day have such cause to regret the indifference with which he treated the illustrious sojourner in the land of the Golden West.

When at last the visitor to the Pacific slope reached his quiet home in the East, he gathered his friends around him and to them he revealed the alleged frauds that had been perpetrated upon them. He told them how, many years ago, he, or some one else, was induced to buy some Shasta daisy seed, enough from which to raise ever so many plants. The plants were planted in a frame and left there to flower. The flowers, when they came, were not good enough, so the order went forth to hoe them up and throw them over the fence. This all happened years ago; but the pilgrim did not think of it before. Some other people in after years got hold of some Shasta daisy seed, but before the plants came into flower the growers hoed the ground around them before they made up their minds to tell the man with the hoe to throw them over the fence. Even if they had made up their minds to order the man with the hoe to hoe up the daisies, they would not add to the order to throw them over the fence; that would not be a methodical way of doing business.

After Mr. O'Mara rested from the fatigue of his journey, he took the pains to read up and find out what all the specialists in Europe and America have accomplished, and when he learns all, he announces to the world that, although in his versatility Burbank introduced some good things, yet, combined, all the specialists of the countries referred to beat him hollow. The horticulturists of the United States surely owe a debt of gratitude to Patrick O'Mara for his fearlessness in his disinterested attack on the Wizard of the Golden West, whose doom is sealed in spite of Harwood, Burpee, Vaughan, and all the rest.

H. P.

Growth of Anthurium Warocqueanum.

Editor Florists' Exchange:

To students of nature it will be interesting to read of the rapid growth of a leaf of one of our most beautiful indoor foliage plants—Anthurium Warocqueanum—very little seen in private greenhouses where sufficient heat is at command. It is easily grown in a well-drained pot, in a rich open mixture of peat, loam, sand and manure, with plenty of waterings and moderate shading. The plant I have was bought 2 years ago from a large commercial establishment, the only one they had. Last Spring I cut it down and grew it in a 9-inch pot all Summer. About two months ago I shifted it into a 12-inch pot in a good rich soil. The result was a noble leaf indeed—38½ inches in length by 13½ inches in width, a gain of 6½ inches in length and 4½ inches in width on the last leaf. The plant has now eight large leaves, and when my first measurement was taken the leaf must have been about eight days old.

Nov. 5, 13 in. x 2½ in.	Nov. 13, 28½ in. x 9¾ in.
Nov. 6, 14 in. x 3⅝ in.	Nov. 14, 30⅛ in. x 10¾ in.
Nov. 7, 16 in. x 4 in.	Nov. 15, 33 in. x 11½ in.
Nov. 8, 18 in. x 5 in.	Nov. 16, 34 in. x 12¼ in.
Nov. 9, 19½ in. x 6½ in.	Nov. 17, 35¼ in. x 12½ in.
Nov. 10, 21¾ in. x 7½ in.	Nov. 18, Sunday.
Nov. 11, Sun.; no meas.	Nov. 19, 37½ in. x 13¼ in.
Nov. 12, 26 in. x 9¼ in.	Nov. 20, 38½ in. x 13½ in.
	Nov. 21, 38½ in. x 13½ in.

OTTO JEKOLIN.

Westwood Replies to Job.

Editor Florists' Exchange:

Under the head of "Reflections on Current Topics," I notice that Job takes to task your New England contemporary for claiming Kirkcaldy as the birthplace of "America's greatest gardener." If Job could see Kirkcaldy now; "it's up the Pith," and Pathhead has become one of the Kirkcaldy burghs, making it perfectly proper to say that the large-hearted gardener was born in the same town as our "ain Adam Smith." A few minutes' walk separates the birthplaces of the two great men.

We agree most heartily with Job that the vote of the Gardeners and Florists' Club of Boston was a complimentary one, and it is appreciated by both candidates. It was a most friendly contest so far as the two candidates are concerned.

I hope that Job has heard of the latest method of the Gardeners and Florists' Club of Boston for the elevation of horticulture?

I have always been led to believe that His Satanic Majesty was buried in Kirkcaldy; but is it possible that Job has not heard of the resurrection that took place there, a great many years ago, when his Majesty came forth from his silent tomb, soared above the house-tops, turned his face toward the west; and the people in the "Auld Toon" have it on record that he is so busy with the cities of New York and Chicago that he has never had time to pay a visit to the Hub of the Universe, dear Boston.

T. H. WESTWOOD.

Registration of Plants.

Editor Florists' Exchange:

It was very gratifying to me to read in the last week's issue of The Florists' Exchange the article on the Registration of Plants. Professor Webber has got the right idea as to how registration should be accomplished. I differ from him, however, in one particular. I think the S. A. F. O. H. is the proper body to adopt his suggestions. This is a national organization, with members in nearly every State in the Union, and has at the present time a system of registration applying, unfortunately, only to the name of the plant, but sadly lacking in description and other things necessary for its proper identification. For the S. A. F. to adopt and carry out Professor Webber's suggestions as to registration would mean considerable expense to the society; but I am sure those applying for registration would gladly pay all necessary expenses attached to the same. Once let the society take the proper steps to adopt the suggestions advanced by Professor Webber, and I believe there will be no trouble in getting the wherewithal to carry on the work. The plants registered, with their descriptions, and wherever possible accompanied with photographs, should be published in the annual report of the society. In this way the S. A. F. can become of more benefit to its members, and at the same time take its proper place as the national society of horticulture in America.

I trust that now the subject is once more before your readers, others will give expression to their views thereon. One thing is certain, if the S. A. F. longer neglects the proper registration; another society will arise and enter the breach, for it is not to be thought that American horticulturists will be long content with the present system of registration of plants as carried on by the S. A. F.

PETER BISSET.

Notes from Pittsburg.

IT WAS CHRISTMAS FLOWERING PLANTS at the Florists' Club meeting the other night (4th inst.), and friend Clark of the Cut Flower Company just tickled our fur the wrong way a little bit. He hit us straight from the shoulder, caring not a fig whom he hurt, and it did us good. He said we could grow cut flowers all right, but when it came to flowering plants in pots Pittsburg was nowhere. He referred to commercial growers only. So far as they go, the Blind Brothers at West View grow fine stock, and A. W. Smith of Sixth avenue grows excellent material, and a young firm out at Cheswick promise nobly, and John Bader's is the emporium of Western Pennsylvania, but all of these are only a drop in the bucket of the demand of this great Smoky City. Then

WHERE DO WE GET OUR POT PLANTS? From New York, Philadelphia and Cincinnati! Representatives from these great cities come to our town with a lot of samples and put up at a first-class hotel and treat us to eat and to smoke—nothing else I guess, for Wm. C. is a rigid teetotaller—then hire a wagon into which they load their sample plants and drive around the city and suburbs from florist's store to florist's store showing their goods and entering their orders. And they go home happy. They declare Pittsburg is a "bully good town." The make big sales at full prices, and their money is sure. Our city people must have pot plants and our florists must supply them, and it is a godsend to us to have those outside growers come to us with their plants. He declared there is

A MAGNIFICENT OPPORTUNITY for a young man or firm in the plant business for the Pittsburg market. But he must grow A1 stock and put it up in attractive, presentable form. He deplored the dirty pots and slip-shod appearance of potted plants often sent to market. Well-grown, well-bloomed, tastily done up plants will always sell and at a good price, but slovenly rubbish is only fit for the dung hill. Right within trolley car distance of this city are lots available, clean, clear air land, where a man could start a plant-growing establishment, then a telephone message in an hour or so would bring in a hurried order, or in a half day a wagon load. Or the city florist needing the plants could jump on a car and run out to the greenhouse and select whatever material he wanted, engage it weeks ahead if need be. Everything is here except the man.

WALTER JAMES. While Mr. Clark was ripping us to pieces near me sat a young man named Walter James. He is now head gardener at the Western Penitentiary, but for years he served as propagator at the Phipps Conservatories and he is a bright, hard-working, energetic fellow and a most excellent propagator and grower of the finer pot plants. Now, if a lad like this had the money and had one or two other equally energetic and skillful growers associated with him, I couldn't help thinking this shoe would just fit his foot.

ARTIFICIAL POINSETTIAS.—A member had the temerity to ask for information about these. Mr. Clark got warm and declared "We've got to have them!" Smith grows his own and he grows them splendidly, and the Blind boys grow some, but aside from these where else can you get a poinsettia in this town? And he emptied his wrath upon a quaking little potted plant he lifted from the exhibition table. When you get them they are of such quality and condition you can't sell them. Poinsettias are just the color and thing for Christmas, that is, if you could get the quality, but what's the use of talking, we haven't got them.

TELL US OUR FAULTS.—Mr. Clark declared it is deception and nonsense when we visit a brother florist's place and find his plants are mediocre or rubbishy to tell how fine they are just for the sake of pleasing him and keeping on the right side of him: then another fellow will come in and tell him the same thing till the man himself believes it. Then he sends the "stuff" to market and the heartless public impresses the truth upon him; it either refuses to purchase his stock or buys it at a ridiculously low figure. Far better be honest with the florist and tell him his stock is no good, and when the next man comes in let him also advise him of the inferiority of his plants and so on. This will set him to thinking, working and aiming at a higher grade, and when he goes to market the quicker sales and better prices will accentuate the truth of his honest critics. But an old fellow present declared that if we should visit a neighbor florist and talk so boldly as this to him, he'd never ask us in or treat us! That ancient must be born again.

FUNNY ABOUT MR. CLARK.—At a previous meeting Mr. Clark was on the floor dilating on chrysanthemums and telling us about the kinds Fred Burki grows and that Fred wouldn't grow anything unless there is money in it. Now Wm. C. is in the commission business, and it is rumored that that is the moneyest branch of our calling, and he showed it, for emblazoned on his portly breast was an usually generous diamonded charm, a Scottish Rite, they say. Some wag, dazzled by the vivid rays, hinted that he guessed Fred wasn't the only Crœsus in the trade. Well, did you observe the other night a complete masonic eclipse held sway? William, don't be so sensitive; no nobler eagle ever screamed: wear it all the time, my boy.

WM. FALCONER.

The Free Seed Fight on Again.

A strong delegation of seedsmen appeared before the House Committee of Agriculture on Wednesday, December 12, in opposition to that feature of the Congressional free seed distribution relating to common varieties of garden seeds. Those who spoke were W. A. Burpee and W. H. Maule, of Philadelphia; C. F. Wood, Louisville, Ky.; Henry W. Wood, Richmond, Va.; and Henry B. Hathaway, Rochester, N. Y. Messrs. Wood appeared in behalf of the American Seed Trade Association. The hearing was continued Thursday morning. Among others present were Messrs. Alexander Forbes and Patrick O'Mara of Peter Henderson & Company, New York; W. P. Stokes, Philadelphia; F. W. Bolgiano of Washington and Baltimore; W. F. Massey, editor Practical Farmer, Philadelphia. They were heard Thursday together with W. W. Smith, Washington representative of the anti-seed movement. A dress suit case of free seeds rescued from a bonfire on Long Island last Summer, with two other suit cases of resolutions and newspaper editorials condemning the distribution were offered as exhibits. Professor Galloway, chief of the Bureau of Plant Industry, Department of Agriculture, will, it is said, endorse the seedsmen's contentions against the purchase and distribution of pumpkin seed, etc.

NEW JERSEY FLORICULTURAL SOCIETY.—The regular monthly meeting and annual election of this society took place on December 7. Final reports were made of the recent Fall exhibition by the secretary and treasurer, showing a deficit of $125, which will have to be paid from the treasury or be met by one or more of the society's patrons.

The annual election resulted as follows: President, W. J. Bennett, gardener for Mr. A. C. Van Gaasbeck; vice-president, Arthur T. Caparn, superintendent estate of Stewart Hartshorne; secretary, Henry Halbig, gardener for Mr. George Graves; treasurer, William Reid, gardener for Messrs. S. & A. Colgate.

The competition running monthly during the past year was closed, and the names hitherto designated by numbers announced: General class: first, Peter Duff, with a monthly average of 92 points; second, William Reid, with 88 points. Special orchid display: first, Arthur Bodwell, with 90 points; second, Lager & Hurrell, with 92 points for only ten months. Special for gardeners without glass maintained for seven months: First, Arthur T. Caparn, with 85 points.

The exhibit of the evening consisted of the usual meritorious display of orchids and chrysanthemums, with specimen Gloire de Lorraine begonia, grown by Peter Duff, and four varieties of carnations—Robert Craig, Mrs. M. A. Patten, Lieutenant Peary and Enchantress—by Philip Cox, gardener for Mr. C. L. Bausher of Montclair, not for competition, and awarded a certificate by the judges—Messrs. William Reid, William Phillips and George von Qualen.

J. B. D.

Sports.

(Paper prepared by Patrick O'Mara and read before the Horticultural Society of New York, Wednesday, December 12, 1906.)

About a year and a half ago I was invited to address this body on the subject of "Sports" in connection with a paper read here from Professor L. C. Corbett. At that time the opportunity was not forthcoming to deliver the address which I had planned, and so the material which was accumulated was lost or mislaid and is not available now. My intention was to address this meeting without the aid of a written paper, and thus possibly it would be more extended, but having been called away on a pressing matter, I was compelled to hastily put something together so as not to disappoint the members and visitors.

It is with much misgiving as to my fitness for the task that I approach the subject, and willingly would I forego it entirely. It is to be hoped that at some future meeting some one competent to deal with it from its scientific aspect will be found who will address this body on the subject and treat it exhaustively, as I believe there are many of us who are intensely interested in it. The possibility that I may say something which will induce a further ventilation of the subject here is probably the motive which impels me to venture into it now.

It is not my purpose to broadly consider the question of sports, but only to confine myself to a few of the leading varieties of cultivated plants which have originated in that manner, with possibly a passing reference to a few noted "seed sports," so popularly designated to distinguish them from these which have been produced by bud variation.

A "sport" as popularly understood among florists and gardeners is that portion of a plant which assumes one or more characteristics essentially different from the rest of the plant, either in flower, foliage or habit. The vexed question among gardeners and florists is how this change takes place, to what prime cause can it be ascribed? I candidly confess to knowing little of what science has imparted on the subject, but that little leads me to believe that nothing definite has been enunciated. The preponderance of opinion, as far as I have sounded it, seems to be that "sporting" is due mainly to conditions of growth, or, to put it in one word, environment. This cause is not accepted by the vast majority of growers as responsible for the phenomenon of "sports;" the general belief is that it lies in the blood, to use the vernacular, or to put it in one word, heredity.

Cause of Sporting.

In his paper presented to this society on March 8, 1905, Professor Corbett said: "Sporting, then, may be encouraged by extreme conditions. Either extreme feeding or extreme poverty may induce plants to sport. Severe changes in climate or soil conditions may result in decided changes in stature, habits of growth and fruitfulness, which are as marked attributes of a sport as are changes in the color of foliage or fruit."

This is undoubtedly true in the abstract, but it is when brought to bear on concrete cases that it fails to fully satisfy. If by extreme feeding is meant the culture given to roses, for example, by florists and gardeners when forced under glass for Winter flowering, the question arises why more sports are not developed? When thousands of growers are forcing the same variety, it is not always the one who is feeding his crop the heaviest that finds the variety produce a sport. The fact, too, that a few varieties alone have displayed sportive tendencies to the extent of producing new sorts strengthens the conviction that the cause lies in the blood.

Sporting Tendency of Some Roses.

The rose Catherine Mermet has been the most prolific in sports of the many which have been grown for cut flowers. Its greatest descendants as sports are the Bride and Bridesmaid, the latter displacing the parent entirely. If feeding was the prime cause, why did not many growers find a Bride and a Bridesmaid? Catherine Mermet also produced the Waban, and I think one or two other sports which have disappeared. Parti-colored sports have appeared occasionally in the Bride, and now a grower has one beautifully striped white and pink, the latter being the Bridesmaid color and largely predominating.

Maman Cochet produced a white sport, and in this connection I would say that when a neutral shade like pink is produced it seems that the combination which produced it carries with it the tendency at some time to produce a white sport. The rose we know as American Beauty has produced two pink sports, American Belle and Queen of Edgely, and it is not too much to expect that from these, if largely grown, would emerge a white sport.

From the rose Safrano came the yellow sport Isabella Sprunt and from Perle des Jardins came Sunset; from the latter I believe came Lady Dorothea; from Golden Gate came Ivory; from Bon Silene came the striped rose American Banner, which in addition to the change in flower showed a marked change in foliage, it being decidedly rugose. The latter characteristic is slowly disappearing under propagation, in fact has almost vanished at the present time. Caprice, Striped La France and other striped roses coming from neutral tinted sorts, coupled with the fact that the other sports enumerated follow in the same line, are sufficient warrant for the belief that the combination which resulted in the parent sorts laid the foundation for the sports which resulted from them, and that the manner of growth had no part in it as a prime cause.

Establishment of W. P. Stokes, Moorestown, N. J.

Bouvardia Sports.

The sporting cycle in the bouvardia is very interesting, and in results it exactly parallels the examples set forth relating to the rose. From B. Hogarth, a deep scarlet variety, issued B. elegans, a lighter colored form, and from that issued B. Davidsonii, a pure white. It is interesting to note that two white sports originated at the same time, one in Greenville, now Jersey City, N. J., with Mr. Vreeland and offered as B. Vreelandii, the other B. Davidsonii. They were identical, and as the Davidsonii was first on the market the other name was dropped. The original stock of B. elegans in both cases was purchased from Peter Henderson, and the conclusion arrived at then was that the elements of change were contained in the plants, and that it would occur under any circumstances. Subsequently a double white and a double pink variety were produced as sports, and later a dwarf variety, White Bouquet, sported from B. Vreelandii with William Bock of Cambridge, Mass., who retained the old nomenclature (Vreelandii), having the same flowers as the parent, but a dwarf, bushy habit, about a foot high when in flower. The fact that these sports were progressive in color leads to the belief that the cause for their appearance was within the plant rather than that their coming was brought about by outside forces. As bouvardias are largely propagated by root cuttings, it strengthens this belief.

Other Sports.

An instance where at a bound a white sport issued from a scarlet variety is found in Salvia splendens alba. From Salvia splendens, at the base of the tube in the latter, is always found a bleached white which extends less or more beyond the sheath, therefore, the white sport seems a natural progression, as the subsequent striped sport is.

The double abutilon, a sport from A. Thompsonii and identical in its variegated foliage and color of flowers, is the only case of sporting which I can recall in that plant, although widely grown.

The carnation sports are numerous, and here again they are progressive. I cannot recall, for instance, where a yellow issued from a red or white, or a white from a yellow or a crimson. It is when neutral shades are reached that sporting begins. The same is true of chrysanthemums and to a lesser extent of dahlias, both of which are very prolific in sports.

In seems to be along well defined lines of color changes then that sporting follows, and the layman may well be pardoned when he arrives at the conclusion that it is in the blood and is not brought about by growing conditions. If the latter theory were correct, it seems to me there would be no limit to sports, while the limitations seem to be arbitrarily fixed, which is not the case with seminal reproduction.

Other Phases of Sporting.

Another phase of sporting is when the habit of the plant is changed, some examples of which I have alluded to previously. Climbing roses issue frequently from dwarf sorts, particularly in the monthly class. As far as I can recall, the flower in such cases is always identical with the parent. In the hybrid perpetual, and hybrid tea classes, too, climbing sports are produced, but there is a difference very marked from the monthly sports. The latter are easily fixed and never "run back," while the others, to the best of my knowledge, are never absolutely fixed, but are constant reversions, temporary and permanent, in individual plants.

The foliage sports are many, but I will only mention one, viz., the Golden Bedder coleus which resulted as a sport from Lady Burrill, a variety with harlequin markings of dark red and yellow. It has never reverted. While on the subject of coleus, I cannot forbear referring to a marked instance of the occurrence, wide apart, of a similar break in this plant. The golden leaved coleus originated in England and was imported by Peter Henderson. Before the plants arrived, seedlings raised from seed saved on the place from the old dark-leaved sorts developed some golden varieties.

Seed Sports.

In Professor Corbett's paper, already quoted from, he says, "Burpee's dwarf lima bean is a good example of a sport where the habit of the plant was markedly changed." This brings us into the realm of seed sports, wider and more complex than the other, and I do not mean to explore it to any extent.

Professor Bailey is authority for the statement that: "Bud variation and seed variation are one in kind," and again: "I am ready to say that I believe bud variation to be one of the most significant and important phenomena of vegetable life, and that it is due to the same causes, operating in essentially the same way, which underlie all variations in the plant world." Again he observed: "I want to express my conviction that mere sports are rarely useful. Sports are no doubt the result of very unusual or complex stimuli or of unwonted refrangibility of the energy of growth, and not having been induced by conditions which act uniformly over a course of time they are likely to be transient." Again: "The vexed questions associated with bud variation are not yet greatly elucidated." Again: "All these conclusions prove the unwisdom of endeavoring to account for the evolution of all the forms of life upon any single hypothesis; and they illustrate with greater emphasis the complexity of even the fundamental forces in the progression of organic nature." Again: "Now this matter of bud variation has been a most puzzling one to all writers upon evolution who have touched upon it. It long ago seemed to me to be inexplicable, but it is no more unintelligible than seminal variation of plants." These quotations from "The Survival of the Unlike" are introduced to show how contradictory even an eminent authority on the subject can be, at least so it appears to me, a layman. If I understand him at all, it is to the effect that all sports are the result mainly of the conditions under which the subjects are grown; that all variations are of a sportive character; that the difference between well cultivated and poorly cultivated plants is a sportive one.

The average florist and gardener is hardly prepared to accept that view; perhaps the reasoning is too subtle for him to follow. He knows that no cultivation of which he is master can make a poor variety as good as a good one; he knows that sports, as he understands them, are sporadic, and many believe that by a careful study of heredity on the part of scientists the law governing sports might be discovered.

But to return to the lima bean. Here again we find a cycle of change. Three sports appeared within a very short time, almost simultaneously, viz., Kummerle's—subsequently called Dreer's; Henderson's, the latter appearing with several growers at the same time, and Burpee's. Of the origin of the first two I have no specific knowledge; they merely happened. But as to the last, the raiser—I had almost said the "creator"—claimed that a horse trod on a plant while it was young, that it never grew to be a climber, and that the beans reproduced dwarf plants. This was generally known in the trade, and more than one grower crippled vine plants in an effort to develop a dwarf, but without success.

The White Plume celery is another notable example of a seed sport, and once the break came others followed.

Fern Sports.

I had almost forgotten to mention the latest and most interesting forms of sporting, viz: the forms which have sported from the "Boston" fern. If I remember correctly, when that variety first made its appearance there was considerable discussion as to what it really was, and it was finally classified as a sport from Nephrolepis exaltata.

Darwin said: "Of all the causes which induce variability, excess of food, whether or not changed in nature, is probably the most powerful." Here again we have the food question. The florist and gardener believes that the amount of food which will bring his crop to the highest perfection is not excessive; possibly he is wrong. The excessive amount is that which will cause deterioration, and it is not under such conditions that sports have appeared with him. It might not serve any useful purpose, yet it seems to promise an interesting field of study, for some of our scientists to thoroughly examine into sports obtained through bud variation under domestication in an effort to clear away the mists which now surround their origin.

Interior View of a Stokes' Greenhouse. Lilies in Foreground.

AMONG THE GROWERS

Around Boston.

J. T. Butterworth has an interesting establishment at South Framingham. Mr. Butterworth's specialty is orchids and he can handle these plants to perfection, as may be seen by paying a visit to his greenhouses at this season where he has a gorgeous display. A house filled with Cattleya labiata had a fine lot of flowers of immense size and handsome colorings. Many of the plants carried thirty and forty flowers in spikes of five and six. Cattleya Trianæ, of which there is a house, is making splendid growths, and will show many fine blooms at an early date. Cattleya Mossiæ were also doing nicely. Some 100 plants of Cattleya Harrisoniæ have been throwing large quantities of bloom. Dendrobiums are beginning to show signs of nice spikes of bloom and Lælia anceps, of which there are some large plants, are going to make an elegant showing soon. Cypripediums in large quantities are grown, and it is nothing uncommon to count fifty blooms on a plant. A batch of cœlogynes are looking well and have bulbs which will insure a quantity of blooms later on.

In addition to orchids Mr. Butterworth grows a general stock of flowers. Two houses are filled with carnations; no fancy sorts are cultivated, but good standard varieties like Queen, Enchantress, Fair Maid and Mrs. M. A. Patten. Bulbs of various kinds are forced in large numbers, two houses being devoted to this purpose after the chrysanthemum season. Lily of the valley is a specialty and the brand grown by Mr. Butterworth is of the best.

At Samuel J. Goddard's place at Framingham may be seen some of the most up-to-date carnations and grown to perfection. Since the writer's last visit another house has been added to the establishment. Among the varieties noted of recent introduction, Rose-Pink Enchantress was very fine, and Mr. Goddard is highly pleased with it. Ideal is a good white, and Lady Bountiful produces splendid blooms, but Queen is yet considered here the best for general purposes and for largest returns. Harry Fenn is regarded as the best crimson, and Cardinal is giving much satisfaction, being thought superior to Victory. Helen Goddard, which was raised here, is grown in number, but at the present time the plants are being grown for cuttings, for which there is a great demand.

At Peter Fisher's establishment at Ellis may be seen some of the latest varieties of carnations in the best possible shape, although some sorts are here not so good as they have been. Lady Bountiful is not doing so well as it did a year ago; and White Lawson at the present time is almost a failure. White Perfection is doing nicely and promises well. Superior so far is giving satisfaction and promises to be heard more of. Elsa and Alma Ward are both doing well. Among the unnamed varieties No. 600 is most extensively grown. It is of a deeper shade than Enchantress. Evangeline is doing fine; it is of an orange salmon color and is a good seller. The one variety that now shows up as the winner is Beacon; it is about to be disseminated, consequently is grown in large quantities. It is the best producer we have ever seen. Those who saw it last year will remember the number of blooms on the benches devoted to it. It is equally as productive now as then. Large quantities of it are being raised, and the first batch of cuttings are now rooted. Among the standard sorts which are still here grown in quantity are Mrs. M. A. Patten, Nelson Fisher and Enchantress.

Mr. Fisher does not seem to have so many seedlings this season as formerly, still there are enough to warrant a further trial of several which probably will be heard from at a future date.

J. W. DUNCAN.

Walter P. Stok s, Moorestown, N. J.

The accompanying illustrations show views of the establishment of Walter P. Stokes, Moorestown, N. J., who is also the proprietor of the Stokes Seed Store, 219 Market street, Philadelphia, Pa.

One of the pictures gives an exterior view of the establishment. The three houses to the left are new, and have lately been finished. They are iron trussed houses, built by the King Construction Company. The two large houses are 28x120 feet each; the smaller house, 16x100 feet. The latter is used for forcing lily of the valley, and has a room at the far end for bunching and packing the flowers. The other photographs show an interior view of one of the large houses; also an interior view, but taken to more clearly give an idea of the iron gutter construction. On each side of the gutter, it will be noticed, the sash bars are set in iron brackets. These are so arranged that they take all the drip, which passes on into the gutter; the water then runs down through the upright pipe supports to an underground drain.

Mr. Stokes is greatly pleased with these houses and very much so with the drip arrangement, as the ends of the sash bars are always dry and therefore should last a long time.

A general assortment of stock is grown on this place, and disposed of among the retail stores of Philadelphia. One whole bench is planted with poinsettias for cutting; then there are a large number of these plants in 4-inch pots for Christmas trade. Another bench is filled with L. Harrisii, which are now being cut; there are also two blocks of these coming on for a succession. Large quantities of Boston ferns are raised; these are mostly in 6 and 7-inch pots. There is also a nice lot of Pteris tremula in 6-inch pots, while the side benches are filled with 2 and 3-inch ferns and small plants of Asparagus plumosus. Large numbers of Paper White narcissus are also raised for cutting. One house is planted with carnations which all look promising; the varieties grown are Enchantress, Governor Wolcott, John E. Haines, Harlowarden and Flora Hill.

DAVID RUST.

Interior of one of W. P. Stokes's Houses, Showing Iron Gutter Construction.

SHADING PLANTS WITH COLORED CLOTH.—In telling of his recent experiences in the "Shading of Plants With Colored Cloth," Professor W. R. Lazenby of the Ohio State University, during the final session of the sixteenth annual meeting of the Ohio Academy of Science, held in Physics hall, Ohio State University, last week, said the best results were obtained in the use of black cheesecloth. His tests with this color were satisfactory, and extensive experiments along this line will be made next Spring at the university. It was his opinion that not only flowering plants but vegetables and germinating seed can be protected from the late frosts by covering them with black cheesecloth. He also believed that the germinating of the seed was materially hastened, without ill effect, through the use of this material.

THE CANADIAN TARIFF.—Among the clauses of the new Canadian tariff that affect the florist trade are the following:

"Florist stock, viz., palms, ferns, rubber plants (ficus), gladiolus, cannas, dahlias, and peonies. British preference, 15 per cent.; intermediate, 22½ per cent.; general, 25 per cent.

Florist stock, viz., azaleas, rhododendrons, pot grown lilacs, araucarias, bulbs, corms, tubers, rhizomes and dormant roots, not otherwise provided for, seedling stock for grafting, viz., plum, pear, peach, and other fruit trees—free.

The act in which the foregoing clauses are included has been presented to the House.

CLUB AND SOCIETY DOINGS.

NEW YORK FLORISTS' CLUB.—Notwithstanding the inclement weather over 100 members turned out to the club meeting on Monday evening, December 10; the drawing card being the election of officers, a proceeding which occupied most of the session. President Scott presided. The following were elected members of the club: Emil Sevoy, Benoit De Meyer, Camile Sierens, and H. D. Darlington. Nominations were made as follows: C. R. Gloeckner, David Howells, John Seligman, Joseph Levy, J. D. Cockroft and Malachi Tierney. Resignations were received from John N. May, C. H. Allen, and E. Steffens. In view of the eminent services rendered the club by Mr. May, who was its first president, also those of Mr. Allen, who held that office for two terms, each of these gentlemen was elected an honorary member.

Patrick O'Mara was appointed inspector of election, and Wm. Duckham and Walter F. Sheridan, tellers. The result of the balloting was as follows: For president, C. H. Totty, who received 72 votes as against his opponent's (J. B. Nugent, Jr.) 29; for vice-president, A. J. Manda, 74, H. O. May, 28; secretary, John Young, 76, A. J. Guttman, 25; treasurer, L. W. Wheeler, 64, C. B. Weathered, 48; trustees, John Scott, 83, W. F. Sheridan, 61, Julius Roehrs, Jr., 66. On motion of Mr. Weathered the election of Mr. Wheeler was made unanimous. Mr. Weathered had held the office of treasurer for nearly twenty years, and in a few words spoke feelingly of his great interest in the club and its affairs, which would remain unabated, he said, although he was no longer an officer. The vote for the offices of president, vice-president and secretary was also made unanimous on motions of the unsuccessful candidates. Each of the newly elected officers made a brief speech promising his best endeavor on behalf of the club.

Mr. Wheeler gave notice that he would present at next meeting the following amendment to the by-laws: "To amend Section 4, Article 5, by adding: 'The treasurer shall furnish a bond equal to the amount in the treasury on taking office, plus 33-1-3 per cent., such bond to consist of three individuals or a surety or bonding company acceptable to the board of trustees.'"

Mr. Traendly called the attention of the club to the death of Mrs. E. V. Hallock; the president appointed the following committee to draw up suitable resolutions thereanent: Messrs. Traendly, Wheeler, and Stewart.

The exhibition tables were graced with a number of beautiful flowers and a splendidly grown plant of Begonia Gloire de Lorraine. The latter was grown and exhibited by H. Turner, superintendent, Castle Gould, L. I. It was in a 10-inch pot, and measured three feet in diameter. The judges awarded Mr. Turner a cultural certificate. Dailledouze Brothers showed a vase of their new pink carnation, Welcome, a sport from Mrs. Thos. W. Lawson, of a beautiful pink shade, which was awarded a preliminary certificate, the judges scoring this variety 89 points. A. Demousy of Brooklyn showed a seedling crimson carnation which had a fine long stem and was of a pleasing color and good size, measuring 3½ inches and upwards in diameter. This variety scored 85 points, and was awarded a preliminary certificate. A. J. Guttman, for John E. Haines of Bethlehem, Pa., staged a vase each of the two carnations now being introduced, Imperial and Pink Imperial. The former scored 82 points and the latter 85 points, receiving a preliminary certificate. M. Tierney, Highlands of Navesink, N. J., exhibited a vase of a new scarlet carnation, Mrs. Robert Hartshorne, which scored 74 points. Anton Zvolanek, Bound Brook, N. J., had some Winter-flowering sweet peas, receiving the thanks of the club and a request from the award committee that he show the varieties later in the season. F. G. Mense of Glen Cove, L. I., showed a remarkably fine bunch of Princess of Wales violets, for which he received a cultural certificate.

L. W. Wheeler

Treasurer-Elect N. Y. Florists' Club.

☞ The New Officers.

PRESIDENT-ELECT CHARLES H. TOTTY, was born in the village of Albrighton, County of Shropshire, England, on September 8, 1873. His people for generations have been in the building business, but he had no taste whatever for that line and took up gardening as a profession. After working three years in a local garden he went to Dickson's, of Chester, to spend a year going through the different branches of that immense establishment. From Dickson's he went to Norris Green, Liverpool, a noted fruit growing establishment; after a year there he came to America, in 1893, at the age of 19. His first position in the United States was at Canandaigua, N. Y., on the estate of Mrs. F. F. Thompson; he left there after a year and a half and went to Madison, N. J., on the Twombley estate, and four years ago engaged in business for himself.

Charles H. Totty

Pres.-Elect N. Y. Florists' Club.

The chrysanthemum has been a hobby with Mr. Totty all his life. When he started in business he naturally turned to that plant, and while he grows roses and carnations, the chrysanthemum is his favorite flower. Mr. Totty has contributed notes on chrysanthemums to the trade press since 1895.

Fraternally, he is a Past Regent of North Jersey Council Royal Arcanum, and also a member of the F. & A. M. and Improved Order of Red Men.

Mr. Totty has served on the exhibition committee of the club the past year with much acceptance. He is greatly interested in the work of the organization, and will, we feel sure, perform the duties of the office to which he has been elected with credit to himself and satisfaction to the association, the high status of which will be maintained under his leadership.

VICE-PRESIDENT A. J. MANDA was born in Bohemia in 1870. He was apprenticed as a gardener in his native country, went to England when 15 years old, and worked in the nurseries of Messrs. Paul & Son, Broxbourne, Herts, for twelve months. Coming to the United States when 16 years of age, he went to work in the Harvard Botanical Garden, Cambridge, Mass., till the firm of Pitcher & Manda was founded in the Fall of 1888, when Mr. Manda went to Short Hills, N. J., to take charge of that concern's hardy herbaceous department. The following January he was sent to England with the stock of Mrs. Alpheus Hardy chrysanthemum, which at that time created quite a sensation, it being the first of the hairy varieties, and to open a branch nursery for the firm at Swanley, Kent, of which he had entire charge and management until the house dissolved partnership, at which time Mr. Manda returned to America and worked in various places till the Spring of 1902. Since then he has had charge of the Pratt Estate gardens, Brooklyn, N. Y.

John Young

Re-elected Secretary N. Y. Florists' Club.

Mr. Manda has served on the exhibition committee this year with President-elect Totty, and is a regular attendant at the club's meetings, a fact which demonstrates his interest in its affairs.

TREASURER-ELECT L. W. WHEELER, was born at Cherry Creek, Chautauqua County, New York, on December 20, 1868. He entered the employ of Vaughan's Seed Store, Chicago, in 1894, and has been manager of the New York branch of that firm for the past six years. Mr. Wheeler became a member of the club about five years ago, and is one of the most regular attendants, taking part in the discussion of every subject brought forward tending to the advancement of the organization. He belives in promoting the social side of the club, and last year was chairman of the outing committee. The large vote polled for Mr. Wheeler against so formidable an opponent as Mr. Weathered testifies to the former's popularity.

SECRETARY JOHN YOUNG needs no introduction to our readers. He has been one of the club's efficient officers since 1891, and his annual re-election to the secretaryship is proof of the high value placed on his services by his fellow members. The

Anthony J. Manda

Vice-Pres.-Elect N. Y. Florists' Club.

fact that there is always a yearly opposing candidate to Mr. Young is the fault of the club's by-laws which call for the nomination of two candidates for each office, and in no way reflects the feeling of the members that any change of the incumbent in the secretaryship is necessary. Mr. Young made the speech of his life on Monday night; his remarks were feelingly uttered and truthful to the core when he stated that the promotion of the welfare of the New York Florists' Club was paramount with him often at the sacrifice of his own business interests.

FOR THE RETAILER

[All questions relating to the Retail Trade will be cheerfully answered in this column. We solicit good, sharp photographs of made-up work, decorations, store interiors, etc., for reproduction here.—Ed. F. E.]

The reign of the horse and Thanksgiving are now history. The horse show is altogether a myth as far as the retail florist is concerned, but Thanksgiving trade seems to gain from a florist's point of view as time goes on.

Debutante Bouquets.

The "social bud," or debutante, is now Queen and rules supreme.

You can walk into any high-class flower store and see all hands as busy as the proverbial bee, all handling nothing but the finest product of the grower. A leading Fifth avenue florist finished seventy-seven bouquets for one fortunate young lady about to make her bow to society, and I have seen a debutante réceive as many as two hundred floral tributes.

Every seasonable variety of flower and combination are used for these, and some startling effects are to be seen.

Pink seems to be the favorite shade for the fair debutante, but the bouquets are by no means confined to that color. The glorious Richmond, the peer among red roses, is much in demand, and is usually the preference of the male purchaser who we find rarely buys pink. A bouquet of Richmond in combination with Cypripedium insigne and lily of the valley was superb. This was tied with a broad sash of foliage green ribbon. Another very rich effect was obtained with about three dozen Richmond roses, and a large cluster of the beautiful golden orchid, Cattleya Dowiana, which has become so popular, and should be more extensively grown. A broad ribbon the shade of old gold put the finishing touch to this work of art. A most elaborate creation was composed entirely of Dendrobium formosum, with long sprays of Vanda cœrulea falling from one side of the bouquet and reaching almost to the ground. Adiantum Farleyense completed this gorgeous affair, ribbon being conspicuous by its absence.

Pink roses such as Killarney, Mme. Abel Chatenay, Mme. Caroline Testout, Golden Gate, and the never failing Bridesmaid are used extensively for this work either by themselves or in combination with lily of the valley, cypripediums, hyacinths, narcissi, or any other small flower.

Bouquets composed entirely of cattleyas, cypripediums or other orchids in combination with gardenias, tied with ribbon to match the orchids, are very pleasing. Adiantum Farleyense should be used if possible, although graceful sprays of Adiantum cuneatum and even Asparagus plumosus are very suitable.

Carnations also deserve a place here, and must not be overlooked. Enchantress is a great favorite. The same combinations can be used as with the pink roses. Carnations are good to fall back on where a less expensive bouquet is required. The red varieties, such as Robert Craig, Victory, and others, are not desirable for debutante purposes, and should never be recommended. Last season at a Fifth avenue home where I had charge of the decorations, I saw a large bouquet of red carnations; it was good by itself, but strictly by itself, for it simply howled and refused to be suppressed. The color scheme and most of the bouquets were pink.

Christmas Decorations.

Any florist will tell you that the one thing that makes the Christmas rush so trying is the decorting. We all have more than enough to attend to n taking orders for plants and cut flowers; nevertheless we must handle cases of holly, mistletoe, hundreds of yards of roping, and enormous numbers of wreaths. It is a good plan to get decorations off your hands as early as possible, but of course Christmas dinner decorations come last, and t a time when we are all willing to go home. Holly rranged in plateaus to suit the size of the tables s very popular; but unless the holly is very good t is better to brighten it up by the addition of a ew sprays of black alder. A few flowers of poinsettia placed on the table in conjunction with holly s very pleasing. Small electric lights are sometimes used and add much to the effect.

A decoration entirely of poinsettias is very attractive and makes a very brilliant table. A large vase filled with these flowers occupies the center of the table; others are scattered over the cloth, forming a design or carelessly, as suits the occasion. There is great danger of poinsettias wilting; this is easily overcome by placing the stems in warm water and leaving them for a few minutes. This forces the sap up to the flowers or bracts, and seals the end of the stem. They should not be cut again after once being treated, or it will be necessary to repeat the operation. If this plan is carefully carried out there will be no such thing as wilting.

Robert Craig or any other scarlet carnations are always in great demand for Christmas on account of their brilliant coloring; but prices at this season make the flowers prohibitive except to our wealthy customers. And even they sometimes refuse to pay the seemingly fabulous figures quoted. A beautiful table, where the family silver could be used to good advantage, is to have a low punch bowl gracefully filled with scarlet carnations and Adiantum cuneatum, loving cups being placed at regular intervals around the table, each one surrounded with a wreath of Cypripedium insigne, and the cup proper filled with carnations as in the center, bold bows and loops of holly ribbon. A corsage of Cypripedium insigne and gardenias for the ladies and boutonieres of red carnations complete the effect.

Euphorbia Jacquiniæflora, with its pretty racemes of red flowers makes a beautiful table decoration, but the plant, is not grown to any great extent in this country. It has long been a favorite in Europe and is extensively cultivated for the London market. I have heard whisperings that an enterprising grower promises to give us Salvia splendens for Christmas; it would certainly be a welcome addition to our supply of red flowers. I hope he may succeed.

D. RAYBUN.

Boxwood Wreath

Artist, Meyer, New York

DIRECTORY OF RELIABLE RETAIL HOUSES

THE WEEK'S WORK.

Timme's Timely Teachings.

Holiday Preparations.

The great amount of business transacted at all the principal holidays by florists, and compressed into but a few days of vehement activity, necessitates timely and thorough-going preparations. There is a good deal of gratifying comfort in knowing that all is ready and in proper shape and place for the coming tidal rush of trade. Christmas is close at hand, the festival of all others looked forward to with high anticipations for many months, with hopes most likely to be fulfilled.

Having the stock with which to meet the increased volume of trade is, of course, of greatest importance. The last moment's survey of the available supply very often reveals the want or insufficiency in this or that line, with barely time to correct matters. The retail florist, to his dismay, not infrequently finds himself short in some important line of goods when business is already in full swing. Few are the growers who on their own places produce all in flowers and plants needed for their holiday home trade, and the lack of some good thing or other that they by all means should have in stock is discovered too late. It is well, therefore, while yet it is time, to do what is possible in completing the stock or in making arrangements for being fully supplied in time with everything needful.

It is not easy to hit things just right as to amount and kind of stock in providing for any one of our holidays, and, indeed, it would be owing to a rare streak of luck were this to happen at Christmas. One of two things is the usual outcome—either a selling out clean with a deal of good trade lost owing to inadequate supply of stock, or a hearty, brisk business commotion to the very end, with good stock left over. It is my opinion that the latter state of affairs is to be preferred in nearly every case as being less annoying and disappointing to dealer and patrons, and curtailing to a smaller extent the sum total of clear profits. A good many of the unsold plants are usually disposed of in the two weeks following Christmas, and the actual loss in stock thus amounts to little.

Packing Plants.

The packing, shipping and delivering of plants and made-up articles is the most burdensome feature in the great stir and bustle of holiday business. Cost of material, time and labor involved make this part a weighty item in the expense account, especially so at Christmas. Heavy and thorough packing then is most needful, and the things to be packed, with few exceptions, require the most elaborate kind of doing up and a deal of careful handling. It is then when a good packer and shipper is most appreciated, very little less, if any at all, than a good grower. The cause of disappointment to customers and annoyance to all concerned may in most cases of the kind be traced to the packing room.

The usual methods practiced in the packing and shipping of plants will not do for the holiday business. Everything is in pots or receptacles of some kind; most of it but partially and some of it not at all established. But every article nevertheless is looked upon as a finished product of the gardener's art when purchased, and is expected to reach its destination in the same full prime of presentable condition. This means that in wrapping and sending the plants must be held in an upright position, and that all crowding and jamming in transit must be carefully guarded against. Many plants, especially high-priced single specimens of the soft-wooded flowering species, should first be subjected to a good staking and tying, calculated to reduce bulk and to shield the crisp growth from being broken in packing. Three or more stout stakes, or a light framework of similar description, securely fixed around the outside of a plant, renders the wrapping up of the most fragile things a simple and easy affair. At Christmas it is necessary to employ several thicknesses in wrapping; first tissue paper around upper growth and crown, next to this a double folding of sheet cotton, tightly wrapped all around pot and plant, and finally a neat finishing off with wrapping paper, held in place by string or twine. This is usually all-sufficient for home delivery or sales over the counter in ordinary cold weather. Several thicknesses of newspaper between cotton and outer wrapper must, however, be added should the weather be extremely cold, or in cases where plants are to travel great distances. In doing up anything in this line for shipping by express a complete boxing in becomes necessary. The boxing or crating, easily and quickly constructed by anyone handy with tools, should be light but securely nailed. The plant basket or other article to be thus prepared for long distance transit must be held firmly and rigidly inside the crating by wire or string fastenings and cleating on all sides, not to forget a good lining of the box inside with paper, cotton, moss or excelsior, as the case may require. The top-piece of box or crating should always be a wide one, tightly nailed, for several good reasons: It is usually the hold by which the package is carried; then it allows of other light articles being placed on top of it by the express people, and finally it affords room for address and directions, which, in every case, should be plain and accurate.

The packing and shipping of plants, when this department is in competent hands or under the supervision of one experienced in work of the kind, is done with precision and dispatch and causes few ruffles in the smooth flow of holiday transactions. But there are so many florists who never do much of this sort of work except at the holidays, and to these it is the greatest of bugbears in the entire business rumpus occasioned by these events. A little practice, however, will soon render the work an easy enough matter and enable any practical workman to do it with considerable facility. All the material needed, boxes and lathing, saw, hammer and nails, shears, paper and twine, each must have its proper place and be in adequate supply.

Decorative Greens.

The enormous quantities of all sorts of greens made use of for decorative purposes at the Winter holidays, baffle all attempts at calculation, all efforts to estimate amount or value. Alone that part of the material produced by careful cultivation under glass, such as smilax, asparagus and ferns, amounts to quantities truly immense. But nature without the aid of man furnishes by far the greater portion of all the verdure which is to adorn many thousands of homes at this the most gladsome of holidays. The wilds of the far North as well as those of the extreme South must share in the production of natural decorative greens, and rarely ever does the supply, large as it is, exceed the overwhelming demand for this most serviceable material.

The profits in handling the various kinds and brands of natural greens are pretty evenly divided among a great number of dealers. Many go into this line of business only for the short period of the rushing holiday activity, offering the greens in made-up form. The ever-vigilant street peddler, in many instances, drops all else for the time being and turns greens vender, to be met with on every hand. All sorts of people lay in store a stock of bells, wreaths and other make-ups as a temporary side line to their holiday trade. Thus a very large amount of the available material is disposed of, mostly of the inferior grades, which make a selling at low figures with a fair margin of profits possible.

Nevertheless a great deal, and this the best portion, of this trading in greens falls to the share of the legitimate florist. It is to his interest to offer something better in quality and make-up than the great horde of his competitors. This is expected and so understood by the public. He has the great advantage over all other dealers in being patronized by the better class of trade. In living up to expectations he makes the best use of an opportunity to add largely to his net returns and possibly, to some extent, in purifying and elevating public taste.

Florists, if ever possible, should make up their own roping, wreaths and garlands. Their wares should be of heavy, substantial make, the wreaths double-faced and finished off neatly with a bow of bright-colored ribbon, not all of the conventional flaring red color. Nor is it at all necessary to use the select best grades of the greens for any of these make-ups. Very much can be accomplished with the short and otherwise unserviceable material, in producing the highest grade of finished goods, that even at double the price easily outsell the flimsily-made, cheap article of the street men. A few red-berried sprays of Winter berry or the like, interwoven in the green of some of the make-ups, greatly enhances the attractiveness and value of such. It also helps to hide defects in too sparingly berried holly. Moderation in the use of it, however, is advisable, though a touch of brightness by its employment is not out of place in some of the best make-ups in green.

There should be enough variety in these articles to afford ample scope for choosing, and in arranging plants and flowers for display some samples in this line should be included. The great bulk of the greens, whether yet in the cases or already made up, must be kept in a somewhat moist and cool place, basement or cellar, or in a dark shed. It should not be exposed to the direct sunlight or drying winds any more than can be helped. FRED. W. TIMME.

New York.

The Week's News.

The manufacturers of the Lehman heaters seem to have a particular good thing in their apparatus for heating florists' wagons; over 350,000 of these are now in use throughout the country. Of course, they are not all used by florists. The danger of delivering plants for decorative purposes about the city during cold weather is such that no florist should be without a few of these Lehman heaters for use in their wagons.

W. C. Krick of Brooklyn is so deluged with orders for his patented letters that he is having to divide his output among his customers in order to keep them going, as he cannot begin to fill all the orders he is receiving. Mr. Krick has also put on the market a new Christmas tree stand that is finding much favor; this is a metal device, and one that will hold any sized tree.

The legislative committee of the S. A. F. O. H., together with interested rose growers from Madison, N. J., will appear before the interstate committee at Washington, D. C., on Wednesday, December 19, with respect to the exorbitant charges made by express companies for the conveyance of flowers. W. F. Sheridan, as a member of the legislative committee of the New York Florists' Club, will attend, as also will L. M. Noe of Madison, N. J., and F. L. Moore of Chatham, N. J.

L. Kuebler, who is associated with his brother William Kuebler, wholesale florist, Brooklyn, had a nasty fall on Monday morning while leaving a restaurant on Sixth avenue. The pavement was covered with ice at the time, and Mr. Kuebler after he fell went into the Coogan building, and took the elevator to the third floor where the Cut Flower Exchange is located. While in the elevator he became unconscious. A doctor was called, and it was found that Mr. Kuebler had a bad cut in his head. After the wound was dressed he recuperated quickly, and was able to go to his home in Brooklyn.

Frank Millang, wholesale florist, 55 West Twenty-sixth street, who for several weeks has been laid up at his home with a broken ankle, was able to go to business on Monday of this week for the first time. His many friends were glad to see him around again.

The delivery wagon of John Scott had a run in with a trolley car on Broadway a few days ago, and while the driver was thrown from his seat and the wagon badly damaged, no serious injury was done to either the driver or the horse—a very lucky escape.

Friends in the trade will be sorry to hear of the death of Mrs. E. V. Hallock of Queens, N. Y., which occurred suddenly last Saturday. The funeral services were held from the family home on Monday forenoon, the interment being private.

Christmas trees have begun to arrive in large numbers, and they are to be seen at their usual market place, West street, between Chambers and Franklin.

The office and factory of the Weathered Company is located at Orient and West Side avenues, Jersey City, N. J., to reach which visitors should take the Montgomery street car from Jersey City to West Side and Orient avenues or C. R. R. of N. J. from foot of Liberty street to West Side avenue station. The post office address in Box 789, New York City.

J. C. Vaughan, Chicago, was in town this week, attending the funeral of Mrs. E. V. Hallock.

The evergreen, princess pine, so much used for retail purposes, is, from present indications, rather a scarce article this year, and for those who use a lot of this material we think it will be good policy to get their orders in early and avoid disappointment.

T. Mellstrom, representative of Sander & Son, St. Albans, England, who has been here on his semi-annual tour, will sail for England to-day (Saturday) on board the S. S. Etruria.

The Lord & Burnham Company, horticultural builders, have received a contract to erect a greenhouse for B. R. Hoffman, Sixtieth street, Philadelphia, Pa.

A burglar pried open a side door at the store of Popkin & Collins, florists, Main street, Orange, N. J., on Wednesday night the 5th inst., and got away with an old coat, two pruning knives and $4 in cash. Certainly not a large haul for all his trouble.

A. Forbes and Patrick O'Mara of Peter Henderson & Company went to Washington Tuesday to speak before the House Committee of Agriculture on matters pertaining to the free seed distribution of 1907.

A. J. Cowee, Berlin, N. Y., was in town this week, and attended the meeting of the New York Florists' Club, of which body he is a member.

The plant auction season of Wm. Elliott & Sons, which is just drawing to a close, has been a very successful one this year.

J. Featherstone, late superintendent of Greystone, Yonkers, N. Y., left New York on Saturday last, by the S. S. St. Paul, to pay his parents in England a visit. Before leaving Greystone he was the recipient of a very handsome silver loving cup, presented to him by the employees of Greystone as a token of their friendship. He will be missed by his numerous friends and acquaintances. Mrs. Featherstone and child accompanied him.

O. V. Zangen, seedsman, Hoboken, N. J., has just recovered from an attack of pneumonia.

Chicago.

News Notes.

Otto Schwill, Jr., proprietor of one of the most progressive growing and retail houses in the middle South, left here last Saturday evening for his home at Memphis, Tenn., after a pleasant visit with his old companion, Leonard Kill.

E. H. Green of Dallas, Texas, was in the city the first of the week procuring material to add 150,000 square feet of glass to his present extensive establishment. After a few days in Chicago spent at the Auditorium Annex most of the time in his horticultural and railroad interests with a side look into political futures, Mr. Green returned to Texas.

A carload of Japanese lily bulbs, after being detained a month or more on the road, reached Chicago last week consigned to Vaughan's Seed Store. All the best of the Japanese varieties were in the lot.

Charles Finch, Jr., of Saginaw, Mich., was a recent visitor, and spent a few days with P. J. Hauswirth.

A telegram reached here Sunday, announcing the death of Mrs. E. V. Hallock, and J. C. Vaughan left immediately to attend the obsequies.

Vaughan & Sperry are receiving daily invoices of Hudson River violets of a quality far superior to any they have previously received from that section, and have contracts sufficient to fill all requirements for the holidays, large orders having already been booked.

Bassett & Washburn are looking forward with pleasant anticipations to the reaping of a Christmas harvest from 2,000 giganteum longiflorum lilies from cold storage bulbs. They appear to be just right for a Christmas crop, with beautiful foliage and a prospect of fine large flowers.

WM. K. WOOD.

Philadelphia.

News Notes.

There is a slight lull at the retail stores—the first let-up in brisk business since the beginning of October. At nearly all the stores quite a lot of boxwood plants, aucubas and evergreens in tubs are seen, and so far, sales of these have been very good. Quite a number of window boxes filled with boxwood are noticed throughout this city. Many of the stores have sample wreaths made of boxwood, and orders are being taken every day, as the wreaths are very effective.

We are very sorry to announce that John G. Whilldin of the Whilldin Pottery Company has met with a great bereavement, in the death of his wife. The loss is a sad one, as they have no family, and had been together since childhood.

The Hugh Graham Company is sending in a very choice lot of plants of Nephrolepis Barrowsii, compact plants, in 6 and 7-inch pans—the best yet seen in this market. This firm also is sending in some dwarf poinsettias in 4-inch pots; the plants are about eight inches high, with large heads.

Edward Reid is in the South, looking up his customers, and at the same time doing a little gunning after game in Virginia.

Mrs. Ellsworth of Allentown, Pa.; and A. N. Pierson, Cromwell, Conn., were in town this week.

Bayersdorfer & Company have received large shipments of moss wreaths and red immortelles by steamers Kaiserin Auguste Victoria, Artemisia and Zaandam, all of which came into New York. As orders are awaiting these goods, this firm has arranged with the United States Express Company to bring them over in sealed cars. In order to keep up with the rush of holiday business the firm started a night force on Monday evening, and will keep it working until all orders are filled.

Robert Kift is selling quite a lot of plants of Ficus pandurata. He keeps a few choice specimens on hand and finds they pay well.

Habermehl's have the decoration order for the first large ball of this Winter; it will take place at Horticultural Hall on December 26.

Dr. Robert Huey, the well-known amateur outdoor rose grower, has received a shipment of seedling roses from Alexander Dickson & Sons of Belfast, Ireland. One of these, which the doctor saw growing the past Summer in the Dickson nurseries, is in his opinion superior to American Beauty for outdoors, if it will do as well here as in Ireland. He still has the two original plants of Killarney that were the first in this country, and this variety he considers one of the leading outdoor roses.

Phil is about again and promises he will heed Job's advice, and be good.

D. T. Connor, Lord & Burnham's representative here, has sold material for one rose house, 22x200 feet, to Alfred Burton, Wyndmoor, Pa., and material for five houses, each 21x150 feet, to Aug. Doemling, Lansdowne, Pa. Both of these orders are for material according to the latest construction, iron gutters, etc.

DAVID RUST.

St. Louis.

News of the Week.

Charles Connon has closed his floral stand in one of the big department stores and is now with the Michel Plant and Bulb Company, having charge of their Maryland avenue store.

J. W. Ross, florist at Centralia, Ill., spent a day last week with the local trade. E. W. Guy, of Belleville, Ill., also paid the craft a visit; he reports good trade.

Charles Wors, formerly one of our wholesalers, now owning a retail store on North Market street, reports that his wife presented him with a fine baby girl last week. His son, Charles, Jr. is now in the employ of Augermuller.

Frank Fillmore, one of the club's foremost members, who has been in business for many years on the South side, has offered his place for sale. Frank wants to get out in the country, build a place, and grow for the market.

The city has started a nursery near the Chain of Rocks Park to grow young stock for the new improvements to be made along King's Highway next year. W. E. Robinson, the head of this department, is busy with a force of men stocking up.

The flower show guarantee fund is growing nicely: Secretary Beneke thinks by the first of the year most of the fund will be raised. The committee—Messrs. Weber, Bentzen and Smith—will make a personal canvass after the club meeting this week Thursday.

ST. PATRICK.

CLASSIFIED)VERTISEMENTS

CASH WITH ORDER.

he columns under this heading are reserved advertisements of Stock for Sale, Stock nted, Help Wanted, Situations Wanted or r Wants; also of Greenhouse, Land, Sec-Hand Materials, etc., For Sale or Rent.

ur charge is 10 cts. per line (7 words to the), set solid, without display. No advt. epted for less than thirty cents.

Display advertisements in these columns, 15 its per line; count 12 lines agate to the inch.

[If replies to Help Wanted, Situation Want- or other advertisements are to be addressed e of this office, advertisers add 10 cents to er expense of forwarding.]

Copy must reach New York office 12 o'clock dnesday to secure insertion in issue of fol-ring Saturday.

Advertisers in the Western States desiring to ertise under initials, may save time by hav- their answer directed care our Chicago office 127 E. Berwyn Ave.

SITUATIONS WANTED

ON WANTED.—At once by married good grower of carnations and all tock. Address, A. G., care The Flo-change.

ON WANTED—By experienced young 0. as gardener and decorator in flower 'an give references. Address, A. D., Florists' Exchange.

ITUATION WANTED—January 1, by young man. Danish, with 1 1-2 years' European experience in general pot plants. Two years' American experience in ferns and general pot plants. Address A. E., care The Florists' Exchange.

SITUATION WANTED—Florist, German, single, 19 years' experience, honest, willing worker for employer, competent to take charge, desires position. Please state wages and how many miles from New York. Address Florist, General Delivery, P. O., Jamaica, L. I.

SITUATION WANTED—As grower of roses, carnations, chrysanthemums, bedding plants, Twenty-seven years' experience, private and commercial. Best of references. Would like a change. Been in my present position as grower for 5 years. Nationality, Scotch. Married, 41 years of age. Address, Alex. Ross, c/o L. C. Howe, Florist, Dover, N. H.

NURSERY FOREMAN

Will be open for engagement after January 1st. Has thorough ornamental nursery training, including herbaceous plants. References. Address A. Z., care The Florists' Exchange.

Mention the Florists' Exchange when writing.

SITUATION WANTED—By a practical up-to-date cut flower and pot plant grower also experienced in landscape gardening, vegetables, etc. Twenty-six years in the business, learning in Germany. 44 years of age, married, best of references. State particulars in first letter. Address E. G., 61 Second Street, Bristol, Tenn.

WANTED

Position as traveling salesman for good reliable wholesale firm, dealing in Plants, Seeds, Bulbs or Florists' Supplies. Have had ten years' experience in the flower and seed business, and can furnish very best of reference. Address, Salesman, care of Florists' Exchange.

HELP WANTED

WANTED—Sober, intelligent man for rose section; one who understands the business. Send references to Wm. F. Kasting, Buffalo, N. Y.

WANTED—Single man for carnation house. State age, nationality, experience and wages expected. Board furnished. Address Box 437, Minersville, Pa.

WANTED—Young man to assist in up-to-date flower store. Must be decorator, of good appearance and able to wait on select trade. Address X. D., care The Florists' Exchange.

WANTED

At once, young traveling salesman thoroughly acquainted with bulb and plant line. Address with full particulars, stating commencing terms expected and references.

JOHN SCHEEPERS & CO.,
2 Old Slip, N. Y.

HELP WANTED

WANTED—At once, night fireman for commercial range; steady position for year; wages $50.00 per month; reply stating experience and references. James D. Cockcroft, Northport, L. I., N. Y.

WANTED—At once, a sober, well recommended young man as greenhouse assistant. One with experience in fern growing preferred. Steady work for a good man. Wages, $10.00 per week to start. Anderson & Christensen, Short Hills, N. J.

WANTED.—First class night fireman thoroughly familiar with high pressure steam boilers, who has had experience with the Vacuum system, to work at large greenhouse plant. Pay good salary. Write, Green Floral & Nursery Co., Dallas, Texas.

WANTED—At once, an able-bodied, intelligent young man of good character to learn the florist business. An excellent opportunity of advancement for the right man. Carnations, violets and bedding plants. Must be able to drive and care for one horse. $20.00 per month, room and board, to start. Send references in first letter. P. O. Box 106, Berwyn, Chester Co., Pa.

Seedsman Wanted

We want a young man as order clerk in our flower seed and bulb department; permanent position. Apply, stating age, experience, etc., to

HENRY A. DREER, 714 Chestnut St., Phila, Pa.

Mention the Florists' Exchange when writing.

SEEDSMAN

Wanted a young man with experience in putting up orders, attending to customers, and general store work. Apply with references, stating wages expected, to **"Seed Store,"** care Florists' Exchange, 2 Duane St., N. Y. City.

Mention The Florists' Exchange when writing.

MISCELLANEOUS WANTS

WANTED—At once, 100 Cyclamen Giganteum in bloom. Address R. A. Ralston, Asbury Park, N. J.

WANTED TO BUY—Greenhouses to be taken down. State full particulars of same when writing. Address, F. W., care The Florists' Exchange.

WANTED—Ulrich Brunner Rose Stock, American grown on own roots or Manetti. The Fernery Greenhouses, Bellona Ave., Govanstown, Md.

WANTED TO LEASE—Commercial place of 8,000 to 10,000 ft. of glass., with one or two acres of land and dwelling. Would take it now or first of April. Must be near New York; Jersey preferred. Address C. M., care The Florists' Exchange.

WANTED—Special prices on the following: 3,000 lbs. mixed sweet peas, 3,000 lbs. mixed tall nasturtiums, 3,000 lbs. mixed dwarf nasturtiums. I also want large quantities of all kinds of garden and flower seed. What have you to offer, and what is your best price? Write at once to William D. Burt, Dalton, N. Y.

FOR SALE OR RENT

Rare Opportunity

For a florist, to establish a good paying business; 16,000 inhabitants; one of the fastest growing towns in State. The grounds are especially adapted for the business. Main Av., on line of trolley. Five minutes from station White Plains, N. Y. For full particulars apply to

GRIGGS & TREUPEL
R. R. Ave. White Plains, N. Y.

Mention the Florists' Exchange when writing.

FOR SALE

A 100 Acre Farm, between Bridgewater and Middleboro, Mass., beautifully situated, southern exposure, 7 room dwelling, barn, outbuildings and good well. The loam is very heavy and rich, extending north to lighter loam and white propagating sand, standing wood in large quantity. This place offers splendid opportunities to start greenhouse and nursery business, and is directly located on electric road. No competition of any description within miles. Will sell on easy terms to party with good references.

CLARENCE A. HAMMETT, Newport, R.I.

Mention the Florists' Exchange when writing.

FOR SALE OR RENT

FOR SALE—Well established retail florist store in near-by town. Inquire Joseph J. Levy, 56 West 28th St., New York City.

GREENHOUSE PLANT, about 35,000 ft. under glass, large boiler, etc., for rent, or would run on shares with responsible party (suitable for garden truck, etc.). For particulars apply to T. Shriner & Co., Harrison, N. J., or John Hutton, 668 Park Avenue, N. Y.

FOR SALE

Des Moines, Iowa, wholesale and retail greenhouse establishment, 29,000 feet of glass, three acres of ground, well located, all in good order, with good wholesale and retail trade. Price, about $8,400; terms reasonable.

VAUGHAN'S SEED STORE
CHICAGO

Mention the Florists' Exchange when writing.

FOR SALE

A well equipped place, consisting of seven greenhouses, over 30,000 feet of glass, a nine roomed house, barn, stock, etc., and eight acres of land. This is a decided bargain and a rare opportunity. For particulars address

S. S. SKIDELSKY,
824 N. 24th St., Philadelphia, Pa.

Mention the Florists' Exchange when writing.

STOCK FOR SALE

100,000 greenhouse grown Asparagus Plumosus Nanus seed; ready about Dec. 15. $4.00 per 1,000. Joseph Wood, Spring Valley, N. Y.

FOR SALE—Rooted cuttings of Enchantress, $2.50 per 100; stock plants of Gold Mine, 75c. per doz.; $5.00 per 100. Riddell & Herrick, Farmingdale, L. I.

WHITE AND YELLOW BONNAFFON, Black Hawk, Enguehard and Maud Dean chrysanthemums. 75c. per doz.; $5.00 per 100. A. D. Kroll, Lansdowne, Pa.

CYCLAMEN plants for Christmas sales, in 5 and 6 in. pots, $6.00 and $9.00 per doz. Selling fast, so place your orders early. Safe arrival guaranteed. Geo. A. Rackham, 880 Van Dyke Av., Detroit, Mich.

BABY RAMBLER ROSES, fine dormant stock, one year, $12.00 per 100; 2 1-4-in. pot plants, extra well rooted, $4.00 per 100; $30.00 per 1,000. Orders booked for delivery now or any time up to late Spring. Samples free. Brown Brothers Company, Rochester, N. Y.

SURPLUS STOCK OF SEEDS—Calliopsis, (California Sunbeams), Golden Fleece; Dahlia Monarch, mixed; Eschscholtzia, Golden West; Freesia, Geranium, Good Venture; Heliotrope, Lemoines'; Ipomea, Heavenly Blue, White Tassel; Nasturium, Butterfly, Jupiter, Saturn, mixed; Poppy, Fayal, Irresistible, Maid of the Mist; Tacsonia Buchananii. Write for prices. Theodosia B. Shepherd Co., W. H. Francis, Mgr., Ventura, Cal.

FOR SALE

FOR SALE—Second-hand, four-inch, cast-iron pipe, hubs cleaned and in good order. Address, Wm. G. Grimm, Cedar Lane, Woodhaven, L. I.

FOR SALE—Ice box, used four months, 16 ft. long, 7 ft. wide and 8 1-2 ft. high. Good for commercial or wholesale florist. Will sell at a sacrifice. Chas. Millang, 50 West 29th St., N. Y.

BOILERS BOILERS. BOILERS.
SEVERAL good second-hand boilers on hand, also new No. 16 Hitchings at reduced cost. Write for list. Wm. H. Lutton, West Side Avenue Station, C. R. R. of N. J., Jersey City, N. J.

FOR SALE GREENHOUSE PIPE

4-inch boiler tubes, second hand, in fine condition, absolutely free from scale and with ends cut square. Sample and prices on application.

KROESCHELL BROS. CO., 33 Erie St. Chicago.

Mention the Florists' Exchange when writing.

FOR SALE

Greenhouse Material milled from Gulf Cypress, to any detail furnished, or our own patterns as desired, cut and spliced ready for erection. Estimates for complete constructions furnished.

V. E. REICH, Brooklyn, N. Y.
1429-1437 Metropolitan Ave.

Mention the Florists' Exchange when writing.

NOTICE

To be sold immediately at great sacrifice, florists' delivery outfit, consisting of two top wagons, three open wagons, two horses with harness, one rubber-tired surrey; all in fine condition. An exceptional opportunity. Apply,

EDWARD HIGGINGS
1 West 28th St. - N. Y. CITY

FOR SALE

BOILERS No. 6 Weathered, round, $60.00. One 11 section Sunray hot water sectional boiler, grate 3 by 3. Price $150.00. New Henderson boilers; send for price on size wanted. One No. 367 Lord & Burnham hot water boiler, 7 sections, 36 in. grate, heat 8,500 sq. ft. of glass, used one season, price $150.00, guaranteed.

PIPE Good serviceable second hand. No Junk, with new threads. 2 in. 7c.; 1½ in. 5½c.; 1¼ in. 4c.; 1 in. 3c.; 2½ in. 10c.; 3 in. 14c.; 4 in. 18c. 4 in. cast iron greenhouse 14c. 2 in. NEW, standard, full lengths, 9½c. ft. All kinds of fittings for 4 in. cast iron and all sizes wrought iron.

STOCKS AND DIES New Economy, easy working. No. 1 cuts ¼-¾-1 in. $3.00; No. 2 cuts 1¼-1½-2 ins. $4.00; Armstrong Adjustable No. 3 cuts ½-1 in. $4.00; No. 3 cuts 1¼-1½-2 ins. $6.50.

PIPE CUTTERS Saunders, No. 1 cuts to 1 in. $1.00; No. 2 cuts to 2 in. $1.30; No. 3 cuts to 3 in. $3.00; No. 4 cuts to 4 in. $4.50.

STILLSON WRENCHES Guaranteed. 12 in., grips 1½ in. $1.10; 18 in., grips 2 in. $1.50; 24 in., grips 2½ in. $2.25; 36 in., grips 3½ in. $4.50.

PIPE VISES Reed's Best Hinged Vise, No. 1 grips 2 in. $1.75; No. 2 grips 4 in. $3.50.

GARDEN HOSE 50 ft. lengths ¾ in., guaranteed; 9c.; for heavy work, guaranteed; 12½c.

HOT-BED SASH New; Gulf Cypress, 3 ft. x 6 ft. 80c.; glazed complete $1.60 up. Second hand sash glazed $1.00 and $1.25, good condition.

GLASS New American, 50 ft. to the box. 10x12 single at $1.90. 10x12, 12x12 10x15 B double $2.65. 12x14 to 12x20 and 14x14 to 14x20 B double $2.85. 16x16 and 16x18 B double $2.95. 18x20 to 18 x 24 double $3.20 per box 6x8, 7x8, 8x10 old, single $1.50. 8 x 10 and 8x14 old, double $1.65. 12 x 14 old single $1.75.

PLATE GLASS MIRROR with white enameled frame 2x7, price $12.00.

Get our prices on second hand wood material. We can furnish everything in new material to erect any size house. Get our prices.

METROPOLITAN MATERIAL CO.
Greenhouse Wreckers
1398-1408 Metropolitan Avenue, BROOKLYN, N.Y.

Mention the Florists' Exchange when writing.

MONTREAL.—At the annual meeting of the Gardeners and Florists' Club the following officers were elected for the ensuing year: President, A. H. Walker; first vice-president, J. Pidduck; second vice-president, J. C. Eddy; secretary-treasurer, W. H. Horobin; assistant secretary, H. J. Eddy; executive committee, W. G. Pascoe, Alf. C. Wilshire, G. A. Robinson, G. Urengde, G. Trussell, Julius Luck; social committee, Joseph Petty, W. S. Watts, J. Prescott. It was decided to hold a chrysanthemum show next year, provided a suitable hall can be secured, and it was also resolved to offer a silver cup for competition at the exhibition of the American Carnation Society, in Toronto next January. The several reports for the year were submitted to the meeting, and were found to be very satisfactory.

GENEVA, N. Y.—Hobart College has received a gift of $500,000 and over from William Smith, for the purpose of establishing a woman's college in connection with Hobart College.

CHANGES IN BUSINESS.

BRENTWOOD, N. H.—Edgar Prescott is building a greenhouse and with his son will start a florist business, the latter having been employed for several years by the late J. T. Smith, florist.

SPRINGFIELD, ILL.—The Crowres Specialty Company has been incorporated; capital, $5,000; truck gardening; incorporators, Edward C. Holzworth, Frank W. Lamey, Samuel A. Wight.

MILWAUKEE, WIS.—The Loveland Floral Company has been incorporated with a capital of $1,500; incorporators, John Krueger, Carl Carlson and Charles F. G. Wegner.

CANADIAN NEWS

TORONTO. — Business continues good with most stock fairly plentiful. Violets are scarce and consequently high. The weather has lately been very dull, so stock opens slowly. The cut of violets for Christmas is likely to be short; the supply of red roses and red carnations will also probably be short. Some fine colored American Beauty are coming in, but not enough to fill all orders; the same may be said of Richmond. Chrysanthemums are still good and plentiful; medium sized flowers sell best; small flowers and large specimen blooms are not much called for. Some good poinsettias are arriving and they are in fairly active demand. But few orchids are now offered. The first azaleas have appeared, but as yet move slowly.

I am sorry to report that W. J. Lawrence lost his youngest boy last week. Mr. and Mrs. Lawrence have the sympathy of all the trade in their sad bereavement.

The finance committee of the Horticultural Exhibition reports that up to date there appears to be a deficit of about $600; this may yet be reduced. The expenses this year were about $2,500 more than those of last year, and the deficit is less than last year's.

Albert Houle, manager of the Bedford Park Floral Company, has two beautiful houses of roses that look just about right for Christmas. He has two beds of Richmond that are much the best I have seen of this fine rose; many of the buds are on stems three feet long, and as strong as American Beauty stems. The blooms are of a fine color. The stock is a credit to Mr. Houle as a grower, for he has been building all Summer and even yet his houses are not finished. He is finding a good market for all his stock.

THOS. MANTON.

Boston.

Impressions of a Traveler.

William Nicholson of Framingham, who recently returned from his trip abroad, gave the writer a few interesting facts of how he was impressed with English horticulture. One of the first florist establishments he visited after reaching Liverpool was that of Mr. Young at West Derby. Mr. Young's specialty is carnations, he having quite extensive greenhouses devoted to their culture. Malmaison varieties he raises to perfection, many of the plants being grown on year after year. American varieties were quite extensively grown, and Mr. Young said that the English varieties have had to give way to them. Mr. Young ships to Covent Garden as well as to Liverpool.

At Blenheim Palace Mr. Nicholson saw some of the finest grown carnations. American varieties that were well done were Enchantress, Mrs. Thos. W. Lawson and Lady Bountiful. Malmaison sorts were here done to perfection.

The most interesting carnation growing establishment visited by Mr. Nicholson was that of A. F. Dutton, at West Drayton. The establishment is in the country, several miles from anywhere; but the whole place is after the style of a modern American carnation growing plant. Mr. Nicholson said that the houses reminded him of his own recently constructed ones, except that they were wooden instead of iron frame. Even the boilers were of American manufacture, being the "Ideal." American varieties of carnations were grown exclusively and were planted and trained as would be done here. Enchantress, Harry Fenn, Governor Wolcott and Fair Maid were all very fine; Victory, Robert Craig and other recent varieties were being tried. Mr. Dutton ships largely to the Covent Garden market where his products command the highest prices. The system used is to pack several dozen in a box, which is made of very thin lumber. The flowers are not unpacked at Covent Garden, but sold right in the boxes, which are charged for on the sales slip, but credited upon return.

At the great Shrewsbury show Mr. Dutton's exhibit of carnations was very fine, and although he lost the first prize for the best collection on a technicality he was awarded a prize equal to first.

At the Shrewsbury show Mr. Nicholson was very much impressed with the extent and perfection of the exhibition. The Eckford exhibit of sweet peas was the finest he had ever dreamed of seeing. He was much impressed with the table decorations and said that some of our exhibition managers could learn much from a visit to one of these shows. At the Edinburgh exhibition Mr. Nicholson was equally taken with the quality and quantity of the exhibits and the interest shown by the public.

While visiting Covent Garden he was surprised at the quantities of foliage material sold there; especially noticeable were the colored oaks, beeches, prunuses, maples, etc. He wondered what could be done with all of it, but learned later that much of it was used for hotel decorations.

Mr. Nicholson says the finest outdoor roses he saw were in Scotland, and the finest trees on any private estate he visited were observed at Castle Kennedy. The best bedding he saw in England was at Hampton Court, but that could not compare with the fine bedding noticed in France at the Jardin des Luxemburg, the Jardin des Plantes, the Jardin des Louvre and the Versailles gardens. The best roses commercially were seen in Paris.

One of the finest sights that Mr. Nicholson saw was the houseboat decorations on the Thames. There are hundreds of these houseboats on the river, each converted into a veritable flower garden, trying to beat its neighbor as it were. Ivy geraniums were largely used and the color effects were great object lessons for the floral artist.

Society Notes.

At the meeting of the Board of Trustees of the Massachusetts Horticultural Society on Saturday, nine new members were elected to the society and the exhibition schedule for the year 1907 adopted. This schedule has no important changes, except that several of the smaller exhibitions during July and August have been eliminated. It was decided to invite the Gardeners and Florists' Club to hold its landscape gardening classes in Horticultural Hall, which would be free of cost to the club. It was voted to invite the State Board of Agriculture to hold its Winter meeting in the halls of the society in December, 1907. A rule was adopted governing protests at exhibitions whereby any exhibitor feeling aggrieved by the awards might have the committee reconsider their action, providing a protest was duly filed with the secretary. The following committees were appointed for 1907:

Finance Committee—Walter Hunnewell, chairman; S. M. Weld, Arthur F. Estabrook.

Committee on Prizes and Exhibitions—J. K. M. L. Farquhar, chairman, W. N. Craig, A. H. Fewkes, Isaac Locke, Wilfred Wheeler and W. H. Spooner.

Committee on Plants and Flowers—A. H. Fewkes, chairman, Robert Cameron, W. N. Craig, William Nicholson and T. D. Hatfield.

Committee on Fruits—Wilfred Wheeler, chairman, Chas. F. Curtis and J. Willard Hill.

Committee on Vegetables—Isaac Locke, chairman, J. B. Shurtliff, Jr. and Duncan Finlayson.

Committee on Gardens—Chas. W. Parker, chairman, Oakes Ames, George Barker, W. N. Craig, S. M. Weed, A. H. Fewkes, J. A. Pettigrew, W. P. Rich, Henry P. Walcott, W. W. Rawson and W. H. Elliott.

Library Committee—C. S. Sargent, chairman, T. Otis Fuller, Samuel Henshaw, C. W. Jenks and Henry P. Walcott.

Committee on Lectures and Publications—W. P. Rich, chairman, J. W. Manning, Edward B. Wilder and J. A. Pettigrew.

Committee on School Gardens—Henry S. Adams, chairman, W. E. C. Rich, H. S. Rand and W. P. Rich.

News Notes.

The landscape gardening classes of the Gardeners and Florists' Club will commence on Friday evening and will be held twice weekly during the Winter.

Hugh Grant, for several years with D. Zirngiebel Needham and more recently with J. Strout of Biddeford, Me., suffered a paralytic stroke and is now in the Boston hospital in a serious condition.

Frank Dolansky of Lynn, is bringing in some fine poinsettias to the Park street market.

A bright little boy arrived to warm up the home of J. A. Cartwright on Saturday, the coldest December 7 on record, with the mercury 5 degrees below zero.

Don't forget the meeting of the Gardeners and Florists' Club Tuesday evening, the 18th inst. W. H. Wyman will be the speaker, his subject "Craft and the Craftsman." Besides it is President Wheeler's last meeting of the term; let us guarantee him a large attendance as in the past.

J. W. DUNCAN.

RUTHERFORD, N. J. — Julius Roehrs has built a new range of houses containing 21,000 square feet of glass. These houses are of Lord & Burnham construction. This range is used exclusively for orchids. Catleyas of different varieties are the kinds grown, and the whole range is in condition to supply the demand for this recherche flower.

RANDOLPH, VT.—The "Green Mountain State," in a recent issue, gives an illustrated description of the establishment of H. E. Totman, which now embraces over half an acre under glass. Mr. Totman recently installed a Kroeschell boiler; the heating plant is on the downhill system. A general collection of stock is cultivated.

REVIEW OF THE MARKET

NEW YORK.—Flowers of all descriptions are in short supply in this market at the present time, and prices are high. Usually at this time of the year there si a diminution of values, as retailers have not very much to do; and while there is not much going on among the retailers just now, the general scarcity along all lines is such that prices are above normal, and the question is being asked, what will be the figures at Christmas time if this scarcity keeps up? The best grade of American Beauty roses are bringing 50c. and 60c., and there is an occasional sale made where the quality is extraordinarily fine and a higher figure is realized. The special grades of Bride and Bridesmaid are at the 15c. mark, and there are times when Bridesmaid, with extra long stems, have run a little above that figure.

Carnations are selling well, and while good, long-stemmed stock brings anywhere from $4 to $6 per 100, there is also a supply that cleared out at $2 and $3 per 100, owing to its inferiority.

Cattleyas are quite scarce, with the exception of C. Percivaliana, and these the buyers do not seem to ask for to any extent.

Lily of the valley is selling well, and some of special grade is coming in that brings $5 per 100; in fact, this high grade stock can be cleared out much quicker than the short-stemmed flowers.

Stevia is in fairly large quantities; and there are still a few chrysanthemums to be seen here and there in the wholesale district, though the supply is indeed a very moderate one compared to what it was a week ago. Gardenias are among the best selling flowers just now, and from 75c. to $1 each is being realized for them. It is expected that there will be a supply of these, with stems two or three feet in length, that will bring $1.50 each for the Christmas holidays.

The supply of Roman hyacinths and Paper White narcissus is about equal to the demand, and the price of $2 flat seems to have become established.

Violets are the one exception to which the remarks we make about high prices cannot be applied; these sell at from $1 down, and there are very few indeed that reach the dollar mark. Lilies are a little stiffer in value than they were, 15c. each being asked for the better grade of blooms. Smilax is not selling as well as it was; on the other hand, Adiantum Croweanum is bringing somewhat better prices by reason of its improved quality.

CHICAGO.—From this point, at the early part of the week, there is little to offer, but about the same old story which appears annually between Thanksgiving and Christmas. It seems difficult to prognosticate absolutely the prospect of stock to be delivered, yet from an extended visitation among the largest growers it is safe to say that Christmas this year will be as fully supplied with cut flowers as the holiday has been in the past two decades. Of tea roses there will evidently be a plentiful sufficiency. American Beauty, Liberty and Richmond, though of good quality and reasonably abundant, will still command a high figure.

Carnations from present appearances are not going to be any too plentiful, particularly in colors. Mrs. T. W. Lawson has not done any too well in this section this year, while Mrs. E. A. Nelson, Enchantress, Harlowarden and a few others of the scarlet, pink, and crimson varieties are holding their own and probably a little better than in previous years under more careful and scientific cultivation. In whites, White Perfection, The Belle, Lady Bountiful and Lieutenant Peary, with White Lawson and Boston Market for shipping, show up the most attractive in Chicago.

Further than this in the flower line it is evident that here will be a shortage, and that prices will hold well up to the high notch. The short crop of all wild holiday greens will tend to support the high price of the greenhouse crop of the various members of the green family. W. K. W.

PHILADELPHIA. — Cut flowers are cleaning up nicely each day; while there is not a large business going on at retail, prices are steadily advancing. As the supply is limited, no doubt the wholesalers think this method an easier way of getting good prices at the holidays; by adding a little each week the advance will not be so noticeable. Of American Beauty roses the supply does not quite equal the demand; $7.50 per dozen is being asked for specials this week. All first class stock of tea roses is held at $15.00 per 100, while $20 is being asked for some specials. Choice Bridesmaid are most in demand, while Killarney is also a very good seller. Mme. Abel Chatenay and Wellesley have a good call, and the best stock sells well at above named figures.

The demand for double violets is not so strong, but the supply is so uncertain that $1.50 per 100 is yet obtained. The large singles are improving in quality and sell well at 75c. and $1 per bunch of 100.

Orchids are in strong demand. The best cattleyas bring 75c. each flower; Dendrobium formosum, 40c. per flower; Lælia albida, $1.00 per dozen flowers; Cypripedium insigne, 15c. and C. Leeanum, $2.00 per dozen.

Bouvardia is a very good seller; pink and red are in greatest demand at $3 to $4 per 100.

Carnations are much firmer with prices still advancing; some extra choice stock has sold at $8 per 100. Enchantress, choice, bring $6; Mrs. Lawson and Queen Louise, $5, while other varieties go at $3 and $4 per 100. Gardenias are scarce in this market; the best flowers are now offered at $9 per dozen and are all sold.

Paper White narcissus and Roman hyacinths fetch $3 and $4 per 100. Asparagus plumosus is scarce, selling at 50c. and 75c. per string; bunches 50c. and 75c. Smilax in fair supply at 15c. Extra choice lily of the valley realizes $5 per 100. DAVID RUST.

FIRMS WHO ARE BUILDIN

CEDAR FALLS, IA.—L. M. Ye market gardener, has completed a n greenhouse, 136 feet long.

BOWDOINHAM, ME.—E. B. Sprag is making extensive repairs on and large addition to his greenhouse pla

Wholesale Prices of Cut Flowers, New York, Dec. 12, 1906

Prices quoted are by the hundred unless otherwise noted

Roses — A. Beauty, fancy—special	40.00 to	60.00
" extra	20.00 to	25.00
" No. 1	12.00 to	15.00
" No. 2	6.00 to	8.00
" No. 3	5.00 to	6.00
Bride, Maid, fancy—spe'l	10.00 to	15.00
" extra	6.00 to	8.00
" No. 1	5.00 to	6.00
" No. 2	3.00 to	4.00
Golden Gate	3.00 to	15.00
Richmond	3.00 to	15.00
Mme. Abel Chatenay	3.00 to	15.00
Adiantum	.50 to	.75
Croweanum	1.00 to	1.50
Asparagus	25.00 to	50.00
" Plumosus, bunches	8.00 to	15.00
" Sprengerii, bunches	8.00 to	15.00
	to	
Callas	10.00 to	12.00
Cattleyas	40.00 to	75.00
Cypripediums	to	12.00
Daisies	to	

Carnations — Inf'r grades, all colors	2.00 to	3.00
Standard Varieties — White	3.00 to	4.00
Pink	3.00 to	4.00
Red	3.00 to	4.00
Yel. & Var.	3.00 to	4.00
*Fancy— (*The highest grades of standard var.) — White	4.00 to	6.00
Pink	4.00 to	6.00
Red	4.00 to	6.00
Yel. & Var.	4.00 to	6.00
Novelties	6.00 to	8.00
Chrysanthemums	2.00 to	6.00
" Fancy	10.00 to	20.00
Gardenias, per doz.	9.00 to	12.00
Lilies	10.00 to	15.00
Lily of the Valley	2.00 to	4.00
Mignonette	to	
Narcissus, Paper White	to	2.00
Roman Hyacinths	to	2.00
Smilax	8.00 to	12.00
Violets	.50 to	1.00
	to	
	to	
	to	
	to	

Wholesale Prices of Cut Flowers—Per 100

Boston Dec. 11, 1906	Buffalo Dec. 10, 1906	Detroit Dec. 8, 1906	Cincinnati Dec. 10, 1906	Baltimore Dec. 12, 1906	NAMES AND VARIETIES	Milwaukee Dec. 4, 1906	Phil'delphia Dec. 11, 1906	Pittsburg Dec. 11, 1906	St. Louis Dec. 10, 1906
30.00 to 50.00	40.00 to 50.00	...... to 50.00	50.00 to 60.00	...... to	ROSES — A. BEAUTY, fancy—special	...... to 25.00	50.00 to 60.00	50.00 to 60.00	25.00 to 35.00
20.00 to 30.00	30.00 to 40.00	...... to 25.00	45.00 to 50.00	...... to 25.00	" extra	...... to 20.00	...... to	30.00 to 40.00	15.00 to 20.00
10.00 to 20.00	20.00 to 25.00	...... to 16.00	30.00 to 40.00	12.50 to 20.00	" No. 1	...... to 18.00	...... to	15.00 to 20.00	10.00 to 12.00
...... to 10.00	8.00 to 10.00	...... to 12.00	...... to	5.00 to 8.00	" Culls and ordinary	...... to 12.00	...... to	6.00 to 8.00	4.00 to 6.00
8.00 to 10.00	8.00 to 10.00	4.00 to 8.00	6.00 to 8.00	...... to 5.00	BRIDE, 'MAID, fancy-special	...... to 6.00	6.00 to 10.00	...... to	6.00 to 8.00
5.00 to 6.00	6.00 to 8.00	...... to	5.00 to 7.00	...... to 4.00	" extra	...... to 5.00	...... to	...... to	4.00 to 5.00
2.00 to 6.00	...... to	...... to	...... to 4.00	...... to 3.00	" No. 1	...... to 4.00	...... to	...... to	2.00 to 3.00
1.00 to 2.00	4.00 to 6.00	...... to	...... to 3.00	...... to 2.00	" No. 2	...... to 3.00	...... to	...... to	...... to ......
...... to	4.00 to 6.00	4.00 to 8.00	3.00 to 8.00	2.00 to 5.00	GOLDEN GATE	3.00 to 6.00	...... to	...... to	2.00 to 6.00
...... to	4.00 to 8.00	...... to	...... to	3.00 to 5.00	K. A. VICTORIA	3.00 to 6.00	...... to	...... to	2.00 to 6.00
2.00 to 15.00	4.00 to 12.00	...... to	...... to	3.00 to 5.00	LIBERTY	3.00 to 8.00	...... to	...... to	...... to ......
...... to	...... to	3.00 to 8.00	...... to	3.00 to 5.00	METEOR	...... to	...... to	...... to	...... to ......
...... to	4.00 to 8.00	4.00 to 10.00	...... to	2.00 to 4.00	PERLE	3.00 to 6.00	...... to	4.00 to 12.00	2.00 to 5.00
...... to	...... to	...... to 50.00	...... to	...... to	ORCHIDS—Cattleyas	...... to	...... to 50.00	...... to	...... to ......
...... to	...... to	2.00 to 4.00	...... to	1.00 to 1.25	CARNATIONS — Inferior grades, all colors	2.00 to 4.00	2.00 to 3.00	3.00 to 6.00	1.50 to 2.00
1.50 to 2.00	2.00 to 3.00	...... to	...... to 3.00	1.50 to 2.00	Standard Varieties — White	...... to	2.00 to 3.00	3.00 to 6.00	1.50 to 2.00
2.00 to 3.00	2.00 to 3.00	...... to	...... to 3.00	1.50 to 2.00	Standard Varieties — Pink	...... to	2.00 to 3.00	3.00 to 6.00	1.50 to 2.00
2.00 to 3.00	2.00 to 3.00	...... to	...... to 3.00	1.50 to 2.00	Standard Varieties — Red	...... to	2.00 to 3.00	3. 0 to 6.00	1.50 to 2.00
2.00 to 3.00	...... to	...... to	...... to	1.50 to 2.00	Standard Varieties — Yellow and var.	...... to	2.00 to 3.00	3.00 to 6.00	1.50 to 2.00
2.00 to 4.00	4.00 to 5.00	...... to	...... to 4.00	2.50 to 3.00	Fancy Varieties — White	...... to	4.00 to 5.00	...... to	2.50 to 4.00
3.00 to 4.00	4.00 to 5.00	...... to	4.00 to 5.00	2.50 to 3.00	Fancy Varieties — Pink	...... to	4.00 to 5.00	...... to	2.50 to 4.00
3.00 to 4.00	4.00 to 5.00	...... to	4.00 to 5.00	2.50 to 3.00	Fancy Varieties — Red	...... to	4.00 to 5.00	...... to	2.50 to 4.00
3.00 to 4.00	4.00 to 5.00	...... to	4.00 to 5.00	2.50 to 3.00	Fancy Varieties — Yellow and var	...... to	4.00 to 5.00	...... to	2.50 to 4.00
5.00 to 6.00	...... to	...... to	...... to	...... to	Novelties	...... to	...... to	...... to	...... to ......
.75 to 1.00	.50 to 1.00	...... to 2.00	1.00 to 1.50	...... to 1.00	ADIANTUM	...... to	...... to 1.00	1.00 to 1.25	1.00 to 1.50
...... to 50.00	15.00 to 20.00	25.00 to 60.00	35.00 to 50.00	25.00 to 50.00	ASPARAGUS, Plum. and Ten	25.00 to 50.00	50.00 to 75.00	35.00 to 50.00	25.00 to 40.00
...... to	15.00 to 20.00	20.00 to 30.00	...... to 35.00	25.00 to 50.00	" Sprengeri, bunches	25.00 to 50.00	...... to 50.00	20.00 to 40.00	25.00 to 75.00
10.00 to 12.00	10.00 to 12.00	10.00 to 12.50	...... to 15.00	6.00 to 10.00	CALLAS	12.00 to 15.00	...... to	...... to	12.50 to 15.00
10.00 to 20.00	8.00 to 25.00	4.00 to 25.00	...... to	4.00 to 25.00	CHRYSANTHEMUMS	8.00 to 30.00	10.00 to 50.00	...... to	15.00 to 25.00
...... to	...... to	...... to	...... to	...... to	DAISIES	...... to	...... to	...... to	...... to ......
...... to 12.50	15.00 to 20.00	...... to	...... to 15.00	...... to 12.50	LILIES	...... to	...... to	12.50 to 15.00	...... to ......
2.00 to 4.00	...... to	3.00 to 4.00	...... to 4.00	...... to 4.00	LILY OF THE VALLEY	3.00 to 4.00	4.00 to 5.00	2.00 to 4.00	3.00 to 4.00
2.00 to 3.00	1.50 to 2.00	...... to	...... to 3.00	...... to	MIGNONETTE, ordinary	...... to	...... to	...... to	2.00 to 3.00
4.00 to 5.00	2.00 to 3.00	...... to	...... to	...... to	" fancy	...... to	...... to	...... to	4.00 to 5.00
...... to 12.50	...... to 15.00	12.50 to 15.00	...... to 15.00	...... to 20.00	SMILAX	...... to	...... to	12.50 to 15.00	12.50 to 15.00
.50 to .60	...... to 1.00	1.00 to 1.50	...... to 1.00	...... to .50	VIOLETS, ordinary	...... to	...... to	...... to 1.25	.40 to .50
.75 to 1.00	...... to 1.50	...... to	...... to 1.50	...... to .60	" fancy	...... to	...... to 1.50	...... to 1.50	.60 to .75
...... to	...... to .15	...... to 1.25	...... to .15	...... to	GALAX LEAVES	...... to	...... to	...... to	...... to ......

Indianapolis.

News Jottings.

A visit to several of the growers disclosed a fine supply of flowers and plants for the holiday trade. Begonia Gloire de Lorraine, lilies, poinsettias, cyclamen, azaleas, and variegated foliage plants are in quantity and of elegant quality. The outlook for cut flowers is promising, the increased area of glass from year to year proves effective at this time.

The December meeting of the State Florists' Association was fairly well attended. It was decided to hold the annual January meeting at the Commercial Club rooms; exhibits of novelties are to be made and certificates awarded. Arrangements were also made for light refreshments. The election of officers will also take place.

Mr. Cary, foreman at the Indianapolis Flower & Plant Company, is to take a position with another firm.

Visitors: Thos. Knipe and W. W. Coles, Kokomo.

Wm. Schilling is on the sick list.

I. B.

FAIRMOUNT, IND.—Joseph Shane, owner of a greenhouse plant in the west end of town, is just now considering himself a fortunate individual in that he, after purchasing a gas well, which is located near his place and formerly owned by the local gas company, which recently quit the field, made a test of the well and found that it had a seven-pound pressure.

Wholesale Prices of Cut Flowers, Chicago, Dec. 11, 1906

Prices quoted are by the hundred unless otherwise noted

ROSES — American Beauty		
36-inch stems.........per doz.	5.00 to	6.00
30-inch stems.......... "	4.00 to	5.00
24-inch stems.......... "	3.00 to	4.00
20-inch stems.......... "	2.00 to	3.00
18-inch stems.......... "	1.50 to	2.00
12-inch stems.......... "	.... to	1.50
8-inch stems and shorts "	.... to	1.00
Bride Maid, fancy special......	10.00 to	12.00
" extra..........	6.00 to	8.00
" No. 1..........	4.00 to	5.00
" No. 2..........	.... to	3.00
Golden Gate..........	3.00 to	10.00
Carnot..........	3.00 to	6.00
Uncle John..........	3.00 to	10.00
Liberty..........	3.00 to	12.00
Richmond..........	3.00 to	12.00
Kaiserine..........	3.00 to	8.00
Killarney..........	3.00 to	6.00
" extra..........	8.00 to	10.00
Perle..........	3.00 to	6.00
Chatenay..........	3.00 to	6.00
Callas..........	.... to	16.00
....	.... to	....

CARNATIONS			
STANDARD VARIETIES	White..........	2.00 to	3.00
	Pink..........	2.00 to	3.00
	Red..........	2.00 to	3.00
	Yellow & var....	2.00 to	3.00
*FANCY (The highest grades of Sta'd var)	White..........	3.00 to	4.00
	Pink..........	3.00 to	4.00
	Red..........	3.00 to	4.00
	Yellow & var....	3.00 to	4.00
NOVELTIES..........		.... to	....
ADIANTUM..........		.75 to	1.00
ASPARAGUS, Plum. & Ten..........		.35 to	.50
" Sprengeri, bunches.		.35 to	.50
LILIES, Longiflorum..........		15.00 to	20.00
HARRISII..........		15.00 to	20.00
Orchids—Cattleyas..........		50.00 to	75.00
SMILAX..........		8.00 to	12.00
LILY OF THE VALLEY..........		2.00 to	4.00
VIOLETS..........		1.00 to	1.50
" single..........		.75 to	1.00
HARDY FERNS per 1000..........		.... to	1.50
GALAX "		1.00 to	1.25
NARCISSUS, Paper White..........		3.00 to	4.00
CHRYSANTHEMUMS per doz		1.00 to	3.00

St. Paul.

News Notes.

Alfred Lemke has purchased August S. Swanson's interest in the Swanson Floral Company and hereafter the business will be conducted by Mr. Lemke and Gust A. Colberg. A short time ago this concern suffered a fire loss, but they are now getting things in shape in the way of painting, etc.

L. L. May & Company have had a busy week: funeral work being indeed heavy. The advance sales of holly, green, etc., through their traveling men, have been good and from present prospects a great deal more will be handled than in any previous year. Lycopodium is not as scarce as was first anticipated, and it looks now as though there would be a sufficient quantity to supply the trade nicely, although the price is up to $6 and $7 a crate. This firm is receiving large quantities of holly.

Gust A. Colberg of Lemke & Colberg is in Chicago, picking up novelties for the holiday trade. PAUL.

Cincinnati.

News Notes.

Rain for the past twenty-four hours will not help produce many Christmas flowers. Stock at the present time is not plentiful by any means, and many more carnations could be used, as well as American Beauty. Tea roses are equal to the demand. Green goods are plentiful; holly is exceptionally fine this year. The carloads now on track sell at $3.50 to $4 per case. Bouquet green is scarce; laurel is a cent higher than last year.

Saturday night was the regular meeting of the Cincinnati Florists' Society; a quorum was present and some business transacted. Next month we will have a "green fly" smoker and a lunch; these should fetch out a good crowd, for when you reach a man's stomach you generally reach his soul. Several papers are to be delivered and a feast of oratory expected. Everybody come.

The H. Weber & Sons Company had their new pink carnation before the committee. Mabelle is the variety's name; it scored 82 points, 85 being necessary for a certificate. This does not say but what it is a fine sort. Many a variety has been discarded because it did not score 85 points when, if the truth were known, it was better than its brother or sister that had scored 85 or 90. It is just this very point which should cause the American Carnation Society to send a committee to see a variety growing before awarding a certificate; then a certificate would be worth something. As it is, all the judges know about a variety is what they see before them.

Frank Ball has gone into the manufacture of wirework on Third street.

Henry Kunzelman has opened a store on McMillan street, Walnut Hills.

Ben George is trying to run two places at the same time.

Mr. Baum, of Knoxville, Tenn., and Chas. Dieterick, of Mayville, Ky., were callers this week.

E. G. GILLETT.

San Francisco.

The Thanksgiving Day trade in this city showed an improvement with the majority of the florists of from ten to thirty per cent. over that of former years.

On December 3 N. E. Hansen, explorer for the Department of Agriculture at Washington, arrived in San Francisco from a tour of the Old World in search of rare specimens of plants and trees that would be of economic value to the farmers of the United States.

Hansen said he went from England to Lapland, Norway, Sweden, Finland, across Russia and Siberia to Vladivostok, and from there to Japan, and that in all these countries he heard references made to Luther Burbank. This explorer brings back to this country a species of cherry which is expected to thrive well in the most northerly latitudes.

On December 1, Edna, daughter of Professor Wickson of the University of California, was married to William F. Kelly. The maid of honor and bridesmaids were her sisters Kate, Ida and Gladys, and the ushers were her brothers Harmon and Guest. In addition to the Luther Burbank bridal bouquet of intermingled orchids and orange blossoms the spacious rooms of the Wickson house in Berkeley presented a fairy picture of artistically arranged Enchantress carnations and ferns, the handiwork of decorators belonging to the floral depot of Florist Seulberger of Oakland.

ALVIN.

SOUTH BEND, IND.—On account of the phenomenal growth and development of the business of the Ideal Concrete Machinery Company they have found it necessary to vacate their present factory building, and have leased the plant formerly occupied by the Bissel Plow Company, which will give them three times their present floor space, and other facilities which will materially assist in promptly taking care of the ever increasing demand for "Ideal" concrete machines.

Christmas Greens Headquarters

Holly $5.00 per case
Boxwood - - - $15.00 per 100 lbs.
Laurel Festooning, extra quality, 5c. and 6c. per yd.
Princess Pine Festooning, $6.00 per 100 yards.

Wild Smilax $3.50 and $7.00 per case.
Laurel Wreaths, extra quality, $2.50 per doz. upwards.
Branch Laurel, - - 50c. per bunch.
Bouquet Green - $7.00 per 100 lbs.

Galax New Crop Bronze and Greer $1.00 per 1000, $7.50 per 10,00(
Ferns, Fancy and Dagger, $1.25 per 100
Leucothoe Sprays, - - $1.00 per 10
Green and Sphagnum Moss, $1.00 pe bbl.

Headquarters for all Florists' Supplies, such as **RED IMMORTELLES**, Wire Designs, Cut Wire, Letters of all kinds, Immortelles, Cycas Leaves, Milkweeds, Sheaves of Wheat, Ribbons, Boxes, Folding, Blue Corrugated, &c. **THE HOUSE THAT CAN SUPPLY THE GOODS ON A MOMENT'S NOTICE.**

HENRY M. ROBINSON & CO., 11-15 PROVINCE ST., 9 CHAPMAN PLACE, BOSTON, MASS

L. D. Tel., Main 2617-2618.

Mention The Florists' Exchange when writing.

SOUTHERN WILD SMILAX

Now ready in any quantity

Book orders now for future delivery. **Beaven's Fadeless Sheet Moss,** $3.50 per bag, delivered. Send for samples. Also **Fancy Holly** for **Xmas** trade. Satisfaction guaranteed. Write for prices.

E. A. BEAVE[N] EVERGREEN, ALA.

Mention The Florists' Exchange when writing.

Fancy or Dagger Ferns

$1.00 per 1000

Galax, Bronze or Green, 75c. per 1000.
Boxwood, No. 1 Stock, 50 lb. cases, $8.50
Laurel Festooning, 4c., 5c. and 6c. per yard. Finest quality
Laurel Wreaths, $3.00 per doz. Cheaper grades if wanted
Southern Smilax, fancy stock, 50 lb. cases $5.50
Laurel Branches, 35c. per bundle

Send your orders for **LAUREL FESTOONING** in now for Christmas, as later we may be unable to fill them.

Telegraph Office: New Salem, Mass. Long distance telephone connections.

CROWL FERN CO., MILLINGTON, MASS.

Mention the Florists' Exchange when writing.

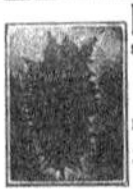

EXTRA FINE NEW CROP FANCY FERN

$1.25 per 1000. Discount on large orders. GALAX, per 1000, $1.25. Green Galax; $1.25 per 1000.

MICHIGAN CUT FLOWER EXCHANGE

WILLIAM DILGER, Manager.

Let us have your standing order for Ferns, we will make Price right all through the season.

38 & 40 Broadway. Formerly Miami Ave. **DETROIT, MICH.**

Send for our weekly price list on Cut Flowers.

Mention The Florists' Exchange when writing.

HOLLY! HOLLY! HOLLY!

Holly Wreaths, Lycopodium and Lycopodium Wreaths

My Man in the Woods with 12 years' experience in packing, can ship you direct, and thus save extra expense in freight. Choice Delaware Holly, well berried, at $3.00 per case. Wreaths $10.00 to $15.00 per 100. Cash with order.

H. T. DUMONT & CO. - 1305 Filbert St., Philadelphia, Pa

Mention the Florists' Exchange when writing.

REED & KELLER 122 W. 25th STREET NEW YORK

Importers and Manufacturers of **FLORISTS' SUPPLIES** Galax Leaves and Decorative Greenery

New York Agents for Caldwell's, Monroe, Ala., Parlor Brand Smilax.

Mention the Florists' Exchange when writing.

THE BEST WAY

to collect an account is to place it with the

National Florists' Board of Trade

56 Pine St., New York

WHY? Because many debtors will pay the Board tearing otherwise a bad rating in our Credit List. Full information as to methods and rates given on application.

Mention the Florists' Exchange when writing.

CUT FLOWER BOXES
EDWARDS FOLDING BOX CO
MANUFACTURERS
PHILADELPHIA, PA.

Mention the Florists' Exchange when writing.

THE AMERICAN CARNATION
Price $3.50. Send for Sample Pages
A. T. DE LA MARE PTG. & PUB. CO., Ltd., 2-8 DUANE STREET, NEW YORK

INSURANCE

of your plants from **FREEZING** in cold weather at a trifling cost. Use a celebrated

LEHMAN WAGON HEATER

There is no danger of fire; no smoke, dirt nor gases to injure plants. They burn **Lehma[n] Coal,** which costs less than ½ cent per hour.

350,000 Lehman heaters are in actual use by **Florists**, Horsemen, Agriculturists a[nd] Physicians. Have you one? Write for new booklet, with prices, to-day.

LEHMAN BROS. Manufacturers 10 Bond St., NEW YORK

J. W. ERRINGE[R] Gen. West. Sales Agent 45 E. Congress St., CHICAG[O]

Also for sale by Henry F. Michell Co., 1018 Market St., Philadelphia, Pa.

BEWARE OF IMITATIONS

N. LECAKES & CO.

53 W. 28th St., NEW YORK

Tel. No. 1214 Madison Square

Stands at Cut Flower Exchange Coogan Bldg., W. 26th Street & 34th Street Cut Flower Market.

SPECIALTIES: Galax Leaves, Ferns and Leucothoe Sprays, Holly, Princess Pine and all kinds of Evergreens.

Green and Bronze Galax Leaves

Mention the Florists' Exchange when writing.

Southern Smilax

If you want **SMILAX**, and you want to get it when you want it, send your orders to

JAS. TOMLINSON - Newton, Ala

Mention the Florists' Exchange when writing.

BRILLIANT
Galax and Leucothoe SPRAYS
Wholesale Trade Solicited
J. L. BANNER & CO., Montezuma, N. C.

Mention the Florists' Exchange when writing.

WIRED TOOTHPICKS

10,000, $1.50; 50,000, $6.25

MANUFACTURED BY

W. J. COWEE, BERLIN, N. Y.

Samples free. For sale by dealers.

Mention the Florists' Exchange when writing.

HAVE YOU USED THE

Perfect Flower Pot Handle and Hanger

It is just the thi[ng] for you to displ[ay] your plants by ha[ng]ing them on wal[ls] etc., especially wh[en] you are crowded [for] room. Also for [lift]ing plants out of j[ar]dinieres; will sust[ain] a weight of [...] pounds.

No. 1 will fit from [...] 5-inch pots 30c. per d[oz.]
No. 2 will fit from [...] 8-inch pots 40c. per d[oz.]
No. 3 will fit from [...] 12-inch pots 50c. per d[oz.]

By mail 10c. ex[tra] per doz. Sam[ple] pair 10c., postpai[d].

W. C. KRICK, 1164-66 Greene Av., Brooklyn, N[.Y.]

HOLLY AND HOLLY WREATHS

Dark Green and Well Berried

CHOICE DELAWARE, per case, $1.00, 2x2x4 ft.
CHOICE VIRGINIA, per case, $3.75, 2x2x4 ft.
HOLLY WREATHS, 10c and 12c.
LAUREL ROPING, 3c. yard.

Cash. Order early, and will ship on any date desi[red].

HARRY L. HUBBS, N. E. Cor. 34th & Cumberland, Commission Merchant, Philadelphia, Pa

BOUQUET GREE[N]

Best quality at **lowest rates.** We gather own **Greens** and bring by our own boat direc[t].

Also **CHRISTMAS TREES**

Northern Michigan Evergreen Nursery.

SCHOONER GEO. L. WRENN, S. W. cor. Clark S[t.] H. Schuenemann, Capt. Bridge, CHICAG[O]

WHOLESALE GALAX and LEUCOTH[OE]

Direct from the woods to the dealer.

Galax, Green and Bronze .... 60c per
Leucothoe Sprays (green only) .... $2.00 per
Ferns (dagger and fancy) .... 70c. per

Special prices on lots of 10,000 and up.
Terms strictly cash, F. O. B. Elk Park, N. C.

F. W. Richards & Co., Banners Elk, N

Pittsburg.

le Notes.

December is society's gayest nth. The last few weeks have n filled with many important nts, and the remainder promises to no less brilliant. Many of the sea-'s debutantes will be presented be-e the New Year, and delightful af-s will be given in their honor. ddings are also quite numerous; or two notable ones took place week and the demands upon the ist were heavy. There was quite all for good stock of flowers, but supply was equal to it. Roses and nations are of good quality. Chrys-hemums are going down and will out shortly. Paper White narcis- are plentiful. Violets are in good nand. Prices seem satisfactory, another week will change things. lant sales are fair. Christmas ens, bells, holly, etc., are every-re and it looks as if the market be stocked up as heavy as last on. Carloads of trees were in sev- weeks ago and many more are he road. Holly is of good quality. isitors the past week were, W. P. ig of Philadelphia, and Mr. Glenn Kittanning, Pa. Mr. Peterson of cinnati was also here with a sam- lot of Christmas plants for which took some nice orders.

. S. Randolph of Randolph & Mc-ments moved into his newly pur-ased home on Stanton avenue last ek.

E. C. REINEMAN.

LEVELAND, O.—J. M. Gasser templates taking a Southern trip the benefit of his health. He may o visit the Bermuda Islands when lilies are in bloom there. Mr. sser has been declared by the rt quite capable of managing his siness affairs.

POUGHKEEPSIE, N. Y.—A local per states the Dutchess County rticultural Society lost over $300 its recent flower show. "Despite is fact the members of the society e happy and they will continue to ve flower shows just as long as the iblic takes any interest in them."

New Orleans, La.

News Notes.

A. Alost, the Gentilly road florist, has just added to his establishment five greenhouses, each 54 x 18 feet and one propagating house, 32 x 10 feet. These are already planted with cucumbers that are doing well, to be followed later by flowering plants and ferns for the market.

Emile Valdejo and wife have returned from Europe, both looking well, and report having had a splendid time in the old country. Mr. Valdejo visited most of the leading establishments while on the other side, and speaks highly of the novelties seen at the nurseries of Lemoine and others. He was especially impressed with a new race of begonias which Lemoine has "created"—a blending of the tuberous and shrubby species, which, he says, are bound to cause a sensation when introduced into this country. Perhaps the most striking thing was the decoration of the private residences with window boxes. He says the whole front of the houses was a mass of flowers, the boxes being apparently filled regardless of cost. He also speaks in glowing terms of the perfectly grown flowering plants to be found at the Parisian flower markets.

On Esplanade street is the garden of Mrs. Joseph Muller, the widow of an old-time Southern florist. This is the only florist establishment in New Orleans carried on exclusively by a lady. Mrs. Muller is assisted by her daughter, Miss Virginia, and they deserve great credit, for in spite of many drawbacks they have made a success of their business. The greatest difficulty is the getting of competent help, so they are thinking seriously of reducing the size of their place. It doesn't matter how busy Mrs. Muller may be, she always finds time to entertain any of her boys, as she loves to call them, when they pay her a visit.

CRESCENT CITY.

No Doubt About It.

You certainly have a first-class paper. THOS. H. WESTWOOD.
Pres.-elect Boston G. & F. Club.

Mention the Florists' Exchange when writing.

WHOLESALE TRADE LIST

ASPARAGUS PLUMOSUS, 2½ inch pots, $3.00 per 100.

ASPARAGUS SPRENGERI, 2 in. pots, $2.00 per 100.

BOSTON FERNS, 5 in. pots, 20c. 6 in. pots, 25c.

CLEMATIS PANICULATA, 4 in. pots, $1.50 per doz., $10.00 per 100; 3 in. pots, 75c. per doz.; $6.00 per 100.

DRACÆNA INDIVISA, 5 in. pots, $2.00 per doz.

FERNS, fine assortment, 2½ inch pots, $3.00 per 100.

HYDRANGEA Thos. Hogg, 4-6 flowering branches, $10.00 per 100; larger plants for tubs, 25c. each.

IVY, Hardy English, 4 in. pots, $1.50 per doz.; $10.00 per 100.

NEW PARIS DAISY, Queen Alexandra, 3 in. pots, $5.00 per 100.

YELLOW DAISY (Etoile d'Or), 3 in. pots, $5.00 per 100.

SANSEVIERA (Zebra plant), 4 in. pots, strong $1.50 per doz.; 3 in. pots, $1.00 per doz.

ROOTED CUTTINGS Fuchsias, 4 varieties, single and double; **Heliotrope** dark blue, **Salvia** Bonfire $1.00 per 100. Coleus Verschaffeltii, Golden Bedder and other showy varieties 75c. per 100.

Alternantheras, best red and yellow, 50c. per 100.

Smilax 2½ inch pots $2.00 per 100.

C. EISELE, 11th & Roy Streets, PHILADELPHIA, PA.

Mention the Florists' Exchange when writing.

The STANDARD VENTILATING MACHINERY

The original machine with self oiling cups; the most powerful, least complicated very compact, with ease of operation.

The New Duplex Gutter over six miles in use and highly recommended; the only drip proof gutter in the market.

The Standard Return Steam Trap has no equal for simplicity or its workings. Catalogue free.

E. HIPPARD, Youngstown, O.

Mention the Florists' Exchange when writing.

"THE BEST INVESTMENT I EVER MADE"

is the verdict of one of the largest rose growers who placed two of these **GREENHOUSE BOILERS** instead of two others of well known make.

Estimates furnished for heating plants erected complete, or for material only.

JOHN A. PAYNE

Horticultural Architect and Builder.

33 Clendenny Ave., Jersey City, N. J.

Sash opening apparatus and all kinds of greenhouse structural material.

Mention the Florists' Exchange when writing.

GREENHOUSES:

MATERIAL FURNISHED AND MEN TO SUPERINTEND ERECTION IF DESIRED.

CYPRESS SASH BARS ANY LENGTH [illegible] OR LONGER.

THE A. T. STEARNS LUMBER CO., NEPONSET, BOSTON, MASS.

Are You Now Deciding

on the details of your new houses?

Write us for Sketches and Suggestions, they will be of interest to you.

A. DIETSCH CO.

Louisiana Cypress and Washington Red Cedar **GREENHOUSE MATERIAL**

619 Sheffield Ave., Chicago, Ill.

Mention The Florists' Exchange when writing.

A. HERRMANN

Manufacturer of Floral Metal Designs

IMPORTER AND DEALER IN FLORISTS' SUPPLIES

FACTORY: 709 FIRST AVENUE, BETWEEN 40th AND 41st STREETS, NEW YORK

OFFICE AND WAREROOMS: 404, 406, 408, 410, 412 East 34th St.

WRITE FOR NEW CATALOGUE

Mention the Florists' Exchange when writing.

THREE REASONS FOR OUR RAFTER CAP

First: It prevents glass breakage—successful glazing in direct contact with iron is out of the question.

Second: It's an insulation against heat absorption in the summer.

Third: It's a non-conductor of cold in the winter.

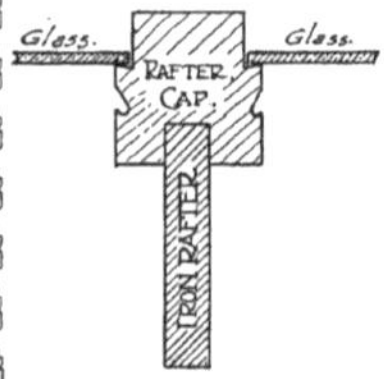

A very little matter — a rafter cap—but it does big things for our iron frame house—the strongest, lightest and longest to last of all constructions. Send for our Iron Frame Circular.

Lord & Burnham Co.

Greenhouse Designers and Manufacturers.

1133 Broadway, corner 26th St., NEW YORK.

BOSTON BRANCH, 819 Tremont Building.

Mention the Florists' Exchange when writing.

REMOVAL NOTICE!

H. Bayersdorfer & Co., Philadelphi

THE FLORISTS' SUPPLY HOUSE OF AMERIC

BEG to announce to their patrons and the trade their removal into ne spacious and up-to-date quarters, occupying the entire building at

1129 ARCH STREET

where with most modern facilities and increased working force, they will endeavor to still further improve their already well established record fo promptness and reliability.

When in Philadelphia, step in. Make the new centrally located stor your headquarters.

ALWAYS WELCOME

Mention the Florists' Exchange when w

HAMBURG VALLEY

Strong Pips for forcing .... $10.00 per 1000
" heavy Clumps .... 18.00 per 100

TULIPS, a few varieties left such as Rex Rubrorum, Due Van Thol, Yellow Parrot, Yellow Prince, Late mix and Double Mixd .... $5.00 per 1000

ROSES

Chas Wood, lilac and red; Paeonia, red and large; Ulrich Brunner, cherry red; Marg. Dickson, white; Perle Blanche, white; Amma de Diesbach, lively carmine; Mons Boncenne, deep crimson; Jules Margottin, carmine rose; Magna Charta, pink; Prince Camille de Rohan, dark red; Baroness Rothschild light pink; Paul Neyron, red; Baby ramblers, Alfred Colomb; light crimson; Fisher Holmes, brilliant crimson; Pius IX, scarlet .... $7.00 per 100

SPIREA JAPONICA ....$4.00 per 100; $38.00 per 1000.
" COMPACTA ...$5.00 per 100; $42.00 per 1000.
BLEEDING HEARTS .... $7.00 per 100
LILIUM SPEC. ALBUM 8x9........ $8.00 per 100
" " RUBRUM .... $7.00 per 100

WM. ELLIOTT & SONS
201 FULTON STREET -:- NEW YORK

Mention the Florists' Exchange when writing.

RAWSON'S FLOWER MARKET STOCK

has been grown for us exclusively for the last ten years and we wish to emphasize the fact that it cannot be genuine, unless purchased direct from us. It is undoubtedly the finest stock for cutting.

THE FOLLOWING COLORS

BRILLIANT CRIMSON	DARK BLUE	DARK BLOOD RED	FLESH COLOR
LIGHT BLUE	ROSE	SCARLET	FINEST MIXED

at 60c. 1-8 oz.; $4.00 oz., and Pure White, at 75c. 1-8 oz.; $5.00 oz.
Sow now, if wanted for Easter. Sow in January, if wanted for Decoration Day.

W. W. RAWSON & CO.

5 UNION STREET, BOSTON, MASS.

Mention the Florists' Exchange when writing.

PACIFIC SEED GROWERS' CO.

109 MARKET STREET
SAN FRANCISCO, CAL.
Specialties:
Onion, Carrot, Lettuce, Sweet Peas

Mention The Florists' Exchange when writing.

ASPARAGUS SEED

1906 CROP	100	1000
Plumosus Nanus, True	50c.	$3.50
Sprengeri	15c.	.75
Cycas Revoluta Seed	$2.50	22.50

Headquarters for all the best flower seeds. 100-page seed buyer's guide free.

MOORE & SIMON, Seed Growers,
339 Market St., Philadelphia

Mention the Florists' Exchange when writing.

QUALITY SEED BULB PLANTS

SEND FOR CATALOGUE
ARTHUR T. BODDINGTON
342 West 14th St., New York.

Mention the Florists' Exchange when writing.

GROW YOUR OWN
TREES
and SHRUBS from
SEED.

Send today for our
TRADE SEED LIST
and also for our *Descriptive Catalog*, which is replete with valuable information.

OTTO KATZENSTEIN & CO.
Wholesale Dept. ATLANTA, GA.

Mention the Florists' Exchange when writing

ESTABLISHED 1884

Bridgeman's Seed Warehouse

Rickards Bros., Props.
IMPORTERS AND GROWERS OF HIGH GRADE
Seeds, Bulbs, Plants, Etc.
37 EAST 19TH ST. *Near Broadway NEW YORK CITY*
Telephone: 4235 Gramercy

W. & D.'s Specialties for Forcing

Mignonette "New York Market"
Sweet Peas "True" Christmas Flowering (Pink and White)
Tomato "The Don" Tomato "Stirling Castle"
Mushroom Spawn "English" and "Pure Culture"
Special prices on application
WEEBER & DON, Seed Merchants and Growers
114 Chambers Street, NEW YORK

Sow Now The True Thing!

Ageratum. Blue Star, the best of all for pots. 6 Tr. Pkts. $1.25; Tr. Pkt. 25c.
Alyssum. Carpet Queen fine extra dwarf strain. 6 Trade Pkts. $1.25 Trade Pkt. 25c.
Begonia. Erfordii, for pots the best rosy pink. 6 Trade Pkts. $1.25; Trade Pkt. 25c.
Begonia. Gracilis Luminosa. Bedder, new with large bright scarlet flowers and ball-shaped habit, unexcelled for pots and outdoors. 6 Trade Pkts. $2.50; Trade Pkt. 50c.
Cyclamen. Giant flow. separate colors. 1000 seeds, $6.00; Trade Pkt. $1.00.
Cyclamen. Giant flow. mixed colors. 1000 seeds, $5.00; Trade Pkt. 75c.
Petunia. Rosy Morn, a fine bedder. 6 Trade Pkts. $1.25; Trade Pkt. 25c.
Petunia. Californian single Giants, extra strain. 6 Trade Pkts. $4.00; Trade Pkt. 75c.
Petunia, double fringed Giants. 6 Trade Pkts. $5.00; Trade Pkt. $1.00.
Phlox, New Cecily, the very best large flowered, real dwarf, compact. Drum. Phlox for pots, mixed colors. 6 Trade Pkts. $2.50 Trade Pkt. 50c.
Salvia, Bonfire. 6 Trade Pkts. $1.25; Trade Pkt. 25c.
Salvia. Fireball, this is a new, real dwarf compact early flowering, fine variety and there is hardly a better one for pots. 6 Trade Pkts. $2.50; Trade Pkt. 50c.
Verbena, Mammoth unexcelled strains; as Auricolor flowered, Scarlet, Striped, Pink, Purple, White, each separate. Oz. $1.50; Trade Pkt. 25c.
For larger quantities special quotations.

O. V. ZANGEN, Seedsman, Hoboken, N. J.

Gold Medal Strain BEGONIAS Tuberous Rooted

	Per doz.	Per 100
Single, Scarlet	$0.40	$2.50
" Dark Red	.40	2.50
" Pink	.40	2.50
" Rose	.40	2.50
" White	.40	2.50
" Yellow	.40	2.50
" Nankeen	.40	2.50
" Orange	.40	2.50
" Salmon	.40	2.50
" Mixed	.30	2.25
Double White	.65	5.00

	Per doz.	Per
Double Rose	$.65	$5
" Orange	.65	5
" Red	.65	5
" Salmon	.65	5
" Dark Red	.65	5
" Yellow	.65	5
" Mixed	.50	4
NEW VARIETIES.		
Duke of Zepplin	1.50	11
La Fayette	2.40	18
Single Giant, Fringed mixed	1.00	8

STUMPP & WALTER CO., 50 BARCLAY ST., NEW YORK

Mention the Florists' Exchange when writing.

FORCING RHUBARB.

Under the greenhouse bench or in any old cellar or mushroom house is entirely practical and an easy proposition.

Send for My Special Florists' Circular on Rhubarb Forcing

It gives ample directions for successful culture. I have a good supply of large **Undivided Clumps.** Prices: $2.00 per doz; 25 for $3.75; $12.00 per 100. $100.00 per 1000. (500 at 1000 rate).

Stokes Seed Stor

219 Market Street, PHILADELPHIA, PA.

XXX SEEDS

Verbena. Improved mammoth, the very finest grown, mixed. 1000 seeds, 25c.
Cineraria. Finest large flowering dwarf, 1000 seeds, 50c.
Phlox Pumila Compacta. Very dwarf and compact; grand for pots; in finest colors, mixed. 100 seeds, 50c.
Alyssum Compactum. The most dwarf and compact variety grown; perfect little balls when grown in pots. 1000 seeds, 25c.
Chinese Primrose. Finest large-flowering fringed varieties, mixed; single and double, 500 seeds, $1.00; half pkt. 50c.
Pansy, Finest Giants. The best large-flowering varieties, critically selected; mixed, 5000 seeds, $1.00; half pkt. 50c.
Petunia. New Star; from the finest marked flowers, extra choice. Trade pkt. 25c.
Cyclamen Giganteum. Finest giants, mixed, 200 seeds, $1.00; ½ pkt. 50c.
Salvia "Bonfire." Finest variety grown, 1000 seeds, 40c.
CASH. Extra count of seeds in all packets.

PRIMROSES

IMPROVED CHINESE. Finest grown, named or mixed, strong, 3-inch. $1.50 per 100.
XXX strong, 3 in., coming in bud, $4.00 per 100.

JOHN F. RUPP, Shiremanstown, Pa.
The Home of Primroses

Mention the Florists' Exchange when writing.

BURPEE'S SEEDS

PHILADELPHIA
Blue List of Wholesale Prices mailed only to those who plant for profit.

Mention the Florists' Exchange when writing

EXTRA CHOICE
FLOWER SEEDS

List free on application.
FRED. ROEMER, Seed Grower,
QUEDLINBURG GERMANY.

Mention the Florists' Exchange when writing

GLADIOLI

For Forcing
All stock guaranteed to be as represented

	100	1000
America, flesh pink	$10 00	$75 00
Shakespeare, light	5 00	40 00
Nezinscott, red	3 50	30 00
White and Light, mix good	1 50	12 00
extra	3 00	25 00

250 at 1000 rate.
5 per cent discount for cash with order.

JOHN LEWIS CHILDS, Floral Park, N. Y.

LILY OF THE VALLEY PIPS

Just arrived and are, as usual, the finest imported into this market no matter under what name. Send for prices.

SPIRAEA

	per 100
Japonica—Extra strong clumps	$3 50
Astilboides Floribunda	4 00
Compacta Multiflora	4 00
Gladstone	6 50

LILIUM LONGIFLORUM

	per 1000	per 100
6 to 8 inches	$27 00	$3 00
7 to 9 "	45 00	5.00
Multiflorum, 6 to 8 inches	28 00	3 00
" 7 to 9 "	50 00	5 50

J. M. THORBURN & CO.
33 Barclay St., through to 38 Park Place, NEW YORK.

Mention The Florists' Exchange when writing

LAST OFFER

Superfine Single Mixed
TULIPS

$ .60 - - per 100
4.50 - - " 1000

Single Mixed Hyacinths. Freesias
Paper White Narcissus
PRICES ON APPLICATION

JAMES VICK'S SONS
ROCHESTER, N. Y.

Mention the Florists' Exchange when writing

Catalog Engraving

and ILLUSTRATIONS
that print EASILY. That's the kind we make — have been since '73

JAS. M. BRYANT, Horticultural Engraving and Printing
706 Chestnut Street, PHILADELPHIA, PA.
Write for our Catalogue of Stock Engraving

Mention the Florists' Exchange when writing

Seed Trade Report.

AMERICAN SEED TRADE ASSOCIATION

Henry W. Wood, Richmond, Va., president; C. S. Burge, Toledo, O., first vice-president; G. B. McVay, Birmingham, Ala., second vice-president; C. E. Kendel, Cleveland, O., secretary and treasurer; J. H. Ford, Ravenna, O., assistant secretary.

The area devoted to canary seed grown in Argentina in 1905 was 21,817 hectares (one hectare equals 2.471 acres); peas and beans, 24,599 hectares, castor beans, 3,949, and fruit trees, 87,269.

The crop bulletin of the Ontario Department of Agriculture gives the following information:

Reports regarding peas differ considerably. Taken all together, however, the crop is an improvement in quality compared with more recent years. The presence of the dreaded weevil or "bug" was reported only at scattered points, and the growing of peas is again coming into general favor.

Corn has turned out to be a remarkably fine crop both as to yield and quality. The plant had most favorable growing weather all along, was well cobbed and fully matured, and for both husking and silo purposes was all that could be desired. Only a little of the latest was caught by frost.

Clover seed.—Winter-killing and Midsummer drouth told on clover fields reserved for seed, and the crop is a rather light one. When correspondents wrote but little of the crop had been threshed, owing to the rush of other farm work. While not at all general, the midge was at work in various localities both east and west. Alsike, however, has turned out well where reported upon.

CHICAGO.—Immortelles cleaned up especially well, particularly red, which came near being a scarcity. Princess pine has held its high price up to $8 and $10 per crate, and there seems no probability of a decrease as all supplies are now in sight.

Messrs. Ward, Bunyard, and other Eastern men are on deck with propositions for bulb orders for 1907.

Advance troubles are seen from the fact that California seed growers are already asking a fifty per cent. increase on price or reduction of delivery on contracts on onion seed.

LOS ANGELES, CAL.—To keep pace with the rapid settlement of this part of the State, we are to have a new wholesale and retail seed house which is to open up for business January 1, at 555 South Main street. The firm is to be known as Morris & Snow Seed Company. O. M. Morris, who for thirteen years was connected with the Germain Seed Company and with Vaughan's Seed Store for the past two years as traveling salesman, brings to the business an experience of California trade conditions that will be helpful to planters. M. C. Snow has been in the nursery business for years at San Bernardino, therefore knows the requirements of the trade here, and the new firm is welcomed to the business life of Los Angeles.

CUYAHOGA FALLS, O.—Matthew Crawford, after due consideration, has agreed to lend his services for an entire year to the Shiocton Garden Land Company, at Shiocton, Wis., eighteen miles from Appleton, and a few miles further on from Green Bay. This company is experimenting on a huge truck farm, embracing some 3,500 acres. Already approximately $150,000 has been spent in the purchase of the land and draining same. The idea is to carry on a sort of experiment station, and to fully see under just what conditions the garden will best produce the largest quantities of all garden truck. The matter of working the big garden in shares has been considered as well as disposing it to farmers generally who would truck it as their own property. In the experiment work, part of the land will be fertilized, part of it used in its natural state. The soil is of a rich loam, several feet deep. Mr. Crawford will also grow gladiolus bulbs here. He will also edit a department in a leading horticultural journal while in Wisconsin. For quite a number of years he has been a member of the Wisconsin State Horticultural Society.

INDIA'S SEED CROPS.—Responding to an American inquiry, Consul-General W. H. Michael, of Calcutta, furnishes information about the Indian product of castor seed and oil and other seed crops of that country, as follows: During the fiscal year 1905, India exported 1,461,000 hundredweight, and during 1906, 1,299,000 hundredweight of castor seed, valued at $35,364,000, most of which went to the United Kingdom. There has been but little increase in the acreage during the last six years. The largest amount of the product was from the crop of 1902-3, which amounted to 1,752,000 hundredweight. In addition to the export of castor seed there is a large annual export of castor oil. During the eight months—from January 1 to August 30, 1906—there were shipped from Calcutta 945,891 gallons.

John Pereboom, representing the firm of D. Nieuwenhuis & Sons, Lisse, Holland, has arrived in New York, and will make a tour of the country, introducing his firm's special lines of bulbs and plants.

One of the novelties Mr. Pereboom will introduce to the trade is a new spirea—White Queen—which has been raised by the firm he represents, and which is a cross between Spirea Japonica and Astilboides floribunda, and throws twice the number of flowers as the old Spirea Japonica.

JOHN PEREBOOM,
Care of MALTUS & WARE,
14 Stone Street, New York

Of the exports of the principal descriptions of seed the values in 1906 were as follows: Linseed, $13,718,333; sesamum, $4,897,666; rape seed, $4,059,666; cotton seed, $3,406,000; castor, $2,622,333; and poppy, $2,007,333. Of the total, Bombay shipped last year $20,393,000, or 57.7 per cent.; Calcutta, $7,739,000, or 21.9 per cent., and Karachi, $3,655,000, or 10.3 per cent. Linseed goes chiefly to the United Kingdom, Germany, and France; rape seed to Germany and Belgium; sesamum and poppy seed to France and Belgium; cotton seed and castor to the United Kingdom and earthnuts to France. [Calcutta dealers in seeds are named by Mr. Michael, and the addresses are on file at the Bureau of Manufacturers.]

NOTES FROM THE CHANNEL ISLANDS.—There has been of late years a growing disposition on the part of British bulb growers to discredit Channel Island bulbs because they are smaller than the Dutch and Fen District bulbs. The Islanders are now remedying this defect (according to English ideas) by sending certain varieties of bulbs, particularly Telemonius plenus and that class, to Holland to be "blown out." There is no gainsaying the fact that such treatment tends to a quicker sale; but as a flower producing medium the bulbs are certainly less reliable than the smaller but more solid ones. English growers may take it as a reliable fact, that, size for size, the Jersey and Guernsey bulbs are heavier than the Dutch; and they are distinctly healthier and have the reputation of being more floriferous. The Dutch bulb merchants know this. The past season witnessed the heaviest sales to the Dutchmen yet known. We have bought largely from them; but much cheaper than they purchased from our growers.

It is certain too that the Islanders are becoming more enamored of certain varieties, Double White, Golden Spur, and the better Ornatus and Emperor types; the best forcing varieties are being sought after. The heavily scented and weighty kinds such as Grand Monarque, Soleil d'Or, etc., are steadily declining in favor. Indeed the situation may be summed up by saying that the Channel Island growers are forcing heavily to come in before the Scilly Isles, and planting outside only the best and most popular sorts. Bazelman minor is clearly gaining in public favor. There is too a sharp inquiry for the rarer and most beautiful "Glads," and the bulbs of the Nerine sarniensis (the beautiful Guernsey lily) is being bought up by the nurserymen.

The wholesale firms using your valuable paper can do a good business if they can place before our tomato growers a really improved variety of the "Large Red." But this does not mean merely a slightly less amorphorus form of the old corrugated red tomato. That had its excellent points, for it was very early, very hardy, forced as well or better than any other variety, was a heavy cropper, fairly short-jointed, and was of a distinctly good flavor. Its drawbacks were the roughness and uncertainty of shape, its great unwieldy size, and its far too luxuriant foliage. The number of "male" seedlings in each batch was a great defect. The Guernsey hothouse growers are now searching for a tomato which shall have most of these good qualities without the defects. All the leading growers declare that the extra weight per plant, and the extra earliness at which the Large Red ripens, much more than compensate for the rather smaller price per pound which that variety fetches. There is therefore a splendid opening for any novelty which can fulfill the conditions.—Horticultural Trade Journal.

FREE SEED DISTRIBUTION.—"To be or not to be?" is the question that at the present time is uppermost in the minds of the seed trade. Along every line competition in this country is so great that none but the strongest can stem the current of trade. Energy, ability and indomitable push are requisite to the success of any enterprise in this country. The seed trade is no exception to the rule. The seedsman has more to contend with than any other class of merchants, and their troubles are not, in most cases, due to want of care in the transaction of their business, energy or industry. They must from necessity depend upon the grower for their supplies, both as regards quantity and quality, and they have but little redress for failure in either case. In addition to competition, which is quite as keen as in any other branch of business, the Department of Agriculture is now a menace to the seedsmen's business interests that threatens total destruction. Again circulars are out asking for proposals to furnish any surplus seed the dealers may have of 1906 crop. The Department asks also for samples to accompany each variety, and that all seeds must be of the highest test of germination, true to name, and subject to the Department's scales for full weight. In case the seeds offered are accepted, the same are to be delivered after July 15, 1907. If the offer is accepted the merchant is bound to deliver the seeds, "provided an appropriation is made by Congress now assembled for payment of the same." This is certainly a one-sided transaction, but on a level with much of the "protection to American industry," for which the Republican eagle is constantly screaming.

The efforts now making to defeat this infamous appropriation must be strengthened, or it will be made. One of two conditions is to be met—the bill must be killed, or the seed trade, as a profitable industry, will be. Which shall it be?

ATLANTA, GA.—So far we have had no Winter; gardens are yet green, peas are blooming, fig trees are budding out. We fear that vegetation will be so far advanced that when the icy waves of your section begin to move down this way in January or February the destruction will be very great. One crop with us is very short, I refer to the cow pea, also known as Southern field or stock peas. This is one of our most valuable crops; it is the clover of the Southern States, as the plant enriches the soil and the vines make a hay equal to clover. The peas are very nutritious and good for man or beast. We deem the white varieties superior to your white Navy or marrow beans, served in the same way. Nothing produces more or better milk and butter than these peas when fed to cows. The colored varieties are generally used for this purpose and must be boiled. Until within the last 15 or 20 years the cultivation of this crop was confined to the Southern States. Now, however, you plant the earlier varieties in your State, and they are planted in almost every State of the Union. The shortness of the crop will be felt far and wide. Excessive rains rotted the peas before they could be harvested, therefore prices will be very high.

There are all colors of them, ranging from pure white to deep black, ring streaked, speckled and mottled, round and kidney-shaped. The names usually applied to them are the White Lady, White Brown Eye, White Black Eye, Wild Goose, Crowder, Redsipper, The Unknown, The Clay, Whippoorwill, The Iron and Java. They nearly all have long vines, only two or three being dwarf—Whippoorwill, Jefford's Early and Davis's White; all, however, are cow peas. They are planted either broadcast, one or two bushels per acre, or in drills. We plant them largely between the corn rows. It is of no use to plant them until the ground is thoroughly warm. It is claimed by some that land planted with these peas a year or so, becomes thoroughly inoculated with bacteria, fitting it for alfalfa and other clovers.

MARK W. JOHNSON.

CATALOGUES RECEIVED.

JOHN BODGER & SONS, Gardena, Cal.—List of Contract Prices for growing Flower and Vegetable Seeds.

DAMANN & COMPANY, San Giovanni a Teduccio, near Naples, Italy.—General Catalogue of Bulbs, Seeds, Plants, etc.

THE BARTELDES SEED COMPANY, Denver, Col.—Illustrated Price List and Descriptive Catalogue for 1907. Includes a full list of Novelties and Specialties. The firm's motto is "Western Seeds for Western Planters." A handy calendar for 1907 is furnished on the back cover of the catalogue.

NURSERY DEPARTMENT.

Conducted by Joseph Meehan.

AMERICAN ASSOCIATION OF NURSERYMEN.
Orlando Harrison, Berlin, Md., president; J. W. Hill, Des Moines, Ia., vice-president; George C. Seager, Rochester, N. Y., secretary; C. L. Yates, Rochester, N. Y., treasurer.

A pamphlet of much interest to nurserymen is Bulletin No. 132 of the Maine Agricultural Experiment Station on the subject of "Plant Breeding in Relation to American Pomology." The bulletin briefly epitomizes the history of plant breeding as applied to the development of American fruits. The subjects discussed are: Beginnings of systematic breeding; the development of American pomology; results of breeding, and unsolved problems. The address of the Station is Orono, Me.

ATLANTIC, IA.—I. N. Brown, formerly with Silas Wilson, and latterly with Stark Brothers here, expects to make arrangements to engage in the nursery business on his own hook, either where the Stark Brothers have had their nursery or somewhere else near the city. The withdrawal of Stark Brothers will leave Atlantic without a nursery as R. D. McGeehon, the only other nurseryman here, expects to quit business after this year.

BROOKINGS, S. D.—C. M. Olston and E. Loken have organized the Sioux Valley Nursery Company. Mr. Olston is a graduate of the agricultural college, having completed his course there some ten or twelve years ago. Since that time he has been in the nursery business in various portions of the Northwest, of late years holding the position of foreman in several. Mr. Loken has given a great deal of attention to horticulture by practical experiments. This company will pay especial attention to the breeding of trees, roses and shrubs that are adapted to the climate of North and South Dakota, Minnesota and Iowa.

MINNESOTA STATE HORTICULTURAL SOCIETY.—I think this society the largest and best in our land. The members have won stupendous victories over old Boreas and moved the apple belt up to Manitoba. The writer was sent for to give an address at the fortieth annual meeting on "Our Unused Capital," showing what possibilities yet lay before those heroes of the North. The meeting opened grandly. One of the large churches was well filled, hundreds of students coming from the Agricultural College. The meeting lasted from the 4th to the 7th of December. Thursday night there was a grand banquet. Many distinguished men from other States were there. The advance made in forty years was a marvel. There was a splendid display of fruit of the finest quality and many promising seedlings.

C. S. HARRISON.

Seasonable Topics.

Cestrum Parqui, known to some as the night-blooming jasmine, is a desirable greenhouse plant to grow in a dwelling in Winter, for the sake of the sweet ordor emitted by its flowers. There are whitish yellow, and when under outdoor culture the plant blooms in Midsummer. Coming from Chili, it will endure a little frost. It used to be common in New York collections.

Corylopsis spicata is one of the earliest of Spring-flowering shrubs the flowers leading the foliage. They are borne in half drooping racemes, slightly fragrant, appearing on the shoots of the previous season. The shrub requires good soil, to promote strong and numerous shoots, then the display of flowers is much finer.

Styrax japonica is a shrub often mentioned as a good one for Winter forcing. We do not remmeber seeing it so used, but its bunches of white flowers are very pretty, and it would make a handsome pot specimen. It is easily raised from seed sown in Spring.

Cornus alba bears white flowers, hence its name. But it had better have been called rubra, for it is far better known for its red stems in Winter than for its white flowers in Summer. It should not be overlooked in plantings, for its blaze of color in Winter is extremely striking.

When sawing off the limbs of trees growing erect, it is best that the cut be a slanting one, as the rain is then better shed and rot is made less easy. When the limbs are of horizontal growth the slant is of no advantage. All large limbs are better painted to keep out moisture, where it is evident it will take time for the healing of the wound.

Rhododendrons may be pruned if desired, but as pruning throws them back a year or more for flowering it is not often done unless the bushes are unshapely or for other good reasons. They will break afresh from old wood. The pruning is best done in late Winter.

One who is familiar with the curing of the black walnut nuts says that much of their desirable flavor is lost by letting them lie with their hulls on so long after they fall. The hulls impart a rank flavor, he says; and the recommendation is to hull the nuts immediately when ripe. In fact, if they are gathered before they have fallen and are hulled at once, the flavor is delicate and much superior to what it is when the hulls are not removed for so long.

The difference between the hazel and the filbert lies entirely in the length of the husk. When the husk overlaps the nut it is a filbert, when it is not as long as the nut, it is a hazel. The leading varieties of fiberts are increased by layering, or by grafting them on others less valuable.

Evergreen Boughs for Covering.

That boughs of evergreens are most useful for covering evergreens and other stock in Winter is a fact appreciated by all familiar with the subject. There is such a thing as being too kind to shrubs that need covering. It is a great mistake to tie up in a close bundle such sorts. Some years ago a new hand in a nursery was given the job to place straw around some yews and other evergreens that are sometimes badly scorched in Winter. This he did, but the evergreens were first tied up tightly and then straw tied around them in the same way. When Spring came and the straw was removed, the evergreens were in a nearly dead condition. The exclusion of air by the tight binding had so weakened them that what frost reached them injured them far more than it would have done had they been entirely uncovered. It should be well understood that good protection consists in giving the plants shade and protection from strong winds. Straw is very good for the purpose, but the branches must be tied together lightly and the straw placed on in the same way, neither being packed so close that air cannot find its way through the mass. Where corn stalks are available nothing better could be used. Their large leaves break the light and yet are so loose that air passes through them, but not to a degree that injury to the foliage occurs, such as it would do were the leaves entirely exposed. Small evergreens in nursery rows are well protected when covered with corn stalks, especially if forest leaves are strewn over the plants first. Dead leaves are excellent, as even when they fall from the evergreen to the ground they are still of value, keeping frost from penetrating to the roots. The essence of good protection is to keep sunlight from the foliage and to protect from cold winds. Treated in this way many evergreens survive cold Winters that would not do it otherwise. Branches of hemlock, spruce and other evergreens can be had sometimes, and these make good covering.

Box Bush for Florists' Use.

The growing use of box bush twigs for florists' use suggests the probable profitableness of setting out a lot of plants of it for the purpose of cutting from. As sometimes seen the leaves of box are not of a good shade of green, but this comes from growing the plants in poor soil—something box bushes abhor. There is no evergreen that rejoices more in good, deep, rich soil than the box. It will make shoots of some length, with leaves of a good size and of a bright green—just the condition in which both florists and their customers like to receive it.

There are dozens of varieties of box, but with very few exceptions they are all to be referred to the common box, Buxus arborescens, the one that goes under the name of tree box commonly. This one is to be preferred because of its making a freer growth, affording the opportunity of cutting shoots of sufficient length to suit a florist's wants. There are other beautiful ornamental sorts in nursery collections—just the thing for pyramidal forms, so much in demand now—but, as said, they lack the free growth of B. arborescens.

Set out box plants in Spring, early, and besides good soil an addition of a mulch of manure would help them.

Weeping Norway Spruce.

Because of the oddity of their appearance and sometimes, too, of their gracefulness, weeping trees of all kinds are always salable stock for nurserymen to grow. There is many a place on a lawn where such a tree fits the position better than any other one would do. The character of the many weeping sorts is so very different that it adds to their value very much. Where a weeper is demanded that makes height there are many well-known sorts to select from, and where no more height than possessed is required there, too, is no lack of sorts to satisfy. The photograph reproduced is of one of the latter kind, one that makes no leader, its growth all being of a lateral, drooping character, the weeping Norway spruce, Picea excelsa inverta.

Picea Excelsa Inverta, Weeping Norway Spruce

It is the grotesque character of this weeping spruce that calls for its planting, not its beauty always although at times it takes on a character of gracefulness which is very pleasing.

There are other weeping Norway spruces; one called Wales' weeping forms a leader and so continues to ascend in growth, weeping as it grows. Our subject makes but little upright growth. There are branches continually springing up at the summit, and although they droop in time there is height gained, so that, little by little, the tree gets taller; and then if a stake be tied to the top and a shoot fastened to it the shoot becomes set in that position in a year or two, gaining height quicker than by the other way.

A singular feature of the growth of this weeping Norway spruce is the decumbent habit of growth peculiar to the twigs. There is a downward tendency at first, followed by an uprising of the ends of the shoots, in a sense the opposite of being inverted.

There are some two dozen varieties of the Norway spruce, as the species is apt to vary greatly. Even in a bed of seedlings many differences will be noticed; but of all the variations, the weeping one is the most striking and the best known.

JOSEPH MEEHAN.

THE WEEK'S WORK.

Timme's Timely Teachings.

The Finishing Touches.

Next in importance to being well supplied with stock is to have this in fine trim and condition at the right time. Nothing so much interferes with the smooth run of holiday business as being constantly held back by duties that could well have been attended to beforehand. Some of the plants will likely need staking and tying. Wherever needed they should be freed of fading flowers and dying leaves. The appearance of foliage plants as, for instance, palms, ficus, pandanus, crotons and dracænas, is heightened and brightened by a good sponging off. Most of such plants anyway need it at this season of the year worse than at any other. The pot or pan of every Christmas plant, in which it is to be sent out, must be clean and should be washed if it isn't clean. All those to be displayed for ready counter trade, or serving as samples, should be decked out in ribbon attachments and suitable pot covers, after being thoroughly watered and allowed to drain off. For the greater part of the stock this can wait until the orders are made up ready to be delivered. Holiday stock at the farther end of the greenhouses should be brought forward, and whatever in the making up of attractive plant combinations can be done now should not be deferred until the last moment.

Much of the stock handled at Christmas will stand a considerable amount of hardening off. Placing it in a temperature from ten to fifteen degrees lower than that in which it was forced and brought to a finish will greatly add to its commercial value. It will better endure the many hardships it is likely to undergo in handling, packing, transit and untoward living room conditions. When there is time to spare at the finishing end of hard forcing for a gradual hardening off, it should be given due attention, this being especially needful at the Winter holidays. Begonias, poinsettias, bouvardias and a few of the hothouse decorative plants resent sudden changes in temperature of any excessive cooling down, and must therefore be handled accordingly. Sweeping cold draughts through store or packing room are to be guarded against.

The value of attractive display in front window and show room on holidays as well as at all other times must be obvious to all conducting a florist's business, be it the most stylish establishment or ever so unpretentious and modest an affair. This feature in the holiday preparations should receive its full share of proper attention. A crowding of stock all about the floor and working counters is to be avoided. There must always be sufficient room for unhampered transaction of business. The most enchanting element in the matter of display—the very soul of allurement on a florist's place—is cleanliness. So much for this week's work; there is enough of it to keep all hands pretty busy. Nothing should be delayed or entirely overlooked that will tend to simplify and render more easy the task of coping with an unusually large amount of business such as Christmas is likely to bring this year to everyone in the trade.

Holiday Delivering.

Very much of what is bought at Christmas from florists is carried away by the purchaser, and these are much-liked customers. But any florist's establishment laying claim to being of any pretensions at all depends for the greater part of its holiday returns on orders that include the prompt delivering of the goods purchased. In most instances this is a single plant or made up pan, basket, hamper or the like article, to be sent to a certain address at a specified time, particular stress being placed on the latter injunction. It is easily seen that the first essential in taking orders, coming in fast and manifold at the busiest rush hours, is acuracy in booking them followed up y systematic and orderly methods in he making up and sending out of these rders, varying largely, as they invariably do, in character, destination and ime limit.

Here then, it would seem, is no lack f good excuse for the making of blunders. So I thought once at a time when he private gardener had turned commercial florist, but the florist not yet nto the the merchant, who must rely n recognized business methods, faithfully observed at all times. Since then have learned that there really is no reater pleasure on earth than to be the thickest of a roaring and rushing usiness, tired to death and gasping for bit of rest. And I have also learned hat there is no need whatever of making mistakes, and if, after all, they are ade occasionally, no need of going into pasms over it.

Lily of the Valley.

Up until now cold storage stock of ly of the valley had to be relied upon or forcing, all that entering into the oliday trade being mainly the remnant f last year's importation. After this he newly arrived pips will be in fit ondition for forcing. A thorough going ver of the new stock, now stored in old frames, will do much toward simlifying matters right along during Vinter wherever extensive and regular orcing is practiced. Unless the time as taken for the assorting of the differing grades when the pips were unacked, it should be done now, so as o be ready with pips most suitable for mmediate use when the new stock is one into.

Years of experience have brought with hem reliable knowledge as to what sort f pips are best for a forcing right after rrival and throughout the first part of Vinter. I am quite safe in recommendng for this purpose all such as appear o have been grown on sandy, gritty soil, sually showing a long crown of pinksh color, gradually decreasing in thickess toward the point, and the longest ost evenly fibered roots. Pips of this escription, especially if they have had ne or two good freezings, can now be orced with good results. But it will ake from eight to ten days longer to ring them into bloom than was reuired in the case of cold storage stock. ily of the valley furnishes no excepion to the rule that the later in the eason hardy bulbs and roots are forced, he less time and heat will it take and he finer will be the output.

Pips intended for early work, after eing separated from the other less suitble grades, should be packed in boxes ith earth under and between the unches, and these boxes be stood closey together in outdoor frames, handy or being carried into the forcing house t any time during the months of Winer in numbers as needed. This is the ost convenient plan in arranging for a orcing in regular successive batches nd much to be preferred to having hem heeled in the soil of the frame. t is best to spread a layer of moss ver the crowns of all the pips, whether acked in boxes or stored in the usual ay.

That part of lily of the valley stock hich is to go into Summer cold storage ay be left in frames until the first r second week in March or may at nce be placed in cold storage rooms, here the temperature, right for this tock, is twenty-eight degrees, rather a rifle lower than higher. Pips grown on eavy land, showing a thick-set, purlish crown and somewhat short, roughy fibered roots, are less apt to shrivel cold storage and hold vital energy ongest, and are therefore the kind easst to be held back and usually show up est after having been retarded for any reat length of time.

In packing lily of the valley for cold torage boxes of an even and convenent size are used. The bunches, after aving been immersed in water, are tood unright in a closely packed tier, ith moss all around them, under, beween and some over the tips. Nailed p with strips of lathing, they can be laced in tiers, thus occupying comparaively little room.

A high temperature in the sand, about 0 degrees, and quite cool overhead, ith an abundance of moisture at the oots and an all around humid atmoshere, are conditions essential in the orcing of lily of the valley. The roots f all pips just brought in for forcing hould be slightly shortened in with a air of sharp shears before planting in ench or trays. A few days' hardening ff of the finished product greatly adds o its commercial value.

Lilium Longiflorum.

It is time to bring in lilies intended or Easter. That holiday comes early, nd it is better to have sufficient time n hand than to be compelled to emloy high power forcing. Lilies in rames should now be showing distinct op growth and well advanced root formation. In this, as usual they will differ greatly, and the headway made will not be uniformly even or alike throughout any lot of lilies. An assorting into at least two grades will at once give a brighter appearance to the stock and, what is more, will enable the grower to treat it according to the respective needs of the varying lots. Those lilies that are farthest ahead in crown growth, and this bleached and colorless from having been under cover too long, should first be stood in some shady place or be covered with paper during the day until the leaves have turned from white to green. Lilies started in small pots must now go into larger sizes.

For a first beginning and until the close of the holiday turmoil the lilies will fare pretty well on any light bench in a cool greenhouse, holding a temperature of from 48 to 53 degrees. Under a bench, however, is no good place for them, unless they display no head growth at all. After New Year's more heat must be afforded to all the grades, a general slow rise in easy stages for the most advanced, so as to ward off green fly as long as ever possible. It is likely that 60 degrees will suffice for all of them until the middle of February, when it will be less difficult to determine on how to proceed further. In conclusion I will remind the lily grower that great heat is a means of bringing the most backward in line, but this only when well furnished with active roots.

Hydrangeas.

Well ripened wood is the principal point to be considered in deciding whether or not a hydrangea is fit for forcing. It is yet early; some of this sort of stock, especially that field-raised and but recently potted up, has hardly had sufficient rest or time to acquire firmness of wood and energy for a fresh start. But it is none to early for arousing hydrangeas into renewed activity if they are to display their huge, gorgeous trusses of bloom the coming Easter. And it is that holiday for which most of them are raised and when they are looked upon with greatest favor. It is then when the small sized and thinly branched hydrangea, the stock most profitable to grow, can be most readily disposed of.

Hydrangeas that were grown in pots all Summer usually ripen their wood sooner and more thoroughly than the field-grown plants. They also are shorter and more compact in shape. It is well to give form and well balanced roundedness to larger specimens now, before growth starts, by staking and tying here and there wherever a sprawling, unshapely plant shows the need of it. The smaller plants also should come in for a little in the way of straightening and tying up now so as to hinder one-sided growth and awkward spread. In doing work of this kind neatness in execution will result in no harm.

The start should not be made in forcing heat. A cool house, with a temperature of between 45 and 50 degrees, is a good place for hydrangeas until a fine break of new growth has been made. Sprinkle much but water sparingly at first. The highest point, about 65 degrees, is reached by a slow and gradual rise not before February. This degree of heat is held until the flowers show the first tinge of rosy blush, when cooler quarters should be chosen for the plants.

Astilbe Japonica.

Other good Easter plants are spiræas. These also should now be started into growth, a cool bench being well enough for them at first. Spiræas will be all the finer for being briught into bloom in moderate heat, a temperature not exceeding 55 degrees at any time. In this they will finish up nicely and in good time if brought in now. Those being heeled in frames should be potted up at once. If the balls of roots seem dry, a good soaking before being potted up will disperse all doubts on this point. Plant firm, using very rich compost for packing. After growth has started it is well to keep the plants at a safe distance from tobacco fumes, since the young foliage is easily damaged thereby and never is troubled by insects. All the varieties of astilbe or spiræa adapted for florists' use, the original type as well as those of recent introduction, are good for forcing, each one possessing its own peculiar merits not to be found all combined in any one variety. But all of them are alike in this one respect, that they, as also hydrangeas, need large quantities of water when making their growth, but especially when under forcing and developing bloom.

Stevia Serrata.

Let us by no means forget to save stock plants of Stevia serrata. I know it is an old-timer, but it has so many good points in its make-up that it would be sinful and exceedingly unwise to do away with it altogether. Though it is somewhat difficult, unless kept very cool, to make it carry its bloom through to the holidays, it is most useful for some floral work right along through Fall, when airily delicate cut material in white is scarce and yet so effective in all sorts of floral make-ups. Besides that, it is one of the easiest things to grow.

FRED W. TIMME.

RED RIDING HOOD, New Scarlet for 1907.

If you want to be in line get your order in early. This is the scarlet you will pay your coal bill with.
Strong, healthy, well rooted cuttings ready Jan. 1st, 1907. This speaks for the healthy condition of our stock winning first prizes on every vase of carnations exhibited at the Chicago Flower Show, 15 in all.
We also have **ARISTOCRAT, WHITE PERFECTION, DAY BREAK LAWSON** a grand variety of the Lawson family in some respects superior to Enchantress, and many others of the best varieties.

SEND FOR COMPLETE LIST AND PRIZES

CHICAGO CARNATION CO. A. T. PYFER, Mgr. **JOLIET, ILL.**

Mention the Florists' Exchange when writing.

Imperial and Pink Imperial Carnations

You Cannot Afford to be Without these Two Excellent Varieties
Price $12.00 per 100; $100.00 per 1000, 250 at 1000 rates, a discount allowed when cash accompanies the order

A. J. GUTTMAN, The Wholesale Florist of New York, 43 WEST 28TH STREET

JOHN E. HAINES, BETHLEHEM, PA.

ROOTED CUTTINGS

	Per 100	Per 1000
WHITE—Queen	$1.50	$12.50
Lady Bountiful	2.50	20.00
White Lawson	2.00	17.50
PINK—Enchantress	2.00	16.00
Lawson	1.50	12.50
Pink Patten	4.00	
Helen Goddard	$4.00	
Ethel Ward	2.00	$15.00
RED—Red Lawson	3.00	17.60
Robert Craig	5.00	
Harry Fenn	2.00	15.00
VARIEGATED—Mrs. Patten	2.50	20.00

QUIDNICK GREENHOUSES J. H. CUSHING, Prop., QUIDNICK, ANTHONY P. O., R. I.
Mention The Florists' Exchange when writing.

UNROOTED CARNATION CUTTINGS

ENCHANTRESS, QUEEN, FAIR MAID, RED SPORT, HARLOWARDEN, pink, white and variegated LAWSON, $10.00 per 1000.
WHITE PERFECTION and VICTORY, $30.00 per 1000.
LADY BOUNTIFUL, $12.00 per 1000.
LIEUTENANT PEARY, $15.00 per 1000.
SCOTTII FERNS, 6 in., $26.00 per 100.
COLEUS, Verschaffeltii and Golden Bedder, 2 in., $18.00 per 1000.

Larchmont Nurseries
Larchmont, N. Y.
Mention The Florists' Exchange when writing.

ROOTED CUTTINGS

February and March Delivery

CARNATIONS and GERANIUMS

Send for list of varieties and prices.

ALBERT M. HERR, LANCASTER, PA.
Mention the Florists' Exchange when writing.

JOHN E. HAINES

The leading scarlet, brilliant color, fine stem, the most productive ever introduced, blooms early until thrown out in July no extra grass, all shoots make flowers. Watch the papers and see what growers say about it. None but well-rooted healthy cuttings leave the place. Rooted Cuttings ready December 15, 1906. Price, $6.00 per 100; $50.00 per 1000.

JOHN E. HAINES, Bethlehem, Pa.
Mention the Florists' Exchange when writing.

CARNATIONS

THE BEST rooted cuttings of the following varieties viz:—
Pink Lawson, Red Lawson, Var. Lawson, White Lawson, Enchantress, Harry Fenn, General Lord, L. Naumann.
Plants clean; healthy and free from rust. Prices right. Address

A. W. WILLIAMS - Highland, N. Y.
Mention the Florists' Exchange when writing.

CARNATIONS

Rooted cuttings ready January 1. Victory, $6.00 per 100; $50.00 per 1000; Enchantress, Bountiful, White Lawson, Var. Lawson, Patten, $3.00 per 100; $25.00 per 1000; Pink Lawson, Boston Market, Queen, H. Fenn, and Fair Maid, $2.00 per 100; $16.00 per 1000. 5 per cent. discount for cash with order.

R. ENGELMAN & SON, Pittsfield, Mass.
Mention the Florists' Exchange when writing.

MABELLE—New Pink Carnation for 1907

Color.—A peculiar shade of lovely pink, with a faint yellow cast; several shades lighter than the Lawson, unlike most pinks, the brightest sun does not injure the color. Size.—Three to four inches in diameter when established. Odor.—Pleasing, but not strong. Stems.—Invariably strong, but always graceful, ranging from 12 to 30 inches during the season. Habit, etc.—A very quick active grower; making specimen plants in a short time, even from late cuttings. On account of its rapid growth, requires supporting very soon after benching. Gets away rapidly, blooms early and gives long stems right from the start. Productiveness.—Prodigious is the best word we know of to use here. It is the most incessant bloomer early and late, we have ever grown. Stock limited. Delivery Jan. 5th to 10th and later. Price, $12.00 per 100, $100.00 per 1000.

THE H. WEBER & SONS CO., OAKLAND, MD.

CARNATIONS

Rooted cuttings ready now of the following varieties: **Victory**, $6.00 per 100; $50.00 per 1000. **Enchantress**, $2.50 per 100; $18.00 per 1000; **Lady Bountiful**, $3.00 per 100; $25.00 per 1000; **Mrs. Patten**, $2.50 per 100; $20.00 per 1000; **Pink Lawson and Boston Market**, $1.60 per 100; $12.50 per 1000. Write for complete list of varieties, including all the best novelties.

JENSEN & DEKEMA, 674 W. Foster Ave. **Chicago, Ill.**
Mention the Florists' Exchange when writing.

CARNATIONS

F. DORNER & SONS CO.
LA FAYETTE, IND.
Mention the Florists' Exchange when writing.

ABUNDANCE

Rooted cuttings of the most prolific white carnation will be ready for delivery in January. Price, $5.00 per 100; $40.00 per 1000; 250 at 1000 rate; 5 per cent. discount for cash with order.

RUDOLPH FISCHER, Great Neck, L.I., N.Y.
Mention the Florists' Exchange when writing.

S. J. GODDARD

Framingham, Mass.
Rooted Carnation Cuttings a Specialty
Correspondence Solicited.
Mention the Florists' Exchange when writing.

GERANIUMS in good varieties 2½ in. pots, ready March 1 1907.
WM. J. CHINNICK, Trenton, N. J.
Mention the Florists' Exchange when writing.

A. B. DAVIS & SON, Inc.

PURCELLVILLE, VA.

Place your orders now for Red Sport cuttings, the best red carnation grown. $3.50 per 100; $30.00 per 1000.
Mention the Florists' Exchange when writing.

CARNATIONS

No. 1 stock rooted cuttings these prices for Dec. and Jan. delivery only.

	Per 1000		Per 1000
Enchantress	$20 00	B. Market	$15 00
L. Bountiful	25 00	Lawson	15 00
Cardinal	25 00	Harlowarden	15 00

100 at thousand rates. Cash with order.

SMITH & GANNETT, Geneva, N. Y.
Mention the Florists' Exchange when writing.

White Enchantress

white sport of Enchantress, rooted cuttings $12.00 per 100; $100.00 per 1000.

E. SCHRADER, NEW SPRINGVILLE
Richmond Borough, N. Y.
Mention the Florists' Exchange when writing.

GERANIUMS

Rooted, then grown in pots over a month. Sent free of soil. **Nutt, Doyle, Bruantii and Buchner**, $14.00 per 1000. **Ricard, Poitevine, Perkins, Viaud**, etc., $16.00 per 1000. Plenty **Nutt** and **Doyle. Coleus**, Verschaffeltii and G. Bedder, 60c. Fancy, fine, 50c. Giant, all grand, 80c. per 100. **Gladioli**, Groff's mixed, 50c. per 100. Cash or C. O. D.

DANIEL K. HERR, Lancaster, Pa
Mention the Florists' Exchange when writing.

All GERANIUMS

Booked for this Month.
PETER BROWN,
LANCASTER, PA.
Mention the Florists' Exchange when writing.

GERANIUMS

Ricard, Doyle, Buchner, Nutt, Poitevine, Brett, 2 in. pots, ready in January. Orders booked now at $20.00 per 1000.

ROOTED CUTTINGS BELOW READY NOW

	100
Fuchsias, best varieties	$1.50
Double Petunias	1.50
Heliotropes	1.00
Ageratum	.75

ERNEST HARRIS, DELANSON, N. Y.
Mention the Florists' Exchange when writing.

ROOTED CUTTINGS Prepaid per 100. Ageratum Gurney, Pauline, Coleus assorted, 60c., Salvia Bonfire, 75c. Vinca variegated, 90c., $8.00 per 1000. Cash.

SHIPPENSBURG FLORAL CO., SHIPPENSBURG, PA.
Mention the Florists' Exchange when writing.

Rip Van Winkle

Has finally got awake, and finds that he has at least 125,000 **Geraniums** in 2 in. pots and in fine condition, and will sell at $18.00 per 1000; composed of the following varieties: **Poitevine, La Favorite, F. Perkins, Viaud, Doyle, D. Grant, Bruantii, Pasteur, Brett, Nutt** and several other varieties. This is to make room "Get a move on you," and get some fine stock.
Cash with order.

J. E. FELTHOUSEN,
154 VAN VRANKEN AVE., SCHENECTADY, N. Y.
Mention the Florists' Exchange when writing.

VEGETABLE PLANTS

CABBAGE New Early and Succession $1.25 per 1000
LETTUCE Grand Rapids, Big Boston, Boston Market and Tennis Ball, $1.00 per 1000.
PARSLEY Moss Curled. $1.25 per 1000.
TOMATOES Lorillard and Mayflower, 40 cts. per doz., $2.00 per 100.

R. VINCENT, Jr. & SON, White Marsh, Md.
Mention the Florists' Exchange when writing.

500,000 VERBENAS

60 Finest named varieties: **rooted cuttings** 75c. per 100; $6.00 per 1000.
Plants, $2.50 per 100; $20.00 per 1000.
Our list is the choicest from millions of seedlings. Order early.

J. L. DILLON, Bloomsburg, Pa
The Floral and Plant Business of the late Mr J. L. Dillon will be continued under his name by his executors. LOUISE H. DILLON, ALICE D. FURMAN, Executor
Mention the Florists' Exchange when writing

POINSETTIAS

Cut and in pans for Christmas. For prices apply to

GEORGE DARSLEY,
176 Claremont Ave. JERSEY CITY, N. J
(Come and see them.)
Mention the Florists' Exchange when writing

GER

Rooted cuttings
Beaute de Poi
rooted and packed
C. F. TREICHL
Mention the Flori

Cineraria

Benary, Cannell and Sutton's Prize Strains dwarf or semi-dwarf, large flowers, all shades and colors, mixed 2½ in., $2.50 per 100. Cash please.
SHELLROAD GREENHOUSES, Grange, Baltimore, M
Mention the Florists' Exchange when writin

LIST OF ADVERTISERS

INDEX TO STOCK ADVERTISED

Contents.

PAGE

The Free Seed Hearing.

How Congress can continue the free distribution of pumpkin and squash seed after the showing in opposition made before the House Committee on Agriculture is beyond comprehension. First came a delegation of seedsmen, among them being W. Atlee Burpee, W. F. Maule and Walter P. Stokes, of Philadelphia; Alexander Forbes and Patrick O'Mara, of Peter Henderson & Co., New York; Henry W. Wood, of Richmond, Va., President of the American Seed Trade Association; C. F. Wood, of Louisville, Ky., Henry B. Hathaway, of Rochester, N. Y., F. W. Bolgiano, of Washington, and others. Then appeared Professor W. F. Massey, of the Practical Farmer, of Philadelphia, and Professor J. T. Jackson, of Richmond, Va., Editor of the Southern Planter, who spoke for the agricultural experiment stations and the agricultural press.

The seedsmen urged upon the committee that the practice of the government in giving away cheap varieties of common seeds was an unjust interference with a legitimate industry. Examples were given where the reckless distribution of such seeds absolutely destroyed the whole seed trade as far as packet seeds were concerned within large areas. Representative Davis, of Minnesota, a member of the Committee, stated that he not only sent out his full quota of 12,000 packages, but went out in the corridors of the Capitol and bought packages from people who made it a business, so that he distributed 30,000 to 35,000 packages a year to his constituents through the county chairmen and postmasters of his district. He thought the seedsmen should not object, as he distributed only one package to each person, although he gave away a total of 35,000 packages in his district alone!

The charge having been made that the seedsmen had attempted to influence the opinions of agricultural editors by offering or threatening to withhold their advertising, Messrs. Massey and Jackson, both editors of agricultural papers, strongly denied the truth of this charge and stated that they had opposed the pumpkin-seed distribution for 20 years because they wanted the money spent in some way to advance the cause of agriculture.

William Wolff Smith, the Washington representative of those opposed to the present method of distributing free seed, stated that the Department of Agriculture, the farmers, the press, the public and the seedsmen all agreed on the proposition that the money now so largely wasted, should be turned over to the Department of Agriculture to be used in securing rare and valuable seed from foreign countries, for breeding and selection of seeds, both foreign and domestic, and for other work of this character. In support of his statements Mr. Smith produced the resolutions of the National Grange, the Farmers' National Congress, the State Granges of New York, Illinois, Kentucky, Ohio, New Jersey and elsewhere, together with hundreds of other local granges, horticultural and agricultural societies. He also submitted the resolu- eties. He also submitted the resolutions of the Agricultural Press League, letters from five hundred editors editorials from one thousand papers, all condemning the present method of distributing free seed.

What probably had the most effect on the committee, however, was the support given the anti-free-seed movement by Professor B. T. Galloway, of the Bureau of Plant Industry. Mr. Galloway supported the movement most heartily. He presented to the House committee matter of the greatest interest to agriculture in general. He showed that the three projects—the wilt-resisting cotton, the seedless orange, and the durum wheat—had increased our products $25,000,000 annually. "Did anything like that ever come from the pumpkin-seed distribution?" asked Rep. Brooks, of Colorado, facetiously. Professor Galloway then produced boxes of dates grown in this country and exhibited pictures of the palms producing them. The committee sampled the dates and found them excellent. He also produced ears of corn and described how the department by a process of selection and breeding was increasing the yield per acre. He described at length the good work done with cotton and tobacco seed, with the hardy orange and other citrus fruits. All told he presented to the committee more than seventy plans, each one carefully worked out, of what the department proposed to do for agriculture along these lines if it had the money. He then advanced the proposition that if Congress would apply the money now expended in sending out old varieties of common garden seeds to this work the department could accomplish much more than it is doing. Professor Galloway also pointed out that the work the department had in contemplation would cover practically every Congressional district in the United States, so that members of Congress would not lose anything, but their districts would be incalculably benefited by the change. Professor Galloway presented an amendment embodying the views of the Department of Agriculture for the "purchase and distribution of new and uncommon seeds, plants," etc.

At the conclusion of the hearings on this subject Mr. Smith said: "Having demonstrated to the House Committee that the farmers, the agricultural press, the daily press, the public, the seedsmen and the public in general, are united in their insistence that instead of wasting this money in distributing pumpkin and squash seed that nobody wants, and are equally insistent that the money should be expended in the securing and distributing of really rare and valuable seed, if Congress does not give ear to the wishes of the country I think all those interested may well despair. We might present a few more letters, a few more editorials, a few more resolutions, but as the sentiment is unanimous already, I don't see how the case could be strengthened."

The prospects are very good that the House Committee will bring in a bill making liberal appropriations for the Department of Agriculture this year. The bill will probably carry about eight million dollars. The total estimates for the Department of Agriculture amount to $7,854,680. Total appropriation for this year is $6,930,440. Some of the proposed increases are as follows: Agricultural Experiment Stations, $803,500 to $842,000; collecting statistics, $108,000 to $123,000; soil investigations, $221,460 to $237,240; Bureau of Entomology, $94,610 to $136,270; and public roads inquiries, $70,000 to $101,000. The greatest proposed increase, however, is in the Bureau of Chemistry presided over by Dr. Wiley. Dr. Wiley wants $750,000 additional to carry out the provisions of the Pure Food Act passed last year. He wants to establish laboratories at New York, Boston, Philadelphia, New Orleans, Chicago, San Francisco, Seattle and Galveston and other cities yet to be designated. Incidentally it is proposed to increase his own salary $1,500 per annum.

Gardenias.

Any attempt to convert Gardenia florida into a tractable subject for Midwinter forcing by having recourse to ordinary, well-worn methods must inevitably result in failure. Cultural conditions and treatment as accorded the general run of Winter-flowering crops do not fully meet the requirements of the gardenia. In every instance where special provisions had not been made for its culture this brought discouraging res ts. From this it must not be inferred that the culture of gardenias is exceedingly difficult or altogether beyond the mastery of the inexperienced grower, for this is not the case. But it should be understood that there is little use of going headlong into the raising of gardenia blooms during the Winter months, unless the grower is fully assured that conditions are just right and not likely to be interfered with by paying attention to the wants of other crops.

We have now reached the most critical period in the growing of Winter-flowering gardenias, a time of the year and a stage in their growth when the truth of the foregoing remarks will be most readily owned up to by all gardenia growers, especially those in the midst of a first attempt. Of late many establishments have added gardenias to their stock for Winter forcing, prompted by the steadily growing demand for anything choice and differing from the stock generally offered. Gardenias, far more than orchids or other varieties, have proved exceedingly profitable wherever they can successfully be grown. There is no doubt but what they will be cultivated under glass for the production of a choice and high-priced article in cut material to a considerable extent in the near future. Gardenias will not bear long-distance shipping as well as most other products of the cut flower grower. A location near a large city and within easy reach of a favorable market, therefore, holds out the best promise to anyone intending to make gardenia culture a prominent feature. Ot several places houses have been fitted up especially for the purpose, and wherever this has been done with the full understanding of the plant's requirements, it has proved a well paying investment and a means of rendering its culture a comparatively simple matter in the hands of any average good grower with some experience in the work undertaken.

The principal agencies very apt to bar success in the Winter forcing of gardenias are the sickening, yellowing or complete dying off of the plants, the reluctance of indoor grown plants to freely set buds and their readiness, after the grower has succeeded in making them do so, to drop these buds before they expand into open flowers—a formidable array of bugbears, indeed, most active and hardest to overcome at this the season of shortest days. Since there is no cure for these evils but timely measures of prevention, I can serve the inexperienced grower best by briefly setting forth those points in gardenia culture under glass which, when faithfully observed, will lead to success.

The equipment as regards heating facilities should be such that the temperature in the gardenia house can easily be held at a steadily fixed point, not much lower than 70 degrees during the coldest days of Winter. The benches must be well provided with piping underneath to furnish a reasonable amount of never failing bottom heat. Benches must be well drained; two inches of coarse but clean material, spread over the bottom, are none too much for this purpose. On the top of this three inches of soil are placed, this to be a mixture of very sandy loam, decomposed horse manure or that from a spent hotbed, leaf mold not over a year old and roughly broken up turfy sods—all as near as possible in about equal preportions.

The planting is done in the latter part of Summer with thrifty young stock, out of 3 or 4-inch pots, not too root-bound or root-hardened. Any yellowish or feeble plants should be rejected for bench culture and be reserved for pots and Summer flowering. If the bench, as advised, has been well provided with drainage material all over the bottom, roughly covering the openings in planking or tiling, there will then be no need of setting the plants on elevations or little hills, as is sometimes done. But care should be had in planting so as not to place the crown of the roots any lower than merely out of sight below the surface of the soil. The working fibers of the roots, when gardenias are healthy and in a thrifty state of growth, will always strive to reach the upper layer of soil and will need a feeding every now and then in the form of top-dressing, this to be the same compost as used in filling the bench. Gardenias are induced to set buds more freely than they are wont to do by reducing root and atmospheric moisture as well as temperature at a time when indications of a seeming let-up in growth are favorable for the formation of buds. But as soon as this is accomplished the regular heat and moisture must again be afforded, all the more necessary now since any lowering in temperature, or lack of moisture at the roots or in the air of the house, in fact, any check whatever, will cause the falling of the rapidly swelling buds before they are ready to expand into the perfect product aimed at.

FRED W. TIMME.

Genista Monosperma.

(108) In the Youth's Companion we saw a picture of a flower called Bridal Veil, or Genista monosperma. We want to know whether it is true that it is almost impossible to propagate it and why, and if there is anybody else propagating it at present.

Minn. O. K.

—Genista monosperma, a picture of which you have sent us, while not extensively grown, can be propagated well enough by those who understand its requirements and have the necessary greenhouse facilities. It is just possible that the plant can be obtained through some of the wholesale plant growers of the country, and perhaps it would be a good idea to write to some of those whose advertisements appear in this paper.

Limed Nitrate of Soda.

(109) In your issue of December 8, Franklin Noble writes about fertilizing with nitrate of soda. Now, what we want to know is the difference between limed and unlimed nitrate of soda, or, more plainly speaking, how to prepare it. We have been trying to find out from our local druggists, but they don't seem to know.

St. Paul, Minn. H. K. & SONS.

—The inquiry for information of how to prepare limed nitrate of soda for fertilizer use illustrates the trouble that may come from confused meaning of the term "lime." Nitrate of soda and caustic lime should not be mixed together. The Rhode Island Station experiments were made with a caustic lime that had been air-slaked six months perhaps, and therefore partially re-carbonated, and to that extent quite different as to action on nitrogen from the original caustic. Then I believe the lime and the nitrate of soda were applied to the soil at different times; possibly some of the nitrate may have been applied a year subsequently.

But if your correspondent will use a true carbonate, such as calcareous marl, chalk, wood ashes, or very fine ground oyster shells, a dry mixture can be made with nitrate of soda readily enough; in fact, a number of commercial fertilizer manufacturers are now using calcareous marl as a filler, or body, to carry the small percentage of nitrogen, potash and phosphoric acid in their product. This fact, however, is concealed from the users of the fertilizer, for the reason that with full knowledge users themselves may buy the marl and such other elements as are wanted, separately, and not buy the manufacturers' ready mixed product.

The carbonate of potash in unleached wood ashes, from its causticity, has a slight initial antagonism to nitrogen, but not like what caustic lime has, so marl or chalk is more desirable. The Caledonia (N. Y.) Marl Company have been quoting this marl, 97 per cent. carbonate of lime and dust dry, at $1.75 per ton in car lots, small shipments at a slight advance. The Marksboro (N. J.) Cement Company may also sell the marl in small quantities.

FRANKLIN NOBLE.

FOUNDED IN 1888

THE FLORISTS' EXCHANGE

A Weekly Medium of Interchange for Florists, Nurserymen, Seedsmen and the Trade in General

Exclusively a Trade Paper.

Entered at New York Post Office as Second Class Matter

Published EVERY SATURDAY by

A. T. DE LA MARE PTG. AND PUB. CO. LTD.

2, 4, 6 and 8 Duane Street,

P. O. Box 1697.
Telephone 3765-6 Beekman. NEW YORK.

CHICAGO OFFICE: 127 East Berwyn Avenue.

ILLUSTRATIONS.

Electrotypes of the illustrations used in this paper can usually be supplied by the publishers. Price on application.

YEARLY SUBSCRIPTIONS.

United States, Canada, and Mexico, $1.00. Foreign countries in postal union, $2.50. Payable in advance. Remit by Express Money Order Draft on New York, Post Office Money Order or Registered Letter.

The address label indicates the date when subscription expires and is our only receipt therefor.

REGISTERED CABLE ADDRESS:
Florex, New York.

ADVERTISING RATES.

One-half inch, 75c.; ¾-inch, $1.00; 1-inch, $1.25, special positions extra. Send for Rate Card showing discount of 10c., 15c., 25c., or 35c., per inch on continuous advertising. For rates on Wants, etc., see column for Classified Advertisements.

Copy must reach this office by 12 noon Wednesday to secure insertion in issue of following Saturday.

Orders from unknown parties must be accompanied with cash or satisfactory references.

The Florists' Exchange wishes all its friends a Merry Christmas and a Happy and Prosperous New Year.

Society of American Florists and Ornamental Horticulturists.

Department of Plant Registration.

Central Park Nursery, Topeka, Kansas, submits for registration canna Magnificent. Foliage green; bloom rich scarlet of extraordinary size; height 4 feet.

Appointment of Director.

Secretary-elect P. J. Hauswirth has tendered to President Kasting his resignation as a director of the Society of American Florists and Ornamental Horticulturists and same has been accepted. President Kasting has appointed Theodore Wirth of Minneapolis to serve as a director for Mr. Hauswirth's unexpired term of two years.

WM. J. STEWART, Secretary.

PUBLICATIONS RECEIVED.

SOCIETY OF AMERICAN FLORISTS AND ORNAMENTAL HORTICULTURISTS.—Report of 22d annual convention, held at Dayton, O.

The report, as usual, is most interesting. It contains a full stenographic account of the proceedings, list of plants registered, plant introductions for 1906, the prize essays on "Marketing Plants and Cut Flowers," bowling and shooting scores, list of members, etc. The life membership now numbers 123, the annual membership 804. The report of the superintendent of the trade exhibition shows a net balance to the credit of the Dayton Florists' club of $846.75. The total receipts for floor and sign space were $2,053.72.

Berberis Repens.

Editor Florists' Exchange:

I herewith enclose leaves of this beautiful plant. Broad-leaved evergreens do not do well in the West. Azaleas, kalmias, hollies and rhododendrons cannot endure our dry air and bright Winter sun. We have this plant, however, the holly-leaved creeping barberry, Berberis repens. This is an evergreen and is beautiful for Christmas decoration. The Rockies and the Black Hills are full of it, and with a slight protection from the sun in Winter it does well. The flowers grow on large spikes. They are clear yellow and of a delicious fragrance. One seems to be wading through billows of it. It should be widely disseminated, especially in the West. Some from the Western coast were planted in England, and like most things from that section did not prove hardy.

York, Neb. C. S. HARRISON.

The San Jose or Chinese Scale.

There has just been issued by the Bureau of Entomology, Department of Agriculture, Washington, D. C., an exhaustive illustrated bulletin (No. 62) on the San Jose scale, prepared by Professor C. L. Marlatt, Entomologist. The history of the insect, its habits, distribution, host plants, remedies, etc., are fully treated upon and the bulletin should prove of the utmost service to all horticulturists.

The San Jose scale is now known to be of Chinese origin. Its name is derived from its first point of colonisation in America, namely, at San Jose, Cal., and is, in a sense, undesirable, says Professor Marlatt, as giving an unmerited notoriety to the district in California which had the misfortune of being the accidental place to first harbor it. The author of the bulletin believes that a more appropriate designation is the "Chinese scale," but it is improbable that a new name will ever be adopted for an insect which has become so thoroughly well known and exploited under its original designation.

The San Jose scale, the ravages of which have become so widespread that but few places in which fruit growing is carried on in this country or Canada have escaped infestation, was first established in the United States in the early seventies at San Jose, Cal., in the grounds of Mr. James Lick. This gentleman was a great lover of plants, and imported from foreign countries trees and shrubs for the ornamentation of his grounds, and it was naturally inferred that in some of these importations he had introduced this insect. Before the investigation as to the origin of the scale was instituted Mr. Lick died, and it was impossible to trace his importations. A list of the hardy trees, shrubs, and vines on which the scale has been found in greater or less number (given in the bulletin) is a most extensive one, embracing the majority of the subjects commonly employed in the ornamentation of gardens and grounds.

The methods of control which have been especially followed in the Eastern States are (1) the lime-sulphur wash, (2) the soap treatment, (3) treatment with pure kerosene, (4) treatment with crude petroleum, (5) treatment with mechanical mixtures of either of the last two oils with water, and (6) petroleum emulsion with soap. All of these methods have proved themselves to be successful against the San Jose scale when properly carried out. As compared with the lime-sulphur wash, the others mentioned are more expensive, and the two oils, unless very carefully applied, are likely to injure the treated plants and are now seldom used. One's choice of method must therefore be governed by availability, special needs, and experience. In the main these remedies, including the lime-sulphur wash, are Winter treatments and may be employed at any time when the trees are in dormant, leafless condition. The weaker oil-water mixtures and the emulsions may, however, be used in the growing seasons. The treatments enumerated are all for trees in the orchard. Nursery stock badly enough infested to require such treatment is best destroyed. For the general disinfection of nursery stock the hydrocyanic-acid-gas treatment is the standard and only satisfactory means.

Registering Carnations.

Editor Florists' Exchange:

As you accuse me in your issue of December 15 of not being just to registrars of new carnations in holding names so that they appear in the trade papers simultaneously, I want to say in my own defence, and I think you owe it to me to make it as public as you have the accusation, that I adopted this plan of holding all matter pertaining to the Carnation Society (registrations and all other matter), so that it should appear in all of the trade papers at the same time, because The Florists' Exchange, several years back, wrote me a letter relating to an article in another paper a week previous to its appearance in the Exchange, and told me very plainly that I should not show any partiality in matters pertaining to the society. If I were to send registrations out from here Monday or Tuesday, The Florists' Exchange would have them one week ahead of the others—certainly partiality for The Florists' Exchange. (Oh no!)

Not being more than human mistakes have occurred at various times in my career as secretary, but I certainly have tried hard to be just and fair with everything pertaining to the Carnation Society.

ALBERT M. HERR.

[It is not a question of partiality or impartiality, but one of right. As we have previously said registration of new plant names should be published at the earliest opportunity, irrespective of simultaneous appearance in the trade papers. The obliging secretary of the American Carnation Society has at all times acted fairly and squarely, in other words, has done his duty in the matter of furnishing material connected with the society to the trade press, for which we thank him so far as we are concerned, and if we did have occasion, which we do not now remember, to call his attention to a case in which seeming "partiality" was shown, it was not, we believe, one associated with registration. We again submit that the rights of registrars of new plants are of first importance; and this we state from no selfish or personal motive, but to obviate happenings of the kind which have called forth this correspondence. Trade papers have to "shoo the fates," and we among others have to take our chances. Once the secretary has despatched the information he desires published, at the earliest moment, his responsibility and that of the society ceases; and this, as we see it, is clearly his duty. Ed. F. E.]

OUR READERS' VIEWS

A Correction.

Editor Florists' Exchange:

Pathhead takes its name in this way. There is a roadway that has always been named "the path." The incline is very steep. The termination of the path is called Pathhead. In my reply to Job it reads "up the pith" instead of up the path. Please make the correction, that your readers may understand what I mean when I say Kirkcaldy "is up the path."

THOS. H. WESTWOOD.

Greenhouse Glass and Present Tariff Relation.

The printed report of the proceedings of the twenty-second annual convention of the Society of American Florists, held at Dayton, Ohio, last August, is now out, and for the benefit of those who were not present at the meeting, they will find on pages 78 to 85, the action which was taken upon the discussion of President Kasting's address, relative to the cost of glass for greenhouse work.

It will be noticed in that report that it was suggested that the first step for practical results would be to find out from the Committee of Ways and Means, what was likely to come up.

The Hon. Butler Ames, one of the Massachusetts Congressmen, stands as a leader and member in favor of tariff revision, and in reply to a letter addressed to him, as to what action would be likely to be taken upon revision by those who favored such course, he makes his reply as follows:

House of Representatives, U. S.,
Washington, D. C., Dec. 8, 1906.

Benjamin Hammond,
Fishkill-on-Hudson, N. Y.

Dear Sir: Congressman Ames wished me to acknowledge receipt of your letter of the 6th instant with its enclosures in reference to the proposed revision of the tariff, and to say in reply that this matter has not yet reached a point where the majority of this Congress have indicated that they are favorable to a revision.

Yours respectfully,
L. A. LEGARÉ, Private Secretary.

It will be seen from the letter received from the Chairman of the Committee of Ways and Means of the House of Representatives, already published, and this letter above shows, that there is no expectation of any real work being done at the present session of Congress. What may develop during the Winter, which will lead up to an extra session next year, remains to be seen, but there is no doubt that if the florists as a body will stand together, their collective influence would have much weight.

BENJAMIN HAMMOND.

The Tariff on Greenhouse Glass.

Editor Florists' Exchange:

The correspondence on glass duty in The Florists' Exchange a week or two ago I sent Herman B. Walker, the able Washington correspondent of the Newark News—one of the leading papers of the country—and you will perhaps be interested in his reference to the subject in the December 13 issue of his paper; some of the points of which article, I should think might be of interest to the readers of The Florists' Exchange generally.

Like the exorbitant rates still retained on third and fourth class mail matter in the interest of the express companies, it does seem that this trusting trust business, by which a common necessity of life, like window glass, is retained at a rate of duty which is virtual robbery to the mass of people who are required to use it, for the benefit of the few in the trusts, has long since reached its limit, and is a matter regarding which the facts I think should be fully understood by the public. And when the facts are understood, I apprehend there will be very little question about a prompt duty reduction and remedy. As with a number of other articles in the present tariff law, there is apparently about 5 per cent. for the protection of labor, and 45 per cent. or 95 per cent. for the protection of the trusts. Hence, the conditions and prices as we find them today.

F. W. KELSEY.

New York.

The following are Mr. Walker's comments on the letter of Senator Payne:

In this letter there is contained three of the four stock, and only, arguments of the standpatter. There isn't time at this session of Congress to revise the tariff. The same thing was said last year and the year before by the Paynes, Dalzells, Cannons and Drydens of Congress. Tariff revision is difficult, because you can't revise one schedule without revising others. If it was a simple thing that anybody could do there wouldn't be any necessity for having able men in Congress, or, for that matter, for having a Congress.

Strange the standpatters don't see the weakness of that argument—the admission that they are afraid they are not big enough and able enough to make a good job of a tariff revision, that they hesitate about touching it because they doubt their own ability to perform the task. There was a panic just previous to the passage of the Wilson tariff, and there have been no panics under the Dingley tariff. This argument, although becoming somewhat frazzled, is still the prime favorite of the standpatters, and they have found it effective, because it is partly true. There was a period of depression and panic in 1893, which had practically disappeared before the passage of the Wilson bill. If the special interests and trusts of the country are opposed to tariff revision there will probably be a period of depression, and possibly of panic, whenever any tariff revision is attempted again, if the trusts think the revision isn't going to be entirely in their interests.

There is no doubt that, if the interests object to tariff revision, they can scare the country into fits on the subject any time it is seriously proposed or contemplated. They have the power. Whether they would exercise it is a different question.

And what does this mean? Does anybody see anything alarming in this sober, definite, proven fact that a handful of men representing billions of capital which control the great interests and industries of a country, can dominate the policy of a government by the threat of industrial panic and depression? That is what it amounts to. There is no other reason for fearing panic or depression because it is proposed to reduce a few tariff schedules which now enable the interests to impose high prices upon consumers and accumulate immense personal and corporate fortunes for the few.

There is, though, one familiar standpat argument missing in this letter of Payne's. He explains, as others have done, how impossible it would be to revise the tariff this year if he wanted to, which he doesn't, but he don't tell the rest of the old, hackneyed, familiar and tiresome story, of how dangerous it is going to be for the Republican party to revise it next year or year after, because of its possible effect upon the Presidential election.

Payne's letter to the florists is a good standpat letter, but how wearisome are its arguments.

Protests Against Burbank Controversy.

Editor Florists' Exchange:

I like The Florists' Exchange except this Burbank business, and I must say it is low and mean and beneath gentlemen to throw mud at a fellow craftsman, as some are doing, prompted seemingly by envy. To my mind they are far beneath Burbank as men, and they are sinking themselves lower and lower in the estimation of good people, while Burbank by his manly silence is rising higher and higher. Burbank never claimed to be a god or to create something out of nothing as these fellows would make us believe. They know what he means by create and creations as he uses the words. Then why lengthen the controversy? I only want to be recorded as standing for the right. S. J. GALLOWAY.

Editor Florists' Exchange:

Why all this useless hairsplitting about that little word "creation?" Is it blasphemy to use it except in connection with the Creator and Preserver of the Universe? Some of your correspondents seem to think so. If they are right, then there is a good deal of blaspheming going on, for one can hardly read an article in a paper without coming across that word in one form or another. I have just read a description of the coming Virginia exposition, and there the words appeared three times, and always in connection with the work of man.

Mr. Burbank is not the first one to call improvements of plants by artificial pollenization creations. About thirty-five years ago the late Dr. Wilhelm Neubert of Stuttgart, Germany, editor and proprietor of "Deutsches Magasin für Garten und Blumenkunde," presented to all the readers of his magazine his steel-engraved portrait, and under it wrote this motto:

"Von der Allmacht Schöpfungs feuer
Einen Funken selbst zu leiten,
Das ist dem Menschen auvertraut,"

which briefly translated means: "It is intrusted to man to guide one spark of the Almighty's fire of creation." In explaining this motto Dr. Neubert said, that he was induced to write it while thinking of the grand results attained by flower-lovers through artificial pollenization. There you have a beautiful sentiment, a platform on which we all can stand. The Almighty's creative power compared to a fire, but one tiny spark of it intrusted to man to create more useful plants and more beautiful flowers.

If Luther Burbank had lived four hundred years ago, he would have been roasted over a fire for calling himself a creator. To-day he receives a roasting in The Florists' Exchange for calling his productions creations. Again I ask, why this hairsplitting over a simple word? It seems to me to be a waste of time and ink.

If Luther Burbank is a humbug, as John Birnie says, let us have it in a few plain words. Burbank certainly has done wrong if he made the world believe he created a cactus without thorns. Thornless cacti have existed as long as the prickly varieties. All epiphyllums that I am acquainted with are thornless. The surprising part is that the whole country seems to have swallowed the story. Those cacti are by no means uncommon. The lovely little Epiphyllum truncatum is in almost every plant collection, however small.

I hope that all will be straightened out, that Messrs. Burbank, O'Mara, Birnie and others will shake hands as Christian gentlemen should, and there will be joy in Heaven. C. EVERLING.

Reflections on Current Topics.

MR. EDITOR.—I have not the pleasure of the acquaintance of Mr. Clark of Pittsburg, spoken of in the notes of William Falconer recently, but he seems to be a man after my own heart, one who believes in calling a spade a spade, in striking straight from the shoulder no matter where the blows fall. It is apparent that the time has come when all right-minded people have become sated with this continual patting on the back, this make-believe style into which correspondents for the trade press and others have fallen. The present procedure seems to be that, when a grower invites a party to visit him, "entertaining them royally," some scribe immediately gives him (the grower) a jolly in the papers in appreciation of the jollification. When a drummer gets an order he immediately rushes into print with an eulogy of the buyer and the grand stock he is growing. When an advertising solicitor secures an advertisement, a gushy write-up accompanies its appearance, with a promise of two or three more such, and occasionally an offer of part of the solicitor's commission as a bonus.

The sun of the "horticultural hyprocrite" seems to have reached its zenith. We want and need more outspoken craftsmen like Mr. Clark of Pittsburg, irrespective of his Scottish rite jeweled badge; more men like Patrick O'Mara or George Watson, for example, who when he speaks, always says something, and says what he thinks—when he does think. To help along the good work of telling the truth as it is found, I suggest the inauguration of a Daniel auxiliary of the S. A. F. from which all members of the Ananias Society, including John Birnie and John G. Esler, shall be excluded. For president of that pressing organization I would propose Mr. Clark of Pittsburg; George Watson as secretary, and myself as treasurer, so that should the society not succeed the funds will be safe at all events. The fees to be pro rata according to the truthfulness of the members.

* * *

The recent annual election of officers of the New York Florists' Club seems to emphasize very strongly that this is the day of the young man. The old chaps, who have borne the heat and burden of the day, may well be permitted to rest on the laurels they have won. Their record is a splendid one; and

The Late Alfred F. Conard.

the younger generation will surely satisfy if they but maintain it. The method adopted by this body of bestowing honorary membership on the old and faithful workers is an excellent one; it's better than oslerising them. The Club should have a life membership, as well; so that the old timers, if desired by them, may still have a chance of contributing their quota to the exchequer, and prevent a rush of resignations by those who think they are old enough and have done enough to be placed on the free list.

* * *

I have read the remarks of President Westwood of the Boston club regarding his birthplace. It seemed to me that he was at sea with his geography; and to make sure I consulted an old and favorite atlas, where I find that the Firth of Forth and "mony a mile" lie between the "Lang Toon" of Fife and Pathhead, the latter being in the county of Mid lothian. The matter is not of very great importance, still I like to put a man right when his statements are "agley." The reported resurrection and flight of his Satanic majesty shows that the Scotch didn't know enough to hold on to a good thing when they had it.

* * *

John Birnie, I notice, comes to the rescue of Pat O'Mara in the "creation humbug." Dictionary definitions don't satisfy John as they do horticultural professors and their critics; he goes right to the fountain head, the Book that was before dictionaries were. There is some hope for a man when he quotes Scripture; but I have heard it said that that is always the last resort of the fellow whose argument is a weak one. There is some excuse for Birnie, though. He says he was "brought up under the refining influence of peat reek." I find "reek" means smoke and I reckon it so beclouded him in his younger days that he has never got over it. Peat "reek" I find, too, is said to have a refining influence on the reputed national beverage of the Scot. Really the properties of "reek" must be wonderfully potent.

I see that O'Mara is now following Burbank's plan and remaining silent, for which he has the congratulations of JOB.

P. S. To my friends, as well as my enemies, I present the compliments of the season. J.

Obituary

Alfred F. Conard.

Alfred F. Conard, president of the Conard & Jones Company of West Grove, Pa., was found dead in bed on Saturday morning, December 15; death was caused by a stroke of apoplexy. He was 71 years old, and leaves a widow but no family.

Mr. Conard was a descendant of Dennis Conard (or Kunard, as the name was then), a German, who was one of the first settlers of Germantown, now a suburb of Philadelphia, in 1683. Alfred was the son of Thomas and Rebecca Shoemaker Conard and obtained his early education in his father's school at West Grove and at Westtown Friends' Boarding School.

After having been associated with Thomas Harvey in the nursery business and having acquired a thorough knowledge of his vocation, Mr. Conard formed the firm of Conard & Brother, but later entered into partnership with Charles Dingee under the firm name of Dingee & Conard. The business formed at that time was largely in the general nursery line and employed agents. There were but two greenhouses in use and the establishment was known as the "Harmony Grove Nursery."

About the year 1867 the firm began more extensively the propagation of roses, Antoine Wintzer having been secured as propagator. At this time Mr. Conard compiled the first mail order catalogue to sell roses and was really the pioneer in this line, having been largely instrumental in organizing the mail order business in flowering plants, which soon extended all over the United States and to foreign countries, establishing a remarkable reputation for West Grove roses.

About 1892 Mr. Conard became separated from the Dingee & Conard Company and established a new business in his own name, and later, in 1897, associating himself with S. Morris Jones, a prominent business man of West Grove and with Antoine Wintzer, who had already made his reputation as one of the most successful propagators of roses in the country and who had worked with Mr. Conard ever since his start in the business, organized the Conard & Jones Co. While it was constantly the aim of this firm to build up a reputation for first class stock in all kinds of ornamental flowers and shrubbery, roses have always held first place and since the incorporation of the company have been grown in large and constantly increasing quantities.

Mr. Conard was a man of very retiring nature, and for that reason not so prominent in the trade generally as his long experience and extensive knowledge of the business would have warranted. He was scholarly in his tastes, methodical and precise in his habits, well read, and well informed, "a gentleman of the old school." He was particularly proficient in those qualities which go to make up a successful mail order salesman. In compiling catalogues, his work was most accurate and thorough.

Mr. Conard was for many years a director of the National Bank of West Grove, and interested in other organizations of a more or less prominent nature. He was a member of the Society of Friends and regular in attendance at its meetings. In 1862 he was married to Lydia C. Hughes, daughter of Samuel and Mary Ann Hughes, and sister of Mark Hughes, of West Grove. He is survived by Mrs. Conard, a sister, Sara C. Satterthwaite, of Kennett Square, and a brother, Pennington Conard, of Philadelphia.

Albert Woltemate.

Albert Woltemate, the well known florist of 5230 Germantown avenue, Germantown, Pa., died suddenly on the 17th inst., it is supposed from heart disease. The funeral was held on the 20th, the body being cremated.

The death of Mr. Woltemate was a great shock to his many friends as he had appeared to them to be in his usual health almost up to the last. He was 51 years of age.

The business he conducted was founded by his father, probably more than 50 years ago, the grounds occupying a square from Germantown avenue to Green street. On his father's death Albert took the business and had conducted it with success throughout. His widow survives him.

Behind a rough exterior Mr. Woltemate hid a manly character that made warm friends of those who knew him well. Hard-working, honest and always reliable his sudden death is greatly deplored. J. M.

AMONG THE GROWERS

Wietor Brothers, Chicago.

It is undoubtedly a fact that Wietor Brothers, Chicago, are fully justified in their claim of being the largest growers of strictly commercial varieties of chrysanthemums in the country, and with their 60 standard sorts, tried and true, which are grown on a large scale and the 83 varieties of novelties or late introductions which this year composed their list and which were grown in sufficient numbers to test the different buds and their various qualities, in all 143 varieties representing a product of one hundred thousand high grade chrysanthemum blooms, it may be judged that this branch of their extensive business is one of no little importance. A recent visit to their plant on High Ridge found the chrysanthemum season fast drawing to a close, in fact, so nearly through that conclusions and deductions on the results of the season could be drawn with safety. Foreman James Psenicka, who was found in his usually receptive mood, talked entertainingly on the chrysanthemum business of 1906. "The early part of the season was," he said, "by far the best for the grower and the large early varieties such as Monrovia (yellow), October Frost (white), Lady Harriet (pink), and Monogram (light pink), the latter one of this year's introduction by Buckbee, all proved profitable and will be largely grown next year. Charlie Cronin, a light buff Japanese variety introduced last year, proved a good early.

"Among other new varieties that we tried this year for the first time which give promise of being profitable commercially, and which we shall grow on an increased scale next year, may be mentioned Mrs. Swinburne (white), Rosiere (pink), Beatrice May (white, mid-season), Marie Vuillermet (white Jap.), Le Payron, a late yellow, in form not unlike Major Bonnaffon; Amateur Rosiers, a good early

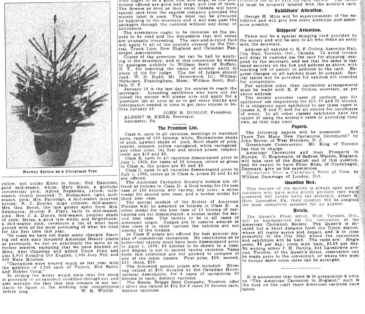

Norway Spruce as a Christmas Tree

yellow, not unlike Kioto in form; Guy Hamilton, good mid-season, white; Mary Mann, a globular commercial pink; Alfred Reganeau, yellow, mid-season, closely incurved; T. Richardson, light, mid-season, pink; Mrs. Partridge, a mid-season incurved bronze; R. J. Brooks, large crimson, mid-season; Mrs. Geo. Beech, the late golden sport from Mrs. Swinburne; Morton F. Plant, early to mid-season, pink; Mrs. J. A. Dunne, mid-season, peculiar shade of pink; Merza, a good late white, and Brighthurst, a mid-season pink, constitute a list of what have proved with us the most promising of what we tried for the first time this year.

"In roses we have not made many changes. Starting out with sixty thousand American Beauty plants as previously, we run on practically the same as in former seasons, excepting that we have doubled on Mme. Abel Chatenay and added Uncle John and also 5,000 Rosalind Orr English, 1,000 Joey Hill, and 500 Kate Moulton.

"Carnations were housed much as last year with the addition of 2,000 each of Victory, Red Sport, and Robert Craig."

In closing the writer would state that the stock is generally in an excellent condition throughout, and also mention the fact that this concern is not unlikely to figure in the seedling rose competitions before long. W. K. WOOD.

An Attractive Christmas Tree.

We send you photo (herewith reproduced) of a little Christmas tree (Norway spruce) for table decoration. In many other ways these nice little trees can be made very effective, and if taken up with a ball of earth and done up with a little moss, they can be placed in an attractive jar so as to give them a finished standard. With a little care these trees will remain green all Winter, and even be suitable for planting out another Spring if they fall into good hands. We offered these little trees last season for the first time, and they took well with the local trade. This year we anticipate a much increased demand. ELM CITY NURSERY COMPANY.

New Haven, Conn.

National Congress of Horticulture.

The National Council of Horticulture has thought it wise to call a meeting of a Congress of Horticulturists of the world to assemble at Jamestown, Virginia, during the latter part of the exhibition to be held there in 1907 to commemorate the four hundredth anniversary of the first permanent English settlement in what is now the United States. The exact date of the meeting and the formal programme has not been decided upon, but will be announced later, but in the meantime we ask that all interested in progressive horticulture plan to attend the Congress and communicate with H. C. Irish, Missouri Botanical Garden, St. Louis, Mo., U. S. A., as to what definite subjects should be discussed.

W. W. TRACY.

CARNATIONS

American Carnation Society.

Everything is in readiness for the meeting in Toronto, Ont., January 23 and 24, excepting the flowers for the exhibition and the attendance. The exhibit ought to be a good one, and large, as the premiums offered are good and large, and lots of them. The flowers as soon as they enter Canada will have special care from the express company provided the society label is used. This label can be procured by applying to the secretary and it will also pass the packages through the customs without any delay or annoyance.

The attendance ought to be immense, as the papers to be read and the discussions that will ensue are unusually interesting. The rate-and-a-third fare will apply to all of the country covered by the Central, Trunk Line, New England and Canadian Passenger Associations.

Copies of the premium list can be had by applying to the secretary; and in this connection he wants to apologize publicly to William Scott of Buffalo, N. Y., for inserting the name of another party in place of his for judge. The list of judges should read: W. N. Rudd, Mt. Greenwood, Ill.; William Nicholson, Framingham, Mass.; William Scott, Buffalo, N. Y.

January 16 is the last day for entries to reach the secretary. Intending exhibitors who have not yet joined the society will please note and apply for a premium list at once so as to get entry blanks and information needed in time to get their entries in before January 16.

JOHN H. DUNLOP, President.
ALBERT M. HERR, Secretary.
Lancaster, Pa.

The Premium List.

Class A, open to all varieties, seedlings or standard sorts, vases of 100 blooms, white, Enchantress shade of pink, Lawson shade of pink, Scott shade of pink, scarlet, crimson, yellow variegated, white variegated, any other color, the first and second prizes, respectively, are $10 and $6.

Class B, open to all varieties disseminated prior to July 1, 1906, for vases of 50 blooms, colors as given in Class A, the prizes are $5 and $3.

Class C, open to all varieties desseminated prior to July 1, 1905, colors as in Class A, prizes $3 and $1.50 are offered.

The American Carnation Society's medals are offered as follows in Class D: A Gold medal for the best vase of 100 blooms, any variety, any color; a silver medal for second best vase; and a bronze medal for third best vase.

The special medals of the Society of American Florists will be awarded as follows in Class E: A silver medal for the best vase of 50 blooms of carnations not yet disseminated; a bronze medal for second best vase. The variety to be in all cases of American origin. Judges are to reserve awards in this class if in their opinion the exhibits are not worthy of the medals.

In Class F prizes are offered for best general display of commercial carnations. No restrictions as to color—but variety must have been disseminated prior to April 1, 1906; 50 blooms to be shown to a vase, and display is not to exceed twenty varieties. Vases from this collection are not allowed to compete in any of the other classes. First prize, $50; second, $30; third, $20.

The following special prizes are included: Silver cup valued at $50, donated by the Canadian Horticultural Association, for 6 vases of carnations, 50 blooms in each; distinct varieties.

The Steele, Briggs Seed Company, Toronto, offer a silver cup valued at $25 for 6 vases 25 blooms each, distinct varieties.

Montreal Gardeners and Florists' Club, Montreal, Que., offers a cup valued at $25 to the exhibitor making the largest display—all vases in all classes being counted as part toward this display.

The R. W. King Company, Ltd., Toronto, Ont., and North Tonawanda, N. Y., offer a silver cup valued at $25 for the best 100 carnations in four varieties, four vases; competition restricted to the users of King's greenhouses.

The H. Dale Estate, Brampton, Ont., offers a silver cup valued at $25 for a vase of 100 blooms of the best carnation to be disseminated during 1907. Cash will be paid for this prize should winner prefer it.

John H. Dunlop, Toronto, offers $10 (gold) for the best vase of white carnations, 50 blooms, distinct from other entries.

W. Gammage, London, Ont., offers $10 (gold) for the best 25 blooms, pink seedling or sport darker than Enchantress and lighter than Lawson, never before winning a prize or medal. Those having preliminary certificates eligible. Entries for this prize will not be eligible to compete for any other prize.

W. J. Lawrence, Eglinton, Ont., offers $10 (gold) for best vase 50 blooms not more than three varieties, open to growers having less than 20,000 feet of glass.

John H. Dunlop offers $5 (gold) for the best vase of 12 blooms carnations, open to private gardeners only.

George Vair, Toronto, offers $5 in cash for best vase of 25 bright red carnations, to be distinct from other entries.

Rules Governing Award of Certificates of Merit.

A variety must have been bloomed not less than three years; not less than fifty blooms must be shown and an entrance fee of $5 is charged for each variety. The variety must be properly labeled with the society's card.

Preliminary Certificate.

This can be competed for by two-year-old seedlings, twelve blooms or more to be shown, and an entrance fee of $2 paid for each variety. The variety must be properly labeled with the society's card.

Exhibitors' Attention.

George H. Mills will be superintendent of the exhibition and will give you every attention and assistance possible.

Shippers' Attention.

There will be a special shipping card provided by the society and will be sent to all who make an entry with the secretary.

Address all exhibits to E. F. Collins, Assembly Hall, City Hall, Toronto, Ont., Canada. To avoid trouble and delay in customs use the card for shipping, supplied by the secretary, and see that the same is fastened securely on the box and address as above, with marking ink or pencil, in addition to the card. Express charges on all exhibits must be prepaid. Special tables will be provided for exhibits not intended for competition.

For exhibits other than carnations arrangements must be made with E. F. Collins, secretary, as per above address.

The society provides vases of uniform size for exhibitors' use respectively for 100, 50 and 25 blooms. It is obligatory upon exhibitors to use these vases in classes A, B and C, and for all entries for certificates of merit. In all other classes exhibitors have the option of using the society's vases or providing their own, as they may elect

Papers.

The following papers will be presented: Are There Too Many New Carnations Introduced? by John Birnie, of West Hoboken, N. J.

Greenhouse Construction. Mr. King of Toronto has this in charge.

American Carnations and their Prospects in Europe. C. Englemann, of Saffron Walden, England, will take care of the English end of this question, and we expect to have Peter Riise, of Copenhagen, Denmark, give us his experiences.

Carnations from a Canadian's Point of View, by William Gammage of London, Ont.

Question Box.

This feature of the society is always open and if members who have some knotty problem they want answered will kindly write the secretary, Albert M. Herr, Lancaster, Pa., their question will be assigned the most competent member for an answer.

Hotels.

The Queen's, Front street, West, Toronto, Ont., will be headquarters for the convention of the American Carnation Society. The Queen's is situated but a short distance from the Union station, where all trains arrive and depart, and is in close proximity to the City Hall where the convention and exhibition will be held. The rates are: Single room, $3 per day; room with bath, $3.50 per day. By writing either J. H. Dunlop, 644 Lansdowne avenue, Toronto, or the Queen's direct, reservation can be made prior to the convention, or where two wish to occupy same room rates can be arranged.

It is announced that there is in preparation a book on "The American Carnation in England," such is the hold on the craft there American varieties have taken.

Carnations at Joliet, Ill.

Although in the passing away of our late friend James Hartshorne the craft lost one of the most affectionate and one of the most beloved members of the profession, it is a pleasure and a delight to state that the plans which he so carefully laid are being carried out here in point and detail to perfection. A few days since it was my pleasure, in company with Uncle John Thorpe, than whom there exist but few better critics and judges of matters horticultural, to spend a day in Jo..et at the houses of the Chicago Carnation Company. The establishment and its divisions have previously been so fully described in these columns that to go into details would be practically a reiteration, but the present management and the floricultural features cannot fail to be of interest to our readers. I hesitate whether to commence with the genus homo or genus dianthus, but will select for the beginning the former.

A. T. Pyfer, the present manager of the Chicago Carnation Company, has been with the firm for the

House of Carnation White Perfection, November 1, 1906
Growers, Chicago Carnation Company

A. T. PYFER
Manager Chicago Carnation Company

past five years in the capacity of bookkeeper until the death of Mr. Hartshorne, who was always very confidential with Mr. Pyfer, they working together in harmony in all business transactions.

Mr. Pyfer was born August 26, 1878, near the city of Freeport, Ill., attended the country schools and Mt. Morris College, where he prepared himself for teacher, afterward taking a business and shorthand course in the Freeport College of Commerce, graduating in 1899. After filling various clerical positions he engaged with John Bauscher, Jr., florist of Freeport, Ill., remaining two years and coming to Juliet in 1901 as bookkeeper for the Chicago Carnation Company. He has always taken an active interest in the carnation industry, becoming acquainted with the trade in general, and is well qualified for his present position as manager.

Mr. Pyfer is a member of the American Carnation Society, also a member of the Masonic fraternity.

Peter Olsem to whom much of the success of the concern is due, is the superintendent of the growing department and has been connected with this company the past five years, always being in close touch with the late manager, whose high ideas of growing the carnation he is carrying out, and is making a good showing, so far, in his new capacity, bidding fair to rank among the leading carnation growers of the country.

Mr. Olsem was born August 11, 1879. Coming to this country in 1892 he engaged in the business with the leading florists of what was known at that time as Rogers Park, now a part of Chicago. He at once selected the carnation as his favorite flower and has been connected directly or indirectly with the leading carnation growers ever since, and has reached a high altitude in his selected specialty. Much of the Chicago Carnation Company's success at the last flower show was due to Mr. Olsem's hard work, and the results speak for themselves. Being naturally energetic, he became interested in the greenhouse building and spent several Summers with Michael Winandy, returning to the growing of carnations each Winter.

A concern, however near perfection cannot succeed by hiding its light under a bushel, nor even can advertising, however judiciously executed, comply with all the requirements of the present day business methods. There must be a live wire on the oad. The Chicago Carnation Company has one. A. F. Longren, traveling representative of the company, was born in the city of Chicago twenty-seven years ago and grew up in the environment of the extensive greenhouses built to the north of the city, beginning his career in the florist business at the age of fourteen, working in the greenhouses in that section. After an apprenticeship of several years, on the inducements held forth in the construction line he engaged in this phase of the industry, with which he has kept in close touch. After an extended experience on the road he allied himself with the Carnation Company and for two years has acted as the traveling representative of the house.

William Hartshorne, who takes charge of an important section of the carnations, is an elder brother of Jim and as foreman has met with great success and his just reward.

Now for the flowers. The Aristocrat is well deserving of its carefully selected appellation. As it grows at Joliet it is simply superb; and if it does as well elsewhere after dissemination as it has done

PETER OLSEM
Supt. Growing Dept. Chicago Carnation Co.

at home it is scarcely saying too much to state that it approaches as near the pinnacle to which all hybridists have aspired as any flower has ever reached. Of this variety 25,000 plants were carefully benched and are in a flourishing condition.

Probably the next attractive feature to a carnaton specialist would be a house of 10,000 plants in perfect form of White Perfection, followed as a good second in whites by several benches of Lady Bountiful. The White Lawson, though late, are now making a good growth and give good promise for early returns.

In colors, Cardinal takes the lead. Red Riding Hood, a seedling known as 49 and put on the market this season as a debutante, is certainly in the scarlet class all that could be desired. The Rose-Pink Enchantress, which goes on the market this year, was also in excellent form, as was J. A. Valentine, which is grown on a generous scale.

The Mrs. Thomas W. Lawson in its various shades were found in abundance. A bench of Pierce's Governor Guild, though attractive, do not promise to outdo other members in its class.

A red sport of General Maceo, small but very free. Harlowarden in excellent condition and many of the old-time favorites were seen. Then in chrysanthemums White Bonnaffon was in perfection, and Golden Eagle, superb in color, equal to last year, but evidently from having been overfed, not in good condition. WILLIAM K. WOOD.

House of Carnation Aristocrat, December 1, 1906
Growers, Chicago Carnation Company

CLUB AND SOCIETY DOINGS.

CHICAGO FLORISTS' CLUB. — The monthly meeting of this club was held at Handel Hall on Thursday evening of last week with a fair attendance. An auditing committee was appointed composed of C. H. Fiske, E. C. Amling, and August Poehlmann.

The annual reports of the treasurer and financial secretary were read and approved.

A motion was carried to the effect that the committee on the Hartshorne booth fund turn the net receipts over to the treasurer of the club, and the chairman of the booth committee with a specially appointed committee be authorized to deliver the receipts as intended.

The election of officers for the ensuing year resulted in two changes from the original nominations on account of absolute withdrawal of the candidates the ticket as elected being: President, H. N. Bruns; vice-president, Leonard Kill; treasurer, Edgar Sanders (re-elected unanimously by a standing vote); financial secretary, E. C. Amling in place of H. E. Klunder, who declined the nomination, and recording secretary, Phil. Schupp, in the place of L. H. Winterson, who absolutely refused to be considered for re-election; trustees, F. F. Benthey, J. F. Klimmer, August Poehlmann, C. H. Fiske, and George Asmus.

The names of John Ewart and Joseph Marks were presented for membership. W. K. WOOD.

ST. LOUIS FLORISTS' CLUB.—The regular monthly meeting of the Florists' Club was held Thursday afternoon, December 13. The meeting was not so well attended, as most of the members were very busy with advanced holiday work. President Irish occupied the chair. W. C. Smith, chairman of the trustees, reported that they had made arrangements for the club to hold its meetings hereafter in the Burlington building, opposite the post-office, this being more centrally located, and the meetings will be better attended. The club's several yearly exhibitions will hereafter be held in some small hall, and the public will be invited to attend them free of charge, so the objections of several of the members have been removed who would not attend meetings in the old hall. Gustave Eggeling's name was presented for membership and he was elected by full vote. The committee, consisting of Messrs. Weber, Bentzen and Smith, who have the flower show matter in hand, made a very favorable report. The chairman, F. A. Weber, reported that $2,500 had been subscribed to the guarantee fund, and that by the next meeting, in January, the fund would surely go to $7,000 and the other $3,000 by the February meeting. This report brought all the members to their feet, ready to lend a helping hand and to work hard to accomplish the desired end. Secretary Beneke reported that subscriptions were coming in daily from business men in the city.

Two essays were read, one by G. H. Pring of Shaw's Garden on "Growing Orchids," the other by A. J. Bentzen on "Growing Cyclamen." Both papers were well received by the members who extended the authors a vote of thanks. H. L. Goodman, who sells pulverized manure for the Union Stock Yards, Chicago, was present and gave us a talk explaining the merits of his goods.

The next meeting will be held on Thursday afternoon, January 10, in the new meeting hall, 810 Olive street, at which a large attendance is expected.

THE COLUMBUS (OHIO) FLORISTS' CLUB held its regular semi-monthly meeting Tuesday evening, December 11, in the rooms at the Brent building. President Stephens was in the chair, and a large attendance of members and their friends was present. Much interest was manifested in an exhibition of plants, for as voted at the last meeting, there will be at each and every meeting, from now until the first one in May, 1907, either plant or cut-flowers, or both displayed. As prize awards for these displays the club has adopted M. B. Faxon's plan of point awards. At each meeting points to a maximum of 25 will be awarded for each entry, be it plant or flower; this plan will be followed until the end of the season, when those members having the largest point totals will be awarded in order three prizes, namely: $5, $3, and $2. Messrs. Currie, Stephens, Hills, and Siebert, and others who enthusiastically seconded this plan; believe that much interest in the club meetings will be encouraged by it. In order to overcome the seeming objection of any large grower putting on exhibition at any particular meeting a great number of entries and thereby causing an uneven and perhaps not wholly fair competition, it was made a condition that each member would be limited to one entry at each meeting. Where there are several members belonging to one firm, the points are to be credited to the individual member whose interest in the club is such that he personally takes the trouble to exhibit a plant or flowers for the good of the club. At this meeting th Fifth Avenue Floral Company was awarded 20 points for an excellent specimen of Gloire de Lorraine begonia; John H. Williams received 15 points for a fine Tarrytown fern; and Sherman Stephens also 15 points for a fine Jerusalem cherry. There will be no regular committee chosen to award these point prizes, but each evening our president will appoint a committee of five members for this purpose. At this meeting Messrs. McKellar, Brust, Butler, Reichert, and Hamm awarded the prizes.

Walter Butler, who is with the Fifth Avenue Floral Company, was elected an active member. The committee appointed to consider the important question, of increasing the annual dues advised the club to make no change for the present.

Vice-president Currie reported that the entry fees received at the recent chrysanthemum show were practically equal to one-third the expenses of the exhibition—a very satisfactory showing indeed (each competitor was charged as an entry fee 10 per cent. of the first prize for which he competed).

At our next meeting there will be a special prize for the best six carnations of any variety. After adjournment Mrs. M. B. Faxon announced that a lunch had been prepared for the members and their friends—it is needless to say that ample justice was done to this part of the program. As our next meeting night falls on Christmas, it was voted to adjourn till Tuesday evening, January 8, 1907. F. W.

PITTSBURG FLORISTS' CLUB.—The December meeting of the Florists' Club was well attended, about 30 members being present. Christmas plants and other topics were discussed and there was an exhibit of plants and cut flowers suitable to the season. John E. Haines of Bethlehem, Pa., showed his two new carnations, Imperial, a pink variegated, good blooms on long stems, a fine flower but one that does not sell well with our trade; Pink Imperial, a good pink of a magnificent color, a de-

H. N. Bruns,
President-Elect Chicago Florists' Club.

sirable commercial carnation. B. K. & B. Floral Company of Richmond, Ind., also staged two new carnations—Puritan, a good white, and Superior, pink. Both seem to be good varieties.

Mr. Price, gardener at Laughlin's private place, showed some fine plants of Begonia Gloire de Lorraine. Randolph & McClements exhibited specimens of decorative plants, among them Ficus pandurata and Phœnix Roebelenii, which were much admired. McRea & Jenkinson had nice poinsettia plants and a few other things. The Phipps conservatories at Schenley Park showed plants of poinsettias and other blooming sorts. John Bader had several sizes of blooming Begonia Gloire de Lorraine, good hardy plants grown in a cool temperature. D. Fraser, gardener to Mr. Henry C. Frick, showed cut blooms of primulas and cyclamen.

W. Clark of the Pittsburg Cut Flower Company was called upon to talk about Christmas plants. He stated that he was not a grower and had been out of the retail business for quite a time, so did not know much about plants, but before he got through it was very evident that he knew a whole lot and was not slow about telling it, although some of our growers perhaps did not like to hear what he said. It was strange, he said, that so few good plants for the market were raised by our growers, when there is such a good demand, particularly for Christmas and Easter holidays. Thousands of dollars' worth of plants are sold by outsiders, who can afford to send their agents here to solicit orders, which they readily procure and entertain their customers handsomely at considerable expense. If these plants could be bought at home, that is the same quality, this would not happen. With but one or two exceptions there are few good plants grown around the city, and Mr. Clark said that when we visit greenhouses we invariably say things we don't mean. We tell the grower his stock looks all right so as not to hurt his feelings, when it would be far better if we would cling to candor and tell him exactly what we know and show up his faults; in the end the grower would soon come to the conclusion that he is working the wrong way. Good plants can be grown in and around Pittsburg as well as anywhere else, and there is a splendid opening for some one to make money in that line, if properly conducted. Good results must come from the efforts of the individual through taking advantage of natural conditions and opportunities. The most of our growers in bedding and other plants try to grow quantity, not quality; that is, they imagine they have quality, but it is a grade of their own. Good quality bedding plants for the Spring trade always bring almost double the price of poor ones, and there are never enough of them, as the growers all know; but very few of them try to improve their methods of growing the next season.

Mr. Crall of Monongahela City was called upon; he stated that conditions were different in his locality as regards the plant trade for holidays. In a small place people will not pay the price and he did very little trade in that line.

The membership of the club is steadily increasing; one member was proposed. It was decided to have a social time next month instead of a meeting. A committee was appointed as follows: B. L. Elliott, John Bader, T. P. Langhans, H. L. Blind, E. C. Ludwig and your correspondent as chairman, who will have full charge of the matter. It will likely be a "smoker," and as our rules and by-laws call for nomination of officers at the January meeting, a short business session will be held at the same time. Those members who are delinquent in dues should come to time, as they will not be admitted unless in good standing, as heretofore.

E. C. REINEMAN.

MORRIS COUNTY, (N. J.) GARDENERS AND FLORISTS' SOCIETY meeting for December was well attended. It was the occasion of the annual election of officers, and we wanted to hear Mr. Totty talk on the new chrysanthemums. The election resulted as follows: President, Richard Vince; vice-president, Percy Herbert; secretary, E. Reagan; treasurer, Wm. Duckham; executive committee, A. Herrington, A. McKendry, Thos. Stokes, J. Heeremans, A. R. Kennedy, Ernest Wild, C. H. Totty, Alex. Brown, O. Koch, R. M. Schultz, Wm. Mühlmichel and H. B. Vyse. The retiring president, Mr. Heeremans, received a rising vote of thanks for his efficient services during his two terms, to which he responded feelingly. The newly elected officers accepted their reponsibilities of office in neat speeches, each promising to do his best.

Three new members were elected—Thos. Wilson, Frank Eskeson, and Wm. McKenzie.

After preparations for the eleventh annual "smoker" had been made, Mr. Totty told us extemporaneously of the new chrysanthemums and how they showed up at the exhibitions this Fall. He spoke of Miss Clay Frick (white Duckham) as the best of the whites, and Miriam Hankey the leader in pinks; the stem foliage and flower, together with their shipping qualities, should make these varieties popular for some time. Mrs. Geo. Hunt, Mrs. Henry Barnes, Kathleen Stoop, Mrs. A. T. Miller, A. H. Lee, and May Godfrey were able to work out their own salvation if given a chance.

The new single varieties, he believes, have a future, being artistic, decorative and relieving. The new French varieties came in for consideration. President Loubet, Sergeant Levy, and Mlle. L. H. Cochet were among those mentioned. Elmer D. Smith's efforts as a hybridizer received high praise, and many of his introductions were well spoken of. The speaker received a hearty vote of thanks for his able efforts, after he had answered many questions.

Wm. Duckham, A. Herrington, C. H. Totty, and R. M. Schultz were chosen a committee on "smoker" which takes place January 9 next. John E. Haines, Bethlehem, Pa., sent new carnations Imperial and Pink Imperial. The latter showed up fine and received a certificate of merit. Imperial suffered in transit and it was requested that it be shown again.

Our treasurer, Wm. Charlton, has been ill a long time and the deepest sympathy is felt for him. He has been treasurer 11 years (since we were organized), able, energetic, and faithful. He has declined to be renominated. E. REAGAN.

BAY SHORE (L. I.) HORTICULTURAL SOCIETY.—The annual meeting of the United Bay Shore Horticultural Society took place at the South Side hotel Wednesday evening. Officers were elected as follows: President, E. P. Strong; vice-president, J. Rogers; secretary, Wm. McCollum; corresponding secretary, A. Paterson; treasurer, D. McTosh; exhibition committee, J. R. Howell; chairman, M. J. Connellan, M. Yesck, W. Stuart, W. Cameron. Later in the evening about one hundred members gathered round the banquet board. Speeches were made by Dr. E. S. Moore, Secretary Neubrandt, of Tarrytown Society; Messrs Burnett, Rickard, Ross, J. T. Scott, Secretary McCollum, and M. J. Connellan. Dr. Moore presented as a gift from the members of the society a handsome gold chain and charm to President Strong, who suitably replied. A very enjoyable evening was spent by all present.

A. PATERSON.

Cultivation of Orchids.

(Paper read by G. H. Pring, of Shaw's Garden, before the St. Louis Florists' Club.)

Owing to the Orchideæ being such a large and varied order, I only intend to deal with the genera which have commercial value as cattleyas, lælias, cypripediums, odontoglossums, cymbidiums and dendrobiums.

Cattleyas and Laelias.

These closely allied genera, with their large and highly colored flowers, are among the most popular, useful, and showy of all orchids. They are natives of Mexico and Brazil, where they are found in the ravines and valleys. In these situations the plants affix themselves indifferently to the trunks and branches of trees, or to the bare rocks in the gorges of the mountains. In this wild state, scarcely any soil is found at their roots, only a little moss and a few leaves which have fallen among the stems.

Culture.—Notwithstanding the enormous extent of territory over which the cattleyas and lælias are spread there is a similarity in the climatic conditions, thus favoring the horticulturist, in his being able to cultivate them in the same glass house, which is usually termed the "cattleya house," the most convenient being a spacious airy building, well ventilated, pointing north and south.

It is preferable to have all orchid houses with a north and south aspect, which enables one to obtain the full benefit of the sun, light being one of the chief items in successful orchid cultivation. In such a house, cattleyas and lælias enjoy a temperature ranging from 55 to 60 degrees F., in Winter, and 60 degrees F., in Summer, with such increments by sun heat as circumstances admit. The compost should consist of peat or polypodium fiber and moss, with an addition of crushed crocks, this keeping the compost sweet. Ample drainage should also be an important item. Pots proportionate to the size of the plants should be selected. Over-potting, with the object of stimulating the plants into more active growth, is one of the greatest fallacies that can be entertained in orchid culture. The plants should always be potted above the rim of the pot as much as possible to prevent them getting water-logged, and should be potted moderately firm.

The best time for repotting is when they begin to emit their new roots, according to the species. During the growing season these plants enjoy a plentiful supply of water at their roots, with a slight spraying overhead. When the growths are mature, the water supply should be gradually diminished, until only enough is needed to prevent shriveling.

The shading of the houses during the Summer should be of some thin material, just enough shade being afforded to prevent injury to the young growths. A plentiful supply of ventilation during the Summer is essential. The best species commercially are—Cattleyas Trianæ, Mossiæ, labiata vera, gigas, Percivaliana and Warneri. Lælias crispa, pumila, purpurata, autumnalis, anceps and its varieties.

Cypripediums.

This is a widely distributed genus, native chiefly of North-east India, being found on the lower parts of the Himalayas, etc., Burma and the islands of the Malayan Archipelago, and also South America, which is the home of the selenipediums; these differing from the cypripediums in having a three-celled ovary, and the latter one-celled, a difference, though, not strongly marked in the inflorescence, the scapes producing a succession of flowers, several being open at the same time.

Culture.—Cypripediums, commonly called "lady slippers" are no doubt the easiest to cultivate. More hybrids of these have been raised by hybridists than of any other genus, the seedlings flowering in the course of two and a half to three and a half years.

When imported plants are received it is advisable to lay them out on damp moss, giving a slight spraying occasionally to induce them to emit new roots. They may be potted without fear in a mixture of peat and moss in equal parts, with a little charcoal added. Such species as Spicerianum, bellatulum, and concolor enjoy an addition of fibrous loam and crushed crocks. They should be given a plentiful supply of water during the Summer, both at their roots and leaves. Heavy shading during Summer is necessary to prevent the leaves becoming yellow through the strong rays of the sun. The temperature should be kept as near as possible in the Winter at from 60 to 65 degrees F., and not less than 65 degrees F. in Summer. Such species as insigne, etc., enjoy an intermediate temperature. A suitable time for repotting is in Spring, about March being preferable. When the plants are in full growth, a little liquid manure applied occasionally will be found beneficial.

Odontoglossums.

This the most popular genus of the cool house orchids is distributed throughout the mountainous region facing the Pacific, extending from Peru to the southern portion of Mexico, the Colombian districts being very rich, yielding the much sought after Odontoglossums crispum and triumphans. It is quite a common occurrence in the London sale rooms for such prices as $5,000 to be paid for single specimens of O. Pittianum and others. Although odontoglossums are indigenous to tropical countries they are found at considerable altitudes, growing on trees, etc., hence the majority are better accommodated in a cool house where an abundance of moisture can be obtained all the year round, combined with a free circulation of air.

The tropical heat here in St. Louis in the Summer is detrimental to the majority of the cool house orchids, although the Mexican species, such as Odontoglossums citrosmum apterum, cordatum Insleayi, grande, Cervantesii and Rossii, which need an intermediate temperature, can be grown successfully with a little attention.

Culture.—A good general compost for potting odontoglossums consists of equal parts of fibrous peat, fresh chopped sphagnum moss, with an addition of crushed crocks and silver sand. The best time for repotting is about the end of September, or in the month of March, according to the condition of the plants. Careful watering is necessary after potting to prevent the growths damping off, especially with such species as Cervantesii and Rossii. During Summer a plentiful supply of water is essential both at their roots and leaves. Heavy shading is necessary for these cool house plants; lath roller blinds are the best, being easily manipulated.

Cymbidiums.

This is a popular, though not a large, genus of orchids dispersed over the Indo-Malayan region, Japan, etc.

Culture.—The cymbidiums are of a robust habit having stout pseudo-bulbs, and thick fleshy roots which are freely produced, provided they have ample pot room for development. The compost should consist of good fibrous loam and peat, in the proportion of two-thirds of the former and one-third of the latter. Ample drainage should be provided, with an abundance of water during the growing season, keeping the plants fairly moist during Winter. A shady corner in the cool house, where an abundance of moisture can be obtained, should be afforded for the successful cultivation of these plants. Repotting should be accomplished after the flowering period when the new growths have started. The most popular species are, Cymbidiums, Lowianum, giganteum, eburneum, Tracyanum and Hookerianum.

Dendrobiums.

This large and most interesting genus of epiphytal orchids has a very large distribution over the Old World, being found chiefly in India, Burma, Assam, and the islands of the Malayan Archipelago, the richest districts being the Burmese, and the lower parts of the Himalayas. The dendrobiums indigenous to these districts are enveloped in a humid atmosphere during their growing period, owing to the enormous amount of vapor which ascends from the Bay of Bengal, which is eventually precipitated as rain. After this comes the dry season, which generally lasts about two to three months, thus enabling the plants to have complete repose.

Culture.—For successful cultivation, these plants require a special house, where, approximately, the natural conditions can be given. The compost should consist of peat and moss in equal parts, with an addition of crushed crocks. During the growing period a plentiful supply of water should be applied to their roots, and an occasional spraying overhead afforded. When the growths are mature the water supply should be diminished considerably; just enough should be given to prevent the growths becoming too shriveled. The temperature during the resting period should be about 50 to 55 degrees F. During Summer the minimum should be 60 degrees F. Repotting should be accomplished after the flowering period when the new growths have started. Shading should consist of some thin material, just enough being given to prevent harm to the young growths. The chief commercial species are, Dendrobiums, nobile, Wardianum, Phalænopsis and formosum giganteum.

Our London Letter.

BY A. HEMSLEY.

CARNATIONS.—Supplies of good blooms have been over abundant in Covent Garden market during the past season. Enchantress and Mrs. T. W. Lawson are most extensively grown, and prices are down from 25 to 30 per cent. lower than a year ago. Growers, however, are still persevering, and I find stock is remarkably healthy with most firms that I have visited.

The show held at the Royal Botanic Gardens under the auspices of the newly formed Winter-flowering Carnation Society on December 4, was in every way a great success. Taking the exhibits they were all good, and quite a large number of visitors attended, most of whom were specially interested in carnation growing, many traveling a long distance in order to be present. I mention this as showing the increasing interest taken in the carnation for Winter flowering. It is chiefly the American varieties that are grown, but we have a few good things recently introduced by English growers. These, however, show that they are related to the American sorts. I must take Britannia first, for it was the opinion of every one that this was the most attractive feature of the show. A first-class certificate was given for it. Its only weak point was a lack of fragrance, but I can say that even in this respect it is better than most scarlets, and blooms which I have received from the raiser (A. Smith) have given off a pleasant odor when the box has been opened, yet in a dry atmosphere it soon evaporates. I must add that this variety took first prize for 36 blooms of any scarlet, and also that a gold medal was awarded for an exhibit of about 33 dozen blooms, which were put up as a supplementary exhibit. Mr. Smith is sending it out early in the year and almost every grower who saw it placed orders.

Another very attractive variety was Mrs. H. Burnett from H. Burnett, Guernsey. This also gained a first-class certificate and took first prize for the best 36 blooms of any blush pink variety, in which class there were seven good exhibits of Enchantress. The latter were all very fine, but in addition to perfect formed flowers, the former is of a more decided shade of color.

Now to come to the general exhibits. Taking whites, a number of varieties were shown and it was difficult to say which was really the best, but the first prize for 36 blooms went to A. F. Dutton for his improved White Lawson, the blooms being very fine. Yet I think White Perfection, from J. Green, who took first prize for 18 blooms, were equally good. Lady Bountiful though not coming in a first prize exhibit was splendidly shown, and we must certainly see more of the others before discarding it. I have referred to blush, or flesh pink varieties, but there is Lady Carlisle, as shown by Mr. Waters, which attracted much attention. This grower took first prize for collection. Here Fiancee was also very good; the color bright and calyx firm. We shall have to recognize this as one of the best, though some have discarded it.

In scarlets Robert Craig was well to the front; it took first prize in one class, and was well shown by most growers. Victory was also good. St. Louis, which recently gained an award from the R. H. S., is another good scarlet. And other older varieties continue to be well grown. It seems difficult to say which is really the best. Yet to go back to what makes the best price in market I must again refer to Britannia. We never see this exposed for sale, for though the grower has several large houses full, all blooms are ordered in advance.

Coming to crimsons it is even more difficult to say which is really the best, but Harlowarden still finds most favor with growers, yet Messrs. Bell & Sheldon secured first prize in the large class with President, but Harlowarden came first in another class. And I am still in favor of selected stock from Harry Fenn. Here I would like to say that much depends upon careful selection. New varieties are always welcome, but many of the older sorts want some beating, where the stock has been properly looked after.

Falling back to scarlets I find that there are two large growers, at least, who still raise large quantities of William Robinson and find it profitable. Fancy or striped varieties find but little favor in our English markets, but I may say that Mrs. M. A. Patten proved to be the best seen at the show. Prosperity was very good, yet it is not a profitable market sort.

English Horticultural Notes.

CARNATIONS.—We have two splendid new Winter-flowering carnations to offer to the American public. You have probably been expecting that something good would arise from the efforts of English cultivators when they seriously applied themselves to seedling raising. Without saying that the newcomers are better than everything else, I must still say that as compared with American varieties in England, they are very telling. Britannia is a new rich, very bright crimson with every quality except fragrance. According to the English standard, it obtained 35 out of a possible 40 points, dropping 5 on scent. It grows vigorously, throws up plenty of large, strong, well-made, smooth flowers; edge moderately fringed. The flower stems average 20 inches at least, and are strong and elastic. It stands up grandly and is certainly an all round, first rate flower:—First class certificate, London, December 4. The stock belongs to H. Smith, The Nurseries, Enfield Highway, London.

The second variety is Mrs. H. Burnett from Mr. H. Burnett, Guernsey. The color is a charmingly soft salmon-flesh, warm and most attractive. For its color alone it is worth growing, but its other qualities may be guaged when I say that it obtained 37 out of a possible 40 points, and won a first-class certificate.

THE WINTER FLOWERING CARNATION SOCIETY held its first annual exhibition on December 4 in the Botanic Gardens, Regents Park, London. H. Mathias, Medstead, Hants, is the honorary secretary. Of course as a first attempt the show was very modest, but there was a good general display. Competition was confined to trade growers for the amateurs are in a minority so far. Another year ought, however, to see a change. There was no conference or reading of papers in connection with the show. Gold medals were awarded to Mr. Smith for his group of Britannia (see above) and to Messrs. Bell & Sheldon, Castel Nursery, Guernsey, who had some promising seedlings, including yellows. Medals of lesser value were awarded to Messrs. Hugh Low & Company, Enfield, London; Cutbush, Highgate; T. S. Ware Ltd., Feltham; A. F. Dutton, Iver, Bucks; J. Green, Reliance Nurseries, March, Cambs.; and B. & V. Haig, Castle Hill Nurseries, Maidenhead. Prizes for a collection (10 ft. x 4 ft.) fell to C. F. Waters, Deanland Nursery, Balcombe, Sussex, and to S. Mortimer, Rowledge, Farnham, Surrey.

J. HARRISON DICK.

Philadelphia.

News Jottings.

All the stores are now engaged in preparing for the rush at the week end. From present indications there will be a large number of plants sold, probably more than ever before. There are certainly two or three times the number of azaleas around than in previous years, and many more poinsettias, while all the various nephrolepis are very prominent.

Pennock Brothers have a very pretty window display this week—all styles of lanterns covered with bark suspended by red ribbons, the bottom of the window filled with pans and baskets which contain poinsettias, A. Farleyense, ericas, etc., all gaily bedecked with colored ribbons.

John Thatcher, for the past ten years in charge of the private establishment of Mr. Edward Le Boutillier and one of our best growers of ornamental foliage plants, leaves that position January 1, for Chester, W. Va., which place is across the river from East Liverpool, Ohio, where he is to take charge of the new place of Mr. C. A. Smith.

At the annual meeting of the Pennsylvania Horticultural Society, held on Tuesday, the following officers were elected for 1907: President, James W. Paul, Jr.; vice-president, James M. Rhodes, Edward Le Boutillier, Henry F. Michell and Rudolph Ellis; treasurer, S. W. Keith; secretary, David Rust; professor of botany, Stewardson Brown; professor of horticultural chemistry, Dr. Persifor Frazer; professor of entomology, Dr. Henry Skinner; professor of biology, Dr. Ida A. Keller. The Spring exhibition will be held March 26, 27 and 28, 1907; the annual exhibition and chrysanthemum show, November 12, 13, 14 and 15, 1907; peony and outdoor rose show late in May; sweet pea and outdoor cut flower show late in June; dahlias and outdoor cut flower show in September; the exact dates to be determined for these exhibitions later, according to the season.

Albert Woltemate, the well-known florist of Germantown, dropped dead on Monday last. For many years he had conducted quite a large business, being both a grower and a retailer, with a store at 5230 Main street or Germantown avenue. He was a member of the Florists' Club and the Pennsylvania Horticultural Society, but had not taken any active interest for the past ten years; in fact, he was seldom seen away from his home. He was about 50 years of age.

DAVID RUST.

St. Louis.

News Notes.

The St. Louis Horticultural Society will hold its next meeting at the home of C. C. Sanders this week and some interesting facts are looked for. The society has issued a very neat circular and membership card explaining its objects, aims, and privileges, also what it costs to become a member. The membership is divided into four classes; first, patrons who shall make a gift to the value of $100; second, life members who shall pay at one time $50; third, active members who shall contribute annually $10; fourth, regular members who shall contribute annually $5. Harry Young is president, Alex. Waldbart, vice-president, F. C. Weber, treasurer, and Otto G. Koenig, secretary. The society will hold monthly meetings for the present at one of the member's homes. President Harry Young reports that the society is progressing, is not antagonistic to the local florists' club as some think, but will work in harmony with it when opportunity presents, as the society is made up of members, mostly all of whom are also associated with the florists' club. The society has the endorsement of Wm. Trelease of the Missouri Botanical Garden; F. W. Taylor, who was chief of Horticulture and Agriculture at the Louisiana Purchase Exposition; and Henry T. Kent, president of the Civic Improvement League. There is room for such a society, similar bodies now existing in Chicago, Philadelphia, and other cities, and so long as it does not antagonize our florists' club, which is of twenty years' standing, and which President Young says he will not tolerate, we wish it every success.

ST. PATRICK.

Cincinnati.

Trade Notes.

Monday we had snow three inches deep. We are just before the Christmas battle, and the questions confronting the commission men are, what will we have and what will we get? All we can do is to wait and see, sell what we can get, and be satisfied, then write to the trade papers and tell them of the immense business we didn't have, or name a certain per cent. above last season.

You will pardon me for using the word "season," as Brother Rudd does not live in Missouri and therefore does not like to see the word in print. But in all seriousness, it does not look as though there was going to be much stock to fill Christmas orders; I hope I may be mistaken.

I am in receipt of the official schedule of the American Carnation Society, and under the heading "Notice," I see our secretary tells us that the one and one-third railroad fare has been secured. However, the Central Passenger Association refuses to grant us Ohio people any such concession, and if this is the case, it will cut out several certificates that would otherwise go to help pull the count up to the hundred mark. It might be well for Mr. Herr to look into the matter, as every certificate helps. The regular fare in Ohio is two cents a mile, and this is the reason the Passenger Association will not issue the certificate.

Henry Lodder, of Hamilton, O., and J. T. Herdeger, of Aurora, Ind., were callers during the week.

I wish all a very Merry Christmas.

E. G. GILLETT.

Auld Nick o' Kirkcaldy.

With apologies to Job and Tam Westwood.

Oh Job! Oh Tam! you shouldna ha'e tel't
That in Kirkcaldy Satan dwelt
Till Scots, like Cain, their brither slew
The Evil One. What else'd they do?
But dead Auld Cloutie widna bide.
In Scotia's land he couldna hide;
So westward wi' his friends he fled.
While we exist he'll ne'er be dead.
In Gotham an' the Windy toon
Auld Hornie's kept a busy loon.
The Smoky City's 'tween the twa,
An' here at times we feel his paw.
Would the Hub were nearer tae us.
From sin an' Satan, Boston, free us!

W. F.

FOR THE RETAILER

[All questions relating to the Retail Trade will be cheerfully answered in this column. We solicit good, sharp photographs of made-up work, decorations, store interiors, etc., for reproduction here.—Ed. F. E.]

Begonia Gloire de Lorraine.

Begonia Gloire de Lorraine seems to be more in evidence this season than ever before, and in spite of its being more or less a failure last Christmas, one large grower has three houses filled with this magnificent plant, which has evidently come to stay. The indications point to large sales of it for the holiday trade. I hear complaints that it does not do well in the store, and lasts no time in the house. This should not be the case if the plants are kept well moistened. If they are neglected they go to pieces very rapidly; this is especially so with the hanging baskets.

Begonia Gloire de Lorraine were used entirely at a prominent society wedding held in Grace Church this week, and the effect was most striking. The chancel was banked with splendid specimen kentias and Cocos plumosus, the tall plume-like leaves of the latter lending a light airy effect to the decoration unobtainable with any other palm. The baskets of Gloire de Lorraine begonias were hung promiscuously to the height of fifteen feet. The bell-like shape of the begonias was most appropriate. They were also used in the body of the church, tall standards about five feet high being erected at every third pew and wound with Asparagus plumosus. A large basket of begonias was placed at the top of each standard, completing a very pretty decoration.

The house was also done in pink. A shell canopy was used in the reception room. This was covered lightly with Asparagus plumosus, and Killarney roses arranged in large clusters, giving the effect of a rose bower. A large mirror in the same room was very effectively done. A fine specimen of Cocos plumosus reached from the floor to the ceiling, forming a natural arch; a tall silver vase arranged with Uncle John roses and a large bow of pale pink ribbon completed the effect. The guests were seated at small round tables, the decoration being a small handle basket filled with Enchantress carnations and Adiantum cuneatum. The handles were wound with pale pink ribbon and tied with a bow of the same hue. The idea is good where the space for decoration is limited, as the baskets take up no more room than a vase of flowers, and are much more decorative. The bride, contrary to custom, carried a bouquet of Killarney roses and a cluster of lily of the valley showered with white silk ribbon and lily of the valley. This is the first time I have seen pink carried by a bride, and it may be the inauguration of a new fashion.

A Unique Dinner Decoration.

A dinner decoration I saw recently at the Holland House is worthy of description here. The entire room was covered with Southern smilax, no part of the wall or ceiling being visible. This was dotted all over with miniature electric lights, several hundred being used. The large, round table had a tank in the center sunk to the level of the cloth. In the center of the tank was an island of glass crystals illuminated by changeable electric lights. A fountain played up through the center. On either bank of this miniature moat lily of the valley and cattleyas were used, forming two large wreaths of flowers. The bottom of the tank was covered with fine white pebbles; small gold fish were placed in the water and miniature swans floated on the surface. Corsages of cattleyas and gardenias tied with orchid ribbon, and Dendrobium formosum for the gentlemen, completed this somewhat elaborate decoration.

Anthuriums.

This week I have observed a few flowers of anthuriums in some of the prominent stores. A. Brownii, A. Andreanum and some of the more showy varieties would form a welcome addition at this season, but from a commercial grower's standpoint, I think, hardly profitable, although some plants come from that source; but the majority of them are sent in by private gardeners. The flowers attract a great deal of attention, and really make a most striking decoration for the dinner table. They are never cut with their foliage, but go splendidly with large fronds of Adiantum Farleyense. Cypripediums are good used in combination with anthuriums. Their scarcity, however, does not permit of their general employment, but some enterprising grower may take them up and do well with them. What our customers want is something new, something odd, and it is a great tax on the ingenuity of the grower and florist to satisfy their demands.

Variegated Stevia.

Variegated stevia has made its appearance in quite respectable quantities and is eagerly purchased by the enterprising buyer. A large wreath of bronze galax and white roses, with the variegated stevia used to fill in instead of Adiantum cuneatum, was quite original and most effective. I do not believe, however, that this plant is destined to be a great rival of the better known variety, which is deservedly popular and always in demand.

D. RAYBUN.

Holly Wreath.

Artist, Myer, New York.

Canadian Tax on Commercial Travelers.

The provincial premiers who recently held a conference with Sir Wilfred Laurier, in Ottawa, Canada, are said to have had a satisfactory consideration of the question of modifying or repealing the tax on nonresident commercial travelers, which is levied by the provinces of British Columbia and Prince Edward Island, and the tax on foreign travelers in Quebec Province. As the tax stands in the province of Quebec, it calls for the payment of $300 per year for those foreign travelers calling on liquor firms; a yearly tax of $100 on those calling on wholesale houses only; $200 per year on those calling on both wholesale and retail houses. A six months' license is sold and cuts these figures in half. British Columbia has a nominal tax of $100 on all travelers representing firms outside the province. Prince Edward Island has a nominal tax of $20 on travelers who represent firms outside of the province. These three provinces are seriously considering a withdrawal of this business restraining tax.

New York.

News of the Week.

Judging from the reports of growers in this vicinity the plant trade for the holidays has been unusually heavy. Both flowering and decorative stock of good quality are about sold out, and as unusual preparations have been made this year, it goes without saying that the present holiday season will see more and better grown plants than have ever been seen before.

We notice in one or two places rather unusual things for Christmas time, namely, salvia and spiræas. Some made-up pans containing salvia and spiræa in flower and Asparagus Sprengeri make a rather pretty appearance, and will, no doubt, sell to good advantage. There are also poinsettias in quantity and in various sizes, ranging from little pans with plants five and six inches high to large plants three and four feet high; and there seems to be a demand for all the various sizes. There is not much use for an artificial poinsettia when such excellent natural stock can be procured as is seen in the New York market.

The meeting that should have taken place between the legislative committee of the S. A. F. O. H. and interested growers and the interstate committee, at Washington, Tuesday, December 11, has been postponed until Friday, January 4.

John Pereboom, representing the firm of D. Nieuwenhuis & Son, Lisse, Holland, arrived at this port on Tuesday, the 11th inst., and will make a tour of the country in the interests of that firm. Among the novelties Mr. Pereboom has to offer is a new white spiræa called White Queen, a cross between S. japonica and S. astilboides floribunda, which was raised by the firm he represents.

Robert Berry, who has been traveling for Frank Darrow, 26 Barclay street, came in from a Western tour this week, having had a very successful trip. Mr. Berry will no longer represent this house on the road.

William Plumb has joined the staff of J. H. Small & Sons, retail florists, Broadway.

O. L. King, of the King Construction Company, Tonawanda, N. Y., was in town this week.

Bonora, the new fertilizer is now being put up in dry form, and is continuing to give complete satisfaction wherever it is used. Gardeners and others who have used this preparation speak with unstinted praise of the wonderful effects it produces when used on plants, both decorative and flowering.

Boston.

Gardeners and Florists' Club.

There was an enthusiastic meeting of the Gardeners and Florists' Club on Tuesday evening to hear Winsor H. Wyman deliver his interesting discourse on "Craft and the Craftsman." Over a hundred members were present notwithstanding that the mercury hovered at zero and many had to stay home to prevent a freeze-up. Twelve new members were elected and sixteen names were dropped from the list for nonpayment of dues.

On the exhibition tables were vases of variegated and pink Lawson carnations from H. A. Stevens Company, the latter receiving honorable mention; and violets from S. J. Goddard which received commendation for their excellent cultivation.

A lively tilt took place when it was tried to amend the by-laws whereby nominations for officers will be made from the floor instead of by a nominating committee as at present. The amendment was finally lost by two votes, it requiring a two-thirds vote to pass it.

It was announced that the January meeting would be ladies' night, and that J. K. M. L. Farquhar would favor the club with an illustrated lecture.

The year just closed has been a very successful one for the club; 125 new members have been elected, and there has been an average attendance at the meetings during the year of 118 members. J. W. DUNCAN.

Newport, R. I.

Christmas Trade Prospects.

Florists are now busy receiving shipments of plants and other requisites for the Christmas trade. As yet no novelty has made its appearance, nor do I think it likely there will be any offered unless Nephrolepis Whitmanii be called a novelty, well furnished plants of which are likely to be quickly disposed of this Christmas. Nephrolepis Piersoni elegantissima and N. Scott'i are here in quantity, and in such condition as warrants them to be quick sellers at prices a little in advance of last year's. Palms are also selling at a slightly advanced figure. Flowering plants are just coming in from Boston, New York and Philadelphia; the same might be said of foliage plants, the most of which are shipped from dealers and growers in or around the cities named. Poinsettias, Gloire de Lorraine begonias, ardisias and solanums are offered in large numbers and of good quality. The dealers who usually handle these most extensively are receiving more this year than last and ask prices a little higher than in previous years for the same class of stock, with indications pointing to them asking a still higher price by the beginning of next week. Araucarias have been favorites from away back and they still more than hold their own. For some reason or other there is a scarcity of fancy foliage plants, such as crotons, dracænas and well grown Pandanus Veitchii. Everyone knows that without an assortment of these a florist is seriously handicapped at this time of the year; it then must be the case that choice stock in these lines commands a higher price in the larger cities, which together with the increased general demand for them accounts for their absence except in limited quantity.

Exhibit of Robert Leupke, Houston, Tex., at Texas Floral Society's Show.

Cut flowers are already in brisk demand. Welch Brothers are shipping larger quantities than usual at this time of the year to local dealers. Violets are surprisingly good and sell readily. Carnations are coming in in splendid condition; so are roses.

Holly and material of like nature is available in sufficient quantity, but luckily not in such superabundance as last year. Christmas trees are as yet rather hard for dealers to bargain advantageously for, but I think by Tuesday of this week these trees will come in in numbers sufficient to meet the demand. Taking everything into consideration I am of the opinion that a much larger volume of business will be done this Christmas than last year, and that the profits will be correspondingly greater. Zeigler told me that he expected to sell double the quantity of stock he sold last year, and that he is ordering goods on the strength of that conviction; other dealers are equally optimistic.

Much interest is taken here in the initiation of a movement to raise funds for a memorial to the late Congressman Adams of Wisconsin in recognition of his valuable services in Congress and out in the cause of agricultural education. It will be remembered that solely through the efforts of Congressman Adams the federal appropriation for the extension of the work of the States experiment stations throughout the country was materially increased. As is very often the case with men of like attainments, Mr. Adams died a poor man. Although it is not yet definitely settled what form the memorial will take, still the fact that the homestead on which the family of the late congressman lives is encumbered leaves but little to guess as to what purpose whatever amount may be collected will be put by the committee having the matter in hand. Professor Wheeler of the Rhode Island experiment station is a member of the committee.

W. B. Leeds has purchased the Fred. W. Vanderbilt estate known as Rough Point. This estate is situated in one of the most picturesque parts of Newport and has always been considered one of the most valuable estates here. It is understood that the price paid by Mr. Leeds exceeded six hundred thousand dollars.

At the municipal election held last week a goodly proportion of the horticulturists who were candidates for the representative council secured election. Among the successful ones were, Thomas Gibson, Joseph Gibson, James J. Sullivan, Patrick F. Reynolds and James E. Sullivan. Bruce Butteron and Andrew Christensen tied with opponents in the wards wherein they were candidates.

Taking everything into consideration, which includes the purchases of valuable estates by rich newcomers recently, and the large amount of work planned and in course of construction, Newport from a horticultural standpoint is entering on the long looked for road that leads to a new era of prosperity.

Patrick Devine, who for many years was gardener on Baroness Seilliere's estate "Inchiquin," has received the appointment of gardener to Mr. Pembroke Jones at Friedheim, the estate he recently came into possession of by purchase from the heirs of the late owner, Theodore Havemeyer.

Extensive improvements are contemplated by Mr. Jones, which include the planting of shrubberies and herbaceous borders.

Thomas Kelley has been appointed successor to Mr. Devine.

D. M.

Indianapolis.

News Items.

Tomlinson Hall market was well supplied with flowers, but the retail sales were disappointing. Nearly all the high grade stock held for Christmas has been wholesaled. Much of the feeling created by the erection of the coliseum has been allayed, as it is reasoned that the many gatherings held there will be a benefit to the florists who retail their output on the market.

John Heidenrich is erecting another house which conforms to the rest of his range in Iowa street.

John Bertermann inspected several establishments at Richmond, Ind., last week; all of them were full of excellent stock. The E. G. Hill Company is cutting sweet peas for the Pittsburg market.

The seed stores report the heaviest business on record in the green goods line.

Visitors: Carl Baum, Knoxville, Tenn.; W. W. Coles, Kokomo, Ind.

I. B.

A Texas Exhibit.

Our illustration gives a partial view of the chrysanthemum exhibit of Robert Leupke, Houston, Texas, one of the pioneer florists of that city, made at the recent show of the Texas State Floral Society. Mr. Leupke supplied something like 600 blooms of the character shown for a local church wedding decoration, which was the most elaborate affair in decorating ever seen in Texas. S. J. M.

CHANGES IN BUSINESS.

PITTSBURG, PA.—George W. Beears has opened a flower store at 53 South Seventh street.

WALTHAM, MASS.—R. L. Goinsalvos has opened a florist store at 100 Chestnut street.

SIBLEY, IA.—A. R. Redshow will build a greenhouse and engage in the florist business here.

KANSAS CITY, MO.—The Alpha Floral Company has moved to larger and more commodious quarters at 1105 Walnut street.

CHARLOTTE, MICH.—The Fuller Floral Company has rented a store in the Foster block and will occupy it as a flower store.

TENAFLY, N. J.—The Mushroom Company has been incorporated with a capital stock of $5,000. Incorporators, F. J. Swain, F. Bertuch, M. Gintzler.

WELLSTON, OHIO.—Walter Butler of Chillicothe has sold his interests in his florist business there and will remove to this place, build greenhouses and conduct a general florist's plant.

The final games in the series between teams composed of New York seedsmen and Madison, N. J., gardeners, were played on Saturday, December 15, at Madison, and resulted in the defeat of the home team, which gave New York the championship honors, thy having won two out of the three matches. The individual scores are as follows:

MADISON.			
Crane	133	167	163
R. Schultz	124	105	105
C. H. Totty	133	137	113
Keating	122	194	131
W. Duckham	150	135	152
Total	662	738	664

NEW YORK.			
L. W. Wheeler	105	140	141
W. Rickards	164	149	130
A. Rickards	145	160	180
Proton	168	200	192
Chadwick	185	175	175
Total	767	824	818

CLASSIFIED ADVERTISEMENTS

CASH WITH ORDER.

The columns under this heading are reserved for advertisements of Stock for Sale, Stock Wanted, Help Wanted, Situations Wanted or other Wants; also of Greenhouse, Land, Second-Hand Materials, etc., For Sale or Rent.

Our charge is 10 cts. per line (7 words to the line), set solid, without display. No advt. accepted for less than thirty cents.

Display advertisements in these columns, 15 cts per line; count 12 lines agate to the inch.

[If replies to Help Wanted, Situation Wanted, or other advertisements are to be addressed care of this office, advertisers add 10 cents to cover expense of forwarding.]

Copy must reach New York office 12 o'clock Wednesday to secure insertion in issue of following Saturday.

Advertisers in the Western States desiring to advertise under initials, may save time by having their answer directed care our Chicago office 127 E. Berwyn Ave.

SITUATIONS WANTED

SITUATION WANTED—As working foreman or section man; competent grower of roses, carnations, chrysanthemums and bedding plants. 18 years experience. State full particulars and wages in first letter. Address B. F., care The Florists' Exchange.

SITUATION WANTED—As working foreman or assistant by expert grower of cut flowers and general stock, also propagator. German, 31 years of age, with 17 years' experience. Thoroughly competent, sober and reliable. South preferred. Address, Ch. H., P. O. Box 41, Aldrich, Ala.

SITUATION WANTED—Young man, 33, married, 15 years experience in general greenhouse and nursery work, and possessing some executive ability. Seven years in present position as working manager of up-to-date place; desires similar position. Address B. H., care The Florists' Exchange.

SITUATION WANTED—By a young man who has had five years experience in carnation growing. A first-class propagator, A-1 with the hose, strictly sober and can furnish reference to that effect from present employer. New York State preferred. Address B. M., care The Florists' Exchange.

SITUATION WANTED—Florist, German, 26 years of age, single, 12 years experience in outdoor flowers, palms, roses, ferns and bedding stock, also landscape gardening, wants position in Florida, near Jacksonville preferred. Private place or florist business. Good, sober and active worker. Best of references. Address A. A., care The Florists' Exchange.

SITUATION WANTED—Any lady or gentleman requiring the services of a competent florist and horticulturist, experienced in all branches of the florist trade, also fruit and vegetables, inside and out, including hothouse grapes, early and late peaches, plums, cherries, strawberries, etc.; early and late forcing. Married; one daughter, 14 years of age. Nationality, English. Aged 45; disengaged when suited. Address B. C., care The Florists' Exchange.

HELP WANTED

WANTED—Greenhouse man; $10.00 per week to start. Emerson C. McFadden, Short Hills, N. J.

WANTED—Single man for carnation house. State age, nationality, experience and wages expected. Board furnished. Address Box 437, Minersville, Pa.

WANTED—A smart, bright, honest boy for wholesale florist; will be given a good opportunity. Address with full particulars to B. O., care The Florists' Exchange.

WANTED—Experienced man by retail florist. Must know how to make-up funeral work and wait on customers. Aged 25 to 35. Chas. H. Fox, 21st and Columbia avenue, Philadelphia, Pa.

WANTED—Foreman for commercial place where roses, carnations and a general stock is grown. Have about 75,000 feet of glass in central state. Give salary and particulars in first letter. Address B. W., care The Florists' Exchange.

WANTED—A good reliable nurseryman, familiar with evergreens, and who understands the propagation of shrubs, perennials, etc., and who has had experience in landscape work. Give full particulars and state salary expected. T. E. Steele, Pomona Nurseries, Palmyra, N. J.

Seedsman Wanted

We want a young man as order clerk in our flower seed and bulb department; permanent position. Apply, stating age, experience, etc., to

HENRY A. DREER, 714 Chestnut St., Phila, Pa.

Mention the Florists' Exchange when writing.

Thirty cents is the minimum charge for advertisements on this page.

HELP WANTED

SEEDSMAN

Wanted a young man with experience in putting up orders attending to customers, and general store work. Apply with references, stating wages expected, to **"Seed Store,"** care Florists' Exchange, 2 Duane St., N. Y. City.

Mention The Florists' Exchange when writing.

MISCELLANEOUS WANTS

WANTED TO BUY—Greenhouses to be taken down. State full particulars of same when writing. Address, F. W., care The Florists' Exchange.

FOR SALE OR RENT

FOR RENT—Three greenhouses, 140 ft. each, stocked with roses. Also dwelling house; will rent cheap. L. Hill, Box 133, Madison, N. J.

FOR SALE—A retail florist store in the best and busiest section of the city. Positively a money maker; good reason for selling. Address B. Y., care The Florists' Exchange.

FOR SALE—4,000 feet of glass, new, in thriving town of 4,000; 24 express trains daily. No competition. 50 miles from large greenhouse. Easy terms. Investigate immediately. Address A. C., care The Florists' Exchange.

FOR SALE OR TO LET—For a number of years, well located in one of the largest New England cities, 16 years established retail business, 11 roomed dwelling, with two stores, about 12,000 feet of glass in splendid condition, stocked with palms and foliage plants, carnations, violets and bedding stock. Small cottage on side street. For further particulars apply to Arthur T. Boddington, 342 West 14th St., N. Y. City.

FOR SALE

Des Moines, Iowa, wholesale and retail greenhouse establishment, 29,000 feet of glass, three acres of ground, well located, all in good order, with good wholesale and retail trade. Price, about $8,400; terms reasonable.

VAUGHAN'S SEED STORE
CHICAGO

Mention the Florists' Exchange when writing.

FOR SALE

A well equipped place, consisting of seven greenhouses, over 30,000 feet of glass, a nine roomed house, barn, stock, etc., and eight acres of land. This is a decided bargain and a rare opportunity. For particulars address

S. S. SKIDELSKY,
824 N. 24th St., Philadelphia, Pa.

Mention the Florists' Exchange when writing.

Rare Opportunity

For a florist to establish a good paying business; 16,000 inhabitants; one of the fastest growing towns in State. The grounds are especially adapted for the business. Main Av., on line of trolley. Five minutes from station White Plains, N. Y. For full particulars apply to

H. W. SPARLING
35 W. 125th St., New York City

Mention the Florists' Exchange when writing.

FOR SALE

A 100 Acre Farm, between Bridgewater and Middleboro, Mass., beautifully situated, southern exposure, 7 room dwelling, barn, outbuildings and good well. The loam is very heavy and rich, extending north to lighter loam and white propagating sand, standing wood in large quantity. This place offers splendid opportunities to start greenhouse and nursery business, and is directly located on electric road. No competition of any description within miles. Will sell on easy terms to party with good references.

CLARENCE A. HAMMETT, Newport, R. I

Mention the Florists' Exchange when writing.

HOW TO GROW MUSHROOMS

Price, - - - 10 cents.

A. T. De La Mare Ptg. & Pub. Co.
2-8 Duane St. New York.

STOCK FOR SALE

100,000 greenhouse grown Asparagus Plumosus Nanus seed; ready about Dec. 15, $4.00 per 1,000. Joseph Wood, Spring Valley, N. Y.

FOR SALE—Rooted cuttings of Enchantress, $2.50 per 100; stock plants of Gold Mine, 75c. per doz.; $5.00 per 100. Riddell & Herrick, Farmingdale, L. I.

SWEET PEAS, Christmas white and pink, $2.00 per 100, fine plants; will exchange for rooted cuttings of geraniums, coleus or canna roots. Geo. M. Cook, Arlington, Md.

WHITE AND YELLOW BONNAFFON, Black Hawk, Engueham and Maud Dean chrysanthemums. 75c. per doz.; $5.00 per 100. A. D. Ezolf, Lansdowne, Pa.

CYCLAMEN plants for Christmas sales, in 5 and 6 in. pots, $6.00 and $9.00 per doz. Selling fast, so place your orders early. Safe arrival guaranteed. Geo. A. Backham, 880 Van Dyke Av., Detroit, Mich.

BABY RAMBLER ROSES, fine dormant stock, one year, $12.00 per 100; 2 1-4-in. pot plants, extra well rooted, $4.00 per 100; $30.00 per 1,000. Orders booked for delivery now or any time up to late Spring. Samples free. Brown Brothers Company, Rochester, N. Y.

SURPLUS STOCK OF SEEDS—Calliopsis, (California Sunbeams), Golden Fleece; Dahlia Monarch, mixed; Eschscholtzia, Golden West; Freesia, Geranium, Good Venture; Heliotrope, Lemoinee'; Ipomea, Heavenly Blue, White Tassel; Nasturium, Butterfly, Jupiter, Saturn, mixed; Poppy, Fayal, Irresistible, Maid of the Mist; Tacsonia Buchananii. Write for prices. Theodosia B. Shepherd Co., W. H. Francis, Mgr., Ventura, Cal.

FOR SALE

FOR SALE—Second-hand, four-inch, cast-iron pipe, hubs cleaned and in good order. Address, Wm. G. Grimm, Cedar Lane, Woodhaven, L. I.

BOILERS BOILERS BOILERS.
SEVERAL good second-hand boilers on hand, also new No. 15 Hitchings at reduced cost. Write for list. Wm. H. Lutton, West Side Avenue Station, C. R. R. of N. J., Jersey City, N. J.

FOR SALE GREENHOUSE PIPE

4-inch boiler tubes, second hand, in fine condition, absolutely free from scale and with ends cut square. Sample and prices on application.

KROESCHELL BROS. CO., 33 Erie St. Chicago.

Mention the Florists' Exchange when writing.

FOR SALE

BOILERS No. 8 Weathered, round, $60.00. One 11 section Sunray hot water sectional boiler, grate 3 by 3. Price $150.00. New Henderson boilers; send for price on size wanted. One No. 367 Lord & Burnham hot water boiler, 7 sections, 36 in. grate, heat 8,000 sq. ft. of glass, used one season, price $150.00, guaranteed.

PIPE Good serviceable second hand. No Junk, with new threads. 2 in. 7c.; 1½ in. 5½c.; 1¼ in. 4c.; 1 in. 3c.; 2½ in. 10c.; 3 in. 14c.; 4 in. 18c. 4 in. cast iron greenhouse 14c. 2 in. NEW, standard, full lengths, 9½c. ft. All kinds of fittings for 4 in. cast iron and all sizes wrought iron.

STOCKS AND DIES New Economy, easy working, No. 1 cuts ¼-¾-1 in. $3.00; No. 2 cuts 1¼-1½-2 ins. $4.00; Armstrong Adjustable No. 2 cuts ¾-1 in. $4.00; No. 3 cuts 1¼-1½-2 ins. $6.50.

PIPE CUTTERS Saunders, No. 1 cuts to 1 in. $1.00; No. 2 cuts to 2 in. $1.30; No. 3 cuts to 3 in. $3.00; No. 4 cuts to 4 in. $4.50.

STILLSON WRENCHES Guaranteed. 12 in. grips 1½ in. $1.10; 18 in., grips 2 in. $1.60; 24 in., grips 2½ in. $2.25; 36 in., grips 3½ in. $4.50.

PIPE VISES Reed's Best Hinged Vise, No. 1 grips 2 in. $1.75; No. 2 grips 4 in. $3.50.

GARDEN HOSE 50 ft. lengths ¾ in., guaranteed; 9c.; for heavy work, guaranteed; 12½c.

HOT-BED SASH New; Gulf Cypress, 3 ft. x 6 ft. 80c.; glazed complete $1.60 up. Second hand sash glazed $1.00 and $1.25, good condition.

GLASS New American, 50 ft. to the box. 10x12 single at $1.90. 10x12, 12x12 10x15 B double $2.65. 12x14 to 12x20 and 14x14 to 14x20 B double $2.85. 16x16 and 16x18 B double $2.35. 16x20 to 16 x 24 double $3.20 per box 6x8, 7x9, 8x10 old, single $1.50. 8 x 10 and 8x14 old, double $1.85. 12 x 14 old single $1.75.

PLATE GLASS MIRROR with white enameled frame 3x7, price $12.00.

Get our prices on second hand wood material. We can furnish everything in new material to erect any size house. Get our prices.

METROPOLITAN MATERIAL CO.
Greenhouse Wreckers
1398-1408 Metropolitan Avenue, BROOKLYN, N. Y

Mention the Florists' Exchange when writing.

Commercial Violet Culture

Price, $1.50

The Florists' Exchange, 2-8 Duane St., New York

FOR SALE

Greenhouse Material milled from Gulf Cypress, to any detail furnished, or our own patterns as desired, cut and spliced ready for erection. Estimates for complete constructions furnished.

V. E. REICH, Brooklyn, N. Y.
1429-1437 Metropolitan Ave.

Mention the Florists' Exchange when writing.

NOTICE

To be sold immediately at great sacrifice, florists' delivery outfit, consisting of two top wagons, three open wagons, two horses with harness, one rubber-tired surrey; all in fine condition. An exceptional opportunity. Apply,

EDWARD HIGGINGS
1 West 28th St. - N. Y. CITY

Mention the Florists' Exchange when writing.

LEGAL NOTICES

A. T. De La Mare Printing and Publishing Company, Limited.—The annual meeting of the stockholders of this Company will be held at the office of said Company, Nos. 2 to 8 Duane Street (Rhinelander Building), in the Borough of Manhattan, City of New York, on the tenth day of January, 1907, at 12 o'clock noon for the election of a Board of Directors and two Inspectors.

J. H. Griffith, Secretary. A. T. De La Mare, President.

A. T. De La Mare Printing and Publishing Company, Limited.—By order of the Board of Directors the Transfer Books of the above Corporation will be closed on and after December 31, 1906, at 12 o'clock noon, to January 11, 1907, at 12 o'clock noon.

David Touzeau, Treasurer. A. T. De La Mare, President.

1906 Florists' Directory

THE AMERICAN FLORIST Directory for 1906 is now ready for distribution. It contains 475 pages, including complete lists of the **Florists, Seedsmen** and **Nurserymen** of the United States and Canada, arranged both by states and towns and all names alphabetically. Also lists of Foreign Merchants, Firms which issue catalogues, Horticultural Supply Concerns, Parks, Cemeteries, Landscape Architects, Experiment Station Horticulturists, Botanical Gardens and other invaluable trade information.

Price, $2.00 Postpaid

Address

A. T. De La Mare Ptg. & Pub. Co.
Limited
2 to 8 Duane Street, New York

Chicago.

News Notes.

And now for Christmas, joy and pleasure for the multitude, but speculation, hard work and overtime for the florist in every department. The experiences of a year ago, so vivdly impressed on the minds of all connected with the business, should be remembered, yet all conditions and probabilities ought to be carefully placed in the balance of consideration before orders are placed with the grower or commission man; and the latter should carefully measure the supply before accepting the order on which the retailer and his customer are to depend. What the week before the holiday is to be meteorologically it is impossible to state at this time when it is just beginning, but the six weeks previous could not have been less satisfactory to the grower, the sky almost continually overcast even when not raining, there being (writing without statistics at hand) probably not an average of one bright, clear day in seven. Of the corresponding weeks last year it may be said they were exactly opposite, being absolutely perfect, forcing everything ahead until the ten days before Christmas, when the alternating current turned on a spell of such gloomy conditions that the development of flowers became stagnated, roses particularly refusing to open.

The practice, which has gone out of vogue to a considerable extent, of strenuously endeavoring to get everything in shape for a holiday will tend to make the supply still shorter at the festive time. The American Beauty is the chief crop in this market, and from the present appearance of the houses it is evident that a week's sunshine will furnish approximately enough to go around, though the best authorities prophesy a shortage in special lines. In other lines at the first of the week, with the exception of princess pine, and scarlet carnations, Richmond and Liberty roses, three floral standards never overabundant at this event, there does not loom up on the horison any abnormal specter of scarcity.

Among C. W. McKellar's other remarkable traits it is probably not generally known that he possesses not a little inventive genius. He has recently patented an article, which, though simple, is certainly of economic value, in the form of a wire broom-holder which, hanging against the wall, holds this useful household article entirely out of the way, brush end up and where it can be readily placed or removed.

Out at Joliet the J. D. Thompson Carnation Company are growing, on quite an extensive scale for an experiment, an undisseminated seedling of Peter Fisher's called Evangeline. They have also a large quantity of Robert Craig, White Perfection, The Belle, and Nelson Fisher. A seedling, Lucille, white slightly overlaid with pink, which has never been shown, will doubtless be heard from in the future.

What is the matter with the Mrs. T. W. Lawson carnation? Is it, like its long line of predecessors, on the decline and decrepit, exhausted with its own beauty and abundance? Certainly in this section it is far inferior to any time since it was sent out with, of course, the exceptions that prove the rule.

N. J. Wietor, Adam Zender and John Muno spent several days last week hunting in the southern part of the State, returning on Saturday rejuvenated and prepared for the Christmas rush. Peter Reinberg also landed at headquarters on Saturday from a similar outing. All reported a delightful time and all the game that true sportsmen would take.

The Poehlmann Bros. Company the first of the week felt confident of being able to fulfil all requirements of their customers with their usual long and strong stock of carnations and roses, and for this season of holiday demand an exceptionally large supply of chrysanthemums and lilies.

At George Reinberg's establishment on the morning of the busiest week in the year there was little to be said: The management, making no prophecies, but resting on their oars, promised to say something later; which, judging from the optimistic appearances of the surroundings, would be of a pleasant vein.

Harry Papworth of New Orleans was in Chicago last week, and it is an unauthenticated statement that it was building material and not Christmas flowers or Christmas presents that he was pricing.

The managers of the J. A. Budlong estate have brought their holiday crop out in a state of remarkable perfection, and those who were fortunate enough to have had an order placed with and accepted by this concern may be assured of satisfaction.

The Lincoln Park conservatories never presented a more gorgeous exposition of floricultural features than at the présent time when the show houses abound in tasteful decoration, combining bloom and foliage in perfect form and arrangement. The Christmas color is manifested in the main by thousands of well grown poinsettias, Begonia Gloire de Lorraine, both pink and white, with an unlimited and yet not overdone stock of decorative plants, complete a wonderful exhibition of horticultural art which is free to those who will but just look. Perhaps the most important department of the show is the superb collection of flowering orchids, embracing the entire Lincoln Park and Selfridge combination of seasonable varieties. Though in no way allied to the trade every man who is interested in his profession should avail himself of the opportunity to visit this beautiful holiday exhibition.

The E. F. Winterson Company are showing some exceptionally fine poinsettias for which they have booked some large orders for this week's delivery, though they expect to have them in stock after Christmas, as they have a large supply to draw from.

Percy Jones, the first of the week, had a few samples of Jeannie Nonin and Yellow Chadwick chrysanthemum graded as small, medium and select at two, three, and four dollars per dozen, which find a ready advance call. He is agent for four houses of these flowers which had not been disturbed until the above referred to specimens were cut.

Mr. Hulsizer of the company bearing his name in Des Moines, Iowa, was in town a few days ago.

At the Peter Reinberg offices may daily be seen a most beautiful shipment of Uncle John roses which they have always found a popular Christmas flower, and this year the concern, according to Mr. Spencer, will have the best Christmas crop of Richmond and Liberty they have ever cut.

Vaughan's greenhouses at Western Springs are making heavy shipments locally and out-of-town of their fine stock of Christmas decorative plants. Incidentally it may be mentioned that at the Randolph street store the windows and the entire surroundings are most artistically decorated for the festive occasion. No expense has been spared and the execution of the work is a decided credit to the artist.

The Central Floral Company in making preparations for Christmas have installed a balcony and made several ground floor changes. Among new features here was noticed an abundance of dried statice, which combined with the Christmas berries in several forms was very attractive.

Wietor Bros. are fortunate in possessing an exceptionally fine stock of American Beauty roses which with Liberty, Uncle John and Bride at the top notch and an ordinarily good stock of their other specialties insures satisfaction to the concern and to their customers.

John Ziska of the Chicago Rose Company is lamenting the loss, which occurred in the market last week, of a handsome 32nd degree Masonic charm which disappeared from his fob, within thirty minutes, but just how, when, or where, he is still only supposing, while hoping for its return.

Mrs. A. Lange has recovered from the effects of a sprained ankle and bursted blood vessel and expects to leave on Monday for the family home in Omaha to spend the holidays.

At the beginning of the week Vaughan & Sperry report more favorable prospects than had been antipated from previous reports both as to supply and demand. They feel safe on the violet question, which is one of their leaders.

William Abrahamson of the supply department of the E. H. Hunt concern has returned from an extended tour of the West and Southwest and reports general prosperity in all sections he visited.

William Breitmeyer of Detroit, Mich., was in town the first of the week and visited some of the interesting points in this neighborhood.

Harry Bunyard representing A. T. Boddington was among recent visitors.

As The Florists' Exchange will not reach our subscribers in the Middle West until a day or two before Christmas, we quote the prices which will then probably prevail; in fact they have practically gone into effect with the opening of the week.

WM. K. WOOD.

PORTLAND, ORE.—George H. Lamberson, secretary of the State Board of Horticulture, died on December 4. He was a native of New York, and was 53 years of age. He leaves a widow and three children.

CYCAS LEAF HOLDER

PATENTED

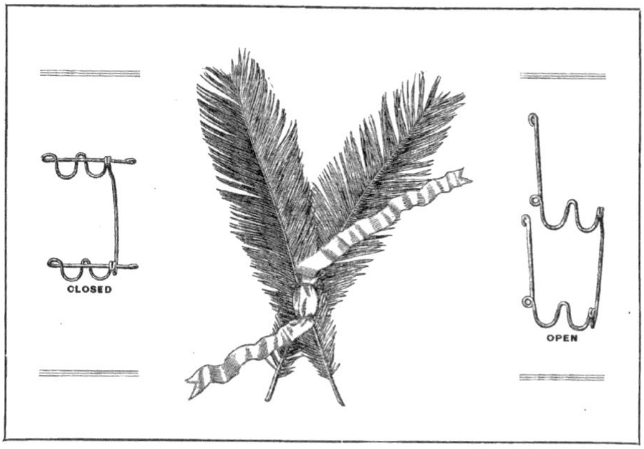

WITH these **CYCAS LEAF HOLDERS** one can adjust two or three Cycas Leaves as shown in center cut above. The device will securely fasten the leaves at the proper angle and prevent spreading. A ribbon may be placed under the catch of the holder, thus enabling the florist to tie an effective bow without destroying or in any way disarranging the teeth of the leaves. The price of the holders is such that no florist can afford to be without such a simple and practical appliance.

Price for 2-Leaf Holder, 15c. per dozen. **Price for 3-Leaf Holder, 18c. per dozen.**
Liberal Discount to Dealers.

...NOVELTIES...

Japanese Swans, $1.00 dozen.
Raffia Flat Boxes for Violets, 50c., 65c. and 75c. each.
Japanese Hanging Ferneries, $1.80; $6.75 per dozen.
China Shoe, Delft.
Watering Cans, Delft.
Bisque Shoes and Figures.
Celluloid Wreaths.
Bisque Wreaths.
Nickel Bouquet Holders.
New Gold and Antique Green Baskets to fit any size Fibre Jar.
Fern Pots, Green and Red, Etc.

We have originated more ideas for the trade than all other supply houses combined.

REED & KELLER, 122 W. 25th St., New York

Mention The Florists' Exchange when writing.

REVIEW OF THE MARKET

NEW YORK.—While there is not a great deal of business doing in the cut flower district, it is remarkable how high prices of most staple flowers are. Of course, always during the week preceding Christmas the cut flower business is dull, chiefly because retailers are getting pretty well supplied with flowering plants of all descriptions, and there is little going on among society in the way of social events. It is the very scarcity of flowers that is keeping up the prices to the pitch they are at the present time, and dealers are free to confess that it is, in the main, unfortunate that values are so high just before a holiday, as it is not so good for the business in general as it would be if stock were more plentiful and prices easier.

There has been a dearth of sunshine for the last two or three weeks, and growers report that while there are plenty of flower buds in sight, both of carnations and roses, they seem slow to develop. There is no telling, however, what a few days of sunshine may bring forth, and if we do have bright weather, it is just possible that the crop of roses for Christmas may be surprisingly large compared with what has been the rule during the last two or three weeks. There is also some evidence here and there in the wholesale district that roses are being held back, which is most unfortunate for the dealer who has to handle them at this time; for while prices are high, it does not mean that retailers are going to pay the top figures for stock that shows evidence of being kept in the grower's cellar two or three days before it has been shipped to the city, consequently such stock is unsalable unless offered at a much lower figure than present ruling prices.

American Beauty roses are quite scarce, and 60c. each seems to be about the ruling figure for most of the special grade stock, though at times some of extra quality will realize 75c. each. Of Bride and Bridesmaid there are a few of superfine quality that bring as high as 20c. each, though this is a little above the average for the ordinary run of special grade stock. Number two grade clears out quite satisfactorily and at good figures; in fact, this grade is easier to handle at the present time than the number one grade.

Carnations continue to sell at good prices, and the small stock, such as can be sold at from $2 to $3 per 100, is in the minority. The general run of carnations coming in are realizing about $4 per 100, fancy grade fetching somewhat higher figures.

Gardenias are not selling quite as well as they were, and there is a supply of extra fine quality coming into the market regularly. The supply of lilies, narcissus and Roman hyacinths seems to be increasing steadily, with no change in prices.

Violets are selling fairly well, and while $1.25 is the price for select grades, an occasional bunch of specials brings 25c. higher.

The orchid trade is not brisk just now, but it is expected these flowers will move much better next week, and we understand there will be a nice supply on hand.

There is much speculation as to what Christmas prices will be, and rumors are abroad that American Beauty roses will touch the $1.50 mark, but as the supply of both roses and other flowers is as yet an unknown quantity, no one can tell what Christmas figures will be until that day arrives. Let us hope, however, that there is no supply of overkept stock, and that when the Christmas business is over on Tuesday there will not be a surplus left in the hands of the dealers, as has been the case too many times before.

PHILADELPHIA.—As is usual the week before Christmas there is quite a lull in the cut flower business. Prices continue to advance steadily; for American Beauty roses, $9 per dozen is now being asked for the best, and $15 per 100 for the best teas. Fancy carnations are at $8 per 100 this week, but there is not much of this kind of stock on hand.

At present the wholesale houses are rather gloomy about the supply for next week. We have had so much cloudy and rainy weather recently that roses and carnations are not blooming and the flowers coming in are soft, with weak stems. Some complaints have been received from other cities to which flowers have been shipped, that roses in particular are arriving in poor condition. DAVID RUST.

BOSTON.—As might be expected flowers are beginning to get scarce and prices are advancing on all sides. It is thought that by the end of the week Christmas values will rule. There are few American Beauty roses in the market at present, and prices have gone up, $7 and $8 per doz. being the prevailing figures for the best grades. Bride and Bridesmaid have also advanced in price, $2 per dozen being the top-notch. Some fine Richmond and Killarney are in and record prices will be asked for some of these fine roses. Carnations are not at all plentiful; either they are in short supply or are being held back for the first of the week. Violets have not changed in price, neither have lilies; but there are not many in. Sweet peas bring $1 and $1.50; Paper White narcissus, $2 and $3. There are yet some chrysanthemums at from $6 to $20. Lily of the valley brings $3 and $4. Asparagus is plentiful at the usual prices. J. W. D.

PROVIDENCE, R. I.—Tea roses of the varieties grown about here are scarce, and first class stock is bringing $12 per hundred. Carnations are not plentiful by any means and sell at from $3 to $5, according to varieties and grade. Violets are of very good quality and enough are coming in for the demand, selling at $1 per 100 wholesale. Mignonette is arriving in limited quantities, bringing $3 per 100. Business is only fair at present. G. A. J.

NEW BEDFORD, MASS.—Trade the past week has been very good, with the stock supply none too plentiful. Carnations sell at 50c. and 60c.; roses, $1.50 to $2 per dozen; violets, $1.50 per hundred. Prices for Christmas will be very high, and flowers quite scarce. There is plenty of Christmas green being brought into the city. Good berried holly is scarce. Princess pine, laurel, etc., are in good supply.

The department stores here are decorating on a large scale, calling for big supplies of evergreens. HORTICO.

ROCHESTER, N. Y.—With Christmas so near every florist here has his hands full. The demand up to the present, for holly, laurel and other greens, has been above normal, and this is a general sign here of a brisk holiday business run. Although we have had no sunshine for the past three weeks, and during that interval heavy winds and cold spells, there seems to be no lack of material for the florists to dispose of. At the commission house of George Hart, news was heard of a scarcity of decorative greens, he already having sold out of his supply, 10 days ahead of last year. There is also a big demand for small palms, Boston and Scottii ferns, the same selling at fair figures. Potted plants in blossom will perhaps be the only notable thing in which the trade will be short, although of cut poinsettias there will be plenty, the J. B. Keller Sons having an entire house devoted to these latter and they are just right. Many evidences of imitation green and red articles are offered for sale, perhaps more so now than in former years. Prices at present are as for Thanksgiving, except in cases of well-grown stock which always sells the best. COCKNEY.

DETROIT.—The demand for flowers here is steadily improving, owing largely to the cold snap which Detroit has experienced. Everywhere there are evidences of extensive Christmas preparations. Carnations are still a little scarce and are cleaned up at a good price. Roses are of much better quality at present and sell readily at $6 and $8 per hundred. Violets seem to be a little scarce still.

The prospects are that Christmas stock will be very high and very hard to obtain this year, as the sun shone only four days in November, and December thus far has been little better.

Gust. H. Taepke has recently bought the land around his Elmwood plant. This land had previously been leased by him almost from the time he commenced business. HARRY.

GRAND RAPIDS, MICH. — The weather has been quite cold the past week; the rainy spell turned to snow, then the thermometer dropped to 10 degrees above zero. Business has been good, especially with the downtown stores. There are still plenty of chrysanthemums and they sell well, helping out the scarcity of carnations, particularly red and pink shades. White is in best supply. Roses are more plentiful, but at present no more than equal to the demand. Paper White narcissus and Stevia are abundant. Out-of-town demand has continued fine all through the Fall, and orders are steadily increasing in size as the season advances.

The outlook for Christmas stock is but fair. There will be the usual shortage of red carnations and roses; in fact, carnations will be awfully scarce while roses may be nearly equal to the demand. In plants there will be the usual supply of seasonable stock. G. F. C.

KALAMAZOO, MICH.—Preparations for Christmas business are chiefly occupying our Kalamazoo retailers. Holly has already arrived and appears to be of a good grade so far as I have seen, which is an item of great interest, as large numbers of wreaths are made up and sold by the florists here every Christmas. These wreaths retail at 25c. and 50c. the latter size being a double one and rather the more popular of the two. The trade in Christmas bells has largely passed out of the hands of florists although they still continue to carry several lines of them. The prospects for a very large cut of flowers are not so bright as usual, the weather having been dismal nearly all the month and not conducive to the growth of flowers. Van Bochove & Brother are expecting to cut a good crop of roses and carnations and will also have a considerable supply of pot plants for sale. Grofvert and DeSmit and also F. W. Meyers will be in well with carnations; and a few days of fine weather will doubtless do a lot to help out a decent cut with the rest of the growers.

H. Fisher will spend a day or two in Chicago picking up stock for his store here. He is employing extra help making up holly wreaths, etc., and has been successful in obtaining some extra good cases of holly.

As our townspeople are all well supplied with plenty of work, etc., there is no reason why the florists should not enjoy their share of the prosperity likewise, so a good Christmas business is confidently anticipated by all. S. B.

INDIANAPOLIS.—The general tone of the flower business last week was much like the weather—gloomy and unseasonable; stock, particularly carnations, suffered, a great deal of it being weak and soft. Much outside decorating is being done by the seedsmen, but the florists have had little for social occasions. Regular counter trade was anything but brisk, so quantities of flowers had to be disposed of in funeral work, which was heavy at times. Customers often bought plants which they meant to keep through the holidays.

Home-grown violets are not in sufficient quantity for the demand, and sales often cannot be made when customers are offered a substitute. Princess of Wales and Marie Louise wholesale at $1 to $2 per 100. Sweet peas sell well at $1 to $1.50.

Poinsettias are earlier and more generally grown this year. Vases of this Christmas flower, well grown, are displayed by the retailers; $3 to $9 a dozen is asked over the counter for them. Lily of the valley has been scarce at $4 per 100, but the deficiency will soon be met. Select mignonette is shipped in at $8 per 100. Stevia of exceptional quality is on the market at $2 per hundred sprays. Home-grown Bridesmaid and Bride of fine quality are being used exclusively at $7 to $8; Liberty and Richmond are now selling at $8 to $10, although Christmas prices of $8 to $25 per 100 took effect the middle of this week. American Beauty are retailing well at $3 to $18 a dozen. Paper White narcissus and Roman hyacinths are plentiful at $4 per 100. Carnations are more numerous than usual, and unless the weather becomes severe there will be enough during the holidays. I. B.

ST. LOUIS.—Business was reported dull the past week, but this is usually the case before the holidays. A few small wedding and some funeral orders constituted about all the business done, sufficient to use up about one-half the stock on hand. Prices were hardly up to those of last report. On Monday very little stock came in, not enough to go around, and it looks as though the growers are holding back for better prices the latter part of the week. In some cases roses have advanced; American Beauty will, by the end of the week, be at $12 per dozen for fancy long, other grades accordingly; Bride, Bridesmaid, Richmond, Killarney, Ivory will advance to at least $15 per 100 for extra fancy; firsts, $10, and seconds $6 to $8. With clear weather we should receive plenty of roses. Carnations are becoming scarce; fancy stock of Enchantress, Robert Craig, Mrs. T. W. Lawson, and Lady Bountiful will be up to $5 and $6 per 100; other grades of these at $3 and $4. California violets will go up to $2 and perhaps $2.50 per 100, and should be plentiful as they now are. Roman hyacinths and Paper White narcissus will go over $4 per 100. Extra fine Lily of the valley will be held at $5 per 100; callas, $15 to $20; sweet peas, 75c. to $1 per 100. Extra fine stevia sells at $1; cut poinsettias, $35 per 100. Smilax continues to drag at $12.50. Common ferns are up to $2 per thousand. Prices on other greens remain the same.

In Christmas greens trade is brisk; nothing is scarce except ground pine, which is up to $15 per crate. Holly is selling well, and is of fine quality and plentiful at $3.50 per case wholesale. Mistletoe is very fine also, and the market has plenty for all demands.

Very fine blooming plants are to be seen at the show houses of uptown florists, and have a big demand; those most in favor include poinsettias, grown to single stem and head, Begonia Gloire de Lorraine, very fine, cyclamen and azaleas; and all seem to be very popular with the plant-buying public. ST. PATRICK.

MINNEAPOLIS.—Business the past week, has been only fair, with the exception of funeral work, which has been quite active with a few of the dealers. Stock is coming in only fairly well, there is nothing on which there is a surplus. Good roses are cut by most of the growers; Bride and Bridesmaid seem to be of much better quality than other varieties. Richmond have not done so well up to the present time; while all of the growers have a large number there are but very few specimen blooms on the market. Killarney, and Kate Moulton appear to have done better with local growers. Carnations are about as good as in former seasons, but the cut does not appear to be very heavy. Violets are a sticker this year; very few are cultivated here and it appears that the growers who were very successful with them last year, have made a complete failure this one. There are still a few good chrysanthemums, but it is doubtful if we will have any for the Christmas trade. Lycopodium is away up, $10 per crate being the universal figure, and even at that price there does not appear to be anywhere near enough to supply the demand. The commission houses are quoting the green wreathing at $3.50 and $3.75 per 100 yards to the merchants, while the florists have no trouble in getting $4.75 and $5 per 100. There appears to be considerable wreathing, but very little lycopodium in crates. Holly is coming in nicely; the quality appears to be very good, but not any better than in previous seasons. Considerable has arrived in a frosted condition. PAUL.

FIRMS WHO ARE BUILDING.

SELINA, CAL.—T. H. Elliott is building a greenhouse 16 x 120 feet.

Wholesale Prices of Cut Flowers, New York, Dec. 19, 1906

Prices quoted are by the hundred unless otherwise noted

Roses	A. Beauty fancy—special	40.00	to	60.00
	" extra	20.00	to	25.00
	" No. 1	12.00	to	15.00
	" No. 2	6.00	to	8.00
	" No. 3	5.00	to	6.00
	Bride, Maid fancy—special	10.00	to	15.00
	" extra	6.00	to	8.00
	" No. 1	5.00	to	6.00
	" No. 2	3.00	to	4.00
	Golden Gate	3.00	to	15.00
	Richmond	3.00	to	15.00
	Mme Abel Chatenay	3.00	to	15.00
Adiantum		.50	to	.75
	Croweanum	1.00	to	1.50
Asparagus		25.00	to	50.00
	" Plumosus, bunches	8.00	to	15.00
	" Sprengeri, bunches	8.00	to	15.00
		......	to	......
Callas		10.00	to	12.00
Cattleyas		40.00	to	75.00
Cypripediums		......	to	12.00
Daisies		......	to	......
		......		......
		......		......

Carnations	Inf'r grades, all colors		2.00	to	3.00
	Standard Varieties	White	3.00	to	4.00
		Pink	3.00	to	4.00
		Red	3.00	to	4.00
		Yel. & Var.	3.00	to	4.00
	*Fancy—(*The highest grades of standard var)	White	4.00	to	6.00
		Pink	4.00	to	8.00
		Red	4.00	to	6.00
		Yel. & Var.	4.00	to	6.00
	Novelties		6.00	to	10.00
Gardenias, per doz.			9.00	to	12.00
Lilies			10.00	to	15.00
Lily of the Valley			2.00	to	4.00
Mignonette			2.00	to	3.00
Narcissus, Paper White			......	to	2.00
Roman Hyacinths			......	to	2.00
Smilax			8.00	to	12.00
Violets			.50	to	1.50
			......	to	......
			......	to	......
			......	to	......
			......	to	......
			......	to	......
			......	to	......

Wholesale Prices of Cut Flowers—Per 100

Boston Dec. 17, 1906	Buffalo Dec. 20, 1906	Detroit Dec. 15, 1906	Cincinnati Dec. 17, 1906	Baltimore Dec. 12, 1906	NAMES AND VARIETIES
50.00 to 100.00	40.00 to 50.00	... to 50.00	... to 12.00	... to ...	A. BEAUTY, fancy—special
20.00 to 50.00	30.00 to 40.00	... to 25.00	... to 10.00	... to 25.00	" extra
10.00 to 20.00	20.00 to 25.00	... to 16.00	6.00 to 6.00	12.50 to 20.00	" No. 1
... to ...	... to ...	... to 12.00	... to ...	5.00 to 8.00	" Culls and ordinary
10.00 to 25.00	4.00 to 20.00	4.00 to 8.00	... to 10.00	... to 5.00	ROSES BRIDE, 'MAID, fancy-special
5.00 to 16.00	... to 15.00	... to ...	... to 8.00	... to 4.00	" extra
4.00 to 6.00	... to 10.00	... to ...	... to 7.00	... to 3.00	" No. 1
... to ...	4.00 to 8.00	... to ...	4.00 to 5.00	... to 2.00	" No. 2
... to ...	8.00 to 15.00	4.00 to 8.00	4.00 to 10.00	2.00 to 5.00	GOLDEN GATE
... to ...	6.00 to 15.00	... to ...	... to ...	3.00 to 5.00	K. A. VICTORIA
6.00 to 25.00	10.00 to 20.00	... to ...	6.00 to 25.00	3.00 to 5.00	LIBERTY
... to ...	10.00 to 20.00	8.00 to 8.00	... to ...	3.00 to 5.00	METEOR
... to ...	10.00 to 20.00	4.00 to 10.00	... to ...	2.00 to 4.00	PERLE
... to ...	... to ...	... to 50.00	... to ...	... to ...	ORCHIDS—Cattleyas
... to ...	... to 8.00	2.00 to 4.00	... to 2.00	1.00 to 1.25	CARNATIONS Inferior grades, all colors
2.00 to 3.00	3.00 to 5.00	... to ...	... to 3.00	1.50 to 2.00	Standard Varieties White
2.00 to 3.00	3.00 to 5.00	... to ...	... to 3.00	1.50 to 2.00	Standard Varieties Pink
2.00 to 3.00	3.00 to 5.00	... to ...	... to 3.00	1.50 to 2.00	Standard Varieties Red
2.00 to 3.00	5.00 to 10.00	... to ...	... to 3.00	1.50 to 2.00	Standard Varieties Yellow and var
3.00 to 5.00	5.00 to 10.00	... to ...	6.00 to 8.00	2.50 to 3.00	Fancy Varieties White
3.00 to 5.00	5.00 to 10.00	... to ...	6.00 to 8.00	2.50 to 3.00	Fancy Varieties Pink
3.00 to 5.00	5.00 to 10.00	... to ...	6.00 to 8.00	2.50 to 3.00	Fancy Varieties Red
3.00 to 5.00	... to ...	... to ...	6.00 to 8.00	2.50 to 3.00	Fancy Varieties Yellow and var
5.00 to 6.00	... to ...	... to ...	... to ...	... to ...	Novelties
.75 to 1.00	... to ...	... to 2.00	... to 1.00	... to 1.00	ADIANTUM
... to 50.00	... to ...	25.00 to 60.00	35.00 to 50.00	25.00 to 50.00	ASPARAGUS, Plum. and Ten
... to ...	... to ...	20.00 to 30.00	... to 35.00	25.00 to 50.00	" Sprengeri, bunches
10.00 to 12.00	10.00 to 15.00	10.00 to 12.50	... to 15.00	6.00 to 10.00	CALLAS
... to ...	8.00 to 25.00	4.00 to 25.00	... to 15.00	4.00 to 25.00	CHRYSANTHEMUMS
... to ...	... to ...	... to ...	... to ...	... to ...	DAISIES
10.00 to 12.00	15.00 to 20.00	... to ...	... to 20.00	... to 12.50	LILIES
2.00 to 4.00	3.00 to 5.00	3.00 to 4.00	... to 4.00	... to 4.00	LILY OF THE VALLEY
2.00 to 4.00	6.00 to 8.00	... to ...	... to 4.00	... to ...	MIGNONETTE, ordinary
4.00 to 8.00	4.00 to 6.00	... to ...	... to ...	... to ...	" fancy
12.00 to 15.00	... to 15.00	12.50 to 15.00	... to 15.00	... to 20.00	SMILAX
.60 to .75	... to 2.00	1.00 to 1.50	... to 2.00	... to .50	VIOLETS, ordinary
.75 to 1.00	2.00 to 3.00	... to ...	... to 3.00	... to .60	" fancy
... to ...	... to .15	... to 1.25	... to .15	... to ...	GALAX LEAVES

NAMES AND VARIETIES	Milwaukee Dec. 11, 1906	Phil'delphia Dec. 11, 1906	Pittsburg Dec. 15, 1906	St. Louis Dec. 17, 1909
A. BEAUTY, fancy—special	... to 25.00	50.00 to 60.00	50.00 to 60.00	30.00 to 35.00
" extra	... to 20.00	... to ...	30.00 to 40.00	20.00 to 25.00
" No. 1	... to 18.00	... to ...	15.00 to 20.00	12.50 to 15.00
" Culls and ordinary	... to 12.00	... to ...	... to ...	5.00 to 10.00
ROSES BRIDE, 'MAID, fancy-special	... to 6.00	6.00 to 10.00	12.00 to 15.00	6.00 to 8.00
" extra	... to 5.00	... to ...	... to 10.00	4.00 to 5.00
" No. 1	... to 4.00	... to ...	... to 8.00	2.00 to 3.00
" No. 2	... to 3.00	... to ...	4.00 to 6.00	... to ...
GOLDEN GATE	3.00 to 6.00	... to ...	... to ...	2.00 to 6.00
K. A. VICTORIA	3.00 to 6.00	... to ...	4.00 to 8.00	2.00 to 6.00
LIBERTY	3.00 to 8.00	... to ...	10.00 to 15.00	... to ...
METEOR	... to ...	... to ...	... to ...	... to ...
PERLE	3.00 to 6.00	... to ...	6.00 to 12.00	2.00 to 5.00
ORCHIDS—Cattleyas	... to ...	... to 60.00	... to ...	... to ...
CARNATIONS Inferior grades, all colors	2.00 to 4.00	2.00 to 3.00	... to 4.00	1.50 to 2.00
Standard Varieties White	... to ...	2.00 to 3.00	6.00 to 8.00	1.50 to 2.00
Standard Varieties Pink	... to ...	2.00 to 3.00	6.00 to 8.00	1.50 to 2.00
Standard Varieties Red	... to ...	2.00 to 3.00	6.00 to 8.00	1.50 to 2.00
Standard Varieties Yellow and var	... to ...	2.00 to 3.00	6.00 to 8.00	1.50 to 2.00
Fancy Varieties White	... to ...	4.00 to 5.00	10.00 to 12.00	3.00 to 4.00
Fancy Varieties Pink	... to ...	4.00 to 5.00	10.00 to 17.00	3.00 to 4.00
Fancy Varieties Red	... to ...	4.00 to 5.00	10.00 to 12.00	3.00 to 4.00
Fancy Varieties Yellow and var	... to ...	4.00 to 5.00	10.00 to 12.00	3.00 to 4.00
Novelties	... to ...	... to ...	... to ...	... to ...
ADIANTUM	... to ...	... to 1.00	.75 to 1.50	1.00 to 1.50
ASPARAGUS, Plum. and Ten	25.00 to 50.00	50.00 to 75.00	40.00 to 50.00	25.00 to 40.00
" Sprengeri, bunches	25.00 to 50.00	... to 50.00	20.00 to 30.00	25.00 to 75.00
CALLAS	12.00 to 15.00	... to ...	... to 20.00	10.00 to 15.00
CHRYSANTHEMUMS	8.00 to 30.00	10.00 to 50.00	20.00 to 30.00	... to ...
DAISIES	... to ...	... to ...	... to ...	... to ...
LILIES	... to ...	... to ...	15.00 to 20.00	... to ...
LILY OF THE VALLEY	3.00 to 4.00	4.00 to 5.00	3.00 to 4.00	3.00 to 4.00
MIGNONETTE, ordinary	... to ...	... to ...	... to 5.00	... to 3.00
" fancy	... to ...	... to ...	... to 8.00	4.00 to 5.00
SMILAX	... to ...	... to ...	12.50 to 20.00	12.50 to 15.00
VIOLETS, ordinary	... to ...	... to ...	1.00 to 1.75	.40 to .50
" fancy	... to ...	... to 1.50	1.50 to 2.00	.60 to .75
GALAX LEAVES	... to ...	... to ...	... to ...	... to ...

St. Paul.

News Notes.

L. L. May & Company have arranged two handsome holiday windows with immortelles, bells, ribbons and novelties of every description. Some of their plant creations are simply beautiful and they expect to sell them in large numbers. They report the booking of a large number of orders for holly wreaths, wreathing, bells, etc.

Alfred Lemke of the new firm of Colberg & Lemke, was married last Tuesday.

August S. Swanson of the Swanson Floral Company has sold his interest in the retail department to Alfred Lemke, son of E. F. Lemke, one of our oldest florists.

Holm & Olson are making big preparations for a heavy Christmas trade.

PAUL.

Minneapolis.

News Notes.

Amundson & Kirschner are doing a very nice business; funeral work, with them the past week has been indeed heavy.

Donaldson's Glass Block are doing a heavy trade; their ice boxes are now so arranged that the firm can handle cut flowers in almost unlimited quantities.

P.

FARGO, N. D.—Two new greenhouses are wanted at the agricultural college, and Professor Waldron and President Worst are going after the legislature when it meets with the object of getting an appropriation to erect them.

Wholesale Prices of Cut Flowers, Chicago, Dec. 23, 1906

Prices quoted are by the hundred unless otherwise noted

ROSES American Beauty		
36-inch stems..........per doz.	.... to	12.00
30-inch stems .... "	.... to	10.00
24-inch stems.......... "	.... to	9.00
20-inch stems.......... "	.... to	8.00
18-inch stems.......... "	.... to	5.00
12-inch stems.......... "	.... to	3.00
8-inch stems and shorts "	.... to	2.00
Bride Maid, fancy special..........	10.00 to	15.00
" extra..........	8.00 to	10.00
" No. 1..........	.... to	6.00
" No. 2..........	.... to	....
Golden Gate..........	12.00 to	15.00
Uncle John..........	6.00 to	15.00
Liberty..........	6.00 to	25.00
Richmond..........	6.00 to	35.00
Killarney..........	8.00 to	12.00
" extra..........	15.00 to	25.00
Perle..........	6.00 to	10.00
Chatenay..........	6.00 to	20.00
Callas..........	.... to	16.00
Poinsettias..........	2.00 to	4.00
Hyacinths, Roman..........	2.00 to	4.00
....	.... to	....

CARNATIONS			
Standard Varieties	White..........	4.00 to	5.00
	Pink..........	4.00 to	5.00
	Red..........	5.00 to	6.00
	Yellow & var..........	5.00 to	6.00
*Fancy (The highest grades of Sta'd var.)	White..........	6.00 to	8.00
	Pink..........	6.00 to	8.00
	Red..........	.... to	8.00
	Yellow & var..........	.... to	8.00
Novelties..........		.... to	....
Adiantum..........		.75 to	1.00
Asparagus, Plum. & Ten..........		.35 to	.50
" Sprengeri, bunches		.35 to	.50
Lilies, Longiflorum..........		.... to	20.00
Harrisii..........		.... to	20.00
Orchids—Cattleyas..........		75.00 to	100.00
Smilax..........		.... to	12.00
Lily of the Valley..........		3.00 to	5.00
Violets..........		1.00 to	1.50
" single..........		.... to	1.00
Hardy Ferns per 1000..........		.... to	1.50
Galax "		1.00 to	1.25
Narcissus, Paper White..........		3.00 to	4.00
Chrysanthemums per doz.		2.00 to	4.00

New Orleans, La.

News Notes.

The Abele Brothers have just received word from Germany of the death of their father. They have the sympathy of all the trade in their great bereavement.

Charles Eble is well stocked with plants for the holidays. He has imported a nice lot of small spruce firs which he has potted up. People, he says, ask often for growing Christmas trees; these look very dainty. At his establishment a fine lot of Poinsettia pulcherrima, with fine well-developed bracts, which he will cut for Christmas, are seen growing out-of-doors.

At A. W. Rehm's place, corner of St. Charles and Napoleon avenue, is to be seen a fine display of plants suitable for the holidays. He is also well stocked with large palms and other plants which are used for wedding and ball decorations, etc.

George Thomas is cutting quantities of sweet peas, with fairly long stems, from out-of-doors; this is remarkable for the middle of December even for Louisiana.

C. W. Eichling's store and greenhouse, which are situated on the fashionable St. Charles avenue, are quite gay at present with Begonia Gloire de Lorraine, both the pink and light varieties, callas, and pot grown poinsettias; also fine specimens of Boston and Pierson ferns, and well grown plants of his favorite Adiantum hybridum. This latter certainly makes a fine attractive gift plant.

One of the most attractive sights in the private gardens of this city at the present time are the large plants of poinsettia. There must be thousands of them scattered throughout the city. Some of the bushes are of immense size, and the brilliant effect can be well imagined. Another very effective plant noticed by the writer was a Bougainvillea Sanderiana in full bloom climbing over the porch of a private residence.

CRESCENT CITY.

Boston.

A Trip to Madbury, N. H.

W. H. Elliott personally conducted a party of some twenty-five of the Boston storekeepers to view his large greenhouse at Madbury, N. H., on Thursday of last week. A special car carried the party in both directions and ample refreshments were served by Mr. Elliott's able assistant, A. Hutson.

This large greenhouse which the writer has formerly described in The Florists' Exchange, is in splendid condition and contains, I think, without doubt the largest number and best looking lot of Richmond roses to be found anywhere. There are twelve thousand plants of this variety grown. Killarney follows with over half that number, while other varieties grown are Wellesley, Mrs. Oliver Ames, Safrano and Bon Silene, the latter two varieties being in demand for special occasions among Boston florists. American Beauty, which it was intended to grow here and which was grown for several years, has been discarded and the space devoted to Richmond. This monster house is 812 feet long by 54 feet wide, is divided into four sections, although there are no partitions. In the first section in the front of the house are three beds of Killarney, which are very fine indeed, being just in crop. Three beds are given up to Wellesley and the other beds in this section are devoted to Mrs. Oliver Ames, Safrano and Bon Silene. In the second section Killarney is again planted at the front, seven beds being filled with it, and the back three beds with Richmond. The third section contains Killarney, in three beds, and seven beds of Richmond. The fourth section is given over to Richmond exclusively. That this latter is one of the best roses ever introduced, there is no question, and as grown here, there is nothing to equal it. The foliage is in perfect condition, the stems rigid and the flowers all that could be desired. In another house adjoining, which is later, used as a propagating house, Asparagus Sprengeri is grown, and is the strongest lot of this variety the writer has ever seen. The party arrived back in Boston in the early evening, and before the North Station was reached a rousing vote of thanks was given to Mr. Elliott for his kind and thoughtful entertainment during the afternoon.

School Gardens.

School gardens was the subject of discussion under the auspices of the Committee on Children's Gardens of the Massachusetts Horticultural Society on Saturday afternoon. H. S. Adams, chairman of the committee, presided and announced a list of prizes to be awarded for school gardens, home gardens and children's garden products by the society the coming year. The speakers were Geo. H. Martin, Secretary of the State Board of Education, who said that a school garden was the most effective laboratory that either an elementary or high school could have.

Professor F. A. Waugh of the Horticultural Department of the Massachusetts Agricultural College, spoke on horticultural education for school garden teachers; W. A. Baldwin, principal of the State Normal School at Hyannis, spoke on school gardens in normal schools and Frank M. Marsh of Fairhaven on children's gardens and the public.

E. H. Wilson, formerly plant collector for James Veitch & Sons, is visiting Boston this week. Mr. Wilson will soon go to Northern China on a collecting trip in the interests of the Arnold Arboretum.

J. W. DUNCAN.

CANADIAN NEWS

LONDON, ONT.—At J. Gammage & Sons' everything is in good shape for the Christmas trade. Begonia Gloire de Lorraine and cyclamen are about the best they have ever had. The outlook is that cut flowers will be scarce for the holidays. F. Dicks is cutting some good roses and carnations.

Gammage & Sons are building a new house, 200 x 20 feet, for young carnation stock. F. C.

TORONTO, ONT.—Business continues good with rose stock still plentiful. Chrysanthemums of good quality are still offered; all our stores have them, and prices are generally reasonable. Violets are still scarce and the demand for them is lively. Princess pine also is scarce, and from what I have heard is likely to be so for the season.

I am pleased to report that W. Jay, Jr., is recovering from his accident, and is soon likely to be around again. The doctors say, however, that he will have to be careful for some months. His father has advertised their retail store on Spadina avenue for sale, and has several offers for it. This will not limit their business much, as their greenhouses are in a fashionable neighborhood and not very far from the store.

The present indications are that cut stock for the holidays will be scarce. Plants, however, will be fairly plentiful, and the prospects for a lively business are very good.

THOMAS MANTON.

JAMESTOWN, PA.—Last week fire gutted the building used by A. R. Catlin as a seed store. His stock of seeds he says was worth about $1,000. It is practically a total loss. His insurance is $800.

Rochester, N. Y.

ade Notes.

Weather conditions the past week have been far from favorable, and zero has been reached twice. This of course has its effect on the grower and all would like to have the assistance of Old Sol for a few days, to relieve the coal bins a little.

Since Thanksgiving, the market has not been very brisk, although enough decorating and funeral work is to be had, which keeps stock moving. There has been no material advance in prices, these being as last quoted. Thanksgiving trade was good, chrysanthemums being the favorites, with a scarcity of the yellow varieties; pink and white moved slowly, the price of these being lower than for yellow.

The Vick & Hill Company has a fine addition to late pink varieties, a sport of Mrs. Jerome Jones, identical with the type, except in color, which is a very pleasing shade of light pink.

The flower department which was started in the big store here has been discontinued on account of lack of a refrigerator, or a suitable place to keep stock over night, although in the near future plans may be discussed to enable the firm to carry a full line of cut flowers and plants.

The shipments of holly that have arrived to date are in good shape, being well-berried, and of good color.

J. B. Keller Sons have the orders for the decorations at the annual dinner of Chamber of Commerce.

COCKNEY.

Los Angeles, Cal.

Trade Notes.

The Knapper family, recently from Philadelphia, Pennsylvania, have opened a flower store at 808 South Spring street. In addition to their natural flower work they carry a fine line of artificial flower designs, which is a new departure in the business in this town.

Rosa Knapper, who had been with Dreer's for several years, is now with Ethelind Lord on Third street. Miss Lord has charge, this season, of decorations at Hotel Raymond, one of the finest Winter resorts on the Pacific Coast.

A. F. Borden, for many years manager of the Redondo Floral Company store on Spring street, has gone into business for himself, opening a store at 118 West Third street.

The first of January the Orange County Nursery and Land Company of Fullerton will begin the propagation of all exotics that will grow in the open in Southern California (and the list is an extensive one), in sufficient quantities to meet the growing demands for that class of stock. Travelers who have a love for plant life have supplied their friends on this coast with seeds, roots, and cuttings of subjects from every part of the world, and now it is possible to find specimens of all these things on private grounds as well as in our public parks. Some of them, of course, are of interest only to botanists, but the great majority are cultivated for beauty or utility, in many cases both.

Rising & Dunscomb Company, Inc., have absorbed the Ocean Park Floral Company, Hollywood Rose Company, and West Park Nursery and have opened a wholesale wareroom at 205 N. Broadway. The Hollywood Rose Company had the unique distinction of sending out such varieties only as proved of value in Southern California after several years' test on their trial grounds and their catalog contains the names of but 47 varieties. The same policy will be carried out by the new management—a good idea. It will save amateurs a lot of expense and disappointment.

P. D. BARNHART.

SPOKANE, WASH.—Orlando G. Cooper, a prominent horticulturist, died on December 6, 1906, of pneumonia. He was 71 years of age. A widow and daughter survive him.

WHITE MARSH, MD.—Friends of Thomas Vincent of the firm of R. Vincent, Jr. & Son, will be pleased to learn that he is slowly improving in health; he has had a long siege of it.

Providence, R. I.

News Notes.

T. J. Johnston is out with a very swell delivery wagon, built by Monahan Bros. of this city, and lettered to artistic perfection. It will be under the guidance of Eddie O'Brien, Mr. Johnston's reliable driver.

Rennie & Thomson, seedsmen, have opened at 35 and 37 Washington street, with all the equipment of a first-class seed store.

Nelson Pierson of Norwood, R. I., is bringing in the best Princess of Wales violets seen here, and he has the knack of bunching them to perfection.

Arthur Zirkman, representing M. Rice & Company of Philadelphia, Pa., was calling on the trade here the past week.

Three of our flower store keepers have received notice to vacate their quarters soon. The owners or landlords need the stores for their own business.

Thos. Curley has been laid up the past week with a very severe cold.

Walter Mott was in town the past week.

G. A. J.

Grand Rapids, Mich.

News Items.

Eli Cross was over in Chicago last week laying in a large stock of supplies and plants so as to be able to properly meet the expected Christmas demand. Mr. Cross has a fine lot of cyclamen timed just right to hit the holidays.

Crabb & Hunter are cutting especially fine Bride and Bridesmaid roses with two to three foot stems.

Henry Smith's Estelle carnations are fine and show what can be done with this variety when well grown.

American Beauty roses are the thing just now with the Grand Rapids Floral Company.

J. A. Creelman, manager of Chadwick's flower store since it was started, has quit, and goes to Los Angeles, Cal., where he has two brothers in business. Mrs. Chadwick has, temporarily at least, assumed the management of the store.

G. F. CRABB.

Baltimore, Md.

Horticultural Society Meeting.

The ninth meeting of the Maryland State Horticultural was held in the Fifth Regiment Armory, this city, last week. The exhibits, consisting of the finest fruit and vegetables of the Maryland farms, the best products of the greenhouses and nurseries, together with the latest ideas in horticultural machinery and implements, were placed under the direction of a committee composed of Professor T. B. Symmons, of College Park, State Entomologist; C. L. Seybold and George Morrison.

The meeting was opened by Cardinal Gibbons, and Mayor Timanns delivered a speech of welcome,

Orlando Harrison, mayor of Berlin, Md., responded to the address, in the course of his remarks he said: "We tillers of the soil of the State of Maryland, produce about thirty-five million dollars annually. I claim that any State that produces so much wealth by means of its farmers and gardeners should be entitled to a building in the great central city of the State, which should be known as the Horticultural Hall. I ask here to-day that some son of Maryland donate a plot of land for this purpose, and ask the State to erect a building for the farmers, truckers and fruit-growers and centralize various office buildings of the State that are located in Baltimore city in one, which will be economy to the State and give the tillers of the soil an opportunity to put their products on exhibition in our city continually. Let us show what we can grow in this grand old State of Maryland. We spend about two and one-half million dollars with you for fertilizers and an equal portion for other necessities, and we are glad to patronize home industries.

"To the people of Baltimore city, you do not know what is in store for you in the country, nearly one-half of our great State yet undeveloped; no State in the Union can offer such varied opportunities in fruit growing as Maryland. We have the rich level land and fertile mountains. Why do you seek investments out of the State when you have greater opportunities at home for investment of capital? Why send your sons out of the State to find profitable employment when the eastern shore soil offers ample opportunities?"

The meeting put itself on record as being opposed to free seed distribution by the U. S. Government.

The decorations of the great drill hall were pronounced exquisite; thousands of palms and foliage plants, with hundreds of spruce trees ranging from 5 to 20 feet in height, were used; the galleries were festooned with evergreens, Southern smilax and bunting. Sixteen circular groups of rare exotics ranging from 10 to 20 feet in diameter were distributed in geometrical balance, giving a harmonious conservatory effect. The fruit and flower tables being lined along the sides of the promenades, the visitors were afforded the best opportunity to examine the exhibits.

The displays of Henry F. Michell Company, Philadelphia, Griffith & Turner, Bolgiano and others, were very complete and interesting. During the day many thousands of school children visited the exhibition.

The judges were Messrs. Wm. Duckham, A. Herrington, and Peter Bisset.

One of the features of the meeting was the illustrated lecture on "Forestry" delivered by Professor F. W. Besley.

The nursery exhibits of I. H. Moss, Franklin Davis and Corse Nurseries were much admired.

Messrs. Kress, Bauer, Morrison, Herman, and others of the Baltimore Florists' Club had excellent displays of cut flowers, specimen plants, and floral designs.

To General Superintendent Manning and the district superintendents of the various parks is due the credit for the elaborate decorations and successful hall arrangements.

The Park Board of Baltimore, with its officials, has taken the initiative by fostering at least one great horticultural show every year; it is to be hoped that the Baltimore Florists' Club will combine with the Horticultural Society to a still greater extent, and aid in the matter of educating the public along this particular line.

The following officers were elected, viz., president, Orlando Harrison; vice-president, C. L. Seybold; secretary and treasurer, Prof. T. B. Symons; members of the executive committee, E. P. Cohill and J. W. Kerr; county vice-presidents—Allegheny county, R. H. Gordon; Anne Arundel, L. J. S. Linthicum; Baltimore county, Richard Vincent, Jr.; Calvert county, F. O. Smith; Caroline county, J. S. Lapham; Carroll county, H. Fuss; Cecil county, C. I. Reeder; Charles county, W. H. Gray; Dorchester county, T. Harry Hopkins; Frederick county, D. H. Hargett; Garrett county, W. McCulloh Brown; Harford county, L. E. Hollingsworth; Howard county, W. S. Powell; Kent county, J. S. Harris; Montgomery county, R. Brentley Thomas; Prince George county, Dr. E. P. Magruder; Queen Anne county, W. Irving Walker; St. Mary's county, Jesse Turner; Somerset county, F. E. Matthews; Talbot county, Dr. Charles Lowndes; Washington county, A. L. Towson; Wicomico county, W. F. Allen; Worcester county, C. M. Peters.

The following are the prizes awarded for flowers:

Roses—American Beauty—First, Geo. Morrison. Red rose other than American Beauty—first, Stevenson Brothers; second, John Cook. Pink—first, Stevenson Brothers; second, John Cook. White—first, John Cook; second, I. H. Moss.

Carnations—Lawson shade—First, I. H. Moss; second, A. J. Tormey. Light pink—first, I. H. Moss. Red—first, George Morrison. Variegated—first, I. H. Moss.

Best American seedling never disseminated—first, H. Weber & Son; second, John Cook.

Miscellaneous Cut Flowers—Mignonette—first, F. C. Bauer. Cypripedium—first, George Morrison.

Flowering Plants—Begonia (not Gloire de Lorraine)—first, George Morrison, Cypripedium—first, George Morrison.

Foliage Plants—Rex begonia groups, first, George Morrison. Foliage plants (six species), first, George Morrison.

Bulbs—Best collection of bulbs and roots—first, R. Vincent, Jr., & Sons.

As a special premium for a group not entered in any class, but as having merit, the judges recommended that a first prize card be given Mr. Edward Herrmann for a group of mixed flowering plants. Special mention was made of the wreath of Camellia japonica exhibited by Mr. Kress.

C. L. SEYBOLD.

San Francisco.

Trade Notes.

Podesta & Baldochi did the decorations for the Bates-Burnham wedding. White and gold were the beautiful scheme carried out in chrysanthemums and fruits. In the drawing-room where the service was read, the hymeneal bower was modeled after the old mission style, made of palms, with the chimes done in tulle wedding bells. The dining-room was a study in golden fruits, masses of oranges and persimmons, with ferns and chrysanthemums perfecting the idea. In the reception hall bamboo was used and again masses of the golden blossoms.

The Pacific Ocean Exposition company filed this week articles of incorporation, with a stated capital stock of $5,000,000, divided into 500,000 shares of $10 each. The incorporators are R. B. Hale, I. W. Hellman, Jr., W. F. Herrin, Rufus P. Jennings, Homer S. King, Hartland Law, William A. Magee, John Martin, W. H. Metson, Percy T. Morgan, Henry T. Scott, Frederick W. Sharon, Harry L. Tevis, F. Tillman, Jr., and Charles R. Beitler, only one of whom, Harry L. Tevis, is a professional floriculturist, but the average wealth of the group is considerably over a million dollars. The incorporation articles set forth chiefly as their object the holding of an international world's fair in San Francisco in 1913, to assist in which Congress has been asked to appropriate $5,000,000.

A wind and rain storm of unprecedented severity caused an estimated million-dollar loss in San Francisco's center of temporarily built shacks during all the night of December 9 and throughout the entire succeeding day; and along the peninsula trees and buildings were blown over. The trade was not overlooked by the wild flight of the storm, many nursery trees being uprooted and many greenhouses dismantled or damaged more or less. After inspection and much inquiry the finding is that it would require an enumeration of the long list of growers on both sides of the bay to embrace all that were more or less damaged.

Santa Rosans entertained last week a large delegation of Washington, Oregon and Northern California nurserymen who stopped en route to the annual meeting at Hanford of the Pacific Coast Association of Nurserymen. Their stop at Santa Rosa was to inspect the walnut orchard of Mrs. E. M. Vrooman, which has become quite famous throughout the Northwest, and to see the "creations" of Luther Burbank, particularly his quick-growing walnut, the thornless cacti and other features.

ALVIN.

David McFarlane, Gardener to Mrs. H. Walter Webb at Scarborough, N. Y., took the trouble to write us his point of view on U-Bar houses—here is part of it: "The hundred foot house erected by you last March is a great success, both for utility and from an architectural point of view." U-Bar reasons are shown in our new catalog. Send for it. Pierson U-Bar Co., Designers and Builders of U-Bar Greenhouses, Metropolitan Building, 4th Avenue and 23d St., New York.

Not Luck or "Happen So"

has been responsible for the remarkable growth of our business and given us so large a number of satisfied customers. It is not the result of getting promiscuous orders here, there, anywhere, anyhow—all profit or no profit at all—it is clearly due to the high quality of our material and the "square deal." Please bear in mind that of the forty years we have been in this business every one has seen an increase of orders. The manufacture of greenhouse material is our whole business—not a side line. We print this in the hope that you will inquire further. Our catalogue will be sent if you are interested.

John C. Moninger Co.
CHICAGO
115 E. Blackhawk Street

THE AMERICAN CARNATION
(Price $3.50)
A. T. DE LA MARE PTG & PUB CO. LTD
2-8 Duane Street, New York.

"Always Safe and Reliable. Ask Your Friends."

The Caldwell Tank and Tower

gives a quality and reliability of service that is peculiarily satisfying to Florists and Nurserymen, who need plenty of water in hot and dry weather and who need it badly when wanted.

Tanks made from Red Gulf Cypress, the imperishable wood from Louisiana, and a tower of steel with the factor of safety great enough for every emergency, are what gives the Caldwell Outfit its reliability, its strength and its freedom from repairs.

It gives ideal service to Florists, and is highly recommended by the many using it. Illustrated catalogue and list of users in your vicinity sent on request.

W. E Caldwell Co., *Louisville, Ky.*

Tanks (Steel-Wood / Galvanized) Towers
Wind Mills—Pumps—Gas Engines

Mention The Florists' Exchange when writing.

Greenhouse Materia[l] of Louisiana Cypress and Washington Red Cedar — Hot Bed Sash

Greenhouse Hardware and Post — Patent V and U Gutters.

OUR GRADE INVARIABLY THE BEST, OUR PRICES RIGHT.

Write for Catalogue and Estimate when figuring on your new houses.

A. DIETSCH CO., 615 to 621 Sheffield Avenue, CHICAGO, ILL.

Mention The Florists' Exchange when writing.

ARE YOU GOING TO BUILD

Assure yourself of **HONEST COMPETITION** figures by obtaining an estimate from me on **Iron Frame** or **Sash bar** greenhouses. My prices are the lowest for the best class of work.

FRANK VAN ASSCHE
(FORMERLY SUPT. FOR WEATHERED)
FACTORY: Fulton and Rose Ave., Jersey City, N. J.

Mention the Florists' Exchange when writing.

THE JENNINGS IMPROVED IRON GUTTER

PATENT IRON BENCH FITTINGS AND ROOF SUPPORTS. VENTILATING APPARATUS. IMPROVED VAPORIZING PANS for Tobacco Extracts, Etc.

SEND FOR CIRCULARS — **DILLER, CASKEY & CO.** — Successors to JENNINGS BROS

S. W. CORNER SIXTH AND BERK STS., PHILADELPHIA, PA.

Mention the Florists' Exchange when writing.

GEO. M. GARLAND
Iron Gutters and Posts
Patented December 27th, 1898.
Send for Catalogue.
Garland's Gutters will keep snow and ice off your glass and prevent breakage.
DESPLAINES, ILL.

A sample of this gutter is on exhibition at Chicago Flower Growers' Market.

Mention The Florists' Exchange when writing.

WEATHERED COMPANY·

Builders of Iron and Cypress Greenhouses, Greenhouse Heating and Ventilating Apparatus.

P. O. Address, Box 789, New York City.

Mention the Florists' Exchange when writing.

PLANT CULTURE

Price, - - - $1.00.

A. T. De la Mare Ptg. & Pub. Co.
2-8 Duane St. New York.

ALL HEART

SUN DRIED CYPRESS

GREENHOUSE MATERIAL

IS THE BEST
WE HAVE LOTS OF IT
SEND FOR SKETCHES
ESTIMATES AND FREE
CATALOGUE
VENTILATING APPARATUS
HOT-BED SASH
FITTINGS &c

FOLEY MFG. Co.
471 W. 22ND ST.
CHICAGO

If you are having delay in getting your roof material, send your orders to us and don't be in trouble. We will handle any order in the time agreed. Try us.

FOLEY MANUFACTURING COMPANY
471 W. 22nd St., Chicago

Mention the Florists' Exchange when writing.

The STANDARD VENTILATING MACHINERY

The original machine with self oiling cups; the most powerful, least complicated very compact, with ease of operation.

The New Duplex Gutter over six miles in use and highly recommended; the only drip proof gutter in the market.

The standard Return Steam Trap has no equal for simplicity or its workings. Catalogue free.

E. HIPPARD, Youngstown, O.

Mention the Florists' Exchange when writing.

FURMAN BOILERS FOR GREENHOUSE HEATING

Valuable Catalogue on Modern Steam and Hot-Water Heating, mailed free upon request. Address

THE HERENDEEN MANUFACTURING CO.
203 Pearl Street, NEW YORK. Dept. F. GENEVA, N. Y.

Furman Boilers have been awarded the Certificate of Merit at Five different Florists' Conventions. Have a record of 20 years. Over 25,000 in use.

SELLING AGENT: EDW. S. DEAN, Bloomington, Ill.

Mention The Florists' Exchange when writing.

N. TONAWANDA, N.Y. — TORONTO, ONT.

KING CONSTRUCTION CO.
GREENHOUSE CONSTRUCTION AND EQUIPMENT
WRITE FOR CATALOGUE AND PRICES

WHOLESALE TRADE LIST

ASPARAGUS PLUMOSUS, 2¼ inch pots, $3.00 per 100.
ASPARAGUS SPRENGERI, 3 in. pots, $2.00 per 100.
BOSTON FERNS, 5 in. pots, 20c. 6 in. pots, 25c.
CLEMATIS PANICULATA, 4 in. pots, $1.50 per doz., $10.00 per 100; 3 in. pots, 75c. per doz.; $6.00 per 100.
DRACÆNA INDIVISA, 5 in. pots, $2.00 per doz.
HYDRANGEA Thos. Hogg, 10-12 flowering branches, $10.00 per 100; larger plants for tubs, 25c. each.
IVY, Hardy English, 4 in. pots, $1.50 per doz.; $10.00 per 100.
NEW DAISY, Queen Alexandra, 3 in. pots, $6.00 per 100. 2¼ in. pots, $3.00 per 100.
YELLOW DAISY (Etoile d'Or), 3 in pots, $6.00 per 100. 2¼ in. pots $3.00 per 100.
SANSEVIERA (Zebra plant), 4 in. pots, strong, $1.50 per doz.; 3 in. pots. $1.00 per doz.
ROOTED CUTTINGS Fuchsias, 4 varieties, single and double; Heliotrope dark blue, Salvia Bonfire $1.00 per 100, Coleus Verschaffeltii, Golden Bedder and other showy varieties 75c. per 100.
Alternantheras, best red and yellow, 50c. per 100.
Smilax 2¼ inch pots $2.00 per 100.

C. EISELE, 11th & Roy Streets, PHILADELPHIA, PA.

Mention the Florists' Exchange when writing.

SUMMER IN WINTER

BY USING

Standard Greenhouse Boilers

One cent gets our catalog.

GIBLIN & CO., UTICA, N. Y.

Evans Improved Challenge

Roller-bearing, self-oiling device, automatic stop, solid link chain make the IMPROVED CHALLENGE the most perfect apparatus in the market.

Write for catalogue and prices before placing your orders elsewhere.

QUAKER CITY MACHINE CO.
RICHMOND, IND.

HEATING
THE GREENHOUSE

thoroughly and economically during the coming Winter is the problem now engrossing the mind of the Florist who takes time by the forelock.

I am in a position to help you to the best solution of this problem, I have done it for others, I can do it for you.

It will be to your advantage to consult me and get quotations on your heating plant either erected complete or for material ready for erection.

I have the largest line of greenhouse boilers on the market and can give prompt shipments.

WRITE ME TO-DAY

John A. Payne
Horticultural Architect and Builder
33 Clendenny Ave.
JERSEY CITY, N. J.

Sash opening apparatus and all kinds of greenhouse structural material.

CYPRESS
IS FAR MO[illegible]THAN PINE
CYPRESS
SASH BARS
UP T[illegible]GER.
GREENHOUSE
AND OT[illegible]TERIAL,
MEN FUR[illegible]ERINTEND
ERECT[illegible]SIRED.
S[illegible]S.
THE A.T. S[illegible] Co.,
NEP[illegible]ASS.

THE HEADER—
OUR IRON FRAME KIND

We make it a combination drip gutter and continuous header, forming a perfect seat for the lower rail of the ventilation sash and taking care of all drip from them. The roof bars extend only to the header, where they are firmly screwed to the sash bar clasp. This arrangement overcomes the double shade of the roof bars and ventilating sash, while in no way weakening the house—a point not possible in any but our iron frame construction.

Simply another case of attention to details—not only attention but hard-sensed, practical improvements, always reducing the shade but never weakening the house.

Send for Iron Frame Catalog.

Lord & Burnham Co.

Greenhouse Designers and Manufacturers.

1133 Broadway, corner 26th St., NEW YORK.

BOSTON BRANCH, 819 Tremont Building.

Mention the Florists' Exchange when writing.

SAVE TIME AND MONEY

OUR GREENHOUSE MATERIAL

CUT AND SPLICED REQUIRE NO MECHANICS

LET US ESTIMATE ON YOUR HEATING VENTILATING APPARATUS HOT BED SASH

Putty **GREENHOUSE GLASS** Points

S. JACOBS & SONS,

1365-79 Flushing Ave., BROOKLYN, N. Y.

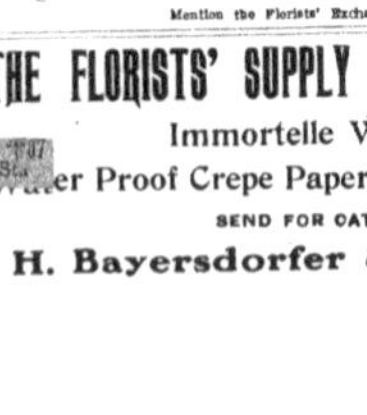

"The test of years is the real test."

Scollay Boilers

ARE BEST

See our advertisement in next issue.

Catalogues sent on application.

JOHN A. SCOLLAY,
74-76 MYRTLE AVE.,
BOROUGH OF BROOKLYN,
NEW YORK CITY.
Telephones 1492-1493 Main.
U. G. SCOLLAY, Manager.

Mention the Florists' Exchange when writing.

A. HERRMANN

Manufacturer of Floral Metal Designs

IMPORTER AND DEALER IN FLORISTS' SUPPLIES

FACTORY: 709 FIRST AVENUE, BETWEEN 40th AND 41st STREETS, NEW YORK

OFFICE AND WAREROOMS: 404, 406, 408, 410, 412 East 34th St.

WRITE FOR NEW CATALOGUE

THE FLORISTS' SUPPLY HOUSE OF AMERICA

Immortelle Wreaths,

Water Proof Crepe Paper, Red Mats for Plants

SEND FOR CATALOGUE.

H. Bayersdorfer & Co., 1129 ARCH ST., PHILADELPHIA, PA.

THE FLORISTS' EXCHANGE

We are a straight shoot and aim to grow into a vigorous plant

A WEEKLY MEDIUM OF INTERCHANGE FOR FLORISTS, NURSERYMEN, SEEDSMEN AND THE TRADE IN GENERAL

Vol. XXII. No. 26 — NEW YORK AND CHICAGO, DECEMBER 29, 1906 — One Dollar Per Year

CONTENTS AND INDEX TO ADVERTISERS, PAGE 799

Seed Trade Report.

AMERICAN SEED TRADE ASSOCIATION

Henry W. Wood, Richmond, Va., president; C. S. Burge, Toledo, O., first vice-president; G. B. McVay, Birmingham, Ala., second vice-president; C. E. Kendel, Cleveland, O., secretary and treasurer; J. H. Ford, Ravenna, O., assistant secretary.

Seedsmen will be interested in Bulletin 37, Bureau of Soils, Department of Agriculture, which treats on the subject of "Experiments in growing Cuban Seed Tobacco in Alabama."

MATTITUCK, L. I.—We hear it rumored that an important change is to take place soon in the Long Island Seed Company, that J. M. Lupton, the promoter and head of the company, is to retire, and that its business will be carried on by Messrs. Barnabas Garvey, Jr., William V. Duryee and P. Harvey Duryee.—Exchange.

IMPORTS OF SEED, ETC.—December 20.—Vaughan's Seed Store, New York, three cases. December 21—Thorburn & Company, New York, 13 pkgs. Vandegrift & Company, New York, 10 barrels. Weeber & Don, New York, one barrel. Enler & Robeson, 375 bags. To order, 93 bbls. seed; 211 bbls. roots.

December 23—McHutchison & Company, ten cases lily of the valley pips; Henderson & Company, five pkgs. seeds; to order, 153 bags clover seed; Crosby Company, 10 bags garden seeds; H. F. Darrow, 6 bbls. seed; J. Dunn, Jr., 2 cases plants; Elizabeth Nursery Company, one case plants; Henderson & Company, 250 sacks of seeds; Maltus & Ware, 18 bags seeds; 25 cases plants, 4 cases roots; McHutchison & Company, 12 cases plants; to order, 100 bags seed.

THE SEED TRADE ON LONG ISLAND.—The drummer for the seed trade this Winter will find Long Island a deserted field within a radius of twenty miles from the City Hall, New York; fully nine-tenths of the lands formerly devoted to the trucking industry have passed into the hands of the speculators for residential purposes, which takes a large proportion of land away from the market gardener. These farms are being rapidly cut up into city lots and broad streets opened up and lots sold on the installment plan, which leaves but little room for the gardener. The only land he can get is vacant lots and the lease of these is subject to their being sold, when immediate possession must be given.

The writer met one of the numerous small seed dealers a few days since whose store is within the city limit of greater New York, who usually buys about four thousand dollars' worth of seeds annually. In speaking of the conditions of trade, he said: "I shall not contract a dollar's worth of seed for another year. My customers have sold their farms at prices which have made them immensely rich, and they have retired from business. The small truckers who have in former years rented small places will continue to work along the same lines, but will be restricted in their acreages, as the owners will not rent but hold their lands for the speculator and builder."

This dealer's experience is the same as that of a score of others of the same class. What of the future? is the question. The natural conclusion would be that the trucker must go farther east on Long Island; but that is impossible, as all the lands under cultivation, within twenty-five miles, have been taken up, and beyond that the distance is too great to haul their products with horses, and the cost of transportation by rail is too heavy to be practical. At present the farmer will not avail himself of the cheap lands of Suffolk County because freight charges are excessive, and the railroad company will not reduce freights because there is so little to carry.

This condition of affairs will not injure the seed trade, as a whole, as produce will be grown somewhere, and many Long Island truckers are now looking to New Jersey for homes and business.

European Notes.

The omission of the word "pansy" from the last notes on flower seeds may puzzle some of your readers who are kindly asked to pardon a very evident lapsus pennæ.

The continuous and drenching rains previously reported have now given place to severe frost and snow which seems likely to continue. This will help us a little with belated shipments, but as the railway and steamship lines are now choked up with Christmas traffic, ordinary traders are treated with scant courtesy.

The miserable remnants of our early beet crops now coming to hand give some of us the nightmare; they certainly beat all records for poverty.

The famous cattle show in London has been held during the present week and has enjoyed the usual share of public support. The display of roots for cattle feeding made by the principal retail seedsmen of the United Kingdom has been simply grand in spite of one of the most adverse seasons on record. No novelty of any importance was exhibited.

The National Potato Society has held its annual exhibition at the Royal Horticultural Hall during the present week, and judging by the paucity of visitors has fallen on evil days. The annual meeting of the society on December 13 was anything but a happy gathering. The annual report of the committee was rejected, an unfavorable balance announced, and in the end the meeting broke up without electing any officers for the new year. The society was started when the potato boom was at its highest point; its decay is in a geat measure due to the slump in the potato market, which, as one well-known grower remarked, "fairly beat the band."

The Veteran J. Comont is back in London hale and hearty.

Alfred Watkins, who has been on the sick list for some time, is back to business once more.

S. B. Dicks, who has had a sharp attack of bronchitis, is progressing satisfactorily.

The writer most heartily wishes all his readers a Happy and Prosperous New Year. EUROPEAN SEEDS.

NOTES FROM HOLLAND. — A continuation of the most unusual Summer-like weather has marked the month of November, and not only have bulb plantings been finished under the most favorable conditions known for years but the Winter covering of bulb fields has been laid without any interruption. With the exception of a single night frost to help the leaves off the trees, fully a month later than any other year, not a single sharp frost has reminded us of the approach of Winter. However, such unusual behavior in nature has not been without effect on the bulbs that had been planted early in the season, and in many places the growth above the ground is already very considerable. Bulb sales have now come to an end and generally very little surplus stock has been left on the hands of the grower. Only the spiræa has moved slowly, but liliums and lily of the valley have sold very well and have been cleared out at satisfactory prices. Seed crops have now nearly all been harvested, and notwithstanding the fine Summer and Autumn, some crops like radish and carrots have not been up to expectation.—Horticultural Trade Journal.

GUERNSEY v. DUTCH BULBS.—I noticed some remarks in your last issue, says a correspondent of the Horticultural Trade Journal, relative to Guernsey grown bulbs in comparison with Dutch, and I am not surprised to learn there is a growing disposition on the part of English bulb buyers to discredit Channel Island bulbs because they are not so large as Dutch grown, but surely the writer only quotes a portion of the cause of the prejudice when he writes of size. In my experience Guernsey grown bulbs are súitable for two or three definite purposes, and for those purposes no finer bulbs can be obtained. Selected stocks grown in the Channel Islands for forcing for very early work are a week or so in front of Dutch given the same treatment. This is no doubt accounted for by the advantage they have in early ripening. Probably when they are lifted and warehoused the fields in Holland are still green and full of growth. Before a bulb can be forced it requires a certain amount of rest, and if by climatic or other influences it can be induced to go to rest earlier so much earlier will it force. A plain example is seen of this in Roman hyacinths: the further south they are grown the earlier will they bloom; and again, if an early ripening season occurs in Holland through hot dry weather the Dutch bulbs always force earlier. The Guernsey bulbs are also fine for a grower who wishes to plant a large quantity outside for stock purposes, for rapidly obtaining a large number of bulbs and for producing a large quantity of bloom for market.

By what I have seen on my few short visits to Guernsey, the soil is much stiffer and heavier and of a more solid nature than Holland, and also much dryer, which tends to produce a bulb smaller in size but more solid, consequently the bulb is more prone to split up and reproduce its kind. According to my observations it is when a bulb has reached its maximum of solidity that it produces an offset, and here is probably the reason why the Dutch grown attain a larger size and yet only produce one or two very large blooms; the natural damp climate an dlight moisture-laden soil grow the bulb to a great size without being correspondingly solid, consequently the largest and finest blooms are obtained from Dutch grown.

It should not be forgotten that almost all bulbs, including narcissus, are to a certain extent aquatic in their nature, consequently the Dutch conditions are the most natural and produce the finest bloom. Judging from the standpoint of size, uniform and reliable growth such as is wanted when designs in beds of private gardens are required to be laid out, and also such as are required to look well in appearance and size for shop window sale, the Dutch grown are still a long way ahead of Guernsey. The former, when used for bedding, if procured from a first-class firm, can be relied upon for every bloom of a variety to be open at the same time and practically every stalk and leaf to be the same height.

I notice that large quantities are being shipped to Holland to be "blown out"; this is just what they want, and if grown in Holland one or two years subject to the refining influence of the Dutch conditions I should imagine no better bulbs would be obtained anywhere. Stocks in Guernsey are, generally speaking, more healthy than Dutch, no fields yet being "bulb sick" as they are in some instances in Holland.

If the buyers used Guernsey bulbs for the purposes for which they are adapted, and used Dutch for the choicer retail work, the prejudice at present existing with some English growers would soon disappear.

I hear a record both in weight and value has been made in shipments to Holland this year from Guernsey which is very satisfactory to all concerned, to the Guernsey man, the Dutch grower and the final buyer in England or abroad.

National Sweet Pea Society, Eng.

Editor Florists' Exchange:

Permit me to supplement the information contained in the reports of your correspondent, "European Seeds," by a brief resumé of the proceedings of the society at its annual meeting on December 6. There was a good muster of members, and the proceedings were perfectly harmonious throughout.

The total income during the past year amounts to £379.13. 8; and after all expenses are paid, including the double schedule for the Ulverston show, there is a balance in hand of about £18. A gold medal was presented to the late secretary, H. J. Wright, and an honorarium of £25 to the present capable and very efficient secretary, C. H. Curtis.

Next in importance to the two shows (at the London show Royalty was present in the person of Princess Victoria) must be classed the extensive trials of the newer varieties at Reading under the superintendence of Charles Foster. Arrangements have been made for carrying on this work on a more extensive scale next year, and raisers of new varieties which it is proposed to put into commerce next year cannot do better than send (at once) twenty seeds of thé same to Charles Foster, Horticultural Superintendent, University College, Reading, England. The first-class certificate of the Sweet Pea Society will in future only be awarded to varieties that have been tested at Reading. A special floral committee of twelve—seven amateur and five trade growers—has been formed to adjudicate on new varieties submitted to the society, and all varieties will be presented to them under number only. An award of merit may be granted to novelties which are submitted to the floral committee on the day of the exhibition; for this award a two-thirds majority will be sufficient.

I earnestly trust, as a member of this committee, that our American friends will be represented at Reading or London, preferably at both; they will be well and properly treated.

Sir George Cowper is the new president and Leonard Sutton, of the famous Reading firm, chairman of committees. The members' roll has increased from 119 in 1901 to 465 in 1906; all parts of the civilized world are represented; every lover of sweet peas is eligible for membership, and as the members' fee, which amounts only to the moderate sum of $1.25, includes a copy of that invaluable work "The Sweet Pea Annual," tickets for exhibitions and the right to compete at them, and other valuable privileges, it is a very profitable investment. A very liberal schedule has been prepared for the 1907 show which is to be held in London on July 16. Prizes of the total value of £215.17.6 are offered for competition, and owing to the generosity of the donors of special prizes, only £50 of this sum will be drawn from the exchequer of the society.

It has been decided not to hold any provincial show during 1907, but the society has donated medals to various horticultural societies in different parts of the country in the hope that it will foster the culture and improvement of the sweet pea.

Any person desirous of joining the society should communicate with the secretary, Charles H. Curtis, Adelaide Road, Brentford, England.

S. B. DICKS.

A NEW HELIOTROPE.—The Fargo (N. D.) Forum thus describes a new heliotrope originated by A. B. Leckenby of Brighton Beach, Wash.

"This new plant was developed from the common heliotrope, being a hardy variety with heavy dark green foliage, but having instead of the typical colored blossoms, flowers of an intense dark blue color, shading to a creamy white center. The variety has still another peculiarity that is even more pronounced than its color, and that is the immense size of the blossoms, which are from two to three times larger than those of any other variety of the heliotrope. It was not until late this Fall that the true beauty of this new species was shown, when the foliage changed to a deep rich brown and the flowers became still darker.

"Leckenby, who resides at Brighton Beach and who is the discoverer of this new plant, was at one time agricologist for the State of California. Later he came to Washington as experimenter and agriculturist for the Northern Pacific railway, which installed experimental stations throughout the Northwest, and while acting in this capacity Leckenby introduced into this Northwest country many grasses and plants which were considered impossible of growth on the Pacific coast. After severing his connection with the Northern Pacific Leckenby received from the Government at Washington, D. C., a roving commission, covering all the territory west of the Cascades in which to carry on his experimental work.

"He has retired from active work and is living on his ranch at Brighton Beach, where he devotes his time to his favorite vocation."

CATALOGUES RECEIVED.

SLUIS & GROOT, Enkhuizen, Holland.—General Price List of Flower, Vegetable and Agricultural Seeds.

W. ATLEE BURPEE & COMPANY, Philadelphia, Pa.—Farm Annual for 1907; will be referred to at greater length next week.

CHARLES H. TOTTY, Madison, N. J.—Catalogue of Chrysanthemums and other Novelties. Fully Illustrated. A complete and interesting catalogue.

W. E. MARSHALL & COMPANY, New York.—Illustrated Catalogue of Seeds, Bulbs, Plants, and Garden Requisites, with an interesting list of Novelties.

MOREHEAD MANUFACTURING COMPANY, Detroit, Mich.—Catalogue giving full information regarding the Morehead Fitting Return Steam Trap, a device that is meeting with much favor among greenhouse men.

California Plant Notes.

Bailey says, "In the American tropics Monistera deliciosa requires a very warm, moist climate for the production of fruit." Experience with this magnificent plant about Los Angeles does not harmonize with that statement. Grown on the north side of the residence of Mr. Homer Laughlin, and well fed, it thrivés luxuriantly. Under a large ficus tree at Singleton Court, in dense shade, it grows with less vigor, perhaps because not so well fed; while the one grown in full sunlight in an angle of The Holleubeck Home, with a southeast exposure, bears more fruit than both the others combined. When the temperature went up to 110 one day in September and the humidity down to 25 per cent., which a few days afterward dropped to 7 per cent., some of the foliage was slightly browned. The fruit on the last named plant began to ripen November 1 from bloom of a year ago. The plant is now in flower, the blossom being curious as well as beautiful, and will so continue until next May. The one grown in the dense shade of the ficus never ripens its fruit; nor does it bloom profusely. The temperature has been as low as 6 below freezing during the outdoor life of these plants, yet they have not been injured, although without any other protection than the tree and buildings afforded.

Bougainviellea interia now coming into bloom, is one of our most attractive climbers. This plant resisted all attempts of propagators about Los Angeles to root cuttings, until this season one of our progressive, persistent firms went at the work in a proper way, and the result is several thousand fine young plants, which sell as soon as large enough to set out, for from $3.50 to $5 each.

B. glabra is a perpetual bloomer here, while B. spectabilis, or splendéns, flowers but once—from March to May. But a well fed plant when in flower, against a background of evergreen trees with dark green, glaucous foliage, is the queen of flowering climbing plants in South California.

Dahlia imperalis is now in its glory. There are two varieties in cultivation—a white and a light lavender colored one. This stately plant, if given plenty of fertilizer and not too much water and plenty of room for development, grows to an immense size in this part of the state—18 to 20 feet high, with a trunk at the base of 12 inches and a spread of top 8 feet with hundreds of pendants, bell-shaped flowers open at once. It is a beautiful sight.

A variety of hemerocallis, the specific name of which the writer is unable to learn, is now coming into bloom and will continue to flower in great profusion until next May. The color is that of H. flava, the petals more pointed, and the flower odorless. It is one of our most desirable Winter-blooming herbaceous plants.

The low temperature which prevailed here the last half of November so thoroughly chilled the poinsettias that the crop of bracts will be very small. Last season they did no better for the same reason, but for several years previous climatic conditions were such that the plants were a blaze of glory; and being easily propagated every one put in cuttings in abundance, only to meet with disappointment at flowering time. At the Hollenbeck Home there are 3,000 poinsettias growing, and when at their best they are a dazzling sight. Two years ago the bracts measured 18 inches across.

Eucalyptus robusta, now in bloom, is one of the most beautiful evergreen trees. The dark green foliage, of large size, on dark red branches, forms a fine background for the great profusion of white, silk-like tassel flowers. The seed vessels of this variety are set so thickly on the branches and become so heavy that they break the branches and mutilate the tree unless they are cut off immediately after flowering.

I have a young plant propagated from a vine of Vitis heterophylla, which shows no variegation in the foliage, although care was taken in selecting the cutting to get the best marked leaves. Is the variety a species or a sport, and has my plant reverted to the original? Who knows?

P. D. BARNHART.

NURSERY DEPARTMENT.

Conducted by Joseph Meehan.

AMERICAN ASSOCIATION OF NURSERYMEN' Orlando Harrison, Berlin, Md., president; J. W. Hill, Des Moines, Ia., vice-president; George C. Seager, Rochester, N. Y., secretary; C. L. Yates, Rochester, N. Y., treasurer.

WESTERN ASSOCIATION OF NURSERYMEN.—The seventeenth annual meeting of this association was held at Kansas City, December 18 and 19. A number of interesting papers were read.

BILLINGS, MONT.—Tighe & McDonald, of the Montana Nursery Company, Missoula, Mont., are making preparations to install a nursery here. They have just purchased 100 acres of land on the big flat near Billings as a site for the nursery and are also making arrangements to erect a warehouse and packing plant. The cost of this plant will be more than $10,000.

TIME TO SOW TREE SEEDS.—Below we give a list of trees. Please tell us through your valuable paper which of the seeds of these trees should be planted during the Winter in a greenhouse, and which should be left until Spring and planted in the open ground. Please give a hint or two as to soil, depth to plant, temperature, etc. The list follows: Abies balsamea, A. concolor, A. Douglasii, A. Nordmanniana, A. sibirica, Chamæcyparis Lawsoniana, Juniperus virginiana, Picea alba, Picea excelsa, Pinus austriaca, Pinus Strobus, Pinus Strobus nana, Pinus sylvestris, Taxus baccata, Thuja occidentalis, Tsuga canadensis, Picea pungens (Koster's), Acer campestre, Acer platanoides, Acer polymorphum atropurpureum? A. B. D & SON.

—There is no reason why all of the seeds named should not be sown in a greenhouse if suitable. Shallow boxes of a size 18 x 18 inches and of a depth of 4 inches, are suitable for use. Sow in January, the seedlings should appear in a month's time. A good rule for covering seeds is to cover them with soil to about their own size. Thus a seed one-eighth inch thick should have one-eighth inch of soil over it. Glass or some covering placed over the boxes after the sowing is well. It keeps moisture in the soil and keeps the soil dark as well, both of great help to the seeds. But little heat is required the first two weeks, as the seeds are absorbing moisture then, but afterwards a temperature of from 50 to 60 degrees in the house would suffice.

When conveniences are at hand better success usually follows the sowing of seeds indoors than outdoors, the elements being under control and the seeds where they can be watched. But all may be sown outside, doing the work the first thing after the ground is in proper condition in the Spring. Should it be decided to follow outside sowing, the acers should be mixed with damp sand now and put in a cold place where they will not vegetate, for kept dry all Winter they will not grow in Spring. One thing more: Seeds of Juniperus virginiana will not grow under a year. Keep them in a pot, or box, mixed with soil and set them outdoors, sowing them next Fall. J. M.

California Fruit Growers in Convention

The thirty-second annual convention of Fruit Growers, the fifth under the auspices of the California State Commission, opened at Hanford, Cal., on December 4, lasting four days. President Elwood Cooper occupied the chair, opening the proceedings, and there was a large attendance. Mayor H. A. Beekhuis welcomed the visitors in a neat speech. In the course of his address President Elwood referred as follows to the scarcity of labor:

"The most serious problem that confronts the fruit grower is labor. Without greatly increased numbers the present area that is planted to fruits cannot be properly managed. California cannot progress without an increased number of workers. We had immigration last year on these Atlantic shores of 1,100,000—and of a class that involves a heavy tax to care for, while the best workers for California are excluded without any organized plan for supplying others. Further planting of fruits should be discouraged."

Governor Pardee then made a telling address.

A number of interesting papers were presented, among them one on "The Growing and use of Eucalyptus," by Dr. W. H. Miller. He advised buying young plants from some reliable nurseryman, rather than to undertake growing from seed.

The second day of the convention was given over to the Pacific Coast Nurserymen's Association, the session being presided over and opened with an address by President F. W. Power, whose talk covered the subject of nursery stock and inspection. H. C. Rowley spoke on "The Fruit Grower's Aim"; Leonard Coates on "The Nursery Business in California," and J. B. Pilkington on "European Methods." Professor E. J. Wickson gave a talk on "Fruit Varieties," and P. H. Dorsett one on "Introductions at Plant Introduction Garden" at Chicago. The latter addressed covered the introduction of new and untried varieties of fruits, nuts, and beans, some of which are adapted to the desert regions, and all of which have a commercial value.

A banquet was given to the visitors in the evening, being largely attended.

In an address on the subject of "Relation of the Nurserymen to the Grower," A. N. Judd said:

"I would enact a law which places a fine for selling unclean trees or those not true to name; this fine I would make equal to the cost of the tree sold, the cost of cultivation, the rent of land, damage to the land for like product (as no apple will grow where one grew before), and the loss of profit that should accrue during the time before the discovery of the criminal mistake was made. It seems to me that the longer the average nurseryman is in business the less interest he takes in the betterment of our fruits, and the more certain he is to combat discoveries, or I might say rediscoveries, which the energetic orchardist makes by reading up or by experiment."

The convention went on record, by adopting a resolution, against the free distribution of seeds by the Government, being of the opinion that "much more good would result if this money was used to aid the Department of Agriculture and the State Experimental Stations in the securing, growing and distributing of rare and valuable seeds and plants,

Thuja Occidentalis Aurea.

which might prove of economical and commercial value to the people of the United States."

They also favored the adoption of a parcels post in the United States.

Horticultural Notes.

The Golden chestnut of California is Castanea chrysophylla. It is called golden because of the appearance of the under side of the leaves when the wind blows. It will endure some 10 degrees or more of frost, rendering it a good shrub for the Southern States.

Why rhododendrons are often disappointing is because of being in limestone soil or where lime is. Sometimes when near dwellings that have been plastered there is lime in the soil. If this is suspected, the soil should be thrown out and fresh light loam or peaty soil substituted for it.

Consular report says the Bavarian farmers note with satisfaction that mistletoe, Viscum album, formerly "a dreaded parasite" on apple trees, has been gradually decreasing by the use of it for Christmas decoration—"a custom lately introduced into Germany."

Bambusa Metake is considered hardy in the vicinity of New York City in ordinary situations, but when subjected to severe cold and high winds its foliage becomes badly browned. A good place for it is in a partly open wood. In such a situation the little protection it gets from the surrounding trees prevents the loss of its bright green foliage.

Pyracantha seeds require a full year in the ground before sprouting. They are best kept in boxes of soil for a full year and then sown. This obviates the using of a bed for them a whole season for nothing, with the labor of weeding, etc., added.

Winter pruning has a tendency to make weak trees and shrubs grow stronger. Wherever a shoot is cut back a new one stronger than before may be confidently looked for. It adds but little to the bushiness of what is pruned. Bushiness is better obtained by Summer pruning.

A writer who has been in Japan mentions Euonymus radicans as having scarlet berries. It has not been our fortune to see it produce any berries here, numerous as are the specimens of it in various situations. In Japan it is said to ascend to the tops of the tallest trees.

Propagating Hawthorns.

This is the season for the securing of hawthorn berries. They hang on the trees until late in the Winter. To increase stock of them the berries are gathered and mixed with damp sand, in which they can stay until Spring if desired. But many prefer to wash them free of pulp after they have been in the sand for a few weeks, when the pulp is rotten, and then replace them in fresh, clean sand, there to remain until Spring, when they should be sown. It is not always that they grow the first year; they often lie in the ground a whole season before sprouting. All the species are grown in this way, but the colored and other varieties are increased by budding or grafting, budding chiefly, on the common stocks. The English, oxycantha is mostly used, but for all sorts our own wild kinds are good, and for varieties of our native sorts such stocks are to be preferred. One reason for the choice of our own species for stocks is, that they are free from the attacks of borers, which cannot be said of the oxycantha, as it is well known to be often killed by borers in the collar of the plants.

Thuja Occidentalis Aurea.

Our native Arbor vitæ is well known as among the most useful of all our wild evergreens. As an ornamental tree it is to be found on everyone's grounds where there is room for an assortment; and then for hedging or screening purposes it has no equal. And it is not only in its own country that it is so esteemed; in the lists of foreign nurserymen it is given a prominent place.

The illustration herewith is of one of its most charming varieties, the golden one known as the George Peabody Arbor vitæ, and which in catalogues that give botanical names will be found under the head of Thuja occidentalis aurea.

This golden American Arbor vitæ is a valued sort for all plantings where an evergreen of its habit of growth and a golden foliaged one is required. Our picture shows a single tree, with no others near it, but it is one of many grouped behind it, forming in all a background to a driveway, the evergreens being the boundary of the pleasure grounds. This specimen was photographed in Midsummer, and it was then a lovely sight. The golden ends of the foliage contrasted nicely with the green foliage behind it; and the whole specimen was well set off by the green sward in which it stood.

We think a great deal of this Arbor vitæ. There are other golden-edged ones, but none the equal of this. Very often golden forms will appear in a bed of seedlings and sometimes a shoot of golden color will be noticed in a large specimen, and whoever finds such a sport should watch it and propagate it, if it promises anything different from what we already have.

There is another golden-edged one, which was found in the Meehan nurseries some years ago, and which is called Meehani. So far as the golden color is concerned, it is not as good as the one we illustrate, the George Peabody. But it makes a desirable variety, especially as it has not the usual Arbor vitæ shape. A specimen of it as tall as the one of our illustration would be very much broader at the base than the latter.

There is a variety of the American Arbor vitæ with silver tips instead of golden. It is called Victoria. It makes an interesting variety, but not so much so as the golden ones, and, further than this, as the specimens get large they appear to lose a good deal of their variegation. The specimen photographed is a fair sized one, as those familiar with Arbor vitæ know, and we but wish that its beauty in gold and green could be portrayed in the picture.

It may not be generally known that the American Arbor vitæ and its varieties do not succeed well in the South, at least not nearly so well as the Chinese Arbor vitæ does. In the sandy soil of Southern New Jersey and along the coast in Delaware it does well. Some of the prettiest hedges of it we ever saw are in the part of New Jersey mentioned. But when it comes to the still warmer States, the Chinese is the one to plant. It is far superior there to the American.

When the George Peabody Arbor vitæ is grown in pots or tubs it makes an excellent decorative plant, and we really think it has then a deeper yellow-edged appearance than when grown as a lawn specimen. JOSEPH MEEHAN.

Boxwood Exhausted

Manetti, for grafting, 3-16 to ¼ inch, $10.00 per 1000.
Manetti, for grafting, 2-16 to 3-16 inch, $7.50 per 1000.

HIRAM T. JONES, Union County Nurseries, Elizabeth, N. J.

Mention the Florists' Exchange when writing.

KOSTER & CO.

Hollandia Nurseries BOSKOOP, HOLLAND

Hardy Azaleas, Box Trees, Clematis, Conifers, Hydrangeas, Peonies.
Pot-Grown Plants for Forcing.
RHODODENDRONS, H. P. ROSES, Etc.
Catalogue free on demand.

Mention the Florists' Exchange when writing.

ROSES

CRIMSON RAMBLER, DOROTHY PERKINS, and other leading climbers. BABY RAMBLER, Hybrid Wichuraiana, Hybrid Sweet Briar, Hybrid Rugosa and Hybrid Perpetual. Large assortment of varieties, fine stock and reasonable prices. Send for catalog or trade list.
BAY STATE NURSERIES, North Abington, Mass.

Mention the Florists' Exchange when writing.

F. & F. NURSERIES

SPRINGFIELD NEW JERSEY

Wholesale Growers — TREES AND PLANTS in full assortment. Trade Catalogue Free

MANETTI STOCKS

Especially for Florists' use. Best French Grown.

Grafting Size, 3 to 5 m-m., per 1000 .... $7.00; per 10,000 .... $65.00
First Size, 5 to 10 m-m., per 1000 .... 9.00; per 10,000 .... 80.00

Newark prices. DUTY PAID. For prompt delivery, order now and avoid disappointment.

ROSES, two years, field-grown, well-rooted

DOROTHY PERKINS .... per 100, $8.00
CRIMSON RAMBLER .... per 100, 10.00
HYBRID PERPETUALS, in good assortment, per 100, $10.00 to $12.00.

Send for our Wholesale Price List of Roses, Clematis, Flowering Shrubs, Conifers, Etc.

JACKSON & PERKINS CO., NEWARK, NEW YORK. (Wayne County.)

Mention The Florists' Exchange when writing.

P. OUWERKERK

216 Jane Street
WEEHAWKEN HEIGHTS, N. J.
P. O. No. 1, Hoboken, N. J.

JUST RECEIVED FROM OUR HOLLAND NURSERIES

Rhododendrons, Azaleas, Spiræa Japonica, Lilium Speciosum, Peonies, Bleeding Heart, Pot-Grown Lilacs, Hydrangea in sorts, Clematis and H. P. Roses in the best sorts.

PRICES MODERATE

SEND TO

THE MOON COMPANY

For Your { TREES, SHRUBS, VINES and SMALL FRUITS

Descriptive Illustrated Catalogue Free
THE WM. H. MOON CO. Morrisville, Pa.

Specimen Nursery Stock

DECIDUOUS TREES and SHRUBS, EVERGREENS, RHODODENDRONS, AZALEAS, over one hundred (100) acres of the choicest varieties.
Send for price list.

COTTAGE GARDENS COMPANY
QUEENS, LONG ISLAND, N. Y.

Holland Nursery Stock

Ask for Our Catalogue. It will interest you.

ENDTZ. VAN NES & CO. BOSKOOP, HOLLAND

LARGE TREES

OAKS AND MAPLES
PINES AND HEMLOCKS
ANDORRA NURSERIES
WM. WARNER HARPER, PROPRIETOR
Chestnut Hill, Philadelphia, Pa.

Mention the Florists' Exchange when writing.

EBBINGE & VAN GROOS

Formerly THE HORTICULTURAL CO.
BOSKOOP, HOLLAND

Hardy Nursery Stock, such as H. P. Roses, Rhododendrons, Azaleas, Clematis, Buxus, Choice Evergreens, Peonies, etc.
Ask for Catalogue.

H. DEN OUDEN & SON,

BOSKOOP, HOLLAND.

Wholesale growers of nursery stock for the American trade. Catalogue free on demand. Also views in our nurseries.

Large Stock of

PEONIES, M. L. RHUBARB LUCRETIA DEWBERRY

Write for Prices
GILBERT H. WILD, Sarcoxie, Mo

Trees and Shrubs

We make specially low prices on nursery stock to Parks, Cemeteries, etc.
Wholesale price list on application.
We carry immense quantities of the finest named varieties of peonies.

PETERSON NURSERY
505 W. PETERSON AVE. CHICAGO, ILL

Not a bloomin' thing

but *roses* to offer you

101 best sorts. Own roots. 2 1-2 and 4 in.
Get our price list. Send your want list

THE LEEDLE FLORAL COMPANY, SPRINGFIELD, OHIO.

Mention the Florists' Exchange when writing.

Beautiful New Pink Rose

"Aurora"

See announcement and full description in Florists' Exchange, Dec. 8 issue.

PAUL NIEHOFF, Lehighton, Pa.

Mention the Florists' Exchange when writing.

Special HEDGE PLANTS Best Varieties

CALIFORNIA PRIVET — DEUTZIA PRIDE OF ROCHESTER — NORWAY SPRUCE
BARBERRY THUNBERGII — TARTARIAN HONEYSUCKLE — AMERICAN ARBOR VITÆ

Full assortment of Ornamentals, Fruits, Roses, Clematis, Vines, Peonies and Herbaceous Plants.

Write for our fall wholesale trade list.

W. & T. SMITH CO., GENEVA, N. Y.

Mention the Florists' Exchange when writing.

Roses! Dahlias! Cannas! Violets!

Miscellaneous Plants!

Roses. We have in stock upwards of 1000 different varieties, consisting of the very latest European varieties, as well as all the leading varieties of American origin. Stock from 2½ and 4 and 5 inch pots, all on own roots. Ask for catalogue.

Dahlias. 25 leading varieties, all under name, guaranteed true, including the best sorts in cultivation, such as Admiral Dewey, Constancy, Gloriosa, Orange King, Prof. Baldwin, Maid of Kent, C. W. Bruton, and Uncertainty. Field clumps as dug, $5.00 per 100; $45.00 per 1000. Catherine Duer, field clumps, $8.00 per 100.

Cannas. 40 leading varieties. $10.00 per 1000 and upwards. Write for list and prices.

Violets. Lady Hume Campbell, Princess of Wales, Swanley White, Admiral Avellan and Luxonne, nice strong plants, from 2½ inch pots, $3.50 per 100; $30.00 per 1000.

Miscellaneous Plants

Ampelopsis Veitchii, nice strong two-year-old field-grown plants, per 100, $6.00, per 1000, $55.00.
Clematis Paniculata, two-year-old field-grown stock, strong plants, per 100, $7.00, per 1000, $65.00.
Cissus Discolor, nice plants, from 2½ inch pots, per 100, $4.00.
Cyperus Gracilis, from 2½ inch pots, per 100, $3.50.
Asparagus Sprengeri, from 2½ inch pots, per 100, $4.00.
Asparagus Plumosus, from 2¼ inch pots, per 100 $4.00.
Weeping Lantana, from 2½ inch pots, per 100, $3.50.
Viburnum Plicatum and a complete list of hardy shrubs, vines and miscellaneous plants of all kinds. Send us your list for prices. Ask for catalogue—it's free. Address.

The Dingee & Conard Co., Rose Growers, WEST GROVE, PA.
Established 1850 — 70 Greenhouses

Mention The Florists' Exchange when writing.

NEW DEPARTURE IN GRAFTING ROSES

SCIONS TO BE FURNISHED BY THE CUSTOMER.

If you are planning to use any quantity of Roses the coming season, write to us for prices. We cannot get enough wood from our plants for all of our orders, but our facilities for grafting are first-class. Write for prices.

EDW. J. TAYLOR Southport, Conn.

GRAFTED ROSES

Fine Stock from 3-in. pots.
Richmond, $2.50 per doz., $15.00 per 100, $125.00 per 1000.
Killarney, $2.00 per doz., $15.00 per 100.
Etoile de France, $3.00 per doz., $18.00 per 100.
Kaiserin, Carnot, Uncle John, Chatenay, $2.00 per doz., $15.00 per 100.
Bridesmaid, Golden Gate, Wootton, $2.00 per doz., $12.00 per 100.

ROSES OWN ROOTS

Fine Stock from 3-in. pots.
Richmond, $10.00 per 100; $90.00 per 1000.
Etoile de France, $12.00 per 100.
Sunrise, Perle, Sunset, Chatenay, $8.00 per 100.
Bridesmaid, Golden Gate, $7.00 per 100.
Asparagus Plumosus Nanus from 3-inch pots, $8.00 per 100; Sprengeri from 3-inch pots, $6.00 per 100.

Send for Catalogue.

WOOD BROS., Fishkill, N. Y.

Mention The Florists' Exchange when writing.

New Pink Rose

Miss Kate Moulton

Is the QUEEN of all Pink Roses
Write us about it
Minneapolis Floral Co., - Minneapolis, Minn.

Mention the Florists' Exchange when writing.

ROSES

EXTRA HEAVY IMPORTED HYBRID PERPETUALS
in all leading varieties, per 10 $1.50, per 100 $12.50
CRIMSON RAMBLER .... " 15.00
BABY RAMBLER .... " 17.50

PERENNIAL GARDENS CO., - TOLEDO, O.

American Beauties

We have them. You want them. We are booking orders for early delivery. Fine stock. Write us for price.

ALDRICH FLORAL COMPANY, 26 E. High St., SPRINGFIELD, O.

Mention the Florists' Exchange when writing.

DAHLIAS

Now is the time to place your order for Bulbs which will insure you getting named varieties in any quantity; delivery to be made this fall or early spring.

DAVID HERBERT & SON,
Successors to L. K. PEACOCK, Inc.
ATCO, N. J.

Mention the Florists' Exchange when writing.

THE AMERICAN CARNATION
Price $3.50. Send for Sample Pages
A. T. DE LA MARE PTG. & PUB. CO., Ltd., 2-8 DUANE STREET, NEW YORK

LIST OF ADVERTISERS

INDEX TO STOCK ADVERTISED

Contents.

PAGE

Boston.

News Notes.

Robert Cameron of the Harvard Botanical Gardens sailed on the Admiral Sampson for Jamaica on Wednesday. Mr. Cameron is on a plant collecting trip to the West Indies for the Harvard experimental station at Solidad, Cienfuegos, Cuba.

Daniel Iliffe is doing the piping and iron work for Don the florist at Beverly Farms in a house he is rebuilding for Summer use.

R. & J. Farquhar & Company are now American agents for Fisher, Son & Sibray of the old Handsworth Nurseries, Yorkshire, England, making a specialty of specimen trees and shrubs.

The landscape gardening classes of the Gardeners and Florists' Club meet now regularly every Tuesday and Friday evening.

J. K. M. L. Farquhar will give a talk on "Southern Europe" at the next meeting of the Gardeners and Florists' Club, which will be Ladies' night.

W. N. Craig is more proud of his Christmas present than any of the boys. 'Twas twins; all doing well.

J. W. DUNCAN.

Chicago.

News Items.

Out on Bowmanville avenue Fred. Weber conducts one of the most successful American Beauty ranges in Chicago. We are pleased to note that on Friday last the stork delivered a boy at the house, making the third in line to carry on the good work.

Lacy Young of the Deamud Young Fern Company was in town during the holidays helping out at headquarters. He reports that early snow and cold weather have considerably impeded their work in the woods.

ROCHESTER, N. Y.—The distinctive new feature of the Christmas trade was the sale of partridge berries in globes. They sold at $1.50 to $2.50, according to size, and all the florists who had them sold out. The volume of business was the greatest ever known here, and the prices were satisfactory. Most dealers say that there was a noticeable increase in the sale of potted plants, though cut flowers sold so well that several dealers were entirely cleaned out. Roses went readily at $4 to $6 a dozen and American Beauty brought from $9 to $24 a dozen. One house that had some extra fine chrysanthemums sold them at $10 a dozen. There was an abundance of carnations at $1 to $2 a dozen and plenty of violets at $4 a dozen. In potted plants poinsettias, begonias and azaleas sold in about the order named. Plant baskets, some running as high as $10 or $15, sold on a more liberal scale than usual. There was plenty of holly at the usual prices; but ground pine and roping were difficult to get at the last. C. R. W.

FIRMS WHO ARE BUILDING.

MOUND CITY, ILL.—Henry Hillerich recently added a modern greenhouse to his plant.

TRAVERSE CITY, MICH.—Frank M. Paine contemplates doubling his greenhouse capacity.

OAKLAND, R. I.—Amos Darling recently completed another large greenhouse and is now installing a hot water heater. He will use this house to raise cucumbers for the market.

CALENDARS RECEIVED.

ARCHIAS SEED STORE, Sedalia, Mo.

Correction.

Through an error made in the telegraph office some stock was advertised by Godfrey Aschmann, on page 770 of our last week's issue, that should have been omitted, as he was entirely sold out, particularly begonias, Jerusalem cherries and cocos.

THE WEEK'S WORK.

Timme's Timely Teachings.

Cinerarias and Calceolarias.

A cold house, such as I have described in these columns some time ago, is now the proper place for much of the stock held in readiness for Spring sales. Needless here to enumerate all the different kinds of stock that would at this season greatly be benefited by being kept in a cold house until about the beginning of February. But cinerarias and calceolarias belong to a class of plants that are positively injured by being kept in the warmth of an ordinary greenhouse. It will not kill them, of course, but they will not be the grand plants at Easter or in late Spring the grower had in mind when he started the seeds. The grower of a miscellaneous collection of stock labors under difficulties if he has no cold house, more so than if he had no hot-house. I might have used the term cool instead of cold, but feared to be misunderstood. A temperature of 55 degrees is considered cool for many things we grow, while it is altogether too hot for others, certainly so for cinerarias and calceolarias. These now fare best in a temperature a few points above freezing, in a house coming nearer to being cold than simply cool.

The plants should now be held a little on the dry side, with just moisture enough at the roots to keep up sprightly freshness. They will need a little water now and then, for they are not resting, but what growth they make will be strong and solid, while, if made in warmer quarters, it would be flabby, long-jointed and preyed upon by hordes of greenfly in spite of all precautions. It is well to place the plants on the best lighted bench, close to the glass, with plenty of space between them.

Geraniums.

Now when chrysanthemums are all gone and Christmas trade also has caused a perceptible clearing out of stock, it is time to remind the grower of bedding plants that nothing is more detrimental to perfect development in the growth of geraniums than crowded quarters. And the most harm from this cause is done before the plants receive their first shift, which, in most instances, is seldom given before February. On many places more geraniums are grown than there is room for, and it is not until almost Spring before they are afforded anything like decent treatment. The question here is pertinent. Does it pay better to raise a lot of well-cared-for and superbly done geraniums or twice and thrice as many, poorly finished and altogether unfit to stand any show against the other in a locality where keen competition rules? I cannot answer this question, for I have never tried both ways. But I abhor any kind of mediocre measures in the culture of anything grown for profit, and it is likely that in this respect I am yet a trifle out of date. For several seasons now I have sold geraniums, 4-inch, in bloom, at $10 per 100 wholesale and at from $1.50 to $2 per dozen retail, and sold out clean every Spring. I can grow them for that and accord them the same good treatment as any other, often less profitable crop. I have now for years practised both the one shift and the two and three shift course of growing geraniums into salable stock of the 4-inch market size. The first lot, propagated in September and at once put into 2-inch pots, will now go into 3-inch and in March into 4-inch pots, after which they will not be cut back any more. This is the main lot, but I propagate geraniums right along until the end of January, these last making good 3-inch stock for shipping in early Spring. Those propagated quite late in the Fall are rooted in the sand, potted up into 2 1-2-inch pots and in February or March into the regular 4-inch size. These are, as far as their value for bedding out is concerned, fully as good as those propagated in September and shifted twice, but they bring less money wholesale as well as retail; still, since they cost less to produce, they are about as profitable as the others. I also sell a good many 5 and even 6-inch geraniums every Spring, in fact all the year around, at prices which I consider ample recompense for the extra shift and room required in their care.

Having thus dwelt at considerable length on my own ways of doing things, I think I have best served the purpose of imparting information to those new in the plant business. At the same time I have shown that I practise what I preach, a sort of coincidence not over-prevalent everywhere.

There can be no doubt that geraniums lose most in commercial value at that period intervening between the time they fill their first pot with a dense network of roots and their next shift into larger pots. It is then when they are packed closest, usually occupying some out-of-the-way spot, and when the grower finds least time to give them proper attention, knowing that they of all others can bear a lot of hardship and confident that they will easily live through it. But if he is wise he will now give them a good overhauling, a cleaning, pinching back, repotting and resetting on a bench, with all the light possible, and traversed by the currents of fresh air on fine days. Good, rich compost, somewhat sandy, should be used for this shift and ordinary, rather heavy potting soil for the last transplanting in early Spring. From now on geraniums must not be allowed to stand still in their growth for the want of water, but must be kept on the go right along until they have filled their last pot with roots. Holding them then a little on the dry course will throw them into profuse bloom, should they evince any reluctance in forming buds. Right after transplanting they want water but sparingly, but after the new break is well forward they call for as much as most other stock, and should have it. Geraniums can get nicely along without sprinkling of foliage, but occasionally, on bright mornings, a good spraying seems to make them appear thriftier. When in bloom all sprinkling overhead should be omitted. A temperature of 55 or 58 degrees at this time is about right.

Reminders.

Growers with more bench room at their hands than they know what to do with—there are such cases—should now plant sweet peas. It is not too late for the securing of an immense crop of flowers in early Spring. On benches with too little headroom for peas a continuous crop of pansy flowers for Winter picking might easily be raised. Early sown and now thrifty plants will do for the purpose.

The seeds of verbenas, lobelias, daisies, pansies and snapdragons for Spring trade should now be sown.

Cuttings of swainsona for Summer blooming indoors can now be put in the sand, as also of Begonia semperflorens, salvia and double petunia for the bedding trade.

FRED W. TIMME.

Rooting Cuttings of H. P. Roses.

(110) How shall I proceed to root cuttings of hybrid perpetual roses?
INQUISITIVE.

—Take half ripened wood and root the cuttings in the propagating bench, the same as is done with tea roses.

Insects on Araucaria.

(111) I enclose a piece of araucaria; please give the name of the insect affecting same. It begins its ravages usually on the lower tier of the plant and works toward the top, killing everything in about four to six months. The portion of the plant attacked first assumes a pale brownish color and a little later turns dark brown and dies. Under the microscope these insects resemble the common wasp, but appear wingless; they are not very rapid in their movements, neither are they very numerous.
INQUISITIVE.

—The araucaria branch had no live insects on it when it reached this office, but from its general appearance, and the description of the insect as seen under the microscope, we are of the opinion that the trouble comes from red spider. Less heat and frequent syringing will soon put an end to this insect.

Propagation of Clematis Jackmanii.

(112) Can Clematis Jackmanii be propagated from cuttings; if so, how?
INQUISITIVE.

—Clematis can be grown from cuttings by taking the young side shoots in Summer and rooting them on the propagating bench in the greenhouse, keeping them shaded fom direct sunshine, and having the sides of the propagating bench protected so that no cool wind strikes them until they have made roots.

Retail Price of Large Kentia.

(113) What would a kentia 7 feet across and 5 feet high be worth at retail? INQUISITIVE.

—The retail price of a palm of the size mentioned depends upon the perfection of the leaves and its general condition. We could not hazard placing a value on such a plant unless we saw it.

Soil for Carnations.

(114) I send you under separate cover a sample of soil I have piled up with manure for carnations next Fall; please let me know if the soil is all right. It seems to be light; do you think I had better add some heavier soil when putting it in the house?
Md. W. A. P.

—The soil sent for examination is much too light and fine for carnations; there is not a particle of fiber in it, and it would pack or become too solid after being put in the benches. We would procure some heavier and fibrous soil if possible, and mix it, in equal proportions, with the heap already prepared.

Pruning Lemon Trees.

(115) When is the right time to prune lemon trees? W. A. P.

—We would require to know how the lemons were being grown, and of what size the plants are before giving any advice about pruning them. Ordinarily a lemon tree needs no pruning until it has become too large for the premises it occupies.

Diseased Lettuce.

(116) We send a leaf of our diseased lettuce. Would you describe through your paper the cause, nature and remedy for same? C. H.
Penna.

—Lettuce disease is of common occurrence, being in some soils more troublesome than in others. When once this disease gets a headway there is no remedy for it. The disease has often been called sunburn, which is a mistaken idea, as usually when there comes a spell of cloudy, muggy weather, the disease spreads much more rapidly than in bright weather. Of course, climatic conditions have a great deal to do with the rapid spread of the fungus. One of the greatest means conducive to the trouble is a too close atmosphere. The aim should be to keep a good, bracing atmosphere in the house. Lettuce delights in fresh air. Certainly when the house goes much over the night temperature, 45 degrees, a crack of air should be put on. According to my experience, the warm then sudden cold spells that we had to contend with in the early part of this present Winter have helped to bring about this trouble. One could pay the strictest attention to watering, airing, etc., and still fail to get the desired results. The soil the lettuce is planted in plays an important part in this respect. Lettuce must have good drainage and a fairly rich soil, rather on the light side than too heavy, so that the plants can get quick root action. But, as stated, if the disease has got good headway, the only remedy is to start afresh. I would recommend new soil, or to sterilize the soil you have. It would be poor policy to replant in the soil that contained the diseased plants. The chances are the next crop would go the same way. But in case one did not want to go to all this trouble, I have seen elegant cauliflower produced in soil where lettuce was a failure. Another thing might be mentioned, if the means were at command, namely, sub-irrigation. By this means the surface soil would be always dry, while the roots would have plenty of moisture. W. TURNER.

FOUNDED IN 1888

THE FLORISTS' EXCHANGE

A Weekly Medium of Interchange for Florists, Nurserymen, Seedsmen and the Trade in General

Exclusively a Trade Paper.

Entered at New York Post Office as Second Class Matter

Published EVERY SATURDAY by

A. T. DE LA MARE PTG. AND PUB. CO. LTD.

2, 4, 6 and 8 Duane Street,

P. O. Box 1697.
Telephone 3765-6 Beekman. NEW YORK.

CHICAGO OFFICE: 127 East Berwyn Avenue.

ILLUSTRATIONS.

Electrotypes of the illustrations used in this paper can usually be supplied by the publishers. Price on application.

YEARLY SUBSCRIPTIONS.

United States, Canada, and Mexico, $1.00. Foreign countries in postal union, $2.50. Payable in advance. Remit by Express Money Order Draft on New York, Post Office Money Order or Registered Letter.

The address label indicates the date when subscription expires and is our only receipt therefor.

REGISTERED CABLE ADDRESS:
Florex, New York.

ADVERTISING RATES.

One-half inch, 75c.; ¾-inch, $1.00; 1-inch, $1.25, special positions extra. Send for Rate Card showing discount of 10c., 15c., 25c., or 35c., per inch on continuous advertising. For rates on Wants, etc., see column for Classified Advertisements.

Copy must reach this office by 12 noon Wednesday to secure insertion in issue of following Saturday.

Orders from unknown parties must be accompanied with cash or satisfactory references.

Registration of Plants.

Editor Florists' Exchange:

Peter Bisset's closing remarks in your issue of December 15—"for it is not to be thought that American horticulturists will be long content with the present system of registration of plants as carried on by the S. A. F."—finds our approval. We have given up registering. August 20, 1902, we registered with the S. A. F. a geranium seedling of ours, Double Dryden (see S. A. F. Report of August, 1903, page 13). We exhibited this variety under the name Double Dryden, at Asheville, N. C., in 1902, and it has been advertised and sold by us since that time. The just closing year, 1906, Vincent, Jr., & Son offered Double Dryden quite largely at $5 per 100. On page 27 of E. G. Hill Company's 1906 catalogue, we find under "new geraniums for 1906," Double Dryden offered at 35c. each!

Registration with the S. A. F. is a farce.

HENRY EICHHOLZ.

Waynesboro, Pa.

The Burbank Controversy.

Editor Florists' Exchange:

Every one has the inalienable right to criticise, and every one is amenable to criticism, even Burbank. Mr. Galloway is evidently of the opinion that Burbank should not be criticised; how he got on that pinnacle Mr. G. does not say.

I have never heard of any "mud" being thrown at Mr. Burbank; only a lot of facts recorded which he has never tried to controvert. Mr. Burbank has never posed as a "fellow craftsman;" he has posed as a creator (golden silence giving consent), also as a wizard; in other words, a male witch. I don't think that any one in his right mind would "envy" Mr. Burbank or be jealous of the niche he fills. Let him come off his perch and meet his "fellow craftsmen" on the level. When he does, he will find that they are not "beneath" him in any way, but considerably above him, judging from the intrinsic value of their introductions, and the comparative uselessness of his. Burbank is no more a creator than the butterfly, the bee, or the meanest bug which by God given instinct carries the pollen from flower to flower.

Mr. Everling's argument that Burbank is not the first to use the word "creation" in connection with plant breeding is no good: two wrongs don't make a right. His explanation of Dr. Neubert's "motto" is nice—full of "sentiment" and poetry; but I have never yet seen it recorded that that "tiny spark of creative fire" was ever transmitted either to Mr. Burbank or Dr. Neubert.

Job seems to be better posted on that "national beverage" than he is on theology. JOHN BIRNIE.

President Kasting of the S. A. F. O. H. sends the Editor Christmas greetings, accompanied with a beautiful thermometer and handy blotter. Many thanks.

The Year 1906.

In the general prosperity of the country which has characterized the year now drawing to a close, the industries represented by The Florists' Exchange have shared in a manner most satisfactory, so much so that no failure of any moment can be recorded.

Business in all lines has been active, and of an increased extent, particularly so at the various festivals, Easter, Memorial Day, Thanksgiving and Christmas. Greenhouse building goes on apace, and the spirit pervading the craft is one of complete optimism. The only cloud that has overshadowed the general brightness has been the awful calamity which befell the brethren on the Pacific Coast, when in April last earthquake and fire devastated the beautiful city of San Francisco, spreading ruin and desolation in their wake. With characteristic American pluck and energy, however, the craftsmen located in the illfated district rose to the occasion, and after but a brief stagnation, business is again fast assuming its wonted activity.

Plant Acquisitions.

The year 1906 has added its quota of new plants. Among those registered with the S. A. F. O. H. may be named the following: Alternanthera aurea robusta (Schray & Son); Cannas—Superior (Schray & Son), quite a list by the Southern Floral Company, Sunburst, Topeka and Magnificent (Central Park Nursery Company), Meteor and New York (Conard & Jones Company). Chrysanthemum—Weber's Chadwick (Weber & Sons). Ferns—Nephrolepis Fruckii and Berryii (Fruck). Orchids—Cattleya Charles G. Roebling (Roebling), Dendrobium nobile Mrs. Larz Anderson (Fabyan), Lælio-Cattleya Bernice (Lager & Hurrell), Lælio-Cattleya W. A. Roebling 2 (Roebling); Roses—Christine Wright, climber; Columbia, climber, (Hoopes Bro. & Thomas), Aurora (Niehoff), Rosa rugosa magnifica (Conard & Jones Company).

New Carnations.

With the American Carnation Society, the following new varieties have been registered: Red Warrior (Anderson), Winsome (Riemels), Pink Imperial (Haines), Abundance (Fischer), Crimson Glow (Dailledouze Brothers), Avalanche (Pye), Pocahontas (Baur & Smith), Welcome (Dailledouze Brothers), Mrs. Robert Hartshorne (Tierney), Splendor (Stevenson Brothers), Harvard, Georgia, and Faust (Cockcroft), Toreador (Weber & Sons), Red Riding Hood (Chicago Carnation Company), Lucille (J. D. Thompson Carnation Company).

Work of Carnation Society.

At the exhibition of the American Carnation Society held at Boston in January last only two new varieties were certificated. These were Winsome (Riemels) scoring 85 points, and Winsor (F. R. Pierson Company) scoring 90 points. The standard in carnations has reached a point which makes the securing of certificates nowadays a difficult matter indeed.

A subject which received considerable attention at the A. C. S. meeting referred to was the inspection of varieties at the establishments of the originators by a competent committee of judges. This plan, if put into execution, will, it is thought, add to the value of the society's certificate, while at the same time rendering the receipt of that award still more difficult. The Carnation Society goes to Toronto, Ont., next January, where the convention presided over by John H. Dunlop, and exhibition, promise to maintain the high standard reached by this progressive association.

It is graftifying to note that American varieties of carnations are meeting with increased favor abroad, particularly in England.

New Chrysanthemums.

The Chrysanthemum Society of American continues its good work in the matter of passing upon the merits of new sorts. Among the varieties certificated during the season of 1906 are the following:

October 13—President Loubet (Hill); October 20—Director Gerard (Hill), Fusee (Hill), Comoleta (Smith & Son), Mary Godfrey (Totty), Mrs. A. T. Miller (Totty); October 27—Mrs. G. A. Lotze (Lotze), Mrs. Westray Ladd (Stroud), Miss Clay Frick (Totty), Mlle. L. H. Cochet (Hill); November 3—Ongawa (Smith & Son); November 6—Mlle. E. Chabanne (Hill); November 10—Charles Ragee (Fries), Mme. Semon Jossier (Hill), Alice Roosevelt (Hill), Detroyat (Hill), General Pecquart (Nichols); November 17—Golden Dome (Macrae); December 1—Mlle. Jeanne Rosette (Hill).

Exhibitions.

The C. S. A. held a very successful exhibition in Chicago in conjunction with the Chicago Horticultural Society. This exhibition, excellent in every particular, was not a financial success. The same report is heard of several other shows throughout the country. Despite this untoward result, however, the enthusiasm of show promoters remains unabated, and already plans are being laid for the holding of exhibitions next year.

And while on the subject of shows it may be of interest to remark that the smaller flowered chrysanthemums, singles, pompons, etc., seem to be gaining in popularity, although in no way affecting the interest in the large flowers. The newer of the larger bloomed sorts do not, in the main, show any great advance over existing varieties, which have held their own well at the various exhibitions.

Work of Societies Generally.

The good work of the various organizations devoted to the advancement of the art continues. Mention has already been made of that of the Carnation and Chrysanthemum societies. The S. A. F. O. H. held a most successful gathering at Dayton, O., under the leadership of President William F. Kasting. Perhaps the most important work done was the setting in motion of preparatory plans for the great national flower show to be held, under the auspices of the society at Chicago in 1908. To further the purposes of this exhibition a guarantee fund of $10,000 is sought to be raised. Every florist interested in his calling should contribute his quota to this fund, as the results accruing from the contemplated exhibition are sure to be far-reaching and generally beneficial to the trade. Next year the S. A. F. goes to Philadelphia, with ex-secretary William J. Stewart as president, the office of secretary being filled by Phil. J. Hauswirth of Chicago. A record-breaking convention in every way is looked for. An interesting feature connected with the S. A. F. this year is the institution of a Ladies' Auxiliary, which is meeting with much success.

The American Peony Society met at Boston this year, with a large and encouraging exhibition. The nomenclature question is still uppermost with this organization, and gradual progress is making. In 1907 the society meets at Cornell University, Ithaca, N. Y., where a large number of varieties are being tested as to trueness to name and otherwise.

Much good work has been accomplished the past year by the National Council of Horticulture in the promulgation, through the daily press, of practical horticultural information. It can, we think, be safely said that the efforts of this body have been considerably conducive to the gratifying increase in the sale of seeds, plants and bulbs which has been a noticeable factor of the past year. Through the means of various appropriations the Council's work, along the lines mentioned, will go on. This organization is planning for a congress of horticulture in connection with the Jamestown (Va.) exposition in 1907.

The American Rose Society held a gratifying exhibition and convention in Boston this year. This organization is making very satisfactory progress, largely through the interest taken by the respective officials. Preparatory plans are making for next year's show to be held in Washington, D. C., in March, with Robert Simpson as president.

The American Seed Trade Association met in Toledo, O., and, as usual, had a most successful gathering. The seed trade continues to fight the free distribution of common seeds by the Government, and its efforts, though not wholly successful, have been decidedly encouraging. The contest continues backed by such a prominent Government official as Professor Galloway, chief of the United States Bureau of Plant Industry; and it is to be hoped that the next year will see the total abolition of a practice which not only is of itself proving an exceedingly harmful factor, but costing the seed trade considerable money in its endeavor to combat it.

The Government also continues to distribute, by circular, the names of seedsmen found to have adulterated certain field seeds. The plan is said to be proving efficacious, though the justice or fairness of it to the seed trade generally is very questionable.

The American Seed Trade Association celebrates its quarter-century anniversary in 1907, and the meeting for next year will likely be held in New York City.

The American Association of Nurserymen journeyed to Texas this year, and, as usual, held an interesting and successful meeting. Considerable good work has been done by this organization in freight classification and other matters. Detroit, Mich., is the meeting place for 1907, with Orlando Harrison as president.

New Organizations.

Among new organizations established in 1906 may be mentioned the Society of Southern Florists and Ornamental Horticulturists, the aim of which is to further and promote horticultural interests in the Southern States. Much progress is making in that district, particularly in New Orleans, in the growing of roses and other plants under glass.

The New England Dahlia Society has been organized to advance the interests of the dahlia, and considerable enthusiasm is being manifested in the work of that body, the membership increasing in a most satisfactory manner.

The Work of Scientists.

Along scientific lines the American Breeders' Association is doing commendable work, and great good is sure to spring from its efforts. There is a likelihood of a conference on Plant Hardiness and Acclimatization—a most important subject—being held in New York in 1907, under the asupices of the Horticultural Society of New York.

Florists' Clubs Continue Active.

It is only necessary to mention that the various florists' clubs continue on their upward course. The work each of these bodies is doing is of incalculable value.

The Death Roll.

The death record for 1906 is, we regret to say, a very large one. Among well known florists who have gone from among us are J. A. Budlong, John Reck, George Wietor, Joseph Kift, Sr., Ferd. Boulon, J. C. Rennison, F. W. Ritter, James Wolfe, Charles Dannacher, Thomas Devoy, Anthony Cook, W. J. Schray, G. H. Rowden, C. H. Kunzman, F. A. Blake, J. J. Wood, James Weir, Jr., A. Emslie, James Hartshorne, E. D. Clark, Roger O'Mara, James Warburton, G. W. Patten, P. R. B. Piersoh, C. W. Turnley, J. L. Dillon, R. J. Mendenhall, Lewis Ullrich, A. F. Conard, and Albert Woltemate. The seed trade has lost Mrs. Theodosia B. Shepherd, S. D. Woodruff, August Rhotert and Herman Rölker; the nursery trade, S. B. Parsons, Sr., George H. Ellwanger, Theodore S. Hubbard, George Ellwanger, and G. R. Moore; the landscape gardening profession mourns the loss of R. Ulrich, Joseph Forsyth Johnson, and William Doogue; the greenhouse building trade, F. C. Moninger. Our European brethren have suffered sad bereavements in the calling away of F. W. Burbidge, Harry Turner and E. Vander Cruyssen.

New Literature.

The literature associated with the trade has been added to by the following works: Names of Roses, revised edition (Semon), Manual of the Phlox (Harrison), Orchid Hybrids, revised edition (Sander & Son), Plant Breeding, revised edition (Bailey), Culture of Water Lilies and Aquatics, revised edition (Henderson), Entomology (Folsom), How to Make a Fruit Garden (Fletcher), and Lawns (Barron).

Miscellaneous.

Among subjects which have interested the trade during the year may be cited: The Degeneration of Forcing Roses, the Birnie discussion on Geraniums, Stove vs. Greenhouse plants, the Increase in Express Rates, the Work of Luther Burbank, and the Registration of Plants.

Noteworthy events recorded are the opening of the new building of the Baltimore Florists' Exchange, the consolidation of the Pennock-Meehan Company, the expansion of Welch Brothers and H. M. Robinson & Company.

The growing interest of employers in their employes has been manifested in the banquets given by the A. H. Hews Company and the Herendeen Manufacturing Company; while the camaraderie existing in the trade generally is exemplified by the numerous outings and club dinners held throughout the year.

The brief, but incomplete, summary of trade affairs here presented shows a wholesome and gratifying condition, generally, which the year on which we are about to enter, from the work planned and hoped to be accomplished, cannot but see maintained and advanced, in the consummation of which The Florists' Exchange will, as has been its practice, these now eighteen years, act well its part.

In closing we desire to extend our thanks for the large and increasing advertising patronage given us during 1906, a continuance of which we shall do our best by all legitimate means to merit in 1907.

The New York Market in 1906.

In looking backward over the year just closing, we can but feel that the florists in general will find much satisfaction in the fact that the demand for flowers and plants has kept equal pace with the output at all times, despite the enormous additions to the glass area for their cultivation constantly making.

Speaking for New York City, the year has been a most satisfactory one. Cut flower growers have met with market prices that, no doubt, will average much better than has been the case for some years. It is a noticeable fact that this market has been in a glutted condition very seldom during the year. The rose growers especially have been favored. It was particularly noticeable that the high prices prevailing around the holidays did not have a serious break until into the month of March. Of course, there are some growers, no doubt, who did not realize the highest market values, but that was no fault of the market, but rather owing to the poor condition of the flowers produced.

So far as varieties go, it can safely be said that the old standards—American Beauty, Bride and Bridesmaid—are holding their own with the various new roses that have been introduced. Mme. Abel Chatenay seems to be gaining somewhat in popularity, and we believe that the red rose Richmond will eventually take its place as the leader in its color. While during the warm Fall months nobody seems to have much use for it on acount of its opening quickly, its presence begins to be felt in November, and from then onward it is a prime favorite. as this rose is much easier to grow than either Liberty or Meteor, it does not seem that, for indoor purposes, there is much use in devoting space to other varieties of red roses.

Killarney has forged to the front, and is now a rose that is much called for among the better class of stores; and, no doubt, it is only a question of time when this variety will share equal honors, so far as being grown in numbers goes, with that old, but well-known favorite, Bridesmaid. Uncle John and Golden Gate have not as yet become large factors in the rose supply of this market; and the new rose Wellesley has not yet appeared in any large numbers. Coming down to the later months of the year we find that the market prices of roses is about all that could be desired, and that careful growers are receiving good returns from all the stock they can produce.

The carnation industry may be said to be flourishing equally as well, or nearly so, as the rose industry. Growers have caught on to the fact that this market is a poor place on which to crowd inferior or poorly grown stock. There has been much elimination of old-fashioned varieties. Growers have provided themselves, after careful consideration, with the best sorts in their respective colors, and it goes without saying that the quality of carnations coming into New York during this year has been of superior grade, and, as a natural consequence, prices have averaged accordingly.

At the present time it would seem that Enchantress leads all other varieties as a favorite in the light pink class, and for cerise pink the variety Mrs. Thos. Lawson does not seem to have been superseded. Mrs. M. A. Patten is grown more extensively than any other in the variegated class; and for scarlets the two varieties, Robert Craig and Victory, are most largely grown. The white varieties mostly seen just now are White Lawson, The Queen and Boston Market.

The demand for violets has probably been more erratic than that of any other flower, consequently we see more sudden changes in the prices for violets than for anything else. While there have been times when the values of violets have seemed to be out of proportion altogether, we are still inclined to think that the returns to the growers have never before been so low, but there was still a profit left, and the great increase in the glass devoted to violet culture, that takes place every Summer in the violet growing district, helps to bear out this statement.

The sale of bulbous flowers—we refer particularly to narcissus in variety, tulips and Roman hyacinths—was probably more satisfactory this year than for some years past. It was noticeable that early in April, and sometimes before, immense shipments of narcissus commenced to arrive from the South, and florists in this vicinity, who are growing bulbs for this market, would do well to bear that fact in mind, as the Southern grown flowers can be sold at a very much lower figure than the home-grown produce, and still leave a good margin of profit to the grower.

Lilies have been in supply practically all the year round. There were times, probably, when they were too plentiful to realize their full value to the grower, yet around Easter they sold to good advantage, and have been bringing quite good figures during the last few months of the year.

The chrysanthemum season this year was a very satisfactory one, indeed. Owing probably to the fact that the outdoor asters were not so good in quality as is usual for this market, the early chrysanthemums met with excellent demand, and the prices realized were far better than have been obtained for several years. The quality of the chrysanthemums throughout the season may be said to have averaged much better than usual, and with the exception of one or two occasions when the supply was a little over-abundant, prices throughout the season were exceptionally good; in fact, growers are free to admit that the recent past chrysanthemum season was one of the best on record.

Lily of the valley has practically been in supply all the year round, and this is one of the staple things of the market bringing good averages at all times.

Orchids are growing in popularity by leaps and bounds; probably in no other flowers has there been such a marked increase in the supply, and yet, with very few exceptions, there has always been a good demand for all the flowers in sight.

Gardenias as cut flowers are growing more in favor until now there are several establishments where complete houses are devoted to them for cut flower purposes. The plants have been benched similar to what is done in the case of roses, and gardenias are being grown successfully and immense crops produced during the darker months of the year.

The business in green material, such as smilax, asparagus and adiantum in variety, is making wonderful strides, and some growers are devoting their whole establishments exclusively to the cultivation of these materials. In addition to this, there have been asparagus industries developed in Florida, whence come shipments to this market every day during the season.

Taking it all in all, the New York cut flower trade during the year 1906 has been eminently satisfactory to those growers who understood their business and had the necessary equipment for producing good stock. The plant trade throughout the city can be said to have flourished equally as well as the cut flower business, and great advancement has been made in the production of flowering and decorative plants, particularly at seasons when they are needed most, such as Christmas, Easter and Memorial Day.

Nothing particularly new has been introduced during 1906, though much improvement is seen in the way of developing older favorites. Begonia Gloire de Lorraine is now being sold by the hundreds, where a year or two ago it was sold in dozens. Camellias and gardenias are being grown more extensively and when in full flower sell readily. Azaleas are still as great favorites as ever they were, though the same can hardly be said of rhododendrons; these latter as pot plants, we think, are losing prestige.

Crimson Rambler roses, together with the white and pink-flowered varieties of this type, have been just as popular as they ever were, though the same can hardly be said of the hardy perpetual roses forced in pots for Easter work. It would seem that with the advent of the Dorothy Perkins and other light colored varieties of the Rambler class, the demand for the hybrid perpetuals is on the wane.

Hydrangeas, cyclamen, geraniums, primulas and ericas, together with dwarf orange trees and solanums, are just as great favorites as ever, and can always be sold to good advantage by the grower who does them well.

In fact, at this, the close of 1906, we feel safe in saying that the plant and flower trade of New York City is in a healthier and better condition than it ever was before, and the cultivation of this kind of stock offers to a practical grower, just as good inducements—better we think—as it ever did in the history of the industry so far as this city is concerned.

Reflections on Current Topics.

MR. EDITOR.—I have just been reading the interesting report of the S. A. F. proceedings at Dayton, O. There is no question but a good deal was said there; and the report even as a bit of current horticultural literature is well worth any man's $3, which amount it costs to be a recipient of the pamphlet. We have now the full text of what each man participating in the various discussions said; and one sentence connected with the canna registration debate is, to me, particularly informative. It is this:

"Mr. G. C. Watson: I think that our registration does give a variety a fictitious value with the general public, and I contend that it is our duty, now when the question is before us, to correct that."

In previous reflections I made the remark that George Watson always says what he thinks—when he does think. Now here is a case where there is no disputing that George "thunk," because he says so, and you have the result. But what was uppermost in my mind as I read the thought, was the awful amount of fictitiousness George, as the self-constituted secretary of the S. A. F. Peony Association, desired to foist on the horticultural public in registering that long list of Japanese peonies! Did he think then as he "thunk" at the Dayton convention?

* * *

Recently I commented on the patting on the back prevalent by certain parties when describing the stock of growers. It seems that the class papers themselves are not averse to a little "taffy," for witness your Boston contemporary's issue of December 22. It is not stated whether or not the various eulogiums appearing there on the worth and work of your contemporary were unsolicited. I presume they were, for it would be but poor policy for any meritorious periodical, real or fancied, to "fish for compliments." Neither am I sure that condemnation should be meted out to the witnesses who have borne the testimony of the kind no doubt desired, if not asked for. But as I read the various testimonials I was reminded of a verse that appeared in a paper adopting a similar plan of laudation of itself as the one under mention, to this effect:

"A luminary of such power
Will greatly of its strength be shorn;
If, hapless, in an evil hour
It wastes its space to blow its horn."

The writer of that verse was evidently a thinking man, although he was dubbed a carping critic, which latter characterization will doubtless be mine.

I was glad to see the fac-simile signature of John Birnie among those of the other "lauders." The chirography is firm, something I hardly expected, but I notice Birnie fails to dot all his "i's." He evidently doesn't believe in cow tail progress; yet I fail to understand his grudge against Burbank unless it be through jealousy over that "ten thousand annuity." The Scot who gave the annuity seems to be a wiser man than his captious countryman, however. The appearance of Birnie's signature in the Boston paper shows his confidence in a few of his fellowmen at least, as regards the safety of his bank account.

* * *

To return to my friend Watson, I observe he has been endeavoring to discover the whereabouts of His Satanic Majesty, unsuccessfully. It may be "ill taste," but I couldn't help being reminded by this circumstance of the title of the novel "Japhet in search of a Father."

"His Nibs," "Auld Clootie," "Nickie Ben," or "Whatever title better suits him," has too, I notice, been responsible for driving someone, signing "W. F." to drop into poetry (?). I can forgive Beelzebub for everything he has heretofore done—giving the Kirkcaldy folks the slip, evading Watson, entering the herd of swine, etc.; but to be the cause of "creating" verse of the W. F. stamp, is to me as unpardonable as delay in, or duplicate registration of plants, seems to be to yourself, sir.

The topics discussed this week are about as pertinent to horticulture as McGorum's Rose House Wisdom is to the cultivation of the Queen of Flowers; but they being "current," the indulgence of your readers is asked by JOB.

The Craft and the Craftsman.

(Excerpts from a paper read before the Gardeners and Florists' Club of Boston, by W. H. Wyman of the Bay State Nurseries.)

Some men men succeed in every business and every legitimate avocation, while some others do not succeed in those same pursuits, under equally favorable conditions. The difference therefore between success and failure does not necessarily lie in the craft but in the craftsman himself. This is axiomatic—a self-evident truth. And it is equally true that no man, however successful he may be, or may have been, in one department of our many sided activities, will succeed equally well in every other or any other.

It is, then, of the greatest importance that every man selects for his craft that which he likes, and likes because of his adaptability thereto. It is my good fortune this evening to address a company of gentlemen who have chosen their craft and are in the earnest pursuit of it. The production of fruits, vegetables and flowers, the decoration of the home, the lawn and the landscape, is an avocation worthy of the best there is in the best of men.

Your field of activity is broad—so broad that the man has not yet been born who can say, with any approximation to truthfulness, he has mastered it.

This fact alone makes your calling one of peculiar interest to a thoughtful man. Mother Earth is so full of mystery, and delights so often in doing the unexpected, that one is kept ever on the alert. He knows that the unexpected is sure to happen. Then again Nature guards so jealously the citadel to her secrets that only observing mortals are allowed to profit from her. The wisest of men succeed only by the most careful observation and practical, persistent application. Every plant has its own peculiarities, it will succeed in one soil and will not in another. It must have its own conditions complied with or no returns are given. Nothing is more capricious and nothing is more exacting than a living plant, and the higher the order the more exacting its demands.

Hence the soil, the temperature and all the conditions that have to do with the plant must be reckoned with before the actual work of production has been begun. The man who does not carefully consider this feature of his problem, acts the part of the man who builds his house upon the sand without giving due regard to the foundation thereof. Disastrous consequences are sure to follow.

The time was when people in general thought that the boy who was stupid at his books, not capable of making a lawyer, or a doctor, or a minister, would do to make a cultivator of the soil. But the time has come when men realize that it takes as good brains to compel Nature to give her best as to do anything else that is worth the doing. It is one thing to cultivate the soil, it is another to compel Nature to do her best.

* * *

The man who would succeed in this department of human activity must understand well the external elements with which he has to deal; he must see the possibilities vested in a tiny seed, the possibilities in a stretch of wild unbroken landscape, or a mound of broken rocks. The gardener must have the imagination of the poet, the fine discrimination of the artist. He must not only produce the material, but he must see that the material is arranged so that there shall be no "war among the roses"—no clashing among the flowers. We have all been in gardens where there was a profusion of beautiful flowers, looked at individually, and yet there was, in reality, little if anything to admire. On the other hand, we have visited gardens where there were only a limited number of plants, of very common sorts, and we were enchanted by them; common every-day plants and flowers, but so beautiful! They all seemed made for each other, and were so arranged that they were a harmonious feature of the landscape, each one doing duty to the whole.

Let us now turn from the work to the workman himself. The sordid question of dollars and cents concerns all of us, for food, shelter and raiment we must have. But the man who never gets above and beyond the money standpoint of his calling, never gets far toward success in the highest degree.

It is the man who becomes engrossed in his work and thinks not of the pay, who is doubly paid. The genius in his craft is the man who has so much in his soul seeking expression that, work hard as he may, he never quite catches up with himself. There is more yet seeking expression and he rejoices at every new day for the opportunity of working out that which is pleading for expression from within. A sense of duty well done is in itself a rich reward, and he who does his full duty is sure of substantial remuneration. Elbert Hubbard says, "Folks who never do any more than they get paid for, never get paid for any more than they do."

* * *

No priest at the altar deals with anything purer than the flowers—the handiwork of God. And he who has part in their creation should feel the dignity of his calling so that none should be found more childlike in straightforward simplicity than he. We must not forget that there are some exceptions, and in some instances, as in Latin, sometimes we thought the exceptions were more general than the rules. How out of place a man of low designs and unbridled passions in a bower of pure fragrant flowers. How a man of coarse unwholesome speech disfigures the landscape. How out of keeping with his surroundings a man looks who has no regard for his personal appearance, who allows himself to go unshaven and unwashed. One feels to say with Hamlet when he heard the coarse jokes of the clown, "Has this fellow no sense of his business that he sings at grave-making?" The true man sees purity in the dew-drops, hears music in the wind as it plays in the branches above his head, and breathes the fragrance of the flowers.

The craft elevates, refines and enobles the craftsman in this your chosen field. It cannot be otherwise. Let me not be misunderstood. I am speaking of the real craftsman—the man inside the clothes we see—whom the world can never see only as he is revealed by the work which he does.

On this line there was a man who spoke of himself—"The works that I do they testify of me." And with as much truth we can each say the same words. It is not true of all gardeners or of all florists that they are pure of character, chaste in speech and temperate in habit. But it is true of many of them. They are among nature's noblemen. The craft is full of inspiration; but, as in all other walks of life, some go at cross purposes with the tendency of their calling.

* * *

There are some who always live in the lowlands intellectually and morally. They cannot appreciate the man who lives upon the highlands, in wholesome air, healthful surroundings, and in God's sunshine. But business is not all sordid and mean. It is what you make it. Your craft is, in character, what you make it. My business is all right. If it is base and sordid it is because the man behind the gun is base and sordid.

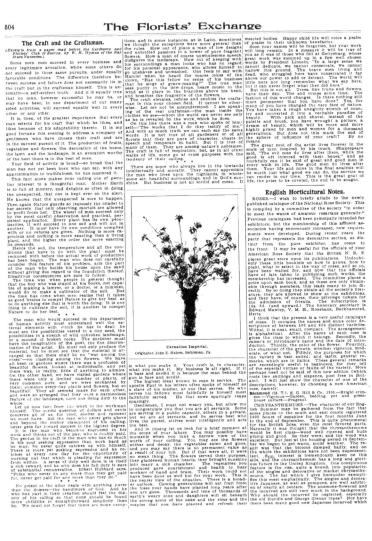

Carnation Imperial.

Originator, John E. Haines, Bethlehem, Pa.

The highest ideal known to man is service. The apostle Paul in his letters often spoke of himself as a slave of his master, as one that serves. He who serves his fellows most faithfully is himself most faithfully served. He that sows sparingly reaps sparingly.

Gentlemen, I must not weary you, but allow me to congratulate you that you are all servants. Some are serving in a public capacity, others in a private, but we are all servants, and he serves best who lives the purest, strives most intelligently and acts the best.

And in closing let us look for a brief moment at the scope of your labors. You may possibly have moments when you take a narrow view of the worth of your calling. You may see the flowers wither and decay, the vegetables eaten and gone, and you may say there is no permanent value as a result of your toil. But if that were all, it were no mean thing. The flowers served their purpose, they gladdened human hearts, they brought sunshine into many a sick chamber. The vegetables you produced gave nourishment and health to busy workers of hand and brain. Their work could not have been done as well but for your work. This is the nearer view of the situation. There is a broader outlook. Coming generations will eat fruit from the trees your hands have planted long years after you are gone. Thousands and tens of thousands of earth's weary sons and daughters will sit beneath the strong arms of the oaks and the elms and the maples that you have planted and refresh their wearied bodies. Happy child life will voice a psalm of praise to their unknown benefactor.

Soon your names will be forgotten, but your work will long remain. In a measure it will be true of you as it was of those who fell at Gettysburg, whose great work was summed up in a few well chosen words by President Lincoln, "In a large sense we cannot dedicate, we cannot consecrate, we cannot hallow this ground. The brave men living and dead, who struggled here have consecrated it far above our power to add or detract. The world will little note nor long remember what we say here, but it can never forget what they did here."

But this is not all. Trees, like fruits and flowers, have their day. The end comes some time. The fashion of this world changes. Is there nothing still more permanent that you have done? Yes, for many of you have changed the very face of nature. You have taken a rough unsightly stretch of country and converted it into a veritable paradise of beauty. With pick and shovel, instead of the palette and brush, you have wrought a picture, a dream of beauty, which will be more and more highly prized by men and women for a thousand generations. But does not this mark the end of the sphere of influence of your craft? By no means.

The great soul of the artist lives forever in the souls of men inspired by his touch. Shakespeare said, "The evil men do lives after them, while the good is oft interred with their bones," and as truthfully can it be said of great and good men in every walk in life. The good men do lives after them. Your life and mine in the final analysis will be worth just what good we can do, the service we can render in our time. This is the great goal of life, the prize to be coveted, the end to be sought.

English Horticultural Notes.

ROSES.—I wish to briefly allude to the newly published catalogue of the National Rose Society. This is compiled by a committee of the society "in order to meet the wants of amateur rosarians generally." Previous catalogues had been principally intended for exhibitors; but the membership of this affluent association having enormously increased, new requirements were developed. During recent years the party that represents the decorative section, as distinct from the pure exhibitor, has come to the front. It may be useful for the officials of your American Rose Society that the British N. R. S. places great store upon its publications. Undoubtedly these little booklets on how to prune, how to plant, what to select in the way of roses, and so on, have been waited for, and now that the officials have of late taken to publishing such works, the membership has increased. The committee places a price upon each book, and as these are only obtainable through members, this leads many to join directly. By so doing they obtain all the society's literature, they are allowed to show at the exhibitions, and they have, of course, their privilege tickets for the admission of friends. The subscription is 10s. 6d. (and upward.) The honorary secretary is Edward Mawley, V. M. H., Rosebank, Berkhamsted, Herts.

I think that the present is a very useful catalogue of roses. It contains the names and some color descriptions of between 500 and 600 distinct varieties. Withal, it is neat, small, compact. The arrangement is alphabetical. After the name of each rose is given the class to which it belongs. Secondly, the raiser's or introducer's name and the date of introduction. Thirdly, the color of the flower. Fourthly, the character of the growth, whether vigorous, moderate, or what not. Fifthly, the purposes for which the variety is best suited; and lastly, general remarks, which are in italics. These general remarks are exceedingly useful to beginners, for they tell of the especial virtues or faults of the variety. More perhaps need not be said of this new edition (which costs two shillings and sixpence, post free in Britain). I will just show the character of one of the descriptions, however, by choosing a new American rose, namely:

Richmond (H. T.), E. G. Hill & Co., 1905.—Bright crimson.—Vigorous.—Garden, bedding, pot and greenhouse culture.—Fragrant.

CHRYSANTHEMUMS.—The character of our English Summer may be gathered from the fact that some places on the south and east coasts registered 1000 hours of sunshine for the four months June to the end of September. This is quite phenomenal for the British Isles, even the most favored parts. Naturally it was thought that the chrysanthemums would be first class—wood well ripened and buds plump and good. So they were; and the wood was excellent. But just at the housing period in September we began to get warm, moist weather. The result was that the blooms damped badly, and on the whole the exhibitions have not been superexcellent. Still, interest is tremendously keen on this side, and the chrysanthemum has a long and glorious future in the United Kingdom. One conspicuous feature is the rise, quite a bound, into popularity, of the singles and decorative or market chrysanthemums. The list which I give hereunder exemplifies this most emphatically. The singles and decorative Japanese, as well as pompons, are well exhibited at nearly all centers. The anemone-flowered and the incurved are still very much in the background. Why should the incurved be neglected, especially the old Rundle and George Glenny types? Nor have there been many good new Japanese incurved which are so justly popular in America. I now give the list of

NEWLY CERTIFICATED VARIETIES.

VARIETY.	KIND.	COLOR.
Algernon Davis	Japanese	Deep yellow
Alice Crate	Single	Deep rosy purple
Annie Hamilton	Japanese	White
Beauty of Weybridge	Single	Chestnut and bronze
Buttercup	Incurved	Yellow
C. H. Hearn	Incurved	Bronzy buff
Clara	Decorative	Better than Carrie
Crown of Gold	Single	Old gold
Distinction	Jap-incurved	Deep buff
Dorothy Gouldsmith	Japanese	Canary yellow
Duchess	Japanese	Soft yellow
Dora Godfrey	Single	Pale yellow
Edith Jameson	Japanese	Flesh pink
Edith Harling	Single	Yellow
Eric	Single (early)	Yellow
Ethel	Decorative	Straw yellow
Fred Duck	Japanese	Deep red
Florence Gillham	Single (early)	White
Galatea	Single	Rosy pink
Glitter	Japanese	Yellow
Hector	Pompon-decorative	Pink
Hilda	Decorative	Rosy red
H. Hampson	Single	———
Jeannette	Single (early)	Pale rose
J. H. Runciman	Single	Terra-Cotta
Jumbo	Japanese	Yellow and crimson
Kathie	Single	Crimson lake
Lizzie	Single	Rosy pink
Madame G. Rivol	Jap-incurved	Bronzy pink
Madame C. Oberthur	Japanese	White
Merstham White	Single	White
Mrs. Andrews	Single	White
Mrs. Thyne	Single	Bronzy yellow
Mrs. Sidney Fox	Japanese	Lilac-pink
Mrs. H. Reddan	Single	Rose and yellow
Mrs. Arthur Beech	Decorative	Bronze
Mrs. J. W. Scott	Japanese	Creamy white
Mrs. R. C. Felton	Japanese	Old rose and buff
Mrs. R. D. Eves	Japanese	Ivory white
Mrs. H. Perkins	Japanese	Light Chestnut, gold reverse
Mrs Norman Davis	Japanese	White
Mrs. Brewster	Single	Russetty brown
Mercedes	Decorative	Pure white
Miss E. Partridge	Single	Rosy pink
Olive Dunsday	Decorative	Pink
Surrey	Single	Rosy cerise
Tapis de Neige	Decorative	White
W. Beadle	Japanese	Violet-crimson and yellow
White Countess	Decorative	Pure white
Total .. 49		

Surely never before have so many singles been certificated. This is indeed the day of the decorative section. For years these were neglected, but they have come forward with a bound. In our table, Japanese are to be understood to be the large exhibition varieties; and decorative kinds are the lesser flowered kinds that are mostly grown for market, for the open garden, or as bush-trained "decorative" plants.

Curiously, the finest exhibition of the year was not that of the National Chrysanthemum Society in London. It was that of the Scottish Horticultural Association in Edinburgh. The show is held from Thursday to Saturday in the Waverley market, a fine architectural building evidently like the hall at Chicago where the recent chrysanthemum show was held. At this dreary season, a great and resplendent show of these magnificent flowers, with music, abundance of light and warmth, attracts the Edinburgh public. The gate takings were £1,000. In part the market, which covers one acre, is turned into a promenade concert "salon," with chrysanthemums as the central feature, if not the central attraction! Edinburgh was the first place where exhibition boards (hardly known in the United States) were totally abolished in favor of vases; and now, for two years, point-judging has been in vogue and the points are published. I give an example:

The chief prize was the City of Edinburgh Victoria memorial, for fifteen vases in fifteen varieties, three blooms of each. Out of seven entries there were six lots staged, and the first place was easily secured by Mr. Lunt, gardener, Kier, Dunblane. This is the seventh time Mr. Lunt has gained this prize; last year he was a half point behind Mr. Nichol, Forgandenny, but this season Mr. Lunt surpassed all previous efforts, and was awarded 140 points for the fifteen vases out of a possible 180. The varieties were as follows:—Mrs. F. W. Vallis, 10 1-2; Madame P. Radaelli, 9; Reginald Vallis, 9 1-2; F. S. Vallis (extra fine), 11; Algernon Davis (very extra), 10; Lady Conyers, 8; Mrs. W. Knox, 8 1-2; Mrs G. Mileham, 7 1-2; Marquis V. Venosta (superb), 11; Jumbo, 8; Henry Stowe, 7 1-2; Bessie Godfrey, 9; Mrs. R. Cadbury, 10; J. H. Silsbury, 9 1-2; Miss O. Miller, 11.

These points are set out on cards for the public benefit. Of course, only the leading classes are treated thus elaborately, and the most skillful judges are necessary. We in this country have not yet learned to stage such huge bunches or vasefuls as you in America; nor are specimen plants or groups of very much account. A grand feature, however, is the decorations in baskets, epergnes, etc. Baskets of Autumn fruits and foliage are truly magnificent at the N. C. S. shows. J. HARRISON DICK.

An interesting article by Uncle John Thorpe, on "To-day's Flower Shop," in which he enumerates the popular plants and flowers cultivated at the present time, appeared in the Chicago Daily News of December 19.

Va.

Our London Letter.

BY A. HEMSLEY.

CHRYSANTHEMUMS.—The last important show has now been held, excepting the market show which comes next week. We have had numerous varieties added, and a few may prove valuable acquisitions. The singles are becoming too numerous, and I doubt much if some that have gained certificates will be worth the attention of those who grow for market. In large Japanese we have some good things, also others which I am sure will prove useful as medium-sized blooms for market. I will make a selection of a few of the best for a later note. It has been a disastrous season for most of those who grow for market. Many planted extensively for flowering in the open ground, and though the weather was so favorable for flowering, the plants did little good owing to all the markets being overloaded. And with this excessive supply, which lasted so late, it crippled those who have second earlies under glass. It has been many years since the markets were so overstocked and prices so low, yet I find that those who grow really useful sorts and keep up a regular succession do not complain so much. This oversupply will have one good effect; it will check those who take up the culture of flowers with the idea that there is a lot of money to be made; and who do not understand what is wanted, and also have no connection with the best buyers. Anyone who goes to our Covent Garden market regularly may learn much. It really comes to this now—the growers who do things best and keep up a succession throughout the season, can do fairly well, but they must also have a connection among the best buyers. I visited one of the best florists' shops the other day and I found that for direct consignments of the best blooms good returns were being made, while the same florist was buying in the market for casual trade, at very low prices. New comers, or those who do not understand the trade, can soon lose money, while those who work systematically will survive. But the most unfortunate part of the business is that the oversupply from casuals cripples the regular trade on account of so much cheap "stuff" being put on the streets, and offered in the streets at less than it has cost to grow it. Take the trade generally it is going through a rather bad crisis. Some who have started and bought in such large quantities are sure to drop out, while others who have a better knowledge of the trade will survive.

Carnation Pink Imperial
Originator, John E. Haines, Bethlehem, Pa.

SWEET PEAS.—Anton C. Zvolanek, sweet pea specialist of Bound Brook, N. J., favored this office with a nice bunch of flowers from some of his newer varieties for the holidays. Included among them were: Mrs. Alex. Wallace, lavender; Mrs. Wild, scarlet; Mrs. Wm. Sim, salmon pink; Mrs. Hanan, cerise pink and Jack Hunter, yellow. Although one does not expect to have sweet peas at their best at Christmas, the flowers mentioned were borne on good long stems and were in other respects equal to those usually seen during February and March—a fact that makes the varieties particularly desirable as Winter-forcing sorts.

CLUB AND SOCIETY DOINGS.

NEWPORT (R. I.) HORTICULTURAL SOCIETY.—The annual meeting of this society was held Tuesday evening, December 11, President Alexander MacLellan in the chair and an attendance of members that taxed the seating capacity of the hall. As usual at annual meetings much interest was manifested in the proceedings, especially in the reports of the officers on the work of the society during the year and the disposition and present state of its finances. The report of the recording secretary reviewed the work of the society and contained many suggestions for future consideration whereby, if adopted, better results still might result. In the report of the secretary special stress was laid on the need of something being done to keep alive the interest of the members in the meetings, and with this aim he recommended frequent lectures on horticultural subjects by men of known ability, and also, with the same end in view, suggested that more attention be given to the social side of the meetings. The success attending the society's offer of liberal premiums to school children was also referred to and the hope expressed that in the coming year these premiums would be increased in number and value. The reports of the financial secretary and treasurer showed the finances to be in a sound condition; over a thousand dollars was awarded in premiums, still leaving in the hands of the treasurer a larger balance than appeared last year. The reading of the roll showed a slight increase in membership, with the general financial standing of members satisfactory.

The election of officers resulted as follows (President MacLellan declined re-election.): President, Bruce Butterton; first vice-president, Samuel Speers; second vice-president, James Robertson; recording secretary, David McIntosh; financial secretary, Joseph Gibson; treasurer, Col. A. K. McMahon; sergeant at arms, William F. Smith; executive committee, Alexander MacLellan, Dr. A. J. Anderson, William J. Matson, John T. Allan, James J. Sullivan, Andrew Christensen, Stewart Ritchie, William F. Smith, John W. Gibson; auditors, Thomas B. Connolly, W. S. Sisson, William H. Young.

The communication from Professor Wheeler in relation to the raising of funds for a memorial to the late Congressman Adams of Wisconsin was very favorably received and a committee was appointed to solicit subscriptions with the result that quite a sum was secured. Bruce Butterton was elected a delegate to attend the meetings of the Association of Societies for Rural Progress; this society will meet in Newport early in the new year. Following the dispatch of business an exceedingly enjoyable social session was entered into when refreshments were served. Among the visitors at the meeting was Walter Mott, representing Messrs. Bobbink & Atkins. The society starts on a new year under very favorable auspices. D. M.

THE ELBERON (N. J.) HORTICULTURAL SOCIETY held its regular meeting December 3. Much interest was shown in a new seedling carnation exhibited by Mr. Tierney of Highlands of Navesink. It was awarded a certificate of merit scoring 90 points. Mr. Tierney has named it Mrs. Robert Hartshorne, in honor of his employer. There was also exhibited by Peter Murry, a beautiful Phœnix Roebelenii, scoring 90 points; carnations exhibited by A. Bauer scoring 90 points; stevias by A. Grieb, scoring 85 points; and violets by Fred Dettlinger, scoring 85 points. A committee was appointed by the society to meet the Board of Education of Oakhurst to arrange for the beautifying of the school grounds with shrubbery and whatever else is required to put the grounds in good condition. The committee appointed is composed of Messrs. Robertson, Grieb, and Dettlinger.

A very large and interesting meeting was held, the feature of the evening being an able paper on chrysanthemums by Chas. H. Totty of Madison, N. J. Mr. Totty gave the society a rare treat, and lots of information. He received a vote of thanks. Some fine flowers and vegetables were staged. Two new members were nominated making a total of about 53 members in good standing. F. W. D.

LENOX (MASS.) HORTICULTURAL SOCIETY.—The regular meeting of this society was held December 15. President F. Heeremans in the chair. Alex Murray of Lenox was unanimously elected a member. It was decided to hold three exhibitions this year—a rose and strawberry show in June, annual and perennial show in August, and the annual chrysanthemum show in October. All committees for 1907 were appointed, viz., employment, essay and entertainment, and arrangements made for schedule and judges for plants and indoor flowers, herbaceous plants and outdoor flowers and vegetables. G. F.

The Seed Business as a Mai -Order Proposition.

As a mail-order proposition, the seed business looks like a "cinch" to the uninitiated. It looks like an easy way to make money, to get up a prettily illustrated seed catalogue; advertise it in leading publications; sit at a desk and open letters containing cash for seeds, and mail out the packets.

The most of the business is done in February, March, April and May, and one can spend the other eight months of the year having a good time spending the profits.

Just so.

But ask the men who have made a success of this "ideal mail-order business" how near the business approaches "ideal" conditions, and let them tell you about the "real thing," and if you are looking for a "soft snap," you will choose something involving less detail, and hard all-the-year-'round-work, and some business that yields larger profits on the capital invested, and that can be learned and mastered more easily.

The mail-order seedsman may sell rose bushes, but he knows practically little about the proverbial "bed of roses."

The history of Chicago seed houses for the past thirty or thirty-five years would be interesting in some ways, but it would be mainly a history of struggle and failure. There are too many cemeteries to make the retrospect a cheerful one, and so we will forget the failures, and recount the successes.

Arrangement of Callas and Adiantum
Artists L. L. May & Co., St. Paul

How many Chicago advertising seed firms have made a success of the business? How many of the dozen or more that have made the attempt to succeed during the past twenty-five years are in existence to-day?

Well, really, we will have to confine ourselves to the singular verb.

Just one. That is, one advertising seedsman whose business is confined to flower, garden and field seeds, bulbs, plants, etc.

Beside the one success in this line that we will name, there is the Albert Dickinson Company, wholesale dealers in field seeds exclusively; the largest in their line in the world. But they do not issue a catalogue, and are not "seedsmen" in the common acceptance of the term. Their success is marked and unique in the business world, and the story of their stupendous achievement may be told in another issue.

The one success above referred to is that of a firm whose head has grown up into the business from a boy, beginning in a small room and soliciting his first trade by written letters or in person, by tramping through Cook, Lake and Will counties, Illinois, canvassing for nursery stock, during the vacation seasons when he was attending High School in Chicago.

The man referred to is J. C. Vaughan, of Vaughan's Seed Store, Chicago and New York.

To tell of Mr. Vaughan's practical study of his chosen business, even to the planting and cultivation of seeds on his trial grounds; of the painstaking thoroughness that has gained for him the national and world-wide reputation of an intelligent and dependable seedsman, florist and nurseryman, would fill volumes.

What we are interested in just now, is how much of Mr. Vaughan's success is due to advertising, and how responsive mail-order seed buyers are to advertisements?

Here's a proposition that would stagger most mail-order advertisers; and this knowledge was gained from the recent interview with Mr. Vaughan.

Catalogues cost about fifteen cents each, including postage.

The average mail order is about $1.50. Add to this the cost of advertising to produce inquiries, plus rent, clerk hire, insurance, taxes, and the cost of seeds, and the profit on each transaction seems very small indeed.

"But then there are the sales over the counter at the stores?"

Mr. Vaughan smiled at this question and said:

"Yes, there have been fairly good seasons when the entire net profits of our central store for the year did not exceed the gross average receipts of five business days during the month of April."

While Mr. Vaughan did not say what the April sales averaged per day, the statement seems rather startling.

And yet, notwithstanding the fact that the average mail-order sales are so small, and that the stores must be run at a loss during eight months of the year, Vaughan and his co-laborers have achieved large success where scores have failed.

Ask Mr. Vaughan as to how it has been done, and he'll tell you:

"The reason for our good luck, so far as paying our bills year after year, lies probably in the fact that we have worked hard and for long hours trying to secure and hold all the trade, wholesale and retail, that is naturally tributary to Chicago, and have added to our offerings Fall bulbs and greenhouse plants, thereby extending the season, and enabling the firm to retain capable help the whole year through."

"What part has advertising played?"

"Oh, as to that! Aside from knowledge of the business, honesty and hard work, advertising is responsible for the whole thing; but advertising in magazines, newspapers, catalogues, and all kinds of printed and written announcements, is only a small item in the advertising game. You know, poor Richard says, 'It's not what I earn but what I save that makes me rich.' Just so it's not the number of new people one makes a sale to, but the number of customers one sells to year after year, that constitutes paying trade; and so dependable goods and honest dealing are advertising; in fact the opposite of this is true, but it is advertising of a kind that doesn't pay.

"And yet, here's a strange thing about the catalogue seed business. You would naturally think that if a customer was well pleased with the goods he purchased by mail last year, that he would send his order right along this year, or at least write for a catalogue, wouldn't you?

"Well, he won't; very few will do that. They will look for the advertisement of your new catalogue, and if they don't see it, they will send for the one they do see advertised, and run the risk of buying from a firm that they know nothing about.

"And that is the radical difference between a mail-order customer that you deal with only once a year, and one who is buying from month to month. People forget lots of things in a year. And then, if you don't advertise, some people may surmise that you have died, or failed, or become rich and retired.

"But remember this: While fair dealing, and seeds that will grow, may not induce a customer who bought last year to write for a catalogue this year—unless he sees it advertised—no amount of advertising will induce a man or woman to send for the catalogue of a seed firm that ever sent them poor seeds. That's one thing that the people don't forget.

"And so, even with mail-order seed buyers, whom you have to nudge once a year with an advertisement, in order to get them to even look in your direction, fair dealing and the best goods procurable are important factors in successful advertising."

Nothing was said by Mr. Vaughan about the thousands of new mail-order seed buyers, who are coming into the market each year, whose trade may be secured by advertising, and the thousands of others, who have bought seeds here and there, who may not as yet have dealt with his house, but who read the advertising columns of magazines and papers where seed advertising appears, and thus are prospective customers for seed firms who advertise.

There are 5,737,372 farms in the United States, the owners or workers of which may be counted as buyers of seeds. Add to these about 3,000,000 other rural dwellers, who have more or less ground that they cultivate in a small way, and who buy seeds from one source or another, and the clientele of the advertising seedsmen is at least 8,656,900. Counting that each one of these may purchase on an average $1.50 worth of seeds per year, we have the snug total of $12,985,350.

Even if the total sales are but one-half of this vast sum, the advertising seedsman has a large opportunity.

In closing, a word should be said about the grand educational work that honest seedsmen are doing for the country at large, for if "he who makes two blades of grass to grow, where but one grew before, is a benefactor," is not he who causes two beautiful flowers to bloom, where but one blossomed before, doubly a benefactor?—Agricultural Advertising, December, 1906.

San Jose Scale.

Editor Florists' Exchange:

Now that it is generally recognized that the San Jose scale is a serious menace to fruit and other trees and shrubs innumerable, a word may be in season in the way of a reminder that this is the time of the year when the most effectual steps may be taken to annihilate this pest. There are many remedies recommended for use in the premises, and probably each one has something commendable in its composition; but every one, I think, has this in its favor, that it can be applied in Winter to outdoor trees and shrubs without danger resulting. Not so at other seasons of the year, however.

The destruction of the San Jose scale is by no means effected by a single application of even the deadliest of preparations; on the contrary, only by persistent worrying can it be got rid of. Another point in relation to this pest worthy of attention is that its presence is occasionally unnoticed until it has accomplished a disagreeably great deal of harm; it then becomes necessary, in order to be on the safe side, to minutely examine everything likely as well as unlikely to be affected, and apply remedies immediately.

M.

OUR READERS' VIEWS

Sports.

Editor Florists' Exchange:

Patrick O'Mara's paper on this subject, recently published in your columns, opens up a fertile field for discussion, and one upon which many people will agree to differ. The scientists seem to be agreed that sports are produced more often by an excess of food than by any other cause. This does not seem to me to work out in actual practice. I incline to the belief that sporting is hereditary because sports often occur in places far distant from each other at practically the same time. In carnations this occurred with white and variegated Lawson, sports occurring the same year hundreds of miles apart. The same thing occurred with the white and deep pink sports of Enchantress. It would seem as though when the psychic moment had arrived in the life cycle of the variety sporting will ensue, no matter under what conditions the plant may have been growing. To this the unbeliever wil probably say, and with truth, If Enchantress was due to sport this year why didn't we all get it as wel as the man who did? and that brings us back to where we started from. Mr. O'Mara's paper presented the views of other people in a very able way, without giving any decided opinion of his own, in which perhaps he was wise.

I have wondered if sporting were, perhaps, reversion or a tendency in the plant to get back to a previous condition. Take for instance the chrysanthemum. The color of the original progenitor of the present day kinds (C. indicum), was yellow, and any white varieties that have sported to my knowledge have reverted to yellow. Mrs. Henry Robinson produced Mrs. O. P. Bassett. Jerome Jones produced several yellow sports. Mme. Carnot also produced two yellow sports. Timothy Eaton produced Yellow Eaton. Nellie Pockett sported to Cheltoni; Mrs. Swinburne to George Beech and so on. Pinks on the other hand always sport to white, as though this were the first step in the act of retrogression, cases in point being Glory of the Pacific harking back to Polly Rose; Maud Dean to White Maud Dean, and the latest, W. Duckham, producing Miss Clay Frick. These sports are all identical with the parents in everything except color. Now we have Yellow Eaton, itself a sport, producing the sport now being sent out as Golden Dome, which shows some variation of foliage as well as shape of flowers. I hear of a precisely similar case this year in the variety Dr. Enguehard; three flowers of the plant were normal, the fourth instead of being pink was white and the character of both flower and foliage is entirely changed.

Sports, so far as I have seen and studied them, seem to be a law unto themselves, and not amenable to any law of nature that I know anything about.

CHARLES H. TOTTY.

Madison, N. J.

Burbank on Liquor and Tobacco.

Some weeks ago the editor of an Eastern paper having some curiosity to know if Luther Burbank used either liquors or tobacco, wrote him about it. In reply she received this letter:

"DEAR MADAM:

"If I answer your question simply by saying that I never use tobacco or alcohol in any form, and rarely coffee or tea, you might say that was a personal preference and proved nothing. But I can prove to you most conclusively that even the mild use of stimulants is incompatible with work requiring accurate attention and definite concentration.

"To assist me in my work of budding—work that is as accurate and exacting as watchmaking—I have a force of twenty men. I have to discharge men from this force, if incompetent. Some time ago, my foreman asked me if I took pains to inquire into the personal habits of my men. On being answered in the negative, he surprised me by saying that the men I found unable to do the delicate work of budding invariably turned out to be smokers or drinkers. These men, while able to do the rough work of farming, call budding and other delicate work 'puttering,' and have to give it up, owing to an inability to concentrate their nerve force.

"Even men who smoke one cigar a day cannot be trusted with some of my most delicate work.

"Cigarettes are even more damaging than cigars and their use by young boys is little short of criminal, and will produce in them the same result that sand placed in a watch will produce—destruction.

"I do not think anybody can possibly bring up a favorable argument for the use of cigarettes by boys. Several of my young acquaintances are in their graves who gave promise of making happy and useful citizens; and there is no question whatever that cigarettes alone were the cause of their destruction. No boy living would commence the use of cigarettes if he knew what a useless, soulless, worthless thing they would make of him.

LUTHER BURBANK."

A Christmas Chrysanthmum.

Our illustration shows part of a house of Jeannie Nonin chrysanthemum, grown by Emil Geschick, Main and Johnson streets, Germantown, Philadelphia. The plants are all grown three flowers to a plant. The entire crop of 1000 plants was brought in for Christmas, the first flowers being cut on December 20.

DAVID RUST.

Chrysanthemum Jeannie Nonin for Christmas.

Grower, E. Geschick, Germantown, Pa.

Where to Plant the Laurel.

Many of those who purchase laurel, Kalmia latifolia, from nurserymen complain that the plants fail to make a satisfactory growth. The plants make but little growth, and what is made is not of the bright green color it should be. These cases occur through planting the laurel in improper situations. Purchases do not recognize that the plant is a shade lover, and that it needs a fine loamy soil or a light one at least. Occasionally when in a bed of mixed evergreens where it gets the shade of other plants the laurel thrives, but rarely as it would do were it in a situation similar to those in which it is found in its wild state. The valley of the Wissahickon, Philadelphia, was in former years a famous place for this laurel. So many plants were there and so large were they that wagon loads on wagon loads of branches were taken from them every Christmas for the making of festoons for local churches. The plants occupied the hills on each side of the creek, and always were near the highest ground, unless where the high ground extended to the water's edge, in which case the plants would be there as well as elsewhere. Both hills are very rocky, but as they are well filled with large forest trees, and have been so always, so to speak, there is abundance of fine mold, formed from decaying leaves and branches, for the laurels to grow in. This is what they like, and then, too, the hills are moist, always, because of their loose surface and the descending moisture. Then add to all the shade the trees overhead provide, and note then how the laurels thrive, and where to plant them is quickly known. It is not essential that they be in a wood, but they certainly require shade during a part of the day, preferably from the noonday sun. On a private place near by there has been a plantation of these shrubs made on the north side of a large wood. The trees do not overhang the laurels, but they shade them nicely in Summer, and how they do thrive!

When evergreens are perpetually in shade their leaves are not as beautiful as they are when some sunlight reaches them. Nature seems to provide the sunlight in Winter, for when the leaves fall in October these laurels and all other evergreens catch the direct rays of the sun until the close of April, and, no doubt, this compensates for the lack of sunlight through the Summer for strengthening the foliage.

When planting laurels give them a sandy soil close to the roots. This settles about the roots better than common loam, much to the advantage of the plants.

Monthly Roses in Winter.

When monthly or any other roses are required for selling purposes in Spring the best way is to dig them up in Fall and heel them in in some cool place outdoors. A cool place is suggested, as a rose starts to grow early in Spring, and if in a shady place on a northern slope buds are not pushed forth as early as if in a warm, sunny spot. On the other hand, orders demand that stock be got out early in Spring at times, and this necessitates that they be in unfrozen ground. It is therefore better that all such stock be heeled in and then covered heavily with leaves, straw or like material to keep them free from frost, that what may be needed may be taken out at any time.

When in the open ground all Winter, monthly roses need some protection for the lower portion of their shoots. They need but about six inches preserved, as from such length the flowering shoots for the season are made. There are various ways of giving this protection. Soil itself thrown around the plants will do; so will long manure, straw, hay, sawdust, ashes, or similar materials, if they but give shade and some protection from the cold. It is during February and March that protection is called for more than at any other time.

Grafting the Rose Acacia.

Beautiful as the rose acacia is as a bush when in flower it is far more admired when grown of more height. As before mentioned the fertile variety is a taller and less spreading grower than the sterile one, and, besides, its crimson haired seed pods adorn it almost as much as do the flowers.

In European nurseries it is quite common to find the rose acacia grafted on tall stems of the flowering or yellow locust, Robinia pseud-acacia. Whether the fertile or the sterile form of the rose acacia is used, I do not know. These grafted plants are much sought for, making pretty specimens, and as the growth of the rose acacia is often almost horizontal its heads are almost drooping when grafted. When on its own roots the rose acacia is prone to suckêr to some extent, and this disposition meets with no outlet when it is grafted.

If strong stocks of the yellow locust, with good roots, can be procured they may be grafted in Spring, but in this and all cases of grafting it is better that the stocks grow a year in the position in which they will be grafted, that they may be well established before the grafting takes place.

Unfair Competition.

A Connecticut nurseryman writes me as under:

"I have just read your comments in The Florists' Exchange of November 10 on unfair competition. An instance came to my notice the past week quite similar in character. Our State forester (a young man with apparently the best of intentions), in a talk on 'Forestry,' stated that last Spring he secured a good many thousands of white pine seedlings, 2 or 3 years old, from a Western grower, at $3.50 per thousand, and sold some of them to farmers in the State at cost price. He further remarked that the State was growing four hundred thousand more which would be ready to plant in the Spring of 1908, and while he did not say so, he left it to be inferred that these could be had at cost."

—The article referred to by our correspondent related to the complaints of Australian nurserymen on the acts of Government officials there who were raising and selling eucalyptus and other trees at a price below what nurserymen could sell them for. In the case referred to by our correspondent the farmers had the benefit of the wholesale rate though buying but a few, making the cost to them lower than that at which their nurserymen could supply stock, and being, of course, to the injury of the nurseryman. This should not be.

JOSEPH MEEHAN.

Victory Has Made Good

Place your orders early for rooted cuttings. Prices $6.00 per 100. $50.00 per 1000.

Guttman & Weber
43 W. 28th St. NEW YORK
Grower, LYNBROOK, L. I.

LEADING CARNATIONS

ARISTOCRAT (Beautiful Cerise)
RED RIDING HOOD (Scarlet)

Also many other good ones. Early delivery of well rooted first-class healthy cuttings. Send in your order early. Catalogue ready Jan. 1st, 1907.

CHICAGO CARNATION CO., A. T. PYFER, Mgr. **JOLIET, ILL.**

Mention the Florists' Exchange when writing.

ROOTED CARNATION CUTTINGS READY NOW

Strong, Healthy and Thoroughly Rooted Cuttings of the following varieties:

	100	1000		100	1000
Victory (scarlet)	$6.00	$50.00	Lieut Peary (white)	$4.00	$35.00
Robt. Craig "	6.00	50.00	Lady Bountiful "	3.50	30.00
Red Sport "	3.50	30.00	White Lawson "	3.00	25.00
Enchantress (pink)	2.50	20.00	Boston Market "	2.00	15.00
Lawson "	2.00	15.00	Queen "	2.00	15.00
Mrs. M. A. Patten var.	2.50	20.00	Queen Louise "	2.00	12.50

Remember we guarantee satisfaction.
250 of any one variety at 1000 rate. Write for discount on large orders.

J. D. COCKCROFT, Northport, Long Island, N. Y.

Mention the Florists' Exchange when writing.

ROOTED CUTTINGS

	Per 100	Per 1000		Per 100	Per 1000
WHITE—Queen	$1.50	$12.50	Helen Goddard	$4.00	
Lady Bountiful	2.50	20.00	Ethel Ward	2.00	$15.00
White Lawson	2.00	17.50	RED—Red Lawson	2.00	17.50
PINK—Enchantress	2.00	15.00	Robert Craig	5.00	
Lawson	1.50	12.50	Harry Fenn	2.00	15.0
Pink Patten	4.00		VARIEGATED—Mrs. Patten	2.50	20.00

QUIDNICK GREENHOUSES J. H. CUSHING, Prop., QUIDNICK, ANTHONY P. O., R. I.

Mention The Florists' Exchange when writing.

Rooted ROSE Cuttings

AMERICAN BEAUTIES	per 100, $3.00;	per 1000, $25.00
KAISERIN	" 2.50	" 20.00
CARNOT	" 2.50	" 20.00
LA DETROIT	" 2.50	" 20.00

BASSETT & WASHBURN
Office, 76 Wabash Ave., Chicago — Greenhouses, Hinsdale, Ill

UNROOTED CARNATION CUTTINGS

ENCHANTRESS, QUEEN, FAIR MAID, RED SPORT, HARLOWARDEN, pink white and variegated LAWSON, $10.00 per 1000.
WHITE PERFECTION and VICTORY $30.00 per 1000.
LADY BOUNTIFUL, $12.00 per 1000.
LIEUTENANT PEARY, $15.00 per 1000.
SCOTTII FERNS, 6 in., $25.00 per 100.
COLEUS, Verschaffeltii and Golden Bedder, 2 in., $18.00 per 1000.

Larchmont Nurseries
Larchmont, N. Y.

Mention The Florists' Exchange when writing.

CARNATIONS

THE BEST rooted cuttings of the following varieties viz:—
Pink Lawson, Red Lawson, Var. Lawson, White Lawson, Enchantress, Harry Fenn, General Lord, L. Naumann.
Plants clean; healthy and free from rust. Prices right. Address

A. W. WILLIAMS - Highland, N. Y.

Mention the Florists' Exchange when writing.

CARNATIONS

F. DORNER & SONS CO.
LA FAYETTE, IND.

Mention the Florists' Exchange when writing.

GERANIUMS

S. A. Nutt, $10.00 per 1000. Well rooted and packed right. Cash with order.

C. F. TREICHLER, SANBORN, N. Y.

Mention the Florists' Exchange when writing.

MABELLE—New Pink Carnation for 1907

Color.—A peculiar shade of lovely pink, with a faint yellowish cast; several shades lighter than the Lawson. Unlike most pinks, the brightest sun does not injure the color. Size.—Three to four inches in diameter when established. Odor.—Pleasing, but not strong. Stems—invariably strong, but always graceful, ranging from 12 to 30 inches during the season. Habit, etc.—A very quick active grower, making specimen plants in a short time, even from late cuttings. On account of its rapid growth, requires supporting very soon after benching. Gets away rapidly, blooms early and gives long stems right from the start. Productiveness.—Prodigious is the best word we know of to use here. It is the most incessant bloomer early and late, we have ever grown. Stock limited. Delivery Jan. 5th to 10th and later. Price, $12.00 per 100, $100.00 per 1000.

THE H. WEBER & SONS CO., OAKLAND, MD.

ROOTED CARNATION CUTTINGS

Good clean, healthy stock, free from all disease. Enchantress, best light pink; Robert Craig, fine red; Nelson Fisher, best dark pink; M. A. Patten, excellent variegated; W. Lawson. Orders taken now will be ready for January delivery. Write for prices.

VALLEY VIEW GREENHOUSES
VELIE Bros., Props. MARLBOROUGH, N. Y.

Mention the Florists' Exchange when writing.

CARNATIONS

Rooted cuttings ready January 1. Victory, $6.00 per 100; $50.00 per 1000; Enchantress, Bountiful, White Lawson, Var. Lawson, Patten, $3.00 per 100; $25.00 per 1000; Pink Lawson, Boston Market, Queen, H. Fenn, and Fair Maid, $2.00 per 100; $15.00 per 1000. 5 per cent. discount for cash with order.

R. ENGELMAN & SON, Pittsfield, Mass.

CARNATIONS

No. 1 stock rooted cuttings these prices for Dec. and Jan. delivery only.

	Per 1000		Per 1000
Enchantress	$20.00	B. Market	$15.00
L. Bountiful	25.00	Lawson	15.00
Cardinal	25.00	Harlowarden	15.00

100 at thousand rates. Cash with order.

SMITH & GANNETT, Geneva, N. Y.

PLANT CULTURE

PRICE, $1.00.
The best book for the plant grower.
A. T. DE LA MARE PTG. & PUB. CO. LTD

S. J. GODDARD

Framingham, Mass.
Rooted Carnation Cuttings a Specialty
Correspondence Solicited.

Mention the Florists' Exchange when writing.

ABUNDANCE

Rooted cuttings of the most prolific white carnation will be ready for delivery in January. Price, $6.00 per 100; $40.00 per 1000; 250 at 1000 rate; 5 per cent. discount for cash with order.

RUDOLPH FISCHER, Great Neck, L. I., N. Y.

Mention the Florists' Exchange when writing.

White Enchantress

white sport of Enchantress, rooted cuttings $12.00 per 100; $100.00 per 1000.

E. SCHRADER, NEW SPRINGVILLE
Richmond Borough, N. Y.

Mention the Florists' Exchange when writing.

ROOTED CUTTINGS
February and March Delivery

CARNATIONS and GERANIUMS

Send for list of varieties and prices.

ALBERT M. HERR, LANCASTER, PA.

Mention the Florists' Exchange when writing.

JOHN E. HAINES

The leading scarlet, brilliant color, fine stem, the most productive ever introduced, blooms early until thrown out in July no extra grass, all shoots make flowers. Watch the papers and see what growers say about it. None but well-rooted healthy cuttings leave the place. Rooted Cuttings ready December 15, 1906. Price, $6.00 per 100; $50.00 per 1000.

JOHN E. HAINES, Bethlehem, Pa.

Mention the Florists' Exchange when writing.

A. B. DAVIS & SON, Inc.

PURCELLVILLE, VA.

Place your orders now for Red Sport cuttings, the best red carnation grown. $3.50 per 100; $30.00 per 1000.

Mention the Florists' Exchange when writing

CARNATIONS

Rooted cuttings ready now of the following varieties: Victory, $6.00 per 100; $50.00 per 1000. Enchantress, $2.00 per 100; $15.00 per 1000; Lady Bountiful, $3.00 per 100; $25.00 per 1000; Mrs. Patten, $2.50 per 100; $20.00 per 1000; Pink Lawson and Boston Market, $1.50 per 100; $12.50 per 1000. Write for complete list of varieties, including all the best novelties.

JENSEN & DEKEMA, 674 W. Foster Ave. **Chicago, Ill.**

Mention the Florists' Exchange when writing.

All GERANIUMS

Booked for this Month.

PETER BROWN,
LANCASTER, PA.

Mention the Florists' Exchange when writing.

Rip Van Winkle

Has finally got awake, and finds that he has at least 125,000 Geraniums in 2 in. pots and in fine condition, and will sell at $18.00 per 1000; composed of the following varieties: Poitevine, La Favorite, F. Perkins, Viaud, Doyle, D. Grant, Bruantii, Pasteur, Brett, Nutt and several other varieties. This is to make room "Get a move on you," and get some fine stock.
Cash with order.

J. E. FELTHOUSEN,
154 VAN VRANKEN AVE., SCHENECTADY, N. Y.

Mention the Florists' Exchange when writing.

GERANIUMS

Ricard, Doyle, Buchner, Nutt, Poitevine, Brett, 2 in. pots, ready in January. Orders booked now at $20.00 per 1000.

ROOTED CUTTINGS BELOW READY NOW

	100
Fuchsias, best varieties	$1.50
Double Petunias	1.50
Heliotropes	1.00
Ageratum	.75

ERNEST HARRIS, DELANSON, N. Y.

Mention the Florists' Exchange when writing.

GERANIUMS

Rooted, then grown in pots over a month. Sent free of soil. Nutt, Doyle, Bruantii and Buchner, $14.00 per 1000. Ricard, Poitevine, Perkins, Viaud, etc., $16.00 per 1000. Plenty Nutt and Doyle. Coleus, Verschaffeltii and G. Bedder, 60c. Fancy, fine, 50c. Giant, all grand, 80c. per 100. Gladioli, Groff's mixed, 50c. per 100. Cash or C. O. D.

DANIEL K. HERR, Lancaster, Pa.

Mention the Florists' Exchange when writing.

MUST HAVE ROOM

Mum Stock Plants of Estelle, Jerome Jones, Mrs. R. Robinson, white; Wm. Duckham, Dr. Enguehard, Mrs. Coombs, M. Liger, pink; Black Hawk, Dazzler, crimson; Col. Appleton, yellow; and mixed varieties at $3.75 per 100.
Rubbers, 4 in., 25c.
Dracaenas, 4 in., $9.00 per 100.
English Ivy, 2½ in., $2.00; 3 in. $1.50; 4 in., $8.00 per 100.
Rose and La Favorite white Geranium, 3 in., $2.50.
Double white Fuchsia, 3 in., $2.60.
Very best double white Petunia, 3 in., $2.50.
Genista, 6 in., $15.00 per 100.
Red and yellow Alternantheras, $1.00 per 100.
Verschaffeltii and Golden Bedder Coleus, 2 in., $1.75; unrooted cuttings, 75c. per 100.
Sprengeri, 4 in., $10.00 per 100.
Guaranteed to be good healthy plants. Cash with order please, or would exchange for a limited number of Azaleas, small Palms, spirea, Vinca Variegated and Primula Obconica, if good. PORT ALLEGHENY GREENHOUSES, Port Allegheny, Pa.

Mention the Florists' Exchange when writing.

CHRYSANTHEMUMS

All Varieties to Suit Everybody.

See Bargain Offers in Previous Issues.
SEND FOR PRELIMINARY LIST.

Nathan Smith & Son, Adrian, Mich.

Mention the Florists' Exchange when writing.

GERANIUMS

in good varieties 2½ in. pots, ready March 1 1907.

WM. J. CHINNICK, Trenton, N. J.

Mention the Florists' Exchange when writing.

Imperial and Pink Imperial Carnations

You Cannot Afford to be Without these Two Excellent Varieties

Price $12.00 per 100; $100.00 per 1000, 250 at 1000 rates, a discount allowed when cash accompanies the order

A. J. GUTTMAN, The Wholesale Florist of New York, 43 WEST 28TH STREET

JOHN E. HAINES, BETHLEHEM, PA.

Chrysanthemums

Stock Plants

WHITE

Early—George S. Kalb, Polly Rose, Willowbrook.
Mid-Season—Miss Minnie Wanamaker, Ivory, Mrs. H. Robinson, Niveus, Queen, Alice Byron, Eureka.
Late—Mrs. McArthur, Timothy Eaton, W. H. Chadwick.

PINK

Early—Glory of the Pacific.
Mid-Season—Pink Ivory, J. K. Shaw, Adela, Mrs. Perrin, Ethelyn, A. J. Balfour, Wm. H. Duckham, Dr. Enguehard.
Late—Maud Dean, The Harriott.

YELLOW

Early—Monrovia.
Mid-Season—G. Pitcher, Col. D. Appleton, Golden Gate.
Late—Major Bonnaffon, Mrs. Trenor L. Park, H. W. Rieman.

RED

Cullingfordii, Matchless.

BRONZE

Kate Bromhead, Mrs. Duckham.

Guaranteed to be strong, healthy plants, $1.00 per doz., $6.00 per 100.

A. N. PIERSON, CROMWELL, CONN.

Mention The Florists' Exchange when writing.

Chrysanthemums

STOCK PLANTS

Testout, Nonin, White Shaw, The Baby, $1.50 per doz., $10.00 per 100.
Ivory, **Bonnaffon, Jones,** white and yellow, **Kalb, Mrs. Duckham, Robinson, Amorita, Smith, Helen Frick, Am. Beauty, Carrie, Godwin,** crimson, **Appleton, White Bonnaffon,** 75c. per doz., $5.00 per 100.

CASH

HENRY EICHHOLZ, Waynesboro, Pa.

Mention the Florists' Exchange when writing.

Chrysanthemum Stock Plants

Mary Mann, $3.00 per doz., C. Touset and Rio de Italia, $1.25 per doz., $10.00 per 100. Mrs. Kalb, Pacific, Estelle, Appleton, M. Bailey Enguehard, Maud Dean, Merstham Yellow, T. Eaton, White and Yellow Bonnaffon, Yellow Jones, $1.00 per doz., $6.00 per 100. 5,000 Ivory, $4.00 per 100.

WM. SWAYNE, Box 226, Kennett Square, Pa.

Mention the Florists' Exchange when writing.

CHRYSANTHE- MUM STOCK PLANTS

Geo. S. Kalb, Polly Rose, Niveus, Robinson, Timothy Eaton, Wm. Duckham, Dr. Enguehard, Robt. Halliday, Col. Appleton, Maj. Bonnaffon. 75c. per doz.; $5.00 per 100.
Cash with order.

EDWIN BISHOP - ROSLYN, MD.

Mention the Florists' Exchange when writing.

Chrysanthemums

JEANNIE NONIN, the very finest white, stock plants, $7.00 per 100; one doz., $1.00. Cash with order.

HUGO PLADECK - Elmhurst, N. Y.

Mention The Florists' Exchange when writing.

CHYSANTHEMUMS, STOCK PLANTS

Jeannie Nonin, large white, best late variety, Nagoya, large late yellow, fine orange color, $1.00 per doz.; 6 doz. for $5.00, Cash with order.

J. McMullen, 8th St. & 4th Ave. Flushing, N. Y.

Mention The Florists' Exchange when writing.

ASPARAGUS

ASPARAGUS PLUMOSUS, 3 in. $6.00 per 100; 4 in. at $10.00, 6 in. at $25.00 per 100.
ASPARAGUS SPRENGERI, 3 in. at $5.00, 4 inch at $8.00 per 100.
BOSTON FERNS, 8 in. at $1.25 each.
PIERSONI FERN, 6 in. at 40c. each.
ASPIDISTRA, green, 6-7 in., 6-12 leaves, at 5c. per leaf.

CHRYSANTHEMUM STOCK PLANTS

Opah, Monrovia, Omega, Lady Harriett, Viviand-Morel, Duckham, Halliday, Robinson, Appleton, Dalskov, Ivory, Dr. Enguehard, Timothy Eaton, Yellow Eaton, White Bonnaffon, Major Bonnaffon $500 per 100 Cash or C. O. D.

W. J. & M. S. VESEY, Fort Wayne, Ind.

Mention the Florists' Exchange when writing.

500,000 VERBENAS

60 Finest named varieties: **rooted cuttings** 75c. per 100: $6.00 per 1000.
Plants, $2.50 per 100: $20.00 per 1000.
Our list is the choicest from millions of seedlings. Order early.

J. L. DILLON, Bloomsburg, Pa.

The Floral and Plant Business of the late Mr. J. L. Dillon will be continued under his name by his executors. LOUISE H. DILLON, ALICE D. FURMAN, Executors

Mention the Florists' Exchange when writing.

2½ in. **ASPARAGUS PLUMOSUS,** $3.00 per 100.
3 in. " **SPRENGERI,** $4.00 per 100.
2 in. **HIBISCUS,** in variety, $2.50 per 100.
2 in. Flowering **BEGONIA,** $2.50 per 100.
2 in. **BOSTON FERN,** $3.00 per 100.
2 in. **TARRYTOWN FERN,** $5.00 per 100.
2 in. **SCOTTII,** $4.00 per 100.
3 in. " $6.00 per 100.
4 in. " $10.00 per 100.

THE NATIONAL PLANT CO., Dayton, Ohio

Mention the Florists' Exchange when writing.

CHARLES H. TOTTY

WHOLESALE FLORIST

MADISON, N. J.

CHRYSANTHEMUM NOVELTIES A SPECIALTY

List Now Ready. Send for it.

Mention the Florists' Exchange when writing.

All NURSERYMEN, SEEDSMEN and FLORISTS

wishing to do business with Europe should send for the

"Horticultural Advertiser"

This is THE British Trade Paper, being read weekly by all Horticultural traders. It is also taken by over 1000 of the best Continental houses. Annual subscriptions to cover cost of postage, 75 cents. Money orders payable at Lowdham, Notts. Address

EDITORS OF THE "H. A."

Chilwell Nurseries, Lowdham, Notts

European Agents for THE AMERICAN CARNATION

Mention the Florists' Exchange when writing.

Araucaria Excelsa

16 to 18 inches High, 4 to 5 Tiers, 50 cents each: $5.00 per dozen.

THE CONARD & JONES CO., West Grove, Pa.

Mention the Florists' Exchange when writing.

Palms, Ferns, Etc.

WHOLESALE PRICE LIST.

Asparagus Plumosus, 2 in., $3.00 per 100; 3 in., $6.00 per 100.
Asparagus Sprengeri, 2 in., $3.00 per 100; 3 in., $6.00 per 100; 4 in., $1.50 per doz.; 5 in., $2.00 per doz.
Asparagus Scandens Deflexus, a beautiful green for wedding and funeral work, 3 in. pots, at $1.50 per doz.
Boston Ferns, 5 in. pots, $3.00 per doz.; 6 in. pots, strong, $6.00 per doz.; 7 in pots, $9.00 per doz. Larger specimens, $1.50, $2.00 and $3.00 each.
ASSORTED FERNS FOR DISHES, $3.00 per 100; $25.00 per 1000. We have a large lot to offer in best varieties.
Aspidium Tsussemense, 3 in., $1.00 per doz.; $8.00 per 100.
Pteris Argyraea, 3 in., $1.00 per doz.; $8.00 per 100.
Pteris Wimsetti, 3 in. 75c. per doz.; $6.00 per 100.
Dracaena Fragrans, 5 in. pots, 50c. each; $5.00 per doz. 6 in. pots, 75c. each; $9.00 per doz.; 7 in. $12.00 per doz.
Dracaena Indivisa, 2 in. pots, $2.50 per 100; 6 in. pots, 20 to 26 inches high, 50c. each; $5.00 per doz.; 7 in. pots, 30 to 34 inches high, 75c. each; $9.00 per doz.
Dracaena Terminalis, 2 in. Nicely colored, $1.25 ped odz.; 3 in., $2.00 per doz.; 6 in., $9.00 per doz.
Pandanus Utilis, 3 in....per doz., 1.50
" " 4 in....per doz., 3.00
" " 5 in....per doz., 5.00
Cocos, for dishes, 2½ in., $1.50 to $1.75 per doz.
Cocos Bonneti large specimens, $40.00 each.

	In.	Each	Per Doz
Kentia Belmoreana	3		$ 2.00
Kentia Forsteriana	....7x	2.50	
" "	....7xx	3.00	
" "	7	2.00	24.00

Phoenix Canariensis, 2 in...per doz., 1.00
" " fine bushy plants. 10 in. pots, $2.50 each. Large specimens.
Phoenix Reclinata, 3½ in. per doz., $2.00
" " 4 in. per doz., 3.00

Aucuba Japonica, 10 in. pots, 3 ft. high, $1.50 each.
Rhododendrons, 50c. and 75c. each.
Boxwoods, 1 ft. high, 35c. each.; $4.20 per doz.
Boxwoods, 1½ ft. high, 50c. each.
Boxwoods Bush Form in tubs, 4 ft., $5.00 each.
Boxwoods, Pyramids in tubs, $2.50 each. 3 ft. high. Larger plants $4.00 and $5.00.
Boxwoods, Pyramids. 3 to 4 ft. $3.00 to $4.00 each.
Boxwoods, Standards with fine heads. About 3 ft. high, $2.50 each.
Primula Chinensis. 5 inches at $2.00 a dozen.

The Geo. Wittbold Co.

1657 BUCKINGHAM PLACE, **CHICAGO**

Mention The Florists' Exchange when writing.

SEED PANSY PLANTS

THE JENNINGS STRAIN

50,000 plants now ready. From finest selected stock, large flowering, fancy colors, in great variety. Stock is first-class in every respect. 100 by mail, 60c.; by express, 500, $2.00; 1000 $4.00; 2000, $7.00; 3000, $10.00. Seed, $1.00 per pkt. of 4000; 1 oz., $5.00; 2 oz., $9.00; 3 oz., $12.00. Cash with order.

PANSIES in bud and bloom, fine plants for winter blooming, $1.00 per 100; $7.50 per 1000.

E. B. JENNINGS, Lock Box 254 **Southport, Conn.**

Grower of the Finest Pansies

Mention The Florists' Exchange when writing.

AMPELOPSIS VEITCHII

Strong, well rooted plants, with 20 to 30 in. tops, $3.00 per 100; 500 for $12.50. Sample of six plants by mail for 50c. Satisfaction guaranteed. Cash with order from unknown parties. Address

CHARLES BLACK, - HIGHTSTOWN, N. J.

1906 Florists' Directory

THE AMERICAN FLORIST Directory is now ready for distribution. It contains 475 pages, including complete lists of the **Florists, Seedsmen** and **Nurserymen** of the United States and Canada, arranged both by states and towns and all names alphabetically. Also lists of Foreign Merchants, Firms which issue catalogues, Horticultural Supply Concerns, Parks, Cemeteries, Landscape Architects, Experiment Station Horticulturists, Botanical Gardens and other invaluable trade information.

Price, $2.00 Postpaid

Address

A. T. De La Mare Ptg. & Pub. Co. Limited

2 to 8 Duane Street, New York

SCOTLAND'S FLOWER

THE HEATHER

Read its absorbing history, its legends, traditions, poetry and songs.

A most acceptable Christmas present for Scotch folk and lovers of things Scotch. Only $1.50.

The book is beautifully illustrated; a spray of heather in natural color forming an appropriate frontispiece.

A. T. DE LA MARE PTG. & PUB. CO., Ltd

Nos. 2-8 Duane Steet, New York

Mention The Florists' Exchange when writing.

Chrysanthemum growers who have a surplus of stock plants should advertise them in THE FLORISTS' EXCHANGE.

Mention the Florists' Exchange when writing.

Cineraria

Benary, Cannell and Sutton's Prize Strains; dwarf or semi-dwarf, large flowers, all shades and colors, mixed 2¼ in., $2.50 per 100. Cash please.

SHELLROAD GREENHOUSES, Grange, Baltimore, Md.

Mention the Florists' Exchange when writing.

CLASSIFIED ADVERTISEMENTS

CASH WITH ORDER.

The columns under this heading are reserved for advertisements of Stock for Sale, Stock Wanted, Help Wanted, Situations Wanted or other Wants; also of Greenhouse, Land, Second-Hand Materials, etc., For Sale or Rent.

Our charge is 10 cts. per line (7 words to the line), set solid, without display. No advt. accepted for less than thirty cents.

Display advertisements in these columns, 15 cents per line; count 12 lines agate to the inch.

[If replies to Help Wanted, Situation Wanted, or other advertisements are to be addressed care of this office, advertisers add 10 cents to cover expense of forwarding.]

Copy must reach New York office 12 o'clock Wednesday to secure insertion in issue of following Saturday.

Advertisers in the Western States desiring to advertise under initials, may save time by having their answer directed care our Chicago office at 127 E. Berwyn Ave.

SITUATIONS WANTED

SITUATION WANTED.—Young man, 20, with experience, wants position in a New York flower store. Rudolph Schoenberger, 309 East 65th St., New York City.

SITUATION WANTED—By single man, grower of roses, carnations and chrysanthemums. Competent worker; temperate. Can take charge 50,000 feet of glass. Address Florist, 270 Seventh Avenue, New York City.

SITUATION WANTED—By a single man who has had 25 years experience both in Germany and America. Desires steady position; can give reference. Address D. W., Five Mile House, Govanstown, Balto. Co., Md.

SITUATION WANTED—As foreman by first-class grower of cut flowers and pot plants. 23 years experience; first-class references. Address J. G. Fleuti, 58 Dey Street, New York City.

SITUATION WANTED—As working foreman or section man; competent grower of roses, carnations, chrysanthemums and bedding plants. 18 years experience. State full particulars and wages in first letter. Address B. F., care The Florists' Exchange.

SITUATION WANTED—As working foreman or assistant by expert grower of cut flowers and general stock, also propagator. German, 31 years of age, with 17 years' experience. Thoroughly competent, sober and reliable. South preferred. Address, Ch. H., P. O. Box 41, Aldrich, Ala.

SITUATION WANTED—As working foreman in first-class commercial or private place; Eastern states preferred. 23 years experience in Europe and this country in the growing of cut flowers and potted plants, also gardening. Sober and honest, capable of handling men. Please state full particulars in first letter when writing. Address Florist, Box 61, Weston, Mass.

HELP WANTED

WANTED—Experienced man by retail florist. Must know how to make-up funeral work and wait on customers. Aged 25 to 35. Chas. H. Fox, 21st and Columbia avenue, Philadelphia, Pa.

WANTED—Foreman for commercial place where roses, carnations and a general stock is grown. Have about 75,000 feet of glass in central state. Give salary and particulars in first letter. Address B. W., care The Florists' Exchange.

WANTED—Young man with some experience in general greenhouse work. Position permanent and good home. State age, experience, references and wages per month with board. Geo. S. Belding, Middletown, N. Y.

WANTED—Assistant greenhouse foreman, accustomed to making rose cuttings, taking charge of section of greenhouses and capable of filling and packing orders. Best of references required. Elizabeth Nursery Co., Elizabeth, N. J.

WANTED—Best opening in the country for practical, capable seedsman. If there is an employee in any seed house who wants to become a proprietor and has the necessary executive ability, I want to hear from him at once. J. A. Everitt, Indianapolis, Ind.

WANTED—A good reliable nurseryman, familiar with evergreens, and who understands the propagation of shrubs, perennials, etc., and who has had experience in landscape work. Give full particulars and state salary expected. T. E. Steele, Pomona Nurseries, Palmyra, N. J.

Seedsman Wanted

We want a young man as order clerk in our flower seed and bulb department; permanent position. Apply, stating age, experience, etc., to

HENRY A. DREER, 714 Chestnut St., Phila, Pa.

Mention the Florists' Exchange when writing.

Thirty cents is the minimum charge for advertisements on this page.

HELP WANTED

WANTED

Experienced Nurseryman and gardener, familar with ornamental stock and garden planting. A good opening for right party. If interested write for further particulars. Address, New England, care The Florists' Exchange.

MISCELLANEOUS WANTS

WANTED TO BUY—Greenhouses to be taken down. State full particulars of same when writing. Address, F. W., care The Florists' Exchange.

WANTED—Large specimen Palms, Kentias, Phoenix, Seaforthias, Raphis or tree ferns. Not to exceed (20) twenty feet in height. (No Cycas or Lantanias needed.) Must be clean healthy stock. Write stating prices to D. D. M., care The Larkin Co., Buffalo, N. Y.

WANTED—Special prices on the following: 3,000 lbs. mixed sweet peas, 3,000 lbs. mixed tall nasturtiums, 3,000 lbs. mixed dwarf nasturtiums. I also want large quantities of all kinds of garden and flower seeds. What have you to offer, and what is your best price? Write at once to William D. Burt, Dalton, N. Y.

WANTED

1,000 **Echeverias.** 1,000 **Red Alternantheras,** strong, rooted cuttings. 1,000 **Yellow Alternantheras,** strong, rooted cuttings for cash or will exchange for strong, healthy rooted **Carnation** cuttings: **Mrs. Thos. W. Lawson, Enchantress** or **White Lawson.**

SCHNEIDER & NOE, Congers, N. Y.

Mention the Florists' Exchange when writing.

FOR SALE OR RENT

FOR SALE—A retail florist store in the best and busiest section of the city. Positively a money maker; good reason for selling. Address B. Y., care The Florists' Exchange.

FOR SALE OR TO LET—For a number of years, well located in one of the largest New England cities. 16 years established retail business, 11 roomed dwelling, with two stores, about 12,000 feet of glass in splendid condition, stocked with palms and foliage plants, carnations, violets and bedding stock. Small cottage on side street. For further particulars apply to Arthur T. Boddington, 342 West 14th St., N. Y. City.

FOR SALE

Des Moines, Iowa, wholesale and retail greenhouse establishment, 29,000 feet of glass, three acres of ground, well located, all in good order, with good wholesale and retail trade. Price, about $8,400; terms reasonable.

VAUGHAN'S SEED STORE
CHICAGO

Mention the Florists' Exchange when writing.

FOR SALE

A well equipped place, consisting of seven greenhouses, over 30,000 feet of glass, a nine roomed house, barn, stock, etc., and eight acres of land. This is a decided bargain and a rare opportunity. For particulars address

S. S. SKIDELSKY,
824 N. 24th St., Philadelphia, Pa.

Mention the Florists' Exchange when writing.

Rare Opportunity

For a florist to establish a good paying business; 16,000 inhabitants; one of the fastest growing towns in State. The grounds are especially adapted for the business. Main Av., on line of trolley. Five minutes from station White Plains, N. Y. For full particulars apply to

GRIGGS & TREUPEL
R. R. Ave. White Plains, N. Y.

Mention the Florists' Exchange when writing.

HOW TO GROW MUSHROOMS

Price, - - 10 cents.

A. T. De La Mare Ptg. & Pub. Co.

2-8 Duane St. New York.

STOCK FOR SALE

100,000 greenhouse grown Asparagus Plumosus Nanus seed; ready about Dec. 15, $4.00 per 1,000. Joseph Wood, Spring Valley, N. Y.

BABY RAMBLER ROSES, fine dormant stock, one year, $12.00 per 100; 2 1-4-in. pot plants, extra well rooted, $4.00 per 100; $30.00 per 1,000. Orders booked for delivery now or any time up to late Spring. Samples free. Brown Brothers Company, Rochester, N. Y.

SURPLUS STOCK OF SEEDS—Calliopsis, (California Sunbeams), Golden Fleece; Dahlia Monarch, mixed; Eschscholtzia, Golden West; Freesia, Geranium, Good Venture; Heliotrope, Lemoinee'; Ipomea, Heavenly Blue, White Tassel; Nasturium, Butterfly, Jupiter, Saturn, mixed; Poppy, Fayal, Irresistible, Maid of the Mist; Tacsonia Buchananii. Write for prices. Theodosia B. Shepherd Co., W. H. Francis, Mgr., Ventura, Cal.

FOR SALE

FOR SALE—Second-hand, four-inch, cast-iron pipe, hubs cleaned and in good order. Address, Wm. G. Grimm, Cedar Lane, Woodhaven, L. I.

BOILERS BOILERS BOILERS.
SEVERAL good second-hand boilers on hand, also new No. 16 Hitchings at reduced cost. Write for list. Wm. H. Lutton, West Side, Avenue Station, C. R. R. of N. J., Jersey City, N. J.

FOR SALE GREENHOUSE PIPE

4-inch boiler tubes, second hand, in fine condition, absolutely free from scale and with ends cut square. Sample and prices on application.
KROESCHELL BROS. CO., 33 Erie St. Chicago.

Mention the Florists' Exchange when writing.

FOR SALE

Greenhouse Material milled from Gulf Cypress, to any detail furnished, or our own patterns as desired, cut and spliced ready for erection. Estimates for complete constructions furnished.

V. E. REICH, Brooklyn, N. Y.
1429-1437 Metropolitan Ave.

Mention the Florists' Exchange when writing.

FOR SALE

BOILERS No. 6 Weathered, round, $60.00. One 11 section Sunray hot water sectional boiler, grate 3 by 3. Price $150.00. New Henderson boilers; send for price on size wanted. One No. 367 Lord & Burnham hot water boiler, 7 sections, 36 in. grate, heat 8,000 sq. ft. of glass, used one season, price $150.00, guaranteed.

PIPE Good serviceable second hand. No Junk, with new threads. 2 in. 7c.; 1½ in. 5½c.; 1¼ in. 4c.; 1 in. 3c.; 2½ in. 10c.; 3 in. 14c.; 4 in. 18c. 4 in. cast iron greenhouse 14c. 2 in. NEW, standard, full lengths, 9½c. ft. All kinds of fittings for 4 in. cast iron and all sizes wrought iron.

STOCKS AND DIES New Economy, easy working, No. 1 cuts ½-¾-1 in. $3.00; No. 2 cuts 1¼-1½-2 ins. $4.00; Armstrong Adjustable No. 2 cuts ¾-1 in. $4.00; No. 3 cuts 1¼-1½-2 ins. $6.50.

PIPE CUTTERS Saunders, No. 1 cuts to 1 in. $1.00; No. 2 cuts to 2 in. $1.30; No. 3 cuts to 3 in. $3.00; No. 4 cuts to 4 in. $4.50.

STILLSON WRENCHES Guaranteed. 12 in., grips 1½ in. $1.10; 18 in., grips 2 in. $1.50; 24 in., grips 2½ in. $2.25; 36 in., grips 3½ in. $4.50.

PIPE VISES Reed's Best Hinged Vise, No. 1 grips 2 in. $1.75; No. 2 grips 4 in. $3.50.

GARDEN HOSE 50 ft. lengths ¾ in., guaranteed; 9c.; for heavy work, guaranteed; 12½c.

HOT-BED SASH New; Gulf Cypress, 3 ft. x 6 ft. 80c.; glazed complete $1.60 up. Second hand sash glazed $1.00 and $1.25, good condition.

GLASS New American, 50 ft. to the box. 10x12 single at $1.90. 10x12, 12x12 10x15 B double $2.65. 12x14 to 12x20 and 14x14 to 14x20 B double $2.85. 16x16 and 16x18 B double $2.95, 16x20 to 16 x 24 double $3.20 per box. 6x8, 7x9, 8x10 old, single $1.50. 8 x 10 old, double $1.65. 12 x 14 old, single $1.75.

Get our prices on second hand wood material. We can furnish everything in new material to erect any size house. Get our prices.

METROPOLITAN MATERIAL CO.
Greenhouse Wreckers
1398-1408 Metropolitan Avenue, BROOKLYN, N.Y.

Mention the Florists' Exchange when writing.

Commercial Violet Culture

PRICE, $1.50

The FLORISTS' EXCHANGE, 2-8 Duane St., New York

LEGAL NOTICES

A. T. De La Mare Printing and Publishing Company, Limited.—The annual meeting of the stockholders of this Company will be held at the office of said Company, Nos. 2 to 8 Duane Street (Rhinelander Building), in the Borough of Manhattan, City of New York, on the tenth day of January, 1907, at 12 o'clock noon for the election of a Board of Directors and two Inspectors.

J. H. Griffith, Secretary. A. T. De La Mare, President.

A. T. De La Mare Printing and Publishing Company, Limited.—By order of the Board of Directors the Transfer Books of the above Corporation will be closed on and after December 31, 1906, at 12 o'clock noon, to January 11, 1907, at 12 o'clock noon.

David Touzeau, Treasurer. A. T. De La Mare, President.

San Francisco.

News Notes.

The trade signs of the times were so promising of Christmas holiday activity as to lure another old-time cut flower dealer into the arena of competition. Ten days before Christmas Wickstrom's Floral Depot, so well known for years when the city was in normal condition as one of the only two flower stores in Market street, reopened in the city's very center of fashionable retail trade, the location being at 943 Van Ness avenue.

A. Duhem, an oldtimer in the business, is with the Wickstrom Floral Depot as overseer.

Two blocks down the avenue from the Wickstrom stand is the Art Floral Company, Inc., V. Matraia, manager. This stand is fortunate in being a corner location; the two busy retail streets being Van Ness avenue and Eddy street. I saw here among the busy employees several I had known before the April disturbance as proprietors of prosperous flower stores who lost not only their stores but their homes, household belongings and personal effects.

Charles Cohn, owner of the flower store in the ferry building, returned last week from a trip to New York, Boston and Philadelphia, he said that he there learned that the florists and growers of those cities had sent to San Francisco a cash donation for the benefit of local florists who lost all they had by earthquake and fire.

December 19 the Oakland fiesta committee decided to commence work at once on a great floral festival to be held in the Spring.

A heavy crop of lily of the valley, a specialty of the Holland Nursery Company of Elmhurst, is being supplied to the florist trade for their Cristmas-New Year's business.

M. V. Brown of Los Angeles is a visitor here. He has just concluded a sale of his nursery and cut flower business to M. L. Helsel.

This week Professor George Compere, head entomologist of the State's university, returned from a successful parasite hunting expedition. His intinerary embraced searching in France, Spain, Algiers, Italy, Australia, China, Ceylon, India and Japan. The citrus growers of the State are and have been spending more than a quarter million dollars annually in destroying by fumigation, red and purple scales. Mr. Compere brought with him from the Canton region in China a few thousand tiny flies, internal parasites, and from them he confidently expects to breed enough to rid the citrus belt of the harmful scales. He also brought with him a collection of ferocious aphis-eating ladybirds for distribution in California orchards.

ALVIN.

BALTIMORE, MD. — The next meeting of the Gardeners' Club will be held in the new hall of the Florists' Exchange. A house-warming, smoker, and general good time are expected. C. L. S.

TERRYVILLE, CONN. — Edward Fenn, florist, High street, is reporte dangerously ill.

TRADE, 1906

From the reports presented in this week's issue it would appear that the Christmas trade of 1906 was generally of a satisfactory nature, showing in some cities an increase over that of previous years. Owing to the dark weather immediately preceding the holiday stock in some localities in certain lines was scarce. In cut flowers carnations appear to have had an almost unprecedented call, and record prices are quoted. Not so many reports of "pickling" are heard, although the commission dealers were handicapped by an influx of consignments at the last moment.

The plant trade was, as usual, active. Nothing particularly new in this line of stock is reported. The weather was rather severe, and a few complaints of frozen plants are recorded. Holly and other decorative greens were, it appears, in ample supply, and generally cleared out. Artificial flowers have been much in evidence this year, but this line meets with no favor with the better class stores. The paper bell, it would seem, has reached its zenith, and appears to be on the wane as a factor at Christmas.

Now for Easter, which falls on March 30, 1907.

NEW YORK.—Christmas has come and gone once more, and the same old story relative to the appearance of unexpected supplies of cut flowers at the last moment, causing a surplus to be left in the hands of the dealers after the business rush was over, has again to be chronicled. Speaking generally, the Christmas business was good; prices all around were high enough to please the most exacting, and everything went along smoothly until well on toward Monday evening, at which time buyers realized that stock was more plentiful than was anticipated. Prices began to waver, everybody got all they required, and there was plenty of stock left over for the next day. As there is not much doing in the wholesale district any more on Christmas morning, there could be only one result, and the general verdict is, that there were too many flowers sent in at the last moment. Without taking into consideration the left-over stock, however, business was good. American Beauty roses sold in quantity at $1.50 each, and Bridesmaid at 25c. and 30c. each, Golden Gate and Killarney reaching similar figures. The red rose of the hour is Richmond, and the best of these went in quantity at 50c. each. White roses did not enjoy the popularity of the pink ones, and had to be disposed of at considerably lower figures.

Probably never before were there so many red carnations in sight for the holidays; some early sales of the best were made at $25 per 100, but the general price ranged from $20 to $15 for choice stock. Pink carnations brought anywhere from $8 to $12 according to quality, with an occasional sale of superfine blooms at 15c. each. White carnations, like white roses, did not sell to advantage, good fancy varieties being at any time obtainable at $6 per 100. There was a large supply of ordinary grade stock, particularly in white and light pink colors, which could be had at from $3 to $5 per 100, and for which the demand was anything but sufficient to clear them out.

Violets brought $1.25 and $1.50, some sales of specials reaching the $2 mark; at the same time many brought but $1 or less, and the supply was such that there was a nice surplus left over.

Orchids and gardenias cleared out fairly well; and lily of the valley was in good demand up to the afternoon of Monday, after which time there was not much call for it. Lilies and callas sold well. Paper White narcissus and Roman hyacinths were plentiful enough for all demands, and no advance was made over ordinary figures. There were a few chrysanthemums here and there, but they were of but ordinary quality and not much sought after.

Green material cleared out fairly well at regular figures, no efforts being made to advance prices on these goods.

The business on Wednesday was remarkably quiet, and it was evident that prices would become about normal again. The weather during the first three days of the week was bitterly cold, and quite a little stock arrived in the market in a frozen condition.

PHILADELPHIA.—It has been a very successful Christmas with all the trade. A large business was done; probably never before were so many plants sold at Christmas. The chief method of selling plants was in made-up baskets, flowering and foliage plants being mixed. We had nothing new in the plant line, but there were a much larger number of azaleas than formerly and fewer Begonia Gloire de Lorraine. Oranges, ericas and ardisias all sold well. Higher prices prevailed for almost everything.

Pennock Brothers did a very large business in rustic baskets; on account of the high prices of cut flowers they pushed sales on baskets and sold over 250.

H. H. Battles used Florentine pottery vases for his plants and these were filled very effective. As usual the prices of all cut flowers went very high. American Beauty sold at from $6 to $15 per dozen, with a scarcity of the $8 and $10 sizes. Tea roses were scarce; flowers that had been selling at $8 and $10 were advanced to $20 and $25 per 100, and many more could have been used. There were some extra prices for choice stock; for Killarney $40 per 100 was paid in one case and $30 in another. Carnations advanced to from $6 to $18 per 100, and unless one paid $10 or $12, the stock received was not worth much. Gardenias and cattleyas were at $9 per dozen. Apparently there were plenty of violets, which sold at $1.50 to $2 per 100, with $1.50 per 100 for the large singles.

Monday was very raw and cold here which prevented free delivery on account of extra wrapping, and nearly all the stores worked later on Tuesday.

A boiler burst at the Floral Exchange greenhouses at Eagely, Pa., Sunday night when the thermometer was down to 7 degrees. The S. S. Pennock-Meehan Company are trying an automobile delivery wagon, this week.

DAVID RUST.

BOSTON.—Every year sees an increase in the flower trade and while changes annually occur in some lines, the tendency is to a particular class of goods for Christmas work. The supply of all kinds of stock seemed equal to the demand; and yet there appeared to be little surplus. There was quite a lot of poor material, especially in roses, but the growers, who had first quality stock had little difficulty in disposing of it at first-class prices. In roses, American Beauty led, $12 to $18 per dozen being the top notch for the extra fancies; others sold at from $1.50 up to $10 per dozen, according to size and length of stem. Richmond went well, reaching $6 per dozen for the best fancies. Wellesley was also a good seller. Other roses realized anywhere from $1 up to $3 and $4 per dozen.

Carnations sold well and reached the limit as to prices, some growers getting as high as $15 and $18 per 100 for extra fancy blooms. The ruling prices for colored varieties were $5, $6, $7, $8 and $10. White varieties sold slowly at $3, $4 and $5. Sweet peas brought $1 to $2; lilies, $1.50 and $2 per dozen. Lily of the valley did not advance much, bringing from $3 to $5. Violets went at from $1 to $2 for some extra fine flowers. Stevia sold slowly. There were quite a few chrysanthemums, but they met slow sale. Greens of all kinds sold well; there was a big trade as usual for wreaths made of all kinds of hardy materials like hemlock, pine, laurel, boxwood, etc. Holly sold in large quantities.

The Christmas plant trade just past was far ahead in this city of any previous year's record. That plants are being used more and more at this season is evident, and that the cut flower trade does not increase proportionately has also been apparent this season. All kinds of plants, if well done, sold; but there were few made-up pieces. The trade here seems to call more for well grown plants of their particular variety. Azaleas were without doubt the leaders in number's disposed of, and it is a peculiar fact that this season the larger plants were very much in demand, while last year it was those of a smaller size. Begonia Gloire de Lorraine is always a winner and sold well. Poinsettias went fairly well; and cyclamen had a great demand. Ardesias were well fruited and sold like hot cakes; while cypripediums carrying ten or more flowers were good sellers. Tulips in pans sold fairly well; while there was a fair demand for well grown Boston and other ferns.

W. H. Elliott had a fine crop of Richmond roses, which just came in right and compared favorably with any blooms ever seen in this city.

Thos. Roland of Nahant had a nice lot of Begonia Gloire de Lorraine and some extra fine cyclamen.

Edward McMulkin had an exceptional lot of ardisias and cypripediums of his own growing. He also did a large business in baskets of fancy fruit, of which he makes a specialty.

A. N. Pierson of Cromwell, Conn., sent some excellent hanging baskets of Begonia Gloire de Lorraine, which sold well.

J. M. Ward of Peabody had a nice lot of poinsettias, begonias and cyclamen and excellent pans of Euphorbia jacquiniæflora.

A. M. Davenport of Watertown had a lot of fine pans of tulips being the first on hand with them this season.

A. Leuthy's specialty was azaleas, of which he grew an enormous stock.

Pierce Bros. of Waltham had an excellent lot of cyclamen and made a specialty of Azalea Firefly. J. W. D.

PITTSBURG.—Christmas trade of 1906 is past and at present it is doubtful whether the receipts are any better than last year's, for quite a few of the retailers did not do as well as they expected. The weather was rather unfavorable for the florist business, but could not have been more suitable for Christmas time—plenty of snow and cold. The thermometer went below 10 degrees on Christmas eve, and it required plenty of work wrapping plants and cut flowers for safe delivery; yet there were a few complaints of customers receiving goods in a frozen condition. A good many plants were half frozen in the markets and store rooms, and the growers were not careful enough in protecting stock against the cold. Even some of the retailers neglected to wrap carefully while making deliveries.

There was a brisk demand for plants and they brought good prices. The variety was about the same as usual for Christmas. Of made-up plants there were not so many. Pans of greens and poinsettias were in the majority, but they suffered from the cold and were not as presentable as they should have been.

In cut flowers the usual variety was handled at good prices. Roses were rather high even for poor stock, some of which was not fit to be offered for sale. Of the good ones about $25 per 100 was the price, and they retailed at from $5 per dozen and better. American Beauty were also up in price, from 75c. up, wholesale, retailing at from $12 per dozen upwards. Carnations ranged from $6 to double that price, the dealers selling them at $2 per dozen and better. The stock was pretty fair, with a good supply. Paper White narcissus sold well, being about the only clean flower, selling at 75c. per dozen at the lowest price. Roman hyacinths and lily of the valley were not much in demand; the latter were not extra good. Violets were in fair demand, retailing at $2 per bunch of 50. There were more chrysanthemums on the market than ever before so late in the season, and a few good ones at that, which brought $1 each at retail. They were mostly all white, and sold fairly well. Stevia was much used and helped to fill up bunches. A few Harrisii lilies and callas were in the market, but not much called for. Sweet peas sold for $1 a bunch—a small one at that. Cut poinsettias sold well at from 50c. up retail; some few home-grown ones were fairly hardy and stood up well.

Christmas greens went about as usual; trade in these goods is so much scattered that the prices have been cut the last few years, and it hardly pays the florist to handle them in quantity as it requires much labor. Trees were too plentiful and did not all sell. Holly went well and was of good quality. Mistletoe was scarce with a better demand than ever before. Pine and laurel wreathing sold at usual prices and a great deal was used for decoration. Needle pines went slowly. There was a fair demand for southern smilax. Christmas bells were handled in large quantities, particularly paper bells; the largest size retailed at from 25c. up. Artificial poinsettias were also much in evidence, being used everywhere for decoration, in some store windows very effectively. The florists made fine displays in their windows, and the stands in the Allegheny market were handsomely decorated, electric lights being used very effectively among the green and bright colors. E. C. REINEMAN.

NEWPORT, R. I.—In my report a week or more ago I said that indications pointed to higher prices for plants and flowers at Christmas than were obtained a year ago; and now late on Christmas eve, when the rush is over and the business incident to the occasion practically finished, I am not only able to verify what I have already said in relation to prices, but I am also able to state that the prices obtained for first-class stock exceeded expectations. As far as plants are concerned I say without hesitation that this was the first Christmas of which I have any recollection when seasonable plants of good quality in quantity where offered for sale. Gloire de Lorraine begonias, poinsettias, ardisias, azaleas, Begonia Turnford Hall, and solanums were all good quality stock, and were in demand in the order named, although perhaps Begonia Turnford Hall would have been in greater demand if offered in larger numbers and of a quality similar to that of Gloire de Lorraine. Ardisias sold at $1.50 to $2; araucarias, $1.25 to $3; azaleas, $1.50 to $3; solanums, $1; cyclamen, 50c. to $2; spruce trees in 8-inch pots, 50c.

In cut flowers, Bride and Bridesmaid roses brought $1.50 to $2 per dozen; carnations, $1 to $1.50 per dozen; Lilium Harrisii, $2 to $3. M.

DETROIT.—Christmas trade in this city has been a huge one in every sense of the word both as regards cut flowers and plants. Everyone seems entirely satisfied with the results obtained during the entire holiday season.

At the Detroit Floral Company, well up in the residence part of town, a steady business was afforded them. The sale of pot plants was larger than in past years, owing to the scarcity and poor quality of cut flowers. Poinsettias found favor with everybody. Basket effects of foliage and flowering plants went well. Jerusalem cherries were not much called for, while Boston ferns sold well. Cut flowers of all kinds were very high priced. Enchantress was the leading seller in carnations.

The Patterson Floral Company, in the Strand, also boast of an excellent trade. Poinsettias and Jerusalem cherries were in demand.

W. B. Brown said more flowering plants were used in his place than were foliage plants, in making up baskets. Immortelle wreaths and Christmas bells proved to be slow sale in his locality. In combination with his Christmas trade, Mr. Brown had a large decoration to attend to. He decorated Strassburg's Hall very tastefully for a Christmas eve ball. The decoration consisted of Christmas trees with diamond dust for snow. The balcony and chandeliers were strung with garlands of holly and ground pine roping.

E. A. Fetters stated that his Christmas trade this year, far exceeded last year's. Poinsettias in pans more than held their own, with cyclamen plants a close second, the latter selling at the popular price of one dollar. Roses sold well at from $3 to $7 a dozen. Small baskets of flowering plants found an exceedingly large demand. With Mr. Fetters as with Mr. Brown, paper novelties are a past number. Boxwood wreaths seemed to catch the eyes of the flower buying public this year.

At J. F. Sullivan's store, trade is reported as being larger than at any of the past holidays. American Beauty went readily at from $18 to $24 a dozen. Violets sold for $5 a hundred. Price, however, seemed a small matter here as Mr. Sullivan disposed of twenty thousand violets. Lots of baskets, made up mostly of flowering plants, proved a great drawing card. His store was stripped of immortelle wreaths. The sale of cut poinsettias was unprecedented throughout. His window display also bore the marks of true decorative genius. It had marble dust on it to represent snow, with a lattice scroll for a background. This was covered with wild smilax and holly. Upon the snow were set boxes of violets and baskets of flowering plants finished in the top notch style for which J. F. Sullivan has acquired a reputation.

B. Schroeter tried his best to maintain his reputation for prompt attention to business and in all probability maintained it. He had plenty of good stock and it went exceedingly well. He profited by last year's complaints about plants dying, by attaching a card, containing printed directions, to each individual plant. These directions for the most part pertained to the watering of plants.

Of the business done by John Breitmeyer's Sons, little need be said except that while it was immense, it was handled with such system that it is hardly possible for them to become pinched for delivery accommodations.

G. H. Taepke said everything was cleaned out. Saturday proved to be an immense day for plant trade, while cut flowers did not move so fast until Monday. Palms and Boston ferns sold exceptionally well as did araucarias. Good cyclamen found a ready market. Baskets sold well, while novelties proved a failure there also, especially birch baskets. "Bells," said Mr. Taepke, "are simply a back number."

Albert Pochelon, proprietor of the Beinb Floral Company, stated that his trade was far beyond his accommodations. With him there was really on one plant having a lead over any other. Cyclamen proved to be in great demand. Christmas bells and wreaths of all descriptions found many buyers in his locality.

At Woodmere the florists are all in a bunch and there is in consequence great rivalry. Their displays were remarkable. Gust. Knoch, who runs in Christmas wreaths and holly to a large extent, had an interesting display consisting entirely of various kinds of wreaths of many varied colors. HARRY.

GREENVILLE, OHIO.—James Frost writes: "Trade for Christmas here was the heaviest ever known. Much more business could have been done could stock have been procured. This town is not heavy on roses, carnations having the call, all home stock being used up early. Shipped stock showed the pickle sign badly. Plants sold better than ever before, the call being for narcissus, hyacinths and primroses. More Christmas trees could have been disposed of. Holly was good, and cleaned up well. Paper Christmas bells have been overdone, and they did not sell. Poinsettias did not take well. Prices were somewhat higher than last year, but we don't seem to get city prices. Roses brought $1.50 to $2.50 per dozen; carnations, 75c. to $1; American Beauty, $4 to $12. Funeral work came in heavy as usual at holiday time."

Wholesale Prices of Cut Flowers, New York, Dec. 25, 1906

Prices quoted are by the hundred unless otherwise noted

Roses — A. Beauty fancy—special	100.00	to	150.00
" extra	40.00	to	60.00
" No. 1	20.00	to	25.00
" No 2	12.00	to	15.00
" No 3	8.00	to	10.00
Bride, Maid fancy—special	20.00	to	25.00
" extra	12.00	to	15.00
" No. 1	6.00	to	8.00
" No. 2	3.00	to	5.00
Golden Gate	3.00	to	25.00
Richmond	6.00	to	30.00
Mme. Abel Chatenay	3.00	to	25.00
Adiantum	.50	to	1.00
Croweanum	1.00	to	1.50
Asparagus	25.00	to	50.00
" Plumosus, bunches	8.00	to	15.00
" Sprengeri, bunches	8.00	to	15.00
......	......	to	......
Callas	10.00	to	20.00
Cattleyas	40.00	to	75.00
Cypripediums	......	to	12.00
Daisies	......	to	......

Carnations — Inf'r grades, all colors	3.00	to	4.00
Standard Varieties — White	4.00	to	5.00
Standard Varieties — Pink	4.00	to	5.00
Standard Varieties — Red	4.00	to	5.00
Standard Varieties — Yel. & Var.	4.00	to	5.00
*Fancy— (*The highest grades of standard var) — White	4.00	to	6.00
*Fancy — Pink	4.00	to	10.00
*Fancy — Red	6.00	to	15.00
*Fancy — Yel. & Var.	4.00	to	6.00
Novelties	15.00	to	25.00
Gardenias, per doz.	12.00	to	18.00
Lilies	15.00	to	20.00
Lily of the Valley	3.00	to	6.00
Mignonette	2.00	to	6.00
Narcissus, Paper White	2.00	to	3.00
Roman Hyacinths	2.00	to	3.00
Smilax	8.00	to	12.00
Violets	.75	to	1.50

Wholesale Prices of Cut Flowers—Per 100

Boston Dec. 24, 1906	Buffalo Dec. 24, 1906	Detroit Dec. 15, 1906	Cincinnati Dec. 17, 1906	Baltimore Dec. 12, 1906	NAMES AND VARIETIES	Milwaukee Dec. 11, 1906	Phil'delphia Dec. 11, 1906	Pittsburg Dec. 24, 1906	St. Louis Dec. 24, 1906
50.00 to 100.00	40.00 to 50.00	to 50.00	to 12.00	to	ROSES A. BEAUTY, fancy—special	to 25.00	50.00 to 60.00	50.00 to 125.00	75.00 to 100.00
40.00 to 50.00	30.00 to 40.00	to 25.00	to 10.00	to 25.00	" extra	to 20.00	to	75.00 to 100.00	50.00 to 60.00
20.00 to 40.00	20.00 to 25.00	to 16.00	6.00 to 8.00	12.50 to 20.00	" No. 1	to 18.00	to	to 50.00	30.00 to 40.00
8.00 to 20.00	to	to 12.00	to	5.00 to 8.00	" Culls and ordinary	to 12.00	to	15.00 to 25.00	10.00 to 25.00
25.00 to 35.00	4.00 to 20.00	4.00 to 8.00	to 10.00	to 5.00	BRIDE, 'MAID, fancy-special	to 6.00	6.00 to 10.00	12.00 to 25.00	15.00 to 20.00
10.00 to 25.00	to 15.00	to	to 8.00	to 4.00	" extra	to 5.00	to	to 20.00	10.00 to 12.50
6.00 to 10.00	to 10.00	to	to 7.00	to 8.00	" No. 1	to 4.00	to	12.00 to 15.00	6.00 to 8.00
to	4.00 to 8.00	to	4.00 to 5.00	to 2.00	" No. 2	to 3.00	to	6.00 to 10.00	to
to	8.00 to 15.00	4.00 to 8.00	4.00 to 10.00	2.00 to 5.00	GOLDEN GATE	3.00 to 6.00	to	to	6.00 to 15.00
to	6.00 to 15.00	to	to	3.00 to 5.00	K. A. VICTORIA	3.00 to 6.00	to	4.00 to 10.00	2.00 to 6.00
6.00 to 35.00	10.00 to 20.00	to	6.00 to 25.00	3.00 to 5.00	LIBERTY	3.00 to 8.00	to	15.00 to 40.00	to
to	10.00 to 20.00	3.00 to 8.00	to	3.00 to 5.00	METEOR	to	to	to	to
to	10.00 to 20.00	4.00 to 10.00	to	2.00 to 4.00	PERLE	3.00 to 6.00	to	8.00 to 10.00	4.00 to 15.00
to	to	to 50.00	to	to	ORCHIDS—Cattleyas	to	to 60.00	to	to
to	to 3.00	2.00 to 4.00	to 2.00	1.00 to 1.25	CARNATIONS Inferior grades, all colors	2.00 to 4.00	2.00 to 3.00	to 4.00	2.00 to 5.00
3.00 to 4.00	3.00 to 5.00	to	to 3.00	1.50 to 2.00	Standard Varieties White	to	2.00 to 3.00	to 4.00	2.00 to 5.00
4.00 to 6.00	3.00 to 5.00	to	to 3.00	1.50 to 2.00	Pink	to	2.00 to 3.00	to 6.00	2.00 to 5.00
4.00 to 6.00	3.00 to 5.00	to	to 3.00	1.50 to 2.00	Red	to	2.00 to 3.00	to 6.00	2.00 to 5.00
4.00 to 6.00	5.00 to 10.00	to	to 3.00	1.50 to 2.00	Yellow and var.	to	2.00 to 3.00	to 6.00	2.00 to 5.00
4.00 to 5.00	5.00 to 10.00	to	6.00 to 8.00	2.50 to 3.00	Fancy Varieties White	to	4.00 to 5.00	to 8.00	6.00 to 8.00
6.00 to 10.00	5.00 to 10.00	to	6.00 to 8.00	2.50 to 3.00	Pink	to	4.00 to 5.00	to 8.00	6.00 to 8.00
6.00 to 10.00	5.00 to 10.00	to	6.00 to 8.00	2.50 to 3.00	Red	to	4.00 to 5.00	8.00 to 10.00	6.00 to 8.00
6.00 to 10.00	to	to	6.00 to 8.00	2.50 to 3.00	Yellow and var	to	4.00 to 5.00	10.00 to 12.00	6.00 to 6.00
to	to	to	to	to	Novelties	to	to	to	to
1.00 to 1.25	to	to 2.00	to 1.00	to 1.00	ADIANTUM	to	to 1.00	.75 to 1.00	1.00 to 1.50
to 50.00	to	25.00 to 60.00	35.00 to 50.00	25.00 to 50.00	ASPARAGUS, Plum. and Ten	25.00 to 50.00	50.00 to 75.00	30.00 to 50.00	25.00 to 40.00
to	to	20.00 to 30.00	to 35.00	25.00 to 50.00	" Sprengeri, bunches	25.00 to 50.00	to 50.00	20.00 to 40.00	25.00 to 100.00
12.00 to 16.00	10.00 to 15.00	10.00 to 12.50	to 15.00	6.00 to 10.00	CALLAS	12.00 to 15.00	to	to 20.00	12.50 to 20.00
to	8.00 to 25.00	4.00 to 25.00	to 15.00	4.00 to 25.00	CHRYSANTHEMUMS	8.00 to 30.00	10.00 to 50.00	20.00 to 30.00	to
to	to	to	to	to	DAISIES	to	to	2/0 to 4.00	to
12.00 to 15.00	15.00 to 20.00	to	to 20.00	to 12.50	LILIES	to	to	20.00 to 25.00	to
3.00 to 5.00	3.00 to 5.00	3.00 to 4.00	to 4.00	to 4.00	LILY OF THE VALLEY	3.00 to 4.00	4.00 to 5.00	2.00 to 5.00	3.00 to 4.00
2.00 to 4.00	6.00 to 8.00	to	to 4.00	to	MIGNONETTE, ordinary	to	to	4.00 to 5.00	3.00 to 4.00
4.00 to 8.00	4.00 to 6.00	to	to	to	" fancy	to	to	to 8.00	5.00 to 6.00
12.00 to 16.00	to 15.00	12.50 to 15.00	to 15.00	to 20.00	SMILAX	to	to	12.50 to 15.00	12.50 to 15.00
to	to 7.00	1.00 to 1.50	to 2.00	to .50	VIOLETS, ordinary	to	to	1.00 to 1.25	1.00 to 1.50
1.00 to 2.00	2.00 to 3.00	to	to 3.00	to .60	" fancy	to	to 1.50	1.50 to 2.00	to
to	to .15	to 1.25	to .15	to	GALAX LEAVES	to	to	to	to

PROVIDENCE, R. I.—Never before was there a better or more satisfactory Christmas trade than during the past week. Some kinds of flowers were very scarce, particularly red carnations, red roses and red flowers of all sorts. Carnations were scarce and high-priced, bringing from $5 to $10 per 100 wholesale, and retailing at from $1 to $2 per dozen. Tea roses brought $2 per dozen wholesale, and sold at $3 to $5 per dozen retail.

What few American Beauty were available brought $24 per dozen retail.

Violets, particularly the single varieties, were plentiful and sold at $1 to $1.50 per 100 wholesale. Narcissus, Roman hyacinths, and lily of the valley, $4 per 100 wholesale.

Azalea plants sold well, particularly the Fire Fly variety. Ardisias went remarkably well, as did Whitmanii fern and orange trees in fruit.

Gloire def Lorraine begonias seemed to be unsatisfactory, either as store or house plants, as they shed their foliage after the slightest change of temperature. There was a good trade in palms, rubbers, araucarias, Boston ferns, fancy ferns and aspidistras.

The paper bell business was overdone as on every corner on the principal business streets' bells were disposed of at 5 and 10c. each. Only one florist about here bothers with this stock.

The evergreen trade was exceptionally good. Creeping Jennie roping brought from $6 to $8 per 100 yards wholesale, and wreaths of the same from $1 to $2 per dozen wholesale. Laurel wreaths went at from $1 to $3 and holly wreaths at from $2 to $6 per dozen wholesale. The boxwood wreaths shown about here were made by the florists and proved a satisfactory decoration for the cemeteries.

G. A. J.

Wholesale Prices of Cut Flowers, Chicago, Dec. 26, 1906

Prices quoted are by the hundred unless otherwise noted

ROSES American Beauty			
36-inch stems.........per doz.	....	to	12.00
30-inch stems .... "	....	to	10.00
24-inch stems........... "	....	to	9.00
20-inch stems........... "	....	to	8.00
15-inch stems........... "	....	to	5.00
12-inch stems........... "	....	to	3.00
8-inch stems and shorts "	....	to	2.00
Bride Maid, fancy special......	10.00	to	15.00
" extra.	8.00	to	10.00
" No. 1.............	....	to	6.00
" No. 2.............	....	to	....
Golden Gate.....................	12.00	to	15.00
Uncle John......................	6.00	to	15.00
Liberty.........................	6.00	to	25.00
Richmond........................	6.00	to	35.00
Killarney.......................	8.00	to	12.00
" extra......................	15.00	to	25.00
Perle...........................	6.00	to	10.00
Chatenay........................	6.00	to	20.00
Callas..........................	....	to	16.00
POINSETTIAS.....................	2.00	to	4.00
HYACINTHS, Roman................	2.00	to	4.00
....	....	to	....

CARNATIONS				
STANDARD VARIETIES	White..........	4.00	to	5.00
	Pink...........	4.00	to	5.00
	Red............	5.00	to	6.00
	Yellow & var....	5.00	to	6.00
*FANCY (The highest grades of Sta'd var.)	White..........	6.00	to	8.00
	Pink...........	6.00	to	8.00
	Red............	....	to	8.00
	Yellow & var....	....	to	8.00
NOVELTIES.................		....	to	....
ADIANTUM..................		.75	to	1.00
ASPARAGUS, Plum.& Ten......		.35	to	.50
" Sprengeri, bunches.		.35	to	.50
LILIES, Longiflorum.........		....	to	20.00
HARRISII..................		....	to	20.00
Orchids—Cattleyas..........		75.00	to	100.00
SMILAX.....................		....	to	12.00
LILY OF THE VALLEY..........		3.00	to	5.00
VIOLETS....................		1.00	to	1.50
" single..............		....	to	1.00
HARDY FERNS per 1000........		....	to	1.50
GALAX "		1.00	to	1.25
NARCISSUS, Paper White......		3.00	to	4.00
CHRYSANTHEMUMS per doz.		2 00	to	4.00

BALTIMORE, MD.—Christmas eve the stores were doing a rushing business and all indications point to a heavy and a very satisfactory Christmas trade in both cut blooms and decorative stock. During the past week we had quite a variety of weather, some snow and plenty of rain and slush; this week, however, was ushered in with beautiful, clear cold weather, ideal for shopping. First-class stock in cut flowers has already been cleaned out by orders ahead; for over a week there will be a scarcity of roses and carnations, as has been expected. Holly seems plentiful and large quantities have been received from all over the State and Virginia. Poinsettias are very popular; and the quality is exceptionally fine. Halliday Brothers have a nice lot of gardenias. Begonia Gloire de Lorraine is much scarcer hereabout than ever before. C. L. S.

KALAMAZOO, MICH.—The Dunkley Floral Company, according to the Gazette, is to be served with notice to vacate all city property about its place.

CHICAGO.—It became evident early in the week that there were not goods enough to go around, and all shippers even as early as Tuesday and Wednesday began to take orders conditionally, and from Thursday to Saturday were refusing the delivery of goods in many lines regardless of price; by Saturday afternoon, it is doubtful if an order of any size at a reasonable figure could have been placed with an assurance of being filled. Carnations and roses both commenced to soar on Thursday, although the grip had been felt earlier; but when the orders began to come in on advertised prices and the trade saw that the goods were not in existence, it soon became a matter of self-preservation and all comers were turned down, so that on Friday and Saturday, high grade Bride and Bridesmaid, which had not been listed at over 15c. brought 25c., and had it not been for the friendly feeling among the members of the trade would have as readily realized 35c. At the same time the best Richmond and Killarney were keeping out of sight of customers at 40c. to 50c.

The carnation situation, though quite as active, the best flowers having been sold between wholesalers, presumably to cover orders, at prices ranging from 8c. to 10c., is looked at with a view of a possible pickle by hundreds of small to medium producers, a fact that was developed by the Sunday market, which produced an abundance of carnations from devious sources to the extent sufficient to carry whites of fairly good quality as low as 3c. All colors held up to 6c. and 8c., and if fancy changed hands readily at a higher price by one or two points.

Later reports may turn the situation topsy turvy, but from the present outlook, it is from my point of view, the hardest proposition which the Chicago market has ever run up against to comply with the requirements of its trade's demands and furnish the goods in quantity and quality as ordered and desired.

Sunday afternoon saw some relief. Prices were so high that intending purchasers withdrew their orders to some extent and an influx of white carnations had a more or less bearing effect, yet everything in color held its ground.

Poinsettias are much in evidence. They are generally well handled, showing that little signs of wilting, having been well grown, carefully cut and hardened.

With the scarcity of everything in the floricultural line, Christmas in Chicago was over-blessed with an abundance of the holiday emblem. Holly was everywhere. Possibly owing to the well-known shortage of green, holly has been delivered in Chicago by the train load. One well-posted authority told me that unquestionably there was four times as much holly put on this market last week as ever before and a good salesman told me Saturday night that he had just sold a hundred cases at twenty-five cents a case and still had four carloads to dispose of, as he put it "to burn, I guess."

The market opened on Monday morning as usual with a surprise and yet it was an expected surprise. Carnations which had been held, particularly white, were in over-supply notwithstanding which the colored sorts held up in price. Fairly good whites sold as low as 3c. and all the colors were in demand at 6c. and 8c., and in some cases higher.

The rose market was absolutely secure and carefully covered.

A tour among the houses that handle the bulk of stock going out of Chicago elicited the following important information.

Peter Reinberg—"By far the best and most satisfactory American Beauty business that we ever had. Much more pleasant than last year, as we have been able to fill all orders to the satisfaction of our customers. Incidentally on Monday morning we received from the houses 3,000 Mrs. Marshall Field roses from our stock of 7,000 plants—a most satisfactory return."

Wietor Brothers optimistically see something above a 20 per cent. advance over last Christmas. Prices held up and stock held out with the possible exception of medium length American Beauty on which some orders were necessarily cut.

C. W. McKellar reports a business more than satisfactory, his specialty of orchids being more in demand than in supply.

Flint Kennicott of Kennicott Brothers Company says that in his twenty-six years of business this Christmas is unquestionably the heaviest in orders and the shortest in supply. "We have been fortunate in having a good supply of carnations and a fair line of stock with the exception of roses."

Knighton & Johnson—"We have had a very good week, fine in every way."

Zech & Mann—"We can safely say that our business is as good again as last year."

E. H. Hunt—"We were compelled to turn down an immense lot of business, the largest in the history of the house, owing mostly to the shortage of roses; yet we made good by satisfying our trade with our full supply of carnations, poinsettias and violets."

J. A. Budlong—"A considerable increase over last year. Stock was a little weak, owing to unfavorable weather. Could have used a lot more of good stock if available."

Poehlmann Brothers Company—"Better than last year's and it looks now as if we could fill all requirements."

Wieland & Risch—"Far ahead of last year, probably 33 per cent. We were in crop both with roses and carnations and have filled all orders."

The J. B. Deamud Company—"A material increase; in other words we believe that we are still living up to the trade mark, 'The busiest house in Chicago.'"

The A. L. Randall Company report general lines well up to former years. Shipping business has been good. The supply business for the first year has been more than satisfactory.

E. C. Amling—"Biggest Christmas that we have ever had. Could have easily doubled the business if we could have gotten the stock."

The Chicago Rose Company—"Best ever. One of the best shipments of roses of the season reached us on Monday morning from our houses. Our wire business has been splendid and we have handled a lot of decorative greens."

Percy Jones—"I call it a fair, ordinary Christmas, the shortage of roses being perhaps the most notable feature."

Vaughan & Sperry—"Everything has gone along as nicely as could be desired. Red roses and red carnations have, of course, been scarce; but our violet business has been very large and satisfactory in every way."

N. C. Moore & Company—"Well pleased with the results."

Sinner Brothers—"Though we were short of stock, we cleaned out nicely; could have sold much more, if we had had it."

Bassett & Washburn—"Very, very busy. We were off crop in nearly all lines, but filled orders, considering the fact that the Christmas demand was the heaviest we ever received."

Benthey-Coatsworth Company — "We never before had such a Christmas as to demand and prices. We had a more than fair cut, exceptionally on Killarney. Our business will run beyond 40 per cent. increase over any past holiday."

E. F. Winterson Company—"Large advance orders booked previous to the opening of the Christmas season and an extremely heavy call after that time realized for us the largest business in our history. We were compelled to turn down some demands for red stock, but in the main, believe customers have been well satisfied with our covering of their orders. Our supply department also was most satisfactory; all lines of decorative greens being cleaned up in good shape."

WILLIAM K. WOOD.

ST. LOUIS.—Stock will be scarce for the holidays. The weather for the past few days has been cold and cloudy, and as a consequence all kinds of cut flowers are very scarce and, of course, the demand great. The retailers have all they can do at the present time. The plant trade is reported very active, with heavy sales in almost every line and good prices. Roses have not been plentiful all of the past week, and indications point to full holiday figures on all varieties. American Beauty sell at $12 per dozen; from that down to 15c. for shorts. For Bride and Bridesmaid, $6 per 100 is the lowest price for shorts; extra fancy, are up to $15 per 100. Richmond and Killarney bring $20 for extra fancy. Other varieties are very scarce. Of carnations there is a fair crop, but prices are up to $8 for fancy, $5 and $6 for next choice, with common held at $4 per 100.

The supply of violets will not exceed the usual receipts; the call is heavy and prices are up to $2, and will probably go to $2.50 for fancy California.

Roman hyacinths and Paper White narcissus will be in fairly good supply, with hardly any advance in prices. Extra fine lily of the valley is up to $5 per 100. Stevia is in plenty and comes in just right to help out.

It is rather early to say anything about the business for Christmas, as to-day (Monday), the rush is on, and all hands are busy attending to the trade.

ST. PATRICK.

CINCINNATI.—The demand for Christmas stock never before was better and the stock never scarcer. The wholesalers sold everything they could get; more they could not do. The retail stores bought heavily out-of-town, for the reason that they could not get the goods at home, and I believe that the retail trade will equal that of any previous year's; but the wholesale end of it will drop behind. Green goods were not used so extensively as in other years. Holly went well; and California pepper sold only in limited quantities.

Prices for New Year's will be equally as high as at Christmas, and unless we get sunshine, flowers will be just as scarce. Nothing new in plants or decorations in this market.

E. G. G.

Davenport, Ia.

The Tri-City Florists met at the greenhouse of Harry Bills on North Brown street last week, and an interesting session was held, there being a large attendance. The advisability of organizing a horticultural society in Davenport or in the tri-cities was discussed, and it was the opinion of the members that such a society would be a good thing. The society would consist of laymen or parties not engaged in the profession.

The question which was up for general discussion at the meeting was "Roses and their propagation; which are the most profitable bulbs, and their culture." It was also decided to adopt a question box.

The programme committee reported and gave the outline of the programme for every month of the ensuing year. The topics which will be taken up during 1907 are as follows:

January—"What are the most profitable plants to grow for Easter trade?"

February—"The making and care of hotbeds. Does it pay to make hotbeds? What are the best plants to grow in hotbeds?"

March—"How is the best way to beautify cities, their lots, boulevards and public places?"

April—"What are the most profitable plants to grow for Spring trade?"

May—"Peony culture—What are the best kinds to grow for cut flowers? Does it pay to grow perennials for cut flowers?"

June—"Rose culture—What are the best varieties to grow for the Summer months; for the Winter months? Does it pay to grow roses out-of-doors?"

July—"Greenhouse construction—Best material for benches. Which is better for heating, steam or hot water?"

August—"Carnation culture—What are the best varieties to grow? Does it pay to grow carnations for out-of-door or Summer blooming?"

September—"What are the best plants to grow for Christmas?"

October—"Ornamental tree and shrub culture—Best trees and shrubs for private grounds—Does it pay to grow hardy roses?"

November—"Chrysanthemum culture—What are the best varieties for commercial use, for pot plants and for cut flowers?"

December—"Heating greenhouses—What is the best and cheapest fuel? How is the best way to decorate show windows?"

Detroit, Mich.

Club News.

The Detroit Florists' Club meeting was well attended December 19. Several out-of-town members were present in expectation of hearing a paper read by Robert Flowerday, who, however, was unable to prepare his paper owing to the serious illness of his daughter. The subject upon which Mr. Flowerday was to speak was, "Christmas Twenty Years Ago and To-day." Inasmuch as no other program had been provided the members spoke of seasonable Christmas stock. From this topic they drifted on to heating under forced circulation. They also spoke about the question of getting good coal and at a reasonable price.

The Wildmere Gardens, a nursery in Highland Park, Mich., formerly owned by Mr. Briscoe, has been turned into a stock company. The corporation has a capital of $10,000.

The L. Bemb Floral Company is rapidly acquiring a larger trade as shown by the new horse and wagon. This new outfit is to be initiated during the holidays. Mr. Pochelon has just remodeled his store, having built stationary ribbon cases in the wall. A new rose room has been constructed in which no ice is used, it being sufficiently cool without it. HARRY.

Pittsburg.

News Notes.

Randolph & McClements have bought the business of Siebert, the East End florist, including greenhouses on Stanton avenue and the lease on the building at Baum and Beatty streets. The lot is 100x120 feet and the present building occupies the front half of it. Randolph & McClements, as their lease is a long one, will erect a large building on the rear half of the lot at Beatty and Commerce streets and will remove their store to that location next Spring.

GERMANTOWN, PA.—At the regular semi-monthly meeting of the Thomas Meehan Horticultural Society held in the plan room of the landscape department's offices, the following officers were chosen for the ensuing year: President, Samuel Baxter; vice-president, William Lamb; secretary, Henry A. Illman.

After an interesting and optimistic address by the retiring president, Warren Chandler, the subject for the evening, "The Winter Storage of Vegetables, Fruits and Plants," was discussed from several points of view. S. Mendelson Meehan gave an address on the storage and preservation of fruits, while the practical methods of the Winter storage of vegetables, flowers, trees and roots were treated in the order named by Messrs. Illmau, Hemming, Lamb and Baxter. The discussion following the addresses was participated in by nearly all the members present, and an interest manifested in the society which the firm of Thomas Meehan & Sons, Inc., encourages for reasons both educational and practical. I.

BLOOMINGTON, ILL.—At a meeting of the Florists' Club of this city, held December 13, preliminary steps were taken toward arranging for the meeting of the Illinois State Florists' Association to be held in this city on Tuesday and Wednesday, February 19 and 20, 1907. J. F. Ammann of Edwardsville president of the State Association, was present and delivered an address upon "Organization." After the address by Mr. Ammann the routine business of the local club, which has a membership of twenty-five florists in Bloomington and Normal, was transacted and the following committee on exhibition appointed: George Washburn, Fred Roe and W. T. Hempstead. A flower show is to be one of the principal features of the meeting of the State Association here next February. The location of the show as well as the place of holding the club's annual meeting have not yet been decided upon. The program is now being prepared and will be ready for publication within a comparatively short time. The State Association has a large membership and the local members expect an attendance of at least 150 delegates.

STREATOR, ILL.—A fire at Newell Brothers' greenhouses entirely destroyed the boiler room and partially destroyed the greenhouses, causing a loss of $1,000 on the building, and $500 on the growing crop of vegetables.

EASTON, PA.—Arthur L. Raub & Company report that they are highly pleased with the Standard pumping engine which they installed last Spring. They state that by the use of this machine they will save, each year, more than twice what the pumping engine cost them.

LYNN, MASS.—Brooding over the death of his brother, and worried because all of his plants had been destroyed by frost, James F. Marble, 73 years of age, the proprietor of small greenhouses, sought to end his life on December 19 by inhaling illuminating gas. The police were notified and hurried the man to the Lynn hospital, where the physicians believed that he would undoubtedly recover. Marble has made a previous attempt to commit suicide while suffering from melancholia.

Always Satisfactory.

We have always been very well paid when advertising in your paper; the class of trade it brings has always been very satisfactory.

VALLEY VIEW GREENHOUSES,
VELIE BROS., Props.

New York.

Trade Notes.

The retail stores of this city made grand showings for Christmas; and so far as we can learn at the present time business, we think, has been entirely satisfactory. The elaborate displays made, particularly by the Broadway stores, seem to grow more beautiful as the years pass and it is most gratifying to note also that with each succeeding year there is less of the artificial to be seen in the make-up of these displays. The introduction of artificial leaves, plants and flowers is, we think, something that every first-class florist ought to do away with. It might be all right for some classes of merchants to make special efforts to bring in a lot of artificial material such as birch, magnolia, holly and poinsettias, but it seems poor taste at the best for those interested in the flower trade to introduce that class of goods in direct competition with natural products. As we said before, we are glad to see that such things have secured but a very poor foothold among the better class of florists in this city.

In speaking of the retail displays as seen here, it is unnecessary to make any invidious distinction, as every florist now appreciates the value of an elaborately dressed window and he spares no pains in securing the best that is obtainable for his trade; arranging the same in the most artistic manner possible.

While we saw no new thing in the way of plants, it can truthfully be said that the many old favorites have not been grown to greater perfection or shown more artistically than has been the case this Christmas. Ardisias, oranges, azaleas, cyclamen, ericas, begonias and poinsettias were the principal standbys, and no store window was without some one of this list of plants, well-grown and tastefully arranged.

The weather was extremely cold for a day or two preceding Christmas, but the art of delivering plants has now reached such perfection that it goes without saying that no retail customer was unfortunate enough to be the recipient of a frozen plant.

Holly and the various kinds of evergreens were not so abundant this year as usual, and prices were higher than the average. It would seem, though, that this shortage did not inconvenience the retail trade to any extent, as very little of the green material was left on hand with the dealers when the holiday business was finished.

The Cut Flower Exchange, on December 18, declared a dividend of 10 per cent. to the stockholders at their offices, 55 West Twenty-sixth street.

F. D. Rennison, representing J. B. Pilkington & Company, Portland, Ore., has been spending a few days in the city in the interests of his firm. Mr. Rennison's chief mission here was to get in touch with some of the importers of Belgian decorative stock.

S. Williams, of Wadley & Smythe, Fifth avenue, advises us of the death of Mrs. H. Williams, wife of Henry Williams, seedsman, Fortis Green, Finchley, England, who is brother to the late B. S. Williams, orchid grower, Holloway, London, England.

On Wednesday, December 19, Anton Zvolanek, Bound Brook, N. J., obtained a judgment of $469 against the company that supplies Summit, N. J., and vicinity with water. It seems that the company in question has the right of way through Mr. Zvolanek's property, and some time last Summer desired to do some excavating through a piece of land on which Mr. Zvolanek had planted some of his new sweet peas. Mr. Zvolanek informed the workmen that they would be liable for heavy damages if they proceeded to dig in that particular place; they went away, but returned during the night following, completed their job and ruined seventy-two plants of new sweet peas, hence the suit.

Bernard Lapp, New Providence, N. J., has a sport from the Bride rose which is striped with pink and white, a very pretty variegated form, and one that should be a winner.

New Orleans, La.

News Notes.

On December 19 the New Orleans Horticultural Society inaugurated a series of lectures pertaining to horticulture. The one on this date was delivered by Professor Newell from the State Experiment station at Baton Rouge, the subject being "Crop Pests." Professor Rosenfeldl of Radford, Va., read a very interesting and instructive paper on the white fly or "mealy wing," which together with the sooty mold which it causes, is a great enemy of the citrous plants of Louisiana. Professor Rosenfeld described the insect very minutely, and gave several formulæ for its destruction. C. W. Eichling spoke of a very satisfactory agent for the destruction of insects on orange trees, namely the Target Brand of Scale Destroyers.

A visit to the Abele Brothers' gardens showed them well prepared for the holidays.

At Gruza's two establishments everything was also found in readiness for the Christmas and New Year's rush.

CRESCENT CITY.

Cincinnati.

News Notes.

Last week a horse and wagon belonging to Sunderbruch, florist, was struck by a large two-seated gray automobile at Green and Bremen streets. The horse was knocked down and so badly injured that it had to be killed. The automobile, which contained the chauffeur and a man and a woman, passed on without slacking speed to see what damage had been done. The police are now looking for the owner. The horse was valued at $200.

DU QUOIN, ILL.—A greenhouse establishment is needed in this town, according to a local newspaper, and William L. Thill, proprietor of the Tamaroa greenhouses, may fill the want, provided favorable conditions can be arranged.

LANCASTER, PA.—B. F. Barr & Co. are installing a Standard pumping engine in one of their houses for supplying water for their entire plant.

CPSIA information can be obtained
at www.ICGtesting.com
Printed in the USA
BVHW04s1412041018
529296BV00017B/519/P

9 781528 56201